THE GREAT WAR

VOLUME XI

This Volume Combines Volume 11, Volume 12 & Volume 13
of an Original 13 Volume Set.

Reprinted 1999 from the 1918 & 1919 editions
TRIDENT PRESS INTERNATIONAL
Copyright 1999

ISBN 1-582790-30-2 Standard Edition

Printed in Croatia

Subject Index to THE GREAT WAR. Vols. I. to XI.

Black Roman numerals indicate the number of the volume, ordinary figures the first page of each chapter.

"The Runner."

THE GREAT WAR

THE STANDARD HISTORY OF
THE WORLD-WIDE CONFLICT

EDITED BY

H. W. WILSON

Author of "With the Flag to Pretoria"
"Japan's Fight for Freedom" etc.

and

J. A. HAMMERTON

Editor "Harmsworth History of the World"

PROFUSELY ILLUSTRATED

VOLUME XI

LONDON
THE AMALGAMATED PRESS LIMITED
1918

CONTENTS OF VOLUME XI

WAR SCENES IN COLOURED PHOTOGRAPHY

PHOTOGRAVURE PLATES

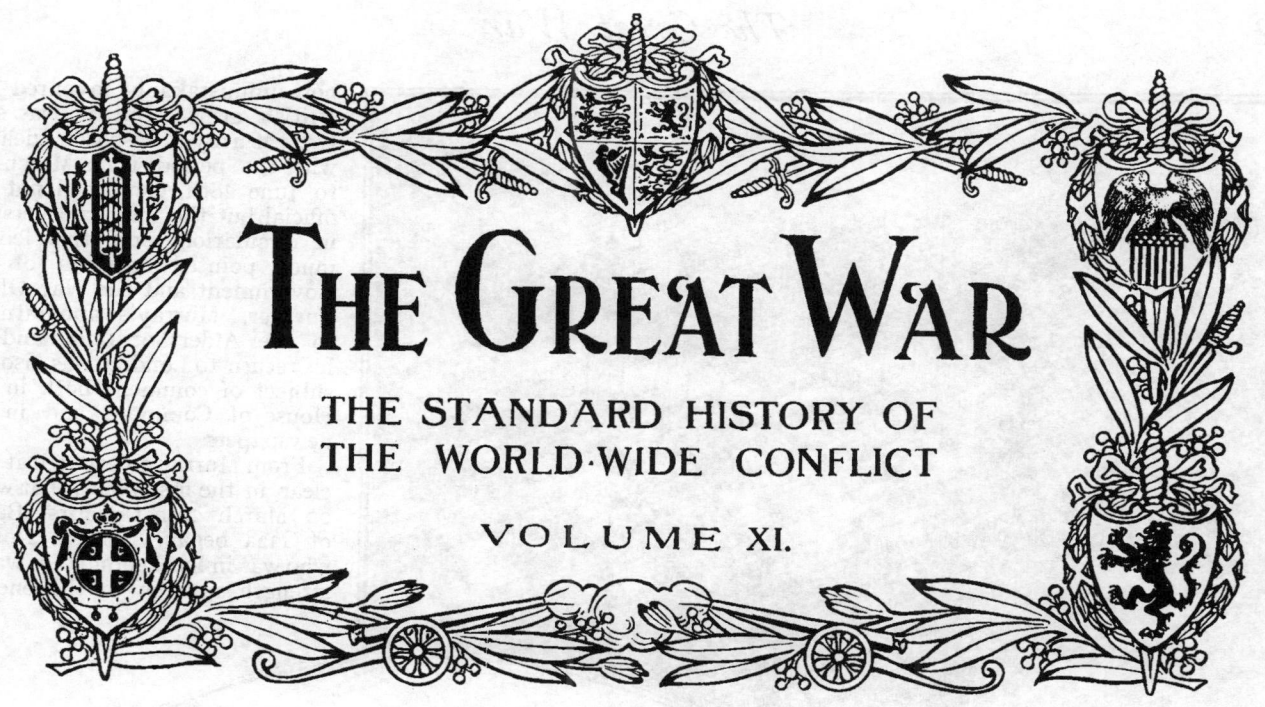

THE GREAT WAR

THE STANDARD HISTORY OF THE WORLD·WIDE CONFLICT

VOLUME XI.

CHAPTER CCXXVII.

ALLENBY'S VICTORIOUS ADVANCE INTO PALESTINE AND THE SURRENDER OF JERUSALEM.

By Robert Machray.

High Interest of the Holy Land—Beginning of the Advance from Egypt—General Murray's Despatch—The First and Second Battles of Gaza—British Co-ordination in Palestine and Mesopotamia—General Maude Co-operates with General Allenby—Falkenhayn's Indecision—Bombardment of Gaza Defences—Brilliant British Victory at Beersheba—Turks' Left Flank Smashed—Scots Take Umbrella Hill near Gaza—Battle of Sheria—Crushing Defeat of the Enemy—Fall of Gaza—Turkish Line Rolled Up—Allenby Pushing On Northward—Magnificent Charge of Midland Yeomanry—British Government's Sympathy with Zionists—Suggests Palestine a National Home for Jewry—Fine Political Move—Germany's Vexation—Allenby's Rapid Progress—Heavy Enemy Losses—Turks Make a Stand—A Futile Effort—British Capture Important Railway Junction—Jaffa Occupied—Advance Eastward on Jerusalem—Turkish Attempt to Hold It—Partial Success—Great Fight for the Holy City—Allenby the Conqueror —His Simple but Dignified Entry on Foot—Jerusalem Delivered from the Turk.

TO Christians everywhere no country had the same high interest as that attached to the Holy Land. Especially was this true of the vast majority of the English-speaking peoples who, familiar with the Bible 'from their earliest years, knew its place-names, with their religious and historical associations, as well as—or in some cases even better than—those of their several counties or neighbouring districts. Consequently the campaign in Palestine derived from the past a significance all its own; but it also possessed an extra-ordinary importance both in itself and in relation to the whole world-war. In Chapter CXCV. (Vol. 10, page 65), which dwelt more particularly on the safeguarding of the Suez Canal by the expulsion of the Turks from the Sinaitic Peninsula, there was narrated the beginning of the advance of the British beyond the eastern frontier of Egypt, and some in-dication was given of

the great possibilities that lay before this new crusade. It was indeed a crusade, yet of a novel kind, for under the ægis of Great Britain and her Allies, not only Christians, but Mohammedans and Jews were to share in its benefits.

Sir Edmund Allenby, who had been in command of the Third Army in France, replaced Sir Archibald Murray as head of the Egyptian Expeditionary Force on June 30th, 1917. On that date, and for about four months afterwards, the position of the British was a few miles south of Gaza, the modern Ghuzzeh, or Ghuzze, in ancient times the chief city of the Philistines, and about fifteen miles north of Rafa, on the Egyptian side of the boundary. By the middle of March, Murray's engineers had pushed on the railway from the Suez Canal, along the coast by way of the old caravan route, to Rafa, where they con-structed a large station some twenty miles from Gaza, and nearly thirty-five miles from

PRIZE OF WAR FROM THE AIR.
Sir Edmund Allenby, K.C.B., Commander-in-Chief in Palestine, inspecting a German aeroplane which had been driven down and captured by a British airman during the fighting in the Holy Land.

[Egyptian official photograph.

BY ONE OF SOLOMON'S POOLS.
British soldiers pumping water from a
Palestine well known as Solomon's Pool.

Beersheba, otherwise Bir Saba,
the Turkish base on his right.
His further operations depended
on the continuation of the line
northwards. To protect its
construction towards Gaza by
the occupation of the Wady
Ghuzzeh, or River of Gaza, five
miles south of that famous town,
and also to capture the town
itself, Murray had attacked the
Turks on March 26th and 27th;
but, after achieving considerable
success, he was able only to attain
the former object. Another effort
was made on April 17th and 19th,
but though some ground was
gained the town remained in the
hands of the enemy.

Known as the First and Second
Battles of Gaza, these operations
were for several months shrouded
in much unnecessary mystery.
When the facts were published, however, it looked rather
as if they had been held up with a view to keeping
bad news from the public—at least till more cheering
tidings of later movements could be communicated. The

Murray's despatch about Gaza — enemy knew what had taken place, and
through the publication of his official
telegrams on the first battle everyone
was aware that he claimed a victory.
At the time it was very generally believed that the
victory was to be credited to Murray and his men, who
had received the congratulations of King George on their
success. Afterwards, as was observed in Chapter CXCV.
(Vol. 10, page 87), a much less optimistic opinion came to
be held, and this opinion was strengthened by what
came out from unofficial sources about the second battle.

It was not, however, until November 20th, more than
seven months after the second battle, that the War Office
revealed what had actually occurred by publishing a
lengthy despatch from General Murray, dated June 28th
and covering both battles. Meanwhile, Murray had been
superseded by Allenby, and the situation in Palestine

now unmistakably favoured the
British arms. But it was seen
that Murray's despatch, dealing
with the period from March 1st
to June 28th, confirmed not the
official but the unofficial versions
in circulation, and this led to
much pointed criticism of the
Government and the War Office.
Further, Murray's appointment
to the Aldershot Command on
his return to London was also the
subject of comment both in the
House of Commons and in the
newspapers.

From Murray's despatch it was
clear, in the first place, that when
on March 26th the First Battle
of Gaza began, General Dobell,
who was in local command, was in
strength superior to the enemy.

[British official photograph.

WINDING WAYS IN THE HOLY LAND.
British Yeomanry marching through the Judean foot-hills during the advance on Jerusalem. An officer
was himself photographed while photographing the column of mounted officers, dismounted Yeomanry,
and transport waggons as they wound their way through the stony country.

The British force consisted of three infantry divisions—
the 52nd, the 53rd, and the 54th — and two cavalry
divisions, the Anzac Mounted Division and the Imperial
Mounted Division, besides the Imperial Camel Corps.
The Turks had between two and three divisions, the
greater part of their troops being some distance from
Gaza, but not so far from it as to forbid the speedy
sending of reinforcements to its assistance. In addition
to the handicaps of the two hours' fog in the early
morning and the lack of water as the day wore on,
which had been reported previously as the reasons why
the town had not been captured, it was tolerably plain
that, if the cavalry work was brilliant, the infantry were
not handled very well, though they fought magnificently.

It turned out that, as night had fallen on March 26th,
Gaza had been enveloped by the British—this was fresh
news. The Mounted Anzacs were round the place on the
north and, struggling gallantly through its thick cactus
hedges, were fighting in its streets. The 53rd Division
was occupying the formidable Ali Muntar position, which
it had stormed, but on its right flank only a thin line of

cavalry held off the columns the enemy was bringing up. The 54th Division held the Sheikh Abbas Ridge, but there was a gap of two and a half miles between its left and the right of the 53rd. The Imperial Mounted Division and the Camel Corps, stretched over a very wide front, were trying to beat back ever-growing enemy forces, which were advancing in strong bodies, supported by artillery, to the relief of the town from the north, north-east, and south-east. The 52nd Division remained in reserve south of the Wady Ghuzzeh, and was not thrown into the battle. At nightfall it seemed as if the Turks, in their augmented strength, might in their turn

[*British official photograph.*
TROOPS IN RESERVE.
Men of an Indian Rifle battalion in their dug-outs in reserve on the Palestine front.

INDIAN OFFICERS IN PALESTINE. [*British official photograph.*
Some of the officers of an Indian Rifle battalion on the well-sandbagged slope of their dug-outs in reserve on the Palestine front. Indian troops greatly distinguished themselves in the course of General Allenby's campaign that led to the capture of Jerusalem.

envelop the Anzacs. To obviate this contingency, General Chauvel, who was leading the Anzacs, was directed to withdraw them during the night to the west of the Wady Ghuzzeh, the Imperial Camel Corps being ordered to assist him. This movement made the position of the 53rd Division untenable, and the 54th was already retiring westwards from Sheikh Abbas. The 53rd, therefore, was withdrawn from Ali Muntar, and the two divisions got into touch in the night.

The Turks were thus able to reinforce the garrison of Gaza with considerable bodies of troops. Next morning the British were hard at work again, and patrols actually seized and occupied the positions up to and including Ali Muntar, which had been captured on the preceding day. But the Turks at once counter-attacked before the patrols were reinforced, and Ali Muntar was lost again, though the other positions were held. These, however, forming a salient, were subjected to heavy artillery fire from three directions, and it was found impossible to keep them permanently. In fact, a general retirement had become inevitable, and the whole British force was withdrawn

to the western side of the Wady Ghuzzeh, where a defensive line was taken up by the infantry to cover the further progress of the railway which then was approaching Khan Yunus.

The cost to the British of the First Battle of Gaza was about four thousand casualties ; on the other hand, the Turks lost twice as many men, according to General Murray's estimate, and they did not try to advance on the 28th, but contented themselves with occupying and strengthening the Gaza defences.

In General Murray's despatch there were two special features. One was the large number of the British casualties — seven thousand—and the other was the removal of General Dobell from local command at the front. Another thing that attracted attention was that the 53rd Division was commanded by Major-General S. F. Mott, whereas in the first battle it had been led by Major-General A. G. Dallas, C.B., C.M.G.

General Murray stated that he had **Murray's plan** instructed General Dobell that upon no **of action** consideration was a premature attack to be made. There were good grounds for this order. It was not until April 17th that the attack began, and in the meantime the Turks had been greatly reinforced, while the defences of Gaza had been rendered most formidable. The strength of the enemy had grown to five divisions of infantry and one of cavalry, and he had constructed works all along his front, which put out of the question any enveloping move by cavalry until after his line had been pierced or broken sufficiently. The attack had to be a frontal one, and it seemingly was carefully prepared. The railway, by April 5th, had its rail-head at Deir el Belah, and a station had been opened there a little south of the Wady Ghuzzeh. Arrangements had been completed for ensuring a water supply by placing in the wady tanks into which rail-borne water was pumped from Deir el Belah. In addition to the 52nd, the 53rd, and the 54th Divisions, Murray now had the 74th Division, with the same cavalry divisions as before, but he was no longer in preponderant strength as he had been at the commencement of the first battle.

The general plan was that the advance on Gaza, with three infantry divisions and two cavalry divisions, should take place in two stages. The first was the occupation of the Mansura and Sheikh Abbas Ridges, timed for April 17th. Then was to follow a short period of further preparation, heavy guns and fighting Tanks being brought up, supplies advanced, and the water supply improved. Next was to come the advance on Gaza itself. The first part of the programme was carried out without much opposition. But there was a different story to tell concerning the second part, which was the more important. The 74th Division did not come into action, as it was

BRITISH GOVERNOR OF JERUSALEM.
Mr. Ronald Storrs, C.M.G., Egyptian Civil Service, appointed Governor of Jerusalem after General Allenby's capture of the city.

The captured ground was consolidated during April 20th, and a long period of trench warfare supervened, lasting till near the end of October.

Meanwhile General Dobell had been relieved of his command. Of this General Murray wrote :

It became apparent to me that General Dobell, who had suffered some weeks previously from a severe touch of the sun, was no longer in a fit state of health to bear the strain of further operations in the coming heat of the summer. To my great regret, therefore, I felt it my duty to relieve him of his command. . . Accordingly on the morning of the 21st (April) I interviewed General Dobell, and informed him of my decision, in which he concurred. I then interviewed General Chetwode, and instructed him to relieve General Dobell in the command of the Eastern Force.

Lieut.-General Sir Philip Chetwode thus replaced General Dobell, ard this led to the promotion of Major-General Sir H. Chauvel to the command of the Desert Column—the two mounted divisions—in succession to the former, while Major-General E. W. C. Chaytor took Chauvel's place as head of the

Major-General E. W. C. Chaytor, C.B., C.M.G., succeeded General Chauvel in command of the Anzac Mounted Division.

Surgeon-General J. Maher, in charge of all branches of the Medical Services in the Palestine operations.
MENTIONED IN PALESTINE DESPATCHES.

Major-General Sir Henry Chauvel, K.C.M.G., C.B., succeeded General Chetwode in command of the Desert Column.

held in reserve. The 53rd Division, on the left, took Samson Ridge after severe fighting, and got within three miles of Gaza along the coast. But the 52nd and 54th Divisions, to which were assigned the assault on Ali Muntar, now made into a much more formidable fortress than in the first battle, were unable to make much headway owing to the accurate fire of the Turks. Such successes as were gained could not be wholly maintained. The fight was continued all day. In the afternoon General Murray instructed General Dobell to hold what ground had been gained, with a view to a fresh assault on Ali Muntar next day. But Dobell, backed up by General Chetwode and all the divisional commanders, sent word to Murray that he was strongly of the opinion that the resumption of the attack did not offer sufficient prospect of success to justify the very heavy casualties which must be expected. General Murray gave way so far as the suggested attack was concerned.

BRILLIANT YEOMANRY LEADER.
Lieut.-Colonel H. A. Gray Cheape, leader of a brilliant charge of Yeomanry in Palestine early in November, 1917.

Anzac Mounted Division, the " steps " got by these fine cavalry leaders being thoroughly well deserved. It had to be said, however, that it was passing strange that General Murray had not discovered that the health of General Dobell unfitted him for further operations until after the second battle was lost ; and perhaps it was not altogether astonishing that Murray himself was replaced, though that was not announced till about ten weeks later.

One of the most satisfactory things in Murray's despatch was his unstinted admiration of the magnificent work of all the fighting troops before Gaza. No praise, he said, could be too high for the gallantry and steadfastness of the cavalry, infantry, artillery, Royal Flying Corps, and all other units which took part in the two battles. He particularly commended the 52nd, 53rd, and 54th Divisions, which, since their reorganisation after the operations in the Dardanelles, he declared had improved out of all knowledge. The Anzacs had lived up to their splendid reputation. He noted that the Camel Corps, "manned by Australian, New Zealand, and British personnel," had proved itself a *corps d'élite*. He also made it known that the Expeditionary Force had been joined by a French detachment under Colonel Piépape, and an Italian detachment under Major da Agostino.

When General Allenby took over the command he found his forces entrenched on a front of about 14,000 yards from Sheikh Ajlin, on the coast, to the north-eastern corner of the Sheikh Abbas Ridge, where their lines turned back towards the Wady

[*Egyptian official photograph.*
EXAMINING A NEWLY-MADE CRATER.
Men of the British forces in Palestine interested in inspecting the crater caused by the explosion of a land mine in the desert sand.

[*Egyptian official photograph.*
PILLAR OF SMOKE IN PALESTINE.
Exploding of a land mine on the Palestine lines of communication. The firing of the charge sent a dense column of sand and smoke into the air.

Ghuzzeh, with their right flank extended to Shellal, towards which a railway was in process of construction from Rafa. Over against them lay the Turks, with their right on the sea, and their left south and east of Beersheba, and their front had been made very strong.

As far back as May, General Murray put the forces of the enemy in the Palestine area at probably eight divisions, six infantry divisions being in the front line, reinforced by artillery and machine-gun units as well as by mounted troops. For the most part the guns were officered and manned by Germans and Austrians. At that time, too, the Turks were building a military railway from El Tineh, on the Central Palestine Railway, towards El Mejdel, about a dozen miles north-east of Gaza. Their Generalissimo

at the time was the German, Kress von Kressenstein. In September it was rumoured that General von Falkenhayn had arrived in Jerusalem, and was to take over the command of the operations against the British, but at the same time it was reported that he was about to begin an offensive against General Maude at Bagdad.

Falkenhayn, with his headquarters at Aleppo, was impaled on the horns of a dilemma. Although widely separated geographically, the operations of the British in the East, whether under Maude in Mesopotamia or Allenby in Palestine, had a very genuine connection with each other. In these areas the war was almost specifically a war against Turkey, who already had suffered very considerably in both, albeit for a while she had been successful at Gaza. In the one she had lost Bagdad and the prestige that went immemorially with its possession, and in the other she was very directly menaced by the British advance from Egypt, which, moreover, had brought into the field against her new and very important opponents. She had now to face the implacable hostility of the Arabs under the King of the Hedjaz, formerly styled the Grand Sherif of Mecca, and other princes of Arabia, who had raised the banner of a fresh Islamic movement against the pretensions of the Young Turks in Constantinople and the " Turanians " generally, and had inflicted serious losses upon her by destroying many of her military posts in their country and by damaging materially a large part of the Hedjaz Railway.

Falkenhayn in a dilemma

In what direction was Falkenhayn to strike? Chapter CXCV. brought the narrative down to August, 1917, the 30th of that month being signalised by an advance of the British line near Gaza on a front of eight hundred yards, at an insignificant expense of life, in spite of considerable hostile artillery and machine-gun fire. During September no incident was recorded of special interest on the Palestine front, but soon the story was to take on a very different colour, for all the time Allenby had been preparing on a large scale for the resumption of the advance.

The efforts of the British forces in the East had meanwhile been closely co-ordinated. The rumours that had credited Falkenhayn with an offensive against Bagdad had not materialised. On the other hand, General

Artillery of English West Country troops advancing through the Judean foot-hills. There are hills a thousand feet or thereabouts high on either side of the road from Jaffa to Jerusalem which, if well defended, would take a bold army weeks to secure. So intense was General Allenby's pressure that the Turks were compelled to abandon one position after another, suffering heavy losses in the course of the operations.

Transport column of English West Country troops on the march, forking and taking alternative roads on either side of a strip of bad ground in the foot-hills of Judea. The British advance was extraordinarily rapid, Sir Edmund Allenby conquering the whole of Southern Palestine in seven weeks. The campaign opened on Oct. 31st, on which day Beersheba was captured, and Jerusalem surrendered on Dec. 9th, 1917.

WEST COUNTRY TROOPS TAKING PART IN SIR EDMUND ALLENBY'S ADVANCE THROUGH JUDEA TO THE CAPTURE OF JERUSALEM.

Maude, whose splendid services will be detailed in a later chapter, had been showing great activity in Mesopotamia, with the object not only of defeating the Turks severely in that region, but of furthering General Allenby's plans by keeping the enemy busy there and preventing his despatching reinforcements to Palestine.

General Allenby in the meantime had revolutionised the situation in the Holy Land. After months of comparative silence it was with what seemed startling and dramatic suddenness that the news reached the public, through the newspapers of November 2nd, that Allenby had captured Beersheba on October 31st. But the event which was thus chronicled, and the other striking events which followed quickly in its train, were the meet reward of a lengthy period of patient and thorough preparation and the careful working out of plans as patiently and thoroughly formed and matured. In these respects the victorious advance of Allenby in Palestine bore a strong family likeness to that of Maude on Kut and throughout most of his Mesopotamian campaign. Both waited till they were quite ready in all respects.

The railway from Rafa had reached Shellal, and on October 24th was being pushed on with all speed towards Karm, six miles south-east of Shellal, on the road to Beersheba, and a light line was being constructed from Kamli, three and a half miles south of Shellal, towards El Buggar, which lay about eight miles east of Kamli on the road to Beersheba. Sixteen miles south of the last-named place detachments were sinking wells at Ecani, Khalasa, and at Asluj, where in May demolition parties of the mounted divisions had destroyed the station on the Beersheba - El Auja railway, wrecking at the same time, in co-operation with similar parties from the Camel Corps, many miles of track up and down the line.

On October 27th the Turks, intrigued by the new railway developments towards Beersheba, made a strong reconnaissance from the direction of Kauwukah, three miles south-west of Tel es Sheria, against Karm with two regiments of cavalry, supported by between two and three thousand infantry and a dozen guns. The men who were busy making the track were screened by a London Yeomanry brigade, which occupied the high ground five miles west of Abu Irgeig, a station on the Central Palestine Railway north-west of Beersheba. Infantry were about to replace the cavalry, but before the change was made the Turks attacked the latter in greatly superior numbers west of the Wady Hanafish, which was **London Yeomanry repulse an attack** described by Mr. Massey, the accredited Press correspondent with the Expeditionary Force, as a rough watercourse with many twisting tributaries in the torrent-torn country parallel to the Beersheba-Gaza road. The Yeomanry, some of whose squadrons were at times threatened with envelopment, fought most gallantly, and in spite of the odds held off the enemy long enough to enable the 53rd (Welsh) Division to get up in time, the Turks in the end being repulsed with great loss.

It was on this same day of October that General Allenby began the attack on the Turkish main line, stretching along the Gaza-Beersheba road from the coast to some

little distance east of Beersheba, in all about thirty miles in length, by a bombardment of the Gaza defences, which steadily increased in intensity. Three days later British and French naval forces, commanded by Rear-Admiral T. Jackson, C.B., M.V.O., joined in the shelling of these defences and also of the road, railway bridges, and the station at Deir Sineid, north of Gaza, on the military railway which the Turks by this time had pushed on through El Mejdel to within a few miles of Gaza itself. The shooting of the warships was most accurate and did much damage. Keeping the attention of the enemy thus fixed on the west, General Allenby struck a **Co-operation by naval forces** quick surprise blow at him on the east, the success of which led to the crumpling up of the whole of the enemy's main line within a week and his rapid retreat to the north.

Allenby had planned the attack on Beersheba for October 31st. By the preceding evening he had concentrated his mounted troops at Asluj, Khalasa, and in the neighbourhood of Shellal, while his infantry lay at Ecani and on the El Fara-Beersheba road, the extreme left forming a defensive flank towards Abu Irgeig, six miles

A TURKISH BOOBY TRAP THAT FAILED AT GAZA.
When the Turks evacuated Gaza they left several traps in which they hoped to catch some unwary British soldiers. One was this table, on which three bottles were left, apparently inadvertently. Anyone touching them carelessly with a view to tasting their contents would have been blown sky high.

from Beersheba, on the road from Gaza to that town. During the night, under a beautiful moon, the cavalry made a turning movement by sweeping round in a wide curve through the desert from the south to the north, and as the day broke reached a point in the hills north-east of Beersheba, threatening the road from it to Hebron.

Deeming that the waste country outlying on that side would be an adequate protection, the Turks had never looked for anything of the kind. In the meantime the infantry also made a night march, and as dawn came deployed opposite the west and south-west defences of Beersheba between the road from it to Khalasa and the Wady es Saba. The supporting artillery were in action as soon as it was light enough for them to see their targets. Standing out of a tumbled sea of small hills, covered with low scrub through which sand showed plain, was the height known as Hill 1,070. In the distance appeared the long white line of the enemy's defences, held by six or seven thousand Turks. Hill 1,070 had first to be taken.

Lying about three miles to the south of the Turkish

AT THE WELLS OF BEERSHEBA.
British soldiers at one of the wells at Beersheba shortly after the capture of that place on October 31st, 1917. The taking of the town was especially welcome on account of the precious water supply of the wells, which, according to Arab tradition, date back to the time of Abraham.

main trenches, this eminence had been made into a very strong redoubt. Its sides were extremely steep and all its ravines were covered by German machine-guns, of which a section had been placed on the top of the hill. At half-past five the British guns vigorously shelled Hill 1,070. The day-breeze had not yet sprung up, and the sand, rising in thick clouds, hung in the still air and hid the height from the view of the gunners, who, after half an hour, had to cease firing till their mark became clear again. At eight o'clock the bombardment was resumed and the wire was cut. Then the Londoners advanced "as if on parade," said an eye-witness, "not a man flinching," despite heavy fire, and at a quarter to nine o'clock they stormed the hill after stiff hand-to-hand fighting, capturing eight officers and eighty men. This important outpost having been secured, the London troops and dismounted Yeomanry moved on to assault the enemy's first line of trenches, and, attacking with great dash, carried them by about ten o'clock. But a harder struggle lay before them in taking the second line, and well did they come out of it. Of this Mr. Massey wrote :

Our infantry made rushes across the open, heeding neither the enfilade fire nor the spasmodic machine-gun fire. In a few places the shells had broken down the wire, and into these the bombers dashed, while others tore down the wire from the iron supports with their hands, and were in upon the Turks before they realised that resistance was futile. This grand work was done by soldiers from English counties, many of them men who had prepared themselves for Great Britain's defence before the war burst upon the world. They showed inspiring courage and resource. Their onslaught on the south-western trenches only served to whet their appetite. After resting awhile, they crossed the rough pebbly bed of the Wady es Saba to reduce the chain of holes and trenches on the western side of Beersheba, which, strongly held, were even more formidable. Fighting for more than twelve hours had not lessened their

determination, and moving steadily and methodically on the same well-thought-out plan which had been so successful throughout the day, they proceeded to capture one length of defences after another, until at half-past nine all the Beersheba stronghold was ours.

While the systems of trenches defending the town on the south and west were being attacked and carried in the course of that long day by the splendid infantry and Yeomanry, the mounted troops on the east and north-east were doing equally magnificent work. By one o'clock the Anzacs had stormed a high hill called Bir es Sakaty, six miles east of Beersheba, which barred their way to the town, and then cutting across the Hebron road and the Wady Itmy effectually closed to the Turks any exit in that direction. Three miles east of Beersheba towered the height, a thousand feet high, known as Tel es Saba, which had been strongly fortified, and was exceptionally difficult of approach by reason of the steep banks of a wady alongside its southern slopes. With all their wonted zeal and gallantry the Australians and New Zealanders tackled this forbidding position, and in the course of the afternoon captured it after a tremendous struggle. Next they **Australians ride** successfully dealt with a group of houses **into Beersheba** between the hill and the Hebron road which was held by a German machine-gun section. By that time darkness was falling, and a line of trenches on the east lay about a mile between them and the town where were wells of the blessed water for the men and their animals, who were now parched with thirst. Dismounting, the 4th Australian Light Horse charged that last line, and, beating down all resistance, remounted and rode cheering into Beersheba, where they succeeded in capturing many prisoners.

PRIMITIVE PUMPING SYSTEM.
Arabs' mechanical contrivance in use for drawing water for the horses of the British force from one of the Beersheba wells. A blindfolded camel, driven round and round by a seated Arab, worked the strange wooden wheels that served to raise the water.

So closed the battle, and thus was the flank of the enemy on the east, which he had judged impregnable, rolled up. The capture of Beersheba was at once a fine tactical, and, what was more, a notable strategic victory. The town had hardly been a great centre in the past. The well-known Biblical phrase, "from Dan to Beersheba," had given it a niche in history which, on general grounds, it did not merit. The loss of the place, however, was in itself a heavy blow to the Turks, to whom it had served as a base for their attempts to invade Egypt through Sinai. It was estimated that of the six or seven thousand men who defended it only about a thousand got away. Nearly two thousand of them were made prisoner. Thirteen of their guns were taken, as well as many machine-guns, in addition to an immense quantity of war material of all kinds which the Turks, never imagining they

TELEPHONING DURING A DESERT ADVANCE.
At a mobile French telephone-post during the advance in Palestine. In his despatch of June 28th, 1917 (published nearly five months later), Sir Archibald Murray announced the addition to the force under his command of a French detachment under Colonel Piépape.

would be unable to hold the town, had either had no time to destroy utterly or left practically untouched. A locomotive in the station had been blown up, but the carriages attached to it were undamaged. Warehouses full of corn were almost intact, though an attempt had been made to burn them down. In view of their gains the loss of the British was light.

Strategic importance of the victory

Important as all this was, the great thing was that the taking of Beersheba put an end to the long period of trench warfare that had supervened on the Second Battle of Gaza. With the capture of the town the left flank of the enemy was uncovered. If, as some supposed, Falkenhayn—or whoever was responsible for the general Turkish plan of campaign—had decided, in face of the double menace of the British in Palestine and Mesopotamia, to consolidate a defensive in the former while directing an offensive in the latter, that plan had been brilliantly brought to nothing. In any case, there was a world of meaning in the telegram which General Allenby sent to General Maude, in acknowledgment of one received from him with congratulations on the capture of Beersheba. "We hope," wired Allenby, "our efforts will assist yours, and that our co-operation will shorten the road to victory." As presently was seen, Maude was again actively co-operating—this time from Samarra on his centre towards Tekrit.

Allenby's troops were ranging north and north-east of Beersheba on November 1st and 2nd. The Welsh (53rd) Division, with the Camel Corps, moved forward towards Ain Kohleh, nine miles north of the town, and his mounted men, pushing up the road to Hebron, came within four miles of Dhaheriyah. Meanwhile, the water supply was organised at Beersheba, and an attack was planned on Sheria. The Welshmen took up a position from Towal Abu Jerwal, six miles north of Beersheba, to Muweileh, four miles north-east of Abu Irgeig, from the station at which place Irish troops dislodged the enemy and compelled him to retreat precipitately. For a few days thereafter there was quiet in this sector. In the meantime things had been happening in the Gaza sector.

The bombardment of the Gaza defences and of the tract of ground north of it had been maintained by land and sea with little intermission. On the night of November 1st the fire reached a pitch of severity that the Turks had never experienced before. It was the prelude to the determined attack of the British early next morning on the whole of the enemy's first line of trenches, stretching from the eminence known as Umbrella Hill westward to the sea, including Sheikh Hasan, or, in other words, the extreme right flank of the entire Turkish position in the south of Palestine.

FRENCH SIGNALLING-POST IN PALESTINE.
Activity at the French signalling-post attached to a flying column in the desert during the advance through Southern Palestine. The seated men were sending and receiving heliographic signals, while mounted comrades were being sent with messages to the flying column.

ON GUARD IN THE HOLY CITY.
Guard of British troops mounted at the Jaffa Gate of Jerusalem after the occupation of the city by Sir Edmund Allenby. The photograph was taken through the ancient gateway.

the 19th Turkish Division, the remains of the 27th, and part of the 16th, in addition to depot troops and the greater portion of his cavalry. In his despatch of December 16th, which was published on January 25th, 1918, General Allenby wrote :

The action of the enemy in thus employing the whole of his available reserves in an immediate counter-stroke so far to the east was apparently a bold effort to induce me to make essential alterations in my offensive plan, thereby gaining time and disorganising my arrangements. The country north of Beersheba was exceedingly rough and hilly, and very little water was to be found there. Had the enemy succeeded in drawing considerable forces against him in that area, the result might easily have been an indecisive fight—for the terrain was very suitable to his methods of defence—and my own main striking force would probably have been made too weak effectively to break the enemy's centre in the neighbourhood of Sheria Hareira. This might have resulted in our gaining Beersheba, but failing to do more, in which case Beersheba would only have been an incubus of the most inconvenient kind. However, the enemy's action was not allowed to make any essential modification of the original plan, which it had been decided to carry out at dawn on November 6th. By the evening of November 5th all preparations had been made to attack the Kauwukah and Rushdi systems, and to make every effort to reach Sheria before nightfall. The mounted troops were to be prepared, in the event of a success by the main force, to collect, as they were somewhat widely scattered owing to the water difficulties, and push north in pursuit of the enemy. Tel Khuweilfeh was to be attacked at dawn on the 6th, and the troops were to endeavour to reach the line Tel Khuweilfeh-Rijm el Dibh.

Alarmed by Allenby's success on their eastern flank, the Turks had resolved on making a great effort to throw him back, but it proved futile, and resulted only in their further serious discomfiture. As the day broke, his attacking force moved from its positions to the south-east of the Kauwukah system of trenches. With splendid dash the Yeomanry took by storm the works on the enemy's extreme left, and then advanced due west by the railway, capturing the line of detached works lying east of it. Soon after midday the Londoners and Irish troops, having brought forward their guns to wire-cutting range, commenced the assault on the Kauwukah trenches, and were completely successful in capturing all their objectives. They also took the adjacent Rushdi position. By capturing Sheria Station before the darkness fell they consummated a splendid day's work. The Yeomanry reached the line of the Wady es Sheria, and the force on the left got close up to the Hareira Redoubt, which was still occupied by the enemy. In the course of a fine performance the troops had advanced eight or nine miles during the day, and had captured a series of very powerful works on a front of nearly seven miles, the greater part of which had been held and strengthened by the enemy for over six months. Six hundred prisoners were taken, as well as field-guns and machine-guns.

The Yeomanry encountered the most stubborn resistance in the early morning, but on the whole the British loss was comparatively slight. According to plan, when it was seen that success was certain, the cavalry were ordered to go on in pursuit and occupy Huj and Jemmameh, eleven and nine miles respectively east of Gaza. Meanwhile, the Welshmen had taken Tel Khuweilfeh, and though they were driven from a height by a counter-attack, they retook it, swung forward, and stormed another hill, which much improved their position. The fighting here was bitter, and the Turkish losses were very heavy, including several hundred prisoners and some guns. At nightfall the Turks were completely defeated, and were retiring from most parts of this sector, with the British at their heels. More than half of the main Turkish line was now rolled up, and under that ever-growing menace the rest was soon to follow.

At midnight, on November 6th, Allenby launched what proved to be the final assault on the very strong works that still covered Gaza ; but, as a matter of fact, the British met with very little further opposition there. Since the capture of Umbrella Hill, and the enemy's first

A tremendously heavy fire was concentrated for some minutes on Umbrella Hill, which was strongly organised, and lay about five hundred yards from the British on Samson's Ridge. Then the Scottish Territorials of the 52nd (Lowland) Division, the guns having lifted beyond the height, sprang over the parapet, rushed into and occupied the enemy's trenches, in which they found few men alive and many dead. The artillery had made easy the capture of Umbrella Hill, its trenches had been reduced to a shapeless mass, and the Scots quickly proceeded to consolidate themselves.

Later, the Lowlanders and East Anglian troops, assisted materially by aircraft, after several hours of fighting among the sand-dunes, many of which, notably one called El Arish, had been turned into formidable redoubts, captured the whole of the rest of the objective Allenby had set out to secure. In the evening and early on November 2nd the Turks, sensible of the importance of the ground they had lost, delivered repeated counter-attacks to regain it, but artillery and rifle fire smashed up each of their attempts, with very severe casualties. Next ensued a few days of comparative calm.

On the east Allenby struck heavily again on the morning of November 6th. Three days before he had advanced north on Ain Kohleh and Tel Khuweilfeh, across very difficult country, and on the 4th and 5th his mounted troops repulsed several strong assaults. The enemy had brought up very large forces, which included

Futile Turkish counter-attack

Capture of Umbrella Hill

Captured Turkish train at the platform of the junction where the Beersheba and Gaza lines branch off from the Damascus-Jerusalem Railway. British soldiers marching along the permanent way exchanged cheering congratulations with the driver and armed guards of the rolling-stock.

Saluting the Union Jack when first hoisted from the Town Hall of Jaffa on the occasion of the formal occupation of the town by Sir Edmund Allenby. On the morning of November 17th, 1917, Australian and New Zealand mounted troops entered the historic seaport of Jerusalem.

Last milestones on the new Crusaders' glorious march to the delivery of Jerusalem.

On December 11th, 1917, General Sir Edmund Allenby made his official entry into Jerusalem through the Jaffa Gate, attended by his Staff, the Commanders of the French and Italian detachments, and the Military Attachés of France, Italy, and the United States of America.

The deliverers of Jerusalem: Sir Edmund Allenby's historic entry into the Holy City.

On the steps at the base of the Tower of David, within the Citadel, a proclamation was read in Arabic, Hebrew, English, French, Italian, Greek, and Russian, promising the population freedom in all lawful business, and protection of every sacred building, spot, pious foundation, and customary place of prayer.

In the Barrack Square Sir Edmund Allenby received the notables of the city. The Mayor and the Mufti were presented, the Sheikhs in charge of the Mosques of Omar and Aksa, the heads of all the religious communities, and the Spanish Consul, who had been in charge of the interests of all the belligerents.

Incidents in the ceremonial celebrating the delivery of Jerusalem after four centuries of Ottoman dominion.

Crowds filling every niche of the Church of the Holy Sepulchre, the most sacred spot on earth to countless millions of people.

The Tower of David and the City Wall, viewed from the clock-tower over the Jaffa Gate in the west wall of Jerusalem.

The Damascus Gate, in the north of Jerusalem, one of the eight that pierce the walls built by Soliman the Magnificent.

Picturesque general view of the City of Jerusalem from the Mount of Olives, overlooking the City Wall and the Temple enclosure.

Sacred spots rescued from Ottoman possession and taken under protection by the British Empire.

line from it to the coast, no outstanding event had occurred in that sector. There had been, however, no cessation of the bombardment of the other fortifications defending the town and of the tract of ground to the immediate north of it. Warships, British and French, from the sea, heavy howitzers and field-guns from the land, poured day after day a terrific fire on the defences and cut enormous gaps in them; but a large part was still sound enough or capable of being repaired. The Turks had no thought, however, of trying to build up the breaches made by the guns. It was rather Allenby's threat, that was ever coming nearer from the east, than his artillery which disheartened them and took all the strength out of their resistance at Gaza, causing them to evacuate it. That night only a few of their men remained in the trenches, and when the troops from the Western Counties and Indian soldiers on the south-east, with East Anglians and forces from the Home Counties on the coast, went " over the top " and moved on to the attack, there was comparatively little of a struggle.

The stronghold was in the hands of the British by dawn, and, passing through it, Scottish Territorials from Glasgow and the Highlands forthwith pushed on along the shore through the sand-dunes as far as the Wady Hesi, eight miles farther north, to which watercourse Indian cavalry also advanced by the coast road. Some Turks still held on to the Atawina Ridge, east of Gaza; but by the morning of November 8th it, too, was in the possession of the British, who then had driven the enemy out of every portion of the Gaza-Beersheba line, which had stood over against them so defiantly all the **General retreat of** long and weary months since the **the Turks** Second Battle of Gaza. The whole Turkish army was in retreat.

Giving the enemy no respite, Allenby's soldiers, horse and foot, pressed on in every part of the field, in spite of the difficult terrain and the frequent lack of water, to say nothing of their having to fight and overcome fairly large bodies in some stubborn rearguard actions which the Turks put up to cover the withdrawal of their main forces. The Hareira Redoubt was captured on the morning of November 7th. The Londoners, after a severe engagement at Tel el Sheria, a steep hill, with a deep wady running in front of it, which they took by a bayonet charge at 4 a.m. that day, pushed forward their line about a mile north of it, several counter-attacks having been repulsed. The Anzacs, sent on from Sheria in company with the Londoners, encountered considerable opposition from strong rearguards, which was finally flattened out next day by a superb charge of the Warwick and the Worcester Yeomanry. Of this splendid episode a War Office communiqué of November 11th stated that a general officer commanding, who was reconnoitring near Huj, nine miles north-east of Gaza, saw a large body of the enemy with guns marching about a mile and a half away in a north-easterly direction, and he ordered the Yeomanry to charge it. The Warwicks and the Worcesters responded at once; notwithstanding an intense fire from "heavies," machine-guns, and rifles, and went forward with a gallantry and dash worthy of the best traditions of British cavalry. Twelve guns were captured, the Austrian crews being killed or wounded, three machine-guns and a hundred prisoners also being taken.

This completely broke the resistance of the Turks, and they abandoned Huj, which had been one of their principal depots. Meanwhile Jemmamch had been occupied; like Huj it was in flames when the British reached it. A smart little affair gave Indian Imperial Service Cavalry Beit Hanum, to which the Turks had extended the railway from Mejdel, and the Scots, who had got across the Wady Hesi and repulsed five strong counter-attacks, took Herbie, higher up the same line. Allenby was now from five to ten miles north of the Gaza-Beersheba position, and his airmen, who had bombed the retreating columns of the

[*British official photograph.*
A CONQUEROR WHO WAS HAILED AS FRIEND.
General Sir Edmund Allenby leaving Jerusalem by the ancient Jaffa Gate, which is known to the Arabs as "The Friend." Its massive iron doors are seldom opened.

Turks, reported that the shattered forces of the enemy were everywhere retiring before him.

While General Allenby was thus prosecuting his victorious advance in Palestine, and General Maude had been playing up to him in Mesopotamia, the British Government dealt the Turks a blow of the deadliest kind, though it was not in the field, but in the region of high international politics, that its effect was felt. In Chapter CXCV. (Vol. 10, page 79) a reference was made to the Hebrew impulse towards the resettlement of the Holy Land which was known as the Zionist Movement, and afterwards a description was given of the sufferings of the Palestine Jews at the hands of the Turks, who were backed up by Germany in this as in **British sympathy** other infamies—such as the massacres of **with Zionism** the Armenians and the Greeks in Asia Minor, and the persecution of the Arabs. Now that the thunder of the British guns might be heard in Jerusalem, the day of reckoning, at least in part, appeared to be approaching, and the thoughts of Jewry throughout the world turned to the ancestral home of the Hebrew race.

It was at this moment that Mr. Balfour, as British Foreign Secretary, addressed to Lord Rothschild, the most prominent of the British Jews and one of their recognised leaders everywhere, a letter conveying, on behalf of the Government, a declaration of sympathy with Jewish Zionist aspirations. This letter said :

His Majesty's Government view with favour the establishment in Palestine of a national home for the Jewish people, and will use

[*French official photograph.*

SUN-SIGNALLING IN SINAI.
Heliographing from a signalling-post in Sinai with comrades who were twenty-five miles away.

their best endeavours to facilitate the achievement of this object, it being clearly understood that nothing shall be done which may prejudice the civil and religious rights of existing non-Jewish communities in Palestine, or the rights and political status enjoyed by Jews in any other country.

Epoch-making was perhaps not too strong a term to apply to this announcement, which attracted universal attention. There were many ways of regarding it. So far as the British Empire was directly concerned, the course of the war had shown that the defence of the Suez Canal was one of its supreme interests, and that it was eminently desirable that Palestine should either be occupied by the British or held by a people who were sincerely friendly to them. And here was enunciated a policy which, at a stroke of the pen, turned the millions of Jews scattered over the globe into friends, as was very evident from the unanimous approval, outside Germany, they gave to it.

This was not the first time that a British Government had shown its sympathy with Jewish national aspirations—though it had never before been in a position to speak as it did now. In previous years it had negotiated with Dr. Theodor Herzl, the great founder of the Zionist Movement, with respect to proposed Jewish settlements at El Arish; and then, when that was found impracticable, in East Africa, though that also was dropped. It now went a great step farther, making in effect an offer of Palestine to the Jewry of the world. That it was playing a trump card was at once seen by the disquietude the letter occasioned in Germany, where the Zionist Movement had many supporters among her influential Jews.

So great an impression did the declaration of the British Government make on the rulers of Germany that they let it be known that, if they won the war, they would go a long way towards inducing Turkey to grant the Jews some form of autonomy in Palestine. But the Jews, as clearsighted a race as any on earth, understood very well what sort of " national home " they would have under a Turco-German régime, and the idea did not entrance them.

There was no mistaking how cordially, how enthusiastically, the Jews as a whole welcomed Mr. Balfour's letter. They hailed it as a veritable triumph. The "Jewish Chronicle," the chief organ of British Jewry, said that amidst all that was dark and tragic in the times there had arisen for the Jews a great light. It declared that the statement of British policy with respect to the future of Palestine was the perceptible lifting of the cloud of centuries, the palpable sign that the Jew, " condemned for two thousand years to unparalleled wrong " was at last coming to his own. He was to be accorded the opportunity and the means whereby, in place of being a " hyphenation, he would become a nation," and that instead of being a wanderer in every clime, there was to be a home for him in his native land. The day of his exile was at an end. This journal also noted that the beginnings of this policy of the British Government were to be found in the negotiations with Dr. Herzl, alluded to previously, and that the developments of the war had merely given that policy a more definite direction.

Palestine for the Jews

It was not only the Jews who acclaimed Great Britain. The Americans in particular, and the peoples of the world in general, not included within the Germanic pale, loudly applauded her. In reply to a question in the House of Commons, Mr. Balfour said that this letter had not been submitted to the other Allies, but he added that he believed that it expressed what they felt in the matter. It was certainly proper that Great Britain

SHADE IN THE DESERT.
Palestine observation-post, where the men on duty had a rustic shelter against the blazing midday sun. Inset : One of the London Yeomanry signallers on outpost duty during the great Palestine advance.

ON SENTRY-GO IN SAND.
Indian soldier on sentry duty in Palestine, armed only with a knife.

should give a lead, for though French and Italian detachments accompanied Allenby's army, that army otherwise was British. The Turks, however, had still to be driven out of the larger part of Palestine, and to that by no means easy task Allenby continued to address himself.

On November 9th the British progressed along the coast, the route taken by Napoleon, and having occupied Ascalon, marched still farther north, operations having reached the stage of a direct pursuit by as many troops as could be supplied so far in front of rail-head. Ascalon, once the principal city of Palestine, and styled the " Bride of Syria," had become not much more than a collection of red-roofed huts, standing amid wells and gardens, and surrounded by the ruins that spoke mournfully of its vanished pride and power. In Biblical times it actually boasted a goddess of its own; much later, under the Seljuks, it was the capital of a province, and issued its own coined money. Famous during the Crusades, Ascalon was taken by Richard Cœur de Lion in January, 1192, but after several changes of rulers it reverted to the Caliphs of Egypt. In the thirteenth century it was destroyed by the great Sultan Baibars, who filled in its harbour. Since that time the invading sands had nearly swallowed it up, and had turned it into a desolation, which its sparse inhabitants with their mean dwellings sharply emphasised. The British entered it unopposed.

The Scots, who had occupied Ascalon, marched on four miles beyond it in pursuit of the enemy's main force, and east of it Allenby's mounted troops swept forward two miles north of Arak el Menshiye, on the central railway, where bodies of Turks from their Hebron line had been gathered together to withstand them. His whole line from the railway to the sea was now from six to ten miles above the Wady Hesi. He estimated that since his offensive had begun the Turks had suffered ten thousand casualties, not counting five thousand men they had lost as prisoners. He reported that the guns captured numbered well over seventy, including several 5·9 in. howitzers, and that the other booty was immense, but could not be detailed owing to the size of the battlefield, its area being about six hundred square miles in extent. On November 10th his men were in the

neighbourhood of Esdud, the ancient Ashdod, whose walls were demolished by King Uzziah (2 Chronicles xxvi.), and the Turks were preparing to make a stand on the north side of the Wady Sukereir, the mouth of which was about four miles beyond the town. At the same time his cavalry and infantry on the eastern flank were advancing towards Hebron.

Operations on November 10th and 11th had shown a stiffening of the enemy's resistance on the general line of the Wady Sukereir, with its centre about El Kustine. The Hebron groups had retired north-east of Arak el Menshiye, and prolonged the enemy's line towards Beit Jibrin. In newly-dug trenches on the farther bank of the wady fifteen thousand men were assembled to attempt to stay the British. The wady, with its steep banks, was in itself a considerable obstacle, but neither that natural difficulty nor the determined efforts of the Turkish

CAMEL TRANSPORT.
Egyptian native employed to look after the camel transport animals under British supervision.

AT AN O.P. IN THE HILLS.
Punjabi observer at his post on the Palestine front during the advance.

soldiers, who, as usual, fought stoutly in defence, held up the advance. Allenby spent the 12th in preparations for the attack, which was set for early next morning. His forces were now operating at a distance of some thirty-five miles beyond his rail-head, and the bringing up and distribution of supplies formed a difficult problem, but it was overcome.

There was trouble, too, about water, which also did not prove insuperable. The troops even succeeded in getting forward two heavy batteries in support of the attack. Never in the world were men more willing than Allenby's, more eager to get at the enemy. On the morning of the 13th the Turkish position, with some twenty miles of front, stretched from El Kubeibeh on the north to the vicinity of Beit Jibrin on the south. The right half of it was roughly parallel to and only about five miles in front of the junction of the branch from Jerusalem with the central railway, which was the enemy's main line of supply from the north. It was on this junction that Allenby had his eye.

Making a combined assault with his mounted troops and infantry, Allenby drove the enemy from the wady, and forced him to retreat to the Wady es Surar, eight miles south of Jaffa. During the 12th the Yeomanry had pushed north up the left bank of the Sukereir, and had

A PRIZED TROPHY.
Australian mounted troopers holding up on their bayonet points a Turkish flag captured by them in Palestine.

seized Tel el Murreh, on the right bank near its mouth. The Scots were close to Burka on the preceding day. On the 12th the Anzacs were pressing forward towards Balin, Berkusie, and Tel es Safi, on the east of the railway. On the 13th the British were on the move, and the attack on the Turks became general. The terrain was open and rolling, dotted with small villages, whose mud walls were surrounded with plantations of trees. The chief feature of the landscape was a ridge on which stood the villages of Katrah (Cedron) and El Mughar, and the Turks had formed it into a strong position.

There was a tremendous struggle first at Burkah, which proved an extremely hard nut to crack. It had been well fortified, and consisted of two lines of perfectly-sited trenches, one behind the other, and about a thousand yards apart. One had to be attacked up a glacis, and then came a stretch of absolutely flat ground leading up to the glacis of the second. The business was efficiently attended to by two Edinburgh and two Rifle battalions. In face of a strong fire the Riflemen swept the foe out of the first line. The Edinburgh men co-operated on the flank, and took a height called Brown Hill, but, twice counter-attacked by very large masses, had to give it up for a while. Going back with Gurkha reinforcements, they quickly had it again. Next the second line of enemy trenches was carried in magnificent style, and the field was strewn with Turkish dead.

Then South-Western County troops and Scots went on to a point eight miles north of Esdud, and from it assaulted

OUSTED FROM POSSESSION.
Turkish troops outside the Church of the Holy Sepulchre preparing to march out of Jerusalem before General Allenby's victorious advance, with a view to taking up a position farther north.

Katrah and El Mughar, these two isolated villages on their rocky eminences standing well out of the plain. In front of the native village of Katrah lay a Jewish settlement, well built and prosperous, and an excellent example of what the Zionist Movement had done and might do for the country. Katrah was admirably suited for defence. Of the action Mr. Massey wrote :

North of Mughar Hill there is a hill with a double crest, just behind which is Sugar Loaf Hill. While the attack was in progress, Yeomanry from two Thames-side counties, and one Southern County regiment, got to Yebna—the Jabneel of Joshua and Uzziah, the latter of whom took it from the Philistines—a big village on the west, between which and Mughar lies a big plain intersected by a wady. The Yeomen galloped across the plain with no cover at all, and got on the Sugar Loaf. Their charge to this position in succeeding waves furnished a spectacle rarely seen in this war. While the Scots were routing out a nest of machine-gunners in a pretty clump of cypresses surrounded by cactus, the Yeomen, under gun and rifle fire, crept over the Sugar Loaf to the double-topped hill, and distracted the Turks' attention a good deal from the Scots' attack. The latter rushed forward and cleared the whole place. The Turks, hemmed in on all sides, were driven into the valley, and fourteen hundred prisoners, twenty-eight machine-guns, and three field-guns were handed over to the Yeomen, of whose assistance the Scots speak highly. They also gave high credit to the West Country English troops, who, during the attack on Burkah, swung round at an opportune moment and threatened the enemy left, a highly creditable movement on the part of the brigadier.

How severe was the fighting in these brisk encounters was shown by the fact that at Katrah the British buried four hundred Turkish corpses. More important than· any of these successes, fine as they were, was that Allenby was all the while closing his grip on the enemy's railway system. On November 13th El Tineh was in his hands. This place was the junction with the central railway of the branch through El Mejdel to Beit Hanum, near Gaza. The Australians took it, with many prisoners, one gun, three aeroplanes, much ammunition, and quantities of stores. At its capture over a thousand Turks were seen looting these stores, but an armoured car swiftly ran in among them, and, killing and wounding a great number, scattered the rest over the plain.

Next day Allenby got possession of the railway in the neighbourhood of Naaneh and Mansura, and occupied the junction with the central railway of the line from Jerusalem, thus cutting off the last named from all communication by rail with Damascus and Aleppo, where it was rumoured that Falkenhayn was concentrating an army for the protection of the Holy City, the fall of which was now seen to be well within the region of probabilities. If the Turkish Army in Palestine, supposed to be at least 150,000 strong, had not been destroyed, it had been very thoroughly beaten, and had lost about 25,000 men, of whom nearly 10,000 were prisoners. But with Mesopotamia also on his hands, Falkenhayn did not appear to be able to despatch very large reinforcements to the Palestine front, however much they were wanted there. With the railway now impossible, his easiest route for supplies was the road from the north through Shechem (the modern Nablus) into Jerusalem, towards which, in the south-east, the British, having captured Dhaheriyah, were also advancing by way of Hebron.

There was no pause so far in Allenby's advance. His operations had broken the Turkish army into two separated parts, which retired north and east respectively. On November 15th his troops—Scots, West Countrymen, and cavalry—marched on up between the railway and the coast, occupied Ramleh and Lydda, and along the shore came within three miles of Jaffa. Lydda, otherwise Ludd, was the reputed birthplace of St. George, the patron saint of England. On that day the heaviest fighting took place at the Abu Shusheh Ridge, near the ancient Gazer, a few miles southeast of Ramleh, whence had run a branch railway to Jaffa which had been pulled up by the Turks. The ridge was the scene of another magnificent charge of the British Yeomanry—one of several such charges,

HADJI GULIELMO OUTSIDE JERUSALEM.
Mr. Spencer Leigh Hughes, M.P., who witnessed the Kaiser's arrival in Jerusalem in 1898, wrote: "The Kaiser had arrayed himself like a Crusader as seen in pantomime—helmet, silk robe, and the other usual trappings for the part."

and all of them marked by effectiveness no less than by dash. Galloping up a steep slope, heedless of violent machine-gun fire, the Home Counties Yeomen stormed the ridge, sabring four hundred of the enemy, and capturing three hundred and sixty men and a gun. The tale of prisoners was ever mounting up. At Lydda the Anzacs took three hundred Turks, as well as four machineguns. On the 16th Allenby's line was pushed forward a little, and in the evening of the same day the Anzacs entered Jaffa, which they found had been evacuated by the Turks.

Jaffa, the seaport of Jerusalem, was the ancient Joppa, from which the prophet Jonah embarked on his wonderful voyage, and early in the Middle Ages pilgrims were shown at Joppa, as others had been for centuries before that, the bones of a gigantic monster which were said to be those of Jonah's "whale." The town figured often both in the Old and in the New Testament, and had a great place in the story of the Crusades. Before the war it had a population of about 50,000, and was famous for its oranges. Along the coast from it stretched the Plain of Sharon as far as Cæsarea, and all about it were vineyards and orange groves. On its east side the groves had been thinned for firewood, but on the south side whole plantations had been wantonly uprooted. The retreating

THEATRICAL ENTRY OF THE KAISER INTO JERUSALEM ON HIS "PERSONALLY-CONDUCTED" TOUR, IN 1898.
Messrs. Thomas Cook arranged the tour which the Kaiser and Kaiserin made in Palestine in 1898. On October 29th the Kaiser entered Jerusalem through a breach in the wall near the Jaffa Gate which had been specially made. "This curious specimen of a pilgrim entered the Holy City armed to the teeth, escorted by troops, with Turkish police thrashing out of the way such natives as had drawn near."

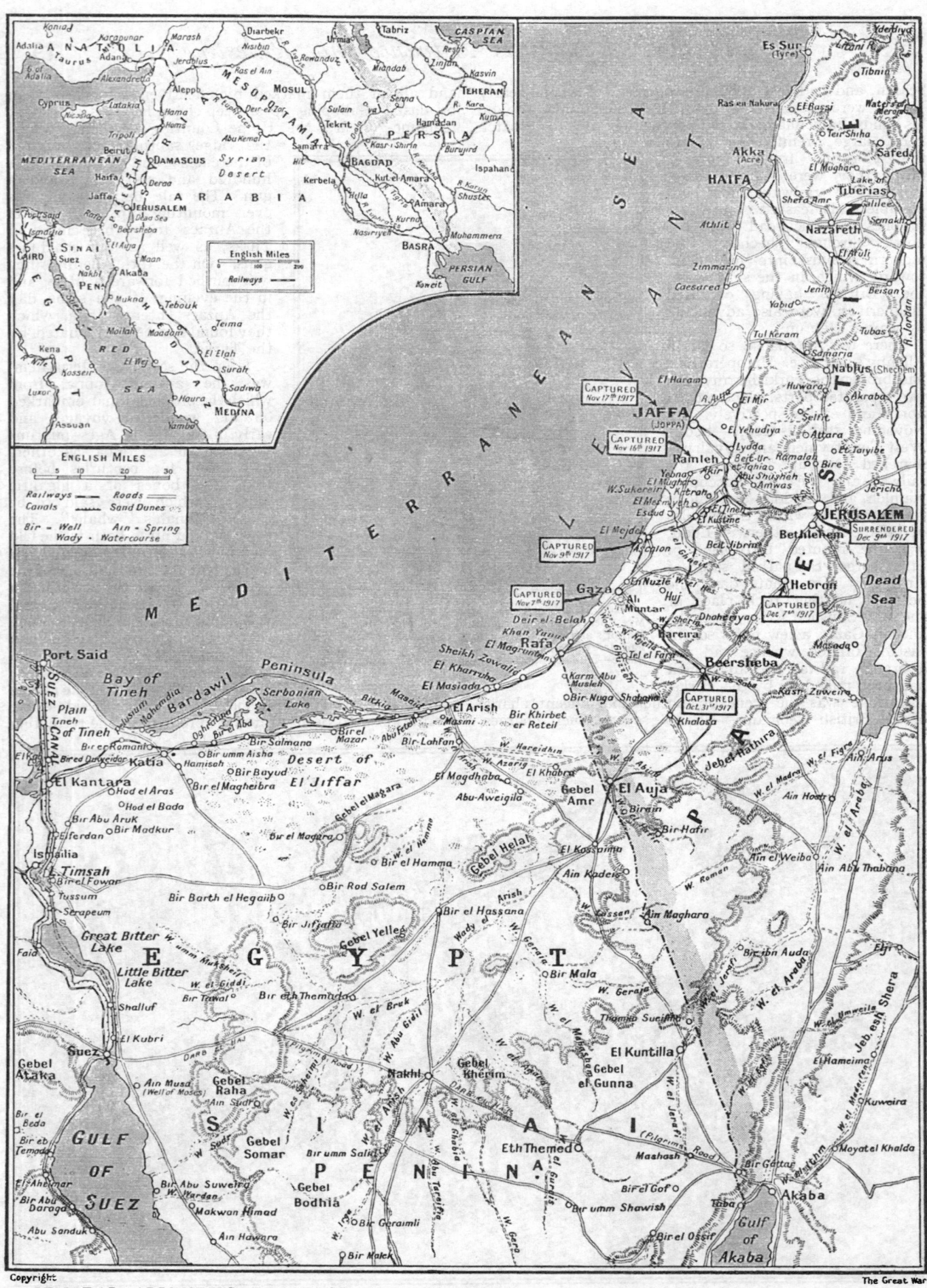

GENERAL ALLENBY'S PROGRESS FROM BEERSHEBA TO THE CAPTURE OF JERUSALEM.

On this map are shown the places taken by the forces of Sir Edmund Allenby during his triumphant advance from the capture of Beersheba on October 31st, 1917, to the surrender of Jerusalem on December 9th, less than six weeks later. The small inset map shows the relation of the area of the Palestine fighting with the Hedjaz to the south and with Mesopotamia to the north-east.

Turks, however, did not try to destroy the town, in which were a few Europeans when the Anzacs entered it. Jaffa had a rock-girt harbour, which, from its small size, was suitable only for ships of slight tonnage, large vessels having to lie outside. The place was prosperous. It was the commercial centre of the Zionists in Palestine, several of whose settlements were only a few miles away. It was also the home of a German colony, with the usual propaganda activities. In Jaffa, as elsewhere throughout the occupied territory, the British were welcomed by the native inhabitants, and in the markets and bazaars business went on with hardly an interruption and in largely increased volume, the merchants quickly realising that they received from the new-comers hard cash in exchange for their goods, instead of the much depreciated currency notes which the Turks had forced upon them.

Turning now his chief attention from the Plain of Philistia, Allenby struck out eastwards in the direction of Jerusalem. The character of the terrain changed from undulating sandy or cultivated ground to steep foot-hills and rocky mountains, with a general absence of roads. Transport was difficult, but rains, long overdue, fell at this time, and lightened the problem of the water supply, though they made the going heavy and temporarily impossible in some localities, great pools accumulating in the nullahs, which turned into streams and flooded the surrounding country. Marching into the hills of Judea, Yeomanry and West Country and Scottish soldiers drove forward the enemy over a boulder-strewn region by persistent attacks with the bayonet. On November 18th the mounted troops, moving through the hills, occupied Beit-Ur-et-Tahia, twelve miles north-west of Jerusalem, and also held Shilta, which lay a short distance north-west of the former place. Beit-Ur-et-Tahia, the Arabic form of Beth Horon the Lower, was on the northern road, which was not much better than a mountain track, from Jaffa to Jerusalem, Beit - Ur - el - Foka, otherwise Upper Beth Horon, being two miles farther to the east. Beth Horon was the scene of Joshua's great battle with the five kings of the Amorites, in the course of which he cried: "Sun, stand thou still on Gibeon, and thou, moon, in the Valley of Ajalon!" Rising to a height of 2,500 feet, the Highlands of Judea began about fifteen miles west of Jerusalem, to which the branch railway passed through the narrow valley of the Wady es Sikkeh. The only good road was the main road from Jaffa to the Holy City, and by it the infantry advanced on November 19th.

In his despatch of December 16th General Allenby explained the situation **Securing the** at this time. The Turkish army, which **British position** had been cut in two by his capture of the railway junction, had retired partly east into the hills in the direction of Jerusalem, and partly north along the coastal plain. The nearest line on which these two portions could unite was that of Tul Keram-Shechem, and the reports of Allenby's airmen indicated that it probably was the enemy's intention to evacuate Jerusalem and withdraw to reorganise on that line. The Commander-in-Chief considered that before the British position in the plain could be regarded as secure it was essential to obtain a hold on the one good road which traversed the

hills from south to north—that from Jerusalem to Shechem—and he, therefore, struck towards it. For a time he stopped his advance in the plain at the Nahr el Auja, and, meanwhile, his engineers were constructing with all possible rapidity the railway northwards through Gaza, so as to give him the necessary supplies, only a part of which could reach him by sea, and that not with certainty owing to the fluctuations of the weather.

Having captured Latron and Amwas **Advance along** on the morning of November 19th, **the main road** the infantry marched along the main Jaffa-Jerusalem road to the Bab el Wad, where they entered a narrow defile which continued for about four miles to Saris. There the road had been blown up in several places by the Turks in their retreat, and the rest of the day was spent in making repairs to enable the troops to reach Saris, which was defended by Turkish rearguards.

On the 20th Kuryet el Enab, farther along the road, and only about six miles from Jerusalem, was carried at the point of the bayonet by the Somersets, Wiltshires, and Gurkhas, notwithstanding organised opposition.

TRANSPORT BY TRYING WAYS.
Hurrying up shells for the guns during the Palestine advance. The horses dragging the limbers along the difficult ground of a sandy wady—or dried-up river-bed—were passing a convoy of ammunition-laden camels halted in the sheltered wady for rest.

In order to avoid any fighting in the close vicinity of the Holy City, Allenby gave instructions to some of the infantry to swing north from Kuryet el Enab towards Bire by a track leading through Biddu, and these were carried out on the following day. In all this storied region a particular interest attached to Kuryet el Enab, for it was the Kirjath Jearim of the Bible, the place where the Ark rested for twenty years before it was removed to Jerusalem. It was also towards Bire that the cavalry were marching, and on November 20th they were in contact with the enemy four miles west of that village, which was situated on the road from Jerusalem to Shechem, and, standing on a hill nearly three thousand feet high, was about nine miles north of the city. By the afternoon of the next day their advanced parties were within two miles of the road, and an attack was being delivered by other mounted troops on Beitunia, where there had been heavy fighting on the 20th. Counter-attacked by much superior forces, they fell back, after a bitter struggle, on Beit-Ur-el-Foka.

Meanwhile the infantry, moving up from Kuryet el Enab, had stormed the Neby Samwil (Prophet Samuel) Ridge, one of the highest points in Palestine, the site of the

AT THE POOLS OF SOLOMON.
One of the most important links in the ancient and modern water supply of Jerusalem, which has always depended mainly on artificial reservoirs to which water is brought from a distance.

ancient Mizpah, and only about five thousand yards from the Shechem road. Mizpah was the scene of the covenant of reconciliation between Jacob and Laban, and afterwards was a place of national assembly for the Tribes of Israel. The Turks bombarded the mosque which contained, according to tradition, the tomb of Samuel, which the British gunners had carefully refrained from shelling.

From the top of the ridge the British obtained their first glimpse of the Holy City, and their hopes ran high. Jerusalem seemed almost within an arm's grasp. But the Turks made a great effort to retain it, and more than a fortnight had to elapse before they were compelled to relinquish it. All the world knew that its fall was imminent, and all the world was watching and discussing what was going on. Germany, through **First view of** her Press, was doing her utmost to mini- **Jerusalem** mise the successes of the British both in Palestine and Mesopotamia. The "Cologne Gazette" said that those in the former sensibly affected and probably threatened with ruin the German colonies in the region that had been overrun, but it prophesied that the many obstacles that lay before Allenby in his path to Jerusalem would prove insurmountable. His advance so far had gone well, because it had been covered by a powerful squadron from the sea; let him but once get away from the protection of the warships, and there would be an entire change of the situation.

Yet it was plain from German journals, published a day or two later, that great uneasiness was beginning to be felt as to the fate of the Holy City. It was reported that the Kaiser had summoned a conference of his leading generals to consider what might be done to save it. Next the German people were prepared for what was about to take place by being told that as Jerusalem was not equipped for defence it might be necessary to abandon it —"a painful loss," said the "North German Gazette,"

in an editorial, "in view of the city's great historical past, but no military change would thereby be caused." The whole German Press lined up—or, rather, was lined up, for it was in the hands of the German Government—to point out that the fall of Jerusalem did not in the least alter the general war situation, which, it asseverated, was unmistakably favourable to Germany, and that if the Turks lost the place the damage done would be far more a matter of sentiment than of anything else. One or two independent writers, however, did admit that the capture of Jerusalem, coming after the taking of Bagdad, would be a serious blow to the Turks and the "Islamic cause." A well-known German professor confessed in an article in the "Kreuzzeitung" that the situation in Palestine was grave, and said that the real question at issue was whether England or Turkey was to rule over the Moslem world.

Stirred to further efforts, doubtless by Germany, the Turks now endeavoured to check the British advance, and not without a certain measure of success. They made a strong stand along **More obstinate** the whole line from the Nahr el Auja, **Turkish resistance** four miles above Jaffa, all the way to Jerusalem, on the high ground west of which they concentrated large forces with powerful artillery. On November 22nd they made two strong counter-attacks on the Neby Samwil Ridge, but both failed. On the 23rd and 24th, however, the advantage lay with them. Determined and gallant assaults on their positions to the west of the Shechem road by the British were ineffective. The enemy, who had been reinforced and had many machine-guns, was able to get support for his infantry from heavy guns placed on the Shechem road, whereas the lack of roads on their side prevented the British artillery from coming up to help their infantry, who had to fall back. "It was evident that a period of preparation and organisation

AT THE POOL OF SILOAM.
Stone steps lead down to the reservoir called the Pool of Siloam, which is filled with waters of Gihon brought along an underground conduit tunnelled by Hezekiah in preparation for the siege by Sennacherib.

would be necessary," said Allenby in his despatch of December 16th, " before an attack could be delivered in sufficient strength to drive the enemy from his positions west of the road."

On November 26th the War Office announced that Allenby's advanced patrols, who were on the north bank of the Wady Auja, had been pressed back to its south side. It also stated that his mounted troops had captured Bittir Station, seven miles by the branch railway west by south of Jerusalem, and Ain Karim (Miriam's Well), between Bittir and the Emmaus road into Jerusalem. On the 29th another War Office communiqué said there was no change in the situation in Palestine, but Turkish official telegrams, which were allowed to be published, made it known that the British had been repulsed in the centre near the Shechem road, as well as at the Auja. In the Turkish Parliament the Minister of War declared that the contest was turning against the British, and that the Turkish position was safe. But he was utterly mistaken.

The Judean foot-hills secured   Allenby issued orders to consolidate the positions gained, and to wait for reinforcements. He rightly pointed out that, though his final objectives had not been achieved at the time, invaluable results had been obtained. The narrow passes into the hills of Judea had rarely been forced, and had been fatal to many invading armies. His swift advance, which had been pressed with such determination, had, however, deprived the enemy of the advantages which would have accrued to him had he been given the opportunity of fortifying these defiles. As it was, the British had won positions in this difficult country, from which another attack that was likely to be successful could be prepared and delivered. In the first week of December Allenby's reliefs in men, guns, and supplies were well forward. Existing roads and tracks had been

OUTSIDE THE GOLDEN GATE.
About Jerusalem's Golden Gate many legends have been told. It is said to have been through it that Christ made His triumphal entry. An old Syrian belief was that when a victorious enemy entered the city by this gate the Turkish Empire would collapse.

greatly improved, and new ones were constructed. The water supply had also been developed. In the meantime the Turks delivered several assaults, but these neither delayed the Commander-in-Chief's preparations nor made any impression on his line ; on the contrary, it was the enemy who suffered materially.

From November 27th to November 30th the Turks were very active on Allenby's front on the high ground north and north-east of Jaffa, on his flank about Beit-Ur-el-Foka, and on the Neby Samwil Ridge. On the night of the 29th the enemy got into an outpost north-east of Jaffa ; but next morning the hostile detachment, numbering one hundred and fifty men, was rounded up and captured by Australian Light Horse. Particularly heavy fighting took place between Beit-Ur-el-Foka and El Burj. Close to the latter village the Scottish Lowland troops   **Sharp fighting at Beth Horon** once more gave an example of their quality by storming a boulder-strewn ridge, which was well fortified. Despite a strong fire that swept through their ranks, they charged up the steep hillsides, and killed, made prisoner, or put to headlong flight every Turk in the place. Near Beit-Ur-el-Foka, which was the scene of bitter combats, Cheshire, Shropshire, and Welsh regiments assailed the enemy in most difficult ground, and thoroughly defeated him, one company taking three hundred prisoners.

One episode vastly redounded to the credit of the Welsh Yeomen. Ordered to take Foka itself, a hamlet on a hill with almost precipitous sides, a company worked round the height, and just as darkness was falling reached the summit, where they found five hundred Turks under a German officer. The Turks laid down their arms and were standing-to when the German, observing the small numbers of the attacking force, shouted " Fire ! Fire ! " to his men, some of whom picked up their rifles and began

IN THE PROMISED LAND.
Mizpah, with Jacob's Pillar of stone, captured in the course of General Allenby's victorious campaign in Palestine. From the rocky coign a wonderfully beautiful view is afforded across the valley.

fighting. Seeing that there was no surrender, as they had supposed, the Welshmen fired indiscriminately into the mass, and for a few minutes there was a fierce and terrible struggle in the small square and little streets of Foka.

The German officer was then bayoneted and killed, as were many of the Turks. The remainder, though four times more numerous than their opponents, had had enough by that time, and gave up.

With weapons changed, this desperate affair might have belonged to the days of the Berserkers and the Vikings. The enemy tried more than once with large forces to recapture the Neby Samwil Ridge, which he felt as a very sharp thorn in his side, but he did not succeed. His most serious attempt on the ridge developed on November 29th, but it was beaten back with comparative ease.

The Turkish artillery, manned by Germans and Austrians, again took as their target the mosque over Samuel's Tomb, a site held in equal reverence by Christian, Jew, and Mohammedan, and after destroying its minaret, reduced it to ruins.

In these various encounters the enemy's casualties were heavy, his loss in prisoners alone being seven hundred and fifty between November 27th and November 30th.

By the end of the first week of December, Allenby was fully ready for the final attack on Jerusalem. His heavy artillery was shelling Beitunia, which covered the enemy's line of retreat from the city by the Shechem road. His airmen, who had been most useful throughout the campaign, were doing good service both in bombing enemy positions and forces and in carrying out observations, to the effectiveness of all of which operations a spell of favourable weather

BRINGING THE TURK TO HIS KNEES.
After the capture of the stronghold of Gaza, General Allenby gave the Turks no rest. They fought stubborn rearguard actions, but these were defeated by Australian and New Zealand mounted troops and by English Yeomanry, who relentlessly pursued the retreating foe and rounded up stragglers in hundreds.

at this juncture greatly contributed. In contests in the air his machines almost invariably proved their superiority over those of the Turks.

On his far right flank Allenby was moving up. Welsh troops, supported by cavalry, advanced from their positions north of Beersheba, on December 4th, and without opposition occupied Hebron, the "City of Abraham, the Friend of God," which lay nineteen miles almost due south of Jerusalem.

For some little time nothing of importance had occurred in this quarter. **British troops occupy Hebron** Patrols had kept working northward from Dhaheriyah in touch with the Turks, whom the pressure west and south-west on Jerusalem had caused to withdraw altogether from Hebron—it was a sign that the end approached. Hebron had played its part in ancient history, but it had long been an insignificant town. In its Cave of Machpelah, Abraham, Isaac, and Jacob were buried, and the Oak of Mamre was still pointed out north of the place, though the tree shown was probably a descendant of the original under whose branches the Patriarch encamped. One of the six Hebrew cities of refuge, Hebron was the temporary capital and military base of King David when he was making ready to capture Jerusalem. And now another soldier, of a people that was not even in existence in the days of David, was about to consummate a similar enterprise.

From Hebron Allenby's troops marched up the road towards Jerusalem, their aim being to reach the line of Bethlehem-Beit Jala by December 7th, and that of Sur Bahir-Sufafa, close to the Holy City on the south, on the following day.

CLEARING THE WAY FOR THE ADVANCE.
British skirmishing line going forward over captured ground during General Allenby's advance towards Jerusalem. The skirmishers looked carefully for any lurking foe as, with rifles ready for instant use, they spread in a thin line across the country ahead of the main force.

On the 7th, however, the weather broke, and rain fell with hardly any intermission for three days in the Judean Hills, which were swathed in mists that rendered air observation and visual signalling impossible. The roads became impassable in some localities, and very difficult in others, thus jeopardising the forwarding of supplies. All this meant a retardation along the whole line from east to west of Allenby's attack, and he arranged to protect his right, in case of its movement south and east of Jerusalem being delayed, as turned out to be the fact. On the rest of his front, west of the city, his troops assembled in their assigned positions on the night of the 7th, and the first stage of the great assault was begun at dawn next morning, notwithstanding the bad weather, by the Londoners and dismounted Yeomanry.

The Yeomen, with their pivot on Neby Samwil, secured their objective early, though their task was extremely arduous. It was to take a system of very strong works in and about the Beit Iksa spur, in face of the concentrated fire of field-guns and many machine-guns, accurately operated by German and Austrian artillerymen. But the brave Yeomen pushed right on through the storm of shells and bullets, took the spur, and captured **Yeomen capture** the village of Beit Hannina, with two **Beit Hannina** hundred prisoners falling into their hands.

The Londoners, who were fighting south of the Jaffa road, assailed a series of defences, equally strong by nature and military artifice, which swept Ain Karim and Deir Yesin with its guns. One brigade made a frontal assault, while another turned the enemy's position by mounting up a spur south-west of the village of Ain Karim. The troops of the latter brigade had first to get down a precipitous hillside into a deep vale, and then had to climb the spur to the Turkish trenches. They were equipped with picks, and made paths as they went along. And all the while they were under heavy fire. When they got to the enemy's first trenches they found a battalion of Turks in possession of them, and after sharp fighting, drove it out, and held the ground thus gained. Then the two brigades combined, and together stormed the main line of works, and by seven o'clock in the morning this whole enemy system was captured. Mr. Massey described what took place next:

From this position the ground rises very steeply to a sharp ridge, covered with large boulders, on which the Jewish colony stands. The turning brigade was unable to get right round, as it

was heavily shelled by a Turkish battery south of Jerusalem in a position quite close to the Holy City. It was impossible to find positions for our field-guns on this steep ground, but two howitzers were brought up with infinite labour, and at four o'clock in the afternoon the brigade making the frontal attack fixed bayonets, and all the battalions charged the ridge and carried it by a gallant rush after a strong fight, the Turks leaving many dead on the field.

As Allenby's right wing, which had been marching towards Jerusalem by the Hebron road, had been delayed, and was still some distance to the south of the city, it became necessary for the Londoners to throw back their right and form a defensive flank facing east towards Jerusalem, from the western outskirts of which considerable rifle and artillery fire was being experienced. This hindered the general advance on the west, and in the

AID FOR A TANK.
Digging out a Tank which had got badly wedged in an awkward bit of ground during the Palestine advance.

afternoon Allenby decided to consolidate the line which had been gained and resume the movement next day, when the right wing would be in a position to exert its weight. By nightfall the British line ran from Neby Samwil, to the east of Beit Iksa, through Lifta, to a point about a mile and a half west of the Holy City, whence it was thrown back facing east. All of the enemy's prepared defences west and north-west of Jerusalem had been taken, and Allenby's troops were within a short distance of the Shechem-Jerusalem road. The Londoners and the Yeomen had displayed wonderful endurance. The former especially had done very well, as, after a night march in pouring rain to reach their

ON TANK REDOUBT AT GAZA.
A Tank which caught fire during the second attack on Gaza had to be left, and gave its name to a redoubt which changed hands several times before the British finally secured it. The Turks had made use of the stranded monster as a machine-gun and observation post.

PALESTINE RE-WON BY THE NEW CRUSADERS.
Map of the southern portion of Palestine, illustrating the advance of Sir Edmund Allenby from the Gaza-Beersheba line to Jaffa and Jerusalem during his victorious campaign in the closing months of 1917.

positions of deployment, they had made an advance of from three to four miles in difficult hills, though confronted by the most stubborn opposition. In the course of the day some three hundred Turks were made prisoner, and a vast number of them killed, while the casualties of the British were light.

When the advance was resumed on the following morning it was soon discovered that the Turks had withdrawn from Jerusalem during the night. The Londoners and the Yeomanry, after driving back rearguards, cut the Shechem road four miles north of the city, and the Welshmen, who had come up, cut the Jericho road, thus isolating Jerusalem. The Welshmen in their march had taken Bethlehem, that little town of infinitely sacred associations being left unharmed.

Surrender of Jerusalem There was a Turkish battery firing at them close by, but they made no reply, for fear of touching one stone of the holy place. They also occupied the Mount of Olives. Then they stretched out eastward in the direction of the Jericho road, but were held up awhile by fog and by the state of the roads, which the enemy had blown up. When they moved on again they drove the Turks down the Jericho road and joined hands with the Yeomanry from the Shechem road. At noon a parlementaire came out of Jerusalem and surrendered it to General Allenby.

The Holy City was undamaged. As King George phrased it in a message of congratulation, which he immediately despatched to the victorious Commander-in-Chief on hearing that Jerusalem had been taken: "By skilful dispositions you have preserved intact the Holy Places." Mr. Bonar Law, in announcing the capture

to the House of Commons, said that the event had been in some degree delayed in consequence of the great care which had been exercised to avoid damage to sacred places in and round the city. The Turks, too, claimed to have respected Jerusalem, for their communiqué which admitted the loss said that, as the British had succeeded in pushing their attack as far as the outskirts, they transferred their own troops from the west and south of the city to the east of it. The fact, however, stood forth that they had been forced out of Jerusalem after having been very badly mauled, and that their prestige had received a shattering blow. It was stated in Parliament that precautions were taken at once against disturbances on the transfer of the city from the Turks, a British political officer and a British governor, accompanied by British, French, Italian, and Indian Mohammedan guards, being sent to safeguard all the Holy Places of the three faiths.

That Jerusalem had been reft from the Turk caused the most unbounded rejoicing among the Allies and throughout all Christendom, save in such part of it as was Germanic. The Pope expressed his satisfaction, though not till some time after the event. As already indicated, there were millions on millions of Mohammedans who were opposed to Turkey, and they, too, rejoiced that the city which had its Holy Places for them, as for Christians and Jews, had been taken from her. The King of the Hedjaz, who had been co-operating with Allenby by repeatedly raiding the Hedjaz Railway, sent his congratulations, as did other Moslem princes and notables. All Jewry was glad. The Chief Rabbi of London said the good

MODERN SURVEYING FROM AN ANCIENT SITE.
British military map-maker at work in Palestine on the site of an Early Christian temple that had been part of a Turkish fort. On the right a seated artist was making sketches of the tessellated pavement.

news that Jerusalem, which for ages had been the magnetic pole of the love and the reverence of the world, was in the possession of the British had reached the Jews on the very day when, two thousand and seventy years before, the Maccabees had freed the Holy City from the heathen oppressor, thereby changing the spiritual future of humanity. "Who knows," he added, "but that to-day's victory may form as glorious a landmark in the history of mankind."

German comment naturally was acid, but it had to admit Allenby's success, though it found some comfort in frequently repeating the opinion that his triumph was moral far more than military. Yet there was no gainsaying the truth that the fall of Jerusalem, whatever might be thought of its military importance, marked a further stage in a singularly

BRITISH AIRMEN ATTACK TURKISH INFANTRY.
Again and again the British flying men gave a good account of themselves during the fighting in Palestine. On more than one occasion airmen on bomb-dropping outings discovered masses of Turkish troops and dispersed them with bombs and machine-gun fire.

brilliant and swift campaign, which had already cost the Turks very heavy losses, including over 12,000 prisoners and more than a hundred guns of various calibres, with twenty million rounds of rifle ammunition and a quarter of a million rounds of gun ammunition. Within seven weeks Southern Palestine had been conquered and Jerusalem taken, in spite of the most determined resistance and difficulties of every kind. It was hard, moreover, to imagine anything more mortifying to the pride of the German Kaiser than that the Holy City should be in British hands. It was impossible not to recall his entry into it in 1898, when, arrayed in helmet and robes, like a Crusader, and amid the blare of trumpets in its beflagged streets, he posed as the Envoy of Allah and the Protector of Islam, albeit the arrangements for his trip to Palestine had been made by Cook's Tourist Agency. In striking contrast was the entry of General Allenby into Jerusalem, which took place two days after the surrender, and was as simple and dignified as the other had been theatrical and vainglorious.

"A purely military act with a minimum of military display," was an apt phrase which characterised Allenby's

appearance in Jerusalem as the victor. He entered the city officially at noon on December 11th, and he entered it on foot, with a few of his Staff, the commanders of the French and Italian detachments, and the Military Attachés of France, Italy, and the United States of America. At the Jaffa Gate he was received by guards representing England, Scotland, Ireland, Wales, Australia, New Zealand, India, France, and Italy. Near the gate, which the Arabs called "The Friend," was the breach in the walls made for the Kaiser's entry nearly twenty years before. Allenby went in by the gate itself, which tradition reserved for conquerors. No thunderous salutes acclaimed the victor. No flag was hoisted, and none was pulled down; but the people, happy to be delivered from the thraldom of the Turk, welcomed him most joyfully. The procession proceeded through the Zion quarter to the citadel. From the steps of the Tower of David, which was standing when Christ was in Jerusalem, a proclamation was read in Arabic, Hebrew, English, French, Italian, Greek, and Russian announcing that the city was placed under martial law for as long a time as military considerations made it necessary, but also stating that the inhabitants were to pursue their lawful occupations without fear of interference. Allenby further proclaimed:

Allenby's proclamation

Since your city is regarded with affection by the adherents of three of the great religions of mankind, and its soil has been consecrated by the prayers and pilgrimages of multitudes of devout people of these three religions for many centuries, therefore do I make known to you that every sacred building, monument, holy spot, shrine, traditional site, endowment, pious bequest, or customary place of prayer, of whatsoever form of the three religions, will be maintained and protected according to the existing customs and beliefs of those to whose faith they are sacred.

Thus was Jerusalem given its charter of deliverance, while British guns were in action on the north and east of the city, from which the enemy was being driven farther and farther away.

CHARGE OF BRITISH YEOMANRY IN PALESTINE.
While carrying out a reconnaissance through difficult country broken by watercourses and ravines, a squadron of British Yeomanry was attacked by Turkish infantry. The Yeomanry charged into the enemy, killing and wounding half of them and capturing the rest.

BRITISH PATROLS ENTER GAZA AFTER THE FINAL SUCCESSFUL ATTACK.

It was on November 7th, 1917, that the second stage in Sir Edmund Allenby's victorious advance was marked by his capture of Gaza, Beersheba having been secured on October 31st. Gaza had already been the scene of considerable fighting, and the Turkish defences had been greatly strengthened after the earlier inconclusive battles for the place. When General Allenby began his attack on the Turkish line his initial success compelled the enemy to evacuate Gaza, but much fighting took place between the first British forces to enter the town and snipers and machine-gunners who were covering the Turkish retreat.

H.M. DRIFTER FLEET

CHAPTER CCXXVIII.

UNDER FULL STEAM.

[British official photograph.

THE GLORIOUS WAR RECORD OF THE ROYAL NAVAL RESERVE.

By Percival A. Hislam.

Historic Mutual Interdependence of the Navy and the Mercantile Marine—The Tudor Navy—Establishment of a Permanently Enlisted Force of Petty Officers and Men in the Mid-Nineteenth Century—Drafting System at Naval Depots—Organisation of the Royal Naval Reserve in 1859—Qualifications for Commissions in the R.N.R.—Mobilisation of the R.N.R., August 3rd, 1914—Enthusiastic Response of the Mercantile Marine to the Call for Volunteers—How Captain Kinneir, of the Ortega, Successfully Defied the Karls-ruhe—Duel Between the Carmania and the Cap Trafalgar—And Between the Alcantara and the Greif—Work of the Auxiliary Patrol—Special Service against German Submarines—The Victoria Cross Awarded to Lieutenant R. N. Stuart, R.N.R., Seaman William Williams, R.N.R., Lieutenant C. G. Bonner, and Skipper Thomas Crisp—General Services of the R.N.R. the Wide World Over—Mine-Sweeping Work of the Trawler Section—Skipper Watts, V.C., of the Gowan Lea, and Skipper Thomas Crisp, V.C., of the Nelson—Indifference of the Mercantile Marine to German "Unrestricted Ruthlessness"—Retired Flag Officers Take Commissions in the R.N.R.—Summary of Honours and Decorations Won by Officers and Men of the Royal Naval Reserve.

IT has been said, and with a good deal of truth, that it was not until within twenty years or so of the outbreak of the Great War that the people of the British Empire began to realise the extent of their dependence upon naval power. One might almost say that, having gone contentedly to sleep after the Napoleonic Wars, the nation virtually lost all interest in the sea—except for one or two incidents which scared it badly, but were soon forgotten—until the publication of Mahan's "Influence of Sea Power upon History" in 1890. From that time onward there was never more than a momentary backward look or faltering step in the development of the British Navy. But it is, in its way, a remarkable thing that, as the country came to realise more and more the all-embracing importance of sea-power, so its perception became more and more dulled to the fact that the Royal Navy—the fighting Navy — can never represent more than a fraction of the maritime power or the maritime ascendancy of such an Empire as the British. It was, no doubt, unconsciously assumed that the mercantile fleets would be held secure from

serious risk under the protecting wing of the standing Navy; that the supremacy of the one would necessarily carry with it the safety of the other; and that trade and transport services would be "seen through" satisfactorily on the broad shoulders of that small fraction of British sea-power represented by the British Navy.

History, however, lent little support to such theories as these, for since the Royal Navy first began it has always in war time been very distinctly the dependent of the merchant service. For the earliest known records of British sea-power we must go back to the days of Julius Cæsar, when a British contingent, fighting side by side with the Veneti in the mouth of the Loire, was destroyed by the Romans with their much more powerfully built galleys; while towards the end of the third century after Christ, Britain was actually wrenched free from the Roman yoke and recognised as a co-equal empire, thanks solely to the effective work of a rebellious fleet under Carausius, who had been appointed to keep in check the pirates of the North. The foundation of the Royal Navy, however, is usually reckoned as dating from the reign of Henry VII. Until then the

[British official photograph.

QUICK OF EYE AND HAND.

Two of the crew of a drifter on patrol standing by the forward gun ready for instant action on first sight of the approach of enemy underwater craft.

GENERAL VIEW OF A CONVOY AT SEA.
Twin services, his Majesty's Navy and his Majesty's Mercantile Marine were absolutely essential the one to the other—warships convoying merchantmen that brought the indispensable supplies to the country, the merchant service keeping the Navy supplied with everything required to enable it to keep the sea.

for defence against the Spanish Armada in 1588, only thirty-four vessels in a total of 192 were " Queen's Ships," the remainder being either hired from or lent by their owners, or specially fitted out and maintained by some public body, such as the City of London. It is not necessary to trace here in full the continuity of this dependence upon the Mercantile Marine ; but it is to a certain extent summarised in the fact that not until after the middle of the nineteenth century did the petty-officers and men of the Royal Navy become a permanently enlisted force. Prior to that time a ship's company was simply enrolled for the commission. The men were paid off at the end of it, spent their accumulated wages as they liked, and, when their money was all gone, looked round for a new ship, with, in the great majority of cases, a supreme indifference as to whether she were a man-of-war or a merchant-man. In those days a popular

country had been content to rely almost wholly for its naval operations in war upon the hire or appropriation of ships from the merchant service ; and as these ships were usually armed for their own defence, and consequently carried a number of trained fighting men, their transition from peaceful to warlike pursuits was simple enough.

It will be seen, then, that under this system the Navy depended so much upon the merchant service that the merchant service was actually the Navy, merely changing over from a series of private concerns to a national weapon when trouble came. In the reign of Henry VII., however, the shipowners formed themselves into a sort of combine, with the object of exacting exorbitant rates for the hire of their vessels ; and it was to render himself and the nation more or less independent of such tactics that King Henry created a standing national fleet.

Nevertheless, this most desirable reform stopped very far short of rendering the country or the Navy independent of the Mercantile Marine in war. So much may be seen in the fact that among the English fleet mobilised

captain in the Navy found no trouble in getting a crew together, while an unpopular one would be left standing for weeks, dependent upon the press-gang or the unwary volunteering of men who did not know the sort of billet they were walking into.

With the establishment of a standing or long-service personnel and the perfection of the drafting system at the three principal naval depots—Chatham, Portsmouth, and Devonport—the commissioning of any ship became a mere matter of clockwork. The necessary ranks and ratings in the various branches were told off from the Drafting Commander's office, and, on the appointed   **Drafting system at depots** day, assembled on the parade-ground, inspected, and marched on board to begin that settling-down process that is the worst part of any commission, officers and men usually being entire strangers not only to the ship, but also to each other. This was the system ruling in the British Fleet at the outbreak of war, each man and each ship being permanently attached to the same port throughout the whole of his or its service. This arrangement was naturally a strong incentive to the men to make their

MERCHANT STEAMERS PROCEEDING TO TAKE THEIR PLACE IN A CONVOY.
Some idea of the efficiency of the protection that was afforded by the Allied Navies to general shipping is furnished by the fact that in 1918, when the U boat " blockade " was at its strictest, between four and five thousand ships entered and left the ports of the United Kingdom every week—at the rate, that is, of twenty-seven ships an hour. German " unrestricted ruthlessness " had no terror for British seamen.

homes, supposing they married, in the ports on the books of whose depot they were borne; and for this reason the incidence of naval casualties was localised to an extent quite unknown in the case of the Army. By the inexplicable run of circumstances, Chatham, though not the largest of the depots, seemed to suffer much more heavily than the others, particularly in the early days of the war. For instance, of the warships sunk from the start of hostilities down to the end of 1914, the Aboukir, Hogue, Cressy, Pathfinder, and Hawke were manned from Chatham, the Amphion and Monmouth from Devonport, and the Good Hope and Bulwark from Portsmouth. In all of these losses the death-roll was heavy.

With the creation of a standing personnel for the Fleet, it was still realised that the country could not afford to maintain in peace such a force as would assuredly be necessary to carry it successfully through a great war. Dependence upon the Mercantile Marine for the provision of a large proportion of our fighting force was seen to be inevitable, and to that end there was established, in 1859, the Royal Naval Reserve. As it existed in peace, this organisation consisted entirely of officers and men who had made the sea their calling, but who had preferred the Red Ensign of the merchant service to the White of the Royal Navy. It would be nearly true to say that this standard was maintained throughout the war; but in some branches—notably the accountant, or **Qualifications for R.N.R. commissions** clerical—even officers were accepted without any prior knowledge not only of the sea, but of the particular work they were about to undertake. In the executive or seaman branch officers were entered either as midshipmen or as sub-lieutenants. Midshipmen were required to have served at least two years in one of the approved Mercantile Marine training-ships (the Worcester in the Thames, or the Conway in the Mersey), and to be specially recommended for one of the commissions allotted annually by the Admiralty to these vessels; or else it was required that they should have served a year at sea in a first-class

DELIVERING DESPATCHES TO A VESSEL IN A CONVOY.
Vessels of all kinds and sizes exchanged the Red for the White Ensign, and acted as tenders between the shore and ships of the Navy and vessels proceeding under their convoy, carrying mails, newspapers, and despatches out to them at sea, and generally acting as "errand-boys."

British merchant ship as cadet, midshipman, or apprentice. Of sub-lieutenants a higher standard of capacity and experience was naturally required, the regulations demanding that a candidate for such a commission " must (a) have served as first mate (or in a superior capacity) of a British steamship of at least 1,500 tons, or a British sailing-ship of 1,000 tons gross tonnage, for not less than one year; (b) possess a Master's Certificate of Competency under the Merchant Shipping Acts; (c) have served as master or first mate of a British ship within six months of making his application for a commission; (d) certify that he intends to follow the sea as his profession." Certificated second and third mates of British ocean-going steamers of at least 3,000 tons, and fourth mates of ships of 5,000, were eligible for commissions as sub-lieutenants in the Reserve, provided that they held their certificates and served at sea for three and a half years, and that they further possessed either a master's certificate or a provisional certificate of competency as master. There is no need to enumerate the training which the officers had to undergo with the Fleet. Suffice it that for those below the rank of commander the regulation periods were one

DAWN BREAKING ON A CONVOY AT SEA UNDER NAVAL ESCORT.
Moving a vote of thanks to the Services in October, 1917, the Prime Minister stated that since the beginning of the war 13,000,000 men had crossed and recrossed the sea, and out of that vast number only 2,200 had been lost through the action of the enemy—a loss, approximately, of but one man in every 6,000. More convincing tribute to the efficiency of the Navy's protection could not be conceived.

The Great War

4

32

month in each of the first three years of belonging to the Reserve, and, subsequently, either two weeks a year or four weeks every alternate year ; while, in addition, there were special courses in gunnery, torpedo, strategy, international law, court-martial procedure, and so on, which officers could attend if they desired.

These details relating to the R.N.R. have been set out because so many people in Britain either did not understand that these officers had any connection with the sea at all, or else conceived the idea that the Navy was being flooded out with incompetent people who entered straight away as officers. It is, unfortunately, the fact that the great reserve of strength presented by the Mercantile Marine was drawn upon by the Admiralty to the detriment of the long-trained and recommended men of the Navy itself, whose claims to promotion were thus brushed aside ; but although that policy was the cause of a great deal of legitimate ill-feeling in the Navy, it should not close our eyes to the fact that in the Mercantile Marine the Admiralty and the nation had a reserve of highly-trained seamen and navigators, to ignore whom in the hour of need would have been the greatest folly. The men of the Royal Naval Reserve were all drawn from the merchant service, and, according to their occupation, were entered as wireless operators, engine-room artificers, seamen, and stokers.

The Royal Naval Reserve was mobilised on August 3rd, 1914, but the commissioning of large groups of ships from the Second and Third Groups of the Home Fleet, together with the immediate appropriation of large numbers of vessels from the Mercantile Marine, showed only too quickly how inadequate even the thus augmented personnel of the Navy was to meet requirements. The Admiralty thereupon issued a special appeal to officers and men of the merchant service to volunteer for work with the Fleet — an appeal which, it is needless to say, was answered with magnificent and immediate enthusiasm—while in practically every case where a merchant ship was taken over for the fighting service the whole of the officers and men went over enthusiastically with it ; so that when the vessel had shipped her guns and ammunition, a commanding officer, and a few specialists from the Royal Navy, she was fully equipped as a fighting unit. Thus did the merchant service of the twentieth century play the game as in the days of the Cinque Ports and of the Armada. By the end of the third year of war the officers alone of the Naval Reserve had increased in number from fewer than 2,000 to close upon 12,000—a fact significant not only of their patriotism, but also of the infinitely harder work—under infinitely more trying conditions—left upon the shoulders of those who, with equal patriotism and in the face of probably greater dangers, remained to carry on the honoured and priceless work of the merchant service. It was not long after his appointment as First Sea Lord that Admiral Jellicoe declared that without the Mercantile Marine the Navy could not exist ; and although he was referring then to the work of the Marine as the indispensable carrier of the nation's and the Navy's indispensable supplies, it is equally true that the direct fighting power of the Fleet would have been vastly and perhaps vitally affected but for the willing assistance that was forthcoming from those under the Red Ensign.

To describe in any detail the work of the Naval Reserve during the war would, for all practical purposes, be

Jellicoe's tribute to the R.N.R.

equivalent to describing the naval war itself, and it will be possible here to select for mention but relatively a few of the affairs in which its officers and men acquitted themselves with particular distinction. One of the first incidents that brought to the public eye the spirit of the merchant service was the escape of the defenceless liner Ortega from the German raiding cruiser Karlsruhe. The war had barely opened when these two vessels sighted each other off the coast of South America, near the Strait of Magellan, and the Karlsruhe promptly ordered the Ortega to stop. What would have happened to her and her passengers and crew if she had been best left to the imagination ; but Captain Douglas Kinnier, the Ortega's commander, was not of the sort that stops so easily. He knew that he could not escape in a straight run, since the German was by some knots the faster ship ; so he headed his vessel for Nelson's Strait, described by one who knows it as "the most gloomy ocean defile in the world, without anchorage, an uncharted channel never before attempted, which no seaman knows or desires to know." The Karlsruhe steamed hard to cut off her intended victim before she could reach the entrance to the strait, but failed, and, even with the Ortega ahead as a sort of pilot ship, dared not follow. Providence smiled on the intrepidity of Captain Kinnier. He brought his ship safely through the strait and safely home ; and the Admiralty, with a promptitude quite unexpected in those days, rewarded him with the Distinguished Service Cross. In those days, too, it was essential that a man should hold his Majesty's commission before he could receive such a decoration, and Kinnier was therefore granted at the same time a commission as lieutenant in the Royal Naval Reserve.

Daring escape of the Ortega

A few weeks later, on September 14th, 1914, there was fought the first high-sea duel of the war, and, strangely enough, the combatants on either side were armed liners. The German Cap Trafalgar, an almost brand-new ship, had been commissioned by the enemy as a commerce raider, while the Carmania, of the Cunard Line, had been fitted out (and commissioned ready for active service nine days from the outbreak of war) as a commerce protector. It so happened that the Cap Trafalgar had not scored a single victim when the Carmania fell in with her near the island of Trinidad—and she had no chance of any afterwards, for at the end of a hard-fought action that lasted an hour and a half, and in which the Carmania was badly knocked about and set on fire, the Cap Trafalgar turned turtle and went to the bottom. The full story of the action is told in its proper place in this history (Vol. II., p. 286) ; but the point emphasised here is that out of forty-three officers borne in the Carmania when she won this fine victory only five belonged to the Royal Navy ; and among the petty-officers and men the proportion was probably about the same. Captain Noel Grant, R.N., was in command, but Commander James Barr, R.N.R., remained in the ship as second in command when she was taken over by the Admiralty, and received the Companionship of the Bath for his share in the fight. Besides the commanding officer, the only R.N. officers in the ship were the first lieutenant, who had joined up from the retired list, two doctors who had taken temporary commissions for the period of the war, and the chief gunner, who was in charge of the armament. The rest of the officers were all

CAPTAIN NOEL GRANT, R.N.
"Well done. You did fine service." Such was the message of the First Lord of the Admiralty to Captain Noel Grant, of H.M.S. armed liner Carmania, which sank the German armed liner Cap Trafalgar off Trinidad on September 14th, 1914.

ON H.M. HOSPITAL-SHIP LIBERTY.
Officers and men of the British hospital-ship Liberty. Commander Lord Tredegar, R.N.R., and Lieutenant G. Herbert, R.N.R., are seen in the centre of the seated row in front.

selves in action with the enemy, or who may, by the character or length of that service, obtain the special approbation of the Lords Commissioners of the Admiralty, will be eligible to receive commissions as officers of the Royal Navy." The first officer of the R.N.R. to be so transferred was Sub-Lieutenant Gordon C. Steele, "for service in action." That was all that was made public as to the reason for the transfer; but the officer had for some time been employed in the submarine branch.

Some of the finest and most invaluable work of the R.N.R. was performed on what was known as the Auxiliary Patrol —a vast organisation surrounding the British Isles and extending far beyond—and consisting of a great number of armed yachts, trawlers, and drifters. Like the greater part of the work that fell to the Navy, that for which these craft were responsible was monotonous in the extreme, yet lacking nothing in hardship and discomfort.

The whole of the seas adjacent to these islands were portioned off into areas, and to each area was allotted its section of the Auxiliary Patrol; and the first and principal business of the small, comfortless craft that patrolled and scoured these areas day and night was

of the Mercantile Marine, who had either taken up commissions in the R.N.R. when the war broke out or belonged to it already. Sub-Lieutenants George H. Dickens and Douglas Colson (since killed), both of the R.N.R., were awarded the Distinguished Service Cross.

It would be a matter of sheer impossibility to record all the incidents in which the officers and men of the R.N.R. distinguished themselves, and even if it were possible the fact would remain that there would be left untouched those monotonous yet supremely vital services upon the efficient discharge of which rested the whole fabric of the Allies' war machine, and at the same time offered little opportunity for striking acts of individual gallantry For example, the 10th Cruiser Squadron—maintaining in perhaps the most inhospitable waters in the world the relentless commercial blockade of the North Sea—was composed entirely of converted liners, manned, like the Carmania, with their own mercantile crews and a thin sprinkling of R.N. officers and men. At the end of the first year of hostilities a distribution of honours was made among those who had been engaged in this monotonous and, to the country, practically unknown work and it is significant that out of ten D.S.O.'s, seven went to the Naval Reserve, as did the whole of the eight D.S.C.'s. In three and a half years of war only one solitary fight fell to the lot of the 10th Cruiser Squadron, and that was on February 29th, 1916, when the ex-Royal Mail Steam Packet steamship Alcantara, Captain T. E. Wardle, R.N., rounded up and fought a duel to the death with the disguised Greif, which, under neutral colours, was endeavouring to creep through on to the Atlantic trade routes. As a result of this fight, in which both ships were sunk, Lieutenant-Commander Frank M. Main. R.N.R., who had already received the D.S.O. for his work in the patrol generally, was specially promoted to commander; the D.S.O. was awarded to Engineer Lieut.-Commander Charles A. N. Williams, R.N.R.; and the D.S.C. to Acting-Lieutenant J. Howell Price, R.N.R. Midshipman Hardress W. D'Arcy-Evans gained the particularly high distinction of a transfer from the R.N.R. to the Royal Navy, under that article of the Reserve Regulations which says: "Officers who, when on actual service in the Fleet, shall have greatly distinguished them-

Honours awarded to the R.N.R.

INTERDEPENDENCE OF SEA AND AIR SERVICES.
British drifter towing an observation-balloon to its appointed place, from which it was to carry out its work searching the air and the surface of the sea for suspicious craft, and its depths for enemy submarines.

the detection and destruction of enemy submarines. The ceaseless watch on bridge or deck for the sign of a peri-scope ; the untiring ear in the wireless-room standing by for a word from a merchantman attacked ; the trained listener at the hydrophone beneath the water-line straining to disentangle the hum of a submarine's motors from the babble of sound coming through the submerged receiver ; these things were part of the daily and nightly work of the one-time merchant seaman, temporarily enrolled in the R.N.R., who ran the Auxiliary Patrol in fair weather and in foul, armed with guns, nets, depth - charges, lance-bombs, and anything else efficient that came to hand for fighting the most insidious and dangerous foe that the Navy —to say nothing of the Naval Reserve—had ever had to con-tend against.

The secrecy persistently maintained in everything con-cerning the details of anti-submarine work prevents the recording of any of the literally innumerable acts of gallantry, resource, and devotion to duty which characterised the work of the Auxiliary Patrol and which played no unimportant part in bringing about the diminution of U boat activity that became so evident in the middle of the fourth year of the war. It is possible, however, to give some indication of the relative im-portance in this connection of the work of the Royal Naval Reserve. The first honours' list affecting the patrol was published in the " London Gazette " of July 14th, 1916, and in a brief appreciative introduction the Admiralty said : " The Lords Commissioners of the Admiralty have received with much satisfaction from the officers in charge of the Auxiliary Patrol areas at home and abroad reports on the services per-formed by the officers and men serving under their orders during the period January 1st, 1915, to January 31st, 1916. These reports show that the officers and men serving in the armed yachts, trawlers, and drifters of the Auxiliary Patrol during the period in question have carried out their duties under extremely arduous and hazardous conditions of weather and ex-posure to enemy attack and mines with marked zeal, gallantry, and success." Then followed the list of decorations. Of seven D.S.O.'s, three went to the Royal Navy (all these recipients having rejoined from the retired list at the start of the war), and four to the R.N.R. Of twenty-four D.S.C.'s, all but one went to officers of the R.N.R., the exception being a chief gunner of the R.N. Sixty-two Distin-guished Service Medals were distributed among the petty-officers and men, fifty-one of them belonging to the R.N.R. In a second honours' list dealing with the further work of the Auxiliary Patrol down to the end of 1916, the Royal Naval Reserve took forty-four awards out of forty-nine.

Work of the Auxiliary Patrol

These figures convey some idea of the part which was played by the Naval Reserve in the vast and

LIEUTENANT-COMMANDER CHARLES FOX.
In command of H.M.S. Mary Rose, convoying merchant ships from Norway in October, 1917, Lt.-Cdr. Fox fought three enemy cruisers, and went down with his ship, its flag flying.

SUB-LIEUTENANT F. W. MARSH, R.N.V.R.
In the great fight of H.M.S. Mary Rose, October 17th, 1917, Sub-Lieutenant Marsh kept the after-gun going when all the other gues had been put out of action. He was one of the few survivors who reached the Norwegian coast.

highly-organised business of fighting the U boat ; but this force took a no less important hand in that more in-dependent and more hazardous phase of U boat hunting known as Special Service—" S.S."—or, in more expressive language, submarine strafing. It involved the use of particular methods against the U boat, and although there are the best of reasons, unfortunately, for believing that the enemy scented them in a relatively short time (though he was never able altogether to overcome them), it is still forbidden to hint at the subject other than very vaguely in this country. **Special Service** The following, **against submarines** however, was printed in an English paper in September, 1917, from the " Nachrichten," of Hamburg : " On a westward run from the coast, in order to lie in wait for the ships destined for England, one of our big U boats, towards nine o'clock in the morning of a cold March day, sighted a smallish steamer of about 1,500 tons, approaching on an east-ward course, which excited remark not only by her high bridge and high deck erections, but also by the meaningless deviations from her route and her wild zigzag course. The submarine put the last torpedo into the tube for the attack, and the torpedo was launched without being noticed. It had scarcely penetrated with a powerful detonation into the centre of the steamer when she began to sink, and after a second explosion in the boiler-rooms she dis-appeared in less than three minutes.

" The large number of the crew standing on deck, who only succeeded, in spite of the utmost exertions, in lowering one boat into the water, seemed to confirm the suspicion that this was a U boat trap. In order to ascertain certainly if this were so, U — went up to the survivors, who were drifting about on the water, and fished out six men who were clinging, half-benumbed, to planks. The men were very well dressed and had a good military carriage, to which one is not usually accustomed in mercantile ships. Ac-cording to their statements the steamer was bound from Africa to England. After denying it for a long time, they at last admitted that they belonged to the Navy. The ship sunk was, they said, the U boat trap Q27, H.M.S. Warner, and the captain and all the officers had perished in the boiler explosion."

For reasons that are sufficiently obvious, the Admiralty, in making awards for services against enemy submarines, never, save in extremely exceptional circum-stances, gave any indication as to the nature of that service. Indeed, it was not until the middle of 1917 that the public were made officially aware that the work of the Fleet against U boats was meeting with any recognition at all, as until then the honours awarded for these services were usually included among the " miscellaneous " decorations, or else issued with no word at all. The first " Gazette " in which any mention was made of " service in action with

The building of the ships: Night work in one of Britain's vast shipyards.

Submarine or mine? British patrol examining floating wreckage found on the sea at dawn.

[Photo by F. J. Mortimer

Unshakable amid the surge of war: British sailormen pulling out to a British lighthouse.

Food for the Homeland: Warships and seaplane escorting a merchantman through the danger zone.

True to her tradition: A torpedoed merchantman going down with the Red Ensign flying.

A R.N.V.R. lieutenant swam to a drifting mine and fastened a line to its ringbolt. It was then towed to smooth water and destroyed.

A mine-sweeping officer and an engine-man boarded a deserted trawler and, at imminent risk, cut away two mines fouled in her tackle.

A patrol ship detected a submarine which had torpedoed an oiler, and rammed it abaft the conning-tower. The U boat rolled over with a violent explosion and vanished in a boiling, bubbling sea. Of two men seen struggling in the water, one was rescued and brought prisoner ashore.

Fine feats in the Royal Naval Reserve's campaign against German mines and submarines.

enemy submarines " was that of July 20th, 1917, and there a very great honour was bestowed on the R.N.R. One of his Majesty's ships—nameless, of course—had so distinguished herself in fighting U boats that, among other distinctions, two Victoria Crosses were allotted to the ship, and as it was impossible for the Admiralty to decide who were the most worthy to receive the honour, the choice was left to the ship's company. As a result of their balloting the V.C. was awarded to Lieutenant Ronald N. Stuart, R.N.R. (who had won the D.S.O. four months previously), and Seaman William Williams, also of the R.N.R. An earlier R.N.R. recipient of the V.C. for anti-submarine work, though the reason for the award was not stated at the time, was Lieutenant W. E. Sandars, whose name was gazetted in June, 1917, " in recognition of his conspicuous gallantry, consummate coolness, and skill in command of one of his Majesty's ships in action." Unhappily, this officer was killed in action two months later, and a few weeks after his death the posthumous award of the D.S.O. was made in the " London Gazette." Two other officers of the Royal Naval Reserve who, down to the end of 1917, had been awarded the V.C. for their anti-submarine work were Lieutenant Charles G. Bonner, who already held the D.S.O., and Skipper

V.C. awards to the R.N.R. Thomas Crisp, who, as will be told later, fell gloriously in the action which won for him the coveted cross.

Some day the full story of all these heroic deeds will be known, but the authorities were never blamed for withholding details of the methods employed which might have been of the remotest use to the enemy. For that reason it is possible to give here no more than an indication, as it were, of the magnificent work of the Naval Reserve against the U boat. Mention must be made of Cedric Naylor, who joined with a temporary commission as a sub-lieutenant in December, 1914. Later on he volunteered for the submarine hunt, and he appears to have had some success. In February, 1917, he was awarded the D.S.C. Three months later a bar was added to this decoration. Another brief interval passed, and he was specially transferred to the Royal Navy in recognition of his very distinguished services ; and within a year of receiving his first award he added to his laurels the D.S.O. in August, 1917, a bar in November, and a second bar in February, 1918. Six such honours as these in one year, and from one Government, must surely constitute a " record." In much the same category are Lieutenant John Lawrie, Acting-Lieutenant F. R. Hereford, and Engineer-Lieutenant Leonard Loveless, all of the R.N.R., to each of whom was awarded the D.S.O. and the D.S.C. with bar, while another officer of the Reserve, Lieutenant Stephen White, received the D.S.C. with two bars.

Turn now to what may be called the general services of the R.N.R. From the first day of the Navy's mobilisation the Admiralty adopted the practice of appointing the more experienced officers to posts of importance. At the beginning of 1918 close upon one hundred and fifty destroyers, torpedo-boats, and similar craft were commanded by them ; and special reference should be made to one of these craft (which must, unfortunately, be nameless), in which the commanding officer and the second in command, both belonging to the R.N.R., had been honoured respectively with the D.S.C. and bar and the D.S.C. with a mention in despatches, while the gunner, R.N., had received the D.S.C., and the engineer in charge (a naval warrant-officer) had been twice mentioned in despatches. We may well regret that the story of such a ship—a 350-ton destroyer launched in 1897—had to be put into cold storage until after the war. For the most part it was to the older torpedo craft that R.N.R. officers were appointed in command, but nearly every new destroyer as she was passed into service shipped a Naval Reserve midshipman as part of her complement, and the sort of work they did when the opportunity arose was

IN COMMAND ON THE LUSITANIA.

Captain W. T. Turner, who was in command of the Lusitania when she was torpedoed by a German submarine, May 7th, 1915. He went to sea again in charge of a ship on Government service, and was again torpedoed, after which, with characteristic British imperturbability, he once more took service in command of another vessel.

splendidly typified by Donald Gyles, of the Broke, in the gallant fight which that vessel and the Swift put up with six German destroyers in the mouth of the Channel on the night of April 20th-21st, 1917. For his conduct on this occasion Midshipman Gyles was awarded the D.S.C. and transferred to the Royal Navy.

Many other ships in important classes, besides torpedo craft, were given over to the command of Naval Reserve officers. These included both submarine-hunters and large mine-sweepers of special design, as well as—in the middle of the fourth year of the war—about fifty armed merchantmen, twice as many mercantile fleet auxiliaries, and whole groups of ships of special classes to which no particular reference was publicly made. Many distinguished themselves in the submarine service, to which the R.N.R. had not been admitted prior to the war, and all over the world officers **Ubiquity of the R.N.R.** and men alike added lustre to the records of a great Service which in the remote past had sprung direct from their own. Indeed, this ubiquity of the Naval Reserve was one of the most remarkable things about its invaluable work, as may be seen from a few illustrations of it, taken haphazard from a somewhat jumbled list of naval honours. Commander R. H. W. Hughes, R.N.R., was awarded the D.S.O. for his services in Cameroon. The official record stated that, at the beginning of the campaign, Commander Hughes superintended the work of clearing a way through the wreck barrage constructed by the Germans, and piloting H.M.S. Challenger to within bombarding distance of Duala, and he subsequently, at considerable risk and frequently under fire, carried out survey work on the Sanaga, Njong, and Campo Rivers, and continuously harassed the enemy's coast outposts. Lieutenant Francis W. Lyte received the

D.S.C. " for his services as pilot of the armed launch Shushan, on May 9th, 1915, when he handled the vessel with the utmost coolness under fire. Lieutenant Lyte has done good work in the Shat-el-Arab operations on many other occasions." Sub-Lieutenant C. J. Charlewood won the D.S.C. for cool and gallant work at Dar-es-Salaam in November, 1914 ; and this is the brief official account of how another R.N.R. officer won the same decoration during the Turkish attack on the Suez Canal in the following February : " A shell struck the fore funnel of H.M.S. Hardinge and completely shattered one of Lieutenant George Carew's legs from the knee down, and broke one arm, besides inflicting other wounds. Notwithstanding this, he continued to advise on the piloting of the ship with coolness and equanimity." Lieutenant Thomas A. Bond, of the Royal Australian Naval Reserve, received the D.S.O. for the following remarkable piece of work : On September 11th, 1914, during the attack upon the wireless station at Bita Paka, in German New Guinea, Lieutenant Bond displayed conspicuous ability and coolness under fire in leading his men through most difficult country and enforcing the terms of surrender while drawing off an attack by another body of the enemy. He showed great daring when, accompanied by only one officer and one man, he suddenly disarmed eight Germans in the presence of twenty German native troops, drawn up under arms, all of whom were then marched off and held prisoner Later he personally captured five armed natives.

MID. DONALD GYLES, D.S.C., R.N.R.
Held up the German boarding-party rushing H.M.S. Broke, in the destroyer fight in the Channel, April 1917.

Another D.S.O. went to Lieutenant John Percival, R.N.R., who was Acting-Director of the Nigeria Marine at the commencement of hostilities, and was largely responsible for the efficient manner in which the vessels of the Nigeria Marine were fitted out for duty with the Cameroon Expedition. The exceedingly successful manner in which the evacuation of the Serbian and Italian troops from Durazzo was carried out between December, 1915, and February, 1916, was recognised by the Admiralty with three D.S.O.'s for the R.N. and ten **Cameroon, Durazzo** D.S.C.'s for the R.N.R., all but three **and Gallipoli** of the recipients of the latter being skippers. For the same operation no fewer than seventy-two skippers were awarded the Serbian Gold Medal for Good Service. Officers and men of the Naval Reserve have further been decorated or mentioned in despatches for their work with the Dover Patrol and at Salonika, while their invaluable work during the trying operations in the neighbourhood of the Gallipoli Peninsula will never be forgotten. To take but a single phase of them—the landing from the River Clyde—one of the most glorious and tragic episodes in our fighting history. The captain of the transport, Commander Edward Unwin had himself been in the merchant service and the R.N.R. before transferring to the Navy as a supplementary

lieutenant. He was one of six heroes who won the Victoria Cross on that never-to-be-forgotten April 25th, 1915, and the others included Midshipman George L. Drewry and Seaman George McK. Samson, both of the R.N.R. The magnificent work of our transports, both in the landing and the evacuation, was generously rewarded by the King.

That feature of the work of the Naval Reserve with which the world was most familiar during the war was the sweeping up of enemy mines. This has been aptly described as " the work that always began again," for there was nothing to which the Germans applied themselves more assiduously than the endeavour to render the narrow seas, and in particular the principal lanes of mercantile traffic, impassable. Mine-laying submarines were principally used for the purpose ; and the ships, the officers, and the men of the merchant service were principally employed in frustrating it.

The full story of the unparalleled heroism and devotion of those employed upon this monotonous and perilous work can never be adequately told. Germany's first act of war at sea—in open defiance of the law of nations—was **German mine-laying activity** to lay a mine-field in the approaches to the Thames, with the sole object of sinking merchantmen— not to mention that there was good reason to believe that the vessel engaged on this work, the Königin Luise, began operations actually before the outbreak of war. The German ship was sunk by a flotilla of our destroyers, but the light cruiser Amphion came to grief on that very mine-field next morning, and from that time onwards the policy of scattering mines broadcast about the high seas, but principally in the most frequented lanes of mercantile traffic, was developed by the enemy for all it was worth. At first, fishing-boats and small merchantmen, under neutral colours, were employed to carry the mines to sea and deposit them, and it is possible that the special mine-layers Nautilus and Albatross, built before the war, and designed to carry four hundred mines apiece, made a few surreptitious trips into the North Sea and dumped their deadly freight into what were considered to be likely spots As time went on, however, the German passion for mines grew. The fast cruiser squadron which dashed across the North Sea in December, 1914, and shelled Whitby, Scarborough, and other places on the North-East Coast, left behind a large number of mines in all sorts of unsuspected places—showing how, even so early in the war, regular warships had been adapted for mine-strewing—and it was in connection with the removal of these snares that the R.N.R. first came into the public eye as the sweeper of our ocean pathways. It needed thirteen days of continuous and strenuous work to clear the mines away, and this is what the official records said of some of the Naval Reserve officers who took part in it : When Trawler No. 99 (Orianda) was blown up by a mine on December 19th, Lieutenant H. Boothby, R.N.R., successfully got all his crew—except one, who was killed—into safety. Lieutenant Boothby was again blown up on January 6th, 1915, in Trawler No. 450 (The Banyers). Lieutenant C. V. Crossley, R.N.R., was sweeping on December 19th, when three violent explosions occurred close under the stern of his ship (Trawler No. 465, Star of Britain). He controlled the crew, and himself crawled into a confined space near the screw-shaft, discovered the damage, and temporarily stopped the leak sufficiently to enable the pumps to keep the water down and save the

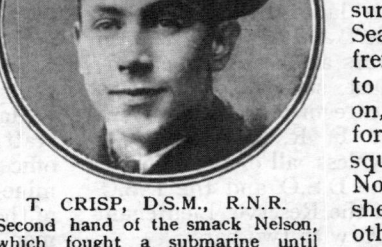

T. CRISP, D.S.M., R.N.R.
Second hand of the smack Nelson, which fought a submarine until sinking, with ammunition exhausted, August, 1917.

ship. Lieutenant W. G. Wood, R.N.R., trawler Restrivo, did excellent work in going to the assistance of damaged trawlers, and performed the risky duty of crossing the mine-field at low water when sent to bring in the Valiant, which had been disabled by a mine. Several skippers were highly commended for their services during those strenuous days, and the Distinguished Service Cross was awarded to two of them. Their names—they were the first skippers to be awarded this decoration—were Thomas W. Tringall and Ernest V. Snowline.

German warships as mine-layers There was good reason to believe that the German ships did not leave behind on the East Coast all the mines they carried, for it was soon discovered that practically all classes of German warships were furnished with at least a few mines as part of their defensive equipment. Quite correctly, the naval authorities in Berlin anticipated that, in the vast majority of cases, whenever British and German warships met the encounter would turn very rapidly into a pursuit, with the British ships in the rear. To meet this more or less invariable state of affairs, the German ships were furnished with a dozen mines or so and a shoot leading down well over the stern, so that the deadly missiles could be dropped in the path of a chasing fleet. Nor were the mines always dropped singly. Often they were tied in pairs, one at either end of a strong hempen cable, so that, drifting apart, they might stretch the cable across the track of the pursuers and add to their chances of destruction. Thanks to good look-outs and excellent manœuvring, this legitimate but rather contemptible practice never achieved any success —at any rate, during the first three and a half years of the war.

As the British patrol in the North Sea became more numerous and efficient, it became more and more difficult for the enemy to use ostensible " neutrals " for the work of surreptitious mine-laying, for our men—and especially the R.N.R. folk, than whom none were better equipped for this sort of thing, having worked among merchantmen all their lives—quickly developed the knack of scenting a suspicious ship at a distance. The enemy, therefore,

had to fall back upon other devices, and by far the most troublesome of these was the mine-laying submarine. Vessels of this type, usually of small dimensions for their special work, could creep into all sorts of places and deposit their infernal spawn at their leisure, so that an area which had been thoroughly swept one day, and carefully guarded against surface craft, would be found next morning to have accumulated a fresh crop of mines, sprung up like mushrooms. One of these special mine-laying submarines, the UC5, went ashore on a shoal near Harwich in April, 1916, surrendered, and was salved ; and, with her damage repaired, was subsequently exhibited in London and New York. The capture of a German submarine was, by the way, a very rare occurrence, since, whatever the condition of the ship when she surrendered, the crew invariably opened the sea-cocks or made some other arrangement which would send her to the bottom soon after they had been taken off. The UC5 carried no other offensive weapons than a dozen mines, but later on the regular ocean-going U boats were served out with an equal or greater number apiece, so that they might be left in the more distant waters visited by them.

[*Russell.*
A STURDY PATRIOT.
Vice-Admiral Thomas Philip Walker, R.N. (retired), temporary captain R.N.R. He was in command of H.M. armed yacht Aegusa when mined and sunk on patrol in the Mediterranean in April, 1916.

Strange things sometimes happened to these submerged mine-layers. A case is on record where two trawlers were proceeding slowly through a suspected area, when the cable stretched between them, and held down to the sea bottom by heavy " kites," was suddenly brought up taut. Certain investigations were made, whereupon the two trawlers, still keeping the cable quite taut against the obstruction steamed slowly a little farther apart. One of them allowed a dangerous-looking canister to slide down the cable ; a few seconds later a button was pressed, there was a violent upheaval of the water, and another German **Submarine mine-layers destroyed** submarine had sown its last crop. Now and again one would be detected at work by a seaplane or a " blimp "— one of those fast and handy little airships that did such useful work on the patrol or as part of the convoy system —and in such cases the detector would either call up by wireless a couple of destroyers or trawlers, or else glide

[*Elliott & Fry.*   [*Russell.*

Rear-Admiral Charles Holcombe Dare, M.V.O., R.N. (retired), commander in the Royal Naval Reserve.   Admiral John Locke Marx, M.V.O., R.N. (retired), commander in the Royal Naval Reserve.   Admiral Sir Alfred W. Paget, K.C.B., K.C.M.G., D.S.O., R.N. (retired), commander in the Royal Naval Reserve.

THREE FLAG-OFFICERS WHO EMERGED FROM RETIREMENT TO SERVE IN THE ROYAL NAVAL RESERVE.

gently towards the surface and let fall a depth-charge. In either case there was little hope for the U boat.

Still another evidence of Germany's belief in the mine—perhaps the most sneaky of all weapons of war—came with the discovery of the building of the Bremse class of cruisers, the first of which appear to have been completed in the early part of 1917. These were vessels of about 4,000 tons, carrying a normal armament of four 5·9 in. and eight 4·1 in. guns, and having the phenomenally high speed of thirty-five knots—the fastest British light cruiser actually in service when the war began was of twenty-five knots. In addition to their guns, however, these German ships were equipped with no fewer than 480 mines apiece, and there is little doubt that the objects with which they were designed were, in the first place, to act as a rear-guard to the German Fleet if ever it should meet the British, and to strew their mines in the path of the latter's approach; and, in the second, to rush out from their bases at selected moments, plant their mines in patches on the principal steamship routes, and return as fast as possible. At least six of these vessels were known to be **Bremse class of** in commission or under construction at **cruisers** the beginning of 1918, representing an aggregate cargo of 2,880 mines; while a number of the earlier light cruisers in the German Fleet had been adapted towards the same end, carrying from 80 to 200 mines each. With the policy of mine-laying carried to such lengths as these, it is no surprise that the British mine-sweeping service grew, until, at the beginning of 1918, it absorbed a total of something like 2,000 craft and 30,000 officers and men, the vast majority of the latter being mercantile officers and ratings serving in the Royal Naval Reserve, while the bulk of the vessels engaged were but little altered from the time when they were following the peaceful pursuit of deep-sea fishing—the finest training-ground for seamen and pluck that any nation ever possessed. The indefatigable sweepers were to be found everywhere—in the Arctic, the North Sea, the Irish Sea, the Atlantic, the Mediterranean, the Adriatic, and at the Dardanelles—where their work won

the highest praise. In each of these seas the waters were parcelled into areas, each with its own base and its own service of sweepers. During 1917 there was an average of one thousand trawlers constantly at work round the British Isles, and every twenty-four hours they swept an area of three thousand square miles. In the course of the year they brought to the surface and destroyed no fewer than 4,600 German mines—representing the possible salvation from destruction or serious damage of just four thousand six hundred ships. How many of the trawlers and of their gallant crews were lost in the process was not made public.

The Mine-sweeping Section of the R.N.R. had been formed in 1911, its officers being largely skippers of their own craft who undertook to place their vessels and their personal services at the disposal of the Admiralty in the event of war. The scheme gave no great promise of success, and when the war began no more than one hundred

FIGHTING THE U BOAT.
Special British patrol boat armed with a 3 in. gun on the look-out for enemy submarines.

and eleven skippers (warrant-officers) had been enrolled. However, events proved that nothing was wanting but the stimulus of war. The number rapidly increased and continued to grow as the war went on, until at the beginning of 1918 it exceeded three thousand. Not by any means all of them were engaged in mine-sweeping. A large number were in command of drifters, whose particular business was the hunting of the submarine; while others, again, were employed as escorts to merchant shipping near home. One feature of this section of the R.N.R. well worth mentioning here was the extraordinary prevalence of Scotsmen among them. For example, at the beginning of 1918 there were sixty skippers who bore the surname of Buchan, which happened to be the name of only one other officer in the

[British official photograph.

MINED, BUT SAVED FROM SINKING.
Trawler that had been brought safely into harbour after having her bows blown off as the result of striking a mine. Many such wonderful instances were seen of vessels that, despite serious damage by mine or torpedo, were yet salved by their indomitable crews.

The transport Aragon (Captain Francis Bateman in command) was torpedoed and sunk in the Eastern Mediterranean on December 30th, 1917. One of his Majesty's destroyers, while picking up survivors from the Aragon, was herself torpedoed and sunk.

In the upper photograph the Aragon is seen heeling over, watched by soldiers on a life-raft and a destroyer standing by. The lower picture shows the end of the liner as her hull blew up. Approximately four hundred and eighty-four lives were lost.

LAST MOMENTS OF THE TRANSPORT ARAGON, TORPEDOED IN THE MEDITERRANEAN.

TORPEDOING OF THE ANDANIA.

On January 26th, 1918, the Cunard liner Andania, outward bound, with about forty passengers and a crew of over two hundred, was torpedoed by a German submarine off the Irish coast and sank on the following Monday. All the passengers and crew were saved with the exception of a boy and an A.B.

Skipper Watt ordered full steam ahead, and called upon his crew to give three cheers and fight to the finish. The cruiser was then engaged, but after one round had been fired a shot from the enemy disabled the breech of the drifter's gun. The gun's crew, however, stuck to the gun, endeavouring to make it work, being under heavy fire all the time. After the cruiser had passed on, Skipper Watt took the Gowan Lea alongside the badly-damaged drifter Floandi and assisted to remove the dead and wounded."

Properly to appreciate this magnificent action it must be borne in mind that the Gowan Lea was armed with only one gun—and that certainly not heavier than a 12-pounder—while the Austrian cruiser, which was one of a flotilla, carried nine 4 in. 30-pounders. The fact that fourteen of our drifters—employed in barring the route for enemy submarines from the Adriatic into the Mediterranean — were sunk in this Austrian excursion, adds further to the admiration evoked by the magnificent conduct of Skipper Watt. This officer had already received the Serbian Gold Medal for Good Service in connection with the evacuation of our sorely-tried ally's army from Durazzo, and his gallantry in the Strait of Otranto fight brought him the Italian Silver Medal for Valour and the honour of a special mention in French Orders.

The second Skippers' V.C. was won by Thomas Crisp in an action that cost him his life. On an August afternoon, says the official account, at about a quarter to three, the trawl was shot from the smack Nelson, and the smack was on the port tack. The skipper was below packing fish; one hand was on deck cleaning fish for the next morning's breakfast, and then the skipper came on deck, saw an object on the horizon, examined it closely, and sent for his glasses. Almost directly he sang out, " Clear for action ! Submarine ! " And he had scarcely spoken when a shot fell about a hundred yards away on the port bow. The motor-man got to his motor, and the deck hand dropped his fish and went to the ammunition-room ; and the other hands, at the skipper's order, " Let go your gear," let go the warp and put a dan on the end of it. Meanwhile, the gunlayer held his fire until the skipper said : " It is no use waiting any longer ; we will have to let them have it."

Skipper Crisp's great heroism

Away in the distance the submarine sent shell after shell at the smack, and about the fourth shot the shell went through the port bow just below the waterline, and then the skipper shoved her round. There was no confusion on board, not even when the seventh shell struck the skipper, passed through his side, through the deck, and cut through the side of the ship. The second hand at once took charge of the tiller, and the firing continued.

whole of the Reserve. Further there were among the skippers 22 named Cowie, 15 Bruces, 20 Duthies, 36 Mairs, 16 Mackays, 23 Murrays, 16 Reids, 23 Stewarts, 20 Watts, and 25 Wilsons, together with a plentiful scattering of Campbells, Mackenzies, and so forth, the whole making as imposing an array of Scottish patronymics as could probably be found in any general list of its kind.

Mine-sweeping, it will be seen, did not by any means exhaust the activities of the Trawler Section. One of the most distinguished of the Scottish skippers was Joseph Watt. He was the first of the rank to win the Victoria Cross, and the story of his amazingly gallant action was thus told in the " London Gazette ": " The King has been pleased to approve of the award of the Victoria Cross to Skipper Joseph Watt, 1206 W.S.A. (that being his official identification number), for most conspicuous gallantry when the allied drifter line in the Strait of Otranto was attacked by Austrian light cruisers on the morning of May 15th, 1917. When hailed by an Austrian cruiser at about one hundred yards range and ordered to stop and abandon his drifter, the Gowan Lea,

COM. ION H. BENN, M.P., R.N.V.R.
Awarded the D.S.O. for services
during the bombardment of Ostend
and Zeebrugge.

SKIPPER JOSEPH WATT, R.N.R.
Received the V.C. for heroism in
command of the drifter Gowan Lea
in the Mediterranean.

All the time the water was pouring into the ship, and she was sinking. One man, the gunlayer, went to the skipper to see if he could render first-aid, but it was obvious that he was mortally wounded. "It's all right, boy, do your best," said the skipper; and then, to the second hand, "Send a message off." This was the message: "Nelson being attacked by submarine. Skipper killed. Send assistance at once."

All this time the smack was sinking, and only five rounds of ammunition were left, and the second hand went to the skipper lying there on the deck and heard him say, "Abandon ship. Throw the books overboard." He was then asked if they should lift him into the boat, but his answer was, "Tom, I'm done. Throw me overboard." He was too badly injured to be moved, and they left him there on his deck and took to the small boat, and about a quarter of an hour afterwards the Nelson went down by the head. It was just drawing into dusk then, and the crew of the boat pulled all that night. Towards morning the wind freshened and blew them out of their course. They pulled all that day, and had a pair of trousers and a large piece of oilskin fastened to two oars to attract attention. Once a vessel was sighted, and once a group of mine-sweepers, but they passed out of sight. At night the weather became finer, and all through that night they pulled until daybreak, when, at 10.30 a.m., they found a buoy and made fast to it. By afternoon they were sighted and rescued. The second hand, who took charge of the tiller after the skipper had been shot down, was his son; and so the great tradition goes on.

One is tempted to repeat that it would be hopeless to pretend to record even a tithe of the heroic deeds performed during the war by officers and men of the Royal Naval Reserve. The best that can be done is to select a few of the finest, and present them as typical, as they truly are, of the spirit that animated the entire force. Nor was it the change from a mercantile into an official uniform that created the spirit, for those who remained to carry on the vital work of the country in the Mercantile Marine faced the same dangers as their brothers in the R.N.R.—and the R.N.—with equal courage and skill. Only a few weeks before the war Admiral Sir Percy Scott, urging the view that the submarine had rendered useless all other types of warships, had said: "Trade is timid; it will not need more than one or two ships sent to the bottom to hold up the food supply of this country." What an amazing idea this was, and yet how typical of the ideas of so many people who had forgotten that the Navy and the Mercantile Marine were twin brothers—not only in their vital importance to the country, but in blood and tradition. In the first year of the German submarine campaign of "unrestricted ruthlessness," which began on February 1st, 1917, more than 1,100 British merchantmen, apart from fishing craft, were sent to the bottom; and yet, at the end of that year, ships were still entering and leaving the ports of the United Kingdom at the rate of about 4,500 a week! Of course, it should be understood that Sir Percy Scott was referring not to the men of the Mercantile Marine, but to "trade"—the shipowners and consigners of freight, who, in his opinion, would decline to risk their goods at sea in war. As for the men, a representative of the Board of Trade, in the course of a public speech, referred to the only case in which one of

SKIPPER T. CRISP, R.N.R.
Awarded the V.C. posthumously
for great heroism. He had already
received the D.S.C.

LIEUT. C. G. BONNER, R.N.R.
Given the V.C. for gallantry and
skill in action with an enemy submarine. Had already won the D.S.C.

LIEUT. T. B. McNABB, R.N.V.R.
Awarded the D.S.C. for swimming
to a drifting mine in a heavy sea
and securing it.

CAPT. T. E. WARDLE, R.N.
Rounded up and fought a duel to
the death with the German commerce raider Greif, Feb., 1916.

GALLANT SEAMEN WHO CARRIED ON THE GREAT TRADITION IN THE GREAT WAR.

(Photo by F. J. Mortimer, F.R.P.S.

HOME AGAIN : THE WIND-JAMMER MOVING TO MOORINGS

(Photo by F. J. Mortimer, F.R.P.S.

ON BOARD A WIND-JAMMER : TAKING IN SAIL.

them, of British nationality, had refused to sail because of his dread of submarines, and this was his account of the incident: " We found it necessary only a short while ago to prosecute a seaman who had failed to join a transport, and there was no doubt that he was technically guilty ; but he set up and successfully maintained a defence which is unique in the annals of the Mercantile Marine. He admitted that he had failed to join the vessel, but he said that his reason for doing so was that his shipmates refused to sail with him because he had already been torpedoed six times. In other words, while they were fully prepared to take the ordinary sporting chance of being blown up, they were not prepared to accept the handicap of having a Jonah on board ! "

It was mentioned in the early part of this chapter that when officers of the Mercantile Marine distinguished themselves when attacked by the enemy, it was necessary to give them a temporary commission in the Royal Naval Reserve before their services could be recognised in the usual way. This was because the regulations under which such decorations as the D.S.O. and the D.S.C. could be awarded laid it down specifically that the recipients had to bear a commission in his Majesty's forces. At the end of 1916, however, a change of policy of the first importance manifested itself, for in December of that year the " Gazette " announced that the King had conferred a number of decorations and medals on officers and men of the merchant service, " in recognition of zeal and devotion to duty shown in carrying on the trade of the country during the war." This was the first of a series of such lists ; and surely no section of the community, even in the enlisted fighting Services themselves, could prove a greater title to such recognition. Another and a very highly appreciated honour conferred upon the Royal Naval Reserve was the appointment of Captain Herbert James Haddock, C.B., to be a naval aide-de-camp to the King.

HEROIC YOUNG GUNNER.
On February 15th, 1918, German destroyers attacked a flotilla of Dover drifters, sinking seven. Seaman-Gunner F. Plane, the sole survivor on his vessel, went on firing his gun till the boat went down under him. He was picked up later.

These appointments had previously been confined exclusively to officers of the Royal Navy, and it was in recognition of the enormous services they had rendered during the war that the R.N.R. and the R.N. Volunteer Reserve were given this honour in July, 1916. Captain Haddock received his first commission in the R.N.R. in 1883, and at the time of his appointment as aide-de-camp had for many years been the senior officer of the Reserve on the active list. It should be mentioned that it was not until a few weeks before the outbreak of war that the rank of captain in the R.N.R. was created. Captain Haddock was for some time in command of a squadron of " dummy battleships,"

" Dummy battleships " employed as a decoy to the German Fleet, the hulls of the ships being merchantmen, with the superstructure of turrets, tripod masts, and the rest all make-believe—mostly wood. This device was employed also by the Germans, but its humour seems to have outlived its usefulness.

Another innovation which went far towards strengthening the bonds between the Royal Navy and the Royal Naval Reserves—bonds which, it is to be feared, had been not too close or cordial before the outbreak of war—was the early appointment to the R.N.R. of a number of retired flag-officers. The Navy always has an extensive

" retired list," and, naturally enough, those officers upon it who were fit offered their services to the Admiralty practically *en bloc*. In spite of the great expansion of the Fleet, however, there was no possibility of giving even to a tithe of the senior officers appointments commensurate with their rank in the Royal Navy ; and, rather than let their energies and abilities run to waste in the hour of their country's need, a number of them applied for and received temporary commissions in the R.N.R. Not only did they thus become members of a " junior " branch of the naval service, but they dropped from two to four places in rank, since they all entered the R.N.R. as commanders — ranking between lieutenants and captains. The names of the officers who were first to place their services so patriotically at the disposal of the country are worth recording, and they are given in the order in which they first appeared in the official " Navy List " : Sir Alfred W. Paget, K.C.B., K.C.M.G. (Admiral) ; Herbert Edward Purey Cust, C.B. (Rear-Admiral) ; John Locke Marx, M.V.O. (Admiral) ; James Startin, C.B. (Vice-Admiral) ; Charles James Barlow, D.S.O. (Admiral) ; Evelyn Robert Le Marchant (Rear-Admiral) ; Charles Holcombe Dare, M.V.O. (Rear-Admiral) ; and Spencer Victor Yorke De Horsey (Rear-Admiral). At the end of 1917 twenty-one retired officers of the Royal Navy were serving in the R.N.R., though by that time they all held the rank of captain.. Some were given the command of bases from which anti-submarine patrols operated, but the majority commanded armed yachts actually employed at sea on the patrol service. One of these, the Aegusa, mined and sunk in the Mediterranean in April, 1916, was commanded by Captain Thomas Philip Walker, R.N.R., whose rank in the R.N. was that of a vice-admiral on the retired list.

It is desirable, above all things, to emphasise the fact that for all practical purposes the war fused into a solid whole the two great branches of the Empire's sea-power, and brought them again into line as the co-equal defenders of our rights and existence. In this chapter a few names have been mentioned, but the truth is that without the Naval Reserve the Navy could never have carried on, while both would have been lost but for the incomparable services of the Mercantile Marine. The British Empire and the allied cause alike rested upon the freedom of sea communications, and no one can draw a line to show where the responsibility of one Service ended and that of the other began, so closely were they knit in the true comradeship of common endeavour. This interdependence of the Navy and the Mercantile Marine soon came to be recognised as a vital **United sea services** factor in British Imperial policy, of which the command of the sea must ever be the paramount objective ; and the war was not very old before the Admiralty began to perfect arrangements whereby, in the event of future wars, the Mercantile Marine would find itself trained and ready at the shortest possible notice to take up the rôle in which it has never failed.

It was mentioned in the early part of this chapter that some of the first deeds of heroism performed in the war by the merchant service were rewarded not only by a decoration, but by the granting of a commission in the R.N.R., without which, under the existing regulations, the decoration could not have been bestowed. This was overcome later—after the Mercantile Marine had been recognised as part and parcel of the Empire's defence and had been honoured with the title of "His Majesty's Merchant Service"—and the establishment of the Order of the British Empire enabled further recognition of the work of the Mercantile **"His Majesty's Merchant Service"** Marine to be made. Among those who were appointed Officers of the Order (O.B.E.) early in 1918 were the following, the accounts of their services being taken from the "Gazette":

Captain E. B. Bartlett.—Has been in command of a steamship during the war and has carried a series of important cargoes. His ship has twice been encountered by enemy submarines, and, by skilful handling of the vessel, Captain Bartlett compelled them to break off their attacks.

Captain Neil McNeil.—In command of a ship conveying troops, passengers, and cargoes to and from this country throughout the war without mishap. By conspicuous ability he evaded capture by the German raider Emden, and later escaped attacks by enemy submarines.

Captain E. W. Bastard.—Has been a master in the service of his company for twenty years, and throughout the war has been passing through the danger area, carrying many important cargoes for the Government. A ship of which he was in command was recently torpedoed, but he got the whole of the ship's company away in safety, and is now master of another vessel which has been sailing through the war zone.

Chief Engineer T. A. Bowman.—Was chief engineer of the Belgian Prince, which was sunk by a German submarine on July 31st, 1917, in circumstances of exceptional cruelty. Mr. Bowman was one of those who had been taken on board the submarine, when she dived and threw the British prisoners into the water, after the majority had had their lifebelts taken from them. He was in the water from about 9 p.m. until about 6.30 a.m. on August 1st, when he was picked up by a patrol vessel.

Captain W. T. Turner.—Was the commander of the Lusitania when that vessel was torpedoed, and he afterwards went to sea again in charge of a ship on Government service, which also was torpedoed by a German submarine. He again took service in command of another ship, of which he is still acting as master.

The following is a summary of the honours and decorations won by officers and men of the Naval Reserve down to the beginning of 1918, with the exception (save in the case of the V.C.) of those who had lost their lives in action ·

Victoria Cross	8
C.B.	3
C.M.G.	1
Distinguished Service Order	66
Distinguished Service Cross	359
Conspicuous Gallantry Medal	10
Distinguished Service Medal	467

In addition, thirty-three officers had been decorated by Allied Governments.

[F. J. Mortimer, F.R.P.S.

A CHEERING MESSAGE ACROSS THE TUMBLED WATERS.
"All's well!" The message sent over the waves from the men of a mine-sweeper to a destroyer in wintry weather in the North Sea. The full story of the unparalleled heroism of the men employed upon the monotonous and perilous work of the Mine-sweeping Section of the Royal Naval Reserve is one that can never be adequately told.

GERMANS AT RIBECOURT

CHAPTER CCXXIX.

[British official photograph.
UNDER SCOTTISH ESCORT.

SCOTLAND'S SHARE IN THE GREAT WAR TO THE END OF 1917.

By Neil Munro.

Race Sentiment and the Fighting Traditions of Scotland—Highlands and Lowlands: The Influence of Romance—In the Retreat from Mons
—Some Typical Exploits—The Loss of the 1st Gordons—The Marne and Aisne—London Scottish Introduce the Kilt to Paris—
Arrival of the Territorials—The Battle of Ypres—Neuve Chapelle and Loos—Deeds of the Scottish Divisions—Borderers and
Lowlanders in Gallipoli—Sir Douglas Haig as Commander-in-Chief—The Scots on the Somme—" Jock " in Artois—Kilts and
Bagpipes—Scots from Overseas—The Arras Offensive—Cambrai—In the Eastern Fields of War—Business Scots in War Councils
—Some Happy Discoveries in the North—Shipbuilding and Engineering—Industrial Scotland's Effort—Agriculture, Deer Forests,
Forestry—A Frugal People's Contributions to the War Chest and to Relief Funds.

T HE welding of three or four different nationalities into one, called British, is so comparatively recent an historical event that individually we still think and speak of ourselves as English, Scottish, Welsh, or Irish rather than as British. While the common flag of the Union has the same meaning for us all, and commands in us equal fealty and affection, our old race nomenclatures prevail as strongly as ever, endeared by tradition, history, song, and story. Of the three Great Powers at war in the west, the French alone appear to sink all territorial distinctions, and accept contentedly the generic name. The Germans, compact of peoples even more recently confederated than the British, are Prussians, Bavarians, Silesians, Brandenburgers, Pomeranians, in the first place, and Germans only in the second—a fact which was duly recognised in the estimates of their character by the troops opposing them, as well as in the adroitly flattering speeches of their Emperor.

A spirit of emulation is fostered by the judicious recognition of the old race sentiments, and the territorial constitution of our Army during the preceding hundred and seventy odd

years had been a recognition of this fact. For that reason it is quite appropriate at this stage to give, in summary, some idea of the contribution made by Scotland and the Scots to the efforts of the Empire in the great war of liberation. It must be done without vainglory, and with due regard for the relative proportions of things ; for, after all, Scotland is but a thinly-populated part of the British Isles, with not many more inhabitants throughout its whole extent than there were in the county of London. Its pride is that in proportion with its population it came to the shock of conflict with as much patriotic fire and endurance as any other part of the realm, and that its troops, during a three years' campaign, markedly distinguished themselves in every part of the world where the armed might of the British Empire was then engaged.

If the martial spirit be a good thing to perpetuate— and, meanwhile at least, the point admits of no controversy — Scotland, when war broke out, was fortunate in being closer to the warlike traditions of the past than any other part of the United Kingdom. The last battle fought in these islands was in 1746, on that melancholy moor that lies between the foot-hills of the Grampians and the Moray

[Painted by William Orpen, A.R.A.
ONE OF SCOTLAND'S GREATEST SOLDIERS.
Field-Marshal Sir Douglas Haig, Commander-in-Chief of the British
Armies in France, was son of John Haig, of Cameronbridge, Fife, by his
wife Rachel, daughter of Hugh Veitch, of Stewartfield, Midlothian.

LT.-GEN. SIR F. W. N. McCRACKEN, D.S.O.

In command of a Scottish division which fought with splendid heroism at the Battle of Loos, September, 1915.

MAJOR LORD GEORGE STEWART-MURRAY.

Black Watch. Second son of the Duke of Atholl, he was wounded at the Aisne and taken prisoner by the Germans.

Firth. The rising of the clans was not so essentially a response to the summons of Charles Edward Stuart as a last acknowledgment of the hereditary power of the chiefs who ordered it; but it was, until now, the final manifestation in Britain of compulsory military service.

The men of the clans were virtually conscripts — willing perhaps, but conscripts not the less — their tenure of the lands they occupied being conditional on their readiness to draw the sword. They still had their weapons, and a rough kind of military policy and organisation, while the rest of Britain had put down the sword, as it thought, for good, and taken up the ell-wand. One natural consequence of Scotland's tardy entrance into the modern life of ell-wands, manu-

the bugle-call. For generations the Highlands and Islands had had close association with the Army and a certain possessive pride in the Highland regiments. The industrial conditions of the Highlands and Hebrides had sent great numbers of the crofter and farming class into the old Militia battalions for training each year, and the fishermen were, in large numbers, in the Naval Reserve. These were, of course, automatically mobilised at the outset, but were followed immediately by volunteers to an extent that is believed to have made the recruiting of the Western Highlands exceptional in the first six months of the war. In the Isle of Lewis, closely populated by the crofter and fisher class, young men became as rare as trees, and the absence

factures, and a seemingly settled peace was that in the Highlands and Hebrides, at all events, military service under the Crown was not, when the Great War broke out, repugnant to a people whose tribal and family histories got all the lustre they had from not very remote deeds of war.

The call to war in August, 1914, nowhere got more immediate response than in the North. In the cities there was an instant rush to join the Colours, and places like Glasgow, Edinburgh, Aberdeen, and Dundee had for months the utmost difficulty in dealing with successive tides of recruits, impelled by a common emotion always more urgent in densely peopled communities than in rural parts. Yet the rural districts of the country were quite as prompt in realising the situation and answering

of trees in the Hebrides is still as marked as when Dr. Johnson was there. Skye — with a record of military enterprise for a hundred and fifty years probably more striking than in any other rural area of the same extent in the kingdom — a nursery of Peninsular commanders, was no less eager to follow the call of the pipes again. The Island and Highland seaboard districts have, long since, published their rolls of honour in extraordinary large volumes — among the most striking documents of the war; some of the more ardent clan associations have done so also, but if the lowland counties postponed such printed records, it was not for want of material, for they, too, rose magnificently to the occasion.

In the flux of modern Scotland, nearly all the old lines of demarcation between Saxon and Gael had broken

Capt. D. N. Miers, Cameron Highlanders, killed at Beaulne, September, 1914.

Lt.-Col. H. P. Uniacke, C.B., Gordon Highlanders, killed, Aubers Ridge, March, 1915.

Lt.-Col. A. S. Koe, King's Own Scottish Borderers, killed at Y Beach, Gallipoli, on April 26th, 1915.

THREE SCOTTISH OFFICERS WHO FELL IN ACTION EARLY IN THE WAR.

down, and the never wholly quenched martial tradition and fire of the clan counties had, for a century back, been shared in more or less degree by Scots of all descents, down to the English border. The blend of intermarriage for at least three hundred years made this inevitable. Yet it was to the kilted corps that Scots—Lowland as well as Highland—most eagerly flocked; the Scots overseas contingents insisted on the filibeg, and the typical "Jock," for the German as for others, was a man bare-kneed. It is a tribute to the powers of romance. For the Lowland Scots regiments, it cannot be too much insisted upon, have records at least as long and brilliant as any of those that wear the tartan. Their origins and their contributions to national history will, on the whole, evoke more unqualified gratitude from the unprejudiced patriot.

But glamour and romance are nowhere more potent than in military affairs; modern Scottish art in song, story, and painting has ever been so admiringly preoccupied with the Celtic element in the national history of the eighteenth and nineteenth centuries that a foreigner might well imagine the picturesque and gallant characteristics of the race were confined to wearers of the kilt and players of the bagpipe. If the Lowlanders feel aggrieved at this, they must lay the blame on men of genius of their own race—Scott and Stevenson and Hogg, and many others who gave romantic mystery, poetic idealism, and all the old primitive graces to the Celts they wrote of, while endowing their Lowland characters too generally

the Army and Navy was the rally of the North confined. Later on we shall touch in a little more detail on her industrial and administrative efforts in connection with the war; but here, in the more general review, it is desirable to allude, however briefly, to them. Great naval bases in the East and North of Scotland, that had been slowly developing up to August, 1914, were now completed with the utmost rapidity by titanic efforts on the part of engineers. They played a great and indispensable part in the command of the sea by the Navy which, for the first time, was now made visible and impressive to the people of Scotland, who hitherto had seen but little of its might, and was, by the end of 1917, to have in its control a Scots First Sea Lord and a Scots First Lord of the Admiralty. Except in the making of ships, and in their engine-rooms, the Royal British Navy had previously made but little demand upon Scotsmen. Like the cavalry, of which Scotland had never more than one regiment in the country (and even that had been withdrawn from her), the Navy was regarded as practically an English concern, as it was necessary to go south to English waters to find it, and only the summer plumage of the Reserve kept the Scot familiar with the bluejacket uniform. In a single season Scotland was to exercise a greater share in the sea-power of the realm than she had done before in all her history. Merchant vessels and their crews were taken over by the Admiralty; tramps, lighters, and trawlers entered

Scotland and the Royal Navy

SCOTS FROM FAR WEST.
Sir Robert Borden, speaking to a battalion of Scots from Canada in their camp in England on Easter Monday, 1917.

with but the humdrum qualities of pawkiness and the moral virtues. High-spirited youth was never yet intrigued with pawkiness, nor much inspired by the contemplation of meek kailyard attributes, and for a hundred years all that had been young and ardent and truly national in the Scottish race as a whole had felt some magic uplift in the sound of the mountain pipe, and its heart "warm to the tartan," a costume once, and not so very long before proscribed as a badge of rebellion.

Not exclusively, however, to the provision of man-power for

upon a new career as naval auxiliaries; a period of dangerous but profitable adventure, On His Majesty's Service opened up for native mariners and fishermen, a bold and indomitable race of men who as mine-sweepers, patrols, etc., did invaluable work under the Blue or White Ensign. The sport of yachting, always extensively pursued in the firths, was suspended in a single day, and from the pleasure fleet went forth thousands of skilful sailors and navigators to join the ships of war.

No less vital, however, was the aid to be given by industrial Scotland — that well - defined

CANADA'S EX-GOVERNOR-GENERAL GREETING A CANADIAN CONTINGENT.
The Duke of Connaught, Governor-General of Canada from 1911 to 1916, watching a march-past of the Canadian Scottish during their stay at an English training camp. With their pipers at their head the Scots from the Dominions were passing through a town near their camp.

HOMEWARD BOUND.
Arrival in London on home leave from the battle-front. A Scottish soldier sending off a telegram at Victoria Station announcing that he is thus far on his well-earned holiday journey.

midland belt of the country in which a great geographical "fault" has concentrated the productive power of the people. The Central Lowlands, as they are technically called, are separated from the mountainous Highlands by a line running from north-east to south-west between Stone-haven and Helensburgh on the Firth of Clyde, and from the southern uplands by an almost parallel line, running from St. Abbs Head to Girvan. Between those two lines the central part of Scotland sank in far-back geologic times before man appeared on the earth, and happily preserved for future ages Scotland's all-important coalfields, on which the prosperity of the country largely depends. Not only the most fertile part of the country, but having by far the greatest proportion of the mining and manufactures, the Scottish midlands contributed most man-power to the war from its teeming population, and was also of vast importance as contributory of new ships, enginery, and munitions.

Great industrial achievement

From the first hour of war the great shipyards and engineering works of the Clyde valley wrought day and night; the marvels of their achievement could not be realised until peace should make possible a full revelation. There sprang up, too, a vast new industry—the manufacture of munitions—and a great many workshops of world-wide reputation whose activities had previously been wholly exercised in products of ordinary commerce, changed their character and set feverishly to the making of shells, aeroplanes, arms, equipment for the Fleet and Army. Gretna, on the border, became a huge arsenal; others on almost as ambitious a scale sprang into existence in other parts of Scotland, where great wooden towns rose suddenly as in an exhalation, among lonely green fields, and were,

in a few months employing hundreds of thousands of women. The provision of torpedoes, of range-finders, and many other vital elements in the material of war concentrated almost wholly in the Scottish midlands.

On Sunday, August 2nd, 1914, when Germany invaded Belgium, Scotland, which had just entered the season during which its tourist and sporting attractions for the realm in general are at their height, realised that the holiday spirit must instantly be suspended. In a day or two hotels, country mansions, and shooting-lodges were deserted, and the mobilisation which quickly followed changed in a single day the aspect and conditions of life in every part of the country. Territorials, who had just completed their summer camp training, were comparatively easily handled; more difficult was it to deal with the unregimented manhood of the country, which promptly rushed to the recruiting offices. For a fortnight there was but hazy speculation as to the situation and aims of the Regular Army. We were to know of it first definitely when it was engaged **First Scots** under Sir John French at Mons, where we **in action** learned the Scots Greys were in Sir Philip Chetwode's 5th Cavalry Brigade; that Scots Guards, Black Watch, Gordons and Royal Scots, Highland Light Infantry, Argyll and Sutherlands, Royal Scots Fusiliers, Scottish Rifles, and Borderers were under Smith-Dorrien and Douglas Haig. It was a stimulating thought to Scotland, and yet fraught, naturally, with anxieties—that already her most famous regiments were in the fray. The list of them was almost complete when the Seaforth Highlanders, with the 4th Division, in which were two Scottish brigadier-generals, Hunter-Weston and Lowthorpe Haldane, came up to the reinforcement of the main body near Le Cateau.

During the retreat from Mons these regiments suffered heavily, yet covered themselves with glory. The Scots Greys were, in English newspapers, reported to have repeated an exploit of their old Peninsular days, and charged with Highland infantry hanging on to their stirrups, with the cry of "Scotland for ever!"—a romantic story at which the judicious smiled. The Greys, indeed, had gone about their charge on more businesslike lines, and with Chetwode's gallant English cavalrymen had gone through the horsemen of the enemy "as if they were blotting-paper," in the phrase of an observing officer.

In the 3rd Division of the Second Army Corps, General Hamilton had the 1st Gordons, 2nd Royal Scots, and 1st Scottish Fusiliers. When this corps on August 25th, on the Cambrai-Le Cateau road, met the German onslaught of seven divisions single-handed, and with both its flanks exposed, it seemed an impossible situation from which to

MEMORIES OF TOSSING THE CABER.
Scottish troops in the Balkans carrying trench-building timbers, which may well have reminded them forcibly of the old Highland game of tossing the caber.

extricate itself, but it did so. The guns against it were five to one; its right flank was turned in the afternoon of the 26th, and while a general retirement was in operation, the 1st Battalion of Gordons, under Colonel W. E. Gordon, V.C., isolated and surrounded in a narrow lane, were, all but one company, killed, wounded, or made prisoners.

That a kilted regiment, recognised to be among the "corps d'élite" of the Army, should be put out of action so early in the campaign stirred the North profoundly, and in a week it could have produced a whole division of Gordon volunteers to avenge the disaster. The surviving company was joined by eager reinforcements before the Battle of the Marne, and was up to its fighting strength again before the move north to Flanders, by which time the ranks were filled by stalwart lads, mainly from the Lews.

Two typical exploits The retreat from Mons had finished at the Marne almost before those at home had realised it was inevitable, and it was very belated intelligence Scots had of the events of that crowded and terrific fortnight during which the prestige, and even the existence, of the whole British Army was at stake. It is known now that every hour of that retreat was fraught with unimaginable hazards and hardships, deeds of endurance and daring as sublime as any in human history, and that every corps and every man shared equally in all that was in it of epic trial. But the mind is incapable of emotionally realising contemporary epics as a whole, and so it concentrates on typical isolated incidents which, in art and history alike, always get a prominence wholly out of just proportion to their background. Two such incidents may be quoted now, because they are typical of countless of their kind that were to be recorded later on in the war.

One of these was the exploit of Private George Wilson, a reservist of the Highland Light Infantry, who, forty-eight hours before the declaration of war, had been selling newspapers in the streets of Edinburgh. On September 14th, when his regiment with the 5th Brigade was in action at Verneuil, he single-handed attacked a German machine-gun position, shot the officer in charge, captured the gun, and shot or bayoneted the six Germans who worked it, a deed for which he received the Victoria Cross.

Another exploit of a Scot on the Aisne was the subject of lurid pictorial treatment in Paris for months afterwards. A guard of Scotsmen with a Maxim gun held an isolated bridge just across the river, where it was unexpectedly rushed by overwhelming forces of the enemy. One by one the Scots were killed until there was only a single survivor, badly wounded. He lifted the gun, staggered

ON GUARD AT SALONIKA.
At the entrance to the British Guardhouse at Headquarters in Salonika. The Scottish soldier on guard duty, his compatriots, and the other British soldiers were pleasantly conscious of the camera.

with it across the bridge towards the enemy to secure a better position, and held them at bay until supports came up, when his dead hand was still upon the lever and thirty bullet wounds were in his body.

On the Aisne the mortality among officers of the Scottish battalions was exceedingly heavy; but this was more or less the case with all units involved. One brigade alone lost three of its four colonels, one of them being Lieutenant-Colonel Adrian Grant-Duff, of the Black Watch. Particularly unlucky were the 1st Cameron Highlanders, who in heavy fighting on September 14th, to the west of the sugar factory at Troyen, lost seventeen officers and over five hundred men. A fortnight later, when entrenched near Beaulne, their battalion head- **At the Aisne and** quarters was blown up, and five officers **the Marne** and some thirty men were lost, including Captain D. N. Miers, then temporarily in command of the battalion, Captain A. G. Cameron of Lochiel, Lieutenant Napier Cameron, and Lieutenant Meiklejohn. "No British regiment," says Buchan's "History of the War," "suffered more heavily in the first two months of war."

The next phase of the war, after the tide of German invasion had been thrown back at the Marne and the enemy was dug in on the Aisne, was the effort of each side to outflank the other on the north, whereby the lines gradually stretched out until they rested on the Channel. It was then for the first time that Scotland fully realised the magnitude of the national effort demanded, and that a long struggle, even of years perhaps, should test the fortitude of the people as it had never been tested before. Vague first impressions that the fighting in France would be carried on by the small Expeditionary

IN COLD QUARTERS IN THE SOUTH.
Soldiers from Scotland in the trenches on the Salonika front. They found it necessary to be warmly clad in the winter, the rigour of which contrasted greatly with the intense heat of summer.

Force comprised wholly of the old Regular Army, while home defence would sufficiently occupy the Territorials, were dispelled in less than twenty-four hours after the story of the retreat from Mons went through the kingdom on a certain Sunday which found British spirits at what was probably their lowest ebb during the whole war.

Almost immediately after mobilisation, the Territorial battalions had volunteered for active foreign service, and the bulk of those belonging to Scotland had been sent into training camps in England. Much as at first they enjoyed their new experience in a country a great many of them individually had never seen before, and among English people whose cordiality and hospitality they vastly appreciated, they had soon chafed at the prospect of the inaction of home defence, and it was with gladness they now got the route for the foreign field.

About the first Territorial corps to cross the Channel was the London Scottish, which was engaged for some weeks on lines of communication, and introduced the kilt to Paris in October, 1914, the first time the *jupe courte* had been seen there since after Waterloo. Before the

London Scottish set a standard

First Battle of Ypres was decided, the London Scottish were sent north from the Seine and thrown into the combat, in which they distinguished themselves by a steadiness and valour that gave our Army Command the utmost confidence in hastening all other Territorial units into action as soon as possible.

The transference to Flanders brought many fresh Scots troops into line. Upon the 7th Division unquestionably fell the brunt of the fighting for the Ypres salient between

October 20th and November 11th, when the final assault of the Prussian Guard was beaten off. It had landed in Flanders on October 7th. Four Scottish regiments were in the division—the 2nd Scots Guards, 2nd King's Own Scottish Borderers, 2nd Gordon Highlanders, and 2nd Royal Scots Fusiliers. For three weeks the division, which in its composition comprised the flower of the old British Army, held the worst menaced part of the salient —against a force six or seven times its strength. Day after day, its battalions sadly bereft of officers and reduced calamitously in its rank and file, it was called upon to renew the unequal struggle, until at last it was almost annihilated.

Scotsmen in the 7th Division

There were three divisions and some cavalry to bar the advance of the enemy along the Menin road. The 1st and 2nd Divisions were on the left of the 7th, and had in their composition four other Scottish battalions—the 1st Scots Guards, 1st Black Watch, 1st Camerons, and 2nd Highland Light Infantry. During the most critical part of the fighting those divisions had against them five army corps, three of them of the first line. The character of the defence may be gathered from an Order of Sir Henry Rawlinson, issued to the 7th Division, in which he mentions that when it was withdrawn from the firing-line to refit there were but forty-four officers left out of the four hundred that had but a month before come from England, and out of 12,000 men only 2,336.

Whole battalions were virtually wiped out in this otherwise futile German onslaught, including the 2nd Royal Scots Fusiliers and the 1st Camerons, who had early

[*British official photograph.*]

SCOTTISH SOLDIERS LEAVING AN ADVANCED DRESSING-STATION IN MACEDONIA.
Scottish battalions, among them Cameron Highlanders, Royal Scots, and Argyll and Sutherland Highlanders, played a gallant part in the operations on the Struma-Doiran front, by which General Milne supported General Sarrail's offensive, farther west, directed upon Monastir in the autumn of 1916.

LIEUT.-GENERAL SIR AYLMER HUNTER-WESTON.
In 1914 a brigadier with the 4th Division, General Hunter-Weston later commanded the 29th Division at the Dardanelles, and the Eighth Army Corps at the Battle of the Somme.

[Portrait by Francis Dodd.

in September been put into the 1st Brigade to replace the Munsters, who were completely put out of action in the Mons retreat. Of the Fusiliers, who went into action over 1,000 strong under Colonel Baird Smith, seventy men and a second-lieutenant were left to answer the roll-call; caught in an untenable position but resolutely fighting on, the regiment had preferred extinction to retreat.

In the successive German assaults on the Yser, on La Bassée and Arras, as well as on Ypres, every Scottish regiment in the " Army List " was represented in the defence; October and November were poignant months for the Scottish people. During those terrific weeks, in which the thin lines of the British stemmed the thrust of the enemy for the sea, Boulogne, the chief medical base, seemed peopled only by wounded, their doctors, and nurses.

In November Scottish Territorial battalions began to arrive in large numbers, and in the next six months they were along the whole British line,
Scottish Territorial engaged in every operation of the
battalions arrive campaign; among them were kilted corps of Canadian Scots, in their tartan and general accoutrements undistinguishable from the home Highland battalions they were affiliated with.

From March 10th to March 15th, 1915, is a period of poignant memory to the North of Scotland, for the Battle of Neuve Chapelle involved battalions of Territorials from those rural shires, and no town or village but had its sorrowful list of killed and wounded. Scots Guards, Borderers, and Gordons, in a charge on the Aubers Ridge under terrific rifle and machine-gun fire, suffered grave casualties among officers and men. For three days little or no progress was made. In a resumption of the attack on the morning of the 14th, Lieutenant-Colonel Uniacke, C.B., commanding the 2nd Gordons, fell, and the command devolved upon Major J. R. E. Stansfield, D.S.O., who

was afterwards wounded. The 6th Gordon Battalion of Territorials, headed by Lieutenant-Colonel McLean of Breda, was in support, and advanced to the charge with the pipes screaming. Heroically Breda fell, also his adjutant, and many gallant men of Banff and Donside. But the impetus of the charge carried one platoon right through the British line and half-way over to the enemy position, where it remained all day and retired only when the dark came on.

Neuve Chapelle failed to accomplish all that was desired, but the story of it will long persist in Highland valleys.

Two months later Festubert gave these Scottish battalions some of " their own back again," though the casualties among them in that well-fought, well-won fight were considerable. Here the Territorials, now pouring up to the lines, were as conspicuous by their deeds as the Regulars, and at least one
battalion of Argylls, new come from **Neuve Chapelle,**
" the Bonnie Banks of Loch Lomond," **Festubert, Loos**
was practically wiped out of existence.

Next among salient days in the diary of the war in 1915 came the Battle of Loos, from September 25th to 27th. The 9th Division and the 15th Division, both of the New Army, proved themselves of the same martial stuff as the older inured " Fighting Seventh." It was one of the greatest battles ever fought by the British Army, second in this war only to the Somme, and specially notable were the achievements of Lieutenant-General McCracken's 15th Scottish Division and the 47th London Division, who between them burst through the German lines and found themselves simultaneously in Loos. Highland and Lowland brigades were in this divisional exploit; when Loos was taken, the Highlanders impetuously swept a mile farther on and over Hill 70. Unfortunately, the dash of these Black Watch, Seaforths, Gordons, and Camerons—one a pioneer battalion—was

[Portrait by Francis Dodd.

LIEUT.-GENERAL SIR JAMES HALDANE, K.C.B.
A Gordon Highlander with a distinguished military record, General Haldane was a brigadier with the 4th Division in 1914; later he was given a divisional command, promoted lieutenant-general, and created K.C.B.

not supported by any reserves, so the unanticipated breach they pierced in the German line had to be abandoned and a shattered but undaunted remnant reluctantly withdrew to the position chosen by the tactics of the fight. Loos was a great battle and a great success; if it fell just short of being a glorious victory, it was due to no lack of spirit in the Scots. Two Black Watch battalions in the Bareilly Brigade of the Meerut Division (for Scots and Indians were there combined) had advanced with their pipers playing at Aubers Ridge, and fought on

WHERE SHIPS WERE BUILT.
Glimpse, from part of its lofty machinery, of a Clydebank shipbuilding yard.

though decimated. The V.C. was won by Piper Daniel Laidlaw, of the 7th K.O.S.B., 15th Division, for the traditional old braggart feat of playing on the parapet.

In General McCracken's division the casualties numbered over 6,000 in two days. The 9th Black Watch came out of the action with only a little over one hundred men and one officer left.

In this summer of 1915 interest and anxiety at home fluctuated between France and Gallipoli, and Scotland was as depressed as any other part of the Empire by the events of July on the Peninsula. The first Scottish troops to land there were a battalion of the K.O.S.B. and the 5th Royal Scots (Lothian Territorials), units of a very fine division. In the landing at Y Beach, on April 26th, the Borderers lost their commanding

officer, Lieutenant-Colonel Koe, and more than half their men. From June 4th to June 28th General Egerton's 52nd Scottish Lowland Division found the heights of Achi Baba a sad and costly obstacle, and the same division, on July 12th, in a resolute attempt to take the Krithia position, suffered grave losses that gave thenceforth the name of Gallipoli a sinister meaning to Clydesdale and the Lowlands generally. In the Gallipoli campaign were involved Scotland's two mounted corps—the Scottish Horse and the Lovat Scouts, first raised for the Transvaal War, but on this occasion employed as infantry. Early at the Dardanelles, too, was a Naval Division, which included many Scotsmen from the Clyde and Forth Division of the Naval Volunteer Reserve, and some Scottish Yeomanry.

Sir Douglas Haig's succession to Sir John French in the Chief Command of the British Armies in France, in December, 1915, was naturally highly agreeable to the sentiment of the Scots at home and abroad. He was the son of a Fifeshire man by a Midlothian mother; so far as heredity and birthplace go, he **Haig appointed** was a Scot of the Scots. "Heredity goes **Commander-in-Chief** down to the rock," in the phrase of an old Gaelic proverb—that is to say, its influence on type is greater than that of environment and personal experience, and though Haig, like so many countrymen of his own class, was educated mainly in an English school and at Oxford, and had served his country for the most part with English cavalry, the salient features of his character remained Caledonian. He was quiet, he was "dour," he was daring, but with that deliberative caution which, in the Fifer, goes generally with great reserves of strength and fires banked down till the hour of crisis. In the Sudan, in South Africa, and in India he had greatly distinguished himself.

When the British Expeditionary Force went to France, in August, 1914, Sir Douglas was in command of the First Corps. It held the right half of the line at Mons, and in the retreat was extricated from an exceedingly precarious position at Mervilles only by the skilful tactics of its

ON THE BUSY BANKS OF CLYDE.
Looking down on a Clydebank shipping yard from one of its monster cranes, with another of these cranes in the immediate foreground. The Clyde in the years 1915-17 was employing far more men than it did in any pre-war year, and was using up a vast deal more material.

commander, who a week later won high praise from French by his opening of the offensive on the Aisne.

" The action of the First Corps," said Sir John, " under the direction and command of Sir Douglas Haig, was of so skilful, bold, and decisive a character that he gained positions which alone have enabled me to maintain my position for more than three weeks of very severe fighting on the north bank of the river."

Day after day, night after night, the enemy's infantry hurled violent counter-attacks against Haig's corps, but never on any occasion succeeded, though the casualties were very severe, and one brigade alone lost three of its four colonels. Of Sir Douglas's work during the First Battle of Ypres, Sir John French's despatch said :

" Throughout this trying period Sir Douglas Haig, ably assisted by his divisional and brigade commanders, held the line with marvellous tenacity and undoubted courage. Words fail me to express the admiration I feel for their conduct, or my sense of the incalculable services they rendered. I venture to predict that their deeds during these days of stress and trial will furnish some of the most brilliant chapters which will be found in the military history of our time."

It was an army vastly augmented in size and power, since the days of the tenuous defensive line in Flanders, that Haig began, in January, 1916, to prepare for the first really stupendous British effort of the war. He had seventy divisions in the field, leaving out of account the troops supplied by the Dominions and by India. All the Territorial corps and the daily growing might of the Army were at his disposal, and the supplies of munitions were on an incredibly titanic scale.

When the assault opened on July 1st, 1916, every Scottish regiment was represented on the front assailed between Gommecourt and Mametz. Unfortunately it was not permissible to specify divisions **The Battle of** engaged or identify battalion units, but **the Somme** what Scotland knew was that the men of her race from Highland glen and Lowland dale and midland city, from the cliffs of Cape Wrath to the Border marches, were in the Somme and Ancre valleys at this supreme hour. In the first day the attack from the left part of the line, between Gommecourt and Thiepval, failed, the fullest power of the expectant and well-prepared defensive being massed there. One Scottish battalion entered Thiepval village, but Thiepval and all to the north of it was not to be definitely won till later on.

The story of the Somme fight, which lasted for over eight months, is not for recapitulation here (see Chapters CXLIX.-CLIV., Vol. 8), but it falls within the purpose of this rapid review of Scotland's part in the war to say that in every phase of that long battle, on virtually every acre of that countryside wrested from the foe by deeds heroic, the Scotsmen manifested every traditional martial quality of their race. Their graves are many in Picardy, the names of its obliterated woods and villages have more poignant memories and associations for a myriad Scottish households than had the name of Flodden. It was on the Somme, in months of preparation in Picardy, that the French people first and best got to know that kilted or bonneted people who had in other centuries been their " auld allies." Hundreds of thousands of them had been there for a year, billeted in the villages behind the lines, training in the fields outside of shell range, thronging the roads with tartan. The French folk liked them, and they—largely themselves being a rural people, or at least of rural birth—liked the French. They entered often into the most cordial relations with the Picardy peasants, helped them in the work of their fields and gardens, and the sound of their mountain pipes at réveillé cheered the morn or closed the day with the tattoo.

On the Somme there were divisions exclusively Scottish ; some of them wholly Territorial, and the more detailed

THE HERO PIPER OF THE K.O.S.B.
At Aubers Ridge in the Battle of Loos, September 26th-27th, 1915, Piper Daniel Laidlaw won the Victoria Cross " for the traditional old braggart feat of playing on the parapet."

history of the future will associate their names with the most sanguinary exploits, the most bitterly-contested points of the great advance. It was a Highland Territorial division which for weeks fought in the splintered, wired, and pitted cockpit of the High Wood ; it was a Scottish division which, after six continuous weeks in the fighting-line, captured Martinpuich in a wild impetuous rush that was not in the official programme for the day ; it was the Highland Territorials, again, who carried the fortress village of Beaumont-Hamel, one of the hardest tasks that faced troops throughout the whole battle ; and Deville Wood is soaked with the blood of South African Scots who, wearing the Murray tartan kilt in honour of their honorary colonel the Duke of Atholl, fought bitterly for every yard of that unspeakably abominable place.

Fricourt and Longueval, Mametz and Delville, La Boisselle and Courcelette **Proud names in** —they became shapeless, almost undis- **Scottish annals** tinguishable, places in the landscape of the Somme, but the names will abide with memories sad and proud in the annals of Scottish regiments. On the farthest point reached by the London Scottish during the battle a large memorial cross was erected not long afterwards. For miles behind and around it was a rolling moorland pitted with shell-holes. The cross is a plain one of two great beams, and stands about eight feet high. At its base is a cairn, in which is embedded a strong block of oak bearing a metal plate with an inscription.

Once more the more furious fire of war drifted north— this time to the Arras sector. The task for the moment was done on the Somme. Bapaume, so long a visionary goal, was won at last ; so was Péronne. In these desecrated towns, so long occupied by the foe and left

H

by him in a state unspeakable, the Scots had but little time to view the ruins, for they had to trek up the Arras road behind their bagpipes to bring in the spring of 1917 and push back the German in the Ancre valley. More closely massed together than before, the Scottish troops—and that only a part of them—far outnumbered the original British Expeditionary Force, and throughout the Arras offensive of the spring of 1917 were wielded by Commander-in-Chief as if he had pinned his faith for this occasion mainly upon his own countrymen.

Without exception the commanders of these Scottish divisions were Englishmen or Irishmen, but Headquarters comprised many Scots in positions of vital importance. Intelligence, for instance, was under Major-General Charteris, and aerial affairs under Sir David Henderson, both Glasgow men; while one army corps, the fifteenth, was commanded by Lieutenant-General **Scotsmen holding high positions** H. S. Horne, C.B., a Caithness man, to whom was attributed the introduction of the "creeping barrage" in artillery fire. For weeks preparatory to the new offensive east of Arras all that part of Artois behind the zone of fire assumed a markedly Scottish hue, as brigade after brigade of the Northerners concentrated in the countryside contiguous to the great highways between St. Pol and the frightfully-shattered town of old tapestry weavers. It is, in many of its aspects, not unlike rural parts of the Scottish Lowlands, though the absence of dikes, fences, and hedges more closely suggests the unbroken farmlands of Manitoba or Saskatchewan. The rural toils, cares, and frugalities of the Artois peasants were, in the main, those of agricultural Scotland. During their concentration and in the periods of rest from the trenches in the course of the battling which followed, the Scots, or "Jocks" as the argot of the war designated them—borrowing a term once associated only with the Scots Guards—entered intuitively into sympathetic rapport with the people among whom they were billeted.

Thackeray, in "Vanity Fair," describes how "Donald the Highlander, billeted in the Flemish farmhouse, rocked the baby's cradle, while Jean and Jeanette were out getting in the hay," during the muster for the Battle of Waterloo, and adds: "As our painters are bent on military subjects just now, I throw out this as a good subject for the pencil, to illustrate the principle of an honest English war." Hundreds of thousands of such scenes could have been found by any sentimental artist in Artois in the spring of 1917, only, with a more modern idea of gallantry, Donald left the women to nurse their babies and worked in the fields himself. It was possible to render considerable assistance to the natives in their farming operations; all their young men were away with the Colours, and the old men and women left behind would probably have had but indifferent crops in autumn but for the skilled and hearty co-opera-**Highlanders help the French farmers** tion of those bonneted lads from the Lothians, Ayrshire, Moray, or Argyll. Whole battalions of them repaired the country roads; in companies, during hours of intermission in their training, they dug in fields and gardens, and introduced some measure of sanitary reform where before sanitation had been as primitive as in rural Scotland of the eighteenth century.

At first the kilt and bagpipe vastly astonished the people, wakened each morning at réveillé by the strains of "Johnny Cope" played through their villages, and unfamiliar with the "garb of old Gaul"; but long before the thunder of British guns on the Ancre, which drummed all day and night, and lit up the evening sky as with the aurora borealis, had receded to the east, the presence of the Caledonians, their dress, and their mountain music had become commonplace. Those French rustics learned to distinguish the regimental tartans better than most civilians could do at home.

By this time there were more varieties of tartan in the field than at any time since the Battle of Culloden, for to the old Regular patterns had been added others unknown to the pre-war Army, old clan "setts" adopted by regiments of Scots from Canada and South Africa. The most vivid of all—the brilliant red of Duart Maclean, worn by the stalwart Maclean Highlanders, half-Canadian, half-United States in their levy—was to come on later.

The kilt, as the uniform of Scottish Highland infantry, had almost been suppressed in the 'eighties, when Childers, at the War Office, proposed the abolition of all distinctive tartans as a measure of economy, and inferentially threatened the extinction of the filibeg itself, a prospect which roused the indignation of Scotland, and was finally averted—by Royal intervention, it was understood—after an indignation meeting of titled and prominent Scots at Stafford House. What sentimental fascination the costume has for the North of the Tweed was proved during the earlier part of the war, when recruiting was still voluntary; the kilted battalions attracted by far the greatest number of men, and in 1917 there were far more kilts in France alone than there were in all Scotland in the clan period.

Apparently the kilt justified itself as a garb suitable for warfare in all climates; it was now being worn on all the battle-fronts of Europe and Asia where the British Army was engaged, and there was not the slightest suggestion that it had any disadvantage either in the winters of France or the heats of Mesopotamia. For at least two years it was considered desirable to "camouflage" the tartan, covering it on active service by a khaki apron. During 1917, however, this device of protective colouration seems to have been regarded as unnecessary under the conditions of trench warfare, and many, if not most, of the battalions by then even advanced to the attack without the apron. The sporran, which, in older wars, contributed, with feather bonnets **The kilt and the bagpipe** and scarlet doublets, to the pomp of the Highland corps, had been left at home; but the general result was that a Scottish soldier in the field during the Great War looked more like the clansman of the period of Montrose, Dundee, and Prince Charlie than he ever did when turned out in "Highland uniform" designed by London military tailors. The universal change to the old flat bonnet, in place of the glengarry, which was quite a modern invention; the use of the steel helmet, approximating pretty closely to the old morion; and, in winter, the resort to buff or goat-skin jerkins, completed an "ensemble" strikingly reminiscent of the old clan days.

The kilt as worn to-day (said Lieutenant-Colonel John Buchan in his "History of the War") has a somewhat formal and modern look suggestive less of Rob Roy than of the Prince Consort. But watch that company of Camerons returning from a route march. The historic red tartans are ragged and faded, the bonnet has a jaunty air, the men have a long, loping stride. They might be their seventeenth-century forbears, stepping on a moonlight night through the Lochaber passes. Here is a battalion from the Borders. The ordinary Borderer in peace-time looks like anybody else, but these men seem to have suddenly remembered their ancestry. They have the lean strength, the pale, adventurous eye of the old Debatable Land.

Another external feature distinguished the Scottish regiments—the bagpipe. For a considerable time it was, save the bugle, the only musical instrument to be heard. Later, of course, the virtue of divisional brass bands was discovered. When the war started, Scottish battalions took with them to the field only five or six pipers each, and these, in actual combat, generally took up an alternative rôle as stretcher-bearers. By and by it was found that the stimulating and cheering effect of pipe music on the Scots was of no little importance, and after two years of war battalion pipe-bands numbered twice or three times as many players as they did at first. English divisional commanders and brigadiers, probably with no

Gallantry that won the Victoria Cross. On September 14th, 1914, Private George Wilson, of the Highland Light Infantry, single-handed attacked a German machine-gun position near Verneuil, killed the officer and six men and captured the gun.

Highlanders marching back from the trenches headed by their pipers. Early in the war every Scottish battalion took a few pipers into the field; later these few musicians, who also acted as stretcher-bearers, were augmented into large pipe bands.

Heroism and music from the Highlands of Scotland that resounded anew through France.

"They that walk in darkness ——": Highlanders leading a blinded officer from the battlefield.

Triumphal progress of the kilt in Italy: A Highland officer the cynosure of all eyes.

Quarters of Italian troops near the firing-line among the Carnic Alps. The work of conveying provisions and fuel to large numbers of men, perched on almost inaccessible ledges like these, presented difficulties that only inexhaustible perseverance and ingenuity overcame.

Convoy of supplies traversing roads constructed in the Alps by Italian sappers. Beyond the point which pack animals could attain, provisions had to be carried on their backs by the born mountaineers who formed a most distinguished part of the gallant Italian Army.

Hardships of war in the snow-clad mountainous highlands of Italy.

musical or sentimental prejudices in favour of the pipes, were significantly the most urgent advocates of this increase.

A massed divisional pipe-band, with its drummers, by the end of 1916 had become a colossal affair, with from four to five hundred men in it. On certain occasions Scottish divisions resting had such band performances, and Sir Douglas Haig was present sometimes when this extraordinary aggregation of drones and sheep-skins drowned the voice of the not far-distant guns.

It was one of the favourite " wheezes " in some of the Scottish divisions that there were—in other divisions than theirs, of course—battalions in kilts who could speak only Dutch or French. If you addressed them in Scotch or Gaelic they would throw up their hands and cry out " Kamerad ! " went the story. The implication was that Boers and "habitants" of the French-Canadian provinces were predominant in those Scottish regiments recruited overseas. It was only a joke ; the kilted regiments sent over by the Dominions were as genuinely Scottish as any in the Army, with more sentiment and fervour on the subject of their nationality than if they had gone to war directly from Glasgow or Glen Urquhart. They represented that passionate patriotism of the exile which finds expression in Caledonian Clubs and clan societies in Cape Town, Winnipeg, or elsewhere by orgies of haggis and bagpipes on St. Andrew's Day or on January 25th. Scottish battalions from overseas were peculiarly fortunate in these respects—that they could always get more fresh drafts of men than they needed, and of the highest standard, and their folks across the oceans made it a pious duty to see that they wanted for nothing in equipment and field comforts.

One might search in vain for the Frenchman from the province of Quebec among the Canadian Highlanders ; though from Glengarry, Ontario, and **Scots from** elsewhere in the Eastern provinces were **overseas** certainly husky-looking men in tartan who spoke " habitant " French—but not quite so fluently as they could speak English or Gaelic. Their names and heredity were Scottish, and, scions of genuine Highland colonies that in Canada still keep up the Gaelic tongue, they very properly counted themselves as Scots " pur sang," though they had never set eyes on these islands till they came over with their contingents. Of course, too, the Dominion kilted corps included large numbers of men who had only in recent years emigrated from Scotland.

Among the South African Scottish soldiers were admittedly fluent speakers of the " Taal," but with them it was a language acquired since 1902. They were, for the most part, Scots who fought as youths with the Imperial Army in the Transvaal, settled down there, and joined the Colours when the Great War began. From that source came a great many officers and instructors, not only for the overseas contingent, but for the Army raised at home. One of the largest and finest pipe-bands at the front in France was recruited exclusively in Africa, and every man in it was a Scot who had learned the art years before in one or other of the regular Highland regiments.

It was with the sound of the pipes still in their ears that in April, 1917, the Scottish division concentrated in and near Arras went out and took up their fighting positions to the east of that shell-shattered town. The Grande Place of Arras " roared with the Highland drone," and for weeks, during which some of the most sanguinary fighting of the war continued, the kilties surged through it like a tide, either going to, or coming back for a brief respite from, the contested ground where they were hurled again and again against an enemy who considered himself inviolable as a cliff of the sea. Day after day were fought engagements to which the fiercest old tribal battles of the North were mere squabbles by comparison ; yet it was many weeks, after the first break-through of

the German lines on April 9th, before it was understood at home that the Army of Scotland was away from the Somme and specially involved in this new exploit. Only one Scottish regiment's name came into the newspaper chronicles of the time, yet all the Scottish regiments were there, with many corps of their countrymen from the Dominions, and no regiment but added to the lustre of its martial traditions.

The most crucial days were April 9th and 23rd. On the 9th, at 3.20 a.m., the Scottish brigades were standing to arms ; at 5.30, the zero hour, under a terrific barrage, they advanced to the attack, and in a very short time carried their part of the first system of enemy trenches. Shortly before eight o'clock they attacked the second objective, which was captured with the assistance of Tanks. So far, the progress made was considered to be comparatively cheaply bought, though we may accept as typical the experience of one **In the Battle** Cameron battalion, which went into the **of Arras** attack with twenty-three officers and five hundred and twenty-one men, and had twelve officers and one hundred and seventy-five men killed or wounded.

In the week which followed, a great many of the German strong points, concentrated in or near villages which had lost all habitable appearance, passed into British hands, and by the time Fampoux was captured, fourteen thousand prisoners had been passed back into the great barbed-wire cages prepared for them on the St. Pol-Arras road.

After a lull, during which the Germans found themselves harassed by the French offensive farther south, the Arras battle was resumed on April 23rd on a wide front on both sides of the Scarpe ; the whole German intermediate line which preceded the " Siegfried " system of trenches was broken through, Gavrelle and Guémappe were captured, and there was another considerable haul of prisoners. Repeated counter-attacks of the most desperate kind made upon the new position at Gavrelle brought serious casualty lists to Scotland, and until well on in May the taking, consolidation, and holding of the Oppy line, Rœux, and Monchy-le-Preux left few hours of respite for the Scottish divisions. The Gordons alone engaged in these operations could have made up two brigades. In the month of April one Scottish division won one hundred and forty medals, though repeatedly it happened that there were neither officers nor non-coms. surviving to report individual deeds as daring as any of those that won due official recognition.

Following the victories of Arras, the Scots were prominent next at the surprise attack by the Germans at Lombartzyde, where Lowlanders of the Highland Light Infantry, by a cool and resolute defence of a gravely threatened flank, checked effectively what would otherwise have been a vastly more serious development. At the surprising Cambrai " push " in the latter part of November, 1917, these **At Lombartzyde** Northerners were again engaged, and **and at Cambrai** battalions of them fought their way into the closest proximity to the menaced town. Following the gaps made by the Tanks they swept, with English and Irish, over the enemy's outposts and stormed the first defensive system of the Hindenburg line on the whole front, then pressed on a mile farther to the second system. Highland Territorial battalions crossed the Grand Ravine and entered Flesquières, where fierce fighting took place, helped to secure the crossing of the canal at Masnières, and captured Marcoing and Neuf Wood. They were Scottish troops who, moving north-east from Flesquières, captured the German defensive lines south-west of Cantaing, and the village itself, together with five hundred prisoners. Later in the day they continued their advance and established themselves in positions more than five miles beyond the former German front line.

While Scottish troops in France and Flanders were

BATTALION OF CANADIAN SCOTSMEN IN TRAINING IN ENGLAND.
The Scottish regiments recruited in the Dominion were as purely Scottish as any that came from the north of the Tweed, being composed of men whose names and heredity were Scottish, scions of genuine Highland colonies in Canada that still kept up the Gaelic tongue.

gaining fresh laurels in the old " cockpit " of Europe, so familiar to their countrymen in the seventeenth and eighteenth centuries, the kilt and bonnet were equally conspicuous in other parts of the world. Gallipoli has already been referred to. After the withdrawal from that peninsula, a host of Scots descended upon Egypt—where the command was entrusted to Lieutenant-General Sir James Wolfe Murray, a Peeblesshire man—Palestine, and Mesopotamia ; their bagpipes hailed the morn in Greece.

Gaza occupied their attention for a long period, and cost them many casualties before it was captured. The hot sands of Ancient Babylonia, with a summer shade temperature of 103 degrees, severely tried some of the regiments transferred there from the rigorous weather of Northern France.

In October and November, 1917, Scottish troops led the van on the left flank in the Staff operations which carried Jaffa. They were, mainly, soldiers of the Lowland Scottish division which had fought the Turk in Gallipoli— men of Glasgow, Greenock, Edinburgh, and Ayrshire. On the night of Hallowe'en they stormed the El Arish Redoubt, " Umbrella Hill," and the " Little Devil " ; some days later they marched through the sand to the Wady Hesi, found the enemy strongly holding its north bank, attacked with the bayonet, and carried the whole position by nightfall. After a week of strenuous and incessant fighting, during which they covered nearly seventy miles, they captured a strong Turkish position in two villages on the Wady Rubin, taking one thousand two hundred prisoners, and next day were striding across the Jerusalem line.

In the Palestine advance

Major-General Hill, commanding the division in the Wady Rubin affair, afterwards wrote a letter to Brigadier-General Pollock, who commanded the attack, in which he described it as " a truly gallant and magnificent achievement illustrating what Scottish grit and determination can do." In a Brigade Order it was stated " without assistance from any other body of troops, except a cavalry demonstration on the left flank, by their determined heroism " the Scots captured an entire position extending to a frontage of 4,700 yards, " one of great natural strength, held by a garrison considerably exceeding the attackers in strength. The defence, with an abundant

supply of machine-guns and some artillery support, had been ordered to hold out to the last by Kress von Kressenstein, the Germany Army commander, who had himself chosen the position."

When Jerusalem was entered on December 11th by General Allenby and his Staff, it seemed peculiarly appropriate to the Scottish that among the forces represented should be the Royal Scots, the oldest line battalion in the Army, with a history so ancient and variegated that it had been humorously designated " Pontius Pilate's Bodyguard " by the country of its origin.

While Scotland contributed her full share to the fighting forces of the Empire—and her dead in the first three years of the war have been estimated in number nearly seventy thousand men—she also took a prominent part in that national organisation essential to support them. Prominent among the Scots whose business or trade experience proved invaluable to the Government may be mentioned the Right Hon. Sir Joseph P. Maclay, a great Clyde shipowner, who was appointed Shipping Controller in the Ministry in December, 1916 ; Mr. Andrew Weir, the shipbuilder, Surveyor-General of Supply at the War Office, and a member of the War Council ; and Sir William Weir, the Glasgow engineer, whose technical experience was of the utmost value to the Air Board from its institution. His brother, Colonel James Weir, of the same firm, who had in the earlier stages of the war

Scottish men of affairs

graduated from an artilleryman to be a flight officer, and latterly to the superintendence of great aeroplane construction on Clydeside, was, towards the end of 1917, made Chief of the Technical Department of the Air Ministry. These were among the happiest discoveries of a Government eager to secure men of unusual experience and qualities. Upon Sir Joseph Maclay and his Advisory Committee depended the drawing up and organising of a programme of standardised ship production to counter the results of the U boat campaign.

To the names mentioned—which were not to be found in any biographical work of reference before the war— must be added those of the Right Hon. Sir Eric Geddes, and his brother Sir Auckland Geddes, Edinburgh men. Sir Eric's management of an Indian railway, and later of the North-Eastern Railway, happily suggested his appointment to the head of British military railways in 1916 ; he did marvellous work in organising the lines in France. In July, 1917, he became First Lord of the Admiralty— a striking tribute to his versatility. Sir Auckland Geddes, who had been a doctor in the R.A.M.C. in the South African War, and was Professor of Anatomy in the McGill University, Canada, when the Great War broke out, entered the Army, and rose to be Brigadier-General in charge of Recruiting in May, 1916. In August, 1917, he was appointed Chief of the National Service organisation.

It has already, if briefly, been indicated that industrial Scotland, from the very first day on which war seemed imminent, took measures to throw all the power of her sinews, all the influence of her master minds into the struggle. Very quickly the competitive antagonism of her greatest business concerns was completely suspended, and the greatest old rivals in trade anticipated all that prudence might dictate to the Government and pooled their knowledge, their experience, their plans, and productive appliances. Into the production of material of war firms, who for long appeared unlikely to derive any commercial advantage from the change, turned their plants, designed for very different purposes, but happily adaptable for the new occasion. Engineers and shipbuilders, whose names and works had been familiar for generations to every part of the world where ships may voyage and railways run, intuitively formed themselves into consultative and advisory bodies, and organised affairs on a colossal scale as disinterestedly as if the age of Communism had begun.

Manufacturers' loyal enthusiasm

The marvellous celerity with which new works all over the country sprang up and began to pour forth the weapons and necessaries of war was largely due, not to any " canny " foresight of possible expansion of personal interest, but to a loyal enthusiasm ; and men gave freely of their time, their counsel, their personal supervision to projects from which they could not hope to derive the slightest personal advantage.

Some labour disputes on the Clyde, at an early stage of the war, created in England, perhaps, apprehension which on the Clyde itself would appear merely laughable in the circumstances. They were purely sectional, arose from misunderstandings principally, were quickly settled, and at no time led to any serious arrest in the output of work. Some unpleasant innuendoes regarding the drinking habits of the Clyde artisans, made by politicians who obviously knew nothing about the subject, were much resented by hundreds and thousands of men whose honest, unflagging, and sober industry, as represented by the

renown of Clyde work for a hundred years, might have shown how absurd was the generalisation. Not for very long, however, could the most temperate inclination to alcoholic stimulants be conveniently indulged on the Clyde and in most parts of Scotland. The consumption of spirits in Scotland has always been less per head of the population than in England, a statistical fact which is not very generally known ; only the enterprise of Northern distilleries has peculiarly associated the name of the country with whisky, a so-called " national beverage," which is really only of comparatively modern use there.

Drinking hours—always much shorter in Scotland than elsewhere in the kingdom—were reduced gradually and rapidly, until at last, either by Government control or the voluntary act of the licensees, public-houses were open only for a few hours each day. The manufacture of pot-still whisky, which comprised by far the greatest bulk of the spirit known as "Scotch," was completely suspended, and the distilleries entered upon an indefinite period of inaction. " Grain whisky," manufactured by the patent-still process by certain very large dis-

Whisky production for explosives

tilling concerns, continued to be produced, but not for the assuagement of any national thirst ; the spirits of high potency which they alone could turn out were found indispensable in the manufacture of certain explosives, and were all commandeered for this purpose. Before the end of 1917 whisky was selling retail at fifteen shillings a bottle in Scotland, a price at which it was manifestly almost out of the reach of the working man.

In the autumn of 1914 the Clyde shipyards had under

WORTHY HEIRS OF THE MARTIAL TRADITIONS OF THE CLANS. *[British official photograph.*
Highland Territorials crossing a captured German trench in the Cambrai battle sector and pressing forward to attack a further objective. Scottish Territorials arrived in France in large numbers in November, 1914, and thereafter were engaged in every operation of the successive campaigns.

construction some of the most ambitious creations of Admiralty imagination, and in naval and mercantile contracts had an enormous amount of work in hand. From 1908 to 1910 there had been dull times; the recovery began in 1911, and was extraordinarily rapid. In 1913 the river had turned out 757,000 tons of new shipping, a record in its history. What the actual production was in three years of war cannot be even approximately stated, but it certainly very much exceeded the output of the old pre-war record year, 1913. Most of this increase was, of course, naval work; every class of fighting ship and every kind of auxiliary craft for the Admiralty's use was on the stocks of those wonderful shipyards set beside a narrow stream running for many miles through pastoral scenery. New yards were opened, old ones were vastly extended, and marine engineering establishments, by the extension and re-organisation of their works, kept abreast of the additional demands upon machinery. The Clyde in 1915-16-17 was employing far more men than it did in any pre-war year, and was using up a vast deal more material, but the calls on the yards and shops were such that in neither case was the supply equal to the demand, and it is questionable if the maximum possibilities in the way of output were nearly reached. Standard ships and concrete barges became features of the work of the river in 1917, though only a very subordinate one.

In the East of Scotland the same activity in relative degree was manifest. The greatest progress on this coast was made at Dundee, where vessels of large size were constructed; but the Forth, awakened to life by the new

SCOTS IN THE DARDANELLES.
[British official photograph.]
Working-party of Highlanders on a Dardanelles cliffside, helping to get the materials for making a break water. In the summer of 1915 some of the Scottish troops taking part in the ill-starred Gallipoli Campaign suffered very severe losses.

presence of the great Rosyth naval base, began to have a larger vision of its destiny, and its schemes and potentialities became enormous. Big new yards were opened at Kinghorn and Alloa; old Leith yards were considerably extended. At Aberdeen the provision of trawlers for work more urgent and onerous than fishing occupied a great many more men than before, and yards and factories were greatly extended in consequence.

Naval bases in Scotland

Rosyth, Cromarty Firth, and Scapa Flow in the Orkneys fully justified the pre-war policy of the Navy, which had decided upon them as commanding bases for the North Sea, and that coast saw more of the power and activity of the Fleet than western waters or the English Channel did.

Iron and coal are no less important in Clydesdale than shipbuilding. The demands upon its steel and iron were constantly ahead of the supply, but the output of the collieries after the middle of 1915, despite the great bodies of colliers who flocked to the Colours from the very first day of war, was invariably, or at least frequently, in excess of the demand, or what amounts to the same thing, in excess of transport—sea and land—necessary for its conveyance. At no time after the commencement of hostilities had there been any real scarcity of coal in Scotland.

Though nearly all but this midland area of the country is rural, it cannot as a whole be described as agricultural, and it quickly became evident that agriculture — brought to the highest pitch in the world, as in the Lothians—had been shamefully neglected throughout great

DECORATED FOR BRAVE DEEDS.
[British official photograph.]
Men of a Scottish regiment on the western front being decorated with medals which they had won by acts of heroism in the field. One Scottish division won a hundred and forty medals in a single month.

areas of the North. The deer forests of the Highlands —those treeless expanses of moor, glen, and mountain, though they had once maintained great resident peasant populations, did so no longer, and were able to contribute to the Army only the very limited number of keepers, stalkers, and gillies they employed. Extensive sheep-runs, too—wide solitudes giving occupation to a mere handful of shepherds in each case, proved as unproductive of recruits. Where the Naval Reserve and the Highland regiments got their recruits from were the old, despised, so-called " congested " crofting areas, in which the ancient Highland polity of small land-holdings still persisted.

Of these crofting districts the Island of Lewis may be quoted as typical. In the first year of the war, out of a population of 30,000, " Loyal Lewis " had given 4,320 men, the equivalent of an infantry brigade, to the Navy and Army. The percentage of the total population was nearly 15 ; of males, over 33. In one district, that of North Tosta, the percentage of total population was 32, and of 400 men, 189 were with the Colours—47 per cent. Had the proportion of enlistments over the whole British Isles been equal to that of the Lews, the fighting power of the Crown would have numbered 6,500,000, and there would have been no Cabinet crisis. The military value of the contingent from this little surviving area of the old Highland world is not fully represented by numbers, for the casualty and honours lists bore ample testimony to the fighting quality of these gallant crofters and fishers.

War brought the sporting estates of the Highlands down to their real economic value regarded from a national standpoint. In the first year shooting rents declined at least 50 per cent., and comparatively few were let at all.

Agriculture and forestry

It became advisable—necessary, indeed—to keep down the herds of red deer which, after an unwonted period of sanctuary, had increased greatly ; shooting parties of quite unconventional character were organised for this purpose, and the aid of good marksmen from the Army was enlisted.

By the autumn of 1917 the cultivated area of Scotland had been greatly increased. With the assistance largely of women, farmers put under the plough and cropped much grassland, and many thousands of acres that had previously been neglected ; the system of small town allotments assumed great proportions in the neighbourhood of every burgh and village. For many years the obvious and exceptional suitability of many parts of the country for afforestation had been pressed upon successive Governments, and the Royal Scottish Arboricultural Society had long endeavoured to get the authorities to recognise the importance of the question, but with very little success. In 1911 the Board of Agriculture for Scotland was created, with a fund for carrying out its purposes, one of these being the promotion of forestry. Nevertheless, the total expenditure in this connection in Scotland in seven years was only £17,500, as against £84,345 in England and Wales, and £117,973 in Ireland — though Scotland offers greater opportunities for afforestation than all the other parts of the United Kingdom put together.

With a history of neglect, indifference, and repression that went back for a generation or two, the timber supply of Scotland was a mere fraction of what might have been ; but still there were estates with fairly considerable areas of trees on them, mainly conifers that grow rapidly and thrive remarkably well in every part of the country save, perhaps, in the Hebrides. Upon these woods, when transport of food cargoes requisitioned shipping that previously had taken over the lumber of Scandinavia and North-West America, the axe of the woodman fell remorselessly. Tradition asserts that Scotland once sacrificed all her mature timber for the construction of a single ship-of-war in the Middle Ages. It is doubtless but a fairy tale ; certain it is, however, that the slaughter of the woods in the first three years of the Great War threatened to leave the land as bare of sylvan features as Johnson professed to find it in his Hebridean journey.

War Loans and Relief Funds

That thrift which, rightly or wrongly, is popularly attributed to the Scotsman—who, to tell the truth, has got the reputation in the past chiefly through his making a virtue of necessity—seemed not wholly an illusion when appeals were made for War Loans and Relief Funds. The results surprised even those best situated to judge of the country's savings and financial resources. A people who in the end of the seventeenth century were beggared by the failure of the Darien Scheme, to whose enterprise they contributed £300,000 of the £600,000, which was all the cash they had, were found capable of cheerfully producing funds which to that age would seem fabulous.

But long before the " sweet simplicity " of Five per Cents. had become attractive to investors, Scotland was contributing on the most generous scale to all the War Relief Funds, and Glasgow by far outstripped any other city in the kingdom outside of London in the magnitude of its offerings. This zeal for the immediate welfare and relief of our fighting men never slackened for a day in Scotland, however much War Bonds might appeal ; the figures of every national fund are eloquent of continuous support from the North on the most generous scale. But beyond national relief funds, the country initiated and maintained relief schemes, agencies, and institutions specially for its own people. Not exactly in this category may be classified the Hospital for Limbless Soldiers and Sailors, of which the Princess Louise became active patron and head, for the hospital and grounds at Erskine House, Renfrewshire, was for men of any British race, but the place itself was the gift of Scots, and was by Scots maintained.

There were many other agencies more exclusively designed for the Scottish soldier and sailor— who, for instance, at Christmas was assured of his " Jock's box " of good things from his own folk, no matter in what part of the world he might be serving his King and country. And at the end of 1917 the Scot, with all the fervour, faith, and dour determination of his country behind him, was fighting on the Belgian and French front, in Italy, in Mesopotamia, in the Holy Land, and in Macedonia ; holding garrisons on the outskirts of Empire and refilling the seas with ships as they were being swept by piracy.

ON GUARD AT SALONIKA. [*British official photograph.*
Representative of the various forces united there against the common enemy—
a Scottish soldier on sentry duty guarding stores on the shore at Salonika. He
was silhouetted against a background in which the ships on which the Salonika
Expedition mainly depended were dimly seen.

Italian coast battery in action bombarding Mount Hermada, the last great natural bastion that barred the Italians from Trieste, in September, 1917, before the reverse that overtook the Italian arms on the Upper Bainsizza plateau necessitated the general retreat to the west of the Isonzo.

Italian armoured train of naval heavy guns, manned by sailors, in action against the Austrians on the coastal heights of the Carso. The railway from Monfalcone to Trieste, running along the shore, enabled these formidable moving forts to be concentrated at any desirable point.

ITALIAN HEAVY GUNS THAT HAMMERED THE AUSTRIANS ON THE ADRIATIC COAST.

CHAPTER CCXXX.

THE DEFEAT AND RECOVERY OF ITALY.

I.—The Carso Battles and Storming of the Bainsizza Plateau.

By Edward Wright.

Italy Still a Nation in the Making—Disturbing Factors of Clerical, Giolittian, and Socialist Forces—Difficult Task of Successors of Cavour—Proposals for Italian-Franco-British Offensive—General Badoglio's Successes in May, 1917, at Cuk and Vodice Ridges—Magnificent Advance of Carso Army to the Hermada Fortress—Italy Stopped from Complete Victory by Lack of Munitions—Violent Austrian Counter-Offensive—Prophetic Defection of an Italian Brigade on the Hermada—Military Bankruptcy of Russia Endangers Italy—Baron Sonnino Visits London for Help—Woeful Economic Condition of Italian People—English Coal Dearer than Bread—The Month of a Hundred Food Riots—Treacherous Intrigues in Turin—The Isonzo Campaign of August, 1917—Fine Victories on the Carso—Second Italian Army's Masterly Conquest of Bainsizza Plateau—Tableland Battle of September 4th Ends in a Draw—General Capello Left with a Perilously Exposed Flank—Pope Benedict's Appeal for Peace.

IN political stability Italy and Russia were the weaker of the Allies, and were therefore subjected to heavier internal trials than Great Britain and France. Continually the Teutons strove to effect by intrigue what they failed to achieve by force of arms. In Russia both the Government and the urban populace were undermined and perverted by subtle enemy influences. In Italy the patriotic House of Savoy was completely immune from maleficent Court intrigues, and it was upon certain political parties and ignorant sections of the people, together with certain clerical and aristocratic circles, that the Germans and Austrians worked their far-reaching and sinister machinery of demoralisation.

Italy did not enter the war as a united nation. Only an energetic and enlightened minority produced the current of popular feeling that swung Italy into the Grand Alliance. The most influential Italian politician, Signor Giolitti, was opposed to Italian participation in the war. Pope Benedict and a majority of the College of Cardinals were also strongly inclined to a position of neutrality, which more or less tacitly favoured the Central Empires. Some considerable part

ITALY'S ARMY LEADER AND BRITISH ARTILLERY.
General Cadorna (centre), the Italian Commander-in-Chief, visiting the British batteries which assisted the Italians in their offensive against the Austrians in 1917.

of the Italian aristocracy was strangely united with many of the leading men in the Italian Socialist movement in supporting as much as possible the Germanic cause.

Thus, in some very essential elements, Italy still remained a nation that was in the making but not yet made. The master factor of disturbance was the Papacy, with its ramifying connections in the aristocracy and its confusion of entangled world-wide interests. The great Catholic block of Austria-Hungary, Bavaria, Baden, Westphalia, the Rhineland, West Prussia, and Silesia largely controlled the mineral wealth and the technical industries of Central Europe, and, with its population of some sixty million souls, formed the principal united Roman Catholic Power in the world.

Italy suffered from the fact that she was both a virile, modern temporal Power and a strong, ancient spiritual Power of universal scope. Of old she had fallen to pieces, because of the distracting and alluring influences of the spiritual Empire that was seated in her capital. For more than fifteen hundred years the grand religious organisation had absorbed most of the finest minds and strongest characters in the nation, not only separating them from the general politics of united Italy, but at times making them hostile towards purely national interests.

To many noble Italian families Italy was only the footstool of the enthroned and universal Power of which, for centuries, they had been the principal ministers. The ambitious men among them looked to exercise their talents, directly or indirectly, in the management of the strongest religious Power on earth, and never ceased to lament that the modern Italian nation was able slowly and arduously to develop upon the ruins of the Papal States. Sincerely they thought that the spiritual destiny of the Italian people was

REST BY THE WAYSIDE.
Italian troops resting along the trench-like banks of a road behind their front line, before the retreat.

INGENUITY IN TRENCH-MAKING.
Communication trench on the Italian Carso front. It was excavated to but little depth, and the sides were then ingeniously built up of stone, topped with sand-bags, providing a protected way across an exposed stretch.

infinitely more important than the immediate national temporal interests. In their view it was a disastrous mistake for their country merely to act as one of the modern Great Powers of Europe, and for reasons of democratic sentiment and territorial rectification side with "infidel" France and "heretic" Britain, Russia, and Serbia, at the time when the fate of sixty million Roman Catholics in Central Europe hung in the balance between bankrupting defeat and reconsolidating victory.

Giolitti and the men of his Machiavellian school had little in common with the clerical party of Italy, but from shrewd calculation of the material advantages of the long-established Italian interest in the Papacy, they were also strongly inclined to work against the war. Giolitti thought that Italy, as a spiritual Power, would

eventually lose more through assisting in the defeat of the Central Empires than she would immediately gain thereby as a temporal Power. He was quite patriotic in his way, and there were many Italian business men, with as little religious belief as he possessed, who agreed with him that the country should make the most of its extraordinary position of spiritual leadership, and negotiate a peace with the Central Empires as soon as opportunity offered.

Some of the Italian Socialists of the Teutonic school were, likewise, sincere in their opposition to the struggle for the unredeemed lands of their country. They were unbought by the gold of Germany and Austria, and they worked for these enemies more effectually by reason of their wild, but genuine, pacifism. Undoubtedly they were strongly influenced by some of the Socialist lackeys of the Kaiser. But it was only because the ideas that the Germans gave them **Italian opponents** fitted into their own frame of mind **of the war** that they vehemently intrigued against the Italian armies and against Great Britain and France.

There were, of course, numerous mercenary traitors working between the three powerful groups of clerical, middle class, and labouring class of "defeatists." Some of them were connected with the wretched gang gathered about Caillaux in France. Others were connected with the pro-German parties in Switzerland, Spain, and Greece. This fungus growth of treachery, greatly as it extended in 1917, the year of disaster, was not of historic moment. It merely flourished upon the rubble loosened from the structure of nationality by the three strong forces of disruption, which were inspired by genuine ideas of policy.

Only by means of a fairly rapid success in the contest with Austria-Hungary could the King of Italy and his military and political lieutenants have tamed and quietened the parties who were throughout opposed to the war. When hope of soon overcoming the enemy, by means of a general allied offensive, vanished in April, 1917, the situation in Italy became perilous. General Nivelle, the French Commander-in-Chief, did not improve matters in trying to offset results of the Russian Revolution by altering the general allied plan of campaign and launching a Franco-British offensive a month before the Italian armies were able to resume their mountain war.

By reason of the partial failure of the French attack on the Aisne, and the alteration this entailed in the principal plan of the British Commander-in-Chief, the operations of the Italian armies became detached and secondary affairs that failed of full effect. Some attempt was made to link them with a renewed Russian offensive in Galicia, but as the Russian Revolutionary armies fled without fighting, the relief they afforded to Italy was temporary and slight.

Never in modern times were men faced with such a task as that which King Victor Emmanuel, General Cadorna, and Signor Bissolati courageously struggled to perform in the spring of 1917. The former work of constructing modern Italy, undertaken by Mazzini, Garibaldi, Cavour, and King Carlo Alberto, though terribly difficult, was less difficult than that which fell upon their successors. The hostile influences in the **Italian Government's** Vatican were stronger, and reached **arduous task** deeper and farther. The Italian middle classes, whose fathers had been the mainstay of the House of Savoy, were to a considerable extent seduced from their allegiance by Germanic commercial and financial interests, and strongly swayed by the attitude of Giolitti and his party. Moreover, the popular element from which Mazzini and Garibaldi had derived their strength was partly diverted from national interests by the novel force of Social Democracy of the Teutonic school.

After the events related by Dr. James Murphy in Chapter CLXXIV. (Vol. 9, p. 91), there was a long pause in all operations on the Italian front. Nothing of importance occurred between the end of November, 1916, and the middle of May, 1917. Snow and ice, low-hanging mist, and frequent tempests imposed a practical armistice upon the millions of men arrayed along the mountain front of four hundred and seventy miles between Switzerland and the Adriatic Sea.

Then it was that Italy profited awhile by the positions of vantage she had gained upon her Alpine ramparts. There can be no doubt that if geographical and weather conditions had favoured an **Winter truce** offensive, Italy would have become the **aids Italy** main objective of the Central Empires immediately after the conquest of the larger part of Rumania. It was the Germanic policy always to strike in concentrated superior force against the weaker nations of the Grand Alliance. Thus, after Serbia and Rumania were almost put out of action, and Russia reduced to a condition approaching moral bankruptcy, Italy became the target of hostile attack.

During the long winter, happily, General Cadorna and his Staff were released from immediate anxiety. Clearly, however, they could foresee that all the mass of manœuvre that Ludendorff could spare from the western front would eventually be hurled against them. So before the Russian Revolution occurred, the Italian Government endeavoured to convince the British and French Governments that the salvation of Italy had become the main problem of the Entente. There was first an allied conference on the

MONTE SAN GABRIELE'S MUCH-CONTESTED HEIGHT.
Village of Santa Caterine, at the foot of the strongly-fortified height of Monte San Gabriele, with the smoke of bursting shells during an Italian bombardment showing above the lower summits. A severe struggle for the possession of this mountain mass took place during the early autumn of 1917, and the Italians had secured a great part of it before the débacle towards the close of that year.

matter on January 6th, 1917, at which Mr. Lloyd George and M. Briand were present. Then in March, 1917, Signor Boselli, the Italian Premier, travelled to Paris and London to advocate the adoption of General Cadorna's scheme for anticipating the Austro-German offensive by means of an Italian-Franco-British offensive directed across the mountain line of the Isonzo towards Laibach. When the military results of the Russian Revolution became obvious, the Italian Staff and Cabinet again renewed, with more urgency, their appeal for large and immediate help. In France General Foch became convinced of the reality of the Italian peril; in Great Britain Mr. Lloyd George also inclined to the views of the Italian commanders and statesmen.

For technical reasons the Laibach campaign was adversely criticised by leading French and British military authorities. As explained in Chapter CCXIV. (Vol. 10, p. 429), the great lengthening of railway communications along the inadequate tracks that crossed the Alpine system between France and Italy formed the immediate ground for the rejection of the scheme. Having been hostile to each other for more than a generation and divided by military alliances and colonial ambitions, Italy and France had left their railway communications in somewhat the same condition as were the Russian and Rumanian railways. They had been designed for mutual attack, and not for mutual defence. Moreover, the extreme wear on locomotives and rolling-stock during the war had diminished all transport facilities in both countries, and the enormous success attained by the intensified submarine campaign against shipping in the spring of 1917 tragically increased the difficulties of moving French and British armies to the Isonzo line and keeping them well supplied with munitions, food, and drafts.

General Nivelle was then practically Commander-in-Chief of both the French and British armies on the western front. He was able to overrule Sir **Nivelle's strategy** Douglas Haig's plan for a Flemish cam-**embarrasses Cadorna** paign, and being confident of the success of his own scheme for completely piercing the German lines, he reckoned that he could best help Italy by speeding up his own preparations. He could not even wait until the snow melted in the Alps and allowed the Italian armies to co-operate in the great western offensive movement. He delivered his attack nearly a month before the date when mountain warfare could be resumed in Northern Italy. It failed in its larger aim, and the position of Italy became, in the view of General Cadorna and his Staff, almost desperate. They had to attack in order to help two of their principal Allies—France and Russia—at an anxious time when they were themselves in need of assistance of every kind. Only by a few days

MODERN IMITATORS OF AN ANCIENT PHILOSOPHER.
Huge hogsheads fitted with stout wooden doors provided convenient and quite comfortable accommodation, of which Italian officers on the Isonzo front availed themselves with philosophical humour.

did they forestall a great Austro-Hungarian offensive on the Isonzo front.

In the second week in May the Italian batteries below the Julian Alps and along the Lower Isonzo opened a furious bombardment of the Austrian positions. The Italian gunners were assisted by British and French artillery and by British monitors in the Northern Adriatic. These reinforcements, however, did not bring the armament at the disposal of General Cadorna to an equality with his available man-power. Great Britain, for example, sent only ten batteries of 6 in. howitzers. In shell-fire power Italy remained by far the weakest of the Great Powers of Europe, by reason of the fact that she possessed no native coal or iron resources, and was inadequately provided with industrial material and machinery by her more fortunate Western Allies. These Allies made the mistake of wasting part of their own abundant munition output, and the output of Japan and the exported war materials of the United States, in a hopeless endeavour to transform the demoralised and mutinous Russian peasant into a disciplined fighting man. Italy, loyal and rich in man-power, was allowed to remain impoverished in armament, with the result that the Germans and Austrians obtained, practically without fighting, the British, French, Japanese, and American munitions sent to unwilling Russia.

In spite of their inferiority in gun-power and shell production, the Italians valiantly succeeded in breaking into the vital mountain positions of the enemy. On May 14th the infantry of the Second Corps, under Major-General Badoglio, forced a series of passages over the twisted and ravined Isonzo, by Zagara, and began a long, arduous drive across the northern mountain rampart above Gorizia. The knife-like crest of the mighty mass of Cuk and the high saddle of Vodice, connecting Cuk mountain with the Santo height, were the principal objectives of the Second Italian Army.

Quickly the Florence and Avellino **Cadorna opens** Brigades worked over the lower slopes **his offensive** of the Alpine wall, blasting away the Austrian works with heavy trench-mortar bombs. South of Vodice saddle another brigade of the Sixth Corps carried the steep face of Monte Santo. But as the victorious column reached the summit it was enveloped and crushed by a fierce counter-attack. The enemy commander had in reserve several divisions from the Galician front, and, under answering bombardments, he poured forth his troops in a tremendous counter-offensive. Cuk and Vodice and the surrounding tangle of mountains and foot-hills smoked and flamed like volcanoes, while the masked infantry clashed together amid tempests of gas-shells, high explosive, shrapnel, and machine-gun fire.

Blue and Khaki : At the Linking of the Lines

From the Photograph of a Scene during the German Thrust for Amiens, March, 1918

Under this terrifying test the warlike spirit of the Italian people shone victoriously. On May 15th some two thousand Alpini and Bersaglieri made a splendid diversion at Bodrez and Lago, on the north-western edge of the Bainsizza plateau. They topped the great strata height, attracted a huge hostile force against them, demonstrated until the night of May 17th, and then withdrew. In the meantime the main Italian forces of attack climbed the crest of Cuk and the mountain ridge of Vodice, and from these commanding positions mowed down the masses of Austrians, Hungarians, Bosnians, Turks,

Italians seize Cuk and Vodice

and Slavs that tried to climb up the reverse slopes. As a considerable number of the Slav soldiers of the Dual Monarchy were in a rebellious frame of mind, they had to be used in dense masses, with machine-guns behind them and brutal officers and non-commissioned officers directing them. The machine-gun fire of the Italians was therefore murderous, yet some seven thousand prisoners managed to find an opportunity of surrendering.

For eight days the Austrian commander, General Lukas, continued his violent counter-assaults against his lost mountain line above Gorizia, while General Capello and General Badoglio in turn launched fresh attacks between Cuk and San Gabriele mountains. The Italians made little farther progress, but held their ground and increased their grip upon the Vodice saddle. There was no reason for them to attempt another leap forward. Not only did they require considerable time to bring their guns forward, but their entire operation had been in the nature of a partial feint. It was to the Third Italian Army, under the Duke of Aosta, that the main attack had been entrusted, and the Second Army, under General Capello, was only clearing the way for the principal action by diverting large enemy forces to the northern sectors.

On May 23rd General Cadorna achieved the surprise he had been patiently engineering. For lack of artillery he could not make a simultaneous movement north and south of Gorizia, as British or French commanders with their superior armament would have done. He had to make a demonstration offensive northward, and then haul his batteries in another direction for the grand battle, before

the enemy also shifted his guns. By a comparatively short bombardment the Italian commander wrecked some of the enemy's positions of importance upon the stony, waterless Carso tableland between Gorizia and the Adriatic shore. British monitors destroyed the railway communications with Trieste, smashing up a troop train, wrecking the track, breaking down a viaduct, and exploding a large ammunition magazine a few miles north-west of the Adriatic seaport. The land artillery, helped by a fine trench-mortar corps, blasted away part of the quarried rock works and the cemented defences from the height of San Marco by Gorizia to the estuary positions of San Giovanni by the seashore.

In the infantry attack that followed, the Third Army of Italy broke clean through the enemy's main line of subterranean rock shelters, achieving as difficult a victory as that which Australian and British soldiers won more gradually above the Hindenburg tunnel in the west. In ordinary land conditions a break-through might have been effected, but on the waterless, rough wilderness of the Carso the task of bringing forward guns, ammunition, and water checked the movement of the victorious infantry. Yet by May 25th the Italians carried the vital Flondar line, broke all the series of fortifications between the Brestovizza valley and the sea, and reached the Gibraltar of the Trieste positions—the Hermada mountain. It rose a thousand feet above the sea, with its five hundred guns screened by a large wood that climbed up the slopes.

The Italian soldiers worked through the trees to the Medeazza Terrace, about half-way up the western incline. Then by the

Attack on the Hermada

edge of the sea they crossed the curious subterranean stream of the Timavo, and approached from San Giovanni, the naval fortress of Duino. They were within gunshot of Trieste.

General Cadorna, however, regarded it as unwise to make an immediate assault upon the honeycombed rock of the Hermada, which had cross-firing connections with the Brestovizza position northward and the Duino fortification southward. The success of the Italian infantrymen had taken their own Staff by surprise, and they were beyond the protection of their main artillery when they

BRITISH HOWITZER IN ACTION ON THE ITALIAN FRONT. [*British official photograph.*]
In the gunpit of one of the batteries of British artillery that were sent to the assistance of the Italian Army in its great offensive of the summer of 1917. Italy was unfortunately the weakest of the Great Powers in artillery, and the lack of sufficient armament was regarded as one of the contributing causes to the failure of her 1917 offensive to reach its full fruition, and therefore to the subsequent retreat.

K

ITALIAN NIGHT AIR RAID ON AN AUSTRIAN NAVAL BASE.

An incident in a great night air raid by Italian airmen in Caproni bombing aeroplanes on Pola, Austria's naval base and arsenal on the Adriatic, during the summer of 1917. No fewer than forty-six machines took part and, leaving their base at regular intervals, bombed Pola for five consecutive hours. On this occasion a parachute bearing a powerful chemical light was utilised for the first time for revealing their objectives to the airmen.

settled down to organise their new line. A furious and sustained effort was required in the rear of the victors, in order to afford them immediate support against the inevitable grand counter-attack that General Boroevic was visibly preparing.

A secret disaster had befallen the armies of Italy. Their guns were running out of shell. In the evening of May 26th, when the Austrians were hurriedly retreating, and the war of movement was beginning above the half-evacuated Hermada Ridge, an astounding order came from General Cadorna suspending the offensive. Through lack of help from her Allies Italy, in the hour of her grand victory, had no shell left wherewith to support her infantry in delivering the final blow against the half-broken and reeling enemy. The Austro-Hungarian losses had been remarkably heavy. More than thirty thousand enemy corpses awaited burial in the new Italian line, and the prisoners taken since May 14th numbered twenty-four thousand. Some four hundred guns were lost by the Austrians, some being smashed by gun fire, others blown up in retreat, and about sixty captured intact. There can be no doubt whatever that if General Cadorna had been provided by Great Britain, France, and the United States with more guns and more shell he would have won a grand success.

His principal aim in the May offensive had been to prepare the way for the Russian campaign in Galicia. He succeeded in destroying most of **Italy's shortage** the hostile forces released from the **of artillery** Russian front, and so wearing down the main Austro-Hungarian Army as to compel the dictator of the German Empire to detach more men and guns from the eastern theatre of war. Naturally, he expected that his success would provoke a most violent reaction, and that all possibly available hostile forces would be extended in fierce action against his men until General Brussiloff was ready to strike.

In the night of June 3rd the grand Austrian counter-offensive was launched from the hills south of Gorizia to the mud flats by the Adriatic Sea. Careful as the Duke of Aosta had been in saving some of his stock of shell, he had not sufficient material left for effective counter-battery work against the thousands of hostile guns. On the northern wing, by the Faiti Hrib hill positions, all the shelters of the Italian infantry were destroyed and the ground overrun by Hungarian and Tyrolese troops. But the splendid Tiber Brigade recaptured the heights in the afternoon of June 4th.

In the centre, about the Brestovizza valley, the battle swayed for three days and nights in incessant fighting in the open field. The tableland was veiled in the smoke of exploding shells, through which the opposing lines and columns drove against **Heroes of** each other. Each side brought up fresh **Hill 219** brigades and divisions, sometimes in motor-vehicles, sometimes in marching order, and all had to get through the wide and heavy barraging fire before coming into action.

There were practically no defences. The old positions were blasted away, and the power of high-explosive shell, bursting on the bare rock and breaking it into a hundred splinters, was incomparably appalling. Between Castagnevizza and the Hermada the Italians emerged victorious. They lost ground, recovered it, lost it again, and again recovered it, between Versic village and Hill 219. When they seemed to have lost Hill 219 finally, in the morning of June 6th, and both sides were so hammered by artillery that neither seemed able to advance farther, General Diaz sent the Italian Grenadiers forward as a forlorn hope. The Grenadiers had been fighting since May 23rd. They had recently stormed Hill 219, between Jamiano and Selo, and, after beating back several counter-assaults, had just withdrawn, apparently spent, from the battlefield. Yet when they were brought out again to relieve the troops who should have relieved them, they stormed back to the hill with all their old fire, held it firmly for two days against all enemy efforts, and when relieved returned to their rest billets scarcely more than a thousand strong. Of them five men in six had fallen. But Hill 219 was theirs.

There was, however, a prophetic local disaster south of the height where the Grenadiers distinguished themselves. On the slopes of the Hermada a fresh Italian brigade was entrenched for defence as well as could be

74

done in the circumstances. The position was far from excellent, as there had been no time to blast and drill the rock into good underground shelters. The enemy's bombardment was heavy, and the flying fragments of stone and steel were numerous and deadly. The brigade, however, had not to endure more than its victorious comrades, yet at the first drive of the Austro-Hungarian infantry some two thousand of the men surrendered, and the other four thousand gave way almost as weakly.

It was not panic fear that broke the Italian line, but the influence of the official Socialist party of Italy. The soldiers had been taught that it was their duty to cease fighting for the nation in order to bring about a defeat in which class warfare could be waged in Russian fashion. The brigade deliberately went on strike against the war, and surrendered in almost as cool a manner as the Russians soon afterwards did on the Galician front.

Gains annulled by treachery   The effect of this act of treachery was to annul one of the most important gains purchased during the May offensive at heavy cost in Italian life. The Duke of Aosta sent forward his reserves, who made a most gallant effort to regain the lost slopes. The fresh troops almost succeeded in retrieving the situation, but, as they were connecting with a large Italian force that had been isolated by the traitors, Boroevic in turn brought his reserves into action and pressed the Italians back from the Flondar line and across the Timavo stream.

Like the heroic garrison of Monte Nero, in the subsequent and grander disaster, the loyal Italian infantrymen near Hermada fought on when completely surrounded and deprived of food and water. Not until all their ammunition

FIGHTING AMONG THE HEIGHTS.
Alpini of the Italian Army leaving their trenches in the high mountains and crawling forward over snow, and behind the cover afforded by rocky boulders, to attack the Austrians on the Isonzo front.

was gone did they surrender. Then it was only a comparatively small body that fell into the hands of the enemy.

In spite of the failure by the Hermada, the series of battles ended in favour of the Italians. They held the Cuk-Vodice Ridge, and were entrenched on the lower slopes of Monte Santo ; they had broken into the enemy's system on the Carso to a depth of about a mile and a half on a front of some six miles ; although they had been driven from the lower slopes of the Hermada, they yet continued formidably to menace this great bastion of Trieste. Fourteen thousand of their men remained in the hands of the enemy, but nearly a third of these were persons of the Bolshevist type, whose loss was rather a gain in moral sanitation. The Austrian prisoners numbered twenty-five thousand, and as the long   Austrians attacked near Asiago   battle had been very severe and the artillery fire exceedingly destructive, the proportion between prisoners and total casualties was larger than usual.

While attack and counter-attack were clashing on the Carso in the second week of June, the Sixth Italian Army in the eastern fringe of the Trentino took up the work of assisting the intended Russian campaign in Galicia, by breaking on June 10th into the Austrian lines near Asiago. Nearly the whole of Monte Ortigara was carried during a violent storm, and two days then passed before the enemy recovered sufficiently to make a vain counter-assault.

For the rest of the month the Italian Commander-in-Chief demonstrated against the enemy by means of whirlwind artillery attacks. Then, on July 1st, the Central Empires' forces, weakened by the Italian, British, and French offensives, were attacked in Galicia by General

ARTILLERY IN THE ALPS.
Italian gunners carrying their weapon in pieces up rocky paths to a new position in the mountain heights. Each separate piece was of a weight to try a strong man even on level ground.

Brussiloff, who was in greatly superior strength in both men and guns. In the middle of July the Third Italian Army again exerted severe pressure upon the Austro-Hungarians on the Carso plateau, by assailing the high land overlooking the Brestovizza valley, which was the main artery of the plateau defences of Trieste. The quarried line was shattered and captured, but before General Cadorna could complete his share of the combined Russo - Italian operations against Austria - Hungary, the hitherto victorious Russian forces repeated on a vast scale the conduct of the Italian brigade on Hermada, and mutinied and fled in the wildest disorder.

CAMOUFLAGE ON THE CARSO.
Network of reeds and other material disposed about and over a roadway to break its line as seen from aeroplanes far above, and so make it indistinguishable from the surrounding country.

ITALIAN ARTILLERY ON A MOUNTAIN SUMMIT.
Gun which Italian artillerists had taken to one of the high points on their front. The work achieved by Italians in mountain warfare was extraordinary, and not least extraordinary was the way in which heavy guns were got to heights whence they could dominate enemy positions.

July, 1917, seemed to be almost as bad as they had been in Russia in February, 1917. A majority of the populace, largely consisting of oppressed Slavs, were in a state of passive rebellion, awaiting only the spark of a great military defeat in order to break out into active rebellion. Even the ruling Teuton and Magyar peoples were worn out by the war, and likely to rise when the despotic military power was relaxed. They took no joy in the overthrow of revolutionary Russia. Rather did they wish that they could imitate the Russian urban classes and shatter the Austrian and Hungarian oligarchies that had led them into utterly ruinous war.

The entire complexion of the war was abruptly changed. Of all the combatant nations of the Grand Alliance, Italy was most seriously endangered by the complete demoralisation of the Russian armies, as well as by the contagion of the Bolshevist movement. Against her, Austria-Hungary would swing practically the whole of her active forces, and as General Pétain was compelled to adopt defensive tactics, making only some short leaps forward to keep the enemy occupied, it was probable that a German army would be released to strengthen the Austro-Hungarians in an attempt to obtain a decision against Italy.

There was nothing for General Cadorna to do but to attack the enemy as fiercely as possible, before the terrible effects of the Russian disaster were fully felt on the Isonzo and Trentino lines. In these circumstances the Italian Commander-in-Chief made his last, despairing proposal for a combined rapid thrust by the Western Allies across the Isonzo mountains towards Laibach. Laibach was a knot of main railway tracks, and its capture would undoubtedly have crippled Austria-Hungary and possibly compelled her to make peace.

Social and political conditions in the Dual Monarchy in

Towards the end of July, 1917, Baron Sidney Sonnino, the Italian Foreign Minister, journeyed to Paris and London to plead for help before help came too late. He was warmly received by Mr. Lloyd George, and heartily welcomed at a public meeting in Queen's Hall, London, on August 4th, 1917. But, from a military point of view, the journey of the distinguished Italian statesman was almost as fruitless as the journey which Thiers made through the European capitals when France was lying under the heel of the Hohenzollern.

British and French military authorities still held that the proposed Laibach offensive could not be properly mounted in time to prevent Germany from swinging strongly down to the defence of the mountain rampart of Trieste and Laibach. Sir Douglas Haig was then hopeful of being able to carry the Passchendaele Ridge by the end of August, and absorb every available German division in a battle for the Flemish coast. General Pétain was still averse to adventure among the Italian Alps, as he had more than enough work to do in repairing the error of General Nivelle and strengthening his

Sonnino visits Paris and London

own line pending the arrival of a large United States army.

The Italian authorities were promised that aid should quickly be given to them if the Germans joined with the Austro-Hungarians in any very considerable number. But in regard to the audacious stroke planned by General Cadorna co-operation was again refused.

It must, however, be remembered that the Chiefs of Staff and Commanders-in-Chief in the Field of France, Great Britain, and the United States were reduced to a very cautious frame of mind by the break up of Brussiloff's armies. They rightly felt they could not then afford to take risks which they would have readily run in the early period of the war. The Grand Alliance had lost, in Russia, its grand reserve of trained men, and although there was a still finer reserve of soldiers in the United States, this latter reserve was composed of half-trained or untrained officers and men, mostly **Result of a miscalculation** lacking arms, who would not be ready for action until 1918. The military authorities of the Western Powers calculated that the severe and continuous pressure of Sir Douglas Haig's armies and the intermittent but fierce local offensives of General Pétain's armies would at least save Italy from any strong attack by the Germans.

Here, undoubtedly, an inaccurate and unfortunate calculation was made. In an indirect yet telling way the clogging mud of Flanders, that delayed for months the British conquest of the German positions round Ypres,

brought about the defeat and panic retirement of the Second Italian Army. All that can be said from this point of view is that the check to the British operations could not be foreseen, and that, from the general military standpoint of the Western Staffs of the Grand Alliance, the course which at the time seemed to be the safest was adopted, because the perilous circumstances had the effect of enforcing prudence and patience upon the men responsible for military policy.

In regard to political affairs, however, the crying needs of Italy were woefully neglected. **Coal dearer than bread** The Italian people were beginning severely to suffer from semi-starvation. The prolonged winter of 1916-17 had tried them to the uttermost, and revealed to them their economic weakness and poverty. The price of English coal rose to 720 lire (£28 10s.), which was nearly thirty times higher than it had been in peace time, when the competition between German and British coal importers kept the price down to 25 lire per ton. Italian money lost much of its purchasing power, and the rate of exchange on London fell, by February, 1917, to 37 lire to the pound sterling, which was about 7s. less than 37 French francs fetched in London.

There was no coal for Italian factories, many of which had to close down, as the Government could only guarantee very limited supplies of fuel even for war industries. A piece of English coal actually became dearer than a piece of bread of the same size. When English wheat in English

RUINS OF THE MONASTERY ON THE SUMMIT OF MONTE SANTO.

Monte Santo, rising almost sheer on the eastern bank of the Isonzo at the southern end of the Bainsizza plateau, was a standing menace while in enemy hands to whatever Power held Gorizia. It was carried by the Italians on August 26th, 1917, after a desperate struggle, in which seven thousand guns, including some British and French, were engaged. In this single battle the Austrians lost about 100,000 men.

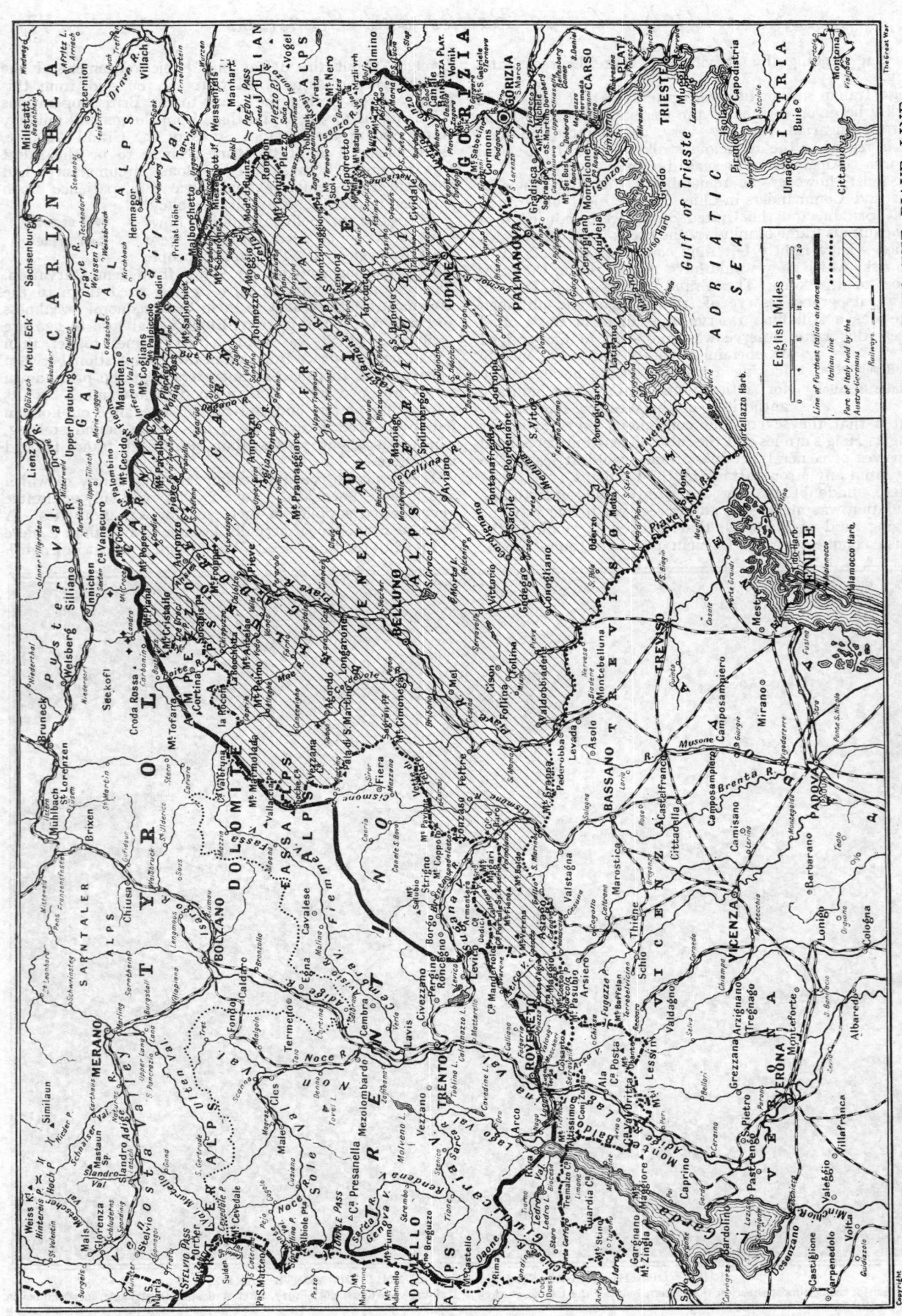

AREA OF THE FLOW AND EBB OF ITALY'S MILITARY SUCCESS: FROM THE CARSO PLATEAU TO THE PIAVE LINE.

markets was selling at £16 16s. a ton, English coal in Italian markets was fetching somewhat more than £28 per ton, reckoning the lire at its native worth. The extraordinary price of English coal enhanced the cost of Italian wood fuel, that rose to £16 per ton. In a country already poor in forests, the few trees that remained were almost all destroyed, and the southern peasantry had to burn their old olive trees in order to cook their food and keep themselves warm.

The lack of coal had a general disastrous effect upon the distribution of the food supplies. Railway traffic had to be cut down in an incredible manner in order to save coal for military transport and munition factories. The result was that even where there were stocks of food available the task of distributing them to the large and widely spread population became extremely difficult. Worst of all, the native production of munitions did not develop regularly and steadily as fresh hands were taken on and trained in increasing number. The output of war material alternated between fits of fierce activity and despairing lethargy according as supplies of coal arrived from England.

In assigning tonnage Italy was handicapped to the profit of France. Proper allowance was not made for the fact that Italy was farther away from British and American centres of supply, so that the ships she used had to make longer voyages, and yet were, by reason of the smallness of the Italian mercantile marine, deplorably inadequate to both her military and general needs.

In the ordinary circumstances of peace time Italy required ten million tons of coal per year. In the extraordinary circumstances of war time, when all her finely-skilled mechanics should have been working at sustained high pressure and imparting their skill to quite a million new assistants, the supply of coal fell disastrously below the normal annual average. For instance, in the first six critical months of 1917, when the Italians were vainly endeavouring to increase their armament, in view of a combined Austro-German offensive, only about two million six hundred tons of coal were landed in the country. The best advice the Italian Government could give to the shivering people was to invite them to warm themselves in the southern sun of Sicily. Some of the idle, wealthy class went south for warmth, but the working people could not leave their work to bask in the natural heat of the southern orange groves.

When the people were suffering from lack of coal and from unemployment, they had to endure the results of bad harvests. The harvest of the autumn of **Failure of** 1916 was a million tons less than the **the harvests** harvest of 1915, and this also was at least two million tons below the requirements of the population. In the summer of 1917 the total deficit of three million tons of grain brought the Italians to the verge of general famine. Bread riots occurred in more than a hundred places, and the Socialists of the pro-German school, along with gangs of wretched traitors, worked with diabolical energy to provoke a general insurrection.

Signor Lazzari, secretary to the official Socialist Executive, sent a circular to all Socialist mayors and town councillors asking them whether they were prepared to resign all together on an arranged date. As these urban authorities were in control of the local machinery of food distribution, their sudden resignation would have disorganised food supplies at a time when railway difficulties, shipping difficulties, and bad harvests had brought the Italian people down to starvation point.

Other methods were employed by German agents to starve the people into shameful defeat. In the important city of Turin the Socialist party began by provoking trouble among the much-enduring working class. In the hope of preventing any serious food difficulties the Commune of Turin was supplied in August with a **Treacherous propaganda** ration of grain consisting of 10,000 cwt. more than had been received in June. Yet formidable riots broke out, and had to be suppressed with considerable bloodshed, and as the populace were actually suffering from hunger, the use of firearms against them left them in a state of menacing and brooding sullenness.

It was afterwards found, however, that while the people were fighting in the streets for bread and falling dead or wounded in hundreds, there were vast quantities of flour concealed in the city, and even larger quantities would have been immediately available for distribution, but

ON OUTPOST DUTY AMID THE ALPINE SNOWS.
Astonishing was the physical endurance of the Italians who endured the rigours of the winter campaigns among the Alps. Hardy mountaineers though many of them were, they were subjected to tests of endurance which might have been supposed beyond the power of human nature to support.

for the fact that one of the most important milling plants had temporarily stopped work owing to the breaking of a pipe, and that another large mill was closed owing to lack of lubricating oil.

The Turin riots were part of an elaborate scheme of treachery that was reported to include the destruction of large ammunition stores behind the battle-front, and to aim at bringing about the paralysis of the internal strength of Italy at the time when the leaders of the Central Empires were preparing to make a mighty concentrated attack upon the Italian armies.

In the meantime a penetrating and far-reaching propaganda was engineered against Great Britain and France. The Western Allies were accused of being the authors of all the economic miseries of the Italian people. France, it was alleged, was keeping Italy weak and dependent, so that she should be the dominant Mediterranean Power and mistress of Northern Africa. Great Britain was charged with battening on the war, profiteering in coal, greedily monopolising shipping, ruining what little financial independence Italy possessed, and reducing the starving country to a position of bankrupt vassalage,

UPWARD BY TUNNELLED WAYS.
Italian Alpini dragging supplies along a way bored upward through the solid rock on their mountainous front. Great ingenuity and perseverance were displayed by the Italians in overcoming the natural difficulties of the terrain on which much of their heroic struggle had to be carried on.

compared with which, so the propagandists clamoured, the generous technical, commercial, and financial assistance that Germany had formerly given was a pure blessing.

In vain did the apologists for Great Britain assert that the bitter shortage in food and fuel and materials was due to the murderous operations of German and Austrian submarines. The reply was made that, even if English coal could not be supplied in large quantity, what little there was available for the people should not be sold at an utterly extortionate price, and that the disastrous depreciation of the foreign purchasing value of Italian money could be remedied by a British loan if the British nation really wished to help Italy. Also the secret of the repeated requests for military assistance leaked out by subtle channels, and aggravated the intense unpopularity of Great Britain.

Slanders on the British soldiers

For the more ignorant elements of the peasantry and urban labouring classes, who could not grasp the details of problems of international commerce and finance, foul slanders upon British soldiers were prepared. It was spread about that the sanguinary repression of food riots in Turin was undertaken by British troops. This rumour reached the Second Italian Army on the Northern Isonzo line, and eventually had a profound effect upon one disheartened force there.

In regard to the Italians of the educated class, a skilful attack upon the British Army was based upon a slight exaggeration of some sound facts given, in the first instance, by sincere admirers of the British genius. These had pointed out, as an example of the magnificent talent of their Allies, that the British soldier was better looked after than any other European combatant. He was fed with meat three times a day, they admiringly said. As Italian soldiers, shivering on Alpine slopes, did not get meat three times a week, the tale only made them think that part of the great resources of British shipping might fairly be devoted to providing them with a daily ration of foreign meat.

The prolongation of the war had greatly reduced the Italian stock of cattle. The country which used to export considerable quantities of butter and cheese had not enough for her own people. In the spring of 1917 butter became practically unprocurable, and most of the cheese was requisitioned for the Services. Meat rose in price to three shillings a pound, and fish also became still dearer, so as to prohibit the poorer classes from obtaining it. Soldiers going home on leave could not help being moved by the privations of their wives and children. The wonder was that the web of treacherous intrigue, spun around the facts of food and fuel shortage, did not entrap a larger number of the embittered fighting men of Italy.

General Cadorna became seriously alarmed. He asked for powers of wider range over the troubled villages, towns, and cities in his rear, and resumed the Isonzo offensive, without the aid of British and French armies, in the hope of disorganising the hostile preparations for a grand attack and of reviving the spirit of his men. On August 19th he showed that the successes he had won on the Carso in May could be repeated with larger results among the Alpine approaches to Laibach.

Bridging the Isonzo

Again he surprised the enemy. The Italian Second Army, under General Capello, managed to throw eighteen bridges across the Isonzo. The river was running strongly between narrow banks, immediately above which towered the steep heights ramparting the Bainsizza plateau. This was a great forested tableland stretching to the wide Chiapovano valley, which was the chief line of enemy communications. The defending army, under General Lukas, was nervously expectant, as the guns of Italy and her Allies had been thundering for twenty-four hours on a wide front of forty miles from the Adriatic shore to the Julian Alps.

The crossing of the Upper Isonzo had already been brilliantly practised as a demonstration at Bodrez and Lago, on the upper course of the river, during the battles above Gorizia in May. The Italians first shattered the enemy's machine-gun redoubts with heavy trench-mortars, sent patrols across the river to form bridge-heads, and then made bridges under cover of continuing increasingly heavy artillery fire.

At the same time the Third Italian Army on the Carso advanced in a violent demonstration against the lower positions of the Hermada fortress system and against the uplands protecting the enemy's mass of howitzers in the Brestovizza valley. In this southern battlefield the struggle became as intense as in the main theatre of attack. The enemy's line between Korite and Selo was stormed, and the steep heights overhanging the Brestovizza valley were gradually reduced by fierce and numerous " dolina " actions. " Dolina " was the local word for the crater-like depressions of soft red earth in the bare rock of the Carso. The Italian Staff was of course well acquainted with every natural dolina, ranging in diameter from twenty to two hundred yards. But when the crossroads at Selo were taken, the attacking troops discovered there were many new artificial doline, all carefully camouflaged from aerial observation, and packed with men, machine-guns, trench-mortars, and scattered pieces of field-artillery.

Furious and close fighting went on day and night for more than a hundred and fifty hours. The slopes of the Brestovizza valley became one of the most horrible scenes of slaughter in the war. Dead Italian Grenadiers and dead Hungarian militiamen stretched under the scorching sun, with their faces blackening and swelling. The Grenadiers had to crawl up the waterless waste of stone and, against a malicious fire, bomb their way into masses of concreted rock, and there arduously reshape the defences under incessant shell fire delivered at exactly marked range by great cross-firing masses of hostile heavy guns.

On both sides the losses were heavy, for the Hungarians were the steadiest fighters in the Dual Monarchy. But the Italians proved themselves the better men. In a terrible week of continuous battle they overran the double trench system, where there were a machine-gun and a crew of four men every six yards of line. Farther south the Flondar positions, that had been won and lost in May, were recaptured, together with the three bastion heights, 146-metre Hill, 145-metre Hill, and 110-metre Hill, that formed the terrace outworks of the large high-wooded rock of the Hermada. The Austrians retained the high eastern positions of the Hermada mountain crest, overlooking the sea, and the other dominating clump of Stari Lokva above Brestovizza. On the northern edge of the Carso, by the Vipacco River, there was another long mountain rampart projecting south of Gorizia. Here the Italians carried Faiti Dosso, bending the enemy back towards the highest clump of mountains.

Along the Isonzo ravine

The advance on the Carso was not, however, pressed with main strength. The more northerly principal Italian offensive proceeded with such remarkable success that General Cadorna required his Third Army only to hold the enemy fiercely down on the southern wing, and prevent the hostile reserves there from marching northward to the Bainsizza plateau.

On the large, rolling, wooded upland between Tolmino and Gorizia the enemy's lines followed the twisting ravine of the Isonzo and formed a high moated salient at the village of Plava. In places the plateau came down to the riverside, at a slope scarcely more than three hundred and forty feet above sea-level. But the great tableland quickly rose behind Plava to the height of twenty-seven

hundred feet, and ended with the Volnik summit, which was thirty-one hundred feet high. In the southern corner of the plateau was Monte Santo, which the Austrians had lost and regained in the May battles, and then more strongly fortified as the outwork to the height of San Gabriele, from which they directly dominated the wrecked city of Gorizia.

General Capello desired to complete his May offensive by the capture of Monte Santo. He held most of the Cuk-Vodice Ridge, fronting the fortified hill, but he knew that he would only sacrifice the lives of his men if he attempted a direct frontal attack upon the enemy's rampart above Gorizia. This was why he had practised in the previous battle the crossing of the upper course of the Isonzo near the riverside town of Canale. His design was to make his main thrust some ten miles above the hill he wished to take, and bring his victorious troops across the Bainsizza plateau in a sweeping, turning movement. His plan was an intricate and difficult one, but

[Italian official photographs.

ITALIAN INGENUITY IN ARTILLERY ADAPTATION.

Monster bomb-thrower which was much used by the Italian Army. Where the human bomb-thrower's cast was measured in yards, this artillery adaptation was capable of throwing its bombs a distance of two miles.

Inset above: An ingenious type of double-barrelled Italian machine-gun which fired twenty-five shots from each barrel at one pull of the trigger. It was carried in a box such as that shown in the foreground.

L

the Alpine troops of the Second Army carried it out in a perfect manner.

The Austrians had transformed the plateau into a vast entrenched camp, defended by zone after zone of tree-screened lines, with masses of guns hidden in the hollows of the high, undulating country. The Alpine troops crossed the river in darkness before dawn on August 19th, and worked behind the range of mountains east of Canale and Plava. When the hill village of Vrh was suddenly stormed, the Austrian flank was turned, and a swift retirement was imposed on the enemy. Losing men in tens of thousands and guns in hundreds, **Monte Santo carried** he conducted a hasty but fighting **by the Italians** retreat towards the Volnik mountain and the Chiapovano valley.

Rearguard after rearguard made desperate stands, with the backing of machine-guns and light artillery, but the Italian troops, invigorated by victory, worked around the flanks of each force that tried to delay them and, rolling up all the main Austrian line, carried Monte Santo by an outflanking attack. The ground thus rapidly won extended on a front of about twelve and a half miles, to a depth varying from three and three-quarters to four and a half miles. In some places the Chiapovano was reached and left behind, the break being larger and more promising than that which the Germans afterwards effected in the Italian lines farther northward.

ON ITALY'S ALPINE FRONT.

[Italian official photograph.

Italian troops advancing on skis in single file across a snowy slope in the upper regions of their mountain front. They carried their rifles slung across their backs, that they might have freedom to use the sticks with which they steadied themselves over the difficult surface they had to traverse.

It was by a new system of nocturnal frontal attack that the Italian successes were accomplished. All the enemy's lines crossing the Bainsizza plateau were turned, and the Italian troops broke into clear country, where no barbed-wire entanglements or concrete forts checked their manoeuvring movements. Theirs was undoubtedly a great feat, and had they possessed more shell and more artillery they would probably have done to the Austro-Hungarians what the Germans afterwards did to them.

Their victory was the most rapid and sweeping success hitherto won in parallel battle on the western and south-western front of war. Neither the French commander nor the British commander had ever driven so deep as four and a half miles into the enemy's zones of fortification. What was then needed, in order to shatter completely the Austrian line and compel a decisive and disorderly retreat, was the immediate presence of a strong army of manoeuvre able to continue the grand drive of the Second Italian Army when the latter were becoming exhausted by a week of incessant marching and fighting in rugged, wooded, and mountain-topped country.

Compared with the very slow and very costly progress made by the forces of Sir Hubert Gough against the Passchendaele Ridge in the same month and under

similar conditions of misty and rainy weather, the rapid and sweeping assault of the forces of General Capello contained the larger promise of a decision. The Italian people might therefore fairly claim that two months before a small body of six thousand of their troops, in peculiar circumstances, showed fatal signs of weakness, their general forces displayed such fine superior qualities as might have won a grand victory, if the organisation of a single military and economic front had effectively prevailed from the North Sea to the Adriatic.

As things stood, however, General Cadorna was unable to crown all his efficient work by a supreme thrust over the high eastern edge of the Bainsizza plateau. The men of the Second Army continued to fight forward for nine days and nights. On August 27th they broke through the last line of Austrian rearguards and came upon the new main front of resistance which the enemy commander had improvised out of the rough system near his original heavy-gun positions. His rearguards had done their duty in gaining time for him to dig in and bring up very large reserves.

Then it was that the bankruptcy of Russia imposed so very heavy a task upon Italy that she required French and British assistance in order to effect a final break-through before the enemy could recall any more troops and guns from the Galician front. The local Italian reserves were thrown upon the tableland for the attack upon mountain crests guarding the great valley-line of Austrian communications. The action opened on August 28th, but after a fierce hand-to-hand struggle with hand-bombs and bayonets, the forces of assault were severely checked. As a matter of fact, they appear to have been less numerous than the great army which the Austrian commander had rapidly collected. Moreover, their artillery, which had to be hauled across the Isonzo and brought around the captured western heights and ridges of the Bainsizza plateau, was markedly inferior in power to the reinforced hostile ordnance.

Immediately after the check to the Italian advance the Austrians delivered their grand counter-attack. It had taken them eleven days to re-organise and strengthen their foot and guns and repair their heavy losses of more than a hundred thousand men, including some twenty-six thousand prisoners. Their new forces, however, were unable to recover the lost ground, as the Italians not only stood firm but slightly extended their line in some places.

The new Italian line was a sound one. South of the great tableland the enemy's key position on the hill of San Gabriele held out stubbornly after the loss of Monte Santo. By means of steady and heroic assaults the Italian troops reached the **Attack on** lower slopes of the height that dominated **Monte San Gabriele** Gorizia northward, but the mass of hostile artillery in this sector maintained so devastating a barrage fire that the machine-gun garrison on the crest was able to repel the valiant but scanty groups of bombers who managed to get through the curtains of shell.

General Capello knew that he could only take San Gabriele by a northern flanking movement similar to that whereby he had captured its outwork of Monte Santo—that is to say, that only by again breaking General Lukas' new front, by the eastern edge of the Bainsizza plateau, could room be won for a sideways drive upon San Gabriele and the line south of it. Had this been

General Armando Diaz, appointed Commander-in-Chief of the Italian Army, November, 1917.

Kobilinaglava   Polubino   Tolmino   Prapetno   R.Iso

Valley of the Isonzo from Kobilinaglava to Ciginj, viewed from Monte Hevnik, west of Tolm

Pasubio   Toraro   Canove   Campolongo   Campo
     Campomolon   Roana
     Spitz Tonezza   M.Erio

View of the Asiago Plateau from Pasubio to Cima Caldiera, seen from Cima Echar, south-east of A

Bečenico   Volzana   S. Maria   Kozařsče   Senski Ciginj

Germans drove across the Isonzo south of Tolmino up towards Plezzo, shown on the next page.

Verena   M. Catz.   Cima Portule Zebio   Val di Nos   Cima Caldiera
M. Interotto   Meata   Basco di Gallio   Cima Undici   Cimon
                                          Cima Dodici   Colombara

...rthern front of the Italian Army protecting the Venetian Plain from invasion from the Trentino.

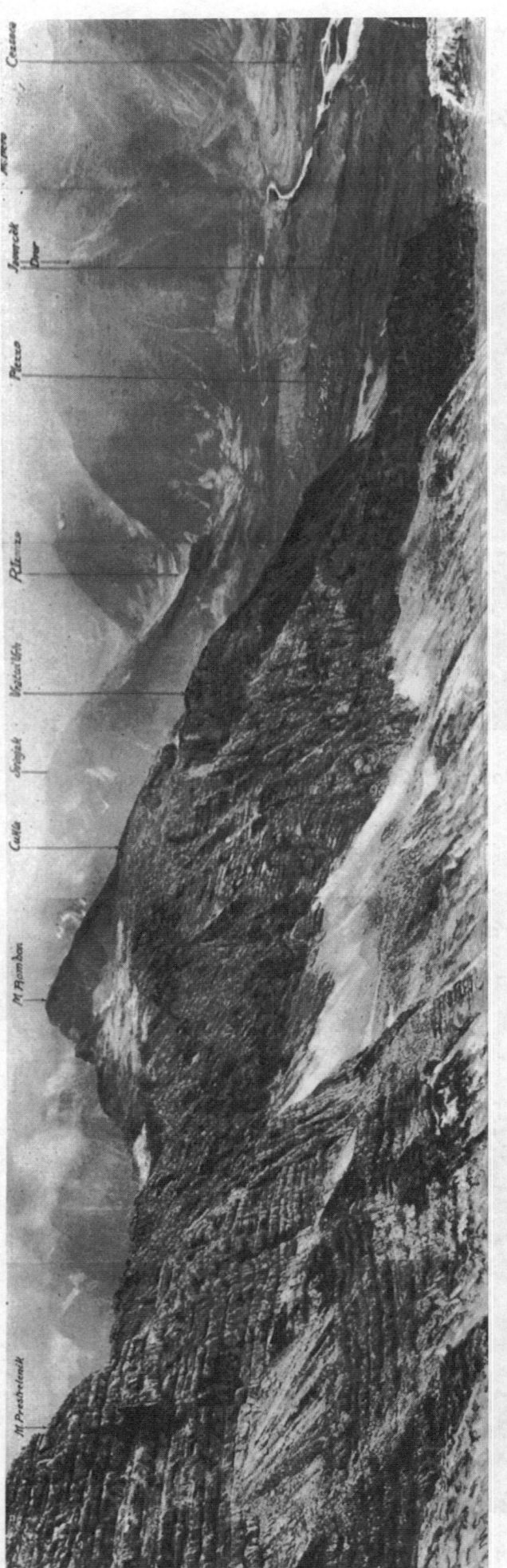

86

Panoramic view of the Valley of the Isonzo, from Monte Prestrelenik to Cezssoca, showing Plezzo.

Continuation of the Valley of the Isonzo south-eastwards through the Julian Alps to the Stol.

done, the Third Italian Army on the Carso would have at last been able to resume its offensive movement in favourable circumstances.

So again General Cadorna strongly demonstrated with his Third Army against the Bresto-vizza position south of Gorizia, and on September 4th he launched his Second Army once more against the enemy's new line on the plateau and the hills north of the city. Almost simultaneously the enemy replied by a grand counter-attack with his southern wing.

He recovered some ground about the Hermada, only to lose it again when the Italians rallied and charged back. But in the critical centre of the mountain line of battle the troops of the Second Italian Army, while winning some important positions, failed to break the enemy's main line and rectify their own perilous new front.

They were in a salient between Tolmino and San Gabriele mountain. Northward they had a long exposed flank, behind which the mountains, ridges, and river-line made communications arduous and slow. Even this exposed flank was not the most serious aspect in the situation of the Second Army, for in its northern rear at Tolmino—which was one of the most impregnable positions in Europe—the enemy had been able to maintain two bridge-heads across the Isonzo, at Santa Lucia and Santa Maria hills.

General Capello's position was good for attack but bad for defence. His forces had driven at a great speed into the enemy's lines. Could the strength of the initial thrust have been not only sustained, but increased, to correspond with the large masses of fresh troops that General Lukas was deploying, the wedge would have broadened and lengthened out into one of the grandly decisive victories of the war. But as there was no powerful and free mass of manœuvre at hand, the Italian general, by reason of his weak artillery power, could not advance farther and did not care to withdraw.

Need of a mass of manœuvre

The question whether it would have been safer to withdraw is one that professors of strategy are likely to debate for generations. From a strictly military point of view, a considerable withdrawal would have been the safest course in the circumstances. On the other hand, the troubled condition of the Italian people and the weakening spirit of one or two brigades, that had been touched by Bolshevist influences, were a source of profound anxiety to the Commander-in-Chief and his lieutenants. They felt they could not follow the example of Ludendorff at Bapaume and recoil in order to fight more strongly. It was one of those situations in which all the elements in the complexion of a nation were suddenly and severely tested.

The work done by the Clerical party, the Giolitti party, the official Socialist party, and the treacherous forces that worked in and alongside them, was quickly turning to the great advantage of the enemy.

BROUGHT DOWN FROM THE AIR AND SALVED FROM THE SEA.
Italian floating crane raising from the waters of the Upper Adriatic an Austrian aeroplane that had been driven down in a damaged condition. Italian flying men showed great daring and resource in battling with the enemy in the air.

By an unfortunate coincidence, Pope Benedict published an appeal for peace and freedom of the seas in the month when the armies of Italy were desperately making their final attempt to anticipate the great Austro-German offensive.

The influence of some leading Austrian Jesuits appears to have told upon the policy of the Vatican. Although there was no ground for supposing that Pope Benedict, the scion of a noble Genoese family with brilliant ecclesiastical traditions, had any idea that he was doing a disservice to his race, it was an incontestable and tragic fact that the time at which his appeal for peace was published suited the military plan of the Protestant dictator of the Central Empires in a manner that could scarcely have been due to pure chance.

The Pope had long desired to make an appeal for peace, and, in spite of the Germanic colour of some of the phrases he used, little serious harm might have been done had his message been published at a moment less critical in the history of the Italian people.

Untimely Papal proclamation

But it came when the urban populations were rioting for bread, when traitors were trying to destroy munition stores, stop the production of war material, and disorganise the distribution of the reduced food supplies, and when one Italian brigade had already gone over to the enemy.

The Italian soldiers were making their last desperate attempts to prevent their country being overrun by the new Goths and Huns. When they failed, in spite of most gallant efforts, to reach and wreck the machinery of invasion, their spirit was lowered by their Pope's proclamation that "the terrible struggle appears to be a useless massacre."

[Italian official photograph.

An Italian battleship leaving Taranto. Italy is ill provided by nature with naval bases. Large harbours at Spezia, in the Gulf of Genoa, and at Naples facilitate the naval defence of Italy's western littoral; but there is no large naval base between Taranto, within the heel of Italy, and Venice at the top of the Adriatic Sea, and the defence of the eastern littoral largely depends upon the coastal railway system.

[Italian official photograph.

Italian battleship entering the inner harbour of the Italian naval base at Taranto. At the end of 1915, the year she intervened in the war, Italy possessed six Dreadnoughts, eight pre-Dreadnoughts, and ten armoured cruisers. Four super-Dreadnoughts, with a displacement of 30,000 tons and speed of twenty-five knots, had been laid down in 1914, designed to carry a principal armament of eight 15 in. and twenty 6 in. guns.

ACTIVITY AT TARANTO, THE NAVAL BASE WITHIN THE HEEL OF ITALY.

GENERAL CAPELLO (CENTRE)

CHAPTER CCXXXI.

WITH HIS STAFF.

THE DEFEAT AND RECOVERY OF ITALY.

II.—From the Break at Caporetto to the Rally on the Piave.

By Edward Wright.

Von Below Assumes Command of the Austro-German Armies on the Isonzo Front—Italian Troops Undermined by Socialist and Defeatist Propaganda—Cadorna's Preparations to Withstand the Impending Grand Assault—German Artillery Superiority—Opening of the Attack, October 24th, 1917—Italian Positions North and South of Caporetto Treacherously Left Open to the Enemy—Alpine Troops Fight to the Death upon Monte Nero—The Whole Venetian Plain Exposed to Invasion—Von Below Marches into Cividale and Udine—Heroic Rearguard Actions of General Diaz's Troops on the Tagliamento Plain Save the Third Italian Army From Being Cut Off—Horrors of the Retreat of the Army and the Population—An Eye-Witness's Story—German Surprise Attack Upon the Italian Rearguard Near Codroipo—Italian Cavalry Save the Main Italian Army—Amazing Achievement of the Fourth Italian Army Retreating from the Carnic, Venetian, and Ampezzo Alps and the Dolomites—Generals Diaz and Robilant Take their Stand Along the Piave—Italy's Fate Dependent Upon the Mental Balance of the Army—Resurrection of the True Italian Spirit—The Partially-Fused Elements of Ancient and Modern Italy Forged Into One Strongly-Tempered Whole.

WHEN the Austrian Jesuits were skilfully playing upon the pacific nature of Pope Benedict, and using their power in the Vatican to sap the spirit of the Italian people, the Government of Austria-Hungary was in a mood of ferocity. The bankruptcy of Russia opened a great field of domination to the Central Powers in the direction of the Black Sea, and the ruling class of the Dual Monarchy began, as their prospects improved, to vie with the Prussian military and industrial caste in the matter of inordinate ambition. The sufferings of their own starving people touched them less than the condition of the cattle on their large estates. As they could buy more cattle when they had extended and consolidated their power, so, they thought, they could by territorial conquests acquire more oppressed races to serve their needs.

As soon as the Austrians had saved their own line from breaking they regarded Italy as their prey. According to their own account, they arranged a grand offensive in September, 1917, immediately after their retreat across the Bainsizza plateau had left the Second Italian Army in an awkward position, with a long exposed flank. But just as

A BRILLIANT ITALIAN GENERAL.
General Luigi Capello commanded the Italian Second Army, which in August, 1917, accomplished the fine feat of throwing eighteen bridges across the Isonzo under intense fire and carrying Monte Santo.

they were prepared to strike, one of the Slav officers in their Army was reported to have gone over to the Italian lines and revealed the plan of operations.

The Austrian High Command became doubtful of its ability to effect a surprise. The discontent in its armies had spread from the Bohemian and Jugo-Slav elements into some Teutonic and Magyar middle-class and labouring men in the forces. Even if the surprise attack were conducted by divisions from which all Slavs were removed, the danger of warning the enemy could not be removed. For the Austro-Hungarian peoples generally then wanted a quick end to the war, and, following the example of the Bolshevists, preferred peace by defeat to peace by victory, because the former was more certain and rapid.

Although the Austrian commander had built up a gigantic armament of concealed batteries out of guns removed from the Russian front, he was afraid to attack the Second Italian Army. He was obliged to appeal for help to General von Ludendorff, and the German dictator, who had closely followed the course of the long negotiations between General Cadorna, General Foch, General Pétain, and Sir William Robertson, at last boldly gambled against Sir Douglas Haig.

Leaving General von Armin to fight upon the Passchendaele Ridge—like Stonewall Jackson in the American Civil War—without any immediately large reserve behind him, the actual War Lord of the Central Empires railed his army of manœuvre down to the Isonzo front.

His original design seems to have been to anticipate a Franco-British expedition, and prevent the utter demoralisation of the Austro-Hungarian peoples. He did not expect that the six German divisions he could spare would be sufficient to achieve an important decision. But he placed them under one of his ablest and most experienced men—General von Below.

Below had shown himself a man of fine military talent in his conquest of the Baltic provinces of Russia. When the Ludendorff-Hindenburg circle climbed to supreme power over the ruins of General von Falkenhayn's schemes, Below had been chosen to conduct the most important of all the new operations—the defensive battles on the Somme in 1916. There he had become thoroughly acquainted with the latest Franco-British methods of intensive gunnery tactics, and he had introduced **Von Below placed in command** the deadly phosgene shell and other new chemical atrocities and perfected the German cage form of artillery barrage.

On arriving on the Isonzo line General von Below took command of the large Austro-Hungarian forces there. To make sure that no soldier under his orders revealed the new plan to the enemy, he withdrew all Austro-Hungarian troops between Tolmino and Plezzo and sent his own shock troops into the battle-line. His main design was to employ against the Italians the methods of overwhelming gun fire he had learnt from the British in France.

He knew exactly the number and quality of guns and number of shells that General Cadorna possessed, and he saw to it that his own batteries and ammunition dumps were enormously superior to those of his opponent. He intended to use far more guns than the Austrians had employed in mountain battles, and to submit the Italian soldiers to a gas-shell bombardment exceeding any they had ever experienced. Only when he reckoned he had worn down the nerves of the Italian troops did he arrange to launch against them his comparatively small force.

There was another, but more important, element of surprise in the German commander's plan. It was an element upon which he did not build, as it was curiously uncertain in quality, but it eventually gave him a far larger victory than he hoped to achieve. A second Italian brigade had been completely undermined by Socialist and other defeatist propaganda. The Prussian commander was in the fortunate position of knowing exactly, before he struck, the position occupied by the Italian troops who were averse to fighting. The brigade in question held some vitally important trenches between Tolmino and Caporetto, and had begun to fraternise with the Austro-Hungarian forces directly in front of it.

Had an ordinary attack been made upon the philosophic cowards the result would have been similar to that obtained in like circumstances below the Hermada. An Italian reserve would have met and stopped the attacking force, which would have gained only a further patch of ground about the bridge-head by Tolmino. General von Below, however, arranged to launch a large and special column of two picked divisions against the comparatively small, treacherous Italian force. Thereby he hoped to reach the sound Italian reserves before these became fully aware of what had happened.

GENERAL BOROEVIC.
Commander of the Austrian army on the Carso that was entrusted with the defence of Trieste.

How far the officers of the two pacifist Italian regiments went in allowing the strange situation to develop cannot be stated, as they were all killed or captured in the disaster that ensued. It is also impossible to affirm whether the Austro-Hungarian force, that first arranged a kind of informal armistice, was as sincere in its action as the Bohemians had been during the first secret preparations for attack in September. In any case there can be no doubt that some of the Austrian officers concerned reported to Headquarters the curious condition of things obtaining by the Plec position in the line below Monte Nero, and that General von Below had sufficient inventive skill to transform the extraordinary situation into a great military advantage. During his terrific bombardment of the Italian lines he carefully spared the Italian Bolshevists, but withdrew the Austrian troops who had made peace with them, and brought up two divisions of the finest German shock battalions to end the armistice in an abrupt and terrifying manner.

In the meantime General Cadorna, with his Headquarters at Udine, with General Capello, the Duke of Aosta, General Diaz, and General Badoglio, made all possible preparations for a determined stand against some three-quarters of a million Austrians, Hungarians, and Germans arrayed between the Predil Pass and the Hermada. General von Below had six German divisions and eight Austro - Hungarian

ONE OF A GREAT MILITARY TRIUMVIRATE.
General Badoglio commanded an Italian army corps in the May offensive in 1917, and directed the operations which resulted in the capture of Cuk and Vodice. In November, 1917, he was appointed with General Giardino to a place in the Italian Supreme Command under General Diaz.

divisions, with some special shock forces, under his command. General Boroevic had his southern army brought up to twenty-three divisions, while the Austrian forces on the Carnic Alps line were composed of only three divisions under General Krobatin. In the Trentino was the Eleventh Austro-Hungarian Army, consisting merely of eight divisions, under General Scheuchenstuel.

It will thus be seen that in actual battalion strength the forces employed for the invasion of Italy were not at all overwhelming. The enemy Commander-in-Chief was unable to arrange to strike in force down from the Trentino on to the Italian rear, as he could not find men enough to make two grand concentrations of striking power. Even in the Julian Alps, from which his staggeringly successful stroke was delivered, the number of divisions was much less than that of the old and new accumulations around Gorizia and on the Carso.

In artillery, however, the enemy was in considerably superior strength. The heavy guns he massed on his nineteen miles of attack, between Plezzo, or **Below opens his** Flitsch, and Tolmino, or Tolmein, com-**bombardment** pletely dominated the two thousand light and heavy guns of the Second Italian Army. The bombardment opened in the fourth week of October with terrific violence and deadliness. As the weather was damp and the air stagnant and misty, the German and Austrian gunners used mainly gas-shells, the fumes of which clung with horrible persistency about the Italian trenches. Such was the strength of hostile gun fire that General Cadorna began to reckon that he would probably lose most of the ground he had won on the Bainsizza

plateau. Of course, he had no inkling of the condition of mind of the fraternising brigade below the Nero mountain.

The enemy's bombardment seemed to be thundering upon all the line of the Second Italian Army. But it was not so. The six thousand pacifists were left to the kind of peace they desired, so as not to excite in them the instinct of self-preservation. While all their comrades were being deluged with high explosive and gas on October 23rd, they were allowed to go on dreaming their gentle dream of an International Socialist Revolution, in which a beautifully murderous class **German shock** war was to put an end to all conflicts of **forces attack** national interest and international law.

About two o'clock in the morning of October 24th they were awakened out of their Russian dream. General von Below had arranged his six German divisions into three great spear-heads of storming forces. One struck in the north at the narrows of Saga ; the second struck at the gorge of the Isonzo opposite Caporetto ; the third did not strike at all. It walked northward along the banks of the river upland from the bridge-heads of Santa Lucia and Santa Maria, and turned all the Italian positions south and north of Caporetto. Throughout the war Tolmino and the stream-girdled mountain behind it had remained a centre of invincible resistance.

Just by the neighbouring village of Santa Lucia the Isonzo was joined by the Idria River and the Baca River. Down the valley of the latter stream there ran a good railway, connecting with two great railway centres, Klagenfurt and Laibach. Tolmino also had some splendid communications with Krainburg and other concentration camps, so

SPREAD OF THE FLOOD OF HUN INVASION INTO THE VENETIAN PLAIN.
On November 6th, 1917, the German official communiqué reported the capture of the Tagliamento line, cavalry supported by motor machine-guns being the first enemy troops to cross the river. Italian cavalry drove the enemy cavalry back, but were compelled to retire before the machine-gun fire.

CONCENTRATED RIFLE FIRE VERSUS AIR RAIDER.
Platform erected over the roof of a house in Venice, with an ingeniously arranged overhead lattice-work, through which a score or so of Italian marksmen were able to bring their rifles to bear, more or less in a single focus, on raiding Austrian aeroplanes.

discussing Utopian politics and reading newspapers kindly furnished them by the enemy.

These newspapers were a remarkable example of Teutonic ingenuity. They were an almost exact reproduction of two of the leading Italian journals, but some strange items of news were inserted amid the authentic text. For example, the Italian soldiers were able to read that fifteen thousand British and French troops were being employed in shooting down the bread rioters at Turin and other places, because the Italian Government could find no Italian forces willing to kill their own countrymen and countrywomen.

Naturally the Italian shortage of food and coal was exaggerated, while the happiness and comfort in which British and French people were living were equally exaggerated. It is highly probable that there were some actual traitors working under the disguise of disgruntled Socialists and Anarchists in the ranks of the forces, upon which the enemy played with forged newspapers and fraternisations, espionage devices, and other methods of demoralisation already practised to perfection on the Russian front.

When in the mist and darkness of the tragic October 24th twenty thousand Prussian soldiers walked over Plec Trench, they had practically no fighting whatever to do. For miles they walked up the river towards Caporetto, under the grey shadowy mass of Monte Nero, looming above the opposite side of the river. When dawn came up and the autumn haze cleared away, the hard-pressed but unyielding Italian garrison on Monte Nero saw to their horror that two enemy divisions were marching across their line of retreat.

Even the situation at Cambrai, when the Germans surprised the British forces holding the southern base of the Cambrai salient, was by no means so tragic as that obtaining around Caporetto when the Prussians got behind the rear of the northern section of the Second Italian Army at daybreak on October 24th. There was no single brigade in reserve to act as five thousand British Guardsmen did against two German divisions in the critical moment of the Cambrai break.

Tragic surprise at Caporetto

For upon the Italian soldiers lay the shadow of the economic miseries of their country, and of all the poisonous intrigues of the three great organised forces of pro-Germanism. Many men there were who did not lose heart, and fought on with heroic desperation. But as their flanks were uncovered by the panic flight of comrades, their gallant attempts to retrieve the great disaster were fruitless. On Monte Nero the Italian Alpine troops held out for days. Completely surrounded and regarded as dead or captured by their own High Command, they were at last seen by an Italian airman still fighting around the mountain-top at a time when the Second Army had

that men and munitions could be rapidly poured into it by three or four channels. This is why the enemy commanding officer at Tolmino was able not only to hold the Isonzo valley, but strongly to maintain bridge-heads across the river.

When Gorizia fell, and in its fall blocked up a similar southern knot of railway and main road concentration channels, Tolmino remained the only gateway of invasion the enemy possessed on the eastern Italian front. The Second Italian Army tried to turn the Tolmino positions by a most gallant thrust from the Caporetto sector to the high dominating crest of Kra, or Monte Nero. From Monte Nero the Austrian positions at the central meeting-place of the river valleys were partly outflanked, but the operation was not regularly developed over the Alpine masses between Monte Nero and the Tolmino mountain. In peaceful holidays it used to take tourists eight hours to climb from Monte Nero to Tolmino, but probably it would have taken the Italian Army eight months to work southward to the castled mountain above the Isonzo, where Dante had written part of his " Divine Comedy." So this operation had been postponed until Gorizia could be firmly secured by the capture of San Gabriele mountain.

The Austrians pretended they did not grasp the importance of their bridge-head and converging communications at Tolmino. For six months they kept so remarkably quiet that the Italians, holding the Plec Trench above the bridge-head hills, were able to spend their time in

vanished and the Third Army was trying to stand on the Tagliamento line.

Meanwhile the enemy gathered from the seeds of treachery, sown broadcast in Italy, such a harvest of military victories as utterly surprised him. General von Below probably swore over the moderate view he had taken of his chances of success. Before him opened a prospect larger than that which Alaric and Attila had contemplated from the same mountain rampart of the Isonzo.

Flat beneath his eyes stretched the plain of Venice. In the western haze was Lombardy, where all the industrial strength of Italy was concentrated, and where the southern flank of France could be attacked with the united victorious forces of the Central Empires. "Eye and have, my Attila," sang George Meredith. All that the new Attila eyed he could have had if his forces had been adjusted in advance to the scope of his victory. The twenty-three divisions that Boroevic was using on and about the Carso were completely wasted. They were in the wrong place, and, moreover, they could not make any progress against the army of the Duke of Aosta, in which General Diaz began to fight one of the most superb rearguard actions in modern history.

Venetian plain thrown open

Below had no need to fight either the Third Italian Army between Gorizia and the sea, or the right wing of the Second Italian Army on the Bainsizza plateau, which was leaning back from its broken centre and vainly searching to make contact with the brigade that had let the enemy through.

The Prussian commander had only to sweep in force down the road from Caporetto to Cividale and Udine, and thence close southward upon the flank and rear of the Duke of Aosta, in order to repeat the success of Moltke at Sedan and Hindenburg at Tannenberg. Had he arranged to attack with twenty-three divisions, leaving Boroevic only fourteen divisions, the envelopment of three Italian armies might have been rapidly effected. For the Fourth Italian Army along the Carnic Alps was in extreme peril, as well as the divided Second and Third Armies on the broken Isonzo line. But General von Below could not take full advantage of the amazing situation.

In ordinary circumstances General Cadorna would have had a very strong second line in the Caporetto sector. Along the original Austro-Italian frontier on the western side of the Isonzo there rose a line of formidable fortified mountains, including the Stol Ridge, the Mia, the Matajur, and the Kolovrat heights. The principal crests towered five thousand feet above the river valley which the enemy occupied. He had only light artillery with his advanced troops, while the Italians had their heaviest pieces on and around their mountainous support line. Yet such was the confusion in the defending forces that a German lieutenant, with a few hundred Silesians, carried the most important height by the gateway to the Friulian plain, while an Austrian rifle division stormed the steep mountain ridge of the Stol. By seven o'clock in the morning of Thursday, October 25th, the army of Below was descending the highway along the Natisone valley to the great plain that began at Cividale.

Caporetto almost another Sedan

A day's march northward all was confusion in the Italian lines by Plezzo. For the narrows of Zaga, which the Italians had been holding valiantly, were carried by the enemy, after he had made his astonishing walk through the Plec position. Between the two points of their wide separated thrusting forces, the six German divisions

CHARGE OF ITALIAN CAVALRY COVERING THE RETREAT.

During the retreat to the Piave the great traditions of the Italian cavalry were finely upheld by the mounted troops, which engaged the advancing enemy long enough to permit of the main army retiring in good order. The Genoa Regiment performed deeds of great valour in a little village near Udine. One troop dismounted, carried their machine-guns to the upper floors of the houses, and fired from the windows, while their comrades with levelled lances charged a line of enemy machine-guns, overthrew it, and captured about thirty prisoners.

rolled up the greater part of the Second Italian Army, and, linking with the Austrian divisions along the uncovered Carnic Alps, they marched quickly down into the plain and endeavoured to get behind the Third Italian Army, the fragment of the Second Army, and the Fourth Army.

What then occurred cannot be described except from the Germanic point of view. The German brigades sent forward scouts on motor-cycles, followed by cavalry and machine-gunners and motor-vehicles, behind which the victorious infantry marched with remarkable pace and endurance. The lowland was threaded by many watercourses, trickling in dry summer through wide beds of dry gravel, which became broad, fierce torrents whenever a tempest washed down from the Alps. Happily for Italy, a torrential rain fell for thirty-six hours. The series of dry watercourses and trickling streams became wide rivers, while marshes formed in the overflow hollows between the network of water-lines near the frontier.

General von Below was seriously delayed by the effects of the great downpour. He could not spread out his forces over the country, but had to march them in columns down the railway track and main road running from Cividale to Udine towards the Tagliamento bridge near the village of Codroipo. In all there were only three crossings of the Tagliamento when it was in full flood, and these three lines of communication had to be carried over many other swollen streams between the Isonzo and the Tagliamento. The Italians destroyed the small bridges and culverts as they fought their way backward, and left the invaders in a region of marshes and torrents.

On Saturday, October 27th, the anniversary of the fall of Metz, Cividale fell

Fountain at Conegliano, thirty-five miles north of Venice. Many houses had been destroyed by shell-fire before the Germans entered the town.

City gate of Vittorio, Treviso, with the white flag of surrender still on it, after the entry of the Austro-German forces.

flaming into the hands of the enemy. On Monday, October 29th, he reached Udine, a most important railway junction, some seven and a half miles beyond Cividale, which had been General Cadorna's headquarters. The possession of Udine gave Below good lateral connections with Boroevic's unwieldly, large southern army, and enabled him forthwith to arrange the grand manœuvre of Codroipo Bridge.

From Udine to Codroipo the distance was only about seventeen miles along the railway track and parallel highway. From the Italian line on the Carso to Codroipo Bridge the distance was about thirty miles. The centre and southern wing of the Third Italian Army had also to cover about thirty miles in order to gain the lower bridge across the Tagliamento at Latisana, near the Adriatic shore. The intention of the Prussian Commander-in-Chief was to strike across the river at Codroipo, and there separate the remnants of the Second Italian Army and the northern wing of the Third Italian Army from the main mass struggling along near the sea.

Then he arranged to sweep down the branch railway behind the river and the bridge-head of Latisana in as triumphant an enveloping operation as Moltke accomplished at Sedan.

A strange and dreadful silence prevailed to the end of October, while the masses of some seven hundred and fifty thousand Teutonic, Magyar, and subject Slav forces were converging in a drive upon the rear and flank and across the reversed front of the jammed and encumbered multitudes of soldiers and civilians whom the Duke of Aosta and General Diaz were trying to withdraw from overwhelming disaster. German reports merely said that good progress was being made. Italian reports stated that

Guns and material abandoned on a roadside by the Italians during their retreat beyond the Tagliamento. (These three photographs appeared in German newspapers.)

ALONG THE LINE OF ITALY'S RETREAT.

the withdrawal of troops continued. The tension was as fearful as that which the world underwent in the summer of 1914, between the fall of Charleroi and Mons and the victory of the Marne.

Narrowly did the Duke of Aosta escape the fate of Napoleon III. The scenes on the lines of retreat were terrible. The population of the invaded hamlets and towns blocked the roads and made dangerous rushes for the bridges when the panic cry ran that Austrian cavalry had been sighted. Railways were at first blocked by long lines of stationary trains, helpless for want of coal.

British and Italian soldiers tramped along without food until they came to Latisana. In other places fugitives looted as they ran, and made supplies difficult for the gallant and orderly forces that were fighting a string of rearguard actions between Udine and Codroipo to prevent a premature irruption by the enemy.

The young flower of the warlike Italian nobility perished on the Tagliamento plain, alongside many Grenadiers and other forces of General Diaz. But they did not fall in vain. They held the enemy off the long, confused, and crawling northern flank of the Third Army and the **Splendid Italian** fragment of the Second Army. Lined out **rearguard action** among the torrents and marshes, in a position stretching below Udine to the Lower Tagliamento River, the Italian covering forces saved their country from supreme disaster. Under their steady and valiant protection the Italian columns moved towards the bridges, while their rearguards made a series of stands against the fierce mass attacks of Boroevic's great army.

The conditions of the retreat were far worse than those of the Belgian withdrawal from Antwerp to the Yser. The Italian Army was much more numerous than the Belgian. It followed mainly a single road near the coast,

occupied by motor-lorries, and a railway track where trains were stationary for lack of fuel. Along the rough, ballasted way families of peasants toiled beside the marching soldiers, while the rain, that was saving them all from capture, drenched them, chilled them, and aggravated their hunger and misery and despair.

The final element of horror was added to the apparent chaos of the retreat by the appearance of enemy airmen They flew low over the packed road and railway track, dropping bombs **Tragedy of** and using machine-guns upon civilians **the retreat** and soldiers alike. The enemy also brought gun fire to bear rapidly against the flank and rear of the fugitives by rushing forward light motor-lorries and firing over the rearguarding forces upon the slow stream of distracted Italian people.

Any detailed description of the sufferings of women and children need not be given. They were not so intense as those of the starving Serbian peasantry, tramping until they died in the snow of the mountains, yet they were so heartrending as to remain for ever a nightmare memory for Italy. There were times when some of the crowds endangered the military operations, and had to be sternly held back with revolver and bayonet. Here and there officerless and panic-stricken soldiers added to the confusion and spread the contagion of blind fear. The British gunners happily saved their guns. They arrived hungry but serene at Latisana, along with some British Red Cross units, one of whose ambulance cars was honey-combed with bullet-holes by machine-gun fire from an Austrian aeroplane.

Perhaps the best method of conveying an authentic impression of the scenes of the great Italian retreat would be to give a description of it that was not intended for

ENTRY OF AUSTRO-HUNGARIAN TROOPS INTO GEMONA.

On October 30th, 1917, the Austro-Hungarian forces reached Gemona, in the province of Udine, during their pursuit of the Italians retreating through Venetia. In this picture a German artist depicted the scene when the invading troops entered the town, and did not scruple to show one of the invaders engaged in the congenial occupation of forcibly taking a fowl from one of the townsmen.

A JUBILANT MOMENT FOR THE KAISER.

Gorizia, taken by the Italians in the earlier fighting on the Isonzo front, was reoccupied by Austro-Hungarian troops on November 28th, 1917, and the Kaiser shortly afterwards paid a visit to that much-disputed town, once more in the hands of his allies. (Photograph from a German newspaper.)

publication. Among the many letters from the Italian forces that succeeded in escaping, we take the following account given by a Red Cross nurse in a letter to a friend, which we have been allowed to translate :

Consider our last days out there. When meeting at meals I studied the faces of the other nurses before daring to ask if there were better news. Each time there were only more names to be added to those we had lost. We were betrayed, betrayed ! But perhaps it was not the soldiers who were most guilty.

The truth may be told to-day, now that we have vindicated ourselves with so much blood and so much heroism. The blow was terrific, and under it we lost our heads. Yet it seems so impossible that they should break through. Only a few hours before we had to evacuate our hospital an order came to us to prepare fresh beds. At half-past seven in the evening I was serving out pillows and mattresses, and helping my orderlies, who were not numerous enough for the work that had to be done. At eight o'clock I went down to dinner, and as I was beginning the soup a cyclist messenger dashed in with orders to evacuate the place at once as best we could.

Think of having to evacuate one thousand patients in a few hours from a hospital that had only been fitted with means for removing two or three hundred patients a day ! It was atrocious ! We had to awaken the wounded and sick men in their beds, make them get up, and send most of them off on foot. We only had enough carts for the very serious cases. The others had to trudge away in a black night under a deluge of rain.

In a few hours the hospital was empty, and we remained with the officers, trying to pack some cases and take down the tents. All the time we could hear the gun fire increasing in volume, with the shells exploding so close that the hospital was likely to be hit at any moment.

It was a night of agonising vigil ! Only towards morning were we able to leave. Our director wanted me to go to the railway-station, hoping we might catch the last train. But our luck was bad, and we had to make the whole journey on foot and by ourselves.

I wept on leaving the hospital, all in good order as it was, with the beds made, the cupboards full of stores, and flowers in all the little rooms. I had five minutes in which to throw my clothes in a bag, which was afterwards left by the roadside, so that I lost everything—my linen, my dresses, my Red Cross outfit, books, necessaries, the photographs of mother, father, and baby—everything !

But all this was nothing to me then. For five days and nights I tramped among carts and military waggons, guns and ammunition vans, among the retreating soldiers, and terrified fugitives carrying their children in their arms. Ah, what a spectacle ! I wept again, and I saw many officers weeping at their helplessness in such a defeat.

I lived with the soldiers, sharing their rough life and eating their rations, when they had any for themselves and the poor fugitives. Three hours after we left our hospital it was occupied by an enemy vanguard, consisting of cavalry that had hurried forward. When we were only eight and a half miles from Udine we learnt that the enemy was already there.

This created a panic among the mob of fugitives, who had already been terrorised. They fled away wildly, shrieking and disorderly, by every possible path. A heart-breaking scene ! I found myself running between horses, through mud and rain, until I was at last picked up by a passing motor-car which, however, was soon forced to stop. The crowd completely blocked the road, and it was impossible to pass.

We all thought we should be captured, but I was then seized by a strange, calm resignation. I took my leave of you all, and blessed you all in my thoughts, but I remember thinking sorrowfully of the pain you would feel. Death then seemed to me near and certain. I don't know why. Perhaps it was because so much evil might have happened to me that the thought of death calmed me and soothed me.

I spent another night and morning in the rain before reaching the Tagliamento. On passing over we found radiant sunshine beyond. While we were making the crossing, enemy aeroplanes appeared overhead and tried to destroy us on the bridge.

But death in this form we also escaped. Our own gallant aviators drove the Austrians away, and we crossed the river in safety. By this time I was so calm that I was able to help several women and children to cross. One of the boys I attended to became as attached to me as my own shadow for the rest of the journey.

Of course, beyond the Tagliamento there were no trains, telegraphs, or ways of getting a message through. I had another three days' tramp, but in comparison with what I had gone through I might call it a pleasure journey if this did not sound harsh and cynical. Just fancy ! I met three of our own officers, personal friends, who joyfully greeted me—you can imagine how touched I was—and took me with them, swearing that no director in the world should take me away from them.

They treated me with the utmost kindness, looking after my needs as far as possible. We ate when we could, and slept more or less in the same manner. But the discomforts suffered in friendly company, and far away from all danger, did not even appear discomforts.

A vivid human document

I was never tired. I was almost happy and gay. We were all young, and it was good to be alive in the world. But the reality, the tragic reality of the facts, was constantly recalled. . . . The search for bread was idle labour. The villages were bare of everything, being invaded by a whole army, and further by a fugitive population.

Happily, the strain on the advancing enemy was almost as great as the strain upon the retiring Italians. The German soldier has always been remarkable for his marching power, and to it Moltke had attributed the victory of Sedan. But amid the torrents and marshes between the Alps and Adriatic Sea the picked divisions of Teutons were almost worn out by the task their commander imposed upon them.

They did all that men could do in the excitement of the great success to bring off the enveloping movement. In the morning of October 31st they were in correct position for the accomplishment of the most rapid decision in the long history of the war. The Prussian Light Infantry, with Bavarian and Würtemberg infantry, deployed by the bridge-head position of Codroipo, and stretching northward for two and a half miles to the village of Dignano were a Brandenburg division and a Silesian division. These all worked down and behind the Italian rearguards, while corps of Austro-Hungarians, directed by Boroevic, pressed forward along the coast in a frontal attack against the Latisana crossings.

At this time there was a gap between the Third Italian Army and the fragment of the Second Italian Army. Into the gap there came some Bulgarian officers, who had been selected originally for espionage work along the Isonzo, because they had learnt the art of war in the Turin Academy, and in the Italian uniforms provided them could speak to Italian soldiers with special experience of their ways and language. Thus did the best educated class of Bulgars reward Italy for having taught them military science.

The Bulgar spies had been attached to Below's army **Disaster befalls the Third Army** for the immediate purpose of creating confusion in the original Italian lines along the Carso. After working there, when the Bolshevist brigade left the river gate open, the Bulgars, assisted by energetic but less well-equipped Austrian and German officers, also in Italian uniforms, found a still more important field of operations in the Tagliamento line by Codroipo.

The Third Italian Army had extended across the Udine road, after fighting rearguard actions at Lavariano, Pozzuolo, and Bertiolo, all well to the north of the seaward line of retreat. But the Bulgar spies, on October 31st, found the gap in the improvised line of defence, and led some disguised forces of Prussians and South Germans to the eastern bank of the river. From this position a strong surprise rear attack was made upon the large Italian rearguard forces around Codroipo village. The tragedy that ensued on the right wing of the Duke of Aosta's army was similar to that which occurred to the centre of General Capello's army by Caporetto. Below managed to bring two of his divisions through the gap in the lines of defence, so that another large Italian force of a hundred thousand men **Fate of the Second Army** was surrounded and killed or captured.

At the same time the surviving units of the Second Italian Army, which had retained sufficient strength to form up by the Tagliamento north of Codroipo, were also again attacked from behind, and swept into the net of the victorious Germans. Over sixty thousand Italians laid down their arms on the Tagliamento line, bringing the number of prisoners captured by the enemy to a hundred and eighty thousand men. Fifteen hundred guns were taken.

In the night of October 31st the bridge-head of Latisana was abandoned by the heroic 1st and 2nd Cavalry Divisions and by the magnificent Lancers of Genoa and Novara, who sacrificed themselves in saving the infantry and the guns. As the Germans and Austrians advanced towards the river, with motor machine-gun batteries and light field-guns mounted on motor-vehicles, one troop of the Lancers of Genoa dismounted and brought their machine-guns into action, while the rest of the men on horseback sheltered behind the houses of the little village until the order was given to charge.

They carried the hostile position and took some prisoners. Then, as fresh forces came down from Udine, they made another charge. When the regiment was reduced to a single squadron, the survivors cut their way

ITALIAN TOWN LOST IN THE RETREAT BEYOND THE TAGLIAMENTO.
General view of Udine, the capital of the province of the same name, which was occupied by the Austro-Germans on October 29th, 1917, during the retreat of the Italians. It was a most important railway junction, which had been the Italian Commander-in-Chief's Headquarters, and the possession of it gave the German commander valuable lateral connection with the large southern Austrian forces.

ON SENTRY DUTY IN A MOUNTAIN SOLITUDE.
Italian sentry at a look-out point on Monte Grappa. The great mountain mass, the highest point of which is Monte Grappa, rises to the east of the River Brenta, beyond the valley of which to the westward is the Asiago plateau. In this region took place much of the stubborn fighting by which the Italians stayed the invaders.

back to the river and crossed it. The Novara Lancers were as gallant as their comrades. Seven times they charged into lines of enemy riflemen and machine-gunners until they compelled a leading hostile division to deploy for action, after its spear-head of advanced skirmishing forces had been driven in. By the time the enemy commander was prepared for an important battle the Third Italian Army had escaped, and was entrenched on the western side of the large, swollen mountain river.

Work of the Italian cavalry

All through the war there had been much discussion as to the value of cavalry under the new conditions of warfare. It was generally reckoned that they had become obsolete; but it was the horsemen of Italy that saved the main Italian Army, even as the British cavalry during the retreat from Mons saved the British Expeditionary Force.

After the Duke of Aosta and General Diaz brought their men across the wide, roaring flood of Alpine rain-water—where there were at times more than ten thousand men crowding along the narrow steel plate of the railway bridge above the frothing spate of the tempestuous river—it still seemed doubtful whether the Third Army would be able to make a stand, and many of the soldiers were so dispirited that their officers did not know whether there was any fight left in them. It was partly in order to stimulate the depressed infantry that the Italian cavalry had sacrificed itself in charging down the attacking forces.

Fugitives of the Second Army were still in panic flight, far in the rear of the Tagliamento line, spreading news of their defeat with all the wild exaggeration of men who had lost courage and were trying to excuse themselves. Anxious observers wondered if the fatigued, sodden, hungry, and cheerless men behind the Latisana and Codroipo wrecked bridges would ever again stand to battle in the heroic spirit they had displayed upon the

Carso. Had the rain continued, the Tagliamento line could have been held for some weeks, as the condition of the ground would seriously have delayed the enemy. Although he had captured some two thousand five hundred Italian guns, with an enormous amount of ammunition, the labour of bringing the pieces into position, when all the ground between the three main roads was like a fen, would have taken so much time as to enable General Cadorna to establish himself on the western bank of the river.

The weather, however, turned against the Italians, after helping to save them from supreme disaster. Rain ceased in the Alps, and the steep beds of shingle rapidly discharged into the sea the flood of water that had come down like tidal bores. The Tagliamento fell as suddenly as it rose, and on Sunday, November 4th, the small northern Austrian army on the Carnic Alps, under General Krobatin, began to force a passage by Pinzano, by the northern edge of the Venetian plain, on a line nearly sixty miles due west from Tolmino. A spear-head German division of Silesians and Schleswig - Holstein Grenadiers burst over the river and advanced by the evening fourteen miles beyond it.

The effect of this manœuvre was to drive a wedge behind the Fourth Italian Army that was retiring from the Carnic Alps and the Dolomite peaks of Cadore. Under General Robilant, the Fourth Italian Army of hardy mountaineers was swinging back towards the far-distant neck of the net that Below was closing behind it by the middle course of the Piave.

The Second Italian Army had practically disappeared. There were left the Third Army, retiring across the Livenza River towards the Piave River, on a front of about thirty-eight miles; then, at a distance of some twenty-five miles westward, the First Italian Army, under General Pecori, was holding the eastern heights on the Brenta River against the forces which the Austrian commander in the Trentino was rapidly accumulating for another grand offensive. Towards the gap between the Duke of Aosta on the Livenza River and General Pecori on the Brenta River, General

MARINE ARTILLERY IN THE PIAVE MARSHES.
Men of the Italian Royal Marines with one of their guns mounted amid a camouflaging screen in the shallows of the River Piave. Along the Piave from the mountains to the sea the Italians held the Austro-German advance. Though the Austrians effected crossings at one or two points, the actions yielded nothing of importance to the invaders.

Robilant, with the Fourth Italian Army, violently struggled to reach the Piave River line and fill the neck of the net there before three hostile armies could encircle his forces.

On November 6th General von Below ceased directly attacking the Third Italian Army, and leaving this work to General Boroevic's more numerous forces, swerved northward towards the valley roads of the Lower Venetian Alps leading to Longarone and Belluno. His intention was to strike upon the flank and rear of the Fourth Italian Army, part of which was some ninety-three miles distant from the point at which it could make contact with the Third and First Italian Armies.

General Robilant had Krobatin thrusting at him from the north, Below breaking in upon him from the south, and Scheuchenstuel driving at him from the east and trying to connect with Below. Had the connection been made, the fate of the Fourth Italian Army would have been worse than that of the vanished Second Army. Only by an amazing achievement on the part of his men did General Robilant escape.

His task was far more arduous than that of the Duke of Aosta, and the country through which he had to work was of infinite difficulty. It was broken by four mighty mountain systems—the Carnic Alps, Venetian Alps, Ampezzo Alps, and the Dolomites, towards which ran only one railway, constructed along the valley of the Upper Piave. A few wandering side-roads branched from this valley and followed the winding tributary streams to the great glaciers and snow-fields of the high Alps.

Happily, General Robilant's troops were among the hardiest men of the world. Some of them made forced marches over the mountains, which were already snow-covered, and when they emerged from the blinding snow-storms they came into rain-shrouded valleys where the rising water made the ground a bog.

At first the men could not understand why they had to abandon the extraordinary positions they had won—the peaks to which they had lifted their heavy artillery, the

ERECTING AN ENEMY GUN-PLATFORM.
Austrian gun-team preparing a position for one of their heavy guns on the Italian front. The men were at work screwing up the revolving platform on which the gun was to be fixed. (From a photograph in a German newspaper.) The Austrians had an immense superiority in heavy ordnance, and used hundreds of Skoda guns against the Italians.

rock galleries in which they had lived above the clouds for nearly two and a half years, dominating the enemy. Strategy was not their forte, and they could not appreciate the need for the instant and vehement race down to the narrowing gap far away in their rear.

First they had to leave a large rearguard on the Carnic Alps, by the Fella valley, to hold back Krobatin's forces. Then behind this first rearguard General Robilant was able to organise a more important temporary line of defence on the Upper Tagliamento, from Tolmezzo to Gemona. Here he stood to battle against the Austrian forces from October 29th to November 7th. His flank at Gemona was only about twelve miles north of Udine, so that if it had been broken the enemy would have had more space in which to manœuvre around the remains of the Second Italian Army and the two intact Italian forces on the mountains and by the sea.

Stand of the Fourth Army

In the end the Alpine rearguard between Tolmezzo and Gemona was enveloped, the enemy claiming the capture of a further seventeen thousand Italians with eighty guns. In the meantime some of Below's German forces made an unexpected swerve away from the main southern battlefield towards the valleys of the Venetian Alps.

By November 6th they were fighting by the town of Sacile for the valley road to Belluno. Sacile, with the hills of Vittorio, was situated midway between the Tagliamento and the Piave Rivers, and upon the railway connecting Udine with Venice. It was a most important position of defence, both for the rear of the Fourth Italian Army retiring from the Alps down the single railway that had fed the Dolomite front and the Carnic front, and for the northern wing of the Third Italian Army that was retreating to the Piave line.

The Italian troops made a most gallant stand at Sacile and the Vittorio hills; but,

NAVAL GUN ON THE PIAVE.
[*Italian official photograph.*]
Heavy Italian naval gun mounted on a pontoon for service on the Lower Piave. When, in the autumn of 1917, the Austro-Germans broke through into Venetia, they announced that they would be in Venice itself by November 20th, but the men who held them back on the Piave line cancelled their time-table and changed their outlook.

ITALIAN AIRMEN DROPPING BREAD TO COMRADES ISOLATED ON A MOUNTAIN PEAK.

A small company of Alpini holding a mountain position found themselves surrounded and unable to retreat through the ring of enemy artillery fire. Determined to resist as long as their ammunition lasted, they held out, and were almost starving when Italian flying men, who had observed their plight, flew over the position and dropped loaves of bread, wrapped in strong netting, among the indomitable heroes.

while they were successfully defending the entrance to the main Alpine valley, Below swung a Würtemberg and Austrian force up the more northerly valley of Barcis. His men followed the course of the Cellina tributary of the Livenza River, climbed over the intervening mass of mountain, and descended upon the town of Longarone, lying in the Upper Piave valley a day's march above Belluno.

They drove right into the centre of the railway communications of the Fourth Italian Army, and captured another ten thousand men and a large quantity of gun material and war stores. All Italian forces in the Upper Piave valley appear to have been cut off. By November 11th Belluno was captured, and an Italian brigade in the Cordevole valley, west of Belluno, also found its path of retreat blocked. This brought the number of Italian prisoners to a quarter of a million, while the lost guns amounted nearly to three thousand.

In spite of these practically inevitable accidents the lengthy retirement from a most difficult mountain front of more than one hundred and twenty miles was effected with remarkable skill and energy by the Fourth Italian Army. The weary men fell back fighting **Fourth Army's** from Feltre and Fonzaso and, still pressed **retirement effected** by General von Below's German divisions, occupied the twelve-mile angle of mountains between the middle course of the Piave River and the Brenta River.

Below did not use his own men to make another attempt to break through the Third Italian Army, which had retreated across the Lower Piave after fighting a series of rearguard actions by the Livenza stream. He left the strongest Italian force to General Boroevic's large Austro-Hungarian masses. These, however, were unable to accomplish anything of importance. In the meantime Below, in person, continually tried to repeat his successful Tagliamento stroke, and wedge through the junction of

the dispirited Italian armies. By this time the Second Italian Army was completely gone. Most of the men who were not killed or captured were spread in disordered flight over a considerable part of Northern Italy. The Third Army had to extend westward to fill part of the gap, while the Fourth Army, in the mountains above Robert Browning's lovely city of Asolo, extended southward to the Piave at Pederobba, and there linked with the force that was directly protecting Venice.

Savagely and incessantly Below drove at the positions to which General Robilant was desperately clinging. The German storm divisions were reinforced by the Austrian army of the Carnic **Enemy attacks** Alps, and the combined forces were **begin to flag** arranged in battering columns, winding through the valleys of the mountain masses between the Brenta and the Piave.

The Italians held firm against the first and most dangerous and yet lightest assaults. The enemy had no heavy artillery with him, and his troops were as fatigued as the men they attacked. They had climbed over Alp after Alp, carrying with them machine-guns and ammunition, in attempts to enfilade the retreating Alpine troops of Italy. They had been in turn counter-attacked in many obscure and unrecorded fights on the ledges, slopes, and pinnacled rocks of the various mountain systems, where opposing companies had fought to the death for some strategic purpose they did not clearly understand.

Like madmen the Germans had toiled in their endeavour to cut off the Fourth Italian Army. When they failed to effect this grand manœuvre their spirit was not so high as it had been. Sheer physical exhaustion began to tell upon them, and their difficulties were soon increased by the abrupt onset of bad weather in the great tangle of mountains they occupied.

Owing to these difficulties, Below could not immediately accomplish by main force the third breaking movement he intended. The process of retirement had greatly increased the strength of the surviving Italian armies by shortening the line of defence. The troops had drawn back into the narrow gap, between the mountains of the Trentino and the lagoons above Venice. The lagoon sector was easy to hold with comparatively small forces, and the length of the main new river-line of the Piave was not much more than forty-five miles. Consequently, the Third and Fourth Italian Armies were able to re-assemble in considerable depth, and until the enemy got his long-range heavy artillery into position, after hauling the pieces some seventy-four miles, there was no danger of an assault in overwhelming strength.

It was about November 8th that General Diaz began to make a stand along the Piave, with the assistance of some of the forces under General Robilant. General von Below and his lieutenants could then only rely upon finding the Italian rank and file in so completely demoralised a condition as to enable them again to break through and pursue the panic-stricken Italians to the Adige River line. The military balance had been skilfully restored by the Italian commanders. It was the **Italy tested** mental balance only that was the dubious **by disaster** factor in the situation on the Piave, upon which the fate of Italy depended.

Upon the frame of mind of the Italian soldier it was clear that the fortune of war would turn. At the beginning of the second week in November, 1917, nobody had any sure knowledge of this matter. The men did not feel quite sure of themselves after the trial through which they had passed; their regimental officers were feverishly anxious, while the Staff officers and the commanding generals awaited the great psychological ordeal with intense solicitude. Throughout Europe men were talking about the disaster of the Italian campaign in

Abyssinia and various untoward episodes in the Tripoli campaign, and wondering whether the emotional, artistic, brilliant, and inventive and fertile Italian people would, in the crisis of its destiny, show that backbone of character without which no nation, whatever its gifts of imagination and intellect, can survive the dreadful test of a great war. Practically the same tremendous ordeal as the French race abruptly underwent in August, 1914, was more unexpectedly imposed upon the Italian race in the third year of the war. Every **Forces of** belligerent people was in turn tested **disintegration** to the uttermost by some grave disaster.

As we have already seen, Italy was still to a considerable extent rather a geographical expression than the home of a race that was entirely true to itself. Religious, political, and economic forces of disintegration worked with extraordinary power to prevent all classes of Italians from combining into a homogeneous nation. There were, moreover, profound differences in temperament between the level-headed, businesslike Northern Italian and the passionate and rather lawless Southern Italian, with his secret societies, his picturesque but degrading poverty, and his Anarchism deriving from traditions of age-long oppression. It was the Northern Italians who had rescued Italy from foreign tyranny and imposed upon the powerful ecclesiastical noble families the modern temporal rule of the House of Savoy.

Were the grand ecclesiastical families Italians first and the seminaries of international religious politicians afterwards? Or were they still bent upon assuring themselves of their spiritual powers of dominion at the expense of the independence and integrity of their country? Were the hard-headed business men of Lombardy, who had been the real masters of such politicians as Signor Giolitti, willing to become the economic and political vassals of the Teutons,

HEROIC ITALIAN GUNNERS' LAST STAND ON THE HEIGHTS BEYOND THE ISONZO.
Loyal Italian troops of both the Second and Third Armies fought a series of magnificent rearguard actions when falling back to the Tagliamento line. This picture by Signor Matania illustrates one of the many examples of supreme self-sacrifice furnished during the retreat—a little company of heroic Italian artillerymen fighting to the last against hopeless odds and letting the enemy pass only over their dead bodies.

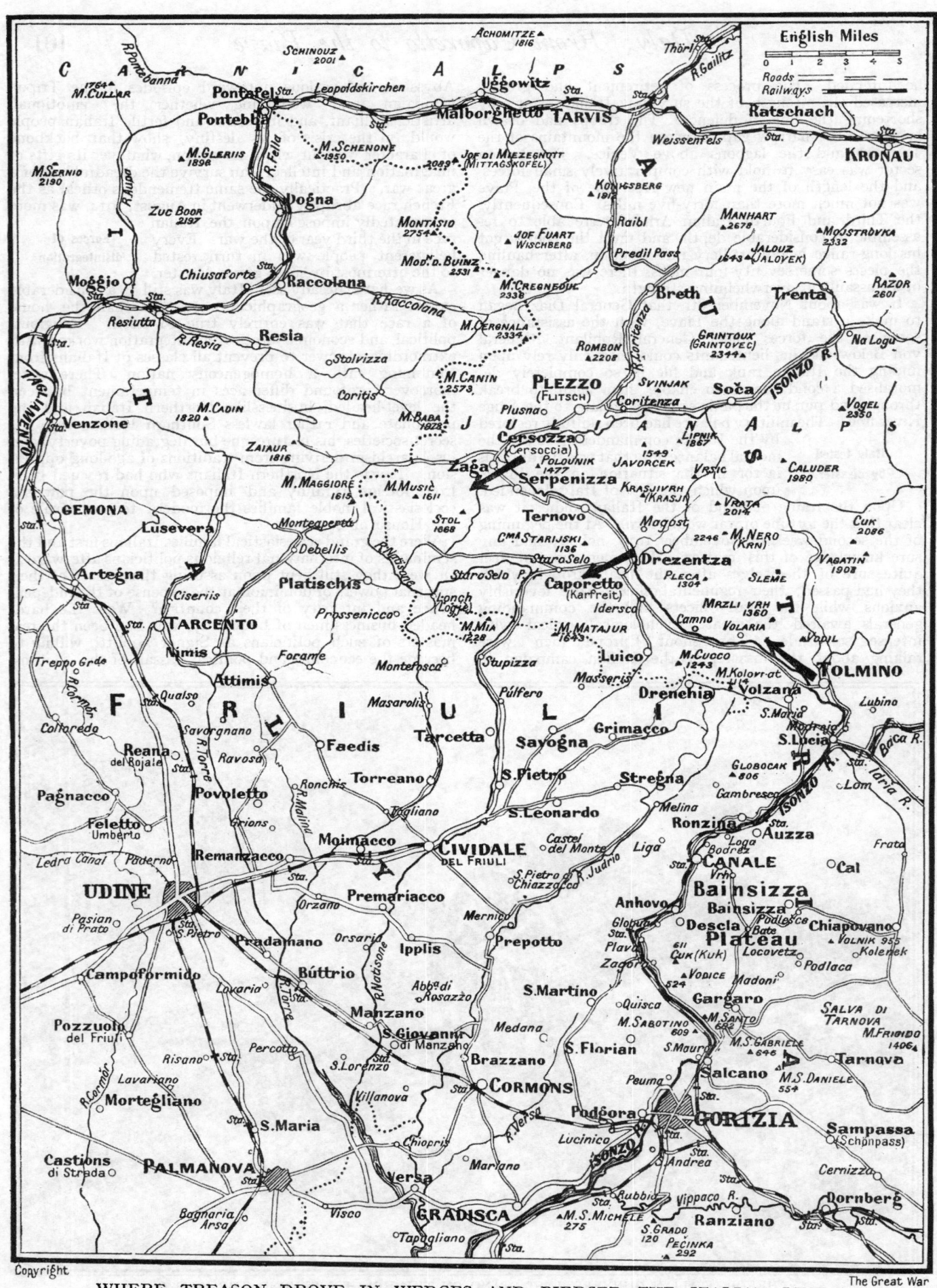

WHERE TREASON DROVE IN WEDGES AND PIERCED THE ITALIAN LINE

The Germans concentrated on Santa Lucia, below Tolmino, on October 24th, 1917, and, marching up the Isonzo valley, poured through the gaps treacherously left open at Caporetto and Zaga, swept over the Friulian plain, capturing Cividale and the important railway junction of Udine. The arrows indicate where the enemy wedges were driven in the Italian positions.

in return for little more than a degraded and shameful existence ? Were the official Socialist mayors of towns and Socialist Commune authorities ready to continue their strike against the war to the point at which they themselves would meet the fate of the Bolshevist Government of Riga ? Such were some of the questions to which a valiant reply was speedily given along the line of the Piave.

It is not extravagant to say that the defeat of Italy was her salvation. What her enemies gained in the temporary occupation of her territory they lost, in manifold proportion, by the effect they produced upon all the old and new Italian forces of disunion.

Tens of thousands of men who had been playing at something like treason were shocked into an anguished sense of national realities by the disaster on the Isonzo front. Even many men of cool, calculating mind, who had been averse to their country entering the war against the Central Empires, were stirred with a passion they did not know they possessed when they learnt that the Goth and Hun had again broken through the Alpine rampart of their ancient and lovely land.

From the north to the south of Italy there was such a resurrection of the true Italian spirit as Mazzini and Garibaldi had not known in the days of the first rebirth of the national genius. Man is a mystery to himself. Often the thoughts to which he gives loudest expression are silently contradicted by the impulses of his instinct. Many Italians had talked loudly of the supreme international interests of their race. The official Socialists of the Teutonic school had made most clamour in this regard, but the quieter, religious politicians had been most hostile to purely national interests. The tragic event at Caporetto, however, brought the instinctive part of their nature into supreme action. They were Italians first, and the doctrinaire play of their intellect was completely numbed at **Fused into unity** the thought of the loss of Venice **by defeat** and the invasion of Northern Italy.

Neither the Austrians nor the Germans conducted themselves in the conquered provinces in a manner calculated to deaden the feelings of all honest Italians that had been opposed the most to the war. The German soldiers were inspired by a new Hymn of Hate more becoming to gorillas than to human beings. They sang that the children of conquered races would become the foes of their own sons if they were not now killed in the cradle, and that women carrying child must be slaughtered to prevent them becoming the mothers of an enemy generation. In the Austro-Hungarian Army wild bands of Mohammedans from Bosnia were deliberately loosened upon that part of the Italian population which had trusted in the civilised and Christian clemency of the invading armies. Belated fugitives carried the tale of the atrocious conduct of the invaders into Northern Italy, and thence the reports spread like flame along tinder throughout the peninsula.

Grey-haired men in civilian clothes hurried to the fighting-line and made impassioned speeches to the troops. They were deputies and senators from Parliament, consumed with the common anxiety in regard to the spirit of the defenders of the country.

Their eloquence was wasted. The Italian private did not need it. The retreat had educated him. At bottom the Italian peasant or working man from the north or the south had always been sound. The way in which he had brought up some of the largest families in Europe, in an age when other proletariats were artificially restricting the number of their children, was really good evidence of his soundness of soul. It was not through ignorance or through chance that he had flooded the United States, Brazil, and the Argentine with his descendants, and become one of the mainstays of labour in both France and Germany. He was virile, and trained by his life as a father to a laborious existence of self-sacrifice.

Along the Piave and upon the mountains between the Piave and the Brenta the soldiers of Italy wanted only rest and food and some grounds of confidence. Confidence they obtained from the happy news that armies of Britons and Frenchmen were hastening to their aid. This completely dispelled all the slanders against their Western Allies, making it clear that no desire for the weakening of Italy as a Mediterranean and North African Power had never been entertained by France, with the tacit consent of Great Britain. The spectacle of troops in sky-blue and khaki crowding through the cities of Northern Italy answered all the Germanic propaganda far better than spoken or written words could do.

The courage of the Italian soldiers rose to a strange ecstasy. Tired battalions fought as they had never fought before, even in their finest actions across the frontier. They had to vindicate the honour of their country, and while they **Italy's honour** were vehemently holding the river-line **vindicated** and the mountain ridge just above the plain of Asola, the scattered remnants of the Second Italian Army gathered in shamefaced small groups which were re-collected into brigades.

The hammer-blows of her enemies, instead of scattering the partially-fused elements of the race, had, by one of the most remarkable instances of historic irony, forged the fragments of ancient and modern Italy into a strongly-tempered whole. Had peace come with victory at the time when Italy was still disunited, the deep, sombre, fratricidal contest would have gone on for at least a generation, and maybe for a century or more.

But the barbaric invader healed with miraculous rapidity the self-inflicted wounds of Italy. When the Vatican was compelled to contemplate the possibility of becoming the veritable vassal of the half-heretic, half-pagan power of Prussia, with the Catholic part of Germany and Austria-Hungary developing a modernistic theology as a political device, while acting as the subordinate instrument of the Hohenzollern suzerain, the old domestic Roman quarrel about the division of spiritual and temporal power in a strong and independent Italy shrank into true perspective and insignificancy.

The barbaric destructiveness of Austrian and German bomb-dropping airmen told in an intense manner upon the mind of Pope Benedict. The Della Chiesa of Genoa was, after all, an Italian nobleman. His Rome was the Rome of St. Peter and St. Paul—the hearthstone of Western European civilisation and the original source of Christian influence in all Western and transoceanic lands.

Clever as Ludendorff had been in sending Below to Italy, he had been so successful that he had overreached himself. Throughout the war the foreign influence of the Vatican had to a considerable extent been one of benevolent neutrality towards the Central Empires. Wherever a powerful Catholic priesthood had been able to go its own way, without fear of immediate **Barbarism defeats** complications, it had worked directly or **its own ends** indirectly for the benefit of Germany.

In Ireland and in Australia, in Canada and Spain, in Chile, Argentina, and other South American Republics, in Central America, and in Italy itself, strange Germanic forces had worked under cassock and mitre. Even in trampled Poland the Catholic Church had united with the selfish, noble, large landowners in discreetly favouring the eventual triumph of the Germanic Powers ; while in enslaved and wretched Belgium there had been a distinct and strong undercurrent of ecclesiastical intrigue against Cardinal Mercier and against the bishops and priests who sided with him and with the overwhelming majority of Belgian people. The hidden basis of this extraordinary condition of things was liable to be sapped by the results of the Germanic invasion of Italy, which seemed at the time likely to become in more ways than one the most fortunate disaster that the Western Allies had suffered.

LINES OF COMMUNICATION OVER YAWNING ABYSSES: THE "TELEFERICA" IN USE.

Italian ingenuity devised the "teleferica" to cope with the enormous difficulty of conveying men, munitions, and supplies to the positions required by strategy and tactics on almost inaccessible mountain peaks. Strong wire cables were stretched between the various points, and along these cradles were drawn on the chain-ferry principle, carrying whatever was required across gulfs that could not otherwise be bridged.

ITALIAN INFANTRY

MOVING FORWARD.

THE DEFEAT AND RECOVERY OF ITALY.

III.—The Victorious Stand on the Asiago Plateau and Grappa Front.

By Edward Wright.

The Rapallo Conference—Versailles Council and Union of Fronts—Peril of Losing Command of Adriatic—Austrian Army Crosses the Piave—Below Concentrates for New Offensive Battering-ram Tactics on Brenta Front—Hötzendorf's Last Chance—Badoglio's Terrible Defence of Asiago Plateau—Magnificent Heroism of Italians on Tondarecar and Fior Mountains—Victorious Stand by Frenzela Ravine—Failure of Austrian Main Army—Below Tries a New Way of Attack—His Intended Death-blow to Italy—Loss of Quero Angle and Break at Fener—Glorious Recovery of Italian Forces—How the Garibaldi Brigade Held the Invaders—Heroism of Calabrians—Arrival of British and French Armies—Recovery of Key Position of Monte Tomba.

N the last week of October, 1917, while the principal armies of Italy were desperately fighting for life, Sir William Robertson and General Foch hastened to the Italian front, and, without waiting for a call for help, arranged with General Cadorna for the despatch of British and French armies of support. In the meantime a new Italian Government was formed of members of all parties except the United Socialists, Signor Orlando becoming Prime Minister.

M. Painlévé, the French Premier, travelled to London with General Pétain, and had long consultations with Mr. Lloyd George and General Smuts. Then, on November 6th, a general conference was held at Rapallo, on the Gulf of Genoa, at which the Prime Ministers of Italy, France, and Great Britain, with their Chiefs of Staffs and other advisers, debated the means of establishing a single military and economic union, in which there would be a powerful allied army of manœuvre always ready for a supreme crisis.

General Foch had long been in favour of close and intimate

GENERAL GAETANO GIARDINO.
General Giardino succeeded General Cadorna in February, 1918, as Italian member of the Inter-Allied War Council at Versailles. He had previously been Deputy Chief of Staff to General Diaz, the Italian Commander-in-Chief.

union with the three great Armies of the Western Powers. General Cadorna was the originator of the plan, and Mr. Lloyd George and General Smuts also approved of it. Sir William Robertson, however, while doing all he could to speed British forces to the assistance of Italy, raised some technical questions in regard to the manner in which general unity of control could best be exercised.

At the time the opposition of the British Chief of Staff was so strong that the Rapallo Conference did not produce any solution of the great problem of a general, unified command. On November 12th, when Mr. Lloyd George was passing through Paris, he delivered a remarkable speech in favour of the proposed new military arrangement. He spoke of the blunders and disasters of the Allies, and contrasted the few miles of ground they had won with the great stretches of territory that Hindenburg and Ludendorff had rapidly conquered.

He proposed that a Supreme War Council should sit at Versailles, closely linking together the Armies of Italy, France, and the British Empire, at which Sir Henry Wilson,

COMRADES IN ARMS ON JOINT GUARD.
Where British and Italian troops were quartered sentry duty was performed by men of both nationalities. A British and an Italian sentry are here shown presenting arms while their respective officers exchange salutes.

General Foch, and General Cadorna should act independently of the General Staffs of their countries. The French and Italian people welcomed the proposal, but there was an immediate current of opposition to it in Great Britain. Perhaps the harsh language deliberately employed by Mr. Lloyd George to sting and arouse the allied nations, told for the moment against the fiery Welsh statesman.

The main difficulty, however, was that the British people felt that their national sovereignty would be invaded in dividing the control of the allied armies by means of an International High Command at Versailles. The experiment of making General Nivelle the Generalissimo of the western front had worked very badly. None of the Allies had produced a commander of exceptional genius, and doubt was expressed whether British troops **British troops** would stand up to temporary reverses **to assist Italy** under foreign control as well as they did under their own generals.

Months were to pass before Mr. Lloyd George carried out his policy, by Sir William Robertson retiring from the position of Supreme Command and Sir Henry Wilson being appointed in his place. In the meantime much of practical importance was done with a view to uniting Italy, France, and Great Britain into a single block of resistant power. A large British army, under one of the most brilliant of British commanders, Sir Herbert Plumer, set out for Italy to hold part of the Piave line by the Montello height. A large French army also moved partly by rail and partly by road—under one of the best French commanders, General Fayolle—to undertake the defence of the mountain rampart above Asolo.

At the same time steps were taken to relieve the food shortage in Italy by restricting the supplies of the British people. The British Government had been foresightful of the needs of its nation, and, while acting in loyal co-operation with French and Italian buyers of wheat and other necessities, had accumulated considerable stocks of provisions in answer to the enemy's submarine campaign and the continually increasing restriction of cargo space consequent upon the transportation of American troops and material to France.

Neither the Italian nor the French authorities appear to have been so long-sighted in the purchase and accumulation of food stocks as were the British authorities. In the tragic winter of 1917 the thrifty Briton had to come to the help of his Allies and straiten himself in food so that his comrades might live. The production of French wheat had fallen considerably, while Italy was by far the worst off of all the Great Powers, and the task of supplying her with food, material, new armament, and armies of support taxed the resources of the Alliance to the uttermost.

On the other hand, much was gained by these measures of establishing economic union as well as military combination. In spite of the sudden resurgence of patriotic feeling that united the Italian people and the rapid moral recovery of the Italian armies, the forces of pro-Germanism still remained strong in the country.

There were signs that Signor Giolitti intended to use his power in Parliament to overthrow General Cadorna, the Commander-in-Chief, and Baron Sonnino, the Foreign Minister, and lead Italy back, chastened and humbled, into the League of Central Europe. At the beginning of 1918 he made his first attempt, by means of a coalition of the **Importance of** forces of disruption, to obtain Parlia- **the Piave line** mentary control of foreign and military policy. He was defeated by the fact that the patriots of Italy no longer fought alone against invasion and famine, but were backed by the arms of France, the general power of the British Empire, and the fields and factories of the United States.

There was, however, a critical period of suspense of three weeks between the arrival of French and British armies and the opening of the new turning attack of General von Below. Great was the danger that the enemy would burst over the mountain rampart between the Piave and Brenta Rivers, destroy the First and Fourth Italian Armies, and compel the Allies to make their intended stand farther back along the course of the Adige River.

The Adige River was certainly a stronger line, as its stream of water, running by Verona and emptying south of the Venice lagoons, was broad, deep, and constant. Venice and Padua and Vicenza would have been lost, and Verona would have been reduced to dusty chaos. Another slice of rich territory would have fallen under the savage tyranny of the barbarians. But, from a purely military point of view, the Adige line would have shortened the work of defence and facilitated it in other ways.

On the other hand, there were reasons that compelled General Cadorna and his Staff to attempt to stand along the shingle-beds of the capricious torrent of the Piave. Not only would the effect of the loss of Venice and Padua have deepened the depression of the Italian people, but the northern waters of the Adriatic would have come under the dominion of the Austro-Hungarian Fleet.

There were no good harbours on the Italian shore of the Adriatic. It had always been a matter of difficulty to conduct naval operations against the enemy from the shallow base of Venice. The loss of the Venetian harbourage would have been a very serious disaster, exposing a long line of coast to hostile naval raids, and perhaps to more serious amphibious operations. The Austrians had an incomparable series of natural defences.

Through the Sunny South: British artillery on the march to the Italian front.

[French official photograph.

Help for Italy's women and children: British reinforcements passing through an Italian country town.

Under the shadow of the Alps: British column on a screened road near the front.

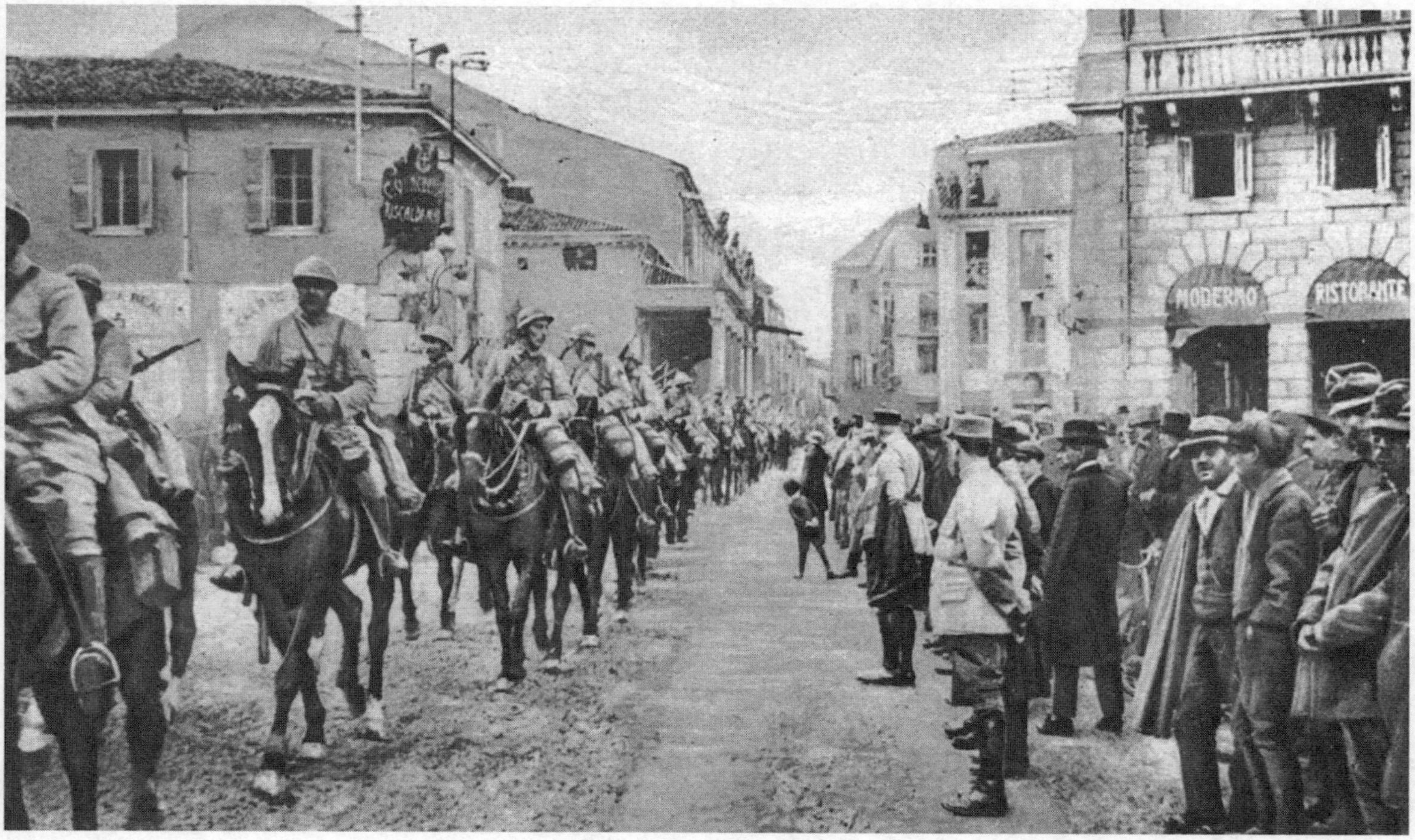

[French official photograph.

Gallant gentlemen in Verona: French cavalry riding to help in the defence of Venetia.

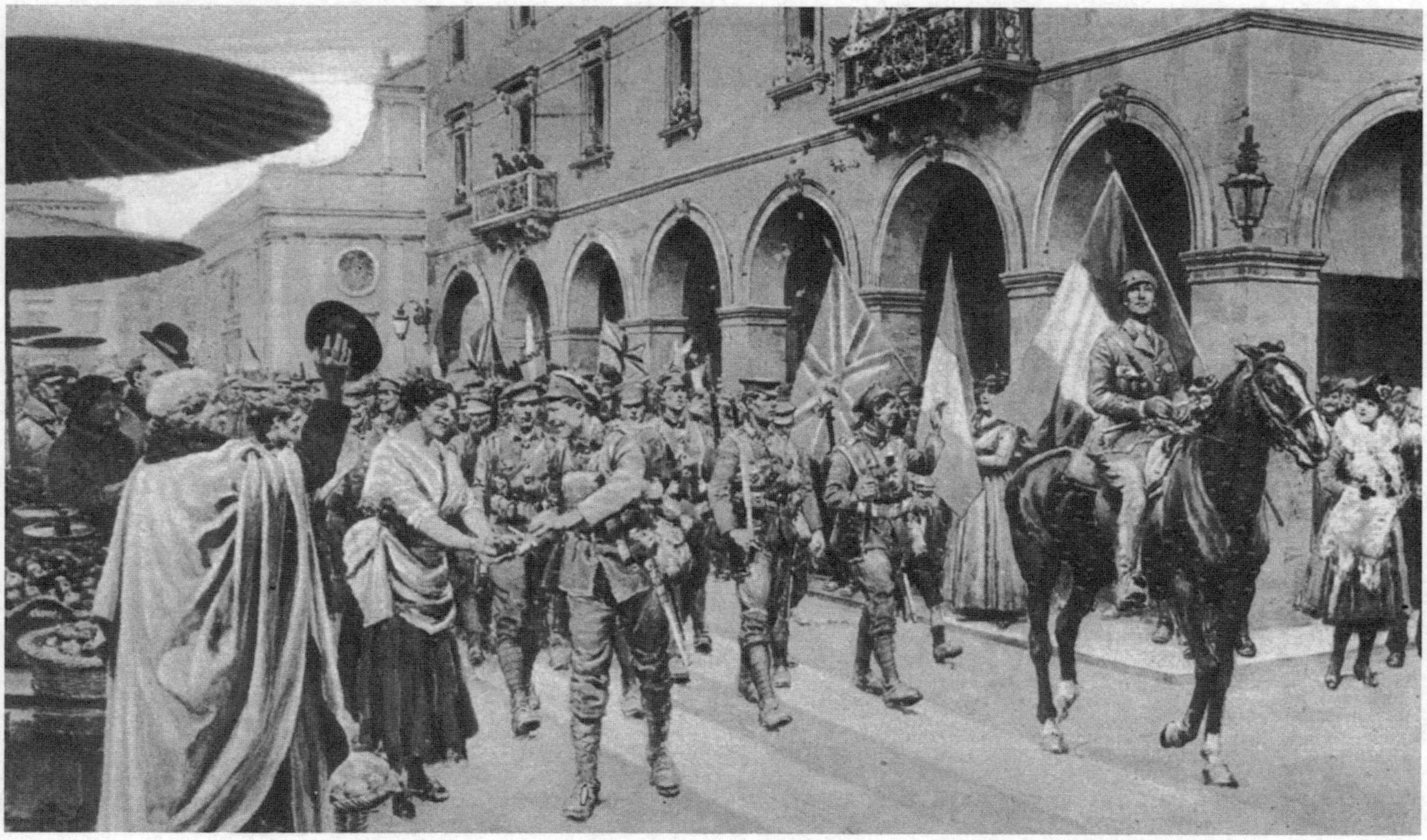

Roses and smiles for allies and friends: Enthusiastic welcome of British troops in Northern Italy.

A treasure of the world which the Hun aimed at destroying: Venice, from the Campanile.

Venice imperilled: Italian sailors taking stores to a destroyer lying in the Grand Canal.

roadways, and shelters along the islanded waters of the Eastern Adriatic.

Their ships could work southward, behind mine-fields, fortified isles and islets, and make sudden dashes to the bare Italian coast, where a system of railway guns and motor-guns had to be devised to hold off attacks until the forces based on Venice swept down upon the enemy's line of retreat. The operations of the British monitors, assisting the Third Italian Army, and the work of all the allied light naval forces that managed to hold the Northern Adriatic, would have been very badly checked if the river-line above Venice had been abandoned.

The Italian Commander-in-Chief therefore held on to the Piave line, in spite of the fact that it was almost as easy to cross as the Tagliamento River, though, happily, much shorter. From the popular point of view, the new battle that opened on November 8th was fought for the glorious monuments of the lovely and romantic Italian city that had once held dominion over the Mediterranean. One hour's bombardment by long-range Austrian artillery was likely to destroy the treasures of ages, which were less a national possession of Italy than the heritage of the human race. The Italian Government did everything possible to prevent Venice from being treated as a place of war. Nobody in uniform was allowed to enter the city, and the civilian population was encouraged to leave by means of a free train service.

As Venice was one of the four principal Italian naval stations these precautions were vain. Nothing would have given the new Goths and Huns fiercer pleasure than an opportunity of excelling the work they **Below resumes** had done in France and Belgium, and **the offensive** dealing with St. Mark and the Ducal Palace as they had dealt with Rheims and Louvain. When prevented from bringing their artillery to bear upon the enchanted city they bombed it by aeroplanes.

In the meantime the thought of the destruction of all the beauty of Venice helped greatly to strengthen the spirit of the Italian soldiers. Quickly they recovered confidence in themselves, and while General Cadorna was busy over the problems of international command, General Diaz, the saviour of the Third Italian Army, was appointed Commander-in-Chief.

General von Below began his new operations on November 10th, 1917. He reached the Piave line from Segusino to the sea, and, driving back the armoured cars rear-guarding the Italian forces, captured the bridge-head of Vidor on the eastern bank of the river. Immediately the large Austro-Hungarian army, under General Boroevic, tried to force various passages of the river and break the new front of the Third Italian Army. In nocturnal operations, begun in a hurricane of wind and snow, the Austrians crossed by the shingle-beds of the rising mountain torrent that remained uncovered, and by November 13th established bridge-heads at Zenson and Grisolera, while making attempts and feints at crossing in other places. Then, on November 16th, the passage of the river was again forced at Folina and Fagare.

These actions yielded nothing of importance to the invaders. Their success depended entirely upon the state of mind of the Italian troops and a supposed condition of demoralisation which did not obtain. The Italians fought with great fury round every crossing they had lost, and either routed and captured the enemy forces or drove them back into the river loops, and there hemmed them firmly in. At Folina the Lecce Brigade killed or captured the Austrians. At Fagare the famous 54th Division, which included the Novara Brigade and the 3rd Bersaglieri, threw the enemy back from the river, while their artillery cut him off from the stream. In the Zenson loop the Austrians were also promptly counter-attacked and thrown back to the river; while in the sea marshes they were checked by Italian Marines and Bersaglieri and the fire of British monitors, at a distance of 20,000 yards from Venice. This was

AIRCRAFT-SHOOTING IN THE ITALIAN FENS.
Anti-aircraft guns mounted on pontoons installed among the marshes surrounding Venice assisted in the defence of the city against attack from the air. Naval guns were also so employed.

exactly the same distance at which the Third Italian Army had been held off from Trieste just a month before.

During the second week of November two Austrian armies gathered along the Lower Piave against the Third Italian Army; but as they were not able to bring up their heavy guns, and got only a small number of 6 in. howitzers into position, they could not maintain the volume of gun fire necessary for sweeping a path across the rain-swollen torrent and the flooded fenland. The evidence of the strength of spirit of the Italian forces made the prospect of any unprepared rush attack look too gloomy. Below refused to agree to it, as the terrain was difficult.

Most of the country was very low-lying and screened by thickets of mulberry orchards and yellowing willows. The sodden ditches, dank cottages, and water-logged fields were six feet below the few **Bad weather** available road embankments, and the **helps Italy** great walls that restrained the river rose twenty feet above the trenched marshes. The conditions were somewhat like those under which the Belgian Army fought, and the diked, inundated fenland, through which the Piave had made two wide beds, was transformed by the winter rains into a stronger system of defence than at first seemed possible. The tempests of the second week of November were a boon to the Third Italian Army, and with the aid of civilian labour the troops constructed a new series of lines that defied all attack and completely stalemated the principal Austro-Hungarian forces.

General von Below was furiously disappointed by the failure of Boroevic. The Prussian commander was well aware of the fact that he had only a short time in which to carry out his plan of conquering Italy. He knew exactly what progress the French and British armies were making in their journey to the Piave line, for his agents in Turin, Mantua, and other places on the route of transportation kept him informed of the march of the allied forces of support.

With a view to accelerating his last great attack, Below abandoned most of the eastern ways of communication to Boroevic. He massed his main forces of Germans, Mohammedan - Bosnians, Hungarians, and Austrians in the mountains between the Piave and the Brenta. His line was formed in a crescent, of which the centre was at Feltre. He had no feeding railway line, as the Udine track branching to Vittorio was damaged; while the Belluno track, running through the Upper Piave valley, was not linked with the Austrian system beyond the Carnic Alps.

Hötzendorf given his opportunity

Closely connecting with Below's personal forces was the Austro-Hungarian army of the Trentino, under General von Scheuchenstuel, who possessed the excellent railway and motor communications that had been constructed for the former offensive against the Asiago plateau positions. It was possible rapidly to feed the heavy and light guns which were already sited on either side of the Sugana valley for the resumption of the offensive against the First Italian Army, the right wing of which was holding a line of mountains between Asiago and Tezze.

Scheuchenstuel shrank into obscurity as soon as the action opened. Field-Marshal Conrad von Hötzendorf, the former Commander-in-Chief of the Austro-Hungarian Armies, was allowed by his German masters a last opportunity for retrieving his many mistakes. He had always been distinguished as a specialist in Trentino operations, and had continually insisted that his original plan of driving down upon the Italian rear from the Trentino was preferable to making costly counter-offensives on the Isonzo line. It had been the ruling passion of his life to invade the rich Lombard plain from the Trentino, and for years before the war he had planned and practised his various manœuvres of feint and thrust.

Defeated by Russky and Brussiloff in 1914, the old Austrian Chief of Staff had been retired by the German High Command, and nominally replaced by archducal figureheads. His Trentino plan had been attempted in 1916, but had failed. He was now given a brilliant German master-gunner as assistant, and strongly reinforced with men and material. Serving him were two railways from Innsbruck and Vienna that united at Franzensfeste and thence ran in a double line to Trento, with a branch line to the Asiago battlefield. From his point of view, the prospects of breaking down the Brenta valley were remarkably good, and in conjunction with Below he opened the battle in much the same circumstances as had obtained at Verdun in February, 1916.

Italians score a first success

Two battering-rams played upon the First and Fourth Italian Armies on either side of the Brenta River. The Austrian Field-Marshal struck the first blow after a long and intense bombardment of the positions around Asiago. His infantry leaped into the town on November 10th, and swept over the mountains by Gallio, where there was a gateway to a short valley cut into the plain of Asolo, in the rear of the Third and Fourth Italian Armies.

The ambitious stroke completely failed. The Italian commander fought a fierce street battle in Asiago, but he did not make any decisive stand for the town, as he found it was too completely dominated by hostile artillery. He merely rearguarded himself by house-to-house fighting, and placed his main forces in dead ground in a large depression south of the city. At the same time he swung his supports northward to the mountains by Gallio. Here his men rallied, and bore the enemy back from the valley gate of the plain, recovering all the positions they lost during the first hostile rush.

[*British official photographs*]

ON THE RIVER-LINE WHERE ITALY TURNED AND STOOD.
Bridge of Vidor, looking across the Piave to the enemy position. Vidor, the bridge-head of which was captured by General von Below in November, 1917, lay to the north of the Montello, which was occupied by British troops before the close of the year. From its neighbourhood Below had, on capturing the bridge-head, delivered what he intended to be the death-blow to Italy. Inset above: Another view across the Piave at Nervàsa.

A NARROW ESCAPE.
Italian transport waggon on a mountainous road in the Trentino. It had been brought to a standstill at a dangerous bend just in time, for its fore-wheels were already hanging over the abyss.

Badenecche, Fior, Castel Gomberto, inner and outer Meletta, Sisemol, and others, which outflanked and enfiladed the ground the enemy had won at Asiago, projecting like a rugged, gigantic buttress into the enemy's new lines.

Owing to the intensity and weight of the Austrian gun fire, and the difficulty of deploying and supplying large numbers of troops upon the roadless mountains, only one Italian division could be maintained in the high salient above Asiago. When the men were settled in their positions it was difficult **Regina and** to relieve them, so that the splendid **Alpine Brigades** Regina and Alpine Brigades, that recovered the heights about Gallio, had to hold out for many days and nights against continual assaults, conducted by a succession of fresh hostile forces.

Their task was similar to that which the immortal 7th British Division performed during the First Battle of Ypres, while waiting for General Foch to arrive with his Ninth Army. By happy chance General Foch was present in the struggle around the Brenta and Piave Rivers, waiting for his army to arrive, together with a British army, and meanwhile assisting the Italian Commander-in-Chief in manœuvring against the Teutonic battering-rams.

The policy adopted by General Diaz was more than bold. He strained his troops to the limit of their powers of endurance in a way that, to anybody who thought the Italians were liable to demoralisation, must have seemed desperately perilous. But General Diaz knew his countrymen as no foreigner did. By imposing terrifying

This skilful re-establishment of the flank of the First Army was the first definite victory won by the Italians since their conquest of the Bainsizza plateau. In both material and moral effect it was profoundly important. It taught the enemy that the soul of Italy was fortified instead of being distracted by all the disasters that had followed the event of Caporetto. It taught the Italian soldier that he was still the master of the fate of his nation, and that the power of the invader could be broken. By saving the great mountain rampart above Asolo from being turned, it reserved for the Italians and the French a strong defensive sector in which the enemy could be fought to a standstill. In the night of November 12th the Austrian Field-Marshal renewed his attack on the Gallio gateway, where the outer Meletta and Longaro mountains barred his way to the critical Frenzela ravine. Immediately above this narrow ravine was a great mountain block, round which the Brenta River curved from the Sugana valley. The mountain masses formed a vast promontory, with Monte Lisser dominating the ancient road of invasion to Bassano and the plain, and linking its fires with the Italian batteries on the Grappa mountain sector. West of the Lisser height was another tangle of mountains, Tondarecar,

[Italian official photograph.
ARMY FIELD DEPOT ON MOUNTAIN SLOPES.
Italian field depot established on the slopes of Monte Pasubio, a height south-east of Rovereto, in the Trentino, and west of the Asiago plateau, on which the Italians made their victorious stand against the invaders.

ordeals upon them, he vindicated the strength of character of his race, and gained one of the finest defensive battles of the war.

His men shattered the attack of November 11th, and although they lost Monte Longaro on November 13th, they returned to the key position of outer Meletta, and held on to it with marvellous tenacity. In the night of November 13th and the morning and evening of November 14th the Regina Brigade and the Alpine troops broke up assault after assault between Monti Fior and Meletta. The situation, however, was very critical, and General Diaz sent one of his best men, General Badoglio, with a division from the Third Army, to hold the side gate into the Brenta valley for another five days. Many more days than five, however, were to pass in terrific warfare before the conqueror of the Sabotino, the Vodice ridge, and the Bainsizza plateau received the men and guns needed to make the Frenzela ravine impregnable against the mightily armed invaders. For weeks General Badoglio had to stand against appalling odds.

Having rail-head close behind him, the Austrian Field-Marshal brought up more heavy artillery and, resuming the attack on November 15th, began to feed his men forward in larger numbers against the mountain line thinly held by the Alpine troops and infantry. The Italian brigade on the outer Meletta and Monte Fior destroyed every force coming in its range with rifles, machine-guns, and Fiat machine-pistols, while the Alpini on Monte
Austrian storming Tondarecar shot down three
forces repulsed successive storming forces. On November 16th the Austrians again advanced against the same mountains and were swept back. The following day the Perugia Brigade made a splendid counter-movement around the outer Meletta, and recovered some advance works that had been lost in the long battle.

General Badoglio continued to press the enemy back from the Meletta sector on November 18th and 19th, deliberately provoking the enemy commander to more violent efforts. These issued in a great and sustained battle on November 22nd, in which Field-Marshal Conrad von Hötzendorf made a last vain attempt to justify the fame as a strategist he had enjoyed in peace time. By this he was becoming little more than the political ornament of a Prussian command, a German general being reported as the real commander on the Asiago plateau.

Employing hundreds of heavy guns against the small portable mountain pieces employed by the Italians, the Austrian commander swept all the Italian front and rear with gas-shell and high explosive, and while the overwhelmed Italian batteries had to remain silent to escape

destruction, he launched an incessant encircling attack upon the heights directly guarding the narrow ravine road. His waves of infantry were continually renewed, each being covered by a dense barrage that splintered the rocks into hundreds of thousands of flying fragments and quarried the mountain sides.

The violence of the gun fire, however, was not altogether an advantage, for the attacking troops could not keep too

[British official photograph.
PREPARING PATHS FOR THE ARMY.
British Royal Engineers building bridges in the rough terrain at the foot of the mountain ranges towering over the Venetian plain, among which the British troops took up their position in December, 1917.

close to its screen of shell because of the wide zone of destructive effect. The Italian troops suffered badly from the continual bombardments, but when they could see the hostile infantry masses they counter-attacked them with invincible fury. Two regiments of the Perugia Brigade and the Alpini lost two-thirds of their effectives, but did not budge an inch. At times they gave ground under gun fire, when their advanced shelters had been

[British official photographs.
ON FORWARD OBSERVATION DUTY FOR THE HEAVY GUNS IN ITALY.
British observation officer in Italy watching the movements of the enemy from the doubtful cover of a leafless, spiny hedge, while a brother officer, ensconced amid the decaying undergrowth, takes careful notes of all he sees. Right : A gunner of a British battery spotting hostile aeroplanes.

blown up, but in their counter-charges they avenged all their losses upon the hostile infantry which, as it broke and fled, was pursued with machine-gun fire and low-flying Italian aeroplanes.

At the end of the dreadful day the mountain line above Asiago was as strong as it had been before Conrad von Hötzendorf opened his great offensive. The town which the defenders had abandoned early in the engage-

STUDYING THE LIE OF THE LAND.

British officers at the foot of the British position on the Montello range scanning the country westwards towards Cornuda. Cornuda, a small town on the main road to Asolo, acquired considerable strategic importance owing to its being a station on the railway line to Treviso.

ment, and the advanced positions from which they had retired, had been only covering works designed to test the strength and direction of the invaders' manœuvres. The main mountain line was indeed held more firmly than it had been in the second week of November, for General Badoglio was already benefiting by the arrival of allied reinforcements, and guns and shell were being despatched to supply some of the tremendous losses in

Italian war material. As the enemy, however, possessed thousands of intact captured guns of all calibres, together with large accumulations of captured shell, in addition to his own vast armament, he was able to bring more pieces into position than the Italian Army commander, and also more rapidly to increase the depth of his massed parks of artillery. By the end of November he had about two thousand five hundred guns on a front of ten miles between the Brenta and the Piave. This worked out at one gun to every seven yards, and as the radius of the concussion effect and the range of steel splinters and fragments of rock were often to be reckoned in hundreds of yards, the gun-power of the attacking forces became appalling.

On the Asiago plateau, where the Austrians and Germans had close railway connection with their depots and factories, the mass of guns was at first much larger **Tremendous Austrian** than that of Krobatin's and **artillery power** Below's armies. Long before Below could bring a 12 in. piece into action, Conrad von Hötzendorf was using hundreds of the great Skoda guns. He had thousands of medium heavy pieces when Below was using a hundred or two hundred 6 in. guns mounted on motor-carriages.

Had the grand struggle in Italy taken place in the plain, the defence would have been completely blasted away, owing to the tragic weakening of the artillery of defence and the strengthening of the artillery of attack. In the mountains, however, it was often very difficult for hostile gunners to place their shells exactly in the hollows and abruptly turning valleys and ravines in which the chief Italian infantry forces were gathered. The exposed steeps and valleys were occupied only by companies of machine-gunners and men with machine-pistols, trench-mortars, and hand-grenades. They had shelters blasted out of the rock, and their positions could not be discovered except by reconnoitring attacks in force, and when the enemy massed against them in clear weather they were often able to slaughter the invaders by the thousand before close fighting occurred.

SPOTTING FOR THE GUNS FROM AN ADVANCED POSITION.

British artillery officer directing the fire of the battery according to the instructions of his forward observation officer. Right: A British observation-post. For some months after the British troops took up their position in Italy the bulk of the work devolved upon their gunners and flying men.

DARING CROSS-RIVER RAIDING BY ITALIAN SOLDIERS.

Trench raiding exploits of the Italians across the Lower Piave were described by an artist on that front as being conspicuously daring among many daring deeds. On the occasion illustrated, " by little short of a miracle, the men got across on their half-submerged craft, without coming under the rays of the searchlights with which the enemy was sweeping the river, and returned safely with a bag of several prisoners."

When a long-sustained assault was launched in misty weather, the strength of the defence was naturally lessened, and though the machine-gunners and sharpshooters maintained a barrage of bullets across the ways of approach, it was usually possible for a persistent enemy division to drive in the Italian covering forces and engage with the main defending forces.

Hötzendorf, like Below, was greatly favoured by the weather. Occasionally a tempest of snow whitened the high, rugged tableland, and at night the wind was often bitterly cold. But for weeks the snow never fell heavily, the season being milder than any the natives of the mountain region could remember. In an ordinary winter there would have been ten feet of snow on all mountain paths and roads, and the movement of the enemy's heavy guns would have become impossible, while the labour of bringing up large shells from the rail-head would have been so enormous as to produce a condition of temporary stalemate. Even a permanent snowfall of a foot or two would have been very useful to the Italians and their Allies, as their reconnoitring pilots would have traced the position of the hostile guns by the patches of bare ground where the snow had melted away under the flame of the charges.

Mild weather favours the foe

In the Trentino, as in the Ypres swamps, Thor, the old sky-god of the Teutons, favoured the less enterprising descendants of his worshippers, instead of giving aid to the Lombards, Franks, and Anglo-Saxons who had shown more of the spirit of adventure and spread themselves far beyond their ancestral forests. General Badoglio had reckoned on having to hold out only for five days, in the middle of November, because he thought that the usual fall of snow would completely check the movement of the hostile artillery and allow time for the French and British troops and guns to get into position and relieve the strain upon the hard-pressed and feebly-armed Italian armies. But the snow did not begin to fall heavily until the last week in November, and by this time the German commanders, who had taken the conduct of the battle

116

out of the hands of the Austrian Field-Marshals and Grand Dukes, had sited by the Piave and Brenta Rivers a number of guns exceeding that with which Falkenhayn had tried to batter into Verdun.

On the Asiago tableland Conrad von Hötzendorf was practically relieved of his command, and one of the ablest of Below's experts in heavy-artillery tactics took control of the eastern field of war. He was a man of ability, and when he opened his offensive in bright sunshine on December 2nd, 1917, he employed British methods of artillery demonstrations and artillery ambushes.

He began with a regular gun fire bombardment, which he increased to the hell fire usual before an assault. Then his guns suddenly lifted, and while the heavy pieces shut down on the Italian rear and ways of communication, his light and medium guns rolled their attacking barrages up the mountain slopes and down the mouths of the valleys. But when the surviving Italian infantrymen rose to repel the waves of assault not a figure was visible, and before they could dart back to their shelters the entire weight of thousands of guns fell upon them, scattering shrapnel as well as high explosive and gas. Then there was a lull— sometimes fairly long and sometimes brief.

Suddenly, all the mechanism of long-range slaughter was again set working by the Teutonic master-gunner. He executed diabolical variations upon his principal scheme, sending out patrols to snatch some important advance work when he thought that he had wearied the Italians with his trick of capturing them in the open. Day and night he proceeded with his ghastly battle practice, inflicting severe losses upon the defending troops, while increasing the skill and precision and combination work of his time-tabled and telephone-directed batteries.

Terrible German artillery practice

As in the best-mounted British offensives, the guns so dominated the field that many of them were able to rest in the open field, where the large patches of dark ground clearly indicated their whereabouts. All the guns of

General Badoglio had to remain silent and concealed, so that those which escaped the enemy's searching hurricanes of fire could help the infantry in the hour of the great ordeal.

In the morning of December 4th the first and second Italian lines were flooded with blinding gas and a new kind of shell containing a powerful emetic. When it was thought that the Italian troops were all occupied in vomiting and crying, with inflamed eyes and disturbed stomachs, their wire entanglements were broken by a trench-mortar bombardment, and behind the rolling barrages there swept large masses of Austrian infantry, headed by storming-parties of German shock troops trained in mountain warfare in Alsace.

All the Teutons, Magyars, Bosnians, and Dalmatians were employed in very dense masses ; for the German commander reckoned either that the Italian artillery had been put out of action, or that he could destroy it as soon as the batteries that had survived his bombardments revealed themselves. On the northern sector of the mountain line his shock tactics were successful. His artillery completely smashed the light mountain guns of the defence, and his divisions, storming the slopes in **Italian gallantry** deep waves, and driving through the **in defence** valleys in columns, moved faster than the survivors in the Italian line could fire.

Most gallantly did the defenders of the Tondarecar and Badenecche mountain sector fight. In the morning they broke attack after attack, and when part of their line was driven in, enabling the enemy to climb on to one of the spurs, they counter-attacked and won back some of the ground, lost it again, and yet charged once more. One runner of the Alpine troops took a message to Headquarters at Foza when his comrades were surrounded. The general could give no help, as he was being pressed back on the other wing and his centre was reeling. All he could do was to send an answering message to his lost brigades, asking them to fight on while they had ammunition left,

and thus rearguard the breaking line while fresh positions were taken up. The scene was one of the most memorable in the whole war, and certainly the most precious example of Italian valour in modern Italian history ; for the Italian troops were men of the Second Army, under the best commanding officer of that army, who had begun life as a doctor, won high fame as a military conqueror, and then lost all that made life worth living when the troops beyond his sector broke on August 24th. Instead of having an army to command, he had only a single division, and most of his men were dead or dying.

But Badoglio's men were of the same stamp as himself. They asked nothing more than to fall in honour on the field of battle ; but before they fell they wanted to vindicate the honour of their race. In **Daring feat of** other words, it was not death or victory **Bersaglieri** for them, but death with victory. After the Austrians turned Badenecche on the south and thrust over the saddle between the summit and Tondarecar in the eve of a day of continual fighting, some of the Bersaglieri fell back on the western slope and there fought all night. In the morning there were eighteen privates left in a sea of Austrians. As the small party skirmished along the valley they found that Monte Fior, in their path of retreat, was occupied by the enemy. They charged up the peak, and by some miracle recovered the great mountain.

It took the Austrians twenty minutes to discover that they had been frightened away by eighteen officerless men. They climbed back to the mountain-top in hundreds and killed seventeen out of the eighteen heroes. But one Bersagliere, though wounded, managed to crawl down the mountain-side and gain the new line running by Monte Spitz, Monte Miela, and the Frenzela ravine.

About the time that Monte Fior was thus strangely recovered for an hour, General Badoglio made an equally astounding recovery of his original line on Monte Tondarecar. He launched two battalions of his Alpine

HEROIC CUTTING-OUT EXPLOIT OF ITALIAN SEAMEN AT TRIESTE.
On the night of December 9th-10th, 1917, a party of Italian seamen, creeping up in small launches in the darkness to the harbour of Trieste, cut the steel hawsers holding the mined harbour-net. They then entered the harbour noiselessly and discharged two torpedoes at the Austrian battleships Wien and Monarch. The former was sunk, but the latter, though hit, remained afloat. While the Italians were carrying out this daring achievement Austrian searchlights played over the heavens in anticipation of attack from the air, and the Italians got safely away.

FRENCH TROOPS EN ROUTE TO ITALY'S AID.
[French official photograph.

Arrival of a motor convoy of French soldiers at Brescia, in North Italy, on their way to the Italian front in the autumn of 1917.   They were being heartily cheered by the car-loads of Italian soldiers on the left.

Foza was the Headquarters of the Italian general, and, like Sir John French in the First Battle of Ypres, he stayed in person to meet the enemy. When his Staff urged him to retire, he said he would wait until the building was hit. But in the night of December 5th-6th the Austrians cut the road between Foza village and the house occupied by the general and his Staff. Thereupon a major of an Alpine regiment collected some stragglers, placed them on the hill behind Headquarters, and shot down the leading Austrian force, while the general and his Staff motored under fire to the Frenzela ravine.

The Austrians also reached the ravine, but few of them returned from it. It was as narrow as an ordinary staircase in places, with two walls of rock rising almost sheer on either side. Here and there were ledges on which Italian engineers had blasted hidden shelters out of the rock. The cliffs seemed absolutely uninhabited when the Austrians approached, but when they reached certain marked ranges a machine-gun barrage brought the foremost men down, and then travelled over the trapped column. There was no path to the plains through the Frenzela ravine. **Austrians trapped in a ravine** Another Austrian division, therefore, tried to work around to the Brenta valley by the Vecchia road to Valstagna. Here, however, another Italian general, who had lost most of his men, improvised a new command out of a considerable number of retiring groups, and with short-ranged machine-gun fire completely blocked the southern road and kept the line below Asiago firm as a wall.

troops, who had been attacked around Castel Gomberto, midway between the old and new Italian lines. It was these troops that had lost Monte Fior, having there been outflanked and threatened with envelopment. But, instead of retiring southward, the Alpini made an utterly unexpected charge forward, using nothing but their own machine-guns to cover each rush they made against the enemy's distant left centre. They recaptured the high mass of Tondarecar, thereby throwing into complete confusion all the operations of the hostile commander. When his line broke at the most critical point, he could not tell in what way the amazing Italian general would follow up his stroke. He had to draw back on his centre, where he was fighting in the ravine road to the Brenta valley, and make a fresh concentration against the survivors of the two thousand Italians who had broken right into his flank. As he had more than a hundred thousand men immediately available on a short front, he was able to recover the lost mountain. By the time he had done so he had lost the battle.

General Badoglio had given ground and sacrificed some sixteen thousand men of heroic temper. But the ground he had lost was of no permanent value, as it had formed a salient exposed to an overwhelming cross-fire of heavy artillery, and useful only for the temporary purpose that it had completely served. It had broken up the final grand offensive made by the enemy on the western bank of the Brenta, and when it was abandoned the attacking forces were so utterly wasted in working over the mountainous outwork that they had no strength in which to attempt their main task.

At Foza village, south of the Meletta height, the position was extremely critical while the Alpine battalions were making their tiger leap back to the Tondarecar.

SUPPLIES FOR MOUNTAIN TRENCHES.
[Italian official photograph.

French supply convoy passing through an old Italian town on the way to their trenches on the mountainous part of the front taken over in the closing weeks of 1917. The French army in Italy struck a splendid first blow at the Austrians in the Monte Tomba sector on December 30th, 1917.

On the southern side of the Frenzela ravine the battle swayed most violently between Buso village, Ronchi valley, Monte Sisemol, and the heights south of Asiago. By reason of his enormous weight of artillery the enemy commander was able to shatter the Italian lines, covering the white summits, the pine-wood slopes, and the patches of bare rock with rolling hurricanes of flame and steel, brick-red shrapnel bursts, and poison gases. When the smoke and fume cleared away the mountains looked as if they had been transformed into huge quarries. The Italian infantry was compelled to give ground and shelter on the reverse slopes. When, however, the Jaegers and other storm troops topped the abandoned summits and crests, the Italian guns that had remained silent through all the bombardments came furiously into action, and the Italian infantry surged back with officers in low-flying aeroplanes leading them on and shooting at the enemy with aerial machine-guns.

BRITISH TROOPS IN ITALY. [British official photograph.
Detachment of British troops on the march from the station in Italy at which they had arrived. They were on their way to their new front, and their appearance excited considerable interest among the peasant women and children of the countryside through which they passed.

Bersaglieri on Monte Sisemol

The 4th Bersagliere Brigade finely distinguished itself by the defence of Monte Sisemol. After the enemy broke over the Meletta defences in the evening of December 5th, and tried to storm into the Frenzela ravine, the Italian centre withdrew in the night from the Ronchi valley. At daybreak on December 6th the parks of hostile artillery sited around Asiago and Gallio swept all the southern Italian line as far as Monte Kaperlaba, and in the afternoon division after division of Austrian infantry tried to sweep down towards the plain by the wider winding valleys below the narrow Frenzela gateway. For twelve hours the two regiments on Monte Sisemol fought the enemy off, standing six great attacks, counter-charging whenever they were forced to retire, and throwing themselves into wild mêlées for hand-bomb and bayonet hand-to-hand combats.

In the meantime the rest of the division was preparing a line in the rear on the Col del Rosso and the neighbouring mass of Monte Melago, under a heavy long-range bombardment by the enemy's big guns. When all was ready for the Bersaglieri to withdraw, some of them either preferred to fight to the death or did not receive the order. Fighting still continued on Sisemol after the enemy had announced the capture of the mountain, and when the last man fell, on December 8th, a long and significant period of quietude occurred on the western bank of the Brenta River. There the principal Austrian army had been so depleted of man-power by a few Italian divisions that the gigantic mass of guns which Conrad von Hötzendorf had sited became as impotent as a steam-hammer with a burst boiler. The Austrian losses were so heavy that the offensive could not be continued, and, like Falkenhayn after Verdun, the former Chief of Staff of the Dual Monarchy faded into the obscurity of disgrace.

Seldom has one great battle so resembled another as the Battle of the Brenta resembled the Battle of Verdun. By the gate of France there is a system of heights cut into two sections by the meandering valley of the Meuse. By the gate of Italy there is a system of mountains also cut into two sectors by the valley of the Brenta. In peace time armoured forts rose on the crests with a commanding field of fire, but when the power

NEARING THEIR NEW FRONT. [Italian official photograph.
British regiment marching along a road near the Piave, on their way to take up their position in the allied line on the Italian front. It was just before Christmas, 1917, that the British troops, in a night patrol over the Piave, captured their first Austrian prisoner.

of the monster aeroplane-directed howitzer was generally recognised, the fortifications were reduced to the position of observation and machine-gun posts, and the defending guns were removed and greatly increased in number, range, and calibre, and concealed in pine-woods and other kinds of screening material.

Under the new conditions of warfare the river-moat increased the strength of the defending forces. Swept by hundreds of cross-fires it formed a death-trap against an invading host attempting a direct frontal attack, and it compelled the invaders to divide and persist in flank attacks. Whenever a height or system of heights on one side of the river was lost, elsewhere along the flank, the gain of ground was of little immediate use to the enemy. For when he occupied it, he was subjected to a furious enfilading bombardment from the unconquered heights on the same line across the river. His next movement could therefore be foreseen and anticipated. He was obliged to shift his main point of attack and undertake, across the river, the reduction of the high positions from which his victorious troops were exposed to flanking fire.

What Dead Man Hill was to Verdun the peaks above the Frenzela ravine were to the Grappa mountain defences. When Conrad von Hötzendorf exhausted the strength of his country in vainly endeavouring to reach the Brenta River at a point some miles behind the north-eastern Italian front, General von Below withdrew with most of his men from Italy, thereby tacitly admitting defeat of his main scheme of conquest.

Before, however, the Prussian commander retired, in angry disgust and violent disappointment, he made a prolonged, costly, and yet ingenious attempt to retrieve the failure of the Austrian Field-Marshal. There was one very important difference between the situation along the Meuse and the situation along the Brenta. The eastern Italian flank did not slope down into a wide plain, but ended abruptly by the Piave River, beyond which were high mountains dotted with battery positions. General von Below placed his own troops of the Fourteenth Army along the Piave River, and lined out the Austrian army, under General Krobatin and General Krauss, on the northern front held by the Fourth Italian Army. At the same time he brought a considerable part of the forces of General Boroevic from the Lower Piave and employed them as a general reserve.

In the matter of men and guns the army of General Robilant was more than outnumbered—it was overwhelmed. It had lost a very considerable number of men and a large amount **Inequality of** of material in the long and difficult retreat **opposing forces** from the Carnic Alps and the Dolomites; and when it turned to make a stand on some twelve miles of mountainous terrain between the Piave and the Brenta, it was half-surrounded by some three armies, each of which was stronger than itself in men and guns. Most of the artillery saved by the mountain troops was of the lightest kind, some pieces being so small as to be portable.

General von Below, on the other hand, possessed many mobile 5·9 in. batteries, consisting of pieces mounted on motor-vehicles. He was able also to bring rapidly into action on the northern front of the corner of the Italian

line many Austrian pieces ranging up to 12 in. calibre, which were moved along the Trentino railways towards Tezze and Primolano.

When the eastern battle of the Brenta opened on November 13th, the Fourth Italian Army stood around Monte Tomatico, below the lost town of Feltre, and extended towards Fonzaso, covering Primolano, and there joining with the First Italian Army by Monte Lisser. In the preliminary action of November 13th the Austrian left wing of Below's **Austro-Germans** crescent advanced in the mountains **capture Primolano** between the Brenta and the Cismon valleys, and occupied the old fortifications on the frontier and the town of Fonzaso.

This movement gave Below command over a good highway running southward towards Primolano, which he vehemently wanted as a central rail-head. Conrad von Hötzendorf and he therefore enveloped Primolano from either side and captured it on November 14th. Then, in strong force, with his columns spread out fanwise and skirmishing forces deployed between the masses in the valleys, the Prussian commander advanced towards the confluence of the Brenta River and Cismon stream, succeeded in outflanking the garrison of Monte Roncone, and carried the Tomatico ridge.

All this part of the work seems to have been carried out by Bavarian and Austrian mountain troops, and it went forward with terrifying speed. After getting the command of Monte Lisser, the four invading armies were able to assail from three sides the advanced positions of the small forces defending the eastern corner of the mountain wall.

A HALT ON THE MARCH. [*French official photograph.*
French transport column halted on a mountain road while on the march through Lombardy and Venetia to reinforce the Italian army taking up its stand on the Tagliamento line after the disaster of October, 1917.

The Italians were swept by fire across the Piave, bombarded and charged along the northern front, and often enfiladed from the Brenta valley. At first it seemed as though the forces commanded by General Alfred Krauss might repeat the Caporetto stroke, and drive down the corridor of the Brenta valley with its two good roads and railway track. But for five days the 9th Italian Regiment held the Brenta Pass with wonderful tenacity and skill. Standing on Monte Cismon, the gallant three thousand broke every attack by fire or by counter-charge, and when the whole line had to bend, the men drew back to the little cluster of stone houses by the tall belfry of San Marino, in the neck of the Brenta gorge. Here they connected, across the river, with the army holding the position above the Frenzela ravine, and with desperate stubbornness kept the enemy back during the most critical phase of the conflict for the mountain corner of the Venetian plain.

Meanwhile the right wing of the Fourth Italian Army was driven in by a terrific blow. Below could be seen arrogantly making open preparations for his grand offensive. His array of forces crowded the roads on the opposite side of the river, moving in plain sight against the background of autumnal hills above Vidor Bridge. Had General Diaz possessed the power of gun fire that General Cadorna employed a month previously on the Isonzo, the hostile movements could have been disastrously blocked in a hundred places. But any attempt at barraging operations by the weakly-armed Alpine force would have provoked a duel of light mountain guns against 5·9 in. howitzers and cannon.

These guns were mounted on motor-chassis and placed on the hill-sides, that twinkled with their flames as they played searchingly upon the Italian flank and rear. A similar bombardment was opened by Austrian gunners on the northern front, until the doubly-assailed garrison of the angle of mountains by Quero was compelled to give ground. The Como Brigade, unrelieved since the opening of the struggle, was pressed back on Quero on November 16th, and the Alpine troops on the more central mass of Monte Prassolan were also compelled to retire before mingled forces of Bosnians, Austrians, and Prussians.

Then, in the evening of November 17th, Below in person, with his enlarged Fourteenth Army, delivered the stroke he intended to be the death-blow to Italy. All day the Austrians had been thrusting with utmost violence on the front of the Fourth Army, while the Germans lashed the rear, where the mountain wall ended and the plain began. As darkness fell the slopes beyond the Piave River blazed with gun fire, and the steeps, inclines, and uplands between Quero and Cornuda smoked and rocked under the exploding shells.

Holding down the Italian garrisons by the riverside

IN COMMAND OF THE FRENCH ARMY IN ITALY.
General Fayolle (seated), Commander-in-Chief of the French forces which aided Italy in repelling the invader. With him is General Barthelemy, his Chief of Staff.

with his intense artillery fire and vicious machine-gun barrages, the Prussian commander wasted no time in trying to bridge the Piave, but sent his men across the stream in a flotilla of boats. Punting and rowing, in about forty of the large, high-nosed river-craft used on the Friuli waterways, several companies of Germans shot into the defenders' searchlights, and endeavoured to win a footing near Fener village by the speed and audacity of this manœuvre.

At Fener the river is split by a long island of shingle, and as the boats rounded the obstacle the Italians swept them with machine-guns and machine-pistols and completely broke up the flotilla. The disappointed enemy commander kept his guns bombarding the opposing positions along the river. He destroyed Fener village, and with a tremendous concentration of his guns ploughed up the ground about it.

At one o'clock in the morning of November 18th he made a stronger essay to form a bridge-head some two miles below Quero. He was successful. A larger flotilla set out, directly opposite Fener village, under cover of a deep, dense barrage, under which the survivors of the local force of defence could not rise. The Germans kept

BRITISH TROOPS GOING FORWARD TO THE TRENCHES ALONG THE PIAVE.
The British force which went to the assistance of Italy towards the close of 1917 occupied the Montello sector of the Piave front, at a point where the river is about a mile wide. It was described as "a broad, flat, and dreary expanse of light-coloured gravel, through which meanders a narrow stream, ridiculously out of proportion to its watercourse." When flood water came down, however, it became a torrent.

VENICE: THE QUAY OF THE DALMATIANS.

Paved with marble and embellished with Ferrari's equestrian statue of Victor Emmanuel II., this quay is one of the most popular lounges in Venice. Connected with the Molo by the Ponte della Paglia, it affords a good view of the Doge's Palace, whence this photograph was taken.

Great as the set-back was, it was retrievable. The enemy could not debouch into the plain, through the narrow gap he had made in the mountain wall, while the Grappa system and all its connections rose above his flank. What should have been done at Caporetto was skilfully and nobly carried out at Monfenera. Standing strong on its centre, and swinging back on its wing to keep good contact with the Third Army, the commander of the Fourth Army held the Prussians back by counter-charges.

Four times, on November 18th, General von Below launched strong forces on the riverside spur to complete his conquest of it and extend over Monte Tomba. In his final attack he succeeded in gaining some important trenches, but the Italians rallied and returned and recovered the position. Then in the night of November 19th a fresh force of Germans threw the Italians back again. In turn, Italian reinforcements renewed the swaying struggle, tiring out the available

close to the wall of thunderbolts, and, winning a footing, rushed the battered trenches. Brilliantly swift were their movements, showing that the operation had been perfectly rehearsed. Scarcely had the leading men reached the village than the sappers were swinging pontoons into position behind them.

Over the bridge, while darkness still held, the shock troops of Below's army passed between Quero and the plain, and stormed up the spur of Monfenera. At Monfenera the mountains ended near the road that ran from Pederroba to Bassano, well in the rear of Monte Tomba, Monte Pallone, Monte Grappa, and the eastern cliffs of the Brenta River. It was the stroke of Caporetto, delivered with direct, downright force, as before, but without any suggestion of co-operation from the men who broke under it.

The immediate effects of this shattering thrust into the Italian rear were far-reaching. The surprised Italian commander had to give ground, drawing his force back from Quero and Alano, and making the central heights around Monte Grappa the base of his defence. The new Italian line still rested partly on the Monfenera spur and its higher western continuation, Monte Tomba.

Thence it boldly curved north in a high salient, enclosing Monte Spinoncia, Monte Salarolo, and Col dell' Orso. Behind these heights was the Grappa mass, 5,827 feet high, forming a system of peaks, saddles, and hollows, and overlooking all the other heights. Tomba and Monfenera were mere hills compared with Grappa. North-west of Grappa the Fourth Army held Monte Pertica and the Berretta saddle sloping to the Brenta.

forces of assault, and winning precious time for the elaboration of new defences and the arrival of more supports.

It was, however, upon the original garrison of the mountain line between the Piave and the Brenta that the supreme task fell — upon Garibaldi's Brigade, the Reggio Brigade, the Como Brigade, and others. The most famous composed the 56th Division, which **Ordeal of the 56th Division** fought on the salient above Grappa, and in a long battle, ending on November 22nd, broke up Würtembergers, Tyroleans, Bosnians, Prussians, and Jaegers. The defenders' losses were heavy in proportion to their numbers, for they were continually raked with medium heavy artillery, against

VERONA: ON THE BANK OF THE ADIGE.

Comrades in arms chatting on the embankment of the river along whose banks Dante walked in the days of his banishment from Florence. In the background is the Cathedral, a Romanesque building of the twelfth century, with a campanile begun by Michele Sanmichele and never completed.

CAPTIVES WHERE THEY THOUGHT TO BE CONQUERORS.
Austrian soldiers being marched as prisoners into an Italian town which they had expected to enter as conquerors. Apart from the occasion when large forces were cut off by the piercing of their line, the loss of effectives by capture suffered by the Italians was smaller than that suffered by the Austrians.

Brigade and its supports digging themselves in on the lower southern slopes, but extending forward over the top of the saddle and the Monfenera ridge. The Italian forces seemed to be in a precarious position, as in clear weather they were overlooked from the Tomba crest. But although enemy observers directed heavy gun fire upon them, no further infantry attacks were made on the mountain edge by the Piave River. After a long pause for fresh preparation, General von Below shifted his German spear-head, and on December 11th stormed against the high salient above Grappa. The new battle lasted for eight days, the Italians, with French batteries assisting, losing some of

which their mountain guns could not reply, and they were subjected to vehement infantry attacks on three sides.

At Monfenera and Monte Tomba the struggle went on, day and night, for nearly a week. On November 22nd the Calabria Brigade, clinging to the heights in hastily made shelters, was hammered in a manner extraordinary in a mountain battle. Below brought up more heavy guns on the hills beyond the river, and with **Calabria Brigade's** both German shell and captured Italian **indomitable pluck** shell devastated the positions. The dug-outs were not deep enough to shelter the garrison, so infantry and gunners were horribly used.

Nevertheless, the Calabria Brigade fought on for twenty-four hours against every force Below could deploy against them. They lost the Tomba crest, and captured the Monfenera summit, lost that, and recovered the other, and lost it again. When the struggle ended in mutual exhaustion, the Prussians and Pomeranians were in the position of having won the ground and lost the battle.

They were settled on the Tomba crest, with the Calabria

A SATISFACTORY MOMENT.
General Maistre watching the 1,392 prisoners taken by the French on Monte Tomba on December 30th, 1917, marching into internment.

the mountain wedge at Monte Pertica, Monte Spinoncia, and Monte Asolone, but once more gaining the victory.

Only on the Asiago plateau, after another considerable pause, did the enemy commander achieve any definite success. On December 23rd the western Austrian wing broke over the Col del Rosso, by the Frenzela valley, and took, farther south, Monte Melago. The Italians recovered the latter height, but failed to return to the Rosso saddle.

This slight loss was more than balanced by a New Year's gift to Italy from France. On December 30th French Chasseurs

AUSTRIANS ON THEIR WAY TO INTERNMENT "FOR THE DURATION."
A substantial batch of Austrian prisoners captured by the Italians during the fighting on the Piave. After General Diaz consolidated his position on the Piave line the fighting continued to go steadily in favour of the Allies, and the Italian official communiqués reported large numbers of Austrians captured.

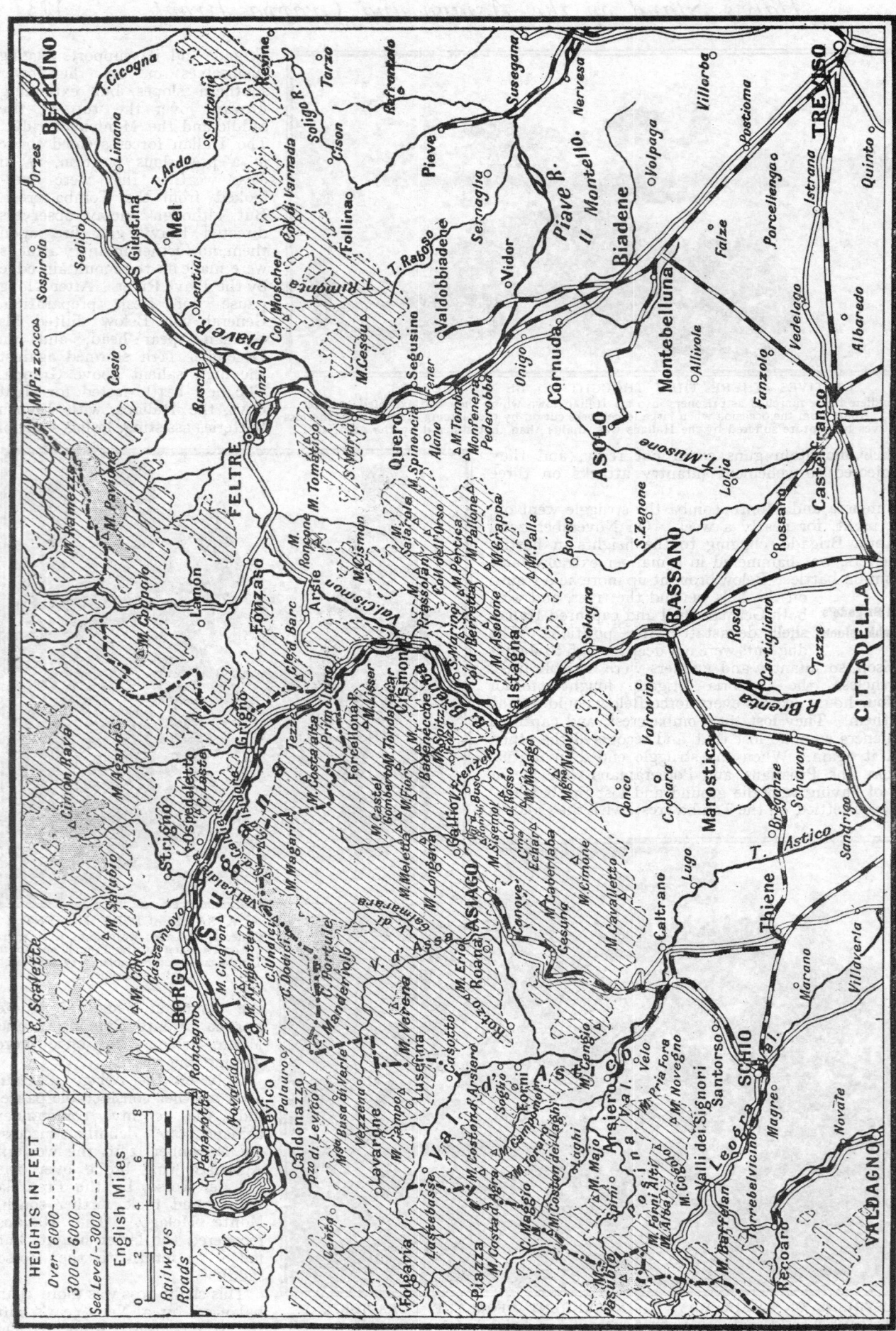

THE MOUNTAIN FRONT ALONG WHICH ITALY MADE HER VICTORIOUS STAND AGAINST THE INVADER.

WIRE ENTANGLEMENTS ON THE PIAVE.
Italian soldiers repairing wire along the Piave front.   Early in November, 1917, the Austro-German forces reached the line of the Piave, but though part of General Boroevic's army crossed the river and established bridge-heads on the right bank, the Italians prevented their making any important use of them.

and infantry of the line, backed by French, Italian, and British guns, carried the summit of Monte Tomba, from which the allied forces could dominate the Piave valley and relieve the troops on the eastern flank of Grappa.

The victorious appearance of the French army of support, on December 30th, was connected with the policy adopted by General von Below; on November 24th, when desisting from operations on the Tomba and Monfenera heights, his men were a week too late in reaching the height immediately above the plain behind the Third Italian Army.   Had the Prussian commander, with his original force of a hundred thousand men terribly wasted by battle, and his Austrian supports still more weakened by the work of preparing Prussian victories, attempted a swift descent into the plain, he would not, in all probability, have escaped destruction.

Franco-British aid arrives

It had apparently taken General Foch and Sir William Robertson, with General Fayolle and Sir Herbert Plumer, a considerable time to reinforce the armies of Italy.   In the age of railway manœuvring, many persons in civilian life, misled by legends of the shuffling of German forces from east to west, expected that a long succession of troop trains, running through Mont Cenis and along the Riviera, would quickly restore the balance of military power in the Venetian plain.

As a matter of fact, the work of carrying two modern armies from Northern and Central France to Eastern Italy was carried out with remarkable speed.   But it took a month.   The movement of the men was comparatively easy.   They marched, entrained, and marched, sometimes over the Alps, sometimes along the Lombard plains.   But they were useless without the vast machinery

of the new warfare.   The guns, shell, charges, smaller weapons and ammunition, entrenching material, horses, mules, carts, lorries, and general supplies of two well-equipped armies were not to be moved in a week.

The number of available locomotives and trucks was limited, as the armies in action and preparing for action required many of them.   The task of arranging the withdrawal and transport of men and material was intricate and huge, and the arrival of the western armies, in the nick of time, was a magnificent achievement in rapid organisation.

When the Britons and Frenchmen crossed the Italian frontier, and marched towards the Piave line, their path was a happy one. The Italian people, moved to deep passion, hailed them as saviours. The Grand Alliance was cemented, and between the people themselves the blood bond was made. The warm welcome and a certain pride at being thought worthy of helping hard-pressed comrades, swelled the hearts of the marching men.

In anticipation of Below's movements, the British army established itself on the Montello ridge, by the Piave, so as to form a strong pivot, in case a fighting and manœuvring retirement from the mountain wall, above Robert Browning's old home at Asolo, was necessary.   The French army settled just above Asolo, to receive Below's thrust from Tomba.   When Below refused to continue his attack, General Fayolle assailed him.   The result was that Below returned to Germany.   Without anything like a battle on a grand scale, the arrival of the British and French forces had, for the time, decided the issue of the campaign.   Below won on the Isonzo; he lost on the Brenta.   By their splendid recovery the Italians saved themselves, and their Allies arrived in time to see the final episodes in their victorious stand.

TWIN CRANES TO RAISE A HEAVY HOWITZER.
Italian artillerymen putting a heavy howitzer in its new emplacement.   The main part of the huge weapon was raised by two powerful cranes for swinging into position, the men pulling the rope attached to the muzzle were able to guide it to the exact position for being lowered.

An ammunition loading-station on the western front. Each projectile, packed within struts, had to be man-handled separately, and the work of " humping " the shells called for great physical endurance. From rail-head the ammunition was taken forward in motor-waggons.

Canadian siege-gun firing into Lens from an emplacement camouflaged with nets strewn with leaves and strips of green cloth. At the moment of discharge the men stopped their ears with their fingers to prevent the drums from being burst by the shock.

FEEDING AND FIRING THE GUNS OF CANADA'S FIELD AND SIEGE ARTILLERY.

GENERAL HORNE

CHAPTER CCXXXIII.

INSPECTING CANADIANS.

HOW CANADA WON NEW GLORY IN 1916-17.
By F. A. McKenzie.

How Canada Kept Her Promise—"Carry On!"—The Position at Ypres—A Picture of Desolation—The Corps Moves South—Contrasts Between Ypres and the Somme—Fight at Mouquet Farm—Some Notable Heroes—How Richardson Piped to Victory—The Fight for Desire Support Trench—General Currie's Picture of the Battlefield—Resignation of Sir Sam Hughes—New Administration in Europe—General Turner's Problems—The Organisation in England—Lord Beaverbrook's Career—The Fight for Vimy Ridge—A Difficult Advance—German Officer and Canadian Corporal—How Canadian Soldiers Fought—The Advance Beyond the Ridge—Fight for Fresnoy—Sir Julian Byng's Promotion—General Currie Becomes Corps Commander—The Fight for Hill 70—Some Glowing Tributes—The Canadians Called to Passchendaele—The Battle of Bellevue Spur—How Lieutenant Shankland Won His V.C.—Another Great Blow—Capture of Passchendaele—Canadian Cavalry at Cambrai—Lieutenant Strachan's V.C. Ride—The Forestry Corps—A Record of Achievement—Why Canadian Railwaymen Went to France—Building a Mile of Line a Day Under Fire—Strength of the Canadian Expeditionary Force—The Situation in Canada—The Return of Prosperity—The Battle for Conscription—Formation of a Union Government—Why French Canadians Remained in Opposition—The New Government's Fighting Issue—An Overwhelming Victory—Financial Support—Amazing War Loan Figures—Canada in the War to the End.

T HE Canadian Army Corps spent the first part of the summer of 1916 in the Ypres salient. Its earlier fighting, culminating in the fierce Battle of Maple Copse and Sanctuary Wood, and its part in the winter raids of 1916-17, have been described in previous chapters (Chapter CXXII., Volume 7, page 1, and Chapter CLXXVIII., Volume 9, page 189).

The people of the Dominion had well redeemed their promise to stand by the Motherland during the war. The First Contingent of 20,000 men had grown to an army corps of three divisions in the field, soon to be increased to four. Up to June, 1916, 334,209 Canadians had been enlisted for overseas service. The Government had spent for war purposes in one year and eight months about £38,000,000, exclusive of the amount to be paid to the British Government for munitions; for the Canadians not only raised and supported their own men, but met the entire charges of their military operations, including the cost of shells fired.

The Governments of the various provinces

IN MEMORY OF BRAVE MEN.
Ceremonial unveiling of the memorial erected by the Canadian Artillery to their comrades who fell during the taking of Vimy Ridge. Canon Scott opening the ceremony with prayer and hymns.

had also helped independently of the Dominion Administration. For example, the Ontario Government spent £100,000 on a military hospital at Orpington, in England, and the city of Toronto raised £400,000 for war purposes. There was scarcely a prominent family in the Dominion that had not given its men for the war. The spirit of the people was splendid. When news came of the loss of sons on the field, parents in many cases hid their grief and gloried that they had been allowed to do something for the cause of freedom. One example of this was in the case of the Hon. A. P. Shaughnessy, son of Lord Shaughnessy, President of the Canadian Pacific Railway. When Mr. Shaughnessy was killed in battle his father, in answer to innumerable messages of sympathy, said:

We are only passing through the same sad experience as thousands of others in every portion of the Empire. If his example arouses a feeling of patriotism and responsiveness in those hundreds amongst us of military age, many of whom are without his family cares, who thus far, through indifference or because of bad leadership or petty local issues, have failed to assume their responsibilities as citizens and subjects, we shall feel that there is additional compensation for the sacrifice.

A RESERVOIR IN THE BATTLE ZONE.
House in Lens used by the Canadians as a shelter for their tanks of drinking-water. The man in the centre was standing behind the tank, not in it, as a first glance suggests.

A mother sent her husband and five sons to the front. News came that the husband was killed in battle. "Never mind," she said bravely, "there are five more to carry on!" With parents and wives showing such spirit, it was little cause for wonder that the soldiers at the front played their part as men.

The position of the Canadian Army Corps in the Ypres salient was in many ways very trying. For considerably over a year they had fought on, in, and near the salient, barely holding their own. To the north they had been obliged, despite the utmost gallantry, to yield considerable territory during the Second Battle of Ypres. Even at Hooge, the miserable little bit of soil which formed the village itself was no longer within the British lines. Farther south the position remained practically unchanged. There had been innumerable skirmishes and raids by day and night, in which the Canadians had proved afresh their fighting qualities. But in place of advancing they had been obliged to remain stationary week after week under the unceasing fire of the enemy.

Canadians in the Ypres salient

Not that the Canadians sat down quietly under the German fire. In the summer of 1916 a number of German regiments had been brought against them from the Belgian Army front. Canadians and Germans were both keen to get at one another. There were constant raids and forays in No Man's Land. Time after time the Canadians crept on the enemy, surprised him, cleared his trenches, blew up his dug-outs, and retired with trophies. They came to know sections of the front not as No Man's Land, but as the Canadian prairie. But while such raids were useful in keeping up the spirit of the men and in worrying the enemy,

their main value was that they encouraged enterprise, aided enthusiasm, and helped to maintain moral.

It is worth recalling Ypres itself as it was in the summer of 1916, before the Canadians left it. The straight road from Vlamertinghe, passing through an area of ever-increasing destruction, reached the railway and "Dead Man's Corner." Thence, leaving on the left the ruined waterworks with the dismantled water-tower, it went through a series of wrecked streets to the central square.

Here was row after row of broken houses. Not a house was whole, and entire areas had been almost obliterated by German shell fire. The tower of the Cathedral had been stripped until only one narrow, broken part stretched heavenwards. Of the famous Cloth Hall nothing but a few tottering walls remained. The fourteenth-century Town Hall had disappeared. The massive Church of St. Peter was as though an earthquake had struck it. The lunatic asylum, a noted asylum in its day, was now a fantastic mass of shell-holes. When in the early days of the war the Germans visited the place, they gathered the lunatics together, drove them out into the town and set them free.

Awful havoc in Ypres

In August, 1916, word went round that the Canadian Corps was moving south. Everyone had been watching the great advance of the British armies on the Somme. The Canadians were to take part in it. And so the three divisions moved out of the line. Meanwhile, the 4th Division arrived in France from England. This division had been in training for some months in England under Major-General David Watson—in civil life a newspaper proprietor and editor in Quebec—who had distinguished

IN CLOSE BUT NOT UNCOMFORTABLE QUARTERS.
Canadians resting in a barn near the firing-line. Wire hammocks were slung in three tiers in a wooden framework, with a narrow gangway left down the middle.

himself by brilliant work as a brigadier. This 4th Division represented, like the others, every part of Canada, from Halifax to the Pacific. Seventy-five per cent. of the men were Canadian born. There were Highlanders with the tartans of the Seaforths, the Douglas, and the Royal Stuart. There were Grenadiers drilled to be worthy of the King's corps after whom they were named.

There were some battalions with characteristics all their own. One of these, for example, was the Pioneers, husky Western giants from Vancouver Island. An officer, Lieut.-Colonel Lorne Ross, had gone back to the West from the front to raise a distinctive battalion. He appealed to none but outdoor men. The people of the West knew Colonel Lorne Ross, and he quickly obtained more volunteers than were required. He sifted them out. There were men in the ranks whose fame had reached far beyond Vancouver. Frank Slavin, the pugilist, served as a private. The battalion wore the Douglas tartan in honour of the great fighting Governor of Vancouver Island. High anticipations were entertained of what the 4th Division would do when it went out, anticipations which were more than realised.

While the 4th Division remained for a time in the Ypres salient, the remainder of the Canadian Corps went on to the Somme. Whereas around Ypres everything told of deadlock, in Picardy everything proclaimed advance. The British had broken through the German lines. They had taken many prisoners. The British trenches were on the other side of what a few weeks before had been German positions. Every man's soul was thrilled by the abundant evidences of advance and of victory. The numbers of German prisoners working on the roadways as the troops approached the fighting-ground were visible proof of the British triumph.

The soldiers coming back from the front returned with German trophies in their haversacks, German postcards, bits of German shells, German war medals and ribbons. The men in the ranks were singing again. Old tunes had been revived, old choruses started afresh. Every battalion moved along with a swing, not

HIS MAJESTY'S PIGEON POST.
Carrier-pigeons returning to their motor "loft" behind the lines on the western front. The birds had been taken out to the front-line trenches and thence sent back as message-bearers.

merely the swing of disciplined marching but the swing of triumphant men. who at last saw what they had long striven for coming within reach. As the Canadians passed under the hanging Virgin of Albert —the great golden figure on the church-tower that had been knocked by shell fire to a horizontal position — they seemed to enter a new world. The roads were lined with troops, guns, and commissariat waggons moving in opposite directions. Everything revealed evidence of minute care. The line of route of every battalion was planned with the utmost attention to detail. Every road had been made wide enough for its work. Each advance was followed by armies of labourers who laid tracks, rebuilt and broadened the old highways, and macadamised them to give them foundation enough to stand their heavy loads. The countryside gave an impression of enormous reserve power, of gigantic strength, and of great and complex organisation.

The 1st Division, the first to arrive, had not, however, much time for contemplation. The troops had barely paused at Albert when orders suddenly came for them to go forward. The men of one battalion were holding a service in the Y.M.C.A. when the

WAR PIGEONS IN THEIR TRAVELLING HOME.
One of the travelling lorry homes of H.M. Pigeon Service on the western front, and (inset above) the pigeons at home in their "loft." Homing pigeons proved of considerable value as war-messengers for carrying information from front-line positions to the rear.

colonel interrupted them with word that there was a big job on hand.

The Australians who had been fighting in this district had moved out to take Mouquet Farm. They wanted a good finish before handing the ground over. After a tremendous artillery fire they found themselves confronted by a very difficult position. Some Canadian troops were hastily sent out to help them. A Montreal battalion was the first to arrive. It had to advance through a hostile

AT A CANADIAN R.F.C. TRAINING-GROUND.
Canadian airmen of the Royal Flying Corps at an aviation camp near Toronto. With the approach of winter the Canadian airmen, in training in thousands, went south, like migratory birds, to where more suitable climatic conditions prevailed, and completed their training at Fort Worth, in Texas.

barrage across open country full of shell-holes. It was closely followed by a Canadian Scottish battalion from Vancouver and by a Toronto battalion. Australians and Canadians occupied the same trenches, and for thirty-six hours they held on against the most dreadful conditions.

This was the beginning of a series of brilliant engagements by the Canadians on the Somme, and the troops under entirely new conditions quickly justified their old reputation. Sir Douglas Haig, writing to Sir Sam Hughes with reference to one of their attacks, said :

It must be a source of pride and satisfaction to you to know that the gallant officers and men who came from Canada to fight for the King and in the cause of the Empire invariably do their duty in a way which reflects the greatest possible credit on themselves and on their Dominion.

By the end of September the Canadians, after continuous hard fighting, had captured over three square miles of territory and counted their prisoners by the thousand ; but in September and October their casualties were over 23,000. The men, however, were imbued with unbroken confidence. One Canadian considered himself good enough to attack a dozen of the enemy, and time after time they did so. "Certain distinct characteristics of the Canadian were speedily apparent to the Germans," wrote one correspondent after a fight.

German dread of the Canadians

They have seen English and Scottish battalions attacking with cool cheeriness, the men even finding time to joke with each other as they threw bombs and plied their bayonets. But the Canadians stalked them silently and with cold ferocity, clearing a crater and leaving it to attack the next with the same grim thoroughness. I do not know which method of uprooting the Boche fills him with the greatest terror, but there is no doubt about his wholesome dread of the Canadian type of foe.

How the Canadians fought on the Somme could be judged not alone by the ground they gained, but by the precise records in the " London Gazette." Cases of men decorated for building roadways under intense fire, for crawling up to enemy positions and remaining there some time, for trench-digging under concentrated bombardment, and the like, were so numerous that it would be impossible to mention them all.

Major H. F. McDonald, of Winnipeg, when carrying out a dangerous reconnaissance under heavy shell fire, had his arm blown off by a shell splinter. He would not, however, allow the stretcher-bearers to remove him until he had reported the result of his reconnaissance. Major J. K. Mackay, of Nova Scotia, in command of a battery, found in one heavy fight that all the men at his observation-post were killed or wounded. He went out himself, re-established the post two hundred yards beyond the front line, and resumed communication with his battery. He remained all day in this exposed position, sending back most valuable information.

Time after time officers refused to retire even when wounded. Lieut. W. J. Holliday, who captured an enemy position with a small party and held it against three attacks, was wounded ; he continued at duty for forty-two hours until relieved. Another young officer, Lieut. W. E. James, was decorated for a similar act. The padres did their part, creeping out in the trenches, attending to and dressing the wounded continuously, under very heavy fire.

Officers, single-handed or with one or two men behind them, attacked and captured enemy machine-gun positions. Lieut. W. M. C. McLellan captured an enemy machine-gun with one man, and brought it into action against the enemy. Later he brought in a wounded man under intense fire. Lieut. A. H. Gilmour, of Winnipeg, led carrying-parties three times with water and bombs to the front lines over 1,500 yards of captured ground swept by machine-guns in daylight. Lieut. A. C. Bowles, of Brampton, fought two machine-guns in the open

Notable courage of all ranks

with great courage and determination, repelling two bombing attacks. Later a large force of the enemy, from six hundred to eight hundred men, came up against his position. He repulsed them, finally killing two of them with the butt-end of his rifle. Lieut. J. A. Hamilton, of Brandon, after being buried by a shell and having several ribs broken, continued in command, inspiring and encouraging his men until another shell rendered him unconscious. Doctors went out to the exposed trenches during the height of battle. Thus Captain T. C. Francis O'Hagan, of Calgary, went out and rescued a wounded officer and five men under very heavy fire.

The men in the ranks rivalled the courage of their officers. Junior men took senior command when their seniors were shot down. Thus Lance-Corporal S. Cole, in a platoon where everyone above him was killed or wounded, took command during a time of particular danger, directed his men for two days, and in the final attack led his company to their objective. Private J. Dawson, of the Royal Canadian Regiment, dressed and carried in wounded without ceasing from the front line and No Man's Land

At a hot corner: A Canadian sheltering behind his motor-car from a bursting shell.

Hun labour lost: Remains of a concrete barricade that was stormed by the Canadians.

Canadian Highlanders marching back to rest billets, headed by their pipers and regimental goat.

Heroes of the charge at Cambrai, Nov., 1917: Lieut. H. Strachan, V.C., with his Fort Garry Horse.

Canadian cavalry machine=gun section riding into action over a rolling down in France.

"Eyes right!": *Canadian troops returning the salute of the guard at a Canadian corps headquarters.*

Canadian narrow-gauge train taking ammunition up the line through a shattered village.

Humming activity at an ammunition dump behind the Canadian lines on the western front.

for fifty hours. Before he collapsed he had attended to one hundred cases. Corporal A. F. Neatby, of the Princess Patricia's, found himself isolated with his Lewis-gun detachment. He guided his men through a stretch of unknown country, nearly 1,000 yards, not away from the enemy but up to them. He planted his guns in advanced shell-holes commanding both the enemy's trench and the ground behind, and remained there for twenty hours, until the trench had been finally taken.

Private J. Nelson, also of a Lewis-gun section, took charge when his officer and non-commissioned officer had been killed. He placed the guns with great skill in a position right in advance of the enemy line. Private C. Parsons, when carrying a despatch, met eleven of the enemy. He promptly attacked them, killed two, and made the remainder surrender. Cases such as these could be given by the score. A corporal in an Eastern battalion had his deeds in the battle for Regina Trench recorded officially as among "the most extraordinary ever known." The battalion captured a line of German trenches, and a small party of the enemy, two officers and twenty men, began a counter-attack. The corporal advanced alone against the whole party. He emptied his revolver, and then picked up first one and then another German rifle, each of which he emptied. He shot down the two officers and sixteen men ; while he was shooting, one of the officers attacked him with a bayonet and pierced his leg below the knee, but the corporal shot him dead. The rest of the enemy attempted to escape, but he shot four and made the fifth a prisoner. Although wounded in two places, he remained in the trenches until his battalion was relieved.

In many cases death in battle prevented men from receiving high honours well earned. One conspicuous instance was in the advance of October 8th, when the Canadians attacked a German position on a frontage of three hundred and fifty yards, and to an average depth of about five hundred yards. A slow bombardment of the enemy trenches had been begun about three days before by the British heavy guns and 18-pounders. On the morning of the attack an intense creeping barrage opened, and the German trenches were heavily shelled. The facing enemy positions were particularly strong and well placed, some being on the reverse slope.

They were protected by heavy wire entanglements. Scouts reported that these entanglements had been destroyed. Observation was exceedingly

Piper Richardson's glorious death difficult, and it became known afterwards that the reports were incorrect. The Canadians moved up in four waves, the distance through No Man's Land being three hundred and fifty yards. They were met by heavy, sustained German machine-gun and rifle fire. The place seemed like a sheet of flame. One observer declared that the machine-gun bullets were so numerous that it was as though a continuous wave of metal was sweeping over him. "They were advancing like the Guards at Loos," said a flying officer, who observed the entire operation from above.

Soon the Canadians found themselves caught in the wire. Without hesitation they set themselves to cut

their way in. Large numbers fell ; others took their place. Here occurred an incident typical of many others. A Western Highland battalion was held up in the wire. Its pipers volunteered to go to the help of the men, and one of them, Richardson by name, walked to and fro playing his pipes while the soldiers hacked and tore at the wire that was holding them. He played with every skirl and every throb of the instrument as calmly as though on parade. Then, when the men got through,

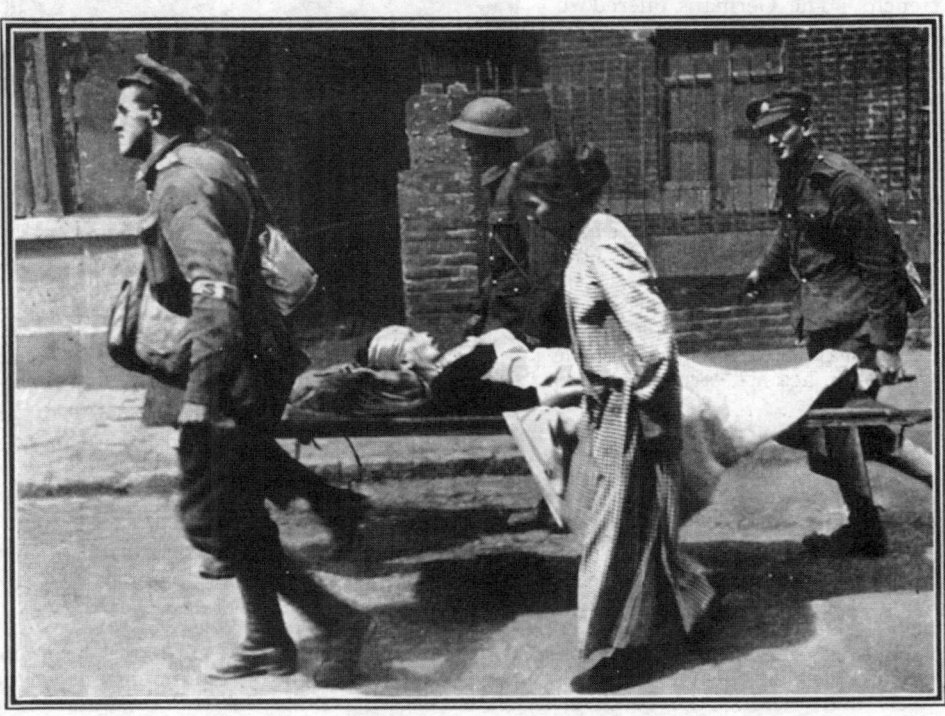

WOMEN VICTIMS OF MAN'S INHUMANITY.
A French woman, wounded during a German bombardment behind the Canadian lines, being taken to a dressing-station. Her stilled figure, and the bowed attitude of the girl accompanying her, form a touching study of the mute suffering of the womanhood of an invaded country.

he marched on with them, still playing, marched on to the enemy trenches, where a shell caught him and killed him.

The troops at last forced their way through, and at one point succeeded in establishing themselves in the enemy trenches. Before they could advance farther strong bombing counter-attacks began, and a heavy bombardment was opened on the newly-captured trenches. The men were gradually forced back. The **Canadians on the Somme** Germans could come down from four roads at this point. Sixty per cent. of the men who tried to bring back bombs were killed or wounded.

The 4th Division, which immediately after its arrival had been sent to the Ypres salient, was moved later to the Somme, and the first three divisions were shortly afterwards withdrawn. The worst that the Canadians now had to face was the weather. Trenches were seas of mud. It became at times practically impossible to move guns up. The soldiers looked mere masses of mud. Doctors put the greatcoats of the wounded on the scales when they were brought into hospital, and in some cases the coats were found to weigh considerably over one hundred pounds each. In the trenches men stood still all day with mud over their middles ; even in the shelters behind, the mud was nearly as bad, yet the men carried on with singular courage and cheerfulness.

A typical instance of Canadian fighting on the Somme was in the advance of November 18th, when men from four battalions moved forward on a front of 2,700 yards to take Desire Support Trench. There had been a fall of snow in the night which wiped out all landmarks. The troops passed the trench. It was so badly knocked about that they could not recognise it. One battalion lost every officer save two subalterns. While these two were discussing what they should do, a shell came and knocked out one of them. The second, a lad in his teens, led his men on, secured point after point, and held on to the last. He and his men drove a body of fifty-three Germans into a corner of a trench. The Germans offered to surrender, holding up their hands, and then, when the Canadians approached, repeated their old trick of throwing bombs at them. The Canadians instantly attacked, the officer himself shooting thirteen men. The punishment was quick and thorough. On this occasion the Canadians made a gain of between eight hundred and twelve hundred yards. They took a very large number of prisoners, and established their position in such a way as to make it possible to hold it against strong German attacks.

The full significance of these operations on the Somme did not appear at the time. The weary struggle from trench to trench, the nibbling away at enemy positions, the test of strength day after day, seemed to many outsiders a mere throwing away of men. Subsequent events proved that it was far from that. The Germans were already a score of miles behind, burning villages, cutting down trees, and making the country desolate, knowing that

TWO FINE SOLDIERS.
Field-Marshal Sir Douglas Haig photographed with General Sir Arthur Currie, commanding the Canadian Corps, on the occasion of a visit of inspection to the Canadians on the western front.

advances such as these would soon force them to retreat a considerable distance.

To the people of Canada the fields of the Somme share interest with the country around Ypres. On the Somme, as in Ypres, many Canadian dead lie buried. Sir Arthur Currie, whose division had done strenuous, costly, and successful work there, revisited, in the summer of 1917, the ground of this fierce fighting. He thus described his impressions in the " Listening Post " :

To-day I rode from Bapaume to Albert, past Destremont Farm, Courcelette, the Sunken Road, with the Zollern Graben, the Hessian Trench, and the Regina Trench in the distance, past Pozières Ridge, the cemetery, and the quarries. Nature, as if ashamed of the madness of man, is fast changing the appearance of the battlefield. The ragged, shell-torn landscape is now covered by green grass and poppies, and nothing seems to indicate that it was a battlefield except the battered villages, the upturned tanks, and the wooden crosses which mark the resting-places of our gallant dead. Dead they are, but not forgotten. Gone, but with their spirit still remaining ; and some time, before returning to our beloved Canada, the Canadian Corps must there erect a monument to their memory. To us those places will ever remain hallowed ground, and as I rode along I breathed a prayer to the Great Ruler of the Universe for guidance—a prayer that we, the survivors and the successors, would ever hold inviolate the great trust bequeathed to us.

An important change took place in November, 1916, in the organisation of the Canadian Army. General

HONOURS FROM BELGIUM'S KING FOR CANADA'S COMMANDER IN THE FIELD.
General Sir Arthur Currie examining the gas-mask of one of his men when inspecting a divisional train.　Right : General Orth, of the Belgian Army, decorating Sir Arthur Currie with the Belgian Croix de Guerre and the Order of the Crown of Belgium.

Sir Sam Hughes, K.C.B., who had been Minister of Militia prior to the beginning of the war, and who had been largely responsible for the raising of the Expeditionary Force, retired. Sir Edward Kemp, a successful business man who had done good work in organising the production of munitions, succeeded Sir Sam Hughes as Minister of Militia at Ottawa. A new office was created, Minister of Militia Overseas, with headquarters in London. Sir George Perley, who had been Acting High Commissioner in London, undertook for a time to serve as Minister of Militia Overseas also. He immediately flung himself into the work of reorganising the British command of the Canadian forces. Here he was fortunate in securing the aid of Major-General R. E. W. Turner, V.C. (afterwards Lieut.-General Sir Richard Turner), who relinquished the command of the 2nd Division in the field to be General Officer Commanding in Great Britain.

General Turner, the senior Canadian commander, had already proved his great organising ability. The best proof of the success of his work in England was that, after his plans came into full operation, it was always possible, however heavy the Canadian casualties at the front, to send out at once drafts from England to keep up every battalion to full strength.

The manner in which the Canadian Corps had been

SONS OF ERIN FROM THE FAR WEST.
The Duke of Connaught (third from the left) inspecting the Duchess of Connaught's Own Irish Rangers of the Canadian Force during their period of training in England. With the duke was Lieutenant-Colonel O'Donohue (second from the left), the commanding officer.

recruited at the beginning, while it brought supplies of men, involved many difficulties for the authorities, difficulties which General Turner had to face immediately. Local leaders raised local battalions. A prominent sportsman in an Eastern city, for example, would appeal for a Sportsmen's Battalion and obtain twelve hundred recruits. He himself would be colonel, and the whole of the battalion would be in effect one big family. The mayor of a small town would raise a battalion there, himself being given the colonelcy. Thus many of the battalions were officered at the start by men who had had practically no military experience. They were tried men of affairs, and had proved themselves leaders in their localities. Capacity for leadership is one of the first qualifications for an officer, and most of these senior officers thus chosen made good. Naturally, however, some did not.

When the battalions arrived in England many of them had to be broken up, their men being required as drafts for the fighting battalions in France. The junior officers were also wanted in France, but there was little room for majors and colonels fresh from Canada. Thus there came a period in England where hundreds of senior officers, who had come out full of military ardour, and who before coming out had raised their companies and battalions, were eating their hearts out in London

WAYSIDE INSPECTION OF CANADIAN CAVALRY ON A FRENCH ROAD.
General Sir Charles Kavanagh, K.C.B., inspecting Canadian Cavalry on the western front. Cavalry from the Western Dominion distinguished itself greatly when opportunity offered, as in the great fighting on the Cambrai sector in November, 1917.

WHERE CANADA'S WOMEN CARRIED ON MEN'S TASKS.
Women war-workers in one of the car shops of the Canadian Pacific Railway.
The women of the Dominion threw themselves with energy into all manner
of unaccustomed-work to take the places of men on military service.

No reference to the home side of the Canadian organisation would be complete without mention of the War Records branch, under Lord Beaverbrook. When Mr. Aitken, the boyish Montreal financier, came to England in 1910 and captured an almost hopeless seat for the Unionist Party at the General Election, he quickly became marked as a man of extraordinary qualities. He soon made himself felt in English political life. He had the great gift of youth, being then in the early thirties. He obtained honour after honour—knighthood, baronetcy, peerage—with startling rapidity. Shortly after the First Canadian Contingent arrived in

or elsewhere, with nothing to do but to draw their pay, and with apparently little chance of seeing active fighting. In the battalions at the front men from all parts were mixed up together. A Toronto battalion might receive reinforcements from Calgary. The territorial system was in danger of disappearing, and with it the local pride and the bond of local knowledge which did so much to maintain the esprit de corps.

Eventually drastic measures had to be taken. The system of receiving local battalions to be broken up on their arrival in England ceased. Each territory was made responsible for recruiting, to keep up the strength of its unit. Each soldier enlisted not so much into a battalion as into the Canadian Army. The large number of unemployed senior officers in England were offered the choice between reverting to the rank

Canadian organisation in England of subaltern and going out to France, or going home and returning to civil life. Many of them doffed their majors' and colonels' distinguishing badges and went out to France as simple lieutenants.

The Canadian organisation in England was very extensive. The Pay and Record Office in Westminster alone numbered its staff by the thousand. There were other large administrative buildings in London, and extensive administrative branches elsewhere. The First Contingent had been housed at Salisbury Plain before proceeding to the front, and spent part of the winter of 1914-15 there under very trying conditions. The later troops were more fortunate. They were stationed in the South-East of England—in Kent, Surrey, and Sussex—distinct commands being under General Sir Sam Steele, a famous Western fighter, Brigadier-General Meighen, and Major-General Garnet B. Hughes. It had been hoped to send the 5th Division to the front, and for months the whole division waited anxiously, expecting at any time orders to cross the water. But it was found during 1916-17 that all the resources in man-power of Canada must be concentrated on keeping the four fighting divisions in the field up to full strength. "Better four divisions fully manned than five weak divisions," was the motto of the Canadian Government and Staff. Events justified this decision.

WAR WORK OF WOMEN.
Canadian women doing heavy work in one of the car shops of the
Canadian Pacific Railway.

England he became Canada's official historian. The War Records Department under him was worked with the utmost thoroughness. It not only issued a popular official history, but it led the way in the use of war photography as an instrument of propaganda.

Out of the very considerable sums earned by the exhibition of Canadian pictures Lord Beaverbrook commissioned some of the greatest living artists to go to France to record permanently Canada's glories. Thus, among others, Augustus John donned khaki as a Canadian major to find inspiration for his brush on the fighting fields of Flanders. Lord Beaverbrook's ingenuity, his financial skill, and his restless energy kept his department at white heat. From the first every possible record of every event connected with the Canadian Army was carefully preserved.

Lord Beaverbrook was so conspicuously successful in this work that in 1918 he was invited by Mr. Lloyd George to take charge of the British official war publicity and to enter the Government as the first Minister of Propaganda.

When, towards the end of 1916, it was agreed that the British should make a serious and sustained attack on the Arras-Soissons front, the Canadians, now joined by the 4th Division, were given a place of honour, the task set before them being to capture Vimy Ridge, a dominating position some 475 feet high, commanding a wide stretch of country to the south-east, east, and north, the story of the taking of which was given in Chapter CLXXXIII. (Vol. 9, page 309).

Vimy Ridge had been held by French, British and Germans in turn. Its height and the valleys around, particularly the Souchez valley, had been the scene of some of the most sanguinary battles of the war. The Germans regarded their position as impregnable. The ridge, which sloped gradually up from the eastern side, dropped sharply to the west. This gave the Germans a sheltered area difficult to locate or to reach with artillery fire, where they could place their heavy batteries. These batteries were protected by ferro-concrete structures, so thick and strong that the Germans evidently reckoned that they would defy the heaviest artillery. In addition, during the winter of 1916-17, they constructed little

TANK VERSUS MOTOR-CAR.
In an exhibition of the power of a British Tank at Toronto the new war monster was made to attack a large motor.

concrete forts so placed that they could sweep every approach with enfilading machine-gun fire. From the heights of the ridge the Germans commanded a view of the entire country for many miles, and they fortified the villages behind them.

The Germans held the top of the ridge. The Canadian lines were lower down the slope. To the north was a series of ruined villages in the valley of the Carency. It was at this point that the great German advance was checked earlier in the war. The villages bore evidences of the tremendous fighting of the past. Souchez, in particular, presented a picture of desolation as dreadful as anything to be seen in the war.

The people in these regions

were among the most charming and delightful the Canadians had yet been among, and did all they could to make the men from overseas feel at home.

The preparations for the capture of Vimy Ridge, elaborated in February, 1917, made even the preliminaries for the Battle of the Somme look small. Every battalion was allotted its part. Company officers were fully informed by their superiors of the details of the entire movement. Every soldier was given a clear idea of what was expected of him and of his company. He knew all there was to be known about the enemy position in front of him. The result was shown in the extraordinary spirit of keenness displayed by all ranks.

The Germans knew that the Canadians were about to attack, and they brought up a number of their best troops to resist them. A significant report was captured after the battle, signed by General von Bachmeister of the 79th Reserve Division, and dated March 30th. "The Canadians are known to be good troops," wrote the German general frankly, "and therefore well suited for assault. There are no deserters among the Canadians."

Canadians capture Vimy Ridge

Early in the latter half of March, 1917, the systematic bombardment of the enemy positions began. The Canadian front was narrowed for the purpose of the attack to about seven thousand yards, and a British brigade co-operated with it. Day by day the artillery fire increased. By four in the morning of Monday, April 9th, the last of the Canadians were at their jumping-off places. The weather was wet and cold. In some places the men were up to their waists in icy, sloppy mud. At 5.30 the British artillery opened. There had never been such a barrage before. The shells, as they burst on the German front, seemed to make a wall of living fire. After three minutes the Canadians quietly went over the trenches and moved forward. Their pace was a little quicker than a dead march. They had a certain time allowed them to complete each stage. If they went too quickly they would get within their own barrage. It was a quiet, grim forward move. Some Highland companies were led by their pipers.

The Canadians advanced in four waves against four successive objectives, the last of which was, at its farthest point, about two and a half miles from the British front

VICTOR AND VANQUISHED.
All that was left of the motor-car after the Tank—to show its power of demolishing an obstruction—had passed over it twice at the Toronto "Victory Loan" demonstration in 1917. Under the pressure of the leviathan the car collapsed like matchwood.

THREE PROMINENT CANADIANS.
Left to right: Colonel A. MacDougall, Major J. Bassett, A.D.C. to the Minister of Militia, and Major Hughes, M.P. In October, 1916, Colonel MacDougall was promoted brigadier-general and given command of the Forestry Corps, developed from the previously existing Forestry battalions.

line. The whole movement was planned to occupy about nine hours.

Along one section of the front the Germans had blown up a number of mines, creating a series of big craters, the narrow paths on either side of which could be swept by enemy machine-gun fire. Along the rest of the front were innumerable shell-holes. The troops had to step from edge to edge of these amid a tangle of broken wires. Any man who was seriously wounded and fell into a shell-hole died. The Germans had protected themselves by an exceptional number of strongly placed machine-guns. As the Canadians moved forward they suddenly saw green and red streaks and balls of bursting golden showers above them. It was the Germans in their trenches sending up signals for their artillery to retaliate. Very soon the German guns began; then their fire mysteriously slackened. The mystery was explained afterwards. The British had placed a number of heavy howitzers in reserve. The moment the German artillerymen began to fire they rained shells on the enemy positions.

When the Canadians reached the first German trench some of them passed it without knowing it. There was scarcely a sign of it save lines of corpses and occasional broken guns. Then they came to the **Canadian platoon** second trench. It was little better; **system justified** but as they went on the fighting grew in intensity.

The machine-guns were the main trouble. Here the platoon system of battalion organisation bore fruit. During the winter the Canadians had carefully cultivated a platoon system under which every subaltern was given his own little group of men, numbering between thirty and forty. The platoon officer, with a platoon sergeant and his men, formed a little company. Every man there knew the men with him, and how he could rely on them. And so, when the German machine-guns began spitting out their fire, each platoon had its own method for dealing with them. Their success against machine-guns was one of the marked features of the day. Within forty minutes of

the opening of the battle practically the whole of the German front-line system had been taken, save that on the left.

When the troops reached Petit Vimy itself, some of the Germans there scarcely realised what had happened. One officer, grasping the situation, called aloud in English: "I surrender. I want an officer of my rank to accept my surrender." A muddied Canadian corporal came up. "I can't deal with you," said the officer haughtily. "I must have an officer to take me." "You're a nice fresh jay, you are," said the corporal. "Give me your weapons, quick! Now you turn and help with the wounded. You're too fresh, my lad, you are." A bayoneted rifle, suggestively pointed forward, made his meaning clear.

The Canadians had won. The little section of the ridge which remained would soon be in their hands. One division alone had captured 1,800 men; another had captured 1,300, and another nearly 700.

Many deeds of heroism were performed that day. Men fought on, despite wounds. One officer, shot badly in the first advance, called for his orderly to help him on and keep with his men, leaning on the orderly's shoulder. The orderly was killed and the officer himself wounded again in the leg. Then he crawled with his men—since

GENERAL LIPSETT AND HIS STAFF.
On October 31st, 1917, the Canadian Government published details of the composition of the Canadian Expeditionary Force serving on the western front, Major-General L. J. Lipsett being at that time in command of the 3rd Division.

he could no longer walk—to their first objective. In the heights around Thelus hundreds of Germans were hiding in the old caves. One officer alone took one hundred prisoners, also machine-guns and bomb-throwing machines, from one cave.

Telephonists went time after time through the German barrage repairing the wires. One telephone operator established himself one hundred and fifty yards in front of the infantry line on the forward slope of Vimy Ridge, where he was constantly under fire from snipers. One lieutenant, a scout officer, took a party of scouts forward with the leading wave of his battalion. The enemy wire at this point was not cut, so he cut a passage through it. Then he crossed the second line of wire, went through his own barrage, and entered a German battery. Returning through this barrage, he waited till it lifted, and then took a party of men up with him, captured the guns, and dealt with the Germans who were hiding in their dug-outs.

A lieutenant worked his way up to a machine-gun that was firing heavily on his battalion and, single-handed, captured it, bombing the crew out. He was wounded in the early advance, but kept on. Another young officer bombed a machine-gun crew and captured the gun and seventeen unwounded prisoners. A Toronto lieutenant found himself held up three hundred yards west of Farbus Wood by a machine-gun from the east edge of the wood. He took four men, skirted round the edge of the wood, captured three prisoners, and silenced the gun. Then he led his platoon into the wood, captured a battery of enemy guns, three officers, and twenty-five men. One well-known officer in charge of a machine-gun company was supposed to stay behind and send his second in command forward. He demanded that he should go forward himself. His second in command refused to give up his right. The two officers settled the matter, according to tradition, over a friendly game. The major won. He led the guns himself, captured one enemy machine-gun, and helped to capture another.

Not only the men in the fighting-lines, but the men behind, showed their mettle. The **Courage of the A.S.C. drivers** drivers in the Army Service Corps did their share. One man was wounded in the leg near Neuville St. Vaast while driving his waggon. He stayed on the driver's seat, however, and completed his task. When he handed over his team he was so weak from loss of blood.that he had to be lifted off his waggon. Another driver was in charge of a horse ambulance loaded with wounded. The enemy was heavily shelling the road he was travelling over. Two of his horses were struck by shell and had to be killed. The

driver then carried all the wounded men to a place of safety —a trench a hundred yards away. Then he went, still under heavy fire, half a mile down the road to secure help. Coming back with the bearers, he assisted them to carry the wounded to the dressing-station. Another driver, wounded in the arm by a piece of shell, had his arm placed in a sling, resumed his place on the driver's seat, and drove with one arm for three hours.

A young doctor did a deed as brave **Devotion of the** as any. He went through gas-shell fire **medical officers** to dress a wounded man. Finding it impossible to perform his work with his gas-mask on, he removed it, and quietly completed his task amid great clouds of poison gas. Another doctor, seeing an aeroplane shot down by the enemy a short distance away, rushed over to help. He was wounded in the head, but still kept on under heavy shell fire, helped one of the wounded airmen from his machine, dressed him, and had him carried back to the dressing-station.

The weather during the attack was appalling. It grew worse afterwards. Snow began to fall, snow which lasted for three days. It was impossible to move guns far forward, and the limit of an infantry advance is always the extreme range of its guns. The troops were exposed to hardships more severe in the days following victory than most of them had yet experienced.

When the gains of the battle began to be reckoned up

TYPICAL VIEW OF THE TERRAIN OF THE BATTLE OF THE SWAMPS.

Canadians in the line at Passchendaele. The Flanders offensive of 1917 was maintained for three and a half months under most adverse weather conditions, in which the low-lying clayey soil torn by shells and sodden with rain turned to a succession of vast, muddy pools and long stretches of bog, impassable for both man and beast except by a few well-defined tracks, to abandon which meant death by drowning.

it was found that the Canadians had taken one naval gun, thirty-five howitzers, many of large calibre, twenty-seven field-guns, one hundred and twenty-four machine-guns, and eighty-seven trench-mortars, in addition to over four thousand prisoners. Sir Henry Horne, the general commanding the First Army, issued an Order of the Day expressing his high appreciation of the splendid work carried out.

By the troops of the First Army (he declared) the Vimy Ridge had been regarded as a position of very great-four strength. The Germans have considered it impregnable. To have carried this position with so little loss testifies to soundness of plan, thoroughness of preparation, dash and determination in execution, and devotion to duty on the part of all concerned. April 9th will be an historic day in the annals of the British Empire.

On the morning of April 10th the Canadians again attacked the Germans on their left and, despite the severe weather, gained possession of the most important points there. It was difficult to do anything on the 11th on account of the weather, but on the morning of the following day an attack was made amid a blinding snowstorm on the last remnants of the ridge left in German hands.

Capture of the Ridge completed

The 5th Prussian Grenadier Guard Battalion had been brought up with orders to hold on at all cost. The Germans still occupied a group of concrete emplacements, or "pill-boxes." The Canadians swept over them, getting right to the edge of the village of Givenchy itself. On the morning of April 13th there were signs that the enemy was beginning to withdraw some way back to the Arleux-Acheville line. One body of Canadians moved out towards Givenchy. Seeing no sign of life, the brigadier-

general, taking a few men with him, moved into the ruins of the village. A sniper got him, inflicting a slight wound, but the sniper was one of the very few enemy left. The village had been deserted. A troop of Light Horse went out towards the Arleux loop, and also towards some quarries, to capture a battery reported to be there, but they found that the battery had withdrawn. This day saw a considerable extension of the British line. To the right the Canadians moved on beyond the village of Willerval.

On the 14th the advance continued, the Germans putting up a stern rearguard resistance. The evening of that day saw the Canadians on an extended line facing Avion and Mericourt, Acheville and Fresnoy. The total advance had been during this period at the widest part close on six miles, and at the narrowest point to the west three thousand yards.

The troops occupying the valley beyond Vimy Ridge had still an arduous task before them. The Germans were strongly occupying a series of mining villages and towns which ran in an almost continuous semicircle from Lens to Oppy. Here they had abundant artillery, despite their losses nearer the ridge. The ruined houses, electric-power stations, mine-heads, and factories formed very valuable shelter for them. The Canadians captured a certain number of German trenches. Mostly they scattered out in the open country, where at first they dug themselves in in little pits; gradually the pits were deepened and joined up, and fresh trenches made. Wherever the enemy thought he saw signs of life he concentrated the fire of his heavy guns, and it was no uncommon thing for a thousand shells to fall on a small area in the course of a single day.

The guns were got forward through the mud with the utmost difficulty, and then the next stage of the fighting began. The German front at Arleux had to be attacked over a distance of about 2,600 yards. On April 25th the British guns again opened **Gallant capture** battle. There was very heavy wire in **of Arleux** front of the German lines. The troops to the right reached their objective after severe fighting, particularly in the village itself. The centre had considerable difficulty in getting through, the Germans resisting to the last.

The Canadians were faced by a strong point consisting of a machine-gun in a sap in front of a small but very deep sunken road. The fighting here was stubborn and somewhat disorganised, but the Canadians won. A battalion attacking at another point with three companies came under a hostile barrage, and was held up for a time by the strong wire in front of it. The enemy machine-

LIGHT LINES LAID BY THE CANADIANS ON THE WESTERN FRONT.
At a junction on a light railway laid by the Canadians for maintaining communications on their part of the front, and (inset above) Canadian railway troops fixing a turntable near Lens. It was the boast of the Canadian railroad battalions that they followed right behind the fighting-line and carried their light railways to new positions in a few days, so that " stations, sidings, and lines appeared as though by magic."

guns were well placed. The Canadians fought them with rifle-grenade and bayonet. One machine-gun to the west of the village enfiladed the battalion. A captain and some men destroyed it with rifles and rifle-grenades.

There were three sunken roads, each strongly fortified and strongly held. Even when the Canadians reached the ruins of Arleux, machine-gun fire faced them at every point. The whole position would have been impregnable to

WINTER NEAR THE WEST FRONT.
Snowstorm in a French village near the Canadian line. To the right a number of men of a Canadian battalion were assembling in the snowy street for their pay parade.

A SOLDIERS' CHURCH.
Canadian troops at St. George's Church, a small wooden edifice which had been erected for them near their line on the western front. They were going to attend their Christmas service, 1917.

any save the best troops. The Canadians, however, drove the Germans out, and by evening the village was entirely in their hands.

The capture of Arleux was followed by an attack on Fresnoy. The dominating point here was a hill, southeast of Fresnoy Wood. There was a valley from Fresnoy to Izel where the enemy could advance to counter-attack. They also held a very advantageous position close to a brewery. The attack opened with a concentrated bombardment by heavy howitzers. While the Canadians attacked on their front, a composite British brigade attacked on the flank. The attack was timed unusually early, 3.45 in the morning. This early start was an undoubted disadvantage. The troops swept into the village and moved ahead, but in the darkness it was impossible to locate all the dug-outs, with the result that the advancing troops were attacked in the rear. Two companies reached their final objective shortly after five o'clock, and over two hundred prisoners, including four officers, were taken during the day.

The prisoners taken at Fresnoy included fresh German troops who had been brought up in order to recover Arleux. Their plan had been anticipated by the Canadian attack. When they were told that the troops who had captured them that day were the same men who had taken Vimy Ridge they refused to believe it, declaring it impossible that any troops could make such

a series of attacks. The village of Fresnoy and part of the ground to the extreme right of the Canadians was handed over by them to other troops. On May 4th the Germans made a very strong counter-attack on Fresnoy. They succeeded in entering the place. They were driven out, but returned in heavy forces, compelling a withdrawal from Fresnoy village and wood. The village was not at this time held by the Canadians.

The Canadians now settled down to prepare for the next stage of their advance.

In June, Sir Julian Byng, who had commanded the Canadian Corps for over a year, was promoted to an Army command. His successor was Major-General Arthur Currie, commander of the 1st Division, soon to be promoted to lieutenant-general, and knighted. The promotion of a man who had been less than four years before a civilian to the high office of the chief command of a fighting Army Corps of four divisions naturally attracted considerable attention.

Sir Arthur Currie
in command

General Currie, born in Ontario, had gone West as a young man, and at the outbreak of war was a dealer in real estate in Victoria, B.C. He had always taken considerable interest in military affairs, having enlisted as a private in the local volunteer artillery, and risen to the command of his brigade. He had gone through military courses and Staff rides, and when the First Contingent was raised he was appointed a brigadier, and came over in command of his men. He did so splendidly in the early fighting that at the first opportunity he was given charge of the 1st Division. He proved himself a soldier

MAINTAINING THE RESERVES OF AMMUNITION.
Preparing a position for a fresh ammunition dump on the western front. Canadian soldiers clearing the wintry ground for one of the accumulations of shells made necessary by the incessant work of the artillery in both offensive and defensive fighting.

KEEPING SMILING THOUGH WOUNDED.

At a Canadian " kitchen," only a hundred yards from the enemy lines near Hill 70. A youthful soldier, though wounded in the leg and arm, smilingly faced the camera while having a drink of hot coffee— not the less welcome though his " cup " was an old meat tin.

of foresight and insight. Of great physique, a tireless worker, with the power of inspiring the men under him, he became more and more recognised among the fighting leaders of the Allies as one of the military discoveries of the war. He quickly justified his selection for the supreme Canadian Army Corps command.

The next objective for the Canadians (as already set forth in Chapter CCXVI., Vol. 10, page 457) was the town of Lens, to the north-east of Passchendaele, a mining centre which for over two years had defied every effort of the Allies to capture it. It was one of a series of small mining towns and villages which ran into each other, a shapeless mass of houses, easy to hold, difficult to take, where troops could fight from ruin to ruin.

The Canadians made raid after raid around Liévin and Avion. They fought over different pit-heads and through swamps which the Germans had created to delay their advance. They unceasingly maintained their offensive, worrying the troops in front of them. Late in July the Canadian front was advanced into the Cité du Moulin, a suburb of Lens. Then Liévin was taken.

Capture of Hill 70
General Currie, however, determined to deliver a bigger blow. In place of fighting from house to house he decided to try in one masterly move to take a dominating position over Lens.

The position selected by him was Hill 70, the spot which had successfully resisted the British attacks in September, 1915, and the defences of which had been greatly strengthened.

At 4.25 on the morning of Wednesday, August 15th, 1917, the Canadian troops went "over the top" and stormed the position. They got as far as the western defences of the Cité St. Auguste, penetrating the German position to the depth of about a mile. They captured the series of strong points and trench lines forming the defence of Hill 70.

The blow was delivered with precision. The Canadians, thoroughly trained and knowing what was before them, went clean through the German positions. They did

what the Germans thought it impossible for any fighting men to do.

" No quarter was asked for or given," said one contemporary account of the fight. " The Canadians were attacked from the rear as well as the front, the enemy having emerged from the cellars which linked up underground works in and around Lens. This hand-to-hand encounter was an incident unparalleled in modern warfare, for the artillery on neither side dared interfere lest they killed friend as well as foe."

Eleven hundred prisoners were taken, and it was estimated that there were fully fifteen thousand enemy casualties.

There immediately began a big series of frantic and costly attempts by the Germans to recover what they had lost. In a short time ten big counter-attacks were launched. German division after German division was annihilated in the effort to get forward, for everywhere Canadian machine-guns and Canadian artillery, Canadian snipers and Canadian bombers, kept the way blocked. The 4th German Guards Division, which made a culminating attempt when many others had failed, was almost wiped out. The story is told that the 4th Guards came across the open country in fours. They walked straight and indifferently into the Valley of Death. When they reached a given point the British guns and machine-guns opened fully on them. " The division was literally cut and blasted by the machine-gun and artillery fire from the field of battle," wrote one onlooker. " What **German Guards Division destroyed** was left of the division withdrew." One machine-gun officer told how he had as his target for an hour and a quarter strong reinforcements of the enemy coming up in columns of four to be used in counter-attacks.

He declared that his men had killed more Germans in the one day than they had seen in the whole of the previous time.

Then the Canadians attacked again, making for a line of German trenches skirting Lens to the west and north-west. They captured enemy positions on a front of two thousand yards. The Germans again launched many counter-attacks, but in vain. More high honours were won for distinguished courage in the Battle of Hill 70 by the Canadians than in any other.

Sir Douglas Haig sent this message to Sir Arthur Currie :

I desire to congratulate you personally on the complete and important success with which your command of the Canadian Corps has been inaugurated. The two divisions you employed on the 15th instant totally defeated four German divisions, whose losses are reliably estimated at more than double those suffered by the Canadian troops. The skill, bravery, and determination shown in the attack and in maintaining the positions won against repeated heavy counter-attacks were, in all respects, admirable.

The Canadians now held commanding positions over Lens on one side. But before they could go much farther they were summoned to take part in the attempt to capture Passchendaele Ridge, a point which had been attacked time after time unsuccessfully by other troops. No higher compliment could have been paid Canada.

East Lancashire Lads Going Forward in France

This meant a change for the corps from the First Army to the Second. General Horne sent a message to General Currie, before the departure of the Canadians, which was greatly appreciated by the whole corps:

As the Canadian Corps is now leaving my command, I wish to express to you my warm appreciation of the good work done by your troops during the time that they served in the First Army.

You have had a great and a glorious year. The discipline, good spirit, and soldierlike qualities displayed by all ranks have enabled you to carry out to completion each task which you have been called upon to undertake.

The importance of successful operations elsewhere calls for your presence and co-operation. I am confident that the same fine fighting spirit which has been shown by all ranks during the operations against the Vimy Ridge and in the Lens area will be again apparent, and I look forward with confidence to your further success. I am very sorry that you are leaving my command, but I hope to welcome you back later on.

The great forward movement on the Western Flanders ridges, which had been so successfully negotiated during the summer of 1917 by the conquest of the Wytschaete-Messines Ridge (described in Chapter CCVII., Vol. 10, page 321), had not been maintained so well as was expected. Bad weather, the most rainy ever known within memory in Northern France or Flanders, had hindered the operations. And so, while a considerable part of the desired heights had been captured, Passchendaele and the country to the north of it still held out. Passchendaele commanded a great stretch of country half-way across to the Dutch frontier.

As readers of Chapter CCXXII. (Vol. 10, page 543) will remember, the Canadians had a man's job in front of them. The stretch of country beyond Ypres to the British trenches facing Passchendaele was little **Canadians move** better than a great bog, and the enemy **to Passchendaele** had to be attacked from lowland swamps. Moreover, the Germans had learned new ways of defensive warfare. These have been described already.

General Currie and his army threw themselves into their task. The Canadian plan of erecting plank roads was adhered to. In an incredibly short time great avenues ran out towards the ridge. Innumerable mules moved through the mud-heaps up to trenches carrying panniers

MAJ.-GEN. SIR DAVID WATSON, K.C.B.
In a statement as to the Canadian Expeditionary Force serving on the western front, issued by the Department of Militia on October 31st, 1917, it was announced that Major-General Watson was in command of the 4th Division.

of shells. When even the mules could go no farther, men carried shells and guns right under the very noses of the Germans.

No attempt was made to conceal from the troops the formidable nature of the task before them. General Currie himself addressed the different brigades before attack. He told them what lay ahead. He told them something of the preparations made to clear the way. He told them, too, how Canada and the Empire relied on them to go through with their job. Every man went into this battle strung up to **Canadian memories** the utmost keenness. Generals were **of Ypres** found in the foremost lines. There were competitions between different platoons and companies as to which should go farthest. The soldiers laughed even at the "pill-boxes." "We will catch Heinie in his little funk-holes like a rat in a trap," they said gleefully.

There were special reasons why this Passchendaele move appealed to Canada. The town of Ypres itself was full of memories for every man, memories of great sacrifice and of many comrades laid to rest. The trenches which they took over, facing Passchendaele, were the very same trenches where, in the spring of 1915, the Germans had attacked them with poison-gas at the opening of the Second Battle of Ypres. High officers who led their brigades and divisions in these trenches had played their part in lower ranks in the previous fight.

The first stage of the battle was against Bellevue Spur to the centre, Wolf Copse to the left, and Dad Trench to the right. For two days drying winds had swept over the country, but shortly before the men went "over the top" a heavy storm and a hurricane of rain broke. There was a thick mist which balked the airmen and made it almost impossible for the different battalions to keep in touch. The wet and the mud so damped the flares that signals could not be readily ignited.

Under a withering machine-gun fire the Canadians to the left moved through Wolf Copse. Some of their trench-mortar troops had carried up their Stokes guns to concealed positions right under the German strong points. They had to creep along to them and to lie flat on their backs while firing.

CANADIAN CAVALRY IN TRAINING IN FRANCE.

After long waiting, some of the cavalry from the Western Dominion had its opportunity in the attack on the Cambrai front in November, 1917, and splendidly made use of it. A squadron of the Fort Garry Horse had charged five miles behind the German lines, when the commander being killed, Lieutenant Henry Strachan took command, attacked and destroyed a German battery, and fought his way back by night through the enemy lines, bringing in all his wounded and fifteen prisoners. He received the Victoria Cross for his exploit, the full story of which is told on page 148.

The Canadian troops to the right, advancing towards Dad Trench, also came under heavy fire. They almost reached the trench, when they were strongly counter-attacked and driven back foot by foot. Officers and men, wounded and bleeding, fought on. Some, who could no longer stand, fought as they lay on the ground.

The centre of the attack moved straight towards Bellevue Spur. It was faced first by a group of "pill-boxes." One of these had been knocked out by the British artillery, and was full of dead men. The second had been somewhat damaged, but the third was intact. The Canadians moved over these, captured and destroyed them. Then one party stumbled up through the mud to the right. Another party stumbled up to the left. The right group reached its position and held its ground for some time. Then, in the thick mists, they received reports that the troops to their right had been driven back to their trenches, while those to the left had all been killed or wounded. There was apparently nothing to do but to fall back, if they were not to be surrounded and captured ; and so the officers reluctantly gave the word to withdraw.

The party of the left centre, however, had not all been killed. After passing the " pill-boxes " a number of men struggled along until they found themselves faced by two half-completed German strong points. They rushed these. There were then twenty of this company left, with one machine-gun. A young officer came up, Lieutenant Shankland, who afterwards received the V.C. for his work

that day. He rallied the men and re-formed them. Some others straggled up with another machine-gun, and altogether he had between forty and fifty men. One of his guns was soon destroyed by enemy fire. Another lieutenant who had got near joined him with four men. The little group held on hour after hour. They quickly realised that they were on the dominating point of the spur. · There were great forces of the enemy below them. In the mist they could not tell the enemy numbers, and the enemy could not tell their weakness. Shankland

BRIG.-GENERAL SEELY.
Right Hon. John Seely, C.B., D.S.O., M.P., was appointed to the command of a brigade of Canadian cavalry in February, 1915.

SIR GEORGE PERLEY AT VIMY RIDGE.
When the new office of Minister of Militia Overseas, with headquarters in London, was created, after the resignation of Sir Sam Hughes, Sir George Perley, who had been Acting High Commissioner in London, took over the duties of the new office as well.

quickly arranged his men, some of them facing the west and some the south, the two points through which the enemy could approach. There they lay, picking off the Germans every time they tried to come up. The long fight surged now this way, now that. At any moment the little group might be rushed off its feet. The men resolved that, at any rate, they would fight to the last.

Hour after hour they waited, expecting reinforcements. At last, taking advantage of a lull, Shankland left his men and plunged down the hillside back into battalion headquarters. Here everyone feared that the day had gone against them. Shankland rushed in. His uniform bore traces of fierce fighting even amid the mud. One bullet had pierced the magazine of his gas-mask, another had cut through his pocket, a third had cut across his back, penetrating a tin of sweetmeats which he had outside his coat and making a slight surface wound. He asked his commander to send up men to support his little company. "I'm holding the top of the ridge. I have fifty men up there. There is some dead ground over which you can come." And he led supports back.

CANADA'S MINISTER OF OVERSEA FORCES.
Sir Edward Kemp (in the centre) with a group of Canadian generals on the western front. In October, 1917, Sir Edward Kemp was appointed a member of the Canadian Cabinet as Minister of Oversea Military Forces.

A new battalion had now come up to reinforce the troops. A big, fresh forward move was determined upon. Dad Trench was again attacked. The Germans had already suffered severely from the persistent rifle fire of the men on the hill-top. They were getting wearied. One officer and four men captured a "pill-box." The troops moving round from Dad Trench and Wolf Copse encircled the spur.

There was still much fighting to be done. Hour after hour, until far into the night, the battle went on around

OLD BRICKS FOR NEW BUILDINGS.
Canadians building themselves quarters in a district newly recovered from the enemy. Plenty of material was available from demolished buildings, and mules were used to bring up the heavier stone.

each "pill-box" and around each knoll. The German troops holding Bellevue Spur were in many ways as good as any the Canadians had ever fought. They were young, high-spirited, and competent. Some of them had apparently come fresh from a long rest. They had just been inspirited by news of their Italian victories. They showed no signs of the war-weariness, the hunger, or the want that some English critics imagined existed in the German Army. Even when captured they retained their confidence. The

whole battle was a sheer, desperate struggle. The end was a Canadian triumph. Every "pill-box" was taken, and a large number of prisoners was secured from them. The hill-side was strewn with the dead of the rival armies.

On the following Tuesday the Canadians struck again. There had been little rest in the interval. The Germans had counter-attacked time after time. Their artillery, from a considerable distance around, concentrated on the desolate country between Ypres and the front lines. The morning opened fine, with a blood-red sky, significant symbol of the day's events, and bright autumn sunshine. There had been a busy night. German snipers had searched the positions constantly. German aeroplanes had visited the rear of the lines, bomb-dropping. There had also been much shell fire. The Canadian barrage opened shortly before daylight. Less than five minutes afterwards the enemy replied with a tremendous counter-barrage. Troops from every part of Canada engaged immediately. The weather changed during the morning, becoming much colder. The clouds gathered, and shortly before noon cold, miserable, continuous rain began, which made the mud worse than ever.

On the right flank the Canadians fought the 364th German Infantry hand to hand, the Germans standing their ground and flinging cylindrical sticks on our men as they closed with them with the steel. The fiercest fights occurred around Meetchele and Goudberg. A number of concrete emplacements round Goudberg were the last to be taken. One young officer turned the fortunes of the day at Meetchele. Here the attacking troops were held up by strong concrete emplacements. At the most critical moment the officer ordered his men forward and plunged on himself at their head. The men got among the "pill-boxes," destroyed eighteen of them, and cleared the way to their final objective. Long before noon it was known at Headquarters that all the objectives had been taken, and that the Canadians stood on the line marked out for them by the Staff before they began.

Fierce fighting around Goudberg

The Canadians were now on top of the Passchendaele Ridge itself and on either side of it. The Germans declared that on that Tuesday they entered the village of Passchendaele and were driven out of it; but this was wrong. Passchendaele was left for the third attack. The Canadians went to the very edge of the village beyond Crest Farm and dug themselves in there. Apparently the Germans, expecting an advance on Passchendaele that day, abandoned it. Furious counter-attacks were launched from beyond Goudberg and from the valley to the right of Passchendaele. Time after time the German reserves

HAVOC IN THE MINING FIELDS OF FRANCE.
General impression of the gradual demolition of Lens while it was the centre of swaying battles in 1917. This photograph was taken while the once prosperous colliery town was under bombardment by Canadian artillery, one of whose shells had just burst in the background.

 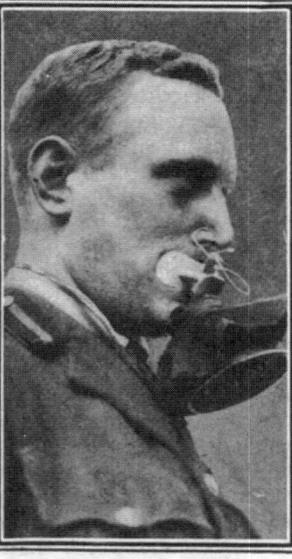

GERMAN GAS-MASKS FROM LENS.
The flexible portion of the first was of leather, suggesting shortage of rubber in Germany. Right: Mouthpiece, nose-clip and chemical-box, used by runners who would be hampered by headpiece and goggles.

came up. Here the Canadian artillery, which had been handled with the greatest skill, came into full effect, though inferior in number to the guns of the enemy.

In their desperate exertions to retrieve their defeat the Germans used more artillery and dropped more explosives on this area than they had ever done in a similar area and time during the war. Their aircraft attacked towns away behind the lines—Poperinghe and its **Haig congratulates** neighbours. On one night alone close **the Canadians** on one thousand bombs were dropped in and immediately around ruined Ypres. Their guns searched the long roads over which the ambulances were sent.

The Germans tried every trick to catch men. Thus, one night a German crept up and started piteous moans and cries, muttering broken words of English. The colonel of a Western battalion occupying that section of the trenches ordered his supports to stand back while he went out to rescue this wounded man. He crept carefully to within twenty yards of him ; then the German, throwing off his pretence, opened rapid fire with his rifle. The colonel dropped quickly into a shell-hole and replied. A bullet caught him on his shoulder, but he knocked out his man and got safely back to his own position.

Despite heavy losses—losses inevitable in such a fight— the Canadians made ready for a final blow. On November 6th their objective was Goudberg, Mosselmarkt, and Passchendaele itself. The troops not only occupied Passchendaele village, but penetrated to a point known as Vindictive Cross-roads. Goudberg, Mossel-markt, and Passchendaele all fell into their hands.

These splendid victories, a welcome relief in a somewhat sombre autumn campaign, were the subject of much congratulation. Sir Douglas Haig visited the Canadian Headquar-ters to convey his felicita-tions in person. "While all the troops did well, and contributed materially to the results achieved," he declared, "the per-formance of the Canadian Division in particular was remarkably fine."

"It is stupefying that anyone should have been able to make such an assault," declared the special correspondent of

MODERN BODY ARMOUR.
A smiling Canadian displaying the body shield which he had taken from a German captured in battle.

the "Matin." "Seeing the conditions, we realise what a fabulous *tour de force* it took to gain this terrain. As the Canadians say, the Germans are now thrown back into their own element, into the mud-holes of the lower ground."

Shortly after the capture of Passchendaele the Canadians again moved on. The 1917 campaign had not, however, quite yet closed. When Sir Douglas Haig made his surprise thrust at Cambrai in November the Canadian cavalry took a prominent part in the move. The Fort Garry Horse led the way, and charged right on into the village of Mesnières, five miles behind the German lines. They captured several villages and took numerous prisoners and a battery of German guns.

They had many adventures on that great ride. The most bril-liant was led by a young officer, Lieutenant Henry Strachan, who shortly afterwards received the V.C.

His squadron was approach-ing the enemy front line at a gallop when the commander was killed. Lieutenant Strachan at once took command, and headed his men through the enemy lines of machine-gun posts. Gathering up the survivors, Lieutenant Strachan made straight for a Germany battery which was firing

ARROGANCE IN UNCONGENIAL CIRCUMSTANCES.
Canadian soldiers bringing in captured German officers. Many of these gentry maintained their Prussian arrogance up to the last and professed a haughty unwillingness to surrender to British rank and file—hauteur of which not the smallest notice was taken.

at point-blank range on three or four British Tanks. He himself, with drawn sword, was in among the gunners, sabring them, and killed seven. His men accounted for the remainder. They were among the gunners before any of them, save one, could destroy their guns. A German sergeant at one end managed to load and to fire with the breech only partly closed. This ruined his gun. "He stood to attention and saluted death." A Canadian tried to rescue him, but in the mêlée he was trampled under foot. Lieutenant Strachan rallied his men and fought his way back by night through the enemy lines, bringing all his own wounded men safely in, together with fifteen prisoners.

Mr. Roland Hill, who visited the Fort Garry Horse shortly afterwards, thus described part of the advance:

The next adventure of the raiders was in a sunken road to the right of Rumilly. There seemed to be a considerable body of enemy troops marching down this narrow country lane to reinforce those in the town. The squadron was making across grass meadows with good going, but the major decided that the discomfiture of these Huns was worth while. Half the squadron veered to the right, where they could ride smoothly down a slope into the road. The remainder got the command to charge and the signal that there was a sunken road ahead at the same time. They knew what it meant. The half hundred horsemen clung to their horses over the miniature precipice right on top of a German machine-gun party, and by sheer luck not a man was unhorsed. It was a massacre. Over fifty Huns were killed, but the rest got into Rumilly and gave the alarm.

The two halves of the squadron joined again. It was decided to await news or reinforcements. From two sides the Hun machine-guns opened on the party, and although the men were comparatively

ROAD-MENDING UNDER SHELL FIRE.
Two of a party of Canadians, repairing a railway under fire, watch the flight of an approaching shell ; their comrades, busy at the moment, took no notice of it whatever.

and that second was fatal. He and his men were surrounded by the now desperate gang. They all surrendered but one, and he was cut down in attempting to escape.

It was now dark, and the Canadian major made the Hun officer act as guide to Mesnières, which was reached without further serious fighting. There the little band found regimental headquarters. The rain was coming down in torrents, but the troopers insisted on getting back to where there were more horses and remounted. They stood by all night, hoping for the chance for further adventures.

Charge of the Fort Garry Horse

It was said that had other cavalry been allowed to follow up where the Canadians went that day, there would probably have been a general German retreat from Cambrai, and the place might have fallen into our hands.

This record would be incomplete without mention of two other branches of the Canadian Army that did noted work in the war—the Forestry Corps and the Railroad Battalions. Early in 1916 the British Government found

safe in the banks of the road, there were severe casualties among the horses.

It was decided, as dusk was coming on, that they should make their way back and meet what British troops were following up. The remaining horses were stampeded in the direction of Cambrai, and immediately the Germans fell into the ruse, thinking that the squadron had galloped on.

With a captain from Montreal, who speaks perfect German, in the lead, and with the order to use sabres in preference to rifles, as being less alarming and giving as good results, the little band started. The first difficulty encountered was a party of infantry halted on the Mesnières side of Rumilly. The Canadians were not challenged, and easily cut their way through to the main road, where in a few minutes they sighted a Tank, which they signalled, and which did splendid work protecting their rear. Then the horseless troopers found a German officer and nine men, who called on them to halt. The Montreal captain joked with the officer, and told him in German that he must have his "wind up" badly. The German hesitated a second at the taunt,

RAILWAY TROOPS FROM THE DOMINION.
Canadians laying a light-railway track near the firing-line. The permanent way was made up with ballast provided by demolished buildings in the neighbourhood. In oval: Bolting the rails to the sleepers at a dump of line sections ready for laying.

CAMOUFLAGE AT LENS.
Canadian gun emplacement at Lens. Netting and sacking cleverly painted to resemble pointed masonry effectively concealed the iron-vaulted sand-bagged position in the basement of a building where the competent gunners lurked ready for instant action.

itself seriously in need of timber. Great Britain had for some years relied on supplies from the virgin forests of other lands. Forestry had become a lost art.

The outbreak of war quickly brought a cessation of these supplies. At the same time it brought an enormously increased demand for timber for Army purposes. Timber was wanted to build plank roads for troops, for sleepers and ties for military railways, for props and roofing for dug-outs, pits, and mines, and for duck-board roads and trench-mats.

It was suggested that the British authorities should cut down their own forests or obtain the use of some of the vast forests of France—20,000,000 acres in all. But there were scarcely any skilled men available. Then Britain turned to Canada. In February, 1916, the British Government cabled to Ottawa, asking for a forestry battalion—or, to speak more exactly, a lumber battalion—of 1,500 men, to be raised and sent to Europe. The Dominion Government called upon Mr. Alexander MacDougall, a distinguished engineer and railroad contractor, who had suc-   **Canadian Forestry** cessfully carried out many big under-   **Battalions raised** takings, to see the matter through.

Mr. MacDougall was appointed officer commanding the new battalion to be raised for lumber work, and was given the rank of lieutenant-colonel.

Colonel MacDougall took the matter up in earnest. The first of the Canadian Forestry Battalions was duly authorised on February 25th, 1916. The first draft landed on British soil on April 28th, 1916. Machinery was already on its way. Suitable timber land had been surveyed in England, and the men were at once despatched to Virginia Water. The erection of the first mill was completed by May 13th. Two other drafts followed, bringing the strength of the battalion, by May 28th, up to 1,609 men of all ranks.

In these ranks were technical experts, skilled labourers, sawyers, edgermen, saw hammerers, millwrights, saw-filers, and the like. Many were over military age ; others had been rejected for the fighting ranks for one reason or another, but were good lumbermen.

The corps did not wait for the delivery of their own machinery, but adapted whatever they could get. They

HOISTING THE ENEMY WITH HIS OWN PETARD.
Canadians firing a German 4.2 in. gun upon the enemy, who had abandoned the weapon when compelled to retreat. In circle : Adjusting a Canadian siege-gun in its elaborately camouflaged position before beginning energetic interference with the enemy's military activities.

made some use of Scottish mills, each with a capacity of about 5,000 to 7,000 F.B.M. feet for a ten hours' shift. The Canadians, however, applied their mechanical ingenuity to these mills, and soon greatly increased their output. As soon as possible they built Canadian mills, these mills doing their 25,000 to 30,000 feet and more in a ten hours' shift. Visitors to the beautiful forest country around Windsor were startled to come suddenly on clearings, to hear the ring of the axes, and to see mills busily at work, resembling scenes in a Canadian forest.

Before, however, the first mill at Virginia Water was opened, Lord Kitchener was pressing that a large proportion of the Canadian lumbermen might be sent to France. The British Government made representations to Canada : " Production now held up by lack of men, and his Majesty's Government would be most grateful if Canadian Government could raise these men on lines of previous battalion." As a result, a **Forestry Corps** second and a third battalion, each **created in 1916** 1,100 strong, was raised, and other battalions quickly followed.

It was soon found necessary to have, not forestry battalions, but a Forestry Corps. This development took place in October, 1916, Colonel MacDougall then being made brigadier-general. By the beginning of 1917 it was found necessary to provide a base, training, and mobilisation camp in England. By the middle of June in the same year the corps in England and France had grown to 15,000, and by January 1st, 1918, there were over 18,000 Canadians enlisted in the corps and at work in England, Scotland, and France, in addition to a very large number of Portuguese, Finns, and others. The corps was further helped by a considerable amount of German prison labour being allotted to it.

The first camp at Virginia Water had grown to thirty-eight establishments in the United Kingdom, from Sutherlandshire to Devonshire. Canadian lumbermen were at work cutting down the forests of great estates. In France there were no less than seventy camps all over the country, from the Jura Mountains in the south-east to the Landes in the west, in the Gironde and the Haute Marne, around Bordeaux, and in the forests of the Somme.

PREPARATION FOR THE REAL THING.
Canadians training in England firing rifle-grenades into dummy enemy trenches during one of a series of most realistic fighting competitions that formed part of their course of instruction.

Some of the battalions worked in country as far removed from the war as could be conceived. Others worked under the shadow of the guns. Battalions operating near the front found themselves frequently under heavy shell-fire and under attacks from German aeroplanes. In January, 1918, several members of one company were given the Croix de Guerre with bronze star for their work under fire.

While the forest lands of England, Scotland, and France were to some extent denuded by the work of the corps, it soon became apparent that the permanent result would be beneficial. Large numbers of the woods that were cut down in France had been already ruined by shell and machine-gun fire. The trees were riddled with bullets, and saws were broken, sometimes as many as five in a day, by coming in contact with metal particles in the wood. The trees would have died slowly because of this. In England and Scotland the clearance of old forests gave fresh life to afforestation, which was quickly taken up as a Government scheme to be carried out on a national scale for national purposes.

The Canadian railroad troops were sent to France not at first at the request of the British authorities, but on the urgent insistence of Canadians themselves. Every Canadian railroad expert who visited the British front in the early days of the war was appalled by the wasteful methods of conveyance used. Large numbers of heavy motor-trucks distributed supplies to the Army, often from the base ports. There was small use even of the available French lines. One train can hold as much as 200 motor-lorries. It employs four men in place of 400, and its use saves the inevitable tearing up of roads which a big lorry service means. The Canadian railroad men pointed out this insistently, but

ON PAY PARADE AT THE FRONT.
Canadians filing up to draw their pay at a table set in the open street that served as pay-office in a village that had been captured on the western front.

received little encouragement. Finally, Lord Shaughnessy, the President of the Canadian Pacific Railway, recruited a Canadian railroad battalion skilled in construction, and sent it to France.

At first it seemed as though the battalion would not be allowed to do anything effective. Then Mr. Lloyd George, at that time Minister of War, appointed an active railway man, Mr. (afterwards Sir) Eric Geddes, to re-organise and extend the system of constructing and operating military railroads in France. From that moment the Canadian railroad men came into their own. Fresh battalions were raised, some by the Dominion railroads, some by leading contractors, and some independently. A famous Western contractor, Mr. "Jack" Stewart, who had the reputation of saying less and doing more than anyone else, became brigadier-general and head of the Canadian railroad men.

Work of the railroad battalions It was the boast of these railroad battalions that they followed right behind the fighting army. A few days after the capture of fresh territory on the Somme, at Vimy, and elsewhere railways were run right up to the new positions—light railways, followed quickly by standard-gauge lines. The railroad troops worked constantly under heavy fire, with steel helmets to protect them from shrapnel fragments, and gas-masks to guard against poison-gas attacks. Heavily-armoured locomotives hauled up their materials. Stations, sidings, and lines appeared as though by magic.

The pioneers would come into new country with bridges blown away, tracks obliterated, and traps everywhere. There were German mines placed in positions to blow them up. Their very engines were sliced by shells, and

"LOGGING" NEAR VIMY RIDGE.
Men of the Canadian Pioneers carrying split logs across the Souchez River, near Vimy. Though their work was timber-cutting, they were sufficiently near the fighting-front to have to wear gas-masks and steel hats.

often enough the battalions had to pay their toll in life for their work. Sometimes they could only work at night. They would employ large numbers of their men at every rush job, 600 men working like one, laying a railway at the rate of a mile a day, building bridges at amazing speed. In one case a bridge, 140 feet long, in a very dangerous position, was started on a Friday and finished on the following Tuesday. The Canadian railwaymen well earned their place of honour. **The Canadian Army in 1917**

Much misapprehension existed in many quarters about the actual strength of the Canadian Army before conscription was enforced. Precise statements were issued in the autumn of 1917 by the Canadian Government. Up to the end of May, 1917, 418,102 men had been recruited, but large numbers of volunteers were discharged for various reasons.

In a statement dated October 31st, 1917, the Department of Militia stated that, while it would be injurious to disclose the order of battle of the Canadian forces in the field, the following facts, while revealing nothing to assist the enemy, might prove of general interest.

The Canadian Expeditionary Force serving on the western front included:

1. The Canadian Army Corps (Lieut.-General Sir A. W. Currie), consisting of the 1st Division (Major-General A. C. MacDonnell); 2nd Division (Major-General H. E. Burstall); 3rd Division (Major-General L. J. Lipsett); 4th Division (Major-General D. Watson); and corps troops (i.e., extra divisional units under the direct orders of the corps commander).
2. The Canadian Cavalry Brigade (Brigadier-General J. E. B. Seely).

The actual number of regimental units engaged at the front or employed on lines of communication were:

Cavalry : 4 regiments.
Artillery : 1 horse artillery brigade, 12 field-artillery brigades, 9 siege batteries, 12 trench-mortar batteries, 2 heavy artillery batteries, 1 anti-aircraft battery, and 5 divisional ammunition columns.
Engineers : 24 companies.
Infantry : 48 battalions.
Machine-Gun Groups : 20.
Forestry Corps : 38 companies.
Railway troops : 10 battalions.

In addition to these were the Signalling Service, Army Service, Medical Service, etc.

The four Canadian Divisions, apart from all other troops, totalled about 75,000 men ; including pioneers, there were 54 battalions of infantry, or some 55,000 men, over 10,000 artillery, from 3,000 to 4,000 engineers, 3,000 medical troops, and about 2,000 Army Service. With a cavalry brigade of some 3,000, this came to just 80,000. In addition there were other troops working with the corps, which brought Sir Arthur Currie's strictly fighting force to nearly 90,000 men.

CLEARING A RUINED WOODLAND.
Canadian Pioneers felling and cutting up shell-shattered trees on the western front. Many saws and axes were put out of action by coming in contact with bullets and shell fragments imbedded in the timber.

The approximate establishment of Canadian troops in France was as follows :

The four divisions and the cavalry brigade	78,000
Fighting corps, troops	11,000
Total fighting troops	89,000
Army Service Corps and Medical Services	8,000
Railway, Forestry, Labour, etc., Services	28,000
Total lines of communication	36,000
Grand total	125,000

There was in England a 5th Division.

Four Divisions in France

It was hoped to increase the Canadian Army in France to five divisions, and this formation was organised. But it proved difficult at one and the same time to bring it up to establishment and to supply the needs of the four senior divisions for men ; then very heavy fighting caused a very heavy increase in the reinforcements needed, and the 5th Division had to send drafts to the elder sisters. Its artillery, which had not been depleted, got across to France as a body, but the infantry and other arms became draft-producing corps. At the beginning of November the 5th Division numbered only some 12,000 or 13,000 men, of whom some 10,000 were infantry.

The 5th Division, established early in 1917, was,

however, broken up a year later and the four-division formation maintained.

There were the sick, wounded, and convalescent, some 15,000 men. The administrative services absorbed some 15,000 or 16,000 men. There were, in addition, reserve units numbering not far short of 40,000 infantry and 25,000 of other branches. In Canada itself there were 20,000 officers and men.

Let us now turn to the situation in Canada itself. From the first there was everywhere outside the Province of Quebec the utmost enthusiasm for the war, an enthusiasm backed by the most splendid sacrifice of men and money. The Canadians, like the people of most parts of the Empire,

hoped at the beginning for a short war. The troops of the First Contingent, when they were delayed on Salisbury Plain in the winter of 1914-15, were loud in their complaints that if the British authorities did not hurry on they would not reach France until the " great push " had begun and the real fighting was over. As month followed month, the realities of the war situation came more and more home to the people.

At the start there was a period of considerable industrial depression, but this gradually righted itself, and by the summer of 1917 Canada was enjoying a time of great material prosperity. The farmers of the West obtained prices unheard of before for their crops. The manufacturers of the East were kept busy producing material of war. Employment was abundant and well remunerated. Farmers came from the United States anxious to take up the waiting lands of the West.

Material prosperity marched side by side with a spirit of sternness and even with a touch of sombreness, for Canada was realising more and more the extent of the sacrifice of her young manhood. After each fight the returns of the casualties mounted up. Victories such as Courcelette, Vimy, Hill 70, and Passchendaele could not be had **Internal conditions in Canada** except at a price. The total of killed and wounded rose from tens of thousands to scores of thousands. Then the hundred thousand mark was reached, and all too soon the hundred thousand mark was left far behind. But there was no weakening of purpose ; people realised that the greater the loss and the harder the struggle the more urgent and necessary the task before them. The spirit of easy optimism was replaced by one of inflexible resolution.

In the early summer of 1917 the Dominion was faced with the possibility of being unable to maintain at full strength the four divisions in the field, much less to send to the front the 5th Division waiting in England.

There had been growing up a feeling that partisan Government should be ended. In the past, party politics had been taken very seriously in Canada ; each side fought for power with a vehemence which left British political passions in the rear. Political partisanship was supported by a widespread patronage system. Government contracts were frankly given out to the friends of the Government, the departments having lists of preferred

WOODMEN FROM THE FAR WEST ON THE WESTERN FRONT.
Canadian soldiers taking brushwood to their billets on the western front, and using horses to drag the bundled branches, as they had been accustomed to do in Canada. In circle : Canadian Pioneers splitting logs on the western front.

contractors. Minor positions under the Government were distributed as a reward for political services. It was a recognised principle that each Government should be "good to its friends." This had built a strong wall of self-interest and self-seeking around the partisan system.

Now came the proposal that partisanship should go, that the old intrigues and backstairs influence should be swept away, and that the best men of the country drawn from both parties should unite together for the Government. When this idea was first mooted few men dared openly to oppose it, but some professional politicians threw their influence on the other scale.

A quiet, hidden fight followed, and for a time it was uncertain what would happen. It was obvious that if Sir Robert Borden, the Premier, were to form a Union Cabinet he must be the head of it. This meant that the

Patriotism v. Partisanship Liberals, who believed that the whole current of political life had set in their direction, should abandon hope of political supremacy. This particularly affected the Western Liberals, who had reached a point where, owing to the growth of population and consequent increase in voting strength, they might be supreme in Canada.

The situation was complicated by another factor. The Union Government must enforce conscription if the Army was to be kept up to full strength. It would, in fact, be created mainly for that purpose. Sir Robert Borden approached the Liberal leader, Sir Wilfrid Laurier, who demanded that there should be a referendum before conscription was enforced. The experience of Australia had shown what a referendum on such an issue meant. In place of accepting this demand, the Government introduced a Military Service Bill to establish a system of selective compulsion throughout the Dominion. The Bill was furiously debated. It passed its second reading in the Lower House, in July, with a majority of sixty-three. The third reading was carried in the Senate without a division, and it was signed by the Governor-General on August 28th. In the same Session the Government passed a number of other war measures, one of them, the War Time Election Act, taking the vote from aliens and giving it to the near women relatives of soldiers and making provision for taking the votes of soldiers and nurses overseas. One Bill for the settlement of soldiers on the land was carried, providing for a grant of 160 acres and a loan of up to £500 for discharged soldiers. Despite the large sums being voted for war purposes, the Government further announced its intention of taking over the Canadian Northern Railway and paying out its shareholders.

Parliament prorogued on September 21st, the negotiations for Union still proceeding. Sir Wilfrid Laurier, backed by a majority of French Canadians, continued his hostility to conscription, but on October 12th Sir Robert Borden was able to announce that a number of leading

Borden forms a Union Ministry Liberals had agreed to join the Government and that a Union Ministry had been formed with himself as Premier, and with the seats in the Cabinet equally divided between Conservatives and Liberals.

This remarkable result, involving as it did the cleavage of the Liberal Party, was due to several causes. The people of Canada as a whole had had enough of old-time politics. They wanted a new and higher era of public life to begin. The very strength of the opposition of the French Canadians in Quebec united and strengthened the English-speaking provinces. When the crisis was at its height the Liberal Press of Canada came out almost unitedly for Union. The leading Liberal papers of Toronto, the "Star" and the "Globe," urged day after day that patriotism must come before party loyalty. They discarded their old leader. "The great body of Liberals throughout Canada, who have thrown themselves whole-heartedly into this war, have no desire or intention to be put in a false position by accepting a leadership that would seem to represent

them as opposed to conscription or to any other measure that may become necessary to the winning of the war," declared the "Toronto Daily Star." The "Manitoba Free Press," the great Liberal organ of the West, noted in pre-war days as the doughtiest of fighters for aggressive Liberalism, now declared that it would know no partisanship until the war was over.

Sir Robert Borden had to shed from his own side some extremists unwilling to have any association with Liberalism. The Liberals who joined him in the Cabinet included Mr. N. W. Rowell, a distinguished lawyer, the leader of the Opposition in Ontario. Mr. Rowell was one of the most influential advocates of the policy of prohibition. He had visited Europe the previous year and had seen military conditions on the front. He returned to Canada a convinced adherent of the policy of conscription. Mr. F. B. Carvell, of New Brunswick, became Minister of Public Works. Mr. A. L. Sifton, the Liberal Premier of Alberta, member of a very famous Liberal family, became Minister of Customs. Mr. James Calder, one of the most influential members of the Liberal Government of Saskatchewan, joined the Cabinet, as did Mr. Crear, a politician of great influence in Manitoba. Major-General F. C. Mewburne was appointed Minister of Militia and Defence, Sir Edward Kemp coming to England as Minister of Militia Overseas.

The Union Cabinet was as representative of both political parties throughout Canada as could possibly have been expected. A small War Council within the Cabinet was appointed, an inner body specially charged with handling war matters.

The news of the formation of the Union Ministry was received by the extremist Liberals, the men who still followed Sir Wilfrid Laurier, with defiance. The General Election was ahead. They resolved to fight the new Ministry to the utmost, but they did not know the spirit of their own nation.

Why was it that the majority of the French Canadians showed at this stage of the war such indifference to the vital nature of the conflict? It might have been expected that, as descendants of the French, when France was fighting for her life, and as members of the British **Question of the French Canadians** Empire with all at stake, they would have had dual reasons for helping. These claims were recognised by some of their people. There were French Canadians in the Army, although proportionately nothing like so many as there should have been, and these fought well. Men like Major Papineau, a descendant of the famous rebel, did their utmost to influence their people on the right lines. Papineau died heroically in the Battle of Passchendaele, dying as he had lived—in the hope that French Canada might be true to her highest ideals.

Generally, however, the French Canadians were influenced by two main reasons. The first was constitutional. "Canada had been brought into this war," they said, "without her people having been consulted. If they were to yield on the point by helping now it might be used as a precedent to force coming generations into England's wars in which they had no interest." Then, many of the French Canadian Catholic clergy were unsympathetic to the Allies, and in few countries had the clergy greater power than in the Province of Quebec. Numbers of the French Canadians regarded the France of their day not with sympathy but with aversion. Their love had been turned to hate by the special legislation instituted by the Republican Government against the religious orders. The France of their fathers had been Catholic and monarchical; the France of their own day was republican and atheistic. Let Germany act as the whip of God to punish it. This feeling, not always expressed, was very widespread and had great influence.

The New Union Government resolved to fight the election on one issue only. Was the Army to be supported or was

British officer attached to the armoured=car section holding up deserters on the Russian front.

Captain Gerrard, Russian interpreter (on right), helping to stop Russians trying to desert.

Guard of faithful Russian soldiers drawn across a road to bar the way to deserters.

British officer, assisted by Russian soldiers, giving a deserter a chance to save his honour.

Loyal Russians who, under a British officer with a Lewis gun, stayed the German cavalry.

Captain Gerrard, of the Russian Army, instructing loyal soldiers as to positions in the retreat.

Medley of Russian horse and foot thronging the roads during the great retreat in Galicia.

Flight of a Russian regiment from its position on receiving tidings of a German onslaught.

it to be let down ? It was announced that the patronage system was to end. Government contracts were to be given out in future on purely business lines. People who were profiteering out of the war were dealt with. Nominees for Government posts were to be chosen by Civil Service Commissions, and not selected by favour. But the one issue emphasised in every speech was this : " Are we going to let down our boys at the front ? "

Sir Wilfrid Laurier protested against the assumption that he was not in favour of winning the war. " I want to win this war. I appeal to everyone to rise up and do their duty." But he wanted to win by voluntaryism and not by compulsion. The Province of Quebec had not, he admitted, done her part in the war as fully as the English-speaking provinces, but he would persuade, not compel her people. The Laurier party attempted to raise the cry of corruption. Some of their spokesmen fought as though the election were being conducted along the old party lines of twenty years ago. They did not realise that a new spirit and a new temper had come over Canada.

In the closing days of the election the friends of the Union Government anticipated a majority of forty. But day by day, as the issue became more and more defined, the prospects of the Union Party rose. The soldiers in Europe voted first. Fully ninety per cent. of them declared for the Union Government and conscription. It soon became clear, as the returns of the voting came to hand that, when the whole of the votes could be counted, the total majority of the Government would be not forty but about seventy. The West, the stronghold of Liberalism, went almost solidly for the Union, and Canada generally showed that for it in this struggle there was only one issue— the winning of the war. The verdict of the nation was absolutely decisive without the vote of soldiers overseas. The vote was, as was expected, overwhelmingly—almost unanimously—for Union and victory.

The spirit and temper of the nation was proved not alone in the General Election, but in the immense financial efforts made throughout the country. City after city set out to beat all rivals in the amount of its patriotic contributions. Toronto, in particular,
Immense financial claimed to lead the way, and did much
effort put forth to justify its boast in the great Red
Cross campaign, in October, 1917, when it aimed to raise £100,000 for the British Red Cross, and topped its own figure by over sixty per cent.

The campaign was opened at a monster rally at the Massey Hall. Lord Northcliffe, Chairman of the British War Commission in the United States, came specially from New York to launch the effort. At that gathering, one of the most enthusiastic that even Toronto had known, the Mayor announced that the City Council had voted £25,000 for the appeal. There were three days in which to raise the money. On the first day £50,000 was raised. Thereupon the organisers promptly increased the sum they wanted. Thousands of telegraphic appeals were sent out, and bands of canvassers went from house to house. Every factory was visited and practically every person urged to give. The Rotary Club and the Retail Merchants' Association, the women's organisations, the Labour Unions, and the city clerks all worked together.

The close of the campaign was made under the most unfavourable weather conditions, owing to very heavy

RUINS IN THE WAKE OF WAR.

All that remained of a big sugar refinery on the Canadian sector in the Somme area after the enemy had been driven eastward. Nothing was left but rubble-heaps of the building about battered remains of the machinery.

rain, but rain was not enough to damp enthusiasm. By noon of the third day a total of £120,000 had been reached. By that night the figure had reached £167,794. Mr. Hamilton Fyfe, the well-known English journalist, described the closing day as one of the most wonderful in his life. " I have yet to witness more dashing energy put forth on the part of any city or spirit of devotion or spirit of self-sacrifice than that which I have seen among the people of Toronto." Toronto found itself hailed by all parts as the most generous city of the Empire. Other cities throughout Canada ran it very close in the amount of their contributions.

Early in 1917 Canada raised a domestic loan for the war. The amount asked for was $150,000,000 (£30,000,000) ; the actual amount subscribed was $260,000,000 (£52,000,000). In November the Victory Loan was floated. Another $150,000,000 was asked for. An elaborate organisation had been built up to ensure the success of this second effort. Armies of men canvassed the people in every city. Many cities were divided out into districts, and formally enrolled volunteer workers pledged themselves to make so many calls a day, so that every home, every store, every shop, every warehouse, and every factory would be visited in the three weeks which covered the period of the campaign.

An airman flew over Ottawa on the opening day, dropping programmes urging every person to support the loan. In many places the campaign was launched by the hoot of steam-whistles, the ringing of every public bell, and the discharge of guns. City bid against city. The Duke of Devonshire,   **Canada pledged**
the Governor-General, made the first   **to victory**
subscription. Within a few hours it was reported that the Hudson Bay Company had subscribed £200,000. Montreal and Toronto bid against one another day by day. In the end, not only were the $150,000,000 (£30,000,000) raised, but a further $258,000,000 (£51,600,000). The total number of applications throughout the country numbered 707,000. Thus between March and December of one year the people of Canada raised for two National Loans no less than £133,600,000.

" Money talks," it is said. In money as in men, with all she had and all she was, Canada was in the war to the end.

Study of the ex-Emperor Nicholas as it appeared after the Bolshevist pillagers had ransacked it. This room had been occupied by Kerensky, whose bed was behind the screen in the corner.

Room which had formerly been used as a study by the Emperor Alexander II. It was said that the Bolshevist fury was directed against the palace of the Tsars because Kerensky had made it his residence.

The room of the Grand Duchess Tatiana in the Winter Palace at Petrograd after the sacking of the palace by the Bolshevists in November, 1917, when Kerensky surrendered to the forces of anarchy.

Work-room of the Empress Dowager, showing a shell-hole in the wall. The mob carried off much, and slashed and damaged everything in the Palace that it did not see fit to take away.

RUIN WROUGHT BY THE FORCES OF ANARCHY IN THE WINTER PALACE OF THE AUTOCRATS.

GETTING AWAY THE GUNS

ON THE GALICIAN FRONT.

THE COLLAPSE OF RUSSIA.
By H. W. Wilson.

Political Personalities Behind the Russian Revolution : Lenin, Trotsky, and Kerensky—Extremism Rooted in the Anarchical Nature of the Russian Races—Organisation of the Soviets—Russian Army Discipline Destroyed by German Propaganda—Disastrous Results of Fraternisation—The Navy Destroyed as a Fighting Force by Mutiny—Reduction of Output of Munitions—Soviets' Hostility to the Allies—Great General Offensive Prevented by the Collapse of the Russian Army—Russian Staff Attempts an Offensive in Galicia under Brussiloff's Command—Successes at Busk, Koniuchy, Halicz, and Kalusz—Victory Thrown Away by Pacifism and Corruption—Shameful Retreat of the Russian Armies—Gallantry of the British Armoured-Car Section—All Galicia Recovered by the Germans—Extremists Attack Petrograd—Exposure and Flight of Lenin—Results of Kerensky's Jealousy of Korniloff and Kaledin—Germans Capture Riga—Kerensky Denounces and Arrests Korniloff and Proclaims a Republic—Germans Exploit the Soviets' Doctrine of Self-Determination to Dismember Russia and Destroy her Piecemeal—Fall and Flight of Kerensky —Winter Palace Seized and Sacked by the Extremists—Lenin and Trotsky Assume Command—Extremists Triumph Throughout Northern and Central Russia—Spread of Civil War—Extremists Open Negotiations at Brest Litovsk—Ruthless Conduct of the Negotiations by the Germans Culminating in the Humiliating Peace of March 3rd, 1917—Betrayal and Collapse of Russia.

THE story of the Russian Revolution in Chapter CLXXV. (Vol. 9, page 117), was carried down to the close of April, 1917. At that date the conflict between the Extremist and the Moderate Revolutionary parties had already become acute. Energy which should have been exerted against the German invaders of Russia was dissipated in political strife, which grew in intensity until it assumed the character of civil war, and brought the break-up of the Russian Empire into a welter of semi-independent or independent States.

Two personalities were in conflict behind these two parties— Lenin and Kerensky. Lenin, the leader of the Extremists, was a typical product of Russia. He was alleged by his enemies to be a German, named Cedarblum, or Zederbaum, who had substituted himself for the true Lenin on the latter's death in exile, and had stolen his papers. In reality he was a genuine Russian

of forty-seven, whose true name was Vladimir Ulianoff, and who came of a landowning family. His brother was executed for complicity in a plot against the Tsar Alexander III. in 1887. He himself was a Revolutionist by profession, a man of unbalanced ideas, a fanatic of the narrowest type, who would turn the whole world upside down to realise his delusions. An exact parallel to him is perhaps to be found among the French Revolutionists in Anacharsis Cloots, who was equally destitute of humour, and likewise held that " the nations are necessarily evil, but the human race is essentially good," and who also strove to wipe out nationality. Lenin's watchword was destruction, not compromise. His influence had brought the collapse of the earlier Revolutionary movement in 1906, as men tired of the anarchy which his methods involved.

He was accused of acting as the paid agent of Germany, and documents were seized and published by M. Kerensky which

WITH THE BRITISH ARMOURED CARS IN GALICIA.
Commander O. Locker-Lampson, M.P. (on the left), who commanded the British armoured cars on various parts of the Russian front. He was with the Russians at the time of their retreat from Galicia, when his cars performed signal service in delaying the enemy advance.

appeared to convict him of such conduct. In 1918 a whole series of papers passed into the hands of the Allies which proved the man to be in German pay—a mere dupe or traitor. Thus on September 12th, 1917, he was paid £10,350 by his German masters through M. Fersen, of Kronstadt.

In 1914, early in the war, the Germans released him—an extremely significant act—after he had fallen into their hands in the Carpathians. In April, 1917, they allowed him to travel from Switzerland to Russia by the German railway system, and Germans flocked to the stations to see him pass, saying to one another, " There's William's man ; now we shall have value for our money ! " The pallor of Lenin, a certain curious cast in his face, and the overwhelming energy of his methods recalled Robespierre ; but Robespierre was an ardent patriot, a hater of disorder, and an enemy of his country's enemies. Whereas Lenin repudiated patriotism, proclaimed himself in favour of civil war, and behaved precisely as the salaried ally of Germany and the bitter enemy of Russian freedom would have acted.

Lenin's fanatical lieutenant, Trotsky   His right-hand man was equally fanatical, and was also proved by documents to have been in receipt of German pay. Trotsky, whose true name was stated to be Lieber Bronstein, or Braunstein, was a Polish Jew. He had been expelled from Germany, France, Switzerland, and Spain as a dangerous Anarchist. At the outbreak of the Revolution he was in New York, and, attempting to return, was stopped by the British Navy and detained at Halifax, N.S. He was only allowed to proceed on M. Kerensky's invitation, and for this he did not forgive Great Britain. He had accepted completely the teaching of the earlier Russian Anarchist, Bakunin. That is to say, he believed in destroying religion, law, order, property, nationality—the very structure of civilisation—in order that evil, which he identified with inequality, might be annihilated and men might all be equal. He worked frantically, eighteen hours out of the twenty-four. He was accessible to all, and could be seen at the Smolny Institute any day in a room the floor of which was filthy with cigarette-ends and the debris of sunflower seeds (chewed by Russians of the lower class).

In him was little sense of reality and no knowledge of history. His mercilessness, his furious zeal for his fantastic creed, his utter want of scruple, made him an incomparable auxiliary for Lenin.

Character of Alexander Kerensky

M. Kerensky, who in the hour of his fall was the most conspicuous man in Russia, was a lawyer of thirty-six who had distinguished himself in the Duma as an extreme Socialist. He was bitterly criticised by his opponents for his weakness, but it is only fair to say that on rare occasions he ventured to tell the people the truth. " This free Russia," he said to a deputation from the front, " is a State of slaves in revolt." The Conservatives declared that he used his lungs rather than his reason, and existed entirely in an atmosphere of talk. The Leninites accused him of living indolently and luxuriously. Like Danton, whom in certain respects he resembled, his life was spent in alternations between spasms of intense energy and complete apathy. He was not bloodthirsty, though critics severely blamed his treatment of Generals Gourko and Korniloff, but his Government wanted courage and decision. He reasoned with people who could understand no argument but machine-guns. He

M. KERENSKY AT RUSSIAN HEADQUARTERS.
Alexander F. Kerensky, who rose to prominence in the Russian Revolution, and succeeded Prince Lvoff as Prime Minister in July, 1917, was also Minister of War. M. Kerensky (in the centre of the group, wearing a light uniform and with his hand upon his breast) was visiting Headquarters for the purpose of reawakening the spirit of resistance in the Russian troops.

opposed polite Liberalism to wild fanaticism. "The Extremists," said Mr. Henderson, the British Minister, a not unfriendly observer, in July, 1917, "have succeeded in making good government in Russia impossible." M. Kerensky, in fact, looked on and left problems to settle themselves. At the most critical moment in Russian history he made speeches and drifted.

One of the reasons why the Extremists steadily gained strength and why anarchy increased was to be found in

A COSSACK COMMANDER.

General Korniloff, who took command of the Russian Army under Kerensky in 1917, was a Cossack of humble birth. In September, 1917, he was marching on Petrograd against Kerensky's Government, but his forces melted away and he surrendered.

the Russian character. The old Byzantine writers a thousand years before had described the races of Russia as above all others "anarchical." Russia's typical product, the gospel of Tolstoy, might have prepared the world for this upheaval, with its unbalanced talk and reversion to barbarism. That gospel rested upon a peculiarly literal interpretation of the Bible, and taught acquiescence in evil by not resisting it ; the surrender of justice by not enforcing it ; the abolition of property, which was condemned as an un-Christian institution ; the destruction of nationality, and the annihilation of the family, as two influences which came between man and his Maker. So Rousseau in France had appeared before the Revolution as the symptom but not the cause of a great change in thought, and had produced similar effects to Tolstoy. The doctrine of either lent

Tolstoy's legacy to Russia itself to perversion in the mouths of fanatics and fools, and what Napoleon said of Rousseau, "it would have been better for France had he not been born," a Russian might have echoed about Tolstoy.

Behind Lenin—generally, though not always—was the Soviet of Petrograd (or Council of Workmen's and Soldiers' Delegates), with similar bodies throughout Russia. The Soviets were well organised, and controlled a force, the Red Guard, a mob of armed workmen, soldiers, and peasants, which could usually be trusted to fight for them. The secret of Russian politics in the eight months before the Leninites openly seized power lay in this : that the so-called Governments were mere shadows with no trustworthy fighting force at their command. They meant well, but were unable to realise their excellent intentions. Thus the nominal Russian Government and the real centre

of authority were apart as the poles. The nominal Government under M. Kerensky for the most part tried to maintain order at home and favoured the prosecution of the war, though it openly declared that peace must soon be concluded. The real authority in the Soviet favoured immediate peace and "class war" at home, and was dominated by men of German names on the German salary-list. The nominal Government on the whole represented the educated class and the heads of industry, wherefore it was nicknamed "bourgeois." The real authority represented the proletariat—the workers, soldiers, and peasants, who knew little of what was at stake, and sought the satisfaction of their immediate desires. The community was divided on class lines into two peoples, of which the proletariat was determined **Origin of the Soviet** to extinguish the other, and this other people, the "bourgeoisie," scarcely troubled to resist. Its fate, like that of the Huguenots in the France of Louis XIV., was either to be extirpated or to take refuge abroad, depriving Russia of its knowledge, business capacity, and leadership.

The origin of the Soviet has been described in Chapter

M. KERENSKY AND GENERAL ALEXEIEFF.

Revolutionary Russia's Prime Minister, M. Kerensky (right), arriving on a visit to the Russian Army Headquarters. In September, 1917, Kerensky placed himself temporarily at the head of the Army, and appointed General Alexeieff his Chief of Staff.

CLXXV. (Vol. 9, page 117). Its executive of eighteen members included no one who worked with his hands, and no soldier, but only lawyers, doctrinaires, journalists, and talkers, several of them accused of being in German pay. The majority of its members were probably well-meaning, but, as in the case of the French Revolution, power rapidly passed into the hands of a very small number of violent extremists, fanatics, or criminals. Taine estimated the number of Jacobins during the Terror in France at five thousand ; the true supporters of Lenin in Russia were probably not more numerous. They exercised an authority far beyond their numbers, and were always for desperate courses.

ARMY DELEGATES AT THE DUMA.
Delegates to the Workmen's and Soldiers' Council holding a meeting in the Duma, whence they issued a stirring appeal to their comrades at the front to fight for liberty.

Throughout May and early June, 1917, the Russian Army continued in a state of ferment, incapable of undertaking serious military operations. Its discipline had been destroyed, and with the destruction of discipline the disloyal elements in the Army became supreme. The Russian soldier earlier in the war had shown himself to be brave, patient, and enduring. He was, however, credulous and ready to believe any story that he was told, and he was wretchedly educated. No one fell a readier prey to catch-phrases. The Germans, from aeroplanes and from emissaries moving between the lines, showered proclamations upon him. They did this because even before the Revolution they had observed how weak was discipline in the Russian armies. These proclamations were printed in Russian, and were read by the clever soldiers to their comrades. Some of them declared that the Tsar was the victim of British treachery, and that Great Britain was forcing them to fight for her and lending Russia money at exorbitant interest, while she was shirking the battle herself. Others told the Russians that Germany, by causing the war, had caused the Revolution, and that therefore the Russian Army ought to be grateful to her, and to cease fighting now that freedom was won. No one appears to have noted that these two sets of German documents contradicted one another.

German craft v. Russian credulity

Between the lines fraternisation began, encouraged by the "Pravda," the organ of the Extremists. Despite a general order issued by the Russian Commander-in-Chief on June 6th, the Russian officers were unable to stop it. The Germans were able to examine the Russian positions; on one occasion, at Baranovitch, they found out where the reserves were stationed and the ammunition dumps

were placed, and then suddenly opened fire, killing or wounding seventy-nine Russians. At another part of the front the Russians received a number of cylinders of gas. They thought it too cruel, and did not use the gas. A couple of days later the Germans showed their appreciation of this tenderness by furiously bombarding the Russian trenches with gas-shells, which claimed many victims.

The German aim was gradually to deprive Russia of her leaders—by compelling them to choose between death and emigration—and to leave her only with peasants and workers who could easily be enslaved. For that reason German agents incited the Russian soldiers to mutiny and kill their officers, who were subject to daily insults and outrage. The greater the officer's capacity, the greater his danger, because the Germans paid head-money for the murder of the most distinguished. General Nogin was shot dead to gain a reward of £1,500. When an attack was attempted, the officers led "over the **Murder of Russian officers** top," and had to fear shots from behind as well as from the enemy in front. Behind the lines they were no safer, for there all pretence of discipline ceased. At Helsingfors, remote from the war, the troops seized forty officers in September. Some they imprisoned, others they took out and killed as angry children kill flies. Generals Vasilieff and Ornoffsky, Colonel Karenius, and seven others of equal rank they dragged to a bridge, flung them into a river, and fired at them as they swam. When Colonel Karenius tried to climb out, they beat in his head with a crowbar. They beheaded another officer in the act of eating his dinner before his family. They chased into the forest and lynched Colonel Djunin, a very gallant Cossack officer. Outrages on the officers at the front only ceased for a short time when the troops were warned that mutineers and assassins would be summarily punished. The artillery and Cossacks

HOLDING CONVERSE WITH THE ENEMY.
Russian soldiers talking to an enemy officer in the German lines on their front. Before the final débâcle, even where the Russians did not exactly fraternise with the foe, many such informal meetings took place.

showed a better spirit than the infantry, and the Russian gunners had often to be protected by wire from their own comrades.

The Navy had already ceased to exist as a fighting force. In May, Admiral Kolchak declared that "the old system of discipline had passed away; confusion and mistrust reigned in its stead." The Revolution was from the first more bloody on sea than on the land. The Extremists, led by a handful of criminals and incited by German agents, took possession of the smaller warships in the Baltic and stirred up a great mutiny. Three of the ablest Russian admirals — Viren, regarded by many as the Russian Nelson, Nepenin, and Nebolsin — were burned at the stake or thrust through holes in the ice and left to freeze slowly to death. Captains and lieutenants were hung up and used as living targets, or were placed in the ice till their clothing froze, and were then hauled to the yard-arms and dropped on the ice. In one case an officer was sawn in two. The widows and orphans of the leaders who thus perished were brutally treated. Wives were constrained to witness the assassination of their husbands. Others saw the bodies of the men whom they had loved torn in pieces or trampled into the snow by a drunken mob. The men, when questioned by English eye-witnesses of these infamous deeds, could give no reason or explanation, but a number of seamen at Helsingfors were observed to have obtained new sources of income—presumably from the German Secret Service funds.

In the Black Sea Fleet a great mutiny broke out in June, but at first was not of a murderous character, as the officers withdrew. In January, 1918, however, there was a wholesale massacre, in which four admirals and more than sixty other officers perished. In the Baltic some were spared. Two hundred were imprisoned at Kronstadt, and fed every other day on bread and water **Mutiny in** by the committees, which explained **the Navy** that officers might be required if the Germans attacked. A few were forcibly released by loyal crews. Others were from time to time murdered. In September, 1917, a savage massacre took place. The crew of the Dreadnought Petropavlovsk killed four lieutenants with deliberate cruelty. Other officers vanished without any further information. Thus the commander of a destroyer which fought with great gallantry in the Gulf of Riga had disappeared when his vessel returned to port. He was not seen to have been killed in the action, but either threw himself overboard

RUSSIAN SOLDIERS IN THE REVOLUTION.
Men of the Russian Army discussing the new state of affairs. When the Revolutionary spirit spread among the soldiers, the loosening of the bonds of discipline was seen to have disastrous effects. In the upper photograph the Revolutionary leader, Boris Georgevitch, is seen addressing his comrades in an attempt to revive in them a spirit of defensive patriotism.

in despair or was stealthily killed by his men. The German were given command of the Baltic without striking a blow, and the operation of the British submarines there were deprived of support.

Both Army and Navy fast melted away, and the dissolution was only delayed by difficulties of transport. Whole regiments deserted when they could, deciding that they had had enough of the war. They returned to their villages or crowded into the towns, where they demanded work and also insisted on drawing their Army pay. A report that a decree had been issued dividing up the land was one of the chief causes of this disintegration of the Russian armies. Even the good and patriotic men were affected; they wanted to be in their own villages to get their fair share of the land. The appearance of masses of undisciplined armed men behind the lines led to constant riots and disturbances.

As the Army dwindled—though it still mustered enormous masses of men, since the old régime had mobilised ten million fighters—so also the output of munitions declined. The works were controlled by committees, and the usual hours were six a day, while work was not done on more than three or four days a week. The munition workers incessantly went on strike and insisted on being paid for the time during which they were striking. They demanded gigantic increases of wages, and at the same time did far less work. In August, according to General Korniloff, the production of shells had fallen by 60 per cent., and that of aeroplanes by 80 per cent. In one typical factory by July the output weekly had fallen from 100 tons to 7½ tons, and three days' rest a week was taken.

In September the immense works at Sormovo, near Nijni Novgorod, closed for want of materials. The frequent fires in munition works were another result of German handiwork, and still further reduced the output. Other industries were affected in an even greater degree. Gradually the businesses and factories in Russia came to a standstill. Employers, unable to pay the enormous wages demanded or to obtain the raw material they required, closed down. By September it was becoming as difficult to buy manufactured goods, even such necessary articles as nails and horseshoes, as it was to purchase bread. Clothes were unprocurable.

So early as May, 1917, the Soviet, under the sway of pacifists and grossly misled by the artful German propaganda, showed distinct hostility to the Allies. With credulous optimism it persuaded itself that the Germans were thirsting for peace, and that the war was being prolonged by the British and French Governments for selfish purposes. Of the British and French sacrifices for freedom, of the holocaust of British dead offered up at the Dardanelles for Russia, it seems to have known nothing. It protested against a Note which Prince Lvoff, the Premier, had prepared, asserting the determination of the Russian people never to conclude a separate peace, but to observe Russia's treaties with the Allies. It repudiated Russia's plighted word in these "scraps of paper," as if to show that extreme democracy can be as treacherous as any tyranny. It forced on the Ministry a statement of policy which contained in modified terms its own formula of "peace without annexations and indemnities." In June its organ, "Isvestia," openly attacked Great Britain and France as "Imperialistic nations." While it more and more absorbed authority, the lawful elected Russian Assembly, the Duma, fell into the background. No one paid any attention to it, because it was suspected of moderation and anxiety to continue the war. The one important aim in the eyes of the extremer Revolutionists was to have done with the war so as to obtain leisure for prosecuting the Revolution and

Animus against the Allies

debating about it. The terrible fact that vast German armies were encamped on Russian soil within a few hundred miles of Petrograd was disregarded by these visionaries.

The "All-Russian Congress of Soviets" met in Petrograd on June 16th, but those who looked to it were disappointed. It took no measures to prosecute the war vigorously, but seemed to be living in dreamland. It pressed the Allies to meet neutrals and Germans in a great Socialist Conference which it proposed to convene at Stockholm, and despatched emissaries to Great Britain, France, and Italy to preach Revolutionary doctrine. The demand for this conference was supported by extreme Socialists among the Allies who were inclined to forget that logic does not convince men in whom there is not a good disposition.

Great general offensive blocked

The Soviets could not be persuaded to take measures for the restoration of discipline in the Army, and thus the elaborate plans which the Allied War Council had prepared in November, 1916, for a great general

offensive, could not be executed. M. Kerensky, the minister of War, made some lukewarm and half-hearted efforts to re-establish order. But when he issued comparatively mild instructions, instituting penalties for desertion and dereliction of duty, he was freely denounced by Lenin and ill-supported by his own followers. M. Tseretelli, one of the most patriotic and enlightened of the Revolutionists, warned the Soviets that inactivity on the Russian front, far from consolidating the Revolution, was imperilling it; but he spoke to deaf ears. The only response to these appeals was the organisation of a battalion of women soldiers by women. They issued a stirring manifesto. "The Germans," they said, "whether in soldier's uniform or in workman's shirt, are all alike fighting for their country and not talking about Socialistic paradises.

BOLSHEVIST DEMONSTRATION IN PETROGRAD.

Gathering of Bolshevists—soldiers and civilians—in the streets of Petrograd at the time when Kerensky was away on the Galician front and the Korniloff rising threatened his Government. In circle : A captain of the 56th Russian Regiment addressing a gathering of Kronstadt soldiers in July, 1917.

or strangling industry and commerce by exorbitant demands." They wasted their breath. The response to their call was by no means enthusiastic. Many women of the upper class came forward, but the men were not to be shamed by their reproaches. The Revolutionists continued their talk of peace, and though a few "Battalions of Death" were formed of male volunteers for desperate undertakings, they were mainly composed of officers from units where the men had mutinied or deserted.

None the less, in mid-June the Russian Staff decided to attempt a great offensive in order to keep faith with the Allies, and M. Kerensky left for the front to

AT THE BOLSHEVIST HEADQUARTERS.
Machine-gun protected entrance to the Smolny Institute, at which the Bolshevists established their headquarters. On duty were members of the Red Guard and of the Petrograd garrison.

GUARDING THE BOLSHEVIST LEADER.
Doorway leading to the room in which Lenin transacted his business during the period of his disastrous usurpation of power. The posting of armed guards outside ensured him against any unwelcome intruders.

address the troops and appeal to their committees, some of which were showing excellent spirit. The original intention had been to attack all along the front, but the troops in some of the army groups were too much demoralised to look for anything from them. It was therefore determined to open the offensive in Galicia by a great movement of the south-western army group threatening Lemberg, and then to attack in the Russian centre opposite Vilna, while finally the Rumanian Army was to strike in. The condition of the Russian armies in Galicia **Offensive organised** was rather better than on other portions **in Galicia** of the front. There were three concerned in the intending operations, which were to be carried out by General Gutor, under the supreme command of General Brussiloff—namely, the Eleventh under General Erdeli, north-west of Tarnopol; the Seventh under General Belkovitch, south-west of Tarnopol; and the Eighth under General Korniloff, before Stanislau. The Second Army was to cover the left flank of the Eighth in the direction of Kolomea and Nadworna. Owing to delay in the transport of artillery and munitions, the three armies which were to deliver the main blow could not act simultaneously. On June 29th, after M. Kerensky and

the commissaries had made fiery speeches to the men and entreated them to fight for the Revolution and peace, the artillery preparation opened on a front of about thirty miles from Busk to Koniuchy.

The country was most difficult for operations, intersected by numerous parallel streams, flowing generally in deep ravines, with wooded banks and strongly fortified forests. The hostile troops opposed to General Gutor's attack were mainly Austro-Hungarians and Turks, but there were five German divisions on this section of the front. The Germans must have known of the Russian intentions. The secret of the im- **Russian troops** pending attack cannot but have leaked **take Koniuchy** out in the fraternisations. Moreover, the German Staff had a perfect spy service, good sources of information in Petrograd, the reports of the airmen who constantly patrolled behind the Russian lines, and also the disclosures made by deserters, who revealed what they knew of General Gutor's plans. But even if the Germans were on their guard, the Russians had a great superiority in men and materials, as they opposed fifty-four divisions (about 750,000 men) to thirty German, Austrian, and Turkish divisions (under 400,000 men).

The German trenches were rapidly reduced to a series of shell-craters, and on July 1st the Russian infantrymen assaulted. Up to the last minute it was always uncertain whether they would advance. M. Kerensky had to expose his own life on one occasion to induce a regiment to "go over the top," and ten divisions, or some 140,000 men, refused to take any part in the fighting. The Russians made great progress south of Zboroff. They fought their way into the squalid little village of Koniuchy, pushing before them Saxon, Rhenish, and Turkish troops, and making numerous prisoners—8,564 in all. They took three lines of trenches and advanced well beyond the village, but then found themselves confronted by the German positions east of the Zlota Lipa, which were of great strength. South of Koniuchy, at the important junction of Brzezany, the Germans generally held their own, though the Russians made some slight progress.

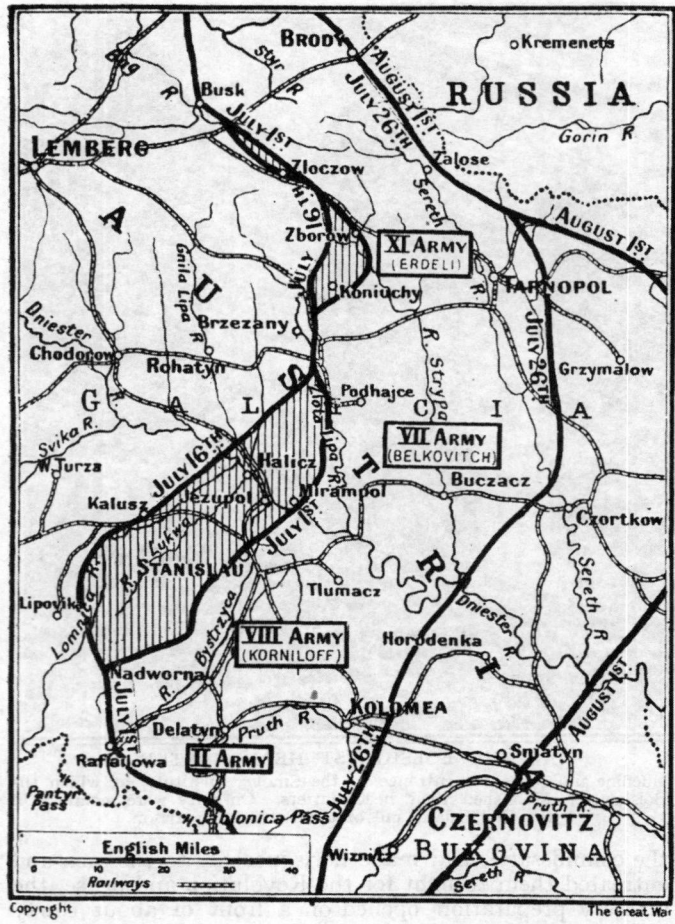

RUSSIA'S LAST OFFENSIVE AND ITS SEQUEL.
On June 29th, 1917, General Brussiloff opened an offensive in Galicia between Busk and Rafailowa. The shaded portion shows the extent of the advance to Kalusz. There discipline was destroyed by pacifist poison, and the armies retreated during the following fortnight, as shown above.

The fortified woods in this direction greatly impeded their advance, and one of the Russian divisions at a most critical moment refused to move, pretending that it had not consented to attack on that day. The Russian infantry suffered considerably as the result of this act of cowardice or bad faith, but very heavy loss was inflicted on the Austrians and Germans, and brilliant work was done by the British armoured cars which were supporting the Russians. The main positions at Brzezany were not taken.

On July 2nd, after a violent bombardment of the German positions near Zboroff, the 4th Finnish Division and a Czech-Slovak brigade, recruited from Austrian prisoners, assaulted with splendid spirit, **Swaying battles** to widen the gap that had been made on **for Brzezany** the previous day and turn Brzezany. The German entrenchments were carried at the point of the bayonet—three lines in succession—and 6,300 prisoners and twenty-one guns were captured. The same day further attacks were made at Brzezany itself, but without any serious change, and the moral of the Russian troops began to show signs of failing. The Guards in particular refused to obey orders, and other units declined to remain longer than a day in the advanced line or to act on the offensive. M. Kerensky addressed his speeches to the recreants, but without much effect, as other emissaries ridiculed him and were received with frantic applause. In the end one regiment of Guards had to be surrounded by artillery and cavalry, and was then compelled to surrender an Extremist agitator who had caused most of the mischief, and was shortly afterwards acquitted " with honour " by a court of Extremists. Several days were

lost in consequence of this mutiny, and the German Staff was allowed to recover from its first alarm and to bring up reinforcements.

On July 6th the effort to turn Brzezany was resumed by attacking near Zloczow, a small place on the railway from Tarnopol to Lemberg. The assault took place in the early morning after a violent bombardment ; three lines of trenches were stormed, but then the Germans hurried up reserves and flung the Russians back after a fierce struggle. German aeroplanes attacked the Russian infantry as it retired, and poured machine-gun fire into it. About Koniuchy there was also furious fighting. After a swaying encounter, which lasted most of the day, the Russians made some small gains. Near Busk the Germans attempted a great counter-attack supported by armed motor-cars, but this was repulsed.

That same day General Korniloff began to move in on the other flank of the German front, near Stanislau, with great spirit. On July 8th he pressed this advance, assaulting the German positions west and south-west of Stanislau, and about noon fought his way through the outer German position, driving the Germans helter-skelter before him, taking Jezupol, and pursuing them for eight miles to the little River Lukwa. In this brilliantly conducted engagement 7,131 prisoners, twelve heavy, and thirty-six light guns were taken by the Russians. On the 9th the Eighth Army continued its onslaught, but met with an increasing degree of resistance as Halicz was approached. The Austro-Germans were gradually forced back in a series of street fights through the villages, so that at nightfall the Russians had **Halicz and** penetrated into the hostile position to a **Kalusz taken** maximum depth of seven miles and had taken 1,000 prisoners. On the 10th they entered Halicz, capturing 2,000 prisoners and thirty guns, with immense quantities of munitions and stores, and they crossed the Dniester. On the 11th the Russians carried Kalusz after a stubborn and protracted engagement, but there the moral of the troops gave way. They pillaged the town, drank all the liquor they could obtain, and rioted madly. About the place fighting continued spasmodically for four days. The Russians were greatly hampered by violent rains which swelled the rivers and rendered the position of the troops at Kalusz critical.

This was the high-water mark of the Russian offensive. By July 15th, 834 German and Austrian officers, 35,809 men, 93 guns, 28 trench-mortars, 403 machine-guns, and a large quantity of war material of other kinds had been taken. The German line had been sharply pressed back and a dangerous angle in it created near Brzezany. The Russians had turned the difficult country north of Halicz where German fortified line succeeded fortified line. In Germany and Austria great reliance had been placed on Lenin's ability to paralyse the Russian armies, and their successes created something bordering on panic, because the Russians now menaced Lemberg and even Hungary. The evacuation of Lemberg and Cracow began. But at this moment, one of the most fateful in the whole war, pacifist poison began to work. Russian troops here and there retired from their positions without orders. They had beaten the Germans in fair fight ; they were now to be beaten by the Germans through treachery. An honourable and glorious peace was within their grasp at this crisis when the British and French were attacking violently and successfully on other fronts ; and they threw everything away. On July 16th the Russian reserves refused to go forward and check a German turning movement against Kalusz. General Korniloff had to let go of his prize, as a regiment deserted its positions, allowing the Germans to penetrate the front.

The German Staff had made all its arrangements with the Extremists in Petrograd. They were to seize the Government there while the German forces routed the Russian Army with the aid of pacifists and of bribery.

On July 18th a German demonstration was made on the line between Tarnopol and Busk, which runs through a rich corn-growing country. The obvious intention was to divert reinforcements from Halicz and Kalusz, which were being attacked. Tarnopol was the point on which the railway system of Eastern Galicia centred, and from it the Russians drew their munitions and food. The Russians at first resisted well, but then the poison began to take effect. The reserves discussed the question whether they should go forward, and finally **Eleventh Russian Army collapses** decided to disobey orders. The men at the front, being badly supported, gave way. A whole regiment marched off, near Zborow, opening a gap in the Russian line. Next, the 6th Grenadier Division deserted en masse, and fled yelling in panic over the country or surrendered to the Germans. At this most critical juncture General Brussiloff removed General Gutor from command of the army group, and replaced him by General Korniloff, whose energy and success in the offensive had been great. He had to hand over the command of the Eighth Army to General Tcheremisoff, and to go for that purpose to Stanislau, leaving the danger-point at Zborow.

The greater part of the Eleventh Russian Army was now in flight, racing for Tarnopol before a moderate German force. Its strength was quite three to one, and with troops of average quality or any loyalty there should have been no danger except to the Germans. Indeed, the Germans never dreamed of such success; and when they had won it they seemed afraid to use it to the utmost. They might have captured some 200,000 men with a vast material had they advanced rapidly, for there was nothing to stop them. Russian troops, ordered to close the gap and to cut off the German force which had pushed through it, instead of marching, held meetings and voted as to whether they should march. The command had passed from the officers to traitors and fools. To cut a miserable story short, on the 21st the Germans reached the outskirts of Tarnopol, where fighting with the Russian artillery and Cossacks began. The rest of the Russian troops for the most part walked or galloped off. The infantrymen even attacked their own guns and seized the horses, cutting the traces and bolting.

The situation was becoming so serious that on the 22nd the Russian group of armies near Vilna was ordered to attack, despite the indiscipline it showed. Some feeble assaults were delivered on that and on the following day, but they collapsed at once, because though the officers gallantly led "over the top" the men did not follow. The Germans were free to exploit their victory, yet they still advancd with the extremest caution.

A few Russian units, supported by the British armoured motor-cars, behaved with extraordinary gallantry, covering the shameful flight of their comrades. The famous British airman, Lieut.-Colonel J. Valentine, was also prominent in efforts to stop the rout, acting in concert with Commander O. Locker-Lampson, who worked brilliantly in command of the British cars. On the evening of the 21st the German heavy artillery began the bombardment of Tarnopol, while in that town prevailed " unimaginable panic," as a Russian witness telegraphed. Two treacherous regiments were surrounded by artillery and Cossacks and ordered to surrender their Leninite leaders and lay down their arms.

After a hundred rounds had been fired into them they obeyed. " Our troops," the Russian Headquarters reported, " have shown complete disobedience to their commanders." Marauders and deserters plundered Tarnopol under the German shells, and set it on fire in several places. The rot had spread from the Eleventh Army to the other armies.

Besides the Grenadier Division, which had behaved so miserably, the 113th, 153rd, and 74th Infantry Divisions deserted en masse. On July 24th the Kaiser, the Austrian Emperor, and Field-Marshal Mackensen made a pompous entry into Tarnopol, which was still aflame and showing pitiful traces of the utter Russian collapse. Stanislau had to be abandoned on July 25th, and Kolomea a day or two later. Most of the Russian material was withdrawn, except near Tarnopol, where the Germans captured great deal of booty, including heavy guns of large calibre made in England, France, and the United States, trucks, locomotives, motor-cars armoured and unarmoured, motor-lorries, ammunition, fodder, and food. Thousands of men gave themselves up, voluntarily for the most part, to the Germans. By the 30th the rout had been stayed as the result of General Korniloff's vigorous measures; and had he been energetically supported, discipline might have been restored and Russia saved from bitter agony. On August 3rd the Germans re-entered Czernovitz. All Galicia, except a narrow strip along the frontier near Brody, and all the Bukovina, had been reconquered after a campaign of a fortnight, in which 22,000 Russians had surrendered and 200 Russian guns had been taken, with but little fighting, though the German reports painted absurd pictures **Germans recover all Galicia** of a desperate resistance on the part of the Russians. The British motor-cars were continually in action with the enemy, and lost heavily, earning General Korniloff's special thanks for their fine conduct, but some of their casualties were caused by Russian infantry who tried to fight their way into the cars.

General Korniloff, as the only means of preventing the criminal element in the Army from completely destroying it, during the rout issued orders to his subordinates to use

THE EX-TSAR NICHOLAS II. AT TSARSKOYE SELO.
Nicholas II., as prisoner of the Revolutionary forces, was at first kept guarded at his palace at Tsarskoye Selo, fifteen miles from Petrograd, where he pathetically remarked : " I am hardly less free now than formerly; for have I not been a prisoner all my life ! "

artillery and machine-guns without hesitation against troops which wilfully deserted their positions, and demanded from Petrograd the restoration of the death penalty. This was formally restored by a Government Army Order on July 25th, though only at the front, and it was to be inflicted even then solely by a court constituted of three officers and three soldiers, chosen by lot. Finally General Korniloff was appointed Commander-in-Chief on General Brussiloff's resignation. The Government received no support from the Extremists or even from the Soviet in its disciplinary measures. The Extre-

Korniloff appointed Commander-in-Chief mists attacked it for restoring the death penalty, and it would go no farther than to issue a spirited proclamation calling on the troops to do their duty, and threatening that " towards cowards and traitors no mercy will be shown." For his part, M. Kerensky suppressed two pro-German newspapers which had been circulated in the trenches by the Leninites, " Justice," and " Justice in the Trenches," but as against this he refused to sign any death warrants, so that the death penalty remained largely inoperative, except where officers ventured to take matters into their own hands at the risk of their lives.

The Government at Petrograd, in the meanwhile, had been fighting for its life. The Leninites, who had planned an attack on the city, carried it out in the midst of a political crisis. On July 15th all the Conservative members of the Ministry had resigned, dissatisfied

ONE OF THE RUSSIAN DREADNOUGHTS UNDER STEAM.
The Poltava, seen in the above photograph, was one of four sister ships that were the special pride of the Russian Navy before the débâcle.

with M. Kerensky because he had too hastily granted self-government to the Ukraine—the vast corn-growing area in Southern Russia between Moscow and the Black Sea. The Extremists intended to seize the Government and to open peace negotiations exactly as they did in November. The garrison was to rise and the fleet to act. The conspirators had even arranged to arrest M. Kerensky, and but for an accident they might have got him into their hands. He at once denounced them as guilty of conspiring with Germany, though he had no force he could trust except a mere handful of Cossacks. On July 16th disturbances began. The Extremists ranged the city in motor-cars with machine-guns, and at first it appeared as though the garrison would support them. But the ships of the Baltic Fleet, which were to have arrived to aid them, were delayed. M. Kerensky had sent orders to Admiral

Verdervsky, who commanded that fleet under the committees, to sink with submarines any vessel that attempted to leave Helsingfors for Cronstadt or Petrograd. The message was intercepted by the Extremist committees, and the admiral was prevented from carrying out the orders. A certain amount of time, however, was lost in discussions by the plotters, and that fact probably saved M. Kerensky. On the 17th three or four thousand armed seamen and workmen arrived from Cronstadt in steamers and tugs, but they came too late to strike the intended blow, and found that the Cossacks had been reinforced with troops loyal to the Kerensky Government.

An apathetic street fight took place in which a number of men on either side were killed or wounded, and after it the seamen re-embarked and the mob dispersed. The Cossacks cleared out the Villa Kshesinkaya, which had been seized by the Leninites and made it their headquarters, but failed to capture Lenin himself. He bolted in disguise, while his friends, Trotsky-Braunstein and Stekloff-Nakhamkes disappeared with him. The mutiny collapsed. The casualties were reported to have been sixty Cossacks and five hundred Extremists killed or wounded, but, according to some eye-witnesses, they were really much heavier.

Admiral Verdervsky was removed and Captain Razvoroff appointed to command a fleet which only obeyed him at rare intervals. Such was the anarchy and such the cowardice and feebleness of the Government that Lenin and his friends found it easy to elude arrest. Lenin himself seems to have gone to Sweden or Germany to consult German agents and to work out a new plan of campaign. A committee was appointed by the Soviet to investigate the charges against him, on which served a number of persons with curiously German names—MM. Gotz, Handelmann, Lieber, Dahn, and Krochmal. It subsequently exonerated him completely. On August 5th **Charges against Lenin published** M. Kerensky published the charges against him, which were of the gravest character—conducting a propaganda with money paid by Germany to hamper military operations, organising an armed rising at Petrograd, and inciting units at the front to disobey. A correspondence between Lenin and a lawyer, Kozlovsky, was also printed, which showed that funds from an unknown

AN IMMENSE RUSSIAN SUBMARINE THAT WAS SUNK.
The Russian Navy, until the rot of Bolshevism paralysed it, had been making rapid progress in the matter of submarines, and this photograph shows the submarine Bars, one of the latest construction, with its torpedoes carried on the deck. This submarine was lost with its officers and crew.

source had been paid to Lenin through this man. A receipt for two hundred pounds signed by Lenin and a letter from him asking for additional payments were reproduced. Koslovsky was said to have £200,000 standing in a Russian bank to his credit, which had been sent him from Germany; it was stated that the well-known German financier, Warburg, was in hiding in a neutral embassy at Petrograd, together with Captain **German support** Boy-Ed, who had made the United States **of the Extremists** too hot for himself. These two financed the Extremist movement and paid the Soviet newspapers and "Red Guard" as they had tried to finance the Anarchists of the Industrial Workers of the World in the United States.

On July 20th, after tedious negotiations, M. Kerensky succeeded Prince Lvoff as Prime Minister with promises of support from all parties. He retained the office of Minister of War and of the Navy, and his Minister of

THE DRY-DOCKS AT REVAL.
The accommodation for naval repairs at Reval is very great, that port being in every sense of the word the Portsmouth of the Baltic. This photograph gives a glimpse of the great dry-docks, with two submarines in process of repairing.

Agriculture was M. Tchernoff, whose proposals for dividing up the land were exceedingly popular with the peasants, but were regarded by Russian Moderates as dangerous to Russian finance and unjust. M. Kerensky had immediate difficulties with various parts of Russia which were endeavouring to secede. He dissolved the Finnish Diet, sent Cossacks to Helsingfors, where there had been serious rioting, and attempted to bridle the Rada, or Council, of the Ukraine, which was demanding virtual independence. He arrested General Gourko and a number of other officers on the pretext that they were engaged

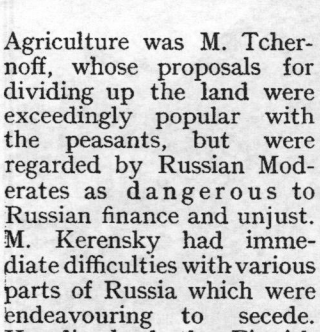

GENERAL VIEW OF REVAL AND THE NAVAL MEMORIAL.
The lower photograph illustrates a famous monument at Reval, where it was the custom to lay a wreath in memory of the crews and officers lost in the Russian submarines. This scene shows the ceremony which took place in connection with the loss of the submarine Bars.

in a reactionary conspiracy, and General Gourko was fortunate in escaping to England. He sent the hapless Tsar to Tobolsk, but there his life was probably safer than it was near Petrograd, and the peasants showed singular respect to him when the train passed. The Soviet's demand for a Socialist Conference at Stockholm to make peace was supported by M. Kerensky. He gave General Korniloff very inadequate backing in his two main demands —for the restoration of the death penalty in the Army at the rear as well as at the front, and for the abolition of the soldiers' committees. All the general's protests and remonstrances were wasted; he pointed out that the drafts arriving were untrained because of the want of discipline at the rear, and that the troops at the front, among whom a semblance of order had been restored, were re-infected by them. A gulf began to open between General Korniloff and M. Kerensky.

The Russian Army had never been so well equipped, if discipline could have been restored. Though after the collapse in Galicia eighty German and forty Austrian, Bulgarian, and Turkish divisions still remained on the eastern front, these troops were the lees of the German Army—composed of the older men and of units which

LAUNCHING A NEW RUSSIAN SUBMARINE FROM THE NAVY YARDS AT REVAL.
Submarine building activity was steadily developing, and indeed had reached its highest pitch when the Revolution broke out. At Reval the accommodation for launching was probably the finest at any navy yard in the world, as it was possible to launch as many as six submarines in one day. In the above scene the submarine Turc has just taken the water, her crew on deck and a large gathering of spectators by the quay.

showed little fighting spirit. The Russian Army was abundantly supplied with material and munitions. Never, said a secret report by General Denikine, had it possessed such a superiority in material and men. The proportion of machine-guns at the front had risen from one or two per battalion (which was also the British figure in 1914) to thirty-two. No longer had the artillery to be placed on an allowance of only four shells per gun per day, as was the case with the British batteries in the First Battle of Ypres and with Russian batteries early in 1915 before Warsaw. The doors into Prussia and Hungary could have been opened at any time in 1917 with a vigorous push. Never had the efforts made by Great Britain, the United States, and Japan to munition and assist

BOLSHEVISTS AT WORK CORRUPTING THE RUSSIAN NAVY.
Scene alongside the cruiser Dwina at Reval while a demonstration of Bolshevists had come to the boatside to urge the crew to rebel against the Government of the Tsar.

works of Southern Russia for steel and iron to make munitions, the rails and loco-motives to replace destruc-tion caused by the enemy and make good wear, could not be provided. Able Canadian and American engineers were sent to advise and assist the Russians, but they were paralysed by the Revolution. In August the Russian Minister of Com-merce admitted that 25 per cent. of the locomotives and 18 per cent. of the waggons had failed, though it was currently reported that the failures were more like 80 per cent. of both. The shortage was complicated by the action of the engine-drivers, who declined to take trains farther than fifty - five miles without relief, reducing the distance covered monthly by locomo-tives from 3,500 miles to 1,900. At the same time a

LOWERING THE IMPERIAL ENSIGN AND RUNNING UP THE REVOLUTIONARY FLAG.
These historic photographs continue the story of the Dwina, and show the crew, after deciding for the Revolution, pulling down the flag of the Imperial Navy and hoisting the red flag of the nebulous anarchical Republic which took the place of the Government of the Tsar.

Russia been so great. A large British tonnage, which could only be spared at the cost of hardship to the British people, was employed in carrying ammunition and guns to Archangel, where the port was administered by British naval officers. The railway thence to Vologda was under British supervision, and, when other Russian lines deteriorated, it remained efficient.

The one serious material hindrance to a great Russian offensive was the state of the railways, which early in the war had been severely strained by heavy troop and supply traffic, and had fallen into disrepair. Owing to the demands on the iron-

MOTHER-SHIP OF BRITISH SUBMARINES IN THE BALTIC.
A view of the Dwina while employed as mother-ship to the British sub-marines in the Baltic. Several of the submarines can be seen alongside.

very marked decrease in the output of coal restricted the supply of fuel.

There was still hope that firm government and the restoration of discipline might follow the National Conference that opened at Moscow on August 25th. It was greeted by a general strike of trade unions at Moscow, as if to give the members an object-lesson in the pleasures of anarchy. Even the waiters stopped work, and the conference could get nothing to eat but sandwiches. General Korniloff had a narrow escape on his journey to it, as the Extremists attempted to wreck his train. Much the most important speech

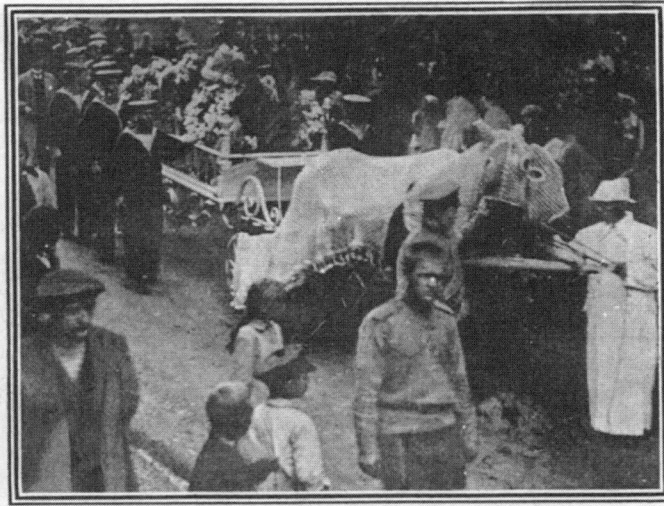

ENGLISH BISHOP OF PETROGRAD OFFICIATING AT THE FUNERAL SERVICE OF A BRITISH SAILOR AT REVAL.
In the first of these two views the funeral service for a British sailor, conducted by the English Bishop of Petrograd, is in progress on board a ship in Reval Harbour. In the second is seen the cortège, accompanied by members of the crew and British officers, entering the place of burial.

was that which he delivered. He spoke of "the terrible evil of disorganisation which is destroying the Army." He strove to shame his countrymen by telling them of the grievous peril of Rumania, who had entered the war under Russian pressure. "The Germans," he said, "are knocking at the gates of Riga, and if our Army does not help us to hold the shores of the Gulf of Riga, the road to Petrograd will be opened wide." He called for three fundamental reforms without which the war could not be prosecuted: restoration of discipline, restriction of the regimental committees, and increased pay for the officers. His final warning was, perhaps, the grimmest of all. In November the supply system would break down, and the Army would be left without food or munitions.

General Korniloff's grim warning

General Kaledin, Hetman (or chief) of the Cossacks, who at that moment alone controlled an organised if weak military force on the Moderate side, followed. He supported General Korniloff, who was of Cossack blood and of humble birth, having risen by sheer energy and merit. He demanded that politics in the Army should be suppressed, discipline enforced at the rear as well as at the front, and the war be energetically prosecuted. He might as well have spoken to stone figures. M. Kerensky was jealous of the soldiers and afraid of them. The Extremists dominated the Convention by their energy and determination. They sat repeating their formulas — abolition of profit, nationalisation of

the land, and peace at any price. The Conference brought no result; union between the Moderate men of all parties remained a mere dream. General Korniloff left Moscow in despair, and the Petrograd Soviet answered his appeals by defeating a resolution in favour of the reintroduction of the death penalty in the Army.

The blow which General Korniloff had anticipated in the region of Riga fell at once. The Germans had long been preparing a move there, with their usual caution, though there was nothing to stop them in the demoralised

THE GOOD FRIENDS OF A BRITISH SAILOR WHO DIED ON SERVICE IN RUSSIA.
The photographs on this page have a unique interest as showing the sympathy manifested for a simple British sailor of the famous submarine E9, who died while on service and was buried at Reval. In the lower view the funeral cortège, comprising various submarine crews, is illustrated, and above is the sailor's grave, with a permanent headstone and flowers of remembrance.

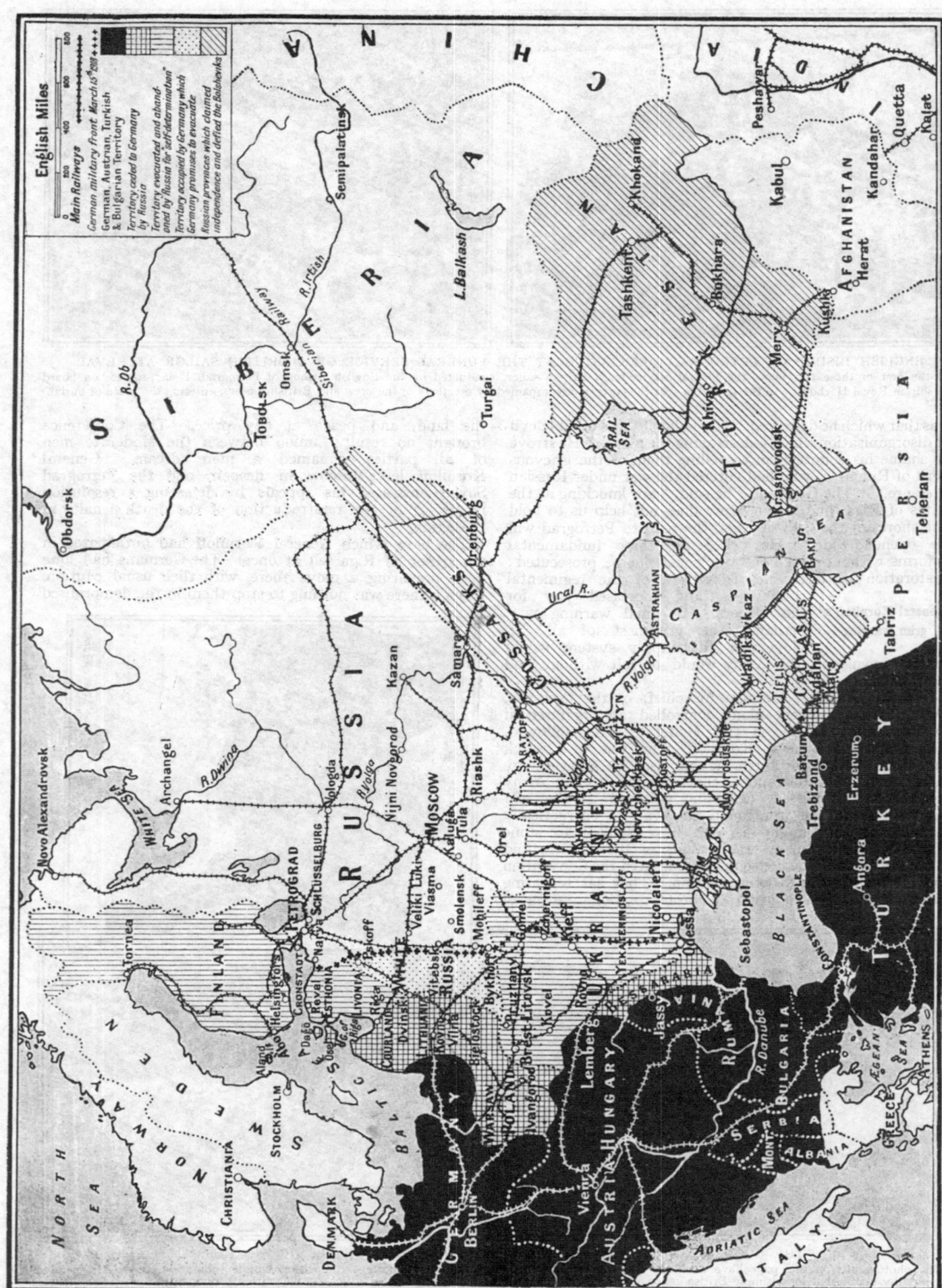

English Miles

Main Railways

German military front March 3rd 1918

German, Austrian, Turkish & Bulgarian Territory

Territory ceded to Germany by Russia

Territory evacuated and abandoned by Russia for self-determination

Territory occupied by Germany which Germany promises to evacuate

Russian provinces which claimed independence and defied the Bolsheviks

The Great War

RUSSIA AS PARTITIONED BY THE TREATY BETWEEN THE GERMANS AND THE BOLSHEVISTS, SIGNED AT BREST LITOVSK, MARCH, 1918.

Copyright

Russian Army. Their light craft had carefully reconnoitred the coast at the mouth of the Gulf of Riga, while their aircraft were almost daily over the islands in that gulf. Late in August General von Below began to move with great deliberation along the coast towards Riga and the mouth of the Aa. There were no difficulties in his way. A Siberian brigade treacherously abandoned its positions without orders and opened the door for him. On September 1st, after a violent bombardment, the Germans crossed the Dwina at Uxkull, eighteen miles above Riga, thus compelling the Russians to choose between evacuating that city or being cut off in it. The Russians retired on September 3rd, blowing up the forts and bridge; and the famous port, the second in the Russian Empire, was in German hands. In earlier times it had been a prize much fought for, with its old-world streets and its Gothic buildings—recalling the days of the Teutonic knights and the Hanseatic League, to which it had once belonged—with its trade **Riga occupied by** in timber, wheat, and hides. Now its **the Germans** distilleries and steel-works were seized by the German Government. Russia had held it uninterruptedly since 1710. Here also the Kaiser made a state entry and reviewed his victorious troops, congratulating Prince Leopold of Bavaria and the Eighth German Army on a success that had been bought from traitors. A Russian deputation from the local Soviet waited on the German general placed in command, and asked him to fix the rate of wages at one pound a day. With Prussian brutality he ordered the deputation to be shot, and fixed the standard rate at a shilling a day. Thus did Germany reward her dupes.

This disaster did not awaken the Revolutionists from their dreams. It was followed by a mysterious incident which aggravated all the misfortunes of Russia. Early in September General Korniloff was informed that M. Kerensky feared another Extremist rising in Petrograd, and wished the general to place a cavalry corps at his disposal on the approaches to Petrograd, when M. Kerensky would proclaim martial law. General Korniloff made the necessary dispositions and issued the necessary orders. On September 7th M. Lvoff, a member of the Duma and an entirely different person from Prince Lvoff, came to General Korniloff and submitted alternative plans of action with M. Kerensky's authority, one of which involved the proclamation of a temporary dictatorship for General Korniloff.

The general said that he thought a temporary dictatorship and the proclamation of martial law throughout the country were the only measures by which Russia could be saved, but he asked that M. Kerensky and M. Savinkoff, both of whom he trusted implicitly, should be associated with him in the dictatorship. M. Lvoff took this message to M. Kerensky and, to his stupefaction, was instantly arrested when he made his report. M. Kerensky alleged that the general had issued an ultimatum, and immediately demanded and received full power to crush him. On September 9th a proclamation was published denouncing General Korniloff on the charge of betraying his country and the Revolution, ordering his surrender of his post and his arrest, and imposing martial law on the Petrograd district. General Korniloff, in utter bewilderment, concluded that he had either been deliberately entrapped and betrayed by M. Kerensky or that M. Kerensky had been overpowered by the Extremists. He marched on Petrograd, invited the Ministers to join him, and gave his word that their safety should be assured. General Kaledin, at the same time, moved against the extreme Revolutionists in Southern Russia, though his arrest had been ordered by the Rostoff Soviet. A number of Cossacks left the front to join him.

If General Kaledin had intended to support General Korniloff he had no opportunity of giving help, though he seized certain of the southern railways and defied the

local Soviets with impunity. The march of the Korniloff troops on Petrograd swiftly collapsed. They melted away, till on September 13th General Krymoff, who commanded them, ordered his men to lay down their arms, and himself proceeded to Petrograd. After a terrible interview with M. Kerensky, in which he accused the Prime Minister of betraying General Korniloff and Russia, he went to his home and shot himself. There was no other bloodshed. Petrograd was mournfully indifferent. General Korniloff was placed under arrest and his trial was ordered. Meantime the Government proclaimed Russia a Republic, and on September 15th announced that supreme power had been placed in the hands of a Council of Five, one of whom was M. Kerensky. A sheaf of proclamations followed, in the evident belief that thus order could be restored in Russia. The troops were begged to cease taking part in political disputes, arresting their commanders, and forming volunteer detachments (which deserted and plundered the country) on the pretext of fighting the counter-Revolution. Thus complete was the demoralisation.

ROMANOFF HOUSE, MOSCOW.
The home of Michael Romanoff, founder of the dynasty that fell in the Revolution of 1917. Elected Tsar by a Grand National Assembly, Michael reigned from 1613 to 1645.

When M. Kerensky issued his proclamation denouncing General Korniloff he was in actual fact preparing his own downfall. This was swiftly to follow, but some weeks of political intrigue and constant change intervened, in which the Extremists steadily gained ground, the desire for peace at any price grew, and anarchy and civil war spread. The iron hand of the earlier Tsars had been needed to make of a chaos of more than sixty-four principalities, sixteen States, and ten races or religions, generally at war with each other, the Russia of 1914. Long before the war the Pan-Germans had proposed to break South-Western and South-Eastern Russia up into a number of petty States and to cut Moscow off in this way from the Baltic, the Black Sea, **Pan-Germans plan** and the Caspian. For that purpose, as **Russia's disruption** they subventioned separatists in the British Empire, in Ireland, in Canada, in South Africa, and in India, so they financed a "Ukraine movement" in the Ukraine. "Holy Russia" had already vanished with the Tsar Nicholas, now prisoner at Tobolsk. It had been dissolved into a multitude of provinces. Some were in the hands of the Germans, and were likely to remain German unless liberated by force. In all, over 100,000 square miles of Russian territory was under the German flag, and twenty millions of the former Russian population were now German serfs. Two millions of Russian prisoners were dying slowly of hunger in German prison camps; three millions had fallen on the battlefield or perished of disease.

MILITARY GOVERNOR OF PETROGRAD.
General Vassilkovski, in the foreground, who at the beginning of August, 1917, was appointed commandant of the troops in the military district of Petrograd in succession to General Polovtsoff.

Three of the seven largest Russian cities (Warsaw, Lodz, and Riga) were in German hands.

The Soviet had proclaimed the right of all nationalities to govern themselves without carefully considering what this meant. This proclamation had been astutely exploited by the Germans to complete their aim of breaking Russia up, cutting her off from the sea, and devouring her piece by piece. The great province of Finland, at the very gates of Petrograd, defied the Government there when it listed. The Ukraine asserted virtual independence, withdrew its troops from other parts of the Russian front than the south-west, and issued a proclamation in which it asserted its desire for peace. Any quarrel with it would bring for the rest of Russia the peril of starvation, as it was now the chief corn-growing area. The province of Lithuania, instigated by German agents, was agitating for self-government; so also were the provinces of Esthonia, Livonia, and White Russia. Bessarabia, in the south-west, set up a Parliament of its own. The Crim Tartars in the Crimea convened a Tartar Congress. The Cossacks refused obedience to the authorities at Petrograd, fearing the seizure of the land which they held as a people of peasant proprietors, and formed a loose confederation of their own. The Mohammedan tribes of the Northern Caucasus and Transcaucasia, which had always been a separate Government under the Tsars, had also Parliaments of their own. In Siberia, on the Amur River (facing Japan), in the Transcaspian territories, other anarchical States appeared.

The confusion was grotesque. Thus Rostoff-on-Don was in territory claimed by both the Ukraine and the Cossacks, and it was usually in the hands of Extremists who obeyed neither. The shore of the Black Sea was intermittently controlled by the Black Sea Fleet, which sometimes obeyed the Petrograd Soviet, sometimes its own leaders, and sometimes the Ukraine Council, or Rada. Scattered through these new republics were many towns which were governed by Soviets in sympathy with the Petrograd Extremists. Accurate frontiers could not be

"Self-determination" produces chaos

drawn. The country changed like a chameleon every month as the tribes and races fell apart, which the Tsars by seven centuries of effort had striven to weld together. No such break-up of a great European Power had been previously recorded in history. Poland, when partitioned, was the feeblest of States and the most anarchical.

In the country districts remote from the towns, where disorder was perpetual, anarchy prevailed. Bands of armed men held up trains in the forest regions and in the wild gorges of the Caucasus. A band of two hundred men broke the line to the Caucasus, near Vladikavkaz, in October, derailed a train and then plundered the passengers, killing or wounding more than a hundred of them in the process. Agrarian trouble spread. The large landowner during the summer was not allowed to harvest his crops, lest by selling them he should bring down the price of the corn which the peasants had grown. His seed was seized, his cattle and horses were killed or carried off; if resistance was offered, hayricks, barns, and country-houses were set on fire. Prudent people handed

APPEAL TO THE RUSSIAN FLEET.
M. N. S. Cheidze, who was leader of the Social Democratic Party in the Duma, became President of the Council of Workmen's and Soldiers' Delegates. When this photograph was taken he was appealing to the sailors of the Baltic Fleet to continue the fight for liberty.

over their land to the peasants for division—though the sale and transfer of land were now forbidden by law—knowing that if they did not their lives would not be safe. The peasants often fought over their booty, and in one such encounter seventeen persons were killed or wounded.

The displacement of the landowners brought famine nearer. The peasant was usually a bad farmer. He knew little or nothing of the science of agriculture. Where he grew ten bushels the landowner on the same area would grow twenty or thirty. The great sugar-growing estates were divided up and their fertility destroyed. Furthermore, when the landowner was dispossessed, his implements and machinery were not efficiently used, and went to ruin. He naturally did not sow where he could not reap, and in the autumn and winter of 1917 the area under crops was enormously reduced. People were too busy with the Revolution to grow food. Russia, however, still contained large supplies, as the produce of the three previous harvests could not be exported and a surplus had been grown in each of these years. But the peasants buried their corn, refusing to sell it at the Government price, as they were paid in paper money, which had depreciated 80 per cent., while everything which they wanted to buy had risen by 800 per cent. In the North of Russia, by early November, famine had appeared. Efforts were made to send corn to the starving districts, but the trains were generally plundered on the way, and the collapse of the railways hampered movements of supplies.

While the country drifted to ruin, through misery and starvation, the holding of conferences continued in the hope that talk would provide Russia with the **German Fleet takes** substitute for a strong man. The Demo-**Baltic Islands** cratic Conference, which met at the end of September, was as futile as its predecessors, though, on October 8th, an agreement was reached between the Moderates and the less extreme Socialists. A Ministry was formed in which M. Kerensky was Prime Minister, and in which there were eleven non-Socialists to five Socialists. But as at the same time the Extremists elected Trotsky-Braunstein to the position of President of the Petrograd Soviet, the signs pointed to immediate danger. No one obeyed M. Kerensky.

A fresh German advance had no effect on the Revolutionists and Anarchists. Fooled by tales that the German Navy had mutinied, Russian seamen were rioting or killing their officers at Cronstadt. Suddenly, on October 12th, eight German Dreadnoughts, forty destroyers, and thirty mine-sweepers and small craft appeared off the Island of Oesel, at the mouth of the Gulf of Riga. The resistance offered was pitiful. An appeal by M. Kerensky to the Russian Baltic Fleet met with no response. On the 13th the Germans attacked the Russian works on the Isle of Dago. A weak Russian detachment—the only ships that could be induced to fight—was caught in Moon Sound on that day, and the old battleship Slava was speedily sunk, though most of her crew were saved. With her the destroyer-leader, Gromky, was sent to the bottom. The other Russian ships were lucky to escape. By October 14th the islands were in German hands, with fifteen thousand prisoners. The relations between the Allies and the Russian Democrats were not improved. M. Kerensky pointedly asked, "Where is the British Navy?"

DR. A. I. SHINGAREFF.
Minister of Agriculture in Kerensky's Provisional Government. He was assassinated by the Red Guard when in hospital as a prisoner of the Bolshevists, on January 20th, 1918.

Another conference, the Council of the Republic, met at Petrograd on October 20th. The Extremists dominated it, having elected the majority by the machinery which they so well knew how to manipulate—that is to say, by the Army Committees and the armed mob of the towns. Many alarmist speeches were delivered with the usual result. The attitude to the Allies was cool. M. Kerensky, on November 2nd, in his last important speech dealing with foreign affairs, declared that "Russia was worn out with the strain, and claimed as her right that the Allies should shoulder the burden." His War Minister in a secret session proposed immediately to conclude peace. He was dismissed by **Fall of** M. Kerensky, who was not yet seemingly **Kerensky.** prepared to go so far as his colleagues.

M. Kerensky's fall was imminent. The Moderates no longer trusted him because of his half-measures. The Cossacks and officers had not pardoned his treatment of General Korniloff. The Extremists derided his weakness. The loyal troops were ill-cared for by him and were left insufficiently supplied with food and ammunition. Knowing an attack on himself was purposed, he took no steps to meet it. The only force that could be trusted to protect the Winter Palace, where he lived, was a detachment of a Battalion of Death, some two hundred women from a woman's battalion, and a number of young officers in Cadet battalions. The corridors of the Winter Palace were no longer crowded with suitors. The populace had tired of his oratory, and it wanted peace, plunder, and bread. Relying on this feeling, the Extremists laid their plans calmly and methodically, though many resolutions were passed denouncing them. Early in November Lenin had reappeared. He now made his first move by instructing the troops in the garrison of Petrograd (which according to the organs of the Soviet included a large number of criminals, estimated at from 18,000 to 70,000) to disregard all orders except those given through the Soviet committee which he controlled.

M. Kerensky, on November 6th, appealed to the Council of the Republic for its support in putting down any disturbances. More than half the members stayed away, and from those who attended he did not obtain the free hand which he desired. Next morning he disappeared,

COMMANDER-IN-CHIEF KRYLENKO.
Sub-Lieutenant Abram Krylenko, an Anarchist, was appointed by Lenin Commander-in-Chief of the Russian Armies, in succession to Dukhonin, in November, 1917.

HEAD OF THE MOSCOW GARRISON.
M. Mooralov, who, from being a private soldier, in the course of a few weeks, during the struggle between the Bolshevists and the Provisional Government, became Commander-in-Chief of the Moscow Military Garrison.

AA

stealing off in disguise. He embarked in a motor-launch on the canal which runs by the Winter Palace, and so reached a point where a motor-car was waiting for him. The Extremists do not seem to have troubled about his arrest. They may have connived at his escape as William III. connived at the flight of James II. He reached Bykhoff, on the railway to Kieff, a little later, and passed out of the story. He had repeatedly proclaimed his determination to fight to the last, but he vanished at the very moment when his presence was most needed.

The end came quickly. That evening cavalry and infantry, under the orders of the Extremists, patrolled the streets, while the public, weary of Revolutions, went home to bed. In the Government Headquarters at the Winter Palace panic prevailed. No one would issue orders, and all discussed unceasingly. **Kerensky Government forcibly overthrown** The Extremist adherents occupied the Central Telegraph Office and the Official Telegraph Agency. They maintained good order and were polite. As the night advanced they seized one strategic position after another, working round the Winter Palace and isolating it. They had an assembly of their own ready in the Congress of Russian Soviets, in which of four hundred and seventy-five delegates they had secured three hundred and thirty-five. By way of a reminder to the terrified Ministers in the Winter Palace, on the 7th, the powerful cruiser Aurora and three destroyers steamed up the Neva and anchored opposite the palace, so that their guns could sweep the streets. In the great Fortress of St. Peter and St. Paul, which rises to the north of the Neva over against the Winter Palace, Extremist troops prepared the heavy guns for action.

All was now ready for the last scene. To the Revolutionists of the Congress of Russian Soviets in session at the Smolny Institute, whence the widows and orphans had been unceremoniously ejected, appeared Lenin himself, accompanied by his right-hand man, Zinovieff (whose real name was Apfelbaum), implicated with him in the charge of taking German money, and mentioned by name in an order issued on March 2nd, 1917, by the Deutsche Bank as one of the " propagandists " in German pay. Trotsky presided over the Soviets, which elected as the officials of the assembly fourteen Extremists, including the above three, and seven less violent Revolutionists. Two demands were made for the peaceful surrender of the Winter Palace, and both were rejected by the Kerensky Government, though it had nothing to fight for it but a few hundred badly-armed people. There was a certain tragic irony in the fact that the last effective stand of the last element of national government in the Russian capital was made by boys and women against Anarchists commanded by aliens. At 9.30 that Wednesday night Petrograd was startled from its apathy by the brilliant scarlet flash and violent detonation of a salvo from the Aurora's guns. **Extremists occupy the Winter Palace** The ship was not as yet firing in earnest; she was discharging blank to frighten the defenders of the Winter Palace, which the Extremists desired to capture intact that they might plunder it at their leisure. Machine-guns were brought up by the assailants, and with them two anti-aircraft guns supplied by French factories, but not for such work as this, and the Extremist infantry joined in the fight. With such effect did the women defenders of the palace fire that they drove back the " Red Guards " in panic-stricken flight. Reinforcements joined the Extremists—two more destroyers, a mine-layer, and several mine-sweepers—but they were careful not to use their artillery, and only one shell was fired into the palace. Meanwhile, in the city perfect order prevailed, and the public, recovering from its alarm at the roar of the big naval guns, went to hear Cheliapin sing at the People's Palace. At two a.m. of the 8th the Winter Palace

surrendered through want of food and ammunition. The smallness of the casualties illustrated the half-hearted character of the fighting. The defenders suffered no loss, and the assailants had only six men killed. Many of the Cadets and women were brutally murdered and flung into the Neva. The soldiers outraged some of the women and beat in the face of one with the butt of a soldier's rifle. If the lives of most of them were saved it was because a British officer, General Knox, intervened on their behalf. The Extremists had not as yet made up their minds to quarrel with Great Britain.

The congenial business of plundering the Winter Palace was now carried out with a thoroughness which German troops might have envied. Pictures were wantonly destroyed. Only one portrait survived, and that was the grim likeness of Count Moltke, which looked down on the litter and ruin. Furniture and treasures were removed by the troops and their wives in motor-lorries. The priceless plate, the magnificent rugs, the embroideries and tapestries, precious as the magic treasures of " The Arabian Nights," were stolen. Historic documents were torn up and thrown about the rooms, which were ankle-deep in correspondence. The Emperor's cabinet had not been overlooked; it was strewn with papers in his handwriting. Cupboards and drawers had been forced. The seats of the chairs were slashed. If certain of the art treasures escaped it was only because they had been previously removed.

Thus Lenin gained the upper hand in Petrograd. Already he had telegraphed to Germany and to the Allies a proposal for a three months' armistice. On November 9th his Government was confirmed by the Congress of Soviets, and the new Ministers at once proceeded to visit their departments. Trotsky, who had become Foreign Minister, descended upon the Foreign Office. He demanded **Petrograd in Lenin's power** the secret treaties; the functionaries declined to obey his orders and left him to find by himself what he wanted, and to search for the documents through a thousand boxes of papers, ready packed for the evacuation of the capital. No clerk would draft a telegram for him, and he was taunted by the women of the staff. In other departments the officials either absented themselves or declined to aid the Leninites. During the 9th many outrages were perpetrated, among them the murder of General Prince Tumanoff in the streets. The Extremists forcibly suppressed the great newspapers, entering their offices and seizing their plant. Nevertheless, many news sheets appeared denouncing the Anarchists.

On November 10th Petrograd heard reports that M. Kerensky, with a force of troops, was approaching. Lenin sent orders to the Central Telephone Exchange to cut off all communication with the south, but as the telephone employees threatened to withdraw en masse if he interfered with them, he gave way. He was indeed too busy in other directions that day, preparing decrees of every kind, to trouble himself about such a trifle. Private ownership of land, forests, mines, minerals, and oil-wells was abolished. All factories were transferred from the owners to the workers, who were to manage them by committees. The municipalities were empowered to seize houses, whether inhabited or uninhabited, and to place in them people who were homeless or who lived in insanitary dwellings. A stay in the payment of rent for small houses and flats was imposed. Power was given to seize the clothes and boots of any person who paid a rent of more than £200 a year. No one was allowed to draw more than £15 a week from the banks. Previous orders had been given that no one was to be allowed to leave Russia with more than £20 in cash. The country was turned into an immense prison, in which the population was being slowly ruined and in peril of dying of hunger.

M. Kerensky's approach led to further fruitless sacrifice of life, while Petrograd looked on indifferently. In

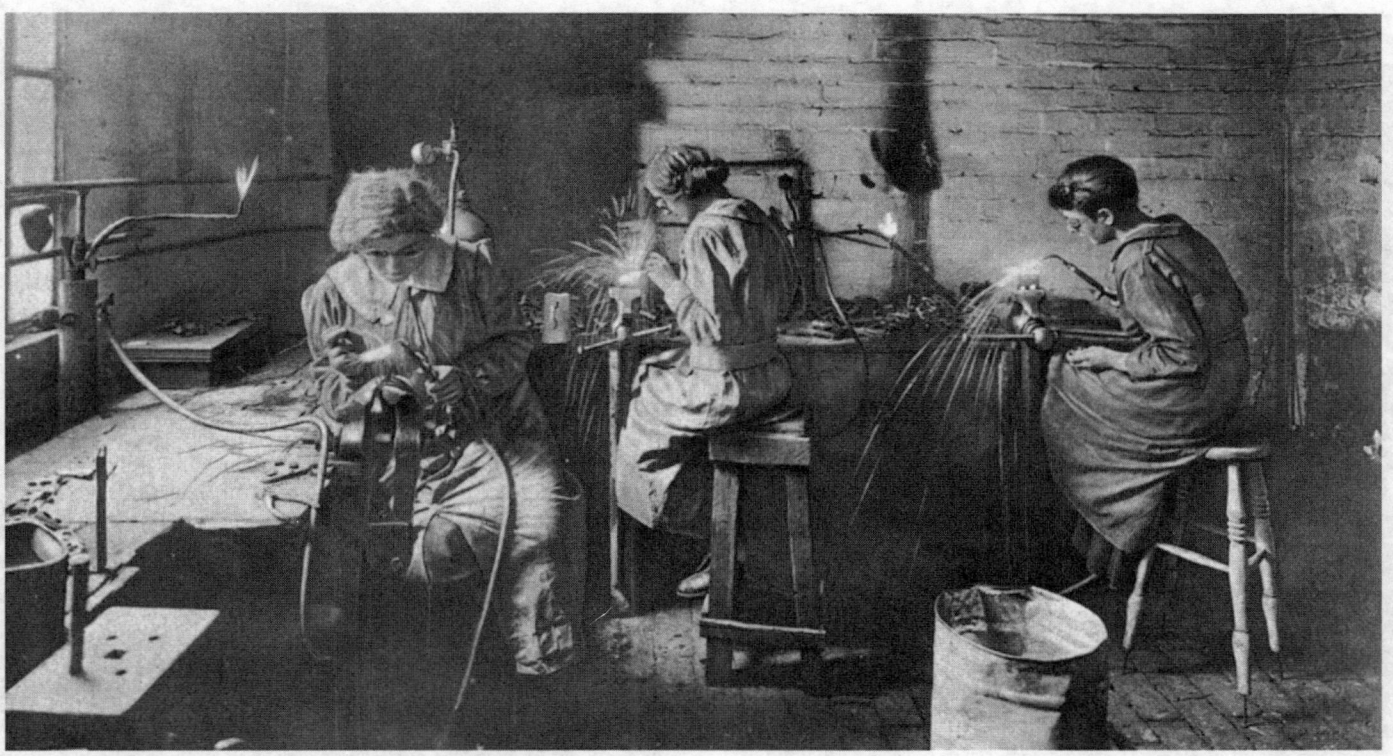

Acetylene welders at work: Their eyes protected by special "goggles" from the intense white heat.

A man's helpmate slotting breech ring forms for 5 in. 60-pounder guns.

The immensely interesting photographs reproduced on this and the three following pages give some idea of the priceless help afforded by the women of the Empire. Untiring in work calling for great physical strength and endurance, and adept in craftsmanship requiring delicacy of manipulation and minute attention, women have proved equal to the task of producing every kind of munition and material required for the war.

Boring inside breech pieces of heavy guns.   Rough turning jacket forging for 6-pounder guns

Women operating radial drilling machines drilling plates for girder bridges.

Doping and ferruling marine engine condensers.

Slotting breech pieces for heavy guns.

Women marking, finishing, and loading boiler tubes in a large Northern works.

Sewing coverings for aeroplane hangings in an aircraft factory.

Doping the wings of aeroplanes that will dominate the air.

Women acting as "mates" to joiners making seaplane floats.

Operating automatic lathes rough turning aero-engine cylinders.

obedience to orders from him the military Cadets occupied the Central Telephone Exchange and the Hotel Astoria, one of the finest in Petrograd, ejecting small parties of Extremists. The Leninites at once concentrated in great force with artillery and machine-guns and attacked these points and the four military schools. The Cadets were hopelessly outnumbered, and had little ammunition. They were quickly overpowered and were treated atrociously. Six or seven of them in an armoured car which ran out of petrol were trampled to death by a furious mob. Others were torn to pieces or shot by their guards. In a few cases, however, the seamen, who preserved better discipline, actually fought to protect them. Throughout the city they were hunted down and killed, till a warning from the Railwaymen's Union that it would not tolerate terrorism stopped these murders temporarily. From November 11th to 14th an engagement proceeded at Tsarskoye Selo, outside Petrograd, which was terminated by M. Kerensky's supporters going over to the Extremists. After this collapse the Leninites took a stronger line with the railwaymen, and as a hint to them imprisoned the director of the Nicholas Railway to Moscow. In this way they forced the union to execute their orders.

At Moscow the Extremists had triumphed as completely as at Petrograd, while the bulk of the population and the troops looked on. They attempted to dissolve the City Council, and they seized the Kremlin on November 10th, murdering thirty Cadets who formed its garrison. A stronger force of Moderates was brought up, and the Kremlin was retaken and held, together with the centre of the city, by 3,000 Cadets and students in the Moderate interest. The Extremists did not hesitate to attack. Two 9 in. guns, under men who were commanded by a German, and two batteries of artillery bombarded the centre of the city from various vantage points and the Sparrow Hills. The National Hotel, close to the Kremlin, was damaged by shells, and the numerous French and English visitors in it were in great danger.

Extremists triumph at Moscow

The Moderates were gradually forced back into the Kremlin, which was bombarded on the 14th with some effect. Russia's Holy of Holies, the famous Cathedral of the Assumption, was struck. The tower of Ivan Veliki and the fantastic Church of St. Basil were damaged. The Kremlin was in imminent peril of destruction, and the peaceable population of Moscow was for a whole week under constant fire and in fearful danger. On November 17th a truce was arranged. The terms were signed by the leaders of eleven different parties, while a private soldier was appointed Governor of Moscow in the Extremist interest. The Extremists did not respect this "scrap of paper," but killed in cold blood several of the Moderates and looted the treasures of the Kremlin. The loss in the fighting was variously estimated, and seems to have been much less than was at first supposed. According to some accounts, over 10,000 men, women, and children were killed or wounded, but British residents in Moscow estimated the casualties at only two hundred.

Lenin and his party were now supreme in the two Russian capitals, and over a considerable area of Northern and Central Russia. Elsewhere their authority was precarious. In the anarchy civil war spread and increased in violence. In Finland, which was attempting to assert its independence, a Moderate majority was returned in the Diet. Thereupon the Extremists, on November 14th, began a general strike, and, aided by the Russian Extremists, fell upon the Moderates, whom in several places they killed. Houses were plundered, men of substance were robbed, cash in the banks was seized, bands of marauders ranged the country. The railways ceased working, and there was no food. In the midst of all this misery Finland proclaimed its independence, and appealed to the Allies to send it supplies, as its population was starving. In the Ukraine a confused struggle began between the

Moderates and Extremists—between the "bourgeois" champions of Ukraine rights and the Bolshevist believers in anarchy. This civil war was complicated by the interference of the "Red Guards" (or Extremist Russian forces) on the one hand, and of the Cossacks on the other, and by the occasional interposition of the Black Sea Fleet. In the spasmodic fighting which went on many estates were devastated, and thousands of people were slaughtered pitilessly. In South-Eastern Russia General Kaledin convened a Cossack Congress at Novtcherkask, and beset Rostoff. A Moderate force under General Alexeieff marched troops into the Donetz valley and threatened Kharkoff. Many officers joined Alexeieff, but he was too weak to do more than hold the Extremists in uncertain check. In the Transcaspian territories civil war blazed out afresh in the neighbourhood of Tashkend, where the Extremists were in strong force.

Civil war throughout Russia

Some of the Anarchist Ministers showed alarm in face of the growing demoralisation. Eleven of them resigned, but this did not seriously affect Lenin's power. His programme was as popular as ever in Petrograd—if not outside it—peace at any price and plunder for all. Yet his difficulties grew fast. The factories were closing. Employers were ordered to keep running and pay fabulous wages, but had not the money to do this. In some cases, as at the Putiloff Works, the Government granted a subvention, and the Extremists were able to find the cash, as they had seized £60,000,000 in gold at Moscow. This was a stroke of luck, because the establishment at Petrograd where the notes were printed had run out of fuel and paper. Still, for all this discovery of gold, the clamour of the troops at the front increased. They were left without boots, winter clothing, or food. The officials in most of the Government departments remained on strike, or did as little as possible. The Allies had naturally stopped the despatch of supplies after Lenin's declaration that he meant to have peace at any price.

Lenin had now to fulfil his promise to secure peace, which was passionately desired by Extremists, soldiers, workers, and peasants alike. On the night of November 20th the Extremists issued peremptory orders to General Dukhonin, the Russian Commander-in-Chief, directing him immediately to offer an armistice to all the nations, hostile and allied, involved in the war. Dukhonin, an honest, courageous, and patriotic officer, asked for certain explanations before acting. He wanted to know what was to happen to the Rumanians, and he inquired whether he was to negotiate with the Germans only or with the Turks as well. The only answer vouchsafed to these very necessary questions was a fresh and yet more imperious order from Lenin to talk no more but act at once. Dukhonin declined to obey, not from contumacy, but for a very practical reason—that successful negotiations for a peace could only be carried out by the Government. Lenin was not a person to tolerate any opposition. He promptly appointed Sub-Lieutenant Krylenko, commonly known as "Father Abraham," an Anarchist of indifferent intellect and morals, to replace Dukhonin as Commander-in-Chief. He further instructed the soldiers themselves, unit by unit, to open peace negotiations with the German units confronting them, and to arrest and guard any counter-Revolutionary generals, "so that lynch law, which is not worthy of a Revolutionary army, cannot take place, and these generals cannot evade imminent justice." The difficulty of conducting such negotiations lay in the ignorance of the Russian soldiers, who believed that the formula "no annexation and no indemnity" meant that the Russian Army was to attempt no offensive and to levy no contribution on Germany. The pressure for peace was increased by the growing want. The Extremists had raised the food ration in Petrograd, neglecting the troops. Though fifty millions sterling, since the rising in November,

Anarchist Commander-in-Chief

BOLSHEVIST HEADQUARTERS IN PETROGRAD.
The Smolny Institute, occupied by the Bolshevists in 1917 as the seat of their Government, was begun by the Empress Elizabeth in 1748 as a nunnery for orphan girls, on the site of a palace of Peter the Great; a school for girls was added by Catherine II. in 1764.

had been allotted to the purchase of supplies, much of it had been embezzled, and the food sent by railway was constantly looted at the stations in the universal disorder. The Army units were dissolving more rapidly than ever, plundering and devastating the country as they retired.

The Extremist diplomacy assumed an air of growing hostility to Great Britain. Trotsky, in a Note which was virtually an ultimatum, issued on November 20th, called on the Allies to make peace, with the threat that if they had not done so on November 23rd, Russia would hold herself free to act alone. In a bitter speech he proclaimed his intention of conducting his diplomacy in public—a declaration which he immediately disregarded—and of sweeping all the secret treaties into the dust-bin. These treaties he published, with no regard for the Allies, but they proved so tame and uninteresting that no capital could be made of them, even by Germany. He demanded from Great Britain the release of two Russian offenders against the British Defence of the Realm Act, Tchicherin and Petroff, and directed that no British residents in Russia should be allowed to leave until they were handed over. To bring pressure to bear on the Allies and compel them to make peace, he threatened to repudiate all Russia's foreign debts. Thus Russia, under the Extremists, was fast becoming the open enemy of the Allies and the ally of Germany.

General Dukhonin held stubbornly aloof from any peace negotiations, but representatives of the Fifth Russian Army, in the face of protests from the Allied Military Mission at the Russian Headquarters, on November 28th crossed the front and conferred with the German Staff. The chief Russian representative was Lieutenant Schneur, a person of German descent, who had conducted a blackmailing newspaper in Paris before the war, and was, a few days after his

negotiations, to be arrested as a former agent of the Russian Secret Police. The Moscow City Council protested against this method of making peace, and the Cossacks did the same. It was of no avail. The Germans were only too well pleased to split Russia up, and they encouraged the Extremists by receiving their overtures favourably.

On December 1st a cessation of hostilities was arranged on the northern and Galician fronts, to take effect from 10 p.m. of the following day, and on December 2nd the Leninite peace delegates arrived. They were ten in number—six members of the Petrograd Soviet, a workman, a soldier, a seaman, and a clerk. As none of them knew anything of military matters, and as it was said that some of them could not even write, they were accompanied by two officers from the General Staff, though General Dukhonin still refused to take any part in their mission. They left for Brest, where they were greeted by Prince Leopold of Bavaria in a haughty and dictatorial speech, and were then handed over to his Chief of the Staff, General Hoffmann. **General Dukhonin** While they were thus engaged another **brutally murdered** devoted Russian officer had been cleared out of Germany's path. On the night of the 2nd General Dukhonin's headquarters at Mohileff was surrounded by Extremist troops. His own troops received no orders, and offered no resistance. At ten next morning Lieutenant Krylenko entered Mohileff in triumph, and then learnt that Dukhonin was at the station in danger. According to his own account, he hurried to the rescue, but was thrust aside. Dukhonin was murdered by the mob, and his body brutally mutilated. That same day General Korniloff, through

COUNTRY LAID WASTE BEFORE THE INVADER.
View of a Russian village in flames, taken by the observer in an aeroplane during the retreat before the Germans occupying Riga in 1917. The striated appearance of the landscape is due to the Continental method of growing crops in broad stretches not intersected by hedges.

the connivance of his guards and the help of certain Turkoman and Transcaucasian troops whose language he spoke, made his escape, with many other prisoners, from the little town of Bykhoff and rode swiftly south-east to join Kaledin. The Moderates of the Ukraine protected him in his flight.

On December 5th the Armistice Conference at Brest began, in the presence of German, Austrian, Turkish, and Bulgarian representatives. The Leninites, on requesting the Germans for a statement of their peace aims, were told that this was a matter which must be left to the politicians. They next asked the Germans to propose to the Allies an armistice on other fronts, but again they were rebuffed. A project was submitted by the Russians under which neither side was to send forces to other fronts, and the Germans were to withdraw from Moon Sound and the islands in the Gulf of Riga. This was peremptorily rejected. The Germans demanded the payment of £300,000,000 in gold, the instant withdrawal of the Russians **Armistice Conference** from Galicia, their retirement from **at Brest** the front, the surrender of certain positions and of the Black Sea coast south of the Caucasus frontier, and even the disarmament of the Russian Army, though this last demand they finally consented to waive. Trotsky, despite his promise of open diplomacy, did not venture to disclose these terms. The Germans treated the Leninites with scant courtesy, but agreed to an armistice till December 17th. They met every request for terms with the remark that they preferred to go on fighting rather than fetter themselves. As a result of these negotiations the

DESTRUCTION RENDERED NECESSARY BY RETREAT.
Bridge blown up by the Russians in the course of a methodical retreat. Such destruction was a means of hindering and delaying the German cavalry in their pursuit, and was a necessary part of an organised retirement.

position of the Rumanians was rendered desperate. They also had to ask for an armistice, or their Army would have been immediately overwhelmed.

The Russian Extremists now began to discover that Germany did not intend to give them the reasonable peace which they had so often promised. The populace and the peasants, however, cared only for one thing—the end of the war ; and any blame for the unsatisfactory conditions could always be laid upon the stubbornness of the Allies. Trotsky and Lenin had no choice. What they had promised they had to perform, at the price of being supplanted by other Anarchists who made yet larger offers, or by the House of Romanoff.

During the negotiations the elections in Russia for the Constituent Assembly had concluded. In every direction the Extremists brought violence to bear. They terrorised voters, they manipulated votes, they announced publicly that any result other than an Extremist majority would be regarded as a " falsification of public opinion," and that fresh elections would take place wherever Extremist voters had any reason to complain of the result. They held up the fate of General Dukhonin as a terrible warning to Moderates. Notwithstanding these tactics, down to January 10th only 158 Extremists were elected as against 261 more Moderate Revolutionists. Meanwhile, Extremist decrees were issued in rapid succession. Trotsky had determined, it was alleged, in some freak of fanaticism to abolish everything in Russia except human life. Religious marriages were swept away, divorce was facilitated ; at funerals no religious services might be used ; the Church treasures and estates were confiscated ; law courts, law, and legal officials were abolished ; the populace was to decide everything at special tribunals by votes, thus returning to the worst methods of Athenian democracy in the old days ; money and landed property were no longer to exist ; balances

TO SAVE AMMUNITION FROM THE PURSUING FOE.
Destruction of ammunition dumps by a Russian army during retreat. In the downfall which followed upon the Bolshevist loosening of all discipline the disorderly retirement of the armies often rendered such safeguarding measures impossible.

IN THE UKRAINE.
Ukrainian soldiers, showing the uniform of the army of the new State formed out of the West and South of Russia.

in the banks and in safes were seized ; houses, buildings, land, and cattle became the property of the State ; Russia was to be dissolved into a number of communities with a central Anarchist authority to make certain that the proper degree of Anarchy everywhere prevailed. The machinery for carrying out these decrees, however, did not exist. The officials in Government departments remained on strike. When coercion was applied to them they did as little as they possibly could, though the Leninites arrested every one who questioned their decrees, and inflicted upon offenders savage punishments, such as deprivation of food-cards (which meant swift starvation), confiscation of property, and ejection from their houses. In every direction men, women, and children were brutally murdered under the pretext that they were "bourgeois." The dragonnades of the Anarchists far surpassed in cruelty and mercilessness the worst deeds of Louis XIV. In the midst of all this confusion and tyranny the supply of food steadily declined and the efficiency of the railways daily diminished.

Persecution of the bourgeoisie

While the Extremists negotiated peace with the Germans they waged war on General Kaledin and his confederates, General Dutoff at Orenburg, and Generals Alexeieff and Korniloff in the Donetz valley. General Kaledin attempted to seize the great railways and prevent the Extremists bringing up supplies and men by them. His strength in men was insufficient for so important an enterprise, and he did not possess the Extremists' boundless supply of munitions, machine-guns, motor-cars, and artillery. Moreover, the Railwaymen's Union showed hostility to him and refused to move his men by train ; while the Ukraine Government was too feeble to give him effective aid or was secretly hostile.

The largest estimate of his forces did not put them at more than sixteen Cossack regiments with twelve batteries, against which there were hordes of Extremist troops fighting to be rid of the war. The " Red Guards " were merciless. Kaledin appears to have been half-hearted in his struggle. Everything in Russia seemed to conspire in the Extremists' cause. It was a sign of the extra-

ordinary revolution through which the world was passing when Chinese troops had to be summoned to Harbin, in Manchuria, to maintain order there, and when appeals were made to Japan for the landing of a military force at Vladivostok to put down riots there. Anarchy was now supreme throughout the Russian Empire, and to maintain its supremacy and make everyone happy Lenin threatened at an early date to set up the guillotine for his political opponents.

The Extremists maintained an obstinate silence as to the course of their peace negotiations, but the Germans announced that on December 15th an armistice agreement was signed at Brest Litovsk which was to last twenty-eight days in any case, **Armistice agreement** and to continue indefinitely if no notice **signed December 15th** of its termination was given. The conditions were not disclosed, but included a promise from the Germans not to move from the eastern front any troops which had not previously received orders to withdraw. The Russian Commander-in-Chief, Krylenko, gave instructions for operations to cease, though they had in actual fact been suspended for many months. The terms were not signed until a brave and patriotic officer, General Skalon, who acted as military adviser to the Extremist delegates, had been found dead. His demand that the Germans should evacuate Moon Sound had led to the failure to reach an agreement at the first series of conferences. He went into a room which the Germans allotted to him, and there his body was presently found with a bullet wound, and the world was invited by the German authorities to believe that he had committed suicide. Who killed him (if he did not kill himself) will perhaps never be known. This is another of the mysteries of the war.

The last days of this terrible year were days of anguish for those who loved Russia best. Any child can destroy the work of years of patient effort, and now the structure of the Russian State, as the result of a few months of

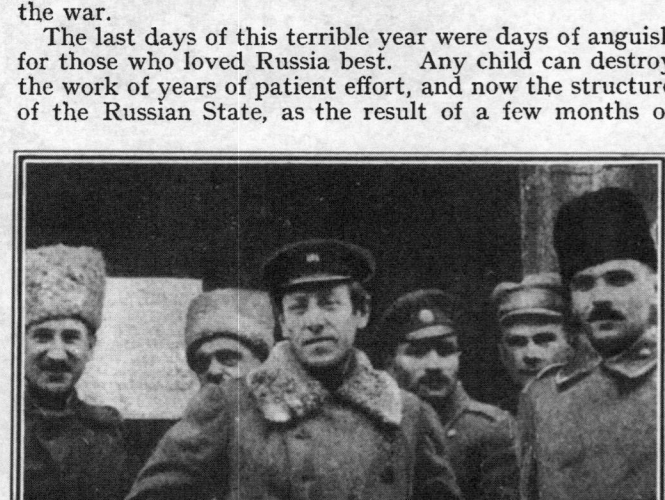

PRESIDENT OF THE RADA.
Professor Grushki, President of the Ukrainian Parliament, or Rada, addressing some of the Ukraine troops before they started for the front.

UKRAINIAN MINISTER OF WAR.
M. Petlura, Minister of War in the Ukraine Government. The Ukraine Parliament at Kieff from the first opposed the Bolshevist rule in Russia, and their troops on occasion fought against the Bolshevists.

government by fools or knaves, lay in the dust. The railways were working uncertainly; the Ukraine and the Don Cossacks were holding back their corn for themselves. Six ounces of bread per day was the ration to all but the privileged workers, and often even this could not be obtained outside Petrograd, though in Petrograd the supply of corn increased in January. Meat had practically vanished except from the tables of the Extremist leaders and their friends. The streets were in filth and disorder. Every man did that which was right in his own eyes. A hundred persons would fight their way into a tramway-car capable of holding one-third that number. Robberies and murders no longer attracted attention. Life was more unsafe than in the worst periods of the Middle Ages. Honesty had disappeared. Enormous sums were stolen from the State. Civilisation was being submerged. In their utter wretchedness men no longer cared for freedom or its catchwords, seeing the use which had been made of them. They yearned for a strong, efficient rule which would restore order, that first necessity of human life. They saw it nowhere but under the German flag, and a host of German agents was now pouring stealthily into the Russian capital to proclaim the blessing of German culture. Outside Petrograd, as the Russian armies melted away, hordes of brigands devoured and destroyed, while everywhere the peasants rioted and burnt.

On December 25th the negotiations at Brest were temporarily interrupted to allow the Extremists to communicate with the Allies. The Germans refused to accept a Russian proposal that "national groups which before the war were not politically independent shall be guaranteed the possibility of deciding by referendum the question of belonging to one State or another or enjoying their independence." This would have given Alsace-Lorraine and Poland some chance of liberation. The Germans

GATHERED FOR A FATEFUL MEETING.
Delegates from Ukraine conversing with German officers outside the Government building at Brest Litovsk. The town in which the Peace Conference met, Brest Litovsk on the River Bug, was once the home of the Polish kings.

replied with a vague and evasive form of words which left no hope for the enslaved races. Trotsky at once denounced what he described as "Germany's hypocritical peace proposal," and talked of resistance. But, as he well knew that the Russian Army was in no state to offer it, this was mere wind. "Protest, protest," said Mr. Kruger on one famous occasion, "you have not got the guns; I have." Such was, in effect, the German answer to Trotsky. Simultaneously, faithful to the plan of playing off one State against another, the Germans recognised the Ukraine and began peace negotiations with a mission from its Government, thus forcing Trotsky's hands. There was a touch of irony in the fact that from the date when the Ukrainian delegates appeared at Brest the Russian Extremists began to get the upper hand in their struggle with the Ukraine troops.

On January 7th the Russian delegates were again at Brest—a sign that their protests were not to be taken seriously—though Trotsky, who was with them, announced that "I will sign only an honourable peace." The practical comment on this was the presence of a large German and Austrian Mission in Petrograd and the arrival of many more German merchants and commercial travellers and of Admiral Kaiserling, a German naval officer, who came to arrange for the use by Germans of a base on the Russian Murman coast, towards which a railway had been built with British aid during the war. Other German agents appeared in Western Russia, beyond the trench line, and began to arrange for the export of food and the import of manufactured goods. The German diplomatists now determined to bring violent pressure to bear. A request for the transfer of the venue of the negotiations to neutral territory was received by Herr von Kühlmann, the German Foreign Minister, with utter scorn. He refused it peremptorily. He insisted that, as the Allies of Russia had taken no action towards peace during ten days' suspension of negotiations, which had been agreed to on December 25th so that they might join in the proceedings, all the conditions previously settled had lapsed. Germany would require Russia to conclude a separate peace or to face the consequences, among which would be war to the

German pressure on Russia

PEACE DELEGATES FROM THE CENTRAL POWERS.
Members of the German and Austrian delegations waiting the arrival of the Russian representatives at Brest Litovsk. An armistice conference began there on December 5th, 1917, and after various adjournments a humiliating and disastrous "peace" was concluded in March, 1918.

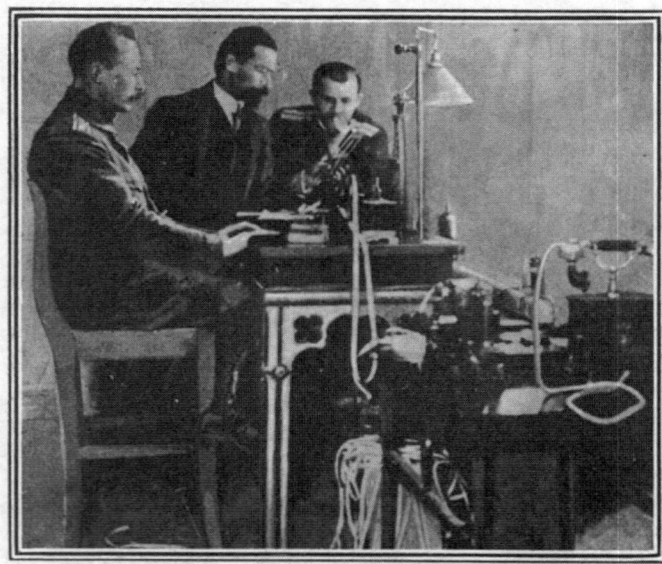

knife. Count Czernin, the Austrian Foreign Minister, followed in much the same terms. If Russia would not conclude a separate peace, he said, " then things will take the necessary course, but the responsibility for the continuation of the war will fall exclusively on the gentlemen of the Russian delegation." The comedy, carefully arranged by the Germans, concluded with a threatening protest from the German, Austrian, Bulgarian, and Turkish Staff against the wireless messages which the Russian Extremists had sent out attacking the German Government and the German High Command. In their simplicity they had supposed that Germany would permit the weapon she had used with such stupendous effect against Russia and Italy to be turned against herself.

The Russian delegates dared not break off the negotiations. Their only chance of retaining power lay in securing peace. Trotsky at once lowered his tone, and the armistice was extended till February 18th, and negotiations were transferred to Warsaw. Meantime, on February 9th, peace was signed between **Ukraine signs a separate peace** Germany and the Ukraine, but on the previous day, according to Trotsky and Lenin, the Ukraine capital, Kieff, was taken by the Russian Extremist troops. The organs of the Extremists abused not Germany but Great Britain, France, and the United States. Mr. Lloyd George and President Wilson were denounced as hypocrites and " Imperialists." Commander-in-Chief Krylenko issued a wild proclamation in whch he summoned Russian soldiers and peasants to " a holy war against the Russian bourgeoisie and that of Germany, France, and Great Britain." He declared that the Russian Army was in no state to conduct this holy war, as it was "tired " and "exhausted," and therefore the struggle was to be conducted by " an army of the people of which the nucleus should be the Red Guard." Some faint, distorted recollection of the French Revolution may have dictated this turgid bombast. In the French Revolution, however, France was saved not by armed mobs, but by the hesitations and quarrels of her enemies and by the genius of the greatest soldier of all time, leading an army in which discipline was enforced by the severest penalties.

The conditions which Germany had granted to the Ukraine were not disclosed till February 13th. The Ukraine became, in effect, a German protectorate. The Germans and their allies were given exceptional commercial privileges, such as before the war they had enjoyed in Russia, with disastrous consequences to Russian industry. They were granted the first call on the foodstuffs and raw materials of the Ukraine, and there was a stipulation to the effect that railway traffic was to be resumed as soon as possible. Each party to the treaty was to permit the prisoners of the other side to return home, so far as they did not decide to remain in the country which had captured them—a provision which enabled the Germans, if they so desired, to use their Ukraine prisoners for forced labour. Provided the Ukraine satisfied its German conquerors, it was to be granted a large slice of Poland—nothing less than the province of Brest Litovsk. But the boundaries of the Ukraine north-eastward and south-eastward were left undetermined. This was a very clever German stroke, as the new vassal State could be extended indefinitely according as events shaped **Ukraine under** in Russia. On the lowest estimate the **German control** Ukraine became a State of 200,000 square miles, with a population of thirty millions. On the largest estimate, and supposing it to extend to the Caucasus, it had an area of over 300,000 square miles and a population of forty millions.

The Russian Revolution had so far produced not a single new idea, not a single ideal. It had been a hunt for plunder, accompanied by destruction, with none of the unselfishness and patriotism which marked the noblest days of the French Revolution. But it might still produce martyrs. Trotsky and Lenin were now to be tried in the furnace. If they had been true men they would have stood firmly to their lunatic creed and died for it, as visionaries sometimes can. They gave no such proof of character. The Ukraine peace was followed immediately by an abject message from the Russian Extremists, dated February 10th, stating :

We could not sign a peace which would bring with it sadness, oppression, and suffering to millions of workmen and peasants.

But we also cannot and must not continue a war which was begun by Tsars and capitalists . . . Russia . . . declares the present war with Germany, Austria-Hungary, Turkey, and Bulgaria at an end. Simultaneously Russian troops receive the order for demobilisation on all fronts.

The idea of Trotsky and Lenin was apparently that they could turn to the more congenial work of civil war, as simultaneously with the order to bolt from the German front, operations against Finland, the Ukraine, and Kaledin's Cossacks were pressed with greater energy. Kaledin, recognising that his position was hopeless, and that the choice in future lay between German rule and Bolshevist anarchy, killed himself. In Finland the Russian Revolutionists horrified the world. A deliberate attempt was made to murder all the male children of their political opponents of twelve years of age **Russian atrocities** and over. The so-called "bourgeois" **in Finland** were killed wholesale where they fell into the Anarchists' hands. A furious struggle raged between the "White Guards," or more moderate Finns, and the "Red Guards," or representatives of Russian savagery and Anarchism. In this the "Red Guards," supported from Petrograd with men and munitions, gained the upper hand, and the country was laid waste until Germany intervened on behalf of the "White Guards."

The Russian Extremists, if they imagined that they could ignore the Germans, and if they were not deliberately playing into Germany's hands, were speedily undeceived. On February 18th the Germans resumed the war, and advanced on the whole Northern Russian front with great rapidity, crossing the Dwina and taking Dvinsk, while a rabble of Russian soldiery fled ignominiously before them,

BOLSHEVIST LEADER AT BREST LITOVSK.
Arrival of Trotsky, the Bolshevist leader, to attend the Peace Conference at Brest Litovsk. He is shaking hands with one of the German officers who received the party. Behind him are Joffe, head of the Russian delegation, and Kameneff.

abandoning guns by the thousand, rolling-stock, thousands of motor-cars, and an enormous spoil of shells, rubber, and copper which the Allies had foolishly placed in Russian hands. Another abject wireless message was sent by Trotsky and Lenin, in which they hurriedly abandoned all their convictions and agreed to sign peace; but of this the German Headquarters took no notice. A written acceptance of the peace terms followed, to be treated as contemptuously. The Russians were peremptorily ordered to withdraw their Revolutionary forces from the Ukraine, from Finland, from Esthonia, and from Livonia. Germany's appetite grew with the eating. All propaganda and all agitation against Germany and her allies were to be abandoned. Russian warships were to be disarmed, and the mines in the Baltic and Black Sea to be removed. The Russian troops, including the "Red Guards," were to be "completely demobilised." Russia was required to accept trade conditions **Bolshevists surrender** which meant her perpetual servitude to **to Germany** Germany. Trotsky and Lenin were made to eat all their bluster and all their fine words. Meanwhile news arrived from the districts traversed by the Germans in their triumphant march that Soviet representatives and "Red Guards" were everywhere being summarily shot or hanged on gallows in the public squares.

Once more Trotsky and Lenin grovelled before the German conqueror. On February 24th, after a debate in the Soviet, in which the Anarchists declaimed, Lenin, pale and repulsive, his face twitching involuntarily, made an interminable speech, advocating instant peace. He said of the Germans:

Their knees are on our chest, and our position is hopeless. This peace must be accepted as a respite, enabling us to prepare our decisive resistance to the bourgeoisie and Imperialism.

At noon that day a dishevelled, frightened-looking Bolshevist proceeded under a flag of truce to the

ARRANGING AN ARMISTICE.
Parlementaires from the Russian Army, who, at the beginning of December, 1917, crossed to the enemy position under a white flag. They were met in No Man's Land, and, with bandaged eyes, were taken to the German divisional headquarters, where they presented their credentials from Krylenko, the Russian Commander-in-Chief.

German lines to hand in Russia's submission to all Germany's demands — immediate and unconditional surrender. He was allowed to pass, but no answer was vouchsafed. Krylenko, the Russian Commander-in-Chief, inquired whether the German High Command regarded the war as ended, and he, too, was ignored. The German troops continued their resistless march. They were now in Reval, the great Baltic base of the Russian Navy; they were in the important railway junction of Pskoff, only eight hours from Petrograd; they were in Vitebsk, another important junction; they were moving towards Bologye, a vital point on the last railway connecting Petrograd with Moscow and the south; they were nearing Kieff; they were reported to be landing in Finland. Simultaneously the Turks were pressing on in Armenia. Trebizond was reoccupied.

Germans advance into Russia Erzerum, Kars, and the whole Caucasian coast were open and unguarded. There was nothing to prevent any resolute enemy of Russia from helping himself. From every quarter ravenous foes were closing in upon the mob of uneducated peasants and ignorant workmen who had sold their birthright in the belief that Germany was thirsting for peace.

In these dreadful hours, which their wickedness had brought upon their country, Lenin and Trotsky and their other associates appear to have cared chiefly for their own skins. They were in peril of seeing their retreat cut off,

and they who had shed so much human blood could expect no quarter. They had disarmed Russia, yet now they themselves took to flight, after calling on the wretched mob of hooligans that had so far obeyed them to fight to the last. On February 25th a proclamation, of the same type as that previously issued by Krylenko, badly printed on discoloured paper, and evidently composed in panic and confusion, was pasted on the buildings of Petrograd. It said:

The damned minions of William and the **General stampede** German Kaledins, together with the White **from Petrograd** Guards, are advancing against and shooting the Soviets, reconstituting the power of the landlords, bankers, and capitalists, and preparing for the restoration of the monarchy. The Revolution is in peril. A mortal blow will be struck against Red Petrograd. . . Workers and all oppressed men and women, you must swell the ranks of the Red battalions. To arms all of you, that the struggle may cease only with your last breath!

But fighting Germans was an occupation much less safe and lucrative than murdering civilians and women. The response of the soldiers to this appeal was a stampede from Petrograd. Germans by hundreds—nominal prisoners of war—were already in the city, and only waiting the order from their Headquarters to seize the Revolutionists. Eastward from Petrograd and north-westward to Finland poured fugitives who had very good reasons for getting out of the Germans' way.

At last, on March 3rd, the Germans condescended to notice the surrender of the Bolshevists. That night their

SIGNING THE CESSATION OF ARMS CONTRACT AT BREST LITOVSK.
Members of the Conference who agreed to a twenty-eight days' armistice on December 15th, 1917. Prince Leopold of Bavaria (10), German Commander-in-Chief in the east, signing the armistice. 1. Kameneff; 2. Joffe, head of the Russian delegates; 3. Mme. Biecenke; 4. Kontr.-Adm. Altvater; 5. Capt. Lipsky; 6. Karachan, secretary; 7. Lt.-Col. Fokke; 8. H. E. Zeki Pasha, Turkish Deputy; 9. H. E. Ambassador von Merey; 11. Gen. Hoffman; 12. Col. Gantschew, Bulgarian Deputy; 13. Capt. Horn; 14. Capt. Roy; 15. Maj. Brinkmann; 16. Maj. von Kameko; 17. Capt. von Rosenberg; 18. Maj. von Mirbach; 19. Dolivo-Dobrowolsky.

PEACE CONFERENCE BUILDING AT BREST LITOVSK.

It was in this timber building at the manufacturing town of Brest Litovsk, in the Government of Grodno, that the Bolshevist delegates met the representatives of the Central Powers at the close of 1917 and early in 1918 for the discussion of peace terms, and found that they had placed Russia in the position of a conquered people and in the power of an arrogant and unscrupulous enemy.

wireless announced that " by reason of the signing of the peace treaty with Russia, the military movements in Great Russia have ceased." They still continued to advance in the vast territories which Germany was tearing from her dupes, and that very day it was known that a large German fleet had seized the Aland Isles in the Baltic. The terms which Lenin and Trotsky accepted placed the Germans permanently within one hundred miles of **Bolshevists accept** Petrograd, and almost shut Russia out **Germany's terms** from the sea. Finland, Esthonia, Livonia, Courland, Lithuania, Poland, and the Ukraine all had to be surrendered to Germany for disposal, or for what the Germans jestingly called " self-determination." In the Caucasus the territory which the Tsars forty years before had conquered from Turkey was to be ignominiously restored to the Sultan. Kars, Ardahan, and Batum, for nearly half a century Russian towns, had to be given up. The Russian Anarchists were once more compelled to swallow their fine words. All propaganda work against Germany was to be stopped by them.

On the economic side they were made to grant Germany all the special privileges she had enjoyed in Russia under the commercial treaty of 1904, and to guarantee the duty-free export of ore. The " conscription of capital " and " nationalisation of all the means of production," which the Bolshevists had pompously proclaimed, were summarily stopped, for wherever Germans owned shares in banks or factories or mines they could claim immunity, and to touch them was to break the treaty.

The full terms of the treaty with the appendices were not published at once, seemingly because Lenin and Trotsky did not dare to confess to a wrecked and ruined Russia what treason they had committed. But, so far as the terms were divulged, they left Russia with a frontier which ran from Narva southward to Dvinsk, and thence to Pruzhany, on the frontier of the Ukraine. The exact area of the Ukraine was left in doubt, but according to German maps it included all Southern and South-Central Russia, and ran to the Caucasus range, and it could be indefinitely extended at the Kaiser's fancy. In addition to the territory which Russia had finally to renounce, a large area remained in German occupation, with a promise of future evacuation; but it was almost daily increased on various pretexts. The German military frontier on March 15th, 1918, is shown in the map on page 174, and extended from Narva in the north-east of Gomel, Zchernigov, and Kieff, to a point east of Odessa. German troops were close to Vitebsk and Mohileff, **Russia's partition** and within striking distance of Moscow **and humiliation** itself, whither the seat of Russian Government was removed on March 10th. Other German forces were at Abo in Finland, where a landing was effected early in March, and there were reports that one of the Hohenzollerns was to receive the Finnish crown. The total territory permanently abandoned by Russia covered an area of over 500,000 square miles of rich and valuable country, and if the Germans extended the Ukraine frontier this might be indefinitely increased. In German occupation were some 70,000 square miles of additional territory, outside Finland, the Ukraine, and the other areas ceded by Russia, and there was no security of any kind that the Germans would not permanently retain this land, since the Bolshevists had destroyed Russia's social organisation, finance, and military and naval forces. Many Russian warships in the Baltic and Black Sea were seized without resistance, though by a sudden counter-stroke of the Black Sea Fleet Odessa was recaptured at the end of March. German agents advanced with impunity into Siberia, and bands of armed and disciplined German prisoners destroyed important points on the Siberian Railway to prevent any action by Japan.

While the Germans acted and moved, the Allied Governments conferred and talked. So grave was the peril to all Asiatic Powers, and in particular to Japan, China, and Great Britain, so easy was the path opened to Germany by the utter collapse of resistance in Russia and the systematic destruction of the Russian educated and civilised class, that a swift occupation by Japan of the Siberian Railway was urgently required to prevent the

TRUE BROTHERHOOD IN ARMS.
In their single-hearted co-operation with Russian troops that did not betray their trust the men of the British armoured car section even volunteered on occasion to help man the trenches. This photograph shows them giving machine-gun instruction to some Cossacks who helped to try to stop the mad retreat.

Germans from making Siberia a new and vast German field of exploitation and supply. Such Japanese action would have been welcomed by patriotic Russians; it might even have steadied the Bolshevists and led them to pause in their cowardly surrenders to the German foe. But, as so often before in critical moments of the war, the Allies at this supreme hour failed in clearness of aim and concentration of effort. They still sunned themselves in the illusion that Russia, after she had committed suicide, could be resurrected swiftly, and that she was vigorous and alive. They did not **Russia out of** understand that where Napoleon had **the war** failed the Kaiser had succeeded; that where Napoleon had destroyed his own fighting strength in an impotent stroke against Russia, the Kaiser had levelled Russia in the dust and made of a once gigantic foe a magazine of man-power and supplies.

Bolshevist Russia had abandoned the war, and had become what Italy was in the eighteenth century, "a geographical expression." Her peoples, who under nobler leadership might have fought resolutely for their national

freedom, bartered it for an easier life and sank to the tragic position of slaves. On the Slav races they brought ruin and agony, and that which is crueller than either—shame—justifying anew Gibbon's taunt, and degrading " the national appellation of the Slavs from the signification of glory [*slava* in Russian means " glory "] to that of servitude." They who might have stood steadfast for their Lord in this conflict of right against wrong, denied Him and passed out into the outer darkness.

No surrender in the Napoleonic Wars **Disastrous** was so terrible to those immediately **consequences** concerned, so disastrous in its ulterior consequences. There is a certain wasp, described by M. Fabre, that attacks large beetles, paralyses them with an injection of poison from its sting, and then lays them up helpless in its nest to be devoured alive by its young. The beetle is enormously larger than the creature which exploits it, and retains life only that it may be useful to its assassin. Such was the fate henceforth reserved for Russia, or what remained of her. She was to be eaten piecemeal by Germany and the German vassal States, and sucked of her blood, since she had surrendered national independence as a child casts away a toy. Never before in her history had she been compelled to abandon everything worth living for, nor had she had to submit to be sundered into fragments and flung back into the disunion of the Middle Ages. Nor was there any promise of a dawn to come in this night which had descended upon her.

The Extremists were left to ruin her till Germany was ready to overthrow them. They who fancied that they were exploiting Germany were themselves exploited by her. The war had thus proved that the real " Sick Man of the East " was not Turkey but Russia. It had ended for at least a century, so able Russians declared, the conflict between German and Slav which began in the Middle Ages. This new triumph, after the capture of the vital line of communication to Constantinople and South-Eastern Asia, was by far the greatest German achievement of the war, An unbroken block of territory, either German or under German influence, now stretched from Zeebrugge to Riga and the Black Sea and Caucasus and the Persian frontier.

Beyond the fortified German frontier line lay a welter of weak States, waiting absorption and liable, from their conflicts with what yet remained of the old Russia, to gravitate to the German side and to fall into the iron clutch of Germany. The check which the presence of a great military Power on the eastern frontier had for four centuries imposed on the Hohenzollerns was removed.

By obtaining control of the great railway routes to Central Asia, Bokhara, and Tashkend, they could menace China and India. The foundations were laid for schemes of aggression far beyond anything of which even the wildest Pan-Germans had hitherto dreamed. The Kaiser's world-empire had indeed become a fact.

CHAPTER CCXXXV.

LIFE IN BELGIUM IN THE FOURTH YEAR OF THE WAR.

By Emile Cammaerts.

It is with more than common satisfaction that the Editors of The Great War present to their readers the following vivid description, by M. Emile Cammaerts, of the conditions of life in Belgium during the German occupation. Although not written in the past tense, according to the strict convention of modern history, the chapter rightly finds a place in this standard history of the war as a contemporary document produced under the stress of intense feeling by an ardent patriot who is also a great poet. In his use of the present tense the distinguished author has adopted the modern idiomatic equivalent of the historic infinitive so often employed by Tacitus, and the device serves to emphasise the poignant actuality of the description of the fortitude and endurance of the heroic Belgian people during the period of their great affliction.

IF we try to imagine the life of the civilians in some big town of the occupied part of Belgium—Brussels, for instance—we must never forget that the far-away rumbling of the guns can often be heard, that at regular intervals the tramping of German patrols resounds in the streets, and that there is scarcely an hour in the day when expectant food queues do not line the pavement in the populous quarters of the city. These constant features of Belgian life will at once give us the atmosphere of the picture which we are trying to sketch. As we have only fragmentary and incomplete evidence to go by, we may exaggerate the proportions of certain figures or miss the right colouring again and again. Sympathy, however burning, imagination however alert, cannot entirely supplement the lack of personal experience, of individual memories.

I have had the opportunity of talking to many who have witnessed these scenes and lived this life. It has become to me a vivid reality, especially at night, when apparently disconnected dreams carry me right into the middle of dear and familiar surroundings. But in such matters we ought to trust neither the visions of our heart nor the suggestions of our brain. The merest scrap of personal evidence is more valuable than the most elaborate description. In attempting to speak of life in occupied Belgium, with the material at my disposal, I feel

that I am bound to go wrong here and there, but whatever mistakes I may indulge in concerning other things, the rumbling of the guns, the tramp of the "field-grey," and the long queues standing for hours in the rain must remain as the background of the picture. This at least is true. It is the obsession of every one, the fundamental groundwork of every life, the source from which every Belgian draws his hope of deliverance, his hatred of oppression, and his dread of starvation.

I.—The Rumbling of the Guns.

The guns sound quite near in the army zones of Luxemburg, Hainault, and Flanders; but when the wind blows from the west, or when some important action is taking place, the drum-fire is heard distinctly as far as Brussels. The years of war have not yet dulled the people's attention to it. They stop in the street to listen to the low murmur. They wonder what is taking place. During the autumn of 1917, when the guns roared for weeks round the Ypres salient, they guessed the truth —that their masters were getting the worst of it. They even believed, in spite of the German communiqués, that the Allies had broken through, and the rumours of a German defeat spread like wild-fire through Brussels.

It must always be remembered that Belgium, from the hour of its occupation, has been practically isolated from the allied countries. The only

[Speaight.

THE KING OF THE BELGIANS.

King Albert's steadfast courage in the face of Germany's invasion of Belgium, and during the subsequent years of the struggle in which the greater part of his kingdom was occupied by the enemy, assured him an honoured place among the heroes of the Great War.

INHABITANTS OF BRUSSELS AWAITING RELIEF.
Men and women of Brussels gathered in the hall of one of the large banks patiently waiting their turn at a distribution of food in 1915. But for the daily pint of soup and loaf of bread served out to them by those who organised the system of relief these people would have starved.

stirs in their hearts. They hardly ever think of the danger which an allied advance may mean to themselves, of the fresh destruction implied, of the misery of leaving their homes and being turned out, once more, on the roads like helpless refugees. Should one of them ask, "What will happen if ' they' are obliged to retreat ? " a hundred voices would answer, " It would mean victory, and victory is worth any price."

For the Belgians may have given up their weapons, they may be invaded, they may even, in certain parts of the country, be driven like slaves to work for the enemy, but they do not consider themselves out of the war. There is something at once pathetic and wonderful in the value they attach to their patriotic resistance. They sincerely believe that they are the vanguard of the allied armies, and that in refusing to work for the enemy, in counteracting their propaganda, in disobeying their regulations, in rendering whatever

news is German or German censored, consequently disbelieved. When information from friendly quarters reaches Brussels through the forbidden Press, or some French or English newspaper, it comes about a month too late. The direct result of such a situation is a state of restlessness easily explained if we remember that in a country like England, for instance, where the public is not nearly so excitable, the most extraordinary rumours have found credence since the beginning of the war, in spite of the fullest information being given in the Press. The only difference is that in free countries such rumours are very often alarming, while in Belgium they are always inspired by the wildest and most reckless optimism.

Since the siege of Antwerp the Belgians have lived in this state of suspense, and though they have been disappointed again and again, they have not lost, after years of German oppression, the extraordinary faculty of creating good tidings and the most extraordinary readiness to believe in them. But whatever they may have imagined, the distant roar of the guns has remained the supreme argument. Every hope, every anxiety has been associated with it. Those who had sons, husbands, or friends in the Belgian Army shivered at the sound, for they knew that any offensive, even if successful, must be costly. To them, nevertheless, the distant voice of battle—the long drawn battle which must decide their fate and that of their country—is the inarticulate message of the outside world brought into their prison on the wings of the western breeze. And the pang of anxiety for the soldier on the Yser hardly subdues the irrepressible feeling of yearning and secret triumph which this sound

service they are able to render to the good cause, they have a considerable share in the success of the allied armies. Even the deportee who has been compelled to work in some German Kommando preserves this extraordinary pride. One man who had been obliged to leave the country in a hurry, being under suspicion, assured me that the work accomplished in Belgium was worth an army corps to the Allies.

Patriotism in passive resistance

This may well be exaggerated, though it seems evident that the resistance of Belgian civilians must considerably hamper German activity in this sector of their front. It may be almost impossible to estimate its importance in terms of men, but it is easy to realise that if Germany

DISTRIBUTING FOOD CARDS IN BELGIUM.
The only lady member of the American Commission of Relief, which succoured the Belgians before the United States became one of the belligerent Powers, said that the endless procession of men and women waiting for their small daily dole of food was something unforgettable.

were able to add 500,000 Belgian workers to her industrial army, to leave the Dutch frontier unguarded, and to reduce to a minimum the personnel of the police, she would derive considerable advantages from such a situation. Instead of this, she has been obliged to deport the men before getting any work out of them, which attempt has proved a failure from every point of view, to demolish industrial plant and remove the machines before using them, to place strong garrisons in the largest towns, to flood the country with spies and secret agents, and to line the Dutch frontier with sentries and two rows of electrified wire. These strong measures did not prevent 30,000 young men from joining the Colours and filling the gaps caused by the first campaign.

Sometimes, however—very frequently in the army zone, less frequently in Antwerp and Brussels—the booming of the guns bursts quite close to the expectant civilians. Londoners

"SOUPE COMMUNALE" UNDER THE STARS AND STRIPES.
Portion of a queue waiting outside a Brussels communal kitchen for the supply of soup in 1915. Men, women, and children lined up with jugs, cans, and other vessels in which to carry away the soup provided by the American Relief Commission.

are accustomed to the alarms and excursions of hostile air raids, but do they realise what the feelings of the Belgian people must be during a friendly attack? It is one thing to see the risk of war brought near to us by German airmen and to listen with satisfaction to the din of the barrage directed against them, and to open one's paper on the next day to read that one or two of the enemy machines have been brought down by our defences. It is another to be bombed by one's own men and to be torn between the natural anxiety for the safety of one's family at home and the greater anxiety for the safety of the pilot of the frail machine surrounded with bursting shrapnel. Mrs. Kellogg, the only American

Torn between two anxieties

woman member of the Commission of Relief, described one of these air raids over Brussels in 1916:

We were at lunch when suddenly the roar of the German guns cut across our talk. We rushed into the street, where a gesticulating crowd had already located the five allied aeroplanes high above us. Little white clouds dotted the sky all about them, puffs of white smoke that marked the bursting shrapnel. Our picturesque Léon [her Belgian servant] slipped over to assure me that this was not a real attack, but just a visit to give us hope on the second anniversary of the beginning of the war, to tell us that the Allies were thinking of us, and that we should soon be delivered. Without doubt they would drop a message of some sort. All the while the aeroplanes were circling and the guns were booming. Then, suddenly, one of the aviators made a sensational drop to within a few hundred metres of the Molenbeek Station, threw his bombs, and before the guns could right themselves, regained his altitude, and all five were off, marvellously escaping the puffs of white smoke before and behind them. This was thrilling, until suddenly flashed the sickening realisation of what it really meant. But to Belgian wives and mothers what must it have been? As they looked up they cried: "Is that my boy, my husband, who has come back to his home this way? After two years, is he there? My God! Can they reach him?" The only answer was the roar of the guns, the bursting shrapnel, and they covered their eyes. I visited Madame ——, whose only son is in the flying corps, at her toy-factory the following day, and realised what the experience had cost her. Her comment, however, was, "Well, now I believe I am steeled for the next."

The explanation of Léon was not altogether fanciful. The few raids over Belgium during the first year of the war were undertaken merely to cheer up the people and to spread comforting news. They provoked the wildest enthusiasm. People ran into the streets or climbed on to the roofs with a complete disregard of the bursting shrapnel, waving their hats and handkerchiefs and shouting themselves hoarse, though, of

FEEDING THE OLDER MEN.
A typical and pathetic scene at one of the food centres in Belgium organised by the American Relief Commission. The old men were able at this centre to remain and eat their allowance of food instead of having to carry it away for consuming at home.

A BELGIAN MEDICAL OFFICER'S QUARTERS.
Utilised as a first-aid post by the German troops during their temporary possession of it, this house was subsequently occupied by a Belgian Army medical officer.

course, the friendly airmen could not possibly hear them. Sometimes even the excitement was such that, in spite of the German decrees, the " Brabançonne " was once more sung in the streets. That small speck in the sky was a message from outside, the man would come again (didn't he say so in the proclamation he had scattered over the town ?), but next time the whole Army would follow him : " Courage, the hour of deliverance will strike soon ! " Nobody dared to question such words, and long after the airman had disappeared in the west the police were not able to clear the streets. People asked " How long ? " And those who suggested another month were scoffed at.

The next day, as might be expected, the **German shells** town was heavily fined, but everybody **in Brussels** agreed that " it was worth it."

After this, the regulations became stricter and the people were obliged to take shelter at once. Do not suggest to an escaped Belgian that such measures may be inspired by the desire of avoiding useless loss of life. The mere idea that the German authorities should think of his welfare seems to him ludicrous. No, if they forbid the people to remain in the streets, it is merely because the traffic might serve as an indication to the raider. Anyhow, it is a fact that, in order to get their regulations obeyed, the Germans used shells instead of shrapnel during one of the first raids (September 27th, 1916). They announced afterwards the names of the civilians killed " by the airman's bombs," but fragments of the German shells which caused the casualties were picked up among the wreckage, and the people understood.

Those who know what life is like in the small towns behind the British front in France will realise what is going on in corresponding districts in Belgium. In Courtrai, Roulers, Bruges, and generally in the army zone, the aerial bombardments have become too frequent and too severe to cause any particular excitement. The civilians accept them with stoicism and resignation. In spite of all their efforts, the Germans have not succeeded in stirring

the people against England, or even in breaking their spirit. A student of Bruges, eighteen years of age, who crossed the wire recently to join the Army, was asked when he arrived at Folkestone why he did not wait another year before enlisting. He explained that his house had been wrecked during a raid, his father was killed, his mother and sister lay gravely wounded in hospital. " There seemed nothing else for me to do." Many of the victims are detained in dangerous spots by the enemy in order to work for him, and when the accidents happen the Germans alone are considered responsible for them.

In March, 1917, the burgomaster and the town of Ghent were condemned to pay a fine of 10,000 marks in the following circumstances : After an aerial bombardment which had caused the death of several civilians, the Kommandantur issued a poster publishing the names of the victims " killed by British airmen." During the night some patriots substituted these words: " Killed by a German Zeppelin."

I cannot say if these words were merely prompted by the " parti-pris " of the ignorant or by the desire, which, thank God! is not yet extinguished in Belgium, to play a practical joke on the **Belgians and the** enemy. But even if they were to be **struggle** taken seriously they would convey some idea of the state of mind of the great majority of the people. The German is not only the oppressor, he is the scapegoat, the cause of all troubles, of all sufferings. I believe that, if the rain spoilt the crops, the Boche would at once be made responsible for it in some way or another. There is a rough-and-ready justice in the popular mind. The peasants know, of course, that no German can spoil the crops, but they know that he can requisition them. The citizens of Ghent know, or ought to know, that it would not pay the Germans to bomb their own lines, even for the satisfaction of killing a few Belgians. But they know also that they started bombing open towns and that, if it had not been for them, there would have been no war—in any case, no war in Belgium. Others may wander from the essential principles of the struggle—they are not likely to do so ; they are too often reminded of them.

It might have been expected that after three years and a half of waiting, and two years of severe privation, a population completely isolated from the rest of the world and fed on German censored news would show certain evident signs of lassitude. In every allied country the Russian collapse, by postponing the prospect of an early settlement, has more or less encouraged pacifist devices.

CAPTAINS AND KINGS OF STAINLESS HONOUR.
King Albert of Belgium presenting his generals to King George on the occasion of one of the visits paid by the latter to his heroic ally in the little strip of country held so doggedly after the first irruption of the German hordes through Belgium.

People realise that they have henceforth to choose between some form of compromise or a prolongation of the struggle and of the hardships it implies. It would therefore be only natural if such a reaction were felt particularly strongly by a nation faced with starvation and feeling all the might of foreign oppression. The Belgians have heard a great deal about the advantages which Germany is going to derive from the armistice in the east. They know very little concerning the reserves in men and in material of the Allies, which are bound to bring about the downfall of German militarism if they are used with determination. They are infected with an intense propaganda which represents King Albert as a prisoner of the British, and the Belgian soldiers as fraternising with the enemy on the Yser.

In spite of this, from all reports received, I think I may safely say that in no country of the Entente is the moral so sound on the war among all classes of the population. This conviction is not based only on the declarations of the determined young men who risk their lives and liberty in crossing the wire, and who might be inclined to judge the feelings of their compatriots by their

Population's sound moral own. It is founded on the declarations of the authorised leaders of public opinion, on the unanimous testimony of neutral observers, and even on the avowal of the Germans themselves. In the two quarters where some international tendencies might have shown themselves, among the Socialists and the Catholics, there has been up to now no sign of weariness.

The official memoir of the Socialist Party, written in July 1917, after the Russian collapse, is one of the most striking documents produced during the year. Already, in December, 1916, the Belgian Socialists had warned their " comrades " of the Entente against the dangers of a premature peace. Now that the Central Empires have been strengthened and that the industrial population has been brought to the verge of starvation, they claim again the restoration of their country in its absolute freedom and independence, the payment by the Central Empires of an indemnity for the damage done in Belgium, and the liberation of the oppressed nationalities in Europe. They repudiate indignantly the policy pursued by the Russian Maximalists and by those who, in neutral and allied countries, "stir up feelings of charity and humanity at the risk of sacrificing the most sacred rights of mankind." They remain convinced that " a satisfactory peace could only be concluded either through the military victory of

A CALL TO THE BATTERY.
Inside the telephone-post of a Belgian heavy battery. The artillery of the reconstituted Belgian Army won the great respect of the enemy by its very high efficiency in practice.

the Allies or through a radical transformation of ideas and institutions among the Central Powers."

As for the Catholics, under the energetic leadership of Cardinal Mercier they have maintained the most uncompromising attitude. The Germans are, for them, outside the pale of nations, and will remain there until they have atoned for their crimes. Again and again, in his pastoral letters and his sermons, the cardinal has developed the idea that only punishment and repentance could wipe out the memory of the outrages committed, and that Divine justice stands above even Christian charity. This sound doctrine has been so readily adopted by the people that, when the Pope issued his Note to the belligerents, not one voice was raised to defend it. The very name of peace could not be mentioned, and it is only since the various declarations of President Wilson and the British Prime Minister that a few moderates have **Uncompromising courage** been allowed to mention the possibility of resuming one day friendly relations with the enemy. But everybody agrees that they must be beaten first.

Such questions and many others concerning the future of the country are discussed every day, for it would be a mistake to think that social life is stopped in Belgium. There are, of course, no "functions" of any kind, and no public meetings are allowed by the authorities, except those of the activists. But behind the closed shutters of the mourning mansions of the aristocracy, in the cafés—at least, in the Belgian cafés, which, by a kind of tacit consent, no German will enter—in the homes of the bourgeois and of the workman, people gather more frequently perhaps than before, because there is more leisure for many, and because it is the way to save light and coal.

War conditions have revived the old custom of the " veillée," when a few friends and neighbours meet in turn in one another's houses. The women knit for the prisoners, or mend the family's clothes—it has become almost impossible to buy new ones—the

FRENCH WAR MINISTER WITH FRENCH MARINES.
General Lyautey, while French Minister of War, made a tour of the Flanders front defended by Belgians and of the strip of coast held by French Marines. He is here shown, with General Balfourier, inspecting the Marines who took part in the defence of Dixmude.

men smoke when some member of the gathering has been lucky enough to secure some tobacco ; and there, around the slow-burning stove, under the lamp, after the last German proclamation has been ridiculed—there is one at least every week—and when the housewives have exchanged recipes concerning some wonderful new substitute, plans are made for the future of the country, and the war is discussed.

I have had the opportunity of hearing several echoes of these small meetings, and never once have I heard that the Allies or the Belgian Government were blamed for pursuing the war. Sometimes people ask : " Is it really not possible to bring about the end of this ? " But they do not wait for the others to tell them that their wishes cannot yet be fulfilled. " Of course we know nothing. We must trust those who can judge. They know better." And, after the wit of the family has told some gossip which he has just picked up about " the tiger " (Von Falkenhausen),

Belgian, perhaps more than of any nation, it would be right to say, " It takes all sorts to make a world." It is unhappily true, then, that in some quarters greed has exerted its humiliating influence. The Germans have been able to buy off a few consciences, and some trades-people have not resisted the temptation to make fruitful bargains with the enemy. There is a small minority, a very small minority, of traitors and profiteers in Belgium ; but, strange as it may seem, there are no pacifists.

When I asked the reason of this para-doxical situation of one of my informers, who, by his position, had travelled a good deal about the country and had been brought into contact with people of all classes, he said :

Confident of the end

The thing which is most amazing for us when we come over here is to meet so many people sceptical about the issue of the war or suggesting the probability of a draw. It is a strange experience to see one's faith questioned by those who live in far better circum-stances and who, but for the losses on the field, have scarcely felt the war at all. You ask me the secret of our optimism. Before my escape from Belgium I should not have been able to ex-plain, but since I have been here I begin to understand. You wonder that we keep up our spirits in our German prison, cut off from the rest of the world. It is precisely because we do not hear too much about the Allies' efforts that we never doubt their success. Good tidings always reach us somehow, while we remain happily ignorant of all the internal difficulties, the petty rivalries, the plots of the defeatists, and the pro-German intrigues. On the other hand, we receive first-hand and trustworthy information concerning the situa-tion in Germany, the food crisis, the growing discontent of the masses, and the disaffection of the soldiers. The old Landsturmers quartered in our towns and the " embusqués " of our Komman-danturen have long ceased to be overbearing. They are fed-up with the war, and a great many are not afraid to say so. We judge the economic condition in Ger-many from our own, and we trust that somehow or other the machine, especially the industrial machine, will not bear the strain.

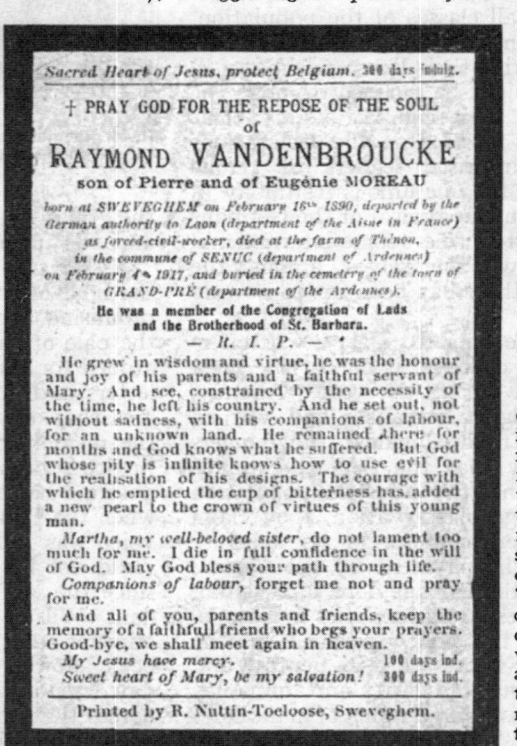

EVIDENCE OF GERMAN CRUELTY AND MENDACITY.
In the above "souvenir mortuaire" of a deported young Flemish man, forced to labour near the German lines in the Ardennes, is to be seen how much of truth there was in the German statement, made within a few weeks of his death, that "No Belgian deportee is working in Northern France behind the front."

or repeated one of the thousand anecdotes which circulate, in typewritten copies, in the cafés, and in the streets, the small party separates on the threshold. " To sleep is to dine," says the old French proverb. Many have to put this into practice, but it does not prevent them from making a joke of it.

I do not want to embellish this picture of Belgian life ; I do not want in the least to convey the impression that all Belgians are either martyrs or heroes. This illusion has already done too much mischief. On the contrary, no people in Europe is more deeply and more openly human, with all the qualities and the weaknesses which the word implies. Whatever the Belgians are, they show it ; they carry their character on their face, and their heart on their sleeve. They are unable to exercise self-restraint and to strike heroic attitudes. There is no classicism, no style about them, and no greater mistake could be made than to compare their action at the beginning of the war with that of Leonidas. The righteous feeling of a publican evicting a drunkard who is insulting his daughter is much more akin to the wild indignation which got hold of the average Belgian on the day of the ultimatum. Of the

Character of the people

I should add that we have no hope whatsoever that the present German Government will ever bend to any compromise without strong pressure from inside. We know their methods and their spirit too well to entertain any illusion on the subject. As far as Belgium is concerned, for instance, they will never give up their "guarantees," and the least of these guarantees is the preservation of the administrative separation of the country which would wreck the whole national fabric. As long as this attitude is maintained the war must go on. It is the right thing to do, since there is nothing else to be done.

The secret of our resistance is that we stand closer to Germany. We do not expect any miraculous concession from the German Imperialistic spirit, but, rightly or wrongly, we are convinced that we are witnessing the decline of this spirit. We do not believe in German organisation and German efficiency, because we can see ourselves how disorganised and inefficient it can be. We do not believe in German cleverness, because none of their tricks ever caught us napping. And we believe in the Allies' success because we see the results of their efforts without thinking of the difficulties they may experience in making them.

II.—The Tramp of the Soldiers.

Sometimes, at night, when people talk quietly of their hopes and miseries, when their thoughts wander towards some Belgian soldier in the trenches or some prisoner in the cold hut of a German camp, footsteps are heard in the street in front of the door. It is a German patrol—a few privates, led by a non-commissioned officer ; and for one

[Translation.]

COURAGE!

Belgians, your dignified attitude, your superb protests, have at last aroused neutrals. If during the last few weeks the foreign Press has not reached us, it is because it is unanimous in protesting against the cruel wrong done to your liberty by the occupying Power. Continue to show to the world the example of a country small in extent but great in moral value, and the unwearied courage of its children. Crushed under the heel of a brutal aggressor, continue to oppose Right to Might. This attitude will win for you the sympathies of all true hearts and the admiration of history.

Let none co-operate directly or indirectly with the crime of the Teuton Passive resistance in all and always, this must be your watchword.

LONG LIVE BELGIUM!

Please copy and circulate this leaflet.

DES ACTES !

Les Évêques ont jeté le cri d'alarme !

La magistrature et le barreau ont flétri les mesures de l'occupant !

Députés et sénateurs ont protesté !

Les administrations communales ont résisté !

Les syndicats patronaux et ouvriers ont vengé l'honneur de la classe ouvrière !

Bravo ! nous avons entendu la voix unanime de la Belgique !

Mais l'heure des protestations platoniques est passée ! L'heure de l'action sonne !

Ni la magistrature, ni le barreau.

Ni les députés, ni les sénateurs !

Ni les fonctionnaires, ni le clergé.

Ni le personnel enseignant.

Ni les employés des banques,

Ni les ouvriers, ni les patrons.

Ni chomeurs, ni non-chomeurs.

personne ne se présentera !

Nous sommes tous solidaires !

Celui qui se présente, soit fonctionnaire ou employé, soit magistrat ou avocat, soit prêtre ou instituteur, soit ouvrier ou patron, soit chomeur soit non-chomeur

EST UN TRAITRE

Il n'y a plus que des Belges qui ne veulent pas être des esclaves !

[Translation.]

DEEDS !

The Bishops have given the cry of alarm !

The Magistrates and the Bar have branded the measures taken by the occupier !

Members of Parliament and Senators have protested !

The Communal administrators have resisted !

The Unions both of masters and men have avenged the honour of the working classes !

Bravo ! We have heard the unanimous voice of Belgium !

But the time of platonic protests is past, and the hour for action strikes !

Neither the magistrates nor the bar, neither deputies nor senators, neither officials nor clergy, neithers teachers nor bank clerks, neither masters nor men, neither employed nor unemployed, *no one will answer the summons !*

We are all of one mind !

Whosoever answers the summons, be he official or clerk, magistrate or lawyer, priest or teacher, master or workman, employed or unemployed—IS A TRAITOR !

We are, above all, Belgians, and we will not be slaves !

COURAGE !

Belges, votre attitude digne, vos protestations superbes ont fini par émouvoir les neutres. Si depuis plusieurs semaines la presse étrangère ne nous parvient plus, c'est qu'elle est unanime à protester contre l'atteinte cruelle portée par l'occupant à votre liberté. Continuez à donner au monde l'exemple d'une nation petite par l'étendue, mais grande par la valeur morale et l'inlassable courage de ses enfants.

Écrasés sous la botte d'un aggresseur brutal, continuez à opposer le Droit à la Force ; cette attitude vous vaudra avec les sympathies de tout cœur bien né, l'admiration de l'histoire.

Que personne ne coopère *ni directement,*

ni indirectement au crime du Teuton :

Résistance passive

en tout et toujours, tel doit être votre mot d'ordre !

VIVE LA BELGIQUE

— *Prière de reproduire et de faire circuler.* —

[Translation.]

HOLD ON !

Citizens of Brussels, hold on !

Neutral Governments are protesting !

The Pope is intervening in our favour !

Dutch papers only reach us at very rare intervals !

The American Trade Unions are rising against the slavery that the Germans would impose upon us !

Citizens of Brussels, hold on !

It depends on your tenacity to save Belgium from slavery and dishonour !

If they want to take us, let them fetch us from our homes, from our garrets, from our dwellings !

Neither master nor workman, priest nor employed, workers nor unemployed, let none answer their call !

Let them arrest us all ! Rather all than a few !

We are all of one mind !

UNION IS STRENGTH !

TENEZ BON !

Bruxellois ! Tenez bon !

Les Gouvernements neutres protestent !

Le pape intervient en notre faveur !

Les journaux Hollandais ne nous parviennent plus que très rarement !

Les *Trades-Unions* américaines se lèvent contre l'esclavage que les allemands viennent nous imposer !

Bruxellois ! Tenez bon !

Il dépend de notre ténacité de sauver la Belgique de l'esclavage et du déshonneur !

Si on veut nous emmener qu'on vienne nous arracher un à un de nos faire de nos mansardes, de nos quartiers

Ni patron, ni ouvrier ni prêtre ni employé ni chomeurs, ni non-chomeurs ! personne ne se présente !

Qu'on nous arrête tous !

Nous sommes tous solidaires !

Plutôt tous que quelques-uns !

L'UNION FAIT LA FORCE !

LA LIBRE BELGIQUE

N° 126 — TROISIÈME ANNÉE — AOÛT 1917

PRIX DU NUMÉRO — Élastique, de zéro à l'infini (prière aux revendeurs de ne pas dépasser cette limite)

FONDÉE LE 1er FÉVRIER 1915

BULLETIN DE PROPAGANDE PATRIOTIQUE — RÉGULIÈREMENT IRRÉGULIER
NE SE SOUMETTANT À AUCUNE CENSURE

ADRESSE TÉLÉGRAPHIQUE
KOMMANDANTUR - BRUXELLES

APRÈS TROIS ANS !

4 Août 1914 - 4 Août 1917.

On the left is a reduced facsimile of the front page of "La Libre Belgique," the original consisting of four pages, each measuring 12 in. by 8¼ in. This paper, destined to be one of the most famous of secretly produced publications, in defiance of the Germans, the heroic Belgians started in February, 1915, and continued to issue from "a cellar on wheels," despite all attempts at suppression. The border, which appears black in this reproduction, is in the original in the Belgian national colours, black, yellow, and red. Bribes to informers, terrible threats, hard sentences passed on patriots suspected of being in any way connected with its production or distribution, and the deportation of anyone found to be in possession of a copy—nothing that the diabolical ingenuity of the German authorities could devise in the way of repression—served to stop "La Libre Belgique," which remained one of the outstanding marvels of unflinching and unquenchable patriotism. On this page also are given facsimiles (and translations) of the spirited leaflets issued from that secret Belgian press which did much to keep up the courageous spirit of a suffering people.

"FREE BELGIUM" AND PATRIOTIC LEAFLETS FROM THE BELGIAN SECRET PRESS.

moment the conversation stops and the women cease to sew. The rhythmic beating of the nailed boots on the rough pavement soon grows fainter. With a sigh of relief the women again bend their heads over their work, the men pull at their pipes, and, without further notice of this small incident, the talking is quietly resumed.

For you never know. At any moment the soldiers may stop, enter the house, and arrest one or more of the party. It might be here or it might be next door. It might be for some offence against the German regulations, or for nothing at all—an anonymous letter, or the denunciation of an " agent provoca- teur." Anybody, at any moment, is liable to arrest. Some have left in the morning for their office or for their work and never been seen again. Once arrested, you are brought straight to the Kommandantur, and, if your cross-examination is not considered satisfactory, sent to the prison of St. Gilles or some other gaol and put for weeks into solitary confine- ment pending your trial by a German military court.

Inquisition and victims

Terrible tales are told about the German inquisition, and one wonders really why the tormentors spend so much energy in torturing their victims when nothing prevents them from deporting them according to their own sweet will. It is true that Burgomaster Max and a few other prominent citizens were never regularly tried, and were simply packed off to Germany as " undesirable." But, as a rule, the oppressor likes to make a show of legality and to extract from the " culprit " a formal avowal, and, what is still of greater value to him, the denunciation of some " accomplices." Every possible means is used for this purpose.

Some people have been deprived of food to compel them to speak, others have been beaten, others were told that their wife or their child was dying, and that they would be allowed to see them if they confessed their crime. The examinations are kept up for hours in order to exhaust the strength of the accused, and when one examining officer is tired, another takes his place. There is a ghastly tale of a pregnant woman who was awakened in the middle of the night by a man of the secret police, an electric torch being flicked in her face to startle her and break her nerves.

I could not vouch for every one of these stories. Few of those who are supposed to have experienced such torture have come back to describe them. Enough is known anyhow to render these rumours plausible, so that the people should live in dread of the German police and the German spies who infest the country, especially in the large towns. They can be found everywhere, in the street, in the trams, in the cafés, in the churches, under any possible disguise. It is their business to find out who publishes and circulates forbidden papers, such as " La Libre Belgique," who brings news from the soldiers to their families, who helps volunteers to cross the wire, who entertains relations with the Belgian Government ; and when their quest remains fruitless, as it often does, to convict of such crime any good patriot who, for some reason or another, finds himself on their black list.

Their work was rendered more easy by the seizure of a certain number of copies of the " Libre Belgique." One of these thrown in the letter-box of any suspect or slipped in a drawer during a perquisition could serve as a pretext for his immediate arrest. A well-dressed gentleman called on the principal of one of the most important free schools in Brussels. He told this cleric that the school had been highly recommended to him, and that he wanted his two boys to be educated there. He insisted on paying beforehand the fee for the first term, and slipped, as he left, a banknote in the principal's hand, whispering in his ear, " For the ' Libre Belgique,' you know," and disappeared, after saying that he would bring his boys the next day.

Work of German spies

Something in the man's behaviour made the cleric suspicious, and he promptly sent the banknote to the office of " La Belgique," one of the German censored

A RUINED TOWNSHIP IN THE VALLEY OF THE YSER.

Dixmude, photographed by Lieutenant Coomans, of the Belgian Flying Corps, in August, 1917, from an altitude of 2,000 feet. The town, on the Yser, was captured by the Germans in November, 1914, and irre- parable damage was done, the Town Hall and fine Church of St. Nicholas. in the Grande Place—seen in the centre of this picture—being reduced to ruins. This is a scene that is typical of the war zone in Belgium.

BELGIAN BISHOP IN ENGLAND.
Monsignor de Wachter, with some of the refugee Belgian children whom he had confirmed. He had been sent by Cardinal Mercier of Malines to visit Belgians exiled in England.

papers subsidised by the "Politische Abtheilung," asking for a receipt. The next day the German agent reappeared, escorted by two soldiers, and declared that it was his painful mission to arrest the principal, since, by accepting the money, he had admitted that he was connected with the publication of a forbidden paper. "Which paper?" asked the priest, showing great astonishment. "The 'Libre Belgique.'" "It is the first time that I hear the name," was the answer. "I thought you meant 'La Belgique.' The money has already been taken there. I am sorry I made this mistake, but perhaps there is still time to claim it. Here is the receipt if you care to go."

The patriot avoided thus a penalty of from ten to twenty years' imprisonment or deportation to Germany. But, for one who escapes, how many fall victims of their confidence?—for the German military courts of Hasselt, Brussels, and Ghent may safely be compared with the "Bloody Council" of the Duke of Alva.

On the rampart of Bruges (writes the correspondent of a Dutch paper) old women wrapped in black cloaks appear from time to time. They do not speak to each other, but they pray in a low whisper. They pray for the dying, according to an old Flemish custom. They know that, behind the high grey walls of the barrack yonder Death is already looking some young people in the eyes. A quick rattle of guns is heard. . . . "It is all over," they say, and the tears run down their cheeks. Soon afterwards a cart loaded with coffins rolls towards the cemetery. This is not a vision of the past, it is the naked and terrible truth in Belgium to-day.

According to German statistics published by the "Deutsche Jurisprudenzzeitung," a hundred death sentences were pronounced in one year (1915-16). Since then we do not possess any official record. A German wireless, however, informed us in January, 1918, that from the beginning of Von Falkenhausen's régime— that is, since April, 1917—120 people had been condemned to death. It is true that the German statement only admitted thirty executions, but trustworthy reports from Belgium, giving the names of the victims and the dates of their executions, do not, unhappily, confirm it. The number of Belgian martyrs may, without fear of exaggeration, be estimated at thirty per month, from eight to ten of which are women. It is as if, every day of the year, a martyr fell, pierced by German bullets, behind the "high grey walls" of the Belgian prisons. Most of them are guilty of no worse offence than that which served as a pretext for the murder of Miss Cavell. They have helped soldiers to cross the wire, carried messages through the frontier, or fallen victims of the wily intrigues of some "agent provocateur." But the German authorities rely on

Martyr roll of Belgian civilians

terrorism to maintain order, and it is understood that "examples" must be made.

Here, again, stories are circulated the veracity of which cannot be easily checked, but I should not give an accurate picture of Belgian life if I did not allude to them. They are widely circulated in the country, and the people believe in them. They largely contribute to create the mixed feeling of terror and hatred which the tramp of the foreign soldiers awakes in every Belgian heart. Every squad may be a firing-squad, every officer an executioner. The two daughters of M. Groneret, a shopkeeper of Liège, were compelled to witness the death of their father and mother. Life was then promised to them if they consented to speak and denounce their "accomplices." The eldest, aged twenty, refused courageously, and was shot beside her parents. Pressure was then put on the younger, a girl of fourteen, but she remained firm to the last, and shared the same fate.

Murder of the Groneret family

There is no doubt about the execution of the Groneret family, but the horror inspired by the death of the two young girls may well have inspired some of the tragic developments of the story. Here, however, is a typical incident which has been reported by a trustworthy eye-witness: On December 15th, 1916, a woman of the Campine district, the mother of two children, came to the prison of Hasselt and asked to be allowed to see her husband. She was told that permission could not be granted just then, and was asked to call again the next day. When she came the porter gave her a parcel containing the clothes of her husband, who had been shot during the night.

Such examples could be quoted by the score. Some

PEACEFUL INDUSTRY IN THE WAR AREA.
Belgian soldier watching one of his brave countrywomen carrying on at her lace-making in one of the partially ruined villages to which many of the inhabitants clung through all the miseries of war.

DD

details may have been added by the popular imagination, but their main features remain true. They weave a kind of tragic background behind the everyday life. They stand as a threatening cloud above every Belgian home. The result arrived at by the authorities when they allow or encourage such cruelties has been attained. The Germans are feared. But hate is stronger than fear. In the street, when obliged to pass before a "field-grey," the Brussels bourgeois will look in another direction ; in the tram, no lady will remain in the car if a German takes his seat beside her. There are Belgian and German cafés, Belgian and German shops, and, in the country, where such arrangements are not always possible, the intrusion of an enemy is invariably followed by dead silence, even orders being given by signs. On August 17th, 1917, when a service for the birthday of the Austrian Emperor was celebrated in Ste. Gudule, the great **Belgian ostracism** church was deserted, and when, three **of the Germans** days later, the German Emperor crossed the town, only his soldiers and policemen were there to greet him. This complete ostracism may relax, to a certain extent, in small country towns and villages where only a few old and mournful men of the Landsturm form the whole garrison, but it is unmistakable and relentless in every town where even those patriots who speak to an enemy with the idea of getting some useful information from him live under a shadow.

The distance between victor and vanquished (a neutral who visited Belgium wrote in the "Nieuwe Courant," July, 1917) is as great to-day as at the beginning of the war. Walloons and Flemings appreciate the amenities of life, but they are also able to endure suffering. They are a stubborn people, more capable of hatred than any other. They have heart and nerve. And the German who dreams of protecting Belgium, dreams of a peace accompanied by the rattle of machine-guns.

The Germans sowed terror, thinking that they would reap the golden crop of submission, and lo! only thistles and nettles grow on the Belgian fields. And they wonder and ask themselves and every neutral they meet : "How is it ? What have we done that we should be hated thus ? "

The Abbé de Voghel, vicar of the Church of La Chapelle, in Brussels, was condemned to twelve years' penal servitude after the prosecution had asked for the penalty of death. He thanked his judges for granting him his life since his greatest wish "was to see King Albert enter his city at the head of the Army," in which the abbé's two brothers were serving. "But if you had given me less I should have been disappointed," he added, "it would have meant that I had not deserved so well of my country." Truly inexplicable behaviour ! But, if the Germans wonder at their failure, they do not alter their methods. They know no other. They no longer publish the names of the patriots sentenced by their courts, since such practice only prompts others to follow their example. They have also ceased to bury the **Savage punishment** martyrs outside the prisons, where people **for small offences** could come and pray on their graves and cover them with flowers, but they go on condemning them, deporting others and fining many more. According to their own admission, 100,000 sentences were pronounced in one year (1915-16), and this figure must be largely increased by now. The disproportion between the offence and the punishment is, perhaps, more suggestive of German terrorism than the most sensational stories of torture and wanton cruelty. Here are a few examples :

Parents are daily condemned to a penalty of three to six months' imprisonment and a fine of one thousand marks for " not having prevented their sons from crossing the frontier." Anybody who, verbally or otherwise, gives news from the soldiers to their relatives remaining in Belgium is heavily fined and deported to Germany. An official proclamation has been posted in Flanders declaring that anybody who should be taken carrying any weapon —even a pocket-knife—would be shot. At Antwerp M.

Gheyssens, a notary, who refused to put up for sale the premises of an English company, was condemned to six months' imprisonment, followed by deportation. A citizen of Hasselt was fined one thousand marks for closing his windows when the military band was playing in the market-place. M. Dejardin, a deputy of Liège, and the curate of Heusay, incurred, respectively, a penalty of one and five years' imprisonment for mistranslating an official document. (The curate had translated the signature : Von Tauchnitz, de vaurien,* and M. Dejardin. a miner, who did not know a word of German, had signed the paper without noticing the joke.) The burgomaster of Mons, for refusing to stand at attention before the military governor of the town, had to pay 7,500 francs, etc.

It is scarcely necessary to recall here the deportation of M. Max, the burgomaster of Brussels, and of his successor, M. Lemonier, whose crime had been to defend their constitutional rights ; or that of Professors Pirenne and Frédericq, whose only offence was that of declining to help the Germans in the creation of the new University of Ghent. For such trivial pretexts at least ten deputies and senators, fifteen burgomasters and aldermen, eminent advocates and well-known doctors, have been banished from the country.

The imposition of collective fines on the communes has become a regular source of income for the German war-chest. Any incident may serve as a pretext to justify such measures—a telegraph-post thrown down by a gale, the successful escape of workmen or recruits, the appearance of an allied aeroplane over the town, or a sympathetic demonstration towards British prisoners. In the summer of 1917 Mons had to pay 500,000 marks after a British air raid, under the pretext that it followed the announcement by a Belgian paper published in Holland that Prince Rupprecht of Bavaria had established his headquarters there. The small commune of Zele, near Termonde, was condemned to a fine of **Collective fines** 100,000 marks because the inhabitants **on communities** had distributed food and cigarettes to British prisoners. Malines was fined 20,000 marks because the local authorities had refused to clear up the wreckage caused by the bombardment of the town by the enemy.

The last example illustrates particularly well the German policy pursued in Belgium. It is not enough that the people should not do anything to help their country, they should also do everything to help Germany. It is not enough that they should refrain from any demonstration of sympathy towards their Allies, they should also exert themselves to further German aims. Malines should clear the ruins wrought by German guns, deportees should be employed on military work, professors should lend their name and reputation to the German University of Ghent, patriots should be compelled to dig trenches and build concrete dug-outs to shelter German soldiers. It is not enough that the tricolour flag should no longer be shown, gold must be painted white, and the Prussian colours fly from every window.

The tramp of soldiers has become especially loud in some Belgian towns. The Germans are not suppressing a rising. They are protecting a little band of traitors against the infuriated population whose patience is exhausted. For the stubborn hostility against the Boches, however burning, cannot be compared to the fierce hatred of the people against the few activists who, with German help and German money, are endeavouring to break up Belgium. There is a traitor in the Belgian tragedy. It is a man who, before the war, was regarded as a failure while he considered himself a success. He belongs generally to the intellectual class. It is a college professor whose head has been turned by the prospect of a chair at Ghent, or a civil servant who could not resist the temptation offered by a directorship, or a doctor in

---

* The German word *tauch* means to cheat, and the French word *vaurien*, a scamp.

Brussels in German occupation: Parade of German troops before the House of Parliament.

German Governor=General's Mounted Guard outside the King's Palace, Brussels.

Panoramic view of the terrain held by the Belgians near Luyghem, west of Houthulst Fores

Belgians damming dike waters to impede enemy.

Belgian refugees on their way to Engl

German trenches in the neighbourhood of Luyghem partially destroyed by Belgian artillery bombar

...g military footbridge over the floods, connecting a Belgian advanced post with the main line.

...ian peasants fleeing before the invasion.

Belgian sentries on a road exposed to German artillery.

...trenches were captured and occupied by Belgian troops in the battles of November, 1917.

Ruins of the Church of Merckem.   *Apse of the Church of Pervyse.*

German sacrilege: Malines Cathedral, showing the temporary screen hiding the wrecked choir.

search of patients, a singer without voice, a painter without talent, a poet without inspiration, or merely a debtor without any money—what the French call a "raté," a man who cannot forgive his country or his Government for the scant attention given to him in the past and who is ready to sell his soul for power, money, and a top-hat.

Such people exist in every country, and it is perhaps one of the worse features of foreign oppression that it gives them a chance to satisfy their greed and their rancour. They may be seen in Belgium to-day lecturing to the empty benches of the Ghent University, filling the most responsible posts of the deserted Flemish Ministries, going in and out of the Kommandantur bent on some cloudy errand. Dressed in brand-new frock-coats, they wander through the streets, trying not to see the look of hatred which follows them everywhere and not to hear the ironic greeting "Traitor ! Judas !" whispered by every passer-by.

In August, 1917, a certain Karl Heynderickx, formerly communal clerk at St. Nicholas, a small Flemish town, now promoted to a general secretaryship in the Flemish Ministry of Brussels and to a professorship at Ghent, was greeted in that fashion, in the market-place of his native town, by an advocate called Thysbaert. Heynderickx, in the hope of putting a stop to the practice, prosecuted Thysbaert before the Justice of the Peace, but Thysbaert was acquitted. The traitor then appealed to the German court, which naturally condemned Thysbaert to pay a fine, but a crowd assembled before the door, and, when the

German activist intrigue exposed

two men came out, the patriot was acclaimed and carried shoulder-high to his house, while Heynderickx was hissed and obliged to run for his life.

Similar incidents happen frequently. The professors and students at Ghent, the new officials at the Flemish Ministry in Brussels, are outside the pale of society. These men were so few, and their propaganda had so little influence, that the patriots never took the trouble to attack them seriously. It seemed scarcely worth while. But the self-appointed " Council of Flanders " proclaimed the " independence of Flanders," in January, 1918, and started a violent propaganda under German protection. In spite of the ridiculously small number of separatists (there are only a few hundred activists among the four million Flemings) this step might have proved dangerous in creating among the German people, and even among allied nations, the illusion that a certain part of the Belgian population wanted to dissociate themselves from the rest of the nation and to receive separate treatment at the peace conference. An " independent " Flanders meant evidently a German-protected Flanders. Though German statements have repeatedly assured us that they do not want to annex Belgium " violently," they might, later on, make the same answer to the Allies about Flanders as they did to the Bolshevists concerning the Baltic provinces : " We do not care to annex an inch of territory, but we cannot decently refuse to protect large provinces, if the people there claim our protection."

This sort of intrigue had, therefore, to be stopped at once. The Belgian people and the Belgian authorities in the country realised it, and decided to oblige Germany to show her hand and to declare openly that the activist movement was prompted and encouraged by her. The street riots at Antwerp, and the arrest and release of the activist leaders in Brussels, definitely exposed the intrigue. In Antwerp, on February 3rd, 1918, the crowd attacked an activist cortège in the street, tore their banners into shreds, smashed their musical instruments, and forced them to seek refuge in a picture-palace, where they remained blockaded for hours. The German police had the greatest difficulty in safeguarding the lives of the demonstrators and charged the crowd repeatedly with fixed bayonets.

In Brussels, a few days later, the Belgian Court of Appeal took the initiative of prosecuting the eleven signatories of a poster proclaiming the independence of Flanders. Two of them were duly arrested, on February 8th, and the judge was cross-examining them when a German major in full uniform rushed into the study of M. Jottrand, the public prosecutor, with great clatter of sword and spurs, and, thumping the table with his fist, demanded the immediate release of the two activist leaders. The scene was so loud that the public assembled outside. M. Jottrand only consented to give the order of release when Major Schauer had given him a written document stating that he took all the responsibility for the illegal measure. And a few moments later the Belgians assembled before the Palace of Justice could see the German officer walking out, carrying the voluminous dossier under his arm, with one traitor on each side. Such a picture was not soon to be forgotten. I need scarcely add that the three presidents of the Court of Appeal were deported as " undesirable," after which all the Belgian magistrates decided to suspend their sittings.

Extraordinary country, where the patriotic judges go on strike hand-in-hand with the patriotic workmen, and where an archbishop and the members of the Supreme Court are counted among the foremost ringleaders !

CARDINAL MERCIER'S PALACE IN MALINES.
Cardinal Mercier was one of Belgium's heroic figures during the war. Under his energetic leadership the Catholics maintained a most uncompromising attitude ; for them, until Germany's crimes were atoned for, the Germans were outside the pale of nations.

It is very difficult to give a trustworthy picture of Belgian life in the spring of 1918 without producing an impression of gloom. The situation of these seven million men, women, and children separated from their friends and relations in the Army or abroad, completely isolated from the rest of the world, left at the mercy of a victor who is exerting all his cunning in order to extract the last ounce of their energy, the last potato of their crop, the last shilling of their money, the last breath of their patriotism, is nothing short of desperate. It would be tragic in any Latin country. It may not appear so, to a superficial observer, in the country of Jordaens, Rubens, and Teniers.

There is no beer, not even tobacco. The people are fed on substitutes when they are fed at all, terrorism is rampant, the whole country, with its wide, rolling plains and capricious hills, **Laughter alive** has become a huge prison ; but laughter **despite terrorism** is not entirely dead. The Belgian's answer to the tramp of the soldiers is his laughter. Not bitter, defiant laughter, rather the broad, good-humoured laughter of a man who, in the circumstances, would rather be ruined or deported than give up a practical joke.

The spirit of Brussels under M. Max, during the first weeks of occupation, is still alive. The yoke has become

HUN INVADERS AT THE PLAY IN A BELGIAN THEATRE.
German soldiers in the auditorium of the Royal Theatre at Liège, the town which made an historic defence against them on the treaty-breaking invasion of 1914. Liège, which became a Belgian possession in 1830, was the capital of the province of the same name.

from hand to mouth. It is not a question for them of being able to obtain butter to put upon their bread, it is a question of obtaining any bread at all.

The Belgian people may be roughly divided into three classes —those who are entirely dependent on relief, mostly industrial workers, small shopkeepers, and a certain portion of the professional classes who have been thrown out of work or entirely ruined by the war; those who are only partly dependent on relief, including a number of the bourgeois class, whose income, though curtailed, allows them to pay the low prices of the " Comité National "; and those who are still entirely self-supporting, including the farmers, some merchants, and the owners of landed property. Out of the seven million people remaining in Belgium about four million are entirely or partly dependent on the work of the Commission for Relief. So that if, for one reason or another, the imports of food-stuffs under neutral control happened to cease, the majority of the population would, from one day to another, be faced with complete starvation.

It does not enter into the scope of this chapter to examine how such a situation has arisen. It is enough to point out that the Germans have failed to persuade the Belgians that the British blockade is in **Germany responsible for starvation** any shape or form responsible for it. This fallacy, propounded by the censored Press, has been repeatedly exposed by Cardinal Mercier and the local authorities who protested against the deportations. The people know that Britain allowed the import of foodstuffs under neutral control, and that, when these do not reach the country, as was the case in

heavier and the shoulders which carry it are slightly stooping now, but the face has kept its grin, the eye its twinkle. Any foreigner who could have witnessed the Antwerp meeting, and the peculiar means of obstruction used by the obstructionists—sneezing-powder, evil-smelling fumes, wild cries of a menagerie—would never have realised that these were patriots defending their national honour under the threat of machine-guns. Thank God! there is still some laughter left in the Belgian people, and, as long as it lasts, no oppression, no treason, can prevail on them. For is not laughter the deepest and dearest possession of freedom?

III.—The Spectre of Starvation.

" I shall never think of Belgium," writes Mrs. Kellogg, " without seeing endless processions of silent men and black-shawled women, pitchers in hand, waiting, waiting for the day's pint of soup. One and a quarter million make a long procession. If you have imagined it in the sunshine, think of it in the rain. A man may shut himself in his house and forget the war for a few hours, but he dare not venture outside. If he does, he will quickly stumble against a part of this line. . . ."

Not margarine queues, mind you, nor meat queues, but food queues in the fullest meaning of the word. If those who are waiting there did not receive their ladle of soup and their loaf of bread, there would be nothing, absolutely nothing, for them to do but to starve. It is the only thing which stands between them and absolute famine. There is no money, no reserve. These million and a quarter—they must be now over a million and a half—live from day to day and

SCENE IN LIEGE DURING THE GERMAN OCCUPATION.
A temporary bridge built by the Germans at Liège after their capture of the town. It was erected to replace the Pont des Arches, constructed in 1860-63 on the site of an ancient bridge. The Pont des Arches had been blown up by the Belgians before the town was yielded to the enemy.

the summer of 1917, it is owing to the torpedoing of the relief ships by U boats. They are also aware that, had Germany consented to submit to the same control regarding raw material, the Belgian workshops might have been kept busy, and half a million men would not have been thrown out of work. Not being able to use Belgian industry, owing to the stubborn refusal of the employers and the men to work for her, Germany has deliberately destroyed it, requisitioning stocks of material, taking away some machines, and destroying the rest of the plant. As early as September, 1916, a correspondent of the " Vossische Zeitung " declared that " the average cost of living was much higher in Belgium than in Germany." Why? Because, if the blockade paralyses German trade and deprives certain German workshops of raw material, these workshops and the workers belonging to them have been utilised by war industries. It is not the blockade which reduces the Belgian workers of Mons, Charleroi, and Liège to the desperate conditions in which they find themselves to-day. It is not even the enormous requisitions in money, food, and raw stuffs made by the enemy. It

The penalty of patriotism is the stubborn and splendid patriotism which made these men refuse to work against their country. Through the misery of German prison camps and Kommandos, through untold cruelties, starvation, illness, exhaustion, the deportees learnt their bitter lesson, and taught it, when they came back alive, to those who had been left behind. The Belgian civilians are starving to-day for the same reason for which they were massacred in August, 1914—because they resist Germany's will.

GERMAN OFFICERS COMMANDEERING STALLIONS IN BELGIUM.
Stock-raising was extensively carried on in Belgium, the animals supplying all the domestic demands, and furnishing an important article of export. The few years immediately preceding the war showed a downward tendency in the number of horses. Most of the live-stock was seized by the Germans.

Some misconception exists abroad concerning the food conditions in occupied Belgium. Some alarming news reached England during the first year of the war, when the scarcity of meat was largely compensated by a plentiful supply of cheap fruit, vegetables, and farm produce. On the other hand, during 1916, when prices were rising fast and the position had become alarming, some superficial observers took upon themselves the responsibility of declaring that the situation in Belgium was not much worse than in England. Conditions change, of course, from month to month and from place to place. It may be assumed that in the country districts, where the German requisitions are necessarily less drastic, and where people can still obtain such necessaries as eggs, milk, and potatoes at a reasonable price, life is far less painful than in large towns. There has been at times a strong feeling against certain farmers who were accused of hoarding food or of selling it to the Germans. But this antagonism, which was to a certain extent fostered by the enemy, has been considerably allayed by the patriotic devotion of country people to their relations and friends in town, or even to total strangers dwelling in industrial districts.

Men and women from the Liège region, unable to support their families, tramp sometimes for days in Hesbaye or Flemish Limbourg in order to obtain food at the farms, and they seldom come back empty-handed. Walloon children by the thousand are found as far as the Dutch frontier in places where they cannot make themselves understood. But the voice of heart does not need translating. It has become a regular custom for anybody feeling the strain of

BELGIAN WOMEN AND GERMAN SLAVE-DRIVERS.
Belgian women and children employed in a mill at Moustier under German military control. This picture poignantly suggests the terrorism under which the people lived—the girls apprehensively awaiting the result of a colloquy between one woman and a soldier, which an officer is grimly watching.

war-life to " take a cure " in some remote village. This last resource, however, will soon disappear, since it becomes more and more difficult for the peasants to protect themselves against the Germans' greed. In the army zones people are dragged to prison for hiding a pound of potatoes, and incur heavy fines if they do not declare everything—corn, hay, eggs, poultry, cattle. In these parts the Germans help themselves, and have long ceased to trouble about payment.

I will not dwell at any length upon the conditions of the working class and the low middle class in large industrial centres such as those of Mons, Charleroi, and Liège. I can only assure my readers that nothing which has been written concerning the starvation of Belgium is exaggerated, as far as these districts are concerned.

Destitution and high mortality The miners are the only workmen who are not thrown out of employment. In Hainault the number of destitutes increased, in 1917, from 60,000 to 400,000. The great majority is dependent on the communal soups and the 300 grammes of bread provided by the " Comité d'Alimentation." This is about half the food necessary to keep alive a man not doing any physical work. The sufferings are increased in winter by the enormous price of coal (over £10 a ton), and of clothes and boots, which are now practically unobtainable. The Germans have commandeered for their " Zentrale " all potatoes, sugar, and fats, only relinquishing a small portion of the material production to the " Comité." The price of other foodstuffs purchased in shops has become so prohibitive that even the well-to-do are strictly rationed. (Eggs cost 1s., coffee 15s. the pound, milk 8d. a pint, a small cabbage 1s. 6d., etc.) The mortality has trebled, and tuberculosis is threatening the very existence of the race. In Brussels alone the number of deaths from consumption, which was 307 in 1914, increased to 308 in 1915, 387 in 1916, and 482 in 1917. Before the war there was an average of 150 births against 140 deaths per week. In 1917 there were only 120 births against 279 deaths.

But the aspect of a town is more eloquent than all statistics. The German correspondents, who only wander through the central " boulevards " and near the stations, may well speak of overcrowded theatres, brightly-lit shop windows and cafés, and the animated crowds which fill the streets. A city where thousands of men come on leave, which is constantly crossed and recrossed by troops going and coming from the front, is bound to be animated. There are German theatres, German concerts, German shops, and German cafés which remain open till twelve at night. But this has nothing to do with the life of the average Brussels citizen, who avoids the centre of the town haunted by the " field-grey " and their female friends, and seeks refuge in his suburb where he lives with his neighbours as in a village.

The fact is that, owing to the presence of the enemy and the difficulties of communication, town life is dead, and only suburbia remains. The Monnaie Theatre, **Belgian town life dead** when not commandeered for some German performance, remains closed. No big concerts are given by Belgian orchestras. A few cinemas are still frequented in winter, partly because it has become cheaper to go out than to stay at home, where fire and gas have to be kept burning, and the cafés have remained what they were before the war—popular clubs where neighbours and friends gather in the evening to drink, to smoke, and to gossip. Even the distasteful war-beer made with horse-beans, and the dull tobacco made with chestnut leaves, have not put a stop to this deep-rooted national custom. For, if the fare is bad, the gossip is more lively than ever. There is the whole world to talk about, and sixty million Germans to abuse.

Those who knew Brussels before the war, the gay city with its noisy streets, loud-speaking crowd, and comfortable life, would be staggered if they could wander to-day about the deserted and silent thoroughfares of the upper part of the town. But for the few cars used by the Kommandantur and the " Comité National," no motors are to be seen ; cycles have vanished ; unemployment has considerably decreased the pedestrian traffic. The tramways, on the other hand, are very active. They are the principal means of transport for public services, all heavy material being conveyed in small open trucks along the line. Even burials take place in that way, the coffin being placed in the first carriage, and the family and friends sitting in the second. A few months ago a few oxen, donkeys, and old horses were still employed by private firms. Now they are seldom to be seen. The dustmen, for instance, must drag their cars along, and it is a painful sight to see these weak men in harness struggling to climb the steep streets. Another remarkable feature, in a town where no household was complete without some pet animal, cats and dogs are quickly disappearing. No regulations have yet been made in Brussels, as in Ghent, for instance, about the slaughtering of dogs, but such regulations have become useless. There will soon be no dogs left.

If there are few passers-by, they can be heard approaching from afar, owing to the wooden soles which replace the old leather ones when these are worn out. Many poor people walk in wooden shoes, and even some policemen are seen wearing this rustic footgear. The women do wonders to look neat and smart, and they succeed to a certain extent. Only their intimate friends know that their new dress is the third edition, modified and converted, of an old pre-war " toilette," and they do not easily confess that their best coat has been made out of an extra blanket. Owing to the requisitions, wool, cloth, and even linen have become so valuable that, in some cases, robbers have taken **Devotion of the " Little Bees "** away the clothes of their victims, reviving the custom of the old highwaymen.

The enemy has seized every kind of brass in the cafés, tramcars, and public buildings, and even in private houses. All the brilliant copper fittings are replaced by dull iron. The shine has gone from the gay city. After the scarcity of food, this want of brightness and spotless cleanliness is perhaps the severest trial of the Brussels housewife. It was the great luxury of the poor in Belgium. Water is still plentiful—it is perhaps the only thing which has not been affected by the war—but a small piece of soap is worth four shillings.

And still through frost and snow, through wind and showers, unexpectedly the queues of " silent men and black-shawled women, pitchers in hand," bar the way, and the wanderer realises that out of 750,000 people who live in Brussels, from 200,000 to 250,000 are destitute. Besides these grown-ups who wait before the " Soups," there are crowds of children who gather at 11 o'clock before the canteens for subnormal children, to take the extra meal provided by the " Petits Abeilles," the private association known in Brussels as the " Little Bees." Twenty-six thousand children are fed by 2,000 to 3,000 women of all classes who have volunteered for this work since the beginning of the occupation, and looked after by one hundred and twenty-five physicians who are giving their services.

The " Little Bees " are all volunteers. They receive a subsidy from the Commission for Relief, and go from door to door to collect alms. They gather in this way, in Brussels alone, £100 a week, besides gifts in food, and bring their honey back to the hive. Their popularity in the town has grown tremendously, and it is believed that it is owing to their untiring efforts that the mortality among children has been kept within bounds.

Queen Elisabeth was the promoter and the patroness of the association before the war. But, in spite of the absence of their Queen, engaged in sterner duty on the Yser front, the workers have remained faithful to their

895

Merckem, in Flanders, west of Houthulst Forest, as it was photographed from the air in 1915, after the first bombardments. Though it had been damaged, the village was still recognisable, the church (seen below the middle curve of the road) having only lost its spire.

Merckem, as it was seen from the air in 1917, after many months of bombardment by artillery had reduced it to a mere tract of shell-pitted ground, the line of the old road through it, and the foundations of the church, remaining but dimly discernible.

SEEN FROM THE AIR: FLEMISH VILLAGE OBLITERATED BY ARTILLERY.

post, and will be able, when the time comes, to render a glorious account of themselves. This is how Mrs. Kellogg describes the rush of youngsters in the canteen :

It was raining outside, but all was white and clean and inviting within. Suddenly there was a rush of feet in the courtyard below. I looked out of the window ; in the rain 1,662 children between three and fourteen years, mothers often leading the smaller ones, not an umbrella or rubber among them, were lining up with their cards, eager to be passed by the sergeant. These kind-hearted, long-suffering sergeants kept this wavering line in place, as the children noisily climbed the long stairway, calling, pushing. One little girl stepped out to put fresh flowers before a bust of the Queen. Boys and girls under six crowded into the first of the large airy rooms, older girls into the second, while the bigger boys climbed to the floor above. With much chattering and shuffling of sabots they slid along the low benches to their places at the long narrow tables. The women hurried between the wriggling rows, ladling out the hot, thick soup. The air was filled with cries of " Beaucoup, mademoiselle, beaucoup ! " A few even said " Only a little, mademoiselle ! " Everybody said something. One tiny, golden-haired thing pleaded, " You know, I like the little pieces of meat best." In no time they discovered that I was new, and tried to induce me to give them extra slices of bread or bowls of milk.

Though they bear other names in other towns, there are " Little Bees " all over the country looking after 253,000 subnormal children, and fighting hard to protect the little ones against tuberculosis and other diseases which are the direct result of the food crisis.

It is almost impossible to give an idea of the efforts made in Belgium to preserve the race and alleviate suffering. The schoolchildren (there are 1,200,000 of them) receive an extra meal at 4 p.m., given them by the school-masters and schoolmistresses. The " Drop of Milk " cares for expectant mothers, and has 53,000 babies under supervision. The Clothing Relief provides several hundred thousand garments, besides giving a few hours' employment a week to 25,000 seam-stresses in Brussels alone. The lace industry—the only industry whose exports are allowed—keeps 48,000 workers busy. The " Restaurant Economiques " provides over 10,000 cheap meals a day in Brussels to the many " Pauvres honteux," who would rather endure severe privations than be seen in the soup queues.

All these foundations are sub-sidised by the communes and the Commission for Relief, and none of them could work for more than a month without the help of volunteers and the con-stant flow of private subscriptions. Mr. Hoover speaks of an army of 55,000 volunteer workers on relief that has grown among the Belgian and French people, " of a perfection and a patriotism **Charity born of** without parallel in the existence of any **patriotism** country." It is " to the growth of the relief organisation, and the demand it has made upon the people's exertions and their devotion, that its moral has flowered in such a fine national spirit and stoical resolution."

The Belgians have refused to work for Germany, but they are working for Belgium harder than ever ; some of them are so engrossed in this new undertaking that they have no time to weep over the past. Their sight must remain clear like that of the pilot of the ship, for there is danger ahead. Never has there been so little money in the country, and never have so many charities flourished.

The Army is worshipped. In many homes the picture of the absent soldier occupies the place of honour in the living-room, and is surrounded with small household treasures. Tapers are kept burning before these shrines during the winter nights, and they are surrounded with flowers in summer. The soldiers' children and the orphans are the object of solicitude of hundreds of associa-tions, such as the " Secours des Enfants de nos Braves," the " Obole populaire," the " Friends of our Soldiers' Children," the " Orphan's Flower," and the prisoners in Germany are not forgotten by " L'Adoption," the " Comité du Soldat Belge Prisonnier," while the disabled are looked after by " La Fraternelle des Soldats Mutilés."

The last escaped civilian I interviewed **Belgian people's** was fifty years of age. He kept a **spirit indomitable** small pork-butcher's shop close to the school where I used to go as a boy. I remembered his face distinctly. He is greyhaired now, and only half his normal size. He explained to me how he had crossed the wire at great risk with his son a month ago, and had come to England in order to enlist in the Army. They had taken his boy at once, but he encountered great difficulty owing to his age and physical condition. " They think I am too weak," he protested, " but I am putting on a pound a week since I have left the country." I asked him how things were going on in his quarter of the town, and what the people thought of the war. He said :

THE DEFENDER OF LIÈGE.
General Leman (in the centre) on a visit to Paris. It was General Leman's heroic defence of Liège against the German onslaught at the beginning of the war which held up the enemy and so gave the Allies some further days to prepare for the attack.

The Russian débâcle coming on the top of the Italian defeat has been a great disappointment, of course. The Bruxellois realise that they are in for another year of it. They begin to wonder how they will stand the joy of seeing the King and the Army enter the town. Will they have enough strength left to bear it ?

It was one of the most heart-rending pieces of eloquence I have ever listened to. His eyes were swimming, and he could scarcely control himself. The patriotic fervour of this old man, who had spent thirty years of his life selling ham and sausages, might well stand as an example to many intellectual sceptics who delight in understanding " the other side's point of view."

" The great characteristic of the Belgian people," writes Mr. J. G. Blieck, in the " Amsterdammer," after spending two years in the occupied provinces, " is the uncon-querable strength of their living spirit, this spirit which remains silent because obliged to do so, but remains untamed, which laughs because inclined to do so and because it knows. Yes, even in the present circumstances, the spirit of Belgium laughs ! It laughs at the incongruities of life, mocking the warrior's sword, mocking its own misery. But laughter means victory ; and it is precisely because Belgium began again to laugh so soon, and has never ceased to laugh since, that she will conquer. She does not even resist the evil spirit, because it has no hold upon her.

" She has remained entirely free. The Belgians laugh in their prison ; the fire which burns their staunch, indomitable souls will not be quenched. They do not allow themselves to be downhearted ; they remain stubborn and proud. They are really strong because, in their unconsciousness, they are above the contingencies of our miserable life. They are strong because they accept their misery, and refuse to admit that they are miserable."

CHAPTER CCXXXVI.

THE ROMANCE OF THE BRITISH CABLE SERVICE IN WAR.

British Submarine Cable System an Instrument of Dominion Over the Seas—The Eastern Telegraph Company—Refusal of Permission to the Western Union Company to Land a Cable in Germany Results in Germany's Complete Isolation—German Attack on Swakopmund—The Nürnberg at Fanning Island—The Emden's Raid on Cocos-Keeling Islands—Flight of the Emden on H.M.A.S. Sydney's Arrival on the Scene—Melodramatic Escape of the German Raiding-Party in the Ayesha—Abortive German Attacks on St. Vincent and Funchal—British Capture German Wireless Station at Duala and Link Up the British Forces in Cameroon with the War Office in London—British Cable Ships at Gallipoli—Abuse of British Cables for Espionage Purposes by Teutonic Agents and by Officials of Neutral Countries—Friction with Sweden and with Holland—Cable Embargo Stops Dutch Traffic with Germany in Sand and Gravel for Military Use.

IN the exercise of sea-power the British Fleet is only one main instrument of dominion. The British submarine cable system, with the British Mercantile Marine, completes the circle of the outer forces of the Grand Alliance. Throughout the war the British Empire and its Allies have continually drawn much strength from the results of the work of inventive British engineers and enterprising British and American capitalists.

Since the English Channel was linked up, in 1852, by seventy-five miles of cable laid between Dover and Ostend, the power of the British cable organisations has extended to the habited ends of the earth. The Eastern Telegraph Company has a line running from Land's End, through the Mediterranean, to Suez, and on through the Red Sea to Bombay, there linking with Madras, Singapore, Hong-Kong, Australia, and New Zealand. Most of the cables surrounding Africa are controlled by the English company, and many of those that cross the ocean to South America are under its management.

Other British companies and Government authorities control important deep-sea electric communications, and a large proportion of foreign cables running beneath the great seas

GERMAN CABLE RAIDERS AT COCOS.

One of the landing-party of Germans—and one of their four Maxim guns—from the raider Emden, which destroyed the cable station at Cocos, in the Indian Ocean, in November, 1914. When the Emden steamed away to meet her fate, the landing-party got away in a commandeered yacht.

is the property of United States corporations. Some time before the war, Mr. Gerard, when U.S.A. Ambassador in Berlin, endeavoured to obtain permission for the Western Union Company to land a cable in Germany. There was only one cable direct from Germany to America, running by the Azores Islands and owned by a German company. By a happy exhibition of greedy selfishness the German company successfully fought against any American invasion of its monopoly. The result was that at the outbreak of war, when the German cable was cut by the British Navy, all full, regular, instant communication between the Teutons and their sympathisers in America was stopped.

Touched with the irony of the affair, Mr. Gerard, in August, 1914, told Herren Ballin, of the Hamburg - American Line, and Gwinner, of the Deutsche Bank, the facts of the situation. Fierce was the anger of the two Germans when they saw how much they might have saved for their country and their companies if there had been an American-owned cable landed in Germany. They complained personally to the Emperor in regard to the corrupt influence exercised by the German Cable Company. A few days afterwards Mr. Gerard was officially informed that the Western Union Company was granted the right to

213

land its cable. But the grant was given too late. The British Fleet, operating at the time in the Bight of Heligoland, had already cut five German submarine cables running from Borkum to Brest, Vigo, Tenerife, and New York. No fresh cables were permitted.

As all the German oceanic cables passed under the English Channel, it was easy to cut them, and impossible for the enemy to repair or replace them. The cutting of six other cables between Germany and Great Britain was a still easier affair. Germany then could not communicate by cable across the oceans.

The messages she tried to send through Holland, Denmark, Norway, and Sweden had to pass through Great Britain and France. All Scandinavian and Dutch submarine lines were landed on the shores of the Western Allies. In the south the Teutons could reach cable stations in the Adriatic and connect with lines in the Mediterranean. There, however, the old long-distance British monopoly came into operation, and the Eastern Telegraph Company remained master of the inland sea and its electrical connections with Africa and Asia. In regard to the Far East, Germany was again blocked, as all land lines passed through either Russia or India.

According to German statistics there remained, after the cutting of German cable connections with North and South America and Africa, some three hundred and thirty thousand miles of submarine cable in **British control** operation. But two hundred and eighty **all cable lines** thousand miles of the total were in British control. Recent advances in wireless telegraphy did not compensate the Germans and Austrians for the cutting of their cables and for the censorship of all messages they sent over neutral connecting lines.

Most fortunately for the Grand Alliance, the marvellous invention of Marconi was still in a state of delicate development. It was possible to maintain a continual attack upon the most powerful German wireless stations, and jam the messages they sent out. Even in ordinary peaceful circumstances the working of long-distance wireless telegraphy across the ocean was subject to strange disturbances.

When to these natural disturbances there was added all the artificial means of interruption the Allies could command, long and regular communications between Nauen in Germany, Sayville in the United States, and Windhoek in South-West Africa became practically impossible. The Germans got through short messages with considerable trouble, but the codes they used were often translated, with some results that were equivalent to a military disaster.

The Germans were almost entirely cut off from direct telegraphic communication with their colonies, and had no means of communication with their great liners in foreign harbours and with their hundreds of trading ships. The great network of their commerce in neutral lands was seriously interrupted. **Isolation fatal to** When their agents in North and South **German activities** America were desperately working to help their commerce-destroyers, and provoke economic and political trouble in neutral countries that were favouring the Grand Alliance, the loss of clear and rapid cable connection probably did more than anything else to lead to the eventual defeat of the enemy's manifold schemes.

In some cases the Germans had to risk their submarines in order to get into short-distance wireless communication with their plotting agents. The history of German

THE BROKEN CABLE.
Lifeboat of the sunken collier Buresk, used for repairing the Cocos-Perth cable. One end of the severed cable is made fast at each end of the boat.

intrigues in Spain might have been very different had it been possible to send long, regular, and swift messages by cable. There were many other remoter States in which German and Austrian propaganda and intrigue were sadly hindered by lack of good communications.

All these facts were frankly admitted in detail in an article published by the authoritative German organ, " Blatter Für Post und Telegraphie." The writer remarked that the British people enjoyed an almost limitless dominion over telegraphic communications, and used their control of submarine cables as a remarkable instrument for the expansion of their position in the world. The superior power of the British Fleet assured the cables against hostile attack,

LINK IN BRITAIN'S GIRDLE ROUND THE GLOBE.
Germans on the wharf at Fanning Island, in the Pacific Ocean, raided by their cruiser Nürnberg in September, 1914. A landing-party from the ship there severed the cable from British Columbia to Australasia —part of the round-the-world cable system—and partially wrecked the instruments of the cable station.

while the cable system, according to German estimate, practically doubled the fighting value of the British Navy.

Naturally the Germans did all they could to destroy or damage the vast British network of electric communications that linked together the British Empire. Directly war broke out, the four British cablemen at Swakopmund, in South-West Africa, who had the misfortune to be in the only British station in German territory, were arrested on the false charge of having communicated with the military forces in Cape Town. The four men were treated as base criminals, and confined, each in a small cell, in Windhoek Gaol. Then, without having anything proved against them, they were removed to an internment camp fifty miles away, from which they were afterwards

DESTROYED DYNAMO-ROOM AT FANNING ISLAND.
In September, 1914, the German cruiser Nürnberg arrived at Fanning Island, in the Pacific Ocean, and sent a party on shore to destroy the cable station. This photograph shows part of the station as the Germans left it.

WRECKAGE AT COCOS CABLE STATION.
Cable-room at the Cocos Island station, in the Indian Ocean, after the landing-party from the German raider Emden had worked their destructive zeal there in November, 1914.

compelled to trek on foot a hundred and thirty miles farther north. Again they were marched a hundred and twenty miles south to Otjiwarango. They were kept on starvation rations, subjected to the insults of angry mobs, marched north and south until they were worn out, and finally released, after nearly eleven months' imprisonment, by General Botha. In the meantime the great Boer general, having captured Swakopmund, repaired the cables there, and linking them with a new telegraph system, directed his enveloping movements with complete electric communications that greatly helped him to rapid and overwhelming victory.

Germans attack Fanning Island Through lack of sea-power the Germans could not thoroughly destroy the Swakopmund cable by dragging it up at various points in the deep sea and cutting it into fragments. They could only damage the shore end and smash the instruments. Their general lack of real destructive power was clearly displayed in the attack upon the Fanning Island station on September 7th, 1914.

Fanning Island is one of a group of lonely coral islets lying in the Pacific Ocean near the Equator, some considerable distance below the Sandwich Islands. From British Columbia the cable runs for three thousand six

hundred miles, in the longest single sector in the world. From the coral island the cable then extends to the Fiji Islands, and thence to New Zealand and Australia, bringing the Australasian Dominions ten thousand miles nearer to Canada than they formerly were, and making, with the Eastern Telegraph lines, a complete British telegraph cable system round the earth.

Admiral von Spee had a keen appreciation of the importance of the British cable system between Australasia and the rest of the British Empire. He detached the light cruiser Emden for raiding and destructive work in the Indian Ocean, sacrificing this important ship to destroy the Cocos-Keeling station. He also despatched the light cruiser Nürnberg for a quicker and less perilous attack upon the Fanning Island station.

The Nürnberg left Honolulu with a collier, on September 1st, 1914, and arrived off Fanning Island early in the morning of September 7th. She came in under a French flag, and the superintendent, Mr. A. Smith, went down to the shore to get the boat off and meet the French commander. He hoped to get a fresh steak and some ice for breakfast, but all that was offered him was a bullet through his head; for a German officer pointed a revolver at him and called upon him to surrender. **Apparatus not wholly destroyed**

The superintendent surrendered very promptly because he could see that he was also covered by a Maxim gun in one of the enemy boats. The Maxim was then placed in such a position as to command the station, while German Marines and seamen entered the compound, stopped the operators working in the office, placed them against the wall with their hands up, and set to work with axes to smash up the instruments.

The work of destruction, however, was not carried out in a thorough manner. A remarkable amount of useful gear was left untouched, because the Germans were more interested in a profitable raid upon the superintendent's office. They found a considerable amount of money and, unfortunately, some private papers giving the position of buried spare instruments. These were discovered after a search and destroyed, as were also the electric-light installation and the refrigerating plant.

The cablemen were unable to convince the Germans that the ice-making apparatus was a harmless necessity of life on a tropical island. The plant was regarded as something to do with wireless telegraphy, and blown up with dynamite. Both the Canadian and Fijian ends of the cable were gun-cottoned at the shore, and then grappled and cut some two miles out. Happily none of the inhabitants of the islands suffered any personal injury from the German landing forces, Admiral von Spee's men being indeed uncommonly courteous and rather apprehensive of their own end.

In the office, where the German visit had been expected for three weeks, a cable message was posted stating that the Nürnberg or the Leipzig was due any day. One of the German officers saw the notice and said with a smile, "Rather interesting, don't you think? I will take this as a souvenir." Some of his comrades also sawed down the giant flagstaff, on the top of which flew the British flag, and annexed this also as a souvenir. In twelve hours the Germans completed their work and steamed away, west-south-west, towards the Marshall

Electricians' fine work Islands. Two days afterwards, however, the Nürnberg returned, to make sure that no repairs had been effected.

For some time Australia, New Zealand, and the principal South Pacific islands held on to the British Empire by one endangered thread of copper running through the overloaded line at Singapore. On September 25th Captain E. L. Tindall, of the steamer Kestrel, arrived at Fanning Island under commission from the British Cable Board in London, with a full cargo of cable material and supplies

GERMAN RAIDERS AT COCOS ISLAND.
Men of the German raider Emden, who formed part of the landing-party at Cocos, in November, 1914, taking commandeered stores to the commandeered yacht Ayesha, in which they got away when the Emden had steamed off on the approach of H.M.A.S. Sydney.

to repair the damage. Thereupon, the staff at once set to work to restore temporary communication.

An operator, Mr. Hugh Greig, who entirely lacked experience in handling or mending cables, boldly undertook to get the Australasian end into working order. He made a grapnel out of an ordinary pickaxe, and thereby succeeded in partially raising the heavy shore end at the place where it had been cut. He then dived and, working under the sea, got ropes round the cut cable, enabling it to be raised above the water, where he buoyed up the ends with rafts made of barrels and planks. There was no possibility of getting the severed ends of the cable together, as the Germans had towed them far apart and there was no spare cable for filling the gap. But Mr. Greig was not to be beaten by a little difficulty of this kind. Having buoyed up the ends, he managed to make a workable connection between them with ordinary covered wire, and in two days Fanning Island was communicating with the South Pacific and Australasian stations.

The station electricians also performed some fine work under adverse conditions. They collected sufficient serviceable parts out of the wreckage to enable them to reconstruct some transmitting and recording apparatus. When the British Columbian end was fished up after some three weeks of work, the men on Fanning Island had reason to feel proud of the way in which they had served the Empire. The total cost of repairs was not great, amounting only to about £5,000; but had the captain of the Nürnberg known a little about submarine telegraphy and destroyed the instruments more thoroughly, there would have been serious interruption of means of communicating with Australasia at a time when the Anzac Expeditionary Force was setting out on its long voyage.

COCOS ISLAND WIRELESS MAST DESTROYED.
Remains of the wireless mast on Cocos, which was destroyed by dynamite by the raiding Germans in November, 1914. The men are (right) the superintendent of the station and the wireless operator, who on the arrival of the Emden sent out the "S O S" which brought along the avenging Sydney.

At a Franco-British Outpost in the Great German Advance, March, 1918

Soon after the Nürnberg had apparently completed her work, the daring captain of the Emden made a very skilful attempt to cut the other ocean cable running to Australia. On September 22nd, 1914, the Emden appeared off Madras and shelled the city, from which the cable ran to Penang on the way to Northern Australia. The German gunners seemed to have a good knowledge of the Madras cable station, but luckily their shooting was not good. No damage whatever was done to the office or to the shore end, and communication over the Northern Indian Ocean remained undisturbed. One shell burst in the roadway, sending a steel splinter across the table where the censor worked. As this official was not at the time in the room, the sudden surprise attack was utterly vain in its main purpose, although the native population was somewhat perturbed by the deadly exhibition of the long reach of the "mailed fist."

For some reason Captain von Müller, of the Emden, did not proceed with his original plan for destroying cable stations. His remarkable successes as a commerce destroyer occupied him for two months. But **Piracy fettered by electricity** after he had captured eighteen British ships and prevented many others from leaving port, he saw he could not continue his work while there was a well-handled British cable station at the hub of his circle of operations.

British cable offices were not only centres of world-wide communication, but valuable points of naval reconnaissance. At the Cocos-Keeling Islands, in the Indian Ocean, there was a cable connection direct with Australia, Java, Madagascar, Natal, Zanzibar, and Aden. In a quick relay India could be reached, while Mauritius and other southern ports were on the same system. Moreover, there was a powerful wireless plant on Cocos Island, which kept in constant touch with H.M.S. Minotaur, H.M.A.S. Australia, H.M.A.S. Sydney, and other warships in the area in which the Emden was working.

The Emden was somewhat like a land force engaging in raids, while leaving unattacked a strong hostile fortress in its rear. Captain von Müller began to feel the invisible pressure **Raiders among** of the British system of electrical **the coral islands** communications. At last, on the night of November 8th, 1914, he made with all steam for the palm-grown atoll of Cocos, and in the grey morning of the following day he anchored off the lagoon and sent out boats with a strong landing-party to take the station by surprise.

He failed to effect a surprise. About 6 a.m. an operator at Singapore was chatting over the cable with the operator at Cocos. Instead of getting an ordinary answer, he deciphered a message: "Emden at Cocos landing an armed party." After that Cocos was silent, but Singapore was active. The head office in London soon received the message from Singapore: "Men getting ready to go to Cocos with stores and new instruments."

All day Cocos remained silent, but in the evening the Singapore operator had the happy idea of seeing whether there was still a feeble current coming through the line. He rigged up one of the old mirror instruments devised by Lord Kelvin in early days, and since displaced by more convenient but less refined devices. The Kelvin instrument magnified almost imperceptible movements of the needle by reflecting the action on to a screen with the aid of a

H.M.A.S. SYDNEY, AFTER SINKING THE EMDEN, WHICH HAD WRECKED THE COCOS CABLE STATION.
The Australian cruiser Sydney, photographed as she was lying off Cocos Island on the morning of November 10th, 1914, the day after her fight with the German raider Emden. While a party from the Emden had been cutting the cables and wrecking the cable station at Cocos Island, the Sydney was seen rapidly approaching from the nor'-nor'-east. The Emden tried to get away, but, after a running fight, was sunk by the Sydney.
FF

brilliant light. Cocos was able to state, when the mirror was set up at Singapore :

> Everything smashed. No light. Will get instrument up at daylight. Report us all well. Emden engaged by British cruiser. Result unknown. Landing-party commandeered schooner Ayesha. Good-night!

This message from Cocos came in at about 9.15 p.m. on the day of the battle. Next morning the cablemen on the island managed to get their instrument up as promised, and sent out an interesting story of their adventures. At 6 a.m. on November 9th, 1914, a member of the staff was leaving office after night duty and met a Chinaman who told him that a ship was lying off the entrance to the lagoon. Climbing on the roof of the office, the operator saw a four-funnelled warship, and as the station had been for some days in wireless communication with the Minotaur, he first thought it was the British cruiser.

Then the doctor of the station climbed to the roof and saw that one funnel was a dummy one, made of canvas, and that the ship was flying no flag. Thereupon a wireless cry for help was sent out : " S O S. Strange ship in entrance," altered presently to : " S O S. Emden here." Messages were also sent by cable, as already described.

While most of the staff was getting out of bed and dressing, the Emden got out a launch carrying Maxim guns fore and aft and towing a couple of cutters. Reaching the jetty, the boats disembarked a landing-party of some forty men, with three officers and four machine-guns. "Where is the wireless, if you please ? " said one of the officers. " We have had plenty troubles with your wireless and cables."

Splitting up into three sections, each under an officer, the landing-party rushed the quarters and office, turned out the operators, and posted guards about. As we have seen, the rush on the cable office was made too late, all communicating stations and London having been advised of the raid. The rush on the wireless hut was also belated. The man at the wireless key continued to send out the call until the second party of Germans discovered him, and although the Emden was trying her hardest to jam the station call with her wireless apparatus, the message that doomed the raider went out clear enough to be received by the Australian squadron, then within steaming distance.

There were twenty-nine Britons at the station, with a few twelve-bores and small arms, against some forty-three

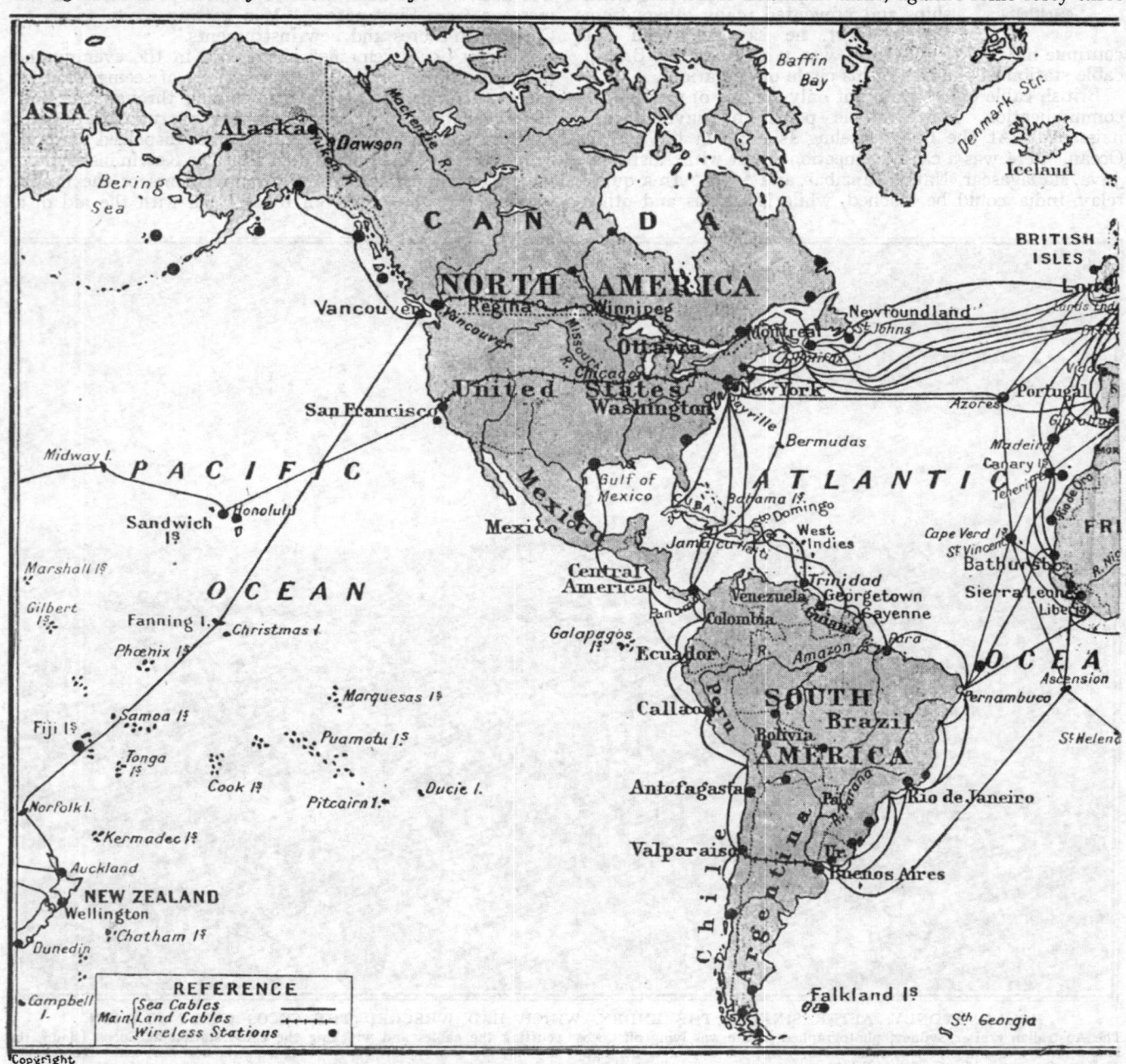

THE WORLD'S LINES OF COMMUNICATION: LAND AND SEA CABLES AND WIRELESS STATIONS—

Germans, all well armed and covered by four machine-guns and the armament of the Emden. Resistance would have been ridiculous. The station-party was put in the mess-room under a guard with a machine-gun, and the rest of the landing-party proceeded to wreck every instrument and electrical appliance they could find.

They dynamited the wireless mast, blew up the engine-room, shattered the dynamos and switchboards, and destroyed more cables than existed. For the Cocos cablemen had rigged up a dummy cable after hearing of the affair at Fanning Island, and upon **Germans destroy** the destruction of this short length of **a dummy cable** line that led nowhere the enemy wasted a disastrous amount of time. As the false cable was thinner and easier to handle, the Germans hauled it in by the hundred yards, chopping it into so many pieces that it seemed that they were making bits to take away as souvenirs.

The dummy cable was the bit of cheese that caught the mouse. While the landing-party was still endeavouring to make certain that Cocos station would not be repaired as quickly as Fanning station had been, the siren of the Emden called three times, summoning the boats. The

officers whistled their men, who struggled down to the jetty under a load of bundles of message wires, baskets of old slips, books and guns, and other spoils of war. The cable staff accompanied the raiders to the jetty and fired a salvo of camera clicks at their courteous enemies by way of farewell.

But the final parting was considerably delayed. At about 9.30 a.m. on November 9th, as the Emden was clearing the island by some five hundred yards, the German ensign flying triumphantly, another warship was seen coming from nor'-nor'-east. She was the Australian light cruiser H.M.S. Sydney, armed with eight 6 in. guns against the Emden's ten 4·1 in. guns. A superiority of two knots in speed seemed to give the Australian cruiser every advantage. But as the action opened an Emden gunner got home a blinding shot. The range-finder in the Sydney was hit by the shell, which also damaged the range-finding apparatus. The result was that the Australian gunners could not get on their target. Shot after shot fell short or went over, until the language of the cablemen grew too violent for publication. The Emden was shooting well all the time, having had abundant battle practice in the Indian Ocean. But as the two ships

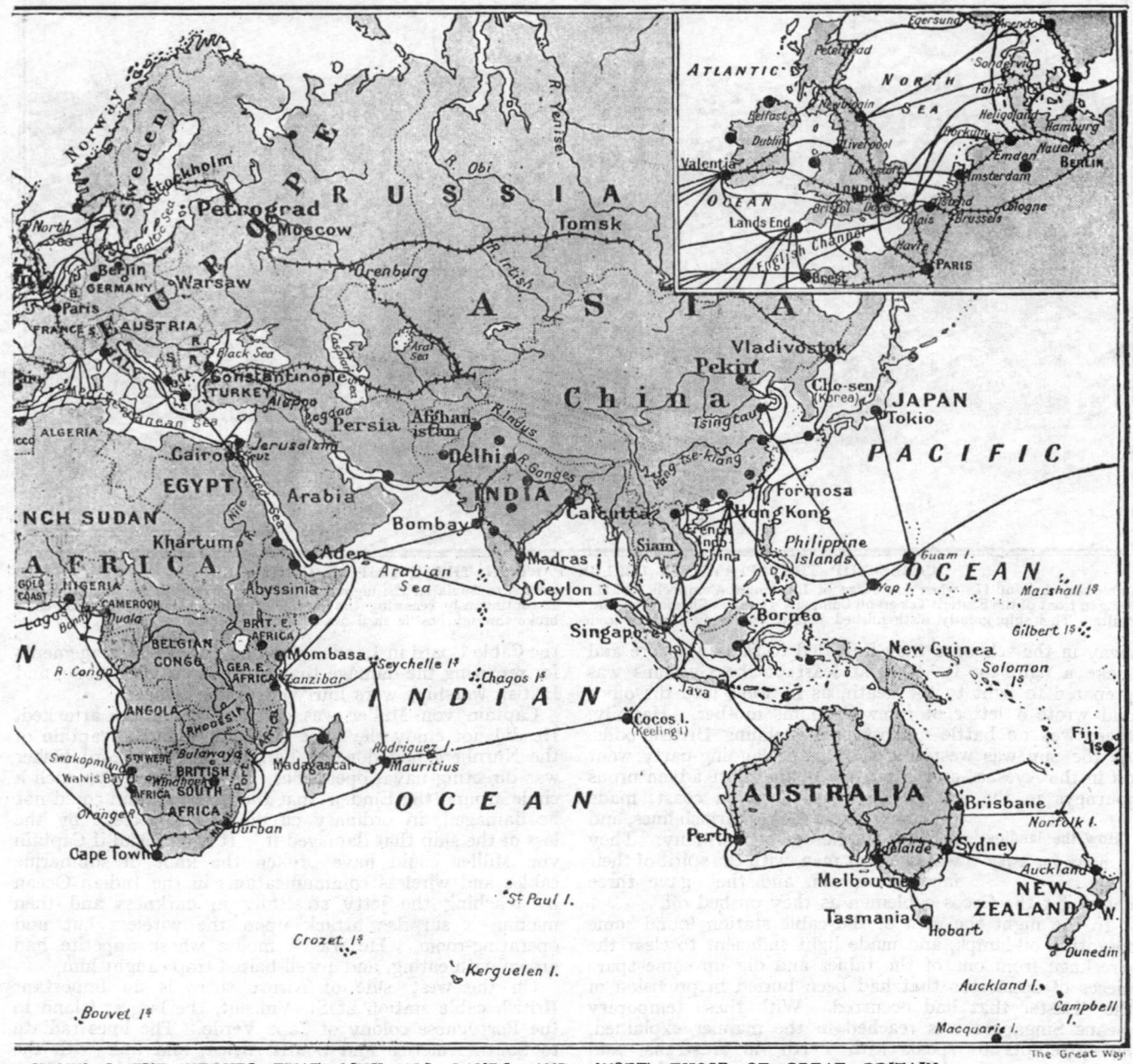

—SHOWING THE NERVES THAT LINK ALL LANDS, AND (INSET) THOSE OF GREAT BRITAIN.

were hull down on the sky-line, the disappointed men on Cocos had one minute of satisfaction. The Sydney had got another range-finder, and her heavier shots were beginning to turn the raider into a sinking heap of scrap-iron.

The last moment of satisfaction for the cablemen was, by another abrupt vicissitude of battle, changed into a scene of trouble. As the Britons were still gazing at the empty sky-line, they were hailed from behind in guttural English. The German landing-party had returned. When the launch and the two cutters were half-way out of the lagoon the Emden had observed the Sydney and, hauling up her anchor, put out to sea, leaving the three officers and their men to their own resources.

The crews again disembarked on the jetty, set up their four Maxims along the path to the station, and informed the cablemen that they intended to commandeer the schooner Ayesha, which belonged to Mr. Clunies Ross, who was the owner and Governor of the islands.

The German party collected half the provisions, and announced that if the Sydney returned before they got

In the morning a more elaborate instrument was dug out from its hiding-place and communication was re-established with Rodrigues. Before half the messages were got through there were more alarms and excursions. Another cruiser was seen making for the island, and the Chinese servants promptly took to the bush. It was the Sydney returning to search for the hostile landing-party, after having piled up the Emden on North Keeling Island, fifteen miles from the main group of the palm-grown atolls. Some time afterwards the Secretary of State for the Colonies congratulated the Eastern Telegraph Company on the work of its staff on Cocos Island, and stated that the prompt way in which the presence of the enemy's ship was notified was, in great measure, the means of bringing about the destruction of the most dangerous commerce-destroyer in the German Navy.

Government praise for the cablemen

There was another businesslike incident in the Cocos Island affair that testified to the efficiency of the British cable service. At 6 a.m. on November 9th, before the first boat-load of armed Germans had landed by the jetty,

CABLE-SHIP THAT PLAYED A USEFUL PART IN THE GALLIPOLI CAMPAIGN.
Cable-ship Levant II., when in charge of Lieutenant Campbell, R.I.M., lying in front of the Eastern Telegraph Company's store at Sliema Harbour, Malta. This ship greatly distinguished herself by laying a cable from Imbros to Suvla on the night of the Suvla landing in August, 1915, and in continuously renewing the means of communication when the cable broke through hostile shell fire or ordinary action.

away in the schooner they intended to remain ashore and make a fight for it. One at least of the Germans was prepared to fight to the death, as he went into the office and wrote a letter of farewell to his mother. Happily, there was no battle against overwhelming British odds. As the sun was westering the hostile landing-party went off in the Ayesha, and, after one of the most adventurous journeys in the war, reached the Arabian coast, made their way safely to the Turkish lines, and became the heroes of Germany. They were gallant men, with the spirit of their famous captain, and they gave three cheers for the Cocos cablemen as they pushed off.

How the landing-party got away

In the night the men of the cable station found some forgotten oil-lamps, and made light sufficient to clear the wreckage from one of the tables and dig up some spare pieces of apparatus that had been buried in prevision of the disaster that had occurred. With these temporary means Singapore was reached in the manner explained, but attempts to speak with Perth, in Australia, and Rodrigues, on the African side, were unsuccessful.

the Cable Board in London was busy making arrangements for repairing the damage that had not yet been done, and British warships were hurrying to the rescue.

Captain von Müller was defeated before he attacked. He did not enjoy the same advantages as the captain of the Nürnberg had done at Fanning Island. Lord Fisher was directing naval operations, and he had drawn such a circle around the Emden that the Cocos station could not be damaged, in ordinary circumstances, except by the loss of the ship that damaged it. It is doubtful if Captain von Müller could have broken the knot of submarine cables and wireless communications in the Indian Ocean by reaching the jetty stealthily in darkness and then making a surprise attack upon the wireless hut and operating-room. He was a mouse whose appetite had grown with eating, and a well-baited trap caught him.

On the west side of Africa there is an important British cable station at St. Vincent, the largest island in the Portuguese colony of Cape Verde. The lines radiate to South America and South Africa, and link with the Cocos station and the Australian and New Zealand offices.

St. Vincent was therefore designed to be attacked by the enemy, and it was the intention of Admiral von Spee to occupy the Falkland Islands and steam across the ocean for an attack on St. Vincent, after his light cruisers had wrecked the stations at Fanning Island and Cocos. Admiral Sturdee's victory, however, saved the main British cable system from serious attack, and some of the German seamen designated for the raid upon St. Vincent arrived there as prisoners when Admiral Sturdee called at the port on his return from the Battle of the Falkland Islands.

Afterwards, an attempt was made on the connecting cable station at Madeira by a German submarine. She entered the Bay of Funchal, torpedoed a French gunboat and a British steamer, and sank the cable-laying ship the Dacia. Then she tried to interrupt the cable service by bombarding the station, but failed to do any serious damage.

Attack on the Madeira cable

Regarding the enemy's operations against the British cable system as a whole, he must be judged to have failed completely. Only at Fanning Island did he obtain even a temporary success, and the magnificent organisation of the Eastern Telegraph system reduced the destruction of the Pacific station to a matter of comparative unimportance.

Had the Germans been more efficient at Fanning Island, and attacked the Cocos station before running amok among British shipping in the Indian Ocean, they might have caused serious inconvenience. For there was a time when the central Singapore station was indirectly at their mercy. On February 15th, 1915, the 5th Light Infantry

Regiment of India broke into mutiny as they were about to embark for Hong-Kong. Under the influence of traitors in the pay of Germany, some of the men brutally murdered their officers, shot down women and civilians in the street, opened the gates of the camp where Germans were imprisoned, and held Singapore for some hours at their mercy. They killed and wounded several members of the cable staff, and officers of the cable-ship, but through lack of German guidance they failed to break the main cable system that ran through Singapore. Had Fanning Island, Singapore, and Cocos stations been permanently put out of action by cutting the

shore ends and towing the line out to great depths, the communications of the Empire would have been wrecked.

The German Admiralty, however, had not properly considered any campaign against the British cable service, and the raiding cruisers were not provided with means of doing very great damage. Admiral von Tirpitz was an imitative creature with a routine mind, who overlooked the possibilities of other weapons besides his neglected submarines. He was all brute force and no finesse and flexibility, and his dismissal from the position of autocrat in the German Marine was a most serious blow to British sea-power.

After having lightly escaped from the enemy's hasty and feeble plan of attack, the British cable service began to work against the enemy in an active manner. The cablemen first distinguished themselves in the autumn of 1914 in the operations in Cameroon. At Duala the Germans possessed a powerful wireless installation, with which they were able to defeat the operator in H.M.S. Cumberland. Whenever the Cumberland tried to talk to the Bonny River station the stronger German wireless plant jammed the messages. There was, however, an old disused cable running to Bonny, and the cable-ship Transmitter joined the naval forces, with the small cable-ship Trojan, and worked at repairing the line. The cable had been cut by the enemy in two places; wrecks had been sunk on it; moreover, it was sadly injured by mine explosions above it and dragging anchors underneath it.

The Transmitter arrived off the Cameroon River in September, 1914, and while coming in under a thick fog, overheard a humorous conversation between the Cumberland and the German wireless station. The Germans were asking: "Shall we send a carpenter down to mend your Dreadnought?" This was a sarcastic reference to the little river gunboat H.M.S. Dwarf, which, after sinking a German gunboat, had run on a mudbank.

Equal to the emergency

The cablemen picked the line up in midstream, and found that they could still get messages through to Bonny. The cable-ship anchored in very strong currents that made it swing at every turn of the tide, and lifted the broken end of the line on board and fixed instruments to it. Then, as soon as Duala was taken, the Transmitter repaired the entire cable and ran in a new shore end. After a week's work Duala was put into regular and rapid communication with Bonny, enabling the British Commander-in-Chief to obtain a better control of all the

OUTLYING CABLE STATIONS OF THE BRITISH EMPIRE.
Picturesque view of the marshes on Fanning Island, in the Pacific Ocean. In oval: The Germans who raided the cable station on Cocos Island, in the Indian Ocean, commandeering the schooner Ayesha for their own escape after they had been abandoned by the Emden running from H.M.A.S. Sydney.

scattered forces under his command. The Transmitter linked him with the War Office in London and with French and Belgian military authorities, as well as with the Nigerian telegraph system. Again the Germans had not been thorough enough in their work of cable destruction, probably because their commanding officers were too supercilious to stoop and ask advice from the humble German cablemen.

In the Gallipoli Campaign there were two cable-ships that played a very useful part. The cablemen laid and **Cable-ships at Gallipoli** repaired lines from the island bases to the Peninsula, often working under heavy fire and being subjected to other dangers. The cable-ship Levant II. especially distinguished herself by laying a cable from Imbros to Suvla on the night of the Suvla landing, and in continually renewing the means of communication when the cable broke through hostile shell fire or ordinary action. Good service was also done by cablemen in other expeditions in which long-distance means of secret communication from sea bases were matters of vital importance.

The Germans and Austrians also found that the world-wide British cable system was very useful for the purposes of military intrigue. The rapidity with which news travelled from Great Britain to Germany gave rise to the suspicion that there was an undiscovered cable running under the North Sea. Any secret powerful wireless installation operated from England to Germany seemed to be unlikely, as the aerial waves could be picked up and detected.

A secret cable, however, was regarded as a possibility. Ordinary commercial cables are of the four-cored type, and heavy in proportion to their fourfold power of working. As a business undertaking a four-core line is alone worth the expense of laying, but it would be a difficult matter to lay a cable of this kind without observation from passing ships. On the other hand, a light single-core line might have been laid in peace time between England and Germany, in readiness for war.

Thorough, however, as were Germany's preparations for land warfare, it is doubtful whether Admiral von Tirpitz had sufficient initiative and foresight to run a sealed secret cable to England, by way of assuring success in the fleet engagement he was always unwilling to accept. It was through neutral agents using secret codes on wires and cables under British control that the enemy conducted his communications overseas.

Some of the spies of Teutonic, neutral, and British stock, working from British war bases, appeared to be interested only in the Scandinavian and Dutch herring trade. All the messages they sent related to barrels of herrings which they wanted either to buy or to sell. One part of their code was:

			CODE WORDS.
Torpedo-boat	..	..	Barrel, 1st series.
British	..	..	First quality.
Norwegian	..	..	Black painted.
Swedish	..	..	Blue.
Danish	..	..	Red.
Russian	..	..	Sixth quality.

Thus a cabled order for "600 barrels first quality, first series," would mean: "British torpedo-boats in square **Espionage use of cable service** 600 on chart." When the strange merchants of herrings were tracked down in British ports, other persons in German employ endeavoured to send information under the North Sea by means of codes relating to other articles of commerce.

All this obvious kind of espionage use of cable service was foreseen and fairly well kept under. Far more important, in more ways than one, was the use to which the cable service was put by the officials of certain neutral States. There can be little doubt that some of the Greek authorities, in the reign of King Constantine, used the Mediterranean cables for the benefit of the military and naval forces of the Central Empires.

Seemingly innocent messages relating, apparently, to commercial matters arrived at Athens and, after being decoded and transformed into a fresh verbal disguise, went over the Austro-German and Bulgarian lines, with sad results to allied troopships and shipping and the military position of the Rumanian and Salonika forces. Until the French and British Governments restored M. Venizelos to power in Athens, the task of distinguishing between honest and treacherous commercial cables to Greece was practically an impossible one.

Swedish officers of State also misused the British cable service. As early as April, 1915, British authorities became aware that their cables were being employed for German purposes by Swedish officials. The matter was brought to the notice of the Swedish Government, with a threat that the sending of Swedish telegrams in cipher over British cables would be restricted unless definite assurance were given that the unneutral practice had ceased.

The Swedish Minister readily gave the required assurance. Nothing to him was cheaper than words. His Government at the time was openly in favour of Germany, and engaged in trying to form a pro-German Scandinavian League, threatening an invasion of Russia if the enormous Swedish commerce in war material with Germany were stopped by the British blockading squadrons.

The formal assurance given in May, 1915, was renewed on July 2nd, 1915; and again on August 10th, 1915, the Swedish Minister for Foreign Affairs stated that no German messages had been sent by Swedish officials over British cables for some months, and that nothing of the kind would occur again.

Yet, as we have seen in Chapter CCX. (Vol. 10, page 367), members of the Swedish Embassy to the Argentine Republic continued to use the British cable system for the purpose of allowing the German Ambassador at Buenos Ayres to promote the murder of **Cable embargo a diplomatic weapon** Argentine seamen and the destruction of Argentine steamers by means of carefully directed submarine attacks. Only the defeat of the Swedish Conservative party by the Liberals and Socialists definitely stopped the dishonourable and dastardly misuse of the British facilities in submarine cable services.

The power of the British cable service was used against the Dutch Government with a view to saving British soldiers from losses in fighting " pill-boxes " and other German concrete fortifications. It was from Holland that the Germans obtained most of the sand and gravel from which they made their concrete machine-gun forts. The quantity of material sent into Belgium through Dutch waterways was far in excess of the ordinary needs of the enslaved Belgian people, and the military use made of it was beyond all reasonable doubt.

The Dutch Government, however, would not agree to interrupt that traffic in war material which had cost many British lives in the Battles of Arras and Ypres. There seemed to be no way of inducing Holland to observe real neutrality except by warlike methods. Happily, the commerce of the Dutch people depended to a considerable extent upon the British cable service, and by way of gently exerting pressure over the sand and gravel problem, the British Government refused to allow Dutch commercial messages to be sent over cables in British control.

Some Dutch firms then endeavoured to escape the inconvenience imposed upon them, by arranging for firms in the United Kingdom to receive and transmit telegrams on their behalf. This tricky evasion of the cable embargo was countered by an official British warning, published on November 23rd, 1917, informing firms in the United Kingdom acting in Dutch interests that they would be severely handled by the censorship authorities. The full pressure of the cable embargo then fell upon Dutch commerce, and in February, 1918, the British Foreign Office announced that an arrangement had been made permitting the embargo provisionally to be raised.

CHAPTER CCXXXVII.

THE CAMBRAI BATTLE OF SURPRISES.

I.—From the British Break-through on November 20th, 1917, to the Check at Bourlon Ridge.

By Edward Wright.

Sir Douglas Haig's Position at Passchendaele—German Miscalculation of Power of Tanks—How the British Army at Cambrai Saved Italy—Startling Irish Devices at Bullecourt—Terrible Task Set to Ulster Division—Magnificent Bombing Advance Through Two Miles of Hindenburg Works—West Riding Division Breaks the Enemy and all Records in Swift Advances—Duel Between Tank and Anti-Tank Guns—Capture of Havrincourt, Graincourt, and Anneux—Highland Territorials Checked at Flesquières—German Gunner Officer Upsets British Plan of Operations—Sixth Division Reaches Noyelles—Eastern County Troops Storm Over Welsh Ridge—Remarkable Adventures of a Tank Amid a German Battery—Conquest of Lateau Wood—Leap-frog Advance of 29th Division into Marcoing and Masnières—Heroic Exploit of Fort Garry Horse—Gallantry of Guernsey Men—Splendid Highland Advance into Fontaine—Yorkshiremen Held at Bourlon Ridge—Lancashires Break the Prussian Guard—Sir Douglas Haig Stands for a Pitched Battle.

AT the end of October, 1917, Sir Douglas Haig and his army commanders were in a position of extraordinary difficulty. The attack upon Passchendaele had temporarily failed, but it was necessary to continue the operations against that place so as to secure a good northern position for the winter and end the bitter, arduous campaign with an inspiriting victory. This had to be done with regiments worn by fighting and at a time when a strong and well-equipped British army had to be sent to the help of the Italian forces.

As he could gather only a comparatively few divisions for the new offensive, while increasing the strength of his attack on Passchendaele, he had to find an important sector of the enemy's front which was liable to break under a surprise assault. He found such a sector near Cambrai, where General von Ludendorff was relying upon the strength of the Hindenburg line in order to detach troops for the grand concentration around Passchendaele Ridge. The Cambrai sector had become a resting-place for German divisions exhausted in the Ypres battles. These tired and wasted troops were confident in the protection

of the forty-feet deep Hindenburg tunnel, and the wide zones of wire entanglement in front of their three great trench systems, which had flanking defensive works built into or along three canals that crossed the main systems of fortification.

Both Ludendorff and his local commander regarded the Cambrai lines as secure against anything except raiding operations. They left this part of the line weak in artillery as well as in men. They calculated that the defensive works could not be smashed sufficiently to enable hostile infantry to pass through, without an intense, prolonged bombardment by many heavy guns. When the bombardment opened, there would be time, they reckoned, to reinforce the defending artillery and bring down to Cambrai fresh divisions to receive the grand British attack.

These calculations were correct so far as they went, but they did not include one new machine of battle that had been employed for more than a year by British armies in France and Flanders. The enemy thought he had defeated the Tank by means of his new infantry guns and his widened trenches. Because the British armoured cars could not operate effectively in large numbers over the quagmires of Ypres, where mud buoys

AT A BATTERY SHELL DUMP.
British soldiers getting shell from a battery dump for an 8 in. howitzer on the western front in France. The weighty missile was placed on a special contrivance by means of which two men could carry it easily.

223

marked the position of sunken guns and vanished Tanks, everybody of importance in the German High Command thought that the race which had invented cannon at Crécy, built the modern big gun, and made the machine-gun had failed in its last great military invention to produce another really effective weapon.

All through 1917, however, the crawling steel leviathans, male and female, were being produced in British workshops by the hundred. They were being produced for a definite purpose. Sir Douglas Haig and his Staff knew exactly what they could do, and prepared to recognise and correct the mistakes in their former employment.

In the Somme campaign in September, 1916, the Tanks had been brought into action hurriedly before their commanders and crews were properly trained. The useful work they did was not the full measure of their powers. They helped the offensive forward, but did not do as well as they might have done had the training of the crews been completed. In the snow and rain of the Arras battle the armoured cars had bad ground, and in the Messines Ridge attacks and in the Ypres swamp battles they were not used in large numbers, for the reason that the terrain did not suit them. Thereupon, **Large production of improved Tanks** the studious and thoughtful German, unaware of all the facts of the case, came to the conclusion that British commanders had no faith in the new British chariot of war, and merely continued to use it as a show piece to encourage the infantry. This was the ground upon which the surprise offensive at Cambrai was built.

As a matter of fact, the power of the Tank had been improved by a year of practical experience. Owing to its ill-luck in other actions it had become a better weapon of surprise than it had been in September, 1916. The enemy did not know what it could do on the dry grass of almost undamaged land between Havrincourt and Lateau

Wood. It was the perfect instrument for making gates of attack through the hundred yards' depths of thickened barbed-wire lacing the Hindenburg line. With its cannon and machine-guns it formed a travelling fortress for action against concreted works and earthen dug-outs. Its master virtue was that it gave the British commander the opportunity of launching an offensive, without first warning the enemy by prolonged gun fire.

On the other hand, there was the difficult technical problem of getting a multitude of Tanks into position very close to the enemy's line, without arousing his suspicion by the noise of the **Careful preparation for surprise** engines or other sounds or sights of preparatory activity. The organisation for the attack had to go on stealthily at night, over lines that, in daytime, had to seem empty of life and new objects.

A little evidence of work was permissible. The Germans were busy making new lines behind Cambrai, in preparation for the next year's campaign. From their point of view they were ready to allow a similar show of defensive preparation along the British front. But the British work that went on, apparently slowly in daylight and energetically swift in darkness, was connected with an immediate attack by part of the Third Army, under the former commander of the Canadian Corps, General the Hon. Sir Julian Byng.

Sir Julian Byng used a very small army. It was formed of the Ulster (36th) Division, the West Riding Territorial (62nd) Division, the Highland Territorial (51st) Division, the 6th Division, the 20th Division, and the 12th Division, with the 29th Division and the 5th Cavalry Division in support. In reserve were the 40th Division, the London Territorial (47th) Division, and a strong force of cavalry. Afterwards, there were brought into action the 2nd Division, the 59th Division, the 25th Division, and the 55th Division, with a division of Guards and other forces,

PREPARING FOR THE CAMBRAI BATTLE AT ONE OF THE BRITISH TANKODROMES IN FRANCE.

In the Cambrai Battle the Tank—which had been introduced on the field of battle rather more than a year earlier—played an important part. Its power had been greatly improved by a year of practical experiment, and all through that year the crawling steel leviathans were being produced in British workshops by the hundred. They were being constructed for a definite purpose, as Sir Douglas Haig and his Staff had learned by experience exactly what they could do, and had been able to recognise and correct any mistakes in their former employment.

but many of these did not appear until the forward movement had been proceeding for some days, and did not enter the surprise operations, in which only seven infantry divisions, all much under establishment strength and worn in the Ypres battles, got within reach of one of the greatest victories on the western front.

Sir Douglas Haig could give Sir-Julian Byng only forty-eight hours in which to gather what fruits of victory the line of Tanks might reap. It was calculated that about two days would elapse between the time when the garrison of the Hindenburg line, with its immediate supports, was overcome with surprise and the time when large reinforcements of German men and guns would turn the action into a pitched battle.

Sir Douglas Haig's original intention was to avoid a pitched battle at Cambrai on the morning of the third day of action He hoped that Sir Julian Byng would be able to get far enough forward to make a pretence at capturing Cambrai so as to attract the German reserves towards the menaced city. It was arranged that, instead of attacking Cambrai, General Byng, if he won a strong position on Bourlon Ridge, should make a conversion on his left; and, striking in the rear **Original plan of the offensive** of the junction of the Hindenburg lines at Quéant, sweep the enemy positions along the Sensée River by a backward movement along the Cambrai-Arras road.

This would have opened a gap of very considerable width in the strongest part of the enemy's field fortifications, where his garrison was small and comparatively weak in artillery. It was hoped that something very great might then be accomplished if all went perfectly in accord with the plans. This ultimate part of the scheme, however, was but the glittering superstructure of a sound, limited local action. The principal design was to stagger the over-confident German High Command and compel it to divert

the further forces intended for action in Italy to the work of filling the breach in the Cambrai lines which Sir Julian Byng's comparatively small force intended to make.

As the Cambrai campaign succeeded in saving Italy from another German attack and caused a severe wastage in German effectives with smaller losses to the British troops engaged, there are no grounds for supposing that Sir Douglas Haig and Sir Julian Byng were at fault in planning and executing the surprise **Cambrai campaign** attack. Even the incidents of the later **relieves Italy** local British reverse, that afterwards occurred in part of the line from which no movement had been made, cannot alter the main result that the strategic genius of Sir Douglas Haig and the executive ability of Sir Julian Byng enabled a little British army to act powerfully at a long distance from the critical Piave and Brenta river-fronts, and take practically a decisive part in the successful stand made by the hard-pressed Italian armies.

The fact that Sir Julian Byng could not repeat at Cambrai the decision which General von Below obtained at Caporetto with fresh troops in no way reflected upon British leadership and soldiership. It merely showed that the German soldier was still a good fighting man, inspirited by the break-up of the Russians.

The superstructure of the British plan of attack toppled into ruin a few hours after the Tanks crawled across the outer defences of the Hindenburg line. Nevertheless, Italy was aided by a small British army on the western front, as Sir William Robertson and Sir Douglas Haig planned it should be.

Early on November 20th, 1917, the ground was favourable to the attack, but the weather, being misty and threatening

TANKS THAT DID WELL IN THE CAMBRAI BATTLE.
British Tank in action, going over rough ground, and (in oval) the same Tank is seen as it was taking a steep bank. In the top photograph another of the wonderful machines is shown on the crest of a rise, just at the point when the "topple," regulated from within, was about to take place.
GG

THE ROAD FROM ARRAS TO BAPAUME.

An impression by Mr. C. W. R. Nevison, one of the British official artists at the front, of the national road from Arras to Bapaume, that ran in a straight line for about sixteen miles, bordered on both sides by trees until these were destroyed in the havoc of war.

rain, impeded the action of the large force of British flying machines secretly collected, at the expense of the Canadian soldiers holding Passchendaele Ridge, for ensuring the local command of the air in the new theatre of assault. Not a gun was fired by British artillerymen while the squadrons of Tanks rose from their hiding-places and, with an alarming whir of their engines, crawled from Havrincourt Wood to Bonavis Ridge, into the enemy's wide fences of barbed steel.

But as the Tanks came out into the open, with files of infantry ready to march through the lanes they made, the guns of the Third Army started a whirlwind bombardment in exceptional circumstances. The gunners had not been able to prepare for battle operations by registering on hostile targets during the previous days. It is a general rule for battery commanders to try **A whirlwind bombardment** one gun at a time upon the places he intends to bombard with full strength. These trial shots he makes as casual in appearance as possible, but it is impracticable, when a large artillery force is practising in this manner, to make an opponent believe that nothing is intended. In fact, thorough registration is one of the best forms of feinting, when the purpose is to alarm the enemy and induce him to concentrate in sectors where no attack upon him is intended.

On the Cambrai front, where the enemy had to be lulled to sleep, preliminary registration would have been a crime against all the laws of common-sense. Therefore, when the bombardment opened, the Army gunlayers and the forward observation officers had to display as quick and precise judgment as Navy gunlayers and fire-control officers in a fleet engagement. They first fired sighting shots by the map, and then, with forward telephone control

and the aid of aerial observers, searched for and got on their targets as quickly as they could.

The enemy had many important batteries in all the dead ground he could find. Guns were sited in partly sheltered positions behind the nearest undulations of ground, ridges, and hills of the chalk country. It was not possible during the brief surprise bombardment to discover and counter-batter all the German guns. Some of these, when the officers were surprised by the suddenness of the offensive, kept silent, and with deadly patience waited for the appearance of the British infantry and the British Tanks.

In the meantime, demonstrations were made on practically the whole of the British front south of the Scarpe River. Over the German lines rolled artillery barrages, followed by dense smoke-screens, behind which were no infantry. In other places gas attacks were made, with whirlwind bombardments, in order to alarm enemy commanders and induce them to telephone for unneeded reinforcements.

There was some substance, however, as well as much show behind all these threats. Between Fontaine and Bullecourt battalions of the 16th Irish Division and the 3rd Division made an assault upon the great tunnel trench and the curved system beyond Bullecourt. This part of the Hindenburg line had been attacked before without success, and the enemy still remained strong in the two thousand yards of tunnel.

When the Irishmen and Englishmen went over on the morning of November 20th the Germans were in considerable disorder, some running up from the tunnel to escape from poison gas, and some rushing down to avoid shell fire. This situation the Irishmen had produced by a peculiar use of certain fireworks of an alarming nature. Charging into the confused garrison, they took the tunnel and seven hundred prisoners with comparative ease, but narrowly escaped being **Irish charge with** blown up with their prisoners. German **fireworks** sappers had heavily mined all the tunnel, but a happy discovery made at the most fortunate moment revealed all the workings of the mines, and the leads were cut before the Germans could fire the charges. There was some hard fighting in the support trench, and in the nine counter-attacks following upon the Irish victory.

In the neighbouring Bovet position, which the Englishmen of the 3rd Division also overran, there was a similar successful surprise rush, ending in fierce but vain counter-thrusts by the division garrisoning the Quéant salient. This division was the 240th, and the side blows delivered against it on its left, at the time when the main British army of attack was thrusting far along its right flank, greatly helped in the general success. Far south, beyond the other end of the main line of assault, West Lancashire Territorials made another demonstration thrust into the enemy's line by Vendhuille, and succeeded in drawing away and holding enemy forces from the field of battle.

The hardest task of all fell to the Ulster Division, acting as the left wing of General Byng's army of attack. The Ulstermen set out, near Hermies, in a bombing and trench-mortar attack upon the great bend of the Hindenburg line running along the Canal du Nord, from a point by Havrincourt towards Mœuvres and Inchy. Unlike all the other attacking troops, the men of Ulster had no Tanks to help them through the zones of barbed-wire and the mazes of concrete forts, entrenchments, and tunnel-ways. Great as had been the output of British armoured cars, there were not sufficient of these new machines of war to aid all the troops engaged in battle. The Ulstermen went forward with hand grenades, Lewis guns, and trench-mortars, and began, at first slowly, to blast their way up the Hindenburg line by means of personal skill and daring. The enemy held a dominating position on a fortified and tunnelled mound, some sixty feet high, formed of earth excavated from the canal. The canal itself was a dry bed, some sixty feet across,

On the highway of war: British troops around a Tank upon the road to Fampoux.

Life in the country towns benumbed by war: Allied troops in occupation of Nesle.

Perils upon once quiet country ways: A long-range German shell exploding near a road.

Tanks passing captured German guns upon the way to the attack on Bourlon Wood.

Bringing in a prize: One of H.M. landships towing a German 5·9 naval gun.

Labour to tax the strength of giants : Moving up the heavy guns over shell-torn, water-logged terrain.

cutting deep through hills in places, with steep, impracticable sides of brickwork or turf. By each bank of the great cutting was the labyrinth of the Hindenburg line, with its burrows, strong works, and alleyways connected by telephone wires with enfilading positions at Graincourt and Pronville.

Close and savage was the fighting up to the mound, but, in vehement bombing combats and trench-mortar bombardments, the 109th Brigade, of the 9th, 10th and 11th Inniskillings, and former citizen volunteers of Belfast, broke down the entanglements, worked through the great line, stormed the mound, and transformed it into a dominating Ulster machine-gun position and observation point.

Then, as the splendid Ulster thrust continued towards the Cambrai-Bapaume road for the remarkable distance of four thousand yards, the German forces on the opposite side of the canal tried to check the Irishmen's progress by enfilading fire. The enemy's flanking positions seemed impregnable, as the wide, deep canal was a perfect moat, protecting the enemy far better than water could have done. Pontoons were useless, and climbing down and up the steep, smooth banks was impossible.

The Divisional Staff, however, had foreseen the difficulty of crossing the dry canal, and had prepared against it. With surprising speed some Belfast shipwrights, serving as sappers, threw a temporary bridge over the cutting, and, passing over the artificial ravine, the infantry cleared the ground of "pockets" of Germans, and enabled the gallant 109th Brigade to battle forward beyond their objective. By four o'clock in the afternoon the Cambrai-Bapaume road was crossed, and the main Hindenburg line was reached at the bend by the outskirts of Mœuvres.

Here the Ulstermen rested all night, with the key position of Mœuvres almost in their grasp. The main Hindenburg line, with the great tunnel, extended from Quéant and Pronville along the southern edge of Mœuvres village to the Canal du Nord, and ran along the cutting, to bend again round the end of Havrincourt, thence stretching south-east below Ribécourt, Marcoing, and Crèvecœur.

Ulster Division's fine performance At an average distance of about a thousand yards was the Hindenburg main support trench. This ran north of Pronville, through the northern end of Mœuvres and the southern face of Flesquières, and then curved above Marcoing. The Hindenburg support tunnel, some thirteen miles long, was forty feet underground, with a concreted roof, and exits at every thirty-five yards. Mœuvres was a combination of two grand fortresses. Wearied by their long, incessant trench battle, the Derry and Belfast men had to pause outside the tunnelled village while fresh supplies of hand-bombs, cartridges, and other munitions were brought up to them. The Germans had magazines of bombs and general ammunition, secretly stored all along the line through which they had retired, and fresh forces were fed up to them through covered ways from Pronville and Inchy. Still, such was the spirit of the Ulstermen, that undoubtedly they could have broken into Mœuvres in the night of November 20th. as they afterwards

did in daylight on November 21st, had General Byng thought it necessary to thrust at once the keen edge of his left wing deeper into the Quéant salient. For reasons we shall afterwards examine, a further attack by the Ulstermen was not considered necessary on the opening day of the battle.

Their advance of four thousand yards was an extraordinarily strong feat of arms. Once more they proved themselves fighting men of magnificent quality. They were the shield of the army of attack as well as one of its keenest swords. For they covered, for more than two miles, the exposed right flank of General Byng's forces,

A RUIN-MAKER MASKED IN RUINS.
German heavy gun in position captured by Highlanders during the British advance in the attack on the Cambrai front; it was well screened by the mere skeleton of the building in which it was placed. The Highland Division had as its objective in the advance the high Flesquières Ridge.

penning the enemy into the new Quéant salient, while breaking him, by downright personal prowess, for miles along the strongest part of his Hindenburg system.

In the matter of depth of attack the Territorial Division of West Riding men excelled the men of Ulster. They pierced the enemy's defences to a depth of seven thousand yards. This was some two thousand yards more than any other British force had reached in an advance through the German lines. The Yorkshiremen, however, were helped by British armoured cars, and fought for a considerable distance over breadths of open ground, instead of having to bomb and blast their way through wire entanglements and sunken and caverned trench systems.

They stormed over the German lines running across their front, while the Ulstermen worked up through connected labyrinths, with no opportunity for open-field warfare for miles ahead. In the circumstances we may fairly regard the **West Riding Division's feat** two achievements as equal. Certainly, the West Riding Division of Territorials, containing in Brigadier-General Bradford, aged twenty-six, the youngest of British generals, was a magnificent set of fighting men, shedding new lustre upon Territorial organisations generally, as did the Highland Territorial Division that fought on its right.

Upon the Yorkshire line facing Havrincourt a battle-line of Tanks operated with surprising effect. The day broke dull and grey, with low-hanging clouds foretelling a fall of rain. Weather experts, however, promised that the rain would keep off for some hours, and the downpour did not begin until midday. On the dry, rolling fields of withering grass and thistles the great line of grey armoured cars, led by a commander with his battle-flag flying, crawled up to the front 300-foot belt of wire without a gun being fired. Wide lanes of flattened entanglements were made at appointed places. Then, as the British infantry began to follow in the wake of the Tanks, the secret concentration of attacking artillery was revealed to the startled, unprepared enemy.

There was a short period of tension, when the entire army of attack wondered whether disaster or victory were its lot. In a previous nocturnal raid the Germans had captured a few prisoners from General Byng's forces, so that it was possible that one of these men might unknowingly have revealed sufficient to put the German Staff on guard. Then, an hour before the attack, a barrage had been flung over part of the British line by some German gunners, apparently as a warning.

Happily, this was only a symptom of vague nervousness. The enemy knew little of what was coming upon him. He expected only an ordinary attack, with **Germans taken by surprise** a heralding bombardment. When the infantry set out behind the Tanks and the supporting artillery crashed upon the hostile defences and all known gun positions, the reply of the opposing ordnance was remarkably weak. Some British battalions had scarcely any casualties during the first phase of the assault. Many German gunners were smothered with gas-shell, and, moreover, were prevented by the mistiness of the atmosphere from seeing clearly the grey forms of the Tanks and the khaki figures on the browning green and withering grey grass.

The West Riding Division put two brigades into action and held one in reserve. The advance was opened on the right by the 185th Brigade, composed of the 2/5th, 2/6th, 2/7th, and 2/8th West Yorkshires. On the left was the 184th Brigade, formed of the 2/4th and 2/5th King's Own Yorkshire Light Infantry and the 2/4th and 2/5th York and Lancasters. They stormed Havrincourt, where parties of the enemy held out in the ruins of the château, and then, with their Tanks, chased the surviving fugitives from the first Hindenburg system across the undulating country towards Graincourt.

There followed some stiff fighting at Graincourt, where the Germans had a splendidly appointed quarters, good enough for an army corps staff, and an elaborate electrical installation. Nests of enemy machine-gunners, along with troops rallied after the break at Havrincourt, endeavoured to check the Yorkshiremen's advance, while against the Tanks two anti-Tank guns in Graincourt came into action.

The duel between the guns in the Tanks and the anti-Tank guns ended in a complete victory for the mobile British fortresses. They destroyed the special artillery designed to destroy them, and helped the infantry into Graincourt. Then some cavalry came into line with the foremost battalions, and Tanks, horse, and foot pushed onward into the village of Anneux, where a bomb and machine-gun fight went on until the following morning.

The cavalry first charged into the village, and were met with machine-gun fire, compelling them to retire and dismount. Thereupon the Tanks went forward, nosing out the German machine-gun positions, while infantry and dismounted troopers beat the garrison down with hand-bombs and Lewis-gun fire. In the interval a fresh

VICTORS ON THE FIELD.
Irishmen in captured German trenches. The Ulster Division broke the Germans by downright personal prowess.

German division, the 107th, brought from the Stokhod River sector of the Russian front, poured down into the caverned village and renewed the strength of the defence.

In the meantime other Yorkshiremen extended along the Cambrai-Bapaume road, maintaining touch with the Ulster Division on one side and throwing out, on the right, a long defensive flank linking with the Highland Territorial Division by the western spur of Flesquières. When night fell, the men of the West Riding had completed an advance of four and a half miles from their original front, overrunning the two principal systems of the Hindenburg line, gaining possession of two villages, and entering a

"FIGHTING MEN OF MAGNIFICENT QUALITY."
Men of the Ulster Division waiting to go into action. The Ulster Division, acting as the left wing of General Byng's army of assault, set out from Hermies and carried their thrust along the bend of the Hindenburg line flanking the Canal du Nord from Havrincourt to Mœuvres.

third. On their way they took, by a chapel, a battery of 5·9 in. guns, and when in the morning of November 21st they easily broke the force that had just arrived from Russia, captured the whole of Anneux village and began to push on to Bourlon Wood, they secured two more 8 in. howitzers by Anneux.

Had all gone as well in the centre as on the left wing, where twenty thousand Irishmen and Yorkshiremen rapidly advanced, the Battle of Cambrai would have ended in a great decision. But the movement of the 51st Highland Division, on the right of the West Riding troops, was definitely checked by the heroic action of a German artillery officer.

BRIEF REST ON CAPTURED GROUND.
Irish troops engaged in the fighting on the Cambrai front resting in and about trenches from which they had driven the enemy. Irish regiments won new glory by their dash and heroism in the Cambrai fighting.

BOOTY FROM THE BATTLEFIELD.
Men of English County regiments—some of them with German helmets on their heads—with a pile of rifles that they had gathered on that part of the Cambrai front from which they had driven the foe.

The Highland Division was formed of the 152nd Brigade of 1/5th, 1/6th Seaforths, 1/10th Gordons, and 1/8th Argyll and Sutherland, with the 153rd Brigade of 1/6th and 1/7th Royal Highlanders, 1/5th and 1/7th Gordons, and the 154th Brigade of 1/9th Royal Scots, the 1/4th Seaforths, 1/4th Gordons, and 1/7th Argylls.

Their objective was the high Flesquières Ridge where, by the village on the cross-roads from Cambrai and Ribécourt, there were screened pits of guns covering the Hindenburg line. Over the lower undulations the Highland Territorials and their squadrons of armoured cars advanced with comparative ease from their position near Trescault. The Tanks drove over the Hindenburg outpost line and crossed the ditched fields, with the attacking infantry in open order chasing the remnants of the German garrison.

When, however, the flanks of this central advance were secured, and the grand surprise stroke was about to be driven home, Tank after Tank fell as it tried to break the way for the Scotsmen. Then men went up the slope against the southern side of the village. Here there was a strong brick wall, skirting the grounds of a château, and

affording excellent cover for a line of enemy machine-gunners. The enemy's plunging fire was impassable by infantry, and the Tanks therefore were deployed, head on, against the formidable obstacle to victory. Some of them were knocked out, at very short range, by direct hits from German field-batteries sited beyond the crest of the hill. But it was a single German artillery officer, remaining alone at his battery and serving a field-gun single-handed, who did most to upset completely the plan of Sir Douglas Haig and the conduct of Sir Julian Byng's operations.

The German gunnery officer was a superb marksman as well as a very brave man. His gun was not a swinging anti-Tank piece of special design, but an ordinary quick-firer of seventy-seven millimetres (little more than 3 in.) calibre. He obtained hit after hit upon the British Tanks, and when at last he fell dead beside his gun the Highland Division had but one Tank left in action. With grim fury the troops cleared all the enemy's works around the village, bayoneting some of the gunners in the eastern gun-pits, but the machine-gun fire from the park wall and the fortified houses held them up all day and night.

By noon on November 20th they had taken all their second objectives, except the village itself; but, owing to the disaster to their armoured cars, there **Key position of Bourlon** remained at the close of the first critical period of the battle a sag in the central sector of the British advance.

Beyond Flesquières Ridge loomed the dark wooded mass of Bourlon Hill, upon which both the West Riding Division and the Highland Division should have been converging, from Anneux and Cantaing, at nightfall on the first day of battle. The dominating Bourlon position was the key to the high strategic operation against the Quéant salient, in view of which the battle had been arranged. It became a question whether Bourlon and the position on each side of it could be captured and strongly reorganised during the shortening period allowed for the arrival of the powerful German reserve forces. This, however, was a problem for the Commander-in-Chief and his lieutenant to attempt to solve the following day.

In the morning of November 20th the tide of tactical successes continued to flow along the line of attack, with the exception of Flesquières Ridge. On the right of the Highland Division was the 6th Division, which drove through the Hindenburg system in the direction of Marcoing. Its 71st Brigade was formed of the 1st Leicesters, the 2nd Sherwood Foresters, the 9th Norfolks, and the 9th Suffolks. In its 16th Brigade were the 1st West Yorkshires, the 2nd Durham Light Infantry, the 11th Essex, and the 14th Durhams. The 3rd Brigade was composed of the 1st Buffs, the 8th Bedfords, the 1st Shropshires, the Northamptonshires, and the 2nd York and Lancasters.

In the opening of the attack the 71st Brigade, with its Tanks, carried the village of Ribécourt, after sharp fighting among the wrecked houses and spacious dug-outs along the two high-roads. Beneath Ribécourt was a subterranean labyrinth, where parties of snipers and machine-gunners wandered about long after the battle was over

and their commander and staff had fled in the direction of Cambrai. Some of the snipers were resolute men, and confident that a swift and powerful counter-offensive would release them. They fired from places about the village, and from ditches and spinneys between Ribécourt and Flesquières, until they were all tracked down in the morning of November 21st.

While the difficult work of clearing up the catacombs of Ribécourt was proceeding on November 20th, the 2nd Durhams and 1st West Yorkshires of the 16th Brigade swung to the left against Flesquières Ridge. There they gallantly helped the Highland Division by attacking and taking a battery **Dragoons capture** at the point of the bayonet and **Noyelles** clearing the ground east of the long rise.

The 6th Division then fought forward with Tanks and cavalry towards the village of Noyelles. A squadron of dragoons, whose appearance greatly demoralised the Germans, took the village at a gallop, in the face of severe machine-gun and rifle fire. The troopers scattered the German garrison, captured forty prisoners in the open, and unearthed ten more from the cellars. Then patrols of infantry arrived and, clearing the valley, held it until the Lancashires of the 29th Division took over the position.

On the right of the 6th Division was the 12th Division, consisting mainly of Eastern County troops. Its 35th Brigade was composed of the 7th Norfolk, 7th Suffolk, 2nd Essex, and 5th Berkshires. In its 36th Brigade

PREPARING THE SIEGE ORDNANCE FOR ACTIVE OPERATIONS.
Putting the finishing touches to one of the heavy siege guns behind the British front in France. Above: Assembling—or putting together—the parts of a British heavy gun preparatory to railing it forward to its appointed position in the artillery line.

were the 8/9th Royal Fusiliers, 7th Sussex, and 11th Middlesex; while the 37th Brigade was formed of the 6th Queen's, 6th Buffs, 7th East Surreys, and 6th West Kents. The enemy's out-lving fortress village of La Vacquerie was the first objective of the leading brigade of the 12th Division. With the help of the wire-breaking and trench-raking Tanks, the village was stormed early in the morning, leaving the aroused Germans still entrenched upon the large and powerful fortifications of Welsh Ridge. Over this long rise the attacking troops fiercely worked, while on their right the 20th Division fought over Bon-avis Ridge and had a wild struggle in Lateau Wood.

In the latter light division were the 10th and 11th King's Royal Rifles, and 10th and 11th Rifle Brigade, forming together the 59th Brigade. Its 60th Brigade was composed of the 6th Oxford and Bucks, the 6th Shropshires, and 12th King's Royal Rifles. In its 61st Brigade were the 12th Liverpools, the 7th Somersets, the 7th Durhams, and the 7th Yorkshire Light Infantry.

To these gallant troops there fell a task almost as hard as that of the Ulstermen. They were the extreme right attacking wing, and as they went forward the German forces on the St. Quentin sector drove into their flank and poured around their front to assist the defending forces in the Cambrai sector.

DRY MOAT DEFENDING THE LABYRINTHINE HINDENBURG LINE.
Men of the Ulster Division clearing up the section of the Canal du Nord captured by them in the Cambrai surprise attack. The canal was a dry bed, about sixty feet wide, with steep, impracticable sides of brickwork or turf, forming a ravine before the Hindenburg line.

There was a time when Lateau Wood seemed likely to check the advance in the way that Flesquières Ridge had done. Not only was the wood strongly garrisoned by machine-gunners and riflemen, but it contained several batteries of field-guns and 5·9 in. pieces. Happily, there was some cover for the attacking Tanks, **Tank charges** and none of the German gunnery officers **a battery** was so heroic a marksman as the man who, single-handed, had held up the British centre. To a British Tank commander fell the honours of war about Lateau Wood. With a degree of skill more amazing than his courage he charged a battery of 5·9's, steering his storming car between two of the guns, and then, turning down the line, killed or scattered the crews. With other Tanks the car of victory then picketed the position, and held it until the infantry arrived.

Sir Julian Byng and his Staff had foreseen that the side pressure on the light division would be tremendous, and that its comrades of the 20th Division would have hard work on the Welsh Ridge. Therefore, leap-frog tactics were adopted. At half-past ten in the morning, when most of the Hindenburg reserve line had been taken, and cavalry was preparing to ride up behind the infantry, the famous 29th Division moved out through the 20th and 12th Divisions towards the canal at Marcoing and Masnières.

The Tanks again acted as path-breakers and advanced forces. Twelve Tanks went into Marcoing, each with a designated point to take and hold. They arrived at the moment when a German party was in the act of running out an electric wire to blow up a bridge over the canal.

The Germans were caught by the machine-guns of the Tank before they could fire the charge, and the important bridge was secured intact. At Masnières, however, the Germans were more fortunate in their work of destruction. Holding up the British patrols with machine-guns that swept the approaches to the crossing, they seriously damaged the bridge carrying the main road; consequently, the first Tank that attempted to cross fell through the structure into the canal. The water was not deep enough to drown the crew; they emerged from the man-hole, leaving their wrecked machine of war protruding above the canal.

The destruction of the Masnières Bridge was a second unfortunate check to general operations. It enabled the enemy to hold out in the northern part of the village, while the 5th Cavalry Division of Canadian, Umbala, and Secunderabad Brigades was moving forward at noon, in the design to pour over the passages which the 29th Division were securing. There was a fierce infantry battle at Les Rues Vertes (or Green Streets), a suburb of Masnières, south of the canal. **Exploit of** After this the 88th Brigade of 4th **Canadian cavalry** Worcesters, 1st Essex, Royal Newfound-landers, and 2nd Hants broke into the main position, crossing at a lock when the bridge had been broken, and engaging the enemy in cellar combats amid the old catacombs of the town.

During the action a temporary bridge was constructed, and in the afternoon a squadron of Fort Garry Horse, of the Canadian Brigade, crossed and charged through the enemy's holding line, captured a battery of guns, broke up a body of German infantry, and did not stop its

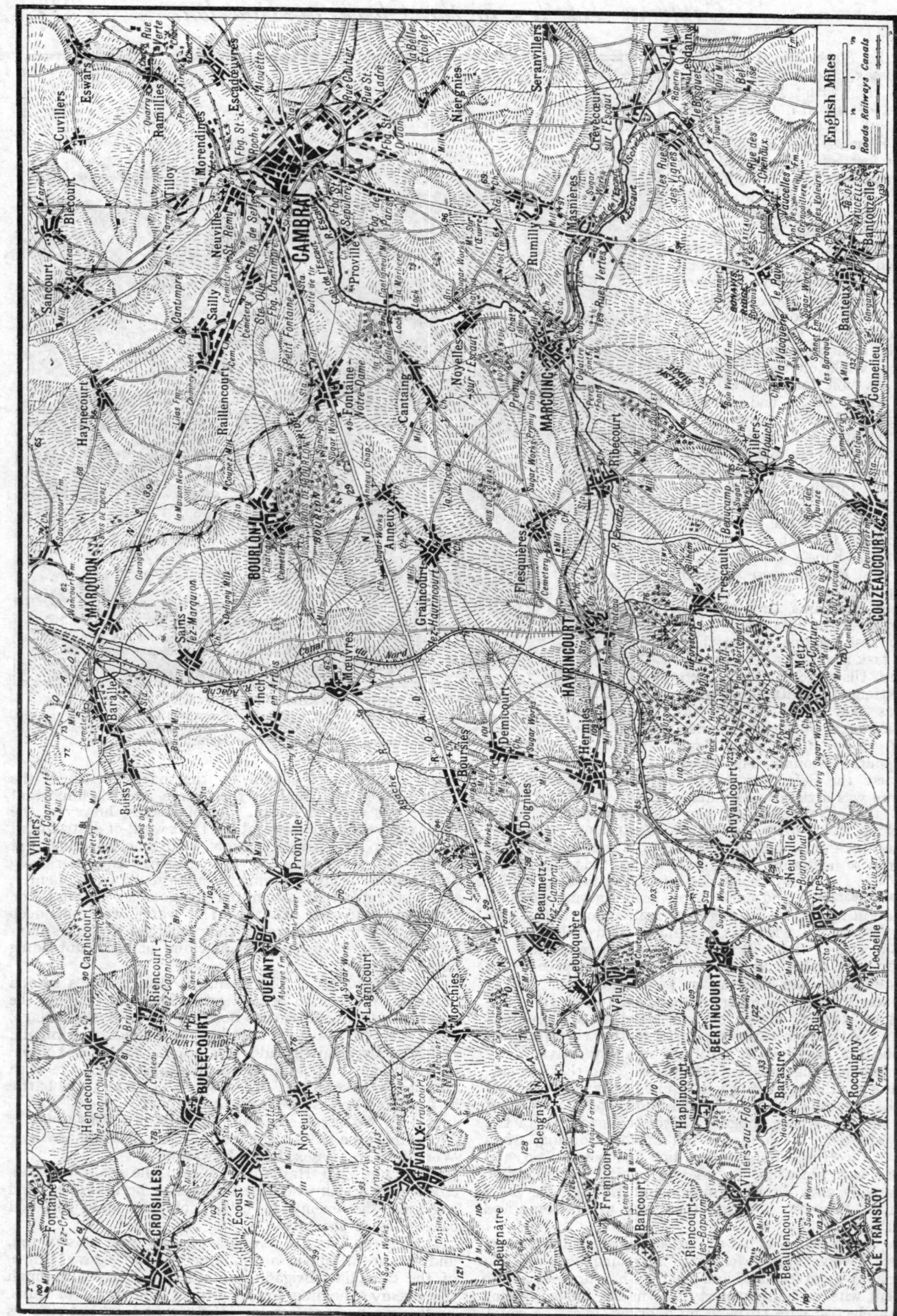

MAP SHOWING THE FRONT OVER WHICH THE BRITISH SURPRISE ATTACK ON THE CAMBRAI SECTOR WAS MADE IN NOVEMBER, 1917.

The Great War

driving thrust until nearly all the horses were killed or wounded. The Canadian troopers then took up a position in a sunken road and, after maintaining themselves there against all attacks until nightfall, cut their way back to the British lines, bringing with them some prisoners they had taken in their gallant and extraordinary action.

Their success showed what an entire cavalry division might have done in dashing into the wreckage of the enemy's last positions had Masnières Bridge been captured intact. The local German commander, however, had been a businesslike man. As we have seen, he held the bridge with machine-guns against the advanced parties of British infantry, and gained time to ruin it before the first Tank arrived. His action was afterwards reckoned by the British Commander-in-Chief to have been one of the two deciding factors in limiting the success of Sir Julian Byng. It ranked in effectiveness with the German gunner's stand on Flesquières Ridge.

In the meantime, the 87th Brigade of 2nd South Wales Borderers, 1st Scottish Borderers, 1st Inniskilling Fusiliers, and 1st Border Regiment stormed into Marcoing against only weak opposition, and extended in a line some fifteen hundred yards from the bridge-head at the bend of the canal. In front of the brigade was the last defence of Cambrai, consisting of the Beaurevoir line. This, however, was so strongly reinforced by the enemy from Cambrai that the splendid Scottish, Welsh, and Irish force could not make farther progress.

The left brigade, the 86th, formed of the 2nd Royal Fusiliers, 1st Lancashire Fusiliers, 16th Middlesex, and Guernsey Light Infantry, fought alongside the 6th Division, and made a very successful attack upon Nine Wood (or Bois de Neuf), lying between Marcoing and Noyelles. The Guernsey force was in action for the first time, having only been a few weeks with the division. In this short period the islanders had worked very hard to attain the standard of skill of the veteran battalions of Gallipoli renown. When they went into action their ruling idea was to prove themselves worthy of their comrades, and they fought with such steady vehemence as won high praise from their general. Nine Wood was captured in the morning, clearing the way for the blow against Noyelles by the 6th Division and for the advance of cavalry forces towards Cantaing.

While the left wing of the 29th Division cleared the ground around Marcoing, its right wing occupied most of the burrows of Masnières and began to extend towards Rumilly. Heroic attempts were made to break into Cambrai, but magnificently as the British infantrymen fought, they could not, unaided, deliver the last decisive blow. Their supporting artillery was unavoidably delayed in the sunken roads that served this part of the new battlefield, while the cavalry that could have made the conditions of the closing conflict equal, by riding down enemy gunners, could not get across the Scheldt Canal in any force.

Heroic efforts to enter Cambrai

The enemy's communications were naturally in good order. They enabled him to improve the defences of his last line while the fight was still going on in the northern part of Masnières. He rapidly succeeded in making the Rumilly and the Beaurevoir line south of this village into a strong and well-supported rearguarding barrier that could not be surmounted in the absence of British artillery.

When night fell, the Third Army, under General Byng, had broken the German system of defence to a depth of four and a half miles on a wide front. The larger part of the thirteen miles of Hindenburg tunnel was conquered, some five thousand prisoners were captured, and only fragments of the last German trench systems, the Beaurevoir and Marquion lines, remained unconquered. From the recovered villages in the rear came streams of women of all ages, old men, and little children, all surprised at the suddenness with which they had been released from Teutonic slavery.

A great day's work

Bearing bundles and pushing handcarts, wheelbarrows, or perambulators, they formed small torrents flowing against the great currents of infantry battalions, troops of cavalry, guns, armoured cars, and transport columns spreading northward over the conquered ground. Probably the most tragic feature among the liberated French people was a man of military age, barely thirty-five, who had lived during the war in a house where

A BATTLE TROPHY FROM THE AIR.
Enemy aeroplane brought down by the British during their advance on the Cambrai front—at a point that was far behind what had but a short time before been the German lines.

German officers had been billeted. He had been kept alive for three years on the leavings of the rations of his baby, secretly conveyed to him by his wife.

Every three months the house was searched, without the man being found. Bloodless and colourless from long confinement in the dark, and feeble from lack of exercise, the man looked like an aged spectre. All food had been requisitioned by the German authorities, and almost every inhabitant of the hamlets and towns had served a term of imprisonment for hiding a fowl, or a sack of flour, or some other edible.

The people had been only kept alive by the American, Spanish, and Dutch Relief Committees, and everything of any value in farms, village dwellings, and manor-houses was removed by the invaders. All pictures, tapestries, good furniture, and bric-à-brac had long since been looted, and the women and girls had been subjected to sinister usage, especially by German officers. In some places the British were kissed when they arrived; in others they were welcomed more practically with cups of coffee—imitation coffee made in Germany, but given in gratitude and drunk in friendship.

"FROM THE FRONT TO CAMBRAI."
British soldiers in a street of Marcoing, about four miles south-
west of Cambrai. Marcoing was one of the principal villages taken
in the rapid British advance on November 20th, 1917.

The escape of the liberated French people was
generally favoured by weather conditions that
went seriously against the victorious troops. It
began to rain about noon, and thereafter, when
the landscape was not veiled by a downpour, it
was shrouded in thick white mist. Hills, trees,
and houses loomed vaguely a hundred yards
away, and the pilots of the Royal Flying Corps
became unable to inform the generals conducting
the attack of the positions and difficulties of the
advanced British forces. Working under low
clouds and in driving mists, with a strong westerly
wind blowing, the British pilots had to fly fifty
feet from the ground. Even at that height they
were at times lost in the fog, and their gallant
attempts to keep in touch with the foremost troops
were often unavailing.

Nevertheless, they attacked German batteries
and small groups of enemy infantry with machine-
gun fire and bombs, losing eleven machines while

**British bad luck
in weather**
skimming over trees and houses and
bumping against hillsides. In the
enemy's rear British pilots assailed his
lorry trains, transport columns, rail-
ways, and aerodromes, and obtained some valuable information in spite of the rain, fog, and gale. There can
be little doubt that the continuance of British bad luck in
regard to battle weather conditions seriously contributed
to the limitation of the first great surprising success.

In the rainy autumnal night energetic efforts were
made to get forward the guns that had stuck in the
sunken roads, and bring up supplies to the divisions
around Cambrai. Then, in the morning of November
21st, the attack was renewed in a race against time,
while the German commander was busy bringing the
Prussian Guard down from Lens and collecting all other
reinforcements immediately available.

The Highland Territorial Division made a glorious
effort to retrieve the check to its force of armoured cars.
The Scotsmen carried Flesquières in a rapid rush, swept
into Orival Wood, taking a battery of 5·9 in. howitzers on
their way, and got in line with the West Riding Division
and the 6th Division by carrying the village of Cantaing.
Around the necks of the embarrassed Seaforths and
Gordons the joyful villagers clung, while the saddened old
parish priest told of the sufferings of his flock.

The capture of Cantaing did not content the furious

Highlanders. In the evening the 4th Seaforths and the
7th Argylls of the 154th Brigade swept northward by
La Folie Wood and, clearing another stretch of country of
enemy forces to a depth of nearly two miles, stormed into
the village of Fontaine-Notre-Dame late in the afternoon.

Assisted by Tanks, the small Highland force cleaned up
the village at the point of the bayonet, and then, in the
strength of two companies, fought all night against the
German battalions launched against them from three
sides. It was not until noon of November 22nd that
the survivors of the five hundred Highlanders withdrew
from Fontaine. All their ammunition was spent, and
they were nearly surrounded by some three thousand
attacking Germans, while the great dominating mass of
Bourlon Ridge was still in the enemy's possession.
Smitten by plunging, flanking machine-gun fire, shelled
from three sides, and attacked by men six times their
number, the Scotsmen drew back from Fontaine, but not
until they had nobly vindicated themselves.

On their left the men from the West Riding completed

A DESERTED VILLAGE ON THE CAMBRAI BATTLEFIELD
Ribécourt—between Havrincourt and Marcoing—captured by the British early on
November 20th, 1917. The photograph was taken immediately after the enemy had
been driven from the village.

the capture of Anneux village, and with a number of
Tanks and squadrons of the 1st Cavalry Division fiercely
worked forward directly upon the wooded hump of
Bourlon Ridge. This ridge was the supreme prize of
battle for which Sir Julian Byng strove with all his
power. It rose above the Cambrai-Bapaume road, overlooking all the battlefield, and affording observation over
Cambrai on one side and the Quéant salient on the
other. It was the grand key position
between Cambrai and Arras, and gave   **Importance of
high military value to Fontaine village   Bourlon**
and La Folie Wood immediately east-
ward, and to the Hindenburg defences between Mœuvres
and Bourlon village immediately westward.

If the British advance ended short of Bourlon Ridge
no great and direct strategic result would issue from the
victory. If, on the other hand, the ridge were taken and
firmly held, the position of the German forces between
Cambrai and the Sensée River would become so desperate
that General von Ludendorff would be compelled to
exhaust his available reserves in a bottle-neck battle
against a deep, enveloping British movement.

At first the local German commander did not divine
the intention of Sir Julian Byng. As soon as the Prussian
Guard arrived from Lens the German commander rushed
them into the defences of Cambrai between Noyelles and
Masnières. There the Guards pressed upon the infantry

of the 29th Division and dismounted regiments of the 1st and 5th Cavalry Divisions, but were beaten off with such slaughter as recalled the early days of the war.

In dense masses the Prussian Guardsmen came over the crest north-east of Masnières, and moved along the railway to Marcoing. So terrible was the work of the 29th Division that the last fragments of the storming battalions of the Prussian Guard dropped into shell-holes, pits, trenches, and gullies, and refused to go on.

The defence of Noyelles was taken over by a company of the 1st Lancashire Fusiliers. The Lancashire men were attacked in a more scientific manner than were most of their comrades. The Prussians gathered **Lancashires against** under the cover of the spinneys, on a **Prussian Guards** stretch of rising ground, worked forward in open order, and closed in sharp, quick rushes. They reached some of the houses, and tried to take the rest with the bayonet.

Like wild-cats the Lancashire men were upon them, smashing them up, and then swaying back themselves as fresh enemy forces surged forward. Middlesex men and Royal Fusiliers reinforced the Lancashires, and by down-right personal skill in combat broke the Guardsmen after two hours of hand-to-hand fighting, and drove them in panic confusion back across the canal.

It was the kind of fighting that the men of the 68th Brigade strangely enjoyed. They did not like mechanical warfare, and it seemed to them rather unsportsmanlike

BATTALION M.O. INSPECTING TRENCH-FEET CASES.
In the earlier periods of the war, "trench feet," due to damp and insufficient care of the extremities, wholly incapacitated a large number of men. Later, carelessness in this respect was made punishable.

to mow the tall Prussian Guardsman down in masses. They preferred him to advance properly in artillery order, and engage in the wild kind of war Rugby match. One post changed hands seven times, remaining at last in the possession of the Englishmen.

"It was a pleasure to smash them," said one of the Lancashire officers. "At first we were up against rabbits, who were all for going into their holes. But the Guards were far better stuff. They put up a good fight."

As a result of the combat the British troops remained in the Beaurevoir line, north of the Scheldt Canal, at a point halfway between Masnières and Crêvecœur. Hence their line ran north-west above Masnières and Noyelles and Cantaing to Fontaine. From Fontaine it bent back westward along the southern edge of Bourlon Wood to the Canal du Nord, south-east of Mœuvres.

The West Riding Division had been unable to take the Bourlon Ridge on the critical day of the battle, November

21st. As they pushed forward in the morning, they came to a trench of the last Marquion line, running along the edge of the high wood. The work was a fine example of the art of camouflage, being covered by a long curtain of green-painted canvas, melting into the colour of the scene. A Yorkshire Territorial, however, was amazed to see faces on the green ground. The anxious Germans showed themselves too much, with the result that the men of the West Riding stormed into the outskirts of Bourlon Wood, and almost achieved a decisive victory about the time when the Seaforths and Argylls were holding the flank at Fontaine.

There were, however, strong German forces hidden amid the trees on the ridge, supported by machine-gunners in an old quarry, and assisted by more machine-gunners near the end of the Anneux road, who poured an enfilading fire upon the storming-parties of Yorkshiremen.

A few Tanks managed to climb for some distance into the high wood, but the infantry could not get through the machine-gun barrage. On the left of the Yorkshiremen, in the evening of November 21st, the Ulster Division bombed and trench-mortared their way into the Hindenburg line, on the southern outskirts of Mœuvres village. Then some five and a half miles of the end part of the Bapaume-Cambrai road was occupied and overlapped by the Third Army, leaving in the hands of the enemy barely more than **Haig's difficult** a remnant of two and a half miles **problem** of the tragic highway of battle.

Sir Julian Byng and his seven divisions had done all they could in the forty-eight hours allotted to them. The check at Flesquières and the delay at the broken bridge of Masnières had prevented them from reaping the full fruits of their surprising victory. And when, in the evening of November 21st, 1917, the effects of the surprise were exhausted, there fell for solution to Sir Douglas Haig one of the most difficult problems in war. He had to decide whether he should be content with all the useful ground he had won, or whether he should open a pitched battle for Bourlon Ridge against the strengthened, alert, and angrily resolute enemy.

In the first case it was necessary to abandon all positions dominated by the Bourlon height, and withdraw to Flesquières Ridge, giving up without a blow villages, rises, canals, and crossings —all associated with a famous victory. This

SOLDIERS FROM THE WEST RIDING.
Men of the York and Lancaster Regiment in the trenches having their small box gas-respirators inspected. Two battalions of this regiment were in the 184th Brigade that stormed Havrincourt in November, 1917.

would have been a remarkable symptom of inherent weakness, inviting from the enemy a violent, sustained counter-offensive against any sector that was likely to give way under attack.

In the alternative it was necessary at once to engage again in a process of intense, grinding attrition with the Germans, who were drawing fresh strength from their eastern theatre of victories in so large a way that they would soon be able strongly to recover the initiative on the western front. For every man that General von Ludendorff lost about Cambrai he could bring three more from his reserves in Russia, until he became stronger than the Western Allies.

Yet, in these circumstances, the British Commander - in - Chief grimly resolved to give battle for Bourlon Ridge. What weighed most with him was the calculation that continued pressure against Cambrai would have a

BRINGING IN GERMAN PRISONERS.
A remarkable feature of Sir Julian Byng's attack on the Cambrai front was the number of prisoners taken. On the night of the "surprise" Sir Douglas Haig was able to report that 8,000 prisoners had passed through the collecting-stations.

larger effect upon the situation of Italy, so that the Italian armies and the Franco-British forces of support would be completely relieved, no matter what local result was obtained on the Bourlon line. It also seemed to him at the time that the enemy was very doubtful of being able to retain the dominating ridge, and was preparing new positions in view of a withdrawal. The enemy, however, could not retire from the high wood without further very serious loss in the lower ground gently sloping to the Sensée and Scarpe Rivers. Both his lines and communications would come under observed artillery fire, and all his positions in the overlooked sectors would be imperilled by well-directed, cross-firing batteries. Tempting was the prize of war still offered in Bourlon Ridge, and Sir Douglas Haig arranged to make a second struggle for it.

ABANDONED "STRONG POINT" IN THE GERMAN DEFENCES.
Partially completed German strong point which was taken by the British during the great Tank advance on the Cambrai front in November, 1917. The steel skeleton was being prepared for its covering of concrete. It was pointed out by the war correspondents that the German trenches of this sector were—especially in the rear lines—very wide, as though designed to hinder the progress of the Tanks, which they failed to do.

THE CAMBRAI BATTLE OF SURPRISES.

II.—From the Capture of Bourlon Ridge to the Retirement to Flesquières.

By Edward Wright.

Enemy Brings up Reinforcements from Flanders, Russia, and Italy—Disposition of the Numerically Smaller British Forces—British Attack Resumed November 23rd—The Ulstermen at Mœuvres and Highland Territorials at Fontaine-Notre-Dame—40th Division Carry Bourlon Wood—Skill and Audacity of British Airmen—Fierce Struggle for Bourlon Wood—Haig Handicapped by Lack of Reserves—Repeated Hostile Counter-Attacks Stemmed—East Surreys Escape from the Trap in Bourlon Village—Great Effort by the Guards and West Riding Territorials—Germans Effect a Surprise on the British Right Flank and Capture Gonnelieu, Gouzeaucourt, and La Vacquerie—Guards, Railwaymen, Tank Crews, and Others Come to the Rescue—Ordeal of the 29th Division at Gouzeaucourt—Serious Situation at Masnières and Les Rues Vertes—Gallantry of the Guernsey Battalion—29th Division Evacuate Masnières—Main Enemy Attack on the Bourlon-Mœuvres Sector—Notable Deeds of Heroism Performed by Men of the 17th Fusiliers, 13th Essex, and 17th Middlesex under Captain McReady Diarmid—Tanks Co-operate with the Infantry at Gonnelieu, Gauche Wood, and Villers Guislain—British Line Withdrawn to the Flesquières Ridge—Material Results of the Three Weeks' Fighting—Sir Douglas Haig's Summary of the Operations.

WHEN, in the evening of November 21st, 1917, Sir Julian Byng received the order to renew the action around Bourlon Wood, he and his Staff were unable immediately to give battle again. The troops were severely strained by constant marching and fighting. It was impossible to send them at once into action against the large fresh forces which the enemy commander was bringing up by three railways and the knot of roads at Cambrai.

Thirty-six hours had to be sacrificed in resting the men and relieving or strengthening those that were most worn. In this period the enemy, who had already brought two fresh divisions and five resting battalions into line, with the survivors of his original forces, railed troops up from the Aisne and from Flanders, besides bringing forces direct from Russia, and turned his main reserve away from Italy towards Cambrai.

A very able cavalry commander, General von Marwitz, was placed in control of the Cambrai front, while the new tactician, General von Hutier, who had been practising leap-frog division charges with special infantry gun fire at Riga, was given command of the St. Quentin sector. Ludendorff prepared for the pitched battle in a very

BRITISH RECAPTURE NOYELLES.
Inhabitants of Noyelles, who had been rescued by the British under machine-gun fire, getting into an ambulance for removal to safety. Noyelles was taken by the British on the second day of the Cambrai Battle, November 21st, 1917.

large way, even bringing General von Below back from the campaign in Italy, in order to get all the best minds in the German Army behind the heavy return blow he was organising near the centre of the western front.

It was the first time that the new German High Command had prepared an offensive movement in the west. It was in the west that first Moltke and then Falkenhayn had broken down, and lost their reputation and their high position. For the Ludendorff and Hindenburg combination the western test of battle was an anxious affair, and the prestige of the defensive capacity of the British soldier shadowed the calculations of the German leaders in spite of themselves. Fine British military traditions extending through centuries had been renewed, and given clearer lustre by the creation of a national army on the Continental scale.

The German War Lords appeared by no means confident of victory, and in an indirect way they tried to open a path for negotiations for peace through Austrian diplomatists, while energetically gathering every available man for the ultimate ordeal of the grand western campaign.

General von Marwitz gave little attention to the direct but feinting thrusts towards Cambrai. He left the 29th

Division almost undisturbed until the end of the month, on the Marcoing and Masnières line, and placed his main counter-attacking divisions at some distance from the Bourlon and Mœuvres critical front. Whenever a British force won any considerable part of ground there, he used his men like human battering-rams, and by downright weight of numbers recovered the key positions.

On the British side the gallant Ulstermen were strengthened by the 56th London Territorial Division. The splendid West Riding Division, which had entered Bourlon Wood and withdrawn after hard fighting, was relieved by the 40th Division. One brigade of the 40th, the 119th, was a Welsh unit formed of the 9th Welsh Fusiliers, the 12th South Wales Borderers, and the 17th and 18th Welsh. In its 120th Brigade were the 11th Lancashires, the 13th East Surreys, the 14th Highland Light Infantry, and the 14th Argyll and Sutherlands. Its 121st Brigade was composed of the 12th Suffolks, the 13th Yorkshires, and the 20th and 21st Middlesex.

British forces outnumbered The 51st Highland Territorial Division, one of the most tried in the field, remained in front of the salient village of Fontaine, two miles from Cambrai. The Guards were being brought up to relieve the Highlanders, and the 2nd Division was moving down to replace the Ulstermen, while the West Riding men, who had fought from Havrincourt into Bourlon Wood, could only be given a short period of rest before they resumed their attack upon the ridge alongside the British Guards.

Again, therefore, the British forces were very small and

SOME OF GENERAL BYNG'S TEN THOUSAND CAPTIVES.
German prisoners coming in from their captured second line near the Canal du Nord and Havrincourt. At the end of November, 1917, after ten days' fighting, the number of prisoners taken by Sir Julian Byng's forces in the operations south-west of Cambrai exceeded 10,500.

worn in comparison with the large fresh German forces rapidly and continually gathering for the pitched battle. The old British standard strength of twelve battalions to a division had not been maintained, through lack of trained man-power. The German commander had another great advantage in the matter of heavy artillery fire, as his undamaged railways and roads enabled him to move his pieces quickly forward, while the British heavy guns were being dragged over the old broken battlefield, soaked with rain and unconnected with the roads and light railways serving the original British front.

By the morning of November 23rd, however, the re-organisation of Sir Julian Byng's forces was sufficient to allow the new attack to be undertaken. In the previous night a battalion of the Queen's Westminsters obtained an important tactical success by storming forward on the left of the Ulstermen and pushing the Germans out of the wooded point of Tadpole Copse, rising west of Mœuvres village. The copse was a valuable spot in connection with the left flank of the Bourlon Ridge, but only when the ridge itself was conquered, with the village, could the military importance of the success of the Queen's Westminsters become fully evident.

The morning attack was made in a line stretching from Tadpole Copse and Mœuvres to the village and hill of Bourlon and the hamlet of Fontaine-Notre-Dame. Four British divisions swung upon and around the great black hummock of Bourlon and against the fortified villages and entrenchments on either side of the height. The 40th Division, with armoured cars in front and Hussars behind, swept up the slopes of the rounded ridge and along the road to Bourlon village, while the indefatigable Highland Territorials again attacked Fontaine-Notre-Dame, and the equally

WOUNDED BOUND FOR HOSPITAL AND BEARERS FOR THE CAGES.
Wounded British soldiers being carried back to dressing-stations by German prisoners over duck-board tracks laid through the woods. Copses and woods were a feature of the terrain of the Cambrai Battle, and added greatly to the difficulties of the British infantry in their attack.

tireless Ulstermen bombed their way back into Mœuvres village, with the London Territorials surging forward on their left flank from Tadpole Copse.

On both flanks there was terrible fighting and little progress. The Ulster and London Divisions had to attack slightly downhill, through the four-square maze of the main Hindenburg line and support line. From Tadpole Copse, a rise slightly above the sunken fortress, the Territorials of London advanced in a double stream towards Pronville, while dominating the enemy's wired and well-defended positions in Mœuvres Cemetery. As they were sternly battling forward and threatening Inchy, the Ulstermen, having Tanks at last to help them, pushed into the double labyrinth of Mœuvres against most determined opposition.

Savage battle for Mœuvres The German garrison was full of fight. They cleared out of the path of the Tanks, but when the armoured batteries had lumbered by, the defending troops emerged from their secret burrows and bombed and sniped the Ulster infantry. In savage rushes the Irishmen carried one cottage after another, routing the Germans out of caverns and tunnels, pinning them against broken walls, and beating others down with the butt of the rifle.

The streets were blocked with wreckage and strewn with grey and khaki-clad bodies. Rain gave way to sunshine, sunshine was blotted out by mist, daylight faded into darkness, and still the dreadful sway of battle went on in the flame and fume of Mœuvres and on the land

about Pronville and Inchy. From the west, the German batteries in the Quéant salient maintained a continual flanking fire ; from the north an ever-increasing number of German batteries rolled barrages up and down the broken edge of the Hindenburg line, in co-operation with the movements of fresh forces of their counter-attacking infantry. Then, as this infantry marched towards the furnace of death, low-flying British machines harried them with machine-gun fire, or directed gusts of shrapnel upon them from the attacking British batteries.

In and around Mœuvres the Germans had several advantages. Not only could they attack on two sides, with both foot and guns, but they could steal back to the village by secret subterranean passages when they had been apparently smashed back towards Inchy in over-ground fighting. They alone knew the secret geography of the two labyrinths of the double Hindenburg system,

UNDERGROUND ADVANCED DRESSING-STATION ON THE CAMBRAI FRONT.
At the entrance to an advanced dressing-station of a Highland battalion during the Cambrai Battle. The dressing-station, deep under ground, was reached by a sloping passage, along which the wounded were lowered or drawn up by means of a winch and cable. German prisoners were assisting at the winch. Inset : View from above of the same entrance, showing a badly wounded man on the tethered stretcher.

and they dodged the Tanks and the Ulstermen and Londoners, and fought like badgers. There were times when Mœuvres seemed to be entirely conquered, but fresh waves of Germans arrived and reinforced the remnants of the garrison, who bore the attacking troops out of the upper part of the village. On the east side of Inchy the Rangers, Kensingtons, London Scottish, Queen Victoria's Rifles, and Queen's Westminsters, with other battalions of the 56th London Territorial Division, were held up on their left by fierce machine-gun fire. On their right, however, they made a gallant advance and greatly helped to relieve the pressure upon the fatigued but indomitable Irishmen, who had fought continually since the opening of the action.

CONTOUR MAP OF THE BOURLON RIDGE BATTLE AREA.

A small patrol of Londoners worked their way into a sap westward of Pronville. This was a daring enterprise, undertaken to test the strength of the enemy. It found the Germans alert and numerous, and under a hot fire the patrol returned. Practically every British movement was answered by violent bombardment and counter-attack. There were occasions, as on November 24th, when an entire fresh German force, some thousand strong, was caught by the British artillery and smashed on the open field, so that none of the troops got into the battle-line.

At the end of the battle, when the 2nd Division relieved the long-enduring victorious Ulster Division, the gain of ground in and about Mœuvres was not important. The German commander, General von Marwitz, would not abandon Mœuvres to save the lives of his men. He lost some five field-guns and had to withdraw division after division, but at the close of November, 1917, Mœuvres remained in his possession. Its cost in life did not trouble him. Troops were already arriving in large numbers from the Russian front, and important tactical points, likely to serve as jumping-off places for a great German counter-offensive, were becoming more immediately valuable than German lives. The same situation prevailed on the other wing of the six miles of bitterly-contested ground around Bourlon Ridge.

Highland Division attacks Fontaine

The village of Fontaine-Notre-Dame was built on a slope below the great high wood. Yet the village position, with its sugar factory, railway-station, and ruined buildings, was a dominating point in the general battle. It stood well above the plain about Cambrai. The buildings on the outskirts of the city were only two miles away, and were used by German observation officers in directing gun fire upon the right flank of the British force. The possession of Fontaine was vital to the success of the enlarged plan of the British Commander-in-Chief. He wanted the village both as an outwork to the Bourlon Ridge and as a distracting menace to Cambrai.

So in the morning of November 23rd the Highland Territorials, preceded by a line of Tanks, made another fierce and sustained attempt to capture Fontaine. Covered by a barrage, to which captured German guns, with large supplies of abandoned ammunition liberally contributed, the Tanks charged the village. Thereupon, the German garrison set fire to the houses and retired. When, however, the armoured cars went right through the flaming ruins, breaking down some of the cottages, in pursuit of the retreating infantry, the Highlanders found that the enemy's flight was only a clever trick. Fontaine had become a warren. A considerable number of the defending troops had merely hidden themselves when the Tanks approached. When the High-landers arrived, Fontaine strangely became alive with Germans, who had machine-guns in cellars, behind broken walls, in the windows, on the roofs of various houses that had not been set alight, and in the shell of the church.

On the northern side of the village the Tanks were attacked by special batteries, and also by machine-guns that were at the time reported to have been provided with a new kind of armour-piercing bullet. Meanwhile, the gallant Scotsmen, who had borne some of the heaviest burdens of the battles since the opening of the offensive, were attacked by the reinforced German garrison, and gradually pressed back to the edge of the village.

As the leading Highland brigade retired in front, there was delivered against the flank of the division a tremendous surprise blow. Along the Scheldt Canal, between Fontaine and Noyelles, the Germans had retained a considerable patch of woodland known as La Folie Wood.

While the frontal battle was raging, the German commander, as British pilots reported, sent large new forces down the western bank of the canal to reoccupy the wood. Then, early in the afternoon, an attack in force was made upon the flank of the Highland Division, apparently with the design to break in towards Cantaing and turn the British line below Bourlon Wood. This design was upset by the Scotsmen, who shattered and dispersed the enemy in La Folie Wood.

Success won by sacrifice

Northward, greater and denser waves of German infantry surged into Fontaine, and when the worn, fatigued yet persistent Highlanders again stormed into the village from the western side, they could not bear up against the fresh hostile forces sent against them. Again their Tanks lumbered about the ruins, squelching through shells of houses and driving down the streets, with blazing guns, until nightfall. Nevertheless, the Germans remained in such force that the village could not be cleared of them. When the battle ended, the Highland Territorial Division, which had taken Fontaine easily with two companies in the night of November 21st, was unable to secure another strong foothold in this critical part of the battlefield.

Yet the sacrifices made by this magnificent set of fighting men were not in vain. By furiously driving at the enemy, in the morning and in the afternoon of November 23rd, they compelled the German commander so to deploy his last available reserves against them that he had not sufficient men to hold the centre of the six-mile stretch of the swaying front of battle. Bourlon Ridge was won in spite of the apparent lack of progress at

Fontaine and Mœuvres. The British wings of battle stretched the enemy beyond his strength, and he broke in the middle under the pressure of the 40th Division.

Bourlon Wood consisted of a mass of thickly-growing oak and ash, under which was a dense brushwood. The forest covered some six hundred acres, and rose about a hundred and thirty-two feet above Anneux and the outskirts of Fontaine. It went up in easy slopes, a huge, rounded, wooded boss, with an old quarry on its southern edge and another quarry, manor-house, and village resting on the corner of the north-western slope, only some sixty-five feet below the tree-screened summit.

The German garrison had not had time fully to fortify the forested height, but they dug trenches along both the front and the reverse slopes, and stretched barbed-wire between the trunks of the trees and excavated machine-gun holes beneath the brushwood. In ordinary circumstances it would have been wild folly for the infantry of a single division to attempt to carry Bourlon Wood in one stride. The German gunners could put a cage of fire around the ridge.

Bourlon Wood ringed by guns They could curtain it off in front by bombarding the British assembly trenches from the direction of Mœuvres and the Canal du Nord, firing across the sides of the British salient. Then they could barrage the western flank of the hill from Inchy, Sains, and Marquion, and put a blanket of shrapnel, high-explosive, and gas shell upon the rear, front, and eastern flank by means of their batteries sited around Cambrai, Neuville, Sailly, Raillencourt, and the long-range positions behind these points.

Forest fighting in such circumstances would have been impossible for the three British brigades, had it not been for the aid given to them by the improved armoured cars. Since their first appearance in Delville Wood, in the Somme campaign, the British Tanks had been made heavier, larger, and generally more formidable. With an increase of motive-power, weight, and stride, these new machines of war had become a practically perfect instrument for a forest battle. No oak-tree on Bourlon Ridge could delay their advance. Far **Tanks as forest fighters** from being an obstacle, the trees and tangled undergrowth of the high wood were the best of cover to the great steel, slug-like things, protecting them from enemy artillery observers and the point-blank fire of the German guns.

The Tanks set out at half-past ten in the morning of November 23rd, at a time when the German commander was fully engaged with the threat to both his wings. Over the Tanks, and over the Welsh, Scottish, and English infantry, spreading out from the paths made by the Tank commanders, were low-flying British aeroplanes, carrying bombs, machine-guns, and signalling devices. A good many of the men in the German division garrisoning the forest fought with desperate bravery. As in other places, they let the Tanks go by them and drive lanes of attack through the trees and brushwood. But when the British infantry appeared the Germans poured streams of machine-gun fire from their various hiding-places. They had machine-gun positions in the boughs of the oak-trees, and in holes between the trunks, naturally camouflaged with withering bramble and the fluttering foliage of saplings.

WATCHFUL AND WAITING IN THE SUPPORT TRENCHES.
British officer on the western front going the round to see that all was well with the men of his section of the support line. On December 16th, 1917, heavy snow fell on the whole front and, as a correspondent put it, the war became snowbound.

All the leading British platoons and their supports had to conduct enveloping operations, or rush attacks upon the nests and burrows of the enemy. But after four and a half hours of close fighting a great British victory was announced by the German guns. For these guns, instead of maintaining their fire upon the approaches to the ridge, altered their elevation and bombarded all the great wooded hummock. German gunnery officers had learnt that their impregnable centre had fallen, and although they could not see where the victorious British troops were, they blindly lashed the forested height, on the chance of doing some damage to the victorious 40th Division and its line of Tanks.

Had the German Air Service been equal in skill to the British, the enemy might have been able to make the victors pay somewhat dearly for their important success. Happily, the British pilots remained the practical masters of the patch of sky around Cambrai, and some of

British airman's daring feat

their achievements were of a remarkable order. In one case a British airman saved a most critical situation. Early in the afternoon, when the Tanks had topped the ridge, and were descending the northern reverse slope, they came upon a strong hostile entrenchment held by enemy machine-gunners using armour-piercing bullets, and backed by some German batteries.

A large number of German infantry had collected around this rallying position, to which the fugitives from the summit were withdrawing. The British pilot flew down and, from a height of less than fifty feet, he and his comrade dropped bombs on each gun, with such good marksmanship that the guns were put out of action. Then "zooming" up and swinging round, he and his observer brought their machine-guns to bear upon the German infantry, and scattered them so completely that the checked lines of Tanks were able to proceed on their victorious course.

This incident again served to show how near the Third Army had been from the first day to a decisive victory. Had the air been clear on November 20th, when the line of Tanks serving

the Highland Territorial Division was held up at Flesquières Ridge, the skill and audacity of the British pilots might have cleared away the obstacles to a complete and rapid success. As it was, in spite of adverse weather conditions, the heroic ability of the Royal Flying Corps was a great contributory factor to the fine general achievement.

During the German counter-attack on Fontaine a British pilot swooped to machine-gun a hostile column of infantry. But his own gun jammed, and a shell burst under his machine, making it turn a somersault, while a fighting German pilot hovered immediately above him. The British officer landed between the opposing forces, and finding his machine was badly damaged, joined the Highland Territorials and worked with them as a stretcher-bearer for the rest of the day. Another pilot, who was brought down when machine-gunning Germans at a height of only thirty feet, picked up a German rifle and, fighting

a single-handed rearguard action, withdrew into the British lines.

Less fortunate was another young British pilot, who combined impudence with audacity. In one of the hottest parts of the battlefield he observed four enemy machine-guns in action against his own infantry. He charged them and, dipping close to the ground, swept them with his Lewis gun, leaving only one German gunner in action.

"Zooming" up on the farther side, the gay young Briton put his thumb to his nose and spread out his fingers. This was a case of what the ancient Greeks used to call *hybris*, the kind of insolence which the gods always punish. At the moment when the officer made his amusingly vulgar gesture his offending hand was shattered by a bullet from the remaining German machine

BARRIERS AND STRONG-POINTS THE BRITISH BROKE THROUGH.
Trees felled by the Germans across the road near Havrincourt in order to obstruct the advance of the British Army towards the Hindenburg line. In circle: Ribs of a German strong-point which the enemy did not have time to complete with concrete in face of the British offensive.

gunner, and when he returned to the aerodrome he somewhat sadly remarked that it was best to be polite, even to the Boche.

In Bourlon village, at the north-western corner of the wood, the conflict was of an extraordinary intensity. The enemy was able to pour in fresh forces from the north, and also to counter-attack continually from the west, between Sains and Inchy. The pressure exerted upon him more to the south and south-west, around Mœuvres and Pronville, was insufficient to exhaust his forces in the Quéant salient. Such was his abundance of troops, some of which were already arriving from Russia since the opening of the Cambrai offensive, that he was able strongly to resist in a concentrated effort in the Quéant salient, at the same time as he brought new forces into battle from the Arras-Cambrai road down to Bourlon village.

No doubt, if Sir Douglas Haig had been well provided

with men, he could have held Bourlon village by opening another action on the opposite side of the Quéant salient at Cherisy and Bullecourt. This is what Ludendorff would have done in similar circumstances. Strong, however, as the British armies on the western front had been at the beginning of 1917, the succession of burdens placed upon them had been too heavy. They had had to help General Nivelle to recover from the effects of his grand scheme of attack; they had to engross all the principal German reserves while Kerensky, Lenin, and Trotsky were reducing Russia to a state of impotent anarchy; and they had to despatch a strong force to the help of Italy. All this had to be done during a period of almost incessant fighting of a wasting kind, when the

enemy was able to gather fresh strength, first gradually, and then rapidly, from his victorious eastern armies.

It is doubtful if the Duke of Wellington ever had such difficulties as those which Sir Douglas Haig steadily and coolly endeavoured to surmount. The Scottish Field-Marshal, with his able lieutenants, did all that was possible to exploit the succession of successes won by skill rather than by strength. The officers and men of the small but incomparable forlorn hope attacking the Bourlon positions were, without any doubt, more than worthy of their leaders.

Seldom have the British Isles produced a breed of fighting men of equal quality. The men of the Welsh borderland and the squires and yeomen of England who fought under Henry of Monmouth displayed a remarkable power of endurance during their march across the Somme and their stand at Agincourt. But they were at least matched by the modern Territorial soldiers, veterans of the Regular Army, and men of the Volunteer and conscript forces who, in strangely small numbers, tried in vain to break through the German line on either side of Bourlon Wood.

Great Britain's fighting breed

The British losses had been heavy in the fighting along the Hindenburg line, in the Battle of Arras, the storming of the Vimy Ridge, and the campaign round Lens, in the actions on and beyond the Messines Ridge, and, above all, in the terrible swamp battles of Ypres. The Commander-in-Chief would have needed men enlisted in 1916, and continually trained in the summer of 1917, to make good his losses and enable him to recover from the effects of the collapse of Russia.

As he did not possess such reserves, his only hope of winning time was to strike the enemy in the brilliant and unexpected way he had done. But straight and true as his stroke was delivered, there had not been sufficient weight behind it. He had required, in order to guard against such checks as that of Flesquières, a larger number of leap-frog divisions, like his gallant 29th Division.

HORSES AND CHARIOTS GATHERED AGAINST THE HUN.
Royal Field Artillery horses sheltered near a ruined church in France. In circle: Tanks parked behind the British lines. Hundreds of these steel leviathans were produced in British workshops in 1917 in the faith, abundantly justified at Cambrai, that they would prove invaluable engines of war.

Lacking such additional storming forces, all he could finally do was to attempt to turn the enemy's line through Bourlon before he was compelled to retire to Flesquières.

When night fell on November 23rd, 1917, the whole of Bourlon Wood was in British possession, but Bourlon village remained in the hands of the Germans. There followed several days of fierce, swaying struggle over the ridge and in the flanking villages, in which English, Scottish, Welsh, and Irish battalions, with Hussars and other dismounted cavalry, did all that men could do to achieve the impossible.

The German commander launched his first counter-attack soon after losing the ridge. He threw in three thousand Guardsmen of the 9th Grenadier Regiment, but they were completely repulsed. In the morning of November 24th strong German forces made another attempt to recover the high wood. **Heavy German counter-attacks** When they were thrown out, in spite of the increasing fury of their barrages, another German force was launched upon the weary Britons. In the north-eastern corner of the wood the enemy made an important gain of ground, only to be blasted and stabbed out of it by the 14th Argyll and Sutherland Highlanders, remnants of the 119th Infantry Brigade, and the dismounted 15th Hussars.

Never did infantry of the line show greater endurance than the battalions of the 40th Division, to which most of the restorers of the front belonged. After the attack on the north-eastern corner of the ridge was broken, the enemy swung another dense force on the high ground west of the wooded height, where more gallant dismounted cavalry shattered the German waves, while the infantry with rifle fire and the covering curtain of shrapnel from their gunners, held off a thrust upon the middle part of the wood.

Then, when the aggressive strength of the enemy was partly worn down, the indomitable 40th Division made a superb effort to complete the great work it had carried out the previous day. Part of the 120th Brigade, including the 13th East Surreys and the 14th Highland Light Infantry, attacked the smoking rubble of Bourlon village, and made themselves masters of the whole of this supreme key position. Roused by his loss to a mood of desperation, as night was falling on November 24th, the enemy commander flung every battalion within reach into the furnace of Bourlon Ridge.

The wooded height smoked and flamed under the gun fire of the great line of German batteries, and behind the last rolling storm of shell fire the German infantry stormed back into the wood. Fierce and wild were many incidents in the twilight battle, but the personal courage of the British soldiers, the assistance of the Tanks, and all the artillery that was hauled up to the new front overcame the enemy. By midnight it **Bourlon Ridge aflame with battle** seemed as though the gate to a success of large strategic importance had at last been won.

The splendid 40th Division, having borne the brunt of the struggle, badly needed relief. The fact that cavalry had to dismount and fight for considerable periods in the front line, as in the First Battle of Ypres, indicated how hard pressed and outworn the infantry were becoming. Sir Julian Byng, however, had no means of immediately strengthening his line on Bourlon Wood and in Bourlon village. Within call was only the West Riding Territorial Division, that had already fought from Havrincourt into Bourlon Wood, and had only been relieved two days before. So the tired and wasted conquerors of the ridge and the village had to be left to stand against the enemy's grand counter-attack.

The German general spent twenty-four hours in organising a more powerful assault. He got more guns into position and brought up strong fresh forces of infantry. Then, in the evening of November 25th, when the ground of approach was screened in mist, he leaped with overwhelming strength upon the gallant 40th Division and its cavalry supports.

Along the high wood the Germans failed. Their storming battalions employed all the tricks of war they had been practising against the Russians, but the shooting of the riflemen and machine-gunners on the ridge, and the brilliant directing work of observation gunnery officers, so shattered the waves of assault that the remnants which flowed into the British lines survived only as prisoners.

In Bourlon village, however, the German enveloping movement was more successful. While the Englishmen and Scotsmen were, like their comrades on the right, warding off the frontal attack, their western flank was broken and some of the troops were surrounded.

It was thought at the time that the garrison of the village had been completely overwhelmed. As a matter of fact, they were enveloped to the number of five hundred men and seven officers, but they were not defeated. They were mostly East Surreys, and in their improvised defences among the broken cottages in the south-eastern corner of the village they held out for two days and then escaped. One of their signalmen, though wounded, managed to slip out of the village and, undetected in the darkness, made his way to the British line in Bourlon Wood. So weary was he that he collapsed after describing the plight of his comrades. Thereupon a Yorkshire officer volunteered to attempt to reach the East Surreys and guide them out of their trap. Creeping out of the wood, he reached the encircled men and led them into safety by the way he had come.

The Territorials of the West Riding Division relieved the 40th Division, and the Guards took the place of the Highland Territorials along the approaches to Fontaine. With the enemy in possession of a shoulder of the ridge by Fontaine, and **Victory in the balance** holding the high western ground of Bourlon village, only sixty-five feet below the summit of the ridge, the British position was a difficult one, with several elements of weakness in it. The enemy had observation over a considerable part of the ground south of the wooded height, and could therefore, whenever the weather was clear, bring well-controlled fire to bear upon movements in the British lines.

The battle was still neither won nor lost. In spite of the enemy's superiority in reinforcing power, he could not attain his end and recover the ridge, and after most of his violent counter-movements he had a period of weakness in which more positions could be snatched from him. There were, however, new signs that he was about to undertake a counter-offensive on a grand scale. German guns of all calibres began to fire ranging shots from new positions, indicating that there was at least one fresh battery in each novel site whose commander was carefully registering for a mighty bombardment. British reconnaissance pilots caught glimpses of large movements of troops and transport far behind the enemy's lines, and there were other symptoms that Sir Julian Byng's little army was likely to be subjected to a counter-offensive of great weight.

Sir Douglas Haig believed that attack was the best form of defence. On November 27th he made his final attempt to carry out his original plan, and thereby disorganise the enemy's preparations. The Tanks again were formed into line and directed against Fontaine-Notre-Dame and Bourlon village. Magnificently did the British Guards swing up the slopes behind the Tanks. The German machine-gunners had a long field of fire between the village and the face of Bourlon Wood. They held many posts along the railway line and behind it; they fired from the sugar-beet factory on the Cambrai road, from the railway-station, and the sand-pits beyond and around the Crucifix on the Raillencourt.

The sowers: British airmen contemplating a bomb which will scatter death among the foe.

R.A.F. pilots and observers marking German positions before going up.

A daytime flight to the battle-front :

British pilot and observer dressing for a night-bombing raid.

Fixing a bomb on a large day-bombing

Constant activity of men and machines of the Royal Air Force on the western fr

taking wing to engage enemy aircraft.

or an excursion over the enemy lines.

Pilots of a day-bombing squadron mapping out an expedition.

R.A.F. bombing squadron observers drawing a gun from the store.

rations for bombing expeditions by day and night over enemy trenches and territory.

Avenging bolts from the blue: Bombs dropping from an Italian aeroplane on enemy objectives.

Death on the wing: Italian aerial bomb falling upon an Austrian position on the Italian front.

But the Guards went on, with grim, hard fighting all the way. They stormed the sugar factory, chased the Germans among the houses and farmyards into the Cambrai road, and searched the cellars and ruins with bomb and bayonet, while the German gunners curtained the village off on one side and the British gunners barraged it northward. The observation officers on either side had a good view, though the air was heavy with a hanging mist.

The Grenadier Guards could be seen fighting through the ruins of the village against an intense machine-gun fire from the enemy parties. On their right were the Scots Guards, working up to the eastern side, under hostile flanking fire from La Folie Wood, while on the left the Coldstream Guards fought into the sugar factory and over the sand-pits, and the Irish Guards, moving towards the shoulder of Bourlon Ridge, faced a terrific plunging fire sweeping down the slopes.

The enemy was well prepared for battle. Behind the garrison of the village were two fresh German divisions that went into action the moment the Guards came forward. When the Guards reached north of Fontaine, the German storming battalions burst upon them, and all the freshly detrained infantry, covering the country west of Cambrai, were rushed into the battle.

At first it seemed as though the Guards would break all their records and accomplish a miracle, so well did they stand on their newly-conquered line against attack after attack. But, as the day wore on, the incessant and severe pressure of more numerous and well-handled forces began to tell, and the British line gradually swung back again through the village. By the evening it was bent back from the Cambrai road, but it still curved farther north of Bourlon Wood than it had been at daybreak.

In the other corner of the battlefield the glorious Territorials of the West Riding once more **Yorkshiremen storm** stormed into Bourlon village. Like the **Bourlon Village** Guardsmen, however, they were then counter-attacked front and flank by much superior forces, and violently pushed back to their lines on the ridge. As the result of five days' constant fighting the British troops still held a promising position on Bourlon Ridge, without having been able to gain all the ground necessary for the security of their high salient. Sir Douglas Haig then resolved to answer the German preparations by organising another offensive movement on a larger scale. Part of the troops engaged was relieved, and some fresh forces were brought up from quieter parts of the front. In the interval of preparation the right flank of the Cambrai salient was improved by the 12th Division in the neighbourhood of Banteux, and the enemy's line north-west of Bullecourt was again attacked by the 16th Irish Division.

At the end of November the number of prisoners taken by Sir Julian Byng's forces in the operations south-west of Cambrai exceeded 10,500. The captured guns numbered 142, the machine-guns 350, and the trench-mortars 70, and great quantities of ammunition, stores, and material of all kinds were taken.

As the British preparations for another attack were going on, the enemy's registering fire became more menacing, and it was seen that his field of activity not only covered all the ground he had lost, but extended southwards towards Epéhy. On the other hand it was clear, from reconnaissance work, that the German commander remained anxious about his Sensée River line, which was endangered by the British conquest of the Bourlon Ridge. Everything pointed to the principal hostile effort being made between La Folie Wood and Mœuvres.

In these circumstances Sir Julian Byng arranged his forces most strongly around the new ground he had won. Part of the 56th (London) Territorial Division, with the 2nd Division and the 47th (London) Territorial Division, held a front of about five miles, extending from the eastern edge of Bourlon Wood to Tadpole Copse, west of Mœuvres. Below Tadpole Copse the left brigade of the 56th Division formed a defensive flank across the Agache Marsh to the old British front line. Linking with the 47th Division in Bourlon Wood was the 59th Division, holding the line south of Fontaine, while the 6th Division at Noyelles occupied the ground it had conquered on November 20th. The 29th Division had not moved from its bridge-heads at Marcoing and Masnières. The 12th Light Division and the 20th Division held the line from Lateau Wood northward, while the 55th Lancashire Division, with the Liverpool Scottish, occupied the old British front beyond about Honnecourt.

For a distance of sixteen thousand yards the British right flank was covered by five British divisions, who had been fighting for several days, but the British commander felt confident that **British right flank** they would prove equal to stopping any **defences** attack the enemy would make upon them. Below the Banteux Ravine the divisions in line were weak, and held very extended sectors. But their defences were more complete and better organised than those of the forces northward, as the ground they occupied had been for some months in British possession, and was, moreover, recently strengthened by the capture of the Bonavis Ridge.

It was expected that a holding attack would be delivered upon the old British front by the southern base of the new Cambrai salient. Orders were given for local commanders from Villers Guislain to the south to take special precautions. The troops were warned to expect attack, patrols were sent out for signs of any hostile advance, while additional machine-guns were placed to secure supporting points and divisional reserves were placed close up.

The reserve divisions immediately available in the area consisted of the Guards Division and 2nd Cavalry Division, both of which had been engaged in recent fighting at Fontaine and Bourlon Wood. They were arrayed behind the villages of La Vacquerie and Villers Guislain, while another much-tried division, the 62nd West Riding Territorials, was placed in a north-westward direction by the road to Bapaume. Still farther back a fresh South Midland Division was assembling, two more cavalry divisions were within two or three hours' march to the battlefield, and another body of horse was a little farther away.

When the battle opened in the morning of November 30th, 1917, the German commander employed the general tactics foreseen by the British Staff. He began by a holding attack upon the British flank. With a view to preventing the British forces there from reinforcing their comrades on the principal northern front, he launched against them some five divisions, with portions of two other divisions. In the **Clever enemy** ordinary way these forces of attack would **artillery device** have been insufficient to make any serious impression upon the old fortified British lines. The defenders' slight inferiority in numbers ought to have been balanced by the strength of their works, and there is no reason to suppose that the enemy commander expected to achieve much more than snatch some trenches from the British troops and keep them engaged while the main battle raged around Bourlon Ridge.

The Germans had no instrument of surprise like the British Tank. Nevertheless, they used a telling method of artillery demonstration which produced results far beyond expectation. Between seven and eight o'clock in the morning the German gunners on the north began furiously to pound the Bourlon sector with gas-shell, and, while this grand bombardment was proceeding, a splutter of gun fire was opened upon the British forces around Gonnelieu and Bonavis Ridge. The degree of shelling

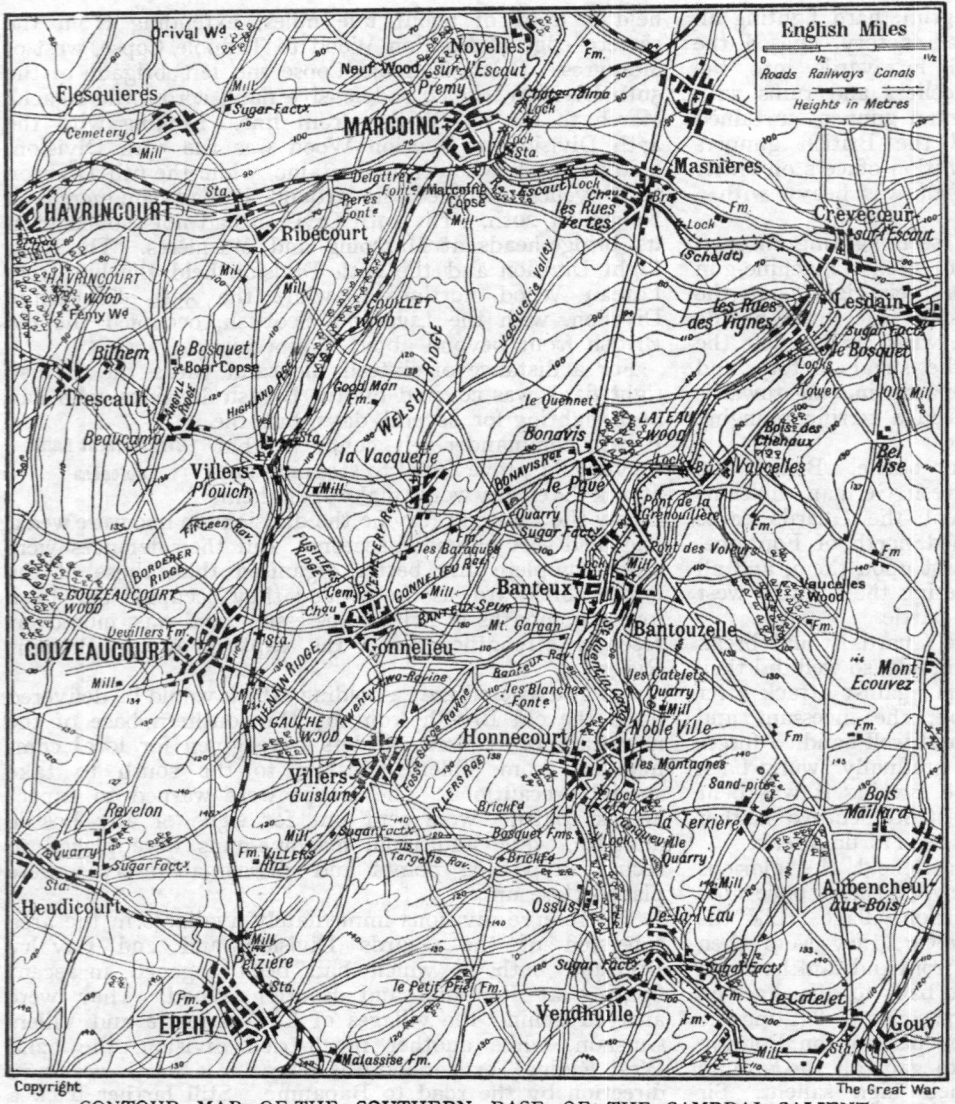

CONTOUR MAP OF THE SOUTHERN BASE OF THE CAMBRAI SALIENT.
On November 30th, 1917, German troops, gathering in the mist, broke over the northern end of Bonavis Ridge, thrust through the ravine between Villers Guislain and Gonnelieu, and captured Gouzeaucourt.

concentrations with knife-like effect. A series of long columns advanced through the mist without any heralding barrage, and, while the infantry of the Lancashire Division was under cover, and awaiting the grand bombardment, the Germans broke into them. At points where any serious resistance was offered the attacking troops stopped and formed a defensive line, while the forces behind them swerved away towards the spot where an opening had been found.

The German staff-work in this operation of testing and exploration of the British line seems to have been excellent. It was similar in nature to—though smaller in scale than—the staff-work of Hutier's army in the great offensive of March, 1918. The directors of the battle waited on events after they had pushed their leading brigades against the British line, and when they learnt that gaps had been made they swung their main forces down the lanes between the blocks of British troops they had failed to surprise.

Then, all the reserve strength of the enemy was suddenly and overwhelmingly brought to bear upon the resisting yet confused lines of British soldiers. In the previous battles in the Cambrai sector the Germans had appeared to be weak in the air, yet around Gouzeaucourt, in the morning of November 30th, there was an extraordinary number of low-flying German aeroplanes raining machine-gun fire upon the defending infantry. The Germans also employed large quantities of smoke, shell, and bombs to blind and bewilder the troops they were surrounding, and to screen their own enveloping movements.

They broke over the northern end of the Bonavis Ridge and made their way through the ravine between Villers Guislain and Gonnelieu. Three British divisions —the 55th, the 12th, and the 20th—were involved. With amazing rapidity the Germans exploited their two successful thrusts, taking in flank and rear the British defences on the ridge and in the villages, capturing Gouzeaucourt at nine o'clock **Enemy pierce the** in the morning and reaching the outer **British line** defences of La Vacquerie. A considerable number of British troops were shattered in little more than one hour, by means of a local surprise as remarkable as that which the British forces had recently effected by means of numerous mobile forts.

Isolated parties of British troops made a gallant resistance. There was a fine stand made in Lateau Wood, and another occurred south-east of La Vacquerie village. Northeast of this village the 92nd Field Artillery Brigade warded off four attacks, in some of which the German infantry approached within two hundred yards of the guns. When the surviving gunners were finally compelled to withdraw they removed the breech-blocks from their pieces.

On the high ground east of Villers Guislain the garrison of the forward British positions held out strongly against the enemy along their front, at the time when the valley

was nicely calculated to keep the troops in the front line under cover without alarming them. Officers stayed in their dug-outs waiting to see whether the gun fire would increase into the fury of an attacking barrage, and many of the machine-gunners and special patrols appear to have adopted the same attitude.

It was a very brilliant device on the part of the enemy. It seems to have been conducted by one of the lieutenants of a very capable man of French stock, General von Hutier, who had been elaborating important new methods of attack against the Bolshevist forces along the Dwina River. Hutier had found a new way of making mass attacks using light guns in Napoleonic fashion in the forefront of battle, and sending his infantry forward in an intensified development of the leap-frog advance, which all armies were practising.

In the country of chalk there were many deep folds and hollows in which large bodies of **Surprise attack** troops could secretly assemble in the **in the fog** night, close to the opposing entrenchments. Early in the morning the autumnal mist still covered them from observation, and screened all the other intense preparations for immediate attack. When the British patrols went out, the German forces were still held back; when the patrols returned, the attackers gathered in the fog. Comparatively small as were the forces of attack, they were used in a few

between them and the village was occupied by large forces of Germans. At Limerick Post, south of the same village, some of the troops of the 1/5th Royal Lancaster Regiment and the 1/10th Liverpool Regiment held out all day long against repeated heavy attacks.

But these gleams of heroism were set against a large dark background of defeat. The last time a well-entrenched British line had given way under sudden attack was at Ypres in April, 1915. The enemy had then employed chlorine gas, while using, in addition, his much superior heavy artillery and high-explosive shell.

His temporary success at Ypres was won by means so vile that it did not diminish the prestige of the British soldier. For, more than two and a half years after the poison-gas surprise, the defensive fighting power of the British races was such that it overshadowed the imagination of Germany, and strongly influenced the plans of the German High Command.

The Germans themselves inclined to the view that, when the British soldier stood firmly on the defensive, the cost of trying to break through his line was too great to be contemplated. In 1916 Falkenhayn had preferred to attack the veteran French Army at Verdun rather than test the new British Army holding the gate to the Channel ports. Ludendorff and Hindenburg had also thought it wiser to permit the British Army to make a succession of attacks, which twice at least brought their own forces near to breaking point—rather than to attempt to enlarge the scope of their submarine campaign—by attempting to drive the British Army down to the sea.

Behind the modern Briton loomed the spirits of his forefathers—from the Saxons who stood with Harold on the slopes of Senlac to the men who **Moral effect** held Wellington's lines in Portugal. **of the surprise** The studious Teuton, who believed in the special virtues of races, had been oppressed by the long tradition of the strength of the British defensive line. The manner in which his mass formations had been repeatedly shattered by British marksmen, since August, 1914, had confirmed him in his view of the impregnability of the British line. He could only maintain his self-confidence by continually asserting that the new British soldier was trained only in trench warfare, and would be at great disadvantage in open-field battle.

The remarkable ease with which the old British fortified line was broken about Gouzeaucourt had therefore a very large indirect effect upon the course of the war. It removed from the mind of the German his long-established fear of the defensive strength of the Briton, incited him to a bold, inventive mood of new aggressiveness, and so led up to the great offensive against the Fifth and Third British Armies in March, 1918.

One German division, the 34th, with some support from other forces, made the thrust through Villers Guislain and Gonnelieu to Gouzeaucourt and beyond, to a depth of more than two and a half miles.

During the hour and a half, when the enemy was advancing into the British artillery positions that covered the battle-front northward at Marcoing and Masnières, nobody in Gouzeaucourt seems to have been informed of the perilous situation. The commander of an unbroken division was almost captured through

lack of communication of the enemy's progress on sectors behind him.

Staff officers were reading over the reports of the previous night, orderlies were making coffee and frying bacon, and one officer at least was taking his bath, when shots sounded very close to Gouzeaucourt, and the enemy was discovered to be inside and all round the village. He then pushed out another five hundred yards, occupying Gauche Wood and attacking La Vacquerie, taking on his way a considerable number of guns and a considerable number of prisoners, until his progress was stopped by the action of local reserves.

The real strength of the enemy forces that broke into Gouzeaucourt was tested at midday on November 30th, when the British Guards came up. The Guards Division might have been **Guards to** regarded as exhausted from previous **the rescue** fighting, for its recent action in Fontaine-Notre-Dame and Bourlon Wood had left it weak in numbers. Scarcely more than a brigade of the Guards appears to have undertaken, with the help of the Umbala and Secunderabad Brigades of the 6th Cavalry Division, to restore the disaster to two other British divisions.

Carrying full packs, with bands playing them on, the Guardsmen whistled and sang marching tunes, and closed upon Gouzeaucourt from the west, while the dismounted Indian cavalrymen filled the gap on the right, and began to work towards Villers Guislain from the south and south-west.

The counter-attack was facilitated by the brave skill of a party of men from the 29th Division, who, with a company of North Midland Royal Engineers, were holding on to a position in an old trench near the quarry at Gouzeaucourt, where their divisional general had been surprised in his headquarters.

A still more remarkable reinforcement of the British line was obtained from the railway line by Villers Plouich and Gauche Wood. Here, when the Germans came over the ridge, some Canadian and American railwaymen and engineers were driving engines, unloading trucks, and doing constructive work. Bursts of high explosive, gas, and shrapnel, with volleys of bullets, drove them through and beyond the village. There, however, they stopped and asked for rifles. Though untrained for the war, many of them were good shots, and there were veterans

CAMOUFLAGING A ROAD LEADING TO THE FRONT.
Soldiers screening a road, along which British troops were being moved up to the fighting-front, by means of wayside nets and overhead lines bearing strips of coloured cloth. These seemingly flimsy devices served to make the line of the road and the traffic on it unrecognisable from high-flying enemy aircraft.

of the Spanish campaign among them. The engineers, with a British battalion of troops engaged on constructive work, went forward with the Guards, and after fighting gallantly and winning the high admiration of their comrades, they helped to picket the lines in the night. The Tank commanders and crews had been engaged in previous actions, and were moving their machines from the Cambrai salient, in order to refit and rest. On receiving news of the enemy's success, the officers and men of the Tank Brigade displayed superb energy, bringing their travelling forts rapidly into Gouzeaucourt, amid the confused overcrowding of the ways of communication by Metz and other places just behind the new fighting-front.

Under the grim pressure of the Guards, who battled into Gouzeaucourt and up the high ground eastward known as St. Quentin Ridge, the victorious Germans suddenly gave ground, leaving a rearguard to cover their retirement. Many British guns were recovered, together with a considerable proportion of men who had been taken prisoner by the enemy.

In the dressing-station of the recaptured village the Guardsmen found British surgeons and dressers tending British and German wounded men, and calmly going on with their work. "Hallo! We were waiting for you fellows!" said one orderly, as his countrymen came in. This appears to have been the most emotional remark made in the strange circumstances. A trophy park of German guns, captured in the first operations, passed back to German possession, and returned in a few hours to the original conquerors, along with some two-thirds of the British guns that the enemy seized but could not retain. So comparatively few prisoners remained in German hands, after the magnificent return thrust of the Guards, that, in order to make out a total of 4,000 British captives, the enemy Staff had to include dead as well as wounded in their deliberately misleading estimate.

Just above the broken line the famous 29th Division, which had been fighting for ten days and nights, had a most terrible and bewildering ordeal. As already explained, its stand was made under very confusing conditions, owing to divisional headquarters being captured by the enemy at the opening of the battle.

Ordeal of the 29th Division The British general and his Staff were in a quarry near Gouzeaucourt, with most of their heavy artillery around them, and in his surprising flank attack the enemy swept over the quarry and the artillery positions without any warning.

Only by forming a rearguard with his cooks, batmen, and orderlies—most of whom were captured—did the general barely manage to escape, through a heavy German barrage and sniping fire. It was some time before he could establish new headquarters eastward of Gouzeaucourt, and resume complete control of his troops on the northerly Marcoing and Masnières line. In the meantime his hard-pressed men, with a considerable part of their artillery temporarily lost in their rear, were making one of the most desperately heroic defences.

Happily the veteran division had not been caught

napping in the misty morning. Soon after daybreak its observers in Masnières reported that they had seen large forces of German infantry in Crêvecœur, a mile and a half away. The alert was sounded, and troops stood to at the alarm posts. At Masnières was the 86th Brigade, with the 87th Brigade holding the line to the Cambrai road, and the 88th Brigade in reserve.

A few minutes after the alarm the 16th Middlesex Battalion, linking on the right with the wing of the 20th Division, reported that the 20th had been driven back. Germans could then be seen coming out of Lateau Wood, behind the lines of the defenders of Masnières and Marcoing. Then strong enemy forces in front in turn swept in dense waves upon Masnières, advancing on both sides of the Scheldt Canal, and trying to cut off the troops on the north bank by seizing the canal crossings and the suburb of Les Rues Vertes. At the same time another fierce enemy assault was made upon the Marcoing positions.

KEEPING THE WAYS CLEAR FOR MEN AND GUNS.
Clearing away the mud on the road to the trenches. Bad weather with, as a result, water-logged ground, severely hampering movement of men and guns, persistently attended Sir Douglas Haig's offensives.

Never for a moment did the officers and men lose their heads. The most serious situation was that in Les Rues Vertes, where the Germans were storming down upon brigade headquarters. As the foremost attackers entered Masnières from the suburb, Captain Gee collected a band of servants and signallers, joined them to two companies of the Guernsey Battalion, and made a tiger-leap back to Les Rues Vertes.

As has been remarked before, the Guernsey men were untried, newly-trained troops when first they entered the Cambrai salient on November 20th. They fought like the best of veterans, plunging into the cottages of the suburbs, and taking the ruins at the point of the bayonet, against machine-gun fire, with a promptitude that completely disconcerted the enemy. Captain Gee was a most inspiring leader. He brought down one German with a heavy walking-stick. Then, after four orderlies had been killed by his side, he charged the last German machine-gun crew in the village. Firing with revolvers in both hands, he slew all the machine-gunners and turned the gun upon the retreating grey figures.

Guernsey battalion's fine achievement

Scarcely had the Germans been thrown out of Les Rues Vertes than a fresh force of them renewed the attack on both sides. The gap on the right of the defending division invited an encircling movement. Yet this movement was not easily made, for on the broken flank there was a group of Britons with Stokes' mortars, and they continually pounded the copse, where the Germans assembled again and again for the side thrust that might have cut off not only the 29th Division but also the larger British force around Bourlon Ridge. After keeping the mortar battery in action until all ammunition was used, the officer in charge threw his mortars into the canal and led a party of infantry, along with his own men, in a counter-assault against a new German force in Les Rues Vertes.

The Guernseys there were still defending the bridge-heads by the canal, and every man who could hold a rifle was in the thinning line around the village. At four o'clock in the afternoon, after many local actions, a great general enemy onset was directed on all sides. It was held and broken. At five o'clock Les Rues Vertes was again subjected to a narrower but sustained thrust, intended to drive by its weight into Masnières. The thrust failed, as the enveloping attacks had done, and, before night fell, Les Rues Vertes was full of enemy dead and wounded, and the bodies stretched along the canal-bank to Crêvecœur, near which the British division maintained an outpost at Mont Plaisir Farm.

Blinded officer's superb conduct On the northern side one of the senior officers was totally blinded by a shell. Despite his torn eyes, this gallant gentleman insisted on remaining at the lock between the villages, and walked up and down the front line, led by an orderly, encouraging his men. The Scottish Borderers sallied from Marcoing and attacked the Germans in a network of sunken lanes, while the Inniskillings held the enemy off on the western edge of Masnières, and some of the South Wales Borderers, supporting the 86th Brigade, did some magnificent close-quarter fighting.

When the infantry action ceased at nightfall the hostile batteries, that had been shelling the division from three sides all day long, continued to rake the canal-side positions. In the morning of December 1st the assault was resumed, while the hostile guns knocked the last houses to pieces in a bombardment of augmented power.

During the night the Germans had thrown a bridge over the Scheldt Canal, between Crêvecœur and Masnières, and, under the intensified barrage, a large body of shock troops endeavoured to get across in a rush. They were allowed to crowd the bridge and form a bridge-head. Then four British machine-guns, in the outskirts of Masnières, opened a mowing fire over the intervening level of ground. At least five hundred Germans were killed, many falling into the waterway.

Abandoning their outpost near Crêvecœur the defending troops gathered in Masnières, while two enemy aeroplanes brought the hostile barrage crashing on the British line. Over the canal bridge at Les Rues Vertes the storming columns broke into the corner of the salient, and appeared to be closing in overwhelming force upon the wasted wing of the division.

The British brigadier calmly walked along the canal bank. "Steady men!" he cried. "Don't fire until you see the whites of their eyes!" The worn-out men gripped their rifles and aimed. As the Germans swarmed over one bridge a platoon of Lancashires counter-charged. A remnant of eighty Germans, with eight machine-guns, was captured from the attacking forces. Nine separate attacks were beaten off by the 29th Division at Masnières in the afternoon and evening of December 1st, and other hostile assaults were broken around Marcoing.

So long as there seemed a possibility of improving the position in the rear of the division, by the recapture of the Bonavis Ridge, the glorious 29th stood its ground, though exposed to incessant attack on three sides. In the night of December 1st, however, Bonavis Ridge

remained in the enemy's hands, and the defenders of Masnières were, therefore, ordered to withdraw to the west of the village. A Staff officer arrived at half-past seven, and the retirement was carried out in excellent fashion, after the wounded had been removed, ammunition taken away or burnt, and the bridge-head defences blown up. The blinded officer, who had held the lock between Masnières and Marcoing, was the last to leave. Still led by his orderly, he trudged back to the more flattened line running down by Marcoing towards La Vacquerie.

The stand made by the 29th Division, after the three divisions south of them had been driven in, was the salvation of the British forces holding the line in the northern and eastern sides of the Cambrai salient. Together with the Guards and the 5th Cavalry Division, the heroes of Gallipoli enabled the men on and around Bourlon Ridge and along the Canal du Nord to turn a moral defeat into a practical victory.

In the German offensive of November 30th the main attack, directed upon the line from Fontaine-Notre-Dame to Tadpole Copse, was not launched until Gouzeaucourt had been taken. At nine a.m. General von Marwitz, excited by the success won against the southern British flank, endeavoured swiftly to smash into the opposite side of the salient, and bring off the capture of all the British men and material between Gouzeaucourt and Havrincourt. There would then have been left such a gap in the original British front between Arras and Cambrai as would have opened the way to a larger enemy manœuvre.

Against the 2nd Division, arrayed between Bourlon village and Mœuvres village, the German formations were flung in extraordinary fashion. Upon the 47th London Territorial Division, holding the gas-drenched forest on Bourlon Ridge, the grey waves also burst in tempestuous force. Against the right brigade of the 56th London Territorial Division in Tadpole Copse, and against its left brigade in the Agache Marsh, the storm also **Storm attack on Bourlon Ridge** broke, but with rather less fierceness than in the north.

After a short whirlwind bombardment some German infantry guns galloped up to rising ground by Bourlon village, and began to fire point-blank into the 1st Royal Rifles of the 99th Brigade of the 2nd Division. One gun fired three shots; the others less. The Riflemen would not allow more. Then two German battalions came out of the ruins in full marching order, and in compact lines moved forward as on manœuvres. The survivors entered the prisoners' cage of the 2nd Division.

Fresh masses came forward against the

MEN AND MUNITIONS THAT MADE THEIR MARK AT CAMBRAI. British working party with some of the shells they had unloaded at a dump in readiness for attack. At Cambrai the element of surprise made it necessary to withhold preliminary gun fire; but as the Tanks came out into the open, the guns started a whirlwind bombardment.

22nd and 23rd Fusiliers and 1st Berkshires, as well as against the Riflemen. The arms of the killers ached with the effort of slaughter.

Seldom had well-skilled soldiers, with rifles, machine-guns, and Stokes guns, such an opportunity of proving the sustained destructive power of their weapons. Wounded men begged their comrades to prop them up, so that they could continue to use their rifles. Scotsmen especially, and some of the 2nd Highland Light Infantry in particular, were inclined to anger when stretcher-bearers approached to take them to the dressing-station. After destroying the attacking forces and capturing two 5·9 in. howitzers, two field-guns, and a mortar, the victors drove into the enemy's territory and there established an advanced line of posts, giving them a wider field of fire and denying observation to the hostile artillery.

Many acts of shining heroism glorified the common courage

GERMAN PRISONERS' AID TO BRITISH WOUNDED AT MASNIÈRES.
The capture of Bonavis Ridge by the enemy on November 30th necessitated the withdrawal of the 29th Division from Masnières. In the cellars were many British wounded and German prisoners, but on the night of December 1st all were evacuated safely, the prisoners helping to carry away the wounded.

of the division. Three at least were of perdurable lustre. When the German batteries opened their hurricane fire, a company of the 17th Fusiliers was withdrawing from an exposed position in an advanced sap-head. With unexpected speed the hostile infantry attacked. Thereupon, Captain W. N. Stone, the officer commanding the company, sent three of his platoons back, and with the last platoon, and Lieutenant Benzecry, held up the weight of the German rush until the main British position had been organised. Fighting to the death, their faces to the foe, the little rearguard saved the line from a surprise thrust.

Somewhat later in the day, another strong body of picked German storming troops broke into the wing of the 2nd Division at a difficult corner. The 6th Brigade, including the 13th Essex, King's Liverpools, 2nd South Staffords, and 17th Middlesex, had probably the hardest of all the fighting. Their line was broken by the great dry moat of the Nord Canal, across which contact could scarcely be maintained. The men had to slide down a fifty-foot wall and climb another steep side by means of ropes, under enfilading machine-gun and rifle fire. Down

Essex men fight to a finish   the brick bed of the canal each side made rushes with bombs, while opposing snipers fired into the sunken scene of struggle from shelters in the banks.

In one of the German rushes a company of the 13th Essex was isolated in a fragment of trench west of the canal. All day the gallant party held out against the circle of enemies, making a fierce and active resistance that greatly relieved the pressure on the rest of the brigade.

Then, at four o'clock in the darkening winter afternoon, a council of war was held by the two remaining company officers—Lieutenant J. D. Robinson and Sec.-Lieutenant E. L. Corps—Company-Sergeant-Major A. H. Edwards,

and Platoon-Sergeants C. Phillips, F. C. Parsons, W. Fairbrass, R. Lodge, and L. S. Legg.

Unanimously they agreed to fight to the last and not surrender. To battalion headquarters they sent two runners to convey their decision, and the runners happily managed to get through and deliver their message. Then, far into the night, the gallant company was heard fighting, and there was little room for doubt that to a man they carried out their great act of self-sacrifice.

Many attempts were made to rescue them, but the enemy's grip was too strong to be broken. When the last of these heroes fell, the battle still raged in the darkness in and about the deep canal cutting. But in darkness or daylight the line was held, fresh ammunition being steadily supplied so that the fire never slackened. Prisoners were amazed to find so few men in the position they vainly tried to take, and the commander of one of the last enemy brigades that failed reported, in order to excuse his failure, that the British garrison had received heavy reinforcements. The floor of the disused waterway was covered with dead and injured grey-clad bodies.

The third deed of remarkable gallantry in the 2nd Division was performed in the afternoon of November 30th, on the extreme right flank. Here, where the 17th Middlesex Regiment connected with the battalions of the 47th London Territorial Division, the large masses of the enemy succeeded in overrunning three of the posts of the 2nd Division, and making a gap between two of the battalions of Territorials.

The Germans penetrated some distance into the line and created a very perilous situation for their opponents. But Captain A. M. C. McReady Diarmid, of the 17th Middlesex, led his company forward through a heavy barrage and broke through the hostile **Captain McReady** force with such shattering effect that the **Diarmid's heroism** German line swung back for a third of a mile, losing on the way many men. Again, on December 1st, a fresh German division broke into a position near Captain McReady Diarmid's company. Forming a bombing-party, the great fighting man, who was a marvellous thrower, killed eighty Germans himself, while his men forced the enemy back three hundred yards. Then he was slain by a bomb, near the spot whence the Germans had started.

At the time Captain McReady Diarmid was, Cuchulain-like, making his first deep drive into the enemy's rank on the extreme right flank of the 2nd Division, another desperate struggle was proceeding beyond the left flank. From Mœuvres westward to Tadpole Copse the enveloping German masses thrust at the 168th Brigade of the 56th London Territorial Division. In one fierce succession of attacking waves they reached battalion headquarters of the 8th Middlesex, who were attached to the brigade. The commanding officer, with his staff, held the Germans off with hand-grenades until more troops arrived and regained the trench. Though reduced in strength by recent battles, and severely pressed by larger forces, the men of the 168th and 169th Brigades beat off all attacks. The Queen's Westminsters, London Scottish, the 1/2nd London Regiment, and the 1/8th Middlesex Regiment were valorous in resistance.

The other fresher division of London Territorials, the 47th, had a nightmarish time among the crashing oak and ash trees of that wood of death—Bourlon Ridge. Less racking high-explosive shell was used than in other high-wood battles. Instead, the deep arc of opposing batteries almost mechanically maintained a vast yet softly sounding cascade of very deadly poisonous gas projectiles. So infected was the air that the men could not remove their masks, the design of Marwitz being to force the Londoners to exhaust either their box-respirators or their powers of endurance. The London Rifles, Post Office Rifles, Civil Service Rifles, Poplar and Stepney Rifles, London Irish, St. Pancras, Blackheath and Woolwich, Surrey Rifles, and Queen's London, with the 1/6th and 1/15th London Regiments, were among those who endured the extreme stress of chemical torture and ferocious, dense infantry assaults.

In the afternoon of November 30th the 1/6th and 1/15th Londoners were forced apart by columnal masses of Germans. The two commanding officers, however, gathered runners, signallers, orderlies, cooks, and battalion staff together, with a reserve company, and leading an immediate counter-attack, successfully closed the gap. All other attacks were repulsed with very heavy losses to the enemy.

Germans suffer crushing casualties On the entire northern area of the Cambrai salient the casualties of the Second German Army, under General von Marwitz, were crushing—bitter fruits of a German defeat outbalancing the small, partial success at Gouzeaucourt. One British machine-gun battery, of eight pieces, fired seventy thousand rounds of ammunition into the successive waves of Germans. Long lines of infantry were raked sideways by British machine-gunners, while being shot down in front. British field-gunners succeeded in achieving what German field and heavy gunners vainly tried to do. They brought their batteries up to the crest line and fired directly at short range upon the hostile masses.

French batteries came into action on November 30th in the Cambrai salient. General Pétain promptly placed some of his troops within reach of Sir Julian Byng, in case of need. Part of the artillery of this supporting force entered the battle in a very helpful way, and although the remainder of the troops were not required, the fact that they were available was of much assistance in assuring the strength of the new dispositions made by the British High Command.

On December 1st the struggle fiercely continued on the whole front. The magnificent British Guards, most effectively helped by the Tank Brigade, stormed completely over St. Quentin Ridge and entered Gonnelieu. At one point, where the infantry was checked by a machine-gun barrage from a German entrenchment, a single Tank clambered up and operated on either side, filling the ditch with dead enemies and silencing fifteen machine-guns. Large targets were obtained by all the Tank crews here, and very severe losses inflicted upon the enemy.

The Tanks also co-operated with the dismounted Indian troopers of the 5th Cavalry Division in the attack upon Gauche Wood. The Germans were resolved to hold this important flanking position at any cost, and engaged in desperate fighting for it. In one spot there were four hostile machine-guns in a space of twenty yards, and German field-batteries were in action close behind. The Indians and the Guards advanced with great determination, but their deadly work was considerably lightened by the assistant Tanks. The huge, crashing, cannonading, bullet-raining steel monsters slaughtered the Germans, smashed their machine-guns, and killed the teams of some pieces of hostile artillery, three of which were captured.

Beyond the memorable patch of hilly woodland, Tanks, Guardsmen, and Indian cavalrymen worked down the hollow joining Twenty-two Ravine, towards the rise of ground on which stood Villers Guislain. Moving against heavy, direct artillery fire, three of the landships reached the outskirts of the lost village; but the troops that tried to follow them were held up by machine-guns, and the Tanks at last withdrew. **Tank attack on Villers Guislain**

By this time General von Marwitz had changed his plan of campaign. Swinging what remained of his principal force from the northern front and western flank to the eastern flank, he endeavoured to enlarge the ground that had been regained between Lateau Wood and Villers Guislain. It was his increasing pressure that compelled the 29th Division to evacuate Masnières.

There then opened to the enemy commander a way of attack running below Welsh Ridge to La Vacquerie. He had the Bonavis-Masnières road and the adjoining Vacquerie Valley for direct operations, and the Banteux position westward and Villers Guislain Ridge southward for cross-firing bombardments and converging movements.

Secure in the possession of the Bonavis Ridge, and with Villers Guislain held against the Guards Division and the Tank Brigade, the tactical advantages of the German commander were important. A very telling moral effect was to be obtained by winning the closing round in a winter campaign. Such an effect Sir Douglas Haig had

MAINTAINING THE LINE OF VOCAL COMMUNICATIONS.
Officer of the Royal Engineers with two of his men engaged in laying a telephone cable along a trench near the fighting-line. The maintenance of telephone facilities between advancing units and their supports was an important element of such a " surprise " forward movement as that on the Cambrai front.

produced in his last victory on the Passchendaele Ridge, and his surprise success had first promised an enormous magnification of this moral effect in the Cambrai operations.

Now General von Marwitz cleverly aimed at a winning close on the Ypres scale. On December 2nd he opened a series of heavy attacks on Welsh Ridge and La Vacquerie village, while maintaining strong holding actions from Marcoing to Bourlon. On the following day he became more aggressive, and with large reinforcements attacked savagely on all the eastern British flank, from the vicinity of Masnières to La Vacquerie village. The village he won, and by his pressure he compelled the British forces to withdraw from the farther bank of the Scheldt Canal. Again, on December 5th, he made a prolonged and costly attempt to storm the Welsh Ridge; but, after three days of fierce fighting, it failed.

The strength displayed by the German commander had a marked influence upon the plan followed by Sir Douglas Haig. It convinced the British Field-Marshal that he would not be able to recover Bonavis Ridge without sustained, severe fighting. On the other hand, the possession of the Bonavis Ridge was **British withdrawn to Flesquières** practically essential to the security of the Bourlon position. Sir Douglas Haig had therefore to decide whether he would prepare another great offensive movement, or evacuate the endangered ground and withdraw to Flesquières Ridge.

Ever since November 22nd the problem of retiring to the Flesquières line had troubled the British High Command. It went against the stubborn Scottish character of the great captain of war to abandon positions gallantly won and heroically held—the sombre mass of Bourlon, the Hindenburg system by Mœuvres, Anneux, and Graincourt, Noyelles, Marcoing, and the Welsh Ridge.

But he had no doubt of the correct course, and gave orders for it to be followed. On the night of December 4th the evacuation of positions was begun. The more important enemy field defences were destroyed, and those guns that could not be removed were rendered useless. In the afternoon of December 5th the German forces started to feel their way forward, and though they showed great caution, groups of them were caught in the open by the British artillery.

Great skill and courage were called for from the covering troops. In the afternoon of December 6th two companies of the much-tried 1/15th London Regiment of the 47th Division were acting as a covering force by Graincourt. Through a hostile attack farther east their flank was turned and they were cut off. Yet the London Territorials broke through the enveloping German line and, after putting many of their foes out of action, arrived in good order on the new British front.

This front, which was completely established by the morning of December 7th, 1917, corresponded roughly to the former Hindenburg reserve line. It ran from a point one and a half miles north-by-east of La Vacquerie, north of Ribécourt and Flesquières to the Nord Canal, one and a half miles above Havrincourt. It was generally between two and two and a half miles in advance of the British line of November 19th. The troops retained an important section of the Hindenburg system, with its excellent shelters and other material advantages.

The material results of the three weeks' fighting consisted in the gain of 12,000 yards of the former enemy front line from the neighbourhood of La Vacquerie to that of Boursies, together with nearly 11,000 yards of the main Hindenburg line and Hindenburg support line, with the **Material results of the battle** villages of Ribécourt, Flesquières, and Havrincourt. A total of 145 German guns was kept or destroyed, and 11,100 German soldiers were captured.

The enemy had taken an unimportant part of the British front line between Vendhuille and Gonnelieu, and captured British guns and British soldiers considerably less in number than his own losses in men and material.

Having regard to its historic interest, it will be best to conclude with the statement that the British Commander-in-Chief made about the operations:

In view of the strength of the German forces on the front of my attack, and the success with which secrecy was maintained during our preparations, I had calculated that the enemy's prepared defences would be captured in the first rush. I had good hope that his resisting power behind those defences would then be so enfeebled for a period that we should be able on the same day to establish ourselves quickly and completely on the dominating Bourlon Ridge from Fontaine-Notre-Dame to Mœuvres, and to secure our right flank along a line including the Bonavis Ridge, Crèvecœur, and Rumilly to Fontaine-Notre-Dame. Even if this did not prove possible within the first twenty-four hours, a second day would be at our disposal before the enemy's reserves could begin to arrive in any formidable numbers.

Meanwhile, with no wire and no prepared defences to hamper them, it was reasonable to hope that masses of cavalry would find it possible to pass through, whose task would be thoroughly to disorganise the enemy's systems of command and intercommunication in the whole area between the Canal de l'Escaut, the River Sensée, and the Canal du Nord, as well as to the east and north-east of Cambrai.

My intentions as regards subsequent exploitation were to push westward and north-westward, taking the Hindenburg line in reverse from Mœuvres to the River Scarpe, and capturing all the enemy's defences and probably most of his garrisons lying west of a line from Cambrai northwards to the Sensée, and south of that river and the Scarpe.

Time would have been required to enable us to develop and complete the operation; but the prospects of gaining the necessary time, by the use of cavalry in the manner outlined above, were in my opinion good enough to justify the attempt to execute the plan. I am of opinion that on November 20th and 21st we went very near to a success sufficiently complete to bring the realisation of our full programme within our power.

The reasons for my decision to continue the fight after November 21st have already been explained. Though in the event no advantage was gained thereby, I still consider that, as the problem presented itself at the time, the more cautious course would have been difficult to justify. It must be remembered that it was not a question of remaining where we stood, but of abandoning tactical positions of value, gained with great gallantry, the retention of which seemed not only to be within our power, but likely even yet to lead to further success.

Whatever may be the final decision on this point, as well as on the original decision to undertake the enterprise at all with the forces available, the continuation of our efforts against Fontaine-Notre-Dame gave rise to severe fighting, in which our troops more than held their own.

On November 30th risks were accepted by us at some points in order to increase our strength at others. Our fresh reserves had been thrown in on the Bourlon front, where the enemy brought **Haig's account of the operations** against us a total force of seven divisions to three and failed. I do not consider that it would have been justifiable on the indications to have allotted a smaller garrison to this front.

Between Masnières and Vendhuille the enemy's superiority in infantry over our divisions in line was in the proportion of about four to three, and we were sufficiently provided with artillery. That his attack was partially successful may tend to show that the garrison allotted to this front was insufficient, either owing to want of numbers, lack of training, or exhaustion from previous fighting.

Captured maps and orders have made it clear that the enemy aimed at far more considerable results than were actually achieved by him. Three convergent attacks were to be made on the salient formed by our advance; two of them delivered approximately simultaneously about Gonnelieu and Masnières, followed later by a still more powerful attack on the Bourlon front. The objectives of these attacks extended to the high ground at Beaucamp and Trescault, and the enemy's hope was to capture and destroy the whole of the British forces in the Cambrai salient.

This bold and ambitious plan was foiled on the greater part of our front by the splendid defence of the British divisions engaged; and, though the defence broke down for a time in one area, the recovery made by the weak forces still left and those within immediate reach is worthy of the highest praise. Numberless instances of great gallantry, promptitude, and skill were shown.

I desire to acknowledge the skill and resource displayed by General Byng throughout the Cambrai operations, and to express my appreciation of the manner in which they were conducted by him, as well as by his Staff and the subordinate commanders.

In conclusion, I would point out that the sudden breaking through by our troops of an immense system of defence has had a most inspiring moral effect on the armies I command, and must have a correspondingly depressing influence upon the enemy. The great value of the Tanks in the offensive has been conclusively proved. In view of this experience, the enemy may well hesitate to deplete any portion of his front, as he did last summer, in order to set free troops to concentrate for decisive action at some other point.

Sir Douglas Haig proved to be correct in his prevision that the principal result of the first surprising success of the British armoured cars would be that the German High Command would hesitate again to leave any part of their lines opposite the British front in a weak condition. General von Ludendorff greatly strengthened his armies, and selected the British front for decisive action because of the lessons he had learnt at Cambrai.

WAR BOND POSTER

CHAPTER CCXXXIX.

AT NATIONAL GALLERY.

HOW BRITAIN RAISED £6,000,000,000 FOR THE WAR.

By George A. Sutton,

Director of Publicity to the National War Savings Committee.

Cost of the War up to July, 1915—Mr. McKenna's Supplementary Budget for 1915-16—Duty on Excess Profits—Mr. McKenna's Budget for 1916-17—Some Financial Milestones of the War—Mr. Bonar Law's Appearance as Chancellor of the Exchequer—Treasury Bills, Exchequer Bonds, and War Expenditure Certificates as a Means of Raising Money—Success of the Five Per Cent. and Four Per Cent. War Loans in January, 1917—Analysis of the National Debt of £5,500,000,000 in January, 1918—Figures of Germany's War Loans—The Problem Confronting the British Chancellor of the Exchequer—A New Departure in National Finance Necessary—Origin and Constitution of the National War Savings Committee—War Savings Committees and Associations—Report of the Committee's Work to March, 1917—Extension of the Committee's Activities in Publicity—National War Bonds—Tanks as Advertising and Collecting Mediums—Business Men's Week—Summary of Work to the End of 1917.

THE financial side of the Great War, the getting and spending of those vast sums of money which Mr. Lloyd George, who in the period then under consideration was Chancellor of the Exchequer, called in his picturesque fashion " silver bullets," was the subject of a previous chapter of THE GREAT WAR (LXXIV., Vol. 4, page 197). Therein something was said about the extraordinary machinations of German financiers to embarrass Britain during those few, full days which preceded the declaration of war on August 4th, 1914, and about the panic on the world's Stock Exchanges. And then followed an account of the policy of the British Government in financing the war down to the flotation of the great loan in July, 1915.

The loan in question, " a great national appeal for a great national purpose," produced, apart from certain small subscriptions, £570,000,000, but although " far and away beyond any amount ever subscribed in the world's history," it was inadequate to finance the war for more than a few months. At that time, Mr. Asquith stated on June 29th, the war was costing the country £3,000,000 a day.

The loan carried interest at 4½ per cent. with a possibility of more, and was repayable at par between 1925 and 1945. It was

subscribed by 550,000 persons, or one in eighty-four of the population, while a further 547,000 persons invested an additional £15,000,000 therein in small amounts through the Post Office. These totals were exclusive of stock issued for the purpose of converting Consols and other Government securities into the new 4½ per cent. war loan.

As far as this chapter is concerned, the story may begin with Mr. Asquith's speech in Parliament on July 20th, 1915. More money was wanted, and he asked for a vote of credit for £150,000,000. It was the third in the current financial year, and it brought the total amount voted for the cost of the war, then not quite a year old, to £1,012,000,000. He estimated that it would carry the struggle on until the end of September.

September came, and with it an unpleasant surprise for sticklers for economy. The House of Commons met on the 14th, and on the next day Mr. Asquith asked it for a further vote of £250,000,000, the seventh since the outbreak of the war. In his speech he stated that from April 1st to June 30th the struggle had cost Britain £2,700,000 a day, from July 1st to July 17th £3,000,000 a day, and from July 18th to September 11th over £3,500,000 a day. Advances to Allies were responsible for most of the increase; the Army was spending more, but the Navy a little less.

ROYAL PRINTING OF NATIONAL WAR BONDS.
King George, accompanied by the Queen and Princess Mary, at the Bank of England on December 18th, 1917. His Majesty was starting the machine for printing the first of a new issue of £5 National War Bonds.

A few days later Mr. McKenna, then Chancellor of the Exchequer, made a distinct innovation in national finance. Hitherto one Budget a year had been deemed sufficient, and the taxpayer could at least be sure of a year's interval before new burdens were put upon him. But so rapidly was the cost of the war mounting up, so quickly were the proceeds of the big loan being exhausted, so distant seemed the prospect of peace, that the Coalition Ministry then in power decided to impose new taxation forthwith, not to wait until the end of the financial year, six months later.

In one direction this supplementary Budget, itself a novelty, introduced a novel idea into national finance; but in others, and especially with regard to the income-tax, it followed precedent, and that precedent just the line of least resistance. The novelty was the excess profits duty. From all sides there came stories, exaggerated perhaps but by no means wholly imaginary, of persons making huge fortunes from the possession of ships, the manufacture of munitions of war, the sale of necessary articles of food, and in other ways; and the Chancellor

[*Langfier.*
SIR ROBERT KINDERSLEY, K.B.E.
Appointed Chairman of the National War Savings Committee on its constitution in 1916.

of the Exchequer could certainly rely upon the support of public opinion when he proposed that these fortunate persons should pay over to him 50 per cent. of their excess profits. Roughly speaking, excess profits were defined as those made in excess of the profits, as shown by the income-tax returns made in the financial year 1913-14. There were, however, various concessions and alterations, too technical for discussion here. The Chancellor counted on £6,000,000 from this new duty for the current financial year, but thereafter on a much greater sum. The returns were soon to show that he had here tapped a very productive source of revenue.

The income-tax was raised, not as usual by so many pennies in the pound, but by 40 per cent., and the new scale came into operation for the financial half-year beginning October 1st. In practice it meant that 20 per cent., the half-year's proportion of 40, was added to every man's assessment. If he had originally been charged £21, he

was now charged £25 4s. To produce still more from this fertile plant, the limit of exemption from the tax was reduced from £160 to £130, and a corresponding reduction made in the amounts allowed as abatements. Farmers were asked in future to pay tax on their full rent, not on one-third of it as before, unless they preferred to be taxed, as other traders were, on their actual profits. The somewhat complex rates of super-tax were revised, the highest being increased from 2s. 8d. in the pound to 3s. 6d., although they were not paid on quite the whole income, but only on its excess over £2,500.

The other changes affected indirect taxation. The duty on sugar was raised from 1s. 10d. to 9s. 4d. a cwt.; tea, tobacco, cocoa, and coffee were to pay 50 per cent. more. Users of motor spirit and patent medicines were asked for contributions, and so were the purchasers of motor-cars, motor-cycles, cinema films, and one or two other things when imported from abroad. The public was asked to pay more for its postages, telegrams, and telephones.

The result of these changes was to add, so the authorities estimated,

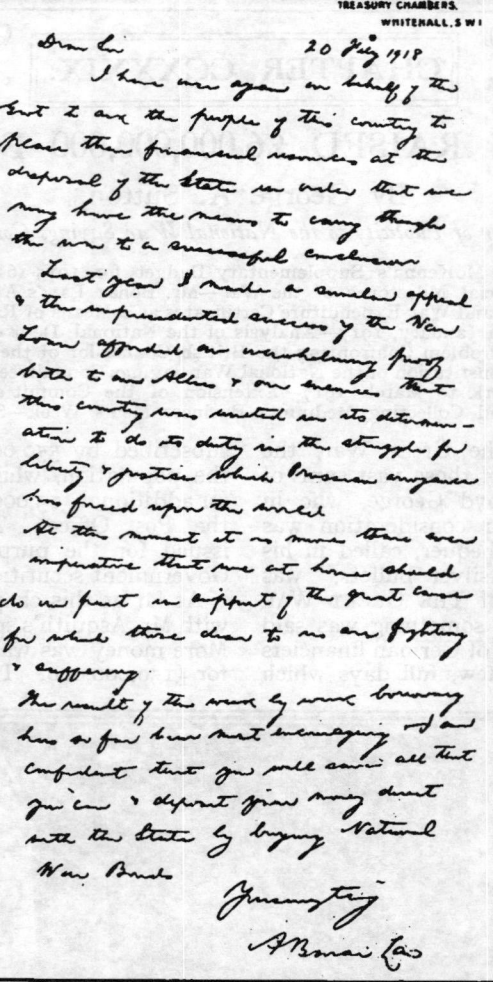

THE CHANCELLOR'S APPEAL.
Reduced facsimile of the appeal to the people of Great Britain to buy War Bonds, issued by Mr. Bonar Law, Chancellor of the Exchequer, in February, 1918.

[*Vandyk.*
MR. GEORGE A. SUTTON.
Appointed Director of Publicity to the National War Savings Committee, November, 1917.

another £107,000,000 a year to the national revenue, but of that sum only £33,000,000 would be collected during the year 1915-16. However, certain taxes were producing more than was forecast in the earlier Budget, and so the total revenue for the year could be put at £305,000,000. So far so good; but on the other side were an estimated expenditure of £1,590,000,000, an estimated deficit of £1,285,000,000, and a net National Debt of £2,200,000,000.

No increase of taxation, however severe, could meet such an outlay, and further borrowing was soon necessary. First of all a little was obtained from the United States. To that country both Great Britain and France owed a good deal of money, and this liability was very detrimental to the rate of exchange, which was then moving steadily against the European countries. Accordingly, a loan for 500,000,000 dollars at 5 per cent. was arranged, the two countries borrowing the money jointly.

But this £100,000,000, of which Britain only got a part,

was merely a drop in the ocean, so fast was the cost of the war increasing. On November 11th—and the story is still only in 1915—Mr. Asquith asked the House of Commons to vote a further £400,000,000, and on that occasion he mentioned £5,000,000, not £3,500,000, as the daily average of expenditure. That sum enabled the Government to conduct the war until February, 1916, and on the 21st of that month the Prime Minister was again asking for more. £120,000,000 was required to take the country on to the end of the financial year, when £1,782,000,000 would have been asked for, and presumably spent.

Mr. Asquith did not, however, stop there. To begin the next financial year he asked for another £300,000,000, the two votes together making a total of £420,000,000, and on this occasion he went somewhat fully into the financial position. In this review the most satisfactory feature was the fact that the daily rate of expenditure had fallen somewhat below the estimate of £5,000,000. Moreover, the expenditure included the sum of £161,900,000 lent to Britain's Allies and her Dominions, and the daily expenditure on the fighting services really worked out at only £3,000,000. It had increased since November at the rate of £400,000 a day, not perhaps an excessive sum when the expansion of the armies in the field is remembered.

AT GLASGOW'S TANK BANK.
The Rt. Hon. G. N. Barnes, M.P. (signing paper), purchasing War Bonds on a Tank's visit to Glasgow in January, 1918.

The time for a new Budget, the nation's annual accounts, was then fast approaching, and on April 4th, 1916, this was presented by Mr. McKenna to the House of Commons. For the year just closed the revenue had reached the unprecedented figure of £337,000,000, the largest item in which was the income-tax, which had produced £128,000,000, more than sufficient to meet the whole of the national expenditure had this remained as it was before the Boer War. But instead of the £117,000,000 of 1898-99, the nation had spent £1,599,000,000, four-fifths of which amount had been added to the National Debt.

SAILORS ON A LANDSHIP.
At a Tank Bank: Handing up cheque for £20,000 to be invested in War Bonds for King George's Fund for Sailors. On the Tank were sailors, all of whom had been in torpedoed ships.

Turning to the coming year (1916-17), the Chancellor dealt only in estimates. The expenditure he placed at £1,825,000,000, all of which save £225,000,000 was directly required for the prosecution of the war, and something

approaching £100,000,000 of the balance for the interest on the debt incurred since August, 1914. He proposed further additions to taxation. Another screw was given to the income-tax. It was to be 5s. in the pound on big incomes—those exceeding £2,000 unearned and £2,500 earned—a year, and was to descend by graduated stages to 2s. 3d. in the pound, its lowest rate. The excess profits' duty, which had so far only yielded a paltry £140,000, but which was expected to produce £75,000,000 in 1916-17, was raised from 50 to 60 per cent.; amusements were taxed, visitors to theatres, cinemas, race meetings, football matches, etc., being called upon to contribute something to the revenue through their entrance tickets; and the duties on sugar, coffee, and cocoa were increased. A new tax was placed upon matches, mineral waters, cider, and perry. With these additions he expected to receive from revenue £502,000,000, which, if correct, would leave £1,323,000,000 to be provided by borrowing.

The Chancellor then dealt with even more stupendous figures. He said that, assuming the war to last so long, by March 31st, 1917, Britain's National Debt would stand at £3,440,000,000. Of this, £800,000,000 would doubtless be recovered, for it had been lent, so the net debt would be £2,640,000,000. The charge for interest on this debt, together with a reasonable provision for its gradual extinction, would absorb £145,000,000 a year, or about the total amount of the annual national ex- **Stupendous figures** penditure between the end of the Boer **for 1916-17** War in 1902 and the outbreak of extravagance in 1909. The same idea can be expressed in a more homely way. Dividing the debt equally among the population, on March 31st, 1917, every man, woman, and child in the United Kingdom would owe £75, and so every household of six would owe £450, in most cases more than the value of the house in which they lived.

The Finance Bill, giving effect to the Budget, passed its second reading in the House of Commons on May 18th, and a few days later Mr. Asquith asked for another £300,000,000. He then estimated the daily cost of the war at £4,750,000, although a careful calculation showed that during the previous fifty days it had been £70,000 a day

AT ONE OF LONDON'S TANK BANKS.
Officer who had been wounded in battle buying War Bonds at the Tank Bank in Trafalgar Square. Though no longer able to fight physically, he was ready to do his part financially.

in excess of that figure. The increase was due to the greater financial assistance rendered to Britain's Allies and her Dominions. Another vote of credit, one for the unprecedented sum of £450,000,000, carried on the war until October, when the Prime Minister called for a further £300,000,000. He then informed the public that the war was costing a little over £5,000,000 a day. There had been, since the previous estimate, no increase in the amount spent on the Navy, and a slight decrease in that spent on the Army; but a great deal more had gone on munitions. This was the thirteenth vote of credit asked for by Mr. Asquith's Government. Before the end of the year that Government had fallen, and one headed by Mr. Lloyd George had taken its place. In this Mr. Bonar Law was Chancellor of the Exchequer.

As Finance Minister Mr. Law made his bow to Parliament on December 14th. He wanted £400,000,000, and, according to figures which he then gave, it was none too much. During the previous sixty-three days the daily rate of expenditure had been £5,710,000; before that period—*i.e.*, before the middle of October—it had been £5,070,000 only. The total expenditure since the beginning of the war had been £3,852,000,000, or—as he did not say—close upon £100 for every man, woman, and child in Great Britain.

It is now full time to deal with a very pertinent question. How was all this money being found? It was all very well for the House of Commons to vote it, but that was the beginning, not the end of the story. The big loan of July, 1915, had produced, roughly, £600,000,000, but that sum was spent before the end of that year. Taxation had been increased, but even if the most sanguine estimates of the revenue were reached it would not provide quite £2,000,000 a day, and at the close of 1916 nearly £6,000,000 was needed. There was a gap for the financial authorities to bridge of something between £3,000,000 and £4,000,000

SCARBOROUGH'S INGENIOUS "SUBMARINE."
Unable to get a submarine moored in their harbour as a "Bank," during the "Business Men's Week," for investing in War Bonds, the people of Scarborough fitted up a tramcar as a colourable imitation of the underwater craft.

a day, nearer the latter than the former figure. During 1916 the bulk of this money was raised by the sale of Treasury Bills and Exchequer Bonds. Treasury Bills are simply promises by the State to pay the amount stated on each at the end of a certain period, usually three, six, nine, or twelve months. They are sold by the Bank of England—the war brought in the practice of selling them day by day over the counter at a fixed price rather than in lump sums by tender, the method which formerly prevailed. The discount varied somewhat, being affected by the state of the money market; but during 1916 it was round about 5 per cent. They are a form of security intended almost entirely for bankers and financial houses, with large sums of money to invest for short periods; they make little appeal to the general public, for whom they are unsuited. They were, and had been for a number of years, a very useful method of raising money, especially money that was only required for a short time; the danger during the war was lest their number and amount should become excessive, and that danger was certainly present in the latter part of 1916. At the opening of the year the amount outstanding was £380,381,000, but twelve months later it had been increased to £1,115,149,000.

Exchequer Bonds were a form of security which made a much wider appeal. They were issued for longer periods, usually three or five years, and were bought by private investors. The usual rate of interest paid on these bonds during 1915 and 1916 was 5 per cent., but in September, 1916, the rate was raised by Mr. McKenna to 6 per cent. Many financial authorities regarded this measure as imprudent and unnecessary; imprudent because it tended to reduce the value of British securities generally, and unnecessary because the money could be raised at a lower rate.

The experiment, however, was but short-lived. At the end of 1916 the amount of 5 per cent. Exchequer Bonds

LIKE GULLIVER WITH THE FLEET OF LILLIPUT.
Sailor arranging the ships of a miniature fleet which was set afloat in the fountain basins in Trafalgar Square during the London Tank Bank rally in March, 1918. Right: One of the ships about to take the water.

The "launching" was performed by Admiral Sims, who was in command of the American fleet in European waters, and the mimic naval display proved a very popular feature during the week of its exhibition.

outstanding was £334,520,000, and of 6 per cent. Bonds £159,200,000. Of the former £180,800,000 had been sold since April 1st, and all of the latter since October 1st. Thus Treasury Bills and Exchequer Bonds, both short-dated securities, had furnished most of the millions borrowed by the Government in 1916. The balance had been raised in various ways: a little, nearly £30,000,000, by War Expenditure Certificates, which were practically two-year Treasury Bills, some by loans from abroad, and some by the sale of War Savings Certificates.

These forms of borrowing could not be continued indefinitely, and towards the end of 1916 there were rumours that a new loan was contemplated. On December 30th the following notices were issued: "The Lords Commissioners of his Majesty's Treasury give notice that no further applications for £6 per cent. Exchequer Bonds, 1920, will be accepted after this date, either by the Bank of England or by the Post Office. The Lords Commissioners of his Majesty's Treasury give notice that no further applications for War Expenditure Certificates will be accepted after this date."

Once again coming events had cast shadows before, and consequently there was no surprise when the official announcement of the loan appeared. The preparations were carefully made; it contained one or two novelties designed to attract investors. In the first place the main part of it was a 5 per cent. loan, and this was a higher rate of interest

A ROYAL EXAMPLE.
Queen Alexandra at Marlborough House releasing a pigeon carrying an application for £500 War Bonds, subscribed for by the Q. A. League for the Treloar Cripples' Hospital.

THE QUEEN'S MESSENGER.
Taking Queen Alexandra's pigeon post order from the messenger bird on its arrival at the Tank Pigeon Loft in Trafalgar Square.

than the British Government had paid for permanent borrowings for more than half a century. There was also a 4 per cent. loan, and investors could take their choice.

An income-tax of 5s. in the pound makes a serious inroad upon incomes derived from investments, for it means that a 5 per cent. security only yields $3\frac{3}{4}$ per cent., and so on. Recognising this, the Government offered to investors a 4 per cent. security free of income-tax—*i.e.*, one of which the full £4 of interest was received by the owner. That relieved him, not only of an income-tax of 5s. in the pound, but of the payment of any increase in the tax.

Investors in this particular security could view with indifference an additional 1s. or 2s. 6d. on the income-tax. They could rely upon a clear 4 per cent. On the other hand, should the income-tax be reduced, these persons would obtain no benefit. It was a sporting offer to the public.

Persons putting their money into the 5 per cent. loan could not claim these advantages, but their tastes were not forgotten; £100 of stock was offered to them for £95, so that their rate of interest worked out at a fraction over £5 5s. per cent.; and moreover, when the loan was repaid, as arranged, between 1929 and 1947, they would receive a full £100 for each £95 invested.

They were liable to the ordinary income-tax, and allowing for this at 5s. in the pound, it was calculated that they would receive £4 2s. 3d. per cent. on their money. Persons with small incomes who paid a lower rate of tax, or no tax at all, would, of course, receive more.

Choice offered to investors

Even with regard to income-tax, however, something was done for the investor in the 5 per cent. loan. The tax was not to be deducted from the interest when paid over to him. He was liable to it, but the "small man" would be freed from the undoubted annoyance of having to claim the return of over-deducted tax from the Income Tax Commissioners and of waiting some months until he got it. Finally, holders of Exchequer Bonds and of Treasury Bills were allowed on favourable terms to exchange those forms of security into the new loans.

Attention was paid to the maintenance, as far as possible of the capital.value of the loan. Provision was made for a

SMALL BEARER OF A LARGE SUBSCRIPTION.
A Battersea firm applied for £250,000 War Bonds, despatching the order by pigeon post to the Tank Bank in Trafalgar Square, and stipulating that it should be acknowledged as part of Battersea's contribution.

depreciation fund. This was at the rate of ⅛ per cent. per month (1½ per cent. per annum), and, to anticipate for a moment, Mr. Bonar Law said nearly a year later that £30,139,220 had been so set aside. Of this sum £27,962,937 had been used to purchase £29,535,000 of the 5 per cent. stock, which had been therefore cancelled. Further, the loan was sold through the Post Office to those who could only invest small sums, £5 being the lowest amount taken, and it was stated that death duties could be paid by the loan, taken at the price of issue. This would probably prevent blocks of it from coming to the market.

The lists opened on January 12th, and remained open until February 16th. Within those five weeks £850,301,000 was applied for and allotted, £30,715,000 **Success of the** of this being in the form of small applica-**1917 War Loan** tions made through the Post Office. No less than 5,289,000 persons contributed to it, a figure which may be compared with the 550,000 who participated in the loan of 1915. Its success was due partly to the help of the banks. These institutions did not, as was the case in 1915, take up large blocks of stock themselves; instead, they lent the money to their customers, taking up the loan for them. It is uncertain how much was lent in this way, but the total must have been considerable, although it was quickly reduced as clients repaid the advances. The annual report of the London City and Midland Bank for 1917 gave some figures which showed the extent to which that particular institution, the largest of the ordinary banks, helped the loan. Its clients applied for £86,000,000 and converted £7,000,000 of Treasury Bills, making a total subscription of £93,000,000. For the purpose of taking up the loan the bank advanced to them £26,813,000, which sum by the end of 1917 had been reduced to £12,645,539.

One small matter and a summary before passing to the financial history of 1917. The 1915 loan had been issued at 4½ per cent., but with the promise that if a further loan was issued bearing a higher rate of interest that

ON PATRIOTIC BUSINESS.
Tank 113 arriving in Holborn to collect the Prudential Assurance Company's investment of £628,000, interest on £25,000,000 already invested by the company in the War Loan.

higher rate should also be paid on the money lent in 1915, the lender having the right to convert into the new loan. That contingency had now happened, and a further ½ per cent. fell to those holders of the 4½ per cent. stock who chose, as most of them did, to convert. The precedent was not perhaps a good one, and might mean additional liabilities of unknown extent to the taxpayer, but Mr. Lloyd George, then the new Prime Minister, said about this time that "so far as we can foresee or control the future, a higher rate of interest than this—(*i.e.*, 5 per cent.)—will not be paid."

Figures about this loan were soon made public,

the most authoritative being those given to the House of Commons by Mr. Bonar Law on May 3rd when introducing his Budget. The 5 per cent. loan, including converted Treasury Bills, amounted to £966,048,000, and the 4 per cent. one, also including Bills converted, to £22,658,000. In addition £821,005,000 of the 4½ per cent. loan was turned into the 5 per cent. security, and £282,792,000 of Exchequer Bonds was likewise transferred. A few holders of this loan and of the Bonds transferred into the 4 per cent. loan, £28,726,000 being the amount of these transactions. Some of the money obtained—the "new money," to use the jargon of the market—was used to repay other borrowings. In the first five weeks of the year £200,000,000 of Treasury Bills was liquidated, and in three months, including the conversions already mentioned, the amount outstanding was reduced from £1,148,500,000 to £464,000,000.

There was no difficulty in spending the rest of the money. On February 12th Mr. Bonar Law asked the House of Commons for £550,000,000, and a month or so later (March 15th) for £60,000,000. The latter was the more alarming of the two. The February vote was for £200,000,000 to carry on the war until March 31st, and the balance of £350,000,000 to open the new financial year with ample credits. The March vote showed that the £200,000,000 was insufficient; in other words, not only was the rate of expenditure rising, it was rising faster than the authorities had expected. In February the daily rate was £5,790,000, against £4,520,000 in the earlier part of the financial year. Small wonder that the expenditure for the year then drawing to a close would be something like £350,000,000 more than the estimates, or that the National Debt on March 31st, 1917, would be between £3,800,000,000 and £3,900,000,000.

So matters stood about the time that the Budget for 1917-18 was introduced. **Budget figures** The only changes in taxation then pro- **for 1917-18** posed were the increase in the excess profits duty from 60 to 80 per cent., and certain increases in the taxes on tobacco and amusements. With these additions the Chancellor estimated his revenue for the year then in front of him at £638,600,000. The expenditure was estimated at £2,290,381,000, of which £1,975,000,000 was for the cost of the war, and another £211,500,000 for interest on debt.

Mr. Law did not on this occasion go very far into the larger question of Britain's total liabilities, but he did state that during the war the country had spent already—he spoke on May 2nd, 1917—£4,318,000,000. Of this vast sum revenue had contributed £1,137,000,000, or 26 per cent., and so £3,181,000,000 remained added to the National Debt, which, with the pre-war figure, then stood at £3,854,000,000. The Chancellor's estimate for the year 1917-18 was that

"A SAFE INVESTMENT FOR MILLIONS."
Sir Thomas Dewey, Chairman of the Prudential Company, speaking from the Tank, said: "We as a company believe that the British Government gives the best security in the world."

the struggle would add another £1,652,000,000 to that figure, making it £5,506,000,000 on March 31st, 1918. If this sum could be divided over the whole world, it would work out at more than £3 each for every man, woman, and child on earth, whether white or black, red or yellow.

On May 9th Mr. Law asked for £500,000,000, the largest request ever made in a single vote, for the £550,000,000 of February 12th was in reality two votes, one for 1916-17 and the other for 1917-18. He then stated that the daily expenditure for the past five weeks had been at the high average of £7,450,000, although loans to Allies and Dominions, just then being made on an extended scale, reduced the net, or real, expenditure of the country to £5,600,000 a day.

The next vote of credit, the largest until then required, was for £650,000,000, and was asked for on July 24th. A longer period—one hundred and twelve days, or sixteen weeks—was then taken by Mr. Law to illustrate his case, and in that the country had spent £6,795,000 a day. During that time £155,000,000 more than the Budget estimate had been spent, £63,500,000 of this being accounted for by larger loans, and £91,500,000 by the greater cost of the Army (£64,500,000), of munitions of war (£12,000,000) and by larger expenditure on food (£15,000,000).

War bill to January, 1918

On October 30th came another of these periodical statements, the occasion being the need for a further £400,000,000. The expenditure for ten weeks, or seventy days, analysed, showed a daily average of £6,414,000, while the increase for the financial year was £222,500,000 over the Budget estimate. The National Debt had risen to £5,000,000,000, of which £1,260,000,000 would, the

ART IN THE SERVICE OF ADVERTISEMENT.
"The Peacemaker," by Rosina M. Gutti, one of the effective reproductions of fine works of art employed as large colour posters to arrest the attention and impress upon the mind the necessity of saving.

Chancellor hoped, be recovered from the Allies and Dominions. A new consideration, and a favourable one, was brought into the account, and this was the fact that £74,500,000 of the increased outgoings had gone on buying raw materials, foodstuffs, and ships. When these were sold this sum would be recovered.

Finally, as far as 1917 is concerned, on December 12th, Mr. Law asked for £550,000,000. The average daily expenditure for sixty-three days up to December 1st, he explained, was £6,794,000, or an excess over the Budget estimate of £1,383,000. Taking a wider survey, he showed that the average daily expenditure for the first thirty-five weeks of the financial year was £6,686,000, or an excess over the Budget estimate of £1,275,000. As, however, recoverable expenditure during this period amounted to £225,000,000, the real excess over the estimate was only £350,000 a day.

With this the House of Commons had voted, in twenty-one

A GENTLE REMINDER—AND AN EXHORTATION.
Whistler's Portrait of his Mother—one of the most famous examples of modern portrait painting—was happily utilised as a poster for emphasising the personal value of loyal investment.

votes of credit, £6,242,000,000 for carrying on the Great War. According to figures given in the "Statist," the actual war bill to January 5th, 1918, was £5,645,000,000, of which £805,000,000, or just over 14 per cent., had been raised by revenue, leaving a National Debt on that date of £4,840,000,000, or adding, as we must, the pre-war debt, one of, in round figures, £5,500,000,000, of which perhaps £1,860,000,000 was recoverable. The assumption, however, was probably open to the criticism that it took too favourable a view of the position in Russia. Some of it, how much cannot be said, had been lent to that country, and time only would show whether she could or would repay it. As some slight set-off against the steady rise in expenditure, it was pleasant to know that between April 1st and December 31st, 1917, the revenue produced £65,000,000 more than the authorities had estimated.

Analysis of the National Debt

The year 1918 opened with a National Debt of £5,500,000,000, of which £650,000,000 was represented by Consols and other securities generally, leaving £4,850,000,000 as the sum raised by borrowings since August, 1914. An analysis of this vast sum shows that £924,000,000 was raised by the two big loans of 1914 and 1915, and a further £947,000,000 by the one of 1917. The net sales of Treasury Bills had produced £1,058,000,000, and of Exchequer Bonds, £623,000,000. These four items accounted for £3,552,000,000, while £896,000,000 had been raised by loans abroad and in miscellaneous ways. Much of the balance of £402,000,000 had been derived from sales of War Savings Certificates and National War Bonds. Among the miscellaneous borrowings should be mentioned a loan for £100,000,000 offered to investors in India in February, 1917.

It is not easy, nor is it at all necessary to our story, to make a comparison between the finances of Britain and those of Germany. The conditions were so utterly dissimilar. The position, however, was examined with great thoroughness by Sir E. H. Holden, Bart., in his annual address to the shareholders of the London City and Midland Bank on January 29th, 1918. His detailed explanation showed how the Reichsbank increased enormously the supply of credit and paper money in Germany without a corresponding addition to its stock of gold, and this proceeding rendered any exact comparison with conditions in Great Britain impossible. He gave the figures for Germany's seven loans, totalling altogether £3,647,000,000, and added :

Germany's total war borrowings

The amount of the floating debt, consisting for the most part of Treasury Bills, at the present time—(*i.e.*, January, 1918)—may be estimated at about £1,450,000,000, so that the total borrowings of Germany since the outbreak of the war appear to be about £5,100,000,000, against total cash borrowings in the case of this country of about £4,900,000,000.

To return after this digression to Britain's war debt. Here was quite enough to tax the resource and ingenuity of the ablest financier that ever lived. To provide the interest on this huge sum, to set aside funds for its gradual repayment, and, most urgent of all, to find some way of dealing economically with the immense floating debt of Treasury Bills and Exchequer Bonds, were problems of the highest magnitude; but, big as they were, Mr. Bonar Law and his advisers had still a bigger one to face, for they had to make some provision for the future. Taking everything into account, remembering the position of Great Britain as the linchpin of the Grand Alliance, it is hardly too much to say that to deal wisely with the problem—so great, so complex, so unprecedented—involved one of the greatest efforts that man had ever been called upon to make. To provide for interest and repayment, to tax heavily without crippling industry or penalising a particular class, and to adjust the claims of the present with those of future generations—these were a few of the difficulties.

Although the country had borrowed, by the end of 1917, no less than £4,850,000,000 for carrying on the war, that struggle was then by no means over. On the contrary, some thought it was only just beginning, while British folk were agreed that, cost what it might, the nation was bound to see it through. It was costing, as we have already seen, some £7,000,000 a day, or nearly £2,600,000,000 a year, and it might easily cost more. Indeed, if the past was any guide, it was fairly certain that this would be the case; £2,000,000 a day might come from revenue, but even the heavier taxation, foreshadowed late in 1917 by the Chancellor, could hardly add £500,000 a day to that sum. In the most favourable circumstances Mr. Law, or his successor, must reckon on having to borrow £5,000,000 a day as long as the war lasted, for it mattered nothing, in this connection anyhow, whether the money was spent or only lent; it had in either case to be found, and both principal and interest to be guaranteed by Britain.

Problem before the financiers

This was the *x* in the difficult equation which the financiers had to solve. Certainly, viewing the position as it was at Christmas, 1917, two years more was none too long if the grim task before the Allies was to be fulfilled; it seemed to many that three years was little enough for its full accomplishment, especially when it was realised that 1918 would be far advanced before America could pull her full weight in the allied boat. Four years was more than a bare possibility, but perhaps it will be sufficient to assume that a prudent financier would make his arrangements on the assumption that three years more were needed to see it through, and that in each of those years he would have to borrow at least £2,200,000,000. Taxation, if it

could be further increased, might possibly save him from adding much to that figure as the months wore on, but the position was undoubtedly grave, and it was made graver by the many demands, not small ones either, by various classes of the community for more money from the national purse, whether in the shape of wages, pensions, or allowances of other kinds. For many of them doubtless a good case could be made out, but as inevitably as day follows night, did one demand bring forth another. In fact, the requests for increased remuneration made by all classes of workers during the Great War were the most perfect, and at the same time the most dangerous, example of the principle of the vicious circle that this generation has known. This, however, is a big subject, and we must turn to the second part of this chapter.

Montreal, once an island meadow and now one of the noblest cities of Greater Britain, had a romantic origin. The story is told by Parkman. The island in the St. Lawrence, whereon rose the hill called Mont Real, had been handed over from one French trading company to another, and Maisonneuve, the representative of the recipient association, asked the Jesuits to take spiritual charge of the new colony. They accepted and took possession with an elaborate ritual. They approached in boats singing a hymn, landed, and raised an altar, kneeled down as the Host was raised aloft. Then the priest spoke : " You are a grain of mustard seed that shall rise and grow till its branches overshadow the earth." The words were strangely prophetic, as the Montreal of to-day proves.

This Biblical simile of the grain of mustard seed may be used, without either irreverence or incongruity, for the National War Savings Committee. We have just said something about the financial position of Great Britain during the Great War, and have spoken of the enormous accumulation of debt, early in 1918 something about £6,000,000,000 sterling, and the possibility—or more truly the probability—of an increase upon even that huge total.

The time was ripe for a new departure in national finance, one which should rank in future years with Pitt's introduction of the income-tax and Peel's abolition of the duties on corn. The old expedients —Exchequer Bonds, Treasury Bills, and then a loan from the investing public, perhaps 350,000 strong—although excellent in their day, were obviously inadequate for the changed situation; as well expect Don Quixote to win kingdoms and dethrone kings with only his own sword and Sancho Panza behind him.

New financial methods needed

There was happily no doubt in the main as to what that new departure should be. Beyond, infinitely beyond, all former wars, the Great War was the affair of the whole people, not merely that of a ruling class and a professional Army. In 1918 one in four of the whole manhood of this country, old men and babes included, was bearing or had borne arms in its defence, and millions of other men, and also of women, were working to provide them with food and weapons. With few exceptions the able-bodied population was directly helping to carry on the war; with still fewer the whole people had a personal interest in its fortunes, that intense human interest that can only come in one way—a husband, a son, a brother, or a lover in the forefront of the battle.

The people were finding the men and the muscle; they must also find the money. By the people we do not mean the few, comparatively speaking, who have a banking account and employ a stockbroker. We mean the 46,000,000 people in the United Kingdom. The burden was too big for any class, however rich and influential, to bear. It must be shared, as was service in the field, by all.

For this change the time had fully come; moreover, in 1917 it was opportune. A variety of causes tended to make it easier than it had ever been before. The introduction, tardy though it was, of compulsory military service had brought home to all the fact that nothing less than the nation in arms was force enough to beat the foe, and the

Decorating the flag of the French Morocco Regiment with the Medaille Militaire.

Men from Fort Douaumont giving latest news to General Dubois, in command at Verdun.

War-tortured heights above the Meuse: Shell bursting on the summit of Froide Terre.

Distant view of Belleville: Within the sheltering ring of Verdun's forts.

Ground consecrate to deathless heroism: Glacis of Fort Douaumont, strewn with litter of war.

Main gate of Fort Souville: The limit attained by the German besiegers in 1916.

Winter scene at Verdun: "The storms of wintry time will quickly pass, and one unbounded spring encircle all."

wide extension of the franchise, especially to women, accepted with marvellously little opposition, had shown how willing the nation was to recognise in this way the brotherhood and sisterhood of service.

The third reason was a material one, but it was perhaps the strongest of all. From the outbreak of the war wages had been steadily rising, and during 1917 especially that rise was enormous. There was another side to this, it is true, the big increase in the prices of commodities—or, as we say, in the cost of living—and the two were bound together as cause and effect, although it was hard to say which was the one and which was the other. But when due allowance is made for this, it is still true to say that the working classes had many millions of income which, without depriving themselves of any necessary article of food or clothing, they could lend to the State.

Let us illustrate this point. In 1915 no less than 3,470,000 people received increases of wages amounting to £677,700 a week, or something like £35,000,000 a year. In 1916 a somewhat similar number of workers received £595,000 a week, or £30,000,000 a year. This total of £65,000,000 is not perhaps very much when compared with the figures mentioned as the cost of the war, but in eleven months of 1917 over 4,330,000 persons received increases amounting to £1,507,500 a week, or £80,000,000 for the year. £145,000,000 of increased wages is something, but there is more to come. The official return from which the above figures are taken says that " these statistics are exclusive of changes affecting seamen, railway servants, agricultural labourers, policemen, Government employees, domestic servants, shop assistants, and clerks." This list embraces quite a considerable section of the community, and everyone knows that they, too, received during the war period, and especially in 1917, substantial additions to their incomes. On January 29th, 1918, Mr. Herbert Samuel said in Parliament, and no one contradicted him, that rail-

General increase in wages

way workers had received an additional £10,000,000 a year, and civil servants £3,000,000. The £20,000,000 given yearly to the miners and the £40,000,000 to the munition workers, mentioned also by him, are doubtless included in the return already quoted, but the £72,000,000 a year added to the pay of soldiers and sailors is not, nor are the millions dealt out by way of separation allowances.

Apart from these classes, agricultural labourers were guaranteed a minimum wage of 25s. a week, increases of pay were given to the police, while clerks, as the reports of the banks and other big institutions showed, did not come off badly. Public officials all over the country shared in the increased wages and salaries; for instance, it was said in February, 1918, that in Liverpool the rates were to be increased by 1s. 6d. in the pound, of which 6d. would go in bonuses to employees, and about the same time the London County Council adopted a most generous bonus scheme. Farmers and certain classes of small capitalists also increased their incomes considerably during the war. In fact, the most succinct way of putting the matter would be to say that in 1917 and 1918, except persons with fixed incomes from investments, the owners of house property, and certain classes of professional men—architects, for instance—the whole community was in receipt of bigger incomes. Moreover, millions of women and girls who before the war were living in the homes of their parents, and had command only of small sums of money, were in 1918 receiving salaries and wages which they themselves in 1913 would have regarded as impossible to earn. No computation of the gross total of these increased incomes can be at all reliable, but enough has been said to show that the £145,000,000 recorded by the Board of Trade must be multiplied by more than one or two. Indeed, early in 1918 Sir William Pearce, M.P., stated that the increases totalled no less than £1,000,000,000 a year. The money deposited in the banks was additional proof of this prosperity. On December 31st, 1917, it was calculated that

the twelve big joint-stock banks held £1,130,000,000 of other people's money, and that of this about £207,500,000 had been added during the year.

In 1918 the money was in the country awaiting investment, and so, happily, was an organisation for collecting it, that being the National War Savings Committee. In Chapter LXXIV. (Vol. 4, page 197) something was said about the War Loan of 1915, and one of its novel features, an appeal to the working classes. For their benefit bonds were sold at the post-offices, and so were vouchers for 5s., which could be exchanged, with a small bonus, into bonds. In this way something over £24,000,000 was raised.

Such was the beginning of the popular appeals, which in 1916 were the basis of Britain's policy for financing the war. In 1915 Mr. McKenna, then Chancellor of the Exchequer, appointed a committee to advise on the question of war loans for the small investor. In its report, presented to Parliament on January 30th, 1916, the members drew attention to the recent increases in wages and to cognate matters, and advised the appointment of:

War loans for small investors

1. A committee to undertake propaganda work and to promote the formation of agencies and investment societies.

2. A central committee to advise upon and approve the financial details of schemes for investment societies and to supervise their working.

These recommendations were adopted by the Chancellor of the Exchequer, and on February 9th, 1916, it was officially announced that two National Committees had been constituted—the National Organising Committee for War Savings and the Central Advisory Committee for War Savings. Mr. G. N. Barnes, M.P., was chairman of the former. These committees were later united and reconstituted as the National War Savings Committee, and its objects were : (1) to stimulate the sentiment and urge the need for economy ; (2) to promote the formation of War Savings Associations ; (3) to secure for the nation, through these associations, a certain amount of the money required for the prosecution of the war.

Of this National Committee the guiding spirit was its chairman, Mr. R. M. Kindersley, a director of the Bank of England. From the very beginning he spared no efforts to make the movement a success, and the knighthood (K.B.E.) conferred upon him in 1917 was a slight recognition of his untiring efforts in directing the organisation in Salisbury Square, London, where the Salisbury Hotel was taken over for its headquarters, when its earlier home in Abingdon Street, Westminster, was found too small for the increasing amount of its work. This committee covered England and Wales only, for Scotland had one of its own.

The report already referred to contained other valuable suggestions, in addition to the one which created the National Committee. Two of these were of special importance. Evidently the Committee had considered carefully one of the prime financial problems of recent years—the steady deterioration of capital value, whether of Consols, house property, or other forms of what are called gilt-edged securities—and the members had reached the conclusion that any new issue of capital must be free from this handicap. They recommended the issue of war savings deposits, or certificates as they soon came to be called. For each one 15s. 6d. should be paid, and at the end of five years one pound should be returned to the investor. This meant compound interest at the rate of just over 5¼ per cent., and, moreover, another advantage, freedom from income-tax. The suggestion was made that these certificates should be limited to persons with incomes of £300 a year and under ; but afterwards a limit less liable to abuse was introduced. No person was allowed to hold more than 500 of them. These War Savings Certificates were first issued on February 22nd, 1916. Similar issues followed on kindred lines in Australia, New

The National War Savings Committee

TO HELP THE WAR LOAN.
British airship over Trafalgar Square in March, 1918. It dropped leaflets in connection with the Business Men's Week.

England and Wales with a network of local committees, and in this matter it received valuable assistance from inspectors and other officials of the Board of Education, men whose professional duties had made them familiar with the special conditions of the various districts. Gradually these committees were established. They were of three kinds. For every county there was a county committee; in cities, boroughs, and urban districts with over 20,000 inhabitants there was a local central committee; and in towns and districts with less than 20,000 people there was a local committee. The work of the county committees was to supervise the doings of the local, but not the local central committees, within their areas, and this brings us to the difference between these two. A local central committee was in direct communication with headquarters in London; a local committee worked through the county committee.

War Savings Committees

These were differences of degree, but between a War Savings Committee and a War Savings Association there was a difference in kind. The report already mentioned had advised the formation of the latter societies, and the committees were but the means to that end. Committees had nothing to do with the collection of money, which was the business of associations. The former were organising bodies only. They were usually formed, on the initiative of headquarters, by calling a meeting of representative men of the town or district, the mayor or chairman of the urban council, the town clerk, the clergy, trade union leaders, big employers of labour, and others. Much depended upon securing a secretary who possessed the necessary vigour and knowledge, and in many cases these were found among the public officials. But whether they were public or private persons, a large number of men and

Zealand, Canada, and India; also in the United States. Germany, too, adopted a War Savings card.

The next problem was how to get these certificates into the hands of the people, and for this end " the organisation on the extensive scale of voluntary savings associations " was recommended. To this task, then by no means a popular one, the Committee set its hand early in 1916.

As a preliminary step, the National Committee set to work to cover the whole of

women were discovered, willing to devote much time and endless energy to the new national movement.

The movement was for the National Committee to stimulate the various local committees, and for the local committees to encourage the formation of associations. To assist them the National Committee planned a number of schemes for saving, and drew up and distributed literature to explain their working. One or two of these did not prove very popular, and after a time interest chiefly centred round two of these, one known as 2a, which utilised an ordinary passbook, or bankbook, system, and the other, known as Scheme 5, based on the purchase of coupons or stamps.

To form a War Savings Association, the first step was usually to call together those **War Savings** interested, to decide upon a name, and **Associations** to appoint a treasurer, a secretary, and a committee. The members agreed which model scheme they would adopt, and then applied for affiliation through the local committee. Each committee and each association was registered under a distinctive number; thus 243/7 referred to the seventh association working in Area 243.

The schemes most generally adopted were 2a and 5, referred to above. Under both schemes associations existed to sell the 15s. 6d. War Savings Certificates to their members, payments being made by instalments. In Scheme 2a this was effected by subscriptions being entered in the member's book; in Scheme 5, by means of coupons purchased from the secretary and affixed to a card. Sixpence was the smallest sum received, and the member's card contained squares for 31 coupons, so when the card was full the member was entitled to a certificate. Supplies of coupons were obtained by secretaries from headquarters, and arrangements were made to enable money to be withdrawn in case of need. There was no obligation to pay subscriptions at any particular time, but most associations collected them once a week, and this was the ideal plan.

In this proceeding there was a certain financial gain, which is not perhaps obvious at first sight. As soon as

AIRSHIP THAT AIDED A TANK BANK.
Gondola of a British airship which was detached and stationed in Trafalgar Square near the Tank in Business Men's Week, March 4th-9th, 1918. Each investor at the Tank received a souvenir leaflet from the gondola.

WAR LOAN LEAFLETS FROM THE AIR.
Interested watchers of a fluttering leaflet dropped from the airship that passed over London on March 8th, 1918. These leaflets, advertising the War Loan, were eagerly scrambled for that they might be kept as souvenirs.

the members of an association had collectively paid in 15s. 6d., which might easily be in a single day, the secretary purchased a certificate at a post-office, and entered it in his books as belonging to the association. This certificate was dated the day of purchase, and was handed over to the member who first completed the payment of 15s. 6d. That member, therefore, received a certificate dated, not the day on which his purchase was completed, but some time anterior to that. Consequently, he would receive his £1 in something less than five years. This principle was applied right through. Certificates were bought with the collective funds as soon as ever possible, and were given out as payments were completed. A member could purchase as many as he pleased, subject only to the limit of 500 imposed by Parliament. When a certificate was handed over, its number was registered in the name of the recipient at a post-office. In form it was a green slip of paper perforated. The narrower, or left-hand part, was pasted into the recipient's book, and the other portion signed and handed in at a post-office.

It should perhaps be said that War Savings Certificates could be purchased without the intermediary of an association, and that larger certificates—representing 25, 50, or other suitable number between 12 and 500 of the 15s. 6d. certificates—were issued by the Treasury in the form of a single document designed to save labour and time. Arrangements were also made to enable school-children and others to invest their pennies in the purchase of War Savings Certificates.

People chafe, and sometimes not without cause, at the endless formalities in public departments, but a moment's thought will show that in the case of the National Committee certain formalities were necessary, for public money was involved. Steps must be taken to prevent unauthorised persons from securing supplies of stamps, while the misuse of certificates must be guarded against. Provision was made to prevent such happenings. Secretaries of associations sent every month an account to the National Committee, and another to the local one, while twice a year their accounts were audited by an independent authority.

The encouragement and supervision of War Savings Associations were not, however, the main work of the National Committee. The Committee on War Loans for the small investor, called, for the sake of brevity, the Montagu Committee—the Hon. E. S. Montagu, M.P., was the chairman—recommended that Exchequer Bonds should be issued in small amounts, £5 and multiples of £5, and sold through the Post Office. The **Results to March, 1917** National Committee undertook to push this sale and during 1916 bonds to the value of £44,000,000 were sold in this way.

The annual report of the Committee, which appeared in 1917, gave a good idea of its manifold activities down to March 1st, 1917. Under its auspices no less than 1,100 local committees and over 26,500 War Savings Associations had been formed ; of the latter 10,000 came into existence in January and February, 1917, the fruits evidently of the vigorous campaign in support of the War Loan. The associations had between two and three million members, "drawn probably in the main from among those who had not previously saved, and who had been induced to do so

AT THE AIRSHIP GONDOLA.
Sir Eric Geddes, First Lord of the Admiralty, making a purchase of War Bonds in Trafalgar Square during the Business Men's Week.

IN THE "CABIN" OF AN AIRSHIP.
Interior of the airship gondola which was exhibited in Trafalgar Square during the Tank Bank Week of March, 1918.

by a system of collective saving." From the outbreak of war to the end of 1916 small investors had lent over £118,000,000 to the State. During 1916 an average of £1,600,000 a week was received from them.

Something about the size and nature of the 26,500 associations should be of interest. They were formed in connection with social groups, such as churches, schools, and friendly societies, and among the employees of mines, railways, munition works, factories, warehouses, and shops of all descriptions. Their membership varied from as few as 10 to as many as 10,000, and only 172 associations had by then been dissolved. There were associations in both the Navy and the Army—in fact in all branches of national life. Perhaps the most hopeful part of all this work was that done in the schools, and about this a good deal could be said. The teachers were **Fine record** among the most zealous and successful **of the schools** of the preachers of the new gospel of economy, in which very often the parent received instruction from the child. Examples of this work are multifarious, but room may be found for one or two taken from "War Savings" for January, 1918. Therein we read how in Walsall, with 17,000 children, there were 37 school associations which, with a membership of 6,397, had subscribed £15,035. A school at Nuneaton had passed the £1,000 mark, and was on the way to £2,000. One at Wigan had done the same, and one at Ashford had a thermometer to record progress, the various class-rooms competing for the first place. A village school in Hampshire, away from the high wages of munition areas, raised over £400 in a year.

The National Committee had many lines of attack. Its publicity campaign included regular advertising in the big newspapers, the supply of information to editors all over the country, and the display of posters on prominent hoardings and public places generally. It issued a monthly journal, "War Savings," and supplied a variety of leaflets, explaining its aims, to local committees and the general public. A big department in the Salisbury Hotel was devoted to making arrangement for lectures and speakers and providing lecturers with lantern slides, while a group of itinerant organisers addressed meetings and in other ways promoted enthusiasm. Over 100,000,000 paper bags were sold to retail tradesmen, one side of the bag being pictorial, the other practically a leaflet.

The year 1917 witnessed still greater progress. Just before it opened, the Chancellor of the Exchequer asked for the assistance of the National Committee in making known the virtues of the big loan to be issued early in 1917. This help was willingly given. A conference of 1,500 representatives of the local committees was held in London on January 11th, and was addressed by the Chancellor. The workers then threw themselves heart and soul into the task, and contributed not a little to

National Committee's publicity campaign the success recorded in the earlier part of this chapter. During the summer the Committee turned its attention to the direction of a campaign for securing economy in food.

It is not surprising that, with a record of almost unbroken success behind it, the National Committee should be asked to undertake new and bigger tasks, and it was in connection with this extension of its activities that, in November, 1917, the present writer was invited by the Chancellor of the Exchequer to assume the position of Director of Publicity. By this time the Treasury authorities fully recognised that publicity was a business proposition; for it is of little use to have an excellent article to sell unless the public can be made acquainted with its merits, and this is as much the work of a specialist as is any other form of professional or commercial activity. Something had already been done in this direction; for instance, the success of the 4½ per cent. loan was partly due to the work of Sir Hedley Le Bas, who was responsible for making it known, and who remained a member of the National Committee. It was, therefore, evident that the contemplated extension of the Committee's work must be accompanied by a corresponding extension of its activities in the direction of Press and other publicity.

The main reason for this increased activity was the introduction in October of a new form of security. Towards the end of 1917 the Chancellor, Mr. Bonar Law, was faced with the task of raising more money. It would have been far from easy to float a new loan owing to the short time that had elapsed since the issue of the big one at the opening of the year, and so recourse was had, perforce, to another expedient. It was in these circumstances that he decided to try the experiment of weekly, continuous borrowing, and for this purpose the War Savings Certificates were not sufficient. After consultation, therefore, a new scheme was devised. New securities, called National War Bonds, were introduced, and were of four kinds. One kind was repayable in five years from 1917, another in seven, and a third in ten. Interest on all alike was at the rate of 5 per cent. per annum, or 1s. in the pound, and on each there was a premium payable on repayment of the capital. This was 2s. on every £5 of the five-year bonds, 3s. for every £5 of the seven-year one, and 5s. for every £5 of the ten-year ones.

National War Bonds This meant that the investor would receive £5 2s. for every £5 invested, if he withdrew the capital at the end of five years; but if he left it for seven or ten years he would receive £5 3s. or £5 5s.

The business of the National Committee was not to sell the bonds, but to make their existence and their virtues widely known. Bonds for £5, £20, and £50 were sold at post-offices and through banks, while bonds for larger amounts, £100 and upwards, could only be obtained through the banks and stockbrokers. The smaller bonds were known as the Post Office issue; the larger as the Bank of England one. Interest on these bonds was payable half-yearly, on April 1st and October 1st, and both bearer bonds and registered bonds were issued. No income-tax was deducted from the interest (except on the bearer bonds), but persons liable to the tax were to pay on the income received in this way. So much for the three kinds of bonds; the fourth was one free from income-tax, but only paying 4 per cent. interest to the investor. It was repayable in ten years, but there was no premium.

At first the success of the new issue was by no means certain, but in a short time the increased activities of the Publicity Department began to make themselves felt. The sale of bonds through the Post Office, which, during October and November averaged between £300,000 and £400,000 a week, jumped up in December to something over £2,000,000 a week. In the first three months of 1918 the total mounted steadily, quite a number of weeks contributing over £1,000,000 each, until by the end of March £25,000,000 had been sold in this way. Sales of the bonds through the Bank of England showed also a steady rise, especially from the commencement of 1918—four weeks' returned sales amounting to over £30,000,000 each, and quite a number in excess of £20,000,000, while the worst week during the three months produced over £16,000,000.

The first campaign to popularise these bonds was associated with a novel kind of advertising. This was the visit of Tanks to the large towns. They created extraordinary interest, and at the same time a certain healthy rivalry between place and place was fostered. It was suggested that a highly practical form of local patriotism was to try and take a high place in the competition as to which town could invest the largest amount per head of its population. Some remarkable figures were reached during the winter of 1917-18. The visit of a Tank usually lasted for a week. In one week of this kind Glasgow raised over £14,000,000. At West Hartlepool £36 per head was contributed. Dundee with £25 per head, York with £18, and Sunderland with £15 per head were other towns that did remarkably well; indeed, Tank Weeks became quite a national institu- **Success of the Tank banks** tion. Here may be mentioned also the big movement for the sale of War Bonds, etc., known as Business Men's Week. It took place in the first week in March (4th to 9th), and during its six days over £135,000,000 was raised. This time London had its Tank Week, the first real opportunity the Metropolis had to show what it could do in this rivalry, and so well did it answer the call that more than half the above total was raised therein. The figures for the week worked out at about £4 for every man, woman, and child in England and Wales.

The National Committee inaugurated other activities, among them a scheme for selling War Bonds and War Savings Certificates by shopkeepers. For this purpose a new kind of bond, called the nominative, was introduced. It was for £5, was repayable in ten years, with a premium of 5s. in addition, and carried interest at the rate of 5 per cent. Some alert person named it the "easy-to-buy bond," and this phrase expressed its essential qualities. It could be bought as easily as a postal-order. The purchaser received it at once on payment of the money, but before he could obtain interest on it he must register it. These bonds were not on sale at post-offices, but at a large number of shops registered for the purpose through the War Savings Associations.

In conclusion, a few figures may be useful in summarising the work done to the end of 1917. There were then in existence 1,623 committees and 37,840 associations, of which 12,000 were in connection with schools. During the year small investors had put £183,000,000 into Government securities, £66,800,000 of which had gone to purchase War Savings Certificates. Altogether, since the fateful August 4th, 1914, no less than £256,500,000 had been subscribed through the various Post Office issues to meet the cost of the war. Of the new National War Bonds, £10,700,000 had been sold to 706,998 persons through the Post Office, and £196,800,000 through the Bank of England, all in two and a half months.

FRENCH VICTORIES OF 1917: AT VERDUN & ON THE AISNE.

By Edward Wright.

General Pétain Debarred from Undertaking a Large Campaign by Political and Military Considerations—Generals Guillaumat and Fayolle Open Heavy Artillery Bombardment—Enemy First and Second Line Works Shattered—Critical Importance of Dead Man Hill and Hill 304—French Infantry Advance, August 21st, 1917—Success of the Moroccan and Southern French Divisions on the Left Bank of the River—French Progress on the Right Bank—Extraordinary Precision and Thriftiness of the French Artillery Work—Second French Army's Successful Thrust to Beaumont and Caurières Wood, August 26th—Chaume Wood Carried by the Monroe Division of Passaga's Army Corps, September 8th—Preparations for the Entire Conquest of the Ladies' Walk by the French Sixth Army under General Maistre—French Attack Opens October 23rd, after Sixteen Days' Bombardment —Germans Demoralised and Defeated—General Retirement of the Germans from the Aisne, November 1st, 1917.

FTER his series of successes along the Ladies' Walk and the Craonne Plateau in July, 1917, with the chronicle of which Chapter CCII. (Vol. 10, page 223) concluded, General Pétain, while adopting an actively defensive attitude until the U.S.A. Army was ready, prepared to help Sir Douglas Haig's large operations by means of a skilful method of limited attacks.

Neither the political situation nor the military position of France allowed him to indulge in a grand campaign. His aim was to recover from the losses of General Nivelle's offensive, steady his troops, and train them in new methods of assault, while awaiting the liquidation of Russian affairs between Kerensky and Korniloff, and attending the results of the British thrust from Ypres.

The Russian contingent on the French front became infected with the moral disease of Bolshevism, and had at last to be disbanded, the loyal men being retained in the rear as army labourers. As there were powerful pacifist forces working in the very heart of France, her military chiefs were anxious in regard to the results of political and plutocratic intrigue,

over which they had no means of control whatever. There was also a strong and widespread system of social machinery for depressing the spirit of the French people, and inspiring them with distrust of their Allies. Persons were paid to create panics, bring munition workers out on strike, and spread wildly exaggerated reports of French casualties.

All this great and ramifying political and social intrigue, which will form the theme of a separate chapter of this history, was the dominant characteristic of the general situation in France in the summer and autumn of 1917. It influenced the policy of General Pétain to a very considerable degree.

Yet, in spite of his difficulties, the great master-gunner and commander of France found means of affording generous aid to the British armies. He was able to send a fine though small force, under one of the best of his army commanders, General Anthoine, to operate upon the northern German flank at Ypres, with results already related in the story of the Third Ypres Campaign (Vol. 10, page 429). In addition to giving this direct help to the Fifth and Second British Armies, the French Commander-in-Chief

HONOUR FOR A HERO OF VERDUN.
General Leconite fastening the cravat of Commander of the Legion of Honour on General Guillaumat, who directed the successful operations at Verdun and on the Aisne in 1917.

arranged to take such action in the most promising parts of his lines as would compel the German High Command to maintain strong holding forces in men and guns along the apparently inactive French front.

As soon as the Germans began to concentrate along the Passchendaele Ridge, in answer to the furious attacks made by the army of Sir Hubert Gough, the old battle-field of Verdun flamed into fierce activity. Two of the ablest of Pétain's lieutenants, General Guillaumat and General Fayolle, began, in the second week of August, 1917, to practise with parks of huge siege-guns sited on both banks of the Meuse.

General Pétain in person went to Verdun, to watch the developments of the methods of gunnery that he had invented in 1915, and practically perfected in 1916. His men had many of the new 15 and 16 in. French guns and howitzers, and the monster artillery and long-range medium pieces were employed in a masterly manner. The bombardment began in the first week of August, and greatly increased in intensity at the beginning of the third week. The Germans took the gun fire at first merely as a

French feint in conjunction with the British offensive; but as the merciless pounding continued and increased in scope, the enemy High Command was faced with a very difficult problem.

German artillery overpowered

General Guillaumat, who was the director of operations, aimed at winning a battle purely by artillery power. He knew that the Germans had sent away a considerable part of the six hundred batteries that had been concentrated around Verdun. Being able completely to overpower the guns that remained, he knocked them out by the hundred in counter-battery work. At the same time he proceeded entirely to shatter the lines of German works on both sides of the Meuse.

On the Verdun sector the enemy retired a day or two before the infantry action. His trenches, dug-outs, concrete forts, and communications on Talou Hill, Hill 344, and Hill 240 were filled with his dead, and made uninhabitable for the survivors of his front-line garrison. He was obliged to deploy his troops in his second zone of battle divisions and keep his supports some miles away at Spincourt and Beaumont.

His new positions, however, were discovered, and the monster French howitzer and high-velocity guns lifted and poured their thunderbolts into Spincourt and Beaumont Wood and other places of concentration for German reserves, while the medium artillery and quick-firers were turned upon the second German zone of defences. The French infantrymen in the meantime did not move. Most of them were under cover, waiting until their own field-artillery had completely counter-batteried the scattered fragments of the German light artillery, which, about August 18th, began to use little except the new irritant gas-shells.

Enemy second line bombarded

The battle was won on the right bank of the Meuse,

WHERE ROADS RE-ECHOED TO THE TRAMP OF SOLDIERS.
Fresh troops marching to Verdun to relieve the battle-worn holders of the sally-port of France. In oval: Walking wounded on their way to an aid-post in the neighbourhood of Verdun, along a road strewn with the litter of war.

IN THE RUINED BUT GLORIOUS REGION OF VERDUN.
French troops engaged in reorganising ground which they had won back from the invader in the neighbourhood of Verdun. Mines and shells had reduced the terrain to a desolate stretch of craters which had to be wired against possible counter-attacks.

a bombardment. Then a third tunnel served the same purpose in another direction.

But the tunnels had been built in the days when German sappers did not know what a 16 in. French howitzer could do. First some middle-heavy French pieces choked the entrances to the tunnels on August 17th. After the Germans had cleared away the earth brought down by the explosions, the 16 in. French pieces took up the work of destruction and merely by straightforward smashes on the chalk above the tunnel roofs closed the galleries from the inside.

By August 19th Dead Man Hill and Hill 304 and the neighbouring heights were bare of grass, weeds, and Germans. Every yard of ground was ploughed up, and all that the German commander accomplished by reinforcing his front line was to double his losses. The bombardment continued the following night, and as day was breaking at ten minutes to five, with a river mist spread over the opposing lines, the French infantry came out and cautiously moved towards their line of shell fire. This suddenly increased in intensity and began to move forward. Thereupon, the German gunners placed their barrage upon the French trenches, completely missing the forces of attack who had already gone forward.

Precise little devices of detail of this kind were a speciality of the French Staff of the Second Army at Verdun. By moving the infantry out in a mist, before their own barrage lifted, they saved thousands of their men from German shell fire. Each French soldier was provided with a new wallet, known as the Pétain wallet, containing rations for six days. He also carried his old receptacle for provisions. This was filled with an extra supply of hand-grenades.

French devices of detail

It was expected that the enemy could bring into action many guns that he had kept silent and concealed, and maintain a blocking curtain fire between his lost positions and the French lines, and then try to press the French infantry back with his reserves. This was why the French soldier took a large stock of food with him and an additional

between Talou Crest and the ground near Chaume Wood, a couple of days before the French infantry moved out to explore and collect and consolidate. On the left bank of the Meuse, however, where the enemy held the dominating observation heights of Dead Man Hill and Hill 304, the action took another course. In this sector the German commander could not withdraw without a strong attempt at resistance. The line his men occupied was of critical importance, and had been won by months of fighting in 1916. So long as he held it he could sweep the ground he had evacuated on the other side of the river and maintain his hold upon Verdun.

Therefore, instead of withdrawing men from Dead Man Hill and the neighbourhood, he brought up larger forces. His hope was that, by crowding his front line, he would ensure sufficient survivors from the dreadful French gun fire to enable him to hold the French infantry back while his reserves could come into action.

To a considerable extent he relied upon the great tunnelled shelters that ran from Dead Man Hill. There was the Gallwitz tunnel, provided with an electric railway and extending for more than six hundred yards into Crow's Wood, possessing at each end four branching passages opening out into well-sheltered ground. There was also the Crown Prince's tunnel, somewhat smaller in length, but equally valuable, both for bringing forward troops through a barrage and for affording shelter for the garrison during

FIELDS ON WHICH ONLY HONOUR SURVIVED.
Part of the country near Verdun where the French long held the foe at bay with unflinching heroism. Over the sodden, tortured ground and between the water-logged shell craters the brave defenders had to pass by means of duck-board paths.

amount of ammunition. The longer he could fight without troubling for supplies, the more work the French counter-battery guns would be able to do, and the more Germans the ordinary French batteries would be able to kill.

There was little hand-to-hand fighting in the first phase of the infantry action. On the left the height covered by Avocourt Wood was taken and the central ridge of Hill 304 was half encircled, while Dead Man Hill, Crow's Wood, and Cumières were being overrun. The Moroccan division and the Southern French division that carried out most of the work on the left bank of the Meuse went through a Brandenburg division with remarkable ease. About a thousand Brandenburgers were in the tunnels, and their officers tried to induce them to take their machine-guns and make a stand while the reserves were coming up. But the crack Prussian division was demoralised by the way in which the French commander had been using the Pétain method of group control for batteries of the heaviest calibre. During the last days of the bombardment the Prussians had been stealing into the French lines by the hundred, confessing they could no longer endure shell of the calibre that their armies had been using since the opening of the war.

Prussian troops demoralised The French infantry could have occupied ground to a much greater depth than it had been ordered to do. Especially did the southern division want to flow round the sides of the highest down, Hill 304, and push onward towards Forges. The general, however, kept his men well in control, and after clearing out the tunnels, he extended only into Crow's Wood and Cumières Wood. Had he occupied the northern side of the main central hill, he would have directly exposed his men to curtain fire from German batteries about Montfaucon.

General Pétain and his brilliant lieutenants were intensely economical of the lives of the French soldiers. Their design was first to provoke all German artillery within range to a duel with their own great guns, using the newly-won crests as much as possible as additional fire-control stations. Only when the German guns were seen to be beaten was another infantry advance intended.

In the meantime the enemy had the choice either of accepting defeat on the field where he had continually boasted of victory, or of diverting down towards the banks of the Meuse some of the artillery which he was moving from the Russian front to Flanders. General Pétain did not mind which of these two courses the enemy adopted, and meanwhile he was careful not to have his own infantry exposed in an unnecessary manner. He was fighting with guns and employing men only to occupy the ground that the guns won. **German High Command embarrassed**

On the right bank of the Meuse the French advance began at Talou Crest and at the village of Champneuville, lying directly opposite Dead Man Hill and Crow's Wood. Hill 344, north of Talou Crest, was also taken with Mormont Farm and 240-Metre Hill, north of Louvemont. Then on the north-east of Louvemont, the German lines, running through Fosses Wood and Chaume Wood, were broken, and parts of the woods were taken. As the enemy commander had withdrawn his front-line garrison, with a view to fighting an open-field battle in the manner employed around Arras in May, 1917, the advancing French forces went forward without difficulty.

When the time came for them to stand up against the main strength of General von Gallwitz's army, the guns of France flooded with deadly gas the woods and hollows in which the German battle divisions were gathered, with the result that the intended grand counter-attack did not take place.

AT WORK IN A CELLAR AID-POST BENEATH A VERDUN FORT.

Vaulted galleries deep down below the Verdun forts, lighted by electricity, were used as aid-posts for the wounded. Here the men were brought, to wait on seats and couches made of boxes and piles of coats, for the military surgeons to give them treatment that would suffice to alleviate their sufferings until they could be removed to greater security elsewhere in the French lines.

Coloured Photo, No. 4.

British Light Cruiser at Full Speed in the North Sea

Again the French troops, composed of two divisions under General Deville and General Caran, could have advanced much farther than the objectives set them. So far as infantry action went they could have captured one of the main positions of the German reserve—Beaumont Wood. But after taking thousands of prisoners, they remained on the line assigned to them on a level with their comrades across the valley of the Meuse.

The combined lines of attack on each side of the river had a total length of about fifteen miles when measured on the map, and about twenty-five miles when all the sinuosities of the downland entrenchments were measured. The enemy had seven divisions in line, four on the left bank, in and around Dead Man Hill, and three on the right bank above Louvemont. One of his divisions was completely destroyed, and the others were so crippled that they could not act against the French advance. Some German forces on the extreme left swung round to counter-attack through Avocourt Wood, only to be raked by the mass fire of the French guns and broken in detail by the advanced French forces.

In more ways than one the battle was a remarkable example of the progress of the new French method of attack. In the spring of 1916 the Germans, in spite of their great accumulation of men and guns, had never been able to arrange to press forward simultaneously on both banks of the Meuse. All they could do was first to hammer directly at Verdun, and, after winning space for flanking fire across the river, to change direction and batter forward against the Dead Man Hill positions. When, in the summer of 1917, General Pétain had completed his artillery organisation, the commander of the Verdun army was able to attack along both sides of the Meuse, while deploying far less infantry on the double front than the Germans had formerly used in one sector.

Moreover, the comparatively small French forces of assault were so handled that they were able to do more work around Verdun than the enormous German forces had accomplished. In the second day of the battle they took Goose Ridge and the village of Regnéville, on the left bank of the river, while on the right bank they conquered Samogneux village and the formidable system of fortifications connecting the village with 344-Metre Hill. Regiments of Southern French troops

Rush through poison gas carried out this advance from Vacherauville across the large hilly bend of the Meuse to Samogneux. They had to go through clouds of poison gas, poured by the enemy on the positions he had evacuated, yet they took ground to a depth of two miles in less than one hour.

The village of Forges, north of the hill positions of Goose Ridge, Hill 268, and Regnéville Down, was also occupied by French patrols at the close of the second day of battle. As a matter of fact, the plan of General Guillaumat did not include the capture of Forges, Regnéville, and Samogneux. Small parties of French soldiers set out to explore the enemy's lines, and found them so

weakly held that the battle moved forward without directions from the victorious commander.

All he at last had to do was to assent to the retention of positions that already had been won. The fact was his gunners had surpassed themselves. Upon Talou Crest, for example, there was none of the vast spread of new shell-holes seen on the Somme battlefield. Instead of the ordinary lunar-like landscape, which for special reasons marked Dead Man Hill and its tunnel connections, the country immediately above Verdun was shelled with precise thriftiness. Mackensen Trench and other lines of works were punctured with such neat regularity that scarcely a shot was wasted. Where deep caverns existed the heaviest kind of French howitzer had been used for breaking the roof. Fine intelligence work, as well as excellent aerial photography and artillery skill, had gone to the making of the French victory.

So widespread was the destruction of the German works and so far-reaching and deadly the bombardment of the German reserves, that the French advance continued for some days after all the original objectives had been attained. Holding the enemy down day and night by overwhelming gun fire, General Guillaumat brought his quick-firers forward and, at dawn on August 24th,

SEARCHING PRISONERS TAKEN NEAR VERDUN.
Youthful Germans taken prisoner by the French in the fighting before Verdun. They were making a heap of their personal belongings and undergoing search for any secreted papers which they might have about them.

sent his infantry forward for another mile and a quarter on the left bank of the Meuse. In a single movement the whole of Hill 304 was stormed, together with the line of forts north of it and the works along the Forges brook, between Haucourt and Béthincourt.

From Malancourt Wood and Montfaucon Wood two masses of German guns had been maintaining, since August 20th, a smashing barrage between Avocourt Down and Dead Man Hill. By means of a high pylon observation station at Romagne, enemy gunner officers had directed a precise and searching flanking fire on their lost ground on the right. But a **French officer's** French observation officer brought one **remarkable shot** of his heavy pieces ranging on the pylon, as soon as Dead Man Hill had been won, and with a single remarkable shot destroyed the hostile fire-control station.

When the enemy's artillery was blinded and beaten down the French troops drove into the outworks of Béthincourt, and established themselves all along the bank of the Forges stream. Then, in the morning of August 26th, after a new and vigorous artillery preparation, the right wing of the Second French Army stormed through Fosses Wood and carried Beaumont Wood and Chaume Wood, finally attaining the outskirts of Beaumont village and the edge of Caurières Wood of heroic memory, where Captain Driant had fallen at the head of a brigade of light infantry in February, 1916.

This fine French thrust into the centre of the hostile line above Verdun was carried out on a front of only two and a half miles. It was calculated to provoke a fierce counter-attack of a similar knife-like kind. This was delivered from Wavrille, and, being expected, was countered by such a hurricane of shell as left the advanced forces of French infantry little further work to do, except to collect more prisoners. Two new German divisions, thrown into Beaumont village, engaged in a savage hand-to-hand struggle in Beaumont Wood. But an army corps of General Passaga, which had been fighting since August 20th, inflicted a complete defeat upon the two fresh German divisions, and by August 27th brought the total of unwounded German soldiers captured on both sides of the Meuse to close on ten thousand.

On September 8th, after the enemy had vainly reacted against the French advance, a part of the forces of the Monroe Division of General Passaga's army corps broke into the deep and numerous shelters of the German camp in Chaume Wood and won the mouths of the ravines eastward. The effect of

this stroke, in which eight **Vain German** hundred prisoners were taken, **counter-attack** was to ease the new French positions about Beaumont and provoke a German counter-attack, delivered by five thousand men, who failed to recover any of the ground. The defending French regiment, under Lieutenant-Colonel Tixier, recoiled under the shock, leaving some advanced forces that were encircled by the enemy, but the regiment returned in a stirring bayonet and bombing charge, rescued its men, recovered its positions, and scattered the enemy.

Throughout September no important French offensive could be undertaken with a view to helping the British armies struggling in the swamps around the Passchendaele Ridge; but when the great Australian and New Zealand attack on Passchendaele failed in October and the presence of General von Below's army on the Italian front was known, General Pétain showed that the long preparations he had been silently making could give him at least a local victory when one was needed. Under the direction of another new French Army commander, General Maistre, the High Command of France had been

DETERMINATION INCARNATE.
Soldiers belonging to General Mangin's division: An interesting presentation of the type of men who vowed, and magnificently made good their vow, that the Germans "should not pass" at Verdun.

Pétain became Commander-in-Chief, twenty-one important attacks or counter-attacks, while the French had made, with more effect, eighteen strong attacks or counter-attacks.

When the long and fearful wrestle ended, with the French forces entrenched on the highest eastern part of the plateau, the general situation was not satisfactory to either side. Indeed, the French positions practically invited the enemy to continue his counter-offensive. He did not do so, because the French commander had covered all the ground with his guns, and showed, when the Crown Prince again tested the line in the middle of September, such an increase of strength as daunted General von Boehm, the man behind the Hohenzollern figurehead, and his lieutenant, General von Müller.

When the complete bankruptcy of Russia was apparent, General Pétain began to prepare for the great battle in the west. As we have seen, he first made Verdun secure by driving the Germans back almost to their original lines. Then, after another seven weeks of steady nocturnal preparation, he employed the Sixth French Army to transform the entire plateau of the Aisne into the position of a grand buttress of France.

The French High Command, brilliantly distinguished in both the history and the actual study of warfare, never intended that the enemy should retain, in the grand natural fortress of France, the means of launching a supreme offensive between Noyon and Rheims. Victorious as the Sixth Army of the Aisne had at last been, at Craonne and along part of the Ladies' Walk, it still remained with its back close to the river and its western **Back to the** flank exposed. When the river **Ladies' Walk** again rose in flood it was not unlikely that the enemy would endeavour to repeat on a magnified scale the stroke that had almost led to a grave French disaster early in 1915.

The entire conquest of the plateau was a matter of absolute necessity to General Pétain. This was recognised by General von Ludendorff. In the fourth week of October, when the German Commander-in-Chief was hard pressed around Passchendaele and left with a small reserve, owing to the despatch of General von Below's army to Italy, he retained strong forces of defence along the Aisne under General von Müller. In the centre were the 2nd and 5th Divisions of the Prussian Guard, with the 13th Division and the 47th Reserve Division on either side. Supporting these four divisions were the 14th and 211th German Divisions,

CARRYING ON UNPERTURBED UNDERGROUND.
The Chief of Police of Verdun and his staff at work in the vaults of the Citadel, whither all the municipal authorities were compelled to transfer their offices during the incessant rain of shells that fell upon the town.

for months siting along the Aisne a very formidable park of monster howitzers.

General Pétain's plan was to complete the long Battle of the Ladies' Walk by a final sudden blow. Between May and July the enemy had used up forty-nine divisions on the Aisne front without being able to push the French army from the top of the great ridge. The Germans had delivered, since the date when General placed beyond the battle zone so as to arrive in time to fill any gap.

General von Müller had full notice of the intention of General Maistre, for a long and very heavy bombardment was needed in order to break a path for the French infantry. The enemy's defence was based upon the caverns and quarries in the limestone heights, and he possessed such strong natural shelters from shell fire as only the 15 in. and 16 in. French guns could wreck.

The only element of surprise in the French plan of attack consisted in the number of monster guns employed in the bombardment. This began in a slow, methodical, but terrifying manner on October 7th. While the battle-planes of France held the air, photographing airmen swooped over each target selected by the French gunners, and recorded the result of the shot. With remarkable speed the photograph was developed and printed, and copies were given to the battery commander and his lieutenants. When it was found that more rounds were needed to achieve what was intended, firing went on against the target until the aerial photograph showed that the mighty thunderbolts had pierced the rock roof of the great grottos.

On account of mists there were few hours of good visibility, but the gigantic work of destruction went on day and night. The Frenchmen had for **Sixteen days'** months been registering on their prin-**bombardment** cipal targets, and when they obtained all the ordnance they needed, they maintained a stream of monster shells, each of which roared away with a sound like that of an express train. The fog was probably of general advantage to the army of attack. It compelled the French gunners to use an enormous number of shells, but the effect of the frightful pounding upon the nerves of the Prussian Guardsmen and German infantry of the line compensated for the expense in munitions.

For sixteen days and nights the bombardment went on. The greatest of the limestone caverns, such as Montparnasse, which could hold an entire division, were broken in from the top and closed at the entrances. The German commander lost so many men that he at last resolved, in sheer desperation, to attack. He hoped he would be able to disorganise the French preparations, and it seemed to him that, in any case, it would be better to lose his men in an active manner than to let them perish in thousands under the tempest of French shell.

This decision, however, was arrived at too late. The German attack was fixed for half-past five in the morning of October 23rd, and **Fierce French** was aimed at the French right wing **attack launched** below Filain village. The larger French attack was launched fifteen minutes before the hostile infantry had orders to move. The result was that the Chasseur Division, on the French right, had a much harder tussle than their comrades, and had to go through a more violent hostile barrage, but the work they did in slaughtering the massed German forces on their sector constituted by far the most important feature of the fighting.

The line of the French attack was unusually short. It covered only the western wing of the German positions, on either side of the dismantled old fort of Malmaison, at the point where the Ladies' Walk ended on the road to Laon. A battle-front of scarcely more than four miles of ground was directly attacked, although it soon broadened out to more than six miles. General Maistre pretended he did not care anything about mere strategy; the use of the word provoked the sharp play of his wit. He was only a good tactician, he informed his Staff; but, as was afterwards proved, his narrow but tremendous thrust was designed with large strategic considerations, and brought about a very important result, with the minimum cost in French life.

The weather was as bad on the high ground of the

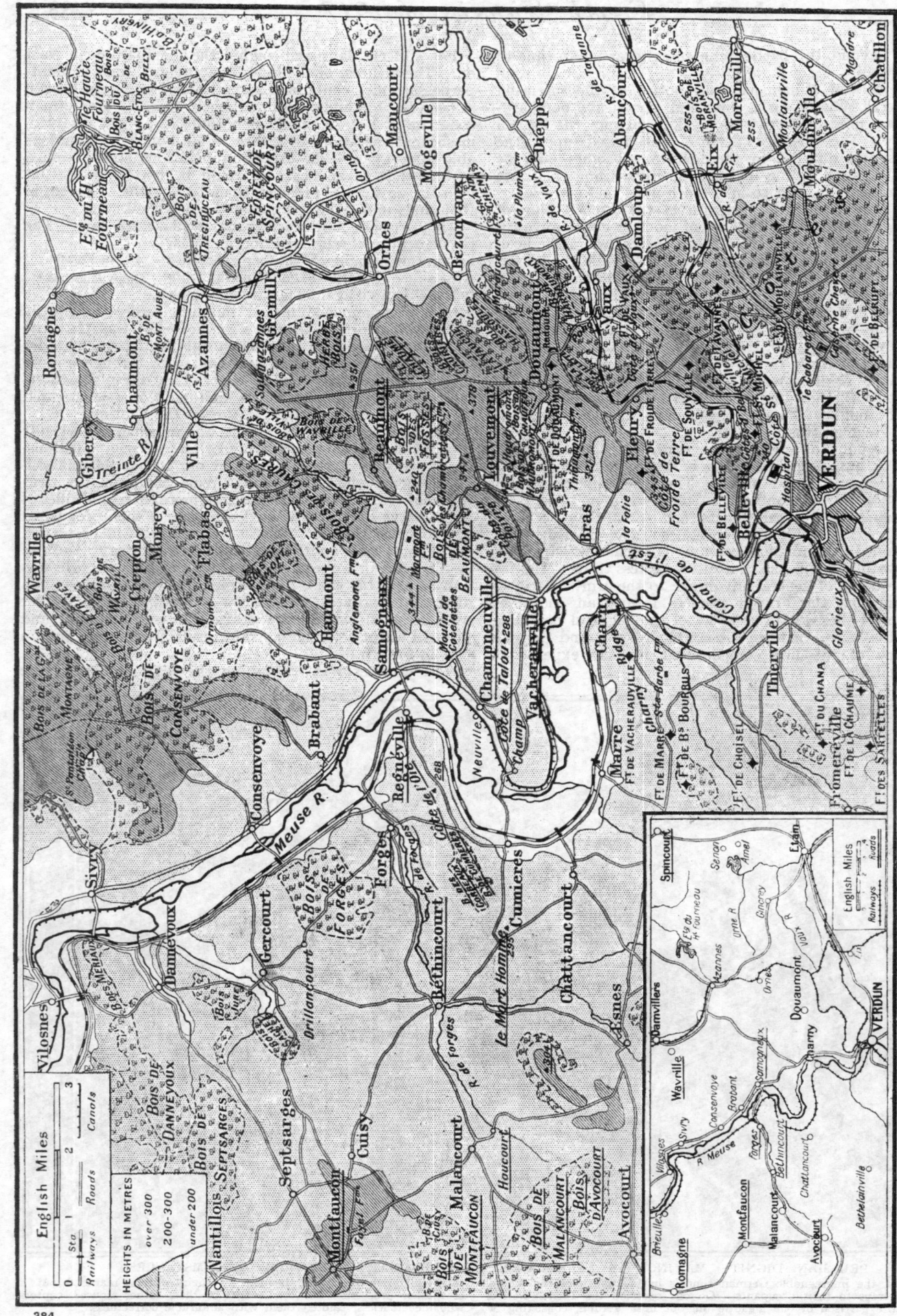

GENERAL AREA OF THE VERDUN FIGHTING ALONG THE VALLEY OF THE MEUSE IN 1917.

The names of the places which were scenes of the fighting described in Chapter CCXL. are underlined in this map.

The Great War

Copyright

Aisne as it was by the Passchendaele Ridge. A dense fog shrouded the plateau, while a heavy drizzle of rain made the slopes slippery and turned the brown-and-white paste around the shell-holes on the Ladies' Walk into clogging mud. It was in such conditions that General Nivelle had failed to carry out his plan for the entire conquest of the plateau in the previous April, but under the perfect Staff organisation of General Maistre the attack developed with such masterly regularity that the fog helped rather than hindered.

Somewhat after the manner of General Plumer's reproduction of the Messines Ridge there had been made, from aerial photographs, a model of the Aisne Plateau and the heights north of it. This had been studied closely by the attacking forces, who had further been trained in a special method of assault. French Tanks, that moved more quickly than the original British Tanks, were skilfully employed to help the infantry in overcoming strong points which the guns had not completely-destroyed.

Behind the Zouaves, Chasseurs, and French infantry of the line were brigades of African natives, who had been found to be the best troops for the difficult work of rapidly and completely clearing out systems of defence over which the first waves of assault had passed. The French negro, armed with steel and hand-grenades, was a terrible man in a loose trench skirmish when the line was going forward victoriously. He took risks which a more cautious European would have declined, and by his quick method of fighting enabled the French field-gunners also to come up with surprising rapidity into the thick front of battle.

On the western side and in the centre the enemy had been so shattered by very heavy gun fire that only a sprinkling of machine-gunners remained in action above ground when the French infantry advanced under cover of the mist. The quarries of Fruty and Bohery were carried in a single storming movement, and soon afterwards the ruin of Malmaison Fort, in which some German machine-gunners were holding out, was conquered by the Zouaves.

Zouaves take Malmaison Fort

Here fell a noble representative of a distinguished French family, Lieutenant de Villebois-Mareuil. At the age of sixty he had been well content with the position of a subaltern of the Zouaves, leading his men to victory with an agility like that of a lad, and falling just as the fort was taken.

Malmaison was not much of a fort. It had been sold by the French Government, and part of the material had been used in building barracks at Laon. Nevertheless, the old work occupied a position of great importance on a dominating knoll on the plateau. When it was strengthened by German sappers, and filled with machine-guns sweeping the long Soissons road and the lower ground directly southward, it stopped for months all French progress round the end of the Ladies' Walk.

But the 16 in. howitzer had eviscerated Malmaison Fort of all the new sources of strength that had been put into it. Owing to the fog the remnant of the German garrison could not see their assailants while the gradual converging assault was in progress. The fort was rushed with

comparative ease about two hours after the infantry movement began.

This was an unexpected stroke of good fortune for General Maistre. He had calculated that the old fort would have been connected with the great cavern of Montparnasse, a little distance behind it, and as Montparnasse was capable of holding at least ten thousand men, it had seemed likely that there would be a long struggle at Malmaison, similar to that which occurred about Thiepval and Mouquet Farm in the Somme campaign.

The Germans, however, had been so confident of the strength of their position that they had not troubled to drive a tunnel from the cavern to the fort. By means

BOATS FOR THE BUILDING OF BRIDGES.
Pontoons of the French bridge-building section of the Engineers on the River Meuse. These pontoons could be used either as boats for transporting men across the river or as the basis over which to lay the planks of a floating bridge.

of carrier-pigeons the news of the fall of the fort was sent to Army Headquarters in about seven minutes, and General Maistre at once enlarged his plan of attack, and sent up fresh forces with more quick-firers. In the meantime excellent progress had been made on the left flank, where the villages of Allemant and Vaudesson were quickly conquered. On the right wing, where the German attack was forestalled and completely disorganised, less ground was won, but the heights above Pantheon Farm and La Royère were taken, giving the French soldiers dominating positions from which they swept with fire the villages of Pargny and Filain.

With both of his flanks strongly placed, General Maistre made another leap forward from his new centre at Malmaison. His infantry, Tanks, and quick-firers forced their way along the Soissons-Laon road into the village of Chavignon, more than two miles north of the line of departure. The success had a larger scope than was at first apparent in the fog. There was a moral quality in the victory which was of more importance than the material gains.

Gallantry of a French cadet

The fog was symbolic of the state of mind of General von Müller's army. A cadet of the 20th Chasseurs, seventeen years old, led three men into action, and with them captured four prisoners. Scouting again through the fog, he discovered a large dug-out containing fifty Germans. Killing the machine-gun crew, the boy and his three men attacked the strong German party and took eleven more prisoners. So long as fighting went on in

IN WAR-SHATTERED VERDUN OF IMPERISHABLE RENOWN.

A very impressive view of Verdun as seen from one of its destroyed buildings during the period when its heroic defenders were pressing back the stubborn enemy. Though much of the town fell in ruins during the height of the German onslaught, the French not only stayed the attackers but, during the fighting of 1917, pressed them farther back from the centre of the ring of famous fortresses.

the fog, the Frenchmen were able to make their enemies think they were being attacked in force. When, however, the captured Germans were being led towards the prisoners' cage, with a single Chasseur leading them, they saw how weak the cadet's party was. One of the Germans drew a pistol and shot the leading Chasseur, wounding him slightly; but so quickly was the villain killed that the other Germans attempted no further resistance.

Germans eager to surrender

A large part of the German forces never came into action. In one cavern near the original French front line three hundred Germans remained undiscovered after the action was over. They made no attempt to defend themselves, and surrendered as soon as they were found near Bohery Quarry. In another shelter an entire brigade surrendered with its commander and all its officers, as also did the remnants of six other German battalions that had been more severely tried by the French artillery.

When the struggle was raging most fiercely, a French non-commissioned officer saw the opening of a grotto, and, without waiting for his men, went forward with a revolver and summoned the Germans to surrender. He made a mistake in regard to the strength of the enemy, and found himself facing forty German soldiers and a commanding officer. There was nothing for him to do in the circumstances but to offer to surrender. "Not at all, not at all!" said the enemy officer, speaking good French. "It is we who are your prisoners." When shown the road to the prisoners' cage, he led his men along it.

Undoubtedly it was the unparalleled length and intensity of the French bombardment that demoralised the German

army along the Aisne. The defending forces consisted of troops of good quality, the Guards especially being men of fine physique. Most of them were, however, suffering more or less from shell-shock, and the garrisons of the first and second positions had often been cut off for days from all supplies and unnerved by the damage done by the great French guns.

At the end of the first day the Sixth French Army had taken eight thousand prisoners from eight German divisions, and had begun to capture men from other forces hastily diverted into the new battle-line. No hostile counter-attack was, however, organised, as General von Müller had completely exhausted all troops within his reach in vain attempts to stay the first French advance. In the night of October 23rd, French patrols began to work forward against the broken German front between Chavignon and the Mont des Singes. They collected as prisoners a considerable German rearguard who did not want any more fighting.

The more the enemy weakened the more fiercely General Maistre pressed him. The French commander did not expose his men in large numbers to the enemy's gun fire, but brought his own overwhelming artillery down upon the German reserve positions, controlling his fire from the new line of heights that had been won, and sending searching-parties and Tanks into the copses and woods to discover what the German infantry strength was.

Enemy retires in haste

But the strength of the German infantry was gone. In the morning of October 25th the enemy commander refused to continue the battle, and surrendering some twenty-five square miles of territory, withdrew in extreme haste from the Forest of Pinon to the edge of the canal connecting the Oise River with the Aisne.

Extreme as was the haste of the enemy, he was caught by the advanced French forces, losing more than two thousand prisoners and another score of guns. This brought the tale of French captures to more than eleven thousand prisoners, a hundred and sixty guns, and several hundred machine-guns.

The last batteries of German artillery were captured intact near the marshy valley below the Aisne Plateau. French patrols shot down the horses with revolvers, chased away or captured the gunners, ending their advance at a distance of five miles from the hill town of glorious, cathedral-crowned Laon. On the right wing the brilliant division of Chasseurs, under General Brissaud-Desmaillet, worked up against the village of Filain and the lake reservoir of the Oise and Aisne Canal, and extended eastward over the plateau above the Chevrigny spur.

There were then indications that the Sixth French Army intended to move forward to a much larger achievement, after winning the grand
French dominate the Aisne plateau observation positions on the northern side of the plateau. The German army was very seriously enfeebled, and although it had been reinforced by five divisions, the artillery power of General Maistre had been practically doubled by the gain of the best observing posts and the destruction or capture of nearly all the light and medium guns of General von Müller.

The general position of the Germans had become unsound. Where they still held on to the Aisne Plateau, above Froidmont Farm, they were in a salient with two exposed flanks. On their western side, in the valley of the Ailette, they were also exposed to attack. Everything was then promising on the western front, and both General Pétain and Sir Douglas Haig were fairly confident of

VERDUN, THAT DREW THE EYES OF ALL THE WORLD.
Members of a Spanish Mission looking over the ruins of Verdun. Rheims and Verdun, as the two hardest knots of the French resistance, were the points on the western front which representatives of neutral countries were particularly desirous of visiting during the war.

achieving very important successes before the new hostile masses arrived from the eastern theatre. But the unexpected rupture of the Italian lines along the Isonzo interrupted the work of General Maistre. He had to depart with General Plumer, whom he equalled in the organisation of hill battles, and assist in the reconquest of the mountain rampart above Asolo.

The needs of Italy were so urgent that some of the best men and officers of the Sixth Army had to be transported over the Alps to the mountain line of the Piave River. At the beginning of November, while General Maistre was preparing to carry out his new work, Ludendorff ordered a general retirement from the endangered positions above the Aisne. He found his forces were unable to maintain themselves at Chevrigny, Courteçon, and Ailles, by reason of the French thrust right through his flank at La Malmaison.

Ever since October 23rd the powerful French artillery had been vigorously bombarding the enemy's positions in the centre of the plateau. The fire steadily increased

BRITISH GENERALS VISITING THE BELEAGUERED GATEWAY INTO FRANCE.
British Military Mission visiting Verdun during the siege. Major-General Scott was in charge of the mission, which included a large number of general officers. Among the party were Generals Cowper, Currie, Uniacke, and Birch, and Brigadier-Generals Armitage, Brind, Johnson, Phillips, and Thorpe.

in intensity and accuracy, as batteries got into position on the conquered ground from which the valley of the Ailette could be enfiladed. The Germans knew that an attack was coming, and feared that if they had to fall back across the marshy valley, under both front and flanking fire from the French guns, a great disaster might ensue.

They therefore retired, about November 1st, leaving a rearguard to maintain a show of activity in the night when the French patrols came forward. At dawn on November 2nd a party of Chasseurs discovered that the German trenches were empty. Large cauldrons of hot soup seemed to show that the German lines had been unexpectedly evacuated; but the Frenchmen had taken part in the advance from Lassigny in the previous spring, and went forward very cautiously.

It was well they did so, for there were many traps. At Courteçon, for example, there was a German helmet on a

armistice prevailed between Gaul and Teuton, with just enough raiding and artillery practice to maintain the show of war while preparations were being made for the critical spring battles.

At Versailles, where the Allied War Council sat, General Foch gradually rose above other commanders into the position of Generalissimo of the western front. General Pétain became subordinate to him, and Sir Douglas Haig was rather reluctantly induced to take over the positions won by General Humbert between St. Quentin and La Fère, and place there the Fifth British Army, under Sir Hubert Gough, at the time when the Versailles Staff foresaw that the supreme enemy offensive would be directed against this part of the allied line.

Foch appointed Generalissimo

As was evident from the concentration of French forces, produced at the cost of perilously lengthening the critical British line, the man-power of the Republic was

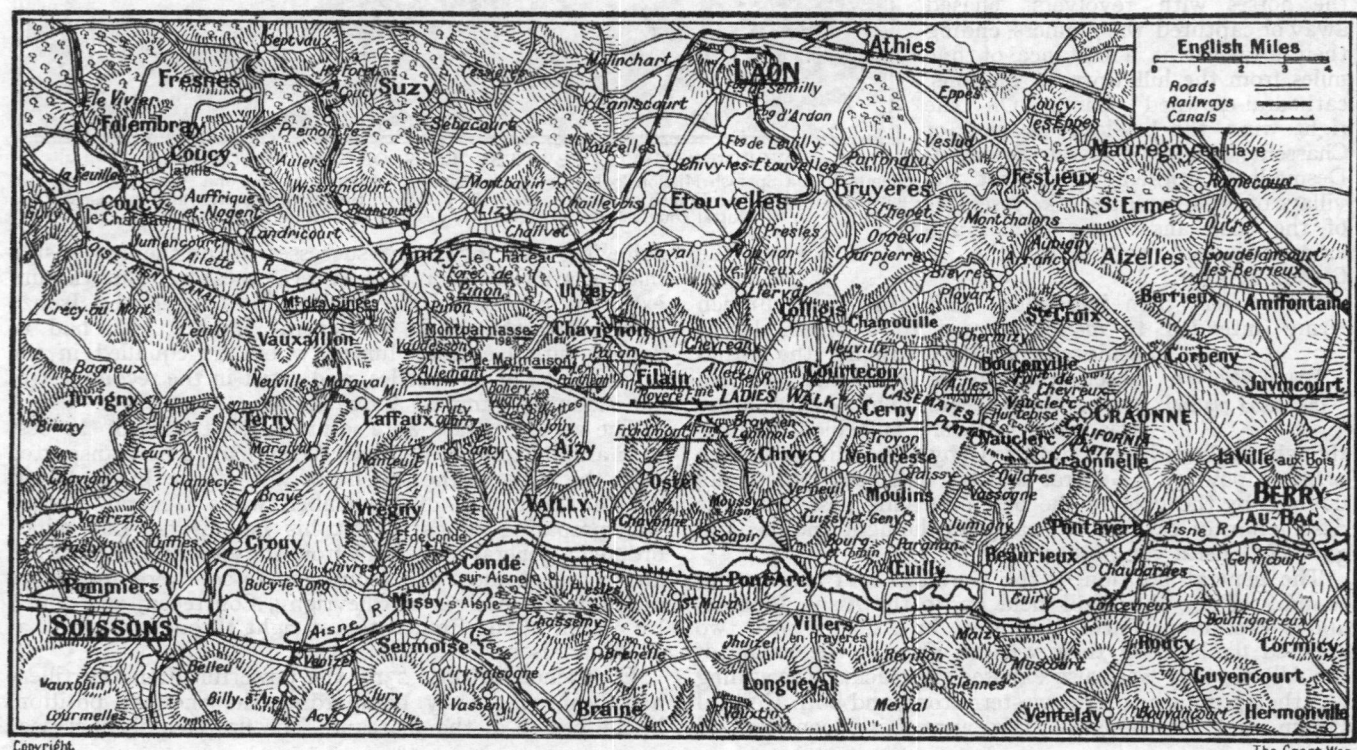

SCENE OF GENERAL MAISTRE'S AISNE VICTORY OF 1917.
In this map may be followed the course of the successive stages of the brilliant French campaign of 1917, which drove the enemy back towards Laon from Fort Malmaison and the Ladies' Walk. The names of places referred to in the account of the operations are underlined.

pole, and down the pole there ran a wire to a mine. All the ground was flooded with mustard gas, and it was not until the French guns severely counter-batteried the German gas-shelling artillery that the entire plateau was occupied. It was an historic moment when the French troops, with the capture of forty more German guns, occupied all the flat top of the great long ridge between the Aisne and the Ailette, and worked down to the southern bank of the small northern stream.

The enemy had clearly regarded the plateau as a position worth the utmost sacrifice, and for six months he had used his best troops in attack and counter-attack. Each side had massed hundreds of guns upon the strip of land on the summit, and their men had clung to the edge of it, being unable to give any ground without losing the entire advantage of the position.

Winter brings an armistice

There was a great raid on the German trenches at Juvincourt on November 21st, 1917, and four days later the army of Verdun made a short leap forward, above Samogneux, storming two enemy systems of deep fortification on the slopes of Caures Wood. Then the winter

wearing under the tremendous strain of the prolonged struggle. The defection of Russia told most heavily upon her old ally in a moral as well as a material manner. The tardy increase in military strength of the British Empire could not fully compensate for the disruption and impotence of the friendly Power that had overshadowed for a century Europe and Asia. And as the United States was not then ready to take the field in grand and complete array, the leaders of France grew troubled in mind and tensely active.

Yet M. Clemenceau, once more in the ascendant as Premier, with his fierce energy and grim gaiety, was symbolic of the indomitable nation he inspired for the supreme effort. His body, that should have shown signs of wearing out, was like a thing of tempered steel, and his mind worked with a reach and mastery of detail never displayed in its apparent prime. He put into thorough execution measures disinfecting the country of the miasma of defeatism; he quickened the prosecution of Bolo and other suspicious personages; and by his example and his exertions he strengthened the country for the ultimate ordeal.

The hanging Virgin of Albert: Finally shot down by the Germans in March, 1918.

Farm buildings occupied by British troops on the western front set on fire by German shells.

Sulphurous smoke uprolling from a British ammunition dump destroyed before retirement.

Cemetery near Lens as it was when the Canadians drove the Germans back in 1917.

Bailleul, April 15th, 1918: Photographed a few hours before the town fell into German hands.

Gas-masked British gunners firing point-blank into advancing masses of the enemy during the German offensive of March, 1918.

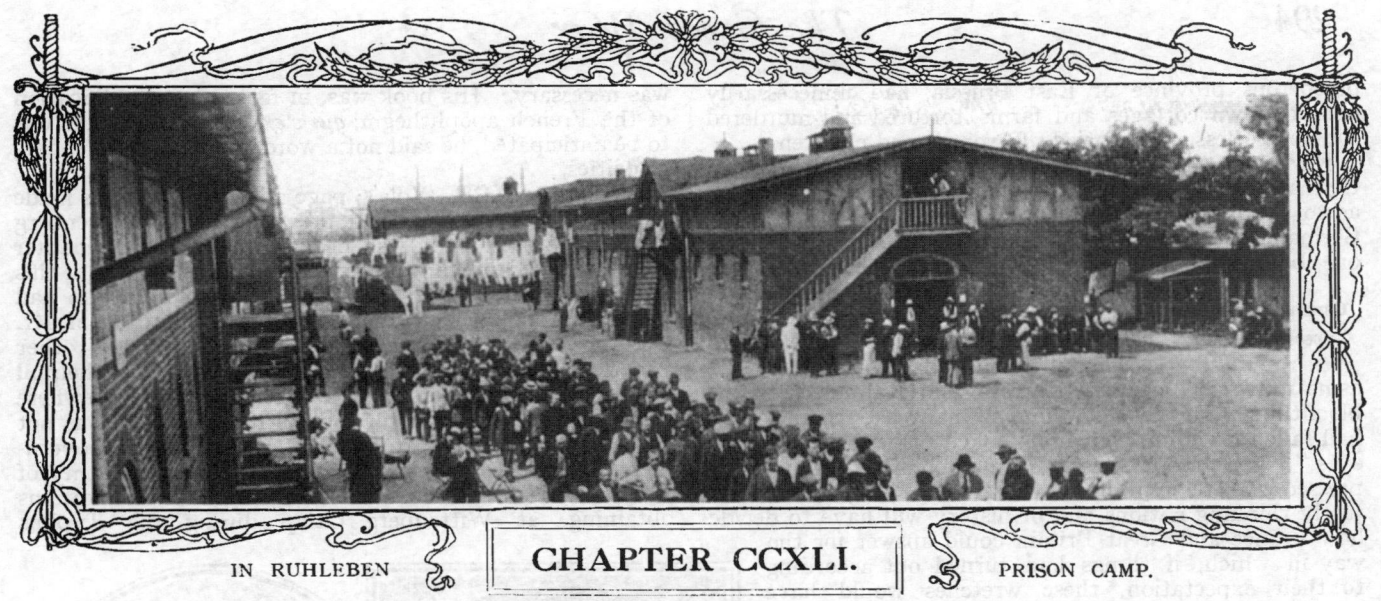

CHAPTER CCXLI.

GERMANY'S CONTINUED ILL-TREATMENT OF BRITISH PRISONERS.

By Robert Machray.

With the exception of the defeat of the enemy, nothing lay nearer the heart of the British people—whether in Great Britain or the Dominions—than the treatment of those whom the fortune of war had made the prisoners of Germany. The manifold evidences of the brutality of the German—and more especially of the Prussian—nature imparted to the subject a character of the deepest anxiety. Some particulars of the savage cruelties practised are recorded in earlier volumes of this History. In Chapter XCII. (Vol. 5, page 250) is given the record of "German Inhumanity to British Prisoners" down to the close of 1915, and in Chapter CLXVII. (Vol. 8, page 453), "The Supreme Development of Teutonic-Ottoman Barbarism," there are further details of the fiendish treatment accorded by Germany and her allies to those who had the misfortune to fall into their power. In presenting this further narrative the Editors would point out that the photographs which illustrate the chapter are necessarily of a general character, as Germany, naturally, did not willingly permit camera evidence of the ill-treatment of prisoners to get abroad ; such pictures as were allowed to get through were obviously intended to give the most favourable impression.

E ARLY in the war the world in general had come to the definite conclusion that the German treat- ment of prisoners of war, whose status as honour- able had been specially guarded by The Hague Convention, was barbarous and abominable in the extreme. So pronounced, so damning, was this verdict that the German Government, then more concerned to gain favour with neutrals than it was later, when the United States of America declared war, authorised the publication, in 1915, at Leipzig, of an illustrated book, by a well-known professor, Alexander Backhaus, in defence of Germany's treatment of prisoners of war. This volume, which was given the widest circulation, was an illuminating example, with its curious special pleading, of the perverted men- tality and strange psychology apparently inseparable from any German view of others. The impression which the professor wished to convey was not only that the Germans were naturally kind and tender-hearted, but that the prisoners who fell into their hands were shown the utmost consideration and even indulgence.

OFFICER PRISONERS WHO ESCAPED.
Captain C. V. Fox, Scots Guards (left), and Captain J. A. L. Caunter, Gloucester Regiment, who, after being made prisoner, succeeded in escaping from Germany. They were received by King George in July, 1917, and the photograph was taken as they were leaving Buckingham Palace.

Had not the whole matter been so serious, such a book would have been merely ridiculous, because of its absurd perversion of some of the facts, and its unblushing mendacity with respect to the others, in the case against Germany. Backhaus had the hardihood to write that German officers and sub-officers did not regard their prisoners as enemies, but as men entrusted to their care ; and that they were glad to give tea, tobacco, chocolate, and fresh linen to such of the poor fellows as received no comforts from home. There could have been no more fanciful picture. Hardly a prisoner returned from Germany to England but said that had it not been for the parcels sent to the former country most of the British would have starved to death. Many Russian prisoners did die of starvation, as did Serbians and Rumanians, for few or no parcels were despatched to them. Aware that the world knew something of the truth, Backhaus attempted to excuse, or at least palliate, the German treatment of the captured Rus- sians by saying that it was not surprising if the Landsturm men at first were not very friendly to them, seeing that they had destroyed and ravaged the

293

prosperous province of East Prussia, had unnecessarily burned down cottages and farms, tortured and murdered the defenceless, and carried off women and children.

Reviewing the position of the British prisoners of war in Germany, Professor Backhaus, who was under no illusions as to the inhuman treatment of these men, justified the German attitude by stating that it was a perfectly natural one, because of the " vexation felt towards England, who for years had planned the isolation of **German professor's** Germany, and without adequate cause **special pleading** had allied herself with the enemies of Germany." He added that it was quite as natural that " negroes, Tartars, and Kalmucks, to the bloodthirsty savagery of whom so many a German soldier had fallen a victim, were not looked on with very loving eyes." A characteristically German point of view was expressed when he went on to state that the judgment of " all justly thinking nations and of history will have to decide how France and Great Britain could answer for the way in which, if things had turned out according to their expectation, these wretches would have overrun the flourishing lands of Germany, and have thrown back European civilisation for thousands of years."

What Europe had to expect from German civilisation had been demonstrated in unmistakably horrible fashion by the appalling outrages and hideous massacres that took place during the first weeks of the war in Belgium and France, and later in Serbia and Rumania. The German treatment of prisoners of war was for a long period on similar lines. To reinforce his argument the professor collected and published a series of photographs of types of the soldiers of the Allies belonging to the coloured races, whose civilisation, though recognised as not that of Europe, could not have been on a lower plane than that displayed by Germany ; but, of course, he did not say so. On the contrary, after boasting that the Germans were intellectually and morally, as well as militarily, the superiors of all their enemies, he declared that these photographs, which had been carefully selected to suit his purpose, pointed out what " sort of vagabonds " they had had to fight, and that he was filled with holy wrath by the thought that numerous highly-educated, promising sons of Germany had been done to death by the rifles or knives of " such hordes." Yet his admissions of the hate Germany manifested towards British and Russian prisoners indicated that he was conscious that an apology

was necessary. His book was, in fact, an exemplification of the French apophthegm, *qui s'excuse s'accuse.* As was to be anticipated, he said not a word about the Wittenberg atrocities.

In Chapter XCII. (Vol. 5, page 263) reference was made to the conditions which had prevailed in the Wittenberg camp for prisoners of war in 1915. When that chapter was published much was known about the horrors of this place from the statements of British soldiers who had passed through them, and from the despatches of Mr. Gerard, then U.S. Ambassador at Berlin, and of other American diplomats, who took a great and most helpful interest in the prisoners, both at Wittenberg and elsewhere in Germany. The full story, in all its blackness, was not revealed until April, 1916, when a "Report by the Government Committee on the Treatment by the Enemy of British Prisoners of War regarding the Conditions obtaining at Wittenberg Camp during the Typhus

PRISONERS WHO WERE REPATRIATED.
Private William Ward (left) and Private E. Knott, wounded British soldiers who were repatriated, and gave evidence as to the brutal treatment meted out to prisoners of war in German camps.

Epidemic of 1915" was submitted to Parliament, and issued as a White Paper (Chapter CLXVII., Vol. 8, page 475). The committee, over which Mr. Justice Younger presided, examined on oath the prisoners, including the doctors of the R.A.M.C., who had been at Wittenberg, and wrote down their evidence. It is not too much to say that, when the report was published, its terrible disclosures of German inhumanity to the prisoners, and of abject cowardice in face of disease, shocked and disgusted all " justly thinking " men and women throughout the civilised world. No African, however benighted in soul, could have behaved worse than did the Germans at Wittenberg. When Major Fox, D.S.O., Scots Guards, who in 1917 succeeded in effecting his escape from Germany, and knew what he was talking about, said, in a speech delivered in November of that year, that the " worst of the cannibal tribes in Africa did not touch our noble enemy the Boche," Wittenberg alone would **Boches worse** have sufficed to confirm his words. **than cannibals** But Wittenberg did not stand alone. The camps at Gardelegen and Stendal had similar dreadful records.

It was no wonder that the eminent Professor Backhaus had nothing to say about Wittenberg. Nor did he touch on the singularly similar stories of the camps of Gardelegen and Stendal. The former was a large camp lying between Berlin and Hanover, and it held about eleven thousand prisoners of war, of whom about two hundred and sixty were British; the rest being French, Russians, and Belgians. In February, 1915, it was swept by an epidemic of typhus in conditions that almost repeated those of Wittenberg. The prisoners of the different nationalities were mixed together in the same way, and the Russians once again transmitted the infection in the same manner to the others in overcrowded

SUFFERERS HAPPY TO BE HOME.
Group of maimed and wounded British soldiers outside the hospital at which they were received on arriving home after bitter experience as prisoners of war in Germany.

compounds. The unfortunate men were half-starved, and all were miserably clothed. Many of them were without boots; of the British, about thirty out of the whole number had serviceable footwear. All were dirty, for there was no soap, and most of them were verminous. All were bullied and knocked about by their German guards. The German authorities, suspecting, as well they might, an outbreak of typhus, sent three British, four French, and one Russian army doctors to the camp. The British medical men were Major P. C. T. Davy, Captain A. J. Brown, and Captain Scott Williams. Describing the place, Major Davy said:

In passing through the camp on the day we arrived I had been struck by the complete silence everywhere. A few prisoners were standing or pacing to and fro, singly and in groups, in complete dejection and apathy. There was no talking or laughter, nobody was playing games. The only sounds were brutally shouted orders of the sentries, who were closely posted in every direction. Now, in passing from one company to another, and talking to the

PRISONERS WHO EFFECTED THEIR ESCAPE.
Mr. Frederick Short, Warwick Regiment (left), who was taken prisoner in July, 1916, but a year later escaped from Germany; and Pte. D. L. Grant, R.M.L.I., who was captured in March, 1918, but made good his escape after two days.

prisoners, one could not but be struck by the gaunt, hunted look they all bore. So much wretchedness and sickness concentrated in such a small area, such a sense of the absence of any sort of human feeling, made one utterly shocked and miserable. It was still sadder to see that what was all so horrible to me in its novelty had for them become so much a part of their life that they accepted it almost without comment.

Colonel Brunner, the German commandant, a man of brutal temper, treated the men in the camp as if they were there for the punishment of crimes they had committed, not as prisoners of war. He told the doctors that they would be dealt with rigorously if they did not obey his orders. They saw Dr. Wenzil, the German medical officer in charge, and were shown by him an overcrowded hospital, ill-equipped with even the commonest medical requisites. When the malady made its presence felt, and it was established that it was typhus, Dr. Wenzil fled instantly from the camp, as did all the other Germans in the place. So far as Wenzil himself was concerned, his flight did not save him, for soon afterwards the disease seized on him, and he died of it. The epidemic lasted for more than four months; it came to an end in June, and out of the two thousand cases of the fever, about three hundred terminated fatally. The typhus was, luckily, of a mild type, and the doctors of the Allies worked magnificently, aided by volunteer nurses from among the soldiers. In the number of those who rendered the medical men great assistance were ten French priests who were prisoners; eight of them took the disease, and five died. Of the British who acted as attendants, twenty caught the infection, but only two succumbed. Of the sixteen doctors eventually in the camp, twelve got typhus, two of them fatally. Very little help in any shape or form came in from the outside. So far from showing sympathy, the Germans, from a safe distance beyond the cordon of entanglements, evinced the utmost hostility.

Typhus outbreak at Gardelegen

Stendal was another camp that in a great measure reproduced the dreadful experiences of the prisoners of war at Wittenberg and Gardelegen. Typhus manifested itself at Stendal about the same time as at the two other places, and the German doctors and guards there took to flight in precisely the same precipitate manner, leaving the sick to doctors of the Allies—in this instance French and Russian—within rows of barbed-wire. The "British Medical Journal," of June, 1916, gave an account of what occurred at Stendal, in the words of Dr. Ribadeau-Dumas, one of the French medical men sent there by the Germans to fight the epidemic. There was the same bad food, the same absence of proper medical treatment and supplies, the same brutality as at Wittenberg. One day the soup was so bad that the French could not eat it. As a punishment they were made to stand motionless in rows for two hours, and then they were herded in a special barbed-wire enclosure with sixty men from Wittenberg suspected of typhus. The prisoners became desperate, so wretched was their state. The German authorities did little or nothing to help them until the disease began to spread outside the camp among the German people of the neighbourhood, and only then did they take some measures to combat the malady.

Typhus epidemics spread deliberately

Owing to bad food, insanitary conditions, and the like, outbreaks of typhus occurred in other camps, as, for example, the camp at Schneidermühl, in Posen. The great majority of the prisoners of war there were Russians, and only a small number were British, who, when they first arrived, had to shelter themselves in holes they dug in the ground, as no buildings were provided for them. Typhus was followed in this instance by cholera; the former claimed fourteen hundred victims, but the latter was even deadlier— in one compound alone three hundred and sixty men died of it. Twenty-one British perished. The German medical men fled, leaving the sick to a handful of Russian doctors, who practically had to fight the epidemics with their bare hands, for they were not provided with drugs and other necessary supplies. At Cassel-Niedzwehren typhus was deliberately brought about in epidemic form by herding prisoners of different nationalities together with Russians. In this camp the outbreak reached prodigious proportions —ten thousand cases, two thousand of which proved fatal. When the commandant at this place was remonstrated

OFFICER PRISONERS AT CREFELD.
Two British officers—Lieut. H. N. Harrington, Cheshire Regt. (second from left) and Capt. H. P. O. Sleigh, Border Regt. (fourth)—with Russian officers who shared their prison confinement at Crefeld, in Rhenish Prussia.

with, he remarked that placing the infected with the uninfected was "his way of fighting the war."

Nothing connected with the German treatment of prisoners of war was a more thoroughgoing refutation of Backhaus's assertions that the Germans dealt mercifully with their captives than a book, which appeared in 1917, entitled "Sixteen Months in Four German Prisons." This volume narrated the impressions and experiences of Mr. Henry C. Mahoney, from July 31st, 1914, to December, 1915, when he was released and returned to London. The four prisons of which he was in turn an inmate were Wesel, Sennelager, Klingelputz, and Ruhleben. Arrested as a spy on his arrival in Germany, through which he was passing on his way to Russia on business unrelated in any way to the war—Great Britain had not then declared war on Germany—he had to endure from the outset the most poignant sufferings at the hands of German officers and guards. Having succeeded in proving that he was not a spy, he was sent from Wesel to Sennelager, where at that moment there happened to be a German of the humane type in command of the camp. But this officer was soon replaced by another of the usual stamp, a Major Bach, who was a "pastmaster in the grim art of conceiving new and novel methods to worry and punish those so unfortunate as to be under his thumb. He was devilishly ingenious and fertile in the evolution of ways and means" to make the prisoners feel their position as acutely as possible.

A favourite punishment with this monster was to order a prisoner to have given him so many hours "at the post." Mr. Mahoney described how this sentence was carried out in the case of a Zouave, who, for insubordination and attempting to strike a guard under the severest provocation, was sentenced to four hours of this horrible torture:

Pte. A. Williams (English).   Pte. O'Brien (Irish).

Pte. A. J. Michie (Scottish).   Pte. J. Davies (Welsh).
Selected by First-Lieut. O. Stiehl to illustrate a description of the national characteristics—English, Irish, Scottish, and Welsh — of the men in a prisoners of war camp in Germany, of which he was the officer in charge.
GERMAN IDEAS OF BRITISH TYPES.

Escorted by four guards with loaded rifles and fixed bayonets, the unhappy Zouave was led to a post. One of the soldiers stood on either side of the prisoner ready to run him through should he attempt to escape or resist. The other two guards, discarding their rifles, uncoiled a length of rope which they were carrying. The prisoner's hands were forced behind his back and his wrists were tied tightly together, the rope being drawn so taut as to cut deeply into the flesh and to cause the unhappy wretch to shriek. He was now backed against the post round which the rope was passed. His ankles were then tied as tightly as his wrists and also strapped to the post, which action drew another yell of pain from the victim. Finally, another length of rope was passed round the upper part of his body, lashing him firmly to the support to prevent him from falling forward. After the Zouave had been strung up for some time I decided to creep out and up to him to ascertain from direct close observation the effects of this treatment upon the victim. . . . The weak wretch was in a fearful plight. The ropes had been drawn so tightly round his wrists and ankles as to cause the circulation of the blood through the hands and feet to cease, while the flesh immediately above the knots was swelling up in a fearful manner. All sense of feeling in the hands and feet having gone, the man was hanging limply, instead of standing against the post. He writhed and twisted in frenzied efforts to secure some relief, but each movement only caused further pain and the unintentional utterance of piercing shrieks. Each successive outburst grew weaker. The body dropped more and

more forward. His head dropped lower and lower on his chest. The struggles and cries grew fainter, until at last his head gave a final jerk. He shrieked no more. Insensibility had come to his relief.

But this insensibility did not save him long. The guards, who had withdrawn, now came up and released him from the post, when he fell like a log to the ground. They dashed buckets of water over the prostrate man until he revived, and then they retied him to the post. Each time he relapsed into unconsciousness this process was repeated until he had undergone the full four hours without counting the intervals of insensibility. "It did not matter whether the man fainted three or thirty times. It was only the instalments of time against the post which in the aggregate were taken to represent the full term of punishment." Mr. Mahoney observed that the first demonstration of this punishment did not fail to exercise a far-reaching influence upon the other prisoners, and that Major Bach was beside himself with delight. This officer conceived a fiendish means of increasing the agony of a prisoner condemned to this punishment—this was to order the poor wretch to be tied to the post at such an hour as the sun beat most fiercely on his naked head, the racking torment of intolerable heat thus being added to the torture of the ropes. Mr. Mahoney also stated that it was the fact that Bach strolled up when the sufferer was passing through this terrible ordeal, and, a couple of paces away, would stand, with his hands clasped behind his back and his legs wide apart, "surveying the results of his devilry with the greatest self-satisfaction," and flinging coarse jokes and gibes at his victim. Not only did this specimen of the "kind and tender-hearted" German officer enjoy this dreadful spectacle, but he took pains to get others to enjoy it also, for he invited the people of the vicinity to come to see the enforcement of this punishment, and they did so, clustering on the path on the opposite side of the road facing the stake, laughing and joking among themselves, and cheering frantically when the trussed man gave an abnormally wild cry of pain.

Bach drew up a regular code of sentences " to the post." The slightest offence was punished with two hours ; the maximum was eight hours. After a while the single post was not enough to satisfy him. Three were brought into use, and Mr. Mahoney testifies that he saw as many as three men undergoing the torture of the post at the same time, their combined shrieks and agonising cries penetrating to every corner of the camp. Such scenes were hard to bear by the comrades of the victims. Mr. Mahoney wrote of this :

On one occasion, when Major Bach was standing as usual before one of his victims, laughing and jeering at his futile writhings and agonised appeals for mercy, a number of British prisoners who were standing around in mute sympathy for the hapless man could not control their feelings. Suddenly they gave expression to fierce hissing of disapproval. Major Bach turned, but not with the mocking triumph that one would have expected. His face wore the look of the characteristic bully who is suddenly confronted with one who is more than his match. He was completely taken off his guard, so unexpected and vigorous was our outburst. But when he saw that he was merely threatened by a few unarmed and helpless Britons, his sang-froid returned, although it was with a palpable effort. He glared at us. There was no disguising or possibility of misconstruing the expression of disgust and rage on our faces. One and all wondered afterwards why he did not sentence every man of us to a spell at the post. Possibly anticipating that things might become ugly, he ordered us to our barracks. We moved away slowly and sullenly, but the guard coming up we were unceremoniously hurried into our domiciles, although it demanded energetic rifle proddings and clubbings from the soldiers who swarmed around us in overwhelming numbers to enforce the order.

Not all Germans were such cruel tyrants as Bach, even at Sennelager. Fortunately for the prisoners of war, the medical attendant of the camp, a Dr. Ascher, was really kind and just, and did what he could for them. He chided the guards for their rough conduct, and on one occasion actually rescued from ill-treatment a body of men, including some British prisoners, who had been set the impossible task of hauling for three miles a huge traction engine which had broken down on the road. Seeing that those who were attempting to move the engine were far too weak and exhausted for such an **One German** effort, he ordered them to desist, and **"white man"** took them to an inn, where he told them to order what they liked, at his expense. "We were so dumbfounded," was Mr. Mahoney's comment, "at this first expression of a 'white man's' action which we had encountered in Germany, that we could not utter a sound. We merely sat like a party of expectant children at a Sunday-school treat." This good doctor saw that the prisoners had a proper meal, and he insisted on their washing it down with beer or lemonade. Then he enjoined a short period of rest in aid of digestion. "You can imagine how we clustered round the doctor, thanking him for his kindness, but he would not listen to our expressions of gratitude. . . . When he next came into the camp," added Mr. Mahoney, "he received such a thundering and spontaneous ovation as to startle him, until at last the reason for this outburst dawned upon him, but he turned it off with his characteristic laugh and joke."

It would have been well for the reputation of Germany if she had possessed many men like Dr. Ascher. There were others of the same type, but they were few and far between, and their efforts were frowned on and discouraged by the authorities, sometimes even punished. An instance of this was chronicled by Mr. Gerard, then American Ambassador at Berlin. He saw a paragraph in the "North German Gazette," the official newspaper, which stated that certain **Humanity a** inhabitants of a small town near the **punishable crime** Danish frontier had been guilty of improper conduct towards prisoners of war, and in consequence had been sentenced to imprisonment and fines, besides having their names printed in the paper, to the end that they might be "held up to the contempt of all future generations of Germans."

Knowing from personal observation and from the reports of his staff how badly the prisoners of war were treated, he not unnaturally supposed that the German Government had at last been aroused to the necessity of protecting them from annoyance by the civil population. Investigation, however, dispelled this illusion. The truth was that some prisoners passing through the place to a camp made signs that they were hungry

and thirsty, and some of the kind-hearted Scandinavian population of the town gave them something to eat and drink. It was for relieving the sufferings of the prisoners that these good people were imprisoned, fined, and had their names pilloried in the paper. "I do not know," said Mr. Gerard, "of any one thing that can give a better idea of the official hate for the nations with which Germany was at war than this."

In the first months of 1916, reports—which reached the British from British prisoners who either had contrived to escape from Germany, or who had been returned home under agreement with the German Government— proved that in many camps there was very little real improvement of the evil conditions prevailing in them, or in the general attitude of the Germans towards their captives. A member of a party of British prisoners, who arrived

BRITISH SOLDIERS INTERNED AT THE HAGUE.
In the summer of 1917 an agreement was made by which some thousands of combatant (officers and N.C.O.'s) and civilian prisoners, British and German, were to be interned in Holland until the end of the war. In this photograph is shown the recreation-room at The Hague of British military prisoners released from Germany. Above: A block of fifteen houses at The Hague placed by the Dutch Government at the disposal of some of the British prisoners of war lucky enough to exchange the conditions of prison life in Germany for those of internees in Holland.

at Tilbury early in January of that year, stated that their common lot was to receive kicks, blows, and abuse. In February upwards of a hundred British soldiers were repatriated. By that date Germany had begun to employ prisoners on an extensive scale in work of all kinds. One of the soldiers told how, when prisoners had been sent to North Germany to build sheds for Zeppelins and had declined to engage in this unpatriotic business, eight of their number were sentenced to twelve months' hard labour in an ordinary prison. A man who had been at Ostrov testified that prisoners were struck with bayonets for slight offences. He instanced a King's Royal Rifleman who, for smoking contrary to orders, was pierced in the stomach and died next day. He mentioned that another soldier had been severely stabbed in the lungs on very inadequate provocation. That same month of February saw a demonstrated case of the brutal treatment of a British prisoner that aroused intense indignation

BRITISH SEAMEN TURN THEIR HANDS TO FORESTRY.
Some of the British sailors who were taken prisoner at the Battle of Jutland on May 31st, 1916, were employed felling timber in a German forest. They adapted themselves to their changed conditions of life with unfaltering determination to make the best of a bad business.

throughout Great Britain—the case of Private Tully, of the Royal Marines.

The case of Private Tully In one of the opening stages of the war Tully was captured at Antwerp, and he was then a fine, big, strong man. He came back to England an utter wreck, a mere ghost of what he had been, and, after lingering a week or two, died in Millbank Hospital. His case was brought up in the House of Commons. Mr. Herbert Samuel, for the Government, said that Tully had been confined in the camp at Döberitz, and that, after working in the wet, he had no means of drying his clothes and could get no underclothes. In July, 1915, Tully was seized with rheumatic fever through going on daily fatigue duty, getting wet through and having no change. He was sent to hospital, where he was convalescent after five weeks, when he was transferred to the camp at Dryotz, a few miles from Döberitz. He had to carry all his kit on the march, broke down, and shortly afterwards was returned to the Döberitz hospital, where he had no treatment, and had to depend for assistance on another British prisoner who was a patient there. Consumption had set in, and when he was exchanged and had arrived in England he was seen to be extremely emaciated and far gone; he was in a hopeless state. The Medical Board, which reported on his condition, stated that it was due to exposure and insufficient food and clothing while a prisoner in Germany.

Tully's case, which was given the widest publicity in the Press, caused much angry feeling in the country, and led to a demand for reprisals. The question of reprisals was one which was repeatedly debated both in Parliament and in the papers, but without result. Many people were opposed to reprisals on humanitarian grounds, and there was always the unanswerable argument that in any competitive policy of reprisals it was impossible for the British, with their ideas of what was right, to equal, far less surpass, the Germans in brutality and callous indifference to suffering.

DINNER-TIME IN THE INTERNED SAILORS' QUARTERS.
With the deft handiness traditional in the British Navy the sailors made their prison quarters as shipshape and comfortable as circumstances allowed. These photographs reached England in the spring of 1918, when the men had been in captivity for more than a year and three-quarters.

AN ALL-POLICE ELEVEN AT DÖBERITZ.
Group of British soldiers, all of whom were ex-policemen, photographed at Döberitz while prisoners of war in Germany. Among the things " verboten " by the notice on the wall were " whistling and singing," and the notice also included the minatory " No waterboiling or cooking."

In Chapter XCII. (Vol. 5, page 250) references were made to the splendid work on behalf of prisoners of war accomplished by Mr. James W. Gerard, the Ambassador of the United States at that time to Germany. After America broke off relations, Mr. Gerard, who, before leaving Berlin had been subjected to indignities in the characteristic German fashion, returned to his own country, and brought out, a few months later, a volume recounting his experiences in the Fatherland, under the title of " My Four Years in Germany." This book, which first was published serially both in Great Britain and the United States, attracted universal attention, and on no ground more than on what it revealed concerning the German treatment of prisoners of war, and especially of British prisoners. It shed a great deal of light on the whole subject. So far as was possible in the circumstances, Mr. Gerard represented Great Britain in Germany up to the beginning of February, 1917, and he did all that was in his power to render tolerable the existence of the British prisoners there. Though he was frequently deceived by the Germans, who " window-dressed " the camps for his inspection, and otherwise bluffed him, he undoubtedly was the means of bringing about many changes for the better in at least some districts.

At the outset Mr. Gerard found the impression that German prisoners of war were treated very harshly in Great Britain. He sent one of his staff to England to see what actually was the truth, and the report of this official—who had soon discovered that there was no foundation for such an impression —helped the Ambassador to obtain better conditions for the British prisoners in Germany. But the notion that German prisoners were not treated well in Great Britain persisted in Germany. Probably, for purposes of its own, the German Government was at no pains to let the facts be known. At any rate, the " Deutsche Tageszeitung," in January, 1917, recorded an incident which appeared to bear this out. It was difficult to imagine that Hindenburg was not thoroughly acquainted with the manner in which his nationals, whether soldiers or civilians, were dealt with—all too tenderly, as a large number of the British people thought—by the British Government. Yet, according to this journal, the Field-Marshal, when visiting a hospital on the western front where some wounded British officers were being nursed by a woman who spoke English, angrily ordered her to go away, remarking at the same time that he was unwilling that the British should be better treated there than were his brave soldiers who had been so unfortunate as to be prisoners of war in England.

From the start Mr. Gerard was **Mr. Gerard's work** hampered in his work of mercy and humanity by the **of mercy** German authorities. Of this he wrote :

After vainly endeavouring to get the German Government to agree to some definite plan for the inspection of prisoners, after my notes to the Foreign Office had remained unanswered for a long period of time, and after sending a personal letter to Von Jagow

BRITISH OFFICER PRISONERS REMOVED TO SWITZERLAND.
By agreement a number of incapacitated prisoners were transferred from Germany to Switzerland. This group of British officers comprised (from left to right) Lieut. Bell, Canadians ; Lieut. Armitage, K.O.Y.L.I. ; Capt. Rose, Lincs ; Lieut. Swan, Northants ; Capt. Field, Warwicks ; and Capt. Bowen, Scots Fusiliers.

(the German Foreign Minister), calling his attention to the fact that the delay was injuring German prisoners in other countries, I finally called on the Chancellor and told him that my notes concerning prisoners were sent by the Foreign Office to the military authorities; that, while I could talk with officials of the Foreign Office, I never came into contact with the people who really considered the notes sent by me, and who made the decisions as to the treatment of prisoners of war and inspection of the camps, and I begged the Chancellor to break down diplomatic precedent and allow me to speak with the military authorities who decided these questions. I said, "If I cannot get an answer to my proposition about prisoners, I will take a chair and sit in front of your palace in the street until I receive an answer." The result was a meeting in my office. . . .

In twenty minutes we managed to reach an agreement, the substance of which, as between England and Germany, was that the American Ambassador and his representatives in Great Britain, should have the right to visit the prison camps on giving reasonable notice, which was to be twenty-four hours where possible, and should have the right to converse with prisoners within sight but out of hearing of the camp officials; that an endeavour should be made to adjust matters complained of with the camp authorities before bringing them to the notice of higher authorities; that ten representatives should be named by our Ambassador, and that these should receive passes enabling them to visit the camps under the conditions above stated. The agreement was ratified by the British and German Governments, and thereafter for a long time we worked under its provisions.

All-powerful corps commandants

This meeting took place in March, 1915, but Mr. Gerard or his representatives had previously visited Ruhleben, Döberitz, and other prison camps, and had done what they could to ameliorate the lot of the hapless British prisoners. This agreement would almost have been a charter of liberties for these unfortunate men if it had been fully lived up to by Germany. After it was signed and sealed, Mr. Gerard was faced by another difficulty. Germany was divided into army corps districts, and during the war the respective corps commanders were clothed with absolute authority, their orders superseding those of all civilian officials, no matter how high their rank. Armed with his agreement, Mr. Gerard went to inspect the camp at Halle for officer prisoners, but found it inoperative. On returning to Berlin he was told that the matter would be arranged; but his second visit to Halle had the same result. On going back again to Berlin, he complained to the Foreign Office, and then was advised to see the corps commander of the district, as he was in supreme authority there. Finally, Mr. Gerard did see this personage, and succeeded in effecting his object. At Berlin there was a Prisoners of War Department, presided over by General Friedrich, but his power was less than that of these corps commanders, who were very jealous of their rights.

As his duties as Ambassador prevented him from visiting many of the camps, Mr. Gerard saw to it that members of the Embassy were constantly engaged in this work of inspection. In his book he recorded a visit which he made of the officers' camp at Hanover Münden, where about eight hundred officers, of whom thirteen were British, were confined in an old factory on the bank of the river below the town. The Russian officers handed to him some arrows tipped with nails which had been shot at them by the boys of the town, and the British drew his notice to the filthy state of the camp. "In this, as, unfortunately, in many other officer camps," said Mr. Gerard, "the inclination seemed to be to treat the officers not as captured officers and gentlemen, but as convicts." He had quite a sharp talk with the commandant of the camp, and not without good results ultimately, for this German officer in the end turned his camp into one of the best in Germany. For some time Mr. Gerard's reports of his visits, or those of his representatives, to the various prison camps were published in White Papers presented to the British Parliament; but before he left Germany the American Government discovered that the publication of these reports irritated the Germans to such a degree that the British Government was asked not to make them

Ill-treatment of officer prisoners

public any more. Copies were always sent to Washington, as well as to London and the Berlin Foreign Office.

Wittenberg was visited by Mr. Gerard after the epidemic of typhus had run its course. He noted that the Germans employed there a large number of "police dogs," not only in watching outside the camp, in order to prevent the escape of prisoners, but also inside it. He stated that the prisoners told him that they had been bitten by these animals. Such dogs—described by several eye-witnesses of their use as really half-bred wolves—were employed in many camps besides Wittenberg. In May, 1917, a White Paper was presented to Parliament giving the evidence of British officers, non-commissioned officers, and men who had returned from captivity in Germany, respecting these police dogs.

Private Richard Marsh (of the King's Own Royal Lancaster Regiment), who had been a prisoner at Stendal up to the end of January, 1916, stated:

The general treatment was very harsh, and as far as my experience goes is getting worse. On December 26th, 1915, we had a very bad time of it. Three shots were fired as a signal for all the prisoners to get into their huts; but we had never been warned about it, and consequently did not know what it meant. The sergeant-major came through the compound in which I was and set the dogs which were with him—big half-bred wolf-hounds—on those who had not gone in. I had the misfortune to be bitten in five places, and finally the dog flew at my throat, and had it not been for a thick muffler I was wearing I feel sure I should have been killed. As it was, I carried the dog some twenty yards holding on to my chest with his teeth. When I complained to the sergeant-major he threatened me with his sword. As a result of the dog's attack I was unable either to sit down or lie down properly for a couple of weeks.

Sergeant Rodman (R.A.M.C.), who reached London in January, 1916, after fourteen months of Wittenberg, said:

The German sentries would bully and insult the English especially. They would go round the companies in pairs, one with a rifle and bayonet, and the other with a revolver and leading a big dog. When they came near an Englishman the sentry would let out the lead of the dog so that he could spring at the Englishman and jump on him and tear his clothes. I have seen a coat with the sleeve half torn out, which, one of the sergeants told me, had been done by a dog. Complaints were made to the Ambassador [Mr. Gerard], and afterwards this was stopped.

Police dogs in prison camps

In his book Mr. Gerard relates how this improvement was brought about by a striking suggestion he made to Von Jagow when talking over conditions at Wittenberg "Suppose," said the Ambassador to the German Foreign Minister, "I go back to Wittenberg and shoot some of those dogs, what can you do to me?" This question was answered by the disappearance soon afterwards of the brutes from Wittenberg. But they continued to be used in other camps; more than that, the German authorities advertised for such dogs—so Major A. S. Peebles (of the Suffolks), who had been a prisoner at Halle, testified, and gave at the same time as frightful an example of German brutality as perhaps was ever recorded:

At Torgau we had seen advertisements asking for dogs to guard prisoners, but it was at Halle that we were to see them actually used. The following illustrates the terrible brutality and utter callousness of the Germans. On several occasions I saw a Belgian soldier leave the camp carrying a number of sacks and accompanied by two "Feldwebels" and several dogs. The Belgian was little more than half-witted. One evening he appeared to be very much upset. I asked him where he went in the afternoon. After much hesitation he told me that he was taken out into the fields, dressed up in the sacks, and baited by the dogs to train them. The man was absolutely terrified. Complaints were made to the commandant, and shortly afterwards he left the camp, as he was told, "for his health."

When the British Government, through Mr. Gerard, entered into a correspondence with the German Government respecting these police dogs, and pointed out that the use of such animals had on no occasion been adopted at internment camps in Great Britain, it said that the practice of employing them was open to strong objection, because, besides exposing the prisoners to serious bodily injury, it placed men who were entitled to honourable treatment on the same footing as criminals.

On December 4th, 1916, the German Foreign Office replied that it had been shown to be of military necessity to keep police dogs in some prisoners' camps in view of the large numbers of prisoners of war in Germany. It asserted that, having regard to the smaller number of prisoners in Great Britain, no comparison could be drawn between conditions in the two countries. It protested that the animals were not "particularly savage," and that it was impossible to regard the police use of them as a breach of the "principles of humane and reasonable treatment of prisoners." This statement, which closed the correspondence on the subject, indicated clearly the official mind of Germany as to what was humaneness in dealing with captives, and was typical of the general German attitude.

Among the features of 1916 was the trial of Sir Roger Casement on the charge of high treason, which resulted in his conviction, degradation from his rank, and execution. In the number of those who testified against him were several repatriated Irish prisoners of war, and they recounted his attempts to win them and their compatriot prisoners over to Germany. The Germans had collected all the Irish prisoners in one camp at Limburg, near Frankfort-on-the-Main, and treated them well in order to induce them, with Casement's support, to become traitors, but only about fifty of them were seduced from their allegiance. Those who stood fast were mixed up with Russians as a punishment. Two of the faithful men, Moran and Dewlin by name, were shot at Limburg, and though the German authorities claimed that these Irishmen had attacked the sentries, the evidence at the trial of Casement suggested that they were killed—in plain words, murdered—because of their declining to join the arch-traitor, and what Mr. Gerard had to say about them tended to show that this was the fact. In his book the ex-Ambassador stated that he received

LORD NEWTON. [*Elliott & Fry.*
Appointed Under-Secretary of State for Foreign Affairs in 1916, Lord Newton conducted the negotiations at The Hague in July, 1917, regarding the release of prisoners of war for internment in Holland and Switzerland, the repatriation of badly-wounded prisoners, and the revision of punishments for attempts to escape.

information of the shooting of one Irish prisoner, and that although the camp commandant had assured Dr. McCarthy, an American medical man attached to the U.S. Embassy in Berlin, that the investigation had been closed and the guard who had done the shooting exonerated, nevertheless, when Mr. Gerard himself visited the camp to investigate the matter he was told that such investigation was inadmissible, as the shooting was still *sub judice* by the German authorities. Mr. Gerard was not permitted to speak to those prisoners who had seen the shooting. When he afterwards learned that another Irishman had been shot by a guard on the day before his visit, he found that similar obstacles to an investigation were placed in his way. In such circumstances the killing of these men had a thoroughly suspicious aspect.

Irishmen shot at Limburg

Speaking generally of the Limburg Camp, Mr. Gerard observed that the Irish prisoners did not bear confinement well, and that many of them who were in hospital were suffering from tuberculosis. They also appeared peculiarly subject to mental breakdowns. He mentioned that two Catholic priests, Father Crotty and Brother Warren,

from a religious house in Belgium, were doing wonderful work among these prisoners.

In the House of Commons in April, 1916, Lord Robert Cecil, on behalf of the Government, said that he could only express profound regret that it had "so underestimated the brutality" of the enemy. What was in his mind at the time was the report on the Wittenberg horrors, as well as the case of Tully. But his colleague, Lord Newton, in reply to Lord Grenfell, towards the end of June of the same year, in the House of Lords, made the public acquainted with another sample of the German treatment of prisoners which proved that the enemy's capacity for brutality had again been underestimated. Lord Grenfell asked what was the truth concerning British prisoners of war at Libau, in Courland, as letters had been received describing the privations which they were suffering there, which they were told were reprisals for the brutal treatment of German prisoners who had been transferred from Great Britain to France. An extract from one of these letters was quoted by him : " We get up at 4 a.m. and return at 6.30 p.m.," wrote a British soldier, who was set to work on a railway, " and we are living on practically nothing, with two thin blankets and no bed. I can assure you it is perfect hell." Lord Newton explained how it had come about that German prisoners had been sent to France from England.

It appeared that at the instance of Lord Kitchener, then Secretary of War, about two thousand Germans had been transferred from British camps to Rouen and Havre to help the workmen at these places in loading and unloading vessels. Lord Newton said that these Germans were not ill-treated, but were supervised by British officers and overseers—the German Government had supposed they were put under the French, whose policy was to deal with German prisoners exactly as French prisoners were dealt with by the German authorities—and were on precisely the same footing as German prisoners in Great Britain. Therefore the German Government had no excuse. The German prisoners in France were far from being treated brutally by the British. This was made perfectly clear, for the British Government permitted the American Embassy in Paris, on behalf of Germany, to inspect these men, whereas, on the other hand, the Germans for months refused to allow Mr. Gerard to send any member of his staff to report on the condition of the British prisoners in Courland.

British prisoners in Courland

It would have been difficult to find a more wretched place than Libau, the inhabitants of which were in rags, and more than half-starved. The food supplied to the British prisoners was scarcely sufficient to sustain life ; parcels did not reach them from home until many weeks had passed, and the resources of the town were so limited that it was almost impossible for them to buy anything. The men were miserably housed in a building which overlooked the harbour, and they slept on bare boards. They were kept unremittingly at work, and they were punished with atrocious severity on the least pretext.

The "post" was a frequent instrument of punishment, and it was reported that it was not an uncommon thing to see twenty prisoners tied up at the same time, and undergoing this hideous form of torture. Among the punishment cells were four so terrible that they were characterised as "absolutely Black Holes of Calcutta." The climate of the Baltic, chill and damp, as well as the privations and sufferings they were compelled to endure, told heavily on the men, and consequently there was much sickness, for which there was little or no medical aid forthcoming. Bad as was the lot of the prisoners at Libau, there was something worse in store for many of them; it seemed always possible for the Germans to "go one better" in the way of remorseless brutality. In February, 1917, five hundred men were picked out and sent to the

Prisoners under Russian gun fire

Russian firing-line to undergo the rigours of an Arctic temperature, on meals reduced to two a day, and with extremely inadequate protection against the bitter cold. For ten hours they were forced to work under fire from the Russian guns. They slept in a tent, hardly warmed at all by small stoves, and some of them had no blankets. Not one had a change of clothing. The solace of smoking was denied them. "It is an awful and most miserable existence," wrote one of the Coldstream Guards there to his wife.

"You are being dealt with in this manner," said the German authorities to these men in the firing-line on the eastern front, "as a retaliation for German prisoners of war being sent into the firing-line on the western front by the British authorities." The German Government would withdraw the British prisoners from the eastern front. Instead of this being the case, she had sent the five hundred men referred to into the trenches, and had, to quote Lord Newton's words, "subjected them to deliberate ferocity." Furthermore, Germany had informed the Government that she had never put British prisoners into the firing-line on the western front, but Lord Newton showed this was not true, the fact being that several bodies of British prisoners had been kept for months, though secretly, within four or five miles of the trenches on the German front, and ill-treated most abominably. It was another characteristic story of German treachery.

What had taken and was still taking place was revealed by three men of the Dorsets, who had been taken prisoner by the Germans at Beaumont-Hamel on January 11th, 1917. They had escaped in the following April, and got back to England, where they made statements which proved the falsity of the German claim. The company to which the three soldiers belonged had raided a portion of the German line and captured two dug-outs, but by a turn in the tide of war it was shortly afterwards surrounded by a far more numerous force of Germans, who made prisoner one officer and about eighty of the rank and file. These captives were removed to Cambrai, where they found between three hundred and four hundred other British prisoners, some of whom had been captured as far back as the preceding November. They had been kept behind the German lines near Trescault, and had been made to work in the zone of fire. Nothing had been heard in Great Britain of these men, and their relatives could thus but have feared the worst. It was not the fault of the men that no word of their fate reached their friends. The absence of news had to be credited to a peculiarly dastardly act of cruelty on the part of the Germans. For, though the prisoners were permitted to write postcards, not one of these postcards ever reached its destination—a thing that was capable of only one explanation: the destruction of the cards by the Germans. Of course, no parcels were sent from home to these men, for their very existence was unknown; they were given no more food by their captors than just kept body and soul together, and they were brutally ill-used in other ways.

PRISONER VICTIM OF TEUTON BARBARITY.
Burial of Seaman John Player Genower, of H.M.S. Nestor, prisoner of war at Brandenburg Prisoners' Camp. Seeking to escape from a burning building, he was brutally bayoneted by the German guard, and thrust back into the flames to die, on March 9th, 1917. In circle: Portrait of Seaman Genower.

alleged that both Great Britain and France had kept German prisoners immediately behind the firing-line, and it asserted that it had done nothing of the same kind with respect to British and French prisoners. This assertion was entirely false, but there was unfortunately some degree of justification for the allegation regarding German prisoners being employed in the zone of fire behind the British line. In a speech in the Lords, in May, 1917, Lord Newton said that some German prisoners who were making roads were wounded by shells from the German guns, and he stated that Germany perceived in this incident a good chance for making reprisals. Germany demanded that the prisoners should be withdrawn thirty kilometres (about nineteen miles) from the line of fire, and the Allies agreed to do so. But she had given the British Government to understand that thereafter she

In the middle of January, 1917, about a hundred of these soldiers, whose condition was worse than that of slaves, were transferred to Ervillers, where, six miles behind the German front, they were set to work on making roads. A month later they were sent to Sauchy-Lestrée, some ten or twelve miles behind the German lines, but by that time about twenty of them had succumbed. Still later they were marched to Sauchy-Gauchy, but their number had been reduced then to sixty. Never a word, never a parcel, came from home for any of them; they were as the dead. The odious farce of allowing them to write postcards which were never despatched was repeated more than once by the Germans. "Nobody there," said one of the Dorsets who had escaped, "received any parcels or letters." Nor did they get any fresh clothing of any sort. "We were not even given a shirt. We arrived back in the British lines in the same uniforms in which we were captured, and in which we had worked in all weathers, rain and sun. There were no means of drying them, and when we got wet we had to sleep in our wet things."

The dreadful stories of the three men of the Dorsets were confirmed from other sources. Prisoners, who effected their escape from Hameln, related how they had seen poor wrecks of soldier-comrades, who had been made to work immediately behind the German front, carried into hospital there so emaciated that they were no more than living skeletons. "I never saw men look so bad as they did, even after they had been in hospital," said a man who got away from Hameln in May, 1917. When these men recovered enough to speak of their· experiences, the tales they told were ghastly. They had been starved, beaten, knocked about, flogged; some of them had been wounded by shells from British guns.

A MURDERED PRISONER.
Private Joseph Barry, Scots Guards, who was brutally murdered by his armed guard at Sennelager Camp in Germany.

A letter, written to his sister by a private of the Connaught Rangers, and published in the newspapers about June 9th, 1917, described the state of a prisoner still kept behind the German front on the west:

Cruel usage of Australians

I am a prisoner of war, but I am not in Germany. I am just behind the firing-line. We are working from morning to night, and within range of the British guns. We are living in an old battered house, and have not enough to eat. Please send parcel of food. Another month of this and we shall all be dead. We are not allowed to smoke, and we are wired in like birds, so you can see how we are fixed in this terrible hole. At night we have nothing to cover us when we lie down.

Further striking testimony to the German treatment of prisoners near the firing-line appeared in a narrative published on May 31st, 1917, and written by Captain C. E. W. Bean, the official Press correspondent with the Australian forces in France. On the 11th of the preceding April, after a great attack on the Hindenburg line, a thousand Australians were cut off by German machine-guns and made prisoner. They were given little food and otherwise badly used; many of their seriously wounded were compelled to march on foot away into captivity in Germany. What occurred was told to Captain Bean by two of the Australians who managed to escape and return to the British lines. After describing the callous and cruel way in which the inhabitants of the French villages, through which the prisoners passed, were prevented from giving them anything to eat or drink, these two men spoke of their treatment at Lille, whither they had been sent by rail. The Australians were packed into the rooms in the upper story of an old fort, one hundred and ten of them being put in each room:

AIRMEN PRISONERS UNJUSTLY SENTENCED.
Lieut. Ewald Scholtz, R.F.C. (left), and Sec.-Lieut. H. C. Wookey, R.F.C., who were taken prisoner and sentenced to ten years' penal servitude for dropping leaflets in the German lines. On the threat of the British Government of reprisals on German officers the monstrous sentence was cancelled.

For five nights and six days one hundred and ten Australians lived in the room where the escaped men were. It is the first time in our country's history that Australians have ever suffered organised torture. The room was about fifty feet by twenty feet. The floor was tiled. For a few minutes each day the men were allowed into the yard for exercise. Their only convenience for all sanitary purposes was one barrel, which stood in the corner uncovered. The windows had to be shut, for they slept on the tiled floor without a blanket, though snow fell at night, and their food was too little to keep life together. They were given one-seventh of a loaf of bread—that is, one slice per man—with some fermented mangolds each day, with one cup of coffee at night and one in the morning. When the man who took the barrel each day downstairs to clean it asked for a glass of water, the guard would not allow it. The cook refused a mark offered for a little bread. They were not once allowed to wash until the last day, when they cleaned up to leave.

Now came the most extraordinary part of the story:

At the end a German corporal came into the room. He asked them if they knew what they were there for. They said "No." He said, "You may write and tell your people and your Government all about it—just what has happened—and say you are here as a punishment. Seven weeks ago the German Government wrote to the British Government about the employment of prisoners near the line, and they have not yet received an answer." The Australians told him it was a lie—there was not a German prisoner within twenty or thirty kilometres of the line. These men had passed hundreds of times in our back areas companies of fat, well-clothed, happy-looking Germans twenty miles behind the British lines, with Australians and British soldiers alike giving them cigarettes, and only the French people, whose homes they have ravaged, showing the least resentment. But they knew their protest would make no difference.

British demand for reprisals

Two hundred and forty Australians were sent by train on that day to work on a dump a short distance from the firing-line. Together with English and Scottish soldiers, forming a double company, they were ordered to unload stores, but they were soon in such a weak state from want of food that many of them collapsed. They received one-third of a loaf of bread, and coffee in the morning, and stewed horseflesh with a few grains of barley in the middle of the day. Such was their daily allowance. Their hunger was so keen that they entreated their guards to permit them to cut anything green that could be eaten—grass, nettles, dandelions, and rape. They picked out and devoured the potato peelings which their captors had thrown away. The knowledge of such facts as these by the general public in Great Britain again led to a sharp demand for reprisals, but nothing came of it. The official attitude was expressed in the Commons by Mr. J. F. Hope, who said that he was authorised to state that the view of the Government was that to enter now on a course of competitive ill-treatment of prisoners in the matter of food would be a policy for which the enemy was better adapted by temperament and tradition than were the British. Meanwhile, negotiations had been going on between the two Governments, and, in June, Mr. Hope announced that an agreement had been come to by which British prisoners were to be withdrawn thirty kilometres from the firing-line.

About 2,000 had already been withdrawn, and it was expected that the rest would speedily be withdrawn, but this was far from being the case. In a report, dated March 6th, 1918, and issued as a White Paper on April 11th following, the Committee on the Enemy's Treatment of British Prisoners stated that, in spite of the agreement, British prisoners, according to the most recent information, were still employed within the thirty-kilometre limit, fed on totally insufficient food, and treated with extreme brutality. This report opened with a striking sentence that said:

The detention and employment by the German armies, behind their firing-line in Belgium and France, of British N.C.O.'s and men captured on the western front has brought upon these

BRITISH PRISONERS WHO ESCAPED FROM THE HUN.
Four Scottish soldiers who had made good their escape from Germany and reached England in the spring of 1918. From left to right : Private Wood, of the Camerons, and Private Davidson, Corporal Dickson, and Corporal Murray, all of the Royal Scots. They were being interviewed by the Earl of Stair, who had himself shortly before been repatriated after having been a prisoner of war in Germany.

prisoners an amount of unjustifiable suffering, for which a parallel would be hard to find in the history, tragic in so many of its incidents as that history has been, of the treatment by the enemy of their prisoners during this war.

In a general review of the German treatment of British prisoners of war, it had to be said that all the prison camps were not equally bad, and it also had to be borne in mind that the ordinary German soldier was brutally treated by his superiors, who were accustomed to inflict severe punishments for even slight offences committed by their own men. As regarded individual camps, much depended on the nature of the respective commandants, some of whom were less inhumane than others. As a rule, the South Germans behaved better than the North Germans. In several camps, as notably at Ruhleben, the prisoners made their lot more endurable by organised efforts. The improvement in many camps at the end of 1915, owing to the hard work of Mr. Gerard and his assistants, was continued into 1916 and 1917. But at best the prisoner of war was always suffering, either physically or mentally, or both. The long confinement was difficult to bear. As Mr. Gerard said, when addressing an American audience in 1917: "You sitting here cannot imagine the horror of living two and a half years in a German prison camp. I know, because I saw." It was a frequent thing for prisoners to become mentally afflicted, their brain breaking down under the incessant strain.

Insanity due to suffering

In the first months of the war prisoners had nothing to do outside their ordinary camp duties, and the comparative idleness which resulted from this was in itself no small trial, leading not a few to volunteer for work on farms and the like. With more than two millions of prisoners on her hands, Germany soon saw the economic value of such a tremendous addition to her labour-gangs, and though it was expressly contrary to military law and usage she set many of these luckless men to make munitions. British prisoners revolted at doing such work against their own country. One of the men who returned from the Friedrichsfeld Camp to England in May, 1916, said that numbers of prisoners were employed underground in pits and quarries, and that some of them had been seriously injured by explosions. He added that British prisoners often refused to do underground work, and steadily declined to do anything that would help Germany to win. Pressure of all sorts was brought to bear on them to induce them to give way. Some were sent to prison, others had parcels and letters stopped, and others again were driven into the pits by German soldiers with fixed bayonets.

Rather more than a year later a party of eleven British soldiers and three French officers, who had escaped from Germany, reached a British port after various adventures. After stating that it was their experience that the British were treated more harshly than other prisoners of war, and that it was a case of their hearing " Gott strafe England ! " every day, they said that four hundred British prisoners were sent to work in the coal-mines in the Rhineland, but that all of them had refused to do so. The Germans thereupon selected men from the number and flogged them with rubber pipes, or struck them with the butt-ends of rifles. In another case, where the British declined to do work which they thought inimical to the interests of their country, the men were lined up against a wall and told they would be shot if they did not change their minds. But not a man flinched. The order to fire was given by the German in command. There was no firing, however, for it had been arranged among the Germans beforehand that there was to be none. The whole thing was an attempt —a plant to break the spirit of these British prisoners, but it was a signal failure. The men were then marched back to camp, having triumphantly come through as severe an ordeal as could be imagined.

Slavery in German mines

In August, 1917, the " Pall Mall Gazette " published what a prisoner wrote to his brother on a postcard, dated July 8th, and despatched from one of the prison work-camps :

News is very bad. I have been at a salt-mine now for the last two weeks, and I am about dead. It is worse than the Siberian mines in Russia. If we cannot make thirty waggons, we are kept down for sixteen hours. I do not think I shall ever see England or Canada again. When we fall down exhausted they beat us with rifles and bayonets.

With respect to the sending out of the prisoners of war to work throughout Germany, Mr. Gerard pointed out in his book that it had one very evil effect. " It has made it to the financial advantage of certain farmers and manufacturers to have the war continued." He showed that the Prussian landowners, or Junkers, obtained four or five times as much for their agricultural produce as they did before the war, and had the work on their farms done by prisoners, to whom they paid only sevenpence a day, though they received from the Government nearly as much for feeding them. In a statement after his return to the United States, he reported that the prisoners were leased or sent out to farms in much the same way as convicts in America were sent in the South. After alluding to the fact that the class which benefited from the sweat and toil of the prisoners was the very class which had the greatest say in the government of Germany, he observed that the "Tageblatt" of Berlin was suppressed for three days for calling attention to the huge profits made by this class in this particular way. As a general thing the men on the farms were better off than most of the other prisoners, though this depended on the goodwill towards them of their overseers, some of whom were brutal enough.

After the United States broke off relations with Germany in February, 1917, the Americans of course were unable to do anything more on behalf of the British prisoners, military or civilian, in Germany. But in 1917 a new factor emerged which was not without a marked influence on the German treatment of these men. In the earlier years of the war the number of British prisoners in German hands far exceeded the number of German military prisoners in British hands. In 1917, however, the reverse was the case, the number of the latter being nearly double the number of the former. By the end of August of that year Great Britain had captured over 102,000 Germans since the beginning of the struggle, whereas her loss to Germany in the same time was only a little above 56,000, including Indian troops. Among the German prisoners were very many officers, and however indifferent Germany might be, and was, to the fate of her rank and file—the "cannon-fodder"—she was really concerned as to what happened to officers. In this lay a certain leverage

Action of the British Government

PRISONER VICTIMS OF GERMANY'S 1918 OFFENSIVE.
This photograph, which appeared in a German journal, was described as representing a batch of British prisoners taken on the Arras sector of the western front during the German offensive which began on March 21st, 1918.

which the British Government could utilise in its negotiations with the German Government with regard to the general treatment of British prisoners of war.

Naturally, the British Government had from the first taken the greatest interest in the fate of the British prisoners, and had done much for their relief in a variety of ways. In the diplomatic field it had made excellent use of the good offices of Mr. Gerard and his staff, as has been seen. Mr. Gerard paid his first visit to a German prison camp as early as August 20th, 1914; this was at Döberitz, and among the prisoners were a few British soldiers. The British Government provided the American Ambassador with generous sums of money to be expended at his discretion for all the British prisoners of war, and also sent clothing. "Nothing was omitted," Mr. Gerard testified, "and every suggestion made by me was immediately acted on, while many most valuable hints were given me from London as to prisoners' affairs." He further bore witness that King George and Queen Mary showed a deep personal interest in the welfare of the British in Germany, and that this concern never flagged during the period of his stay in Berlin. The Government also made use of the good offices of the Americans in negotiations for the release of civilians and the exchange of diplomatic and consular officials, as well as the release of incapacitated military and naval officers and civilians. By virtue of these negotiations over six hundred British subjects returned home between December, 1914, and May, 1916. Lord Newton, who made this announcement, also said that an agreement had been reached between the British and German Governments for the transfer of British and German incapacitated soldiers to Switzerland. The French had

BRITISH SOLDIERS FALLEN INTO ENEMY HANDS.
In March, 1918, the Germans launched their offensive, seeking to break the Franco-British line at its point of junction, and though they failed in their object they succeeded in taking a number of prisoners. This photograph of some of the prisoners appeared in a German newspaper.

made a similar arrangement some time previously, particularly with respect to those suffering from consumption, a disease which had seized on many prisoners because of the bad food and the other privations to which they were subjected.

This agreement marked a great step forward in the treatment of the most unfortunate of the prisoners of war. The first party of British soldiers, between three hundred and four hundred in number, arrived in Switzerland on May 11th, 1916, and were given the heartiest welcome by the Swiss authorities and people. The place to which they were going was Château d'Oex, and on the day before they reached it the chief magistrate of the place, to mark its pleasure in receiving them, gave instructions that its inhabitants were to wear gala attire. Flowers bedecked every house, and the streets were gay with flags and wreaths. It was high festival in Château d'Oex, and the feelings of the poor prisoners, many of whom had come from worse than Egyptian bondage, were profoundly affected; the men cried like children, and some swooned from sheer emotion. "It's like dropping right into heaven from hell," said one of them, addressing Mr. Grant Duff, the British Minister,

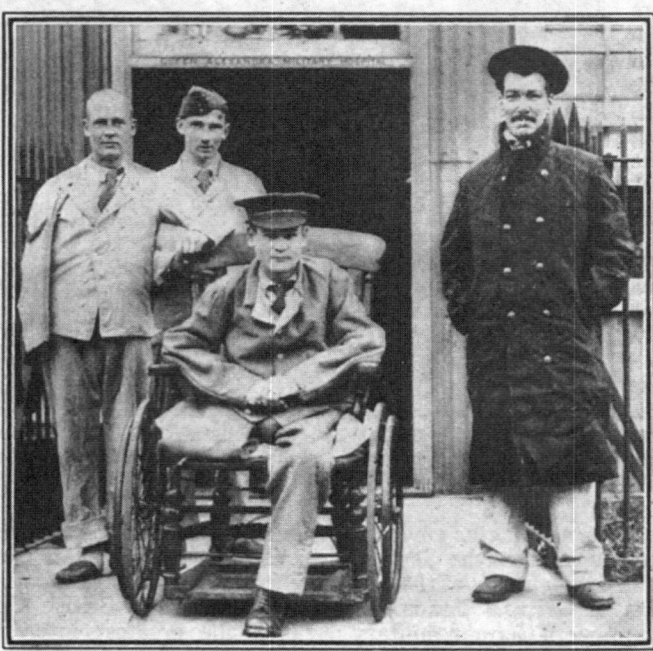

MEN WHO HAD SUFFERED IN GERMAN HANDS.
British prisoners of war repatriated from Germany who were able to give evidence as to the ill-treatment which was meted out in German prisoner of war camps.

who had been most active in furthering the arrangements for their comfort. Soon other parties followed the first, and all were most warmly greeted by the Swiss. The subjoined letter, written from Switzerland by a private in a Highland regiment to his wife, and published in the "Dunfermline Journal" on September 2nd, 1916, was typical of the attitude of the men interned :

Just a few lines to let you know that I have at last got clear of the pigs. I will know a difference after twenty months of torture. [He had been taken prisoner on November 11th, 1914.] I could never put anything in my letters or postcards—if we mentioned anything about our treatment or the quality of our food, our letters were immediately destroyed. You have no idea what we have suffered, but they will pay salt for it all after the thing is over. They have managed to knock me up a bit, but I will get over that now. I think the rough treatment we got at Gardelegen put the peter on me. I have never been the same since. What with getting the boot and butt-end of their rifles it was a time. They have killed a large number of our boys, shooting them for the least thing, and starvation has put a large number of our lads under. But I am clear of it all now, thank God! I will not be long in getting back my strength here.

By April, 1917, about fifteen hundred British prisoners had been transferred under the agreement from Germany to Switzerland, and an equal number of German prisoners from Great Britain to Switzerland. The men thus transferred were

REPATRIATED WOUNDED PRISONERS.
Two British soldiers who had been taken prisoner, and who on returning home gave evidence as to the treatment of prisoners of war in Germany.

selected by commissions composed of Swiss doctors, who went up and down the prison camps in the two belligerent countries, and after a strict examination issued certificates entitling the prisoners who had been given them to enjoy the friendly internment of the Swiss Government, which facilitated in every possible way the carrying out of everything for their benefit. The deliverance —for it was nothing less—of the British prisoners from the German camps was hailed with rejoicing in Great Britain, and many British journals sent representatives to describe the scenes taking place when the men arrived there, as well as to hear from their own lips particulars of their treatment at the hands of the Germans. Lord Northcliffe, who had gone to Switzerland to greet them, made a suggestion which bore good fruit. His idea was that it would be a great thing for them if arrangements could be made by which they might be enabled to be visited by their wives. It was an idea that appealed to the public generosity, and the funds were provided for its very successful realisation.

Through Mr. Gerard an agreement was arrived at by the British and German Governments by which permanently disabled men were repatriated, and the Dutch Red Cross co-operated most effectively in carrying it out. The repatriated soldiers had lost limbs or were otherwise incapable of ever appearing in the fighting-line again. Similarly, the severely wounded were exchanged between Germany and Russia, and in "My Four Years in Germany" Mr. Gerard said that he believed that this particular exchange was the factor which prevented the entrance of Sweden into the war. As the men traversed the whole length of Sweden in the railway, they presented such a spectacle to the Swedish population that the Swedes were effectually kept "from an attack of unnecessary war fever." Some of the repatriated British were so changed that their nearest and dearest were unable to recognise them.

In August, 1916, the British Government proposed to that of Germany the repatriation of civilian prisoners over forty-five years of age, and after some discussion on special points an agreement to that effect was come to in the following December, with a proviso that not more than twenty persons might be retained in either country for military reasons. The agreement determined that neither Government had the right to claim the repatriation of its nationals who did not wish to leave, and that British and German retired naval and military officers who were not in the receipt of pay, ships' officers, and merchant seamen should be regarded as ordinary civilians. Between six hundred and seven hundred British were affected as against about four thousand Germans; it was the sort of one-sided bargain that pleased Germany. The British Government had learned that Germany would not consent to an equal exchange, and from motives of humanity the former agreed to the setting free of all civilians over forty-five, the main consideration being the deplorable mental condition of many of the older men in the internment camps.

In the early part of 1917 there was in Great Britain an agitation, which was strong for a time, in favour of an exchange of civilian prisoners on the " all-for-all " basis. It was represented that of the four thousand in Ruhleben many, unless speedily released, would die, become insane, or be permanent invalids, and the British Government was urged to take action for their immediate exchange, even if that exchange should involve setting free all German civilians who were interned. But there were 26,000 civilian Germans interned in Great Britain, and to that number had to be added, according to the view of the German Government, about 11,000 more, who were interned in the rest of the British Empire, to make the suggestion acceptable. The thing was evidently disproportionate in the extreme; the British military authorities keenly opposed the idea, as giving an unfair advantage to Germany, and the matter dropped. In intimating the decision of the Government, Lord Newton said in the Lords that the exchange was a bad one for Great Britain. At the same time he announced that the exchanges which had been proceeding under the existing

Negotiations for exchange

agreements had been stopped, and that the situation, so far as German action was concerned, showed a relapse into barbarity. The real inwardness of this was manifest when, in June, Lord Newton stated that the Germans were more anxious to sink ships than facilitate the exchange of prisoners. A month or so previously Dr. Kriege, of the German Foreign Office, had said in the Reichstag that " naval reasons "—in plain terms, the submarine campaign—prevented exchanges. In the course of the same sitting he made, however, an important admission, though it was intended far more to allay German fears for their kin's welfare than for any other reason; this was that the treatment of prisoners of war was " better in England " than anywhere else.

Conference at The Hague

In March, 1918, there was a similar agitation, but it, too, resulted in nothing, and for exactly the same reason —viz., that the all-for-all proposal gave Germany far too much the best of the bargain.

Lord Newton, with the official position of Assistant Under-Secretary of State for Foreign Affairs (unpaid), was the head of the Prisoners of War Department of the Foreign Office, and he had worked hard and unweariedly on behalf of the British prisoners in Germany, both civilian and military. In 1917 he took a step which had great results. On his initiative a conference between representatives of the British and German Governments on prisoners of war was arranged to be held at The Hague by the Dutch Government, the Embassy of which at Berlin had taken the place of the American Embassy in looking after the interests of the British prisoners in Germany. The first meeting took place on June 24th, 1917. The British representatives were Lord Newton, Lieut.-

WELCOME HOME! ARRIVAL OF A VESSEL WITH PRISONERS OF WAR FROM GERMANY.
Scene at Boston, Lincolnshire, in February, 1918, on the arrival of a vessel with a number of repatriated officers and men who had been freed from German prison camps. The people who thronged the shore gave a hearty cheer of welcome to the men on board, who cordially responded—glad to be home at last after their terrible experiences. The Mayor of Boston gave them a public reception.

General Sir Herbert Belfield for the Foreign Office, and Sir Robert Younger, the chairman of the Government Committee on the Treatment by the Enemy of British Prisoners of War. Germany was represented by General Friedrich, whose position was somewhat analogous to that of Lord Newton, and by two other German officials. Dr. Baron van Vredenburch, nominated by the Dutch Government, presided, and acted as intermediary, neither the British nor the Germans holding direct speech with each other. After several days' debate an agreement was reached on July 2nd which rescinded previous agreements, but gave much greater prospects than any before.

To start with, this new agreement—which was presented to Parliament as a White Paper in July, 1917—declared that the Dutch Government was ready to intern in Holland, till the end of the war, a number of British and German combatant or civilian prisoners of war **Provisions of** not exceeding 16,000, of whom 6,500 were **the agreement** to be officers and non-commissioned officers and 2,000 invalid civilians, the remainder being sick and wounded combatants. Here was a novel and most promising feature. Among other things, the agreement provided that more lenient schedules of disabilities were to be drawn up, that very bad cases were to be sent home at once from Switzerland, that punishments for attempts to escape were to be reduced to fourteen days' military confinement, except in instances where property had been damaged, when the sentence was to be not more than two months, and that all reprisals against individuals were to be cancelled, all further reprisals not going into effect till after four weeks' notice to the Government of the nation affected. One of the most striking features of the agreement was that all officers and non-commissioned officers, irrespective of rank or number, and whether under punishment or not, so soon as they had been in captivity for at least eighteen months, were to be interned in Switzerland or other neutral country, unless they preferred to stay where they were.

In August, 1917, Lieut.-General Sir John Hanbury-Williams, who had been Military Attaché at Petrograd, went to The Hague to superintend, in co-operation with the Dutch authorities, the arrangements for the reception and accommodation in Holland of British prisoners of war from Germany under the agreement, but owing to obstacles put by Germany in carrying it out, it was not till well into November that British prisoners began to move out of the German prison camps in considerable numbers. On November 27th 94 officers and 331 men were sent from Germany into Switzerland; a still larger contingent followed a month later, the numbers being 75 military officers, 9 naval officers, and 554 men. The first contingent for internment in Holland, where it was cordially welcomed, did not arrive in that country until December 19th, and the first of the prisoners to be repatriated did not land in England—it was at Boston—till January **5,000 British** 6th, 1918. Up to the spring of 1918 **freed from Germany** many hundreds more prisoners had either been repatriated or interned in Holland and Switzerland. The agreement was working well, and Lord Newton was to be congratulated heartily on the success achieved. The total number from Germany of British released or interned in Switzerland and Holland since the outbreak of war was then about five thousand.

Direct Government action on behalf of British prisoners was reinforced in various ways. Reference has been made to " The Government Committee on the Treatment by the Enemy of British Prisoners of War " as responsible for the White Paper which disclosed to a horror-stricken world what had been the conditions in the Wittenberg Camp. That committee had been appointed by Sir John Simon in September, 1915, to collect, verify, and record information from those who had been prisoners in Germany and the other enemy countries. With Sir Robert Younger, a Justice of the High Court, as its head, the committee included representatives of the War, Foreign, and Home Offices, with Mrs. Darley Livingstone as its honorary secretary. The committee carefully examined every man who had returned home, and sifted all statements made, but only published some of them from time to time, when they were very effective in their revelations of German cruelty. Many people, however, thought that a much larger use might have been made of such statements for propaganda and other purposes ; but the view of the committee was that, as a general thing, the interests of the men who still were prisoners in Germany would not be furthered by such publicity.

In 1915 purely voluntary organisations did much for the relief of the necessities of prisoners through regimental and other committees, but there was a good deal of overlapping. A census of parcels passing through the Post Office was made in June and July, 1916, and it showed that while the quantity of food sent to prisoners in Germany was excessive, the distribution of such food among individual prisoners was very unequal, some receiving a superabundance—even up to sixteen parcels per fortnight—and others little or nothing. Accordingly, the War Office developed, in September, 1916, out of " The Prisoners of War Help Committee," a body which it had recognised in 1915, an organisation called " The Central Prisoners of War Committee," which was based on the Joint War Committee of the British Red Cross Society and the Order of St. John. The first chairman was Sir Starr Jameson, and he was supported by a strong committee. On the death of Sir Starr, in 1917, the Earl of Sandwich was appointed to the vacant place.

This committee undertook to send food and clothing in sufficient quantities to every British and Indian prisoner of war in Germany, Austria, Turkey, and Bulgaria. It abolished the sending of parcels, except to officers, by private persons or local **Central Committee's** associations, unless the parcels had a **excellent work** special label on them issued by itself. This action led to many protests, and the committee modified it to the extent of allowing people to despatch goods from well-known stores and shops. The committee arranged for supplying bread from Copenhagen for prisoners in Northern Germany, and from Berne for those in Southern Germany ; but the result, though generally good, was not always satisfactory. In 1917 a Joint Committee of Parliament was appointed to inquire into the methods of the Central Committee, and its investigations led to some improvements, but it also praised the organising capacity and the zeal manifested in what had grown to be an undertaking of great magnitude conducted most creditably and successfully. It also spoke well of the Regimental Care Committees and other authorised associations. In the beginning of 1918 the Central Committee was—directly through its packing department, or indirectly through Care Committees and authorised associations—responsible for seeing that three parcels of food and a sufficient quantity of bread went each fortnight to every British prisoner in Europe. In January of that year it began the publication of a monthly journal, " The British Prisoner of War," which gave much valuable information, such as the kind of parcels that could be sent to those interned in Holland and Switzerland, and how to send money to prisoners. The Central Committee was doing fine work, and doing it in a fine way.

By the end of 1917 Germany had lost every one of her colonial possessions, but before they had passed from her she had achieved in them, wherever possible, a record for inhumanity to prisoners, particularly British prisoners, which was on a par with that in Europe. In a White Paper, presented to Parliament in September, 1917, statements were published respecting the treatment by the Germans of British prisoners and natives in German East Africa, already touched upon in Chapter CLXVII. (Vol. 8, page 453). As had been the case in South-West

At the heart of desolation: Ypres in 1918, viewed from an altitude of 1,100 feet.

Australians in the crazy ways of Ypres: A typical scene in the mangled town.

Passing through a town near the battle-front: Troops on their way to "take over" in the line.

Soldiers at the doors of typical dug-outs beneath the ruined buildings of Ypres.

Going up: An observation balloon of the splendidly efficient Australian Flying Corps.

Australian soldiers marching past the ruined Cloth Hall of Ypres.

Australian machine-gunners posted beyond a French military cemetery repelling German infantry advancing on Villers=Bretonneux.

Africa, the British who were made prisoner by the Germans in East Africa were ill-fed, badly-housed, and habitually ill-used. Great pains were taken by their captors to humiliate them in the eyes of the natives. The Rev. Ernest Spanton, principal of St. Andrew's College, Zanzibar, said : " As a result of our treatment by the Germans, we were generally spoken of by the natives as slaves ; the Swahili word ' mateka,' which they used, is a particularly offensive one from an African point of view, and is never used by one African to another unless he wishes violently to insult him." Nothing, in fact, was left undone to degrade the British before the natives. A long sworn statement by Archdeacon Woodward, Vicar-General of the Diocese of Zanzibar and East Africa, gave numerous instances of the manner in which the Germans did this, many of them being so disgusting as to be quite unfit for general reading. In a word, the Germans in East Africa were true to type.

As 1918 opened there was an impression—what with the successful operation of the agreement come to at The Hague and reports of better conditions in the German prison camps—that the hard lot of British prisoners of war in Germany would show considerable improvement, and that the German Government would manifest less inhumanity than in the past. This idea was rudely shattered when it was announced that two British airmen, Lieut. E. L. Scholtz and Second-Lieutenant H. C. Wookey, who had been captured by the Germans, had been savagely sentenced to ten years' imprisonment in a German gaol for dropping propaganda leaflets in the German lines, though the Germans themselves had never hesitated to drop propaganda leaflets in the allied lines when they had a chance—a fact of which there was plenty of proof. The British Government acted promptly, and told the German authorities that unless **Effective threat of reprisals** these sentences were quashed, two German officers of high rank, who were prisoners in England, would, as a reprisal, be removed from their quarters and confined in an ordinary camp. This threat was sufficient, and the two airmen had their sentences cancelled. But the Germans had shown that there was no real change in them.

This was further demonstrated by statements made in May, 1918, to a correspondent with the American Army in France by a Frenchman, who had escaped from Hameln, in Hanover. This man said that he had talked with an American soldier sent to that camp after being so emaciated and weakened by excessive work in the Harz salt-mines that he could hardly cross a room without leaning on pieces of furniture and supporting himself on boxes piled there. In these mines, the American reported, Englishmen also suffered severely. Three out of nine, sent like himself to Hameln utterly worn out, died. The food they had had was practically starvation—a thin soup made from barley or cabbage, and sometimes eggs, salt cod, and other fish, but quite uneatable. There was little bread or potato, and no parcels from home ever reached them. The punishments included beating with a rifle-butt or the flat side of a bayonet, and confinement in a dark cell known to these nine prisoners as the " hot chamber " from its being heated with steam at a high temperature. After the men had been kept in this place of torture for some time they were turned out into the snow, where they had to stand to attention—also for some time. Deaths were frequent—and no wonder ! The Frenchman declared that he could confirm what the American said, because he had seen an Englishman at Hameln who had returned from these mines with not enough strength even to hold a cigarette.

In May, 1918, the question of the exchange of prisoners of war suddenly underwent a fresh and at the same time a most promising development. The Hague Agreement had done a good deal; but only for officers and non-commissioned officers ; it did nothing for the rank and file. Early in the month Lord Newton announced that

the British Government, in order to bring about an improvement in the conditions of British prisoners in Germany, and not for purposes of revenge, had adopted the policy of reprisals. This had all along been the policy of France ; she treated German prisoners in precisely the same way as Germany treated French prisoners, and she took care to let the enemy know it. The success of this policy could not but seem to be confirmed when, just about the very time Lord Newton made the above statement, the " Times " made public the fact that an agreement had been concluded between France and Germany for the internment in a neutral country of non-commissioned officers and *men* who had been prisoners for more than eighteen months. In commenting on the agreement this journal drew attention to letters which had appeared previously in its columns from British officers interned, under The Hague Agreement, in Holland, who **Franco–German** insisted on the contrast between their **Agreement** own release and the continued detention in Germany of their men, subjected in many cases to still almost inconceivably inhuman treatment, and these officers asked indignantly whether nothing was being done to help them.

Nearly a fortnight, however, passed before there was any British official reference to the Franco-German Agreement. On May 14th Lord Burnham, in the House of Lords, called attention to it, and contended that if something of the kind was not done for British prisoners the charge of official callousness as to their fate would be justified. In reply, Lord Newton stated, with the authority of Lord Milner (who shortly before had become Minister of War), that the Government was now prepared to reconsider the whole question of an exchange of prisoners. He admitted that the men had ground for complaint in being excluded from previous agreements between Great Britain and Germany, but protested this exclusion was not due to callousness on the part of the British Government, but to the fact that the German Government looked on the ordinary prisoner as nothing better than a beast of burden. He explained that the view of the War Office, the Admiralty, and the Cabinet hitherto had been that the more they exchanged prisoners the more they prolonged the war, but he acknowledged that the agreement between the French and the German Governments completely altered the situation, and intimated that the matter would now be gone into by the War Cabinet.

Lord Newton confessed that the agreement had come as a surprise to him, but next day he was able to give particulars, of which the most important were :

1. All non-commissioned officers and men were to be repatriated, head for head and grade for grade, if they had been in captivity for eighteen months.
2. Officers who had been in captivity for eighteen months were to be interned in Switzerland head for head regardless of rank.
3. Officers, N.C.O.'s, and men taken prisoners before November, 1916, and interned **330,000 men** in Switzerland on the grounds of ill-health, **involved** were, with certain exceptions, to be repatriated without regard to rank or number.
4. Invalids were to be repatriated, or interned in Switzerland under the Berne Agreement of March 15th, 1918.

Lord Newton said that the Franco-German Agreement involved in all about 330,000 men, including civilians. The Marquess of Salisbury, taking note of the figures, gave expression to what was obviously the general feeling by declaring that public opinion would be profoundly dissatisfied if French prisoners could be exchanged in large numbers and nothing corresponding could be done for British prisoners. Strong emphasis was added to this when, almost simultaneously, it became known that negotiations were taking place between Italy and Germany for an exchange of prisoners on a basis similar to that of the Franco-German Agreement.

Anzac Memorial Service, held on the Show Ground at Sydney, New South Wales, April 25th, 1917, Anzac Day. The Archbishop of Sydney conducted the service, and soldiers, sailors, and vast throngs of civilians gathered to honour the memory of those who had fallen in the cause of freedom.

Part of the military parade which was included in the 1917 celebration of Anzac Day (April 25th), in Sydney, New South Wales. The photograph shows a portion of Macquarie Street, with some of the soldiers who had returned from fields on which the word "Anzac" had been brought into being, to become generally accepted as a synonym for magnificent heroism and dogged endurance in a great cause.

HEROES WHO WERE NOT WITHOUT HONOUR IN THEIR OWN COUNTRY.

COMMISSARIAT CAMELS

CHAPTER CCXLII.

CROSSING THE DESERT.

THE ANZACS' GREAT RECORD DURING 1917.

By Keith A. Murdoch,

Special Correspondent of the " Sydney Sun " and the " Melbourne Herald."

Distinctive Types of the Australian and the New Zealand Soldier—Bitter Climatic Conditions on the Somme During the Winter of 1916-17 —The German Retreat Discovered—Australian Pursuit to Bapaume and the Hindenburg Line at Quéant and Bullecourt—First Attack at Bullecourt Unsuccessful—The Homeric Thirteen-Day Second Battle of Bullecourt Ends in Australian Triumph— Pleasant Interval of Rest in the Valley of the Ancre—Conscription Rejected by the Commonwealth—Australians Engaged in the Offensive at Messines under Sir Herbert Plumer—Astonishing Labours and Heroism of the Australian Tunnellers—The Australian Flag Planted on Hill 60—Australia's General War Contribution—All the Anzacs Gathered Together for the Attack on the Flanders Ridges in September, 1917—The Battles of the Menin Road, Polygon Ridge, and Broodseinde—Australian Front Line Withdrawn after the Splendid Failure at Bellevue Spur and Passchendaele—Generous Co-operation with the Canadians—German Moral Shaken by the Superiority of the Anzacs—General Birdwood—Some Other Distinguished Commanders of the Australian Troops— Distinctive National Organisation of the Anzacs—Australian Troops in Great Britain.

THE individual story of the Australian and New Zealand forces in Gallipoli and the Battle of the Somme, which sent tales of the Anzacs' prowess ringing round the world, has been intimately described in this history (Chapter CXXXVIII., Vol. 7, page 348). Their deeds during 1917 continued to be as distinctive and as impressive. While their Light Horse divisions, famous as the most mobile and dashing mounted troops produced by the war, played a leading rôle in the desert and Palestine offensives of Generals Murray and Allenby, their infantry and artillery were to be found where fighting was thickest in France and Flanders. Sir Douglas Haig set great value on these troops, and their special qualities in attack were feared and written about among the Germans. Though they fought through many a battle, and their thoughts of home became more and more distant memories, the Anzacs never lost their verve and fire in attack, their moral and muscular endurance and capacity in trench-holding and defence, their confidence in complete victory over their enemies.

The original landing brigades at Anzac had been a picked band of twenty thousand sternly-trained young athletes. Now

HONOURS FOR AUSTRALIAN CADETS.
Major-General the Hon. Sir James M'Cay, K.C.M.G., C.B., V.D., general officer commanding the Australian Imperial Forces in Great Britain, presenting decoration to one of the Australian cadets qualifying for commissions at Cambridge.

the forces were different. They were still extraordinarily young in appearance, yet they seemed to have become hard, war-bitten, veteran soldiers. Two hundred thousand mothers were now wondering what their boys, so long away, were like—330,000 men had been enlisted in Australia, and nearly 100,000 in New Zealand. The forces had become an appreciable part of the Empire's armies, but they maintained in every way their distinctive organisations. They were Australia's effort, New Zealand's effort, in a cause vowed as sacredly by the peoples of these outer Dominions as by those older British peoples living at the threatened heart of the Empire; the very distance over which they travelled at the call of the race proved their ardour, and the interest with which their friends at home followed their doings was never less than a deep national faith in them.

Australian soldiers called the Canadian, for whom and the Scottish troops they had an ardent liking, " the Tommy who had a chance in life." The phrase has a good deal of truth, and it applied equally well to " Billjim " from " down under." He was the Englishman, Scot, or Irishman who had grown up under extraordinarily generous conditions. He had come from a country where food, warmth, and clothing were liberal, where a free, secular, and compulsory education opened the mind and heart, where rigorous military training was enforced, working hours were regulated by the State, and healthy sport was a general interest. He had lived much in the open air, under a friendly sky which permitted man and beast to sleep at night in the fields. He was a child of the bush, which demanded labour and resourcefulness in return for its manifold joys ; or a child of a garden city,

UNDERGOING SEARCH BEFORE INCARCERATION.
German prisoners being searched by their Australian captors on the western front. In circle : Disclosure of the contents of the prisoners' capacious pockets was watched with interest tinctured with amusement.

where every street was wide and sun-swept, and every suburb had its playing-fields. The Australian and New Zealand soldier had been, pre-eminently amongst those who fought in Europe, the darling of Nature ; she had showered her gifts upon him, and the result was height and strength, physical endurance, and magnificent tone. It was sometimes urged against him that, so free was he in his mind and bearing, he would own no man as master. But there were a thousand stories—stories of sunken transports, of charges into death, of stern fighting in surrounded positions which proved the truthfulness of Australasian discipline.

Each Dominion produced a distinct type. The same British qualities shone out in action. But in appearance and in leading characteristics the types were always recognisable. The Australian's height maintained a

Dominion troops' distinct types. higher average than any other Army ; he was a tall, lanky, loose-knit, but wiry man, the limbs swung freely, with the easy grace of a natural athlete ; the shoulders sloped, the arms were strong and long ; the face strikingly frank, open, and confident. The New Zealander was more stockily built, more staid in character ; the Canadian buoyant, wide-awake, and optimistic, with a never-failing sense of humour. They all fought with the same generosity which characterised their homelands, spending their blood on the fields of France and Flanders on the same scale of liberality as that on which they lived.

The conditions in which the Australians fought during the winter of 1916-17 were as bitter as these warm-blooded men from Southern sunshine could imagine. Few had seen snow before it fell about them on the bleak

plains of the Somme country or in the open trenches before Messines and Wytschaete. They knew about tropical heat, variable winds, even tornadoes and typhoons ; they had been in Gallipoli through tempests which washed dead Turks into their flooded trenches and chilled them to the bone. But this frigid European winter was a new experience added to all the hardships and hazards of battle and the sorrows of exile. It is difficult for the people of Great Britain, inured to their climate, and accustomed to see their soldiers amongst them regularly on leave, to picture the burden placed upon Anzac during these months.

It was the place of honour in the British line—the centre of the Somme battlefield. And here the full fury of the winter was gathered. What trenches existed were immature. Roads were broken, railways were few and scattered. Artillery was concentrated on each side in **Winter on the Somme** great array, and the aftermath of the Battle of the Somme was seen daily in heavy firing upon saps and lines of communication. The battlefield was a sea of mud. Wind and rain lashed it into a thin and fumy slush. It was nothing for horses to disappear into shell-holes, nothing for wounded men to be smothered in mud. "We lost a gun to-day," wrote an Australian general at the time ; "it

disappeared into the ground, and I have a boy standing at the place to mark it." Another Australian general, brigadier of the 12th Brigade, was mortally wounded in the front line, and though the saps were cleared for his removal, it required thirteen hours to have him carried to the rear.

The four Australian divisions of General Birdwood's corps had been brought back to the Somme from Ypres early in November. The world was still ringing with the hammer-strokes of the great battle ; the armies of Prince Rupprecht were reeling under them. They had perhaps reached their highest intensity during the previous visit of the Anzacs to this region, when on the rolling ground about Pozières and Mouquet Farm all the weight, strength, and force of both sides had contested every advance with the bitterness of great determination. The Australians were never men to be satisfied with easy fighting, and though winter was now clogging the offensive, they maintained aggressive tactics through all their stay in the south, varying mere aggressive trench and outpost warfare with assaults on German positions on a big scale.

Their resource and initiative, those qualities which had made a fortress of their slender hold on the cliffs of Gallipoli, were brought to bear on the problems of winter. General Gough had all sections of his Fifth Army at work on consolidation, and large and small gauge railways, saps, roadways, hutments, and supply organisations began to appear in all directions. The Australians formed from their labour companies and infantry a light-railway corps, which "found" substitutes for ballast, sleepers, and even locomotives, and laid tracks across and through the shell-holes. A good trench system was dug, provided with dug-outs, and revetted; the communication trenches were extended for miles. The science of shell-hole defences was studied and applied. Throughout the winter the line was held thinly, but in great depth, and the outermost defenders were the garrisons of small shell-hole outposts, sometimes deep into No Man's Land. There were frequent encounters. The German line was steadily pushed back. Now it would be a German strong point stormed by Australian bombers at Flers, the next time an advance of a few hundred yards at Warlencourt or Flers.

High rate of sickness

These long winter months on the Somme were as severe a tax upon the Australian Corps as any great offensive. What could be done for the men's comfort was done. Alone amongst the British armies they received double issues of blankets. "Tommy cookers," the delight of all dug-outs, were provided in such quantities as could be obtained. The men had wonderful supplies of socks, knitted by their patriotic womenfolk in Australia; and they were trained in methods of protection against trench-feet by the use of whale-oil and constant care of boots and socks. Despite this, the rate of sickness was high. The difficulties of the area accounted for many casualties,

but casualties were far outnumbered by cases of sickness, which had a high percentage of serious illnesses.

Gradually, as the frost came, the troubles of this battle-racked district began to disappear. When the Australians arrived, every particle of supplies, every cartridge, every duck-board, every sheet of iron had to be carried seven miles by hand. But by the close of the winter light railways transported not only shells and rations, but troops. A deep system of defences had been organised, living conditions had become dry and sanitary, and though the combination of severe cold and wet was still a source of illness, the health of the troops had recovered from an ordeal which had cost more than all the dysentery of Gallipoli, and was never again to be faced.

Ready for new effort

A steady stream of reinforcements had been flowing through the Australian camps in England to the stricken field of the Somme, and when the earliest days of spring broke upon General Birdwood's corps, it was, though tired and worn, still capable of the great tasks thrust upon it. These tasks were the following up, harassing, breaking, and hastening of the German forces throughout

AUSTRALIAN TROOPS MARCHING THROUGH ALBERT.

Soldiers from the sunny island continent of the South passing the battered church of Albert in wintry conditions, and (inset above) an Anzac transport waggon passing over a snowy road. The conditions in which the Australians fought during the winter of 1916-17 were as bitter as these warm-blooded men from Southern sunshine could imagine. Few of them had ever seen snow before it fell about them on the western front.

the great retreat to the Hindenburg line, described in Chapter CLXXXII. (Vol. 9, page 285).

The commencement of this retreat was discovered by a young Australian officer who, during an early morning patrol, explored a German line and found that the enemy had decamped. Together with the evacuation of Gallipoli, this retreat will rank as one of the great surprises of the war. For the Australians a period of widely-extended village and open fighting followed, and commanders and men were given unique opportunity for their qualities of initiative and manœuvre. The Australian sector was the rolling country, thickly studded with villages, to the south of the Albert-Bapaume road, beginning with the gloomy and ill-omened Butte de Warlencourt and ending five miles to the south in the village of Gueudecourt. Pushing forward across this area, the corps kept constantly in touch with the German rearguards, finding some villages empty and others strongly defended. It drove the Germans from many defended positions, and so hurried the retreat that the enemy was frequently compelled to counter-attack, and failed **Anzacs harry** even to complete some of the lines of **the German retreat** halt he had marked out in series of half-dug trenches.

By March 16th the Australians had arrived on the edge of Bapaume, and it and the villages near it fell next day without much fighting. The Germans had devastated the country in much the same way as the Russians had despoiled their land before Napoleon. Buildings of every description had been blown up, fruit trees were demolished, delay-action mines had been placed in cellars and beneath roadways. Brand-stick and powder had been freely applied. One of the first to take effect was that under the old Town Hall of Bapaume, which with its fine tower, a relic of 1610, was destroyed with all its inmates. Happily few men were quartered in the building, but two French deputies had taken up their abode there for the night. From prisoners the Australians learnt that the Germans had counted upon a divisional headquarters being established in the cellars, but happily the many dug-outs and cellars wrecked along the line of retreat in this way brought few casualties. The Australians soon learnt to avoid the traps. The German ingenuity had been exercised to its fullest in their manufacture, and even pencils left lying about were filled with explosives, so that soldiers who

sharpened them would lose their hands. Such clumsy tricks profited them little. Even their mines in roadways were badly planned, and the Australians, now moving across unbroken country and along roads little affected by the war, kept constantly driving the enemy before them.

The retreat ended, at the end of March, by the Germans dodging, like scared and chastened rabbits, into the deep trenches of the broad Hindenburg line hinging upon Quéant and Bullecourt. But before they nestled into its snug security they had been compelled to accept action a dozen times, and each had been costly. A typical fight was that at the village of Beaumetz, which the 15th Brigade (Victorian), by a converging attack, stormed far in advance of the German time-table. Here the Germans counter-attacked, as though the commander feared reproof. He sacrificed his men without avail. On March 26th the 7th Brigade, comprising battalions from junior States of the Commonwealth, found the storming of Lagnicourt an arduous problem, compensated for by the killing of four hundred Germans; and the capture of Noreuil on April 2nd by the 13th Brigade, and Doignies by the 14th, brought the Australians up against the Hindenburg line.

ANZACS AT M.G. DRILL.
Lewis machine-gun battery of an Australian division at drill with their weapons behind the lines on the western front.

Visitors to this desolated Somme country found among the chief interests of that fascinating and moving scene the strong defensive positions, thick with concrete shelters and wire entanglements, which day by day the Germans abandoned before the Australian pursuit. Their railways lay twisted and ruined through the country. Their successive lines of trenches and strong points showed months of labour. Yet their devastations and destructions were as thorough as their previous defensive work. The country was laid bare. Every house was a mere ruin. Even their soldiers' graveyards had been gone over, and names cut out from the wooden crosses, lest

BATHING PARADE AT A REST CAMP.
Soldiers of one of the Anzac divisions on the western front marching to a bathing-place on a small river near their rest camp well behind the lines.

the pursuers should identify the units which had fought there.

The fighting now passed into the two fierce battles of Bullecourt, in which once again the Australian soldier's dash and endurance won even the grudging praise of his enemies. General Allenby's Third Army had been swinging down from the north-west, in a series of successful drives from the Scarpe to Chérisy; and in conformity with Sir Douglas Haig's general strategic plans, based largely upon the coming offensive of the French under General Nivelle, the Australian divisions got ready to sunder the Hindenburg line.

Here, between Bullecourt and Quéant, it was deeply implanted in a hillside rising behind to the farming village of Riencourt;

BOUND FOR THE FIRING-LINE.
Squad of Anzacs marching forward to take their places in the front trenches. In France, as in Gallipoli, where they had won their immortal nickname, these men of Britain's daughter States fought magnificently.

READY TO GO ANYWHERE.
Australian machine-gun, with its supply of ammunition, etc., neatly arranged for rapid transport on a pack-horse. The men from "down under" proved themselves masters of resource and initiative.

the well-grassed lands, studded here and there with trees, were not unlike the Australians' own rolling country, as yet untouched by shell fire; the early days of spring were bringing back to these young soldiers the colours of home, and they looked from their positions on either side of Quéant over wide and apparently peaceful scenes into which might have fitted the pastoral and farming tasks about their own settlements.

Their first attack was made on April 11th. A blizzard had blotted out their vision. The air was bitterly cold, with snow and fierce wind. The attack had been timed for the previous day, but the dozen Tanks, on which the whole assault was to hinge, had lost their way, and the men had to be brought back at the last moment from their starting lines to wait until next morning. When the 4th and part of the 12th Brigades went over at dawn against the Hindenburg line, the Tanks failed in their objects, and proved actually a handicap, for artillery could not be used as protective barrages owing to the impossibility of knowing where the Tanks were. The

men did more than any chief could have asked. They knew the wire belts of the German lines were uncut, so they took over mats on their backs, and these they laid upon the barbs. Both lines of trenches were broken through along the whole front of attack—the redoubtable Hindenburg line was sundered. But the failure of the Tanks meant that the Fifth Corps, on the left, which was to have taken Bullecourt and linked up with the Australians, could not storm the bastion. The Australians were attacked frontally and from each side. Enfiladed, they worked their machine-guns from left rear right round their front to right rear. They fought heroically, meeting attacks with the bayonet, and even leaping from their trenches to meet the shock of the assaulters. Their supply of bombs gave out. Nothing could be brought to them over the bullet-swept zone between them and their original line.

At last they were ordered back. Officers waited to show their men the way through the German wire. A most gallant officer, Major Percy Black, V.C., D.S.O., directed his men at the gaps, and was shot dead as he himself moved through the wire.

The greater Battle of Bullecourt **Homeric Battle** came within a few days. On May 3rd, **of Bullecourt** in conjunction with British forces extending over a front of sixteen miles to the north, the Australian Corps again assailed the Hindenburg line, again broke it, and again found themselves with both flanks fully exposed and masses of Germans concentrated against them. The storming troops on this occasion were the Victorians of the 6th Brigade and the New South Wales men of the 5th. The battle brought a glory to Australian arms no less than that which embellished them at Gallipoli and at Pozières; men counted their lives as nothing compared with the objectives their commanders had set them; valour and self-sacrifice could have had no more moving expression.

The attack was launched at dawn. Behind a barrage deeper and more intense than anything they had seen in the Battle of the Somme these brave soldiers from Australian desks, Australian workshops, Australian farms and pastoral stations—men who had never thought of war until Great Britain called for their assistance—leapt with a cheer into Hindenburg's line. For days the

WAGGON LINES OF AN AUSTRALIAN FIELD-BATTERY IN A FRENCH WOOD.

It was claimed by Australia that her troops were the best equipped Army ever put into the field. At her own expense she provided everything for its service, meeting not only the cost of every unit, but even that of the shells fired over the heads of her troops by British artillery attached to her corps.

heavy guns had been pounding the wire. It was cut to shreds. The Australians passed through it as though it had ceased to exist. And though the German barrage, registered accurately upon the trench line, found them at once, no losses could daunt their spirit. Within sixty minutes of the zero hour they had gripped both trenches of the line. A third wave passed on, as arranged, towards Riencourt on the hill. It went over a sunken tramway line and reached a hedged road. There it was like a leaf that had fluttered from a rose. For neither on its left side nor on its right did the supports arrive. The wave wilted. The British barrage was moved back behind it, for the ill-fortune of other sectors of the attack called for a defensive line of shells at places better suited for a stand. These men were the high-water mark of the tide of the Battles of Arras. Few got back.

Such desperate fighting had seldom been seen as that in the Hindenburg line and around Bullecourt. By all the rules of war the Australians' narrow hold on the German works was untenable. They held an insecure perch of some four hundred yards in a trench **Deadly hand-to-hand** system which the enemy prized beyond **fighting** the cost of divisions. But they held on. Brigades were moved up a narrow sap bravely dug by the engineers during the first hours of the attack—a sap so heavily fired upon that lines of dead were on either side. From each flank of the Australian position parties moved down the trenches in the most deadly of all hand-to-hand fighting—bombing. Great supplies of bombs had been gathered in accessible positions, and the men steadily fought their way down through the Germans, beating them by sheer superiority, until the gains had been increased to a solid 1,200 yards. That night furious counter-attacks were made. At one moment the outlook seemed hopeless. Storm troops of the 3rd

Prussian Guard, with waves of men bearing flame-throwers, debouched from Bullecourt and Quéant, after fierce artillery preparations. The Australians were attacked from either flank; they were enfiladed, fired on from the rear, and heavily pressed in front. The right side gave way. The Germans even reached the sap, which alone connected the new positions with the old line and the sources of supply. Back in the old line, every man was posted to a defensive position, and the brigadier seized a rifle. But the 6th Brigade, though now a remnant, held. As so often happens at such times, the word to retire was passed round. The heroic men flung it back. "Who said 'retire'?" they asked. "What officer of ours gave that order?" The night was one of ceaseless fighting, but dawn saw the Australians still there. During the day the 1st Australian Division recovered by another prolonged and bloody bout of bombing all the trench works lost during the night.

"Who said 'retire'?"

The fighting at Bullecourt raged for thirteen days, and was constantly an Homeric conflict. General Gough brought up the 7th Division to storm Bullecourt itself, and a series of night attacks at last cleared this bastion. During all that time the Australians were under the enemy's concentrated artillery fire, clearly marked as a target in the two trenches of the Hindenburg line; they were the aim of fifteen counter-attacks, some delivered after new methods, such as that of waves of men diving forward from shell-hole to shell-hole like a school of seals; they were called on for advances against the south-eastern strong points of the village. A great day was that on which the gallant Gordons, storming forward through the shattered houses of Bullecourt, linked up with the Anzacs, who bombed down the trenches to meet them, thus establishing at last a continuous line.

320

In the final attack upon Bullecourt men of the 5th Australian Division, following a hail of trench-mortars and Stokes bombs, rushed the German strong points on the eastern side, and the British line was thrown round the village.

For most of the Australian force many weeks of rest followed the final assault upon Bullecourt. These were sunny, happy days. The divisions were grouped in pleasant billets within reach of French cities. Training was maintained and large-scale manœuvres were practised. The opportunity was taken to send a large percentage of officers and men through special courses of instruction. The Anzac Corps School, which had been founded in a few hutments on the banks of the Ancre, grew to the size of a township. In the chalky valley, amid woods which rang with the axeman's strokes, it reminded its homesick occupants of a mining camp at home. A steady flow of reinforcements was coming across the seas from the Australian preliminary training camps, and these brought the divisions up to full strength. These days were among the most pleasant spent by the Anzacs during their wanderings. They found the sympathetic French life entertaining, they found sport in the fields, on the rivers, in the canals ; they found time to study and read, and, above all, to deal with those masses of correspondence which kept so tight the ties between Australia and her **Pleasant days in billets** soldiers. The Australians were famed as letter-writers, and "mail day" was as great an event in the Army as it was in the distant bush settlements, where the folks at home waited anxiously for the ever-fresh written signs of affection.

At home the question of reinforcing the Army was arousing feverish controversy. Mr. Hughes' great effort to secure conscription at the end of 1916 had failed. Since then recruiting had been sufficient to maintain the forces in the field. Out of a total population of five millions, about 450,000 men had offered their services at the recruiting offices, and some 330,000 had been found medically fit. Nevertheless, the conscience of the community was uneasy, and the movement for conscription became insistent. New Zealand had early in 1916 adopted by Act of Parliament a measure of conscription, providing for the reinforcement of her existing brigades by compulsory draft, chosen by ballot. Mr. Hughes gradually carried the country forward to another conscription referendum. His Ministry had been returned by an overwhelming majority at the elections in May, 1917, and the prospects of securing an affirmative vote seemed good. After a whirlwind campaign, in which both sides professed their thorough loyalty to the Empire's war aims, and the anti-conscriptionists claimed that they were differing from Mr. Hughes merely on a question of procedure, the electors again rejected **Australia again** compulsory service. The arguments— **rejects conscription** that Australia's vast work in supplying the Allies with food, wool, and metals, and that her own defensive interests could not be reconciled with a more searching form of reinforcement—won the country.

The echoes of Bullecourt had not died when the Second Anzac Corps became engaged as part of Sir Herbert Plumer's Second Army in the great offensive of Messines. The corps had been stationed here throughout the winter, and their strong, aggressive tactics had made the period little less trying and wearying than that of their countrymen on the Somme. Though the work was mainly preparatory, and though the 3rd Australian Division had arrived only in November from their training depots on Salisbury Plain, the corps maintained a hot pace in raiding, sniping, and artillery shoots. In particular, a great raid was made by the 10th Brigade of Victorians, when nearly a full battalion went "over the top," eight hundred Germans were killed, and many prisoners taken. The area from slightly north of Messines to the River Douve, close to the manufacturing city of Armentières, was subjected to the closest study, and experimental shooting or infantry work against all the German posts was carried through, so that their strength could be ascertained and the offensive planned accordingly. Much of the success was due to this thoroughly scientific planning of the barrages and the infantry advances.

KING GEORGE VISITING HIS NEW ZEALAND TROOPS IN FRANCE.
At the end of March, 1918, King George visited many of his armies along the French front who had been sternly engaged in staying the great German offensive. During two crowded and inspiring days his Majesty travelled over three hundred miles by motor-car among his troops, and in the photograph is seen on a visit which he paid to some of the New Zealand forces in the fighting area.

Meanwhile, great mines had been made by British, Canadian, and Australian mining companies. The battle was the prelude to the greater offensives designed for the Ypres front later on, for it was necessary to clear the Messines Ridge before the ridges alongside it could be attacked. From this ridge the Germans had dominated the Ypres salient for nearly three years ; they had been able to look down into the streets of the city and mark the movements of every living thing. How easily, therefore, could they with enfilading fire and flank counter-attack hold up and bring to naught the heavy offensive which Sir Douglas Haig intended to make the greatest British stroke of the year. The left of the Messines battle-front actually touched that from which the Ypres assaults were launched later. It was here that an Australian mining company blew up Hill 60 and a neighbouring height called the Caterpillar. The achievement was that of a moment ; but it required eight laborious months of pre-paration. Galleries had been laid by the Canadians. The Anzacs' part was to complete and defend them. And defence meant a deep network of tunnels and mines,

AT A ROYAL INSPECTION.
Troops from Australia in training in England marching on to the parade ground at an inspection by King George.

CADETS FROM "DOWN UNDER" AT CAMBRIDGE.
Australian cadets in training at Cambridge being inspected by Major-General the Hon. Sir James W. M'Cay, K.C.M.G., C.B., V.D., who was accompanied by the Right Hon. Andrew Fisher, High Commissioner for Australia. Sir James M'Cay commanded the 2nd Australian Infantry Brigade at Gallipoli.

driven under perilous conditions. In this counter-mining and camouflage mining the Germans were as active as the British. They knew that somewhere in the neighbourhood great mines were being made. They drove in this way and that, and it was the Australian mining company's duty to lead them off the track, trap them, and "blow" them before they could damage the vital works.

The long struggle beneath the ground had its aspects as hard and dangerous as anything on the earth or in the air. It had its surprises, its sudden gusts of explosion, its disappearance of men. There were ninety-eight "blows" before the final explosion that shattered whole companies of Germans and strong defensive positions. Many of these were German mines that threatened the system. Scores of thousands of pounds of ammonal were lying ready in the mine chambers for the offensive ; at any time the Germans might have discovered them and rendered the system harmless. A few days before the great day they did indeed destroy a gallery, and record digging was required to restore it. The Australians had a reputation

on both sides of the line as quick diggers, and in making one defensive tunnel, six feet by three feet, they averaged twenty-nine feet a day for seven days.

All such work had a special tincture of heroism. It was laborious warfare in the bowels of the earth, in vitiated atmosphere, in darkness, under conditions that restricted movement and made noiselessness imperative. The tunnellers secured electric power from their comrades the Australian Electric Company, who installed fans and pumps. But in the main there could be no relief from strain of war-mining on the western front. Such mines would be closed in Great Britain or Australia by the inspectors of mines, and the directors would be rebuked. War conditions necessitated absence of ventilation, muffling of sound, and removal of all spoil at night. Yet above the general high level of soldierly work shining deeds arose. Donning life-saving appa-ratus when gas was bad, men went down into the worst places to rescue or to encourage. The listeners, stationed for lonely vigils where even whispering was not allowed, lived under intense strain, interpreting the sounds into the picking, trucking, timber-ing, or tamping of neighbouring Germans. Their listening instru-ments were not unlike the tin cans and medical stethoscopes improvised by the Anzacs at Gallipoli. There were cases of Australians meeting Germans underground, with spades or picks as weapons. A typical case of gallantry was that of Sapper T. Earl, of New South Wales, who **Australian miner's** was buried by a German explosion at **great gallantry** the end of an Australian gallery. The Germans were within six feet of him, and he could have saved his life by letting them know. But such a craven course was not for an Australian miner. Though wounded, he dragged himself into the best position for listening, and here he lay for forty hours, with little hope of rescue, but with grim determination to leave by him a clear story of what the Germans were doing. When his mates reached him they found a complete record of what he had heard, with the time of each sound. He himself was exhausted and died.

Among the first to climb the parapets on June 7th were volunteers from the tunnellers. Many had begged permission to "go over" with the infantry. The scheme provided that eight should accompany one of the late waves, to prepare and repair dug-outs for battalion headquarters. Yet somehow thirty-one Australian tunnellers found themselves in the first wave, and first on Hill 60, and they put a flag up there—an Australian flag—and claimed this work as theirs. In particular, a young Victorian miner played an heroic part. He dug three British soldiers out of a collapsed trench in full view of the enemy, standing on the parapet, with bullets whistling past him. Twice the spade was shot from his hand; twice he was wounded. A less conspicuous but equally noble deed was that of a tunnelling sergeant, who controlled the carriers, standing in an exposed position for three nights, with the certainty that sooner or later he would be shot. He was killed on the third night, and his successor was shot on the night succeeding.

So well had these secrets been kept, that Australians waiting for the advance on their assembly points wondered, when the terrific explosions rent the ground before them, and the air for miles around them, whether their last hour had

"BY NEBO'S LONELY MOUNTAIN."
Australians having a brush with the enemy when proceeding to the capture of Neby Musa, the Nebo of the Bible, on the way to Jericho. On Neby Musa, a lonely height west of the Jordan, is a rude mosque reverenced by the Mussulman world as the tomb of Moses.

come. They were, however, soon following a great barrage well into the enemy territory. The opposition at first was patchy. The barrage had driven the first lines of Germans out of the first trenches, or killed them. The Australians and New Zealanders found nothing but dead and evidence of flight. Bits of food lay in shell-holes and dug-outs, with kit and bombs. One man had taken off his socks and trousers there, and left them. A bit farther back lines had rallied, and machine-guns began their pit-a-patter. The swift whip and crack of bullets past the ears began to be noticed. But the Germans had little stomach for the fight. Many had cowered low in their line of shell-holes, and when the hail of shrapnel passed over them and our men advanced quickly with the bayonet they put their hands above their heads with "Mercy, Kamerad!" or they ran. There were lines of trenches behind hedges, and several farms converted into concrete redoubts caused considerable trouble. The determined Anzacs stalked the points they were unable to rush, and the New Zealanders were in and beyond Messines, and the 3rd Australians up to their objectives to the south, in accordance with time-table.

Anzacs on the Messines Ridge

Mr. C. E. W. Bean, the official Press representative on the Australian front, wrote of an incident typical of the day:

It became realised that the Germans must be holding some sort of a position behind the hedge bank. One or two men bolted from a trench in front, several fell as they ran, but several made for the hedge and ducked behind it. A machine-gun chattered at an angle. But practically an endless line of determined men, swarming up the hill with lines upon lines to follow after it, is almost a hopeless thing to stop. While the German was shooting at one another was working round him. Moreover, the shooting of these particular Australians was very good indeed, their training had been a long and complete one, and it told in this fight. For German after German was found lying there afterwards with clean bullet wounds through head or chest.

A Victorian officer, looking carefully, saw the pull of dust from that machine-gun. The Germans build in almost all their trenches very solid steel and concrete shelters for the crews of their machine-guns. Many of these had been smashed by heavy shells, but here and there one held good. One of them could be seen behind a row of big trees a little behind the hedge. The whole thing was carefully screened with green and brown network to look like dead leaves. In the block-house itself nothing could be seen. But behind a certain tell-tale tree in that row there appeared always a wisp of dust.

The officer with several men crept through the hedge, from shell-hole to shell-hole. The Germans had their hands full with

CARRYING ON AT YPRES.
Australian soldiers gathered at the old barracks at Ypres; the building had been reduced to an empty shell, but the men accepted its cover with the philosophy of old campaigners.

GENERAL BIRDWOOD RETURNING TO HIS HEADQUARTERS ON THE WESTERN FRONT.

In this striking drawing by Major William Orpen, A.R.A., one of the official artists with the British armies in France, is indicated the desolation in which headquarters were frequently established near the fighting-front.

General Sir William Birdwood was the trusted and capable leader of the Australian force, having been appointed commander of the 1st Anzac Division before native Australian generals had acquired experience.

the crowd already overlapping, and this party slipped past. It worked round the side of the little grey block-house, and the gunners must have heard or seen it. By the time they were in the rear of the place they saw eight or ten of its crew bolting towards one of the farm hedgerows. The Australians seized the gun, turned it round, and fired part of the unfinished belt at the running men. Then they turned it round and blazed into the backs of the Germans who were still holding out in some shell-holes behind the hedge from which the stand had first been made.

Masses of artillery had been concentrated by the Germans in expectation of the offensive, and the Australian positions were soon under a deluge of shells, little less deadly than those singing above their heads towards the enemy. During the approach march before dawn the advancing battalions had been under a heavy fire of gas-shells, and the men had been compelled to stumble along in their gas-masks. The earliest heroism of the day was that of young officers who went along these gas-laden roads without their masks, so that they could guide their men and have them ready at the appointed moment. The big barrage with heavy guns came as a result of the observations of two enemy aeroplanes, which spied out and signalled by flares the Australians' new lines.

A fine strategical stroke was launched during the after-noon. The 4th Australian Division had been brought, unknown to the Germans, from the **4th Australian** Bullecourt zone. It passed through the **Division's advance** New Zealanders and British troops in front of Wytschaete, and made about mid-afternoon, under cover of its own artillery, a further great attack on the German positions, driving all before it for another two miles. Tanks were used with good effect, and when they could be of no more assistance above ground, the Tank crews took their machine-guns into the trenches beside the Australians, and fought there for the next three

days. By midnight the Australians were holding half the new battle-front. The Germans attempted several counter-attacks, but only one could be formed up suffi-ciently for an advance across the open, and it melted under machine-gun and artillery fire. There were frequent prolonged bursts of hurricane bombardment upon the British lines, and throughout the next thirty-six days during which the Australians held their line the artillery fire from each side was consistently heavy. But the Germans could not succeed in counter-attacking, and the battle was closed **Victory after** with the honours undivided, the 9th **thirty-six days** Brigade of New South Wales men making a clean advance on July 31st as the flank movement of the great opening attack in the Battle of the Ridges.

A word should be said here of Australia's general war contributions. She ever aimed at a complete Army. She wished her national effort to be thorough, and she looked forward to the day when her experienced sons should return as guardians and as teachers of the future guardians of their Southern homes. She had placed her Navy, headed by its Dreadnought, as a complete unit at the Admiralty's disposal on the first day of war, and it did its part in all the seven seas. She added unit after unit to her Army, improvising, borrowing instructors, buying material, until she had many squadrons of aero-planes—fighting scouts as well as artillery observers—batteries of heavy guns, mining companies, and railway operating companies. She had her own troupes of enter-tainers, such as the "Anzac Coves," who cheered many hundreds of men nightly in the improvised theatres, and went into the back areas, suffering losses like other units.

The Australian Flying Corps, which at once established a high reputation for dash and efficiency, was recruited mostly from the ranks of the A.I.F. It had its own training establishments in Australia and England, and soon grew to five full squadrons. One young airman who, after daring reconnoitring at a low height on the opening day at Bullecourt, was badly wounded and shot down, insisted on being driven to the Anzac Corps Headquarters to make his report before going to hospital. Frequently Australian flyers in the R.F.C. were engaged on Australian fronts, such as the two Australians who were forbidden to ascend on October 4th at Passchendaele owing to the high wind, but who did valuable work, crashed, and yet got back to Ypres to report what they had seen.

Daring Anzac airmanship

The Commonwealth Government met the cost of the A.F.C., as it did that of all its war units, including even the shells fired over the heads of its troops by British artillery attached to its corps.

In September all the Australian and New Zealand divisions were gathered for their greatest battle on the western front. Nothing in their past exceeded, nothing in their future could equal, the scope and intensity of the fighting for the Flanders ridges. The divisions were overflowing in numbers. Their spirits were at their highest after the long rest of summer. Their confidence was supreme. They were at last together in one extensive battle order. For the first time in the history of the war they were brought into the same army, given one united task. These men gloried in their distinctive identity—they prized their Australasian comradeship above all else. And they tackled the desolate slopes of the Passchendaele

ridges with all the greater determination because the task had been made one of Southern Britons against the German.

Once again Sir Douglas Haig gave to the Anzacs the most honoured place in the line. They were set to storm the rising ground of the Polygon Ridge, and as with each successive assault the British forces moved up the slopes, the Anzacs' front was changed, so that before these superb storming troops there should always be the rising ground. After Polygon there was Broodseinde, and, after Broodseinde, Passchendaele. The men never failed to do their part, and they claim it as a privilege that at least on one occasion they were able to turn aside from their own work and help neighbours who were hardly beset by counter-attacks.

Some of the Australians had seen and defeated the German "pill-box" and redoubt system at Messines; to the majority it was new. To realise what they began to do at dawn on September 20th one must picture them waiting in the enemy's barrage for the signal to go out against lines of concrete to redoubts stuffed with men and machine-guns, protected by trench systems and wire entanglements—surrounded by the bodies of gallant men who had failed to storm them in the bitter battles of August.

Storming the Passchendaele slopes

The ridges were broken by shell fire, but still green; white villages—Zonnebeke, Broodseinde, Gravenstafel—still nestled on their sides; the famous woods of Polygon, the Hanabeek, and Zonnebeke still waved their full-leafed branches in the winds; the long, straggling, red-and-white township of Passchendaele still looked across into Ypres over verdant fields and pleasant pasture land—the wooded playing-grounds of the Flemish people for centuries.

FROM BENEATH THE SOUTHERN CROSS TO FORESTRY WORK NEAR THE WESTERN FRONT.
New Zealand troops who were engaged in forestry work in France. They had erected neat shanties of rough timber for billets near the scene of their operations. The work of the forestry detachments was one of very considerable importance, and was carried on sometimes close to the fighting-front where the timber was shattered by shells, and sometimes many miles away from the battle-line in such sylvan scenes as this.

The blast of war was to wither it all—up, into, and beyond Passchendaele itself. And with the blast went, for the greater part of the way, the Australian and New Zealand divisions. More than anything previous it was an artillery battle. By the time the first day of attack had come the Anzacs had completed far-flung preparations. They had moved their artillery audaciously close to the German lines. Emplacements for heavy guns, howitzers, and field-guns had been made by night under the very noses of the enemy. Roads had been built, duck-board tracks laid, railways and tramways constructed. In this work the full labour strength of General Plumer's Second Army was used. The Australian tunnellers made battle headquarters, dug-outs, shelters ; the pioneers and engineers built their saps. A devoted corps staff plotted out the lines of marches and systems of relief. Strange places were turned into shelters for troops on the march. Supplies were stacked at accessible places along the communications—even supplies of comforts, for Australian public funds had their commissioners always working with the men in the battle zones and seeing to their needs.

And so, as light broke on September 20th, the 1st and 2nd Divisions stormed across and through the Polygon Wood, while British troops on either side advanced also to their objectives.

It was the Battle of Menin Road. Such a barrage had never been seen. It was some three times as deep and intense as that of Messines. The heavy guns pounded the German back areas and points where the enemy left his motor-vehicles for the march to the front; machine-guns played ceaselessly on his saps, light guns of all calibres threw a broad curtain of explosives upon his front lines. As each objective was reached, the great belt of metal rolled forward, preparing for the next advance. One, two, three times the dreadful barrage halted, churning the earth into spraying mud and sand and sweeping it with shrapnel ; until after the third advance it had tucked the infantry, as it were, into their new positions, and had nothing more to do than play about the German lines, break up their counter-attacking parties, and hold itself ready to descend again in full force in front of the new British lines whenever an S O S signal called for the artillerymen's help.

The success of the battle was complete. Brilliant weather favoured it, and the going was easy. On sections of the front little opposition was encountered. There were cases of officers, single-handed, or with small parties, taking scores of prisoners. The Australian scouting-parties, sent out ahead of the final objective to clear up shattered obstacles in front, made remarkable hauls. One party of an officer and two men from the 8th (Victorian) Battalion returned with two German officers, two machine-guns, and forty-eight men. Several battalions had found stores of cigars in the trenches of their first objective, and the men advanced behind the barrage smoking them. The 5th Brigade had a redoubt named "Anzac" in its objectives, and raised an Australian flag upon it.

Victory of Menin Road

Nothing could have exceeded the battle spirit of these Australians. They had the confidence of their own muscle strength, the assurance of superiority, the decisiveness of determined men. Most had been "over the top" before, nearly all were specialists in some weapon or fighting method, and all had the true offensive spirit. It was an occasion when the individual initiative of these sturdy,

independent civilian soldiers was invaluable. Casualties meant that privates had to take command of platoons, non-commissioned officers of companies. Some redoubts had to be stalked. Snipers were put to fire upon the slits in the walls through which the German machine-guns played, while parties worked round the flanks and rear. Little posts of tenacious Germans had to be rushed with the bayonet by small parties hurriedly organised. But the success of the attack lay in one thing above all others— the closeness with which the men followed the barrage.

Throughout the Battle of the Ridges, even amidst its most galling times of clinging to and consolidating hard-won positions under terrible shell fire, the Australians showed their peculiar sense of humour. The barrage they praised as "real dinkum," or a "bonza." "I leant up against it, and, when it suddenly shifted forward, fell over," was one saying. "I lit my cigarette on it," was another. They were known among the Germans as "souvenir kings." "Your men rob while they fight," was one German officer's complaint "You would have shot me if I had had it," said a German lieutenant, when a young Australian officer ordered him up from his dug-out, and then demanded to know why he had not brought up his revolver—a prized souvenir. "I will shoot you if you don't go down for it," was the Australian's answer. One man, after Zonnebeke had fallen, went into the ruined church to seek some souvenir of Hun occupation, and a chance shell buried him in bricks. "It is the first time I have been in church for twenty-seven years," was his remark when dug out, " and then it is thrown around me."

On September 26th the 4th and 5th Divisions attacked in the Battle of Polygon Ridge. On the previous day the 5th Division had been through a severe ordeal. After a succession of heavy shoots the Germans at dawn threw down a barrage little inferior to that under which the British line had gone forward on September 20th. It fell with particular severity on the British troops on the Australians' right. And then the very division against which the Anzacs had been placed on arrival in France—the 50th Prussian Reserve Division—came forward in masses to attack. The Germans had

Battle of Polygon Ridge

seen the arm raised again to smite, and this was their desperate effort to parry the blow. All day fighting as fierce as any in the many terrible battles of the Polygon Wood raged around the Australians and their flank. The line to the south of the Anzacs was driven in, and part of the flank lost, but recovered by a dashing counter-thrust in the afternoon. Into the evening the attacks and counter-attacks continued. All day German troops were seen moving in omnibuses along the Menin road. They came under artillery fire as they massed for their final attack, about 5.30. But they came on in waves. The Australians' right became hideously exposed, and until nearly mid-night the Anzacs were holding on, outflanked, enfiladed, constantly attacked, amid a fury of artillery fire.

Yet at dawn they leapt from their places. The British barrage had descended like a wall, the whole line had begun to move on once more. It was a bitter day, especially on this southern sector. Similar lines of "pill-boxes" and redoubts, similar trenches and machine-gun emplacements and snipers' nooks, had to be rushed as the barrage lifted. The 4th Division proceeded steadily to its mark. But the 5th was working with its flank fully

|Elliott & Fry.

MAJOR-GENERAL SIR JOHN MONASH.
In command of the Australian 3rd Division, he had been a civil engineer before the war revealed his ability as a military leader.

WAYSIDE REST ON A DESERT MARCH.
Australian troopers in the Palestine campaign having a rest during an advance. While their horses enjoyed a nose-bag feed many of the men took the welcome opportunity that was afforded them for indulging in a quiet smoke.

of the events which made it historical for ever for the Anzacs. The Australian front was moved northwards to bring the divisions opposite the next ridge—that of Broodseinde; and the Second Anzac Corps, containing the 3rd Australian Division and the New Zealanders, was brought up to the left of General Birdwood's line. When at dawn the Anzacs went forward they were in greater array than they had ever been before. Four great divisions moved shoulder to shoulder against the Germans. The centre of the British advance was thus occupied by a solid phalanx of Australasian soldiers greater in numbers than any previous Dominion attacking force. Much of the dash that marked that day came from the stirring of national pride and enthusiasm for the comradeship of the South.

The supply columns had worked day and night to bring up the shells and ammunition. Tracks had been pushed forward, horse and mule teams, with panniers of shells, or loads of bombs and food, had moved in never-ceasing stream to the batteries and dumps. The guns had been dragged on over the pounded and pitted fields. A great barrage, little less effective than that prepared with all the wealth of weeks of labour for the first assault, accompanied the Anzacs on their way. These artillerymen, these labour companies and supply services, saw nothing of the assaults which carried the flag another two thousand yards forward and drove the Hun from yet another ridge. But the day owed much to their labours, their endurance, and casualties, and they shared its glory.   **The Battle of Broodseinde**

Not for a moment did the fortunes of this day waver. The men were irresistible, and they swept the Germans from the ridge. They reached exactly the point decided, and there stopped. New Zealanders stormed the Abraham Heights; the 3rd Australian Division took the rising ground towards Passchendaele; the 2nd Division captured

exposed, high " in the air." A pitiless machine-gun fire came from its right wing, and snipers played havoc with its lines.

One of the prettiest bits of manœuvre work done by Anzacs in France was carried through this day. The outlook was as formidable as could well be imagined. But a deflection of two battalions to the right, into territory which had not been marked out for the Australians, gradually secured this area. And reserve troops completed the frontal advance. These were decisions taken on the spot, and showed the capacity of Australia's civilian generals to manœuvre at the height of battle. But as usual the glory rested with the young platoon commanders and sergeants—the mere boys who, fresh from school or from office desk or farm, faced the ordeal of leadership and won the day.

Holding on during those days, when all objectives had been secured, was as dire a trial as anything that had gone before. The lines were weak, and the positions so exposed that supplies could be brought forward only with the utmost difficulty. German aeroplanes swooped down frequently and fired bursts of machine-gun bullets upon the poor trenches and shell-hole defences; the men brought down one with rifle fire. And this curious contest between machine-guns in the air and rifles upon the exposed ground went on for days. The survivors of the battalions got down to their last small stores of provisions. The iron rations were eaten with shell-hole water. The last cartridge was within sight. Relief came none too soon.

But the line was held, and, when others came to take it over, all was ready for the greatest of all the battles of the ridges—the Battle of Broodseinde. October 4th was clear and bright, worthy

IMPROVISED BRIDGE-BUILDING BY ANZACS.
Anzac engineers constructing a temporary bridge in Palestine by using canvas reservoirs lined with timber for pontoons. They were also making a roadway approach across the muddy deposits. At this point, in the flood season, the water rose as much as ten feet.

Broodseinde ; the 1st took the high ground to the south. Few stories are more dramatic than the tale of the Victorians of the 1st Division there.

These gallant men of the 2nd Brigade had reached their starting-points when an enemy barrage thundered down, full forty-five minutes before the hour for the British attack. They were awful minutes for all who knew that brave men were lying out beneath the shells. Many of the platoon commanders had got their men dug into deep shell-holes, with walls of earth rising on each side of their narrow shelters. But even these provided poor protection from the explosives that pounded down, searching, apparently, every part of the starting-line.

" Now, then, The barrage extended, until it had passed
Australians ! " nearly to the left side of the Australian front. It was a formidable hail of shells, sometimes " crumping " like the beats of a kettle-drum, sometimes seeming less intense, but always carrying its message that the attacking troops were being blasted by a terrible fire. Happily, on the left, where the troops of the 3rd Division had been compelled by the curious windings of the Ravebeek stream to mass on a narrow and exposed strip of territory, it passed just overhead and buried itself in the ground behind. But on the right the men came under its full fire. One battalion lost a third of its storming officers before it had advanced to the attack. Yet the barrage had to be suffered in silence.

Some critics spoke of the Australians' discipline as though it were inadequate. But such times as these told how, when the supreme test of discipline came, the Australians never failed to respond. At the appointed moment in the Battle of Broodseinde, though racked and battered by the German barrage, the Australians went forward as one man. Their officers climbed from the shelters with a cheery " Now, then, Australians ! " And the men did not loiter. The British first barrage had opened, and the German artillery, which before had filled the air with its explosions, could now scarcely be heard. British shells whistled overhead, making a continuous shrill sound as of a great wind. And as they exploded about the enemy's positions and burst around his redoubts they crowded his lines with reeking craters and enveloped them in smoke.

As the men on the right stumbled forward they could just discern, some thirty yards away, lines of others groping about in the darkness. It was an astounding sight. They were as yet far from the enemy's positions ; it seemed unthinkable that Germans should be here. " They must be our men," muttered some. " They're Fritz," said others. At places officers advanced nearly to touching distance. At others whispered demands for the night's countersign was given Then the strange fact dawned on Australians and on Germans alike that both sides had planned a great attack for the same moment.

The Australians dashed straight at the German storming troops. Here and there a cool-headed Lewis gunner got to work with his gun. The Germans hesitated, some firing, others turning. Then their line
Hand-to-hand broke. They were mowed down by
between the barrages rifle and machine-gun fire, thrust down with bayonet, scattered and slain by the British barrage as they ran frenzied into it. The Australian lines passed through them as though they were a wall of paper. Men, hearing of the strange event, when Australian and German met on equal terms, both arrayed for offensive work in the quietest zone of all that night—the zone between the barrages—went up when the wave of battle had swept past this place to see the spot. And though German dead, still bearing the full offensive equipment of the German storming troops, were there in plenty, only one Australian soldier lay stretched on the ground as the price the battalions had paid for their amazing victory. Captured orders showed that the Germans had indeed planned a big

attack for that morning. It was intended, like the counter-attack of Polygon, to strike a day before the British had planned to advance and to disrupt the British plans by seizing a vital assembling point. The accidents of the day had worked well for them. They had timed their barrage to begin long before the British. Yet their scheme fell to ruins against the wall of Australian resolution.

Few Germans waited even to defend their redoubts. They seemed dazed and dispirited by the barrage and fled up the ridge. Shells ploughed the ground about them, shrapnel descended upon them from mid-air. And behind them came, in a great rush, soldiers who knew how to get full value out of every weapon in the modern armoury. The Germans were, indeed, beaten before the first lines advanced against them. "What could we do," asked a young German afterwards in the prisoners' cage, " against these big, brave Australians ? " At places the German officers tried hard to rally their men. Along the top of the ridge ran a sunken road, and here, and in folds of trenches on either side, the last attempts to hold the hill were made. On the right flank non-commissioned officers gathered. Gallant but ineffective bands of " die-hards," they had machine-guns, but could get no men to stay with them. The Australians swept on and dug new lines on the farther side of the ridge. A wonderful vista had been opened to them. They looked, from the points from which for three years the Germans had dominated Ypres, and observed every living thing that moved within it, deep into the green and fertile occupied territories. Such a scene had not been before them since they had, after bitter fighting, climbed the heights of Gallipoli in August, 1915, and seen stretched ahead the promised land. Here were the grassed and wooded fields of Flanders, with villages clustering along the white roadways, and the spires of cities rising
from the plains. The great regret of   **Anzacs reach the**
the day was that orders prohibited far   **highest ground**
deeper penetration of the invaders' lines.
The Anzacs, flushed with success, felt that the whole power of the German Army was tottering. They came under heavy fire as they dug their trenches, and snipers' bullets played about them. But they would have welcomed still more adventurous tasks.

Next day came the rain, and the story changed. The fine spell of weather had been worth divisions. The prolonged storm, bringing heavy rains day after day, cost all that the sunshine had saved. Water transformed the battlefields into quagmires. The pounded earth, which in places had been turned over and over again by the shells, became a sticky slush. At first the mud was ankle-deep, mere surface slipperiness. But soon every shell-hole filled with water, tracks broke up, and the work was carried on under most distressing conditions. Storm and rain swept and reswept the sector. Heavy showers chased one another over the backs of these hundreds of thousands of fighters and workers, while intervals of wild, wind-swept blue sky seemed but to mock. At night movement was slow and dangerous —very near to impossible. Men struggled through mud, at places waist-deep, into assembly positions for advances across zones as deeply stricken. The troubles became infinite. Guns could not be dragged forward over the morasses, roads were cut to pieces and became impassable, tracks became patches of duck-board interspersed with stretches of knee-deep mud. Movement became ten times more necessary, for more supplies were needed, and all possible repairs had to be made to communications ; at the same time it was ten times more difficult. And the men in the line and approaching to it found their special troubles multiplied. The pace in an advance had to be slower—the barrage was apt to get far ahead. Rifles and Lewis guns choked where opposition showed itself ; the fighting was far more arduous

Australians hunting for Turkish snipers over rocky ridges in Palestine.

[Photographs by Captain Hurley, Australian official photographer in Palestine.

Camel transport laden with bags of bread ready for the men in the front line.

[Photograph by Captain Hurley. Australian official photographer in Palestine.

Following the Israelites' old road to victory: Australian Light Horse passing through Bethlehem to the capture of Jericho.

[Photograph by Captain Hurley, Australian official photographer in Palestine.

Tents of the Anzacs pitched in a depression in the Judean foothills in the Valley of the Jordan.

[Photograph by Captain Hurley, Australian official photographer in Palestine.

New Crusaders under the walls of the Holy City: Australian Light Horse riding between Bethlehem and Jerusalem.

for men tired with dragging their feet through heavy mud—stopping frequently to help some mud-bound comrade, perhaps themselves losing a boot or puttee in the clinging morass.

Thus the battles for Passchendaele entered into a new phase. The programme of leaps had not yet included Passchendaele itself—the height that dominated all. Yet Passchendaele must fall, if the great battlefield were not to be left under the Germans' direct observation for the winter. And the very mud through which British troops floundered emphasised the need for gaining the high ground, so that at least Germans should winter amid the slush and water of valleys, while the British enjoyed the dryness of the heights. Sir Douglas Haig decided that, despite all the new handicaps, the offensive should be pushed on.

In the first of the new series of bad weather pushes the Australians played a small but a glorious part. It was confined to flank operations in woods which will be remembered as occasioning a severe test of Anzac endurance. These shattered, mud-bound belts of tree-stumps, named Daisy and Dairy Woods, were on the eastern slope of the ridge; behind them stretched a waste of mud, connecting Broodseinde Ridge with that of Keiberg—the last of the heights. In these woods heroic fighting took place on October 9th, after which the Germans retreated across the mud and established themselves in the lines and redoubts of Keiberg. The charge here was made by the 2nd Australian Division, which had five days of difficult and arduous trench-holding since its great assault on October 4th. The men were near the last ounce of strength. Their sufferings in the bitter weather and heavy fighting had been intense. But their spirit was still equal to an offensive—their third within three weeks. And they found

Anzac attempt on Passchendaele strength to push on through the woods, and even to cross the death valley of the Ypres-Roulers railway, and storm there some redoubts which were enfilading them. A great impression was made in Australia by the story of these heroic lads' fighting against superior forces after the severe privations and casualties of the week; it pricked the conscience of Australia to think that such men should be weakened through lack of reinforcement, and the event had much to do with the second attempt to secure conscription by referendum.

In the next blow, struck on October 12th, the Second Anzac Corps had great objectives. The 3rd Australian Division and the New Zealand Division stormed forward on the slopes leading to Passchendaele. Before the New Zealanders were the swollen stream called Ravebeek and the sinister height called Bellevue. Along this Bellevue spur ran high ground into Passchendaele itself, while opposite the Australians, on the New Zealanders' right, were morasses and crowded shell-holes reaching up to the nearest houses of the township, with the shattered white stones of the Passchendaele church bulking large among them. Across the railway were battalions of the 4th Division, who were to guard their comrades' flank—a task perhaps more hazardous than being engaged in the main advance, for it meant a bulging effort under the observation of the German machine-gunners of Keiberg. The barrage that day was thin, the gun-carriages dug into the mud, making accurate, sustained fire impossible; the task of getting supplies of shells and of moving up the batteries along those broken and congested mud tracks had proved more than all the willing helpers of the infantry could accomplish. But the men pushed on at dawn, and the story of their splendid failure is as moving as any of their victorious exploits.

The New Zealanders came at once under heavy fire. They had to cross a morass, in which wounded men sank into the ground and heavily-loaded men could scarcely stumble. Wave after wave passed on—wave after wave came to the flooded stream. Here the Germans had laid down their main barrage. It splashed into the waters at the fords and tore up the mud for many yards behind. The stream had flooded over into the shell-hole area, and was at parts an impassable sheet fifty yards wide. The New Zealanders struggled to find passages. A stone road, now flush with the water, became the main path. Wounded and dead fell here, and the dauntless living had to press on over the bodies of their comrades. On the other side they rushed uphill. But each wave, as it re-formed and advanced, came up against impenetrable barriers of wire entanglements, while across the wire they could see the sinister redoubts, with machine-guns spitting out protection across the barbs. This wire was of extraordinary thickness and strength, and stretched in two deep belts in front of the attackers. "The only thing that can stop the Anzacs," a great British general said once, "is uncut wire." The New Zea- **New Zealanders'** landers tried it, once, twice, thrice. **splendid failure** Brave men attempted to crawl beneath it. Some reached the second belt before falling to the enemy snipers. One got through the whole belt, crawled to the side of the main redoubt, and was about to throw in bombs through the machine-gun slits when a rifle-grenade unhappily struck him. That brave act might have been the turning-point of the day. Such single-handed adventures are sometimes the difference between victory and defeat. But the sheer physical difficulties of their task proved beyond even the Anzacs' strength. The waves marched forward, wading through the mud, stepping as best they could over the dead bodies of their comrades, right into the wire. That was the high-water mark. The New Zealanders gave that day an example of devotion to duty, of splendid death, as noble as any that has occurred. They showed how soldiers could accept the sacrifice of their lives in place of the victory that was not to be. Rough lines were dug in front of the wire, and it was hoped that a further great effort would yet crown the division's unbroken series of victories in France and Flanders with the greatest victory of all. But at night the lines were withdrawn to allow of heavy bombardment of the wire. Further rains came, and the task had to be postponed for the Canadian Corps, then on its way from its scene of victories at Vimy and Lens to the great magnet of the Ypres offensive.

So stout a position as Bellevue could not but have its effect upon the whole battle-line. The 3rd Australians accomplished their approach marches through darkness, over broken and muddy tracks, to time, and the men moved forward as soon as the barrage opened. The New South Wales troops of the 9th Brigade advanced far towards Passchendaele. The Victorians of the 10th Brigade came at once under a murderous enfilading fire from Bellevue and Graf Farm—a nest of redoubts farther up the Bellevue spur. The Ravebeek, which turned sharply to the north, and divided Australians from New Zealanders, had converted all the **Australian front** left flank into impassable morass; the **line withdrawn** Australians here had to scramble round it. All the time the deadly machine-gun fire and the rifles of the snipers played upon them. Yet men did that day get into Passchendaele. They advanced far towards their final objectives. And had it not been that every point in their line was overlooked by the concrete defences of the Bellevue spur they might have held on. It was a most gallant effort, the cost of which in travail of spirit and body can never be estimated from a library chair. Much of the territory gained that day was held. But, in conformity with the changed line, the outlying positions won were abandoned, and the front line withdrawn to posts from which the next attack could be launched

Heavy days of trench-digging, trench-holding, and consolidation followed; the line had to be sorted out—no easy task on such a vast and broken battlefield. The weather in peace time would have driven all people

UNLOADING STORES FOR AUSTRALIAN TROOPS IN PALESTINE.
Conveying stores from a transport off the coast of Palestine. The stores had to be brought from the vessel to the shore in surf-boats, and were then carried up the beach by coolie labour.

indoors. Here it had to be endured in open shell-holes, day and night, or on the shattered duck-board tracks of the wilderness, where there was so much deep mud and so little firm soil that every wounded man required relays of stretcher-bearers, six to each stretcher ; every load of rations, or timber, or gum-boots, meant many hours' travail for the carriers, and shelling was always heavy. There were new names which arose these days around this old-world countryside — "Death's Gully," "Hell-fire Track," "Suicide Corner," and so on—the battlefield names which betoken the hazards and difficulties that continued long after ground had been gained in an offensive. Eager fighting went on day and night for the new No Man's Land. This was work in which the Anzacs legitimately prided themselves. "We own No Man's Land," was their claim wherever they went. The 5th Division had many days in the line opposite, and in the valley of Keiberg, and their patrol work was never excelled. Time and again they brought in Germans. They explored the enemy's outer positions, daily inflicting loss. They assailed his patrolling-parties, capturing or killing them. There were days when the artillery fire on this sector reached battle intensity, so strong a pace did the division force in patrol and local fighting.

Anzacs help the Canadians Meanwhile, Canadian generals and Canadian Staff officers, in the good Canadian way, would appear in the early morning and make their way past Anzac positions to the front shell-holes. "You will have some breakfast ?" was an ordinary question in those days, when Canadian divisional or brigade commander arrived soon after dawn at an Australian headquarters. "Nothing, thank you—except a guide," would be the reply. And so generals and guides went forward through the heavily shelled areas, found the points of vantage nearest the enemy, and studied out the difficulties ahead of the Canadian men. As the divisions

began to trickle through that vast armed camp behind the battle-lines the men of the three Dominions studied each other closely—and saw much to admire. The capture of Passchendaele had been from the first a task principally for Dominion men, and the sight of the great Dominion armies gathered about Ypres was one of the wonders of the war on the western front.

The great exploits of the Australians and New Zealanders on the ridges were nearing an end. They were given no further work to do in mass. But the help they gave the Canadians brought some of the most intense individual fighting seen on the battlefield. Twice part of the 1st Division was sent forward to win new territory and protect the Canadians' flank. On each occasion the German showed fight, and bitter and costly bouts resulted. Man met man ; Australian and German were found side by side, each bayoneted by the other ; redoubts yielded only to stern bombing attacks, snipers maintained their fire until killed at their posts. Death was not questioned on either side ; only victory was sought. The Australians pushed forward their lines always to their objectives. There were sad hearts that the final assault on Passchendaele, and the glorious capture of that redoubtable stronghold, should belong to the Canadian records. But the Australians delighted in their comrades' success, and gloried also in the fact that they should still be in the fight at the finish.

Bitter fighting man to man

To estimate the work accomplished by the Anzacs on the ridges it must be remembered that the Russian collapse had given Germany an opportunity to gather here the flower of her Army. Constantly she brought new troops to the zone ; ceaselessly she augmented her concentrations of guns. She never seemed to lack men or shells. And she had a wealth of strong concrete positions. How far back these lines of redoubts went it was impossible at the time to say. What was certain was that the general military situation was enabling Germany to use her full strength in the defence of the ridges. Yet she was steadily and ruthlessly pushed from them. Each time she saw the arm raised to strike the blow; her airmen told her how and where it was to be delivered; her artillery and infantry were strained to the utmost to ward it off. Yet each time she had to take it full and square in the face. It would scarcely be believable now how much her armies reeled under the hammering. Yet the evidence of her discomfiture was complete. Each battle was followed by frantic orders from Army commanders for more resistance. The tactics were changed—first counter-

"POT-SHOT" AT AN ENEMY AIRMAN.
Australian Lewis gunners at a post formed of a shell-destroyed tree. The man behind the gun was training his weapon on an approaching German aeroplane.

attacks were tried, then considerable strengthening of the forward lines with machine-guns, then the use of specially-selected and tried troops. What could be described only as a wailing arose from the German Army. The intensity of the British battle fire brought forth from the rank and file piteous letters home, and some of the diaries found in the dug-outs made pathetic reading. The place became in the German mind a huge and unescapable graveyard. One division mutinied and was withdrawn from the line. Some troops refused to advance. On occasions, especially when good weather favoured the preparations for the British barrages and the speed of the attack, the bulk· of the enemy forces surrendered as soon as the British assailants got within striking distance. There was in truth good basis for the growing conception of the German infantryman as a poor muddled soldier, with his hands above his head, crying "Kamerad!"

Superiority of Anzac moral Had winter not closed on the scene these battles would certainly have produced a widespread retreat of the German forces. For the Germans had reached a lower stage of moral than even that which marked the close of the Somme offensive. They very badly needed their winter refitting and rest.

It was natural that the Australians should take away with them to their new winter zone—that of Messines and Wytschaete—a sense of strong superiority over the Germans, mixed with some little contempt for the German infantrymen. Australians and New Zealanders were never more convinced that the German infantry, when given the arduous and testing tasks of great offensives, would prove a poor hand in battle. They went into the winter of 1917-18 confident of their capacity to meet whatever might come against them in the changed conditions of 1918. And as they spent the winter days and nights, seeing to their defences and peeping occasionally also

TO THOSE WHO FELL AT POZIÈRES.
Cross erected on the battlefield with the inscription: "In Memory of the Officers and Men of the 1st Australian Division who fell in the taking of Pozières, July, 1916."

into the enemy's lines, they were well satisfied with the prospects. The winter was infinitely more pleasant than the preceding one had been for the force. Casualties were few, sickness became rare, and the conditions were more settled. All the divisions from the two Dominions were ready again for hard fighting when the summons of the spring came.

During good and bad days, during rest and hard soldiering, General Sir William Birdwood was ever the trusted and capable leader of the Australian force. The duality of his position was sometimes embarrassing. As General Officer Commanding the Australian Imperial Force **General Sir William Birdwood** he was the direct servant and representative of the Commonwealth Government. To Australia, and Australia alone, he was responsible for all the administrative side of the vast organisation. He had full powers of appointment and control in all units of the A.I.F. whether in Palestine, in England, or in France. And for all he did as administrator he had to answer to the Government in Melbourne, which in turn had to answer to the electors of the Commonwealth. On the other side Sir William Birdwood was answerable to Sir Douglas Haig for the fighting of the First Anzac Corps, as its corps commander. The British Government provided the Corps Staff, of which General Birdwood was the head.

NEW ZEALANDERS IN FRANCE.
The officer commanding the New Zealand force on the western front holding an inspection of the rifles of a company of his men.

This arrangement arose in the early days of the war, when Australia did not feel capable of corps leadership. That it continued was in itself a high testimony to General Birdwood, for as Australian-born generals developed with experience opportunities came for fulfilling a very natural national desire—that Australian troops should be commanded in the field by an Australian-born officer.

General Birdwood's prestige, capacity, and success were so unquestionable that there was never the slightest movement towards meeting the desire. He was an indefatigable worker, ever courageous, whether on the field or in the more delicate difficulties of his office; his sympathies with his men were intense, and he understood them through and through. He went constantly into the firing-lines, and his cheerful insistence on moving amid shell fire was always a source of anxiety to his personal Staff.

Other Australian commanders The strain upon him will be understood when it is remembered that he had to lead an Army fighting twelve thousand miles from home, on foreign soil, in trying climate, under conditions involving constant hardship, heavy fighting, and serious losses; only a remarkable man could have succeeded. General Birdwood's prestige was a valuable asset to the force. The men all knew and admired him. They had grown up in small communities where personal freedom was general. Some would shout to him as he passed, "Hallo, Mr. Birdwood!" thinking it the height of friendly and respectful salutation. He gauged all his men at their true worth, and they never failed him.

Australia was fortunate in her other commanders. In Major-General C. B. B. White, Chief of Staff to General Birdwood, she had a bright and able young officer destined to go far in his profession. A Queenslander, he was one of the most successful General Staff officers on the British front, and the Corps Staff became famous for the excellence of its staff-work. The 1st Division was long under the command of General Sir Hubert Walker, an Indian Army officer, who had his men's high esteem and was in all ways a strong, hard-hitting leader.

Major-General Sir John Monash, commander of the 3rd Division, was a civil engineer before the war, but showed that outstanding ability could make of a civilian a successful and competent military leader. The other Australian-born divisional commander was General Sir J. T. Hobbs, in whose hands the 5th Division worked with unvarying success. The training camps in England were commanded by Major-General Sir James M'Cay, whose career included many remarkable successes. He had been a successful lawyer, politician, Minister of Defence, and banker before the war called him to field command in the Army.

Some special advantages accrued to the Anzacs for their distinctive national organisation. Australia lavished her wealth upon her troops. Her **Australia's care for her troops** contributions to the British Red Cross and Belgian Relief totalled more than four million pounds. But for her own men she cared with an unceasing anxiety. Government action was always on a generous scale. The Australians drew higher pay than any other troops in France, they were splendidly equipped with all-woollen garments, with all the fighting needs that money could buy. And private action supplied them with many comforts. The women of Australia sent them millions of home-knitted socks and vast quantities of gifts. Every festival was marked by the distribution of parcels from home. The Australian Red Cross attended to sick and wounded, while a national organisation, which sprang from a Sydney public fund, supplied the needs of the fit men. It sent its delegates to every firing-line; it established cocoa and coffee stalls under shell fire, where working-parties could get their refreshment. Tobacco was specially imported from Australia, trench stoves were supplied; the men's comfort was studied as no troops' had been in the past. There were countless private societies at work—here a gathering of mothers of a battalion, there a little working-party organised by a battalion commander's wife—which worked ceaselessly for the comfort of special bodies of men, forwarding funds to their regimental accounts, or sending them clothes and "goodies." It was claimed with some pride by Australia that her troops were the best-equipped, best-fed, best-mothered army ever put in the field. This prevision extended to Egypt and Palestine, and included all units.

Similarly the Anzacs remained the special care of many public-minded and hospitable people in Great Britain. Their visits to England and Scotland during leave days, or while polishing their training at Salisbury Plain, were full of interest, and as far as possible British people filled them with pleasures. Country homes were opened to them. Free railway warrants carried them to the most distant part of the kingdom. Hospitality was organised, so that all should share it to the full. There were long lists of people who were seldom without Anzac soldiers as their guests. Some of the finest houses in the country became convalescent hospitals dedicated to Anzac officers and men.

There were organised facilities for sight-seeing, and these days of sojourn in the land of their fathers made a lasting impression upon the soldiers, and seemed destined to have an important Imperial effect. They not only established individual bonds between the British people and the Australians, but had an immediate and widespread educative influence.

That the Australian Army owed much to the British people and the British war organisation would never be denied by an Anzac. Much of their equipment was necessarily purchased **Knitted bonds** from British stores. Some of their **of Empire** leading officers belonged to the British or Indian Army. The Mother Country had for many years been generous in placing what military science and military material she had at the disposal of the Commonwealth.

The Australian force was very largely fashioned on the British model. Moreover, some of the finest camp sites on Salisbury Plain were allotted to the Australians and New Zealanders. Here all the Australian drafts were put through from eight to twelve weeks' training before being sent to France. The men were placed in large camps of wooden huts, and, in addition, special schools and depots were established at Weymouth, Grantham, and elsewhere.

The administrative Headquarters of the Australian force remained always in London, where it worked as part of the Australian organisation under Brigadier-General Griffiths, C.M.G., D.S.O., a devoted servant of the force.

The Australian force thus had its tentacles scattered in many directions. Its organisation included special flying corps training stations, engineers' camps, nurses' homes, and a wide medical system; while in France it maintained bases at Havre and Etaples, and its full share of general hospitals and casualty clearing-stations. It was noticeable that Australian doctors suffered to a higher percentage in casualties than those of any other force. The casualties as a whole were testimony to the rigours of the tasks.

Up to the end of 1917 the Australians had lost 43,000 killed, 115,000 wounded, 67,000 sick, and 4,000 prisoners and missing.

CHAPTER CCXLIII.

THE ORGANISATION OF YOUTH IN THE WAR.

By Sir Robert Baden-Powell and E. K. Nugent.

Increase of Juvenile Delinquency Due to the War—Character as a National Asset—Importance to Boys of a Healthy Environment Outside School—The Boys' Brigade : Its Contribution to the Forces of the Crown—Some of the Work Done and Honours Won by the Boys' Brigade—The Church Lads' Brigade—The Cadet Movement—The Boys' Naval Brigade—The Boys' Life Brigade—Standardisation and Co-ordination of the Work of Boys' Clubs and Girls' Clubs—The Boy Scouts' Movement—Readiness for Immediate Service on the Outbreak of War—Provisional Guarding of Communications—Tribute from Mr. Lloyd George, Lord Kitchener, and Lord Derby—Preliminary Training of Elder Boys in Military Duties and in Elementary Knowledge Necessary for the Air Service—The Sea Scouts on Coastguard and in the Navy—Boy Cornwell, Midshipman Gyles, and Boy Ireland—Admiral Jellicoe's Praise of the Scout Training—The Girl Guides—Development of the Boy Scouts' Movement in Other Civilised Countries—The Consequent Sense of Brotherhood Among the Young Generation of All Nations a Guarantee for Future Peace.

DURING the progress of the war a flagrant case was thus reported in the Press police news :

> At —— two small boys appeared on remand charged with housebreaking and setting fire to the residence of Mr. ——. It was stated that they had got into the empty house, and had there remained

for five days, during which they had lit a fire in every grate, burning books, etc.; they had slept in every bed in the house and had littered jam and flour all over the place. The Chief Constable reported that the interior of the house was a veritable pigsty. It was estimated that the total damage amounted to £350. The inspector of the Society for the Prevention of Cruelty to Children reported that the elder boy had stated that he had acquired the art of burglary from seeing it practised on the film.

Splendid fellows ! They were possessed with the spirit of high adventure ; had the cinema shown examples of gallant deeds of life-saving, they would probably have devoted themselves to that kind of activity with equal gusto. As it was, they must have had a simply glorious time. What heroes they must have been to their schoolmates !

But there were, during the war, too many heroes of this kind, for one serious outcome of the national crisis was the notable and steady increase of juvenile so-called crime in almost every city of the United Kingdom.

In Manchester, as a typical centre, the chief constable reported the existence of " Black Hand Gangs " and " Red Hand Gangs," groups of boys organised for mischief under their own boy leaders, and composed of lads filled with the romance of crime. The reformatories throughout the

country generally became full, and the prevalence of juvenile delinquency increased steadily.

In this Great Britain was not alone, for in Germany, too, a similar trouble grew up. It was an outcome of the war, due probably to the unrest of a dramatic time, also to the slackening of parental control owing to fathers being away on service and mothers on munition work ; to the shortage of school teachers, to high wages and easy employment, and more especially to the absence of the elder brother at work or on service.

Thus the boys were left in a lawless environment during their spare hours. This was a danger to the State since, in view of the critical time lying before the country, those who were to be future citizens required a more effective training in character than had ever been available before, to fit them for the great responsibility ultimately to rest upon their shoulders.

For this, character was the most important equipment of all. One result of the war was to expose in a remarkable degree the value of national character. A nation possessed of certain inherent characteristics of individual manliness and initiative, coupled with a sense of playing the game, though untrained in war, showed itself capable of standing up—and of standing up successfully — to another which for generations had been collectively organised and drilled under military ideals for war. The results of the respective trainings were on the one hand a cheery patriotism, coupled with chivalry in the field, as against forced service with a reversion to brutish savagery in action.

LIEUT.-GEN. SIR ROBERT BADEN-POWELL, K.C.B., K.C.V.O.

In 1908 Sir Robert Baden-Powell founded the organisation of Boy Scouts to promote good citizenship in the rising generation, and in the Great War the members of that organisation proved of great value.

337

It was apparent that the worst the British nation could suffer through the war was the loss of that character which is an asset alike good for it in peace and in war.

How to maintain that character became the quest of educationists and patriots with an eye to the future of the race. It may have been said, possibly a little vaingloriously, that character is a national asset of the Briton; but all the same, it is one which may be lost. It is too valuable an acquisition to be left to chance. How it can be adequately fostered and developed among the citizens of to-morrow is the question for each generation.

The boys in public schools and boarding schools have it instilled into them to a certain extent by the actual discipline of boys among boys, such as good form and of playing the game, of sacrificing their own individual desires for the good of the whole, and of obeying the unwritten laws of what is expected of an honourable man. These and many other points are incul-

Primary object of cated in the ordinary life of the public-
boys' organisations school boy. But the day-school boy does not get the same advantages. So soon as he is released from his lessons he goes out into his own environment, on his own line outside the school wall. Thus the character of a large mass of British boys has always been dependent on the chance nature of their environment outside school.

It is to supply a healthy environment that so many boys' organisations have been instituted by men interested in the lads and in the welfare of the nation.

We have been asked to write some account of the doings of the Boy Scouts' movement in this regard and of their work in the war, but it would scarcely be just to omit mention of the fact that equally good work was done by other voluntary organisations for boys. Most of these, if not so large in numbers, were senior in institution, and had for many years been doing the pioneer work and laying the foundations of that splendid spirit of devotion to duty which has distinguished

our men at the front. It was the combined efforts of all that had notable effect, firstly, in the production of a very large leaven of recruits for the service who as boys had been already trained to discipline and patriotism; secondly, in preventing a considerable amount of juvenile delinquency which would otherwise have been rampant during the war; and finally, in preparing a goodly number of the rising generation of citizens for the enhanced responsibilities which in a few years would rest upon their shoulders.

It was only natural, therefore, that early in the war, when juvenile crime began to show itself so pronouncedly, the Home Secretary called in the help of these societies and invited their co-operation. Thus to them came unlooked-for opportunity of extending their work into national war service, both in checking the rising tide of delinquency by extending their membership and in preventing it by providing healthful and useful war work, and also in preparing the lads through moral, mental, and physical development for more efficient citizenship later on.

The national effect of this work is probably not generally

BUILDING STABLES.
Boy Scouts of Birmingham building an extensive range of stables. Those in the foreground were fixing mangers.

realised any more than the devotion of the men who carried it out. These men worked double tides, since the demand for their effort was increased, while their number was reduced by half owing to the needs of the Service. But those who were left rose nobly to the occasion and, in many cases sacrificing prospects of highly paid billets, did what they deemed their duty for love— love of country and of the boy.

The Boys' Brigade—founded in 1883 by Sir William Smith, with the following object: "The advancement of Christ's Kingdom among boys, and the promotion of habits of obedience, reverence, discipline, self-respect, and all that tends towards a true, Christian manliness"—had, on the outbreak of the war in 1914, already passed through its ranks something like 750,000 to 800,000 officers and boys trained in

UNLOADING UPRIGHTS FOR HUT-BUILDING.
Part of a detachment of two hundred Birmingham Boy Scouts who erected extensive stables and huts for the War Office. Here they were unloading some of the materials from a tractor, with (in the background) one of their buildings nearing completion.

elementary military drill and discipline, and out of this number, during the first year of the war, 250,000 joined the forces of the Crown, and formed an invaluable addition to them. They were rapidly promoted, and, in addition to securing commissions in very many cases, they supplied drill instructors and non-commissioned officers for the New Army.

Number 4 Company of the 13th Battalion Rifle Brigade was formed within fourteen days after the declaration of war entirely by London boys of the Boys' Brigade. The week following the declaration of war London companies supplied orderlies, foot-messengers, and cyclists to carry orders and despatches from

MARCH-PAST OF KENTISH MAIDS.
At a great rally of Boy Scouts and Girl Guides at Foot's Cray, Kent. Marching past Brigadier-General Appelbe, C.B., who is seen to the left, saluting.

QUEEN MARY AND THE GIRL GUIDES.
On March 23rd, 1918, when King George and Queen Mary paid an informal visit to the Victoria Working Men's Club, Richmond, the Queen showed special interest in a detachment of the Girl Guides. The Guides are here seen saluting her Majesty.

various headquarters of Territorial regiments to the War Office and Government departments, and the same thing was done all over the country. In Glasgow the 16th Battalion of the Highland Light Infantry, known as the Boys' Brigade Battalion, was formed almost entirely of ex-members of the Boys' Brigade.

In Aberdeen twelve bearer-parties from ex-members of the Aberdeen battalion were accepted in September, 1915, by the Red Cross Commissioner to act in connection with 1st General Hospital, and the battalion president was appointed transport officer for the North-East of Scotland.

For work at home large numbers of boys collected waste-paper, bottles, old metal, etc., for the Prince of Wales's and other funds. The record collection of bottles for one battalion was as follows: Over half a million bottles collected, value £1,650, for the local Soldiers' and Sailors' Help Society.

The first Red Cross Day in Scotland was organised in October, 1915, entirely by the Glasgow battalion and other Boys' Brigade centres throughout Scotland, and realised over £15,000.

Many companies undertook the cultivation of plots of ground, and in this way increased the food production of the country.

The boys throughout the brigade contributed for the provision and carrying on of two large huts for sailors and soldiers, one at Rouen and one at Edinburgh.

In connection with air raids in London, orderlies and messengers at police-stations, Tubes, and certified raid shelters were supplied regularly, also orderly buglers to sound the " all clear " signal. Ambulance squads attended for work at raid shelters, and rendered useful assistance where damage and injury took place.

A special decoration was issued to every boy who gave a total of not less than a hundred hours of voluntary and unpaid service in connection with the war, performed out of school or business hours, and up to April, 1918, 2,650 badges had been won.

A large quantity of books and magazines were collected for the use of the Army and Navy, and assistance was given very largely in connection with flag days, messenger work for hospitals, recreation and rest huts, and railway canteens. **Honours won by the Boys' Brigade**

The number of officers and ex-members who joined the forces between the outbreak of war and April, 1918, was estimated to be 350,000.

Although it is impossible to get anything like a complete record of all the distinctions won, the record up to the last-named date showed the following :

V.C.	..	..	..	8	Military Medal	..	..	132
D.S.O.	..	..	..	20	Médaille Militaire	..	.	9
D.C.M.	..	..	..	71	Mentioned in Despatches	..		57
Military Cross	..		..	73	Various (Belgian, Russian, etc.)			44

These records show to some extent the service rendered by the Boys' Brigade in the supreme hour of trial.

The Church Lads' Brigade—a Church of England movement combining military organisation with moral and religious instruction—was also fully organised before the war, and had in 1917 a membership of 60,000 boys.

On the outbreak of war an entire battalion was formed, and accepted, for service in the Army, composed of ex-members of the C.L.B. This battalion did good service in France, and a large number of distinctions were won by its members.

CADETS OF A FAMOUS CORPS.
Major-General Lord Scarborough (on left), Director-General of Volunteer Forces, inspecting the London Scottish Cadet Corps at Westminster.

The Cadet movement extended its work among boys of all grades. A typical instance of the war work of cadets was that of the 7th London Regiment Cadet Corps. The corps was formed in 1914, with the object of capturing the lads by appealing to their desire to " do their bit " for the country.

Companies were formed in the various London districts, and, in addition to the ordinary drill and shooting, signalling and photography, woodwork, map-reading, and telegraphy were held out as attractions.

Useful war service was done in various ways by the cadets in connection with the National Registration scheme. Some cadets took part with the Boy Scouts in the work of air-raid buglers ; they also carried out trench work on the London defences. Sections of them assisted local Red Cross associations and ambulance stations in raid work, and other sections were trained in the air service. Excellent reports were received from commanding officers, and commissions and promotions were quickly obtained by cadets drafted to the senior Services.

The Boys' Naval Brigade—a branch of the Navy League, with its naval uniform—aimed **The Boys'** at capturing the boys with a leaning **Naval Brigade** for the sea, and, without forcing them to join the Navy, gave them every assistance whenever they desired to do so.

During the first three years of the war the brigade sent over a thousand officers and boys into the Navy, a like number into the Army, and over five hundred into the Mercantile Marine. Records show that many decorations and promotions were won by these boys.

Those who were not of an age for service did useful work as messenger-boys to the Admiralty and other Government offices. The movement extended on good lines during the war in South Africa and Canada.

The Boys' Life Brigade, although essentially a non-military organisation, carried out valuable war service for the country. During the first year of war about 21,000 of its members joined the forces.

A special feature of the work of this brigade was " life-saving." Prominence had always been given to instruction in first-aid to the injured, with the result that some thousands of its members were trained and ready to take up service with the Red Cross Society and the St. John Ambulance Association.

One or two instances will **The Boys'** show the nature of the war **Life Brigade** work done by the brigade. One battalion (at Oldham) raised over £100 for the support of a bed at the St. John Ambulance Brigade Hospital in France. In Manchester the brigade V.A.D. dealt with seventy trainloads of wounded.

As in all other boys' organisations, many companies found themselves without leaders, but the boys were, in most cases, able to step into the breach and keep the training going, and also to assist in public service duties.

The Shaftesbury Society and Ragged School Union, established in 1844, continued its valuable work during the war, and, in spite of a greatly depleted staff, took upon itself additional work in the care of the children of fighting men. The various moral, religious, and social agencies worked in connection with the society were kept going under great difficulties.

The good work which the Boys' Clubs and Girls' Clubs had been carrying out before the war came into greater prominence, and the club doors were opened wider than ever before, in spite of the absence on service of so many officers and senior boys.

Their work was standardised and co-ordinated by such

LINKED WITH AN HISTORIC PAST.
The Duke of Atholl inspecting the Guard of Honour of the Leith and Edinburgh Boys' Brigade at Holyrood Palace, Edinburgh, the historic shrine of Scotland's national spirit.

societies as the London Federation of Working Boys' Clubs, and in Liverpool the Union of Boys' Clubs. This linking up enabled the various clubs to work in touch and sympathy with one another without friction or overlapping, and facilitated the organisation of games, matches, and competitions.

The Boy Scouts' movement was founded in 1908 with the aim of developing good citizenship among boys by the inculcation, through attractive methods, of character and intelligence, handicraft, service for others, physical health and development. A notable feature about the Boy Scouts during the war was their ability to take the place of men called away on service, and to take upon themselves new duties demanded by the times.

War was declared at the time of the August holidays in 1914, which for the Scouts was the normal time for going into camp. They were thus ready in considerable numbers to take the field with camp equipment, trek-carts, etc., in all parts of the United Kingdom. Their services were in instant demand. It was known that among the many thousands of German residents in this country there were many charged with the duty of destroying communications in order to hamper the mobilisation of our forces on the declaration of war.

Coloured Photo, No. 5

Defiance Beneath its Defensive Web: Camouflaged British Howitzer

Thus telegraph and telephone wires, railway bridges and culverts, waterworks, marine cables, etc., had to be watched and guarded, and within a few hours this duty was being effectively done by troops or patrols of Scouts in every part of the country. They faithfully carried out their charge on demand of the chief constables, day and night, until military forces were available.

It is a remarkable fact that, as a result, no interruption of communications occurred at this eventful time.

Mr. Lloyd George wrote : " I do not think I am exaggerating when I say that the young boyhood of our country, represented by the Boy Scouts' Association, shares the laurels for having been pre- **Official praise** pared with the old and trusted and tried **and thanks** British Army and Navy. For both proved their title to make the claim when the Great War broke upon us like a thief in the night."

At the Admiralty, War Office, and other Government departments, Boy Scouts, whose training had specially fitted them for it, were taken on in numbers as orderlies and messengers. The extension of military establishments in many districts caused a further demand for their services, which was effectively supplied by the Scouts. In many cities the Scouts' headquarters were transformed into stations for supplying messengers to the police, hospital, and municipal authorities.

Similar duties were carried out in a minor degree, according to their distance from the theatre of war, by Scouts in the Overseas Dominions and in foreign countries.

Scouts were used as orderlies and buglers by the police in London and other centres for air-raid duties.

For their services in connection with recruiting during the early days of the war the Scouts received the appreciation and thanks of both Lord Kitchener and his successor, Lord Derby, as Secretary of State for War.

In common with cadet and other boys' organisations, the Scouts' Association arranged for the training of elder boys in military duties in anticipation of their being called up for service. But they went farther in that they carried out the instruction at no less than nine schools of training in the preliminary knowledge necessary for the air service.

In country districts the Scouts did much useful work in the collection of eggs for the use of hospitals, and in food production by helping the farmers and others. They also made themselves useful in the distribution of War Bonds and other Government circulars.

By their own efforts they raised a handsome sum of money, chiefly by working for it, since no begging or touting was allowed. They were thus enabled to send seven motor-ambulances to the front, and to set up and equip and man six recreation huts for soldiers in France and Italy.

The variety and value of their war services is fairly indicated by the testimonials received from the heads of the many different departments which they served.

A popular branch of the Boy Scouts' organisation was that of the Sea Scouts, boys specially trained in boat handling and the **Sea Scouts** elements of seamanship. At the moment **mobilised** when war was declared, a large force of these was assembling with a view to a great camp in the Isle of Wight for regattas and practical training.

They were thus mobilised when the call came for their services, and within a few hours they were on their way to take up duty at all the coastguard stations from John o' Groats to Land's End.

Their normal organisation, in " patrols " of six or eight boys under a senior or " patrol leader," lent itself specially to this distribution, a patrol being sent as a self-contained unit to each station. The Royal Naval Coastguardsmen were thus immediately relieved and enabled to join the Fleet for service afloat.

To the boys were assigned the duties of watch-keeping,

MARCH-PAST OF THE YOUNGEST MEMBERS OF THE SENIOR SERVICE.
Admiral Sir Rosslyn Wemyss, K.C.B., First Sea Lord, inspecting units of the Boys' Naval Brigade on the Horse Guards Parade in May, 1918. Inset above : Sir Rosslyn Wemyss speaking to one of the youngest of the boys of the brigade, which in the first three years of the war had sent over a thousand boys both to the Navy and Army, and five hundred into the Mercantile Marine.

patrolling, cyclist despatch-riding, telephone duty, and signalling, under the petty-officers in charge of stations. They were granted a messing allowance by the Admiralty, the boys doing their own catering and cooking.

The variety of their duties may be judged from the following log extract noted in the inspection of one small section of coast : " Warned a destroyer off the rocks in a fog." " Sighted and reported airship going S.S.E., five miles distant." " Provided night guard over damaged seaplane, which was towed ashore by drifter." " Light shown near —— at 3.15 a.m. for seven minutes, and again from apparently the same spot at 4.35 a.m." " Trawler No. —— came ashore. Permits all in order, except J—— M——, who had none. Took his name and address to police superintendent at ——." " Floating mine reported by fishing-boat No. ——. Proceeded with the patrol boat, which located and blew up the mine." " Provided guard over wreck and stores three days and nights in —— Bay."

In some parts of the coast the stations had no naval officer or man in charge, but the duties were none the less efficiently carried out, the " patrol leader " being given sole responsibility for their proper performance, and in no case was this trust misplaced.

Another gratifying point about the whole thing was that the sympathy and support they received was earned by the Scouts on their own merits. When they first

DINNER-TIME IN AN ITALIAN SCOUTS' CAMP.
Boy Scouts of Milan drawing rations when in holiday camp. The Italian Boy Scouts were officially utilised for auxiliary service with the Army during the war. They were given non-combatant duties, and by taking these released many able-bodied men for Army service at the front.

took over the duties there is no doubt that they were in most places unpopular ; the local men thought they were being deprived of the chance of Government pay by these boys coming to take up the duty of coast-watching, and they disliked them accordingly. They also thought that, being only boys, it would be easy to evade their instructions or to cow them, but they soon found their mistake. The lads carried out their duties with all the sense of responsibility and with all the determination of trained police, and were loyally backed by their officers when they made their reports to them.

The consequence was that the men soon found themselves shamed by these youngsters, who were doing their work for mere patriotic reasons, and doing it with a strict sense of duty that stood against all bullying and all underhand methods. Then their habit of doing good turns to their neighbours by helping in the gardens and houses around them, and helping on the farms or with the fishermen at their work, soon brought them favour, and they became popular at every station. It is a splendid result, and one of which not only the boys, but also their Scoutmasters and trainers may be proud.

This is what the naval officer in charge of this service on one part of the coast wrote concerning

BOYS WHO KEPT ALIVE THE SOUL OF INDEPENDENT SERBIA.
Serbian Boy Scouts at drill and (above) enjoying a boxing match in camp. Mobilised and attached to the Army as despatch-riders and orderlies on the outbreak of war, the Serbian Boy Scouts did particularly good work during the great retreat from the country, and afterwards, during the exile, they kept up their organisation and training so as to be ready for use directly opportunity offered.

FRENCH APPROVAL OF ENGLISH SCOUTS.
A rally of Boy Scouts, three thousand five hundred strong, paraded for Church Service at St. Paul's Cathedral, was inspected by Major Blanchard, of the French Army, in the courtyard of Guildhall.

the conscientiousness and reliability of the Sea Scouts:

They are doing excellent work *entirely by themselves.* . . . . They have never failed to patrol the coast and railway line and to carry their despatches through by night since August 4th, 1914, although, as you can well understand, the weather conditions on some occasions in these parts are very bad.

In addition to the coastguarding service, numbers of Scouts were employed as signallers, bridge-boys, and orderlies on the transports, hospital-ships, colliers, and mine-sweepers. Over a thousand were drafted into the Grand Fleet, since the special nature of their discipline and active intelligence, as encouraged by the Scout training, appealed with special force to the officers of the senior Service.

Many of the lads gained personal distinction in the performance of their duties, the more noticeable incidents being Boy Cornwell, whose pluck and endurance when mortally wounded gained for him the Victoria Cross; Midshipman Gyles, the hero of the hand-to-hand fighting with German boarders in the Channel; and Boy Ireland, who refused to leave his captain when the Britannic was sunk in the Ægean Sea.

Of the Scout training, Admiral Jellicoe wrote: " Discipline produced by this system is unquestionably that which is required by the Navy." And, in speaking of the ex-Boy Scouts in the ships under his command, Sir David Beatty said : " They are a credit to the form of training which has made them what they are. . . . I am glad to hear that the educational authorities are taking up the curriculum of the Sea Scout training— that is indeed a step in the right direction."

One of the wonderful developments of this wonderful war was the extent to which women came to the fore. Thanks to their splendid spirit, they rose to the occasion, and from highest to lowest a vast number of them took up war work in one form or another. What they may have lacked in trained capability they made up in adaptability. They very soon learned what was necessary, and were able to replace men in almost every trade and industry ; not only that, but in many cases they improved on the work and the output of their predecessors.

But it was evident that the ordinary school

education of the girl previous to this time had not brought out the qualities which lay within her. Although a good deal had been done for the boys in the way of Brigades, Scouts', and Cadet Corps, little had been done for the girls beyond the establishment of a few working-girls clubs and the Girl Guide movement.

The Girls' Friendly Society had a wide membership, as had also the Young Women's Christian Association, both excellent movements, but more for older girls and young women, and rather for their moral benefit than for their education.

The Girl Guides was practically the only institution which had for its definite aim the training of the girl outside the school walls in complement to what was taught within the school. The object of the Guide movement was to promote the same principles as those of the Boy Scouts—namely, the development in the girl of character and moral sense, handicraft and skill, health and hygiene, and service for others.

This was encouraged through a scheme of games, competitions, and badge-earning. Having been started only two or three years before the war, the number of girls trained through this agency was comparatively small, but the war work of even those few showed that the training was on the right lines for meeting the needs of the times ; and the movement, instead of suffering through the exigencies of the war, went ahead at a remarkable rate in its expansion. This went on not only throughout the British Isles, but in the Overseas Dominions and other countries as well.

Work of the Girl Guides

The need of such common-sense training was evident, and the spirit of the times made the girls eager to join and to practise service in the form of " doing their bit " in the war. Thus, although only schoolgirls, as a rule, and therefore more restricted in their activities than their brothers, large numbers of them in the capacity of Guides took up the work of acting as assistant ward and house maids at the hospitals, as land-workers and harvesters on farms, as messengers for the War Office and other Government offices and Ministries, besides carrying out egg-collections for hospitals and waste-paper collections, and other work by

IN THE LAND OF KNIGHTLY SERVICE.
Japanese Boy Scouts in their picturesque uniform being reviewed at Tokyo by General Fukushima, Vice-Chief of the General Staff of the Japanese Army. Above : The distinguished general addressing the Scouts after the inspection.

In the United States of America the development of this movement had been the greatest, and its national work was on the most extensive scale. Numbering close on 300,000 boys, it was organised for special work, particularly in the direction of distribution of War Liberty Loan literature and canvassing and propaganda work in connection with this. For this service the boys received the cordial appreciation of the President of the Treasury. So, too, in the food production they earned the praise of the director of that department for their organised campaign under the slogan of " Every Scout to feed a soldier."

In France the Scouts did valuable work as messengers to the Army offices, in some cases also serving in British Staff offices. Also they were employed as orderlies in the hospitals, where their services were much appreciated.

One Scout stood as an example of the spirit in these lads. When captured by Germans, he refused to give away the position of a French party which was known to be in the neigh-   **Martyrdom of a** bourhood. He was accordingly placed   **French Scout** against a telegraph-post and shot for his patriotism. One of the German officers went so far as to admit it was a pity that he should have to be killed.

King Albert's two sons became Boy Scouts, and the movement was strong in Belgium before the war. The Scouts of Antwerp particularly distinguished themselves in the early days of the war by their valuable work in carrying out communication work and sending supplies between that city and the outlying defences. In the withdrawal of the Belgian Army they were attached to the Army Headquarters, and played a useful part as cyclist orderlies both then and subsequently in the campaign in Flanders. Scouts were also useful as orderlies

WELCOME TIDINGS BUGLE-BORNE.
Boy Scouts in the City of London receiving their instructions at a police-station before setting out to sound the " All Clear " through the streets after an enemy air raid had been finally repelled.

which they were able to raise funds and establish and equip a fine recreation hut for the men in France, and send out a motor-ambulance, which, in their name, was presented to the Army by Princess Mary.

The overseas branches, more especially in Canada, also gave useful aid in the provision of comforts for the men at the front. For these the Guides supplied a recreation hut and workers, as well as a motor-ambulance.

The American branch of the movement—strongly organised and ably administered by Mrs. Low—rendered useful service of a similar kind in the United States.

If the war had done no other good, it, at any rate, gave an immense opportunity to woman.

Guide training was designed to ensure that the spirit engendered among the young generation should be continued when there was no longer the   **Purpose of** glamour of war work to arouse it, and   **Guide training** that the girls should be trained in character, in discipline, and in general capability to meet what would be expected of them in their time.

But, though tending to make citizens of them, the training was not therefore intended to make men of them. Their womanliness was to be preserved, and their efficiency in homecraft helped, so that they might in fact as well as in name be the best guides as well as better mothers for the succeeding generation.

While dealing with the question of the share of juveniles in the war, it may not be out of place to note very briefly what our Allies in other countries did at that time.

The Boy Scout movement had been adopted in almost every civilised country before the war, and this fact had an after-war possibility that is not without its significance when considered in conjunction with what boys did during the war.

ON DUTY AT A RAILWAY TUNNEL.
Early in the war Boy Scouts did good service guarding places where enemy agents might have wrought damage. Two Scouts were here watching a railway tunnel while others were being posted above.

to certain of the hospitals, one of their duties being the care and repair of surgical instruments.

The Italian Boy Scouts, at whose head was the Crown Prince, early in the war did some good but unassuming work. They attracted the notice of the authorities, and later on the Ministry of War utilised the Scouts for auxiliary service with the Army. They were given non-combatant duties, but by taking these they released able-bodied men for Army work at the front. Some served as orderlies to British Staff officers.

The Serbian Boy Scouts had as their chief the Crown Prince of Serbia. Very early in the war they distinguished themselves by their useful work as orderlies and first-aiders at the hospitals. Then, when their country was invaded, they were mobilised and attached to the Army as despatch-riders and orderlies, and did particularly good work in the retreat from their country. During their enforced banishment the Scouts kept up their

NAVAL OFFICERS IN THE MAKING.
Cadets of the Royal Naval College, Keyham, Devonport, receiving instruction in navigation. Taking sun sights with the sextant to determine the exact position of their ship.

HEAVING THE LEAD.
Instruction in seamanship on board H.M.S. Elf. One of the cadets in training at the Royal Naval College at Keyham, Devonport, engaged in heaving the lead to ascertain the depth of the water beneath the vessel.

for internment, and the same was the case with the Scouts in Holland.

Very friendly relations, with interchange of greetings, was also maintained with the Boy Scouts in Spain, in whose uniform the King himself appeared as their chief; and so, too, with the Scouts of Denmark.

In China some of the Scouts volunteered and proceeded to France as interpreters and managers of the Chinese Labour Corps.

It is evident that possibilities underlie this association which exists among the boys and girls of the various nations inspired with a common ideal. **Comradeship in**
Their feeling of brotherhood **many nations** has been cemented by the comradeship of war duties, and strengthened by mutual sympathy and intercorrespondence. If this spirit can be developed, as is the hope of the promoters, it will no doubt form not merely a useful incentive to efficiency for the rising generation, but also a bond such as will hold them in close relationship with their neighbours, and will be the best guarantee for good, mutual understanding towards the permanency of peace in the years to come.

organisation and training, ready to be of use to their country as soon as opportunity offered.

In Rumania the Scout movement, though of recent origin, was utilised during the war for co-ordinating the services of boys with Army requirements as orderlies, etc., and in the enforced retirement of the main forces to the north-east corner of the country the Scouts did further valuable work in the direction of food production.

Scout movement In Greece the Boy Scouts of Athens, **world-wide** among other things, showed kindness and hospitality to their British brother Scouts when some of these were rescued from the hospital-ship Britannic at the time when she was torpedoed off the coast.

The Scouts of Salonika did splendid work in the great fire there, and in the course of this six of them lost their lives.

The Scouts of neutral countries, in more than one place, did exceedingly good service during the war. Thus, in Switzerland, they made themselves of great use in the reception and guiding of prisoners of war arriving there

TAKING THEIR BEARINGS.
Cadets on board H.M.S. Elf gathered round the compass for instruction in taking the bearings of the sun, and so determining their vessel's course.

One of Britain's floating workshops: A naval repair-ship, thrashing her way out to the assistance of a cruiser temporarily incapacitated by engine trouble in mid-ocean, greeted as she passes by an armed yacht also flying the White Ensign.

To the aid of a neutral flying signals of distress: A small British patrol cruiser standing by to take off the crew of a neutral wind-jammer which has struck a mine and is on fire forward and sinking by the head.

REPAIR AND RESCUE WORK AT SEA BY SHIPS OF GREAT BRITAIN'S NAVY.

NEW MEN AND NEW METHODS AT SEA: THE BRITISH NAVY ADJUSTS ITSELF TO THE SUBMARINE.

By H. W. Wilson, Author of "Ironclads in Action," etc.

Indecisiveness of the Naval Operations in the Early Years of the War Due to the Antiquated System of Control—Conditions Revolutionised by the Development of the Submarine—The Lines of Destiny—Facts and Figures Relating to the German Blockade of Great Britain—Vital Importance of the Strait of Dover—Operations against Germany's Naval Bases in Flanders in 1917—Commodore Tyrwhitt's Energetic Action on the Belgian and Dutch Coasts—Savagery of German Submarine Crews—Squadron-Commander Savory's Flight from Great Britain to Constantinople—British Activity in the Bight of Heligoland and off the Coast of Jutland—Nine Neutral Merchantmen and Two British Destroyers Sunk by German Cruisers off Shetland—German Attacks on Convoys off the Tyne and the Norwegian Coast—Three British Destroyers Torpedoed off the Dutch Coast—Admiral Sir Rosslyn Wemyss Appointed First Sea Lord and the Admiralty Reorganised—Breslau Sunk off Imbros and Goeben Driven Ashore—Adventures of the German Raider Wolf—German Destroyer Raids in the Strait of Dover—British Official Disclosure of the Tonnage Losses Inflicted by Submarines—Zeebrugge and Ostend Sealed Up by British Naval Forces—The Price of Victory.

IN Chapter CLXXX. (Vol. 9, page 233) the history of the naval war was carried down to the close of May, 1917, at which date the British Admiralty was being slowly remodelled. A series of changes had then been made. The General Staff that was so urgently needed to anticipate the enemy's moves, and use to the highest advantage the immense force available, had not yet been created. The history of the next months of the naval war was to be mainly a record of continued submarine depredations at sea, and in Great Britain of the progress towards a better and more efficient Staff system, the necessity of which was recognised by most of the younger British naval officers. Without it the British Navy lacked a brain and was at a dangerous disadvantage against the German Navy, in which a General Staff, modelled on that of the German Army, had existed for many years and functioned admirably.

Experience shows that modern war is too complicated to be

MAJOR-GENERAL A. S. COLLARD, C.B., R.E.
In November, 1917, General Collard, who had been Director of Inland Waterways and Docks, was appointed Deputy Controller for Auxiliary Shipbuilding, and in March, 1918, was given powers to devote himself exclusively to the development of the new national shipyards and further to extend the existing private yards and engine shops.

conducted by a single man, however gifted. Napoleon was the last soldier who attempted thus to direct large-scale campaigns, and though his was certainly the greatest genius that had ever devoted itself to military problems—though he was young and endowed with almost superhuman energy—his methods broke down fatally in Spain, in Russia in 1812, in Saxony in 1813. He complained himself that with his one-man system "nothing is foreseen." The Germans, after the close of Napoleon's wars, studied his strategy, and believed that they had discovered a means of avoiding his mistakes. It was to concentrate the control of operations in the hands of a small body of men who represented not influence or rank or birth, but the highest ability and intelligence. Five men under the old Moltke, three of them only lieutenant-colonels, and one a mere major, directed the strategy of the German armies in 1870. The same system, revised and improved, was employed in the German Army in the Great War. German Staff officers were carefully prepared for their duty by a close and prolonged study of the history of war, corrected by constant practice in the use of all its weapons. Work at Headquarters alternated with work in the field or at sea.

In the British Navy, down to 1918, operations were directed by officers who were capable administrators, but were not noted as students of strategy. The control of the whole vast machine, which included some five thousand vessels of various types, manned by 450,000 men, was centralised in the hands of a single person, the First Sea Lord. This system was the product of an age

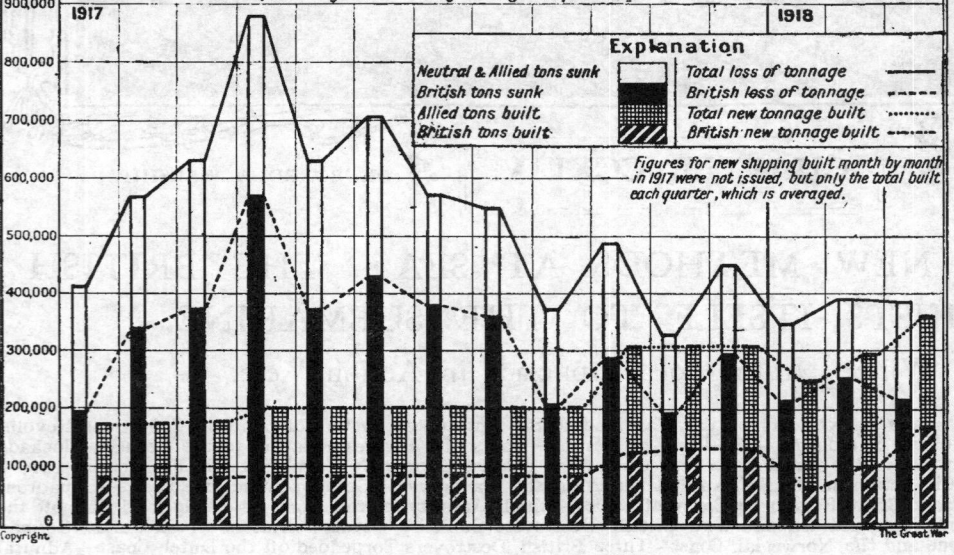

THE LINES OF FATE AT SEA.
Diagram comparing the shipping losses of Great Britain and of the Allies and neutrals in the submarine campaign month by month with the new tonnage constructed. If the line of loss remained permanently above the line of new construction, the defeat of the Allies was inevitable.

of peace in which the Navy had seen no serious fighting. It was not the system under which the British Navy had defeated Napoleon's Navy. The First Sea Lord was not left free to devote his mind to strategy. On the contrary he was overwhelmed beneath a mountain of detail. On his desk every morning would be found a pile of some fifteen hundred letters and telegrams, all of which he was expected to answer personally. From early morning he was lost in this jungle of correspondence, and if he ever emerged from it it was with energy exhausted and brain wearied. The indecisiveness of the operations at sea in the earlier years of the war arose not from any inherent defect in the officers in charge of the Admiralty; on the contrary, one at least of them, Lord Fisher, was penetrated to the highest degree with the offensive spirit, and had foreseen the peril of the submarine before the war and the need for an energetic policy in the Baltic. The failure arose from a system which was out of date.

Through the first two years of the submarine campaign the British Navy followed the plans that had been drawn up without reference to the submarine. **Navy fettered by** Lord Fisher had warned the Government **obsolete system** of the danger in 1912 and 1914, but had been regarded as an alarmist, in precisely the same way that Ministers were certain before the war that the Germans would never venture to bomb London from the air. The submarine was not a factor that could be ignored. It had revolutionised conditions at sea. Its growing power required a complete revision of the allied strategy, yet the professional head of the Admiralty was without the leisure needed for the work of revision, and he had at his elbow no strategist to help in his judgment. When Lord Fisher, after his brief term of administration, left the Admiralty in May, 1915, on the ground that ships which were required in the North Sea were

being despatched to the Dardanelles, his vast offensive plans were tacitly discarded, as there was no one with the intense energy needed to prosecute them. A purely defensive policy was followed, on the line of least resistance, which was to parry the enemy's strokes and not to strike the enemy. The British Navy was strong, and its officers and men were penetrated with the finest spirit, or the results of this strategy might have been much more serious. The Germans had a system which could succeed without genius at the top. The British, down to 1918, had a system which was liable to fail from faults of organisation, even if it were in the hands of a genius.

For the Navy to change its whole system of High Command and strategy in war was a critical measure. It was the more dangerous because any change was opposed by honest conservatism and by many good officers who had grown up under the old system, and could not believe in the possibility of improving it. The real test of organisation, however, is success. The business of the High Command in war is to win victories. Nothing else matters.

If victories are not won with superior force, if, on the contrary, reverses recur, then reform is needed, When the organisation is sound, as it was in the British Navy at Trafalgar, the consummate commander at sea (in the person of Nelson) and the great strategist at the Admiralty (in the person of Barham) work together, and then the result is " not victory, but annihilation."

The safety of the Allies and the fate of Great Britain depended on two lines. The first showed the shipping sunk by the submarines. The second showed the new shipping completed. These were the lines of destiny. If the line of losses remained continuously above the line showing new shipping com-   **The lines of** pleted, the collapse of the Allies could   **destiny** only be a question of time. Obviously, however, the building of ships to replace those sunk was a mere passive measure of defence. A far better policy was to adopt methods which would prevent submarines from getting to sea at all, or, if they did, would enable the Allies to attack and sink them. A hunted submarine has no leisure to destroy merchantmen. Before the war 1,900,000 tons of shipping had been launched in Great Britain's best year, but by 1916 the output had fallen to 542,000 tons. In 1917 this was distinctly improved, and 1,163,000 tons were launched. In 1918 it was hoped to construct 1,800,000 tons, and eventually to reach an output of 3,000,000 tons a year. But many difficulties arose. Shipbuilding was conducted by the State and taken over from private firms, and the State made many mistakes, with serious consequences. The steel needed for an enormous programme of shipbuilding left so much less for offensive weapons, for the construction of guns and shells and warships. The labour needed had to some extent to be taken from the fighting ranks, as women could only be employed to a limited degree. The plant necessary had itself to be created, and this made further demands on the supply of material and men. The cost to Great Britain, whose shipping suffered most, was grievous, and was aggravated by the conduct of some workers in her shipyards who frequently struck work, and by the slackness of others who, when their wages were

[Laffan.

[Val L'Estrange.

[Russell.

REAR-ADMIRAL S. R. FREMANTLE.
DEPUTY CHIEF OF NAVAL STAFF.

REAR-ADMIRAL SIR A. L. DUFF.
ASSISTANT CHIEF OF NAVAL STAFF.

REAR-ADMIRAL G. P. W. HOPE.
DEPUTY FIRST SEA LORD.

[Russell.

[Russell.

VICE-ADMIRAL SIR H. L. HEATH.
SECOND SEA LORD.

ADMIRAL SIR ROSSLYN WEMYSS.
FIRST SEA LORD AND CHIEF OF STAFF.

REAR-ADMIRAL L. HALSEY.
THIRD SEA LORD.

[Elliott & Fry.

[Bassano.

[Elliott & Fry.

MR. ARTHUR F. PEASE.
SECOND CIVIL LORD.

REAR-ADMIRAL H. H. D. TOTHILL.
FOURTH SEA LORD.

RT. HON. E. G. PRETYMAN.
CIVIL LORD.

Personnel of the Board of Admiralty as reorganised and rearranged in January, 1918.

The portraits in the top row are of the admirals engaged with the First Sea Lord in the "operations" duties of the Admiralty. Those on each side of Sir Rosslyn Wemyss and in the bottom row are of officials engaged in "maintenance" duties.

German picture of a U boat submerging to attack the convoy seen on the horizon

Always ready: Battleships of the British Grand Fleet lying at anchor with steam up

Suspense: The Spanish mail steamer Infanta Isabel de Borbon held up by a U boat off Cadiz.

"Good luck!": Incoming British destroyer (on left) greeting a submarine going out on patrol.

On board one of H.M. ships at Kola Inlet, North Russia.   Right : Taking coal aboard from a collier in the Arctic.   These picturesque photographs illustrate one aspect of the arduous conditions in which the British Navy carried on its work during the war.

Breaking up the ice around a frozen-in ship in the Dwina River to keep the highway clear. The important Russian port of Archangel lies at the mouth of the Dwina, where it empties itself into the White Sea.

Under the White Ensign in the white regions of the Arctic.

raised, did less, increasing the stringency. This attitude was in signal contrast with that of the ununiformed, unmedalled heroes of the British merchant service, who faced privation, wounds, and death, and the indomitable devotion of the Royal Navy and its auxiliary services. Those who suffered most by the war never uttered a complaint, but went faithfully about their duty.

Each ship lost in this period of the war counted more and had a much graver effect than in the earlier period. For now the available tonnage had been so greatly reduced that there was no surplus of any kind. First one thing and then another had to be eliminated from the British imports as the noose tightened about Great Britain's neck. Paper, sugar, fattening materials for cattle, manures, wine, petroleum, petrol, one after another these articles had to be so reduced in quantity that the life of the nation began to feel the pressure. The short-sightedness of the politicians who in the half century before the war had permitted British agriculture to fall into decrepitude was cruelly punished. The momentary cheapness for which self-dependence had been sacrificed cost the people dear indeed. A full account has been given in Chapter CXCVI. (Vol. 10, page 91) of the strenuous efforts made in 1916-17 to increase the output of food, and of the success which attended it despite many great difficulties that had to be overcome and numerous mistakes which were perhaps inevitable in so gigantic an enterprise. Whatever the activity of the submarines, it was proved that with ordinary foresight in administration Great Britain could never be starved. She could grow enough potatoes if their culture was not discouraged by fixing too low a price, and she could obtain enough fish to maintain her population if she had the will to suffer and endure before privation, increasing loss, and the sacrifice of her manhood. The storm darkened visibly about her, but she set her back to the wall, though one by one the lights of her life were extinguished. She was losing the world and recovering her soul.

Growing strain on British shipping

The German blockade of Great Britain was not, like the earlier British blockade of Germany, largely illusory and nullified by qualms of diplomacy. Its effect was felt in a growing shortage of every imported article. Tonnage had to be concentrated on indispensables—a bare sufficiency of food, munitions, and raw materials for munitions. In mid-1917 a fresh strain was imposed on British shipping. To move the new American Army to Europe and keep it supplied meant immense new demands for shipping, which in 1916 and early 1917 none of the Allies had foreseen. The American Government, as far as it possibly could, used American ships or the German vessels seized in American ports for the transport of its forces, but the American tonnage had previously been conveying supplies to the Allies in Europe, and now became unavailable for that purpose. Another factor which augmented the pressure on Great Britain was the comparative failure of the harvest of 1917 in France and Italy, which the British people had to make good, and the almost complete failure of the American plans for sending food and supplies to Europe in the early weeks of 1918 through the severe weather which deranged the American railways. The Allies in their fierce struggle had not only man against them, but in these most critical hours they had to suffer ill-fortune as well. No such storm as that which in early January, 1918, visited the American seaboard and Eastern States had been known for decades.

Before the war the ocean-going vessels in the British merchant service totalled nearly 18 million tons, of which 3 millions were engaged in trade between the various dominions and foreign countries, while the remaining 15 million were engaged in trade with the United Kingdom. In mid-1917 the British ocean-going tonnage had fallen to 15 million tons, of which 14 millions were employed in home service. Of this nearly half was allotted to the needs of the Navy, the Army, and the Allies, so that only about 7 million tons remained to carry on in war the traffic which had demanded the service of 15 million tons in peace. Nor was this all. Before the war vessels could make more voyages in a given time. They were not delayed loading or unloading ; they had not to wait for mine-fields to be cleared or convoys to arrive, nor had they to follow a devious course at sea so as to elude the submarine. What time was actually lost from these causes does not appear. But it would probably not be incorrect to state that the carrying power of each ton of shipping was reduced by them to the extent of 25 or 30 per cent., and perhaps more. So that the 7 million tons of shipping would only do as much work as 5 or 6 million tons before the war, and the carrying power available for Great Britain had been reduced by two-thirds. Before the war Great Britain imported annually goods of the weight of 58 million tons, of which 43 million tons were raw materials and luxuries. In 1916 these same imports had been reduced to 15 million tons. In this figure material imported by the Government was not counted.

German railway system secure

The far-reaching effect of the submarine blockade has already been indicated in the chapter dealing with the Italian reverses (vol. 11, page 69). In the second stage of the great duel between sea-power and land-power, which filled the last half of 1917 and the early months of 1918, land-power consistently gained. The German railway system was consolidated and assured. At no point were the Allies able to menace it. To the vast system which linked Zeebrugge and Hamburg with the Balkans, Constantinople, the Bagdad front, and Palestine was now added another series of systems placing Germany in land communication by railway with Petrograd, Moscow, Kieff, Kharkoff, the Black Sea, Transcaucasia, and even farther afield with Siberia, Turkestan, and the North-West of India. At the same time the strain on the German railways was relieved by the complete control of the Baltic and the partial control of the Black Sea which the German Navy gained through the collapse of Russia. Both these seas from the end of 1917 onwards could be used by shipping under the German flag, some considerable part of which had been British. Through a want of foresight at the Foreign Office on the eve of war (and, in the case of the Black Sea, during the early weeks of the struggle) this shipping had been permitted to enter these dangerous waters, and had been virtually handed over to Germany.

Sea-power menaced by the submarine

While Germany was able to move troops, munitions, and supplies without any hindrance over these two closed seas and over the gigantic system of railways which spanned Europe and Western Asia, and while she had now easy access to the most fertile areas of the world, British naval communications remained precarious and exposed to attack by two species of craft—submarines and surface raiders. While Great Britain largely depended on imported goods which had to be conveyed over the treacherous water, liable to attack at each moment of the voyage, Germany was self-dependent and could draw what she wanted overland without fear of hostile attack. Sea-power had sustained a tremendous blow as the result of the illegal employment of the submarine and the difficulty of the Allies in adjusting themselves to the new conditions. Air-power might to some extent have undone the mischief, but between 1914 and 1916 (except for the brief interlude of Lord Fisher's administration) the British strategists and Ministries had rather regarded aircraft as subsidiary weapons, and the advocates of unlimited air war as faddists, and it was not till the submarine campaign was far advanced that they altered their policy. Throughout the Great War democracy, though it was fighting for right and its life, was more conservative, more averse to resolute thinking, large ideas, and quick adaptation ; more sluggish in action, more inclined to those half or quarter measures which in war notoriously and inevitably spell unsuccess, than the syndicate of clever men which controlled German policy. Germany listened to her able experts. The German Staff was supreme, and it concentrated its entire attention on the defeat of the Allies. The allied statesmen, owing to party exigencies, devoted half their time to purely internal questions and political disputes, and thus could not always act quickly and completely.

The Germans throughout the later months of 1917 were completing submarines at the rate of from six to seven per month. At what rate the Allies were sinking them was not disclosed. Probably towards the end of the year the German losses were almost as great as the number of new submarines completed. According to a semi-official German statement, between February 15th and June 1st, 1917, only fifteen German submarines failed to return to their bases. This figure would show a loss of only about three boats per month in that period, or less than one per week.

In November Sir Eric Geddes, who was then First Lord of the Admiralty, announced in Parliament that "from the beginning of the war between **Estimated losses of** 40 and 50 per cent. of the German sub- **German U boats** marines commissioned and operating in the North Sea, Atlantic, and Arctic Oceans" had been sunk. By the close of January, 1918, the German losses were estimated by a British authority at 100 boats, which was not far from half the total strength of their force. Most of these boats were destroyed with all their crew, meeting the fate which they thoroughly deserved.

The line of British losses in merchant shipping fell considerably between June, 1917, and the spring of 1918. But even in 1918 the loss remained serious. It fluctuated

ROYAL VISIT TO DOCKYARDS.
King George inspecting the crews of auxiliary vessels and mine-sweepers during a visit which he paid to the naval establishments at the Nore on May 23rd, 1918.

slightly from week to week, rising when the weather favoured the Germans and their best submarine captains were at sea. Convoy by surface warships was largely employed by the Allies, but was not always a complete protection.

The German submarines occasionally attacked convoyed vessels with success, as in the case of the transport Tuscania, torpedoed with American troops on board, on February 5th, 1918. Convoy, however, decreased the risk, because an attack made on a convoyed ship or squadron in daylight usually meant the destruction of the submarine, and few German captains at this stage of the war were eager to face this.

This system of convoy, coupled with a great system of patrol, necessarily involved a very severe strain on the Navy and its auxiliaries. According to figures given by Sir Eric Geddes, British warships during a typical month in 1917 had steamed a million miles in home waters, while

SURVIVORS OF THE TORPEDOED AMERICAN TRANSPORT TUSCANIA.
Public reception at Southampton of a thousand American soldiers, some of the survivors from the transport Tuscania, which, although proceeding under convoy, had been torpedoed by a German submarine about ten miles off the Irish coast on February 5th, 1918. The vessel, an Anchor liner built in 1914, had 2,397 people on board (including 2,011 officers and men of the American Army), of whom 210 lost their lives.

HEROES OF THE DOVER PATROL.
Three of those who received medals at Dover on March 3rd, 1918, from Admiral Sir Rosslyn Wemyss for having greatly distinguished themselves in the work of the Dover Patrol. They were (from left to right): Deckhand A. Holt, Engineer T. H. Walkerley, and Seaman A. Chambers.

little time to submerge. Sometimes the U boat dived too late. In one case a seaplane caught a German submarine on the surface, and before she could submerge dropped a bomb on her stern which made a large hole in her deck. Immediately after there emerged from a stratum of mist three more German submarines accompanied by three German destroyers and two seaplanes. All these vessels opened fire on the British seaplane, but without effect. The British pilot turned and dropped a second bomb on the damaged submarine and saw her sink in the midst of wreckage in a film of oil. He made good his retreat after this very fine piece of work.

The waters most frequented by submarines were those in which the depth conditions were most favourable, ranging from 100 to 200 feet. There a large submarine could safely " sit " on the bottom with engines stopped, and without any risk of surface ships colliding with her. She would require a depth of 40 feet or so completely to submerge her, and on the top of that at least another 30 or 40 feet of water to take ships clear of her; a greater depth was desirable if she was not to be seen and reported by aircraft or troubled by heavy seas. On the other hand, below 250 feet the pressure became **Waters frequented** severe, and though British submarines, **by submarines** and probably also German boats, during the war descended to greater depths, there was some danger and considerable inconvenience in so doing. In deep water a submarine had to remain on the surface or to keep her engine running if she submerged, and this both used electricity and was apt to disclose her presence. These facts will explain why the German boats cruised mainly at certain points, such as the entrance to the English Channel, the Bristol Channel, and the Irish Sea. The depth of water there was favourable, and moreover

naval auxiliary forces had steamed six million miles. In the North Atlantic and Arctic Oceans the examining squadrons achieved " the almost incredible feat of intercepting and examining every single merchant ship trading with neutral countries." In that work the Royal Naval Air Service co-operated with signal results. It had increased during the war from 700 men to 41,000. In September, 1917, its patrols covered 170,000 miles— 90,000 by seaplanes and 80,000 by airships. On seven occasions in that month seaplanes received appeals for help from ships which were being attacked, and arrived in time to drive down the submarines. The Germans learnt to dread these swift and terrible dragons of the air. Whereas the destroyer in the most favourable circumstances could not come at a call at a speed of more than 30 knots (if that), a seaplane could proceed to the scene of action at 70 or 80 miles an hour, giving the submarine

KING GEORGE AT A MARCH-PAST OF HIS NAVAL FIGHTING MEN.
The King at Harwich, on February 26th, 1918, where he inspected naval forces and visited various training and air establishments. His Majesty received a large number of officers of the Fleet. These photographs show, on the left, King George holding a review of hundreds of men who had fought in almost every naval engagement of the war; and, on the right, some of the men marching past.

BRITISH SUBMARINE IN THE MAKING.
Interior view of a British submarine in course of construction. Some idea of the size of the underwater vessel may be gathered by comparing with it the size of the men who were at work in it.

them was therefore one of the aims of British strategy, and this involved a great barrage, lavish use of mines, and a powerful force of patrols. As sufficient destroyers were not available for the work of patrolling, drifters and other small fishing craft, to the number of a hundred or thereabouts, were used to watch the strait. These were not fighting vessels, and their weakness invited constant attack from the German destroyers.

To keep the Zeebrugge destroyers under control was thus one of the most important tasks of the British Navy. Early in June a series of operations was carried out against the German bases in Flanders. The first stage of the attack was a

these were the points on which sea traffic concentrated, giving the Germans a better chance of finding targets.

To deal with the invisible pirates, science was called in. A new instrument, known as the hydrophone and described in the French Press, enabled allied vessels to hear the sound of the submarine's engines and screws in the water when she was moving. Other new instruments indicated her presence when she was at rest on the bottom. To destroy or disable submarines, depth charges were still largely used. As has already been explained, they were bombs containing a large quantity of high explosive, dropped to the depth at which the submarine was supposed to be lying, and detonated, if possible, in contact with her hull. If her position was not exactly gauged her hull would be only shaken and her crew frightened, and though her outer tanks might be damaged and oil escape to the surface, the inner skin of the vessel might not be pierced or her seaworthiness be destroyed. Improved construction

Importance of the Strait of Dover

had made the German submarines very much safer for their crews than the earlier craft had been. Vessels of the Deutschland class, modelled on the boat which had crossed the Atlantic in 1916, were most generally employed in 1917. They were not far from 300 feet in length, had good sea-keeping qualities, and were capable of standing rough usage. But as the boats improved the crews declined in efficiency, owing to the heavy loss inflicted by the British Navy.

Though in this period of the war Zeebrugge was not much used by the larger German submarines, because of the mining and bombing operations of the British flotillas and aircraft, it was a matter of extreme importance for the Germans to be able to pass the Strait of Dover. It was a laborious and dangerous undertaking to navigate submarines round the North Coast of Scotland through stormy waters and violent currents and tide-rips. If they could steal down the coast of Holland (voyaging for a considerable part of their run in neutral waters), and then dash through the Strait of Dover at night, they gained, according to trustworthy calculation, from ten days to a fortnight in reaching their favourite cruising grounds in the Channel. To close the Strait of Dover to

NEARING COMPLETION.
External view of a submarine being constructed in a British shipyard. In the foreground the first deck-plates were being fitted, while in the distance expert workers were engaged in the task of fixing the periscope.

vigorous bombing by R.N.A.S. aeroplanes of the German seaplane base at Zeebrugge and of the shipping in port there, on the night of June 3rd-4th, to cripple the German aircraft and prevent them from interfering with subsequent operations. This air bombardment was accomplished without any loss of British machines, and was exceedingly successful.

The next stage was a naval bombardment, on June 5th, of the German basins and docks at Ostend, whither the Germans had been forced by the air attack to remove certain of their undamaged submarines. The bombardment was carried out by a considerable force, which fired a large number of rounds at long range. The ships taking part in it were out of sight of the coast, and their fire was controlled by British aircraft.

The results were good. Photographic reconnaissance showed that most of the German workshops were destroyed or badly damaged. The entrance gates to the dockyard basin and the submarine shelter were wrecked. Several vessels were sunk, and a destroyer was crippled, while the

British vessels sustained no injury, probably because of the efficiency of the aircraft co-operating. As had been expected, the German torpedo craft in the harbour put to sea to escape the shells. They were able to get out because the weather was hazy and the British squadron was at some distance. The Germans found the British waiting for them in another direction. During the night Commodore Tyrwhitt, who was so constantly in action in the North Sea, had moved out to the Belgian coast with a powerful force of light cruisers and destroyers. His difficulty always was to get the German craft far enough from their bases to be able to reach them. They were fast and wary; on the slightest sign of a British vessel appearing above the horizon they were apt to retire. On this occasion he sighted six vessels of the S type, destroyers of 555 tons, built shortly before the war, with a speed of 32½ knots, and manned by about 100 officers and men. As usual, they steamed off at their fastest when his racing cruisers came into view, but he was able to get within extreme range of them and to effect several hits on two of them, and perhaps

Six German destroyers engaged to damage others. The S20, last in the German line, was sunk, and seven of her crew were picked up in the water by the British. There were no British casualties, and no damage to the British vessels.

The British naval losses were heavy all through the early summer. The most notable are tabulated at the end of this chapter. On May 26th the hospital-ship Windsor Castle, with 600 wounded on board, was wantonly sunk by two torpedoes. Six of the crew perished, but all the wounded were saved; and all on board behaved with magnificent gallantry, the captain in particular, Commander Wilfrid, setting an heroic example. On July 9th a terrible calamity befell the British Navy in the destruction of the Dreadnought battleship Vanguard. She was lying at anchor with the fleet when she suddenly blew up. All on board her perished, a total of 804 officers

AIR BOMBARDMENT OF BEYROUT.
British seaplanes' attack on storehouses and railway sidings at Beyrout Harbour. A direct hit had been obtained on the railway offices, seen on fire in the centre, while sheds on the right had also suffered.

EVIDENCE FROM THE AIR OF INSTRUCTIONS DULY CARRIED OUT.
Further photographs of the attack by British aeroplanes on the storehouses and railway sidings of Beyrout Harbour. Inset above is a copy of the photograph that was issued with the airmen's operation orders. That hits were obtained at A, B, and C was immediately revealed by the photographs taken indicating the results. The lower photograph shows the effect of the bomb that was dropped at A.

and men. Her loss fell in the same class of mysteries as that of the mine-layer Princess Patricia, the battleship Bulwark, and the armoured cruiser Natal, all destroyed by internal explosion. She displaced 19,250 tons, mounted ten 12 in. guns, and had been launched in 1909.

In the North Sea, which was now being slowly closed by mine-fields, the British Navy had left a wide channel free of mines off the Dutch coast, out of deference to Dutch susceptibilities. German shipping, however, made such constant use of this channel that Germany rather than Holland profited by its existence. The Germans laid mines where they listed, in neutral and open waters, without saying a word and without receiving a remonstrance. The British **Smart capture of** announced to neutrals the exact **German merchantmen** location of their mine-fields, and for this received not gratitude, but protests. German traffic between Zeebrugge and Heligoland was systematically conducted through the safe channel, and German merchantmen took to carrying freight from Rotterdam and the Rhine ports to Hamburg by it, thus relieving the strain on their worn-out railways. The British Government tardily announced its determination to close this channel by a mine-field which would have stretched across the North Sea to a point near the Yorkshire coast. It modified its plans when the Dutch protested with a violence they had never displayed in dealing with the brutal outrages of the German submarines on their own ships. On July 16th Commodore Tyrwhitt struck a sharp blow at the traffic. At 1 a.m. that day a number of German merchantmen left Rotterdam

MONITOR AGAINST SEAPLANE.
Anti-aircraft gun in action from a well sand-bagged position on board a British monitor off Trieste. The monitor had been attacked by an enemy seaplane.

for Heligoland. At 4.30, when they were proceeding comfortably on their course, they sighted a considerable force of British cruisers and destroyers. The British stood in between them and the shore, and immediately hoisted signals to "stop and abandon ship," enforcing them by shots across the bows of the German vessels. The Germans disregarded the order. Two vessels made for the Dutch coast and reached it near Bergen, but in so doing were badly damaged by the British fire. Four others were cut off and captured by the British destroyers, which brought them away under their own steam, two of them with their German crews on board. Several shells from the British flotillas unfortunately reached the coast, but the attack was delivered by the British at a distance of four miles from it, and therefore outside territorial waters, which only extend three miles from the coast. Dutch war vessels arrived as the action was over and as the British were steaming off, leaving the two German ships which had stranded, one of them badly on fire. The damaged German vessel was subsequently floated and repaired.

A cry of rage went up from Germany at this skilful and successful attack, and the Dutch Government, under German pressure, protested strongly on the theory that the British had violated **Impudent complaint** Dutch territorial waters. The fact, how- **by Germany** ever, was that the action had taken place four miles from the coast, as we have seen. In any case, the use by one belligerent of those territorial waters as a corridor was a flagrant violation of the essence of neutrality, and ought certainly to have been stopped at the outset, not to have been tolerated for three years. The Germans had the less right to complain, because they themselves showed not the slightest respect for neutral waters. Twenty cases in which they had made submarine attacks within Spanish waters between April and July, 1917, were mentioned by the British Foreign Office.

The savagery of the submarine crews might have been expected to rouse all civilised men against Germany. A fresh atrocity was perpetrated on July 31st, when the steamship Belgian Prince was sunk. The vessel was stopped 200 miles from the land, and her crew was ordered to take to the boats and come on board the submarine. The captain was sent down into the submarine a prisoner.

THE FLYING MAN'S MESSENGER.
British airman, having brought his seaplane to rest on the surface of the water, releasing one of his carrier-pigeons with a message to his base.

GERMAN PRISONERS TAKEN AT SEA.
Some of the captured crews of the ten armed German trawlers which were sunk by British naval units during a " sweep " of the Cattegat on April 15th, 1918.

The rest of the crew, 41 in number, were mustered on deck. The Germans stripped all but eight of their outer clothing and life-belts, smashed the boats, and removed the oars. Then, leaving the British on deck, they closed down the hatches and proceeded two miles, when they suddenly submerged, flinging their hapless victims into the sea to drown. Most of the 41 went down with the submarine, but three, after eleven hours in the water, were rescued, and survived to tell the horrible story. On such a scale had the Germans murdered human beings in their campaign of piracy that down to June 30th, 1917, as was officially stated in the House of Commons, 9,748 non-combatants, of whom 3,828 were passengers—many of them women and children—had been killed by them in British merchant ships. By May, 1918, the number of non-combatants murdered afloat by the submarines had risen to 15,000. Cases in which submarines fired upon unarmed crews in boats, after the ship had been sunk, multiplied fast. Eleven such were recorded by the International Conference of Merchant Seamen in 1917. In four instances the crews of neutral ships were **Ruthless savagery of** thus treated, and no satisfaction was **German pirates** given by Germany. Moreover, lists of 14 Norwegian and 28 Swedish ships which had been sunk " without trace," in accordance with a telegram sent by Count Luxburg to the German Government, were drawn up and published. In these vessels all on board had been ruthlessly slaughtered. All rights and laws of the sea had been transgressed, and the world had been swept back to the morality of the Stone Age. The neutrals remained submissive and humble.

A remarkable feat which showed the excellence and range of British aircraft was performed in July by the R.N.A.S. A large Handley-Page aeroplane flew from Great Britain by Italy and Albania to Mudros, in the Ægean, making the flight of 2,000 miles in 31 hours 34 minutes, with certain brief stops on the way. This machine was commanded by Squadron-Commander K. S. Savory. On the night of July 8th it proceeded to Stenia Bay, Constantinople, where the German battle-cruiser Goeben was lying. The Goeben was found ablaze with lights as the great machine dropped to a height of only 800 feet above her and discharged a first salvo of four bombs. These missed the ship, but hit a submarine and

a destroyer which were alongside her. The lights went out very quickly, and a second salvo struck her forward, " causing a large explosion and a big conflagration." After this brilliant work the British machine bombarded the steamer General, which was used by the Germans as their headquarters, and made two hits on the afterpart of that vessel. The Turks admitted the hits on the General and damage to a destroyer, but denied that the Goeben had been injured. In actual fact she was not seriously harmed, as she continued afloat and active.

Two changes took place at the British Admiralty during the summer. Sir Eric Geddes, who had been Controller in charge of naval construction, replaced Sir Edward Carson as First Lord in July; and in August, Vice-Admiral Sir Rosslyn Wemyss **Changes at the** replaced Sir C. Burney as Second **Admiralty** Sea Lord, receiving increased powers and the duty of acting as chief of the Operations Division which planned offensive operations. So long, however, as the First Sea Lord continued to be overburdened with details the Admiralty machine was not equal to the strain on it.

While food in Great Britain was slowly becoming scarcer, in Germany the position had slightly improved. On August 13th the German bread ration was restored to 4½ lb. per head per week, which was in excess of the British voluntary ration, and was almost the quantity fixed when bread was first rationed in Germany, in February, 1915. On the other hand, Germany was in want of many requisites which were tolerably abundant in Great Britain. Leather was

NETS FOR FINLESS MONSTERS OF THE DEEP.
Attaching the floats to nets used in fighting the U boats. The floats were made of glass of a light sea-green colour, and covered with a netting of wire or rope.

damaged her engines. She was towed into port by a Spanish torpedo-boat; portions of her machinery were supposed to have been removed, and her store of oil and her torpedoes were placed ashore. The commander gave his word of honour to remain in port, and repairs were executed by Spanish workmen. A month later the value of a German officer's promise was illustrated when, on October 6th, this vessel suddenly made good its escape. The Spanish Government directed that all the officials concerned should be tried by court-martial, but it took no effective steps to secure the return of the submarine, which resumed its attacks on allied shipping.

failing, and was reserved for the Army. Soap was strictly rationed on a very low scale. Woollen materials were almost unprocurable. For want of cotton and wool, factories in all directions had closed. Coal was running very short. In the spring of 1918 the German bread ration was reduced, and conditions deteriorated again.

At short intervals the British carried out reconnaissances in the Bight of Heligoland, where the mine-fields—British as well as German—were constantly increasing. On August 16th a number of British light craft scouting in these waters sighted a German destroyer and attacked her. She fled, and though she was hit repeatedly and seen to be on fire, she escaped in misty weather through the German mine-fields.

STURDY REPRESENTATIVES OF THE R.N.A.S.
Men of the Royal Naval Air Service at rifle drill, and (above) marching home to their quarters. In 1918 the R.N.A.S. was amalgamated with the R.F.C. as a single service under the style and title of the Royal Air Force, controlled by the newly created Air Ministry.

Another brush took place on September 1st, when a British light force detected thirteen or fourteen German minesweepers, mostly of the armed trawler type, off the coast of Jutland, and attacked them with such effect that four ran for the Danish coast and beached themselves there, two of them in flames. A few days later, possibly as a reply to this, a German submarine appeared off Scarborough in daylight on September 4th, when large numbers of people were on the parade. At 6.55 p.m. she opened an erratic fire on the town with two of her guns, from a range of four miles, and continued her fire for ten minutes. Three persons were killed, and a girl was wounded, while some material damage was inflicted. The submarine escaped by submerging when British vessels hurried to the spot on hearing the firing.

Submarine raid on Scarborough

In early September the badness of food in the German Navy caused a mutiny at Wilhelmshaven which was rapidly and mercilessly suppressed. The responsibility for it was placed by Admiral von Capelle, the German Naval Minister, upon the handful of German Socialists who showed independence of the Government.

On September 10th a German submarine bearing the number U293 (which was a "camouflage," as at that date Germany had certainly not completed 293 submarines) arrived off Cadiz making signals of distress, and claiming she was short of lubricating oil and had

The system of convoying merchant craft, adopted by the Allies, not only led the German submarines to concentrate, but also, in waters which could be reached from German ports, invited attack by German surface ships. This was only to be expected. In the old French wars convoys were not infrequently the cause of battle. The First of June, 1794, was fought by the British to destroy a French convoy, and had the British on that occasion gained a complete success revolutionary France might have been forced to surrender. The most vulnerable of British convoys, because it moved nearest the German Fleet, was that which at regular intervals crossed the North Sea to the Norwegian coast. It included many neutral vessels from whose crews the Germans were probably able to ascertain the force employed by the British and the methods followed. Such a convoy of twelve steamers left the Norwegian coast on the afternoon of October 15th, bound for the Shetlands. As an escort against submarine attack two British destroyers, the Mary Rose, Lieut-Commander C. L. Fox, and Strongbow, Lieut.-Commander E. Brooke, with three small armed vessels of the trawler class, only one of which was equipped with wireless, were attached. No provision was made by the responsible naval authorities against attack by surface ships. Early on the 17th the armed trawler which was fitted with wireless fell back to screen a ship that had dropped behind owing to the shifting of its cargo.

The weather was foggy, and day had not broken when, some 65 miles from the Shetlands, two large vessels appeared. They seem to have been disguised as British warships, but they were in reality large and very fast German cruisers of a type that had been built since the war. Against them the British destroyers were at a terrible disadvantage, inferior in speed, in steadiness, and, most of all, in gun-power, where they were enormously outmatched. There could be no real battle when the odds were such ; it was as an encounter between children and grown men. By some obscure chance or by surprise the Germans were able to put the wireless out of action in both destroyers before the alarm could be given. On this point the official account is not clear. What is certain is that the officers and men in both British warships prepared to sacrifice themselves for the honour of the Navy. The Strongbow was first attacked and subjected to a terrible fire, which speedily crippled her. She made an heroic fight and sank with the colours flying. Forty-

Heroic defence of a convoy

seven officers and men went down in her ; the rest of her crew were rescued by neutrals. The Mary Rose fared even worse. One of the earliest shots from the German cruisers struck her magazine, causing a violent explosion, and she, too, sank with the flag, still defiant, defeated but not dishonoured. Of her crew only ten escaped death in the tempestuous sea that was running by clinging to two large lifebuoys until they could struggle to a lifeboat floating near them.

The crowning act had still to come. The Germans, after destroying the two British warships, which was a perfectly legitimate deed of war, fell brutally on the convoy. At a range which did not exceed 200 yards, according to the depositions of survivors, they fired on these neutral ships. They were seen to aim deliberately at two women in one vessel who were waving a white flag. No sort of warning was given. It was cold-blooded murder. Three vessels of the convoy were able to escape because they were some distance off in the fog, and because of the gallant resistance offered by the British destroyers. The others, five Norwegian, one Dane,

Cold-blooded murder

and three Swedish vessels, all of them unarmed, were sent to the bottom and no attempt was made to rescue their crews. On the contrary, the German cruisers fired at several of the boats in the water. The crew of the Norwegian steamer Kristine, twelve in all, had taken to their boat at the first alarm. A German shell, fired at the boat, sank it and killed nine men. The other three struggled back to the wreck of their ship, where they were again shelled till only one was left, and he fell back into the sea.

The total of lives lost in the merchantmen was about 85. The affair was over in little more than half an hour, and the German cruisers immediately made off at full speed. They had a distance of nearly 400 miles to cover if they returned to the German North Sea base, and some 350 miles to steam if they made for the Baltic. Soon after they had disappeared small British patrol vessels arrived and rescued all who were left alive in the water. The British cruiser forces had not engaged the Germans on their approach and failed to intercept the Germans when they retired. According to an official statement,

[Photo by F. J. Mortimer, F.R.P.S.

WASHING-DAY ON BOARD A BRITISH WARSHIP WHILE LYING IN HARBOUR.
British sailors busy over their laundry work during an easy spell. Some of them, with trousers rolled above the knees and sleeves rolled above the elbows, knelt upon the decks to rub their jumpers, while others were soaping or rinsing theirs at the water-tubs.

SCARS OF SERVICE.
On board the Iris, formerly a Mersey ferry-boat which took part in the great raid on Zeebrugge, showing her riddled funnel and fire-swept deck.

and nine destroyers, intercepted, off Halmstad in Sweden, a German armed steamer, the Maria, Lieut.-Commander D. R. Deuterbach, mounting 6 in. guns, and with her ten small patrol craft. The Maria received a heavy fire, and in a few minutes was ablaze. The other patrol craft were quickly disposed of. In striking contrast with the behaviour of the German Navy in the convoy affair, the British rescued sixty-four Germans from the water before they retired without having suffered any loss.

A more important affair occurred in the Bight of Heligoland on November 17th. According to the German account, six large vessels of the battleship or battle-

" no message reached the Admiral commanding the Orkneys, the Commander-in-Chief of the Grand Fleet, or the Admiralty, that the convoy had been attacked until the surviving ships arrived at Lerwick." The destruction of the wireless installations in the two destroyers was blamed for this.

The action, though glorious to the officers and men of the two warships engaged, who behaved heroically, was unfortunate. It weakened the confidence of neutrals in the British Navy. The " Cologne Gazette " sneeringly remarked, " England can neither guard her own waters nor those of her Allies." It deepened the feeling that the Admiralty and War Staff needed

POST OF HONOUR ON THE IRIS.
The captain's bridge of the Iris after the gallant vessel returned from taking part in the great exploit of St. George's Day, 1918. The Iris suffered heavily both in attempting to make fast to the Mole and in the later stages of the engagement.

thorough reorganisation and a change of personnel, and that the old methods had broken down. An inquiry was promised. The official account stated that " the enemy raiders succeeded in evading the British watching squadron on the long dark nights both in their hurried outward dash and homeward flight." This was not reassuring, as, in effect, it was a confession that the feat could be repeated any winter's day—which it speedily was.

Minor action in the Cattegat The usual protests followed the brutal conduct of the German Navy, and were treated by Germany with her invariable contempt. The Norwegian Government in a Note said : " A profound impression has been made upon the Norwegian people by the fact that not only have the German submarines continued to sink peaceable neutral merchant ships, paying no attention to the fate of their crews, but that now even German warships have adopted the same tactics."

The German Navy in early November displayed some activity, and on November 2nd a minor action took place in the Cattegat. That morning British light forces which, according to the Germans, consisted of six light cruisers

cruiser type were engaged on the British side in addition to numerous cruisers and destroyers. The British report made no mention of these large ships, but said that the British forces, shortly before 8 a.m., sighted four light cruisers on a northerly course, accompanied by destroyers and mine-sweepers. The mine-sweepers dashed off northwest, but did not all escape, as one was sunk by gun fire from a British destroyer, and a lieutenant and five men of her crew were rescued. The account continued :

The enemy light cruisers and destroyers turned off towards Heligoland, and were pursued by our advanced forces through the mine-fields. A running engagement took place under a heavy smoke-screen until four enemy battleships and battle-cruisers were sighted. Our advanced forces broke off the engagement and turned back to meet their supports outside the mine-field. Owing to the presence of mine-fields it was necessary for our vessels to keep to the line taken by the enemy ships, and consequently this area was too restricted for the supporting ships to manœuvre in. The enemy did not follow our vessels outside the mine-fields.

The report concluded with the statements that one enemy cruiser was seen to be on fire, a heavy explosion was observed in another, and a third cruiser dropped behind, evidently damaged, but that " the destruction of these ships was prevented by the presence of the enemy's large vessels and by the proximity of Heligoland." The British and German reports differed, as did the two accounts of the Battle of Jutland, but the definite fact remained that no German warship of any importance was destroyed. The handling of the British light cruisers and destroyers was, however, daring and skilful, and they did their utmost to bring off a great stroke, such as the destruction of four German Dreadnoughts would have been.

There were some brushes during the autumn off the Belgian coast. On September 21st the dockyard at Ostend was thoroughly bombed by British aircraft, and on the following day it was bombarded at long range by British monitors, which remained out of sight of the coast while

SCENE OF ONE OF BRITAIN'S FINEST NAVAL EXPLOITS.
View of the Mole at Zeebrugge, the great curving structure of solid masonry which runs out a mile and a half into the sea, sheltering the entrance to the Bruges Canal and docks. The main breakwater was connected with the shore by a viaduct on piles.

their fire was controlled from the air. Satisfactory results were obtained. In the action three German seaplanes were destroyed. On November 3rd the Germans made the first publicly recorded use of a new weapon in the shape of a boat which was steered by electricity and carried a heavy charge of high explosive. This craft was driven by an oil engine, and paid out astern a wire which connected it with a shore station and worked the rudder. An aeroplane controlled its movements by reporting them to the shore station. This device was used against a British cruiser patrolling the Flanders coast with little effect, as it was immediately detected and destroyed.

German "barred zone" extended In November the German Government announced its decision to extend the so-called "barred zone," within which neutrals were to be sunk remorselessly. This was a matter of trifling importance, as the Germans spared no ship which they encountered whether it was within or without the zone. The changes made were the closing of the "free channel" to Greece; the narrowing of the "safety avenue" round the Dutch coast from twenty to seven miles, and the creation of a new danger-zone round

the Azores. The practical comment on this proclamation was supplied by the Germans themselves. Their destroyer V69, which the Dutch, in contravention of the laws of neutrality, had repaired for them and restored to them when she had been put out of action by the British, immediately after sank five Dutch fishing-luggers in the "safety avenue."

On December 12th occurred a double repetition of the convoy affair—off the Tyne and off the Norwegian coast. In the night of December 11th-12th a south-bound convoy was proceeding down the British coast when two neutral steamers, which belonged to it and had dropped some distance astern, were attacked by three large German destroyers. Both were torpedoed; one sank at once and the other broke into two halves which were ultimately salved. The Germans then steamed up to two trawlers which were fishing off the Tyne and sank one of them and damaged the other, killing eight men. They made good their retreat without being brought to action or molested in any way. The other affair took place in broad daylight that morning, and affected a convoy bound from Scotland to Norway. It consisted of six ships—one British, two Norwegian, two Swedish, and one Danish—protected by an anti-submarine escort, the destroyers Partridge and Pellew and four armed trawlers. According to neutral reports the attacking force consisted of four large German destroyers supported by very fast and powerful light German cruisers. At 11.45 a.m. the Partridge sighted strange destroyers coming up, and immediately went to quarters and engaged them. The British were once more exposed to overwhelming force. The Partridge, offering a most gallant resistance, was severely hit early in the action; soon after an explosion took place in her hull and she sank. The Pellew was badly damaged by hits below the water-line; her engines were partially disabled, and she was crippled though she was not sunk. The convoy was then

GERMAN COAST BATTERY OF MACHINE-GUNS AT ZEEBRUGGE.
All along the Flanders coast the Germans sited artillery, from 15 in. guns to machine-guns, a battery of which is shown in this photograph from a German paper. The British kept them on the alert, and pinned to the sea-front large forces which otherwise could have been employed more effectively elsewhere.

attacked and all the vessels in it destroyed, including the four armed trawlers. Fortunately another convoy in the neighbourhood escaped, probably owing to the brave defence of the British destroyers. The Germans showed no particular sign of haste. They rescued 24 officers and men of the Partridge's crew and 26 of the crews of the other British vessels sunk, and they offered to save some of the neutrals whose ships they had destroyed. Several survivors reached Norway in boats, and 100 men, 88 of whom were neutrals, were rescued by four British destroyers which arrived after the Germans had vanished. They were part of a squadron that, according to the official statement, "was hastening to the scene."

Long-distance observation failure

The escape of the Germans after the previous convoy affair had been ascribed to the destruction of the wireless in both the British warships engaged, and to the long, dark nights. In this case the Germans do not seem to have damaged the wireless in the convoying vessels before signals could be made, and they appeared in daylight. The previous attack had been a "tip-and-run" affair; in this case a certain deliberation was manifest. A court of inquiry reported that "all possible steps" were taken by "the other forces that were at sea for the purpose of giving protection to the convoys." The system of long-distance observation the British Navy adopted was clearly attended by serious risks. One result of that system was that it left the submarines free to come and go, and the North Sea open to German raiders. New men were needed to work out a new strategy. Changes at the Admiralty had long been necessary, and now at last they were made, after war had proved the old Staff methods and organisation faulty.

They were hastened by a sad incident which seems to have been one of the inevitable mischances of war. At 10.30 on the night of December 22nd-23rd a number of British destroyers, which had been engaged in protecting a convoy on its voyage to Holland, were waiting for a return convoy, laden with food in the shape of cheese and butter, in foggy weather off the Dutch coast, when they were attacked by submarines. One of the vessels in the escort struck a mine but was not sunk, and was able to return to port. Four destroyers were in line with her. Immediately after she had been damaged, the second British destroyer in the line went up in a sheet of flame and steam which rose from her amidships. The destroyer next astern of her very gallantly steamed close to her, to save

Three British destroyers sunk

her crew, and was also torpedoed and sunk. Meantime, the leading destroyer had turned; as she came round a third torpedo struck her with deadly results. The fourth destroyer in that welter of sinking ships and dying men was handled with consummate coolness and devotion by her commander. She quickened to full speed, zigzagged to avoid any further German torpedoes, and worked round to the points where the other destroyers had sunk,

H.M.S. VINDICTIVE BACK IN HARBOUR AFTER GLORIOUS SERVICE AT ZEEBRUGGE.
Appearance of the deck of the Vindictive after the return from Zeebrugge. It was on April 23rd, 1918, St. George's Day, that the Vindictive, with Commander Carpenter in command, formed the chief of the heroic company of British vessels of all kinds that made a surprise attack on Zeebrugge. The vessel, which returned battered but triumphant, had well earned the admiral's signal, "Well done, Vindictive!"

WHERE ONE OF TEN SURVIVED.
Fighting-top of H.M.S. Vindictive after her return from Zeebrugge. Of the three officers and seven men in the top only one man survived, and he had served his gun right through the engagement.

of Staff (or operations) duties from routine (or maintenance) duties. The new offices were grouped thus :

OPERATIONS.
First Sea Lord, Admiral Sir Rosslyn Wemyss.
Deputy Chief of Naval Staff, Rear-Admiral S. R. Fremantle.
Assistant Chief of Naval Staff, Rear-Admiral A. L. Duff.
Deputy First Sea Lord, Rear-Admiral G. P. W. Hope.
MAINTENANCE.
Second Sea Lord, Vice-Admiral Sir H. L. Heath.
Third Sea Lord, Rear-Admiral L. Halsey.
Fourth Sea Lord, Rear-Admiral H. H. D. Tothill.
Civil Lord, Right Hon. E. G. Pretyman.
Controller, Sir A. G. Anderson.
Second Civil Lord, Mr. A. F. Pease.

From the nature of things this change could produce no instant revolution in the operations against the submarine. The U boat danger had been allowed to develop to such lengths that only gradu- **Preventive policy** ally could it be brought under. The real **to be adopted** test of efficiency would be the method adopted after due time had been given for preparations. Experiment after experiment seemed to show that there was only one certain cure—namely, to prevent the submarine from putting to sea. Building of merchant shipping to replace the tonnage sunk, convoy, deviations from the ordinary routes—these were only at the best palliatives and not remedies. "To stop the holes " was the real cure, but that policy was accompanied by great difficulties and risks because it had been so long delayed and involved such enormous preparations and diplomatic embarrassments. Presently it was seen that the War Staff was working along the right lines. The Germans were now displaying an increased tendency to use their submarines for random bombardments of coast towns. On December 12th a

dropping boats, lifebelts, and everything that would float to help the men in the water, until the submarines near her had been driven off. No German craft was distinctly seen, but in the darkness and stormy weather this was no cause for surprise, and the Germans claimed the three vessels as torpedoed, not mined. A total of 13 officers and 180 men perished in this tragic mishap. The three destroyers lost brought up the total of British vessels of that class sunk in 1917 to 18, 11 of which went down in the grim North Sea—losses which were not heavy when the extraordinary work performed by the British destroyers and their incomparable crews is taken into account.

On December 26th it was announced that Vice-Admiral Sir Rosslyn Wemyss had succeeded Admiral Sir John Jellicoe as First Sea Lord, Sir John receiving a **Reorganisation of** peerage in recognition of his work. Early **the Admiralty** in January the reorganisation of the Admiralty was completed by a number **of** important changes. The First Sea Lord was relieved of the routine work of administration, and was left free to deal with important questions of policy. Under him was a Deputy Chief of the Naval Staff, Rear-Admiral S. R. Fremantle, concerned with operations against the enemy in home waters ; a Deputy First Sea Lord, dealing with all operations against the enemy outside home waters ; and an Assistant Chief of the Staff, dealing with the anti-submarine war. It was announced that in the appointments to these posts merit and not seniority was considered. The system thus set up was parallel to that of the Army, and was unquestionably a great advance on that which had existed previously. It speedily bore fruit in a much more vigorous and intelligent prosecution of the war. One of its best features was the separation

A COMPANY OF HEROES.
After the raid on Zeebrugge. Some of the officers and crew of the Vindictive who had been in the action. To the left is Captain Carpenter (with his arm in a sling), and near him Gunnery-Commander Osborne.

RESCUING THE WOUNDED AT ZEEBRUGGE.
Bringing men wounded in the attack on the Zeebrugge Mole down the gangways on to the false deck of H.M.S. Vindictive during the action. This work was carried out with magnificent heroism, and it was stated that all the wounded were rescued.

large German submarine shelled Funchal, in Madeira, wrecking the Church of St. Clara, and killing or wounding a number of people. On January 14th a German vessel, probably a submarine, fired fifty shells into Yarmouth, killing four persons and injuring ten. On April 9th a German submarine bombarded Monrovia, the capital of Liberia, on the West Coast of Africa, for an hour, inflicting several casualties and destroying the wireless and cable stations.

The collapse of Russia and the shameful peace which her Revolutionists concluded affected the allied naval position considerably by withdrawing from the war the Russian naval forces and freeing the Germans from all anxiety in the Baltic and the Black Sea. In the Black Sea the German warships Goeben and Breslau, which, early in the war, through a want of foresight and energy had been allowed to reach and remain in Turkish waters, were now free to operate in the Mediterranean. On January 20th, 1918, at 5.20 a.m., the British destroyer Lizard, on patrol duty off Imbros, about seventeen miles from the entrance to the Dardanelles, sighted two ships steaming rapidly to her. The leading vessel was made out to be the Breslau; a mile

astern of her followed the battle-cruiser Goeben, mounting ten 11 in. guns. There were no large British or allied ships available at this point to meet the Germans, but the Lizard opened fire on her big antagonists. They replied with such accuracy as to prevent her from closing and using her torpedoes, though she was handled with singular skill and resolution. In Kusu Bay, at Imbros, were two British monitors, the Raglan, mounting two 14 in. guns, and M28, a small vessel mounting one 9·2 in. gun. The Goeben attacked these with her powerful battery, and as at the best they could only oppose two heavy guns to her ten, and moreover it would seem that they were surprised, they could effect little. A second British destroyer, the Tigress, now joined the Lizard and attempted to draw a smoke-screen between the Germans and the monitors, though in so doing she and the Lizard were subjected to a violent fire. The Raglan was badly hit and sank; the M28 caught fire amidships and blew up about 6 a.m. The Germans, having inflicted this severe loss, turned south, followed by the gallant British destroyers and by British aeroplanes which had gone up. The British aircraft were so active, however, that they forced the Breslau to zigzag, and edged her into a British mine-field off the south-eastern point of Imbros, where she suddenly sank after four explosions had torn her open.

The Goeben turned towards the Breslau and circled round her, but then steamed southwards away from the Dardanelles. At that moment four Turkish destroyers emerged from the Dardanelles, accompanied by a Turkish cruiser. The Tigress and Lizard ran at them, vigorously attacked them, and drove them back after making several hits on the rearmost and setting her on fire. Meanwhile, as no British vessel of her own class appeared to engage the Goeben, British aeroplanes kept up an attack on her and dropped bombs with such effect that she turned and headed for the Dardanelles. As she did so she struck a mine. The big battle-cruiser settled down aft with a list of 10 or 15 degrees and her speed fell considerably. She reached the entrance, however, and there she was met by the Turkish destroyers and by several German seaplanes. The British **Goeben bombed,** aircraft continued their pursuit and **mined, and stranded** bombed her once more, making two hits as she entered the strait. A little farther up the current runs very strong off Nagara Point. Here was the opening left by the Turks in the boom closing the strait, close to the Asiatic coast. At this point the Goeben ran ashore on a gravel bottom, and there, in those famous waters which had seen the clash of so many races over so many centuries, she was again hit twice by bombs from British aircraft, which continued their dashing attacks upon her despite a heavy fire from her guns and from the Turkish works.

The Turks claimed that they shot down one British machine. Meanwhile, the Lizard and Tigress had been compelled by the Turkish fire to retire. As they fell back they drove off a German submarine and rescued a number of survivors from the Breslau in the water.

In command of the Raglan was Lord Broome, nephew of the first Earl Kitchener and heir to the title, but he was not among the casualties, which were 133 killed and 27 wounded. Constant air attacks were made upon the Goeben for several days, and in all sixteen direct hits were effected upon her. On the 22nd she was struck amidships, and steam and smoke were seen pouring up from her, but as the bombs employed were not heavy the effect was not so great as could have been wished, though the attacks were made with splendid energy and courage. An attempt was made by submarines to torpedo her on the night of January 27th, 1918. She lay in so unfavourable a position for underwater attack that the enterprise was of a desperate nature and only resulted in the loss of submarine E14, Lieutenant-Commander G. S. White, with all the British crew except seven, who were taken prisoners. On the 28th the British aircraft reported that the Goeben had been got off and taken to Constantinople. The Turks declared that her injuries were not grave.

In February the German raider Wolf succeeded in returning to Kiel after a prolonged cruise of fifteen months. It was at first falsely announced that she had slipped into Pola, in the Adriatic. As a matter of fact, she proceeded far north, into the Arctic circle, and then stole down home through Norwegian territorial waters. The Spanish steamer Igotz Mendi, which she had seized during her lawless operations and converted into an auxiliary cruiser, stranded near the Skaw Lighthouse, on the Danish coast, with a German prize-crew and a number of British prisoners on board; thus the true facts became known. The Germans were interned, the steamer salved and seized, and the prisoners liberated by the Danish authorities. The German Admiralty published fabulous accounts of the Wolf's exploits. With the help of her auxiliaries, one of which was the British steamer Turritella, captured in February, 1917, she had, it declared, destroyed or greatly damaged 210,000 tons of allied shipping, sunk the Japanese Dreadnought Haruna, and crippled a British or Japanese cruiser. The truth was that she had behaved with singular prudence in her fifteen months at sea, and had inflicted in that time less damage than many enterprising submarines caused in a few weeks. She made in all only fourteen captures, in addition to which half a dozen vessels were damaged or sunk by the mines which she laid. The Turritella came to an early end, as her crew sank her to

Exploits of the German Wolf

avoid recapture by the British, and were made prisoners. The Wolf left Germany in December, 1916, and proceeded by way of Iceland down the Atlantic to the East, laying mines off all the important coaling stations on the route; off the Cape, where she was the cause of the injury to the Tyndareus (see Vol. 9, page 257); in the Gulf of Aden; off Bombay and Ceylon; on the Australian coast, where her crew professed that a seaplane which she carried made a trip over Sydney Harbour; and between the North and South Islands of New Zealand. The standard of morals had been so debased by the Germans in this war that no one indicted the cruel act of placing mines in remote seas, where no real military object was to be gained, but at best a few hundred neutrals or non-combatants might be murdered.

For many weeks the Wolf remained in a safe, land-locked harbour in Dutch New Guinea, which was never visited by whites, repairing damage to her machinery. She employed her seaplane to reconnoitre and bring ships to. Thus the seaplane suddenly approached the British steamer Wairuna and dropped a message to her: " Stop immediately; take orders from German cruiser. Do not

GREAT EXPLOIT OF BRITISH SUBMARINE HEROES.
Lieutenant R. D. Sandford, R.N., leaving an obsolete submarine loaded with explosive beneath the viaduct of the Zeebrugge Mole. He and his companion, though the target of German machine-gun and rifle fire, got away in their dinghy, and the submarine blew up, destroying a great part of the viaduct.

use your wireless or I will bomb you!" The Wairuna defied this order, when a bomb was dropped close to her, and the Wolf came into sight steering to head her off. She surrendered perforce. The German readiness to employ new methods and weapons was illustrated by this incident. The Wolf finally laid a mine-field off Singapore, and sneaked back to Europe with 400 prisoners and a valuable cargo. As a rule her prisoners were fairly treated.

The vigilance shown by Vice-Admiral Roger Keyes, who had taken over the command at Dover after the Admiralty reorganisation, soon compelled the German destroyers to move. He guarded the Strait of Dover so carefully that the German submarines found it increasingly difficult to run through, and the Germans determined to attack the small British craft watching the strait with their surface vessels. Very early in the morning of February 15th, 1918, five or six large destroyers made a dash from Zeebrugge for the strait. Probably they had obtained information of the British dispositions from spies or neutrals. The fighting which followed was brief and unequal. For half an hour through the dark and misty night the noise of rapid firing was borne in to the British coast, as the Germans caught and sank in succession eight little drifters or trawlers, manned by indomitable fishermen and engaged in the anti-submarine work. The crews of these small

German destroyers in Dover Strait craft behaved with their accustomed magnificent valour. They had no prospect of success, and help from the warships did not come, through one of those mischances of which the history of war is full. The German destroyers closed in to a range of only fifty yards. "The only thing I can compare this action to," said one of the men engaged, "is an attack by a cruiser on a man in a small open boat, armed with a popgun or revolver."

In this fierce but one-sided affair sixty men perished, and seven drifters and one trawler were sunk, fighting to the last. The survivors were publicly thanked and deservedly honoured for their superb conduct. On the night after the attack eight other armed fishing vessels replaced the vessels destroyed, and other fishermen calmly took up the task of the dead. And thus once more a whole class of men were proved by the stern test of war to have in them "not merely the ordinary virtues of common life but something high and resplendent which is associated with the stories of old saints and heroes." The one unsatisfactory point of the episode, in which such devotion was displayed by the British crews, was the escape of the Germans without hurt or punishment. On the following day a German submarine fired some thirty rounds at Dover under cover of darkness, and retired after killing a child and injuring seven persons. A further attempt was made by the Germans to repeat their blow on March 21st, with disastrous consequences to themselves. On that day, not long before dawn, the two British destroyers Botha (Commander R. L'E. M. Rede) and Morris (Lieut.-Commander P. R. P. Percival) were patrolling the

GERMAN NAVAL BASES IN FLANDERS.
Map of the Belgian coast from Nieuport to Zeebrugge, showing the canal system linking Bruges with Ostend and Zeebrugge.

BLOCKING UP OSTEND HARBOUR.
On May 9th, 1918, H.M.S. Vindictive was taken, loaded with concrete, and sunk as a blockship in the channel leading to Ostend Harbour.

eastern end of the Channel with the French destroyers Mehl, Magon, and Bouclier, when flashes were seen and firing heard off Dunkirk. The Allies steamed rapidly to that point and sent up star-shells to light up the water, but they could discover no trace of hostile craft. They altered course and made a fresh search, when a star-shell suddenly showed the dim shapes of a large number of destroyers moving stealthily through the darkness. After a swift challenge the allied vessels opened fire. The Germans threw out a smoke-screen, and under cover of it tried to retreat, firing torpedoes, which, fortunately, failed to hit. Suddenly, in the gloom, the Morris sighted a large German destroyer close to her, and at only five hundred yards fired a hissing torpedo at it. A great spout of smoke and flame and spray rose from the German destroyer, which heeled over and sank stern foremost. The Botha received a shot through her main steampipe, yet she contrived to fire two torpedoes at the two leading German destroyers, though she seems to have missed them. Her speed was falling through her injuries, but her captain, with splendid resolution, turned and drove in his ram on the fourth German, cutting the destroyer clean in two as the collision came. The Botha then cleared the wreck and endeavoured to repeat this deadly manoeuvre against the next German boat astern, but failed, as her speed was now too low.

The German vessel did not escape. It was caught by the French destroyers, and received from them a series of **Destroyer fight in the Channel** salvos till it was seen by them to sink with a great fire burning fiercely in its hull. The other German vessels effected their escape, and the Botha was towed back to port. One small and two large German destroyers were certainly sunk, and it is possible that a fourth vessel was also destroyed, as the French reported pouring a heavy fire into it, and observing signs that it had gone down. The trials of the Germans were not over when they extricated themselves from the allied destroyers. On their return to Ostend they were attacked by British aircraft from Dunkirk, which bombed them and threw them into disorder. A number of German seaplanes came out to support them and were severely handled by the British. A single British pilot brought down three German machines, and one other was accounted for by the rest of the British airmen. Finally, as the Germans were entering Ostend, the stern of one of their destroyers was struck by a torpedo fired from a British craft which had eluded observation. Prisoners captured stated that eighteen German vessels had taken part in the fighting. A very sharp lesson had been administered by the allied destroyer leaders and the British airmen.

Among the many outrages of the German submarines, the attack made on the hospital-ship Glenart Castle in the Bristol Channel, at 4 p.m. on February 26th, was specially noteworthy for its savagery. The vessel had all her lights burning and the proper marks. She had no patients on

WING-CMDR. F. A. BROCK
DEVELOPED THE FOG SCREEN.

CMDR. R. S. SNEYD D.S.O.
BLEW UP H M S. THETIS.

CAPT. HAMILTON BENN.
MOTOR-LAUNCHES AT OSTEND.

CMDR. VALENTINE GIBBS.
H.M S IRIS.

SURGEON PAYNE, SURGEON CLEGG, COMMANDER OSBORNE, CAPTAIN A. F. B. CARPENTER, STAFF-SURGEON
McCUTCHEON, ASSISTANT-PAYMASTER YOUNG, GUNNER COPLEY.
OFFICERS OF H.M.S. VINDICTIVE WHO SURVIVED THE ATTACK ON ZEEBRUGGE MOLE AND HARBOUR ON ST. GEORGE'S DAY.

CAPT. E. BAMFORD.
ROYAL MARINES.

CAPT. H. C. HALAHAN.
BLUEJACKETS' STORMING-PARTY.

LT.-CMDR. GORE-LANGTON.
H.M.S. PHOEBE.

COL. B. N. ELLIOT.
ROYAL MARINES' STORMING-PARTY

Heroes of the glorious naval raid on Zeebrugge and Ostend, April 23rd, 1918.

Marines and bluejackets springing up the gangways from H.M.S. Vindictive to storm the Mole.

Landing from H.M.S. Vindictive on the upper wall of the Zeebrugge Mole.

Glorious end of H.M.S. Vindictive, successfully sunk at Ostend Harbour, May 9th, 1918.

H.M.S. Iphigenia, the obsolete cruiser that blocked Zeebrugge Canal.

Iris and Daffodil, used as boarding-steamers at Zeebrugge Mole.

H.M.S. Vindictive at Dover after her return from the successful raid on Zeebrugge Harbour on St. George's Day, 1918.

board, but of her crew and staff, including several women nurses, one hundred and fifty perished. From the wounds on the bodies and injuries to the boats which were afterwards recovered, it was clear that the Germans must have fired on the boats to complete their crime. The master of the ship, Captain Burt, faithful to the immortal traditions of the merchant service, went down with her.

In March, 1918, the British Government decided to divulge the tonnage figures showing the losses inflicted by the submarines. This decision was dictated by the failure of the shipbuilding yards to turn out the new tonnage promised month by month. It had been hoped to complete 150,000 tons of new vessels every month. Unhappily, the figures steadily fell for many weeks, from 130,375 tons in November, 1917, and 115,752 in December, to only 58,588 tons in January. The output rose again to just over 100,000 tons in February, and to 161,000 tons in March, but dropped again in April to 111,000 tons. It thus continued dangerously below the enemy's sinkings and the monthly average which the Government had hoped eventually to reach, though in March Lord Pirrie was appointed Controller of Shipbuilding with special powers.

The total allied and neutral merchant tonnage lost through military action in the war to the end of 1917 was, for the United Kingdom, 7,079,000 tons, and for foreign countries, 4,748,000 tons. The new tonnage built by Great Britain was 3,031,000 tons, and the enemy tonnage captured and taken over, 780,000. Foreign countries had built 3,574,000 tons, and captured or taken over, 1,809,000. Thus while foreign countries had made a net gain of 635,000 tons, Great Britain had suffered a net loss of 3,268,000 tons, to which a net loss of 367,000 in the first quarter of 1918 had to be added. Almost the entire burden of this frightful struggle had therefore fallen upon Great Britain, and to the stupendous sacrifices which she had made in her noblest blood were added enormous losses of material. The highest level of submarine destruction was reached in April, 1917, when 893,000 tons of shipping (of which 555,110 were British) were sunk ; but after that the losses slowly declined to a figure of 305,000 tons in April, 1918. The serious fact was that the British new construction entirely failed to keep pace with the British losses. On British shipping depended the very life of the Alliance. The various armies and nations fighting in the allied cause received their munitions and food through the merchant fleet of Great Britain. The American Army and all its requirements had to be conveyed to the front almost exclusively in British merchant vessels, while the merchant service had also to provide the greater part of the patrol service and naval auxiliary cruisers. The work of navigation, moreover, fell on officers and men who faced all the perils and privations of combatants with little of their glory, and who were too often overlooked by Parliament and administration, though it was their lot to do and die, often in the most frightful circumstances. To the eternal glory of the race, in these hours of trial, the moral of the British seaman did not suffer. "With a pluck and bravery beyond all praise," said the chairman of the Peninsular and Oriental Steam Navigation Company, on December 12th, 1917, "they go to sea to-day as they did before the war. . . . Even those who have undergone the shock of having their ships torpedoed soon get tired of their rest, and apply to go afloat again." It was as though the whole British merchant service had been touched with the fire of the men who died for freedom at Thermopylæ.

The grim resistance of Great Britain, the iron tenacity of her merchant seamen, the steadfastness of her fishing population, the patience and endurance of her Navy, surprised the rulers of Germany and led to many German explanations in the closing months of that terrible fourth year of the war which had witnessed the failure of so many hopes. The German experts dealt

Tonnage losses in the war

VIEWING THE BATTLE-SCARRED VETERAN.
Party of privileged visitors being shown over H.M.S. Vindictive on her return home after the great part that she had played in making history in the attack on Zeebrugge Mole on April 23rd, 1918.

in statistics which they had carefully garbled, but beneath their figures was the truth that, until British new construction surpassed British losses, the position must deteriorate. On April 17th, 1918, Admiral Capelle, the German Secretary of State for the Navy, declared that "the danger point for England has already been reached and the situation of the Western Powers grows worse from day to day." A few days later, however, Captain Kühlwetter, of the German Admiralty, made the important admission that "the protection given to (American) transports is so efficient that the danger to the submarine is too great to be worth the risk" (of attack), a notable tribute to the British Navy.

Right of "angary"

In March the Allies decided to take over a number of Dutch steamers which were lying in various allied ports unused. This incident led at the time to much controversy, though it was in accord with the right of "angary," which the Germans had themselves invoked in the Franco-Prussian War of 1870 when they seized a number of British steamers in a French port, then in their possession, on the ground that they needed them.

The first visible indication of the change produced by the Admiralty reorganisation was the excellent Staff work and boldness of conception which marked the British raid on Zeebrugge and Ostend, carried out on April 23rd (St. George's Day), 1918. The object of the operation was to close these two ports by sinking ships filled with concrete in the narrow entrances to them. Such an enterprise involves the very highest demands on the skill and resolution of seamen. Many similar attempts were made in past wars, but never, since the introduction of effective artillery, with much success. The Japanese in

pilework of a viaduct that connected the land with the landward end of the Mole. The whole attack on the Mole was a diversion to keep the attention of the Germans off three of the blockships, which were to steam in during the uproar and sink themselves in the canal entrance. At Ostend the plan was simpler ; there was to be no diversion, but two blockships were to steam right in and place themselves in the very centre of the Channel. The approach of the British both at Zeebrugge and Ostend was to be covered by a violent bombardment from monitors and other craft and by dense clouds of smoke or artificial fog, spread by motor-vessels with special appliances which were the invention of Commander. F. A. Brock. Vice-Admiral Keyes was in command, supported by Sir R. Tyrwhitt (who had been specially promoted to the rank of Rear-Admiral in January) with his famous light squadrons. The crews of the blockships and the landing-parties were all volunteers, and had been systematically trained beforehand, so that each man knew exactly what he had to do.

Twice in April the expedition, which comprised seventy vessels of varying speed and sea-keeping capacity, started and found the conditions unfavourable. On April 22nd it once more

1904 repeatedly tried to block the entrance to Port Arthur, but failed each time, though they displayed extraordinary heroism. In the war of 1898, between the United States and Spain, Lieutenant Hobson had endeavoured to seal the Spanish port of Santiago by sinking an American collier in the channel leading into it. He also failed. On the Flanders coast was an artillery of terrific power, far surpassing that mounted at Port Arthur or Santiago. The Germans had multiplied guns of every size, from the monster 15 in., capable of hitting at twenty miles, to 6 in. guns and machine-guns. One hundred and twenty heavy weapons could concentrate on any vessel at a range of sixteen miles. It was into this German citadel, bristling with guns, that the British Navy now proposed to penetrate by a deed of breathless daring in order to stop the holes from which the piratical submarines issued.

Six obsolete cruisers and two old submarines of the C class were to be used in the operations. Five cruisers, the Brilliant, Iphigenia, Thetis, Sirius, and Intrepid, were converted into blockships, filled with concrete so that their hulls would be difficult for the Germans to destroy, and were fitted with mines so that they could be swiftly sunk. The sixth cruiser, Vindictive, was specially equipped for carrying a storming-party to the great curving Mole at Zeebrugge which ran out one mile and a half, sheltering the entrance to the Bruges Canal and docks. She was provided with eighteen gangways which could be swiftly lowered, with flame-throwers, with Stokes guns (trench-mortars), and with three howitzers for close action against the German batteries on the Mole. With her were two Mersey ferry-boats, Iris and Daffodil, similarly equipped. The two submarines were loaded with high explosives in the bow, and were to be taken in and run against the

Details of a daring scheme

ABOARD H.M.S. VINDICTIVE AFTER THE RAID.
Hole made by a shell in the Vindictive when coming alongside the Mole. In circle : One of the crew with a piece of the ship's armour-plating riddled by shrapnel. Above : Sorting out debris after the engagement.

set out. The night was hazy and overcast, with a high tide; the wind was in the right quarter to blow the artificial fog in on the Germans; the wash of a gale was still felt. It was not a night on which aircraft could operate. By the plans both Zeebrugge and Ostend were to be attacked simultaneously at midnight. As arranged, the monitors opened fire and the small craft spread artificial fog, so thick that the Germans afterwards complained that they could see nothing through it. The Vindictive worked up to full speed to dash in to the Mole, and as she did so Admiral Keyes made her the signal, "St. George for England," to which her captain, Commander A. F. B. Carpenter, replied, with ready wit, "May we give the dragon's tail a damned good twist." Through the German mine-fields she went, as a great searchlight at Zeebrugge swept the horizon, till suddenly a puff of wind lifted the fog and disclosed her. Every German weapon that would bear opened on her; star-shells went up; and she replied with all her guns. A storm of projectiles swept the deck as Commander Carpenter, from the unprotected bridge, laid the stern of his ship against the stonework of the Mole, anchored with a rattle of cable, and signalled to the Daffodil to butt her hull in, while the Iris went

ahead to grapple the Mole. There was a choppy sea, and in it the ships rolled heavily, crashing against one another and against the Mole.

Commander Carpenter, when the Vindictive had reached her station, moved to a lightly-armoured structure protecting the large flame-thrower which she carried. This became the target for many German shells, and was soon riddled and put out of action. He was wounded, and nearly all in it were killed or wounded. The two leaders of the storming-party, Captain H. C. Halahan, of the Navy, and Colonel Elliot, of the Marines, were killed before the order to land had been given. The gangways were dropped—such of them as remained—but the ship rolled and bumped, and they now rose high above the parapet of the Mole, and now crashed down on it, so that it was a matter of great peril to cross them. Up them, however, moved, with unfaltering heart if with cold sweat in their hands, the steady procession of seamen and Marines—laden with machine-guns, flame-throwers, bombs, helmets, gas-masks, and all the heavy accoutrement of modern battle—reached the tip of the gangway, and then dropped down into a hell of fire to the parapet, swept by German machine-guns, and then from this again, with another drop of sixteen or twenty feet, **Storming the** **Zeebrugge Mole** to the surface of the Mole. Grievous loss was suffered and magnificent heroism was displayed in this landing. The very dying cheered the men up those plankways of death. Lieut. H. T. C. Walker, with one arm shot off, shouted "Good luck!" to the procession as it passed over him. Thrice the fore-howitzer in the Vindictive was manned as gun-crews were mown down. The foretop was struck early, and all in it killed or wounded, but Sergeant Finch, of the glorious Royal Marine Artillery, himself wounded, kept up a fire from it.

The Daffodil nobly performed her duty of holding in

SURVIVORS OF THE SPLENDID NAVAL FEAT.

One of the crew of the Vindictive in a sand-bagged position on the deck. In circle: Machine-gunners in their post upon the cruiser. Above: Survivors sorting out the effects of comrades killed in the exploit.

the Vindictive against the Mole, and maintained twice the normal pressure in her boilers in doing this. Sheltered by the Vindictive she did not suffer severely, but her commander, Lieut. H. Campbell, was wounded. The Iris was the target of a great concentration of German guns. Her grapnels would not hold or span the parapet. Lieut.-Commander Bradford and Lieut. C. E. V. Hawkins climbed from her to the parapet and sat on it under fire endeavouring to hold the grapnels fast. Both these heroic officers were shot down; they reeled and fell between the Mole and the ship. The Iris's bridge was struck; her captain, Commander V. F. Gibbs, was mortally wounded, and Lieut. Spencer, who was navigating her, was also severely wounded, but remained conning the ship from a fragment of the bridge that was left. Lieut. Henderson took over the command. Two large shells caused fearful loss. One came through the upper deck, accounting for every man in a party of 56 Marines who were waiting to go ashore. The other killed or wounded 30 men in the sick-bay. Her position became so critical that she was ordered to shift her berth to a point astern of the Vindictive where **Mad fighting** there was more shelter. When she **on the Mole** crawled out, a battered wreck, it was with 77 dead and 105 wounded on board.

On the Mole a fierce struggle was in progress as the British surged forward with bombs and flame-throwers to destroy the sheds and buildings and a battery of six German 4 in. guns at its seaward end. Another party pushed landwards to a point where barbed-wire crossed the broad roadway, with machine-guns mounted beyond it, and swept through this obstruction. Thereabouts perished Commander Brock, leading most gallantly. Some of the stormers caught sight of a German destroyer lying alongside the Mole, and attacked her crew with bombs,

causing a violent explosion and setting her on fire. There was a wild fight, as the Germans fled into underground chambers with steel sliding-doors, out of which they were bombed. While it was at its height the whole structure rocked and the air was red with flame which leapt to an immense height. One of the submarines had safely reached the viaduct and exploded several tons of explosive in the exact position intended. All the British cheered as they heard the din of the explosion and the rattle of splinters and fragments from it. It was one of the most gallant acts on that wonderful night that the submarine crew had performed. **Blowing up** Commanded by Lieut. Sandford, five **the viaduct** picked volunteers drove their C boat against the pilework with a tremendous jolt. As they came in towards their goal every gun fired at them, and on the roadway above they could see and hear Germans, some jeering in the belief that they had missed their course and were trapped, some firing at them. The submarine carried a small boat fitted with a motor-propeller. Into this the crew scrambled after the fuse had been lighted which was to detonate the charge in the submarine's bow. In getting clear, however, the propeller was broken, and with only two minutes to spare, the six, under a murderous fire, had to row for safety. They were but 200 yards off when the explosion took place, and masses of concrete, splinters of steel, and fragments of Germans rained about them. A gap of 60 feet to 80 feet had been blown in the Mole, so that no reinforcements could reach it from the shore. In the very nick of time the submarine crew, every man of it wounded, was picked up by a boat from the fleet. The second submarine grounded and could not reach the Mole; she was therefore towed off, as the first had done its work so well.

Behind the Mole the water was swarming with German

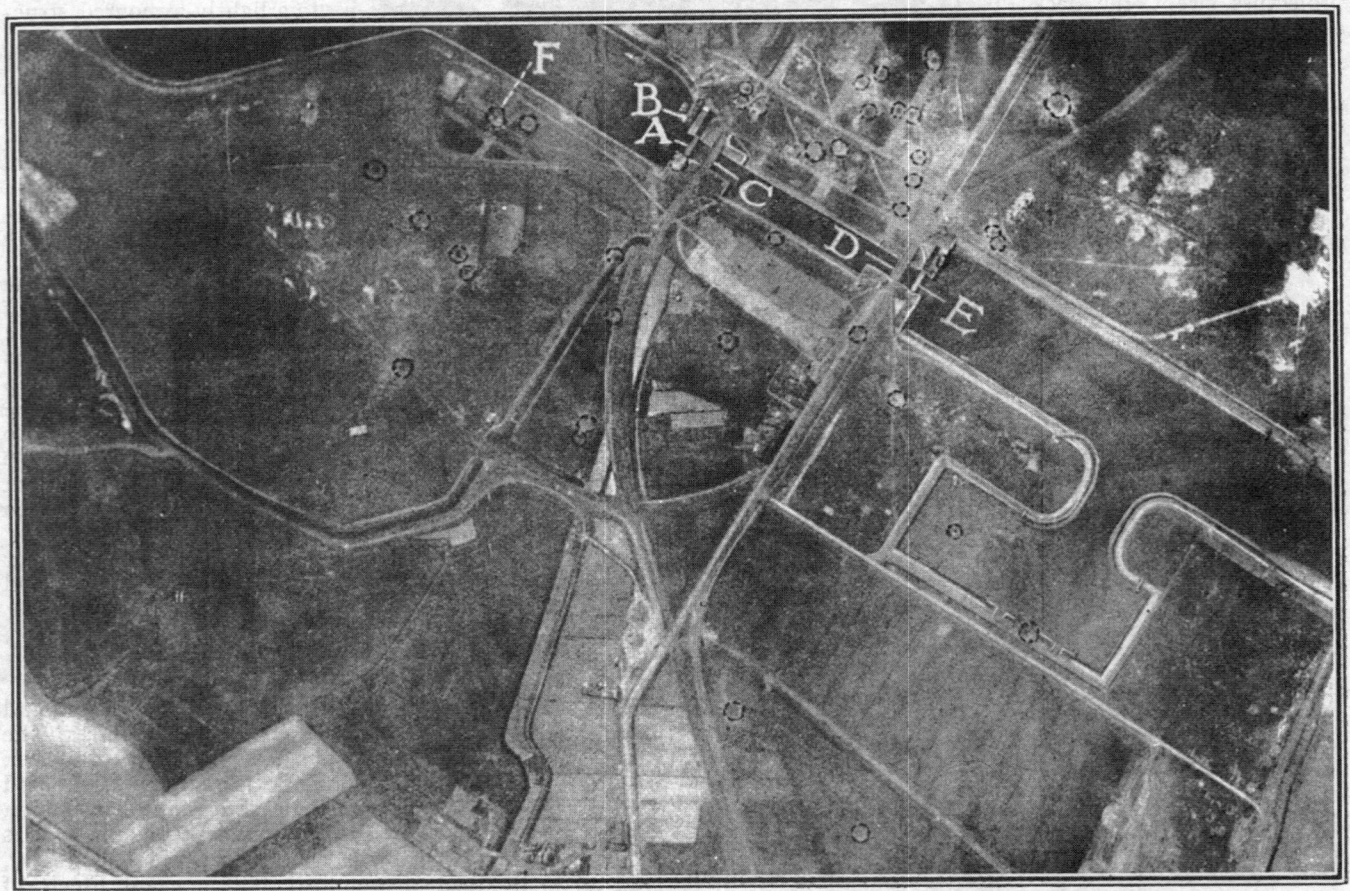

CANAL WORKS AND DOCKYARDS AT ZEEBRUGGE AFTER A BRITISH NAVAL BOMBARDMENT.
Photograph taken from the air of the entrance to the Bruges Canal at Zeebrugge after a long-range naval bombardment in 1917. The dotted circles indicate where hits had been obtained on the dockyards and canal works. A and E mark the caissons of the lock; B, a spare caisson; C and D, bridges at each end of the lock; and F, a storehouse. The width of the lock was forty yards.

COMMODORE H. LYNES,
C.M.G.
Directed the operations when
H.M.S. Vindictive was sunk at
the entrance to Ostend Harbour
on May 9th, 1918.

small craft, and on these the British destroyers North Star (Lieut.-Commander K. C. Helyar) and Phœbe (Lieut.-Commander H. E. Gore-Langton), with several coastal motor-boats, delivered a dashing attack, sweeping round the seaward end of the Mole. Two German motor-launches were sunk by shells. A German destroyer was torpedoed and probably sunk, and much damage was inflicted on other vessels. On the other hand the North Star was hit in her engine-room by a shell from the shore, and her speed was so reduced that she became an easy mark for the German guns. They riddled her boats and pierced her hull so that she began to sink. The Phœbe, in the midst of the turmoil, swept through the splash of the shells to her aid, and attempted to take her in tow. She was sinking too fast to be brought away, and the Phœbe could only remove her crew and withdraw. The North Star was the only vessel of any size lost by the British Navy. Two other small coastal motor-boats and two launches were sunk, but not until they had torpedoed the steamer Brussels and two more German destroyers.

All the while the blockships were steaming in unseen. The Thetis led. As she rounded the Mole the smoke-cloud lifted and showed her to the Germans. Under heavy fire she rammed her way through the numerous obstructions which guarded the entrance to the canal, but unfortunately one of her propellers fouled a net and she became unmanageable. She ran aground, was hit repeatedly, and began to sink in the channel. To complete her destruction the mines in her were fired, but not until valuable instructions had been signalled to the blockships which followed her. The Intrepid came next, under Lieut. S. Bonham-Carter. Working all her guns, she passed between the breakwaters at the canal entrance, and swinging round right across so as to block it, she was skilfully sunk. Lieut. Bonham-Carter escaped with difficulty on a float, the target for a violent German fire. The Iphigenia brought up the rear. Steaming into a dense cloud of smoke, she rammed and sank a dredger and caught a barge across her bow; then she, too, entered the canal and was cleverly sunk across it by her captain, Lieut. E. W. Billyard-Leake, effectually sealing it. The gallant crews of these two ships escaped, some in a motor-launch which stood in under a terrific fire, others in their own boats.

The object had been attained. Zeebrugge was sealed up, and it now remained to withdraw the ships which had grappled the Mole, if it were possible to get them away. The Vindictive's siren was sounded repeatedly as the signal of recall. Back over

the battered gangways came the survivors of that heroic night, bruised and bleeding, while through the din the siren trumpeted again and again its call.

For twenty minutes with admirable staunchness Commander Carpenter remained, till it was reported that no one was left who was capable of staggering to the ship. Then came some minutes of extreme peril. The Mole had protected the hulls of the ships, but as they drew clear of it a veritable tornado of shells lashed the water about them, until in the dense fog of the smoke-screen all three vanished, the Vindictive bearing with her a quarter of a ton of masonry, from the Mole, which fell on board. For the splendid conduct of all her crew she was honoured with a signal by Vice-Admiral Keyes, "Well done, Vindictive!"

At Ostend the operations were conducted by Commodore Hubert Lynes with equal gallantry, but with less success, because of an unlucky touch of wind which at the critical moment blew the smoke-screen aside, and because the Germans had moved the buoy which marked the channel to the entrance. The blockships Sirius and Brilliant could not reach the entrance to the harbour; they were blown up some little distance from it, and their crews were withdrawn in motor-launches and boats.

The total loss was 188 officers and men killed or mortally wounded and 384 wounded, while only 16 were missing. Those engaged received the special congratulations of the King, who stated: "The splendid gallantry displayed by all under exceptionally hazardous circumstances fills me with pride and admiration." Vice-Admiral Keyes was created a K.C.B., while Commander Carpenter was promoted to captain's rank. The Admiralty recorded its

Zeebrugge Canal sealed up

high admiration of the perfect co-operation displayed, and of the single-minded determination of all to achieve their object. The disciplined daring and singular contempt of death places this exploit high in the annals of the Royal Navy and Royal Marines, and will be a proud memory for the relatives of those who fell.

The Germans professed that the entrance to Zeebrugge was not closed, and their statement had this much of truth in it: that there remained a ship-canal from Bruges to Ostend by which German vessels could still get to sea from Zeebrugge via Ostend. Still the splendour and daring of the exploit remained. It deserved complete success, it came within an ace of achieving it; and in an hour of sorrow and depression it put new spirit and determination in the nation's heart. The long period of passive defence at sea was over. The men who died so gloriously had not given their lives in vain.

Admiral Keyes speedily showed that persistence in attack was his settled policy. On the night of May 9th-10th he directed another gallant and dashing attempt to complete the blocking of Ostend. On this occasion

THE BLOCKSHIPS AT ZEEBRUGGE.
Photograph which appeared in a German newspaper, showing the Intrepid and Iphigenia, which had been loaded with concrete and sunk by the British on April 23rd, 1918, at the entrance to Zeebrugge Harbour.

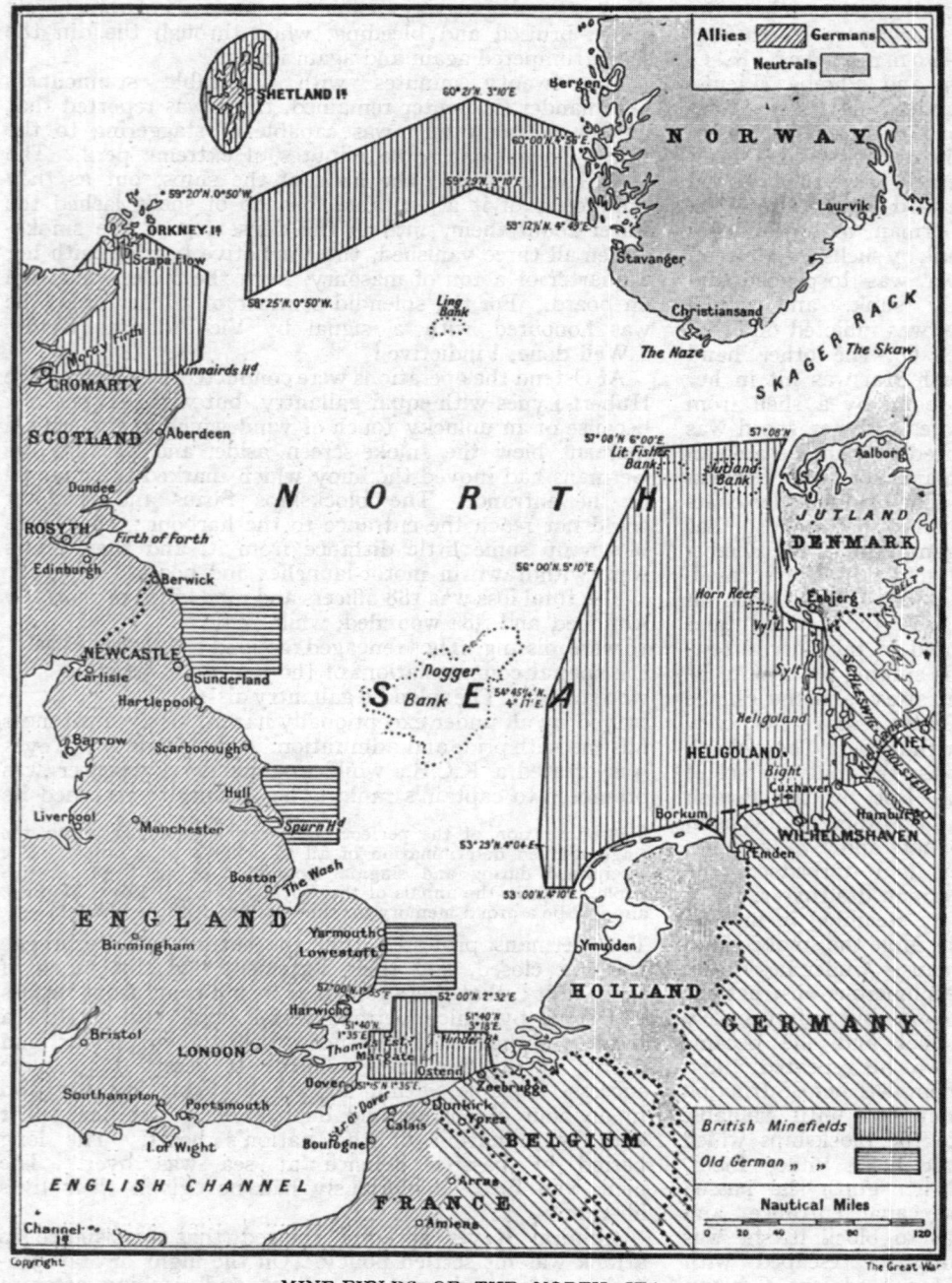

MINE-FIELDS OF THE NORTH SEA.
In this map are shown both the old mine-fields laid by the Germans off the English coast early in the war and the later extensive mine-fields laid by the British, including the "danger zones" created off the Scottish coast to the Orkneys and round the Shetland Islands. The chevron-shaped mine-field between the coasts of Scotland and Norway was established in the middle of May, 1918.

several minutes the Vindictive groped in this for the entrance, then a puff of wind lifted the fog and showed the piers; a motor-boat laid a flare between them, and the Vindictive pushed in under a terrific fire. Commander Godsal laid her nose against the eastern pier and prepared to swing her hull across the channel when came a second mishap. A shell struck the conning-tower, outside which he was standing, and killed him instantly. Lieut. V. A. Crutchley, inside the tower, tried in vain to bring the ship round; she was hard and fast, and would not be moved. Here, as before at Zeebrugge, there was a strict time-table to be followed, and he could not wait. He therefore ordered the charges in the hull to be fired and the vessel to be abandoned, and this order was skilfully carried out. Before he left he searched the wreck for the body of Commander Godsal, but of that gallant officer no trace could be found.

The total loss in this affair was eight officers and men killed, ten officers and men missing, and twenty-nine officers and men wounded—a total of only forty-seven. One motor-boat had to be destroyed owing to damage to its engines. The entrance to Ostend was not completely blocked, and the Germans a few days later managed to drag the Vindictive's wreck towards the eastern pier, so that a channel about thirty feet wide remained clear. Through this small craft (destroyers and submarines) could pass, though not without some difficulty. Sir Roger Keyes and the officers and men concerned received the warm thanks of the War Cabinet for their gallant work. As welcome were the tributes of praise which poured in from the Allies, who marked with enthusiasm the persistent offensive of the British Navy.

A few days later the sealing of Zeebrugge was rendered even more secure when a German destroyer was sunk close to the entrance by a 350 lb. bomb discharged from a British aircraft which struck her bow.

A feat similar to that accomplished at Zeebrugge was brilliantly performed by the Italian Navy early on May 14th, when an Italian motor-craft, under Lieut.-Commander M. Pellegrini, **Austrian** with three seamen, penetrated into Pola **Dreadnought sunk** and fired several torpedoes into a great Austrian Dreadnought of the Viribus Unitis type, sinking her in the harbour. The ships of this type displaced over 20,000 tons and were armed with twelve 12 in. guns in triple turrets. This was the second enemy Dreadnought put out of action in 1918, as a battleship of the Rheinland class was wrecked on the coast of Finland and badly damaged, if indeed she did not become a total loss.

The British measures against the submarines received

the Vindictive was used as the blockship, and several hundred tons of concrete were run into her hull. Commodore Hubert Lynes planned and executed the operations in which it was hoped to take the Germans by surprise. Aircraft and monitors were to co-operate, and the heavy British artillery in Flanders was to direct counter-battery work on the German guns. The night of the 9th seemed all that could be desired—windless and moonless, with no visible sign of fog. The Vindictive stood in, handled by Commander A. E. Godsal. She was preceded by destroyers and motor-craft which were to spread a smoke-screen and place a flarelight for her to steer by. As she passed into the darkness the monitors bombarded, the aircraft hovering above the town released their bombs, and the British guns on the Flanders front opened fire. At this critical moment misfortune once more befell the British. Wet sea fog suddenly came up, hiding everything. For

The funeral procession passing through Market Square, Dover, on the way to the cemetery. Right : The local ministers of religion at the graveside.

On Saturday, April 27th, 1918, the seamen and Marines who fell in the raid on the German naval bases in Flanders were buried with all the pomp of a great naval and military funeral service in Dover Cemetery. This fine photograph records the closing scene of the impressive ceremony, which was attended by the relatives of the fallen heroes and by the officers and men of the Fleet and garrison.

HEROES OF THE NAVAL RAID LAID TO REST IN ENGLAND.

a further development on May 15th, when a large new mine-field was laid obstructing the northern exit from the North Sea. The southern passage through the Strait of Dover was now mined and closely watched. The new mine-field stretched from Norwegian waters to a point near the Shetlands. At the same time new danger-zones were created off the Scottish coast, reaching to the Orkneys, and round the Shetlands. The work of mining the submarines in and creating effective barrages against their passage was now proceeding in real earnest, and the Germans began to discover that mines were weapons which could be turned against themselves. The vast system of British mine-fields in the North Sea can best be studied in the map on page 378. The enormous field off the German coast was for the most part laid in January, 1918, but was only gradually completed. The new northern mine-fields could not be rendered effective at once, but they slowly became more and more dangerous to German vessels. While the British Navy was busy with these immense operations, the German submarines continued their plan of random mine-laying near British harbours and in the highways of traffic, but no longer with the old success. The German submarines were at last being sunk faster than they could be completed; new allied shipping was at last being completed faster than it could be sunk. A new departure in tactics, the use of British submarines of large size to convoy shipping, hampered the pirates considerably and caused the loss of one of their large submarines in May. The tide at sea was slowly turning, and the new policy of the Admiralty was being abundantly justified by results.

The Price of Victory.

List of the British naval losses and of the most important British and allied shipping losses. Ships are British unless otherwise stated :

1917.
June 2	..	Cameronian, transport, torpedoed, 63 killed.
June 13	..	Avenger, armed merchant cruiser, torpedoed, 1 killed.
June 22	..	Himalaya, French steamer, torpedoed, 28 killed.
June 27	..	Kleber, French cruiser, mined, 38 killed.
,,	..	Armadale, transport, torpedoed, 11 killed.
July 4	..	Destroyer, mined, 18 saved.
,,	..	Mine-sweeper, mined, 10 killed, Mediterranean.
July 7	..	Destroyer, torpedoed, 8 killed.
July 9	..	Vanguard, battleship, blown up, 804 killed.
July 22	..	Otway, armed merchant cruiser, torpedoed, 10 killed.

July 26	..	C34, submarine, sunk, all crew killed.
July 29	..	Ariadne, cruiser, torpedoed, 38 killed, Channel.
Aug. 15	..	Destroyer, mined, 46 saved, North Sea.
Sept. 19	..	Orama, armed merchant cruiser, torpedoed, no loss.
Sept. 22	..	Destroyer, torpedoed, 50 saved, Channel.
Oct. 16	..	Begonia, mine-sweeper, considered lost with all crew.
Oct. 17	..	Strongbow, destroyer, sunk in action, North Sea.
,,	..	Mary Rose, destroyer, sunk in action, North Sea.
Oct. 24	..	Destroyer, sunk by collision, 23 saved.
Nov. 4	..	Small monitor } sunk by submarines on Palestine Destroyer } coast, 33 killed.
Nov. 18	..	Patrol ship, torpedoed, 9 killed, Mediterranean.
Dec. 1	..	Châteaurenault, French cruiser, torpedoed, Mediterranean.
Dec. 6	..	Jacob Jones, American destroyer, torpedoed, 37 survivors.
Dec. 11	..	Naval airship destroyed, 5 killed, North Sea.
Dec. 12	..	Naval airship interned, Holland.
,,	..	Partridge, destroyer, sunk in action, North Sea.
,,	..	Four armed trawlers, sunk in action, North Sea.
,,	..	Destroyer, sunk in collision, 2 killed.
Dec. 22	..	Three destroyers, mined or torpedoed, North Sea.
Dec. 24	..	Furness, boarding-steamer, torpedoed, 101 killed, Irish Sea.
Dec. 30	..	Destroyer, torpedoed, 10 killed, Mediterranean.
,,	..	Aragon, transport, torpedoed, 611 killed, Mediterranean.
Dec. 31	..	Osmanli, armed merchant cruiser, 199 killed, Mediterranean.
1918.		
Jan. 1	..	Grive, boarding-steamer, torpedoed, no loss.
,,	..	Arbutus, mine-sweeper, torpedoed, 9 killed.
Jan. 4	..	Rewa, hospital-ship, torpedoed, 3 killed.
Jan. 9	..	Racoon, destroyer, wrecked, Irish Sea, all lost.
Jan. 12	..	Two destroyers lost in storm with all hands, except 1.
Jan. 20	..	Mechanician, escort vessel, torpedoed, 13 killed, Channel.
,,	..	Raglan, monitor } sunk by Goeben at Imbros, 224 M28, monitor } killed.
Jan. 21	..	Louvain, boarding-steamer, torpedoed, 224 killed.
Jan. 27	..	E14, submarine, sunk off Dardanelles, 7 prisoners taken.
Jan. 28	..	Hazard, gunboat, sunk by collision, 3 killed.
Feb. 5	..	Tuscania, transport, torpedoed, 210 killed, Atlantic.
Feb. 8	..	Boxer, destroyer, sunk by collision, 1 killed, Channel.
Feb. 15	..	Eight drifters, etc., sunk in Channel by German destroyers, 60 killed.
Feb. 26	..	Glenart Castle, hospital-ship, torpedoed, 150 killed.
March 1	..	Calgarian, steamer, torpedoed, 48 killed.
March 22	..	Mine-sweeper, mined, 66 killed.
March 23	..	Destroyer, sunk by collision, 2 killed.
March 27	..	Destroyer, mined, 41 killed.
March 28	..	Tithonus, boarding-steamer, torpedoed, 4 killed.
April 1	..	Destroyer, sunk by collision, no loss.
April 4	..	Destroyer, sunk by collision, all lost.
April 23	..	Destroyer North Star, sunk in action, Zeebrugge.
,,	..	Two coastal motor-boats and two launches sunk in action, Zeebrugge.
April 25	..	Cowslip, sloop, torpedoed, 6 killed.
,,	..	Torpedo-boat No. 90, foundered in storm, 13 killed.
,,	..	French submarine Prairial sunk in collision.
May 1	..	Mine-sweeper, sunk, 26 killed.
May 14	..	Destroyer torpedoed, 2 killed.
May 23	..	Moldavia, British armed merchant cruiser, torpedoed, 56 American soldiers killed.

COUNTING THE COST OF A MOST SPLENDID VICTORY.

Roll-call after the brilliant naval attack on Zeebrugge and Ostend on St. George's Day. The total loss of officers and men killed or mortally wounded in this most daring enterprise was 188, and, in addition, the extraordinarily small number of 16 were reported as missing. The wounded numbered 384. Although these casualties were heavy in proportion to the numbers engaged they were justified by the results obtained.

CHAPTER CCXLV.

BOMBING BIPLANE.

THE SWAY OF BATTLE IN THE AIR, 1917-18.
By Edward Wright.

General Von Höppner's Effort to Win Mastery in the Air—Reformation and Extension of the German Air Service—German Methods of Fighting with Large Formations and Use of the Decoy Trick in Attack—Capture of Captain Leefe Robinson, V.C.—British Thrust into Lens Defeated, and General Nivelle's Thrust towards Laon Impeded by Inferiority in the Air—Opportunity for Pursuing Policy of Reprisal Raids Lost Owing to Lack of Official Prevision of the Needs of British Airmen—Fine Work of British Naval Airmen—Further Reorganisation of the British Air Service Begun—Some British Champions in the Air: Captain Albert Ball, Major Avery Bishop, and Captain A. M. Wilkinson—Practical Franco-British Predominance in the Air Secured—Great Air Contests During the Preparations for the Battles of Messines-Wytschaete Ridge—America's Preparations for Aerial Warfare—Astonishing Feats of British Airmen in the Third Battle of Ypres—Development of Nocturnal Aerial Operations—The Battle of Cambrai and First Appearance of the Australian Flying Corps—Creation of the Air Ministry and Establishment of the Royal Air Force—Systematic Attack upon German Territory Begun—Part Played by Aircraft in the German Offensive begun in March, 1918.

WHEN the British Air Board was established in January, 1917, as related in Chapter CLX. (Vol. 8, page 275), Germany had entered upon a large scheme of reorganisation and expansion. General von Höppner, Chief of Staff to General von Below in the Somme campaign, was so impressed by the British recovery from Fokker superiority that he resigned his command in the field to make a supreme effort to win mastery in the air for his country, and by the winter of 1916 was exerting a pressure in the air that caused anxiety to the British and French Commanders-in-Chief. He brought out improved types of fighting machines, together with workmanlike imitations of the Handley Page bombing machine, and developed a special form of aerial attack.

The British Flying Corps largely relied upon the native spirit of sportsmanship, and sent out single fighting pilots, like Captain Albert Ball, V.C., who fought against any odds.

The Prussian commander employed science instead of sportsmanship. He made his best fighting men, such as Captain Baron von Richthofen, the leaders of large formations, most of the men in which were trained to shepherd allied airmen into positions where a matador stroke could be delivered. The design was always to bring superior strength to bear upon the gallantly adventurous British and French pilots. The special German formations were unattached to any sector or army, and travelled all along the front, using the power of numbers to destroy any small allied force they encountered. These tactics were a practical application of the classic military principle of concentration, and so numerous were the successes it effected that Captain von Richthofen alone was credited before he fell with a personal destruction of eighty allied machines.

So long as the British and French Armies fought alongside each other by the Somme their air chiefs were able to answer the enemy's massing of force by combined swoops over his lines. When, however, in the spring of 1917, General von Ludendorff retreated from Bapaume and Roye, and the French and British forces, under the direction of General Nivelle, selected widely-separated fields of attack, Von Höppner was well rewarded for his foresight in reforming and extending the German Air Service and developing the method of fighting with large formations.

By combining most of his battle squadrons for action on one critical sector, the enemy general was able to sweep the air with destructive effect. From an aerial point of view the distance between the new French front on the Aisne and the new British front around Arras was negligible. From their central position in the

ROYAL VISIT TO AIR-TRAINING CENTRE.
King George viewing an aerial gun during a visit which he paid to the Royal Air Force Armaments School. With his Majesty are Lord Cromer, Brigadier-General Hearson, and Commander Sir Charles Cust.

AAA   381

great western salient German pilots could turn in less than a couple of hours from the French to the British front, and break a path for reconnaissance in any direction.

General von Höppner brought out in large number a small German machine of the Albatros type, and with it exercised the same blinding pressure in the spring of 1917 as the Fokker fighters had exercised in the spring of 1916. The successful manner in which the German Army conducted its withdrawal in the middle of March, 1917, was no doubt due to the fact that the British and French Flying Corps no longer held any decided mastery of the air.

Sir William Weir, the new Director of Supplies, by personal enterprise and official encouragement of the private manufacturing resources of the country, gradually provided aeroplanes of which Sir Hugh Trenchard, commanding the aerial forces on the western front, was desperately in need ; but, meanwhile, casualties among British airmen rose from fifty-six in January, 1917, to one hundred and nineteen in February, and to one hundred and fifty-two in March, while on a single day in April one hundred and seventeen casualties were reported. By the end of April the British losses considerably exceeded three hundred, and the damage done to the German air forces was to a considerable degree less than was later inflicted when better British machines were available.

Casualties among British airmen

The enemy chaser squadrons, that saved the retiring German armies, had various methods of attack. One of the most common was to send a single decoy machine below a British machine and let the crack German pilot, hiding high in the clouds, swoop on the tail of the Briton when the latter was trying to attack. When a few British fighting pilots were escorting a bombing squadron of old, slow aircraft, the German circus—or formation—leader would send down a few machines which would make a

pretence at attack, and quickly retreat, fiercely pursued by the British battle-planes. Then upon the unprotected bombing machines the main force of the German circus would close.

There were a few first-rate British machines on the western front in the spring of 1917, but, according to an estimate given in the House of Commons, the machines of the most up-to-date kind represented only four per cent. of the material with which Sir Hugh Trenchard and his officers were compelled to work.

The result was that when a first-class but small squadron of good British battle-planes attempted to clear the air above their old, slow reconnaissance machines, the conflict opened with a tremendous advantage on the side of Captain von Richthofen, or Captain von Bülow, who directed the two principal German massed formations.

Decoy trick of attack

The decoy trick was usually employed by the enemy. Keeping his main force hidden in the clouds, he would send out two or three machines in order to lure half a dozen British aeroplanes to the appointed place of destruction. When this place was reached, from twenty to thirty enemy machines would envelop the small British squadron, cutting it off from the British lines, and, if possible, leading it over batteries of German anti-aircraft guns. After the guns had done what work they could, the formation would close for action, using from four to five machines against every British machine. Richthofen himself would hang above the conflict, and make his swoop usually upon some easy victim who had been forced into a position of disadvantage by the subordinate German pilots.

One of the most remarkable struggles of this kind

ARMS AND THE MEN IN THE AIR.
Handing out machine-guns to British battle-plane observers, and (in circle) filling the machine-gun drums with cartridges. Above: Passing loaded drum to an observer aboard a battle-plane.

occurred over Lens between six special new British machines and the entire force commanded by Captain von Richthofen. Captain Leefe Robinson, V.C., the distinguished Zeppelin destroyer, was trapped and completely outfought by the great German formation, being shot down by Sergeant Festner and made prisoner, while three other pilots in the new machines were brought down, making the enemy a present of the latest examples of British improvements in aeromotor and aeroplane design. Only two out of the six new battle-planes landed in British territory.

Successes of Baron von Richthofen In an action over Douai, on April 14th, Captain von Richthofen claimed the destruction of an entire British squadron, and Sir Douglas Haig admitted on that day that many of his machines were missing. The Canadian-British divisions were then endeavouring to develop the advantages they had won on Vimy Ridge by making a grand thrust into Lens. Had the German gunners been blinded by the destruction of their spotting aeroplanes, and had all British reconnaissance machines been fully protected by their battle-planes, General Horne might have been able to smother the enemy batteries and break a path into the tunnelled mining city.

General von Höppner, however, held the mastery in the air. He saved Lens, and enabled it to be converted into a vast underground concentration place, equal to tunnelled Arras, for opening a grand surprise offensive. After stopping the British advance between Lens and Quéant, the German air controller proceeded to show that the striking force of air-power could be made as disconcerting to an overpowered opponent as was the striking force of sea-power.

He turned to the Aisne and Champagne front when General Nivelle tried to break through to Laon, on April 17th, and greatly helped to diminish the effective strength of the heavy guns which the French Commander-in-Chief had accumulated.

The great German aerial formations were probably not superior in number to the combined totals of French and British fighting aeroplanes, and in personal quality such officers as Captain Ball and Captain Guynemer indisputably excelled the best German airmen. Yet by means of a more scientific application of the principle of mass attack in regard to specific actions, and the employment of the short interior line across the salient of Lens, La Fère, and Moronvilliers, where separate allied armies were fighting at a wide angle to each other, the concentrated German Flying Corps victoriously exploited its means of very rapid movement from the British to the French front.

When a fighting force holds interior lines, and can move at the pace of two and a half miles a minute, between two great battlefields from eighty to ninety miles apart, it doubles its striking power in theory. In practice, however, General von Höppner trebled the power of his corps; for he left the British corps **German kite-balloon** seriously weakened at the time when he **decoys** was massing against the French pilots.

One of his formation leaders turned the German kite balloons on the French front into decoys. As a French squadron swooped on the balloons a larger German fighting formation, that had been hiding above the clouds, attacked the attackers, and brought many of them down, while the German observation officers, in the only two balloons that had to be sacrificed, descended safely in parachutes.

April 14th, the day on which Richthofen won his greatest success against the British corps, was also memorable as the date of the last British raid into German

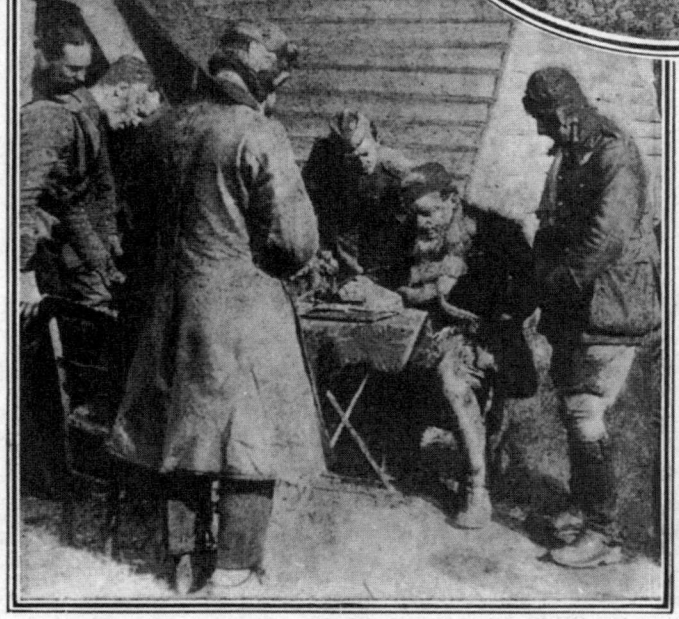

FLYING ACTIVITY ON THE WESTERN FRONT.
British pilots bringing in their reports as to enemy positions, and (in circle) a member of the R.A.F. with a big bomb. Above: American airmen over one of their aerodromes in France.

UNIT OF GREAT BRITAIN'S AERIAL LIGHT FORCES.
Starting off for work over the German lines in conjunction with the British artillery and infantry. Extraordinary co-operation between the three arms in the first week of June, 1917, was largely responsible for the success of the British Second Army on the Messines Ridge.

turn against their lords when rigorous and incessant measures of terrorisation were maintained against them. Probably nobody knew this better than the officers commanding the British naval bombing forces. They were, however, unable to continue the work they had begun at Freiburg.

All their available chasers, bombing machines, and pilots that could be detached from the Dover Patrol and anti-submarine work and general naval reconnaissance were absorbed in the task of assisting the armies in the field. Owing to lack of the best material the military wing of the Royal Flying Corps had to call for immediate help from the naval wing. Naval raids over Germany, which should have increased in number, range, and destructive quality, were completely stopped in the year in which London and other parts of England were suffering most severely, as already described in Chapter CXCVIII. (Vol. 10, page 125).

territory made for some months. Under Lieutenant-Colonel Charles E. H. Rathborne, wing-commander in the R.N.A.S., a considerable number of British naval airmen combined with a French flying force in a destructive bombardment of Freiburg. Two daylight attacks were made with material and moral results of a remarkable character. Large important buildings were shattered, and a feeling of contagious terror spread all along the Rhine. Wealthy Rhinelanders who were able to do so moved into Switzerland, while the business and working populations clamoured either for complete protection or for a treaty with France and Great Britain for the abolition of all air raids beyond the immediate fighting-fronts.

It was a grand occasion for pursuing with the utmost rigour the policy of reprisal raids which had been generally advocated since the opening of enemy attacks upon non-combatants. The dubious German movement for peace, that gathered way in July, 1917, would have had an enormous addition of popular sentiment behind it had there been hundreds of Handley Page machines with Rolls-Royce motors available in the spring and summer of that year for bombing attacks upon the Rhineland cities and the Westphalian industrial centres.

But no further British raid on veritable German territory took place for many months. Sometimes the lost provinces of France were attacked, but British bombing machines never droned over the servile tribes who worked for the Prussian squires and for the industrial and financial magnates allied with the oligarchy of which the Hohenzollern was only a gramophone figurehead. Of all races in the world the Germans were most subject to break and

The naval airmen serving with the military wing finely distinguished themselves. The most remarkable of their fighting pilots was Flight-Sub-Lieutenant Joseph Malone, who rose to **Naval airmen's** fame in the evening of April 23rd, **splendid feats** 1917. He attacked a hostile scout and forced it down, turned upon another German machine, killed the pilot, and wrecked the aeroplane. Then at a range of twenty yards he shot down, completely out of control, a third enemy scout, and ran out of ammunition while engaging a fourth machine. Returning to the advanced landing-ground he obtained more supplies, flew against another German formation, and forced down his fourth machine, that fell out of control.

ANTI-AIRCRAFT GUNS IN ACTION IN FRANCE.
Anti-aircraft guns which brought down a huge German aeroplane in France in 1918. Apart from the daily toll of enemy aeroplanes exacted by flying men, anti-aircraft guns had a very successful record in 1918. Thus, in the first week of June, French guns brought down thirteen enemy machines.

Flight-Lieutenant James Gobie also showed extraordinary skill and aggressiveness on numerous occasions, and Flight-Commander B. C. Bell and R. H. Little gallantly outfought all German airmen they met. Flight-Lieutenant Raymond Collishaw brought down four machines in one day, sending the first down in a nose-dive, shooting the second down out of control, crashing a third in a spin, and shooting away two of the planes of the fourth machine.

Yet the diversion of naval air forces to direct Army work remained a very remarkable success for Germany, and for Great Britain a disaster of which the political issue was of immeasurable magnitude. It was due neither to Sir Hugh Trenchard and his fighting pilots nor to Sir William Weir and the new Air Board. It can only be attributed to the men in high position in the summer of 1916 who failed to anticipate the needs of British air forces by the spring of 1917.

One result of the startling German victories in the air was that the further reorganisation of the British Air Service was begun. On April 10th, **Reorganisation taken in hand** 1917, it was announced that Brigadier-General Brancker was appointed Deputy Director-General of Military Aeronautics, and that Colonel Charlton was promoted brigadier-general and made Director of Air Organisation. A few days afterwards the King was pleased to become Colonel-in-Chief to the Royal Flying Corps, as a special mark of his appreciation of the courage, skill, and devotion of the badly-equipped but indomitable airmen.

The Germans did not prevent observation work, although they made it costly for the flower of British youth. Prac-

TESTING THE VOCAL COMMUNICATION WITH THE BATTERY.
R.A.F. kite-balloon observer testing his telephone before ascending. Besides enabling the observer to communicate with the guns, the telephone was often vital to him if his balloon hid attacking aeroplanes from his vision; then his battery told him when he must take to his parachute.

tically all the batteries captured in the British advances were found in the exact positions previously located by aerial scouts, and the successful counter-battery work by which British infantry were protected was largely due to spotting done by pilots and observers using machines that gave them no chance against enemy battle-planes and little protection against hostile ground fire. In gallantry British airmen excelled their most adventurous forefathers, making the age in which they briefly lived more spacious than any other in the history of their race.

What can match the courtesy in death of one officer who took part in the April offensive on a day when Richthofen held dominion in the air? Returning alone from a long journey over the enemy's lines, the British airman was enveloped and forced into a tight corner. By supreme agility and marksmanship he escaped, and, landing awkwardly in his own lines, apologised for the way he had come down. His foot was smashed, one eye was shot out, there was a mortal wound in his body, and his machine was a thing of rags and splintered wood. Yet he begged pardon for a bad landing, made his report, and died.

The Germans took to using machine-gun fire against British troops, according to the tactics invented by Sir Hugh Trenchard. The British cavalry, when attacking Monchy, were charged by German aeroplanes which swept troopers and horses with machine-gun fire in a way that showed that conditions of aerial warfare had changed since the Somme campaign. Enemy machine-gun attacks from the air were also delivered at Gavrelle in the last week of April, the fact being proudly announced by the German High Command.

R.A.F. KITE-BALLOON OBSERVER IN PARACHUTE HARNESS.
Kite-balloons, as the eyes of the guns, were singled out for attack by enemy artillery and aircraft. If they were set on fire the observer's sole chance of life was to jump from the car, and observers never went up on duty until attached to their parachute.

FRANCO-GERMAN DUEL IN THE AIR.
Photographs of actual combats in the air were rare, as other aviators present were naturally intent on other things than cameras. This picture of a French airman engaging a German Albatros was secured by a French observer.

to destroy the Germans. At the speed they went over enemy positions their marksmanship with bomb and machine-gun was seldom good. But their presence had a very depressing effect upon the hostile soldiery and a cheering influence upon their own infantry.

The British infantryman at the time needed cheering. When in the front line he saw many of the actions between old-fashioned British machines, usually in small number, and up-to-date German machines generally in large number. He saw his own airmen crashing from the skies, driven down out of control or descending to save themselves, and the spectacle did not inspire him with comforting thoughts. Then, when the enemy adopted the Trenchard system of aerial attacks on infantry, while making a successful stand with large fresh reserves and new mobile batteries along the Hindenburg line from Fresnoy to Quéant, the British soldier sadly contrasted his experiences in the Somme Battle with those of the Battle of the Rivers.

Captain Albert Ball, who had been sent home to train apprentice pilots in his methods of fighting, returned to the front on April 7th. Single-handed he attacked from twelve to fourteen machines, destroying ten in his first two weeks. On April 26th he assailed a formation of twenty German machines over Cambrai, and, though surrounded, broke his way out, crashing two of the Germans. Even when he fought with his British squadron, he had only five machines against the twenty or thirty that Richthofen and Bülow manœuvred. Yet he attacked the Germans on sight, whatever their strength was, and his example was a fine stimulus to his comrades. On almost every occasion when he and other pilots met the enemy the British were outnumbered, and the Germans

British airmen, however, still remained superior in this moral form of offensive. During the fighting round Lens three British machines, flying near the level of the roofs above the main street, scattered with bombs a German regiment filling the road. Then two airmen, missing their way after a great fight near Douai, spied a squadron of Pomeranian Hussars and a gang of a hundred infantrymen unloading trucks by a railway-station. One pilot dispersed the cavalry, after killing about a score of them, while the other caught most of the men by the railway. This form of air work was not much esteemed by the pilots. They carried it out more to encourage their own infantry than

laid all manner of traps to catch the champion Briton. After he had brought down at least forty-three German machines, he was ambushed by Lieutenant von Richthofen, a relative of the best enemy pilot, and killed over Lens in the evening of May 7th, 1917. Captain von Richthofen disappeared temporarily about the same time, being apparently wounded, but returned later in the year.

A young Canadian cavalry officer, Major W. Avery Bishop, V.C., succeeded Captain Ball as British champion in the air. Both were young men of small stature, quick ways, and full of a curious, nervous energy. Both preferred

British champions in the air

CAPTAIN P. F. FULLARD, M.C.
With a record of forty-two enemy machines destroyed, Captain Fullard won the sobriquet of "The Wizard of the Air."

MAJ. W. A. BISHOP, V.C., D.S.O., M.C.
Major Bishop succeeded Captain Ball as British air champion, destroying at least fifty German machines.

FLIGHT-COM. K. S. SAVORY, D.S.O., R.N.A.S.
Commander Savory flew from London to Constantinople, July 9th, 1917, and bombed the German battleship Goeben and the Turkish War Office.

to roam as free-lances through the sky, and trust to their personal spirit of daring skill rather than to the scientific enveloping manœuvring of a formation. The most remarkable achievement of Major Bishop was an attack upon a German aerodrome. He shot down four German pilots as one by one they tried to climb up to fight him. In the number of successes achieved in a single day, Major Bishop was excelled by Captain A. M. Wilkinson, who shot down and destroyed six machines in a day. But in the total of his achievements Major Bishop was supreme among British pilots. With the same astonishing

pilots, the system under which they worked was not so good as the German system of massed formations. There were, for instance, occasions when Captain Ball had to work from half-past two in the morning until half-past nine at night. Under such a tremendous strain, young men with the finest constitutions became exhausted, and in work in which steadiness and nerve were everything, many good men fell because they needed rest. Their best machines were also overworked, and often very badly damaged, so that they had to be withdrawn for repairs.

| Lieut. Erwin Böhme, killed on the western front the day before the Kaiser awarded him the Ordre Pour le Mérite. | Lieut. Wissemann, who had killed Capt. Guynemer, was shot down by Lieut. Fonck. | Lieut Voss, credited with having " brought down fifty adversaries," was killed in a fight by a British airman. | Baron von Richthofen, killed after having himself claimed over sixty victims. | Capt. Baron von Tutschek, one of Germany's "star" airmen, shot down by a French adversary over the enemy lines. |

FIVE OF GERMANY'S LEADING AIR FIGHTERS KILLED ON THE WESTERN FRONT.

deadliness as Captain Ball, the Canadian airman engaged in all manner of combats, in most of which the odds were against him, and by destroying at least fifty German machines he became the greatest of all living masters of the air.

German successes exaggerated   There is considerable doubt whether Major Avery Bishop was not the absolute aerial champion. Although Captain von Richthofen was credited with a larger number of complete victories, there were grounds for supposing that the German method of record was designed to inflate the fame of its champions. Many machines that were forced down were not destroyed, and in British and French figures of the successes of crack pilots no victory was counted unless there was evidence that the hostile machine was seen to crash. In many cases, where an allied pilot fought single-handed against heavy odds, he destroyed machines that were not included in his record.

There was complete proof that the total German claims in regard to the destruction of allied machines were very considerably exaggerated. For all these reasons the official German figures of the victories of Richthofen were regarded as dubious, and although the German baron was undoubtedly a cool, deadly fighter of the scientific school, it is more than probable that he was excelled by Captain Ball until the time when Ball fell, and that he was surpassed by Major Bishop, who had the happiness to survive the worst period of the aerial struggle, and become the hero of Canada and the instructor of hundreds of fresh pilots.

Yet great as were the achievements of Major Bishop, Captain Ball, and other champion British

"You don't know what a beastly game it is when nothing is going as it should, and you have not got enough men to do the jobs," said Captain Ball in one of his last letters on May 3rd, 1917.

But while Captain Ball was making his last and most gallant struggle to help the Allies recover the mastery of the air, the terrible stress of defeat lightened and changed into a balance of forces, and finally into a practical Franco-British predominance. In May, 1917, seven hundred and thirteen machines were reported to have been brought down on the western front. This was four less than had fallen the previous month, when the enemy was at his strongest. Germany lost four hundred and twenty-two machines, according to allied reports; while Great Britain and France lost two hundred and seventy-one machines, according to German reports. British losses were sixty-one fewer in May than in April, French losses were sixteen more, and German losses were seventy-three more. Of enemy machines brought down, two hundred and forty-three were destroyed by the British and one hundred and ninety-nine by the French.

Germany loses air domination

Sir Hugh Trenchard also greatly increased the enemy's unrecorded losses by developing a system of nocturnal raids on hostile aerodromes in France and Flanders. Then, by using flares and other illuminating devices, British bombing machines were able to pursue the German infantry from the fighting-line into rest billets, and thunder upon the sleep of the fatigued troops. This intense and immediate development of bombing operations, by day and night, was the principal compensation for the long and

GERMANY'S AIR CHIEF.
General von Höppner, made head of Germany's air forces when it was decided to combine the aerial and anti-aircraft departments under one control.

serious interruption of British naval air raids into Germany.

About this time the British air commander answered the German attempt at infantry attack by an extended use of aerial machine-gun fire. In the later phase of the Arras Battle there had occurred a telling example of the moral effect of aerial co-operation with infantry. A large,

OUT ON OBSERVATION DUTY.
British biplane taking observations from some thousands of feet high in the air over the enemy lines on the western front. The photograph was taken from a companion machine in flight, part of the lower plane of which is to be seen on the left.

fast-flying British squadron was returning from a long patrol and, seeing infantry in action, swooped down upon the German force, raked it, and, by means of remarkable climbing power, escaped all injury from ground fire.

The German losses from this lightning-like aerial assault were probably small, as the pilots flew too swiftly to take good aim. Yet the effect upon the struggling British troops was wonderful. They had been fighting at a disadvantage with grim resolution, but they flamed out in battle fury and, cheering their unexpected airmen, fought onward with a refreshed vehemence quite out of proportion to the aid that came to them from the sky.

Therefore, in the preparations for the action on the Messines-Wytschaete Ridge on June 7th, 1917, Sir Hugh Trenchard made a splendid effort to show Sir Herbert Plumer's army that Britain was again mistress of the air. By June 3rd the German aerial losses were double those of the British. Then, on June 4th, eighteen enemy machines were destroyed against the reported loss of five British aeroplanes. On June 5th sixteen hostile machines were brought down, while only seven British aeroplanes were missing.

Grand air contest at Messines

June 6th was the day of the grand contest. General von Höppner massed all his available chaser squadrons upon the Second British Army. He employed five battle wings, some of which were formed of more than thirty machines. As the entire German organisation of chaser squadrons then numbered four hundred and eighty machines—some being used to protect German territory, while others operated along the French front and quiet British and Belgian sectors—the large formations that tried to hold dominion of the air between Lille and Ypres were the utmost measure of Germany's fighting aerial strength.

At the end of the day six British machines were missing, but the German battle wings were dispersed with heavy casualties, including the loss of at least eighteen machines. Then, on June 7th, when the ridge rocked with artificial earthquakes and smoked and smouldered under rolling hurricanes of shell, the German battle wing made a last desperate attempt to blind Sir Herbert Plumer's forces. Twenty enemy machines were destroyed and fourteen British machines were missing, but the British loss was light in comparison with the results obtained.

The sky was cleared of flying Germans, and infantry and artillery were excellently served by British pilots and observers. The hostile infantry was swept by aerial machine-gun fire unparalleled in warfare, and all the German rear organisation, to a depth of many miles, was seriously damaged by bombing and machine-gunning squadrons. Aerodromes were blown up, trains were wrecked, ammunition stores were exploded, and reinforcements pursued and scattered.

Night brought no relief to the enemy, when the loss of aerial power, which he had laboured so long and industriously to maintain, was abruptly overset. Across the flaming battle-sky there droned the night raiders of the British Empire—soldiers and seamen, Australians, Canadians, and New Zealanders, all intensely trained to the difficult work of rising and landing and keeping their course in the darkness. Some of them reached the railway-stations, where there were long lines of rolling-stock filled with ammunition for the hard-pressed German Army. Until dawn the sky blazed and thundered, and little was left of the trucks and their contents when clear daylight enabled a survey to be taken.

If Sir Douglas Haig and General Plumer had not arranged the movement of men and guns entirely with a view to a battle with limited objectives, all the enemy's lines between the Lys and the Menin road might have been overrun when the Royal Flying Corps recovered with practical completeness the mastery of the air. It was not, however, possible to change the method of advance as soon as the enemy was blinded and thrown from the ridge. The pilots could have done much more than they did had preparations been previously made for larger movements of their infantry and artillery.

Sweeping victory of the R.F.C.

There remained some gallant German pilots who succeeded in worrying some of the Australian gunners in the later action below the eastern slopes of the Messines Ridge, but in a general way the battle in the air at the end of the first week in June, 1917, ended in a sweeping British victory for all arms of the new service. The contact pilots were magnificent both in number and in skill. They set an entirely new standard in aerial attack upon infantry, and in order to induce German pilots to take the same risks General von Höppner had afterwards to bring out a special machine with armour protections.

In the third week in June there was a remarkable reduction in British aerial losses. On some days no machines were missing, on others only one or two; while the number of German aeroplanes crashed or sent down out of control often amounted to ten or fifteen. Through the rest of the month the effects of the great British

Tuning=up an immense R.A.F. machine before departure on a bombing raid into Germany.

Duel à outrance: French aeroplane driving a German seaplane down in flames into the Channel.

In reprisal: A squadron of French double-engined Caudron aeroplanes dropping bombs upon Karlsruhe.

British fighting aeroplane starting out to engage enemy machines during the German offensive.

Fiery end of a German aeroplane brought down by British airmen behind their lines.

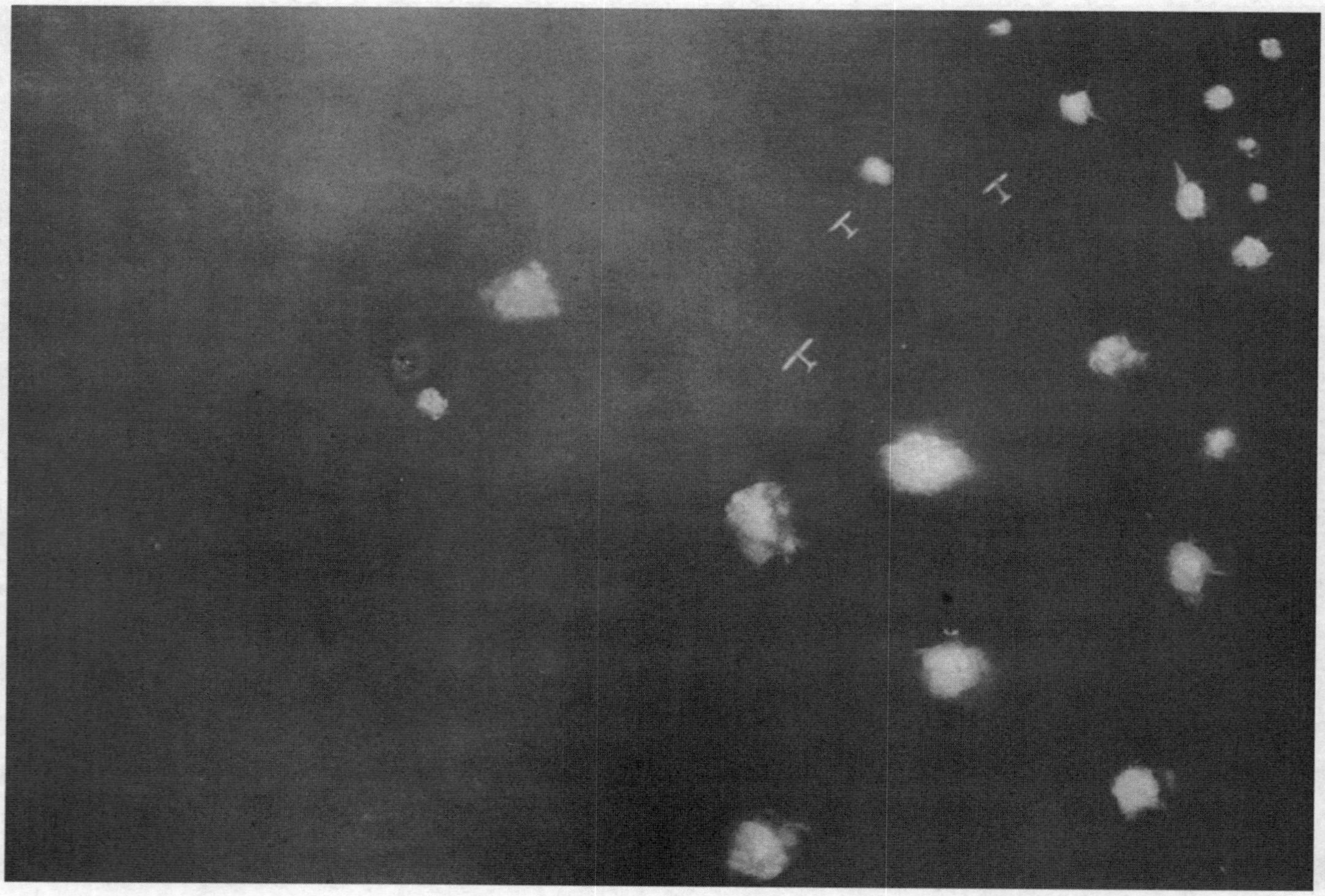

[From a picture by C. R. W. Nevinson, one of the official British artists at the front

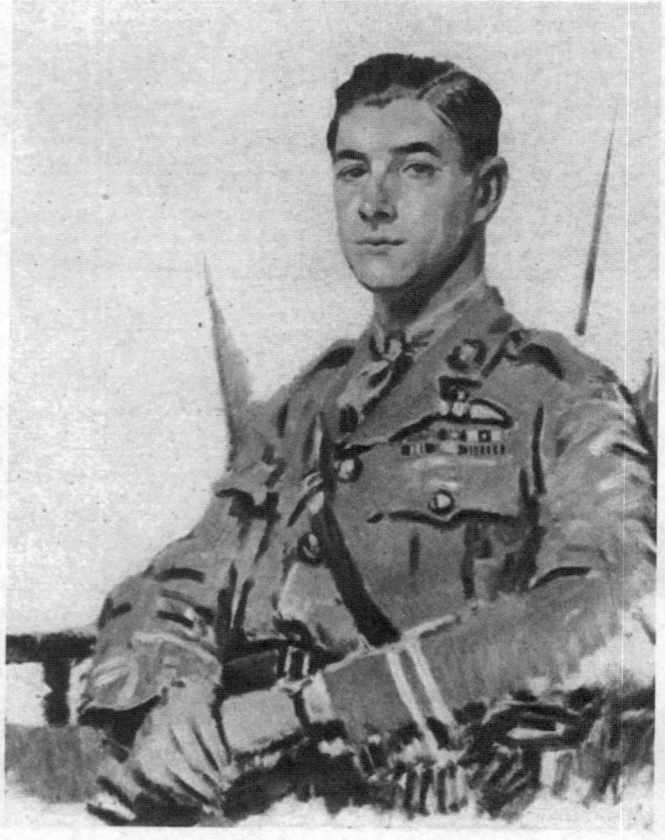

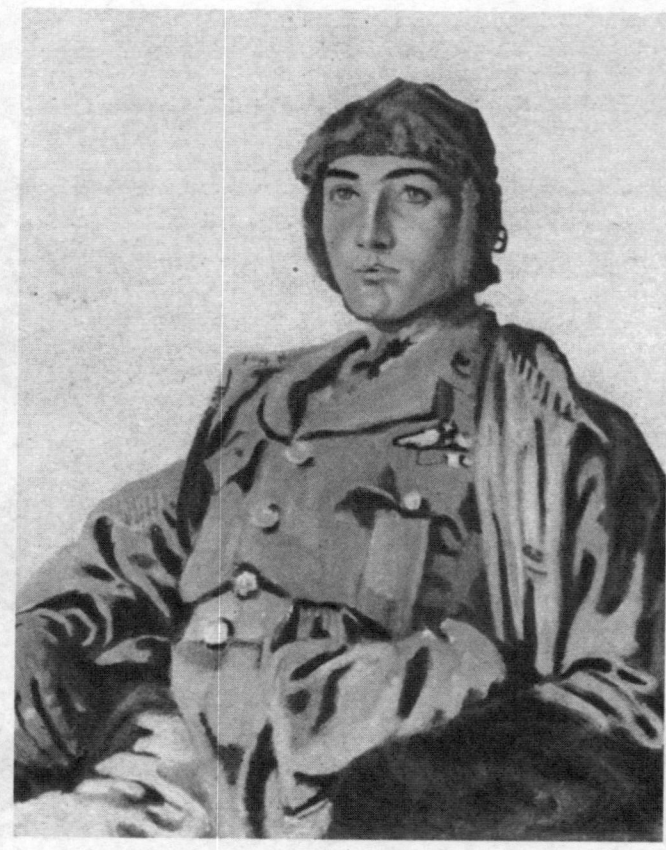

"Archies": Shells from the anti-aircraft guns bursting round aeroplanes.

[From portraits by Major Sir William Orpen, K.B.E., A.R.A., one of the official artists on the western front.

Capt. J. T. C. McCudden, V.C., D.S.O., M.C., and Sec.-Lieut. A. P. F. Rhys Davids, D.S.O., M.C.

victory told on all operations along the western front. The destruction of the German battle wings compelled the German air chief to weaken his chaser squadrons guarding German territory, and, profiting by this situation, French airmen extended their raids as far as Essen in the first week of July and obtained a local predominance on the Aisne front and around Verdun. In July, 1917, Captain Baron von Richthofen returned to the battle zone where his wing, under Lieutenant Voss, had suffered very badly. The German champion brought with him many new pilots whom he had been training, and made his first new kill on the third of the month, when the British lost one machine and the enemy nine. At the same time the Germans became more enterprising in night raiding —due, no doubt, to months of practice on lines indicated by the more inventive Briton. On July 6th, for example, one hundred and forty-four bombs were dropped by night in the British lines, but the British bombing machines more exactly placed nearly three times that number of bombs upon German targets.

As preparations for the Third Battle of Ypres proceeded every form of aerial activity developed intensely. Large fighting formations clashed in the high altitudes, while reconnaissance, photographic, spotting, and bombing aeroplanes worked, dodged, and fought in the lower air. The French forces on the left of the British were served by Captain Guynemer, the famous champion, who won his fiftieth victory on August 1st, and was killed the following month over Poelcappelle by Lieutenant Wissemann, who in turn was slain by Lieutenant Fonck, the friend of Guynemer and his successor as leader of the wings of France.

This was a period of gigantic effort in all aerial work by the principal combatant nations. In Great Britain the methods of the new Air Board began to tell upon the course of the war. A novel system **U.S. preparations** of training was adopted by which skilled **for aerial warfare** pilots were produced in much larger numbers in less time. Considerable supplies of new British machines of a superior type arrived on the western front just in time to counter another great and sustained offensive movement by General von Höppner.

The United States Congress voted the huge sum of £128,000,000 for aviation purposes. A new aeromotor, the Liberty engine, was also advertised in the United States Press as a marvel of rapid inventiveness and standardised production. These two American contributions to the aerial power of the Grand Alliance did not, for a considerable time, have any direct influence upon the struggle in the air. There was indeed delay in the execution of the American programme, yet the tremendous scale upon which the United States planned its preparations served further to stimulate the other warring nations in organising aerial warfare. First by platoons, and at last by divisions and army corps, the contending peoples took the air, and moved towards the fulfilment of Tennyson's prophecy of the ghastly clash of great aerial fleets.

The summer of 1917 was a memorable period in the history of military aviation. Sir Hugh Trenchard maintained his dominating position in the air against the fierce lunges of the German Flying Corps, and when the First French Army was ranged alongside the Fifth British Army,

with the best French pilots operating with the enlarging forces of the British Empire, another stage of terrible progress was reached in the employment of aerial power.

The aeroplane had broken up the system of connected fortified lines. It had chased the infantry out of vast tunnels and forced them to scatter in screened shell-holes and concealed works of concrete. Under the eye of the aerial observer, gunners had been compelled to disperse, as, in spite of all difficulties in maintaining telephone communication, batteries had to keep wider apart, and use smoke-screens when firing, besides dodging by night to new emplacements to escape destruction.

When the struggle for Passchendaele Ridge opened

SPOILS OF WAR FROM THE AIR.
Body of a giant aeroplane that was brought down inside the British lines on the western front being taken away on a trolly by men of the Royal Flying Corps from the spot where it fell. The machine was painted all over with hexagons of various tints.

on July 31st the new superiority of the air force of Great Britain was reflected in the strangely empty appearance of the German advanced line and battle frontier. Nothing could be seen. The old, clearly marked entrenchments, so easily photographed from the air, were left merely to draw the fire of the British guns. The German Army was skilfully scattered in an invisible manner, and its battery sites were enormously increased and largely vacant.

By the manner in which they met the British offensive at Ypres the Germans frankly admitted they had been reduced to a position of inferiority in the air. Industriously and ingeniously they made the best of their bad case, and brought all the devices of camouflage and concealment to practical perfection before they finally abandoned trench warfare and vigorously turned to a more mobile kind of struggle.

Unexpectedly helped by a prolonged period of curtaining rain and smothering mist, the Germans avoided some of the gravest disadvantages of their complete loss of mastery in the air. By refusing to delude themselves with false hopes, and by **British cavalry** searchingly examining the aerial odds **of the air** against them and basing their new plan of defence entirely upon their aerial weakness, the alert and businesslike Teutons succeeded in eluding complete defeat. Never was sound, workmanlike Prussian military practice so well displayed as in the Third Battle of Ypres.

When the struggle began in the rain and fog the occupation of British airmen seemed gone. Instead, however, of remaining in their aerodromes, they hummed out under the low-lying storm clouds, and invented another form of aerial offensive. They became the

BROUGHT DOWN IN FRANCE.
Type of German machine-gun on an aeroplane that was brought down on the French front. It will be observed it was fed by a notably large drum of ammunition which was attached to the fuselage.

one remarkable attack upon German aeroplane sheds a British pilot came down on the flying ground, taxied across the grass, fought a German machine-gun, routed the gunners, and harried them when they fled into the sheds.

One British lad of eighteen dropped to twenty feet above a road and engaged in a duel with a German officer in a motor-car. He killed his foe, chased another man into a cottage, and fired at him through windows and roof. These extraordinary operations were not conducted by a few venturesome pilots, but by scores of flying advanced forces. There were two units that flew for more than three hundred and ninety-six hours, firing over eleven thousand rounds of machine-gun fire on ground targets. Many other units did almost as well.

When a spell of clear weather came, nocturnal aerial operations developed in an extraordinary manner. Both armies possessed new and heavier machines, enabling greater weights to be carried, and the bombs grew larger as well as more numerous. The night sky blazed with firework effects when the opposing formations of bombing machines hummed over the lines in the moonlight, amid the crash of great air barrages, the uprush of deadly rockets, the rattle of machine-guns, and the abrupt, roaring bursts of the large high-explosive bombs.

Development of night flights

cavalry of the air, and, flying over the enemy's country, spread terror there. As aerial infantry they had attacked enemy trenches in the Somme campaign. Now, as aerial cavalry, they more particularly ravaged his rear areas.

Far behind the enemy's lines they swooped upon the roads, and squirted machine-gun bullets down chimneys, through roofs, and into front doors of cottages containing enemy reinforcements. They scattered marching German columns, bombed the German camps and aerodromes, flying so low that their wheels nearly brushed the grass, and were seldom much above the tree-tops.

When counter-attacked at a disadvantage the new aerial light forces took refuge in a rain-cloud, put fresh drums on their guns, and made another swoop. In

German pilots, who had played at being chivalrous knights of the skies, in imitation of the sportsmanlike Britons, threw off all pretence of decency when they were thoroughly defeated. They deliberately selected, in their stealthy nocturnal raids, hospitals crowded with wounded soldiers, and dropped, or tried to drop, upon them bombs

SIGNAL FOR TAKE ACTION AT A FRENCH ANTI-AIRCRAFT STATION.
Men of a French anti-aircraft section hurrying to their posts on a sudden alarm having been given of the approach of enemy aeroplanes. The outlook man was pointing to the quarter from which the machines were coming. The anti-aircraft guns at this point were stationed, with a goodly extent of open country around, on a railway-siding platform, from which the gunners could command a wide field of fire.

CAPTAIN GUYNEMER.
Brilliant French fighting airman who had gained his 54th victory when he was killed on September 11th, 1917.

SEC.-LIEUT. FONCK.
French airman who distinguished himself by crashing six enemy machines to earth in a single day's fighting.

containing two hundred and fifty pounds of their latest high explosive. German prisoners admitted that this violation of international convention was consciously and studiously carried out, observation machines being employed to find the hospitals and trace the route by which they could be reached at night by the bombing machines.

At sunrise and sunset smaller German machines began to practise the tactics of aerial cavalry work that Sir Hugh Trenchard had developed. Night or twilight was the time chosen by the enemy for flights over the British lines. By day the British pilots were much the more active, and even at night they dropped upon the enemy far more bombs than were loosed upon British areas.

Occasionally Captain Manfred von Richthofen, leading the main German battle wing, would endeavour by a sudden, intense concentration to sweep the sky. He achieved some temporary successes, enabling his formation to claim its two hundredth victory on August 19th, after seven months' work. The British and French combined air forces, however, steadily maintained a general predominance, and while the French aviation service bombed Frankfort and the Lorraine mines, the Royal Naval Air Wing made several German aerodromes in Flanders untenable by continuous attacks, and helped in the military operations around Ypres.

Never a fine night passed without great fleets of bombing machines speeding over the enemy's lines for an attack upon railway-stations, rolling-stock, waggon transport, and ammunition dumps. The German Gotha machine was clean surpassed by larger and more powerful British raiders, which, in spite of unfavourable weather, continuously worked over the hinterland of the German front, adding another ghastly terror to all the wearing, racking elements of modern warfare.

German airmen showed an absolute lack of initiative and enterprise. They never attacked British airmen had broken many of their columns on the march and cleared trenches by diving so close that their wings nearly brushed the parapets. British pilots were the first to make long-distance raids on a large scale, and they also were the first to strike directly at the heart of their enemy by

SUB-LIEUT. NUNGESSER.
One of the many daring French flying men who qualified as "Aces" by bringing down more than five enemy airmen.

subjecting hostile aerodromes to such incessant attack that certain German squadrons were unable to continue their work.

When General von Höppner obtained more machines and men and built new sheds, he in turn sent out night raiders against British aerodromes. On clear days German reconnoitring machines were sometimes heard flying far behind the British lines, so that it looked as though the allied superiority in the air was a fiction. Pilots on each side could, in certain conditions, roam far over hostile territory. The conditions, however, were severely limited for German pilots over British territory. They had, as a rule, to keep very high in the air in clear daylight, and trouble usually occurred if they descended to take good photographs of British rear positions. Even when they kept at a high altitude and made long detours over the Belgian front in their journeys to the British rear they ran considerable risk in daylight expeditions in clear weather.

In September the superiority of the Franco-British formations became overwhelming. The enemy was more completely blinded than he had been since the opening of the Somme campaign. In the middle of the month British spotting aeroplanes brought their batteries upon seven hundred German guns, while the German artillerymen could do little more than vaguely scatter shells over positions that seemed likely to be used as battery sites.

Two hundred and seventy-four enemy machines were destroyed by the British forces during the month; one hundred and thirty-nine were crashed, one hundred and twenty-two were sent down out of control, and thirteen were shot down from the ground.

Occasionally one of the enemy battle wings, reinforced by some Gotha bombing machines, endeavoured to answer a frenzied call for aerial reconnaissance made by General von Armin. The more fiercely the crack German pilots challenged the British mastery in the air the more they became weakened. Richthofen's famous assistant, Lieutenant Voss, was killed on September 23rd when endeavouring to win a field of vision over the British lines. The German champion was flying a new Fokker triplane, which was a copy of the Sopwith triplane engined with a copy of the Rhône motor. He manœuvred with extra-ordinary ability, but was trapped and shot down.

In October, when a great victory was narrowly missed owing to the British artillery being unable to find a firm footing in the swamp, the scene between Ypres and Passchendaele strangely revealed the effect of the British mastery of the air. On and about the Zonnebeke road, for example, British guns were so crowded together that their muzzles lifted over the breeches of those in front. Never was there such a target for enemy batteries. If German spotting aeroplanes could have held the air, under the guard of Richthofen's or Böhme's battle wing,

INSIDE A BRITISH GIANT BATTLE-PLANE.
The largest aeroplanes in use in 1918 had sufficient space for the airmen to stand upright, and were provided with windows as well as a skylight. The airmen depicted here were watching an enemy machine crashing.

the artillery behind the Australian and New Zealand forces could have been smashed into scrap steel in one brief, hurricane bombardment.

The aerial situation, however, was such that the principal force of heavy German guns was drawn far back and left without effective observation machines. The hostile shell fire against the guns along the Zonnebeke road remained fairly light, and in spite of the enemy's essays in night bombing and in twilight attacks with machine-gun fire, a decisive break would have been made in the enemy's front, largely through the efforts of the Royal Flying Corps, had the ground been dry enough for the guns to have been brought forward at the speed required by the Anzac infantry.

Air offensive shifted south

When Passchendaele was at last won there was an apparent change in the conditions in the struggle for the air. Much to the disgust of the victorious Canadians, German airmen seemed to increase in number and aggressiveness, while British pilots appeared once more to be hard pressed and reduced in strength. Men lying out in shell-holes on the ridge had continually to dodge the machine-gun fire of enemy machines, and although German observation aeroplanes were still prevented from

becoming too familiar with the British side of the battle-field, they yet appeared to be gradually gaining more power of vision. The explanation was that Sir Hugh Trenchard had shifted the point of the British aerial offensive in correspondence with Sir Douglas Haig's preparations for the Battle of Cambrai.

In the operations that began on November 21st a fine new air force made its first fighting appearance in Europe. The Commonwealth of Australia had been building up an aerial fleet, and its first squadrons had already done splendid work in Mesopotamia and Palestine. The Dominion of Canada had given many excellent men to the Royal Flying Corps, and won—in the person of Major W. Avery Bishop—the championship of the air. As in naval matters so in aerial policy, it suited the great Dominion to contribute in an immediate way to the main fighting strength of the Empire by allowing its men and material to enter the British battle organisation. The Union of South Africa and New Zealand followed the same course as Canada, and sent many fine pilots directly into the British flying force.

Australia, however, was moved, largely by geographical considerations, to organise independent forces on sea and in the air, and her distinct flying corps, represented in the Cambrai Battle by a purely Australian squadron commanded by one of the earliest Australian airmen, made a glorious start by winning in one day's fighting an extraordinary number of decorations.

But for the misty weather the aerial forces of General Byng's army would have changed the course of the war on November 21st by showing, in an absolute manner and for the first time, what aerial cavalry could do in favouring circumstances against a surprised enemy. Owing to the thick autumnal mist, however, little effective work could be done. Although the pilots **British airmen at Cambrai** took extreme risks, flying very low above the troops and getting at times mixed up in tree-tops, the admirably prepared blow from the air failed to complete the stroke delivered by the battalions of Tanks. German gunners were able to check the British mobile forts at a critical point in the centre of the battlefield, where in clear weather less than half a dozen British machines would have brought a devastating smother of shells upon the half-broken Germans, and then descended and raked them on the surface of the ground by machine-gun fire.

When at last the air cleared, during the struggle for Bourlon Ridge, the energy, skill, and audacity with which the attacking pilots worked showed clearly of what victorious help General Byng's army had been robbed by fog in the opening of the battle. British airmen were ubiquitous. One of them saved a Tank from being destroyed and captured by swooping down upon the enveloping hostile force and scattering it. Other pilots fiercely held the air against the new concentration of German chaser squadrons, and enabled their reconnaissance machines to bring the British guns abruptly upon large bodies of hostile reinforcements.

Even when Ludendorff completely recovered from the British surprise thrust, and gathered an overwhelming number of fresh divisions against the small, tired forces under General Byng, his main design was defeated by British air-power. As his armies were in a practical condition of blindness, he had to wait for misty weather to ensure that the British Army would also have to fight in obscurity.

On November 30th the effect of the successful British reorganisation in the production of machines and training pilots was displayed in the enemy's battle arrangements. Once more he frankly admitted his inferiority in observation and general aviation work, and ably planned a new form of warfare to escape from the disadvantages imposed upon him. He made his concentrations at night, and kept his main striking force at some distance from his lines.

MAJ.-GEN. W. S. BRANCKER,
Controller-General of Equipment.

MAJ.-GEN. F. H. SYKES, C.M.G.,
Chief of the Air Staff.

COMMODORE SIR GODFREY PAINE, K.C.B.,
Master-General of Personnel.

REAR-ADMIRAL MARK KERR, C.B.,
Deputy Chief of the Air Staff.

RT. HON. SIR WILLIAM WEIR,
Secretary of State and President of the Council.

MAJ. J. L. BAIRD, C.M.G., D.S.O.,
Parliamentary Under-Secretary of State.

BRIG.-GEN. GUY LIVINGSTON, C.M.G.,
Deputy Master-General of Personnel.

BRIG.-GEN. E. L. ELLINGTON, C.M.G.,
Dep. Director-Gen. of Military Aeronautics.

MAJ.-GEN. J. M. SALMOND, C.M.G., D.S.O.,
Commander of the Royal Air Force in the Field.

PRESIDENT AND MEMBERS OF THE AIR COUNCIL OF THE BRITISH EMPIRE IN APRIL, 1918.

Portraits by Swaine, Hoppe, Lafayette, Heath, Elliott & Fry, Bassano, and Langfier.

RECEIVING THEIR FLYING ORDERS.
Pilot and observer of a British aeroplane on the western front receiving instructions by plans and photographs at the moment of starting out on a reconnaissance over the German lines.

number of new formations, and the Army was combed out in order to increase the personnel. An ample number of recruits for bombing work was obtained, but first-rate scouting pilots appeared to be growing fewer in number in proportion to the general increase of the force. The enemy's air service had suffered severely, the losses in machines and expert airmen being very great in the Flanders and Laon areas. Yet Captain von Richthofen survived, and, both as an inspiring instructor and as an energiser of apprentice pilots, he remained a valuable personal force for the Central Empires.

The strength of the United States did not begin to tell upon the course of the struggle for the

Then, after waiting for the friendly covering of a mist, he marched his battle divisions forward, and broke through the British flank by the weight of unexpected numbers, yet failed to do more than make a dent in the British front, for the reason that his victorious troops could not clearly see where they were going. By suddenly concentrating a large number of low-flying machines against the disordered British flank he added considerably to the immediate weight of his blow at Gouzeaucourt, but even on the field of his victory he could not maintain the air superiority he needed.

As soon as the mist cleared, British pilots met the hostile battle wings and contact forces, and, in a long struggle, reasserted their superior power, so that at the end of 1917 the British flying force was in a much better position than it had been at the close of the Somme campaign.

By December all combatant peoples were generally alert to the great advantages of air-power, and to the urgency for organising every possible element of national strength

British Air Ministry formed in invention of new flying devices, in production of enormous quantities of machines and engines, and in the raising and training of hundreds of thousands of men for aerial work of various kinds. No longer was it possible for one far-seeing man, like General von Höppner, to surprise opponents by the extent and speed of his preparations. In both manufacture and training the contest became a downright dogged test of general resources, energy of the workers, inventive skill, and airmanship qualities.

In Great Britain the ferment of preparation brought about new changes in the Air Board, which was transformed and expanded into an Air Ministry. The military and naval wings were amalgamated into a single Royal Air Force. A special Air Minister was appointed in the person of Lord Rothermere, Major-General Sir Hugh Trenchard was made Chief of the Air Staff, Rear-Admiral Mark Kerr became Deputy-Chief of the Air Staff, with Commodore Godfrey Paine as Master-General of Personnel, Major-General Brancker as Controller-General of Equipment, and Sir William Weir as Director-General of Aircraft Production. Major-General J. M. Salmond succeeded Sir Hugh Trenchard as commander in the field.

In Germany steps were taken to form a considerable

AFTER A DAYLIGHT RAID.
Observer of a British aeroplane, on returning from a daylight bomb-dropping raid over enemy territory, handing over the photographic plates on which he had secured evidence of the results.

air during winter preparations for battles in the spring of 1918. American designers of engines and machines appear to have been flushed with hope rather than fully equipped for the great task they had proposed to themselves. Vast as were their resources for standardised production, the quality of commercial American work was somewhat different from the quality required in the highly specialised, delicately wrought battle machines of Europe. The American fitter had to be educated in order to become equal to the French or British fitter, and for many months, while his education was proceeding, the United States Expeditionary Force was compelled to borrow fighting machines from the French and British Air Services. On the other hand, Great Britain was no longer a burden upon France in the matter of aircraft requirements. There had been a large and free development in British aeromotor design and manufacture, and although perhaps rather too many types of engines were in use, the way was clear for the evolution of an aerial prime mover with power and general efficiency commensurate with the prestige and needs of the Empire.

Under the masterly direction of Sir William Weir, who later succeeded Lord Rothermere as Air Minister, the production of thousands of machines of superior qualities proceeded with such effect that the delay in the execution of the American programme had no disastrous result upon the allied command of the air. A remarkable invention solved one of the last grand problems in practical air-power, and, by greatly augmenting the value of the machines, helped to save the Allies from complete overthrow when the British line broke on March 21st, 1918, between Epéhy and La Fère.

In the meantime the definite British recovery of aerial superiority was displayed by an extension of raiding operations. The range of the Handley Page machine, with its Rolls-Royce motors, had been proved on July 9th, 1917, when Flight-Commander Savory, Flight-Lieutenant McClelland, and Lieutenant Rawlings travelled from London to Constantinople, with a stop at Rome, and bombed the German battleship Goeben and the Turkish War Office.

With such bombing aeroplanes as these, the systematic attack upon German territory was at last begun in the autumn of 1917, and continued with increasing severity into the spring of 1918. Between October, 1917, and the

MOBILE ANTI-AIRCRAFT GUNS IN FRANCE.
British soldiers, on their way back from a spell in the fighting-line on the western front, passing a battery of mobile anti-aircraft guns by the wayside.

middle of March, 1918, there were thirty-eight British raids into Germany, in the course of which forty-eight tons of explosives were dropped. Two hundred and fifty flights were made in these operations, at a cost of ten British machines.

Mannheim was one of the principal targets of British bombers, and the great Baden dye works, which were of high military importance, were at last wrecked, the flames being visible at a distance of thirty-five miles. The remoter industrial centre of Stuttgart, the seat of Bosch magneto and Daimler motor manufacture, was reached and badly damaged, while many important Rhineland cities, such as Freiburg, Mayence, Coblenz, Cologne, and Düsseldorf, with Frankfort and other outlying places, were almost panic-stricken by British as well as French air raids. From Southern Germany and Westphalia petitions were sent to Ludendorff and Hindenburg, begging either for better aerial defence or for the opening of negotiations with the Allies for the restriction of air attacks to definite military objectives.

Air raids into Germany

Vain were the efforts made by the reorganised and enlarged German battle wings to win something like a working equality on the western front. The British flying force produced, between the winter of 1917 and the spring of 1918, a successor to Captain Ball, and a rival to Major Bishop, in the person of Captain James Byford McCudden, V.C., who had started his magnificent career as an air mechanic. By April, 1918, Captain McCudden had brought down fifty-four German machines. Twice he destroyed four four-seater enemy aeroplanes in a single day.

Another British pilot, comparable with Lieutenant Fonck and Lieutenant Nungesser, of France, was Captain Philip F. Fullard, who brought down thirty-two enemy machines in four months, while Lieutenant A. P. F. Rhys Davids and Captain Maybery were also pre-eminent as destroyers of German machines and of the moral of the German Flying Corps. Lieutenant T. C. Hoidge, with a record of fourteen successes in three and a half months, was a champion in the making. The German air chief lost nearly all his best fighting and squadron leaders in a prolonged endeavour to complete Ludendorff's plan of attack by recovering the freedom of the air. Böhme, the successor to Bölcke, was overcome and killed. Then Captain Baron von Tutschek, who claimed twenty-seven victories,

A TRAVELLING TELEPHONE EXCHANGE.
Telephone exchange fitted up in a lorry, for maintaining communication with the Royal Field Artillery kite-balloons—"the eyes of the guns"—on the western front.

THE HANDLEY PAGE BOMBING BIPLANE.
This, one of the best known of the British bombing machines, made its first appearance in 1916, and did very valuable work, particularly in the bombing raids carried out over enemy aerodromes and docks. In 1916 a "Handley Page" took a pilot and twenty passengers to a height of 7,000 feet.

was slain, and finally the hero of Germany, Captain Baron Manfred von Richthofen, crashed down dead in the Australian lines on April 21st, 1918.

Midway in this series of disasters, in which the fall of nearly every famous German formation leader told of the maiming or practical destruction of a battle wing,

British secure air supremacy General von Ludendorff succeeded in again overcoming his disadvantage in aerial power, and delivering with complete surprise effect a breaking blow against the British front.

Suiting his tactics to the difference between the opposing air forces, the German commander elaborated a gigantic system of camouflage. He constructed vast systems of new offensive preparations in Alsace, Lorraine, Champagne, Picardy, and Flanders. He allowed allied airmen to watch large bodies of his troops practising the methods of the Cambrai counter-attack, with the support of German Tanks; yet, by keeping his grand mobile reserve between the French front in Champagne and the British front in Picardy, Artois, and Flanders, he gave no indication of his principal attack.

Once more he selected a misty day for the opening of battle, and under cover of night marched his army of manœuvre with un-expected rapidity against a lightly held part of the British front. As in the action at Gouzeaucourt, he increased the effect of his general surprise by a mighty concentra-tion of air forces. After the British battle positions between Epéhy and La Fère were pierced on March 21st, 1918, the re-treating, desperate forces of the defence, outnumbered by three to one on land, were assailed from the air by extraordinary multi-tudes of low-flying enemy aero-planes. Nevertheless, it is not extravagant to say that it was

the allied aviation service which mainly prevented a great local disaster from developing into a general catastrophe. General Pétain despatched large forces of fighting pilots, who arrived between the Oise and Somme on March 23rd and 24th. Together, the allied airmen made the main roads down which the enemy was advancing difficult for large move-ments. They bombed his rail-heads, they broke up his supply trains, and machine-gunned his long marching columns.

Night brought little or no relief to the overcrowding masses of the victorious German Army. Over them flew huge squadrons of bombing aeroplanes, illumina-ting them with falling flares and then loosing among them wide-spread, roaring death and scat-tering upon their means of movement crashing destruction. The waggon-horses and pack-mules of General von Hutier's forces were destroyed in large numbers, and so many of his tractors were wrecked that they blocked the road to Bapaume.

The strength of the German Air Service was, for the time at least, exhausted by a violent, fruitless effort to disengage the checked forces of attack from the claws of the eagles of the Grand Alliance. Three hundred and thirty-nine German machines fell in the vain attempt to clear the way for the intended thrust beyond Amiens to the unbridged estuary of the Somme at Abbéville.

The conditions of conflict between air-power and land-power abruptly changed when some forty German divisions of infantry, with thousands of guns and vast supply trains, emerged from the shelter of concealed and semi-subterranean fortifications and moved in clearly visible masses on the open ground. The first grand display of the striking force of the new service was of classic scope and quality. It definitely marked a new era in warfare.

A BRITISH NIGHT-BOMBING MACHINE.
This, the F.E.2D., an aeroplane of the "pusher" type, having its engine placed behind the pilot and observer, was used to a considerable extent for night-bombing expeditions behind the enemy's lines.

Pining Times of War: London Scottish Returning to Rest Camp After Heavy Fighting

CHAPTER CCXLVI.

WELFARE WORK FOR THE SOLDIERS FROM BASE TO BATTLE-FIELD : A RECORD OF SPLENDID ACHIEVEMENT.

By F. A. McKenzie.

Condition of London when Invaded by British Soldiers at the Outbreak of War—Clubs, Huts, and Rest Houses Supervised by the General Officer Commanding the Forces in London—Special Establishments for Canadians and Australians—Railway Buffets and Hostels —Private Hospitality for Soldiers, Particularly from Overseas—The Young Men's Christian Association Takes the Lead in Welfare Work for Soldiers—Practical and Intelligent Broadening of the Movement by Mr. Virgo and Sir Arthur Yapp—Emergency War Committee Organised—Generous Financial Support by the Public—Extension of the Work of the Y.M.C.A. in France, Gallipoli, Egypt, and Mesopotamia—Great Educational Campaign for the Army—Work of the Canadian Y.M.C.A.—And of the Australian Y.M.C.A.—Some Notable Workers—The Aldwych Theatre—Work of the New Zealand Y.M.C.A.—Help for the Wounded Con-valescents—Concerts and Entertainments for the Men at the Front—Activity of the Young Women's Christian Association— Social and Religious Work of the Salvation Army—Its Mission of Mercy and Its Ambulance Corps—Enormous Development of the Church Army's Activity—Work of the Roman Catholics for the Soldiers—The Catholic Women's League.

IMMEDIATELY on the outbreak of war plans were set afoot in the United Kingdom, and throughout the Empire, to aid and to send comforts to soldiers in the camps at home and at the front. A vast net-work of activities sprang up —apart from the work of the Army chaplains and of the Red Cross—a network covering every phase of the soldier's life.

London, the heart of the Empire and the centre to which most of the troops came, either on duty or on furlough, led the way, and the example of London was followed by every city and town, large or small. There was scarcely a village with a camp near it which did not at least have either a hut or a house arranged specially to receive the soldiers and care for them when off duty.

On the various fronts, from Flanders to German East Africa, these efforts continued on an even larger scale. Philanthropy invaded the very field of battle itself. In fight after fight Y.M.C.A. workers were to be found close to the front lines, under the heavy shell fire of the enemy, working with the Red

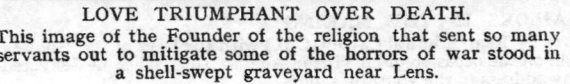

LOVE TRIUMPHANT OVER DEATH.
This image of the Founder of the religion that sent so many servants out to mitigate some of the horrors of war stood in a shell-swept graveyard near Lens.

Cross, providing cocoa and other aids for the wounded and the stretcher-bearers. Volunteer workers helped in every rest camp to organise sports, to provide lecture courses, and to give concerts. Big theatrical and concert-parties from England, including many musical stars, regularly visited the fighting troops. Ladies devoted themselves to the wounded soldier, providing comforts for him in hospital. The journeys of near relatives from the United Kingdom to visit the dangerously wounded at the French base were system-atised, and care, sympathy, and attention provided for them. Even when men died far from home there were organisations to visit their graves on behalf of the mothers, wives, and sweethearts who could not come, to put wreaths on the coffins and to gather some flowers from the graves and to send them to the mourning relatives. Most of these agencies were actively encouraged—and in some cases regularly em-ployed—by the authorities, who recognised that such work made for the greater efficiency of the Army.

London set an example to the whole Empire in its

efforts. Men from all parts of the world flocked to it. Bloomsbury was thronged with New Zealanders, Westminster with Australians, and the Charing Cross district with Canadians. Home troops poured in week after week by the ten thousand. Men from Halifax, Nova Scotia, and Halifax, Yorkshire, made acquaintance in the Strand. The Londoner might often enough find himself in theatre, omnibus, or restaurant with a soldier from Tasmania on one side of him and a soldier from Pretoria on the other. There were times when fresh arrivals from British Columbia and New Brunswick, Southern New Zealand and Rhodesia, seemed to annex the region around Piccadilly Circus. The dullest onlooker learned to appreciate the different types of Empire manhood—the marked contrast between the antipodean men of Otago and their neighbours of Sydney, and the distinction between the soldier from Montreal and his fellow from Vancouver.

The presence of these armies of men, especially the men from the Dominions with plenty of money to spend, attracted the agents of vice and crime, who were unceasingly active. Secret gambling clubs opened in the West End, and dens of all kinds in back streets between Victoria and Euston. Women and their "bullies" hung around the main railway-stations awaiting their victims. Some of them were adepts in drugging and robbing. Young girls, swept away in the moral upheaval which accompanies war, flung themselves in the way of the men. Soldiers from outlying parts of the Empire where prohibition prevails, who had never tasted liquor before, were faced by the attraction of London's bars.

Indictment of London

Some complaints were heard from overseas about the condition of London.

"No attempt was made to guard and cherish our gallant kith and kin from overseas," said these critics. Mr. W. G. Jamieson, Honorary Commissioner of the New Zealand Y.M.C.A., voiced these complaints in detail in a statement on his return home at the end of 1917.

"When the overseas lads arrive in London," he said, "they arrive in hell. No care is taken of them, absolutely none. They might arrive at a railway-station early in the morning and were told to find rooms. . . .

"Go along the Strand night after night and you will see sights that would turn you sick. Nothing is being done.

The fringe has only been touched of what might be done. On Sunday nights you will see the bars crowded. No other place is open to them, and at 9.30 they are turned out into the streets. . . . The thing is damnable, and should be stopped at once, not only for our own troops but for the Canadians and Australians. Men walk from one end of London to another without a place to stay at except a public bar, or some place that is practically a brothel, where they get charged huge prices. The thing is awful, and the Government has done nothing." **Charges disproved by facts**

Mr. Jamieson's statement was emphatically repudiated by his New Zealand colleagues. The best answer to it is a straightforward record of what had been done.

Tens of thousands of troops from the front and from the camps in the United Kingdom arrived in London on furlough each week. Some of these were merely passing through, going straight from Charing Cross or Victoria to Euston or King's Cross and catching the first train to their homes in the North. Very many, however, remained. Numbers had never been in London before or had no friends or relations here. They had their leave pay in their pockets. They were mostly in a mood of reaction from the drab and hard experiences of camp or trench. They were craving for brightness, cheerfulness, good company, and change

FAITH AND WORKS.
The Bishop of London, at Stoke Newington in May, 1918, dedicating two motor-ambulances for service at the front.

Every train bringing soldiers in any number to London was met by volunteer workers, nearly all of them business men over military age and working at war pressure at their own occupations. These gave the new-comers all the information they required, conducted them to clubs if they wished to go to clubs, and assisted them in whatever way they could. There were free refreshment stalls at many of the stations, at which they could obtain food and drink. At night there were motor-cars, freely lent by their owners, to take the men wherever they wanted to go. There was no need for any man to wander around the streets seeking for company, or to go wrong for want of a friendly hand. Then there were no fewer than ninety clubs, huts,

BRITISH SAILORS IN THE MAKING.
The Bishop of London (standing in the centre by Rear-Admiral Cayley, C.B.) with the boys of the Shotley Naval Training establishment, near Harwich, on the occasion of his visit in August, 1917, when he delivered a very stirring address to the youthful sailors.

rest-houses, and the like, all properly controlled, supervised, and approved by the General Officer Commanding the Forces in London. Most of these rest-houses were of a considerable size, some containing five hundred or six hundred beds, or even more. Sleeping accommodation was provided amid comfortable surroundings, usually at a very low price, which the man who had nothing but the pay of a private soldier could offer. The average hut was a spacious and cheery building with billiard-rooms, smoking-rooms, concerts, and entertainments of all kinds. If a man arrived without money, having spent his all, maybe, foolishly, he still found shelter. It was a rule in many of the hostels never to turn a man with an empty purse away.

Special entertainments and festivals were arranged for special seasons. At Christmas, for example, most of these huts acted as the main dispensers of London's hospitality to the soldier, freely entertaining tens of thousands of troops to Christmas fare and giving them a Christmas welcome, with music and song and often dancing as well, with Christmas-trees and presents and everything that possibly could be done to convey the spirit of home. Every soldier, however strange to London, was aware of these places. Big notices in the railway-stations and all over London advertised their addresses. The troops were officially told of them before they left camp. There were information bureaux in the most prominent places, as, for example, the Châlet, in Trafalgar Square. Some of these establishments were for all troops. Some were for special sections. The Canadians had an admirable series of Maple Leaf Clubs, in big mansions in the West End, where, thanks to the work of Lady Drummond and other prominent Canadian women, there was a real home for every Canadian. The Australians had, in addition to other places, the Aldwych Theatre, which was turned into a popular club and a theatre with a continuous performance from three every afternoon until late in the evening for all troops, Australians or others, who cared to come.

Whole-hearted work of London women The most prominent night club in London, Ciro's, in Leicester Street, was taken by the Y.M.C.A. and transformed into a social institution where there were constant entertainments, and where the soldier could receive his lady friends amid comfortable surroundings. Nor was provision made for the private soldier alone. A number of clubs, social rooms, and hostels catered for the young officer. The most splendid club in London, the Automobile, in Pall Mall, became an Overseas Officers' Club.

Ten thousand London women of all classes were regularly enrolled for service in the hostels, giving their time freely. Some of them, women of means, worked during the daytime, serving as waitresses, darning uniforms, scrubbing floors, washing up, and doing everything they could to serve the men. Young women engaged

AFTER CHURCH IN THE WAR ZONE.
Canadian soldiers leaving a wrecked building which had been adapted for use as a place of worship on the western front. Frequently the chaplains made use of such ruins for holding services for the benefit of men in the front lines.

in business or professional work during the day regularly came in the evenings. Still others did the work during the night. There was nothing amateurish or half-hearted about their effort. The women workers were, in nearly every case, required to pledge themselves to certain hours and to keep them. Those who were not willing to do everything that was necessary were not allowed the privilege of keeping on. These English gentlewomen set the tone of the places. The men were quick to appreciate the atmosphere they created. No one who went the round of these hostels could fail to be struck by their cheerfulness and happy air. There was nothing narrow and nothing institutional in their atmosphere. Most of them were real homes.

As one Canadian woman writer said: " These women are not employed in converting and proselytising the soldiers nor in restraining their liberty ; they are engaged in providing comfort and entertainment and in translating into work of practical service the gratitude and affection which all decent people feel towards the soldiers."

The railway buffets and the hostels near the railway-stations were among the sights of London. Throngs of men would arrive at the buffets fresh from the front lines in France, with the mud of the trenches still on them, with steel helmets tied behind their backs, and with rifles still in hand. Their immediate needs satisfied, they

WAYSIDE CANTEEN NEAR MENIN ROAD.
British soldiers gathered at a Y.M.C.A. station in the neighbourhood of the Menin road and under constant shell fire. Many of the association's centres were within a mile of enemy trenches.

others drew their supporters from wider fields. The Young Men's Christian Association stepped at the beginning of the war to the very foremost place in work for the soldiers, and retained its lead all along.

When war broke out the military authorities appealed to it to provide recreation centres for the troops in the camps at home, mostly large marquees. Within a fortnight two hundred centres were started. By the beginning of 1918 these had grown to over two thousand centres under the British flag, reaching from Jaffa to Ypres and from Bagdad to Aberdeen. In France alone there were five hundred centres, many of them close to the front lines and under constant shell fire from the enemy. The tents which were

would flock to the huts while waiting for their trains, and there, many a night, could be seen crowds of men filling every seat, men in rough sheepskin coats and leather waistcoats, with thick strong boots, heavy with the mud of Flanders, recalling experiences with old comrades, dozing, eating, sending telegrams, waiting for the morning trains.

A great deal was done to provide private hospitality for soldiers, particularly overseas soldiers on leave from the front. Thousands of families gave in their names as always willing to welcome soldier guests, and thousands of families had one place at their tables waiting for a stranger. Various organisations undertook to keep registers of such offers, and to put the people offering hospitality and the soldiers in touch. Citizens of London, proud of the record of their city, volunteered to act as guides to strange troops, and day after day parties would set out in chars-à-bancs, exploring the sights of old London. Everywhere they were welcomed. Theatres made it a rule to give large numbers of free seats to wounded soldiers, and some places of entertainment even advertised that wounded men were always welcome to seats in their houses.

Free concerts for soldiers

A popular actor-manager started a plan of Sunday evening concerts for men in uniform at the Princess's Theatre, concerts where the only ticket of admission required was the khaki uniform. This idea was taken up by others, notably by the Victoria Palace, near Victoria Station. The best proof of how the men appreciated the entertainment was given by the crowds that attended every performance.

Some of the leading and most exclusive West End squares were handed over by the freeholders to the Y.M.C.A. authorities for the erection of recreation and dormitory huts, and in some cases the inhabitants of the squares paid the cost of the huts and saw to their maintenance. Hostels were opened for officers, and thousands slept there, needing and appreciating them as much as soldiers did huts.

Special efforts for soldiers were undertaken by numerous organisations, some of them representing particular religious groups, such as the Roman Catholic Church, the Church of England, and the Salvation Army, while

CANADIAN Y.M.C.A. CENTRE IN FRANCE.
Begun by six workers at Valcartier in August, 1914, the work of the Canadian Y.M.C.A. grew—under the sanction and support of the military authorities—until, in 1918, £400,000 was needed to carry it on.

first erected gave place to more permanent buildings, and over £1,000,000 was spent in three and a half years on these buildings alone. The initial work of providing comforts grew into a hundred diverse agencies. In East Africa the Y.M.C.A., at the request of the authorities, provided the entire canteen arrangements for the army. At the bases in France the Y.M.C.A. workers met friends going to visit the wounded and dying, conducted them to their destinations, housed them, and fed them. There were Y.M.C.A. huts in prison camps, and the Y.M.C.A. acted as a leading relief agency for British soldiers when they emerged from Germany to internment in Switzerland and Holland. Y.M.C.A. agents provided shelter for men passing through London on leave, and eighteen thousand men slept in the different Y.M.C.A. huts in one week in London. The association was responsible for numerous lecture schemes for the troops in France, and out of this grew a great educational movement for the soldiers, with the vice-chancellors of the great universities serving as active members of the committee making the arrangements

AT NIGHTFALL IN THE BATTLE AREA.
The padre of an Irish regiment having a quiet chat with a squad of the men before they turned in for the night. Their burrowed quarters were in a sector of the line near St. Quentin, which had been taken over by the British in the autumn of 1917.

Y.M.C.A. libraries provided reading for the troops everywhere, and the association was responsible for a regular scheme of entertainments of all kinds for the British soldiers in every field of war. Most extraordinary of all to those who knew the movement in its older days, it encouraged and helped dramatic clubs among the troops in France, where the soldiers could learn to train their own companies and present famous plays properly mounted and acted by themselves.

Up to the outbreak of war the Y.M.C.A. in England was openly regarded by the outside public as a narrow, purely religious organisation. Gilbert's sneer at " the Y.M.C.A. young man " represented the common attitude. This attitude was not altogether without reason. The Y.M.C.A. had for some years been controlled by a group of men who had not kept fully in touch with the younger generation. They carried the narrower religious practice of the middle of the nineteenth century into the twentieth century. For example, they regarded smoking with abhorrence ; men who smoked were looked upon with suspicion, and it was only after a long struggle that they

permitted smoking in certain rooms in their institutions. Some of them, although by no means all, were not too favourable to athletics. A billiard-room was anathema. Their efforts were mainly aimed at one particular class—the young shopman and warehouseman, particularly the young men in the drapery trades. In other lands, notably in America, in India, and Burma, and in the Dominions, the Y.M.C.A. had focused the social activities of the general community for the young man. In England this was not the case.

This narrowness was encouraged by the system of organisation. Each Y.M.C.A. was a separate unit in itself, with complete self-governing powers inside the constitution of the movement. There were district councils and a National Council, but the National Council had no power to control the smallest local body. Each Y.M.C.A. was administered by a committee, and these committees were usually composed of prosperous older men, more or less imbued with the ideas of their generation.

But young men in touch with youth were rising up in the association itself. The old British leaders looked longingly to the wider activities overseas, and when a forward movement was begun by the opening of large new premises in Tottenham Court Road, London, a very successful Australian secretary, Mr. J. J. Virgo, was called to direct it. An energetic young Englishman, Mr. A K. Yapp (afterwards Sir Arthur Yapp) became National Secretary. The movement reached into **New era of the Y.M.C.A.** new fields ; very practical work was undertaken in various ways, more particularly in the summer training camps of the Territorial Army. The young men were feeling their stride. They gradually acquired larger power in the committees, which had hitherto been dominated by the rich seniors. Some of the older leaders passed away, full of years and honours ; some of them saw the necessity of new ways for new times.

And so at the beginning of the war the Y.M.C.A. had

REPRESENTATIVES OF THE CHURCH MILITANT FROM ACROSS THE ATLANTIC.
The Bishop of British Columbia, who served as chaplain of the 72nd Canadian Battalion, talking to one of his men up the line. Right : The chaplain and choir of an American regiment in France practising hymns for the Sunday service in the open air near their village quarters.

reached the psychological moment when it was prepared to go ahead on lines which would have seemed strange to some of the oldest supporters. Its leaders put before them the idea of practical service. They turned to their older friends. "The devil can make a bad use of anything good," declared Mr. Virgo. "But that surely is no reason why Christians may make no good use of the same good things. Which is better—billiards at the Y.M.C.A. or over in the public-house?" The young men urged that the way to win people to keep in the right path was not to preach at them but to help them. The old restrictions about smoking, secular games, and entertainments were almost wholly swept by the board. All kinds of people, anxious to help the soldiers, found that the Y.M.C.A. presented a ready agency through which they could serve. Leading actors lent their theatres to raise funds for it, and themselves came to the huts to serve the men. Everyone, from the King to the youngest recruit, who studied the movement learned to admire it. The music-hall star found as warm a following in a Y.M.C.A. hut as when he was entertaining soldiers in the biggest variety palace. The preacher from overseas found in a score of camps great audiences of men such as he had been able to obtain

MR. WILLIAM HAINES,
Lieut.-Colonel in the Salvation Army, in charge of its work among British troops in France.

nowhere else. Nothing was too big and nothing was too small for it to attempt, provided the work was of practical service for the soldier. New machinery was necessary to meet new conditions. A fresh central body was created, the Emergency War Work Committee, which took all responsibility for the war work, raising funds and administering them. The chief organiser was Sir Arthur Yapp, who revealed such administrative ability that

MISS MARY BOOTH,
of the Salvation Army, who worked untiringly in aiding and comforting the wounded and dying in hospitals in France.

MISS MARY MURRAY,
Secretary to the Naval and Military League of the Salvation Army, who did much good work among the troops.

later on he was given the direction of the National Food Economy Campaign. Sir Arthur Yapp was backed by an admirable colleague in the Assistant National Secretary, Mr. F. J. Chamberlain, C.B.E. The chairman of the committee was Sir Thomas Sturmey Cave, the well-known engineer. The financial organisation of the war movement owed much to a famous Anglo-Indian, Sir Henry E. E. Procter. Having proved in his own affairs his great financial ability and organising skill, he applied this same financial exactitude to the control of the Y.M.C.A. war funds. At first a modest special fund of £25,000 was asked for. Early in 1918 the voluntary gifts for the work amounted to £1,250,000, and the daily expenditure had risen to £1,850.

Perhaps the most remarkable feature of the support given to the Y.M.C.A. was not so much the amount raised as the way in which it represented the entire nation. Every class of the community subscribed to it. The King, its patron, sent a message saying how the organisation had "worked in a practical, economical, and unostentatious manner, with constant knowledge of

MAJOR W. McKENZIE, M.C.
Salvation Army chaplain to the Australian troops.

those with whom it had to deal." Army commanders wrote urging its claims. Some ragged boys, pushing themselves into the Euston Hut, when asked what they were doing there, said that they had come to see how their money was spent. Their school had subscribed its pennies to help. Between King and street-boys the whole community joined in, the heads of the universities, the chapters of cathedrals, the lord mayors and mayors of cities, the heads of the Navy and the Army, the theatrical and musical professions—all made common cause.

The churches naturally gave it generous aid. But this aid was by no means confined to Protestant communities. When the Jewish Chief Rabbi returned from a visit to France he wrote to the "Times" appealing for aid for the Y.M.C.A. and testifying to its magnificent work. In the East End of London the Jewish community subscribed and built a hut in the Mile End Road for the Y.M.C.A., with a public notice telling what it was—a gift from Jewry to Christendom in a cause which made both one. Jews in the Midlands gave three huts for the Y.M.C.A. in Jerusalem! The Jews even started a Jewish Y.M.A. in co-operation with the parent movement.

At the commencement of the war the first idea was to erect recreation marquees and centres for the men. The marquees were replaced by huts, and these huts tended to grow more and more elaborate as they were more and more used, until there were some that cost £6,000 each, and even more.

Gradually from England the work extended to wherever the British Army was found. A number of huts were built in France, where Mr. Oliver McCowen, C.B.E., K.I.H., LL.B., formerly Y.M.C.A. secretary in Burma, was chief organiser. The map of the region covered by these huts was a very remarkable one. Starting at base depots on the coast, they went from Dixmude to Ypres, from Ypres to Armentières, around Loos and behind Souchez, in Arras and Albert, everywhere right up with the fighting troops. Some of the centres were in barns and semi-ruined buildings, some in cellars when under bombardment, some in dug-outs in the trenches. The service done in these different depots included not merely the provision of warmth and comfort, but the creation of real centres of life for the men. Here they could get out of touch for the time with the drab misery of war. Here they found food different from regulation rations, warmth, light, friends, books, chairs to sit on, lectures and concerts to attend; in camps there were billiard-tables.

When the British Army went to Gallipoli the Y.M.C.A. went with it, and did good work in the hill caves. The work in Egypt presented some of the most spectacular sides of the Y.M.C.A. campaign. In Cairo the famous Esbekieh Gardens, skating-rink, and open-air theatre were taken over and made into a great centre of social life. The movement spread to wherever the British Army went around the Peninsula. Y.M.C.A. men accompanied the Army across the desert to Palestine, and a Y.M.C.A. branch was opened in Jerusalem not many hours after the British general moved through. At the Khargeh Oasis, away west of Mersa Matruh towards the Tripoli frontier, the Y.M.C.A. planted itself with the British outposts. It had its stations all along the Suez Canal, and Tel-el-Kebir, of famous memory, was an important depot. There were many camps around Alexandria, and at Sidi Bishr there was a very large rest camp for men exhausted by their desert work. The Imperial aspect of the work came out in the very thorough campaign among the Indian troops and in India. In Mesopotamia the Y.M.C.A. shared the glories and trials of the troops, and established itself there

from the Persian Gulf to Bagdad. In short, east and west it marched with the Army wherever the Army marched, and it helped the Navy at every station where the Navy made its home.

In addition to the work for the Army, a very extensive campaign was opened for munition workers. A farm colony was established for tubercular patients. In Holland and in Switzerland there were big Y.M.C.A. centres for the prisoners of war. In many military hospitals the Y.M.C.A. hut and the Y.M.C.A. officers' sections were among the best appreciated resorts.

The work grew in different ways naturally and inevitably. Libraries, mainly of fiction, were established at different stations. It was soon found that there was a demand for other books than fiction, and these were provided. There were popular lecturers and preachers and teachers of all types travelling through the camps in Britain and France and elsewhere to speak to the men.

Here again the authorities found a growing demand for more serious subjects than had perhaps at first been anticipated. It took time to realise that with a fresh opportunity for service a fresh duty was emerging. Here was an army of young men, civilians taken for a few years from their civilian life, temporary soldiers who when the war was over were to return to their civilian avocations. Could not the Y.M.C.A. use its machinery to educate the men and to prepare them for their return to civilian life? Out of this idea grew a scheme which

in the end was to overshadow many of the other Y.M.C.A. activities—the great educational campaign for the Army. The work was very largely in the hands of the Rev. Basil Yeaxlee, but he had associated with him many of the leading educational authorities of the English Universities' Extension Movement and Workers' Educational Association. It soon became evident that there could be no question about the demand among the men themselves. Thus, in the early months of 1918, a new step was taken of the greatest moment.

The work of the Canadian Y.M.C.A. for Canadian troops was not at first as widespread as might have been expected. The men in charge were left largely to their own resources. They had no considerable funds to draw on, save what they could raise by themselves. Each man carried out his task as best he could **Work of the** and in what way he saw fit. It was not **Canadian Y.M.C.A.** until the spring of 1916 that the workers came together in a definite organisation, and that Canada prepared to back them as it should. Despite this early want of cohesion and organisation, admirable work was done from the first.

The Y.M.C.A. officers were men of the right type. They won the confidence of all ranks in the Army. One prominent instance proved this. When the troops from Alberta were called upon to elect two representatives for their new Provincial Legislature, they chose at the head of the poll Captain R. Pearson, one of the most active Y.M.C.A. secretaries in France.

When the First Canadian Contingent was raised in August, 1914, and stationed at Valcartier before proceeding to England, six Y.M.C.A. workers started their

"IN REMEMBRANCE."
Miss Mary Booth placing a wreath on a British soldier's grave in France. In oval: French military hospital at Lyons. It had been a Salvation Army shelter for homeless men before the war, and in it members of the Salvation Army continued to render good service.

great task. All kinds of small traders flocked around the camp, starting little businesses to supply the soldiers, and charging extortionate prices, such as 10d. for a loaf, and 10d. for an ordinary 3d. packet of cigarettes. The military authorities asked the Y.M.C.A. to open a canteen, selling everything at ordinary rates. Within twenty-four hours this was done, and the outsiders were ordered to close down. This work at Valcartier was so much appreciated that, at the request of Sir Sam Hughes, then Minister of Militia, seven Y.M.C.A. secretaries were selected, given military rank, and sent with the First Contingent to Salisbury Plain, where their efforts did something to relieve the exceedingly arduous conditions which prevailed during the winter of 1914-15. When the Canadian troops moved on to France difficulty was experienced in obtaining permission for the

Y.M.C.A. men to accompany them. They were virtually smuggled in on the roll of different battalions, and they existed practically on sufferance. They had to use their own personal money or what money they themselves could obtain, purchasing supplies and helping to cater for the troops. This method continued for about a year. Then Canada began systematically to back them. Gradually an efficient central headquarters was established in London, with Lieutenant-Colonel Gerald W. Birks, the head of a well-known Montreal jewellery firm, in command; Major F. T. Smith supervising England, and Major J. H. Wallace supervising France. Colonel Birks, himself a man of considerable means, used his own money freely and enlisted the support of others. In 1916 £60,000 was

arrangement was made with the shipping authorities to permit the importation from Canada each month of two hundred tons—6,500 cases—of sweetmeats, candies, fine preserves, and other luxuries wanted by the Army. It was not long before it was known everywhere that the Canadian Y.M.C.A. huts throughout France had good things on sale that could be secured nowhere else. Under an arrangement made with the military authorities the Y.M.C.A. paid five per cent. of the gross receipts to the units in France, these sums being used for the benefit of the soldiers.

On the Somme the Canadians had forty-two centres. During the winter these were increased to fifty, and the number continued to grow. The majority of these were within range of the enemy guns, and ten to fifteen were right within the trench area. The Y.M.C.A. men were found working amid the ruins of Ypres, and away up in dug-outs beyond that city, sharing the life and the dangers. At battle after battle the Y.M.C.A. officers worked right in the battle area. At Vimy the officer with the 4th Division had three places within five hundred yards of the front line. The men with all the divisions followed up the advance of April 9th, carrying up their supplies and comforts by night to fresh centres. Sometimes the centre would be the ruins of a house, sometimes a hole in the ground, and sometimes two or three bits of corrugated iron put up to make a little cover. In the severe fighting around Lens the Y.M.C.A. carried on its work in such heavily shelled areas as the villages of Calonne, Liévin, and St. Pierre. When the Canadian troops moved up from Lens to Passchendaele they found that the Y.M.C.A.

BIBLES FOR AMERICAN SOLDIERS AND SAILORS.
Every soldier of the American Expeditionary Force and every American sailor on active service was supplied with a khaki-covered Bible. This photograph shows a packer packing the volumes for despatch to the Army and Navy chaplains and the Y.M.C.A. depots at the front.

raised in Canada to support this work. In 1917 £220,000 was raised; and for 1918 the sum aimed at was £400,000. The staff of 37 officers in France and England in 1916 grew to 112 in 1917. The 54 centres of work were increased to 157, and the staff of 136 grew to 545. London was at first left practically outside the scope of the Canadian work, but late in 1917 the Little Theatre in John Street was secured, and the foundations were laid of big temporary premises on the site of the old Tivoli Theatre in the Strand.

It was when the Canadians moved from the Ypres salient to the Somme, in the late summer of 1916, that the Y.M.C.A. authorities saw the beginning of their full opportunity. Here the troops, Imperial and Dominion alike, living in a sea of mud, found it almost impossible to obtain adequate canteen supplies. The troops were short of cigarettes and short of sweetstuffs, the **Luxuries in the front area** two great items that the soldier craves for when at the front. Y.M.C.A. dug-outs and shelters right up in the forward area were open day and night. It was an ordinary thing to find a queue of a hundred men waiting outside to be served, and the few officers and their staff were taxed to the limit, scarcely having time to sleep or eat. The work here was by no means limited to Canadian troops.

Soon the problem of obtaining supplies arose. How could it be possible to secure the necessary canteen stuffs in Britain or France? It was soon found that with the growing food shortage it could not be done, and so an

had gone before and had opened depots en route, ready day and night to serve the passing troops. During the Battle of Passchendaele, in the long and dangerous route between Ypres and the front, a route under continuous bombardment day and night from German artillery and German aircraft, the Y.M.C.A. had depots at regular intervals, providing cocoa, biscuits, and other refreshments for passing troops, **Casualties in the** for wounded, and for the stretcher- **Canadian Y.M.C.A.** bearers. Eleven places were opened up in front of Ypres itself, a number later increased to eighteen, every one being run day and night.

Such service obviously could not be maintained without some losses. In the fighting at Lens one officer and four of the staff were gassed, three were killed, and twelve wounded. At Passchendaele one officer and several men were wounded. At Calonne the Y.M.C.A. moved one day from a ruined house to a cellar next door. A few hours afterwards three shells fell on the old house, smashing it to bits. A few weeks later, after it had been evacuated, the cellar was also smashed up. Such incidents were taken as a matter of course. The Y.M.C.A. officers during all engagements did special work for the wounded.

In January, 1917, the Canadians made a fresh departure. Up to this time it had been the rule to charge 1d. for a large cup of coffee or tea, but it was now determined to give free tea to any soldier at any time at all their places in France. In a few months this service grew so that the cost of teas was over £1,000 a month. In the fighting

Caring for the soldiers at the front: Y.M.C.A. hut in the heart of ruined Arras.

"Into Thy hands ———": Chaplain speeding the parting soul of a dying hero.

Bombardment of Rheims: Removing the famous statue of Joan of Arc to a place of safety.

In a temple not built with hands: Holy Communion in a chalk cave in France.

Sacrilege : Interior of a church deliberately shelled by the Germans on the western front.

Salvage : British soldiers rescuing sacred objects from a ruined church in Armentières.

at Lens in thirty days free tea to the value of over £3,600, in addition to biscuits, chocolates, and cigarettes, was given to the fighting men. At Passchendaele in five weeks the amount distributed cost £8,000.

The work was planned to cover thoroughly all men going to and coming from the trenches. Some of these men had been for days without a hot drink, particularly in the strenuous fighting periods, and were really as much in need of this comfort as many of the wounded soldiers.

In the autumn of 1917 thirty-nine fresh huts, each a hundred feet long, were erected in France. There were nine cinemas, each giving two shows nightly, all the shows being free. The Y.M.C.A. reckoned to provide one hundred entertainments weekly for the Canadian fighting corps. In practically all of these entertainments the performers were the troops themselves. A big hut was set aside for training concert and theatrical parties. A musical and theatrical expert was placed in charge. Parties of picked men would come down from each unit and would be put through a quick course of forced training as musicians, singers, or as players. Scenery and make-up would be provided for them, and these men would produce plays or give concerts of very real excellence. They would give their shows in camps and towns behind the Canadian fighting-front to the troops resting there, often amid the thunder of the guns.

From the first the Y.M.C.A. officers were the organisers of athletics in the rest camps, some of them being noted athletes. They not only organised the men, but obtained supplies on a wholesale scale. Baseball sets, for example, were practically unobtainable in England and France, save in small quantities and at artificial prices. The Y.M.C.A. brought them over from Canada by the car-load. The amount set apart for athletic supplies for the Canadian troops in 1918 was £20,000, and the goods provided on loan for the troops included 500 complete baseball sets, 12,000 baseballs, 6,000 indoor baseballs, 3,000 bats, 60 complete sets of lacrosse, 55 cricket sets, and 15,000 sets of sporting knickers, shirts, and shoes.

Sports and books for the troops

Gradually the need of educational work among the men became evident. Libraries containing stocks of books were established at every possible place, and were lent on a simple system.

Each soldier paid a franc deposit when he borrowed a book and was reimbursed the franc when the book was returned. He could, if he wished, keep the book. As the demand for more serious literature grew, libraries of an educational type were placed in every centre. A number of educational classes were established in England, which were soon attended by thousands of men. Out of these educational classes grew a still wider scheme. Many of the young soldiers had come fresh from the universities, and had not been able to take their degrees. Dr. Tory, Head of the University of Alberta, was called in, and he framed a big scheme for a Khaki University, a thorough educational system for men at the front, which would enable them to take up courses in practically every branch of learning, starting each man off according to

his proficiency in the subject chosen, or continuing his university studies, so as to graduate and be ready for the future when peace came.

In all this work the religious side was not forgotten. Each Sunday evening at each centre a service was held, which was usually conducted by a chaplain attached to one of the units in that district. But, in addition, in all the camps and centres in England and France there was every night what was known as a "Good-night" service, a feature remarkably popular with all classes of troops. The men would flock into the Y.M.C.A. room for a few minutes, one or two old hymns would be sung, a chapter from the Bible read, and a simple word of prayer uttered. The whole service occupied only a few minutes, but

WOMANLY INTEREST IN WELFARE WORK FOR MEN.
Queen Mary inspecting one of the Y.M.C.A. huts that bore her name at the base in France. Her Majesty publicly declared her appreciation of the useful work carried on by the association in its many different centres for the benefit of the soldiers and sailors.

multitudes of men declared that they found it a real strength and help in anxious days.

The Australian Y.M.C.A. had worked in the Army training camps for some time before the outbreak of war, and when the first troops were raised for service overseas it was taken as a matter of course that this work should be continued in Australia itself. But it was considered impossible for Y.M.C.A. officers to accompany the troops to the front, and permission was not obtained until Mr. Wheeler, the secretary of the Adelaide branch and one of the foremost Australian workers, went to Melbourne, interviewed the Minister of Defence, and secured assent to the despatch of five secretaries with the army going to Europe. From these five men the Australian work grew in a little over three years to a staff of one hundred and forty abroad, of whom forty-two were in France. The Australian people, irrespective of creed, rallied to the support of the movement and raised over £600,000 for it. In some cases people gave far more than was asked. Thus in the summer of 1917 an appeal was made to New South Wales for £50,000, and a special collection day, "Red Triangle Day," as it was called, was fixed. The sum raised was £182,000.

Work of the Australian Y.M.C.A.

The Australians were unconventional. They did not believe in being tied down by precedent. They were going to try whatever was likely to benefit the men, and they did so.

The financial side of the work was supervised by some

AUSTRALIAN Y.M.C.A. LEADERS IN FRANCE.
Members of the Australian Y.M.C.A. engaged in forward area work in January, 1918. Back row (left to right): J. T. Massey, A. E. Forrest, Peter Fleming, and F. J. King. Middle row: J. P. Hamilton, G. Stan Arthur, H. A. Wheeler (Chief Executive Officer), L. J. Greenberg, and A. Charlesworth. In front: H. Peake and J. R. Falconer.

of the most eminent business men of Australia. Mr. W. E. Sargood, member of a well-known wholesale house, undertook the direction of business affairs in France. Mr. James Allan left his business at Brisbane at the call of the National Council, and settled in London as Chief Honorary Commissioner here. Mr. Roy Clack, the General Secretary of the Melbourne Association, came over as Field Secretary, and Mr. H. A. Wheeler, of Adelaide, after doing magnificently in organising the war work from Australia, came to England as Chief Executive Officer.

The main work among the troops was carried out by very young men. The association was not only for young men, but was led by them. Thus one of the most prominent workers in France, Mr. Stan Arthur, who had been an officer in the Territorial forces but had been unable to obtain permission to go to France because of a heart affection, was only twenty-four **Splendid men's** years of age. Forbidden to reach the front **splendid work** as a fighting man, he went as a Y.M.C.A. leader, and showed a prevision, grasp of affairs, and an energy beyond praise. The second in command was Mr. Len Greenberg, aged twenty-five, and a third was Mr. Albert Charlesworth, of the same age. One typical story was told of Mr. Charlesworth. During a battle an Australian officer came back to Headquarters, bringing a message from Mr. Charlesworth asking for more supplies. The supplies were handed to a runner, who wanted to know in which direction he was to go. Just then a shell burst away ahead. "You see where that shell burst," said the officer, "you make for that place. Charlesworth's just by there."

Another of the group of young men leaders was the Rev. Peter Fleming, director of the evangelistic work. In peace time he was one of the most prominent of the younger clergymen of Australia, and minister of Flinders Street Baptist Church, Adelaide. Mr. Fleming was an orator. His addresses, dealing with the origin, cause, and real meaning of the war, were so appreciated by the authorities that in camp after camp the troops were paraded on week days to hear him. "No one could understand," said one Australian, "what speeches like his meant to us. Here we were living in mud and grime, seeing nothing but

the burden of war, the losses, the misery, and the endless work. Then Fleming came along; he reminded us of the things we had been apt to forget—why we were at war, why we were putting up with all this, what it meant for us and what it meant for the world. His speeches were the finest tonic the soldiers could have." Hence the encouragement given to Mr. Fleming by the authorities.

Another agent who must be mentioned is Mr. Will Owens, from Sydney, who directed the work in Egypt. It was said of him that he had painted the desert red with the Red Triangle of the Y.M.C.A. The catholicity of the Y.M.C.A. can be judged

IN A LONDON Y.M.C.A. HUT.
American sailors and British men of the Royal Flying Corps at "The Eagle," the Y.M.C.A. hut in Aldwych, which was the headquarters hut for the use of the U.S.A. forces in London.

by the fact that one of the active agents was Mr. Harold Boaz, a Jew, a leading architect at Perth, W.A., and son of Rabbi Boaz, of Adelaide. Mr. Boaz had as his special work to look after the interests of the Jewish soldiers. He did it in the most thorough fashion, working in the closest accord with his Christian colleagues. They were accustomed to describe him as "a first-class Christian in everything but creed."

The theatre in Aldwych, the most prominent part of the Australian work in London, has been referred to earlier in this chapter, and is worthy of further description. The Australian leaders felt that it was necessary to have a big place on fresh lines, something that would be an outstanding feature for all troops coming to London. Accordingly, the Aldwych Theatre, a very short distance from the Australian Government Headquarters in London, was secured and carried on as a continuous attraction for the troops at a total cost of about £15,000 a year. Part of the place was made into a restaurant. One section of the foyer was specially set aside for wounded and convalescent troops, and here day after day the Red Cross workers brought wounded men to tea and to entertainments. A hairdressing saloon was opened to save men from being robbed, as many of them had been robbed. Man after man told the Y.M.C.A. leaders that, coming fresh from the front, they had been charged 6s. 6d., 7s. 6d., and 8s. 6d. for a shave, haircut, and shampoo. In many cases the authorities secured redress through the police; but at last Mr. Burridge, of Perth, W.A., the business manager of the Aldwych enterprise, determined to strike at the root of the trouble, and opened his own barber's saloon. The Australian troops were encouraged to go to the Aldwych Theatre when they arrived in London, to deposit their money there, and to draw it out as they wanted it, rather than wander about with large sums in their pockets, which might be lost through a very brief spell of folly or misfortune. It was an ordinary thing for the Aldwych authorities to hold in their safe hundreds of pounds for men on leave from the front, money which the men had returned to them, usually at £1 a day, to cover their expenses and spendings in town.

But the outstanding feature of the Aldwych Theatre

AT THE SIGN OF THE MAPLE LEAF. Cheery Canadians passing one of their Y.M.C.A. dug-outs near to the fighting-line on the western front.

was the continuous performance, which started at three o'clock each afternoon, and kept on till late in the evening. These performances were free to every soldier in uniform, Australian or otherwise. The theatre had its own orchestra, and for an hour each evening there was a cinematograph performance. Leading actors, music-hall performers, and concert groups of all kinds volunteered their services, and night after night the theatre was packed from pit to gallery with pleased and appreciative throngs of troops.

The work in England and in France included the usual features of huts and entertainments. A great deal was done in the way of distributing free drinks and

supplies. From January to June, 1917, £15,000 was spent in this free distribution. In the fighting at Passchendaele there was a great demand for some special food supplies for the Australians before they went "over the top." It seemed impossible to obtain them, but the Y.M.C.A. stepped in and arranged to serve out a four-ounce block of chocolate to every soldier before he set out. This little enterprise cost £1,100.

The libraries of the Y.M.C.A. were specially appreciated by the Australian troops. Naturally, the great demand was for fiction, and authors like O. Henry, Rex Beach, and Jack London were in chief request. But these were not the only favourites. One author who rivalled the most popular novelist was an American, H. E. Fosdick, who in book after book, such as "The Challenge of the Present Crisis," restated the great moral issues of the war. In one library there was a copy of Thomas à Kempis's "The Imitation of Christ." Month after month this book was continuously out, and on one occasion there were no fewer than thirty names on the waiting list for it. The thumbed copy which the present writer examined showed how carefully the book had been read. Those who judged the Australian soldier on the surface by his free language **Books read by Australians** or, in many cases, his easy profanity, might have seen him, from incidents such as this, in a very different light.

The liberal support given by the people of Australia to the Y.M.C.A. movement for the troops was mainly due to the letters received from the soldiers themselves, telling of what had been done. One party which proved a great success, not only in raising funds for the Y.M.C.A. but also in bringing recruits for the Army, originated in a very simple way. When the first troops returned home from Gallipoli, and were waiting about in Adelaide and other capitals, with nothing much to do, the Adelaide Y.M.C.A. arranged a recreation house for them on Henley Beach. The men were taken down there day after day in chars-à-bancs, entertained, and given something to occupy them. This rest-house grew into a permanent club-house, named after Lady Galway, wife of the Governor, and herself a prominent leader in the work. The work of the club-house was so good that the military authorities requested that convalescent soldiers might go there. One group of returned soldiers, appreciating what had been done for

SEARCH AMID THE DEBRIS OF A DESTROYED CHURCH. Officers near the remains of the church of Boesinghe, about four miles north of Ypres, searching for documents and other things that had been hastily buried there. They had succeeded in unearthing from amid the rubbish some of the old civil registers, somewhat damaged by damp.

FLOWERS TO WHISPER HOPE AND COMFORT MAN.
A British chaplain decorating the altar in his church in the line. The hut which served as church stood in a clump of trees barely two hundred yards from the front line, and the shrapnel helmet on the form was a necessary part of the chaplain's daily attire.

which was £31,000. Before many days the £31,000 figure was left behind, and the target was then raised to £40,000. Eventually £46,000 was subscribed within fifteen days. As a result of such liberality the representatives of the association with the Army were able to lay their plans with the primary consideration of not what things would cost, but what things were required. "We know that if we can show our people in New Zealand that anything is really needed for the soldiers they will give us the money to provide it," said one of the chief New Zealand workers.

The New Zealanders were thus able in their work in Egypt, in England, and on the western front to make provision on an ample and generous scale. In the ten centres in England the houses taken were good buildings in good quarters of the towns, and the huts were large and very comfortably equipped. In some of these places New Zealand ladies themselves organised cooking and waiting staffs, and cooked and prepared all the food sold for the troops. Thus at Hornchurch, where a large Y.M.C.A. hut was established in the **New Zealand** grounds of the convalescent camp, the **Y.M.C.A. to the fore** convalescent soldiers were provided by their own womenfolk with cakes and comforts which the rich men at that time could not command in the best West London restaurant.

them, asked if they could do nothing in return. They formed a concert-party, and set out to raise £1,000, to build an annex to the club-house. They raised £10,000, and they were so successful everywhere that people clamoured to hear them. They went all over Australia, stimulating enthusiasm, raising money, and bringing out fresh recruits for the Army.

The New Zealand Y.M.C.A. earned a reputation for daring and initiative in the war equal to that of the New Zealand Division ; higher praise it is impossible to give. The association was fortunate in its workers and in its methods. Its agents on the fighting-fronts were young men, and most of them very young men. They were backed by the people of New Zealand, not only with sympathy but with funds in the most ample measure. A striking example of the generosity of the people of New Zealand was shown in Auckland. On one occasion the community set out to raise £15,000 for the Y.M.C.A. This sum was raised so quickly that it was resolved to increase the total asked for to £25,000. When this figure was reached someone suggested that Auckland should attempt to rival the record of any other place in Australasia,

In France the New Zealanders earned a reputation, even amidst their keen friendly rivals, of pushing up their buildings to the foremost point possible at the front. They put up their huts and ran them in places where the rest of the community were content to live in cellars. More than one of these huts were blown to bits, and more than one of the New Zealand Y.M.C.A. men badly hit by shells. Still they kept on. At the end of 1917 they took the most daring step of all. A New Zealand division was then settled around one of the most devastated ruins on the western front. It was a place constantly shelled by the enemy and regularly bombed by aircraft, which sometimes rained down many hundreds of bombs in a

UNCONVENTIONAL PLACES OF WORSHIP IN THE WAR ZONE.
French chaplain outside his sand-bagged chapel on the French front on the Aisne, with the clergy-house conveniently adjacent. Right : His Eminence Cardinal Bourne outside the barn which served as the Roman Catholic church of the Irish Brigade on the western front.

night. The bravest soldier reckoned it a matter of ordinary precaution to keep well down in shelter in this place, for it was a favourite target for the Germans. The New Zealanders erected a hundred-feet hut as a recreation centre there, and the hut had months of successful life.

This was typical of the New Zealanders. Their work, under the general direction of Mr. George W. W. B. Hughes, supervising secretary, covered the usual features of huts and entertainments and the supply of comforts to the troops wherever New Zealanders were.

They originated the trench-comforts scheme of taking up cans of cocoa and other supplies for the men in the trenches. Their only complaint was that the commanding officers would not in every case let the Y.M.C.A. men carry the supplies into the trenches themselves. Wherever they could do so, there were plenty of volunteers to go.

Another striking feature of the New Zealand work in France and England was the " Brotherhood of Men of Good Intent," a kind of inner league of men who banded themselves together for betterment. There was only one condition of admission—the man must be aiming at better things.

The New Zealanders, like others, were greatly concerned with the problem of the soldier after the war. What could be done during the war to help him for his return to civil life? Two measures were taken. The first was a big educational scheme for the fit men. The second was a remarkable scheme for the convalescent and partly disabled.

A scheme was worked out at the great convalescent camp at Hornchurch and at the two other stations at Brockenhurst and Torquay for helping convalescent men. Many of these men had partly lost the use of limbs. A man, for example, whose arm had been for many months in splints, found, when the splints were removed, that the muscles and nerve centres had to greater or lesser extent lost co-ordination; he had not command of his fingers. The same thing applied to other parts of other limbs. There were certain formal gymnastic exercises to help the man to recover the use of these limbs, but the Y.M.C.A. authorities thought that something more could be done.

Help for the convalescents

At Hornchurch an Arts and Crafts Department was opened under the direction of Mr. Fawcett, of the Y.M.C.A. Here the men were taught basket-making, wood-carving, metal work, stained-glass making, and various other crafts. Working in close co-operation with the doctors, the man whose legs were injured or weak was given work at which he could sit down. Practice in basket-making or at wood-carving, and still more at metal work, was found to restore suppleness and full co-ordination of the fingers as nothing else could do, with the addition that the man's mind was occupied as it was not while he was at more mechanical gymnastics.

The primary idea was occupation for the mind. Here was something to take the minds of convalescents from themselves. They were set to work at cabinet-making, carving, carpentry, producing things under the most agreeable conditions. The medical benefits were such that before very long it was found by the doctors that much of the formal gymnastics for weakened fingers or limbs could be dispensed with; the use of those parts in producing things was so much more effective.

A third aspect of the work soon emerged. There were a number of men who had lost the physical power of earning a living in their old way. They were weakened or broken, or they had lost necessary limbs. Many of these men were exceedingly depressed, for they saw nothing before them but a life of hopeless dependence. One such example is typical of many. A man had lost one arm and the other was injured. His wounds healed as far as they could be healed. He was sent to the convalescent camp, where no one could fail to notice his depression. He made no secret of the cause of it. There was nothing for him to do. He went to the Arts and Crafts School, and was taught sign-painting with his left hand. He soon reached a point where he was a trained worker. It was like a breath of new life to the man. Good spirits and good hope returned to his life, and when he left for New Zealand it was with the prospect of being able to earn at least something in regular work.

In London the New Zealanders made their headquarters at what was in many ways the most outstanding Y.M.C.A. hut in the metropolis, the Shakespeare Hut in Gower Street. This hut was built by the British Y.M.C.A. on the site taken by the Shakespeare Memorial Committee

CARDINAL BOURNE ADDRESSING IRISH TROOPS.
Towards the close of 1917 Cardinal Bourne, Archbishop of Westminster, paid a visit to the Catholic Irish troops on the western front. He is here seen addressing men of the Dublin Fusiliers.

and Tercentenary Committee to erect a Shakespeare Memorial Theatre. The work of building the theatre had to be postponed until after the war, but the committee lent the site to the Y.M.C.A. and headed the movement for building the hut. A very extensive range of premises was constructed, exceedingly picturesque from without and very comfortable within. In addition to a number of entertainment and living-rooms, billiard-hall, dining-rooms, quiet writing-rooms and the like, there was sleeping accommodation for several hundred men. The **The Shakespeare Hut in London** New Zealanders raised a considerable part of the funds for construction of the whole, and made it their headquarters. The New Zealand Army had its chief offices just by, and Bloomsbury swarmed with New Zealanders. The British Council, feeling that it would be a good thing to have a Dominion centre for troops in London, handed over the Shakespeare Hut to the New Zealanders as they did the Aldwych Hut to the Australians. Hence this was their deal site.

The theatrical profession was specially interested in this hut, as was perhaps natural. The entertainments were under the direction of Lady Forbes Robertson, and leading players of all classes—Miss Ellen Terry, Sir George Alexander, and others—came to entertain the men. Some of the leading lights of the variety stage spared time between their turns at the West-End halls to give an extra turn at the Shakespeare, and they declared that the audience there was the best **Y.M.C.A. section** they had. The Shakespeare Hut was **of the N.Z. Army** one of the brightest and most cheerful spots in London.

The New Zealand Y.M.C.A. was a fully recognised part of the military establishment of the Dominion. Its officers did not take rank as the Canadians did, but were treated as officers without rank. They were a formally recognised part of the Army, their section in the establishment being known as the Military Services Department (Y.M.C.A. Section).

The organised provision of concerts and entertainments for the men at the front, an effort widely appreciated by the whole Army, started in a very small way. In February, 1915, it was suggested by the Ladies' Committee of the Y.M.C.A. that the soldiers in rest camps might welcome the diversion

FRENCH SOLDIERS' CHURCH.
Chapel of Our Lady of Hope, near Auberive, built of rough logs, and decorated by a French soldier who had won the Prix de Rome. In circle: Tiny wooden chapel built for the French soldiers close to the firing-line.

of concerts. It was noticed that men at the front were writing home asking for children's mouth-organs, and that gramophones were much in demand. Why not organise a concert-party and give them good music ? Miss Lena Ashwell, the well-known actress-manager, was behind the new scheme. The Y.M.C.A. took up the idea. Permission was secured from the authorities. Some apparently great difficulties were cleared away, and in that same month the first party went over to France. The whole thing was an experiment ; no one was quite sure if the troops wanted such entertainment or not, and it was impossible to be certain of the type of entertainment they would prefer. The first item on the programme of the first concert laid all doubts to rest. From the beginning to the end the first concert-party received an almost overwhelmingly cordial welcome, and was an outstanding success. The only difficulty was that the performers could not sing enough or appear often enough to satisfy the demands of the men.

A second party set out in the next month. From that point the work grew, until the Lena Ashwell Concert Parties became a recognised part of life at the different bases in France.

The parties usually consisted of six performers. Their journeys were anything but holiday times. There would usually be a hospital concert each afternoon, and two camp concerts in the evening. Often there were long journeys in the intervals. It was no uncommon thing for the concert-party in France to go fifty miles out and fifty miles back in a day, driving in an open car in winter time. In fifteen months over two thousand concerts had been given, and from France and Flanders the parties went still farther—to the Mediterranean and to the Near East. This number was soon doubled.

A still further advance was made when the authorities, yielding to repeated demands, permitted the concert-parties to go up the line right under the fire of the guns. Here, in barns and amid ruins, in places where at night-time no light could be shown lest it drew the enemy fire, the entertainments went on. The performers carried gas-helmets, **Lena Ashwell** and were ready at any moment, as were **Concert Parties** their audiences, to clap on their protection against a German gas attack. In an account of these performances Miss Lena Ashwell wrote :

Very early in their travels the peaceful concert-party found themselves in a little village which was bombed with lyddite by German aircraft for twenty-three hours. However, not German Taubes nor artillery actions interfered with the success of the concerts. The British soldier out there can enjoy a cello solo or a song while shells are whistling overhead, and our own artillery are replying in an impromptu accompaniment. And it is only fair to recall that the nerves of the performers seem to have been as equal to the occasion as those of their more experienced audience. Only at the first terrific unexpected crash were the performers visibly startled—to the joy of the noise-hardened audience. One concert was given among the guns during an artillery action, and in the words of one of the artistes: "It was a weird experience listening to lovely music to the sound of the cannon." At any other concert the experience would surely have been inverted ; and any other audience would have been more likely to be listening to the cannon than to the sound of the music ; but there the men's brains are weary of the roar of the guns and the scream of the shells, and that is why the concert-parties are such an immense boon.

It was difficult to make any, save those who were

present, realise what the service of these concert-parties meant to the lads at the front. Some of them had not seen a woman who spoke their own language for many months, and to them the mere sight of a lady from their own land was like a breath of new life. The songs, old and new, the sound of women's voices in music again, the relief from the strain of war, were an indescribable comfort. " I am a Puritan, with a Puritan's views on the theatre, and you know what a deep prejudice that is," said a chaplain from overseas to the leader of one of the concert-parties, " but I cannot tell you how grateful I am that my boys should have this hour of happiness. You do not know what it means to us." And there were tears in his eyes as he spoke.

Work of the Blue Triangle

The campaign of the Red Triangle was followed in due course by the activities of the Blue Triangle, the symbol of the Young Women's Christian Association. When women began to take a more prominent part in the war, first in munition-making, and then at the bases in France, at all kinds of work—as transport drivers, telegraphists, telephonists, clerks, book-keepers, and the like—it became evident that special provision must be made for their comfort also. Something was done by the existing agencies, but the Y.W.C.A. was felt to be the organisation to specialise for the young women.

Between 1915 and the beginning of 1918 the Y.W.C.A. opened over two hundred huts, canteens, and hostels in the munition areas for munition workers, and in other areas for Government clerks and workers. In many cases these hostels were opened at the request and with the assistance of the firms employing the people. These canteens were feeding, roughly, 130,000 girls a week. Several hostels were opened near large military hospitals

IN A RECREATION HUT.
British and French soldiers enjoying a " sing-song " in one of the Church Army huts on the western front.

number of girls were sent out on to a marsh in Wales picking moss for chemicals; they were looked after. There were Belgian clubs for Belgian women in London, and many similar enterprises.

The problem of housing munition workers—a difficult one at the best—was doubly difficult where young girls were concerned. In towns where munition works were opened all possible accommodation was usually quickly taken up. It took time before houses specially built by the Government could be ready. The Y.W.C.A. opened clearing hostels, where the girls were temporarily housed until suitable accommodation could be found for them. One trouble found in many cases here was that the girls did not want to go when accommodation was found. They implored to be allowed to remain on at the hostels.

Y.W.C.A. help for the W.A.A.C.

When the Women's Army Auxiliary Corps was established, the Commander-in-Chief of that body asked the Y.W.C.A. to do for the women in khaki what the Y.M.C.A. had done for the men. Over twelve centres, with huts and clubs, were started in France for them, under the joint auspices of the Y.M.C.A. and the Y.W.C.A., the two triangles, red and blue, being displayed side by side, and many more in English camps. The problem of aiding the girl in khaki was one of very considerable complexity. The Women's Corps included large numbers

THE CHURCH ARMY AT ROUEN
One of the buildings erected in France by the Church Army for the use of the troops.

for the relatives of wounded and dying men. Clubs for nurses were started at Basra and Bombay. One section of the association dealt with the girls employed on agricultural work in England, providing them with accommodation and food. When numbers of women workers poured into districts where there was no accommodation for them, it was to the Y.W.C.A. that the authorities turned time after time for aid. One hundred flax pullers had to be helped in Somerset. A

THE FRIENDLY HUT IN A BRITISH CAMP.
Hut at Cayeux, near the mouth of the Somme, maintained for the use of the British soldiers in camp there by the Church Army in conjunction with the Church of England Missionary Society.

of the very pick of the womanhood of the country. But they were taken, one and all, right out of their usual surroundings, away from the usual influences of their lives, and found themselves entering on a new life altogether. In the early days extreme independence was rather encouraged than discouraged among the khaki girls. Such a time of transition had its obvious dangers, and the work of the Y.W.C.A. in the camps, both in France and in the United Kingdom, was exceedingly useful at a time when it was most necessary. The extent of the need for this work in England alone can be judged by the fact that by the end of 1917 there were already one hundred camps to which women were going, most of the largest lying isolated far away from towns and villages on high stretches of open country. In the Aldershot Command alone it was planned to employ approximately ten thousand women and girls.

Work of the Salvation Army　　The Salvation Army had, previous to the war, undertaken a great deal of special work for the troops, under the direction of Miss Mary Murray, the daughter of a well-known British general. Her efforts on behalf of the troops in South Africa during the Boer War were widely appreciated. Early in 1915 establishments were opened in France, the first a hut at Rouen, and the second a house at Boulogne. These establishments grew, until by early in 1918 there was a chain of them from Dunkirk to Havre. In some centres the agencies were of the most varied kind. Thus, at Havre, in addition to a number of huts for the British and Imperial troops, there were several hotels and restaurants in the city, where British soldiers passing through were well catered for. At Dunkirk itself the local officers in charge had many exciting experiences. Dunkirk, during 1917, was the object of constant attacks by the Germans—attacks by air and bombardment from one or more big guns concealed in the dunes somewhere behind the German lines. On one occasion a German fleet appeared outside the port and for about a quarter of an hour rained shells into it. So the Salvationists found at this stage that the old public buildings which they had taken, and very admirably transformed at the request of the authorities into a great hostel for soldiers, afforded unexpected advantage on account of the cellars, where refugees of various races crowded.

The Salvation Army huts and hostels laid themselves out for general social work. Where it was permitted to sell food to the troops, practical women officers set themselves to cater for the lads in real homelike style. Here the Salvation Army undoubtedly reaped considerable advantage from the fact that many of its workers were drawn from the same class from which the majority of the troops had come. They worked among them, not as fine ladies, but as their own folk, who could mother them as their own mothers would. Some of these women workers, living in base camps frequently exposed **True Christianity in practice** to enemy aeroplane attacks, earned a wide reputation among the British Army. One of the best known was Mrs. Huish, at Etaples, who, although by no means justifying her title by her age, was known as "Ma" by soldiers everywhere. Soldiers by the hundred thousand passed through her station each year. The hut over which she and her husband presided was crowded night after night. Mrs. Huish worked at a very practical religion. It was her business to look after the boys in place of their own mothers at home, to buy the best food she could for them, to let them have it as cheaply as she could, to help lads fresh from the trenches to get clean clothes, to nurse up the raw young soldier who was suffering agony from blistered feet or aching muscles, to give a special Christmas treat to others, to sew on the lad's buttons, or to prepare him a cup of coffee of the kind he got at home.

And thus she might be seen day after day presiding over her group of assistants, herself cooking great stacks of fresh herrings which she had bought earlier in the day, or frying eggs in great pans of fat, frying them so deftly that strangers would come to watch her. She often cooked two thousand eggs a day. Then from kitchen and frying-pan she would turn to the spiritual side of her work. She would go to a room where hundreds of men would be waiting, and would reason with them and talk to them of their homes, their hopes, and their future. A work such as this is difficult to appraise by ordinary statistics, but no one who witnessed it could doubt its good effects on men of all classes in this Army drawn from all parts of the Empire. In eleven months 1,300 men pledged themselves in this hut, in front of their comrades, to lead a new life.

The Salvation Army, unlike some other agencies, consistently kept the religious side of its work foremost. The comforts of the huts and the meals, the provision of sleeping accommodation, entertainments, and the like, were all used as parts of religious propaganda, not to make the soldiers members of the Salvation Army, but to appeal to their spiritual side. And it was found, in nearly every part of France, that the men flocked to the religious meetings. The old idea of the fighting man as a heedless rapscallion was long out of date. These men were up against the greatest forces men can confront. They were ever face to face with death. In every gathering it could be safely said that a certain proportion, before many weeks were over, would be killed in battle and a larger proportion wounded. The meetings were at times held under fire from bombs from enemy aeroplanes. Men in such circumstances are apt to be either strongly attracted to or altogether repulsed from religion. The Salvation Army meetings showed by their crowds how many were attracted. There would usually be a band of musicians drawn from the soldiers themselves. The speakers would often be soldiers, and the whole tone of the gatherings would **Religious spirit of the troops** be in harmony with their surroundings.

The work for the troops in France, begun by Brigadier Murray, passed after a time into the hands of Colonel Haines, an Englishman who had served for many years in responsible positions in his organisation in Scandinavia and on the European mainland. At the outbreak of war Colonel Haines was one of the heads of the Salvation Army in Germany. He was one of the last to be allowed to leave the country. He immediately plunged into Belgian relief, and from there was transferred to the military work in France. In Colonel Haines the Salvation Army had a very practical, genial leader. A man able to command and to enforce his commands, he had a gift of "enthusing" all under him. Nearly all his staff came from England, men and women selected because of their practical skill in dealing with men and in administering affairs. It was very remarkable how people lacking knowledge of France or of French ways, but gifted with abundant common-sense, would go down, take over practical control in a district, and win the confidence not only of the British, but of the French with whom they had to have unceasing business dealings.

Two branches of the Salvation Army work require special mention. The first of these was the mission of mercy undertaken by Miss Mary Booth and a group of co-workers among the wounded and dying in the base hospitals. Miss Booth came on a visit from her English work, intending to stay a few days. She started to visit the wounded in the hospitals around Wimereux. She found many men there anxious and wanting things done; some of them could obtain no news of their wives and families, and some were troubled in soul. There were husbands fearing for their wives, men entering the Valley of the Shadow of Death who wanted to hear a word of cheer and confidence, men who had lost their bearings in the battle of life and sought to find them again.

And so the work began. Associated with Miss Booth were some other ladies who visited hospitals all along the base. Notices were issued in Britain stating that the Salvation Army would attempt to obtain information for people seeking news of their men-folk at the front. With the co-operation and hearty sympathy of the hospital authorities, doctors, and nursing sisters alike, the work rapidly grew. Miss Booth's stay of a few days lengthened to a stay of years. At her headquarters at Wimereux she daily received large numbers of letters from people at home asking for news, something more than the official tidings, about their wounded or their dead. In the hospitals there were men anxiously seeking news of their kith and kin at home.

The success of such a work as this depends entirely on the spirit in which it is carried out. Officialism and formalism would kill it. The people at its head and the workers throughout must be full of sympathy and pity. Happily, the workers here were naturally well suited for their task. They started with a feeling of ample love and admiration for the British soldier. They came to help him in his hardest hour of life, and the gospel they preached was a gospel of help and hope.

Service of love and comfort When they came across a man in hospital anxious because he had no letters from his family, they wrote personal letters to the mother or wife telling them where the man was, how he was, and how he was longing to hear from them. When the man, blinded by high explosives, or so feeble from lung wounds that he could hardly speak, panted his anxiety about sweetheart or mother or wife at home, they wrote for him, telling just what mother or wife was wanting to know. They would bring the man comforts. If he died, they would go to his grave. If possible, they would be present at his funeral, and they would see that a little stone was put there to mark his resting-place, and that some flowers were laid on the grave in his honour. They would gather some of the flowers, press them, and send them to the people at home as a memorial of their dead.

Such things may seem trivial matters to those who made no sacrifice of their kindred in the war. Any who had brother or sister, father or husband, lying in French or Flemish soil knew otherwise. To many thousands of grieving families the work of Miss Mary Booth and her colleagues came as comfort and consolation in the darkest hours of life.

The second branch of the Salvation Army work calling for special mention is the Ambulance Corps. Almost immediately after the real fighting started around Mons it became apparent **Salvation Army's ambulance corps** that the old British ambulance system was hopelessly out of date. Organisations of all kinds started to supply with the utmost speed motor-ambulances for the wounded. The Salvation Army sent a group of cars out under three officers, Messrs. Aspinall, Taylor, and Pentecost. At first these three officers worked as stretcher-bearers in shifts of from ten to twenty hours, carrying men on their backs up gangways set at forty-five degrees, loading ships, unloading trains, and the like. Then, after three weeks at the base, two of them moved on to the line. Here a year was spent with the glorious 7th and 8th Divisions, after which the Salvation Army cars were moved down to Boulogne for base work.

In all, up to early in 1918, the Salvation Army sent over twenty-five cars and about fifty drivers to France. All of these were " Class A " men, taken from general service. Their work received the warmest appreciation from the British Red Cross. Time after time Major Paget, the Commissioner at Boulogne, emphasised in the strongest possible way the remarkably good influence of the Salvation Army drivers on their colleagues, their high moral, and their admirable discipline. Adjutant Taylor, who subsequently took charge of the Ambulance Section, did a great deal of social work for the Red Cross drivers in the Boulogne base. Attached to his section

FREE REFRESHMENTS FOR THE TROOPS ON VIMY'S BLOOD-STAINED RIDGE.
Prince Arthur of Connaught (in group on the right) with some French and Canadian officers on Vimy Ridge. The corrugated iron building on the left was one of three Y.M.C.A. coffee-stalls on the historic battlefield where hot tea and coffee was supplied without charge to troops going up to or coming out of the trenches. This gratuitous service cost the Canadian Y.M.C.A. £1,000 a month.

EEB

was one of the finest brass bands in France; there were twenty-four instrumentalists, twelve of whom had been bandmasters or musical leaders. At Christmas, 1917, this band played carols to twenty thousand wounded—a record unequalled. The appreciation of the British Red Cross was shown by its urgent demand that the Salvation Army should increase its ambulance work. In response to the demand, a new Salvation Army motor-ambulance unit with twenty drivers was created. "Wherever Salvation Army men are helping," wrote the Hon. Arthur Stanley to General Bramwell Booth, "we hear nothing but good reports of their work. Sir Ernest Clarke tells mè that your ambulance sections in France are quite the best of any in our service."

Next in the extent of its operations to the Y.M.C.A., came the Church Army, which by the second year of the war was spending £240,000 a year on enterprises for the soldier, and a year later had eight hundred huts, tents, and centres in operation. This society was established in 1885 by the Rev. (afterwards Prebendary) Wilson Carlile, with the primary idea of having a movement inside the Church of England on somewhat the same lines as the Salvation Army, using military organisation and titles for evangelistic work. It had grown very considerably up to the time of the outbreak of war, and had established a number of social and relief agencies among the poor. When the war began it concentrated its efforts in the new direction. Tents and huts were established in military centres at home. These were much appreciated not only by officers and men, but by the highest authorities in the Army. Mr. Lloyd George warmly praised them, and Lord Derby declared that the work had conduced materially to the physical and moral welfare of the troops. One special feature of these tents and huts was the partitioning off of a small space in each for prayer and devotion.

War work of the Church Army

Thanks to the cordial co-operation of the Anglican chaplains, the Church Army was able to open a number of stations in France and Belgium, not only at the base depots, but very far up in the front lines. Soon there came a friendly rivalry between the Y.M.C.A. and the Church Army as to which should be nearer the front trenches. On the western front about two hundred of the Church Army huts or shelters were within range of

A "DUG-OUT" IN LONDON.
Model "dug-out" built near the Y.M.C.A. establishment in the Strand as an advertisement for "Hut Day," when a street collection was made to provide more huts for the troops abroad.

the enemy's guns, and by the autumn of 1917 no fewer than a dozen of these had been destroyed or damaged by shell fire. The Church Army men on the Somme had their own periodical, "Sometimes: Being the Somme Times and War Zone Chronicle."

Kitchen cars were sent over to France to travel about among the troops—big, covered motor-cars, with material and appliances for preparing and cooking food for troops on the march and for the wounded. Some extracts from the log-book of one of these cars will best show their experiences:

"7 Jeudi. Fête Dieu. Arrived here 4 p.m., found things lively. Got into working order; visited the marquees, gave the wounded drink and cigarettes, made them feel quite happy. Some sad cases—had to pull myself together or would have failed. Settled now and going strong." "Moving at 6.30 a.m. A very busy day—four trains with very bad cases, a great many German wounded." "A visit by General Sir Douglas Haig. . . . Orders to clear hospital at once—considered too dangerous. Four trains . . . passed through on this day, also forty-three hospital cars . . . each wounded man left with either drink, biscuit, or cigs. —the men cheerful.. The hospital having cleared am awaiting orders. Eight wounded men brought in by mistake—looked after them well." "A bombardment of the hospital in the night." "Heavy bombardment in the night, assisting the doctor's stretcher-bearers." "Orders to evacuate. Instructed to attach myself to —— M.G.C." "Left under orders for —— Farm, very mild spot. Arrived 5 o'clock. Well received. . . . Field ambulance." "Opened out with lemonade and cigarettes to troops passing. Most of them coming out of the trenches seemed . dog tired. . . .

AT THE SIGN OF THE RED TRIANGLE IN THE STRAND.
General view of the Eagle Hut in the Strand, the American headquarters of the Army and Navy Y.M.C.A. in London, where American soldiers and sailors found a home while away from home.

BUSY ON WORK OF MERCY.
Salvationists in New York preparing medical dressings for despatch to the troops in France, where the general ambulance work of the Salvation Army won special commendation from the authorities.

Mr. —— visited us and was surprised to find us so near the front line. Our efforts much appreciated." "There has been shelling by Fritz almost night and day since we came; very heavy to-night." "Carrying on the work. The men very cheerful. The cup of tea or lemonade, together with a cigarette, doing the needful. Heavy bombing all round the camp—most tantalising." "Still carrying on. Heavy shelling during the day." "An officer of the M.G.C. called to arrange for over sixty men to have refreshment; promised to accommodate them at 10.30 p.m. and another party at 12.30 a.m." "Very heavy shelling; a labour company came to seek the needful . . . attended to the walking wounded. Went through thirty-eight gallons of lemonade and twelve gallons of tea." "A very busy day from 7.30 a.m. until 11.15 p.m.; arrangements made to meet two M.G. companies, one at 2 a.m. and the other at 3 a.m." "Roused at 2 a.m. for another M.G. company, Australian, coming down; they were dog tired and thoroughly appreciated the refreshment provided. . . . Terrific bombardment by Fritz."

"Bombardment continued all night; a shell burst about twenty yards from the van at 9.30 a.m." "Up at 1.45 a.m., met party, and retired at 3 a.m.; up again at 7 a.m., and after a very busy day with troops going in and coming out of the trenches, retired at 11.15 p.m.; real good work. Complimented by Australian officers on our work." "Roused at 3 a.m. for a party of M. gunners. . . . More compliments; the officers enjoy the drink and smoke quite as much as the men." "Fritz opened up a violent bombardment at 11 a.m.; and we were continually under shell fire until 5 p.m. . . . the number of shells must have been over seven hundred—heavy stuff." "Had to close down at 9.30 p.m., ran out of water. Heavy artillery fire on both sides. . . . Used one hundred and sixteen gallons of water in twenty-four hours."

The work soon extended beyond the western front. There were Church Army workers in Italy and in Malta, with the armies in Egypt, with Allenby's advance in Palestine, in Macedonia and Mesopotamia, in East Africa and in India. One centre was in the prison vault of a famous war city; some of the workers were to be found in barns and dug-outs, and one on a barge on a Flemish canal.

A Church Army hospital was opened by Lady Bagot in August, 1914, at the Observatory, Brussels. It had to retire before the advancing Germans to Ostend. A little later on it was shelled out of Ostend, and from there, after a temporary stay at one other place, it settled at Caen, at the Ecole Première Supérieure on the Bayeux road. The staff hoped when they reached France to be able to nurse British wounded. They found, however, that their services were most needed for French soldiers, particularly since the French medical service was almost wholly overwhelmed at the beginning of the war by the magnitude of its task. Eventually, the field of fighting moving on to other areas, the necessity of the hospital became less, and it was then resolved to close it and to transfer its staff to Scotland, to Dungavel, the mansion of the Duke of *Peregrinations of a* Hamilton, which had been opened for *C.A. hospital* wounded and invalid sailors. After continuing for a short time, the Church Army, however, decided that it would be advisable to hand the hospital over to the Admiralty to run it for themselves. It had been the means, while under them, of helping many hundreds of wounded and sick men back to health.

Fifty ambulances were fitted up and sent out to the western front. Some of them were manned by clergy. At the end of the period for which the Church Army had promised to run these ambulances, it found itself unable to continue the work under the new directions of the War Office, and so the ambulances were handed over to the military authorities.

When, soon after the outbreak of the war, the public conscience at home was aroused over the treatment of our wounded prisoners of war and the lack of food in Germany, the Church Army stepped into the breach to help in providing large numbers of parcels for these men.

A CHANGE FOR THE BETTER.
Canadian Y.M.C.A. hut established in a German concrete gun-pit, on the western front, of which the enemy had been dispossessed. Many of the Canadian centres were right in the battle areas, three, for example, being within five hundred yards of the front line on Vimy Ridge.

It aided not only the British, but also Russian prisoners in Germany, whose lot was specially bad. Here, again, the work was modified after a time, owing to the entire supervision of prisoners of war aid work being formally and officially placed under the British Red Cross. While not sending parcels direct, the Church Army continued, however, to help the prisoners on its books through the Red Cross. In the summer of 1917 it had about ten thousand men on its register.

In London several hostels were opened. Perhaps the most interesting of these was a large part of the Buckingham Palace Hotel, which was placed at the disposal of the Church Army as a recreation camp and canteen, mainly for troops arriving at Victoria from France. The King granted the use of a portion of the riding school attached to the Royal Mews, which is practically opposite the hostel, and so it was possible

C.A. hostels in London to sleep some six hundred soldiers at a time. The former Central Labour Home in Marylebone Road was transformed into a soldiers' hostel. There was a third hostel in Artillery Row, Westminster, and a fourth was opened in November, 1917, in Great Peter Street, Westminster, in what a short time before had been a common lodging-house.

Special agencies were enlisted for munition workers, and particularly for women, including canteens and hostels, where every provision was made for the comfort of both day and night shifts. There were rest huts for women and girls in their off-duty hours. There were homes in garrison towns for the wives of soldiers, and holiday homes for soldiers' wives and children. One exceedingly useful task was undertaken on behalf of the children of soldiers who had lost their wives, or whose wives had abandoned their little ones. The Church Army agreed to take the entire charge of such children until the end of the war. Another special scheme was a farm in Essex where disabled and discharged soldiers, especially those suffering from shell shock or nerve trouble, were given three months' training for work on the land.

While the services of the Roman Catholic chaplains were very greatly appreciated by men of all Churches, the Catholic community did not enter into the work of providing comforts for its men on the same wide scale as many others. The most prominent Catholic work was organised by the Catholic Women's League. The initials of the organisation stood for its motto—Charity, Work, Loyalty. This organisation had twenty huts in all, four of them being in France. In England there were huts at Ripon, Bramshott, Salisbury, Codford, Richmond (Yorkshire), and several other places. The Codford Hut was almost entirely for Australians, and the Bramshott Hut for Canadians.

In London there was a large hut at Ashley Gardens, with sleeping accommodation for eighty men. In most camps the huts were also used as chapels, where there was no Roman Catholic chapel.

The Catholic Women's League The huts were not run in any narrow spirit. They were open to men of all creeds, or of no creed at all, and some, at least, of the workers in the huts were non-Catholic. The whole spirit in which they were managed was in the highest degree admirable. There was an absence of rules, freedom from restraint, a cordiality and friendship which the soldiers were quick to observe and quick to appreciate. "Give me some pineapple and cream," said a new arrival brusquely to one of the lady workers. Another soldier sitting by glanced at the first speaker. "In this place," said he, "we usually say 'please' when we ask for a thing." And the men lived up to the tone of the place. One great night, which was long remembered, was at the hut at Codford when a great Christmas dance was arranged and the girl partners were brought in from the neighbouring towns in omnibuses. The thing was an overwhelming success. One of the

Australian soldiers showed his appreciation of it in the most practical fashion, for shortly afterwards he sent a donation of fifty pounds to the funds in remembrance of the occasion.

The hut in London was open day and night, and soldiers could obtain a hot meal there at any hour. A great point was made of having everything as little institutional as possible, and of giving the whole place the same thought and care that would be given in a well-kept private home. The food was nicely cooked and served; the rooms were kept well dusted and fresh and clean; the lady workers did everything they could for the men—darning their socks and mending their clothes, keeping their parcels for them on their return to the front, and maintaining regular correspondence with them when on active service. In short, their work was to "mother" the men; and "mother" them they did in the best sense.

Attached to the hut was one room looked upon as a kind of club, which was started at the request of many men who had been out to the front but were sent back to London on light duty. They came to the hut for all their meals, and had this one room reserved for them. There were two large dormitories and several cubicles. Each of the cubicles had been furnished by people in memory of brothers, sons, or friends who had fallen in the war. Many men stayed for weeks at a time, and some were there for months. From one thousand to twelve hundred men passed through this hut every day.

The authorities sent a great many Irish troops here on their way through London. One night there came a telephone message that a considerable party of Irishmen would arrive. When they reached the hut it was discovered that they were **Orange and Green forgather** Ulstermen. There happened to be several very vehement Nationalists in the hut at the time, and everyone looked forward to a real Irish "shindy" when the Northern Unionists and the Nationalists came to argument. The Ulstermen were somewhat glum and reserved at first, but soon all became great friends, and everything passed off very well. Shortly after they left, the superintendent received a note thanking her for all her kindness, and telling her how the men would send all their friends to her.

One of the first war works of the Catholic Women's League was to place twelve thousand Belgian refugees in homes and institutions within twenty-four hours of their arrival in England. Their chief centres in France were in Boulogne and Calais.

The movement to help the soldiers, starting with the simple and natural desire to provide comforts for men placed in conditions of considerable physical hardship, thus grew to a great national and Imperial task. The progress from recreation to education was a natural one. In the course of time old prejudices were laid aside, new methods attempted, and the movements developed in ways which those who started them never contemplated.

The organisers of progress throughout the Empire were united as they could be in no other way; Canadians and New Zealanders, Australians and British, found themselves working as one. The young men from the lands of the seven seas brought their freshness of vision and broadness of view to men trained by more ancient ways in other lands; the men of older lands brought their longer training and experience to the commonwealth. A great link was created between the homes of the Empire and the men in camps and fighting fields. Soldier and private citizen were taught by common association their unity. The homes of England were opened to scores of thousands of overseas men. Even during the war it was possible to see that the spirit of goodwill and kindness had by its practical outcome created a strong bond of Empire reaching wherever British people were; strong not because of formal ties, but because it was the outcome of the spirit of service, sympathy, and goodwill.

THE VICTORIES OF PROGRESS IN MESOPOTAMIA.

By Edward Wright.

Improved Health of Army in Summer Heat—Surprise Swoop Upon Ramadiya—Great Sandstorm Interferes with British Operations—General Brooking's Classic Victory on the Euphrates—Total Destruction of Turkish Force—Magnificent Development of Wheatlands of Mesopotamia—Opening of the Hindiya Barrage Irrigation Works—The Conqueror Who Came with the Horn of Plenty Into the Desert—Breaking Into Enemy's Hill-Screen by the Diala Gorge—Splendid Scottish Attack on Tekrit—Hussars and Lancers Roll Up Turkish Wing—New Cœurs de Lion in Saladin's Home—General Maude's Tragic Courtesy—The Cup of Cholera Tea—Smashing Victory of Khan Bagdadiya—Terrific Pursuit of Armoured Motor-Cars—Effect Upon the Bedouin Tribesmen—Converging Movement on Tuz—Turkish Forces Enveloped—Kurds Join British—Dramatic Possibilities of the Situation.

AFTER the highly-successful operations around Bagdad, related in Chapter CLXXVI. (Vol. 9, page 141), Sir Frederick Stanley Maude left the scattered Turkish forces alone, and began sending a considerable proportion of his troops on leave to India. The furnace summer heat imposed an armistice upon the principal combatants. Only the marauding Bedouin, inured to tropic life, continued some show of activity, and the Indo-British Expeditionary Force reluctantly saved itself from complete idleness by some successful punitive operations against the wilder tribesmen of the Upper Tigris and Euphrates.

In the burning glare of the sandy wastes the Turk from the Anatolian highlands probably suffered as much as the Briton and more than the Indian, especially as he lacked ice-making plant and other conveniences for mitigating the climate. During the first trying fortnight in May, 1917, there was a welcome decrease in summer sickness among the Indo-British troops, a reduction of nearly sixty per cent. over the corresponding period of 1916 being effected. Even when in the height of summer the temperature rose high above all records of recent years, the health of the troops was admirably maintained, showing that the British

medical organisation had been greatly improved since the tragic breakdown in the attempt to relieve the garrison of Kut.

So complete was the new system of ice and pure water supply that Sir Frederick Stanley Maude was able to make some surprising thrusts into the desert at a time when the Turks were prostrate from the heat. In May, 1917, his patrols skirmished around Deli Abbas and other northern hill outposts, capturing a hundred and twenty-five prisoners. Then, in June, a British garrison worked along the caravan route between the Diala River and the Mandali petroleum wells to the marsh of Beled Ruz, to guard the rear flank of the Bagdad army, which had become exposed by a Russian withdrawal.

General Baratoff and his Cossack force, which had come down from Persia to the Diala River, were compelled to retire far into the highlands of Persia at Kirmanshah. The summer climate in the river valley had so undermined their health that they had to break all connection with the British troops and leave a great gap, through which the Turks might have turned the British flank at Bagdad had the enemy been able to overcome transport difficulties and endure the heat. The British occupation of Beled Ruz guarded against this turning movement.

SUCCESSOR TO A CONQUEROR. *[Elliott & Fry.*
When Sir Frederick Stanley Maude, the conqueror of Bagdad, died, November 18th, 1917, Lieutenant-General Sir William Marshall succeeded him as Commander-in-Chief of the British forces in Mesopotamia.

425

Owing to the remarkable development of the British system of transport, General Maude was master of the situation in Mesopotamia so long as the Russian army in the Caucasus continued to press against the principal Ottoman force. When, however, there were clear signs that the rhetoric of Kerensky was proving powerless against the active disintegrating influence of Bolshevism, the British commanders in Mesopotamia and Egypt had completely to alter their plans, and provide against a struggle with the main Ottoman forces. The former German Chief of Staff, General von Falkenhayn, took over the command of the Turkish armies, and, fixing his head-quarters at Aleppo, began to concentrate

Interplay of the British armies there large forces of men and muni-tions, threatening equally Sir Frederick Stanley Maude and Sir Edmund Allenby.

The successor to Field-Marshal von der Goltz occupied at Aleppo the favourite Teutonic central position between two widely separated hostile forces. He could strike along the Gaza line or along the Euphrates line, apparently before any combined British movements on these fronts could be conducted against him. It became known that he had decided only to demonstrate strongly against the far-flung defences of the Suez Canal, and to make his main effort against Bagdad by means of a flanking attack from the Turkish position behind Ramadiya, on the Euphrates.

Falkenhayn's advantage of position between the two British armies was, however, an illusion. Only in theory

Imperial Chief of Staff, Sir William Robertson, in tele-graphic collaboration with Sir Charles Monro in India, Sir Frederick Stanley Maude in Mesopotamia, and Sir Edmund Allenby in Egypt. Slow and roundabout as this cablegram system of collaboration seemed, it proved of superior efficiency to that of the enemy, and led to the complete upsetting of Falkenhayn's plan of attack on Mesopotamia.

General Maude was saved, without having to give battle against the main army of Falkenhayn. He was relieved from all the enemy's intended pressure by a

"TWENTY-EIGHT-IN-HAND" IN MESOPOTAMIA.
Driving a lengthy team—consisting of no fewer than fourteen pairs of mules—across the sandy desert of Mesopotamia. In oval above : Supports in a dip of desert ground awaiting their order to advance and reinforce cavalry engaged in attacking the enemy in Mesopotamia.

did he occupy good interior lines. His railway system was inefficient and incomplete, while the British system of marine and river transport between Great Britain and India on the one hand and Egypt and Mesopotamia on the other hand was, in spite of the long distances, admirable in speed and general volume.

The principal movements in the campaign against General von Falkenhayn were arranged in London by the

strong thrusting movement of Sir Edmund Allenby's army, that compelled Falkenhayn to move his principal forces southward, where they were broken and scattered beyond Jerusalem. This remarkable interplay of long-distance forces must be borne in mind when following all the events in the Tigris and Euphrates valleys after the British capture of Bagdad.

Every British movement was designed and executed with far-reaching aim. Especially after the complete bankruptcy of Russian military power in July, 1917, the situation on the Middle East battlefield became intricately delicate. Every symptom of augmenting weakness in the Russian army of the Caucasus was reflected in an increase of either caution or audacity on the part of the commanders of the British forces opposing the Turks.

Sometimes the British general made a daring stroke at the nearest hostile force **Alternate caution** before this could be strengthened by **and audacity** Turkish forces brought from the Cauca-sian front. At other times he retreated from the scene of a swift victory, because he knew that the enemy was receiving reinforcements, and that his own men would be placed at a disadvantage if they fought another battle far away from their own river base. It was by magnificent rapier play that Sir Frederick Stanley Maude and his able successor, Sir William Marshall, saved the army of Mesopotamia from very severe pressure during the long, difficult period between the development and failure of Falkenhayn's plan and the new situation created by the later Turkish advance through Russian territory into Northern Persia.

SIGNALLING-POST IN THE DESERT.
Signal section of advanced headquarters heliographing orders to the artillery during a forward move in Mesopotamia. The pillar of rock afforded a commanding position for the signaller and his instrument.

No doubt Falkenhayn selected the Euphrates line for his main movement of concentration because of the apparent facility of river transport from the Aleppo railway, along the Upper Euphrates, down to the country below Hit, where the great waterway of the desert swerved within twenty-five miles of Bagdad. Immense, however, were the difficulties of conveying material down the meandering Euphrates, for some five hundred miles of bends and twists, without proper modern craft.

On the map General Maude was much farther from his bases than Falkenhayn was. But the great new British

supplies of ice and water. Making their final movement under cover of night, the troops completely surprised the heat-wasted Turks, and in an action lasting from four till a quarter past eight o'clock in the morning of July 11th, captured the enemy's advanced positions.

Just as the final assault was about to be launched, under conditions that seemed to ensure a decisive victory, everything was thrown into confusion by the intervention of the hand of tropical Nature. As the barren hills occupied by the enemy blazed in the heat, part of the sky-line darkened, and a blinding sandstorm overwhelmed the contending forces. Visual observation was impracticable, while land wires and wireless instruments would not carry messages, so that the **Sandstorm stops** direction of the harmonised movements **a battle** of the attacking forces became impossible. The operations had then to be abandoned, and the alarmed, half-vanquished Turks were able to strengthen their lines and obtain considerable reinforcements.

Yet, as soon as the heat abated, General Maude prepared another attack upon the southern Turkish front at Ramadiya. Under Major-General Sir H. T. Brooking, a stronger attacking force, of two infantry columns and cavalry, was again concentrated within striking distance of the Ramadiya dunes and canals.

The Turkish position was very strong. It was based upon a rise of ground known as the Mushaid Ridge, rising sixty feet above the desert plain and moated on the north by the Euphrates River, and on the south by the

AN INDIAN CONVOY CROSSING THE DUSTY DESERT.
Indian troops with the British forces in Mesopotamia. The mule-drawn army transport carts raised clouds from the " desert's dusty face " as the animals plodded steadily on. In oval above: British troops on the march through a dusty desert way in Mesopotamia.

engineering works in Lower Mesopotamia, the new riverside railway line, and the comparative abundance of engined river-craft made the British commander master of the situation. For he enjoyed the advantage of a central position, with interior lines, against the three Turkish forces about him, by the Persian frontier northward, the Tigris river-head north-westward, and the Euphrates river-head westward. He could suddenly concentrate in superior force against separated enemy divisions, although the Turks generally outnumbered his men. Often he was able to anticipate the movements of the German strategist and so quash them that Enver Pasha and the Young Turk camarilla refused at last to allow Falkenhayn to waste their forces alike in Palestine and in Mesopotamia.

British leap on Ramadiya   Such was the superiority of British means of movement that, even in the most terrible period of summer heat, Sir Frederick Stanley Maude could speed his forces across the desert in a surprising way. On July 8th, 1917, for example, he made a leap up the Euphrates from Feluja, and, at a distance of twelve miles from his outpost line, arrived within striking distance of the important Turkish entrenchments at Ramadiya. In spite of the fact that a heat wave of unexpected intensity made the desert intolerable, an Indo-British attacking column traversed the flaming wilderness and engaged the enemy.

In ordinary circumstances no troops could have survived the long, quick march; but the Indo-British force moved in an extraordinary way, being partly transported by motor-vans and motor-lorries, and provided with special

salt lake of Habbaniya. About three miles behind this formidable ridge position the German engineers with the Turkish force had constructed a large crescent of main entrenchments, extending about a mile round Ramadiya. The eastern front was protected by the valley canal of the Euphrates, while the southern front was still more strongly reinforced by a line of large sand-dunes in which machine-gun positions had been constructed.

ON A BAGDAD TRAMWAY ROUTE.
Western locomotion adapted to Eastern ways. Indian troops, travelling on small horse-drawn tramcars in the neighbourhood of Bagdad, passing a compatriot sentry standing at ease at the wayside.

In so flat a country as the river lands of Mesopotamia the sixty-foot altitude of Mushaid Ridge was of great observation value. It was worth more than a mountain would have been in Europe, and, after the abortive British surprise attack of July, the German and Turkish officers had carefully measured and marked all the artillery ranges on and about their advanced ridge position.

General Brooking, however, had made all allowances for the enemy's increase of strength in ground and men. He bridged the Euphrates and openly prepared an attack upon the enemy's river-line in the morning of September 26th. In the evening, however, the two infantry columns and the cavalry made a night march around the southern flank of the ridge. A small infantry force worked along the northern edge of Habbaniya Lake in the darkness, and before day broke these enterprising troops captured the dam across the valley canal, which was passable by all arms, and occupied the ground behind the ridge.

General Brooking's fine manœuvre

Then, at dawn on September 28th, General Brooking executed as fine a manœuvre as Marlborough did at Ramillies, or Hindenburg at Tannenberg. Comparatively small in scale as the battle was, it was of classical perfection. As soon as the light was clear he threw a fierce barrage upon the outflanked ridge. The enemy commander withdrew his infantry, and in turn lashed the ridge of sand with a tempest of shrapnel, expecting to catch the storming waves of British and Indian troops.

But these troops did not attack; they manœuvred. The cavalry rode from the right flank to the left, crossed the conquered dam, and pushed across a canal running behind Ramadiya, reached the road to Aleppo in the afternoon, and occupied a line of dunes stretching to the riverside, right in the rear of the trapped Turkish army.

While this astonishing movement was beginning, the left infantry column closed southward upon the enemy with magnificent and distracting vigour. The Dorsets and the 5th Gurkhas especially distinguished themselves in the thrust into the enemy's southern front. While the Turks were furiously but vainly fighting against this left Indo-British column, General Brooking again made a great change in his dispositions. He swung his right column away from the Euphrates and around the scene of action, and again struck the enemy on his southern flank, by a line of dunes.

As the two Indo-British columns worked forward and round the enemy, across the bare, coverless stretch of sand to the low pebbly rises, the enemy artillerymen swept the ground with intense flanking fire, while hostile riflemen and machine-gunners poured a frontal rain of bullets upon the attacking waves. Nevertheless, the British and Indian soldiers gallantly won to the high ground, and there dug themselves in. When night fell, the enemy was held down from the river and along the southern edge of the desert, and cut off from all retreat by the Aleppo road. He had no bridges to enable him to escape to the other side of the Euphrates, and he would not have gained anything had he attemped flight in this direction.

Enveloped Turkish troops surrender

Ahmed Bey, who commanded the enveloped force, had fought the British along the Euphrates since the action at Shaiba, in March, 1915. His Turkish troops were reduced to a few thousands by disease and battle. Many Bedouins, who had answered the call of the Ottoman Khalif, had either gone over to the more victorious of the combatants or retired into the waterless sands, where they knew of secret oases in the dry stream beds, by which they could live undisturbed by Turk or Briton, and sally out to plunder the side that lost. They were the supreme terror for all exhausted fugitive remnants of a broken army.

Ahmed Bey recognised that his wasted troops were likely to become the prey of these human vultures, and in the night of September 28th he made an effort to escape from the British net as commander of an organised retreat. He moved his men from the east and south toward the western road to Aleppo, and about three o'clock in the morning of September 29th endeavoured to break out between the Euphrates and the sandhills held by the Indo-British cavalry. No Turks, however, got closer than fifty yards to the entrenched horsemen. They were caught by shrapnel gusts from the Horse Artillery, raked by Hotchkiss fire, and finally broken, just before dawn, by the Hussars and a squadron of Indian cavalry.

As soon as the sky lightened, General Brooking put an end to the convulsive movements of the trapped enemy by launching the 39th Garhwalis and the 90th Punjabis from the southern front. The Garhwalis stormed the canal bridge-head by the Aleppo road, while the men of the Punjab drove into Ramadiya. The Indo-British cavalry, watching the action from the western dunes, saw the Turks advance in a mass against the Indian battalions, and expected a wild struggle.

To their amazement the Turkish guns became silent and white flags went up from the hostile multitude. It was a general surrender of Ahmed Bey and his division. Three thousand two hundred and sixty-five unwounded officers and men were taken, with thirteen guns, two steam launches, several miles of railway tracks, parts of five unassembled engines, and a large quantity of equipment. Only a score of Turkish infantrymen, with a small detachment of cavalry, managed to escape by swimming the Euphrates.

The victory of Ramadiya was of more importance than the number of troops engaged in the action appeared to indicate. The smallness of these forces was due to difficulties of desert transport, and the forces represented the outstretched power of the opposing Empires at a critical point in the Mesopotamian river system. Ramadiya was Falkenhayn's proposed jumping-off place for a return swoop on Bagdad. It was also a central place from which the desert tribes could be controlled, and the blockade enforced against the Turks by stopping supplies from the Lower Euphrates from reaching them.

Reclaiming the Garden of Eden

Finally, the possession of Ramadiya and its canals was necessary to the development of the great Euphrates irrigation scheme, which, neglected by the Turks, became the glory of the new conquerors of Mesopotamia. Hundreds of disused canals were cleared and connected with the new irrigation works by the Shatt-el-Hilla, and three hundred thousand acres were rapidly brought under cultivation, with the promise of the greatest harvest since the days of Haroun al-Raschid. The land by the Shatt-el-Hindiya was also irrigated. Vast quantities of seed grain were planted in the newly-watered territory, and the agricultural renaissance of the birthplace of civilisation filled Lower Mesopotamia with a strange spirit of energy and confidence.

Friendly Kurds, descendants perhaps of the Assyrians, secretly opened negotiations with the redeemers of the parched and desolate ruins of Eden, begging Sir Frederick Stanley Maude to invade their country and liberate them from the Ottoman. Across the Persian marches came a wilder cry for help, from tribesmen wasted by the invading Turk and reduced to utter famine amid their burnt and plundered homes. All old rumours of British achievements in food production and orderly government in India and Egypt were enlarged into magnificent legends when the tribesmen and borderers heard of the explosion of the islanders' creative energy and skill in the wilderness of Irak.

A conqueror coming with a horn of natural plenty into one of the great deserts of the world, and spreading fields of green wealth over the sands he passed, was a marvel of marvels in the Orient. No longer did the patient East bow down in deep disdain when the invading legions

Formal entry of the British troops under General Maude into Bagdad, March 11th, 1917.

Bagdad under the British Flag: Indian troops and mule transport passing along Khalil Road.

Turkish soldiers escorted as prisoners through Bagdad under the gaze of the emancipated populace.

Indian troops of the victorious army marching along a street in process of reconstruction.

Crowds of natives thronging a Bagdad thoroughfare to watch the British troops march by.

Representatives of Britain's power near Bagdad Municipal Offices.

Live meat rations and transport crossing the Diala River.

Indian camel transport crossing a pontoon bridge at Bagdad.

Indian cavalry patrol occupying Khanikin, north-east of Bagdad.

thundered by, for it seemed as though the dim old tradition of the return of the golden age was being actually realised.

The mosquito-bitten, fly-tormented, thirsty British soldier, suffering from prickly heat, did not regard himself as a hero ; yet the work he did at Samarra, Shinaflyah, Hilla, Feluja, and many other places swiftly eclipsed all that accomplished by hundreds of conquering forces between the age of Sargon and the age of Alexander. Inheriting the genius of the race that gave mankind the gigantic powers of steam, the Briton in Mesopotamia was really what the Teuton vainly pretended to be—the superman.

He outflew the bird with his aeroplane, he outspeeded the Arab racehorse with his motor-car, and there was a legend, brought by folk from the Persian Gulf, that he could outswim any fish and move through the depths of the sea. He overwhelmed the Bedouin by the exhibition of powers exceeding those of all magicians in "The Arabian Nights' Entertainment"; and, after commanding awe, elicited, if not downright affection, at least that kind of gratitude consisting in a lively sense of favours to come. Moreover, quite a considerable number of troops in the Ottoman forces almost loved the Briton; and, though good fighting men themselves, rather enjoyed an honourable opportunity of surrendering to him. Proud when victorious, yet rather pleased when captured, they blamed Enver Pasha and the Young Turks for having separated them from their old and esteemed ally and placed them under the control of the irritating German.

It was largely due to this prevailing frame of mind among the Ottoman soldiery that the Turk, when outmanœuvred, surrendered in multitudes. He could not be made to fight against the Briton with the racial and religious ardour with which he battled against the Russian. This was one of the reasons why the **Pro-British feeling among the Turks** Germanic controllers of the Turkish armies were unable fully and immediately to profit by the melting away of the Russian army of the Caucasus during the sinister Bolshevist régime.

The Turks were not unwilling to reoccupy the Caucasian territory lost in former wars ; and, when there, it was fairly easy to move them by stages towards Persia and the northern overland route to India. But it was very difficult for either General von Falkenhayn or his successor, General von Liman Sanders, to arrange for a strong, direct reconcentration of the Ottoman forces, on strict strategic lines, against the Indo-British Army around Bagdad.

There was, however, always a strong possibility that the German commander of the Turks would try to retrieve the disasters on his Palestine and Euphrates fronts, by drawing a considerable part of the eastern Ottoman army down through Mosul for a direct resumption of the Bagdad battle along the Tigris. In the Jebel Hamrin, a long range of low hills running from the Diala River to the Lesser Zab River, the enemy had a screen behind which he could manœuvre, threatening the northern British flank. On October 16th, 1917, there was begun a converging British movement of liberation from this menace, and, two days afterwards, Deli Abbas was taken, and the Turks were outflanked by a night march. They would not stand to battle, and slipped away across the river along the northern road to Kara Tepe, giving Sir Frederick Stanley Maude all the important ground at remarkably little cost of life.

While the British commander was obtaining control of the Diala Gorge, which was the northern gate of invasion of the fertile Bagdad region, the Eighteenth Turkish Army Corps, on the Tigris at Tekrit, endeavoured to relieve the British pressure against the northern hostile force by a counter-movement down the river. The Turks advanced some twenty miles along the waterway, cautiously entrenching at Dur and Huveslat, and extended within striking distance of the Indo-British outpost. But it was not they who struck. General Maude made a series of peculiar leaps upon them that carried him to Tekrit.

He began by a nocturnal surprise swoop on Huveslat on October 24th, but drew back to his own base at Samarra. At the end of a week of quietness, when the enemy reckoned the British were content with having made a counter-demonstration, another remarkable night march again ended in a staggering Turkish defeat. At dusk, on November 1st, two Indo-British columns concentrated at Samarra, and set out on both sides of the river in the darkness. There were no natural landmarks to guide them, but by good scouting on the part of the advanced guards, and fine endurance on the part of the main forces, twenty miles of obscure, difficult country was covered by all arms by four o'clock in the morning of November 2nd.

Against the stealthy manner of approach of the special scouting patrols the Turkish pickets were powerless. They were surprised **Dur carried by assault** and slain. The enemy's main position was carried by assault, under a British barrage from field-artillery that supported the advance throughout, and by ten o'clock in the morning the Turks were fleeing from Dur, having been turned out of their very strong position by an enveloping movement.

Protected by a rearguard, the enemy fell back on Tekrit, the birthplace of Saladin, transformed into a fortified modern camp of great strength. The mediæval town rose from the river on bold bluffs, and from its ruins, roofs, and domes enjoyed wide prospect over the alluvial plain. Round the town enemy engineers had designed a belt of lines, seven miles long, with both ends resting on the high river banks. Kut was not comparable in strength with Tekrit, and the commander of the two Turkish divisions operating on the Tigris fancied he could beat off the British attack.

It was, however, with extraordinary ease that the home of Saladin was stormed by the new Cœurs de Lion. The infantry opened the assault in the morning of November 5th, after another night march from Dur. First, the enemy's centre was drawn in by a splendid dashing advance over 1,200 yards of ground. Then, in the afternoon, a Scottish force, with some sturdy Indian troops, slowly walked over 700 yards of flat plain on the enemy's left, screened only by a barrage from the sweeping fire of the defence.

When the Scotsmen halted, seventy yards from the Turkish line, for their own barrage to lift, the Turks saw the familiar tartan, and scrambled over the parados. But the Scotsmen would not let them flee, and, risking the last seconds of the barrage, doubled with the bayonet into the great entrenchment, taking most of the garrison captive, and further thinning out with rifle and machine-gun fire those that fled into the moving curtain of British shrapnel.

The second line of the Tekrit defences was rapidly reached and taken ; then, on the extreme left, where dismounted horsemen had been containing the enemy and keeping down his fire, **British troops enter Tekrit** the Hussars and a squadron of Indian Lancers completed the panic in Tekrit. They jumped the trenches, and, with the point, charged the flank of the Turkish masses that were retreating in confusion before the infantry. For a thousand yards, through the scattering hostile brigades, the Hussars and Lancers rode, until they were swept at close range by machine-gun and field-gun fire. Wheeling about, the cavalrymen dismounted and covered their withdrawal.

The Turkish right was broken, and rolled back on the river under heavy fire from the British centre. Over the town, smoking with the explosions of British shell, abruptly rose columns of denser fume, indicating the firing of hostile ammunition and supply dumps. Late in the afternoon the victorious force delivered another thrust, and entered Tekrit with slight loss and little opposition, while the

TRENCH-MORTAR CORNER IN THE DESERT LINES.
In the flaming wilderness of Upper Mesopotamia existence in the trenches would have been intolerable but for the perfect transport system with special supplies of ice and water.

and tilling between battles, General Maude was chiefly anxious to place a series of wide barriers between the enemy and his own civilising, busy forces camped upon the vast tract of good earth which he had just recovered from ruin and savagery. In particular, he wanted all the rampart of hills of the Jebel Hamrin to secure the outer defences of Bagdad, and fully control the head-works of the canal watering a considerable and rich part of the country.

As soon, therefore, as he had completely disorganised the Ottoman forces on the Tigris, he withdrew towards Bagdad, and began to make a new concentration northward along the Diala. But, by a strangely unhappy

Turks were retreating up the river. When day broke, white flags fluttered from every roof, and the townspeople welcomed the conquerors with joy.

Their joy was natural but short-lived. They looked forward to a life of plenty and prosperity, during which they would be able to sell their produce to the army, instead of having it seized in Turkish fashion. Order and commerce, they thought, would at once begin to obtain and flourish in Tekrit as in Bagdad. Sir Frederick Stanley Maude, however, arranged matters otherwise by making a complete withdrawal to Samarra as suddenly as he had made his advance.

The Tekrit position was too dangerous to hold at a time when the Turks were free to move their eastern forces from the Caucasus to the Upper Tigris. Tekrit was open to flanking rear attack from the north-western part of the Jebel Hamrin hill screen, as well as to frontal assault down the river. All that the British commander had designed was to protect his river-line by destroying the enemy's base of operations. When this measure of active

Death of Sir Stanley Maude

defence had been admirably carried out, the Indo-British columns retired to their river-head at Samarra, with the gratifying feeling that they had placed another serious obstacle across Falkenhayn's route to Bagdad and the Persian Gulf.

The situation on the Tigris and Euphrates then was one of apparent military stalemate—and political success on the British side. The main opposing forces were too far apart for the delivery of any rapid blow, and all preparations made for the march of a Turco-German army from Aleppo to Bagdad, which should have taken place at this time, according to Falkenhayn's scheme, ended merely in a slow trickle of reinforcements and additional supplies towards the enemy's broken Euphrates river-head.

The army of Mesopotamia had no occasion to run into risks for the sake of fighting. Its strength had been nicely proportioned to its task of containing the Turks in the river-threaded wilderness; while the army of Egypt, with shorter and more ample communications and larger forces, broke the enemy's principal divisions in Palestine.

Like the leader of a great colonising Roman army, fighting for good cornland against a fringe of barbarians,

INDIAN SAPPERS LAYING TELEPHONE WIRES.
Communications were not easily maintained in Mesopotamia: On one occasion a blinding sandstorm rendered visual signalling impossible, and put all the land wires and wireless instruments out of action.

stroke, General Maude died of cholera on November 18th, 1917, with all his plans for the salvation and reconstruction of Mesopotamia only half executed. Enemy agents had made several frustrated attempts to assassinate the great British conqueror, who was carrying out in the desert of the great rivers a work larger than that accomplished by Lord Kitchener in the wastes of the Upper Nile.

The prestige of Sir Frederick Stanley Maude had become a valuable element in the moral power his country exercised over the stretch of troubled Moslem lands between Afghanistan and Arabia. The romance of his avenging victory at Kut, the glory of his swift conquest of the imposing city of Bagdad, and the later series of shattering blows he dealt the Ottoman, with all the magnificent and rapid engineering and irrigation work executed by his troops, made him a figure of wonderful influence. In effect he succeeded—if he did not indeed surpass—Lord Kitchener as an impressive, dazzling incarnation of British genius in the Orient.

Great, therefore, was the loss to his men and his country when he perished, at the prime of his power, through a graceful act of courtesy towards a native of Bagdad. During a simple school ceremony he was offered a cup of tea, into which some cholera-infected milk seems to have been poured. Rather than appear unbending, Sir Frederick took the cup and drank, and, not having been inoculated against the disease, he died with appalling suddenness.

His able lieutenant, Lieutenant-General Sir William R. Marshall, succeeded to the command of the forces in Mesopotamia, being marked out for the position by the considered judgment of his late chief and the record of his achievements.

A Sherwood Forester officer, Sir William had learned the art of warfare on the Indian frontier,

IMMEMORIAL MUSIC IN THE EAST.
Indian troops on their way to the trenches led by their bagpipes—modern equivalents of the dulcimers whose strains rang in the province of Babylon when Nebuchadnezzar was king.

CURIOSITY TEMPERED BY CAUTION.
British Staff officers examining types of bombs left behind by the Turks after one of the defeats they suffered at the hands of the British in their advance north of Bagdad.

and earned a lieutenant-colonelcy in the South African campaign. He had commanded a brigade in France in January, 1915, so successfully that in five months he was given a division, arriving at last in Mesopotamia, after the retreat of General Townshend, at the head of an army corps. His coolness and decision, his bold methods and rapid execution, were mentioned and praised by General Maude.

Sir William Marshall promptly set his troops moving to cheer their spirits by fighting activity and forestall the enemy's manœuvres. He sent Sir R. Egerton northward to force the passages of the Diala and Nahrin Rivers, in the Jebel Hamrin range, and capture the passes; while an independent cavalry column worked up the Adhaim River towards the centre of the long stretch of hills, threatening to get on the flank of the Turks.

The operations began towards the end of November, 1917, when a Russian detachment, unaffected by Bolshevism, was able to give valuable help in strengthening the British right flank. Once more the Turks were manœuvred out of hill positions of great natural strength, being forced

back to Kifri by December 5th. The victorious troops made another leap forward, destroyed all enemy stores in a wide belt of country, and then, as at Tekrit, drew back towards their base.

This, however, was at last fixed along the line that General Maude had endeavoured to secure in April, 1917, when his cavalry failed to reach it through lack of water. The passes of the mountain range were retained and fortified, a bridge-head was constructed at Kizil Robat, and Khanikin (near the Persian frontier) was occupied, together with the Pass of Takigirra. Winter weather conditions on the Persian highlands prevented any further operations on a large scale there. Bad roads needed repairing, the Turk-ravaged, perishing mountaineers required food; so that the main work of the victorious force consisted in fighting the famine among the Persians and borderers by bringing up some of the produce of the newly-irrigated tracts between the great rivers. The conflict with the Turkish divisions that had fled to Kifri had to be postponed until the spring of 1918.

Storm centre shifts westward

One reason for this was that the half-demoralised Kifri force was no longer a menace to the northern flank of Bagdad, while the westerly river-head, at Ramadiya on the Euphrates, was again becoming a storm centre. Throughout early winter the successor to Ahmed Bey, established by the bitumen fields of Hit, received reinforcements and huge quantities of artillery and rifle ammunition.

Neither the newly-arriving infantry nor the new gunners were in number proportionate to the munitions stacked in their widespread encampments. The fresh troops appear to have been only the advanced guard of the long-delayed host of desert campaigners. At any rate, they were insufficient to guard the vast accumulation of military stores from the characteristic leaping attack of the Indo-British Euphrates columns.

The new Turkish commander endeavoured to avoid the fate of his predecessor by splitting up his forces. He kept his main strength fifteen miles upstream from Hit, and when this malodorous, dirty village—hung with the heavy smoke of pitch-fires, and leprous with its sulphur marshes—was approached by British patrols on the

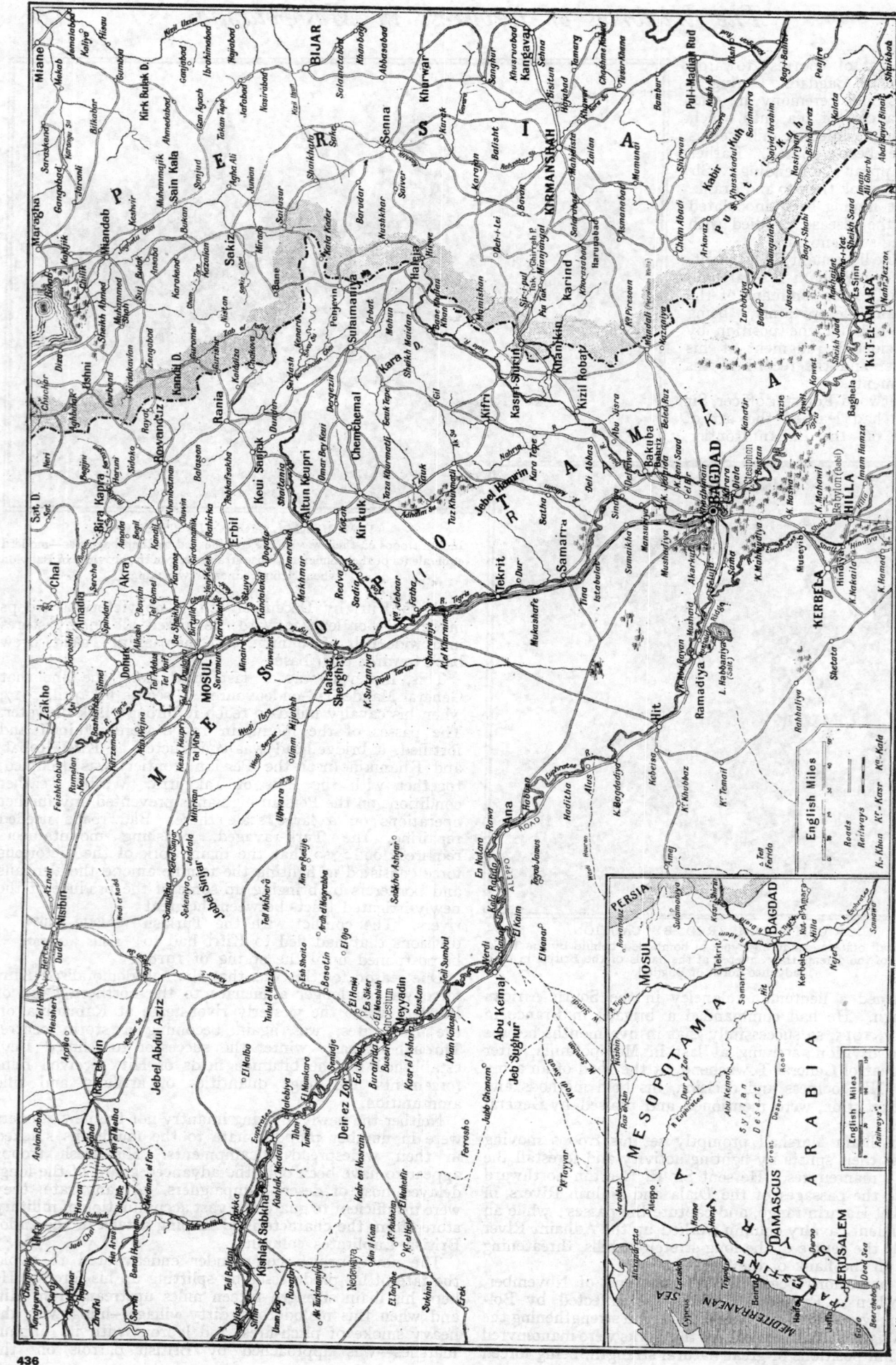

UPPER MESOPOTAMIA, WITH KEY MAP SHOWING THE INTER-RELATION OF THE OPERATIONS IN MESOPOTAMIA AND PALESTINE.

morning of March 9th, 1918, they entered the legendary mouth to the infernal regions without opposition.

Both the rearguard and main body of the Turkish army of the Euphrates were retreating at high speed to Khan Bagdadiya, along a road climbing the barren hills like a staircase cut out of rock. So bad was the road that, at the end of the twenty-two-mile march, the enemy commander rashly reckoned he could stay a while at Bagdadiya village. His troops had been severely shaken by a strong aeroplane pursuit. The British airmen bombed and machine-gunned the long hostile column at heights varying from two thousand five hundred to only one hundred feet, inflicting heavy casualties on the dense ranks and filling many troops with panic.

Probably it was necessary for the enemy commander to attempt to make a stand, in order to revive the spirit of his men as well as to defend the great preparations for the proposed Turco-German campaign. The British general seemed rather slow in continuing his operations, in spite of the fact that Sir William Marshall's orders were that the enemy should be driven as hard and as far as possible. The apparent delay, however, veiled a fortnight of intense and far-reaching preparation in attack and pursuit.

When, on March 26th, 1918, the British and Indian infantry moved forward in waves of assault, under cover of machine-guns and artillery, victory had been organised. As at Ramadiya, the Indo-British cavalry was used as an enveloping wing. The troopers made a long, arduous detour through the desert, and, arriving right across the path of retreat of the Turks, entrenched again on the caravan road to Aleppo, along a stony valley where many ancient battles had been fought.

It may seem extraordinary that the new Turkish army of the Euphrates should have allowed itself to be trapped and destroyed by practically the same simple manœuvre General Brooking used against the former Turkish army on the same river. The explanation was **Triumph of** that, though the manœuvre was simple **armoured cars** in theory, it was so immensely difficult in practice on this occasion as to seem quite impossible to the Turkish general. The journey through the horrible wilderness was a bitter ordeal, yet not only did the cavalrymen bring their horses through it, clean round the enemy's lines to the water's edge upstream, but a strong squadron of armoured motor-cars succeeded in getting over the stony waste on to the Turkish rear.

The employment of armoured cars in desert warfare had been magnificently illustrated by the Duke of Westminster's squadron in the pursuit and final action with the Senussi army on the Egyptian frontier in 1916. It had taken a considerable time for the British forces in Mesopotamia to find a way of using a modern flying column of this kind with complete effect. But at Khan Bagdadiya, in 1918, the new chariots of war, racing over the rough ground where the ancient Assyrian charioteers manœuvred into battle, achieved a victory of a specially brilliant kind.

The course of the action proceeded on the lines of the Ramadiya encirclement. The stubborn Indo-British infantry assailed the enemy's left front, and by the evening took the village. Thereupon the Turkish commander frenziedly concentrated in the darkness on his right, and at midnight tried to break through the cavalry-held line by the Aleppo road. Losing more than a thousand prisoners, as well as many men put out of action, the remnants of the Ottoman force trailed upstream for twenty-two miles to Haditha, where a ruined bridge partly connected a castled island in the stream with both banks.

Fierce and close behind the fugitives came the pursuers. Haditha fell on March 27th, and the Turks continued their flight along the dreary, monotonous river-line, patched with mud-built farmsteads, with occasional villages in palm-groves, set, for security against Bedouin raids, on

islands in midstream. There was no escape, under the new conditions of British warfare, and General Maude's terrifying chase of the enemy between Kut and Bagdad was wildly surpassed.

For a distance of one hundred and thirty miles the pursuit continued at a marvellous pace. When the British and Indian infantry tired, the troopers rode down the Turks. When all the horse were exhausted, the armoured cars pressed onward, belting with machine-guns through every rearguard, overtaking distant detachments guarding the river route against Bedouin raiders, and sweeping all scattered bodies and parties of stragglers into the net of victory.

INDIAN CAVALRY ENTERING KHANIKIN.
Crowds of Kurds watching the entry of Indian troops of General Marshall's army into Khanikin. The town of Khanikin was near the Persian border, about ninety miles north-east of Bagdad.

Only when no formed bodies of the enemy were seen from aeroplanes to be left within striking distance of the armoured cars, that reached a point seventy-three miles above Ana, were the remarkable operations of the flying column stopped. The cars brought the armies of Mesopotamia and Egypt within three hundred miles of each other and, approaching the great desert road running from the Euphrates by Palmyra to Damascus, opened for a transient glimpse a vista of possibilities of linked, sweeping action.

Shadowy at the time this great menace was. Yet even the shadow of it shook the Germanic control of the Ottoman power by filling the leaders of the Young Turk party with strange foreboding. **Lurking menace** Falkenhayn vanished; German troops **of Arab hate** were hastily moved down towards the Jordan and the railway lines to Arabia, to counter the daring raids of Sir Edmund Allenby's troopers and the Arab forces distantly co-operating with them.

In the desert was a grave, hidden danger to the Turco-Germanic league, against which Ottoman and Teuton had long been obscurely yet energetically striving. The source of this danger was in the region through which the armoured-car squadron raced with so amazingly spectacular and practical effects. Between the Tigris and Euphrates, above Bagdad and Hit, was the territory of the Shammar Arabs, the ruling sheikh of whom was kinsman to the Shammar princes of Nejd. Before the war the Shammar sheikh shared with the Aneza sheikh the lordship of Mesopotamia, and regarded the Ottoman with smouldering hate.

In Western Arabia the King of the Hedjaz, with a national army, had, for a distance of 800 miles, cleared the Red Sea coast of Turks, broken the enemy's military railway, and advanced northward to the Dead Sea, almost getting in touch with Sir Edmund Allenby's raiding patrols. The Turks had lost 40,000 troops and one hundred guns in defeats by the Arab army. In Eastern Arabia the larger part of Nejd had won to independence and become allied to Great Britain and France, and there was profound unrest in the tracts of country over which the Ottoman still actively exercised dominion.

It had been hoped, when Sir Archibald Murray first attacked the Southern Palestine front at Gaza, that the

AT BAGDAD RAILWAY-STATION.
A train with British soldiers at Bagdad —one terminus of the line with which the Germans had hoped to link Berlin and Bagdad.

WAYSIDE STATION IN THE DESERT.
Railway-station, which had been built as a fort, on the Mesopotamian section of the Berlin-Bagdad Railway. When the British captured Bagdad in March, 1917, they secured also a substantial section of this line.

Shammar, Aneza, and other tribesmen would co-operate by a swoop upon Eastern Palestine. The Turk and Teuton, however, cleverly managed to rally the northern Shammar Arabs against their southern kinsmen, thereby wrecking the general scheme for a grand Arab movement. The Aneza, like the neighbouring powerful tribe of Jebur, could not be induced to show much active hostility to the Allies, but they were kept at least neutral by handsome bribes and temporary marketing advantages offered them in traffic with hungry Turkish armies on either side of their deserts.

Being economically· dependent upon Palestine and Mesopotamia, the wandering Bedouins of the north were doubtful of the success of the Allies,

Dash towards the Persian frontier and disinclined to provoke the Turks, whose strength at Aleppo and elsewhere was displayed to them. But the marvellous rush of Sir William Marshall's advance force up the Euphrates, carried British arms victoriously in the midst of the black tents of the multitudinous Shammar and Aneza tribes at the critical period of springtime, when the great annual tribal gatherings were being held between Bagdad and Hit, Tekrit, and the Damascus road.

Thus, from the enemy's point of view, there were serious possibilities of a northern Arab rising, consequent upon

the second overwhelming disaster to the Ottoman forces on the Euphrates front. Everything tended to excite the predatory passion of the Bedouins, and lead them to harass Turkish outposts and advanced lines of communication, while the great spoil taken by the British offered a means of providing modern armament to the descendants of the Saracens. The Turkish prisoners taken in the Khan Bagdadiya operations numbered 5,232 officers and men, including the commander and staff of the 50th Division. Fourteen guns, fifty machine-guns, thousands of rifles, with all the superabundant ammunition forwarded for the intended march on Bagdad, fell into the hands of the victors.

As this great material and moral success was brought to a close early in April, 1918, immediate preparations were made by Sir William Marshall for another stroke of similar weight against the distant, separated Turkish right wing, extending near the Persian frontier. Between the towns of Kifri and Kirkuk, behind the half-won range of Jebel Hamrin, the enemy's forces were scattered in a loose and feeble manner. If any Teutonic strategist controlled the distribution of Turkish troops there, he was surprised amid some incomplete paper scheme that was suddenly burnt up in the flame of defeat.

The new operations began towards the end of April, 1918, at a time when the crops were ripening in one of the most fruitful regions of supply in Mesopotamia. Yet again the Indo-British cavalry —surely one of the best mobile forces ever employed in large strategic movements. —completely took the enemy by surprise by the unparalleled sweep of its enveloping ride.

The Turks at Kifri expected the attacking horse to cross the Jebel Hamrin Pass in their rear, and they therefore hastily evacuated the town in the morning of April 27th, 1918. But this did not save them. The tireless and swift cavalry were making a far wider movement designed to close upon the retreating force at Tuz Khurmatli, on the road to Kirkuk. When the Turks were still in Kifri, the Indo-British horse, with no support within twenty miles, arrived within six miles of the trapping place. A Turkish detachment, guarding communications, endeavoured to escape, but was caught in a crescent of charging sabres, above which aerial machine-gunners operated, and very few escaped to the hills, after one hundred and fifty had been killed and five hundred and thirty-eight captured.

In the meantime four other columns of attack pressed the main enemy's force and shepherded it out of Kifri, Ain Faris, and Chaman Keupri, towards the appointed place of doom. In these preliminary operations two hostile battalions broke out of the net and took to the hills, only to be caught and disarmed by the Kurds,

Barge in process of construction by the British Inland Water Transport Service for navigation on the Tigris, on whose waterway the traffic increased enormously when the British conquerors took in hand the reconstruction and development of the occupied towns.

Busy scene at an Inland Water Transport dockyard constructed on the foreshore of the Tigris to facilitate the development of the natural resources of Mesopotamia, which was part of the Imperial work energetically begun by the conqueror, Sir Frederick Stanley Maude.

DEVELOPMENT OF WATER-BORNE TRANSPORT IN MESOPOTAMIA UNDER THE BRITISH.

THE BURIAL OF SIR STANLEY MAUDE.
The flag-draped coffin containing the body of General Sir Frederick Stanley Maude, followed by his mourning comrades, passing into the cemetery at Bagdad through lines of British and Indian troops.

and a fresh battalion from the Kirkuk road entered the battle.

On April 29th the net was closed around the 2nd Turkish Division that had entrenched along the stream by Tuz Khurmatli. Lancashire troops, working against short-range artillery fire and machine-gun barrage, broke into the enemy's right flank and compelled him to abandon Tuz. Then upon the rear of the flying masses thundered the cavalry, a troop of Hussars under a subaltern riding down a hostile machine-gun party, entrenched on a hill, that endeavoured to check the pursuit.

With very slight loss on the British side the battle was won in three hours, leaving only fugitive remnants of Turks to be overtaken on the Kirkuk road. The

WHERE A GREAT WARRIOR RESTS.
Grave of General Sir Frederick Stanley Maude, conqueror of Bagdad, in the British military cemetery outside the town with whose old historic name his name has become imperishably connected.

pursuit was again conducted at extraordinary pace over a remarkable distance until a hundred miles had been covered, Kirkuk and Altun Keupri being taken, and the Lesser Zab River crossed.

Along the Tigris, Tekrit was again captured, and the river advance was continued for another forty-five miles to Fatha, near the junction of the Lesser Zab and main river.

Then Sir William Marshall drew his chasing force slowly backward, leaving Altun Keupri and Kirkuk to the enemy, and concentrating about the Tuz region, where he had taken 3,000

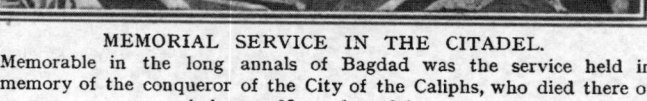

MEMORIAL SERVICE IN THE CITADEL.
Memorable in the long annals of Bagdad was the service held in memory of the conqueror of the City of the Caliphs, who died there of cholera on November 18th, 1917.

prisoners, sixteen guns, twenty-eight machine-guns, and large military stores.

The five victorious northern Indo-British columns opened negotiations with the Kurds, chafing under Ottoman extortion, at the time when the equally victorious western columns were in communication with the strong Bedouin tribes of the Middle Euphrates. The general situation, however, was of exceeding complexity, being produced by a tangle of racial, economic, military, and social forces that often worked in obscure ways.

On the surface the position of the British armies was promising. Sir William Marshall had profited to the utmost by the local weakness of the Turks on the Tigris and Euphrates, and had won all the room he immediately required about **General results** Bagdad and Hit. He had been helped **of the campaign** awhile by the Armenian rising at Erzerum, and afterwards by the desire of the Ottoman forces in the Caucasus to exploit the bankruptcy of Russia by an advance through Kars.

The campaign conducted by General Maude and General Marshall in an unbroken succession of brilliant victories had transformed Mesopotamia from the darkest into the brightest of the fields of war of the Grand Alliance. Yet the defection of war-weary Russia laid a heavy burden upon the British forces in the Middle East. The decaying Ottoman Empire, with its medley of discontented subject races, drew new strength from sources of ancient Turcoman life across the vanished Russian frontier. There were strange, dramatic possibilities on either side when, in the summer heat of the desert, operations slackened again between the rivers running between a dead world, of which scarcely the ruins were visible, and a new world, of which only the promise of existence could be seen.

CHAPTER CCXLVIII.

THE TERRIBLE PROGRESS IN BATTLE MACHINERY.

By Edward Wright.

Teutonic Superiority in First Reorganisation Period—Fire-Extinguisher Becomes a Flame-Projector—Lesson of Hohenzollern Redoubt Action—Mr. Hale's Rifle-Grenade—Sir Wilfred Stokes and the Marvellous Stokes Gun—How the Lewis Gun Contributed to British Victories—German Commanders Plead for Light Machine-Gun—Revival of Body Armour—Colossal Industry and Ingenuity of Hostile Trench Fortifications—Hindenburg Adopts British System of Fieldworks—Strange Developments in the Art of Camouflage—Hutier's Success in Concealing His Preparations for Attack—The German Mist-Making Machine and the British Fog-Box—Enemy's Superiority in Instruments of Vision—Parachute Flares and Progress in Nocturnal Reconnaissance—Grand Secrets of the French Gun and French Shell—High-Velocity Cannon : Their Advantages and Defects—Krupp's Colossal Long-Distance Gun—German Use of Poison Gas—Failure of British Gas Experiment at Loos—Blinding, Sneezing, Nausea, and Mustard Gases—High-Explosive Gas Shell Used by Enemy on March 21st, 1918—Laboured Birth of British Tank and Its Many Midwives—The Light French Tank, the Teutonic Tortoise-Like Land Cruiser, and the New, Rapid, Turreted British Car of Assault—Great Feat of French Armoured Motor-Cars in Battle of Amiens—French Inventiveness in Aeroplane Design and German Imitativeness—Marvellous Progress in Aircraft—The Pomeroy Missile and the Zeppelin—The Aerial Barrage of London.

SOME of the British triumphs of science and invention in the war were dealt with in Chapter CXXV. (Vol. 7, page 67). Later, the pace and range of the evolution of weapons of death were extraordinary. Under the continuing stimulus of the bitterest of all struggles for life, the leading industrial and scientific races of the earth produced an explosion of intellectual energy that was without a parallel.

They changed their ways of living, their methods of working, and their ways of thinking, altering the framework and spirit of their productive organisations in order to become more efficient in the manufacture of battle machinery. In times past, intellectual power of a military kind was principally displayed in improvements in training troops, in arranging conditions of battle and ways of bringing men into action. Very rare was it that a decision was obtained by the sudden introduction of some new powerful weapon.

It was, for example, by new infantry tactics that the Spaniards in the sixteenth century obtained a fiercer fire power than any other race, and almost conquered the world. It was by a more massive use of artillery that the French, towards the end of the eighteenth century, prepared the means of victory for Napoleon. About this time Great Britain, by superior

AN INSTRUMENT OF VICTORY.
Sir Wilfred Stokes with one of the rapid-fire trench-mortars of his invention and some specimens of the projectiles that were thrown by it.

seamanship, held the command of the sea against France, who was nevertheless better in shipbuilding and theory of gunnery.

The great nations kept practically equal to each other in the development of war material. Their commanders were usually men of a conservative temper, averse to any striking novelties, because of the difficulty of educating troops in untried weapons. This conservative frame of mind, however, was changed in the winter of 1914, when the effect of the German and Austrian secret preparations for the conquest of Europe was generally appreciated.

The Central Empires failed to achieve the rapid decision for which they had been working since 1909. Their military authorities had underestimated the amount of munitions required, and there was a serious shortage in shell in November, 1914, that nearly led to a German disaster. The Germans, however, recovered more quickly than their opponents from the bankruptcy of the scheme of their High Command. With remarkable energy and alertness they improvised new means of defensive warfare in the west, while constructing an extraordinary new mass of material of attack in the east. In this first period of thorough reorganisation of armament the Teuton completely surpassed his principal Continental enemies. He was not able to equal the Briton in accelerated production of naval

MAN-MADE EARTHQUAKE ON THE BATTLEFIELD.
Explosion by the Allies of a mine in a wood occupied by the enemy. preliminary to the advance of the infantry to storm and capture the shattered defences of the position.

IMPENETRABLE BARRIERS OF SMOKE AND FLAME.
Photograph taken during some experiments with French flame-throwers on the western front. The liquid, stored in a portable apparatus, ignited automatically on leaving the pipe, and was projected to a distance of about fifty feet.

material, but in the means of rapid improvement of land warfare he excelled the Frenchman for a time, and permanently eclipsed the Russian.

For trench warfare the German did little more than adapt various instruments he had already devised for special purposes in open field fighting. Some time before the war a Nuremberg fireman transformed into an incendiary device an air-pumping machine for ejecting extinguishing chemicals on a fire. His invention was accepted by German military authorities, together with the device of incendiary tablets, for use in house-to-house fighting in villages, or for quickly setting houses on fire in order to terrorise non-combatants. When trench warfare began, the flame-projector was manufactured in larger quantities, with a longer-ranged jet, and for nearly a year its horrible efficacy in burning allied troops out of advanced entrenchments of high tactical value could not be countered by any weapon or instrument possessed by the British or French. It was first employed

442

in a large way against the British at Hooge, near Ypres, in July, 1915.

In the use of trench-mortars and hand-grenades the Germans were likewise in advance of the Western Allies. They appear to have learnt from the Russians in East Prussia the value of high-explosive hand-bombs. The Russians used these missiles as weapons of open field attack against machine-gun positions in farm buildings, villages, and temporary log-built barricades. Some of the German troops under General von François, the predecessor of Hindenburg, were badly scared by the Russian method of hand-bomb attacks. Thinking that what had proved bad for them would be bad for the Briton and Frenchman, the Germans quickly introduced a hand-grenade into trench warfare in the west, where the British soldier had to fight for months with jam-pots filled with explosive, and known as " Tickler's artillery," until after many experiments he was provided with the Mills bomb, which was one of the most perfect things of its kind.

The fight for the Hohenzollern Redoubt in October, 1915, marked the triumph **Early German** of the German bomber. Gallantly, but **success with bombs** vainly, did the riflemen of the 1st and 2nd Guards' Brigades attempt to hold back the new German grenadiers. Bombers were supreme in a deep trench, and at this period the enemy possessed an undoubted technical superiority in bombing operations. It must, therefore, be allowed that in the first phase of the war the enemy showed greater power and alertness in the organisation of battle material. The British commanders in the field were full of good ideas, which were shown by their advocacy of the Madsen gun, but they do not appear to have been sufficiently supported by authorities at home until the new Ministry of Munitions began, as Mr. Lloyd George put it, "to deliver the goods."

The British War Office should not have been slack in appreciating the value of the revived weapon of the hand-bomb. For the first revival of this weapon of the old Grenadiers occurred in 1885, when the British were fighting against the Sudanese tribesmen. Afterwards, in the Manchurian campaign, the modernised hand-grenade had become an infantry weapon second in importance only to the rifle.

Filled with picric acid, trinitrotoluene, or some other high explosive, or with poison gas or incendiary chemicals, the hand-bomb was for long one of the master weapons in the parallel battle in the west. In an improved form, as a perforating grenade, the enemy tried to use it as an anti-Tank weapon during the renewal of open field fighting in the spring of 1918.

TUNNELLERS OF THE FRENCH ENGINEERS.
French miner at work blasting a mine under an enemy position on the western front. Mining was carried to extraordinary lengths in the Great War, notably by the British at Messines in 1917.

The Germans at first went too far in increasing the weight of the hand-bombs, some of which they made so heavy that it was often impossible for the thrower to fling the missile to a sufficient distance to escape himself from the danger zone. But a British engineer, Mr. Hale, had, in 1911, found in advance a remedy for this condition of things. His invention consisted of a heavy grenade, with a long stem fitting into an ordinary rifle, and furnished with a safety device that prevented the projectile from exploding accidentally. Most of the early grenades were of a simple type arranged to explode when they struck. This arrangement, however, did not make them deadly enough, and various forms of time-fuses were employed, with an increasing precision of mechanism that made a perfected missile, such as the Mills bomb a terrifying instrument of slaughter.

Evolution of the Mills bomb

The grenade was further developed in weight and range by means of improvements in trench-mortars. It swelled into the large mine, fitted with feather-like devices to steady it like an arrow, which became known as an aerial torpedo. This was used at first for smashing up front-line machine-gun positions and other strong works, until it was largely replaced in the British Army by the bombs of various types used in the Stokes gun.

This was a rapid-fire trench-mortar, remarkable both for its power and for the manner of its invention. It was designed by a civilian with no first-hand experience of the requirements of soldiers. Sir Wilfred Stokes never thought of becoming a military inventor until a relative, returning from the fighting-line during the period when the German battle machinery dominated the western field, talked about the impossibility of breaking through the opposing lines. He described all the difficulties of cutting the belts of barbed-wire that had held up Field-Marshal French's army at Neuve Chapelle and Aubers Ridge, and the depth and strength and intricacy of the German trenches, with their crossing system of machine-gun fire.

On this information Sir Wilfred devised a handy trench-gun, capable of firing large bombs as fast as they could be placed in the barrel. By good training the rate of fire was made much superior to that of the breech-loading French quick-firing gun, and as the short-range projectiles of the Stokes mortar had a far greater destructive effect than any shell from a field-gun, the power of the new weapon in favouring circumstances was tremendous. The Stokes gun became one of the great instruments of victory in the British armies, and was adopted for many purposes. It could be used as a wire breaker, as a smasher of machine-gun positions, as a trench breaker, a block-house destroyer, and as a projector of poison gas, burning oil, and incendiary chemicals.

The Stokes trench-mortar

The only serious limitation to its use was the difficulty of bringing up the heavy projectiles during an infantry advance over broken ground swept by hostile barrage fire. The gun itself was fairly mobile, but the bombs, which it could fire at the rate of forty a minute, were so heavy that it was often impossible to get them up in time to help infantry detachments which had been checked at some camouflaged concrete work. The number of men needed to work and feed a Stokes gun in a confused action

LOADING A TRENCH-HOWITZER.
British soldiers on the Balkan front engaged in loading a light trench howitzer with its heavy missile. The extensive use of bomb-throwing weapons was one of the marked features of trench warfare.

ARTIFICIAL FOG DEMONSTRATION ON THE IRIS.
An officer of the old Mersey ferry-boat Iris, that was used in the blocking up of the Zeebrugge Canal in 1918, turning on the tap to release the smoke. The smoke—or, rather, fog—screen devised by Wing-Commander Brock, was an important feature in the success of that brilliant naval feat.

of acquiring a new firearm for which great claims were put forward. Some time before the war a Danish inventor designed a machine-gun, with the weight of only fifteen pounds, which was five pounds heavier than a rifle. The new gun was really a machine-rifle, with interchangeable barrels for cooling purposes, yet it was estimated to produce a sustained fire of eighteen hundred rounds. Jamming, the common vice of the machine-gun, was impossible. The rate of fire was four hundred rounds a minute, and as the gun was almost as easy to handle as a rifle, marksmen could be taught to use it in about twelve hours, and get off a hundred rounds in the time a Hotchkiss gun was preparing to get into action. It was said that military and naval men of high practical experience maintained that two thousand men, with the improved Madsen gun, could hold up thirty-six thousand men on a limited front.

As early as May, 1915, Lord French was understood to

in the heart of the enemy's lines could often be better employed in fighting with hand-bomb, rifle, and bayonet.

As a matter of fact, when the German High Command dissolved its trench system into practically invisible zones of concealed crater positions, hidden forts of armoured concrete, tunnels, and camouflaged communication and assembly trenches, the Stokes gun declined for a time in importance, while a new variety of hand-bomb became the principal anti-block-house weapon of the British soldier. The new hand-bomb was filled with chemicals that produced a dense, suffocating smoke. When one was pitched or dropped into a " pill-box," blockhouse, cavern, or tunnel, the garrison had to come out, if they had no secret exit, to escape from the suffocating fume.

Claims for the Madsen gun

Long before the Stokes gun was accepted by the military authorities the British Army had the opportunity

have asked for Madsen guns, as a counter to the enemy's enormous increase in guns of the Maxim type, but the Army Council decided to do without the new weapon, and not until June, 1918, after strong public and Parliamentary agitation, was the question of adopting the Madsen gun seriously taken up by the military authorities at home. In the meantime the military authorities of Germany had begun to make some Madsen guns, although they also had shown some unreadiness to appreciate the new weapon at the value placed upon it by its advocates.

German commanders in the field were most anxious to obtain a lighter and handier machine-gun than their Maxim type. In 1916 General Sixt von Armin, during the First Battle of the

SUCCESSFUL INVENTIONS FOR WARFARE AT SEA.
One of the small fast French boats used in the Mediterranean, chiefly for pursuit of enemy submarines, with her torpedo-tube in position to launch a torpedo. Above : The Telemetristes, a device placed well aloft on warships to detect the sound of submerged submarines and measure their distance away.

BRANDT GRENADE-THROWER.
Grenades with stems fitted into ordinary rifles were succeeded by other devices, like the Brandt, worked by compressed air, which had a range of five hundred yards.

Somme, earnestly begged for a lighter machine-gun ; but, when he took over the defences of the Passchendaele Ridge, Armin obtained only an ordinary modification of the German Maxim.

Meanwhile, a substitute for the Danish weapon was found in the weapon designed by Colonel Lewis, of the United States Army, and vainly submitted by him to the Great Powers of Europe in the days before the war. Fortunately, the Birmingham Small Arms Company took up the Lewis gun, which consisted of a modified rifle barrel, firing cartridges from a revolving drum. The entire mechanism weighed twenty-eight and a half pounds, against the sixty-eight pounds of the Vickers gun, the twenty-eight pounds of the Hotchkiss gun, and the fifteen pounds of the Madsen gun.

Value of the Lewis gun   The sustained rate of fire of the Lewis gun was not remarkable, owing to the time lost in putting on new drums : but the handiness and lightness of the instrument made it very serviceable, especially during an advance and the organisation of the captured ground against the usual counter-attack.

There were some experienced British infantrymen who still preferred the light type of Vickers gun in all conditions of battle, because of the superior firing power and ease and range of traverse of the tripod-mounted standard British machine-gun.

The light Lewis gun became the favourite weapon of the British airman, against the Parabellum gun of German pilots and fighting observers. From the point of view of the British airman the interruption of his firing power, while replacing a used drum by a full one, was a somewhat serious but an apparently inevitable effect. He would

have completely triumphed over enemy pilots had he been able to maintain an intense stream of bullets while manœuvring above, below, and around an enemy. As it was, he often had to swerve away in order to put on a fresh drum. Nevertheless, the Lewis gun was, in the circumstances, a weapon of very considerable value. It helped the British infantry to hold back masses of the enemy in the opening phase of the war, and became one of the most important instruments of attack and defence during the long period of trench warfare.

The German machine-guns were more remarkable by their number than by their quality. During the first three years of the struggle they were, as General von Armin admitted, too heavy and cumbersome, and for some curious reason their **French and German** traverse was often limited. The ordinary **machine-guns** German machine-gunner could not swing his weapon in full circle so as to be able to fire quickly at an enemy behind him. The traverse of his gun was only about fifty degrees. The probability is that, in the case of many machine-guns which were at first an important element in the cross-firing system of German trench defence, the traverse of the gun was limited so that, if captured, it could not be readily swung round to assist in the further development of the attack. For the spring offensives of 1918, however, the Germans produced vast numbers of light machines-guns with an all-round traverse. The French machine-gun was of the air-cooled type, unlike the water-cooled type of the British and German Armies.

Automatic rifles and automatic pistols, of which the British Webley was a first-rate example, were employed by most of the combatants. The revolver was usually an officer's weapon, though sometimes used in a general way in trench combats before the hand-grenade was fully developed. The revolver,

SNIPERS' WEAPONS AND DEFENSIVE ARMOUR.
British officer giving instructions in sniping. In circle : German sniper's mask made of half-inch Krupp steel ; its great weight suggested that it was only used when the chin-piece could be rested on some support.

however, had a very serious defect. The propellant power behind its bullets was comparatively small, so that its range was limited and its projectiles could not penetrate good modern armour.

The revival of the use of armour was one of many modernisations of ancient material of warfare. The enterprising Germans, who had outraced both Great Britain and the United States in the discovery of hardened and tempered steel for armouring warships, for covering the domes of land fortresses, shielding the breech of light artillery, and other defensive purposes, seem to have been first to employ infantry armour. They devised armour-plates for covering observation places in their trench parapets, and made helmets and shields for both snipers and snipers' observers. The shield was fairly good, but the helmet had certain disadvantages, and when it was generally adopted as a shrapnel head defence in the German armies it did not prove quite as efficacious as had been expected.

Helmets of the several armies The French helmet was uncommonly beautiful in shape, and produced with remarkable celerity for common use, while the military authorities of other nations were hesitating whether to employ head armour. But in protectiveness the British shrapnel hat, with its maximum of glancing surface and its freedom from everything likely to arrest a bullet and cause it to penetrate instead of fly off, was a masterpiece of utility. After examining all existing and newly-proposed varieties of helmet, the United States authorities adopted the British design.

No body armour, light enough to be worn by infantrymen in the toil of battle, could resist the direct impact of bullets from rifles or machine-guns. Chest and back protectors, and sometimes stomach protectors, were made by private manufacturers, but at best the varieties of modern body armour were serviceable only against shrapnel, revolver bullets, shell splinters, and bayonet and lance thrusts. All military staffs experimented with them, but could not advocate any national provision of these means of protection.

The German authorities at one time furnished body armour to their advanced forces, but apparently found that the comparative protection was purchased too dearly by loss of mobile **Mobility versus** activity. Increased driving and bursting **body protection** charges in shrapnel shell, in high-explosive shell, in trench-mortar bombs and hand-bombs tended to make light protective body armour scarcely worth its weight. Generally speaking, from a national point of view there was more loss than gain if, in a long battle in which the men were worn down to the point of exhaustion, a certain amount of body protection was won at the cost of a man's strength in the closing, decisive phase of the struggle.

Men often had to fight for days without sleep, while carrying a considerable burden of weapons, ammunition, entrenching tools, water, and food. The well-balanced shrapnel hat did not, in the crisis of their physical strength, seriously aggravate their burden. Body armour, on the other hand, became an enfeebling rather than a strengthening thing. The principal metallurgists of the combatant countries tried to find some light, impenetrable alloy, but they did not succeed. The striking power of modern

EXPLOSION OF A GERMAN FOG BOMB TO OBSCURE A LARGE AREA.
Smoke fires as instruments of warfare were developed on a large scale by modern means during the Great War. Smoke screens for infantry, first employed by the British at Loos in 1915, were a feature of many of the offensives launched by both sides, and shells were manufactured with chemicals capable of spreading a thick mist over a large area for the space of a quarter of an hour or more.

chemicals was greater than the resisting power of modern steel alloys. It was reckoned that even a heavily-armoured super-Dreadnought could be sunk by thirty shells from her own guns at ordinary battle range, provided that each shell got home in a vital part.

In the British rifle penetrative power seems to have been sacrificed somewhat to rate of fire. This was one of the reasons why the enemy experimented with body armour against the British Army. It was also the reason why the Lee-Enfield was rejected by American military authorities. The American troops were provided with a rifle of greater striking power, yet it remains doubtful whether the Lee-Enfield, by reason of the abundant resources for its manufacture, should not have been preferred to the improved Springfield rifle.

In war, as in many other things, practical efficiency was often an affair of compromises. Sometimes what was best for the individual in a short point of view was not best for the Army in a long point of view. Also a superior system of defence sometimes meant an inferior system of attack. It was especially difficult to adjust individual and national interests in the matter of field fortification.

Moved by the personally sound instinct of self-preservation, in the opening of trench warfare, every soldier—except the French soldier—wanted as much shelter as possible. Turenne, in the seventeenth century, remarked that Frenchmen were bad diggers, and so they remained in the twentieth century. Neither commanders nor men thought of digging any kind of cover in August, 1914. When, in the later part of September, 1914, the French were held up by the German entrenchments, they very reluctantly took to the spade, and made trenches along the Aisne only about two feet deep. Under bitter experience the French deepened and extended their lines, but they hated mole warfare.

The German troops had been well trained in trench-digging, and when the German High Command arranged to stand on the defensive in the west while attacking in the east, it encouraged the natural burrowing

Opposing ideas in field fortification instinct of its western divisions. Under the rule of General von Falkenhayn especially all the modern arts of defensive engineering were intensively developed. General von Ludendorff continued the same course, improving the labyrinthine works of his predecessor by extraordinary tunnels and still more remarkable systems of concrete and armoured concrete forts, patterned out in zones of remarkable depth.

In colossal industry and detailed ingenuity the German system of entrenchment was unique. It was unique, however, because the Western Allies decided it would be a mistaken policy to adopt similar measures of protection. The British Army was trained to dig, and its

INTERESTED STUDENTS.
Serbian officers on a visit to the western front watching a liquid-fire demonstration.

WRESTED FROM THE HUN.
French soldier testing the weight and working of a portable German apparatus for throwing liquid fire captured on the western front.

engineers were equal to the German sappers in technical talent and organised industry. There was also abundant British Portland cement of the finest quality, available for building shell-proof works on the German scale had it been thought advisable to do so. The excellence of British mining work, from the saps in the Ypres swamp to the terrific explosions in the Messines Battle, was testimony to the general British talent in trench labours.

Both Lord French and Sir Douglas Haig, however, along with Marshal Joffre, General Pétain, and General Foch, had ideas in regard to field fortification different from those of the enemy. They kept their troops above ground as much as possible, and one of the most common of shelters was the British shelter, consisting merely of an arch of corrugated iron, above which sand-bags and quantities of earth were placed. The earthen cushion was sufficient to stop bullets or shrapnel splinters, but the smallest high-explosive shell could pierce and wreck the shelter.

There were numerous underground caves where men could sleep safely, and where telephone operators and Staff officers could work securely in a bombardment. In places of great importance and peril the British system of tunnelling and cavern-making was equal to that of the enemy, and there were some vast subterranean cities in the British lines served with electric railways, and provided with as many appliances as existed in the Hindenburg tunnel.

Yet, generally speaking, the apparently weak British shelter and the apparently strong German cavern or armoured concrete block-house were representative of opposing ideas in fortification. The British commander did not want the spirit of attack in his men to diminish. He did not desire to see his troops grow into pale-faced cave-dwellers, inclined to go deep into their burrows in the crisis of an action. The additional casualties from direct shell fire could be almost or quite balanced by the superior physique of an open-air life, while the careful fostering of the spirit of attack pursued by the Western Allies in the ordering of their lines was a thing of high value, as Hindenburg in person at last recognised.

After the completion of the Hindenburg tunnel the German High Command ordered no more protective tunnels to be made. Most of those existing were condemned to be either destroyed or partly closed, mined, and ready to be blown up. The German troops were re-educated in the art of holding their lines, and taught to rely rather upon the chance of escaping shell fire than upon getting from ten to sixty feet below ground during artillery fire. Except that the system of block-house shelters was retained to some extent by the enemy, he ended, in the third year of the war, by adopting the British idea of slight coverings and open-air life, reserving his burrows mainly for sleeping, for telephone exchanges, and Staff work.

Probably the development of poison-gas attacks by

ERECTING CAMOUFLAGE FOR A HEAVY GUN ON THE OISE FRONT.
Camouflage, one of the grand technical sciences of the war, was first taken up seriously by the French. It was at last brought to such perfection that vast military works were constructed, and large movements carried out without visible alteration of the landscape or detection by reconnaissance pilots and observers.

means of whirlwind bombardments of gas-shell helped the German to appreciate the value of light and airy cover. But the general change in his method of holding a line was mainly due to the feeling for the superiority in spirit of troops that had been accustomed to live dangerously. When Falkenhayn was retired, Ludendorff brought to the western front many generals accustomed to open field warfare in the east, and anxious to inspire the western divisions with vehemency in attack.

Germans discard the tunnel system They condemned the great tunnels, the large caverns, and the profusion of bomb-proof forts. The success they won in the Second Battle of Cambrai confirmed them in their views.

In the end both sides approximated to each other in the matter of field fortification. At certain places, and for special reasons, the allied armies had intricate and immense subterranean galleries and halls, with surface outlets protected by anti-gas curtains. Places of this kind could shelter many divisions, and by means of new excavating machine-tools fresh assembly places could be constructed with surprising rapidity. Lens, Arras, Rheims, and Verdun were among the more famous of these shelters.

In the new kind of semi-open field warfare, that began in 1917 and developed in 1918, the science of protective devices became of more importance than the art of building concrete works. Camouflage was indeed one of the grand technical sciences of war. It began with scene-painting on a large scale, in which use was made of the latest discoveries and tricks of impressionist and futurist schools of art. Raw primitive colour was splashed on guns, roofs, vehicles, and screens of canvas, while strings of coloured tags of cotton, stretched above battery positions, important railway centres, and unloading depots, changed the aerial view of all spots and knots of activity. The French seem to have been the first to take up the science of camouflage in a serious manner, but they and the British were at last completely excelled by the studious, patient, and industrious Teuton.

The Teuton seldom originated, but when he recognised the value of a thing he displayed, to use his favourite epithet, "colossal" energy in winning a practical leadership. General von Hutier, the inventor of the new German infantry tactics, recognised that the new military art of camouflage could be made the crowning feature of his new system of attack as well as of defence. At immense cost in material and labour he constructed new, invisible roads of concentration against the Fifth British Army by camouflaging each proposed route before he began making his tracks.

When all the new roads and railways were built, together with numerous new depots, scarcely any visible alteration of the landscape was perceived by British and French reconnaissance pilots and observers. The concealment devices used by the enemy were very simple. He merely strung up rags above the ground he was disturbing, so that when he broke the white chalk or yellow clay no new ribbons of colours could be seen winding through the brown-green countryside.

In ancient times, as Shakespeare tells us, Macbeth could never be vanquished until great Birnam Wood to high Dunsinane should come against him, but the wood strangely began to walk towards the hill when Malcolm reached Birnam, and gave the order:

Let every soldier hew him down a bough,
And bear't before him; thereby shall we shadow
The numbers of our host, and make discovery
Err in report of us.

All the art and mystery of camouflage was thus briefly expressed by the English poet, but his countrymen, after finely practising the **Camouflage made a technical science** art of concealing an attack in their attempted drive at Cambrai, in November, 1917, were not equally successful in finding means of penetrating the enemy's use of the same craft.

Smoke fires, as instruments of warfare, were developed on a large scale by modern means. Smoke screens for infantry seem first to have been used by Sir Douglas Haig on September 25th, 1915, at the Battle of Loos, but the enemy perfected the smoke camouflage, under pressure of the superior aerial observation that the British at last won.

The Germans began with the ingenious device of chemical smoke furnaces, placed about their more important battery positions, to create an artificial fog when the guns were

Victims of their own vile inventions: Germans caught in clouds of poison gas.

Liquid fire, first employed by the Germans, successfully adopted by the Allies.

French aerial torpedoes for use in the Flanders offensive.

British Lewis gun in a sand-bagged redoubt at Hill 70.

Serbian rocket-man on duty in a trench on the Salonika front.

Frenchman laying ground mines to scatter enemy night raiders.

French instructor explaining the method of using fuses.

Power-driven trench digger used by the French Army.

Constructive ingenuity applied to the invention of destructive weapons

French mitrailleuse for defending balloons against aeroplanes.

Park of Canadian armoured motor-cars carrying machine-guns.

Battery for firing rifle-grenades in a trench near Verdun.

French soldier learning how to use and fire rockets.

Portuguese with a Stokes mortar in a front-line trench.

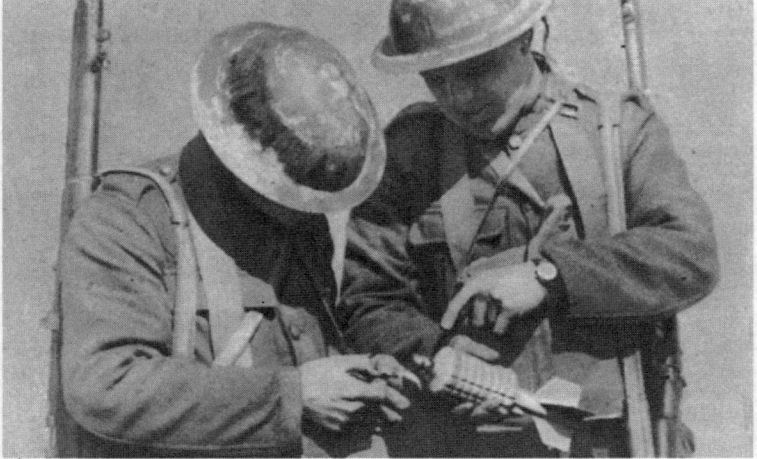

British soldiers examining a small German aerial torpedo.

Appliances and artifices in use among the allied armies on land and in the air.

British Tank of the earliest type, as used at Cambrai.

Improved French Tank first used in Champagne in 1918.

British light Tank, of 1918, with turret action and high speed.

German land battleship captured in 1918 on the western front

firing, so that British counter-battery work, with aeroplane spotting, was impeded. Then, when General von Hutier elaborated his new storming tactics under cover of mist, German chemists provided him with means of making suitable weather for attack at any time.

Nebelmaschinen, or mist-making boxes, were manufactured in large numbers in preparation for the spring offensive of 1918. They contained chemicals capable of spreading a mist over a large area for the space of a quarter of an hour or more. Wing-Commander Brock's naval fog machine, with which Zeebrugge and Ostend were blocked, was a more powerful instrument than the Nebelmaschinen, but it was not ready for use by the military forces in 1917 when battles might have been won by its aid.

At the time the Germans succeeded in hiding the movements of hundreds of thousands of men, thousands of guns, and tens of thousands of supply vehicles, they likewise perfected means of discovering such movements themselves. No system of camouflage, however vast, could screen such a gathering of striking force by daylight in clear weather. Only in the darkness of night — Nature's camouflage that man had employed since the Stone Age—could immense columns march without being seen from the air.

All through the war the Germans had been forward in the production and employment of illuminating devices, such as Verey lights and other flares, rockets, electric beams, and star-shells. They could turn profound gloom into dazzling brilliance at a time when British military authorities, being unable to get sufficient British searchlights, were ordering them from loyal German-American optical instrument makers. The German industrial supremacy in optical glass, electric appliances, and chemical products of fine quality was of high importance in all the visual machinery of the battlefield.

Long did it take the British Army to win to something like a partial equality in powers of vision. In the meantime the enemy developed his trench periscope into a giant observation tube, manufactured great telescopes, and improved his range-finders. His gunnery became excellent, not only on land but at sea. The events of the first phase of the Battle of Jutland Bank, when Admiral Hipper was retreating from the superior forces of Admiral Beatty, were a rather staggering display of the increased power of vision the enemy obtained by means of his superiority in optical devices. The shooting of the small German battle-cruiser squadron more than stood comparison with the gunnery of the large British cruiser fleet, because between the Dogger Bank action and the Jutland Bank action the Germans much improved their instruments.

Superior German optical devices

At the opening of the Battle of the Somme the new national armies of Great Britain were not quite so good in gunnery as had been expected. Neither in counter-battery work nor in the destruction of entrenched positions was the shooting generally exact. On the other hand the German gunners, though losing most of their observation balloons, maintained their ranges with deadly effect, due not only to experience but to perfected instruments of observation concealed in the western hillsides.

This very serious defect in British material of war was

gradually remedied, yet in the spring of 1918 the Germans were again leading in a novel method of observation. They merely developed the parachute flare they had first employed for ordinary night work. They made it larger and stronger, used more illuminating material, and dropped the flares at night from reconnoitring aeroplanes.

This was the way in which they solved the problem of nocturnal reconnaissance flights over large stretches of camouflaged country. They invented the problem and they also found the solution to it. To the energy of mind with which they applied themselves to these special matters of detail their amazing sequence of successes in March, April, and May, 1918, was largely due.

In regard to artillery the Germans and Austrians began

THE MANUFACTURER OF THE EARLIEST TANKS.
Sir William Tritton at work in his office with a model of a Tank on his desk. He was a director of the firm of Foster, Tritton & Co., who constructed the earliest Tanks and worked out many of the practical details of this most successful collective production of British inventive genius.

with a marked superiority over the French and the Russians. This superiority was an intellectual affair rather than a display of productiveness. The German and Austrian Staffs perceived the possibilities of aeroplane control of long-range siege-guns. Using at first only slow machines, dropping smoke-bomb signals, they were yet able to devise ways for registering their large guns upon important targets. Their armament firms constructed for them siege-howitzers of very large calibre, the most important of which were the Skoda 12 in. howitzer, the Krupp 16·8 in. howitzer, and the long-distance Krupp weapon.

Quick-firers or siege-howitzers?

With these powerful new instruments of destruction the enemy changed his view of the value of ordinary fortified entrenched camps. The French Staff, on the other hand, though aware of the existence of the new hostile howitzers, were of opinion that their fine, light, handy 3 in. quick-firer, with its wonderful secret principle of construction, would defeat the enemy in the open field, while he was wasting time and force in detached siege operations. The Russian Staff appeared to be of the same opinion.

The rival theories were put fully to the test at the Battle of the Marne, in circumstances favouring the Western Allies. Belgium and France lost some of their entrenched positions far more rapidly than they had expected, and some French armies suffered severe local reverses that disarranged the plan of General Joffre. These accidents, however, did not alter the execution of the main scheme for an offensive return by the Allies. But in the critical week the French quick-firer, in spite of its superb qualities, could not decisively prevail against the more cumbersome, heavy German artillery, even when this artillery was running short of shell.

The French manœuvring wing, under General Maunoury, was severely checked by the long-range, medium heavy German ordnance, with the result that,

Secret of the French gun   although the French quick-firer broke the German centre, the Germans were able not only to retreat in good order, but to take up a position of magnificent strength from which they immediately resumed the offensive. They were finally checked by the unparalleled rate of fire of the much-abused British Lee-Enfield rifle which, in spite of its inferior penetrative power, proved in the hands of marksmen the real mistress of the European battlefield. Had the French possessed such a rifle, instead of their old-fashioned magazine Lebel rifle—firing nine rounds rapid and only one round afterwards—their quick-firer might have been sufficient to achieve the victory that hung in the balance in the autumn of 1914 and for years afterwards.

Although the Germans captured some hundreds of French guns in August, 1914, it took them nearly two years to make a gun with similar qualities. The reason for this was that when a French gun was taken to pieces the secret of its construction vanished. There was an hydraulic device to take the recoil, and a pneumatic recuperator that used the recoil to bring the barrel back to its exact position. The two were combined in a liquid and an empty space. But the empty space was full of air, occupying a part of the mechanism in which there were no joints. The joints occurred in the part where the liquid rested, because it was fairly easy to make waterproof joints but extremely difficult to make joints permanently tight against a strong air pressure. The liquid and air acted by means of a single piston rod, with a simplicity that concealed an immense ingenuity.

When, early in the war, the Germans opened a French gun, the compressed air escaped, and the expanded liquid covering that had covered the joints seemed to be the only working material. It was late in the war before German guns of the French type appeared. In the meantime many of the Allies were using the hydro-pneumatic device

which the French had adapted to rapid-fire artillery of medium and heavy kinds. The problem of getting an air-tight joint for the recuperator was solved by the French alone when the war began, and the solution gave them by far the best field-gun existing.

The French were also the first to use high-explosive shell. In this matter also they had a secret process. They definitely displaced gunpowder by picric acid in 1886, and were followed two years afterwards by the Germans. In 1890, however, the French invented a shell with thin walls, enabling them to use a larger quantity of picric acid as a bursting charge. The Germans, on the other hand, kept the walls of their shells thick, because they used an inferior metal and were afraid that, if it thinned, it would not stand the enormous pressure of the firing charge.

When the war opened the enemy had not discovered the ingenious process of shell manufacture that enabled the French to use thin-sided shells containing safely an extraordinary quantity of high-explosive. It was not the French steel alloy but the mysterious treatment it received that made the metal wonderfully resistant to the gases   **High-explosive shells and fuses**   that impelled the projectile. Only in the middle of the struggle was the enemy enabled to make a thin-walled shell containing a large bursting charge.

The French also had the best high-explosive fuses, while the British possessed the worst, and the Germans the second best. The French fuse was simple, while the German fuse was intricate. It could be set to fire the bursting charge immediately on striking a resisting surface, such as walls, armour, or the earth. It could also be arranged to go off at the slightest touch from yielding things, which gave it great wrecking force against barbed-wire. Finally it could be set for delayed action, so that the shell exploded after ricochetting on the ground, or entering sand-bags or earth cushions. Then there were ordinary armour-piercing shells, such as all the Great Powers used, for breaking into concrete works. They were more thickly built in front, and the fuse had a delayed action.

The British lyddite shell had a very awkward defect. It went off, at times, under rough treatment. This was why British gunners began the war with a strong prejudice in favour of shrapnel, which they were able to burst above an enemy mass, on the open ground, in an uncommonly effective spraying manner. They were the best shrapnel users in the world, but their infantry suffered badly in the first period of trench warfare from the fact that they had not the same proportion of good high-explosive shell as French and German gunners possessed. It was first patent at Neuve Chapelle on March 10th, 1915, that a great increase in British artillery was needed to break through the enemy's wire entanglements and entrenchments.

Eventually the British recovered the ground they had lost in gunnery, through Mr. Lloyd George's energetic courage in following the advice which he had received, and arranging for the production of an immense number of big siege-guns. The German infantry was hammered by light and heavy pieces, the German artillery was daringly counter-batteried by heavy guns, while the enemy's communications were barraged by long-range cannon and big howitzers. When the shelling of back areas of the

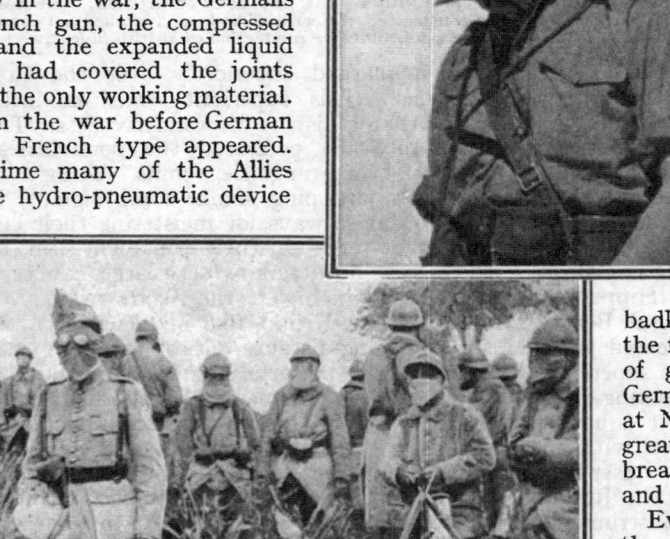

WAR'S HIDEOUS VISAGE.
French soldiers wearing the masks, fitted with goggles and respirators, that rendered them immune to noxious gases. Inset above : Half-length portrait of an officer with the British forces in Mesopotamia wearing his gas-mask.

The Terrible Progress in Battle Machinery   455

battle-front became common in both attack and defence, the high-velocity gun increased in importance. There was nothing novel in high-velocity firing in land battles. It was merely an adoption of naval practice. Additional velocity could be imparted to a shell by increasing the force of propulsion behind it. A gun with a long barrel and a heavy charge would give higher velocity to a projectile than a gun with a short barrel and a light charge. Owing, however, to the heavy charge, a high-velocity gun wore out rapidly. Its use in large numbers was therefore a question of expediency for the Commander-in-Chief to settle.

British and French commanders preferred to keep, as a rule, to low-velocity shooting. By so doing they not only lengthened the life of their long-range guns and saved cordite for bombarding the enemy's infantry and artillery positions, but they avoided ranging upon German billeting places, where French and Belgian people were living. The merciless, terrorising Teuton employed high-velocity guns in continually increasing numbers, because he reckoned that the waste of his material was more than balanced by the moral effect of his swift, unexpected shells upon the civilian population behind the hostile lines.

After bombarding with high-velocity guns many quiet, busy towns that formerly seemed to be out of his range, the German in March, 1918, won a grandiose yet easy triumph by means of an expensive Krupp gun designed for very long-distance firing. Again there was nothing novel in the enemy's piece. The French Government constructed secretly a somewhat similar long-distance gun in 1902, in connection with researches into smokeless powder and general ballistics. Extreme care was taken to keep both the experiments and the valuable deductions therefrom unknown to other Powers; but apparently German agents discovered something of what was going on. The Krupp firm then built an experimental long-distance gun, purely for the purpose of scientific research. When, however, the aggressive plans of the German High Command were revealed to the armament makers, the directors of Krupp constructed, some time before the war, three long-distance guns, for which they asked a quarter of a million pounds sterling each.

Krupp's long-distance guns In the late autumn of 1914, when the lines of the parallel battle in the west were fixed, a suggestion was made that Paris should be bombarded from some point above the Aisne. General von Falkenhayn, however, did not think the result would be worth the expense. There was another consideration. The highly-skilled labour, powerful machinery, and valuable material that Krupps proposed to expend in the manufacture of long-distance guns could all be better employed in the construction of more numerous ordinary heavy pieces of great and direct military importance. It was not until

COMRADES IN DISCOMFORT.
Special masks were devised for the horses. They were quickly adjustable over the muzzle, and were accepted patiently by the animals.

READY FOR THE EMERGENCY.
French soldier with one of the French Army dogs, both masked against enemy gas attack.

in Italy, in Rumania, and Russia, Below and Mackensen proved to be more rapid munition-makers than British mechanics, by capturing more than ten thousand Italian, Rumanian, and Russian guns—many of them fine examples of French and British construction—that Ludendorff allowed Krupps to carry out their proposal. The destruction of one of the first three guns by an ordinary French high-velocity gun at Fismes, and the accelerated exhaustion of the remaining pieces, threw Krupps' programme of construction out of order. There was a pause of twenty-five days between the end of the first phase of the long-distance bombardment and its resumption.

The Krupp long-distance gun was directed against England as well as against France. Its grand target was the mind of the uninformed English public. This was why the first long-distance high-velocity shells were fired when the Fifth British Army was breaking. It was intended that the English people should be dismayed by the prospect of losing the command of the Channel narrows, and the nightmare possibility of having the fire of hundreds of new Krupp guns raking the Kentish ports, the Kentish towns, and falling into London.

Yet in the use of poison gas the Germans had long since obtained some remarkable successes, because other nations had not thought it worth while to experiment in the matter. At the Hague Conference, Admiral Mahan stated that the United States Government refused to agree to the prohibition of the new deleterious gases in warfare for two reasons. In the first place the American view was that slaughter by asphyxiating gas was less cruel and inhuman than drowning by submarine attack. In the second place the American delegate stated that his Government was not inclined to limit the scope of the military inventiveness of its citizens by consenting in advance not to use gases. Lord Fisher, one of the British representatives at the Hague Conference, was of the same opinion as Admiral Mahan, and neither of the Anglo-Celtic Governments adhered to the European

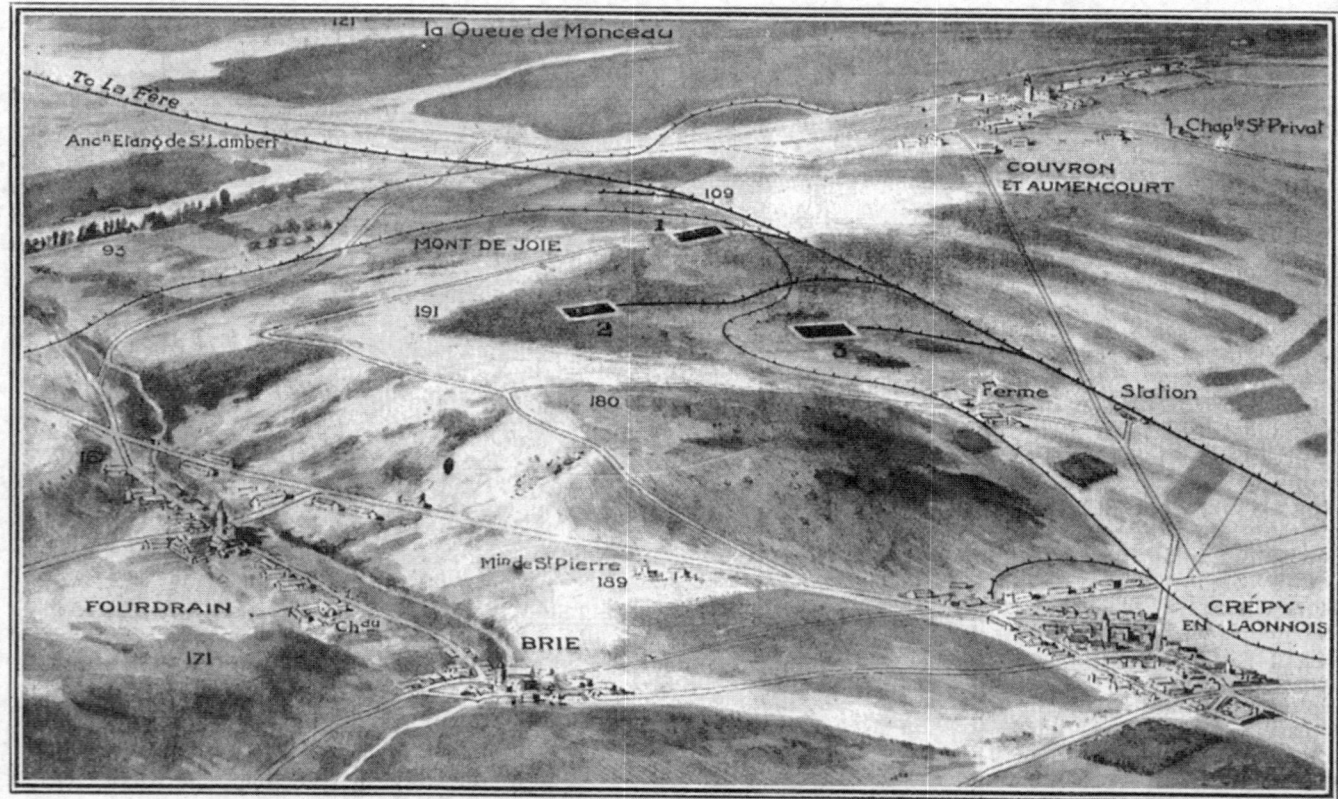

POSITION OF GERMAN LONG-RANGE GUNS THAT BOMBARDED PARIS.

General view of the country near Crèpy en Laonnois where the Germans sited the "Big Berthas" with which, from a distance of about seventy-four miles, they began the deliberate bombardment of the French capital on March 23rd, 1918. The positions of the guns—marked 1, 2, and 3 in the middle of the drawing—were discovered by French airmen, from whose data the three drawings on this page were made.

agreement in regard to the prohibition of asphyxiating gases. The British Government, however, having reserved the right to use suffocating gases, took no steps whatever to make experiments and devise machinery. The Germans, on the other hand, energetically began making experiments and devising gas instruments in 1909, ten years after their Government had signed and sealed a declaration to abstain from using poison fumes. They tried machines for burning sulphur, in imitation of Admiral Cochrane's rejected war plan. As they failed to find an asphyxiating gas which could only be counteracted by oxygen helmets,

they devised various acid poisons that could be neutralised by breathing through alkaline preparations and charcoal.

The surprise which the enemy effected round Hill 60 on April 19th, 1915, and round Langemarck three days later, was accomplished by placing liquid chlorine in steel cylinders, in shells, and in bombs, and using a few other chemicals such as bromine. He thus produced a low, rolling, yellow-green cloud, in which men could have lived had they been provided with simple antidotes. Straw fires would have lifted the poison cloud, stretches of damp hay would have absorbed the poison, while respirators

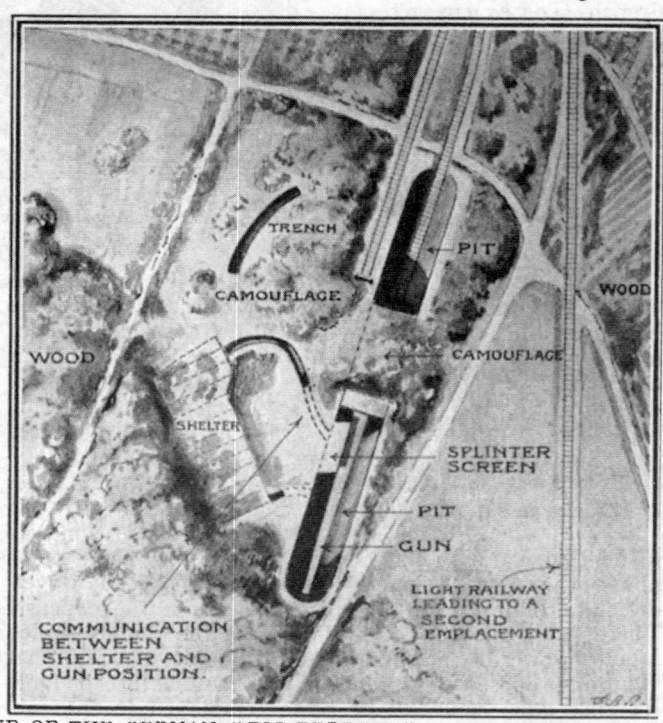

DETAILS OF THE EMPLACEMENT OF ONE OF THE GERMAN "BIG BERTHAS."

The drawing on the left shows the position, as it was ascertained by the observation of French airmen, of one of the long-range guns with which the Germans bombarded Paris during the spring of 1918. The drawing on the right presents an approximate detailed reconstruction of the same emplacement.

steeped in alkaline liquids would have neutralised the chlorine in breathing. The Germans' use of so torturing a medium as chlorine was a vilely barbaric thing, but there would scarcely have been a logical case against them had they employed a gas that killed quickly.

The Germans were badly placed in regard to gas warfare, as the prevailing westerly and south-westerly winds blew against them. Yet, owing to the lack of good Staff work of a scientific kind in controlling the gas employed in the Battle of Loos, the first British experiment with the new German instrument was a failure. Full and exact knowledge of the use of gas by British officers might have been acquired between April, 1915, and September, 1915, had a system of intensive training been adopted. British sailors could have taught British soldiers the art of getting weatherward of the enemy, so as to put gas upon him at nicely calculated sectors.

In the meantime the use of the gas-cloud was almost abandoned by its originators, except on the eastern front. Recognising that they had the wind against them, the Germans devised means of warning and protecting their troops against either visible or invisible, slowly-moving rolls of poison fume, and devised gas-shells that could be cast either with or against the wind in any required direction. Energetically the German chemist laboured to find what gas or mixture of gases would spread with deadliest effect from the small containing space of a medium shell. The gas had to be heavy, so that it would not quickly disperse into minutely harmless quantities. It had also to be as colourless as possible, so that hostile troops might

Constituents of poison gases walk into it. Prussic acid was tried for a considerable time, but in the Somme Battle the deadlier phosgene gas was used. It was followed by other poison gases, to which British and French chemists replied by the deadliest of all preparations of a directly poisonous kind.

The constituents of the Allies' gases were kept secret, but the later German mixtures of an ingenious kind were soon known both by their results and by actual examination. The Germans tried to blind troops before attacking them by shelling them with gases causing rapid inflammation of the eyes. They also produced a sneezing gas to compel men to take off their masks, in readiness to swallow the dose of poison that followed. In one battle they also used a gas that penetrated the mask and produced vomiting. But their masterpiece of chemical ingenuity was the hyperite gas, or mustard gas, that acted on perspiring skins, causing a serious illness until means were found of bathing patients back to health. The smothering of the population of Armentières with mustard gas, at a time when the treatment was not fully developed, was an act of cruelty of a peculiarly German kind.

In March, 1918, when Hutier, Marwitz, and Below were

FRENCH LONG-RANGE GUN IN ACTION.

Firing one of the 13·6 in. guns with which the French successfully put out of action some of the costly " Big Berthas " with which the Germans had bombarded Paris. The French had first discovered the possibility of firing at great distances, and had constructed a long-range gun a dozen years before the outbreak of the war, but it was left to the Germans to use such weapons against distant peaceful towns.

standing ready to break through the British line, their gunners were provided with a new kind of gas-shell that proved one of the main instruments of the enemy's success. It contained a gas that could be stopped by the British mask, but by the simplest of devices it surprised the British divisions against which it was used. There was a great difference between a high-explosive shell and a gas-shell. One exploded with a terrific noise, the other opened and let out its contents with nothing more than a soft plop.

Soldiers trusted their lives to their ears, and when a shell made little or no noise they did not wait to see whether it was a dud, but rapidly put on their masks and sucked at the mouth-pieces. In the opening offensive of 1918, however, the German gas-shell was mainly formed of an ordinary fuse, con- Gas combined with high explosive necting with a quantity of ordinary high explosive. In the high explosive was a bottle containing liquid poison gas. When a hurricane bombardment opened, over both British infantry and British artillery, the shells burst with the usual high-explosive report, and threw up the ordinary smoke of explosion. Many soldiers, therefore, did not trouble to breathe through their respirators, as this was an inconvenient process and interfered with their working ability. They were therefore caught with the bottled gas ; some were killed, and many more received just enough to put them out of action.

The new combination shell of high explosive and gas completed the terrors of modern warfare. It compelled all soldiers to wear gas-masks in battle, which was a misery to mortal flesh. Both sides endeavoured to annul the mechanism of the various types of respirator by maintaining so long and continual a downpour of gas that the filtering apparatus was at last choked. Here, however, British inventiveness proved superior to the German method of colossal use of well-known devices.

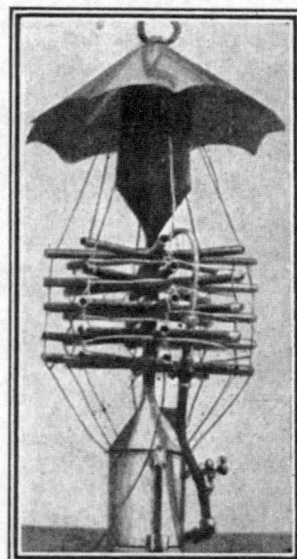

A "LIGHT UMBRELLA."
German "Leuchtschirm," constructed for firing forty rockets automatically.

Charcoal was one of the principal things in a respirator box, and the gas-absorbing power of the best charcoal was rather limited. It was, however, discovered that a new kind of charcoal, made out of the shell of the coconut, had an extraordinary absorbing capacity. Coconut shell had the advantage of being plentiful and cheap, and as a poison-gas filter it promised to defeat the enemy's wasteful method in gas bombardments, as well as subjecting him to new inconvenience. He had no free supply of coconuts, and it was possible to extend the intensified naval blockade system to this new vital raw material of modern battle machinery. German **Stimulus to** charcoal was made out of alderwood and **British chemists** other common porous woods that could not absorb the tenth part of the poison gas that charred coconut shell could. It is doubtful if the enemy derived any permanent advantage from the introduction of deleterious gases into warfare. The high development of his chemical factories gave him some superiority at the beginning, by reason of the fact that he had the largest trained body of technical chemists in the world. His research work was more thorough and wider, and, what was of supreme importance, his general processes of manufacture were of incomparable fineness. Great Britain also had large chemical industries, but they dealt with alkalis rather than with acids, and, with some exceptions, lacked the fineness of technique and the profundity of research that was the mark of German chemistry.

In intellectual power, however, the leading British chemists were equal to the leading German chemists. What the British sadly lacked was, so to speak, a complete system of conduit pipes between the fountain of new ideas produced by their originating minds and the unirrigated fields of routine practice directed by their industrial manufacturers. Under the stimulus of urgent military needs the British began to train a large secondary class of chemists, operating midway between the great men of science and the manufacturers. As this reorganisation of practical British chemistry extended and deepened, Germany suffered in more ways than one. Not only did her troops in the field feel the growing power of British chemical warfare, but her great dye and drug makers had reason to know that the universal monopoly they had enjoyed before the war was being undermined and wrecked.

GERMAN TWOFOLD TRENCH WEAPON.
Combined rifle-rest and grenade-thrower used by the Germans on the Somme front. It was captured by the French and exhibited in Paris with many other enemy engines of war.

Every Great Power at war with Middle Europe took the most natural, effective steps in reprisal for poison-gas attacks. Immediately, in defence of their armies, and indirectly in an attack upon the German chemical industries, they organised great systems of research and technical production, which not only served a military purpose, but inflicted defeat upon the German chemical industries. German dyes and German drugs were likely to find British, French, Italian, and American markets

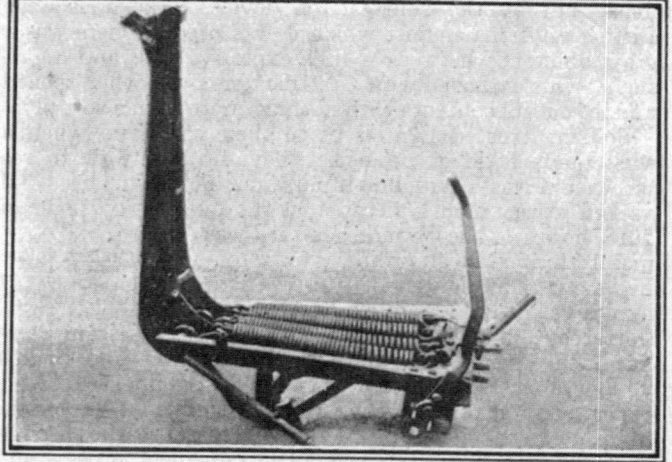

ADAPTATIONS OF EARLY WARFARE EMPLOYED IN MODERN FIGHTING.
Grenade and bomb throwing devices used by the German troops during the fighting in France. The photograph on the left shows a grenade-thrower, which was designed with a series of powerful springs to throw three grenades at once. On the right is a heavily-made catapult which the Germans had devised for the throwing of bombs, thus making use of one of the earliest manifestations of machinery in warfare.

closed to them after the war, and an intense competition for the neutral markets preparing against them.

All the Allies saw clearly the menace that had underlain their dependence upon German chemists for coal-tar dyes, coal-tar medicines, picric acid, and other chemicals. As a measure of national defence they required factories for the production of peaceful commodities, which could quickly be converted to military uses. The erection, staffing, and efficient working of such **German chemical** factories was the direct result of the **industries menaced** enemy's employment of poison gases, and it was not likely that any additional State aid to the German chemical industries would enable those industries to recover the ground they had lost through their use of torture gases.

All the principal German military inventions were more or less routine developments of things existing before war was declared. The British race showed far more genius in striking out into unexplored regions of power, and devising machinery more novel than the shrapnel shell that made for victory at Waterloo. In the autumn of 1914, when the power of the machine-gun was clearly displayed, several British officers found inspiration in a short story by Mr. H. G. Wells, concerning a travelling armoured fortress. Colonel R. E. Crompton, of the Royal Engineers, began to work directly on Mr. Wells' idea, and even employed the Diplock pedrail, which had been an important feature in the land battleship of the brilliant novelist. The pedrail mechanism, however, could not overcome the obstacle of the deeply-dug German trench system.

In the meantime, Lieutenant Macfie, of the R.N.V.R., designed a mobile fort of large size, using the endless wheel or caterpillar process of movement employed on two American agricultural tractors, the Holt and the Killen-Strait. A demonstration of the Killen-Strait tractor was the main working inspiration in regard to the improvement of the Government design, while Lieutenant Macfie's scheme appears to have been worked out some time before the official experts abandoned the Diplock pedrail in favour of the endless wheel movement.

GERMAN TRENCH-MORTAR.
Heavy trench-mortar used by the Germans, with one of the shells it fired.

LIGHT GERMAN "MINE-THROWER."
"Minenwerfer" of a light kind packed on horseback ready for transport. The Germans specialised in mine-throwers of various calibre.

Mr. Winston Churchill, who was then at the Admiralty, took up the idea, and while Colonel Swinton, known in the literary world as "Ole Luk Oie," and Colonel Stern, were stubbornly persisting in improving the design, the then First Lord of the Admiralty brought Mr. Tennyson d'Eyncourt, the inventive naval constructor, into the affair. The travelling fort was armoured according to the best naval practice, fitted with a Daimler engine, and entrusted for manufacture to Messrs. Foster, Tritton & Company, who worked out many of the practical details.

It is thus impossible to say who was the inventor of the famous "Tank." It was a collective production of the unexhausted British genius in practical invention.

Unhappily, the new chariots of war, at their first appearance, were sent into action in small number, with crews who do not appear to have been given time to complete their training. The effect they created, when hurriedly employed to reinforce the British attack upon Courcelles, Martinpuich, and Le Sars, was merely the

MEDIUM AND LIGHT "MINENWERFER" IN TRANSPORT AND IN ACTION.
Types of German mine-throwers. The picture on the left shows four soldiers harnessed to a medium-sized weapon, and that on the right a weapon of a lighter type in firing position and about to be loaded. (The photographs on this page are all from the German Press.)

shadow of the victory that might have been won by them. Sir Julian Byng, a neighbour and friend of Mr. H. G. Wells at Dunmow, the " only begetter " of the landship, was the British Army commander who displayed most receptive activity of intellect in regard to the possibilities of the mobile fort. Although he failed to turn the Sensée River line from Bourlon Ridge, and so upset Ludendorff's preparations for a counter-offensive in the west, he revealed for the first time, in November, 1917, the full and surprising power of the new machine.

Meanwhile, the French Army had adopted the new car of assault, and their engineers had constructed a more rapid kind that was first used by General Nivelle in April, 1917, in the attempt to break through to Laon. British designers also made a lighter, faster Tank, of which large numbers were secretly collected behind the British front in March, 1918. The new light Tank differed in shape from the old heavy Tank, and with its turret action and its surprising rapidity, served somewhat as a real land cruiser in the battles west of Amiens.

The German Tank, called the " land cruiser," was too closely modelled in constructional principle upon the heavy type of British machine to act as a veritable cruising force. It was rather a land battleship, and with its low turret and its armour descending almost to the ground,

it looked like a great, hump-backed tortoise. It had the tortoise-like quality of slowness, and in spite of its formidable armament of cannon, machine-guns, flame-projectors, with anti-gas devices enabling it to cross a poison fume zone, the Teutonic land cruiser that appeared in battle at Villers-Bretonneux on April 24th, 1918, was defeated by the new mobile British Tank.

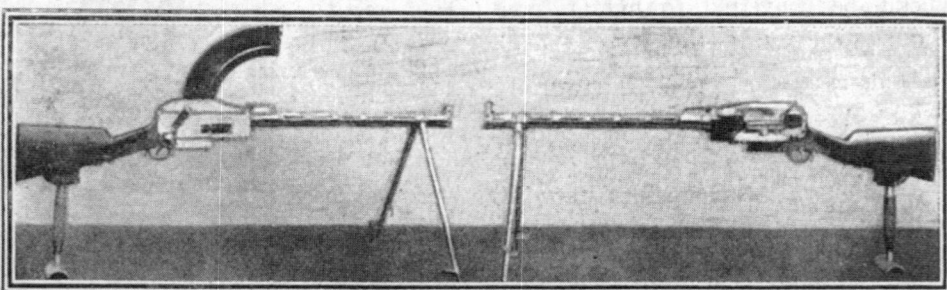

VIEWS OF THE MADSEN GUN ON ITS TRIPOD. [*From the " Engineer."*]
The Madsen gun, about 44 inches long, and weighing 20 lb., could be fired from the shoulder or automatically on a tripod, then discharging about 400 rounds a minute. The front legs of the stand folded up along the barrel, the rear leg fitting into a groove in the stock.

The improved French Tank completely displayed its remarkable battle power during the great counter-attack of June 11th, 1918, on the German lines south-east of Montdidier. More than one hundred of the machines charged in advance of the French infantry, and at comparatively slight cost in casualties proved more effective than an artillery barrage in breaking the enemy's resistance, surprising him in the midst of preparations for another hammer-blow in the direction of Paris, and bringing his new offensive to a standstill. The recapture of the key position of the Méry plateau was one of the supreme triumphs of the fast French Tank.

By the summer of 1918 the Tank was in somewhat the same stage of development as was the aeroplane in the autumn of 1914. It was a thing changing in type and in manner of use, full of defects and virtues. Petrol motor-power was a serious disadvantage, by reason of the danger of fire, and an improved oil-engine of equal efficiency was urgently required. The heat in the fighting chambers, closed during action save for swift glances through peep-holes, was very trying. With the engine working at top power, the quick-firers flaming out as fast as they could be loaded, and all the machine-guns barraging the ground to protect the advancing infantry behind the Tanks, life was more exciting than pleasant in the narrow, complicated interior of a modern chariot of war.

Development of the motor-car

While both the British and French Tanks developed qualities superior to those of the German Tank, the armoured motor-car, that had been neglected by Teuton and Briton on the western front, suddenly became a mighty instrument of battle in the hands of the French. To M. Loucheur, the new French Minister of Munitions, the resurgence in force of the motor-car seems to have largely been due.

In desert battles on the North-Western Egyptian frontier, and along the Middle Euphrates and the tributaries of the Tigris, General Lukin and General Marshall won a series of remarkable victories by means of light-armoured motor-cars, equipped with machine-guns and piloted by aeroplanes.

It became clear that the armoured car was a magnificent cavalry instrument on suitable ground, and the French cavalry was strengthened by numerous cars of a light and heavy type. The light type carried machine-guns, and the heavy was equipped with quick-firing cannon. Attending the cars were motor-bicycles with a single machine-gun, such as had generally been used in open field warfare.

WAITING THE MOMENT TO THROW.
Releasing the pin, the bomber threw the bomb at the last moment compatible with his own safety. If thrown too soon it might be caught and returned by the enemy.

The difference between the French cavalry motor force in 1918 and in 1914 resided in greatly increased number of units, larger proportion of motor artillery, improved engine power and armour design, and that perfected technique of aeroplane control which had been first employed in a capable manner by the Royal Naval Air Service wing at Doullens in 1914. When the Fifth British Army broke between St. Quentin and La Fère, in March, 1918, under a concentration of hostile power that surprised General Pétain as much as Sir Douglas Haig, there was no time to bring the foot and guns of France from Champagne to close the road to Paris.

General Pétain sent cavalry, aeroplanes, and most of his motor force. The motor-cars were the speediest of all instruments of defence, with the exception of aircraft, and they were detached from all parts of the French front and driven at top speed to the Oise line. The 1st Division of Foot Cuirassiers acted with the French motor and aerial forces and with the French cavalry that followed the cars.

It was in optimistic mood that M. Loucheur and the French High Command had laid down the new programme of armoured motor-cars. They hoped to reach behind the enemy's lines the open country suitable for the new cavalry instruments. When, in the **Armoured motors decide a battle** course of events, the cars reached the kind of ground they required, behind the British lines, the idea underlying their reorganisation proved sound. In conjunction with aerial reconnaissance they decided the course of battle between Chauny and Noyon, and prevented an outflanking movement of General Pétain's line and an early thrust towards Paris. The motor artillery proved of special importance, as the large enemy infantry forces had advanced too rapidly to bring guns with them.

No Tanks, in the circumstances, could have been as useful as were the swift armoured cars. In the great retreat, in fact, Tanks were a cumbersome, traffic-blocking nuisance when not sacrificed in rearguard actions. On the whole, at the stage of development attained in the summer of 1918, Tanks were valuable as preliminary instruments of an attack or counter-attack, while armoured motor-cars were, in the first place, useful as a pursuing force when the hostile front was completely broken, and in the second place very effective in the defence of rear areas when the enemy had broken through.

There is a country proverb that two heads are better than one, even if one is only a sheep's head. None of the members of the Grand **Interplay of the** Alliance was of sheepish mind. The **Allies' talents** varied interplay of the national talents of France, Great Britain, Italy, the United States, and Belgium in the improvement of the machinery of warfare was a fruitful source of common strength. The French sense of the permanent importance of the apparently obsolete armoured car was a striking example of the truth that two heads are better than one. The Germans might have won a decisive victory, at the broken junction of the British and French forces, had they quickly brought into action armoured motor-cars and great cavalry forces. They, however, imitated too closely, while improving upon, the British method of offensive surprise, and thus were countered by the original development of the French system and material of war.

France for long led the way in the development of the aeroplane, that changed the conditions of trench warfare in a remarkable manner. The Germans were ahead of all other nations in the technique of the production of large rigid airships. They were repaid for all the work done on the Zeppelin and the Schütte-Lanz by the power of reconnaissance they won in the North Sea and the Baltic. Not only did German airships act as rapid scouts to battle-cruiser forces and battle divisions, but they became and long remained excellent pilots for enemy submarines during the difficult traverse of the dangerous stretch of water between Germany, Denmark, Scandinavia,

NIGHT ATTACK UNDER BURSTING SHELLS AND LIGHT ROCKETS.
British troops on the western front making a night attack on enemy trenches, the position of which is defined by the flashes of fire that can be seen through the shattered tree-trunks and the smother of bursting shells. Rockets were sent up by the enemy that they might gauge the strength of the attacking force, and also to indicate to their supports that they were in urgent need of assistance.

III

ANTI-AIRCRAFT BARRAGE SHOWN IN DIAGRAM.
In this diagram is graphically indicated something of the character of the barrage system of gun fire employed in the defence of London against German aeroplane raids. The anti-aircraft guns, working according to a concerted plan, served to keep the hostile machines in the upper regions of the air.

The Gnome, the Le Rhône, and the Clerget were remarkable types of French aeromotors of varying power. The Green, the Beardmore, the Coatelen-Sunbeam, and the Rolls-Royce were fine examples of British designs. The enemy paid the Le Rhône the compliment of imitation, using a copy of it in the best chaser aeroplanes in the winter of 1917 and the spring of 1918. He also profited much by one of the earliest examples of the new Rolls - Royce aeromotor, The German Emperor, indeed, is said to have admitted that, if his engineers had not examined the Rolls-Royce lubricating device, the construction of giant German bombing machines, with the power of long-distance flight at high altitudes, would have been impossible.

In aeroplane production the enemy began with the advantage of a policy of preparation. He had fostered the erection of factories even by some British manufacturers, calculating justly that they would be serviceable centres for expansion during war. His great motor-car works, such as the Mercédès and Benz, became aeromotor producers on a great scale, and brilliant foreign designers, such as the Dutchman Fokker, were more encouraged by him than by any of the Allies.

At first, however, the German machines were overtaken by British pilots armed with rifles and using chain-shot and other missiles. But the superior organisation of the enemy told on the aerial situation, and, in spite of the better designs of the best British and French manufacturers, he gradually won for considerable periods a predominance in aerial material. For example, a French pilot, M. Garros, invented a method of firing a machine-gun forward through the propeller, by means of synchronisation of gun and engine. Both the machine and the firing method of Garros were adopted by the enemy, who turned out his copies in extraordinary numbers, and by means of them reigned in the sky.

The Handley Page machine became the inspiration for the enemy's large bombing aeroplanes, such as the Gotha. From the Italian Caproni load-carrier, with its multiple engines, the Teutons also obtained ideas, and when bomb-dropping operations increased greatly in direct military importance the size of both allied and enemy multiple-engined cargo-carriers became enormous. Under the wings of the latest giant aircraft men were dwarfed into ant-like proportions. Flying machines were made that could safely cross the Atlantic ocean, and routes were arranged bringing the length of possible journeys between England and Australia down to five days. Landing parachutes, first generally employed for escaping from damaged observation balloons, were adapted as an emergency device in flying machines to increase their safety.

Growth in size of aeroplanes

and Scotland. One of the merits of the large naval airship was that it afforded a steady platform for wireless apparatus that could receive as well as send out long-distance messages.

German submarines, emerging with a sky-line clear of hostile ships and aircraft, also had an ingenious method of long-distance wireless telegraphy. Strong kites were sent up, attached to a conducting wire, which wire became the aerial of the wireless plant on the submarine. By this means the piratical crews were able to communicate over great distances either with their airships or with their proper or secret bases.

The motive power of the German airship was derived from engines, such as the Maybach or Mercédès, developed in German motor-car practice. Great Britain possessed, in such motors as the Rolls-Royce and the Coatelen-Sunbeam, prime movers as capable of improvement for aerial propulsion as were the German engines. During the first years of the war, however, the great British industrial nation, though in undiminished plenitude of power, had to rely upon the French for the engining of the speediest aeroplanes used by the British Army.

An A.B. at the anti-aircraft gun which destroyed the Zeppelin L30 at Salonika. Right : Canadian anti-aircraft guns in action on the western front. The use of aircraft in the war led to a specialisation in weapons for meeting the new menace.

Motor for holding and controlling French observation-balloons and for serving as a station for exchange of messages with the officer on observation duty aloft.   Right : Officer directing the firing of a mitrailleuse upon German airmen flying over the French trenches.

Machine for testing aeroplane engines and (right) specimens of the gas cylinders supplied for filling balloons.   How vast an equipment and how large a staff was required for the Air Service may be estimated from the fact that a single squadron of twenty aeroplanes employed one hundred and fifty men.

TYPES OF GUNS, GEAR, AND REPAIRING OUTFIT USED IN ANTI-AIRCRAFT WORK.

AN EXPERIMENT IN BALLISTICS.
American experts testing a gun employing centrifugal power, a revolving
wheel automatically releasing many hundred bullets a minute.

At the same time, sheer speed in aerial flight was more
especially developed in the light, chaser, or fighting
machines, that gradually changed from monoplanes to
biplanes, and then to triplanes,
like the Sopwith and its Fokker
copy used by Captain Baron von
Richthofen. A pace of two miles
a minute was soon attained,
with remarkable climbing and
manœuvring power. T h e n,
under the pressure of enemy
attempts to recover superiority
in aerial battle machinery, the
already marvellous progress in
allied design and output was
clean surpassed.

After considerable disappointing delay United States engineers
realised their plan for a tremendous, standardised manufacture
of a powerful aeromotor, and
began to specialise in bombing
machines, rumours of which soon
disturbed the people of Western
and Southern Germany. In the
meantime, British and French
designers proceeded further to
improve their fastest machines,
while building giant cargo-carriers
and long - distance submarine-
hunting seaplanes.

Within the space of less than
four years there took place a
revolution in aircraft similar to
that which it had taken centuries to produce in seacraft.

The great airship, of which the Zeppelin was the best
example, was abruptly reduced to a position in regard
to the flying machine similar to that which the sailing-
ship occupied in regard to the steamship, after Mr. John
Pomeroy, a Colonial inventor, had finely distinguished
himself by the production of a special missile against
enemy airships, which gave the smaller, swifter flying
machine a grand advantage in attack.

When provided with multiple engines and an enormous stretch of sustaining surface, the heavier-than-air
machine excelled the floating gasbag. Continually its
chief factor of danger, the inflammability of its material,
was lessened. In some makes woodwork was almost
entirely displaced by steel and other metal work, until
only the dope-varnished linen fabric and the petrol fuel
were liable to be set on fire by incendiary missiles. The
petrol appeared to be the only inevitable flaming peril,
as there were means of making the covering material of
the planes non-inflammable.

Yet as the machines increased in speed of travel and
climb, range of action, carrying capacity, and machine-gun-
fire power, the land defence against the new aerial fleets
also augmented in scope and strength.
The development of the anti-aircraft gun   **Development of**
and its projectiles and manner of employ-   **counter-agents**
ment were almost as wonderful as the
evolution of the giant bomber. For example, the aerial
barrage that protected the vast, straggling streets of London
was one of the grand improvisations of the war, which,
in conjunction with a force of counter-attacking aeroplanes,
achieved an astonishing success.

Restricting the view in this chapter to the development
of the machinery of land warfare, it seems, on the whole,
that the Western Allies were superior in inventiveness to
the Teutons, and gradually approaching them in organising
capacity by the summer of 1918. Only in the use of
poison gases did the enemy display any large, surprising
originality. His strength chiefly consisted in the faculty
of appreciating new instruments that the Allies were
hesitatingly employing, manufacturing them on a grand
scale, and devising tactics for their complete exploitation.

A FIRE-CURTAIN IN THE THEATRE OF WAR.
French infantry facing German curtain fire in front of Fort Vaux, near Verdun. Barrage fire by batteries
working in concert over accurately ranged areas was brought to perfection in the Great War.

Coloured Photo, No. 7

Men of America's First Million : Review of United States Troops in France, March, 1918

CHAPTER CCXLIX.

AMERICA'S ACHIEVEMENTS IN PREPARATION AND IN ACTION, 1917-18.

By F. A. McKenzie.

Complex Problem Confronting America of Maintaining a Self-contained American Army in France—Stupendous Preliminary Work of the Engineers—Arrival of the First American Contingent Drawn from the Regular Army, the National Guard, and the Marines—French Military Decorations Won by American Troops—Institution of Special American Decorations for Distinguished Service—Criticism of America's Army Preparations and the Hon. Newton Baker's Reply—Effect of the German Advance in March, 1918, upon American Opinion—Reinforcements Speeded Up and American Troops Brigaded with British and French Units—American Prowess in Battle All Along the Fighting Line—Report by the Military Affairs Committee of the Senate Concerning Aeroplane Supply—Extraordinary Development of American Training and Transport of Troops After the First Anniversary of U.S. Intervention in the War—The First Million : Their Magnificent Physique and High Character—Capture of Cantigny, May 28th, 1918—American Successes at Chateau Thierry, Bouresches, Cherambauts Wood, Belleau Wood, and Vaux—International Celebration of the Anniversary of the Arrival of American Troops in France and of Independence Day.

T HE American declaration of war against Germany was signed on April 6th, 1917. Less than ten weeks later, in circumstances related in Chapter CCV. (Vol. 10, page 285), General Pershing, the Commander-in-Chief of the American Overseas Forces, and his Staff arrived in France. On June 27th the advance guard of the first American division landed. In October, 1917, the American troops had moved into the trenches, and in the spring of 1918 they definitely took charge of a section of the Lorraine front.

In the latter part of the first year after the American entry into the war there was a feeling of impatience in America, and of disappointment in Europe, with what was actually accomplished. This feeling was due in great measure to a lack of knowledge of the difficulties of early American intervention in force. The people of France, in particular, expected to see an army of millions of Americans land on their soil within a few months of President Wilson's declaration. Every American soldier was greeted with the utmost

enthusiasm. When the millions did not quickly arrive there was a reaction. The public of the allied countries and the public of America itself did not realise that before a country without a great military establishment —like the United States—could prepare and equip a vast army much work was necessary. The American Navy could and did take its place in the fighting-line on the days immediately following the declaration of war.

There was a general and passionate desire among the American people that an over-whelming American force should be enlisted and despatched at the earliest possible date to fight with the Allies, and particularly to fight by the side of the French. At the outbreak of the war it was the needs of France that appealed most to American sentiment. The American people had not yet forgotten French aid in the War of Independence. " I come to help to pay our debt to you for Lafayette and Rochambeau," said a young American who volunteered to enlist in the French Flying Corps in the early days of the war.

Even before General Pershing arrived in

ARMY LEADERS OF TWO GREAT REPUBLICS.
General Foch, Commander-in-Chief of the French Army and co-ordinator of all the Allies' military operations, with General Pershing, Commander-in-Chief of the American Expeditionary Force in France.

ON A ROUTE MARCH IN FRANCE.
American troops, marching along a highway behind the lines on the western front, exchanging greetings with a party of their British comrades enjoying a roadside rest.

France a number of Staff experts had reached Europe for consultation with the Staffs of the Allies. In particular many prominent American business organisers, engineers, and the heads of great concerns who had been called up for the United States Reserve of Officers, had been despatched to Europe to make arrangements for the reception in France of an American Army of two million men.

The American experts found themselves confronted by a very serious problem. America aimed to send most of her Army direct to France, landing on French soil, with their bases in France, and having the entire provision there necessary for their maintenance. The British and French General Staffs earnestly advised them to see that the machinery of war which they were creating should be capable of expansion, and that there should be ample provision for the secondary services that are essential if an army is to be efficient.

The problem of America in maintaining an expeditionary force in France was entirely different from that **Complex problem** of Britain. When Britain resolved to despatch an army she had her bases **before America** ready within a few score miles of the French front. Her arsenals for repairing the weapons of war were within easy reach of the battle-line. She could store in her warehouses on the South Coast of England ample food to supply the armies overseas. Her transports, making short journeys, could easily convey almost any number of men over to France. In France itself the distance between the landing-place of the soldiers and their stations on the fighting-front was, for most of the way, considerably under sixty miles. Most of this section was in the war zone, where the roads and railways were entirely at the disposal of the military authorities. In the case of Canada, which sent 350,000 men overseas, the troops had the British establishments ready for them on their arrival.

The problem of America was much more complex. The Americans' aim at first was not to send small sections of men to work under or be dependent on other armies, but to have a complete army of their own, completely

equipped and self-contained. To reach France these troops had to undertake an average journey of three thousand miles. Arrived in France, their landing-place was naturally on the Atlantic coast, some four hundred miles distant from the seat of war. There was no machinery in France capable of handling their men. They found that they would have to build fresh ports or extensions of old ports to receive their ships when they arrived. They would have to build warehouses. All the food of the Army, or practically the whole of it, would have to be brought over from America, and it was realised that unless food sufficient to last the Army for some weeks was held in store, an unfavourable turn of the war might produce a very serious condition of affairs. An examination of the railways between the

GOING FORWARD WITH BOMBS.
Soldiers of the American Expeditionary Force—with bags of hand-grenades slung about them—creeping forward in a bombing attack during their final training in France.

Atlantic coast and the front showed that it would be impossible, without vast additions, to deal with the American traffic. New cities must be built, arsenals and foundries for the artillery, air cities for the thousands of airmen, towns for salvage work to deal with the necessary repairs and with the utilisation of the waste of war. The most that could be expected from America was that it should send the material and foodstuffs over. Repairs, renewals, reconstruction, and storage had to be done in France.

Thus the problem of the American Army in France was at first not only a military, but an engineering one. The foundations had to be laid before the structure could be built. And so, quietly and unremittingly, saying nothing and doing much, the American engineers set to work. During the winter of 1917-18 the world began to ask what the American was doing. A certain number of American troops had come over to France and England, but where were the vast armies that had been expected? The Germans, in particular, waxed facetious over the Americans. The American was a bluffer and a pretender, they said. He talked much but did nothing. The American armies were mere phantom armies. When some German prisoners saw a group of American soldiers in a town in France they mocked at them. " You are not real Americans," they said ; " you are Englishmen dressed up as Americans to deceive us. We know that there are no American troops here." As it happened, one of the Germans who spoke had been a bar-tender in St. Louis. An American soldier in the group came from the same town, and recognised him. " I am American enough to know where you came from," he said. " I recognise you, friend Fritz, for you have served me many a drink in the —— saloon."

While the outside world criticised, wondered, and doubted, the Americans began to build up their new war-machine in France.

They started at the ports, extending them in such a way as to create what were virtually new dockyard cities. In one place four great piers were built, each pier capable of taking and unloading, at the same time, four of the largest ships afloat. These piers were equipped with the newest and most effective machinery for handling freight. Attached was a series of ten docks ; an area equal to four square miles, extending for nine miles along the front, was planned out for a series of one hundred and eighty warehouses, 50 by 400 feet, and eighty warehouses, 240 by 500 feet. These warehouses were divided into six sections. Twenty lines of track threaded the roadways between them or ran into them. To make room for these places, villages were cleared away and the country-side transformed. A hill of one million cubic yards was excavated to straighten out part of the position.

Vast dockyard cities built

The labour problem was a serious one. A camp had to be built for the thousands of workmen. Of these men, some were negroes from America, who adapted themselves readily to the conditions of life in the new land. The American negroes especially liked France, because there was no colour question there, and the black man was treated the same as the white. Labour was secured from as far afield as Morocco and Greece, and East and West could be seen working happily together side by side in the old French town.

Next came the problem of the railways. The French railway system running on the Atlantic coast ranked among the most efficient and best managed in France ; but to impose upon it the strain of carrying the provisions and munitions for two million men was not to be contemplated. American railwaymen who came to France to study the situation found the French anxious to co-operate with them. French railway methods and American railway methods were different. The French primary idea was safety, the American idea was speed. The Americans—by sidings, ample terminal facilities, and the quick despatch of trains—carried at least 50 per cent. more goods over a single line than the French could. Then the French railway tunnels were not large enough to pass the great freight cars brought over the Atlantic. A number of these freight cars had to be discarded. The Americans, with the permission of the French, did away with many of the turntables, and set about extending the terminal facilities and constructing branch lines and double tracks for certain sections. In all, the Americans constructed within a year about one thousand miles of fresh track in France, and imported large numbers of hundred-and-fifty-ton locomotives and twenty-ton freight cars for use.

Railway system reorganisation

A salvage city was constructed in the heart of France.

LOADING ONE OF THE GREATEST AMERICAN GUNS ON THE WESTERN FRONT.
American gunners sliding a heavy shell into the breech of one of the largest of their guns, preparatory to firing it into the German lines eighteen miles away. Men of the American artillery entered into action with the utmost enthusiasm and determination, some of the gunners who first got into the line working with indefatigable zeal and energy for thirty-six hours at a stretch to get their guns into position.

One building in this had 107,242 feet of floor space, and was solely devoted to repair machinery for shoes, harness, clothing, rubber goods, and metal equipment. Another large building was full of laundry machinery. There was a disinfecting section sufficient to disinfect the clothing of an army, and three buildings for supplementary work which had 90,000 feet of floor space. The camp for the personnel of this salvage city was able to accommodate two thousand persons. It was a model town, with its own sewerage and water systems and electric-light plant, with shower-baths attached to the houses, and everything for the comfort of the staff.

The Americans were resolved to use automobiles to the utmost extent in their legitimate sphere. They did not propose to employ the automobile for heavy freight work, which could be more economically done by railways, but for every possible service motor-cars were **Marvels wrought by engineers** to be provided. The first provision was made for 60,000 motor-vehicles, and a staff of three thousand men was centred in one town to keep these in repair and supply necessary parts. A great mechanical bakery was erected, with two buildings, containing 100,000 square feet floor space each, to bake 500,000 rations of bread per day. It had its own turbo-generating power plant; high pressure super-heated steam from its water-heated boilers. This plant was obtained from an English firm, Messrs. Baker, of Willesden. One section of engineers planned and built a large artillery repairing shop, where field-guns and guns of all sizes up to the largest used by the Army in France could be relined and renewed.

The Americans had to bring over all their own oil, and immense tanks had to be built for its storage. Oil by the hundred thousand barrels could be sucked direct from the tanks to the oil-steamers, and could be run off at once into barrels or into tank-cars, of which there were six hundred, for transfer to other storage centres in other parts of France. Refrigerating experts were employed to build vast meat storage rooms with half a million cubic feet capacity. Some of these refrigerating plants were capable of holding thousands of tons of meat, and could produce hundreds of tons of ice daily. The largest building was about a thousand feet long. Three railway lines ran on one side of it, and one on the other. There were only two larger plants in the United States—one at New York and one at St. Louis.

In all, the American Government undertook works of preparation in France during the first year of the war involving an expenditure of $400,000,000 (£80,000,000).

The first troops to land in France were drawn from the Regular Army, the National Guard, and the Marines. The Regular Army, a small, highly-trained body, had been greatly strengthened immediately after the outbreak of the war by large numbers of young volunteers who rushed to join it. The physical bearing of the **Arrival of the first contingent** men, their discipline and organisation, greatly appealed to all skilled military critics; the only adverse comment passed was that some of the senior officers were rather older than was good for active war, and might not be able to stand the strain of a campaign. General Pershing recognised the justice of this criticism. Every officer, old and young, had to undergo at intervals a physical examination. Those who could not show their fitness were invariably transferred behind the lines or to home duty.

The National Guard differed from the Regular Army in being a volunteer militia, organised by States for interior State protection in times of peace, but subject to calls for special service. Immediately on the outbreak of war the Government had called up the National Guard and raised it to war strength.

The Marines, who formed the third section of the first arrivals, need to be specially mentioned because they rank among the foremost fighting corps of the United States. "Wherever America is in a scrap in any part of the world the Marines are there," was a saying in the days before the Great War. This reputation secured for them, when war broke out, the pick of the very highest type of recruits, many of them drawn from the universities of the Middle West, who eagerly competed to be allowed to join as private soldiers.

The National Army, the new force of a million young men raised under the draft law, did not begin to arrive in Europe until the summer of 1918.

These first arrivals left a very definite impression of efficiency and admirable fighting qualities on all observers. People were surprised at their modest tone. It had been thought that they might come to Europe boastingly. On the contrary, the very opposite spirit was shown from the highest to the lowest. "There is about General Pershing none of the cocksureness, none of the readiness to belittle in a superior manner the methods of the French and British officers; none of the 'we are going to show you how to do it' spirit which one might possibly expect to find in a professional observer who has watched from the outset the mistakes that have been made and the lessons that have had to be learned," wrote one observer. "On the contrary, he is a man who approaches the war with a strikingly complete knowledge of its difficulties, and yet with all the humility of a learner and inquirer." This was the spirit of the Army.

"We have no delusions," said the American officers, "about ourselves. If you find any one of our boys shouting that he has come here to finish up your job for you, knock him out. Most of us understand that we are here to help in a very big business. We realise something of what Britain and France have done. We know how big the task is, and how hard you have worked at it. We want to help you. We are going to learn from you because you have had experience of this game, and we have not. We are studying **Efficiency of the American soldier** what you have done, and what you have discovered, and we hope, when our opportunity comes, that you will find us good fighting stock. We think you will, because our boys' hearts are really in this business."

Written at the time, after studying these new troops at first hand, the following first impressions of them were only deepened by subsequent study:

Efficiency! That is the impression the American soldier leaves on me. This efficiency extends in many directions. For example, in the battalion that I have been with, not a single man is on the sick list. It has mastered the problems of health. Its officers show its soldiers the main causes of disease and explain to them how disease can be avoided. Every man has had impressed on him that preventable illness is a military crime, and that the concealment of illness when it can be cured is unpermissible. The men are treated as men, and not as children, and the result stands revealed in their high standard of accomplishment.

General Pershing and his Staff settled down in Paris. They found almost immediately that it would be necessary for them to have their own telegraph and telephone systems if they were to conduct operations without delay. This involved the construction of a complete set of lines from various points on the Atlantic coast right through the heart of France to Paris, and then on to the Lorraine border. Another direct wire connection was made with London, where Staff work rapidly grew. These lines were put up with great rapidity, and it was interesting to note along many of the Routes Nationales of France the fresh wooden posts with their taut wires and the marks U.S.A. on them, running parallel with the older and slacker French wires. In October, 1917, the American troops, who had been steadily increasing in numbers, began to move to the front, and towards the latter part of that month they took their places in the line acting with French troops. The American Headquarters then moved forward.

The immediate aim of the Americans was to have five

Motor-lorries leaving the dockyard with the mail for the American troops in France. The lavish employment of motor-vehicles for every legitimate purpose was one of the most notable evidences of America's concentration on economy of time and labour.

One corner of the harbour showing among the fishing-boats and coasting vessels a yacht equipped as a submarine-chaser with a gun forward and, half-mast high, a look-out platform with an electric searchlight.

Sketches by a French artist of American activity at a naval base in France.

Morning scene at an American port in France: Soldier-labourers arriving in motor-cars to unload cargoes.

Arrival in France of the U.S. transport Leviathan, the one-time German liner Vaterland, with 12,000 American troops aboard.

German prisoners shovelling sand from the sea-shore to be employed in building barracks for American troops in France.

American tank-car for motor spirit. The American Expeditionary Force also employed large numbers of these for petrol and drinking water.

Leaving for camp after disembarkation. Type of the American cavalry and horse-drawn baggage trains that came to France with the American Expeditionary Force. Inset above : One of the American military police, armed with a heavy automatic pistol.

America's co=operation with the Allies : Varied activities of U.S. forces at a French port.

divisions in the fighting-line, and to have for the start half a million men in France. Some of the divisions which came over brought a reputation of their own with them. Each of the divisions of the Regular Army had its special traditions going back to the Civil War; the National Guard went back still farther. The New England Division, for example, had in its ranks the direct descendants of the Minute Men of the Revolution and of Ethan Allen's mountaineers. Their officers, when reminded of the Boston "tea-party," where one of their companies first had its start, declared that they had come to Europe for a very friendly tea-drinking. The Rainbow Division was so called because it was drawn from eighteen different States of the Union. Its men believed and hoped, as did every battalion, that they were to be the first in the line and where the hardest fighting was to be done.

The first published information about the position of the American troops in the line came from a German official statement announcing the capture of some American soldiers in a raid in French Lorraine in February, 1918. Shortly afterwards the American Government confirmed the fact that the Americans were on the Lorraine front. They occupied at that time sections of the front between Verdun on the north and Baccarat on the south. As is usual with new armies, they were not at first given the control of their whole front, but were brigaded with French troops. Then their brigades were placed next to French troops, so that French and Americans worked side by side. The Americans from the first had the highest appreciation of the spirit and discipline of their French allies; but the language difficulty was very keenly felt. Neither the French nor the Americans are good linguists, and the number of American troops who could speak intelligible French was very small indeed, while in the French regiments the men who could speak English were few and far between.

American positions in the line   The country in which the Americans now found themselves included some of the most historic fighting-ground in France. They were opposite the lost province of Lorraine, and from some of their positions they could see the smoke coming from the factories of Metz itself. South of Verdun was the St. Mihiel salient, held by the Germans, projecting, like two sides of a triangle, into the French front. Immediately around it was a country of woods, hills, and valleys. Important military cities like Toul, Nancy, and Epinal lay behind, cities that were the constant objective of German aeroplanes. The great Saffais plateau formed a natural barrier which had saved the French line in this part of the front in August, 1914. There were towns like Lunéville which had been overrun by the Germans in their first advance at the opening of the war, and which still showed, in their blown-up bridges and their burned-out houses, what German occupation meant. Two fast-flowing rivers—the Meurthe and the Moselle—ran through the country behind. There were great iron-mines here, but the dominating note of the country was rural and agricultural rather than industrial. The forests to the north, in particular—forests which had not suffered so much destruction as those in some other parts—gave a pleasant note to the land. This was in times of peace one of the most prosperous, fertile, and prolific parts of France, and in one section of it was to be found one of the most famous health resorts of Europe.

The American troops entered the fighting zone with the utmost enthusiasm and determination. They were out to win the war. They wanted to hurry things on. When some artillerymen first got to the line they worked for thirty-six hours at a stretch to get their guns into position. There came some delay in the arrival of the shells. They hurried back to the French officer responsible, begging and imploring him to hurry up. "We are losing time," they said. "What's the hurry?" asked the Frenchman.

"The Germans have been waiting for three years. A few days more or less will not make much difference." The Americans did not see it in this way. They wanted to "get a move on." And so it was that wherever they settled down they began to plan offensives against the enemy. "We want to get away from trench war to open war," they said. They devoted themselves to their musketry, and specially prided themselves on their skill with the rifle, believing, with the leaders of the British Army, that the rifle and the bayonet are the main weapons of the soldier.

One fine regiment, occupying one of the first sections of the line taken over by the Americans, came in for a very trying time. It was shelled by the Germans day and night, gas-shells being largely used. Some of the troops, new at the work, found it difficult to remember to keep their gas-masks always by them. This increased the casualties. Yet when, after a few days, the authorities resolved to have a raid to clear the Germans out of the position, every man, down to the cooks and the orderlies, volunteered for the undertaking.   **Americans' first offensive action**

This section of the line, although it had witnessed much of the bloodiest fighting of the late summer of 1914, had become comparatively quiet. The Germans were concentrating their attack elsewhere. They had Landwehr battalions to hold the front, and the most exciting experience some time before the Americans arrived was when a flock of wild-geese flew over part of the line, and French and Germans jumped on their parapets to fire at them. But the Americans soon altered all that. The Germans, finding themselves affected by numerous raids and by increasing artillery fire, began to reply in kind, and the American sector soon became a very "lively" spot.

The American Army's first offensive action was in the middle of February, 1918, when, on a Wednesday afternoon, the American batteries took part in the artillery preparation for an attack by the French at the Butte du Mesnil. The French attack was completely successful, capturing a position which had held up the French advance in September, 1915. The work of the American batteries was a considerable factor in it.

The work of the American troops at this stage was a severe test of soldierly qualities. This holding the line meant living under almost continuous artillery fire, often in cellars of ruined villages, being shelled and gassed and raided at every opportunity. The German gas-shell, the fumes of which settled low down, clung about uniforms and made cellars and places of ordinary shelter uninhabitable for long spells at a time, added a fresh torment to life. The troops could, at least, console themselves with the knowledge that they were sending more shells and worse gas than the Germans were firing on them. The Germans time after time flung considerable forces in raids against the Americans. The soldiers from across the Atlantic were able justifiably to boast at the end of some weeks that they had held their own line against all attacks, and each time, mainly by the use of the rifle, they had driven the Germans back.   **Decorations for great gallantry**

Large numbers of the troops won decorations from the French Government during these trying weeks. On one occasion alone, in March, forty-eight Americans were awarded the Croix de Guerre for gallantry in action. All of these had been engaged in the sector east of Lunéville. They represented all ranks, from colonels to privates.

Lieutenant-Colonel Matthew A. Tinley, of Council Bluffs, Ia., was decorated for the brilliant way in which, during a violent enemy attack, he succeeded in keeping the line intact in spite of the efforts of the enemy. During the raid of March 5th, north-east of Badonviller, when the Germans knocked the American positions almost to pieces by shell fire and then attacked in waves, Colonel Tinley gathered his men together, re-formed the line, and poured

AMERICA'S WAR MINISTER ON A TOUR OF INSPECTION IN FRANCE.

The Hon. Newton Baker, Secretary for War in the U.S. Government, paid several visits to France to study the requirements of the American Expeditionary Force, and inspect the working of the organisation provided to meet them. This photograph shows him seated between General Pershing, on his right hand, and Brigadier-General Walsh, studying the plans for an engineering project at a transportation centre.

so strong a fire on the German infantry that, after a short fight, they were obliged to withdraw.

Major William J. Donovan was decorated for his fine example of bravery, activity, and presence of mind during a violent bombardment. "He is the best officer under fire that I have ever seen," said a French officer. Colonel McArthur, when participating in a French attack with French troops, advanced in such fashion that he succeeded in bringing a Bavarian officer back with him. Lieutenant Henry A. Peterson was working a trench-mortar when all of the crew were killed. He continued firing, in the face of the enemy attack, until all the ammunition was exhausted, shattering the enemy storming columns which were trying to advance. Two sergeants from New York took possession of machine-guns which the Germans were trying to smash, turned them against the German troops, and smashed up their defensive front line. Lieutenant A. W. Terell was directing his battery of the artillery during the fight when a number of men were badly wounded, including himself. When the doctors came he refused to allow himself to be attended to until his men were bound up, although he was so severely wounded that later his leg had to be amputated.

Early in April Corporal F. H. Helmar was given the Médaille Militaire, the most prized of French military decorations. "Although buried in a fallen dug-out, caused by the explosion of a high-powered shell," said the French citation, "he continued to encourage his comrades while the rescue was being organised. Having been rescued from the debris, with several contusions, he refused to have his wounds dressed, and, instead, set to work rescuing his comrades from the wreckage. He spent the whole night digging in the terrain, giving a remarkable example of devotion, fortitude, and courage."

It may seem unnecessary to mention in detail such cases in a war in which great gallantry was the rule among the soldiers of the Allies, but the instances are remarkable as showing the real spirit of the American troops. Every

Notable courage and devotion

observer of these men in the fighting-line at that time— the present writer among them—was struck by the remarkable resource and daring of the men.

The American Government found that it had no adequate means of decorating men who had performed acts of conspicuous bravery, or of recognising the acts of allied troops. It was possible to bestow the Medal of Honour, which was regarded as the supreme decoration for any man. This was bestowed by the President himself, the Commanding General of the Expeditionary Force cabling his recommendation for immediate action, and presenting the medal when the recommendation was approved. Only in the case of a person apparently fatally wounded, or so ill as to be in danger of his life, was the Commanding General authorised to give the medal without the President's previous approval. This Medal of Honour could be awarded posthumously.

The need of an additional award was so much felt that in February special American decorations were authorised —the Distinguished Service Cross and the Distinguished Service Medal. A bronze oak leaf and a silver star were additional citations; war service chevrons and wound chevrons. The Distinguished Service Cross was in bronze, and was to be awarded by the President or, in the name of the President by the Commanding General of the Expeditionary Force, to any person who, while serving in any capacity with the Army, distinguished himself or herself by extraordinary heroism against an armed enemy of the United States. The Distinguished Service Medal was to be a bronze medal bestowed upon any person who had distinguished himself or herself in exceptionally meritorious service to the Government in connection with the military operations. The war service chevron was for each enlisted man who had served six months in the war zone. A chevron was to be awarded for each wound. Both the Distinguished Service Cross and the Distinguished Service Medal could, like the Medal of Honour, be bestowed posthumously. The first Distinguished Service Crosses were

Special American decorations

awarded to Lieutenant John O. Green, Sergeant William Norton, and Sergeant Patrick Walsh, " for extraordinary heroism in connection with military operations against an armed enemy." The despatch of the general commanding their division in which he recommended these first decorations is of historic interest :

I recommend that the Distinguished Service Cross be awarded to the officer and men named hereafter, who distinguished themselves by acts of extraordinary heroism.

Lieutenant Green, while in a dug-out, having been wounded by an enemy hand-grenade, was summoned to surrender. He refused to do so. Returning the fire of the enemy, he wounded one and pursued the hostile party.

Sergeant Norton, finding himself in a dug-out surrounded by the enemy, into which a hand-grenade had just been thrown, refused to surrender and made a bold dash outside, killing one of his assailants. By so doing he saved the company's log-book.

Sergeant Walsh followed his company commander to the first lines, in spite of a severe barrage. The captain being killed, he assumed command of the group and attacked a superior force of the enemy, inflicting a severe loss upon them. Though of advanced age, he refused to leave the front.

About this time a certain amount of criticism was heard

![photograph]
ACQUIRING KNOWLEDGE AT FIRST HAND.

Mr. Baker examining a heavy gun. On January 10th, 1918, he announced that the American Army in France was, and would continue to be, provided with all the artillery it wanted as rapidly as it could use it.

concerning the state of the American preparations. The military work of President Wilson's Cabinet was violently attacked by many of his critics in America itself, while a number of by no means unfriendly observers in England and in France began to ask more and more insistently what America was really doing. " When Britain had been in the war for a year she had fought three great campaigns," said these critics. " Before she had been in the war a month she had an Army of over 100,000 men fighting in France. What battles has America fought in her first year of the war ? " As shown earlier in this chapter, such comparisons were unfair, and the people making them did not understand the fundamental differences in British and American circumstances.

Criticism of America's work Mr. Baker, the Secretary for War, appeared in person before the Senate Committee on military affairs on January 10th, and gave what was described as an absolutely frank statement of America's war preparations and the results attained up to date.

In the course of this he said that the United States would have five hundred thousand men in France early in 1918, and one million five hundred thousand more men ready to go in that year. Critics of the Army had made much of the fact that America's first artillery was largely dependent upon the Allies.

It is fair to say (he declared) that the American Army in France, large as it is, and the American Army to be sent there, large as that is, are and will be provided with artillery of the type they want as rapidly as they can use it.

Our problem was to get it over, and at the enemy. It was not for us to map out an ideal plan. Our problem was to get into co-operation with Great Britain, France, and our other friends in the most immediate and efficient way. The problem could not be decided here. It is so extraordinary and so vast that it must be seen and studied on the ground before it can be comprehended at all.

The main points Mr. Baker put before the Senate Committee were as follows :

1. A large Army in the field and in training, so large that further increments to it can be adequately equipped and trained as rapidly as those already training can be transported.

2. The Army has been enlisted and selected without serious dislocation of the industries of the country.

3. The training of the Army is now proceeding rapidly, and its spirit is high. The subsistence of the Army has been above criticism. Its initial clothing supply, which was temporarily inadequate, is now substantially complete, and reserves will rapidly accumulate. Arms of the most modern **Statement by the War Secretary** and effective kind, including artillery, machine-guns, automatic rifles, and small arms, have been provided by manufacture or purchase for every soldier in France, and are available for every soldier that can be gotten to France in 1918.

4. A substantial Army is already in France, where both officers and men have been additionally and specially trained, and is now ready for active service.

5. Independent lines of communication and supply, vast storage, and other facilities are in process of construction in France.

6. Great programmes for the manufacture of additional equipment, and for the production of new instruments of war, have been formulated.

7. No army of similar size in the history of the world has ever been raised, equipped, and trained so quickly. No such provision has ever been made for the comfort, health, and well-being of an army.

Mr. Baker said that he made this statement on America's Army preparations for two reasons :

ADMIRING A BIG GUN'S WAR-PAINT.

Mr. Baker and General Pershing interested in some camouflaged heavy ordnance. By January, 1918, artillery was available for all the American troops that could be got to France during that year.

SCENE OF A STREET BATTLE.
Rue Carnot, Château Thierry, after the American troops' successful fight there on May 31st, 1918.

1. Because the American people were entitled to know the splendid effectiveness with which democracy had been able to organise the man-power and the material power of the United States in the great cause.

2. Because the American Army in France under General Pershing and America's Allies were entitled to have the benefit resulting from a depression of the enemy moral which must come when the Germans realise that American democracy has neither blundered nor hesitated, but has actually brought the full power of its men and resources into completely organised strength against their military machine.

Mr. Baker visited England and France in March, 1918, and had conferences of far-reaching import with the heads of the British and French Governments. The Allies very keenly desired that the Americans, in place of keeping their Army as a separate organisation, should as a temporary measure, brigade American regiments with French and British troops. They could in this way acquire a knowledge of war which older battalions had obtained in the field, and they could be more immediately available. The Americans had a very strong objection to this; they wanted to keep their Army as their Army, under American direction

Americans brigaded with the Allies and doing things in an American way. They believed that while it might take longer to bring the whole force into the field in this way, it would be a much more effective weapon in the end.

But the whole outlook was changed by the German advance on March 21st, 1918. The Americans were among the first to realise that a new problem now confronted them. General Pershing and General Bliss, the Military Representative of America with the Supreme War Council, in co-operation with Mr. Baker, agreed on a new line of policy which had President Wilson's approval. General Pershing, in a message to the French Command, offered, on behalf of the President and the people of the

United States, all the troops in France to be used as General Foch directed, in whatever way he thought fit.

On April 1st it was officially announced that, as a result of communications and deliberations between the different parties, the American Government had agreed that such of its regiments as could not be used in divisions of their own might be brigaded with French and British units so long as the necessity lasted.

The shock of the March disaster to the allied cause aroused the American people. Up to now they had been inclined to regard an allied victory as a certainty. Now they saw the possibility of a German triumph facing them. Britain and France told them that the one great need of the

THE BRIDGE AT CHÂTEAU THIERRY.
On May 31st and June 1st, 1918, when the Germans made a desperate attack on Château Thierry, on the Marne, American troops took a brilliant part in its defence. They blew up the bridge, which they were more particularly defending, but before doing so waited until German troops were actually on it.

moment was men. There were vast armies of men in America almost ready to come over. President Wilson took into his own hands the direction of the effort to get these men over. He swept away all obstacles, and in an incredibly short time a fleet of transports of a magnitude such as the Atlantic had never before seen was crossing the seas week by week, every ship crowded with Army men and munitions of war.

Before June arrived fresh reserves were coming in to Europe—to England and France—at the rate of between two and three score thousand a week. By May Mr. Baker was able to announce that America had 500,000 soldiers in Europe. By June he was able to say that the number had risen to 700,000, and to intimate that before many weeks were over it would be 1,000,000.

"The decision of the United States Government is both generous and wise," declared the "Times" when news came that the Americans had consented to the brigading of their troops with allied units.

It is generous, because the natural aspirations of our great

American ally is to see its rapidly-growing Army operating in the field as one cohesive whole. This distribution of operation of its units, even though the expedient will be only temporary, implies a spirit of chivalrous sacrifice in the face of stubborn necessity. It is wise, because the needs of the Allies in France are urgent, and because it has become imperative that the training of the American units should be accelerated. . . . It seals the bond of brotherhood which unites the European Allies with the United States in the common cause of civilisation.

The placing of the Americans under the supreme command of General Foch caused immediate developments. One division of American Regulars at once moved up from the Lorraine front to help the Allies farther north. Other divisions that had just come out of the lines for a rest were hurried back there. French troops were relieved in the Lorraine sector, and Americans were given entire charge of a considerable part of the line here.

This decision meant that the large number of Americans pouring into Europe could go at once to sections of the fighting-line without waiting for their own secondary services. They could thus immediately reinforce the British Armies, which had suffered so heavily, and the French on the eve of their great conflict.

Every section of the British Army desired that the Americans might be brigaded with it.

The Canadians sent imploring messages to America. "Come and join us," they said. "We like you, and we believe you like us. We'll do everything we can for you. We want you with us." Canadian **American mettle** officers were already contemplating a **proved in battle** possible enlargement of the Canadian Corps when, by fresh American troops being attached to it, the four divisions which had done so nobly might grow to eight.

Meanwhile the American soldiers were showing their mettle more and more in the fighting. A considerable engagement took place in mid-April, when 1,200 German shock troops attacked the American position west of Remieres Wood, south-east of Verdun. They captured the village of Seicheprey, but the Americans vigorously counter-attacked and retook the place. The engagement was declared by General Pershing to have been the most

severe in which the Americans had yet taken part. " The enemy's losses were much greater than we anticipated, as was evidenced by the fact that more than three hundred dead were left in the American trenches and No Man's Land."

" It's better than baseball," said the Americans, setting their teeth tight.

Farther down, immediately before the Seicheprey engagement, the Germans endeavoured to take another section of the line. They opened a very heavy barrage fire and attacked four times during three days, but they **Croix de Guerre** never got past the American wire, and **for a U.S. regiment** several hundred of the men were killed.

The French military authorities marked their sense of the American fighting strength in a very striking and novel way.

The regiment which had been fighting was cited in the French Army Orders and had its colours decorated with the Croix de Guerre by the French commander under whom it was serving. After the colours were decorated, one hundred and seventeen soldiers of all ranks, from colonel to private and from chaplain to N.C.O., were decorated by the French.

Word came from the north that the division which had moved upwards from Lorraine was entering the firing-line. It had spent seven days at special training, every part of its equipment being thoroughly overhauled and the men put through the new open war drill. Then it marched for five days into the battle zone and took up its position.

Early in May there came word from these troops. Some of them had taken up positions south of Grivesnes and west of Montdidier, with French divisions to the right and left of them. They were violently attacked by the Germans after a heavy bombardment of two hours. Three German battalions advanced. There was a heavy fight, and the American casualties were by no means inconsiderable ; but in the end the Germans were driven back, leaving the lines heaped with dead and several

AMERICAN TROOPS MOVING UP TO TAKE THEIR PLACE IN THE FIRING-LINE.

With a French cyclist as guide, a column of troops of the American Expeditionary Force is here seen as it marched along a sunken road in the war zone on its way to the trenches. It formed part of the first of the United States forces to enter the fighting area, and its arrival evoked considerable interest among the French soldiers who had eagerly awaited the men of the Western Republic.

French children cheering a regiment of United States troops passing through a village on the way to the front. The American Army's first offensive action was in the middle of February, 1918, when American batteries took part in the capture of enemy positions at the Butte du Mesnil. From that time onwards its force in the field was felt more widely as it played an ever more important part in the hostilities.

American infantry, with French Tanks in support, leaving their trenches to attack Cantigny, which they captured, with two hundred prisoners, at the end of May, 1918, their first "big success," in the war. Advancing in two steady waves, they crossed the intervening zone to their objectives, a depth of nearly a mile, in exactly forty minutes, and there dug in and continued to hold the position.

AMERICA'S IRRESISTIBLE MIGHT FLOODING FORWARD IN FRANCE TO OVERWHELM THE TEUTON INVADER.

prisoners in American hands. This, the first sign that the Americans were joining in the great battle now being fought in the north, aroused great interest everywhere.

The Germans quickly renewed their attack. A day or two later they launched a very heavy bombardment of mustard-gas, sending over thousands of gas-shells. It was at this time that the American force in the field began to be felt. A month or two before the Germans had been sneeringly demanding what had become of the Americans. Now they seemed to be every-where. In addition to the army holding the Lorraine front, an ever-increasing force appeared in Picardy, where the great battle for Paris was going on. When

TAKING NO RISKS.
American soldiers searching the ruins of Cantigny for lurking Germans after capturing the village on May 28th, 1918, the first large enterprise in which they proved their quality as cool and steady fighters.

AMERICAN SOLDIERS SMOKING OUT THE HUNS.
Germans emerging from the smoked-out cellars and underground retreats in Cantigny to surrender to the victorious American troops. The enemy, who surrendered freely, were chiefly young Silesians and Brandenburgers.

Paris itself was threatened, word came up that a strong American force had already arrived to help to protect it. At the beginning the desire of the American people was to work with the French rather than with British troops, it being thought that this would be more useful. Now this plan seemed to disappear, and all along the British lines American regiments were to be found brigaded with British divisions. The moral effect of this arrival of the Americans was very great. The armies of the Allies had been pressed hard. The losses of both British and French since the opening of the German offensive had been very heavy; at the very moment when they were almost bending under the strain these hosts of men—well armed, well found—came and stood by the side of them.

In May the British and French Press were allowed to announce that a new American army had arrived; in other words, the National Army which had been training for months, the pick of the young manhood of America, was reaching the field of war.

"Your men remind me of British soldiers," said the English visitor to General Pershing. "Your boys make me think of Canadians at every turn," said the Canadian

visitor. But the Americans, while having many of the characteristics of both, had yet distinctive characteristics of their own.

When the new armies arrived in Europe they had their experience yet to get, but no one could doubt their spirit, their temper, or their deter-mination, and it was soon found in fight after fight that the Americans, hard pressed, hard driven, and often outnumbered, yet held their own, driving back enemy attacks, holding their ground, and turning threatened defeat into victory.

In handling his troops in Europe, General Pershing showed a mixture of severity and liberality. Certain crimes were crushed without mercy. Every army, however carefully selected, has a certain small proportion of undesirables. The first American soldier who was guilty of an offence against a woman was promptly given a sentence the severity of which rang through the Army. Crime was very rare indeed. Even military offences were few in number. In the front lines the worst punishment that could be given was to send a man out of the fighting zone into the lines of communication. A corporal **American Y.M.C.A.** guilty of some minor offence was **and Red Cross** ordered to go back and do duty in the rear. He went to his commanding officer imploringly. "Take my pay for six months, but let me stay here and fight the Hun," he begged.

The Army was much more liberal in its use of the work of philanthropic organisations than some European forces. The Y.M.C.A. was virtually a branch of the service, independently conducted. It had almost unlimited funds behind it, and at the request of the authorities it took charge of the post canteens. This was a step of very doubtful wisdom, for in attempting to run these post canteens without too heavy a loss it had to charge higher prices than soldiers had been accustomed to pay, and thereby incurred a certain amount of unpopularity. But the Y.M.C.A. did magnificent service in many ways. It organised hostels for officers and men behind the lines, and its representatives were found in cellars up in the front lines, often working with their gas-helmets on, preparing coffee, cocoa, and other refreshments for the boys who were fighting.

The American Red Cross, which had done great work in aid of the French homeless and wounded from the very beginning of the war, was tireless in its efforts to help the soldier.

The Salvation Army, which was kept behind the lines in the British Army, was allowed to go forward with the Americans, and the work of the Salvation lassies was very widely appreciated. They made doughnuts and "cookies" for the boys; they repaired their clothes for them. In many of the officers' messes the attendants

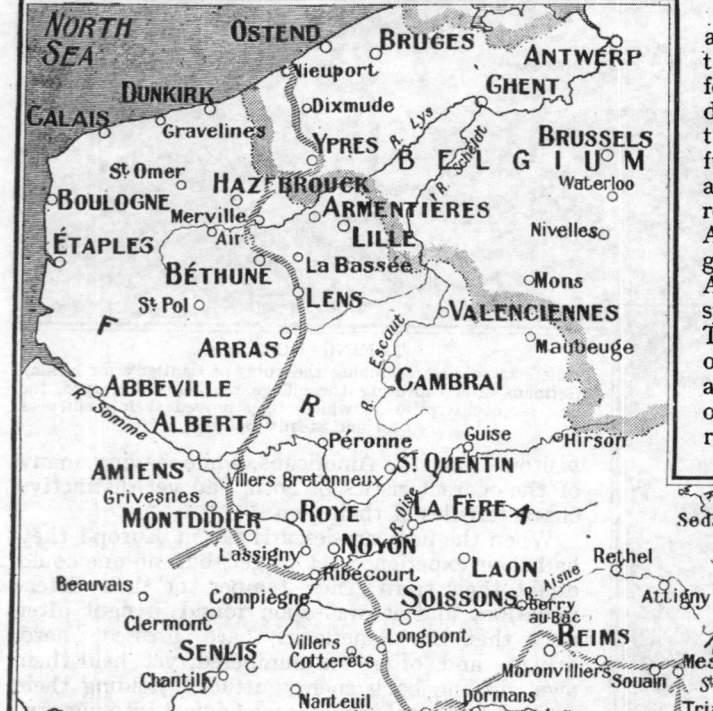

WHERE AMERICANS FOUGHT IN THEIR FIRST YEAR.
Map of the western battle-line as it was on July 14th, 1918. The arrows indicate positions that had been held by United States forces up to that date.

were American gentlewomen, who, unable to fight themselves, came to the front to do that which they could in helping to serve the men.

A large number of the American troops came from prohibition States where the majority of them had neither seen nor tasted liquor. In France, a wine-growing country, it was thought by many that they might suffer heavily from intemperance as a reaction from former conditions. It was found that many of the men tried to drink French wines at first. The vast majority of them found that they did not like them, and went back to water and coffee. The amount of intemperance was much less than in armies of men who had always been able to obtain intoxicants.

American plans in aviation

Responsible leaders of American flying were sent to France, and a big flying and training ground was built in the heart of France. So many young men volunteered for the Flying Corps that it was possible to pick out the recruits with the utmost rigidity. The Americans adopted the plan of the British Army of having all pilots officers, and not the French plan of using N.C.O.'s and men as pilots.

The type of man aimed at as the flying officer was the young, athletic college man with quick perceptions, clear eye, and steady brain. The difficulty was not to obtain these, but to select from among the number of those who wanted to join.

The authorities responsible for the production of aircraft resolved that they would have an engine surpassing any in the world—the Liberty engine. All the noted aeroplane and automobile engineers were brought together into conference; when it was agreed that each should reveal his own special secrets of efficiency, that the best points of all might be combined in the national engine. Theoretically the idea was excellent; actually the idea worked out far from well.

Individual points of excellence need to be synchronised and harmonised when they are brought together in one machine. The conferences of the committees led to long delays. When plans of the different types of engines were decided upon, it was found that further delays occurred in production. Greatly to the annoyance of the American flying men and of the responsible American aviation corps, certain people in America made absurd boasts about what America was going to do. Some of these promised that 20,000 American aeroplanes would be in flight in Europe in the spring of 1918. One or two put the figure at 50,000. They did not realise the vast equipment for each squadron of a score of aeroplanes—the staff, the repairing plant, and the like. A squadron of twenty aeroplanes employs one hundred and fifty men, and has a fleet of cars, repairing cars, and the like for its requirements.

Delay in aircraft production

In place of there being 20,000 aeroplanes in flight in the spring of 1918, the first batch of engines had only arrived in France for testing. The Americans, in order to help the Allies, sent large numbers of men—trained aeroplane mechanics—to the workshops of the United Kingdom.

They had also sent a number of their own men, qualified pilots, to the Air Forces of England and France, where they were doing admirable work. The American flyers were still depending on European-made machines, and it was impossible to obtain an adequate supply of these owing to the demands of the Air Services of the European countries themselves.

The Military Affairs Committee of the Senate investigated the reason for this shortage of aircraft, and issued a report on the matter in April, 1918. It dealt, among other things, with the Liberty motor.

It is apparent from the evidence that the twelve-cylinder Liberty motor is just emerging from the development or experimental stage. Since the original design and the setting up of the first completed motor in July, 1917, a large number of changes have been found necessary, many of them causing delay in reaching quantity production. Within the last two months changes of considerable importance have been made which, it is hoped, will make the motor serviceable for combat aeroplanes of the defensive type and for bombing and observation aeroplanes.

Twenty-two thousand five hundred Liberty motors have been ordered, 122 have been completed for the Army, and 142 for the Navy. Four have been shipped overseas. Some of those already delivered are being altered to overcome the defects ascertained during the last few weeks. It is understood, however, that these alterations will consume but a very short time.

Report on the Liberty motor The production of Liberty motors to date is, of course, gravely disappointing. The Government officials having the manufacture of the Liberty motor in charge have made the mistake of leading the public and the allied nations to the belief that many thousands of these motors would be completed in the spring of 1918.

The production of combat aeroplanes in the United States for use in actual warfare has thus far been a substantial failure, and constitutes a most serious disappointment in our war preparations. We had no design of our own, neither did we adopt any one of the European designs until months after we entered the war.

The committee summarised its conclusions very reasonably in one sentence: "Much of the delay in producing completed combat aeroplanes is due to ignorance of the art, and the failure of organising the effort in such a way as to centralise authority and bring about quick decisions."

At the start of the war the United States Government had purchased altogether 'less than two hundred aeroplanes in its entire history. The Signal Corps had arranged during the year for the making of about 11,500 combat aeroplanes in the United States, and had sent vast quantities of material to France to have aeroplanes made there in French factories.

April 6th, 1918, was the first anniversary of the entry of the United States into the war. Let us review what it had done in that time.

Review of the first year's work

The strength of the fighting Army had been multiplied nearly eightfold, as the following comparison will show:

		Officers		Men
APRIL, 1917.				
Regulars	..	5,791	..	121,797
National Guard	..	3,733	..	76,713
Reserve Corps	..	—	..	4,000
Total	..	9,524		202,510
APRIL, 1918.				
Regulars	..	10,698	..	503,142
National Guard	..	16,893	..	431,583
Reserve Corps	..	96,210	..	77,360
National Army	..	—	..	516,839
Total	..	123,801		1,528,924

Of this Army close on 500,000 men were in Europe, a number to be doubled within the next three months,

CAPTURING GERMAN PRISONERS FROM CANTIGNY DUG-OUTS.
"Smoking" enemy troops from their cellars and hiding-places beneath wrecked buildings in Cantigny. In May, 1918, the Americans took part in the fighting near Montdidier, and on May 28th they advanced on a front of a mile and a quarter to the north of that place, stormed the enemy lines, and attacked and captured the village of Cantigny, taking nearly two hundred prisoners, as well as a quantity of material.

LLL

CHARGE OF AMERICANS TO THE CRY OF "LUSITANIA!"
United States troops going forward in a bayonet charge in the early summer of 1918. An Australian officer recorded that again and again he heard the shout "Lusitania!" on American lips in the charge, as though memory of that German crime nerved American arms in the long-looked-for hour of dealing punishment.

and which, it was announced, would be quadrupled before the end of the year. The American troops had up to that time suffered a total of 2,368 casualties, as follows:

Killed in battle	..	..	..	163
Died of disease or accident		..		957
Lost at sea	..	..	..	257
Died of wounds	..	..	..	52
Other causes ..	..	..	..	47
Missing and prisoners		..	..	63
Wounded	..	..	..	829
Total	..	..	..	2,368

The Ordnance Department increased its staff in a year from ninety-seven officers to over 5,000 officers. Its eleven Government arsenals—none of any very considerable size—grew as though by magic to a vast munition production organisation. It enlisted 1,400 privately owned manufacturing establishments, some of them on the most enormous scale, to help it. It built many new plants itself.

Germany awaking to the facts

Germany was now beginning to realise what American intervention must mean. The German Press was slowly admitting the truth. "It is certain," said the "Berliner Tageblatt," "that before very long North America will succeed in preparing masses which must in all circumstances be a very valuable support for our enemies. . . . We will hope that the offensive in the west will now lead to a result that will exclude North America's participation in the war, so that there will be no second year of war with America."

The occasion of the first anniversary of the American entry into the war was celebrated by all the Allies, and long statements were published in America showing what the country had done in the year.

But the real feeling of the American people was one not of exultation, but of severe introspection. The events of the previous fortnight in the great Battle of Amiens had revealed the new strength of Germany. A few more battles such as this and America would find herself fighting with the enemy in possession of the continent over which the war was being waged. American people were mortified that, though they had been in the war a year, they were only able to play a comparatively small part in this Armageddon, holding one section of the line apart from the main battle-front.

The American people passionately and enthusiastically desired the success of the allied cause. Each day for months past had made it more and more their cause. They knew something of the vast preparations on their side, of the hosts of young men called up, of the hundreds of thousands of soldiers already sent to France. What they wanted was that this force, which had been growing for a year, should now come into immediate use.

America impatient for quick action

Where were the American aeroplanes? Where were the American guns? Where was the American fighting army? These were the questions put, not by America's Allies but by the American people themselves. The resolution of the people swept the nation from the Executive Mansion to the smallest sections or their community—"Speed up!"

Then followed events which soon became the marvel of the world. They would, of course, have been impossible had there not been a year of solid work behind. The troops had already been raised, equipped, and drilled. They were waiting—a million of them—to move across the sea. The shipping policy had helped to obtain the ships ready for them; vast supplies had already landed in Europe; adequate methods of transportation had been evolved.

Now had come the hour to drive—a drive only possible with a well-equipped and well-prepared team. The cry went up from the Allies to America for help. Britain was taxing her own resources to the full. She was ready to let her harvest go waste, if need be, in order to obtain a few thousand more men from the land. The Dominion of Canada was enforcing methods of recruiting more drastic and far-reaching than at one time appeared possible. France—bleeding, suffering, yet indomitable—looked across the seas for aid.

The war organisation of America, by which the President is virtually autocrat for all war purposes, was shown in its real strength. President Wilson himself took a direct part in the shipping situation. Vast armadas, such as had never sailed the seas before, quickly assembled at various Atlantic ports. Monster German liners were transformed into American troopships. Luxurious ocean-travel ships were gutted and fitted with bunks and men packed in them by the thousand. The number of American troops coming to Europe rose within a few weeks from 100,000 a month to an average of 10,000 a day.

The passage of these ships was so carefully guarded by the American and British Navies, working in the closest and most cordial co-operation, that half a million soldiers crossed the sea with scarcely the loss of a life by enemy attack. One unfortunate exception to this rule was on May 23rd, when H.M. armed mercantile cruiser Moldavia was torpedoed and sunk with American troops aboard, and fifty-six of the soldiers were lost. In June it was possible to announce that 1,000,000 American soldiers were in Europe. By July plans had been already completed for the landing of a force of between 2,000,000 and 3,000,000 men before the year was out.

What was mostly remarked on was not the number of these troops, but their quality. Military critics had spoken highly, and with reason, of the first batches of Americans who arrived —the Regulars, the National Guard, and the Marines—but without in any way diminishing the praise given

TRYING ON CAPTURED ARMOUR.
Men of the American Red Cross Service, who were among the early arrivals on the French front, trying on German body-armour which had been picked up on the battlefield in the Verdun region.

to the pioneers, it must be added that these new troops, the National Army, surpassed every expectation. These men of the West were mostly tall and of magnificent physique. In build it was noted that they strongly resembled the Austra- lians. They were all of them young, in the very crowning years of early man- hood. They landed in Britain ready for battle, every man with his steel helmet and gas-mask and full equipment. They came modestly, without boasting. And it was easy to see that they came in a temper far more dangerous than any boast- fulness could be. They and the mighty nation which they represented had reached the conclusion that while it remained in its present mood, Germany must be treated as men would treat a deadly rattlesnake.

Quality of the National Army

Their standard of conduct was very high. They were surprisingly stern, set, grim. It had taken them some time to make up their mind as to how they should regard the German. Now their minds were made up. Little instances showed their attitude. It was told at one of the ports how the Americans had resolved to take a certain number of prisoners they had captured over to America in one of their returning boats. The prisoners, who had been under British care, drove down to the ship-side and marched aboard, laughing, joking, and smoking fat cigars. An American captain took them in charge. He immediately ordered them to form in line, to stand to attention, and throw their cigars overboard.

One German officer sneered contemptuously as he did so. "Put that man in irons!" the captain ordered. A second grumbled a protest. "Put that man in irons," said the captain quietly to his guard. When that was done, he added, "Now take the others and lock them up in their cells."

The first section of the new National Army arrived in England in the second week of May, 1918, and on Saturday, May 11th, a regiment, consisting of 2,700 men, under the command of Colonel Whitman and Lieut.-Colonel Wagner, marched through London and was received by the King.

Only short notice had been given of the coming of the American troops, but the notice was long enough to attract great crowds. From Waterloo Station to Wellington Barracks dense throngs of cheering people were to be seen everywhere. The American flag flew from public and private buildings, and "Old Glory"— perhaps for the first time in British history—was freely worn in the buttonholes of Londoners in their own city. The King sent a stirring message to the officers and troops, a facsimile copy of the King's letter being handed to each officer and man at Wellington Barracks, where they were resting after their march. The King's letter read as follows :

The King's letter to U.S. troops

AMERICAN SOLDIERS IN GERMAN "FLAMMENWERFER" HARNESS.
Men of the American Expeditionary Force wearing some of the liquid fire throwers which had been captured from the Germans during raids on their trenches. In the front view, on the left, are seen the long nozzles and hose of these barbaric devices introduced by Germans into modern warfare; in the photograph on the right are shown the containers, as worn on the shoulders of those taking the machines into action.

FRANCE'S TRIBUTE TO PRESIDENT WILSON.
American troops marching past the President of the French Republic on July 4th, 1918, when the Avenue du Trocadéro was formally renamed Avenue du Président Wilson.

Soldiers of the United States,—The people of the British Isles welcome you on your way to take your stand beside the Armies of many Nations now fighting in the Old World the great battle for human freedom.

The Allies will gain new heart and spirit in your company. I wish that I could shake the hand of each one of you and bid you God-speed on your mission.

April, 1918.   GEORGE R.I.

The scene at Buckingham Palace as the troops marched by was picturesque and impressive. The King was waiting for them, talking in the forecourt of the palace with General Biddle and other American officers. When distant cheering was heard announcing the coming of the regiment, King George walked down the forecourt and stood on the edge of the broad pavement with the Queen, Queen Alexandra, and other members of the Royal Family behind them. The Guards' Band led the way, and, following the young troops, came a small company of American veterans of the Civil War in London, carrying a banner inscribed "Not for ourselves, but country."

"The build and bearing of the troops," said a writer in the "Times," "roused constant admiration. One spectator would say, 'They look a tough lot'; another, 'They are a fine lot'; a third, 'They are an even lot'; while a fourth could only express his praise in a shout of 'Good boys!' or 'Go it, boys!' It is worth noting that when the colours passed many men **London's greeting** received them with bared heads, and **to the Americans** that 'Off with your hats!' was heard now and then in admonition of a civilian. Considering that the custom of so honouring the colours of British regiments is still far from universal, this may be accepted by Americans as a rather remarkable tribute.

"Three things were striking in these Americans—their youth, their seriousness, and their modesty. The first quality is easily conceded to America; we all think of her as young. Those of her sons whom London scrutinised so keenly came under arms only last summer. They were officered chiefly by men who then passed through the officers training corps, though the commanding officer and the lieutenant-colonel belong to the old Regular Army.

IN HOMAGE TO WASHINGTON.
Statue of George Washington in the Place d'Iéna, Paris, where the Presidential stand was erected for the Independence Day celebration in 1918.

They might, therefore, be expected to deserve the name of boys, by which they were affectionately called. But it was their presentation of the idea of youth, of the quintessence of youth, which struck the spectator. Nor was it modified by the suggestion of dead-earnestness which accompanied it, and might seem to clash with it. The qualities in combination distinguished the American battalions from any young British regiment, which strikes the observer as at once older and more light-hearted. Not that there was really any lack of hilarity about the Americans in their hours of ease. The one who sang a comic song in front of the barracks before parade had a joyful heart, and was certainly a joy to the Londoners who stood listening to him. As for the men's modest demeanour, it ought to dispose of the notion that the Americans cherish any intention 'to show us how things should be done '—if that suggestion is not long since dead."

It soon became evident that relations between the British and Americans in war operations were to grow more and more intimate. The greatest gratification was afforded to the British people by the announcement in May that the Americans proposed henceforth to send numbers of their wounded to England. Up to this time the American idea had been to build large hospitals in France. King George gave a magnificent site in Richmond Park for a fully-equipped hospital of five hundred beds for the wounded Americans, which was presented as a free gift from the British Red Cross Society and the Order of St. John. The first intention was to have the hospital at Windsor; and in a resolution it was stated:

That this Joint Committee of the British Red Cross and the Order of St. John hereby offer to the American Red Cross a fully equipped hospital of 500 beds, which, by the gracious permission of his Majesty the King, will be erected in Windsor Great Park, and which it is hoped to complete and hand over early in the autumn.

The Joint War Committee, in asking the American Red Cross to accept this gift, desire to mark their admiration of the devoted work which the American Red Cross performs for the cause of humanity, and at the same time their gratitude for the generous help and warm-hearted co-operation which the American Red Cross extends to the British Joint War Committee in Red Cross effort common to both nations.

The Americans launched their first considerable offensive on May 28th, 1918. It was well known that immediately following the placing of the American troops under the supreme command of General Foch one body of Americans was sent north through the Lorraine sector. The position of these troops was revealed when, on that May Tuesday morning, they advanced on a front of a mile and a quarter north of Montdidier, stormed the German lines, and attacked and captured the village of Cantigny, taking 170 prisoners and a quantity of material. Their blow came at a critical moment, for the great Battle of the Aisne was then at its height. The German Crown Prince's forces, sweeping over the Chemin des Dames, had carried the northern heights of the river east of Soissons along a front of more than twenty miles. From there they had pressed on, and had advanced twelve miles from their original lines.

AN AMERICAN "ACE."
Baylies, one of the first American flying men to qualify for the title of "ace" by bringing down five enemy machines.

In the fight for Cantigny, after an hour's heavy firing from the allied batteries, there came a final crushing concentration of artillery of all kinds. Then at a quarter to seven in the morning, the Americans jumped up from their trenches—to use the description of spectators — "smiling as if they were going to play baseball," and followed a well-directed rolling barrage in two waves. It took them forty minutes to reach their objective, a depth of nearly a mile. They were preceded by twelve Tanks, all of which safely returned.

The resistance was at first not so heavy as might have been expected. The Germans were not in great strength at this point, and the tremendous artillery fire had knocked the heart out of many of them. There were, however, a number of individual fights in the streets of Cantigny, and no fewer than 250 German dead were counted there. Many of the Germans were still in dugouts when the Americans came up, seeking shelter from the artillery fire. The whole move was carried through with the greatest precision and exactness.

It was symbolical and significant that at the hour of German triumph the Americans should strike back. This attack was, of course, a very small affair compared with other happenings in the battle, but it gave good proof of the American qualities. The Germans did not appreciate the American move. They showed their annoyance by counter-attack after counter-attack, but each counter-attack was brilliantly and successfully repulsed. One attack, on the morning following the American capture, was preceded by a very heavy bombardment. Large bodies of German troops

then advanced, but the allied artillery, concentrating upon them, held them up before they reached the American position.

The growing seriousness of the German advance spurred the American people to still further efforts. General March, Chief of Staff, told the members of the Senate Military Affairs Committee early in June that the situation was serious, and that the rapidity of the German advance was unexpected by virtually all of the allied military experts.

The situation emphasised the necessity for the urgent transport of American troops abroad. He was able to add that, under the brigading arrangement with the other allied armies, the percentage of actual combatants in the units shipped abroad was much higher than under the previous American plan. The House of Representatives marked the national realisation of the position by voting unanimously an Army Appropriation Bill for £2,400,000,000, and gave President Wilson unrestricted authority to increase the Army without limit. He was formally authorised "to raise large drafts, the maximum number of men which may be organised, equipped, trained, and used during the fiscal year for the prosecution of the war until it shall have been brought to a successful conclusion."

Carte blanche for President Wilson

The Allied Supreme War Council issued on June 4th a statement about the position, in which it emphasised the gravity of the situation, its faith in victory, and the more and more important part the Americans were playing in the war. It described the German aim as "now seeking to gain a position in Europe by a series of desperate and costly assaults upon the allied armies before the United States can bring its full strength effectively to bear.

"Thanks to the prompt and cordial co-operation of the President of the United States, arrangements which were set on foot more than two months ago for the transportation and

A FAMOUS AMERICAN FLYING MAN AND A FIGHTING MACHINE.
Packing up one of America's big fighting aeroplanes for transmission to the western front. Above: Major Raoul Lufbery, America's champion flying man in the summer of 1918. He was shot down on May 19th, 1918, while engaging a German triplane, carrying two guns.

brigading of troops will make it impossible for the enemy to gain a victory by wearing out the allied reserve before he has exhausted his own."

The Germans made desperate efforts to prevent American troops crossing the Atlantic. The German people were assured by their rulers that the Atlantic would be closed. Finding it impossible, except in one or two cases, to attack the transports when on their way to Europe, the Germans watched for and succeeded in sinking some of the transports on their return voyages

SCENES OF EARLY AMERICAN FIGHTING.
In May, 1918, the American troops attacked and captured the village of Cantigny, north-west of Montdidier, and in June took part with the French in heavy fighting in and about Château Thierry on the Marne.

when empty. Early in June two German submarines appeared in American waters and began a fierce attack on every American passenger ship they met. They had a day or two of sheer destruction. Even here, however, they could not approach the transports, and had to content themselves mostly with small, undefended vessels—a liner, schooners, passenger steamers, and the like. They sank some small ships, killed some people, and inflicted a certain amount of hardship on others. But they completely failed to prevent the despatch of reinforcements to France. What they did succeed in doing was in tremendously stimulating the American war spirit.

The German troops, pressing on towards Paris, had reached Château Thierry, only about forty miles away. The American Marines, who had done very notable service in the fighting on the Lorraine front, were sent to this place ; and, in co-operation with the 9th and 23rd Infantry and other infantry forces, and also with French troops, they did some strenuous and notable work. In **Americans at** nine days' fighting they advanced at **Chateau Thierry** points over two miles, took four hundred prisoners, and captured three 7 in. heavy mortars and a number of machine-guns. They entered Château Thierry, where they met and fought the Germans and drove them out of the place with heavy loss, unofficial American estimates placing the German casualties at fully one thousand. The Germans came back next day in heavy force, when orders were given to the Americans for retirement. Château Thierry was on the north of the river. The bridge on the other side of the Marne was

blown up before the Americans got across, leaving them cut off on one side of the river with the German hosts advancing on them. They moved through the town and along the banks of the river until they reached the next bridge, where they got over. In this fight an American corporal swam across under the machine-gun fire and shell fire and rescued a French officer.

A few days later the Americans attacked and captured the Veuilly Wood, a hill on the Ourcq, and re-entered Château Thierry, taking over one hundred prisoners in co-operation with the French. The Germans counter-attacked, but the Americans met them with such concentrated fire that they could go no farther. Then the Americans jumped out to counter-attack. The Germans, however, although held up, by no means lost their power to strike. They greeted the Americans in turn with a heavy barrage and destructive machine-gun fire, but they failed to keep them back. One unit of the Americans took the village of Bouresches, another occupied the triangle south of Bouresches and Cherambauts Wood.

The Belleau Wood was a centre of keen fighting, and the Americans secured a commanding part of it, and from this point they proceeded step by step. The position was strongly defended by the Germans, who had numerous strong machine-gun nests in it. By Wednesday, June 12th, the American Marines had captured the last of these machine-gun positions, and the Marines, working around it, bayoneted the defenders and seized over a dozen machine-guns. **Twelve days'** The place proved to be very stoutly **fierce fighting** defended, being placed among rocks and having an elevator arrangement for bringing the machine-guns into use and protecting them from artillery fire.

"The Americans have been fighting continually for twelve days," one correspondent wrote when this capture had rounded up this stage of the defence; "they have passed through the severest tests, and have proved that they can fight as well as any troops in the world." Intense shelling, heavy barrages, frequent gas attacks, all failed to affect the Americans' hold. The German counter-attacks on Bouresches were so terrific that it seemed at the time as though the place could not be held.

Reuter's correspondent with the Americans related one typical incident. A report was received that Bouresches had been occupied by the Germans. A major went down from Headquarters to discover the facts of the case, and fell in with the officer who had been entrusted with the defence of the village.

"Are the Boches in Bouresches ?" he inquired hastily. "Yes, sir," was the reply. There was a lurid interlude, and the Staff officer was then understood to inquire whether the order was not that no Germans were to be allowed to remain in Bouresches. "Yes, sir," was the stolid response. "Then why the hell have you left them there?" came the hot demand. "Burying-party not yet arrived, sir," was the quiet answer.

The Mayors of Meaux and the neighbouring districts, in a letter to the commanding officer of the American forces on the Marne, said: "The civilian population will never forget that, since the beginning of June, when their homes were threatened by the invader, the —— Division victoriously stepped forth and succeeded in saving them from the impending danger. The Mayors, who were eyewitnesses of the generous and effective deeds of the American Army in stopping the enemy advance, send this heartfelt expression of their admiration and gratitude."

Pausing for a moment to gain breath after the fighting about Bouresches, the Americans, in close co-operation with the French, continued to attack the German lines. Very careful preparations were made for an attempt to capture the village of Vaux, which was held by the Germans. The Americans here adopted the plan largely used by the Canadians in their advance, of taking the rank and file as fully as possible into the confidence of their officers. The men were practised in what was expected of them, and they were given plans of the village. Every man had his own particular task allotted to him. He knew where he was to go, what he was to do, and how he was to do it.

The attack opened with heavy artillery fire, which smashed up the communications far in the rear and prevented reinforcements from coming up. While the rear lines were thus being cut off, a growing volume of shell fire concentrated upon the village itself. Then the Americans flung themselves forward. A hill, a wood, and the village were their objectives. They made their way through the wood. They got into Vaux. House after house was bombed, and by the evening the whole line was taken and four hundred and fifty prisoners captured.

It was notable in this

IN THE CAUSE OF LIBERTY.
Captain Bealey, of the British R.A.F., addressing American officers and men about to start for Europe from the foot of the famous Statue of Liberty at the entrance to New York Harbour.

fighting that the American airmen were playing a more and more prominent part. The American Air Force, hampered as it had been at the beginning by its lack of machines, never lacked brave men to fly what machines were available, and it was now coming into its own kingdom, a kingdom which promised to be as great and as glorious as that of any branch of the allied Services in this war.

The first anniversary of the arrival of the American troops in France was naturally fittingly celebrated by the French people. The President of the French Republic sent two telegrams of congratulation, one to President Wilson and the other to General Pershing. The message to President Wilson read:

I cannot allow the anniversary of General Pershing's arrival in France with the first units of the American Army to pass without expressing to you my admiration of the magnificent effort accomplished since then by the great sister Republic, and my warm congratulations to the fine troops who are beginning to give daily proofs of their valour on the battlefields.

The Allies, who at this moment have to keep in check the forces considerably increased by the Russian capitulation, are passing through the most difficult hours of the war. But the rapid formation of new American units and the incessant increase in maritime transports, are surely bringing us to the day on which the balance will at last be restored. When the scale turns in our favour, the allied armies, fraternally united, will take decisive revenge on the enemy, and, by their common victory, will found a peace in accordance with the principles solemnly laid down by you, assuring, with the necessary guarantees, the reign of right and liberty of the nations.

The message to General Pershing was:

The anniversary of your arrival in France affords me the happy opportunity of addressing my heartiest congratulations to you and the valiant troops under your command who have borne themselves so admirably in the latest battles. I beg you to accept all my wishes for a continuance of their successes.

General Pershing sent the following in reply:

Allow me to thank you, Monsieur le Président, for the kind message which you have sent me on the occasion of this anniversary. The enthusiastic welcome which Paris accorded us a year ago to-day has since been extended to the American Army by all your nation.

To-day our armies are united in affection and resolution, and are full of confidence in the final success which will crown the long struggle for the liberty of civilisation.

July 4th was approaching, and the Americans had resolved to mark the date worthily. In this all their Allies were eager to help them. Mr. Baker, Secretary of War, was able to announce two days before that 142nd anniversary of the American Declaration of Independence that over one million American soldiers had then sailed for France. President Wilson in a statement wrote:

Good news for the Fourth of July — I have to-day received the following letter from the Secretary of War, which seems to me to contain information which will be so satisfactory to the country that its publication will be welcomed and will give additional zest to our national celebration of the Fourth of July:

More than one million American soldiers have sailed from the ports in this country to participate in the war in France. In reporting this fact to you I feel that you will be interested in a few data showing the progress of our oversea military effort. The first ship carrying military personnel sailed on May 8th, 1917, having on board Base Hospital No. 4 and members of the Reserve Nurses Force. General Pershing and his Staff sailed on May 20th, 1917. The embarkations in the months from May, 1917, to and including June, 1918, are as follows:

1917.		1918.	
May	1,718	January	46,776
June	12,261	February	48,027
July	12,988	March	83,811
August	18,323	April	117,212
September	32,523	May	244,345
October	38,259	June	276,372
November.. ..	23,016	Marines	14,644
December	48,840		

Total, 1,019,115.

The total number of troops returned from abroad, lost at sea, and casualties is 8,165. Of these, by reason of the superbly efficient protection which the Navy has given to our transport system, only 291 have been lost at sea. The supplies and equipment in France for all the troops sent are, by the latest report, adequate, and the output of our war industries in this country is showing marked improvement in practically all lines of necessary equipment and supplies.

To which I replied:

Your letter of July 1st contains a very significant piece of news and an equally significant report of the forwarding of troops during the past year to the other side of the water. It is a record which I think must cause universal satisfaction, because the heart of the country is unquestionably in this war, and the people of the United States rejoice to see their forces put faster and faster into the great struggle which is destined to redeem the world.

Mr. Baker, Secretary of War, to-day said that progress in shipping troops oversea had been so well maintained that the United States was six months ahead of the original programme.

It would be strange, indeed, if the allied peoples had not attempted to celebrate American Independence Day in worthy fashion. They required no spur or incentive to do so. All the doubts and wonders of a few months earlier had been swept away. America had revealed herself in her full strength. People had come to know what the coming of this new ally meant. France treated the day as a new national festival. In England, **England celebrates Independence Day** King George led the celebration, being present at a baseball match at Chelsea between teams of the American Army and Navy, and handing over a ball bearing his autograph. This baseball match was very remarkable. London had seen nothing like it. Enormous crowds were present, and the scene showed England what America at play can do.

There was a thrill in the air in London on that Liberty Day. Two nations, strained at times through minor misunderstandings, were coming to know each other as they really were. The Stars and Stripes and the Union Jack floated side by side everywhere. The man who did not wear the American flag in the lapel of his coat was an exception. Every American soldier in the streets—and there were many of them—was greeted by the people as a friend. The vast area of the Central Hall, Westminster, was packed in the morning with the crowd gathered to voice the sentiments of England. Many of the people carried Stars and Stripes which they waved at every opportunity. When the band of the Coldstream Guards struck up the American National Anthem, all the people joined in. "The Star-Spangled Banner" was becoming a familiar tune to the English people.

Major-General Biddle, commanding the United States forces in England, and Vice-Admiral Sims, commanding the American Navy in European waters, sat side by side with Dominion statesmen like Mr. Arthur Meighen and Sir George Perley. Lord Bryce presided over the gathering. What had been a day of anger on one side and of grief on the other had, he declared, been turned into a day of rejoicing and affection for both.

Mr. Winston Churchill re-echoed the allied determination to see the war through to the end. "The essential purpose of this war," he said amidst loud and repeated cheers, "does not admit of any compromise. This war is becoming a conflict between Christian civilisation and scientific barbarism. The struggle is between right and wrong, and as such is not capable of any solution which is not absolute. Germany must be beaten. Germany must know that she is beaten, must feel that she is beaten. Her defeat must be expressed in terms and pacts which will for all time deter others from committing her crimes, and which will make it impossible for her to renew them."

While the young British statesman was speaking in this way in London, **America pledged to final settlement** President Wilson was echoing similar sentiments on behalf of the American people in a speech delivered on the historic spot of Washington's tomb.

The past and the present are in deadly grapple, and the peoples of the world are being done to death between them. There can be but one issue. The settlement must be final. There can be no compromise. No halfway decision would be tolerable. No halfway decision is conceivable.

The celebration of July 4th makes a fitting close for this chapter. A new chapter was opening in the war, in which America was to play a still greater part. No man of British blood could pass through those days without deep emotion, and without feeling a kindling of warm affection and appreciation for the kith and kin across the sea who had thus come to his aid in this darkest hour. Britain had fought her great battles. There was no need and no room for jealousy concerning the great part awaiting America. With the aid of her full manhood this war could have but one end. Come soon, come late, that end must come. And even in Germany, while a drilled and disciplined Press was proclaiming news of German advances, men were slowly coming to see their certain doom.

The Star-Spangled Banner came to the Allies as a messenger of hope and victory, and to the Germans as a harbinger of doom and punishment.

Europe, reeling under the blows and desperate struggles of Germany to secure the decision, saw in the coming of this new ally a strong comfort and the assurance of victory. The spirit of the American people themselves, enthusiastic as it had been at the beginning, was now steadily reaching to greater heights. There was an impatience of what had been done—the noble impatience due to the fact that the people wanted more done. No sacrifice that could be asked was too great. From Maine to Oregon, from the soldiers in the fighting trenches in Lorraine to the German-bred people of the Middle West whose fathers had escaped from Prussian tyranny, the one word went up: "We are in this fight to a finish. We are not going to lay down our arms till Kaiserism is ended once and for all."

Anglo-Saxon brotherhood in arms : American troops led by a British band marching past a British general in France.

Men of the Royal Naval Volunteers on the look-out for suspicious craft or possible enemy raiders.

One link in the encircling chain that barred the coast of Britain to foreign invaders: Sentry on shore duty.

On duty at a look-out station: A cycling battalion taking part in coast patrol work.

Boy Scouts performing coast-guarding duties on a Martello tower dating from an earlier time of threatened invasion.

Britain's Home Defence: On watch and ward around her coast.

England's only kilted Volunteers: "A" Company City of London National Guard on parade.

London's 20th=century trained bands: Fifth Battalion City of London Volunteer Regiment at Guildhall.

Left to right. Back row: Lt. H. W. Stansfeld, Lt. R. Graefe, Lt. F. Hanchard, Lt. C. C. Robson, Lt. J. M. Bathe, Sec.-Lt. W. G. Bousfeld, Lt. H. C. Russell, Lt. F. Barclay, Lt. C. S. Lambert, Lt. T. G. Forbes, Lt. R. Sungar, Lt. C. F. Newington, Sec.-Lt. H. N. Lubbock, Lt. C. M. Howard, Lt. I. Cooke. Second row: Sec.-Lt. P. Nevill, Lt. C. de V. Barrow, Lt. R. B. Brierly, Lt. Count T. Riccardi-Cubitt, Lt. W. I. Whitaker, Lt. P. T. Johnson, Lt. F. W. D. Gwynne, Lt. W. Y. Strang-Watkins, Lt. C. Forbes, Lt. C. Gaskin, Sec.-Lt. Knowles, Lt. E. H. Risley, Lt. J. M. Gibson-Carmichael, Lt. Lucas, Lt. S. M. Monkland. Third row: Capt. A. F. Baynham, Capt. W. E. Hansel, Capt. P. Arnold, Capt. C. L. Thompson, Capt. S. Austin, Capt. R. G. de C. Anderson, Lt. W. H. Homan, Lt. A. F. Berridge.

Lt. E. V. Barker, Capt. W. Wilson, Capt. A. Eve, Capt. H. A. Barton, Lt. C. W. Stockman, Lt. E. C. Wigan, Sec.-Lt. C. W. Lyon. Fourth row: Lt. T. L. Tapper, Lt. E. H. G. Cayley, Lt. F. A. Rhodes, Capt. C. W. Fosbery, Maj. T. H. Cooper, Maj. T. D. Challoner, Maj. J. G. A. Baillie, Capt. A. P. Copplestone, Capt. H. J. Powys-Keck, Capt. F. B. Andrus, Maj. A. P. Raven, Capt. L. A. Routledge, Capt. H. Hayward, Capt. H. Parker, Lt. E. Cheshire. Front row: Maj. J. A. Arrowsmith, Maj. R. M. Hutchinson-Lowe, Maj. W. J. MacQueen, Maj. T. A. Chalk, Maj. H. R. L. Pym, Major T. H. Manners-Howe (Assist.-Commandant), Col. J. G. L. Searight (Commandant), Col. A. T. Swaine, Lt.-Col. C. G. F. Fagan, Lt.-Col. C. Healey, C.M.G., Lt.-Col. F. A. S. Steele, Maj. F. H. Lehmann, Capt. H. A. Meredith (Adjt).

[*Photograph by Bassano.*]

Portrait Group of the Commandant and Chief Officers of the Royal Defence Corps, London Division.

THE SCOTS COMPANY

CITY OF LONDON (V.)

THE ORGANISATION OF BRITISH HOME DEFENCE UNDER FIELD-MARSHAL VISCOUNT FRENCH.

By Charles Lowe, M.A., Author of "Our Greatest Living Soldiers," "Battles of the Nineteenth Century," etc.

Viscount French Appointed to the Command of the Home Forces, December, 1915—Necessity of Preparing Against Possible Invasion—Complication of the Problem due to Submarines, Air-War, and Other Agencies—Coastal Roads the Best Fortification—" The Principles of Home Defence "—Test Mobilisation of the Guards by Motor-car in 1909—Organisation of Motor Transport as an Auxiliary to Home Defence—Motor Volunteer Corps under the Supervision of the Territorial Force Association—Viscount French's Statement on the Volunteer Force and its Motor Auxiliaries, November, 1917—Forces Available for Home Defence—The Volunteer Act of December, 1916—Resources of British Man-Power Available For Home Defence Apart from the Volunteers—Subsidiary Purposes of the Home Defence Forces—The Sinn Fein Outbreak of 1916—Enemy Raiders' Bombardments of the Coast—Viscount French's Statement with Regard to Anti-Aircraft Defence, December, 1916—War Cabinet's Report for 1917—Marked Improvement of Anti-Aircraft Defence After the Raid on London, July 7th, 1917—Creation of the Air Board and Successful Development of the Home Defences.

IT was well said that, before ever a shot had been fired on the western front, Field-Marshal Sir John French, who was appointed to command the British Expeditionary Force, had already done good work for his country by the swift marshalling of his men.

Yet the post of Commander-in-Chief was one from which Sir John himself seemed at first inclined to shrink. His maiden speech in the House of Lords, after becoming Viscount French of Ypres, took the form of a eulogy of Lord Kitchener who, " coffined in a British man-of-war " —to quote the striking words of Lord Derby—had just " passed to the Great Beyond " ; and this speech referred to his relations with the deceased soldier in South Africa.

At that time (he said), and during later years, I became so impressed by his great qualities, and my estimate of him was so high, that when I had reason to believe that I had been selected for the chief command in the field, I went to Lord Kitchener very early one morning and urged him to see the Prime Minister and endeavour to arrange that he himself should take the place, and that I should accompany him as his Chief of the Staff. Although at that moment he had no idea of taking over the position of Secretary of State for War, I could not prevail upon him to do this.

Therefore Sir John himself submitted to the burden

imposed upon him and bore it manfully, wisely, steadfastly, and valiantly for about eighteen terribly anxious months, when he asked to be relieved of it about the middle of December, 1915. His request was granted, and he was then appointed to the supreme command of the Home Forces—a post which might be said to have been almost in the nature of a new creation, through the co-ordination and concentration in one hand of several authorities not hitherto centralised.

Having stemmed the tide of German advance towards the Channel ports with an Army superior to the enemy only in respect of its bravery and endurance, but vastly inferior in numbers, armament, and munitions, Lord French addressed himself to the task of securing the United Kingdom itself from the peril of invasion, which he himself regarded as a very possible and serious one.

Addressing a meeting of motor-owners in November, 1917, on the subject of motor-volunteers, he said :

The first thing I was taught as a soldier—all soldiers are taught it, but I am afraid do not altogether take it in—is that what happens in war is the unexpected. If any war has ever taught the people that lesson, the present war has. It has been one string of surprises from August, 1914, up to two or three days ago. They have occurred to friend and foe

LONDON VOLUNTEERS ON GUARD DUTY.
Men of one of the London Volunteer battalions changing guard at the southern entrance to the Thames Tunnel. Such duty as this was the earliest officially allotted to the new force that sprang into existence on the outbreak of war.

493

alike, to the Germans, the French, the Austrians, and the English. We have all had the greatest surprises; the latest one you know of. It is going on now, perhaps the greatest of all. It is what is going on in North Italy. [The débâcle on the Isonzo.] We may quite possibly have another surprise; it is invasion. I want you to realise that it is quite possible, and the lesson we have to learn is that we must be prepared for everything.

Lord Roberts, for one, was never tired of warning his countrymen against the possibility of invasion by the Germans, who might conceivably succeed in their object in spite of a defence such as had never before been offered to any invaders of these islands.

There were several invasions of Great Britain, large and small, from the time of Julius Cæsar to that of Wolfe Tone and Napper Tandy in 1797-98, but only one was opposed on the shore.

This was Cæsar's first landing (55 B.C.), when the Britons, who had gathered on the cliffs of Dover to give him and his legions a hot reception, scurried across to Deal—his real objective—to engage in a brief and unsuccessful encounter with the legionaries on the beach.

Cæsar's second landing at the same place next year met with no resistance at all—that is to say, with just as little as was opposed to William and his Normans, who were to wade ashore from their galleys at Pevensey Bay in 1066.

In the interval there had been scores of landings by the Scandinavian sea-rovers, to whom, as a rule, the only resistance offered was after they had disembarked.

Some sporadic French incursions by small bodies afterwards aimed at burning the Cinque Ports and shipping; but, after the Norman Conquest, the next serious attempt was that of the Spanish Armada, which was utterly defeated by the Blue Water School of sailors —the Drakes, Howards, and Grenvilles—who anticipated the maxim of Nelson that attempts at invasion must be foiled on the sea.

Napoleon was only restrained from attempting invasion

F.-M. THE DUKE OF CONNAUGHT.
On the recognition of the Volunteers as part of the military forces for home defence purposes, the Duke of Connaught was appointed their Colonel-in-Chief.

by the fear that his Villeneuve would meet with the fate of Philip's Medina Sidonia.

Exactly a century after the Armada, in 1688, Dutch William, with a fleet of five hundred transports and an escort of over fifty men-of-war, landed at Torbay, where his disembarkation was not even opposed by a corporal's guard; but it was all a question of wind—on such slender and capricious accidents did the fate of nations then depend. For the north-easter which blew the Prince of Orange over from Holland also bottled up in the Thames the Stuart fleet under Lord Dartmouth, who was waiting to sally out and attack him.

In 1797 a French force of fifteen thousand men, under Generals Hoche and Grouchy, headed for Bantry Bay to make a landing in Ireland, for the conversion of that country into a republic. But it all went to sand, water, and ruin, under pressure of the elements; and when, in the same year, another and a smaller French force landed at Fishguard, in Pembrokeshire, it was forced to capitulate; and this was the last time that the soil of Britain had been trodden by the foot of an invader.

Apart from these smaller invasions there had been since the Norman Conquest something like fifty successful small raids on our shores — by French, Dutch, Spaniards, and others — though momentary success attended them only from the fact of their having been in the nature of surprises, and therefore unopposed.

When he was at the War Office (December, 1911) Lord Haldane gave his reasons for believing that a surprise invasion was altogether out of the question, since the Committee of Imperial Defence had come to the conclusion that a force exceeding seventy thousand men "had no chance of getting through unobserved." As chairman of that committee in 1905, Mr. Balfour said in the House of Commons: " I trust I have convinced the House that, even in these suppositions, unfavourable as they are [to us], serious

Lord Desborough, President of the Central Association of Voluntary Training Corps, was a zealous worker in organising and establishing the Volunteer movement.

General Sir O'Moore Creagh, V.C., G.C.B., Commander-in-Chief in India 1909-14, who became Military Adviser to the Central Association, V.T.C.

Mr. Percy Harris, M.P., who immediately on the outbreak of war, proposed the raising of a volunteer force for home defence, became secretary of the Central Association.

LEADERS IN THE ORGANISING OF THE VOLUNTARY TRAINING CORPS.

WOMEN POLICE MARCHING TO BUCKINGHAM PALACE, JULY 6TH, 1918.
In 1916, the Commissioner of Police employed as auxiliaries some of the women patrols started earlier by the National Union of Women Workers to look after the welfare of the girls of England. They were so useful that a Corps of Women Police was formed later, some of whom are shown here.

invasion of these islands is not a possibility which we need discuss."

On the other hand, Lord Roberts was very positively of the contrary opinion, and spent his time when out of office in calling the attention of his countrymen to the necessity of improving their system of military service and home defence.

In reasoning thus Lord Roberts had a main eye to the possibility of a German surprise in time of peace. The problem assumed a totally different aspect when the outbreak of war practically eliminated the element of surprise.

Problems of a possible invasion Nevertheless, an attempt at invasion became a possibility which had to be reckoned with, and that was why an experienced soldier like Lord French was entrusted with the task of preparing for it.

The problem was complicated by the innovation of submarines, air-war, and other agencies, and the fact that an overwhelming predominance of surface battleships was no longer a guarantee of the victory which would have formerly resulted from such preponderating strength.

Without a Channel tunnel whereby, free from submarine attack, unlimited food supplies might be secured from France, the Germans, as temporary masters of the sea, might blockade the nation into starvation and submission,

or attempt a landing in order to accelerate the process of subjugation.

A landing from the sea in presence of an enemy is one of the rarest and most difficult operations in war. Yet that it is feasible, even in circumstances apparently the most adverse and impossible, British soldiers and sailors had repeatedly proved. Apart from minor operations, mainly of the naval kind, such feats may be mentioned as the landing at Aboukir, near Alexandria, in 1801, when Abercromby's army was rowed and waded ashore in the teeth of heavy musketry and cannon fire, and in a subsequent battle beat their opponents.

In the case of the British expedition to the Crimea, in 1854, its landing at Eupatoria (Old Fort) was not opposed by so much as a Cossack patrol. Again, in 1860, a mixed force under Sir Hope Grant landed in the face of heavy Chinese fire and captured the Taku Forts at the mouth of the Pei-ho, though a similar attempt in the previous year had ended in disaster and repulse. Perhaps, however, the most outstanding operation of the kind was the allied landing at Gallipoli in April, 1915, under heavy Turkish fire, though at the end of the same year the enterprise had to be abandoned.

How, in turn, were the British to meet and deal with surprise descents, supposing that an invading force could manage to get inside and behind the naval guard ? How

DECORATING SPECIAL CONSTABLES WITH SILVER STARS FOR LONG SERVICE.
Sir Edward Ward, Director of Voluntary Organisations, inspecting a force of more than 7,000 Special Constables, paraded in Regent's Park in May, 1918, to receive the Silver Star awarded to all Special Constables who enrolled prior to January, 1915, and had served continuously since. Above : Sir Edward Ward shaking hands with officers of the Headquarter Division after conferring the decoration upon them.

KEEPING IN TOUCH.
Signalling to a trawler with a searchlight set on an improvised platform on a cliff.

were the land forces to be concentrated to deal with such a descent at any given point ? The answer might be expressed by one word — mobility, the power to pass from one point of the coast to another with the least possible delay.

The very best kind of fortification with which the shores could be fenced would be— not a Chinese wall, or a Roman rampart, or a chain of Martello towers such as were erected during the Napoleonic era, or a series of detached forts such as exposed the entire Franco-German frontier to heavy gun fire, causing the Germans to invade France by the roundabout way of Belgium—but simply a good, broad, serviceable road.

It was not enough to be able to convey home defenders

Teutonic invasion ? A corresponding change of side is, however, to be found in the case of a Prussian officer who lived for many years in London as a military instructor, and passed through his hands thousands of young British officers ; who used to set tactical schemes for the manœuvres of Volunteer and Territorial battalions all over the kingdom, and supervise their execution on the spot ; who, under the pseudonym of " Promptus," wrote a little volume on " The Principles of Home Defence," which was pronounced by one of our highest authorities to be the best thing on the subject, and another, under his own name, on " Tactical Principles " ; who, when the war began, returned post-haste to Germany and was at once reinstated in the Army, in which he fought against the Allies in France and was given the Iron Cross ; after which, on being transferred to the Russian front, he was wounded, taken prisoner, and sent to the safe seclusion of far-off Turkestan—there to relieve the tedium of his captivity by resuming his studies on the defence of England, in which he had previously sought and found an asylum. Such was the varied and adventurous career of the man—a modern Dumouriez on a lesser scale— who for nearly twenty years had been entrusted with the task of teaching young British officers how best to defend their native land against invasion.

Motor transport in home defence

" The Principles of Home Defence," by " Promptus," was published in 1904, but, to a great extent, its schemes and arguments were antiquated, or at least deprived of much of their force, when motor-power became supplemental and ancillary to railway transport. Indeed, the expression " motor transport " does not once occur in his treatise.

As far back as 1909—or five years after " Promptus " wrote—the attention of the country was aroused by a practical experiment to the vast importance of motor-transport as a new agency of war. On St. Patrick's Day of that year a composite battalion of Guards was hastily mobilised and hurried down from London to Hastings to repel the assumed landing of an invader. For

WATCHING AND WAITING FOR ENEMY RAIDERS.
Royal Naval Air Service dirigible patrolling the sea-coast, itself protected by powerful anti-aircraft guns that could repel any aeroplanes swooping upon it from the blue.

from military centres to any given point on the coast which might be threatened ; it was necessary to be able to transport them, by bicycle or motor-vehicles, from this point to any other—from the pretended to the real place of landing—without the loss of time involved in moving on circuitous lines.

The idea of a coastal road was strongly advocated by General Dumouriez, one of the earliest and most brilliant generals of the French Revolution. He quarrelled with his employers, and sought refuge in England, where he spent the rest of his life as a pensioner of the Government in devising schemes for the defence of the country against French invasion, dying at Henley-on-Thames, where he lies buried in the parish church.

What would have been thought of a German general— Bernhardi, for example, or Von Kluck—who had fallen out with the Kaiser, if he had come over to England to offer his services in devising means to enable her to repel a

" OUR ANTI-AIRCRAFT GUNS CAME INTO ACTION."
Battery of anti-aircraft guns manned by both naval and military men in hot action against enemy aeroplanes attempting to cross the coast.

this purpose about three hundred motor-cars, of private or pleasure kinds, had been placed at the disposal of the authorities.

It had been calculated by the Guards' officers that the journey from the Crystal Palace to Hastings, a distance of fifty-four miles, would bring the head of the complete column, travelling at twenty miles an hour, into Hastings at 1 p.m. Some doubts were expressed among experienced motorists as to the possibility of a column of two hundred and eighty-six motor-vehicles, exclusive of cars for Staff and other officers, guests, and journalists, maintaining that speed. But the military forecast was justified; punctually at one o'clock the cars of the Headquarters Staff were speeding along the front at Hastings.

This experiment was made exclusively with private motor-cars, each carrying four to six men only at the utmost; but as commercial lorries of all kinds sprang into existence they revolutionised the means of transport and their value for home defence became incalculable.

In the case of the Hastings experiment each car may have carried at a pinch an average of half a dozen men, but lorries could be loaded up to thirty and more, and the difference in speed was not material. To what extent this kind of motor transport could be utilised in the seat of war was shown on several crucial occasions, but more especially at the Battle of the Marne, when a part of General Maunoury's reserve army behind Paris was thus shot from its concealment and quickly thrown on the German right flank with important results.

As an auxiliary to home defence the organisation of this new means of transport soon began to take form throughout the country. In the London area several motor volunteer corps quickly took shape, such as the County of Middlesex Motor Volunteer Corps, the County of London Motor Volunteer Corps, and the City of London Motor Volunteer Corps.

Motor Volunteer Corps formed

At a London dinner, in the spring of 1918, to celebrate the second anniversary of the motor transport volunteers, Sir J. Lister-Kaye, the honorary president, said the corps had a strength of 520 men and 433 vehicles. They had conveyed 668,000 men of the forces who had come to London on leave or were returning to the front. In 1916 they carried men by hundreds; by 1918 they transported them by thousands, the weekly average being from 10,000 to 15,000. The corps then formed part of the recognised Volunteer Force for the defence of the country.

This motor-transport movement quickly spread to the counties, in response to a private appeal from the Army Council, which expressed the wish that the owner of every commercial motor-car should enrol his vehicles in a recognised motor volunteer corps for use in the event of threatened invasion and for occasional work in connection with the transportation of troops and material.

Soon there were few or no counties which had not provided themselves with M.V.C., consisting of motor-transport sections and companies, or groups of sections. Each of these county M.V.C. was given its O.C., who in turn was subject to the county commandant of Volunteers for the district, the whole being under the general supervision of the Territorial Force Association of the county,

ANTI-AIRCRAFT ACTION AGAINST A RAIDING ZEPPELIN.
Officer and men of an anti-aircraft detachment who claimed to have fired the successful shot which brought a Zeppelin down into the Thames. On October 24th, 1917, it was officially stated that from the beginning of the war to that date the British Air Service had brought down sixteen Zeppelins.

which continued to act, as before the war, as a sort of organising agency for recruiting. On the creation of this national network of M.V.C. Viscount French had mainly set his heart.

When he took office practically the only perfect piece of administrative organisation at his disposal was the series of enactments known as the " Defence of the Realm Act," under the provisions of which, as already explained in THE GREAT WAR (Chapter CCVI., Vol. 10, page 309), it was a serious crime to publish details relating to military, naval, and aerial movements unless they had been sanctioned by the censor. Suspected persons could be interned or deported. Speeches against recruiting could be prevented, and those who sought in any way to hinder the country's efforts in war could be punished by long terms of imprisonment.

But Lord French wanted much more than this Act to help him in the execution of his new task. In an official review of his first year's activity at the Horse Guards, he wrote (December 31st, 1916) :

When I assumed command of the forces in the United Kingdom I was directed to review the situation as it affected home defence with a view to deciding whether defensive requirements were met by the system then in force.

According to these instructions I made an exhaustive study of the situation, and came to the conclusion that modification was necessary, in view of the most recent experiences we have gained in the conduct of war under existing conditions.

The Army Council agreed generally to the proposals submitted, and a reorganisation on the new lines has since then been carried into effect.

Nearly a year later (November 6th, 1917), at another motor-volunteer meeting in the City, the Field-Marshal said, with a special eye to the Volunteer Force and its motor auxiliaries :

Viscount French on mobility

When emergency arises, the motor volunteers will be fully organised to take up at once the transport duties of the Volunteer Forces. For such a force as the Volunteers, and for such objects as they have to attain in case of invasion, mobility is the one great essential, and it is to the motor volunteers that we look to provide them with that mobility. It may, indeed, be justly said that the motor volunteers are absolutely essential to the effective defence of these islands in case of threatened or actual invasion.

The latest regulations governing the use of motor-vehicles will seriously affect the motor volunteer corps unless owners of

VOLUNTEER CAMP KITCHEN.
Field-kitchen at a summer camp of the Second City of London Volunteers (Corps of Citizens). The members of the corps did the whole of the camp work themselves.

motor-vehicles agree to the recommendations which we are putting forward. The new rules lay down that licences will only be granted where cars and drivers are placed at the disposal of the military authorities for use in the event of national emergency. . . .

The motor volunteer corps is absolutely essential to the maintenance of a Volunteer force in this country, if that force is to be kept useful and efficient.

Passing from the motor volunteers to the force itself, which they were intended to supplement and subserve, the Commander-in-Chief said:

During the present year [1917] the use and efficiency of the Volunteer Force have been greatly enhanced and increased. I do not quite see how we can undertake the defence of the country now without the Volunteers. I very much regret that there are still people who sneer and jeer at them, and say they are playing at soldiers. I hope everyone will try his utmost to discourage that foolish kind of talk—these ridiculous and unpatriotic ideas. It is nothing less than wicked to give expression to them, and I cannot find words too strong to condemn them. It was reserved for the present war for the Volunteer to show what he was made of. They stood between this country and disaster. It is our patriotic duty to support the Volunteers to the utmost of our power, and encourage them in the work which they may have to perform. Do not make any mistake about it, they may have to perform the work.

Speaking at Chertsey a little later in the same year, General Sir Edward Hutton—the organiser of Mounted Infantry—who had in turn commanded the Dominion Militia, as well as organised and directed the military forces of Australia—laid the greatest stress on the value of our citizen-soldiers, saying that "every **500,000 Volunteers called for** effort should be made to swell the numbers of our Volunteers up to half or three-quarters of a million, and thus constitute a splendid home defence force. A huge force of Volunteers would be the salvation of this country, and would have more effect on our enemies than anything else."

Strictly speaking, the forces available for home defence may be grouped under three general heads:

(a) The Volunteers.
(b) Men under training for the front, including Dominion troops.
(c) Men on leave from the front, of whom, for example, there were some 600,000 during the last four months of 1917, or an average of over 150,000 for each month.

Some one having complained that soldiers on leave from the front were compelled to carry their full trench kit with them, it was officially explained that this was necessary for a military reason of the first importance. The soldier on leave would, in the case of invasion or threatened invasion, be called upon to take the field at once.

The Volunteers, who may be said to form the largest and most permanent element of home defence, were drawn from several sources:

(a) Old Territorials, who had not in one or another capacity gone to the front.
(b) National Reservists, as they were called, consisting of veterans in any combatant force of the Crown.
(c) Home Service Employment Companies.
(d) Men composing the National Guard and Royal Defence Corps.

The last-named body, which was created in April, 1916, consisted mainly of old soldiers invalided from the fighting fronts. They were utilised principally for guard duties at prisoners-of-war camps, and also for the protection of vulnerable points such as railways and bridges.

At the head of the Volunteers was placed the Duke of Connaught, as Colonel-in-Chief, and at one of his first inspections—in Somerset—he said the Volunteers were resuming their old importance—the importance they used to have before the Territorial Force was formed. It was especially for the defence of their country, in case of attack, that the Volunteers were required, and he assured them that the War Office and the Government attached great importance to their number and efficiency.

Under the Volunteer Act of December, 1916, volunteering became a more serious thing than it had ever been before. The great majority of **Military status of the Volunteers** the men were now, to all intents and purposes, trained soldiers. They were well grounded in drill, musketry, trench-digging, and bombing, while many specialised in machine and Lewis gunnery.

It may be well to quote the clause of the Act defining the status of the Volunteer:

(1) The King may accept the offer of any member of a Volunteer corps to enter into an agreement for the duration of the war.
(2) A breach of such agreement is an offence (equivalent to absence without leave) under the Army Act.
(3) A Volunteer, while employed or engaged under the terms of such agreement, is subject to military law.

On the passing (April, 1918) of the Act raising the age of military service to fifty, some little apprehension was felt lest the absorption into the Army of the Volunteers thus made available for oversea service should tend to deplete and almost skeletonise the Volunteer Force. But a corrective, or counter-weight, to this cause of

IN A SUMMER TRAINING-CAMP.
Corner of the Surrey camp of the United Arts Rifles (1st Battalion Central London Volunteer Regiment), one of the earliest of the Volunteer battalions that were raised in the autumn of 1914.

diminution was promptly devised by the Lords, who inserted a clause in the Bill providing that every man granted a certificate of exemption should join the Volunteer Force for the period of the war.

Lord Lansdowne declared that by this means the force might easily be raised to the strength of 500,000 men; while Mr. Percy Harris, M.P., hon. secretary of the Central Association of the Volunteer Training Corps, committed himself to the statement: " I believe we could raise, not 100,000 men, but from 500,000 to 1,000,000 soldiers ready to take their place in the fighting-line to prevent the enemy from effecting a landing on these shores."

DEFENCE, NOT DEFIANCE.
Men of the 5th Battalion Essex Volunteers carrying spades and implements to the defence works at their training camp.

READY TO CONTEST THE LAST INCH OF GROUND.
Colonel Colvin inspecting men of the 5th Essex Volunteers while engaged in trench digging. Every week-end battalions of Volunteers went into camp to learn trench-digging, the making of wire entanglements, and general military routine.

As inferential proof of the resources of British man-power of various kinds available for home defence—apart from the Volunteers—it may be mentioned that after the reverse to the Fifth Army in the Somme region on the launching by the Germans of their great offensive on March 21st, 1918, reinforcements to the number of something like 240,000 men were rushed across the Channel within eight days, at the rate—said Lord Curzon in the Lords—of 30,000 per day—a rate of transport, as Mr. Lloyd George added in the Commons, which had never before been reached—and this without impairing home defensive power.

On British resources in this respect considerable light was thrown by the various " Reports of the Select Committee on National Expenditure," which began to be issued towards the end of 1917. In the first of these it was stated:

A great expenditure is being incurred through the maintenance of very large forces in the United Kingdom. . . . Whether the number of Army units maintained at home, having regard to the existence of the Volunteer Force, is excessive or not, is a military question on which your committee can express no

opinion; but we are impressed by the magnitude of the number.

The second report, issued December 13th, 1917, contained this reference to military expenditure:

That expenditure, excluding the cost of men in hospitals or convalescent establishments, is no less than two-thirds of the present cost of the Navy, including construction and all auxiliary services. Besides these forces there are in the United Kingdom at any one time some tens of thousands of fully-trained men, home on leave from the armies in France, who are required to bring their equipment with them so that they could be called up to strengthen existing units in the event of any attempted invasion. There are, further, considerable numbers, as a rule, of Dominion troops in this country under training.

The main object of the Home Defence Force was to prevent foreign aggression, but it also served the subsidiary purpose of coping with domestic insurrection, whether prompted by the simple spirit of rebellion, or instigated and subsidised by our declared enemies. It was, for example, clearly proved that German money and the German military mind were at the bottom of the Sinn Fein rising at Easter, **German designs** 1916; while the arrest and imprisonment **upon Ireland** of all the Sinn Fein leaders in May, 1918, was also due to the fact that the Government had again discovered proof that the Sinn Feiners were allowing themselves to be used as the dangerous tools of German designs on Ireland.

The Sinn Fein outbreak of 1916 took place at 12.15 p.m. on Easter Monday, April 24th, and by 5.20 p.m. on the same day a considerable force from the Curragh had reached Dublin to reinforce the garrison there, while other troops were on their way from Athlone, Belfast, and Templemore. " The celerity with which those reinforcements became available," wrote Lord French in his despatch on the subject, " says much for the arrangements which had been made to meet such a contingency. I was informed [at the Horse Guards] of the outbreak by wire on the afternoon of the same day (April 24th), and the 59th Division at St. Albans was at once put under orders to proceed to Ireland. . . ." Two of the brigades actually reached Dublin within the next two days—quite a notable feat.

Concluding his despatch to Lord Derby—covering that of General Sir J. G. Maxwell, the new Commander-in-Chief in Ireland, detailing the suppression of the outbreak—the Field-Marshal begged—

French's despatch on the rebellion To bring to your notice the assistance afforded to me by the Lords Commissioners of the Admiralty, who met every request made to them for men, guns, and transport with the greatest promptitude, and whose action enabled me to reinforce and maintain the garrisons in the South and West of Ireland without unduly drawing upon the troops which it was desirable to retain in England.

In another despatch, reviewing the first year of office at the Horse Guards, Lord French, in alluding to the rising at Dublin, wrote :

. . . I will only add that both in England and in Ireland the military arrangements for its suppression proved everywhere adequate, and reflect great credit on all concerned.

At the same time, from the German point of view, this Sinn Fein rising at Easter, 1916, undoubtedly had the effect of causing the Government to increase the garrisons in Ireland, and thus lock up, or immobilise, troops urgently needed at the front.

Several letters having appeared in the Press suggesting that General Sir Robert Baden-Powell should organise the Boy Scouts to take part in some form of coast-watching under Government approval, the Chief Scout hastened to reply : " I may say that the practical idea thus suggested has been in operation, by Coastguards, Sea Scouts, and fishermen working together under the direction of the Admiral Commanding Coastguard and Reserves, ever since the outbreak of war, from John o' Groat's to Land's End." Sir Robert Baden-Powell dealt fully with the subject in THE GREAT WAR (Chapter CCXLIII., Vol. II, page 337). Hitherto, in treating of home defence, reference has been made only to invasion by an armed force. But dangers threatened from the sea as well as from the air, without any actual landing of the enemy.

That a surprise descent—on a small scale, at least—was possible seemed to be proved by the frequency with which the Germans in the first four years of the war succeeded in bombarding the English coast from submarines as well as surface ships, though without ever doing serious military damage, as the attacks were invariably directed on undefended places such as Scarborough, Whitby, Hartlepool, and Yarmouth.

This was nothing new. " The control of the sea, however real," wrote Mahan in his " Influence of Sea Power upon History," " does not imply that an enemy's single ships or small squadrons cannot steal out of port, cannot cross a more or less **Coast-watchers around Britain** frequented ocean, make harassing descents upon unprotected points of a long coast-line, enter blockaded harbours. On the contrary, history has shown that such evasions are always possible to some extent to the weaker party, however great the inequality of naval strength."

As for Yarmouth—where a monument to Nelson looks down upon the beach from which he embarked to assert Britain's sea supremacy—it was bombarded three times up to the beginning of 1918—in November, 1914, on April 25th, 1916, the day after the Sinn Fein outbreak in Dublin, and again in January, 1918, when several destroyers threw a score of shells into the town and then all scathless made their escape.

German submarines made similar attacks at Whitehaven, on the Cumberland coast, in August, 1915, Seaham (Durham), Southwold, Scarborough, Funchal (in Madeira), Bayonne (in the Bay of Biscay), Monrovia (the capital of Liberia), and even at Dover, when, soon after midnight on February 16th, 1918, a German submarine opened fire on the leading British port of entry, and rained shells on it for several minutes " The shore batteries replied," reported Lord French next day, " and the enemy ceased fire after discharging about thirty rounds."

After all, however, it was the primary business of the British Navy, more than of the Army, to deal with those daring sea-raiders. But there was still another form of enemy attack which had meanwhile been more and more claiming the attention and arousing the energy of home defenders.

This was attack from the air. All other arms of the British combatant service had been of slow and gradual development, but the art of airmanship, by comparison, might almost be said to have been a sudden creation. Blériot's flight across the Channel in July, 1909, may be taken as the first revelation of the power of the new arm. Five years later this arm had become one of the most important and revolutionary weapons of war.

In his despatch to the Secretary of State for War, dated December 31st, 1916, reviewing his first year of office as Commander-in-Chief of the Home Forces, Lord French wrote :

At the time of my assumption of command the question of the anti-aircraft defences of the country was under consideration.

On February 19th it was decided that the London defences should be handed over to me, and on February 26th it was further decided that I should be responsible for the whole of the anti-aircraft land defences of the United Kingdom.

Previous to this I had given considerable attention to the subject of anti-aircraft defence, and I submitted a scheme for consideration, which was approved and has been carried out.

During the winter there was little hostile activity in this direction, but since I assumed charge of these defences enemy airships and aeroplanes have invaded the country whenever conditions admitted. **Anti-aircraft defence in 1916**

In all, nineteen raids have been made by German airships and seventeen attacks have been made by aeroplanes.

The damage done has been comparatively small, and nothing of any military importance has been effected.

Taken as a whole, the defensive measures have been successful. In very few cases have the enemy reached their objective. They have been turned, driven off, seriously damaged by gun fire, and attacked with great success by aeroplanes. Seven have been brought down, either as the result of gun fire or aeroplane attack or of both combined.

The work of the Royal Flying Corps and of the Gun and Light Detachments, including the Royal Naval Anti-Aircraft Corps, has been arduous, and has shown consistent improvement ; the guns and lights have been effectively handled, and the pilots of the Royal Flying Corps have shown both skill and daring. All are deserving of high praise.

To the foregoing may be added a statement in the " War Cabinet's Report for 1917," as to responsibility for home defence against air raids as distinguished from the control of lighter-than-air craft :

The former is under the control of the Field-Marshal Commanding the Home Forces, and the Air Council is not responsible for it. Aircraft, anti-aircraft guns, and searchlights for the defence of London have been united under the immediate command of a single general officer.

Elsewhere in the United Kingdom the guns and lights are under the local general officer commanding-in-chief, while the aircraft has been grouped under the general officer commanding a brigade.

From Lord French himself no review for 1917 was forthcoming corresponding to that for the previous year, but this omission was supplied by the War Cabinet's Report for 1917, which gave a somewhat detailed account of the enemy air raids culminating in that of June 15th, when a powerful squadron of enemy airmen took advantage of almost perfect conditions to make a dash for London. They dropped bombs freely on the City and the East End, entailing a casualty list of 157 killed and 432 injured.

This raid was followed on July 7th by one still more audacious, if happily less successful in respect of casualties, which amounted to but 59 killed and 193 wounded. Nevertheless, the circumstances of this second great raid on London caused much public uneasiness and anger—feelings thus expressed by the " Times " :

The German air raid on London on Saturday has produced much anger in the public mind, and the Government must be prepared to face widespread indignation. . . . At least twenty German aeroplanes appeared over London. Their advent was heralded by a large number of warnings privately given, though by no general warning. They hovered over London for a considerable time, descending to a much lower altitude than on the last occasion. They left in no great haste, and the four enemy machines which were ultimately brought down were all hit while they were recrossing the sea.

Still more outspoken, the " Daily Mail " wrote :

Since the Dutch burned Chatham, two hundred and fifty years ago, making mock of the miserable system of passive defence which the feeble English Government of that date had organised with Stuart slovenliness, there has not been a more discreditable event in our military history than Saturday's raid. There is not a single redeeming fact. The story is altogether humiliating. . . . The raid of Saturday is no isolated incident. It is one of a series of events all almost equally disgraceful to all concerned—Admiralty, Horse Guards, and Air Service commands. All are so heavily involved, and the position is so grave, that the men who have failed should at once be called upon to resign and be replaced by younger, more active, more energetic minds. Our airmen, who are the best in the world, may well complain that they are being made a laughing-stock to the enemy.

Commons in secret session

So widespread was popular anger caused by this raid, and so serious the situation it created, that the Prime Minister ordered a secret session of the House of Commons to explain the position, since—as he said—there were certain facts and figures which it would be undesirable, and even dangerous, to disclose, except under the veil of secrecy. His explanation simply came to this—that more flying machines were wanted, and that the claims of our Army in the field came first.

The fatal casualties (he said) which had been suffered by the civilian population in the last raid were very regrettable, but unless our troops at the front were supplied with aeroplanes in sufficient number to secure a proper knowledge of the German trenches and positions, and to guide the artillery barrage, their losses might easily be not 28 but 28,000. . . . If the Germans knew that by bombing English towns they could force us to withdraw fighting squadrons from France there could be nothing which would encourage them more. Nothing could be more disastrous to the conduct of military operations than anything which encouraged the Germans to believe that by these raids they could excite such a clamour in this country that the Government could not resist the demand for the withdrawal of aeroplanes from the front. If the aeroplanes could be provided both for the front and for our defence against raids, that would, of course, be done. If not, the Army must come first, and it was vitally important that the Germans should know it.

Statement by the Prime Minister

The unfortunate raid on London of July 7th, 1917, might be regarded as the turning-point in the British Air Service. After that there was a marked improvement in every direction, especially in the construction of new aeroplanes, though on this subject, as remarked by the War Cabinet Report for the year, " the writer is at once confronted by the fact that the information desired by the country is precisely the information desired by the enemy."

Public curiosity was to some extent gratified by Mr.

CYCLIST VOLUNTEERS ON SCOUTING DUTY IN AN ENGLISH WOOD.
Cyclist scouts of the Willesden Battalion Middlesex Volunteer Regiment creeping stealthily through a wood during practice manœuvres. Apart from their particular functions as a regimental unit, these cyclist scouts, with their intimate knowledge of the country, were in a position to render valuable service in intercommunication work as despatch-riders and visual signallers should other communications be cut by an enemy force.

Winston Churchill who, in the Commons (April 25th, 1918), said that since the Ministry of Munitions—in the previous year—had been entrusted with the construction of aeroplanes and aeronautical appliances of all kinds :

We have delivered more than twice as many aeroplanes as have ever been made before. We are now making in a single week more than we made in the whole of 1914 ; in a single month more than we made in 1915 ; in a single quarter more than we made in 1916 ; and we are going to make this year several times what we made last year.

At sea, and more particularly at the Battle of Jutland, their airships had given the Germans facilities of observation not at the disposal of Sir John Jellicoe or Sir David Beatty. Otherwise,

PRIVATE CARS PLACED AT THE PUBLIC SERVICE.
Parade of National Motor Volunteers at the Wellington Barracks for inspection by General Sir Francis Lloyd. By the spring of 1918 the London Corps had a strength of 520 men and 433 vehicles.

WOMEN AUXILIARIES TO THE VOLUNTEERS.
Major-General Sir Francis Lloyd, Commanding the London District, inspecting the Women's Section of the Green Cross Motor Transport Reserve and men of the National Motor Transport Volunteers.

the recurrent operations of the Zeppelins over land had only inspired the minds of Britons with an intense detestation of the German name and acted as a stimulus to recruiting. As a writer in the "Times" remarked on the death of Count Zeppelin, these monster aircraft of his devising had been diverted from their legitimate sphere of observation into one of wanton, aimless massacre of innocent civilians, "and in so far as the count acquiesced in their perversion he has helped to make the German name a byword throughout the world."

Zeppelin armada dissipated   Up to the time of Count Zeppelin's death in March, 1917, at least a score of his expensive monsters of the air had been lost to Germany ; while seven months later (October, 1917) at least five out of a squadron of enemy airships which had invaded England, and even dropped bombs on London, were brought down or otherwise disposed of on their devious return journey. In flying over England they kept to such a high altitude that no aeroplane at that time could reach them ; but their machinery got frozen and out of gear, and when—blown thither by an adverse wind—they reached France they were crippled, flying low in daylight, and afforded a fine target. The Royal Flying Corps came into existence in May,

1912, with naval and military wings, and, as already related in Chapter CCXLV. (Vol. 11, page 381), these ultimately became the Royal Air Force, with an Air Ministry and Air Staff behind it. Henceforth the Germans were made to realise that for Great Britain the most vigorous line of home defence was on the Rhine, on the principle that the best parry is ever the thrust. Several months previous to the creation of the Royal Air Force the policy of reprisals, for which public opinion had insistently called—but with which, according to the War Cabinet's Report for 1917, the Government at first " would have nothing to do "— had been vigorously urged, almost in identical terms, by both General Smuts, at a luncheon given him by the Associated Chambers of Commerce (October 4th, 1917), and by Lord Rothermere, Chief of the Air Ministry, at a banquet in honour of the Air Service given by the Benchers of Gray's Inn (December 14th, 1917), when he declared, amid loud cheering : " At the Air Board we are wholeheartedly in favour of air reprisals. It is our duty to

SEA SCOUTS BRINGING IN A MESSAGE.
Immediately upon the outbreak of war the Sea Scouts, a branch of the Boy Scouts organisation, took up duty at all the coastguard stations, under the direction of the Admiral Commanding Coastguard and Reserves.

DIRTY WEATHER IN THE GREAT CITY.
Sentry on guard on the Thames Embankment, wearing oilskins and a sou'wester—a figure that became familiar near bridges, piers, and anti-aircraft gun stations along London's waterway during the war.

avenge the murder of innocent women and children. As the enemy elects, so it will be the case of 'eye for an eye, and a tooth for a tooth,' and in this respect we shall slave for complete and satisfying retaliation."

A month before this, General Smuts had said :

The enemy is now in his impotent rage more and more striking at us through our non-combatants, our women and children. Aerial warfare against the defenceless is the new weapon.

I venture to predict that this weapon will not only fail, but will prove a terrible boomerang to the enemy.

We are fully alive to the danger of the new night attacks by aeroplanes. We have set about the aerial defence of London along somewhat novel lines and with a great measure of success.

Our defences will continue to develop, and the public may rest assured that nothing will be left undone which may tend to the more complete protection of this nerve-centre of the Empire.

The turning-point of the new policy—of reorganisation as well as of reprisal—was marked by the night of Whit Sunday, 1918, when London, for the first time since the beginning of the great German offensive on March 21st, became the object of some score of Gotha machines operating in two columns, one by way of

Kent and the other by way of Essex. Their toll of 37 killed and 161 injured was offset by the loss of seven of their machines, which were brought down either by aerial counter-attacks or the fire of anti-aircraft guns.

By this time the nation was beginning to reap the fruits of its new air organisation, which drew cordial appreciation from the Press. The "Daily Mail," for example, wrote :

Our airmen and the London air defences between them accomplished an excellent piece of work on Sunday night in destroying certainly five and probably seven German aeroplanes, several of which were brought down in flames. This is a most welcome improvement, though the proportion of German casualties is probably not yet sufficiently heavy to prevent the Huns from visiting us again. The ideal will always be an organisation which can account for most of the raiders.

Colonel Repington also wrote :

Most of these attacks I have witnessed from London itself, but this last effort I observed from a point outside London, and was able better to appreciate the immense development of the aerial defences of the capital, which have been steadily improving during a period of many months. On no other occasion have the anti-aircraft defences been so complete. The barrages set up by the outer and inner defences, the great display of powerful searchlights which dazzle and confuse the hostile airmen, and the fruitful activity of our own Air Service were all very much in evidence, with the gratifying results that London was spared the heavy damage and loss of life that must have occurred with less perfected arrangements to defend it. Best of all was the constant evidence displayed throughout of the intimate co-operation of all parts of the defensive system, and we must conclude that those responsible for the air defence of London have not wasted their time.

Improvement in aerial defences

Lord French—to whom this great improvement of British anti-aircraft defences was largely due—had been denied the personal satisfaction of recording in a communiqué this first conspicuous result of his organising work, as he had meanwhile (May 6th, 1918) been transferred from his post as Commander-in-Chief at the Horse Guards to that of "Lord Protector," so to speak, at Dublin. His successor was General Sir William Robertson, whose title, "General Officer Commanding-in-Chief, Great Britain," was evidently intended to show that his authority did not extend to Ireland.

TAKING NO CHANCES OF SURPRISE.
Soldiers belonging to a Hants Territorial Battalion on sentry duty on the shore enlisting the aid of the telescope of a coast watcher of the Royal Navy to identify a suspicious object.

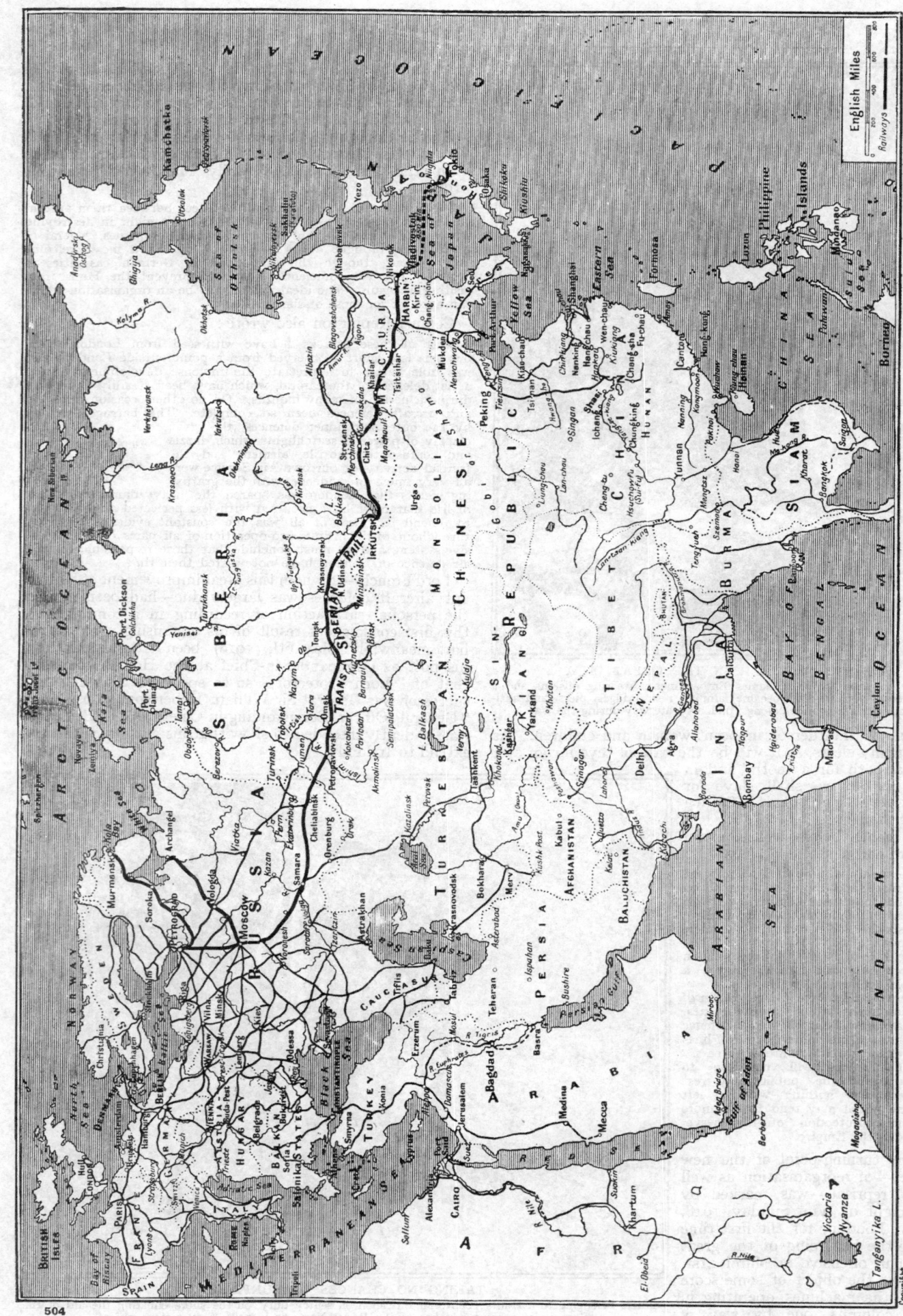

The Great War

MAP OF SEA AND LAND COMMUNICATIONS BETWEEN EAST AND WEST, ILLUSTRATING THE AREA OF JAPAN'S NAVAL ACTIVITY AND THE TRANS-SIBERIAN RAILWAY LINK BETWEEN VLADIVOSTOK AND THE ARCTIC SEA.

CHAPTER CCLI.

THE FAR EAST IN THE WAR: FROM THE AUTUMN OF 1916 TO THE CHINO-JAPANESE CONVENTION.

By Robert Machray.

Japan's Change of Attitude Towards China—A Friendly Policy—Effect of Russian Revolution in the Orient—China's Internal Troubles —Passing of Yuan Shih-kai—German Intrigue in Peking—The Tuchuns and the Rise of Tuan Chi-jui—America's Influence in the Far East—China Breaks Off Relations with Germany and Declares War on Germany and Austria—How the Allies Gained —Japan's Continued Fealty to the Cause—Her Destroyers in the Mediterranean—Bolshevism in Siberia—China's Firm Action in Manchuria—Allied Landing at Vladivostok—Question of Japanese Intervention—Japan and China Sign a Military Convention and Pool their Armies and Navies Against the Enemy.

J APAN'S share in the war to the autumn of 1916 was the subject of Chapter CXXXI. (Vol. 7, page 206). The Island Empire of the Far East was then in possession of Tsing-tau, the rest of the district of Kiao-Chau, and nearly all Micronesia — the Marianne (or Ladrones), the Marshall, and the Caroline Islands—from which the Germans had been expelled. Her fleets, in conjunction with those of the Entente, were controlling the Pacific and Indian Oceans. In addition, she was supplying the Allies with munitions and equipment on a large scale, and lending monetary assistance to the common cause. As 1917 opened, a loan to Great Britain of ten millions sterling was successfully floated in Tokyo.

Two reasons caused Japan to declare war on Germany. One was her determination to avail herself of the opportunity of extirpating German influence in Eastern Asia, which she regarded as essentially her sphere. The other, and more immediately compelling, was the request of Great Britain for her help, under the terms of the Anglo - Japanese Alliance, which provided that if Great Britain or Japan were involved in a war, arising from unprovoked attack or aggressive action by any Power or Powers, the other party to the treaty should at once come to the military assistance of its ally.

Among other things, the Alliance provided for the maintenance of the independence and territorial integrity of China. As was noted in Chapter CXXXI., page 208, some of the Japanese disapproved of the Alliance, because they thought it circumscribed the action of Japan with respect to China, whose fate, they asserted, was for her the biggest of all questions in the world. They strongly advocated a "forward" policy, for which the absorption of Europe in the war seemed to give an unusually favourable chance of success, and they were profoundly disappointed that the agreement between Japan and China which was signed on May 25th, 1915, did not satisfy all the twenty-one demands that had been made by their diplomats, though, as a matter of fact, China was compelled to make large concessions.

On the other hand, there were Japanese — and these were among the most prescient in the land — who considered that this forward policy if persisted in would jeopardise the Anglo-Japanese Alliance, tie Japan's hands in the war, and in all probability

[Bassano.

MILITARY REPRESENTATIVE OF A GREAT ALLY.
Major-General N. Hibiki, Quartermaster-General of the Japanese Army, visited London during the fourth year of the war to confer with the British Headquarters Staff.

completely alienate America, part of whose people, unaware at the time of the extent to which German intrigue affected their views, were already unfriendly. These considerations, reinforced by outside advice, had led to the withdrawal of the demands which appeared most to impair the sovereignty of China. But the

Two schools of Japanese opinion

Japanese Jingoes were loud in their protests, and continued their agitation for a " firmer " dealing with China, towards which, however, the wiser statesmen of Japan had determined to adopt a very different line.

Count (afterwards Marquess) Okuma was Premier of Japan when the agreement of 1915 was concluded. On his resignation, an outcome in 1916 of the political struggle between the two schools of Japanese opinion, a crisis developed which became acute when the Emperor, on the recommendation of the Genro, or Elder Statesmen, sent for Field-Marshal Count Terauchi to form a Government, instead of Viscount Kato, whom Okuma had named as his successor. Denouncing the interference of the Genro as unconstitutional, a new party, headed by Kato, was formed, under the title of Kensei-kai, in October of that year, and drew to itself other political elements, particularly the Kokuminto, or Nationalists, which gave it an absolute majority over the Seiyu-kai and other followers of Terauchi in the Diet, or Parliament. The Field-Marshal took as his platform the vigorous prosecution of the war and " Hands off China ! " When the Diet met on January 23rd, 1917, he delivered an address in which he said that Japan's part in the war was the closest co-operation with her fellow " participants " ; and he also stated that Japan enjoyed the most cordial relations with neutrals, particularly China, with which, he observed,

" We shall not spare our efforts to cultivate relations of mutual confidence and assistance." It was plain, nevertheless, that the Opposition would be too strong for him ; and in order to avoid defeat he obtained the assent of the Emperor to an immediate dissolution, to be followed shortly by a General Election, an edict to that effect being promulgated next day.

In the electoral campaign which ensued it soon was apparent that the bulk of the Japanese people rallied round the Terauchi Government and its twofold policy. The most conspicuous exponent of that policy with respect to China was Viscount Motono, the Foreign Minister. In a remarkably frank speech in the Diet on January 23rd he admitted that the past actions of Japan had created an unfavourable atmosphere for her in China, and he declared that for the welfare of both this must be dissipated. He went on to remark that no one denied that Japan possessed great political and economic interests in China, but he pointed out that these did not give the Japanese the right to intervene in the internal affairs of China, as some of them had done, taking sides with this or that faction among the Chinese—with consequences that were deplorable, as the results were animosity to Japan and a misunder-

Viscount Motono's frank speech

standing of her real intentions, which, instead of being hostile, were most friendly to China. He closed his observations by reminding his countrymen that, though Japan did occupy a special position in China, the fact could not be ignored that other Powers had vast interests in that country which must be respected by Japan, which, moreover, was bound by agreements with these Powers and, besides, was associated with these Powers in the war.

PICKED INFANTRY OF JAPAN: THE IMPERIAL GUARDS DIVISION ON THE RIFLE-RANGE.
Men of the Japanese Imperial Guards Division practising at the perfectly equipped rifle-range at Tokyo. The infantry of the Guards were recruited from men selected from the whole country, unlike the other divisions, which were supplied with recruits from their own districts. The arm of the Japanese infantry at the time of the Great War was the improved Arisaka rifle, calibre 6·5 mm., a Mauser with an altered chamber.

POISED ON THE WAVES LIKE A RESTING GULL.
One of the many hydroplanes employed by the Japanese Navy to direct the gun fire of battleships. From the moment when Japan first organised her Navy on European lines with the object of becoming a first-class sea Power, she kept abreast with every development of science and invention.

break off relations with Germany and eventually to line up with the Allies—a political move in itself of such vital importance to her as to usher in a fresh stage, it might be a new era, in her long and wonderful story. Two months prior to America's declaration of war, President Wilson, because of Germany's announcement of unrestricted submarine warfare, severed relations with that Empire, and asked the other neutrals to adopt the same course. China was included in the invitation, and accepted it, though after some delay, due not to the merits of the case but to dissension among her leaders, who were quarrelling bitterly among themselves.

When the war broke out in 1914 Yuan Shih-kai was President of the Chinese Republic. In the previous year his troops, under the command of General Tuan Chi-jui, of whom much more was to be heard, had suppressed with ease an armed insurrection of the Cantonese, or Southern, faction, and he appeared to have a firm grasp of the reins of power. His strength lay mainly in the North, which was conservative if not reactionary, and he had scant sympathy with the Radicals of "Young China," who had a large following in the South. His guiding principle was to govern the country according to its old autocratic traditions, which he sincerely believed were the most suitable for the Chinese people. Rejecting the provisional Republican Constitution, which had been the work mainly of the Southerners, and practically abolishing the Parliament that had been set up under it, Yuan framed a new Constitution, concentrating in himself the executive authority.

Yuan Shih-kai for some time proved an able administrator of the country's internal affairs, but he showed

This and similar appeals to the good sense of the Japanese had their due effect. The prosecution of the war against Germany, on which Terauchi and Motono insisted, and not interference with China, stood out as supreme. The result of the General Election in April, 1917, was a majority for the Government. At the end of May, Terauchi, speaking to the prefectural governors,

New era in China's history

was at pains to tell them that Japan's main business in the world was to support the Allies and cement friendship with China. So far as the latter was concerned, this involved a complete reversal of Japanese policy.

Meanwhile, there had occurred two of the greatest events in the war, perhaps in the history of mankind. March saw the Revolution in Russia, which swept away the Tsardom; April, the declaration of war on Germany by the United States of America. Both events had a tremendous influence on the Far East. The great change that was coming over Russia took months to develop, and therefore did not immediately affect the situation in Eastern Asia materially, but as the break-up of that Empire proceeded, with disorder spreading throughout Siberia, it was seen to hold a significance for that part of the globe almost impossible to exaggerate. The intervention of America in the war had much the more marked effect at the outset, and very soon brought about a profound and radical alteration in the whole aspect of Far Eastern affairs.

For some time previously China had been looking hopefully towards America for support and guidance; in the end, like her, she enrolled herself in the League of Nations embattled to overthrow the common enemy. Other factors played their part, but, more than anything else, the incitement and example of the United States induced China to

CHINESE OFFICERS ON VERDUN'S HISTORIC BATTLEFIELD.
Officers of the Chinese Mission visiting the western front at Verdun with General Corvisart, of the French Army (on the left). They appeared to find amusement in being photographed in the shrapnel helmets which all visitors were compelled to don when taken up to the front line.

very little grasp of the situation externally, and failed to take into account Japan and her "forward" policy as it was at that time. In the negotiations over the twenty-one demands put forward by Japan in 1915, he strenuously opposed most of her claims as derogatory to China's sovereignty and as invalidating the treaty rights of other Powers. After these demands were modified, in accordance with the suggestions of the Allies, he still declined to accede to them; but presented with a two-days' ultimatum he yielded, as the military weakness of China gave him no option. But this did not strengthen him in the Presidency, and he had incurred the hostility of Japan, which, in any case, remembered against him that formerly he had withstood her with regard to Korea and had favoured Russia.

Already an autocratic ruler, Yuan had determined in 1914 to make himself Emperor of China, as was indicated by his decision to perform the Imperial **Question of** Sacrifice in the Temple of Heaven, a **the monarchy** service reserved for the sovereign alone. For the most part the mandarins sympathised with the restoration of the monarchy, and in the beginning supported him. On the other side stood the Southerners, who were Republicans, led by Sun Yat Sen, and organised by the political association known as the Kuo-min-tang. In August, 1915, the movement for the restoration of the monarchy, with Yuan at its head, took on a more definite form, but it had now to reckon with Japan, whose interests, both political and economic, in China had been vastly increased by the acceptance of most of the twenty-one demands, and who did not look on Yuan personally with too friendly eyes.

In October the question of the monarchy was referred by the State Council, a creation of Yuan, to a vote of the provinces, but Japan intervened before a decision was taken and advised against the restoration. Yuan replied that the matter must abide by the vote, which, in the upshot, was nearly unanimous for his accession to the Dragon Throne, though there was much doubt whether those voting were genuinely representative, as they were nominees of his or of his friends. When Japan again counselled him not to proceed with his scheme, Yuan answered that he had no intention of dropping it, but would delay putting it into execution till the New Year. A revolutionary outbreak, however, at Shanghai caused the State Council to memorialise him to end the prevailing unrest by proclaiming himself Emperor immediately. With many protestations of his unworthiness, he agreed, the monarchy was proclaimed on December 12th, 1915, and his coronation set for February 9th, 1916.

To Yuan the moment seemed ripe for the realisation of his project, but events soon showed that he had made a tragic mistake. Insurrections broke out, and several provinces renounced their allegiance. If **Sudden death of** Li Yuan-hung, the Vice-President, who **Yuan Shih-kai** had led the forces of the revolution which had established the Republic, refused to take sides, General Feng Kuo-chang, who had been Yuan's right-hand man, pronounced for the continuance of the Republic, as did General Tuan Chi-jui. When Yuan's troops began to fraternise openly with the rebels it was plain, even to himself, that the tide had turned against him, and in January, a fortnight before the day appointed for his enthronement, he announced officially that the reinstitution of the monarchy was indefinitely postponed.

By this time Yuan had been deserted by many of his adherents, and two months later his few remaining friends besought him to resign the Presidency; but he declined. Then more provinces seceded, and more of his supporters abandoned him. It was clear that his plans had failed, and when he made a last effort to retrieve himself in April by transferring all civil authority to a Cabinet, of which Tuan Chi-jui was Premier, it was too late. The Southerners proclaimed Li Yuan-hung as President, and formed a Provisional Government at Canton. Without success Tuan tried to appease them by a declaration that Parliamentary government would be re-established. Yuan had drafted his resignation, when his sudden death cleared the political atmosphere. Li Yuan-hung became President, Feng Kuo-chang Vice-President, and Tuan Chi-jui remained on as Premier.

Yuan Shih-kai's passing was a great loss to China. He was the strong man who understood what his countrymen required in the way of a government. Soon after his hand was removed China presented a dismal picture of confusion and internal strife, of jarring politicians and warring military chiefs, of bankrupt finance and impeded commerce. Tuan Chi-jui's Cabinet consisted of members of all parties, but there was no real unity. The Parliament which had sat in 1913 was convened in August, a move which it was believed would conciliate the Southerners; but it did nothing of the kind, as they maintained that Tuan was at heart as monarchist and as militarist as Yuan had ever been. When Parliament met, the Southerners showed they were hostile to Tuan, but they were powerless. As a whole the country was dominated by the Tuchuns, or military governors of the provinces, with their individual armies. Most of them supported the Premier, but for the nonce they tolerated the Parliament and permitted it to blow off steam.

In the beginning of 1917 China was described by the Peking Correspondent of the "Times" as "simply drifting," because of the lack in the Government of really strong men inspired by patriotism. The war was hardly an issue. According to a prominent Japanese writer, the idea of bringing China into the struggle was first broached by Great Britain in 1915, when Yuan Shih-kai was still supreme, but was not persevered with because of Japanese opposition. Early in 1917 America took the lead in the matter by directing her Minister at Peking to try to get China to **German intrigue** sever diplomatic relations with Germany. **in the Far East** For some time before, a few Chinese, among whom was the influential Tuan, the Premier, had been in favour of China's throwing in her lot with the Allies. Though Li, the President, was not anxious to endorse the action of the United States, and Vice-President Feng was doubtful about it, the Cabinet, aided by foreign advice, took the view that China should do so. Accordingly, on February 9th, 1917, the Chinese Government sent a Note to Germany protesting against the unlimited submarine campaign, and threatening to break off relations if the protest were disregarded. Germany replied that she was driven by necessity to make war on neutral ships, but promised adequate measures for safeguarding Chinese lives. Meanwhile, with the object of preventing China from withdrawing from her attitude of neutrality, German agents conducted the most unscrupulous propaganda, accompanied by wholesale bribery, in Peking and other centres.

As far back as 1895 the Deutsch-Asiatische Bank, whose headquarters were in Berlin, had been established in China, and it succeeded in associating itself with the Hong-Kong and Shanghai Banking Corporation, the principal British institution of the sort in the land, but this was an arrangement which in the end did not work out well for British interests in the Far East. When the war began, Germans were largely in control of the foreign finance, commerce, and industry of China; they were predominant even in the Crown Colony of Hong-Kong—it and the German concessions in the treaty ports were hotbeds of German intrigue.

The Chinese Government's need of money and the disputes among the political rivals and factions gave Germany an opportunity which she did her best to exploit, German missionaries circulated pamphlets full of lies about the British, and from Shanghai carried on a campaign of misrepresentation which struck at the Allies all over the East. In 1915 the Germans organised a

Major Prince Amoradhat of Siam (in light coat) with American, British, French, and other allied officers on Vimy Ridge.

General Phya Bhijar (seated on left), of the Siamese Mission, with his Staff on a visit to the western theatre of war.

King Rama VI. of Siam with his Headquarters Staff. The King, who succeeded to the throne in 1910, was educated at Sandhurst and Christ Church, Oxford, and had strong personal ties with Great Britain. Siam declared war upon Germany July 22nd, 1917.

Siam, " The Kingdom of the Free," rallied to the defence of the world's freedom.

King George inspecting a contingent of Japanese sailors in a British port.

Ashes of Japanese sailors killed in action being taken ashore for transmission to Japan.

Native artillery of 1st and 2nd Divisions marching past President of the Chinese Republic.

Interesting group of Chinese military and naval officers in their Westernised uniforms.

Chinese labourers filling motor-lorries with sacks of corn from a dump at a rail-head in France.

Chinese serving with the British Army in France drawing oats from a depot for use up the line.

Picturesque crowd in a corner of a Chinese labour camp on the western front.

Chinese working under Canadian Engineers getting loose stone from a quarry for making roads.

Chinese serving with the British Labour Corps in France.

East helping West to fight the Hun: *Chinese serving with the British Labour Corps in France.*

great cinematograph propaganda, the film pictures which toured the provinces being of such a nature as impressed the natives with her tremendous military power. From China men such as Hentig and Pappenheim, of the German Legation at Peking, proceeded to Afghanistan, Kashgaria, Mongolia, and Yarkand to stir up trouble for Great Britain and Russia.

Germany did not hesitate when an occasion presented itself to support the provincial authorities against the central Government. She gave her blessing to the Tuchun of Yunnan when he declared his province independent, and she stood behind the curious monarchist movement under Chang Hsun, which was a sensational feature of the summer of 1917. Her object was to embarrass the rulers of China to such a degree as to keep them from committing their country to the side of the Entente.

Germany failed in this effort, though for some weeks she succeeded in staving off a decision by precipitating a political crisis. In the meantime she offered to cancel certain monetary claims she had against China, and she distributed large sums in bribes among the officials. She did not get Tuan to change his mind. He was strongly in favour of breaking off relations with Germany, and demanded immediate action of President Li, who, however, declared that Parliament alone could decide the question. Opposition developed more and more between Li and Tuan, and time passed without anything being done.

After consulting leading men at Peking and in the provinces, Tuan and his Cabinet, in the beginning of March, resolved to break off relations with the German Government, and to issue instructions to the provincial authorities in that sense; but Li refused to sign the instructions, whereupon Tuan resigned the Premiership and left the capital for Tientsin. Li soon found that Tuan was supported not only by the Cabinet, but by a majority of the political and military leaders, as well as of the Members of Parliament, and he sent Feng, the Vice-President, to bring him back. **Relations severed with Germany** Ultimately, a reconciliation was effected, and Parliament voted approval of Tuan's policy, in spite of the objections of the Southerners.

On March 14th the German Minister was given his passports, and the German Consuls were dismissed. Further, the Chinese Government interned the German ships at Shanghai and Amoy, and sent about their business more than five hundred Germans whom it had employed in various capacities. It also took measures which had an important bearing on the finance of China, inasmuch as it repudiated the German share of the Boxer indemnity, and suspended payments on German loans.

These measures gave some relief to China's financial position, which had become very bad. The weakness of her Government was largely due to its lack of funds, which was caused by the refusal of the provincial authorities to remit the customary subsidies to the capital. One of the causes which had helped on the success of Tuan's policy of breaking with Germany was that on February 28th the Allied Ministers sent to him a memorandum which promised that, if relations with the enemy were broken off, their Governments would consider favourably a suspension of the payments on account of the Boxer indemnity, as well as a revision of the tariff in order to give China a larger revenue.

Originally the Boxer indemnity, which was imposed in satisfaction of the losses incurred by foreign States and their nationals through the Boxer rising in 1900, was about sixty-seven millions sterling, but through deferred interest and other charges it had increased to nearly twice that sum. Of the indemnity, Germany's share was twenty-two millions, and most of it was still unpaid. With the exception of Russia, Germany had a bigger share than any other nation. America had had the least; after converting the amount of it she had received into a trust for the education of young Chinese in her colleges and schools, she had cancelled the balance. The Allies' share came to two millions a year, a large sum for China to find in her impoverished condition, and the suspension of such an onerous payment would be a great matter to her.

China stood to gain even more from the revision of the tariff. This was a Customs tariff, which the commercial treaties with the various foreign Powers entitled China to impose at the rate of five per cent, *ad valorem* on all exports and imports. In 1902 the tariff was converted into a specific duty on the basis of prices ruling in the three years prior to the Boxer outbreak. In the years that followed prices altered so disadvantageously for the revenue that in practice the tariff, still nominally five per cent., yielded little more than three and a half per cent. In 1913 China had given notice of her desire that the tariff should be revised so as to make the rate an effective five per cent., but nothing was done at the time. The promise of the Allied Ministers that the matter would **Tuan Chi-jui and his critics** be taken up was a strong inducement to China to break off with Germany, for when that promise was carried out the increase in the Chinese revenue would be upwards of three and a half million pounds.

Having succeeded in getting relations broken off, Tuan Chi-jui next strove to push the business to its logical conclusion by having war declared on Germany, but although the Chinese as a whole were in favour of it, several months passed before he was triumphant. Internal political dissensions prolonged the delay, and German money was not wanting to inflame the spirit of faction. The Japanese and other Allied Ministers gave Tuan what support they could, and America's declaration of war in April was not without its influence. On the 26th of that month a conference of Tuchuns at Peking voted for an immediate declaration, and early in May the Cabinet passed a resolution unanimously to that effect.

When the subject was debated in Parliament most members pronounced for declaring war, but opposition was strong against Tuan personally and the "militarists" with whom he was identified. It was asserted that in defiance of Parliament he was bent on establishing a military despotism, and an insistent demand was made for the reorganisation of Tuan's Cabinet. A stronger reason, perhaps, for the hostility shown to Tuan and his supporters was that the Southerners, who were anti-militarist, as well as some others, did not wish him to reap the benefit of those financial advantages which the Allied Ministers had suggested might accrue, and were certain to accrue if war was declared. After a riotous session Parliament voted not to declare war while Tuan remained in office, but he stood to his guns and urged President Li to dissolve it. Li, however, dismissed Tuan, who again withdrew to Tientsin.

As the Tuchuns demanded Tuan's reinstatement, and began mobilising **The U.S. Note to China** their armies, civil war was imminent. Several provinces declared their independence. At this juncture Li asked Chang Hsun, the commander of the armed forces at Hsuchowfu, and one of the most powerful of the Tuchuns, to go to Peking with a view to a compromise. Chang marched to Tientsin, where immediately afterwards a Provisional Government was set up by these military governors. The rumour spread that the Manchus were to be restored. When Chang arrived in Peking with his army he at once occupied the Fengtai railway junction and other strategic points, and under this pressure Li dissolved Parliament.

It was at this time that President Wilson addressed a Note to China which, though designed with the best intentions, had the unfortunate effect of giving umbrage to Japan. This Note expressed the hope of the United States that factional and political disputes would be set aside, and that all parties would work to "re-establish and co-ordinate the Government and secure China's position among the nations." It said that in view of the distracted state of the country its entrance into the war was secondary to a restoration of its national unity.

Regarding her place in the Far East as predominant, Japan did not like this direct American speaking to China, and thought that at least she should have been consulted beforehand. It turned out that the Note had been despatched to Peking not only without consulting Japan, but without consulting Great Britain, France, and Russia, all of whom were vitally interested. Official circles in Washington admitted there had been inadvertence, and declared there was no intention on the part of America of undermining Japanese influence in China. This closed the incident; which was well, for the enemy had all along been trying to create and foster bad feeling between the United States and Japan by his usual methods of intrigue.

Germany had assured America that Japan was determined to obtain the mastery of the Pacific, and that the latter had already gained a footing in **Zimmermann's Mexican intrigue** Mexico with a view to operations against her. The Kaiser told Mr. Gerard, then U.S. Ambassador at Berlin, that the Mexican Army was officered by Japanese colonels. At the same time the enemy sought to inflame Japan, through her Jingoes, against the United States, and probably offered to assist her. Extremely significant, at all events, was the despatch from Zimmermann, the German Foreign Secretary, to Eckhardt, the German Minister to Mexico, which was intercepted by the American Secret Service and published by the U.S. Government (Chapter CLXXIII., Vol. 9).

This famous, or rather infamous, despatch proposed an alliance between Germany and Mexico in the event of the United States not remaining neutral because of the unrestricted submarine warfare. Germany and Mexico were to make war together on America, and Mexico was to reconquer " her lost territory in New Mexico, Texas,

CANADIAN CHINESE IN FRANCE.
Many of the Chinese in France came from Canada. Above: A scene in a labour camp, showing a Chinese missionary reading on the occasion of a native celebration.

and Arizona." Then it was suggested that the President of Mexico, on his own initiative, as it was intended to appear, should communicate with Japan, inviting her adherence to the campaign, and should offer to mediate between Germany and Japan.

The making public of the Zimmermann letter did much to unite the Americans against Germany; but it had the ill effect of increasing American suspicion of Japan, which, however, was allayed greatly by Japan's declaration immediately afterwards that she was absolutely loyal to her Allies and the cause for which they were fighting. Field-Marshal Terauchi, the Japanese Premier, said that the German plot, whereby Japan was to ally herself with Mexico in an attack on the United States, only proved to what a degree of aberration German ignorance could go in **Japan repudiates the German scheme** gauging the aspirations of other nations. "Japan," he added, "would commit a veritable act of madness against her own interests if she were to attempt to violate her pledged word."

This was in March, 1917, and the American Note to China was delivered early in the following June. Japan saw that it was very much her affair to arrive at a good understanding with America. As it happened, a Japanese Mission, similar to those sent to Washington by Great Britain and other Allies (Chapter CCV., Vol. 10, page 285), was on its way to the United States, and discussion was postponed till its arrival.

With regard to China herself, the American Note, by its advice that the securing of national unity should precede a declaration of war on Germany, appeared rather to support the policy of President Li as against that of Premier Tuan, and somewhat played into the hands of the opposition to the latter. But Li had become virtually a prisoner in Peking, where Chang for the moment was supreme. Towards the end of June, Li consented to a

CELEBRATING THE CHINESE NEW YEAR.
Two Chinese labourers from Canada at a joss-house on the western front praying for Good Luck at the beginning of their New Year.

redrafting of the Constitution and the election of a new Parliament, which was to be composed of fewer members than had been its predecessor. Some of the military leaders seemed to be satisfied, and it looked as if a basis of compromise had really been obtained that would put an end in large measure to the dissension so long rampant, when there supervened suddenly and unexpectedly one of the most curious tragi-comedies of all history.

On July 2nd the world was startled by the extraordinary news that on the previous day Chang had proclaimed the restoration of the monarchy, that the boy " Manchu Emperor," Hsuan Tung, had been **Tragi-comic** placed on the throne, and that President **"restoration"** Li had taken refuge in the Japanese Legation. Chang acted as Dictator under the title of Grand Secretary, but in this his brother Tuchuns, on whom in point of fact he had stolen a march, would not submit to him. The coup d'état had the further result of joining up all the contending factions in common opposition to Chang. Tuan advanced an army from Tientsin ; he was supported by Feng Kuo-chang, the Vice-President, and other generals. Sun Yat-sen was put at the head of the Navy. From the Japanese Legation Li ordered Feng to assume the Presidency, with Tuan as Premier. Chang's rule was short. After enduring a

THE ROLL-CALL.
Roll-call in a Chinese labour camp. The names of the men were inscribed on streamers revolving on a pivot.

short siege his troops capitulated on July 12th, and Chang found an asylum in the Dutch Legation. The twelve-year-old Emperor abdicated, solemnly explaining that as he was only a child he had had nothing in reality to do with the affair. So closed this astonishing episode, which beyond doubt owed something to German inspiration.

On July 18th Feng Kuo-chang consented to be President, and a strong Cabinet was formed under Tuan, Premier as before. Feng's acceptance of the Presidency was a blow to the Southerners, who again became very active against Tuan and his "militarism." For the time Feng co-operated with

Tuan, and on August 3rd the Cabinet unanimously resolved to declare war on Germany and Austria. On the 14th the official declaration was issued, signed by Feng and countersigned by Tuan and the other Ministers. The declaration was accompanied by a statement abrogating all treaties, agreements, and conventions with the Central Powers, as well as such parts of international protocols and understandings as concerned their relations with China.

At Shanghai the Chinese naval authorities took over three fine Austrian steamers. The Austrian soldiers and sailors who had been employed at Tientsin were interned, and Austrians working for the Chinese Government were discharged. All the offices of the Deutsch-Asiatische Bank were sealed up, and foreign bankers, in conjunction with a Chinese official, were instructed to liquidate its affairs. With regard to enemy subjects in the country, China pursued the same course as Great Britain ; they were compelled to register, but such as were considered unobjectionable were allowed to reside in their homes and carry on business under police supervision. Though the Southeners, **China's declaration** again openly recalcitrant, would not **of war** acknowledge the "Peking Government," they, too, declared war on Germany and Austria ; in this, at any rate, the North and South were united, but their disunion extended to everything else, and soon was seriously intensified.

Tuan's Government immediately benefited by the declaration. Japan at once arranged to advance a million sterling to meet its most pressing needs. On September 9th the Allied Ministers announced that, in recognition of the step, there would be a postponement for five years of the Boxer indemnity payments, except on the part of Russia, who was to make a postponement in proportion to her share, which was twice as big as that of any of the others. Later it was arranged that after the period of postponement had elapsed China was to settle about the indemnity with each of the Allies separately. Regarding the revision of the tariff, the Ministers pledged their best endeavours to bring the rate up to a real five per cent., but difficulties arose as to details, and as late as June, 1918, a commission, composed of Chinese

ENTRANCE TO A CHINATOWN ON THE WESTERN FRONT.
Before China declared war against Germany, on August 14th, 1917, thousands of her coolies, organised under allied officers, did excellent work behind the fighting-lines. Later their numbers were increased till, by March, 1918, over 200,000 were so employed.

and allied representatives, was still sitting in Shanghai endeavouring to resolve them. With the money obtained from Japan, Tuan consolidated his position against the South, as the Southerners had foreseen, but were unable to prevent.

From the international point of view China gained enormously by her declaration of war on the Central Powers, for it gave her a standing among the Allies such as nothing else could have done. That standing among the Allies carried with it a standing in the world, an amount of elbow-room, an independence even, which she had for years ceased in practice to possess. As an American writer shrewdly observed, she had in effect transferred " the responsibility of maintaining her political integrity from her own shoulders to the collective shoulders of the Allies," and simultaneously had given herself a title to a voice in the final settlement that must come after the war. Japan was in sympathy with China's action. Such was the result of the reversal of the forward policy. She showed what that change in her policy meant in several ways. Thus she withdrew her troops from Cheng-Chia-Tung, in Manchuria, a town which she had occupied because of fighting that had occurred there between some of her own guards and Chinese soldiers. Also, when China sought her opinion as to the advisability of asking the consent of the Allies to increasing the tariff, she had expressed herself ready to accede to such increase, if the other Powers would agree to do

Chino-Japanese rapprochement the same. By her attitude of disinterestedness politically the way was being prepared for an entente with China.

On their part the Allies gained by this bettering of the relations between Japan and China. They gained, too, by the Chinese declaration of war on the Central Powers, though not from the military standpoint, for the Chinese Army, if nominally 800,000 strong, was split up under the provincial military chiefs, and was far from reaching the standard required for effective participation in the struggle, while the Chinese Navy was a negligible quantity. Even had the Army been fit for service, transport was lacking. But the Allies gained much morally; the prestige of China, still considerable in Asia, had its effect on their behalf. As regarded shipping, there was the substantial advantage of securing the 30,000 tons of the enemy vessels that were seized by China, and handed over on lease to the British for the general purposes of the Entente. It was, however, by her enormous contribution in labour that China rendered most material assistance to the cause.

Before her declaration of war, thousands of her coolies,

organised under allied officers, had been doing excellent work behind the fighting-lines, and after the declaration their numbers were vastly increased. In the spring of 1918 there were nearly a hundred thousand Chinese employed in many ways in support of the British armies in France, with about an equal number co-operating with the French, and five thousand with the Americans, while Chinese labour was also being used extensively in Mesopotamia and in East Africa.

Though mainly composed of coolies, these vast industrial forces, in all not far short of a quarter of a million men, comprised trained mechanics and competent artisans, many of them from the arsenals at Hanyang, Hankow, and Canton, and **China's help to** these were at work chiefly in the French **the Allies** munition factories, some of which were entirely manned by them. Chinese dockers held the record at Boulogne; at Dieppe nearly all the dockers were Chinamen. Many Chinese were sailors on British ships, and while thus engaged more than a hundred of them lost their lives, while others were submarined three or four times. In the United Kingdom all sufficiently qualified Chinese medical students volunteered for duty in the hospitals, and Chinese doctors became house surgeons and physicians in the hospitals of London, Edinburgh, Liverpool, Bristol, Plymouth, Portsmouth, and other centres. Wealthy Chinamen subscribed handsomely to the war loans and

war charities, besides presenting aeroplanes and ambulances.

Hand in hand with Japan's policy of sincerely friendly relations with China went that of establishing a thorough understanding with America. As mentioned previously, the latter was one of the objects of the Japanese Mission, which, like the British Mission and other Missions of the Allies, visited Washington in the course of 1917. The head of the Japanese Mission was Viscount Ishii. His speeches impressed the Americans by their fine oratory, but, far better than that, by their perfect exposure of German intrigue, which had

FAR EASTERN VISITORS TO THE BATTLE AREAS IN FRANCE.
Group of Chinese students photographed as they were about to start for the trenches. Above : Officers of the Chinese Mission to Europe in 1918 passing down the Meuse aboard an electrically-driven pinnace.

tried and was still trying to keep America and Japan apart, and by their unconditional assertion of the loyalty of Japan to the cause. With respect to China, Japan's reversal of the policy of encroachment had given Viscount Ishii an excellent case.

In the first week of November, 1917, Notes were exchanged between Mr. Lansing, United States Secretary of State, and Ishii, dealing with the relations of Japan and America, as between themselves, with regard to China, and with Japan's own relations

EASTERN WORKERS IN A WESTERN FIELD.
Chinese Labour Battalion en route to a sector of the western battle-front, for a spell of road-making and trench-digging, led by a British officer and sergeant.

CHINESE AID FOR CANADIAN ENGINEERS.
Men of a Chinese Labour Corps working at a crusher by a quarry where Canadian Engineers were obtaining stone for road-making on the western front.

with China. The Notes showed that Japan and the United States had reached a common basis.

They stated that in order to silence mischievous reports it was desirable to announce publicly the position taken by the two Governments. On her side America declared she recognised that Japan had special interests in China, particularly in that part to which her possessions were contiguous, but America also said that the territorial independence of China was to remain unimpaired, and that the open door was to be maintained. On her part Japan accepted as her own this exposition of the policy of the United States. The two Powers further declared their opposition to the acquisition by any Government of special rights in China, which would affect her sovereignty, or deny equal opportunity to all in her trade and commerce.

Mr. Lansing and Viscount Ishii

From a supplementary official statement issued by Mr. Lansing it appeared that Japan pledged herself to do everything in her power for the suppression of Prussian militarism, and that complete and satisfactory agreements concerning naval co-operation in the Pacific, for the purpose of attaining the common object against Germany and her allies, had been reached after discussion in Washington by representatives of the American and Japanese Navies. Mr. Lansing went to the root of the matter when he went on to observe that there had been

growing up a feeling of suspicion between Japan and America, as a result of a campaign of falsehood adroitly and secretly carried on by Germans, whose Government, as part of its foreign policy, desired to alienate the two countries. He stated that the Notes, which had been exchanged, cleared all this away. Taking cognisance of the Notes, the Chinese Government intimated that it did not regard as binding on China agreements between or among other nations, but that China scrupulously observed such compacts as she herself made with others.

In 1915, 1916, and 1917 the question of China was the chief preoccupation of Japan. Her Jingoes relegated the war to a secondary place. Not a few of them thought, and some of them openly expressed the opinion, that Japan would have done better to keep out of the conflict altogether.

Germany naturally took advantage of this state of things, and incessantly intrigued to bring Japan over to her side. She whispered that the Anglo-Japanese Alliance bound Japan to Great Britain, whose interests were far from being the same as those of the Japanese, and suggested that a **Japan's work for** separate peace and an Alliance with her **the Entente** would be to their mutual benefit, but particularly profitable to Japan—which, being interpreted, meant that she was willing that the other should have a free hand in China. These things were said in secret.

Openly through her newspapers—all rigorously controlled by herself—Germany spoke to Japan in language which was a mixture of bullying and cajolery. She professed that she saw in what she called the " oscillations of Japan's action in the war " that Japan was half-hearted in the matter. Other people, who certainly were not Germans, were inclined to think that Japan might have done much more. Japan had a ready answer for Germany and for all others who made light of the part she played in the war.

Japan's reply was that she had entered the war against Germany because she was bound to do so under the terms of the Anglo-Japanese Alliance, which provided that in certain eventualities Japan should take counsel with Great Britain as to action. These eventualities had materialised, and counsel had been taken together, with the result that Japan's part had been decided between the two contracting Powers as the taking of action by her in the Far East, Japan's natural sphere, and in the Pacific and Indian Oceans. Japan pointed out that she had stood by the decision, had taken Tsing-tau and the Micronesian Islands, and that her fleets controlled the

Eastern seas. She claimed there had been and there was no half-heartedness, as she had fulfilled and continued to fulfil what had been agreed upon. She proclaimed her unaltered and unalterable fidelity to the Alliance, which she stated was and would remain the pivot of her whole world-policy.

Japan, however, did more than what had been arranged between herself and Great Britain. Though it was not known at the time by the Japanese or the British public, Japan—in February, 1917—in view of the unrestricted submarine campaign of Germany, despatched a flotilla of destroyers to the Mediterranean to co-operate with the warships of the Allies in that U boat haunted sea. It was not till May, 1917, that Lord Robert Cecil, the Foreign Under-Secretary, made announcement in the House of Commons of this further and most welcome contribution to the cause by Japan. This Japanese squadron, which was commanded by Admiral Tetsutaro Sato, consisted of a considerable number of destroyers, gunboats, and other mosquito craft. In August of the same year it was reinforced by several units, and proved of great service.

Of the British soldiers and nurses saved from the transport Transylvania, torpedoed in the Mediterranean on May 4th, 1917, the great majority owed their preservation to

GENERAL FENG KUO-CHANG, who became Acting-President of China in 1918.

Sato's ships, which raced to the rescue, lay alongside the sinking vessel, and succeeded in getting most of the troops off her. Later in 1917 Japanese destroyers in the same area saved the passengers and crew, numbering in all five hundred and fifty souls, of a torpedoed liner, and successfully defended simultaneously a transport from attack. Several times this Japanese fleet reported that it had sunk enemy submarines. To all this had to be added that Japan's work at sea for the Allies included that of her merchant marine, which did practically all the carrying between Asia and Europe. In 1918 she lent many thousand tons of shipping to America.

Among the Allies in Europe the idea was frequently mooted that Japan should be invited to place a large number of her troops on the front, preferably in France; but no official request to that effect had been made by the Entente Powers. Japan's statesmen, however, let it be known that such a request, if sent, would receive the most sympathetic consideration. But they pointed out that, as Japan herself did not possess the transport required for the huge army that alone would be worth while despatching to Europe, the problem of obtaining the tonnage needed was, in the circumstances of the time, extremely difficult, if not impossible, of solution. Besides the question of tonnage, another thing had to be taken into account—the great distance of Japan from France (about ten thousand miles) or other parts of Europe; a Japanese army there would be very far from its base. These obstacles were not insuperable. A situation might conceivably arise which would render it essential that they must be overcome, but the situation had not arisen, and until it did arise—which was very unlikely—Japan's Army was best at home, keeping watch and ward over the Far East and protecting the interests of the Allies generally in the Orient. So Japan reasoned, and the march of events proved that this reasoning was sound.

YUAN SHIH-KAI, President of China, October 6th, 1913-June 6th, 1916.

Towards the close of 1917 the main preoccupation of Japan shifted from China to Russia. The Russian Revolution (Chapters CLXXV. Vol. 9, page 117, and CCXXXIV, Vol. 11, page 161,) was then in its third phase. The first saw the downfall of the autocracy and the formation of a Provisional Government under Prince Lvoff co-operating with the Allies against Germany. The second phase began and ended with the rise and fall of the Kerensky régime, which also was hostile to the enemy, but was unable to make headway against him because of the Bolshevist disintegration of the Russian Army. The third was that of the triumph of the Soviets, or Bolshevist, organisations, with Lenin and

Left : General Li Yuan Hung, who succeeded Yuan Shih-kai as President.   Centre : General Chang Hsun, who led the monarchical movement in the summer of 1917.   Right : General Tuan Chi-jui, the Premier, under whose influence China declared war on Germany and Austria in 1917.

PROMINENT PERSONALITIES OF THE CHINESE REPUBLIC.

Trotsky in control at Petrograd, and later at Moscow. During the second phase the demand had become prominent for a peace without annexations and indemnities, and based on the right of peoples to determine their own destinies; but the Government of the day showed no desire to cut the lines attaching Russia to the Allies, though the increasing demoralisation of the Russian Army gave little hope of its being able to co-operate effectively with the Entente.

Japan and the Allies stood waiting to see what would happen, the former viewing with apprehension the spreading disorganisation of Siberia, in whose cities and towns the Soviets made their influence supreme. Bolshevism was opposed to every instinct of Japan, and as it came nearer to her she could not but be moved to deep anxiety, which was not lessened as the third phase of the Revolution developed, with the Soviets, under Lenin and Trotsky, in power, and acting — consciously or unconsciously — as German agents. Among the earliest features of that phase were the throwing over of the Allies, the demobilisation of the Russian Army, and the beginning of negotiations at Brest Litovsk for a separate peace with the enemy. The grave concern felt by Japan was reflected in special meetings of the Council of Ministers, and on the excited exchanges of Tokyo and other financial centres of the country by falls in the prices of all securities.

As was natural, it was mainly on the route of the great Trans-Siberian Railway that the activities of the Bolshevists were manifested in Siberia, for even a short distance away from it the country was sparsely settled and the roads were indifferent. Before the Revolution the line had been the scene of a tremendous traffic, scores of trains passing westward daily with munitions and other supplies for the Russian front. The Revolution paralysed the railway, the result being that stores accumulated at the large central points and at Vladivostok, the terminus on the Sea of Japan.

In the autumn of 1917 half a million tons of military and other stores—sent there by the Allies, but chiefly by Japan and the United States, to enable Russia to carry on—lay at the Pacific port. After the seizure of power by the Soviets, Japan withheld further supplies, and America diverted to Japanese ports her ships on passage to Vladivostok with cargoes of war materials. Besides the question of the fate of the vast accumulations at Vladivostok, the question of the fate of that city itself,

which was within forty-eight hours' steam of her own shores, rose into great importance to Japan, who felt that through Bolshevism the German menace was being brought very near her there.

To the other Allies, no less than to Japan, the question of the fate of the whole Trans-Siberian Railway became a matter of the utmost significance owing to the persistent advance, in spite of the Brest Litovsk peace negotiations, of German forces into European Russia, and the high probability that German agents were hard at work in

TYPES OF CHINESE INFANTRY.
The modern Chinese Army was inaugurated in 1905. At the end of 1916 over 500,000 men were under control of the War Office, in addition to troops in Yunnan and Sze-chuan. Types of the men are shown above, the smaller photograph indicating how equipment was adjusted for field service.

their insidious way all along the line. One of the features of the position in Siberia was the presence there of many thousands of German and Austrian prisoners of war who, under the Bolshevists, were permitted practically to be at large, and therefore had plenty of opportunities for disseminating the German poison. The Czecho-Slovaks among the Austrian prisoners were not hostile to the Allies, but every German officer was a rallying-point against the Entente, and reports were current that he and his like were organising armed forces for what could be only one object—the penetration and exploitation of Siberia by Germany. Further, it was impossible not to see that if the Bolshevists in Siberia should openly side with Germany, and permit themselves to   **German menace in Siberia** be drilled, disciplined, and led by these Germans, Siberia might quickly and easily pass under the control of the enemy, which would be a disaster of almost unparalleled magnitude to the Allies, but more especially to China and Japan.

The Bolshevists, however, did not side openly with Germany, but they soon raised serious disturbances in that part of China known as Northern Manchuria, through which ran the Trans-Siberian Railway and over which Russia had certain rights by treaty, in much the same way as Japan had over Southern Manchuria, though both regions were still Chinese territory. From Manchouli Station on the western frontier to Suifenho on the eastern frontier of Northern Manchuria—a distance of nearly six hundred miles—the Trans-Siberian Railway was called the Chinese Eastern Railway, a denomination also applied to the branch from Harbin, on the main line which, passing southward, connected at Changchun with the South Manchurian Railway. The Chinese Eastern, like the rest of the Trans-Siberian, was in Russian hands, and it was guarded by Russian troops. In the same way the South Manchurian was managed by Japan and guarded by Japanese soldiers. The headquarters of the Chinese Eastern Railway were at Harbin, and the Russian General Horvat, in command of the troops stationed there and along the line, was the director-in-chief of the railway. At Changchun the Russians were in contact with the Japanese. As well as China, Japan therefore was affected by changes in the position of affairs in Manchuria brought about by the Bolshevists. But it was China who actually took the steps to quell the local Soviets.

Meanwhile the internal situation in China had not improved. In September the Southerners had instigated a revolt in Hunan, which met with considerable success at the start. The Allied Ministers in Peking counselled Tuan Chi-jui to compromise matters with the South, but instead of doing so he sent additional troops to the scene of the fighting. He was determined

UNITS OF THE CHINESE ARMY AS REORGANISED ON WESTERN LINES.
Chinese cavalrymen who were being trained in scouting duties. Above : Chinese gunners with a German mitrailleuse. On January 1st, 1916, a modified form of conscription came into force in China.

It was at this juncture that the Bolshevist disturbances in Manchuria came to a head and turned the attention of the warring Chinese political factions from their domestic conflicts to the situation in Siberia, which they could no longer ignore. What was happening in Siberia affected all Outer Mongolia as well as Northern Manchuria, but it was the latter that felt it most seriously. Harbin was the scene of grave disorders caused by the Bolshevists, and at a conference of Chinese officials with the Allied Ministers at Peking it was agreed that China should send troops there to deal with the trouble. Accordingly two Chinese regiments were moved up from Kirin, and took control of the town after some fighting with the Bolshevists, who were supported by two regiments of railway guards.

By December 25th the Chinese had disarmed their opponents and had deported them beyond the frontier. General Horvat, the Russian who had been in command alike of the railway guards and the railway, was anti-Bolshevist, helped the Chinese, and remained to manage the line, from which all the other Bolshevist railway guards, including a regiment at Hailar, were removed and sent across the frontier. China put in all about ten thousand of her troops into Northern Manchuria, and effectively prevented the Bolshevists from using the railway for any military purpose.

West of the Chinese Eastern Railway the route of the Trans-Siberian Railway continued to be the scene of terrible occurrences. At Irkutsk, some miles west of Lake Baikal and a comparatively short distance from the Manchurian border, great riots were engineered by the Bolshevists, who slaughtered indiscriminately all who were against them or were accounted " counter-revolutionaries." There were similar dreadful happenings on the Amur Railway, the line which, branching off from the Trans-Siberian at Karimskaia, ran eastward to Habarovsk, and thence southward to Vladivostok.

to crush the insurrection, but President Feng did not fully support him, and the Tuchuns of Mid-China—the great Yangtse River region—held aloof. These facts led Tuan to resign, but Feng soon recalled him. President and Premier, however, did not long pull together, and the latter again retired from office. The Northerners split into two factions —one under Feng and the other under Tuan—and in these circumstances the South made some progress in its campaign against them. In December a Cabinet of a non-party character was formed, but some of its members were pro-German, and as the Allied Ministers objected to them—which was not surprising—Feng next set up a War Council, making the indispensable Tuan its chief as Minister of War.

At Vladivostok itself there was much confusion, with frequent thefts and murders, which the local Soviet was either unwilling or unable to bring to an end. A rumour that Japan had landed forces there in December proved incorrect, but as she could not be indifferent to the state of things in that port little surprise was felt when it was officially announced that in January, 1918, she had despatched a warship thither for the protection of her own interests as well as those of her Allies. Great Britain took similar action, and the town somewhat sobered down. But disorders persisted under the Bolshevists in other parts of Siberia, and in the various outbreaks numbers of Chinese and Japanese lost their property, and some of them their lives.

China was again entangled in the strife of faction, but Japan took a grave view of what was taking place in the Russian Far East. In the Diet, Count
Terauchi warns Terauchi, commenting on the situation,
the Bolshevists warned the Bolshevists that Japan, if her interests were threatened, would not hesitate to resort to such measures as were required. On their side the Bolshevists showed a minatory attitude, to which further point was given by repeated and apparently circumstantial statements to the effect that two hundred thousand German and Austrian prisoners of war had been armed by them. As February closed, Japan was discussing intervention with her Allies. In European Russia the sky had darkened still further. Alarmed, as it appeared, by the advance of the Germans towards Petrograd, Lenin

and Trotsky, the Bolshevist chiefs, had thrown up the sponge and had specifically declared that Russia was out of the war. A separate peace was signed, and the German menace grew more and more formidable, casting its shadow far across the Orient. Speaking in the House of Commons on March 14th, Mr. Balfour, the Foreign Secretary, envisaged the probability of decisive action by Japan, but as the friend and not the enemy of Russia, who, he said, " lay absolutely derelict on the water," and unless assisted would be Germany's easy victim.

At the time the negotiations for **President Wilson's** the intervention of Japan came to **attitude** nothing, as America did not see eye to eye with the Allies. In a message to the Congress of the Soviets in January, President Wilson had declared that " the treatment accorded to Russia by her sister nations in the months to come will be the acid test of their goodwill, of their comprehension of her needs, as distinguished from their own interests, and of their intelligent and unselfish sympathy." Taking his stand on this statement, Mr. Wilson declined to endorse the suggestion of Japanese intervention, even if that intervention were made in conjunction with forces of the other Allies.

While the question of intervention was still being considered by the Allies in March, China took a remarkable step. The Cabinet decided to co-operate fully with Japan with regard to the external situation, which it now recognised as dangerous, and delegates were sent from

BUSHIDO RIDES OUT AGAINST KULTUR: JAPANESE CAVALRY ON THE MARCH.

In 1918 it was estimated that the Japanese active Army included twenty-seven regiments of cavalry, divided into eighty-nine squadrons, her total mobilisable land forces approximating to 1,400,000 men. Service in Army or Navy was compulsory, liability for service commencing nominally at the age of seventeen, but actually at twenty, and extending to forty. Japan's military budget of 1917-18 was equivalent to about £10,500,000.

Peking to confer with the Japanese military authorities at Tokyo with respect to the measures they should take in common against the enemy. It was Tuan Chi-jui who was most influential in bringing about this striking change in Far Eastern affairs, which in itself besides was a new and memorable departure in the history of the world.

In April sanguinary riots broke out in Vladivostok. Armed bands of Bolshevists attacked buildings occupied by Japanese firms, committed extensive robberies, and killed three Japanese. It looked as if the city would be given up to murder and pillage, as had been the case with other places of importance in Siberia, and it seemed as if the vast stores that had been piled there by the Allies would be destroyed. On April 5th Admiral Kato, in command of the Japanese naval forces in the port, landed several hundred Marines to quell the disturbances and protect life and property. Later in the same day British Marines were disembarked for the same purposes. The Bolshevist Government and the local Soviet protested angrily, but the two Allies explained that their action had been taken with the object of maintaining order in the town; that, in fact, the Marines were a police force who had done, and would continue to do as long as it was necessary, the special work assigned to them, and that the landings had no connection with the general situation elsewhere in the Russian Far East.

About the end of April, 1918, Viscount Motono resigned on account of illness, and was succeeded by Baron Goto as Japan's Minister for Foreign Affairs. Goto had been Minister of the Interior, and was a mainstay of the Terauchi Government. As rumours circulated that his new post signified a change in policy, he took occasion on May 1st to say these were unfounded, and that Japan was loyal to her engagements. The Anglo-Japanese Alliance, he said, continued to be regarded as of supreme importance, and the fealty of Japan to the Allies was inalienable. Speaking of Russia, he declared that the situation there had afforded an opportunity to the enemy of increasing his malevolent propaganda with a view to an estrangement between Japan and Russia, as well as between Japan and America. Russia was a Power which was endeavouring to reorganise a machine that was temporarily out of order, and Japan desired to encourage and assist that reorganisation. He stated that Japan sought the friendship, co-operation, and help of China, whom he begged to disentangle herself from her old prejudice, which had been fostered by the common enemy. His words concerning China were underlined by the fact that a couple of days previously a syndicate of Japanese banks, supported by the Japanese Government, had advanced two millions sterling to the Chinese Government, and by the still more significant fact that it was now well known that a military agreement was on the point of being signed between the two countries.

Preceded by an unofficial, but probably accurate, statement that Japan had offered to mediate between the North and South in China, the terms of the agreement

Baron Goto's appeal to China

were published, with some necessary reservations regarding details, on May 30th, in Tokyo as well as in Peking. The agreement took the form of a military convention, which was signed on May 16th, and a naval convention, signed three days later, making arrangements for the co-operation of the Armies and Navies of Japan and China in common defence against the enemy. The Japanese Foreign Office published an explanatory comment, in which it said that, owing to the steady penetration of hostile influence into Russian territory, China and Japan had recognised the imperative necessity of co-operation. As a result, Notes had been exchanged on March 25th, and subsequently Japan had sent to Peking military and naval commissioners to confer with the Chinese authorities. The negotiations had progressed smoothly, and the two conventions were the result. To counter misrepresentations the Japanese Foreign Office added that all reports that Japan would take over the control of China's forces, ships, arsenals, railways, and finance were absolutely unfounded. The Notes exchanged contained a provision that the matters to be arranged would be put into execution at such a time as the two Governments might eventually decide, and it was further provided that the conventions were for the duration of the war, Japan pledging herself to withdraw her troops thereafter.

Siam joins the Allies

In the Far East the summer of 1917 saw another country and people at war with Germany and Austria. On July 22nd of that year Siam, announcing that her object was to uphold the sanctity of international rights in general, and of small States in particular, ranged herself on the side of the Allies, seized nine enemy ships which were in her ports, arrested all Germans and Austrians, whether in her Government service or otherwise, and shut down all enemy businesses.

A FAR EASTERN ALLY OF CIVILISATION.
Somdetch Phra Ramadhipati Srisindra Maha Vajiravudh, known as Rama VI., King of Siam.

The King of Siam had British sympathies, as he had been educated at Eton and Oxford, had studied at Sandhurst, and had been attached to the Durham Light Infantry. When he ascended the throne Siam had no army, but in 1912 he established the beginnings of one by forming a corps of scouts, who locally were called "Wild Tigers." When Siam entered the war her Army on a war footing numbered about forty thousand men, besides about twenty thousand Marine infantry recruited from the coast population. She had no navy. From the military point of view her adhesion to the Entente was not of much significance, but from another point of view it was of great importance. German intrigue had been active in Siam, whence it reached out to India; this was entirely stopped. German trade in the Orient was dealt another shrewd blow, as German writers admitted when discussing Siam's declaration of war. In September, 1917, Siam called for volunteers in connection with proposals for sending an expeditionary force to the western front. Early in 1918 a Siamese Military Mission arrived in Europe, with Major-General Phya Bijai Janriddhi, commander of the 4th Siamese Division, at its head, and proceeded to the battlefields of France.

U.S. MARINES MARCHING

CHAPTER CCLII.

TO EMBARK FOR EUROPE.

THE RAPID EXPANSION OF AMERICA'S SEA-POWER.

By Percival A. Hislam.

America's Naval Decline in the Dreadnought Era—Putting the Lessons of the War Into Practice—The Great New Shipbuilding Programme of 1916—State of the Navy in Ships and Men in April, 1917—The Arming of Merchantmen and the First American Shot at Sea—Encounters between Merchant Ships and Submarines—The Transport and Convoy of the American Army—Von Capelle's Boast and What Came of It—How the Shipping Problem was Tackled—Famous German Liners Converted Into Transports—Submarine Efforts to Cut the Lines of Communication—The Marvellous Safe Passage of the First Million and Britain's Part in It—U.S. Destroyer Flotillas in European Waters—Co-operation with the British and French Fleets in the U Boat Hunt—A Dreadnought Squadron Joins the Grand Fleet—Actions and Losses in European Waters—Submarines Appear off the American Coast—Loss of the San Diego—The Vast Growth of America's Naval Effort.

THE entry of the United States into the war —a subject already dealt with in Chapters CCIV., CCV., and CCXLIX.—followed very closely upon a brief but notable period in the history of American naval development, during which the American nation had registered in concrete form its keen appreciation of the lessons taught by a conflict which, until the spring of 1917, was practically confined to European Powers.

During the closing years of the pre-Dreadnought era the United States Navy had been increased so rapidly and systematically that it stood comfortably in the second place among the fleets of the world ; but—and it is really a most extraordinary thing — as soon as the Dreadnought appeared, stimulating to a remarkable degree the fever of naval rivalry and activity in Europe and the Far East, American enthusiasm on the subject of sea-power fell away and died out almost completely.

What actually occurred is strikingly illustrated by the facts, taken over a period of some years, relating to the naval construction of the United States and of Germany, which, as will be readily understood, was the nation to replace

[*Bassano.*
AMERICA'S ADMIRAL COMMANDING-IN-CHIEF.
Vice-Admiral William Sowden Sims, an officer famous as a gunnery authority and tactician, was appointed to the Command-in-Chief of the U.S. Naval Forces in European waters in 1917.

America as the world's second naval Power. In the five years from 1905 to 1909 inclusive there were passed into service with the United States Fleet thirty armoured ships with an aggregate displacement tonnage of 438,180, while Germany in the same period completed only fourteen armoured vessels totalling 182,940 tons.

It was in the year 1909 that the first Dreadnoughts were completed for navies other than the British. From 1910 until the outbreak of war, a period of more than four and a half years, there were completed for the American Navy only six armoured vessels of 149,650 tons, against an addition to the German Fleet of nineteen ships of 430,250 tons. Add to this that the United States, even down to the time of its own break with Germany, possessed no battle-cruisers, no fast scouting cruisers, and only a very inadequate force of torpedo-boat destroyers, and it will be seen that the Fleet had fallen very far behind indeed.

The war had not been long in progress before the American people awoke to the vital part that sea-power must play in any great world conflict. Mr. Josephus Daniels, Secretary of the Navy, had been responsible for the "Wine Mess Order," prohibiting the consumption of

AMERICAN ADMIRAL CO-OPERATING WITH ADMIRAL BEATTY.
Admiral Rodman, U.S.N. (fourth figure from left), commanded a battle
squadron from the Atlantic Fleet that took station with the Grand
Fleet under Sir David Beatty in the North Sea.

in the Lion—while the armament
consisted of ten 14 in. and twenty
5 in. guns, and eight 21 in.
torpedo-tubes. No fewer than
seven funnels were provided to
carry off the smoke and gaseous
products of the oil-fired furnaces,
three of them being on the middle
line of the ship and the others in
pairs abreast. It was estimated
that the cost complete of each
vessel would not be short of five
millions sterling. The names
selected for the first five were
Constellation, Constitution,
Lexington, Saratoga, and Ranger.

The scout cruisers, 550 feet
long, 55 feet in beam, and displacing 7,100 tons, were to have
a maximum speed of 35 knots,
but a standard sea speed of 25

alcoholic liquors by officers on board ship or in any naval
establishment, a regulation that was resented in some
quarters. He was also accused of impairing the discipline
of the Fleet. Nevertheless, there was no doubt about
his irrepressible enthusiasm for the great Service of which
he was the administrative head, and although the war
must rank first among the influences that brought about
America's naval awakening, the untiring energy with
which Mr. Daniels kept the subject of the sea constantly
before his countrymen must be given no small share of
the credit.

The combined result of these influences was that on
August 29th, 1916, President Wilson put his signature
to the most ambitious Naval Appropriation Bill ever
sanctioned. It covered the naval construction of three
years, and provided for the building of ten battleships,
four battle-cruisers—later increased to six—four scout
cruisers, fifty destroyers, nine fleet submarines, fifty-eight
coastal submarines, three fuel-ships, one repair-ship, one
transport, one hospital-ship, two destroyer tenders, one
submarine tender, two ammunition

U.S. Naval plans, ships, and two gunboats. Each class
August, 1916 of vessel was to represent the embodiment of the essential characteristics
proved by the war to be most desirable ; and as the
United States had for two years been neutral, and therefore to some extent able to survey the work of the
opposing fleets from both standpoints, the characteristics
decided upon are especially worthy of note.

In the first batch of vessels to be begun the battleships were to be of 32,600 tons, with a speed of 21 knots.
Their main battery was to consist of eight 16 in. guns,
firing projectiles of 2,100 lb., while eighteen 5 in. rapid-
fire guns were provided for defence against torpedo craft,
and four 3 in. automatic weapons as an anti-aircraft
battery.

The battle-cruisers, the first ever designed for the
American Navy, were in every respect most remarkable ships. Their length over all was 874 feet—more
than 200 feet longer than H.M.S. Lion, flagship of the
British battle-cruiser force—and their beam 91 feet, the
calculated displacement being 34,800 tons (Lion, 26,350).
The speed aimed at, with turbines of 180,000 h.p., was
35 knots—as compared with 70,000 h.p., and 28 knots

BRITISH HONOUR FOR AMERICAN ADMIRAL.
King George on the quarter-deck presenting Rear-Admiral Hugh Rodman,
of the United States Navy, with the insignia of a Knight Commander of
the Most Honourable Order of the Bath.

knots was to be their acceptance test. Their armament
comprised eight 6 in. and two 3 in. guns, the latter for
anti-aircraft purposes, and they were also to be equipped
with means for housing, launching, and recovering four
seaplanes of the most effective type. In the case of the
destroyers, 35 knots was again the contract speed, and
they were to carry, in addition to four 4 in. and two
smaller guns, twelve torpedo-tubes, mounted in four sets
of three each. The latest British destroyers in commission
when the war began carried only three torpedo-tubes.

No details were allowed to become public as to the progress of work upon this programme, but it was suggested
early in 1917 that, in view of the generally satisfactory
position of the allied fleets as regards Dreadnoughts, and
of the urgent need for merchantmen, and for small craft
to join the submarine hunt, it might be desirable to postpone for a time the construction of the capital ships in
America. Such a course was adopted earlier in France.
It was officially stated in America, however, that the
battleships following those already described would be of
42,600 tons, and armed with twelve 16 in. guns ; and as
a further earnest of America's new-found enthusiasm in

the matter of sea-power, Mr. Daniels announced late in 1917 that plans had been prepared—for use whenever they might be necessary—for the biggest and most powerful battleship that could get through the Panama Canal. This vessel would be 975 feet long and 108 feet in beam, displacing 80,000 tons—just about four and a half times the tonnage of the Dreadnought of 1905. She would have a speed of 25 knots, a complete armour-belt 16 in. thick, and an armament of fifteen 18 in. guns. Incidentally, every such ship would cost, in round figures, £10,000,000.

The fighting strength of the United States at sea as it stood at the moment of its transference from a peace to a war footing may now be summarised. No reference will be made in this summary to the new programme already dealt with. In the forefront of the line stood the battleships Pennsylvania and Arizona, the former flying the flag of Admiral Henry T. Mayo, Commander-in-Chief of the Atlantic Fleet. These **America's fighting strength at sea** two ships, completed in 1916, were of 31,400 tons, and carried twelve 14 in. guns (1,400 lb. projectiles), with a torpedo defence battery of twenty-two 5 in., their main protection consisting of a belt of armour 14 in. thick. There were under construction, and of the same general type, the New Mexico, Idaho, Mississippi, California, and Tennessee, the first three to be completed in 1917-18, and the others in the following year. Behind these powerfully-armed ships came a quartette with ten 14 in. guns apiece—Nevada and Oklahoma, 27,500 tons,

completed in 1916, and New York and Texas, 27,000 tons, completed in 1914.

This brings us back to the era of the 12 in. guns, the last ships of this period being the Wyoming and Arkansas, carrying twelve guns apiece, displacing 26,000 tons, and completed in 1912. There were four Dreadnoughts with ten 12 in. guns—Florida and Utah, 21,825 tons, completed 1911; and Delaware and North Dakota, 20,000 tons, 1910; while at the end of the line were the first "all-big-gun" battleships built for the United **The pre-Dreadnought** States Navy, the so-called "baby Dread- **battleships** noughts" South Carolina and Michigan, which carried eight 12 in. guns each on a tonnage of 16,000. They were completed in 1910.

The principal characteristics of American armoured ships built before the Dreadnought era and still capable of useful service under war conditions are shown here:

BATTLESHIPS.

Kansas, Vermont, Minnesota, New Hampshire, Louisiana, and Connecticut. Tonnage, 16,000; completed, 1906-8; armament, four 12 in., eight 8 in., and twelve 7 in. guns.

Virginia, Georgia, New Jersey, Nebraska, and Rhode Island. Tonnage, 14,948; completed, 1906-7; armament, four 12 in., eight 8 in., and twelve 6 in. guns.

Ohio, Missouri, and Maine. Tonnage, 12,500; completed, 1902-4; armament, four 12 in. and sixteen 6 in. guns.

Alabama, Illinois, and Wisconsin. Tonnage, 11,550; completed, 1900-1; armament, four 13 in. and fourteen 6 in. guns.

Kearsage and Kentucky. Tonnage, 11,520; completed, 1899; armament, four 13 in., four 8 in., and eighteen 5 in. guns.

BUSY SCENE ABOARD A U.S. NAVAL REPAIR-SHIP IN BRITISH WATERS.

Modern developments in warship construction involved an equality of expansion in the means of making good worn or damaged machinery. The repair-ships of the United States Navy—from one of which an inside view is given above—were models of efficiency. Like other kindred departments, they multiplied with the extraordinary increase of America's sea-power. America's fighting ships in foreign waters, said Secretary Daniels in 1918, were "self-supporting, with the assistance of repair ships, with the exception of major repairs and dockings."

ARMOURED CRUISERS.

North Carolina, Montana, Seattle, and Memphis (wrecked August, 1916; salvage doubtful). Tonnage, 14,500; completed, 1906-8; armament, four 10 in. and sixteen 6 in. guns.

St. Louis, Charleston, and Milwaukee. Tonnage, 9,700; completed, 1905-6; armament, fourteen 6 in. guns.

South Dakota, San Diego, Frederick, Pittsburg, Pueblo, and Huntington. Tonnage, 13,680; completed, 1905-8; armament, four 8 in. and fourteen 6 in. guns.

There were, as already stated, no up-to-date scout cruisers in the Fleet, the only vessels of any **Where the U.S. Fleet** value at all in this connection **was weak** being the Birmingham, Chester, and Salem, which were completed in 1908, had a nominal speed of 24 knots, and carried two 5 in. and a number of smaller guns on a displacement of 3,750 tons. The destroyer flotillas aggregated seventy-four vessels built and building, all save twenty being of good, ocean-going types ranging in displacement from 700 to 1,100 tons, in armament from five 13-pounders and three torpedo-tubes to four 4 in. 33-pounders and twelve torpedo-tubes, and in nominal speed from 28 to 30 knots. In the submarine branch there were forty-seven vessels in service and half that number in hand, none calling for special mention.

The general position of the Navy on the material side was that it ranked high in battleship strength, but that, in consequence of the neglect of other types, the Fleet was in effect a group of battleship squadrons rather than an assembly of self-contained and well-balanced fighting units. There were no battle-

READY WITH A REPLY.
Gun team on a United States torpedo-destroyer about to fire at a German submarine.

cruisers, and no scout cruisers of the type found so eminently useful—and multiplied in consequence — by the British Admiralty, while the number of destroyers would normally have been inadequate even to afford anti-submarine protection to the battle fleets when cruising at sea. These deficiencies had been well taken in hand in Mr. Daniels' great programme, but, as we shall see, their existence did not prevent the United States from taking an immediate and effective part in the waging of offensive warfare upon the common enemy.

The personnel of the Fleet was, of course, obtained entirely by voluntary enlistment. The idea used to be very prevalent that American warships were manned for the most part by deserters from other navies; but this was never anything but a stupid fable, and the facts at the beginning of 1917 were that 96 per cent. of the enlisted men were native-born Americans, 2 per cent. were naturalised, while the remaining 2 per cent. was made up principally of natives of the Philippines, **Points about the** Samoa, and Porto Rico. Pro- **Fleet personnel** motion from the ranks was not very strongly encouraged, being, in fact, less practised than in the British Navy; but one of the first measures taken on the declaration of war was the selection of nearly five hundred warrant officers of all branches and their promotion to commissioned rank, to help to meet the increased needs of the Fleet. The rate of pay was naturally higher than in the European fleets, owing to the higher prevailing wage standard on the other side of the Atlantic, and there were other

LOADING-UP AND LEARNING THE ROPES.
Lowering a torpedo into the hold of an American submarine. In circle: Boys having a lesson in sail-hoisting on one of the training-ships established by the United States Shipping Board in connection with America's mercantile marine.

Coloured Photo, No. 8

Sir Edmund Allenby Entering Jerusalem, December 11, 1917

YOUNG SAILORMEN.
Boys at practice in furling sails aboard one of the United States Shipping Board training-ships.

ways in which the American seaman fared considerably better than his " opposite number " under the White Ensign.

In the summer of 1914 a small squadron of American ships was in European waters for what was known as a " Midshipman Practice Cruise." The original " Bill of Fare for General Mess "—that is, for the lower deck—of the battleship Illinois for the week ending July 11th will show how good the catering was, taking the menu for two days —Monday and Friday, which in working-class circles such as those from which seamen are mainly drawn are not usually feast days. Nor were they so in the U.S.S. Illinois, being merely typical of the whole week's arrangements. Here are the menus:

Monday, July 6th.—Breakfast: Preserved prunes, scrambled eggs, potato cakes, toast, coffee. Dinner: Hot roast beef, Spanish sauce, boiled potatoes, chow chow, bread pudding, coffee. Supper: Hamburger steak, fried potatoes, coldslaw, dough-nuts, iced tea.

Sailormen fed like fighting cocks
Friday, July 10th.—Breakfast: Fried bacon, fried eggs, French toast, coffee. Dinner: Broiled steak, onion gravy, roast potatoes, vegetable salad, mayonnaise dressing, coconut custard pudding, coffee. Supper: Cold salmon, baked macaroni with tomatoes, pumpkin pie, cocoa.

Truly, America's sailormen were fed like fighting cocks.

On April 6th, 1917, the date of the American declaration of war, their total strength, including officers, was 69,046, with a further 13,692 officers and men in the Marine Corps. It is typical of the enormous expansion of the naval forces of the United States that exactly a year later the regular naval personnel had increased to 199,490 and the

Marine Corps to 39,946. In the same period the relatively youthful Naval Reserve Force grew in strength from approximately 10,000 to 88,228, and the National Naval Volunteers from 9,000 to 15,822, the total increase being little short of a quarter of a million officers and men. In addition, the number of workers employed in the Navy yards rose from 35,000 to 73,000, there being within the same period a very great expansion in all branches of private shipbuilding and marine engineering enterprise. **Figures of a year's expansion**

The warlike operations of the United States at sea fall more or less naturally into three parts: (1) Local defence, in which may be included the arming of merchantmen; (2) the convoy of the American armies and their impedimenta to Europe; and (3) participation in what may be described as the general naval offensive against the enemy. With regard to the first of these, quite early in 1917 —following immediately upon the German declaration of the " ruthless " submarine campaign— the United States Government decided to arm its merchantmen for self-defence. In the initial stages of the war America had taken a very cramped view of the rights of merchantmen in this matter, inclining to the opinion that vessels so armed were in fact warships, and therefore not entitled to use American ports for ordinary trading purposes. Regulations were afterwards issued laying down the conditions under which defensively armed ships would not be regarded as having lost their

ACQUIRING PROFICIENCY IN SEAMANSHIP AND MARKSMANSHIP.
American Marines at rifle practice aboard ship. The American Marine Corps, officially rated as a "land and sea organisation," ranked among the very best of the United States fighting forces. In circle: Training-ship boys learning navigation.

mercantile status. Their guns were not to exceed 6 in. in calibre, they were to be few in number, and mounted only in the after part of the ship, and the quantity of ammunition carried was to be " small." The vessels were to be manned by their usual crews, the officers being as far as possible the same as were on board before war was declared ; while only "slow " ships were to be armed at all, the faster ones being, presumably, expected to rely solely upon their speed for avoiding submarine attack.

With the opening of the ruthless U boat campaign, however, America lost no time in arming her own merchantmen, or in putting trained naval crews on board to man the guns ; nor was this decision surprising in view of the oft-proved utility of a defensive armament in beating off submarine attack. Statistical records published **America arms her** about this time (about the beginning of **merchantmen** 1917) showed that out of 78 armed merchantmen attacked by German submarines, 72—more than 92 per cent.—made good their escape, while out of a total of 100 unarmed steamers attacked in the same period only seven got away in safety.

Curiously enough, the very first shot fired at sea by the United States after their entry into the war was fired from an armed merchantman, and by all accounts it was a very remarkable shot indeed. The first vessel of this type to cross to England after the opening of the " ruthless " campaign was the American liner St. Louis, which arrived at Liverpool towards the end of March after a totally eventless voyage. On April 2nd, 1917, however, the defensively armed steamer Aztec, 3,727 tons, was sunk by a German submarine off Brest, this being actually the first armed American ship to be sunk in the war, though America herself was not at war until four days later.

United States naval gunners had to wait until April 19th for the first opportunity of striking a blow at the enemy. In the afternoon of that day a U boat was sighted from the bridge of the freight steamer Mongolia, Captain Emery Rice, as she was steaming through waters close to the British Isles. The captain was on the bridge with Lieutenant Bruce Ware, who was in command of the naval party in charge of the armament, when a submarine was sighted off the port bow. The U boat was in the act of submerging, evidently with the intention of taking up a more favourable position for the discharge of a torpedo ; but the Mongolia was immediately headed towards the spot where she had disappeared, and when she again rose to the surface she was immediately astern of the steamer and about a thousand yards distant. By a combination of skilful judgment and good fortune, the stern gun happened to be trained on the precise spot where the U boat broke surface. Said the captain :

Lieutenant Ware gave the command, and the big gun boomed. We saw the periscope shattered, and both the shell and the submarine disappeared. It was a fine exhibition **" Teddy " fires the** of efficiency on the part of American naval **first gun** men. Lieutenant Ware knew before his shell struck the submarine that he had made a hit. There was no guesswork about it—it was but a case of pure mathematics. It must be remembered that the whole affair occupied only two minutes. We did not stop to reconnoitre after the incident, but steamed away at full speed, for it was not improbable that another submarine might be about. That's about all the story excepting this : The gunners had named the guns on board the Mongolia, and the one which hit the submarine was called the Theodore Roosevelt, so " Teddy " fired the first gun in the war after all.

According to a statement issued later, the shot smashed the conning-tower of the submarine and killed its commanding officer, though the vessel herself was able to get back to port.

Many other encounters between defensively armed merchantmen and German submarines occurred during the early stages of America's participation in the war.

The liner St. Louis was reported to have rammed and sunk a U boat on May 30th, but this was almost the last occasion on which the name was announced of any vessel believed to have successfully engaged a hostile craft. The reason for abandoning the practice—which had long been relinquished by the British authorities--was that if such vessels happened at a later date to be overcome by a U boat, the crew of the latter would in all probability consider themselves justified in taking vengeance for the earlier success of their prisoners, as in the notorious case of Captain Fryatt.

One or two stories of such " anonymous " successes may be given. Captain Walter O'Brien, commanding an American merchant steamer with a naval gun crew on board, declared that he was attacked on June 16th, 1917, in the Bay of Biscay by a submarine whose torpedo missed his ship by only a yard. Captain O'Brien swung his vessel round so that her stern gun bore on the submarine when she came to the surface, and after four rounds sent her to the bottom. " What makes the destruction of the submarine doubly agreeable," said Captain O'Brien, " is that she was the same one which sank the big oil steamship John D. Archbold, of the Standard Oil Company."

On June 23rd the Navy Department made public the report of Chief Boatswain's Mate O. J. Gullickson, commanding a gun's crew on a merchant steamer, concerning the apparent destruction of a submarine that attacked the ship. The report stated that about 6.30 in the evening a torpedo was sighted coming towards the ship, which was at once headed for the torpedo with the object of deflecting it. The torpedo struck the ship immediately abaft the beam, but glanced off, went round the stern, and sank, evidently without exploding. Immediately afterwards a periscope was sighted off the starboard beam, and fire was opened at once from the forward gun at a range of about 2,000 yards. The ship was headed towards the periscope. One shot struck the U boat just forward of the periscope, compelling it to submerge, **Oil-tank steamer's** and a light blue smoke came up from **splendid fight** the stern of the submarine. The periscope appeared again at a distance of about 600 yards, when a shot from the after gun hit it square on the water-line, tossing up a shower of steel splinters and causing a great commotion of bubbles in the water. Apparently the submarine was either sunk or badly damaged, as nothing further was seen of it.

Of course, the armed merchantmen did not have things all their own way, even when they were attacked by gun fire by submarines cruising on the surface. For instance, the oil-tank steamer Campana was attacked in this way on August 16th, 1917. She was a large, slow ship, and she put up a splendid fight against her assailant ; but the latter had the advantage of superior armament and speed, and was able to keep almost out of range while the Campana fired away the whole of her supply of ammunition—180 rounds—after which the U boat closed up and sank her without any trouble. Most of the ship's company were ultimately landed safely at a French port, but Captain Oliver, master of the Campana, Chief Gunner's Mate James Delaney, commander of the armed guard, and four members of the guns' crews were made prisoner and taken on board the U boat.

One result of this experience was that the Navy Department ordered the supply of ammunition on board all armed merchantmen to be doubled.

From the very beginning it was realised, not only by the Allies but also by their enemies, that the transportation of the American forces from the other side of the Atlantic to the battlefields of Europe would be one of the most stupendous operations of the whole of the war. Before the vast new American armies could strike a blow at the enemy they had to be carried across some four thousand miles of water, over every mile of which the transports were liable to be attacked by hostile submarines. The German Press from the start

"Old Glory's" answer to the Black Flag: American battleship engaging a German U boat.

American bluejackets at debarkation drill: Assembling, loading, and firing a gun.

U.S. battleship Texas, super-Dreadnought of 27,000 tons displacement, carrying ten 14 in. guns, leaving New York Harbour.

"Hail, Columbia!" From the notable picture by Bernard F. Gribble, shown in the Royal Academy Summer Exhibition, 1918.

American sailors swarming to the fighting-top and bringing anti-aircraft gun into action.

professed a profound scepticism as to whether America would ever be able to take a hand of any consequence in the fighting in Europe, nor were they without some evidence to support their view.

America came into the war at the beginning of the second quarter of 1917, at the moment when the U boat campaign against shipping reached its gravely threatening climax. In the second quarter of 1916 the total loss of British, allied, and neutral mercantile shipping amounted to 522,289 tons. By the last quarter of the same year it had risen to 1,159,343 tons. In the second three months of 1917 it was 2,236,934 tons. The rate of destruction had thus been doubled in six months and quadrupled in a year. Every 1,000 American troops landed in France would need to be supplied with 5,000 tons of stores a year, brought from oversea. There was considerable excuse for those in Germany who anticipated that by the time the American Army was raised and trained there would be practically no shipping left in the world to carry it, to say nothing of maintaining it. Indeed, in the spring of 1917, Admiral von Capelle, the German Naval Secretary, took upon himself the responsibility of asserting definitely: " We are not frightened of America's much-talked-of million Army. It is out of the question that our men in the trenches will ever have to face them. The United States may raise as many troops as it likes, but it cannot bring them over here. Our submarines will see to that." How foolish such boasting looks in the light of subsequent events !

Happily, there were three factors which enemy optimists either overlooked or could not foresee. The first was the fact that in the progress of the submarine campaign the second quarter of 1917 was for the Allies the darkest hour preceding the dawn. New defensive methods were being brought into being, and, of still greater importance, new and vigorous measures of offence against the U boats ; so that by the second quarter of 1918 not only had the rate of tonnage destruction been reduced 50 per cent. as compared with a year before, but the enemy was losing his submarines a good deal faster than they **The darkest hour** were being turned out. Secondly, no one **before the dawn** in Germany seems to have had even the remotest conception of the energy with which the United States, having decided to send a great army to Europe, would set about the construction of tonnage to carry the men and their supplies and to create as big a margin as possible for the general purposes of the Allies.

In this connection it will be appropriate here to quote a few illuminating details from a speech delivered on March 24th, 1918, by Mr. Hurley, Chairman of the United States Shipping Board. He said: " When we took hold of this job (the construction of national merchant shipping) we found there was no shipyard in existence with which we could place an order. Seventy per cent. of the space of the old shipyards was taken by the enlarged naval programme. The remainder was taken by orders placed by American owners and by foreign owners. We had to locate on waste ground many new shipyards. This was the first and the biggest task of the job that faced us."

There were (he continued) 37 steel shipyards in America at the time of our entrance into the war. We have located 81 additional steel and wood shipyards, while 18 others have been expanded. We are building in the new and expanded steel yards 235 new steel slipways, or 26 more than at present exist in all the steel shipyards of Britain. The men in the yards fought a bitter winter. They had the same spirit, and demonstrated the same pluck and unselfishness as the men in the trenches. They have virtually completed the job of building America's new shipyards. . . . Nearly as much tonnage has been constructed in American waters during the past three months as by all other maritime nations of the world combined, and we have also placed in our and the Allies' war service 112 first-class German and Austrian vessels, representing a carrying capacity of nearly 800,000 deadweight tons. At the outset the 37 old steel yards began increasing their capacity, until now they have 195 ways as against 162 eight months ago. Thirty additional

new steel shipyards are being erected, with a total of 203 shipbuilding ways. Thus we have now, in the aggregate 67 steel shipyards either wholly or partly engaged in Fleet Corporation (cargo tonnage) work. Of these, 35 yards with 250 ways are on the Atlantic and Gulf coast, 19 yards with 66 ways on the Pacific, and 13 yards with 84 ways on the Great Lakes.

Our programme for building wooden ships has been beset with many difficulties and handicaps. A year ago we found 24 old wooden shipyards with 73 slipways. Now we have 81 wooden shipbuilding yards, with 332 ways completed or nearing completion. Assuming that those ways each produce two standard ships yearly, we should turn out about 2,300,000 deadweight tons of wooden ships annually. These 332 wooden shipbuilding ways now nearing completion, added to our 398 steel shipbuilding ways, give us a total of 730 berths upon which to build steel and wooden ships. When you consider that we had only 235 a few months ago, an increase is shown of 495 wooden and steel berths on which we can build ships. With our total of 730 we shall have 521 more berths than Sir Eric Geddes in his recent speech stated Britain has at the present time. As further evidence of the organisation effected, let me **Tackling the** say that in 1916 there were less than 45,000 **shipping problem** men employed in all the shipyards of the country, and on March 2nd, 1918, we had increased this number to 236,000, of which 170,589 were working on actual ship construction and the remainder in yard construction and other branches of the industry.

This brings me to a point where I desire to make a brief reference to what have been termed our three " fabricating " shipyards (where the standardised parts of ships were delivered to be put together), located at Hog Island, Newark Bay, and Bristol (Pennsylvania). We are confident that this new method will be a means of adding millions of tons to our merchant marine. These three assembling yards, with their 50 ways at Hog Island, 28 at Newark Bay, and 12 at Bristol, will, when they are in full operation, produce in a single year more ships than Great Britain, the greatest maritime nation in the world, has ever been able to turn out in the same length of time. When the high point in the curve of production is finally reached. the magnitude of America's shipbuilding programme will be realised. No nation can be great commercially unless it has its own manufacturing and shipping, and this is the goal which will be passed in peace if we can reach it in war. There is no doubt that we are destined to be one of the leading shipbuilding nations of the world. We shall build ships in such large numbers and at such fair prices that we shall become the Mecca of the shipbuilding trade of the world.

We need not stop now to consider, from the British point of view, the prospect opened up by the concluding passages of this statement. In its bearing on the war outlook the account of the marvellous development of American shipbuilding ranks among the most depressing cold douches the U boat optimists had ever received. Another severe blow to German *amour propre* was the appropriation for war service of one sort or another of all the enemy shipping that had been lying in the hitherto neutral ports of America since August, 1914. There were in all 98 German ships, with a total gross tonnage of 614,575, and 14 Austrian vessels of 67,817 tons. In a large number of cases the interned German crews living on board had damaged the machinery by smashing it about with hammers, roughing the bearings, firing the boilers while they were empty, and so forth, hoping thereby to render the ships useless for further service ; but they did their work **Bitter pills for** badly, for within five months practically **the Germans** every ship was fit and ready for sea.

Perhaps the bitterest pill for the Germans was the announcement, issued by Secretary Daniels in August, 1917, that sixteen of the finest liners had been appropriated for the transport service, the statement even showing the number of troops that each vessel would carry. Thus the famous Vaterland, of 54,282 tons, at one time the property of the Hamburg-Amerika Line, was fitted to carry 800 officers and 8,000 men, her name being changed to Leviathan. It is said she actually carried 12,000 troops on her first voyage to France in May, 1918.

The smaller but, in her time, equally famous Kaiser Wilhelm II., renamed Agamemnon, was fitted up for 430 officers and 3,400 men. Other vessels thus taken over and fitted out—their new names, if any, being given in parentheses—were the President Grant and President Lincoln, 200 officers and 5,000 men apiece ; George Washington, 350 officers, 4,500 men ; Amerika (America), 4,500 men ; Cincinnati (Covington), 4,000 men ; and the Grosser Kurfürst (Æolus), 3,000 men. All told, these sixteen vessels alone were capable of carrying 2,865 officers and 55,400 men. The German commerce raiders Kronprinz Wilhelm and Prinz Eitel Friedrich, which sought refuge in American ports early in 1915, were respectively renamed the Baron von Steuben and the Baron de Kalb, in memory of German generals who aided Washington in the Revolution.

Having thus dealt at some length with the second factor in the transport problem, which promised well for the Allies, brief mention may be made of the third—the extraordinary care and success with which, from the very start of the war, the whole business of troop transport had, in spite of the activity of enemy submarines, been managed by the allied fleets. In the report of the British War Cabinet for 1917 there appeared the following :

> The record of what has been done by the transport services for the armies of the Allies shows a stupendous amount of work accomplished which constitutes one of the brilliant achievements of the war. There had been transported overseas up till the end of August [1917]—the last date for which statistics are available—some 13,000,000 human beings—combatants, wounded, medical personnel, refugees, prisoners, etc. ; 2,000,000 horses and mules, 500,000 vehicles, 25,000,000 tons of explosives and supplies for the armies, and also some 51,000,000 tons of coal and oil fuel for the use of our fleets, our armies, and to meet the needs of our Allies. The losses in personnel, out of the 13,000,000 men who have been transported, amount to only about 3,500, in spite of the isolated and unpreventable mishaps which occur occasionally. It is a figure which speaks for itself. Of these 3,500 casualties, about 2,700 were caused by the action of the enemy (and it must be noted that this number includes 542 in hospital-ships), while the remaining losses occurred through the ordinary perils of the sea.

Brilliant transport record

With such a record as this to look back upon it is no wonder that those responsible for the maritime safety of the American Army should have looked to their task with confidence. There was more work to be done, but there was the addition of a great Navy to share in it ; and although occasional losses were, humanly speaking, inevitable, having in mind the length and vulnerability of the line of communication and the energy with which the enemy might be expected to prosecute the attack on the transports, this confidence was completely justified by the event. The

first American troops landed in France in June, 1917, having crossed the Atlantic without incident; and it was a few days later that the first intimation was afforded of the enemy's intention to oppose the crossing to the best of his ability. A portion of the First United States Expeditionary Force was on its way to France, convoyed by a squadron of American warships under the command of Rear-Admiral Albert Gleaves. The Germans delivered their attack on the night of June 22nd, while the fleet was still far out in the Atlantic, in circumstances already referred to in Chapter CCV. (Vol. X., page 295).

The enemy made a very special and particular effort to inflict loss upon this, the first great American military convoy sailing for Europe, and his failure was a significant and happy **Attacks on lines of** augury for the future. Many months **communication** went by without any loss, or even attack, upon eastward-bound transports being recorded, though on October 17th the Antilles, homeward bound, was torpedoed and sunk with a loss of 67 of those on board, 6 being Army details.

There is no reason to believe that during any part of this period the German efforts to destroy the transports and dislocate their sailings were in the slightest degree relaxed, though it may well be that the American authorities, after due consideration, decided to publish no details of the unsuccessful attempts that were made. At the end of January, 1918, however, Mr. N. D. Baker, Secretary of War, in the

course of his weekly review of the situation, took the opportunity to warn the American people that the Germans were preparing a great submarine offensive against the American lines of communication with France, saying that the decline in the destruction of mercantile tonnage then taking place was due to the withdrawal of submarines for the approaching thrust. Mr. Baker said :

> As the time draws near when once again the enemy will endeavour to strike a decisive blow in the west, it must be emphasised that he will not be content with mere military operations on a large scale. During the past fortnight enemy submarines have been recalled to their home ports to be refitted, and the most powerful submarine offensive hitherto undertaken may be expected to be launched against our lines

FIRST FRESHETS OF AN OVERWHELMING FLOOD.
These two photographs show the arrival at a French port of transports bringing the first contingents of American troops to fight in the Great War. In May, 1917, the embarkations from America were 1,718. In June, 1918, they were 276,372, completing a force despatched of 1,019,115 men.

ARREST ON SUSPICION.
New York Harbour police arresting suspicious characters taken from a barge in the crowded port.

of communication to France in order to interrupt the steady flow of men and munitions for our own armies and the food supplies for our Allies.

In an interview a day or two later with an American correspondent, Sir Eric Geddes, First Lord of the Admiralty, spoke of this particular menace. He stated that there was no evidence in the possession of the British Admiralty to support the view that U boats were being withdrawn from their regular service to prepare for a grand assault on American communications; but he added: "There is no doubt that the U boats will bend every effort to attack American transports, and if you are to bring across the Atlantic the number of troops that you plan, there will be losses, and probably heavy ones, for life-saving in mid-Atlantic is not easy. I do not doubt that Mr. Baker had good grounds for his statement."

By one of those coincidences that occur more often than most of us remember, the first successful torpedoing of an east-bound American troopship took place within a relatively few hours of the publication of the First Lord's statement.

Anchor liner The vessel was the Anchor liner Tuscania, Captain Peter McLean, forming part of a large convoy which, at the moment of attack, was passing within a few miles of the Irish coast.

Tuscania torpedoed It was just nightfall when a torpedo from an unseen submarine struck the vessel full amidships, while a second torpedo was seen to pass just astern. The Tuscania immediately took a big list which prevented most of the boats from being launched, and many men jumped into the water. After the first momentary confusion, however, the superb discipline and courage of the troops asserted themselves. Without a trace of panic and in splendid order the men went to their stations, and such boats as were capable of being launched were lowered from the almost

AUTHORITY THAT WOULD NOT BE DENIED.
Police boat searching a suspicious launch that failed to stop when ordered. An officer stood on the top of the cabin ready to use his machine-gun at the first sign of forcible resistance.

perpendicular deck. Life-saving rafts were thrown overboard, but the darkness rendered the work of the rescuing destroyers exceedingly difficult, and many men were several hours in the water, clinging to anything that would support them until the coming of the day enabled them to be seen and picked up. A large proportion of the men had never seen the sea until they were marched on board the Tuscania in her American port of departure, but the conduct of everyone throughout was **Only 166 lost** exemplary, and the dominant **of 2,401** sound during the night over those dark, stricken seas was the refrain of a popular American song, "Oh, boys, oh, boys, where do we go from here?"

There were on board the ship when she was torpedoed 76 officers and 1,935 men of the United States Army, the crew making up the total complement to 2,401. That only 166 were lost, including, no doubt, many who were killed by the explosion of the torpedo, is an eloquent tribute both to the organisation existing on board and to the good work of the rescuers.

So far as the records available at the time of writing show, the Tuscania was not only the first steamer lost in carrying American troops to the battlefront, but the first British ship lost in carrying troops from the American continent. Over 400,000 Canadians had, in fact, been brought across without the loss of a single man.

It was nearly three months after this incident that Captain von Kühlwetter, a semi-official naval scribe in Germany, took it upon himself to answer the question, "Why is it that the U boats cannot stop the transport of American troops to Europe?" "If a submarine succeeds in torpedoing a transport," said he in explanation, "the troops can always be saved by the warship which

MAULED BY THE TALONS OF THE AMERICAN EAGLE.
German submarine lying interned in a Spanish port. She had been badly damaged as a result of an encounter with a United States patrol yacht, but managed to escape.

accompanies the steamer. These warships are extraordinarily strong and fast, and are protected by special devices which render it difficult and dangerous to attack them."

It had formerly been the practice of the U boats, when they had torpedoed one ship, to wait about in the vicinity for the chance of torpedoing any vessel that might come up in answer to the victim's distress signals. "The work of sinking these transports," concluded the captain, "would claim too heavy sacrifices. The aim of the submarine warfare can be attained by the sinking of other steamers. It would suffer too much by fighting the transports!" The best consolation he could offer his readers was that possibly troopships were

credit for this marvellously successful piece of work cannot in fairness be monopolised by any one navy, a fact which General Pershing generously acknowledged when he said, in November, 1917: "Thanks to the efficacy of the protection afforded by the British, French, and American Navies, the enemy's submarines could not boast of having caused the loss of life of a single American soldier embarked for conveyance to France." It was also publicly acknowledged a few weeks later by Mr. Franklin Roosevelt, the Assistant Secretary of the United States Navy, that no less than sixty per cent. of America's first million were brought across in British ships under the escort of British men-of-war, which meant for Britain the sacrifice of 200,000 tons of essential cargoes a month.

Curiously enough, although two important transports were sunk about the middle of 1918—the President Lincoln, 18,168 tons, on May 31st, and the Covington (ex-Cincinnati), 16,339 tons, on July 1st—they were both homeward bound from Europe, and so had no troops on board.

U.S. DREADNOUGHTS AND SUPER-DREADNOUGHTS IN FORMATION.
A division of the American Atlantic Fleet at sea. The first four ships are, in order, the Wyoming, Nevada, Arkansas, and Delaware, of which the Nevada was a super-Dreadnought, mounting ten 14 in. guns, and the others Dreadnoughts with ten 12 in. guns.

We have now to set on record such details as are permissible of the earlier stages of the American Fleet's participation in what may be called the inner offensive against the enemy. It has already been pointed out that the United States Fleet was by no means strong in destroyers and like craft, that there were, indeed, not by any means enough to provide the necessary flotillas for attendance with the battle fleets. It therefore created not only great surprise, but the most intense admiration for the war spirit of the United States, especially among those able to look at these things from a professional point of view, when it was announced on May 17th, 1917, that a flotilla of American

destroyed without the fact being made known by the German Admiralty.

As a matter of fact, a vastly significant series of figures published by Mr. Newton D. Baker, U.S. Secretary of War, on Independence Day, 1918, showed that down to the end of June, out of a total of 1,019,115 American troops and Marines sent across the Atlantic, the number lost at sea was no more than 291. The work of transportation had then been going on for only a week short of fourteen months — the first ship carrying military personnel left on May 8th, 1917. Taking the high average of two thousand men per ship per crossing, five hundred separate voyages were involved, each one being across some four thousand miles of ocean, with enemy submarines prowling from one end of the line to the other. The loss in personnel amounted,

Safe passage of the first million nevertheless, to about one-sixth of a single ship's complement, representing nearly one man for every 3,500 carried.

The U.S. War Secretary very properly thanked "the superbly efficient protection which the Navy had given to our transport system," but it should in justice be remembered that the main and most important lines of defence for shipping in the Atlantic were to be found at the exits from the North Sea and in the Strait of Gibraltar. Had it not been for the increasingly effective grip maintained upon those avenues from German bases to the high seas, American transports would have had several U boats to deal with for every one they actually encountered. The

destroyers had recently arrived in European waters to co-operate with British naval forces in the prosecution of the war.

On the arrival of the destroyers at Queenstown, which was assigned to them as their base, Admiral Sir David Beatty, Commander-in-Chief of the Grand Fleet, telegraphed to Admiral **U.S. destroyers in** H. T. Mayo, Commander-in-Chief of the **European waters** U.S. Atlantic Fleet: "The Grand Fleet rejoices that the Atlantic Fleet will now share the task of preserving the liberties of the world and maintaining the chivalry of the sea." To which Admiral Mayo replied: "The United States Atlantic Fleet appreciates the message from the British Fleet, and welcomes opportunities for working with the British Fleet for the freedom of the seas." Rear-Admiral William S. Sims (promoted to Vice-Admiral on May 28th, 1917) was appointed to the general command of all United States naval forces in European waters, his nominal flagship being the Melville, an unpretentious destroyer depot-ship of 7,150 tons launched in 1915; but the admiral was often in London, where plans for the employment of the American forces were co-ordinated with the British naval authorities.

Secrecy was naturally observed as to the force sent by the United States to European waters, but it may be stated that within six months of America's entry into the war there were thirty-six destroyers operating in the British seas; more than thirty armed yachts, and a small flotilla of destroyers were working from French ports in the

Sudden emergency in mid-Atlantic: United States ship despatching a boat to another vessel to fetch a doctor whose professional services were urgently required.

Spray shield fitted in an American warship to protect the mechanism of the forecastle gun when the ship was plunging through high seas. In circle: Front view of the spray shield and of window fittings to the bridge, another striking device in United States warships.

View of the forecastle gun and bow of a United States warship and (right) American sailors training a gun. In July, 1918, the United States Navy had two hundred and fifty ships of all classes co-operating with the Allies in European waters, from the White Sea to the Adriatic.

GUNS AND GUN DEVICES ON WARSHIPS OF THE UNITED STATES NAVY.

convoy and patrol services, while a similar but rather smaller force was based on Gibraltar. These forces were being continually supplemented as new craft were made available in the American shipyards, and in the spring of 1918 it was announced that a battle squadron from the Atlantic Fleet had "taken station" with the Grand Fleet under Sir David Beatty in the North Sea. This squadron was under the command of Rear-Admiral Hugh Rodman, and although its composition had not been disclosed at the time of writing, authorised drawings in the American Press showed clearly that a vessel of the Pennsylvania class (31,400 tons, twelve 14 in. guns) was at its head.

U.S. Navy's first material loss There was, too, in the British style, much secrecy as to the actual work of all the ships, for their principal function was the hunting of the submarine, and that, as long experience had shown, was best done in as deep a silence as possible. The first definite piece of news was the announcement that a patrol vessel, unnamed, had foundered on October 4th, 1917, while on service in foreign waters. Fortunately the whole of the crew was saved, but it was the American Navy's first material loss in the war. A month later—in the early morning of November 5th—the armed yacht Alcedo, employed on patrol in European waters, was torpedoed and sunk by an enemy submarine, 1 officer and 20 men being lost out of the crew of 92. She was the

LAUNCH OF H.M.S. EAGLE.
On June 18th, 1918, with the express sanction of the King, Mrs. Page, wife of the American Ambassador, christened the British warship Eagle, this being the first occasion on which any person not of British nationality had performed such a ceremony.

A HAPPILY-NAMED UNITED STATES CARRIER-BOAT.
U.S.S. General Pershing, built for the American carrier service to take supplies to the American forces in France. In March, 1918, America had 236,000 men employed in shipyards, as against 45,000 in 1916.

first American warship to fall a victim to the U boat. The Germans were made to pay dearly for these losses. Early in October the periscope of a submarine was sighted from the Fanning, employed on convoy duty. It was visible only for a few seconds, and was no more than a foot out of the water, but the destroyer headed straight for the spot, and about three minutes after sighting dropped a depth charge. The Nicholson, another destroyer, also made for the submarine, which by her track appeared to be making towards a merchant vessel in the convoy, and dropped another charge. At that moment the submarine's conning-tower appeared on the surface between the Nicholson and the convoy, and the destroyer fired three rounds at it from her stern gun. The bow of the submarine came up rapidly; she was down by the stern, but righted herself and seemed to increase her speed. The Fanning now headed for the U boat, firing from her bow chaser, and at the third shot the crew of the sub-

marine all came on deck and held up their hands. The periscope had been sighted at 4.10, and at 4.20 the submarine surrendered.

Efforts were made to take the U boat in tow, but she quickly foundered, doubtless because the seacocks had been opened before the Germans came up on deck. Many of the latter were thrown into the sea as their vessel went down, and one was in such a condition when he came to the surface that he could not even hold the line that was thrown to him. Two American seamen thereupon jumped overboard and secured a line under his arms, but although every effort was made to resuscitate him, he died shortly after being hauled on board. The rest of the crew — 4 officers and 35 men — were made prisoner, but they were treated so well on board the Fanning that, when they were put ashore in small boats under guard, they raised three cheers for their captors.

At the end of 1917 there were made public details of actions in respect of which the British Admiralty proposed to confer a number of decorations on officers and men of the American Navy. **Notable actions against the U boats** In the case of one destroyer, the Admiralty report was to the effect that the vessel was convoying a merchantman when the periscope of a submarine was sighted about 800 yards away. The destroyer immediately increased speed and headed towards the submarine, which submerged, but reappeared shortly afterwards travelling in the opposite direction. The U boat next passed close to the starboard side of the destroyer, which released a depth charge, probably causing serious damage, if not destruction, to the submarine. Praising the excellent organisation, preparedness, and discipline on board the destroyer, as well as the quick decision of the officer of the watch, the British Commander-in-Chief proposed to recommend Lieut.-Commander Charles A. Blakeley, the commanding officer, for the D.S.O., and Ensign Henry N. Fallon for the D.S.C.

In the other case the destroyer was one of a number escorting troopships, and was cruising in station in formation when the wake of a periscope was sighted about 1,800 yards off the port bow. The executive officer rang for full speed, and altered the destroyer's course to head for the periscope, and the commanding officer then manœuvred the vessel so as to get her into a favourable position for dropping a depth charge. The charge was dropped when the destroyer was about twenty-five yards directly ahead of the periscope and in the direction of the submarine's advance. After the explosion of the charge debris was seen to rise to the surface, accompanied by large bubbles and discolouration of the water. For his services in this engagement the British Commander-in-Chief recommended Lieut.-Commander George F. Neal for the D.S.O., because it was considered the efficient way the attack was launched was due to his prompt and decisive action and the vigilant look-out maintained on the destroyer. Lieutenant Frank Loftin was recommended for the D.S.C., and Quartermaster W. H. Justice and Chief Machinist's Mate R. G. McNaughton for the D.S.M. Under the laws of the country, however, persons belonging to the naval and military forces of the United States are not permitted to receive medals, decorations, or any other form of reward which might be tendered by foreign Governments, so that the British proposal had of necessity to be declined.

Sinking of the Glenart Castle

There is no doubt that but for this regulation the British Admiralty would have rewarded generously the splendid services rendered by the U.S. destroyer Parker on the occasion of the sinking of the British hospital-ship Glenart Castle on February 26th, 1918. The vessel was torpedoed at four o'clock on a winter's morning, and the Parker, picking up the call for help many miles away, hurried to the scene and proceeded to search for survivors.

The first—a solitary man on a raft—was sighted at one o'clock in the afternoon, and as it was impossible for the destroyer to stand by in waters where U boats were active, she slowed down, and a line was thrown to the man. He was too weak from exposure to handle it properly. It pulled him off the raft, and he was badly cut about by the propellers, but managed to scramble back on to his raft.

The Parker then circled round, and as she did so, Quartermaster J. C. Cole jumped overboard, swam to the raft, and succeeded in bringing the man on board the destroyer; but he was so badly injured and exhausted that it was impossible to save his life. During the afternoon the Parker continued her search, and three more groups of survivors were found clinging to wreckage or drifting on rafts, and in each case men from the destroyer jumped overboard to their aid, the men who thus risked their lives being Boatswain's Mate R. E. Hosses, Machinist's Mate David Goldman, Coxswain Jerry Quin, Yeoman F. W. Beeghley, Ship's Cook W. W. Mathews, and Seamen J. Newman and T. F. Troue. Complimenting the vessel on her work, Vice-Admiral Sims telegraphed: "The work done in wintry seas and gales by all the destroyers' crews has been inspiring, but none more so than the Parker's."

American rescue work in wintry seas

The matter was raised in the House of Commons by members who were evidently unaware of the American Government's prohibition of foreign decorations or the acceptance of rewards of any kind. Dr. Macnamara said in reply: "The Admiralty profoundly appreciate the seamanship and very great gallantry displayed by the United States destroyer," and added, "we have already expressed our very great gratitude to our American friends; nevertheless, if we can make any suggestion to them which they will consider a proper one, to enable us to recognise in a substantial way our opinion of this act of gallantry, certainly we will do so." There the matter had perforce to remain for the time being.

Towards the end of the year the American fleet in European waters suffered the loss of two destroyers. It

AMERICAN DESTROYER ZIGZAGGING THROUGH A DANGER ZONE.

Remarkable photograph, taken from the stern of a destroyer, showing the wake of a United States vessel of this class passing at top speed in zigzag fashion through a danger zone in European waters. To these vessels fell the task of escorting transports and food-ships, and the further onerous duty of saving life—now from a torpedoed transport under escort, now from a vessel miles away sending up wireless appeals for help.

was announced on November 20th that the destroyer Chauncey (420 tons, launched 1901), had been sunk in collision in the war zone with a loss of twenty-one lives. On December 6th the much more modern Jacob Jones (1,050 tons, launched 1915), was torpedoed and sunk by a German submarine, the explosion of the torpedo detonating the depth charges lying in their racks at the destroyer's stern. The incident occurred only thirty miles from land, but one of the boats of the Jacob Jones had to be rowed twenty-three miles before assistance was found.

From the very beginning the British and American forces had worked together in the closest harmony and co-operation, a fact strikingly demon-
War carried into strated when, in June, 1917, the
American waters British Commander-in-Chief on the coast of Ireland (Vice-Admiral Sir Lewis Bayly), being temporarily indisposed, his command was transferred for the time being to Vice-Admiral Sims, whose flag was duly hoisted at Queenstown. Such an incident was unique in the history of the British Navy, and the magnificent spirit that prevailed was further evidenced in the messages exchanged between various high officials on May 4th, 1918.

Towards the end of May, 1818, the war was carried for the first time into American waters. On the 25th of that month a German submarine stopped the schooner Hattie Dunn off the Delaware Capes by means of three rounds fired at her, and, after taking off the crew, sent the vessel to the bottom. It is a matter of uncertainty whether one or two submarines were at work; but, at any rate, the sinkings continued for some days, practically all the victims being sailing vessels of the type common in American coastal waters. The last sinkings, in what may be called the first series, were reported on June 17th; but whether they ceased because the U boat or boats had completed their programme and returned to Germany, or because they had been accounted for by the counter-measures that were promptly put into operation against them, cannot here be declared.

After a short interval the sinkings were renewed—possibly by the same U boats, refreshed and revictualled at some secret base; possibly by others sent out as reliefs. Mines were laid off the American coast, and on July 19th, 1918, the armoured cruiser San Diego ran into one of these and sank, after remaining afloat long enough for everyone, including a few wounded, to be taken off, though six were killed in the explosion. Perfect discipline was maintained, and as Captain Christy, in command, left the vessel a few moments before she sank, the men in the boats cheered him and sang the " Star-Spangled Banner." The San Diego, sunk ten miles off Fire Island and about fifty miles from New York, was the first warship to be lost during the war in American waters. She was laid down in 1902 as the California, and carried four 8 in. and fourteen 6 in. guns on a displacement of 13,680 tons.

By creating a new theatre of war on the other side of the Atlantic the Germans hoped first of all to throw America into such a panic that the
German submarine whole coast would have to be armed
policy fails against bombardment, and even against the possibility of aerial attack from machines carried on board the submarines; and she hoped also that America, seeing her shipping endangered on her own coasts, would stop sending her destroyers to Europe and retain them for defensive purposes on the other side.

This typical piece of German " cunning " failed dismally. The necessary precautions for the protection of harbours were taken—anti-submarine nets for their defence had been prepared before America came into the war—but with the experience of England before them,

lying relatively speaking within a stone's-throw of the enemy's bases, the Americans were never for a moment likely to be seriously concerned at the prospect of bombardment or aerial attack, though the possibility of such incidents was fully appreciated.

As for the mobile counter-offensive against the submarines, that, too, had been taken in hand, and no half-digested measures were necessary, nor was a single vessel diverted from the main anti-submarine campaign in European waters. Before America's entry there had existed a Volunteer Coast Patrol of yachts and other craft suitable for anti-submarine work in local waters, and this had been organised on the lines of the British Auxiliary Patrol by Captain Henry B. Wilson, U.S.N., formerly commanding the battleship Pennsylvania. Over and above these craft there was the residue of the destroyer flotillas—for not all of them had been sent to Europe—as well as a large number of 110-foot " chasers " which, though not sturdy enough for ocean-going work, were excellent craft for hunting the submarine up to a hundred miles or so off shore.

To conclude this record of the early stages of America's contribution to the naval side of the war, one cannot do better than quote a statement made by Secretary Daniels in reviewing the first year of his country's co-operation :

The United States Navy (he said) has in European waters not only a force of destroyers, but also battleships, cruisers, submarine tenders, gunboats, coastguard cutters, converted yachts, tugs, and numerous vessels of other types for special purposes. We have furnished every possible aid which the countries allied with us in the war have requested. We have worked in the closest co-operation with them. Our forces have played an important part in the war against the submarines, and have aided materially in the marked reduction in the sinking of merchantmen as compared with the sinkings of a year ago, and in the no less notable increase in the number of submarines destroyed.

There are no less than 150 naval vessels, not including a considerable number of submarine chasers, operating on the other side. Over 35,000 officers and men are now serving in European waters, and this number does not include the personnel of troopships, supply vessels, armed guards, signal men, radio men, etc., who go into the war zone on recurring trips.
Our fighting ships are self-sustaining, with the **Independence Day**
assistance of repair-ships, with the exception of
major repairs and dockings. Schools and **figures, 1918**
barracks have been established to house
the new men who, when trained, go aboard ships, eventually relieving nucleus crews of men who are sent home to bring out new units. Commanding officers are trained in the war zone, and other experienced officers are returned to America to command new vessels and bring them into the war zone as quickly as possible. Ships are continually supplied with stores, provisions, spare parts, and fuel. Warehouses and depots have been established in Europe to house supplies. Torpedo stations have been established abroad. Ample hospital facilities have been created.

Aviation bases have been established in Europe, and members of the Naval Flying Corps have been for months in active service. The first of the regular armed forces of the United States landed in France were naval aviators, who arrived on June 8th, 1917. The Navy has made a record of which we may well be proud, but much more must be done. Ours has been a modest accomplishment in comparison with the achievements of the Allies, but our contribution has been considerable and is rapidly increasing.

The rate of this increase is strikingly indicated by some figures given on Independence Day—three months later— by Vice-Admiral Sims. The American Navy had then 250 ships of all classes co-operating with the allied fleets in European waters. They had a personnel of 3,000 officers and 40,000 men, and were serving from the White Sea to the Adriatic. "The number of destroyers this year," he said, " will be three times the number now serving. Very soon 150 submarine chasers will be on duty in the war zone; more than a half are there now."

With the vast expansion of her shipbuilding industry— she had nearly overtaken Great Britain in the output of mercantile tonnage in the first half of 1918—and the vigour of her naval construction, especially in the building of submarine chasers, there was already no doubt that America was destined to play a leading part in carrying the naval campaign to a successful issue.

THE ROLL OF HONOUR, 1917.

Outliving Posterity—Casualties in the Navy—The Totals Month by Month—Variations Therein—The Vanguard and Other Losses—Navy Casualties Analysed—Proportion of Officers to Men—Britain's Military Casualties—Her Available Man-Power—The Total of the Dead—Prisoners and Missing—The Losses and the Population Compared—Sir Bernard Mallet's Opinions—The Registrar-General's Report—The Losses Illustrated—Germany's Casualties—Herr Bleibtrau's Figures—A Criticism and an Estimate—Casualties to Nurses and Seamen—Women and Children Murdered—The Losses of 1917—A Comparison with 1916—High Proportion of Officers Hit—Losses in the Various Theatres of War—The Numbers at the Front—Canadian and Australian Casualties—Generals on the Roll of Honour—Heavy Losses among Subalterns—The Share of the Infantry—The Cost of the Year's Offensives—Losses among Politicians—Mr. Primrose and Mr. Redmond—Peers and their Sons in the List—Poets and Scholars—Fallen Athletes—Universities and Schools—Casualties among the Clergy.

IN 1794 Edmund Burke lost his only and fondly loved son Richard. Arrangements had just been made to raise the veteran statesman to the peerage as Lord Beaconsfield, but as soon as Richard's death occurred he declined the honour. A few months later, smarting under a personal attack, he wrote that "Letter to a Noble Lord," the Duke of Bedford, which has been described as the most splendid repartee in history. Therein he referred to his recent loss. "I live," said he, "in an inverted order. They who ought to have succeeded me have gone before me. They who should have been to me as posterity are in the place of ancestors."

During the Great War, and especially during its concluding stages, when so much of the young manhood of the British race lay dead upon the fields of battle overseas, thousands of parents must have felt that, like Burke, they lived in an inverted order. They, too, had outlived their posterity, not one or two, but in many cases three and four sons; they, too, had none to succeed them, and they, too, could say with the old statesman that they had no one to meet their enemies in the gate.

In a previous chapter (Chapter CLXX., Vol. 8, page 533) the record of British casualties during the Great War was carried down

"HE DIED FOR FREEDOM AND HONOUR."
Memorial bronze plaque for presentation to the next-of-kin of those who fell in the Great War. The design, that of Mr. E. Carter Preston, was the one selected early in 1918 from among the many sent in in an open competition.

to the end of 1916. To that date we estimated Britain's total military losses at 1,200,000 and the net loss—after making due allowance for those wounded more than once—at about 1,000,000. Of these something like 330,000 were killed. The naval casualties for the same period came out at 27,000, of whom 20,000 were dead.

After the early part of 1916 the authorities ceased to give information about the number of British casualties. All they did was to issue daily to the Press the names of the killed and wounded. Nothing was said about the place where a casualty occurred, so that none knew, except in the vaguest possible way, what were the losses in the various theatres of war. The authorities, however, did not abolish the first lesson taught in the arithmetic books — simple addition—and although on a large scale this process is tedious it has proved extremely useful in this connection. Day by day and month by month the "Daily Telegraph" gave the total number of casualties reported during the day or month in question, and to the editor of that journal we are indebted for permission to quote them. First we will deal with the losses in the Navy, the senior Service, and will then pass to those of the Army, a much greater total.

COMMANDER LORD ABINGER.
Royal Naval Volunteers.

CAPT. W. H. EVE,
Hussars.

The total for the twelve months shows this result :

Month.		Officers.	Men.	Total.
January	..	76	210	286
February	..	62	1,151	1,213
March	.. ..	123	1,423	1,546
April	.. ..	116	313	429
May	.. ..	177	2,347	2,524
June	.. ..	36	1,234	1,270
July	.. ..	138	1,338	1,476
August	.. ..	97	787	884
September	..	100	614	714
October	..	137	1,013	1,150
November	..	133	2,141	2,274
December	..	89	470	559
		1,284	13,041	14,325

A comparison with similar returns for 1916 may be of interest. There is no great difference in the totals—14,853 in 1916, against 14,325 in 1917, but a closer inspection reveals a result which gives rise to one or two interesting reflections.

Losses in patrolling the seas The 1916 casualties included two exceptional items—the losses in the Battle of Jutland, something like 7,000, and those incurred by the Royal Naval Division on the Ancre, perhaps 2,000. The ordinary losses in the continuous and perilous work of patrolling the seas may, therefore, be put down at 6,000 in 1916. In 1917 they were almost certainly greater, for there was no outstanding item nor, as the above table shows, any outstanding month.

There were, however, considerable variations in the monthly totals. May and January stood at the extremes, with November and April respectively next them. The average loss per month was just under 1,200, or 40 a day, and February, June, and October were nearest to this figure. Curiously enough, the two darkest months of the year, January and December, showed very low losses, while May showed very high ones, and those of both June and July were above the average.

MAJ. E. A. DE ROTHSCHILD,
Yeomanry.

MAJ. V. FLEMING, D.S.O.,
M.P., Yeomanry.

The proportion of losses between officers and men worked out as near as possible for the year at 1 officer to 10 men, but there were extraordinary variations in the several months. In January and April, for instance, the proportion was less than 1 in 3, while in June it was 1 in 34, a tenfold difference. One explanation is to be found in a fact mentioned before in these pages. The figures are those reported, not those incurred, during the month in question ; very often casualties to officers were reported earlier than casualties to men, and so it may have happened that the former were included, let us say, in the May returns, while the latter fell into those of June.

Another circumstance which makes comparisons of various kinds difficult is that from time to time naval men fought on land, and yet the casualties incurred in such fighting were returned in the naval lists. A **Naval casualties in land fighting** brilliant part was taken by the Royal Naval Division in the Battle of the Ancre in November, 1916, and fighting in the same region certainly accounted for a good share of the casualties reported. For instance, this division was mentioned more than once by Sir Douglas Haig in his long despatch which appeared on January 9th, 1918, and dealt with the British offensives of 1917. In fact, a glance at the diary of the war will doubtless throw as much light as anything else on the variations we have indicated.

The figures for January may be taken as the minimum of day-by-day casualties for a Navy which consisted of

DR. ELSIE INGLIS,
Founded Scottish Women's Hospitals.

NURSE DAISY COLES,
Voluntary Aid Detachment.

500,000 men and innumerable ships of every kind and patrolled every ocean of the world except the Baltic. For such multifarious work it was indeed a low figure. On January 8th the Cornwallis was torpedoed in the Mediterranean, but only 13 lives were lost. Two events swelled February's total—the fighting in France in which the Royal Naval Division participated and the loss of a destroyer on the 8th ; with the destroyer all the officers and all the crew save five went down.

March was very like February. A destroyer was lost with all hands in the North Sea, its crew consisting doubtless of about 100 officers and men, and many casualties in the Royal Naval Division were reported. April **R.N.D. in France** represented normal losses plus 80 or so casualties on a destroyer mined in the Channel at the end of March. May produced a heavier roll of dead and wounded men. One officer and 61 men were lost when, on the 2nd, a destroyer was mined in the Channel ; and a larger number a fortnight later when fourteen British drifters were sunk in the Adriatic and the Austrians claimed 72 prisoners. The majority, however, seem to have been incurred by the Royal Naval Division and the other naval men who fought in the April battles in France. For instance, on May 2nd the Admiralty reported casualties to 28 officers. Of these 21 were in the Royal Naval Division, 9 being killed, 11 wounded, and 1 missing. Of the remaining 7, 5 were in the Royal

Navy proper, and 2 in the Royal Naval Reserve. There were no purely naval losses which would have accounted for anything like the 2,524 casualties reported. The same remark appears to be true for June, for when the armed merchantman Avenger was sunk on the 16th only one life was lost.

July witnessed the heaviest naval loss of the year—the destruction by an internal explosion of the Dreadnought Vanguard. This accounted for about 850 of the month's casualties—1,476 in all. In August a destroyer was mined, but nearly half the crew were saved, and 39 deaths were reported from the torpedoed Ariadne. In September another destroyer lost half its crew ; October's bigger total
July's heavy total was swollen by the losses in the fight between two British destroyers, escorting twelve Scandinavian vessels, and two German raiders, altogether 135 officers and men, and by the 19 losses when the Drake went down. November's total needs more explanation, but this is almost certainly found in the fighting around Cambrai, as lists of casualties in the Royal Naval Division and the Royal Marine Light Infantry were reported by the Admiralty. About the same time, to refer again to Sir Douglas Haig's despatch, the naval men assisted the Canadians in their terrible fighting for Passchendaele. December showed a return to the normal.

A glance through the lists reveals one or two outstanding features. In January 29 officers and 53 men were returned

CAPT. THE HON. NEIL PRIMROSE, M.P., Yeomanry.

CAPT. THE HON. H. A. V. HARMS-WORTH, M.C., Irish Guards.

April, and December, in which they were presumably almost wholly of that kind. They work out as follows :

Casualties.	Officers.	Men.	Total.
Killed	74	341	415
Accidentally killed	10	13	23
Died of wounds	5	25	30
Died of injuries	5	11	16
Died	17	22	39
Drowned	38	119	157
Wounded	51	129	180
Injured	47	—	47
Missing	17	211	228
Missing, believed killed or drowned	11	107	118
Prisoners of war	6	15	21
	281	993	1,274

The year's figures included certain losses in air warfare, the Air Service being still divided into naval and military branches. Reference has been made to a list of casualties issued on May 2nd, in which were the names of 5 officers of the Royal Navy proper. But every one of these officers **Classification of** was described as " Flight Sub-Lieu- **casualties** tenant," and 4 out of the 5 were returned as missing. Evidently they were the "costs" of some enterprise undertaken by naval airmen.

The Admiralty gave the names under a large number of headings—in August, for instance, there were 21—but they can be reduced without difficulty to 3—killed, wounded, missing, and prisoners. Obviously "killed" included "died," "died of wounds," "accidentally killed," "missing, believed killed," "drowned," "accidentally drowned," "died as prisoners of war," and "died of accidental injuries." The wounded included "accidentally injured," "accidentally wounded," "injured," "slightly injured," "slightly wounded," "gassed," "suffering from shell-shock," and "suffering from shell-shock and immersion." The missing included : "Prisoners of war" and "believed prisoners of war."

[Lafayette.
CAPT. P. R. O. TRENCH, R.W. Surrey Regt.

CAPT. A. C. DINGLEY, North Stafford Regt.

as drowned ; perhaps they were on the sunk transport Ivernia. In February 20 officers and 279 men were killed, and 170 officers and 418 men wounded, the proportions of killed to wounded pointing evidently to some fighting on land ; but to what can 309 men, no officers, "missing, believed killed or drowned," refer ? March has the same facts, and clearly the same solutions, or want of them—40 officers and 328 men killed, 29 officers and 595 men wounded, and 1 officer and 184 men "missing, believed killed or drowned." April had no outstanding feature, simply a collection of small miscellaneous casualties. May with 36 officers and 629 men killed, 52 officers and 1,374 men wounded, and 45 officers and 167
Destruction of men missing, evidently meant more
H.M.S. Vanguard fighting on land. June had a large number of men, 621, returned as missing. In July the 46 officers and 807 men accidentally killed refer clearly to the destruction of the Vanguard. Both July and August had figures which suggest fighting on land, August especially ; and the same is true of September and October.

In November this was still more certainly the case ; 23 officers and 480 men being killed, 59 officers and 1,462 men wounded, and 13 officers and 124 men missing. December was a month of small miscellaneous losses.

To get some idea of the losses on the high seas, it will not be amiss to take the returns for three months, January,

[Lafayette.
CAPT. HON. L. U. KAY-SHUTTLEWORTH, R.F.A.

CAPT. E. F. WILKINSON, M.C., W. Yorks Regt.

Adopting this classification the year's total works out thus :

Casualties.	Officers.	Men.	Total.
Killed	632	6,199	6,831
Wounded	479	5,357	5,836
Missing and prisoners ..	179	1,561	1,740
	1,290	13,117	14,407

The slight discrepancy between this total and the preceding one is accounted for by corrections in the original lists. A missing man had rejoined, or a wounded man had been wrongly reported, or some other alteration had been found necessary.

The proportion of officers to men works out at almost 1 in 10, both in the gross total and in the three separate

A summary of the twelve monthly totals shows the following results :

Month.	Officers.	Men.	Total.
January	953	32,498	33,451
February	1,216	16,277	17,493
March	1,765	28,709	30,474
April	4,381	31,619	36,000
May	5,991	107,075	113,066
June	3,601	84,667	88,268
July	2,490	68,858	71,348
August	5,264	52,404	57,668
September ..	2,938	109,200	112,138
October	6,205	80,195	86,400
November.. ..	4,906	124,896	129,802
December	3,984	59,031	63,015
	43,694	795,429	839,123

Neither these figures nor those for the Navy are official. Every care, however, was taken to make them accurate, and to secure that end careful note was taken of all modifications and all alterations of casualties reported from time to time.

To the end of 1915 official figures gave Britain's military casualties as 549,467 ; for 1916 the monthly computations of the " Daily Telegraph " made a total of 660,071 ; and now there comes the addition for 1917 of 839,123, making a grand total of 2,048,661. In this immense figure, however, it must not be forgotten, many individuals appeared more than once, and the number of such was an increasing one. It was, for instance, negligible in 1914, fairly small in 1915, but considerably larger in 1916, and especially so in 1917.

When discussing the figures to the end of 1916 we estimated this total at 200,000, and it will not be excessive to put it down for a year later at 448,000, and so to make the net casualties—*i.e.*, the number of individuals who were killed, wounded, or taken prisoner during the Great War to the end of 1917—at 1,600,000 or thereabouts.

FOR THE MEMORY OF THOSE WHO HAD FALLEN.
British soldier-carpenter shaping simple wooden crosses which were to mark the resting-places of comrades who had fallen in France in the terrible struggle for the maintenance of freedom and progressive civilisation.

classes. This means that the losses fell proportionately far more heavily upon the officers than they did upon the men, for the ratio of the two in the Service is nearer 1 in 30 than 1 in 10.

A " Navy List " of 1914 reveals the fact that the Black Prince then carried 35 officers, and most of the destroyers appear to have had five or six. The number of men carried is not given, but the Black Prince would have something like 800, and a destroyer perhaps 90. Taking the Navy as a whole, there might be 1 officer to every 25 men, but certainly not more than 1 to every 20 men. Assuming this to be roughly correct, the risk run by a naval officer was just about double that run by one of his men ; probably it was more.

Coming to the losses in the Army, it may be well first to put on record those for the year specially under consideration. This will lead to some estimate of Britain's total in

Army losses of 1917 the Great War to the end of 1917 ; and to some comparison in this matter between 1916 and 1917, and, as far as possible, with those of the enemy. Other points in connection with the losses of 1917 can then be discussed, before passing to say something about the various classes of society which suffered and the notable individuals who fell. The magnitude of Britain's sacrifice can in this way be made plain to all.

This figure does not include the Navy's losses. In 1914 and 1915 these were about 13,000 ; in 1916 they were 14,853 ; and in 1917 were 14,325, making a gross total of just over 42,000. Adding this to the military total, we have an aggregate of almost **Losses and** 2,080,000, a figure which represents some **population compared** 1,600,000 or 1,700,000 individuals. This total does not include the casualties among the Indian soldiers, at least as far as 1916 and 1917 are concerned.

The population of the United Kingdom in 1917 was something like 46,000,000, to which must be added 8,000,000 for Canada and 4,000,000 for Australia. Adding the white inhabitants of New Zealand and South Africa, we may say that the loss was levied upon 60,000,000 people, and worked out at 1 in 36. If the slight discrepancy in the proportions of the sexes is ignored, the white males of the Empire may be put down at 30,000,000. Then arises the further question as to what proportion of these were fighting men, and here the population of England and Wales, as given in the census of 1911, may be used as the basis for a simple calculation.

In 1911 there were in England and Wales 9,020,657 males between the ages of 18 and 55, which may be taken as the extreme limits of military efficiency. In addition there were 999,386 youths between 15 and 18, and these, therefore, passed within our limits before the end of 1917. The total is so conveniently near 10,000,000 that the odd figures can be ignored. For Scotland, Ireland, and the Overseas Dominions the proportion would be similar, meaning the addition of 6,500,000 to the 10,000,000. This total of 16,500,000 constitutes the body of men from whom the Empire's soldiers were drawn during the first three and a half years of the war, and is just ten times the net number of casualties incurred during that period. If the Empire had undertaken before 1914 to send 1 in 10 of her manhood to do battle in Europe, it would have been hailed everywhere as a remarkable effort, by many even as unnecessary and extravagant; how much greater than that the actual achievement was is revealed in the proud statement that 1 in 10 became a casualty there or elsewhere for the same cause.

To this reflection, however, may be added the reminder that, apart from deaths in battle, there will be an appreciable number of deaths of men of all ages in three years. The total of 16,500,000, moreover, must be taken as **Britain's total** including imbeciles, cripples, and the like, **of man-power** as well as a large number who, although able to go about their ordinary work, are unfitted for any severe physical strain. For these classes some authorities would deduct 25 per cent., and others as much as 33⅓ per cent. If the latter percentage is taken, the net or real white man-power of the Empire would be 11,000,000 ; if the former, it would be nearer 12,500,000.

Here, indeed, everything depends upon the severity of the medical tests ; but some such conclusion as the following would represent the position at the opening of 1918. Britain had mobilised 6,000,000 or 7,000,000 men, of whom a quarter had become casualties, including those invalided out on account of illness, as well as those killed or disabled by enemy action. If everything had to be thrown into the scale, commerce sacrificed, and munitions made entirely by women, she could have mobilised as many again.

The next question to consider is the number actually killed, for, as was remarked before, the distinction that matters to human affection is that great one which divides the living from the dead. An analysis of the monthly totals of losses in the Army shows the following results, the total of the killed in battle and died of wounds being swollen by those returned as "died,"

AT A MESOPOTAMIAN GRAVE.
British officer engaged on Graves Registration duty recording the last resting-place of an officer who had been buried in the parapet of the trench at Sanna-i-Yat, where he fell.

"accidentally killed," "drowned," "missing, believed killed or drowned," and "died as prisoners of war":

Months.	Officers.	Men.
January	291	8,779
February	333	5,274
March	503	8,746
April	1,129	7,777
May	1,599	25,477
June	879	17,539
July	563	13,979
August	1,296	10,709
September	743	19,593
October	1,660	16,356
November	1,319	24,725
December	971	11,693
Total	11,286	170,647

The figures for the three periods to the end of 1917 are, therefore, as follows :

Year.	Officers.	Men.
1914-15	7,801	120,337
1916	8,560	130,176
1917	11,286	170,647
Total	27,647	421,160

To these must be added the Navy's losses in killed. These were 634 officers and 6,203 men in 1917, and 803 officers and 9,140 men in 1916. For 1914 and 1915 there is an estimate only, for the official figures were only down to November 5th, 1915. For that period they were 589 officers and 9,928 men, and the addition is this:

Year.	Officers.	Men.
1914-15	589	9,928
1916	803	9,140
1917	634	6,203
Total	2,026	25,271

Something must be added for the concluding weeks of 1915, so perhaps a total of 2,100 officers, and 26,000 men will be not far from the mark. This makes, naval

"FOR EVER ENGLISH GROUND."
In a cemetery where British soldiers who fell in Mesopotamia were laid to rest. The Graves' Commission, charged with the pious duty of tending the burial-places of these fallen heroes of Britain, had erected a permanent concrete cross over each of the graves.

and military together, a loss in killed alone of 30,000 officers and 460,000 men. Just before the Great War the total strength of the Regular Army was 7,940 officers and 170,377 men.

To this figure of 490,000 something must be added, for a certain proportion of the missing men were certainly dead, and the question of missing and prisoners may now be considered. For 1914-15 the War Office stated that 68,046, 2,145 of them being officers, were missing and prisoners. Of these some 32,000 were captives in Germany, and perhaps 12,000 more in Turkey, so it may be assumed that nearly 25,000 were dead. In 1916 the number returned as missing amounted to 50,858, but undoubtedly some of these were prisoners of war. The majority, however, for reasons given in a previous chapter, were not in that condition; they were dead, and there seems no need to revise our former estimate that 40,000 of them had fallen on the field, but that their identity disks had not been returned. That dreadful July Saturday, when the British infantry dashed in vain against the German barriers between Gommecourt and Fricourt, accounted certainly for a large part of this total.

As regards 1917 we are on somewhat surer ground. The "Daily Telegraph" figures give 2,725 officers and 45,808 men as missing, and 71 officers and 1,929 men as prisoners of war, and this shows how the first returns were made. Early in 1918, however, it was stated by the War Office that 28,379 British had been taken prisoner during the previous year. As the prisoners and missing together amounted to 50,533, it is safe, using round figures, to say that 20,000 of them were dead. This, together with the other figures, makes 85,000 to add to the number of Britain's dead, and brings it up to 575,000 for the period of the war between its opening in August, 1914, and the end of December, 1917.

These figures are "the cost of the war"—a glib and familiar phrase—but they only represent a part of it. The cost in money can be stated and explained, as has been done in an earlier chapter (Chapter CCXXXIX., Vol. 11, page 261), and the cost in life can be estimated with some degree of accuracy, but as for its cost in suffering, mental and physical, in the deterioration of mind and body, in the waste of the world's wealth, and in the delay and perhaps the destruction of hopes for a more healthy, educated, and leisured humanity—at this cost no man can guess. Knowledge has neither speech nor symbol with which to express it.

The effect of this loss on the population was discussed by Sir Bernard Mallet in a paper read before the Royal Statistical Society on November 20th, 1917. He mentioned one very striking fact. "In round **Some striking** numbers," he said, "200,000 persons **vital statistics** were married in England and Wales between August, 1914, and June, 1917, who, in the ordinary course of events, would not have married." It is fair to assume that the offspring of these marriages, and of similar ones in other parts of the Empire, would be some set-off against the loss of 575,000 lives.

Sir Bernard referred to the fall in the birth-rate, one of 11 per cent., when comparing 1906 with 1913; but to balance this there was a drop in the rate of infantile mortality—from 108 to 91 per 1,000 in England and Wales, from 110 to 97 per 1,000 in Scotland, and from 97 to 83 per 1,000 in Ireland. His conclusion was that the net result of all causes affecting births and deaths showed that during 1915, 1916, and the first half of 1917 the excess of births over deaths in England and Wales was 590,000, in Scotland 83,000, and in Ireland 41,000, making a total for the United Kingdom of 714,000. Adding the increase for the war period of 1914, he placed the total excess at over 900,000.

Adjusting these figures to meet the scope of our chapter, the result is somewhat as follows. The addition required to bring them down to the end of 1917 will be 140,000, making a total of 1,040,000, and some- thing must be added for the rest of the **Increase in** Empire. The ratio is 14 to 46, which **male population** gives, roughly, 310,000 more, or a grand total of 1,350,000. Approximately half of these were boys— say, 670,000—and from these 575,000 must be deducted.

We are left, therefore, in spite of the dreadful toll of war, with an increase in the male white population of the Empire of something like 100,000 to the end of 1917. The vague general opinion that the end of the war would see the Empire to some extent depopulated seems, therefore, to be a delusion. Indeed, in 1918 a very plausible case could have been made out for a very different theory.

Many financiers thought at one time that the want of money would make wars, at least wars on the grand scale, very short. But after a time the balance of probability seemed rather with those who argued that want of money alone could never produce that desired end. Similarly it seemed doubtful in 1918 whether the lack of fight- ing men would become sufficiently serious without other factors ever to stop the war.

Britain, at all events, was producing boys more quickly than her men were being killed, and there was no evidence that any of the belligerents were losing on balance between births and deaths sufficient to bring about a real shortage. Faster, as fast—or, at the worst, only a little less fast—than the men were being killed the boys were growing up. The serious point about the losses, as far as vital statistics are concerned, is that they would accentuate the discrepancy between men and women, and so raise social problems of a new and difficult kind.

The report of the Registrar-General on the vital statistics of England and Wales in 1916, which appeared in February, 1918, bore out most of the above conclusions. The deaths of children under one year old numbered 71,646, or 91 per 1,000, the lowest rate ever recorded, and the excess of births over deaths was 277,303. Roughly speaking, half of these were boys, and if to them are added the number of white boy babies born during the year in Scotland, Ireland, and the more distant parts of the Empire, it is evident that the total considerably exceeded the number of those killed in battle, a number estimated in these pages at 190,000 for the year in question. Of the other side the Registrar-General says: "The German statistics record 1,331,000 deaths in 1916, apparently exclusive of at least the great majority of fatal war casualties, as against 1,103,000 births." This was serious but not yet crippling.

This return affords in one particular an interesting com- mentary on Sir Bernard Mallet's conclusion about war marriages, which were specially numerous in 1915. After that there was, for some reason or other, a remarkable fall.

We have thus the curious phenomena, that of an unprece- dentedly high marriage rate in 1915 succeeded by an almost unpre- cedentedly low one in 1916. The flood of marriages which set in

CAPT. H. S. O. ASHINGTON,
East Yorkshire Regt.
[*Bassano.*

CAPT. C. E. STUART,
Suffolks, attd. York and Lanc. Regt.
[*Swaine.*

CAPT. V. G. TUPPER, M.C.,
Canadian Infantry.

CAPT. ALBERT BALL,
V.C., D.S.O., M.C., R.F.C.

CAPT. M. L. YEATHERD,
Lancers.

CAPT. N. G. CHAVASSE, V.C.,
M.C., M.B., R.A.M.C.

CAPT. P. WARD, M.C.,
South Lancs Regt.

CAPT. C. H. BODINGTON,
Household Battalion.

CAPT. J. N. F. PIXLEY,
Grenadier Guards.

CAPT. C. A. BRADFORD,
Yorks, attd. Nigeria Regt.

CAPT. W. A. VERSCHOYLE,
Royal Irish Fusiliers.

CAPT. E. CROMBIE,
Gordon Highlanders.

CAPT. W. J. FORSTER,
East Lancashire Regt.

CAPT. M. L. HILDER, M.C.,
Royal Fusiliers.

CAPT. G. H. BAILEY, M.C.,
R.H.A.

CAPT. H. O'CONNOR, M.C.,
K.S.L.I.

CAPT. G. H. STAVELEY,
K.O.Y.L.I.

CAPT. SIR JOHN S. DYER, M.C.,
Scots Guards.

THE ROLL OF HONOUR, 1917.

Photos by Speaight, Lafayette, Elliott & Fry, Walter Barnett, Bassano, Chancellor.

with the second quarter of 1915 did not ebb until a year later, so that considerably more marriages were registered in the first quarter of 1916 than in the corresponding quarter of any previous year.

These violent changes appeared, we were told, to be giving place in 1917 to a less abnormal state of affairs.

This hard and dreadful fact, however, remains, and statistics are as powerless as sophistry to charm it away: 575,000 young and healthy British lives—more than all the males in Glasgow or Liverpool, more than all the people in Toronto or Leeds—were sacrificed in less than three and a half years because a group of ruthless militarists wished to impose their arrogant will upon a world at peace, and by them the Empire and the world were and are the poorer.

Two illustrations may help to press home the seriousness of this loss. In March, 1917, Mr. G. N. Barnes, then Minister of Pensions, gave in Parliament some **Minister of Pensions'** facts about his department. At that **notable figures** time the Ministry had charge of 62,796 widows, 188,294 children of widows, and 29,832 other dependents of deceased men. In addition there were 125,000 widows who had not reached the pension stage. Nearly 200,000 widows, and almost the whole of 1917 to come!

The other illustration is an extract from a speech made early in 1918 by the chairman of the Prudential Assurance Company. "At about age 21," said he, "the mortality rate in 1915 was five times that of our pre-war experience; for 1916 it was nine times, and for 1917 about twelve times that of our pre-war experience."

Our knowledge of Germany's casualties has passed through three stages. In the first the Imperial Government issued their own figures, which may be regarded as approximately accurate. After a time they ceased to do this, but still the names were officially published, and industrious persons could make totals thereof. For a time this was done by the British War Office, and at the end of 1916 a total of just over 4,000,000 was reported. The third stage began about the middle of 1917, when the German Government prevented their official lists from reaching enemy countries, and consequently reduced the question to little more than guesswork.

In April, 1918, however, a certain military writer, Karl Bleibtrau, gave, in "Das Neue Europa," some estimates of the German losses. The first report of this in the English papers stated that it dealt exclusively with the killed and the prisoners; but as he gave a total of 4,089,511 for the period from August 2nd, 1914, to July 31st, 1917, it was obvious that there was something wrong somewhere, for no one could possibly believe that over 4,000,000 Germans had been killed or made prisoners in that time. However, the fuller text of the article showed where the error lay.

The writer had included the wounded and even the sick and, taking down the story to **Estimates of** January 31st, 1918, had put down the **German losses** total loss at 4,456,961, of whom his estimate was that 1,500,000 had been killed. He gave totals for each month down to July 31st, 1917, and also divided his figure (to then 4,089,511) between the western and the eastern fronts. The former accounted for 2,604,961, and the latter for 1,484,550.

With the "Manchester Guardian" the present writer believes that the figures are "almost certainly under the mark"; but, on the other hand, he cannot accept that journal's own estimate: "A total German casualty list up to the present (April 25th, 1918) of from 2,250,000 to 2,500,000 killed, prisoners, and died of wounds or sickness, and from 5,000,000 to 6,000,000 other casualties, making over 8,000,000 in all."

The main objection to this total rests upon the size and vigour of the German offensive in 1918. Reference has been made to the man-power of the British Empire, with its white population of 60,000,000. The German Empire's population was, in 1911, about 67,000,000—one-tenth greater than that of its chief foe—and other conditions were very similar. The proportions of the sexes and of the unfit can have differed very little in the two countries, and other factors would be much the same. If, therefore, the extreme limit of Britain's man-power was 12,000,000, Germany could not possibly put more than 13,000,000 men into the field, if as many, and at the same time maintain her tremendous output of munitions. To reduce Germany's man-power by 8,000,000, was to leave 5,000,000 men, or at the very outside 6,000,000, available for the offensive and all the work which it entailed.

Germany may probably have organised things better than Britain did at the time when, according to Mr. Churchill, it took six men to produce one with a bayonet on the parapet; but even if her proportion were one in three, her striking force from the North Sea to the Alps would be hardly 2,000,000. In view of what happened in the spring of 1918, this suggests a *reductio ad absurdum*.

There are other explanations perhaps. Many of the casualties had probably returned to the front, while prisoners were used to do much of the auxiliary work of war. These may be allowed for; but, as heretofore, we prefer to give our own estimate and the grounds on which it is based.

In the end of July, 1917, the German totals, as counted by the British authorities, came to 4,624,256. This represented an average of about 110,000 a month, but included the losses at Verdun, which were undoubtedly extremely heavy. An average of 100,000 a month would be sufficiently high for the remaining five months of 1917, and would give a grand total of just over 5,000,000. Something should be added to cover the delay in announcing casualties, but for this 500,000 would be excessive, and it will be better, therefore, to say that the Germans had suffered *at least* 5,000,000 casualties to the end of 1917.

Of these, how many were dead? Bleibtrau said 1,500,000, but he was apparently trying to get at Germany's absolute loss in men, the **German killed,** number permanently removed from her **1,500,000** fighting strength, and he included therefore those who died of sickness, and possibly the prisoners. To the end of July, 1917, the War Office, reckoning from enemy casualty lists, gave 1,132,963 as the number of German dead, and a further 267,237 as missing, the vast majority of whom were almost certainly dead. This makes a total of 1,400,200, while something must be added for the remainder of 1917. For these five months 125,000, or 25,000 a month, will be sufficient, making a total of 1,525,000. This is curiously near Bleibtrau's estimate; but if, as may be imagined, he included prisoners, he was certainly guilty of an understatement. It was also Mr. Gerard's estimate, to which he added 500,000 for the permanently disabled. At 1,500,000, therefore, compared with Britain's 575,000, the matter may be left.

In spite of what imaginative journalists, and inspired but anonymous correspondents speaking on "high authority," have said about masses of German corpses and the enemy's preference for being killed wholesale rather than individually, it is certain that in the period under review the Allies lost many more than the Central Powers. Many proofs could be given, but one must suffice. It can be given by way of parable.

Once, when Napoleon entered a small German town, no salute was fired in his honour. Angry at the slight, he summoned the burgomaster before him and inquired the reason. The official blandly replied that he had ninety-eight reasons for the omission, and would state them. The first was that he had no cannon. "That will do," said the Emperor. The parallel is precise. There are many proofs of the statement made above, and the first is that in 1918 the war was still raging. Had the slaughter been on anything like the scale Britons were led to believe, it would have been over by then. The other reasons, like those of the burgomaster, are superfluous.

British transport advancing in France past a graveyard where rest some of their fallen comrades

Memorial service to men of the Quebec Regiment who fell gloriously on Vimy Ridge.

MAJ. G. E. S. YOUNG.
IRISH GUARDS.
[Swaine.

LT.-COL. E. B. GREER.
M.C., IRISH GUARDS.
[Lafayette.

BRIG.-GEN. C. B. BULKELEY-JOHNSON.
A.D.C.
[Walter Barnett.

LT.-GEN. SIR F. STANLEY MAUDE.
K.C.B., C.M.G., D.S.O.
[Maull & Fox.

LT.-GEN. R. G. BROADWOOD.
C.B.
[Bassano.

BRIG.-GEN. F. E. JOHNSTON.
C.B.
[Bassano.

MAJ. W. REDMOND, M.P.,
ROYAL IRISH REGT.

MAJ. F. H. JOHNSON.
V.C., R.E.
[Bassano.

LT.-COL. G. E. HOPE.
M.C., GRENADIER GUARDS, ATTD. LANCS FUS.
[Elliott & Fry.

Officers who laid down their lives for their God, King, and country in 1917

BRIG.-GEN. J. A. TANNER.
C.B., C.M.G., D.S.O., R.E.
[Elliott & Fry.

MAJ. J. B. T. LEIGHTON.
M.C., SCOTS GUARDS AND R.F.C.
[Lafayette.

MAJ. A. G. McNEILL.
M.C., R.E.
[Lafayette.

BRIG.-GEN. C. G. RAWLING.
C.M.G., C.I.E.
[Lafayette.

BRIG.-GEN. F. A. MAXWELL.
V.C., C.S.I., D.S.O.
[Elliott & Fry.

BRIG.-GEN. A. F. GORDON.
C.M.G., D.S.O.
[Walter Barnett.

MAJ. C. H. GREEN.
S. STAFFS REGT., ATTD. NIGERIA REGT.
[Swaine.

LT.-COL. R. O. KERRISON.
R. REGT. CAVALRY, ATTD. AUSTRALIAN ARTILLERY.
[Bassano.

MAJ. MILES BARNE.
D.S.O., SCOTS GUARDS.

"Be thou faithful unto death and I will give thee the crown of life."

551

"In sure and certain hope ——": Girl gardeners attached to Q.M.A.A.C. tending graves of British soldiers in France.

In one particular there is a close similarity between the British and the German figures. In the former, it will be remembered, a total casualty list of 2,080,000 was the estimate, and of these 575,000 were dead. This is just over one-quarter, and the German proportion, 1,400,200 out of 4,624,256, is near it. To be more exact, 27 per cent. of the British casualties were dead, as were 33 per cent. of the German. The correspondence between the two figures, reached by very different paths, is close enough to be noteworthy, and it may be assumed as a well-established conclusion that the proportion of killed on the world's battlefields in the Great War was between 1 in 3 and 1 in 4 of the total casualties.

To return to the British loss of 575,000 lives. Even this colossal total is not quite the whole tale. The Germans gave a new meaning to the word war; they enlarged the area of its activities until in their view every man, woman, and child became a combatant and every place a fortress. The most ruthless of mediæval warriors did not make a practice of warring upon women and children, while sanctuary was respected even in the case of the most hardened criminal. But all this was changed.

The Roll of Honour in the Great War was not confined to the soldiers and the sailors of the Fleet. It included nurses shelled to death while at their work of mercy, or left to drown in an ice-cold sea. The war extended to men and women travelling peaceably from one country to another, and not those of belligerent countries only; and to seamen who, in pursuit of their ancient and lawful calling, had to face a danger from which they had hitherto been free—that of murder by an unseen hand. It extended also to the men, women, and children of peaceful homes which, through the skill of the devotees of the new warfare, might in a moment be reduced to gaping ruins and their sleeping inmates to charred fragments of humanity. It was on such warfare that the German Emperor asked the blessing of Almighty God.

Some women victims

In April, 1918, a service held in St. Paul's Cathedral commemorated 350 nurses—women who had perished during the Great War, and without whose names the Roll of Honour would be incomplete. Eight with their matron went down with the Glenart Castle; 183 members of the V.A.D. had been stormed at by shot and shell, bombed from above or torpedoed from below, for in the long list of names were many given as drowned, and some as died of wounds.

In this list there were quite a number of familiar names—Mrs. Harley, Mrs. Percy Dearmer, and Edith Cavell, for instance; but, as far as 1917 is concerned, perhaps the most important was that of Dr. Elsie Inglis, a woman physician of marked ability and reputation. She founded the Scottish Women's Hospitals, and in 1915 went to Serbia to fight the typhus epidemic there. Afterwards she was a prisoner of war, and later still did her work of mercy among the Rumanian troops. The mention of Serbia is a reminder that in 1917, also, Mr. and Mrs. Claude Askew were drowned in the Mediterranean as a result of German submarine activity.

The German submarines had many victims, and these too deserve a place on the Roll of Honour. In a war remarkable for heroisms and super-heroisms of every kind, nothing was more remarkable than the quiet way in which the seamen went about their work. The menace of the submarine did not seem able to persuade a single one to stay at home. But the peril was not the less a very real one. On May 15th, 1918, Sir Albert Stanley, President of the Board of Trade, said that 12,500 seamen had lost their lives during the war, while Mr. Havelock Wilson placed the number at 15,000. Grimsby alone, so it was stated in December, 1917, had lost 545 fishermen in this way.

Eight small booklets issued by the Admiralty are eloquent testimony on this point. Each is entitled "Roll of Honour of the Mercantile Marine," and a sub-title says it is a list of officers and seamen in British merchant and fishing vessels whose deaths had been attributed to enemy action, reported to the Board of Trade.

Each document gives the name, the rank or rating, the last place of abode, and the date, or supposed date, of death. The pages are numbered, and in the eight lists there were altogether 118 pages. A page contains about 35 names, so here, down only to March 3rd, 1917, are something like 4,000 victims of German barbarity. There was a good deal said during the war about "indispensable men." Generally they were persons who passed their time in offices, initialing documents, and doing other work of the kind—doubtless of the highest importance to the Empire. But a people trained, as Britons had not been, to face the actualities of life instead of heeding the unreal vapourings of vote hunters, would have known at once that the real indispensables are the men who bring them their food. The seamen are the indispensables. The clerks could all go and none be the worse, but take away the seamen and the country starves.

Losses among merchant seamen

The balance between the 4,000 or 5,000 seamen here and Sir Albert Stanley's figures of 12,500 is not easy to explain. The most likely explanation is that he was wrongly reported, and that he really included all lives, passengers as well as crew, lost in merchant and passenger ships. Anyhow, a considerable number of passengers were lost, and here again the word murder, unusual in legitimate warfare, is the right one. To June 30th, 1917, it was stated in Parliament, 9,748 persons had been killed by the enemy in British merchant ships. Of these 3,828 were passengers, and a large number were women and children. In the same category must be placed those killed in air raids. To July 30th, 1917, there had been in London alone 366 victims of this kind of warfare.

To return to the military and naval casualties, this chapter would be incomplete without some comparison between the figures of 1916 and those of 1917. The monthly figures already given in tabular form will be a useful guide, although they represent the losses reported, not those incurred, during the period in question.

In 1917 the gross total of military casualties was rather more than in 1916, which included the costly British offensive on the Somme. It was 839,123 against 660,071. In the earlier year the worst month was August, when the casualties in the opening stages of the Battle of the Somme were being reported; in the latter it was November. In 1916 and 1917 alike the best month was February, which had 15,700 casualties in 1916 and 17,493 in 1917. In each year there were three months in which reported casualties exceeded 100,000, or 3,000 a day; in 1916 they were August, September, and October; in 1917, May, September, and November. The losses of November, 1917, were the heaviest reported during any one month since the Great War opened, and made all the memorable battles of British history—Crécy, Agincourt, Blenheim, Albuera, Inkerman, even Waterloo — look like petty brawls.

Comparison of 1917 with 1916

For the two years, separating, as is usually done, officers and men, the totals are as follows:

	Officers.	Men.
1916	32,254	627,817
1917	43,694	795,429

The disquieting fact here is the increase in the proportion of officers. In 1916, 4·9 per cent. of the casualties fell upon them; in other words, for every officer casualty there were 19½ men. In 1917 the percentage rose to 5·2, or 1 officer to 18 men. In 1914-15 it was 4·5 per cent., or 1 officer to every 22 men. The proportion, therefore, appears to have been a steadily rising one, from 1 in 22 to 1 in 19½, and then to 1 in 18. But after all this, perhaps, is what might have been expected.

LIEUT. J. G. WILL,
R.F.C.

LIEUT. W. J. O'MALLEY,
R.F.A.

It is no reflection on the gallant lads who went out in thousands from civilian occupations to fight Britain's battles to point to the original Expeditionary Force as the finest Army the world had ever seen. Indeed, a high German authority, who saw the men in training just before 1914, said publicly that it was the most highly-trained force since Cæsar's legions. When these men bore the brunt, the loss in officers, although high, was at a minimum. The succeeding troops were equally brave, but their training had been far shorter, and, as the proportion of them in the Army rose, so did the casualties among the officers.

As regards the killed, the proportion does not seem to have varied so much. In 1917 it was 1 officer to every 15 men, and in the previous periods it was 1 to 15½ (1914-15), and 1 to 15 (1916).

After the withdrawal from Gallipoli at the end of 1915, and the surrender of Kut in the following spring, the great bulk of the casualties were incurred on the western front. The War Office gave practically no particulars about the location of the various casualties during 1916 and 1917, but as regards the latter year there is a glimmer of official light.

A War Office return gave some details about prisoners of war taken and lost in 1917. Great Britain lost 28,379, and 27,200 of these losses were incurred in the west. In Palestine the losses were 610 ; Mesopotamia, 267 ; Salonika, 202 ; East Africa, 100. The proportions must not be pressed too closely, for each total is affected by local and other circumstances, but they may serve some useful purpose here.

		Per cent.
Western Front	..	95·82
Palestine	..	2·16
Mesopotamia ..	..	·94
Salonika ..	..	·72
East Africa ..	..	·36

Applying these proportions to the total casualty figures for 1917—839,123—we find that something like 800,000 were incurred on the western front. Palestine **2,300 casualties a day** would account for about 17,000 of the remainder, leaving another 17,000 for the other three theatres—say, Mesopotamia, 8,000 ; Salonika, 6,000 ; and East Africa, 3,000.

In 1917 the British losses worked out at almost exactly 70,000 a month, or 2,300 a day, and this is perhaps the easiest way to visualise the price paid in flesh and blood for freedom to live without the menace of Prussian

LIEUT. L. N. KINDERSLEY,
Hussars.

LIEUT. THE HON. ESMOND ELLIOT,
Scots Guards.

militarism over the world. A long procession of dead and wounded men—nearly a hundred every hour, nearly two every minute—were borne by their comrades to the grave or the hospital, or limped painfully to the dressing-station, or fell, dead or wounded perhaps, into the hands of the enemy. Each day, before a single man could be added to the fighting strength of the armies, over 2,000 had to be taken over from England as reinforcements. A year without such reinforcements and an army of 1,000,000 men would practically cease to exist.

No one outside a small official circle knew exactly how many men were serving under Sir Douglas Haig in either 1916 or 1917, but it is tolerably certain that nothing like 5,000,000 British soldiers were ever in France at one time. Indeed, the Prime Minister stated definitely in Parliament on May 9th, 1918, that the British Army in France numbered 2,000,000 ; therefore, allowing for the men in other theatres of war, allowing for men on leave, for soldiers doing a great variety of work behind the lines—from commanding a base depot to cleaning a hospital—we may take the figure of 3,000,000 as an approximate total for 1917, and may say that the loss of 840,000 men fell upon a force of 3,000,000 or somewhat less. It worked out at 1 in 3 or thereabouts, certainly it was not less severe than 1 in 4.

In December, 1917, it was stated in Parliament that, since the previous July 31st, 76 per cent. of the total British casualties had fallen upon English troops, 10 per cent. upon Scottish troops, 8 per cent. upon Overseas troops, and 6 per cent. upon Irish troops. These proportions would not hold good for the whole course of the war, but they are not without their value. On this subject little more was known. In nearly four years of war Australia had suffered almost 190,000 casualties, of whom 47,000 were dead, while in June, 1918, Sir Robert Borden said that Canada's total was 152,000.

The extent to which the losses fell upon the various ranks can only be obtained after careful examination of the casualty lists, but something may be said here of the generals who fell during the year. Lieut.-General Sir Frederick Stanley Maude fell a victim to cholera in Mesopotamia. Lieut.-General Robert George Broadwood was **British Generals who fell** killed in the west in June. Of generals in charge of divisions, the New Zealander Major-General William Holmes was killed in July while conducting Mr. W. A. Holman, Premier of New South Wales, round the trenches.

On brigadier-generals the losses fell more heavily. In addition to Lord Binning and Walter Long, the following may be mentioned : John Arthur Tanner, C.M.G., of the Engineers, and Alister Fraser Gordon, C.M.G., in July ; Francis Aylmer Maxwell, V.C., in September ; Cecil G. Rawling, C.M.G., in October, and another V.C., Roland Boys Bradford, in November. Charles B. Bulkeley-Johnson, C.M.G., was killed while leading his cavalry in April at Monchy, and others were Charles Gosling, C.M.G., Godfrey E. Matthews, C.M.G., C. H. J. Brown, the New Zealander, killed in the Battle of Messines, Malcolm Peake.

C.M.G., Ronald C. Maclachlan, Vincent A. Ormsby, Francis Earl Johnston, and Arthur C. Lowe.

As regards the casualties among the officers below the rank of general and the proportions in the different arms of the Service, the bulk of these fell as ever upon the infantry, and second-lieutenants suffered more, both absolutely and relatively, than any other class of officer. In September a somewhat sharp rise in the casualties among artillery officers was noted, and this was ascribed to the newer methods of defence adopted by the enemy.

Analysis of casualty lists

For some little light on this subject let us take the officers' casualty list issued on Monday, April 23rd. It represented losses in the Battle of Arras, and contained 494 military names, of which 271 were those of second-lieutenants, and a further 135 were lieutenants. Only 88, therefore, fell on captains, majors, colonels, and generals, of whom there were 3, and, of these 88, 2 were chaplains.

The artillery, including trench-mortar batteries and machine-gun corps, had 47 casualties, the flying men had 41, of whom 31 were missing, and the cavalry had 34, a number which evidently represented their losses at Monchy. Six losses fell on the engineers, and 4 on the medical service, leaving 362, or almost exactly 3 out of 4 for the infantry. Apart from the losses in the cavalry, which were exceptional, the above figures were fairly representative of those of the year as a whole. However, they may be compared with those of another list, and so tested.

On November 24th the military casualty list contained 288 names. Of these 71 were second-lieutenants and 160 were lieutenants, all the Canadian subalterns, who suffered heavily at this time, being of the latter rank. Thus 231 casualties, or nearly 5 out of 6, fell on these two classes; in April it was 406 out of 494, or practically the same proportion. Of the losses, 50 fell upon the artillery, 22 upon the flying men, 9 upon the engineers, 8 upon the cavalry, 6 upon the medical men, and 3 upon the chaplains. This leaves 190 for the infantry, and proportionately it is somewhat lower than that in the earlier one. The artillery losses were much higher — 50 out of 288 against 47 out of 494 — and those of the cavalry were lower. In both these casualty lists about 8 per cent. of the losses fell upon the flying men.

The course of the war during 1917 may probably throw some light on the variations in the casualty list. Reasons of space make it necessary to confine ourselves to the western front. This, however, is not a very serious handicap, as the only heavy fighting in the outer theatres was in Palestine—at Gaza in March and around Jerusalem in the autumn—with a little in Mesopotamia.

The offensive campaign in the west began on April 9th with the Battle of Arras, which lasted for about a month. On June 7th Messines was attacked, and on July 31st the Third Battle of Ypres began. The second attack there followed on August 16th, and the third on September 20th, after which the battle lasted until the capture of Passchendaele on November 10th. Towards the end of that month came the sudden victory at Cambrai, followed by a British reverse.

With these facts before him, will the reader glance at the table of military casualties earlier in the chapter, and also at the one dealing with the killed alone? In the first three months of the year there was little doing, and yet the total casualties worked out at 81,000, just under 1,000 a day, and this may be taken as the usual cost of holding a hundred miles of line—10 men per mile per day. The figure is important because, roughly speaking, it means that all losses in excess of that average may be put down to some special cause.

In April the special cause was very distinctly present as far as the officers were concerned, but not as regards the men. The losses in officers rose suddenly from 1,765 in March to 4,381. This was obviously due to the casualties in the Battle of Arras, and in May those of the men there were brought in. They rose with equal rapidity from 31,619 in April to 107,075. Allowing something for the losses at Gaza we can estimate those at Arras as follows.

Battle of Arras

In April and May the total casualties came to 149,066. Something like 60,000 must be deducted for the ordinary toll of stationary warfare, and perhaps 10,000 for Gaza. It is not, therefore, unreasonable to state that Arras cost 80,000 casualties, a quarter perhaps being dead.

The heavy fighting did not die down appreciably, for almost before Arras was over Messines had begun. The June and July casualty lists would seem to point to the fact that this was a less expensive victory than Arras. Its price cannot, however, have been much less than 50,000 casualties included in the figures for June and July.

The officer casualties for August, over 5,000, 1 to every 10 men, are a clear intimation of another offensive, and this indeed began on July 31st and lasted until November. The September figures give some idea of its initial cost, but in October there was evidently very heavy fighting also, for that month shows the highest number of officer losses. November was the worst month of the year, and putting the two together it is evident that the fighting round Passchendaele at the end of October and the beginning of November was the most terrible of the year. Indeed, as the "Times" said: "The sufferings and hardships of our troops in this determined advance exceed anything endured in other actions of the campaign."

In October a Swedish paper gave some figures, the point of which was to show that the losses of British officers had

LIEUT. R. B. SAYER,
Royal Fusiliers.

FLIGHT-LIEUT. F. PEMBER REEVES,
R.N.A.S.

[*Lafayette.*
LIEUT. A. G. HARPER,
R.F.A.

[*Lafayette.*
LIEUT. J. E. RAPHAEL,
K.R.R.C.

been at that time unusually severe. The British War Office thought this important enough to reply to, and issued some figures about August and September. During the two months the losses reported from all theatres were 8,860—5,678 in August and 3,182 in September. The enumeration by the " Daily Telegraph " of those made public during the two months was 8,200, the difference being accounted for by the inevitable delay in issuing the names. The official statement said that the officer losses averaged 183 a day in August and 186 in September. The Swedish journal gave it for August as 511. The British figures included all casualties, however slight, and many of the officers had returned to duty before their friends heard that they had been wounded.

After all, men are more than numbers and aggregates of numbers. They are individuals, and it is as individuals— husbands, fathers, sons, and brothers —that their loss is really felt. The horror of a casualty list is not in the number, 32029 or 2013, attached to the name—not so much in its length—as in the names themselves. Boston, H. (Congleton), and Robinson, W. (Barnsbury, N.), mean grievous sorrow in some homes.

Outstanding political names

Each year the Roll of Honour contained names borne by the leaders of the State. A young man bearing the name of Gladstone was one of the first Members of Parliament to fall, while among living statesmen, Lord Lansdowne, Mr. Asquith, and Mr. Bonar Law lost sons, and nearly every other some more distant relative, perhaps even several. In the year under review the outstanding political names were those of Redmond and Primrose. The death of Major W. Redmond, M.P., aroused much sorrow when he died of wounds on June 7th. Everyone recognised the value of the lead he had given to Ireland, for though fifty-six years old he had taken a commission in the Royal Irish Regiment, and was fighting in its ranks when he fell; no mere lip service to the cause, but the real and abiding devotion of an heroic figure.

Mr. Neil Primrose, M.P., who was killed in Palestine later in the year, while leading his yeomen to the fight, inherited many of the brilliant gifts of his father, the Earl of Rosebery. Willingly he had given up his position in the Government, had left his young wife his wealth, and the high social and political position which was undoubtedly his, to go forward to danger and as it proved to death. It would be difficult to name two men more deservedly popular in the House of Commons than Mr. Redmond and Mr. Primrose, so that assembly, like the rest of the country, gave its best to meet the soldier's death. Two other Members of Parliament fell during the year. The Hon. F. W. S. McLaren, a son of Lord Aberconway, was accidentally killed while flying, and Major V. Fleming, an Oxfordshire member, was shot at the front.

Cabinet Ministers' losses

Early in the year Mr. Walter Long's son, Brigadier-General Walter Long, was killed in Greece, and Mr. Bonar Law, who more than most men shrouded his griefs from the public eye, mourned the loss of two. Brigadier-General J. E. B. Seely lost his eldest son, an officer in the Hampshires, and so did his brother, Sir C. H. Seely, Bart., M.P. Other members who lost sons during 1917 in the war were Sir George Younger, Bart., Mr. H. J. Tennant, Mr. H. Nuttall, the Hon. D. Carnegie, Mr. W. O'Malley, Mr. C. B. Stanton, the outspoken labour member, Mr. A. W. Soames, and Mr. E. Smallwood.

The House of Lords did not suffer quite as heavily in 1917 as in the earlier years of the war. Still, its losses were by no means negligible. Four peers—the Earl of Suffolk and Berkshire, the Earl of Shannon, Lord Abinger, and Lord Gorell—lost their lives, and so did the heirs of many more. Lord Binning, had he survived, would have been Earl of Haddington. Viscount Molesworth, Viscount Buxton, Lord Chelmsford, Governor-General of India, Lord Ashcombe, Lord Treowen (formerly Sir Ivor Herbert), Lord Barnard, Lord Shuttleworth, and Lord Gisborough, better known as Colonel Challoner, M.P., lost their eldest sons. Lord de Blaquière lost his heir, the second to die in the war, when the Laurentic went down.

Lord Rothermere's eldest son, Captain the Hon. H. A. V. St. George Harmsworth, of the Irish Guards, whose brother was killed while leading his men on the Ancre in 1916, died in February of wounds received in the Battle of Cambrai. Mr. Denis Buxton and Mr. L. U. Kay-Shuttleworth belonged to that group of young men of good family who had proved the possession of wide mental interests and generous social sympathies, the very negation of class feeling and class interests. A few weeks after his first loss, Lord Shuttleworth lost his remaining son, who was killed while cycling.

Lord Basil Blackwood, heir to his brother the Marquis of Dufferin, was a man who had played many parts in literary and political life, and who possessed varied social and other gifts. The Earl of Minto lost his brother and heir, the Hon. Esmonde Elliot, while Lord Robert Manners, killed while commanding a battalion of the Northumberland Fusiliers, was brother of the Duke of Rutland. The Earl of Airlie, the Earl of Portarlington, Lord Hastings, Lord de Freyne, and Lord Avebury were other peers who lost brothers during the year. Peers who lost younger sons included the Earl of Albemarle, the Earl of Denbigh, whose son, like nearly all the Feildings, was a Coldstream Guard, the Earl of Bradford, Lord Norton, Lord Langford, and Lord Kinnaird, who had lost his eldest son at an earlier period of the war. Lord E. B. Seymour, of Lord Strathcona's Horse, was a son of a late Marquis of Hertford.

Losses in the peerage

At least three baronets were killed or died on active service: Sir R. B. N. Gunter, Sir J. Swinnerton Dyer, of the Scots Guards, and Sir B. R. Williams. Baronets who lost their heirs in addition to Sir George Younger, M.P., and Sir Charles Seely, M.P., included Sir G. W. Truscott, (late Lord Mayor of London), Sir Hercules Langrische, Sir Bryan B. M. Leighton, Sir E. G. Loder, Sir William Osler, Sir Eustace Fiennes, M.P., Sir A. C. Churchman, Sir J. H. Strange, and Sir John Horner.

General Sir Edmund Allenby lost his only son, Sir C. H. Tupper lost a son, and so did Sir Victor Buxton, Bart., and Mr. E. Shortt, the Irish Secretary. The Bishop of Liverpool lost in Captain N. G. Chavasse, of the R.A.M.C., one whose glory it was and is to have won the V.C. on two separate occasions.

How universal and unsparing were the claims of the battlefield may be seen from the names of a few men, eminent in very different walks of life, who lost sons in 1917. Sir R. M. Kindersley, of the National War Savings Committee; Sir Thomas Barlow, the physician; Sir Edward Schäfer, F.R.S.; Mr. Justice Eve, Sir Francis Villiers, Sir David Semple, Sir Vincent Raven, Sir Emsley Carr, and Sir H. Crichton. Others include Mr. A. H. F. Lefroy, K.C., and Professor G. M. Wrong, both of Toronto; Mr. Lincoln Springfield, "London Opinion"; Mr. H. H. Statham, editor of the "Builder"; Professor W. H. Young, F.R.S., Rev. W. Hudson Shaw, Mr. Hartley Aspden, late of the Amalgamated Press; Mr. C. A. Vince, of Birmingham; Mr. W. Pember Reeves, Mr. Albert Gray, K.C., Sir Daniel Hall, Sir H. Montagu Allan, of Montreal; Sir George Adam Smith, Sir Marcus Samuel, Bart.; and Sir W. J. Lancaster.

Another class of men to suffer heavily was those who owed their position rather to their own gifts and qualities, athletic or literary, perhaps, than to any family connections. At the head of these should surely stand the name of Captain Albert Ball, V.C., the champion airman, for ordinary success in the Air Service, to say nothing of such a career as Ball's, needs unusual gifts of both mind and body.

Like earlier years, 1917 saw the deaths of several men who had made an impression upon the literary life of their time—the Sidneys of a later age—such as Edward Thomas,

LIEUT. N. O. DINGLEY,
Worcestershire Regt.

LIEUT. H. F. PICKER, M.C.,
R.F.

LIEUT. H. S. BLACKWOOD,
London Regt.

LIEUT. G. W. W. DENMAN-
DEAN, Royal Marines, R.N.D.

LIEUT. P. H. C. PYE-SMITH,
The King's (Liverpool Regt.).

LIEUT. HON. A. E. G. KEPPEL,
Rifle Brigade.

LIEUT. F. S. CARSE,
Australian Field Artillery.

LIEUT. HON. A. G. CUBITT,
Hussars.

LIEUT. F. TRUSCOTT, M.C.,
Suffolk Regt., attd. R.F.C.

LIEUT. C. H. E. BOULTON,
Q.O. Cameron Highlanders.

LIEUT. J. L. FOWLIE,
Highland Light Infantry.

SEC.-LT. R. COOPER,
Royal Warwickshire Regt.

SEC.-LT. W. H. HURST-
BOURNE,. R.F.A.

LIEUT. H. G. COLLINS,
R.F.C.

LIEUT. HON. A. M. KINNAIRD, M.C.,
Scots Guards.

SEC.-LT. G. G. SAMUEL,
West Kent Regt.

THE ROLL OF HONOUR, 1917.

Photos by Lafayette, Swaine, Bassano, and Speaight.

of the R.G.A., a man whose eyes were always opened to the fair beauty of England, an eager successor of Jefferies and Borrow, as well as a novelist, a critic, and the possessor of a singular charm of character. R. E. Vernède, of the Rifle Brigade, known as the creator of "Mr. Faviel," delighted thousands by the felicitous character of his verses written at the front, and no anthology of the war's poems would be complete without his "England to the Sea," "Before the Assault," and "To our Fallen."

To this company must be added the names of Francis Ledwidge, the Irish poet—who after fighting in Gallipoli and Serbia, fell in Flanders in July—Eugene Crombie, and Eric F. Wilkinson. Robert C. Jackson, of the Buffs, was no poet, but as a publisher of poetry he appreciated and encouraged those who were, and by his death his friends and the world of letters are the poorer. Ivan Heald was a notable writer, while N. M. Goddard, who wrote as Mark Darran, and W. H. Hurstbourne were journalists of great promise.

Poets and scholars who fell An enormous number of the fallen, as a cursory glance at any list of biographical notices showed, had already given proofs that they possessed qualities which would take them far on the road to success as scholars or professional men, but the great majority of these were able to do no more than this when the call came. Some few, however, had been already recognised by their fellows as masters in some branch of intellectual effort. Such were F. W. Hubback, lecturer in classics at Liverpool University; E. W. Webster, an authority on the Basque language, and Fellow of Wadham College, Oxford; C. N. S. Wolff and C. E. Stuart, Fellows of Trinity College Cambridge; A. H. Sidgwick, Fellow of University College, Oxford; and Charles Sproston, Fellow of Peterhouse, Cambridge. The latter was not only a most brilliant scholar, but also a distinguished athlete. C. D. McCourt was a chemist who had done great things in a short life, and the same may be said of a doctor, Major Sydney D. Rowland, a leading authority on vaccination. Captain A. B. E. Hillas, of the Gordons, was one of the outstanding scholars of Trinity College, Dublin. P. H. Shaw Stewart, Fellow of All Souls College, Oxford, was a loss to classical scholarship, and so was G. J. R. Brown, Fellow and Lecturer of Pembroke College. This was the third brilliant son lost during the war by Dr. John Brown, of Glasgow, a former Moderator of the Church of Scotland. A. G. Harper, also of Oxford, had been Professor of Botany at Madras, and E. S. Cardos, of the Buffs, had exhibited several pictures at the Academy. Such losses may give some idea of the type of men who fought and died for Britain. Captain J. G. Wilson, killed on February 1st, was the son of a colonel whose father fought at Waterloo, and whose great-grandfather fell at Minden. It was these picked men and not the weaklings whose lives were demanded by the insatiable god of war.

Some eminent "Blues"

The year 1917 added many more to the long list of fallen athletes. For instance, by October, Cambridge had had no fewer than 117 "Blues" killed. One of these was that fine athlete H. S. O. Ashington, who won three events in the University sports of 1913, this being a record feat, the more so because one of them was to beat C. B. Fry's famous long jump of 23 ft. 5 in. To match him Oxford lost J. E. Raphael, a great cricketer, but perhaps greater as a Rugby three-quarter. Other noted Rugby players to fall included T. A. Nelson, once the Oxford captain and a Scottish International; Lieut.-Colonel E. R. Mobbs, of Northampton, an English International; and Captain W. T. Forrest and the airman J. G. Will, two more Scottish Internationals. Others were Major Leonard Parker, Captain C. D. Baker, and L. C. Blencowe, Oxford Blues;

and B. R. N. Lewis and W. H. B. Baxter, Cambridge Blues. Famous rowing men to die were Lieut.-Colonel G. E. Hope, of the Grenadier Guards, a nephew of Lord Rosebery, who rowed for Oxford, 1906, and twice won the University sculls. Lieut.-Colonel R. O. Kerrison and Captain A. B. Close-Brooks, of Cambridge; the Australian, Mervyn B. Higgins, R. P. Hankinson, and A. G. Kirby, of Oxford. Of professional football players, Donald McLeod, the Scottish International, and Edwin Latheron, R.F.A., the English one, were killed in action. Harold A. Sloan was one of Ireland's finest amateur players at the Association game, eight International caps being his. Captain A. S. Taylor, R.A.M.C., had represented Ireland, and J. Y. M. Henderson had represented Scotland at the Rugby game, while Lieut.-Colonel Eric Greer, of the Irish Guards, was both a sportsman and an artist.

The losses fell upon every class of society, and although the story dwells of necessity upon the more familiar names, those of humbler and less prominent, but certainly not less gallant or patriotic, should not be forgotten. Their names, a legion, were in the papers day by day, and in many cases one of them represented the third or fourth sacrifice in a single home.

The losses of societies of all kinds may begin with those of two universities, Cambridge and Manchester. To June, 1918, Cambridge reported 2,269 men killed out of some 12,000 serving, and a little later Manchester gave 300 out of 2,000 as its figures, old and new, therefore, showing up equally well. So it was throughout. It was said in July that 302 solicitors and 200 of their articled clerks had fallen, and later that 162 barristers had met a like fate. Of the employees of the London County Council, 532 had lost their lives. The Prudential Assurance Company had lost 357 **From office,** members of its outdoor **church, and school** staff, and the "Times" 150 of its employees; 231 members of the Metropolitan Police Force had fallen, and 1,042 of the Artists Rifles. As a sample from a wider area, the small band of Rhodes scholars had lost 14 of their number.

FLAG-COM. THE HON. R. O. B. BRIDGEMAN, D.S.O., R.N

Reference has often been made to the public spirit of those who come from the homes of the clergy, but in the Great War many clergymen and ministers made the sacrifice themselves. In May, 1918, it was stated in Parliament that 86 chaplains had been killed. Of these 57 were Anglicans, 19 Roman Catholics, and 4 Presbyterians. Of these, perhaps, the best known was the Hon. M. B. Peel, vicar of Tamworth, and a son of the late Viscount Peel. Beyond these a certain number fell as actual combatants, these including the Rev. R. A. C. MacMillan, of the Seaforths, a most brilliant scholar, and at the time of his death minister of St. John's Presbyterian Church, Kensington, and the Rev. R. B. Sayer, the young minister of the Congregational Church at Herne Hill. Of clerical families the Bishop of Lincoln lost a son, and the Rev. Joseph Jackson, vicar of Bampton, Oxon, had two sons killed on the same day.

A writer in the "Times," musing over his old school's Roll of Honour, calculated that of his comrades there the war had taken 1 in 8, and that proportion is not an exaggerated one if the figures given by the various public schools are to be trusted. Eton gave 1,032 boys and 4 masters as her contribution; Dulwich 264 boys and 3 masters; the losses of Haileybury were 423, of King's School, Canterbury, 110; of University College School, 176; and of St. Paul's, 366. Bedford School had lost 330, the Leys 121, the Merchant Taylors 210, and the Oratory School 71. These figures are just a few taken at random, but they show how widespread was the national loss. It is quite certain those in the elementary schools were equally large.

SEC.-LT. LORD BASIL
BLACKWOOD,
Grenadier Guards.

SEC.-LT. E. H. ASPDEN,
Royal West Surrey Regt.

SEC.-LT. H. TENNANT,
Dragoon Guards and R.F.C.

SEC.-LT. A. L. SPRING-
FIELD,
Somerset Light Infantry.

SEC.-LT. R. C. JACKSON,
Machine Gun Corps.

SEC.-LT. THE EARL OF SHANNON,
Royal Fusiliers.

SEC.-LT. A. CROPPER,
Wiltshire Regt., attd. R.F.C.

SEC.-LT. I. AP R. OWEN,
R.F.C.

SEC.-LT. D. N. O'N.
HUMPHREY-DAVY,
Hampshire Regt.

SEC.-LT. J. M. PRESTON-MUDDOCK,
Yeomanry.

SEC.-LT. E. FOSTER,
Royal Fusiliers.

SEC.-LT. N. M. GODDARD,
S. Staffordshire Regt.

SEC.-LT. E. G. GOODMAN,
Dorset Regt.

SEC.-LT. J. C. TREDGOLD,
Royal Scots.

SEC.-LT. F. C. CARR,
Machine Gun Corps.

SEC.-LT. G. H. T. ROSS,
Essex Regt.

THE ROLL OF HONOUR, 1917.

Photo by Claude Harris, Lafayette, Bassano, Swaine, Walter Barnett.

LEADING EVENTS IN THE FOURTH YEAR OF THE WAR

For Earlier Events readers should consult the Synchronised Chronology at the end of Volume IX.

1917.

August.

4.—Beginning of the fourth year of the war.
10.—British capture Westhoek Village and Ridge.
14.—China declares war on Germany and Austria.
Battle of Marasesti (Rumania).
15.—**Canadians capture Hill 70.**
16.—British capture village of Langemarck.
18.—Italian offensive: Monte Nero to the sea.
19.—Italian advance on the Carso.
20.—Great French victory at Verdun.
Italian offensive on Isonzo and Carso.
22.—British advance near Ypres-Menin Road.
23.—Russians retire on Riga front.
24.—Italians carry Monte Santo.
French carry Hill 304 (Verdun).

September.

3.—**Germans take Riga.**
Gotha moonlight raid, Sheerness and Chatham.
4.—Gotha moonlight raid on London; 73 casualties.
8.—French carry Chaume Wood.
Kerensky-Korniloff crisis, Russia.
14.—Korniloff surrenders to Gen. Alexeieff.
15.—Russia proclaimed a Republic.
20.—**Great British victory Menin road.**
Germans capture Jacobstadt.
24.—Gotha raid on English coast and London.
25.—Airship raid on Lincoln and Yorks coast.
Gotha raid Kent, Essex coast, and S.E. London.
26.—Renewed British offensive east of Ypres.
28.—**British victory at Ramadie (Euphrates).**
29.—Gotha raid on London; 93 casualties.

October.

1.—Gotha raid on London; 48 casualties.
2.—H.M.S. Drake torpedoed.
4.—British victory Broodseinde Ridge.
6.—Peru and Uruguay break with Germany.
9.—Franco-British success east of Ypres.
Death of Sultan of Egypt.
Belgian troops capture Mahenge (G. E. A.).
11.—British occupy Ruponda (G. E. A.).
12.—Heavy fighting Passchendaele Ridge.
German troops occupy part of Oesel Island.
17.—Whole of Oesel in German occupation.
German naval victory Gulf of Riga.
British occupy Nyangao (G. E. A.).
German raid on convoy in North Sea.
19.—Zeppelin raid E. and N.E. Counties and London.
20.—Disaster to Zepps in France; five lost.
22.—Allied advance N.E. of Ypres.
23.—Great French thrust towards Laon.
24.—**Austro-Germans break through on Isonzo.**
25.—French advance on the Aisne.
Italian retreat from Plezzo Basin-Tolmino line.
28.—**Fall of Gorizia.**
29.—Fall of Udine.
First American shots fired in France.
30.—New British thrust on Passchendaele Ridge.
31.—Gotha raid London and S.E. Coast.
Italians fall back to Tagliamento.
British capture Beersheba.

November.

1.—Count Hertling German Chancellor.
Italians withdrawn behind the Tagliamento.
2.—Germans abandon the Chemin des Dames.
British naval success in the Kattegat.
5.—Enemy cross the Tagliamento.
British occupy Tekrit on Tigris.
6.—Italians fall back towards line of Piave.
Canadians capture Passchendaele village.
British capture Gaza.
8.—**Lenin's coup d'etat in Petrograd.**
British retire from Tekrit.
9.—**Supreme Allied Council created.**
General Diaz Italian Commander-in-Chief.
10.—Enemy captures Asiago.
12.—Enemy across the Piave.
15.—M. Clemenceau to form a Cabinet.
17.—**Jaffa (Joppa) occupied by British.**
Naval fight in Heligoland Bight.
18.—**Sir Stanley Maude dies at Bagdad.**
20.—**Great British Surprise Victory at Cambrai.**
21.—British capture Fontaine Notre Dame and Cantaing.
22.—Germans retake Fontaine Notre Dame.
23.—Severe fighting for Bourlon Wood.
26.—Lord Rothermere President Air Council.

December.

1.—British retake Gonnelieu.
German East Africa clear of enemy.
5.—British evacuate Bourlon Wood.
7.—General Allenby occupies Hebron.
U.S.A. at war with Austria.
9.—**Jerusalem surrendered to British.**
10.—Panama at war with Austria.
11.—Cuba at war with Austria.
12.—Germans raid convoy North Sea.
14.—Italians yield Col Caprile.
15.—Russo-German armistice signed.
16.—Italians win back Col Caprile positions.
18.—Civil war in the Ukraine.
21.—Italians recapture Monte Asolone.
22.—**Peace negotiations opened Brest Litovsk.**
23.—Austrians take Mt. di Val Bella.
25.—Fourth Christmas of the Great War.
27.—Sir Rosslyn Wemyss First Sea Lord.
29.—British advance north of Jerusalem.

1918.

January.

4.—British hospital-ship Rewa torpedoed.
6.—Day of National Intercession and Thanksgiving.
9.—H.M.S. destroyer Racoon sunk off N. coast of Ireland.

1918.

January.

11.—New campaign against Germans in Portuguese East Africa.
14.—British air raid on Karlsruhe.
New Man-Power Bill introduced.
Yarmouth bombarded by torpedo-boat destroyers.
Italian advance east of Brenta valley.
18.—Bolshevists dissolve Constituent Assembly.
20.—Breslau sunk, Goeben damaged, Dardanelles.
26.—Announced British line extended to south of St. Quentin.
27.—British air raid on Treves.
28.—Gotha raid on London; 231 casualties.
29.—**Italians capture Monte di Val Bella.**
30.—Gotha raid on Paris; 255 casualties.

February.

3.—Mtarika, in Lujenda valley, occupied.
5.—U.S. transport Tuscania torpedoed.
9.—Central Powers sign peace with Ukraine.
10.—Ex-Sultan of Turkey, Abdul Hamid II., dies.
15.—German destroyer raid in Dover Strait.
16.—Sir William Robertson resigns.
17.—Gen. Sir Henry Wilson appointed C.I.G.S.
18.—Sir W. Robertson accepts Eastern Command.
20.—British occupy Khan Abu Rayat.
21.—**Fall of Jericho.**
24.—Russia accepts Germany's terms.
Trebizond falls to Turks.
25.—Germans occupy Reval and Pskoff.
26.—Hospital-ship Glenart Castle torpedoed.

March.

1.—H.M. mercantile cruiser Calgarian torpedoed.
2.—**Peace Treaty signed at Brest Litovsk.**
5.—Preliminary peace signed between Rumania and Central Powers.
7.—Moonless Gotha raid on London; 65 casualties.
8.—Fighting at Houthulst Forest.
Gotha raid on Paris.
9.—British occupy Hit.
11.—Austrian air raid on Naples.
12.—Zeppelin raid on Yorkshire coast.
Germans occupy Abo (Finland).
Turks retake Erzerum.
13.—Germans occupy Odessa.
Zeppelin raid on Hartlepool.
21.—**Great German offensive towards Amiens.**
Naval fight off Dunkirk.
22.—British retire to line of Somme.
Allenby's troops cross the Jordan.
23.—Long-range gun shells Paris.
24.—Peronne and Ham lost.
British air raid on Cologne.
25.—Bapaume and Nesle lost.
French evacuate Noyon.
26.—Germans take Roye and Chaulnes.
British victory at Khan Baghdadie.
27.—German rush checked.
French lose Montdidier.
28.—Germans repulsed Arras and south of Scarpe.
29.—British holding firm north of Somme.
Paris church hit by long-range gun.
30.—Germans checked north and south of Somme.
31.—Franco-British troops recapture Hangard.

April.

1.—Hard fighting between the Luce and Avre.
3.—Germans land at Hango.
4.—Allied retreat continued east of Amiens.
5.—Germans attack near Albert.
Allied marines land at Vladivostok.
7.—Arab troops occupy Kerak.
9.—**Great German attack north of La Bassee.**
10.—Enemy established left bank of Lys.
British evacuate Armentieres.
11.—Germans capture Merville.
12.—Germans capture Neuve Eglise.
Zeppelin raid over Midlands.
British take Medo Boma (East Africa).
13.—Germans driven from Neuve Eglise.
Fall of Batum to Turks.
14.—Germans retake Neuve Eglise.
General Foch Commander-in-Chief in France.
15.—**Fall of Bailleul and Wulverghem to Germans.**
British fleet sweeps Kattegat.
16.—Germans take most of Messines Ridge.
17.—British unable to hold Wytschaete.
Bolo Pasha executed in Paris.
Belgian success near Bixschoote.
18.—French success on Amiens front.
Lord Derby Ambassador to France.
Lord Milner Secretary for War.
19.—British gains around Givenchy and Festubert.
20.—Naval skirmish in Heligoland Bight.
23.—**Naval Raid on Zeebrugge and Ostend.**
25.—Villers-Bretonneux regained from enemy.
26.—**Germans gain Kemmel hill.**
Sir William Weir Air Minister.
27.—Germans driven from Voormezeele.
British capture Kifri.
30.—Germans completely repulsed Third Battle of Ypres.
French regain Locre.

May.

1.—British capture Es Salt.
Germans occupy Sebastopol.
2.—French carry the Baume Wood.
5.—Lord French Lord-Lieutenant of Ireland.
7.—Peace signed between Rumania and Central Powers.
British occupy Kirkuk.
9.—**Vindictive sunk at Ostend Harbour.**
Italians storm Monte Corno.

1918.

May.

17.—Prominent Sinn Feiners arrested.
18.—**British daylight raid on Cologne.**
19.—British occupy Nanungu (German East Africa).
Gotha raid on London; 223 casualties.
Gotha raid British hospitals, Etaples.
25.—Italians take Monticello Pass.
27.—**Great German attack between Soissons and Rheims.**
28.—Germans cross the Vesle.
Americans take Cantigny.
29.—Germans capture Soissons.
30.—Germans capture Fère-en-Tardenois.
31.—Germans reach the Marne.

June.

1.—Germans take Neuilly St. Front.
2.—German advance Ourcq Valley.
3.—German onslaught held up.
4.—German submarines off American coast.
6.—Franco-American success in Veuilly-la-Poterie-Bussiares region.
Hospital ship Königin Regentes mined.
7.—British regain Bligny and French Veuilly-la-Poterie.
8.—Hague Conference on Prisoners.
9.—**Germans' Montdidier-Noyon offensive.**
10.—Germans take Méry, Belloy, and St. Maur.
11.—Brilliant French counter-stroke between Rubescourt and St. Maur.
12.—Germans reach south bank of Matz.
14.—Montdidier-Noyon offensive closed.
15.—**Austrian offensive from Asiago plateau to sea.**
16.—Austrians reach west bank of Piave.
17.—Austrians checked in mountain section.
18.—Austrians fail to progress on west bank of Piave.
German attack on Rheims fails.
20.—Severe fighting on the Piave.
22.—Austrian offensive at standstill.
23.—**Austrians retreat in disorder.**
24.—Italians recover whole of Montello.
25.—Allies in Italy take 20,000 prisoners.
27.—Destroyer action off Belgian coast.
Hospital-ship Llandovery Castle torpedoed.
28.—British gain east of Nieppe Forest.
29.—British raid on gas factory at Mannheim.
Italians regain Monte di Val Bella.

July.

1.—American troops carry Vaux village.
2.—Italian success on Monte Grappa.
3.—French advance between Autriches and Moulin-sous-Touvent.
Death of Lord Rhondda.
Death of Sultan of Turkey.
4.—Australians and Americans capture Hamel.
6.—Piave delta finally cleared of enemy.
Franco-Italian offensive in Southern Albania.
Count Mirbach murdered at Moscow.
8.—French gain east of Villers-Cotterets.
Italians win passage of Vojusa, Albania.
9.—Resignation of Von Kuhlmann announced.
Admiral von Hintze German Foreign Minister.
Mr. J. R. Clynes Food Controller.
Gen. Horvath forms new Siberian Government.
12.—French take Castel and Auchin Farm.
Announced allied force on Murman coast.
14.—Czecho-Slovaks capture Kazan.
15.—**Great German attack east and west of Rheims**; to east enemy held by Gen. Gouraud's armies; to west they advance to depth of three miles, crossing Marne at Fossoy.
16.—Germans gain ground towards Epernay: Americans recover ground north of the front St. Agnan-la Chapelle.
Ex-Tsar Nicholas of Russia shot by Bolshevists.
17.—Germans reach Nauteuil and Pourcy.
18.—**Great French counter-attack** from Fontenoy to Belleau, west of a line between Soissons and Chateau-Thierry.
Gen. Gouraud retakes Prunay.
19.—Further French and American progress towards Soissons-Chateau-Thierry Road.
British airmen bomb Zeppelin base at Tondern.
20.—**Germans recross the Marne.**
Liner Justicia torpedoed and sunk.
21.—**French retake Chateau-Thierry.**
22.—Allies cross Marne at Chassins and Passy.
French and Americans reach line Bezu-Epieds.
Gen. Gouraud reoccupies all his old positions between the Suippes and Massiges.
23.—Continued French advance towards Fère-en-Tardenois.
French advance towards the Avre Valley.
24.—Progress north of Chateau-Thierry for two miles.
25.—Allies win Forest of Fère and La Croix Rouge Farm.
Oulchy-le-Chateau taken.
26.—Germans give way on Marne towards Epernay.
French recover Reuil.
27.—**German retreat extending.**
28.—Allies force passage of the Ourcq and take Fère-en-Tardenois.
29.—French advance N.E. of Oulchy-le-Chateau and take Grand Rozoy.
Allies win Sergy.
30.—German resistance stiffening.
Allies take Ronigny and St. Gemme.
Australians capture Merris.

August.

1.—Allied advance north of the Ourcq.
2.—**French retake Soissons.**
British advance west of Ancre River.
3.—Germans withdraw to north bank of Vesle.
Ambulance ship Warilda torpedoed.

END OF VOLUME XI.

THE GREAT WAR

VOLUME XII

Subject Index to THE GREAT WAR. Vols. I. to XII.

Black Roman numerals indicate the number of the volume, ordinary figures the first page of each chapter.

A Glorious Day for Britain's Navy

Admiral Beatty acknowledges the cheers of his men, after receiving the surrender of the German High Sea Fleet.

THE GREAT WAR

THE STANDARD HISTORY OF
THE WORLD-WIDE CONFLICT

EDITED BY

H. W. WILSON

Author of "With the Flag to Pretoria"
"Japan's Fight for Freedom" etc.

and

J. A. HAMMERTON

Editor "Harmsworth History of the World"

PROFUSELY ILLUSTRATED

VOLUME XII

LONDON
THE AMALGAMATED PRESS LIMITED
1919

CONTENTS OF VOLUME XII

COLOURED PLATES

THE GREAT WAR

THE STANDARD HISTORY OF THE WORLD-WIDE CONFLICT

VOLUME 12

CHAPTER CCLIV.

THE FOURTH YEAR—THE DARKEST HOUR BEFORE THE DAWN— VICTORY AT LAST IN SIGHT.

By H. W. Wilson.

Russia's Collapse and Germany's Increased Strength—Unequalled Gravity of the Problem before the Allies—Effects of Military Conservatism and Political Drift—Conflict between Brute Violence and the Laws of Humanity and Justice—All Free Nations Enrolled in Defence of Right—Moltkeism, Marxism, and Bolshevism—The Mailed Fist in Finland—Examples of German Devilry—Murders of Prisoners and Outrages at Sea—Tourist Picnics to Scenes of Teutonic Crime—Perfidy of German Diplomacy—Crœsus on the Throne and Crœsus on the Funeral Pyre—Britain Transformed—Ludendorff's Boast and German Dreams of Victory—The Cyclone of March, 1918—Benefits Seized from Disaster—Allied Command Unified—The Third Great German Offensive—Austria's Failure on the Piave—The Worst Hours Over—Foch's Irresistible Counter-stroke—Developments in Siberia and Central Asia—The Dawn in Sight.

THE fourth year of the war was one of the most terrible twelvemonths through which civilised man has passed. When it opened, the Russian Revolution was in full swing and the rout which had sealed the doom of the old Russia had taken place on the Galician front, though the Peace of Brest Litovsk had not been made. If a nation is that for which its sons will die, Russia had ceased to be such. This Russian collapse vitally affected the Allies in the west. Their offensives were beginning to break down before the increasing resistance of the German armies, heavily reinforced by picked men and masses of artillery—much of it traitorously surrendered—from the eastern front. On the Carso and Isonzo, General Cadorna's troops, in the positions which they had taken up to render the maximum of support to Russia by engaging as large as possible an Austrian army, were now themselves in peril. The American forces

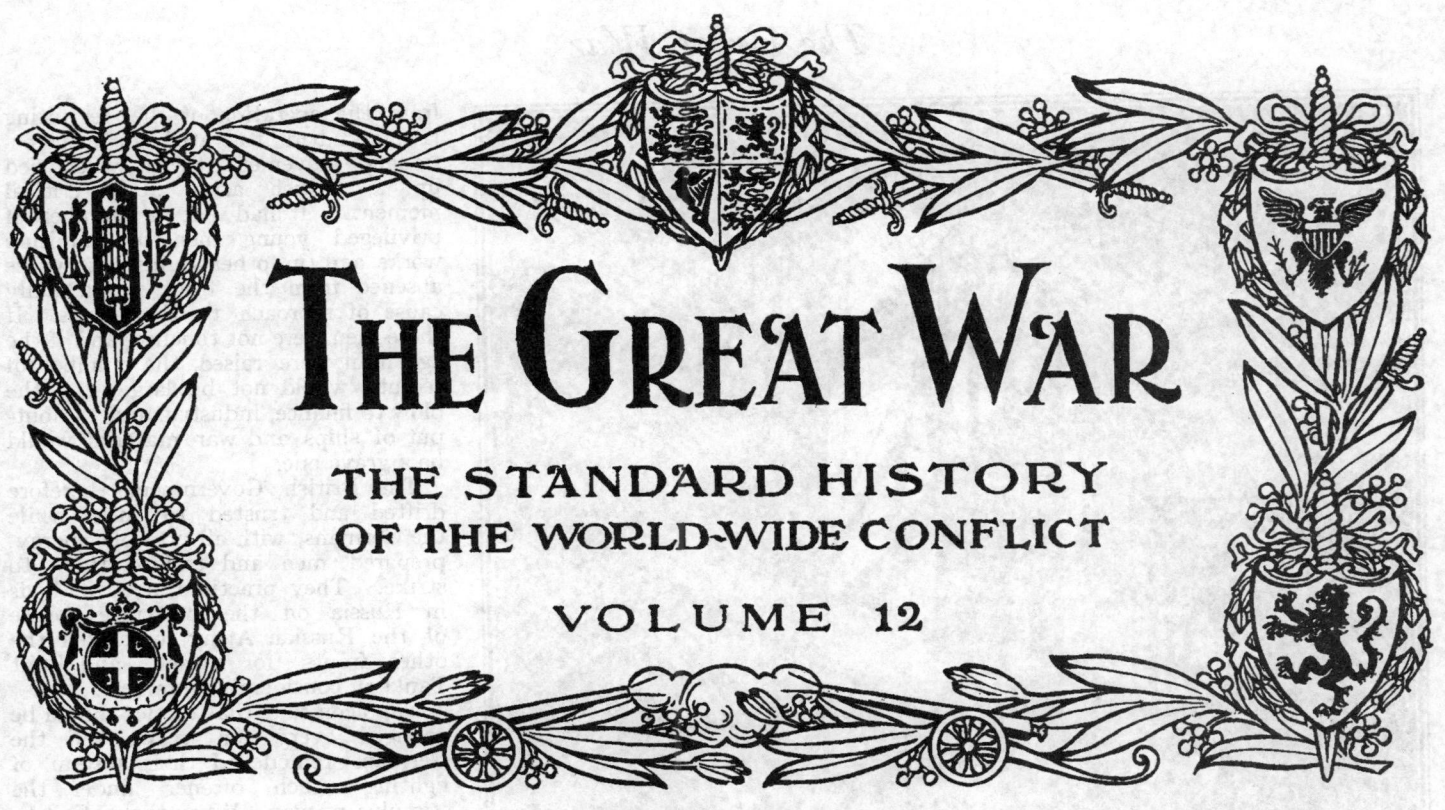

SURRENDER OF JERUSALEM.
Historic photograph taken on the morning of December 9th, 1917, when the Mayor (with walking-cane and cigarette) and his white-flag party met the first British outposts before Jerusalem.

were only beginning their training, and though a small American army had appeared in Europe the problem for the Allies was one of unequalled gravity. It was to resist the German legions, strengthened as these were by the armies which had hitherto been occupied on the eastern front, until the American units could complete their equipment and training and could arrive. The problem was complicated by the utter uncertainty which attached to the submarine position. No one could say what the submarines might do. The British Admiralty, then unreformed and ill-organised for modern war, had failed to deal energetically with a situation which was full of peril. The night was indeed black, and the safety of the Allies was further endangered by an agitation proceeding openly or stealthily in Great Britain, in France, in Italy, to provoke such anarchy as had ruined Russia, paralyse the armies, and by giving the battle to Germany to destroy for ever human freedom.

A

GERMAN METHOD OF HONOURING GOOD FRIDAY.
Interior of the Paris church of St. Gervais, hit by a shell during the long-range bombardment of the capital on Good Friday, 1918. One hundred and fifty worshippers were victims of this attack.

from the operation of the recruiting law, and had tolerated an insurrectionary movement there which tied up a British army at a critical moment. It had left a number of privileged young men in munition works and in other industries whose absence from the front was a daily cause of reproach to themselves. If these men were not touched, and if the age limit were raised, the number of recruits would not be large, and the blow to finance, industry, and the output of ships and war material would be a grave one.

The British Government therefore drifted and trusted to luck, while the Germans, with all possible energy, prepared men and trained them to strike. They practised new methods in Russia on the prostrate corpse of the Russian Army, organised the other fronts for attack, and built Tanks in considerable numbers.

Napoleon said that tactics should be changed every ten years, and the Germans remodelled their system of fighting much oftener under the stimulus of war. When their effort to " waltz through France " and gain a swift and decisive victory on the Marne broke down, they introduced trench war on a colossal scale and perfected the instruments for it with wonderful ingenuity, holding up the Allies for years. Tanks and aircraft might have enabled the Allies to break through, but, unfortunately, both these new forms of weapons were at the outset distrusted by military conservatism in the allied councils. Each side had increased the number of machine-guns and automatic guns to such an extent that a comparatively small force of infantry and machine-gunners could hold up any attack if they were not taken by surprise or outflanked. The artillery strength of each side was so nearly equal, and the ground in most sectors was so torn by projectiles, that all movements became most difficult except at points where the soil was firm or there had been little fighting. It was as though the armies had been sundered by an all but impassable morass.

The best soldiers on both sides deplored the system of trench warfare with its habituation of men to the defensive. "Troops who get used to holding immensely strong positions like these with what is, as war goes, a minimum of danger, must . . . lose the aggressive spirit," wrote one able British officer from France. "What one would like is two or three months of really savage fighting, followed by **Drawbacks of** by peace. . . . This sort of war is ruinous **trench warfare** to troops. They necessarily lose marching power and the charging spirit. This trench life in any case is not good for moral. How does anyone suppose the troops will face the open after it ? "

The Germans found that their dug-outs were too comfortable and secure. They were so safe that the men were reluctant to emerge from them when attacks came, despite the iron discipline which prevailed in the German Army. Nor were the losses in trench war really small. Day after day and week after week men became casualties or were invalided ; the wastage was continuous, and it brought no result. The German Staff therefore cast about for the best method of

All the factors in those sad hours seemed to work in the German cause. The weather itself appeared to obey the bidding of " the old Prussian God," and to serve William II. the Treaty-Breaker. Each recurrent allied offensive was wrecked by unfavourable conditions. The British Government failed to realise the consequences of the Russian collapse and to take timely steps to meet the danger from the increased strength of Germany.

The gradual exhaustion of the nation's man-power had left most of the British units seriously below their establishment. It became necessary, failing a **Problems of** change in the recruiting law, to break up **man-power** one of the four infantry battalions in each British brigade and use it for drafts. The strength of the British brigade was thus reduced by one-fourth, and the burdens which each battalion had to endure were correspondingly augmented.

At the same time the Government was faced by serious difficulties. It had not the courage to enforce compulsion equally and evenly. It had unjustly exempted Ireland restoring the war of movement, arrogantly confident in its generalship and system.

The problem was to surprise the enemy and bring up masses of men without allowing hostile airmen to notice their coming. This was a business demanding ingenuity and skill. M. Abel Ferry, a former French Under-Secretary for War, said in 1918 that when, in 1915, 1916, and 1917, the French Higher Command was urged to adopt surprise tactics the Staff officers uniformly replied : " How do you expect us to conceal from the enemy the concentration of 300,000 men ? " The Germans, however, in 1918, solved the problem which the Allies had previously believed insoluble.

A few weeks later Marshal Foch, the new Allied Commander-in-Chief, turned the German methods against themselves with such remarkable success that his great counter-attack upon the front between Soissons and Château-Thierry caught the German Staff entirely off its guard ; and on August 8th Sir Douglas Haig's sudden onslaught on the enemy upon the Somme repeated Marshal Foch's feat. So that surprise, which as an **Transformation** element seemed to have vanished from **of war in 1918** war with the development of the allied and German air forces, was restored, and generalship was given new scope for action.

This was the great transformation which war underwent in 1918. The details of the new German methods are set forth in the succeeding chapters dealing with the great offensive, which shows how the German Staff treated the problem. General Ludendorff, however, was very greatly helped by the treason of the Bolshevists. This provided him with a very marked superiority in men, and the chance of giving the special training which his troops required for the attack. Some forty divisions, after a thorough training, were gradually brought to the west and added to the one

hundred and sixty divisions already there. Only thirty-five German divisions were left in Russia and the Ukraine, and these were composed of old men and ineffective material. Until the Allies adapted themselves to the new German form of attack, and until the German advantage in numbers passed with the arrival of American troops, the situation was one of particular danger ; there were weeks and months when the fate of freedom trembled in the balance. But the transformation of war had this result. It proved that with generalship and a sufficiency of men any front could be broken through. It gave a new certainty of ending the struggle if only the Allies could hold till the Americans arrived. The new American **Coming of** Army would be just such a force as the **the Americans** Allied Supreme Command would require to strike the deadly blow. It was composed, as Captain von Salzmann wrote in the German Press in July, " of fresh young men with unshaken nerve," not of worn and middle-aged men who had spent years in the trenches under fire. It had never acquired the spirit of the defensive. It had reaped all the benefit of British and French experience. It was provided with the finest weapons which the ingenuity of the Allies could devise.

The British, French, and Italian Armies, after long years of desperate war, fighting continuously, had slowly worn down the German strength, exhausted the German energy, and killed the pick of the German officers and soldiery. Their frightful sacrifices had not been in vain. Over the graves of their dead the new armies were to march to victory, and those dead had made the road.

If an enduring peace was to be assured, freedom to be protected for a generation from further treachery, and if, as President Wilson said, the world was to be made safe for democracy, a final trial was necessary, in which the German

SCOTTISH TROOPS TAKING PART IN A FRENCH CORPUS CHRISTI CELEBRATION.

Procession through a small French town in celebration of the Corpus Christi festival of May 30th, 1918. A detachment of the Catholic members of a Highland regiment stationed in the neighbourhood took part in the festival. At the request of the Vatican the British abstained from making any bombing raids on Cologne and other German towns on that day, though the Germans did not thus reciprocate this consideration.

END OF A TORPEDOED TRANSPORT.
Remarkable photograph of a British transport torpedoed by an enemy submarine in the Eastern Mediterranean. Taken at the moment that the vessel was sinking, with members of the crew still swarming down the ropes.

"'Might is right' must be the motto of every intending colonist. Friendly persuasion will never induce a native to carry a tin box for you. He will only do it if he knows that his refusal will result in his hut being burnt down." No Englishman could have written that passage, which explains Germany's utter failure as a colonising Power. "Torture," says Bishop Weston, who had seen the Germans at their work, "is a recognised method of dealing with Africans." The German naturalist and ex-official Schillings, in 1912, estimated that in the German colonies no fewer than 200,000 natives had been mercilessly shot down in a few years as insurgents. The German massacres in Belgium and Northern France were anticipated in China, in South-West Africa—wherever the German flag flew.

Never had the conflict between brute violence and the laws of humanity and justice proceeded to such lengths.

Staff should put forth all its strength and be worsted at its own game. Behind this struggle between the two Staffs, between the free armies in the west and the forces of Germanism, an even deeper conflict proceeded between two hostile conceptions of life, which had to be fought out to the bitter end. No compromise between them was possible. The German conception was that force knows no limits of right, ruth, or humanity, and that the State is above all law. The Germans had seized upon and perverted the doctrine of Machiavelli that there are two worlds in man—one the world of force or matter in which morality does not exist, which is ruled by the principle "war is war," in which gentleness and restraints are manifestations of sheer imbecility; the other, the world of the spirit, in which morality does exist, but which is entirely outside the sphere of statesmanship. The German asked not "Is this right or wrong?" but "Is it profitable to Germany?" The free nations had passed through the discipline of Greek and Roman thought. "Their strength," said Dr. Mühlon of the Romans, in his famous Diary, "lay not in their armies, but in their unswerving sense of justice." Britain and France and Italy had been Roman or Roman provinces, and the Roman habit of mind, with its reverence for law and eternal justice, underpinned their seemingly chaotic system.

Teuton doctrine and allied ideals

It is not to be pretended that at every moment in their national history they had acted upon the ideal; but the ideal was always there, burning before their eyes, and no Government of theirs could have existed which did not generally conform to it. It swayed them in their treatment of intellectually inferior races. They acted not as masters, but as trustees—as men who themselves would be held responsible for their acts if they fell away from justice. An impassable gulf yawned between their ideas and the ideas expressed by German statesmen and colonisers.

"Germany," said Dr. Mühlon, "knows no other power on earth but compulsion." "It is impossible to get on in Africa without cruelty," said General Liebert, Governor of German Africa. "I felt embittered against the red-tapists who sit East in their comfortable offices and preach humanity," wrote the Duke of Mecklenburg in his account of his African travels.

IN READINESS FOR ACTION.
British warship at sea, with her heavy guns and secondary armament trained out. During the fourth year of war the Navy was engaged in breaking the force of the submarine campaign and covering the passage of American troops.

If Germany had triumphed after her violation of Belgian neutrality, after the series of falsehoods which she urged as her pretext for beginning war, if she who, as Colonel Feyler, a neutral, said, "made war with a lie," had succeeded, then force would have been enthroned as right and the world have passed into a night so black and terrible that the mind shrinks from contemplating it. Each successive violation of the law by her brought, however, fresh antagonism. The attack on Serbia—lawless and wicked as it is now known to have been, planned at Miramar by William II. and the Archduke Francis Ferdinand, reconsidered in its details at Konopischt, carried out with ruthless violence and unequalled perfidy after the famous Crown Council at Potsdam on July 5th, 1914—brought Russia into the field. Because Russia was involved, Germany attacked France to prevent her from helping her ally. But to defeat France rapidly the German Staff decided that it was necessary to move through Belgium, because the French frontier was too strong to be penetrated in such a swift onslaught as the German Government intended. When Belgium was assailed, Great Britain was inevitably drawn in. The cry of agony went up from Belgium and Northern France when the German Staff, in pursuance of its own doctrine, that war knows no laws and restraints, with deliberate cruelty violated all the conventions that centuries of progress had imposed. It was not without effect upon Italy and the United States. Italy entered the field, in one of the darkest hours through which the Allies had passed, with a spirit such as informed Dante and Mazzini—Mazzini,

All free nations banded together who protested against " the immoral indifference that gives Europe up to the dictatorship of force." Then came a long pause while the tide of battle rolled backwards and forwards, and, finally, Germany, spurning all restraints at sea, with a savage disregard for right and wrong, and as the sole means of vanquishing Great Britain, in whom she now recognised, as one of her newspapers said, " the most terrible and stubborn of enemies," turned to her submarine campaign. This inevitably brought in the United States. Throughout the fourth year of the war, for the first time in history, all the free nations were enrolled in the defence of right, and the process could go no farther. " The verdict of the whole earth is just." St. Augustine's famous saying was true. The League of Nations had come into visible existence. Twenty-one peoples were banded together to secure peace. Against them, on Germany's side, were retrograde States with a record of treachery, cruelty, and injustice— Austria - Hungary, whose whole system was built upon the fraudulent manipulation of various nationalities and votes; Bulgaria, whose people had turned upon their liberator Russia and their kindred Serbs with shameful perfidy ; and Turkey, red with the blood of massacres.

Of the two forms of German attack upon freedom and justice, the first was Moltkeism, or Militarism, and it achieved extraordinary results before the turn of the tide came in mid-1918. The other form was Marxism, or Internationalism, and it was not less perilous to freedom, seeing that it caused the suicide of Russia in early 1918. The principle of Marxism, or Internationalism, was in essence the same as that of Moltkeism. It was that force, not righteousness, rules the world, and that war is the only conceivable condition for men. Both doctrines obtained a certain passing countenance from Darwinism as it was distorted by German pedants, who made of it a merciless and unrestrained struggle between all living things for the survival of the strong. The weak man and the weak nation were to be destroyed. The devil was to take the hindmost. But whereas Moltkeism preached war between nations as the means of reaching the goal, Marxism preached war between classes. With Moltkeism the strongest nation was to survive ; with Marxism the strongest class was to devour the others. The German exponents of Marxism were very careful to exempt Germany from the operation of their principle. All classes in Germany were to co-operate in destroying other Powers. Marxism was an article made in Germany for consumption by foreign dupes and traitors. The German Marxists, on the **Moltkeism and Marxism** outbreak of war, did their best to paralyse France and Belgium. They sent Herr Müller, the German Socialist deputy, by motor-car to Paris on August 1st, 1914, to persuade the French Socialists to refuse the French Government war credits, and thus stop the French mobilisation when German mobilisation was already well advanced. Three days later they voted the German war credits *en masse*, showing, as Professor Ramsay Muir aptly remarked, that " they not only had not the power to act, they had not the will." A few weeks later, quite unabashed, they sent three Socialist members of the Reichstag and Dr. Foster, editor of an important Socialist newspaper, to Brussels to persuade the Belgian Socialists to

" IT IS FREEDOM AND PEACE THAT WE BRING."
Some of the 15 in. guns of a British warship. Inset : Forecastle of a British battleship speeding through the North Sea. At the top : 15 in. naval guns seen from above.

ITALIAN GUNNERS' SACRIFICE.

An incident of the Italian retreat under Austro-German pressure in the autumn of 1917. To prevent the enemy from capturing their gun, the Italian artillerymen hurled it from its mountain height into the valley below.

ease Germany's task by submitting. "You ought," said these worthies, "to have let us pass. You would have been handsomely compensated by our Government. National honour is mere middle-class idealism with which Socialists have nothing to do. International treaties do not hold in the event of war."

This German origin of Marxism will explain the powerful support which the Germans everywhere received from the International Socialists, many of whom were Germans or of German origin and connection, and all of whom were the slaves of German ideas, rhetoric, and catchwords. The apostles of brute force, feeling themselves outcasts in a world which rejected their doctrines, drew ever closer together. A vast propaganda, subventioned from Germany, infected the Allies.

Insidious German methods In Russia, so far back as 1905, the German Staff had decided to assist the Anarchists. It as certainly maintained similar relations with the same sections in Italy, France, and the United States, and probably—though here definite evidence is lacking owing to the inertia and timidity of the British Government—in Great Britain. Proof of such support was obtained in France in the Bolo and Duval trials; in the United States in the multitudinous secret documents seized by the American Government; in Italy in the treason trials. The Germans not only used the Marxists, Internationalists, and Anarchists to gain their ends, they also worked both through them and with other means upon a different class of men, for whom they coined the expressive word "softies"—sentimentalists, busybodies, politicians of the meaner type, and persons whose mania it was to advertise themselves. Through these people they spread the idea that an allied victory was out of the question. Clausewitz once said that there were two ways of securing triumph in war. The first was to beat the enemy's armies in the field. The second was to convince the enemy population that there was no hope of success. Moltkeism practised the first ; Marxism the second method— both German militarists and allied defeatists converging on the same result, the triumph of Germany and the replacement of freedom by despotism.

As Moltkeism was visibly doomed at the close of the fourth year of the war in the military sphere, so Marxism had been tried and had failed decisively in the political sphere in the winter of 1917-18. The régime of Lenin and Trotsky proved a nightmare of tyranny and human agony. Its principle was thus brutally expressed by the German Professor Rohrbach, one of the persons responsible for its introduction : "Great Russia for the Bolshevists, and the Bolshevists for us." Freedom of speech, freedom of the Press, freedom of thought, freedom of life were suppressed with a savagery never witnessed before under even the vilest despots. There was something infinitely tragic in the domination of a once great people by such miserable miscreants. The benefits which they had promised, when class war was kindled on the most gigantic scale and civilisation wrecked within their country, did not arrive. On the contrary, Russia wallowed in famine, pestilence, wretchedness, and bloodshed. Germans, Bolshevists, Ukrainians, Cossacks, Caucasians, Tartars, Turks, Constitutionalists, Finns, White Guards, Czecho-Slovaks, Austrian and German prisoners, fought over her rotting carcass. German troops drenched with gas-shells villages whose peasants had flattered themselves with the hope that by making peace they could seize the landowners' estates and enjoy the plunder. A fearful picture of the result which followed when a whole country was handed over to German emissaries and homicidal maniacs was painted in a proclamation issued on June 5th, 1918, to the Peasants' Councils by the Bolshevists :

Russia's awful tragedy of "peace"

Brother peasants, brother peasants, we are starving. We in the towns are receiving only two ounces of bread, and even that is not secure. Our children, our wives, our mothers are starving. . . The enemy has cut off many of the provinces in which grain exists. The enemy has robbed many rich provinces. . . If you do not send grain to the towns the workmen's authority must perish.

In July the Bolshevist newspaper " Izvestia " stated that the supply of bread had fallen to one quarter of its former figure, that the whole population of the northern provinces was starving, that the bread ration was nowhere more than from 2¾ to 5¼ ounces a day, and in several districts was less than one ounce. A German expert who investigated the position reported in July that the people in the Russian towns were in a state of physical weakness from want of food, which could only be understood by those who had actually seen them. They would fall ready victims to cholera and typhus as these pestilences spread. Such were the economic results of Marxism when it was tried in Russia. They were not alluring to other nations.

The German propagandists and the Internationalists had ceaselessly repeated the fable that it was a matter of indifference to the worker what flag flew over him, and whether he was controlled by William II.'s armed legions or by capitalists of his own kin. Here again the Germans had confuted their own falsehood. They applied in Russia, Northern France, and Belgium the methods of the slave-driver. On June 25th, 1918, Herr Haase, a German Socialist, denounced the German Government for practising the worst cruelty on the Russian population :

At Riga some hundreds of persons have been thrown into prison. Among these political prisoners were six women, one of them with a child of two. Children of ten were sentenced to some years' imprisonment for concealing arms. A lad of fifteen was sentenced to death because he had distributed a proclamation, as was alleged. There was no proof against him. Two sisters named Datt were condemned to death on the same charge, and one of them, Julia, was shot.
More terrible still are the tortures which the German authorities inflict in prisons. A man was arrested because he was found with a number of circulars. As he declined to state where they had been printed, two men beat him on the head for several minutes. He still refused to answer, and they undressed him and with a long whip of wire thongs covered with indiarubber beat him all over the body, making him hold his arms above his head.

Explanation
Farthest German Advance up to Battle of the Marne, Sept. 6th 1914.
After Battle of the Aisne, and Allied Retreat from Antwerp, Oct. 19th 1914.
After Hindenburg's Retreat on the Somme, March 19th 1917.
Before Great German Offensive, March 21st 1918.
After Second Battle of the Marne, July 18th 1918.
The Great German Offensives of 1918
Battle for Amiens, March 21st
" " Channel Ports, April 9th
Great Thrust for Paris, May 27th
Battle of Montdidier-Noyon, June 9th
" " Reims, July 15th
Note.- The line here given indicates the farthest German Advance in each battle
Battle-Line on August 1st 1918. (Coloured Green)
English Miles
Railways
Canals
NORTH SEA
ENGLISH CHANNEL
STRAIT OF DOVER
ENGLAND
HOLLAND
FRANCE
GERMANY
LUXEMBOURG
BRUSSELS
PARIS
Copyright
The Great War

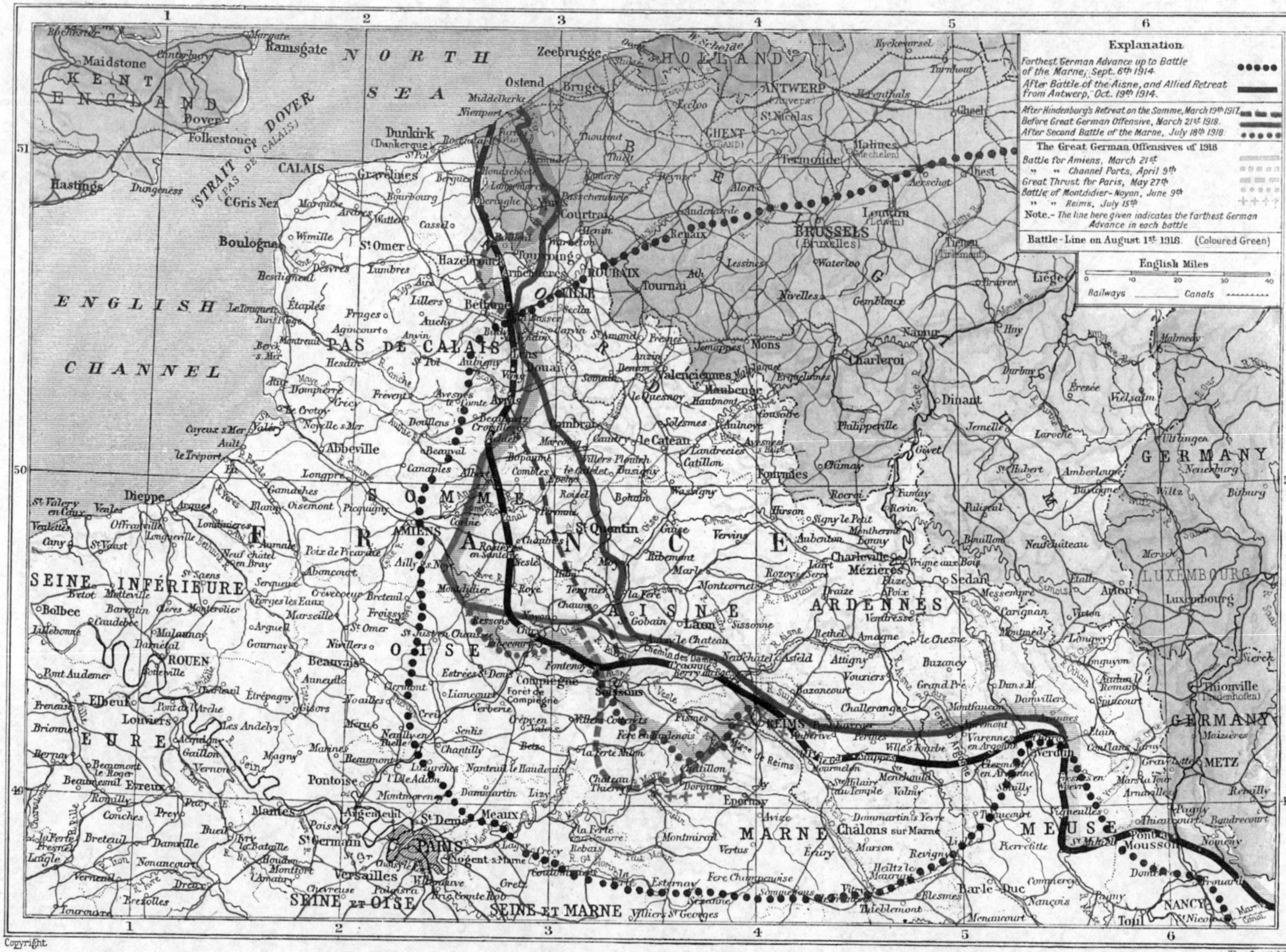

THE MAIN BATTLE LINES OF THE WESTERN FRONT, 1914–1918.

Having beaten him until he was helpless, they fastened him to a bench and beat him till it broke beneath the blows. They then threatened that they would hang him to the ceiling by his feet if he did not reply. They left him to recover consciousness, and from 9 p.m. to 1 a.m. thrashed him till his body was one large wound. On February 16th he was sentenced to death by court-martial, neither counsel nor witnesses being present.

He managed to write to us, and his letter reached us. This is what he wrote : "Friends, my last greeting. I ask one thing only before I die. Can you not reveal to the world the truth about the part played by 'German liberators' ?"

Yet after this the German Socialist party in the Reichstag voted the German war credits in July, 1918.

German barbarism in Finland and Belgium In Finland the Germans seized 73,000 workers and shot hundreds of them, deporting others to forced labour (or slavery) in Germany. They arrested fifty Socialist members of the Finnish Parliament and shot them all. In the Ukraine their cruelties were so great that the peasants rose in insurrection, and in July, 1918, 75,000 men were in the field, offering a feeble resistance in scattered bands. Prisoners taken by the Germans were instantly shot or led away to slavery. In Belgium the same methods were still applied, though there the Germans had no excuse of Anarchism or armed resistance. The appeal of the Belgian workmen to the Socialist parties denounced the Germans as the most cruel and merciless of slave-dealers :

Every day a new district sees the slave-raiders at work. A formidable array of machine-gunners and soldiers conducts a pitiful warfare against the poor Belgian workpeople.

The whole working population of Belgium is threatened with slavery, brutalisation, and death.

Do you know what kind of a wage is flung to their victims by the Germans ? Fourpence a working day ! And the food ! The Belgian civilians who have come back from Germany after three months of detention have lost one-third of their weight. They are unrecognisable, anæmic, ill.

"Germany," said Dr. Mühlon, "needs not only a new brain but also a new heart and a new hide. Europe was beginning to adopt a nobler religion, but she continues in her pagandom."

Thus it is true to say that, as the fourth year closed, the war had more than ever become a holy one—a struggle against the kingdom of hell. "Germany," wrote a neutral observer so far back as 1915, "is the most absolute synonym of evil that history has ever seen." No sign of repentance was shown by the German nation or by its rulers. As they had begun, so they continued. There was no mitigation in the fourth year of the cruelties which they had systematically practised since its outbreak. It is now known from Dr. Mühlon's Diary that the terrible order to murder prisoners in 1914 emanated from William II. himself. "The Kaiser himself said in the presence of an assemblage of officers that he had enough prisoners ; he hoped the officers would see to it that no more were taken. This news is quite trustworthy. What a sequel to the Kaiser's earlier order to his troops in the China expedition : 'Quarter must not be given ' ! "

The Kaiser orders murder From every field evidence continued to pour in of fresh crimes perpetrated by the Germans —crimes such as had never been known before in war between civilised races. The French troops in the victorious counter-offensive of July, 1918, captured the following general order issued by General Ludendorff :

The enemy must in no circumstances be permitted to bury his dead or recover his wounded in front of our lines, not even under the Red Cross flag. If the enemy should attempt this a warning shot must be fired to make him desist. If this has no effect, the enemy will be ruthlessly engaged at once.

This fiendish order was obeyed. German murders of prisoners continued. Two French prisoners taken at Anthenay on May 31st, 1918, managed to escape after witnessing a deliberate massacre by the Germans of captured

ON THE TRAGIC LINE OF ITALY'S RETREAT IN THE AUTUMN OF 1917.

When the Italians had to retreat and form a new line far behind that which they had held on the Isonzo many such scenes as this were witnessed. The soldiers pressed on day and night, with but little food or rest, in their effort to save their guns from the pressure of overwhelming numbers. Crossing the Friulian Plain they were accompanied by large numbers of civilian refugees fleeing from the menace of the ruthlessly barbarous Austro-German invaders.

French troops, some of whom were wounded. Another escaped prisoner in the same region on May 30th saw the Germans fix bayonets and kill four unarmed Frenchmen who had surrendered.

At sea the German submarines continued their wholesale murders with new refinements of devilry. A German submarine deliberately torpedoed the British hospital-ship Llandovery Castle, and then, in the words of one of the very few survivors:

> We saw the submarine rushing about amid the wreckage, and I thought she was trying to ram any other boat that might be afloat. It was quite plain that she was acting with some such purpose. Our boat got away, but for the next fifteen minutes we heard heavy reports and shells passed whizzing over us. I counted twenty shots, and concluded that any survivors in the water were being fired upon.

The screams of the drowning Canadian sisters and nurses rang in the ears of those who witnessed this horrible outrage.

Sinking of the Llandovery Castle Some two hundred and thirty-four persons were murdered, a deed which filled even the neutral Vatican with " profound repulsion." But from Germany came not a word of condemnation for the men who had been guilty of such an atrocity.

A few weeks later a German submarine in the North Sea repeated the crime that had been perpetrated against the crew of the British steamer Belgian Prince, and placed eight fishermen who had been taken from fishing-boats on her deck, closed down her hatches and submerged, drowning four of the eight. Day after day cases were reported and verified in which German submarines had not only sunk ships mercilessly, but had then fired on the survivors in the boats, sometimes till all of them were killed. So diabolical were these outrages, so beyond the ordinary conception of civilised man, that the British Seamen's and Firemen's Union pledged its members to maintain a boycott of German seamen and shipping after the war, unless the British Government took steps to punish the criminals. In the successive German advances and retreats in France all the outrages that had been committed in Belgium in 1914 were repeated in the summer of 1918. Women were violated; civilian property was stolen systematically or wantonly destroyed. At Château-Thierry the houses, large and small alike, were wrecked:

> These [larger] houses were magnificently furnished. . . . To-day there is nothing that has not been destroyed [telegraphed Reuter's correspondent with the American Army on July 27th, 1918]. The tapestries have been hacked to pieces, the pictures slit from corner to corner, the leather and other chair coverings have been ripped from their frames; all the delicate marqueterie and the irreplaceable examples of craftsmanship of past centuries have been smashed. . . . There is not a mirror that has not been broken. . . . The costly carpets have been fouled and rent in every possible way, and inkpots flung at the silk papers on the wall. This vengeful fury has been carried even to the extent of smashing nurseries and dolls' houses. The dolls' houses have been trampled on and torn to pieces, a rocking-horse was cleft with an axe. . . . The fashion in which beds and rooms have been defiled is difficult of description.

On everything these unspeakable beings placed their mark.

Teuton savages in Château-Thierry In one house [says the same witness] there was a valuable library, including hundreds of rare old books, a great number of wonderful bindings, illuminated missals, and ancient manuscripts. There was not a single volume or missal which was not mutilated. . . . Some foul liquid was poured over the illuminations which had defied the fading of time for centuries.

As if to flaunt their defiance in the face of civilisation, the Germans organised tourist picnics in 1918 in places where Belgians had been murdered in 1914. At Famines, for instance, they appeared in noisy processions shouting over the Belgian graves and ruined houses, " Glory to the Kaiser! This is the fate from which he saved our German towns!"

The Germans still claimed to be the great civilising race. One test of this claim should suffice. In 1814, General Müffling, on the German Staff, reported that the Rhine province, which was then under French rule, had been so thoroughly reconciled to Napoleon's policy that in a few years it would have ceased to be German, and even then preferred to be French. This was the result of less than twenty years of French rule. Alsace-Lorraine had been

German for over forty years in 1914, and yet when the French in their transient advance occupied certain of its towns they were welcomed by the people everywhere as deliverers. Through all the four years of agony, from 1914 to 1918, Alsace-Lorraine still looked to the Tricolour for delivery. Not one of the States or territories which Germany had conquered in the first four years of the war had been won over to her. In every one fierce resentment or active resistance smouldered. In the Ukraine, in Poland, in Lithuania, in Belgium it was the same. From all the oppressed and enslaved populations, treated though they were with the most desolating barbarism, went up one cry of hatred for the principle of evil which German rule embodied.

German diplomacy took every opportunity during the fourth year to prove its complete perfidy. Herr Haase, in the Reichstag on June 25th, 1918, stated that the German Government had treacherously violated the terms of the treaty of peace which the Bolshevists had concluded with them. Count Mirbach, the German representative in Moscow, shortly before his assassination, opened negotiations with the Russian Constitutionalists, and then, like another Iscariot, betrayed them to Trotsky and Lenin, who murdered them without mercy. The very speeches which German statesmen made in the Reichstag were falsified. One version would be issued for foreign consumption and another for home, as in the case of Count Hertling's notorious announcement that Belgium would be held as a German pawn.

" The god of brute force must this time and for ever be broken and burned in its own furnace," said Mr. Lloyd George. The constantly recurring evidence of German cruelty and wrong steadied the Allies and steeled their determination in the darkest hours of 1918, even when freedom seemed to be fighting a losing battle. " It is better for us to perish in battle than to look upon the outrage of our nation and our altars; as the will of God is in heaven, so let Him do," ran the words of the old English order of prayer. Never before had the British nation made such efforts or submitted to such sacrifices. Never before was **British fortitude and sacrifice** its fibre subjected to so tremendous a test and its institutions so continuously rocked and shaken as by an earthquake. Six and a quarter million men were raised by it for service in the Navy or Army. Britons of middle age were suddenly summoned from their peaceful vocations to the slaughter of the battlefield. British troops bore unflinchingly the whole burden of the war with Turkey on four different fronts—in Egypt, in Palestine, in Mesopotamia, in Persia—where one and a quarter million British subjects drew rations in the field. In France an army of nearly 2,000,000 British was constantly hammering the German line, or being hammered in the German offensives; and yet, after terrible slaughter and suffering, it remained steadfast and capable of hitting back. In the snows of the Alps, on the Italian front, in the malarious precincts of Salonika, in the swamps and wild forests of the Murman coast, on the Caspian, in Turkestan, in Siberia, in the jungles of East Africa, the British race confronted the same savage foe. On the high seas 420,000 British seamen in the Navy were engaged in breaking the force of the submarine campaign and covering the passage of the American troops. Another 200,000 maintained with sublime heroism the work of the merchant service, and never quailed under the constant menace of a terrible death. These men not only faced danger, but refrained from taking advantage of it to secure high wages. Mr. Havelock Wilson, not without well-merited pride in the British merchant service, declared in July, 1918, that its men had worked for £11 or £12 a month when they could easily have obtained £30. Women took up the task of replacing men to an ever-increasing extent as the man-power of the country began to run low, and confronted peril in hospitals, in hospital-ships, and in munition works with a devotion that stirred the heart. The educated girl of 1918 bore the drudgery of field work on the land with the same spirit. If to the great are given the great trials and sorrows of life, then the claim of the British race to its place in the world was established. There was no land over which the tide of battle passed that was not red with British blood. The

General Sir Henry Horne inspecting a British machine-gun battalion on the western front.

Forward with the guns: Battery of the Royal Horse Artillery galloping into action.

British in Jerusalem: Changing the Mohammedan guard at the Mosque of Omar.

Jaffa under the Union Jack: British band playing in front of Government House.

In the Balkan cockpit: Serbian refugees returning to a village liberated from the invader.

The Mesopotamian campaign: British troops crossing the ridge between Deli Abbas and Kifri.

11

Motor-borne up mountain roads. Italian reserves, heartily cheered by comrades they passed, being conveyed in crowded lorries camouflaged against enemy aircraft by branch-strewn tops.

For the mountain batteries. Italian soldiers loading ammunition-boxes on mules for transport by steep roads and narrow bridle-paths to the high-perched guns upon the Alpine front.

Patrol passing through barbed-wire entanglements destroyed by artillery fire. The men carried sticks to help them on the rough way and to free themselves of clinging strands of wire.

Despatch-carrier delivering a message in a mountain trench on the Piave. In the summer of 1918 the Italians drove the enemy back across the river on the whole of the Piave front.

"Italy shall be free!": Along the rocky ramparts where Italy held and drove back the invader in the summer of 1918.

British martyrs, the Cavells and Fryatts, rose resplendent in their victory over death. The British common soldiers, prisoners in Germany, and subjected to every torture that malice and cruelty could inflict, with the very rarest exceptions refused to bow the head to Baal.

In that endurance of burdens, in that trial of common suffering, all classes were united as never before. While it was being proved on the battlefield that democracy, though it has many points of weakness, is no vain and evil thing, so in the quieter paths of domestic policy and economic change Great Britain underwent a transformation greater than any people had voluntarily accepted. A French critic has not unjustly praised the loyalty, the fairness, the self-abnegation which the British brought to their financial effort. Property submitted cheerfully to yet more stupendous sacrifices. The " rich " not only gave of their lives, they gave abundantly of their substance as well. In this atmosphere of devotion, property began to look upon wealth as a means rather of serving the nation nobly than of procuring self-enjoyment. Conscription was applied to money in this sense : that a man was not permitted to invest where he would ; that he could not hold foreign securities or send remittances out of the country—laws that could easily have been evaded if there had not been goodwill, but which in actual fact were cheerfully obeyed. In 1918 the "rich" paid one-third, or even one-half their income in taxes, and with all they could save of the rest helped the Red Cross. The old idea of life as a merciless competition, in which the weakest should be destroyed—that idea for which Germany stood—was rooted out when it was seen how sublimely upon . the battlefield behaved many of those who would have been classed among the weakest. Thus England, after long decades of prosperity, entered an age of unsurpassed storm and stress.

With that storm and stress came back the shadow of the precariousness of human existence which had always haunted the ancient world. The Greek mind dwelt on the swift transition from Crœsus on the throne to Crœsus on the funeral pyre, beaten and ruined ; on fallen cities and vanished peoples, and was obsessed with the thought that man abides not long in any stay. Now in a few days, weeks, or months cities were wiped out, kingdoms destroyed, nations enslaved, the wealth of generations swept pitilessly away. Of Ypres even the very ruins had perished. The greatest of Russian painters died miserably of starvation at the height of his fame. Millionaires in Belgium or Russia had to beg their bread. Famous generals in the Russian Army sold newspapers in the streets. Officers acted as scavengers ; heroes were hunted down and shot. Nowhere were these transitions more tragic than in Russia, where the Bolshevists, as Professor Rohrbach remarked with German complacency, destroyed the very springs of Russian national life, repudiating the National Debt, seizing the bank deposits, and with their German auxiliaries burnt, hanged, plundered, and tortured. Nicholas II., Tsar of All the Russias, who with all his faults had remained constant to the Allies and had spurned German approaches, was shot and his body thrown upon a dunghill. In a few months, from his country's sovereign he became its victim. Between William II., on July 16th, exulting in the slaughter and destruction of the Second Battle of the Marne—to outward vision still the conqueror of the world—and this last Romanoff, buffeted and spat upon by the guards who led him out to death that same day, what a gulf ! And yet the Romanoff, for all his many evident failings, holds the respect of mankind. To die in an immortal cause is itself a title to immortality.

Amidst earth-shaking events the Germans marched towards their goal. After immense preparations which had been in progress many months a great offensive was opened on the Italian front. The Italian armies were not well placed, because General Cadorna had loyally striven to occupy the attention of the largest possible Austrian force and thus to relieve the strain on Russia. Their position became precarious when Lenin and Trotsky betrayed the Allies, and the Austrian Staff could concentrate all its best troops on the Isonzo and reinforce them with Germans. On October 24th, 1917, after a short but violent artillery preparation under cover of mist,

The reign of tragedy

FROM A DESERT OUTLOOK.
British soldier among the ruins of a caliph's house in the Mesopotamian desert. Such ruins as these, where they were available, served all the purposes of ready-made dug-outs.

the Austrians, aided by nine German divisions, broke through the Italian front between Plezzo (Flitsch) and Tolmino, and in three days claimed 100,000 prisoners and over 700 guns. The Italians had to retreat precipitately to save their armies on the Carso and at Gorizia. Some part of their forces had been infected by an Anarchist propaganda which had been vigorously conducted by German agents. The hope of General Ludendorff was that they would be annihilated and compelled to make peace, and the initial success seemed to justify his expectations. But the Italians did not collapse. With fearful losses, fighting resolutely, they fell back ; they lost the Tagliamento ; they reached the Piave and Venice and the noble cities of the Venetian Plain were in extreme peril. In that hour Italy rose to the emergency. " Mother of heroes," as Wordsworth had called her eighty years before, with the sure prophetic note of the great poet, her people rallied with heroism and faith to the defence of their eternal cause. Before the reinforcements, which were moving fast to their aid from the British and French armies, could arrive the Italian troops arrested the German thrust on the Piave in a series of violent engagements. The decision which Germany sought was not obtained, though a tremendous blow was inflicted upon the Allies. On the contrary, it was demonstrated that the Alliance was something which, in its spiritual greatness, rose superior to defeat. The Bolshevism which wrecked Russia did not overthrow free and united Italy.

The winter intervened to prevent further activity by the German armies in Italy, and General Ludendorff used it to prepare a similar attack upon the British front in France. The portion of the front selected was between Cambrai and St. Quentin, where the Fifth British Army was stationed. This army was weak, numbering only fourteen divisions, many of which were far below their nominal establishment.

Italy—" mother of heroes "

The German intention to attack was loudly proclaimed beforehand. The whole of Germany was informed that a decision was now about to be reached in the west, and the British were to be defeated and driven into the sea. A victorious peace with the exaction of an enormous indemnity from Great Britain was predicted before the end of May, 1918.

Forty German divisions at full strength, numbering 600,000 men, were employed. On March 21st they advanced swiftly, under cover of mist, penetrating the British front, capturing immense accumulations of stores and ammunition, but incurring in their onrush heavy losses. They swept like a cyclone over the Somme battlefields, drenched and re-drenched with British blood. For a brief moment they overpowered the Fifth Army by sheer weight of numbers, despite its heroic resistance, and drove a wedge into the line. At this crisis General

Unity of the Allied Command Pétain flung French troops and masses of aeroplanes into the gap, and it was filled.

The front was re-formed, though only with grievous loss of ground. Under the pressure of calamity, greater than the most pessimistic had foreboded, the British nation did not dissolve in anarchy. As in Italy, the forces of disruption within were overpowered, the strikes which were proceeding or threatened, stopped. Here also the German thrust did not obtain decisive results.

Out of this disaster came good. The Allied Command was unified at last. All the armies were placed under the supreme control of General Foch, who by his character, attainments, and achievements was the greatest of leaders on the side of the Allies. Over 350,000 men were hurried in a month from Great Britain to France. President Wilson at the same time ordered that American troops should be temporarily brigaded with British and French troops, and took steps to accelerate the despatch of reinforcements to Europe, brilliantly seconded in this by the British Admiralty. The effect of the new unity of command was only gradually felt, after the confusion caused by the furious German onslaughts had been overcome, but it was a harbinger of victory. Everything

now depended on the movement of American troops to Europe. There were 400,000 in France early in March, but of these many were not combatants. In the next few months they were moved at the rate of 200,000 a month, so that each month General Foch had at his call a new army. For this great feat, entirely without precedent in the whole history of war, and the more remarkable because it was in large part the work of the British merchant service, depleted though this had been by the enormous submarine losses, posterity will not refuse the British Admiralty and the British nation a large share of the credit. The British people had to suffer hardship and privation; the British Navy worked with magnificent energy. And the end was attained.

Before the situation could change the Germans struck, first at Arras, where British troops repulsed them after a bloody struggle, and then in April towards Armentières and Ypres. French assistance was given, and this offensive also died away in local fighting after the Messines Ridge and Kemmel Hill had been taken by the Germans. Calais was not reached; the decision was not obtained. On May 27th the Germans delivered their third great offensive, attacking on a twenty-five-mile front on the Chemin des Dames, north of Soissons and Rheims. They launched twenty-five divisions against eight British and French, crossed the Aisne, took Soissons, pushed swiftly forward to the Marne, and reached Château-Thierry and Dormans, throwing more and more men into the battle. Rheims was in acute danger; Paris was more directly menaced than ever

before, as the thrust to the Marne was followed by a fresh effort to gain ground near Compiègne. But though the Crown Prince in all employed 750,000 men and approached within forty miles of Paris, for the third time the Germans failed to obtain decisive results. The worst hours of the war were over when, on June 14th, the Germans were unable, from the exhaustion of their reserves, to drive home the blow they had dealt. The goal had not been won. With each German triumph it receded and eluded the German Staff, though now the weeks of the campaigning season were passing fast, and the American armies were pouring in at the rate of 10,000 men a day. Then came a first reminder that General Foch could not be wholly overlooked. A counter-stroke delivered by him at the end of June recovered some important ground.

William II. and his advisers, like

BRITISH NAVAL MEN IN THE FAR NORTH.
Naval officers awaiting the opening of a store in Kola village, at the head of Kola Inlet, North Russia.
Above: Naval officer interpreter in talk with the Lapps at a settlement on the Varsuna River.

IN FREEDOM'S CAUSE.

M. Poincaré, President of the French Republic, presenting colours to a battalion of Czecho-Slovaks on the western front in the summer of 1918. By that year the Czecho-Slovaks in France, many of whom had joined the French forces early in the war, had grown to an army corps.

Pharaoh of old, hardened their hearts. All through these offensives they bombarded Paris with guns of enormous range, and on Good Friday, at the most solemn hour of the most solemn day in the Christian year, made one hundred and fifty victims in one of the Paris churches. In mid-June a fresh offensive was begun by forty Austrian divisions on the Piave to break the last trace of Italian resistance. It issued in complete failure. The Italian armies were on their guard, and after violent fighting drove the Austrians back across the river, inflicting heavy losses on them and taking many prisoners. This was the first battle in which, without aid—for the British and French forces present were comparatively small—the Italians had met and defeated the whole strength of Austria-Hungary. Their victory was a magnificent achievement—the reward of splendid services—and it was yet another sign of the turning tide.

In early July neutrals were informed by the German Staff that a new offensive would open in a few days in France which would exceed in violence any previous attack and bring the decision. The date originally fixed was July 8th, but on that day the weather broke, and the attack was postponed till July 15th. At 1.10 a.m. that day, like a new Xerxes, as overweening in his pride and lawlessness, William II. took his place on a wooden watch-tower, whence he was to survey the triumph of his troops under his son. The German divisions, instead of surprising the French, were themselves surprised and swept by a terrific artillery fire as they moved into position. Nevertheless, the battle at first seemed to go well; the Marne was crossed, German troops headed towards Epernay to cut off Rheims, and with one more effort it looked as though Rheims and Châlons might fall and the immense forces under the Crown Prince wheel to the right for the final march on Paris. But then the German onset was held. After tremendous fighting on the night of the 17th the French Staff reported that Paris and Epernay were safe, and released a great counter-attack which had been prepared by Generals Foch and Pétain. On the flank of the German advance between Soissons and Château-Thierry the French struck furiously and penetrated quickly. As if visibly to mark the change of fortune a great thunderstorm masked

the roaring of the French Tanks and the march of the French infantry into their positions. The colossal German offensive, prepared with so much art, had issued in a failure even greater than that of the Austrians on the Piave. The pledge which General Ludendorff and William II. had given to the Reichstag before it rose, that victory and peace should be won before November, 1918, was never destined to be fulfilled.

For four years the Allies had groped for leaders who could manœuvre large masses of men. They had now in General Foch (created Marshal after his victory) the man, and with the coming of the American millions they would have the men. The greatness of Marshal Foch's achievement lay in this—that with forces inferior to the Germans he had met them at their selected point and driven them back, after the greatest battle which up to that date had taken place in the history of the world. He had outwitted the German Staff at its own game. The military qualities on which it prided itself were now proved to be no prerogative of the German officer but to be fully shared by the free nations. The Allies had thus won three victories in the summer of 1918—the first, the counter-stroke between Montdidier and Noyon; the second, the Italian defeat of the Austrians on the Piave; and the third, which destroyed the Crown Prince's reputation, upon that river of fate—the Marne.

As the tide turned in the west in the same way that it had turned during the American Civil War at Vicksburg and Gettysburg, so it turned in the east, though much more slowly and less obviously. **The turn of the tide** The tyranny of the Bolshevists tottered towards its doom execrated by the Russian people. German generals and officials in Russia were assassinated. The Czecho-Slovaks, Austrian Slavs, who had voluntarily joined the Russian Army in its nobler days, and whom the Bolshevists had proposed to hand over to the Austrian executioner, formed a centre of resistance in Eastern Russia and Siberia. They were opposed by a motley host of Red Guards (whose value, as a German newspaper remarked, could be seen from the fact that 10,000 of them were mown down by a single weak German brigade at Taganrog), German

FROM THE FAIR LAND OF POLAND.

Men of a Polish regiment formed in France swearing fealty to the French Republic and the cause of the Allies before taking their places on the western fighting front. Many Poles fought heroically on the side of the Allies, knowing that on the Allied success depended the freeing of all oppressed races.

armed prisoners, and other mercenaries in the service of the Bolshevists, but they gradually increased their power, though its basis remained precarious, on the shifting sands of Russian feeling. In the Ukraine the revolt against the Germans extended as the peasantry realised the fate in store for them and rose against their German officers. On the Murman coast and at Archangel the sparse population invited allied aid, and it was given.

The overwhelming importance of preventing German access to Siberia and Central Asia was understood in France, whose Government, even in 1917, exerted every effort to secure Japanese intervention. Japan was willing to .act on a mandate from the Allies, but in these critical weeks allied diplomacy was feeble and its statesmanship hesitating. It was not clearly realised that on the solution of the Siberian and Russian problem depended the position of the British forces in the west. If the Germans could strike at the Indian frontier through Persia and Transcaspia, at the Persian Gulf through Mesopotamia, or at the Suez Canal through Palestine, Great Britain must transfer forces to the Near and Middle East, and by the shipping which she would require for such transference she must correspondingly reduce the movement of American troops to France. It was, therefore, of paramount necessity that Japan should act as swiftly as possible on the Siberian front and enable the sound factors in Russia to recover control of the great railways and rivers. Japan had the force, and it could be used without drawing on British or American shipping. But week followed week without any decision being reached. At last, in August, it was announced that a small—and, in the opinion of judges

The Kaiser as a new Sisyphus on the spot, a quite inadequate — allied force was to be despatched to Siberia. This was, however, a beginning. It was one more sign that the pacification which the Germans imagined they had effected in the east by fraud, treachery, and violence was being overthrown. The task of William II. was becoming that of a new Sisyphus. The stone of German tyranny had perpetually to be rolled uphill, but when the summit was reached it always recoiled.

In the air the position of the Allies was improving fast in mid-1918. The pick of the German pilots and youths had been killed. In machines the German Air Service was still, perhaps, ahead of the Allies owing to the disastrous strikes which had interfered with deliveries in Great Britain. But in courage and skill the British, French, and Italians had the superiority, and the date was at hand when the new and large American air forces would enter the fight and drive the war home by continuous large-scale attacks on German cities and munition factories. The Germans had

introduced the practice of bombing towns remote from the front, and they were now to suffer for their crimes. A cry of alarm went up from the Rhine centres at the prospect, and the German Staff was forced to divert from the front a large force of machines and airmen for defence of the threatened centres.

Even at sea the tide was turning by mid-1918, though not as yet very plainly. All risk of starvation in the allied countries had passed. A larger tonnage of new shipping was being completed monthly than was being sunk. The British Navy had not overcome them mainly because in the decisive hours, after the opening of the German offensives, its efforts had to be concentrated upon the safe convoying of American troops. As the price of General Foch's victories it had, therefore, for the time being to leave the aggressive war upon the submarine, and **The dawn** to devote its attention mainly to the task **in sight** of defence, protecting the great convoys which week after week safely arrived. It was not to be supposed that such a record of security could be indefinitely maintained. That it was maintained in the crisis of fate was an achievement the glory of which will never fade.

Thus, though long months of battle lay before the allies when the fourth year closed, the dawn was in sight—" eastward, not now very far." The most terrible foe that freedom had ever encountered had done his worst, and he had not prevailed. He remained still powerful for evil, with immense forces in the field. But the new Marathon, the new Salamis, had not been lost. The living generation, as it looked back on those months of bloodshed and suffering, could, with sure faith, echo the words of the American Battle Hymn:

Mine eyes have seen the glory of the coming of the Lord,
He is trampling out the vintage where the grapes of wrath are stored.
He hath loosed the fatal lightning of His terrible swift sword ;
　　　His truth is marching on.

In the beauty of the lilies Christ was born across the sea,
With a glory in His bosom that transfigures you and me ;
As He died to make men holy, let us die to make men free,
　　　While God is marching on.

And as the cadence to which these noble words were sung had first been heard on the battlefields of Virginia, where men had marched to end the slavery of man, so it now sounded in Europe triumphant with its note of confidence and hope above the carnage, where the free nations gathered for their last fights, shoulder to shoulder in unity and loyal comradeship, striving by deeds and by sacrifice to realise the great aim which Mazzini first embodied in speech as the far-off goal of democracy, " the similitude of that Divine society, where all are equal and where there is one love, one happiness for all."

WITH THE FIRST BRITISH ARMY ON THE FOURTH ANNIVERSARY.
Commemoration service on the British western front in France of the First Army on the fourth anniversary of the outbreak of the war. That fourth year had been one of the most terrible twelvemonths through which civilised man had passed, but its close was held to mark the turning of the tide —" the most terrible foe that freedom had ever encountered had done his worst, and he had not prevailed."

CHAPTER CCLV.

THE GREAT BATTLE FOR AMIENS.

I.—The British Retreat from the St. Quentin Line.

By Edward Wright.

Ludendorff's Four Million Men and Increased Artillery—Inferiority in Number of Western Allies—Foch's Reserve Formed by Fifth British Army Taking Over French St. Quentin Line—Britain's Lack of Recruits to Balance Russian Defection—Winning Novelty in Enemy's New Infantry Tactics—Why the British Line was Selected for Attack—Germany on the March—Extraordinary Secrecy of Hostile Concentrations—Germans Estimate their Gun-Power Four Times Stronger than the British—Colossal Bombardment between Arras and Tergnier—Enemy Masses of Assault Veiled by Thick Mist—Nothing Visible beyond Fifty Yards—Magnificent London Stand in the Keep—West Kents and East Kents Vie in Desperate Gallantry—English Line Wheels Back to Crozat Canal—Wedge Driven between Scotsmen and Irishmen at St. Quentin—Gunners Save Line below Essigny—Manchester Men Hold to Death Manchester Hill—Yorkshiremen Fight against Envelopment at Roupy—Bedfords and Scots Fusiliers Cut their Way Through—Inniskillings' Great Counter-Attack at Douchy—Splendid Recovery at Jussy and Stand at Tergnier—Fall of Ham and Flank Attack on Ulstermen—Superhuman Efforts to Hold Amiens Road—Hungry Scotsmen and German Soup—Sagging British Front Saved from Breaking—General Foch Appointed Allied Generalissimo.

IMMEDIATELY after the Battle of Cambrai in December, 1917 (described in Chapter CCXXXVIII., Vol. 11, page 241). General von Ludendorff published his intention of opening a decisive campaign in the west. For four months the threat was repeated by organs directly or indirectly in the service of the German Staff. The blatant iteration, with the prolonged delay that accompanied it, gave rise to some doubt among the civilian population of the Grand Alliance as to the execution of the threat.

This was exactly the result that Ludendorff intended to produce. He affected not only the uninformed British public but the well-advised British War Cabinet. Only a few weeks before the British line was broken Mr. Bonar Law stated that he was sceptical in regard to a grand offensive by the enemy, who, he said, possessed no dangerous superiority in either men or guns.

General von Ludendorff then had about two hundred divisions on the western front, and, according to the British Minister of National Service, there were about one million six hundred thousand German troops remaining in the eastern theatre of

war or in German depots, the larger number of whom might be brought to France and Flanders. The total number of trained men at the disposal of Ludendorff was therefore much greater than the total number of French, British, Belgian, and American troops standing to battle along the western front.

The German High Command had in 1916 established a general system of industrial conscription, while combing out of factories, farms, and distribution services every man that could possibly be spared for work in the field. The result was that while the united populations of France and Great Britain were larger than the population of Germany, the Germans, in the spring of 1918, still had more fighting men ready for battle on the decisive field of war.

France had continually done all she could to resist the much superior pressure of the enemy. From August, 1914, she had used all fit men between eighteen and forty-eight years of age, and suffered so heavily that it needed a generation at least to restore her vital energies. By temperament and circumstances French commanders were as alert to the advantage of concentration as were the Germans. They balanced

THE WORK OF HIS GUN.
British artillery sergeant on the western front copying into his notebook, from a blackboard well covered with technical particulars, some of the details concerning the firing of his gun.

their expeditionary forces in Greece and Italy by means of a magnificent army of Arabs, Berbers, and negroes, which was employed directly against the Germans from the outset of the war, and fed with hundreds of thousands of gallant and well-handled recruits. Great Britain had not called out her men of middle age, similar to the Territorials of France and the Landsturmers of Germany. She also continued—and no doubt inevitably—to expend part of her British man-power in winning successes in theatres of second or third rate importance.

The establishment by the Supreme Council of War at Versailles of a system of international military control among the Western Allies did not seem to have any marked effect upon civilian minds in the British War Cabinet. Between the Battle of Cambrai and the Battle for Amiens there was sufficient time for British statesmen to re-establish the balance in military power that had been definitely upset by the Bolshevist anarchy in Russia in November, 1917; but it did not seem that everything was done to bring up the British armies in the field to the required standard of additional strength.

The drafts that arrived in France to make good the heavy losses of 1917 were balanced by a prolongation of the British line. The French front between the southern outskirts of St. Quentin and the marshes of the Oise River by La Fère was taken over in January, 1918, by the Fifth British Army under Sir Hubert Gough. The new Imperial Chief of Staff of Great Britain, Sir Henry Wilson, anticipated that the main German effort would be directed against this St. Quentin-La Fère line; but when what he had foreseen happened the allied reserve behind the most endangered part of the front was not strong enough for the terrible task that confronted it.

Man-power on the western front The fact was that General von Ludendorff outplayed his opponents in many of the opening movements of the German offensive. He was only firmly countered in the Arras sector, where his preparations were discovered. In all other important fields of conflict the allied resistance was dissolved into a soldiers' battle, in which the superhuman personal courage of overwhelmed units, who bore up against and finally checked the strategy and tactical methods of the German Commander-in-Chief, had to compensate for the lack of immediate reserve power.

Ludendorff appears to have had immediately available on the western front about half a million more men than the Allies had placed in the field. This number was not sufficient to enable him to undertake the grand offensive in a sound manner. But he was saved from the risk of breaking under a general counter-offensive by the Allies by his large final reserve of men in Russia. As was afterwards seen, he was able to reduce his forces in the eastern theatre to half a million German and Austrian troops of inferior quality without at once endangering his hold upon Russia and Rumania.

The enemy Commander-in-Chief was also terribly strong in artillery power. From his Rumanian, Russian, and Italian fields of victory he brought some ten thousand pieces of captured ordnance and great trains of motor-vehicles for serving the guns with shell, together with an immense stock of projectiles and charges. The larger part of the armament of Brussiloff's armies, which had been magnificently organised by Great Britain, France, and the United States, fell into

German hands long before the rifling of the guns was worn or the stock of shell exhausted. It was the vastest and most complete material of war that the Russians ever possessed, being much superior in both quality and quantity to the battle machinery provided by the old Imperial Government of Russia. What part of it the Bolshevist soldiery did not abandon when they marched out of the firing-line to take part in the plunder of private Russian estates was soon afterwards sold to Teutonic agents at prices that rarely amounted to more than a few shillings for each piece.

In addition to all this immense booty, Ludendorff commandeered for the western battle a considerable part of the heavy artillery of Austria-Hungary, and employed all the output of the German munition factories. Instead of having to apportion guns and shell nicely between the eastern and western fronts, he was able to transport all the intensified production of German war material into France, and there combine it with the existing armament, the material captured in the eastern and south-eastern fields of battle, and the artillery and ammunition dumps of the vassal Empire of the Hapsburgs. The result was that he became as prepotent in artillery power as he was in concentrated, trained man-power.

And having recovered the means of exercising the initiative in France and Flanders, which Falkenhayn had lost in 1916, he displayed remarkable talent in devising a new method of attack that promised to become irresistible.

GERMANY'S COMMANDER-IN-CHIEF ON THE FRENCH FRONT.
General Ludendorff, in chief command of the great German offensive on the western front in the spring and summer of 1918. (This portrait of him in his office at Main Headquarters is from a German newspaper.)

For months his divisions could be seen by allied airmen openly practising the new tactics on the training-grounds at Sedan and elsewhere. Under the direction of officers who had maintained and developed the traditions of open field warfare of manœuvre on the loose eastern front, the German troops were shaken out of the habits of trench fighting and exercised in rapid, flexible waves, changing direction according to the opportunities of instant action.

The hand-grenade became obsolete. Rifle fire and machine-gun fire, employed to the limit of effective range, formed the main instrument of advance. Heavy artillery was used to break down hostile entrenchments and smother hostile gun positions in the manner of trench-smashing operations in 1915, 1916, and 1917. Yet the big gun, which had been mistress of the battlefield, was much diminished in importance by the people who had first employed it in a large way. They knew by repeated experience that it limited every movement of the infantry, so they decided that the infantry should be drilled to make the final thrust through an opposing front with little or no artillery support.

As a matter of fact, a special infantry gun was provided for German battalions of assault. This was a French idea, clearly sketched by General Pétain in 1915, and executed by a mining engineer, M. J. Archer, in the same year. **New German tactics of assault**
For forty months and more commissions of Frenchmen, to the number of eighteen, examined hesitatingly the possibilities of the Archer gun and of General Pétain's scheme for its employment. Meanwhile Ludendorff, whose secret service was not inefficient, heard of the idea, welcomed it as the crowning feature of his new system of tactics of assault, and constructed six infantry guns for each attacking battalion by the time he began to train his troops to work forward beyond all supporting barrages.

The infantry gun, however, was more of moral support

than of material assistance. Like the British Stokes mortar, it helped in the earlier stage of the conflict, but the difficulty of getting up ammunition when the distance lengthened and the confusion of battle increased made the new gun of little avail in the supreme crisis. This had been foreseen by Ludendorff and his lieutenants. They relied on infantry power alone when it came to the turning-point in their line-breaking operations.

The reversion to almost unaided infantry power was the winning novelty in the enemy's new tactics. At dreadful yet deliberate cost to his troops he avoided the ordinary pauses in attacks against fortified lines, which had been caused by the necessity for hauling guns forward to break the way anew for the foot soldiers. At the point at which all action in parallel battles had temporarily ended the German infantry was trained to continue the struggle, with rifle and machine-gun alone, against all the remaining hostile machinery of slaughter.

It was no wonder that Ludendorff imperturbably allowed allied airmen to watch his divisions practising the new tactics. He would not have diminished his chances of success had he published an outline of the new system. For it seemed impossible, after the best manhood of Germany had been destroyed by forty-four months of warfare, in which the power of artillery had continually augmented, that an infantry of second-rate quality could, without the usual escorting shell barrage, break through a series of modern battle positions.

A terrifying prospect

It was a terrifying prospect. From a professional military point of view the success of the method fully justified the extreme rigour of the Prussian method of discipline. It displayed the stronger side of the spirit of Zabern. The Potsdam drill-sergeants had first transformed the conquered Slav races between the Elbe and the Niemen into fine soldiers. They had then done the same thing to the Teutonic tribes of Low Germans and High Germans, with the exception of the Bavarian stocks that had extended into Austria. Finally, when most of their first-line troops were killed or maimed, and many of the best second-line troops were also out of action, they took the remnants of the fit, adult German males, and all lads who were approaching the age for military service, and hammered them into a stronger and more flexible fighting machine than the original German armies had formed.

Ludendorff's new plans

All this was not accomplished in the four months elapsing between the Battle of Cambrai and the Battle for Amiens. Quite a year was spent in training men in the new method, beginning with forces in Russia, who were encouraged to develop initiative and to manœuvre in sensitive lines of sharpshooters and advanced machine-gunners by actions in sectors where the opposing artillery was weak. It was indeed the weakness of Russian gun-power that inspired the new school of German tacticians—such as Ludendorff, Hutier, Marwitz, Boehn, and Below—with renewed confidence in well-handled rifle and machine-gun fire used to the limit of range.

The striking victory won on the Isonzo and the partial success obtained at Cambrai encouraged Ludendorff to believe that by a general use of the new tactics he could achieve the grand decision. He concluded that the British line could have been completely broken at Gouzeaucourt

"THE KAISER AND HIS STAFF ON THE WAY TO FLANDERS," APRIL, 1918.

In this effective picture of a railway-saloon interior a German artist depicted the Kaiser and more than a dozen members of his Staff on their journey to the front at a time when German hopes ran high. The great offensive, opened on March 21st, had driven the allied armies back miles to the westward, and the important centre of Amiens seemed seriously threatened, while plans for the thrust towards Paris were doubtless under consideration on November 30th, 1917, if the numerous divisions wasted against the central Bourlon Hill positions had been secretly arrayed under cover of mist against the British flank, so as immediately to follow up the comparatively small force that pierced to the opposing artillery positions.

The ease and speed with which the British line had been broken was also important in deciding the strategy of the enemy commander. For certain political as well as military reasons he was at first inclined to follow the same course as Falkenhayn had taken and strike at the Army of France. He chose the Aisne front as the sector in which he could best surprise General Pétain, and made all preparations there for a swift thrust towards Paris and an astonishing long-distance bombardment of the French capital.

Yet, misjudging the manœuvring power of the new British armies, which, inured to trench warfare, seemed to him to be incapable of acting in rapid cohesion on the open field, he resolved to strike **Decision to attack** first at what appeared to him **the British** to be the weaker of the two main forces of the Grand Alliance. No doubt the fact that a French general was exercising control over the dispositions of both French and British Armies induced Ludendorff to attack the British line.

He hoped so to defeat the British as to leave them cut off from assistance from General Foch's common reserve. Keenly alive to his own advantages as practical Generalissimo of Middle Europe, he wished to prevent the Atlantic and Mediterranean League from collecting all its powers during the final phase of the struggle by establishing a similar unity of military control.

Meanwhile, as his men by the million practised the new tactics, Ludendorff took large yet simple measures for demonstrating against the French and British forces. He had to mislead the allied commanders as to his intention, so that their principal concentrations of resisting power should be made well away from the Oise and Aisne lines. At huge expense in labour and material he constructed a most formidable

organisation of attack upon General Pétain's main army in Champagne, and extended it round Verdun and St. Mihiel to Lorraine and Upper Alsace.

Consequently, the French Command felt certain that the principal weight of the enemy would again be hurled against its forces. In the same way the British Command was led to expect that an intense effort would be made to recover the Vimy Ridge by a turning movement from Fampoux, Monchy, and the Quéant and Cambrai sectors, and a northern stroke from the Lille Ridge. Then, apparently for the purpose of subsidiary, distracting operations, the organisation for attack was prolonged against all the allied front.

In ordinary circumstances so stupendous a scheme of new communications would have been impossible of execution. But when Count Mirbach became the practical anarch of Russia, with the Soviet as his instrument of anarchy, the German Staff was able to relieve their steel-making works

of the task of providing new light railways, engines, and trucks by removing and transporting much of the dense network of new military lines in Galicia, Volhynia, Podolia, and the Russian Baltic provinces.

As already explained in Chapter CCXLVIII. (Vol. 11, page 441) Ludendorff employed protective devices on a colossal scale to conceal his principal organisations for an offensive movement north-west and south of Laon. He constructed many of his new roads and tracks through country that had been camouflaged beforehand, and built innumerable supplementary emplacements, into which he introduced fresh artillery just before opening action.

TO FACE THE GERMAN OFFENSIVE.
British ammunition-cart taking up supplies to the guns by a short cut over a bad bit of ground on the western front, and (in circle) moving up British field-guns to meet the onrush of the enemy offensive in March, 1918.

When the roads at night were so thronged with traffic that the troops themselves were astonished at the wide front on which they moved, and joyfully proclaimed that "Germany was on the march!" everything worked smoothly in spite of the star-shells dropped by British nocturnal aerial scouts. The precautions in regard to cover were well observed, and although Sir Hubert Gough knew there was a concentration around St. Quentin, and Sir Julian Byng traced many of the new batteries placed in the Quéant sector, Ludendorff's chief surprise stroke was delivered with entire success.

About March 18th, 1918, most of the enemy divisions, that were being rapidly swung forward, had the nature of the coming operations explained to them. They were told that three huge armies were to make a general advance in a westerly direction to the estuary of the Somme at Abbeville, where lack of bridges over the widening stretch of water

direction of Arras, and thereby guard the flank of the first main attacking army.

This army, directed by General Otto von Below, the victor of Caporetto, was known as Michael I., and was launched against Croisilles and Bullecourt. Immediately south of Michael I. was the army of General von der Marwitz, which was called Michael II., and directed against Bapaume and Péronne.

Then about St. Quentin was the Michael III. group, consisting of the great army of General Oskar von Hutier, into which were fed, and that with extraordinary rapidity, most of the reserve divisions of the Crown Prince of Prussia, who was pretending to menace the Champagne front.

The day of attack was known as Michael Day. The name was used as a symbol for the German day of revenge upon the **Germany's "Michael Day"** hated Briton, Michael being a Teutonic national figure similar to John Bull and Uncle Sam. The date of Michael Day was, of course a supreme secret, and regimental officers could still only make a guess at it when the great western march began. Some armies began moving at a pace of twelve to fifteen miles a night about March 14th, and then thought that the offensive had opened and the British line had been broken, and that they were being speeded up to exploit the break-through.

But on March 18th the secret of the date became a fairly open one, and the British Staff learnt something, at least, of what was impending, and drew some troops from the Vimy area of demonstration to strengthen the pivoting point of the line behind Croisilles and St. Leger, while bringing forward some additional artillery for the further strengthening of the Third and Fifth Armies.

According to a published German estimate, the attacking gun-power still remained four times stronger than the defending artillery. Even the demonstrating Mars group, for example, had sixty-eight batteries and several

would leave the British Army separated from the French. It was explained that, as France would quickly come to terms when left to bear the whole weight of the German forces, it was necessary first to direct the grand blow against the British.

So thoroughly had all preparations been planned that failure was regarded as an impossibility. Yet it was arranged that if the attack should be held up at any point operations should cease there, and the troops be moved to another sector. Four groups of forces were arrayed between Arras and La Fère. The most northerly was known as the Mars group, and was detailed to meet and parry any counter-stroke from the

BRITISH TROOPS TAKING OVER THE ST. QUENTIN SECTOR.
British officers at some of the dug-outs which they occupied on taking over the St. Quentin sector of the western front from the French in January, 1918; and (in circle) British officers wading through the slush of a front trench, on the same sector, where the marshland aggravated the normal discomforts of a winter campaign.

C

upon all the British zones of defence was of a subtle deadliness as well as of shattering force. Gas was the enemy's grand medium for smothering all opposition, and, as has been explained in Chapter CCXLVIII. (Vol. 11, page 441), the gas was often placed in a bottle in a high-explosive shell, so that when the rolling, smoking explosions occurred the British troops might not think it necessary to rely wholly upon the gas-masks.

In the dark, stagnant, foggy air the gas as it settled clung about the ground. Many of the German gunners were firing for the first time on the front and at invisible targets, without aerial or any other control. There was thus a large haphazard element in their work, and it was to make up for this that gas-shell was used in an

hundred trench-mortars and infantry guns behind every two regiments waiting for attack. This amounted to the staggering proportion of nearly one piece of artillery to every ten infantrymen in the first phase of the assault. Of course, as the fresh divisions of the grand reserve marched through the first attacking forces, and, without relieving them, made a further thrust onward, the general proportion between the artillery and infantry diminished. Yet the fact remains that the enemy, on his own showing, opened battle with one piece of ordnance to every ten men in the shock regiments.

The final concentration was favoured by the weather. March 20th was a day of rain and low-lying clouds, during which the German front was veiled from British flying observers. Something was seen, however, about St. Quentin.

ALONG THE BRITISH LINES OF REINFORCEMENT.
British troops passing forward through a French village, and (above) marching along a winding bank-protected road through open country, on the way to aid in holding up the pressure of the German offensive.

The British artillery in the neighbourhood bombarded the town with gas-shell, and in the following night many of the British guns were moved to new positions to avoid the hostile counter-battery fire that was sure to come. Also in some of the sectors of the Third Army, where the battle was expected and the troops in line prepared for it, the ground which they had been holding was suddenly changed, so the men might escape the worst effects of the preliminary bombardment.

Considerable injury was inflicted upon some of General von Hutier's leading forces when the British suddenly deluged St. Quentin with gas-shell; but as the **An unparalleled bombardment** German commander had some thirty divisions immediately available for action, and still more in reserve, his plan was in no way disarranged by his preliminary losses. They were, indeed, more than compensated by the arrival of the kind of weather required for a tremendous mass attack.

After the warm weather of early spring the rain rose from the ground in a dense mist and, only gradually thinning away under the sun, allowed a field of vision of fifty yards in the later part of the morning of Thursday, March 21st, 1918. About an hour and a half before day broke, the colossal masses of German howitzers, cannon, high-velocity guns, trench-mortars, and infantry guns opened a bombardment of unparalleled violence and depth. Places some twenty-eight miles behind the firing-line were struck by the high-velocity shells, and the hurricane of high explosive and gas that fell

enormous way so as to produce a completely drenching effect. More than fifty miles of the British front, from Monchy to Tergnier, was flooded with poison gas. All known or possible gun positions were especially inundated, with the aim of weakening the defensive shell curtain and counter-battery fire, and all ground likely to be sheltering reserves was smothered. Then, before the German infantry began their movement, pure high-explosive shell was employed in vast swirls of ploughing, roaring death. The shells were so placed as to blast the gas away from the ground the attacking troops intended to occupy. Immense care was taken in regard to all valleys and winding hollows likely to hold gas and to contain strong garrisons.

They were flogged and winnowed by masses of guns until they looked like long bursts of volcanic activity. Resistance in anything like strength was impossible in such positions, and was not attempted. The British line had been arranged in a flexible manner, somewhat after the model of Ludendorff's system along the Hindenburg line in the previous year.

There was an outpost zone, occupied by detached parties. Behind the observing-posts were machine-gunners, and behind the machine-guns was the first infantry line of any continuity and strength. All this formed what the enemy termed the foreground position. At a certain depth behind it, varying according to the nature of the ground and the scheme of defence, was the battle zone, in which it was intended to fight a pitched battle when the enemy had been compelled to reveal the forces and methods he was employing.

In places the British had advanced strong points, screened by protective devices, and serving both as enfilading machine-gun positions against German forces working through the outpost line, and as artillery observation centres from which, by sunken telephone cables, large groups of guns could be closely directed upon hostile waves and columns striving to reach the battle zone. Southward, in the marshland below St. Quentin, a system of block-houses had been organised after the line had been taken over from the French in January, 1918.

It was only possible to delay the enemy in the thinly held advanced positions, but in addition to their direct, confusing effect upon attacking formations, the outpost forces lessened the power of the bombarding artillery, by greatly increasing the depth of the ground that had to be searched by fire, and also exposed the multitudes of hostile infantry to more prolonged countering gun fire during their struggle to reach the zone of critical conflict.

By choosing a misty morning, and thickening the mist in difficult places by means of smoke-boxes, the German general avoided his worst disadvantages in attack. As his

however, thrust with equal force all along the fifty-mile front, but made knife-like attempts to cut between certain sectors and envelop parts of the line he did not directly assault.

In some ways the general situation had a certain analogy with that obtaining at the opening of the British offensive in the First Battle of the Somme. The British attack was then held and defeated **German success** in the northern part of the line because the **around St. Quentin** defenders were amply prepared there, but was successful in the south, where the troops were taken more or less by surprise.

In the German offensive, proclaimed as Michael's revenge for the defeats he had suffered at the hands of the British, the northern attacking armies failed in an absolute manner. Far from turning the Vimy Ridge line, they failed to approach the pivoting point of Arras or even to recover all the ground evacuated in the retreat to the Hindenburg line. But in the south, above and below St. Quentin, the tremendous weight with which the Germans maintained their assaults resulted in the greatest success they had obtained in parallel battle since the breaking of the Russian line at Gorlice in the spring of 1915.

From all points of view the southern battle was the more important. In it the enemy won at Vermand, a few miles from St. Quentin, the fine straight highway running to Amiens towards his grand goal of Abbeville. He also obtained four or five other roads trending in the same direction. Moreover, he broke the British and French forces asunder at their delicate point of junction, and while pursuing his principal plan of advancing towards the Somme estuary at Abbeville he was immediately able to improvise a formidable, distracting secondary offensive in the direction of Paris.

men could seldom be seen at more than fifty yards distance in the marshlands of the St. Quentin area, and were often invisible when closer than that, British forward observing officers could only direct most of their guns upon known ways of approach and known or suspected emplacements, while maintaining a defensive barrage of shrapnel over No Man's Land and the enemy's unseen lines.

This was far from being sufficient to shatter so gigantic an offensive movement in its opening stage. In clear weather the German superiority in gun-power would probably have been balanced by the British superiority in air-power and by the large field of aimed fire afforded to the defending machine-gunners and riflemen. In misty weather the resisting strength of the fortified lines was much diminished, while the driving force of attacking massed infantry was considerably augmented.

The enemy advanced in masses, so as to get considerable bodies quickly through the shrapnel curtain, and rapidly overwhelm the advanced guards and artillery observers in the foreground positions. He did not,

OPEN-COUNTRY FIGHTING ON THE WESTERN FRONT.
British troops holding a position along a railway when, in the spring of 1918, the early success of the German offensive transformed the conditions from those of trench to open warfare. Above : British troops passing Tanks as they marched through a village near the fighting front.

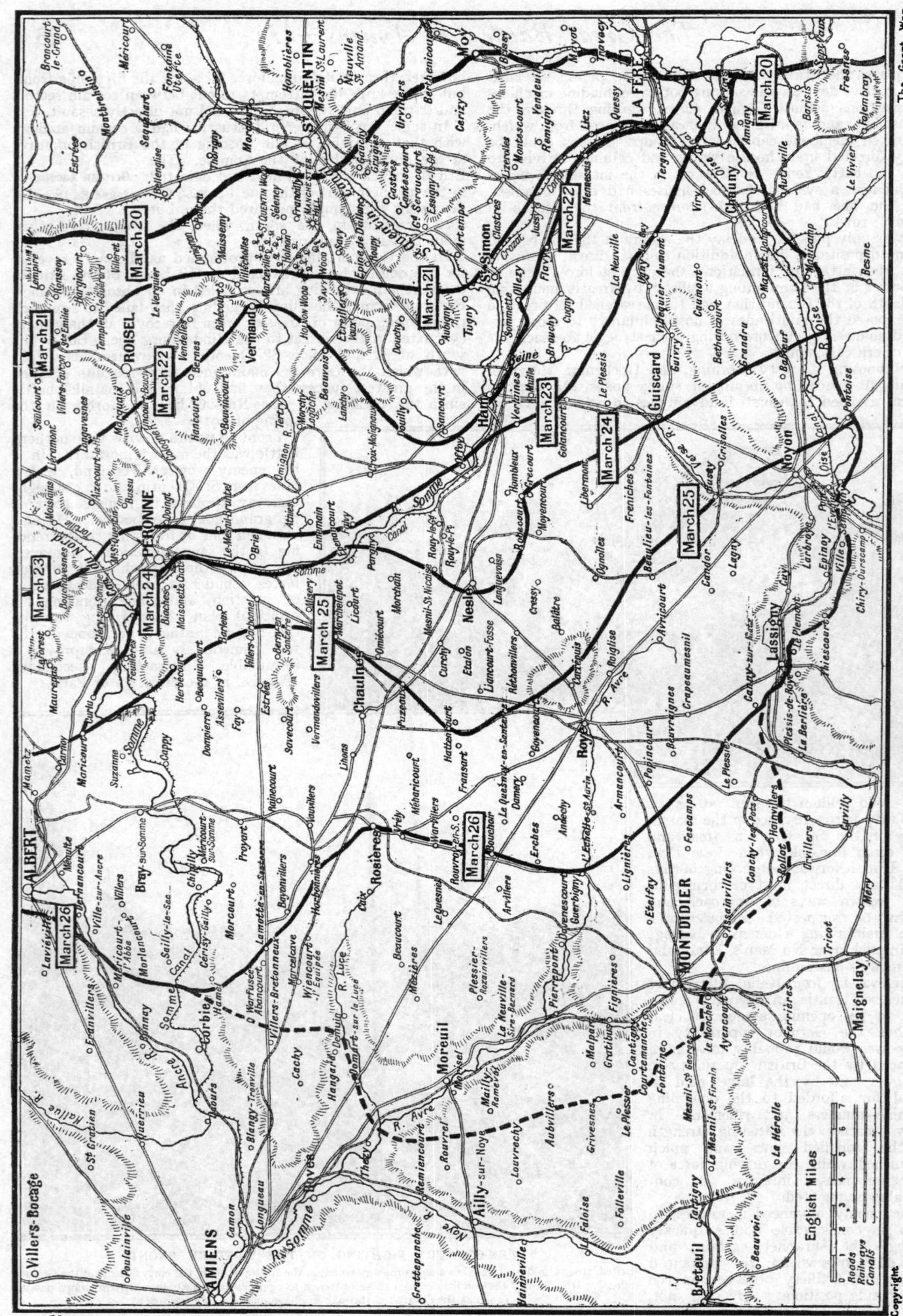

FIRST STAGES IN THE GREAT BATTLE FOR AMIENS.

Map specially drawn to illustrate the waves of the offensive by which in March, 1918, the Germans hoped to capture Amiens, divide the British from the French Armies, and "drive the British into the sea." The line of March 26th indicates approximately where the cyclonic Teuton storm met the fiercest resistance. The broken line marks roughly the limits to which Ludendorff was able to penetrate before the tide of invasion was turned.

24

Against the fourteen divisions of the Fifth British Army, under Sir Hubert Gough, were launched forty German divisions of the Eighteenth German Army, under General von Hutier. At the opening of the action the extremity of the British line rested by the Oise River at Tergnier, close to the hill town of La Fère, which remained in the enemy's possession in March, 1917, owing to his device of inundating the marshy country around. Some of the seventeenth-century fortifications of La Fère were, however, won by the French and handed over to the British. Chief among them were Vendeuil Fort, north of the town; Liez Fort and Garde Fort, north-westward; and the new works constructed by the railway junction of Tergnier, about four miles west of La Fère. Though useless as artillery positions, the old La Fère forts were admirable as machine-gun and observation posts. They became, in British hands, the foundations of a block-house system that extended through the marshlands, and with simpler works, including some that had been first organised by the enemy, formed a chain of redoubts that covered the approaches from St. Quentin.

London troops held the southernmost advanced works, including the fort known as the Keep, opposite La Fère, and the Liez Redoubt, on a chambered rise of ground. A company of the Buffs garrisoned the old fortress of Vendeuil, constructed by Vauban, the architect of the Verdun works. Above the Buffs a Scottish force held the line near Urvillers, and men of the Ulster Division manned the Racecourse Redoubt, built on the spot where the townsmen of St. Quentin were used to amuse themselves with sport. Farther north was a hill that had been taken by the Manchesters in the battle along the Hindenburg line, and called in their honour Manchester Hill. Transformed into a work dominating the western approach from St. Quentin, it was again occupied by Manchester men, who were resolved that they would defend their famous redoubt until the last. Still farther north was the Enghien Redoubt, a strong point in the sector occupied by the 61st Division.

Chain of redoubts near St. Quentin

Upon the chain of redoubts the weight of the German attack first fully fell. When the enemy came forward in the morning—at times varying from seven o'clock to ten minutes to ten, according to the local condition of the mist, the state of the ground, and other circumstances—he was faced by the line of works, arranged several hundred yards apart, belted with wire entanglements and each garrisoned by a company of infantry whose machine-guns were arranged to sweep all the ground.

By the time the gigantic bombardment lifted from the British foreground to the battle position there were some gaps made in the chain of earthworks, and the German infantry stormed out to find the gaps in close waves, with the men scarcely more than a pace apart in the main bodies. Some of their sharpshooters cut the wire that had not been broken by the bombardment, and their best machine-gunners dashed forward and began to send out a barrage of bullets to keep down the British fire while the masses of the shock divisions rushed forward like gigantic human battering-rams. In two main concentrations they endeavoured to break from Moy and La Fère, encircle everything in the nine-mile space between, and then block the path of retreat of the Scottish force north of Moy. The British post at Travecy, between La Fère and Vendeuil, was surrounded early in the struggle, when the fog was thickest, and communications with it became very difficult. But the Londoners in the Keep at La Fère made an heroic resistance. They caught every German force that tried to bridge or boat across the stream, and the struggle went on until the enemy corpses made small islands near the bank, and yet no footing was won.

Meanwhile, Germans tried to strike upon the rear of the Londoners in the Keep by forcing a passage southward, where the waterway swerved by the marshes of La Frette round the British flank. Stealing out under cover of the bombardment and foggy darkness, enemy sappers threw four pontoon bridges across the stream. Over the bridges rushed a Landwehr brigade in an attempt to break by surprise into the English rear, while a Jaeger force was trying to work round the northern side past Liez Fort.

A COIGN OF VANTAGE NEAR THE FRONT LINE.
Machine-gun party of a Scottish regiment watching the progress of the German offensive from a support line. The leader had climbed a tree to give the others instant intimation of the appearance of the Boche.

It was the Landwehr brigade that was surprised. The bridges had been seen and a trap prepared. From the high ground above the marsh British field-guns swept the La Frette position with shell, while the London infantry drove the Germans back to the river. Hutier, however, had many brigades to spare. He sent forward more divisions, and after terrible losses his masses began to work around the Keep. Having delayed for many critical hours the enemy's most menacing thrust at the junction point of the allied armies, the men of the London Regiment had to withdraw hastily from the La Fère Keep, leaving their dead and many of their wounded behind. They fell back on Tergnier and the Crozat Canal line.

Northward the West Kents gallantly stood against the multitudes of Germans, who continually attacked all the morning with increasing forces. The last message that came through ran: "Holding out till 12.30 p.m. Boches all round within fifty yards except rear. Can only see forty yards, so it is very difficult to kill the blighters."

Heroism of the West Kents

Marvellous it is that under such conditions the redoubt was not surrounded soon after daybreak, as occurred with some other outposts. It may have been that the fog was denser and slower in thinning out in the southern marshlands than it was in the hollows of the undulating chalk, where the field of vision enlarged in the course of the morning to four hundred yards. On the other hand, it is possible that the new German mist-making machine was largely used in keeping such redoubts as that of the Royal West Kents blanketed until Thursday afternoon, so as to allow the German gunners to maintain for hours almost a point-blank fire upon the works, during the many intervals in which fresh infantry was marching up to attempt rush attacks from three sides.

The East Kents in Vauban's fortress had the same experience. Owing to the dense fog, the unceasing waves of attack were able to get round the fort early in the morning, and thus bring an enveloping fire on the garrison. Again

HOLDING A ROADSIDE OUTPOST.
On the alert against enemy movements. The men had taken up a screened position by the roadside, the trees on the right evidently having been cut to ensure them from surprise attack on that side.

any price in lives of his men to achieve a decision. He used German divisions against Irish and Scottish battalions—ten men against one, the ten men being backed by four guns against one. Fierce as had been his lunges over the Oise marshes by La Fère, they seemed directed rather to attracting reserves and, if possible, giving the neighbouring French army urgent work to do in helping to save the allied junction than to making a lightning break-through—that is to say, they generally covered the supreme design for striking a shattering blow from St. Quentin in the direction of the roads leading towards Abbeville, which was the distant goal, and the main railway communication between the British and French Armies, which was the immediate objective.

From around St. Quentin the German commander struck with shattering force, and then sent in fresh divisions to pass between the successful troops and carry the attack clean through the battle zone. The British line about the famous old city was held by Scotsmen along the Oise towards Itancourt. Thence the Ulster Division occupied the ground running from the edge of Neuville St. Amand to Gauchy by the Somme Canal, and the fortified knoll, Epine de Dallon, commanding the Somme marshes. On the left of the Ulstermen was a British division **Fog that favoured** composed of Manchesters, Scots Fusiliers, **the enemy** Bedfords, King's Liverpools, South Lancashire Pioneers, and other units. The British outpost positions on Manchester Hill, Epine de Dallon, St. Quentin Racecourse, and other high places seemed to make the line as impregnable as was Vimy Ridge. They commanded all the open country over which the Germans had to work; and had Ludendorff been so foolish as to open battle on a clear day, his massed divisions would have been annihilated as they moved out of the city.

In the fog, however, they effected a complete surprise. At least one British redoubt had a strong patrol groping about No Man's Land vainly trying to get in touch with the enemy at the time when the redoubt itself had been surrounded. The patrol was not captured because of the mist, and, after marching for two days through territory that the enemy overran, it rejoined the army.

It seems to have been about ten o'clock in the morning that most of the first attacking divisions in St. Quentin moved forward behind their skirmishing groups, after a bombardment of six and a half hours. Even at this late hour in the day, when visibility had increased to four hundred yards around Arras, the fog remained so dense between the Oise and Somme that the men could not see more than fifty yards from the trenches. Many of the block-houses were surrounded before the garrisoning companies knew they were being attacked

and again the Buffs managed to sweep the grey flood from their rear, but in the afternoon their strength was so diminished that they could not prevent themselves being firmly hemmed in all round. Nearly every officer or man who was then still handling a machine-gun or rifle was wounded, some of them more than once. Yet the Buffs held out. They held out all the afternoon, and when the evening mist thickened and turned twilight into early darkness, a remnant of the invincibles was still holding out; for their signal-lamp was seen about six o'clock above the Remigny road, telling their comrades retreating to Jussy and the Crozat Canal line that the great tradition of the Buffs, famous in English poetry, was again heroically illustrated.

When in the night the last of the Buffs company fell, the southernmost outposts in their earthworks and Vendeuil Fort had nobly accomplished their desperate task. The pivoting point of the entire line was still firmly held at Tergnier, and as the London men, men of Kent and Kentish men, the Rifle Brigade, Surreys, and other Home County battalions wheeled back to Jussy and the Crozat Canal, the forces above them swung down to the moat of the waterway.

Early in the day the situation between Moy and St. Quentin had become extremely grave. Here it was that Hutier made the most tremendous of his efforts to break swiftly and completely through the British line, offering

A MESSAGE FROM MARS.
Incident during Ludendorff's advance against Amiens. When the photograph was taken, the building, in the occupation of the British, had just been set on fire by a German shell.

and the main British forces holding the battle positions do not appear to have known or to have been warned that the infantry contest had been opened.

The enemy masses, therefore, escaped much of the intense barrage of shells, machine-gun bullets, and rifle fire, for the production of which all the defensive works had been skilfully organised. On the south-eastern flank a wedge was driven between the Ulstermen and the Scotsmen soon after the action opened, with the result that the Ulstermen's battle position on the high ground between Essigny and Contescourt was partly turned.

At half-past ten a message was received from the Race-course Redoubt that strong attacks were proceeding there, and although communications were cut off immediately afterwards, the Ulster garrison continued to hold out until the evening. In the meantime the splendid Irish division most gallantly endeavoured to hold on to its main battle position against overwhelming forces of Germans working down to Grand Seraucourt, more than five miles behind the Gauchy front. All hope of saving the line was lost at two o'clock, when the Germans advanced from Essigny village to the railway-station, and began to trickle onward along paths, hedges, and watercourses towards the canalised Somme.

Gallant stand at Essigny On the entrenched hill by the railway-station an Ulster detachment continued fighting when completely surrounded, but there was a large gap in the British line at this point, and only a small number of infantrymen to hold it. Happily, a young battery commander had his guns on the eastern side of the railway running down from St. Quentin, and in the critical afternoon the fog cleared sufficiently for him to mark all that happened on the slopes by Essigny. He blew the Germans out of the railway-station, smashed them up in the village, and shrapnelled every detachment of any size that tried to work downward.

As in some other sectors, the gunners held the line practically alone. It was ten o'clock at night before they ceased firing, and until they prepared to fall back across the Crozat Canal to Jussy and Flavy-le-Martel no more ground was won by the enemy round the hills by Essigny.

But above Essigny a hasty retirement had to be carried out in the morning of the tragic March 21st. At twenty minutes past eleven Grugies valley was lost, in spite of the fact that the Ulster trenches there were bristling with machine-guns and covered by reinforced groups of batteries, which had been carefully registered. Before noon a considerable number of the guns at Contescourt had to be blown up, and the gunners turned to cut their way back through the enveloping flood of Germans.

FRIEND AND FOE UNDER THE RED CROSS.
Stretcher cases—wounded British soldiers and their German prisoners—awaiting removal at a British dressing-station in the vicinity of the fighting-line during the progress of the German offensive.

In the afternoon clerks, servants, and signallers were armed, together with any available labouring forces, so as to provide men for the continual rearguard actions in the long, heroic retreat. Facing the enemy with a weak line that yet was never broken, the men of Ulster fought till nightfall, and then crossed the canalised Somme by Artemps in good order, and blew up the bridges behind them.

The British division on the left of the Ulstermen had much the same experiences in the same thick weather. At ten o'clock their reconnaissance parties could not find the enemy in the fog; at half-past ten most of their own outpost positions were in course of being surrounded; at twelve o'clock their battle zone in front of Etreillers was penetrated. The earthwork on Manchester Hill, connected with the main line by a sunken cable, was the scene of a feat of arms comparable with the defence of Rorke's Drift.

For five hours the Manchester men fought the enemy from the hill that their fellow-townsmen had captured a year before. The officer commanding was wounded, but continued to direct the action and to telephone to Headquarters how the struggle was proceeding. In his last message he said that practically all his men had been hit, swarms of Germans were round the redoubt, and were entering it in places. "Yet," ran his final sentence, "the Manchester Regiment will defend Manchester Hill to the last."

SHELTER IN A STORM OF WAR.
Mules of a British ammunition column, with their drivers, under the lee of a protective haystack. Meanwhile, the supplies they had brought into the field were being employed to thin the ranks of the advancing foe.

The men were enlisted from the same mills and warehouses; they had worked together before they fought together in a "Pals Battalion"; and together they died, with four hostile divisions strangling them, by choking weight of numbers.

By such magnificent delaying actions as that of the Manchesters and that of the Yorkshires in another advanced position there seemed just a desperate chance of saving the battle-line. The Bedfords and Scots Fusiliers, with other Manchesters and Yorkshires, King's Liverpools, and South Lancashires, made a murderous stand in Holnon Wood and Savy Wood, while the line above, that first threatened to break, was restored by a magnificent counter-attack at Villécholles. All day and all night the British worked

SAVING STORES THREATENED BY THE ENEMY ADVANCE.
Loading a barge with provisions from a forward British supply store during the early stages of the German offensive. The progress of that offensive made it necessary to remove such material farther back to prevent the possibility of its falling into the enemy's hands.

slaughter among the German masses that continually endeavoured to overwhelm them.

At three o'clock on Friday afternoon, March 22nd, the division's battle position was still partly held, though the wasted defending battalions had been so pressed back on both flanks that the triangle they presented to the enemy was being shaped into a circle. The troops on their left were compelled to retire at noon on Friday; while on their right, where the Ulstermen were retreating towards Ham, a most gallant remnant of Yorkshires were fighting like tigers in Roupy, with their line ending in the air, and the Germans working round it into the headquarters of the division.

The Yorkshires just escaped complete envelopment. The Bedfords were surrounded, but broke through the German net. The Scots Fusiliers assembled and marched away as though on parade, but left behind a platoon, through the runner being killed while carrying the order to retire. There was still a good deal of mist on the southern-

Escapade of brave most field of conflict on the second day of
Scots Fusiliers battle, and the platoon was missed by the
enemy. The subaltern and his men did not observe the Germans marching aside and behind them. When night fell the young officer tried to connect with his battalion, found nothing British anywhere about, formed his platoon in fours, and marched them down the road towards Péronne.

The way was clear, but the fields on either hand were full of figures, some resting, some moving. "Wer da?" cried a sentry. The Scot mumbled something as guttural as he could make it, and passed on. Thrice he was challenged, "Who goes there?" But he led his men right through the

enemy's lines, and by the morning reached the British outposts at Beauvois, rejoining his battalion two days later.

Below the road to Beauvois and below the line at Roupy, where the dauntless Yorkshires hung on, the wing of the Ulster Division, represented by the indomitable Inniskillings, won breathing space for themselves and comrades by a fine counter-attack at Douchy, north of the main road to Ham, while the Royal Irish Rifles distinguished themselves by magnificent fighting. The old towered town of Ham, rising in a girdle of marshes by the Somme, was valiantly defended by a rearguard at the canal bridge-head of Tugny, and by Dragoons, Scots Greys, and other cavalry at Ollezy, to give time for the unfortunate townspeople once more to abandon their homes and for the sadly reduced infantry divisions holding the Crozat Canal line to dig themselves in.

The enemy commander endeavoured to make another break-through at the canal town of Jussy, between Ham and Tergnier. By remarkable rapidity and precision of movement his immense infantry masses converged in the misty morning of Friday, March 22nd, upon Jussy and occupied the town. But by an impetuous counter-attack a single British brigade recovered Jussy. The Germans then struck again more to the east, and won a footing across the canal between Jussy and Tergnier. The defending troops, steadily contesting all the critical ground, and maintaining union with the French Army, swung to the railway line between Ham and Tergnier.

Immediately behind them was a stretch of wooded hills, some twelve miles long and five miles deep, with the town of Chauny in the rear, and the moat of the Oise River and the embankment of the Tergnier-Noyon railway protecting the eastern flank of the clump of forested heights from all the savage enemy thrusts delivered from the La Fère base.

It was not until Saturday, March 23rd, that small forces of French dismounted Cuirassiers, with motor machine-guns and motor-cannon, arrived above Chauny to strengthen slightly the line which the English and Scottish troops were still stubbornly contesting against the swarming hordes of Germany.

Not until the evening of March 23rd were **Struggle on the** the positions along the western bank of **Crozat Canal** the Crozat Canal carried by some three German army corps, into which fresh divisions had continually been fed. By this time some allied reinforcements had arrived, with whom the remnants of the British battalions were brigaded, and in murderous rearguard actions, amid the tangled high woods and long slopes of the block of hill country, the British and the French, with some Americans, wrought great havoc among the dense waves and columns of attack, and fell back at last to the south-west of Tergnier and the north-east of Guiscard.

In the meantime, however, Ham had been lost. The Germans poured down in two tremendous forces, one speeding along the two roads through Roupy and Tugny, so as to turn the old fortress town from the north, while the other thrust along the St. Simon road, endeavouring to outflank alike the troops defending Ham and the forces holding the hill country above Chauny. There was wild and terrific fighting below St. Simon, where the Ulstermen fell back in the evening of March 22nd, covered by the cavalry. Some of the Scots Greys, after being entirely cut off, spent the night in adventures among the Germans, and escaped across the canal in the early morning of March 23rd.

The cavalry fought their first actions on foot, but a labour battalion succeeded in bringing up their horses, each plucky,

Crowded ways of war: British troops and transport on the way to meet the German offensive.

Brief respite after strenuous action: British troops from the fighting front resting in a French village.

To rest camp after battle, April, 1918: Warwicks returning from the Forest of Nieppe.

To stay the massed offensive of March, 1918: British field=guns getting into action.

Saluting the brigadier: British reinforcements setting out for the hard-pressed line, April, 1918.

"Sledge-hammer strokes of the heavy guns": British artillery shelling the advancing enemy.

Work of duty and of mercy: Field stretcher-bearers in the zone of fire.

To break the German offensive: British Tank going forward to the battle-line.

inexperienced man struggling along through the darkness with fifteen excited beasts tied together on one rope. When the cavalry sat their mounts they felt ripe for the wildest of exploits. A party from each unit was detached and formed into a kind of irregular force of horse, which conducted actions on its own initiative throughout the rest of the long retreat, and accomplished extraordinarily good work in hindering the movements of the enemy.

The rest of the troopers attached themselves to sections of infantry and, sometimes on horseback, sometimes dismounted, took a main part in all the fierce, quick fighting between Ham and Noyon. For one night Ham was held by the units of the British division from the west of St. Quentin, while the Ulstermen were resting on the road to Roye. But the enemy drove the cavalry rearguards back on the right, and, fanning out from the Crozat Canal, pushed forward again around the flanks of the northern Irishmen. Under a one-armed Staff officer, who had lost his limb at Hooge, orderlies and batmen arrayed themselves in a defensive flank by the Beine River, while fragments of the exhausted battalion of Inniskilling Fusiliers were collected by a brigade major on horseback, and led northward to Brouchy Château, where the line had been badly broken. After bringing his men within storming distance of the lost position, the officer dismounted and, leading the charge against heavy machine-gun and rifle fire, killed or routed all the force in and about the château. This saved the Ulstermen's flank from being pierced, and, stiffened by the recovery of certain units that had been detached for other work, the noble 36th Division held their new line until French troops arrived to relieve them. Little relief, however, did the Ulstermen or the English and Scotsmen alongside them obtain. The French were not in sufficient force to form a solid front, and the men, who had been fighting without sleep or rest since the morning of March 21st, had to line out across the Amiens road by Andechy to prevent a large force of German cavalry from pushing through the gaps to the open country and clearing the way for the great German drive to Abbeville.

Nothing like a line could be held by the remnants of the two divisions that had fought day and night from St. Quentin to the neighbourhood of Montdidier. While the Ulstermen and their French supports were scattered in outpost work west of Roye, the remnants of the Bedfords, Scots Fusiliers, Manchesters, King's Liverpools, and South Lancashire Pioneers conducted a prolonged nightmare-like chain of actions from Ham through Roye to Bouchoir on the way to Amiens.

The struggle about Ham

They it was who held Ham during the night while the Ulstermen were resting. They obtained there small reinforcements from a training school and from entrenching detachments. When the Germans stormed into Ham, the Englishmen and Scotsmen fought a glorious rearguard action at Verlaines. Then, widening their line to counter the enemy's double flanking movement, they made another stand between Nesle and Guiscard, mowing the enemy down in masses on March 25th at Robecourt and Grecourt. The Germans tried to throw bridges across the Nord Canal, but as each detachment appeared with rafts or sections of pontoons, it was annihilated with aimed and controlled fire.

Like the Ulstermen, the Englishmen and Scots were then relieved, and sent to sleep in billets west of Roye. Like the Ulstermen, they awoke to learn that in their absence the line had not held, and that the enemy was marching behind them in great strength on the road to Amiens. There then followed a medley of adventures and battles, in which the Ulstermen, English, and Scotsmen, with the independent detached force of British cavalry, strove by superhuman efforts to hold the southern Amiens roads until General Humbert and General Fayolle could bring up an important French force to safeguard the southern routes to Amiens.

An Ulster brigade headquarters at Guerbigny, near Montdidier, was surrounded by a patrol of two hundred Germans. The brigade staff turned out and fought the enemy off, and the general, with a runner standing at his side, wrote a message for help, pen in one hand and rifle in the other, firing between the words he wrote. When the enemy was beaten off, smaller patrols continued to worry the Ulstermen all night, occasion-

TO HINDER THE ADVANCING FOE.

Engineers removing a temporary plank bridge over a canal on the British western front in France for the purpose of delaying the German advance in the spring of 1918 while the heavily pressed allied line was being strengthened and stabilised.

ally sweeping up a few prisoners and dashing away again. They captured two battalion commanders and a divisional staff officer, who had set off in a motor-car from Guerbigny to examine an endangered rearguard position. Another cavalry patrol captured an ambulance driver near the spot where the empty motor-car remained, but were in turn surprised by a British cavalry patrol. The driver escaped, in a running fight, recovered his ambulance, attached the empty motor-car, and, towing it back, spent the rest of the night in carrying away wounded.

Above Guerbigny the English and Scots division, that had fought alongside the Ulstermen from St. Quentin, again entered into action at Bouchoir, on the Amiens road. Their orders were to hold the line at Le Quesnoy, on the Amiens road, but while marching out there they found the enemy already in possession. The German main army was still moving forward with extraordinary speed, and behind the strong screen of cavalry and infantry, which was trying to push through the Ulstermen on the right, the roads were full of transport, all hurrying forward in the darkness. *Confused fighting in the dark*

The survivors of the great British division—that had covered quite sixty miles of fiercely-contested battleground in its manœuvring retreat from the western outskirts of St. Quentin—were not appalled by the new, heavy task set them. The enemy had trained them in the art of fighting one against ten. They sat down at Bouchoir, on the Amiens road, and there met and threw back a strong German force. In the confusion a column of hostile waggon transport, that had been moving behind the broken troops, took a wrong turning and, instead of proceeding south, went west towards Bouchoir.

The Scots Fusiliers lined the highway, and planned to let the column pass and make an entire capture of it. But one man was too eager, and, opening fire at twenty paces, shot one of the drivers down and alarmed the others, stampeding the train in terrorised confusion. All the Scotsmen then attacked, shooting down more Germans and taking six of them prisoners. But, in the circumstances, the most valuable thing captured was a field-cooker, containing a hot meal for the front-line enemy troops above Guerbigny. The Scots Fusiliers found it very pleasant and comforting, and, with renewed vigour, arranged another ambush on the Amiens road and trapped a German cavalry patrol.

By this time the original scanty divisions that had held the southernmost line on March 21st were utterly outworn. Brigades had shrunk to the strength of battalions, and the men were so dazed by fatigue that many were barely able to move or understand orders. Almost mechanically their thin, ragged line swung a little forward and then a longer distance backwards, and but for the fact that the Germans were growing nearly as tired as the British, the gate to Abbeville might have been pushed open. Yet when the enemy, with incomparable reserves of power, made a dogged spurt onwards, life flickered back into the deadened defending troops, and, with no possible reserve of strength save the numbed spirit within them, they made again and again what appeared to be yet one last effort. Then was it that leadership supremely counted, as well as mettle of race.

British line bent but not broken

They won through. Big was the sag in their line when they were relieved, yet the line was unbroken. Along the roads down which they desperately fought—St. Quentin to Roupy, Roupy to Ham, Ham to Amiens or Noyon—a British force had passed in retreat at the end of August, 1914, after the action of Le Cateau. Where the Yorkshires and Inniskillings stood and charged the enemy, to rearguard the retirement over the Somme, stragglers from Mons had been kept from falling asleep by the roadside by the music of a penny whistle and a toy drum.

Little was the difference in courageous endurance between the long-service Regular soldiers of 1914 and the hastily-trained New Army men of 1918. The Old Contemptibles were better shots than the New Indomitables, largely for the reason that the new infantryman had in the long trench campaign become too much of a bomber, and did not always regard his rifle when used in aimed rapid fire as the eternal mistress of the battlefield.

The old Regular troops, having only an ordinary amount of light field-artillery behind them, had been naturally more accustomed to fighting a battle of manœuvre with little artillery support. This characteristic had recently been acquired in intensive training by the German soldier, who, after the second day of the battle, worked rapidly forward beyond the range of his own guns, and employed long-distance rifle and machine-gun fire to keep his opponents down while he was manœuvring around them.

Yet, in fundamental character and extraordinary resilience and adaptability under tragic conditions of battle, the new British soldier and the old were men of the same quality. It must be borne in mind that the overwhelmed yet unsubdued Fifth British Army had not been in a position to undergo that process of retraining in rifle fire and open field warfare to which the enemy forces owed their success.

Renewed value of the rifle

Sir Hubert Gough's men practically represented all the available reserve that Sir Douglas Haig possessed after fighting the great battles of 1917 and sending an expeditionary force to Italy. When, in order to create an allied mass of manœuvre to be used by the Supreme Council of War at Versailles, the Fifth Army had to take over the St. Quentin-La Fère line, the strain upon the whole British force in France and Flanders increased.

In the absence of the new British recruits needed to balance the enormous German reserve that came from the Russian front, the men holding the line, under continual menace of the great hostile offensive from December, 1917, to March, 1918, had not sufficient time to spare for intensive training in rapid,

aimed rifle fire and open field manœuvres. The result was that many of the later class of soldiers, and in particular those who had been brought in as conscripts, tended, from habit, to rely on bomb-throwing when they should have been using their rifles.

One young but experienced sergeant, belonging to a division that did uncommonly well, lamented the fact, as stretcher-bearers were carrying him away wounded, that he and his fellow non-commissioned officers had not had another three weeks' time to train the men in the old and minutely accurate rifle fire.

When the mist lifted on Saturday (he said), Jerry still came on in such masses that no rifleman could have wanted better targets ; but some of the men in my company wasted too much time in fussing about with bombs, instead of chucking them all away and sticking only to the rifle. Time and again, when Jerry came over the crest, a platoon of real marksmen could have knocked out a battalion.

In spite of the tendency in places to rely upon grenades instead of upon rifle fire, the English, Irish, and Scottish divisions around St. Quentin accomplished all that could have been expected in the circumstances. When British battalions had to fight against German divisions, which could scarcely be seen at forty yards distance, the small force had to give ground. The enemy was too numerous and too close to be killed quickly enough. By giving ground the defending troops generally maintained their power of slaughtering the hostile masses, and their own losses, though these were very heavy, were completely eclipsed by the terrible toll they took of the hostile multitudes.

Had the allied mass of manœuvre been so nicely placed behind the front on March 21st that it could have been thrown strongly into the Battle of St. Quentin at the moment when the defending British divisions had fully done their work of enormous slaughter, the issue might have been different. But, as the French military writer, General Cherfils, afterwards remarked in his review of the operations, " Champagne, on March 23rd, was still looking to see if Picardy were on fire."

The enemy's preparations for another offensive in Champagne were then practically so complete that the allied mass of manœuvre was held in hand for some very critical days, until it was tragically evident that Ludendorff was employing all his available strength to turn the French line at Noyon, as well as to throw the British armies across the Somme estuary. So completely did he outmanœuvre the Council of War at Versailles that to attain an equal rapidity and single-mindedness in control the imperfect mechanism of the Versailles Committee was changed for one-man direction.

Allied unity of control

General Ferdinand Foch, famous for his victories on the Marne and on the Yser, was appointed to the supreme command of the Allied Armies on the western front. General Pétain, Sir Douglas Haig, General Pershing, and King Albert, with all their army commanders, became the tactical local directors of the plan of steady, patient resistance that General Foch adopted in view of the exigencies of the moment.

The situation somewhat resembled that which obtained along the Yser River in October, 1914, when General Foch acted as director of the small resisting forces of Belgians, British, and Frenchmen. The new situation was of greater magnitude and larger peril. Instead of having to save from an enemy in overwhelming force the remnants of the small Belgian force and the small original British Expeditionary Force, General Foch had to bring his mass of manœuvre round to the Somme and the Oise Rivers to prevent the large national armies of the British Empire and the reorganised Belgian Army from being completely separated from the French and American forces and driven into the sea.

At the same time he had to protect the French capital from being attacked, and reserve sufficient force to counter any swift thrust by the enemy against the eastern and central French armies. While General Foch was saving the southernmost part of the line between Montdidier and Noyon, Sir Douglas Haig, with his able lieutenant, Sir Julian Byng, fought a magnificent battle of defence between Arras and the Somme, which is the subject of the succeeding chapter.

MARSHAL FOCH
In Supreme Command on the Western Front

MARSHAL FOCH
In Supreme Command on the Western Front.

CHAPTER CCLVI.

THE GREAT BATTLE FOR AMIENS.

II.—The Fighting Retreat From the Cambrai Salient to the Somme.

By Edward Wright.

Marwitz and his Two Battering-Rams—Terrific Gun Duel around Quéant—Magnificent Stand by the 21st Division at Epéhy—Enemy Breaks the British Flank at Hargicourt—Lancashires' Heroic Rearguard Action—West Surreys Hold Out to Last Man—24th Division Resurges at Hervilly—Terrible Menace at Roisel—Byng Manœuvres his Divisions across Battlefield—Stand of Highland Territorials on Bapaume Road—Gordons and Odd Men Save the Line—Kathen Breaks Over the Tortille—How the 17th Division and Naval Division Escaped Destruction—Race to Le Transloy and the Ancre—Scotsmen and Englishmen Fill the Breach by Péronne—Two Brandenburg Divisions Try the Matador Stroke and Fail—Depression in Germany and Admission of Failure—Battling by Moonlight on Old Somme Fields of War—Heroic Stand at Bray and Marcelcave—Canadian Motor-Guns to the Rescue—The Glorious Achievement of Carey's Force.

ABOVE St. Quentin, at dawn on March 21st, 1918, the British line extended in three salients towards Cambrai. In the south was a small outward bend between Hargicourt and Villers-Guislain, which was formed by the enemy's gain of ground in the second phase of the Battle of Cambrai. Then along the Flesquières Ridge, between Gouzeaucourt and the Cambrai-Bapaume road, was the wide, central British salient, extending over a considerable length of the original Hindenburg line, overrun by the Third Army in November, 1917. The third British salient consisted only of a slight indentation by Quéant, made in continual efforts by Australian and British troops in the early part of 1917.

General von der Marwitz, the German commander on the Cambrai front, planned to capture the larger part of the Third British Army by leaving its central salient unattacked in a serious manner, while making terrific battering-ram blows upon the Hargicourt and Bullecourt bends. Like his opponent, Sir Julian Byng, Marwitz was a brilliant cavalry officer with a characteristic vehemence in assault. He had conducted operations against the demoralised Russians in Volhynia in 1917.

As Von Hutier did at Riga, he practised and developed against the Russians the new infantry tactics, on which Ludendorff was partly relying to obtain a decision in

"THE MAN WHO HELD THE GAP."
Major-General George Charles Sandeman Carey, C.B., who when the Germans broke a gap in the western line at the end of March, 1918, closed it with an improvised "scratch" battalion. For this invaluable service he was promoted from brigadier-general.

France before the United States forces could strongly co-operate with the Western Allies. In the counter-offensive from Cambrai in 1917 Marwitz had essayed a new method of attack directly against Sir Julian Byng. He then failed, however, to make any impression upon the Third Army commensurate with his effort and his losses, because his main long mass of assault was placed by Bourlon Ridge, and could not exploit the results of the surprise break at Gouzeaucourt.

In the spring offensive of 1918 the German commander at Cambrai made no mistake in the disposition of his masses of assault. He brought at least an additional hundred batteries to bear against one British position by the Cambrai-Bapaume road, and he arranged a similar sudden strengthening of his machinery of attack just below Gouzeaucourt. His final preparations, however, were observed, in spite of the rainy weather and the care with which his men covered their new roads and railways with litter, ceased telephoning over a depth of seven miles along the front, and exercised all the arts of camouflage.

Sir Julian Byng knew that he would be attacked on either March 20th or March 21st. He moved some of his heavy guns back, shifted some divisions, and when, in the foggy darkness of the morning of battle, the German bombardment opened with floods of poison gas and earthquake high-explosive effects, the Third British

MENACED BY THE ENEMY OFFENSIVE.
Footbridge over a canal near the western front in France. The soldiers in the foreground were wiring the bank and a fallen tree to hold up any attempted enemy crossing during the push forward.

Army, though completely outnumbered and outgunned, began one of the finest defensive actions in military history.

The gun fire began about a quarter to five, slackened at seven o'clock, partly to allow enemy patrols to examine the British wire, but mainly to lure the defending troops out for infantry action, so that they might be caught by the stupendous hurricane of explosive shell following the gas bombardment. Under the increased intensity of the incomparable bombardment parties of Germans began to test the British line in places, but the main attacks were not delivered on the Cambrai front until nine o'clock in the morning.

The white mist was then still very dense, but, save in some of the watered valleys and hollows, it allowed far more visibility than obtained on the marshy battlefields of St. Quentin. Many British machine-gunners and riflemen were able to open aimed fire at four hundred yards, and although this range was sadly insufficient for the artillery observation officers trying to break the enemy masses before they could close, the Germans did not escape from wholesale artillery massacre.

For, in spite of the thick weather, British observation machines went over the clouded front of war, and pilots planed down over suspected concentration places until their observers were able to discern through the mist the movements of great bodies of men. Thereupon a wireless message, in secret code, brought all the striking power of groups of British batteries down upon the packed columns of hostile infantry.

Air observation through mist

Great as were the advantages the enemy enjoyed by reason of his sudden and able concentrations of enormous masses of men and guns, these advantages were partly balanced by serious disadvantages. For example, in the valley of the Agache River, just above the Cambrai-Bapaume road, and in the neighbouring valley of the Hirondelle brook, the ground was so crowded with bombarding batteries that the gunners disdained all cover for themselves and their pieces and from the beginning of the battle fought in the open.

Although the barrage which they put down was unique in both raking strength and depth, each British gun that remained in action, with the crews working in gas-masks, amid a smothering barrage of poison gas, had a target that could scarcely be missed. A shell that missed a German piece or its stack of shell scattered splinters of steel among the gunners or ammunition-carriers. When the British

batteries shifted on to infantry targets there was a shock battalion to every thousand yards of ground about the Bapaume road and between Gouzeaucourt and Hargicourt. Close behind the shock divisions was a series of massed reserves, strung one behind the other in as small a space as was needed for the utmost rapidity in deployment.

In order to make their huge weight tell instantly, the German attacking masses were arrayed in echelon, one behind the other, for leap-frog progression.

As soon as the first division was too much weakened by its losses to maintain its original thrusting power, the remnants gathered in groups and kept up as fierce a machine-gun and rifle fire as possible, while the second division, immediately behind, poured up between the firing groups,

BARRING THE WAYS OF ADVANCE.
British engineers fixing a cheval de frise of barbed-wire across a narrow road threatened by the German advance in the spring of 1918. Such obstacles, defended by comparatively few men, served to delay the enemy's progress.

threw out its own skirmishing machine-gunners and sharpshooters, and then attacked in complete strength and with all possible speed.

Exhausted in turn, sometimes after a struggle for a few yards of terrain, the second division gathered together in broken bodies and spent its ammunition in producing a general, aimless, long-range barrage of bullets, while a third division leap-frogged over it and introduced into the enemy operations another great, fierce spurt of attacking fury.

All this necessitated a crowding of the German lines, which, especially in the sectors from which the main attacks were made, was of an extraordinary nature. The enemy forces were organised to endure very severe punishment, and they certainly received it on the southern wing of the Cambrai Battle.

On Thursday morning, March 21st, they attacked in immense strength between Maissemy and Gouzeaucourt, breaking against the Scotsmen and South Africans of the 9th Division, the Lincolns, **British stubbornly** Leicesters, Northumberland Fusiliers, **hold Gauche Wood** Durhams, and other troops of the 21st Division, and against an Irish force, and the Queen's, and other battalions of the 24th Division. Around Gauche Wood the Germans surged in waves all day long, only to be destroyed or thrown back by the 9th Division in terrific fighting, like that with which the same Scotsmen and South Africans had held Delville Wood. Assault after assault completely failed, and when night fell Gauche Wood was held as firmly as it had been in the morning.

Below this wood the Leicesters, Lincolns, Northumberland

Fusiliers, and other men of the 21st Division withstood the masses of nearly four German divisions at Chapel Hill, Peizière Station, and other points about Epéhy village. At one point, by Vaucelette Farm, the enemy waves managed to break into the British line under cover of the fog. They flowed around the farm, in which was a party of Leicesters, who fought on when surrounded completely. The strong point was not taken until every man in it was either killed or so wounded that he could fight no more. This heroic, forlorn hope checked the inundating enemy multitude, so that the Durhams, who were behind the farm, were enabled to defeat the attack.

In the meantime the centre of the 21st Division had been apparently broken before the battle became general all along the line. Some time in the morning a hostile storming-party crept up in the fog to Peizière Station, and by means of flame-projectors burnt the garrison out of the ruins. Then, through the opening, the main German forces worked their way into Epéhy village and Lampière. By a glorious counter-attack, two companies of Leicesters, supported by two Tanks, fought back into Peizière. There a fresh German division attacked — ten thousand men against less than four hundred — and, surrounding the ruins, cut off the remnants of the forward company of Leicesters. Instead of surrendering, the Englishmen charged through the double line of Germans and reached their own main force.

Peizière and Epéhy practically formed one large village, and the men of the 21st could only keep their ground by counter-attacking each large German mass just before another storming multitude could leap through it. While the British troops were winning back Epéhy, two of their field-batteries

IMPROVISED PATHS ACROSS THE WATERWAYS.
Temporary footbridge laid by the Engineers across one of the canals behind the British western front. Such bridges were improvised in various fashions, in this instance of duck-board sections supported by floating barrels.

maintained for four hours gusts of rapid fire practically at point-blank range.

With a mist allowing visible space for only about four hundred yards, there was no need for slow and scientific shooting by means of telephone control. The gunlayers knew fairly well the position of their own infantry, and merely waited for the long, shadowy outline of a dense hostile formation to loom before them. Then, with open sights, they worked their guns as fast as they could load them, blasted the enemy away, and cleared the way for a counter-attack.

At one time the gunners were enveloped by some able German commanding officer, who dribbled his men around the artillery position, instead of trying to carry it by a mass attack. Even this did not silence the guns, for by some miraculous point-blank shooting the British artillerymen swept all the ground round themselves, and did everything they could to re-establish the old line. Two of the guns were smashed, two more they had to blow up, the others they kept in action.

Meanwhile, at Chapel Hill, the Lincolns and Northumberland Fusiliers broke all enemy attacks throughout the day. When evening fell, through thickening haze, the 21st Division had nobly vindicated itself, and fully avenged the reverse it suffered in November, 1917, during the German counter-offensive at Cambrai.

There can be little doubt that, had the rest of the line held, Epéhy would have been a complete victory against heavy odds for the 21st Division. Unfortunately, on the right, by Hargicourt, another defending force had its front badly broken by a surprise attack in the mist. As at Peizière and other places, some of the German shock forces crept forward through smoke barrage and fog while the bombardment was going on

MAKING THE WAYS UNSAFE FOR THE ADVANCING ENEMY.
An incident during the German offensive of 1918. A British officer attaching an explosive charge to a bridge in readiness to blow it up should the approach of the enemy make demolition necessary. Right : British Engineers connecting wires for exploding a road mine on the line of the German advance.

BRIEF REST IN TIME OF ACTION.
Wayside rest of British soldiers in a French village during the German 1918 offensive, the passing transport-waggon and Tank suggesting the strenuous times in which such rest was but a necessary pause.

held out to the last man on Friday, March 22nd, in the battle for Le Verguier.

Great was the achievement of the West Surreys. It might well have decided the course of the campaign between Péronne and Arras, for other battalions of the same division made a magnificent stand in manor-houses, farms, and woods, infantry and machine-gunners doing their ghastly work upon the dense lines and charging columns of assault until arms and bodies ached with fatigue. Keeping in touch with the troops on the other side of the Omignon River, the 24th Division at last gave the enemy all the high ground, and in the evening of Friday, the second day of battle, made a new line by Hervilly, in front of the railway junction of Roisel.

This was the stage in the struggle against terrible odds at which the

and filtered through the line north of Hargicourt. As their guns lifted, the main forces of assault poured along the path that had been made through the British system, and turned sharply southward and westward in one of those skilful enveloping movements which were characteristics of the new Teutonic tactics.

Fine, flexible, intensive Staff work was the instrument of the enemy's success. He had in and about the fighting zone an extraordinary number of liaison officers and men, so that, when any small part of the British system seemed to be weakening, the attacking forces for some miles along the line ceased their general operations and instantly began to gather upon the weak spot. Partly this was the **Great stand of** result of the prolonged battle practice in **the Lancashires** which the troops had been trained to move around hostile strong points instead of trying to carry them by repeated frontal assaults and leave the reduction of them to supporting forces with mobile artillery, while searching for ground held only by forces that might be rushed. The rapidity and strength with which the huge, overcrowding forces of attack changed direction, and thrust through the weak spot at Hargicourt towards Templeux le Guerard, formed a masterly example of Staff work.

Lancashire men made a magnificent stand in the old chalk quarries in front of Templeux le Guerard, breaking the new waves of attack in a day-long struggle; but in the continuing haze other enemy forces worked round the gallant defenders, and compelled them by the evening to fall back from Templeux. Night brought no relief to the two defending divisions holding the battle positions between Ronssoy and Maissemy against some ten attacking divisions. Darkness served merely as cover for continually fresh concentrations of thrusting power by the enemy commander. He turned the flank of the 24th Division at Villeret, and at dreadful sacrifice gained Fervaque Farm and Grand Priel Wood, against the steady resistance of the British troops.

Nothing of any importance, however, was lost in this most critical sector, which was just above the western battlefield of St. Quentin, where the Manchesters, Bedfords, Yorkshires, and Scots Fusiliers were fighting with desperate valour. The superb men of the 24th Division drew their line in at Le Verguier, and while their southern comrades held on to the direct Amiens road at Vermand by successful counter-attacks against superior numbers, a body of the Queen's West Surreys

GETTING TO WORK WITH THE GUNS.
British field-artillery going into action. Great tenacity and courage were displayed by the artillery in holding back the enemy masses in their great offensive. Once the field-gunners waited until the Germans were within twenty-five yards before limbering up and retiring.

heroism of the rearguards at Le Verguier and Caubrières Wood and Vendrecourt Château promised at first to fructify into a great British defensive victory. Flushed with the gain of the high ground, and reckless of what it had cost them, the Germans pursued the wasted British battalions, and broke into them at Hervilly village and Hervilly Wood and reached in the rear to Roisel.

But the ease with which this apparent success was won, at a critical point in the British battle zone, was disastrous to the overweening enemy. There was a fresh force of defence gathering behind the tried single division that had almost worn out the strength of at least five hostile divisions. As the Germans made what they **Tank counter-attack** thought was a decisive break-through by **at Hervilly** Roisel, the original British screening troops fell back, met their fresh supports, which were accompanied by ten Tanks, and with them returned to Hervilly village and to the patch of wooded country about a mile eastward.

The Germans were in immense numbers, coming in deep, close lines through wood and village. But they were no longer preceded by an overpowering artillery fire, having left their guns behind them, and relying on the speed and sweep of their movement to keep the retreating British ordnance from organising in strength against them. The Tanks took them by surprise, and, shattering the machine-gun power they were using to clear their way, opened paths for the counter-attacking British infantry.

After great slaughter the British line was re-established

at Hervilly against an enemy so beaten that the new front could have been made permanent, so far as the men occupying it were concerned.

Unfortunately, these troops of the 24th Division and its supporting force were weakened by the same circumstances that had prevented the men of the 21st Division from holding on to Epéhy the day before. The division between the 21st and 24th had been compelled to give so much ground behind Hargicourt that the entire line of the Third Army had to swing back. In the evening of Thursday, March 21st, strong hostile forces, continually fed from General von der Marwitz's huge reserves, were already working down the hollows from Hargicourt towards Villers-Faucon and Roisel.

Villers-Faucon was well in the rear of the 21st Division at Epéhy, and far on the rear flank of the 9th Division at Villers-Guislain and of the Naval Division and other troops on and about the Flesquières Ridge. Roisel was well in the rear of the 24th Division, and horribly far on the right flank rear of the garrisons of the central salient of the Third British Army. In the evening of the first day of battle General von der Marwitz's forces, advancing towards Roisel, were but half as far from Péronne and the Somme bridges as

Filling the gap at Hargicourt

were the Scotsmen and South Africans in Gauche Wood. This was due to the fact that the British front, in following the Hindenburg system, did not extend southward in a straight line, but made a great bend eastward.

The situation in the gap made at Hargicourt, between the 21st and 24th Divisions, was partly and temporarily remedied by an Irish force that succeeded in forming a rear-guard line in the broken sector. The enemy forces were held on Thursday night west of Ronssoy, and although they took St. Emilie, threatening Villers-Faucon and Roisel and the flank of all the centre of Sir Julian Byng's army, they could not break into it. Villers-Faucon was temporarily

lost, but it was recovered by a counter-thrust headed by Tanks.

Angrily, the victorious Leicesters, Lincolns, Northumbrians, and other men at Epéhy fell back to Saulcourt and extended on the right to reinforce the defence of the centre's flank. Then, as we have seen, the great 24th Division, on which the entire movement pivoted, held the enemy at Le Verguier, and by the victory of Hervilly, apparently, made the Roisel defences secure on Friday evening, March 22nd.

By this time, however, the Germans had pressed back the Irish defensive line. It was impossible for the British army commander to save his flank, especially as all the southern front about St. Quentin was giving way and exposing the Roisel position to a turning movement. Instead **The enemy's grand stroke** of attempting to hurry reinforcements up towards the breach, Sir Julian Byng placed a reserve force by Tincourt, behind Roisel, and, with a strengthened defensive line between St. Quentin and Péronne, drew his men as rapidly as possible from the Flesquières salient towards Bapaume, Péronne, and Albert.

For the break that had occurred at Hargicourt seemed in itself to be of only secondary importance, compared with the struggle that was taking place on the northern side of the Flesquières salient. From the Cambrai-Bapaume road to the southern approaches to Arras, General von der Marwitz was combining with General Otto von Below in an explosion of artillery and infantry power of attack that was without parallel in any enemy or allied operations.

Indisputably this more northerly battle—in which Michael I. army group, with some help from the Mars army group, united with the larger part of Michael II. army group in an endeavour to rupture the left wing of the Third British Army, preliminary to turning the first British Army on Vimy Ridge and dividing the forces of Sir Douglas Haig—was the

GERMAN PRISONERS UNDER ESCORT BEHIND THE BRITISH LINES.

"Walking cases" among the Germans taken prisoner during the early stages of the offensive in March, 1918, being helped along by their more fortunate comrades. Though the Germans in that offensive succeeded in overrunning a goodly tract of territory, one of the prisoners who had been captured by the British declared that the ground they had taken was not big enough to serve as a cemetery for their men killed in taking it.

"BONNIE FECHTERS" WHOM THE GERMANS LEARNED TO DREAD.

Scottish troops going forward to reinforce the front line in March, 1918, when the German offensive was launched. The 9th Division (a Scottish one) and the 51st Division of Highlanders were among the troops which were mentioned by Sir Douglas Haig in the early days of that offensive as having especially distinguished themselves in the resistance which they offered to the German onslaught. They were troops the enemy dreaded most to face.

grand stroke for a decision in Ludendorff's scheme of linked actions.

On it he employed his two most successful commanders and his largest masses of men and guns. As soon as the terrific pressure he was exerting could be measured, Sir Julian Byng answered it by marching the 19th Division from the southern salient flank, at Gouzeaucourt, across the centre to the Cambrai-Bapaume road. Deliberately the British commander weakened his line between Cambrai and St. Quentin in order to strengthen his front between Cambrai and Arras, altering his dispositions in the fog and tumult of battle, while his lines were being swept by thousands of guns and his battle positions endangered both right and left.

Sir Julian's manœuvre with his 19th Division was doubly significant. By it he not only strengthened his left, into which he soon poured also his main reserves, but he also facilitated the evacuation of the Flesquières salient, against which the enemy was then only demonstrating. There was one division less to crowd the roads behind Roisel when the southern crisis came. It was a fine move, showing a swift grasp of Ludendorff's design, and, in spite of the accident that afterwards occurred in the long withdrawal from the Cambrai salient, it

Sir Julian Byng's fine move made a general defensive success by the Third Army practicable in the most adverse circumstances.

The famous Highland Territorials of the 51st Division held the sector towards which the 19th Division moved. They were entrenched on the high ground of the Cambrai road, with the Black Watch on Louverval Rise overlooking the hostile Pronville Valley so far as the fog would allow, with the Seaforths on Boursies Hill, and the Argylls by the dominating wreckage of Demicourt village. The height of the positions was no advantage, under the conditions of weather for which Ludendorff and his sixty military meteorologists had patiently, keenly waited.

The German gunners had precisely registered upon the long slopes during actions in the spring of 1917, and in indirect fire, with aeroplane control, had ranged exactly on the reverse declines and hollows, where the artillery supporting the Highlanders was sited. When, therefore, the tremendous bombardment opened in mist and darkness, the German gunner general was able by almost mechanical means to use the hundreds of new guns, placed in position a night or two before action, with nearly as much effect as the pieces that had been sited at the time the Hindenburg line was finished.

For four hours he drowned the Highlanders and their artillerymen in poison gas, and battered them with blasts of high explosive and splinters of phosphorous steel. There was something deadly also in the bullets poured in a barrage upon the defenders, for all the wounds dealt by the enemy were more septic than had previously been noted. **Fierce attack on the 51st Division** Yet he did not have things all his own way, even when he brought an apparently surprising number of guns to bear upon the Highlanders' positions. Forward and aerial observation officers on the British side had traced many of the new batteries, enabling their artillery to reply with searching counter-fire to the great bombardment.

The opposing gunners on either side did not know what results they were obtaining, owing to the fog. Even when, between nine and ten o'clock in the morning, the fog over the rolling chalk country diminished into a mist and the main wrestle of the infantries began, the effects of the counter-battery duel could only be indirectly discerned. Heavy as the enemy's artillery losses were, his guns were so enormous in number that sufficient survived to lift with crashing force upon the Scotsmen's position at Beaumetz-lez-Cambrai, while the struggle for the foreground works was raging.

One remarkable success, however, was won by the parks of crowded German guns north of the Cambrai road. They shot away the British defences in the valley between Lagnicourt Hill and Louverval Rise, and almost the first news of the German infantry movement that the Black Watch in Louverval Wood received came from their rear.

The battalion commander was standing at the door of his shelter, talking to a chaplain and a doctor, when machine-guns opened fire at him from his own support line. His companions tried to get back, but were captured. Scarcely two minutes before this a gunner observer in a forward post reported he could see the enemy gathering in the reserve line, adding immediately that they were also in his trench and bombing him. No doubt the Germans had been creeping forward for hours during the early part of the bombardment when the fog was thickest, and, as at Hargicourt and several more southerly points, they carried some outpost positions before putting in motion their deeply-set divisions of assault.

It was to the high credit of the Highlanders that, though completely surprised on a most delicate part of their line, they made a glorious rally, and as their situation continued to grow more desperate, their stubborn valour and quick-minded skill rose to meet it. The division **Highlanders' glorious rally** above was hammered out of its string of posts, and seriously threatened with penetration of its battle system, and, as the contending forces swayed above the Cambrai road, the Highlanders were exposed to a terrific side thrust against their left flank rear, where some of their heavy guns were.

Yet they fought the battle out with such success that they at Doignies, and the 24th Division at Le Verguier, became the strong, steadying northern and southern pivots on which the centre of the Third British Army swung back from the Cambrai salient and made a line between Arras

and the eastern approaches to Amiens, against which Marwitz entirely spent first all his huge attacking forces and next all the divisions of the grand German reserve that Ludendorff could bring forward in pursuit of his principal aim.

The Black Watch, though surrounded at Louverval, fought an heroic delaying action. The Seaforths at Boursies had cannily taken precaution to fire-step one of their communication trenches commanding the valley down which the Germans were working. Manning this trench as a defensive flank, they swept back each enemy mass as it became visible, and with the Black Watch and the Argylls they fought **Swaying fight for Doignies** the enemy from Doignies until two o'clock in the afternoon. At noon the Germans attained the pulverised summit that had once been a hill village, but the Highlanders came charging back and recovered the important crossways.

Again the machine-guns of the Argylls, Black Watch, and Seaforths got in a position to send the plunging fire down upon the continual German waves of attack that surged upward as fast as they were broken. One Scottish machine-gunner alone used forty belts of cartridges, not in a blind barrage, but in aimed fire at a range of four hundred yards at most, and much more frequently at a hundred yards or less.

When, in the afternoon, the enemy had organised the foreground of the Scottish position for his own purpose, and was able to bring his own men forward with more rapidity until they could not be shot down quickly enough, Doignies was again lost. Yet the general position was saved, as it was later

REST INTERVAL FOR INDOMITABLE MEN DURING A TIME OF GREAT TRIAL.

British troops resting in a French village after being in action during the German offensive of March, 1918. The men's power of endurance was severely tested. One Press correspondent said: "The infantry which bore the brunt of the attack were called on to support a strain which has seldom fallen on men in battle; it could scarcely have been believed that they could have 'stuck it' with the incomparable spirit which they displayed."

on the other flank at Hervilly, when the resisting power of the gallant 24th Division seemed to be utterly spent. The English division that Sir Julian Byng had manœuvred across the battlefield when the action opened was known to be close at hand at the moment when the Highlanders were giving ground and letting the enemy through.

As the enemy came through they were met by the same combination of undaunted front-line battalions, supporting troops, and Tanks as achieved a defensive victory at Hervilly. Doignies was recovered by the crawling, flaming forts of armoured steel, the indomitable Gaels, and their English comrades. Until the evening the slaughter went on, by which time one of the Argylls was heard to complain that shooting Germans down was getting rather monotonous.

If all had been well elsewhere, the Germans could have been pushed back to the valley of the Agache River. But, on the left of the Highlanders, Morchies had been lost after a gallant defence by the next division in line. When the supporting English troops recovered Morchies, and thus prevented a turning of the Scottish flank, the general situation remained such as to compel Sir Julian Byng to proceed with that retirement of his centre which he had prepared when the battle opened. Doignies was therefore abandoned, and on Friday morning, March 22nd, the neighbouring village of Hermies, where the Highlanders linked on with the 17th Division, became the pivoting-point of the British action. Hermies, however, was firmly held against attack after attack, and under cover of this rearguard action the heroic 51st Division began its long fighting retreat, which was conducted under seemingly impossible conditions. After being driven out of Morchies, the Germans made a still more dangerous thrust into Vaulx-Vraucourt, which was in the rear of both Morchies and the Highlanders' battle-zone. On Friday night tractors were

brought up to Beaumetz-lez-Cambrai to haul away the heavy British artillery.

Without losing a gun, except those that had been shattered by enemy fire, the Highlanders retired on March 23rd to Beugny. This was a village on the Cambrai road in line with Vaulx, and from it the Scotsmen extended in a covering line southwards towards Ytres. By this time General von der Marwitz had all his men moving as fast as possible against the retiring Third Army. Every force that remained fit for action, or could be reorganised on the field, gathered with the fresh divisions in dense waves, with the men scarcely a pace apart, and little more than a hundred yards between each rolling grey surge. Marwitz could not tell at what point he might find an opening, so he maintained a fierce, incessant, testing pressure along the whole front.

On the left flank of the Highland Division the Germans swarmed down from Vaulx in close co-operation with another mass thrusting along the Cambrai road. The combined multitudes met about Beugny, where the Gordon Highlanders fought one of the finest actions in their splendid history. The single wasted battalion had too few men to hold the enemy back on both front and flank, but the colonel collected every Briton within call — sappers, pioneers, and odd units —and, making a line around the village, inflicted such overwhelming losses upon the German mass formations that the Highlanders' flank was, by a miracle, saved. In another part of the field the Argylls again had reason to complain of the monotony of their work of destruction, in which they also were assisted by sappers and camp servants.

This was merely the beginning of the nightmare horrors and immortal achievements in endurance of the Scotsmen. While they were holding the enemy back by the Cambrai road, the Germans, on Saturday, March 23rd, broke through the

STEEPED IN SLEEP OF EXHAUSTION.
During the retreat from Cambrai some British units fought for five days and nights on end. When the strain on their endurance was relaxed the men dropped in their tracks and plunged into profound slumber.

BRITON AND TEUTON ALIKE WORN OUT BY THE WEARY WORK OF WAR.
German prisoners with their escort resting on their way behind the British lines. Right : British cavalryman, tired out by many hours on patrol, snatching a few minutes' sleep, undisturbed by the noise of Army waggons rattling over the paved roads.

British line farther south, and, under a brilliant corps commander, General von Kathen, began to march over the Tortille River and across the old battlefield between Bapaume and Albert. The centre of the Third British Army had to change its manner of retirement. While some forces raced down to fill the gap that the enemy had made, others swung back as swiftly as possible, in the design to unite again before the enemy could completely divide them.

The Highlanders retired to the south-east of Bapaume, and made another stand about the approaches to that town and to Le Transloy. But they could win neither relief nor even time to rest upon the ground. Another German regiment, which had advanced across another part of the British lines, broke through eastward, and the

A SUBSTANTIAL PRIZE.
British officer emerging from the German Tank "Elfriede," which had been captured intact, after inspecting its mechanism.

GROOMING THE PACHYDERMS AFTER THE BATTLE.
Washing down Tanks in a British tankodrome after their return from action. From the Battle of Cambrai onwards the new war-machine devised by British ingenuity played an ever-increasing part in warfare, the small "whippet" type, with a speed of fifteen miles per hour, proving especially effective.

across the Tiber. It was a strangely pleasant, picturesque incident in a terrible ordeal. The proudest of all Prussian regiments had reason to appreciate the fighting power of more than one Celtic element of the British Empire, for the Cockchafers had been broken by a Cymric force on Pilkem Ridge before being checked by the rearguarding Gaels between Albert and Bapaume.

The 17th Division, that held the line in front of Hermies and Havrincourt, and the Naval Division, which prolonged the front in the Flesquières salient, had an ordeal somewhat similar to that of their Highland comrades. On the first day of battle their lot was happier than that of the men of the 51st Division. In spite of the enemy's frightful bombardment only a hundred and fifty yards of trenches were lost when the German infantry attacked in seemingly overpowering force. Six assaults against Hermies and seven against Havrincourt were broken, and after felling the attackers in groups the defenders counter-charged them and recovered practically all their foreground positions. When, in the night of March 22nd, the Scotsmen were compelled to retire, through events that occurred higher up the line, the evacuation   **Ordeal of the 17th Division** of Beaumetz-lez-Cambrai seriously threatened the flank of the central British divisions, which kept in touch with the Highlanders and withdrew through Bertincourt to Barastre.

This was a movement of great difficulty, as the Germans got into a wood on the left of the troops, and, partly outflanking them, tried to rush their gunners behind Bertincourt. The British rearguard, which had blown up the lock of the Canal du Nord and was covering the withdrawal of the main force, was cut off, and had to fight its way back, while strong German infantry detachments with machine-guns were making short rushes upon the artillery far in the rear.

The enemy commander did not spare his men when so large a prize was visibly within his reach. Using as a base of concentration Velu Wood, in which were gathering the forces that had attacked the Gordons and other Highland

outflanked Highlanders retreated towards Courcelette, only to find that there they were in still greater danger of being rapidly enveloped. They swerved round to Pys, and crossed the Ancre to Miraumont, walking the desolate scene of former British victories in a condition approaching utter collapse.

In appearance they were like tottering, drunken men emerging into daylight after a long nocturnal debauch. Many of them could scarcely move along, and they were kept upright and in motion only by holding hands like children, so that the flicker of general strength served to balance each individual tendency to fall down and sleep. For five days and nights they had worked to the utmost of their power, and by their wonderful endurance they extorted praise from the last German force that fiercely but vainly tried to break them.

As they staggered by the tragic fields of little white crosses on the rolling moorland of the Somme ridges, a paper balloon came drifting through the shower of shells flung at them from the neighbourhood of Bapaume. When shot down the balloon was found to contain a message written in English from the Cockchafer Regiment of the Prussian Guard: "Good old 51st! Still sticking it! Cheerio!" the extraordinary message ran. Some Prussian officer, or officers, felt as the Tuscans did when they saw Horatius swimming to safety

units, he sent wave after wave of shock troops up the hill behind Bertincourt and along the valley of the stream behind the hill. But all the men he deployed were either shot down or demoralised in a fierce, short-range combat. The victors limbered up their guns, recovered their rearguard, and, in a strangely happy frame of mind, dug themselves in at Bus. Then it was that Marwitz's system of maintaining a general pressure of the utmost intensity almost brought about a British disaster.

While the victors of Bertincourt were about to dig themselves in at Bus, another force, which had suffered heavy losses from the enemy's gun fire but had fought on superbly, passed through the new line to take up a position at Ytres. But the enemy broke through the Ytres flank, and with the same remarkable gathering of men in mass to exploit the small local success, concentrated a great force to enlarge the gap he had made by the Tortille River. The design was to envelop both the 17th Division and the Royal Naval Division and then roll up all the Third Army while driving on to Amiens.

British generalship and the stubborn spirit of the troops prevented Palm Sunday, March 24th, 1918, from becoming the blackest Sabbath in British annals. One British force formed into columns and marched in front of Bus, in face of enemy masses trying to break through, and arrived at Eaucourt-l'Abbaye and High Wood, full of **A critical** high tragic memories like the neighbouring **Palm Sunday** scenes through which the Highlanders were passing at the same time. The men marched in parade order, with absolute steadiness and precision, throwing out flanking guards with machine-guns.

With multitudes of Germans on their flanks and German machines harrying them from the sky, they went across the Somme battlefields, finding food in some of the huts at Le Transloy, which the commander burnt down himself, as his men passed, whistling tunes to the tramp of their feet, after having been thirty-six days in the Flesquières salient.

In the meantime the other British division, terribly imperilled by the enemy success at Ytres, had to race to the gap at Le Transloy against the overwhelming German forces that were striking across the Tortille River and reaching Morval and Lesbœufs for a large enveloping movement. It was a race for Le Transloy. If the enemy got there first, all was lost. But the British divisional general moved his men with remarkable skill, withdrawing first one group and then another against two great German forces, one trying to pierce eastward from Ytres and the other furiously endeavouring to make a breaking thrust southward from Combles.

He brought up pioneers and engineers to cover his transport, that galloped through a fire of shell below Bapaume, while the scratch rearguard maintained a magnificent defence. Then he had to detach some of his men to strengthen the line of another force by Gueudecourt, which was bitterly pressed

PREPARATION FOR ACTION.
Canadian motor machine gunner on the British western front in France fixing a belt of ammunition to his weapon in readiness for meeting the enemy.

by another large force of Germans, who had also come across the broken line of the Tortille River. The men he lent did not rejoin their division until the withdrawal to the new front was completed.

Winning the race to Le Transloy, the British general worked across the old Somme fields of war, making further stands at Mametz Wood and Fricourt. Then his men had to hold the line of the Ancre, west of Albert, in order to allow the weary Highlanders of the 51st Division to sleep their fatigue away. Instead of going to billets on March 26th, the forces from the Flesquières salient had to be roused at night from the first rest they **Across the old** had had for nearly a week, and sent to **Somme fields** Martinsart, where the Germans were breaking through. Hostile machine-gun bullets were already pattering on the general's sleeping hut as he was putting his boots on, but a gallant counter-attack drove the enemy back.

While the Highlanders and 19th Division in support, and the 17th Division, and the Naval Division were withdrawing towards Albert, other forces about the Flesquières salient retired by way of Péronne. Among these were the 9th Division, the 21st Division, and the 24th Division, whose splendid fighting in the first days of the battle has been described.

The Scotsmen and South Africans fell back slowly from Gauche Wood in line with the Leicesters and other battalions of the 21st. German machine-gunners, however, quickly reached the high ground commanding the valley in the direction of Fins, and swept with violent gusts of fire the thin screen of rearguards who were maintaining connection between the two British divisions and preventing a gap being formed between them.

Here, as elsewhere, the extremely alert enemy, finding a weak spot, massed against it with very workmanlike speed. Then began those short, leaping rush attacks, under cover of long-distance musketry and machine-gun fire, which were the speciality of the new Ludendorffian tactics. There was really nothing novel to British

"OBSERVATION CAR" FOR MILITARY PURPOSES.
Interior of an observation car constructed on the western front by Canadian light-railway troops. It was fitted as a living and working room for the officers on duty.

regular soldiers in this method of advancing. It was the way men fought in the retreat from Mons.

Some of the new British soldiers in the 21st Division were rather too much given to the trench heresy of smashing, heavy artillery barrages followed by grenade combats. In circumstances in which the older soldier instinctively raised his rifle, they took up a hand-bomb. While they waited, the enemy's long-distance musketry and machine-gun fire often produced results.

But experience teaches. Although the enemy provided the experience, the Briton, whether regular, volunteer, or conscript, was quick in learning the old lesson regarding the everlasting value of the rifle. Thin as the screen was at Fins, the coolness and gallantry of the men composing it prevented the enemy from breaking through. The 21st Division fell back to Liéramont, which they held till March 23rd, when they fell back on Templeux la Fosse, with the 9th Division on their left. The fighting at this time was beyond description, for the two reduced forces were arrayed along the lower part of the Tortille River, through which Marwitz was using his utmost power to break, **Temporary German** converging upon it from the north and from **air mastery** the east, with two apparently unending masses used like gigantic piston drills.

The weather changed when the British battle positions were evacuated. All the mist disappeared on Saturday, March 23rd, and the sky continued to afford wide power of vision to the many German pilots, aerial observers, machine-gunners, and bomb-droppers hawking over the new British lines. General Sir Hugh Trenchard could not at the time spare officers and machines to keep the German Air Force from

practically holding the mastery of the sky in the area in which General von der Marwitz aimed at shattering the centre of the Third Army. There was more urgent need for British airmen above the Fifth Army, and the men of the 21st and 9th Divisions, with their comrades, had to try to keep their thinning line intact under the eyes of swarms of German airmen, who not only observed their movements but swooped and attacked them.

British brigades were reduced to composite battalions, with only a few commissioned and non-commissioned officers left, while the aeroplane-directed enemy masses were moving forward so quickly that they **Heroic gamble** seemed to grow larger every time they were **with death** blasted away while coming over the crests.

As a rule, breathing space was always to be won by quickly ambushing the first German wave. Many of the enemy brigadiers and generals—no doubt under orders from their High Command—were so eager to press on and deliver the final shattering stroke that they no longer used the cautious scouting line of skirmishers. They tried to carry everything by the main force and marching pace of their troops.

It was possible to work great and rapid slaughter by waiting on a slope until two or three waves came over the other crest, and then sweeping all the ground the enemy covered with musketry volleys, Lewis-gun fire, and the more sustained hose of bullets from the Vickers gun.

This, however, became rather an heroic gamble with death than a business-like stratagem, owing to the great wastage and increase in fatigue of the original British front-line divisions. They were at last well content to give the enemy

BRITISH MACHINE-GUN TRANSPORT GOING FORWARD ON THE WESTERN FRONT.

British machine-gun transport moving along a French road. The development of the machine-gun, and its ever more extensive use both in attack and defence, was one of the notable features of the Great War. "To it," said a war correspondent in 1918, "was due in large part the German success in the March offensive, and to it we owed more than to any other factor our success in bringing the enemy's rushes to a standstill."

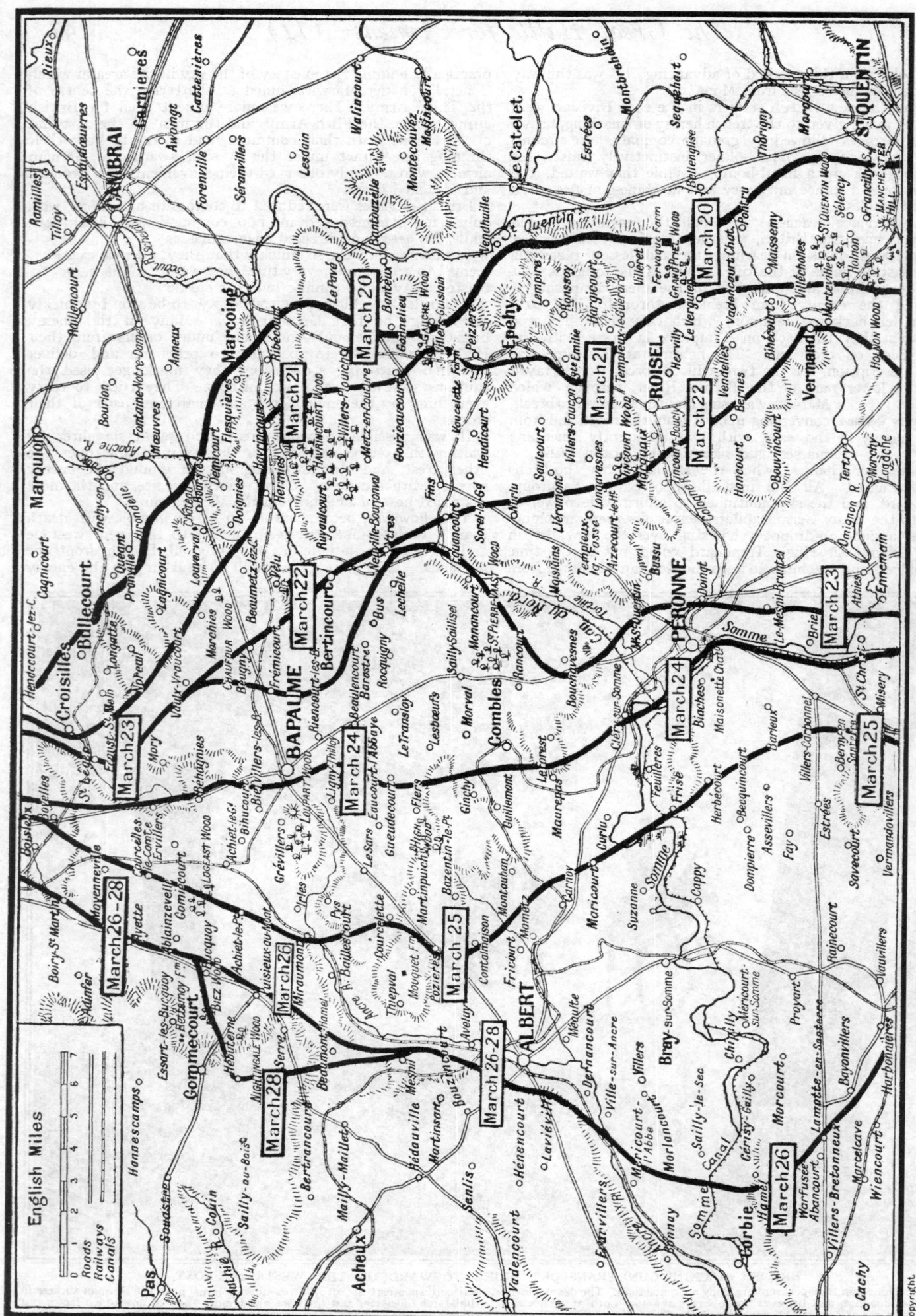

The Great War

PRESSURE OF THE GERMAN OFFENSIVE IN MARCH, 1918.

In this map is shown part of the terrain over which the British troops were forced to retire in the days immediately succeeding that on which the great German offensive began on March 21st, 1918. The black line to the right running from near to St. Quentin in a north-westerly direction to Bullecourt shows the position of the battle-front before the German offensive began. The succeeding lines show the extent to which the British armies retired on successive days up to March 28th. The tract of country south of St. Quentin affected by the offensive is shown in the map on page 24, illustrating the preceding chapter.

46

something to think about by raking his first wave of assault, and enabling him to withdraw before his main forces were loosened and engaged. The series of partial breaks that occurred in the retreating British line seemed generally to have been due to trying to kill too many Germans at once, instead of checking the main bodies and making the enemy Staff officers anxious.

There was, however, a fresh British force — the Black Watch, Sherwood Foresters, Sussex, Cheshires, Riflemen, and Hertfordshires—coming into action to the right of the 21st Division, and the new division took full advantage of the German commander's habit of pushing an attack to exhaustion when more than one wave was engaged. They were in support at Tincourt Wood, behind Roisel and Villers-Faucon, and from a hastily-dug trench they held the Germans on the second day of the battle north of Péronne.

The Germans fell in battalions, but continued to surge forward all day in the same dense formation that they used when trying to break through worn and reduced front-line British divisions in retreat. As in practically all places at which supporting troops were set against the wearying German horde, the line could have been held; but through the break on the Tortille stream another retirement became necessary.

The British front swung back on the front of Mont St. Quentin and the Péronne marshes where the Tortille joins the Somme. The men of the wasted 21st Division and their comrades were temporarily relieved, going to billets in Bray for a rest that unhappily proved to be exceedingly brief. On March 24th, after a fierce action around Mont St. Quentin, and along the upper course of the Somme, the British forces crossed the river, after clearing the evacuated country of supplies and saving all their guns, with the exception of some field-pieces lost on the first day.

A hundred thousand Germans, excited by the news of the Tortille victory in the centre of the grand advance in the south, moved in pursuit behind the retreating rear-guards. Reaching the Somme, on March 24th, they made numerous attempts, between Péronne and Nesle, to force a series of passages between Nesle and Cléry-sur-Somme. Excellently prepared they were, for the lieutenants of Ludendorff had hoped to reach the Somme before the time they did, and had provided everything necessary for a swift crossing. Heavy artillery in very considerable strength was hauled forward by Tanks and tractors so as to assist the field-guns in rapidly destroying all defences on the opposite bank of the stream. Fleets of rafts were brought up, together with the sections of ordinary pontoon bridges, and on Palm Sunday the Second Battle of the Somme opened.

In the narrows over which the Germans continually tried to force a passage and win bridge-heads the British gunner was master. He shot the pontoons to pieces and turned the rafts into wreckage, and drenched the eastern reserves with shrapnel, while British machine-gunners and riflemen put the Germans out of action by more detailed operations. Ludendorff claimed in his communiqué that his men had crossed the Somme. They did so, and tried for half an hour to hold a bridge-head, before they were wiped out.

The next morning two Brandenburg divisions came forward as fresh spear-head forces to the baffled and wearied masses. Attacking and feinting along a great stretch of the river,

Second Battle of the Somme

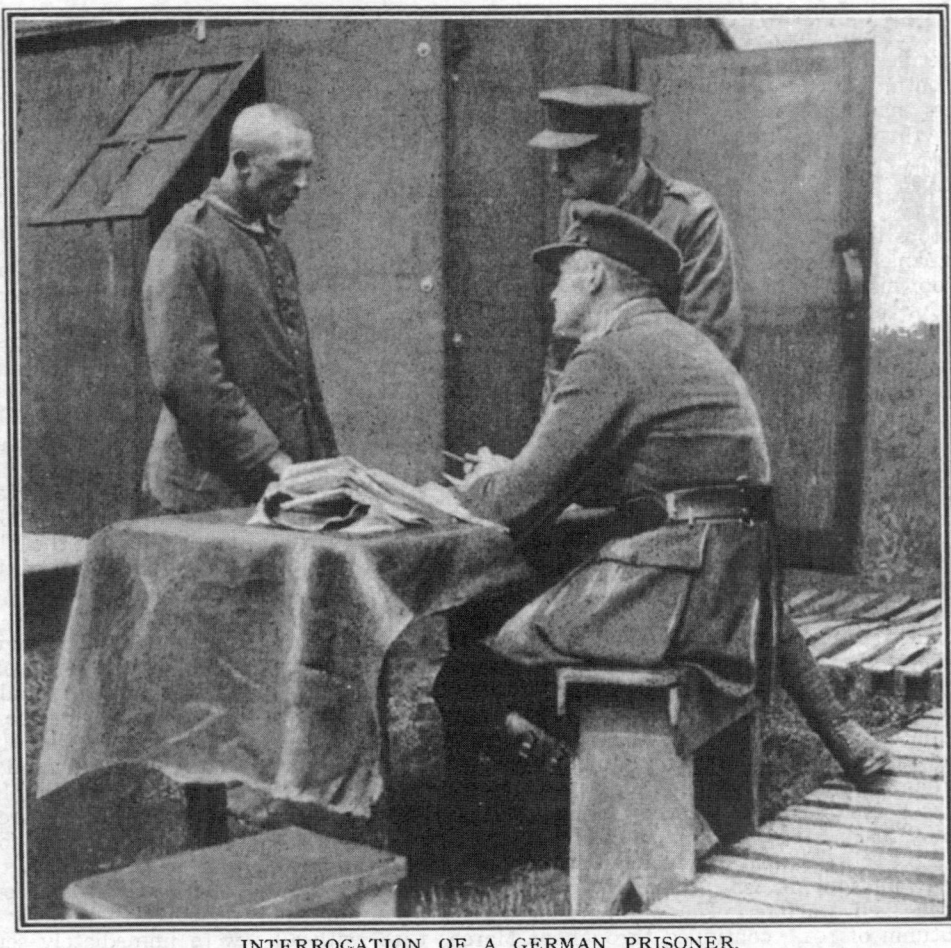

INTERROGATION OF A GERMAN PRISONER.
Canadian Intelligence officers questioning a prisoner who had just been brought in on their sector of the western front. Information gathered from prisoners was frequently of considerable importance, and raids on the enemy trenches were often made with that end in view.

the Brandenburgers, after hard fighting by St. Christ and Falvey, crossed the Somme on March 25th and, after suffering heavy losses at every rush forward, attacked Morchain, Mesnil, and Rouy.

The British line by Chaulnes bent under their resolute assaults, but the defending troops rallied, and in the gallant counter-charges pushed the fresh Prussian forces back, taking a hundred and two prisoners. By this time Marwitz had used thirteen of his divisions against four of Sir Julian Byng's divisions in the middle Somme sector. Above this sector, as the "Frankfurter Zeitung" reported at the time:

Three German army corps, besides the troops of two other commands, were necessary to drive the English back through Bapaume. The real German advance is still checked by the obstinate hostile defence. So long as the enemy occupy chosen positions and with reserves repair the gaps in their dam, no operative movements are possible.

It would have been comforting to many British in the field to hear this shrewd German criticism of Ludendorff's campaign, for their own position was most desperate. The Teutonic dictator of Middle Europe had broken his partnership with Hindenburg because the old Field-Marshal had refused to agree that decisive victory in the west was needed at any cost. He wished Germany to arrange peace, with eastern profits and western surrenders, within limits, as he calculated that the price required in German life for completely breaking the Franco-British front was more than his country could pay if it wished to remain strong in manufacturing and breeding power.

Hindenburg v. Ludendorff

It appeared to the men of the Hindenburg school that the great battle was taking the course they had sadly foreseen, and the criticism in the "Frankfurter Zeitung" was partly inspired by Kühlmann. Ludendorff, however, had the support of the Kaiser and the Crown Prince, and, as absolute master of Germany, and partial War Lord of Austria-

Hungary, he acted on the Somme as Falkenhayn had acted at Verdun, but in a larger way. Where Falkenhayn had sacrificed men by the hundred thousand in the course of a month, Ludendorff sacrificed them by the half million in less than a week.

When the centre and the right flank of the British Third Army steadied on the old entrenchments by the Somme River, Ludendorff threw in another large portion of his main reserve, bringing the number of his closely-engaged attacking troops to well over a million men. He was no longer a cool, capable strategist, but a frenzied gambler trying to recover from his losses by wildly increasing his stakes.

As the men of the Hindenburg school began to point out to him, he had made a profound mistake in organising and delivering his attack between Arras and La Fère. Instead of the two British armies there occupying the ordinary series of three widely spaced lines, they held a front seamed with old and new systems that extended back in places to a depth of more than twenty-five miles. Every line dug by French, British, and German troops, between the heights west of Albert and the slopes east of Flesquières, helped to prevent the attacking masses from changing the nature of the battle from a struggle round entrenched positions into a swift manœuvring action on the open field.

British helped by German works

There was no open field. By the irony of fate it was mainly the German works, evacuated by Ludendorff in his retreat to the Hindenburg line, that saved the British forces from disruption. Always, as the Germans themselves admitted, the British were able to fill every breach made in the vast network of scientific ditches from which they fought. When they lost one trench, there was always another well-placed system, made by the Germans themselves, on which to fall back.

Save for a comparatively small stretch of country immediately in front of Amiens, trench warfare never changed into open field warfare. The old parallel battle, begun in the autumn of 1914, continued throughout March, 1918, with all the enormous wastage imposed by fieldworks upon the attacking forces, until those forces were brought completely to a standstill and obliged to dig themselves in after the old manner.

On Palm Sunday, March 24th, when the three huge armies of assault of Ludendorff were completely entangled in the spider's web of old lines between Arras, Albert, Frise, Chaulnes, Roye, and Noyon, the enemy army commanders took advantage of the full moon and the clear nocturnal sky to deliver their mass attacks as strongly by night as by day. They reckoned that the moonlight, while sufficiently bright for the proper control of the troops, would, by diminishing visibility, serve somewhat like a thin mist for crawling storming-parties.

This method was undoubtedly of some utility. Had all trench systems been passed, it would probably have greatly helped towards a decisive victory. But British troops were well practised in every kind of nocturnal patrol work and night raiding, and as the enemy's advance forces had to grope forward in the moonlight, over ground that had changed since they occupied it, and could not use the intense box barrage, by means of which trenches were usually taken in the night, they suffered crippling losses without effecting anything like a decisive success.

German mass attack by night

Of course, by weight of numbers and persistent pressure they won some points of importance, but the depth of the old battle-lines was too great to enable them to pierce the British line. Round Péronne, on Palm Sunday, they surprised some Sussex and Cheshire men by stealing from Cléry, on the Somme, across the river towards Frise. But the splendid division that had fought around Roisel and Mont St. Quentin made another great stand by Frise, where on Monday, March 25th, they inflicted terrible losses on the enemy divisions that were then forcing the river-line in great strength.

Once more the Englishmen and Scotsmen retired, crossing the No Man's Land of the first Somme battle, and taking cover along the old French support-line by Proyart. Here they broke the new waves of assault in a struggle lasting for forty-eight hours, in the course of which their line was partly shattered by a flanking surprise attack and then mended by a battalion of pioneers, whose counter-attack could not have been excelled by veteran soldiers.

On this occasion, however, the indomitable British held on rather too long to their new front. In many ways it was the most important sector of the battlefield, as it covered, by Proyart, the broad, straight highway connecting St. Quentin with Amiens. Thus it was necessary to hold it to the last extremity, and this the Englishmen and Scotsmen could have done had their left flank by the Somme been absolutely secure.

But due north across the river the British line began to give around Bray, where the 21st Division had abruptly to return to action. As a matter of fact, the 21st was no longer a division, nor even the skeleton of one. It had wasted into an improvised and weak brigade. Yet the men and their officers were in good heart after their brief rest of a day, and if the enemy had been still fighting without artillery they would have held him.

But along the straight, short Amiens road and down the Cambrai-Bapaume-Albert road, and other well-made communications of the Third and Fifth British Armies, he brought forward artillery with the same remarkable speed as he had launched his infantry through the wilderness on only two days' iron rations. Using hundreds of thousands of prisoners of war and enslaved civilian labour from the occupied territories, Ludendorff's Chief of Staff began to extend his broad and narrow railways, and remake roads through the battle zone almost as soon as the action opened. The ends of the German railways were rapidly prolonged during the foggy days of March 21st and 22nd, and when the weather cleared, with the British forces in full retreat across the country over which Ludendorff had retired in the spring of 1917, Ludendorff was as well prepared to follow them by railway and by road as he had previously been to check them from pursuing him.

Vast stacks of material were ready behind his front, and it was reported that many unwounded prisoners were immediately set to work in the rear areas of the battle, in defiance of definite international agreements made during the war. The Prussian Dictator was hard on everybody. He worked his own men absolutely to exhaustion, and also starved them while making them fight to the death. His restrictions in the matter of sick leave and convalescence for wounded were as brutal as his revised methods of mass attack. Nobody he spared while victory seemed within his reach, and the prolongation of his ways of communication proceeded with both celerity and efficiency. He worked men until they dropped, both behind the line as well as in the firing-line.

Ludendorff's relentless rule

That was how he brought a surprising volume of gun fire to bear upon the remnants of the 21st Division at Bray on March 26th. On the same day he poured a tempest of shell into Albert and all the British line running up the Ancre towards the Serre plateau. Breaking in and past Bray, fresh German forces crossed the Somme by Cérisy and began to envelop the Scotsmen and Englishmen at Proyart.

A German battery opened fire at a range of two thousand yards; but the British field-gunners were quicker on their targets. They knocked out the German guns and, limbering up, galloped off. Then the Sherwood Foresters, Black Watch, and Hertfordshire men formed a defensive flank by the Somme, while the division fell back to Marcelcave, just in front of Villers-Bretonneux, where at last the grey German flood was definitely dammed and defeated.

But the single wasted British division was unable to turn the tide back at once without assistance. After the thrust across the Somme had failed under the direction of Marwitz, General von Hutier, acting in intense close operation, in the last stage of the battle for Amiens, swung another large mass of attack against the gallant division from the line of the Luce stream. Yet again the survivors of the division retired to Villers-Bretonneux, where the Australians finally came down from Plug Street to take part in the last and victorious phase of the great battle. All Australians, however, had not been absent in the Second Battle of the Somme. Some of them, belonging to non-combatant units, had finely distinguished

Field=Marshal Sir Douglas Haig inspecting a Canadian battalion on the western front.

"From the front line": British runner delivering a message to a company in reserve.

French infantry out from the trenches passing a British battalion resting by the roadside.

Interlinking of the allied line: British and French in action side by side.

French cavalry patrol working with British infantry during the great German offensive in 1918.

Mutual help and admiration: French troops going up to the front past British comrades.

Two peoples united in a single purpose under single control: British and French troops marching in column.

themselves in a rearguard action on the strangely historic ground of Pozières, where their countrymen had fought one of the hardest of Australian battles. The Canadians also, though far removed at the time from the graves of their comrades at Courcelette, contributed in a very helpful manner to the successful defence of the approaches to Amiens.

At the suggestion of a French-Canadian of great ability, several wealthy Canadians had provided their divisions with a number of armoured motor-cars with machine-guns. The guns could either be worked in the cars or taken out and employed by the crews on the ground. British military opinion, apparently, did not then favour the use of swift armoured motor-cars in the parallel battle along the western front. Cars seem to have been regarded as old-fashioned, cumbersome things, serviceable against Turks and Senussiyeh, but not worth garage space when compared with the new light Tanks that did not need roads on which to travel.

As will be seen in a later chapter, French military opinion differed from the British in regard to the use of armoured cars. It was only through the channel of an independent French-Canadian mind that the Canadian motor machine-gun unit was available for service in the evening of March 21st, when Sir Julian Byng was wondering what cavalry forces he could get from other British armies to fight his rearguard actions.

In reply to his telegram, two of the Canadian motor-batteries set out at midnight, and the others followed by five o'clock the next morning. On Palm Sunday, the day before Albert fell, the grey cars came tearing in clouds of dust down the road by the Somme, and went into action immediately at Maricourt, checking the spread of the large hostile forces working through Cléry and over the old battlefield. The Canadian gunners were asked to jump out with their guns and rearguard the line, while a number of heavy guns and Tanks were being saved from capture by the enemy.

It was a long job getting the guns and monsters of steel away, and the Canadian gunners, after breaking all attacks against their front, were outflanked and shot down. Only three men—a sergeant and two privates—remained unwounded. One of the privates jumped on a motor-cycle to fetch the cars, while the sergeant and the other private kept a couple of guns going and held the Germans up. Then, still under cover of their fire, the cars came up and all the wounded were rescued. After having one of his arms blown off, the commander of the battery got all his men, guns, and cars away, having collected about a hundred and fifty infantry stragglers to extend the line in front of the heavy-gun positions.

Canadian motor-batteries' success

Wherever the armoured cars went they greatly strengthened the rearguards of the great retreat. Two of them, pushing up to the edge of a rise, perceived the Germans massing in a dip of dead ground, opened fire upon them at short range, and threw them into confusion. While engaged on this work one of the cars was hit by a shell, and as it was found impossible to tow it back, further damage was done to it before it was abandoned. In the action at Cérisy an entire German battalion, that had crossed the river in a surprise attempt to outflank the men who were holding Proyart, was shattered by sweeping machine-gun fire along the cross-roads they tried to pass.

Then at Lamotte, just below Cérisy, a body of hostile cavalry tried to charge through the British rearguard holding the highway to Amiens, a few miles from the city. It was the kind of rush attack that the British cavalry had frequently made successfully during the advance from Bapaume to the Hindenburg line. The tactics were for the horse to make such a whirlwind movement that neither machine-gunners nor riflemen could get on the targets. When, however, the Uhlans charged, they were met by grey armoured cars that could overtake horsemen while flashing out a scything rain of bullets through which nothing could get alive. The enemy commander never attempted again to use cavalry against the Canadian motor-batteries.

The Villers-Bretonneux sector, in which the Canadian motor machine-gunners saved the line from the German

THE "LITTLE GUNNERS" GETTING INTO ACTION.
Canadian cavalry machine-gun section on the western front. Having galloped forward to a convenient spot, the gunners dismounted and rapidly got their weapons into position for pumping bullets into the advancing enemy.

cavalry, was for long the storm-centre of the main battle. And strange was the composition of the British force that last held the enemy when he was in sight of his first decisive goal —Amiens and the railway running through it and connecting the British and French fronts. When the splendid force of Black Watch, Cheshires, Sussex, Sherwood Foresters, and Hertfordshires, which had fought itself to remnants between Roisel and Marcelcave, was again turned by a southern German thrust, news came in that this was only the beginning of Marwitz's and Hutier's combined grand movement in strength upon Amiens and Abbeville.

Fresh enemy divisions were being added to all attacking troops still fit for action, and as the northern bank of the Somme had been gained by the Germans, who were pressing into Albert and Sailly-le-Sec, it was clear that the supreme drive at Amiens would need a fresh defending force to withstand it. In the night of March 26th the barbaric Prussian began to bomb from the air the old capital of Picardy, that contained in its cathedral one of the most perfect works of man—the Parthenon of French Gothic. One more day's good fighting, the enemy thought, and his guns would be able to range upon Amiens. But before dawn the next morning a fresh British force had been raised to meet the German stroke. Its appearance would have excited the derision of Marwitz and Hutier. It consisted of some three thousand odd men—men from labour battalions, American engineers, field surveyors, signallers, electricians, mess attendants, grooms, sanitary service men—anyone who could handle a rifle.

Sandeman Carey's scratch battalion

They were commanded by a gunner officer, Brigadier-General Sandeman Carey, who obtained from an infantry training school some regimental officers and led his force, in the afternoon of March 27th, down to the line south-eastward from Villers-Bretonneux. The new recruits dug themselves in well, this being work at which the labour men were expert. Then they were asked to hold their front at all costs for two and a half days, to the night of March 29th, when the French were expected to arrive in relief.

All that arrived for some time were fifty British cavalrymen and some guns. In the meantime the fate of Europe and the world largely depended upon the cohesion and skill of the least-trained mob of men with rifles that ever stood to battle against a strong, veteran, victorious army since the French mob of Revolutionists met the Prussians at Valmy.

Again the highly-trained Prussians, who of all military races most despised the untrained man with a gun, did the testing. They did it far more thoroughly than at Valmy. But, as in the famous battle that opened a new era in Europe, immediately behind the untrained men were very capable **A new Battle of Valmy** Regular officers, worked up to a high power of mind and character by the sheer desperateness of the feat they were attempting.

It came at the end of a week in which hundreds of intensively drilled and experienced British battalions had been compelled to retreat before the fierce, sustained, scientific pressure exerted by a million enemies with a new method of attack. Yet three battalions of men who had never acted together before, and never fought, were resolved not to retreat, because the line was reached at which a British retirement would have meant a terrible Franco-British disaster.

The Germans quickly gathered and, under cover of shell fire, attacked. Beaten back, they renewed their assault, with that increasing vehemence which is the mark of the Prussian military character. In large degree the Prussian leaders in war won through by a sort of gambling resoluteness, piling up their losses until either success covered them or their strength was utterly spent. One of their reasons for this way of doing things was that, if victory were won, at no matter

EVACUATING GERMAN WOUNDED.
British R.A.M.C. men helping a wounded prisoner into a compartment of an ambulance train.

what loss in life, the moral of the surviving troops could be maintained and handed on by them to new recruits.

In this case there was a high strategic end, worth any sacrifice of life from the Prussian point of view. More guns were brought up when the composition of Carey's force was known, so as to play on the nerves of the new recruits. But the general was continually in the line with his men, and the officers of the training school were always in close control. There was no danger of panic flight. The men knew they had to stand to the death, and grimly and quietly they bore themselves. But they desired to feel, through the strain of each hostile rush, that they were under alert, practised guidance. It increased their confidence in themselves, and therewith their fighting power.

This gain was overset by the effect of prolonged mental tension and physical fatigue. The odd men fought for two and a half days, shattering all enemy attempts to break through. But the French battalions never came to take over the line. In such circumstances the best of soldiers would have tended to grow depressed, under the influence of weariness of body and mind. Transformed themselves into the best of soldiers, by personal spirit and inspired leadership, the scratch troops struggled against hopelessness as well as against the enemy's open attacks and treacherous tricks.

In the morning of Saturday, March 30th, they lost some ground, and under a heavy bombardment, drew back towards Villers-Bretonneux. Help was then at hand. An Australian brigade arrived with some squadrons of lancers and drove the Germans back, and at last rest was given to Carey's force—surely the most glorious of small bands of men that ever decided the issue of one of the great battles of the world.

When Carey's force took the field the spiritual issue that hung in the balance was of more importance than the immediate military issue. A gallant stand for a few hours, followed by a hasty retreat through Amiens, would have been a crowning triumph for the enemy. He would have remarked that the great improvised British forces were suffering from a lack of discipline, which discipline could only be firmly implanted in the characters of men by generations of military service.

Even so friendly a critic as the distinguished French writer, M. Maurice Barrès, suggested at the time that the steadiness and ability with which the French line had held under the shock at Verdun, compared with the way in which the British line around St. Quentin had given under hostile attack, was attributable to the results of a century of conscription informed by the Napoleonic **Moral defeats discipline** tradition. Events on the Aisne afterwards altered the elements of this comparison, and by a common misfortune brought Briton and Frenchman closer together again in temper and outlook as well as in policy.

Yet that which happened on the Aisne, like that which happened on the Somme, made Prussianism look still more triumphant. Although from a military point of view the enemy's successes were due to the foresight and skill with which he massed and handled large reserves there were critics who began to think that, under modern conditions, the spirit of liberty was less powerful than the spirit of Zabernism. Brigadier-General Sandeman Carey did not think so, and he had three thousand grounds for his opinions. A new Battle of Valmy had been won and the tide was turning.

IN PERIL WHILE ON MERCY BENT.
Stretcher-bearers hurrying to the field of action along a shell-swept road on the western front. That it was an "unhealthy" area is suggested by the tree in the foreground, the trunk of which had been gashed recently by a flying shell.

THE GREAT BATTLE FOR AMIENS.
III.—The British Victories of Defence Around Arras and Vimy.
By Edward Wright.

Von Below and his Two Army Groups—Discovery of German Design and Rearrangement of British Forces Around Arras—Terrific Fighting at Croisilles, Noreuil, and Lagnicourt—Gallant British Divisions Fall Back on their Battle Positions—How a Subaltern of the Buffs Saved the Line by Vaulx—British Rifle Fire Proves Victorious Against the New German Infantry Rushing Tactics—Moonlit Night Battle in Tangle of Downlands—Magnificent Rally on Beugny Line—Leicesters Save the Situation at Mory—Dead Man Down and its Valley Death-Traps—Great Stand by 3rd Division on Henin Hill—The Dam on the Cojeul River that Defeated Von Below—Battle of Bapaume and Gallant Defence of Beugnâtre Hill—Ludendorff Changes his Plan and Resolves to Break Through by Arras—British Retirement to Ervillers and Sapignies—Engineers Save the Line at Achiet-le-Grand—East Lancashires' Great Counter-Attack along Arras-Bapaume Road—West Riding Territorials Played into Action—Defeat of Prussian Guard at Gommecourt—Master Gunner's Defence of Vimy Ridge—Decisive Victory Around Arras—Invincible 3rd Division and the Guards Complete the German Disaster.

AS we have seen in the previous chapter, the Germans admitted they had made a very grave mistake in concentrating mainly against the British troops arrayed along the old Hindenburg line. The three new British battle zones between St. Quentin and Cambrai extended back to the last of the old German battle zones between Albert and Roye. Then, westward of the old German lines, ran the former British and French zones and battle preparations of the 1916 campaign.

From the ordinary point of view a grand German attack seemed more likely to result in a decision if directed against some important part of the British line which had not been advanced over a great depth of organised country. In some respects Lille was a promising sector from which to deliver a mighty assault, and if Ludendorff had originally selected it as a place in which to use his main reserve power he might have won to the Strait of Dover. But this prospective gain possibly did not seem to him commensurate with the gigantic effort he was making. He only feinted from Lille by a great show of preparation there.

His genuine aim was not merely to force the British armies to retreat from their northern sea base. He wished rather to bring about a final decision in the western

theatre of war. Therefore it was expected that he would attack immediately in front of Arras, and prolong the line of battle to the neighbourhood of Bapaume. At Arras the British advance line was only about four miles from the city, and there was no vast network of old positions in the rear to serve as a rallying ground. South of Arras there was a gradually widening tract of old organised ground, across which the German line had wheeled during the withdrawal from the Somme. Yet in the upper part of this tract the depth of the old defences was scarcely more than that adopted in designing a series of widely-spaced battle positions in the new style.

Between the southern end of Vimy Ridge and the hills above the Ancre there was room for making a grand attempt at a break-through, while strong attacks were being made in other favourable sectors. In this case a rapid German success in the assault of entrenched positions would have led to those operative movements by large manœuvring masses on the open field which the German Staff hoped to conduct.

Ludendorff, however, was over-confident of his strength. He reckoned he could break through in the south so quickly that the British forces there would have no opportunity of using the old positions. Then, while thrusting towards Abbeville, he

BOUND FOR BILLETS AFTER WORK.
Canadian pioneers on the western front returning in a Canadian cart from their work in the front line to their billets.

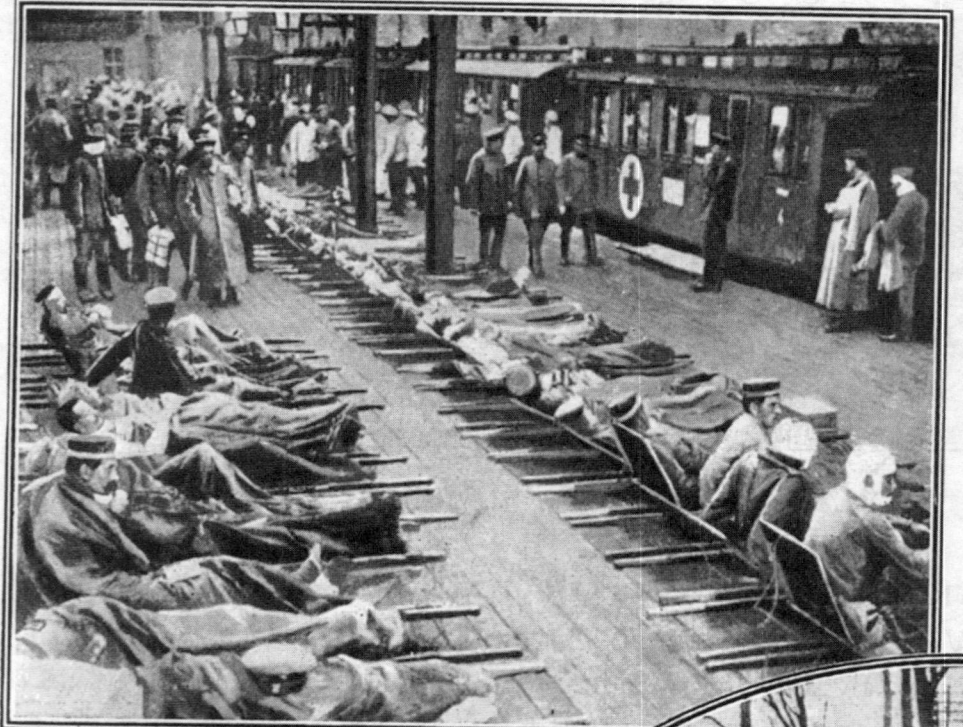

SOME ENEMY CASUALTIES.
Germans wounded in their spring offensive of
1918 being entrained in ambulance coaches.

was placed between Fampoux and Oppy. Here the Guardsmen worked with tremendous energy, strengthening their defences, which they finally brought to such perfection as made them proudly to regard their line as absolutely impregnable. This the enemy recognised by changing the direction of his intended attack. Thereupon, the British Guardsmen were withdrawn from the Fampoux line, which was taken over by the 4th Division, with a fine London division, the 56th, on their left.

On March 21st the Guards, with the 31st Division, were held in immediate reserve at Arras. The battle-line was formed by the 4th Division, that faced the German Mars group and connected with the 3rd Division that held the line along the Sensée stream, while the 34th Division was entrenched about Croisilles, and the 40th Division prolonged the line towards Lagnicourt and, with the 25th Division that came into

intended to outflank the Arras-Vimy line, without losing men in an attack upon the famous ridge. Only in case of lack of definite success in the drive from Cambrai and St. Quentin was the northerly German force to be strengthened from the reserve and employed against the Arras-Vimy line.

In the meantime the German army known as the Mars group, though completely mounted for a great action, waited quietly from Fresnoy to the Arras-Cambrai road near Monchy, with its supporting divisions stretching far behind it through Valenciennes. The design of the German Army commander, Otto von Below, whose Chief of Staff, Krafft von Dellmensingen, had helped him in his successful Italian campaign, was to swing large main forces southward to Bapaume, and there join with the northern wing of Von der Marwitz's army in breaking around Arras towards Doullens.

GERMAN PRISONERS TAKEN NEAR LA BASSÉE.
Queue of German prisoners captured by the British near La Bassée during the enemy offensive. They were
being marched up for interrogation at an Intelligence officer's quarters.

He opened action with the group of armies known as Michael I., arrayed between the Arras-Cambrai and the Bapaume-Cambrai roads. As Von Below only demonstrated with his right wing in the direction of Guémappe, his real front of attack was small when compared with that of the armies of Marwitz and Hutier. The reason for this was that Von Below was

Von Below fails to effect surprise

expected to achieve the supreme success of the battle, his forces being packed in great density so as to produce an overwhelming persistence in the movement of assault.

The design of Von Below was, however, clearly discovered in advance by the British commander, with the happy result that no surprise whatever was effected by the enemy on this part of the battle-front. Things were so arranged on the British side that even the mist, lighter around Arras than around St. Quentin, did not help the attacking masses to escape from slaughter.

Some time before the battle opened, a direct drive against Vimy Ridge was expected, and the division of British Guards

action across the Bapaume road, connected with the Scottish Highlanders, whose great struggle along the Cambrai-Bapaume road was described in the preceding chapter.

Several of these divisions and their supports had finely distinguished themselves in the first great struggle around Arras in the spring of 1917. The men of the 4th Division had then taken Hyderabad Redoubt and fought their way into Rœux just beyond their Fampoux position. Their comrades of the 34th Division had, in the early campaign, stormed all the works about the height of Point du Jour, immediately above Fampoux, and close to the line at Croisilles, which the 34th was holding in the 1918 action; and the 50th Division had captured Wancourt Tower in one of the most brilliant episodes of the campaign. In the new battle the 50th Division was in immediate reserve farther south, while the 42nd East Lancashire Division and the famous 62nd West Riding Division, heroes of the former Cambrai battle, were ready to support the line below Arras.

The supreme element in the British defences around the shattered capital of Artois consisted of machine-gun nests, cleverly concealed and often placed so as to be secure against hostile artillery fire. There was an outpost line, held by parties of infantry, with machine-guns in the rear, working between the posts and strong infantry supports at some distance behind the machine-gunners and the advanced guard. Then between these foreground positions and the main battle positions were the special hidden machine-gun redoubts, often placed in dead ground, which were to prove an invincible obstacle to the enemy.

The enemy's gun fire at early morning on Thursday, March 21st, was tremendously heavy all along the line, Von Below using his artillery to demonstrate down the route by which the Vimy Ridge could be turned as well as to shatter the lines he intended to storm. When the infantry battle opened he continued to demonstrate against the British 3rd Division around Henin, sending against them shock troops that were beaten back. His main attack, how-

BEHIND THE SOMME FRONT.
Street in a Somme town behind the line on which the German 1918 offensive was stayed.

A WATERY BARRIER.
British soldiers on duty at the edge of a flooded area on the Somme front during the spring of 1918, when the Germans launched their massed offensive.

valley of the Hirondelle stream running by Noreuil, while the slopes running up to Lagnicourt were covered by grey swarms. Von Below's tactics were the same as he had employed against the Italians on the Upper Isonzo. He went back to the old Prussian method of attack by masses concentrated on a narrow front, with a long series of closely-packed waves following the spear-point of storm troops that was to penetrate the line.

As the mist cleared somewhat and allowed range of vision of some four hundred yards, the German infantry could be seen marching forward in tranquil order, as though manœuvring under the Kaiser in time of peace, with no hostile artillery to teach their Imperial master that the mobile thin wave was better than the solid mass of frontal assault.

ever, fell first upon the 34th Division by Croisilles and the 40th Division by Lagnicourt. In these sectors the enemy's hurricane of gas and high-explosive shell was irresistible. The Bullecourt salient was smothered in flame, smoke, and earth, with the effect of a volcanic eruption.

The long hill stretching between Noreuil and the Bapaume road, with the crossways of Lagnicourt on the top of it, was hammered with innumerable guns from the Quéant undulations of ground.

No resistance seemed possible under the enormous machinery of slaughter that Von Below had organised. In less than four hours the British wire entanglements were blasted away, earthworks were wrecked, communication trenches blocked up, and both the advanced forces of defence and the main battle forces were drenched with poison gas, which the enemy allowed to collect in all the rear valleys and hollows which he was not able immediately to attack. Then, under a barrage of high-explosive, that cleared of gas the positions they intended to occupy, the Germans came out in masses, striking down the valley of the Sensée River between Henin Hill and Croisilles, and through the hollow by Ecoust village and the

This, however, was, as the German Press afterwards proclaimed, the Kaiser's battle, and his commanders had, for apparently good reasons, returned to the method of sacrificing men in tens of thousands on a line of a few hundred yards. From Fontaine-lez-Croisilles to Quéant, a distance of about ten thousand yards, nearly a hundred thousand German infantrymen were **Opening of the** launched against some twenty thousand **Kaiser's Battle** British foot soldiers. Then from the Lagnicourt road to the Bapaume road another flood of hostile infantry was rolled upon the British defences.

On Henin Hill the men of the 3rd Division held on even to their outpost positions, counter-attacking the shock battalions launched against them. Their artillery curtained off the attacking swarm, which was then broken in fierce, close combats. But some of the other British forces could not kill the Germans quickly enough, and it was to meet this condition of things at the critical points in the line which the enemy selected for his main attack that all the ground had been carefully arranged and measured. All heavy British guns had been removed from the Bullecourt salient, leaving

FARMYARD SITE OF A BRITISH BATTERY.
British gunners at work in a farmyard in France during the prolonged and intense rearguard action that
successfully covered the retreat of the Allied armies under the pressure of the German offensive in the early
part of 1918.

there only a few field-batteries to assist the advanced infantry forces in temporarily checking and confusing the enemy. As soon as the German pressure became irresistible the British force in Bullecourt swung back to a new position, and on the line they abandoned there fell a curtain of British shell fire, the long delayed but terribly effective reply to the enemy's whirlwind bombardment.

There was to be no victory in the Caporetto style for Otto von Below. The mist had begun to thin out at seven o'clock in the morning, and when about an hour and a half later the German infantry movements began there was a range of about a quarter of a mile over which British forward

**Artillery duel
in the mist**

observation officers could work. As many of the British guns had been shifted to hidden new positions, the enemy's counter-battery work went on in a groping manner. In fact the thin haze on the absorbent chalky ground between Arras and Bapaume was more serviceable to the defence than it was to the attack. For when the centre British divisions fell back to their battle positions, the German gunners, with their thousands of guns, could only guess at targets during the decisive phase of the main engagement and generally continue to work by the map, smothering places where troops were likely to collect and maintaining barrages over all communication ways of which aerial photographs had been obtained. The British gunners, on the other hand, had the easier task of keeping up as fierce a fire as possible upon their abandoned foreground, every yard of which was known to them. Then, when the enemy masses came nearer, directing officers in hidden posts on the slopes marked the Germans down at ranges that had been noted in advance, and by keeping the guns on the large moving targets, wrought such slaughter as fully avenged all the British losses on the entire line of battle.

Yet the gaps torn in the compact lines of assault were filled by inexhaustible supports rising out of the smoke and flame. A British observer said the Teutons were like waves of the sea, rippling through the whirlwind of defending gun fire. Bodies of their

dead and wounded littered the brown, scorched fields, filled the hollows and sunken roads, and covered the slopes of the succession of 100-metre heights between the Sensée River and the Bapaume road.

Fresh masses of men, striding over tens of thousands of fallen, continued to pour against the thinning British line. About noon Croisilles, Ecoust, Noreuil, and Lagnicourt were lost. Yet the British foreground defences were not by that time entirely won by the enemy. By Lagnicourt, English County battalions made a prolonged and most effective stand before withdrawing to Vaulx-Vraucourt. They expected the Germans. All night they stood to, and they had look-outs in the craters of No Man's Land. One patrol of twenty-five Norfolks checked the packed enemy battalions before the British positions were visible to the attackers, while the Durham Light Infantry broke and pursued the first wave of assault and captured four machine-guns.

Some Yorkshires held an advanced post until four o'clock in the afternoon, and another part of the outpost line on the crest was defended until evening fell, with the Germans pouring along the Noreuil Down on the left and passing in masses down to Lagnicourt through a break made in the more northerly part of the line. Other small stubborn rearguards, though ferociously pressed, stayed the German advance in main force until seven o'clock in the evening. Then, covered by the return of the white mist, most of the gallant survivors withdrew, facing the enemy and ambushing him when he became too adventurous. But among those who did not retire was an officer of the Shropshires, holding a work with twenty men, and telephoning the enemy's movements to the guns. When last seen he and his men were charging into the Germans.

One Essex officer barred the road to a great force of Germans by collecting stray groups of men and making them into an alert and deadly rearguard. One of them, a gunner-major in a gap, shot the Germans down with his 60-pounders at a range of five hundred yards, assembled his battery crew with rifles and, though wounded, marched off to the assistance of the Buffs.

DEAFENING DEFIANCE FROM STEEL-THROATED MIGHT.
French heavy gun in action near the point of junction of the Allied armies, through which the German High
Command sought to break. Moving on railway lines from point to point, these monster pieces of ordnance
continually surprised the enemy artillery positions all along the line.

The Buffs had a young officer in the brigade bombing school, who, when the overwhelming pressure of the masses of attack made the situation critical, led on the staff of his school, collected some three hundred strays from seven regiments, and with them rearguarded the division. When, in the night of March 21st, the new battle forces of Von Below stormed into an important part of the main British position, the subaltern, with a picked party of bombers, crawled through an intense barrage of machine-gun fire and bombed the attackers out of an entrenchment on high ground.

Then, with the wounded gunner-major, the subaltern of the Buffs, in the morning of Friday, March 22nd, worked around Vaulx Wood and Vaulx-Vraucourt village, the storm-centres of the incessant struggle, and with his continually diminishing band of dogged dare-devils counter-attacked and checked the advance of an army.

The English division at Lagnicourt could have held their front line as strongly all day as did the Scotsmen on the other side of the Cambrai road; but, as at the opening of the Cambrai battle, the left flank of the English was turned by the obliteration of both troops and works. In the Hirondelle valley the long, indomitable stand made by the County battalions, though saving the forces in the Cambrai salient, imposed a terrific strain upon the unyielding division when it was swinging back to its invaded battle position by Vaulx-Vraucourt.

Its own losses were heavy, for the enemy artillery reached in great strength to the Vaulx line. Its effect was heightened by the extraordinarily dense machine-gun barrages which the German infantry maintained from the high ground they had won. Yet the Englishmen, like all other defending forces on Von Below's front of battle, remained in grim good heart throughout their dreadful ordeal.

The sufferings of the German multitudes, from Henin Hill to Lagnicourt Down, were visibly so terrible that the almost overwhelmed British were satisfied with the work they had been doing. It seemed to them that no army, however large, could for long continue to waste as Von Below's army was

LONG-RANGE BOMBARDMENT OF GERMAN BACK AREAS.
British heavy gun sited in a French village to maintain an intense bombardment of the enemy's back areas. By long-range fire of this kind immense havoc was wrought in the German billeting areas and over their lines of communication, seriously impeding their advance.

wasting. High as was the price which Ludendorff had arranged to pay for success, his best commander far exceeded it in the opening stage of the battle.

Von Below's preliminary losses were heavier than those incurred by the British Army on the Somme in the fruitless northern attack against the Gommecourt line. Unlike the British commander, Von Below did not stop his action when it had at least served the purpose of holding considerable British forces around Arras and preventing them from strengthening the yielding southern line.

As was seen from German documents afterwards captured, the victor at Caporetto sustained his prestige by pretending that he had won another great victory around Croisilles. **Von Below's serious reverse** Thereby he obtained a free hand and huge reinforcements from Ludendorff's grand reserve in the apparent design to exploit the break he had made. What he really did was to employ the fresh forces allocated to him in a tremendous attempt to transform a very serious reverse into a victory.

The British divisions had fallen back on their battle-line at St. Léger, Vaulx-Vraucourt, and Morchies, throwing out a new outpost line towards the lost villages. Late in the afternoon Von Below launched another general offensive from Fontaine Wood to the Bapaume road, sending his fresh divisions through his shattered forces against the new line of 100-, 120-, and 111-Metre Hills, on which the defending troops, strengthened by their supports, made an incomparable stand.

Never was there such a killing of Germans since the war began. It was the first time since the First Battle of Ypres that the enemy had tried to burst by sheer weight of numbers through the British line. He used larger masses in extraordinary depth, by means of an improved organisation that enabled him to crowd the ground more quickly and also more densely than he had done in any other battle from Verdun to Cambrai.

The combination of speed and mass was Von Below's Caporetto recipe for victory, and against the British line he used at least three times the number of divisions he had employed against

AN IRON DAM AGAINST THE ONCOMING FLOOD.
Battery of British howitzers in action. A thick hedge along which the guns were lined served as a screen for the position which the artillery occupied temporarily while delaying the enemy's advance until the last possible moment before it withdrew to the next convenient point.

the Italians. No artillery could keep the Germans back. There were not guns enough and immediate stocks of shell enough to maintain curtains of fire to shut the German infantry off. Like swarming insects they buried ordinary opposition with their bodies, and marched over their dead in a high spirit of self-sacrifice, hoping to end the war by a single, prolonged, frenzied effort.

From their point of view they were fighting for a quick peace. All their aching weariness of war became a stimulus to self-sacrifice. Their spirit was thus very high, and the fearless way they went to their death won praise from their opponents. There was no doubt that the German could fight. He had the passive endurance of the Slav when he acted in mass, and much of the alert vigour in manœuvring of the Western Europeans. Indeed, he was largely a Germanised Slav.

He persisted through all artillery barrages, he swamped all works with machine-gun zones of fire, such as that which for a time imprisoned him in Lagnicourt ; then, **Foe advance in swarming myriads** with fresh waves of force continually surging through and reviving his line of attack, he renewed his advance in a manner that seemed irresistible. But the British soldier had yet one weapon—the much-criticised Lee-Enfield rifle—which, when expertly handled, could stay the deepest mass of assault.

Happily, the English division holding one of the most critical points in the northern line had been kept at rifle practice by a commander with foresight and also power of persuasion. While his men were necessarily becoming jacks-of-all-trades, specialising in pitching hand-bombs, and losing many of their best marksmen through the development of the machine-gun force, the commanding officer continued, with something of the insistence of the fanatic, to preach the gospel of salvation by rifle fire. " In the end," he told his men, " you will find the old rifle is still your best friend."

So it proved in the low riverside village of Vaulx and on the bare, climbing meadows around it that ended in the useful patch of cover by Vaulx Wood lying at the foot of one of the spurs of the Lagnicourt Down. One company of one battalion used in the course of the day a quarter of a million cartridges.

None was wasted in mere barrage fire, but in steady-aimed shooting, mostly on large targets at short range. When the second grand assault on Thursday afternoon was broken, enabling the British troops to establish themselves firmly in their battle positions, the struggle did not follow the usual course and slacken into a sort of armistice in the night, for the weather became peculiarly favourable for the kind of operations in which Von Below was expert.

Along the two extensive winding valleys of the Sensée River and the Hirondelle brook the white mist of early morning returned and gathered thickly in the twilight. The haze spread more thinly over the bare chalk downs, yet reduced the field of aimed fire in a manner that protected the re-forming and strengthening enemy masses. Above the white rivers of mist, in the hollows and the thin screen of haze on the hills, the orbing moon shone brilliantly, allowing **German double army's effort** the German Staff to array and direct its huge machinery of attack better than it could have done in clear daylight under far-reaching observation of British machines.

In these favouring circumstances Von Below used his immense double army of the Mars group and the Michael I. group to extract every possible advantage out of his position of much superior numbers. Most of his guns were able to reach the new British line without shifting, and his field-pieces, infantry cannon, and heavy mountain machine-guns were easily moved forward a couple of miles so as to fire from the newly-won line of downs upon the hollow in which Vaulx was built. Then, while the English position again rocked and flamed under the renewed intense bombardment, the Germans swarmed out in the evening behind their barrages.

They endeavoured to achieve so decisive a break as would bring them to Bapaume in the morning. All night long the struggle went on, from the central position at Vaulx to Henin Hill on the left and the high ground about the Cambrai road on the right. The centre was breached but repaired, again

menaced, and again secured. On the immediate right the continuous German masses created a situation of great peril by carrying the Morchies spur, from which an enveloping movement was begun against the forces in the Flesquières salient.

But the Englishmen and Scotsmen on each side of the Cambrai road had held the enemy so long and so firmly that supporting forces were in position immediately behind them. These immediate supporting forces consisted of the Cheshires, Worcesters, Wiltshires, Gloucesters, and other noted battalions of the 25th Division. Morchies was recovered by a fine counter-stroke from 120-Metre Hill behind Beaumetz. This assured the safety of the divisions which were beginning to evacuate the southern salient. Thereupon the German commander shifted the point of his main thrusting forces farther north, and in a more ambitious but more difficult plan endeavoured to strike farther downwards towards Bapaume by breaking into Vaulx and the neighbouring village of Mory.

When day broke, with the fog still choking the valleys and the mist still screening the downs, the wrestle between the gigantic German forces and the scanty British divisions proceeded with the same sustained violence of the nocturnal struggle. There was some lessening of the volume of fire poured out by the enemy's parks of artillery, indicating that the shell dumps in the battle zone, prepared for only a single intense bombardment, were being depleted ; but the resources in German infantry power appeared to increase rather than diminish under the staggering wastage forced by the British defence.

The British commander, however, was not lacking in reserve power, and although he often made his men work almost to breaking point, with local odds of sometimes more than ten to one against them, there was much practical wisdom in his frugal method of using his forces.

The fewer men he employed, the fewer targets he presented to the enemy's tremendous artillery fire which groped for its target on the downs, and the more troops he retained for the grand crisis, **Grand crisis of the battle** which could be seen approaching from the south where the line had been pierced. Only one fresh English division was moved up towards Vaulx in the early morning of March 22nd to strengthen the Englishmen who had been fighting in battalions against divisions for twenty-four hours.

At first it seemed as though the reserve troops had arrived too late. The enemy rolled forward in a grey flood, from the Lagnicourt and Noreuil positions, in an ordinary frontal attack, while attempting a thrust into the English rear from Ecoust. By noon on Friday he succeeded in carrying the front of the British battle position at Vaulx, and there getting a flanking line of attack upon the approaches to Bapaume.

This made things tragically difficult for the Highlanders who had been holding the edge of the Flesquières salient. They found themselves, when making a stubborn, orderly withdrawal from their own lines, violently rushed in the rear below Vaulx. Happily, the situation at Vaulx itself was not so bad as it seemed. Some of the defending troops did not know that they were beaten, outflanked, and in danger of envelopment. They held on to the distillery and other works on the south-western edge of Vaulx, and there became the immovable pivot on which swung one of the finest rallying movements in British military history.

From the distillery the half-broken and badly-bent line had been pressed towards Beugnâtre, scarcely more than a mile and a half from Bapaume. Bapaume was the point at which the armies of Von Below and the army of Marwitz were designed to meet. Had they then met, the fate of the British forces in France and Flanders would probably have been decided, and with them the fate of France. But Vaulx was not yet conquered by the enemy. While the German commander was organising a final attack upon the men in the distillery, the defending lines swung back from Beugnâtre, connected with the rearguard of Gordons farther up the Cambrai road, and swept back triumphantly to Vaulx-Vraucourt.

This recovery of the British battle position, near the Quéant salient, more than twenty-four hours after the Michael I. army group had broken through the British foreground positions, marked the definite defeat of General Otto von Below. Abruptly he fell from the rank of the most successful leader of German armies since Hindenburg broke the Russians at Tannenberg to the position of the most spendthrift and discredited commander since Falkenhayn. Indeed, he had wasted in a single day more men than Falkenhayn used up in a month.

As was afterwards seen from diaries found on his regimental officers, men who had served under him in Italy lost all trust in him, and hoped that they would get under Hutier. Only the unused divisions in the Mars group and the divisions still pouring out from Ludendorff's grand reserve seem to have maintained some illusion of success as they were marched up to relieve Von Below's original shattered forces.

Von Below partly missed his chance through the fault of some local commander at the moment when Vaulx was almost occupied. Instead of throwing all available weight in one direction towards the Bapaume-Cambrai **German commander's** road, the local commander endeavoured **tactical blunder** to win advantages on both flanks of the yielding British position.

He thrust westward at Mory village, over 120-Metre Hill, so as to get another enveloping line of attack due north of Bapaume, at the same time as he pushed half his forces down the Bapaume-Cambrai highway and invaded the flank of the British divisions retiring from the direction of Flesquières. Had he struck in one direction with all his might, something would undoubtedly have broken. By attempting too much he accomplished nothing. West of

Vaulx his troops overran Mory village, but they were not in sufficient force completely to conquer it.

A most gallant band of Leicesters hung on in a single cluster of ruins while their comrades—Staffordshires, Middlesex, Lincolns, and others—fought all night around the village, and continued to hold the enemy on Saturday morning, March 23rd. **British line at** Then a fine Scottish division of Low- **Mory saved** landers and Highlanders, including the Royal Scots Fusiliers and the Highland Light Infantry, marched up to take full advantage of the long check to the German advance.

Fighting forward together, the tired Englishmen and the fresh Scotsmen swept over the thread of water of the Upper Sensée River, and breaking into the tangle of ruins at Mory, re-established the British line at this very important junction of roadways, where eight highways, country roads, and cart-tracks met among three highly important downs, some three miles in the rear of Vaulx. Below Vaulx, which the Germans had meanwhile recovered, the British defence system was formed out of a tangle of old works known as the Beugny line, constructed by the Germans in the previous year to hold the Australian troops back while the Hindenburg line was being completed.

Above Vaulx, which was smoking like a volcano from British artillery fire, the line of the victorious British defence extended by St. Léger and Boyelles to Henin. Henin Hill was lost on March 23rd, but it was not regretted. The Germans had purchased it at such a price as they paid for Dead Man Hill in the Battle of Verdun. Instead of using Falkenhayn's system of extended instalments, Ludendorff's ablest lieutenant had again poured out German lives in

MOVING FORWARD THE HEAVY GUNS ON THE WESTERN FRONT.
Heavy artillery drawn by eight horses passing through the ruins of a French village. Six was the number of horses usually allotted to heavy guns not drawn by machinery, but the state of the roads in bad weather frequently necessitated the use of an extra pair.

tens of thousands during the course of one day in order to gain ground of which he could not make any use.

Henin Hill had been neglected by Von Below on the first day of battle, probably in the hope of turning it rapidly after reaching the Arras-Bapaume road in the evening. But after the capture of Croisilles and the advance to St. Léger his northern-most forces of assault were again checked by the weakened but indomitable 34th Division, which, like the other original defending troops of the northern line, held on to its battle position against every available force the German commander could bring into action.

There was a great German assault in the after-noon of March 21st, another in the evening, a third in the night, and a fourth in the morning of March 22nd. So savage and sustained were the German

BUILDING A BARRICADE.
British troops in a French village during the pressure of the German offensive. They were engaged in erecting a barricade across the village street, behind which a few men could delay an advancing mass.

IN A STREET OF BAILLEUL.
Barricade built up of all sorts of things, from wheelbarrows to wastepaper baskets, chairs, forms, and shutters, in Bailleul, to stay the advancing foe.

attempts to break through between Arras and Bapaume, at a point where the Vimy Ridge could be turned, and the Third British Army caught in the claws of Von Below and Marwitz, that the British Guards Division were brought up to St. Léger to reinforce the splendid 34th Division, which was fighting to the very death and refusing to give any ground.

St. Léger connected with Vaulx-Vraucourt by an upland position bearing the famous name of Dead Man Down. The rounded height rose one hundred and sixty-five feet above the Sensée valley, and stretched for some miles north-east-ward close to Bullecourt. The enemy climbed on to it in the opening phase of the struggle; but although the high ground he won was scarcely more than thirty feet below the crest line which formed the British battle position his situation was then a bad one. For some four miles the upward western

slope was so gradual that the ground, from the attackers' point of view, was a level upland. In the misty weather they could not see what was before them.

The defending troops, on the other hand, had somewhat clearer air on the crest. From the high slopes around it they could generally get a glimpse of the enemy formations in time to pour a hail of bullets and a storm of shell into them. The enemy's artillery, though brought forward with great speed, had to fire blindly, the main positions of the British troops behind their new foreground line being practically undiscoverable. General Otto von Below made a serious mistake in limiting his attack in the north to the wide, deep, high down of the Dead Man and to the Sensée valley by St. Léger, that vainly seemed to promise the means of turning the skilfully fortified mass of chalk.

The German losses were enormous, and nothing was gained by them. What little ground the Germans won in Croisilles and a mile or two farther around St. Léger merely carried them deeper into a death-trap.

Crossing artillery fire and machine-gun fire with Dead Man Down was a somewhat similar though rather lower block of short-grassed chalk, engineered into a strong British fortress, dominating the northern side of the Sensée valley for five miles from Chérisy by Fontaine-Croisilles, St. Léger, and Ervillers. **British fortress on Henin Hill** This was the famous Henin Hill, held by the 3rd Division. At St. Léger the width between Henin Hill and Dead Man Down was scarcely three-quarters of a mile. In clear weather the riflemen on either slope could easily get a bull's-eye on any target moving in the open by the river bottom.

Even in the misty weather, giving a range visibility of five hundred yards on either side, British machine-gunners, communicating with each other from either slope, completely barred the valley, and, with their artillery observation officers, who sent rolling barrages rolling with murderous precision down the Sensée stream to Croisilles, transformed all the ground which the enemy won into a huge slaughter-house for his troops.

Von Below was thus compelled to widen his front of assault. Recognising at last his error in merely demonstrating against the British 3rd Division on Henin Hill, rising a hundred and thirty feet immediately above the ground he had won at Croisilles, the German commander on the second day of battle, Friday, March 22nd, turned all his heavy guns in the north-western side of the Quéant salient upon the down in front of Henin. Under the bombardment he endeavoured to carry the height by a direct frontal attack through the centre above Croisilles. The slopes of the down were here comparatively steep, rising quickly in contours of thirty-five feet to the crest-line of a hundred and thirty feet. For plunging machine-gun fire defence the lie of the ground was perfect.

Although the Germans had used more than a thousand guns, and had tried to plough up every yard of the chalk, the mist prevented them from observing the effects of their fire, and as chalk was easy to burrow in, the British machine-gunners and outpost infantry detachments did not suffer as seriously as they would have done in clear weather, under a prolonged bombardment laboriously directed by the new method of aerial photography.

The German commander employed the usual method of sending his attacking brigades forward in masses, in the hope that his first division would choke the British defence and allow his leap-frog second division to penetrate deeply. But this did not work out according to plan, and the attack came to a standstill by the exhaustion of the enemy's local reserves.

By this time, however, Henin Hill had become, in the German view, a key position for the immediate possession of which no sacrifice would be too great. About half-past nine in the morning, an hour after the British 3rd Division had won a victory above Croisilles against part of the Michael I. group, the picked shock forces of the Mars group, moved the previous day from the Vimy front, **Struggle for the** were launched against the same British **key position** division on the northern narrow end of Henin Hill by Chérisy and Fontaine.

This German attack was successful. In four hours' fighting the heavy grey waves of assault, surging upward under a hurricane barrage of shell, slowly conquered the outpost line of the magnificent 3rd Division. As the main British infantry force swung back to its first battle position at Henin, which movement compelled the British Guards Division and the survivors of the 34th Division to retire from St. Léger, Henin Hill yet strangely remained unconquered.

It had been too long in the possession of the British Army to be occupied rapidly by the enemy, with whatever force of men and guns he attacked. British engineers had spent just a year in fortifying the great down, whose finger-like bastion spurs spread out to the enemy's lines from the central height. Every novelty in defensive works suggested by the campaigns of 1917 had been introduced into the fortification of Henin Hill. It was one of the most important outworks of Arras, the city being in turn the gate to the possession of Vimy Ridge.

When the British garrison retired, leaving something like twenty-four thousand Germans struggling to overrun the summit and sweep down the slopes to the Cojeul River, twelve Britons completely held up this corps of the Mars army group. The twelve men had machine-guns and a large store of belted cartridges. **Twelve Britons** They occupied a line of excellent shelters **hold an army** on the road running from Croisilles to Henin and crossing the narrow neck of the flat top of the down. For three hours the extraordinary struggle of twelve men against an army went on.

In vain did the Germans try every trick in tactics, from mass attacks by brigade to crawling lines of sharpshooters, with the covering machine-guns in support. In the early spring the grass on chalk downs is short, and when a good field of fire has been carefully arranged in advance, and the ground prepared where necessary, attacking either in numbers or in skirmishing parties is likely to be costly to the attackers.

Only when the twelve British soldiers were outflanked on both sides did they retire with all their war material. Then the massed British guns, by the Cojeul River, so completely curtained Henin Hill that in the last glimpse before night fell no living enemy force could be seen on the down.

In the mist and moonlight of the night of Friday, March 22nd, General Otto von Below, whose Christian name should be mentioned to distinguish him from his less famous relative Fritz von Below, commanding an army on the Aisne front, continued his despairing, convulsive attempts to pluck the flower of victory from the pit of defeat. His lack of success against the British battle positions was having a serious effect upon the operations of General von der Marwitz. He

IN PREPARATION AGAINST THE ADVANCING ENEMY.

British soldiers on duty in a French village at a street barricade from behind which they could maintain a delaying rearguard action. This barricade was typical of many such erected to stay the German massed offensive in the spring of 1918. The enemy coming round the bend a short distance up the street would be caught at a considerable disadvantage, whatever their numbers, and suffer severely before they could rush such a position.

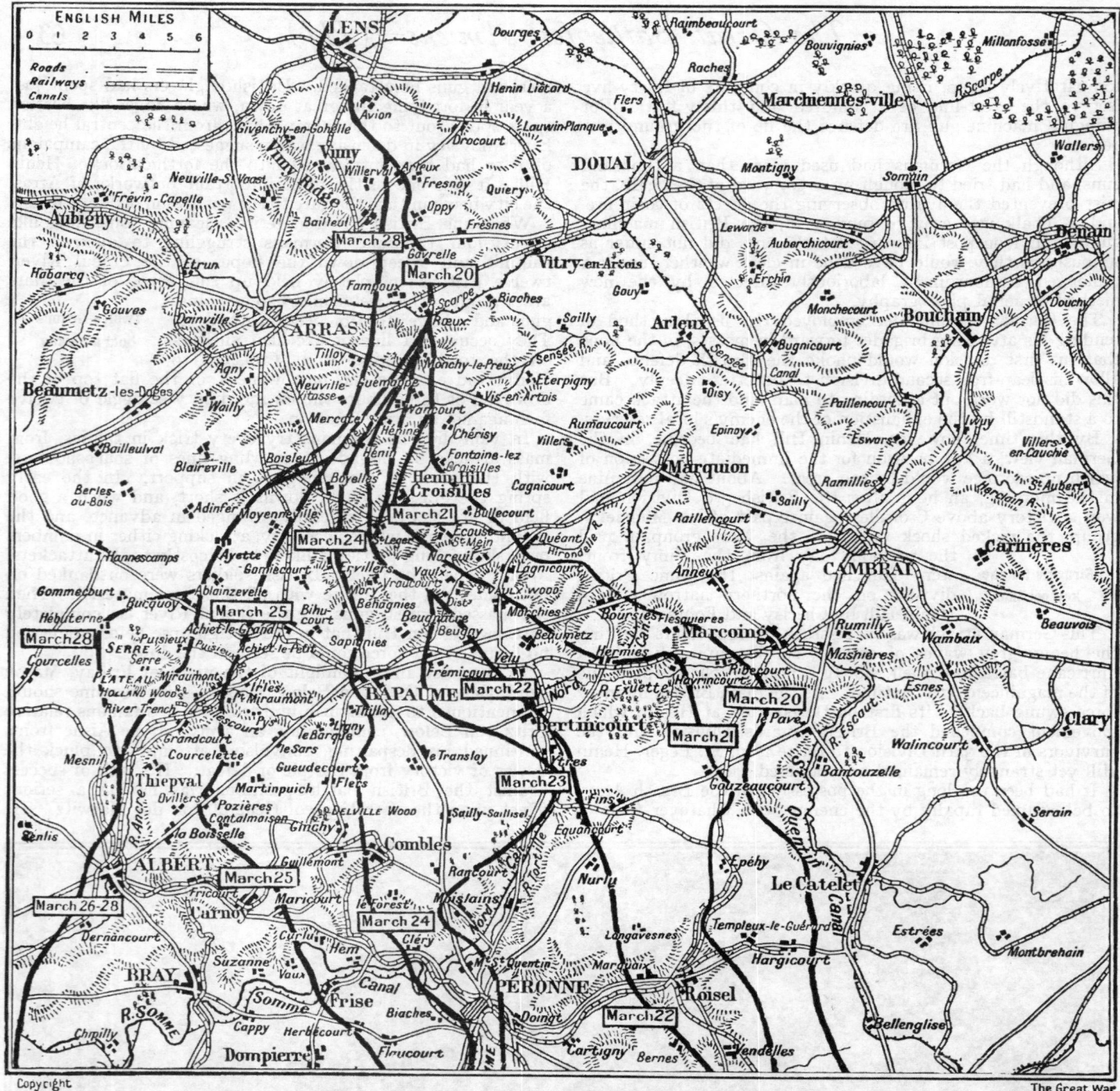

ENGLISH MILES

Roads
Railways
Canals

Copyright

The Great War

GERMAN THRUST FOR AMIENS: NORTHERN PORTION OF THE BATTLEGROUND.
The black line to the right shows the battle-front before the commencement of the great German offensive on March 21st, 1918, and the other lines indicate the positions reached on the successive days up to March 28th, when the line became more or less stabilised.

made it necessary for the commander of the Michael II. army group also to continue to incur debilitating casualties for strategic ends, which, according to plan, should have been easily reached had Von Below, with the strongest of the three hosts of assault, been only moderately successful.

All night long, from the Cojeul River to the Bapaume-Cambrai road, the commander of the two northern German army groups continued the battle with incessant violence. When, however, his right wing was reinforced to exploit the dearly-bought gain of Henin Hill, the forces working forward in the night brought back information showing that the general officer commanding the British 3rd Division had completely outplayed his opponents. Henin Hill was useless. During the misty weather British engineers had dammed the Cojeul River behind it, making a fire-swept flood of water across which during the remaining period of the first critical southern battle all the British line pivoted.

For the second time in two days Von Below had made a grave mistake. He had first tried a turning thrust in enormous strength through the valley at Croisilles, and had

his men shot down in masses from the neighbouring high ground, Henin Hill. Then when, at increasing cost in weakness to his armies, he captured Henin Hill he found that his turning thrust was again frustrated, and that it was necessary to use his Mars group in assailing Fampoux and the southern end of the Vimy Ridge. This was what he should have done on the first day of battle. He could not attempt it on the third day, having diverted, within the limits of safety, almost every available division in the Mars group to the field of combat of the Michael I. army, and that without any result but defeat.

When dawn came up in a clearing sky on Saturday, March 23rd, the battle-line of the northern British forces ran along the Cojeul River from the Cambrai-Arras highway to the Arras-Bapaume highway, with the 3rd Division grimly resting by the lake it had made, the Guards Division extending in front of Boyelles, the gallant survivors of the 34th Division gathered around Ervillers, and the English and Scottish forces, already mentioned, fighting on the height by Mory, with their comrades desperately struggling in the Beugny works to save the

64

flank of the Highland Division, 17th Division, and Naval Division retreating southward of Bapaume.

Dead Man Down still remained the tempest centre. For Von Below, having cleared his right flank from enfilade fire by the capture of Henin Hill, and being definitely in possession of the Vaulx-Vraucourt road of approach, tried with all available power to break across the Arras-Cambrai road and sever the left of the Third British Army; while Marwitz was beginning his tremendous swift thrust into the right and rear of Sir Julian Byng's forces south-west of Bapaume.

As Von Below conducted his main operations by Mory, he co-operated more and more with Marwitz's successful divisions above and below the Cambrai-Bapaume highway. His two armies, at their farthest points of advance, were separated only by six miles of ground, on every rood of which they pressed in unending waves of assault, while their densest formations operated continuously like gigantic mechanical claws, trying to tear through the last organised line of the British defence, so as to meet behind Bapaume at the time when the two similar claws of Marwitz's army groups were closing behind the Tortille River through gaps made at Ytres and Bouchavesnes.

But the men who held the high western part of Dead Man Down were immovable. They broke every enemy mass launched against them in ceaseless battle for thirty-six hours. Mory village guarded the back entrance to the Upper Sensée River, the front entrance to which was by Croisilles and St. Léger. The Upper Sensée River valley wound around Dead Man Down, enabling the forces that won it to carry the great height which, Gibraltar-like, was impregnable to frontal assault. Mory therefore remained the scene of fiercest conflict. After the English and Scots had retaken it, it was again lost and again recovered.

On the high land south of Mory, Royal Fusiliers, West Surreys, Hampshires, Durhams, and Kents fought all day on Saturday, March 23rd, against the German swarms pouring against Beugnâtre Down. They came into action at early morning on March 22nd, and never gave a yard until ordered to retire in the night of March 24th. They checked the general pressure of the enemy and withstood six separate attacks in force.

Rapid rifle fire again proved the triumphant counter to Ludendorff's new system of assaulting tactics. This English division had practised musketry all the previous winter. It helped to save the Third Army, as also did other divisions whose musketry practice had been maintained at all costs.

In the meantime the double pressure of Von Below's and Marwitz's forces began seriously to affect the British line immediately west of Bapaume. As related in the previous chapter, there occurred, on Saturday, March 23rd, a dangerous position at Beugny village, where the Gordon Highlanders, with an heroic force of odd men, made a gallant resistance against an unexpected flank attack from the north. Supporting troops were sent through Bapaume to Frémicourt, and while they were furiously battling against the hordes of Germans, inspired to a frenzy of self-sacrificing valour by news of victory after victory in the south, the British line again seemed about to break in more places than one under the strain of the overwhelming forces pressing and striving, grinding and thrusting against it.

British near to breaking point

The Battle of Bapaume went on increasing in intolerable intensity on Saturday night. The northern rampart of Dead Man Down was carried by the double enveloping movement

from St. Léger and the Mory cross-roads. The Scottish and English garrison of the Upper Sensée River line fell back to Ervillers, while the English division on their right began to retire to Béhagnies and Sapignies, on the Arras-Bapaume road, which they reached in the night of Palm Sunday, March 24th.

Bapaume then was still covered by a British rearguard, under whose prolonged and desperate shelling resistance the Highland Territorial Division, the 17th Division, and the Naval Division, and other important central British forces were retiring in a most intricate movement from the German masses pouring through the breaches in the Le Transloy-Péronne line.

By daring skill on the part of the fresher British troops, and

ESTIMATING THE WHOLE FROM CAPTURED PARTS.
German prisoners taken in Champagne being paraded for identification, to discover what German units were in that section of the line. Before operations of any magnitude were begun both sides conducted trench raids for the express purpose of getting prisoners from whom useful information might be obtained.

superhuman endurance on the side of the exhausted men, the forces withdrawing towards Albert and the Ancre succeeded in escaping destruction and, re-forming, held the northern approaches to Amiens. To win time for them the troops about Bapaume had to struggle from the morning of Saturday, March 23rd, to the night of Sunday, March 24th, and all through Monday, March 25th, against terrific numbers rolling on in continual attack.

Ludendorff had intervened in the conduct of the battle, and altered the direction of important forces of General von der Marwitz. When the British line was broken between Bapaume and Péronne on Saturday, March 23rd, there were two routes by which the pursuit could be carried against the wearied, retreating central British divisions— a short, direct route immediately north of Bapaume and a long, roundabout route through Bouchavesnes.

Ludendorff's new plan of attack

Ludendorff, while supplying Marwitz with fresh troops from the grand reserve to exploit the break, did not allow him to use them all in an attempt at encirclement. The area of operations of the Michael II. army group was extended northward, so as to overlap the downland sector of the Michael I. army group, in which Von Below had met with nothing but reverses.

For the short distance of four miles along the Bapaume-Arras road, from Bapaume itself to Ervillers, some of the Mars group of divisions, with all the remaining Michael I. group of forces and a very considerable number of the reserve divisions of the Michael II. group, were combined in a ferocious effort to break the critical part of the northern British line.

Ludendorff's new system of attack moved to admiration the British and French commanders who suffered badly from it. French military writers went so far as to claim that Ludendorff was, in technique, a pupil of Foch. The

CLEARING A WATERWAY.
British engineers on the western front in France raising a heavy temporary wooden bridge across a canal, by means of baulks and heavy levering logs, to allow of some boats passing through to safety.

supreme concentration of striking power he achieved was certainly that of Palm Sunday, 1918, when, transforming his difficulties around Bapaume into a source of inspiration, he combined the two army groups of Von Below with the reinforced right wing of Marwitz, and made the breaking of the British front below the Vimy Ridge seem as certain an event as human calculation and organising ability could arrange.

In the south General von Hutier was beginning to lose much of the enormous momentum of his drive from St. Quentin. His troops were fatigued by the long, rapid marches across the Somme, and thus liable to be checked by the gathering French forces, who had the Paris-Amiens railway and the Compiègne line to give them quick service.

Hutier had to spend time in strongly bridging the Somme, in order to get his heavy material across in the huge volume required for the final phase of the Amiens battle. By trying too persistently to speed up his men, he tired them out by the time they met fresh allied troops. Marwitz's original main forces, as was also soon evident, were becoming exhausted through continual heavy punishment, and the labour of battling day and night, with wearying changes of point of attack, requiring rapid marching.

The simplicity of Ludendorff's new Ervillers-Bapaume design was a classic quality. Like Napoleon's greatest strokes, it unravelled many complexities, **Enlarged scope of** and suddenly enlarged the scope of the **the campaign** campaign. Ludendorff was no longer content with his plan for driving the Fifth British Army through Amiens and penning all the British forces north of the Somme estuary by Abbeville. He saw his way, as the apparent difficulties of his first scheme increased, to accomplish something greater.

This was to break through the northern resistant wing of the Third British Army, and thus envelop from the north both Sir Julian Byng's and Sir Hubert Gough's retreating forces, while continuing to press them on the southern line. While these two British armies were being broken and taken, Ludendorff intended to turn Arras and the Vimy Ridge, and to swerve on the flank the other British armies, while breaking perhaps into their northern front between Ypres and La Bassée.

Grandiose the new plan was, but the means of carrying it out were practical. Before he opened battle Ludendorff had about a hundred divisions in line and a hundred in reserve, with a large potential final reservoir of effectives in course of transport from the Russian front. All he had to guard against, when the entire British front was endangered, was a great counter-offensive by the French armies, likely to be undertaken almost as an act of despair to relieve the weight against

the British troops. Rightly or wrongly, Ludendorff retained less than a half of his grand reserve to meet this expected blow.

Against the comparatively short battle-line between Noyon and Arras he used at the outset some eighty-five to ninety divisions, including those in action when the conflict opened. Nearly half his available force was concentrated with amazing rapidity against two British armies less than one-third the strength of their enemies. Moreover, owing to Ludendorff's remarkable ability in making swift local gatherings of deeply-arrayed divisions, the power he brought to bear on short but highly critical sectors often gave the attack a

NICELY CALCULATED.
Barge passing under the canal bridge, which has been sufficiently raised to allow of its clearing it with the narrowest margin of head-room between the upper part of the boat and the bridge.

superiority in numbers varying from six to one to ten to one against the defence.

So it was in the last phase of the Battle of Bapaume. The British commander directed his forces with skill and patient caution, adjusting the incessant calls upon his small, immediate reserves with cool, steady head, risking at times a new break in one place in order to fill an actual gap in another. Down the Albert-Bapaume road he sent Tanks to help in holding the Germans from the city until the troops retreating from the Flesquières salient could get their guns down to the Ancre line. The Tanks did some good rearguard work, as the enemy admitted in his official report.

When night fell the British line on either side of the city was wearing dangerously thin. The German generals of division and colonels of brigades used no finesse. They were in too violent a hurry, being grimly content to lose ten German lives to take one British life; because of the vast harvest of victory they hoped to reap above the graves of their dead they launched their men in extraordinary density and depth.

There was science, too, in their intensified and seemingly barbaric swarm operations. They had brought many medium-heavy guns forward from the Quéant salient, the distance of six miles having been easily traversed in the four days elapsing since the opening of the battle. The extension of the military railways from Cambrai was energetically proceeding, together with the construction of new roads.

The British heavy guns, on the other hand, were being hauled as rapidly as possible down to Albert and beyond, every midway position being threatened by the German advance through the flank at Cléry and Maricourt. Only a few field-guns remained by Bapaume for rearguard purposes, and they were swept by hurricanes of gas, high explosive, and shrapnel shell from the powerful hostile artillery. The German moving barrage that screened the attacking infantry masses was as heavy as that in a pitched battle.

Indeed, the new British soldiers in this sector were in a more hopeless plight than the old British regular troops had been in the First Battle of Ypres. Through the inevitable circumstances of the retreat they were submitted to a tremendous bombardment to which they could not reply with anything like equal artillery power.

Many of the new high-explosive shells did not, when they missed a man in direct impact, leave a deep hole in which he could shelter and shoot at the next wave of storming troops.

NEWS FROM THE FRONT.
British soldier inquiring of men in a French armoured car as to the latest news.

Shells of the new model were made to burst sideways when touching the earth and scatter their leaden missiles or steel fragments low over the ground. The impression the explosion made in the soil was often curiously slight. The Teuton had no monopoly in the production of this ghastly novelty of military chemical science. But the benefit of it largely accrued to him in actions in which he possessed a preponderance of gun-power.

Between the sledge-hammer strokes of his artillery and the swinging, battering-ram movements of his infantry masses the rearguard British line gave way north of Bapaume just as the city was being evacuated after an heroic, terrible, and successful holding conflict. One of the leading enemy generals appears either to have timed his final stroke with the precision of genius or to have persisted in unceasing assault in overwhelming strength until his perseverance was, more by chance than by skill, crowned with success.

The battalions of Royal Fusiliers, Queen's, Durhams, Hampshires, and Kents, that had fought for days without giving ground on the high land between Mory and Bapaume, began to wheel back in the night of March 24th-25th in order to keep in contact with the troops retiring above them from Mory to Ervillers. Admirably handled like pieces on a chessboard in the hands of a master of the game, the division withdrew to Béhagnies and Sapignies—two villages on high ground on the Arras-Bapaume road—without giving the enemy an opportunity of rushing its changing front.

Immediately below the division, however, the line suddenly broke. Enemy masses struck the British front between Sapignies and Bapaume at its period of greatest weakness, rushing the rearguard machine-gunners and breaking between the moving companies of battalions.

It was the recurrent crisis in the arduous retreat of an army heavily burdened with all the machinery of siege warfare. Actions could not be broken off with the quickness with which the men of Mons had manœuvred to the Marne. Ludendorff's great masses, while far exceeding in weight the five army corps that Kluck commanded, were yet handled more alertly and more fluidly. They exercised a sort of hydraulic pressure, flowing instantly into any hole temporarily left in the British line when its units were moving back over a tangle of hills and hollows.

Recurrent crisis in retreat

But, as has been already remarked, this fluid sensitiveness of German divisional and regimental staff had its disadvantage. When after a rush forward a sudden check was felt, the forward body of enemy infantry, being without artillery support, waited in the nearest fold of ground for orders and supports from the army commander. This was the reverse side of the minutely detailed system of centralisation by which fluidity in directed movement was obtained on the ground from which the attack was launched.

When a successful German brigade rapidly penetrated the British line to a considerable depth, after a prolonged and very wasting struggle, the ubiquitous British stop-gap, composed of a line of heroic odd men, could generally compel the German Command to hesitate.

LINKS IN THE ALLIED LINE.
French armoured cars and cavalry passing along a paved road near a French village on the way to join up with the hard-pressed British during the German offensive.

Strong, crushing counter-attacks by British reserves were not uncommon, and had, in fact—especially in Von Below's field of operations—transformed several promising local German successes into general reverses. The German Staff, therefore, did not encourage local initiative in the supreme crisis of the conflict. It preferred to make sure of its gain and then organise another massive force to exploit it.

Between Bapaume and Achiet-le-Grand some sappers and pioneers, under a divisional officer commanding the Engineers, filled the broken flank of the Arras road positions. Meanwhile four officers collected every fighting man within reach and formed a force of four hundred and fifty men, who beat off the Germans in a fierce struggle ending in hand-to-hand fighting. When night fell the Achiet-le-Grand line was still intact, and fresh British divisions were moving up for the final tussle against the usual German force used in the supreme moment in the turning-point of a great battle—the Prussian Guard.

Scratch force saves the line

The gallant English division that had saved itself by its pioneers and sappers then fell back to Gomiecourt for a short rest, and an English army corps composed of men of the White Rose and the Red came into action along the Arras-Cambrai road. They were the troops of the 42nd East Lancashire Division and the 62nd West Riding Division.

The Lancashire men were the first to arrive, and they came only just in time. On Monday, March 25th, Ludendorff was gathering in leaping strength below Arras, and when the Lancashire Division was engaged in the delicate operation of relieving the outworn troops the enemy in great force broke into the confused line from Ervillers to Sapignies. Sapignies was already lost, but was recovered by a vehement counter-attack, lost again, and yet once more cleared of the enemy.

In the meantime another German mass, launched from Mory, worked across the Arras road above Sapignies and climbed Gomiecourt Down, a mile and a half in the rear of the Lancashire lines at Ervillers and Sapignies. But the reserve brigade of the division was coming up, and meeting the too adventurous Teutons, drove them back with heavy losses by Béhagnies.

In this village, round which fighting had been going on during the Bapaume battle, the Lancashire Fusiliers made a glorious stand. The Germans were still attacking with the bludgeon weapon of overwhelming numbers, and the Lancashire Fusiliers, though excellent marksmen like their predecessors, found they could not shoot quickly enough. The German waves gathered on the slopes by Mory and then, reaching the 120-metre level of the plateau on which the Arras road ran, came forward in such rapid succession, under cover of a fierce barrage, that rapid rifle fire, Lewis gun bursts, and the steady stream of lead from the Vickers gun could not completely shatter them.

Had the Lancashire Fusiliers been as tired as the men they had relieved they might have been overrun ; but they were fresh and angry. Rising with the bayonet, they met charge by counter-charge, and by muscle and steel saved Béhagnies.

By this time the enemy Staff, having felt the strength of the Achiet-le-Grand defensive flank, which the former English division had held with its odd men, delivered an assault in the grand manner, breaking into Bihucourt, two miles behind the Lancashire positions on the Arras-Bapaume high road.

Lancashire men to the rescue

The British general expected this blow. He had Tanks in reserve near Bihucourt, and the Manchesters counter-attacked with their crawling steel slugs, and in the afternoon of March 25th cleared the enemy out with the bayonet. The other point of weakness in the line hastily taken over by the Lancashires was Ervillers. This, however, was held by a single machine-gun company.

Squatting on the hillside above the Upper Sensée River valley, the gunners for the greater part of the day enfiladed wave after wave of Germans who tried to work along the hollow.

This resolute line of British odd men checked the enemy, though he was in overwhelming strength. So often was he trapped in thousands in the maze of the entrenched downland that he readily accepted a sudden gust of fire upon his first wave as a warning that the ground was registered and covered for the purpose of shattering any force that could be crowded on it.

The Arras-Bapaume road positions were, however, unsound. The long defensive flank by Achiet-le-Grand was exposed to all the southerly forces of Marwitz's army, working from Courcelette, and joining early on Monday morning with the northerly forces coming through Bapaume. The positions were maintained only by fierce counter-lunges against both Von Below's and Marwitz's troops in an action of the open-field order. When time had thus been gallantly and adroitly won to enable the divisions along the Ancre firmly to establish themselves, and to allow heavy guns, Tanks, and war material to be removed from the Arras road, the 42nd East Lancashire Division swung back under cover of night.

The Germans again nicely timed the British withdrawal. They maintained their swarm attacks through the night, seeking for some joint in the Englishmen's line as they felt it moving back. The difficulty with troops retiring at night over hilly country is to arrange for them to preserve an even defensive front across crests, slopes, and hollows. On the occasional lack of perfect linking in rearguard units in a nocturnal retreat over broken country the enemy depended for his openings when pushing forward strongly and generally in pursuit.

But the British divisional general manœuvred backward in a superb manner, with a three-step movement. Fighting heavily in the moonlight, each unit withdrew under covering fire from another. When the enemy charged in pursuit of rearguards, he came under a barrage of bullets from the troops whose next turn it was to make a fighting retreat. The range was never more than five hundred yards, and often less. The East Lancashires had to use their pioneers, engineers, and miscellaneous troops to hold their right, as the former division on the same field had done. Also, they had to call out the survivors of the old division to help in beating the enemy off in the last stage of the battle.

Preparing for the last round

Though their own losses were heavy, it was with an economy of force, marvellous in comparison with the wastage imposed on the enemy, that the Lancashire men defeated Ludendorff's grand design, and in orderly strength established themselves by Bucquoy and Ablainzeville for the final struggle.

Alongside them, on their right, the West Riding Territorials came into action at Achiet-le-Petit, with their band playing them into a combat surpassing, in the heroic qualities it elicited, even their prolonged attacking effort in the Cambrai salient. For thirty-six hours the Duke of Wellington's Regiment, the West Yorkshires, and the Yorkshire Light Infantry held the line above the old battlefield of the Ancre. Then the division, in consonance with the general retirement to the strongest line within reach, withdrew to Puisieux, on the famous dominating level of the Serre plateau, and thence extended in front of Bucquoy, immediately behind which was Gommecourt of tragic memory, with Nightingale Wood and the old network of German works and caverns.

It was far from the thought of Ludendorff and his lieutenants to place the West Riding and East Lancashire Divisions in a position in which they should be inspired to fight with supernatural power. But had they wished to bring out completely every reserve of strength in the spirit and character of the British soldier, the enemy commanders could not have done better than arrange the decisive action along the old line of the Somme battles of 1916 and 1917.

The British line between the Somme and Arras on Tuesday, March 26th, was apparently dangerously weak for a considerable length on the southern sector. There was the skeleton of the 21st Division at Bray, and survivors of forces that had swayed in fierce conflict in front of Albert were entrenched around the town, with men of the gallant 17th Division and Naval Division arranged along the Ancre valley.

About the Serre plateau the West Riding Division was hard put to it to find men to man all their front, and, according to

Into action at the gallop: Royal Horse Artillery going forward on the western front.

Over rough ground: R.H.A. gun bounds in the air as the horses gallop forward.

On August 15th, 1918, a solemn Mass was held in Amiens Cathedral to commemorate the liberation of the city from the menace of the German guns. Our illustration shows the officiating clergy, one of them an Army chaplain, and the congregation in the chancel on that occasion.

Chancel of Amiens Cathedral in August, 1918, showing the high altar arranged for the Thanksgiving Service and the walls of sand-bags that had been raised over the beautiful choir stalls to protect them from bombardment by the infuriated and defeated Huns.

"The Parthenon of Gothic Architecture": Cathedral of Notre Dame, Amiens, rescued from the invader.

Hun handiwork in Amiens. Mr. Hamilton Fyfe reported in August, 1918, that in whole blocks not a building had escaped. " Blackened by fire, scarred by shell-bursts, hundreds of beautiful old structures have been turned into heaps of charred timber, shattered brickwork, or mere dust."

Red ruin wrought by shell fire in Amiens during the struggle for its possession that ended after four months' swaying conflict in the defeat of the Germans by the Allies' counter-offensive in July, 1918, and the enemy's enforced retreat to the Hindenburg line.

Shattered, but free: Amiens in August, 1918, after the Germans had been driven away.

Ready at the bridge: British field gunners guarding a canal crossing in France.

Alert at the outpost: British riflemen in anticipation of an enemy attack.

the new custom, had to set sappers and pioneers to garrison nearly a mile of old trenches. Above them the men of the East Lancashire Division, sadly wasted by their intense, close fighting on the Arras road, were again lined out by Ablainzeville, with the victorious 31st Division connecting with them by Moyennville, the British Guards at Boisleux, the invincible 3rd Division still fighting day and night along the Cojeul River, and the 4th Division waiting events below the Vimy Ridge alongside the London Division.

The British commander still kept his strongest forces immediately below Arras, and apparently regarded the Albert sector, though one of the main gates to Amiens and Abbeville, as of secondary importance. The Albert-Bapaume road, though lost by the British, was not won by the enemy. A cloud of British aeroplanes held the air above the old field of victories of General Rawlinson and General Gough. In continuous action by day and night they dropped seventy-four tons of bombs upon German traffic columns and fired something like half a million rounds of machine-gun ammunition from low heights into German infantry in close formation and into columns of cavalry and transport.

In particular, Von Below's lines of road and railway from Fricourt and Ervillers and Chérisy to his detraining places beyond Valenciennes were assailed from the air in daylight and darkness in a manner hitherto unparalleled in war and very disturbing to the methodical minds of the German Staff.

In their large tracts of newly-won territory the German armies had neither time nor foresight to establish an efficient system of anti-aircraft defence. The incessant vigour and destructive scope of the British, French, and American Flying Corps took the enemy command completely by surprise, and apparently confirmed Ludendorff in his belief in the advantages of his new direction of attack.

He still fought forward along the northern bank of the Somme with the forces that General Marwitz had swung across the Tortille stream, so as to extract from these large but wearying masses of troops every **Awful slaughter** tactical advantage which they were **on the Ancre** still capable of producing. Their losses, however, were the deciding factor in the southern action of Tuesday, March 26th, when they were sent rolling down the deep ravine of the Ancre brook above Albert.

They were caught as they descended, raked as they climbed the bank, shattered again on the long western slopes. Although they were in such numbers that detachments of them succeeded in penetrating far into the British line by such positions as Colincamps, from which the Arras defences could have been turned, the ubiquitous Tank, kept in reserve as the grand rearguard, managed with the help of a small number of British infantrymen to save the situation.

The ruins of Albert were attacked by four German divisions and held by one British division. The grey swarms came down the slopes in the twilight by Ovillers, La Boisselle, and Pozières like an army of ants, presenting in their close, orderly array and mechanical kind of movements a target such as machine-gunners and forward observation artillery officers never dreamt of.

At five o'clock in the evening they were in such multitudes as to colour the hills eastward of Albert. Thereupon the British barrages of machine-gun bullets, rifle bullets, and shrapnel practically ended the battle. Albert, lying in a hollow, exposed to plunging fire from the German positions, was only held until the stores had been removed. Then it was abandoned so that the enemy should occupy it and be bombed and bombarded. From all the lower river ground the British rearguards retired in the night of March 26th, leaving the exhausted enemy fixed for months in an inferior position from which he at last retired without waiting for a pitched battle.

When the remnants of Marwitz's huge main forces were fought completely to a standstill along the Ancre brook and began to swerve across the Somme, to co-operate with the more successful armies of General von Hutier, Marwitz and Von Below entirely devoted themselves to the task of executing Ludendorff's scheme for transforming their failures into a larger victory than had been originally designed. Two divisions of the Prussian Guard were brought up to deal the matador stroke to the West Riding Division, which was being subjected to a fierce preparatory process of exhaustion by less famous but very determined enemy shock divisions.

After being held in leash until they could finish in one tremendous effort what other fresh storm troops had begun, the 1st Prussian Guard Reserve and 3rd Guard Division were loosed upon the Yorkshiremen on March 26th in an action that lasted until March 28th. About Bucquoy the Yorkshiremen on the first day of the Prussian Guard's onslaught beat off five attacks, and then in prolonged night fighting began to retire to Gommecourt and Hébuterne. They had to give ground steadily and coolly in order to enlarge their field of fire against the enemy when, by rush attacks in great force he **Yorkshiremen meet** tried to close and use his fresher strength **the Prussian Guard** and superior numbers in close fighting.

Fatigue was the gravest source of weakness in the defending troops. They had been prevented from getting any sleep for two days before the Prussian Guardsmen were let loose upon them. The company commanders endeavoured to win snatches of rest for their men by leaving patrols out on the moonlit downs to check the pressure and give warning of attacks in force. But the Prussians answered this movement by the rapid employment of large half-moon patrols creeping forward in a crescent, rushing the English advance posts, and then signalling for their main masses to attack. By Wednesday, March 27th, the men of the West Riding were hemmed in on two sides, and in the evening the hostile Guardsmen made a gap in Nightingale Wood, where a gallant platoon of the defence was found, when the ground was afterwards recovered, in attitudes indicating it had died fighting to the last man.

As the enemy was working through the wood to the old front-line fortress of Gommecourt Down, and siting his machine-guns among the dead tree-stumps which were all that remained of the foliage of 1916, the wearied Yorkshire infantry were reinforced by Tanks, the original mobile British artillery that was proving more generally useful than the new German infantry cannon. Even the Prussian Guardsmen retained the old panic fear of the travelling British forts, and a hasty retreat from Nightingale Wood was imposed upon them.

Again on Thursday, March 28th, the attack was renewed with extreme violence. This was the day of decision according to the plan of Ludendorff. All his available forces were then launched in a grand offensive around Arras and Vimy Ridge, from Hébuterne to Fampoux and Bailleul.

The breaking of the British line at the southernmost point of assault seems to have been regarded as a certainty. From prisoners they had captured the German Staff knew that men had seldom been tormented by the lack of sleep to such a degree as the heroic survivors of the West Riding Division were struggling against. Being attacked, however, was the only thing that kept the men awake. They seemed to be miraculously fit so long as they were fighting. It was when the tension ceased that it became almost impossible for their officers **Victory to the** to keep them from falling to sleep stand- **West Riding** ing up wherever they happened to be.

In the great final battle the Prussians certainly did all they could to keep the Yorkshiremen awake. All the morning they came over in dense waves, and with a driving power that enabled them at last to close with the Yorkshiremen. There was constant in-and-out fighting in the old German works; but, against all calculation, it was not the twenty thousand Prussian Guardsmen but the outworn, half-shattered somnambulists from Leeds and other towns and villages of the West Riding who rested victoriously asleep on the field of battle at the end of the day. Their dead were surely with them in that hour—the men of London who fell in July, 1916, as well as the comrades who had newly fallen between the Achiet line and the old-new front by Hébuterne.

FRENCH INFANTRY "DIGGING-IN" ON THE WESTERN FRONT.
Advance of French infantry in extended order. Each man carried an entrenching tool as part of his field equipment, and hurriedly hollowed a depression in which he could get partial shelter before the next dash.

On March 27th the greatest crisis on the western front since the first week of September, 1914, seemed to be over. Around Amiens, Montdidier, and Noyon strong French reserves were coming gallantly and skilfully into action under the leadership of renowned French commanders of armies, directed by General Fayolle, the lieutenant of General Foch. But Ludendorff had expected this great allied rally, and, recognising that for the time being both Amiens and Paris were beyond his reach, he had been for some days preparing a second grand offensive against Arras. The supreme crisis was not over. All the early actions above Bapaume and above Albert were merely preliminary to the great stroke of March 28th.

Second offensive against Arras

Ludendorff reckoned that he had compelled Sir Douglas Haig to place every available division in line on the southern British sectors of the Third Army, which was worn out by fighting since March 21st. Of the British divisions defending Arras and the south-western slopes of Vimy Ridge there was only one which was not wasted and tired by continual battle.

Some of Ludendorff's divisions of the Mars group were also suffering from fatigue and losses, but he had kept others fairly fresh and strong to meet a possible British counter-offensive. Furthermore, he still had, now that General Foch's mass of manœuvre was definitely placed between Noyon and Amiens, more fresh divisions that could be safely spared from his own grand reserve.

Altogether Ludendorff brought about a hundred thousand bayonets with thousands of machine-guns and thousands of guns into action around Arras, seven divisions being engaged north of the river against Vimy Ridge and the city, with three more in the region of the marshes, together with all the old forces under Von Below and Marwitz that resumed the struggle in the downland from Gommecourt Hill to Henin Hill. It was as great an enterprise as that of March 21st, and was expected to yield larger results.

The overpowering German bombardment opened in the moonlight at early morning. The whirlwinds of high-explosive shell thundered about in a curious way, endeavouring to stamp out one outwork after another, while

the usual downpour of gas-shell flooded every known or suspected British battery position. About three o'clock in the morning German trench-mortars began to shatter the wire entanglements, and the preparatory work of destruction went on until from the British outpost line by Gavrelle one British soldier staggered back to the battle position, the only survivor of his company.

As in the St. Quentin battle, advanced enemy storming-parties worked forward during the early bombardments to outflank foreground works of defence and prepare a way for the sweep of the grand formations of assault. But on March 28th weather conditions and other circumstances were not as they had been on March 21st. Visibility was good, and British generalship was alert to the lessons of the great retreat. On Vimy Ridge was Sir Henry Sinclair Horne, the master-gunner of Great Britain.

At twenty minutes to seven in the morning all the British heavy artillery, ranged upon the concentration places of the German artillery, many of which had not escaped the recording lenses of flying photographers. While the crowded German shock battalions were suffering badly some of the British troops withdrew to their battle positions, thus increasing their field of fire against the thick grey waves of Germans.

Very slowly the enemy troops moved across the open ground from the three villages at the foot of Vimy Ridge. Ludendorff had overburdened his troops. To prevent them from failing to penetrate deeply through lack of food he had given them six days' rations to carry, instead of the two days' rations provided for the storm troops around Cambrai and St. Quentin. The Germans also carried two blankets and an extra pair of boots, wire-cutters, hand-bombs, and as much ammunition as they could stagger under.

The German Staff was on this occasion defeated by its thoroughness. Everything necessary for victory had been provided, except the physical strength of a pack-mule. Being only men, the Teutonic infantry crawled rather than walked. Consequently, they could not use anything like a true mass action against the line of British riflemen and machine-gunners. Wave did not follow wave quickly enough to take proper advantage of the ground won by the sacrifice

FOLLOWING THE "WHIPPETS" INTO ACTION.
British troops leaving their shell-hole shelters to go forward in support of an attack by the light "whippet" Tanks. These Tanks, first brought into use in March, 1918, proved of decisive value in the Battle for Amiens.

of the leading troops. Some Germans who fell wounded did not rise again, their cumbersome kit weighted them down, and they were trampled to death by their comrades when they might have survived in hospital.

All day long, from the neighbourhood of Vimy village, through Willerval and Bailleul to Fampoux, on the Scarpe River, the succession of attacks continued. In the early afternoon the Germans had not reached the objectives fixed for the early morning. As the sun was setting the most stubborn of all the German divisions had advanced barely a mile. With one flank in the air it was clinging to the trenches at Willerval and Bailleul, having utterly spent its force in toiling all day across a patch of farmland between Oppy and Gavrelle. The Germans had not reached the edge of the lowest slope of Vimy Ridge. The ground immediately above them was bright with little tongues of flame coming from machine-guns which they could not attack.

The troops of the 4th Division and the London Division, holding the slopes, were like men sitting at a window and shooting into a crowded street. Beside the machine-gunners and riflemen there were many observation gunnery officers on the ridge studying everything that moved in and behind the German lines and directing tempests of shrapnel, high-explosive, and gas-shell upon every target. When night fell small groups of grey figures, representing the survivors of the seventy thousand who attacked Vimy Ridge, crawled out of the death-trap villages at the foot of the plateau and, still under fire, drew back towards Douai.

Such was the confusion of the defeated enemy that some Westminsters, who had been surrounded by the first waves of assault in the morning and managed to hold out magnificently all day, succeeded in stealing between the Germans and regaining their line.

At Rœux the Seaforths made an immortal stand. They held the ruins of the chemical works on the slight rise of ground by the Douai railway, over which men had died in thousands during months of conflict at the close of the First Battle of Arras. The enemy had remained close to the ruined factory since the spring of 1917, and he opened the second battle of 1918 by leaping in overwhelming numbers upon the small

A QUIET MOMENT IN WAR'S LOUD TRAGEDY.
British machine-gun position outside a farm, which was further protected by a stream. The men were taking advantage of a lull in the fighting to overhaul their gun and to enjoy a rest under the pollard willows.

Scots garrison. The Scotsmen were overrun but not overwhelmed. When cut off they fought the Germans back on all sides and seriously interrupted the tidal flow of grey waves along the western approaches to Arras. When their works were breached, the Seaforths bombed, shot, and bayoneted their way back to the battle position east of Fampoux.

Fampoux was only a foreground clump of wreckage, held, like its advanced post at Rœux, as an obstacle to the enemy masses. The neighbouring, overlooking height of Monchy had, in spite of its apparent value in observation, been evacuated as soon as it was evident that a grand attack was coming. Values in terrain had changed since Sir Edmund Allenby's cavalry took Monchy at the gallop. A wide, clear field of fire between outpost line and battle line was worth more than a mountain rising directly above enemy trenches—at least to an army standing on the defensive.

The invincible 3rd Division

The abandonment of Monchy, though necessary for various reasons, bore hard upon the advanced companies of the indefatigable and invincible 3rd Division, still holding, after a week of day and night fighting, the inundated valley of the Cojeul stream. Their flank at Wancourt, by the Arras-Cambrai highway, was somewhat dominated from Monchy. The division had been in line for fifty-two days when the battle began. Yet on March 28th its reduced battalions fought with an enduring courage and skill in manœuvre more wonderful than the high qualities they had shown around Henin Hill when they were fresher and stronger.

The German commander paid them the compliment of using heavy odds against them. The enemy masses were so dense that, in spite of the slowness of their advance, they broke into two battalion headquarters. One belonged to the Northumberland Fusiliers, who for eight hours rocked in a hand-to-hand struggle, driving back the enemy swarms several times with revolvers, rifle butts, and anything handy. The troops had prepared a position behind Neuville Vitasse, but they stayed in ditches and gullies and other places where they could rest their machine-guns and rake the grey, charging lines at short range. It was late before they

DRIVING THE DESTROYER FROM THE RUIN HE HAD MADE.
Highlanders in action amid the wreckage of a village in France. Taking cover behind the mounds of bricks, they were sniping Germans who had not yet been driven out of the outskirts of the village.

settled in their prepared line. Single machine-gunners, inspired by the Henin Hill achievement of the twelve against the twenty-four thousand, stayed behind in noble acts of self-sacrifice and met the compact German lines, steadily mowing them down until surviving troops broke away to cover.

Between Wancourt and Tilloy some of the Suffolks were surrounded. Forming up back to back and ignoring calls to surrender, they stabbed with the bayonet through the first cordon of enemies, and thrust through the successive overlapping forces that blocked their path. The Scots Fusiliers at Henin also gave ground slowly against enormous numbers, felling the enemy in heaps during their retirement.

The British Guards, still linking with the 3rd Division; were also attacked by grey columns winding through the sunken roads of the chalk country, and then springing up in short rush attacks. Sometimes the British Guardsmen had solid waves of the enemy in front of their rifles, at a range of less than a hundred and fifty yards, and

MUSIC TO CHEER THE MARCH.
British troops marching forward on the sector of the front between the Aisne and the Oise, singing popular songs to the accompaniment of their regimental band.

broke them completely. At other times the enemy was too close for shooting, and the Guards used the bayonet.

After the mass attacks were broken the local enemy commander tried the method of infiltration. But the Guards were not to be moved. The attacks against them continued until March 30th, when their machine-gunners stopped the movement as it was gathering its strength, and the enemy retired with heavy losses.

This was the end of Ludendorff's second great offensive. On April 6th some of the spent but not entirely exhausted divisions of the Mars and Michael I. groups were sent out to be slaughtered around Hébuterne. This, however, was only an operation of a holding order, designed to prepare the way for the third great German offensive between Kemmel Hill and Aubers Ridge. Having failed either to separate the British Army from the French or break its centre, Ludendorff endeavoured to drive in its northern flank and attract the rest of Foch's reserve divisions while preparing a great stroke directly against the forces of France.

WAR'S TURBULENT STREAM IN SPATE IN A FRENCH TOWN.
This photograph, taken in a town in the Somme sector of the western theatre of war, vividly reproduces the scenes daily enacted in countless towns of France throughout the Great War:—British and French soldiers, indissolubly cemented together in friendly alliance, pausing on the pavement to watch French and British troops marching towards the front, the whole street given up exclusively to constant manifestations of military activity.

FIRING SHELLS FROM

CHAPTER CCLVIII.

A BRITISH HOWITZER.

THE GREAT BATTLE FOR AMIENS.
IV.—The Final Franco-British Victories of Defence.
By Edward Wright.

British Hold on Unaided—German Divisions Increased to Seventy-eight—Pelle's Divisions Arrive, but are Outflanked—Franco-British Problem of Paris and Amiens—Situation Saved by Enemy's Lack of Cavalry—General Humbert's Manœuvres between Oise and Avre—Magnificent Work of French Armoured Cars—Battle of Porquericourt Ridge—British Cavalry Bolt the Noyon Gate to Paris—General Foch becomes Commander-in-Chief of the Allied Forces—French Infantry Turned by Roye—Heroic Retreat of Cavalry to Montdidier—Fate of Amiens Decided by a Skirmish—Why Ludendorff Changed his Plan—Resumption of Attack towards Paris—Breaking the Enemy on the Thiescourt Hills—Fierce Struggle for Calais-Paris Railway—Gallantry of Dragoons and Canadian Squadron—Villers-Bretonneux Lost and Recovered—Action between German Land Cruisers and British "Whippets."

IN the three previous chapters we have followed the main course of action, from La Fère to Arras, between two British armies and the four German army groups with which General von Ludendorff tried either to break or turn the entire British line. To complete the story of the successful stand made by men who were never outnumbered by less than three to one, and more often by four to one, we must return to the delicate situation along the Crozat Canal, by La Fère, on the night of Friday, March 22nd, 1918.

The canal line was held by the gallant remnants of two English and Scottish divisions, that wheeled back from the Oise River in an effort to rejoin the Ulstermen retreating towards Ham. These British made a most skilful and gallant attempt to hold their long new line. They fiercely counterattacked the enemy at Jussy, and after recovering this bridge-head town from him, and preventing thereby an outflanking towards Guiscard and Noyon, they fell back to the railway line between Ham and Tergnier. There with desperate valour they checked General von Hutier's left wing. For more than forty-eight hours the survivors of the British garrison of the Tergnier line had, unaided,

to contend against the continually increasing forces of the enemy. A few days before the opening of the battle there had been seventeen German divisions in line or in immediate reserve between the Scarpe and the Somme Rivers. By rapid nocturnal concentration movements the German divisions were increased to the number of seventy-eight. Little more than half a dozen of the new divisions were held in hand as army reserves. In the course of a few days all were thrown into the battle, being in fact relieving divisions rather than a strategic reserve. The real reserve consisted of some twenty additional divisions which Ludendorff allocated between Hutier, Marwitz, and Von Below according to his special view of the requirements of the general situation.

At the beginning of the war of rapid movement beyond the St. Quentin sector, General von Hutier, as the most successful of the three German commanders, attracted the largest number of fresh divisions from Ludendorff's reserves. He was Ludendorff's brother-in-law. His success was designed to be the most spectacular of the three combined German operations, so that a new Ludendorff-Hutier partnership, with a firm family basis, might replace the dissolving Hindenburg - Ludendorff union. Hutier's forces were fed directly from the armies of the Crown Prince of

BENEATH A PROTECTIVE WEBBING.
British soldier passing along a well-camouflaged trench on the western front. Such vertical hangings of coarse netting or canvas, strung at intervals, served to render a trench or road indistinguishable to enemy observers from the air.

Prussia, as well as from the immense echelons of marching and entraining columns that extended far into Germany and there connected with the movement of troops withdrawing from Russia and Rumania.

The immediate result of this condition of things was that the weakened British forces between Tergnier and Ham were subjected to incessant pressure that augmented after every successful stand they made. Of all British troops they and their comrades the Ulstermen most deserved the swiftest help from the allied mass of manœuvre controlled by the Supreme Council of War at Versailles.

This mass of manœuvre had been directly created by the release of a French army between La Fère and Tergnier. This line, as the British representative at Versailles pointed out, had been the sector against which the grand German stroke was most likely to fall.

All that General Pétain could do was to send, between Tergnier and Ham, three divisions of infantry under General Pelle. These troops came into action on the third day of battle. General Pelle's force consisted of the 1st Division of Cuirassiers-à-pied and the 9th and 10th Infantry Divisions.

Pelle's divisions arrive At eleven o'clock on the night of March 21st the order was given for them to proceed to the help of the southernmost British force. They entrained at noon on March 22nd, detrained in the evening of that day, and by forced marches through Beaumont, Genlis, and Frières Woods on the morning of Saturday, March 23rd, they arrived in the line of action between Ham and Tergnier. One division was sent to Tergnier, where by a brilliant counter-attack it threw the Germans back from the pivot of the Franco-British forces.

Meanwhile, the outworn heroic remnants of British brigades met the shock of the German masses and withstood them until the afternoon of March 23rd, when, covered by a French supporting division, they drew back to the Oise line immediately below Tergnier and entrenched at the bridgeheads below that town and Noyon.

Very difficult was the task of organising the British and French troops into a single command during the toil and confusion of continuous conflict. The half-broken line of battle was overrun by enemy spies. For the most part the German agents **Enemy tricks of masquerade** were able and dauntless officers who had been partly educated in England, and by purity of accent and intimate knowledge of British military ways could pass themselves off in the fog of the retreat as British officers. Among them were also men who had specialised in French dialects and rural ways of life. These persons mingled with the refugees from farms, villages, and towns, and entered into operations with other secret agents who had been working behind the French and British lines since the opening of the war. They blocked some important roads by spreading panic rumours among the civilian population and giving them orders to withdraw in all haste towards Paris.

The German spies seem to have been able quickly to discover all the information needed by their High Command, as was afterwards clearly proved by events around Armentières and around Rheims. The methods by which the movement of every British division was rapidly communicated through the reorganised Franco-British front to the German Staff were not traced until July, 1918, when General Mangin was able to collect his forces in such secrecy as surprised the enemy High Command.

During the last critical week of March the improved

ON FRANCE'S RIVER OF DESTINY.

A view across the Marne—the river which in 1914 and again in 1918 witnessed the downfall of German hopes at the very time that they seemed on the point of realisation. There was something of poetic justice in the Allied armies' repeated defeat of the modern Huns on the very river on which the ancient Huns under Attila had been overthrown nearly fifteen hundred years before, when in 451 they were sanguinarily defeated at Châlons.

IN AN OUTPOST LINE.
Highlanders holding an advanced position with shallow pits in the chalky soil for earthworks.

West of Villeselve, as has already been related, Ulstermen, Englishmen, and Scotsmen were still fighting, with a rearguard of British cavalry, and escaping complete destruction only by a continual succession of miracles. Hutier's forces alone were rapidly increasing to thirty divisions, containing three hundred thousand picked infantrymen, machine-gunners, and infantry-gunners, behind whom were energetically toiling forward the light and medium artillery forces of the Michael III. army group.

In these circumstances Hutier was able continually to increase the forces of his thrusts westwards towards Roye and Amiens, while bearing still heavily southward upon General Pelle's small Franco- **Third French Army** British forces and threatening a movement **in action** upon Paris. In the clear moonlit night of March 23rd and the settled fair weather of the early morning of March 24th Hutier's corps commanders went on with their tremendous wave-like attacks down the roads and winding lanes leading to Chauny. The guns of the French army under General Duchene, entrenched behind the right bank of the Oise, helped to save the British survivors of the shattered wing of the Fifth Army. But beyond the reach of the artillery on the original French front the enemy's swarming pressure of infantry beat back the central French division and compelled the western division to fall back towards Noyon.

Palm Sunday, March 24th, was a day of extreme tension on the southern battlefield as well as on the central field of

German system of espionage, with its scores of new, eager, and desperate recruits of the highest order, worked with deadly effectiveness between the yielding points of the British and French Armies.

Use was also made of the old trick of taking uniforms from the British dead to dress up German infantry detachments under officers speaking English and talking French with an English accent. Some French forces were seriously endangered when attempting to rush to the help of an apparently small body of troops in khaki that seemed to be heroically struggling to reach their line. Officers in the uniform of British forces known to be fighting in the neighbourhood would approach a French commandant with despairing requests for help in disengaging their men, and then lead the rescuers into a machine-gun ambush.

It was partly to avoid such traps as these that the French commander brigaded with his own forces most of the British troops retreating from the St. Quentin-La Fère line. As soon as a strong liaison system was established under an alert French Staff, the enemy's tricks of masquerade were turned against him, although his espionage activities were not fully checked for some months.

In the meantime General Pelle was outflanked at Ham. This occurred on Saturday morning, March 23rd, some hours before the French forces were able to reach and strengthen the thinning British line below the Crozat Canal. After devoting one of his three divisions to the vital task of holding on to Tergnier, the French general had to place another division in observation at Villeselve, south-west of Ham. This left him only ten thousand Frenchmen, with remnants of fatigued British infantry and artillery, to meet the ferocious German mass attacks between Villeselve and Tergnier.

DEFENDING THE LINES OF COMMUNICATION.
British infantry arriving at a railway embankment which they had been told off to defend during the German advance in the spring of 1918. One result of the massed offensive begun by the enemy on March 21st had been to change the conditions of fighting to "open" warfare on some parts of the front.

conflict. The Germans cleared all the hilly wooded country between La Fère and Guiscard, drove in the centre of General Pelle's force, and took Chauny, Guiscard, and Nesle. Then it was that the need of some stronger central direction than the Supreme Council of War at Versailles was desperately felt.

The Council of War at Versailles could only co-ordinate in lengthy discussion the ideas of the allied military representatives. As in nearly all committees, co-ordination became in practice the acceptance of something like a common denominator between the different ideas, and the rather slow adoption of what seemed to be the most prudent measures.

The strengthening of the French defensive flank at Noyon was the measure adopted. General Humbert, with some of the advanced forces of the Third French Army, began to extend and strengthen the yielding line upon which General Pelle was fighting. But though his forces were brought into action with a celerity that would have been remarkable in ordinary conditions of warfare, General Humbert was unable to cope forthwith with the masses that Ludendorff was manœuvring forward with surprising speed. The new German system of accelerated concentration could not, when it had effected a great break, be countered by methods of cautious prolongation of the broken flanks.

The British reserves were completely exhausted north of the Somme, where Sir Douglas Haig was striving to save his Third Army by moving the Fourth Army down to the river of many battles. The Fifth British Army could only be saved by immediate help from the allied reserve. Even the southern wing of the Third Army, pierced **Enemy's lack of** by General von Kathen on Saturday, **cavalry** March 23rd, by the Tortille River, was divided into retreating fragments, some of which, retiring across the Somme towards Amiens, were reduced to a condition of complete exhaustion.

When Ludendorff insisted upon drawing all the good infantrymen and nearly all the good gunners from the eastern front, Eichhorn, Schultz, Mackensen, Kirchbach, and other leaders refused to guarantee their hold upon Russia unless practically all the available cavalry forces of the Central Empires were left with them. They required speed and movement to balance their growing weakness in striking strength. The spaces over which they had to work, when trying to extract corn from the rebellious peasantry, were so great as to make the use of a very large cavalry force an absolute necessity throughout the eastern fields of operations.

Consequently, General von Hutier and General von der Marwitz had no strong bodies of mounted troops capable of riding down the last thin line of weary British rearguards and odd-men forces which with desperate gallantry continued to hold the immediate approaches to Amiens. Ludendorff and his lieutenants and Staff had made a series of miscalculations in regard to the means by which they expected to win the final decisive action around Amiens.

They had no light, quick Tanks and no speedy armoured motor-cars. Their general supply of draught horses was insufficient for their infantry and artillery, and their mechanical system of traction, on which they most relied, could not work properly until roads were repaired and railways prolonged.

The lack of cavalry was the deciding factor in the situation. In its absence the German infantry was worked and marched beyond its strength. In all operations between the Oise and the Somme the enemy, by great feats of marching, managed to present apparently overwhelming masses of men against each slowly arriving French force.

The French first estimated that they were outnumbered by ten to one, then by eight to one and six to one, and that they still had odds of at least three to one against them when they fought the enemy to a standstill. In the circumstances, however, numbers were not everything. The French troops were able to use the network of railways running immediately into the line of battle. In addition, they had a magnificent system of perfect roads along which they rolled in solid divisions on motor-lorries.

Hutier's men had from thirty to forty miles of war-wasted country to traverse between their base of supplies and their extreme fighting-line. The French, on the other hand, usually had only a mile or two to walk **Rearguard action** between their motor-lorry stopping-place **before Noyon** and the scene of action. In some cases their vehicles were able to advance behind a screen of cavalry and armoured cars, and place well-fed, well-rested troops directly in the battle-line against the hungry, tired, disheartened swarms of Germans.

The rations carried by the enemy troops were exhausted by the evening of March 22nd. All the roads were then so crowded with the columns of Ludendorff's reserves that the troops in the front line had nothing to eat, except the little they could seize from stores abandoned by the retreating British Army. As Quartermaster-General of Germany, which still was Ludendorff's nominal position, his organising work was distinctly bad. He sacrificed food and armament to speed and mass, with the result that one well-fed and well-supplied

Frenchman was able to hold in check from three to ten Germans.

It was not until March 28th that the German infantryman was given more than two days' rations; it was not until March 26th that German soup-kitchens began to appear around Noyon, Roye, and Chaulnes to hearten the hundreds of thousands of troops there with a good hot meal. In the meantime General Humbert fought a great rearguard action in front of Noyon, and sent his light forces forward on the left in an attempt to rescue the Ulstermen and Englishmen and Scotsmen around Nesle and cover the arrival and deployment of the First French Army.

The period of extreme tension lasted from March 24th to 27th. The way in which General Humbert during these days played his scanty forces forward, backward, and sideways in the large field of manœuvre between the Oise River and the Avre River proved that his genius in war had not diminished since he led the Morocco Division victoriously into action in the First Battle of the Marne.

He relied largely upon the old-fashioned armoured motor-car, carrying machine-guns or quick-firers, which General Pétain rightly regarded as one of the finest weapons of cavalry action. The French cars had been especially manufactured, in optimistic mood, for working behind the German front when this was broken by an allied offensive. A famous French armament-maker had recently designed a light Tank for the same purpose, and after his invention had been unanimously condemned by military authorities in Paris, he had brought one of the machines to the front, and, dressed in a mechanic's overall, had manœuvred before some of the fighting French commanders, and obtained an enormous order for the accelerated production of his novel light cavalry machine. It was not, however, ready when the break in the British line occurred. Yet the fact that the new Tanks were in potential reserve in large numbers enabled General Pétain to sacrifice his considerable force of armoured cars in blocking the roads to Paris and Amiens, **Light Tanks and** and in keeping the enemy in play until the **armoured cars** allied mass of manœuvre was gradually brought into position. Possibly the armoured cars might not have been highly successful when used as designed behind the German lines. The broken roads in the battle zones would have been extremely hard to traverse. But in the conditions of the hasty British retreat the French motor-artillerymen and machine-gunners enjoyed some remarkable advantages. None of the roads and lanes over which they worked was hammered by German guns. The surface was in excellent order, having been constantly tended by the white and coloured labour battalions of the British forces, who had constructed many new ways of communication, with new cross-tracks for later movements of British troops.

The advanced German masses were practically without artillery, and were extended in dense waves for the purpose of flowing around every centre of resistance. Woods, for example, were seldom taken by direct attack, even when held only by a few machine-gunners. The Germans swung round all such obstacles, and when they could not find a gap they continually extended north-westward, until their superiority in number enabled them to continue their overlapping movement.

The result was that the light striking forces brought into action by General Humbert were often able to make up in speed what they lacked in weight. British and French cavalry acted as a covering screen, while French, British, and American airmen closely studied the enemy marching columns south of the Somme, and brought back a stream of information out of which General Humbert rapidly wove plan after plan.

One of the most common tricks of the defence was to arrange for a rearguard line to break and let an enemy mass in a pocket and then bring motor-guns and machine-guns to bear upon the ambushed infantry force, with a line of charging cavalry to complete the rout. On other occasions the cars would manœuvre for a surprise swoop, directly under aeroplane guidance, in the manner first devised by Wing-Commander Samson and his small naval force at Doullens.

The adventures of the French motor artillery were among the most extraordinary personal events of the war. Like the similar but smaller force of Canadians operating in armoured cars between Péronne and Amiens, the French officers and their men were constantly engaged in preventing grave little local disasters by transforming apparently hopeless situations into triumphant defensive actions.

Parties of cyclist machine-gunners also performed services out of all proportion to their numbers. One good motor-cyclist, combining judgment with audacity, was often worth more than a battalion of tired infantrymen. He was one of the quickest of all scouts and messengers, as well as a man carrying a machine-gun at a speed of fifty miles an hour. Owing to the fine state of the roads even the ordinary cyclist with a rifle was a soldier of uncommon power. He was less conspicuous than a cavalryman, and although he could not work away from anything more uneven than a cart-track, he could often get rapidly into positions in daylight, from which the enemy's movements could be watched over a considerable stretch of country.

Work of the cavalry — The cavalryman, however, was the main element in the successful defensive campaign. He fought on horseback and on foot, and in motley squadrons of sky-blue and khaki, formed according to chance occasions that brought Frenchmen, Britons, and Canadians together. Behind him were improvised artillery supports formed out of the gunners of the Fifth British Army and the artillerymen of the French armoured cars, with the more slowly arriving, but eventually very powerful, gunners of two crack French armies. General Humbert, whirling about the battlefield in a motor-car,

addressing his men and keeping them in good heart by using the language of sense as well as of sentiment, rapidly organised his diverse forces into a flexible weapon of both attack and defence.

He relieved the remnants of the British divisions around Nesle and Roye, and although he was soon compelled to bring them back into action, he saved them from falling into the enemy's hands through complete exhaustion. Then, with his dismounted cavalry, armoured motor-cars, cyclists, and the indefatigable British artillerymen, he tried to hold the enemy between Nesle and Roye, and **Defence of the Noyon line** endeavoured to push his line directly northward to Chaulnes and get a strong connection with British troops fighting backward from Péronne and Pargny.

Monday, March 25th, was a great day for the small Franco-British force under General Humbert. By this time the original three French divisions were exhausted by continuous fighting against tremendous odds and by the forced marches necessary in meeting the enemy's enveloping manœuvres. With British regiments on their right, holding the Oise bridges at Condren, Amigny, Sinceny, and Autreville, the French infantry swung back to the neighbourhood of Noyon, covered by a division of British cavalry—Lancers, Hussars, and a Canadian squadron. The British cavalry came up and placed themselves under the orders of the French commander, at the moment when the Noyon positions, the key to Paris and pivot of the entire lines of defence, seemed lost.

General Humbert had ordered his troops to resist at no matter what cost, stating that the Noyon line must be held, even if it were outflanked. But by midnight on March 25th

KING GEORGE LEAVING AMIENS CATHEDRAL.

Early in August, 1918, King George paid a nine days' visit to his armies on the western front, arriving there auspiciously three days before the opening of that great allied attack in the Somme area which undid all that the enemy had achieved in the Battle for Amiens. During the stay in France his Majesty paid a visit to ruined Amiens and its damaged, long-threatened cathedral, the menace to which was removed by the triumphant advance of the Allies.

I

FOOTBRIDGE FORMED OF BOARDS AND BARRELS.
A well-constructed temporary bridge across a small river behind the Australian lines in France. The military engineers of the various British forces erected bridges of the most varied materials and the most diverse character.

the line was not merely outflanked but broken in the centre. Then it was that the British horse rose to a magnificent height of effort. The squadrons had been fighting day and night since March 22nd, when they rearguarded the Ulstermen at Ham. They saved the flanks of Irish and British divisions, then energetically assisted the French troops of General Pelle, and after bitter covering actions by Guiscard and Guivry, were holding the bank of the Oise by Pont l'Evêque, south of Noyon.

General Humbert asked them to recover the ridges westward and north-westward of Noyon. The troopers—Lancers, Hussars, Scots Greys, Dragoon Guards, Canadian Horse, and an irregular detachment — rode out in the darkness at whirlwind pace, but found the enemy had occupied the ridge. Dismounting, they advanced up the slopes, and in a glorious feat of arms conquered the highest part of Porquericourt Hill and forced the German masses back to Essarts Wood.

Pressing onwards in daylight on March 26th the British cavalry division worked against much superior numbers through the woods on the hill-tops, with the Canadian squadron and irregular troops on the left, and a French force holding Mont Renaud on the right. The troopers were in a fair way to win all the heights when the French commander decided to withdraw. He had been fighting for time to entrench just below Noyon, and the British cavalry had won him all he needed, and after again covering his infantry while the Germans were resuming their infiltration method of advance, they cut their way back to the new positions in front of the Divette stream.

The Noyon counter-attack was one of the greatest achievements in the history of British cavalry. In conjunction with the superb stand made by a small French infantry force on Mont Renaud, it prevented a Franco-British disaster. Indeed, it may be said that, after the first divisions of the Third French Army had done all that men could do to save the Fifth British Army, the British and Canadian cavalry succeeded, when apparently spent by a hundred hours of rearguarding actions between the Somme and the Oise Rivers, in repaying General Humbert and General Pelle by saving the French forces and the gate of Paris.

As a direct consequence of the sustained charge of the British cavalry force, General Humbert's defensive position became one of the strongest that any army had occupied during the war. The stretch of Thiescourt Hills, on which he rested, between Noyon and Lassigny, was called " Little Switzerland." From the point of view of modern warfare the terrain had many of the natural advantages of mountain defence, without the impracticable slopes and pathless wastes of mountain country.

Few of the hills were much more than three hundred feet above the valleys across which the Germans attempted to drive, and most were less than two hundred feet above the northern hollows. Yet the **French hold firm** intricate nature of the great stretch of high **on Mont Renaud** ground enabled it to be rapidly transformed into a powerful and extensive system of fortification owing to the many old French and German works that had been constructed during the early struggles around Lassigny and Noyon.

Noyon town, in the low Oise River valley, was evacuated and abandoned to the enemy, but the small neighbouring detached rise of Mont .Renaud was firmly held by the French as the outwork of their formidable fortressed block of the Thiescourt heights. The enemy masses, strengthened by fresh divisions, continued to try to break through towards Compiègne. They failed to do so, and in the evening of March 26th the French line was still firm along the Divette stream, that formed a ditch in front of the great clump of entrenched heights.

By this time, however, General von Hutier was only demonstrating along the Oise River and the road to Paris. His main effort was made in the direction of Montdidier, in co-operation with General von der Marwitz's thrust towards Amiens.

Lord Milner, a man distinguished by his remarkable power of decision, came post-haste to France and, in an interview

FOR FEEDING THE GUNS.
Unloading shells for Canadian heavy artillery from railway trucks at a dump on the western front in preparation for the great allied counter-offensive, which followed on and negatived the gains which the Germans had made in their advance towards Amiens.

with M. Clemenceau, arranged for the British and French Governments to appoint General Ferdinand Foch to the position of actual Commander-in-Chief of the Franco-British Forces on the Western Front. By urgent cabling to President Woodrow Wilson, generous permission was obtained for United States troops to act as a general reserve force, and be brigaded as occasion required with French and British divisions. The Belgian Government agreed readily to the appointment of General Foch as Allied Commander-in-Chief, and the Italian Government also accepted for its armies the arrangement made by Lord Milner and M. Clemenceau.

The power given to General Foch was larger than that exercised by General von Ludendorff. In the first place the French man of genius had no mighty rival standing immediately behind him, as Hindenburg stood behind Ludendorff, and fighting against him directly and indirectly, as Hindenburg did through Kühlmann and other German politicians. In the second place General Foch was able, in friendly collaboration with General Diaz, to exercise direct military control over the allied forces in Italy and, at need, to place Italian troops in the battle-line in France. Ludendorff, on the other hand, could exercise only indirect **Foch in supreme command** political pressure upon the Austro-Hungarian High Command, which was reluctant to open another grand offensive in Italy until it was convinced that the strength of the Western Powers was rapidly declining. Ludendorff was not Teutonic Commander-in-Chief in Italy as well as in France and Flanders. The work done by his lieutenant, Otto von Below, had really made the Austrian Court feel more independent. Grudgingly it allowed some artillery to be sent to the western front during the period in which operations were difficult in the Italian mountains; but this measure of assistance had far less strategic significance on the enemy's side than the appointment of General Foch to supreme command on the allied side.

The French commander, however, lacked the material power of his opponent. In personal genius he was superior to the Teutonic dictator, and he had an incomparable record of defensive and offensive victories, from the Battle of Morhange in August, 1914, where he saved the French front with a single army corps, to the Battle of the Piave in the autumn of 1917, where he was co-ordinator of the Italian, French, and British armies of defence. He had broken the German centre in the Battle of the Marne, and saved Ypres in November, 1914, when Sir John French's forces were exhausted. He had carried the approaches to Vimy Ridge in 1915, and acted as co-ordinator of the French and British

PEACE AND WAR BENEATH THE WILLOWS.
British gun in action by willow-bordered water during the German offensive in France in March, 1918. The soldier in the foreground was getting water from where it was deepest and likely to be purest.

forces of attack on the Somme in 1916. His skill in fighting against tremendous odds had been even more remarkable than the persistency and manœuvring power in assault which he had ever shown when circumstances permitted.

Perhaps General Pétain was equal to General Foch as a master of war. Yet the saviour of Verdun lacked that large and varied experience in handling medleys of French, British, Belgian, and Italian troops which the older commander possessed. General Pétain, indeed, had not had anything like the immense practice, in both offensive and defensive campaigns, of General Foch. So often had Foch extricated himself from positions of extreme peril, not of his own making, that he had more caution than some of his brilliant army commanders; yet, when he decided to attack, he excelled the younger men in swiftness and resoluteness of stroke.

Even Marshal Joffre had not such claims upon the affectionate confidence of both British and Italian troops as had the man who had saved the Channel ports in 1914 and the Venetian naval base in 1917. And for some tragic months General Foch required to draw largely upon the confidence of all the allied soldiers. The situation which he had to retrieve was worse than that obtaining after the Battle of Morhange, in which he had first distinguished himself. Once more the Western Allies were outnumbered, outgunned, outmanœuvred, and thrown back with a breaking front. There was no Russia left to undertake immediately a great diversion and compel the German Command to rail eastward forces that might have turned the balance of decision. The available trained

AN INEVITABLE INCIDENT OF RETREAT.
British officer from behind an old tree-bole watching the exploding of an ammunition dump rendered necessary by retirement during the progress of the German offensive. Such destruction was an essential feature of an orderly retirement under the pressure of preponderating forces.

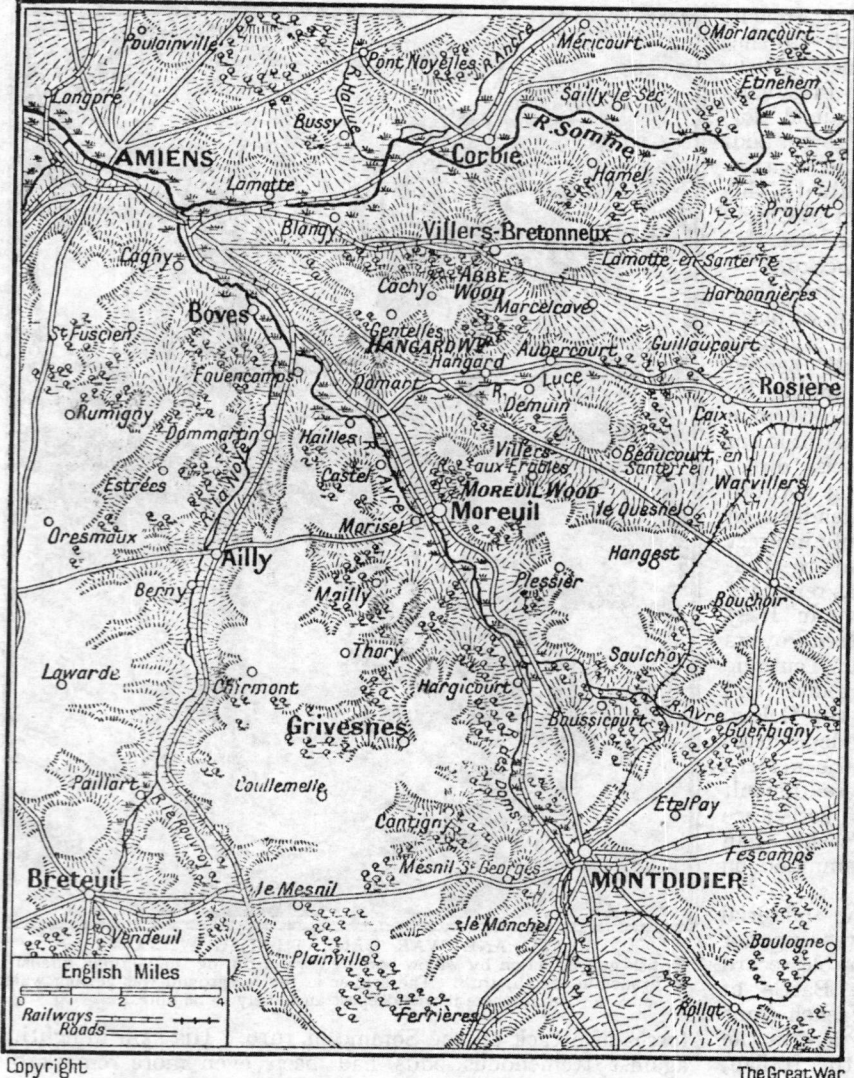

WHERE THE ATTACK ON AMIENS WAS STAYED.
Map showing the country, wooded hills and river valleys, along which the German offensive against Amiens in March, 1918, was finally held up by the French and British armies.

like the great Frenchman, alongside whom he had fought in the First Battle of Ypres, he endeavoured to patch up the Amiens front, at as little cost as possible in the period when strong American help was lacking, before putting everything to the test of a decisive battle.

In some ways the situation between Albert and Lassigny in the evening of March 26th, 1918, resembled that obtaining in Flanders towards the end of October, 1914. Once again the Germans were driving in tremendous force towards the sea, and while an outnumbered British army was holding them in terrible battles in the northern sector and slowly and stubbornly giving ground, the French forces, also outnumbered, were racing up from the south and trying, by overlapping and detaining actions, to reach the British in time to solidify with them into a strong new battle-line.

But two days had been lost ere the allied mass of manœuvre began fragmentarily to come into action. General Foch could not recover the lost time, except by setting his advanced divisions tasks of superhuman valour. On March 27th the first of the new French forces was brought up in motor-lorries to the village of Rollot, between Lassigny and Montdidier. But this fresh force could not spread immediately in strength north-westward towards the country through which the last of the most gallant remnants of the Ulster Division were retreating from Guerbigny. The situation was still very dangerous about Lassigny, and infantry reinforcements had at once to be sent to the dismounted cavalrymen, who were defending Canny and Conchy and the low-lying land through which the enemy was trying to thrust in the design to turn the Thiescourt heights.

The French and British cavalry, mounted and dismounted, had to fight like demi-gods rather than like men, while the fresh infantry forces were gathering to strengthen the bending, lengthening line. Theirs was the finest effort in the war, according to the considered judgment of the High Command. Above Rollot, for example, the cavalry had to carry out an extraordinary series of actions, surpassing the Battle of the Ridges at Noyon, in order to win time for General Foch's reserve to arrive. Moreover, the British and Canadian troopers, who had counter-attacked in front of Noyon, after rearguard fighting all the way back from Ham and St. Simon, had again to fill the gap in front of Amiens and counter-attack Marwitz's forces after checking Hutier's masses.

The story of this single, wasted, mounted division of the British Army links together the achievements of its own heroic, much-enduring foot and guns and the defensive victories of the Third and First French Armies. Partly it was the range of action of these mounted men that brought them into battle after battle all along the most critical sectors of the southern front; but it was not their horses that won the victories.

Enemy thrusting into Roye

While they were still fighting, on March 26th, round Noyon, the French cavalry division, with whom they were later to co-operate, arrived in the neighbourhood of Roye after a march of forty-four miles.

The enemy was thought to be twenty miles away. As a matter of fact, the energetic, swarming Germans had turned the flank of the French infantry and were thrusting into Roye, rousing the resting British soldiers from their billets. Some of the fresh French cavalry came, with amazing unexpectedness, upon enemy columns marching in the moonlight of early morning, and barely escaped from them. A French army corps commander, coming forward with a Staff officer to study the ground before his men arrived, narrowly escaped

forces of the United States were small and untried, and it was far from certain that the immense potential reserve of American military power could be trained, transported, and brought into action in time to alter the critical condition of affairs.

General Foch could not find any opportunity for displaying his greatest powers of mind. He had to adopt the same wary, patient methods of resistance that he had used in the autumn of 1914 in the battles along the Yser and around Ypres. Aroused to the extreme danger of the position around Amiens, which had indeed become patent to all the world, the new commander began to move the First French Army, under General Débeney, into the gap on the left of the Third French Army, under General Humbert; while the Fourth British Army was moving southwards to range alongside the First French Army.

General Fayolle, who had been French Army group commander under General Foch in the Somme battle of 1916, where he had worked with General Rawlinson, was made strategic commander of the Amiens front during the strange, heroic hours when General Carey's brigade of odd men was the only force between the enemy and his grand goal.

Cautiousness was the master characteristic of the new French Commander-in-Chief, but his economical manner of bringing forward small French forces to check the hostile hordes was only an expedient. Behind it was a grim resolution to put everything to the touch before allowing the British and French Armies to be decisively separated. Sir Douglas Haig was moved by the same desperate determination, but,

"Sunshine and Dust near Neuville St. Vaast"

capture, and lost his Staff officer, who was killed while saving the general.

The French cavalry general formed a desperate resolution. He prepared to recover Roye by a vehement counter-attack, thinking this would at least clarify the situation by compelling the enemy to pause and reconcentrate. But the older and higher French commander, who was waiting for his corps, saw the danger.

He opposed the counter-attack on Roye, and ordered a steady, holding action along the highway from Roye to Montdidier. Even this was impossible. On March 27th the French infantry, on the right, was driven in above Rollot, and the French cavalry was attacked through the gap. Covered by some of the ubiquitous British gunners, who had fought continually from St. Quentin, the Frenchmen made a fighting retreat through Montdidier, and in the night of March 27th the small force began to dig itself in upon the hill of Mesnil St. Georges, between the Avre River and the Calais-Paris railway line below Amiens.

In appearance the struggle for Amiens was practically concluded. Before day broke on March 28th the conquering German forces in Montdidier spread across the Avre and, on a battle-front of six miles, climbed the Mesnil Hill. The French cavalry and infantry, with their British **German end almost attained** gunners, were driven back for a mile and a quarter, and the apparently irresistible enemy had but to make another advance of six miles in order decisively to sever railway communication between the British armies and the French armies.

The city of Amiens in itself was not the first objective of the enemy. To him Amiens was merely a railway-station on the line he wished to reach, and by striking at the Calais-Paris railway between Amiens and St. Just he attained his first decisive objective by the easiest path. Standing immediately above the weary Frenchmen was the still weaker collection of armed non-combatants commanded by Brigadier-General Carey. As has been shown in a previous chapter,

Carey's force was fiercely and persistently attacked for several days, but there were not directed against it such tremendous numbers of Germans as were poured through and around Montdidier upon the French line.

It was unlike the Teuton to attack soldiers when he might have continually concentrated against non-combatants. There was a good reason, however, for the southward direction of his main attack. North of Montdidier was the widened marshy bed of the Avre, complicated by the long swamp of the Luce stream. Above these two natural moats were the broad, meeting marshlands of the Somme River, the Ancre stream, and the Hallue **Ludendorff's** brook. Between this great system of **new stroke** streams and morasses rose the large hill of Villers-Bretonneux, behind which was another important height with wooded cover, forming together a grand, natural moated fortress protecting the front of Amiens.

At Montdidier, on the other hand, there was only the Doms brook, a small tributary of the Avre, which, though somewhat swampy above the picturesque, old terraced town, narrowed into little more than a ditch below it. Except for the cover given by a railway line and some patches of brown woodland, there was no obstacle to the rapid deployment of hundreds of thousands of men. What small obstacles existed were overcome before daybreak on March 28th; but as the Germans were almost within reach of the vital French railway line, Ludendorff gave over the struggle for Amiens. As has already been recorded in the previous chapter, he made instead a most desperate and costly attempt to break a new path to the sea over Vimy Ridge and through Arras.

At the same time General Foch, who, seemingly, was on the point of being utterly defeated, informed M. Clemenceau that the worst was over, and that one of the most important defensive battles in the history of the world had been won. As in the most classic example of Turenne's strategic victories, there was no pitched battle. A skirmish of advanced forces decided the day.

CANADIANS' MILITARY PRIDE IN THEIR HORSES AND HARNESS.
Morning work in the transport lines of a Canadian battalion during a period of comparative quiet on the western front. On the right the officers' chargers are seen leaving the lines, in the centre men are cleaning harness, and on the left the picketed horses are being groomed.

No doubt Ludendorff's improved Secret Service system had acquainted him with the fact that his troops had arrived too late at Montdidier. While remnants of the original British forces, with a fresh French cavalry division and some outworn French infantry, were fighting for two days over the ten miles of country between Roye and Montdidier, the southern part of the Calais-Paris railway had been working as it had never been worked before. In conjunction with fleets of motor-lorries, marching columns, and supply-carts, it had become General Foch's instrument for outmanœuvring the enemy commander. The French Army was getting into position. It threw out reinforcements by motor-lorry at Rollot on March 27th, and in the morning of March 28th, when the last Franco-British rearguards were falling back

ENGLISH TROOPS OF WORLD-WIDE RENOWN.
Royal Fusiliers going into action. Many battalions of the Royal Fusiliers were recruited mainly from London, and these superbly upheld the honour of the capital city of the British Empire.

from the hill of Mesnil St. Georges, they met a fresh infantry division of General Débeney's army, and, joining with it, made a counter-attack that decided the happy fate of the railway communications of the Allies.

In extent the ground won was not important. It was about a mile and a quarter in depth and six miles long; but as it included the upland of Mesnil St. Georges, and left the enemy in the valley of the Doms brook, with no observation over the trunk railway line, the gain of ground was the most important made on the western front since the reconquest of Douaumont Down. It was because Ludendorff saw Foch's first great stroke coming, and could not get men up quickly enough to meet it, that he spent the larger part of his distant available reserve divisions in attempting another great offensive around Arras.

German commander's costly mistake The enemy commander's change of plan lost him the campaign. At all costs he should have continued to concentrate against Amiens. Even loss of time between his strokes would have been compensated by a continuing intensity of effort. But Ludendorff without Hindenburg was like Gneisenau without Blücher. He had cleverness of mind without downright force of character. Being clever, he saw the mistake he made in opening his grand campaign across the vast systems of entrenchments between St. Quentin and Noyon and Cambrai and Albert. Instead of persisting in the wrong course in which he was deeply engaged until he righted himself—as Hindenburg or Blücher might have done—Ludendorff tried in another direction, and, failing, wasted the reserve strength that might have brought him victory.

The enormous, startling power in numbers the Germans

displayed, after forty-four months of heavy warfare on two long fronts, was artificial rather than natural. It was not derived from the native strength of the people, but from captive and enslaved labour. The German loss in man-power was temporarily more than balanced by the work done by prisoners of war, deported civilians from occupied territory, and peoples working in conquered lands. Prisoners of war were estimated to number more than three and a half millions, while the controlled civilian labour—westward in Belgium, Northern France, and Luxemburg; eastward in Russian Poland, the Baltic provinces, and parts of Russia proper; northward in Finland; and southward in Rumania—must, directly and indirectly, have amounted to much more than twenty million adult persons.

We must allow, of course, for men withdrawn from military service by their own Governments, for persons needed to supply the necessities of life to their own countrymen, and for the toll of increased disease and malnutrition. Yet, under so hard a slave-driver as the Teuton, the direct and indirect use of conquered people was developed to the utmost, as in the case of the factory and farm hands in Russian Poland.

In some ways the German people profited by the Assyrian policy of their rulers. They were becoming a nation of warriors, served by the captives of their sword. As the war went on their strength in the field increased, in spite of their increasing losses. With every dead German more than half a dozen serfs were purchased, enabling other Germans to enter the Army. There

AN IRON DAM AGAINST INVASION.
French naval gun on the Oise sector of the western front. Batteries of these monster guns poured formidable broadsides which broke up many enemy batteries directly these disclosed their position.

were, however, special limits to this process. It made any serious likelihood of popular revolt alive with a strange peril, of which the action of the Czecho-Slovak prisoners of war in Russia was but a dim foretokening.

Ludendorff allowed Marwitz and Hutier two days to re-form their original forces, which were strengthened by the last picked forces from the enemy general reserve—the Prussian Guard. Then, on Saturday, March 30th, the grand battle was renewed on a front of some fifty miles, from the Somme near Villers-Bretonneux to the Oise River below Noyon.

North of the Somme a strong subsidiary holding attack was delivered between Albert and Arras, making the battle-front with all its windings some eighty miles long. There were two

STRAINING UPON THE START.
French soldiers awaiting the order to cross a canal during their heroic resistance to the advancing foe.

CARRYING WOUNDED UNDER FIRE.
Men of the French Red Cross carrying a wounded comrade through a battered village against which the German offensive was directed. Two of the stretcher-bearers had turned to watch a shell bursting dangerously near the route they were following.

main thrusts. One was directed against the Thiescourt plateau between Noyon and Lassigny, the other against the Amiens railway line near Montdidier. Thiescourt plateau was by far the strongest position on the new French line, for the reasons already given, and the assault upon it was, like General von Below's attack upon General Horne and the First British Army, a military mistake.

Hutier's design was evident. He intended to prevent the new Allied Commander-in-Chief from co-operating with the British High Command by directly menacing the French capital. The idea of this stroke seems to have been based upon misinformation regarding differences in views between the French and British Commands.

General Foch had left only a small garrison on the Thiescourt hills. Against a French regiment holding Plémont Hill, overlooking Lassigny, the German commander launched two divisions directly, while swinging another strong force in a south-westerly encircling movement through the village of Plessis and the brook-threaded hollow running to Plessier Château. While the defending machine-guns were mowing down the frontal wave of attack the enveloping enemy force succeeded in working across a marsh into the grounds of the château. Then from this flanking position the enemy masses

manœuvred against the French Colonial troops at Canny, on the left, and against the wooded crest of Plémont Hill on the right.

Plémont was not conquered. On the northern slope the Germans overlooked two French telephone operators, who called up their colonel in his headquarters. But the commanding officer had only half a dozen odd men on his staff, the rest of his regiment being furiously engaged in battle. Yet he came forward, revolver in hand, and with his six men fought his way back to the summit and, placing a machine-gun there, kept the Germans at bay until half-past four in the afternoon.

Meanwhile, the Colonial regiment at Canny, although it had only a few companies available for counter-attack, began to drive forward as soon as the enemy's strength was felt to be weakening. The Colonial troops advanced upon Plessier Château from the north, and met in the village a force of Chasseurs who were making an encircling movement on the other side. The Germans had mounted machine-guns upon the walls of the park, but the machine-guns were facing the wrong way.

The linking French forces broke in the rear of the apparently successful enemy, and while their artillery barraged all the approaches from Lassigny they killed or captured every German engaged in the early encircling movement. Then on Plémont Hill, where the colonel and his six men were still holding out in the centre of the plateau **Repeated enemy attacks broken** and bedevilling the enemy's operations, another comparatively small counter-attacking force was organised by half-past four in the afternoon. It broke up the German attack completely, and ended in a hot pursuit down the hill and half across the plain to Lassigny.

At Mont Renaud yet another small French force broke some ten great attacks in force, in a struggle lasting far longer than the general battle of the rest of the fortressed hill country. The reason for this was that through some mistake on the part of a subordinate, Ludendorff, at the end of the grand battle, claimed in his official report to have conquered the small outlying knoll from which Noyon town was directly dominated.

He ordered his errant local commander to make good his false claim to victory. But General Humbert then took measures to prevent any German force from taking the hill. He ranged his guns on every yard of approach, and devised rapid means of communication between observation officers on the hillside and all batteries within bearing distance. The local German commander brought his own field-guns forward to a distance of less than one mile from the rise, and under blasting hurricanes of shell sent his men surging forward for nearly a fortnight. But the garrison of Mont Renaud was not to be shaken. It required a great German offensive movement, that took months to prepare, to make good the enemy's claim to victory.

Fifteen divisions against three The first great German attack on the Thiescourt plateau failed as completely as the attack upon Vimy Ridge. The defending artillery in each case had dominating observation and favouring weather, with remarkable visibility. Little more than a screen of infantry was required to check the remnants of the enemy masses of assault after the guns of the defence had done with them.

There was, however, much less artillery power behind the forces of the Grand Alliance in the second and more important sector at which Ludendorff thrust with all available strength. While endeavouring vainly to distract General Foch in the south, the enemy Commander-in-Chief belatedly returned in the west to his original objective, and struck again from Montdidier and Rosières in the direction of the Amiens sector of the Calais-Paris railway. There were still only three French divisions arrayed upon the hills between Moreuil and Monchel, on either side the road leading to the railway.

Behind this small French force was a smaller, wearier British reserve, formed of the British and Canadian troopers who had rearguarded the Ulstermen from the country north of Ham, protected General Pelle's forces, and saved the Thiescourt plateau for the Third French Army. The tired and wasted British cavalry division had been moving upward as a mobile reserve to all the new French line, and when about to rest, in the night of March 29th, received orders to ride northward with all speed and help cover the approaches to Amiens. The squadrons reached St. Boves at midnight, and, in the early morning of March 30th, they were widely scattered in desperate rearguard fighting from Marcelcave to Moreuil.

Marwitz and Hutier skilfully combined their main forces for a decisive drive into Amiens. There were fifteen German divisions deployed against the three French divisions for the turning movement across the Doms brook, and another overwhelming number of divisions of assault were launched against the scanty British forces by the Somme River and Luce stream.

All through Saturday, March 30th, the French and British troops struggled to maintain the natural defences of Amiens against the continuous swarm attacks of the enemy. While the hostile commander repeatedly withdrew and renewed his units, the small defending forces—most of **Surge of battle about Mesnil** whom had already been fighting for days and nights without relief—could only snatch sleep between the periods of attack. On the crest of Mesnil St. Georges one infantry battalion, with some platoons from a neighbouring unit, shattered five successive attacks made by an entire German division. North of Mesnil there was a continual surge of battle by the Doms valley and the slopes of the western hills. While maintaining a terrific pressure on this part of the allied line, the Germans made frenzied attempts to get a short cut to the trunk railway by advancing in the angle between the Luce and Avre Rivers between Moreuil and Hangard. At the junction of the two small streams, by Hailles village, there was barely more than a mile and a half of ground to cover before reaching the railway. Indeed, an advance of a mile would have been sufficient, as it would have brought the enemy to a dominating hill from which he could have shelled the railway line rapidly

into ruin, and barraged the country beyond for his intended turning movement south of Amiens.

At ghastly sacrifice of life he reached Moreuil and the neighbouring wooded hill dominating the angle between the Luce and Avre Rivers, and affording magnificent observation and cover for a direct advance to the railway by the northern short cut. But as the small, overwhelmed French garrison was slowly and stubbornly retiring, the Canadian troopers, attached to the most famous of all British cavalry divisions, galloped up and, in a mounted charge, forced an entrance into Moreuil Wood. Dismounting under cover of the budding trees, they fought forward on foot, and by noon all the wood was theirs, and they were strongly established along the road running towards Demuin.

In Demuin and along the roads to the Somme the fighting was equally desperate. The Germans entered the vitally important hamlet, which outflanked the Villers-Bretonneux positions, and again the indefatigable and indomitable cavalrymen had rapidly to spread forward, dam the grey flood, and send it ebbing backward. Dragoons and Lancers galloped into the breach, and held the ground until fresh battalions arrived.

The attack against the left wing of the French troops, between the Luce River and the Avre, did not fully develop because of the heroic resistance of British Dragoon Guards, with the Royal Horse Artillery and other units. The Dragoon Guards did splendid work around Hangard in the early morning of March 31st. Then, with their comrades, they made 104-Metre Hill, rising between Hangard, Demuin, and Moreuil, as famous in cavalry annals as Porquericourt Ridge above Noyon. In three waves, twelve hundred cavalrymen stormed into the woods on the downland. The first wave reached the fringe of brown trees ; the second wave went half-way through the woods ; the third wave surged out on the farther side, over the dead and wounded of an enemy brigade.

Then from the hill-top another fresh enemy brigade was seen pouring northward over open ground into the battle. Up to the crest the Horse Artillery galloped into action. One battery fired fifteen hundred rounds, another two thousand **Complete enemy check** rounds, every shot being aimed at the large, close target. The mass of three thousand grey figures hesitated, and, in partial disorganisation, neither advanced nor broke and scattered. Only a remnant straggled back, leaving the ground dark with their maimed and dead.

This complete check, in front of the shortest approach to the decisive railway line, compelled the German commander to concentrate for the rest of the day against the French centre, some eight miles southward, between Moreuil and Mesnil. He worked division after division across the Doms brook, at the point where the green cliff of Grivesnes rose, between two hanging woods, above the trickle of water. Helped by travelling curtains of shell fire and covering barrages from massed machine-guns, his storm troops gradually mastered the steep slopes and won the long stretch of high ground running up to Grivesnes village.

The banderillos of Germany then made way for the great matadors—the 1st Division of the Prussian Guard, most famous of all Teutonic fighting men. The Guardsmen fought magnificently. They were told that the greatest victory in history was within their reach, and they did all that men could do to conquer the great down overlooking the railway. After hours of fighting they succeeded in entering the village, only to be thrown out by French bayonets. They returned, and wore down the garrison until there were only five hundred French soldiers, under a colonel, holding the barricaded manor-house in the park by the village. The commanding officer fought at one of the windows, rifle in hand, and after weakening one of the Guard brigades by defensive fire, he came out with his two companies and cleared the park.

General Débeney, however, was not relying upon his outworn, outnumbered troops being each equal in killing power to eight fresh Prussian Guardsmen. His defence was based upon magnificent defensive positions, terrible crossing artillery fires, and especially upon good roads. Down the roads, when the screen of valiant infantry could hold out no longer, came

Men of the West Yorkshire Regiment returning from action after repulsing the Germans near Rheims.

British troops fighting through the wooded country in the valley of the Somme.

Death amid the corn: French soldiers clearing the Courcelles=Tronquoy road.

French soldiers "going over the top" for a daylight bombing raid on enemy positions.

French officers and Canadians watching the enemy lines from behind a German ammunition waggon.

Australian artillery supporting the infantry attacking just ahead while restoring the line east of Amiens in April, 1918

British troops going up to support lines in captured German light-railway trucks drawn by Canadian armoured tractors.

the ubiquitous armoured motor-cars. They broke into the 1st Grenadier Foot Guards, cutting them to pieces with terrifying effect. The motor machine-gunners pursued like cavalry, throwing the Grenadiers into panic confusion.

This was not allowed by Prussian tradition. Guardsmen—and the 1st Division of Guards, above all—could not leave a battle in panic rout. At seven o'clock in the morning of April 1st the survivors were re-formed, and sent up the hill again for final punishment or retrieving success. They were punished, cruelly punished, and those who were lucky enough to be able to surrender told their victors that the French armoured car was worse than the British Tank. Their view, however, was not well founded. It was based only upon the large, slow, heavy mobile forts of the old model, and some days after the first fierce struggle around Grivesnes the greatest machine of surprise in the history of modern warfare was sprung upon the enemy.

On March 27th Australian and British forces of the Fourth Army began to relieve the veterans of the great retreat on the lines about Amiens. By April 4th, when Ludendorff's lieutenants resumed the struggle for the trunk railway, fresh allied forces were well entrenched upon the hills by the network of marshes and waters. It was a day of mist and rain, and as the enemy had brought up his heavy artillery and registered upon his targets, he was able to blast away portions of the Franco-British foreground positions by weight of shell, and then hold the bits of ground he had won by pressure of numbers.

Some fourteen German divisions were employed between the Somme and Montdidier, and among them was the re-formed 1st Guards Division, the 4th Guards Division, and the Guards Reserve Division. Troops of this quality were not used for demonstrating purposes, and although, in the light of later events along the Lys, Ludendorff seems partly to have designed a new Amiens action to pin the Franco-British forces down, there can be little doubt that he also hoped to reach his great objective—the railway.

Cavalry again save the line The attack against the British troops was pushed with ferocious energy. New South Wales battalions, in and around Villers-Bretonneux, were hammered by a violent, terrific bombardment that tore the streets to pieces, and then assailed on the southern flank by troops storming up from the lost French position at Hangard. In spite of their desperate resistance the Australians were gradually driven back and the town was occupied by the enemy. At the end of the afternoon some Dragoons and Lancers, from the greatest division of cavalry that ever rode horse, came to strengthen the New South Wales line.

It was the same cavalry force that had rearguarded the Ulstermen by Ham on March 22nd, and continually saved other infantry of the Fifth British Army, the Third French Army, and the First French Army from Guiscard to Noyon, and from Moreuil to Hangard. Now, with the splendid fresh troops of the Fourth British Army, they again saved the line, magnificently battling forward, with the New South Wales men, until one o'clock in the morning of April 5th, when the vital Villers-Bretonneux position was regained.

While the situation at Villers-Bretonneux still looked dismal, the First French Army, connecting with the Australians of the Fourth British Army, was attacked on the old battlefield of Grivesnes, on a front of ten miles. Round the Franco-British junction point, where the enemy in great force pressed directly towards Amiens, General Débeney lost some of the villages in the river valley, including Castel and Morisel. Yet he held firmly to all the important high ground, inflicting upon the enemy such losses as definitely brought the struggle for Amiens to a close.

On April 5th the German commander shifted his point of attack and endeavoured to obtain a northward line of approach to Amiens. He struck across the Ancre at Dernancourt, to which the new Australian front extended. Again the line was driven in by massed gun fire and rapid waves of assault, and at noon there was danger of an outflanking movement. By a splendid counter-attack, however, the Australians met, wave against wave, the closing assault with

which the enemy hoped to conquer the hills. Fierce leaping lines of men with bayonets clashed against the German shock troops, until by nightfall the enemy was fought to a standstill.

On April 6th the French front was rectified between the Oise River and the Ailette stream by a gradual fighting withdrawal through the Lower Coucy Forest and past Coucy Castle. This removed a dangerous salient, in which there was no room between the marshes and the forested upland of St. Gobain for the deployment of a strong force of defence. Early in 1917 it had been hoped to turn the dominating St. Gobain position by a Franco-British movement around St. Quentin. When the St. Quentin line was lost, the marshy corner became dangerous to hold, and by a strong demonstration with some five divisions a new German Army commander, General von Böhn, occupied the salient and prepared another great surprise offensive **Rectification** along the Aisne. In the meantime the **of French front** British Army was again involved in serious defeat around Armentières and the Messines Ridge. The ground about Amiens then became only a demonstration ground, across which Foch and Ludendorff feinted at each other for several months, while the clashings of their main forces were taking place at a distant point. There was, however, no certainty that the German commander had abandoned all thought of fighting out a decision around Amiens.

The possibility of his resuming the struggle was for long the chief anxiety of the Allied Commander-in-Chief, who was relieved rather than perplexed when he discovered, in the second week in April, that Ludendorff was seriously expending a considerable part of his unused and still superior strength in a violent and sustained attempt to reach the Channel ports.

Throughout all the worry caused by the secondary and somewhat eccentric German offensive on a grand scale, General Foch was carefully arranging with Sir Douglas Haig and General Pétain to transform the Amiens front of defence into a strongly organised line for a great return attack upon the enemy. This scheme had the advantage of being both a measure of prudence, strengthening the weak junction point of the allied armies, and a means for engineering a tremendous surprise as soon as the United States effectives altered the balance of power in Europe. The Germans adopted around Amiens an arrogant attitude of careless strength that turned the tide-mark of their victories into a slope upon which their feet could be made to slip. They did not deeply entrench, but lived on the open field, as though only pausing before they delivered their final smashing blow.

For some weeks after the action of April 4th the fighting around Amiens was concentrated in and about the small angle of ground south of Villers-Bretonneux between the Luce stream and the Avre River. Hangard, a village on the Luce, formed a delicate salient in the Franco-British line, being at the corner of the small curve where the Fourth British Army and the First French Army connected. It was held variously by British troops and French soldiers, and sometimes by Moroccans and Australians side by side. Continually it was lost and recovered, being a point of supreme importance which the losing side violently coveted.

It was a fortified ford on the national **Bitter struggle** road from Noyon and Roye to Amiens. **for Hangard** The enemy therefore had excellent communications in arranging each attack. From the Luce valley on the south and the Aubercourt and Marcelcave hills on the west he could bring a cross-fire of guns to bear upon the low-lying corner, and also send his waves of assault forward in a double encircling movement. While the small, gnawing, incessant action between battalions and brigades was going on at Hangard, the German High Command, on April 24th, 1918, endeavoured to break through to the railway by Boves, and made a whirlwind attack upon Villers-Bretonneux. The enemy troops were enjoying one of their temporary sojourns in Hangard, which opened inviting approaches to the southern flank of Villers-Bretonneux, and enemy gunners gave warning that something was impending by continually searching for the British artillery positions.

Early in the morning of April 24th Villers-Bretonneux was drenched with gas-shells for nearly four hours. When the German guns lifted, the 4th Division of the Prussian Guard with a division of Rhinelanders began to work forward from Hangard Wood and Marcelcave against the Berkshires, Northamptons, Middlesex, East Lancashires, and other British troops holding the village.

Behind the two leading enemy divisions were two other German divisions in full strength, all crowding upon a single English division, the men of which had been living for four hours in clouds of poison gas with their masks on. But the German Staff followed its sound rule of making certainties more certain. Besides using the odds of four men against one, it brought into action for the first time the new monstrous Teutonic Tanks known as land-cruisers. One Tank went over the Middlesex position and—crawling onward, its big guns firing and accompanied by bodies of infantry—forced the Middlesex and West Yorkshires backward. Other Tanks and troops pressed the East Lancashires out of the village. When night fell the British troops were in a position similar to that of the Australian forces on April 4th. They were holding out in Abbé Wood, but Villers-Bretonneux was a German fortress, crammed with machine-guns and full of men flushed with victory, and immensely proud of their possession of the biggest, strongest Tanks in existence.

In the night two Australian brigades came forward to attack, after the English troops had driven the enemy out of the eastern woods. It was bad weather for a nocturnal operation. The moon was veiled in a thick, wet mist, and neither of the main counter-attacking forces knew the ground. The design was for one brigade to advance from the north-west, while the other was to work forward from the south-west, both sweeping past and beyond

UNDER THE SHADOW OF THE GERMAN MENACE.
Civilians in the Somme area in flight—conveying such household gear as they could remove by barrow, truck, and perambulator—before the menace of a ruthless foe's advance. Above: Two poor old French refugees crossing a bridge over the Marne.

the village in the darkness, and linking eastward of it, with the enemy forces enclosed. English troops —Northamptons, Durhams, and others—were to fight through the village.

With no artillery preparation to warn the enemy, the encircling movement began with Victorians, Queenslanders, Western Australians, and South Australians as the pincer forces. They won forward, with bayonet rushes, machine-gun duels, and bomb attacks, through unknown country at night, with the enemy all round them. The colonel of the Queenslanders was met at dawn by a German officer with a message from the commander of the 4th Division of the German Guards. The message was: "You are completely surrounded by three divisions of the German Guards. If you do not surrender, the heavy artillery will immediately be put upon you, and you will be annihilated." A later pencilled message ran: "Officer commanding troops must come at once with German soldier.—Commander, Von Linsingen."

The Australians did come with many **"Whippets" enter the fray** German soldiers, by moving a company back through the town, fighting and collecting prisoners, while the main forces of the superb counter-attack connected at daylight eastward of the village after a series of amazing adventures. Then, as the extraordinary condition of affairs became clear to both sides, and men ceased to wander into hostile camps, there was a battle between the Tanks.

Four of the colossal land-cruisers came upon two British Tanks of the "female" kind, armed only with machine-guns. Bristling with cannon, the monstrous enemy tortoises had easy sport, and crippled one of the British Tanks. But a third British Tank of the "male" gender, with a quick-firer, speeded into the action, and

HELPING HANDS FOR THOSE IN DISTRESS.
On a road in the area threatened by the advancing Germans. British soldiers assisting French refugees in the removal of some of their worldly goods to safety.

by pace in manœuvring knocked out one of the land-cruisers and chased the others away. It was like an action between four cumbrous galleons and one quick-turning small English warship.

This was but the beginning of the first display of power of the new light model travelling fort. By Cachy hamlet, on the southern flank of the Villers-Bretonneux positions, masses of the Rhineland and Westphalia infantry of the 77th Division were seen forming up for a dangerous side-thrust. Steering almost as easily as motor-cars, the small, fast "whippets," as they were called, charged into the enemy ranks, sweeping men down with fire, ramming them and trampling them.

With deadly skill and daring the pilots and gunners carried out their work of carnage with incomparable effect. Prisoners said that entire companies were destroyed by them. They made all the losses of the English and Australian troops, though somewhat heavy, seem light in contrast with the losses of the four broken German divisions, and parts of two other enemy divisions engaged in the final battle. A seventh German division also suffered heavy casualties in a fruitless attack on the French line at Castel.

So ended portentously the long and stupendous struggle for the Amiens railway and the Franco-British lines of communication. By failing completely to reach his first important objective, Ludendorff saw all his costly tactical local successes merged into a great strategic reverse. Severely had he punished the Fifth British Army, and he had inflicted heavy losses upon the Third British Army. He claimed to have taken between Vimy Ridge and the Ailette River 95,000 prisoners, with 1,300 guns, from March 21st to April 25th, 1918. Some of his figures were known to be exaggerated. He claimed to have captured more guns than had been lost!

His material spoil of war, however, was undoubtedly great. In personnel he recovered his wounded quickly, and tended them in a careful, scientific way, while in the first part of the British retreat many seriously wounded defending troops fell into the enemy's hands and swelled the German list of captives. Yet the German loss of soldiers was much heavier than that of the Allies. So staggering indeed was it that, as early as March 27th, Ludendorff personally tried to calm the feelings of the German people by stating that his casualties were within ordinary limits, and that the proportion of slightly wounded was from sixty to seventy out of every hundred. To counter the revelations made by convalescent troops he admitted that at some vital points he had been compelled to incur serious losses. But his extraordinary public apology belied the words in which he framed it.

Enemy's great strategic reverse

In spite of various miscalculations among the Allies, no British or French soldier had died in vain upon the old and new battlefields of the Somme River. Ludendorff, with his Emperor, Staff, nobility, and industrial magnates, had clearly made the greatest of all miscalculations. At best he had devised an intensified process of mutual attrition between the German and Austro-Hungarian and the British, French, and Italian peoples, which would work towards the final victory of the Grand Alliance, as the vast reserves of man-power and manufacturing power of the United States came into action against the Teutons and Magyars.

When the struggle for Amiens ended, the dreadful crisis of the British and French peoples was far from over. Kemmel Hill was then falling, and Calais was in danger of becoming a hostile submarine base. When Calais was saved, Paris was threatened.

Meanwhile, the railway communications of the British, Belgian, French, and United States forces were impaired about Amiens. Usually the line could carry four divisions a day; but, being brought under enemy gun fire, its traffic was reduced for a time to about one-fourth.

This was not a permanent disadvantage, as an additional line was constructed west of Amiens. Yet during the battle below Ypres great efforts were needed to bring supporting troops northward in time, and then keep them supplied with their special war material. It was partly because Ludendorff reckoned he had at least seriously diminished the carrying capacity of the Calais-Paris railway that he selected a weakened northern British sector, farthest from the French and American fronts, as his next point of attack. The Battle for the Channel Ports was the direct sequel to the struggle around Amiens.

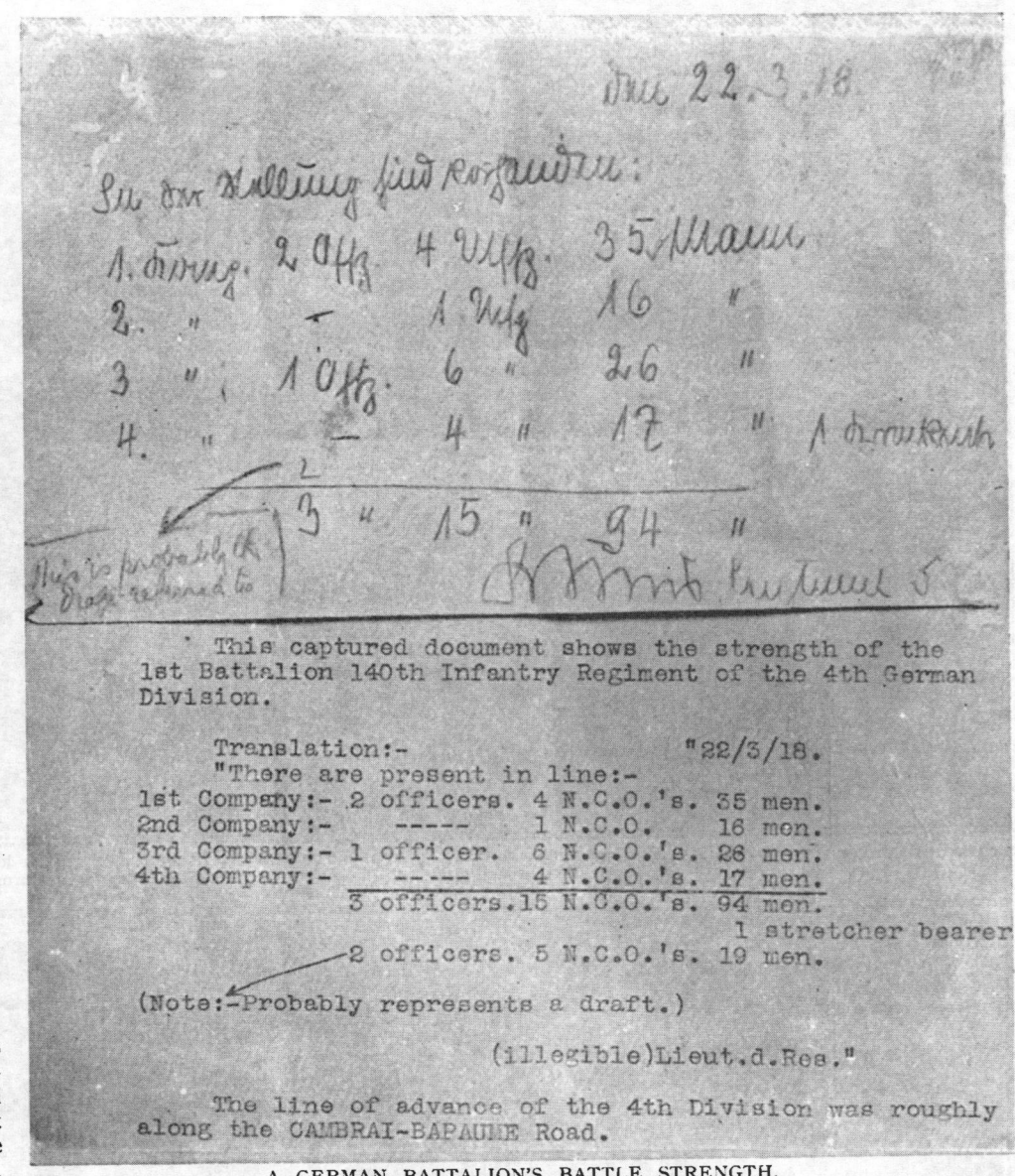

This captured document shows the strength of the 1st Battalion 140th Infantry Regiment of the 4th German Division.

Translation:— "22/3/18.
"There are present in line:—

1st Company:—	2 officers.	4 N.C.O.'s.	35 men.
2nd Company:—	-----	1 N.C.O.	16 men.
3rd Company:—	1 officer.	6 N.C.O.'s.	26 men.
4th Company:—	-----	4 N.C.O.'s.	17 men.
	3 officers.	15 N.C.O.'s.	94 men.

1 stretcher bearer
2 officers. 5 N.C.O.'s. 19 men.

(Note:—Probably represents a draft.)

(illegible)Lieut.d.Res."

The line of advance of the 4th Division was roughly along the CAMBRAI-BAPAUME Road.

A GERMAN BATTALION'S BATTLE STRENGTH.
This document, captured during the German offensive, is interesting as showing the strength of a particular battalion of German infantry on March 22nd, 1918, the day after that offensive began. The war strength of a Prussian battalion should be about a thousand men.

Stripped British gunners at work loading a big gun on the western front. The heavy shells were prepared for loading on the ground, and then raised by a small crane and guided to the breech by the men on the gun-platform.

The same big gun—boldly lettered by its crew with the name of "Bunty"—at the moment of firing its great shell into the distant enemy lines. In the upper photograph is shown light camouflage netting for covering the mighty weapon from aerial observation.

LOADING AND FIRING A BRITISH HEAVY GUN ON THE WESTERN FRONT.

FRENCH GENERAL OFFICER

CHAPTER CCLIX.

DIRECTING OPERATIONS.

THE BATTLE FOR THE CHANNEL PORTS.
By Edward Wright.

Ludendorff's Double Objective in Advancing from the Ridge in Front of Lille: First the Coal-Fields of Béthune, and Finally the Channel Ports—Disposition of the Weakened British Forces between Ypres and La Bassée—General von Quast's Attack Launched between Armentières and Lens, April 9th, 1918—Portuguese Lines at Laventie Broken—West Lancashire Territorials' Defensive Triumph on the Givenchy-Le Touret Line—Gallantry of the 50th Division along the River Lys and of the 51st Division along the Lawe— Failure of Bernhardi to Secure the Béthune Coal-Fields—Ludendorff Diverts his Main Attack upon the Railway Junction of Hazebrouck—Battle Area Extended from Armentières to Hollebeke—Messines and Wytschaete Lost—Haig's Historic Order of the Day—Colossal Enemy Forces Launched in Vain Against the Cassel-Kemmel Hill Line—Bernhardi Outgeneralled by Plumer—Fall of Neuve Eglise and Bailleul—Opening of the Second Great Kaiser Battle—Ludendorff Fought to a Standstill in the Mud of Flanders—French Garrison Overborne on Kemmel Hill—Locre Captured by the Germans and Recovered by Splendid Horsemanship and Gallantry of French Cavalry—Ludendorff's Farewell Fight for the Channel Ports on April 29th Ends in Complete Disaster.

OTH Helmuth von Moltke and Erich von Falkenhayn had endeavoured to turn the northern flank of the Western Allies by attacks upon the lines around Ypres. On April 9th, 1918, General von Ludendorff followed the course of his predecessors, and, after failing to break through at Amiens and at Arras, made a sudden drive in the direction of Dunkirk, Calais, and Boulogne from the ridge in front of Lille.

This strong enemy position had been a constant menace to the northern British forces and the Belgian Army. Prolonged and costly attempts were made by Sir John French, in the spring of 1915, to advance from the marsh-land at Neuve Chapelle and Laventie to the rampart of Lille defences rising between La Bassée and the Lys River. The conquest later of the more northerly ridges at Messines and Passchendaele did not compensate for the early failure to win the high ground east of Neuve Chapelle. The British line there remained weak, and its weakness was of more than military importance. Immediately behind the dominated section of the British front were the coal-fields of Béthune, from which the French managed to continue to extract a considerable quantity of fuel of vital value.

The remnant of the northern French coal-fields, in which miners still gallantly worked in spite of long-distance hostile artillery fire and aerial bombardment, helped to relieve the strain upon British

MOURNFUL GRAVESTONE OVER A DEAD CITY.
Continuous shell fire reduced Ypres to a mass of bricks and rubble laid amidst desolation, and this sign was required to show where the beautiful mediæval city had stood.

mines and British collier-ships. Thus the German commander had an immediate objective of importance in an advance from the Lille Ridge, as well as a final objective of supreme value in the chain of French Channel ports running down to the narrow Strait of Dover.

He began by demonstrating upon the neighbourhood of Lille in the first week of March, 1918, and on the 18th of that month his lines between the Lys River and La Bassée were remarkably active. This activity, however, was but the closing phase of a long and clever feint. When the Battle for Amiens opened, some of the finest of Sir Douglas Haig's forces were collected on the Flemish front in much the same way as the strongest of General Pétain's forces were gathered on the Champagne front.

When the Fifth British Army broke, Australian divisions, which had been arrayed by the Lys River, moved down as quickly as possible to cover the eastward and north-eastward approaches to Amiens. At the same time English and Scottish divisions, which had been collected in the north, were moved with all speed to the Arras-Albert line, together with the New Zealanders. Into the quiet northern sector, from which the fresh British forces came, many of the outworn and wasted divisions of the Third Army were sent.

There was no means of giving the tired and depleted veterans from the Amiens struggle the rest they badly needed. The problem of British manpower had been but partly

MECHANICAL WAR MARVEL OF GERMAN ORIGIN.
French listening-post fitted with an elaborate sound-detecting apparatus first devised by German ingenuity. The Allies adopted it after they had obtained working specimens of the instruments in captured positions.

Ridge, the Sixth German Army, under General von Quast, was suddenly launched in an attack on Tuesday, April 9th. At first only a diverting effect seems to have been intended by the enemy. He wished to warn General Foch and Sir Douglas Haig that he would not allow the northern British sector to be used as a resting-place for weary and battered divisions. The immediate battle-ground had no point of importance, with the single exception of the rise of dry earth at Givenchy. In front of the enemy was a stretch of wasted marshy lowland, seamed by ditches and watercourses from which dwelling-places had disappeared.

Neuve Chapelle, Festubert, Laventie, the Richebourgs, and Fleurbaix were gone, and the woods between them had also disappeared. Estaires, on the Lys, was the nearest place of habitation, and the enemy had some four miles of boggy ground to cover before reaching it ; but General von Quast was remarkably successful in the first phase of his drive.

He announced his intention by several days of unusually heavy shelling, and it was to meet this demonstration that the tired British divisions were hurried forward. Then, from eight to twelve o'clock in the night of April 8th, a tremendous number of gas-shells, with all varieties of poison, were distributed over trenches, battery positions, billeting areas, and ways of approach. Mist gathered thickly in the night, and about four o'clock on April 9th a whirlwind gun fire lashed all the British front from Armentières to Lens, and continued for six hours to smash and drench different parts of the line.

The bombardment was heaviest upon the Portuguese front. It lasted only an hour, yet in effect equalled in destructiveness the hurricane barrages at the opening of the St. Quentin battle. While searching unceasingly for the Portuguese Headquarters, communications, and railways, the hostile gunners suddenly lifted in the fog, about five o'clock in the morning, and let their storming battalions rush into Fauquissart and other advanced posts. With flame-projectors the Germans worked around broken parts of the Portuguese first line, and by seven o'clock in the morning were attacking the second line.

Less than four hours afterwards the **Splendid stand** third line at Laventie was broken in **by Portuguese** places, in spite of the fact that one gallant Portuguese battalion stubbornly clung to its last advanced position at La Couture, fighting until all ammunition was expended, and then holding out with the bayonet in the hope of getting boxes of cartridges through the enemy's barrage. The depleted division lost 317 officers and some 7,000 men in the action between Neuve Chapelle and the River Lys.

The Lys line was the battle zone of the British Army, but the enemy drove forward with such speed that he seemed likely to carry the main position in a single rush. Much of the credit for preventing a complete penetration was due to the West Lancashire Territorials of the 55th Division. Pivoting on Givenchy Hill, immediately on the right of the broken Portuguese force, the Lancashire men fell back on the village line, leaving the attacking forces in a maze of sunken roadways and connecting trenches.

It was puzzling ground for strangers, and while the German forces were exploring it the Lancashires returned by short cuts and roundabout routes and killed or captured thousands of their attackers. Their prisoners numbered nearly a thousand, but this number represented only a fragment of the trapped attacking force. Some of the men of the King's Liverpool Regiment, for instance, were compelled to withdraw from a strong point among the marshes, and an enemy garrison of some two companies occupied the keep in the afternoon in preparation for another leap forward. In the evening, however, the Liverpool men made a counter-attack, in which all the German garrison was killed, with the exception of two men who were captured.

When the German infantry broke through the Portuguese positions on the left, the Lancashires formed a defensive flank running from Givenchy through Festubert to Le Touret. At

solved by the civilian authorities, and the military chiefs were left, in the grand crisis upon the western front, with a force insufficient to counter the enemy's blows. Among the few fresh divisions by the Lille Ridge were the 55th West Lancashire Division, holding the Givenchy positions, and the Portuguese 2nd Division, arrayed on a front of seven and a half miles at Neuve Chapelle and Laventie. Even the Portuguese division was below strength to the extent of some five thousand eight hundred men, and was about to be relieved by a British force

The relieving and supporting British forces consisted of war-worn troops emerging from the southern furnace of battle. The 9th Division of Scotsmen and South Africans, who had made a violent fighting retreat from Gauche Wood, were arrayed from Hollebeke towards the Messines Ridge. In and about Ploegsteert was the heroic and wasted 25th Division that had saved the line by the Cambrai-Bapaume road. In Armentières was the gallant 34th Division, which, at very heavy cost, had broken Von Below's shock battalions by Croisilles. The Highland Territorial Division (51st), the survivors of which had come out of the great retreat reeling like drunken men, was in support of the Portuguese by the Lawe stream. The 50th Division, recently withdrawn from a week of continuous fighting south of the Somme, was brought into action on the Lys River line, while the 31st Division, the 4th Division, and the Guards Division, with the 19th and 21st Divisions, though exhausted by their magnificent and victorious actions around Arras, were set again in terrific battle between Béthune, Hazebrouck, and Ypres.

Attack by Sixth German Army

Ludendorff and his Staff were, of course, well aware of the weakened condition of the British front between Ypres and La Bassée. They knew that Sir Douglas Haig had no reserve, and was compelled to use his worn forces in holding apparently quiet parts of the line while moving fresh forces down to the Somme.

Having everything mounted for an offensive from the Lille

French and British soldiers preparing barbed-wire for defensive works before positions which the Allied troops were holding conjointly.

War-brambles in a once peaceful cottage garden. Portable wire entanglements collected for removal to points where they might be needed.

British soldiers wiring trees which had fallen across a canal, and (in circle) fixing wire on portable racks for erection before trenches.

Canadians practising wiring while resting behind the line. Barbed-wire, destructible only by high explosive and Tanks, was the most effective defensive device used in the Great War. It was said to be the only thing that could stop British troops in an offensive.

FENCES TO KEEP THE TRAMPLING HERDS OF "BLOND BEASTS" AT BAY.

one time both Givenchy and Festubert seemed lost, but were completely recovered by the West Lancashires, who then held on for six days of almost continuous fighting to the Givenchy-Le Touret line.

According to a German order found on all officers and under-officers of the 4th Ersatz Division, the West Lancashires were troops below the average quality and fit only to hold a quiet sector. Six of the English companies were attacked by three German brigades, but the men who were regarded as being "below the average quality" completely broke all hostile attacking forces when, by a feat of heroic endurance and fighting power, they saved the French coal-fields and Béthune town and prevented a local reverse from spreading into a disaster.

At Fleurbaix, on the right of the Portuguese 2nd Division, the British line held as firmly as at Givenchy.

German swoop upon Fleurbaix An hour after the battle began some of the British troops were fighting in the German front-line trenches in a most successful counter-charge. Where the Portuguese trenches were over-run, however, the Germans made a flanking swoop upon Fleurbaix, and at eleven o'clock in the morning some of the Suffolks were almost surrounded on three sides by Canteen Farm, where, nevertheless, they beat the enemy masses back for six and a half hours. At the same time the Yorkshires stubbornly clung to their foreground positions by Bois Grenier, preventing the enemy from turning Armentières directly from the south. Not until eleven o'clock at night did the heroic men of Yorkshire fall back and cover the gas-drenched town.

Meanwhile, the broken ends of the British line were joined together by the glorious 50th Division and the indomitable 51st Division. Both these forces, as we have seen, had fought to utter exhaustion between the Hindenburg line and the Somme River. Before the toxic effects of sleeplessness and overwork were removed from their systems, the Englishmen and Scotsmen had again to bear the extreme ordeal of human endurance in another prolonged effort of resistance against overwhelming masses of fresh hostile troops.

In the enlarging gap left by the Portuguese the Highlanders of the 51st Division rushed forward to prolong the defensive flank of the West Lancashires above Béthune, by the Lawe stream and the Lawe Canal around Vieille Chapelle, three miles west of Neuve Chapelle. The men of the 50th Division extended above the Highlanders along the shallow, canalised River Lys, which, with its wooded bridges, iron drawbridges, and fordable places, was a weak obstacle to an attacking force of one hundred and ten thousand men.

The task of the 50th Division was extremely difficult. At some distance beyond the river was a line of posts, five hundred yards apart. These posts were swiftly surrounded and carried by the enemy, and while he barraged the river approaches, the Durhams, Northumberland Fusiliers, East Yorkshires, and Middlesex had to race his attacking masses to the Lys line, and cross it and throw out bridge-head forces, while improvising a defensive system amid all the pressure of a hurried retirement.

The grand rearguarding division had some serious losses in coming through the German fire curtain, but the men won the race to the Lys, and with their machine-guns, trench-mortars, and rifles held the enemy off while the bridges were being destroyed. Some of the Durhams excelled Horatius. They checked the enemy waves until the bridge was destroyed, and then swam the river under murderous fire. Some of the East Yorkshires refused to retire when their flank was turned by the Germans crossing by Bac St. Maur. They decided further to delay the enemy, and fell fighting.

Durhams excel Horatius

At the drawbridge by Estaires the masses of assault were held for an hour until the great structure of steel and concrete was blown up. But the explosives used did not completely shatter the bridge. Some Germans crossed, yet only to perish, and Estaires when night fell was still held by the Northumberland Fusiliers and Durhams.

Below Estaires the troops of the famous military writer, General von Bernhardi, were incessantly launched all the afternoon and night in a turning movement upon Béthune.

But the headway they made—at terrible cost in strength—was of little importance. At one place two and a half divisions of attack were employed against one brigade of defence, and yet were checked and weakened in a terrifying manner. The English and Scots divisions around and above Béthune were experts in victorious defence. They had practised it a fortnight before upon the armies of General von der Marwitz.

It took Bernhardi nearly three days to break across the Lawe stream, and by that time another superb veteran British division, the 4th, was coming forward at Robecq, fresh from its victory on Vimy Ridge, to help to bring the southern German movement to a standstill, while the 5th Division arrived west of Merville to help stay the enemy's centre advance. In the meantime the Highland Territorials of the 51st Division proved themselves yet again, after their actions at Cambrai in November, 1917, and along the Hindenburg line in March, 1918, among the finest fighting men in history.

They definitely checked all the German attempts to advance by Vieille Chapelle. A party of the Gordons—the battalion distinguished by its rearguard fighting on the Cambrai-Bapaume road—held out by Vieille Chapelle with the Germans entirely round them, and continued for days to slaughter the enemy. When the attacking troops worked through below Estaires, the Highlanders fell back to the old Lawe rivulet, which was little more than a ditch running by Locon. Here the battle was extremely furious, the headquarter staffs of the two brigades in the fighting-line having to fight most desperately against tremendous mass pressure. One of the Scottish brigade commanders was last seen rallying his orderlies in a counter-attack against one of Bernhardi's swarms.

Yet the Highland line was held, with superb assistance from the field-gunners, the batteries leaving each a gun firing at point-blank range during each step in the slow withdrawal between the Lawe streams. By noon on April 12th the 3rd Brigade of the 51st Division still checked the German advance north of Béthune, while the 55th Division marvellously survived on shell-swept Givenchy Hill and broke attack after attack at Festubert.

In the night of April 12th Bernhardi seemed to have Béthune and the coal-fields within his grasp. Using fresh divisions like battering-rams against the wasted defending battalions, he drove under cover of the foggy darkness into Locon northward, and broke into the La Bassée Canal line eastward. Locon, however, was recovered by a fine counter-charge, and the Béthune Canal defences restored; while by the Lys the British forces swung back from Estaires to Merville towards the Forest of Nieppe.

Hazebrouck railway threatened

Bernhardi, though the greatest of literary fire-eaters, was a failure as an army commander. Consumed with hatred for the British, he conducted the action in ferocious bull-like rushes, in which his men were spent, without any gain whatever of strategic importance. By reason of his failure, Ludendorff had on April 13th to alter his plan of campaign. Instead of trying directly to exploit the Neuve Chapelle success in the direction of the French coal-fields and the northern Vimy line, the enemy Commander-in-Chief turned the direction of his main attack northward and north-eastward.

His immediate goal was the railway junction of Hazebrouck, along which the main communication-line of Sir Herbert Plumer's army around Ypres ran through the Flemish hills, between Cassel Mount, Steenvoorde Hill, Mont des Cats, Mont Noir, and Mont Rouge, the Scherpenberg, Kemmel Hill, and the Wytschaete-Messines Ridge. This long range of heights, dominating the lowland plain for many miles in clear weather, was the key to all the northern positions of British and Belgian forces; the rampart of the Channel ports, enormously strengthening the moat formed by the inundated River Yser.

In the evening of April 9th a clever German subaltern, Lieutenant Diebing, succeeded in gaining a bridge-head on the Lys at Bac St. Maur, enabling his divisional commander to pour a large mass of troops over the river to Croix du Bac, far in the rear of Armentières, and on the road to Bailleul and the Hazebrouck-Ypres railway.

Though checked by a gallant counter-attack, the reinforced German troops continued to press forward towards Steenwerck, threatening Armentières with envelopment at the same time as they menaced Bailleul and the hill country. Royal Scots, Highland Light Infantry, and Scots Fusiliers stubbornly held the enemy on the left, along the northern part of the Bailleul-Fromelles road, winning back ground by a great charge at Le Mortier.

Ludendorff, however, introduced a powerful new factor into the situation when he decided to devote his main forces of a quarter of a million of men to an attack upon the Cassel-Kemmel Hill line. In the morning of April 10th, in continuously foggy weather, the Fourth German Army, under General Sixt von Armin, came to the help of the Sixth German Army, under General von Quast, and prolonged the front of conflict from Armentières to Hollebeke. The Scotsmen and South Africans of the 9th Division were fiercely assailed in front of the Wytschaete slopes, while the Wiltshires

Armentières to Hollebeke and Staffordshires of the heroic 25th Division were attacked in the wild waste north of Ploegsteert Wood, and the Lancashires and Cheshires were rushed by Ploegsteert village.

The 25th Division had broken the centre of the German forces on the Messines-Wytschaete Ridge in the summer of 1917. Upon them—when worn out by magnificent fighting in the Amiens battle and brought to "Plug Street" for a rest—there fell the heavy task of preventing the heights they had conquered from being turned. With desperate valour the Lancashires counter-attacked, yet could not restore the situation by the village. Nevertheless, some of the Cheshires,

with Wilts, Staffords, and King's Royal Rifles, hung on for two days in front of the wood, with the enemy behind them and the line of defence twisting at an apparently impossible angle. Encircled battalion commanders, taken unawares in their dug-outs, escaped and returned with counter-attacking machine-gun parties.

While the wood was full of contending infantry, other enemy forces forked out on either side towards the rear of Messines Ridge and the rear of Armentières. By noon Messines and Wytschaete were lost, and the Germans were digging themselves in on the crest. Then was seen one of the **Messines and Wytschaete lost** finest of rallies. The 9th Division extended its front for five hundred yards, the Scotsmen flinging their flank back by the White Château, while the South Africans drove the enemy from the high part of the ridge in a great charge along the crest road.

Between Ploegsteert Wood and Hollebeke General von Armin gained nothing of importance, but he won a partial success by his lower thrust between the famous wood, that had been the British training-school of trench warfare, and the battered, gas-flooded weavers' town of Armentières. The men of the 34th Division, who had held Croisilles against Von Below's terrific gas artillery, survived the still more extraordinary inundations of poison fume in the low-lying river town of French Flanders. Northumberland Fusiliers and Royal Scots were almost cut off at Houplines, after a great fight against heavy odds. While they were making a battling retreat, with the enemy gathering on their flanks, another hostile force entered Nieppe village, well in

MEN OF THE MAPLE LEAF RESTING AFTER BEARING THE BRUNT OF BATTLE.
Canadian troops gathered in a town close behind the line on the western front during the German offensive of the spring of 1918. They had been taking part in severe fighting and some of them were waiting to have their wounds attended to.

PORTUGUESE INFANTRY ON PARADE.
When the German thrust for the Channel ports began, Portuguese troops held part of the allied line between Neuve Chapelle and Laventie.

The German battle director was, however, largely governed by his knowledge of the fatigued condition of most of the British divisions arrayed between Ypres and Béthune.

Ludendorff, therefore, reckoned that he could, by using another considerable part of his grand reserve, completely and rapidly wear down the veterans of the Amiens battle before French and American reinforcements arrived along the shell-battered Calais-Paris railway line. Also, the German Emperor, with his sense of naval opportunities, was keenly alive to the value of the coast-line by the Strait of Dover.

The pocket formed by the Anglo-Portuguese withdrawal had a curious fascination for the enemy. It had the natural appearance of a great trap, with its hill rampart northward by Ypres, its forest cover westward by Hazebrouck, and its network of watercourses and

their rear, on the road from Armentières to Bailleul.

Ludendorff's design was to enclose Armentières and the 34th Division by meeting movements of his Fourth and Sixth Armies. The two great attacking forces nearly joined over the Lys River, but General Plumer and his lieutenants were not to be trapped by so simple a manœuvre in force. Violent British counter-attacks on Quast's advanced front by Steenwerck prevented him from co-operating with Armin, and the point of Armin's thrusting force, that just reached to Nieppe and Bailleul, was blunted with little difficulty. Meanwhile, the brigades in Armentières withdrew, about noon on April 10th, to Erquinghem and then to Nieppe village, on the Bailleul road, where, for more than twenty-four hours they broke every enemy assault. Ludendorff's claim to have taken 3,000 men in the town was a foolish exaggeration. Only odd stragglers were taken, the evacuation having been carried out in excellent order.

When night fell—with furious fighting going on in the darkness on the Wytschaete-Messines Ridge, Ploegsteert Wood, Hill 63, Nieppe, the Becque tributary of the Lys, Merville, and the Lawe brook—nothing of importance yet was lost by the tired British divisions who had come for a rest from the Third Army, under Sir Julian Byng, to the Second Army, under Sir Herbert Plumer. The diked,

Sir Douglas Haig's Special Order ditched, watery lowland, over which the enemy had advanced in the centre for seven miles at very heavy cost, was among the least favourable ground in Europe for a grand offensive. Its difficulties had been notorious for centuries, and in the rains of spring-time the laborious movements of attacks over shell-broken brooks and canals, under incessant defensive barrages and frequent aerial bombardments, were more wearing than the organisation of assaults on the old Somme battlefield.

In ordinary circumstances the enemy commander might have been content to exploit the sudden breaking of the Portuguese line for its distracting effect. When Sir Douglas Haig was concentrating for the defence of Aire, Hazebrouck, and Béthune, Ludendorff might have struck somewhere else.

SUPPLIES FOR THE PORTUGUESE IN THE TRENCHES.
The Germans made so fierce an onslaught on the Portuguese positions that in the action between Neuve Chapelle and the River Lys, on April 9th, 1918, the Portuguese Division lost 7,000 men and over 300 officers. One battalion particularly distinguished itself by stubborn resistance at La Couture.

fortified works southward by Béthune. But Ludendorff and his Emperor reckoned that the spring of the trap was so weakened they could break it.

They gambled against the staying power of the English, Scotsmen, and Welshmen who were being pursued by fresh shock divisions from the Cambrai, Somme, and Arras fronts to the Flemish hills and woods. As was afterwards seen on the Aisne, when some of the same tired British divisions were again pursued, on Secret Service information, in an attempt at final annihilation, the German Command greatly relied to achieve a grand decision on increasing the physical strain upon the British troops.

Sir Douglas Haig was naturally anxious when blow after blow in terrific force continually fell upon those of his men for whom he vainly tried to find quiet, recovering sectors. Instead of giving them the rest they needed, he had to employ them once more in one of the fiercest struggles in history, in order to preserve his strength around Amiens, where the peril still remained greatest. In the following Special Order of the Day he called upon his much-enduring troops to fight to the end, in words like those with which Marshal Joffre rallied the French armies in the First Battle of the Marne :

To all ranks of the British Army in France and Flanders :
Three weeks ago to-day the enemy began his terrific attacks against us on a fifty-mile front. His objects are to separate us from the French, to take the Channel ports, and destroy the British Army.

In spite of throwing already one hundred and six divisions into the battle and enduring the most reckless sacrifice of human life, he has as yet made little progress towards his goals. We owe this to the determined fighting and self-sacrifice of our troops.

Words fail me to express the admiration which I feel for the splendid resistance offered by all ranks of our Army under the most trying circumstances. Many amongst us now are tired. To those I would say that victory will belong to the side which holds out the longest.

The French Army is moving rapidly and in great force to our support. There is no other course open to us but to fight it out. Every position must be held to the last man; there must be no retirement. With our backs to the wall, and believing in the justice of our cause, each one of us must fight on to the end. The safety of our homes and the freedom of mankind depend alike upon the conduct of each one of us at this critical moment.

When this moving appeal was published the situation seemed very sombre around the lost town of Armentières. Ludendorff had decided to attack with all available strength. He appears originally to have had some forty divisions more than the Western Allies possessed in France and Flanders. This enabled him to rest his men considerably between the main actions, and distribute their heavy losses so as seldom to leave any good force in a dispirited condition. The drafts he obtained from Russia saved him from breaking up shattered divisions to keep others up to strength, with the result that, although half of his Grand Army had been severely

this immense improvisation of means for carrying the attack against the line of hills. Already, by April 11th, nearly three hundred thousand German infantrymen, with tens of thousands of assistants, were gathering against the 9th, 25th, 34th, 50th, 51st, 55th British Divisions and the comparatively small forces immediately in support. The Scots and South Africans still held to the crest of the Wytschaete Ridge, while the battalions of the 25th Division were retiring from Ploegsteert Wood towards Neuve Eglise and the outer defences of Kemmel Hill. The men of the 34th Division swung back in line towards the rising ground by Bailleul, while their comrades **Enemy's advantage** had their machine-guns covering the **in numbers** Steenwerck-Merville road, from which the line swung round the Clarence to Neuve Chapelle, where the Gordons held out grandly, and Givenchy, where the West Lancashires were immovable.

Along the whole of this large marshland bend, Armin and Quast incessantly launched their troops in dense waves, covered by machine-gun skirmishers and stealthy, crawling sharpshooters. Each local issue largely depended upon the resource of the opposing machine-gunners and the quickness with which the British riflemen detected movements of creeping storming-parties preparing positions for covering

fire for a coming mass attack. Sometimes the hostile advanced force was rushed and thrown back to the stronger machine-gun line screening the main infantry, as the Warwicks did in the brickfield between Merville and Nieppe Forest. It was often better, however, to watch the enemy's preparations, especially in clear weather, and mark the ranges at which an assault in strength could be chopped up by the British gunners, leaving the British infantry only broken pieces to reduce to complete disaster.

So long as the Lys plain was covered in mist, lingering in moist, stagnant air befouled with every variety of poison gas, the enemy commander continued to derive great advantage from his high superiority in numbers. Concentrating secretly by day as well as by night, he avoided losses from artillery curtain fire

TRAINING OF THE MACHINE-GUNNERS.
Transport arriving at night at a machine-gun school in France. The horses were startled by the flashlight by which the photograph was taken, but their riders had them well in hand.

punished by the British forces, he still had something like three-quarters of a million unused troops in the field, as well as a large number of rested men who had won successes.

The artillery power which the enemy commander employed seems to have exceeded even that used by Von Below, Marwitz, and Hutier. Behind every German attacking division were one hundred and thirty batteries, with three hundred trench-mortars and infantry guns. By April 13th a new concrete bridge was constructed across the Lys, and many new, direct roads were rapidly made to run from east to west, and thus provide the communications of attack which had purposely been omitted from the British lateral system of defensive communication extending only north-east to south-west.

No pause in the operations marked

MACHINE-GUNNING AT NIGHT.
British machine-gunner with his weapon in position for traversing German communication trenches on the western front. The work of the "little gunners," as men of the machine-gun detachments were called, became of increasing importance as the war proceeded.

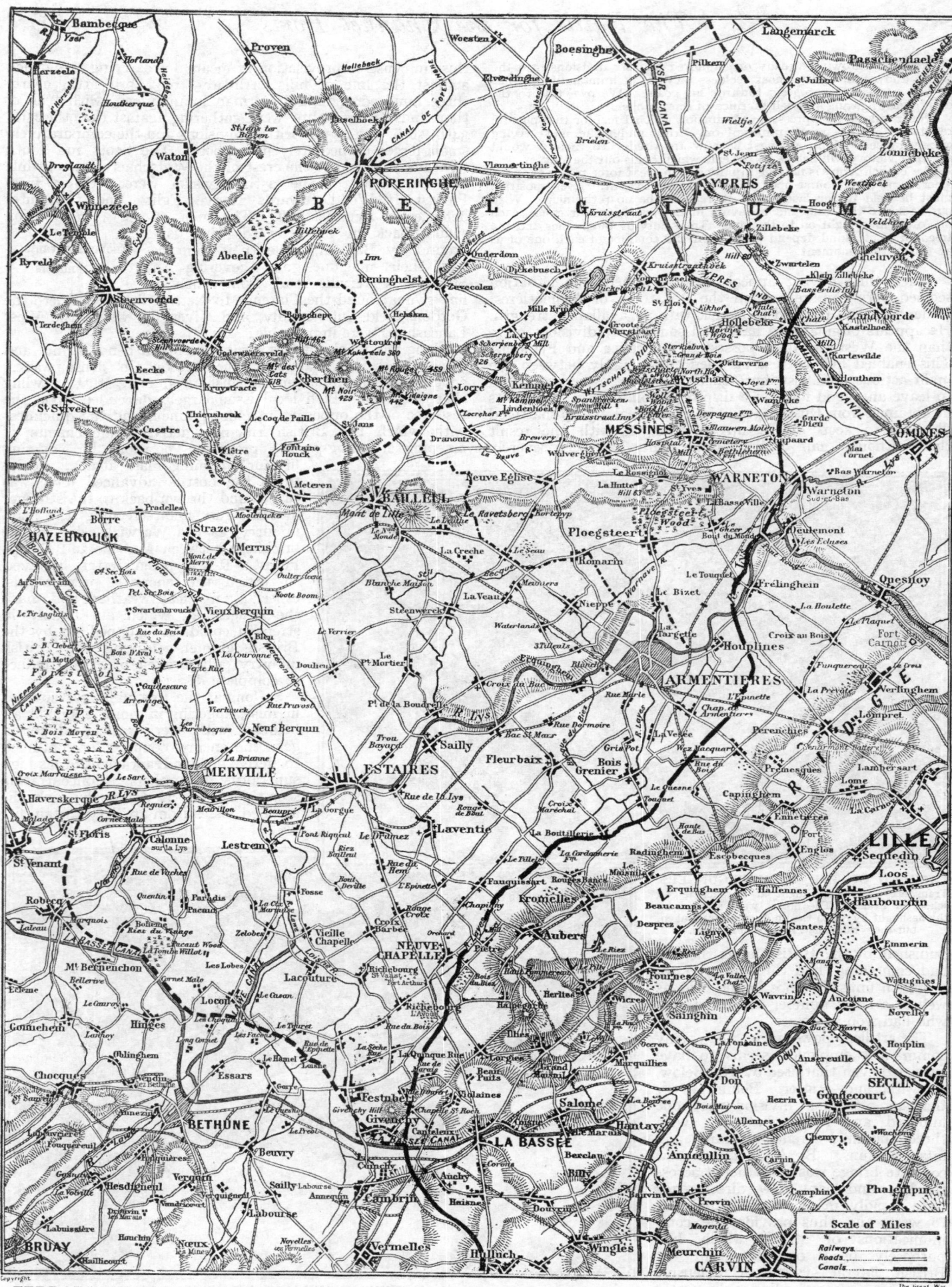

TERRAIN COVERED BY GERMANS IN THE STRUGGLE FOR CHANNEL PORTS, APRIL 9TH–29TH, 1918.
On April 9th, 1918, General von Ludendorff opened the second great German offensive of that year with a drive from the Lille Ridge in the direction of Dunkirk, Calais, and Boulogne.   On April 29th he was fought to a standstill on the broken line shown above.

and machine-gun barrages, until his grey lines shadowed out of the haze, under a tempest of shell and lead covering all possible British positions on the terrain attacked.

Pilots on both sides had to fly as low as two hundred feet above the lowland in order to detect movements of forces on April 9th and 10th. Only in the late afternoon of Thursday, April 11th, did the air begin to clear, when there was a great aerial conflict in which the enemy's squadrons were defeated, with the loss of thirty-five machines against a British loss of only four aeroplanes.

At any cost in aerial warfare the enemy endeavoured to obtain observation control for the vast artillery power he had been hauling forward in the fog. He blasted his way into Merville, obtaining by this Lys town another way of approach to the forest defences of Hazebrouck, employing the extraordinary number of twelve divisions of infantry to win the town his artillery had gassed and shattered.

This was General von Bernhardi's last shadow of success. At an appalling rate of wastage his multitude of one hundred and twelve thousand men, forming a sea of waves on the narrow southern front, surged at last over the Clarence River, between the outskirts of Nieppe Forest and Béthune, and approached St. Venant. But the gallant Durhams, Northumberland Fusiliers, and other battalions, who had been fighting between Estaires and Merville and along the Lys and Clarence streams, had done their work.

Other veteran divisions from the Amiens battlefield arrived in the nick of time at the corner of the great German salient. The 31st Division, which had recovered Mory and held the line south of Arras in the last week of March, arrived on April 13th by the approaches to the Nieppe Forest, and there made a line of defence which, with the help of the British Guards, was not shaken throughout the rest of the fierce battle on the British centre. The Guards relieved the 50th Division on April 11th along the Hazebrouck-Estaires road.

At Robecq, between the forest and Béthune, the 4th Division —fresh from its victory by the Vimy Ridge—came into action soon afterwards, and made itself famous by a defence and a counter-attack even more costly to the enemy than his action below the Vimy slopes. In other parts of the field were the 19th, 29th, 33rd, 5th, and 8th British Divisions.

Sir Herbert Plumer would not give any further ground to Bernhardi. Not only were the Béthune coalfields of high military value, but any widening of the southern corner of the salient of attack would have allowed the enemy to begin a flanking manœuvre around the supreme central obstacle of Nieppe Forest. By throwing strong reinforcements above Béthune the British commander did more than defeat and discredit the literary champion of Prussianism. He compelled Quast to break his strength against **Veteran divisions'** a stretch of woodland five miles long and **unshaken defence** three miles deep, where nicely-spaced machine-gun posts, with screened infantry forces and artillery behind, proved impregnable against the greatest German masses of men and guns that Ludendorff could spare from his general reserve.

The German Commander-in-Chief adopted the sound, ordinary course of alternate or simultaneous blows against the sides of the salient. Between Givenchy and Hollebeke the Germans occupied some twenty-one miles of the British line, and there had room for movement. But by the Nieppe Forest their line of attack was only ten miles long, and subject, therefore, to enfilading gun fire from both flanks, as well as to frontal fire. Naturally, Ludendorff strenuously endeavoured to win more room on either flank, but Sir Herbert Plumer answered this hostile plan by gradually giving ground in the direction skilfully chosen by him and valorously confirmed by his soldiers.

By tremendous efforts of endurance and superior fighting power the wonderful British divisions, with many battalions again reduced to companies and companies to weak platoons, shepherded the grey masses of the most numerous fighting force then in the world to the line of northern hills, where the enemy's strength could be definitely broken at least cost in life to the Allies.

In front of Kemmel Hill only the unaided men of the 25th Division, who had suffered seriously in the Ploegsteert action, held the first gate to the rampart of the Channel ports. It

FRENCH GUNS IN ACTION.
A battery of French 75's firing on a part of the western front where the allied forces were linked together. Three British soldiers were watching the operation from behind the gun in the foreground.

was impossible to relieve them and also keep the central and southern part of the line strong. To find troops to replace outworn forces and extend the critical front when the salient was widened northward, Sir Herbert Plumer began to draw in around Ypres and yield to the enemy Passchendaele Ridge, Poelcappelle, Zonnebeke, Langemarck, and other scenes of bitter actions from October, 1914, to November, 1917.

It was a grave thing to abandon ground consecrated by the most dearly bought of British advances. But the spirit of the British soldier hardened under this sacrifice of positions for which many of his **British valour** comrades had fallen. It reinforced the **under adversity** influence of Sir Douglas Haig's call for a fight to the death and evoked all the grim stubbornness of character of the island race that had seemed so easy-going in the days of peace.

Just as the Ypres retirement was quietly beginning, the men of the hard-pressed 25th Division excelled all their long, splendid record of great achievements by their defence of Neuve Eglise and the approaches to Kemmel Hill. The Cheshires first took the weight of the attack on Friday, April 12th, when a great phalanx of picked enemy divisions tried to break into the hills between Bailleul and Wytschaete. There were some 140,000 German infantrymen arrayed on the narrow front after the new telescoping tactics of assault that was Ludendorff's remarkable contribution to military science. The forces moved into and through each other in a terrific continuity of effort, clashing at last into Neuve Eglise, after complete failure at Bailleul and Wulverghem on either side.

At Neuve Eglise six vital roads met, including the lateral communications along the lower hillside and the upward routes to Kemmel and Ypres and Dranoutre and Locre. Holding the knot of ways, the enemy could take the eastern heights from the rear while developing an attack on the middle hills. Sir Herbert Plumer speeded up his withdrawal on Ypres, but time was finely won for him on Saturday morning, April 13th, by the Worcesters, Sherwood Foresters, Yorkshire Light Infantry, and other troops, who recaptured the village and cross-roads, and for the time also relieved the pressure on Bailleul.

The enemy returned, covered by a blasting bombardment of guns of all calibres, and through the Englishmen's machine-gun barrage and answering artillery fire the survivors of his continuous waves gathered together for more rush attacks. Fifteen divisions were deployed on both sides of Bailleul, together with special storm troops, including men of an Alpine corps. On the enemy's side there was also a strayed bull, maddened by the whirlwinds of fire, that charged a machine-gun post.

The defenders had not slept for days and could not snatch a brief rest, for fresh enemy brigades stormed upward as others fell back broken. At one time the Cheshires, Worcesters, Wiltshires, and Staffords, who had fought since March 21st, were in a hollow square around the village, with only a frail connecting line by the Dranoutre road. Finally the King's Royal Rifles gallantly rearguarded a withdrawal towards the hills, but the commanding officer of the Worcesters —a regiment famous for saving the line

Fall of Neuve Eglise in the first action about Ypres—was the **and Bailleul** last man to leave Neuve Eglise, about which his men had piled the enemy dead.

The definite fall of Neuve Eglise exposed the Wulverghem and Bailleul positions to flanking attack and involved their loss. Bailleul fell on April 15th, together with the strong, high line of Mont de Lille and the Ravelsberg, which were the outer defences to the high hills. South Staffordshires, Notts and Derbys, Lincolns, and other fine troops made a fine stand about Bailleul, where they directed a plunging fire upon the successive forces of attack. They took severe toll of the Alpine corps and two other picked divisions, that eventually carried the falling, smoking wreckage of the picturesque hillside town, with the fine market-square and friendly inns of both happy and sad memories.

The thinning yet still resilient British line ascended the slopes of the hills from Wytschaete, still held in continuous action of a hundred and twenty hours against the Fourth German Army, to the rugged approaches to the Mont des Cats, by Meteren, and the direct, short route to Hazebrouck, by Strazeele, upon which the Sixth German Army was with violent persistence endeavouring to advance.

All round the salient the old marksmanship with the British rifle became the governing factor of the battle. It mastered the enemy south of Ypres in as deadly a fashion as it had mastered him east of Ypres in October, 1914. The men who had grandly come through the latest Arras and Somme battles **Battle for the** were the peers in rapid, aimed musketry **northern hills** fire of the long-service Regular soldiers.

It was more difficult to obtain the old fire effect when the enemy compelled gas-masks to be worn, screened his waves of assault with smoke barrages, and kept down the defending troops with travelling, tricky curtains of shell, mingled with a rain of lead from massed machine-guns. Yet it was against the machine-gun, which the enemy had ever regarded as the master weapon of infantry and continually developed in tactical use and number, that the British rifle often prevailed. In a new kind of volley effect, in which each shot was particularly aimed with great, intensive results, the German machine-gun opposition was frequently beaten down when it was of massive powerfulness.

At the opening of the supreme battle for the northern hills there was a terrific struggle between Meteren and the northern edge of Nieppe Forest. The German centre, after the tussle with the British Guards, endeavoured to avoid the woodland conflict by outflanking the forest along the north. Scottish Rifles, Highland Light Infantry, West Surreys, Worcesters, Middlesex, New Zealand diggers, dismounted Tank Corps men, with other troops and odd men, succeeded in making the approach to Hazebrouck, above the forest, a German cemetery.

But having advanced to the foot of the hills, the German commanders prepared for another great general action under the eyes of their Emperor. On April 16th, when the fog again veiled the battle plain, fierce ramming blows were struck at Wytschaete and the height of Spanbroekenmolen

ALLIED CAVALRY ASSEMBLING TO TAKE AN ACTIVE PART IN AN OPERATION.
Long deprived by conditions of trench warfare of opportunity to display his horsemanship and prowess with his proper weapon, the cavalryman came into his own in 1918, and was an important factor in the successful defensive campaign fought from March to July that year. French, British, and Canadian cavalry fought together in motley squadrons of horizon-blue and khaki, more than once recovering positions that seemed hopelessly lost.

near it, along which the original British line had run. Both crests were lost, enabling the enemy to strike sideways as well as frontally at Kemmel. At the same time Meteren, by the upper corner of the salient, was also stormed by the enemy, so that he had positions of vantage at both ends of his line of attack against the hill rampart. Counter-attacking forces recovered both places, but the enemy continued the struggle for them the following morning.

GENERAL VON BERNHARDI.
Germany's famous military writer, in command of the army that attacked across the Lawe stream in the attempt to break through the British front in April, 1918.

On the same day, April 17th, Ludendorff tried suddenly to break through the Belgian line north-east of Ypres, and thereby throw into confusion General Plumer's forces retiring from the Passchendaele Ridge. Attacked on a front of four miles by the forces of some four divisions, the greatly outnumbered Belgians gave ground; but, counter-charging almost immediately, recovered their line, taking some six hundred prisoners from the seven brigades used in opening the movement. This dashing exploit by King Albert's men was of great assistance to the British troops. It had a cheering effect as well as high material value.

The second great Kaiser battle was beginning. Under the anxious eyes of his master—from whom the Amiens failure could not be hidden—Ludendorff was trying to redeem his losses by showing that he had reduced the British armies to a condition of weakness. Apparently he did not yet believe any great British reserve existed, and counted it evidence of extreme enfeeblement that lads were being sent over the Channel to meet his highly-trained shock forces.

The first French reinforcement had just appeared on the eastern hills in the struggle around Kemmel, and Ludendorff desired to strike decisively with all possible strength before General Foch could help Sir Herbert Plumer with more of the allied mass of manœuvre. Once more he swung two tremendous masses alternately against the two sides of the salient. After a heavy bombardment he attacked in knife-like thrusts from Nieppe Forest to Wytschaete, entering Meteren for the second time, and getting a footing again on Wytschaete Ridge, but failing at Dranoutre and Kemmel Hill.

The next day, after a night-long artillery duel, the southern offensive was resumed on a curve of fifteen miles from Nieppe Forest to Givenchy. Against the British 1st Division, that had relieved the West Lancashires, three German divisions poured, but again the enemy masses were trapped in the works and ditches by the hill of victory.

Then Béthune was assailed through Hinges and Robecq. A German division came in four waves towards the veterans of Vimy Ridge. It was shot down as it fled back to Pacaut Wood. Two other divisions then endeavoured to work forward, but only left prisoners in the hands of the British. Seven other divisions were deployed, mainly on open ground in costly, fruitless attempts to reach the canal between Festubert and the neighbourhood of Béthune. All that the Germans accomplished was to throw a bridge over the canal by Hinges, and walk across in the attitude of surrender, to escape the dreadful sweep of the defenders' fire.

Ludendorff could not accept defeat. In order to win along the north he had to widen the salient, and free his centre from the cross-fire that poured on his medium artillery and forced his howitzer batteries to withdraw from good attacking positions. In the night of April 17th both the German artillery and infantry between Givenchy and Merville were strongly reinforced, and in the morning of April 18th the weight of fire upon the 1st Division was enormous.

Great damage was done to the defences, against which 11 in. shells were used; yet the defensive power of the troops was unbroken. They fought in the open, with machine-guns, rifles, bayonets, and bombs, from nine o'clock in the morning until eight o'clock at night, losing only two outposts by Givenchy and Festubert. Once more, above Béthune, the 4th Division justified its terrible fame for killing. In the darkness the men raked the enemy's gathering-places, such as Pacaut Wood, demoralising the first wave of assault before it moved out. It quickly broke in panic. Five minutes afterwards a stronger force came out, with a pontoon illumined by star-shells. A Royal Engineer corporal annexed the pontoon when the surviving Germans ran, and afterwards picked up a drifting British pontoon.

Ludendorff begins to waver

Then he bridged the canal, and took over a detachment of English and Scottish troops, who, in an action of three hours, captured some hundreds of Germans by Pacaut Wood, completely ending the offensive movement there. On the northern line the routine attacks from Nieppe Forest to Kemmel Hill were early broken. The German troops of the best quality—such as the Alpine corps from Von Below's mountaineering forces in the Italian campaign—were dispirited by severe losses, amounting to one-half of some battalions, and by lack of regular food. The German supply columns

GERMAN WAR LORDS ON THE WESTERN FRONT.
A German artist's representation of the High Command during the offensive on the western front. At the camp-table in the foreground are seated the Kaiser (pointing out something on the map before him), Field-Marshal von Hindenburg, and General von Ludendorff (looking through field-glasses). On the extreme right is the Crown Prince.

were wrecked by the guns of the defence, the marshes being sown with bogged waggons and lost rations.

For the first time in a month of continual actions at extreme pressure, Ludendorff was constrained to pause. It had rained, and his experience of Polish mud was completed by a deep acquaintance, under offensive conditions, with Flemish mud. Flemish mud, combined with British gun fire from dominating hills and short-range and long-range British aerial bombardments, proved an obstacle of terrible hindrance. Snow fell amid the rain, and the wind grew bitter, especially for ill-fed soldiers, who had been heavily punished.

Ludendorff began to waver. It seemed as though he and his Staff had miscalculated the immediately available reserve strength of the British armies, as well as the personal endurance

INGENIOUS DEVICE FOR REGULATING TRAFFIC IN THE WAR AREA.
The words "Go" and "Stop," plainly lettered on large disks, were visible at a considerable distance and prevented congestion at the junction point when pressure on lines of communication was heavy.

of the British soldier. He thought of using his last elements of superior numbers in a supreme test of the French armies and, indirectly, of the United States reinforcements; but, while the new preparations were in train, he could do nothing more than improve his machinery of attack in Flanders.

Fog came on April 24th, and the armies of Armin and Quast reconcentrated under its cover, and, with more new roads crossing the Lys, advanced upon the hill line from the neighbourhood of Ypres, at Vierstraat and St. Eloi to Locre. The high wood of Kemmel Hill was saturated with poison gas, and on April 25th the heroic French garrison was overborne. For eight hours or more the blue force, after being encircled by a flanking movement, was seen by an aerial scout still holding the crest. He reported that the French had made a successful counter-attack, but he was mistaken. They were making their final stand, having sworn beforehand they would never leave Kemmel to the enemy while they lived. The loss of the great observation-post, five hundred feet high, in a country of low-lying, marshy land, was a serious matter at the time. The allied line was drawn back to the Grand Bois by Wytschaete and the Lower Vierstraat, rising again by the Scherpenberg, where Locre, at a junction of roads between Kemmel Hill and Mont Rouge and Mont Noir, was a very important key position which the French reinforcing troops had taken over.

Critical position at Locre

Royal Scots, Camerons, and Black Watch, after a violent action in the mist with strong enemy forces, held on to the ground by Wytschaete and closed a gap by Kemmel, where the victorious Germans were breaking through. Then supporting British troops made two relieving counter-thrusts into Kemmel village, the second of which was successful.

Ground was lost on the left, where the famous Bluff by the Ypres-Comines Canal was taken by the enemy when the Germans renewed their general attack on the hill line on April 26th.

The critical position was, however, Locre, which the French troops guarded. If the line of heights were riven in the middle after the loss of the eastern Kemmel Hill the situation for the forces about Ypres and along the Yser would be grave.

Spurred on by a keen sense of his instant opportunities, General Sixt von Armin and his army commanders, General Sieger and General von Eberhardt, made a series of extreme efforts to reach the gate to victory. On Friday, April 26th, they captured Locre, but their success was achieved too late. Locre returned to the possession of the French. A magnificent cavalry force rode hard for sixty miles northward and, alighting, gave battle, preferring rather to attack the enemy before he firmly dug himself in than to rest. This was a feat of horsemanship likely to be as memorable as the deeds of British cavalrymen which were performed some weeks previously between Ham and Villers-Bretonneux.

Defeated, finally, before Amiens about the time when he failed to pierce the northern line of heights in Flanders, Ludendorff had to recognise that all his grand strokes against the wings and centre of the British forces had failed of strategic effect. At a common loss to Teuton and Briton, which told eventually against the Teuton in a threefold manner, the enemy commander had won two largish patches of useless ground, both of which he was soon ready to evacuate to save his man-power. He had united the Allies under the supreme, direct control of a man of high character and mind. He had provoked the complete strength of the British and American peoples, and heightened the temper of the Allies so that Mr. Lloyd George and President Woodrow Wilson raised the age for military service of their countrymen in 1918. He accelerated, by the threat of his temporary superior numbers, the gathering in France of a huge United States army, and weakened his own forces in a critical manner, while the Allies were growing generally stronger.

A great success against the French in the direction of Paris, while some of their forces were assisting the British by Ypres and by Amiens, was the last desperate measure of retaining the initiative that Ludendorff could conceive. He prepared to spend his final reserve of striking power in this adventure, while urging the Austro-Hungarian Command to co-operate by an offensive on the Italian front.

Ludendorff's thrust for Paris

He fought a farewell fight for the Channel ports on April 29th. His troops attacked from Meteren to Zillebeke Lake against the British and French positions and also assailed the Belgian line north of Ypres. The unfaltering 25th Division, with the West Riding Territorials of the 49th Division and 21st Division, famous also in the previous Amiens and Cambrai battles, were among the forces of defence. Against a succession of assaults they held their lines, and the French on the Scherpenberg positions and Mont Rouge, after giving some ground, recovered Locre, inflicting heavy losses on the enemy, as did also the valiant Belgians. All the slight gains made by the German masses under cover of morning mist were lost in the counter-attacks of the Allies. In the confusion of a complete disaster, proving that the attacking troops were dispirited, the Battle for the Channel Ports came to an end. The ground was then only used for demonstrating purposes while an offensive against the French centre was being mounted.

Removing the sixteenth=century door of St. Vulfran, Abbeville, to safeguard it from Hun savagery.

Before the war: Façade of the Hôtel de Ville in the Petite Place, Arras, in 1914.

After four years of war: View of the same quarter of Arras in March, 1918.

When open campaigning succeeded to trench warfare: French infantry in their individual rifle-pits.

French machine-gunners aligned along a roadside in positions dug beneath the apple-trees.

Vivid impression of the terrific struggle for Armentières in April, 1918 : Holding up a German attack on the Lys Canal.

CHAPTER CCLX.

THE GREAT THRUST FOR PARIS AND SECOND VICTORY OF THE MARNE.

By Edward Wright.

Battle-worn British Divisions on the Aisne—French Troops Overwhelmed by Enemy's Mass Attack—Flank of North-Country Territorials Exposed by Craonne—Heroic British Rearguard at Gernicourt—How the Cheshires Held Bligny Hill—Foch Leaves His Centre Weak and Strengthens His Wings—Germans Win Local Mastery of the Air—Sway of Attack and Counter-attack—Terrific Forest Fighting and Check to Enemy's Advance—Hutier Opens New Western Drive on Paris—Mangin's Massacre on Méry Hill—First Great Victory of French Tanks—Final Enemy Offensive of July 15th—Gouraud Retreats to Victory in Champagne—Böhn's Desperate Advance Across the Marne—American Counter-attack and Italian Stand—How the French Cavalry Trapped the Enemy—Mangin's Grand Counter-stroke on German Flank—New Enemy Army Interposes—British Contingent Strikes at Hostile Flank—Magnificent Scottish Advance Decides the Struggle in the Marne Salient.

AFTER using considerably more than half of his forces on the western front, in attacking the southern British wing on the Somme in March and the northern British wing on the Lys in April, 1918, General von Ludendorff began to devote all his attention to the French centre. As the organs of his Staff put it, his new plan was to exhaust the strategic French reserve.

Great Britain, it was tacitly admitted, had survived the ordeal imposed upon her. She had indeed emerged stronger from the battles that had definitely weakened Germany. The British Cabinet, alarmed into a keen sense of the supreme importance of the Flemish-French front, poured out its large home reserve, raised the age of military service, and "combed out" even vital industries such as coal-mining, and so brought the infantry forces of Sir Douglas Haig fairly up to strength.

Even so the strain upon British man-power in May, 1918, remained terrible. Ludendorff was able to retire his best shock divisions for nearly two months' rest, while bringing them up to strength and training the new drafts. None of the best forces of General von Hutier were kept in action in all grave battles; they were not even kept in line or in support, but withdrawn towards Hirson and Mézières for repose, varied by exercise in improved tactics of attack

On the other hand the Allied Commander-in-Chief could not afford to rest any of his men. All he could do for the British divisions was to endeavour to find easy sectors for them to hold.

Some of the most tried of British divisions, when relieved along the Lys River, were moved down to the Aisne by Craonne, Berry-au-Bac, and the neighbourhood of Rheims, in order to fill out the French line. Alongside these worn British forces were placed French and French Colonial divisions that had likewise borne the burden of the great battles.

The Aisne positions were chosen as a place of rest, because of their apparent impregnability. The line ran from Pinon Forest in the Ailette valley, which was covered by a system of strong block-houses and dominated by guns around the hog's back of the Chemin des Dames. This line was held by a veteran force of Normans, Vendéans, and Bretons. Then towards the end of the Ladies' Walk, the famous California plateau, for which Teuton and Gaul had fought for months, was occupied by the gallant British 50th Division of North-country Territorials, distinguished by their long stand by Dead Man Down, below Arras, at the end of March, 1918, and by their superb defence of the River Lys line immediately after the Portuguese Division was broken on April 9th.

The new line of the 50th Division extended to Craonne and the summit of the great Aisne plateau, and connected with the sector of the British 8th Division, also hardly tried in the northern battle, and now extended by Berry-au-Bac. On their right was the heroic British

GENERAL SIR HENRY HORNE, K.C.B.
Corps commander on the Somme in 1916, Sir Henry Sinclair Horne was later promoted to the command of the First British Army. A great artillery expert, he invented the creeping barrage.

21st Division that had fought from Epéhy to Bray, on the Somme, while wasting away to much less than a brigade.

The line of the 21st Division ended about Bermicourt, where it linked with the sector of a fine French Colonial division that had also recently fought to exhaustion. Immediately in support of the British forces was the renowned 25th Division, which had recently fought from Ploegsteert to the slope of Kemmel Hill, staying the enemy at last by square formation. The British 19th Division, distinguished in the Cambrai road actions and the Lys battles, was available as a second reserve.

As soon as these tired forces were settled along and below the Aisne plateau, Ludendorff made his new plan of attack according to his policy of pursuing the war-worn British divisions. He placed his main reserve above Laon, threatening equally the Champagne front, the Aisne line, and the Oise and Somme lines. It was expected that he would either strike against General Gouraud, commanding in Champagne, or that he would again **Self-confidence** swing westward upon General Humbert or **of Ludendorff** General Debeney and General Rawlinson on the Amiens front.

In the last week of May, however, it became known that the Ailette and Aisne sectors would be assailed, either as a demonstration in the main offensive or as a direct attempt to break southwards. So difficult was the hilly country between the Aisne and the Marne, with its long slopes, lateral rivers, and restored towns, villages and farmsteads, that it seemed impossible for the German commander to think of reaching Paris by the road along which Kluck had returned. Yet this was the astonishingly bold scheme of Ludendorff.

Such was his confidence in his technique of attack that natural difficulties of ground counted less with him than his view of the condition of the opposing troops.

He had in line along the Aisne seventeen divisions under General von Böhn and General Fritz von Below. He greatly strengthened the artillery of these two armies, and under cover of night rushed down fifteen of the best shock battalions that had fought under General von Hutier. Close behind these picked troops came eight more German divisions, ready to enter into action when the shock troops had broken the allied line and needed to be **Allies outnumbered** withdrawn before their aggressive spirit was **by five to one** broken. Only three British divisions and two French divisions, stationed on a front of twenty-five miles between Vauxaillon and Bermicourt, were available to meet the first thrust of the enemy. Even when the British 25th Division and a crack French division in reserve entered into action the odds against the allied soldiers were five to one.

The struggle opened at one o'clock in the morning of Monday, May 27th. From the enemy's enormous parks of artillery there was thrown a barrage two miles deep that rolled over the chalk heights and down the misty valleys, filling the caves, quarries, works, and buildings with poison gas. It was with a deluge of gas that Ludendorff's lieutenants tried to transform the natural caverns and artificial underground galleries of the chalk country into death-traps for the garrisoning troops.

The bombardment lasted only some four hours, yet such was the extraordinary number of guns employed that the wide, deep stretch of heights and the river-courses that seamed them were flooded in poison fume. When the

ALONG THE INTERMINGLED ALLIED LINE.
French and British troops halted together by a roadside in France when forces of the allied armies were brigaded together to withstand the tremendous German onslaught in the spring of 1918. In his historic Order of the Day to his troops, Sir Douglas Haig said : " The French Army is moving rapidly and in great force to our support. . . With our backs to the wall, and believing in the justice of our cause, each one of us must fight on to the end."

bombardment was at its height, with trench-mortars and other infantry guns busy smashing up the foreground works, another colossal use was made of a simple battle device.

A large number of special batteries began to fire smoke-shells, in order to make a great pattern of floating screens upon the Franco-British front. Not only were many of the defence forces curtained off from each other, but the infantry in action on the great plateau was so completely veiled from its own artillery that signal rockets could not be perceived by the gunners through the German smoke barrage.

Stealthily, between three and four o'clock in the morning, patrols of enemy machine-gunners and sharp-

GREAT BRITISH BRIDGE-BUILDING FEAT.
Big trestle bridge completed on the western front in one week by British Engineers as part of their great task of laying a broad-gauge railway at the rate of a mile a day.

RAPID RAILWAY CONSTRUCTION IN FRANCE.
Men of the British Engineers carrying forward the rails during the accomplishment of their feat of laying a mile a day of a broad-gauge railway in maintaining the lines of communication in France.

shooters began to work through the covering defences of the Allies. In the French block-houses in Pinon Forest three French battalions were completely encircled. Heroically the troops held out, fighting for two days, and occasionally getting carrier-pigeons through to the receding allied line. Practically these Frenchmen were volunteers for death, having been aware that their works would be overrun and cut off, but resolute either to fight to the end a delaying action or to hold the enemy until a victorious counter-attack relieved them, they nobly carried out their work. It was their example that afterwards inspired other French volunteers on the Champagne front to turn the tide of war.

In the meantime the heroes of Pinon Forest were not striving in vain. By holding the outer block-houses they prevented the German advance from spreading immediately towards the Soissons sector. But on the Middle Ailette valley the French defence was completely broken by a series of swift and skilful mass attacks. By eight o'clock in the morning some of the German shock battalions had reached the Aisne, by Pont Arcy, on the road to Fismes.

This German success was certainly one of the most remarkable things in the western campaign. The attacking troops had to climb the long, high, northern slopes of the Chemin des Dames ridge, and then fight downward over caverned and excavated ground, where there were grottos

capable of sheltering thousands of men. Yet the Germans worked forward at a pace of more than a mile an hour, through one of the mightiest natural fortresses in Europe. From September, 1914, to April, 1917, British and French troops had been held up by the great northern plateau of the Aisne even as other hosts of armed men had been since the days of Julius Cæsar.

The Germans merely marched from the Ailette to the Aisne, and the ease of their advance was in no way due to any weakness on the part of the French division. The Normans and Bretons fought to the riverside with desperate valour, and there, reduced to the strength of a brigade, they swung back sideways to the plateau south-east of Soissons, and held out for six days in all against continually increasing forces of the enemy. Their stand below Soissons was one of the decisive events in the war. The ground they defended, on the flank of the extending hostile advance, became the grand pivoting point for the first great French counter-offensive when the time came for General Foch to take the initiative.

But in the early morning of May 27th the retirement of the French division from the centre of the Chemin des Dames exposed the English North-countrymen of the 50th Division to a terrible ordeal. The **Fresh ordeal of** Durhams, Northumberlands, and other **the 50th Division** veteran Territorials had stood firm against all the enemy's rush attacks from the California plateau to the village and summit of the historic Craonne peninsula. German machine-gunners and sharpshooting patrols could find no gap in the bombarded and gas-drenched English line, and the enemy was compelled to resort to his old method of mass assault in dense waves, with Tanks in close support, creeping barrages, and all other known methods of line breaking.

The Englishmen did not waver against the frontal attacks. When, however, the French retired on the left by Troyon, and the Germans worked round the back of the connecting English brigade, a rapid retreat had to be conducted. The British general at first endeavoured to relieve the pressure on the French force by making a counter-charge against the advancing centre of the German line. But General von Böhn, who had distinguished himself in the retreat from the Somme to the Hindenburg line, was prepared for a movement of this kind. He employed Tanks against the sudden onrush of the Englishmen, and by this means checked the assault on his centre, while developing along the path of the French retreat his outflanking movement against the 50th Division.

Happily, on the right of the North-country troops, the offensive conducted by Fritz von Below around Rheims was as unsuccessful as had been the offensive conducted by

In Béthune under fire, showing the damaged tower of the church on the right. The Germans, in their attempt to reach the Channel ports in April, 1918, failed to get past the barrier town of Béthune.

British artillery resting by the roadside. Superb assistance was given by the field-gunners to the infantry during the critical period of the German offensive. Though overworked to the extreme limit of physical endurance, they broke up the enemy's preparations for numberless assaults, on some occasions leaving the infantry little more than fragments to reduce to complete disaster. Inset above : A British roadside outpost on the Ypres front.

WHERE THE ENEMY WAS HELD FROM YPRES TO BÉTHUNE IN HIS OFFENSIVE OF APRIL, 1918.

Otto von Below around Arras. The Franco-British artillery observers were especially quick in detecting unusual signs of activity in the enemy's lines on the evening of May 26th. During the night they heavily bombarded the hostile organisations, striking the enemy in the open when he was assembling to attack. Then, during the German artillery preparation, the French and British guns, between Rheims and the hills by Berry-au-Bac, strongly answered the German batteries. The upshot was that Fritz von Below's army failed completely. Its shock divisions were held up and shattered by the French Colonials and by the British troops of the 21st and 8th Divisions, that contained very many young soldiers who came into action for the first time.

When the flank of the 50th Division was turned below Craonne, and the North-countrymen had to retire across the Aisne towards the ridge of Guyencourt, between the Aisne-Marne Canal and the Vesle stream, a difficult manœuvre had to be executed against overwhelming numbers of the foe. The Franco-British Rheims line, that stretched north of the city, had to be moved back to the north-west and thence bent south-west, to keep contact with the French forces retreating towards the Marne. Both Von Below's and Von Böhn's shock divisions made sustained and violent efforts to break through the allied line during the great Franco-British manœuvre.

The French left, by Vailly, was saved by the fine division immediately in reserve, which arrived at Pont Arcy while the Franco-British forces were still struggling on the northern river bank. By heroic counter-attacks the fresh division, often fighting at close quarters with Germans six times their number, held the hostile masses and prevented them from spreading out along the southern line. Thrice the enemy crossed the river, but the French held out until midnight, and allowed time for their countrymen to swing back by Vailly. But at Pontavert, the critical point on the left British flank, the gallant French counter-attacking force, extended beyond its strength, could not save the situation. The enemy worked over the river, and again began to encircle the 50th Division. At Gernicourt Wood there was then a memorable rearguard action, comparable with anything in history. Some of the youngest English

Heroic episode at Gernicourt Wood troops made a stand alongside some of the oldest French Territorials, who were merely a labouring party. Boys of eighteen and men of fifty, they fought to the death; all the English troops fell, and only a few of the Frenchmen escaped.

During the arduous task of recrossing the Aisne the brigades of the 50th Division were for a time cut off from the French force on their left and the 8th Division on their right. But the 25th Division came finely up in support, while an English cyclist battalion reinforced the French centre by a splendid action at Fismes, on the Vesle. The main British forces swung steadily back on the St. Thierry ridge, and with the river valley of the Vesle in their rear, giving the enemy a way of approach behind them, made a glorious resistance on the outskirts of Rheims.

Happily, Rheims itself was really impregnable. Its immense system of wine vaults and new tunnels driven through the chalk, its wired and barricaded streets, sandbagged and loopholed houses, with the crescent of observation heights curving above the city, and the Mountain of Rheims, a large forested clump of nine hills, rising behind, composed a stronger military obstacle to the enemy than the caverned and buttressed high cliffs of the Aisne had proved.

On the westerly outskirts of Rheims the British forces

gained an important victory alongside the French. The Britons formed the moving wheel of the defence and the Frenchmen the axle. The Frenchmen stood firm between Thilloy and Pompelle Fort, and, after a fine counter-attack northward to lighten the general pressure, ended their action by capturing four German Tanks, destroying five more, and taking prisoner the enemy troops that entered Pompelle works.

The British divisions—with a constantly endangered left flank, which the enemy continued to attempt to turn every time the French centre gave ground between Fère-en-Tardenois and Verneuil—fought and manœuvred on the long wedge of high ground between the Vesle and Ardre streams. To strengthen the French centre the British force at first extended

ALLIES WHO SHARED ALL THINGS IN COMMON.
British soldiers going up to the front line in French transport waggons—a frequent incident on the western front, especially when troops of different nationalities were brigaded together after the Allies had inaugurated the system of unity of control in 1918.

across the Ardre, and held the hills above Ville-en-Tardenois, winning time for General Foch to bring his reserves strongly into action by the beginning of June.

The strain upon the British troops, who were not reinforced by their 19th Division until May 29th, was intense. Ludendorff and his Staff had, since March and April, again improved their devices of assault. Each German battalion now had sixteen machine-guns in company groups, and an additional twelve guns that went to form a special brigade machine-gun corps. Each brigade also had three companies of infantry guns. The companies worked forward in line, with one company in support, and the machine-gunners covered the ground in front of the skirmishing patrols with a sheet of lead. When working forward in ordinary circumstances the line of scouts was protected by **Improved German** linked machine-gun fire that swept the **method of attack** onward path. The brigade machine-gunners held the places against which counter-attacks might be expected, or concentrated upon obstacles it was intended to rush.

Personal bravery alone could accomplish little of importance against this flexible and mighty instrument of fire-power. The highest skill and instinct for team-work in the individual soldier, as well as in the regimental and Staff officers, was required by the defending forces in order to cope with the superior numbers of attackers employed. The enemy machine-gunners needed more frequently to be mastered by aimed rapid rifle fire than had been the case by the Somme and the Lys. Yet many of the veterans of the recent battles were either dead or wounded, and their places were filled by untried youths.

RUNNING THE GAUNTLET OF DEATH UNDER THREAT OF ENEMY BARRAGE.

French soldiers passing across a bridge while under heavy fire on the western front, an action which called for nerves tempered like finest steel. Not one of the men could fail to realise that enemy observers had probably located the pontoon bridge, and to know that a smashing barrage was likely to be directed upon it at a moment's notice. Conscious that such barrage was probably withheld until troops should be crowding upon the bridge, the men went over it running at several paces apart in Indian file, so that as many as possible should be able to occupy the farther bank before the inevitable happened and the barrage fell on the bridge.

Nevertheless, qualities of race told. Marksmanship was an affair of visual gift. Either the Briton acquired this visual gift by the practice of games, or his zest for cricket and football was created by some quick, native play of limbs, eyes, and brain. As the French remarked at the time, the baseball-playing American had the visual gift in the same measure as the Briton. When he became well acquainted with his rifle, what he could see he could shoot.

Thus it came about that the apparently weakest divisions in the British Army proved of formidable strength. They held on to the Ardre line on May 30th, when the Germans had reached the Marne, beating back in incessant action day and night the increasing masses of the enemy. The enemy corps commanders had soon to abandon their method of machine-gun penetration and resort to the shock of infantry masses. Still the British line guarding the critical flank of the Mountain of Rheims—on which depended the French army of Champagne and, less directly, both Paris and Verdun—held against all attacks, while **Struggle for the** slowly wheeling back to conform with the **Mountain of Rheims** continuing recession of the French centre.

On May 31st the point of the German wedge flattened and spread eastward along the Marne to Verneuil, giving scope for an attack on the Mountain of Rheims. Guns in considerable number were brought forward, and on June 2nd there opened a fierce struggle, between Rheims and Verneuil, for the approaches to the mountain.

The Germans were then some twelve miles south of the line held by the army of Champagne, and some fifteen miles south of the Rheims salient. Between them and the rear of General Pétain's main forces was the Mountain of Rheims. Between them and the mountain were the survivors of the British divisions, many of whom had been fighting for eleven days and nights. The fresher French forces were not sufficiently numerous to hold the line.

The enemy commander attacked the French to prevent them reinforcing the British, and then poured his divisions of assault upon the islanders. The Allies gave ground, counter-charged, fell back again, and again surged forward. The line held. At the end of four days the remnants of the German divisions were re-formed and employed in a final action to prepare the way for a grand attack by fresh troops.

The Hill of Bligny, rising 600 feet, and commanding the course of the Ardre, was required by the enemy commander before he loosed his new forces. The Cheshires, after repulsing the enemy's first waves, were compelled to retire. They, however, returned with the Shropshires, and in an irresistible bayonet charge cleared the hill, opening ground beneath by which the Staffordshires, forming the right of the gallant 19th Division, were able to recover Bligny village.

This fine success proved decisive in regard to the position on the eastern side of the new Marne salient. General von Böhn did not continue his attempts against the Mountain of Rheims, but for more than a month attacked westward and northward in the hope of finding it easier to enlarge the salient in other directions. Throughout the first phase of what may be termed the Second Battle of **Paris organised** the Marne the position of the French centre, **for resistance** retiring to the river, was extraordinary. When the British divisions swung back and round Rheims, and the French force withdrew on the plateau below Soissons, only a hard-pressed covering line of a few thousand French troops, with less than a thousand British cyclists, connected the allied wings, across some twenty miles of notched ridges, through which the enemy was continually pushing in strength of a hundred thousand men.

The situation was calculated to test to the uttermost the character and qualities of General Foch. The French people at first could not believe their own crack regiments of Normans and Bretons had broken on the Chemin des Dames, and attributed the disaster to the war-worn British divisions. Enemy agents widely endeavoured to create bad feelings in the French against the British, using the false rumour with a view to provoking disorders similar to those which had occurred during the struggle along the Aisne in the spring of 1917.

Both from a military and a political point of view the outlook seemed grave. Once more Paris had to be organised for active defence as the great pivot of allied resistance. Measures were soon taken to safeguard, by removal, industries of vital importance, and place in security women, children, and old people already tried by the enemy's long-distance bombardment. The abrupt, gloomy change in the life of the capital told on the spirit of the population, but scarcely in the way the enemy expected.

Clemenceau's bitterest opponents, the Socialist Deputies, began to rally to the Government's Committee of Defence, and the people stood to the event in grim mood, strangely lightened by memories of the part Foch had played in the First Battle of the Marne.

As Foch's reserves arrived in strength he left a mere covering force along his broken centre, allowing the Germans to reach the Marne on May 30th. Thereby he gave up the main railway line connecting Paris directly with the army of Champagne, together with large quantities of shell and general material of war stored in the Tardenois region north of the Marne. General Gouraud, commanding in Champagne, had to be served with fleets of motor-lorries, and the railway that fed and munitioned Verdun was strained in maintaining an increased volume of supplies.

The Allied Commander-in-Chief was obliged to remain weak somewhere. He elected to fight with all power on his wings, and when the pressure of his troops there became strong, General von Böhn responded to it, and in turn neglected the central Marne front. Not until June 6th did the enemy attempt to force the passage of the river, and only a movement of reconnaissance was made by the men of a battalion, who were counter-attacked by French and American troops and driven back to the northern bank.

Germans reach the Marne again

The allied scheme of defence was based upon the Mountain of Rheims on the east and the Forest of Villers-Cotterets on the west, Compiègne Forest connecting the Villers-Cotterets positions with the woods below the Oise River line. In leafy spring-time the great western system of woodlands was the most perfect of military positions for either attack or defence. The forest trees and brushwood formed the best machine-gun positions, being easy to wire and naturally screened. Light covering forces could thus cushion the shock of charging masses and win time for the full power of the defence to act. Then, under the vast tent of foliage, armies could collect and appear in unexpected places, in spite of the activity of hostile reconnoitring aircraft.

The enemy at first had everything his own way in the air. In their first prolonged storming movement the German shock divisions reached the allied aerodromes and completely disorganised the local aerial service. Meanwhile, the unopposed, massed squadrons of flying Teutons, collected from the entire western front, made life a nightmare for the retreating Franco-British troops. All day foot, guns, horse, supply trains, and railway communications were machine-gunned and bombed, and every manœuvre of defence was detected. Night brought little relief. More German machines arrived, with a new device of a clockwork flare parachute, that illumined a wide circle of ground for two minutes, while the attacking and observing aeroplanes droned invisible against the clouded sky. The great depth of country which the French had to abandon, ridge after ridge, in their first retreat since September, 1914, was largely lost owing to the superiority the enemy exercised in the air as well on the earth.

Allied scheme of defence

German aerial predominance, however, was merely a transient, local matter. British and American pilots flew to the rescue, arriving with the large main forces of the French Air Service. Although by this time the enemy infantry and artillery had won many woods as cover, the German ways of communication were much restricted, and carried over rivers and streams. By bombing pontoons and stronger bridges, and swiftly carrying the allied counter-offensive in the air to the railway bases of the armies of assault the Franco-British-American squadrons did much to check both the direct advance of the invader and his violent efforts to widen the sides of the Marne salient.

BRITISH AIRMAN'S COUP FROM BEHIND THE CLOUDS.

Surprise attack on German troops paraded in the market-place of a battered town behind their lines. They had gathered for the purpose of listening to an exhortatory address from their general on the subject of moral. Suddenly from behind low clouds emerged a British airman with his large bombing aeroplane. He dropped his bombs on the massed troops, while his escorting machines followed up the attack by machine-gunning the confused crowd.

Between Soissons and Château-Thierry the struggle was more severe than it was on the Rheims and Ardre line. Ludendorff, after the defeat of Fritz von Below, gave the latter little further help from the grand reserve, but sent his fresh divisions to General von Böhn, who spent most of them around Soissons. On May 28th, by a series of fierce, costly actions, he won the high, broken ground at Condé, Vregny, and Terny, and, closing from the north and east, in the night, on the old city of many battles, captured it, in ferocious street fighting, on May 29th. The indomitable French recovered it by a magnificent counter-attack, against apparently overwhelming numbers. But Böhn wanted Soissons at any price, and, launching a great Brandenburg force, solidly occupied it.

There then followed a long sway of attack and counter-attack down the Soissons-Château-Thierry road, with the original French garrison of the Ailette line **Sway of attack** holding on to the hills immediately below **and counter-attack** the lost city, and strong reserves working eastward, while the diminishing troops of the cavalry division that had saved the line below the southern bank of the Aisne fought down to the Marne.

Even these last troops were in good heart, although General Foch was placing upon them the heaviest burden of the battle. Some of the men almost quarrelled for the right to sacrifice themselves in machine-gun rearguard actions. Others carried on when badly wounded, until they dropped from loss of blood and fatigue, bringing up ammunition after being disabled for fighting. The men did not, of course, understand why few reserves arrived in their sector, but in cold, personal anger they fought against the enemy's incessant mechanical pressure, using every art of fence, especially at Château-Thierry, the historic riverside town through which the heroes of Mons had swept when they turned in pursuit of the First German Army. American machine-gunners, ably helping by the Marne, marvelled at the French soldier.

On May 30th came the first French counter-attack that enabled Foch to hold on to the straight eastern highway between the Aisne and the Marne. Ludendorff answered it by extending his front of battle fifteen miles, and launching another army northward from the Aisne to the Oise. His movement, however, had been expected, and the northern French force had already begun to wheel back towards the Carlepont Wood just below Noyon and Choisy Hill, by the wooded outskirts of Laigue Forest, from which the new line ran, over hilly ground, towards the great Villers-Cotterets Forest.

By shortening his northern sector, between the Oise and the Aisne, General Foch saved men. While he was carrying out this operation the struggle increased in fury in the German salient. Fresh French forces made a superb leap forward between Soissons and Château-Thierry, driving the Germans over the Crise stream and up the Ourcq on May 31st. Ludendorff poured out more men, until there were fifty enemy divisions in action against the **Great struggle in** Franco - British - American forces. After **the German salient** trying to hold the Allies, by fierce, narrow thrusts from Noyon to Rheims, the German commander on June 2nd delivered the blow intended to shatter the defence.

He struck at Carlepont Wood and failed there. He took Choisy Hill and lost it five times, and left the French Colonials still holding this important key position. At the same time he sent his troops storming into Château-Thierry, and battered once more upon the British and French line by the Mountain of Rheims.

All these actions, though heavy and sustained, were designed to hold and test the forces that Foch had generally disposed along the front of battle. The enemy's grand blow was directed against the Villers-Cotterets Forest. It was anticipated. The French commander made all possible use of the foreground villages, such as Faverolles and Longport, shredding the enemy masses out there by artillery barrages and machine-gun fire, and then launching quick infantry counter-assaults under cover of closely-directed light gun fire.

The villages were recovered, and lost again at night. In the darkness the enemy hoped to equalise the conditions of attack and defence in forest fighting, and, bringing up at evening the last of his immediately available unused divisions, he entered for the second time in the campaign the deadly maze of Villers-Cotterets woodland and was trapped in it. The French returned to the covering line of machine-gun positions, accompanied southward by a United States force of fine quality that strenuously worked forward from Veuilly Wood towards Château-Thierry.

When the first phase of the Second Battle of the Marne ended the best part of half a million of picked enemy soldiers was enclosed in the Marne salient, with flanks more than thirty miles in length, and a centre from which it meant disaster to attempt to advance.

Only one shattered railway, under assailing gun fire, ran through the rough terrain, and the roads were few, the best being liable to be lost in a strong counter-offensive, as it was immediately in the German battle zone. Ludendorff was pre-eminent in the art of making awkward salients for his army commanders. Not content with the two he possessed by Amiens and Hazebrouck, he had made a third—and weakest—along the Marne.

One by one his illusions were falling from him. He had tested severely the young recruits of the British "home army," and found them full of the mettle of their race. He had also had a strong foretaste of the qualities of the armed manhood of the United States, which was rapidly building up an army of a million effectives in France, with little interruption from submarine attack. His exposed flanks, in unorganised country, beneath the Mountain of Rheims and along Villers-Cotterets Forest, taught him once again that General Foch was a master of strategy.

The only way in which the enemy commander could save his flanks was to continue to attack. He had to set a battle in movement on another front before the allied commander could gather men and material for a counter-offensive. Amiens no longer tempted him. Like Falkenhayn in the Battle of Verdun, Ludendorff was **Ludendorff's** bent on reducing the strength of the French **two courses** Army to the point of exhaustion. He reckoned that Foch had made a grave mistake in sending French forces to help the British armies, and that he could yet break through the French front. So long as his numbers and organisation for offensives in series enabled him to retain the initiative, he was, he thought, with his Staff and army commanders, secure against the dangers he ran round every salient he made.

He could not, however, leave the Marne salient as it remained. He saw he had limited his freedom of action, and that only two courses were open to him. Being compelled for his own safety to strike either immediately east or to the west of his line of advance from the Aisne, he arranged to thrust in both directions alternately.

Then it was, after months of patient resistance to the enemy's will, that the Allied Commander-in-Chief began to display the active side of his genius. Marshal Foch, who won his baton by the operations now described, made sound preparations to meet Ludendorff's moves.

He left his own fine army commanders, Generals Débeney and Humbert, along the Amiens salient to prepare, under Sir Douglas Haig, to take advantage of the enemy's weakness on the western line as soon as the occasion arose. In the south a new army commander appeared in circumstances that only M. Clemenceau's advent to power admitted. He was General Mangin, one of General Pétain's lieutenants at Verdun, the grimmest thruster in the French Army, and as skilful in fence as in thrust, who had been retired with General Nivelle in 1917.

With General Mangin, whose return to army command, first in the neighbourhood of Montdidier and then at Villers-Cotterets, was very significant, were General Berthelot, assistant to Marshal Joffre in the First Battle of the Marne, and General Degoutte, another commander of proved ability, with General Mestre, the former conqueror of the Aisne plateau, and General Fayolle.

British Food Ships under Naval and Aerial Escort
From a Water-colour by C. M. Padday

On the Champagne line was General Gouraud, distinguished by his defence of the Argonne Forest and his actions in the ravines of the Gallipoli Peninsula. He was aware of the storm that would break upon his front, and had a surprising method of defence in secret readiness. General Humbert, on the Noyon sector, was also prepared to receive Ludendorff's shock divisions, and upon him the first of the final strokes of the enemy fell.

At midnight on June 8th General von Hutier bombarded all the French line from Montdidier to the Thiescourt Hills, and with a host of a quarter of a million men endeavoured to remove both the Amiens and Marne salients by connecting them in a rapid advance on a front of twenty-two miles to Compiègne Forest and the Méry plateau. From the Méry position he could complete his work of the March offensive and definitely cut the Calais-Paris railway. From Compiègne Forest he could turn the Villers-Cotterets line, and with General von Böhn's armies move in a vast crescent towards Paris.

Very ambitious was the plan of the brother-in-law of Ludendorff, but the strength to execute it was lacking. The drain on the enemy's main reserve was at **Hutier attacks along the Matz** last beginning to tell, and in two ways. Many of his best troops were killed or maimed in his shock divisions, and his general numbers, though still exceeding those of the allied forces, were insufficient for his way of fighting. This was clearly seen in the conduct of the new battle by Hutier, the leader in the new tactics.

He began superbly by getting his men to creep down the valley of the Matz stream, below Lassigny, and make a surprising swoop on Gury Hill, on June 8th, before the pitched battle opened. Then, with tremendous gusts of poison-gas fire and high explosive, his gunners ploughed and drenched the river valley to a great depth, as they had done with the hollows held by the Ulstermen and Scotsmen around St. Quentin. The French troops gave ground to a depth of four miles. In the special circumstances this was the only answer to the enemy's overwhelming attack. Hutier then had a central corridor of advance, from which he had only to expand on both sides in order to turn the Méry plateau westward and the Thiescourt Hills eastward. But all the French commanders concerned—from **French Command's elastic defence** Marshal Foch, General Pétain, General Fayolle, General Humbert, down to the battalion commandants—had been expecting the grand struggle, and when the Matz valley surprise occurred knew when and how it would begin.

The defending forces were therefore arrayed in great depth, with a wide covering zone, held only by battalions on divisional fronts, but supported with a considerable number of quick-firers as well as infantry guns and machine-guns. There was no sentiment about losing guns or ground so long as the light cannon did their work. The French generals cared for nothing except saving the lives of their men, and artillery-men were disabused of the old idea that their guns were their colours. French munition factories, supplying the United States Army in addition to the French with artillery, could quickly replace lost guns. Only men were irreplaceable.

So France deliberately gave guns to the enemy as well as land. Hutier used his forces in massive thrusts, with the usual infiltrating detachments questing and testing the ground between them. Smoke screens divided the troops of the defence, while barrages of special shell rolled over them and their telephone lines. But Foch's lieutenants did not require

BRITISH TROOPS CLEARING THE BEATEN ENEMY OUT OF A CAPTURED WOOD.
Young German soldier coming up from a dug-out to surrender. The wooded districts in Champagne, in which machine-guns and earthworks were easily concealed, enormously increased the task of clearing lurking enemies out of captured ground. As a rule the defeated Germans showed no reluctance to surrender.

to be set the same problems in tactics twice in a fortnight. They had the solutions.

All along the line, from the valley below the Méry upland to the low ground by Renaud Hill, their gunners caught the German waves of assault in the rolling fire of "75's" and heavy guns. They furiously and skilfully counter-batteried the hostile parks of artillery with long-range pieces, made a general curtain of shell along the front with medium ordnance, and used the light quick-firers by hundreds in the covering zone as infantry guns.

There were about one hundred and forty thousand German troops of the shock-division class exposed to terrific gun fire at short range, with machine-guns playing through the shell tempest. They faltered on the wings of the battle-front below Noyon and below Montdidier, where even the French advanced posts held. By the edge of Méry plateau the post on the slope at Courcelles remained unconquered, though the swarming forces of attack worked at last around it. On Plémont Hill a dismounted cavalry battalion was overrun yet unshaken, and behind

HELP FOR A HARD-PRESSED LINE.
French troops passing through a town to reinforce their comrades who were holding up the advancing Germans. Such scenes were common along the front where the enemy struck southwards for Paris after his attempts on Amiens and the Channel ports had been brought to a standstill.

French rally on the Aronde — them the main wooded clumps of the Thiescourt Hills formed a battle rampart both against flanking forces spreading along the Matz valley and against the frontal divisions of attack. By nightfall Hutier had done little more than exploit his preliminary success on the Matz River by widening the corridor to the extent of four miles. This merely brought him to the opposing battle positions of a single divisional sector, at a price of his strength in men that left him weak when the crisis came. Using up more men, he increased his pressure throughout the night, and by extreme violence tried to achieve a decision the following day.

Crowding his men along the Matz valley and the Gury road, he broke through the centre battle zone at Marquéglise and drove the French to the Aronde River. It was a spectacular advance to a depth of ten miles, enabling Hutier to plan a rapid turning movement past Laigue Forest into Compiègne Forest. General Foch prepared for such a movement by ordering the army on the eastern side of the Oise River to withdraw from Choisy Hill and Carlepont Forest down to the outskirts of Laigue Forest. On the western side of the river the Thiescourt Hills and Dreslincourt heights were abandoned, and the line drawn down to the level of Laigue woodland.

This was done to economise the blood of France, by avoiding close fighting at Hutier's strongest point. But the German commander's new plan was completely spoilt. For in the meantime, by the Aronde stream, the French rallied magnificently, broke his men, and pursued them for some three miles.

This glorious recoil marked the turn of the tide in the affairs of the Grand Alliance. In numbers the French force was much inferior to the enemy masses it broke, and moreover, instead of being part of the general army of reserve, as Ludendorff stated in his daily report, it was formed of rallied troops and their last local supports. Foch and Fayolle were waiting until their men in action had worn a quarter of a million Germans down as low as possible before launching a force from the general reserve. This force was ready and close, but kept concealed. It would have been wasted by the Aronde on June 10th.

For some of the detachments in the covering zone were still distracting and enfeebling the enemy. On Plémont Hill the cavalry was fighting greatly, and after breaking fourteen assaults a remnant cut its way back. At Courcelles the advanced guard did not even attempt to escape. It fought with the enemy all round. It fought when it lost its position, counter-charging

WITH THE GUNS IN A FIGHTING RETREAT.
Removing a battery of French artillery before the advancing enemy. In some sectors of the battle area, during the enemy thrust for Paris, the French generals, for tactical reasons and to save irreplaceable lives, deliberately abandoned replaceable guns. This policy was adopted during the operations in the Matz valley.

SOLDIERS WHO FEARED NO SUPERIORITY OF NUMBERS.
French infantry passing through Ribécourt, Oise, after fighting against odds of three and four to one. Early in June, 1918, the Germans began a thrust for Compiègne with many fresh battalions, but met with invincible resistance, especially on their right in the direction of Ribécourt.

The depth of ground won was not remarkable. It covered only the lost strip of the Méry upland to the outskirts of St. Maur, Courcelles, and Le Frètoy, reaching a mile and a quarter in the centre. But the slaughter that took place on the edge of the great block of chalk was terrible. The new Tank had indicated what it could do, when the Australians recovered Villers-Bretonneux in the last week of the previous April. But where the British Tanks had dealt with men by the thousand, the French storming cars dealt with them by tens of thousands, shooting them and trampling them, while the grim French infantry and artillery worked behind and alongside.

Many of the Germans resisted bravely; many fled; but the number of prisoners taken — 1,000, with ten guns — gave, like the extent of the ground covered, no indication of the importance of the victory. The Tanks had to keep to the upland, for on the slopes facing the German artillery they would have come under controlled, massed fire. The victorious infantry had likewise to refrain from appearing in large targets under direct observation of enemy gunners. This limited the success in appearance, but not in effect.

forward, and recovering the ruins, instead of hacking its way back to its withdrawn battle-line on the western side of the Méry upland.

The men of Courcelles had their reward on June 11th. The sudden French retirement on Hutier's left prevented him from striking in force there immediately, as it was designed so to do. It further induced him, also according to General Foch's plan, to devote his attention to the Méry upland, on which he had won a footing and incurred a smarting check. The German commander, feverishly eager to use his remaining reserves with the utmost expedition, organised a terrific drive over the plateau.

That effect was at once visible. Hutier was put completely out of action. He made one demonstration against the Méry upland, which was checked by gun fire.

Then he stood still until August, 1918. The **Counter-offensive** general action around the delicate Marne **with mobile Tanks** salient was resumed, by means of a new thrust by General von Böhn, directed between the Aisne west of Soissons and the northern side of Villers-Cotterets Forest. It could be accepted as an attempt to turn the forest from the north, but it was rather a defence of the

He deployed his divisions each on a front of some 750 yards, which was about three times as close as the common German practice, and four times as dense as the French formation for shock effect. Upon his forces moving into action thus packed there fell the first great stroke of surprise that Ludendorff and his captains had reeled under since Sir Julian Byng showed how Tanks could be used at Cambrai.

The Tank was again the instrument of victory, but it was the car of assault of the new light, mobile model. On a front of seven and a half miles, from Rubescourt, south of Montdidier, to St. Maur, south-west of Lassigny, Foch's mass of manœuvre opened a counter-offensive instead of the routine counter-attack. Overlapping the oncoming enemy mass, and hiding itself in undulating ground until it topped the rise which the German advance parties were approaching, the first veritable army of the allied reserve paralysed and smashed the reinforced army of General von Eben, who was one of Hutier's best men. General Mangin was in command, and rode the enemy down with the new storming cars.

The French Tanks had a speed of seven and a half miles an hour, and were in large numbers, like mechanical cavalry, between the waves of infantry.

MEN WHO BORE THE BURDEN OF GREAT BATTLES.
Chasseurs d'Afrique, on their way back from action on the River Ailette, watching French infantry pass up to the firing-line in motor-lorries. French Colonial troops covered themselves with glory in some of the stiffest fighting of the war, as at Verdun and in the defensive battles from the Ailette to the Marne in 1918

communications from Soissons to the Marne line. The French commander replied by a counter-thrust, and while, for more than a month, little besides skirmishes and demonstrations occurred, matters slowly moved to the grand crisis.

Ludendorff had been staggered by the Méry action. He waited for General Foch to reveal his strength in some other sector, confident that he had preserved sufficient reserves to stand firm in his own battle positions. There were several weak sides to German salients, new and old, at which the allied commander could have struck with effect. But he saw no reason for using men up in attack and immobilising them. He could wait until the United States forces served completely to balance the total enemy forces in the west and allow a larger margin of manœuvring power. In the meantime, it was for Ludendorff to move.

The German commander tried to escape from his difficulties by inducing the Austrian High Command to open a grand offensive on the Italian front. He hoped it would result in a sudden call upon important divisions of Foch's army of reserve. But by the end of June it was clear that the Austro-Hungarian Army could not disturb the plan of operations which the captain of the Entente Powers was calmly pursuing. Italy was an increasing source of strength instead of a factor of weakness to her Allies, and Italian soldiers took over part of the French line by Rheims, as also did the United States troops.

Ludendorff had to attack or retreat. At the beginning of July the American troops nibbled at the corner of the Marne salient at Vaux; in the second week the First French Army

OBTAINING INFORMATION FROM THE ENEMY.
Italian officer interrogating a German prisoner on the western front. During June, 1918, Italian forces took over part of the allied line on the Rheims sector.

nibbled at the Amiens line at Cassel, while the very active Australians were developing important advantages they had won at Hamel and along the Somme. On July 15th the enemy Commander-in-Chief launched the last of his great offensives, with the remaining surplus of capital in man-power and material with which the Bolshevist dictators of Russia had provided him.

His front of attack extended for fifty miles, from Château-Thierry to the Champagne down known as the Hand of Massiges. On the Marne line General von Böhn endeavoured to reach in force across the river valley and carry the Mountain of Rheims. On the Champagne line General von Mudra, who succeeded Haeseler at Verdun in 1916, and General von Einem, who had long held the downland country, tried to break through the lines of General Gouraud, while Böhn turned his flank below Rheims.

The principal and frontal assault, by the reinforced army groups of Mudra and Einem was a disaster as complete and almost as swift as an earthquake. It cost Germany more than any action she had lost since Auerstädt. It was the new Auerstädt, of which, it seemed, the sequel of a new Jena was gradually to follow. General Gouraud won by a trick as simple in seeming as a throwing turn of the hand from an expert wrestler, and as difficult.

Absolutely unknown to the enemy, he drew back his line from the strong system of hills which had been slowly gained by his predecessors in the Champagne command by costly offensives. He abandoned the Moronvilliers heights, Auberive, Tahure Down, and the Hand of Massiges. He left only a thin screen of dauntless volunteers to deceive the enemy and

FRENCH STORMING CARS THAT SERVED AS MECHANICAL CAVALRY.
Small French Tanks of the "whippet" type passing a balloon on their way to the front. It was with such storming cars that General Mangin rode down the enemy in June, 1918, and recovered the strip of the Méry upland, when the turn of the tide began on the western front. These light French Tanks had a speed of seven and a half miles an hour, and were used in large numbers, like mechanical cavalry, between the waves of infantry.

check the forces of assault. His army fell back to Prunay, Prosnes, Souain, and Le Mesnil, with his guns covering all the ground evacuated.

The German bombardment was of marvellous intensity. The lost hills were searched most cleverly, and battered and stained with patterned explosions and torrents of poison. Having possessed the heights and originated the works upon them, the enemy knew where the resistance was likely to be strongest, and on these places he especially concentrated howitzers of every calibre. It was a happy escape for the army of Champagne, but from both a personal and military view the spectators were anxious for their forlorn advanced parties.

It looked as if none could survive Ludendorff's finale of artillery effects. He claimed to have taken more than a thousand guns from the French and British since the last week in May, and he certainly had captured hundreds, with a store of half a million shells. His complete tale of artillery, taken in battle or acquired through the comrades of Lenin and Trotsky, was staggering, and there had been time to replace breech-blocks and damaged parts of many captured

on the masses in movement. Then as the Germans, working apparently against ordinary opposition, reached their line of doom, parks of quick-firers raked them in front and curtained them in the rear, while a great, fixed howitzer barrage shut down between their lines and the original French positions.

Dislocated by the French machine-gunners in the advanced posts, the leading masses of a hundred thousand Germans withered under the unexpected shell fire which caught them when they thought they were standing victorious upon the main French line.

Hesitation and confusion over the bankruptcy of their programme of attack aggravated the dispiriting effects of their heavy losses. Tanks were employed in considerable numbers in the Villers-Bretonneux and Méry actions.

Enemy masses broken and routed

But in the early daylight of summer morning, on the broad zone of approach prepared by the French commander, the cumbersome machines of the old type could not avoid the fire of the forward guns of the defence.

So complete was the disorder in which the enemy masses were thrown that the French advance guards, in their thirty-foot caverns, often became encumbered with prisoners. Prisoners were also taken in the tunnels extending from General Gouraud's battle system. Shelter at any price was what the Germans sought when their Tanks were smashed around them and they themselves were broken and routed by the fire of the French guns and the machine-gun barrages of the defending troops. Only at Perthes and at Prunay, by the marsh of the Vesle, were the French battle positions reached in any force by remnants of the enemy masses. On the Moronvilliers ridge the French foreground block-houses, held by only two or three machine-gunners, broke the German waves of assault for two hours or more. At least one of these posts was holding

pieces. Yet not only did the main French forces, with their Italian and American contingents, suffer little loss, but the advanced guards lived through the heaviest of all bombardments.

When the German infantry cautiously came forward to explore, before the drives in mass were made, the French forlorn hopes produced a telling imitation of a broken army making a last defence. Some were quickly surrounded, and fought to the death; others managed to carry out the programme of a fighting step-by-step retirement, that gave the last touch of verisimilitude to the scheme of deception. Out into the open ground swarmed the shock divisions, numbering fifteen, with ten ordinary divisions behind them to carry on their work, and fifteen more in reserve.

Front-line French and allied observers reported the movements of the enemy by various means, while the heavy French artillery, that had been firing all night in counter-battery work and in disorganising whirlwind blasts on assembly places, settled more heavily

ITALY'S GUNS SENT TO THE AID OF FRANCE.

Italian artillery passing through a French town in which British soldiers were billeted, and (in oval) another view of the arrival of guns and gunners from Italy to aid in defeating the Germans in their attempt to reach Paris in the summer of 1918.

MEN WHO HAD FOUGHT SIDE BY SIDE.
British troops that took part in the French victory in Champagne in July, 1918, marching past General Berthelot.

initiative in attack to General Foch and the western armies of the Grand Alliance.

At first the tremendous importance of the victory of the army of Champagne was not discerned by the general mind. Its significance was largely a technical affair of staff calculations of enemy effectives remaining fit for immediate action, and of British and American reinforcements of untried troops, whose quality was still unknown to German Headquarters. General Foch and his lieutenants alone possessed full knowledge of all the elements of the situation, and while Ludendorff was still gambling on a victory on the French centre, the masterly Allied Commander-in-Chief prepared one of the greatest surprises in the campaign.

out at five o'clock in the evening after a struggle of more than twelve hours, as some of the British block-house parties did in the St. Quentin battle.

But the difference between the conduct of the actions by General Gouraud and Sir Hubert Gough showed what progress had been made in the art of defence against Ludendorff's new system of attack between March and July. General Gouraud was heavily outnumbered, there being a quarter of a million enemy effectives immediately deployed against his line; but when night fell the new wire entanglements he had secretly erected in front of his withdrawn positions were for long stretches littered with German corpses. At least fifty thousand Germans were killed or maimed out of a total deployed force of two hundred and fifty thousand. The French sappers had placed the new wire fields by the pine-woods on the Champagne downs, so that the fire of concealed machine-guns and field-guns converged upon the close formations with which the enemy endeavoured to carry the main French line.

Some of the slight dents in the French line were quickly straightened, and the French troops, amazed at the ease with which they had won a decisive victory of defence, ranking next in importance to the hard-fought First Battle of the Marne, cheered their commander when he reviewed them. From the cellars of Rheims, which they had saved, thousands of bottles of fine wine were provided to all the troops by the grateful vintners. The total French losses, including the men who voluntarily sacrificed themselves to hold the front-line positions, were remarkably light in comparison with the effects on the man-power of Germany. There was not a French division that needed to be relieved.

General Gouraud's decisive triumph

Ludendorff's mass of manœuvre, which British, French, and American troops had been grinding down since March 21st, was definitely and permanently weakened in the Battle of Champagne by the middle of July.

It had fallen to the happy lot of General Gouraud to deal the stroke that hamstrung the forces of Germany, throwing Ludendorff at last upon the defensive, and giving the

TRIBUTE FROM FRENCH TO BRITISH FIGHTERS.
General Berthelot shaking hands with General Godley when arriving to review British troops that had fought on the Marne and Vesle. Addressing them on behalf of the French Army, he said: "Your French comrades will always remember with emotion your splendid gallantry and your perfect fellowship in the fight."

General von Böhn was at the time co-operating with extraordinary energy with Generals von Einem and von Mudra. At great labour of an intense kind the conqueror of the Aisne plateau had organised an offensive along the Marne. The work was certainly carried out with a speed and power astonishing in the difficult circumstances. For in spite of his bad communications in the Marne salient, Böhn succeeded in bringing into action as many troops as Einem and Mudra handled. Probably the fact that half a million French shells had been captured in the great magazine between the Marne and the Vesle enabled the German army group commander to accelerate his final offensive by using the shells and the hundreds of French guns also taken since the March battles.

In the early morning of July 15th Böhn opened on the Marne front as stupendous a cannonade as his fellow-generals employed against the Champagne downland. Between Château-Thierry and the western slopes of the **Germans cross the Marne** Mountain of Rheims his massed guns dominated the broad, shallow valley of the Marne. The French and American advanced guards, while maintaining a strong resistance, fell back, and in light bridges and boats the Germans crossed the river and formed protecting bridge-heads, while many pontoon bridges were erected between Fossoy and Dormans.

The passage of the river was afterwards described by the

Germans as infernal. As in Champagne, the French battle-line had been withdrawn, and many of the light field-guns and all the machine-guns of the defence were concealed during the terrific artillery duel. They came into action only when the masses of German infantry were clearly visible behind the skirmishing, exploring lines of machine-gunners and sharpshooters.

General Berthelot, commanding along the Marne, had designed a subtler trap for the enemy than General Gouraud was working. He wanted the enemy to cross the Marne, and therefore met him there with a covering force of infantry and artillery, that gave ground during the course of the day to a depth of some three miles immediately west of the town of Epernay.

Epernay and Montmirail were the objectives Böhn expected to attain in the course of a day with his reorganised army of a quarter of a million men, and it might have been worth while to let him approach closer to the scenes of old French victories in view of the design that General Mestre, directing the three allied armies around the Marne salient, was working out.

Scarcely enough ground was offered the enemy as a bait, especially in the direction of Montmirail. Here the United States troops counter-attacked with great fury, driving the enemy back to the river. On the other hand General Foch and General Mestre had to play their game with extreme caution in the opening phase, and until they were absolutely certain that Gouraud's victory on the Champagne front was decisive they could not give Ludendorff another large opening nearer Paris for the employment of his divisions of reserve. There were in all some eighty-four enemy divisions either directly engaged in the offensive or ready to come into action—almost half the German forces in the west—as in the offensives against the Third and Fifth British Armies the previous March.

As soon, however, as the success of Gouraud's victory was appreciated Böhn was allowed, within limits, to develop the advantages he seemed to have won in forcing the passage of the Marne. He was checked on his wings by the vine-clad hills north of Condé and by the western slopes of the Mountain of Rheims ; but his central masses, consisting of eight divisions that had crossed the Marne and a similar force working above the river in the direction of the upland behind Rheims, won some six and a quarter miles of ground by the evening of July 16th.

The ground, however, was not really won. It was given. General Mestre and his lieutenant, General Berthelot, held the southern approaches to Epernay merely with the best retreating division in the French Army. It was formed of the hussars, dragoons, and other dismounted cavalrymen who had shielded the Irishmen, Scotsmen, and Englishmen of the Fifth Army in

the action around Roye and Montdidier in March, and broken the German offensive along the Avre, afterwards rearguarding between Fismes and the Marne the broken French centre in May and June. These most gallant and skilful dismounted horsemen were arrayed by Montvoisin to act in an elastic way and encourage the enemy while really holding him.

There was some danger to the Franco-Italian line below Rheims, but it was more apparent than real, as a splendid Scottish and English force was available as a reserve if urgently required. General Mestre, however, did not wish to use the British divisions in defensive work, and he therefore gave more ground for strategic purpose than he need have done under compulsion. In the result he accomplished one of the most remarkable congestions of enemy forces known in history.

Ludendorff, perturbed by the failure of the Champagne offensive and the equally decisive though veiled defeat of his Marne operations, misunderstood the general situation. Following his old course of shifting enormous masses against a weakening sector, he directed General von Mudra to cease action on the Champagne front and swing his remaining reserves westward of Rheims to co-operate with the eight divisions that Böhn had passed over the Marne. At the same time some ten picked **Carnage on the** divisions were borrowed from the armies of **Mountain of Rheims** the Crown Prince of Bavaria and transported with all speed to Laon, whence a railway ran over the Aisne plateau towards Missy.

While this fresh army from the north, brought up to the strength of fourteen divisions under General von Eben, was still on its way south, Mudra and Böhn made a tremendous combined effort to win the ground between Rheims and Château-Thierry, which Ludendorff required for the final attempt to carry Rheims and its mountain and Epernay, and drive deep upon the flank of General Gouraud's forces, while thrusting towards Paris.

There was terrible fighting on the slopes of the Mountain of Rheims, against which Mudra's troops poured along the valley of the Ardre. The Italians lost Pourcy, rallied, and recovered the village. Hill 265, forming the outer work of Epernay, was also lost and regained by the French, and all the allied line, including the important sector held by the American troops, swayed under the tremendous shock of extraordinary masses of German armies.

On the morning of July 18th some of the German troops were still fighting with the utmost violence on the Mountain

INVESTITURE OF FERDINAND FOCH WITH THE INSIGNIA OF MARSHAL OF FRANCE.
On August 23rd, 1918, President Poincaré (centre) accompanied by M. Clemenceau (on his right) attended at the Headquarters of Marshal Foch and presented him with the baton of a Marshal of France. **Above:** Marshal Foch wearing the seven stars on his sleeve, indicating his new dignity, and holding the baton.

of Rheims, more than thirty miles in direct line from their railway base by Missy, on the Aisne. In the Marne salient were at least thirty-three German divisions, with bad communications and in difficult country, exposed to continual aerial attack and long-range fire, and thrown along the fighting-front into considerable confusion and dismay by the massacring they had endured.

In the night there was a great thunderstorm, and the noise of it drowned the engines of the great counter-offensive that the allied commander was engaged in launching. General Mangin, who had conducted on the Méry upland below Montdidier the first important light Tank operations on the French side, had secretly been gathering a French, African, and American mass of manœuvre under cover of the Forests of Compiègne and Villers-Cotterets. With this army were Tanks in extraordinary number, the French Department of Munitions having established a standardised method of production, eclipsing that of the Ford Car Works in America. Tanks at the rate of a thousand a month were in course of production, and General Mangin was able to employ them against infantry as armoured knights had been used in the Middle Ages against unprotected pikemen. Below Mangin's army was another strong striking force of Frenchmen and Americans, under General Degoutte, who also had a large number of Tanks, including many British " whippets."

Mangin's counter-offensive launched

Covered by the thunderstorm and screened by the rain the two Franco-American armies completely surprised the enemy by breaking into General von Böhn's western defensive flank between the Aisne and the Marne. Böhn had expected a strong attack in this direction. It was the routine answer to his violent southern thrust. With the idea of making sure that his offensive operations would not be checked by a drive into his flank threatening the roads and the railway in his rear, the enemy commander had erected a double chain of hill fortresses from the plateau below Soissons to the heights around Château-Thierry. This front of twenty-seven miles was held by first-rate divisions aligned in great depth. But the weight and speed of the allied Tank assault, especially in the northern sectors, completely upset all the enemy's preparations.

General Mangin's army had the more important work and the greater striking power. No artillery preparation was made. When the troops advanced in the thunderstorm the French and American artillery used a rolling barrage, behind which Tanks, infantry, and cavalry rushed the German defences with staggering effect. On the northern edge of the new battlefield Paris Hill and the upland dominating Soissons were carried, and the outskirts of the city reached by exploring patrols. Vauxbuin was stormed, and below this important village the attack was pushed over the Soissons-Château-Thierry road to the Crise stream. An American division took Vierzy and made a further advance of three miles, cutting the neck of the German communications in the crowded Marne " pocket."

The allied success was of a most remarkable nature. In ordinary circumstances it would have brought about a decision. The German line was broken as far as Buzancy, and allied cavalry forces were working in the German rear some thirty miles behind the hostile fighting-front south of the Marne. The enemy's local reserves had in places to come into action without artillery, and were slaughtered by the Tanks and the accompanying cavalry.

Allied success below Soissons

Below the Ourcq River the Franco-American army of General Degoutte also drove beyond its objectives. The Americans took Torcy in forty minutes, reached beyond Belleau Wood, famous for an action in which the United States Marines had shown their high quality, conquered Givry, and progressed beyond it. There was a fine American charge through Cresnes Wood, and a magnificent feat of arms at Courchamps. The southernmost thrust, directed by General de Mitry, who had held the line along the Avre in the March offensive, after narrowly escaping a German cavalry patrol in the action around Roye, brought the United States force into a dominating position around Château-Thierry.

Above General de Mitry's forces the rest of Degoutte's army fought along the Ourcq towards Neuilly St. Front, threatening the centre of the enemy's communications at Oulchy. This part of the allied operations was, however, contributory to General Mangin's impetuous drive below Soissons. The southern army was farther away from the enemy's line of communications, and its fine success served the purpose of holding General von Böhn's troops and preventing them from hastening backward to meet Mangin's men. Similar fierce holding actions were opened by General Berthelot along the Marne and by the Mountain of Rheims, in the same design to check both Böhn and Mudra from moving troops back towards the gap by the Aisne.

Yet the gap was filled. Eben's new army came into action in the evening, and by close, desperate fighting with massed columns against the French and American advanced forces recovered some of the high ground about Buzancy, and cleared the Soissons-Château-Thierry road by a stubborn action on the Hartennes plateau and the ridge of Grand Rozoy.

At the end of the great German counter-attack the French, African, and American troops still held the heights by Soissons, together with the Chaudun plateau and the hill of Vierzy, with a series of important positions running down to the Ourcq River above Neuilly. Great in numbers as was the new German army suddenly interposed between the bankrupt forces of Hutier and the imperilled masses of Böhn, it was yet unable to rob Mangin's men of one of the most important victories in the war.

The advent of the new German army had not been unexpected, for Foch, Pétain, and the French Staff, were well aware that they had not yet exhausted completely Ludendorff's mass of manœuvre. All that had been hoped was that General Mangin might definitely consolidate himself on the conquered positions before the enemy's grand counter-attack opened. When it was clear that this could not be accomplished, General Mestre, working with General Fayolle and General Pétain under the Allied Commander-in-Chief, devised a more subtle, slower, and larger plan of action.

Ludendorff had only saved the armies of Böhn by sacrificing the new army of Eben, and bringing the number of German divisions in the Marne " pocket " to forty-nine or fifty. With the continual reinforcements received from the half-shattered and inactive enemy forces on the Champagne front there were about half a million Germans in the triangle of Soissons-Château-Thierry and Rheims. Some of these Germans were dead, some of them were wounded, and some had been lost by capture. Yet the remaining total of men of all arms and services still approached four hundred thousand, owing to the large reinforcements received from other parts of the western front. In direct line the distance between Soissons and Rheims was about forty miles, and the distance between Soissons and the southernmost point of the salient below the Marne was thirty miles.

400,000 Germans in Marne " pocket "

The organisation required to push four hundred thousand men into this angle of ridged and tortuous country, and provide them there with water, food, and ammunition, was tremendous. The Germans had made new roads across the valleys, and had profited by the routes constructed by the French for their Aisne offensive of 1917, but every road required several bridges and ran over exposed places, and the concentrated aerial forces of France, Great Britain, and the United States bombed by night and day everything visible between the Aisne and the Marne and Laon and the Aisne. The British Independent Air Force gave a respite to the Rhineland cities in order to co-operate in constant attacks upon the half-encircled German forces in the Marne salient.

In the meantime General Mangin's army was strengthened and General Berthelot was given fresh forces, and the struggle for the initiative between Foch and Ludendorff was resumed with a violence and persistence beyond all parallel. No doubt the total forces engaged were smaller than in some other great battles, for the fighting-line was shorter than in the First Battle of the Marne and in some of the actions in the eastern field of war. As a matter of fact the critical fight was concentrated on the two corner sectors by the Crise

Battery of 6 in. guns in action on the Montdidier section of the western front.

Shell bursting on Mont Renaud on the Noyon=Montdidier battle=front in March, 1918.

All that remained of the Church of Combles after the final repulse of the Hun.

Ruins of the Church at Lassigny when recovered by the French in 1918.

Grande Place, Péronne, twice occupied by and twice wrested from the invader.

French gunners on the march from Villers=Cotterets to the relief of Soissons.

French infantry in action outside a village near Noyon in the summer of 1918.

Battery of 75's in position near Montdidier during the great Battle for Amiens.

stream and the Ardre stream. Here General Foch supplied Mangin and Berthelot with the means of intensifying the struggle. In the south-eastern corner, where the Italian detachment was fighting resolutely in defence of the Rheims-Epernay road, after a withdrawal from Bligny Hill, British reinforcements arrived on the evening of July 19th.

The British force had been despatched in haste to take part in the Battle for Paris. When it arrived Paris was secure and the German north-western flank driven in. The French commander at once launched the Scotsmen and English on the north-eastern flank of the enemy, just below Rheims. Passing through the gallant, weary Italians, who had destroyed an entire German division and severely handled several others, the British made a menacing thrust towards the Rheims-Dormans road. On a front of some seven miles they struck along the Ardre River valley at Marfaux, won it, lost it, then partly regained it, and captured Courton Wood.

Strong German forces from the Champagne army fiercely reacted from the Bligny plateau and checked the British left, but the British centre and right fought onward with majestic power. Against an enemy entrenched with an extraordinary quantity of machine-guns on dominating high ground the Highlanders and Yorkshiremen fiercely and skilfully worked, winning St. Euphraise village and Bouilly across the Rheims road, and approaching the main German route of communications running from Fismes and the Ardre valley to Dormans and the Marne front.

On the night of July 19th, as soon as the British pressure was felt in the Ardre valley, the Germans, for the second time in the war, began a rapid retreat across the Marne. Both these retreats were directly effected by the unexpected pressure of the British forces. Böhn and Eben were acting by the Ourcq as Kluck had acted against Maunoury and Franchet d'Espérey, answering the sudden French flank by a terrific counter-attack, while maintaining the struggle on their front.

The German Staff had miscalculated the British reserve strength in men, just as the same Staff, under Moltke, had miscalculated the personal endurance of the British soldier. When it was evident that Sir Douglas Haig was strong enough to despatch some of his best fighting men from local reserve to the Rheims line, the enemy Commander-in-Chief at once ceased his desperate attempts to storm the Mountain of Rheims and to maintain his initiative in attack by a flanking assault against the Fourth French Army in Champagne.

Turning point of the war

The unexpected British movement completely brought to an end the vast scheme of operations which the enemy had begun in March. By an historic coincidence the Scottish Highland Territorial Division, which had met and checked the enemy's first grand attack on March 21st, helped gallantly to deliver the stroke which on July 19th definitely and finally changed the complexion of the war by throwing the enemy entirely upon the defensive.

Ludendorff's forces, however, were still very numerous. In effectives he retained a certain superiority, though much less than that with which he had endeavoured to achieve a decision. His troops were strong in body yet growing weak in spirit, resembling in this respect the forces with which Helmuth von Moltke, after the retreat from the Marne, endeavoured to turn the allied flank by the sea. The enemy commander never thought at the time that he had lost the initiative, and his organs of opinion in the German Press proclaimed that his armies were merely retiring on a shorter line in order to be able to strike another smashing blow upon the allied front.

It was not until September that the representative of the German Ministry of War candidly explained, in Main Committee of the Reichstag, that the offensive operations on both sides of Rheims had failed through the foresight of Foch, Pétain, and their lieutenants. The statement ran:

From the situation as a whole we were entitled to calculate that our offensive operations on both sides of Rheims would lead to success. The decisive factor was to have been surprise, and our preparations were made accordingly. The surprise did not succeed. Our intentions were known to the enemy. He was able to devise his counter-measures, and he devised them well.

Absurd, however, was the suggestion of the Germans that they lost this decisive battle through information given by some of their soldiers captured in a raid on July 14th. Not from such belated and uncertain sources of knowledge was the mighty instrument of counter-offensive mounted in readiness. General Gouraud had prepared since March for an assault on his army. The movements of the first French mass of manœuvre from the Méry plateau in June to Villers-Cotterets Forest early in July was largely due to the initiative displayed by General Fayolle. Then, on July 12th, three days before the final German operations began, the French army commanders round the Marne "pocket," with their immediate director, General Mestre, and General Fayolle as adviser, elaborated the details of the plan of action which was followed. The plan was immediately sent to General Foch for his approval, and quickly returned approved by his assistant General Weygand. The attempted German surprise was therefore no surprise at all. It was foreseen, overreached, and transformed into an opportunity for a counter-offensive some days before the battle commenced.

Victory due to French foresight

The only unexpected element that entered into the situation was the new German army under General von Eben. This was obtained largely from reserves on the British front, where General von der Marwitz drew back from Albert to get a stronger line and save men; while General von Hutier withdrew under pressure from some of the low land by Amiens to protect himself by watery ground from another Tank surprise.

At the time the enemy expected the opening of a Franco-British offensive around Amiens and Albert, and the troops of General Rawlinson and General Debeney strongly demonstrated by a series of fierce front-line attacks. These had the effect of holding the forces of Marwitz and Hutier, while the proper answer to the creation of Eben's army was made by sending more British forces southward towards the Aisne. When the retreat of Böhn's divisions across the river of many victories was discerned on July 20th, the French army commanders and their chiefs, Mestre, Fayolle, Pétain, and Foch, all acting together like a band of brothers, made a new plan of operations.

It may be admitted that it was a plan that failed if regarded from one point of view. Yet from the Allies' general standpoint it created the chain of successes of unparalleled magnitude. The plan was to envelop Böhn's armies, during the confusion of their retreat, by pressing the British counter-attack up the Ardre valley and resuming the French advance under General Mangin between the Aisne and the Ourcq. In incessant, terrific fighting the French and British forces, by the bases of the enemy's salient, tried to reach the communications of some four hundred thousand Germans, while the French and American forces on the southern line below the Ourcq and below the Marne pressed upon the enemy's receding rear in continual woodland actions against machine-gunners and other rearguarding forces.

The affair was rather a test of the enemy's nerve than a scientific attempt at envelopment. The Franco-British-American forces were not only inferior in number to the enemy but also in advantages of position. Their strategic direction was magnificent and it alarmed the German leaders, but the tactical opportunities were not great. General von Böhn was the Teutonic expert in the art of retreating, and he had lost none of his coolness and skill. His flanks were threatened chiefly from the Bligny plateau by the Ardre, already famous in the annals of the Cheshire Regiment, and from the Hartennes upland and the Grand Rozoy ridge between Soissons and Oulchy. Böhn met these threats when he turned his front into his rear by sending the divisions he retired from the Marne towards Bligny and Hartennes. He turned his withdrawing front into a source of strong reinforcement for his menaced flanks.

Böhn's skilful fighting retreat

The result was that, although the Scotsmen and Englishmen in the Ardre valley continued to thrust forward at the top of their skill, endurance, and general fighting power, winning high admiration from their French comrades, they could not make any decisive gain of ground against the stream of German divisions that moved backward to meet them. With the gallant French Colonial force on their right that drove into Vrigny they fought through Rheims Wood towards the German line of communications by Ville-en-Tardenois. But the Germans held until their troops in the south arrived roughly in line with them.

This action, however, helped to expose Böhn's other flank to successful attack by drawing north-eastward large masses of the retreating enemy. Hard had been the fighting around Oulchy-le-Château by the Ourcq heights, where the wings of the armies of Generals Mangin and Degoutte had been checked even in the surprise offensive of July 18th. On the Hartennes plateau the enemy forces had the cover of a wooded height with a deadly field of fire in every direction. South of Hartennes the landscape changed in character, being crossed by the great ridge of the Grand Rozoy, running from west to east at a height of some six hundred and fifty feet, and in clear weather dominating the whole region between the Aisne and the Ourcq. On these heights the Germans had long slopes of open country running down to the French lines, and behind them were the solid positions of the Tardenois hills.

Enemy stand upon the hills

It was the design of General von Böhn to hold the western tableland and ridge, together with the Tardenois hills, in order to safeguard Soissons and the new German battle positions on the heights around Fismes.

There was an enormous accumulation of shell and other material in the Tardenois, and the German commander required some weeks of reorganisation work to get his new line into order. His railway over the Aisne at Missy was under the fire of long-ranged French guns and subjected to constant aerial attack, which together made it very difficult to shift backward the great material of war collected for an advance on Paris. The German forces in Champagne again helped in holding the Ardre valley against the British and French thrusts, but the task of defending the upland flank of the central Tardenois hill positions became increasingly difficult.

As the Germans retreated over the Marne the Franco-American forces closed round Château-Thierry, entering the town on July 21st, and advancing towards Fère and Oulchy by a southern flanking movement through La Croix, Rocourt, and Epieds on July 22nd and 23rd. North of the Ourcq the outskirts of Oulchy were reached and the Soissons road crossed in a swaying battle of thrust and counter-thrust.

Allies capture Chateau-Thierry

The Germans held strongly to the heights above Oulchy, but the French and Americans widened their ground below the village, after losing Epieds and recovering it. They broke through the enemy's rearguards on July 24th, and swept ahead for two miles, taking Oulchy the next day, and working deeply into the Forest of Fère and Riz Wood below it. At the same time the Villemontoire positions were carried, some seven miles north of Oulchy, after a week's fighting, by General Mangin's army.

There then remained only the seven-mile block of high land formed by the Hartennes upland, the Grand Rozoy ridge, and the Beugneux height between Mangin's army and the German centre. This clump of commanding ramparts had, however, become more a formidable obstacle than it had been on the first day of the Franco-American offensive. After a week of continual battle between the army of General Mangin and the armies of Böhn and Eben, the enemy tested and strengthened

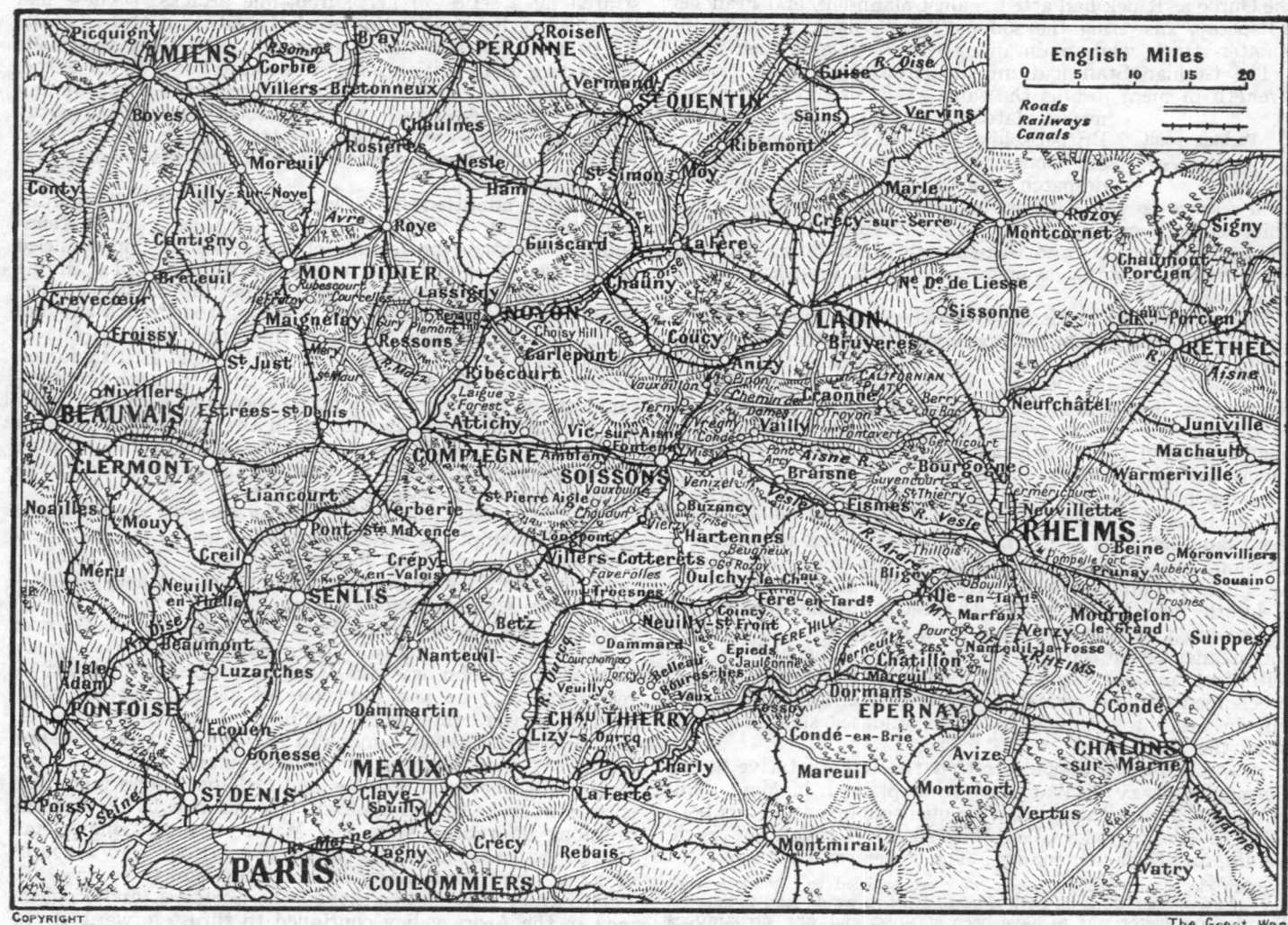

MAP OF THE COUNTRY OVER WHICH THE GERMANS THRUST TOWARDS PARIS IN 1918.
Within the triangle—Compiègne, Rheims, Château-Thierry—the enemy advanced towards the French capital in his attempt of July, 1918. A considerable force of Germans even crossed the Marne, but when the allied counter-offensive began they were driven back across that river as in 1914.

his high positions, and sited behind and upon the ridge and connecting heights the artillery withdrawn from the Château-Thierry sector of the Marne "pocket." There was indeed a treble reinforcement of the Hartennes-Grand Rozoy positions. Böhn's original holding forces were first increased by the arrival of Eben's army, and then enormously augmented by the foot and guns retiring from the southern battle.

This was the reason why Böhn considered he had definitely stopped the Franco-American advance on his flank. On July 27th he drew in all his front from the north bank of the Marne, by Dormans and Chatillon, and stood to action on the Grand Rozoy ridge, the Fère hills, and the wooded heights south-west of Rheims. Then it was that another British force was interposed on the critical Soissons flank line with magnificent results.

The 15th Scottish Division was attached to General Mangin's army and placed on the left of the 17th French Division north of Oulchy. The Scotsmen entered the struggle on July 28th, and acted as flank guard while the fine French force carried the Butte de Chalmont, a high, coverless hill immediately above Oulchy. On July 29th it was the turn of the High-landers and Lowlanders to make the principal assault, with the French division guarding their flank. The Scots had crossed the Soissons road from the hollow of Le Plessier-Huleu, and in front of them was the ridge of Grand Rozoy. Above them the Germans were waiting, as on a balcony, with machine-guns bearing down the inclines, and gunnery observation officers watching for signs of movement. The British soldiers, under heavy bombardment, fought through the woods beyond the Soissons road, and stormed the flaming ruins of Grand Rozoy village. The 17th French Division came into action on the right of the ridge, and carried a farm, but could not reach the crest by Beugneux. The Germans held the high line in strength, and were resolved to make it a stronghold.

In the afternoon, however, the Scotsmen opened another storming attack that filled their comrades with admiration. Over absolutely open ground, gradually rising to the German ridge positions, they went upward, with the German guns playing on the village in their rear and thundering in black smoke on their path, while cross-firing defending machine-gun barrages were directed down upon them. Yet they worked upward to the shelter of some woods, and extended to the high ground above. Clinging to this position in the evening, while the French troops supported them, and Tanks and artillery came up the ridge, they advanced

The 15th Scottish Division's triumph again on August 1st, driving for two miles through the enemy's strongest positions above Fère-en-Tardenois. A monument erected by the 17th French Division to the 15th Scottish Division now stands on the historic height.

In direct consequence of the Scottish victory, General von Böhn abandoned all the Soissons-Grand Rozoy line and the country behind it. French Chasseurs entered Soissons, and other allied forces crossed the Crise stream, while the Franco-American centre advanced through the Fère hills. The fortified heights of the Upper Ardre valley were occupied, and Thillois was recovered by the outskirts of Rheims. The allied movement was continued along the Aisne to Venizel, where the plums had been dangling ripe when the 2nd British Division passed through in September, 1914. There were no orchards left in Venizel in August, 1918, but the fruits of victory were gathered there, after men had been fighting in tens of millions against each other for four age-long years.

Fismes was carried by storm by the impetuous troops of

THE ENEMY HOIST WITH HIS OWN PETARD.
An incident in the fighting on the western front in the summer of 1918. British gunners turning a captured gun around so that they could fire the weapon at the enemy who had been forced to abandon it, and with it a goodly supply of shell.

the United States, who took 8,400 prisoners and 133 guns in the course of the operations, the total allied gains amounting to 34,000 prisoners and more than 400 guns. But the usual proportion between the men taken from an enemy and his general losses did not obtain. The French army in Champagne had taken few prisoners, yet had inflicted crippling injury upon two German army groups. Again, in the long, close struggle by the Mountain of Rheims, many hostile divisions had been ground to skeleton forces by General Berthelot's army, that yet took only two thousand prisoners.

Ludendorff's aggressive strength was exhausted. The renewed striking power won by three years' operations in the east had been spent in the west in four months. Even the picked German forces were so weakened by disappointments, as well as by casualties, that their commander could no longer rely upon them to endure in attack.

Hindenburg had again to be brought forward, by press-agent methods, as captain for a defensive war. The Hindenburg systems, with their half-forgotten Wagnerian names, were advertised in more **Ludendorff returns** detail than in the spring of 1917, with a **to the defensive** view to staying the decay of the spirit of the German people, appalled by losses and embittered by frustrated hopes. Ludendorff did not go the way of Helmuth von Moltke and Erich von Falkenhayn because there was no brilliant successor available, and his disgrace would, as a patent confession of defeat, have further tended to the demoralisation of the Germans and to the immediate loosening of some at least of the Middle Europe alliances.

The retirement of Ludendorff could not in itself have produced any great change. The armies were directed by

"THE LION OF THE ARGONNE" ADDRESSING HIS TROOPS.
The French army of Champagne, under General Gouraud, held steady east of Rheims when the Germans thrust downwards to the Marne. With confident prophecy, when that thrust first threatened, the general had finely said, "You will break the assault, and it will be a great day."

men of his choice, mainly eastern commanders, and the governing class of the country, whom he represented, remained content with his ability in a defensive war of attrition. The ruling class of Germany and General von Ludendorff reckoned that their recent misfortunes merely proved that, under fairly equal conditions of effectives and armament, defence was better than attack.

By returning to the defensive system of 1917, which Hindenburg favoured, Ludendorff still confidently hoped to wear the Grand Alliance down to acceptance of a peace by negotiation, by which Germany could obtain large direct and indirect gains in the east more than com-

German hopes in the east

pensating her for any adjustments in the west. Great efforts in corn-growing, oil production, and mining were being made in the border States of Russia, and the gradual Germanic reorganisation of Russia, under friendly, practical successors to the Bolshevists, was an important part of the enemy's new scheme.

India was to be menaced from the Transcaspian Railway, and a submarine base for Atlantic operations established northward in a Teutonic kingdom of Finland.

While elaborating, in early Napoleonic fashion, the romantic design of recovering from adventures in the east the power lost in the west, Ludendorff

was startled into an appreciation of his immediate peril in the main theatre of war by a new offensive launched by General Foch from Amiens during an artillery duel along the Vesle River. The Allied Commander-in-Chief gave his opponent little time for day-dreaming and less for thinking.

Before General von Böhn could with any confidence report that the divisions released by the shortening of his line along the Aisne and Vesle would not be at once required in another great battle between Soissons and Rheims, two other principal German armies were reeling along the Somme, broken and in disorder.

By this time, however, the situation in France had been strongly influenced by a happy turn of the war in Italy, and with the delivery of the Austro-German offensive there on June 13th, that terminated nine days later in the Allies' great victory of the Piave, we must first deal before proceeding to relate the triumphant progress of allied arms in the field in which a complete decision at last seemed attainable.

VICTORIOUS AT VERDUN AND ON THE MARNE.
General Mangin, who outgeneralled and outfought General von Böhn, the directing force in the Crown Prince's army on the Soissons-Marne sector of the front. He had previously played a principal part in the discomfiture of the Crown Prince at Verdun.

General Berthelot, commander of the Fifth French Army that repulsed General von Below in the Marne-Rheims sector of the western front.

General Debeney, commander of the First French Army under Haig's direction in the advance east and south-east of Amiens.

General Degoutte, who served with General Mangin in the successful operations against General von Böhn between the Marne and Soissons.

THREE FRENCH GENERALS WHO DROVE THE HUNS AWAY FROM RHEIMS, AMIENS, AND SOISSONS.

THE GREAT WORK OF SALVING WAR MATERIAL.

By Edward Wright.

British Necessity the Mother of British Economy—Why the Engineers Wanted Jam-Pots—Little War Charity that Grew into Great Government Repair Works—Strategic Importance of the Boot Sole—Saving a Hundred and Fifty Thousand Pairs of Boots a Week—Gun Hospitals and Convalescent Homes for Motor-Lorries—Teutonic Thoroughness in Scavenging—Fighting the British Blockade by Rag and Bone Merchantry—Ghastly Climax of Corpse Utilisation Factories—Increasing Pressure of the Submarine Blockade of Britain—Connection between Army Cooks' Fat-Box and Supply of Cordite—Mr. Andrew Weir Hustles the Army into Intensive Salvage—Strange Advertisement Campaign in the War Zone—Soldiers become Enthusiastic Salvagers—"Two Little Round Hats" and a Company Dump—Grand National Problem of the Tin Can—Marvellous Work in Salvage Aerodromes—Ford System of Turning Broken Motor-Lorries into New Vehicles—How the British Salvage System Was Affected by the Enemy Offensive—Permanent Results of Campaign for Economy—Winning Victory by Maximum of Output and Minimum of Waste.

NOTHING in the world is so spendthrift as an army. After being trained in economy in peace time, by quartermaster-sergeants presiding over stores with a maximum of red-tape routine, an army on the field of battle is forced into the wildest wastefulness.

When two men are busy fighting each other one does not stop to pick up a button or a penny. Both often throw off their coats and waistcoats in order to free their limbs for the work of combat. So it is with armies. Some Treasuries and Parliaments starve their military forces in peace time, but for every penny then saved taxpayers have to pay pounds after the outbreak of hostilities. There was no thought of salvage during the first period of the war, when the armies were manœuvring against each other and trying at all costs rapidly to achieve a decision. Everything was sacrificed to quickness in the delivery of the blows. The first phase of the battle in the west concluded with the contending forces impotently gazing at each other, in December, 1914, with munitions on both sides almost exhausted, and the ground over which they had struggled littered with the things they wanted.

The British Army was the first to start collecting waste material, for the reason that it was less well equipped than the German Army. British sappers opened up a branch of the rag-pickers' trade by displaying an intense interest in empty jam-jars, bully-beef tins, and sardine-boxes. The troops lacked hand-bombs, and the Royal Engineers had to improvise out of empty jars and tins short-range

WAYSIDE ECONOMY IN THE WAR ZONE.
Roadside advice on the British lines in France. The picking up of nails was doubly important in that, while they might prove of service again, if left on the roads they caused trouble to both horse and motor transport.

high-explosive missiles that could be pitched into the German trenches.

The penury of material transformed the last of the heroic British Regulars into the best exponents of the art of salvage the world had seen since the days of Hannibal. Hannibal, it will be remembered, was starved of military supplies by the senators of Carthage. Trying to save pence, they did not merely lose pounds—they lost Carthage and the empire of the world.

In the British Army hundreds of thousands of recruits worked for months in civilian clothes and trained with imaginary rifles because of the shortage of both khaki and Lee-Enfields. Even among the ragged, wet, vermin-infested men in the ditches around Ypres there was not sufficient clothing, as new uniforms did not arrive as quickly and as abundantly as might have been expected from the country with the largest wool-weaving industry in the world.

But two wounded British officers, unfit for further active service, had the happy idea of helping the forces in the field and finding work for refugee women by opening a repairing shop in France. They began by gathering a few seamstresses together and collecting badly-torn uniforms, and they developed their establishment into a splendid salvage organisation that helped the khaki mills, and also served to inspire salvage work on a large scale in other directions.

Although it does not seem to have been clearly known at the time, the saving of soldiers' clothes often meant the saving of his health. He needed frequent and complete change of underclothes

IN A REPAIRING SHOP.
Mechanics of the Royal Air Force repairing the fabric of a damaged British Experimental aeroplane.

STUDYING ENEMY AEROPLANE CONSTRUCTION.
British officer in the R.A.F. examining the broken wing of a Gotha bombing aeroplane, which had been brought down during one of the German air raids on England in 1918.

and uniform to free him from vermin-carried trench fever and other diseases. It took some years for men of science to trace trench fever to body vermin, and devise changes of impregnated clothing for the troops; but the salvage work begun as a little war charity in the first months of the struggle was the base of all that followed.

Boots were even more important than clothes. After less than a fortnight of fighting, Sir John French's men were in desperate need of boots. When trench warfare settled in its long course, many regimental officers either started repairing shops of their own or engaged contractors to keep the battalion well shod. The boot, however, was too important a thing to be left to individual officers. On it depended the marching power of the Army, and for this reason it engaged the concern of the Commander-in-Chief, who in June, 1915, appointed Major-General Sir John Steevens, the Army salvage expert, to organise large central repair shops.

One was opened in Calais in the autumn of 1915, another was founded at Mudros during the Gallipoli operations, and afterwards removed to Salonika. Later a shop was erected at Alexandria for the army of Palestine; while the army of Mesopotamia had its boots repaired at Basra. Other works were organised in England and Scotland, and these, with the Calais shop, were at last saving 150,000 pairs of boots each week.

Instead of the Army having to purchase new boots at the rate of a quarter of a million pairs a week, only 100,000 were required. Large as was the economy in money, this was of secondary importance. The great thing **Saving of the** was the saving in the stock of available **leather reserve** leather, upon which all the Allies constantly needed largely to draw. Moreover, the British manufacturing plant for Army boot-making, when partly released from service for the New Army, was able to work for millions of allied troops.

By the summer of 1918, when the United States Army was attaining enormous size, most of the civilian population of the British Isles would have been wearing wooden soles and canvas uppers if the military forces had not been exercising for three years remarkable care and organising capacity in turning old boots into new, and also providing repaired Army boots for farm-hands and other workers.

Another general advantage was derived from the working of the Command Repair Boot-shops. As doctors in a hospital discover from the study of disease how illness can be prevented, so the military boot salvagers, through whose hands millions of outworn pairs passed, were able to study ways of making boots with a longer life than any footwear possessed when the war broke out. They designed new technical details of construction, and experimented with linings and other material, until by 1918 the British Army boot was becoming as near perfection as thousands of practical critics could make it. The men worked in teams of five, receiving ordinary pay up to thirty pairs of boots a day, and a bonus, shared among them, on all boots repaired over that number. Under this scheme each man increased his power of work, turning out nine hundred pairs of boots a year more than before.

The repair of guns was taken up about the same time as the repair of boots. In the matter of artillery the British Expeditionary Force was so completely overwhelmed by the enemy that necessity again became the mother of economy. Too much time had been lost by sending slightly damaged guns back to England for repair, so the army in France and Flanders did all it could to save time and transport. Works were erected there at which small repairs could be effected. Then larger plant was obtained and special workmen were taken over the Channel, until the artillery repairing establishments became a great help, not only to the Army but to the hard-pressed and imperilled steamers for which more cargo was waiting than could be transported.

Repair shops for motor-vehicles formed another early branch of salvage work. Even when a chassis was completely smashed up the engine was useful, and those handy men of the Army, the Royal Engineers, whose jobs became immense in number as well **Repair shops for** as in scope, could find good ways to use **guns and motors** many things that seemed no longer serviceable. The Engineers "fagged" for the Army, mended for it, and invented for it, and did most of the early salvage work.

When, however, the new British armies arrived in the field in the summer of 1916, with a startling abundance of war material provided by the new Ministry of Munitions, the general spirit of economy rather diminished. In clothing, boots, and a few other articles that quartermaster-sergeants could control, the saving system was maintained and developed. Systems of repairing firearms, guns, and motor-vehicles were also extended. In other directions the waste far surpassed that which had occurred during the early battles of manœuvre in the open field. A remarkable proportion of bad material, due partly to the inexperience of the new munition-makers, was the principal cause of waste.

In the summer of 1916 the Germans were the grand exemplars of the new art of combining battle operations with the rag-pickers' business. Under the pressure of the partial naval blockade maintained by British ships the Germans began to develop the idea of salvage to its fullest extent. They applied it to the armies in the field, and to civil populations at home and in occupied territories, directing their

Damaged aeroplane being lifted off the lorry that had taken it to an R.A.F. "hospital," and (left) removing the engine of a damaged machine for examination.

Assembling an aeroplane that had undergone repairs, and (left) testing an engine that had been salved from a damaged machine. Far behind the lines there were salvage aerodromes to which broken machines were conveyed for repairs or utilisation of intact parts.

Removing engine from a damaged aeroplane for examination and the carrying out of any repairs that might have become necessary, and (right) testing an engine that had been taken from a damaged machine to discover the extent of its injury.

BROKEN WINGS MADE WHOLE: WORK AT A ROYAL AIR FORCE "HOSPITAL" IN FRANCE.

activities to the recovery of metals, clothing material, and foods and fats.

Articles of lead, tin, copper, aluminium, and other valuable metals were gathered by house-to-house collections. Damaged machinery was broken up, and even good machinery was taken to pieces, so that parts made out of rare metal might be replaced by parts made out of common metal. Millions of empty tins were carefully collected and sent to Essen and other centres for the tin to be extracted by chemical processes. Old tins were also collected in neutral countries adjoining Germany, and brought over the frontier to the tin-extracting works.

All clothing supplies were controlled by the German Government. Outworn woollen material had to be given to the authorities, and mattresses containing woollen or cotton stuffings were commandeered, and returned to their owners stuffed with paper, seaweed, or shavings. The small German stocks of leather were rigorously conserved for Army purposes, and substitutes were devised for industrial and civilian use. The skins of dogs and rabbits were tanned, fibres were woven from nettles and wood pulp, and prolonged and intense experiments were conducted in the hope of finding practical substitutes for sole leather and rubber.

Ludendorff, Hindenburg, and Mackensen were, however, the best of German salvagers. On each occasion when they forced the Russian and Rumanian forces back they made a rapid yet careful collection of all cloth and leather articles, in either good or bad condition, and despatched this valuable spoil to special salvage depots. The rubber, copper, linen, and canvas which the eastern Allies left when they retreated were also gathered by the careful Teutons, who likewise managed to acquire some copper-mines in the course of their offensive in the east.

At home they arranged a systematic collection of fruit kernels, from which oil could be extracted, and began that strange and apparently ridiculous quest for fat at which the Allies ceased to laugh when they, too, found that fat was one of the grand problems of the war. The Teuton started with extracting fat from his horses and mules that fell on the battlefield or died of overwork or disease behind the front. He also collected fat in his Army and municipal kitchens, for fat was the raw material of nitroglycerine, which in turn was the explosive element in modern gunpowder.

Enormous quantities of fat were also necessary for making lubricating oil to save machinery and rolling-stock from wearing out. At the same time fat was **Fat essential in modern warfare** needed as human fuel in the hard winter weather of northern Europe, and as through lack of fodder the Germans had been compelled greatly to reduce the number of their pigs, they were at last hard put to it to obtain the fat they required. In their extremity, before the conquest of Rumania and the practical subjection of Russia opened new sources of supply to them, they endeavoured to develop their Corpse Utilisation Works into human fat extraction works.

At first they took a sinister pride in this dreadful exhibition of Teutonic thoroughness in salvage processes. One of the German authorities in China is said to have told the President of the Chinese Republic of the establishment of the Corpse Utilisation Factory, by means of which nothing on the battlefield was allowed to go to waste. One of the most distinguished

of German war correspondents on the western front referred in gratified tone to the factories, and a German Army Order was found, as already related in Chapter CCI. (Vol. 10, page 198), dealing with the supply of corpses and carcases for fat extraction. Only when the universal expression of amazed indignation echoed over Germany was an attempt made to conceal the later developments in the fat-extracting works by pretending that only animal carcases had been sent there.

To some extent the enemy's famine in fat and other materials of war was relieved by his conquest of the Rumanian oil-fields and large tracts of Russian territory. He restored the Rumanian oil-wells to working order, and, with the help of the Turks, began to get control of the Baku petroleum works, and also obtained more copper and other valuable metals.

By the time that the blockade of German commerce in the west was transformed from a demonstration into a reality, by the entrance into the war of the United States and Brazil, the Germans had saved themselves from exhaustion in raw material by their vast and intensive salvage system and their progress in the east. Although the Central Empires did not obtain all the corn they hoped to grasp in Rumania and the Ukraine, they acquired a vast amount of material of direct military value, together with such opportunities of getting a succession of regular quantities of the things they

SAWDUST FOR WAR SERVICE.
Men of a Canadian forestry battalion filling sacks with sawdust, to be used in the erection of rifle-butts for stopping the bullets.

most needed as enabled their High Command to contemplate the prolongation of the war with arrogant confidence.

In the meantime Great Britain, France, and Italy began to suffer from the submarine blockade. The rate at which shipping was destroyed by the enemy in the spring of 1917, and the rate at which the process of destruction continued through the summer, produced symptoms of somewhat serious shortage in all imported materials.

There was a shortage of steel in the countries of the Western Entente, and a poor harvest, in conjunction with a weakened mercantile marine, led to a shortage of food in Italy, France, and **Enlisting the soldier's interest** Great Britain. This in turn produced, as in the first hunger crisis in enemy countries, a shortage of fodder, with the result that pork fat, animal fat, and butter grew scarce in the period when the ocean-borne supply of vegetable fats was diminishing.

So long as her marine power was intact Great Britain had remained fat collector, soapmaker, and glycerine manufacturer to the world. She had at that time merely to make larger quantities of soap for her export trade in order to obtain all the glycerine needed by herself and her western allies for the use of her guns. When, quite unexpectedly, in the third year of the war, fat became scarce in Great Britain, it was clear that the Briton would have to fight the Teuton on the potato-patch as well as on the battlefield, and also endeavour to beat him in the vital, new national business of rag-and-bone merchantry.

Then arose the problem of inducing the British soldier to take an interest in salvage work. By nature he was a careless person, representative of a race used to working hard and spending quickly, and, except for part of the Celtic fringe, never remarkable for its thrift. Its carelessness was the obverse side of its venturesomeness, and only when it felt itself in a desperate situation did it fully exert its powers of both body and mind.

As a perfunctory salvage worker the Briton was not a remarkable success. He began collecting the waste of the battlefield towards the close of the Somme campaign in 1916, but as a rule his officers had to go out and oversee him if they wanted their division to distinguish itself in the eyes of the Quartermaster-General.

Yet, as the Guards Division afterwards showed, when it was set salving on the field of its victory by the Pilkem Ridge, during the Third Battle of Ypres, the easily recoverable waste was enormous. The Guards picked up one million rounds of unused small-arms ammunition, in addition to many intact cases. The cartridges had loosened from the clips into the pouches, and then jolted to the ground. The Guardsmen reckoned that they paid the cost of their division, including all wives' and children's allowances, by their recovery of the waste of one action on one sector.

Salvaging in the lake of mud between Ypres and Passchendaele Ridge, however, was often an impossibility. When sunken guns could only be indicated by improvising buoys above them, the smaller material remained buried, for the Flemish peasant to go on recovering in rusty fragments, for generations. What with unexploded shells and unused cartridges and bombs, the battle swamp was likely to be a dangerous place to plough and harrow in the years of the coming peace.

While the wrestle in the mud went on at Ypres, salvage operations were begun on a grand scale in the large tract of temporarily recovered country between the Somme and the Hindenburg line. In the autumn of 1917 Mr. Andrew Weir, the new Surveyor-General of Supply, visited France in connection with the formation of an Army Salvage Branch. Splendid work had already been accomplished by the

A MASTER OF THE SCIENCE OF SALVING.
Mr. Andrew Weir, who, as Surveyor-General of Supply, formed a special Army Salvage Branch to co-ordinate the collecting of material with the work of disposing of waste.

military authorities. From army kitchen refuse sufficient tallow was derived to provide Army, Navy, and Government Departments with soap, and sufficient glycerine to propel twenty-three million shells, and from worn-out clothing woollen material worth £1,000,000 was annually derived. Mr. Weir, however, was bent on fighting the enemy's submarine campaign by devising new ways of saving tonnage. He had reorganised the military supply services in an enterprising manner, but all that he had done did not seem to him sufficient to meet the needs of the situation.

When tonnage was lowest the need for tonnage was highest. A great increase in transporting power was required to bring the United States Army to France and to maintain it there. The special feature of Mr. Weir's plan for saving the economic strength of the Grand Alliance was a system of intensified salvage, conducted directly in places where material was most lavishly used. Unless the private soldier could be induced to take up the work in a hearty manner, the vast sea of recoverable material would only be skimmed.

Mr. Weir was a hustler of the scientific school, whose doctrine was "the maximum recovery of material with the minimum expenditure of time, money, and labour." He formed the Army Salvage Branch to co-ordinate the military operations of collecting material with the commercial work of disposing of waste. Special efforts were made to prevent large quantities of stuff being gathered together without order, as such accumulations were found to result in heavy losses through deterioration. Far-seeing arrangements were necessary to obtain rapid circulation of recovered material and make the best use of the small shipping space available for the return of salvage.

METAL LOOTED BY GERMANS IN AN OCCUPIED DISTRICT OF FRANCE.
Great dump of metal objects collected from French villages by the Germans for removal to their munition factories. It was not, however, so removed, for the Canadians, advancing in the summer of 1918, salved the miscellaneous accumulation from the predatory enemy. Bells and bedsteads, pipes and cisterns, stoves, tea-urns and boilers, all manner of metal articles, had been removed by the Germans from French homes within their reach.

MOTOR-CAR CLEARING-STATION.
Damaged cars at a depot awaiting repair and return to service or scrapping for "spares."

When, however, the new machinery of organisation was set in working order, the motive power behind it remained somewhat slack. There was a Board in London, consisting of the Quartermaster-General, Sir John Cowans, the Surveyor-General of Supply, various representatives of the War Office and Ministry of Munitions, together with men with special knowledge of disposal and transport. Major-General Atcherley was appointed Controller of the Executive Department, and one of the first new steps of importance taken was to induce the Army in the field to use old material to a larger extent than had hitherto been considered desirable from a military point of view.

But the British soldier, upon whom the burden of the business fell, was exhausted by the series of grand offensives conducted throughout the year, from the closing battle on the Ancre to the disastrous end of the Cambrai campaign. Divisions had been reduced in strength by three battalions ; veterans of scores of battles had had little leave, and on many occasions the short period of rest in billets had been interrupted by urgent military requirements. There had not been time enough to train new drafts in the latest battle practice, and after shouldering the heaviest task in the European War from April, 1917, to December, 1917, the tired and wasted British battalions could hardly be expected to take much interest in picking up things on the field of battle.

Their sense of duty held them to their job on being sent out in parties under an officer, and the salvage dumps became larger and of more varied composition. Yet the work went against the grain of many non-commissioned officers and privates when they were told off on scavenging jobs during periods in which they reckoned they were entitled to rest. Somebody with a talent for advertising endeavoured to make salvage work popular by adorning the

sinister theatre of war with appealing placards resembling the War Loan posters at home. Columns tramping to and from the firing-line had flung at them at intervals along the roadside the question :

"WHAT HAVE YOU SALVED TO-DAY?"
Motor-lorries running up to the gas-alert zone had the demand lettered upon them.

But the divisions that at last threw themselves with ardour into salvage work were little moved by placarded exhortations or lectures on the value of waste material. Some enterprising major-generals touched the mainspring of action in the minds of their men by arranging a competition to which the best of prizes was attached. It was apparently a sporadic movement, for the Guards Division and others do not appear to have been affected by it. Yet where it was instituted salvage work became an absorbing interest of non-commissioned officers and privates from the winter of 1917 to the spring of 1918.

The scheme was worked by brigades, in each of which the battalion that did best obtained most points for leave. It became at last possible for every man to look forward to getting fourteen days' leave in every eight months if salvage team-work was excellently carried out. Where, for example, the ordinary leave in a brigade was ten men a week, it was possible to increase it to twenty men a week. That meant that every man's turn came round twice as quickly.

Each company competed by means of salvaging platoons that worked as hard as possible when at the front, and received as compensation lighter duties than the others when in rest billets. About December, 1917, some of the companies started wagering with each other over the results of the race in salvage work. "Two little round hats" was the Army slang

INSIDE A MOTOR-LORRY REPAIR SHOP.
Repair shops for motor-vehicles formed an early branch of Army salvage work that was gradually extended to a most elaborate system. Above : A stack of radiators awaiting repair.

for the usual price of victory between the contending sergeants of rival companies. The little round hats were the tin coverings used on the new beer-bottles instead of corks.

Working-parties looking after trenches or wiring-parties had the best chance of big salvage. Barbed-wire and screw pickets for fixing wire were often scarce stores, yet there was usually plenty to be recovered in the land between the opposing posts. There were sectors in which extraordinary zest was displayed for patrol work, until wary officers, alert to the danger of the German half-moon patrols, wondered why their men were so eager to go continually out on adventure between the lines. The reason usually was that one of them had found a store of valuable stuff, which he wanted his company to get into the battalion dump.

Eighteen-pounder cases were excellent tickets of leave. They were made of solid drawn brass, and cost only about three-halfpence to straighten into material worth eight-and-six. Howitzer charge-cases for the 4·7 in. gun were also useful, and there was much in the form of equipment, rifles, and ammunition to be picked up in certain places which the enemy afterwards overran.

One party near Epéhy made the remarkable salvage haul of three field-guns, together with a store of shells. Often a platoon would have two or three men working all day and all night, and the sergeants saw that the men who worked best were especially well treated. After a man had done all his work as a soldier holding the line he needed some encouragement to induce him cheerfully to carry sand-bags full of tins to the salvage dump.

Where, however, the new competitive system obtained there was a great pile of material collected by each battalion when the brigade quartermaster came round to do the pricing. There were tin dumps, waste-paper dumps, food-container dumps, and, where the brigade was happily situated for exploring purposes, there were dumps of brass cases, charge cases, small-arms ammunition, and general equipment. German rifles were especially useful ; they could be converted into

FOR RAPID REPAIRS IN THE FIELD.
British motor workshop, which by keeping in touch with an advancing army could effect certain repairs to material with the minimum loss of time. When at rest the sides could be let down to add to the scanty floor available for the workers.

material for some of the Allies, even as the Turkish rifles salved on the Gallipoli Peninsula had been converted into arms for the reorganised Serbian forces.

Each company saved its fat and sent it through divisional headquarters for manufacture into cordite. All soups were skimmed ; the fat from bacon was carefully gathered, and the meat was usually stewed, so as to get more munition material into the biscuit-tins in which the cooks kept their special salvage. Soldiers who used to jump over shell-cases, leave rifles sticking out of mud, and chop up duck-boards to make fires in the trenches, became the most painstaking of savers when the fatigue work of salvage was glorified by competition for leave.

Platoon dumps were priced week by week, or at any time, but the grand ceremony of umpiring the main salvage collections took place usually at monthly intervals. Practically everything had some value. From cardboard containers, for example, there could be extracted wax of the value of £100 per ton, with wood pulp suitable for paper-making or for direct munition purposes. The collection, in return and repair of such minor articles as containers, oil-drums, and boxes, meant a saving of £5,000,000 a year, and a rapid recirculation of package material that saved shipping and facilitated the supply services.

The tin canister became a grand national problem. It was closely related to the steel shortage, the tin famine, and general lack of shipping. It was also a touchstone of the real efficacy of the new movement for economy. In every country in which English was spoken the tin can had been, for a generation at least, a nuisance and a sin. It was a nuisance because it could not be thrown on the fire like a piece of paper ; and when buried, instead of rusting away, it was dug up again to the general annoyance. In Northern America it was one of the main elements of unsightliness. In Great Britain it perplexed municipal authorities and worried the public by its indestructibleness.

The careful, ingenious Teuton, on the other hand, loved

BRITISH FACILITIES FOR THE REPAIR OF GUNS AND MOTORS IN FRANCE AND ITALY.
Reassembling and repairing guns at one of the travelling repair workshops that were employed on the British western front in France. Right : The "store-room" at the Mobile Repair Unit with the British forces in Italy, where standardised parts for motor repairs were kept ever ready for an emergency in separate numbered pigeon-holes, so that the men in charge could provide anything required at a moment's notice.

the tin can. One of the reasons why it had not been so immense a nuisance in Great Britain as in the United States was that the German firm of Goldschmidt collected British tins, desoldered them, and shipped them to Germany, where the cleaned sheet-steel was returned to steel-works, after a valuable chemical, tetrachloride of tin, had been extracted for use in silk manufacture. When Herren Goldschmidt ceased to act as scavengers for Britain, the empty, disreputable tin can enormously increased in number owing to the import of bully beef and other tinned articles for military and general use. There were armies that could have erected pyramids from the tin cans for which they could find no use, yet solder was increasing in value and rarity, tin was becoming priceless, and steel was growing short.

So long as the tin can was neglected it could not be maintained that the application of science to the utilisation of waste material had been thoroughly undertaken. For it was clear that the Briton had not reached the degree of technical efficiency that the Teuton had attained in his detinning works long before the outbreak of war. The order restricting the supply of tin-plate to **Importance of** the British civilian population was but a **the tin can** measure of palliation. What was needed was an undertaking similar to that which Herren Goldschmidt had established in Germany for cleaning and baling the steel and extracting the tin and lead. Before the war 150,000 tons of used tin steel-plate were exported yearly from Britain to Germany, and the Germans also obtained large supplies from tin cans conveyed from other countries as ballast in trading vessels.

In France it was accounted a wonderful feat when an army could salve two thousand tons of steel from the field of its victories. But in the old tin cans, which were an accumulating nuisance to that Army, there was far more metal available for foundries and for the release of overburdened ships. There were three ways in which old tins could be dealt with. In the first place the tin can could be cut up for making smaller canisters. In the second place the cans could be

returned in their original packing-cases to British manufacturers, who then required a much smaller number of new tins in which to circulate their goods. In the third place the cans could be placed in washing-tanks, immersed in a soda solution, and subjected to electrolytic treatment for the recovery of the tin. The solder could be extracted in a desoldering furnace, and the steel then pressed into hundred-weight blocks for despatch to the steel-works.

British steel-makers, however, were for long averse to taking the scrap. Their prejudice was largely due to the results obtained by British municipal authorities, who used an inferior method, in which all the tin was lost and a very poor kind of steel left. Not until the national salvage movement was strongly organised were large measures taken to equal the enemy in this important matter of saving waste. It was an affair intimately connected with the complete industrial efficiency of the country after the war, as well as with the immediate necessity of overcoming the shortage in metal. If, when peace was made, Herren Goldschmidt found that the field was still open for them, to send every year 150,000 tons of steel and 15,000 tons of tin of extraordinary cheapness from Great Britain to Krupp and other German steel-makers, one of the supreme lessons of the war would have been lost upon the British people.

In the meantime the armies in the field made good progress in some of the most intricate forms of salvage. Far behind the lines were salvage aerodromes, to which everything that tumbled from the air was brought in motor-lorries. There were utilisation factories for the carcasses of crashed enemy bombing and fighting aeroplanes, as well as hospitals for damaged British machines. The aeronautic doctors were masters of the art of reconstruction. Out of two maimed structures they would make a sound one, and often repair a second aeroplane from part of the remaining wreckage.

Daily miracles in utilisation were performed by means of commonplace but intense orderliness.

Every part of a usable thing was placed in finely arranged stores, which became a reservoir of spares for squadrons and a fountain of supplies for the salvage shops, where new or rebuilt machines were turned out in

USEFUL WASTE FROM THE BATTLEFIELD.
Dump of British shell-cases by a roadside behind the lines in France; they had been collected in readiness for returning them to England to be made over anew. In oval: At a great salvage depot in England. Opening boxes of salvaged shell-cases that had been returned from the western front.

regular quantities. Some of the wood-working shops were informed with daring ingenuity. They would not let badly damaged spars go to the waste heap, along with the tattered linen and crumpled steel, for final utilisation. The broken stuff was cut up and, with only a small amount of new material, fashioned into machines that often did better than any of the aeroplanes to which the original parts had belonged.

Like Young America, the aeroplane salvage works
Grew strong through wants and shifts and pains,
Nursed by strong men, with empires in their brains.

Devised on the battlefield to help immediately in winning the empire of the air when there was dire shortage of machines, energised by the overseeing presence of experienced pilots,

Fine work in aeroplane salvage usually convalescing, who knew better than anyone what was wanted in a machine, even if they did not know how to make it, the salvage aerodrome had an atmosphere of inventiveness and activity strangely different from some other departments of State.

The British workman behind the battle-line in France, with hostile reconnaissance aeroplanes sometimes sweeping above his shop by day, and enemy bombing machines searching for it occasionally by night, was a worthy mate of the soldier. The glow in his eyes, when from some salvaged fragment he skilfully made a good new part, was a reflection of the fire in his mind. As machines of first-rate type grew happily common there was a loose kind of standardisation which facilitated the admirable work of the salvage aerodromes.

In this respect, however, they could never hope to attain the ease and rapidity of reconstruction of rifle, machine-gun, and artillery salvage works. The precise standardisation of parts in firearms and ordnance made the work of repairing and rebuilding this highly important material largely an affair

SALVING LEATHER AND LINEN IN FRANCE.
Mountain of boots and shoes worn out by American soldiers in France consigned to a workshop for repair and re-issue. Above: British soldiers collecting the soiled linen of a casualty clearing-station.

of the organisation of plant. From mobile hoists for lifting damaged guns from the battlefield on to motor-trucks, under cover of night, to the powerful machinery in the gun hospitals organisation was everything.

Here the French had many advantages, as they were immediately backed by their great munition works, yet they had something to learn about salvage from their English-speaking Allies. And the Americans had some methods of their own from which the British could derive benefit. In the salvage of motor-vehicles the American Army began in a slow, large way to attain express speed.

Instead of turning each injured car over to a small party of mechanics for repair, in the individual European way, the American erected a great plant for wholesale salvage on

OVERCOMING THE SHORTAGE IN METAL: TREASURE IN OLD TIN CANS.
Placing empty tins in a kiln to extract the solder, and (right) a stack of tins collected for desoldering. Old tin cans, once a serious nuisance to the Army, contained an enormous amount of metal available for foundries. The solder was extracted in furnaces, the tin recovered by electrolytic treatment, and the steel pressed into blocks and despatched to the steel-works. Before the war this use of old tin cans had been almost a German monopoly.

the Ford system. Each ordinary working group did one thing only, without moving from one spot to another. It was the damaged parts that moved, in travelling clutches or other devices, until they were ready to be assembled in a repaired or reconstructed vehicle. Great as were the labour and expense of erecting and equipping such establishments, they not only quickly saved their cost but they had a profound effect upon the French mind. They were indicative of the strength and staying power gathering behind the American preparations.

There was naturally a great set-back to general salvage operations when the successful enemy offensives began in the third week of March, 1918. It was the Germans who best answered the placarded question on the roads by the Somme : "What Have You Salved To-day ? " For a time, General von Hutier, General von der Marwitz, and General von Quast completely eclipsed Mr. Andrew Weir in organising the collection of battle material.

Soldiers in action and marching to action were too desperately occupied in saving the situation to think of saving anything else. The salving of Western Europe was the absorbing task. Brigade quartermasters had little leisure for pricing competitive dumps.

Yet amid the shattering, disordering tumult of the struggle, the main part of the scheme for saving shipping, material, and labour by saving waste increased in importance. The first intensive British salvage operations had followed upon the enemy's period of success in submarine piracy. They had contributed to help the country over the most dismaying stress in shortage of tonnage. When, in the third week of March, 1918, the Allies began to lose the extraordinary mines of metal, and all the treasure-trove of unused or slightly damaged material

found on their victorious battlefields in 1917, the hostile submarine campaign was being held and the production of new shipping was being increased. The great campaign of economy had not lost interest for those soldiers who had taken part in salving competitions for points in regard to leave.

To them the tin-can dump was still a romantic memory during the fierce battles when only a "Blighty" wound could earn a fighting man a little rest at home. In camps and bases in the main theatre of war the new salvage movement went on, and spread to the remoter fields of struggle in Palestine, Mesopotamia, and Salonika. It was something to have reduced to practice a system of conservation and scientific recovery of material before the enemy resumed the grand battle in the west. For it would have been impossible to have popularised the salvage idea among the soldiers after the resumption of open-field warfare, when British divisions were fighting with their backs to the sea and French reserves were sandwiched between them, with long, intermingling routes of supply reaching from Ypres to Rheims.

Yet when, in the summer of 1918, the tide of battle turned, between the Marne and the Somme, the salvaging forces of the Army soon had enlarging fields of victory on which to carry out their work, with the enlarging methods of intensive recovery of material practised during the previous winter. The combination of a new rapidity of advance with a new system of salvage enabled the Western Allies partly to lessen their demands for cargo space during the turning months of the war, when the United States forces were in need of every possible ship to swell the convergent currents of victory in France.

Once again battlefield after battlefield became a great,

SALVING SMALL-ARMS AMMUNITION.
"Pick me up and pop me in. I may kill a Hun one day ! " Notice stuck upon a camouflage supporting post behind the British lines in France to emphasise the importance of saving unconsidered trifles amid the wastage of war.

MEANS TO THE SAVING OF MILLIONS OF POUNDS.
"Save Our Stores ! " A significant S O S of the systematic salvage organisation behind the British lines on the western front. A sergeant is drawing the attention of some of his comrades to the importance of the appeal. Right : Two British soldiers bringing in a goodly sheet of corrugated iron in accordance with the boldly-lettered counsel, which none could ignore, reminding them of the familiar truth that every little thing saved was of importance.

Divers attached to the Salvage Branch of the Admiralty preparing to descend to investigate a partially submerged merchant vessel, and (right) officers and men engaged in salving a merchant ship sunk in shallow water in the English Channel.

Three officers of the Salvage Branch of the Admiralty. In the centre is Captain F. W. Young, Director of Naval Salvage; left, Commander Kay; right, Commander Bate, D.S.C. Right: Merchant ship that had been partially raised and beached near the shore.

Signalling from a partially raised merchant ship to the tug that was gradually towing it into shallower water, and (right) the powerful motor of a submersible pump, with a pumping capacity of 800 tons an hour, that was lowered into the hold of a sunken vessel.

WORK OF THE SALVAGE BRANCH OF THE BRITISH ADMIRALTY.

SHELL REPAIR IN THE FIELD.
British soldiers, at work at a shell-repairing dump behind the line on the western front, making faulty shells fit for " active service."

immediate metal mine for the Allies. Fiercely pressed in their retreat, the surprised Germans left large tracts of country littered with highly valuable waste of war. The booty of weapons, shells, trains, and timber was scarcely of such importance as the vast masses of salvage spoil which gradually were sorted out and sent to feed the famishing foundries and metal works of France and Great Britain. After all, Marshal Foch proved a greater salvager than General von Ludendorff. By throwing the enemy back he recovered, in broken railway-lines, shattered guns, bridges, hutments, motor-lorries, and other material of war, an amount of metal and timber that saved the carrying capacity of a great mercantile fleet and the labours of a host of miners and woodmen.

The general need for intensive salvage was, however, increased rather than diminished by the magnificent series of victories of the Grand Alliance. The great and sudden augmentation of the armed forces of Great Britain, followed by enormous preparations for enlarging the expeditionary force of the United States,   **Need for national** aggravated the strain upon the shipping   **salvage work** power of the Allies. This, in turn, made it absolutely necessary that salvage operations should be intensified generally, both among civilian persons in their houses and at their works and among sailors at sea and troops in camp and in billets at home and abroad. There was fine scope for municipal enterprise in many directions. Four hundred and fifty thousand tons of bones a year were being wasted, together with other refuse that would have served as food for half a million pigs. Cinders, worth 18s. a ton, were still being thrown away, and sent at considerable expense to farmers for ploughing into heavy clay-land.

By August, 1918, the nation was far from having followed the example set by the Army. Indeed, in comparison with the general, scientific salvaging efforts of the German people, the British people remained ignorant, careless, and ruinously spendthrift.

The fact was that we were still wasting an almost incalculable amount of useful material at a time when our shipping was so reduced by enemy submarine operations that British shipbuilding yards could not for years replace all losses. Yet the more clearly it was seen that every ounce of strength, and material would be required to win the war, the greater became the general interest in the direct problems of salvage. Only by combining the maximum of output with the minimum of waste could victory be won and the great reconstruction of peace be carried out with results of permanent efficacy.

SALVAGE IN AND BEHIND THE FIGHTING-FRONT.
Some of the gleanings gathered from the region of a modern battlefield after the collecting of waste material had been thoroughly systematised. Odds and ends of all kinds were brought together at specially-arranged dumping points, where they were classified, and then distributed to centres where they could be used anew. Inset : At a British dressing-station on the western front in France. Collecting the kits of soldiers who had been brought in wounded.

Ammunition mules going up with supplies in the country between Cambrai and St. Quentin.

British artillery moving their guns along the shell=smashed Canal du Nord near Cambrai.

Trophies of Canada's military prowess gathered on the Arras front during the Allies' counter-offen

Canadians resting in a roadside ditch, their stretcher-bearers sheltered behind a "whippet" Tan

...erman field=guns, machine=guns, and trench=mortars taken between July and September, 1918.

Canadian infantry marching to the attack, covered by the machine=guns of an armoured car.

British infantry going forward in the advance on Cambrai which resulted in its capture on October 9th, 1918.

SOUTH AFRICANS

CHAPTER CCLXII.

MARCHING PAST.

WAR RECORD OF THE UNION OF SOUTH AFRICA.

By Robert Machray.

Racial Difficulties—Loyalists and Nationalists—Excellent *Pro Rata* Contribution in Man-Power—How South Africa Raised Ninety Thousand Men—The South African Airmen—Formation of Overseas Springbok Brigade—Fine Work in Egypt—Heroic Defence of Delville Wood—Great Achievement in Battle of Arras—Splendid Capture of Redoubts near Ypres—Magnificent Stand at Gauche Wood—Defence of Messines Ridge: One of the Glories of the War—Financial and Economic Participation.

I N previous chapters due recognition was accorded to the splendid work for the common cause which was done by the military forces of the Union of South Africa, first under General Botha in the territory of the Union itself during the Rebellion (Chapter LII., Vol. 3, page 135); secondly in the conquest of German South-West Africa, under General Botha again (Chapter LXVIII., Vol. 4, page 53); and thirdly in the conquest of German East Africa, under General Smuts and General Van Deventer (Chapters CXXIX., Vol. 7, page 160, CLXXIX., Vol. 9, page 207, and CCXXIV., Vol. 10, page 577). From time to time incidental references have been made to the magnificent achievements of the South African Brigade in Egypt and on the western front, but no presentation has so far been attempted of the war effort of the Union as a whole since the outbreak of hostilities. The present chapter focuses that effort, and adds some further description of the remarkable exploits of the "South African Overseas Expeditionary Force" in France and Flanders in 1916, 1917, and 1918, up to July of the last-named year.

As was shown by the Rebellion in 1914, the internal situation of the Union of South Africa had difficulties inherent in it, the like of which were not to be found in any other of the great self-governing Dominions of the British Empire.

These were mainly racial difficulties, and derived from the days of Boer

MEN WHO DEPRIVED GERMANY OF A COLONY.
Lieut.-Col. F. A. Jones, D.S.O., seated on left, and officers of the South African Scottish Infantry. All went through the campaign in German South-West Africa, October, 1914—July, 1915. Lieut.-Col. Jones fell in action at Delville Wood in 1916.

independence in the Transvaal and Orange Free State, which came to an end with the annexation of those republics in 1902 as the result of the South African War. Under the South Africa Act, 1909, the Cape of Good Hope, Natal, the Transvaal, and the Orange River Colony were united, May 31st, 1910, in a legislative Union under one Government under the name of the Union of South Africa. The political freedom conferred on South Africa was on all fours with that enjoyed by Canada, Australia, and New Zealand, but it did not satisfy a considerable portion of the Boer population. These dissidents styled themselves Nationalists, and clamoured for separation from the Empire and complete independence. The Rebellion of 1914 was made by them, or a part of them, influenced to a great extent, it should be added, by German intrigue.

After the suppression of the Rebellion the Nationalists, with General Hertzog as their chief leader, continued as a political party within the Union, and they secured twenty-seven seats at the General Election of October, 1915, as against fifty-four seats held by the South African Party, which was headed by General Botha, and consisted of Boers who stood loyally by the Union as constituted under the Act, and forty seats held by the Unionist Party, which was "solid" for the Union. In their attitude to the Great War the Boers divided themselves into three groups. The first was heart and soul against Germany, and was prepared to fight with the

153

IN MEMORY OF SOUTH AFRICAN HEROES.
Drumhead service held near Delville Wood, on the Somme, on February 17th, 1918, in memory of the officers and men of the South African Brigade who fell in action there in July, 1916.

Botha brought to such a speedy and triumphant conclusion, the Union mustered about 76,000 men. For the campaign in German East Africa under Generals Smuts and Deventer, both South Africans, it placed in all approximately 38,000 men at their disposal; at one time Smuts had about 20,000 South Africans in his command, and the conquest of that vast enemy territory was largely due to the South African troops, particularly in the operations directed by General Smuts. Most of the men —practically all—who took part in "German East" had also fought in German South-West Africa. Up to July, 1918, the Union had raised 22,000 men for service in Egypt or on the western front as members of the "South

Allies against her anywhere. The second also was ready to take part in the struggle, but in Africa only. The third stood aloof from the war altogether. The first and second groups belonged to the South African Party, the third was Nationalist. Of the total white population of the Union—which in round figures was one and a quarter millions—a quarter of a million, or one-fifth, was Nationalist, and would take no share in the war. In considering the whole war effort of the Union regard must be had to the Nationalist handicap, and in a survey of its effort in Europe the fact, too, that very many Boers would not fight outside Africa must be taken into account.

Composed almost altogether of loyal Boers, who formed the majority in the proportion of about two to one, and of people of British birth or descent, the million of the population who supported the prosecution of the war had contributed to the actual fighting forces of the Empire, by the summer of 1918, more than 90,000 men, or not far short of ten per cent. of their entire number. In the circumstances this was a superb figure, and taken *pro rata* compared very favourably with the effort of any other of the Dominions with respect to man-power put into the field.

Fine contribution in man-power

Before the war the Union had a Defence Force consisting of the Permanent Force, the Coast Garrison Force, the Citizen Force, the Royal Naval Volunteer Reserve, and Special Reserves. The Permanent Force included five regiments— the South African Mounted Riflemen—and each regiment was five hundred strong. There were also Permanent Batteries, with their appropriate personnel. After the war broke out and while it continued the Permanent Force still had to be maintained for police and other purposes, while the Coast Garrison Force and the Royal Naval Volunteer Reserve had to be kept, at any rate in part, for local service. Of course, the Defence Force acted as a nucleus for the whole war effort of the Union, but it had to remain in being as a distinct organisation, and the men required for it must be deducted from the number available for work in the field. It is plain, however, that this Home Guard was in effect performing valuable co-operative work, which should not be lost sight of in the record.

Recruitment for the considerable forces the Union put into the field was absolutely voluntary, and in view of its internal situation could not well be otherwise. Naturally, in suppressing the Rebellion the Defence Force was largely made use of, as also in German South-West Africa, but far the greater number of men serving were volunteers. For the campaign in German South-West Africa, which General

AT A BROTHER'S GRAVE.
A South African nurse placing a wreath on the grave of her brother on the Somme battlefield. The padre standing by had been the fallen soldier's school-teacher.

African Contingent." Most of them had gone through the campaign in German South-West Africa; they were veterans.

To these men, as representing the overseas war effort of South Africa, must be added from 8,000 to 10,000 South Africans who at various times arrived in the United Kingdom, and enrolled themselves in the British Army, not as South Africans but simply as recruits. The first of these volunteers reached London a month after the declaration of war; they numbered twenty-seven, and belonged to what was known as the People's Legion of South Africa, an organisation for collecting a force of fighting men to go overseas. The **Lt.-Col. Sherwood-Kelly, V.C., D.S.O.** Legion sent some two hundred men, paying all their expenses; but, besides these, thousands of South Africans journeyed to Great Britain entirely at their own charges, and became officers or privates in the Army. Not a few of these men rose to distinction. Lieut.-Colonel John Sherwood-Kelly is a case in point. Hailing from Lady Frere, he had been a B.S.A. policeman. Coming to England, he enlisted as a trooper in King Edward's Horse, and steadily rose in rank until at the beginning of 1918 he was major of the Norfolk Regiment and acting lieutenant-colonel in command of a battalion of the Inniskillings. Several times wounded, he had received the

D.S.O., and was made C.M.G. In January, 1918, he gained the V.C., in circumstances thus officially recorded:

> For most conspicuous bravery and fearless leading when a party of men of another unit detailed to cover the passage of the canal by his battalion were held up on the near side of the canal by heavy rifle fire directed on the bridge. Lieut.-Colonel Kelly at once ordered covering fire, personally led the leading company of his battalion across the canal, and, after crossing, reconnoitred, under heavy rifle and machine-gun fire, the high ground held by the enemy. The left flank of his battalion, advancing to the assault of this objective, was held up by a thick belt of wire, whereupon he crossed to that flank, and, with a Lewis-gun team, forced his way under heavy fire through obstacles, got the gun into position on the far side, and covered the advance of his battalion through the wire, thereby enabling them to capture the position. Later he personally led a charge against some pits from which a heavy fire was being directed on his men, captured the pits, together with five machine-guns and forty-six prisoners, and killed a large number of the enemy. The great gallantry displayed by this officer throughout the day inspired the greatest confidence in his men, and it was mainly due to his example and devotion to duty that his battalion was enabled to capture and hold their objective.

The stories of men like Colonel Sherwood-Kelly belong to the records of the British Army rather than to a chapter of the war effort of the Union of South Africa, but such a chapter would be very incomplete without some mention of what was done by these gallant soldiers from South Africa. Both as a Union and through individuals South Africa also gave a large number of airmen to the British Army. At a presentation, early in July, 1918, of two aeroplanes, one of which had been given by the Benoni (Witwatersrand) branch of the Overseas Club and the other by a Durban gentleman, Major Baird, Parliamentary Secretary for the Royal Air Force, stated that at that time there were upwards of three thousand South Africans in the force, and that South African airmen had rendered valuable services—first in German South-West Africa, then in German East Africa, and *South African airmanship* also on the western front. Mr. Burton, Minister of South African Railways and Harbours, and representing South Africa on the War Council, was present, and in the course of a speech said that South African airmen, from their life on the veldt, possessed special qualities required of aviators, including good eyesight and nerves. He also remarked that the commanding officer at Hendon had told him that he was very well satisfied with the work shown by the South African members of the Air Force.

It was not until after the termination of the campaign in German South-West Africa that the Union as the Union was in a position to do anything to help the Empire outside Southern Africa. During the summer of 1915 the great bulk of the South African forces which had still remained in the former German colony returned home. There was *The "South African Contingent"* a suggestion that the Union should supply a contingent for service overseas, and Lord Kitchener telegraphed that the idea was a welcome one. Then the Union offered its batteries of heavy artillery and a force for Europe, and the British Government gladly accepted the proposal. The first unit consisted of five heavy-gun batteries, which arrived early in the following year.

The "South African Contingent" accordingly was formed. It consisted of four regiments—The 1st South African Infantry, under Lieut.-Colonel Dawson, from the Cape; the 2nd South African Infantry, under Lieut.-Colonel Tanner, from Natal and the Orange River; the 3rd South African Infantry, under Lieut.-Colonel Thackeray, from the Transvaal; and the 4th South African (Scottish) Infantry, under Lieut.-Colonel Jones, drawn mainly from the Transvaal Scottish Regiment, which Lord Tullibardine (son of the Duke of Atholl) had been instrumental in establishing at Johannesburg after the South African War, and which was in itself a survival in some sort of Tullibardine's famous "Scottish Horse," that,

YPRES: WHERE BRITISH TROOPS HELD THE GATEWAY TO THE SEA.

In the fighting to the east of the martyred town of Ypres, in September, 1917, the South African Brigade added to the glory it had gained at Delville Wood the year before. It was on September 20th that the "Springboks" went forward and quickly secured a series of strong points, including the Borry, Vampire, and Bremen Redoubts, and later the more formidable Potsdam Redoubt, where they met with desperate and prolonged resistance.

in its turn, was an echo from the British 77th Regiment of Atholl Highlanders of long ago.

Commonly called the "Springbok" Brigade, the South African contingent mustered in all about 4,500 men, the Scottish Regiment being the largest of the four. The 1st, 2nd, and 3rd Regiments had uniforms of khaki of the usual type, with "SOUTH AFRICA—INF—ZUID AFRIKA," and the number of the regiment in brass on their shoulder-straps; the 4th Regiment was dressed in the same manner, with the exception that it wore kilts of Murray (Atholl) tartan and glengarry caps. The Union also furnished several six-gun and four-gun batteries of heavy artillery. In 1918 it had six batteries, with a personnel of nine hundred men, on the western front, and three batteries in Egypt, where,

PRESENTATION CEREMONY ON THE SOMME BATTLEFIELD.
Brigadier-General H. T. Lukin, C.B., D.S.O. (in centre with stick under his arm), presenting decorations on the Somme battlefield to South African soldiers who had distinguished themselves by exceptional courage in the terrific fighting that accompanied the great British offensive on the western front in 1916.

further, it had a Cape Coloured Regiment of 1,500 men, the expression "coloured" signifying men of mixed blood, and not natives. The Union supplied a Native Labour Corps, composed of aborigines from the Cape, Transkei, Transvaal, Zululand, Basutoland, Bechuanaland, and Swaziland, to the number of fifteen thousand for the western front, but experience proved that they could not stand the climate, and the corps came to an end.

Formed in 1915, the South African Brigade had been renewed four times, and the personnel of the heavy artillery twice, up to July, 1918, owing to casualties in the field or through sickness, mostly the former. The casualties were more than 13,000, of which 3,000 were killed, 8,600 were wounded, and about 1,300 were wounded and unwounded captured. These sad, yet glorious, figures bore emphatic witness to the valour of the brigade in action. Rather more than two hundred men had died from disease. Except for the number of men who perished from disease, these figures were far above those of the casualties suffered by **Many honours** the Union forces in the campaign in East **and casualties** Africa. For instance, in that campaign nearly 1,600 men died, but more than a thousand of them died from disease—from the fevers that strike down whites in a blacks' country. The Cape Coloured Regiment had been renewed twice within the same period. All these figures, taken together, are eloquent of the strength and steadiness of the war effort of the Union on the western and Egyptian fronts. The list of honours won by the South African Brigade in Europe testifies to the courage and devotion of its members—2 V.C.'s, 27 D.S.O.'s, 38 D.C.M.'s, 257 M.M.'s, 25 M.S.M.'s, 89 M.C.'s, 1 K.C.B., 1 C.B., 5 C.M.G.'s, 1 C.B.E., 4 O.B.E.'s, 1 Legion d'Honneur, 12 Croix de Guerre, and many other foreign decorations.

In the early part of the winter of 1915-16 the South African Brigade made its first appearance, away from Southern Africa,

in Egypt, under the command of Brigadier-General Lukin, afterwards major-general, at the head of the 9th Division of the Third British Army, the division generally known as the Scottish Division—also characterised as the "Fighting Ninth"—and the division in which the brigade was incorporated after it arrived on the western front. In Egypt, during the campaign against the Senussiyeh in the desert wastes, the 2nd and the 4th South African Regiments were in action, the 1st and 3rd being held in reserve. A narrative of the magnificent performances of General Lukin's column was given in Chapter CXVIII. (Vol. 6, page 474, *et seq.*), entitled, "The Defence of Egypt." After the overthrow of the Senussiyeh, the brigade was moved to the United Kingdom, and in the summer of 1916 stood on the western front. By that time its organisation had been completed.

Besides artillery and infantry, the Union provided several units, all of which rendered excellent service. These included the South African Medical Corps, comprising a general hospital establishment, which after its arrival in England was increased to furnish a general hospital in France, and also supplied the staff of the South African Hospital in Richmond Park, a feature of interest there being the Re-educational School, that was practically the first of its kind and was a wonderful success, under Lieut.-Colonel E. N. Thornton. Another unit was a signal company, composed almost entirely of professional men from the South African Posts and Telegraph Department, under Colonel Harrison. The South African railways also contributed three sections—one workshops company and two operating stations. In addition the Union maintained two "coloured" regiments, the Cape Auxiliary Horse Transport and the Cape Coloured Labour Battalion, both of which established records in their different scenes of work.

The brigade was called on to play a great part in the Battle of the Somme during the second phase of that great epic struggle which began on July 14th, 1916, and lasted nearly a fortnight. The front selected for attack was from a point south-east of Pozières to Longueval and Delville Wood, a length of about four miles. The French co-operated by firing on Ginchy and Guillemont with heavy guns. To the Thirteenth Corps had been entrusted the arduous task of capturing Bazentin-le-Grand and of **Epic battle for** carrying Longueval and Delville Wood, and **Delville Wood** the South African Brigade formed part of this corps. On the 14th the greater portion of Longueval was taken, and next morning the South Africans, who were commanded by General Lukin, and had been held in reserve, were ordered to clear Delville Wood, which was an extensive tract of forest, but with all its trees stripped and torn by shot and shell. By noon on the 15th Lukin had the whole of this wood in his hands, but later was forced back. A narrative of the contest for this wood, one of the most splendid episodes in military annals, was presented in Chapter CLII. (Vol. 8, page 103).

On August 19th, 1916, "South Africa," a weekly paper published in London, quoted the following letter, dated from France on August 2nd, and written by a member of the Head-quarters Staff who visited Delville Wood to obtain information about his son, a South African soldier. No better account could be given of the sublime achievements of Lukin's men.

The dead lying in Delville Wood were still unburied when I was there, because burial was impossible under the fire going on. Men lie in layers. The South African heroes lie underneath. I wonder whether history will do them justice? Will it tell how, ordered to take and hold the wood at all costs, they took it? Then began one of the most heroic defences in the history of war. For three days they were subjected to continuous bombardment by guns of all calibres. They

British soldier on daylight patrol into Albert taking a shot to try to silence a sniper hidden in the ruins.

Officer commanding a British battalion firing from behind the cover of a wall at a spot whence shots were coming.

Men of a daylight patrol stalking the enemy in Albert over debris which provided well-concealed positions for machine-guns.

Two British soldiers dragging a wounded comrade into shelter. They had to lie flat on the ground to avoid drawing a sniper's fire.

PERILOUS WORK ON DAYLIGHT PATROL INTO ALBERT BEFORE THE FINAL RECOVERY OF THE TOWN.

held on with very little food or water. Over and over again they were attacked by overwhelming enemy forces. The gallant fellows fell fast under the terrific bombardment and attacks, but not a man wavered.

Finding them immovable, the Germans at last, on the 18th, concentrated a terrible bombardment for seven hours on what was left of these splendid men, and then, about 5 or 6 p.m., launched an attack by three regiments on the survivors. The front trench was attacked in front and on each flank. My son's trench was attacked from back and front. Our gallant, splendid men, reduced to a mere skeleton of what they were, beat back the Brandenburgers. It was during this awful time that my dear boy fell. They died, our noble South Africans, but they held the wood. Thank God, they held the wood, and, thank God, they kept up the traditions of our race! And my splendid boy helped. He took no inconsiderable part either.

I want the South Africans to get the credit they deserve. If you have any friends who can spread the news of what they did, let it be told. I resign my dear son, who was very, very dear to me, into the safe keeping of my Maker, who gave him to me. It is very hard to part with him, but I glory in his glorious end, my splendid, chivalrous boy; and if his example inspires others, he will not have died in vain. Use this letter as you like, in order to let the world know what the South Africans did. I want these heroes to have some—they can never have all—of the honour due to their glorious memories. What a theme for some painter's brush or some poet's inspiration!

Among those killed in the Delville Wood fighting was Colonel Jones, in command of the South African Scottish. The wood was the scene of numerous extraordinary incidents. For example, Lieutenant W. J. Hill, with a small party of South Africans, was entirely surrounded in the north-west corner of the wood by the enemy, and all were made prisoner. After being prisoners for four days, Hill and his men overpowered and captured their guard, but when they were retiring with their captives they were surprised by a large body of the enemy, and had to leave their prisoners behind them, and escape, which they did. When what men remained of the brigade were relieved on July 20th, they marched from the wood with the pipers of the South African Scottish at their head, piping martial strains. In a special order General Lukin expressed "his high admiration of the splendid gallantry and dogged determination exhibited by all ranks in capturing and holding for three days and nights the Delville Wood," and added that "South Africa may justly be proud of her representatives with the British Expeditionary Force."

New laurels won at Arras

After Delville Wood the brigade had to be renewed and refitted, and it did not appear in action again till April, 1917, when it took part in the Battle of Arras, and added to the laurels it had won at Delville Wood. Of the South Africans' participation in this battle an account was given in Chapter CLXXXIII. (Vol. 9, page 323), and illustrated with a very complete map of the district. Two or three days before the attack began by the British, General Smuts, who was on a visit to the western front, inspected the South African Brigade, and expressed his satisfaction with it. From Givenchy-en-

Gohelle in the north to a point near Croisilles in the south the front of attack was about fourteen miles in length. The South Africans formed part of the Seventeenth Corps, which was commanded by Sir Charles Fergusson, and lay between the Canadians, lined up under Sir Julian Byng against the Vimy Ridge and the Scarpe, where it joined up with the Sixth Corps, opposite Arras, under General Aylmer Haldane.

At half-past five in the morning of April 9th, Easter Monday, the South Africans went "over the top" in the opening assault, each of their regiments being led by its own colonel. So quickly did the attack get off the mark that, according to Reuter's correspondent, one regiment actually reached the first line of enemy trenches without a single casualty. **Three German lines carried** The second line, a regular fortress, was carried with a rush. Scaling embankments which in places were fifty feet in height, the South Africans pushed over a mile in depth into the German system of defence, and then they took the third line. On and off they were fighting all through the battle, which did not come to an end for several weeks. Of their performances early in the battle the "Times" war correspondent wrote:

Besides the Canadians, the other oversea troops engaged in this battle are the South Africans, who behaved with extreme gallantry, and have shown themselves worthy of their record at Delville Wood. The division of which they form a part captured no fewer than 2,200 prisoners, with fifty-two officers, including a brigadier and his staff, thirty-seven machine-guns, seventeen 5·9 in. guns, and two 8 in. howitzers. This was a grand bag, in which the South Africans did their full share.

In the thick of the offensive the brigade attacked in the midst of a snowstorm, over ground ploughed up with shells and encumbered with wire and debris. Under heavy fire from the enemy, who was perched on the crest of a ridge, the South Africans went forward to the

assault as calmly as if on parade, as calmly as they had marched past General Smuts a short time before. The Germans, who were Bavarians, supported by the Grenadiers of the 4th Guard Division, fought stubbornly after the first surprise was past, and many hand-to-hand encounters took place. But the Springboks would not be denied, and after a while threw the enemy into confusion on the very first day of the battle, and many of the Huns, thinking to propitiate them, held out watches, knives, and other articles, and begged for food.

An amusing story was told of a soldier in the South African Scottish. A brigadier of another division who was passing along the front spoke to this man, and not recognising his Murray tartan, asked him, "From what part of the Highlands do you come, my lad?" The soldier

WHERE SOUTH AFRICAN NATIVES WERE NURSED IN FRANCE.
Parade of the staff of a South African native hospital behind the British lines on the western front in France, and (above) a general view of a South African native hospital in France.

presenting arms, replied, "From Bloemfontein." The fighting spirit of these grand troops was illustrated in the case of a man who was wounded early in the attack and was carried back to a casualty clearing-station. As soon as he came to after the effects of the anæsthetic passed, he said: "The barrage was great. Have we won the third line?" On being told that the South Africans had gained a complete victory, he cried: "Thank God, the Hun has got hell at last, and Delville is avenged."

In September, 1917, the South African Brigade again covered itself with glory during the operations to which was given the name of the

WHERE THE "SPRINGBOKS" GAINED NEW GLORY.
On the way to Gheluvelt, between Ypres and Menin, showing something of the devastation wrought by artillery fire. Here the South Africans won fresh laurels in the autumn of 1917.

KEEPING IN TOUCH WITH THE GUNS.
British artillery signallers at work sending flashlight messages from the bank of the Canal du Nord during the victorious fighting towards Cambrai in September, 1918.

Third Battle of Ypres. Of the South Africans' share in that battle an account was given in Chapter CCXVIII. (Vol. 10, page 499). A map accompanying the letterpress showed the precise position of the South Africans in the front of attack, which reached from Langemarck in the north to Klein Zillebeke in the south. This phase of the Third Battle of Ypres opened on September 20th. The chief feature in the south part of the Zonnebeke heights was Hill 35, and on the ridge in front of the hill was the formidable Bremen Redoubt, which dominated the valley of the Upper Steenbeek, and the Germans held strong redoubts west of the stream at Borry Farm and at a point known as the Vampire.

North of the Ypres - Zonnebeke - Roulers railway the crossing of the Steenbeek was barred by an intimidating, highly-fortified position known as the Potsdam Works. In line with the West Lancashires it was against these fortresses that the South Africans were thrown in the wet and slush of that September morning.

Sweeping over the country east from Frezenberg the Springboks quickly took the Borry, Vampire, and Bremen Redoubts, as well as other unnamed strong points. Bremen Redoubt had been expected to give them serious trouble, but with great dash the Natal Regiment captured it with comparative ease. The stiffest fighting took place on their right, where were the Cape and Transvaal Regiments, in the fighting for the Potsdam Redoubt, which the Germans defended for a

long time with the utmost stubbornness. To quote the words of Reuter's correspondent: "Potsdam Redoubt maintained a prolonged and desperate resistance, but Britons and Boers, fighting together very much more fiercely than they had ever fought against one another, finally overcame the enormous natural and artificial defence of the place and broke down the German resistance." This correspondent noted that block-house tactics were a valuable reminiscence to the South Africans, whose marksmanship was high, and who plied the bayonet with a deftness and strength which resulted in a big and ghastly harvest. They went into action with more than two hundred cartridges each, and most of them went back without a single one. In the day the brigade took upwards of three hundred prisoners and about thirty machine-guns.

Among the striking incidents of this struggle was an attack made by a South African N.C.O. and two men on a redoubt, which they captured, together with seventy of the enemy. The war correspondent of the "Times" expressed no more than the truth in writing of the brigade's share in this battle when he said: "It altogether was as fine a performance as they or any troops have ever done." Fortunately, the casualties of the Springboks were surprisingly few in view of the nature of the operations.   **The Third Battle of Ypres**

On March 21st, 1918, the Germans delivered their great attack on the western front which they had long promised to make, and the main blow fell upon the Fifth British Army on a thirty-five-mile front facing the towns of Cambrai, St. Quentin, and La Fère, and lying between the Scarpe to the north and the Oise to the south. That day saw the beginning of the most tremendous battle in history, and the South Africans were in it from the very start. In the initial assault forty divisions of Germans drove against the fourteen British divisions, one of which was the 9th Division, and included in it, as usual, was the South African Brigade, under the command of Brigadier-General Dawson, C.M.G., previously head of the Cape Regiment—the 1st South African Infantry. The "Fighting Ninth" was somewhere on the line of Villeret-Hargicourt-Gouzeaucourt, and the Springboks, with some Scottish troops, held that part of it lying around Gauche Wood and behind Villers-Guislain.

Attacked by three German divisions, moving forward in masses, the South Africans and the Scots fought and checked them in a combat which lasted all day. Hour after hour the enemy came on in wave after wave, and several times succeeded in getting into the edges of the wood, but only to be wiped out or thrown back. Recalling the glories of their stand in Delville Wood, the resistance the South Africans maintained, in the face of the heaviest odds, at Gauche Wood on the opening day of that terrific struggle was one of the most memorable features of the whole contest. They repulsed every assault, inflicting enormous losses on their opponents, and in the evening held the wood as firmly as in the morning, but owing to the retirement of the troops on their right they were unable to continue to hold it. In the night they evacuated the position and withdrew to the line west of Gouzeaucourt.

On March 22nd the fighting was resumed at Heudicourt, to which the South Africans had retired, and again the combat was of the fiercest character, the Germans in their massed attacks suffering terribly. "At one place," said a non-commissioned officer, "the enemy lost 1,500 men—that was at Revillon Farm. Our field-guns and machine-guns caught them, and scarcely a man survived." "Whole companies of the Germans were destroyed in a few seconds **In the German** of time," said another eye-witness of the **offensive, 1918** scene. But ever more and more Germans came marching across the field of carnage, and the South Africans, far outnumbered, but still fighting valiantly, had to quit Heudicourt. During the night of the 22nd they retreated towards Sorel. Next day, and the next, they withdrew farther and farther back, but still fighting for all they were worth, though their numbers had been seriously diminished and they were short of every kind of supply.

Among their losses was their leader, General Dawson, who was taken prisoner and, as was afterwards learned, sent to the officers' prison camp at Karlsruhe. Through what one of them described as very heavy going for "four days of hell," they showed that they were the "bonnie fechters" which the "Jocks," their comrades of the 9th Division, had called them at Delville and Arras. On March 26th the gap through which the Germans expected to advance on Amiens, was closed; then followed the Second Battle of the Somme, with small gain to the enemy, and the first week of April saw the fighting in Picardy die away, but within the next few days a great battle, the Battle of Armentières, began farther north, and the South Africans were in it.

On April 10th, 1918, the South African Brigade added fresh lustre to its already shining record of service in the field. The German front of attack stretched from Givenchy in the south to Hollebeke, with Ypres threatened in the north, Armentières being nearly in the middle, and the British troops assailed were, from south to north, the 55th Division (the West Lancashires), the 51st Division (the Highlanders), and the 9th Division (the Scottish, including, as formerly, the South Africans), and the last-named held the famous Messines Ridge. When the Germans attacked the ridge and made some progress, a brilliant **Springboks on the** counter-attack by the South Africans **Messines Ridge** along the Messines-Wytschaete road restored the line, and higher up the Scots drove the enemy back, his losses being very heavy. When the tide turned again, and the British, pivoting on Wytschaete, had to withdraw somewhat, the Springboks fell back to conform with the general movement of retirement southwards. Days of fierce fighting ensued, and the South Africans did splendid work. The ridge was lost in the end, but they made a magnificent stand.

In the Union House of Assembly, General Botha read a cable message from General Smuts, in which the latter said: "Success of South African Brigade at Messines Ridge is one of the glories of this war. As a unit its reputation is unrivalled." Sir Thomas Smartt, the Leader of the Opposition, said that an appropriate reply should be sent on behalf of the Assembly and the country, expressing deep appreciation of the services of the brigade, and this was agreed to unanimously.

When the Germans were held, and the struggle had flickered out, Sir Douglas Haig telegraphed to the G.O.C. and all ranks of the 9th Division his admiration of the "great gallantry displayed by them during many days of severe fighting north of the Lys," and he stated that, "In the stubborn struggle for the ridge of Wyschaete, with which their name will always be associated, as well as on many other occasions, they had shown the same high fighting qualities which distinguished them throughout the battle south of Arras, and have trustworthily upheld the traditions of the British Army." This was great praise, but not more than was deserved by the South Africans and the Scots of the famous division.

Not that other regiments, brigades, and divisions did not deserve praise, but as the South African Brigade had not a special correspondent to record its achievements, it should be said that its fine work hardly received from the general public the recognition it merited, and very little was heard of the equally fine work of the South African Artillery. A glorious incident, typical of the latter, was the following:

The Germans were attacking in great force, and their infantry swarmed up to within a few hundred yards of the South Africans' guns, which were firing point-blank into the advancing grey masses, and tearing great lanes through the enemy's formation. All communication with Headquarters had been severed, but the gallant commander continued to fight with unabated vigour. Enemy machine-guns were trained on the South Africans, who replied with their machine-guns. All spare hands were ordered to fix bayonets and stand to defend the guns to the last. Officers assisted in the loading, laying, and firing of the guns while enemy shells burst round them in profusion. Nothing could stop the gunners, and their guns kept up a perfect inferno, coughing and spitting death and destruction, till at last the Boches had had enough, wavered, broke, and fled. That front was saved, and soon afterwards the infantry counter-attacked and retook all lost ground, besides many prisoners.

In addition to its military contribution the Union of South Africa gave support to the cause in other ways. At the start of the war its people, like people in other parts of the Empire, sent many gifts to the **Financial and** Home Government for the Services or the **other support** Red Cross, including money, ambulances, wine, fruit, maize, eggs, and tobacco. Very early was established the South African Gifts and Comforts Organisation, the business of which was to provide South African soldiers with something more than the bare necessities in time of war —the something more, and it was very considerable, was obtained in South Africa itself. As the complement of this organisation was a body, known as Lord Gladstone's Committee, with headquarters in London, which raised £60,000 for the same or similar objects, and took special care of those South Africans who had the misfortune to be prisoners in Germany, besides doing much for the South African Hospital in Richmond Park.

From the financial and economic point of view the part played by the Union was by no means insignificant. An official statement of its actual and estimated defence and war expenditure from August 4th, 1914, to March 31st, 1919, showed a total of nearly £35,000,000, part of which was incurred for the South-West Africa Protectorate, formerly German South-West Africa, and administered after the conquest by the Union. Of the large figure mentioned, about six millions were from revenue, the rest being raised by loans.

In the estimates for 1918-19 there appeared a grant-in-aid to the Imperial Government for general war purposes of a million sterling. Further, the Union was of great assistance in supplying coal from the Natal and Transvaal mines for the Navy, and in providing wool and maize for the United Kingdom. Not the least of its services was given in the shape of wattle bark for tanning hides into leather. All these, but its military contribution in especial, go to make up its glorious war record.

"THE SNIPER."

CHAPTER CCLXIII.

BY JAMES McBEY.

THE INFLUENCE OF THE WAR ON ART.

By Frank Rutter.

How the War Affected Art and Artists—The State of British Art in 1914—Sobering Influence of War on the Younger Painters—The Return to Realism—Art and Ideas—Value of Pictures as an Educational and Civilising Influence—Premonitions of the War in Modern Painting—Violence and Post-Impressionism—The Intellectual Bankruptcy of the Royal Academy—Opportunities Afforded by the War to New Talent—Poster Artists and the Recruiting Campaign—The First Bairnsfather Cartoon—Will Dyson's War Satires—The Rise of C. R. W. Nevinson—His Remarkable Interpretation of the Movement and Mechanism of Modern Warfare—Muirhead Bone Appointed First British Official Artist—Eric Kennington's Picture of " The Kensingtons at Laventie: Winter, 1914 "—Orpen's War Pictures—The Arrival of Paul Nash—A New Vision of a New World—The Desolation of the Battle-Scarred Landscape—The Great Air Raid Picture by Walter Bayes—The Canadian War Memorials Fund—Australian Artists and the War—How Artists Have Increased the Efficiency of the War Machine—The Art of Camouflage—Captain Derwent Wood's Masks for Facial Wounds—The War in Sculpture—Canada's Golgotha.

NO history of the Great War can afford to ignore its tremendous and far-reaching influence on British art. The tragic cataclysm which drenched all Europe in blood and changed so many features in the normal social life stirred up primitive emotions latent in mankind which found their fitting expression in the revelations of a new art and a new literature. For just as the heaviest burden of the war fell on the shoulders of the younger generation, so its chief glories, in art as well as in action, were denied to the old and given to the young. When the outworn conventions of the Royal Academy failed, on the whole, to convey any adequate impression of this mighty world - conflict, young artists hitherto unknown rose from the ranks, seeking after and finding new methods of expression.

It may be argued that new movements in art were visible before 1914. That is true, but it was the war that gave balance and sanity to these tentative experiments. Scornful of old ideals and traditions, young artists of talent were inclined in the days of peace to stand on their heads in an endeavour to be fresh, unconventional, and original. The war set the best of them firmly on their feet. Eccentricities and extravagances, the d r o s s of genuine feeling and legitimate ambition, were purified away in the fiery ordeal of modern battles.

"THE ROYAL NAVAL DIVISION, CRYSTAL PALACE, 1916."
By Sir John Lavery, A.R.A.

Further, the war not only restored the younger men to sanity and inspired their pictures, it prepared a public to accept and understand them. It gave these new men their chance. Boy artists, who in peace time might have struggled on to advanced middle age before their genius was recognised and admitted, made themselves famous within the space of a year or two. Nothing but the war could so quickly have broken down the wall of prejudice which is erected by contemporaries between the spirit of a new genius and their own understanding.

Though it is not necessary for every picture to tell a story, it is necessary that every picture should contain an idea and communicate an emotion. That legacy of the decadent 'nineties, the doctrine of " Art for Art's sake," was found unconvincing and unsatisfying in the twentieth century. In its place was substituted a new gospel of " Art for an Idea's sake," and it was gradually realised that the great value of art as an element of education and social progress was because nothing else in the world could impress an idea so vividly and lastingly on the human memory as a great work of art. Though recognised always here and there by the few, but certainly not among many of the professional art critics, this perception of the true function of art became much more general during the stress of war.

During the first decade of the

twentieth century art collectors had been prone to overlook the general lack of ideas in contemporary art, and to derive enjoyment from displays of technical skill. The realities of war soon made even the connoisseur impatient of mere cleverness. A nation living under the strain of war was not to be imposed upon by any juggling with pigment and paint-brush that told the spectator nothing but the painter's satisfaction with his own dexterity.

The state of European painting in 1914 was curiously interesting to the historian and psychologist. The logical development of centuries by masters who laboriously and reverently had conquered province after province of Nature's fairyland was amazingly interrupted by group after group of revolutionary artists. From Giotto in the early fourteenth century to Claude Monet and Pissarro at the close of the nineteenth the art of the Great Masters had been firmly anchored to Nature. They had had many and various aims, but truth of vision had always been one, whether it was the true appearance of forms, the true effect of distance, the true subtlety of light and shade, the true glory of sunrise and sunset, or the true tints of prismatic **Premonitions of** colour in shadows. Artists always painted **war in art** what they saw, or believed they saw, till the experimentalists of the twentieth century began preaching a new gospel that artists should paint not what they actually beheld but what they felt or thought about.

From about 1900 down to the outbreak of the Great War the art world was deluged with theories and "isms." Impressionism, the last of the natural progressive movements in painting—for its essence is the rendering of the true colour of prismatic sunshine and of the exact tint of colour in shadows—was succeeded by " Post-Impressionism," " Cubism," " Expressionism," " Futurism," " Vorticism," and what not. All these were reactionary movements, the earlier ones reacting to archaic forms, the later ones tending towards an abstract ideal that would reduce a picture to the intellectual level of a Turkish carpet or a design for chintz. They would seem unimportant and wholly unrelated to the war but for one most significant fact. Whatever theories these revolutionary painters might hold, their practice showed, as some of them openly asserted, their belief that " strength is beauty," and the one adjective that could properly be applied to all their work was " violent."

Now art is admittedly the mirror of life, and though many of the strange things in frames which elbowed their way into picture exhibitions since 1910 showed nothing at all very

"THE ONLY ROAD FOR AN ENGLISHMAN."
This dignified " recruiting poster," designed by Spencer Pryse, was one of the finest examples among the many posters issued in connection with the war.

clearly, they did reveal one thing—the mentality of their authors. It is a remarkable fact that, in the spring of 1914, P. Wyndham Lewis, the leader of the English vorticists, began a series of abstract paintings with titles taken from military text-books. His " Plan of Campaign," shown in the 1914 Salon of the Allied Artists' Association, was based not on landscape and figures but on the diagram of a battle disposition that we may find in any history book.

The particular case of this young officer typifies the general effect the war had on British art. Before the war Mr. Lewis had painted incomprehensible abstract pictures which none but the initiated can understand. In 1918, after two years' experience with the artillery in France, he returned to London on special leave to paint " The Gun Pit " for the Canadian Government, a splendidly sane record of his remembered experience with the big guns and of the sinewy, massive men who worked them.

Still earlier in 1914 the Russo-Polish painter, Wasilly Kandinsky, the founder of " Expressionism," produced violently coloured canvases in which the trained eye could detect distorted traces of cannon and puffs of smoke. This quasi-subterranean interest on the part of painters in the appurtenances of war, coupled with the extraordinary rage for violence in the presentation of more normal subjects, long escaped the attention of professional

"REMEMBER BELGIUM."
In this striking poster Frank Brangwyn, A.R.A., contributed one of the most notable of artistic recruiting appeals to the series of such that were issued by the London Electric Railways.

art critics. It was recognised, however, by Professor Michael Sadler, Vice-Principal of Leeds University, who in the winter of 1915 delivered a lecture on " Premonitions of War in Modern Painting"; in this lecture Dr. Sadler stated that he had been so impressed by Kandinsky's work that he had asked the artist whether he had any clear vision of the imminence of war in Europe. The painter replied that he had not actually foreseen the outbreak of hostilities, but that he had been conscious of an immense conflict of forces in the spiritual world, and that his endeavour had been to record that consciousness in his pictures.

On the principle that coming events cast their shadows before, European art was undoubtedly affected by the spirit of unrest and lawless ambition that agitated Central Europe before the war. It is significant that the principal buyers of cubist, futurist, and other extreme paintings were to be found in Germany. Always barren in invention and sterile in great art since the time of Dürer and Holbein, modern Germany could not produce even the freak artists of her choice, but with her instinctive love for the brutal she could and did patronise the violent wherever found. The violent distorted visions which Poles, Spaniards, Italians, and some Frenchmen produced she was ready to cherish and barter. With the German exodus from Paris in the first days of the war went the art dealer Kahnweiler, who specialised in cubist paintings.

A sinister violence and subterranean unrest became manifest in European art before it exploded in European politics and precipitated the war. Abroad, and slightly even in England, the wild men of painting had already betrayed in form and colour the spirit of greed and merciless aggression which eventually provoked Armageddon. The art of France had been profoundly affected by this invading spirit; on British painting it had touched but lightly, and long months of war elapsed before it became apparent that a new art was arising, and that art also could help a nation in its hour of need.

The first recognition of the artist's value to the State in war time, of his power to drive home an idea, came in connection with the recruiting campaign of 1914-15. During this period close on a hundred posters were commissioned from various artists by the Parliamentary Recruiting Committee, and two million and a half copies of these were distributed throughout the United Kingdom. It cannot be maintained that many of these posters had any serious pretensions to be considered as examples of the fine arts, but they were undoubtedly striking and efficient. Alfred Leete's " Kitchener Wants You!" was a poster not easily forgotten, and among a number of effective silhouette posters the one showing two

"HUMILITY." BY WILL DYSON.
The Professor : " I am sorry we have no further openings for instructors!" Mephistopheles : "Ah, you misjudge me—I come as a pupil!"

soldiers with fixed bayonets charging a hill and lettered, " Don't stand looking at this, Go and Help!" may be cited as a poster both efficient and artistic.

In addition to these official posters, generous contributions were made to the campaign by several private firms. The recruiting posters issued by the London Electric Railways will be remembered alike for their efficiency and their high artistic value, the most important of them being the " Remember Belgium," by Frank Brangwyn, A.R.A., and Spencer Pryse's "The Only Road for an Englishman," which, by its dignity of design and noble appeal, may be regarded as the finest poster issued in connection with the war. These posters are reproduced on the opposite page.

In connection with the later War Savings Campaign the use of Whistler's famous masterpiece, " Portrait of the Artist's Mother," as a gentle reminder that " Old Age Must Come," was an interesting acknowledgment of a growing belief on the part of authority that the best and most artistic picture is in the end the most efficient poster (reproduced in Vol. II, page 267).

Simultaneously with the appearance of the recruiting poster on the hoardings came the war cartoon in the newspaper, another instance of how artists by the practice of their art gave material assistance to the national effort. As the war lengthened out, the necessity for active propaganda on the part of the Allies became more and more evident to the British authorities, and there is no form of propaganda so concise and telling as the newspaper cartoon. Excellent work in this direction was done by the " Punch " artists, L. Raven-Hill and Bernard Partridge; by Edmund L. Sullivan,

"GOING UP: OUTSIDE VAUX."
One of the vivid sketches taken at the front by Will Dyson, after he had been appointed official artist with the Australian forces.

"THE FIGHTING-LINE FROM YPRES TO THE SEA."
One of the striking bird's-eye landscapes of war scenes by W. L. Wyllie, R.A. It was exhibited at the Royal Academy in 1915.

great impression in America, in Spain, and in other neutral countries. In Mr. Dyson the British Empire was able to claim an artist of international reputation and lasting fame.

His exhibition of "War Satires" at the Leicester Galleries in January, 1915, was the first of a series of exhibitions which enhanced and widened Mr. Dyson's reputation; and later in the war, when he was appointed official artist with the Australian forces, he expressed the valour and endurance of the Australian fighting man as ably and vividly as he had exposed the ruthless brutality of the German. With the exception of Will Dyson, however, it could hardly be claimed that the first four years of war revealed any new political cartoonist in England.

In humorous art it was another matter altogether, and a real discovery was made when on March 31st, 1915, the "Bystander" published the first cartoon by Captain Bruce Bairnsfather. His first effort, "Where did that one go to?" (reproduced on page 180), was succeeded by a long series of amusing drawings which instantly installed themselves as first favourites among both soldiers and civilians. His intimate knowledge of life at the front, and his whimsical sense of humour in the lesser tragedies of life, carried Captain Bairnsfather to a height of popularity he could never have won by pure excellence of technique. It is what he draws rather than how he draws it which becomes the centre of interest, but his drawings certainly form as characteristic a record of the Great War as those by Cruikshank are of the age of Dickens.

By the spring of 1915 the war was absorbing the activities of all the best black-and-white artists in the United Kingdom, and it had revealed one humorous artist of genuine individuality and talent. The case of the painters was altogether different, and the works they sent to exhibitions in London and the provinces varied little from their usual pre-war practice.

The heads of the profession, as well as the rank and file, were most generous in their gifts to Red Cross Funds and similar charities, but they did not alter their style and they were slow to change their subjects.

Toward the close of January, 1915, a great art exhibition in aid of the Red Cross Society was opened at Burlington House, but though it was well supported by Royal Academicians and by members of other recognised art societies, the paucity of war pictures was very noticeable. Only one called for comment, because the historian is not concerned with paintings that have merit; he is concerned with paintings that have significance. Walter Sickert's "The Integrity of Belgium," painted in October, 1914, and showing Belgian soldiers defending a street barricade, was the first oil painting exhibited of a battle incident in the Great War. Still more significant than either of these, though only a prelude to what was later to follow from the same brush, were Christopher R. W. Nevinson's three contributions to the exhibition of "The London Group," held in March at the Goupil Gallery. Before the war Mr. Nevinson was known to the few as a young artist of promise, an ex-student of the famous Slade School, who had attached himself to Severini and the Italian futurists, and was painting according to the rather bewildering ideals and practice of that group of reformers. His three pictures at the Goupil Gallery— "Returning to the Trenches," "Taube Pursued by Commander Samson," "Ypres after the Second Bombardment"—still showed signs of futurist influence, but they were perfectly intelligible and based on what the artist had actually seen while driving his motor-ambulance behind the Belgian front

Nevinson's first war pictures

whose book of cartoons, "The Kaiser's Garland," was equally notable for its message and its art; and by many other well-known black-and-white artists.

Previous to 1914 the Australian artist Will Dyson had attracted attention by the brilliant and original qualities of the cartoons which he then contributed to British Labour publications. After the outbreak of hostilities Mr. Dyson definitely set himself to wage war by his pen and pencil, and no draughtsman exposed German cant, brutality, and inhumanity with more passionate power and greater mastery. Mr. Dyson's view of German methods was well exemplified in his cartoon entitled "Humility," reproduced on the preceding page. This shows Mephistopheles approaching the portals of the German Imperial Academy of War Kultur. "I am sorry," says the professor on the doorstep, "we have no further openings for instructors." "Ah, you misjudge me,' Mephistopheles replies, "I come as a pupil." The connoisseur will observe the marvellous way in which with each subject the artist's technique corresponds to the thought. Mr. Brangwyn, A.R.A., in 1917 unhesitatingly pronounced Will Dyson to be "an international asset in this present war," and the extent to which "Dysons" were reproduced abroad suggests that they must have created a

line. It should be recorded that Nevinson, though subsequently invalided on account of rheumatic fever, was one of the first British artists to go on active service in Flanders during the autumn of 1914. His experience of the realities of fighting proved a wholesome corrective to the will-o'-the-wisp of artistic theory, but his vision of the new realism was informed by a knowledge of all the good that was to be gained from the most advanced artistic theory.

Influence of Italian futurists Just as Dr. Johnson maintained that there was some good to be got out of every book, so it may be urged that there is some good to be got out of every artistic theory. The particular good thing to be got out of the work of the Italian futurists was their successful rendering of the suggestion of movement. This was obtained by a generous use of slanting lines in the composition, and this convention not only gives life and movement to such a painting as "Returning to the Trenches," but used regularly and with an avoidance of curves it also tends to suggest the movement of a vast machine rather than of individual human beings. It was the peculiar distinction and triumph of Mr. Nevinson to leave aside all the extravagances of futurism and snatch from it the two things that helped him to render realistically a new world in a new way. From the very first he stood apart from all other painters of the war by reason of these two things: his extraordinary power and success in suggesting movement, and the implication in all his pictures that modern war is not the affair of human individuals but the creaking progress of a complicated machine. The early picture, "Returning to the Trenches," illustrates in its lower half what Mr. Nevinson was doing before the war, and it may be admitted that it is not clearly intelligible. The upper half of the picture shows what he learnt from the war and the direction in which he was afterwards to develop, and though strange and curious it is perfectly easy to understand. These French soldiers, with their packs on their backs and their bodies and rifles sloping in the direction in which they are marching, are not painted as we see them; they are certainly not painted as the camera would see them, but they are indisputably alive and moving. There is no attempt here to give portraits of a collection of single soldiers, the endeavour has been to express the onward rush of an advancing army, and that impression is both vividly and irresistibly conveyed.

When he wanted to paint portraits, as in "A Group of Soldiers" (page 174), Mr. Nevinson was perfectly equal to the task, but he would not flatter. He must tell the truth, and the great truth about the British soldier after 1915 was that he was simply the British working man in disguise. Mr. Nevinson with unerring eye penetrated to the man behind the khaki and deliberately unveiled the son of toil. The hands of the foremost figures may be exaggerated (but probably are not), and in any case they emphasise the essential truth that these men belong to the horny-handed class. They may not be beautiful, but they are strong,

upright, reliable, and good-natured, and the face of the rearmost is clearly stamped with that appreciation of humour which is one of the most characteristic and delightful qualities in the British soldier.

In landscape as well as in portraiture Mr. Nevinson's aim was always to get at the reality behind the thing seen. "The Road from Arras to Bapaume" (Vol. 11, page 226) does not in the least resemble the view that a camera would take of the scene, but it gives the essential truth of a remembered impression. All inessential details have been suppressed, with the result that the main recollections of the truth—the white switchback track of Roman straightness, the lopped down tree-trunks, the moving traffic, and the limitless expanse—are recorded with increased strength and vividness.

These, of course, are later pictures, but though Mr.

"THE ROADS OF FRANCE."

C. R. W. Nevinson's masterly series illustrating the campaign in Northern France, and rendering a sense of movement and strained energy such as no photograph could possibly convey.

"VISCOUNT FRENCH OF YPRES."
By Sir William Orpen, K.B.E., A.R.A.

"BRIG.-GENERAL J. E. B. SEELY, C.B., D.S.O."
By Sir William Orpen.

Nevinson enjoyed greater facilities and privileges when he returned to France in July, 1917, as an "official artist" than he had done as a motor-mechanic in 1914 and 1915, the essential quality in his pictures, while gaining strength and clarity, remained the same.

The power of suggesting movement and the irresistible progress of the war-machine, which dominated his earliest efforts at painting the war, found perfect and balanced expression in his masterly series "The Roads of France" (page 165) and other paintings exhibited in March, 1918, at the Leicester Galleries. As the Parthenon Frieze commemorates the Greeks' campaign against the Persians over two thousand years ago, so the four paintings of "The Roads of France" illustrate the Allies' campaign in Northern France. By his device in seizing a bending road for his subject, Mr. Nevinson in the first painting of the series conveys an impression of the endless chain of vehicles going up to the front through country unravaged by the war. The very poplars diminishing in the distance all add to the suggestion of infinity. In the second painting the big guns are seen passing through the area of aeroplane observation and frontal light railways. The third shows infantry and horse artillery, beyond the dumping grounds, passing over country recently recaptured. The emphasis on the diagonal lines of the advancing infantry is more subtle here than in the earlier "Returning to the Trenches," but the method is the same, and an admirable suggestion of movement is again the result. Equally successful is the treatment of the gun-team, the taut legs of the animals eloquently conveying

166

the strain of the load they are dragging forward. This realisation of movement and strained energy is something no photograph could possibly convey, nor could the truth be expressed by an artist who drew miniatures of each horse as it would appear if seen closely. It must be remembered that these scenes are viewed from a distance, and that distance materially affects the apparent shapes of objects.

Four hundred years ago the great Italian master Leonardo da Vinci discovered that objects at a distance lost their thinnest portions. "Thus with a horse," he wrote, "it would lose the legs sooner than the head, because the legs are thinner than the head, and it would lose the neck before the trunk for the same reason. It follows therefore that the part of the horse which the eye will be able last to discern will be the trunk, retaining still its oval form, but rather approximating to the shape of a cylinder."

Mr. Nevinson has good authority, then, for the omission of detail, and, remembering the wisdom of Leonardo, it would be foolish to criticise the fourth and last painting of this series because we cannot see every feature in the faces of the little parties of soldiers who are now cautiously entering upon the immediate vicinity of the front trenches. The men here have ceased to be individuals, they are only human atoms crawling about the desolate waste of war.

From a purely artistic standpoint there are two ways in which a painter can make history—he can discover a new way of painting an old subject, or he can discover a new subject. It was Mr. Nevinson's peculiar good fortune to be able to do both. Though different in scale and kind from any

"HEAD OF A GERMAN."
From a drawing by Sir William Orpen, one of the official artists on the western front.

preceding war, there were troops marching along country roads and fighting in trenches centuries before 1914. With regard to scenes of this description Mr. Nevinson may be said to have discovered a new way of treating an old subject. But never before, save in the brains of romancers, had there been a war in the air, and the aeroplane provided the artist with a new subject of which Mr. Nevinson was quick to take advantage. "Taube Pursued by Commander Samson" was the first of a series of pictures illustrating phases of aerial warfare, of which one of the largest and most important is here reproduced (page 174). "Air Battle: Winning of V.C. by Captain Bishop," was painted by Nevinson in the summer of 1918 for the Canadian War Memorials Fund, and is historically accurate even to the position of the two other aeroplanes when the victorious airman destroyed his first enemy, who is here shown crashing to ruin.

In this new field Mr. Nevinson was by no means alone. The Royal Academy Exhibition of 1915, though disappointing in the paucity and poor quality of its war pictures, contained a real novelty in W. L. Wyllie's bird's-eye landscape of "The Fighting-Line from Ypres to the Sea," as viewed from an aeroplane. This was a most interesting experiment which Mr. Wyllie often repeated; and though these bird's-eye views are open to the criticism that they are more like maps than pictures, there is always a possibility that pioneer work in this direction may be the means of helping other artists to discover new and hitherto unexplored beauties of design in Nature.

The art of W. L. Wyllie

A souvenir of the Battle of Jutland was contributed by the same artist in his marine painting, "Bringing in the Wounded Lion," showing Admiral Beatty's flagship being towed into harbour with a heavy list. Other echoes of the war were Herbert A. Olivier's semi-official painting (reproduced on page 169) of King George's visit to King Albert at the front, "Where Belgium Greeted Britain, 1914. At the frontier post on the road from Dunkirk to Furnes, December 4th, 1914"; the large painting of a string of Belgian refugees, entitled "Homeless," by Richard Jack; and Sir John Lavery's "Wounded: London Hospital, 1915" (page 169), a beautifully painted interior of a long ward, with the spring sun streaming through the windows on to rows of beds, and glittering on the

"READY TO START."
Portrait of himself as an official artist on the western front. By Sir William Orpen.

array of medicine-bottles, glasses, and flowers. Charming in colour it was also cheering in its contents, for though there was no shirking of the fact that pain and suffering were there, an incident in the foreground—a nurse dressing the arm of a kilted soldier—proved that throughout the artist laid his accent not on pain but on its alleviation.

The most memorable picture, however, in the 1915 Academy was not a work of realism but a work of imagination. The large allegorical painting entitled "Renaissance," by George Clausen, R.A., was essentially a war picture, though free from the slightest taint of "militarism" (see page 175). On one side of the picture Mr. Clausen showed us a pile of noble ruins, crouched at the foot of which were three figures, monumental in their simplicity and dignity—a woman prone on the ground, a man in black, sorrowful and dejected, an old peasant with his head bowed in his hands. Without the adventitious aid of any cheap symbolism or an added word in the catalogue, the thoughtful instantly recognised in these figures the types of Belgium, Northern France, and Poland — downtrodden, despoiled, and victimised by barbarous and criminal oppression.

On the other side of the picture, amid a field of crocuses, stood the hopefully erect, nude figure of a beautiful youth, behind whom was seen an illumined landscape warmed to renewed fertility by grace of sunlight. This picture, so redolent of gentleness and beauty, by one of England's greatest living painters, fitly symbolised the national view of Hunnish atrocities

"THE FALLING BOMB."
One of Sir William Orpen's war pictures which, though on a subject that even civilians could appreciate, is seen to be more like an illustration to the Apocrypha than an actual transcript of war.

THE CONQUEROR OF JERUSALEM IN BETHLEHEM.
The news spread that Sir Edmund Allenby, the Commander-in-Chief, was in Bethlehem, and the excited inhabitants thronged round him. "One of the happiest days Bethlehem has ever seen," said a native. (From a drawing by James McBey, official British artist in Egypt and Palestine.)

painter of promise, in whom William Nicholson took an interest, and who had contributed some capable paintings to the Exhibitions of the International Society at the Grosvenor Gallery. As a Territorial of the 13th Battalion London Regiment ("The Kensingtons") Private Kennington went out to France **The Kensingtons at Laventie** on November 3rd, 1914, after only three months' training in England since the outbreak of war. He returned to England in 1915, when he was discharged unfit for further service, and then began to paint this picture of a typical moment in his life at the front. His platoon—No. 7 C Company—had served for four days and nights in the fire-trenches enduring the piercing cold of twenty degrees of frost and almost continuous snow. The moment chosen for representation was when the battalion had been relieved, had emerged from the communication trench terminating in a ruined farmyard, and was forming up as a battalion along the ruined village street.

At the time of its exhibition the artist kindly supplied the Committee of the British Women's Hospital with a detailed description of the picture, in which each figure is an actual portrait. From this we quote:

and the invincible optimism, even during the dark days of 1915, of the great spirits of the Empire. While the nation reeled under the horrors of war and stood aghast at undreamt of inhumanities, a poet-painter took heart to give his promise of a blessedness to come. By the simple symbol of a crocus Mr. Clausen nobly reminded the nation of an eternal truth, that even the bitter winter of war passes and spring comes again.

Mr. Clausen's picture was undoubtedly a great work, the greatest that had been seen at an Academy for many years; but it was not strictly a war picture, and so far as the rendering of modern fighting is concerned, no serious rival to Nevinson arose among the younger men till April, 1916, when a large and important painting, entitled "The Kensingtons at Laventie: Winter, 1914," by Eric H. Kennington, was exhibited in Regent Street for the benefit of the "Star and Garter Building Fund." Before the war Mr. Kennington was only known to a few critics and connoisseurs as a young

Corporal J. Kealey is about to give the order "Fall in, No. 7 Platoon," and will see that the men in his charge are correctly lined up in their fours. The stragglers are helped to their places. The fit men support their exhausted comrades. The strong carry the rifles of the sick. Now will commence the march of five miles to a billet which is out of the shelling area. Many, from exhaustion, frozen feet, rheumatism, and other ailments, will fall out, and must wait by the roadside for the next motor-ambulance, or attempt to make their way slowly back to billet, hoping that the regiment is not marching to a fresh one. In the first four—reading from right to left—are Pte. Slade, resting with both hands on his rifle; Lce.-Cpl. Wilson, Pte. Guy, and Pte. McCafferty, who is turning to look at the other men falling in behind. He is hitching up his pack by grasping the shoulder-straps, and is carrying two rifles, one of which belonged to Pte. Perry, who was shot beside him by a sniper.

On the extreme left is Pte. H. Bristol, who has since taken a commission. Directly behind Pte. Guy are two men in waterproof sheets;

"THE UNDERWORLD," BY WALTER BAYES. EXHIBITED AT THE ROYAL ACADEMY, 1918.
This vigorous and haunting painting had for its subject a "Tube" station during an air raid. Designed as a mural decoration, there is an appropriate monumental treatment of the alien figures characteristically sprawling about the platform, waiting with semi-Oriental languor for the "All clear."

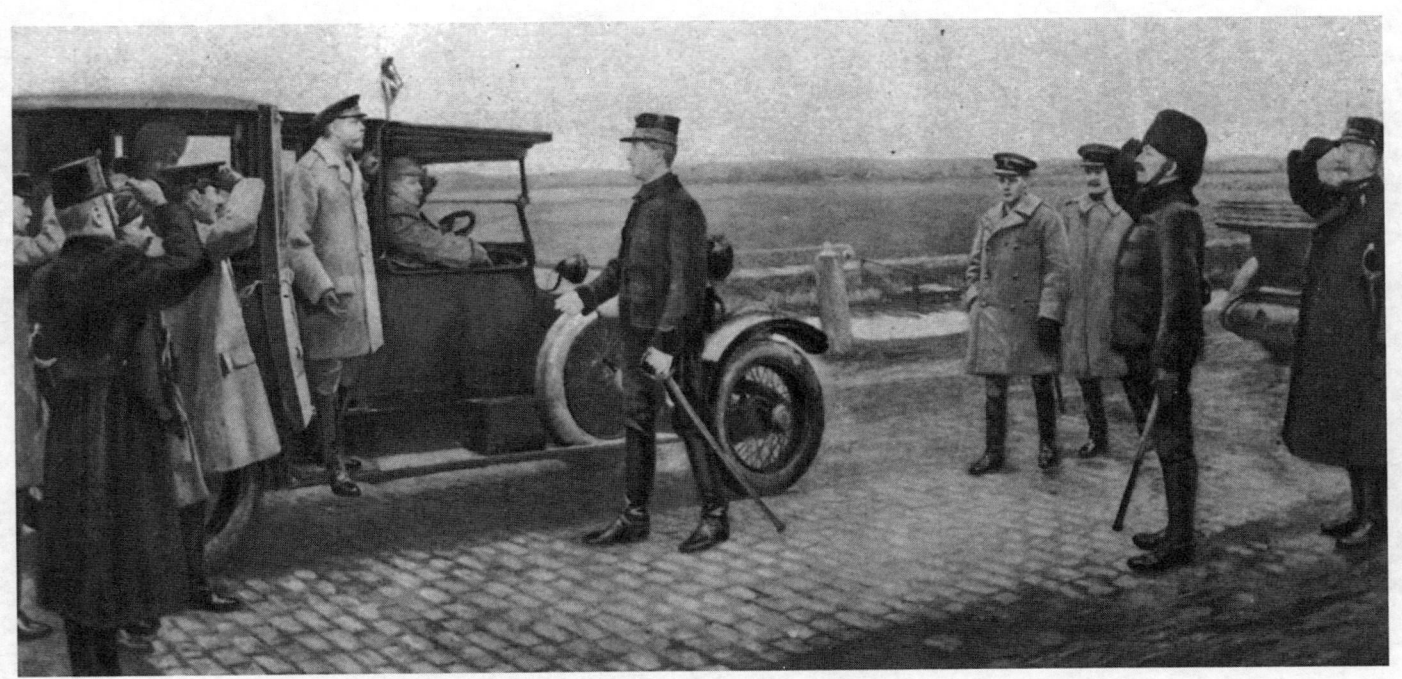

"Where Belgium Greeted Britain." By Herbert A. Olivier.

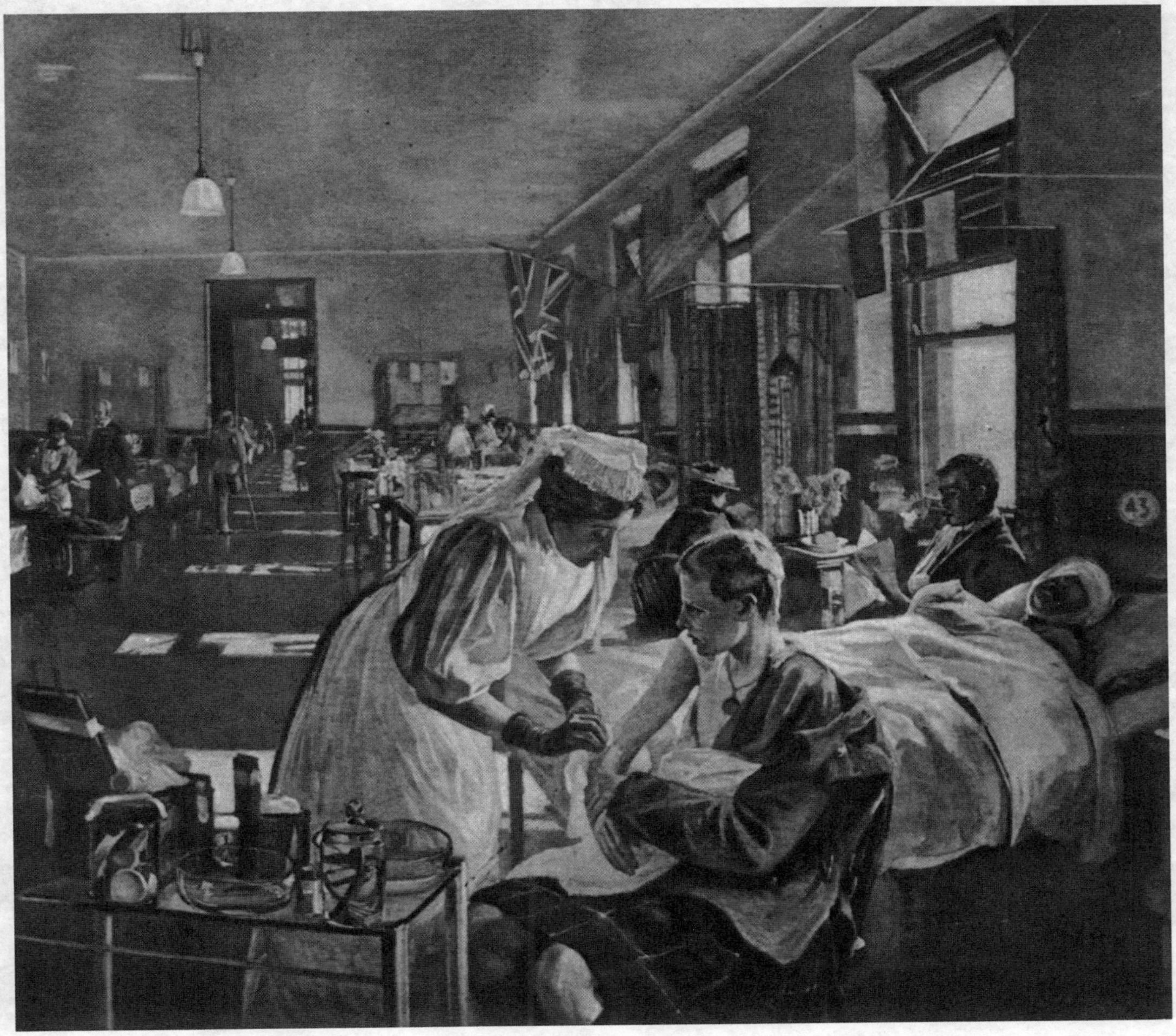

"Wounded: The London Hospital." By Sir John Lavery, A.R.A.

(These two pictures are reproduced by permission of the Fine Art Society, 148, New Bond Street, W., owners of the copyright.)

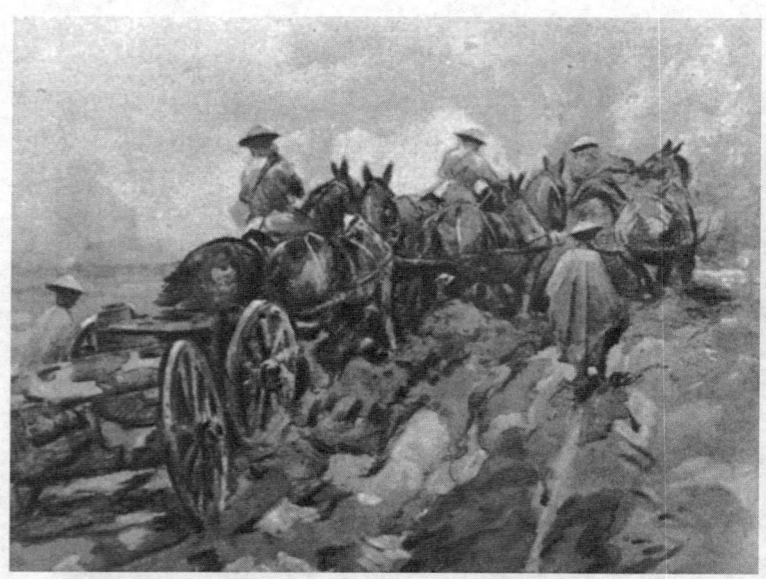

"Australian Artillery Going Into Action."
By H. S. Power.

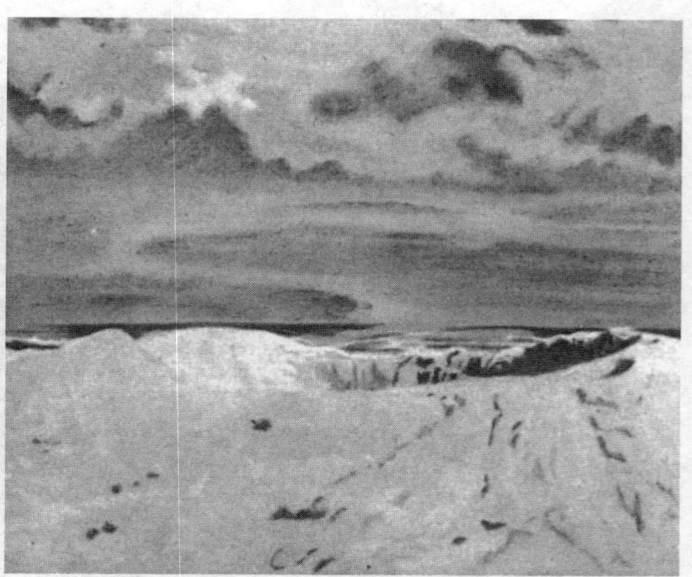

"The Great Mine: La Boisselle."
By Sir William Orpen, K.B.E., A.R.A.

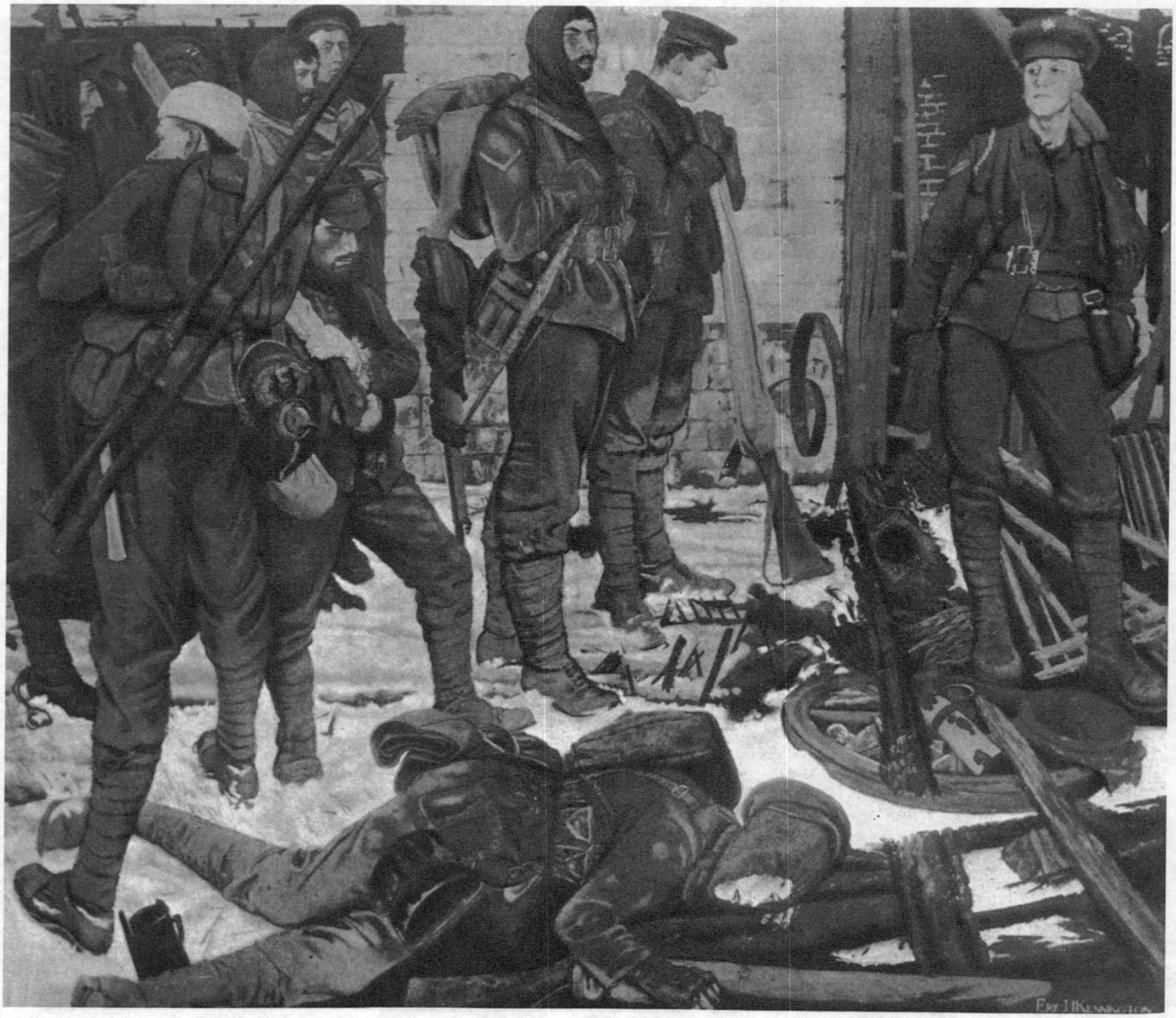

[*By permission of Lady Cowdray.*

"The Kensingtons at Laventie." By Eric Kennington.

"The Little Gate, Ypres."
By Fred Leist.

"An Aerodrome."
By Sir John Lavery, A.R.A.

"Canadian Foresters in Windsor Park." By Gerald Moira.

"The Second Battle of Ypres." By Richard Jack, A.R.A.

Pte. Kennington, in a blue trench helmet, and Pte. W. Harvey.

Pte. Kennington had the ill-luck to be the victim of an accident by which he lost a toe, resulting in unfitness for further service abroad. Fortunately, it was not the right hand which suffered, or this record of the 13th would not have been painted.

On the ground is Pte. A. Todd, better known in the regiment as "Sweeney." He has fallen exhausted by continual sickness, hard work, lack of sleep, long hours of "standing-to," and observing.

A soldier behind McCafferty has the number 77 stuck behind his cap badge. Some few days after our arrival in France we encountered on the march a regiment of French Territorials whose caps bore that number. The 13th and the 77th exchanged greetings and cap badges, many "Kensingtons" carrying the number 77 for months.

This fine work is reproduced on page 170, by kind permission of the owner, Lady Cowdray, and, in addition to its high value as a clear, stately record of quiet heroism, it possesses a technical interest of a rare kind. For this elaborate picture, with the figures nearly two-thirds life-size, was painted on glass. The advantage of this is that the pigment is hermetically sealed, and so long as the thick plate-glass endures unbroken the colour will remain as fresh centuries hence as on the day when it was painted. The disadvantage of this method is only apparent to the practising painter, for it means that the whole picture has to be painted backwards; not only has the subject to be reversed, but even the very process of painting, so that what would have been the last touch must be put on first, and what on an ordinary canvas would have been the first brush-stroke must be laid on last.

When we realise the infinite difficulties of this process, and the apparent ease with which the whole picture has been painted, we cannot consider it otherwise than as a very great achievement, a *tour de force* that is a completely successful masterpiece.

When the Royal Academy opened in the following month (May, 1916) it was at once evident that it contained no war picture that could approach the rank taken by Mr. Kennington's work. W. L. Wyllie, R.A., contributed another bird's-eye landscape, "The Hooge Salient," showing the ruins of Ypres and the surrounding country as seen from above. Lettering on **The older artists** the frame indicated the position of Hill 60 **and the war** and other notable points, and while its worth as an historical document was indisputable, its charm as a wall decoration was open to debate. Of the naval pictures shown in this Academy, Napier Hemy's "A.D. 1915," a spirited rendering of a sea-fight between British destroyers and a German submarine, was decidedly more convincing and pictorial than Mr. Wyllie's "A Fight to a Finish: Off Coronel, November 1st, 1914."

Richard Jack's "Return to the Front: Victoria Railway Station, 1916," was exceedingly popular, and as an illustration of a leave-train scene there was little exaggeration, save, possibly, the hyper-sentimentality of the lonely Highlander squatting in the foreground; but both in painting and colour it was unsatisfactory to critical eyes. Admirable portraits by Orpen, Lavery, and Charles Shannon, charming landscapes by D. Y. Cameron and Clausen, saved the Exhibition from irretrievable dullness and mediocrity, but it was perfectly clear by 1916 that, so far as the war was concerned,

"CANADA'S GOLGOTHA." SCULPTURE GROUP BY F. DERWENT WOOD, A.R.A.
Almost the only work of sculpture that the war had directly inspired up to that time, this important group was conceived, executed, and practically completed in the summer of 1918, although the eminent sculptor was otherwise fully occupied in the Masks for Facial Wounds Department, which he had originated.

the Royal Academy, like the Bourbons, had learnt nothing and forgotten nothing.

The failure of the older artists to grapple with the situation is perfectly explicable, perfectly understandable. Some of them really knew very little about painting, and none of them knew anything about war. When they endeavoured to be topical they envisaged this war after their memory of Napoleonic and Crimean war pictures, repeating the arrangements, but changing the uniforms into khaki. Their sword-waving officers, swaggering cavalrymen, and neatly-brushed infantrymen might still deceive the civilian whose knowledge of war was limited to an occasional air raid, but the men from the front knew better, and laughed their pretensions to scorn. "How absurd!" said a wounded New Zealander, standing before an Academic painting of a cavalry charge. "Why, one man with a machine-gun would wipe all that lot out."

If the Royal Academy failed as a whole, the rival societies did no better. After two years of war the Royal Society of British Artists still filled its galleries with the old goods—"Susannah and the Elders," "An April Morning," "Springtime at Kew," and so forth.

It was probably the general failure of the known and orthodox painters to deal with the war that led the British

Government to select a black-and white artist as the first "official artist." Before the war Muirhead Bone enjoyed a great reputation among connoisseurs for his drawings and etchings of architectural subjects. In the earlier days of the war he devoted a great deal of his time to the interpretation of British war industries, sketching, in his distinctive scholarly style, "The Yards on the Clyde," "The Building of a Liner" (see page 176), and similar subjects. It was no doubt Mr. Bone's known ability to make memorable designs from demolitions and scaffolding that led (in August, 1916) to his official appointment and to his being given special facilities to visit the western front and draw what he saw there.

The regular publication in parts, from the offices of "Country Life," of collections of reproductions of his drawings began a new era in the pictorial treatment of the war. But Mr. Bone's reputation was not made by the **Appointment of official artists** war—it existed before, and he was picked out as the best possible man for the work. Drawings like "The Ruined Tower of Bécourt" and "The Great Crater, Athies" (see page 176), show how splendidly he achieved his task of presenting with truth and dignity the actual aspect of wasted landscape and ravaged buildings. What the war did for Mr. Bone was to increase his public admirers from a select few to a multitude, and the unexpected popularity and wide demand for his books of sketches convinced the authorities that there was room and to spare for other official artists.

In April, 1917, James McBey, another scholarly artist akin in style to Mr. Bone, was appointed official artist for Egypt and Palestine, and in the same month Sir William Orpen, was sent to France.

"A GROUP OF SOLDIERS."
After 1915 the British soldier was simply the British working man in disguise, and in this picture C. R. W. Nevinson, with unerring eye, penetrated to the man behind the khaki, and deliberately unveiled the son of toil.

Orpen is one of the most brilliant of contemporary portrait painters, as may be seen by a glance at his portraits of Lord French and General Seely (see page 166); he could paint figures to perfection, but he could not paint war. He missed its reality and horror in his fascination with its aspect as a spectacle. He never got behind the actual appearance, as Nevinson did, and that is why there is an artificiality about all the pictures Orpen painted in France. His picture of "The Warwicks Entering Péronne : March, 1917" affects us as something seen on a stage. It is "magnificently

"AIR BATTLE: WINNING OF THE V.C. BY CAPTAIN BISHOP." Painted by C. R. W. Nevinson for the Canadian War Memorials Fund, this picture is historically accurate, even to the position of the two other aeroplanes when the victorious airman destroyed his first enemy, who is shown crashing.

produced," of course ; but it is not war. It conveys no sense of the elation of conquest or the human joy of triumph. To be so detached a spectator of modern warfare verges upon the inhuman. "The Falling Bomb" (page 167), though a subject that even a civilian can appreciate, has such a far-away, old-masterly air that it is more like an illustration to the Apocrypha than a transcript of war in 1917. Similarly, "The Great Mine, La Boisselle" (page 170), might be an Alpine landscape. And so the list might be continued indefinitely, the argument being, of course, not that these are bad paintings, but that they are not truly significant of war. When the artist looks in the mirror **Limitations of** and paints himself as "Ready to Start" **Orpen's work** (page 167), leaving behind him his siphons and whisky-bottle, he tacitly confesses that his pictorial attention is limited to the appearance of things, and that he is not greatly concerned with what they really are or with their significance. Like Rembrandt, Orpen could always take an immense delight in painting himself in any sort of "get-up," and in the tremendous fun of painting he altogether forgot the ghastliness of war.

Two months after Sir William Orpen was officially sent out to France, a small collection of water-colours of "The Ypres Salient," by a young soldier, Paul Nash, was placed on exhibition at the Goupil Gallery. Hardly anybody had heard of him, though both he and his brother, John Nash, exhibited at the Friday Club and at the New English Art Club before the war, and their naïve water-colours had charmed several shrewd collectors of modern art. The exhibition passed almost unnoticed at the time, but it aroused the keenest excitement in two or three of the leading art critics, who recognised in Paul Nash a new genius fashioned by war to give a new vision of a new world.

Paul Nash's pictures of the war are the very antithesis of those of Orpen, for he is less concerned with the superficial aspect of things than with their reality and significance. Yet, for all their strangeness, an incontrovertible mass of evidence attests that Nash's paintings are true. Men who had been through what the artist had been through declared "this is how things are in Flanders, this is how the land looks in the fighting-line." It may be admitted that "Inverness Copse" (see page 180), "Eruption," and "Meadow with Copse: Mount Kemmel in the Distance" look more like hell than earth; but then modern warfare is more like hell than anything else we can conceive. As Captain C. E. Montague very truly wrote, in his introduction to the book of water-colours published by "Country Life":

Realism of Paul Nash

In drawing strange places so strangely Mr. Nash contrives to bring back to the mind the strange things felt by men who were there at moments of stress. One does not see with the eyes alone, but with brain and nerves, too, and if these are worked upon in unusual ways, then the messages brought in by the little waves of light that break on delicate shores in the eye are changed—some may say disturbed or blurred; others may say refined into an uncommon rightness,

not to be had at other times. If an artist succeeds in expressing effects of such changes, his work may well delight some of those who have felt the changes go on in themselves. It is sure to scandalise some of those who have not.

Nobody who has not actually beheld the scene painted by an artist can pronounce whether it is true or not. Condemnation on this ground of Mr. Nash's picture by a person who had not seen Inverness Copse is not worthy of a moment's consideration. Among the men who had seen it there were only two opinions—some said it is absolutely true, others that it is a bit exaggerated, but "about right." Granting that it does contain exaggerations, the important point is that only the actual characteristics of the scene are exaggerated. These lumps and holes in the foreground are not more than a pointed commentary on the deeply pit-marked earth exposed to constant shelling. The barbed-wire may be out of all proportion in "Landscape, Year of Our Lord, 1917," but it does loom largely in the mind of the soldier who has shortly to advance through and across it, and it does curl about in extraordinary ways after it has been broken up by gun fire. Mr. Paul Nash always painted his subjects as seen by the mind's eye as well as by the physical organ, and the mind of man ever enlarges that which it has good cause to fear. These paintings may not be true as the camera sees truth, but they are true to the memory of nerve-racked fighting men.

True record of mental vision

"RENAISSANCE": ALLEGORICAL PAINTING BY GEORGE CLAUSEN, R.A.

In this picture—the most memorable one in the Royal Academy Exhibition of 1915—the artist symbolised the national view of Hunnish atrocities and the invincible optimism which held true in the darkest days of the war. On the left are figures typical of Belgium, Northern France, and Poland despoiled by barbarous oppression; on the right the youth amid crocuses was a reminder that even the bitter winter of war would end and spring return again.

Happily, many who read this chapter will never have seen a " Shell Bursting." Those who have not, if they have a spark of imagination, can form a very fair idea of what it means to the neighbourhood, and to the man who sees it, by looking at Mr. Nash's picture.

Paul Nash, a most sensitive and emotional artist, truly painted in each one of these pictures not only what he had seen but what he had felt. And what he felt, above all, was the abomination of desolation caused by war. He felt it as Blake might have felt it, and each picture is a cry from the heart that war is accursed, a black crime to earth and man. They are the most moving and powerful plea for peace that the war produced; yet, perhaps, people who have not experienced the terrors of a bombardment can never fully appreciate them.

The opposite to Orpen, Nash is also very different from Nevinson, for whereas the last continually shows us soldiers as cogs in the war-machine, the second presents his beloved earth as a tortured and violated human being. These two painters—the one a great realist, the other a great imaginative artist, each of them created, formed, and inspired by the war—are mutually the complement of each other. Nevinson shows us the complicated, man-driven machinery **Nevinson and Nash** of war; Nash its awful devastating effects. **compared** That extraordinary nightmare, "Night in the Ypres Salient" (see page 179)—with the working-parties in front of the firing-trench lit up by the enemy's star-shells—and the deeply pathetic " Graves, Vimy " are the inevitable sequel to the material resistance counterbalancing human pressure shown in Nevinson's " Ramming Home a Heavy Shell " and the same painter's dynamic impression of " A Tank." Every city of importance in the United Kingdom was permitted its glimpse of a Tank, but peaceful citizens, who only knew the machine as a counting-house for War Bonds, had to thank Mr. Nevinson for any knowledge of its awful and terrible aspect as it surged forward into action.

By midsummer, 1917, it was perfectly clear to those experienced in judging the merits of artists that, if there were to be any official artists, the two who had most to say on the war were C. R. W. Nevinson and Paul Nash. Representations were made to the proper authorities, with the happy result that during the next few months Nevinson, Eric Kennington, Sir John Lavery, and Paul Nash successively received their appointments as " official artists." Sir John Lavery, as became his age and position, was enlisted, so to speak, for " home service," and " An Aerodrome " and " The Royal Naval Division, Crystal Palace, 1916 " (page 161), are excellent

"THE BUILDING OF A LINER."
One of the many scholarly interpretations of British war industries to which Muirhead Bone devoted much of his time and skill in the early days of the war.

examples of the war pictures—charming in their delicate colour and atmosphere—which he was able to paint without crossing the seas. All the other three went to the western front, where they had already served their apprenticeship as soldiers.

The Academy of 1917 contained one exceedingly popular war picture, Frank O. Salisbury's painting of " Boy 1st Class John Travers Cornwell, V.C." (see Vol. 9, page 175), painted for the Admiralty on board H.M.S. Chester, and illustrating, with scrupulous fidelity to detail, an unforgettable act of heroism and devotion to duty. Walter W. Russell showed a scholarly painting of " Ypres in March, 1916 "; Mr. Wyllie contributed two more bird's-eye views, " The Battlefields of the Ancre " and a " Battle in the Air "; and Bernard F. Gribble a painting of " The Wrecked Zeppelin : A German Airship Brought Down in the Channel " (Vol. 9, page 176). But, as a whole, the collection was distinctly poorer than that of the previous year, and utterly devoid of any war pictures approaching the importance of those shown in 1915.

In June, 1917, British painting suffered the gravest loss it had yet experienced in the war when Captain Gerard Chowne died of wounds at Salonika. Though still a young man, he was widely recognised as a master

"THE GREAT CRATER, ATHIES."
A splendid example of Muirhead Bone's genius in presenting with truth and dignity the actual aspect of the wasted landscape and ravaged buildings on the western front.

of flower-painting and a portrait painter of rare promise, while the delicacy and refined distinction of his water-colours were clearly indicated by his " View from the Trenches, Salonika," " Lothian Ravine," and other drawings included in the memorial collection shown during the autumn at the New English Art Club. Had he lived to become an " official artist " of the war, Gerard Chowne would undoubtedly have taken a high rank among the new men.

Apart from the work of Nevinson, Paul Nash, Dyson, and Eric Kennington—whose respective one-man shows attracted increasing respect and appreciation—the 1917 exhibitions did not reveal any remarkable development of new talent. This year, however, the British Government began to treat art and artists with a seriousness born of increased respect.

On March 5th the Imperial War Museum was instituted, and several important acquisitions were made before the end of the year. During the summer of 1917, also, the Canadian War Memorials Fund was founded by Lord Beaverbrook and Lord Rothermere, who, acting under competent expert advice, soon accumulated a collection of pictures notable alike for its wide scope and high quality. Within a year of its foundation over one hundred and fifty works had been acquired by purchase or presentation, or had been commissioned, the artists represented ranging from popular favourites like Edgar Bundy

"A SHELL FACTORY."
Women-workers in a shell factory, depicted by Charles Ginner. Some of them are wheeling the bogies laden with shells.

and Richard Jack to new men like Nevinson, Paul Nash, Wyndham Lewis, and Charles Ginner.

The number of official artists appointed during this year was further evidence of the curious way in which the war was not only influencing art but persuading a business Government to treat it with more seriousness and consideration than it had yet received in Great Britain. Further additions were made to the list during the following year, and in the spring of 1918 Professor William Rothenstein, a member of a Jewish family long settled in Bradford—was sent out officially to the Péronne front, where he made a number of pictures which were later exhibited in London. One of these, showing the bizarre, serpentine painting of a camouflaged gun, is reproduced on this page.

In addition to those appointed by the Imperial authorities, official artists were working during this year for the Dominion Governments, war pictures by Dyson, Fred Leist, H. S. Power, and others being shown at Australia House, while a number of talented painters were busy on pictures of various subjects for the Canadian War Records. These ranged from such home subjects as the " Shell Factory," painted by Charles Ginner, and reproduced on this page, to " The Gun Pit," by Wyndham Lewis, and other actual scenes of war.

One war painting, and one alone, made the Royal Academy

"GUN IN ACTION AT MARTIGNY FARM."
In this striking picture Professor William Rothenstein showed the bizarre, serpentine painting of a camouflaged gun in action on the western front, whither he was sent as an official artist in the spring of 1918.

of 1918 memorable, the colossal canvas entitled "The Underworld" (page 168), by Mr. Walter Bayes. This vigorous and haunting painting, quite in the new manner, had for its subject a "Tube" station during an air raid. Designed as a mural decoration, there is an appropriate monumental treatment of the alien figures who characteristically sprawl about the platform. The faces are not English faces, it is true, but they are typical of the faces seen in the underworld on such occasions as that which Mr. Bayes commemorates, and their attitudes and dishevelled condition are equally characteristic. Be it noted there is no fear or terror expressed, and this also is true to history, but only the infinite weariness, boredom, and languor of these semi-Orientals waiting for the "All clear" signal which would tell them it was safe to return to the surface.

In placing on permanent record the scenes caused and emotions evoked by the greatest war the world has ever known, British artists have rendered their Motherland a service which posterity will know how to value and appreciate; but while it is of importance to recognise that the young artists served the State well in their capacity of painters, it should not be forgotten that they also quitted themselves well as men.

Comparatively few people are aware how greatly artists, by reason of their special gifts, helped to increase the efficiency of the British Army as a scientific fighting machine. To begin with, every artist is a trained observer; his profession has taught him to use his eyes more keenly than the ordinary man, and consequently the artist-soldier is particularly valuable for all reconnaissance and observation work. His ability to draw rapidly and accurately is found helpful for many military purposes. A number of artists, soon after their enlistment, were discovered to be the best material available for mapping instructors.

Landscape painters, in the ranks or holding commissions, were found invaluable when panoramic views of positions were wanted for artillery and range-finding purposes.

Artists, again, were wanted for and satisfactorily employed in making enlarged drawings of enemy positions from photographs taken from aeroplanes.

Camouflage, which played so great a part in modern warfare, whether for defence or

"WHERE DID THAT ONE GO TO?"

This was the first of a long series of amusing drawings in the "Bystander" by which Bruce Bairnsfather established his reputation as the supreme humorous artist of the war.

to screen a contemplated advance, was almost wholly organised and practised by soldier-artists. It is not in any sense derogatory to the splendid work of the engineers to say that, had they been left to themselves, their camouflage would have been a failure and an index to the enemy.

Fortunately, from its inception, the engineers had the support and assistance of the artists. A great debt of gratitude was due from the Army to Solomon J. Solomon, the well-known Academician, for his invaluable help when camouflage was in its infancy. Depending, as it does, so largely on design and texture as well as colour for its success, the professional painter comes to camouflage with a special knowledge of which the engineer has little. It was the artists who organised and systematised the first stage of camouflage, based on the protective colouring of insects and animals.

It was an artist who discovered the defects in this system and brought camouflage to its second stage of development, based on tone rather than colour, on how things look to the camera rather than how they look to the human eye. The Army's debt to Solomon J. Solomon is only equalled, if not exceeded, by its debt to the young portrait painter Alan Beeton, who was the pioneer of the subtle and highly scientific camouflage practised in 1918.

If the most successful camouflage officers in the Army were the artists, the Navy was not less fortunate in securing Norman Wilkinson, Jan Gordon, and other recognised painters for similar work.

One other remarkable activity on the part of a soldier-artist remains to be chronicled. In May, 1915, F. Derwent Wood, A.R.A., enlisted as a private in the Royal Army Medical Corps. Later he was promoted sergeant and placed in charge of the splint-room, where his skill and experience as a sculptor showed itself in the plaster casts which it was his duty to take of certain specific splints prepared for exceptional wounds. The sensitive spirit of the true artist was naturally distressed, not only by the pain and suffering he saw but by the thought that men recovering from severe facial wounds could only view themselves with horror in the mirror, and hardly dared to go into the street lest the passer-by should shriek at their visible agony.

"THE BOLSHEVIK."

This striking picture, by C. S. Jagger—an implicit criticism of the Revolutionary movement that brought disaster on the Russian armies—was a notable exhibit in the Royal Academy of 1918.

"LANDSCAPE OF THE YPRES DISTRICT, 1917."

One of the pictures painted by D. Y. Cameron, A.R.A., for the Dominion Government's Canadian War Memorials. Mr. Cameron was one of the older school of artists who rose to the occasion brought by the war and produced fine war pictures.

"NIGHT IN THE YPRES SALIENT."

An extraordinary nightmare rendering by Mr. Paul Nash of the horrors of the Ypres front, showing working-parties in front of the firing-trench, the whole scene strangely lit up by the enemy's star-shells.

"THE ATTACK."

One of the notable pictures of actual war scenes painted by Wyndham Lewis in his capacity of official artist on the western front for the Canadian War Records.

It occurred to Sergeant Wood that an artist might still do something for these poor fellows when the surgeons could do no more. His ideas were listened to with sympathy and interest by his superior officers, and eventually out of that splint-room grew the "Masks for Facial Wounds Department,"

Art in the service of surgery of which Derwent Wood was in 1918 the director. Nobody but an artist, and a consummate artist, could undertake this delicate work of restoring a human face to something like its normal appearance before it was ravaged by wounds.

In every stage of its making the mask required the utmost delicacy of touch and skill in handling. First a cast of the wounded portion of the face had to be

taken, and then this cast was built up by plasticine or clay, and moulded to correspond with a pre-war photograph of what the face had been.

Further casts were taken as the modelling approached perfection, and finally a thin electrotype plate of pure copper was obtained, which was enamelled and coloured to match the patient's complexion. All this work, in each case, was done by Derwent Wood himself, with one assistant, a lance-corporal, who before the war had been a modelling assistant in his own studio.

Many medical students and doctors have become artists, some of them very good ones, and several like Henry Tonks and Henry Lamb, of the New English Art Club, reverted to their old profession for Red Cross work after the outbreak of hostilities, but it may be doubted whether any doctor or any other

"INVERNESS COPSE, SUNRISE."

One of the remarkable paintings in which Paul Nash contrived to bring back to the mind the strange things felt in moments of stress by men who were at the battle-front.

artist rendered such immense service to the State and humanity as was that of Derwent Wood, the sculptor.

Fully occupied though he was with his newly-invented æsthetic surgery, Derwent Wood yet found time to conceive, execute, and practically to complete in the summer of 1918 the important group entitled "Canada's Golgotha" (reproduced on page 173), the greatest and almost the only work of sculpture that the war had to that time directly inspired. The theme which the artist has poignantly recorded is that of the abominable outrage perpetrated by the Germans in the fighting near Ypres in 1915, when they crucified a Canadian sergeant who had fallen into their hands.

PORT OF LONDON: CONVERTING A CUNARD STEAMER INTO AN AUXILIARY CRUISER.
Painting by John Everett illustrating the use of camouflage, or "dazzle," painting applied to ships.

PANORAMIC VIEW | CHAPTER CCLXIV. | OF EPERNAY, MARNE.

THE GEOGRAPHY OF THE WAR.
By Sir Harry H. Johnston, G.C.M.G., K.C.B.

It is easy for the lay mind to be wise after the event, but the extent to which geography in relation to strategy was ignored by the War Offices of the Allies before the outbreak of the world-war is only approached by the singularly meagre output of works on the subject written during the first four years of the colossal conflict. It is with special pleasure, therefore, that the Editors of THE GREAT WAR are able to place before their readers the following chapter by so eminent an historiographer as Sir Harry Johnston, G.C.M.G., K.C.B., D.Sc., whose work in geographical science is of world-wide repute, and who has had wide experience as both explorer and administrator, particularly in Africa. Sir Harry Johnston is the author of many valuable works, including a "History of the Colonisation of Africa by Alien Races" and a "History of the British Empire in Africa," and his wide travels before the war had made him familiar with much of the country he describes in this chapter, while he has also visited most of the scenes along the western front during the course of the war. To the problems dealt with in the appended chapter he has brought the results of long years of study and the capacity of a trained thinker and observer, and what he has to tell the reader has the quality of permanent as well as immediate interest.

N war, while it is true that what conquers is not Nature (geography) but the will of man overcoming both topographical and human obstacles, especially the will of man when it embodies justice, it is also true that earth surface, air currents, the configuration and currents of the sea, meteorology, and the presence, absence, and extent of railways and inland waterways must be closely studied before victory can be achieved. The railway factor was dealt with especially in Chapter CV. (Vol. 6, page 133). Here it is proposed to discuss the larger problems connected with geography and strategy in their relation to the war.

In all probability the geography of what was to be the greatest war in history had been far more thoroughly studied in Germany by the military and political authorities than by British statesmen, generals, admirals, and others in authority. The British had, previous to August, 1914, their Intelligence Division of the War Office in London, thinly staffed and poorly housed; they had also their remarkable Royal Geographical Society, recently installed by the energy of Earl Curzon in a magnificent building, and further helped by a modest subsidy from the State to assist it in carrying on its work of geographical instruction. But it is to be feared that

much of the information regarding what turned out to be the principal theatres of the war in Eastern Europe, Asia, and Africa remained unutilised in the map-rooms and archives of that society, and did not, until the third or fourth year of war, penetrate to the Government offices most concerned with strategy. The British Intelligence Division was hampered by lack of space and of suitable accommodation for both storage of maps and papers and compilation of maps and reports; most of all by lack of funds for independent, secret, and adept research.

Geography played a very small part in the entrance examinations for Army (or Navy) officers in Great Britain. A considerable proportion of the Front Bench statesmen in the House of Commons knew no foreign geography, little or nothing of Imperial geography, and either avowed this ignorance as a graceful social trait, indicative of no pedantry, or showed it by their speeches and their decisions. Much the same condition of affairs had been apparent in 1899 and 1900 in reference to the South African War and to the actions of British officers in India, and had been bitterly commented on in the Press of 1902, when impelled by the writings of Professor Spenser Wilkinson and Dr. Miller Maguire to review the scope of approved military studies.

GERMAN-BUILT DIKE IN FLOODED FLANDERS.
Western Belgium lies low and flat, in places seven feet below sea-level, and the Belgians used inundations for defence. Above is shown one of the dikes built by the Germans to dam the water flooding part of the area of their operations.

Yet there is no branch of knowledge more necessary to those who serve the British Empire on land or sea than geography: in other words, a realisation of the surface relief and geological formation of the land, the existence and nature of rivers, swamps, or arid deserts, the position of escarpments, hill-ranges, dunes, and isolated natural forts, the altitude of hills and mountains, the practicability of passes, the presence of springs, the quality of herbage, the configuration of the coasts, depth of harbours, direction and force of currents, seasons of rainfall, prevailing winds, character of indigenes, resources of local food supply, type of forest trees; in short, a practical mastery of the hydrography, ethnography, phytography, zoography, meteorology, and geology which, in common with the understanding of a relief map above and below shore-level, must go to make up a sound knowledge of geography.

NATURAL BARRIERS BETWEEN FRANCE AND GERMANY.
French motor convoy crossing the mountains on the way to Alsace. The Vosges form a natural barrier to an enemy advancing from the east—the more gradual slopes being those to the west, while each successive range has a far steeper face towards the flat Rhine Valley.

Obstacles to the Rapid Seizure of Paris.

To every student of military geography and strategy it must have been apparent that, once war broke out between Germany and France, Germany would attempt to pass through Belgium into North-East France for a rapid seizure of Paris. The direct route to Paris from the German frontier would start from Metz and proceed more or less by Châlons and Epernay, but such a march of the invading army would expose it to several risks of severe defeat, or to appalling, crippling losses. The Paris Basin, the Ile de France, is rather like a saucer, with Paris nearly in its centre and with the rim abrupt towards the east, north-east, and south-east, though scarcely perceptible when approached from the centre.

The routes to Paris

Beyond this eastern rim of the Paris saucer, moreover, there was a succession of steep escarpments if Paris were approached from due east or from the south-east. Firstly, coming from the direction of Metz, there would be the clayey, swampy Woevre Plain to cross under a galling fire from the Verdun heights (a long, narrow plateau running a little west of north and south and protecting the eastward approach to the Meuse valley); next, the menace of the Forêt d'Argonne, commanding the climb up into Eastern, or "Wet Champagne*"; then, again, the successive ascents of the cliffs which constitute the eastward buttresses of the drier regions of Champagne about Châlons and the entry into the basin of the Lower Marne River.

Finally, there would be encountered the intricacies of the Petit Morin and the Ourcq Rivers, and the crossing of the Marne "trench" near Meaux, before the outskirts of Paris could be reached.

Though this "direct" route to Paris might be only 170 miles in approximate length, and the way through Belgium considerably longer (270 miles), the material obstacles of the Belgian route would be distinctly less serious and costly in time and in soldier-life. The Meuse would have to be crossed at the Liège gateway, but the new German artillery could dispose of the Liège fortifications, as of those surrounding the key fortress of Namur. With the fall of Namur the Sambre might, without too great difficulty, be crossed near its junction with the Meuse, and then the German Grand Army would meet no great natural difficulty in its path north of the Oise River towards Compiègne and Paris.

Moreover, the advance through Belgium would, at the same time, paralyse Holland and Great Britain. Holland would thus be surrounded on the land side and Great Britain forestalled where she might most effectively (with her small Army) attack the right flank of the German armies.

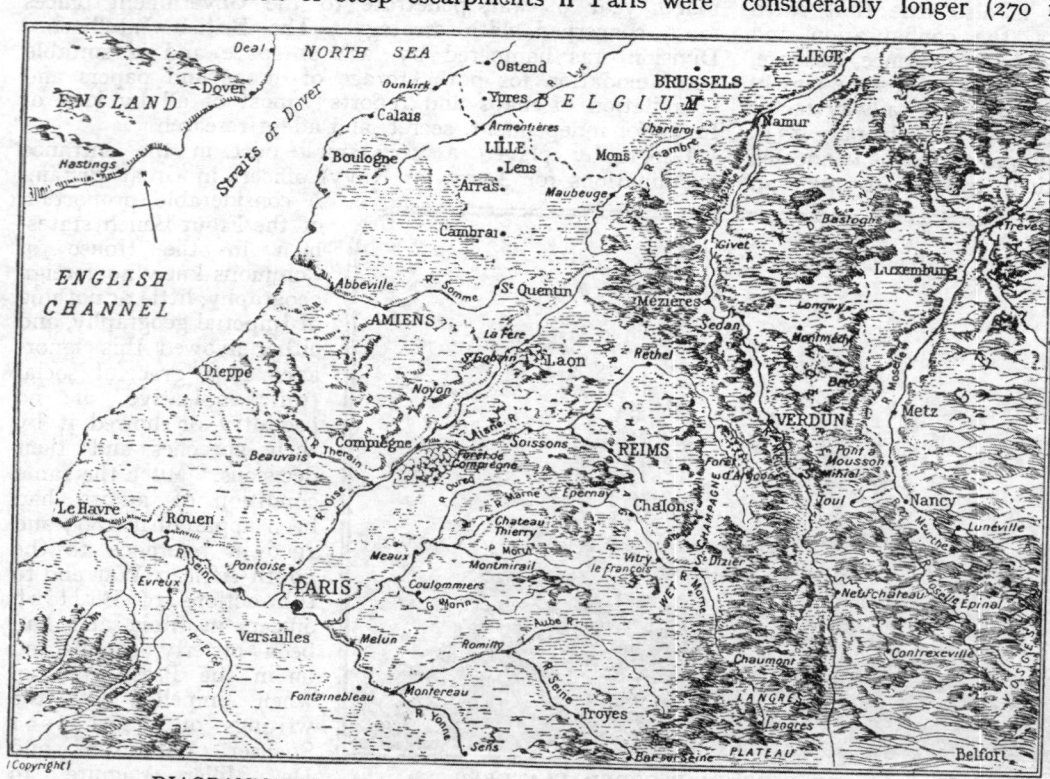

DIAGRAMMATIC VIEW OF THE NATURAL DEFENCES OF PARIS.
In this contour sketch of the western theatre of war are shown the principal plateau belts, river valley trenches, and series of eastward-facing cliff escarpments which lie between the Isle of France, or Paris Basin, and the German frontier, all natural obstacles to the westward advance of an invader.

* This portion of Champagne is distinguished from the western part of this wine-growing district by its clayey soil, retentive of moisture. "Dry Champagne" has a light, porous, chalky surface.

THE RHINE AT ST. GOAR.
Gorge of the Rhine through the slate mountains of Western Germany, showing the level sky-line of the highlands.

It can hardly be denied, therefore, that, from the spring of 1912, both the British and French military authorities might have concerned themselves more than they did with the probabilities of a German attack on France through Belgium, and have sought by their dispositions of defence effectually to provide against it. To this end too much reliance was placed on the fortifications of Liège, Namur, Charleroi, and Maubeuge, and on the extraordinarily defensive qualities of the great hill salient of the Ardennes, between the Meuse and the Sambre, coming to a point or spear-head with the fortress of Namur. Here the deep trench valley of the Meuse was a moat, which might, it was thought, protect the Franco-Belgian defence force to an extraordinary degree. The Meuse between Mézières and Sedan was a

continuance of this barrier, and the Sambre between Maubeuge and Namur its northern complement. The dikes and canals of low-lying Flanders, between Ypres and the sea, and a British expeditionary force garrisoning the uplands west and south of the Belgian frontier, were considered to complete the French defences against an attack coming across Belgium.

Unfortunately, neither the French nor the British Intelligence Divisions appear to have realised that by the triumphs of Krupps' manufacture the fortresses in Eastern Belgium and North-East France were utterly outclassed, mere trumpery obstacles capable of holding up the German armies for three or four days at most.

Crises of Marne and Ypres.

The natural defences of the Verdun heights, of the one-to-two-thousand-feet-high hills and plateau sides between the sources of the Aire and the forts of Toul and Nancy, the low ridge of the Montagne de Rheims, the steep sides of the Marne and Ourcq and Great and Little Morin Rivers aided General Joffre and the heroic French armies in saving Paris from capture and France from being overwhelmed in the autumn of 1914 and the spring of 1918.

On the other hand, it was the natural moat of the Aisne River, the surface quarries and vast subterranean excavations of the Laonnais, of the Aisne Department, which alone saved the German army under Von Kluck from an overwhelming disaster in September, 1914.

The minute study of the geography of North - East France which the Germans made prior to 1914 had caused them to realise the defensive qualities of the Aisne Department, and prepare cemented gun platforms and make other local arrangements and plans for the housing and defending of an army which might be foiled in its first swoop on Paris.

BATTLEFIELD IN "DRY CHAMPAGNE."
The Champagne plain is divided into "Dry Champagne," a semi-desert of porous chalk, where the rain sinks below the reach of plants, and "Wet Champagne," where a belt of impervious clay keeps more moisture on the surface, stimulating vegetation.

PLAINS WHERE INVASION WAS EASY: MARSHES THAT STAYED ITS COURSE.
Typical landscape in the level plain of Belgium, swept by the first flood of the German invasion. The smoke seen in the distance was rising from bombarded Audegem, between Ghent and Malines. Right: The Marsh of St. Gond, source of the Petit Morin, at the foot of the first escarpment protecting the Paris Basin. The few routes through the marsh were rendered impracticable for the invaders by the destruction of the bridges.

NORTH-EAST FRANCE BEFORE AND AFTER 1871.
Before 1871 the Rhine formed the Franco-German frontier for a considerable part of its course, the frontier line turning in a north-westerly direction away from the river to the east of Weissenburg. The shaded portion shows the tract lost to France by the treaty of 1871.

Belfort and the Vosges.

The geographical configuration of Eastern France, after the new frontier had been fixed in 1871, enabled France to command the Vosges Mountains. The approach to this comparatively lofty range of "real" mountains —no mere hills, in several places over 4,000 feet in altitude—is easy from the French side, from the west ; whereas it is remarkably abrupt if ascended from the level valley of the Rhine.

After the declaration of war the French easily mastered the summits and passes of the Vosges, and sent a comparatively weak army down for the premature release of Alsace, while the brave Leman was holding up the German host before Liège. This

Importance of Mont St. Salbert French army in the plains of Alsace had to retreat from Mulhouse (Mülhausen), though the French still continued to hold portions of German Alsace in the Vosges Mountains.

But an even more disastrous result might have followed from this reverse, and from the simultaneous recall of the bulk of the French forces to defend Paris and thrust the Germans back across the Marne. Had it not been for Belfort—and less for the fortifications of Belfort itself than for the natural fortress of Mont St. Salbert behind it, barring the way to the Doubs valley—the German armies of the Rhine might have poured down through the Doubs Valley to the Rhone and threatened Lyons, and even Marseilles and Mediterranean communications. The hills at the back of Belfort scarcely exceed 2,000 feet. Many of the great episodes of the war have been concerned with monticules and hill-crests of from 600 to 2,000 feet, and not infrequently it is the shape and the surface petrology of the eminence that mark it out as a natural fortress resistant to modern artillery rather than mere altitude.

The Pan-Germans who directed German policy

had demanded an advance to the Channel and open sea. Thence followed the great Battle of Ypres and other desperate attempts to drive the British into the sea, sever England from easy contact with France, and reach Calais. The British at that time were aided in resisting the terrific and repeated attacks of the German Army by the geography of West Flanders—the canalised rivers, the dikes, the flooded land, and behind these the little hills and ridges, dunes, and downs of from one hundred to six hundred feet in height above the plain— natural fortresses difficult to batter down. But it was the will of man, inspired by high purpose and maintained by unflinching courage, that throughout the awful ordeal enabled the British to use these topographical aids to turn the invading tide.

From the Baltic to the Rumanian Frontier.

The next theatre of war to occupy British attention, after the crises of the Marne and of Ypres were over, was in East-Central Europe, from the Eastern Baltic shores to the Rumanian frontier with Hungary. Here Russia was attacking Germany and preparing to attack Austria-Hungary. It was mainly in the dismembered kingdom of Poland that these operations took place prior to the spring of 1917.

Region of the Masurian Lakes

The Russians at first advanced from the Suwalki province of northernmost Poland into East Prussia through the difficult and dangerously intricate region of the Masurian Lakes. (See map in Vol. 3, page 68.) They had got well into East Prussia, to the vicinity of the town of Allenstein, when they were met by the redoubtable Hindenburg and disastrously defeated at or near Tannenberg, a spot already celebrated

OBSTACLES TO THE INVASION OF GERMANY.
Diagrammatic picture map of the Rhine " trench " and the westward thrust of Germany along the right bank of the Rhine. The Black Forest ridge rises with the steep escarpments on the west and the more gradual slopes to the east—practically the reverse of the Vosges formation.

for a famous battle in 1410, when the fortune of war turned the other way. On that occasion the Slavs (Poles) utterly defeated the Germans, the Teutonic Knights.

The Russians were confronted by great physical difficulties, while Hindenburg was aided materially by the German railway system and got across the Russian line of retreat owing to Mazedoieff's treachery. A somewhat detailed review of the whole geographical problem as between Russia and her western assailants was given in Chapter XVI. (Vol. 1, page 289).

The Russian rout at Tannenberg was followed by a retreat into the mazes of lakes and swamps known as "Masuria," wherein some 80,000 Russians were engulfed. After the further attempt made on East Prussia by the Tenth Russian Army late in 1914—an attempt again betrayed by Mazedoieff — the course of the fighting turned more to the south, where the Austro-Hungarians proved a far less resolute and skilful foe.

The northern part of the Kingdom of Poland, which, like Western Russia and Prussia, has no natural frontier of any kind, is very flat and traversed in all directions by big rivers, sluggish streams, and marsh-forming rills of water. Roads are sometimes reduced in districts as large as Surrey to a single narrow causeway raised above the surface of what is swampy fenland in summer and autumn, and frozen marsh in winter. This is, likewise, a prominent feature in Suwalki, that northern peninsula of Poland which extends into Lithuania. The character of the ground explains why, even after their victory of Tannenberg, the Germans were for long unable to follow up their success and effect an entrance into Russia through Northern Poland and Lithuania.

Southern Poland, especially all that part known as Galicia (or, properly, Halicz), is a very different country. Near

Poland, Northern and Southern

IN THE HEART OF SOUTHERN POLAND.
Bird's-eye view of Przemysl, in Galicia, or Southern Poland, showing the River San. Southern Poland is known in contrast with the northern part of the Kingdom, as the "pleasant" part of Poland. It possesses a far more genial climate, has little or no swamp, much better roads, and its plateau forms the broad base from which rise up the lofty Carpathians in a vast semicircle to the south.

the confluence of the San and the Vistula (from this important point, it should be noted, there is uninterrupted steamer communication for hundreds of miles down the Vistula into the Baltic) the land rises in a series of terraces or "rims," not unlike those that defend the Paris Basin on the east. This is the "pleasant" part of Poland, with a far more genial climate, little or no swamp, much better roads, good farming, abundant orchards, and the broad base from which rise up the lofty Carpathians in a vast semicircle to the south of Galicia.

The Carpathians, though the altitudes of their principal passes are not so very high (1,900 to 3,300 feet), are so arranged in a series of gigantic natural trenches, with such abrupt ravines and such protecting screening forests, that it is little wonder the Russians, even when most formidable, failed to penetrate in any great force into the Hungarian plains, though the superior railway facilities of the enemy were a factor of considerable importance.

When through treachery and lassitude the Russians fell back before the final German rush of 1917, it was only in one direction that the German armies succeeded in penetrating to any great extent the Russian territories beyond Poland.

This course was taken through the non-Russian countries of Courland, Livonia, and Esthonia. Here, owing to a former Germanisation, the influence of Sweden on the north and Poland on the south, there was more civilisation, there were better and more numerous roads, and the swamps and fens were less frequent.

The people were either Lithuanians (Letts, etc., or of Finnish stock), and had no great liking for the true Russians, being of different speech and mainly of the Lutheran faith. The aristocracy was largely of Teutonic stock and made common cause with the invaders.

IN THE PRUSSIAN AND POLISH LAKE COUNTRY.
Where Northern Poland joins East Prussia the country is an extensive maze of lakes and swamps, known generally as Masuria, or the Masurian Lakes. This great tract of country offered formidable obstacles to any military movement on a large scale.

After the so-called Peace of Brest Litovsk the Austrians entered the province of Podolia, an attractive region of well-populated, cultivated plateau land, with a singularly large local breed of cattle, and the Germans, more or less in alliance with the Little Russians (Ukrainians), reached Kieff, the capital of Ukrainia.

The people of this comparatively vast country of " Little Russia," the Ruthenians, came to look on the German and Austrian invaders—to some extent, at any rate—as allies
against the hated rule of Great Russia, a
Ruthenian hatred burden made more intolerable still under
of Russian rule the mad Bolshevists. This also accounted
for the facilities with which, in 1917-18, the German troops overcame physical obstacles which would have been insurmountable to any invader of Russia who had had a united people fighting against him.

In Poland, Lithuania, Little Russia, and Western Russia the aims of Germany were from the first facilitated, and the Russian strength of resistance greatly diminished, by the intense rancour and the subtle intrigues of the strongly pro-German, pro-Austrian Jews of Russia, Ukrainia, and Poland. " Remember Kishineff " was a cry which reached from Bessarabia to the United States. The Pripet Marshes and the winter cold were thus, to some extent, nullified as geographical defences by the spirit of man fighting against injustice.

GENERAL VIEW OF THE CITY OF KOVNO.
This ancient city, situated on the River Niemen, is the capital of the Government of Kovno, North-West Russia. The Kovno country is a well-watered plateau, about one-fifth of the area of which is covered by marshes and forest.

severance of Russia from the west, in the configuration, climate, people, and means of communication of the Grand Duchy of Finland and the adjoining Russian Murman coast.

ROADS AND RIVERS OF THE NORTH POLISH PLAINS.
Typical landscape of Northern Poland, where the roads are frequently no more than narrow causeways raised above ground which in summer is swampy fenland and in winter frozen marsh. Right : View across the Narev, looking towards Ostrolenka, about sixty miles to the north-east of Warsaw. The Narev, one of the big streams that traverse the flat tract of Northern Poland, flows into the Bug about twenty miles to the north of Warsaw.

Russia's Isolation from Western Europe.

After the Russian Revolution in March, 1917, came a further cause for Western European interest in the physical

CATHEDRAL AND ROYAL PALACE OF CRACOW.
Cracow, the capital of Austrian Galicia, and one-time capital of the kingdom of Poland, is a fortified town on the Vistula. It occupies an important strategical position, commanding the river approach to Silesia and to the Danube Valley by way of the " Moravian Gate."

In the early and later stages of the war the command of the Baltic was in German hands, and Germany and Austria, by their success in diplomacy and arms, having secured the alliance of Turkey and Bulgaria, the defection of Greece, and the conquest of Serbia and Northern Albania, the means of direct communication between France, Great Britain and Russia were virtually restricted to the passage through Norway and Sweden or the sea journey round Scandinavia to the White Sea. The only alternatives were transport through Persia—then convulsed by German intrigues, revolts, and Turkish invasions, and entirely without speedy and sure means of land transport—or the seven-thousand-mile-long Siberian Railway, which kept up communications with the United States through China and Japan.

Passengers and mails might, with occasional interruptions from German submarines, pass fairly quickly across the Scandinavian peninsula to the Finnish coast
or round the north of Finland, at the head of **The ice-free port**
the Baltic Gulf of Bothnia. Thence Finnish **of Kola**
railways carried them to Russia. Munitions
of war, however, could not proceed by the Scandinavian route, but had to be taken all the way by sea to Archangel, a port on a great gulf of the Arctic Ocean known as the White Sea.

Archangel is not far outside the Arctic Circle, and between November and May the White Sea is blocked with ice. Sheer necessity, prompted by British energy, led to a careful investigation of the Murman coast close up to the Varanger

Fiord, belonging to Norway. Here, on the Russian side of the frontier, were found an inlet and harbour sufficiently influenced by the warm water of the Gulf Stream to remain—as does Norway's coast—free from obstructing ice all the year round. A railway constructed with all possible speed and paid for with British money eventually connected Kola, on the Kola inlet, with the Russian railway system.

Then further geographical difficulties arose. Finland, loyal to Russia through the first three years of the war, found herself, by the rise to power of the Soviet, at war with Red Russia, with the murderous plundering Red Guards. Communication therefore ceased or became very difficult between Sweden and Russia through Finland. In her agony Finland turned to Germany for help against the Russian anarchists.

The German forces entered Finland and expelled the Russians, but took over the virtual control of the country. They next attempted to reach to the Murman coast and tried to sever the railway communications between Kola and Petrograd. Their geographical ambitions took higher flights; they contemplated, from a naval base on the Murman coast, seizing and annexing the Spitzbergen Archipelago with its valuable coal deposits, dominating the Arctic Ocean, establishing themselves in Iceland, and even Danish Greenland, and thence bidding defiance to the other "Arctic" Powers—Britain and the United States.

Germany's geographical ambitions

Moreover, the virtual subordination of Finland gave them a land frontier with both Sweden and Norway, and the occupation of the Åland Archipelago, those islets midway between Finland and Sweden which are a standing menace to Stockholm and give the occupying Power the means of closing the Gulf of Bothnia and of throttling Northern Sweden.

This was one of the unfortunate consequences of the Vienna

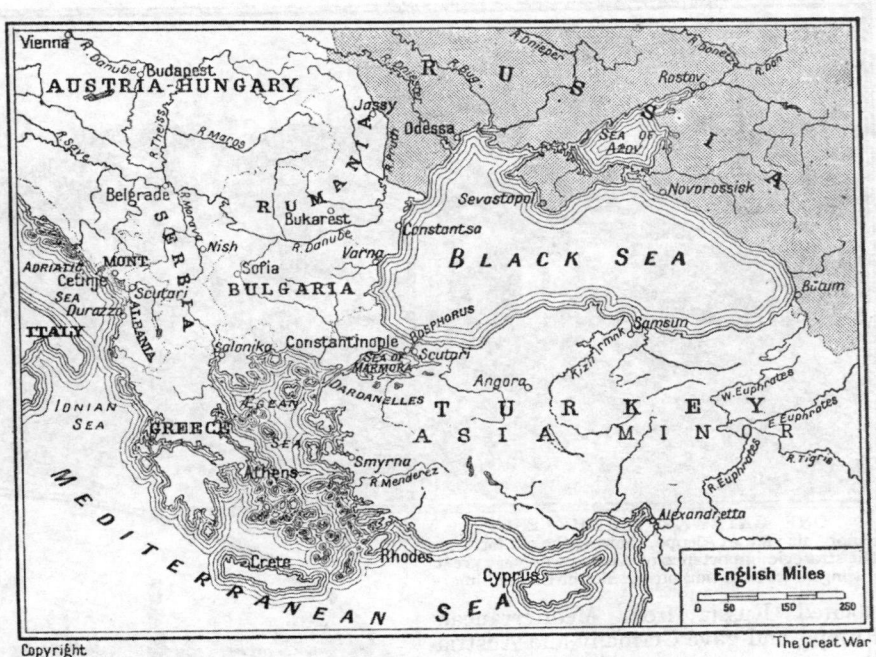

THE DARDANELLES AND THE BLACK SEA.
The great geographical fact about the war in South-East Europe was the existence of the fortifications on the Dardanelles. When Turkey and Bulgaria joined with the Central Powers, Southern Russia was at once cut off from any communication with the Mediterranean.

Conference of 1815. At that assemblage of European Powers the Grand Duchy of Finland—originally an appanage of the Swedish Crown, a people Lutheran in religion, Swedish in culture, in customs, and partly so in race—was, against its will, handed over to Russia as one of the prizes of victory over France. For many years, however, the Tsars of Russia respected the Finnish Constitution and its semi-independence. But under the last of the Tsars, and under some provocation from the Finns, who really abused their Constitution, blundering attempts were made to incorporate Finland into the Russian Empire and to abolish her representative institutions. The outbreak of war in 1914 found Finland, like Poland, half hoping that some reverse to the Russian arms might be the means of her securing release from the Act of the Vienna Congress—independence, or the former connection with Sweden. Then promises of complete autonomy from the Tsar's Government won over the Finns to the Russian cause. These promises were set at naught by the Bolshevists, and Finland underwent such months of horror in 1917-18 that a counter German invasion seemed by contrast a relief from absolute ruin. She had indeed appealed to Sweden to come to her rescue, and Sweden by so doing might have secured for herself the Åland Islands and have made Scandinavia a Great Power. But Sweden was afraid; she hesitated; the Germans came instead.

Sweden's lost opportunity

The Turkish Theatre of War.

The great geographical fact about the war in South-East Europe was the existence of the fortifications on the Dardanelles. If Turkey joined Germany and Austria and coerced Bulgaria into an alliance, Southern Russia was at once cut off from communication with the Mediterranean; her immense supplies of corn and mineral oil were withheld from Western Europe, and she in her turn could not get arms, ammunition, and other war supplies by the southern route, really her only sea outlet after the closing of the Baltic.

The failure of the Mediterranean Fleet of Britain to intercept the Goeben and the Breslau, and prevent those German warships from reaching the Dardanelles and Constantinople, was at least a factor in Turkey's decision to throw in her lot with the Central Powers. Turkey's attitude warped the loyalty of Greece towards Serbia and determined the policy of Bulgaria. The adhesion of Turkey and Bulgaria

ICE-FREE ACCESS TO NORTHERN RUSSIA.
In this map the lined portions of the northern seas are those which are frozen over during a large part of the year; the white portions are those free for navigation all the year. The port of Archangel being ice-bound from November to May, a fresh port was established at Kola, and a railway constructed thence to connect with the Russian railway system.

ONE GATEWAY TO THE EAST.
Panoramic view of Aleppo, showing the old fortress. The strategic importance of Aleppo was very great owing to its situation on the Berlin-Bagdad line.

to cut off Turkish Asia Minor from Syria, Arabia, Armenia, and Mesopotamia. Communication with Russia in Transcaucasia might have been opened up via Bitlis and Lake Van. The Mesopotamian and Palestine Expeditions could then have taken place, and might have been far more easily accomplished if due allowance had been made for the seasonal differences in the Mesopotamian river depths. The Turkish power in Arabia would then have died of inanition.

The Balkan States.

The Turkish theatre of war can scarcely be separated geographically from that of the Balkan States, the affairs of all these countries having

isolated Russia from Mediterranean Europe, and gave Germany and Austria the means of conquering Serbia, of seriously threatening Egypt, of attacking Aden, mining British shipping between the Gulf of Suez and the coasts of India and Ceylon, and of invading Persia and intriguing with Afghanistan.

One way of dealing with the Turkish menace in its inception, that commended itself to some critics, was the landing of an overwhelmingly strong British or British and French force at Alexandretta, the seizure of the Bagdad Railway and Aleppo, and the garrisoning of Diarbekr. Certainly the wealthiest provinces of Turkey lay to the **Strategic value** eastward of Alexan-**of Alexandretta** dretta, but the topography and the strategic difficulties of this part of Turkey are best explained by a diagram (see page 190). The passage of the zigzag Dardanelles might have been made with little damage by a British fleet if it had gone in immediate pursuit of the Goeben and Breslau; but not some months afterwards, when German engineers had strengthened the fortifications and mounted new artillery.

As much bravery and persistency as went to that ill-fated attempt to invade Turkey where she was strongest might have availed, with the then possible co-operation of the Russians,

A KEY POSITION IN THE BALKANS.
Adrianople, as seen from the Great Bridge. Occupying a key position on the Turco-Bulgarian frontier, the possession of Adrianople by Turkey largely influenced Bulgaria to ally herself with the Central Powers.

been so interdependent after the outbreak of war. It might be considered to begin on the north-west in the kingdoms of Serbia and Montenegro. Both are very mountainous, like the neighbouring country of Albania and South-West Bulgaria; but Montenegro is so small that it is little more than one huge mountain mass—the " Black Mountain "—which commands the southernmost coast of Dalmatia and specially the " four-fingered " harbour of Cattaro. Serbia is divided into two unequal parts by the long Morava River, with its twin sources, the Upper Morava, that flows through Nish, and the

PLACES OF IMPORTANCE AND INTEREST IN THE TURKISH THEATRE OF WAR.
Main street of Alexandretta, the principal port of the Aleppo region. Some authorities held that the Turkish menace might have been disposed of at its inception had a strong allied force landed at Alexandretta, seized the Bagdad Railway and Aleppo, and garrisoned Diarbekr, thus severing Turkish Asia Minor from Syria, Arabia, and Mesopotamia. Right: Remarkable ruins of an ancient bridge across the Tigris near Diarbekr.

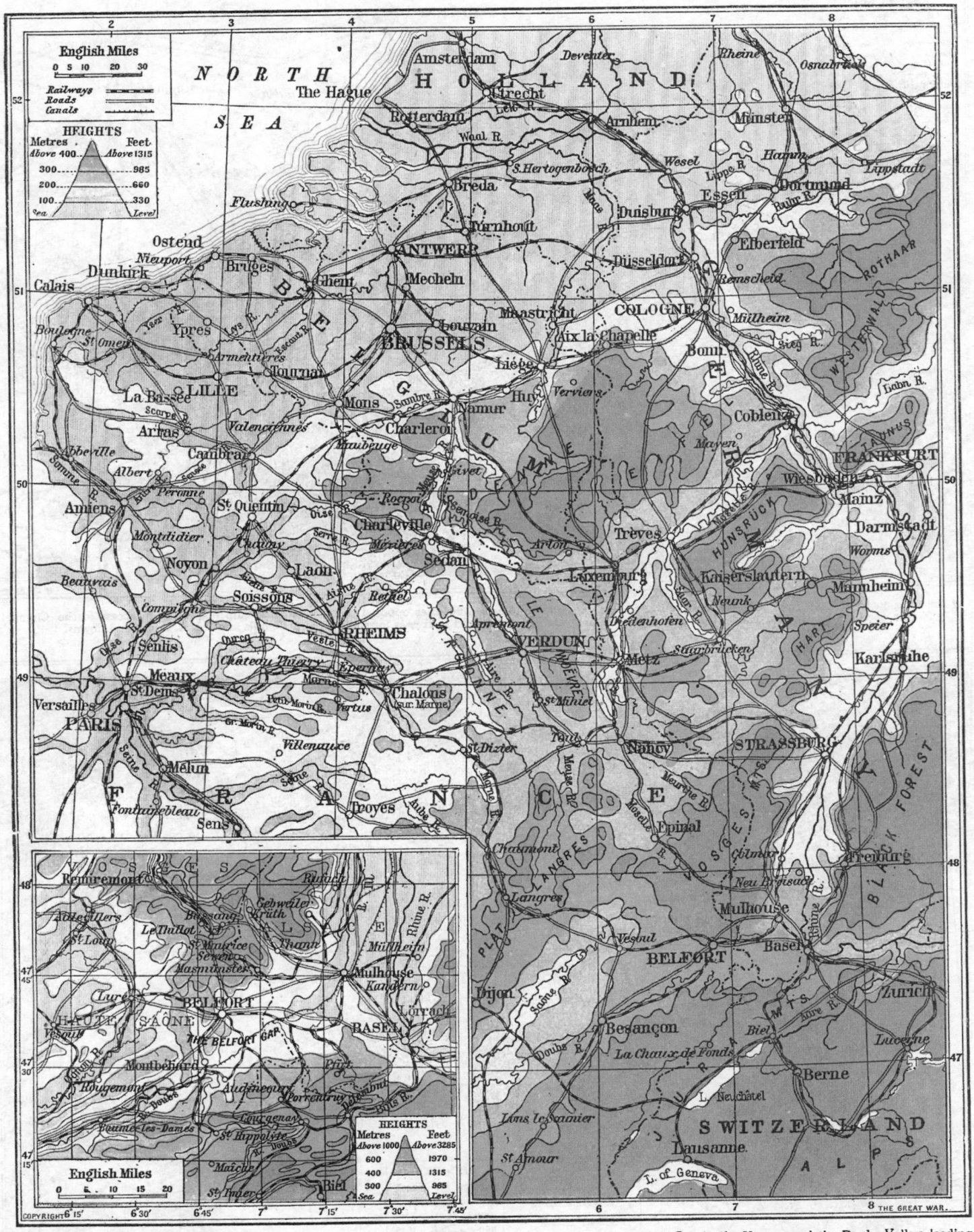

Contour map of North-East France, Belgium, and the Rhineland, showing the natural difficulties of direct approach to Paris from Metz, by way of Châlons and Epernay, as compared with the route through the Belgian plain. The inset map shows the Belfort Gap in the Vosges, and the Doubs Valley, leading from the Rhine Valley to the Rhone, and opening access to Lyons, Marseilles, and the Mediterranean communications.

GEOGRAPHICAL FEATURES OF THE WESTERN FRONT THAT DETERMINED THE INVASION ROUTE.

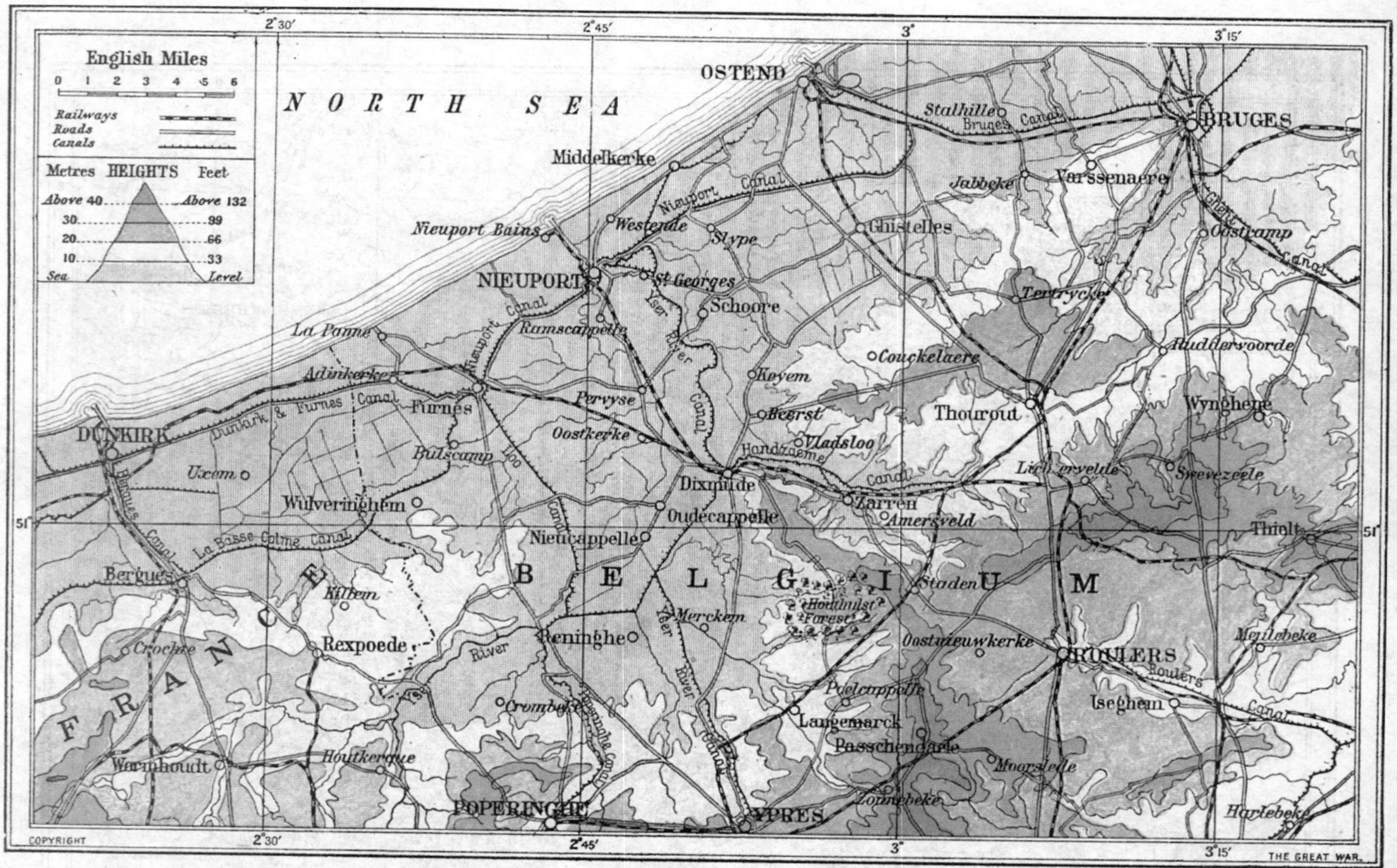

Map of the Belgian coast belt from Ostend to Dunkirk, showing the topographical difficulties opposed to an invader attempting to secure access to the Channel and the open sea by the canalised rivers, dikes, flooded land, and by the natural fortresses formed by the little hills and ridges, dunes and downs.

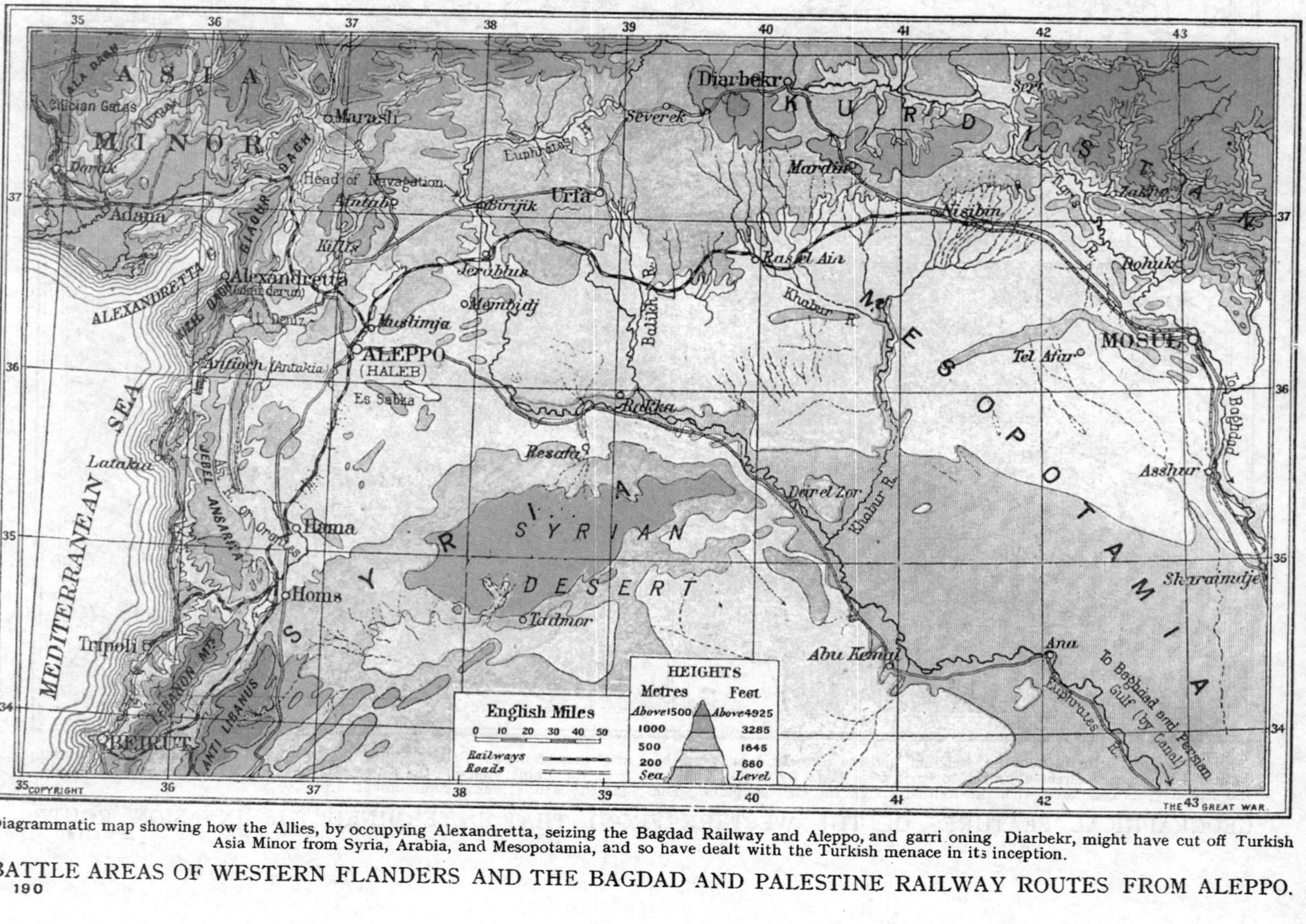

Diagrammatic map showing how the Allies, by occupying Alexandretta, seizing the Bagdad Railway and Aleppo, and garrisoning Diarbekr, might have cut off Turkish Asia Minor from Syria, Arabia, and Mesopotamia, and so have dealt with the Turkish menace in its inception.

BATTLE AREAS OF WESTERN FLANDERS AND THE BAGDAD AND PALESTINE RAILWAY ROUTES FROM ALEPPO.

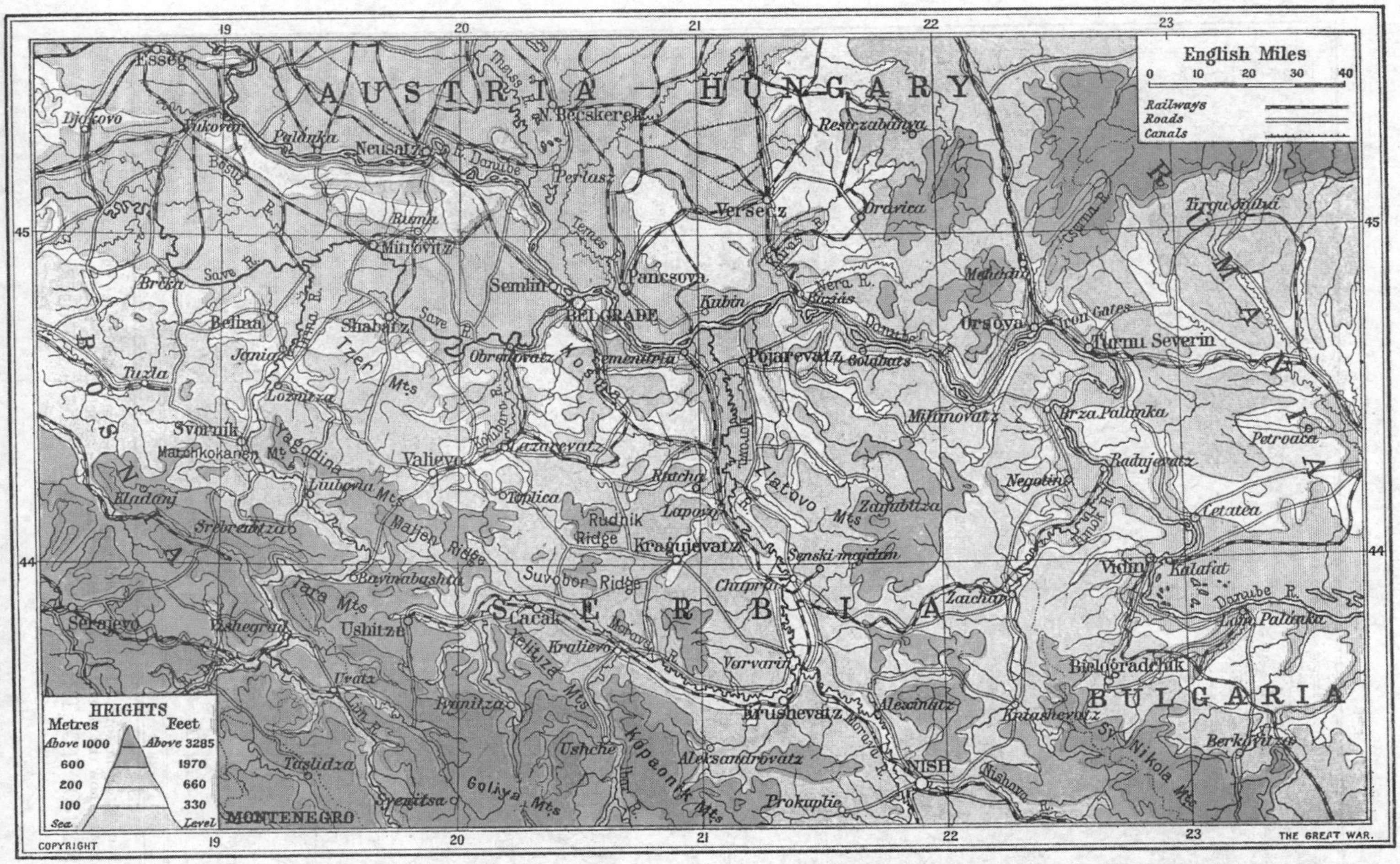

Contour map of Serbia, showing the valley of the long Morava River which bifurcates near Varvarin into the Upper Morava, flowing through Nish, and the Serbian Morava, rising in North Albania. It was mainly up the valleys of these rivers that the Austro-Germans first penetrated in their conquest of the country.

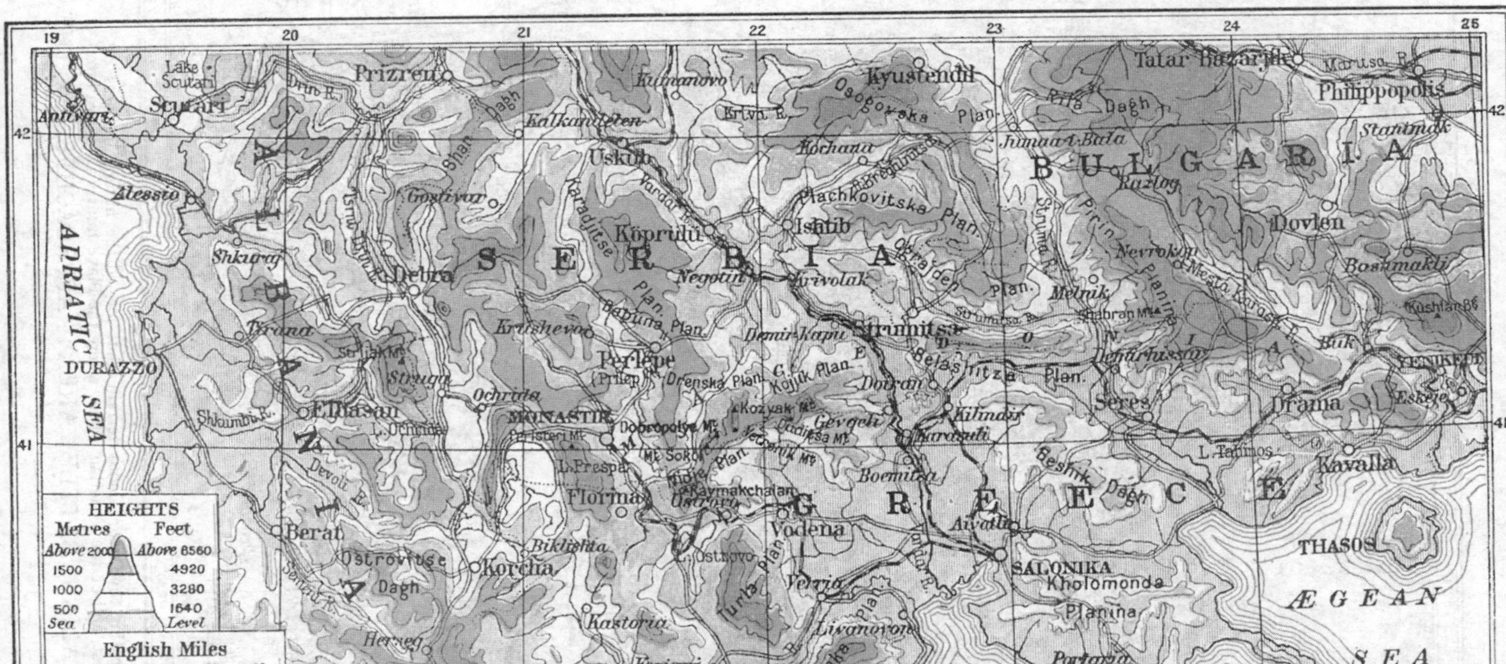

Map of the Salonika front from Durazzo to Yenikeui, east of Kavalla, showing how the mountain barrier on her south-west frontier for a long time protected Bulgaria from any serious degree of invasion on the part of the Western Allies.

CONTOUR MAPS OF SERBIA AND THE BALKANS BATTLE AREA OF THE ARMY OF THE ORIENT.

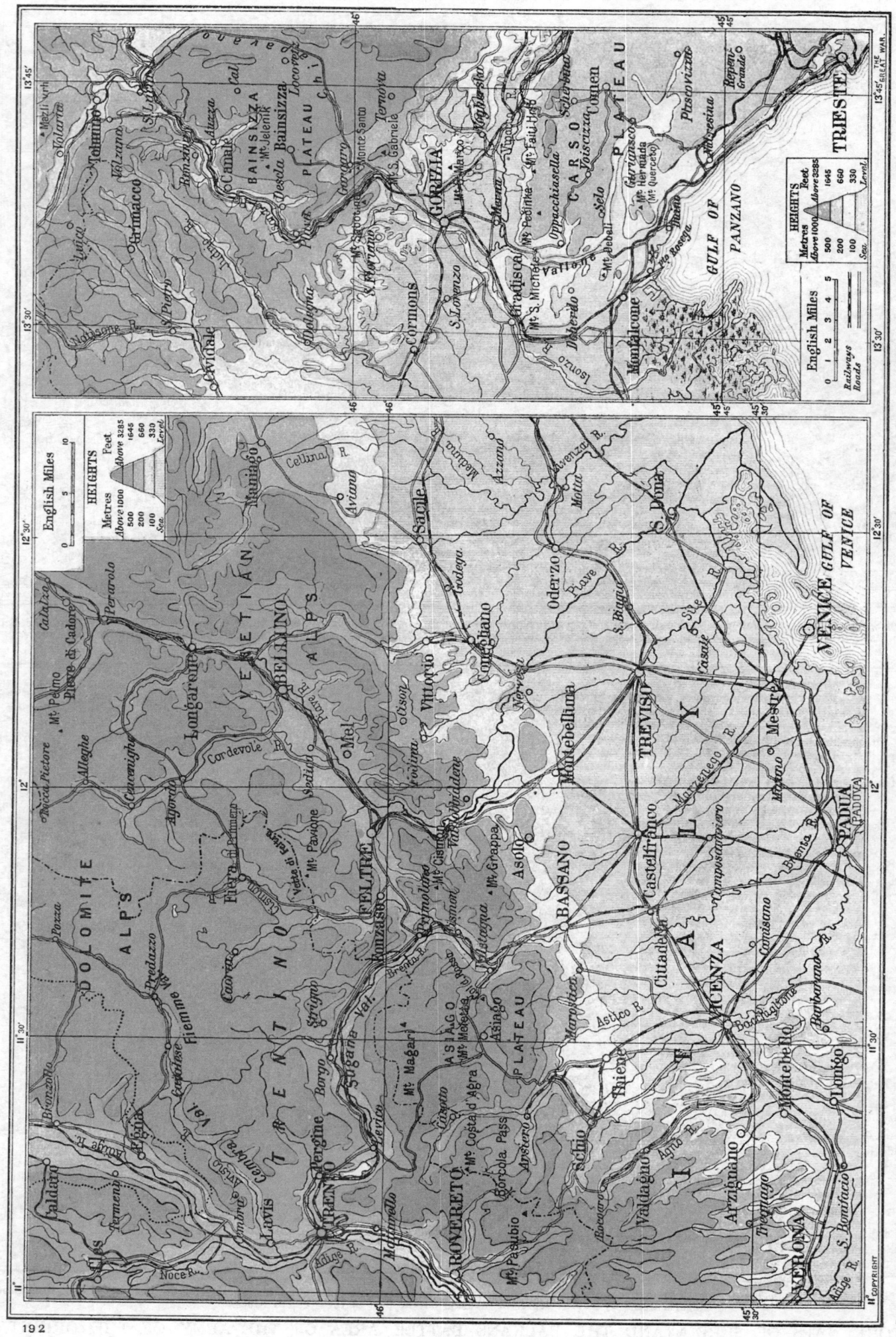

Contour map of North-East Italy, indicating the mountainous terrain that formed the natural defences of the Trentino against attack from the west, and of the Venetian Plain, where the Piave front was drawn after

the Italian retreat in 1917. In the smaller map on the right are indicated the physical features of the Isonzo front, showing how the Bainsizza and Carso plateaux serve as bulwarks of Trieste.

THE ITALIAN BATTLE AREA: APPROACHES TO THE TRENTINO, TO TRIESTE, AND THE PIAVE FRONT.

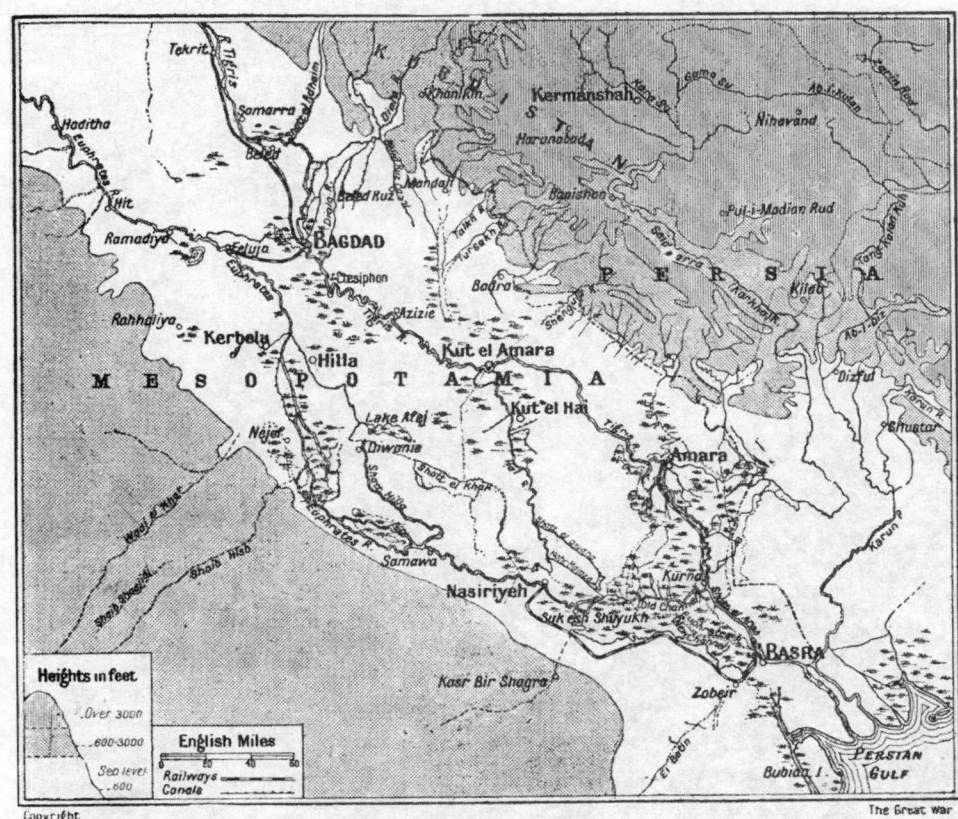

RIVER SYSTEM OF MESOPOTAMIA.

The Euphrates and Tigris, uniting in one estuary, and further interconnected by natural offshoots and artificial canals, were navigable from the Persian Gulf, eight or nine hundred miles inland, to the mountains of Kurdistan and the vicinity of Northern Syria.

it is not improbable the presence of the British and French at Adrianople might have restrained Bulgaria from open enmity.

Asia Minor is only of geographical interest in connection with the war in that its Mediterranean coasts afforded Germany, no doubt, means of carrying on her submarine campaign against allied shipping in the Eastern Mediterranean. Otherwise this peninsula, with its rugged ranges of southern, eastern, and western mountains, its interior salt deserts and bitter lakes, its climate of extremes—broiling heat in summer, deadly cold in winter—its relative absence of good roads and only one trunk railway, scarcely entered into the strategy of the campaigns as a means of reaching the Bosphorus overland from the east. Eastward of Constantinople it was only at Iskanderun, Aintab, Diarbekr, and Bitlis that smashing blows could have been delivered at the Turkish Power—protecting Persia, freeing Armenia, and forcing Turkey to abandon Syria, Mesopotamia, and Arabia.

The Syrian coast lands from Antioch to the Sinai Peninsula consist of parallel ridges of mountain, rising to snowy heights on Lebanon and Hermon, to altitudes of five and six thousand feet in the Jebel Hauran, and to over three thousand feet in the mountains of Judæa. **River system of** This region consti- **Mesopotamia** tuted, on the whole, the least trying and climatically disagreeable portion of the war area. Water, vegetation, and local food supplies were fairly abundant. Portions of the land, except for accidental devastation, were comparative paradises in contrast with the deserts of Sinai and Northern Arabia, the broiling plains or fetid swamps of Mesopotamia.

But one great strategic feature of Mesopotamia in favour of the British invasion was the river system. The two great, nearly parallel rivers, Euphrates and Tigris, uniting in one estuary and further interconnected by natural offshoots and artificial canals, were navigable from the Persian Gulf inland, eight or nine hundred miles, to the mountains of

Ibar (or Serbian Morava), rising in North Albania. It was mainly up the valleys of these rivers that the Austro-Germans were first able to penetrate in their conquest of Serbia.

The mountain barrier on her south-west frontier for a long time protected Bulgaria from any serious degree of invasion on the part of the Western Allies. Another factor in favour of Bulgarian resistance, which was maintained up to the end of September, 1918, was the unhealthiness of the Ægean coast districts, in the neighbourhood of the big river mouths and deltas, especially those of the Struma (the virtual frontier of the Bulgarians) and the Vardar. Enormous numbers of mosquitoes spread the germs of malarial fever.

Turkey was only open to a paralysing attack from the Mediterranean in two directions : (1) At the head of the Gulf of Saros (alongside the Gallipoli Peninsula), and (2) at Alexandretta, or Iskanderun, already referred to. An army like that despatched by the British for the capture of the Dardanelles—say, a force of six hundred thousand men—might have succeeded better if it had been disembarked at Avrasha and had quickly seized the neck of the Gallipoli Peninsula, which is also the southern end of the Tekir Ridge, a range of mountains 1,600 to 2,900 feet high. This, with Saros Island, could have been occupied to safeguard the holding of Saros Gulf. From such a position an attack on Adrianople, the Vienna-Constantinople railway, and the Black Sea coast *might* have been quite possible undertakings, to be followed by Russian co-operation (in 1915 and 1916) and the taking of Constantinople. Again,

IN A LAND OF SAND AND STONES.

British reserves in Mesopotamia going into action. Broiling plains and fetid swamps formed a considerable part of the Mesopotamian terrain. The country, however, possessed in its great, nearly parallel rivers, Euphrates and Tigris, a strategic feature in favour of the British invasion.

One of the Turkish positions to the west of Jerusalem where the Turks vainly sought to stay the British advance on the Holy City. The photograph indicates something of the natural obstacles that General Allenby's forces met with on their victorious progress through the Judean Hills.

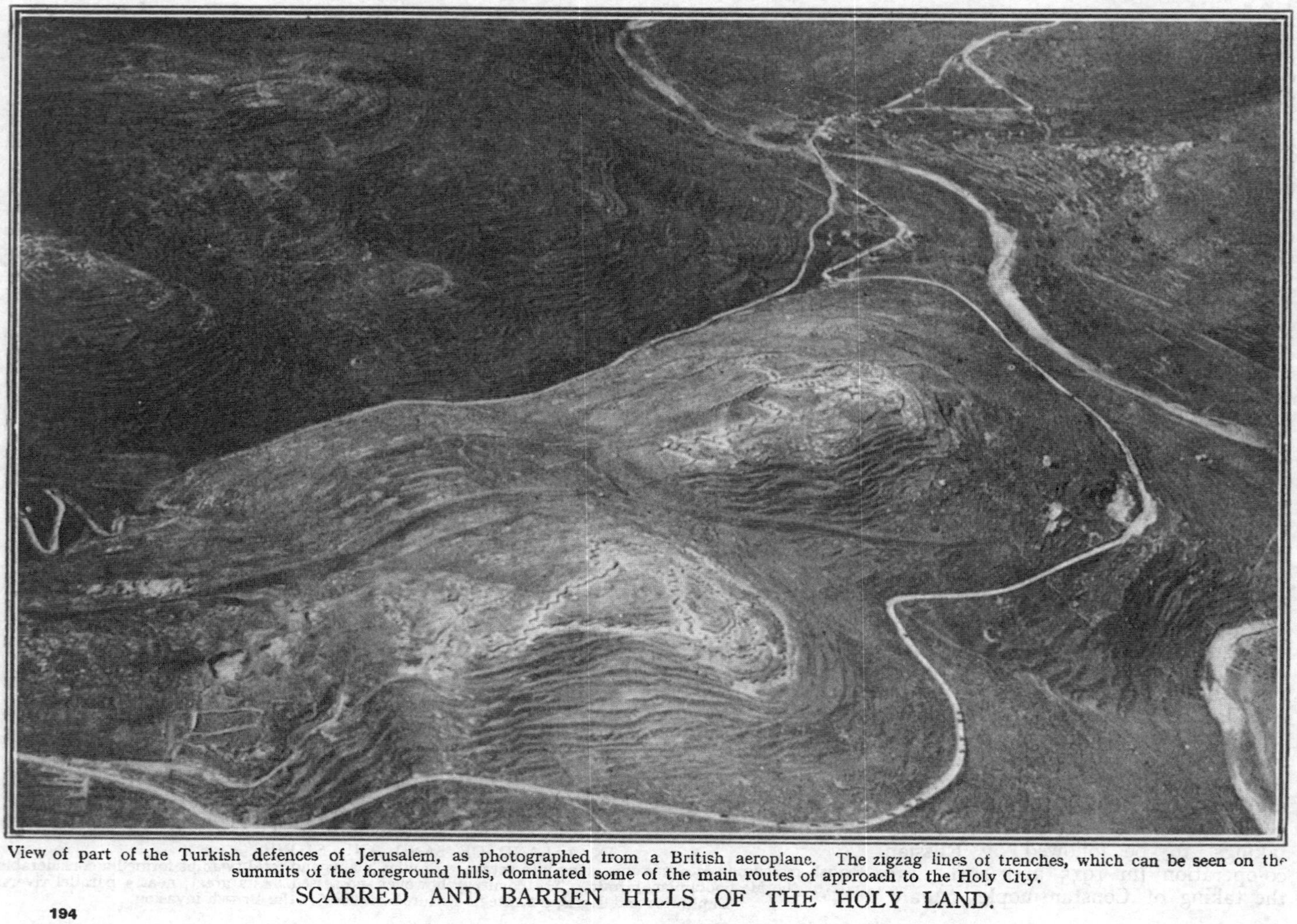

View of part of the Turkish defences of Jerusalem, as photographed from a British aeroplane. The zigzag lines of trenches, which can be seen on the summits of the foreground hills, dominated some of the main routes of approach to the Holy City.

SCARRED AND BARREN HILLS OF THE HOLY LAND.

Kurdistan and the vicinity of Northern Syria. Thus India was connected by water communication without a break with Basra, Bagdad, and Mosul, with Hit, and with a point on the Euphrates nigh to Aleppo. Moreover, the Karun affluent of the Shat-el-Arab (Euphrates-Tigris estuary) was navigable up-stream into Southern Persia and the vicinity of the oil-wells of Dizful and Shuster.

The native peoples of these regions of man's earliest civilisation are of diverse stocks and religions, but of sympathies on the whole preponderating in favour of Western European intervention in their affairs. They had a hearty dislike of Turkish rule. There is the Armenian population on the north, with its big noses and facial

GOLD-MINING AREA OF EASTERN SIBERIA.
Rich in minerals, all of which are worked, Siberia's principal gold-mines are situated to the east of Lake Baikal, on the River Olekma, and on the Altai Mountains.

LINES OF COMMUNICATIONS WITH THE FAR EAST.
Railway-station at Tomsk. A branch line connects the important capital of the Government of Tomsk with the great Trans-Siberian Railway at Taiza.

resemblance to the Hittites graven and sculptured on rocks and amid the ruins of forgotten empires. There are the Kurds of the mountains on the Persian border-line, very "Nordic" often in facial feature, hair-colour, and complexion, speaking a corrupted Aryan language, but fanatically Mohammedan and bent on the perpetual massacre of the Christian Armenian. There are the Arabs of more—or less — pure descent ranging through all Mesopotamia and the eastern part of Syria, the sole, scanty population of the intervening deserts.

Syria and Palestine have a very mixed population, some tribes descended from prehistoric races, others more distinctly Semitic, like the vanished Phœnicians and the modern Arabs and Jews. There are the Druses, of mixed race and a mysterious religion—old, old broken faiths grafted on to fanatic Mohammedanism; there are the Christian Syrians (Maronites), the Christian Chaldæans (chiefly of Northern Mesopotamia), the Jews and Samaritans of Palestine, colonies of Circassians and Tatars, Albanians, and German mongrels.

In the region about the Euphrates Delta may be found remains of the original Gipsy tribes from India, and in Southern Persia one encounters a Negroid type of people descended from the ancient Elamites, and really seeming to represent the relics of the Asiatic Negroes that once dwelt almost uninterruptedly in the lands between Egypt and Malaysia.

In the land of Sinai, where such history-making battles took place between British and Turks—first to repel the Turco-German invasion of Egypt and next to reconquer Palestine from the Turks — the land is sandy desert in the north, and bare, sun-scorched rock and mountain in the south. The loftiest summits of Sinai reach to altitudes of nearly 10,000 feet, and their scenery, if desolate, is very imposing to the eye. Moreover, as they do attract some rain, and even snow, they supply enough moisture to pasture native flocks of goats and sheep and herds of wild ibex. **Topography of the Near East** These again maintain the existence of a few lingering leopards of large rosette markings, somewhat similar to the Persian leopard.

North from Sinai and the narrow Gulf of Akaba runs the extraordinary rift of the Dead Sea and the Jordan Valley. This gorge, from above the Lake of Gennesaret to near the Gulf of Akaba, is below sea-level. In the Jordan waters a dwarf variety of the Nilotic crocodile is still found, and the fish of these lakes and connecting river—those which so

THE LARGEST CITY OF SIBERIA.
View of Tomsk from Mount Vozkressenskayo. Linked with the Siberian Railway and possessing good steamer communication along the Obi River with the Urals, Tomsk, with a population of over 100,000 inhabitants, is a city of great industrial importance.

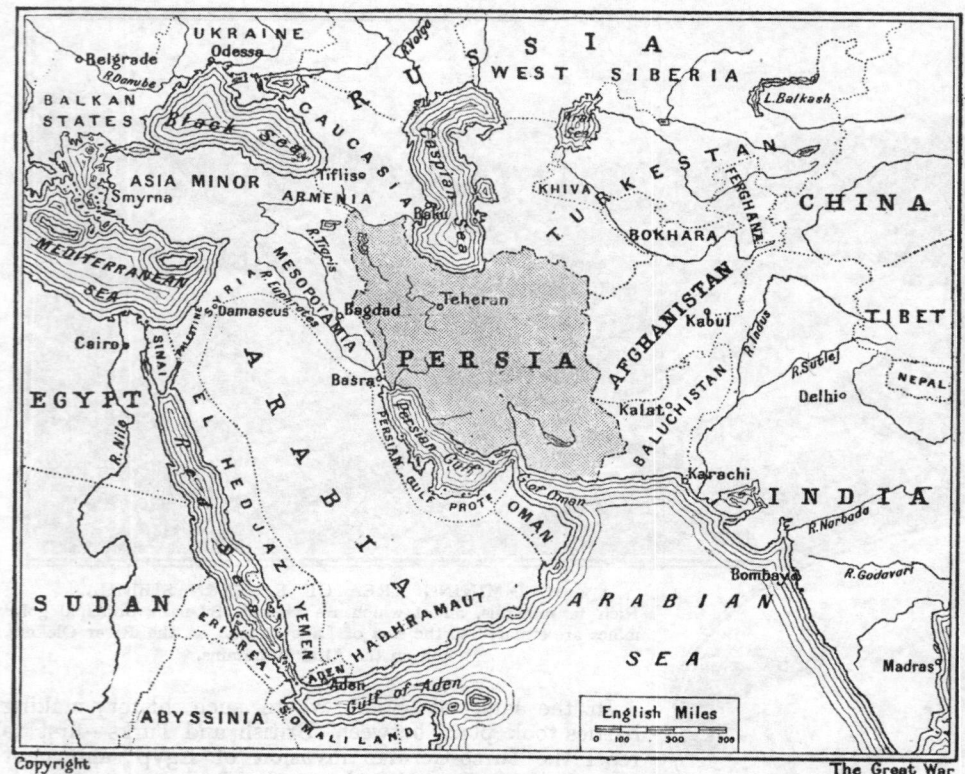

THE IMPORTANCE OF PERSIA.
Lying between the Indian Ocean and the Caspian Sea (with its Russian and Siberian communications and its highly important oil-fields at Baku), Persia is the isthmus that joins India to Arabia and the Mediterranean countries. The country was the centre of much intrigue by the Germans, who sought through it to interfere in Afghanistan and India.

frequently are mentioned in the Gospels—belong, like most of the birds of this hot, sunken valley, to African genera.

The region of Western Arabia came within the war area, for the Arabs of the Holy Places of Islam seized the opportunity to throw off the yoke of the Turk—in Mecca and its neighbourhood, at any rate. Across the elevated, dreary, stony desert tablelands of Midian, and along the dry river valley of Kháibar, the Hedjaz Railway had been constructed by the Turks before war broke out. This railway was repeatedly attacked and torn up at various stations on the way to Medina, where it stops, one favourite place for attack being Maan, about halfway in an easterly direction between the Dead Sea and the Gulf of Akaba. South of the Hedjaz, that region of Western Arabia which is lifted above the sandy deserts of the interior and which consists mostly of volcanic rock and old lava flows from long extinct volcanoes, is the far more delectable country of Yemen—"Arabia Felix"— with ten-thousand-feet-high mountains, a certain rainfall, and an approach to tropical vegetation. Coffee, introduced centuries ago from Abyssinia, has long been cultivated here in terraced plantations on the mountainsides.

This—and the "Himyaritic" country, the land of Hadhramaut, east of Aden —is the region producing incense and other perfumed gums. Here are to be seen ancient cities with cliff-like houses of many stories, and fantastic castles, altogether worthy of "The Arabian Nights," of jinns and black magicians, of subterranean treasure-houses, of the old Minæan civilisation which had so much to do with the first revelation of the East African coast to the commerce of Europe and Asia. Yet it has been involved in the world-war through the action of Turkey.

When she had joined the Germans, Turkey lost no time in making terms with the chiefs of Yemen, who had long disputed her authority and had oft-times been helped by the British authorities at Aden when Turkey would have pressed too hard on them. The Arabs of Mokha and Sana were too fanatically Mohammedan to resist the opportunity of making war on a Christian Power, so Turks and Arabs alike, from the north-west of Aden, attacked that small protectorate, and for a time wrenched the little Sultanate of Lahij from British control.

Siberia and the Far East.

Siberia became involved in the war, in 1918, by the attempts of the Germans to secure control of this vast North Asiatic territory through their Bolshevist allies. Against them, on the other hand, especially in Eastern Siberia, fought a few Russians opposed to the Soviet, or Anarchist, Government, and—strange episode of the war—a host of Austrian war prisoners, captured by the Russians in the days when the Tsar's armies overran Galicia and Bukovina.

These "Austrians" were in reality Slavs from Bohemia and Moravia, who regarded Russia as the upholder of the Slavic peoples.

When the Bolshevists tried to arrest them and hand them over to Austria they threw themselves *Slav assistance in Siberia* on the side of law and order in Eastern Siberia and determined to fight against the Germanisation of the Russian dominions.

Japan, as the ally of Great Britain, declared war against Germany very early in the struggle, and with assistance from British and British Indian troops and a few ships from the British Navy, after desperate fighting and resort to some of the latest devices in artillery fire, captured the principal German stronghold on the Chinese coast. This was the city of Kiao-Chau, which, with a considerable area round it in the province of Shantung, had been leased by China to Germany for a hundred years. Japan simultaneously (and acting in concert with Australian forces and ships) occupied the German archipelago of the Mariana (or Ladrone) Islands

NEAR KRASNOVODSK, ON THE CASPIAN SEA.
Krasnovodsk, on the eastern shore of the Caspian Sea opposite the valuable oil district of Baku, is the seaport terminus of the Transcaspian Railway to Bokhara.

inhabited by a Micronesian race—that is to say, Polynesians of more Mongoloid aspect than those of the other Pacific islands. The Mariana Archipelago was secured by Germany from Spain in 1898. The islets are rich in tropical produce and have a very healthy climate for the tropics. But the only good-sized island in this group—Guam —is the property of the United States. Their relative proximity to the outlying parts of the Japanese Empire (Bonin Island and the Liu-kiu group) gave our ally of the Far East a special interest in their eventual disposal.

Germany's Island Colonies.

On the other hand, the Caroline and Marshall Islands, conquered by the British Australian Fleet, seem destined to become a part of the Australian Commonwealth, together with the Solomon Islands, New Britain, New Ireland, and Northern (German) New Guinea; while Samoa may pass to the control of New Zealand, the destined mistress of Fiji, the Gilbert, Ellice, and Tonga Islands.

Northern Papua (as the Australians prefer to call New Guinea) is a land of 70,000 square miles in extent, of dense tropical forest, and possessing some of the most wonderful among the Birds of Paradise. Its native inhabitants, who for the most part welcomed and assisted the Australian and British forces, are almost entirely of the Papuan race, a branch of the Oceanic Negro stock. There are also the traces of former Polynesian or Indonesian settlements of a higher and more refined semi-Caucasian people, and in the central mountains (nearly reaching to snow levels) there are Negritos, or Pygmy Negroes.

The peoples of the Admiralty Islands and of the large islands of New Britain and New Ireland and the adjacent Solomons are of the highest interest to

THE CONTRASTING COAST-LINES OF THE ADRIATIC.
This map illustrates the contrast between the almost harbourless Adriatic coast of Italy and the opposite eastern coast with its numerous deep-water, well-sheltered ports. It also indicates the projection of the shore of Southern Albania to within forty-five miles of the Italian Cape of Otranto, whereby a hostile Power holding Valona could close the Adriatic to Italian shipping. The map further shows in tint the eastern possessions of Venice down to 1798.

the ethnologist, some for their extraordinary physical resemblance to African Negroes, a few because they represent survivals of the ancient Indonesian immigrants to the Pacific, the originators of the Polynesian type —of comparatively fair skin, European cast of features, and remote European descent (via India and Indo-China).

The Samoans are typical Polynesians —that tall, handsome blend between the ancient white man stock, the Mongol, and the Negroid Melanesian. Samoa will always be interesting to the English-speaking peoples as the last home and resting-place of Robert Louis Stevenson.

Persia and the Caspian Sea.

In discussing the topography of the war, Persia cannot be altogether overlooked, because a portion of the struggle was fought out there. But in this connection the main fact for Great

IN THE HEART OF THE TRANSCAUCASIAN OIL DISTRICT.
General view of Baku, chief town of the Russian Government of that name in Transcaucasia. Situated to the south of the Apsheron peninsula, which is the seat of the great oil-fields, Baku is an important harbour for the Transcaspian trade and the chief station of the Caspian naval flotilla.

ON ITALY'S MOUNTAIN FRONT.

View of the Isonzo near the eastern frontier of Italy, and (above) among the rocky heights about the Tonale Pass in the Trentino. Much of the border line between Austria and Italy consisted of towering precipices and unscalable walls of rock. Austria, when Italy had been almost a suppliant in such matters, had so fixed the border line that Austria was everywhere able to dominate the entries into Italy.

agreed with Russia to leave Persia alone, provided equally that no other Power attempted to interfere with its concerns. Lying between the Caspian Sea (with its Russian and Siberian communications) and the Indian Ocean, geographically speaking, Persia is the isthmus that joins India to Arabia and the Mediterranean countries.

The Adriatic and the Alps.

The mutiny of the Swedish officers and the Persia gendarmerie occurred before Italy came to the help of the Western Powers. Moreover, what Persia was to the illumining of Asia after the first devastating rush of Islam, that mediæval and renaissance Italy was to Europe after the invasions of Goths and Huns, Magyars and Vandals, Germans and Bulgarians ; and mostly after the warped Christianity of the Byzantine Empire had submerged the science of Athens, Alexandria, and Rome.

It needed no common courage on the part of Italy to declare war

Britain in the summer of 1918 was that, with Russia destroyed, there was nothing between Germany and the Indian frontier; nothing between Germany or German-governed Turkey and the oil-wells of Baku, on the Caspian. The possession of this wealth of petroleum might conceivably tip the balance in favour of the Central Powers' success.

The Persia of the middle nineteenth century had grown hostile to the British rulers of India. She intrigued with Afghanistan and seemed ever and again to be the cat's-paw of Russia. The Russian Empire, in fact, impinged so much on Persia that, in order not to be at war with Russia, Great Britain had to consent to some definition and partition of interests in that country which should at any rate save Persia from complete absorption into the Tsar's Empire.

Thus arose the 1907 agreement which the Persians construed into a division of their anarchically governed country between Russia and Britain.

The British in no way abused the advantages of their position in Southern Persia. But as soon as war broke out it was seen that Germany—acting perhaps through the Swedish traveller Sven Hedin—had won over the Swedish officers of the international gendarmerie (which was to maintain law and order in Central and Southern Persia); and this force, led by its Swedish officers, forthwith attacked and cruelly maltreated the British telegraph officials, Consuls, traders, and employees of the Persian Government, the Persian power being incapable of controlling them. Consequently the British Government, as a war measure, and to ward off Turkish or German interference with Afghanistan and India, had to organise a new police force (the South Persia Rifles) under the leadership of Sir Percy Sykes.

But all along and repeatedly the British Government asseverated that it desired most *not* to have to interfere with Persia. If the Russians would have consented to a "self-denying " ordinance, the British would have willingly

Persia as a gate to India

on Austria in 1915. It was at a time when the fortunes of the Triple Entente (as it then was) were none too brilliant. Belgium was almost completely overrun, and North-East France was in the firm grip of the invader, who ever and again made a feint or threw out a suggestion of treating Switzerland as he had done Belgium, or of aiming at Lyons and severing the French contact with Italy. But the Italian people realised that the success of the Teuton attack on the liberties of Europe would be fatal to Italian destinies, except as a subordinate part of a Germanised Central Europe.

The Adriatic coast of Italy is in singular contrast to that of Dalmatia and Albania, being almost entirely without harbours, whereas the opposite coast of Dalmatia and Albania is a maze of islands and deep, secure, sheltered passages with unnumbered seaports. This western fringe of the Balkan Peninsula (indicated in tint on the map on page 197)—Istria and Dalmatia, Ragusa and Cattaro—had once belonged to the vanished republic of Venice, and been saved by Venice from incorporation in Turkey or Serbia during the slow destruction of the Eastern Empire. Hungary, it

Coast-lines of the Adriatic

is true, had acquired an access to the Adriatic at Fiume, and the Holy Roman Empire of Austria-Germany had secured Trieste when Venice was taking up the control that the Constantinople Emperors were losing to Slavs and Turks.

But between the fifteenth and the eighteenth centuries the Adriatic Sea was an Italian lake Italy, which had struggled against German envelopment in the ninth, tenth, twelfth, eighteenth, and nineteenth centuries, was not minded to let the insidious attack succeed in the twentieth. The dominions of Venice had been transferred to Austria by the Congress of Vienna. The southernmost part of the Tyrol was a sovereign bishopric, an Italianate State of the "Holy Roman Empire," from the Middle Ages. **Vital importance of Valona** Austria annexed it in 1814, and it became a threatening protrusion of Teutonic power into Northern Italy, a constant menace of armed intervention in Italian affairs.

It was therefore towards the Trentino and Trieste, Istria and Albania, that the Italian attack turned when war with Austria (and Germany in the background) proved inevitable.

The Albanian coast bulges out southwards so as to approach within forty-five miles of the Italian peninsula of Otranto (see map on page 197), and whereas the latter has only the one indifferent port of Brindisi, Southern Albania possesses the magnificent harbour of Valona, partially sheltered and defended by the islet of Sasseno. The territory of Valona is bordered on the south by Epirus, the northernmost prolongation of Greece. If the Teutonic Powers had succeeded in securing Albania as one of their principalities and had fortified Valona, they could have closed the Adriatic at their pleasure.

Having made this point secure, the Italians turned their attention to the Trentino and Trieste.

All along the frontier of North-East Italy, Austria, when Italy was almost a suppliant in such

matters, had so fixed the border line that Austria was everywhere able to dominate the entries into Italy and to defend access to her own territory—and much of it territory really Italian in race and tongue—by towering precipices and unscalable walls of rock.

Nowhere was warfare to be so amazing, so spectacular, as this struggle between Italy and Austria in the high Alps, much of it at an altitude of ten thousand feet. "The wildest regions of the Vosges, the most difficult mazes of the Balkans' ranges, the most formidable barriers of the Carpathians"—to quote Professor Douglas Johnson— were tame compared with the precipices and icy peaks of the Trentino Alps. The Italian soldiers had sometimes to climb a mountain wall that was nearly vertical and five thousand feet up, and could only do so by driving rings and iron pegs into the rock and hauling themselves up by ropes and ladders.

There were broad glacier trenches of old-time river valleys that led northward from Verona to Trent and Bozen (the

DEFENCES OF ITALY ALONG MOUNTAIN AND STREAM.

Italians constructing shell-proof shelters along a mountain trench above Gorizia, on the Isonzo, and (inset) where the Piave flows through the mountains. To reach Austria through her most vulnerable part—Trieste—it was necessary for Italy to seize and seal the mountain gateways, for no army could be safe on the Isonzo front while its lines of communication, which crossed the Piedmont Plain just south of the Trentino, were threatened from the heights.

ON THE MARCH ABOVE THE SNOW-LINE.
Alpine troops of the Italian Army advancing on skis across a snowfield among the mountains. In circle: Italian patrol among the Alps, wearing white overalls to render them less conspicuous against the snow.

limit of Italian ambition), but, naturally, they were blocked by artillery. Another way northward was up the Ampezzo valley and over the Monte Croce Pass, or eastward by a still more Alpine route, the Tre Croci Pass, through which at one time the Italians hoped to reach the valley of the Drave and get into the heart of Austria.

The more spectacular point of attack, however, was in the direction of Trieste. The fall of Trieste would have a resounding effect on the Austrian Empire; it would entail the capture of the whole Istrian Peninsula and the naval stronghold of Pola, and thus permit of Italy bringing help to Serbia and menacing Hungary. So towards Trieste the main Italian objective was always addressed between 1915 and 1917. The Italian frontier was here drawn so as to give Austria the whole valley of the Isonzo River down to its marshy outlet into the Adriatic. Immediately east of the Isonzo the natural defences of Trieste were tremendous, almost insuperable, with a strong army and the most modern artillery defending them. First there was the town of Gorizia

Natural defences to be taken—Gorizia, overhung almost by **of Trieste** the abrupt and lofty tablelands of the Bainsizza and Ternovano. But Gorizia, taken by the Italians on August 9th, 1916, was comparatively a side issue. The real defence of Trieste was the parched and porous limestone plateau of the Carso and the jutting-out Gibraltar of Hermada Mountain, an untakable natural fortress commanding the coast road into Trieste. These barriers long held Italy at bay. The geographical aspects of the case were dealt with in some detail in Chapter CLXXIV. (Vol. 9, page 91 *et seq.*)

But if the Alps and Dolomites stayed the frantic assaults of the Italians and saved Austrian territory from invasion, they similarly acted as deterrents to German invasions of the Lombard and Venetian plains. They offered so many obstacles to the passage of the protective artillery; they were impassable in the snows of winter, dangerous in the land-slides, torrents, and mists of spring and autumn. And when Germans and Austrians did break through and commence debouching on the plains their advance laterally from east to west was held up by the hundreds of great and small streams and rivers flowing in parallel courses from the mountains to the Northern Adriatic.

200

The Danube and Transylvania.

The Danube and its tributaries played a considerable part in the geography of the war. It was the first river to be brought within the range of hostilities. At the end of July, 1914, the Austrians had commenced to attempt crossings of the Save, Drina, and Danube, and enter Serbia. But their difficulties were tremendous and very costly. Serbia seemed to be girt about by wonderful natural moats, far too deep at all times to wade through, usually approached on either side by nearly impassable swamps. The few bridges were destroyed by the Serbians.

Even when a temporary occupation of Belgrade was effected in December 1914, the Serbians elsewhere succeeded in driving the Austrian armies into the rivers or the marshes; and when the war was more than a year old they stood with their heroic country intact, without a single Austrian being left upon Serbian soil.

"*Feeding the Guns by Shell Pack-Horses*"

From an Oil-painting by Lieut. H. S. Power, R.O.I., Australian Official Artist

Similarly the Danube, in conjunction with the Transylvanian Mountains, seemed to guard Rumania's neutrality, and to make it safe for her to enter the war on the side of the Allies with her south front protected against Bulgaria, and her north by the Russian armies occupying the Bukovina. Germany and Austria were at a deadlock. They could not communicate directly with Turkey and ensure her co-operation ; they could not force the river guard of Serbia with the full Serbian Army to face them. Then Bulgaria and Greece were won over by Germany to make a dastardly attack on—or fail to defend —Serbia on the east and south. But for this traitorous stab in the back Serbia might have succeeded, with her rivers and mountains as defence, in keeping the Germanic Empires at bay till the end of the war. As it was, the remnant of the Serbian Army had to retreat into Albania and to Salonika.

Rumania, when it came to be her turn to enter the lists—urged to redress the balance in the Balkan Peninsula, upset by the Bulgarian attack on Serbia—did not read aright the lessons of her geography.

Rumania—a combination of the old provinces of Moldavia and Wallachia, with a semi-Tatar district, the Dobruja, added after the Russo-Turkish War of 1877, and enlarged by cessions from Bulgaria in 1913—was a kingdom in 1916 of 53,400 square miles. Her boundary with Russia was the Pruth River to its junction with the Danube estuary ; her only land frontier with Bulgaria consisted of a not very lengthy line between Ekrene on the Black Sea and Turtukai on the Danube. Fifty miles north-east of this was the twenty-five miles of railway between Constantsa on the Black Sea and the bridge-head of Cerna Voda on the Danube. Thence, westwards of Cerna Voda for over three hundred miles, the great Danube (often breaking into marshes from five to twelve miles wide) separated Rumania from Bulgaria. *The Danube was not bridged for a length of five hundred miles between Belgrade and Cerna Voda.* On the north-west and west, towards Hungary, Rumania was bounded by a southward extension of the Carpathians, the Transylvanian Alps, a rugged, lofty chain of mountains, rising into heights of 8,000 feet in the south, and 6,000 feet in the north, and only crossed by roads for wheeled traffic over a few passes.

IN THE VALLEY OF THE MORAVA.
The long Morava River—formed of the flowing together of two main streams, the Upper Morava and the Serbian Morava, or Ibar—reaches the Danube a few miles to the east of Semendria. The Morava-Vardar valley possesses a strategic value, providing a clear course through a rugged mountain barrier.

So splendidly defensive a position was the Hungarian frontier of Rumania that it would have sufficed to leave at most two hundred thousand men to defend it against the Austro-German Army, especially as the Russians were in possession of Bukovina on the north, and able to threaten diversions in Northern Hungary. Between the foothills of the Transylvanian Alps and the Danube flowed, almost at right angles to the great river, many large and deep affluents, each one of which might be made a costly barrier to any army that crossed the mountains to march on Bukarest.

Obviously, the strategy required of Rumania, when she came into the war in 1916, was to invade Bulgaria through the Dobruja and march straight on Varna, the great Bulgarian seaport, hand that over to Russia for the landing of Russian contingent forces, then make for Tirnovo and cut the Constantinople railway at Philippopolis. With the support of the Western Allies attacking Bulgaria from the south, and a Russian army landed at Varna, the Rumanians might have had the glory of taking Constantinople and ending the war. Instead of which the Rumanian Army, insufficiently furnished with the necessary artillery, flung itself into Transylvania, was forced to retreat, was followed up, and, very insufficiently backed by Russia, was unable to save the bridge at Cerna Voda, for the Bulgarians and Germans had in their turn invaded her through the Dobruja.

Criticism of Rumanian strategy

Only the long trench of the Sereth River and the Northern Transylvanian Alps saved Rumania from coming completely into the enemy's possession. Once again the victory of the Allies was deferred through a lack of geographical knowledge or an insufficient appreciation of the importance of geography as applied to military strategy, though it has to be remembered that Rumania was led to believe that Bulgaria had had enough of war, and would not attack her if she did not attack Bulgaria.

War Topography of Africa.

Our survey of the war's topography must now turn to Africa. The first resort to arms on that continent was probably the hostile action by Germany on the northern frontier of Cape Colony, but it was almost immediately followed by the seizure of the German Government steamer the Von

AMID THE STERILE HEIGHTS OF THE BALKANS.
Serbian battery moving forward through the mountains. The broad belt of mountains which lies between the Morava-Vardar depression and the shore of the Adriatic is one of the most imposing topographic barriers in Europe—serving as a wall cutting off Central Serbia from its Italian neighbours.

Y

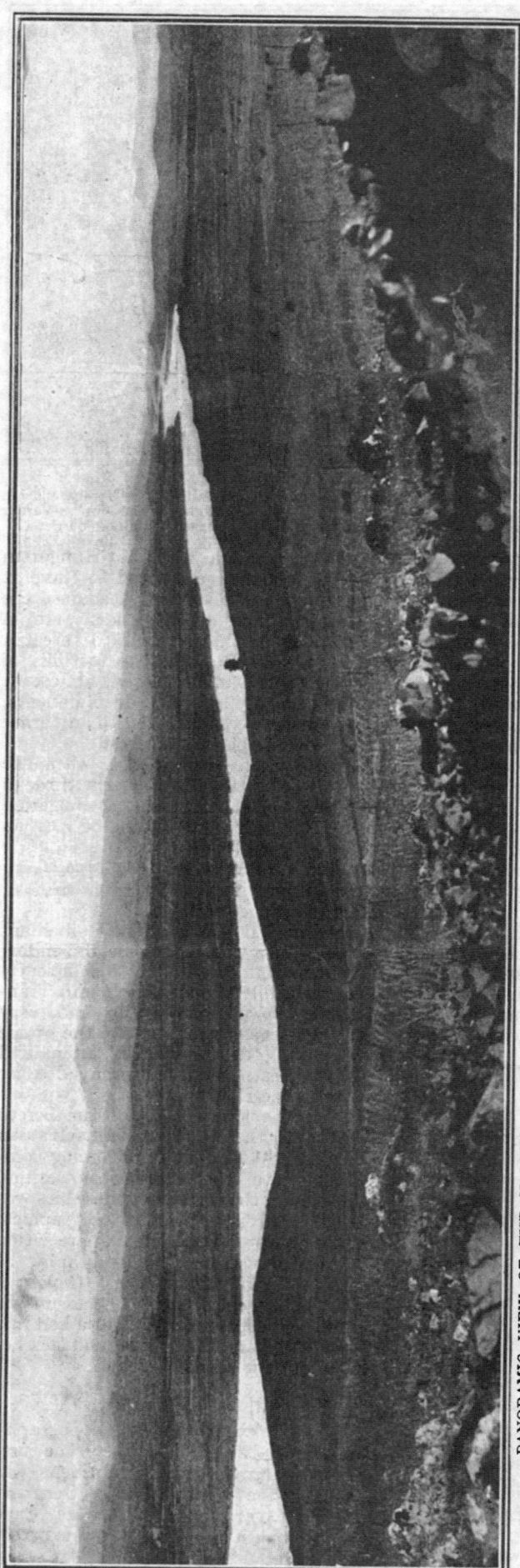

PANORAMIC VIEW OF THE VALLEY OF THE RIVER VARDAR: THE SOUTHERN HALF OF THE GREAT NATURAL TRENCH THROUGH SERBIA.

View northward up the Vardar River, showing in the foreground the wire entanglements before the Allies' position. In the middle of the picture can be discerned the town of Gevgeli, on the west bank of the river, and in the background the mountain ranges which dominate the valley trench, those to the right running eastward to the Bulgarian frontier, those to the left forming part of the physical barrier between Serbian and Greek territory. The great trench cut across Serbia from north to south by the Vardar and Morava Rivers is a main feature of the natural defences of Serbia from attack by her eastern neighbours.

Wissmann on Lake Nyasa, and the British and French invasion of Togoland, in West Africa. Togoland was an elongated State (33,700 square miles in extent), with a bottle-neck only thirty-two miles broad, which Germany had built up in the later 'eighties of the last century, midway between the British Gold Coast and French Dahomey. It was an artificial collocation of three districts, somewhat diverse in history and ethnology, with an absurdly inappropriate name derived from some portion of the "beach," or narrow coast-line.

The eastern half of Togoland belonged ethnically and linguistically to Dahomey, and was formerly under the rule of that bloodstained native kingdom ; the western half, in British occupation, was related in people and language to the northern territories of the Gold Coast—or, in the south-west, was what is termed semi-Bantu. That is to say, the speech of the natives has an affinity with the tongues of the Kaduna basin or the Central Benue in British Nigeria, and those of Sierra Leone and Portuguese Guinea.

      Togoland and Dahomey

Politically speaking, Togoland had no claim to separate existence ; one half should have followed the fortunes of the Gold Coast, and the other those of Dahomey. One half had been already Britannicised (through the missionaries and their education), and the other half similarly Frenchified, before the Germans forcibly acquired it. Consequently, when war broke out, the natives of Togoland showed respectively such decided preference for British or French rule that the German forces surrendered after very little resistance, and the native chiefs wrote quite well-expressed letters in English or French announcing their satisfaction at the change of control. Indeed, some of the Togoland people enlisted in the French Senegalese battalions and came to defend French soil, while others found their way into the Gold Coast regiments sent to Cameroon. Togoland is a valuable part of West Africa, tolerably high and healthy, with no more than a moderate rainfall in the interior. It produces abundant supplies of palm-oil, ground-nuts, and live-stock.

Germany's three great possessions in Africa—almost entirely within the tropics—were (1) Kamerun, or Cameroon, (2) South-West Africa, and (3) German East Africa—Zangia, as it might be called, seeing that it arose from the former dominions of Zanzibar, on the Zanj (or Zangian) coast.

Kamerun consisted, like Togoland—only on a much larger scale, for it had an area of 191,130 square miles—of several regions, four in all, dissimilar in character as regards their ethnology and political affinities. It was a country wholly lacking in homogeneity such as there is in British Nigeria, in Congoland, or Somaliland. Its name—Kamerun—was simply a Germanising of the British seamen's name of "Cameroon," (or "the Cameroons") which, again, was derived from the Portuguese word *camaroes*, and only meant "prawns."

The Portuguese discoverers of this coast noticed the abundance of large shrimps in the estuary of the Wuri, or Duala, River. This trivial term "Cameroon" therefore had to cover in course of time: (1) A region which in the north lay between the basins of the Upper Benue, the Logon, the Shari, and Lake Chad, which was low-lying, unhealthy, peopled by semi-civilised Mohammedans, and ethnically part of Eastern Nigeria ; (2) a central plateau country dotted with great mountains rising to 10,000 feet,[*] fairly healthy, and possibly suited in some degree to European colonisation ; (3) in the west one of the most rainy, heavily-forested parts of Africa, the home of Bantu Negroes, forest pygmies, and great apes, especially the gorilla ; and (4) in the south-east an important section of Congoland, the basin of the Sanga River, and contact with the great main stream of the Congo and with its most important affluent, the Wele-Mubangi.

      German South-West Africa

German South-West Africa, though also on the Atlantic side of the continent, was a widely different land in outward aspect. Its area was even larger—322,200 square miles. It extended between the south of Angola and the Kunene

---

[*] The Cameroon peak on the coast (Ambas Bay) is an isolated quiescent volcano, 13,000 feet high, quite unconnected with the mountains and table-lands of the interior.

River to the frontier of Cape Colony at the Orange River. It is sometimes written of as lying "outside the tropics," but as it is much broader in the north than in the south, two-thirds of it lie to the north of the tropic of Capricorn. The northernmost portion, Ambo Land, is comparatively low-lying, and in general level much below the lofty tableland that comprises nearly all this former German colony, a tableland from which again rise—to heights of between 4,000 and nearly 9,000 feet—ridges and peaks of mountains.

The coast region is almost unmitigated sandy desert, in which, however, some very interesting plants are found growing, such as the weird-looking welwitschia, a "dicotyledon which has never grown up." Ambo Land has a tropical climate and heavy rains in its summer season. Consequently it is unhealthy for Europeans, and exacted a fearful toll in deaths from its early explorers. But the rest of the country has a climate

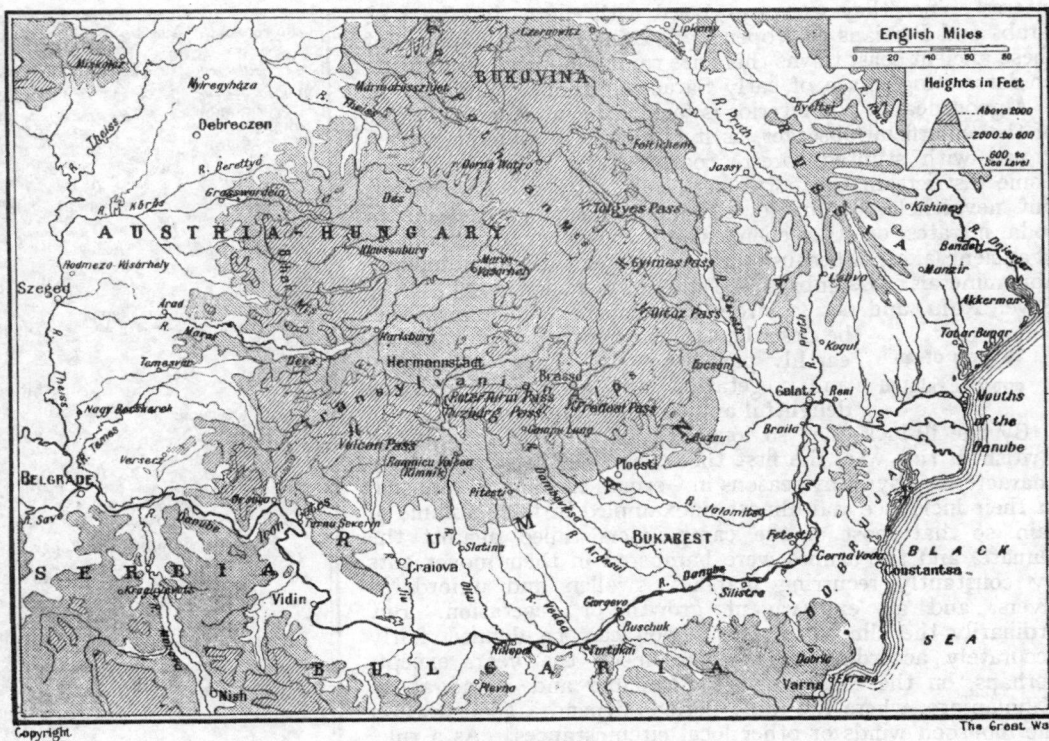

RUMANIA AND ITS BOUNDARIES.

Contour map of Rumania and its immediately neighbouring countries, showing the course of the Danube from where the Theiss flows into it from the great Hungarian plain and the Save joins it at Belgrade. The Hungarian frontier of Rumania was such that two hundred thousand men could have defended it against the Austro-German Army.

sometimes described as "superb," and certainly conducive to health and stamina among its white colonists. The rainfall is rather scanty, but water is seldom far from the surface, and by means of wells, dams, storage, and systems of irrigation, a good deal of tropical and sub-tropical agriculture can be carried on.

As regards natives, the southern part, which is the most arid—though wealthy in diamonds—has, besides European settlers, only a few thousand Hottentots and Hottentot half-breeds, and this is also the case with the sterile coast-belt up the Kunene River. But Ambo Land is rather abundantly populated by Bantu Negroes; and Damaraland, in the centre of the country, at one time maintained several hundred thousand Ovaherero, a fine-looking Bantu people, with—like so many of the Bantu tribes—a hint of ancient Hamite intermixture in their physique. By long wars with the Hottentots and Hottentot half-breeds coming up from the south, and later by conflicts with the Germans, they were reduced to only twelve or thirteen thousand in number.

A long tongue of German South-West Africa extended eastward to Zambezi, a very artificial arrangement which was never recognised by its indigenous Negro tribes whose affinities lay with the people of the Zambezi valley.

Geography of German East Africa

German East Africa was 384,000 square miles in extent, in the Equatorial zone of Africa between 1° and 3°, and 10°40' of south latitude, reaching from the Victoria Nyanza Lake in the north to Tanganyika in the west, and Nyasa and the Rovuma River in the south. It included, by a special loop, the whole of the mighty snow-crowned, twin-summited volcano of Kilimanjaro; it extended to the other snow-capped volcanoes of Myfumbiro in the north-west, to Mount Rungwe and the Livingstone Mountains in the south. Running nearly parallel with the hot coast-belt are ranges of mountains of varying names, with heights of six and seven thousand feet, offering many an uninhabited tract with tempting conditions of soil and climate, rainfall and vegetation, to the foreign settler. Immediately east of the northern parts of the Tanganyika coast there are pleasant plateaus where rises the ultimate source of the Nile, and these might well become the homes of white men. The coast has a number of good harbours, some of them of historic

CAMEROON AND NEIGHBOURING STATES.

One of Germany's three great possessions on the African continent, Cameroon has an area of over 190,000 square miles, and consists of four dissimilar regions, the contours of which are indicated on this map. On the part of the British and French special geographical knowledge was needed to grapple with the tremendous physical obstacles of the country.

interest, since they were associated with the early efforts of Arabs and Persians to "open up" East Africa. At some of these ancient coast towns there are ruined mosques, exhibiting an interesting phase of early Saracenic architecture.

A good deal of the interior is lacking in interest to the eye of the superficial observer, as it is merely a wilderness overgrown with stunted forest, coarse grass, and euphorbias. Some districts in the north-east and centre are arid desert, but nevertheless valuable, either from surface deposits of soda, nitrates, or other chemicals derived from the drying up of ancient lakes, or because their sun-baked rocks contain valuable minerals. Usambara, the mountain region north of the River Rufu, and not far from the Zanzibar coast, may well be described by the hackneyed phrase, "an earthly paradise." Its beauty of scenery and vegetation are accompanied by a delightful and equable climate.

Effects of an unusual rainfall

By the ill-luck that so long dogged the footsteps of the British in this war, the first three years of the struggle were characterised by rainy seasons in German East Africa unusual in their incidence and almost unexampled in their volume of rain, so that most of the campaigners railed against the climate, and the armies were hampered in their movements by constantly recurring marshes, swollen and unfordable rivers, and an extravagant growth of vegetation. But ordinarily the climate of this region can be defined fairly accurately according to the season of the year, except, perhaps, on the coast opposite Zanzibar and round about Kilimanjaro, where the rainy periods depend a good deal on the monsoon winds or other local circumstances. As a rule, the dry season commences in May and continues till the end of October; the heavy rains occur during January, February, and March; the lesser rains in November and December. Yet one side—the north—of a great mountain, or a range of mountains, may be dry and almost wanting in vegetation when the south or west is dripping with moisture and clothed with magnificent forest.

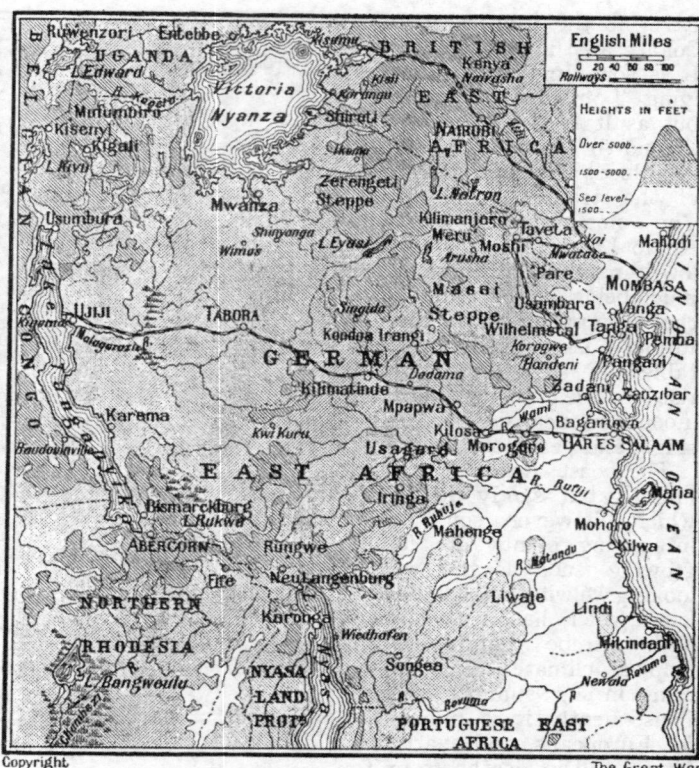

GERMAN EAST AFRICA.

Contour map of the largest of German possessions in Africa. German East Africa, 384,000 square miles in extent, stretched from one degree south of the Equator to the Rovuma River. The British armies were hampered by constantly recurring marshes, swollen and unfordable rivers, and an extravagant growth of vegetation.

In Togoland no strategy or application of geographical knowledge to military plans was needed, as the conquest was a walk-over, largely because of the natives withholding all support from the Germans, or beginning hostilities on their own account. But in Cameroon geographical knowledge —and ethnological as well—was needed to grapple with tremendous physical obstacles and to win over the very decisive influence of the natives. Fortunately it was present in the officers commanding both British and French, and when the story of the conquest of this vast and varied region of West Central Africa is fully told, great credit will devolve on its organisers and conductors; on the officers of the British Navy as well as of the Army; on the French Senegalese soldiers and the British Hausas, Yorubas, and Gold Coast troops. The rapidity with which this extremely difficult campaign was conducted to a successful issue was really amazing.

Of South-West Africa, much the same must be said. General Botha avoided the obvious, and fell into none of the traps laid for him. His march overland from the Middle Orange River, through the upland desert of Namaqualand, and thence to his goal in the Damara Mountains, was a masterpiece of good organisation and good generalship, made possible, we must remember, by the loyalty of the Cape Boys, the Negroes of Basutoland, and the Cape Colony Kafirs. Forty thousand of these yellow and brown-skinned men cheerfully trudged over the desert, carrying loads or driving carts and waggons, and performing every service asked of them. Thus the invading army, which had been expected to arrive by sea, and to march into the ambushes laid for it, and drink of the wells carefully poisoned for its undoing, came into Windhoek by the back door, and wound up the whole campaign in three or four months.

General Botha's march to Windhoek

The East African war was another matter. In this region the Germans were more numerous, and their black army likewise. The latter had been well drilled, and was recruited from local races that loved fighting for its own sake; also from the former slave-holding, slave-raiding Arabs and Arab half-breeds, who hoped the régime of slavery was to return

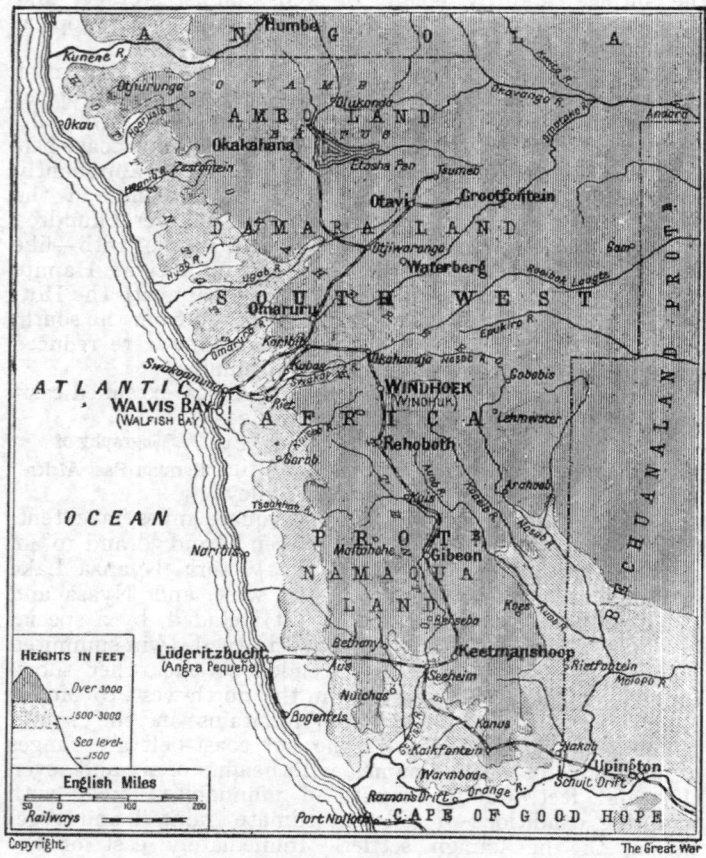

SOUTH-WEST AFRICA.

German South-West Africa—the contours of which are indicated in this map—was the second largest of the Teuton colonies on the African continent, having an area of over 322,000 square miles. General Botha began his campaign by marching overland from the Middle Orange River.

with a German victory. Such men—more often Negroes than Arabs in reality, for the pure-blooded East African Arab is rather anæmic, and not over strong physically—threw in their lot with the Germans, and stood by them with an obstinacy that calls for some admiration, even following their officers into the hopeless struggle in the wilderness of Portuguese East Africa that followed the expulsion of the Germans from their own domain.

Unfortunately, at the beginning of the war the British authorities were at fault in their East African policy. Not only in matters of military strategy, such as the first attack on Tanga, but even more so in not winning over the whole-hearted support of the

MOUNT GEMMI, IN TOGOLAND.
Togoland, 33,000 square miles in extent, was one of the smallest of Germany's African possessions, a narrow strip of territory running north from the Gulf of Guinea.

THE MARKET STREET OF LOME.
Lome, the capital of Togoland, is situated on the very narrow strip of coast that the Germans held. It was a town of about five thousand native inhabitants.

ten millions of indigenous Negroes. Foolish articles and letters appeared in the London and the South African Press, proposing either that German East Africa should be given to Japan—to colonise—or that it should be carved up into "farms" to reward the thousands of South Africans who

NATIVE QUARTERS, DUALA.
Duala, near the mouth of the River Duala, one of the chief towns of the German colony of Cameroon. It had an estimated population of 22,000.

might volunteer to serve under the South African generals who were to—and who did—repeat in East Africa the success they had achieved in Namaqualand and Damaraland.

Suggestions such as these were carefully noted by the Germans, were translated (with exaggerations) into Swahili and circulated among the many natives who, thanks to the Arabs and still more to the European missionaries, could read. The idea got abroad during the first twelve months of the war that the expulsion of the Germans would only be followed by the land being taken away from its native holders and handed over to a foreign people, white or yellow. No effort

was made by the home authorities to employ in or send out to East Africa persons who could speak one or more native languages, and who could be trusted by the natives to tell the truth and to reassure them as to their future after the war. Consequently, whole tribes—whose defection from the Germans might have paralysed their resistance to the Allies, or their escape from the allied forces, as it had done in Cameroon —remained sulkily neutral.

But it is a long lane that has no turning. Expert knowledge came into play at last, and great services were rendered to the allied cause by the Belgians and their Negro army from Congoland. They had first by prodigies of valour, aided by a British naval contingent, driven the Germans from Tanganyika; they next captured the real capital of German East Africa, Tabora, situated in the plains of Unyamwezi. But the most desperate fighting took place between the British, South African, and Rhodesian armies, under Boer and British generals, in the neighbourhood of Kilimanjaro, in the harsh country **Great services of** of Irangi, on the heights of the Nyasa- **the Belgians** Tanganyika plateau, round about the north end and south-east end of Lake Nyasa, and up and down the Zangian coast from the intricate maze of the Rufiji delta to the great Rovuma River. Only a small remnant of the German East African Army (which at one time must have numbered 25,000 Negro, Arab, and Negroid soldiers, under some 7,000 German officers) escaped across the Rovuma to be finally rounded up by the British and Portuguese.

ON A CAMEROON RIVER.
River scene near Duala. The early Portuguese explorers of the coast found an abundance of large shrimps, or prawns, in the estuary of this river, and from their word for each, "camaroes," was formed the name Cameroon.

ENTRENCHED BRITISH CAMP IN GERMAN SOUTH-WEST AFRICA.
Wide deserts in the uplands of Great Namaqualand and mountain ranges in Damaraland were the natural features which the Germans expected would protect their South-West African territory from invasion from the south-east. The British, however, marched overland from the Middle Orange River.

The topography of the war, when it is fully described in detail, must include the remote archipelago of the Falkland Islands, near the southernmost extremity of South America, off which was fought one of the decisive naval battles of the war.

Then Caucasia and its snow-crowned, glaciated mountains, its valuable forests and oil-wells, was fiercely fought over by Turks and Armenians, Georgians and Tatars, Russians—renegade and loyal—Mongolians and Circassians; and, lastly, by a truly amazing British force which crossed Persia and seized the Western Caspian shores and the region of the oil-wells.

Even the hermit State of Tibet was affected by the war, declared its sympathy with Great Britain, and afforded some assistance. China watched with anxiety and precaution the fate of Central Asia, to which she could not be indifferent. Liberia—the Negro republic in West Africa—had her capital shelled by a German submarine for siding with her creatress, the United States; Abyssinia's dynastic revolution and deposed young Emperor are said to be related to German intrigue, which had won over the grandson of Menelik to action against Britain and French interests.

Scarcely one Pacific island or atoll but felt the war somehow, saw German raiders, or witnessed their destruction by avenging ships from Britain, Japan, or the United States. The great Libyan Desert, west of Egypt, was the scene

of tremendous exploits by "fleets" of armoured motors dashing at astonished Berber or Arab cavalry officered by Turks or renegade Germans. British airships quelled German-incited rebellions amid the peaks of the Hindu Kush and the sun-scorched mountains of Northern Baluchistan. Madagascar sent her blend of Negro and Malay to fight or work for France in France.

Annam contributed her gallant little soldiers for the same purpose with signal success; so did British Fiji; so did Bhutan and Nepal; Argentina had her ships "spurlos versenken" by the Germans, but refrained from returning blow for blow. Brazil, on the other hand, was not slow to resent such treatment, and showed herself navally a very useful belligerent on the side of the Allies. Guatemala, Costa Rica, Cuba, and Honduras came into the war on the side championed by the United States.

Portugal contributed an army of respectable size to fight in France, and forces to fight the Germans in East Africa, and as one result had her towns in the island paradises of Madeira and the Azores bombarded by submarines. Morocco, still in parts unexplored, still a land of unexhausted romance and unsolved mysteries, only fighting against the French twelve months before the war broke out in Europe, nevertheless contributed to the French Army soldiers so resolute, so fierce, so hardy that they won respectful notice from the enemy and admiration from the Allies.

ON THE FRONTIER BETWEEN BRITISH AND GERMAN EAST AFRICA.
View taken from an aeroplane of the snow-crowned, twin-summited volcano, Mount Kilimanjaro, and the surrounding mountain country in the north-east of Germany's East African possession. In the immediate foreground is Ugula Gap. In circle: Typical hill scene in German East Africa.

I.W.T. DEPOT.   **CHAPTER CCLXV.**   WHARF AND QUAYS.

THE WONDERFUL WORK OF THE INLAND WATER TRANSPORT.

By Robert Machray.

A Great but Little-Known Service—Its Picturesque Side—Fighting the German Canals—Immense Developments in France and Belgium—How the I.W.T. was Organised—Its Expanding Home Base—New Town and Port Created—Fleet of Four Thousand Vessels—The Splendid Train-Ferry Across the Channel—Romance of I.W.T. Voyaging to the Middle East—How General Maude was Helped in Mesopotamia—Magnificent Tigris Achievements—Basra Turned Into an Ocean Port—The Fine New Hospital Ships—Manifold Activities in Other Theatres of the War: Egypt, East Africa, Salonika, Taranto, Corfu, Valona, and Russia—Whence the Force was Recruited—Training Men in the Schools—Distinguished Directorate in Command.

THE marvels of the British Transport Service on the western front were described in Chapter CLXVI. (Vol. 8, page 431.) Incidentally, references were made to canal transport in France, and some glimpses were given of the activities there of the soldier-bargees who had been recruited from the rivers and canals of the United Kingdom. The present chapter is devoted to an appreciation of the splendid organisation generally termed the Inland Water Transport, which rapidly grew into a tremendous force, but the basis of which was found in the British bargee and his humble barge. The I.W.T., as it was called for short, was one of the most interesting as well as most successful improvisations of the war, in every theatre of which it carried on important operations. In some areas its work was of incalculable value, as, for instance, in Mesopotamia, where the conflict with the enemy was largely a river war. Of all this the public knew scarcely anything, probably because the I.W.T. was so new a body, or still more because it was so little in the limelight. In the following account of its multifarious efforts, the greater part of the information—which brings the story up to the autumn of 1918, and was obtained from an authoritative source—appears for the first time.

It has been well said that the "I.W.T. was in the war wherever there was water"; but the phrase, though happy, requires filling out. The I.W.T. did all sorts of things that, though correlated and interdependent, were hardly suggested by its name, which, owing to the enormous development of the organisation, had, in fact, become rather a misnomer. The field of action covered not only the operating and maintaining at home and abroad of vast fleets of river and canal craft, including the building of barges and light-draught vessels in considerable numbers, but also the construction of camps, shipyards, and docks, as well as other engineering work, and the manufacture of machinery and equipment of different kinds for Army services. Among the most

SIR SAM FAY.   [*Vandyk.*
Appointed Director-General of Movements and Railways in 1917. It was to the head of this department that the Director in command of the Inland Water Transport was responsible.

notable of the I.W.T.'s contributions to the military effort of this country were the creation and the carrying on of the cross-Channel "train-ferry," the daily transport of ammunition and ordnance stores in huge quantities to the armies in France, and the import and distribution of salvage from the battlefields. The very large personnel necessary was got together in many ways, and from many countries, but the I.W.T.'s own training schools for unskilled and semi-skilled labour were constantly adding to its strength.

All this sounds extremely practical and utilitarian—as it was, and as indeed it needed to be. Problems of transport are always among the most formidable in any war, and can only be solved on rigorous business lines; never were they more formidable than in the Great War, and in its own extensive sphere the I.W.T. proved itself extraordinarily capable and efficient in dealing with them. It would be a mistake, however, to suppose that its achievements were devoid of all colour and picturesqueness. Adventure, excitement, danger were often implicit in the story. Of course the I.W.T. was a non-combatant force, but its members frequently were near enough to the front to be under fire. Though ostensibly "inland navigators," not a few of them knew the meaning in those days of the perils of the mighty deep. If the tale could be told in detail, the voyages from British shores to Eastern waters of the sailing-masters of the I.W.T., in what might well be called cockleshell boats, would be seen to be instinct with romance, and to deserve a high place in the stirring annals of the sea. Special interest attached to another side of the work of this admirable body — the tender care it took of the wounded, for whom it provided floating hospitals, well equipped in every respect.

In the United Kingdom before the war canals held a subordinate place in its general transport system, which was practically monopolised by the railways. Many of these canals were owned or controlled by railway companies, who allowed them for the most

Transport was placed under the Directorate of Movements in the Department of the Quartermaster-General, and early in 1915 a Deputy-Director of Inland Water Transport (Lieut.-Colonel—afterward Brig.-General—G. E. Holland, C.M.G., C.I.E., D.S.O.) took charge of the section's operations in France. The I.W.T. broadened out very rapidly in that area, and in October, 1915, it was constituted a separate directorate overseas, remaining under General Holland until his death on active service in June, 1917, when the charge passed to Brig.-General C. M. Luck, D.S.O., the Director when this chapter was written in the autumn of 1918.

As the British Army expanded its Transport Service expanded too, and with the ever-enlarging requirements of the I.W.T. in France, its organisation at home grew more and more. Eventually, in September, 1916, when a new branch of the War Office was established under the title of the Department of the Director-General of Military Railways, afterwards changed to Movements and Railways, the I.W.T., with its own Director in command, formed a part **Modest start of the I.W.T.** of it. The Directorate of Inland Waterways and Docks, as the headquarters of the I.W.T. later was styled, was charged not only with the control of Inland Water Transport work in the various theatres of the war, but also with the supply of personnel and material for the equipment and working of docks overseas, and for construction and other objects at various ports.

At the start the organisation of the I.W.T. at home was on a very modest scale, its depot sharing the quarters of the Railway Troops at Longmoor, in Hampshire. Next a small store was set up at Dover to meet immediate requirements abroad ; and from Dover as base, barges, after being equipped and manned, were despatched to France. But suitable

part to fall into disuse. Many of these formerly busy inland waterways had become choked with weeds and topped with thick yellow-green slime. The case was very different on the Continent, where the canals and canalised rivers were the scenes of incessant and considerable traffic. "At the present moment we are fighting the canals of Germany," said Mr. Lloyd George, replying to a deputation from the Trade Union Congress Parliamentary Committee, which waited on him on March 20th, 1918, to present resolutions passed at the Blackpool Trade Union Congress respecting railways and canals, among other things. These German canals, he observed, " are part of the weapons with which we are confronted; but," he added, "luckily we have the fine canal system of France." It was realised by the British authorities very early in the war that it was necessary to take the fullest advantage of the canal and river systems in France and Belgium to supplement transport by rail and road.

IN A MACHINE-SHOP OF THE I.W.T.

In addition to the varied labours more directly associated with its name, the Inland Water Transport service carried out a great deal of important construction work. In these photographs are seen a corner of the machine-shop, and (above) the mechanical stokers at a great I.W.T. base.

These waterways therefore were developed energetically, and steps were taken to form an organisation to control those in the British zone of operations and maintain them efficiently. Suitable craft were collected from all available quarters. Just as the big London motor-omnibus was seen on the French roads, so the lumbering, crudely-painted Avon-and-Kennet, or other British barge, made its appearance on the French canals, but rather later.

To take over and develop this branch of transport the Inland Water Transport Section of the Royal Engineers was formed as part of the Railway Troops in December, 1914. At the War Office the administration of the Inland Water

barges were hard to procure, and this shortage led to the construction at various places in this country of a number of these craft, which were towed to Dover and fitted out for work in France. When the tonnage problem in the United Kingdom, combined with congestion at French ports, became acute, it was decided to relieve the situation by shipping cargoes in these barges from England through the French canal system to inland depots without breaking or handling en route. Owing to the restrictions imposed by the fact that it was an important naval base, and that the tides made the entrance at times difficult and even dangerous for barges and similar craft, Dover was found to be unsuitable as a base for the I.W.T. Accommodation for stores was limited, and

Women and children welcoming the Liverpool Irish on their arrival in the outskirts of Lille.

Population of Lille in the Grand' Place cheering their British liberators, October 17th, 1918.

October 25th, 1918: An ever memorable day of victory and joy in Flanders, liberated from the inv

…phal re=entry of their Majesties the King and Queen of the Belgians into the city of Bruges.

The sea=front at Ostend, October 17th, 1918, showing the dug=outs left by the Germans.

View of the deck of H.M.S. Vindictive, lying in the entrance to Ostend Harbour.

could not be extended because of the Navy's needs. For a time a store was opened at Ashford for heavy material, but this move involved railing to the port of loading, and soon proved inconvenient in many ways. Meanwhile, demands from overseas increased rapidly, and in March, 1916, it was seen to be imperative that the organisation should have an adequate and independent base.

After careful investigation an excellent site was found on the South Coast. Work was begun on it in June, 1916, and with a view primarily to the barge services, which later increased to large dimensions, was pushed forward with the utmost speed. At this stage Mr. Lloyd George, then Minister of Munitions, visited the depot, and at once perceived the possibilities of this mode of transport for the carriage of munitions. This resulted in a great development. A scheme was approved by the Cabinet authorising the extension of wharfage accommodation, the provision of complete mechanical equipment, and the establishing of schools for training men for the work. A special type of barge was designed and built which was seaworthy and at the same time of the right size for entering the French canals. Apart from the relief of seagoing ships, the advantages of this mode of transport were the dispersal of marine and war risks into smaller units, facilities of loading, the relief of dock congestion owing to the barges passing right through the docks into the interior, the saving of double handling, since the

RAILWAYS IN AID OF THE WATERWAYS.
Engine of the Inland Waterways and Docks Service, and (above) lengthy wharf at the chief I.W.T. base. Here, on what had been a salt marsh, arose a town with a port, the whole combining a military establishment with a great industrial enterprise.

barges discharged at destination, the saving of railway carriage in France, and the comparative immunity of the barges from enemy attack because of their shallow draught. The service was begun in December, 1916, and proved of the greatest value to our troops in France. "Water-heads," the I.W.T. equivalent of rail-heads, were established as near as possible to the artillery, and inland depots set up all along these northern waterways.

In addition to the waterways on the western front, which the Inland Water Transport controlled almost from the outset, every advance of the British in that area brought fresh waterways into its sphere. Demolitions and obstructions due to enemy action were dealt with, and emergency repairs and replacements in the rear of the lines were carried out. All the time the I.W.T. maintained and repaired all its waterways, and also was responsible for the movable bridges that crossed them. For this work salvage units **Vast traffic on** were formed, with floating cranes, piling **foreign waterways** plant, pneumatic machinery, salvage pumps, and other equipment. After the administration of the docks was undertaken, a large amount of plant and material was supplied for operating the docks and for port construction, the personnel consisting of organised dock stevedore companies and port construction companies, trained for the purpose in Great Britain. How vast was the traffic under the I.W.T. on the French and Belgian waterways may be judged from the fact that in one month it aggregated upwards of a quarter of a million tons, and necessitated the employment of a fleet of more than nine hundred craft. This

fleet included ambulance barges, which were in reality small floating hospitals that were used for the conveyance of serious cases unable to stand the jolting and strain of railways or roads. Such wounded received expert attention from the moment they were taken on board till they reached the base. On an average three thousand such cases were dealt with each month.

In 1918 more than four thousand vessels of various kinds were in the service of the Inland Water Transport at home and abroad. For the work of the organisation really suitable craft were for a considerable time not obtainable, but the best that could be done was done with makeshifts. Shipyards were full up with Admiralty and merchant shipping orders, and could not cope with the demand. In these circumstances the Directorate of **Barge-building** the I.W.T. resolved to build the vessels **extraordinary** required. At the new base a barge-building yard was established, and the necessary plates, angles, and other material were procured from concerns not engaged in ship construction. Many vessels were built, re-erected, or repaired in this yard, where an innovation was adopted by which electric welding replaced riveting, with beneficial results as regards speed and economy of material and labour. Apart from the construction of special types of craft for the Admiralty, a notable development was the building of 1,000-ton barges of steel and concrete, as the limit of the canal capacity had been reached with the smaller barges. These big barges had to be discharged in dock, and therefore had not the advantages possessed by the craft that went into the canals; but, on the other hand, they distinctly were a direct relief to shipping.

Meanwhile the new base, which in 1918 it was deemed inadvisable to name, had been growing. Out of what had been a salt marsh arose a town, with a port, the whole combining a military establishment with a great industrial enterprise. Its workers wore the King's khaki and were under military discipline, but what they did was seen in the extensive wharves and quays, in the miles of sidings, in the numerous shops humming with machinery, in the power-stations, in the

AT A DESERT DOCKYARD.
Slipway at an I.W.T. Mesopotamian dockyard, which a year earlier had been but barren desert. In Mesopotamia the I.W.T. made magnificent use of its great opportunity, under Brigadier-General W. H. Grey, R.E.

was an electrically operated landing bridge carrying a double line of rails, which could be raised or lowered to engage with the deck of the ferry according to the state of the tide. The loading and unloading of one of these ferries took about twenty minutes. Complete trains of loaded waggons, locomotives, and heavy war material on wheels were by means of the train-ferry transported straight on to the French railroads.

In addition to all the work described above, the I.W.T. acted as contracting, carrying, and distributing agent for other Services, and its depot was in effect a general base workshop for Army supplies as well as a huge transport centre. Other Services had their store-sheds and warehouses at the port, where also great masses of the salvage of the battlefields, brought back as " imports " by the barges, were

foundries, and later in the barge-building yard. As an electric-power supply was needed for that yard, plant and buildings were erected to supply it and the wharves, shops, and camps as well. The camps consisted of wooden and concrete huts, regimental and other buildings. There were dining-halls and institutes for the men. A spacious hospital was provided for the sick and injured. With the establishment of the shops and plant, though originally meant only for barge construction, a large amount of work was done at the depot which otherwise would have been placed with civilian engineering concerns. Special mention must be made of the supply of cranes, which were essential for the efficient handling of traffic. Cranes for practically all the services of the British Army, as well as for some of our Allies, were provided from the depot, many hundreds having been acquired, or specially built, to meet their ever-increasing needs. King George visited the base on June 5th, 1917, and was received by Brig.-General (then Colonel) A. S. Cooper, the Director of the I.W.T. at the War Office. With the greatest interest the King inspected the works, craft, stores, camps, hospital, and personnel. He launched three vessels that had just been completed, and was shown many signs and tokens of the activities of the force in all the theatres of war. In 1918 the commandant of this base and main depot in the United Kingdom of the I.W.T. was Brig.-General A. J. Allen Williams, C.M.G., who in private life was a well-known civil engineer.

Train-ferries of the I.W.T.

An important development of the I.W.T., and one which marked a departure in British methods of transport, was the institution of the train-ferry service, which, operating between various ports, proved of great military value. The train-ferry was no novelty in Northern Europe or in the United States, and as a matter of fact the invention was British, one of the earliest train-ferries being that which ran across the Forth to Burntisland before the Forth Bridge was built. The Directorate of the I.W.T. made a careful and exhaustive study of the working of the train-ferry system in all parts of the world before adopting it. The I.W.T. ferries were specially designed and constructed. The necessary shore works included lifting bridges and railway access, and at the base the dredging and straightening of the entrance channel. These ferries had several lines of rails on their decks, upon which loaded trains, locomotives, or other heavy-wheeled material were run on deck from the shore, and run off at the connecting terminal. At each terminal

TYPE OF HOSPITAL-SHIP ON THE TIGRIS IN 1918.
The I.W.T. took the Tigris transport operations in hand in August, 1916, and rapidly brought them to a fine state of efficiency. By the summer of 1918 it had in Mesopotamia a force of upwards of 47,000 Europeans and natives.

received, sorted, and sent to inland points. The I.W.T. besides carried out a great deal of important construction work. All said and done, its chief feature was its barge service. From the inception of that service until August, 1918, over one million tons deadweight had been exported by its means from the principal home base. Some further idea of the work of the I.W.T. in other theatres of the war is to be derived from the fact that an aggregate of a million tons was handled each month.

Besides the principal home base—the town and port which came into existence as if by magic—the Inland Water Transport established depots at various places on the coasts of the United Kingdom. Early in 1917 one of these was formed at Glasgow for the equipping, victualling, and manning of all craft for service in the East. Officers and men completed their training there before being drafted overseas as crews of Mesopotamian and other craft. It was in connection with this special service that the sailing-masters of the I.W.T. started in their light craft on adventurous voyages. Owing to the stringent limitations necessarily imposed during the war on the narratives of "those that go down to the sea in ships"— or, for that matter, in tugs and barges—few details could be given of their experiences. It may easily be imagined, however, that a long voyage through waters infested with submarines and strewn with mines, to say nothing of other risks, for small craft such as I.W.T. tugs, barges, and shallow-draught river vessels, was hazardous in the extreme. Even in less exciting times a tug with its tow proceeding to an Eastern port might have incident enough before reaching its destination. The following, quoted from the report of a sailing-master, gives an indication of this phase of the I.W.T.'s work :

On the afternoon of the 12th inst., at 4 p.m., I was in charge of the "H.P.6," in tow of the "H.S.47," proceeding from Malta, when a report was brought to me that a submarine had been sighted in the glare of the sun on our starboard quarter. I put on my shaded glasses and found the report to be correct, and opened fire. In order to give myself and the tug freer action for manœuvring, I slipped the tow-rope. I then ordered the chief officer to signal to the tug to turn stem on to the submarine. I cannot say whether the signal was understood or not. The tug sheered off on our starboard bow, and brought her gun into action ; after firing a few rounds she proceeded on our port bow at about three miles away. The action between the submarine and ourselves was continuous all this time. Shortly after 5 p.m. the firing from the submarine ceased. She was then broadside on, and stationary, clear of the sun, and had evidently been stationary some

time. One attempt only was made by her to overtake us, which only lasted a few minutes, the remainder of the time she was broadside on to us. The course of the "H.P.6" was slightly zigzag from N.E. to E.S.E., and the speed, owing to our using the smoke-clouds, was down to three knots. The distance of the submarine during the whole of the action appeared to me to be about 4,500 yards. The action ended about 5.20 p.m., when the tug slowed down and cruised around us.

What a picture ! A similar incident, which also had a satisfactory ending so far as beating off an attack was concerned, and had a pleasant sequel, was suggested when the Lords Commissioners of the Admiralty awarded £100 to the master and crew of the "S.P.6," an I.W.T. craft, in connection with an attack made by a U boat on a certain November 12th. Unfortunately, other encounters with the enemy had less happy terminations, which was not surprising, in view of the

comparative frailty of the I.W.T. vessels. Crews who parted in sorrow from their small boats on the high seas at length arrived after many adventures to tell their tales before the court of inquiry always held on such occasions, or they did not return, and the rest was silence. Taken altogether, the casualties in men or shipping engaged in these perilous trips were relatively very small. But what courage, endurance, and resource were shown by these sailormen, whose business took them far from their "inland waterways"! With every sense on the stretch, and taking advantage of all imaginable devices to elude the submarines, they fearlessly did their duty on the deep in all weathers, as did their brothers of the Navy and its fringes and the Mercantile Marine.

In Mesopotamia, perhaps even more than in France, the Inland Water Transport had a great opportunity, and magnificently did it rise to it. The most superficial study of the military operations in that area showed that the master-key was the river transport. The country was practically destitute of roads, and from the first advance towards Bagdad to its eventual capture the campaign was essentially a river war. The Tigris conditioned both attack and defence, and more than once intervened decisively in the issue. Men, equipment, food, and supplies had all to be conveyed by the river craft, which also had to bring down the sick and wounded, as well as prisoners, to the base. Lack of transport was largely responsible for the check at Ctesiphon and for the sufferings of the troops. To quote the Report of the Mesopotamia Commission, shortage of river transport was "the foundation of all the troubles."

River transport in Mesopotamia

In July, 1916, the War Office took over this transport from the Indian Government and reorganised it. To this action, and the remarkable development of the service which followed, was due in a large measure the victorious advance to Bagdad, culminating in the capture of that city in March, 1917.

When the War Office took control it sent out Lieut.-Colonel (afterwards Brig.-General) W. H. Grey, R.E., of the I.W.T., to investigate and report to the Army Council. He arrived at Basra on July 31st, 1916, and soon found that such craft as were available were badly found and indifferently navigated ; that buildings, wharves, and equipment were inadequate ; and that tools, machinery, and labour were lacking. Besides, divided responsibility and conflicting orders produced confusion and inefficiency. Although not specially trained for

WHARF OF THE I.W.T. IN MESOPOTAMIA.
Riverside depot of the I.W.T., and (in circle) oil-barges in Mesopotamia. Lack of transport had been largely responsible for the earlier failures of the British forces in Mesopotamia; but after the placing of that transport under the I.W.T., in 1916, conditions were rapidly and favourably altered.

View of part of the camp of the Inland Water Transport at a home depot, one of several established at various places on the coasts of the United Kingdom. The principal base had grown by 1918 into a considerable town. The camp comprised wooden and concrete huts, regimental and other buildings, dining-halls and institutes for the men, and spacious hospital accommodation for the sick and wounded.

The Directorate of the I.W.T. established a large barge-building yard, where many vessels were built and repaired. Electric welding replaced riveting, with beneficial results as regards speed and economy of material and labour. Besides special types of barges at once seaworthy and of the right size for entering the French canals, 1,000-ton barges of steel and concrete were built, providing a direct relief to shipping.

PANORAMIC VIEWS OF A CAMP AND BARGE-BUILDING YARD ESTABLISHED IN THE UNITED KINGDOM BY THE DIRECTORATE OF THE I.W.T.

the duties postulated, the officers of the Indian Royal Marine struggled as best they could against these difficulties. Within a week Colonel Grey cabled home a report proposing drastic reforms, among which were the absorption of this force in the Royal Engineers, and the placing of the whole transport service under one organisation and control. His suggestions were approved, and on September 4th he took full charge of the river transport service in Mesopotamia. Thus was the I.W.T. brought into that distant theatre of the war. In a despatch Sir Stanley Maude, then Commander-in-Chief, said:

The Directorate of the Inland Water Transport was created, and men and material arrived from overseas, as well as additional river craft, while the influx of adequate and experienced personnel for port administration and conservancy work, railways, supplies, and transport, etc., enabled these services to cope more adequately with their responsibilities in maintaining the field armies.

Suitable craft was the first matter to engage attention. When the I.W.T. took the whole transport operations in hand in August, 1916, the number of vessels in commission on the Tigris was about one hundred and thirty, consisting of steamers, hospital craft, tugs, and barges, in addition to a varying flotilla of launches. No provision existed for the erection of craft. As the result of local inquiry Colonel Grey came to the conclusion that vessels based on the lines of those successfully run by Messrs. Lynch on the Tigris for many years were the most suitable, and such craft were built. For the pressing immediate need the Directorate of the I.W.T. organised the resources of both the United Kingdom and India, and collected special craft from all quarters, including Canada, South America, Egypt, and West Africa. In Great Britain orders were placed for more than two hundred vessels. In India officers of the I.W.T. co-operated with the Government, which instituted a Rivercraft Board, to act in conjunction with the Indian Railway Board and the Indian Engineering Association. In the meantime machinery and engineering shops, with the necessary gear, plant and stores, engines and boilers, electric-power supply units, pile-driving equipment, cranes, railway tracks, and rolling-stock, pumps, and timber were sent out from home.

Ships were useless, however, without men, and labour was scarce in Mesopotamia. Men were urgently needed not only to man craft, but for construction, engineering, and ship-building. The men were found—in itself no small achievement. Natives accustomed to river work were recruited in Nigeria. India and Egypt were ransacked for skilled and unskilled labour, shipyard personnel, with skilled supervising staff, being transferred en bloc. Large numbers of Chinese also were secured. Special attention was **Basra made a great port** given at the home base to training officers and men for Mesopotamia, schools of instruction were instituted, and by the end of January, 1917, one thousand seven hundred officers and men had been sent to Basra. In the summer of 1918 the I.W.T. had in Mesopotamia a force of upwards of forty-seven thousand Europeans and natives. What it meant in tact, skill, patience, and hard work to weld this large and varied assortment of humanity into one efficient and smooth-running machine was known only to the officers in charge.

Having solved the craft and labour problems, the I.W.T, set about fitting the main base locally, which was Basra, and subsidiary depots on the Tigris, for the great part they were to play in the campaign of General Maude. Basra was transformed from a place of small intrinsic value, devoid of

all modern shipping and industrial facilities, into a busy port with extensive quays and docks. In 1918 it was becoming one of the great ports of the world, with the certainty of a splendid future, and it will remain a monument to the I.W.T. for all time. In August, 1916, a start was made with the construction of docks, wharves, jetties, and warehouses; slipways were planned at Maghil, in the immediate neighbour-hood. Shoals were dredged away. The Tigris was charted, buoyed, and lighted. Pilots were trained in view of the coming operations; depots were established at Ashar, Kurna, Amara, and other points; the banks of the river were revetted and built up where necessary; piers were reconstructed, and large jetties erected at various places. India gallantly seconded the local efforts. Bombay had been

LANDING-BRIDGE OF A TRAIN-FERRY TERMINAL LOOKING SEAWARDS.
Included in the varied work carried on by the Inland Water Transport service was that of establishing and maintaining the train-ferry system, by means of which complete trains of loaded waggons, locomotives, and heavy war material on wheels were transported straight on to the French railroads.

the port from which supplies had gone forward to Mesopotamia, but a scheme was developed for utilising Karachi, which had advantages over Bombay, as a base for collecting, re-erecting, and repairing craft obtained in India or at home. Its port facilities were extended, and a shipyard was built and quickly manned. As a link in the chain, skilled officers and men of the I.W.T. went to Egypt to organise traffic at Red Sea ports.

The Mesopotamia river fleet grew to considerable propor-tions. At the opening of General Maude's campaign all was in smooth working order, and the I.W.T. met every demand with the utmost **I.W.T. river-heads** promptitude. As the British forces **up the Tigris** advanced up the Tigris the Service pushed forward its river-head to within a few miles of the positions which Maude successively occupied, and supplies arrived steadily and punctually. The troops were practically on full rations on the operations scale throughout, and the wounded and prisoners were evacuated to the base without hitch or delay. Besides food, supplies of munitions and material and fresh drafts of men and camp followers were constantly sent up the river.

On March 11th, 1917, the British entered Bagdad; on March 20th the I.W.T. established a river-head there and performed its functions with the utmost efficiency and regularity. As the military correspondent of the " Times " noted, the transport was perfect, all the wants of the Army being met with commendable celerity. Testimony to the value of the work of the I.W.T. was borne in Parliament, and on March 5th, 1917, the War Cabinet expressed its appreciation of the services rendered by the organisation. The plain truth of the matter is that the I.W.T. made

Native sailing craft in the service of the I.W.T. in Mesopotamia.

Stern-wheeler steamer used on the Mesopotamian rivers.

Salvage steamer built in England especially for service in Mesopotamia.

Self-propelled floating crane, capable of lifting 30 tons at a radius of 60 feet.
TYPES OF CRAFT EMPLOYED IN MESOPOTAMIA.

possible the great victories of General Maude, and no praise of it can be too high.

In the great river fleet of which the I.W.T. disposed in Mesopotamia in 1918 perhaps the most interesting type of vessel, in view of the medical difficulties in 1915 and 1916, was the hospital-ship, which itself was a new type, and was justly described as a triumph alike for medical science and of ship-building skill. These vessels, built to the order of the Directorate of the I.W.T., were designed under the supervision of Major (afterwards Lieut.-Colonel) R. M. Carter, C.B., I.M.S., the very medical officer who so trenchantly exposed the original breakdown in Mesopotamia, and it was equipped according to the best expert advice. True to its policy of enlisting the highest talent wherever discoverable, the Directorate secured the **Hospital-ships** services of Major Carter in assisting in the **on the Tigris** work of medical transport reorganisation.

One of this type of hospital-ship was inspected by the King before its launch, and was at work in Mesopotamia early in 1918. As its draught was only 3 feet 6 inches it could navigate shallow waters. It was about 160 feet long, and had four decks, three being chiefly used for the treatment of cases, of which it could accommodate two hundred. The main and upper deck were adapted for those that were most serious, and formed two hospital wards, which could be used either for European or Indian patients. To facilitate treatment great care was shown in the

ANCIENT BOAT WITH MODERN PROPULSION.
Motor-bellum employed on the Tigris. One of the many kinds of boats made use of by the I.W.T., the ancient bellum was brought up to date by conversion into a motor-boat.

disposition of the cots, and there was free access to every bed. To meet the peculiarities of the Mesopotamian climate the vessel was equipped with a system of ventilation which enabled all the wards to be continuously supplied with fresh air. There was an ingenious distribution of electric fans. In each ward every group of four beds had a separate fan for circulating currents of air, while to meet the severe cold of the winter the ventilation system provided for a delivery of warm air through the ship. A perfectly-equipped operating-theatre, with a preparation-room adjoining, was on the upper deck. The "flying deck" above was arranged for light cases and convalescents.

An interesting sidelight on the work of the I.W.T. in Mesopotamia was that, in order to safeguard the health of the troops in that area, floating and stationary shore water-filtration stations, of a total capacity of about 34,000 gallons an hour, were sent out **Water-filtration** from home. Some of these were installed in **barges and tanks** the various camps and posts on the Tigris lines of communication, and it was fair to assume that the comparatively low rate of sickness prevalent among our men in "the Land between the Rivers" was due to the foresight and care taken in evolving these plants of the I.W.T. To enable the advancing forces to benefit by the provision of these filtration stations, twelve tank barges, each with a capacity of about 10,000 gallons, were despatched to the scene of operations to act as tenders to these installations, and so ensure an ample and continuous supply of pure water.

While its work on the Tigris had necessarily been directed by the compelling necessities of war, the activities of the Inland Water Transport in Mesopotamia were not confined to river transport work pure and simple. These were manifested in the port of Basra, the improvement of the Shat-el-Arab and of the Tigris, and all the equipment that had been set up, and they remained as valuable assets. When Mesopotamia, in the happy days of peace shall have realised the great destiny foretold for her by Sir William Willcocks and others, it will perhaps be found that the work of the I.W.T. contributed in no small degree to that result. In May, 1917, General Grey returned to Europe, and was succeeded by Brig.-

Work in other theatres of war General R. H. W. Hughes, C.S.I., C.M.G., D.S.O., who was the Director in Mesopotamia in 1918.

In other theatres of the war the Inland Water Transport did excellent service. In Egypt its work included extensive use of the Nile and the canal system of Lower and Upper Egypt, and also the lighterage of ships at the principal ports, the base of supply for the army in Palestine being amongst them. The re-erection, repair, and maintenance of barges in that area was also naturally its affair. In East Africa its operations were small as compared with those in other theatres, but these were very useful in port engineering and lighterage. At Salonika it undertook the loading and discharging of ships, and at Taranto, the eastern terminus of

Motor-dinghy used by the I.W.T. on the Mesopotamian rivers.

PURE WATER FOR TROOPS IN MESOPOTAMIA.
Water-filtration barge, with a total capacity of 34,000 gallons per hour, worked by the I.W.T. in Mesopotamia, with an attendant tank barge of 10,000-gallons capacity which served the advancing troops.

the railway that ran from the Channel across France and Italy to the Adriatic, it supplied and maintained all craft for use at that port, besides cranes and other equipment. Earlier in the war it was most helpful in the Adriatic, personnel taking part in the work of the British Mission in connection with the reorganisation of the Serbian Army. Constructional operations were carried out at Corfu, Valona, and elsewhere. In 1918 the I.W.T. made its appearance at the new bases established by the Allies in Russia.

Who were the men who did the wonderful work of which all written here is little more than a summary? The Port of London and the lower reaches of the Thames had known them. Many waterside and longshore haunts round the coasts, as well as the canals, as indicated above, contributed their quota of "amphibians." To these

How the I.W.T. was recruited must be added skilled mechanics and their mates from every trade; seamen, dock, wharfside and general labourers, clerks, and workers in almost every branch of industry. Mr. Harry Gosling and the Dockers' Union, reinforced by many a willing helper, recruited energetically for the force. With respect to its officers the I.W.T. was fortunately able to draw freely upon the ranks of expert engineers and contractors, and others with organising and administrative experience gained both at home and abroad. To assist the good work men, many of whom had resigned important posts, returned from Nigeria, South America, China, and the East, and indeed from all quarters, and joined the I.W.T. It was under such

Hospital-ship built for the I.W.T. for service in Mesopotamia.

I.W.T. motor-tug. The length of this boat was 54 feet, and her maximum service draught 3 feet 5 inches.

Gunboats operated by the Inland Water Transport for defence purposes.
VARIOUS VESSELS IN THE SERVICE OF THE I.W.T.

IN HOME WATERS.
Men of the I.W.T. nearing a lock on an English canal. The horse that had been towing the two barges had just been released from the tow-rope.

LEAVING A CANAL LOCK.
Barges with their khaki-clad barge-men preparing to leave the lock, and (in circle) carefully guiding a barge under a bridge.

influences that the force was built up—no light task—into a compact and efficient organisation, and it was due largely to the same skilled direction that the system of training men in the schools, which were among the most interesting features of the principal base, was a pronounced success. The average weekly attendance at these schools in 1918 was over 1,100. In two years more than 5,000 skilled and semi-skilled men were made proficient as pile-drivers, divers, crane-drivers, motor-boat drivers, fitters, turners, machinists, smiths, strikers, acetylene-welders, tinsmiths, wood-machinists, carpenters, riveters, platers, caulkers, drillers, shipwrights, riggers, painters, and plumbers—a list which in itself afforded a very fair notion of the manifold activities of the I.W.T. These trained men were employed at home or drafted overseas as required. In increasing numbers women took a part in the work of the force.

To use the military phrase, the Command of the Inland Water Transport was exercised by its Director, who was responsible to the Director-General of Movements and

Railways. The first to hold the latter position was Sir Eric Geddes, 1916-17, and when he became First Lord of the Admiralty he was succeeded by Sir Guy Granet, the head of the Midland Railway, who had been Deputy Director-General. At that time Sir Sam Fay, the head of the Great Central Railway, was Director of Movements; he became Director-General of the Department on the resignation of Granet in 1917. The first Director of the I.W.T. was Brig.-General (afterwards Major-General) A. S. Collard, C.B., C.V.O., who had been in charge of its affairs, under the Director of Movements, since its inception. On his transfer to the Admiralty in June, 1917, he was succeeded by Colonel (afterwards Brig.-General) A. S. Cooper, C.M.G., who was Director when this chapter was written in September, 1918. Both Generals Collard and Cooper were officials from the Colonial Civil Service, the former being the head of the Survey Department in Northern Nigeria, and the latter the General Manager of the Nigeria Railway.

MATERIAL FOR THE IRON ROAD.
Hired transport discharging sleepers and other heavy material at a quayside somewhere in the East for use in the construction of railways on the Mesopotamian lines of communication.

LAUNCH OF A BARGE
Large sea-going barge about to be launched under the White Ensign. Down to August, 1918, over 1,000,000 tons dead weight had been exported by means of I.W.T. barges from the chief home base.

KING VICTOR EMMANUEL III.

CHAPTER CCLXVI.

INSPECTING BRITISH TROOPS.

THE GREAT ITALIAN VICTORY ON THE PIAVE.

By Edward Wright.

Russia's Death is Austria's Resurrection—Hapsburg Aims at Independence against Hohenzollern—Hesitation in Co-operating in Ludendorff's Schemes—Field-Marshal von Arz Misled by Events on the Marne—"Hunger Offensive" Opens in Disaster—Tragic End of Attack on Alpine Pass—How the Slavs Helped the Italian Staff—Austro-Hungarian Plan Wrecked by Allies and Surprise Bombardment—British Contingent Holds the Northern Flank of Defence—Englishmen in Nocturnal Combat in Pine Forest—Gallant Stand by Oxford and Bucks and Victorious Charge by Warwicks—The Steel-Trap of the French Line—Glorious Italian Rally on Asiago Heights—Terrific Charge and Counter-Charge on Grappa Positions—The Importance of Browning's Asolo—Bludgeon Work of Austrians and Rapier Play of Italians—The Great Ambush of the Montello Ridge—Enemy's Desperate Attempts on Venetian Defences—The Manœuvre of the Mist and Counter-Manœuvre of the Rain—Piave Rises in Defence of Venice—Hungarian Army Starved by Snow-swollen Torrent—Frenzied Preparations for General Retreat—Piave Falls and Enemy Wades Back.

FROM the complete downfall of Russia the Teutons and Magyars of Austria-Hungary profited in proportion to their numbers more than the Germans did. To a considerable extent they freed themselves from the direct military dominion of their stronger allies. Their forces were no longer closely brigaded with German troops and immediately directed by German generals. With the men, guns, and material detached from the eastern front the main Army was reorganised, greatly strengthened, and restored to Austrian control.

After the events related in Chapters CCXXX. to CCXXXII. (Vol. II), General Otto von Below went with his German divisions to France, taking with him some Austrian guns and gunners. Field-Marshal von Arz became Commander-in-Chief, without archduke in nominal —or Prussian general in practical— position above him. Only the Arch-duke Joseph remained as a Royal figurehead to an army group. For the rest professional soldiers, such as General von Scheuchenstuel, General Wurm, General von Henriquez, and Field-Marshal Conrad von Hötzendorff, were in control. The Court of the young Emperor Charles was resolved that the old Germanic Empire should be as remarkable in military efficiency as the new, so that the Hohenzollern should have nothing left to teach the Hapsburg.

The reorganisation of the Army was a measure of national independence. Although it produced a force scarcely half as strong in numbers as the German force, the re-formed Army of the Dual Monarchy was, in some ways, relatively more powerful.

ITALY'S VICTORIOUS COMMANDER-IN-CHIEF.
General Armando Diaz, appointed in November, 1917, to the supreme command of the forces on the Italian front in succession to General Cadorna, was a junior major-general when the war broke out.

Germany was opposed by France, the British Common-wealth, the United States, and Belgium. Austria-Hungary was opposed in full strength only by Italy. Against the Italians were some seventy-one divisions, each usually of 10,000 infantrymen, with 7,500 guns. They represented the whole of the first-rate troops remaining in the Hapsburg dominions, the other twenty-one Austro-Hungarian divisions being either infantry of lower quality or cavalry urgently needed in Russian and other occupied territory.

Field-Marshal Von Arz was able to plan a tremendous attack upon Italy by half a million men, with another hundred thousand in immediate reserve and eleven divisions available in the last resource from quiet sectors. In massive effect his plan equalled Ludendorff's greatest schemes. Austria, however, was far more inclined to employ her renewed strength as an instru-ment for diplomatic victories than as a weapon for a military decision. So grateful and comforting was her sense of recovered power that she was loath to risk it again in the fortune of war.

Her oppressed Slav races—Bohe-mians, Moravians, and men of Old Serb stock—were in a fierce mood of revolt, and some of them, in Russia, Greece, and Italy, were desperately fighting against her. It was increas-ingly difficult to keep Slav levies in action, even by means of military police using machine-guns and artillery as methods of persuasion. As the various Slav peoples of the Empire outnumbered the ruling Teutons and Magyars, it had never been an easy task to find sufficient soldiers of the governing races to keep Slav forces from surrendering in action.

After the destruction of Russia the men who had connived at the murder of one Hapsburg and charged the crime upon Serbia to provoke the conflict they had plotted with the German Staff, were apt for any additional treachery to the throne that would further their ends. The course was then adopted of preparing to accept the rule of the Hohenzollern in place of that of the Hapsburg.

Yet the men of the school of Count Tisza had to pay in military strength for their ferocious selfishness. Force was their argument, and in order to obtain real striking force the Hungarian troops had to undertake the principal work of attack. When, therefore, the intricate and difficult task of policing the hostile Slav elements was completed, the picked forces of assault immediately

BRITISH GUNNERS IN ITALY.
Man-handling a gun into a new position on the Italian front. The artillery was the first arm of the British forces to go to the help of the Italians.

Only against the Italians, from 1915 to 1917, had some of the Slavs of the Dual Monarchy been personally inclined to fight. The Southern Slavs had been embittered by certain Italian claims over the Eastern Adriatic shore, and had fought hard along the Isonzo for Austria and Hungary, thinking they were also fighting for themselves. But when the new Italian Government of Signor Orlando, formed after the Caporetto disaster, came to friendly terms with the Southern Slavs, a profound though hidden change took place in the re-formed and strengthened Austro-Hungarian main Army.

In this Army there were about twenty-five men of Slav and other oppressed races to every score of men of Germanic or Hungarian stock. When the Southern Slavs began to see, after their hopes in Serbia and Russia seemed broken, that they could eventually win to independence by making common cause with Italy, the real striking power of Field-Marshal von Arz was diminished by more than half. He could rely only on his Teutonic and Magyar units for sustained attacks, and the more of them he sacrificed the weaker grew his hold upon the rebellious Slav forces. The great, generous change in the policy of the Italians, who had been taught by Mazzini that the Middle European Slavs were their

Rebellious Slavs in Austria's Army natural allies, helped to compensate for the tyrannic treachery of the Russian Bolshevists. It gave the Grand Alliance another army of some 400,000 men. The fact that these new men were in the enemy's lines did not make them valueless—quite the contrary.

The closest advisers of the young Emperor Charles recognised the change in the situation. They tried to meet it by reorganising the Empire into separate Teuton, Magyar, and Slav Governments. Had this measure been honestly carried out in the spring of 1918 it might have appeased the revolting peoples. But the young Hapsburg was not strong enough to establish a triple federal system. He was defeated by the Austrian and Hungarian magnates, whose personal power and wealth were founded on the secular oppression of the Slavs of the Dual Monarchy.

ENEMY AIRCRAFT IN SIGHT.
British mobile anti-aircraft gun among rocky uplands on the Italian front. The men were loading it in readiness for attacking an approaching enemy aeroplane, kept under observation by the man on the right.

available for a grand offensive were not remarkably large. The immense Austro-Hungarian Army on the Italian front somewhat resembled an imposing façade, partly of armoured concrete and partly of lath and plaster. It was magnificent for diplomatic negotiations but dubious for military action. May, 1918, was originally fixed as the month for opening the intended decisive campaign against Italy. Yet the snow melted from the Alpine slopes, the water in the Piave River swelled to a mile-wide torrent and again shrank into a stream trickling through sun-warmed gravel beds, and no movement of attack occurred.

The men who stood by the Emperor Charles were cynically following events in the western field of war. Every failure by Ludendorff to reach his objectives in the struggle with the British armies made the Austrian High Command less inclined to renew the attack upon Italy. Indirectly the British were fighting for Kaiser Carl against Kaiser Wilhelm. For the weaker the Hohenzollern grew, the stronger the Hapsburg became, so long as the grand army between the Trentino and the Adriatic did not move.

Alternate menaces and appeals from the Court and camp of Prussia to the camp and Court of Austria produced for months little effect. It was not until the French front along the Aisne was broken by Böhn, at the end of May, as abruptly and completely as the British front by St. Quentin was broken by Hutier in the third week of March, that the men about the Emperor Charles took a fateful decision. It seemed then to them that the course of the war was determined by Germany, and that nothing was left but for the Hapsburgs to remain subservient to the Hohenzollerns.

Ludendorff's Staff ambassadors exploited fully the moral effects of the great western successes. Flattering Von Arz and his army commanders, they remarked it was the new method of attack, first used at Caporetto and practised by all the Austro-Hungarian forces, which had shattered the British and French fronts. The able Austrian High Command had only to use the same method again, while Foch's mass of manœuvre was absorbed in the defence of Paris, and Italy, with all her imported food stocks, growing crops, and glorious treasures, would lie at the foot of her former conquerors. Partly seduced by Mephistopheles and partly by the wealth of Marguerite, the Austrian Faust resolved to act. But though Italy retained her "fatal gift of beauty," it was not, in the event, to be fatal to her.

In the meantime Ludendorff prepared the way for a great Austrian victory by launching Hutier's armies between Montdidier and Villers-Cotterets in an **Allied reserves** offensive that engaged the allied reserves **pinned in France** in France and made it difficult for General Foch to send in the middle of June, 1918, any further reinforcements to Italy. This was all the German commander could achieve in the circumstances, and it fell much below his earlier promises. For he had first arranged to despatch Otto von Below with another hundred thousand shock troops to break far behind the Italian front from the western side of the Trentino. The Third and First British Armies had intervened in this scheme, leaving Below too severely maimed to move, so Ludendorff had to pretend he

was destroying Foch's mass of manœuvre, as a better alternative to a despatch of shock divisions likely to be followed by French, British, and American reinforcements for Italy.

Having regard to the fact that Hutier's new offensive was completely mastered by General Mangin's counter-offensive on the Méry plateau, by June 11th, it is clear that Field-Marshal von Arz was, at the critical moment, deceived in his view of the complexion of affairs in the west.

The Austrian offensive opened with an **Austrian offensive** attempted surprise against the left Italian **launched, June 13th** flank by the Swiss frontier. At dawn on June 13th the scanty outposts on the wild heights about the Tonale Pass were assailed by a division of shock troops. The attacking force was brought up the Alpine valley with the usual secret swiftness in motor-lorries, and sent up the mountains under cover of mist. The ground allowed only a small force to be employed, but when the pass was rushed, with the upper valley approach to the Plain of Lombardy, other troops were ready to exploit the advantages gained.

The brigades advanced in columns that spread into a succession of storming-parties, and in rapid, trickling movements, according to the best Ludendorffian pattern, tried to work over the northern Alpine ramparts of Lombardy, between the Orteler and the Adamello glaciers. They were set to win the high gate to Italy by the evening. They won nothing but appalling death. Caught on the mountain ledges and high counterscarps by raking, crossing machine-gun fire, swept by gusts of shrapnel when they topped a crest, they tumbled by hundreds into the flowering hollows beneath the white Alps.

After sacrificing one of his best divisions against the remote end of the Italian line the enemy commander hoped at least to distract an important defending force from the scene of

BRITISH TROOPS ON THE MARCH ALONG AN ITALIAN MOUNTAIN ROAD.
Although some of the men sent to the help of Italy in November, 1917, had only just come out of the line on the western front, all were delighted with the new adventure, and thoroughly enjoyed the change of scene, the unfamiliar surroundings, and the delicate golden sunshine of the Italian autumn.

AMID MOUNTAIN SUMMITS.
General view of Monte Grappa, between the valleys of the Brenta and the Piave. The line of the roadway made along the face of the rocks can be seen on the left.

ITALIAN OUTPOST ON THE ALPINE BARRIER.
Small wayside Italian post on Monte Grappa, on one of the wonderful roads cut along their rocky mountain front by the Italian engineers. The edges of the tents were weighted down with lumps of stone.

his main effort. But his feints were as vain as his great scheme of camouflage. The Slav had intervened in the conflict. General Diaz moved northward neither a gun nor a man. He knew at what points Von Arz would strike, and at what hour. One very able Slav officer had penetrated entirely into the scheme of the attack and had communicated the details to the Italian Staff.

His Secret Service work, carried out with deadly keenness of judgment, was

Slav-Italian Secret Service

the first fruit of the Slav-Italian entente. In practical value it was worth the help of a Jugo-Slav army. It enabled General Diaz to forestall the most dangerous part of the enemy's plan, and so assured him of victory. As revealed to the Italian Command the enemy's design was simple and massive. It consisted in an immense frontal attack on a line of forty-three miles, along the Piave River and the heights rimming the Venetian Plain above Asolo, Bassano, and Vicenza.

The merit of the straightforward, commonplace Austrian scheme was that it allowed an intense artillery concentration, with terrific cross-firing effects, upon the weak bend in the Italian line by Monte Grappa. On the heights thus swept on front, flank, and rear the Italians, British, and French could not afford to retire to a battle position and let the enemy waste his shell, as General Gouraud did in the Champagne Hills. They were so close to the plain, having been pushed to the edge of the mountain wall in previous attacks, that they had to stand to battle against any forces the enemy brought against them.

Their commander, however, when informed of the final arrangements of the attack, was able to save his men and Allies on the critical mountain flank. In the night of June 14th the Italian, French, and British guns made a sudden whirlwind bombardment of the enemy's lines from the Piave

River corner to the Asiago plateau. Between these points the armies of Field-Marshal Conrad von Hötzendorff and General von Scheuchenstuel were thronging into assembly trenches under cover of a misty night.

The allied blasts of fire, travelling deep into the hostile zone, had a disordering effect. Enemy battery positions and gun crews were caught unaware with gas-shell, and the crowded works in the infantry lines were shattered with high explosive. Along all the high land between the Adige River and the Piave River the Allies' surprise bombardment hamstrung the forces of attack as these were crouched for a leap.

The work of preparing a grand offensive along a front of forty-three miles was an intricate and delicate affair. Every movement had to be exactly time-tabled, and if it faltered a series of connecting movements was deranged. Extraordinary was the weakness of the masses of half a million Austro-Hungarians when they were making their final preparations. The gunners could not try to save themselves and their infantry by opening a grand artillery duel. This premature action would have upset the programme. The armies of assault could only silently endure the fate that had fallen upon them, and work as steadily as possible upon their own half-wrecked plan.

About half-past three in the morning of June 15th the Austrian guns at last opened fire from the Lagarina valley to the sea. Using an enormous quantity of gas-shell according to the Ludendorff method, they poured a deluge of poison over the Italian lines, and reached with special artillery all the towns and villages behind the battle-front. The Teutonic gas-shell, however, was becoming more a nuisance than a general peril. The india-rubber gas-mask of the Allies was so superior to the leather protection used by the Middle Europe forces that the parks of artillery shooting forth the gas did far less damage than they might have done had they employed only high-explosive shell. One by one all the elements of surprise in Ludendorff's new system of tactics were being exhausted, and the Austro-Hungarians, who reckoned they were using novelties, **Fierce attack upon** were outplayed by the liaison officers **the British** of the Italian Staff, who had carefully studied on the western front all the new Germanic mechanism of battle and fully prepared their men against it.

About six o'clock in the morning, when the mountain line was still covered in mist and the opposing batteries were thundering at each other behind protective smoke barrages, the attacking infantry began to use their special devices for screening their advance. They had smoke-bombs thrown from trench-mortars upon the allied machine-gun posts, together with mist-making machines, and the ordinary rolling white clouds produced by a shell used by part of the field-artillery.

The British forces, under Lord Cavan, which had removed from the Montello bastion of the Piave defence to the old

German territory of the Seven Communes of Asiago, were subjected to the same kind of stifling, blinding attack as had overcome the Ulstermen, Scotsmen, and Englishmen on the low hills and ravines by St. Quentin. The enemy rolled his artificial mists over them, filled the hollow where the railway line ran from Asiago, by Cesuna, with poison gas, and after ploughing the lines with a tornado of high explosive, sent four Austrian divisions forward like battering-rams against the 23rd and 48th British Divisions.

The landscape in this important British action, by the extreme left flank of the Italian front of defence, was very interesting from both a military and historic point of view. It consisted of a wide basin of rolling country, encircled by the last high foot-hills of the great Alpine system. The native population were Germans, formed of a Swabian garrison brought down to the rampart of the Venetian Plain by the Hohenstaufen Emperors.

When the mediæval German Empire was shattered, leaving exhausted Germany broken into warring fragments like modern Russia, the Swabians of the Seven Communes strangely remained an island of Germanism in the returning tide of Italian life.

The people kept their language, customs, and character, and in the nineteenth century still had Swabian clergy. They lived by cutting timber on the forested heights around Asiago, and hauling it to Valstagna for floating down the Brenta River to the Plain of Venice. Amid the pine

FIELD HOSPITAL.
British field hospital in a stony valley behind the front line in Italy.

woods they had planted on Lemerle and neighbouring steeps were the new British works, extending for some seven and a half miles, linking on the left with the defences of an Italian Alpine corps, and on the right, by Canove, combining with the Franco-Italian positions stretching to the Brenta River.

The British works were not easy of attack. The first battle position was screened by the dense growth of pines, and behind this sharp forested incline was a depth of some three to five miles of mountain country, through which the Austrian forces had to fight before reaching the plain above Vicenza. The enemy commander, however, opened battle in a very confident mood. Apparently he reckoned on meeting only a weak British force along the high pine woods.

A British brigade had lost a man on patrol at one end of the line, and afterwards had another man killed on patrol at the opposite extremity, to which the brigade was suddenly shifted. It thus appeared that there were only a few British battalions, thinned out as an advanced guard, and that the main battle would be fought on the crests in the British rear. Thereupon the Austrian Command devised the manœuvre of pressing the supposed British covering force back to the high crests, advancing down the Cesuna valley, and winning space from which decisive flanking attacks could be launched against the Franco-Italian positions on the eastern side of the Asiago basin. Should the French and Italian forces give way the Brenta River would be won, enabling the

WITH THE BRITISH RED CROSS IN ITALY.
Model field ambulance dressing-station near the British front line in Italy, and (in circle) bringing in a wounded Austrian. This dressing-station was erected among the pine-trees by men of the R.A.M.C.

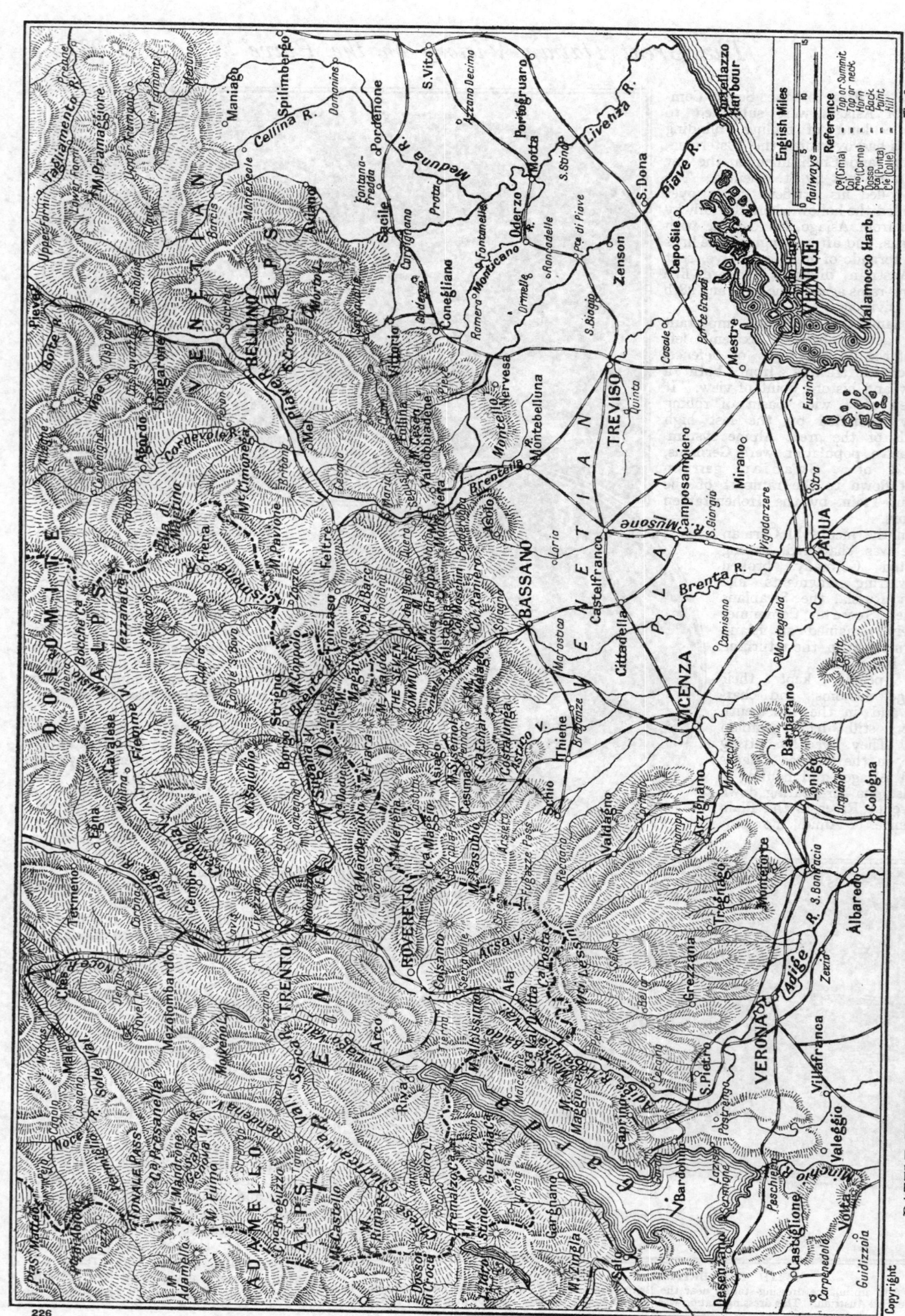

BATTLE-GROUND WHERE IN 1918 ITALY SMASHED THE MILITARY POWER OF THE AUSTRO-HUNGARIAN EMPIRE.

The design of the Austrian offensive was an immense frontal attack from S. Dona, near the mouth of the Piave, to the Montello, and along the heights rimming the Venetian Plain above Asolo, Bassano, and Vicenza, with an intense artillery concentration on the bend in the Allies' line near Monte Grappa. The British forces were in the Seven Communes, near Asiago, with French forces on the heights below Monte Sisemol connecting with an Italian army at Costalunga. Another Italian army was entrenched on the heights about Montenera, Asolo, and the Montello, between the Brenta and the Piave Rivers.

The Great War

mountain rampart above Asolo to be turned, and therewith the main Italian line along the Piave River.

But General Diaz had not moved the British force from the magnificent works it had constructed on the frontal key position of Montello to the flanking key position of Cesuna in order that the British should avoid action by giving ground. It was the high duty of Lord Cavan's corps to act as the extreme pivoting force of the defence, and, like the Lancashire Division at Givenchy, hold the enemy back from the plain at any cost.

When the battle opened between the infantry forces, about six o'clock in the morning, a British patrol became lost in the enemy's smoke barrage and was overrun by the masses of attack ; but the officer kept his rear open and brought his men back to the pine wood. There he climbed a tree from which he could oversee the hostile movements, directed an attack upon some machine-gunners who had worked behind the little force, and ended his little separate fight by capturing the guns.

Then, along the greater part of the British line, forty thousand Austrians, with some of the hardy, ignorant shepherds of Bosnia, who had not awakened to the Southern Slav movement, were caught in the curtain fire of the guns of the defence and raked by the machine-guns and rifles on the concealed infantry positions in the forest. On the front of the 23rd Division the attack was completely repulsed, and though the 48th Division, holding the western sector, lost some of the valley approach, the enemy was held by the switch-trench system, and there broken.

At one point the Sherwood Foresters were obliged to give ground, but without waiting for supports they rallied in a splendid counter-attack and restored their front. Only one serious gap was made by the Cesuna hollow, where an Oxford and Bucks battalion had a hostile rise of ground in front of it. Under this rise an entire enemy division massed, and by driving through a screen of smoke forced back both flanks of the men of Oxfordshire and Buckinghamshire. The Northumberland Fusiliers bent their flank back to keep in touch with their half-surrounded comrades, and a great struggle opened amid the pine-trees, where there was little clear space for machine-gunners and riflemen to act on either side. The men had to fight with bomb and bayonet in a salient a thousand yards deep, running up the columned twilight of the climbing pine wood, fiercely pressed on three sides by men ten times their number.

Bayonet fighting amid the pines

For centuries Great Britain had usually sided with the Austrian Power in wars on the Continent, especially against the French in the days of the Bourbons and Napoleon. It was thus an historic event when Briton and Austrian met in deadly combat in the pine forests of the Seven Communes. When in the night the Warwicks came up to help the Oxfords and Bucks and made a splendid counter-charge on the flank of the salient, it was a completely beaten army that rolled backward from the wooded steeps down to the Asiago hollow. It lost 7 guns, 72 machine-guns, and 1,060 prisoners, and fled in panic with the British in pursuit.

The French forces—below the Sisemol height, connecting with the Italian army by Costalunga—gave ground as soon as the enemy's pressure was fully felt ; then, when the Austrian divisions were crowding into the front positions, the terrible French light batteries opened their rolling fire and the French infantry came forward with the bayonet. Technically it was a counter-attack, but practically it was an assault, beginning with the feint of a withdrawal that induced the enemy to gather on the open field.

The difference in British and French tactics must have been a trial for the Austrians, as they were not, like the Germans, accustomed to the varying methods of the Western Allies. The French still used their small field-guns like machine-guns, having been, early in the war, the originators of the elastic system of defence that Ludendorff afterwards developed. There was veritable and instant elasticity in their flexible line. It gave and then swung forward, ejecting, like a great spring of tensile steel, the screaming, scurrying remnants of the swarms of attack. All the Austrian imitations of Ludendorff's tactics—scouting parties of sharpshooters, worming bodies of machine-gunners, detachments using long-distance covering rifle fire, and lastly the dense, successive waves of the grand assault—were overwhelmed in common confusion. The French troops at the end of the action found only four

ITALY'S KING WITH HIS BRITISH HELPERS.
King Victor Emmanuel, on the extreme left, walking with a British brigadier-general during a visit which he paid to the British forces taking part in the operations on the Italian front.

of their men missing, while a dozen of their bomb-throwers returned with more than a hundred and fifty prisoners.

The Austrian official report on the Asiago battle was remarkably frank, summing up the result of the struggle correctly. It ran :

In the forested zone of Asiago our regiments encountered a mass of attack which had been preparing for action some days previously. Their counter-attacks compelled us to withdraw from part of the ground we conquered.

In other words the enemy commander was anticipated and outmanœuvred. Later it was learned from prisoners taken after the action that attempts made to rally the broken, dispirited forces of Austrians and Hungarians led to violent disorders, which so tended to end in general mutiny that the operations were brought to a close. In these circumstances, but for the enormous power of the Austrian artillery, a counter-offensive would have been practicable ; but the general position of the Allies was not yet favourable to action of this kind. While Germany was still strong in attacks of a very menacing sort, it would have been a waste of the allied reserve to attempt to pursue the Austrians in difficult mountain country.

Result of the Asiago battle

The Italian forces in the Seven Communes were as successful as their comrades. Their gunners gave skilful assistance to the British flank, where their Alpine troops were also of high service as a reserve to Lord Cavan's 48th Division. By the Brenta River there was an enormous concentration of artillery and infantry of the attack. While the British and French contingents were fully engaged, the main forces of the Eleventh Austro-Hungarian Army, under General von

Scheuchenstuel, were driving against the high salients held by the Italians on both sides of the Frenzela ravine.

Famous had been the defence of the ravine in the battles of the previous autumn, but in magnificent tenacity the Italian Army excelled itself now. As on the British front, the troops were compelled to give ground, under the fire of a thousand guns massing upon some four miles of mountainous land and breaking a path for an unceasing swarm of attacking troops. Yet even when the Italian line bent, bodies of men remained on the lost heights, islanded in a sea of enemies, yet indomitable. Some of them managed to hold out until rescued by the great counter-attack; all of them were architects of victory, playing a noble part in continually hampering the hostile movements against the main line of defence on Echar crest.

The river positions by Valstagna held, under conditions of extreme anxiety, when the line gave eastward over the Brenta. On the Asiago forested mountains the army of assault was counter-attacked as it was slowing down. The gallant Frenchmen, having finished the enemy on the Pennar sector, moved forward on their right towards the Costalunga spur, in co-operation with the Italians, who won back ground in prolonged day and night fighting between the Frenzela ravine and the Melago valley. It was a complete victory for the defending forces. As Signor Orlando remarked:

"SPOTTING" FOR THE GUNS.
British artillery observer on the Italian front. Having climbed on to a ledge of rock on which he could kneel, he trained his telescope along the flat surface of the boulder.

On the uplands of Asiago an army of three nations fought with such concord, such brotherly fusion of spirit, plan, and manœuvre as could not be surpassed in a national army. There was, perhaps, this difference—that the flame of emulation burnt still more intensely and incited to rivalry in valour, a wonderful rivalry in which none of the three could surpass the others, so equal were the tenacity of resistance and the fury of attack.

Yet the unaided Fourth Italian Army, holding the most endangered section of line and the most important, was as magnificent. It was entrenched between the Brenta and

Piave, on the mountains, ridges, and slopes to which it had made a splendid fighting retreat the previous autumn. Its front ran in a series of salients, following the contours of the heights about the dominating clump of Monte Grappa, which had been retained by Italians and Frenchmen in the former battle.

At Monfenera there was only an edge of high ground, with a quick incline to the road running by Robert Browning's once lovely town of Asolo, now a wrecked and poisoned target, rising in the immediate battle zone for hundreds of Austrian guns to aim at across the Piave.

Asolo with its hills, filling the gap between the northern Grappa mountain rampart and the eastern riverside ridge of the Montello, was becoming more famous for military worth than for poetic glamour. It was a mighty artillery position on the side of the defence, that strengthened the forces clinging to the Monfenera ridge and the garrison of the Montello. Yet its guns could not prevent the more numerous enemy batteries across the river from taking in the rear the right wing of the Fourth Italian Army, cutting off supplies and reserves, and, with the great northern arc of hostile ordnance, ringing it with shell fire.

Since Below failed with 6 in. pieces against the Monfenera and Grappa positions, matters had not improved from the Italian point of view. The Austrians had brought their heaviest siege-guns forward in astonishing number—in thousands—exceeding in concentration of gun-power even Ludendorff's intensest effort. After the Italians had received all help from the Allies they could only dig for deeper cover and steel themselves to endure the most appalling of bombardments in the hope of recovering the advantage in the infantry action.

That was what happened. By devastating gun fire pouring from two sides the enemy commander swept some of the Italian garrisons away. His own infantry then broke far

WITH THE BRITISH FORCES ON ITALY'S ALPINE FRONT.
British soldier—with a basket of messenger pigeons in place of the usual pack—walking up a stony path on the Italian front. He used an alpenstock to help him on his way. Right: Laden pack-mules with the British forces on the Italian front setting out for a post in the heights.

"Forward to victory!" Italian general addressing his men before action.

Commanders of the British and French forces in Italy: The Earl of Cavan and General Graziani.

After a strenuous day: British transport drivers cleaning motor-waggons by an Italian stream.

Ingenuity of veteran campaigners: Tops of old lorries converted into tents by British soldiers.

Arduous work of the Italian artillerymen: Moving a heavy gun in the mountain battle area.

Mule transport crossing a pontoon bridge constructed by Italian engineers over the Isonzo near Bodrez.

Waging war amid the mists: Military encampment on the slopes of an Italian mountain.

Italian cavalry swimming their horses across a deep though narrow stream during an advance.

into the Grappa front, overrunning the western heights and storming over the fortified promontory in the centre. For a time Grappa was outflanked, and westward across the Brenta ravine the Allies' main positions on the Asiago upland were in danger of being turned.

The leading invaders could have had sight of Bassano and the open plain had the weather been less misty. They were checked by some very gallant gunners by Raniero peak, and impeded by desperate rearguards around the Grappa, but this did not stay the onward mass movement. Only the forefield of the battle had, however, been taken. The Italian commander had his reserves in sheltered positions, and as they came rapidly into action all the line rallied, and in exasperated vehemence resurged upon the enemy.

This was not an heroic improvisation but a manœuvre organised long before the battle by much study, engineering work, and special training of troops. The Italian mind had a fineness like that of the French. Far from trying in a sudden crisis to retrieve by impetuosity what should be carried out by patient preparation, General Diaz and his army commanders had forged beforehand the rapier-like method with which they met the bludgeon attacks of the Austrian Command.

What was spontaneous was the spirit with which the whole of the Fourth Army, tired troops as well as fresh troops, executed the counter-offensive. Preceded by a finely devised system of flanking gun fire bearing across the Brenta in a manner similar to General Pétain's flanking fire across the Meuse in the Battle of Verdun, the soldiers of Italy fought back to the Moschin ridge, saving the men on the Asiago sector from being outflanked. Then, with the Brenta front reconsolidated, they swung around the Grappa and recovered its outworks on the Asolone and the Orso heights.

All this was done on a very misty day, in which aerial observation was at first very difficult and at last impossible.

ON A LONELY OBSERVATION-POST.
Vedette post on a rocky bastion on the mountain front where Italy long held the Austrian invader at bay.

Nearly all the allied machines left the mountain battle-line because the air was so thick they could not work there, and massed along the Lower Piave where the atmosphere was somewhat clearer. Observing officers on the Grappa crests could not follow the action in the shrouded hollows, and when the darkness of night completed the obscurity the task of maintaining the recovered initiative against an enemy in much superior masses taxed all Italian commanding officers.

Yet the initiative was retained in spite of the new masses of troops that Conrad von Hötzendorff, directing Austrian operations on the Grappa front, wildly poured forth all night. His men were disheartened. They had been promised in a long, rhetorical order that at the end of the day they would be standing in the Italian plain, with an abundance of captured food before them. They had given the name of "The Hunger Offensive" to the new campaign, and when, after horrible fighting, their picked divisions fell back to their own lines with half their strength gone, the reserves of lower quality that relieved them were in no mood of aggressiveness. They allowed Italian patrols to recover the original machine-gun outposts, where these were intact enough to be worth reoccupation, and as on the western side of the Brenta, only the weight of the Austrian artillery—which remained enormous despite the daring Italian counter-battery work—prevented the successful counter-thrusts from being driven into the hostile lines.

There was, however, another factor of caution in addition to the enemy's massive gun-power. The situation of the main Italian forces along the Piave River line was not so strong as that of the victorious defenders of the mountain front. Von Arz had arrayed two mighty armies between the Montello curve of the Piave in the north and the seaward bend by Capo Silo and the lagoons and marshes above Venice in the south. The Archduke Joseph nominally commanded

LINED UP AND AWAITING ORDERS: BRITISH MOTOR TRANSPORT IN ITALY.
At a Divisional M.T. workshop behind the British lines in Italy, showing a large number of transport lorries lined up in the yard with their drivers standing by in readiness to proceed to any part of the front. Motor transport became so important a feature of the war on all fronts that extensive workshops were essential for the carrying out of the frequent repairs rendered necessary by active service in frequently rough conditions.

THE MONTELLO GROUP OF MOUNTAINS ON THE PIAVE FRONT.

Mountain range of the Montello, which is on the right bank of the Piave at about thirty-five miles from that river's mouth. The line of the Piave is to be seen just above the house in the left foreground. On June 24th, 1918, the

Italian commander was able to announce that from the Montello to the sea the enemy, defeated and pursued by the Italian troops, were recrossing the Piave in disorder; and by the next day the west bank was cleared.

in the Montello action, and for this Royal battle, which was to restore the personal military lustre of the Hapsburgs, he had the largest and best forces in the reorganised armies. Behind him was also the grandest of all the concentrations of the seven thousand five hundred guns.

His capable Chief of Staff seems to have engrossed most of the heights rising across the river north-east of the Grappa for the purpose of enfilading the hog's back of the Montello on the north, while ploughing it up directly from the east with howitzer fire and sweeping its southern slopes and approaches with cannon and high-velocity guns.

The scheme of attack on the Montello, by reason of the immense machinery behind it, was sound and very promising. Sir Herbert Plumer, an expert in storming ridges and defending them, had transformed the last great hump of earth between Venice and the barbarian into an inland Gibraltar. When he returned to battle for the Flemish hills, and his successor Lord Cavan removed with the British contingent to Cesuna, the capable engineers of Italy went on with the task of consolidating and strengthening the works.

Vast importance of the Montello

The ridge was some seven and a half miles long, with a height of seven hundred feet in the middle, increasing to more than a thousand feet at the western end. Its eastern cliff jutted over the enemy's lines, with the uncertain moat of the waters of the Piave at the foot, and in clear weather commanded all the country, including the Asolo hills on the Italian side, and the Conegliano rail-head and road junction on the Austrian side. It was the hinge of the defence. If it fell Venice fell with it, and with Venice the means of commanding the Northern Adriatic waters.

The weatherwise enemy began the struggle with many advantages. He raked the nearest slopes with high explosive, flooded the positions of support with poison fume, and with it filled all hollows likely to contain guns. Then, while his smoke screens were thickening the nocturnal haze, he bathed the long ridge and its communications with tear gas. Observation power was, under the conditions of

234

modern warfare, the great virtue attaching to the occupation of the height, and by selecting a misty night and using blinding gas in stupendous volume the Austrian commander designed to make his overwhelming infantry forces tell in decisive fashion.

The first part of his scheme was successfully carried out. On June 15th, over the shrunken Piave at Nervesa, his troops crossed in a screen of dense smoke, and in a double movement reached both the northern and southern sides of the promontory. Pushing out sharp-shooters and machine-gunners, the two forces united on the summit above Nervesa, and with the flame and thunder of their barrage as herald tried to sweep the ridge from east to west.

Strain on defence of Venice

When day dawned the enemy had a floating bridge and a great traffic of small boats on the Piave, and two crack storming divisions holding and widening their bridge-heads on the high granite fortress of Italy. The attackers had no artillery with them, but they captured many Italian guns in the forward position, and their promising success was immediately supported by a movement in huge numbers to force another passage of the river on a front of some ten miles below the Montello.

By this time the Piave line had been bent on the southern-most sector, by the lagoon and lake defences of Venice and by the road and line running to the Treviso junction of communications. The strain on the defence seemed intolerable, and Von Arz, feeling all the river-line giving, troubled little about the complete check on the mountain flank, but issued orders that progress was rapidly to be made across the Piave at any cost in life. All reserves were rushed to the Archduke's army group, where Field-Marshal Gorgenger was leading, and to Wurm's army that had won several bridge-heads on the Venice front.

Diaz and his lieutenants had to judge finely and quickly at what points they would react with strength. They counter-attacked most strongly on the southern side of the Montello, a little distance from Nervesa, pinning the invaders between the Brentella stream and the Piave. Their troops also threw the enemy back along the middle reaches of the river. Ground was given only by the seaward marshes, fourteen miles from Venice, and along the northern side of the Montello, eight miles from Asolo.

And this ground was not given lightly. The Italians were full of splendid daring and subtle fierceness; the epic spirit of their Sicilian seaman Commander Rizzo, who sank a battleship from a motorboat, was incarnate in them. They came into action singing, and from the twenty-four roads that crossed the Montello from north to south and made it a checkerboard for manœuvring, they took the swarming enemy frequently by surprise, in spite of his scouting patrols and linked machine-gun posts. Weatherwise was the Italian Staff as well as the Austrian. When mist came down from the Alps to the seaward plain in early summer, long, heavy rain was likely to follow. Field-Marshal von Arz had based his attack upon the opportunity of mist; General Diaz, in turn, was founding his defence upon the certainty of rain.

Absolute command of the air was his immediate need. British, French, and American squadrons joined the numerous Italian airmen over the Piave, and cleared the low-hanging sky of clouds of enemy machines. Then in the haze and the rain the allied bombing aeroplanes and aerial machine-gunners conducted a remarkable struggle for the river against Austro-

HERO OF A DASHING EXPLOIT.
Captain Luigi Rizzo aboard his motor patrol launch in which he attacked and sank an Austrian Dreadnought and put one of the ten destroyers escorting her out of action.

Hungarian anti-aircraft batteries and against the Austrian and Hungarian sappers.

As fast as bridges were constructed they were destroyed. Forces still crossing in boats were machine-gunned, columns marching on footbridges were bombed. The Montello trap was thus made difficult to enter at the time when it became most tempting and most dangerous. On June 16th the rain began to wash the snow down from the Alps, and all the hostile forces soon saw that they were set in a race against the rising torrent. This was the reason why the Austrian sappers worked with amazing energy and determination against the swooping squadrons that broke their bridges, and why Wurm and Kirchbach and other southern army commanders spent their entire strength in the maze of river works and the labyrinthine marsh and lagoon system.

The southern forces were trying to save the army of the Archduke by a releasing turning movement on Treviso. But every thrust they made was answered by a counter-thrust. When the Austrian official report was loud with praise of the Slav elements in the army of assault, Bohemians and Moravians were victoriously charging their oppressors between the Sile stream and the Piave and saving Treviso.

The Austrian and Hungarian leaders made many attempts to deal with their unwilling Slav troops as David dealt

ITALIAN MOTOR PATROL LAUNCH TORPEDOING AN AUSTRIAN DREADNOUGHT.
On the night of June 9-10th, Commander (afterwards promoted Captain) Luigi Rizzo, of the Italian Navy, while cruising with two small patrol launches near Pola, sighted two Austrian Dreadnoughts amid a destroyer flotilla. Dashing to within two hundred yards of the leading Dreadnought, he fired both his torpedoes and sent her to the bottom. He then put one of the pursuing destroyers out of action with a depth charge, and got clear away.

with Uriah. Under machine-gun pressure the men were shepherded into line for attack, where field-guns were laid on them by way of persuading them to fight forward. Those who escaped surrendered to their new allies the Italians. Consequently, while the waters of the Piave were widening under the rain-curtained battlefield, where the confusion was so great that a raiding-party of Italians were able to reach and shoot a Hungarian general of division, only the men of the governing races could be effectively used.

It was the Hungarians who were sacrificed. They were sacrificed by the hundred thousand in the interests of the Hapsburg dynasty, which their magnates wished to abandon

Magyars sent to their death for Hohenzollern rule. It was partly done because they were stout fighting men, likely to force the Italian line and prevent a great disaster ; but, as was afterwards angrily observed in the Hungarian Parliament, there seemed to have been dark reasons of State as well as military urgencies in the orders that sent the last strong multitudes of Magyars to their death.

Bitterly the Magyars fought. In the south they won, by June 17th, a three-mile salient and a longish strip of the western bank of the river. Instantly the special assault troops of Italy, the Arditi, drove into the northern side of the small wedge, while powerful Italian naval guns on floating platforms lower down the river broke the bridges behind the sodden, cheerless, ill-supplied attackers. When only two footbridges remained the Hungarian engineers constructed a cable ferry by San Dona, but could not get reinforcements and supplies over in time to strengthen their weakening forces.

In continuous battle from the Treviso approaches to the lagoons General Wurm endeavoured to relieve the Royal army on the Montello. By June 19th he gained a somewhat longer strip of the western bank, but the more men he passed over the swelling river the more his difficulties increased. Footbridges were becoming the frailest of human works. Aerial bombers wasted scarcely any time upon them, but dropped their missiles in scores of tons upon bodies of hostile troops.

For the Piave was the governing force on the field of battle. On the wide, deep torrent the pine-trees came down from the Alpine slopes with torpedo-like effect. They smashed into the enemy's light bridges, over which some twenty-five divisions at last had to be fed and munitioned. So long as the enemy was attacking, sky, river, and Alps fought for Italy. When the enemy was defeated the sky cleared, the river fell as quickly as it had risen, and the Alpine forests ceased to send down their missile pines.

With strange fatuity the enemy High Command announced that " the fall of the greater part of the Piave front " had taken place on June 19th, which was the day of supreme triumphant progress for the Italians. The army of the Archduke Joseph was then covering the northern half of the Montello and stretching to the railway from Montebelluna. Its position was menacing in appearance, but weak in reality, and by converging routes the Pisa Brigade, with Aosto, Piedmont, and other forces, struck across the ridge and along its southern foot.

In storming columns the Italians worked, submitting to no check and striking mainly across unfortified ground, where

Italian cavalry charge by night the Magyars had little or no cover against the rolling barrages of the returning garrison. Italian gunners who had lost their pieces in the early action accompanied the infantry of attack, bringing ammunition for the guns they were certain would be recovered. Won back many of the pieces were before the enemy could destroy them, and employed once more against him. By the evening the Hungarians were pushed into a salient on the north-eastern part of the ridge, and there were more slowly slaughtered by artillery fire and aerial bombardment.

There was also a fine success at Zenson, on the lower course of the river, where the cavalry of Milan and a lancer regiment ended the fierce fluctuations in the action for the Venice line by a nocturnal counter-charge that drove the enemy to the waterside. With dawn on June 21st came the crisis to which

General Diaz had worked with the patience and science of a great commander.

The enemy had then employed about forty-five divisions. Of these four hundred and fifty thousand effectives, more than one-third, were killed, drowned, or wounded, and the rest of those still in action on the western bank of the Piave were weary and depressed. Unfortunately, the weather was improving in the Alps and over the plain. The steep Piave shot its vast flood of rain and melted snow into the sea, and narrowed and shallowed, leaving broken pontoons, holed boats, trees, and the light wreckage of war upon the resurgent belt of gravel. By June 22nd the stream was fordable in places.

No doubt many Italian soldiers were pleased with fine weather. It had been trying work fighting in pouring rain and mist in an enclosed countryside, offering every means of ambush and surprise. But their commanders were not pleased. Their hopes of turning the enemy's grave reverses into a decisive disaster fell with the falling Piave. An Austrian council of war, presided over by the Emperor Charles, was reported to have determined on a withdrawal on June 20th, when the Italian counter-offensive was proving successful.

Though the victors maintained intense pressure on the hostile forces, especially on the Montello, while arranging their artillery for the final stroke, the beaten forces prepared more quickly their means of escape. The fords were practicable on the night of June 22nd, and soon after midnight the host, that would have been slain or taken had it still needed footbridges to cross the river, waded back to the lines from which it had set out on June 15th.

Rearguards were left on the Montello and in the San Dona salient to cover the removal or destruction of heavy material. On the ridge at daylight Italian patrols discovered what was taking place, and an attack was launched that saved the last of the lost guns from being blown up by the enemy. Many of the pieces were full of explosive when recovered, but the Magyars fled without firing the charges, and

left a few of their own guns behind. By the river prisoners were taken as they tried to push off in boats, and the Italian cavalry **Moral effect of the victory** crossed the water and raided the country towards Conegliano. But there was no real pursuit beyond the river-line. The hostile artillery remained very formidable, little of it being lost owing to the impossibility of transporting the pieces over the Piave during the first phase of the action. The San Dona salient was then evacuated, and by June 25th there were no foes on the western bank of the river, except some twenty thousand prisoners, and a considerable proportion of them were Slav soldiers who had willingly surrendered. The enemy's losses were estimated to amount to 200,000 men, while the Italian casualties were known to be less than 40,000.

The moral effect of the victory of Italy was profound. In Austria it led to riots, in Hungary to a serious attempt at a general strike, in which military police had to occupy important factories and use firearms. The reactionary Ministry dissolved into a Government of official Micawbers, which, while waiting for something to turn up, was bankrupt of ideas and palsied in power. Skoda, the gunmaker, remained the best servant of the Hapsburgs. His artillery was a framework of steel on which the Army was again reconstructed and carefully conserved.

In Italy a people already welded by reverse was annealed by triumph. To its strength was added resilience. Grimness went, and a blithe courage allowing play of mind came, with an inventive audacity which made the Latin race again an incalculable force. To France, Great Britain, and the United States the success of Italy over her ancient foe brought both inspiration and succour. It relieved the tension of spirit, and enabled General Foch to use the mass of manœuvre he had been keeping in hand for all eventualities between the North Sea and the Adriatic, in a stroke that changed the course of the war in the principal theatre of conflict. By the fine economy of force with which he won a great victory General Diaz directly contributed to the recovery of the Allies' striking power on the common front, and opened the way for the glorious series of western advances that began in August, 1918.

CIRCULATING LIBRARY

CHAPTER CCLXVII.

FOR SOLDIER READERS.

INFLUENCE OF THE WAR ON ENGLISH LITERATURE.
By Walter Jerrold.

Times of Great Stress Call for Expression in Literature—A Quickened Interest in Poetry One of the First Effects of the Outbreak of the War— Early Flood of Newspaper Verse—The Napoleonic Wars and Literature : The Later Renaissance—Mr. Thomas Hardy's " Song of the Soldiers "—The Poet Laureate's Call to Action—Mr. Rudyard Kipling on the Hun at the Gate : His Impressive Accounts of Naval and Military Activities—" Mr. Britling Sees It Through " : Mr. H. G. Wells's Spiritual History of the Nation in Fiction Form—A Prose Epic of Gallipoli from Mr. John Masefield—The War Poetry of Mr. Laurence Binyon—Fine Appeal to American Sentiment from Mr. Alfred Noyes—Moments of Imaginative Experience Fixed in Verse—Sir Evelyn Wood on Educated Soldiers— " A Student in Arms "—Poets who Became Soldiers and Soldiers who Became Poets—Captain Julian Grenfell's " Into Battle "— Rupert Brooke's " 1914 "—An Eager and Discerning Critic—Charles Sorley, another Writer of Rare Promise who Fell in the War— Frequency with which Fiction Founded in War Experience was Shot Through with Humour—Ian Hay's " First Hundred Thousand "— Legends of the War—The Steps Taken for a Literary Entente among the Allied Nations—The Inspiring Passion for Humanity.

A T the close of an earlier chapter of this history (Chapter CXCII., Vol. 9) something was briefly said of the way in which the war quickened the poetic spirit, and that especially among the young men who had answered the call from school and university : but the subject of literature and the war demands special treatment for a variety of reasons, perhaps the outstanding one being that any great period of emotional stress or action ever calls for expression, either in the individual or in that aggregation of individuals which forms a nation. The stress may be such as to sharpen and clarify thought and its presentation, or it may have the opposite effect, and history is concerned with the extent to which it does the one or the other. Furthermore, that very stress of the time that tries the soul of a person or a people may well prove a fresh source of inspiration, an awakening of dormant capacity, even a revelation of new power. The place of literature in civilised life is so important that to omit any record of the way in which it was affected by the Great War would be to leave out consideration of the very thing that links the period of the war with that future which its events will have served to mould and modify.

This chapter is mainly concerned with the literature of the war which is commonly, but by no means satisfactorily, termed 'imaginative, for it is rather a presentation of actuality shot through with vision, or vision so felicitously rendered, as a poet has

"FOR EVER ENGLAND."
Grave of Rupert Brooke, one of the most brilliant of the younger poets of his time. He died on service in the Ægean, April 23rd, 1915, and was buried in the island of Skyros.

put it, that the description springs the reader's imagination with a touch. The greatest literature is that which does this in the simplest terms.

One of the first effects on literature of the outbreak of the war was an extraordinary outburst of newspaper poetry. Verses of patriotic rhetoric, songs designed for the purpose of aiding recruiting, satires on the Teuton breakers of the world's peace, contemplative sonnets and lilting lyrics, poured into every newspaper office as though the whole of Britain had become a nest of singing birds. This spirit which sang on the outbreak of war was a perfectly healthy spirit ; it was almost like a national expression of relief at the fact that the long foretold storm had burst ; it was a way of facing " the unknown with a cheer.' Looking back on that flush of verse which reached the public through the daily and weekly Press, it can be said that the average quality was distinctly high, even though a goodly proportion of it might have been described, in the words of H. G. Wells, as a " mere automatic response of obvious comments to the stimulus of the war's surprise."

Within a very short time after the outbreak of war the question was gravely asked : What effect will the Armageddon conflict have on literature ? It was pointed out that the same question might well have been asked a century earlier, when Europe was nearing the climax of the Napoleonic Wars, and the pertinent comment made that comparatively little of any definite impress of the conflict is traceable on literature

The one poet who was directly moved to great utterance by the time in which he was living was William Wordsworth—the one writer whose work could be found glowing and inspiring a century after it was written, when his country was once more at death-grips with recrudescent tyranny on the Continent. It is, however, worthy of note in passing that the long war-period which came to an end on the field of Waterloo was followed by the breathing of something of a new spirit into literature, that within the next decade and a half was comprised much of the work of Wordsworth and Coleridge, most of that of Byron, and all the lyric spontaneity of Shelley and Keats, and this is to take note of poetry alone, for in prose the change—later renaissance, as it might be termed—was scarcely less marked.

Although it might be tempting to institute comparisons between the first quarter of the nineteenth century and the first quarter of the twentieth, any such comparison could in the nature of things be but inconclusive. Conditions had changed greatly if men had not. Then war was a far-off thing concerning, it seemed, some thousands of people. The Great War was something grimly menacing everyone. The relations of war and letters, too, had become entirely different. In 1815 the Poet Laureate "pilgrimaged" to Waterloo that he might write a poem about the battle with appropriate local colour; by 1915 soldiers were promoted poets on the field by the shock of experience. Among the changes that may be noted during the intervening century, there was, with the Crimean War, the

"literature of the war" as including any printed matter dealing in any way with it. Anything so comprehensive as that would need a very large history to itself, even though it consisted of little more than mere mention of the many thousands of items that would have to be included. Therefore it is that this survey of the field is designed to treat more especially of the literature which is described as imaginative, ignoring for the most part all such topical works as were rather the materials out of which the future literature of the war will be developed. The power of rapid reading and instant memorising of a Coleridge and a Macaulay combined will be required by the Gibbon who shall essay the task of making use of all those materials.

The extent to which established writers responded to the new stimulus to expression afforded by an event that transcended all experience was by many regarded at the time as disappointing. It should not have been. Some of the ways in which such writers were moved may be shown as representative of the whole; to cite all would be to reduce history to a catalogue.

Mr. Thomas Hardy, O.M., had written in "The Dynasts" one of the greatest war-inspired poems of the language, but of a kind that could only be written after the lapse of time. In his poetry of the war which befell in the years of his age there was something of the feeling of the seer expressed in the rhythms of one who moved uneasily in "the gewgaw fetters of rhyme," but in the closing stanzas of his "Song of the

POETS AND MEN OF LETTERS WHO PROVED THEMSELVES MEN OF ACTION:

Leslie R. Bumpus, lieutenant in the Australian artillery, whose tender verses, "Passing By" were widely popular.

Alan Seeger, an American poet, who fell in action as a member of the French Foreign Legion.

Thomas M. Kettle, M.P., an Irish writer, who fell in action as an officer of the Dublin Fusiliers.

Rupert Brooke, a gifted poet, who died while on service as an officer in the Royal Naval Division.

coming of the descriptive "war correspondent," and, in Tolstoy, a yet more significant phenomenon, the coming of the realist on to the battlefield. In the American Civil War a great poet first penned battle pictures of painful, poignant, and searching realism. It was not, however, until some years later that Walt Whitman published his "Specimen Days in America," in which the stark ugliness of war was made plain. It is, by the way, worthy of note that though there are people who think a great war necessarily productive of great literature, the American Civil War does not support the theory, for there was in the United States no succession to the great writers — Emerson, Thoreau, Lowell, Longfellow, Whittier, Whitman, Holmes—who had already reached their prime at that period.

Speaking in November, 1916, Lord Curzon indicated something of the secret of what may be termed the immediate effect of the war on literature. Men went out as soldiers who had already made reputations as writers, others who were but just feeling the impulse to write, and yet others who were first impelled to expression by the cataclysmic change which had swept them from the daily round into circumstances so entirely new. But the literature of the war that Lord Curzon thought would become one of its greatest monuments was by no means all produced by men who served at the front. Few were the established writers who were not moved to writing of the war in one form or another.

Here the term literature is used in its stricter sense, not in the all-comprehensive way in which some spoke of the

Soldiers," Mr. Hardy tersely expressed the spirit out of which the first British armies grew:

In our heart of hearts believing
  Victory crowns the just,
  And that braggarts must
  Surely bite the dust,
March we to the fields ungrieving,
In our heart of hearts believing
  Victory crowns the just.

Hence the faith and fire within us
  Men who march away
  Ere the barn-cocks say
  Night is growing gray,
To hazards whence no tears can win us;
Hence the faith and fire within us
  Men who march away.

Much of that which was written in the earlier months of the war was of a rhetorical or exhortatory character, in which reason and thought sought to find expression in the natural form of fire and passion. Mr. Robert Bridges, the Poet Laureate, wrote, with fine simplicity of phrasing but somewhat staccato utterance, his appeal, "Thou Careless, Awake!"

Thou careless, awake!
  Thou peacemaker, fight!
Stand, England, for honour,
  And God guard the Right!

The monarch Ambition
  Hath harnessed his slaves;
But the folk of the Ocean
  Are free as the waves. . . .

Thy mirth lay aside,
  Thy cavil and play:
The foe is upon thee,
  And grave is the day.

Up, careless, awake!
  Ye peacemakers, Fight!
ENGLAND STANDS FOR HONOUR,
  GOD DEFEND THE RIGHT!

When the war came Mr. Rudyard Kipling was regarded as the unofficial laureate of the Empire. His early contribution to the literature of the war gave, in its closing lines, what became at once a familiar quotation. Taking its title from the opening words, the poem was a finely conceived and expressed utterance of that which the nation felt, to which the most truly Imperial of its poets was alone capable of giving adequate form :

For all we have and are,	No easy hopes or lies
For all our children's fate,	Shall bring us to our goal,
Stand up and meet the war.	But iron sacrifice
The Hun is at the gate !	Of body, will and soul.
Our world has passed away	There is but one task for all—
In wantonness o'erthrown,	For each one life to give.
There is nothing left to-day	Who stands if freedom fall ?
But steel and fire and stone. . .	Who dies if England live ?

Mr. Kipling wrote, too, in prose, often linked with appropriate verse, of " The New Army in Training," of " France at War," of " The Fringes of the Fleet," of the doings of the British submarines—" Tales of ' The Trade ' "—and of " The War in the Mountains," where Italy withstood her ancient enemy. Though these works were in the nature of pamphlets, they included such vivid descriptions, or such accurate realisations, that they were of more than topical value. How surely this was so was shown when the pamphlets on the different branches of naval activity were grouped into a single volume, " Sea Warfare."

Another writer of established repute whose work inspired or influenced by the war was looked for with special interest was Mr. H. G. Wells, an author whose novels of modern life were as remarkable for their understanding of different people as his romances of adventure had been remarkable for presenting improbabilities (such as the war had made

prose and poetry, bearing the stamp of literary achievement. His poem on " August, 1914," was one of the more notable utterances in verse of the early days of the war. In his small book " Gallipoli," the epic story of a failure by which the men of the British Empire won undying glory, was set forth for all time with poignant feeling and in stately prose. Though an actual record of the war, it deserves singling out from the vast number of such records for its quality. In " The Old Front Line," he wrote also a remarkable guide to the old front line of the Somme.

Among writers of already established reputation, Mr. Laurence Binyon was of those most markedly touched to new strength by the war. His volumes of poems on the war— " The Winnowing Fan," " The Anvil," and " The Cause "— maintained a high level of inspiration and craftsmanship. Much fine rhetorical stuff had been written on the coming of the war, but Mr. Binyon's work penetrated deeper than rhetoric. There was something that went beyond the appeal to any superficial or temporary passion or emotion in such pieces as this on " The Fourth of August " :

> Now in thy splendour go before us,
> Spirit of England, ardent-eyed,
> Enkindle this dear earth that bore us,
> In the hour of peril purified. . . .
>
> Endure, O Earth ! and thou, awaken,
> Purged by this dreadful winnowing-fan,
> O wronged, untamable, unshaken
> Soul of divinely suffering man.

WRITERS WHO GAVE THEIR LIVES FOR THE CAUSE THEY GLORIFIED.

Donald Hankey, author of " A Student in Arms," killed on the Somme when lieutenant in the Warwickshire Regiment. — Leslie Coulson, author of " From an Outpost and Other Poems," sergeant in the Royal Fusiliers. — Francis Ledwidge, the peasant poet of Meath, killed in action as lance-corporal, Inniskilling Fus. — R. E. Vernède, author of " War Poems," second-lieutenant in the Rifle Brigade, fell at Havrincourt Wood.

actualities) or impossibilities with the sense of reality of a Jules Verne, and with greater literary power. A writer of extraordinary capacity and fecundity, he wrote much directly or indirectly inspired or influenced by the war, his most remarkable work being the powerful story, " Mr. Britling Sees It Through." In this Mr. Wells gave " the spiritual history of the nation during the most searching trial it has ever experienced," and did so in a way that makes the book not only one of the most valuable of the social studies in fiction form produced during the period of the war, but one of a kind of searching revelation. Taking one " sample Englishman," Mr. Wells sought to present his thoughts and feelings, emotions, and resolutions when faced by the war, and he succeeded to an almost uncanny degree. His faculty for presenting fiction as though it were but filmly veiled autobiography was perhaps in part responsible for the way in which his absorbing study seemed to give form and expression to the vague thoughts and feelings of all. Certainly, in " Mr. Britling Sees It Through," he produced the most remarkable sustained achievement in fiction, inspired by the subject of the war and informed with its spirit.

Few of the novelists of acknowledged eminence failed to write one or more stories to which the war formed a dramatic background—Mrs. Humphry Ward in " Missing," Mr. W. J. Locke in " The Red Planet," Mr. E. F. Benson in " Up and Down," and many others. These, however, were for the most part novels, in which the war was utilised as a theme, rather than works in the deeper sense born of the war.

From Mr. John Masefield the war evoked work, both in

In the dark days of the retreat from Mons Mr. Binyon's poet-faith held true, and the same strong spirit rang in his fine " Ode for September," in closing which he stoutly foretold the final overthrow of that force which had seemed for the time being to be triumphing :

> O children filled with your own airy glee
> Or with a grief that comes
> So swift, so strange, it numbs,
> If on your growing youth this page of terror bite,
> Harden not then your senses, feel and be
> The promise of the light.
> O heirs of Man, keep in your hearts not less
> The divine torrents of His tenderness !
> 'Tis ever war ; but rust
> Grows on the sword ; the tale
> Of earth is strewn with empires heaped in dust
> Because they deemed that force should punish and prevail.
> The will to kindness lives beyond their lust ;
> Their grandeurs are undone ;
> Deep, deep within man's soul are all his victories won.

In a short prose play, " Bombastes in the Shades," Mr. Binyon in prescient fashion gave as it were the judgment of history on the German Kaiser, where he showed him suddenly struck to the Shades. Happening upon Socrates, Heine, Bayard, and Queen Elizabeth, the Imperial bully is seen at first in the blustering, arrogant mood in which he had been struck from the earth.

Turning to the work of a poet who had in pre-war days written of war as only a devout lover of peace could do— " Lucifer's Feast " is one of the most damning indictments of militarism ever penned—it will be seen that Mr. Alfred Noyes used his fine mastery of rhetoric, indignation, and aspiration in many poems. The one which he read at Harvard University in 1915, " The Trumpet of the Law," had many fine passages ; its closing lines embodied an appeal to all that was best in American sentiment and feeling :

And they, who did this deed, had they been wronged
Were offered Justice, and not once, nor twice,
But many times ; and they rejected it
For this, to slaughter and to crucify.
O, yet in this dark hour of agony
Those thin sad outstretched arms conquer the world.
And we believe, help Thou our unbelief,
That since the noblest part of man is less
Than that eternal Fount from which it came,
There is a Power above the mightiest State,
The unconquerable minister of law,
Which shall dispense the justice they deny
And show the mercy that they have not shown.
And you, O land, O beautiful land of Freedom,
Hold fast the faith which made and keeps you great.
With you, with you abide the faith and hope,
In this dark hour of agonised mankind.
Hold to that law whereby the warring tribes
Were merged in nations, hold to that wide law
Which bids you merge the nations, here and now,
Into one people. Hold to that deep law
Whereby we reach the peace which is not death,
But the triumphant harmony of Life,
Eternal Life, immortal Love, the peace
Of worlds that sing around the throne of God.

Mr. Alfred Noyes also wrote a terrible poetic tragedy of the German devastation of Belgium, " Rada." Among his striking lyric utterances of the war mood—of the solemn national consecration, rather—one of the most successful was that on " The Searchlights," with the motto, taken from Germany's apostle of militarism, Bernhardi, " political morality differs from individual morality, because there is no power above the State." The concluding stanzas are :

Not far, not far into the night,
These level swords of light can pierce ;
Yet for her faith does England fight,
Her faith in this our universe ;
Believing Truth and Justice draw
From founts of everlasting law.

Therefore a Power above the State,
The unconquerable Power returns.
The fire, the fire that made her great
Once more upon her altar burns.
Once more, redeemed and healed and whole,
She moves to the Eternal Goal.

The articles which Mr. Noyes wrote on the trapping of enemy submarines, that had appeared in newspapers all the world over, were formed into a volume, " The Mystery Ships," but the weird and wonderful working of the censorship caused that volume to be recalled on the morrow of its publication. The similar articles—formed into a volume, " Open Boats "— which he wrote as to the fate of the crews of unarmed merchant vessels sunk by German submarines, will long be remembered, terrible in their simplicity, among the living documents of the war.

From Mr. T. W. H. Crosland came war poems of bitter irony and searching satire and, in " A Chant of Affection," one of the most memorable of the replies to the German Lissauer's " Hymn of Hate," a fine piece of scorn, fashioned and phrased in lasting literary form.

James Elroy Flecker—who had sung with something of a fine riotous beauty of the vague mirage-like fascinations of the caravan and of Persia—died of consumption during the war. The most notable of his poems that grew out of the war, " The Burial in England," though marred by unmelodious blank verse, has forceful, unforgettable lines :

Our foes—the hardest men a State can forge,
An army wrenched and hammered like a blade
Toledo wrought, neither to break nor bend,
Dipped in that ice the pedantry of power,
And toughened with wry gospels of dismay ;
Such are these who brake down the door of France,
Wolves worrying at the old World's honour,
Hunting peace not to prison but her tomb.
Yet is not Death the great adventure still ?
And is it all loss to set ship clean anew
When heart is young and life an eagle poised ?

The pre-war fame of Mr. Maurice Hewlett had been largely that of a master of the art of tapestried romance. In " Sing Song of the War," he achieved considerable success with pieces written somewhat in the manner of the old-time verses and ballads ; and in " The Village Wife's Lament " he sought to make vocal the emotion of a simple country-woman whose shepherd husband had been killed in the war. One of his short pieces, " For Two Voices," presents memorably in dialogue verse the glamour of militarism as seen by heedless youth, and its bitter significance as realised by experienced maturity :

" O mother, mother, isn't it fun
The soldiers marching past in the sun ! "
" Child, child, what are you saying ?
Come to church. We should be praying."

" Look, mother, at their bright spears ! "
" The leaves are falling like woman's tears."
" You are not looking at what I see."
" Nay, but I look at what must be."

" Hark to the pipes ! See the flags flying ! "
" I hear the sound of a girl crying."
" How many hundreds before they are done ? "
" How many mothers wanting a son ? "

" Here rides the general pacing slow ! "
" Well, he may, if he knows what I know."
" O this war, what a glorious game ! "
" Sin and shame, sin and shame ! "

Many of the men who went to the war, and were impelled to write of it in prose or verse, masked the horror and bestiality of it with humour. It was as if, with Montaigne, they some-times smiled that they might not weep. At times, too, the literature of the war was marked by a kind of grim humour, well exemplified in the brevities which Mr. Wilfred Wilson Gibson wrote under the title of " Battle." These verses, brief as the epigrams of the Greek Anthology, but possessing neither the beauty of poetry nor the point of epigram, in their rounded completeness formed something new, individual, and memorable. They might be described as moments of imaginative experience instantaneously fixed in words as a scene is caught by a camera. " The Messages " illustrates the economy of verbal means by which the poet attained his impressive end :

" I cannot quite remember . . . There were five
Dropt dead beside me in the trench—and three
Whispered their dying messages to me . . ."

Back from the trenches, more dead than alive,
Stone deaf and dazed, and with a broken knee,
He hobbled slowly, muttering vacantly :

" I cannot quite remember . . . There were five
Dropt dead beside me in the trench—and three
Whispered their dying messages to me . . .

" Their friends are waiting, wondering how they thrive—
Waiting a word in silence patiently . . .
But what they said, or who their friends may be

" I cannot quite remember . . . There were five
Dropt dead beside me in the trench—and three
Whispered their dying messages to me . . ."

There is something of a haunting quality about that tragic monotone. In it the stunned, dazed feeling of the survivor, with his pained realisation that the messages which he has received he cannot recall, is rendered with something of the rare combination of nature and art which produced " The Old Familiar Faces " of Charles Lamb.

Many, indeed, were the established writers who contri-buted poems or passages to the great volume of the lasting literature of the war. Some lines of Sir William Watson's panegyric of Mr. Lloyd George as " The Man Who Saw,"

No fabled Merlin, son of mist
And brother to the twilight, but a man
Who in a time terrifically real
Is real as the time,

and some of his sonnets of the war will continue to be remembered.

Mr. Frederick Manning in "Eidola" included pieces of grim power in that new irregular verse form, which lent itself in his hands more especially to the rendering of the ugliness and horror of war. Another writer who, turning from the lyric ease of his earlier work, wrote of the war in a new form was Mr. Ford Madox Hueffer. His "Antwerp," with its broken harshness of phrasing, possesses curiously and lastingly impressive qualities :

> With no especial legends of marchings or triumphs or duty
> Assuredly that is the way of it,
> The way of beauty—
> And that is the highest word you can find to say of it.
> For you cannot praise it in words
> Compounded of lyres and swords,
> But the thought of the gloom and the rain
> And the ugly coated figure, standing beside a drain,
> Shall eat itself into your brain :
> And you will say of all heroes : "They fought like Belgians."
> And you will say : "He wrought like a Belgian his fate out."
> And you will say : "He bought like a Belgian
> His doom."
> And that shall be an honourable name ;
> "Belgian" shall be an honourable word,
> As honourable as the fame of the sword,
> As honourable as the mention of the many-chorded lyre,
> And his old coat shall seem as beautiful as the fabrics woven in Tyre.

To its close, with its haunting suggestion rather than description of the refugees' arrival at Charing Cross, the poem gives, as it were, in a succession of tragic etchings the story of the martyrdom of Belgium. Again in "On Heaven, and Poems Written on Active Service," Mr. Hueffer used the free metre with great effect in "Old Houses in Flanders."

Mr. Gilbert Frankau, turning from his happy pre-war Byronic narrative verse, wrote in somewhat Kiplingesque style of the war, as he saw it as an officer of the Royal Field Artillery. In "The Guns," and in "Signals," and also in "The Judgment of Valhalla," for example, he worked this vein in vigorous fashion, the result being wonderful instances of descriptive power employed in verse, but hard and metallic in effect. In "The City of Fear" he wrote impressively, in such irregular form as that of Mr. Hueffer's "Antwerp," if with less of telling terseness, yet with something of the same thrill of realisation :

> This is the City of Fear !
> Death
> Has ringed her walls with his sickle, has choked her streets with his breath ;
> In her cellars the rat feeds red
> On the bodies of those whom their own roof-beams betrayed to him as they fled—
> For none live here
> Save you that shall die, as we died, for the city, and we, your dead,
> Whom God for the sake of our one brave dream has garnered into His hand.

The most successful work was still that in which the music of words was employed in the old time-honoured ways. From Mr. Neil Munro, among other war writings, came a series of "Bagpipe Ballads," some of which will be remembered as long as are the great deeds of his countrymen on the fields of France and Flanders. Such stanzas as these,

closing the ballad of "The Pipes of Arras," are among the triumphs of the lyric form :

> Up then and spake with twitt'rings
> Out of the chanter reed,
> Birds that each spring to Appin
> Over the ocean speed,
> And in its ruined castles
> Make love again and breed.
> "Already see our brothers
> Build in the tottering fane !
> Though France should be a desert,

> While love and spring remain
> Men will come back to Arras,
> And build and weave again."
> So played the pipes in Arras
> Their Gaelic symphony,
> Sweet with old wisdom gathered
> In isles of the Highland sea ;
> And eastward towards Cambrai
> Roared the artillery.

When writing an introduction to a reprint of "Sir Ian Hamilton's Despatches from the Dardanelles"—military documents which attained a high level of literary distinction—Field-Marshal Sir Evelyn Wood said that he had been asked early in the war if the men who were fighting were of the same fighting value as the soldiers of his early experience, and he replied, "Yes, just the same at heart, but with better furnished heads." The Army was no longer divided into "common" soldiers and caste officers ; it had been in subtle fashion democratised and was less an Army than a nation in arms, and of its experience was demonstrated anew the adaptability of the race whose men of letters could become soldiers, whose men of action could in the very terrors and trials of unprecedented warfare become articulate.

Among the most significant of the books which revealed something of that which was best in the soul of the nation at war were the writings of Donald Hankey, who, dying in action, will live in literature as "A Student in Arms." In the autumn of 1914, while Hankey was a sergeant in the Rifle Brigade, his first volume had appeared in the form of an appeal for a unifying simplicity in the Churches ; then came a series of papers, fresh, thoughtful, individual, which—collected in volume form as "A Student in Arms" and "A Student in Arms : Second Series,"—were seen to be the work of a rare and winning personality, one who brought to his task as a soldier a spirituality of mind, combined with something of a passionate love for his fellows, and that understanding which is born of love. As a lieutenant of the Warwickshire Regiment, Hankey fell in battle on the Somme, on October 12th, 1916, leaving in his first anonymous "Student" book, and the material for a second one, some of the imperishable literature that has grown out of the war. Every page of his work bears the stamp of the writer's originality in the handling of his theme, whether that of the relation of the Church to modern life, the democratising of the Army, the qualities of leadership, or the need of the dramatic sense. It is told how Hankey, before leading his men "over the top," asked a chaplain to say a prayer, and then calling his men to follow, said : "If wounded—Blighty ; if killed—the Resurrection." The incident should be remembered as is Sir Philip Sidney's—"Friend, thy need is greater than mine !"

Mention has been made of the way in which the great experience touched into poetry many of those who went to the front, and there is a deep, peculiar, and pathetic interest in the small sheaves of verse which were collected—the living

Ronald A. Hopwood, a captain in the Royal Navy, who wrote fine stirring verses on naval themes.

[Vandyk.
"Ian Hay" (John Hay Beith), author of "The First Hundred Thousand."

[Luca Commerio, Milan.
Gilbert Frankau wrote forceful verses of the war as seen by a captain in the R.F.A.

Boyd Cable, a war-made writer who wrote of Armageddon in vigorous and impressive fiction form.

POETS AND NOVELISTS WHO WROTE OF THE WAR BY SEA AND LAND.

record of young lives destroyed by the blind machinery of war. Not all the verse so produced was poetry, though much of it was indubitably rich in promise for the literature that was to come after the war.

The work of poets who had become soldiers, soldiers who had become singers, was inherently interesting as a manifestation of the idealist spirit that informed the men engaged in the stupendous reality. It was said that the way in which men at the front—even in the trenches—wrote proved the falsity of Wordsworth's dictum that poetry is the result of emotion remembered in moments of tranquillity; it would be truer to say that it proved that statement to be a generalisation rather than the enunciation of a law. If there was little of tranquillity for the soldier-poets, it is certain that the themes that moved them to song were as often those of remembered emotions as they were those directly inspired by immediate surroundings. The work inspired by those surroundings was frequently of a humorous or whimsical character.

Looking through the volumes that were written by men actually engaged in the conflict is to be impressed by the fact that so many of the young men of the time were capable of writing verse. Some of them, it is true, had already become writers, and others would have doubtless turned to the writing of verse in any case. The call to action in a cause known to be great, the ever-imminent prospect of death, often strengthened them to utterance far beyond the mediocrity of that verse-writing which is frequently but a passing symptom of intellectual development.

From among the many it is only possible to particularise a representative few. In April, 1915, Captain Julian Grenfell, D.S.O., wrote while in Flanders what is by many regarded as one of the finest poems inspired by the war, " Into Battle." This strong, sincere, and deeply-moving utterance was by a pathetic coincidence published on the very day, May 28th, 1915, on which its author's death from wounds was announced :

> The fighting man shall from the sun
>   Take warmth, and life from the glowing earth ;
> Speed with the light-foot winds to run,
>   And with the trees to newer birth ;
> And find, when fighting shall be done,
>   Great rest, and fullness after dearth.
>
> All the bright company of Heaven
>   Hold him in their high comradeship,
> The Dog-Star and the Sisters Seven,
>   Orion's Belt and sworded hip. . . .
>
> The kestrel hovering day by day,
>   And the little owls that call by night,
> Bid him be swift and keen as they,
>   As keen of ear, as swift of sight.
>
> The blackbird sings to him, " Brother, brother,
>   If this be the last song you shall sing
> Sing well, for you may not sing another ;
>   Brother, sing." . . .

The death of Julian Grenfell was one of the many literary tragedies of the war, and another of the tragedies of poetic genius cut short was that of Rupert Brooke, whose poetry, less spontaneous than that of Grenfell, had rare beauty of artistry. His sonnets, " 1914," reveal an intense personality, and yet, seeming to speak for the young manhood of Britain, have a sure place among the treasures of poetry. The following, " The Soldier," welcomed by one young critic as the most authentic battle-song produced by the war, has something of poetic prophecy, for the young poet died in the Ægean, while on service, on the anniversary of Shakespeare's death, 1915 :

> If I should die, think only this of me :
>   That there's some corner of a foreign field
> That is for ever England. There shall be
>   In that rich earth a richer dust concealed ;
> A dust whom England bore, shaped, made aware,
>   Gave once her flowers to love, her ways to roam,
> A body of England's, breathing England's air,
>   Washed by the rivers, blest by suns of home,
> And think, this heart, all evil shed away,
>   A pulse in the eternal mind, no less
> Gives somewhere back the thoughts by England given ;
>   Her sights and sounds, dreams happy as her day ;
> And laughter, learnt of friends ; and gentleness,
>   In hearts at peace, under an English heaven.

Dixon Scott, the young critic referred to, was himself one of the eager and discerning men of letters of the time who made the supreme sacrifice in the war, a critic of individuality, of penetrating discernment, and master of a brilliant prose style. Apart from passages in " Men of Letters " inspired by Rupert Brooke's poems, he wrote little that was touched by the war in which his youth was all too early closed, for after a brief while at Gallipoli he died of dysentery in a hospital-ship on October 23rd, 1916—six months to a day after Rupert Brooke had passed away in similar circumstances.

Another poet of remarkable gifts who fell in the war was Charles Sorley, killed in France while leading his company of the Suffolk Regiment on October 13th, 1915. His small volume, " Marlborough and Other Poems," bears the stamp of achievement ; a passage from one of the letters written to a friend, which appeared in the " Times " shortly after his death, shows him something more than a youthful versifier, a man capable of deep thought and of expressing himself with that sincerity of individuality which is one of the first essentials of true literature :

> The chess players are no longer waiting so infernal long between their moves, and the patient pawns are all in movement, hourly expecting further advances whether to be taken or reach the back lines and be queened. 'Tis sweet this pawn being ; there are no cares, no doubts ; wherefore no regrets. The burden which I am sure is the burden of ill-temper, drunkenness, and premature old age— to wit, the making up of one's own mind—is lifted from our shoulders. I can now understand the value of dogma, which is the General Commander-in-Chief of the mind. I am now beginning to think that free-thinkers should give their minds into subjection, for we who have given our actions and volitions into subjection gain such marvellous rest thereby. Only, of course, it is the subjecting of their powers of will and deed to the wrong master, on the part of a great nation, that has led Europe into war. Perhaps afterwards I and my like will again become indiscriminate rebels.

Something of the earnestness, sincerity, and high promise of Sorley's work was revealed in this scrap of his prose not less than in his poems ; in his " Expectans Expectavi "— written just before leaving England for the front—it found expression in a form worthy of the best of the meditative and devotional poets of the seventeenth century :

> From morn to midnight, all day through,
> I laugh and play as others do,
> I sin and chatter, just the same
> As others with a different name.
>
> And all year long upon the stage
> I dance and tumble, and do rage
> So vehemently, I scarcely see
> The inner and eternal me.
>
> I have a temple I do not
> Visit, a heart I have forgot,
> A self that I have never met,
> A secret shrine—and yet, and yet
>
> This sanctuary of my soul,
> Unwitting I keep white and whole,
> Unlatched and lit, if Thou should'st care
> To enter or to tarry there.
>
> With parted lips and outstretched hands,
> And listening ears Thy servant stands ;
> Call Thou early, call Thou late,
> To Thy great service dedicate.

Some remarkable poems were written by Alan Seeger, a young American who, in the autumn of 1914, with a number of his compatriots, joined the French Foreign Legion, and fell, at the age of twenty-eight, on July 4th, 1916, in the attack on the village of Belloy-en-Santerre, in the opening stages of the great Somme offensive, nine months before his great country ranged itself as a belligerent Power against the brutal might of Prussia. The volume of his " Poems " revealed a talent of fresh and distinct quality, and in " I Have a Rendezvous with Death " he wrote one of the enduring poetic memorials of the war :

> God knows 'twere better to be deep
> Pillowed in silk and scented down,
> Where Love throbs out in peaceful sleep,
> Pulse nigh to pulse and breath to breath,
> Where hushed awakenings are dear . . .
> But I've a rendezvous with Death
> At midnight in some flaming town
> When Spring trips north again this year,
> And I to my pledged word am true,
> I shall not fail that rendezvous.

Another writer, revealed a poet by the war in which he fell, was Robert Ernest Vernède, who had already established a reputation as novelist when, in his fortieth year, he answered his country's call. As second-lieutenant in the Rifle Brigade, he fell leading his platoon in an attack on

Havrincourt Wood in April, 1917, and in the best of his "War Poems" gave fine expression to the thoughts with which thousands of Britain's peace-loving sons became soldiers, and some pieces of a penetrating simplicity which makes them of enduring value. "Before the Assault" is perhaps the best of his poems from the larger view, but the simple, manly lines of dedication to his wife, with their tenderness and sincerity, touch a note which will find response in every heart:

> What shall I bring you, wife of mine,
>   When I come back from the war?
> A ribbon your dear brown hair to twine?
>   A shawl from a Berlin store?
> Say, shall I choose some Prussian hack
>   When the Uhlans we overwhelm?
> Shall I bring you a Potsdam goblet back
>   And the crest from a Prince's helm?
>
> Little you'd care what I laid at your feet,
>   Ribbon or crest or shawl!—
> What if I bring you nothing, sweet,
>   Nor maybe come home at all?
> Ah, but you'll know, Brave Heart, you'll know
>   Two things I'll have kept to send:
> Mine honour, for which you bade me go,
>   And my love—my love to the end.

There were many poets who had scarcely revealed their gift of song when they fell as soldiers—each of whom might contribute an immortelle to anything like a complete anthology of the war—Francis Ledwidge, whose early songs had caused him to be hailed as "an Irish Burns," though his poems written under the stress of war were but little touched by its spirit; Robert W. Sterling, whose volume of "Poems" gave evidence of a true literary gift; Richard Dennys, Wyndham Tennant, Henry L. Field, Bernard White, Leslie Bumpus, of the Australian Artillery, Ivar Campbell, and others. The "Passing By" of Leslie Bumpus, though simple, colloquial verse in form, was infused with the glow of poetry, and combined grim realism with tender sentiment in a way that was widely appreciated.

A small sheaf of verse—"The Volunteer and Other Poems," by Herbert Asquith, son of the then Prime Minister, showed in striking fashion that questioning spirit which found utterance in so many forms among the young men of the time:

"BARTIMEUS."

L. da Costa Ricci, Pay-master, R.N., author of "Naval Occasions," and other notable books.

> Have we lost our way,
> Or are we toys of a god at play,
> Who do these things on a young spring day?

he asks in "After the Salvo." From him also came expression of that renewal or revival of faith in immortality which may be traced in much of the literature that was produced under the direct influence of the war, and more especially, perhaps, in that produced by men actually in the field. It was as though, to those engaged in conflict, the horrors of mortality incident to slaughterous war made immortality a necessity.

Among those moved to poetry of real meditative beauty by their personal experience in the war, E. Armine Wode-house may be cited as one most finely representative. His "On Leave: Poems and Sonnets," marked throughout by a deeply serious note, included in "The Temple of Sorrow: To England in Mourning," a noble sonnet-sequence in memory of England's dead. With a fuller and more sustained note than that of most of the soldier-poets, Mr. Wodehouse wrote poems of tense feeling and thought-ful earnestness; he faced the new domination of horror and terror, the amazing demonstration of heroic self-sacrifice, with no merely conventional utterances on his lips. Such a poem as his "Before Ginchy: September, 1916," must have proved a revelation to many people

accustomed to having war tricked out in terms of "glory," and most of its horrors ignored or slurred over. It remains one of the great poems produced during the time of action, revealing the course of that change which was marked in men who had returned home.

In "The Temple of Sorrow" and its complement, "The Ancient Path," Mr. Wodehouse wrote a sonnet-sequence—for the two are as parts of one whole, the path but leads to the temple—that for sustained beauty and dignity, and that rare soul-comforting which belongs to the finest devotional poetry was unexcelled by any of the literature born of the war. One sonnet must here be taken as representative of the whole:

> He?—Who is he—O, mourning mother-heart!
>   Wherever in this land thou be, thou know'st.
>   Whose is the shape which haunts thee like a ghost?
> Who standeth at thy side where'er thou art?
> Thou widow'd wife! thy bosom's aching smart
>   Tells me thou knowest him, too. Whoe'er hath lost
>   A dear one, knows!—for lo! he is an Host;
> And every several loss is but a part
>   Of that wide woe—to-day which mourneth him.
>   Wherever, in this England, tears are shed;
>   Wherever English eyes are sore and dim;
>   Wherever droops the bow'd and stricken head;
>   Wherever unborn hours loom cold and grim;
>   Lo! he is there! For he is England's Dead!

From the same poet, too, in "There was War in Heaven," there came an ode on the ideal for which mankind was suffering that is not unworthy, for inspiration and expression, of a place beside Wordsworth's great "Ode on Intimations of Immortality."

It was a noticeable fact that much of the work written by the poets of action showed the extent to which the writings of Mr. Rudyard Kipling had influenced his younger contem-poraries. Again and again came echoes of his manner in rhythms, his tricks of expression. They were to be found in one of the more striking volumes that came from the Navy, "The Old Way and Other Poems," by Ronald A. Hopwood; as in "Our Fathers," which begins:

> Though the seaplane, soaring upward, may betray the submarine
> To the oil-fed super-Dreadnought steaming nervously between;
> In pursuance of her mission, she'll be well-advised to shun
> Any interfering cruiser with the newest seaplane gun.

"SAPPER."

H. C. McNeile, captain in the Royal Engineers, author of "Sergeant Michael Cassidy, R.E."

In the "Ballads of Battle" of Joseph Lee, while there was also much to be found reminiscent of Mr. Kipling's verse, there were also many pieces, some of them penned during the period of a bombardment, which illustrated the way in which, while they felt and thought deeply, the soldier-poets often masked their gravity with humour and whimsicality. He also struck a solemn note in such short, memory-haunting poems as this "Invocation: Night in the Trenches":

> Creator of the stars
>   Great and Little Bear—
>   Have us in Thy care.
>
> Thou Who set Orion,
>   Watch and ward to keep—
>   Guard a soldier's sleep.
>
> Hand that swung the Spheres.
>   Strawed the Pleiades—
>   Have pity upon these.
>
> Hand that sways the Plough;
>   Will that stays the Pole—
> Sow Thy good seed now,
>   Guide an errant soul.

In a subsequent volume, "Workaday Warriors," Mr. Joseph Lee was again successful in rendering things seen and mused over by the fighting man.

"From an Outpost and Other Poems," by Leslie Coulson, a sergeant in the Royal Fusiliers, showed the way in which the Great Adventure, as it was euphemistically termed, caught up those whose every instinct was for peace, whose very souls revolted at all the abominable hideousness of war, and who yet went out to play their part with a nobility—if there could be degrees in the matter—greater than that of those who were fighters by instinct. Here was a gifted youth whose lyrics of country lanes and of the simple joys of natural beauty and of daily life seemed far removed from everything associated with strife, who joined the Army, passed through the inferno of Gallipoli, and fell fighting in France. His last poem, written in the field but a few days before his death, probably without any final revision, is of peculiar interest as a further indication of the way in which the war was awakening a new questioning spirit in the young manhood of the nation. It is entitled " Who Made the Law ? "

> Who made the Law that men should die in meadows ?
> Who spake the word that blood should splash in lanes ?
> Who gave it forth that gardens should be boneyards ?
> Who spread the hills with flesh, and blood, and brains ?
> 　　　　Who made the Law ?
>
> Who made the Law that Death should stalk the village ?
> Who spake the word to kill among the sheaves,
> Who gave it forth that Death should lurk in hedgerows,
> Who flung the dead among the fallen leaves ?
> 　　　　*Who* made the Law ?
>
> Those who return shall find that peace endures,
> Find old things old, and know the things they knew,
> Walk in the garden, slumber by the fireside,
> Share the peace of dawn, and dream amid the dew—
> 　　　　*Those who return.*
>
> Those who return shall till the ancient pastures,
> Clean-hearted men shall guide the plough-horse reins ;
> Some shall grow apples and flowers in the valleys,
> Some shall go courting in summer down the lanes—
> 　　　　THOSE WHO RETURN.
>
> But who made the Law ? the Trees shall whisper to him :
> " See, see the blood—the splashes on our bark ! "
> Walking the meadows, he shall hear bones crackle,
> And fleshless mouths shall gibber in silent lanes at dark.
> 　　　　Who made the Law ?
>
> Who made the Law ?　At noon upon the hillside
> His ears shall hear a moan, his cheeks shall feel a breath,
> And all along the valleys, past gardens, croft and homesteads,
> HE who made the Law,
> 　　　　He who made the Law,
> He who made the Law shall walk along with Death.
> 　　　　WHO made the Law ?

Many, indeed, were the soldier-poets whose work inspired by the war appealed to something more than the limited and temporary interests of a friendly circle. That the man of literary instincts and tastes may also on occasion prove himself the man of action was abundantly proved. The popular idea of a poet as a man of an inert or flabby type should have been for ever destroyed by the war ; the " artistic temperament " as an apology for weakness should thenceforth have no hearing. Among those who won the Military Cross for great daring in the field was Mr. Siegfried Sassoon, and that he was a poet of unusual gifts was finely shown in a delightful volume, " The Old Huntsman and Other Poems," and again in " Counter-Attack and Other Poems." From among the variedly grim and beautiful pieces in that volume these lines on " Absolution " may be cited as an interpretation of the significance of the great struggle :

> The anguish of the earth absolves our eyes
> 　Till beauty shines in all that we can see.
> War is our scourge ; yet war has made us wise,
> 　And, fighting for our freedom, we are free.
>
> Horror of wounds and anger at the foe,
> 　And loss of things desired ; all these must pass.
> We are the happy legion, for we know
> 　Time's but a golden wind that shakes the grass.
>
> There was an hour when we were loath to part
> 　From life we longed to share no less than others.
> Now, having claimed this heritage of heart,
> 　What need we more, my comrades and my brothers ?

From time to time after the first portions of the British Expeditionary Force had marched off to the jaunty and inspiriting jingle of " It's a long, long way to Tipperary," scraps of fresh songs were heard of as being sung by the British soldiers at the front. These, however, did not appear to strike any very remarkable note ; they were mostly little more than meaningless choruses which, shouted in unison, afforded vocal variety to the monotony of marching. The mere words of the generality of the actual soldiers' songs were

described by Mr. Patrick MacGill as " ' dud ' shells which drop harmlessly near their objective," and he went on to say that such songs were in reality very few. His own " Soldier Songs " were on the whole somewhat disappointing to those who had built high hopes on the boyish promise of the " Gleanings " of a few years before the war ; many of them did no more than follow certain Kiplingesque conventions. Somehow the greatness of things did not move him greatly in verse. Mr. MacGill's work as a prose realist was the more remarkable part of his contribution. He had before proved himself a singularly impressive master of the art of realistic fiction in stories based on the earlier experiences of his checkered career, and in " The Red Horizon " and " The Brown Brethren " he utilised his gifts in presenting stories, episodes, talks, in which his fellow-riflemen of the London Irish figured. In these books, by a kind of cumulative effect rather than by the self-conscious artistry which concentrates on " purple patches," the author made his readers realise the character of some typical men from among the masses who doggedly carried on through the long agony of the war ; strong to do and obey, heroic in action, yet lacking any betrayal of enthusiasm for the great task in which they were engaged. These books represent the war as experienced by a group of companions in arms, and in their general effect do so in a realistic fashion which makes them seem transcripts from a diary rather than essays in fiction based on experience with the grimness and horror of things modified or tricked out in verbal treatment, as was much of the war fiction even of those who had gone " through it." Of the arrival in the firing-line, Mr. MacGill wrote :

> We were alone and lonely, nearly every man of us. For myself I felt isolated from the whole world, alone in front of the little line of sand-bags with my rifle in my hand. Who were we ? Why were we there ? Goliath, the junior clerk, who loved Tennyson ; Pryor, the draughtsman, who doted on Omar ; Kore, who read " Fanny Eden's Penny Stories," and never disclosed his profession ; Mervin, the traveller, educated for the Church, but schooled in romance ; Stoner, the clerk, who reads my books, and says he never read better ; and Bill, newsboy, street arab, and lord knows what, who reads the " Police News," plays innumerable tricks with cards, and gambles and never wins. Why were we here holding a line of trench, and ready to take a life or give one as occasion required ? Who shall give an answer to the question ?

Mr. MacGill's method was, on the whole, one that revealed the reality, the sordidness of war ; he was among those writers of fiction who brought details of the actualities of the war home to thousands of readers in a way that official despatches and correspondents' telegrams could not do.

The whole thing was so stupendous, the issues so vast and so vital, that it was those who sought to throw light on the whole by emphasising what were comparatively minutiæ, rather than those who tried to deal with the whole who achieved literature, and among those thus successful it was the writers with humour who did so in the way that proved most widely popular.

The human mind in moments of stress has a curious habit—an instinct, perhaps, for the preservation of sanity—of fastening on lesser or irrelevant matters so that these impress the memory, and certain it is that of the fiction produced during the war it was that shot through with humour which proved the most generally impressive. Possibly it was so in accordance with that characteristic national habit of masking feelings with immobility or disguising them with manifestations of their antithesis. One of the most notable of the works of this kind was " The First Hundred Thousand," by " Ian Hay " (Mr. John Hay Beith), a book in which one who had already achieved distinction as an author of comedy-novels rendered with an abundance of spontaneous humour the story of one of the units of " Kitchener's Army " in a series of masterly sketches. In this book, with its gaiety, its whimsicality, and its spirited account of the doings of certain individuals in training and in action, the author gave literary embodiment to the spirit which responded to the call of battle, which sent men at first by the hundred thousand and then by the million from civil occupations not only to military life,

Hospital Ship under Escort of Destroyer and Coastal Motor-Boat

Specially painted for "The Great War" by C. M. Padday

but to military life that it was known would lead, after but few months of training, to the battlefield and the likelihood of early death. "The First Hundred Thousand" so presented this, so truly revealed the mass through the unit, that it was, in its particular kind, one of the most significant as it was one of the most popular contributions of the war to literature. It was followed by a scarcely less notable sequel, "Carrying On."

If Captain Beith was one of the authors whose literary talent was if anything heightened by the war, others who revealed the essential realities as experienced by individuals became soldiers first, and developed their literary gifts in the crucible of action. "Sapper"—H. C. McNeile, Captain in the Royal Engineers, and winner of the Military Cross in the Second Battle of Ypres—wrote some of the most revealing, and also some of the most poignant, of war records in the guise of fiction in "Sergeant Michael Cassidy, R.E.," "The Lieutenant and Others," "Men, Women, and Guns," and "No Man's Land." "Boyd Cable," too, was another war-made writer who presented glimpses of the field of Armageddon in fiction form of abiding interest in "Between the Lines," "Grapes of Wrath," and other vigorous works. The realities of naval service were similarly recorded, with that union of knowledge and sympathy of which the heavenly twins, Humour and Pathos, are born, by Paymaster L. da Costa Ricci, a writer who chose to remain hidden in the incognito of "Bartimeus," and by another pseudonymous writer, "Klaxon," equally remarkable in prose and verse. Other pseudonymous authors who wrote finely of their experiences in fiction form were "Vedette," in "The Adventures of an Ensign," and "Contact," in "An Airman's Outings."

Certain legends of the war, which arose during the course of it — arose none knew whence, and spread none knew how—should perhaps be mentioned in that they are likely to find their echo in the literature of the future. There was the appearance of St. George and attendant angels guarding the British during the great retreat from Mons of the first inadequate Expeditionary Force. That story, firmly held as a fact by some, appears to have owed its origin to one of the

JOSEPH LEE.   [*Hoppe.*
Author of "Ballads of Battle," written while on active service in the Black Watch.

earliest pieces of war fiction, Mr. Arthur Machen's "The Bowmen." The evidence as to its origin in that clever little piece of imaginative work seemed to many irrefragable; but there were not wanting those who in their wish to believe in supernatural intervention believed in it. Another legend which arose was that of thousands upon thousands of Russian soldiers that passed by train through Britain, bound for France and the holding up of the advancing horde of Germans. Somebody had, maybe, surmised that Russian troops could thus be brought round from Archangel, and that which had been conjectured by one as a possibility was accepted as a fact by the majority of the people; everybody's neighbour had a friend who had actually seen "the Russians" of this myth army. Another of the war legends was to the effect that Lord Kitchener did not die when H.M.S. Hampshire went down on June 5th, 1916, and that in due time he would return. This legend, similar to those long extant of King Arthur, Charlemagne, Barbarossa, Drake, and other great leaders, was but testimony to the hold which Kitchener had over the imagination of the people, and the feeling of dependence upon his leadership. Yet a further legend was that the deposed and assassinated Tsar Nicholas II. had escaped from Revolutionary Russia, and sought refuge as a poor immigrant in America.

Such legends, widely believed in, could not fail to find literary treatment, arising as they did from that innate feeling for the romantic and the dramatic which is at the base of much literary inspiration.

One very striking instance of the indirect but significant influence of the war upon literature that calls for mention is the formation, on the initiative of Mr. Arthur Maquarie, Honorary Foreign Secretary of the Royal Society of Literature, of a Committee for Promoting an Intellectual Entente among the Allied and Friendly Countries. This committee, which was duly established in October, 1916, consisted of the following members: The Right Hon. A. J. Balfour, O.M., Secretary of State for Foreign Affairs; Dr. A. C. Benson, C.V.O.; Bishop Boyd-Carpenter, K.C.V.O.; Professor W. L. Courtney, editor of the "Fortnightly Review"; Mr. Harold Cox, editor of the "Edinburgh Review"; The Marquess of Crewe, K.G., P.C.; Professor

E. ARMINE WODEHOUSE.
An officer-poet who produced some of the finest poetry written during the war.

HERBERT ASQUITH.   [*Swaine.*
He wrote some notable meditative pieces inspired by his experiences at the front.

    [*Painting by Glyn Philpot, A.R.A.*
SIEGFRIED SASSOON.
Author of "The Old Huntsman and Other Poems," and an officer whose courage gained for him the Military Cross.

    [*Elliott & Fry.*
FORD MADOX HUEFFER.
Who wrote very impressively, in the irregular form of vers libre, of war scenes.

PATRICK MACGILL.
A novelist who wrote with strong realism of typical soldiers in action.

    [*Emery Walker.*
WILFRID WILSON GIBSON.
Author of "Battle," brief poems remarkable alike for their novelty and for their grim humour.

Walter de la Mare, the Right Hon. H. A. L. Fisher, President of the Board of Education; Professor J. Fitzmaurice-Kelly, Professor M. A. Gerothwohl, Mr. Edmund Gosse, C.B.; the Earl of Halsbury, Mr. Thomas Hardy, O.M.; Dean Inge, Professor F. B. Jevons, Professor W. P. Ker, Dr. J. W. Mackail, Sir Philip Magnus, Bart., M.P.; Mr. Arthur Maquarie, Sir Henry Newbolt, Sir A. W. Pinero, Dr. G. W. Prothero, editor of the "Quarterly Review"; Dr. J. Holland Rose, and Sir John E. Sandys.

The end which this committee had in view was that in the future it should not be possible "for one race to attempt the mental domination of others by a highly artificial penetration based upon the prostitution of literature and science under State control and maintenance." Its objects were thus summarily formulated:

To act as a centre of suggestion and co-ordination in this country in all matters likely to promote an Intellectual Entente among the allied and friendly nations, and to serve as a single channel of communication with similar efforts abroad.

To strengthen and increase the ties between the academies, associations, and centres of culture generally in the allied and friendly countries.

To encourage the knowledge of English thought and literature in those countries, and reciprocally to assist a corresponding movement in our own Empire.

To acquaint societies and public bodies with the importance of the movement, to invite them to study in what way they can most effectively assist, and generally to develop action and to correlate efforts.

To take all steps that from time to time may seem desirable for increasing the intellectual intercourse among those nations upon whom depends the shaping of the path of human progress after the present struggle.

The war broke out at a time when self-conscious efforts after a new "note" in the arts had become so strained that anything which was sufficiently unconventional was more or less assured of notice. In literature there had been attempts to render in words the eccentricities of ruggedness, angularity, and singularity which had been manifesting themselves in other arts, though liking for such eccentricities had not spread far beyond the circles of those experimenting in them. There had already been noted something of an awakening and widening of the public interest in poetry, such as encouraged those who remembered Meredith's dictum, as to a capacity for laughter being promise of wit to come in a people, to hope that an increasing regard for poetry might be evidence of a new power of poetic expression. This quickening of interest was accompanied or caused by—for interrelation of supply and demand in such rare stuff as that of literature what economist shall determine?—something of a fresh poetic impulse revealed in the writings of half a dozen or so of poets who were putting the new century's thought and feeling into new words and new forms before the outbreak of the war.

Through all the agony of the war literature was produced, and literature of which history can confidently say that it was worthy. At the outset fears were expressed that the production of books would dwindle to nothing. Those fears proved ill-founded, even though the war was a far longer and far sterner task than the prophets had believed possible. The fear was also expressed that war-produced literature might prove to be little more than a literature of text-books, an emphasising of the material. It has been shown here, and illustrated by passages and poems that demonstrate the truth of the showing, that in imaginative literature much of note was produced, and of a quality which might well raise hopes that the quickening of spirit would give birth to a literature as remarkable as was that of the years that came after Waterloo.

The analogy of the periods does not, of course, hold closely, because of the difference of scale on which the Great War and the Napoleonic Wars were fought. Had such conditions as Britain had to face in the world-wide war obtained a century earlier, Byron, Shelley, Keats, Scott, Lamb, and Landor would all have been liable to have been drawn into the Army before the date of Waterloo. In Brooke, Grenfell, Sorley, Coulson, and others known and unknown, may have fallen the flower of the singers of their generation, who should have carried on the great tradition of British literature. Instead, they carried on that other great tradition of British readiness to defend not only herself, but the cause of freedom wherever such was menaced, and so carrying on, died leaving imperishable memories. With them in mind may be recalled one of Mr. Walter de la Mare's contributions to the literature of the war —"How Sleep the Brave"—applying particularly that which he intended generally:

> Nay, nay, sweet England, do not grieve!
>   Not one of these poor men who died
> But did within his soul believe
>   That death for thee was glorified.
>
> Ever they watched it hovering near
>   That mystery 'yond thought to plumb,
> Perchance sometimes in loathed fear
>   They heard cold Danger whisper, "Come!"
>
> Heard and obeyed. O, if thou weep,
>   Such courage and honour, beauty, care,
> Be it for joy that those who sleep
>   Only thy joy could share.

One of the writers who fell in battle, Professor Thomas M. Kettle, M.P., put into a memorable sonnet, written in "the field before Guillemont, Somme," something of the secret which turned writers into soldiers, and made of soldiers writers long to be remembered by their work. It was not the flamboyant call to fight for flag or titular ruler that did this thing, but something far deeper—it was the realisation that the fight was one for the very foundations of modern civilisation and for the very hopes for the future of mankind. The sonnet, addressed to the author's infant daughter, was included in Professor Kettle's "Poems and Parodies," collected as a memorial volume shortly after his death:

> In wiser days, my darling rosebud, blown
>   To beauty proud as was your mother's prime,
>   In that desired, delayed, incredible time,
> You'll ask why I abandoned you, my own,
> And the dear heart that was your baby throne,
>   To dice with death. And oh! they'll give you rhyme
>   And reason: some will call the thing sublime,
> And some decry it in a knowing tone.
> So here, while the mad guns curse overhead,
>   And tired men sigh with mud for couch and floor,
> Know that we fools, now with the foolish dead,
>   Died not for flag, nor King, nor Emperor,
> But for a dream, born in a herdsman's shed,
>   And for the secret Scripture of the poor.

It was more especially poetry—as may be gathered from this survey of some of the representative work produced under the emotional stress or the actual experience of war—that was influenced; and this was not altogether surprising, for the simple elemental things of life have throughout the ages generally got themselves sung rather than said. While prose may be regarded as the vehicle of thought and reason, poetry is the natural language of those deeper feelings which transcend reason and thought. The Great War called upon the manhood of the nation to fight for everything for which the nation stood, for the good it had achieved, the ideals towards which consciously or subconsciously it strove, and, doing so, stirred the feelings in which those ideals are based.

> Into the night all we her children go:
> The roads are past; the paths are lost; a sea
> Roars round us in the darkness drearily;
> Bleak from the bitter east the tempests blow:
> Our limbs totter; our feet stagger; we tread
> Blind across rock and pitfall to our end—
> Our only guide and friend
> The starlight overhead. . . .
> The stars of the Ideal—there they shine!
> The sentinels divine.

Thus did one of the poets of the war—Mr. R. C. K. Ensor— put it in one of the "Odes and Other Poems," in which he strongly and impressively sang of that passion for humanity which, as it was the inspiration, however blurred and obscured, of the Allies in their defence of Democracy against resurgent Mediævalism, was also to be found a dominant note recurring again and again throughout the literature which played its many parts in comforting, strengthening, and sustaining during the years of agony.

CHAPTER CCLXVIII.

THE TURN OF THE TIDE IN THE WEST.

I.—The Franco-British Victories of the Somme and Avre.

By Edward Wright.

Hindenburg Resumes Control and Tries to Recover Initiative—Arrangements for Tremendous Drive Into Calais—Sir Douglas Haig Prepares to Strike First—Marshal Foch Recalls His Great Thrusters to France—Rawlinson's Grand Surprise in the Last Battle of the Somme—Canadians' Secret March from Arras to Amiens—Amazing Four Minutes' Bombardment—Australians and Canadians Attack through Dense Fog—Infantry Open their Line for Tanks, Cavalry, and Armoured Cars—Australians Reach Lihons Ridge—Extraordinary Manœuvre by Canadians on the Luce—Tank and Artillery Duel by Rosières Ridge—Canada Unlocks the Gate of the Great Victory—Remarkable Step Formation Advance of Australians, Canadians, and French—First French Army Encircles Montdidier—English Troops Fight Into Chipilly—Australian Battle for Lihons Ridge and Canadian Cavalry Charge towards Roye—Humbert with Third French Army Breaks Down the Matz Valley.

AFTER the retreat from the Marne of his armies of attack at the beginning of August, 1918, as related in Chapter CCLX. (Vol. 12, page 113), the German Chief of Staff expected to be assailed in turn. Field-Marshal von Hindenburg had resumed his position, and his unsuccessful Quartermaster-General, General von Ludendorff, though still actively engaged in the business of the Great Staff, and continuing to sign the communiqués, had less overruling power than before. There was, however, no apprehension of disaster on the part of the restored Chief of Staff.

Hindenburg rather welcomed than feared an allied grand offensive. Throughout it had been his policy to stand on the defensive in the west, where, as he consistently held after Falkenhayn's and Haeseler's failure at Verdun, an attacker could be made to bleed to death. He regarded his position as somewhat similar to that of Helmuth von Moltke after the first retirement from the river of defeat in September, 1914. Like his early predecessor in the German Command, he arranged to stand for a while on the defensive and use his gigantic artillery power and machine-gun power in maiming the strategic French reserve. Above all, the definite loss of the initiative was something he did not admit. Moltke had recovered the power of attack

at Ypres and along the Yser in October, 1914, a month after he had been beaten back from the Marne. Hindenburg hoped to be able to renew the struggle for the Channel ports, if these were required in the course of the new submarine campaign, for which larger and more powerful craft were almost ready. But he was not inclined to engage even in a local offensive before he had won a great defensive victory.

Ludendorff had arranged a tremendous attack upon the Second and Fifth British Armies between Ypres and La Bassée. The movement was to have opened on July 23rd, by which time the enemy expected his operations in the Marne and Champagne sectors would have absorbed all the reserves of the Associated Powers. With extreme courage and audacious loyalty Sir Douglas Haig had answered this threat by leaving his front weak and sending some of his best divisions to counter the enemy's preliminary and secondary operations by Rheims and Soissons. Consequently, the German Commander-in-Chief still maintained against the northern British armies and the right wing of the Belgian Army a great concentration of force. The corps he had sent from the Lys River front to the help of General von Böhn, General von Mudra, and General von Einem were balanced, in proportion, by the divisions which Sir Douglas Haig had sent to aid General

EXAMINING A BATTLE TROPHY.
Tank officer and men interested in a captured German anti-Tank rifle. It was designed to fire a 5 in. bullet for penetrating the mechanical pachyderm of the modern battlefield.

247

Berthelot and General Mangin. Therefore, no attack of importance was expected from the British forces.

At first Marshal Foch no more anticipated a successful new British offensive than did Hindenburg and Ludendorff. Friend and foe knew that Sir Douglas Haig had not the strength proper for a grand assault. Many of Sir Douglas Haig's veteran men and highly-experienced officers had fallen in the campaigns of 1917, when the British Commonwealth sustained, with the Italian kingdom, all the main weight of the results of the Bolshevist betrayal of Russia and the perturbing attempt made by certain Frenchmen to betray France.

After helping the French armies the British forces were so reduced in strength that by the spring of 1918 they were only about one-fourth as numerous as the German forces in

TAKEN CAPTIVE BY THE WAYSIDE.
Great German howitzer, one of the many weapons that were captured by the advancing British during the hurried retreat of the enemy on the western front. The Germans were compelled to abandon much of their artillery under the resistless pressure of the allied armies.

the west. In March, 1918, Sir Douglas Haig had fifty-four divisions, each reduced to ten battalions, while the German commander had some two hundred and eight divisions, also reduced. Instead of the British armies being prepotent at the end of three years from the opening of hostilities, as Lord Kitchener had originally hoped, they were in the critical field of the struggle in marked inferiority as regards both foot and guns at the end of four years.

Allowing for sickness, there had been scarcely five hundred thousand British infantrymen to withstand the attacks of nearly a million and a half German infantrymen in March and April, 1918. The result was that the strength of the Fifth, Third, Second, and Fourth British Armies was seriously impaired. Only the First Army on Vimy Ridge remained fairly intact. The other four organisations of battle became amalgams of battered and often scanty veterans and fresh soldier lads. The gallant youngsters proved their power of resistance in the latter part of the struggle for the Channel ports, but their qualities had yet to be tested in the intricate and highly-skilled work of a modern offensive.

Difficulties of the British Staff

The invisible pressure of overwhelming enemy forces, maintained against the British front from the end of April to the end of July, 1918, increased the technical difficulties of the British Staff. Always the crippling of Foch's mass of manœuvre seems to have been, in the German intention, preliminary to the renewal of decisive attack on the British armies, which was designed to be completed by submarine operations, with improved U boats acting in the English Channel from conquered French ports against both British and United States troopships and supply boats.

In face of this continual and increasing danger to his line, Sir Douglas Haig and his army chiefs had a hard task to find time and opportunity for fully training their fresh troops and re-formed divisions. Harder still was it to discover means for practising to perfection all that Staff craftsmanship in the minute direction of attacking movements, of which the enemy was master.

While completing his withdrawal from the Tardenois Hills, between the Soissons plateau and the Ardre valley, Hindenburg rearranged his forces on the western front. By the Belgian coast and the flooded Yser, Admiral von Schröder remained in command of the German Marine Corps, as part of the army group under General Sixt von Armin, whose Fourth Army was still very strong round Ypres and Kemmel Hill. Along the Lys River the Sixth German Army, under General von Quast, was also in remarkable strength, but the new armies under General von Carlowitz and General von Eberhardt, which had been collected to make the break-through to Calais, were removed to the Aisne and Champagne front.

General Otto von Below, much lessened in force, extended below the Vimy Ridge to Arras. From the Ancre to the Avre, General von der Marwitz, also reduced in strength, guarded both banks of the Somme. Immediately below him was the army of General von Hutier, likewise weakened by heavy losses and by the drawing off of forces for action along the Aisne.

Hutier was being rapidly and greatly reinforced, General von Böhn pouring men and guns towards Noyon, Lassigny, and Montdidier as fast as he could draw them over the Aisne plateau. Hutier, as brother-in-law to Ludendorff, had lost his importance in the decline of his kinsman's authority. Böhn was regarded as the better man, and in recognition of his success in escaping envelopment in the Marne operations was appointed army group commander between the Crown Prince of Bavaria's and the Crown Prince of Prussia's armies. The reduction in the nominal power of the Hohenzollern prince was one of the signs of Hindenburg's return to authority.

The new armies of General von Carlowitz and General von Eberhardt, two former corps commanders who had achieved most **Disposition of the German armies** success in the operations against the British forces in the spring, were used in strengthening the wasted armies of General von Mudra and General von Einem from the Oise River to the Argonne Forest.

The concentration of defensive power against General Gouraud and the Fourth French Army was eloquent testimony of the abiding effect on the enemy of the first great victory that Marshal Foch's lieutenants had achieved. Round Verdun, in a condition of considerable anxiety, was General von Fuchs, whose forces were removed from the control of the Prussian Crown Prince and placed in the army group command of General von Gallwitz, an eastern commander who had fought in the First Battle of the Somme, in which Böhn rose to high rank. Below Gallwitz's sphere of influence was a group of strong armies defending the Vosges line and the Alsatian valleys, under nominal command of Duke Albrecht, the heir to the Würtemberg throne.

On the Allies' side of the parallel battle King Albert of Belgium acted as army group commander from Nieuport to the River Lys. Under him and his military adviser was the gallant Belgian Army, commanded by General Gillrain, together with the Second British Army, directed by Sir Herbert Plumer, and the French mass of manœuvre which, under General Degoutte, had fought between the Ourcq and the Marne in July, 1918. Most of the United States divisions, which

On one of the highways of war's unceasing activity: Canadian limbers passing motor-lorries.

Praise from the chief: Sir Douglas Haig congratulating a Canadian battalion after action.

British machine=gunners going forward in lorries during the victorious advance upon St. Quentin in 1918.

New Zealand artillery coming into action within a few minutes of taking up a new position.

One of mangled Flanders' war=rolled roads, flanked with shell=snapped trees and field=telephone wires.

War=time traffic in Hourges in 1918 : British Tanks moving forward and German prisoners coming in.

This heap of stones, captured by the British, was Meteren.

Stretcher-bearers taking a badly-wounded man across a trench.

Plight of a Somme village when re-won for France.

Casualties receiving first treatment at a regimental aid-post.

had formed a notable part of General Degoutte's new army, were detached, and did not come under the personal direction of King Albert.

On the right of General Plumer's men there appeared, in grim resurrection, the Fifth British Army. It was commanded by Sir William Birdwood, whose promotion from a corps command in the Fourth Army had a happy sequel, to which we shall refer later. The task of the Fifth British Army was to watch the Lille ridges and the movements of Quast's diminishing forces. Something was designed to happen when Quast's special divisions of assault were urgently required elsewhere.

Below the Fifth Army, Sir Henry Sinclair Horne with his ever-victorious First Army stood expectant on and around Vimy Ridge. It was somewhat shorn of attacking strength, yet eager to advance. Sir Julian Byng, who had won his high command on Vimy heights under General Horne, remained with the Third Army between Arras and the Ancre, on the line where he had stayed the German Mars groups at the end of the previous March.

Connecting by Albert with General Byng's troops were the Australian divisions that Sir William Birdwood had trained and directed from the days of Egyptian route marches, through Anzac battles on tragic Gallipoli, to Pozières slaughter work, Hindenburg line actions, and the tragic struggle for Passchendaele Ridge. At Passchendaele it had been the fierce desire of the men of the Commonwealth to equal the double achievement of the Canadians on Vimy Ridge by taking the heights and winning army commander rank for their beloved British general. Deeply they wished for an Australian commander, but they would have been the angriest of men had Sir William Birdwood left them for anything less than an army command like that of Sir Julian Byng.

In one way the attainment of the desire of the Australian Imperial Force was more remarkable than that of the Canadian divisions. The Canadian democracy found a brilliant, inventive commander in an estate agent, Sir Arthur Currie. The Australian democracy produced a Jewish leader in war in the person of Sir John Monash, who in the days of peace had been a civil engineer specialising in concrete construction.

General Rosenthal, in Sir John Monash's old 3rd Division, was another Australian Jew of military genius, whose commanding position was calculated to annoy the German military caste, that would not admit Jews to rank of regular officers.

Allied Staffs in consultation

The Australians also took high pride in their final, supreme offence against the aristocratic spirit in military affairs. They arranged that all further officers they required should be men who had advanced by merit from private to commissioned rank.

It was a magnificent force both in defence and attack. Men and officers were more daring in manœuvre than the best enemy shock troops. Sir Henry Rawlinson, as commander of the Fourth Army, and Sir John Monash began to experiment in shock tactics at Hamel and Morlancourt and other points of local importance on the Amiens front. As the result of the experiments a scheme of attack was drawn up by General Rawlinson, approved by Sir Douglas Haig, and discussed with General Debeney, General Humbert, General Mangin, and the western French army group commander, General Fayolle, and General Pétain. Finally it was referred to Marshal Foch.

That was the way in which the Allied Commander-in-Chief often worked. Large and intense was the play of mind among army commanders and their Staffs. Continually they worked out, with the utmost economy of means, plans for taking the enemy by surprise. The schemes were discussed with neighbouring army Staffs and examined by group controllers, national Commanders-in-Chief and their General Staffs.

The scheme which Sir Henry Rawlinson elaborated with Sir Douglas Haig had to undergo considerable criticism because of the presumed weariness of the old elements of the British forces and the inexperience of the new elements. Happily, however, it was accepted. Measures were adopted to use the attack as a strong demonstration if it did not succeed as well as its authors expected, but steps were also taken to exploit fully any great advantage won. For this purpose the French line was altered in character. General Debeney, commanding the First French Army between

GERMANS CAPTURED DURING THEIR GREAT RETREAT.
Prisoners, taken by British troops on the western front in France in August, 1918, being marched back to the cages. They were passing a couple of British anti-aircraft guns.

Morisel and Montdidier, was removed temporarily from the direction of General Pétain and placed under British control. He became for the time an army commander under Sir Douglas Haig. General Humbert, with the Third French Army below Lassigny and Noyon, was also partly connected with the British High Command.

General Humbert, following the fashion, had elaborated a great attack by his army, and had secretly made immense preparations. He began to be more open in his final dispositions, and thereby hastened General von Böhn's movement of reinforcement of Hutier's army. At the same time, under the influence of the British scheme, General Mangin, with the Ninth French Army, wheeled back from the scene of his victories below Soissons and concentrated openly against the Oise River and Chemin des Dames line on Böhn's flank.

Along the Aisne and Vesle the successful Fifth French Army continued to demonstrate vigorously while considerably changing in composition. The American and British units were withdrawn, and General Berthelot, a great expert in Army organisation, was detached for special work and replaced by General Guillaumat a highly-successful commander of the army of Verdun, who was recalled from his new command at Salonika, where he had prepared a great manœuvre which his successor afterwards decisively executed.

Foch's choice of commanders

Marshal Foch's recall of General Guillaumat was highly significant. Like the return of General Mestre from the Italian front, and the restoration of General Mangin to Army command, it showed that the Marshal of France wanted the most skilled of thrusting generals, with the latest experience of the developments of warfare, at the head of his forces.

RECONNOITRING WAR CHARIOTS.
British armoured cars setting out on a reconnaissance on the western front, the lower photograph showing the observers emerged from their gun-turret. These modern war chariots proved immensely serviceable on every terrain.

The essence of the British scheme was, of course, surprise. This was greatly facilitated by the enemy's view of the weakness of the forces of attack. Hindenburg and his Staff, to which Ludendorff was for months still attached, reckoned that the Third French Army, under General Humbert, would open the offensive movement, with the First French Army and the Ninth assisting. This was the sound, easy method of retaining and extending the advantages won in Champagne and the Tardenois. From the Fourth British Army demonstrating gun fire was expected, and General von der Marwitz's corps on the Somme were warned to prepare good cover.

General Rawlinson's main problem in the new Somme battle was, therefore, the same as it had been in the summer of 1916. He had to concentrate in

With the exception of Sir Edmund Allenby in Palestine, and General Nivelle and Sir Hubert Gough in retirement, all the allied leaders in the new tactics of hurricane offensive were banded against the waiting foe. General Gouraud was particularly menacing along the Champagne front, leaping back on ground from which he desired to organise a strong advance. With admirable adroitness and economy in life he kept three German armies stretched to parry his blow, but while brandishing his victorious power delayed to strike. By Verdun, General Pershing built up the First American Army from divisions released by General Mangin, General Degoutte, and General Berthelot. Screened by the Second French Army, preparing to withdraw, the American commander, with his able lieutenant, Major-General Hunter-Liggett, who had led the United States troops in the Marne action, quietly arranged a series of staggering surprises for the Gallwitz group of enemy armies.

Along the Vosges, General de Castelnau played a telling part as organiser of a flank thrust through Alsace. His task was to alarm Duke Albrecht of Würtemberg. By skilful, open preparations, the gathering of United States troops still in training, and a well-conducted Press campaign in France, the allied armies of Alsace attracted the attention of the German Staff.

Planning the supreme surprise

In the meantime the British commander and his Staff, with the general officer of the Fourth Army, had the most difficult of all tasks to perform. They had to accomplish a miracle of intellectual effort, and, with forces inferior in number to those of the enemy, defeat him. Absolute perfection in all staff-work was a vital necessity. British officers of the Regular class, trained in Colonial warfare, and British officers of the extemporised class, who like General Monash and General Currie had learnt as they fought, had alike not merely to equal the German officer in the business of Continental warfare ; they had clearly to excel him.

The lessons of the retreats of March and April had been studied by quiet men with a steady flame of anger in their minds. There was a general commerce in new or improved ideas, relating almost to every instrument of attack, from aeroplanes as smoke-screen makers to the use of massed artillery as infantry guns. The inventive genius of the race was in a condition of exasperated fertility, and it produced so astonishing a series of deadly novelties as convinced friendly critics on Allied Staffs that the British must have their way.

overwhelming local strength, without disturbing the enemy. He had done this in the first Somme campaign by constructing a roofed road, strong enough on top in places for a few vehicles to ply over, under the eyes of enemy observers, while below divisions of attack were invisibly marching into action. It was this original British method of camouflaged approach that General von Hutier had imitated at St. Quentin, and that General von der Marwitz had in vain tried at Cambrai. It was against Marwitz that the device was again used, after he had been detected in its employment and thereby checked.

General Rawlinson strengthened the Fourth Army by borrowing part of General Horne's First Army. The Canadian Corps was moved from Arras to Amiens, so as to set General Currie's men alongside General Monash's men for generous emulation. It was a most promising combination of exciting competitiveness and **Commonwealth and** historic fellowship in battle between the **Dominion rivalry** Commonwealth and the Dominion troops.

Success depended first on the secrecy and speed with which the Canadians were moved, and then on the intricate Staff arrangements for manœuvring into action the infantry, cavalry, Tanks, and armoured cars of the transported forces, and for making the artillery work of the new gunners proof against errors.

The march of the Canadians was conducted with perfect skill. The men and their trains hid by day and moved by night to an unknown destination, that neither the enemy's flare-dropping nocturnal aerial scouts nor his espionage agents traced. They arrived in darkness south-east of Amiens at the end of the first week in August, and took the battle position prepared and supplied for them by Gentilles Wood.

This movement did not give all the strength required for rupturing the hostile front. The Australians also concentrated for attack. For months they had been holding all the direct approaches to Amiens, both north and south of the Somme, by Morlancourt and Villers-Bretonneux.

It was but natural they should be relieved, and London, Sussex, and other troops took over their northern sector, on the tongue of high ground between the Ancre and the Somme, where an important position had been won at the end of July, for the intended offensive along the Corbie-Bray road. Instead of going into billets the northern Australian force crossed the Somme and increased the depth of strength of Sir John Monash's men around Villers-Bretonneux.

There was, however, one accident in the smooth working of the great secret organisation for one of the most important battles in history. General von der Marwitz **Sharp fight for** had suffered many indignities from the **upland positions** aggressive Australians, losing to them village after village, with woods and heights of much value. He had, moreover, surrendered several bridge-heads by the tributaries of the Somme in order to escape surprise attacks by the new storming cars. But he could not allow the high ground snatched from him between the Ancre and Somme to remain in British possession.

It gave another opening for Tank operations below Albert, just when he had sacrificed land north of the town to make his disturbed infantry secure against another local action like that at Villers-Bretonneux. He brought forward one

of the best German shock divisions, the 27th, to recover the ground between the rivers, before the newly-arrived English troops became familiar with their position.

In a fierce local action at dawn, on August 6th, 1918, the enemy commander regained the high ground and took some prisoners. The following day the Englishmen counter-attacked, and won back most of the upland. Their position, however, was not so good as it had been. They no longer had ordinary infantry of **British infantry** the line against them in average defensive **heavily bombarded** strength and unsuspecting frame of mind, but first-rate troops, alert and aggressive, who were further being reinforced because of a mistaken idea on the part of the enemy army commander.

General von der Marwitz knew that his General Staff expected a great attack between Montdidier and Soissons. He thought it likely that the Australians had been relieved by the English, so that a local action between Albert and the Somme might be started during the British artillery demonstrations in order to wrest all the riverside upland from his men and thereby increase the distracting effect of the British feint. To guard against this eventuality the German commander increased his forces of men and guns between the Ancre and the Somme, and opened abrupt, strong bursts of fire at night. To these the British gunners could not reply in any strength without alarming the enemy. The bombarded English infantry had, therefore, to endure the attacks.

Against the imminent Australian-Canadian main offensive General von der Marwitz and his local corps commanders took no counter-measures whatever. The men did not even

ARTILLERY TROPHIES TAKEN BY THE FRENCH FROM THE RETREATING GERMANS.
Scene in Villers-Cotterets in August 1918, where a few of the guns taken from the enemy had been brought together. The guns were so numerous that they filled the towns behind the line of the advance. Often the weapons were taken with ammunition, enough to throw against the retreating enemy for some time—" to pip him with his own squeak," as a British gunner said on ordering a German gun to be turned round to fire at the foe.

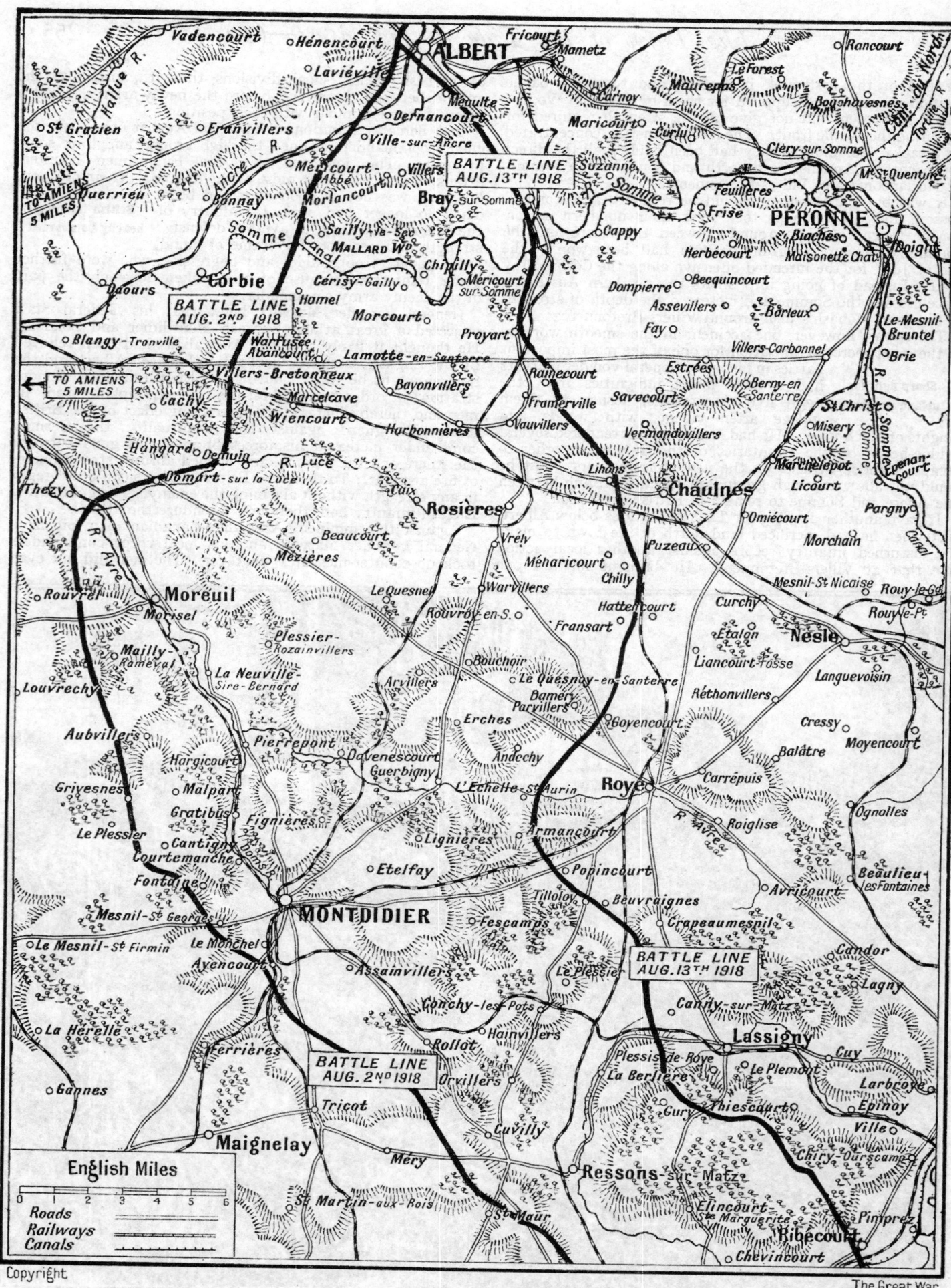

Vadencourt · Hénencourt · Fricourt · Mametz · Rancourt
St. Gratien · Franvillers · Laviéville · ALBERT · Carnoy · Maurepas · Boghavesnes
Querrieu · Bonnay · Mericourt-Abbé · Villers · Méaulte · Dernancourt · Maricourt · Curlu · Suzanne · Clery-sur-Somme · Mt. St Quentin
TO AMIENS 5 MILES · Ville-sur-Ancre · Somme · Feuillères · Frise · PERONNE
BATTLE LINE AUG. 13TH 1918 · Bray-sur-Somme · Cappy · Herbécourt · Biaches · Maisonette Chat. · Boisdu
Corbie · Daours · Sailly-le-Sec · MALLARD W. · Chipilly · Mericourt-sur-Somme · Dompierre · Becquincourt · Asseville · Barleux · Le-Mesnil-Bruntel
BATTLE LINE AUG. 2ND 1918 · Cérisy-Gailly · Hamel · Morcourt · Proyart · Fay · Brie
Blangy-Tronville · Warfusée Abancourt · Lamotte-en-Santerre · Rainecourt · Estrées · Berny-en-Santerre · Villers-Carbonnel · St. Christ
TO AMIENS 5 MILES · Villers-Bretonneux · Bayonvillers · Framerville · Savecourt · Vermandovillers · Misery · Somme R.
Cachy · Marcelcave · Wiencourt · Harbonnières · Vauvillers · Lihons · Marchelepot · Penan-court
Hangard · Demuin · R. Luce · Caix · Rosières · Chaulnes · Licourt · Pargny
Thezy · Domart-sur-la-Luce · Beaucourt · Vrély · Puzeaux · Omiécourt · Morchain
Rouvrel · Rouvroy · Morisel · Mézières · Le Quesnel · Warvillers · Rouvroy-en-S. · Méharicourt · Chilly · Hattencourt · Mesnil-St Nicaise · Rouy-le-Ga
Moreuil · Plessier-Rozainvillers · Fransart · Curchy · Etalon · Rouy-le-Pt.
Mailly-Rameval · La Neuville-Sire-Bernard · Arvillers · Bouchoir · Le Quesnoy-en-Santerre · Goyencourt · Liancourt-Fosse · Nesle · Languevoisin
Louvrechy · Pierrepont · Damery Parvillers · Réthonvillers · Cressy
Aubvillers · Hargicourt · Davenescourt · Erches · Andechy · Carrépuis · Balâtre · Moyencourt
Grivesnes · Malpart · Guerbigny · L'Echelle-St Aurin · Roye · Ognolles
Le Plessier · Gratibus · Fignières · Lignières · Armancourt · R. Avre · Roiglise · Beaulieu-les-Fontaines
Courtemanche · Cantigny · Dons · Etelfay · Popincourt · Avricourt
Fontaine · Mesnil-St Georges · MONTDIDIER · Fescamps · Tilloloy · Beuvraignes · Crapeaumesnil
Le Mesnil-St Firmin · Le Monchel · Assainvillers · Le Plessier · **BATTLE LINE AUG. 13TH 1918** · Candor · Lagny
Ayencourt · Conchy-les-Pots · Canny-sur-Matz · Lassigny · Cuy
La Hérelle · Ferrières · Rollot · Hainvillers · Plessis-de-Roye · Le Plemont · Larbroye · Epinoy
Gannes · **BATTLE LINE AUG. 2ND 1918** · Orvillers · La Berlière · Gury · Thiescourt · Ville
Tricot · Cuvilly · Chiry-Ourscamp
Maignelay · Méry · Ressons-sur-Matz · Elincourt-Ste Marguerite · Pimprez
English Miles · St Martin-aux-Bois · St Maur · Chevincourt · Ribecourt

0 1 2 3 4 5 6

Roads
Railways
Canals

Copyright   The Great War

LINES OF BATTLE EAST OF AMIENS IN THE FIRST HALF OF AUGUST, 1918.

From where the western line had become finally stabilised, south-west of Albert, after the great German offensive of the spring of 1918, the allied forces at the beginning of August initiated a series of smashing victories which

256

before the middle of that month had resulted in the line being carried forward until it ran in a south-easterly direction from Albert, directly threatening the three important centres, Chaulnes, Roye, and Lassigny.

carry out orders to make more shelter against heavy gun fire. In regard to all defensive work they were uncommonly careless, especially for so industriously self-protective a race as the German. This was apparently due to their confident belief that they would be able to resume open-field warfare against the weakened British Army as soon as Böhn and Hutier had broken the French attack.

From the end of March to the beginning of August the enemy commander and his Staff had not troubled to see that proper works were constructed. The troops were in shell-holes and shallow trenches, some being engaged in cutting the ripened crops on the Santerre plateau between the Somme and the Avre, instead of digging dug-outs as Hindenburg —careful man—had ordered. Contempt for the British forces was one of the mother causes of all the long series of German disasters that followed. The feeling of contempt did not last long, but it was fatal to the contemners.

The attackers were admirably favoured by the weather. There were four days of rain that completely screened the final preparations for the offensive, and when there was nothing left to do but for the Canadians to end their nocturnal march and come into line the rain ceased, allowing the ground to dry. Then, on the morning of the assault—August 8th, 1918 —a remarkably thick summer fog blanketed the battlefield.

British military authorities were at last paying very special attention to the science of weather forecasting as a decisive branch of staff-work, and were magnificently rewarded therefor. Meteorologists began to abound in the British armies as they had long since abounded in the German. It was hard to get the Briton to learn, but when he was set to it he became a pacemaker. He had received costly lessons in meteorology at Ypres in the summer and autumn of 1917 and at St. Quentin and Neuve Chapelle in the spring of 1918. He fully repaid the learned Teutons all they had taught him when he in turn surprised them in a dense fog between the waters of the Somme and the Luce. Less than half the British guns were registered, having hurriedly been concentrated from other parts of the front. No enemy targets were visible. But on the artillery Staff of Sir Henry Rawlinson were wonder-workers. The Teuton had nothing left to teach them ; they had made themselves in two years the master-gunners of the world. Amazing was their programme. In the Somme bombardment of the summer of 1916 they kept the guns furiously in action for a week, yet failed to break the hostile works. In the Somme bombardment of the summer of 1918 their guns fired only for four minutes, and produced complete destruction on the southern side of the river.

Gunners and gunner officers were little more than gun tenders in the foggy twilight of the morning of action. They had Staff instructions regarding the pointing of their pieces, weight of charge, rate of fire, and so on, and had to work to programme with the blind but organised energy of stokers in a battle-cruiser in action. It was a dramatic four minutes. For a length of twenty miles the artillery thundered in fog so thick that the flame of the charge could not be seen thirty yards away. The attempted answer of the German barrage was swallowed up in an instant, and the tense, packed troops in the centre of the line of attack were freed from a deep anxiety.

English prisoners had been taken by the enemy in his swoop along the northern bank of the Somme two days before. All the Army were hoping that the captured men would not unwittingly reveal anything important. They did not. The main attack, at 4.20 a.m., was a complete surprise. Along the river the Australian divisions under Sir John Monash went forward with Tanks, and found the garrison of the hostile line dead or fled in many places. Some battalions advanced half a mile before encountering any resistance. Then, in the mist, the infantry and fast Tanks began working into machine-gun positions, while the daring guns of the assault closely followed the foot.

After three hours of blind questing and fighting the fog gradually thinned as the attacking forces reached the enemy's heavy-gun positions. Over the wheat-covered ridges the storming cars charged the batteries, and in most cases captured the guns entire, with ammunition stacked beside them.

Battle opened in thick fog

ON THE EDGE OF A SHELL-CRATER.
Thousands of pits formed by explosion of mines and heavy shells, and often full of water deep enough to engulf a battery, presented appalling difficulties to the advance of the British artillery.

Australian trench-mortar men, accompanying the infantry, turned some of the German pieces on the fleeing Germans. In the clearing sky were multitudes of British aeroplanes exercising strange and far-stretched dominion of the air. Inventive minds among them had greatly increased their power over the land. There were, for example, special squadrons attached to the Tank brigades that piloted the cars to enemy positions and then covered them with a defensive smoke barrage against German field-guns by dropping smoke-bombs. Other pilots discovered fresh enemy troop movements and led the forces of attack in their ambushing operations.

At eight o'clock in the morning an enemy brigade, just relieved, was overtaken. It surrendered, as did also many enemy units resting in reserve areas. By noon the Australians had driven nine miles into the hostile lines, and one of their battalions at the farthest point of the advance had only three casualties ! The Commonwealth troops were, through no fault of theirs, checked only by the river-side promontory of Chipilly, where the enemy fired across the valley upon the audacious field-gunners who came to the forefront of the battle.

Nine miles for three casualties

At mid-day the gallant infantry opened their line, and British cavalry and armoured motor-cars, piloted by the ubiquitous aeroplanes, passed through to exploit the amazing victory. Cars and horse caught up with a train bearing off a railway gun. Farther on they captured a train arriving with reinforcements, and another train was wrecked by aeroplane bombardment.

By a gully the cars of pursuit found more strong enemy forces, but, leaving them for the cavalry to collect, sped into Framerville, chased a German corps commander, who escaped in his shirt, after losing his Staff officers, and surprised more enemy forces lunching in a village. At the end of the great adventure two cars, finding no formed body of Germans before them, went down the road to Péronne. There they were stopped. One had a wheel shot off by a solitary field-gun, the other was disabled on the road. The crews then captured a final batch of Germans, who dragged the disabled chariot of battle to the new British line. This ran in front of a detached ridge near the town of Lihons, about twelve miles from the Australian positions at Villers-Bretonneux.

By Lihons the old French lines made in the early Somme actions from 1914 to 1916 enabled fresh enemy forces, carried forward with extreme speed from the vicinity of Arras, to prevent the attackers from clearing the entire Santerre tableland in the great bend of the Somme. The roads to Péronne were thronged with men and transport streaming

CAUGHT UP AND CAPTURED BY MOTOR-CARS.
German light-railway engine captured by British cavalry and armoured motor-cars while hauling a trainload of reinforcements to the front line—one of several taken in the vigorous opening of the offensive in August, 1918.

in panic haste from the scene of the greatest German disaster since Jena. Over the fugitives flew British aeroplanes, pouring down machine-gun fire and bedevilling confusion into chaos. It would have been possible to have driven still deeper into the enemy's territory, but Sir Henry Rawlinson was well content with his decisive gains, and, by reason of the issues depending on them, preferred to make sure of keeping what he had won.

At the close of the day the Australian line ran from the neighbourhood of Cérisy towards Proyart, Rainecourt, and Lihons Ridge, close to Chaulnes. The men could clearly see the old familiar line of trees topping the Péronne road. Their losses in this marvellous advance were little more than those of an ordinary day in many parts of the line. The enemy had not fought his machine-guns with his usual determination, and nearly all his artillery were taken on the main front of the advance. The victors were in tremendous spirits. They had excelled everything done by friend or foe since September, 1914. As a movement in trench warfare their feat was unparalleled. The Australian nation, less in number than the Belgian, yet set, like its early kinsmen in the New England States, to fill a continent, had consecrated itself as an heroic democracy.

Intricate march of the Canadians

One other young race only equalled it, and that was beside it, brotherly, in the battle. Real and strong democracies are rare in recorded history. Nearly all States of democratic colouring, ancient and modern, are easy-riding oligarchies of money power, industrial power, and landowning power. Like new stars big with influence in the sky of human fate, Australia and Canada blazed in incomparable glory, alongside the equally pure radiance of New Zealand and the more troubled but clarifying glow of South Africa. Of the two leading young nations the Canadians had the more difficult task.

They came in secret haste and darkness to country with which they were not acquainted, and there began by executing an intricate manœuvre. By the windings of the Luce stream the ground rose steeply with hanging woods, and owing to

the contortions of the terrain the Canadians had to cross the water south-eastwards, swing northward again along the river flat, and once more turn southward so as to assail the forested height of Dodo Wood unexpectedly and directly from the north. Moving in the figure of an S, along ground which German gunners dominated, and bringing with them Tanks which had stealthily been worked over the enemy's river moat in darkness, the Dominion troops, under General Currie and his masterly Staff, executed the snake advance in the blinding fog with victorious perfection.

The Australians made the longest thrust in modern trench warfare, while the Canadians carried out the most complicated and decisive of tactical approaches. On the immediate passage of the Luce depended on one side the length and value of the Australian drive, and on the other side the entrance into action of the First, Third, and Tenth French Armies. Canada unlocked the gate through which the eternal barbarian was driven out of France.

Passage of the River Luce

After forcing the passage of the Luce the troops of the Dominion met with fierce resistance in the woods above Hangard, where the Canadian Highlanders broke the enemy with the bayonet. But they swung into line with the men of the Commonwealth on schedule time, and, helped by their more forward comrades, let the cavalry and armoured cars through by Weincourt, under

FIGURING OUT THE LINES OF ADVANCE.
British officers, seated on a heavy trench-mortar just captured from the enemy, studying a map of the Somme district over which their men were making their finally victorious advance.

a sky loud with aeromotors and propellers and aerial machine-gun fire. Unlike the Australians, whose horse were far away, doing famous things between Bethlehem and Nazareth, the Canadians had their cavalry behind them. Some of their troopers had already distinguished themselves on the Santerre upland, as had also the pioneer Canadian armoured-car detachment. When the infantry opened, the horsemen and charioteers worked speedily along the roads and over the cornfields towards Rosières. When the cavalrymen were checked by machine-guns in a wood south-east of Marcel-cave, the "whippet" Tanks crashed into the trees and over the Germans.

In overcoming the numerous small defensive positions in the undulating country, which positions were the enemy's principal rallying-points, the new storming cars saved the lives of thousands of men. Crews and vehicles suffered from gun fire, for on the last ridges below Rosières were gallant

German artillerymen inspired by the officer who, single-handed, fought General Byng's Tanks from Flesquières Hill.

The Canadian cavalry also came under heavy fire by the approaches to Roye. For the troopers had great traditions of audacity, and they accepted no demonstration of power from the enemy, but put him fully to the ordeal of battle in charge after charge. Skilled vehemence was the required quality in the Canadians. They were path-breakers for the French armies, acting in the rear of the strengthened, crowded forces of General von Hutier. As, with the magnificent lead of the Australians, they routed General von der Marwitz's southern wing, they came upon the unengaged reserves in the rear of Hutier's forces. The resistance the Canadians encountered was a tribute to their success. They shook to the ground much of the fruits of victory which their French comrades gathered for many days afterwards. By the evening of August 8th their advance reached a depth of eight miles.

Path-breaking for the French

During the Canadian operations in the Luce valley the First French Army did not move. Its guns merely bombarded the hostile lines for forty minutes after the British infantry attack had started. It was much too costly for the French foot to attempt to advance before the enemy positions on the Avre were turned by the subtle, meandering attack of the men under General Currie. The best men in France were on the right of the Canadians—the light infantry division of General Brissaud-Desmaillet.

As soon as the Canadians wound through the gate of the Luce and opened it, the French troops gradually began

battle around Morisel and Moreuil on a front of only two and a half miles. The underlying design was to refrain from greatly alarming General von Hutier until the peril to his forces was increased by the rout of General von der Marwitz's corps on his flank. Hutier was being taken in the rear, above Montdidier, and the less he was disturbed during the enveloping operations the more men and guns he would lose. Naturally, his corps commanders, by the breaking end of the line, were alert to the local danger, and the French had to fight as hard as the Canadians.

It was not until eight o'clock in the morning that the storming division took the Avre bridge-head of Morisel. By fine ingenuity and courage the infantry crossed the steep river valley, with its forty-five feet of water, bringing their Tanks with them. They encircled Moreuil, and then put on pace to keep in place on the great spear head of allied forces furiously thrusting towards the old Chaulnes-Roye line. Australians, Canadians, and French were in a kind of step formation, the first helping the second, and

the second helping the third. Being more advanced than the French, the Canadians could on occasion swerve and take in flank German forces resisting General Debeney's men.

In the meantime, as he felt the enemy resisting, General Fayolle, in consultation with Sir Douglas Haig and General Pétain, began to press the enemy by the southern side of the Amiens-Noyon salient. Along the Avre, where the First French Army was maintaining a tremendous gun fire, infantry action developed on a wider front towards the neighbourhood of Montdidier. This intense pressure against Hutier's front facilitated the progress of the forces along his rear, and enabled the left wing of General Debeney's army to thrust to a depth of six and a quarter miles behind Montdidier, with a marvellous economy of life. It cost France only 87 men killed and some 180 seriously wounded to break the German front by Roye and take 2,000 prisoners and 70 guns. The Canadians were nearly two miles in advance of the French, and the Australians a mile ahead of the Canadians. In the night of the first day of battle there was no doubt as to the fall of Montdidier. The only question was the number of troops and guns likely to be cut off before they could retire. The French were in Mézières, the Canadians were by Le Quesnel, where "pockets" of Germans were holding out in the village, and the Australians were in front of Lihons Ridge. The original enemy front on the Doms brook was broken at Hargicourt, and violently bent just above Montdidier. Across the new and very narrow salient the allied gunners poured a continuous double barrage.

Fierce thrust on Montdidier

The only temporary check to the combined operations occurred by the upland north of the Somme, where, as we have seen, Marwitz was strongly prepared for a local action. Here his gunners opened heavy fire in the night upon the assembled English troops, and answered the great attacking barrage with an impeding curtain fire. Most gallantly the troops endeavoured to carry out their part of the programme of the offensive and win the Chipilly spur by the riverside.

GERMAN "LITTLE BERTHA" ON EXHIBITION IN PARIS.
Big gun—11 in., weighing 149 tons, with a barrel 25 feet long, and firing a 620 lb. shell—captured by the Australians near Corbie, on the Somme (whence it had bombarded Amiens) on August 8th, 1918. Named "Little Bertha" by its captors, it was placed on exhibition at the goods-station of the Champ de Mars at the close of the month in which it was captured. Above: French officers inspecting the trophy.

One brigade carried Mallard Wood by desperate fighting, taking five hundred prisoners and guns, while another brigade moved on Chipilly. In the dense fog in the river bottom some British Tanks and infantry lost direction and turned north-westward. Others gallantly persisted on the right line, and by the evening fought their way into the village, but were not in strength to hold it.

In the evening of August 9th, however, the English troops fought into Chipilly. Three Tanks took Morlancourt, and a fresh enemy battalion engaged in relieving the garrison. The men of Chicago, acting as reserve to Sir Henry Rawlinson's army, played a gallant part in this northern victory that released the Third and First British Armies for action, and sped the Australians on the way to the Tortille River conquest. The United States troops were marching forward to help, but were likely to arrive too late for the opening of the action.

Fighting into Chipilly　They ran for a league, reaching the line a few seconds after the hour of attack, and without stopping one battalion went straight into and through the German works, completing a long march and wearying run by a victorious charge and several hours of hard fighting and hard work in consolidating the conquered position.

In the meantime the Australians, Canadians, and Frenchmen of the First Army vigorously resumed pressure upon the new enemy forces south of the Somme. By a prolonged and fierce thrust a Victorian brigade worked up the Lihons Ridge. Men and Tanks went out into the open, under direct fire from hostile batteries, shot down some of the gunners, and by Friday night, August 9th, reached the top of the isolated hill swelling some hundreds of feet above the tableland west of Lihons.

During the night the Germans brought up more reinforcements from Cambrai, and at eight o'clock the next morning (August 10th) the tireless Victorians again opened battle. Coming at once under heavy fire they opened out and, with the enemy enfilading them from Rosières railway and sweeping them in front, won a mile of most difficult ground. As they were then brought to a standstill, the Canadian infantry relieved them by a general attack on their right.

The men of the Dominion made a glorious spectacle as they advanced; over the open terrain they went, passing the Victorians' flank. Then other Australian troops attacked the Lihons Ridge from the north, took the wooded summit, and entrenched on the eastern slope, after capturing the enemy field-guns that had tried to break them. By the afternoon of August 10th the ridge was partly won. Darkness fell, with field-kitchens steaming with supper, and Australians and Germans still facing each other on the disputed ridge. At the same time the Australians took over part of the attack north of the Somme, and won the important position of Bray Hill. South of the river an operation conducted by their Tanks was discovered by enemy aeroplanes that attacked with bombs and helped to check the advance by Proyart.

Glorious Canadian advance　By this time General von Böhn, hastily called eastward to save both Marwitz and Hutier, succeeded in temporarily staying the Australian-Canadian advance. He got guns into position in front of Chaulnes and Roye to replace the lost batteries, and at Bouchoir, on the Roye road, the Canadians had a fierce struggle with an enemy division brought by motor-omnibus from the Soissons sector. Böhn's task was to save the corps in the Montdidier salient from encirclement. He prevented another complete disaster by beginning the Montdidier retreat in the evening of August 9th, when Debeney's army was well behind the town at Hyencourt and Frêtoy; but his loss in men and material, when Montdidier fell on August 10th, was tremendous.

What saved the German armies from absolute rout was the old Somme fortified line. There were extant enemy machine-gun positions, which had been British show-places before March 21st, 1918, that served him again with great effect. Some of these, by the Amiens-Roye road, nearly midway between the two cities, were an obstacle to one of the finest cavalry charges in trench warfare.

On Saturday afternoon, August 10th, General Currie made a gallant attempt at another sudden break through the re-formed hostile front. A great multitude of British aeroplanes opened action by bombing, machine-gunning, and smoke-blinding the fresh German forces, while fighting both hostile formations of aircraft and directing the land forces of attack.

These consisted of dragoons, hussars, lancers, and Canadian Horse, with Tanks co-operating. The Tank commanders could defy machine-guns that were mortal to the cavalry; the cavalry could ride down cannon that were often fatal to the Tanks. The enemy machine-gunners, in a quarried wood by the source of the Avre River, succeeded in checking this remarkable essay in new tactics, so far as it was an attempt to cut a way into Roye with the old weapon of the sabre and the new instrument of mobile artillery in armour casing. But the cavalry, Tanks, and infantry continued to work forward towards Roye, with the French Chasseurs on their right, the Australians working beyond Lihons towards Chaulnes on August 11th, against the continual counter-attacks of outnumbering enemy forces.

On August 10th every fresh German division diverted to the broken Somme front cleared the way for another victory for the Grand Alliance. For General Humbert, with the Third French Army, was then making in unexpected fashion the attack which the German Staff had been for a fortnight and more expecting. He gave no warning of his opening of battle.

By a magnificent programme of detailed staff-work the French infantry went out silently, with a delayed, overwhelming barrage suddenly thrown before them when they were already in action. Again it was a general's battle, conducted with infinite precision of prearranged details. The high, broken upland of the Thiescourt Hills, famous in many struggles between September, 1914, and March, 1918, was the objective **Result of the smashing victories** of the French commander. It blocked the road of his flanking direction of attack against the rear of the Roye-Chaulnes fortified lines.

General Humbert demonstrated on his right directly against the Thiescourt heights, but flung his main force alongside the wing of the victorious First Army. He broke into the Matz valley, down which Hutier had attacked him in June, carried Rollot and Conchy in a six-mile advance, in which eight thousand prisoners and three hundred guns were taken. Then, with the armies of General Rawlinson and General Debeney, his divisions completed the concentric enveloping movement on Roye and the upper line of the Somme River, which was being already heavily bombarded by British, Australian, and Canadian artillerymen.

From Gury, General Humbert's men worked round the Thiescourt tangle towards Plessis de Roye and the outskirts of Lassigny. By August 13th his patrols were within a mile and a half of this key position between Roye and Noyon. The First French Army were then in the outskirts of Roye, at Armancourt and Tilloloy; while the Fourth British Army partly encircled the same city from the north and cut the Roye-Chaulnes railway by Chilly. The Australians won Proyart, and the Canadians took Damary and Parvillers. The German prisoners numbered 38,500, with more than eight hundred guns. The Fourth British Army took 21,844, the First French Army 8,500, and the Third French Army more than 8,000 prisoners.

One result of this series of smashing victories was the sudden retreat, in the second week of August, of General von Lossberg's last divisions of assault from Merville and the Lys River line. The designed advance on Calais was abandoned, and the commander of the northern German Army group cautiously put more water between his outposts and the ground of advance of British Tanks. His forces were being weakened by reinforcements for the Somme front, after having been diminished to save the Aisne and Champagne line. The power of the initiative was definitely possessed by the Allied Commander-in-Chief. Without giving the enemy Chief of Staff time to recover from the last blow, Marshal Foch brought the Ninth French Army, under the redoubtable General Mangin, again into victorious action.

THE TURN OF THE TIDE IN THE WEST.
II.—The Final Victories on the Oise, Ancre, and Somme Lines.
By Edward Wright.

Böhn Withdraws to Concealed Battle Positions—New Zealanders Rush Puisieux—How Mangin Tricked Carlowitz—Germans Attempt Too Late to Counter-Attack—Great French Victory between Oise and Aisne—British Guards Break Over the Arras-Albert Railway—Heroic Action by Manchesters at Dovecot, on Ancre—Fourth British Army Resumes Its Drive on the Somme—Byng's Boys Encircle Bapaume —Tanks Break Enemy's Front by Dead Man Down—North-countrymen and New Zealanders Take Achiet-le-Grand and Loupart Wood —Swimming Adventures of the Lancashires—Secret Manœuvre by Canadian Corps—Magnificent Endurance of All British Divisions —Australians Outflank and Storm Bray—Welsh and Yorkshiremen Carry the Great Somme Ridge by Surprise—The King's Company of Grenadiers Hold Mory Headland with the Bayonet—Böhn Withdraws Across the Somme and Stands to Battle by Delville Wood and Longueval—New Zealanders Enter Bapaume and Marshal Foch Opens His Third Pair of Pincers.

IN one week, from August 8th to August 15th, 1918, as related in the preceding chapter, the Fourth British Army, the First French Army, and the Third French Army had destroyed the great enemy salient near Amiens and the Calais-Paris railway and driven thirty German divisions back to the 1914 line between Albert and Lassigny. Along the new line of attack the British, French, and United States forces rapidly organised the means of another pitched battle, and with their heavy artillery interrupted the enemy's communications across the bending river behind Nesle, while keeping his columns under continual aerial bombardment over a great depth of country.

It could not be concealed from the Germans that the Australians under Sir John Monash, the Canadians under Sir Arthur Currie, and the Brissaud-Desmaillet, Delville, and other fine French divisions, under General Debeney and General Humbert, were again warming up for a grand attack. In spite of the strength and vehemence with which the Allies held the air, adventurous German scouting pilots at times reconnoitred the Amiens area almost as far as the sea and discovered the French and British preparations.

But they also perceived that new French and British blows were coming from both flanks of the Somme line. Sir Julian Byng, with

the Third British Army, was about to strike towards Bapaume, while General Mangin, with the Tenth French Army, had been reinforced with some of General Gouraud's best divisions for a turning movement around Noyon. Marshal Foch was opening his second pair of pincers.

In these circumstances General von Böhn endeavoured to save his wing by employing the device of withdrawal on concealed battle positions, such as General Gouraud had used with smashing effect on the Champagne front. The Seventeenth German Army, between Arras and the Ancre, fell back from Beaumont-Hamel towards the railway embankment and cutting at Achiet-le-Grand. At the same time the new German army, under General von Eberhardt, containing elements of the old Seventh German Army, which Böhn had originally directed on the Aisne, created a deep foreground position by the ravine of Audignicourt, between the Oise River and the Ailette stream.

Success in these manœuvres for a great ambush of the attacking forces depended on secrecy. Secrecy, in turn, depended partly on superiority in the air, but largely upon the determination and skill of the scanty troops left in the firing-line to check and delude the masses of assault. For these reasons the intended manœuvres against men of such aggressive temper and subtle mind as Sir Julian Byng and General Mangin completely failed. The New

THREE FAMOUS FRENCH GENERALS.
In the autumn of 1918 General Debeney, in command of the French army fighting side by side with the British armies, was decorated by General Pétain with the insignia of a Grand Officer of the Legion of Honour. From left to right : General Pétain, General Fayolle, and General Debeney.

Zealanders, under General Byng, discovered the withdrawal of Below's forces before the movement was completed, and in violent and agile skirmishes took the high ground by Puisieux which the enemy commander had arranged to be held. The German battalion that had retired too hastily was ordered to recover Puisieux. The men almost mutinied, and when compelled to deliver a counter-attack made only the feeblest of demonstrations.

On the southern Noyon flank General Mangin began his operations in strength some days before Sir Julian Byng opened his offensive movement. The two allied commanders acted in closest co-operation, for they had a common objective removed from all geographical considerations. They were set to attract and destroy the new defensive mass of manœuvre which Hindenburg was creating with utmost speed by the reduction of Ludendorff's armies of attack.

General Mangin's hard task Every night large German forces were poured into General von Böhn's group of armies to enable him to make a long stand between Arras and the heights above Soissons. Böhn had to stand to battle for the reason that his line covered an enormous accumulation of almost priceless material of war. The Germans had already lost in less than a month seventeen hundred guns by capture, and the number of batteries destroyed by the Allies' counter-battery firing between Ypres and Verdun made the enemy's total loss in artillery almost double that of the captured guns. Böhn had been set the task of withdrawing thousands of other imperilled guns back to the Hindenburg line and to the Alberich line above the Ailette River, together with an immense amount of ammunition, railway material, and general supplies.

Although Field-Marshal von Hindenburg was very near to the supreme crisis in German man-power, with a total casualty list of more than seven and a half million men, including lightly-wounded men and sick men temporarily out of action, his need for conserving the machinery of battle was more immediate than his need for saving effectives. His front had narrowly escaped from being completely pierced, and it was necessary to initiate delaying actions on the 1914 line in order to carry out a strong fighting withdrawal to the line of 1917.

Marshal Foch, on the other hand, was only demonstrating for the time being against the new German front. His great aim was to reach the enemy's 1917 line immediately, by a series of pincer movements broadening out from either side of his successful straightforward thrust of the Fourth British Army. First of all, General von Böhn was to be shaken and broken on his flanks, so as to facilitate the task of driving in his weakened centre.

Of all the allied army commanders in action General Mangin was set the hardest task. He had to break directly into the Alberich line by Laon, and turn on his way Noyon on the left and the northern Aisne plateau on his right, and then conquer the enemy's central fortress in France, consisting of the great hill forest of St. Gobain. This movement would save Marshal Foch the cost of storming over the Aisne heights.

The army under General Mangin was increased in strength and used with extraordinary skill. **German trap skilfully evaded** At first the French commander appeared to be about to fall into the trap the enemy had prepared for him. In the middle of August he opened a tremendous bombardment on the German line between the Oise and the Aisne. In the morning of August 16th the French general increased his gun fire to its utmost power, and his opponent drew back his main forces and covered with his silent artillery all ways of approaching the battle positions.

But Mangin was not to be caught by an imitation of his comrade Gouraud's fighting. As we have observed, he had some of the best of Gouraud's men under him, in particular the fine division which had ambushed the enemy in the middle of July below the Moronvilliers heights.

French patrols went out feeling for the enemy, and when he withdrew they rushed his machine-gun posts by Moulin-sous-Touvent and occupied some three miles of ground. The next day the same division sent out more patrols and seized another important stretch of country, while the left

APPROXIMATE ENEMY AND ALLIED COMMANDS ON THE WESTERN FRONT, AUGUST, 1918.

FIELD-MARSHAL VON HINDENBURG.

PRINCE RUPPRECHT OF BAVARIA.

German Marine Corps on Flemish Coast. (Admiral von Schröder.)	IV. German Army. (Sixt von Armin.)	VI. German Army. Lille Sector. (Von Quast.)	XVII. German Army. Vimy to South of Arras. (Otto von Below.)	II. German Army. Somme Sector. (Von der Marwitz.)	XVIII. German Army. Roye Sector. (Von Hutier.)

GENERAL VON BÖHN.

New German Army. Oise to Aisne. (Von Carlowitz.) — IX. German Army. Oise to Aisne. (Mangin.)

CROWN PRINCE OF PRUSSIA.

New German Army. Vesle Sector. (Eberhardt.)	Army of Champagne. (Von Einem.)

Allied side:

KING ALBERT. COMMANDING-IN-CHIEF.

Dover Patrol of Flemish Coast. (Admiral Keyes.) — Belgian Army. (Gillrain.) — French Army in reserve. (Degoutte.)

SIR DOUGLAS HAIG, COMMANDING-IN-CHIEF.

II. British Army. Ypres Sector. (Plumer.)	V. British Army. Lille Sector. (Birdwood.)	I. British Army. Vimy to Arras. (Horne.)	III. British Army. S. of Arras to Arras. (Byng.)	IV. and Part of I. British Army. Somme Sectors. (Rawlinson.)

MARSHAL FOCH.

GENERAL FAYOLLE IN ARMY GROUP COMMAND.

I. French Army. Montdidier. (Debeney.) — III. French Army. Noyon Sector. (Humbert.)

GENERAL PÉTAIN, COMMANDING-IN-CHIEF.

IV. French Army. Champagne and Argonne. (Gouraud.) — V. French Army. Vesle Sector. (Guillaumat.)

General Sixt von Armin controlled the German Marine forces under Admiral von Schröder on the Belgian coast and the Fourth German Army extending to Kemmel Hill. General von Quast's control was extended to Lys River and round Lille with an enormous army of attack that melted away as Generals Carlowitz and Eberhardt and other generals went south to save the line. General Plumer had arranged to fight him and Armin for Calais, but his forces were lessened when the southern German line broke. General Otto von Below's command faced Sir H. S. Horne's army, that temporarily lost strength through secretly reinforcing Sir Henry Rawlinson's army group. General von Below's line of attack partly overlapped Sir Julian Byng's forces, which in turn partly overlapped the northern wing of Marwitz's army. Against Marwitz's centre and southern wing General Rawlinson had part of the First British Army, all the Fourth British Army, and part of the First French Army. General Fayolle, in close co-operation with the British commander, directed first General Humbert's Third Army and General Mangin's Tenth Army, and then took over as well the command of the

First French Army, which was relinquished from Sir Douglas Haig's and General Rawlinson's control after the first victorious advance from Amiens gave the allied commanders a tremendous pressure of work. General Berthelot, commanding on the Vesle, was an expert in army organisation, who restored the Rumanians after their defeat. After his victory at Verdun and Salonika, took command of the and General Guillaumat, the organiser of victory another special task, Fifth French Army. General von Hutier and General von Marwitz almost vanished in defeat, and General von Böhn conducted operations on their retreating fronts. General von Carlowitz and General von Eberhardt were the corps commanders in the spring offensive, who achieved most success on the Lys and at Kemmel Hill, and were promoted to command the new armies in the intended drive on Calais at the end of July. They came south to help Eben, Mudra, and Einem. Carlowitz superseded Eben, and took command as well of Böhn's forces, while Eberhardt superseded Mudra.

wing of the Tenth Army cautiously moved forward into alignment with the successful skirmishers.

General Mangin merely stole ground from the enemy without adventuring against the new fortified positions prepared against him ; instead of entering the ambushes, he annexed them. For four days and nights his patrols worked forward, drawing the enemy's artillery fire at each success, but presenting him with no large or easy targets. There was scarcely any infantry fighting, and the French losses were remarkably light, but the tremendous artillery fire of the attackers destroyed an average of one German battalion in each brigade. They were smashed in their battle positions.

Without anything in the nature of a pitched battle the Noyon flats were dominated by the capture of a hill south of Carlepont, and the Oise lowland was brought further under fire by a trickling advance above Autreches. Furious at being outplayed in this manner, the enemy commander decided to open a counter-attack before the grand offensive occurred. He was, however, too late.

By the early morning of August 20th General Mangin had his artillery sited in the stolen enemy outpost lines. **Enemy's counter-attack too late** Twenty minutes before the German attack was due his great barrages fell upon the assembled hostile troops, and his main infantry, accompanied by numerous Tanks, moved up the high broken ground of the forested slopes between the Aisne and Oise Rivers.

In some sectors of the front of twenty miles were scenes of slaughter like that which General Mangin had wrought on the Méry plateau and the hills below Soissons. In the centre the formidable gully of Audignicourt was carried in the early morning by a force of sharpshooters, accompanied by a battery of quickfirers. As soon as the gunners reached the

heights they began to smash another path of advance. Above Soissons, Tartiers Hill was stormed by nine o'clock, and a German force equipped with anti-Tank rifles was captured, clearing the way for another movement by the Renault storming cars towards the Ailette River, in the rear of the famous ridge of the Chemin des Dames.

In the meantime an extraordinary movement was made by the fine division that General Gouraud had lent to General Mangin. These troops started from positions south of Belfontaine, which they had **French advance on** gradually won from the enemy. From the **Mont Choisy** narrow salient which they occupied they spread fan-wise out into the wooded defiles of the fortified hill system of Mont Choisy and the Blerancourt Downs. The ground was too difficult for their artillery thoroughly to search, and the men had to fight forward with rifle, bayonet, bomb, and machine-gun, with storming cars in immediate support and gallant field-gunners closely following.

Struggling through thickets flaming with hostile machine-gun fire the Frenchmen reached the high wood below Choisy. There they fiercely demonstrated against the citadel of the hostile system while executing a brilliant turning movement on the right. They turned the Blerancourt Hill and linked with the force that had fought through the Audignicourt gully. This gave General Mangin the village of Cuts and the centre of the enemy's important lateral communication— the highway connecting Noyon and Coucy.

Then the attack was pressed on Mont Choisy, the commanding hill position south-east of Noyon. Resolutely the German garrison fought, answering charge by counter-charge, and helped by flanking fire from forces in Carlepont Wood whom the attackers were driving into a narrow salient by the Oise. The gallant Frenchmen were forced back, but returned, and in a series of separate actions around quarries and strong

DAYLIGHT PATROL PASSING THROUGH THE RUINS THAT HAD BEEN ALBERT.

It was in the mist of the early morning of August 22nd, 1918, that Surrey, Kent, Essex, London, and Australian troops worked across the Bray upland into Happy Valley and through Méaulte, and then in fierce rushes some of them entered Albert, where the golden statue of the Virgin and Child had at last fallen upon the church, battered into a shapeless red hummock used as cover by numbers of enemy machine-gunners.

The Hôtel de Ville, Noyon, as it was when recovered by the French, August 29th, 1918. Nothing was left of the fine mediæval building but these fragments of the beautiful Renaissance façade.

View in Noyon, taken from the theatre. For eight days after their evacuation of the town the Germans shelled the place, and when driven out of gun range bombed it from the air.

Place de l'Hôtel de Ville, after the German evacuation of the ancient square, nothing but a heap of ruins. Right: Front of the cathedral, the only prominent building that escaped complete destruction. In centre: French engineers removing the mines and traps left by the Germans. Some of these were fired by means of electric contact, which was operated from the enemy's power-plant at Crisolles, three miles away.

WANTON HAVOC WROUGHT IN NOYON WITH SHELLS, MINES, AND AIR BOMBS BY THE GERMANS WHEN WITHDRAWING IN AUGUST, 1918.

MINES
DANGER DE MORT
DÉFENSE D'ENTRER

points took one German battery at the point of the bayonet and conquered all the hill by eleven o'clock at night.

The next morning General Mangin sent his attacking forces more strongly forward on his right, and battled over the Aisne heights to the Ailette valley near Coucy-le-Château. At the same time he advanced his centre to Bretigny, on the Oise, three miles from the **Recovery of Lassigny** town of Chauny. Noyon was out-flanked and its eastern communica-tions severed.

General Mangin's army took 13,000 prisoners and 300 guns while chasing the broken enemy across the Oise and the Ailette Rivers. As Böhn's left wing fell back in shattered confusion a single division of the Third French Army, under General Humbert, stormed the Thiescourt Hills, which had been outflanked in a previous action conducted in co-operation with the Fourth British and First French Armies. Lassigny was recovered on August 21st, and Noyon half-encircled westward from the Divette stream in the night, when the city was outflanked on the east.

At daybreak on August 21st—as the German army group commander was sending strong fresh forces down to the heights above Soissons, in a vain endeavour to break into the great new salient General Mangin was making—more instant work was provided for all the reserve divisions that General von Böhn could obtain. The Third British Army, under Sir Julian Byng, attacked on a front of ten miles, from the ruins of Moyenneville, south of Arras, to Beaucourt, north of the Ancre stream.

A dense fog hung over the mazy wilderness of the old Somme battle-field, upon which four great actions had already been fought. It was a tangle of rusted wire, zigzagging ditches, hidden pits, and broken works of all kinds from which the main forces of the Seventeenth German Army, under General von Below, had withdrawn to a battle position running by the railway line at Achiet-le-Grand, three and a half miles from Bapaume.

The German commander was thoroughly alert to the attack, as was shown by his withdrawal to his battle positions. Yet on a part of the front his men were surprised by the British tactics. Sir Julian Byng did not employ the method of a hurricane bombard-ment such as General Rawlinson and General Humbert had used. His gunners steadily fired for two hours on the German positions, which were screened by a thick fog, for which, under the advice of its weather experts, the Third Army had been waiting. The fog was deepened by in-numerable smoke-shells, and just as dawn began to glimmer over Gommecourt and the milky sea of vapour below, the infantry attack opened. For a distance of about ten thousand yards English troops swung forward towards Moyenneville, Courcelles, Ablainzeville, Logeast Wood, and the railway junction near Bapaume.

On the eastern sector New Zealand and Lancashire and Yorkshire troops waited for an hour until the northern attack had developed, so as to come into line of assault for their nearer objectives along the Ancre valley. The foggy ground was the chief trouble, as it undulated in swells of a hundred and fifty feet, over one of the most laboured of all fields of war, to the embankment and cutting of the Arras-Albert railway, which the enemy held as his battle-line.

SAFETY FOR CIVILIANS.
French people who had suffered for four years under the German occupation being sent into safety by the advancing Canadians.

FROM THE BATTLE-FRONT.
Inhabitants of the recovered village of Saudemont being removed to a safe distance behind the fighting-line.

Preceded by the line of storming Tanks, the first divisions of attack —English infantry of the line of the 2nd Division and Guards—worked in wide order over the deep maze of the hostile outpost zone railway line beyond Moyenneville. Some of the Guards broke rapidly through the main German line and entered Hamelincourt. Below Moyenneville there was fierce fighting at Courcelles, where the Berkshires distinguished themselves, and in Logeast Wood. But these intricate machine-gun positions were outflanked and en-circled, about a thousand men and two battalion commandants being captured, together with Austrian field-gunners brought from the Italian front to strengthen Below's line. Fog, gas, and smoke impeded the attack more than the resistance of the enemy did, all these elements being either manufactured or selected by the British forces. Areas in which British gunners had gas-shelled hostile batteries were thick with fume when the assailing infantry and Tank sections arrived, and in the mist and smoke that hung about till noon some units lost direction. By six o'clock in the evening, however, the northern part of the railway embankment was occupied, and outposts were advanced more than a mile eastward in places.

Stronger opposition was encountered on the southern line of attack between Achiet- **Heroic Manchesters** le-Grand and Beaucourt, on the Ancre. Here **at the Dovecot** it was that the German army commander used his reserves with the utmost determination. He had to save the flank of the weakened, reeling forces by the Somme which his battle director, General von Böhn, was trying to withdraw with all guns and material. The chief knot of hostile resistance in the forefield of battle was an old German machine-gun redoubt on the high down of Beauregard, mid-way between Puisieux and Miraumont.

Known as the Dovecot, from a pigeon-house standing there in the first Somme campaign, this work covered the railway as it swung south-west towards the Ancre. Late in the afternoon the Manchesters cleared the Dovecot, only to be driven out by a fierce German counter-attack. Under a heavy barrage the Manchesters and their comrades fell back from crater to crater in the wild nocturnal battlefield illumined by bright moonshine. Then, before the Germans could get all their new machine-guns into position, the Englishmen returned with the bayonet to the Dovecot.

But a fresh enemy division, released from the Lys front by the great withdrawal going on there, stormed the Dovecot just before dawn on August 22nd. Even this did not discourage the tireless men from Manchester and the other English troops alongside them. They attacked the fresh German division at seven o'clock in the morning, and for the third **Ninety miles of** time carried the Dovecot, and for **raging conflict** another spell resolutely held it, while the battle which they had opened widened and intensified into the greatest of all struggles in the war.

The movement by the Third British Army, under Sir Julian Byng, at a time when the Fourth British Army, under Sir Henry Rawlinson, the First French Army, under General Debeney, the Third French Army, under General Humbert, and the Tenth French Army, under General Mangin, were all in action, made a line of raging conflict of more than ninety miles between Soissons and Arras. The general offensive of Marshal Foch was developing in tremendous weight and scope. There was a subtle and intricate interlocking design on the part of Sir Douglas Haig.

While General Pétain, with General Fayolle's group of three French armies, was strenuously absorbing the fresh forces that Böhn gathered on his left wing, Sir Douglas Haig was using only two British armies, the Third and Fourth, to exhaust the large reserves being hurried down from the Lys

to strengthen Böhn's centre and right wing. As soon as the Third Army had broken across the Arras-Albert railway the Fourth British Army resumed its great drive on either side the Somme between Albert and Chaulnes. In the mist of early morning of August 22nd, Surrey, Kent, Essex, London,

'MID THE RUINS OF BAPAUME.
It was on August 29th, 1918, that Sir Julian Byng's plan for encircling Bapaume, after some very severe fighting, led to the withdrawal of the enemy and the recovery of the ruins of the town by British troops.

and Australian troops worked across the Bray upland into Happy Valley and through Méaulte. In fierce rushes some of them entered the ruins of Albert, where the golden statue of the Madonna and Child had at last fallen upon the church, battered into a shapeless red hummock, used as cover by

BRITISH CAVALRY PASSING THE "RED HUMMOCK" THAT HAD BEEN ALBERT'S CHURCH.
Of the wonderful allied advance during the latter half of August, 1918, the "Times" correspondent said that the most interesting incident was the reoccupation of Albert, shattered by shell fire almost past belief. Referring to its church, he said : "The great mass of the nave still stands, but I can describe it best by saying that so a toy cathedral made of wax and painted red would look if it had been half melted in the fire."

enemy machine-gunners. Above Albert the enemy answered this pressure by heavy counter-attacks against the new line of the Third Army. At night, in the moonlight, the great struggle fiercely continued, and under a rolling bombardment between Arras and Chaulnes the two British

MAIN STREET IN BAPAUME.
Hardly had the enemy been driven out of the town than British labour battalions came up to make the road good again and pile all the debris in pathetic orderliness by the roadside.

armies continued to thrust into the enemy's defences. Along the Ancre the English and Welsh troops sent patrols up the river valley, where the German garrison was still strongly holding out on the hills by Miraumont, and with reserves hidden in the folds of ground counter-attacking

against the Dovecot work, which again changed hands. While the New Zealanders, Lancashires, and Yorkshires were pressing forward towards Bapaume, General von Below, in the evening of August 22nd, endeavoured to restore the situation by a grand counter-attack on the northern embankment of the Arras-Albert railway.

Sir Julian Byng, however, had more rapidly prepared another grand attack. His Tanks and infantry stormed into the village of Gomiécourt, under raking field-gun and anti-Tank fire from batteries along the Arras-Bapaume road around Achiet-le-Grand. The assembled hostile infantry was swept by the British barrage, and so broken by the attackers that one of the fresh divisions, brought up for the abortive counter-attack, was thrown into complete confusion, battalions and companies losing direction, so that sections came into action a mile apart. Before midnight Gomiécourt was conquered, a mile and a half above the German pivoting position of Achiet-le-Grand.

Capture of Gomiécourt

This great success was followed up, at dawn on August 23rd, by a general attack between the Cojeul River and the large plateau of Dead Man Down above Bapaume. The British Guards, with other fine divisions alongside them, struck at the northern part of the Arras-Bapaume road by Boiry-Becquerelle, Boyelles, and Ervillers. In front of the highway by Hamelincourt was a fresh Saxon division, brought up to reinforce the Prussians and Bavarians. The new troops had a strong position on the downs, but after one of their battalions ran into the Guards and the "whippet" Tanks and was badly cut up, there was little fight left in the Saxons. Some of them surrendered and others fled, pursued by the British storming cars and infantry patrols, that took the larger part of Ervillers Down and approached within six

MILITARY TRAFFIC CROSSING THE BRIDGE OVER THE DESTROYED RAILWAY OUTSIDE ALBERT.
The Arras-Albert railway was the real core of the battle which resulted in the final recovery of the latter town from the enemy on August 22nd, 1918. It presented a formidable obstacle to the British troops, being infested with machine-gun posts, which had to be cleared out by the infantry, assisted by heavy artillery firing along its length and by Tanks swinging down some of its sections. The viaduct and the railway-line were destroyed.

hundred yards of the village, from which Bapaume was only four miles distant.

Above this important scene of action the Tanks led the way into Boiry and Boyelles, and then advanced along both slopes of the Cojeul River valley and across the hill rising above the Sensée River at St. Léger. Nearly all St. Léger Down was won, the victors dropping into shell-holes half a mile from the village, under machine-gun fire and artillery fire from the Germans on Dead Man Down—a famous pivot of British resistance during the enemy's grand offensive in the spring of the year. It was the British Guards who had stayed the enemy's advance on the hills about St. Léger, and they knew the ground on which, in turn, they attacked the Germans, after five months of defensive fighting and reorganisation.

The Guards had lost heavily during the period of German superiority of numbers and armament. When rapidly moved, in April, from the Arras sector to the forest approaches to Hazebrouck, one brigade had made, at great sacrifice, a successful stand against the extraordinary odds of one against twenty. Many of the surviving veterans had only, recently recovered from the wounds of the previous battles of the defence, and the ranks were filled out with numerous new men, yet the Guards displayed a skilled determination in attack that made them once more the admiration of their comrades.

Brilliant work of British Guards

Fiercely and persistently as Sir Julian Byng continued his thrust around Bapaume towards the old Hindenburg line his general casualties were light in comparison with the results obtained. It was estimated that he lost only one man to every four men that General von Below had had put out of action. The fast, light Tanks proved master weapons against the German machine-gun defences, and although some of them were crippled by short-range artillery fire and armour-piercing bullets, the new chariots of assault were used in such large squadrons by the English army commander who first specialised in Tank tactics that they terrorised the enemy infantrymen.

Byng's thrust around Bapaume

After the victory of the Arras-Bapaume road the Tank lieutenants pursued the broken Saxon and Prussian forces, guided by low-flying British airmen, who smote the fugitives while signalling their movements. Some of the storming cars broke clean through the Upper Sensée valley defences, and then charged up the side of Dead Man Down, reaching the road to Croisilles well in the rear of the rallying garrison of Ervillers.

Had it been possible to sustain this adventurous thrust a break-through might have been immediately effected. By this time, however, the Tanks had got into the enemy's main artillery positions and were exposed on the lower part of the bare hillside to a tremendous converging gun fire at very

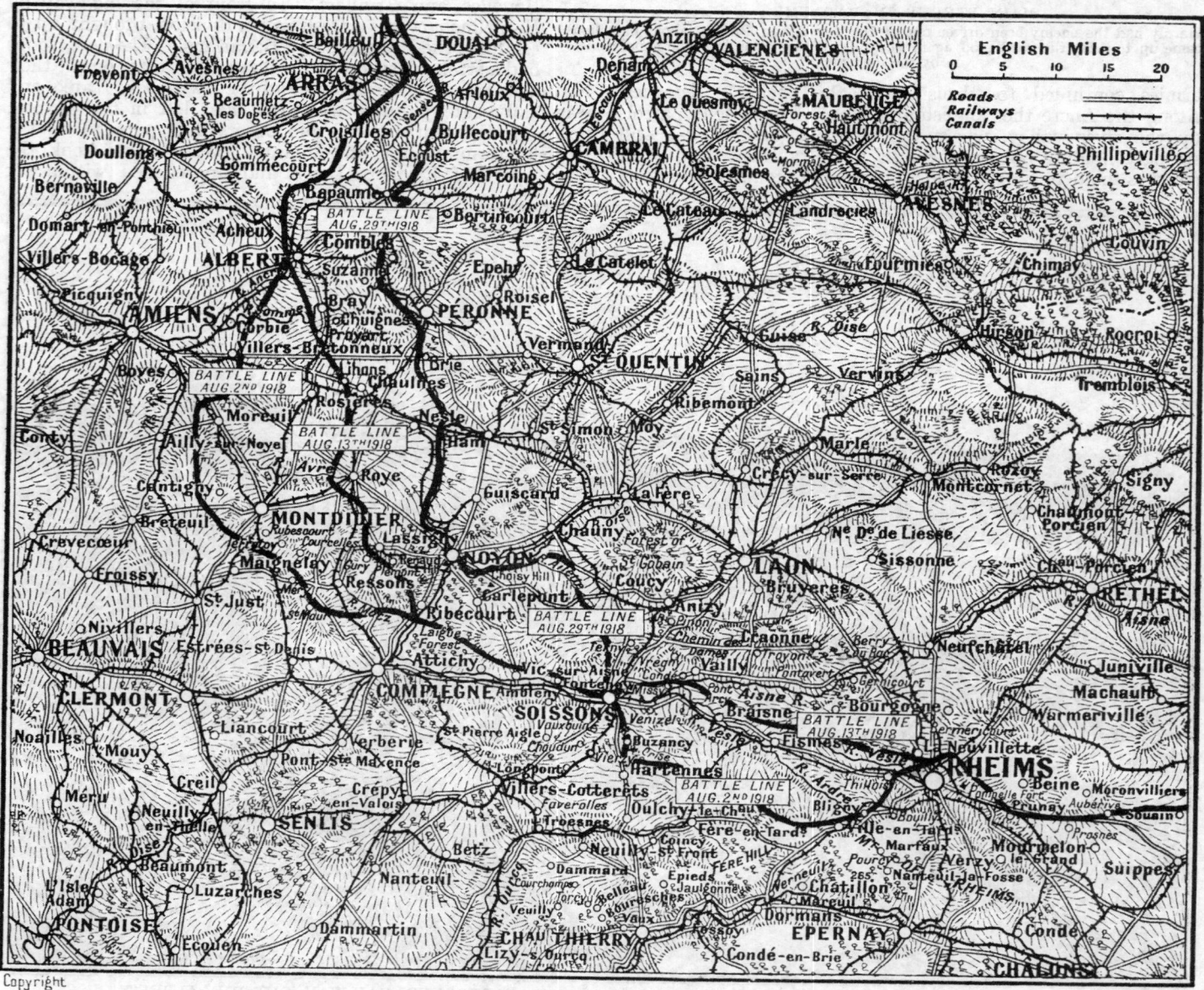

The Great War

TERRITORY INVOLVED IN THE SECOND PINCER MOVEMENT OF MARSHAL FOCH'S OFFENSIVE IN AUGUST, 1918.
The successive battle lines of August 2nd, 13th, and 29th, traced above, show how the great German salient towards Amiens was further straightened out in the second phase of the Allies' counter-offensive, British troops moving on to Bapaume while French troops made a turning movement around Noyon.

Bourlon village in October, 1918, demolished in the terrific fighting for the recovery of Cambrai.

The chateau at Bourlon: One of the stately homes of France, battered and broken by war.

General Plumer, commanding the British Second Army, held up by traffic on the lines of advance.

Canadian transport thronging a sunken road just captured from the Germans.

Liberators of Denain: Canadians marching past the Prince of Wales and General Sir Arthur Currie.

The Prince of Wales (in centre of chancel) at the Thanksgiving Service in Denain Church.

271

Wounded Germans, captured at Chuignes, crossing the German cemetery at Proyart.

German prisoners carrying their wounded conquerors to an advanced dressing-station on a battle day.

short range. Only with a great force of cavalry immediately at hand could the unexpected weakness of the enemy's infantry have been decisively exploited.

Yet the success remained great, and with other victories all along the British line it decided the struggle with General von Böhn's armies, compelling him to speed up his preparations for a retreat from the Somme. For the surprising thrust at St. Léger and Dead Man Down was immediately followed, at eleven o'clock in the morning of August 23rd, by the sudden breaking of the enemy's defensive flank at the fortified gully by Achiet-le-Grand and the Irles Ridge.

Here a fine North-country division, on the left of the New Zealanders, accomplished one of the most difficult tasks in the campaign. The Achiet-le-Grand line was of intricate strength, with the embankments and cuttings of the three railways that met by the village, and the ruined houses and sheds, screening machine-gunners and anti-Tank artillerymen. During the British retreat in the spring a few hundred odd men had been able to hold the Achiet line against the joined forces of Below and Marwitz, largely by reason of the strength of the railway works on Hill 120 and the neighbouring heights.

destroyed six of the new storming cars. The tradition of the German gunner officer on Flesquières Ridge, in the autumn of 1917, was of incomparable value to the German armies.

In order to carry Miraumont, some Lancashires at last swam the flooded stream by Grandcourt and made a fierce advance along the high southern side of the watercourse, by the old German trench system extending to Pys. The enemy was then furiously engaged on the Thiepval Ridge, and the Lancashire troops stole forward in the rear unperceived. But their audacity was countered by a strong encircling movement as soon as the Germans were aroused.

Swimming adventures of Lancashires

Completely cut off, the gallant adventurers received strange inspiration from the sky, one of their airmen dropping a message telling them to hold out as relief was coming. Hold out they did, and when released, by the main surge of the British offensive sweeping over the old high Thiepval-Pozières upland on their right, they cheerily joined in the chase of the retreating enemy.

Miraumont, however, did not fall until the morning of Saturday, August 24th, after a siege of seventy-eight hours.

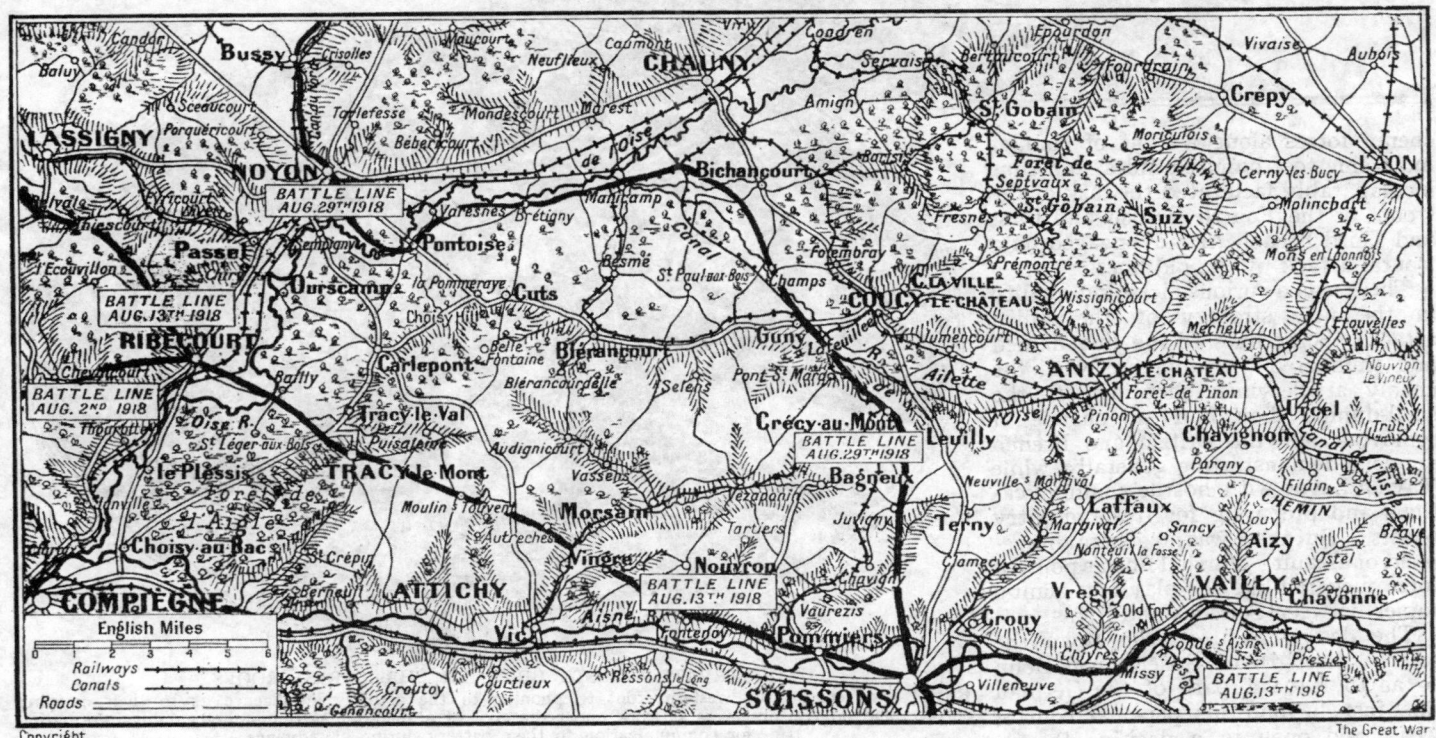

AREA OF THE SOUTHERN HALF OF THE ALLIES' COUNTER-OFFENSIVE IN AUGUST.
General Mangin's French Army provided the lower claw of the pincers opened by Marshal Foch in the second phase of the August battles. Thrusting towards Laon on August 13th, he encircled Noyon on his left, and dominated the great hill forest of St. Gobain on his right front.

The victorious Englishmen pressed along the Ayette-Bapaume road to Bihucourt village, two miles and a half from Bapaume, which in the burning August sunshine was at once brought under short-ranged, observed gun fire from the arc of conquered downs northward and north-westward. Then the New Zealand Division, which had been battling for three days by Puisieux, was also able to strike across the railway towards Loupart Wood and close upon Bapaume from the west.

The enemy garrison of Miraumont was the only remaining obstacle to a general British advance between the Ancre and Cojeul streams. There were men of high **North-countrymen** bravery and skill in this strong outpost of **at Achiet-le-Grand** the Bapaume front, and it was mainly because they held out with unusual determination, after the long swaying action around the Dovecot on the commanding down above them, that the southern wing of Sir Julian Byng's army had its progress delayed for three days. There was a German gunner sergeant-major at Miraumont, handling a single field-piece left behind as a protection against Tanks, who stopped every "whippet" that tried to break into the village. He was reported to have

So long as the famous Somme Ridge south of it was unattacked, continual reinforcements could be collected in the folds of ground eastward, and trickled forward as steadily as British artillerymen allowed. In order to take the old main rampart of the Bapaume defences, upon which the apprentice national armies of the British Commonwealth had struggled for eight months in 1916 and 1917, and there at heavy cost learned the mastery of trench warfare, it was necessary to repeat some of the strategic operations of the former campaign.

In particular, a movement of co-operation was required along both banks of the Somme River. The Australian Imperial Force took the place of the French army which, under Marshal Foch, had assisted in the early siege battle. The Australians, however, were not so far forward as the French had been, and the English and Scottish forces on either side of them were some miles from the Franco-British front of the summer of 1916. Happily, general conditions were different from those under which the First Battle of the Somme had been started.

The last Battle of the Somme was opening with a succession of surprising flank offensives, which continually tested all

the Grand Alliance, according to the traditions established by the men of Marlborough and Wellington, he had to work and fight with indefatigable energy. To save him from wearing out from death or wounds, the new tactics of Tank charges through curtains of smoke had been elaborated by the British Staff. By this method of camouflaged, mechanical attack the heaviest burden of infantry actions was thrown upon enemy divisions, which were forced, on all critical points, to charge against machine-guns in the continual counter-attacks needed to gain time for orderly withdrawal of material.

In the meantime the work that fell upon the unrelieved yet ardent British divisions of attack was a supreme test of the qualities of the race. Often they

enemy forces along a front of conflict increasing to a hundred miles, and thus incomparably facilitated the task of the troops of the Fourth British and First and Third French Armies engaged on a frontal attack by the old lines.

There was a curious flickering quality in the new strategy of the allied attack. Sometimes all the line flamed and thundered with gun fire, with the enemy artillerymen shooting off the shell-dumps they had no chance of removing, and the British and French gunners demonstrating generally, while playing havoc with hostile communications and preparing for fresh infantry onsets. But there was no general movement of assault. Marshal Foch's point of force flickered like the play of a giant's rapier between Soissons and Arras.

The design was to wear down the reserve strength of General von Böhn so as to leave a part of the German line just beyond his personal control weak and open to a decisive thrust. Sir Douglas Haig it was who thought out this part of the operations. He adopted a certain scheme devised by Sir Henry Horne, the leader of the First British Army, and by a secret manœuvre, very similar to that employed in breaking the line of the Second German Army near Amiens on August 8th, the British Commander-in-Chief was on August 23rd busily engaged in rounding off his first series of final victories.

Sir Douglas Haig's secret manœuvre

The Canadian divisions had then retired from the sector immediately north of Roye, after driving the enemy back for fifteen miles and taking 10,000 prisoners and 167 guns. Naturally, the German Staff concluded that troops which had done so much intense day and night fighting required rest. But no British divisions of attack were resting after labour. They were going onward towards the Wagnerian lines of the Hindenburg defence system in one of the most effective feats of sustained fighting and enduring power known in history.

In the new advance as in the old retreat the British soldier, insular or continental, fought, on an average at least, three Germans. Although reinforced with troops of the youngest class, he was still greatly inferior in numbers to the enemy in the western theatre of conflict, and in order to carry out his noble part in the main military operations of

OBSERVATION-POSTS BENEATH SHATTERED ROOFS.
British signallers on the western front telephoning to the artillery intelligence as to their creeping barrage, and (above) observers at work under the roof of a shell-damaged building gaining information for communication to their battery during an advance.

fought onward for three or four weeks, took ten days' relief while standing-to at an hour's notice, then returned to action for another long spell. The Canadians took their relief in the form of long nocturnal marches, with their guns and material, from the neighbourhood of Roye to Arras and the hills between the Scarpe and the middle course of the Cojeul streams. As in the first part of the month, this multitudinous movement of the army of a young nation escaped the eyes of enemy observers and spies by reason of the infinite care with which it was organised and executed. In spite of the fact that the full moon illumined the undulating country in the British rear, across which the Canadians moved from the Fourth Army back to their comrades of the First Army, no Teutonic night-hawk glimpsed what was happening.

This lessening of the weight of attack against the Somme line was concealed from the enemy commander by the activity displayed by the allied forces remaining there. The First French Army, under General Debeney, which had taken the important position of Beauvraignes, midway between Roye and Lassigny, opened a furious bombardment that seemed to herald another infantry assault. The Australian forces, with Scottish, London, and East County regiments, did more than demonstrate. They were bound for the Hindenburg line by the shortest route, running over the Tortille stream above Péronne, and they had to break their path over the section of the Somme battlefield where the French Army had been checked two years before.

They began operations in the morning mist on August 23rd, when the German line was breaking above Bapaume. On the southern side of the Somme, along the tableland of Santerre, the men of the Commonwealth stormed the Ridge of Chuignes and the spurs commanding the river valley as far as Suzanne, where the British troops on their flank advanced in line above Lihons. In a wood beyond Chuignes the men of New South Wales found a gigantic gun that had been employed in bombarding Amiens. It was completely wrecked, the monster barrel having been blown off the carriage and tumbled downhill into a gully. It was no doubt this disaster that had saved Amiens Cathedral.

Having in daylight outflanked Bray across the river, and brought guns on to the dominating Chuignes rise, the Australians in the night stormed Bray, and, with the returning sun, pushed on to the high ground by Suzanne, completing, with the prisoners they took there, a total of 12,000 Germans captured since August 8th—a number far exceeding all casualties of the victors. Then, against small hostile rearguards, composed of machine-gunners with a single quickfirer for action against scouting storming cars, the Australians worked onward towards Péronne, while the German artillery flooded them with gas from the shell-dumps that General von der Marwitz had stacked vainly in the hope of a great offensive victory.

As soon as the Australian line, with its fine British prolongation, swung strongly towards what had been the old French front of attack in the First Somme Battle, the extreme right wing of the Third British Army in Albert also moved, by Bécourt and Bécordel, towards the old British assembly trenches. But instead of striking out by Fricourt, where the first grand offensive had been confined in narrow space, the Briton, with all his old audacity enhanced by **Somme Ridge** masterly skill and new inventions in battle **carried by surprise** machinery, stormed at once over the end of the famous Somme Ridge.

Thiepval Down and the valley of the Ancre, where the Ulstermen had heroically fought and fallen in July, 1916, leaving the position to be carried by costly siege operations lasting four months, was taken in a sharp walk in the morning of August 24th. The difference between the old and new processes of attack was not due entirely to improvements in methods and machinery of war. The temper of the ordinary German soldier was changing. It was often becoming possible for adroitly daring men to take liberties with him.

This was what Yorkshire, Welsh, and Lancashire troops did in the night of Friday, August 23rd. They swam or waded the inundated Ancre brook and, without the help of Tanks or following artillery, rushed the sombre slopes of Thiepval. Then, after a short rest, they went on, in early morning on August 24th, to Courcelette and Pozières. The Yorkshiremen played a leading part in this remarkable exploit, penetrating the hostile lines to a depth of six thousand yards, across a position of immense natural and artificial strength, against which army corps had broken in previous actions.

Although Thiepval had become more accessible, owing to the conquest of Beaucourt and the outflanking movement by Grandcourt, it was mainly due to the weakening of the general German moral that the amazingly rapid success in the opening of the last Battle of the Somme was achieved. The weary divisions that had fallen back desperately fighting from Thiepval crest and the site of Pozières windmill in the spring of the year had an important share in the victory of final reconquest. They had done most to wear the Teuton down to the mood of depression in which he could be easily surprised by unaided infantry.

It was, however, only in patches that the enemy forces were disastrously weakened in spirit. There was fierce, prolonged resistance by the old mine-craters at La Boisselle, where English troops cleared the way to Contalmaison in the early morning of Sunday, August 25th. By this time Mametz was taken, and in the old jungle of Mametz Wood a Welsh force was again established and working up to the central crest by Bazentin, after a magnificent swimming rush over the Ancre.

There was a great strategic change in the direction of attack between the first and second Welsh advances into Mametz Wood. In the first week of July, 1916, the British forces generally advanced from the south; in the last week of August, 1918, they came down on the enemy from the north and north-east, along practically the entire length of the Bapaume-Albert road. Instead of withdrawing north-eastward on Bapaume, the Germans retired over the vast, wild moorland in a south-easterly direction across the Tortille stream.

On August 24th the New Zealanders, in a vehement and resolute advance, broke into Loupart Wood, where a Bavarian garrison met the charging Tanks with a hail of fire, until they were almost trampled by the agile steel monsters. Then the defenders surrendered in a body, and the New Zealanders took the stronghold **New Zealanders at** beyond the wood, fought through Grevillers **Loupart Wood** and Biefvillers to the outskirts of Bapaume, and widened the line of the southerly flank attack against the Péronne and Tortille route of retreat.

Above them, the superb North-country division, which had carried the Achiet junction, pressed the enemy back to Sapignies, on the Arras highway. This was a difficult position to hold, as the British Guards and 2nd Division above the point were well across the road, and engaged in preparing an attack on the famous key position of Mory, by the Upper Sensée River and Dead Man upland. General von Below was alert to the peril to this part of his line.

He had lost St. Léger, on the northern side of Dead Man, and English and Scottish divisions were closing on Croisilles and the approaches to the Hindenburg system. Henin Hill was conquered, commanding the Sensée valley near the old German front. Little remained to Below of the ground he had won, at crippling cost to his Mars and Michael army groups, in March, 1918. Yet he had to cling to the four miles of high ground between Mory and Vaulx in order not merely to win time to put his original defences in effective condition, but to save the flank of the army of General von der Marwitz from being turned, far in the rear, by the Bapaume-Cambrai road.

All the fresh forces he could apparently safely spare from army reserve he sent towards the hills above Bapaume, intending by a great counter-attack to throw the tired British Guards and North-country divisions back to the railway embankment. At the same time Sir Julian Byng arranged for the menaced troops to resume their advance and open the way for the New Zealanders to encircle Bapaume.

On Saturday, August 24th, the extraordinary pitched battle opened, with the opposing forces both in attack. Bavarians of the 36th Division first engaged both the Guards and the North-countrymen and pressed them back. On the headland by Mory, forming the projecting pivot on which the British forces were designed to swing forward, the ground for covering the operations against Bapaume was lost by the Guards. The King's Company of Grenadiers recovered the important headland with the bayonet, and extended savagely beyond it.

The North-countrymen, after resisting with equal fury at Sapignies, worked forward in the evening towards the village of Favreuil, in the hope of breaking through the weakened line by Bapaume. British **The Grenadiers** airmen, however, perceived hostile reinforce- **at Mory** ments marching from Beugnâtre. They were men of the 111th Prussian Division, originally intended to drive in the British front by Sapignies, after the Bavarians had recovered the Mory headland. The airmen badly upset the Prussian force by bombing and machine-gunning it at close range. As scattering troops took cover in the ruins of Favreuil, and began to re-form for attack, the British barrage fell upon them.

Behind the heavy, thrashing shell fire came the English infantry with Tanks. The troops took the village at the point of the bayonet, and in the night worked across the hillside against the enfeebled enemy, reaching Beugnâtre, on the

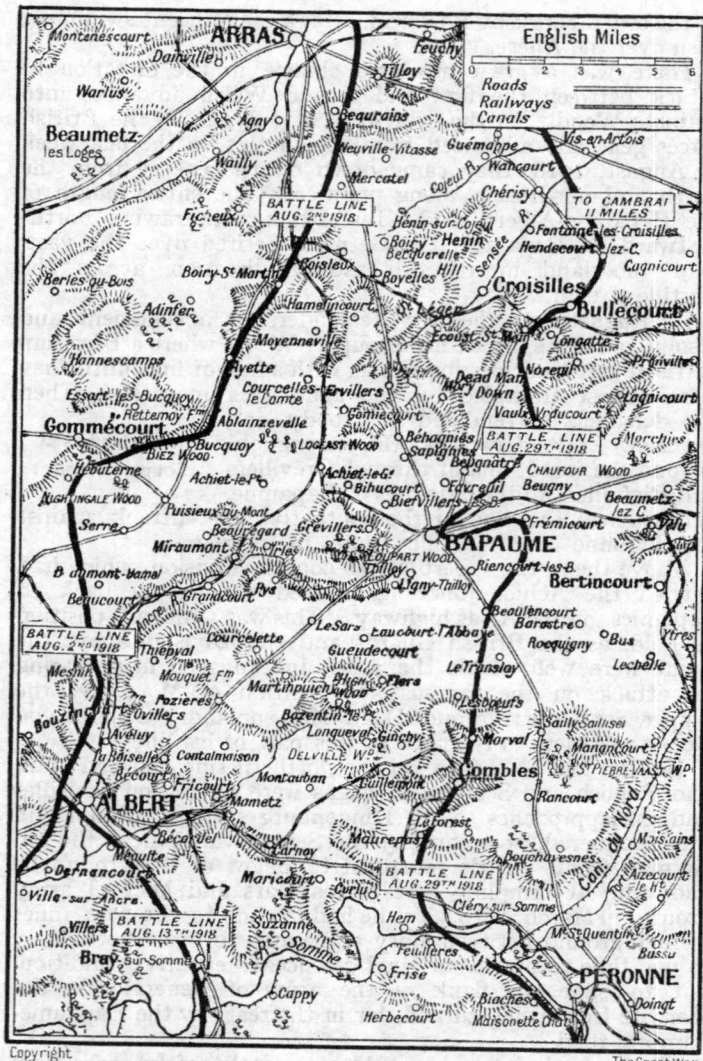

TERRAIN OF THE FIGHTING FOR BAPAUME.
Northern half of the area involved in Marshal Foch's second pincer movement, where the British Army under Sir Julian Byng closed in upon Bapaume, while General Mangin, further south, turned Noyon.

Bullecourt road, some two miles behind Bapaume. Under cover of this wide outflanking movement the New Zealanders tried to carry the ruins of the city, but found the enemy was still maintaining many machine-gunners in the wreckage, with strong artillery protection against Tanks. There was, indeed, a very good German gunner officer in Bapaume, who claimed to have destroyed more Tanks than the gunner sergeant-major at Miraumont, and reinforcements of the general garrison were numerous.

Bapaume did not fall until August 29th, when the entire hostile line between the shattered city and the Somme withdrew in considerable confusion, after another greater attempt at a counter-offensive made across the Bapaume-Péronne road by the army of General von der Marwitz. Yet this attempt was, though tactically strong, but an acknowledgment of strategic defeat. The powerful forces that broke upon the British line, running sideways across the old battlefield by Thilloy, Eaucourt, Martinpuich, High Wood, Longueval, and Montauban, were largely obtained by a general withdrawal across the Somme of the armies which had been fighting by Chaulnes and Roye. Enemy rearguards left Roye on August 24th, and Noyon on August 29th.

This wide, sudden movement of retreat by General von Böhn's centre, in which a vast quantity of material was lost by firing or capture, was produced by the terrific pressure on his wings from the Third British Army and the Tenth French Army. It was accelerated by another British thrust, in which the manœuvring Canadians took a leading part.

The moat of the Middle Somme enabled Böhn to hold lightly for some days his withdrawing centre, and before he evacuated the Roye line he retired his main forces over the river and sent them as reinforcements on the Bapaume-Péronne front, thus aggravating the already difficult task of the British divisions fighting down from the Ancre towards the Tortille. For four days, from August 25th to August 28th, there was a fierce, long, swaying line of conflict over the old fields of carnage by Thilloy, Gueudecourt, Flers, Delville Wood, Longueval, Montauban Ridge, and the broad valley running into Combles hollow. It was Böhn's way of ensuring against a rupture of his flank and keeping men and guns usefully employed there, while all roads behind them were congested with traffic under an increasing storm of aerial bombs, varied by gusts of Lewis-gun fire from British and French machines.

It was on the fields above the Somme that Böhn had won distinction, along with General von Lossberg, the directing mind behind the Royal figurehead of Prince Rupert of Bavaria. He knew the ground, and in several shrewd thrusts in out-numbering strength his strengthened lieutenant was able to drive back for a few hundred yards the New Zealanders at Bapaume, the Lancashires south of the town, and the York-shires, Welsh, East Anglian, London, and other British troops.

The losses inflicted on the enemy commander's freshly-engaged divisions, however, were out of all comparison with the small, transient recoveries of ground made in front of Le Transloy and Combles. Always the British troops returned to the attack, with Tanks, smoke-screens, and augmenting artillery power, recovering at times the undisturbed shell-dumps they had left in the retreat of the previous March. Grimly they wore the fresh enemy forces down, and when, on August 29th, Sir Douglas Haig claimed that his men had consummated the operations begun on the 8th of the month, and " rendered the enemy's positions on the old Somme battlefield untenable," more had been effected than appeared on the surface of things. Between Péronne and Arras the German armies were so exhausted that the Australian divisions and Canadian divisions, placed on the wings of three British organisations of attack, were once more able to open another great movement of victory.

The capture of Bapaume

When the New Zealanders entered Bapaume on August 29th, 1918, the tale of prisoners taken by British forces since the opening of Sir Julian Byng's flank offensive on August 21st was 21,000. In the slightly longer period of General Mangin's similar flank offensive, the French forces had taken some 15,000 prisoners. From the Sensée River to the Ailette River, between which Sir Julian Byng's and General Mangin's men operated, with the armies of Sir Henry Rawlinson, General Debeney, and General Humbert, the allied line ran from the Hindenburg system at Hendicourt and Bullecourt, by Ecoust and Vaulx-Vraucourt, through Bapaume, and Frémicourt, Beaulencourt, Morval, Combles, and Maurepas.

Australian, Scottish, and English divisions stretched across the Somme by Hem to the western bank in front of Brie and Péronne. The First French Army held the western bank of the river of battle beyond Nesle, and skirted the Canal du Nord between Nesle and Noyon ; the Third French Army held the cathedral city of the Oise and the slopes above it, while the Tenth French Army, with gallant United States reinforcements, had thrown forces across the Ailette by Champs, and entrenched on Crécy-au-Mont, Juvigny Down, and the hills above Soissons.

But all these lines of victory, running almost entirely through territory which the British and French had lost in the spring of the year, were not so immediately significant as the preliminary movement of menacing advance of the First British Army by the Scarpe River into fortified country the enemy had strongly held since October 1914. Marshal Foch was opening his third pair of pincers. With this operation, that began on August 26th, overlapping some of the fiercest actions of the Third British Army around Bapaume, we shall start the next chapter.

THE TURN OF THE TIDE IN THE WEST.
III.—The Breaking of the Wotan Line and Storming of Mont St. Quentin.
By Edward Wright.

Below's Faith in Works Rather than Men—The Secret Tunnels of Arras and Horne's Plan—Lossberg Retires on Both Wings and Stands on Somme Battlefield—He is Completely Surprised by First British Army—Canadians Break the Hindenburg Line—Scottish Highlanders Return to Greenland Hill—Londoners Fight Back to Bullecourt—Scots and English Storm the Scarpe Bank—Bullecourt Lost for the Last Time—Magnificent Resilience of London Men—Heroic Tenacity of Liverpool and Manchester Troops—Australians' Amazing Swoop Across Somme—Mont St. Quentin Taken by Three Hundred New South Wales Men—Currie's and Fergusson's Corps Shatter the Wotan Line—The Day of the Tanks—Battle of Dury Hill and Cagnicourt—Lancashires' Break Into Quéant Maze—Naval Division Marches Fourteen Miles Straight into Battle—Great Turning Movement by Pronville—Extraordinary Sandwich of Opposing Forces by Mœuvres—Australians Force North Canal and French Encircle Ham—Enemy's Last Attempt at Blackmailing Savagery.

AS a result of the extreme pressure which the Third British Army, under Sir Julian Byng, exercised upon the enemy forces around Bapaume, the German commander in the last week of August, 1918, was compelled to guard his unattacked left flank by Arras with a division unfit for active work. These troops were placed in the old British lines at Monchy, Guémappe, and Wancourt. Behind them ran the tunnelled Siegfried line of the Hindenburg system, in the rear of which was the Wotan switch-line, extending upward from Quéant to Drocourt.

General von Below seems to have reckoned that amid triple fortifications so strong and extensive as those around Arras troops of even third-rate quality could at least hold out until good counter-attacking forces arrived. His Intelligence officer reported that no signs of a British movement on the weakly-held flank were evident, and that the Canadian Corps was still absent from the First British Army.

For the spring offensive in 1917 Sir Edmund Allenby had constructed beneath Arras a great system of tunnels, with electric railways, by which large forces could be secretly and swiftly moved close to the hostile lines. During the enemy's offensive in the spring of 1918 Sir Henry Horne, who with the First Army extended down to the line formerly held by General Allenby, drew his front back towards the opening of the tunnels, intending to make use again of the underground series of communications for a surprise attack. He even relinquished the very valuable observation position of Monchy Hill in order to win

GAUGING THE WIND.
British soldiers in France ascertaining wind direction and force. Having released a small balloon, one man observed its movements, another noted the time, and the third made the necessary record.

more power in recoil for the amazing forward spring which he intended to make.

There was delay in the execution of his plan, but through being laid by it ripened, as the sound fruit of an inventive mind often will. Instead of being a strong diversion calculated to force the enemy to cease attacking the British wings, the scheme became the culminating surprise in the system of offensives that Sir Douglas Haig and General Pétain arranged under the direction of Marshal Foch. The development in importance of the plan for the stealthy leap of the First British Army was indeed remarkable proof of the efficacy of the completely centralised High Command of the Associated Armies.

All the allied forces in action in the last week of August, 1918, were apparently in a situation of grave difficulty. Under the skilful direction of General von Böhn the enemy armies between Arras and Soissons were repeating the manœuvre of the withdrawal to the Hindenburg system. They had line after line of Sir Julian Byng's, Sir Hubert Gough's, General Humbert's, and General Mestre's former battle positions on which to rest. Behind these trenches, dug-outs, and block-houses were the Siegfried, Wotan, Alberich, and other German systems of ditched and concreted mazes, arranged for interlocking machine-gun fire. Ludendorff was suffering from an attack of neurotic paralysis, with choking and vomiting symptoms, that left him alternately timid and desperate, but Hindenburg had found another man to carry out his original plan for winning the war with stalemate by attrition

SALVING ABANDONED GERMAN STORES.
Australian troops in a town on the western front which they had just recaptured. They were engaged in salving some of the useful material which the enemy had been compelled to leave behind.

by the Highland Territorials of the renowned 51st Division, returned from fierce action by the Mountain of Rheims, and by the Canadian Corps, secretly and swiftly moved from its field of victory by the Somme. They took by surprise the divisions holding the old British positions between the Scarpe and Cojeul streams. The Highlanders followed their line of attack of the spring of 1917, when they had the Canadians on their left, and broke back to the chemical factory of Rœux, the approach to Greenland Hill, and the ruins of Gavrelle.

The most gallant Scotsmen worked along the Scarpe River to Pelves, protecting the left flank of their old battle comrades the Canadians, who had an amazing success against the weakest German division. Setting out two divi-

in the west and checkmate by economic conquest in the east. General von Lossberg, the man behind Prince Rupert of Bavaria, was given practical control of the operations.

Lossberg had made his reputation in the first Somme campaign, and had enhanced it during the defence of the Passchendaele Ridge. With Böhn as his lieutenant, he began by energetically remedying Ludendorff's salient mistakes. By the end of the month he retired his northern operative wing from Bailleul, Kemmel Hill, and **Lossberg retires on both wings** Estaires, thus escaping from attack by Sir Herbert Plumer and Sir William Birdwood. The leaders of the Second and Fifth British Armies had to reorganise the devastated marsh of the Lys valley before they could threaten the Fourth and Sixth German Armies.

Lossberg also refused his southern wing. For a fortnight after its great victory between the Oise and Aisne the Tenth French Army, under General Mangin, was opposed in tremendous strength, the forces of General von Carlowitz being increased by a hundred thousand men. Marshal Foch had in turn to send strong United States brigades to reinforce the French and African troops of the Tenth Army in order to prevent the enemy from successfully counter-attacking from the heights above Soissons. But as soon as General Mangin was again in predominant power the army of Carlowitz evacuated the Ailette valley and the marshes of the Oise, and withdrew into a fortress system on the wooded mass of St. Gobain, leaving the Franco-American forces the heavy task of reorganising a new offensive from low-lying, wasted ground.

Time was what Lossberg required, and by retiring his wings and massing strongly against the French army of Champagne, under General Gouraud, he meant to make a fighting withdrawal from the Somme to the Hindenburg system and save and rest some eighty divisions of attack for the final contest. He expected Marshal Foch to drive in strength along the front of his recent victories, and thereby exhaust the allied mass of manœuvre. In this case the new German battle director intended to open a final offensive by Nancy. These were the circumstances in which the long-prepared plan of Sir Henry Horne matured into decisive execution.

At three o'clock in the morning of August 26th, 1918, in cloudy gloom, with bursts of moonshine, action was opened

AFTER WAR'S HURRICANE HAD PASSED.
Château and park of Goyencourt, about two miles to the north-west of Roye, which was recovered on August 27th, 1918, during the rapid advance of the Allies along the Somme front.

sions strong from the end of the Arras tunnel, they met at first with scarcely any resistance, and sweeping through Guémappe stormed the flank of Monchy Hill, disconcerting the enemy gunners, who were prepared only for a frontal attack. Before breakfast-time most of the ground was won. Then, however, a fresh German fighting division of Baden men made a stand in the old Hindenburg line and on Wancourt Hill. Stubbornly the Canadians still fought forward, winning the tower and upland of Wancourt in a long, fierce action ending in the early morning of August 27th.

At the same time the Canadian Corps swung forward from Monchy Hill and, reaching farther than any British forces had done in previous actions against the Hindenburg line, seized the southern side of **Great advance on the Scarpe** the village of Pelves just as the vehement Highlanders conquered Rœux and took the northern side of Pelves. This glorious combined advance along both sides of the River Scarpe solved the problem of attack, for which no solution had been found in the spring of 1917.

Desperately General von Below and his corps commanders endeavoured to retrieve the mistake of their Intelligence Department. Down the Lille and Valenciennes railways fresh divisions were hurried for a grand counter-attack. In the evening the Canadians were pressed back a few hundred yards in front of Monchy, but a considerable body of the Germans refused to advance, and the Canadians and the Highlanders rapidly prepared, from the vantage ground they had won, a stronger thrust. The men of the Dominion stormed into the village of Boiry-Notre-Dame and, encircling Vis, waded the Cojeul stream and captured Chérisy—positions for which the Third British Army had heroically but vainly struggled in the spring of the previous year.

Above the Arras-Cambrai road the Highlanders surpassed their former achievements by taking the whole of Greenland Hill, while on the right of the Canadians another fine Scottish force of Lowlanders, the 52nd Division, which had skilfully turned Henin Hill the previous day, broke across the Hindenburg line into Fontaine. The Lowlanders were unpractised in Western trench warfare, having come from Palestine, but their skill proved as superb as their courage. At the same time the London (56th) Division, which had broken Below's troops on Vimy Ridge at the end of March, made a resolute thrust across the downs to Croisilles, and after four days fighting, in which the Lowland Scots helped them by the turning movement at Henin, advanced towards the memorable battlefield of Bullecourt, while the British Guards were sweeping across Dead Man Down and threatening the flank of the Hindenburg system.

Highlanders take Greenland Hill

Wonderful was the difference between the situation when Sir Henry Horne and Sir Edmund Allenby were trying to pierce the German defences and when Sir Henry Horne and Sir Julian Byng renewed the attempt. In the first battle of the Hindenburg line, in the spring of 1917, the strategy of the Allies was defective owing to the failure of the Allied Commander-in-Chief, General Nivelle, to carry out the French part of his plan.

In the late summer of 1918 the new Allied Commander-in-Chief completely succeeded in drawing away the enemy's main forces from the line the British suddenly attacked. Instead of General Pétain needing help from the British armies, he was able to assist indirectly in the successful thrust towards Valenciennes by holding vast German forces in play from Verdun to Nesle.

It was because the main burden of the war no longer rested on the British armies that they were able to shoulder their way through the enemy's front at remarkable speed in offensive after offensive. The British again became the main force of the Grand Alliance.

Enemy held from Verdun to Nesle

In the afternoon of August 27th, while an English division on Vimy Ridge was helping the Scottish Highlanders by storming into Arleux-en-Artois, General von Below made another violent essay to prevent the coming disaster. By dividing his large reinforcements into two battering-rams, he struck along the Douai railway against the 51st Division and over the hills between Ecoust and the Bapaume road against the Guards, North-country men, and New Zealanders. The Highlanders gave a little ground on Greenland Hill, while holding their new line in resilient strength. Around Bapaume the fresh enemy forces were so completely broken that the English troops stormed into Beugnâtre. Then, while heavy fighting went on by the historic ruins of Vaulx-Vraucourt and in the Hindenburg line between Fontaine and Bullecourt, the united wings of the First and Third British Armies struck with shattering force upon the main Siegfried and Wotan switch-lines of the Hindenburg system.

On August 29th the men of London of the 56th Division

GERMANS STRANDED IN FRANCE BY THE TURN OF THE TIDE.
Prisoners taken by the Canadians arriving in the cages. Between July 18th and August 31st—that is, the first six weeks of the Allies' great counter-offensive—the allied armies captured no fewer than 128,302 prisoners, over 10,000 of whom fell to the Canadians alone.

returned to Bullecourt, after fighting their way to it for a week from Boiry-Bequerelle. Londoners had first entered Bullecourt village in the battles of 1917, only to be hammered out of it by Ludendorff's men. Above them West Lancashire troops, after bitter fighting, stormed into Hendecourt-lez-Cagnicourt, above Bullecourt, and made an advance towards the catacombed hill position of Riencourt, where the Australians had been held in the early battle. The successes of the English troops brought them into line with the Canadians, who had been waiting for a straighter flank and passing the time by completing the conquest of Pelves, Boiry, Rémy, and breaking German counter-attacking forces.

Above the Canadian Corps, under Sir Arthur Currie, English and Scottish troops also vigorously prepared the coming grand stroke by advancing along both banks of the Scarpe River towards Plouvain, Eterpigny, and Hamblain. Hour by hour the fighting increased in fury as Lossberg poured men down to Douai and Cambrai in the hope of preventing the line from being completely broken. Once more Bullecourt became an inferno of poison gas, blasting explosions, flame, and smoke, in which bodies of grotesque masked figures fought over the old tunnel, with monstrous shapes of steel spitting fire and death, and the roaring barrages churning the ground once more into chaos. Portions of the villages of Bullecourt and Hendecourt were for the last time lost and with them the rising ground of Riencourt.

Savagely fighting, the Middlesex and London Regiments and other metropolitan battalions clung to some of the ruins of Bullecourt, and with bayonet and bomb gradually drove the enemy forces out of the factory and station works by Saturday, August 31st. Greatly helped by "whippet" Tanks that worked close to the redoubts, firing on them with light guns, the Londoners completed nine days of continual battle by an important victory. On their right Liverpool men and Manchester men stormed back to the positions of Ecoust and Longatte, which East County troops had conquered and then lost in the great enemy counter-offensive. On their left other English forces, including heroic Lancashires, recovered Hendecourt, and made Bullecourt secure by driving the enemy from Riencourt rise.

Londoners' nine days' battle

When night fell the British forces stood to battle between the conquered Siegfried line, through which the Hindenburg tunnel ran, and the virgin Wotan switch-line, behind which the thronging enemy had, in the deep, dry cutting of the North Canal by Mœuvres, a third system of strong defences. Some thirteen German divisions were packed into their second zone of works, including at least two divisions immediately released from the Lys front by the evacuation of Kemmel Hill and Bailleul. Hundreds of additional guns were brought down from the north with the fresh infantry, until the attacking forces were in the extraordinary position of being considerably outnumbered by defending forces occupying the strongest modern works in the world.

Sir Arthur Currie, the Canadian commander, had a harder task than that he carried out at Passchendaele Ridge or along the Luce stream by Amiens. He put two fresh divisions in line, if troops could be called fresh after prolonged victorious fighting along the Somme, followed by night marches back to Arras.

Sir Arthur Currie's hard task

Sir Charles Fergusson, commanding the Seventeenth British Corps, which was in action alongside the Canadian Corps, placed the Lancashires and Scots on the right of the Dominion troops, who had on their left an English division to which they were particularly attached.

Everybody in the British Army appreciated the high importance of the action that was opening. Sir John Monash and his Australians were deeply moved by news of the impending stroke by the Dominion troops. There was a very happy union of generous emulation and passionate comradeship between the armed democracies of Canada and Australia.

When Canada was leading the fighting in one of the supreme pitched battles in the war Australia had to help her. Everybody was, indeed, eager to help. Sir Herbert Plumer, with the Second British Army, including an American contingent, began to press the retreating enemy on the Lys front to prevent him detaching more divisions for reinforcing the central battlefield. Sir William Birdwood, with the Fifth British Army, wading back to Neuve Chapelle, struck at the ground by La Bassée and carried it, by way of warning General von Quast that the Lille defences had to be strongly held.

Sir Julian Byng and his victorious Third Army was deeply engaged in the central battle. Some divisions were battling in and around the Hindenburg system, while others were strongly struggling towards it against the main power of Germany. At the end of August the tireless New Zealanders were driving beyond Bapaume towards Haplincourt; the English division alongside them was smashing towards Villers-au-Flos, and other British troops were closing on Le Transloy and Bouchavesnes.

NEW ZEALAND BATTERY MOVING FORWARD TO A NEW POSITION.
The New Zealand Division came in for heavy work during August, 1918. At Puisieux, for example, they had three days' fierce fighting before they were able to strike across the railway to Loupart Wood and close upon Bapaume from the west.

Commonwealth troops. The Omiécourt peninsula was carried, while exploring patrols were vainly trying to discover a practical path for troops through the morasses by Péronne.

In the morning of August 30th the river was passed by Omiécourt, and then, in a long wrestle lasting till midnight, Cléry was won and nearly a mile of ground beyond it. At night more bridges were erected and fresh troops crossed and continued the heavy fighting by Cléry, at the same time linking with other forces to the north.

Storming of Mont St. Quentin

At 5 a.m. on Saturday, August 31st, the main action opened with an extraordinary movement. The enemy expected attack, and had strongly garrisoned the menaced front with men of the Alpine Corps among others. He thought that Sir John Monash would follow a routine course and advance from the south and the west. This course was taken, but at the same time some New South Wales troops made a long march northward and obtained a new way of attack.

Mont St. Quentin was one of the most formidable heights in France. Dominating all the country, it was screened on its south-eastern slopes by a thick wood, protected on the south

Along the Somme, General Debeney, with the First French Army, was fiercely pressing across the river and the Nesle-Noyon line, and, above the Oise, General Humbert was striving to open a path for his cavalry towards Guiscard. Both the First and Third French Armies were converging towards Ham.

In the meantime the Tenth French Army, under General Mangin, gallantly tried to facilitate the success of the First British Army by suddenly resuming the offensive against the army of Carlowitz. General von Lossberg, as has been remarked, avoided the need for reinforcing the Oise and Aisne sector by arranging for his army commander to make a deep, devastating withdrawal to the Hindenburg works by La Fère, St. Gobain, and Craonne. The men he thus immediately saved went to increase the forces with which General von Below endeavoured to defeat the assault on the Wotan line between the Scarpe River and the Hirondelle brook.

"MOPPING UP" IN THE ENEMY TRENCHES.
Daylight patrol of Seaforth Highlanders at the entrance of a German dug-out during an advance on the western front, and (inset) another party entering a dug-out in search of lingering Germans. The soldiers themselves applied the term "mopping up" to this work of clearing captured positions of lurking enemies.

The Australian Imperial Force was in no favourable position to make the enemy Commander-in-Chief despatch a large part of his mass of manœuvre against them instead of against the Canadians. Sir John Monash's men had reached the end of the blind alley on the Santerre plateau, where in the summer of 1916 Marshal Foch's forces had been compelled to wait for the enemy's retirement in the spring of 1917. They were in the old French trenches at Biaches and La Maisonette, facing Péronne, with the marshes and waters of the Somme making a wide moat, across which German machine-gunners maintained a raking fire. Behind the town, from the historic artillery position of Mont St. Quentin, severe gun fire was directed day and night upon the Australian lines and communications. But being faced with an unfavourable position, the inventive, daring Australian commander transformed it into a means of surprising the enemy.

Capture of Cléry

There was a hostile bridge-head at Omiécourt, opposite Cléry, on August 29th, serving as a delaying point against any attempt at a turning movement. It did not delay the

by the wide marsh where the Tortille stream joined the Somme, and covered by the winding tributary along the other flank. In the Franco-Prussian War, as in the later greater struggle, the height had been the key to all the Péronne area. It had saved Péronne from capture and Bapaume from encirclement in 1916.

Yet it took only three hundred Australians, thrusting from the north by Feuillaucourt, to take six hundred and fifty of the garrison of 1,500 troops and break their resistance, while another small body of attackers stormed up from the west and made two hundred and fifty prisoners, and a third force struck between the hill and Péronne and increased the toll of captures. In little more than two hours the New South Wales men were moving on the crest, surveying the rear of the hostile lines behind the unbroken sectors of the Somme front.

This amazing feat of swift audacity provoked at once a panic retreat from Péronne. But the enemy corps commander did not lose his head completely, as had happened in the Santerre battle. He turned every available gun on the lost height and on Feuillaucourt village that English troops had taken, and as the attack had been made without a covering barrage, there having been no time to bring up sufficient guns

GG

THROUGH A BREACHED BARRICADE.
British motor-car by the German barricade erected across the main street of Quéant. Barricade and Quéant were both taken when the Hindenburg line was broken through on September 2nd, 1918.

and arrange the details of a travelling curtain of fire, the strong hostile artillery had the better of it.

In the afternoon, while the hill was made to smoke like a volcano, the collected German reserves stormed back. They recovered Feuillaucourt and attained the summit of the lost pivot of their line, but they could not shake the hold of the New South Wales men on the high slopes. All night the attackers, weary with marching as well as with fighting, clung to their great prize of victory until they were relieved by Victorian troops, who resumed the assault at dawn on September 1st, regained Feuillaucourt and St. Quentin village, and in heavy fighting throughout the day extended over the hill-top.

After a short stand in the quarry the Germans broke and ran, and were overtaken by artillery fire. New South Wales infantry worked into Péronne during this operation, and the hinge of General von Böhn's manœuvres between the neighbourhood of Bapaume and the vicinity of Noyon was wrenched away with alarming violence.

The enemy army group controller had been arranging to make a general stand in front of the North Canal, running from the Hindenburg line at Mœuvres towards Péronne, and extending thence by Nesle to Noyon. By losing Mont St. Quentin he lost the Tortille River line and the canal just by it, and the rear of his forces facing the First French Army was exposed.

Troops from five divisions were captured, including Prussian Guardsmen and men of the Alpine Corps, who had volunteered to hold the height against any attack. British brigades at once exploited the Australian break-through and made a rapid advance to Moislains, in the direction of the former Cambrai salient, while St. Pierre Vaast Wood and Azincourt were taken.

On September 2nd, while the enemy High Command was perturbed over the far-reaching results of the Australian victory, the Canadian Corps and the Seventeenth British Corps broke into and **Vital Wotan** through the strong and more vitally im- **pivot pierced** portant Wotan pivot of the German front.

The Lancashire troops who opened the battle for the Hindenburg switch-line were a pattern of sustained strength. Coming into action towards the end of August, in the violent struggle for the enemy's first line of works, they attacked five times in four days, and made good their advance each time.

In order to get in line with the Canadians for the great pitched battle they had to start the offensive on September 1st by clearing Hendecourt of nests of enemy machine-gunners and snipers, and regaining Riencourt village, to which the Germans had returned in a strong counter-attack.

The Lancashire men closed around Hendecourt at dawn on September 1st, and in the evening of that day they stormed into

Riencourt, winning all the positions needed as jumping-off places. They spent the night in clearing out concealed "pockets" of enemies and organising the great attack; yet at five o'clock in the morning of Monday, September 2nd, they were ready to sweep out on the right of the Canadian divisions through the Drocourt-Quéant, or Wotan, line.

Under so expert a gunner as Sir Henry Horne the artillery work of the forces of attack of the First Army was magnificent. Over ground conquered within a day or two, and so broken that cavalry could not be used, his men brought many heavy guns, as well as numerous field-pieces, skilfully sited them, and stacked ammunition for a tremendous barrage. In the same brief period a very considerable number of Tanks were got into positions of attack in the awful waste of the shattered Siegfried line.

The Germans were also straining to

ONE OF THE RUINED FANES OF NORTHERN FRANCE.
Péronne Cathedral as it was on September 1st, 1918, the day on which the swift, audacious feat of a small force of Australian troops to the north caused the enemy to make a panic retreat from the town. Inset above: The square of Péronne photographed immediately after the Germans had been driven out.

complete their preparations for a great counter-offensive, and they had three fresh divisions assembled, with ten other divisions that had been fighting at Bullecourt, Bapaume, and the neighbourhood, and Staff clerks and odd men of every kind.

The defending forces outnumbered the attacking forces, but the spirit, speed, technique, and material power of the assailants made them irresistible. They clean outraced the enemy in organisation, and overwhelmed him with gun fire and blinded him with **The day of the** smoke. The German gunners put down **Tanks** a heavy barrage, but not in the right place. The Canadian, English, and Scottish infantry were well away, and the German shells burst behind them and behind their storming cars.

It was the day of the Tanks. Without them the battle could not have been won, save at crippling cost. They rolled down paths through belt after belt of heavy barbed-wire, they wrecked machine-gun works, and, reaching over the enemy's special anti-Tank trenches, twelve feet broad at top with space enough at bottom for a horse to travel along, they terrorised the German infantry. General von Below was afraid of the Tanks, and still more apprehensive of their demoralising effect on his men. He had arranged an anti-Tank barrage of armour-piercing bullets and shell, and from every rise of ground his gunners fired at the armour-clad mounted artillery of the British Army. Tanks were maimed or smashed, but many survived, and by the deadly skill of their commanders and gunners made the strongest fortified

AN OBSTACLE THAT VALOUR OVERLEAPED.
Barricade across one of the entrances into Péronne, forced by the Australians when storming into the town on the morning of September 1st, 1918.

including many of the picked men detailed for the intended counter-offensive, were unnerved by their losses under the tremendous Horne barrage and by the appearance of a nightmare multitude of Tanks. Thousands of Germans were thankful to pass as prisoners through their own gun fire.

In the support system the defence was stronger. Yet at Dury village, in the centre of the attacked line, Canadians found the enemy town major and his staff asleep, and surprised by capture a German officer leisurely riding with an orderly back to the line after a period of leave. There was a check of half an hour by the oblong hill by Dury, and the cart-way hollowed into the chalk slope behind it. This sunken lane was lined with caves and rimmed with machine-gun positions, but the Dominion troops carried it, with the windmill, after hard fighting.

At eight o'clock in the morning Dury Hill, commanding the Arras-Cambrai road at a point more than a mile in the rear of the Wotan line, was Canadian property. At this distance in the enemy's communications Canadian light-gun batteries were blazing in action, and half an hour afterwards the traffic of the Dominion transport was proceeding along the highway a thousand yards behind the last ditch of the Wotan

line in the world useless for the purpose for which it had been laboriously constructed.

On a winding front of some twelve miles, from the Scarpe River by Biache-St. Vaast to the Agache stream by Pronville, Englishmen, Canadians, and Scotsmen went forth with their Tanks. The travelling line of shell, just ahead of them, was as perfect as the inventor of the creeping barrage could make it. The Wotan line consisted of two groups of parallel ditches, forming the main and support systems, complicated by machine-gun rear positions in sunken roads in the north, and by a triangle of trenches, pits, and tunnels in the south.

The main system, showing in a line of dull white behind red hedges of rusted wire, was in places about half a mile from the British assembly positions, and for the greater part was carried with remarkable ease and rapidity. The front-line enemy troops,

PÉRONNE: CLEARED OF THE INVADER.
General view of the main square of Péronne as it appeared on September 1st, 1918, when New South Wales infantry worked into the town. In oval : An Australian front-line post in Péronne. The bodies of two German patrols killed by British Lewis gunners were still lying in front of the houses.

works. As Dury Hill rose some two hundred and fifty feet above the field of conflict its tactical importance was great.

South of it, and below the Cambrai road, the Canadians stormed over another long stretch of the second Hindenburg system, which had been hastily constructed in the early spring of 1917, when the first system was partly broken by British attacks. The villages of Villers and Cagnicourt, with the woods of Loison and Bouche, were carried, at a distance of a mile and a half behind the defences which both Ludendorff and Lossberg had regarded as impregnable.

North of the Canadian front of attack English troops admirably facilitated the main thrust. Above the Scarpe River some adventurous Lincolns worked into Valley Wood and fought at the power-station of Biache St. Vaast. The enemy protected the approach to Douai above this point by damming the river and flooding the countryside. He was also secured at Douai from a southern turning movement by the large natural morass of the Sensée stream near Leclus. Here English and Scottish troops overran the

AUSTRALIAN INFANTRY IN ACTION.
Shooting at fleeing Germans under a barrage fire during the attack of the Australian infantry on a portion of the Hindenburg line on September 18th, 1918, and (above) some of the men at the end of that day's advance.

Riencourt. They crowned their victorious career by swerving southwards from the right of the Canadians into the triangular maze by Quéant. The Scottish Lowlanders, who had been fighting forward for a considerable period, also did great work by the intricate junction of the main and switch zones of the Hindenburg defences. When these two worn divisions, including men and officers who had fought day and night without sleep, had broken into the hostile works the Naval Division came decisively into action after a forced march of fourteen miles.

Wotan line by Etaing and Eterpigny, after the Canadian advance, and swung alongside the oversea troops in a further drive towards Récourt Wood and the Sensée Marshes.

Lancashires at Bullecourt

These northern operations, however, were of a gradual, cautious nature, developing an actively defensive flank that served to attract enemy reserves from Douai and guard from any violent side thrust the national army of Canada in the hours of its supreme triumph over the most efficient of military despotisms. The conquerors of Vimy Ridge, Passchendaele Ridge, and the approaches to Roye were no bad judges of the importance of a victory. They regarded their achievements in the final Battle of Arras as something that overshadowed all they had previously accomplished.

Lancashire troops played a great part at Bullecourt and

The endurance of the naval men transformed a serious German reverse into a tragic German disaster. When they arrived the enemy had fallen back from the upper part of the switch-line towards the great cutting of the North Canal. He was inclined to attempt to retrieve his position, even at heavy additional cost in life. Large fresh forces were brought to the rail-head of Marquion, where they formed under the protecting wings of a formation of seventeen fighting aeroplanes. It was evident that they were ordered to make a counter-attack along the Cambrai-Arras road against the Canadian centre. But they did not advance. The German army commander recognised that an irremediable catastrophe had occurred, and he saved his reserve force as his only insurance against complete penetration.

The Naval Division arrived in the afternoon and entered

REMARKABLE PHOTOGRAPH OF THE ATTACK ON THE HINDENBURG LINE.
Attack by Australians on the Hindenburg line on September 18th, 1918, showing the infantry firing at those of the Germans who became visible to them through the smoke and fumes of the bursting barrage shells. The Australians fought forward on that day to the farthest limit of their objective, and even beyond it, and carried the forward trenches of the Hindenburg system beyond Hargicourt, nearly midway between St. Quentin and Cambrai.

"Australian Cavalry"

From a Painting by Lieut. H. S. Power, Australian Official Artist

COLOSSAL GERMAN DUG-OUT.
Elaborate subterranean head-quarters constructed for a German general that became British.

Sir Julian Byng, which for thirteen days had been pressing back the southern wing of the Seventeenth German Army, under General von Below, lengthened again the line of its vehement offensive. In extreme desperation the enemy attempted a counter-attack toward Vaulx, some six miles outside his lost Hindenburg line. Thereby he increased his losses, which included at the end of the day some ten thousand prisoners and about a hundred guns.

When night fell the Seventeenth and Second German Armies began a general retirement to the North Canal for a length of some twenty miles from the Sensée Marsh below Douai to the spur of Mont St. Quentin above the Somme. The terror of the Tank was upon the enemy High Command, and General von Lossberg regarded the deep cutting of the great unfinished canal as the best anti-Tank defence.

Third Army's offensive

The enemy's attack of nerves was a happy event for the men of the Canadian and Seventeenth British Corps. They could have been compelled to conduct a hard and costly struggle in the unbroken country between the rear of the Wotan line and the front of the North Canal front, for they were out of touch with their own heavy batteries and assisted only by some forward light guns, with a four-mile belt of chaos that supply trains had to cross in bringing up shell from the British lines by Arras.

the deep salient created for them above Quéant and the Agache valley. Fighting onward, far ahead of artillery or Tank assistance, and enfiladed from the north, the Drakes, Ansons, Hoods, and Hawkes, with Royal Marines and Royal Irish Rifles, went far and fast. From Inchy Wood they worked steadily forward in the evening towards Inchy village, behind the two zones of the Hindenburg line between Quéant and Mœuvres, and likewise behind the Quéant-Drocourt switch-line. The garrison of Quéant fled without a struggle, but when the Drake Division closed on Pronville some prisoners were taken. The naval men were checked in front of Inchy, and Mœuvres for some days remained, as regards part of its square mile of underground fortress works, in enemy possession.

But the Briton of genius who had thought it worth while to send the Naval Division into battle after a very tiring march was not wholly concerned with the local aspect of the situation he had shaped. As will be seen from a map, the general position was of an extraordinarily paradoxical kind. The British forces were inside both the main and switch systems of the Hindenburg works, while the old British positions outside, by Boursies and Lagnicourt, were occupied by Germans who were still fighting on the Vaulx-Vraucourt hills.

Naval Division's fine work

The enemy forces outside the conquered lines had hastily to retire. Their motor-lorries, guns, and carts crowded along the Bapaume-Cambrai highway towards the bridge across the North Canal below Mœuvres. A considerable number of British gunners had their pieces registered upon the bridge section, and when it was thronged with enemy traffic they opened rapid fire, with observation aeroplanes watching the trapped Teutons and signalling.

Meanwhile, the northern wing of the Third Army, under

With the British forces in such circumstances, Ludendorff, in the days of his power, would have used fifty thousand fresh troops against the temporarily half-spent victors, and kept his guns close to the new line of battle. But Lossberg, suffering from Ludendorff's spendthriftness in German life, had to husband his resources in view of the critical, final phase of the struggle, and his lieutenant withdrew to avoid another action.

For the first time since the Tank offensive at

WITHOUT AND WITHIN.
Front door of the German headquarters, and (in oval) the mess-room of the general and his staff. The dug-out was roofed with huge tree-trunks and concrete ten feet thick.

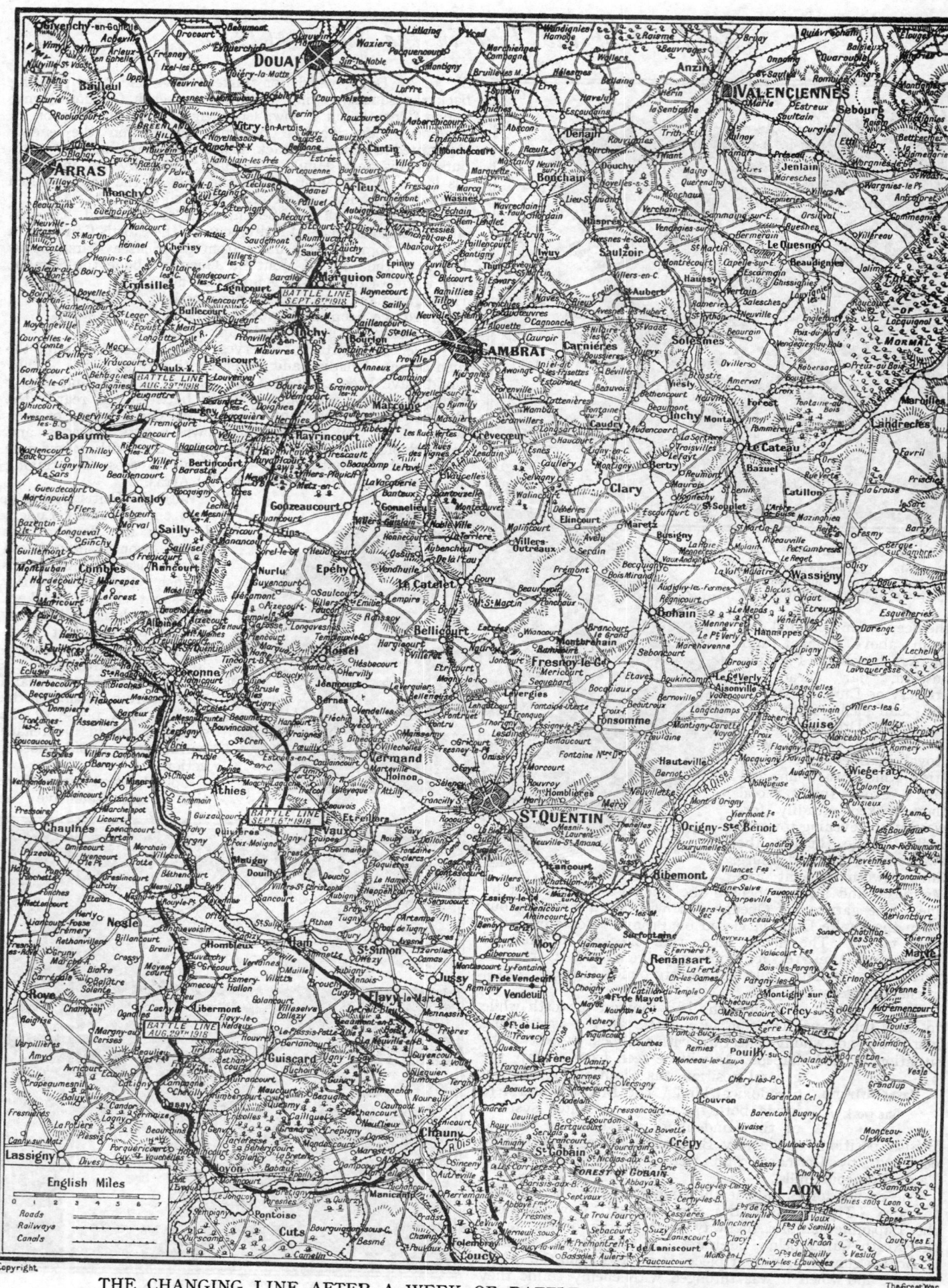

English Miles

Roads
Railways
Canals

THE CHANGING LINE AFTER A WEEK OF BATTLE, AUGUST-SEPTEMBER, 1918.

The closing days of August, 1918, and the opening days of the following month marked important stages in the great eastward movement of the Allies in France. On September 1st Australian troops attacked and captured

286

Mont St. Quentin, immediately north of Péronne, whereupon the enemy retreated from that town. On September 2nd came the dramatic breaking of the Germans' "impregnable" Drocourt-Quéant, or Wotan, line.

Cambrai the British troops advanced into a land of unruined hamlets and farmsteads, and there liberated French civilians who had not seen any allied soldiers, except as prisoners, since the summer of 1914. Saudemont, Rumaucourt, Ecourt St. Quentin, Buissy, and Baralle were taken through the screen of machine-gun rearguards with which the enemy vainly endeavoured to hold the ground.

By September 4th the British line was established along the west bank of the North Canal, and the last objective in an extraordinary series of grand victories was attained.

The Canadians were fighting in Sains, a memorable position on the flank of Sir Julian Byng's early thrust into the Hindenburg system. The Naval Division was meeting with

MERCY AMONG THE RUINS.
British soldiers bringing in a wounded comrade on a wheeled stretcher to a dressing-station in a wrecked building on the western front.

FLOTSAM AND JETSAM FROM AN ADVANCING TIDE.
Busy scene at a Canadian field dressing-station and prisoners' collecting-station in a French village from which the Germans had been driven a few hours before, during the allied advance in the autumn of 1918.

strong opposition from the open slope of the dominant mass of the historic Bourlon Wood. In the burrows of Mœuvres, the scene of heroic exploits by Ulstermen, action was once more proceeding in the old familiar way, with enemy parties working through secret underground passages back to positions from which they had been driven on the surface.

Inchy village was taken, the North Canal was crossed, and a corner of Havrincourt Wood was reached. Southward, by Neuville Boujonval, the troops of the Third Army had a large bridge-head over the canal, which was also crossed between Etricourt and Manancourt by forces that had advanced across the Bapaume-Péronne road. At Moislains the British had another bridge-head over the enemy's canal defences, and the great fighting men of Australia were working forward to the junction of Roisel.

The southern wing of the Australian Imperial Force developed the success of their northern wing by crossing the Somme at St. Christ and Brie and heavily fighting their way to the line of the Péronne-Ham road at Athies. Generally, however, the three victorious British armies, under Sir Henry Horne, Sir Julian Byng, and Sir Henry Rawlinson, resumed an apparent immobility in trench warfare. The exhausted Germans made no counter-attacks of importance, and behind the appearance of quietness a tremendous amount of organising

work went on at fierce speed over the great stretches of conquered ground.

While the new offensive movements were being brilliantly carried out, the Second British Army, under Sir Herbert Plumer, attacked the Fourth German Army, under Sixt von Armin, and made it pay for the mistake of sending too many reinforcements down to General von Böhn. As the Germans were continuing their leisurely retirement towards the Messines Ridge and Armentières, English and Irish troops drove them towards the famous tract of Ploegsteert Wood, and on September 4th captured the tunnelled mound of Hill 63, an observation position of high importance, and recovered the village. There was heavy fighting on the Wytschaete slopes, and the Second and Fifth British Armies swung back to the old front between Ploegsteert and Givenchy, which they began to reorganise for a grand offensive on a surprising scale.

While the five British armies paused to work after fighting, the First, Third, and Tenth French Armies resumed their general pressure upon the half-dazed and staggering masses of invaders. In the night of September 4th General Debeney's men forced the passage of the Somme on a line of six miles by Offey, and, in co-operation with the Australians on their left, battled forward against strong opposition to the Péronne-Ham road. They reached a point four miles from Ham and twelve miles from St. Quentin. In a linked movement the centre of General Fayolle's army group, composed of the men under General Humbert, made an outflanking thrust along the Autrecourt uplands and carried the town of Guiscard. Humbert's cavalry rode into Chauny and extended the advancing line of the Third Army to the same distance from St. Quentin as was the converging force on their left.

General Mangin, whose men were drawing through the lower Forest of Coucy and organising the deep stretch of recovered ground by the Ailette stream, renewed his pressure against the enemy retreating masses. On September 5th the French commander ordered a great bombardment of the

MAIN JUNCTION OF THE HINDENBURG LINE.
General view of Quéant, where the Drocourt-Quéant, or Wotan, switch-line connected with the main Hindenburg line. The intricate triangular maze of fortifications at this junction was decisively broken into by English, Scottish, and Canadian troops on September 2nd, 1918.

wooded slopes in which five German divisions had for a week been fighting against one French division. The enemy forces broke under the gun fire and retreated to the shelter of the main line of the Hindenburg system that stretched down from St. Quentin to the St. Gobain Forest.

This lower Hindenburg line ran in an arc along the western side of the St. Gobain upland from La Fère to Laffaux. Five miles eastward of the St. Gobain summit rose the cone-like hill of Laon, crowned with the glorious cathedral, and grimly surrounded with strong enemy defences. Southward, the ridge of the Chemin des Dames protected it with the Upper Ailette stream and the Aisne and Oise Canal.

Westward was the flooded marsh of the Oise valley, northward the Serre line, and

eastward a Hindenburg switch-line. Against the strongest sector of this intricate circle of defences the Franco-American forces of General Mangin pressed with such effect that the Germans openly acknowledged the great danger to their line, and brought a succession of fresh divisions of high quality to resist the thrust of his army.

When General Mangin's left wing was prevented from giving continual battle by the enemy's withdrawal to the Hindenburg line, on the St. Gobain Hill, he turned again with his right towards the end of the Chemin des Dames, and once more furiously pressed the enemy in a swaying action by Laffaux. In effect, he forced General von Böhn to place his available reserves by the Aisne plateau, so that they could not be used against the French and British forces in front of St. Quentin.

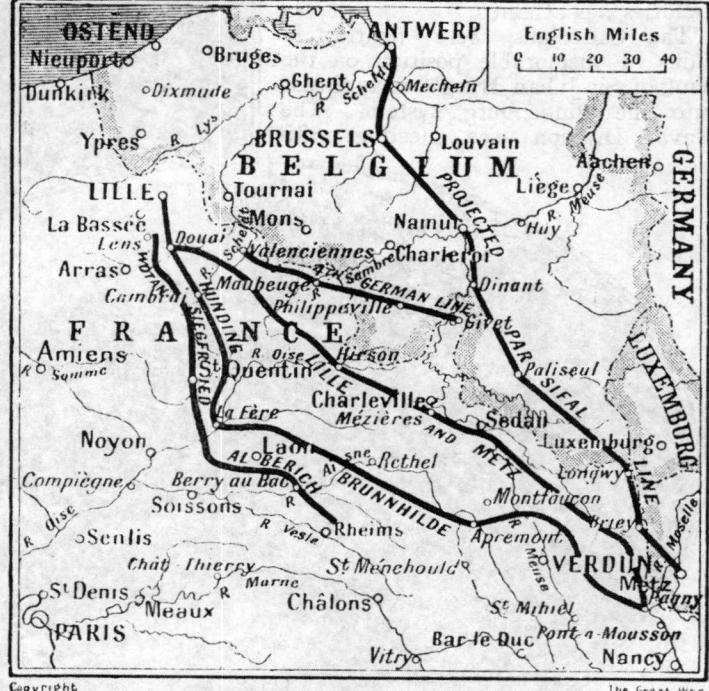

GERMAN DEFENCES IN THE INVADED TERRITORY.
Sketch plan of the five main defensive lines scored by the Germans across France and Flanders. The Siegfried and Alberich lines together constituted what was known as the Hindenburg line. The fourth, the Valenciennes-Givet line and the Parsifal line, were not completed, and their strength remained untested.

In the meantime General Debeney and General Humbert moved their men forward on either side of Ham on September 6th, and the historic old town was recovered. The next day Humbert's troops entered Tergnier, the southernmost point held by the Fifth British Army on March 21st, 1918, and broke over the hills between Tergnier and Ham. The Germans fell back to the Crozat Canal, but their positions were immediately out-flanked by an advance from Ham, achieved by violent fighting along the St. Quentin waterway by Artemps.

Ham was the theatre of a scientific system of destruction. The Germans had spared the picturesque town in their retreat of the previous year, but before they withdrew their main forces from it on September 4th they placed infernal machines in all the houses and connected these with electric firing lines running across the bridges. Long after the last German soldier had crossed the Somme, buttons were pressed miles away, and as the bridges blew into the air the vast conflagration started and gutted every building in the town.

The Germans announced that they intended during their retreat to raze to the ground everything standing on the French soil they occupied. They used the system of electrical control in villages, and in the cases of important buildings they arranged for delayed-action mines to explode when the firing-wires were cut.

COMPREHENSIVE VIEW OF MARSHAL FOCH'S "PINCERS" STRATEGY.
Diagram drawn on map to explain Marshal Foch's strategetic plans in 1918. The inmost pincers comprised the British attack on St. Quentin and the French upon Rheims; the centre pair included the British operations about Cambrai and the French in Champagne; the outermost, largest, pair embraced the Anglo-Belgian offensive in Flanders and the American and French assaults upon the Meuse.

On the road from Puisieux to Bapaume, wrecked in the fierce battles of August, 1918.

General Sir Arthur Currie, the Canadian Corps Commander, inspecting an artillery column.

Fighting in the heart of Valenciennes: Canadian trench-mortar in action.

Entry of Canadians into Valenciennes: Crossing the Scheldt Canal under heavy fire.

Hand in hand in liberated Valenciennes: French childhood's trust in the Canadian soldiers.

Canadian patrol advancing in Valenciennes, covered by a Lewis gun sited amidst the ruins.

Canadian brigadier, off on a reconnoitring tour in a "whippet" Tank, issues parting orders.

The brigadier sets out in his Tank, which was heavily shelled during his reconnaissance.

CHAPTER CCLXXI.

THE TURN OF THE TIDE IN THE WEST.
IV.—The Opening American Victory at St. Mihiel.
By Edward Wright.

British and French Armies Break North Canal Line—German Infantry become a Force of Gunners—Rain Checks Allied Advance—Austria Tries to Open Peace Negotiations—President Wilson Calls for Three Million More Men—The New "Contemptibles" of General Pershing Prepare an American Battle—Foch Requires Paris-Nancy Railway Line—Importance of St. Mihiel Salient to Enemy —Enormous German Defensive Works Strengthening Extension of Metz Positions—Teutons Trapped while Removing their Guns —Skilful Converging Thrusts on Thiaucourt—Blinding of Mont Sec and Storming of Rupt de Mad—Brilliant Work of American Tank Brigades—Hard Fighting for Cliffs of Lorraine—Austro-Hungarian Division Breaks and Surrenders—Aerial Attack on Jammed Fugitives on Vigneulles Road—General Pershing Menaces Metz and Prepares New Surprise Across the Meuse.

THE Canal du Nord, or North Canal, which the enemy adopted as his principal line of defence in the first week of September, 1918, was almost completed just before the war broke out. It was constructed to carry English coal from the Channel ports to Paris without sending barges round by St. Quentin. The canal was some fifty-four miles long, with a bottom width of thirty feet and a water depth of seven and a half feet. The first section of twenty-five miles ran from Arleux, on the Sensée Canal, to the Somme Canal below Péronne. This was the new line on which the enemy endeavoured to stand against the First, Third, and Fourth British Armies after his Wotan system had been pierced by Canadian, English, and Scottish forces.

The second section of the North Canal ran from the neighbourhood of Péronne to the neighbourhood of Ham for a distance of twelve miles. It was broken after a fierce and long struggle by the First French Army, under General Debeney. The third section stretched for seventeen miles from the Somme Canal below Ham to the Oise River at Noyon, and was an obstacle to the Third French Army, under General Humbert. Strong rearguards, that interlocked their fire and used single cannon as infantry guns, defended the canal.

The German armies still remained remarkably strong in the machinery of battle. A light machine-gun of

the Maxim type operated by two men became the weapon of the infantry. With every machine-gun there were two gunners and six riflemen, whose duty it was to protect the gunners and to take their places if they were killed or wounded. Automatic rifles were largely used as an answer to the Lewis gun. Heavy machine-guns were employed as before by special machine-gun corps, but the lighter weapon, for the standardisation of which steps had been taken immediately after the First Battle of the Somme, was produced by the hundred thousand for the purpose of transforming all the German infantry into a force of gunners.

Had it not been for the progress made by the Allies in the standardised output of light, fast Tanks and in the training of tens of thousands of officers and men as commanders and gunners of the new storming cars, the extraordinary use which the enemy made of light machine-guns with a sustained power of fire might possibly have saved him from defeat.

When, at the end of the first week in September, on the central battlefield, the Germans reached the manifold British defensive systems used by the Third and Fifth British Armies in the spring of the year, the resistance of the enemy became strong and determined. The countryside was admirably suited to machine-gun defence, as indeed he German armies learnt in he previous March, when they lost most of their best men through the sweeping

GENERAL HUNTER LIGGETT.
The First American Army in France was formed under General Pershing's command in August, 1918. Two months later a second army was formed, when the first was placed under General Liggett, General Pershing remaining Commander-in-Chief.

SUPPLIES FOR AMERICAN FIGHTING MEN.
Convoy of American supplies going forward along a road in the back areas to where the men of the First American Army had taken up their positions in the battle-front.

fire of the Vickers and Lewis guns of the British infantry. It was a land of rolling downs, seamed with winding cloughs, the local French name for which was " riots." The North Canal ran down one of these cloughs, and beyond it were the broad inclines and rounded summits of chalk, dappled with considerable stretches of woodland, like Havrincourt Wood, Holnon Wood, and Bourlon Wood.

The German machine-gun parties thus had wide fields of fire, and the task of driving them back without serious loss in attack was one of considerable difficulty. In a general way British and French machine-gun and rifle patrols steadily and cautiously worked forward against the enemy rearguard line, while the wilderness between the Somme front and the Hindenburg system was being rapidly crisscrossed again with railways and good roads, and dotted with shell-dumps, Nissen huts, store places, and other camouflaged preparations for the continuing offensive.

The enemy gunners won time for their sappers to make trip-mines, delayed-action mines, and a variety of booby-traps similar to those placed in the same **Rain checks** country immediately previous to the retire-**allied advance** ment to the Hindenburg line in the spring of 1917. The Germans, however, had less time at their disposal than they had won eighteen months before, and they were forced back so hastily that they left long stretches of conquered roads in good condition.

Rain, however, set in on September 7th, 1918, and after first pleasantly laying the foul, choking dust, it broadened the dammed brooks and streams, which the enemy was using as protection against Tank attack, from the Trinquis brook below Douai to the marshland of the Oise River at La Fère. The downpour continued for a week, and seriously hindered the movements of the allied forces. Aerial operations at times became impossible, and traffic, especially along the parish roads and farm-tracks, where battery teams were hauling the guns forward, was impeded.

The forces of the First British Army rested by the upper section of the North Canal, preparing for a grinding advance towards Cambrai. Divisions of the Third Army moved up to attack the hills and woods between Havrincourt and Epéhy, while the Australian and British divisions of the Fourth Army worked towards the railway line connecting Cambrai and St. Quentin, where old British positions by Holnon Wood connected with a new, strong outwork system of the Siegfried line.

At Vaux, some two miles below Holnon Wood, the

Fourth British Army connected with the First French Army which had encircled Ham. As General Debeney's highly-skilled troops approached the old battle positions of the Fifth British Army there was no further room for the deployment of the splendid Third French Army, under General Humbert, which had done so much to save the situation in the previous March.

General Humbert, therefore, began to withdraw his forces, and Marshal Foch detached his Third Army for service as a mass of manœuvre, leaving the First French Army to swing round St. Quentin and along the Oise, in line with General Mangin's Franco-American divisions, that remained one of the principal spear-heads of the Grand Alliance, still directed against the St. Gobain Massif.

PRESIDENT POINCARÉ IN REWON TERRITORY.
The President of the French Republic chatting with some old Frenchwomen when visiting a town recently freed from enemy occupation. The women had remained throughout the occupation and the subsequent fighting.

At the beginning of the second week in September, as the Germans were carrying out their retirement in steady order, under increasing artillery and machine-gun fire, the Australians and British troops of the Fourth Army made a leap upon the important railway junction of Roisel. They took all the line of the railway as far as Vendelles in the south, near Vermand, and began to encircle Vermand at Villevèque, due west of St. Quentin.

Above Roisel the line was again broken, and the old battle villages of the 16th Irish Division and the 21st British Division —Villers-Faucon and Sainte-Emilie—were reconquered. The co-operating French forces closed on Etreillers and Fluquières, which also were British battle positions during the fighting in the spring of the year, and half encircled St. Quentin below Contescourt, a former Ulster position, and by Essigny Station.

The rain increased to a tempestuous deluge on September 9th, but instead of further hindering British and French operations it helped them. Using the windy, drenching downpour in the same way as a fog or smoke barrage, the English and New Zealand forces of Sir Julian Byng's Third Army advanced against the long ridge between Havrincourt Wood and Peizière village. Here the enemy was reinforced by a fresh division, as he expected that General Byng would exploit the victory on the Wotan line by resuming the operations against Cambrai from the direction of Havrincourt Wood.

On a front of some nine miles the indefatigable British divisions, which had advanced from the Ancre and Bapaume areas, came into touch with strong German forces, and attacked them in the driving rain, taking Gouzeaucourt Wood and entering the village, storming up Chapel Hill, and increasing the stretch of conquered ground in Havrincourt Wood. A fresh German division, the 201st, was ordered to counter-attack with a dismounted German cavalry division, and at first refused to do so. When at last it was led forward it recovered some of the ground, but lost it again when the British and New Zealand troops returned to the attack. Another enemy force was then employed to recover the lost spurs, but it failed completely to get through the machine-gun and artillery barrage thrown before it.

Enemy's delaying counter-attacks   The following morning the British advanced forces resumed their exploring attacks, and drove in towards Epéhy, but as the Royal Air Force was blown from the sky by a gale, and prevented from photographing the enemy's positions by thick weather, operations were suspended.

Thereupon, General von der Marwitz in turn resumed his delaying counter-attacks, and in places forced the British line back from Epéhy, after being defeated in Gouzeaucourt Wood. At dawn on September 11th the advanced forces of the Third Army struck again, and at Trescault reached the old British trenches running along the crest of the ridge. But some German machine-gunners on a spur between

Trescault and Beaucamp maintained a sweeping fire that prevented the gain being extended to Villers-Plouich.

On the right of the British front the Australians carried the line forward to Holnon Wood, on the slopes overlooking St. Quentin, and closed round the end of the long, straight road from Amiens at Vermand. Here the enemy continued to give ground to both the British and French forces, but he stood in determined strength by Havrincourt Wood and Gouzeaucourt, remembering with what ease Sir Julian Byng had broken the Hindenburg line in this sector in the previous November. His long-range guns searched the British back areas for a distance of thirty miles, **Austria's peace overtures** showing he was again organised for a pitched battle, and raiding-parties tested the lines of both the First and Third British Armies along the upper section of the North Canal and in the Gouzeaucourt-Epéhy sector.

This was the time when the Foreign Minister of Austria-Hungary, in collaboration with Admiral von Hintze, the new German Secretary for Foreign Affairs, made an attempt to open negotiations for a peace by compromise. The Majority parties in the Reichstag proposed a return to the pacific ideas they had abandoned after the Brest Litovsk treaty of conquest with the Bolshevist leaders of Russia. It was known that General von Ludendorff was beginning to despair, and that Hindenburg and Lossberg, though much less subject to oscillations of temperament, were growing anxious about the increasing strength of the United States armies. From their point of view they had to recover the initiative before the American forces were fit to conduct a great battle.

DETACHMENT OF AMERICAN TROOPS LEAVING CAMP FOR THE FRONT.

In the middle of the second week in September, 1918, trained American troops were arriving in France at the rate of about three hundred thousand a month. By the same date thirteen million more Americans registered for service, from whom three million recruits were selected, bringing the total number of men trained and in training in the forces of the United States to over five millions. It was then that Austria tried to open peace negotiations.

FOLLOWING UP THE RETREATING GERMANS.
Heavy American artillery passing through a shattered town in France, on its way to take up new positions for harrying the enemy retiring before the relentless pressure of the allied armies.

President Woodrow Wilson called for more men, and enlarged the age for military service to eighteen years and forty-five years. By the middle of the second week in September another thirteen million Americans registered for service. From them were selected three million more recruits, bringing the total number of men trained and in training in the forces of the United States to more than five millions.

Trained men were still arriving in France at a rate of about three hundred thousand a month, outbalancing every eight weeks the utmost recruitment that Germany could obtain in a year from the boys she gathered in her barracks.

Indeed, the number of picked trained men in the prime of life who every month entered the finishing training schools in France constituted a finer fighting force than the German Command could hope to organise in the course of a year from growing lads reaching the age for military service. Germans realised that their country would fail in manufacturing and feeding power, in the coming peace, if the High Command exhausted the boyhood as well as the manhood of the nation. This was the reason why Admiral von Hintze, acting as agent of the directors of the General Staff, endeavoured to open negotiations with the Allies. His attempt
German Staff to arrive at a peace by compromise was
still confident utterly vain, for the Teutonic governing classes, while intriguing in all directions, were still bent upon ending the war in a profitable manner, according to Prussian tradition.

Large as were the arriving forces of United States troops, they excited no immediate apprehension in the enemy. For various reasons the German military authorities affected to contemn the newly-armed people of the most powerful of republics. In the first place, they regarded the expedient of brigading American troops with French and British troops as a practical confession by the most experienced allied commanders of the inferiority of American cadres and staff-work. Far from seeing in this arrangement merely a temporary measure for meeting a perilous situation, the German Staff reckoned that it gave them the true value of the new American armies.

The vehement fighting power shown by the United States forces in the Second Battle of the Marne was, in the enemy's opinion, explained by the fact that the small Regular Army had been sent into action before any considerable part of the large National Army was ready for action. This was what had happened in the case of the British forces.

An interval of nearly two years had elapsed between the engagement of the regular British divisions and the opening of a grand offensive by the new British armies. Great progress in intensive training had been made since then, and the German authorities did not expect that two years would elapse before General Pershing set a great army in motion; but they calculated that the American Commander-in-Chief would accomplish nothing of high importance with his men until the ground dried in the spring of 1919.

Unfortunately for the enemy's calculations, the American troops that had been in action, from Cantigny to Juvigny Hill, at a cost of 50,000 casualties, were largely composed of freshly-trained men. The regular soldiers formed a general framework. The new men had suffered in places

LINKING UP WITH THE ADVANCING LINE.
American linemen fixing up their telephone wires in a French village for the maintaining of the most rapid means of communication with troops that were moving forward on the western front.

from lack of experience, as friend and foe had done when beginning, but they had been quick to learn, and without abating their impetuosity in attack, which had elicited the admiration of veteran Australians co-operating with them along the northern bank of the Somme, they acquired the wariness needed to defeat the hopes the enemy had founded upon his adoption of the light machine-gun as the general infantry weapon.

With their enormous machine-gun fire power the enemy High Command not merely hoped to shatter the American waves of attack in another and greater Gommecourt battle, but eventually to pierce the Lorraine front of the Franco-American forces, and thereby convince the Associated Powers that a settlement by negotiation was inevitable. The extraordinary strain under which General von Lossberg allowed his divisions to struggle against the British and French armies between the Scarpe and Aisne Rivers was endured with the ultimate object of saving men for a mass of manœuvre to break through to Nancy.

During the first Somme campaign General von Lossberg, with General von Armin and General von Böhn, had let part of the German forces be worn down almost to exhaustion, yet without breaking, in order to obtain men for invading Rumania and renewing the attack on Russia. Lossberg was once more attempting to economise defensive force along the Hindenburg system, and although his second essay was not very successful in the troubled period when he took over control from Ludendorff, neither he nor Hindenburg was inclined to despair of recovering the initiative.

This scheme of the enemy did not, as it developed, escape the attention of Marshal Foch. While incessantly pressing the Germans between the Yser and the Meuse, and there extending the pincer form of attack against them, the Allied Commander-in-Chief prepared a terrific, direct counter-stroke to the threatened blow from Lorraine. In the meantime he set the First American Army the task of clearing the ground along the northern sector of the eastern frontier. Between the entrenched **First American Army's task** camps of Verdun and Toul the enemy had driven a wedge across the Meuse at St. Mihiel on September 25th, 1914, when the main French forces were occupied in meeting a turning movement on the Somme.

Road and railway were cut between Toul and Verdun, and the enemy obtained control of some of the most important French lines of communication. Verdun was left with only a narrow-gauge line of supply, which condition provoked a prolonged assault on the fortress in 1916, during which a new railway was constructed by Révigny. But the hostile salient of St. Mihiel was a menace rather to Toul and Nancy than to the northern frontier fortress, and as such the enemy seems to have intended to use it for the action he designed in Lorraine.

The Paris-Nancy trunk line, feeding the central sectors of the French front, was cut by Commercy by hostile batteries in the St. Mihiel wedge. The traffic had for years to be diverted southward by Gondescourt, taking more time and diminishing the French railway power, especially during enemy aerial attacks on lines of communication. Marshal Foch needed the **Paris-Nancy** Paris-Nancy main line in full working **railway line** order to increase his power of conducting offensives from Verdun and from Nancy. The American operations against St. Mihiel, though apparently of local importance only, were a declaration of a return to strategic aims of an alarming kind.

There was an implied threat of cutting the German armies from their chief Lorraine base. This had been one of the original schemes of Marshal Joffre that he attempted in August, 1914. Marshal Foch, who as commander of the Twentieth Corps had fought his first battle in Lorraine and won an army command by preventing complete disaster there, had it in his mind to arrange to fight his last battle in Lorraine. Marshal Joffre had returned to his Lorraine scheme, after the defeat of the enemy's first operations for the Channel ports. But the French commander could not, for lack of heavy howitzers, reconquer the St. Mihiel

MAINTAINING THE CONSTANT STREAM OF MEN AND MATERIAL FROM THE UNITED STATES.
Motor transports, laden with baggage, moving off from the ship's side at a European port of arrival of American troops. The steady flow of United States forces to Europe was maintained at a high level and without any diminishing when, in the early autumn of 1918, came signs of the enemy's approaching collapse. The American effort was maintained at its high pitch while any element of doubt remained as to the attainment of the end in view.

positions, and so clear the way for a resumption of the eastern offensive.

In the winter of 1914 and the spring of 1915 the generals of the French armies along the heights of the Meuse made strong attempts to conquer the salient, and the fighting in the Bois le Prêtre, Apremont Forest, and Les Eparges Hill was of fierce intensity. But the slight dents formed at heavy cost in the enemy's line were of little importance. The Allies had not the means of breaking the German front, and when they obtained heavy artillery, Marshal Joffre and his lieutenants preferred to concentrate in Champagne. St. Mihiel remained an obstacle on the eastern border, and until Marshal Foch arrived at supreme command no further strength was spent in essaying to remove the check to operations against Metz and the threat to the Nancy sector.

As soon as the first United States forces were ready to go in line the commander of the Allies placed them between St. Mihiel and Pont-à-Mousson, where the enemy attacked them at Seicheprey and was checked by a gallant counter-attack. For months part of the American forces studied, by observation

FRENCH FLAGS IN ST. MIHIEL AFTER FOUR YEARS.
Children of St. Mihiel escorting French officers through the town and waving the Tricolour. The enemy drove a wedge across the Meuse at St. Mihiel on September 25th, 1914, and the salient remained in German hands until swept by the American army under General Pershing on September 12th, 1918.

and aerial photography, every detail of the difficult wooded hill country between them and Metz. On their right they were only ten miles from the forts of the enemy's great camp, but the ground in front of them was of a terribly strong nature.

The Teutons, after holding it, by methods of open-field warfare against the forces of two French armies, employed all their growing science in fortification upon this extension of the Metz defences. Their last work of importance was the construction, in the spring of 1917, of a Hindenburg line along the base of the salient, to guard against a surprise offensive reaching the most important of their railway centres and the ironfields by Metz, from which their material for munitions was largely obtained. Metz and its neighbourhood formed the most sensitive sector of the German front.

General Fuchs grows anxious

Owing to the extraordinary development in machinery and methods of assault no salient was safe from being rapidly overrun. General Fuchs, commanding the enemy forces between Verdun and Metz, became anxious in regard to his advanced positions, as the divisions of Major-General Hunter Liggett, in command of the First American Army, collected from the Ourcq, Marne, and Aisne along the heights of the Meuse.

Either by design or mischance, an inkling of the intended movement round St. Mihiel reached the Germans. It was talked about too freely, and in the second week of September the German commander began to prepare an evacuation of the salient by withdrawing his heavy artillery towards the rear of the Hindenburg line at Pagny. He had a division of picked Austro-Hungarian troops to strengthen his right flank below Combles, but a large body of German infantry remained in the menaced salient when the guns of the attack opened a tremendous fire in the early morning of Thursday, September 12th, 1918.

It was at 1 a.m., in rain, wind, and darkness, that the American artillerymen revealed the skill they had acquired in the handling of guns of all kinds. Across both sides of the salient, round a line of some thirty-three miles, they hammered the garrison of sixty thousand men for four hours. When the action of the American infantry and caterpillar-cars opened at 5 a.m. the enemy's defensive barrage was of exceptional feebleness. The Germans were trapped in more ways than one.

They were caught with both their heavy and light guns crowding in motion along the two roads, by St. Benoit village and Thiaucourt town, that led from the overwhelmed salient to the extension of the Hindenburg line above Jaulny and Dampvitoux. Many pieces were damaged by the prolonged tornado of shell, and few were able to turn about and maintain anything like curtain fire owing to the immediate lack of ammunition. Fresh shell-dumps were being arranged behind the Hindenburg line,

MARKET-PLACE, ST. MIHIEL, AFTER THE LIBERATION.
By mid-day of September 13th, 1918, M. Clemenceau, with General Pershing, General Pétain, and Mr. Baker, the United States Secretary of War, were able to visit the town, and found the liberated population singing and weeping for joy in the market-place.

BIRD'S-EYE VIEW OF AN AMERICAN CAMP IN THE WOODED ARGONNE.

This singular photograph was taken from an aeroplane flying over the Forest of the Argonne when a period of trench warfare was giving way to one of movement. It shows an American encampment upon a steep slope once covered with coppice growth, but now boasting only a few shrivelled trees.

and old dumps were being removed from the valleys between St. Mihiel and Thiaucourt. In the meantime the gunners were practically impotent.

Instead of being able to cover the retreat of the infantry they had to ask the foot to fight and save the guns. The nice timing of General Pershing's operations saved his men from the German guns, and also compelled the German infantry of six divisions to remain and fight without artillery support. The Americans first advanced on a front of some twelve miles against the southern side of the salient, between the Moselle River by Pont-à-Mousson and the dominating promontory of Mont Sec by Xivray village.

Near the Moselle were large, deep quarries which the enemy had so strongly organised that they could not be

Skilful thrusts on Thiaucourt

carried by direct assault. They were outworks of the Pagny line, and made especially difficult of access by the mass of unmoved artillery immediately protecting the girdling forts of Metz. American troops, however, gradually worked round the quarries, clearing the way for a further advance over the Norroy cliff by the river.

For the most part the ground over which they had to fight was unknown to officers and men, but their businesslike Staff had prepared map sections drawn in clear detail, with bright colours, showing every feature in a manner easily understood. A remarkable system of telephone communications, with the best women operators from New York and Chicago working the central exchange, kept divisional and other staffs in close connection with the advancing forces. Team-work was also promoted by the activities of the largest gathering of aircraft collected for battle on any front. In addition to United States squadrons and French formations, there were British and Italian airmen, and the Royal Independent Air Force powerfully assisted.

In spite of the rain and high wind, the allied airmen went up, and under the roof of cloud, broken in the course of the day by bursts of sunshine, held the air. Some Germans were equally adventurous, and in a new Fokker machine of remarkable quality tried to check the aerial operations. The American champion, Lieutenant Putnam, was killed near Thiaucourt by a German whose machine he had set on fire ; but hundreds of other allied pilots continued his work and quickly cleared the sky above the battlefield of enemy aeroplanes and kite balloons. It was on this day that the Liberty motor was first put to a great test.

Preceded by contact machines, the infantry waves and lines of Tanks drove into the ravines, through the fir woods, and over the ridges. On the left of the quarries by the Moselle the progress of the storming cars was hindered by a wooded steep, but the troops battled onward without the help of their travelling artillery and won their objectives. The light Tanks, however, were of high general service. Farther along the line, where the land was more open, they manœuvred upon enemy machine-gunners, riflemen, and front-line artillerymen, and broke a path of victory towards the Thiaucourt road. Forty-five minutes after the infantry and cars began to struggle through the streaming mud the first villages were taken.

One of the hardest routes of advance was the Rupt de Mad,

Blinding of Mont Sec

a clough running to Thiaucourt from Seicheprey, between the large ridge by which St. Baussant hamlet nestled, and the sombre, majestic mass of Mont Sec. Mont Sec was a natural fortress, 1,200 feet high, from which the enemy commanded all the country as far as Pont-à-Mousson, and by artillery fire cut for four years the Paris-Nancy railway. It overlooked the American positions by Seicheprey and, by reason of its deep shelters and long fields of plunging fire, enabled some Germans to resist and save the central line of retreat by the Vigneulles road. French gunners, however, kept Mont Sec completely blinded by a smoke barrage while the American attacks converged on Thiaucourt.

There was also heavy fire, from machine-guns and automatic rifles from the St. Baussant promontory, against the right flank of the Seicheprey force. This was beaten down

as daylight broadened. With light railways of supply working to extreme capacity, feeding guns of all kinds, that were loaded with rhythmic intensity, an enormous torrent of shell blasted away opposition. Most of the shells were fitted with the new fuse that prevented the high explosive from excavating a deep hole and directed the force of the expanding gas over the surface of the ground.

It would have been awkward for Tank drivers if their own creeping barrage transformed the enemy's territory into a moon-like crater land. It would have been equally awkward for the infantry of attack if their gunners had to abandon the use of high explosive against strong, deep entrenchments, and return to showery demonstrations of the primitive age of shrapnel bombardments, in order to leave the ground undisturbed for operations by the new chariots of war. The new fuse, of which the enemy had made large use in his spring offensive, was a perfecting element in the Allies' new Tank tactics.

After serving their apprenticeship in the craft of Renault car offensives under General Mangin and other French masters of war, the United States Tank brigades greatly distinguished themselves in the St. Mihiel battle. One victorious force of forty-five cars lost only one of their number by the time they reached their objectives, and this one was not lost but only stuck in the mud.

With the aid of Tanks, contact aeroplanes, a mighty mass of stationary batteries, and numerous guns that moved behind them, the southern American divisions achieved a decisive success at half-past eleven in the morning of September 12th. They reached close to Thiaucourt, one of the two key positions near the base of the salient by the Meuse.

The enemy's rear was enveloped by the Rupt de Mad. The longer he resisted along the upper part of the ravine the more men he would lose. General Pershing was not wanting in the art of enticement. He was an American of French stock, mingled by generations of marriages with the British element in the United States. He used the fierce impetuosity of his men in a temperate manner, allowing them full career in the direction of the communication of Thiaucourt, but rather holding them back in the neighbourhood of St. Mihiel.

Brilliant U.S. Tank brigades

Immediately round St. Mihiel, where the enemy had a small bridge-head over the Meuse River, the American Commander-in-Chief employed French Colonial troops. They had little to do but to wait and help gather the harvest of victory. They began to worry the German garrison by raids, some three hours after the southern American attack opened, but they refrained all the day from breaking into the town. On the western side of the salient, stretching from Fresnes to the Meuse River, another French contingent formed part of the First American Army in the first of its great engagements.

These French crack troops, including the Chasseurs-à-Pied, who had helped the Fifth British Army between the Somme and the Oise, were actively employed. The dismounted cavaliers of France were all practically volunteers for death. Officered by the best modern blood of the country, such as sons of Maurice Barrès and Clemenceau, they were originally attached in separate bodies to each large French formation for use in supreme emergency. Alongside United States forces they attacked on a front of eight miles by Les Eparges, Combres, and the Grand Tranchée Calonne. The opening of this operation was delayed for a period of three hours by order of the American commander, who did not wish to alarm the enemy on both sides of the field of battle until he had won a position of advantage in the southern sector.

By eight o'clock in the morning the situation was ripe for the second movement of envelopment. This second movement was more difficult, and the delay in carrying it out was partly designed to draw General von Fuchs' local reserve towards the Thiaucourt ground, where the success of the attack was assured, and thus facilitate the thrust into the cliffs of Lorraine, between the Orne River and the Verdun outworks.

The German had tunnelled into the high hills and burrowed beneath the upland forests. Since the fierce wrestle in the early part of 1915 he had not only elaborated his works but had enlarged his ground by pressing towards Verdun from the south-east during the prolonged action of the northern line. General Pershing and his soldiers had therefore in some ways a more difficult task than that which General Sarrail and his men of the Army of Verdun had tried to carry out. But the American commander possessed more troops and larger reserves, and they inherited all the improvements in tactics and in mechanism which the Allies had purchased in the struggles of four years.

General Pershing had not been greatly pleased when his First Army was temporarily scattered as a reinforcing material among French and British organisations. He wanted to launch his corps in action as soon as possible, under their own Staff, for various reasons. A great American victory was calculated to produce a profound effect upon the mind of the German people, in conjunction with the statements of the immense regular monthly arrivals of United States forces in France. It would **Moral effect of** dissipate all the legends of American ineffec- **the victory** tiveness which the German authorities were still busily spreading. By an ironic coin- cidence, Admiral von Hintze was oratorically endeavouring to convince the Austrian public of the worthlessness of the new American Army on the day of the American victory. Moreover, General Pershing had a duty to his men and nation. His troops had to give battle in their own way, directed by their own Staff and controlled by their own commander, as a matter of honour, prestige, and continuing tradition.

When we have lost a hundred thousand men (wrote an American private from the bloody field of the Ourcq River, where Joyce Kilmer, the poet, fell) we shall have trained our new officers. Then you will see what we can do.

By the time the American Commander-in-Chief had his way his forces had gained by their lengthened period of amalgama- tion with the veterans of the Grand Alliance. They combined veteran qualities with a comparative freshness of temper, making them consciously superior to the average German. In the attack upon the Lorraine heights, which was at least as difficult a job as the conquest of Dead Man Hill on the other side of the Meuse, that held the strongest of German armies up for months in the spring **Teutonic troops** of 1916, the Americans and their French **quite outclassed** comrades were magnificently successful. A German Landwehr division attempted a strong move- ment back to the old battle hill of Combres; but the terrific machinery of the forces of assault, joined to the valorous persistence of the men, completely overcame the German and Austro-Hungarian garrison. The Austro-Hungarians were much praised in official reports for their stubbornness in defence, but this praise was merely lubricating oil for the wheels of German intrigue in Vienna. Picked though the troops of the Dual Monarchy were, they were completely and quickly overthrown, half the division being captured.

All the morning the critical struggle went on against the many machine-gun positions among the hills between the Combres cliff and Seuzey ravine. Progress was delayed for some time, yet the vehement storming troops got ahead of their programme, and early in the afternoon reached their objectives for the day. Everywhere the Americans were well ahead of the step-by-step time-table of advance arranged by their commander. By half-past four on Thursday afternoon the battle was won, and the only remaining problem concerned the number of prisoners and guns that could be taken by the pincers closing from Dommartin and Thiaucourt.

The enemy was everywhere in retreat, and making desperate efforts to get his artillery along the Vigneulles road. It was an impossible task. The rains of the previous days, which

AWAITING THE ORDER TO PRESS FARTHER FORWARD IN PURSUIT.
American troops and supply waggons halted in a well-nigh obliterated town in the eastern half of the St. Mihiel salient in September, 1918. They were waiting for the word to go on in support of comrades who were "pinching" the enemy out of the salient before pressing him back along the Moselle.
II

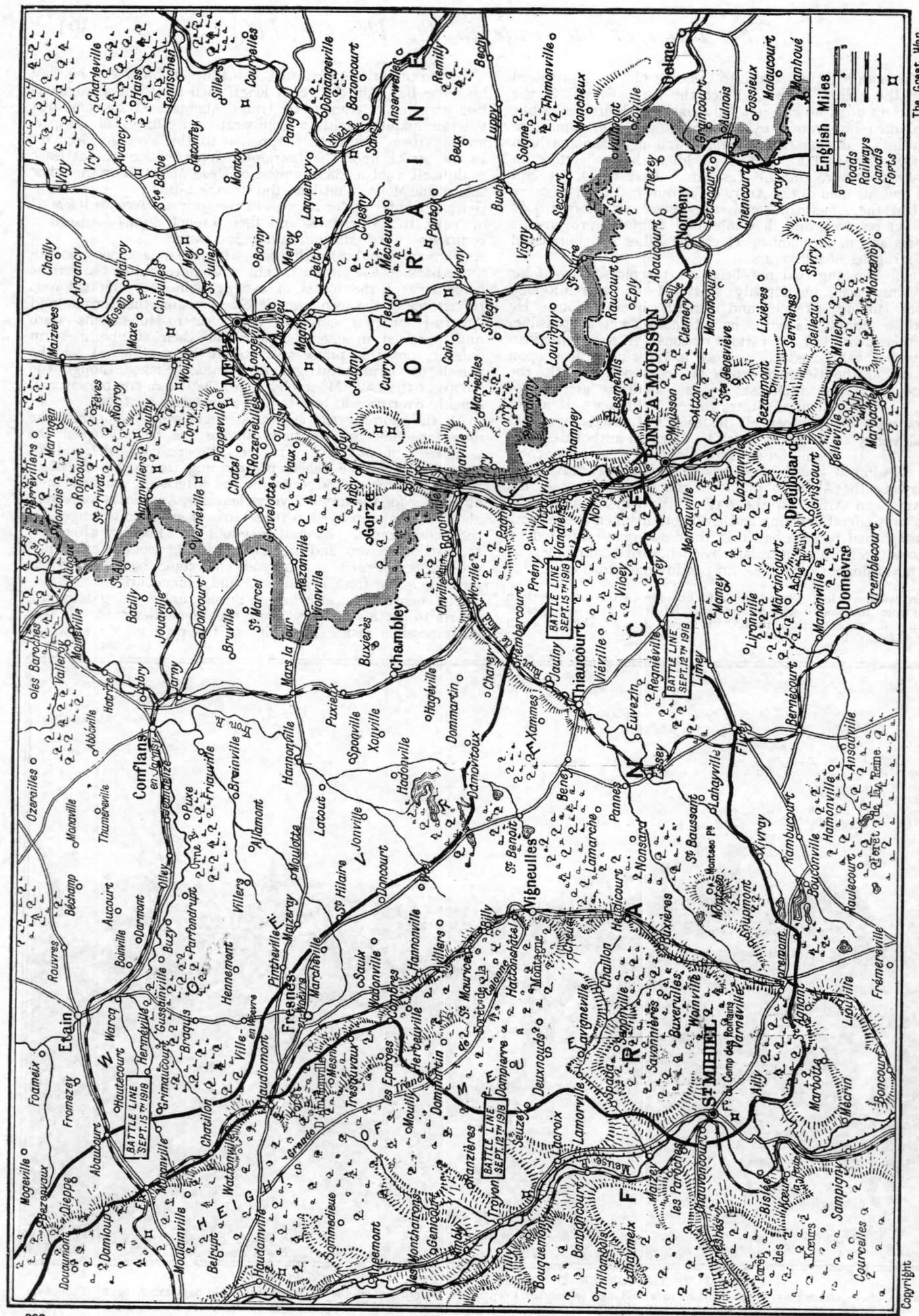

BATTLEFIELD OF ST. MIHIEL, WHERE THE FIRST AMERICAN ARMY, UNDER GENERAL PERSHING, WAS VICTORIOUS IN SEPTEMBER, 1918.

On September 12th, 1918, General Pershing attacked along both sides of the German salient at the apex of which St. Mihiel stood. Securing possession of the Meuse Heights on the west and the Montsec-Thiaucourt line on the south, the Americans commanded the enemy's main artery of communication between Vigneulles and Chambley. Our map shows the area recovered by the Americans in four days' fighting.

The Great War

BRITAIN'S KING HONOURS U.S. SOLDIERS.
King George paid a visit to the armies in France in August, 1918, and took advantage of the opportunity personally to decorate American officers and men for gallantry and distinguished conduct.

had hampered the movements of some of the Tanks, made the roads in bad condition. The roads, moreover, were incessantly swept by artillery fire from both sides of the narrowing strip of the salient.

As the congested transport of troops and guns was struggling towards St. Benoit, through a storm of shell, a hundred and fifty American airmen, carrying each a load of small bombs and five hundred rounds of ammunition, swooped over the highway and bombed, shot, and fired men, horses, and waggons. Limbers exploded, horses fell, men ran for their lives, leaving the only road of escape blocked by a jumbled mass of guns and carts and other vehicles, towards which the attacking troops worked with the energy of victory in the night.

At eight o'clock in the evening St. Mihiel was evacuated by the Germans without a struggle, and into the strangely intact town French patrols began to work. At daybreak the remaining population of two thousand women and children, with a few aged men, were

St. Mihiel freed after four years rescued by their countrymen. At noon, on September 13th, M. Clemenceau, general organiser of victory, with General Pershing, General Pétain, and Mr. Baker, the United States Secretary of War, were able to visit the town, where the people were weeping and singing in the market-place round a French military band, and staring at the unfamiliar blue uniforms of the French troops.

Two hours before St. Mihiel was emptied of the enemy an evening Tank attack completed the fall of Thiaucourt. Here a remarkable prisoner was taken in the person of Professor Otto Schmeernkaze, one of the ornaments of German chemical science. He was the enemy's gas specialist, and the exploiter of chlorine as an instrument of Kultur. He had played a considerable part in combining chlorine with sulphur and other elements, and was very busy experimenting with a new chemical, directed against the United States Army, when he was taken by American soldiers.

FOR GALLANTRY.
The King on the western front pinning the Military Cross on the breast of an American officer.

At midnight the victorious northern American force broke across all the Lorraine heights and entered the central village of Vigneulles. There they fought for three hours against the German forces they were enveloping, winning the village and the road early on Friday morning. The southern American divisions, which had been fighting from the Rupt de Mad into the woods in the heart of the salient, also emerged on the Vigneulles road about eight o'clock on the same morning. The pincers closed twenty-seven hours after their movement began. Large remnants of two German divisions, with more than a hundred guns, were at once enveloped. The line of the heights of the Meuse, connecting Verdun with Toul, was occupied, and the main American operations began.

The famous Second French Army of Verdun, which had had the most glorious of histories under a brilliant succession of commanders, moved down to Alsace under General Hirschauer, and the citizen forces of the United States took over offensive operations around Vauban's frontier citadel. While energetically preparing a grand attack along the western bank of the Meuse, in conjunction with the Army of Champagne under General Gouraud, General Pershing exploited his victory at St. Mihiel by a thundering demonstration against the Metz line.

Immense forces of allied machines, increasing in numbers every day, concentrated on the railway system around Metz, the lines beyond, and on the enemy aerodromes. The enemy Command tried to save the situation by using motor-lorries in the manner in which General Pétain had saved Verdun when his railways were wrecked. But the motor columns were also chased and bombed, and practically no counter-attack of importance was delivered while the work of cleaning the salient and reorganising the heights of the Meuse line went on.

In places the enemy had fled in panic, leaving his bridges intact ; and, where they

U.S. "DARKIES" AS FIGHTING MEN.
Some of the men of an American negro regiment in the trenches in France, where they proved themselves worthy soldiers of the great Western Democracy, behaving in action, as it was recorded, with remarkable sang-froid.

were broken down, French and American sappers quickly erected structures that would bear artillery. One German regiment was taken with its commander and staff ; and, after surrendering, the colonel asked for a roll to be called, so that he might see how heavy his losses had been. Everybody answered to his name in the three battalions, except one officer and one private. The German commander then remarked that his regiment was so complete that he would like to march it into captivity.

It moved off the field of battle under its own officers, guarded by a few American troopers. The 10th German Division, which had fought hard against the Americans at Soissons, and had been sent for a rest to the Meuse, was expected to be formidable, but proved the weakest of all the garrisoning forces. The men surrendered by the thousand rather than fight the Americans again. Most of the 31st Division was trapped in the salient, together with a considerable part of the 5th Landwehr Division. Other forces nearer the Hindenburg line saved themselves by retreat.

Nevertheless, fifteen thousand officers and men, representing one-fourth of the garrison, were captured, and at least half the hostile force was put out of action. Two hundred guns were taken, a large proportion being discovered by Jaulny and the Hindenburg line, when the American troops on Saturday and Sunday were straightening their

front between the Moselle and St. Benoit. In the north the Germans fell back to the Orne River by Etain, and another large area of ground was recovered above Fresnes. The enemy's railway junction at Conflans was brought under short-range fire, and the guns of Metz had to engage, in unfavourable circumstances, in an intense duel with American and French heavy batteries at a range of five miles.

General Pershing intensified his bombardment throughout the third week in September. Had he been a German commander he could have wrecked Metz as completely as the enemy had destroyed Ypres or Rheims. Naturally he refrained from damaging the old lost French city which he and his men were victoriously working to recover. But the tremendous fire brought to bear over the extension of the Hindenburg line upon all the German military positions, while the British Independent Air Force was smashing the enemy's communications, and American, French, and Italian airmen concentrated on his front, convinced the German commander that the Americans were bent on developing a grand offensive directly against Metz along the line of their preliminary success. It **American troops** was the kind of thing a new, enthusiastic **before Metz** army was likely to do under the impetus of its first victory. But General Pershing was no mean strategist. While playing up to the enemy, he brought his Second Army into line under General Bullard, and swung his veteran troops of the First Army across the Meuse towards the approaches to Montfaucon.

Enjoying an absolute command of the air, he was able to manœuvre a quarter of a million men into a new, unexpected position for attack by the time that Marshal Foch timed the new stroke to occur. In the interval the indefatigable British armies struck once more with surprising speed around Cambrai. Foch's pincers were growing larger, and General von Lossberg, battered in the centre, and threatened from the Yser to the Meuse, had to shuttle his reserves more quickly from side to side.

Instead of being able to give all withdrawn divisions a month's rest, he had to send his troops repeatedly into action at intervals of a week or a fortnight. His men were wearing out. The problem was to follow them up with blow after blow until they became as war-weary as their 10th Division at St. Mihiel.

WITH FLAGS FLYING AFTER A GREAT EXPLOIT.
American engineers who had borne their share in the great work on the front of the St. Mihiel salient returning after the successful accomplishment of their task in September, 1918. Inset above : American soldiers in France practising fighting the enemy with his own liquid-fire weapon.

Photo, Russell & Sons

GENERAL JOHN JOSEPH PERSHING,
Commander-in-Chief of the United States Forces in France.

THE TURN OF THE TIDE IN THE WEST.
V.—The Breaking of the Aisne Pivot and the Victories of the North and Scheldt Canals.
By Edward Wright.

Ludendorff's Folly in Scattering His Forces—Enemy's Fruitless Proposal to Escape from Belgian Salient—Yorkshiremen Return to Havrincourt—Mangin's Terrific Attack on the Alberich Line—Single Platoon of Verdun Natives Conquer Laffaux—Subterranean Fight to the Death Under Monkey Mount—Enemy Command Begins to Gamble at Enormous Risk—Marwitz and Below Arrange a Great Counter-Offensive in the Cambrai Style—Corporal Hunter and Six Men Decisively Hold Out in Mœuvres—New South Wales Men Annex the Trap in which They Are Caught at Cologne Farm—Southern Section of Hindenburg Tunnel Partly Overrun—Gallant Thrusts by Scotsmen and Englishmen Above St. Quentin—First French Army Works Under Haig towards St. Quentin Suburbs—Magnificent Leaping Advance by Yeomen of England—East County Troops Checked at Epéhy and Londoners Held Up in Peizière—Remarkable Exploit by Wiltshire Battalion—Tireless 17th Division Works into Gauche Wood—Below Opens His Great Counter-Offensive—The Dog-Fight Above Ronssoy—Storming of the Great St. Quentin Quadrilateral—Marshal Foch Opens His Last Pair of Pincers.

HEN, in the middle of September, 1918, the First American Army on the Meuse began bombarding the defences of Metz the turn of the tide of victory in the west was completed. Henceforward, it was on a flood of important successes in all theatres of war that the forces of the Associated Powers surged upon the crumbling armies of their enemies. Just as General Pershing finished his first operations on the Meuse, on September 15th, the Bulgar and German divisions in the Balkans were pierced and routed by the Allied Army of Salonika, under General Franchet d'Espérey. Then, before Turkey could establish a line to guard her European territory, one of her best armies was broken and captured in Palestine by Sir Edmund Allenby, who quickly extended his operations by the destruction of another Ottoman army.

At last it was clearly seen that Ludendorff, in the folly of his pride, had thrown upon his country heavier burdens than it could bear. He had scattered a very considerable part of his best forces in secondary schemes of conquest before achieving decisive victory in the main theatre of conflict. He had sent troops across the Baltic and across the Black Sea, marched them over the Ukraine and settled them along the

Danube, while despatching continually increasing numbers of picked non-commissioned officers and regimental and Staff officers into Asia. He equalled the British politician of the eighteenth century in the dispersion of forces in a variety of political objectives.

Each of his commitments became so important from a political or economic point of view that it could not be annulled, without very serious general consequences. There was a good fighting force in Finland, under General von der Goltz, which might have turned the tide of a battle in the west. As it was being used to transform Finland into a German kingdom from which the Scandinavian nations could be dominated, this force was not withdrawn across the Baltic until a considerable time after the great disaster had occurred.

In Rumania was Field-Marshal von Mackensen, whose military capacity was questioned, but who had a record of unbroken victories. Under him were some six divisions in a condition of high efficiency. Yet he and his men could not be employed as a strong reinforcement in the western battles for the reason that Ludendorff had imposed upon the Rumanian people a state of economic slavery that made an insurrection certain if Mackensen and his men departed.

PASSING A ROADSIDE DERELICT.
British cavalrymen going forward during the advance towards Cambrai. They were passing a German heavy gun, one of the many which had been abandoned by the enemy as he was being driven finally eastward.

305

PRISONER STRETCHER-BEARERS.
German prisoners bringing in casualties during the victorious British attack on the Hindenburg line in September, 1918.

new and powerful offensives on either side of the Hindenburg lines which made the forcible reconquest of Belgium a certainty. The fresh British hammer-stroke was to be followed by great blows from the American, French, and Belgian Armies.

The new operations began with a series of preliminary movements on September 12th, the day of the first American attack. The splendid York-shiremen of the 62nd Division, their ranks filled out with young recruits after their battle losses in the Ardre valley by Rheims, advanced for the second time into the Havrincourt position, and on the field of their victory the previous November broke the fresh German forces. Then, with other troops, they reoccupied the main Hindenburg line, stretching by the old Cambrai salient to the North Canal.

Mackensen could not even help the Bulgars, Hungarians, and Austrians, owing to the justly angry temper of the Rumanian nation. There was also an affair of personal jealousy between Ludendorff and Mackensen that helped to keep the Prussian of Scottish origin helpless in the month of disasters. After his early successes in Russian Poland, Mackensen had been promoted by Falkenhayn, the temporary rival of Ludendorff, to a leading position in the eastern theatre of war. When Ludendorff succeeded to supreme power he reduced Mackensen to a very subordinate command.

After his fall Ludendorff remained at General Headquarters at Spa, in the Belgian Ardennes. For neither Field-Marshal von Hindenburg nor General von Lossberg, the virtual successor of Ludendorff, could disen-tangle the threads of the many schemes of the fallen dictator. Hindenburg seems to have been ready to acknowledge defeat and strive to obtain terms before his armies were put out of action. General von Lossberg continued to hope, until the end of the last week in September, that he could extricate the German armies from the net in which Marshal Foch had entangled them, and towards the middle of the month an attempt was made to solve the

Overtures to Belgium

problem of the retirement from Belgium by opening through Switzerland informal negotiations for the evacuation of Belgian territory.

As usual, the Teutons endeavoured to veil their admission of growing weakness by adding to the proposal arrogant conditions which they designed to abandon if negotiations took place. King Albert and his Government rightly rejected the offer, knowing well that Belgium had become a vast salient in which the invader had trapped himself, so that he could not attempt to withdraw without an inevitable general disaster.

It was the progress of the First and Third British Armies through the Hindenburg systems between Douai and Cambrai that direly imperilled the great German salient in Flanders. Marshal Foch had already devised a series of

TANKS THAT STORMED THE HINDENBURG LINE.
Cars of assault, driven by men with great experience, were employed in the attack by the Third and Fourth British Armies in September, 1918, to overcome the many new entanglements erected by the enemy.

In the evening the enemy made an extraordinary counter-attack. As his shattered troops were not capable of attempting to return to Havrincourt village and wood, a formation of low-flying aeroplanes swooped upon the men of the 62nd Division as they were altering the conquered positions. The aerial counter-attack was beaten off. But the next day a grand assault was launched against the new British line, from Mœuvres and Havrincourt to Gouzeaucourt.

The enemy returned to the use of liquid fire, and behind his flame-projector parties were strong bodies of machine-gunners and charging infantry, who succeeded in breaking into the British positions. Havrincourt and Trescault were entered by the enemy, but in hard fighting, that lasted in places until nightfall, the Germans were driven out, leaving a considerable number of men captive amid their dead.

This was the last serious reaction against the general British advance between Douai and St. Quentin. All old British battle positions bending round this famous city were gradually won by the Fourth British Army and the First French Army. Maissemy was carried on September 15th, and on the following day the Australians, with their inveterate aggressiveness, broke over the country towards the historic pivot ridge of Le Verguier.

While the British and French forces were making their preparations for another great thrust in strength, General Mangin endeavoured to weaken General von Böhn's reserve by a flanking attack against the Chemin des Dames, or Ladies' Walk, running along the northern Aisne ridge.

With his French, American, and African troops, General Mangin had arrived at the end of the old Hindenburg line, running down from the rear of St. Quentin to the dominating upland knolls by the Laon road and the end of the Ladies' Walk. Almost within bomb-throw of his troops were the limestone caverns, quarries, and rocky dug-outs, against which the strongest of French armies had been checked in April, 1917. General Mangin had been in command of the operations on the Aisne under General Nivelle, and he held that if he had been properly supported by the Government of the period he could have broken through and won in a grand victory full compensation for the heavy losses he had incurred. All that afterwards happened showed that his judgment had been sound, and that he was the inspirer of the enemy's tremendous efforts at a break-through.

General Mangin, however, had changed his tactics as soon as he saw the tactical possibilities of the light French Tank

This was exactly what General Mangin had designed the enemy should do. He had already captured more than forty thousand officers and men from the opposing forces, largely owing to the fact that the enemy's method of deploying in depth had dispersed his force of resistance and enabled the quick, light storming cars to penetrate rapidly into the hostile artillery positions. When the enemy commander attacked with machine-gunners almost as close as ordinary riflemen, and packed the works at the end of the Alberich line, General Mangin returned to his Verdun tactics. With parks of heavy guns, far exceeding in power those employed at Verdun in 1916, he **Verdun defenders'** smote all the German system between the **fierce offensive** St. Gobain Forest and Vailly, on the Aisne.

The French gunners had the advantage of being intimately acquainted with the smallest features of the knife-like ridge and its knolls, spurs, and gullies. They had hammered the enemy out of the ground in 1917, and sited their pieces in the hollows the Germans reoccupied. They knew the ground absolutely to a yard, having large aerial photographs upon which their former bombardments had been based.

In a hurricane of thunderbolts, mingled with shrapnel for shelling the enemy's posts, the forces of assault stormed towards the Laffaux plateau. A regiment recruited from Verdun, with French Marines and light infantry, fought against five of the best enemy divisions. The Brandenburgers who had taken Douaumont were attacked by the division which General Mangin originally commanded, and with which he had recovered some of the chief downs by Verdun.

In the great Aisne battle almost everything was in the enemy's favour. His main front-line forces had enormous caverns and underground workings in which to shelter, and his machine-gunners and artillery observers rested in dominating positions. The French soldiers below them often fought knee-deep in an inundation formed to prevent Tank attacks. One French battalion fought in the water for twenty-four hours before clearing the slope above it. Yet the men of

of the Renault type. Instead of trying to end the war suddenly by one great stroke, he tricked and worried the enemy into concentrating against him, and then massacred the invaders by mechanical means before sending out strong patrols to annex the ground. This was somewhat the way in which General Mangin had first distinguished himself under General Nivelle and General Pétain in the active phase of the defence of Verdun; but his machinery of attack had since been enormously strengthened by British and French inventors.

On September 14th he opened the struggle for Laffaux Mill, Monkey Mount (Mont des Singes), and other key positions on the Aisne Ridge. General von Carlowitz knew that an attack was coming, and having continually failed to check the Tenth Army by a deployment in depth of some twenty-five divisions, the Germans stood to battle in a strong front zone based upon the Hindenburg system around Laffaux.

HIS MAJESTY'S AUXILIARY LANDSHIP HARWICH IN COMMISSION.
One of the auxiliary Tanks that attend the fighting Tanks in the field, supplying them with munitions and oil, and carrying spare parts for effecting urgent repairs during action. In oval: The Harwich, escorted by pioneers of a Scottish regiment, on road-mending work.

EQUAL CARE FOR FRIEND AND FOE.
Canadian and German wounded receiving first attention to their wounds in a captured German shelter converted into a Canadian advanced dressing-station. The Germans confronting the Canadians fought stubbornly and well, and every evidence confirmed the fact that they suffered enormous casualties.

The position of General von Carlowitz was such as to incite him to the most desperate measures of counter-attack. His situation reflected upon the ability of his army group commander, General von Böhn, and the German High Command. He was astride the Vesle Ridge and astride the Aisne River, and extended across the Aisne Ridge and the Ailette valley with a tremendous French artillery flanking all the ridges and hollows he occupied, and also pitching torrents of shell from the south. Along the Vesle line the Fifth French Army, under General Guillaumat, was waiting tensely for the pursuit to begin. As soon as General Mangin's men reached the Malmaison plateau, dominating the last German road of retreat at Chavignon, the Vesle line would give and Guillaumat and his men drive forward.

Undoubtedly, General von Carlowitz and his superior commanders had placed too much confidence in the strength of the Alberich end of the Hindenburg system. They did not expect General Mangin to attack with such adroit and inexhaustible power. When the Hindenburg defences were breached and several of the great cavern shelters were captured, the enemy commander had to use up the last fresh reserves of the Böhn group of armies and send these forces across the open ground in incessant counter-attacks. These counter-attacks were so costly in life that their failure did much to bring the war to an end.

Back to the Ladies' Walk

Verdun took Laffaux by an audacious turning movement, conducted merely by a platoon, and cleared the caverns of Allemant ravine at great speed. The dauntless attackers worked so close that the opposing artillery had to lift from the fighting-front and barrage the rear positions. All day the close wrestle went on, and when night fell, giving the French troops somewhat more cover from observation on the rear, the conflict increased in intensity. Yard by yard the indomitable, indefatigable flower of French valour won ground on the high pivoting point of the vast German quadrilateral of the Hindenburg defences.

The strongest of the German points was Monkey Mount, north of Vauxaillon. It had been transformed into a series of subterranean fortresses, which were held by Germans of magnificent mettle. The garrison had to be killed almost to a man, in one of the most terrible of all trials of strength between Teuton and Gaul. When, however, Monkey Mount was won, the victors had under view and fire the enemy's route of supply and reinforcement running along the Ailette valley to Anizy and Laon.

Carlowitz made tremendous efforts to recover the lost rise, but the forward French guns were able to help the successful infantry. Both sides employed field-guns at a range of a few hundred yards ; these practically became super-machine-guns.

While the main flanking thrust towards the end of the Chemin des Dames was maintained by General Mangin with extraordinary tactical skill and persistent strength, the end of the high ridge was also partly turned by a drive upward from the Aisne. Here Vailly was taken at the same time as the Laffaux upland was captured. Through the deep and steep ravine by Jouy the lower flanking movement went on, while the main French force bombed and bayoneted its way by Fruty quarries towards the high crest at Cologne Farm, which was only a few feet lower than the last supreme dominating point at Malmaison.

By September 17th Mangin's men were within storming distance of the Malmaison summit, the key position to all the ridge and northern valley by which the Chavignon road to Laon ran. Some of the positions had been won and lost five times, but against all fresh counter-attacking forces the French front steadily moved forward, flattening out the high corner by the Chemin des Dames, on which the invaders' power of resistance was based.

The ground on the Aisne Ridge, as was openly admitted by

HUN CAPTIVES WATCH THEIR CAPTORS MARCHING ON.
German prisoners watching Canadian Highlanders going up into action on the western front. In a Special Order, dated October 3rd, 1918, Sir Arthur Currie stated that the Canadian Corps took over 7,000 prisoners in five days, bringing their total capture from August 8th to that date to 28,000 prisoners.

Cambrai, October, 1918: British guns going forward to the battle-front.

Infantry advancing in single file over rough ground in the great advance at Cambrai.

" One great area of devastation ": The square of Cambrai systematically destroyed by the Hun.

Canadian troops of the First British Army entering Cambrai on the morning of October 8th, 1918

Canadian engineers trying to stop the fires caused in Cambrai by the retreating foe.

Explosion of German mine in the Place d'Armes, Cambrai, after the Canadian entry.

Patrol of North Lancashires marching into Cambrai from the south.

Canadian motor machine=gun section awaiting orders on the Cambrai road.

the enemy Staff, was more important than even the St. Gobain Massif, against which General Mangin also continually demonstrated. The Hindenburg quadrilateral was endangered at its southern apex as well as on its north-western side. General von Böhn had to procure more reinforcements from the reserves of the army group of the Crown Prince of Prussia. This was what Marshal Foch was waiting for. He had another pair of pincers ready.

Lossberg was still bent on creating a mass of manœuvre for action in Lorraine, where the Second American Army, under Lieutenant-General Bullard, was seriously interrupting main communications by means of a heavy fire from 16 in. naval guns. In the hope of being able to gather force for shattering the menacing power of the American armies, by a thrust through the Lorraine gap between the heights of the Meuse and the Vosges Mountains, the enemy High Command took enormous risks.

Strengthening Below's forces The forces north-west of Verdun were left comparatively weak, and the armies in Champagne were not strengthened properly. Craonne and the Vesle line were weakly held in preparation for retreat. General von der Marwitz's Second Army, with the remnant of Hutier's forces, upon which General Rawlinson and General Debeney were closing, was left without strong reinforcements. Most of the men that could immediately be spared, after Carlowitz had been strengthened, were placed under General von Below along the Flesquières Ridge, in the old Cambrai salient, for a counter-offensive against General Byng's Third Army.

General von der Marwitz was reckoned by his High Command to have acted in a very able manner in defence of the lower part of the Siegfried line, between the neighbourhood of Gouzeaucourt and the outskirts of St. Quentin. The German Army commander constructed a great new outwork between Holnon Wood and Fayet, in order to cover the northern

WHERE THE ENEMY WENT TO EARTH.
German camp established in a quarry, in which there was the entrance to a passage-way that ran for hundreds of yards through the chalk. It was captured by the British during the advance in the autumn of 1918.

approach to St. Quentin. The new defence was in quadri-lateral shape, excavated and built at uncommon speed after the breaking of Marwitz's line by the Somme.

The third of the successive defeats of Marwitz occurring in one month, when the Australians stormed Mont St. Quentin, caused him further to accelerate the construction of new defences. He took the three British battle positions on the ridges near the Scheldt Canal, reversed them, made new machine-gun emplacements, and erected zones of barbed-wire along what had been the rear of the British lines. The greater part of this work was done during the week in which the German rearguards were **Marwitz's new** holding or receding from the temporary **defensive works** line of the middle part of the North Canal.

While the former positions of the wings of the Third and Fifth British Armies were thus being strengthened and transformed along the undulations of chalk by Epéhy, Hargicourt, and Francilly, General von der Marwitz dragged his artillery across the moat of the Scheldt Canal and placed it well behind the old Hindenburg system, extending eastward of the waterway. He then had his grand battle position protected by the Siegfried line, by the cutting and tunnel of the Scheldt Canal, and by three entrenched and thickly-wired systems, successively dominating each advance by the Fourth British Army.

There was a depth of more than four miles in places between the enemy's first outpost zone and his grand battle position. The only disadvantage in this scheme was that the masses of German field-guns and medium artillery were removed so far away from the deploying ground of the assailing forces that they could not effectively curtain off the assault. Marwitz, however, remedied this defect by obtaining from his High Command an unparalleled number of high-velocity guns. With these guns he was able to create barrages to a depth of ten miles or more within the attacking lines.

GERMAN TRAP TO CATCH BRITISH TANKS.
A British soldier inspecting a sunk trap set by the retreating enemy as a means to delay the progress of the Tanks, which played a considerable part in his final discomfiture and defeat.

His design then was to stand on the defence with the Second German Army, and mow down the men of the British Army with machine-guns, infantry guns, and high-velocity barrages, and to inform the Seventeenth German Army, under General von Below, of the moment when a counter-offensive from the Flesquières Ridge could be launched against the weakening Britons. In general outline the scheme was similar to the enemy's counter-offensive at Cambrai at the end of November, 1917, in which Marwitz had played an important part. The scale of it, however, was much larger, and with the line of resistance against the First French Army and the Fourth British Army, and the line of attack against the Third British Army, it covered a thirty-miles stretch of country.

No mean strategist was the man who devised this double operation of defence and attack. The quality **Marwitz's strategy** of it, with the special factor of surprise in **brings promotion** the use of massed high-velocity guns, showed that the mind of Lossberg had been working on it. But Marwitz had his tarnished reputation brightened by the part he played in the suggestion and execution of the plan. Although he failed of success, he was at once promoted to the most important command on the western front, and sent to defend, with the Fifth German Army, the communications between Metz and Mézières against the First American Army, under Lieutenant-General Hunter Liggett.

Sir Julian Byng, whose forces were again threatened with penetration, when a portion of them were engaged in attacking a strongly reinforced enemy, was generally alert to danger. His corps commanders were careful to stand strong on each main position they won while preparing for the next forward movement. With every increase in the scope of the allied offensive, the peril of a great secret counter-offensive grew, for **H.L.I. heroism** it was clear the enemy would have **at Mœuvres** to attempt violent reactions on some part of the line if he wished to save himself. As the supreme crisis was approaching the enemy's counter-stroke was due.

General von Below had lost the poise and patience of his Caporetto days. As soon as reinforcements enabled him to recover from the blow that had sent him reeling from the Wotan line, he began to try to worry back to all the North Canal line. On September 17th his men drove the Highland Light Infantry out of the pivoting point of Mœuvres. This was loud warning of something more to follow, and the British Guards, the 3rd Division, with special memories of Mœuvres, and the 37th Division, who were holding the neighbouring sector, became grimly expectant.

Even in Mœuvres the enemy was not entirely master of the maze. Corporal Hunter, with six men, overrun and

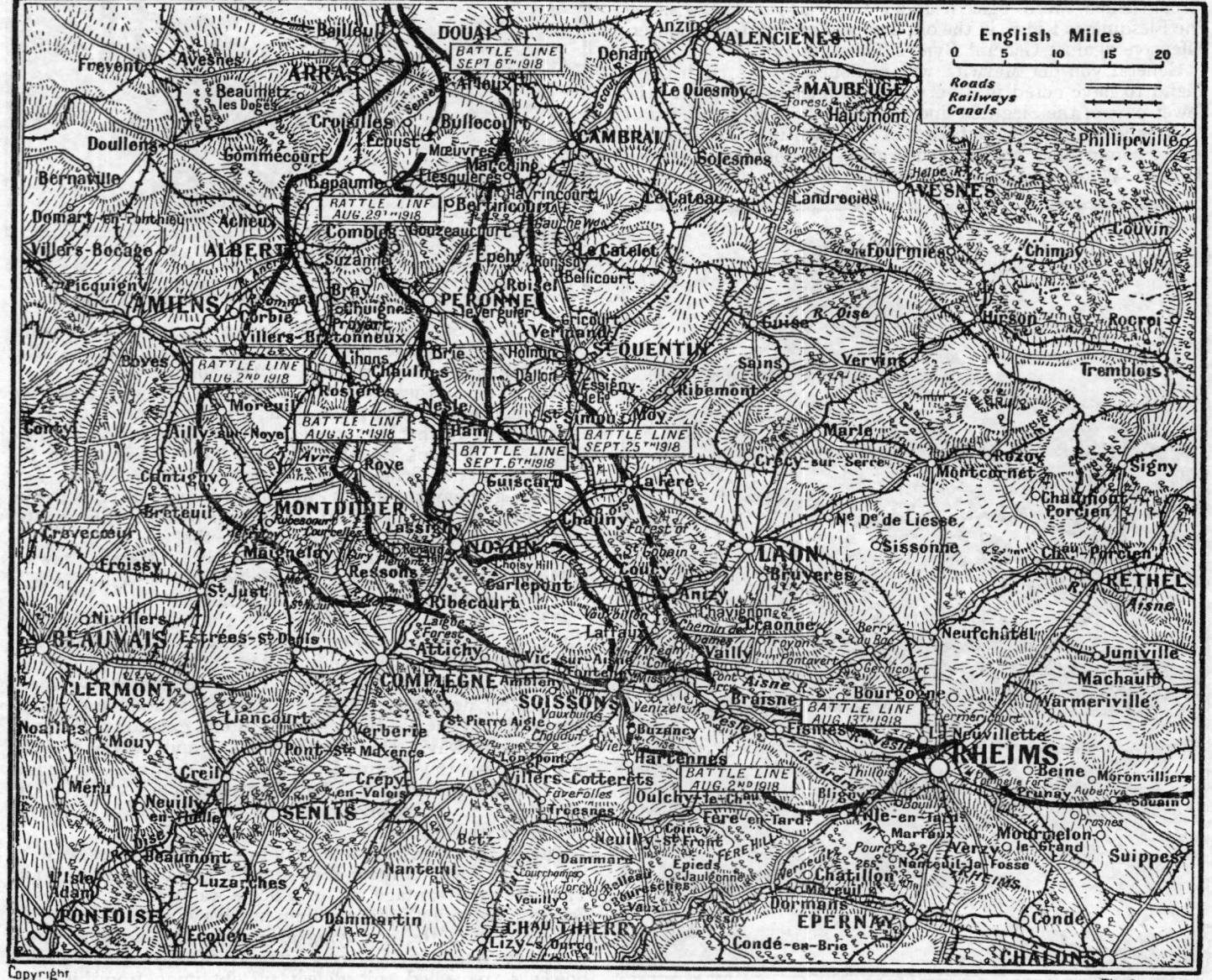

Copyright

The Great War

REDUCTION OF THE GERMAN SALIENT DIRECTED AT AMIENS.

Between August 2nd and September 25th, 1918—in a series of gradually lengthening battle-lines—the allied forces drove the enemy back from the positions that he had gained in his great offensive of the spring. In something less than six weeks of fighting the great salient had been reduced, and the allied forces were directly threatening Laon, St. Quentin, Cambrai, and Douai.

BRITISH TROOPS LEAVING THE TRENCHES TO GO FORWARD IN SUPPORT OF AN ATTACK.
Superb spirit characterised the advance of the infantry over the moorland wastes of thistles and rank corn that lay in front of the wide belts of wire of the Hindenburg line. In some sectors the troops were so eager to reach the enemy that they passed through their own barrage and rushed the hostile positions.

encircled by the Germans, held out with invincible spirit and skill. For the best part of three days and nights the little band fought in the old, battered labyrinth, withstanding such a siege as lifted them, as soon as they were relieved by a returning British advance, to the rank of fighting men of romantic renown. Wide over the Empire spread their fame, and the popular instinct that immediately raised them to a position of symbolic splendour was sound. They were a thorn in the foot of the enemy that made him limp in his last race for the initiative.

While the seven heroes of the Highland Light Infantry held out by the North Canal, where the Germans wanted room for their intended manœuvres, the Third and Fourth British Armies opened the attack which the enemy was waiting to turn to his purpose. Heavy rain fell at two o'clock in the morning of September 18th, 1918, and thereby upset an important element in the attack. Numerous storming cars had been brought up by drivers with deadly experience, in order to overcome the many new entanglements the enemy had erected and break into his many strong points, with the great strength of which the Britons were peculiarly acquainted in virtue of their having been original constructors of the works.

The streaming rain, however, made the undulating chalk country so slippery that the caterpillar wheels of the cars failed

Tanks impeded to grip with their usual speed and power. **by heavy rain** It was the same kind of terrain on which the old heavy Tanks had first proved their surprising ability, and as the weather had been abnormally hot for autumn, drying the porous chalk as in a furnace, the field had seemed very promising when the order of battle was fixed for the use of numerous "whippets." But the heat produced thunderstorms and deluges.

Under a deluge at dawn the men went forward from Gouzeaucourt to Holnon Wood on the British front, and from Holnon and Essigny-le-Grand on the French front. In the centre were New South Wales men, South Australians, Queenslanders, South and West "Aussies," Victorians and Tasmanians. Their achievement was similar to that of the

Canadians in the Wotan line, and they accounted it one of the most successful actions in all their victorious experience.

Before them, on the ridge of Le Verguier, an historic scene of British resistance in March, was a German garrison with orders to hold out to the last man. The attackers covered them with a smoke barrage which added so to the mist already veiling the country that it was an affair of anxious skill to keep direction and knowledge of the situation.

Compass in hand, youngsters piloted platoons and companies, steering partly by the flashes and crashes of their hurricane barrage. Right under the shrapnel the men **Capture of** **Le Verguier** worked, and officers had to get farther into the fire, walking backward in it, so as to face their men and watch they did not get too far forward. As a result the Australians arrived with the shell-lighted fog cloud in the ruins of Le Verguier, and many of the hostile machine-gunners, who had been set to repeat the forlorn gallantry of General Gouraud's volunteers in the Battle of Champagne, fired a few shots and fled. Their guns, lining the parapets of the high entrenchments, behind uncut wire, were abandoned.

There were some sharp struggles in the old system southward, but the village was quickly taken, and five hundred prisoners collected. Above this ridge, at the crest by Villeret village, a company of South Australians ran into a fierce machine-gun barrage, but worked round by a wood and took a hundred Germans with a field-gun and all the worrying machine-guns. At Hargicourt, where the British line had broken in the mists of March, the attackers again met with strong resistance, but could not be denied. After breaking through the village a New South Wales battalion was checked by the obstacle of Cologne Farm, as famous a name of difficulty on the British front as on the front General Mangin's men were attacking.

At Cologne Farm the New South Wales men were so delayed that their artillery barrage thundered away towards the Hindenburg line, leaving the infantry to fight forward unaided. The enemy turned field-guns upon the attacking force, which was caught between two ridges, both manned

315

PART OF A GREAT CANAL BARRIER.
British troops on the steep bank of the St. Quentin Canal. This waterway, which formed part of the strong Hindenburg line system of
defences, was crossed by men of the 46th Division wearing life-belts.

Yet in the returning hour of his ordeal General von
der Marwitz could not bring fresh forces forward
quickly enough to save the front of the Hindenburg
system. All the afternoon the Australians continued
to test, thrust, and penetrate, winning position after
position. They went on fighting when night fell,
and an hour before midnight the 4th Division of Sir
John Monash's corps entered the struggle for the
system Ludendorff had built in the winter of 1916.
Extending the gains of the day, they took all the
rest of the advanced works in their zone of assault.
Practically every Australian battalion
had fewer casualties than prisoners, **4,000 prisoners for**
and some counted a number of **1,200 casualties**
captives larger than their own
strength. In spite of the ground, the Tanks gave them
good aid, some of the cars cruising on the northern
line as far as the Hindenburg works.

When day broke, the irresistible men of the Commonwealth were lying out on a crest by Bellicourt,
overlooking a brown, rolling waste of thistles and
rank corn, on the opposing slopes of which could be
seen the white parapets and wide belts of wire of
the main Hindenburg system. Southward there rose
against the sky-line the great roof tower of the
Cathedral of St. Quentin. The Australians took a
little more ground with some hundreds of prisoners
to straighten out their line, bringing the number of
their captives to more than four thousand, with some
forty guns, at the cost of a casualty list of twelve
hundred—the record in major operations.

On the right of the Australian divisions there was
very stubborn fighting above and round the great
new advanced work covering St. Quentin. English
and Scots battalions, including Buffs, Shropshires,

with Germans firing down with rifles, machine-guns,
and cannon and howitzers. By superb steadiness and
agility the Australians broke out of the trap and
annexed it. Their Lewis gunners shot the enemy
artillerymen, and the infantry captured six quickfirers
and four howitzers, while rounding up many Germans.

Meanwhile, the lost barrage was resting on the
original advanced line of the Siegfried system. When
the leading Australian division, the
Rapid advance of 1st, recovered in clearing weather
Australians the old British outposts, the guns of
victory again lifted and sent their
shells slowly travelling towards the Hindenburg works.
Over the moorland the Australian artillerymen came
with remarkable speed, with their gun teams in little
columns, urgent to support the foot in another successful
drive.

Some of the infantry, however, were too impatient even
for the fastest of gun movements. Feeling the Germans
before them were demoralised, they would not lose time, and
passing through their own barrage they rushed the hostile
trenches by the most sensitive of sectors of defence. It was
where the Scheldt Canal ran underground, depriving the
Germans of their moat against Tank surprises. On ridges
three and a half miles westward defending garrisons had been
given many forward guns, and ordered to resist to the death,
because of the lack of water protection by Catelet and Estrées.
And between these points the enemy had exceptional facilities
in communications; thence had been launched, in the
spring offensive, the waves of attack that broke into the flank
of the Third Army and almost turned the Fifth Army.

IN THE HINDENBURG LINE.
Men of the British forces at the entrance to a great tunnel of the St. Quentin Canal.
The tunnel indicates something of the formidable nature of this part of the long-
prepared enemy defences which were broken through.

Sherwoods, Norfolks, and Durham Light Infantry, fought
from Holnon Wood to Fresnoy, while the Camerons and
Black Watch groped in the mist and smoke towards
Berthaucourt and Bellenglise. Again some of the Germans,
men of the 119th Division, ran away in utter demoralisation;
but there were many others who fought their machine-guns
desperately in the copses dotting the undulating moorland.

The Scotsmen took Berthaucourt, by the Hindenburg
system, with ease. But there was hard fighting on the way
to Fresnoy, where thick belts of entanglements had to be
crossed under raking fire, and earth fortresses and linking
trench systems reduced piecemeal. There was a quadrilateral by Gricourt, formed of a difficult complication of
trenches, somewhat similar to the work captured by the Tanks
in the First Battle of Arras. Here it was that the deluged,
slippery ground left the attacking infantry with less assistance

than usual from storming cars. When night fell the maze still held resisting groups of Germans.

By Holnon Wood, where the British and French lines joined, there was an extension of the formidable work, in which the enemy gallantly stood his ground and had to be rushed and turned and tricked and worn down. The French troops were less than four thousand yards from St. Quentin, but between them and the city rose the two great bastions of Round Hill and Manchester Hill, the latter already dedicated in battle after battle to the immortal glory of the men from whom it took its name. Between the hills and in front of Francilly village in the hollow was **French advance by** a formidable trench system, another part of **infiltration** the quadrilateral, with innumerable minor works about it. Sunken roads extended to St. Quentin, and with their high banks gave admirable shelter to both their machine-guns and artillery. Only a great Tank offensive in favouring weather could have enabled troops to break quickly, without crippling loss, the outskirts of the cathedral-crowned town.

Happily, a deep thrust was not needed by Sir Douglas Haig, who was directing operations. All that he required of the gallant French divisions was that they should form a defensive flank for the central advance, and occupy the Germans' attention around St. Quentin, to prevent them from concentrating along and over the tunnel section of the Scheldt Canal.

General Debeney used the method of infiltration which Ludendorff had copied and expanded from General Pétain. His strong patrols worked forward under short, heavy, covering gusts of gun fire, and met dense groups of Bavarians and Prussians. These were captured in fifties and hundreds, but only after long, bitter combats. The French had to work up a long glacis, against a general barrage of heavy artillery and local cross-fires of bullets and small shell. Only the manœuvring power and endurance of the attackers saved them from winning their victories at too heavy a cost in life. Yet, without in any way lessening their thrusting power in future operations, the divisions broke into Fontaine-les-Clercs and entered the ruins of Epine de Dallon, less than two miles from St. Quentin. On the south they worked into Contescourt, reached Beney and Essigny-le-Grand, and linked with General Mangin's army round the moated position of La Fère.

On the right of the Australians, near the point at which they reached " Farthest East," the Yeomanry division made a fine advance against the 2nd Division of the Prussian Guard and against a much stronger fighting force of Thuringians. The Yeomanry had a very hard opening task, as their route ran through Templeux and **Yeomen beat the** its large area of quarried ground, where old **Prussian Guard** pits and refuse-heaps gave such opportunities of defence that even the Germans captured in preliminary attack boasted the quarries could never be taken. Britons had made a fine stand in the cover of Templeux in March, and there, indeed, saved their line from complete penetration. The Germans had greatly increased the fortification, yet the Yeomen of England, by means of artificial fog and leaping rushes, stormed the quarry, and one party of forty Germans surrendered to the groom of a brigadier, who was merely waiting for his commander to return from a tour of observation.

In the first advance by Ronssoy the Suffolk Yeomanry

BRITISH TROOPS WHO WON THEIR WAY ACROSS THE ST. QUENTIN CANAL.

Men of the 46th Division—South and North Staffordshires—who got across the St. Quentin Canal in life-belts in the wonderful advance over that great obstacle at the beginning of October, 1918. The crossing the canal, as the "Times" correspondent put it, "was a most dashing achievement, with the assistance of hastily-made rafts and ships' life-belts." Some of the hundreds of men seen here are still wearing their life-belts.

took four hundred prisoners, and the Devons a hundred ; but as the brigades were advancing to the next objective, the battalions on the left were for a time checked by a difficulty encountered by other troops with whom they had to keep in close touch.

Very dramatic was the incident that temporarily put the division of Yeomen out of the time-table connecting them with the Australian advance. A strong force of Germans emerged for a counter-attack at a time when some East County troops were resuming their thrust. The two advances began at exactly the same minute and clashed in the open. While the wing of the English division continued stubbornly to battle forward against the fresh German force, the Yeomen on the right of the action poured in a flanking fire of the old, intensive kind. Under this the German force withered up on its left, enabling the attacking waves once more to roll forward. Meanwhile, the right brigade of the Yeomanry fought onward in step with the Australians, and arrived with them at the outpost zone of the Hindenburg line, taking on the way ten guns. The Yeomen's prisoners amounted to more than twice the number of their own wounded, and many of these were only lightly hit. Their achievement with that of the Australians formed the decisive advance of the day.

After the Yeomen had taken Ronssoy with a large number of prisoners, almost in a stride, the enemy's

IN ST. QUENTIN.
The Place de l'Hôtel de Ville, as it was when the town was recaptured.

THE NOTE OF TRIUMPH.
Band of the 137th Brigade playing amid the ruins of Bellenglise, which was captured by the 46th Division in the course of its fine achievements on September 29th, 1918.

resistance increased at Epéhy and Peizière. East County troops and London men attacked these storm-centres of many battles, and in the fog and smoke some companies lost direction. At Epéhy there were dug-outs, with earthworks reinforced by iron girders, through which no trench-mortar shells could break. A force of the Alpine Corps fought with high gallantry in this formidable redoubt, standing out until late in the afternoon, and so checking the Englishmen's advance that the enemy had the opportunity of launching the counter-attack that clashed with the last English movement and gave the Yeomen an opportunity for enfilading fire.

In Peizière the Londoners left behind them in the fog more of the men of the Alpine Corps. These hid in five redoubts, commanding the approaches to the village, and then emerged and kept their machine-guns in continuous action, shooting along the ruined streets with murderous effect. When tackled, the desperate Germans fought like badgers. It took all day and part of the night to clear them out, and it must be admitted that they succeeded in carrying out the tactics of Marwitz's plan and seriously hampered part of the British advance.

By the old railway bend by Peizière and Epéhy was the Larkspur Ridge and the line of Vaucellette Farm, Chapel Hill, and Gauche Wood. Here the 21st Division, that had made so fine a stand at Epéhy in the March battle, with the 17th Division and another fighting force of high fame, combined in a drive

A FINE OLD TOWN HALL WHICH ESCAPED DESTRUCTION.
The beautiful thirteenth-century Hôtel de Ville of St. Quentin as it was found when the enemy was drive out by the French on October 1st, 1918. The highly-decorated façade remained almost intact.

HAVOC AT ST. QUENTIN.
Railway bridge destroyed by the Germans before evacuating St. Quentin, to retard pursuit.

back to the old British front line by Villers-Guislain.

Along the deep ravines and up the steep ridges, battalions of renown— Lincolns, Leicesters, Wilts, K.O.Y.L.I., Manchesters, Lancashire Fusiliers, Dorsets, and West Yorkshires, among others—fought one of the greatest fights in the war. The Lincolns carried Vaucellette Farm, the Leicesters and Wiltshires stormed into the Meath and Limerick posts in an operation with a dramatic turn like that above Ronssoy. The enemy at once came out in strength for his counter-attack, and met the Wiltshires at close quarters in Linnet valley. The Englishmen, without halting, went into the German waves of assault, wiped them out with machine-gun, rifle fire, and bayonet, and steadily continued their programme work towards their objective.

Meanwhile, on the left of the Lincolns and, Wilts, the K.O.Y.L.I. and other Yorkshiremen fought onward to the outskirts of Villers-Guislain. In front of the ruins a German howitzer battery was sent galloping furiously into action, as a desperate measure for breaking the English advance. The Yorkshiremen surrounded guns and limbers and captured officers, men, and material of the battery. Then the Leicesters and Wiltshires in turn raced forward, after the scene in Linnet valley, and reaching the enemy artillery positions, took eight field-guns. At this point the amazing men from Wiltshire had a total casualty list of six men lightly wounded, and behind them

three hundred enemy dead were afterwards counted, and there were many wounded and unwounded prisoners.

The 17th Division, which had fought for twenty-three miles from the Ancre, practically without relief, carrying on their way Thiepval, Schwaben Redoubt, Pozières, Courcelette, Martinpuich, Flèrs, Gueudecourt, Le Transloy, and Beaulencourt, and the bridge-head of the North Canal, topped this marvellous tally of victories by storming into Gauche Wood. It was a long and most violent struggle with which these wearied and wasted troops crowned their career of reconquest.

The Lancashire Fusiliers and Manchesters began with very hard fighting for old positions. The Germans were in superior strength, and the fighting became so mixed that, as parties pushed that way and this along the trenches, men were often prisoners one minute and captors of their conquerors the next. One officer took a group of prisoners, who spied reinforcements, turned on their captor and took him. The Englishman, before he could be removed, was reached by his men and resumed control of his prisoners. Yet again, a German reinforcement swept officer and men back to the road to the prison cage ; but for the fifth time more English stormed forward, and in the final change the officer emerged with a hundred and thirty prisoners.

Slowly, resolutely, the

A RUN IN THE GREAT WARREN.
Entrance to one of the tunnels in the Hindenburg line by which the German machine-gun teams escaped when the defensive system was overrun by the British.

NEW ZEALANDERS GOING FORWARD INTO ACTION.
Men of a Canterbury battalion of the New Zealand Force making their way along a trench to come into action. New Zealanders came in for some terrific fighting south of Cambrai in October, 1918.

THE HERO OF MŒUVRES.
Corporal David Hunter, who received the V.C. for his great exploit on September 17th, 1918, when with six comrades of the H.L.I. he beat off the encircling enemy for over forty-eight hours.

derelict British Tanks were converted by the enemy into machine-gun posts, and nine German battalions were used in continual counter-thrusts, leading to a prolonged and apparently confused tangle of combats calculated completely to wear down the tired Englishmen. Yet Gauche Wood was added to the victories of the 17th Division, and at the end of the fight the Lincolns and their comrades had thirteen hundred prisoners.

Along the gully between Gauche Wood and Gouzeaucourt there was only a short advance to form a defensive flank during the advance over Chapel Hill. **British Guards'** Welsh and English troops encircled **iron defence** Gouzeaucourt village from the south and prepared with their registered guns to shatter any counter-thrust by the enemy against the left of the main forces of the assault. All the heavy counter-attacks that General von der Marwitz launched, with increasing violence in the evening, formed part of the counter-offensive arranged by the enemy High Command.

About four o'clock in the afternoon General von Below launched his long-prepared attack from the old Cambrai salient towards Mœuvres, Havrincourt, and Trescault. The main weight of the assault was thrown over the North Canal towards the Wotan line. On the left the British Guards held their line intact, so completely crippling the German forces in front of them that they could leave them in peace to recover. The Guardsmen then turned on their right, where they could see every figure in the moving masses marching from Flesquières Ridge towards the canal line by Havrincourt.

With rapid, aimed fire the Guards felled each wave of assault. The main attack was broken before it reached the positions of the 3rd Division. Two parties entered the British trenches north of Havrincourt, and another detachment straggled across the canal into a heavy barrage, and surrendered.

Little more than a hundred prisoners were taken by Havrincourt, and the victors did not appreciate the scope of their achievement until they learnt from their captives that quite a strong attempt had been made to recover the Hindenburg defences.

As a result of the offensive of the Third and Fourth British Armies and the counter-offensive by the Second and Seventeenth German Armies, ten thousand Teutons went into happy captivity to a country where food was

troops of the 17th Division fought up Chapel Hill, in an action lasting through the night and continuing the next day. As the Dorsets and Yorkshires went on to their next objective they were counter-attacked by a fresh German battalion coming forward in a sunken road. They followed the same course as the Wiltshires, and afterwards conquered the ground assigned to them.

In the meantime the Lincolns and other troops entered Gauche Wood, and waged once more a grim battle among the destroyed trees and old, ruined Tanks by which the South Africans had fought. Four of the

still abundant and the treatment of captives of war such as became a civilised people.

With the failure of the enemy's attempt to repeat his success of the early Cambrai operations—a failure mainly due to lack of strength in numbers as well as strength in spirit—the war rapidly marched towards a decisive close. For a week minor operations went on between the North Canal and the Scheldt Canal. The enemy made local counter-attacks and the British replied. The undaunted Alpine Corps and Thuringians remained on the battlefield waiting relief by the 121st Division; and the Londoners, Eastern County troops, and Yeomanry resumed the tussle with their old opponents at dawn on September 21st.

With a view to straightening out the British line on the left of the Australians, the Englishmen went out over the slippery ground between Ronssoy and Gauche Wood and fought into the Hindenburg outpost system. By mid-day the English infantry **Dogged battle** was apparently successfully established in **in bad weather** the enemy's advanced line on a length of nearly three miles, with some two hundred prisoners. Then heavy counter-attacks developed. The Alpine troops and men of Thuringia, with fresh forces of the relieving division, stormed out from the Hindenburg main line, released their comrades who had been captured, recovered farm after farm, and by nightfull whittled down the English gain of ground to a quarter of a mile.

In the rain and darkness the action continued. Once more old British trenches and ditches repeatedly changed hands. Meath Post was lost and regained, and other points in the Villers-Guislain gullies returned into the eddy of battle.

At midnight the Londoners and County troops made another attack from Epéhy and Ronssoy, took and lost one redoubt, held another, remaining at daybreak in a fragment of about a mile of outpost line. Day and night the rain fell and the mud deepened. In a return to old-fashioned trench warfare the troops of the Fourth British Army and the First French Army tackled the great quadrilateral between Holnon and Fresnoy, gathering some fourteen hundred prisoners. On September 25th the sky brightened, and hot sunshine began to dry the ground. This was the weather for which Marshal Foch had been waiting, and he struck such a rapid succession of blows from the Meuse to the Yser as prostrated the German Great Staff, filled it with panic fear, and led it to order the Imperial Chancellor, Prince Max of Baden, to secure peace immediately on the best terms obtainable.

ROAD-MAKING DURING THE LAST GREAT ADVANCE.
British troops engaged in cutting a roadway through a war-devastated tract of France, for the maintaining of communication with the fighting forces that were moving rapidly forward during the early autumn of 1918.

THE BALKANS: FROM THE DETHRONEMENT OF CONSTANTINE TO THE SURRENDER OF BULGARIA.

By Robert Machray.

Situation in 1917—Reorganisation of the Rumanian Army—Fine Rumanian Offensive—Brilliant Work of Avarescu—Rumanian Attack on the Sereth Stopped by Russian Reverses in Galicia—Mackensen Seizes the Opportunity—Magnificent Rumanian Defence of Cosmesti Bridge-head—Russian Defections—Great Battle of Marashesti—Mackensen Beaten—German Propaganda in Vain—Rumania Betrayed by the Bolshevists—Forced Into an Armistice—Union with Bessarabia—The Tragic "Peace of Bukarest"—The Salonika Army under a New Leader—Development of the Greek Forces—Italian Offensive in Albania Partially Successful—The Great Allied Final Assault in Macedonia—Magnificent Serbo-French Victory in the High Mountains—Bulgar Centre Broken—The Gap Widened —Heavy Fighting on a Hundred-Mile Front—How the British, with the Greeks, Materially Helped—Epic Struggle near Doiran— Favourable Result for the Allies—Swift Advance of the Serbians and Jugo-Slavs—Bulgar Armies Sundered—Overwhelming Defeat of the Enemy—Bulgaria Asks for an Armistice—Granted on Unconditional Surrender—Bulgaria Out of the War.

THE tangled story of the Balkans, including Rumania, was brought up to June, 1917, in Chapter CLXXXIX (Vol. 9, page 429). At that time Constantine was deposed and Prince Alexander, his second son, had become King, but the real power in Greece was in the hands of Venizelos, the great patriot and statesman who had never wavered in his hostility to Germany, and who had become Prime Minister under the new regime which the Allies had set up. The Salonika Army—or, as the French called it, the Army of the Orient—in co-operation with Italian forces on the west, lay on a solid front from the Ægean to the Adriatic, and no longer feared a sudden stab in the back from a treacherous neutral.

Bulgaria occupied Eastern Greek Macedonia up to the line of the Struma, and with Germany and Austria held all Serbia, except the district of Monastir, which the Salonika Army had reconquered in 1916. Austria was in possession of Montenegro and Albania to the line of the Vojusa. In Rumania all Wallachia was in the grasp of the enemy, who, standing on the line of the Carpathians on the west, and on the line of the Putna, the Sereth, and the Danube on the south, threatened Moldavia; the Dobruja also was his.

With the accession to power of Venizelos, the Provisional Government at Salonika, which had played a most useful part in the struggle, disappeared; and one of his first acts, after he had regularised his position

as the virtual ruler of reunited Greece, was to break off relations with the Central Powers, Bulgaria, and Turkey, and range his country definitely on the side of the Allies. Otherwise little of importance fell to be chronicled in the Balkans till July 22nd, 1917, when the Rumanians undertook an offensive against the Austro-Germans in Moldavia.

After the retreat to the Sereth the major part of the Rumanian Army had been withdrawn from the front to be refitted and reorganised, its place meanwhile being filled by the Russians, of whom, with those already in line or in reserve, there were about half a million. The remainder of the Rumanian forces, consisting of the Second Army, under General Avarescu, stood on the line in the Oitoz district, and was strengthened as opportunity served. It comprised six divisions, and its fighting quality was high.

General Presan, who had shown great ability in the Battle of the Neajlov, was given the task of reorganising the other armies. In this he received very material assistance from the French Military Mission, at the head of which was General Berthelot, with Colonel Petin as his Chief of Staff. Included in the Mission were large numbers of French officers. During the winter and spring they sedulously devoted themselves to training the Rumanian troops, and by April the excellent result of their hard work was manifested in the fine appearance of every Rumanian regiment. They paid special attention to the Rumanian

KING ALEXANDER VISITING THE BRITISH SALONIKA FORCE.
King Alexander of Greece (centre of first three), with the British Commander-in-Chief on the Macedonian front, General Milne, on his right, arriving on the parade ground for an inspection of the British Salonika Force.

Air Force, of which there was scarcely a single unit in existence before Rumania entered the war.

Great Britain, which had a Military Mission, under General Ballard, in the country, and France contributed both aeroplanes and personnel, as well as guns, mortars, shells, and other munitions in large quantities. These were sent through Russia. By the end of June the reorganised Rumanian Army mustered twelve divisions, six of which composed the First Army, with General Christescu, who previously had done well in the operations on the Danube, in command, the other six being the Second Army, with Avarescu at its head. In addition were three divisions in reserve, but without adequate artillery or complete equipment. Under King Ferdinand, General Shcherbacheff, the Russian leader, was in chief command, with General Presan as Chief of Staff.

For the offensive the Russo-Rumanian forces numbered nearly 700,000 men, but—and it was a very ominous but— the Russian part, still about half a million **Russo-Rumanian** strong, was already penetrated by Bolshevist **army positions** influences, and, as events proved, was not to be relied on thoroughly. On the west, from about Dorna Watra, on the frontier of the Bukovina, to Ocna, in the Trotus valley, stood the Ninth Russian Army, linking up with the Second Rumanian Army, which held the front as far as the Putna. Both faced the Austro-German army of the Archduke Joseph along the line of the Carpathians. On the south, from the Putna to Focsani, on the Sereth, the Fourth Russian Army took the line eastwards from the mountains ;

from Focsani to about Namoloasa, half-way to Galatz, stood the First Rumanian Army, and from Namoloasa to the Danube and the sea was the Sixth Russian Army. Against these forces was arrayed the army of Field-Marshal Mackensen, composed of Austrian, Bulgarian, and Turkish troops, with a proportion of German soldiers. In numbers the Allies surpassed the Austro-Germans, who, however, held very strong defensive positions, and, moreover, probably counted on being assisted by **Russian collapse** Bolshevists in the province of Moldavia in **in Galicia** the same way as they had been in Galicia.

It may have been intended originally that the Russo-Rumanian offensive should synchronise with that of the Russians in Galicia, but it was not launched till that movement, after a wonderful initial success that astonished the world, was breaking down in utter disaster, owing to the defection of various Russian units. Thanks to Bolshevism, Tarnopol, which had been in Russian hands since almost the beginning of the war, was partly occupied by the Austro-Germans on July 21st. It was on the very next day that Avarescu, with the Second Rumanian Army, began the attack in Moldavia by an intense bombardment of the enemy's front from the Casin to the Putna, his fire being particularly heavy against Marasti, near the Susitza, where the Austro-Germans had erected strong fortifications, including four redoubts, armed with many machine-guns, which were held by a division under General von Gerok, who was in local command of this whole area.

BRITISH FORTIFIED POST THREE THOUSAND FEET ABOVE THE LEVEL OF THE STRUMA.
British defence work—a machine-gun and gunner are to be seen to the right— on a height overlooking the valley of the Struma, which lay on the right flank of the British forces in Macedonia. The River Struma itself can be seen as a faint line serpentining in the distance on the left. This position was on a height three thousand feet above the river level, with a beautiful prospect over the hills of the Macedonian-Bulgarian frontier.

Avarescu massed no fewer than sixty batteries against Marasti, and shelled it without intermission for two days. In the night of July 23rd-24th several broad gaps were made in its defences. Early in the morning of the 24th his infantry advanced to the attack, and, fighting with great dash, took the place by storm within four hours, notwithstanding the most determined opposition. The Austro-Germans suddenly broke and fled in disorder, the commandant escaping in his slippers and without his cap. Reinforced by troops sent by Mackensen from Focsani, they attempted to make a stand in the mountains, but were driven back by the victorious Rumanians. Desperate and sanguinary encounters took place on July 26th and 27th, but the Rumanians pushed forward, taking three thousand prisoners and eighty

BULGARIAN INVADERS IN SERBIAN TOWNS.
Bulgarian artillery passing through a Serbian town near the frontier of the two countries, and (above) a Bulgarian patrol in Krushevo, about twenty-five miles to the north of Monastir. (These photographs from an enemy source were taken before the Bulgarian debacle which followed hard upon the allied offensive that opened on September 15th, 1918.)

guns, besides large quantities of machine-guns, hand-grenades, and ammunition. So great was the success of Avarescu that he was able to reoccupy the whole district to the frontier. Meanwhile another of his divisions was moving swiftly southwards towards the Putna, and increasing the pressure on the enemy.

These operations on the Carpathian front were planned as part of a general offensive, and on July 26th a strong artillery preparation was begun along the line of the Sereth, and for this the infantry, both Russian and Rumanian, were held in readiness for a powerful assault. The first series of the enemy's entrenchments was destroyed, but six hours before the time appointed for the assault, General Shcherbacheff received a telegram from M. Kerensky, the head of the Provisional Government in Russia, telling him of the disastrous turn of events in Galicia, and requesting him on that account to postpone the purposed offensive.

Accordingly, the offensive was put off, which was unfortunate, as it appeared to have every prospect of success; on the other hand, it had to be said that the failure of the Russians in the north made the position of the allied forces in the adjacent area in Moldavia one of danger, and this had to be provided against, all the more because the Ninth Russian

Army, holding the line of the Carpathians there, was regarded as Bolshevist, and therefore untrustworthy. To meet the emergency Rumanian troops were despatched from the Sereth to that quarter. Mackensen somehow heard of this, and he decided to attack the Sereth line thus weakened.

His plan was to strike a heavy blow which would permit him to cross the Sereth and cut in two the Russo-Rumanian armies. With this end in view he directed his main attack against Marashesti, an important railway junction, in the district north of Focsani, while the crossing of the river was to be forced at Cosmesti. For these operations he concentrated from ten to twelve divisions, and hoped further to profit by reason of the instability of the Russian troops, of which doubtless he was well informed by his spies. It was against these Russians that, on August 6th, he began his attack near Cosmesti, carrying four lines of their trenches, though they fought well. Their commander sent for help, and by one of the chances of war it came, and came immediately, from a Rumanian division that was actually on the march to the threatened area in the north, as mentioned in the preceding paragraph.

Without waiting for orders from Headquarters, the Rumanian general brought his guns into action, and throwing forward a brigade, made a bridge-head at Cosmesti, which held up the attack. South of Cosmesti **Epic defence** fierce fighting raged for three days, the **of Cosmesti** Rumanians bravely continuing the struggle, in spite of the defection of some of the Russian units. But the most terrible and sanguinary contest was at Cosmesti itself. Day after day the Austro-Germans assailed it with their best troops—the Alpine Corps, the 89th Prussian Division, and the 12th Bavarian Division. Eight times in a single day did the mountaineers and the Bavarians deliver a strong attack, and eight times were they repulsed by the gallant Rumanians, who were determined to hold the position at all costs, as they knew its loss would be fatal.

Among the really great episodes of the war, the defence of Cosmesti was maintained with success until August 10th, when Mackensen withdrew a short distance away. It was.

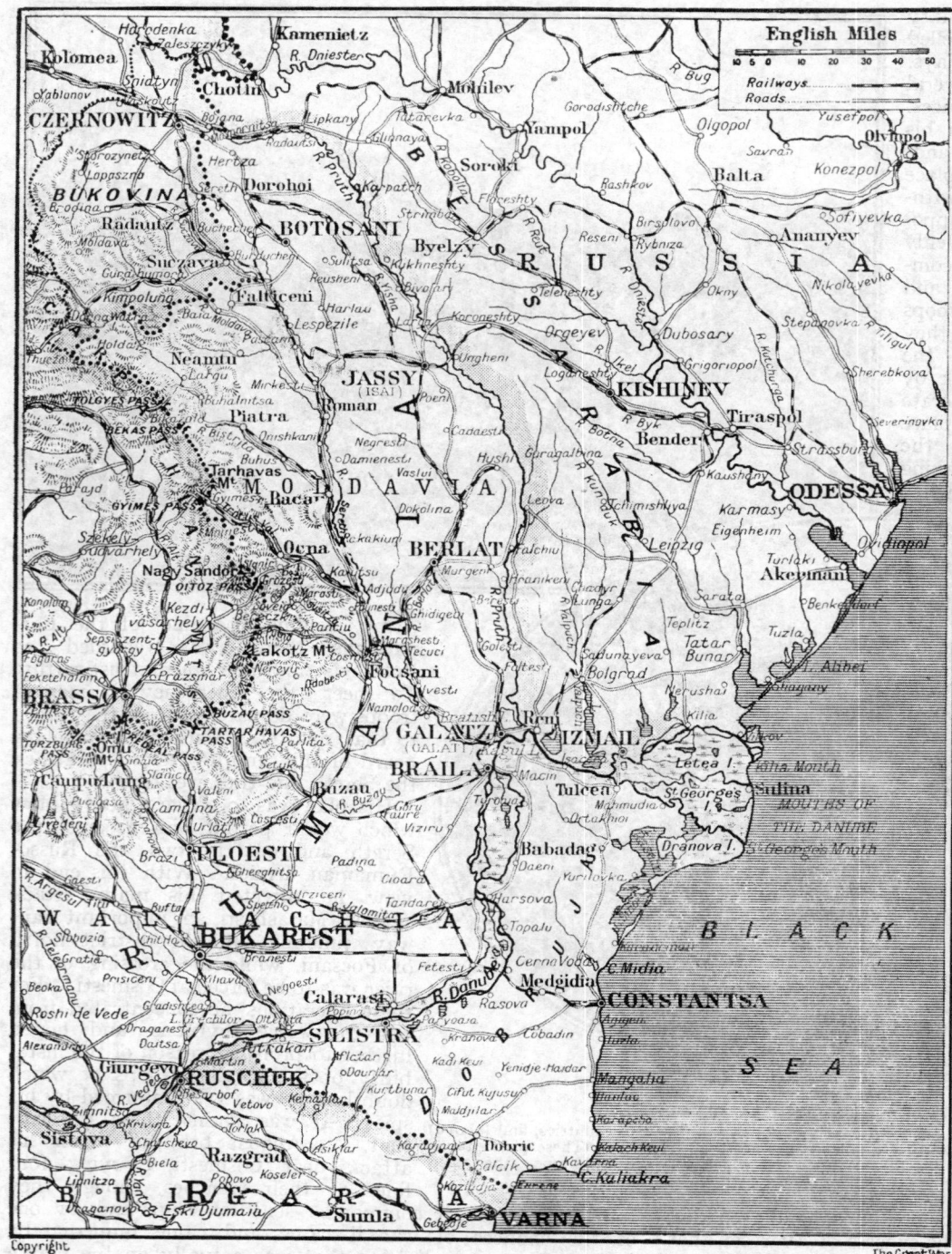

BATTLE-LINE IN THE RUSSO-RUMANIAN OFFENSIVE, 1917.
The Ninth Russian Army extending from Dorna Watra to Ocna, with the Second Rumanian Army southward to
the River Putna, faced the Austro-Germans along the Carpathians. Thence the Fourth Russian Army extending
eastward to Focsani, the Second Rumanian Army to Namoloasa, and the Sixth Russian Army to the Danube
and the sea, confronted Mackensen's Austro-German-Turco-Bulgarian troops.

replacing General Christescu, and being put at the head of the combined First Rumanian and Fourth Russian Armies. Grigorescu began a vigorous counter-offensive on August 12th, but from the start it was compromised by the unreliability of some of the Russian regiments. In one section, where the Rumanians were attacking with brilliant success, a whole Russian division gave way and exposed their left flank, the result being that the enemy immediately poured all his available reserves into the gap and with them played havoc among the Rumanians, who lost 10,000 out of 14,000 men before the action closed. Grigorescu was still attacking on the 13th, but, because of his heavy losses and the untrustworthiness of the Russians, he made no progress, and this second phase of the battle came to an end on that day.

In the meantime Mackensen had been preparing to resume the attack, in which the Archduke Joseph was to co-operate by an assault on the Second Rumanian Army on the Carpathian front. When Mackensen's attack came it was directed along the line from Marashesti to Stravani, above Panciu. It began on August 15th with a tremendous artillery preparation, Marashesti in particular being shelled with great severity for six hours. In the infantry assaults which followed the fighting was extraordinarily desperate. The Rumanians made a splendid stand; officers and soldiers died fighting rather than surrender.

The Austro-Germans were in superior strength, and pressing forward with resolution captured in the afternoon the village of Baltaretu and the Cosmesti bridge-head, but failed to get across the river, to the east side of which the Rumanians had retired, and where they were on higher ground. Between Marashesti and Adjudu, Mac-

a very costly affair to him. The 12th Bavarians had only two thousand men left out of the entire division, and the Alpine troops stated that not even at Verdun had they experienced a more stubborn resistance. Mackensen had gained a little ground, but had failed in his main object. On the Rumanian side the losses also were heavy. When the division that had gone to the rescue was withdrawn at the end of the four days it was found that its regiments, which had been from 3,500 to 4,000 strong, mustered no more than 400 men.

In the most critical stage of the combat news came that Von Gerok had broken in the front of the Russians in the Trotus valley, and had forced them back to Ocna. Undismayed, the Rumanians went on fighting magnificently at Cosmesti, and the bridge-head was saved. After August 10th there was a lull, and during it King Ferdinand made some changes in the commands—General Grigorescu, for instance,

kensen was more successful in his attack on Panciu, but this was only because the Russians withdrew from the part of the line which they had been given to defend, either after a slight resistance or with none at all, and took to the neighbouring woods and villages. Panciu was a serious loss to the Rumanians, as it imperilled the railway junction at Adjudu, from which supplies went up to Ocna, but even more serious was the fact that, as the majority of the Russians were no longer to be counted on for support, the brunt of the defence was thrown practically on the Rumanians alone. Mackensen's capture of Panciu threatened to drive a wedge between the First and Second Rumanian Armies, but Grigorescu sent up reinforcements and filled the gap between them. Thereupon the Rumanians counter-attacked, and with the courage of desperation succeeded in

*Panciu captured
by Mackensen*

forcing the enemy back, though they were unable to recover Panciu.

Fighting continued around Marashesti to August 19th, on which day the Austro-Germans captured the station, but failed to get into the town. The centre of the struggle shifted on that day, too, to the line above Panciu, on the railway from Focsani to Adjudu. Mackensen brought to the assault fresh troops that considerably outnumbered the Rumanians in that sector. After a heavy bombardment, lasting the greater part of the day, he launched his infantry early in the evening of the 19th on the north-west of Panciu towards the village of Paunesti, and there ensued one of the most bitter struggles of the war. Though numerically inferior, the Rumanians fought with superb courage and endurance, which were heightened, moreover, by the presence of their King and the Crown Prince, who watched the swaying struggle from a divisional commander's observation-post.

Six times the attackers came on in great waves of men, and five times were beaten back with terrible slaughter, but the sixth time they managed to get a foothold in the Rumanian trenches.

SERBIANS BRINGING IN THEIR WOUNDED.
Serbian stretcher-bearers carrying a wounded comrade in a village close behind the fighting-front. When the offensive began in the middle of September, 1918, it was the Serbian troops, in conjunction with the French, who opened the attack, going forward on a nine-mile front in the face of immense difficulties.

At that moment the one Rumanian regiment which had been held in reserve, the other reserves having already been thrown into the fight, came forward at the double, and charged with such wonderful dash that the enemy, who had thought victory secure, was taken utterly by surprise, broke, and fell back in disorder. The Rumanians had gained the day, and with it had won the whole great Battle of Marashesti, for afterwards only small engagements took place on this part of the front. Mackensen was beaten. It was a wonderful triumph for the Rumanians—by far the greatest for them in the war, and, for that matter, in all their history as a people. Their reconstituted Army, with its much smaller forces, had worsted Mackensen and his picked troops who had so often been victorious. Yet this event, obscured by other events happening elsewhere at the time, passed almost unnoticed by the rest of the world.

As had been planned, the Austro-Germans under the Archduke Joseph, in the Carpathians, had been attacking while the great battle in the south had been in progress. Their primary object was to prevent Rumanian forces from moving thence to the Marashesti section of the front. In the Carpathians, Avarescu was at the head of the veterans of the Second Army, but at this time the army consisted of only five divisions, whereas the enemy had at least eight divisions. The archduke started his offensive on August 10th, and, as the Rumanians were much outnumbered, the situation at first was extremely critical for them.

The battle for Grozesti

Making a feint on the Rumanian right wing in the Trotus valley, the Austro-Germans directed their main assault against the Rumanians in the hilly country lying between the Trotus and the Putna, and for two or three days they attacked in that district with the utmost violence. The little village of Grozesti was the chief scene of the struggle. The place derived strategic importance from its being the key to the railway just above it—the railway from Adjudu to Ocna and the line of the Trotus. After frantic efforts the Austro-Germans succeeded in taking part of Grozesti, but the repeated counter-attacks of the Rumanians kept them from gaining the north part, which was near the railway and vital to its defence.

Farther south Avarescu, whose forces had been much depleted by his counter-attacks, and who had little or nothing in the way of reserves, withdrew his line about Soveia to a position which gave him the advantage of a shorter front, and there held the enemy. But at the time Mackensen was attacking on the north of Panciu, the Austro-Germans in the Carpathians shifted their main assault to Slanic, about six miles south of Ocna. For this fresh effort they had been strengthened by German reinforcements, and fierce fighting began on August 16th, with the Rumanians being pushed back very

GERMAN GUNS AND SUPPLIES FOR THE CAMPAIGN AGAINST SERBIA.
On the Serbian bank of the Danube. A German picture showing the landing, from the pontoon ferry-boats by which they had crossed the great river, of men and supplies for stiffening the Austro-Bulgaria resistance to the threatened allied attack.

GERMAN PHOTOGRAPH OF A BULGARIAN ADVANCE AMONG THE HILLS NEAR MONASTIR.
In this photograph a Bulgarian force is seen going forward during fighting among the rugged hills of the Monastir district. Shells can be seen bursting at the foot of the nearer slope. The picture gives a vivid impression of the country in which the war was waged along the southern Serbian front.

slowly, as they hotly contested every inch of the ground, until August 19th, when the enemy made much more rapid progress, owing to the exhaustion of the Rumanians, and captured the Slanic glass factory.

It looked as if the Rumanians must give way completely, but at this juncture two regiments, that had made a forced march through the mountains, came up and, without any rest and with the scantiest refreshment, threw themselves on the advancing foe and retrieved the situation. Next day the fighting perceptibly lost in intensity, and gradually died away, except for local affairs of comparative unimportance. On September 9th Avarescu captured some positions near Slanic as well as that village, but his strength was insufficient to hold them when the Austro-Germans counter-attacked with fresh troops.

Stimulated by the demoralisation which was spreading apace in Russia, and for which they themselves were largely responsible, the German authorities came to the conclusion that there was an easier way to subdue the Rumanians than by fighting them in the field, and they organised a great propaganda campaign with the intention of disintegrating the Rumanian Army. Besides distributing lying leaflets and pamphlets to mislead the Rumanian soldiers, most of whom were ignorant peasants, though brave enough, the Germans sent representatives from among their men **Insidious German** on the front to fraternise, or try to frater-**propaganda** nise, with these Rumanians. Among other insidious methods of propaganda the enemy fired each morning from trench-mortars parcels of news-papers which had been printed in Bukarest and contained the grossest misstatements regarding King Ferdinand and his Government, as well as about the Allies in general. But the Rumanians were proof against these assaults on their fidelity, nor did they give heed to the cajoleries and enticements of the Russian Bolshevists among them. Bolshevism, however, did have a baneful effect on the fortunes of the country.

As has already been noted, the Russian armies in Rumania had become during the summer of 1917 a danger rather than a help. As the year drew on, masses of the Russian soldiers left the front, and with the institution of the Leninist Government after the fall of the Kerensky regime in November, the remaining Russian forces in the country disappeared as quickly as the armies in Russia. In December the Soviets, or Councils of Workmen's and Soldiers' Deputies, on the Russo-Rumanian front, joined with Germany in compelling Rumania to adhere to the armistice which was arranged by the Germans and the Bolshevists at Brest Litovsk.

In point of fact Rumania, short of being completely eaten up and destroyed, had no option. She was cut off from her Allies as absolutely as if they had ceased to exist, and they could render her no assist- **Rumania forced** ance. In this crisis of fate their sympathy **into an armistice** availed her nothing, and very much against her will she was obliged to yield to sheer *force majeure*, and agree to the armistice. In the meantime the Russian troops, to the number of about 400,000 men, left the country, selling off en route their guns, rifles, motor-cars, and equipment for trifling sums to anyone who would buy them.

As they passed through the country the disorganised Russian troops committed various outrages, besides carrying on a Bolshevist propaganda. The Rumanian authorities took steps to meet the situation, and by doing so incurred the wrath of the Russian Bolshevist Government, which threw into prison the Rumanian Minister at Petrograd, and even decreed the arrest of King Ferdinand himself. On the joint representations of the allied diplomatists in Petrograd the Rumanian Minister was released. On January 28th, 1918, the "Commissioners of the People," as the Lenin-Trotsky Government called itself, broke off relations with Rumania, impounded the Rumanian funds which were kept in gold in Moscow, and denounced General Shcherbacheff as an enemy of the Revolution. The Rumanian Minister to

Russia was sent, with his staff, back to Rumania. At the same time it was announced that the Commissioners were highly incensed with the Bessarabian Popular Assembly for having invited Rumanian troops into Bessarabia for the suppression of anarchy—*i.e.*, of Bolshevism. By one of the numerous ironies of the war, the action of the Bolshevists in Bessarabia led to the union of that province with Rumania.

An outcome of the break-up of the Russian Empire was the formation of an independent Government and a " Council of the Land " in Bessarabia, and on December 15th, 1917, these bodies proclaimed their definite separation from Bolshevist Russia, styling their country the Moldavian Republic, and asking assistance from Rumania against the Bolshevists, who were interfering with their ordering of affairs. This call for help was most natural, as the vast majority of the Bessarabians were Rumanian. In 1856 the Treaty of Paris gave Southern Bessarabia to Rumania, but it was taken from her by Russia in 1878, an act which she had always resented, though she received some compensation by being permitted to annex the Dobruja. In January, 1918, the Rumanian Government agreed to send a force into

Bessarabia unites with Rumania

Bessarabia for the purpose specified, but it was influenced also by the fact that there were great quantities of stores belonging to Rumania in that country, which the Bolshevists threatened to destroy. A further reason was the hope of reopening communications with the Allies in the west.

Rumanian troops consequently were sent into Bessarabia, and after some unimportant fighting they arrived at Kishinev, the capital, on January 26th. Negotiations thereupon were entered into with a view to the union of Bessarabia with Rumania, and on April 9th the Bessarabian Parliament voted a treaty of union by eighty-six votes to three, the terms including full local autonomy for Bessarabia, with adequate representation in the Government and Parliament of Rumania, and the future adoption by Rumania of equal and universal suffrage, which already prevailed in Bessarabia. Germany acquiesced, because, according to the " Cologne Gazette," " as Rumania was to be permitted to exist, she must be kept in a condition of vitality."

This gleam of good fortune for Rumania had meanwhile been more than counter-balanced by the action of the Central Powers. Early in February, Germany, through Mackensen, intimated to the Rumanian Headquarters that peace was about to be concluded with Russia, and that as the armistice

The " Peace of Bukarest "

with Rumania was at an end, Rumanian delegates should at once be sent to Focsani to see what could be arranged. When the delegates reached Focsani they soon found that the only arrangement was that Rumania was given four days to decide whether or not she would treat for peace—of course, on the terms of the enemy. A Crown Council was held at Jassy, and the question was discussed, but Rumania had really no choice. If she refused, and resumed hostilities, she could hold out, the majority of her generals declared, for perhaps a month at most. Bratiano and Take Jonescu were in favour of continuing the struggle, but they were outvoted, and they resigned their offices.

King Ferdinand asked Avarescu to form a Ministry, and the general undertook the tragic business of getting together a Peace Cabinet. Meanwhile negotiations had been going on with the Central Powers, and at Bufta, on March 5th, a declaration was signed between M. Argetoianu for Rumania, Von Kühlmann for Germany, Count Czernin for Austria, Dr. Momtchiloff for Bulgaria, and Talaat Pasha for Turkey, which was the basis of the " Peace of Bukarest," signed and

BRITISH PATROLS REACHING A VILLAGE ON THE MACEDONIAN FRONT.

During the apparently quiet state of the Salonika front which preceded the final allied offensive minor hostilities were continuous. Raiding and patrol parties frequently went forward testing the enemy trenches and positions, specially at the extremities of the line. When patrols reached such villages as that shown, the enemy usually started shelling them, but nevertheless many prisoners were taken during these sudden raids.

sealed on May 7th. On March 12th Avarescu, under German pressure, resigned, and was succeeded by M. Marghiloman, a former Finance Minister, and more or less a pro-German, according to common account. If he was, he was unable to obtain less onerous terms.

Summarised, the Bukarest treaty was as follows:

Until the conclusion of a general peace Rumania remained in the occupation of the armies of the Central Powers, and had to maintain these armies at her own expense. She ceded to Bulgaria the part of the Dobruja which had fallen to her under the Treaty of Bukarest, 1913, and to the Central Powers the part of the Dobruja north of the other to the Danube. She agreed to a rectification of her frontiers in favour of Austria-Hungary (a loss of 3,000 square miles). On the other hand, the Central Powers bound themselves that she should have an assured trade route to the Black Sea via Cerna Voda and Constantsa. With respect to the Danube, Rumania agreed to the abolition of the European Danube Commission, and its replacement by a body consisting of representatives of States on the Danube or the European coasts of the Black Sea—this excluded the Allies. All parties renounced war indemnities.

Terms of the Bukarest Treaty

A supplementary treaty made Rumania renounce indemnifications for damages caused by the Germans, but she had to undertake to indemnify the Germans for damages suffered by them. Under a second supplementary treaty exclusive rights for working oil in Rumania for ninety years were given to the Oil Lands Leasing Company, an organisation controlled by the Central Powers, and a monopoly of trading in all mineral oil production in Rumania was given to a Monopoly Company, also controlled by the Central Powers ; in the one case the Rumanian Government was to participate in the profits after eight per cent. dividend had been paid, and in the other that Government was to take up twenty-five per cent. of the founders' shares. Under the treaty religious liberty and political rights were given to Roman Catholics, Greek Uniates, the Bulgarian Orthodox, Protestants, Moslems, and Jews.

By the "Peace of Bukarest" Rumania lost nearly one-fifth of her territory. The value of the forests in the mountains and tracts ceded to Austria was put at more than one hundred millions sterling. Rumania also lost about one-tenth of her population. Though she had no indemnity imposed on her in cash, the writing off of the enemy requisitions cost her fifty millions sterling. The value of the oil and other concessions she was forced to give was beyond computation. As the Allied Ministers pointed out in a memorandum, dated May 16th, the monopoly in the exploitation of the forests and the sale of timber, as well as in the export of cereals, set up by the treaty to the profit of Germany, represented a war indemnity, the payment of which would weigh heavily on Rumania for many years.

The Rumanian Army was reduced from 250,000 to 30,000 men and only one hundred and sixty rounds of ammunition were allowed per rifle, a German Demobilisation Commission being appointed to supervise everything. The Army became merely a sort of police force. Beyond a comparatively small amount, war material and munitions were to be stored in the occupied territory under German control. As there was nothing to compel Germany to evacuate the occupied territory, inasmuch as she could postpone indefinitely the ratification of the treaty, though Rumania had to complete it at once, there was little prospect of Rumania being free for a long time to come.

Commenting on the treaty, the Allied Ministers said:

Germany, by the treaty she has imposed on Rumania, has cynically ignored her own declarations. The treaty provides for the spoliation of the public lands, for the scarcely concealed annexation of the whole country, and, after the peace, for its barbarous exploitation, and for the draining of its resources to the profit of the conquerors. It turns Rumania into a veritable convict settlement, where the entire population is condemned to hard labour for the benefit of the conquerors. It is a fair example of a German

Allied comments on the "Peace"

peace. We (the Allies) should consider it all the more closely, inasmuch as the German delegates informed the Rumanian delegates, who were appalled at being required to accept such conditions, that they would appreciate their moderation when they knew the terms which would be imposed on the Western Powers after the victory of the Central Empires.

Among the demands put forward by the Germans at the March conference was one that Rumania should give facilities for a German force to pass through Rumanian territory to Odessa, the great port on the Black Sea. On March 10th, a considerable time before the "Peace," a German battalion moved from Galatz into the Ukraine, and three days later the German occupation of Odessa was announced from Berlin. The Black Sea, like the Baltic, was to be Germanised,

Following on the "Peace of Bukarest" a General Election was held in Rumania, and on June 17th the new Parliament met at Jassy, which was retained as the national capital while Mackensen ruled at Bukarest as dictator. In the Speech from the Throne King Ferdinand referred to the recent "hard decisions," and said that they had been come to because the prolongation of armed resistance would have exhausted the country to the point of destruction. The King's position was a difficult one, as Germany openly desired his abdication, and would have insisted on it had it not been that Austria stood in the way. The King twice offered to abdicate, but neither the Parliament nor the people wished him to do so.

The election had resulted in a Parliament which was largely pro-German, or at all events was amenable to German influences. This was shown by its action with respect to Bratiano and the Ministers who had brought Rumania into the war. On July 18th the Chamber of Deputies, with only two dissentients, voted for the impeachment of the ex-Prime Minister and his colleagues. It had been proposed to try them in the courts, but that idea was dropped, as it was felt the judges would never convict them. So strong was the German pressure that Bratiano and some of the members of his Cabinet were, in spite of their protests, placed under preventive arrest. News of this monstrous treatment did not reach London till well past mid-September, but by that time things were happening farther south in the Balkans which, in conjunction with the changed situation on the western front, were to make all the difference in the world, not only to Rumania but to all the belligerents. By the end of that fateful September Bulgaria had been compelled to surrender unconditionally as the result of a great offensive by the Salonika Army,

Chapter CLXXXIX. (Vol. 9) chronicled the doings of the Salonika Army on the front from the Ægean to the Adriatic up to the close of the short allied offensive in June, 1917 (page 449). For about a year after that time nothing of outstanding importance took place on that front ; fighting was of a desultory character and apparently uninspired by any other than a defensive plan ; there were many raids both by land and through the air, but no great battles, no movements of wide significance.

Work of the British forces

On November 14th, 1917, a despatch was published from General Milne, the Commander-in-Chief of the British Salonika Force, which gave an account of the operations of the British troops in Macedonia from October 9th, 1916, to October 1st, 1917, and it furnished many interesting details, not previously authoritatively narrated, of the assaults made on the Bulgarian positions around Lake Doiran in the preceding April, and especially on the "Petit Couronné" heights a month later. Early in the summer Milne, in order to maintain the health and efficiency of his forces during a period when malaria and dysentery were more or less prevalent in the low-lying areas, withdrew from his forward positions in the Struma valley to the right bank of the river, and to the south of the Butkova valley. The general reported that on the whole the health of his troops was satisfactory, largely owing to the instruction of all ranks in the value of field sanitation and the prevention of disease in the field. Good work was being done with a view to the future. Some of the villages in the plain beyond the Struma were reoccupied by the British in October.

Towards the end of 1917 General Sarrail was replaced as Generalissimo of the Allied Forces by General Guillaumat. In a semi-official statement issued at Paris it was announced that Sarrail, who had had "to cope with great difficulties, and had rendered great services to the country," would be appointed to a new post when circumstances permitted. In June, 1918, General Guillaumat, who had been made Military Governor of Paris, was succeeded by General Franchet d'Espérey, one of the brilliant French commanders on the western front. Before leaving the Balkan front General Guillaumat made it his business to draw attention to the

King Alexander of Greece with General Milne inspecting British troops on the Salonika front.

General Franchet d'Espérey, Commander-in-Chief of the Allied Armies in the Balkans.

In the Salonika hinterland: British motor=convoy assembling on a main line of communication.

Soldiers of the French Army of the Orient watering their horses at a Macedonian stream.

Under canvas in Macedonia: British encampment by the road leading north from Salonika.

Old monastery near the British Balkan front, screened with brushwood and used as a canteen.

French infantry attacking a fortified farm in Macedonia.

Mountain road near Salonika, made by British soldiers.

striking development of the reorganised Greek Army as a combatant part, on a large scale, of the Salonika Army. At the end of May and in the beginning of June there had been some lively fighting in and about the Skra di Legen, the centre of the struggle being south of Huma, eleven miles west of the Vardar. In this action the Allies took several lines of trenches and nearly 2,000 prisoners, but the brunt of the fighting was borne by the Greeks, who, according to a Bulgarian communiqué, had "Venizelist divisions, reinforced by a division of the Greek Regular Army," in that sector. Guillaumat telegraphed to Venizelos :

> I witnessed the splendid attack this morning. Bravery is traditional in the Hellenic Army, but the troops which I saw proceed to the assault of the Skra di Legen knew how to combine method and discipline in the fight, which combination alone leads to victory. The capture of thirteen kilometres (about eight miles) of the enemy line constitutes a very fine war operation. This is the sentiment of our soldiers, who applaud whole-heartedly the success of their Hellenic comrades, by the side of whom they have been fighting for the last twenty months. I feel sure that the new divisions which in turn are arriving at the front will derive from this success, which must fill the whole of Greece with legitimate pride, still greater ardour for work and combat. It is thanks to you that the Hellenic Army is fighting on the side of the Allies ; it will know, thanks to you, how to take a large part in the final victory.

To the Greek statesman, who had done, dared, and endured so much for the cause, as well as for Greece, this tribute was no more than his due, but it was not the less welcome. Since becoming Prime Minister under King Alexander he had performed a great work for the Allies by bringing all Greece into line, and the Allies reciprocated this by extending to him a far larger share of their confidence than was perhaps possible before. In July, 1917, they handed over to him the Greek Fleet, and later in the year they helped him much by advancing money and supplying food to Greece. In August of that year he issued an important White Book, which showed how shamefully Serbia had been betrayed by Constantine, and among his first acts of major importance

Tribute to Greek valour was the renewal of the alliance with Serbia. In the course of the next six months the ex-Ministers and officers who had very nearly brought Greece to ruin by upholding Constantine in his unconstitutional policy were impeached, or brought to trial, and punished.

Venizelos was not without bitter enemies, and in January, 1918, they tried to discredit him and inflame the Greek people by spreading a report that the Allies intended to withdraw their forces from the strongly fortified front in Macedonia and place them behind the lines of the entrenched camp of Salonika, the way thus being left open for a descent on the Greek capital of a Bulgaro-German army, which, it was rumoured, was to be led in person by Constantine himself. The Allies categorically contradicted the report, and Venizelos shortly afterwards mobilised the Greek Army. In June, when the Greek troops, who were supported by the French, stormed the Bulgar trenches on the Skra di Legen, Greece had 150,000 men at the front, and other contingents were coming forward as they were trained.

For more than three months after the Greek success there was quiet, broken only by the usual episodes of trench warfare, on the whole allied line, except in Albania. In the mountainous district north of Valona (Avlona) there had already been sharp fighting between the Italians and the Austrians, the former, helped by the French, gaining a few miles of ground and pushing their outposts towards the Semeni. In July the Italians began a regular offensive, which at the start and for some little time afterwards met with much greater success than they had anticipated and prepared for, and this explained their loss later of some of the territory they had occupied in their advance.

On a front of about seventy miles the Italians—with French forces on their right, and supported from the sea on their left by British monitors, with British and other allied aircraft along the whole line—attacked the Austrian positions near the Voyusa, the assault being particularly intense in the region of the mouth of the river, some fifteen miles north of Valona, on July 6th. After a bitter struggle the Italian

infantry carried the heights between Levani and the monastery of Poyani. The Italian cavalry by a quick movement got between the western slopes of the Malakastra range and the sea, daringly attacked the enemy in the rear, and destroyed the bridges on the Semeni at Metali. Pressing on, Fieri fell into their hands on July 7th.

In the centre, lines of entrenchments south of Berat were taken by storm, and a determined effort on the right gave the Italians a series of heights situated near the head-waters of the Tomoritse. Farther east, between that river and the Devoli, the French drove the Austrians from several fortified peaks. Except in the plain beside the sea the terrain, a jumble of mountains and narrow valleys, was exceptionally difficult, but on July 8th and 9th the advance proceeded with a rapidity that was amazing in the circumstances. The Austrians, losing heavily in prisoners, guns, and material, fell back behind the Semeni, under cover of rearguard actions. On July 10th the **Franco-Italian successes** Italians entered Berat, where they were hailed by its people as the liberators of Albania, and had everywhere reached the Semeni. North-east of Berat the French pushed up the right bank of the Devoli, and captured the village of Mecan.

Telegraphing from Berat, Mr. J. M. N. Jeffries, in the "Daily Mail" of July 23rd, gave a vivid picture of the campaign :

> This is a gallant war here,.in the olden style, with cavalry charges, and towns falling, and a flying enemy, and a general taking leagues of territory and coming, as he did this morning, with his suite, amid a clashing escort of lancers, over a crescent-shaped Roman bridge to the red roofs and minarets of Berat, and bringing with him peace and contentment. Everything that the Near East can provide was there to greet General Ferrero (in chief command of the Italians)—Orthodox priests and cadi and mufti, beys in Stamboul frock-coats, and tiers of Albanians on the hillside and riverside, clad in their stained white, or in torn fragments of the spectrum, shouting "Long live Italy !" and waving fezes of all colours and materials. . . . General Weiss (in chief command of the Austrians) set an example to his officers by fleeing (from Berat) twelve hours before his wife, who was left behind to pack their belongings. Officers poured into their quarters in and around Berat from positions twelve miles away or more, gathered what they could of their belongings, and fled.

This allied offensive had the general result of straightening the Franco-Italian front all the way from Lake Ochrida to the mouth of the Semeni. In the fourth week of July the Austrians began a counter-attack in some force, and compelled the Italians to withdraw their advanced posts, their front afterwards running about four miles north of Berat. Higher up the coast allied aeroplanes repeatedly bombed Durazzo, and did the enemy much damage ; British machines took a considerable part in these operations. For two or three weeks the new front on the Semeni was in a condition of "unstable equilibrium," and then, on August 22nd, the Austrians, now commanded by General von Pflanzer-Baltin, developed an offensive with forces and guns that much outnumbered those of the Italians, who had to retire from Fieri and Berat, and withdraw to their prepared positions north of the Malakastra range. The net gain from the July operations was an improved defensive line for the Italians well to the north of Valona, and better tactical positions for the French on the east. **British capture Bulgarian salient** The Italians took nearly 3,000 prisoners, and the French more than 1,000, while thirty guns were captured. The retirement of the Italians after August 22nd was executed with great ability, and their losses were very slight, while those of the Austrians were heavy.

On September 1st the British carried out a very successful local operation west of the Vardar and immediately south of Gevgeli, capturing five hill-tops which formed an advanced Bulgarian salient that was strongly fortified. Next day the Bulgars made a desperate effort to recover the lost ground, but were repulsed. During the first and second weeks of the month there were various raids and encounters, with much artillery fire, but nothing to indicate the extraordinarily sudden and dramatic change this whole front was to undergo before the month closed. Even on the day before the great allied offensive began a communiqué, typical of many which had appeared from time to time, was issued stating there was lively artillery fire on the whole of the front, that a British raid was successful in the Doiran sector, that an enemy raid was repulsed, and that British, French, and Serbian airmen had dropped large quantities of bombs on various objectives.

The first intimation to the British public of what was toward was contained in a speech made by Mr. Balfour on September 16th, at a dinner given to a Greek commercial delegation then in the country. He announced that the offensive on the Greco-Bulgarian front had begun, French and Serbian troops advancing on a front of ten miles, taking two lines of trenches, and capturing eight hundred prisoners and ten guns. He said this was a prelude to still greater successes in which Greek and British troops would bear an equally glorious part.

According to a statement in the " Matin " of Paris, General

" MACKENSEN BRIDGE " AT NISH.
A Serbian soldier—after the return of the Serbians to Nish—guarding the bridge which the enemy had constructed there in 1916. They were compelled to leave it to the Serbians in 1918, when the surrender of Bulgaria was rapidly followed by the retirement of all enemy forces from long-suffering Serbia.

Guillaumat in the summer had submitted to the French, British, and Italian Governments a plan for this offensive which he had worked out in conjunction with Marshal Mishitch and the Serbian Staff. This plan was approved by these Governments, and when General Franchet d'Espérey succeeded to the Chief Command, he proceeded as soon as possible to carry it out, with results that probably went far beyond the most sanguine anticipations of success based upon it. The plan was to make a strong frontal attack on the Bulgarian line west of the Vardar, and break it, in which event a strong frontal attack was to be made east of the Vardar with the object of pinning down the Bulgarians there, and of preventing them from sending reinforcements to the other side of the river, thus permitting the Allies on that side to consolidate their gains and pursue their offensive.

After a day's artillery preparation the allied offensive—the complete success of which within a fortnight

Great allied assault opens

was the first indubitable indication that the end of the Great War was approaching— opened at eight o'clock in the morning of September 15th with a powerful infantry assault. The section of the front chosen for attack was the most difficult in Macedonia — a mountainous region, with peaks towering to a height of upwards of five thousand feet, lying almost midway, in a tremendous mass about ten miles in length, between Monastir on the west and the Vardar on the east. From west to east the chief mountains were Sokol, Dobropolye, Kravitsa, Vetrenik, Kukuruz, Golobilo, and Kozyak, and some of these were already famous in the war as the scene of

heroic fighting, in which Serb and Bulgar, the two protagonists of the Balkans, had been almost exclusively engaged. The bitter struggle, which had behind it an intensity of racial feeling perhaps unparalleled in the world, was now renewed, the French aiding the one and the Germans the other.

Commanded by the Voivodes (Marshals) Boyovitch and Stepanovitch respectively, the First and Second Serbian Armies held this part of the Macedonian front of the Allies. These two armies, the whole fighting strength that was left of the Serbian nation after six years of warfare, consisted of six divisions, five of which were purely Serbian, and reproduced in their names their aforetime territorial designations— as, for example, the Morava Division, or the Shumadia Division. The 6th Division, which was a part of the Second Army, was composed of Jugo-Slavs from Bosnia, Herzegovina, the Banat, Dalmatia, and Croatia—not a few had come from America. Thoroughly trained by Serbian officers, it had as its commander the Serbian Colonel Voyislav Jivanovitch. Keen soldiers as were the Serbians themselves, these Jugo-Slavs proved even keener.

As was noted in a previous chapter, a division of similar composition had fought as a part of the Russo-Rumanian forces in the Dobruja in 1916, and had acquitted itself most gallantly in the face of the most discouraging circumstances. The bravery and endurance exhibited day after day by the Jugo-Slavs in the struggle that began on that September 15th was even more remarkable. The total strength of the two Serbian armies was about 90,000 men, and of these 22,000 were Jugo-Slavs. In close combination with the Serbs were two French divisions. Such was the force to which D'Espérey had entrusted the hard but glorious task of breaking the front of the Bulgars and of driving them from their strong positions in these rugged and lofty Macedonian mountains. And right well did it execute that task.

The rest of the allied front was held as follows. On the right of the Franco-Serbian force, from about the Skra di Legen eastward to the Vardar, and across that river to Lake Butkova and the Struma, stood the British Salonika Army and several divisions of the Greek Army, a Greek division being on the immediate right. On the Franco-Serbian left were French, Greek, and Italian divisions reaching west to Monastir and the Baba Mountains beyond to Lake Prespa— the Russian contingents that had once been on this line had disappeared, just as they had disappeared from the western **Dispositions of the forces** front. West of these composite forces, all the way to the Adriatic, were French and Italian divisions, with Albanian detachments about Korcha (Koritsa). The whole allied strength from east to west was approximately 400,000 men, with powerful artillery and commensurate munitionment.

Over against the Allies in Macedonia lay the First Bulgarian Army, on the west side of the Vardar, and the Second Bulgarian Army, on the east side of the river, the whole consisting of sixteen divisions—each Bulgarian division, if at full strength, being more than twice the size of the usual division on the western front. The Bulgarians were reinforced by detachments from the Eleventh German Army, which was quartered in Serbia. In Albania a considerable Austrian army was arrayed against the Italians and the French. The total strength of the enemy was probably at least equal to that of the Allies. After the offensive had culminated in the overthrow of the Bulgars, it was said that their moral was low, because of their being tired of the war and because of other reasons, but at the outset they showed no sign of anything of the kind. They struggled gamely enough, but they were outfought and outgeneralled; on the first day they were fighting as hard and well as they had ever fought.

For three days the battle was extremely violent. Stepanovitch began by driving against the heights of Sokol, Dobropolye, and Vetrenik, which formed the south-west rampart of the front attacked. On two former occasions the Serbs had stormed their way some distance forward, but only to be beaten back. Under German teaching the Bulgars for more than two years had brought every imaginable device to bear to strengthen and fortify their line, so steep was the ascent to which that, according to a correspondent, they dropped bombs from the parapets straight on to the heads of the Serbians below. Some distance behind this formidable sector the enemy had constructed a railway from Prilep to Gradsko, on the Vardar, with roads leading up to the front. That railway line now became the Allies' objective. So irresistible was the onslaught of the Serbians, in union with the French, that before the evening of September 15th Sokol, Dobropolye, and Vetrenik, which the Bulgars had deemed impregnable, were carried.

It was a hot, clear day, and as the assault progressed, French and Serbian aircraft effectively supported the advance of the infantry, and bombed the enemy's communications. Notwithstanding the difficulties of the ground, the whole of the first Bulgarian position was broken for a length of seven miles. Next day a Sofia official despatch admitted the defeat, and added that in order to avoid the sacrifice of the Bulgarian troops they had been " withdrawn to new positions situated farther north," after an " obstinate struggle in which the Allies suffered heavy losses." As a matter of fact, the losses of the Allies were much below what had been anticipated.

Meanwhile, heavy fighting had been going on farther north and east from above Gradeshnitsa to Bahovo. On September 16th the Serbians carried the fortified zone between Sokol and the Gradeshnitsa, and forcing the crossing of that stream, threw back in disorder the Bulgars, who were caught by machine-gun fire from the **First Bulgarian** Allies' aeroplanes as they were retreating **position broken** across the bridge at Rasimbey. East of the Vetrenik height, allied forces took by storm the massifs of Chelm and Golobilo. And, best of all, the Jugo-Slavs, whom nothing could check, took with magnificent dash the Kozyak peak, the second Bulgarian line of defence, and the highest point in the whole range.

The Bulgars put up a strong defence, and they had German supports, but they were swept out of their trenches. On that day, too, the breach made in the Sokol-Dobropolye-Vetrenik district, both on the west and the east, was widened in length to ten miles and in depth to about five miles, while the number of prisoners materially increased. In the two days' fighting more than 4,000 officers and men, including a colonel and his staff, above thirty guns, many machine-guns

TRENCH-FIGHTING ON A MOUNTAIN SLOPE IN SERBIA.
Serbian soldiers firing from a shallow trench along the slope of a mountain side, and (inset above) types of the Serbian Army as it was reorganised for the long-delayed but triumphant offensive which was destined to restore their country to the Serbians. The well-laden soldier to the right was a machine-gunner.

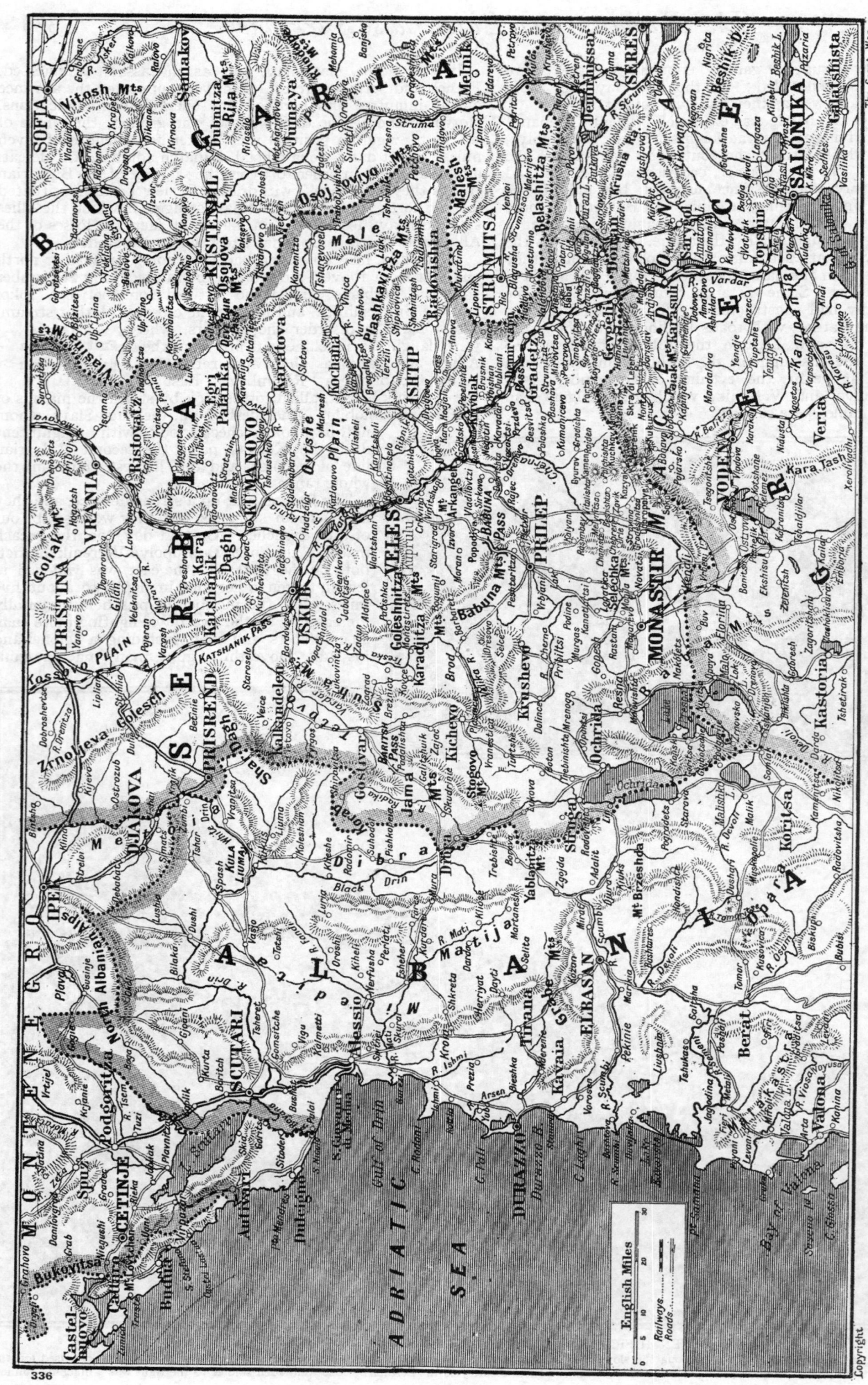

336

The Great War

Copyright

THE MACEDONIAN BATTLEFIELD WHERE THE ALLIED ARMIES COMPLETELY DEFEATED THE CENTRAL POWERS IN THE BALKANS.

The centre of the Balkan front, in the mountain region east of Monastir, was held by a Franco-Serbian force. On the right, from Skra di Legen across the Vardar to Lake Butkova and the Struma, stood the British Salonika Army, with several Greek divisions. On the left French, Greek, and Italian divisions extended from Monastir over the Baba Mountains to Lake Prespa. West again to the Adriatic were French and Italian divisions, with Albanian detachments at Koritsa. The First Bulgarian Army held the centre of the front west of the Vardar. The Second Bulgarian Army lay east of the Vardar. In Albania a considerable Austrian army was arrayed against the French and Italians. By separating the two Bulgarian armies and cutting their main lines of communication the Allies compelled Bulgaria to surrender unconditionally.

and bomb-throwers, and quantities of other booty, fell into the hands of the Allies. Of these operations General d'Espérey reported:

Serbian troops, fighting with splendid moral, rivalled in endurance, courage, and the spirit of sacrifice the French units in repulsing the Bulgarian counter-attacks, which were carried out with the utmost vigour, and in carrying in sheer fighting, in spite of the stiffest resistance, positions which the enemy had been fortifying for three years on ground at an average height of 5,500 feet, comprising a series of wooded and steep heights, some of which had appeared to be impossible to scale.

In hot haste the Bulgarians rushed up reinforcements, amongst which were German detachments, and their cries for help were beginning to be heard in Berlin and Vienna; but in neither of these centres was the urgency of the case realised; if they had realised it, neither was in a position to give material assistance. Notwithstanding the enemy reinforcement, thrown desperately into the new lines that had been taken up, the allied offensive continued with success on September 17th, all the objectives fixed for the day being reached. Another factor now made itself felt on the side of the Serbs and the French. A despatch from Athens, dated September 16th, had noted that Greek troops had effected an advance of from two to three miles on a front of nineteen miles, and had occupied several villages, dislodging the enemy by a bold movement which had taken him completely by surprise, and had caused him sharp losses. Later the Greeks, whose forces were brigaded with those of the other Allies in various sectors, and did not operate independently, captured the heights Zena and Porta. Hellenic detachments co-operated with the Serbs and French in taking, after a severe struggle, the fortified villages of Zovik, on the Cherna, and Stravina, as well as the heights of Polchishta and Beshishta, to the north of the Gradeshnitsa, and the place of the same name, which was fiercely defended by the enemy, who had received orders to hold on there whatever the cost.

In the centre the Allies progressed on the ridges beyond Kozyak, and got a footing on the Kuchkov Kamen; the Serbs took Melynitsa, Vitolishta, and Rasimbey, on the Cherna, about fifteen miles from Prilep, and cut the communications of the Bulgars east of the river with that town, which was the advanced base of the First Bulgarian Army. New Bulgar regiments, placed in the field that day and supported by German units, failed to check the onrush of the Allies, who had advanced twelve and a half miles from their starting-point. Next day the advance had grown to twenty miles, for Serbian cavalry rode into Poloshko, on the Cherna, a few miles south of Vozartsi and Kavadar, both places which leapt

KING BORIS OF BULGARIA.
Ascended the throne October 5th, 1918, consequent upon the abdication of his father King Ferdinand.

into fame during the Franco-British attempt to help the Serbians in 1915.

By September 18th a deep gap had been cut through the Bulgarian front, and the Bulgars, with their German friends, were retreating in disorder. The gap had been broadened as well as deepened. On the east Blatets and Rojden had been stormed, and the Belashnitsa crossed, while the high mountainous zone of Gyurov Kamen had fallen to the Allies, who, in the centre, had gained complete possession of the great ridge of the Kuchkov Kamen. On the north-west the Cherna, from south of Zovik to north of Rasimbey, was being crossed, and the Serbians, marching on Prilep, threatened the envelopment of the Bulgars in the Selechka Mountains.

Setting fire to his stores and camps, the enemy made haste to retreat, but the swift, unrelenting pursuit of the French and the Serbs, particularly of the Jugo-Slavs, gave him no opportunity of throwing up fresh lines of defence, and his retreat rapidly turned into a rout. By this time he had lost 5,000 in prisoners alone, and the number of his killed and wounded was very heavy.

Again he cried to the Central Powers for help, and even approached Turkey, but from neither did assistance come. In these circumstances he sought to move up his troops from other parts of his front, and more especially from the east side of the Vardar, but the British and the Greeks had expected this action, and had taken steps to prevent it.

At five o'clock in the morning of September 18th the British, under General Milne, and the Greeks, under General Orfanides, attacked the positions of the Second Bulgarian Army, which was commanded by General Lukoff, on the front west and east of Lake Doiran. Describing these positions, Reuter's correspondent wrote before the assault began:

On the west side the Bulgar lines, which had been properly compared in previous offensives to a mediæval stronghold consisting of a bastion and a flanking bastion, rise in successive strength to the famous Dub, at the summit of the Pip Ridge, and on to the Grand Couronné, which might be called the keep of the fortress. These are of enormous natural strength, reinforced by all the ingenuity of modern warfare, and are held by an enemy who never fights so stubbornly and courageously as when on the defensive. The ground on the left looking north is dominated by the Pip Ridge, each projection of which seems intended by nature for defence. In the centre and on the horizon is the Grand Couronné, over 2,000 feet above sea-level and a thousand feet above our starting-point. On the right broken hills rise above Lake Doiran, and to win these hills and reach the eastern support of the Grand Couronné one must first pass Jumeaux Ravine and Petit Couronné, the Bulgars' strong allies in our previous offensives.

General Lukoff, Commander of the Second Bulgarian Army.

Dr. G. Radeff, of the Bulgarian Foreign Office.

M. Liaptcheff, Bulgarian Minister of Finance in M. Malinoff's Cabinet.

General Teodoroff, Acting Commander-in-Chief of the Bulgarian Armies.

BULGARIAN SOLDIERS AND STATESMEN WHO NEGOTIATED THE UNCONDITIONAL SURRENDER, SEPTEMBER 30TH, 1918.

On the north-east of the lake the ground over which we had to attack is a flat plain, broadest at the foot of the Krusha Balkans, and tapering and curving round the lake. It is menaced from the north by the massif of the Belashitsa, on the lowest slopes of which are defences which must be overcome if progress is to be made in the narrow plain, which, to the north of Lake Doiran, is less than two miles broad.

An intense bombardment, lasting forty-eight hours and smashing into fragments the Bulgar trenches and wire entanglements, preceded the infantry assault on September 18th, the principal part of the fighting being borne by the 22nd Division, the 77th Infantry Brigade, and the Greek Seres Division. On the eastern slope of Pip Ridge British infantry drove the enemy back, but he brought up his reserves, and a ding-dong struggle of great desperation ensued. In the centre British and Greek troops took the Bulgars' first line of trenches and Sugar Loaf Hill after strenuous fighting. The Greeks enveloped Petit Couronné and stormed Hill 340; a Bulgar counter-attack drove them from the hill, which they retook with much gallantry.

Greco-British gallantry

By the evening the Allies held Doiran town and a considerable extent of the enemy's first and second lines, but had not maintained the ground they had captured early on the left, the operations. there, however, of the British making the work of their comrades and the Greeks easier in the centre and on the right. The Allies took eight hundred prisoners; the Bulgars, on their side of the account, laid claim to five hundred unwounded British and Greek prisoners.

On the east of the lake British and Greek forces advanced by night from the foot of the Krusha Balkans across the plain, and early in the morning captured by assault Akindjali and its strongly-fortified position, proceeding thereafter

north-west to Nikolitch, which they entered in the afternoon.

Heavy and sanguinary as the struggle had been on the 18th, it was not less so next day, the purpose of the Allies being not so much the gain of ground as the retention of the Bulgars on that front. The British again tried to win Pip Ridge and open up the way to the Grand Couronné, but on the ridge, though they pressed forward with the utmost determination, they were at length held up by nests of machine-guns, and had to retire. They formed up again, and made a second effort, but in spite of their courage were unable to take the position. Yet their main object—that of pinning the Bulgars of Lukoff's Second Army to the east side of the

ALLIED COMMANDERS AT SALONIKA.
General Guillaumat (right), Commander-in-Chief on the Salonika front from the end of 1917 to July, 1918, with General Mishitch (centre), and General Milne (left) in command of the British and Serbian forces there.

Vardar—was completely accomplished. As was afterwards pointed out in a British official statement, the enemy had to use his reserves to restore his front, and no troops were able to leave the line in front of the British for the purpose of opposing the Serbs and the other Allies between the Vardar and the Cherna. In brief, the Greco-British offensive was a most material and effective contribution to D'Espérey's offensive in general.

That offensive west of the Vardar had continued, and on September 21st was seen to be developing into a really great victory. Advancing with extraordinary rapidity considering the mountainous nature of the country, the Serbians, after breaking the serious resistance set up by Bulgar rearguards, reinforced by German troops, passed through Vozarci and Kavadar, and reached the Vardar in the direction of Negotin and Demircapu, thus cutting the railway in the valley of that river. This brilliant achievement indicated an advance from the starting-point of upwards of forty miles, and was full of menace for the Bulgars, not only on the west side of the Vardar but on the east side as well. Forthwith they began to destroy their stores and material at Gradsko and in the whole region of the Vardar and Lake Doiran.

In the eastern part of the Cherna Bend they began to fall back, and the Allies captured Chaniste and Orle, having crossed the Cherna at Chebren on the previous day. North and north-east of the Dzena Ridge the Greeks, supported by

SERBIA'S CROWN PRINCE IN THE FIELD.
The Crown Prince of Serbia (with field-glasses) watching operations during the autumn offensive of 1918; General Hanrys (with raised stick), a French commander, Lieut. Prince Murat, and Col. Damyanovitch (left).

French troops, made further progress. Meanwhile, more immediately east of Monastir the Italians, under General Mombelli, had been attacking the enemy, who also was commencing his retirement in that sector; but on September 21st they caught him in the midst of his withdrawal, assaulted him with determination and success, and throwing him into wild confusion made him retreat precipitately with very heavy losses in men and material. By this time the Bulgarians were in full flight on a front reaching from Monastir to Doiran, a distance of about a hundred miles, and at all points the allied pursuit was being methodically and energetically carried out, despite the opposition of the Bulgaro-German rearguards, the allied airmen rendering splendid assistance.

By September 23rd there was no shadow of doubt as to the overwhelming victory of the Allies. From Mogila, above Monastir, their line reached north-easterly to Kanatlartsi and Kalyani, south-east of Prilep. Farther north the Serbs, marching on Prilep and the Babuna Pass, had reached the Vardar from Demircapu to Gradsko, some of their detachments being thrown across to the east bank of the river. South-east of the Serbians, Greek and British troops had advanced beyond Koynsko and Gurinchet, and occupied Gevgeli and all the first enemy line as far as Lake Doiran. The British communiqué stated:

As a result of the attacks and continual heavy pressure by the British and the Greeks, in conjunction with the French and Serbian advance farther west, the enemy has evacuated his whole line from Doiran to west of the Vardar. He has set on fire Hudova Station (ten miles from Demircapu Station), Chestovo, and Tike and Tatarli dumps, and his troops and transport are crowding along the road northwards, heavily bombed and machine-gunned by our R.A.F. Our troops are advancing, and have reached the line Kara-Ogular (on Lake Doiran) Hamzali (about half a mile south of Bogdantzi), and west of the Vardar they are advancing on Mrzentsi in touch with the Greeks at Gurinchet.

Bulgarians in full flight Thus the First and Second Bulgarian Armies, heavily attacked by land and from the air, were falling back in disorder everywhere. But bad as that was for the Bulgars, it was not the whole truth—which was that the Serbians, by the brilliant rapidity of their movements, had completely separated the two Bulgarian armies, and there was no longer any cohesion between them. In about a week the whole military situation in the Balkans had been changed—transformed. Most of the credit for this great achievement was due to the brave and indomitable Serbians. Only a short time before the German Emperor had said that Serbia and Montenegro were out of the war. Yet here were these non-existent Serbians astride the Uskub-Salonika railway, and masters of the railway from Gradsko to Prilep, which they had cut on September 22nd, and which had been the chief line of communication of the Germans in that area. It was no wonder that the Serbian communiqué observed that the "strategical consequences of cutting both the two main lines of the enemy communication and piercing the enemy front are now enormous."

On September 24th the Bulgars and Germans, closely

"CAGED" AND ON THE WAY TO THE CAGES.
Bulgarian prisoners taken by the Greek Army on the Balkan front, with two of their captors to the right; and (inset above) Greek soldiers bringing in a batch of Bulgarian prisoners along a communication trench.

followed by the allied advance guards, and harassed by cavalry and aeroplanes, were falling back in the greatest confusion towards Veles (Kuprulu), Ishtip, and Strumitsa. On the left wing the allied forces, debouching from the Monastir front, were driving back the enemy on the Albanian roads. French cavalry entered Prilep, found the town intact, and seized immense quantities of stores. North-eastward the Franco-Serbians were beyond the Prilep-Gradsko road, and were threatening Veles. On the Vardar the Serbs established a large bridge-head east of Gradsko-Demircapu, and northward, on the line of the Bregalnitsa, were threatening Ishtip.

Farther east the British and the Greeks had advanced to Smokvista, on the west bank of the Vardar, and to Furka and Pazarli on its east side; British cavalry were marching on Strumitsa. More German troops were now rushed up to assist in stemming the rout, but they did not stem it—the rout continued and grew more and more decided. The chief event on September 25th was the capture by the Serbs of the Popodiya Massif, to the east of the Babuna. Within the next twenty-four hours they held the famous pass, together with Veles and Ishtip, and took great quantities of booty, including a number of heavy guns; at the station at Gradsko, which was defended by German troops in vain, they discovered large stocks of welcome food and other supplies. Meanwhile the British had entered Bulgaria at Kosturino, six miles from Strumitsa, and with the Greeks were advancing on the south-west slopes of the steep Belashitsa range. By this time the Allies had taken 12,000 prisoners and more than 200 guns.

On the morning of September 26th the British entered Strumitsa, and British and Greek troops stormed the heights of the Belashitsa range, north of Lake Doiran. Moving up the valley of the Bregalnitsa, Serbian cavalry reached Kochana, about twenty miles north-east of Ishtip, and then pushed on towards the Bulgarian frontier, with the idea of reaching the Struma and enveloping the Bulgars in that area. Allied forces, advancing from Prilep, threw back the left wing of the Eleventh German Army on the mountainous region west of Krushevo. On the 27th General d'Espérey announced that the Vardar railway and the road from Monastir through Prilep to Gradsko were completely. cleared of the enemy, who was being unremittingly pursued northwards.

His statement with respect to the Vardar railway indicated that the valley of the Vardar was no longer under the fire of the Bulgars and Germans. On that day the general advance of the Allies was everywhere pressed. On the west the resistance of the enemy between Lakes Prespa and Ochrida, and to the north-west of Monastir, was beaten down ; from Krushevo the Allies were marching on Kichevo. In the centre the Serbians from Veles were making a strong effort to reach Uskub, and had come within about twenty miles of it, notwithstanding a last despairing attempt of the Bulgars to hold them up ; on their right Serbian cavalry had pushed on to within half a dozen miles of the Bulgarian frontier. On the east the British and the Greeks were advancing north of Strumitsa and the Belas range.

Bulgaria seeks an armistice

It now was very evident that Bulgaria's military position was not a hopeful one, and Bulgaria, realising this to the full, did the best thing for herself that she could possibly do in her circumstances by making overtures for an armistice. On the night of September 26th a superior Bulgarian officer, under a flag of truce, arrived at the Headquarters of General d'Espérey, and requested, on behalf of General Teodoroff, in chief command of the Bulgarian armies in the absence of General Jekoff, the Commander-in-Chief, who was ill and undergoing treatment in Vienna, an armistice for forty-eight hours to permit the coming of two delegates with a view to defining the conditions of an armistice and eventually of peace. The delegates were to be M. Liaptcheff, the Minister of Finance, and General Lukoff, the commander of the Second Bulgarian Army. They were stated to have the authority of the Bulgarian Government behind them, as well as that of King Ferdinand.

From General d'Espérey's reply it appeared that Teodoroff's letter was dated September 25th, and was sent to the Allied Generalissimo through the intermediary of General Milne. Suspecting that the Bulgarian request might be a *ruse de guerre* to allow the regrouping of forces or the bringing up of reinforcements, General d'Espérey answered that he could not grant either an armistice or a suspension of hostilities, which might interfere with the operations in progress in the field, but that he was willing to receive with befitting courtesy the duly accredited representatives of the Bulgarian Government, and he directed them to appear, accompanied by an officer bearing a flag of truce, at the British lines.

It was announced in the British Press on September 28th that on the previous day the British Government had received from an official and authorised source an application from Bulgaria for an armistice. The expression " official and authorised source " gave the lie to reports

Terms of Bulgaria's surrender

which appeared in the German Press to the effect that M. Malinoff, the Bulgarian Premier, was acting on his own accord, without the assent of King Ferdinand or of the Bulgarian Army Command. Remembering the treachery of Bulgaria in the not distant past many people were disinclined to believe in her sincerity now, but the British Government, with good reason, took her request seriously, and Mr. Bonar Law and Mr. Balfour left London to confer about it with Mr. Lloyd George, who was recruiting his health in the country. There was a general consultation among the Allies, and an agreement was reached as to the line to be taken with Bulgaria. On September 28th three Bulgarian plenipotentiaries—those previously mentioned, and a third, M. Radeff, an ex-Minister and an experienced diplomatist—arrived at Salonika. General d'Espérey, who had received instructions from M. Clemenceau, the French Prime Minister, acting as spokesman of the Allies, told them what Bulgaria must do, and at noon on September 30th they signed with him an armistice, which, it was arranged, was to continue until the final peace settlement. The terms on which the armistice was granted can be summed

up in a sentence—the unconditional surrender of Bulgaria. In more detail the main terms were : The immediate evacuation of the territories which belonged to Serbia and Greece ; the immediate demobilisation of the Bulgarian Army, with the exception of three infantry divisions and four cavalry regiments—the arms, munitions, and material of the demobilised troops were to be given into the custody of the Allies, who were to store them at specified centres ; the placing at the disposal of the Allies of all Bulgarian means of transport, including the railways and the ships and other craft on the Danube and in the Black Sea ; the opening of Bulgarian territory for the operations of the Allies against the enemy, and the occupation of strategic points in Bulgaria by British, French, or Italian troops ; and that Bulgaria ceased henceforth to take any part in the war, except with the Allies' consent. Among other things the terms included the restitution to Greece of the material of the Fourth Greek Army Corps which was taken when the Bulgarians occupied Eastern Macedonia, and a provision that Bulgarians serving in the Eleventh German Army were to lay down their arms and become prisoners of war. An important clause stated that all allied prisoners in Bulgaria were to be released immediately, but that Bulgarian prisoners were to be kept and employed by the Allies till the final peace settlement.

The agreement embodying the armistice was essentially military, and dealt with the immediate situation, other matters being left till the Peace Conference. Among these matters was the question of the Bulgarian occupation of the Rumanian Dobruja, but, as it fell out, that was settled long before the Peace Conference. At the moment the most notable feature of the agreement was that, by placing the through German route to Constantinople under the control of the Allies, Turkey was sundered from the Central Powers, except in so far as they could maintain communication with her by the Black Sea. Apart from Turkey the surrender of Bulgaria had other great results. For one thing, it destroyed the grandiose Mittel-Europa project;

Results of the surrender

the Central European League was dead. For another thing, that other grandiose project which was wrapped up in the famous phrase " Berlin-Bagdad Railway " crashed in utter ruin. And, further, the agreement suggested great possibilities for allied action with respect to Austria, Rumania, Southern Russia, and Caucasia.

Up to the signing of the armistice the allied operations continued against Bulgaria. The day before it was signed the " Cologne Gazette " announced that Germany was sending a powerful army to help Bulgaria, but Bulgaria knew well enough that Germany was not in a position to do anything of the kind. On September 29th Italian, French, and Greek troops, on the left wing, pursued the retreating enemy towards Kichevo, and north of Ochrida advanced, reaching, on the west of the lake, the road to Elbasan, in Albania. The most striking success was recorded in the centre, where Uskub was taken by French cavalry. Some days earlier this body of French cavalry had co-operated with French infantry in overcoming the resistance offered by rearguards at Veles. Turning the defence of that town by following almost impassable mountain paths, it daringly penetrated into the Bulgarian lines and carried Uskub.

Among the booty were four hundred prisoners, half of whom were Germans, seven heavy guns, a large number of horses and cattle, and a train laden with corn consigned to the Central Empires. Farther east the Serbians, supported by French and Greek forces, were moving on to Kumanovo, Egri Palanka, and Djumaia. In Albania the Austrians, pursued by the Italians, were retreating towards Montenegro, under cover of strong rearguards. During September 30th, up to 12 a.m., the hour fixed for suspending hostilities, the Allies went on with their advance. In the west Kichevo was occupied and Struga captured. In the centre the Serbs, after heavy fighting, stood on the Bulgarian frontier ; in the evening they marched into Kumanovo as the Bulgars withdrew from it under the terms of the armistice. On the east British and Greek forces were near Petritch. At noon Bulgaria was out of the war.

THE CONQUEST OF PALESTINE AND SYRIA.

By Robert Machray.

In the Middle East the War a Conflict with Turkey—Allenby Safeguards His Front—Advance on the Coast—Turks Fail in Attempt to Retake Jerusalem—British Gain Ground—Zionists Plan for the Future—Jericho Captured—Dashing Raids Into the Land of Gilead—British Divisions Withdrawn to Western Front—Replaced by Indian Troops—Allenby Prepares for Vigorous Offensive—Attacks whole Enemy Line—Great Assault from East Flank—Still Greater Assault from West Flank—Turkish Lines Smashed for Sixteen Miles—Magnificent Advance of the Infantry—Splendid Swift Encircling Movements of the Cavalry—Turks Hemmed In on the North—Fine Work of the Arabs on the East—Shattered Turkish Armies—A Debacle—Thousands of Prisoners—Hundreds of Guns Lost—Enemy Caught East of the Jordan—Ten Thousand Men Surrender—Palestine Conquered—Fall of Damascus and Aleppo—Syria Overrun—Turkey Out of the War.

GENERAL ALLENBY'S victorious advance into Palestine, with the surrender of Jerusalem on December 9th, 1917, followed by his quiet but dignified entrance officially into the Holy City two days later, formed the subject of Chapter CCXXVII. (Vol. 11, page 1). Hailed throughout the world, save by the Germans and their friends, as one of the great events of the war, the capture of Jerusalem by the British marked a definite stage in their operations against Turkey.

At the time a feeling was general that, with the exception, perhaps, of the conquest of all Palestine, their progress in that area would show nothing more striking in the way of military achievement. The idea was reinforced by the fact that this particular military achievement was distinguished by a political and religious significance which added enormously to its importance as well as to its interest. Yet when the conquest was actually undertaken it was consummated so rapidly and completely, and with such vital loss to the enemy, that from the military point of view it far transcended the fall of Jerusalem, and, considered as a contribution to the common cause, was certainly one of the factors that led to the final triumph of the Allies.

In the Middle East the war was practically a struggle between the British and the Turks, its centres being Palestine and Mesopotamia. By December, 1917, it was clear, after the break-up of the Russian Empire, consequent on the Revolution and its subsequent Bolshevist developments, that the British

would have to carry on the conflict single-handed in Mesopotamia. Though they had some welcome assistance from the French, and to a larger extent from King Hussein and his Arabs of the Hedjaz, they bore the brunt of the contest in Palestine from start to finish. To such a degree did they bear it that the conquest of Palestine, with the accompanying conquest of Syria, was to all intents and purposes British. It was the work of a British general, whose name, in any other period of history, would have been on every lip as that of one of the greatest captains that ever led armies to victory. Nor was it any detraction from the British achievement to say that the majority of the troops Allenby commanded were drawn not from the United Kingdom itself but from the Empire. When the day of reckoning came, thousands of Australians and New Zealanders and a hundred thousand Indians stood in the British ranks—all under the same flag of pride and glory.

Rather more than nine months were to pass before that day of reckoning came, and in the interval many great events took place elsewhere in the war, some of which had their influence in Palestine. In a despatch, dated September 18th, 1918, and published on November 6th following, General Allenby gave an account of what occurred under his command after the capture of Jerusalem till the first-mentioned date, which, singularly enough, was the very day on which he began the great offensive that resulted in the delivery of Palestine from the Turks.

On the day on which he made his modest official

BRITISH VESSELS OFF THE PALESTINE COAST.
View of the treacherous Jaffa coast, taken from the wharf. The straight coast of Palestine is almost harbourless, and even at Jaffa—a port which dates from the time of King David—the shore is fringed with rocky shallows.

UNDER CANVAS IN ARABIA.
Camp of friendly Hedjaz Arabs at Kalat el Akaba, at the northern extremity of the Gulf of Akaba.

had fought for the Dardanelles, and who had marched across the desert wastes of Northern Sinai under General Murray — crossed the Auja in three columns and took the enemy completely by surprise. The left column forded the river near its mouth, where it was about four feet deep, and captured Tell er Rekkeit, more than two miles north of the right bank.

Crossing on rafts and pontoons, the centre and right columns rushed at the point of the bayonet Sheikh Muannis, Khurbet Hadrah, and the high ground overlooking the Auja. Four important villages were soon captured, and by break of day the new British line ran from Khurbet Hadrah to Tell er Rekkeit, the Turks, who lost upwards of three hundred prisoners as well as ten machine-guns, being deprived

entry into the Holy City—nnostentatiously on foot — and at the very moment when the proclamation, which was the charter of the freedom of its people, was being read, his and the enemy guns were in incessant action no farther than four miles away on the north and east. Naturally, his first care was to provide more effectively for the security of Jerusalem by driving the enemy to a greater distance from it, and generally to strengthen his whole front to the sea, straightening the line where necessary or desirable. The length of his front from east to west was about fifty miles.

At this time Allenby's forces comprised the 10th, 52nd, 53rd, 54th, 60th, and 74th Divisions, Territorial Yeomanry, the Australians and New Zealanders in their famous Mounted Division, as well as other troops. Of

HELPING HANDS BY THE WAY.
Natives of the Holy Land, well disposed to the Allies, on the road between Jerusalem and Shechem (Nablus), helping a New Zealander to saddle up a pony which he had captured from the Turks.

these forces the 52nd and the 54th Divisions formed his left wing, immediately south of the Nahr el Auja, the river flowing a short distance north of Jaffa (Joppa), across which the British had advanced on the occupation of that town, only to be pressed back again after heavy fighting late in November. During the operations which ended in the taking of Jerusalem there was little change in the situation on the Auja; the British and the Turks consolidated their respective positions, and made or repulsed raids, none of which was of special importance. To protect Jaffa and its harbour, and give additional security to his hold on the Jaffa-Jerusalem road, Allenby determined to drive the enemy from the north bank of the stream and occupy a stretch of country just beyond it.

52nd Division cross the Auja

The forcing of the Auja was a matter of considerable difficulty, as it was fordable only in places, and was commanded by two heights, known respectively as Sheikh Muannis and Khurbet Hadrah, the steep, abrupt terminations of spurs running from north to south, and coming within five hundred yards of the river. Material for the passage had to be accumulated without being perceived by the Turks, which was no easy business in the circumstances; but this was successfully accomplished, and on the night of December 20th-21st, rafts and bridges having been prepared, the 52nd Division—the old and much-tried Scottish Lowlanders, who

of all observation from the north over the valley of the river. A British warship co-operated by raking the enemy trenches with its fire. Later, the Lowlanders pushed farther north, and occupied El Jelil and El Haram, the latter lying about twelve miles above Jaffa. This advance brought Mulebbis, one of the oldest of the Jewish colonies, well within the lines. Many of the inhabitants of Jaffa who had been forced to leave the town were released by the British and returned to their homes.

Having greatly improved the position of his left wing by the brilliant feat of forcing the Auja, Allenby turned his attention to that of his right, which rested on Jerusalem, and which for strategical reasons had to be moved farther north. The weather at the time was most unpropitious, and delayed his preparations for the advance, the objective of which was the Beitin (Bethel)-Nalin line, this forward movement being projected on a front of twelve miles to a depth of six miles immediately north of the Holy City. The operation was entrusted to the Twentieth Corps, which was just about ready for the assault when the Turks suddenly attacked in force astride the Shechem (Nablus) road, it presently becoming evident that they were making an attempt at nothing less than the recapture of Jerusalem.

During the night of December 26-27th four attacks were made on the British pickets at Ras el Tawil, three and a half miles above the city, and east of Bir Nebala, a mile and a half north of the famous Nebi Samwil Ridge, and near the site of the ancient Gibeon. The pickets were driven in, and several determined efforts followed. By 1.30 a.m. on December 27th the 60th (London) Division, which was holding the northern front, was engaged all along the line, while the 53rd (Welsh) Division, on the front east of Jerusalem, was being heavily attacked at various points.

Pressed with great determination, the assaults of the Turks were made by picked bodies of troops. Attacks were repeatedly directed against Tel el Ful, a conspicuous hill overlooking Jerusalem and the intervening ground, but only at one point did the enemy succeed in reaching the British main

A FAMILIAR EASTERN FIGURE.
Water-seller filling his skins at a fountain in the native quarter of an Arab town.

LIBERATORS OF "THE LAND OF PILGRIMAGE."
Djeddah Jalmond Bey (second from left), Minister of War to the King of Hedjaz, with French officers serving with the Sherifian forces that fought against the Turks in Western Arabia.

local counter-attacks, carried out at once, completely restored the situation. This big assault proved to be the final effort of the Turks to retake the Holy City. Some time earlier in the morning Allenby had launched a general counter-offensive by the 74th and the 10th Divisions, and by mid-day this movement was making itself felt, the men advancing in fine style over the broken and boulder-strewn hills, and, hammering the enemy's reserves, deprived him of the initiative. Seeing that the Turkish offensive was spent, Allenby ordered a general advance northward the next day. But the Turks, to do them justice, were still full of fight, and offered a strenuous opposition at most points. The battle continued throughout the whole of December 28th, and did not conclude till the evening of the 29th.

On the first day the British drove the enemy back, and advanced their line on a front of about thirteen miles and to a depth of two miles, in spite of the rough ground and the mountainous nature of the country, which made all movement arduous. On that day Ras Arkub es Suffa, four miles from Jerusalem, and a mile north of the Jericho road, Er Ram (Ramah) on the east side, and Kulundia on the west side of the Shechem road, five or six miles north of the city, and Beitania, were captured. General Allenby reported that Irish troops met with considerable opposition, which they overcame with determination, notwithstanding the **Victorious British counter-attack** difficult terrain, more than 2,000 feet above sea-level, with heights rising to 3,000 feet. The enemy's machine-guns were well posted, and it was not easy to locate them. At one point called Shab Salah the British came under heavy rifle and machine-gun fire from a precipitous hill overlooking the high-road, but the troops of the 60th stormed the hill and cleared the Turks out of it.

Allenby pressed home his counter-attack on December 29th, the second day of this battle, and it developed into a complete defeat of the Turks. The British, beating down a stubborn resistance, for the enemy was still fighting gamely, advanced for a distance of more than three miles along the Shechem road, and occupied Bireh, the ancient Beeroth,

defensive positions, and then he was immediately counter-attacked and driven out by the local reserves. The most severe fighting was east of the Shechem road, and the enemy suffered serious losses. On the extreme right, east of Jerusalem, at Deir Ibn Obeid, a company of Middlesex troops was surrounded by a Turkish force seven hundred strong and supported by mountain artillery. The Middlesex men had no artillery help, but they put up a most gallant resistance against the tremendous odds, and held out until they were relieved on the morning of December 28th.

None of the assaults of the Turks on the 53rd Division was any more successful. About eight o'clock on the morning of the 27th there was a lull in the struggle on the northern front which lasted to nearly one o'clock, when the enemy launched a fresh assault, in unexpected strength, once more against the whole line of the 60th Division. Before the lull the British on the left had pushed back the right flank of the Turkish attack, and gaining ground north and north-east, had penetrated to about two and a half miles on a frontage of about nine miles. Another big effort of the enemy had not been anticipated, as his losses had been very considerable.

This fresh assault in force, which also was pressed with the utmost energy, was powerful enough to reach the British main line of defence, and that in several places. These small successes were, however, short-lived, for in every case

AEROPLANE VIEW OF THE HOLY CITY OF JERUSALEM.

It was early in December, 1917, that Sir Edmund Allenby's brilliant campaign in Palestine was marked by the capture of Jerusalem, the Turks having been forced by his able generalship to retreat from the city without its having to be directly besieged. The capture of Jerusalem, one of the holy cities of three religions, was one of the most dramatic and widely impressive of the episodes throughout the course of the war.

just east of the road on a hill 2,930 feet high, and nine miles north of Jerusalem; while a little farther west, on the other side of the road, the high ridge of Ram Allah was taken.

East of the road Hizmeh (Asmaveth), Jeba—the Gibeah of old, where Jonathan surprised the Philistines—and Burkah were stormed. In the centre Allenby's mounted troops reached Khurbet Ibn Harith, four and a half miles north of Upper Beth Horon. During all these operations and those of the preceding day the British air forces successfully co-operated with the troops. On December 29th enemy infantry and transport in the neighbourhood of Jufna, Beitania, and El Balua, on or near the roads leading north from Bireh, were bombed and machine-gunned by the Royal Flying Corps. By nightfall the Turks, giving up the battle as lost, were falling back everywhere.

Writing of this battle, General Allenby, in his despatch of September 18th, 1918, said:

The Turkish attempt to recapture Jerusalem had thus ended in crushing defeat. The enemy had employed fresh troops, who had not participated in the recent retreat of his army from Beersheba and Gaza, and had escaped its demoralising effects.
Crushing defeat of the Turks The determination and gallantry with which this attack was carried out only served to increase his losses. . . . Seven hundred and fifty prisoners, twenty-four machine-guns, and three automatic rifles were captured during these operations, and over a thousand Turkish dead were buried by us. Our own casualties were considerably less than this number.

As the aftermath of the battle the British, on December 30th, occupied Beitin, the ancient Bethel (the House of God), so named by Jacob after his vision—surely one of the loveliest ever dreamed—of the ladder reaching from earth to heaven, with the angels ascending and descending by it. This place was two miles north-east of Bireh. At the same time El Balua, one mile north of Bireh, on the Shechem road, El Burj, a mile west of Balua, Janiah, and Ras Kerker, six and seven miles respectively north-east of Bireh, were

entered by Allenby's troops. On the next day some further ground was gained. The net result of the effort of the Turks to recapture the Holy City, which no doubt was inspired by Germany, and helped to some extent by German contingents, particularly gunners, was the loss of valuable territory north of Jerusalem, besides their loss in men.

By January 1st, 1918, the British at Bethel were about twelve miles north of the Holy City, held a string of villages on both sides of the important Shechem road, and had secured the ridge of Ram Allah commanding the cross-road leading by the Wady el Kelb towards **New British** the sea. Allenby had, in fact, obtained the **front secured** front which it had been his design to reach when the enemy began his attack. The British consolidated their new positions, and during January made an advance of a mile or more along the Shechem road in the vicinity of Durah, which itself lay between that road and a branch road leading north-westerly to Gilgal. On the 18th of that month British aeroplanes dropped eighty bombs on a railway-station west of Samaria and on camps in its neighbourhood.

A month passed on Allenby's front unmarked by operations of consequence. There were the usual patrol encounters and an occasional raid, as well as a certain amount of aerial activity, this being much circumscribed, however, by the bad weather, heavy rain or thick mists swathing the hills and uplands, rendering flying well-nigh impossible. Early in the year General Allenby was in Cairo, where he was the guest of the Sultan of Egypt, and was given a splendid reception by the people. For the greater part of his journey he travelled by the new railway from Jerusalem to the capital of Egypt. Soon after the beginning of February, as was announced by Lord Curzon in the House of Lords, the line was completed and in working order. This bridging of the Desert of Sinai was, in its way, one of the most interesting developments of the Great War.

Shortly after the fall of Jerusalem, General Allenby, who was already K.C.B., was made a G.C.M.G., in recognition of his distinguished services in the field. A pleasant feature of the New Year was the conferring of honours on Allenby's Commanders and Chief of Staff " for valuable services rendered in connection with the military operations culminating in the capture of Jerusalem." Major-General (Temporary Lieut.-General) E. S. Bulfin, C.B., C.V.O., was made a K.C.B., as was Major-General (Temporary Lieut.-General) Sir Philip Chetwode, K.C.M.G., C.B., D.S.O., while Major-General L. J. Bols, C.B., D.S.O., was made a K.C.M.G. ; Major and Brevet Lieut.-Colonel W. H. Bartholomew, of the Royal Artillery, and Major and Brevet Lieut.-Colonel E. T. Humphreys, of the Lancashire Fusiliers, both of whom held the temporary rank of brigadier-general, were promoted to brevet-colonel for the same excellent reasons.

As was noted in the two previous chapters which dealt with the war in Palestine, all Jewry followed the progress of the British in that country with joy and **British Government approves Zionism** expectation. References also were made to the Zionist Movement and the Jewish settlements or colonies that had been established in the Holy Land by the Zionists before the war. Early in February, 1918, Dr. Weissmann, a recognised leader of the movement, announced at the annual conference of the English Zionist Confederation, held in London, that the British Government, which, in a letter written by Mr. Balfour, had approved of Palestine as a national home for the Jews (Chapter CCXXVII., page 15), had also approved of a Commission of Zionists, whose business was to go to the Holy Land as soon as possible to investigate as to the most

necessary measures for strengthening the Zionist colonies there. He stated that the Government had given facilities for the reopening of the Anglo-Palestine Company, a Zionist financial and commercial organisation, and that the British military authorities were already making use of it for banking purposes. A further interesting announcement was that the Government had empowered the Commission to make full investigation respecting the feasibility of the scheme for founding a Jewish University in Palestine, and, provided military and political **Foundation of Hebrew University** exigencies permitted, to take steps for beginning the undertaking. As a matter of fact, plans had been practically completed before the war for starting a great Hebrew University in Jerusalem.

Two months later Dr. Weissmann, as head of the Commission, was himself in Jerusalem discussing with its Grand Mufti the problems of the near future. And before the summer was over the ceremony of laying the foundation-stone of the university had taken place on a site purchased before the war at Mount Scopus, in the environs of the Holy City. The ceremony was attended by General Allenby, by officers of the French and Italian detachments then in Palestine, by a representative gathering of leading Jews of the country as well as of Jews from Egypt and elsewhere, and by the heads of other communities in the city and land. Twelve stones, symbolical of the Twelve Tribes of Israel, were laid, the first by Dr. Weissmann, the others by representatives of the various branches of Jewish life in Palestine and of the Dispersion.

It was stated in the course of the proceedings, which were of an enthusiastic character, that the new university would

RUINS OF THE GRAND MOSQUE AT GAZA.
The extensive Grand Mosque at Gaza was used by the Turkish army defending that town as a storehouse for its ammunition. Thus it was that when the building was hit during the British attack it was wrecked. Gaza was taken by General Allenby's forces on November 7th, 1917, after terrific fighting, and the capture of the ancient stronghold opened the way for the subsequent rapid advance to the north.

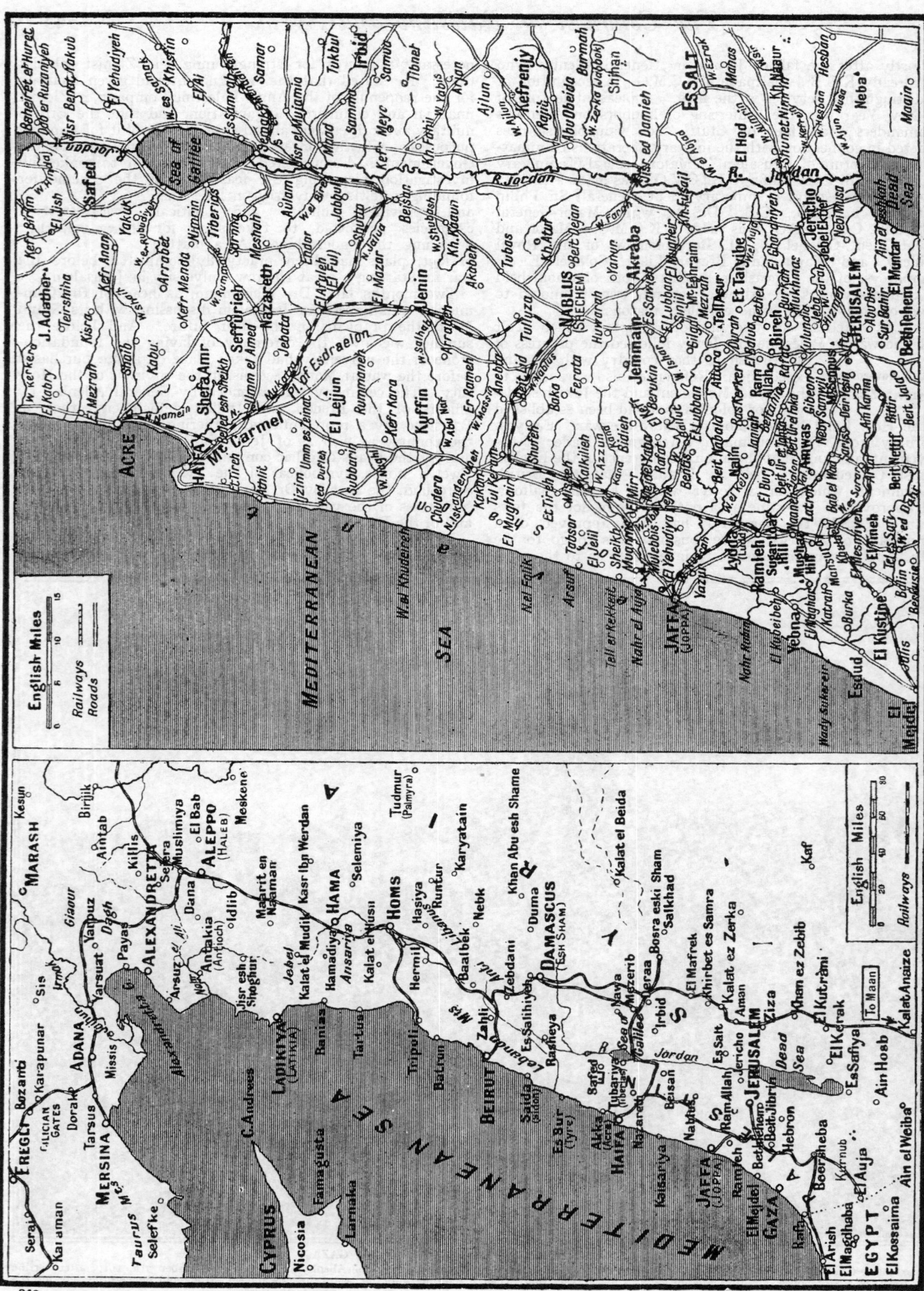

Copyright. The Great War.

WHOLE AREA OF THE BRITISH PALESTINE CONQUEST. RIGHT: LARGE SCALE MAP OF THE JERUSALEM AREA OF MILITARY OPERATIONS.

have professorial Chairs for all the arts and sciences, and would include one of Arabic. "The Hebrew University," joyfully exclaimed Dr. Weissmann, "is no longer a dream—it has become a living reality." In connection with the university was another great project which was called "The City of the Book," meaning by that phrase the foundation of a university press for the printing of Hebrew literature, not only for Palestine but for the whole Jewish world.

These unique developments, which were made possible by the action of the British Government, with the cordial approval of the Allies, were still in the future when Allenby, on February 19th, began a fresh movement on his right, east of Jerusalem, towards Jericho, with a view to making more secure that flank, and also to get into closer touch with the Arabs. The forces of King Hussein were persistently raiding the Hedjaz Railway and cutting the Turkish communications. On January 26th they inflicted a considerable defeat on the enemy on the Seil el Hessa, eleven miles north of Tafile, towards which town the Turks were moving a body of troops from El Kerak, the ancient Kir of Moab, about twenty miles north-east of the southern end of the Dead Sea.

In this battle the loss of the enemy was four hundred killed, three hundred prisoners, including the Turkish commander, two mountain guns, and eighteen machine-guns, besides eight hundred rifles and two hundred horses and mules. Significant of the growing co-operation of the British and the Arabs in this area was a successful air raid, carried out by Australian flying units on February 12th, when over 1,000 lb. of bombs were dropped with good effect—fourteen direct hits being observed on the station buildings, track, locomotives, and rolling-stock at El Kutrani, on the Hedjaz Railway, eighty miles north of Maan. El Kutrani was the station for El Kerak, in whose neighbourhood the Arabs were operating.

As a preparation for his advance east of Jerusalem, Allenby on February 14th moved his line forward on a front of six miles, to an average depth of two miles, on either side of the village of Mukhmas, in the hill country about twelve miles north-east of the city, and met with little opposition. The Turkish left **Stubborn fighting** wing, which covered Jericho, went from **among the hills** about Mukhmas south-easterly to the Dead Sea, Mukhmas itself lying ten miles north-west of Jericho, and being connected with it by a mountain road. During the night of February 18-19th a column marched from Mukhmas, and, after a struggle, took by nine o'clock in the morning Ras et Tawil, a height dominating a wide district. Immediately east of Jerusalem the British front ran from Anata and Ras Arkub es Suffa across the Jericho road south-westerly to Abu Dis, its length being about twelve miles.

At dawn on the 19th Allenby's forces began the main attack—on this occasion they consisted of the 60th and 53rd Divisions, the Anzac Mounted Division less one brigade, and the divisional artillery—and before evening all the objectives selected had been secured to a depth of two miles, despite the immense difficulties of the terrain. El Muntar, a bleak hill over 1,700 feet high on the south-east, was soon taken; on the north Irak Ibrahim, a couple of miles above the Jericho road, was stormed. Along the road itself and on the high ground running eastward, where the resistance of the Turks was very determined, the advance progressed, but more slowly, yet the enemy's whole line was in the hands of the British by three o'clock in the afternoon.

Describing the character of the country and the splendid achievements of the troops, Mr. Massey, the accredited Press correspondent with the forces, said:

No one who has not stood on the Mount of Olives, and looked out on the rugged, barren, twisted country falling away to the Jordan and the Dead Sea, can realise the tremendous effort required to turn out an obstinate enemy from the trenches cut and blasted out of the ridges and spurs of these gaunt hills. The whole country is one succession of hills and valleys until it reaches the marshy flats over 1,000 feet below sea-level. There is scarcely a flat place in the whole sixteen miles from Jerusalem, and throughout their magnificent advance the Londoners were either climbing up steep slopes and stony ridges, or moving along wady beds worn in the rock-faced hills by the torrents of centuries. One place, the Wady Farah, has perpendicular sides five hundred feet high. In this broken terrain the Londoners were set the task of ousting their dug-in foe, who fights best behind entrenchments. That they succeeded with comparatively little loss places them even higher than their previous glorious record in this campaign. I watched them scaling the boulder-strewn hillside, getting

MODERN ARAB VILLAGE OF BEITIN ON AN ANCIENT SITE.
Beitin is the ancient Bethel—or "House of God"—so named by Jacob after his vision of angels ascending and descending by a ladder reaching from earth to heaven. The village, which is about twelve miles to the north of Jerusalem on the Nablus road, was captured by the British forces on December 30th, 1917, after the complete defeat of the Turkish attempt to retake Jerusalem.

over crests, and advancing over open ground in the face of the rapid heavy thuds of the mountain guns and the whirring rap of the machine-guns, and I can say that their gallantry is unsurpassable and their spirit unconquerable. No obstacle was too great to tackle; nothing beat them.

Allenby continued his advance next day, though, in addition to the negotiation of the difficult terrain, the troops were retarded by heavy rainstorms. During the night the column on the south had moved forward to the long ridge at whose northern end lay Talat ed Dumm, the key to Jericho, with the highway winding up and over the hill known to the Arabs as the Hill of Blood, and showing the remains of an old castle of the Crusaders. As day broke, the hill, which was well fortified, was vigorously shelled, and then it was assailed by the Londoners. Before their assaults the Turks fled, but, re-forming, attempted a counter-attack, which was speedily broken by the London men, who were masters of the hill by eight o'clock that morning. The southern edge of the ridge was formed by the huge mass of the Jebel Ektief, from the **Londoners carry the** side of whose precipitous face branched **Hill of Blood** great spurs, with deep ravines in between.

From El Muntar detachments had marched towards this formidable position, which the Turks held in considerable strength, with quantities of machine-guns cunningly sited. After the place was bombarded the British carried the first line of trenches with a rush, and then there ensued much severe fighting, as the result of which Ektief passed to the attackers in the course of the afternoon. North of the Jericho road the Turks made a stubborn stand near Ras et Tawil, but were driven on eastward. On the evening of February 20th the 60th Division had reached a line four miles west of the cliffs overlooking Jericho.

In the meantime the mounted Anzacs had been working south of the infantry in a turning movement eastwards, the plan being that, having dislodged the enemy from a strong point called Neby Musa, they should strike up into the Jordan Valley and take him in the rear. Two miles south of Neby Musa, which was situated near the Dead Sea, the Turks had entrenched some high ground, the approaches to which were so narrow that the mounted men had to move in single file to attack it. The Turks, who had the range accurately, shelled the Anzacs in these defiles and materially delayed their advance, but by two o'clock in the afternoon of the 20th this position was stormed. The further advance of the New Zealand Brigade, which was greatly hampered by the difficult terrain, was checked at a wady in front of Neby Musa.

South of the New Zealanders, however, an Australian mounted brigade discovered a crossing over another wady, and towards dusk reached the Wady Jufet Zeben in the Jordan plain. During the night the enemy evacuated Jericho, and early in the morning of February 21st the Australians entered that town. According to Mr. Massey, there was not a Turk left between Jerusalem and Jericho. As the operations had proceeded, Welsh troops on the north had made a strong demonstration, with the object of preventing Turkish reinforcements being despatched thence to the east. West of the Shechem road ground was gained to a depth of a mile on a front of four miles.

Jericho entered by Australians

Co-operating with the advance on Jericho, the Air Service carried out effective bombing raids against the enemy camps and depots on the east bank of the Jordan near Shunet Nimrim, the ancient Beth Nimrah, which lay five miles from the river on the road to Aman (Rabboth Amon) and the Hedjaz Railway. From Shunet Nimrim a good road ran north, connecting above Samaria with the Palestine Central Railway. On February 21st the Australians marched on from Jericho and established themselves on the line of the Jordan and its tributary, the Wady el Auja (not to be confounded with the Nahr el Auja, previously mentioned). The capture of Jericho was a gain of considerable strategic importance. Allenby's right flank was safeguarded, and it was open to him now to advance northward by the Jordan Valley road, as well as by the Shechem road in the centre and the road along the coast. As the junction of several roads the town had been an advanced base of the enemy and a supply depot. From it and the Jordan Allenby's threat to the Hedjaz Railway became more pronounced.

In early Biblical times the strategic importance of Jericho lay in the fact that it stood at the entrance to the passes of Palestine from the Jordan Valley. The Israelites under Joshua invaded the Promised Land from Jericho, whose walls, according to the Bible narrative, fell down at the sound of trumpets. The place itself was destroyed and laid under a curse. Some six hundred years elapsed before it was rebuilt in the days of Ahab by Hiel, the Bethelite, who laid the foundation with the loss of Abiram his first-born, and set up its gates with the loss of his youngest son Segub, as Joshua had spoken (1 Kings xvi. 34). Afterwards Jericho figured more or less frequently in history, and in the time of Christ was a flourishing city. Herod erected large buildings in it, and it continued to be a place of importance till the Jewish wars, in the course of which it was completely ruined and left a desolation. In the first Christian centuries it was regarded as a semi-sacred spot, probably because a neighbouring hill was supposed to be the scene of the Temptation, and as such, was visited by pilgrims, who found in it some anchorites and monks. When the Crusaders occupied it several monasteries were established there.

Strategic importance of the victory

The modern Jericho, a mere village, lay a short distance from the site of the ancient city. In the days of Christ Jericho was a beautiful place, surrounded with gardens, and with such an abundance of palms that it was known as the City of Palms; but that even then the road from it to Jerusalem had an evil reputation, on account of the difficult country with its facilities for concealment, was shown in the parable of the Good Samaritan and the man who fell among robbers. Doubtless, they sprang on him from their hidden dens in the rocky defiles. Of this rugged region Allenby wrote:

> On no previous occasion had such difficulties of ground been encountered. As an instance of this, a field-artillery battery took thirty-six hours to reach Neby Musa, the distance covered, as the crow flies, being only eight miles.

With his right flank secured, General Allenby decided next to obtain a base sufficiently broad to permit of operations being carried out east of the Jordan against the Hedjaz Railway. This involved taking the high ground which covered the approaches to the Jordan by the road leading from Jericho towards Beisan, as well as the high ground farther west, that stretched across the Mount Ephraim range south of Sinjil, and thence in a north-westerly direction, the length of this front being about twenty-six miles. Here, again, the terrain was one of great natural difficulty—a succession of high and rocky ridges, many with precipitous sides, separated by deep valleys, the whole affording a series of positions of immense strength to the defence. In some places the tracks were mere ledges of rock open to the enemy's fire; in others, the slopes were terraced, and men had to pull or hoist each other up. Every position had to be separately reconnoitred, and the subsequent assembling of troops was necessarily a slow business. In such circumstances no movement could be rapid. On March 2nd and 3rd the British had advanced, with slight opposition, their line north of Jerusalem till their front was nearly halfway between the city and Shechem. Allenby launched his new attack on March 9th.

In the course of the night the Londoners crossed the Wady el Auja, north of Jericho, and on the morning of the 9th seized a position astride the road to Beisan. They encountered strong opposition in occupying Abu Tellul and Beiyudat, and as they advanced across the broken country they had to face heavy fire from the east side of the Jordan; but they gained their objectives, and commanded the ford across the Jordan near the mouth of the Auja. Next day they consolidated their new line, and there remained for a time. Meanwhile larger operations had been going on west of them, where the 53rd and other divisions were engaged, the scene of the fighting being the Shechem road and the districts on both sides of it. On the west side of the road, the centre of the struggle, which was of the most bitter character, was Tell Asur, a hill 3,318 feet high, and the most commanding position in Palestine. The Turks had entrenched it to the summit and lined it with machine-guns; but the gallant men of Middlesex took it. First they captured its trenches, one after another. Next there was hot bombing work by both combatants.

Struggle for the Shechem road

Presently the Middlesex bombing stopped. The Turks, thinking that here was their opportunity, came rushing down; but, swept back by the deadly fire of Lewis guns, they incontinently retired. Thereupon the Middlesex men, pressing after them, swiftly advanced and drove the Turks from the hill. The enemy tried repeatedly, but in vain, to recover this dominating position. On the extreme left, west of the Shechem road, the Turks counter-attacked the 10th Division in the deep vales of the Wadys el Nimr and el Jib—in some places in the latter there was a sheer drop of ninety feet; but the troops fought magnificently and beat the enemy back.

During the night of March 9th and throughout the following day the northward march of the British continued astride the Shechem road, progress being made to a depth of about 3,000 yards on a front of twelve miles. The fighting in and about the pass to Shechem was desperate. Commanded by heights east and west, the road descended to the Wady el Haramiyeh—the "Robbers' Valley," shut in by steep hills, partly covered with olive trees and traversed by the bed of the torrent leading to the "Robbers' Spring." Such a locality gave ample scope for hiding machine-gun nests. Allenby, in a communiqué at the time, observed that the advance went on "in the face of obstinate resistance, the enemy employing numerous machine-guns from concealed positions."

Hebron, " the City of Abraham," entered by General Allenby, December 7th, 1917.

Indian Lancers in the picturesque Syrian port of Haifa, taken by the British, September 23rd, 1918.

British Yeomanry in ancient Damascus, "a rose-red city half as old as Time."

Australian Light Horse entering the Square of Damascus, October 1st, 1918.

Australian mounted troops resting in the main street of Es Salt, Palestine.

London Scottish marching through Es Salt, taken by the British in September, 1918.

Pontoon bridge built by the British over the Jordan at El Ghoraniyeh.

Nearer view of the bridge at El Ghoraniyeh when it was being tested for traffic.

On the west side the high ridges on the north bank of the Wady el Jib were secured, while on the east side three counter-attacks launched against the section of these ridges between Sheikh Saleh and Burj el Lisaneh were repulsed, with great loss to the Turks. The Burj el Lisaneh (the Tower of the Tongue) was a ruined castle perched on the summit of a hill looking across the Robbers' Valley. The British progressed during the night of the 10th, and, advancing throughout the 11th, stood twelve miles from Shechem on the morning of the 12th. On the last-named day East Anglian, South English, and Indian troops attacked the enemy in the coastal area, and gained ground to a depth of three miles on a front of twelve miles, capturing the villages of El Mirr, Bentis, El Lubban (not to be confused with the place of the same name on the Shechem road), Deir Ballut, and Mejdel Yaba, on the Wadys Abu Lejia and Deir Ballut, both of which streams were forced.

To most observers at home it looked as if Allenby was making a general forward move, with Shechem as his central objective, but this was not his design. What had been in his mind was a raid in some force on the Hedjaz Railway in conjunction with the Arabs on the east, who were under the command of the Emir Feisul, the third son of King Hussein. Allenby's operations now enabled him to undertake this raid, which, if successful, would, he hoped, give Feisul a good opportunity of attacking Maan, an important Turkish point on the railway. Allenby's objective was Amman (Rabboth Amon), lying in a direct line some thirty miles east of Jericho, or about twenty-five miles beyond the Jordan, in the Bible land of Gilead, the "Region of the Rocks."

Early on March 22nd the British crossed that river despite the strong current, and having thrown bridges across, established themselves on its east bank, thereafter marching on for some distance, notwithstanding considerable opposition from the Turks. Fresh bridges were built across the Jordan on the night of March 23rd, and by the evening of the next day the troops had advanced from the **Across the Jordan** marshy region of the river, then swollen **to Es Salt** with rains, into the mountainous country towards Es Salt, the Ramoth of the Old Testament, south of which town Allenby's mounted men took the bridge at El Howeij. Among the prisoners taken from the Turks, who stoutly but ineffectively tried to bar the progress of the British, were several Germans. A brilliant attack by a London infantry battalion resulted in the capture of an entire battery. Es Salt, 3,000 feet above the level of the Jordan, itself 1,000 feet below the level of the sea, was occupied in the night of March 25th, and next morning the Turks were driven down the mountain road towards Aman.

In the afternoon of the 27th both infantry and cavalry were converging on Aman, where the enemy, who had been reinforced, held strong positions, but Allenby did not press the attack against it. While his infantry fought containing actions there, his Anzacs and camelry blew up the bridges and culverts on the Hedjaz Railway on both sides of the town, and demolished several miles of track. Having effected this damage, the British withdrew on March 30th to Es Salt.

After stating that his operations were delayed by bad weather, and that before Aman could be attacked in strength this delay had enabled the Turks to concentrate 4,000 men, with fifteen guns, in its neighbourhood, while another 2,000 were threatening Es Salt, General Allenby explained the retirement:

To have driven the enemy from his position, without adequate artillery support, would have entailed heavy losses. Owing to the marshy nature of the country, it was only possible to bring up mountain artillery, and I therefore ordered a withdrawal, which was carried out without serious interruption. . . . Considerable losses were inflicted on the enemy, and in addition fifty-three officers and nine hundred other ranks were taken prisoners, including several Germans. The raid also enabled a considerable number of Armenians to escape and find a refuge west of the Jordan.

In Constantinople the British retirement, which continued to the Jordan, was mendaciously reported to have assumed the character of a complete defeat. A fancy picture was drawn of the Turks advancing victoriously on the British as they tried to get away along the impassable roads. Es Salt was stated to have been "reconquered," and British reinforcements were said to have been forced to fly in disorder before the charges of Turkish cavalry.

Recalling, perhaps, the misgiving felt in the United Kingdom after the official statement respecting the First and Second Battles of Gaza, the War Office issued a denial of the Turkish allegations, and said that the only indication reported by General Allenby of the energetic Turkish pursuit mentioned in the Constantinople communiqués was the fact that on April 1st his rearguard was attacked by some 500 Turks, who were easily beaten off. In April Lord Robert Cecil, speaking in the House of Commons on the services rendered by the Arabs, said that the Emir Feisul's force, which had advanced its front from Mecca to Tafileh, on the shores of the Dead Sea, a distance of some 800 miles, had been assisted to maintain its position by General Allenby's raid.

An advance on April 9th in the region of Mount Ephraim, where the villages of El **Turco-German** Kefr and Rafat were captured, brought the **general offensive** British front west of the Shechem road fairly level with the front in the coastal area, which, east of the Plain of Sharon, next day was heavily attacked by the Turks, with German supports, who, after penetrating into some advanced positions, were ejected by determined counter-attacks, which were delivered by West Country, Irish, and Indian troops. The thick of the fighting was at Berukin, a place about eighteen miles north-east of Jaffa. The Turco-German attack in this quarter was evidently part of a general offensive, for on April 11th the enemy made an assault on Allenby's front astride the Shechem road, which slight gains had brought within about ten miles of the town, and on the same day directed a powerful attack against his positions on the east bank of the Jordan in the vicinity of El Ghoraniyeh, where a bridge-head was defended by Australian Light Horse. The effort of the enemy in the centre was repulsed. For that on the Jordan the Turks had concentrated a force of 5,000 rifles at Shunet Nimrin, six miles from the bridge-head, and their attacks extended from the Wady el Auja southwards.

The battle began in the foot-hills about nine miles north of the Jordan, where the Imperial Camel Corps lay entrenched, and after two hours of hard pounding the enemy, here numbering 2,000 men, was driven off. The main Turkish force marched from the hills east of the Jordan by two roads on El Ghoraniyeh, and got within three hundred yards of the line of the Australians, but there it was held up by a withering fire, and what was left of it made its escape during the ensuing night. In the morning 367 German and Turkish dead lay in front of the Australian wire. The Turco-German offensive ended in utter defeat.

General Allenby now determined to destroy the enemy force at Shunet Nimrin and to reoccupy Es Salt until his men could be relieved by the Arabs. His intention had been to undertake this in the middle of May, but representations from the Beni Sakhr tribe induced him to strike a fortnight sooner, and the operation was begun early on April 30th. His plan was that the Londoners of the 60th Division were to attack Shunet **Turkish success** Nimrin, while his mounted troops, having **at Shunet Nimrin** first moved northwards, were to make a flanking attack south on Es Salt, and cut off the Turks at the former place. Part of the scheme was that the Mounted Division was to leave a force to protect the crossing of the Jordan at Jisr ed Damieh, about eighteen miles north of the Ghoraniyeh bridge-head. The Turks held the west bank at Jisr ed Damieh. General Allenby gave, in his despatch of September 18th, the following account of what took place:

The 60th Division captured the advanced works of the Shunet Nimrin position, but were unable to make further progress in face of the stubborn opposition offered by the enemy. The mounted troops moving northwards rode round the right of the Shunet Nimrin position, and by six p.m. had captured Es Salt, leaving an Australian brigade to watch the left flank. [Allenby was writing of what happened on May 1st.] This brigade took up a position facing north-west astride the Jisr ed Damieh-Es Salt track. . . . At 7.30 a.m. on May 1st this brigade was attacked by the 3rd Turkish Cavalry Division and a part of the 24th Division, which had crossed from the west bank

FORTRESS OF ANCIENT AND MODERN CRUSADERS.
British sandbag-built post by an ancient fortress on the site of Antipatris, built by Herod the Great. Remains (and, inset above, a more distant view) of the castle at Ras el Ain, about ten miles north-east of Jaffa, used as a fortress by the mediæval Crusaders.

of the Jordan during the night at Jisr ed Damieh. The enemy succeeded in penetrating between the left of the brigade and the detachment on the bank of the Jordan. The brigade was driven back through the foot-hills. During the retirement through the hills, nine guns and part of its transport had to be abandoned, being unable to traverse the intricate ground.

By bringing up a much superior force from Shechem, the Turks had scored a success. On May 2nd this force crossed to the east bank of the Jordan at Jisr ed Damieh, and advanced to attack the British at Es Salt, which also was assailed by two Turkish battalions from Aman, but the enemy was completely repulsed. The 60th Division, however, was unable to make any substantial progress at Shunet Nimrin. Meanwhile the assistance which had been looked for from the Beni Sakhr Arabs had not materialised, and as additional Turkish reinforcements were coming up, Allenby in these circumstances decided to withdraw his whole force to the Jordan crossings. Against this was to be set the fact that heavy loss had been inflicted on the enemy, fifty of his officers and nearly 900 other ranks being made prisoner by the British. As was natural, the

British withdraw to the Jordan Constantinople communiqués made the most of this second retirement from Es Salt and of the captured guns, but the casualties of the Turks were far greater than those of Allenby.

In the meantime considerable changes, necessitated by the situation on the western front, had been made in his command, with the result that operations on a large scale were out of the question for some time. During the first week in April the 52nd Division embarked for France, its place being filled by the 7th (Meerut) Division, which had been sent from Mesopotamia. The 74th Division left Palestine during the second week of April, and the 3rd (Lahore) Division came from Mesopotamia to replace it, but it was not until the middle of June that its last units disembarked. In addition to the two divisions withdrawn, nine Yeomanry regiments, five and a half siege batteries, ten British battalions, and five machine-gun companies were taken from the front, preparatory to going to France.

By the end of April the Yeomanry had been replaced by Indian cavalry regiments, which had come from France, and the British battalions by Indian battalions despatched from India. These Indian troops had not, however, seen service in the war, and therefore lacked the experience of the British troops whose place they took. In May fourteen other British battalions were despatched to the western front, and only two Indian battalions were available to replace them. During July and the first week in August ten more British battalions were replaced by the same number of Indian battalions, the personnel of the British battalions being used as reinforcements.

During June the British slightly advanced their front in the coastal area by some minor operations, but hardly any fighting of importance took place until Allenby's great offensive in September, except in the course of July, when an increased number of Germans were found in the Turkish forces. On July 14th the Turks took the offensive on both sides of the Jordan. West of the river they made a sudden attack at 3.30 a.m., captured Abu Tellul, and surrounded some advanced posts. An hour later they were victoriously counter-attacked by the Australian Light Horse, who by five o'clock had Abu Tellul in their hands again. Caught against the advanced posts, all which, save one, had held out, though enveloped, the enemy lost severely, 276 Germans, including twelve officers and sixty-two Turks, being made prisoner.

While this struggle was proceeding the Turks were seen to be concentrating on the east side of the river, midway between Ghoraniyeh and the Dead Sea. A counter-attack was immediately organised by the officer commanding the 1st Australian Light Horse, and, taking advantage of the ground, he moved up his force within charging distance before it was observed by the enemy. The Australians then charged home. Ninety Turks were speared, and ninety-one prisoners, with six officers, besides four machine-guns, were captured. The remainder fled, and effected their escape only because the places they reached were impassable for cavalry. In his account of this action General Allenby stated that the Jodhpur Lancers played a distinguished part. In the month of August and during the first half of September little of military importance was recorded. Then, with even greater and more startling suddenness than was the case in the Balkans, almost simultaneously, the whole situation was transformed by as brilliant a campaign as any in all history.

Making excellent use of the quiet weeks that passed on the front, Allenby saw to the thorough organisation of his forces, old and new. Great pains were taken with the intensive training of his troops for the offensive he planned. For the success of his operations secrecy was essential, and as the hour set for the attack approached his men marched towards their assigned positions under cover of night, and lay hidden during the day amid the olive-groves. This concealment was helped, too, by his mastery of the air, for his flying machines fought off and effectively prevented the enemy scouts from seeing any changes they otherwise might have noted in his dispositions. On the other hand his aerial observers, ranging far and wide, had photographed and mapped out for him the terrain across which his advance was to proceed.

By the night of September 18-19th his preparations were complete and the assault began. Opposed to him were the Seventh and Eighth Turkish Armies, between the sea and the Jordan, and the Fourth Turkish Army, east of the Jordan, their total strength, including considerable German contingents, being about 100,000 men, of whom about 40,000 were combatants. Their Commander-in-Chief was the German Liman von Sanders. Their defensive lines, on which they had been working all the summer, were very strong.

At the moment of attack the British line ran east from the Mediterranean, a few miles south of Arsuf, the ancient Apollonia, across the Plain of Sharon, to a point south of Jiljulieh (Gilgal of old), and thence south-easterly through Rafat and the district of Mount Ephraim to the Shechem road, about ten miles south of Shechem; from the road it passed north of Tell Asur to Beiyudat, on the north side of the Wady el Auja, and struck eastward through the hills to the Jordan, along which, by El Ghoraniyeh, it reached southward to the Dead Sea. Away on the east side of the Jordan lay the Arabs, under the Emir Feisul, who had been assigned a certain rôle, and played it well. Allenby's carefully thought-out and well-matured offensive started its development on both flanks —on his right, in a local attack between the Shechem road and the Jordan, which was more than a feint, for it was designed to secure certain roads; on his left, in the main attack from the sea to Mount Ephraim, a distance of about sixteen miles. Allenby's plan, at once masterly and simple, was to pierce the Turkish front on his left, get behind it, cut it off from the north, and roll it up against the Jordan, the fords of which he proposed securing, while far on the north-east the Arabs at Deraa junction cut the main railway from Damascus and stopped all communication with Aleppo.

On the right, east of the Shechem road, the attack was conducted by a brigade consisting of Welsh and Indian troops, with a Cape (coloured) battalion. During the night of September 18-19th this force marched across the difficult hilly country, passed the watershed, drove the Turks out of their positions, and captured El Mugheir, on the road from Shechem to the Jordan, and commanding several of the fords of that river. Another brigade, operating more to the west, stormed a series of fortified hills north-east of Tell Asur, and advanced to a point about three miles east of Turmus Aya, which lay two miles from the Shechem road. While these movements, rendered most arduous by the mountainous nature of the ground, were going forward with marked success, Allenby struck his main blow, and struck it with all his might, on the west, particularly close to the sea, on the coastal plain, the great highway to and from Egypt which had been traversed by former conquerors of

Palestine and Syria, and of which he had already won the key in the south by his capture of Gaza.

At half-past four o'clock in the morning of September 19th Allenby, after a short but terrific bombardment, launched his main attack from the coast to Rafat, while British warships co-operated from the sea with their fire. As soon as the guns belched forth, the infantry swarmed "over the top," and had gone a long way towards the enemy entrenchments before the Turks, taken completely by surprise, could put down a barrage. Close to the coast London and Indian troops swept on irresistibly over the sand-dunes and turned the Turkish flank. On the right of the Londoners other Indian soldiers, fighting with fine spirit, assaulted and carried a deep series of trenches well placed among low hills. East of these Indians, West Countrymen, with still more Indian troops, broke through the Turkish lines, and early in the day pushed on as far as Miskeh, a short distance from Et Tireh, **Allenby's main attack launched** one of the enemy's strongholds, which was captured afterwards.

Farther along the front British and Indian troops stormed the trenches before them, and, joined by East Anglians, who had routed the Turks immediately opposed to them, stormed Kalkilieh, in spite of a most stubborn defence. Still farther east, at the end of the front thus heavily assailed, French contingents, fighting with their customary gallantry, worked north of Rafat towards the Wady Azzun. Everywhere rapid progress was made, and in three hours the entire hostile defensive system was over-run; in places it was smashed to a depth of five miles; everywhere the Turks were retreating, having already lost many hundreds in prisoners.

By half-past seven o'clock that morning the infantry had cleared the way for the cavalry, who were eagerly awaiting their opportunity. British Yeomanry, Australian Light Horse, and Indian Lancers, moving forward quickly, pressed on into the open country beyond. A

PRIMITIVE DEFENCE THAT FAILED BEFORE NOVEL ATTACK.
Pointed stakes—such as the Ancient Britons used against the Romans—employed by the Turks in Palestine; behind these were metal hoops, pools of water, more stakes, and then barbed-wire. This multiple defence proved inadequate against British valour supported by modern artillery and the newest engine of war— the Tank. In oval: British Tanks in a palm-grove in Palestine.

magnificent opening, designed by a general who was a cavalryman himself, had come for the cavalry, and they knew how to take full advantage of it.

Starting off at a gallop, the Yeomanry and the Indian cavalry rode northward along the coast over roads deep in dust and sand, got across the Nahr-el-Falik, and presently were over the Nahr Iskanderuneh, another big wady farther north. By mid-day they were at Likteria (Hudeira), a road junction, about twenty miles from their front in the morning. Passing over the branch railway, with its northern terminus at El Marah, they advanced north-eastward among the hills south-east of Mount Carmel, and marched on towards the Plain of Esdraelon, the Armageddon of the Apocalypse, their objective being Nazareth. A second cavalry column, also composed of Yeomanry and Indians, moving a little east of the first column, passed over the Turkish lines at Tabsor, and made off in the direction of El Afuleh (El Fule), the junction of the Central Palestine Railway with the railway from Haifa and Acre. During the night it was marching through the Musmus Pass.

Meanwhile the Australian Light Horse had reached the main Tul Keram-Messudieh railway and road in the vicinity of Anebta, cutting off large bodies of the **Tul Keram** retreating enemy, with guns and transport. **Junction occupied** At the same time part of the infantry, swinging eastwards of the ground they had conquered, were advancing on the railway junction of Tul Keram, occupying that important strategic point in the course of the afternoon. Nor for the Turks was all this the full tale of the day's disasters, which included the loss of upward of 3,000 in prisoners alone. East of the Jordan the Emir Feisul, with a strong force of Arabs, descended on the Hedjaz Railway junction at Deraa, according to plan, and severed the Turkish communications leading north, south, and west.

By the evening of September 19th it was plain that Allenby's plan, to the working out of which his Staff brilliantly contributed, was developing into a sweeping victory with amazing rapidity. Next day's operations, which practically concluded the Battle for Palestine, for it was nothing less, made Allenby's tremendous success still more apparent. The pressure of his infantry was mainly exerted towards Shechem. West of it the troops advanced in the direction of the town, beating down all opposition, until in the evening they stood on a line almost due north and south, from Bir Asur, through Messudieh, Beit Lid, and Baka to Bidieh, about five miles above Rafat. A stern struggle took place for the possession of Beit Lid, a height 5,000 yards from the station of Messudieh. After it had been captured it **Converging movement** was decided that a move should be made **upon Shechem** on the station, but this involved taking another dominating hill. In the moonlight a battalion of Sikhs stole up its slopes, and surprising its defenders, who included German machine-gunners, rushed the position, and captured two hundred prisoners besides. While Allenby's left wing had thus got astride the railway and the roads converging on Shechem from the west, his right wing, marching over the very trying country west of the Jordan, and overcoming considerable resistance, reached a line stretching from Khan Jibeit, north-east of El Mugheir, and about five miles east of the ancient Shiloh, to Es Sawieh, on the west side of the Shechem road, three miles above the village of El Lubban, and some eight miles from Shechem itself.

These movements, which so closely threatened Shechem, which the Turks had been at pains to turn into a highly-fortified centre, were made even more significant than they unmistakably were by what had taken place on that day north and north-east of the town, where Allenby's cavalry had done wonderful things.

During the night of September 19-20th the column of Yeomanry and Indian horsemen, who had advanced into the hills east of Mount Carmel, reached the Plain of Esdraelon, and, marching across it in the early morning of the 20th,

GERMANY'S KAISER DEPICTED IN A JERUSALEM CHURCH.
This ridiculous mediæval-looking picture was painted by a German artist as part of the ceiling decoration of the church of the German hospice built at Jerusalem on a site on the Mount of Olives. This site was presented by the Sultan to the Kaiser when he and the Kaiserin visited the Holy Land in 1898.

GENERAL SIR EDMUND ALLENBY, G.C.M.G., K.C.B.
Deliverer of Palestine and Syria from Turkish tyranny

moved across the plain to El Afuleh, which, with its garrison of 1,500 men, was soon captured. At this railway junction an immense amount of booty was taken, the spoil including eight locomotives, two complete trains, forty lorries, and a large quantity of stores. A portion of the column then marched up the Valley of Jezreel to Beisan, occupying the railway and taking about a thousand prisoners. Another detachment struck up north, and got into Jisr el Mujamia, on the Jordan, and about six miles south of the Sea of Galilee (Lake Tiberias), with a view to preventing reinforcements from reaching the Turks from that direction. Many of these cavalrymen had marched seventy miles in the two days—a great record in the circumstances.

By eight o'clock in the evening of September 20th the enemy resistance, General Allenby reported, was collapsing everywhere, except on the Turkish left in the Jordan Valley. All avenues of escape for the defeated Turks were closed, with the exception of the fords across the Jordan between Beisan and Jisr ed Damieh, and on the north the cavalry were collecting the disorganised masses of the enemy and their transport as they arrived from the south. Already more than 8,000 prisoners and 100 guns had been counted among the booty, in which also were immense quantities of both horse and mechanical transport, four aeroplanes, many locomotives, and much rolling-stock.

The general noted that his aircraft had inflicted very severe losses on the Turks in their

climbed the height on which Nazareth stood. The Turks put up a fight, but the cavalrymen beat them, and, surrounding the town, took it with 2,300 prisoners. The mayor, in surrendering Nazareth, stated that Liman von Sanders, the German Generalissimo of the Turkish forces in Palestine, had quitted the town the previous evening when he had heard that the British cavalry were across the Nahr Iskanderuneh. Among the prisoners were many German telegraphists, mechanics, and other technical troops. In this area Allenby's cavalry covered upwards of fifty miles in twenty-four hours, and not without stiff fighting at several points.

Not less remarkable was the performance of the second column of Yeomanry and Indian Horse, whose objective was El Afuleh. After successfully traversing the Musmus Pass during the night, this force encountered and routed a strong body of the enemy at El Lejjun, the ancient Megiddo, on the edge of the Plain of Esdraelon, and about eight miles south-west of El Afuleh. Advancing into the plain, a regiment of Indian Lancers, acting as advance guard, was given such an opportunity as all cavalrymen desire. Mr. Massey described the action:

A Turkish battalion was lightly dug in on a flat about two miles from the entrance to the pass. The Lancers dashed out of the narrow defile, extended, and, galloping over this part of the Plain of Armageddon, crashed into the infantry machine-gunners with the lance, killing ninety and wounding as many more. They took four hundred and ten prisoners. The charge was most brilliantly executed. The cavalry had to gallop over exposed ground against heavy rifle and machine-gun fire, but they never faltered, each wave of horsemen riding through the enemy. Those who were not killed threw up their hands.

After this smart affair the column

WITH ARMY ANIMALS IN WADY AND SANDY WASTE.
Watering the horses of the Australian Light Horse in a wady in Palestine. In circle : Mules of a transport section of the British Palestine force with their native drivers, and (above) some of the animals in sandy dug-outs, arranged for localising the effect of possible shell fire.

retreat along the difficult roads. His airmen not only dropped bombs on the enemy, but shelled them with their machine-guns from low altitudes. The roads by which the Turks fled were, in consequence, littered or choked with the debris of war—dead men and dead horses, smashed guns, and wrecked transport of all kinds. The great battle was ending in much more than a defeat; it was becoming a debacle. There was no doubt about this next day, when Allenby made further gains, and the number of prisoners rose to 18,000 men, but the victory was already won, and all that remained to be done was the gathering up of the fragments of the Seventh and Eighth Turkish Armies.

In the evening of September 21st the infantry of Allenby's left wing, having swung round from Bir Asur, extended its line east as far as Beit Dejan, about ten miles south-east of Shechem, and was shepherding the Turks on and west of the Shechem road into the arms of the cavalry operating south from Beisan and Jenin. The latter place, on the railway and a centre of roads, about twelve miles almost due south of El Afuleh, was attacked both from the north and west by Yeomanry and Indians and by the Australian Light Horse. On the western outskirts the Australians, using the swords with which they had been armed a short time before, charged an entrenched Turkish battalion, sabring many of the enemy and capturing a thousand prisoners. Jenin, in which were not a few Germans, held out for a time, but was in British hands completely early on September 22nd.

From Shechem some Turkish contingents vainly attempted to escape into the Jordan Valley in the direction of Jisr ed Damieh, which was still held by the enemy, but they were caught by Allenby's airmen and thrown into wild disorder. Presently the New Zealanders seized Jisr ed Damieh and closed this exit, which was the last open, taking eight hundred prisoners, among whom was the Staff Commander of the 53rd Turkish Division. On September 22nd Shechem was entered by French mounted troops and the Australian Light Horse, infantry occupying it later.

On September 22nd Allenby announced that the Seventh and

Two Turkish armies annihilated

Eighth Turkish Armies had virtually ceased to exist, and that their entire transport was in his hands. By nightfall that day the tale of prisoners had mounted to 25,000 and of guns captured to 260, but many more prisoners had still to be counted, and there was a great deal of booty to be detailed later. It was a victory as complete as it was glorious. King George expressed the feeling of his peoples when he telegraphed to General Allenby that he was confident that this success, which he truly declared had effected the liberation of Palestine from Turkish rule, would rank as a great exploit in the history of the British Empire, and would stand for all time as a memorable testimony to British leadership and to the fighting qualities of British and Indian troops.

As Emperor of India there was a peculiar appropriateness in the King's reference to the Indian troops of Allenby's command. It was the universal opinion that one of the striking features of the battle was the magnificent dash of the Indian soldiers, many of whom were young and untried in action. The veterans lived up to their high reputation, but the new troops fought like seasoned fighting men, and gallantly responded to every call made on them. Of the Indian troops Mr. Massey wrote:

Divisional commanders tell me they are delighted with the valour of the Indians under all conditions. Forty-seven hours' continuous fighting and marching tested them to the utmost, but they behaved superbly, their only fault having been an eagerness to push on in Thursday's (September 19th) tremendous attack against the coastal defences. Their officers had to restrain them from rushing into our artillery barrage. These Indians, who took the place of some Londoners that were sent to France, were tremendously keen to preserve the record of their division. The Indians, with the Londoners, who

ADVANCE THROUGH THE HILLS TO ES SALT.
Stretcher-bearers using camel transport marching to Es Salt, which, having been earlier taken and abandoned by the British, was finally captured by them on September 23rd, 1918. Above: British camp by a Palestine brook on the way to Es Salt.

COAST END OF GENERAL ALLENBY'S LINE.
Sand-bag defences at the sea-shore end of the British front line in Palestine before General Allenby began his final triumphant advance of September, 1918, which led to the surrender of Turkey.

were the first into Jerusalem and the first over the Jordan, wanted to be the first through the coastal defences. They succeeded, and then went on and secured the crossing of the Wady Falik for the cavalry, afterwards advancing north-eastwards to Tul Keram, and covering the astonishing distance of twenty-two miles in twelve and a half hours, including trench fighting and actions in the open.

On the north the cavalry occupied Haifa and Acre on September 23rd, after slight opposition. Both were towns of historic interest, and the latter was memorable particularly as being the place where Napoleon, after a siege of two months' duration, during which British sailors under Sir Sidney Smith successfully co-operated in the defence, definitely failed in his Palestine - Syria Campaign of 1799. Haifa, the ancient Sycaminum, had seen, like Acre, the Crusaders and the great Saladin. Protected from the Mediterranean winds by Mount Carmel, its harbour is the best natural haven on the coast of Palestine; furthermore, the railway had increased the prosperity of the town. Two or three days later Allenby's cavalry occupied Tiberias, Semakh, and Es Samrah, on the shores of the Sea of Galilee, notwithstanding the determined resistance of their Turkish garrisons. Especially at Tiberias the enemy struggled hard but fruitlessly. The deliverance of the Holy Land, except on the east side of the Jordan, was now nearly complete, and Syria lay open to invasion. Damascus, its capital, the great city of immemorial age, which formed the Turkish base, was only seventy miles away.

WHEN THE TURK WAS DRIVEN FROM DAMASCUS.
Arab regular soldiers searching Bedouin suspects at one of the entrances to Damascus, and (above) General Allenby—in front seat to the right—setting out by motor-car from the city which his army had taken on October 1st, 1918.

First, however, Allenby dealt with the Fourth Turkish Army on the other side of the Jordan. On September 22nd signs were not wanting that it was retreating from the river towards the Hedjaz Railway, by which it expected to escape to the north. The pursuit was taken up by Australian, New Zealand, West Indian, and Jewish troops, the last - named consisting of the Jewish battalions of the Royal Fusiliers, which had been raised in London during the previous winter, and recruited further by Palestinian Jews after their arrival in the country. The Anzac Mounted Division, whose former experience of the terrain stood it in good stead, got into Es Salt by a movement across the hills that threatened the enemy's flank, and occupied that town after slight fighting on September 23rd, capturing more than 600 Turks and Germans, and a long-range naval gun which intermittently had shelled Jericho for months.

Next day the Anzacs were marching on Aman, the Australian Light Horse advancing on the wings, with the New Zealand Mounted Rifles in the centre. One party got astride the railway above Aman and derailed a train full of troops. Storming the crest of a dominating height, the New Zealanders rushed this central point on the railway on September 26th in the face of heavy machine-gun fire. The Turks, with whom were many Germans, fled along the railway northward, with the British in hot pursuit.

Fourth Turkish Army split up

With the capture of Aman the Fourth Turkish Army was broken in two. One part of it was hemmed in between the Arabs on the north at Deraa and the British at Aman, and the other was penned in between that town and Maan on the south, which the Arabs had taken two or three days before. South of Maan the Turkish forces along the railway to Medina were hopelessly cut off. Up to the evening of the 27th, 5,700 prisoners and twenty-eight guns had been captured in the Aman district. On the 28th the British turned south from Aman, and advancing about fourteen miles reached the station of Kustul, where they were in touch with the part of the Fourth Army which was retreating northwards from Maan. Next day this force, stated by its own commander to number 10,000 men, surrendered at Ziza, another station on the Hedjaz Railway, a few miles below Kustul. North of Aman, Allenby's cavalry shepherded the Turks into the arms of the Arabs, who

GATEWAY TO "THE OLDEST CITY IN THE WORLD."
With their entry into Damascus on October 1st, 1918, on which occasion they captured 7,000 prisoners, the British forces took possession of a city which had remained a centre of human activity for thousands of years.

had gained possession of Ezra and Ghazale, stations on the railway north of Deraa, on the 26th, Deraa itself, together with Sheikh Saad, sixteen miles to the north, falling into their hands on the following day with 1,500 prisoners. On the 28th Allenby's cavalry linked up with the Arabs in that area, and swept on up the railway towards Damascus.

Meanwhile the British were also moving forward in the direction of Damascus, but in the region north of the Sea of Galilee. In an effort to stay Allenby's march a Turkish force, which had been despatched in hot haste from Damascus, destroyed the bridge over the Upper Jordan at Jisr Benat Yakub (the Bridge of the Daughters of Jacob), the spot at which the road from Palestine to Syria had for unnumbered centuries crossed the river. But a brigade of the Australian Light Horse swam the stream with the horses farther south and forced the passage, while another Australian brigade got across on the north. On the morning of September 28th the enemy was driven from his positions on the Upper Jordan. On the south-east side of the Sea of Galilee the cavalry, having overcome the Turkish resistance at Irbid and Er Remtheh, drove the enemy confronting them northwards through El Mezeirib. By this time the number of prisoners taken by Allenby and the Arabs had swollen to upwards of 60,000, and the guns captured were more than 330. These great results had been obtained at comparatively small expense. On September 26th General Allenby reported that the total British casualties in this offensive to that date from all causes amounted to less than one-tenth of the number of prisoners taken.

Damascus captured by the British

The advance on Damascus progressed throughout September 29th, both by the road from the Jordan and along the railway, and by the evening of the next day cavalry had established themselves on the north, south, and west of the city, having disposed of the enemy rearguards who tried to bar their way, and taking 1,000 prisoners in the process. During the night of September 30th-October 1st the Australian mounted troops were in the suburbs, and at six o'clock in the morning a British force, in conjunction with a part of the Arab army of King Hussein, occupied the far-famed, old-world city—it was in existence before the Book of Genesis was written, and is hundreds of years older than Jerusalem. In the operations that ended in the fall of Damascus to the British upwards of 7,000 prisoners were taken. After the surrender all the allied troops, with the exception of the necessary guards, were withdrawn from the city, the administration of which was left to the local authorities. The people of Damascus received the British most joyfully. " I was amazed at the heartiness of the welcome accorded the British uniform," wrote Mr. Massey, an eye-witness of the scene : " when a soldier appeared in the streets he was surrounded by an excited and delighted throng."

Most worthy of note was it that on the day when the occupation of Damascus was announced an official statement was issued to the effect that the Allied Governments had decided formally to recognise the belligerent status of the Arab forces fighting as auxiliaries with the Allies against the common enemy in Palestine and Syria. King Hussein Ibn Ali, then Grand Sherif of Mecca, had since he raised the standard of revolt against Turkey on June 13th, 1916, been of most material assistance to the Allies, through the campaigns of his sons, the Emirs Abdulla, Feisul, Ali, and Zeid. In 1916 they held Jedda and Taif, besides Mecca, though they failed to take Medina. Helped by the British Navy—the " Red Sea Patrol "—they captured Wejh, and by mid-February, 1917, had cleared the Turks from the whole of the northern end of the Red Sea. In July they captured Akaba.

Hedjaz Arabs' valuable help

Meanwhile, aided by British officers, at whose head was Colonel E. T. Lawrence, who acted as Staff officer to Feisul, and soldiers of the Egyptian Army, Feisul—the leading spirit among the sons of the King of Hedjaz—formed something like a regular army out of his Arabs and others who supported him. By incessant raids on the Hedjaz Railway he greatly harassed the enemy, and in this he was assisted by British airmen, especially in the neighbourhood of Maan. Moving northward, Feisul made a series of daring raids on the railway between Aman and Deraa. As already noted, the Arabs scored a victory near El Kerak in January, 1918, and in the following April Feisul occupied El Kerak. In August he was preparing to co-operate with Allenby's offensive, and the cutting of the railway at Deraa, with the subsequent march to Damascus, showed his fine leadership. On October 3rd Feisul in person was in Damascus, which by one of the most wonderful turns of fortune's wheel had once more become an Arab city and the capital of the Arab race.

From Damascus Allenby pressed on towards Aleppo. On October 2nd his cavalry charged and captured an enemy column near Kubbet el Asafir, seventeen miles north-east of the city, securing 1,500 prisoners, two guns, and forty machine-guns. North and north-west the mounted troops scoured the country and brought in 15,000 prisoners. Zahleh, on the north-east, was taken on the 6th. The Turks evacuated Beirut, which was occupied on October 8th, and the British marched into Sidon (Saida) without any opposition. Baalbek, the ancient Heliopolis, at the foot of the anti-Lebanon range, was entered by British armoured-car batteries on October 9th. The Syrian Tripoli was occupied on October 13th without resistance, as two days later was Homs, on the railway, about halfway between Damascus and Aleppo. Allenby's advance became a swift, triumphal procession, and on the morning of October 26th his cavalry and armoured cars were in Aleppo after slight opposition.

Aleppo—called Beroea and Khalep in former times—is an old city like Damascus, and like it has seen many mutations. As a place of considerable strategic importance its defence by the enemy had been regarded as a certainty, but Liman von Sanders, feeling no doubt that the game was up, had withdrawn from it a day or two before the arrival of the British, and had gone to Alexandretta. From Aleppo the cavalry rode on to Muslimiya, the junction of the Syrian systems of railways with the Bagdad Railway, and occupied it. The conquest of Syria was virtually complete. It had been a whirlwind affair. In what direction would Allenby strike next was the question : north-westward towards Constantinople, or eastward along the Euphrates ? The question was answered for him.

Turkey capitulates to the Allies

On October 30th Turkey capitulated to the Allies. Doubtless her action was influenced by the unconditional surrender of Bulgaria, which had taken place a month before, by the hammer-blows Foch was dealing the Germans on the western front, and by Marshall's progress towards Mosul, in Mesopotamia ; but the crushing defeats, with the loss of three of her armies in Palestine, she had suffered at the hands of Allenby must have counted for much in bringing about her decision. In no other theatre of the war had the enemy been caused to endure such utter disaster, and Germany's growing weakness made impossible any hope of retrieving the situation.

A fortnight after the armistice was signed the Turkish Government, which no longer was ruled by Enver Pasha and the other Young Turk leaders—most of whom were fugitives —was required by the Allies to withdraw all the Turkish forces westward of Bozanti, north of Adana, by December 15th, and this withdrawal was to be followed by immediate demobilisation in Syria and Cilicia. The Turks had to surrender all their artillery and machine-guns, with their ammunition, in Northern Syria and along the railway as far as Missis, west of the " Cilician Gate," and these demands meant the removal of all Turkish troops from the plains to the east and south-east of the Taurus.

The port and town of Alexandretta were occupied by British and French troops on November 9th, and that was the final operation of importance. Thus were the Turks, after centuries of misrule, cleared out of Palestine and Syria. The administration of these countries was left for future decision, but the prospect before their peoples was bright with promise.

CHAPTER CCLXXV.

"FOR VALOUR": HEROES OF THE VICTORIA CROSS IN THE FOURTH YEAR OF THE WAR.

Number of V.C.'s Awarded in the Fourth Year—Analysis of the List—Crosses Won by Sailors—The Men of Zeebrugge—Bishop and McCudden—Canada's Nineteen V.C.'s—Australian V.C.'s—Two Heroes from New Zealand—The Indian Awards—The Artillery and the Cavalry—Eight Gallant Guardsmen—The Engineers and the R.A.M.C.—A Double V.C.—Machine Gun Corps and Tank Corps—Rev. T. B. Hardy, V.C.—The Ninety-three Infantry Heroes—The Lancashire Fusiliers at the Top—The London Regiment and the Royal Fusiliers—The Royal Lancasters, the Rifle Brigade, and the Worcesters—The Sherwood Foresters—Twenty-one Regiments with Two V.C.'s Each—"No-Surrender" Buchan—Another Twenty-one Regiments with One V.C. Each.

IN almost every country of the world the Great War produced the most remarkable, far-reaching, and often unexpected changes. But in one matter there was no change—human valour, frequent though it was, still commanded the homage of mankind, and here, as elsewhere, Britain held no secondary place. The Victoria Cross remained the most coveted distinction a soldier or sailor could win, and many millions of people knew that the few score who gained it were men with rare and wonderful qualities. They read the stories of their deeds with unflagging interest, as men and women will as long as high and generous thoughts endure. In Chapter CCXXVI. (Vol. 10, page 601), those of the third year were described, and the story is continued here.

During the fourth year of the war—August 4th, 1917, to August 4th, 1918—the Victoria Cross was won one hundred and sixty-eight times; but as one man, Captain N. G. Chavasse, had already won it in the previous year, the net total is one hundred and sixty-seven, for in the official list a name can only appear once — the second award being a bar to the existing cross. Nine crosses were awarded to the Navy; four were won by airmen. Thirty-two were awarded to men of the Overseas Dominions —eleven to Australians, eighteen to Canadians, two to New Zealanders, and one to a South

ONE OF INDIA'S V.C. HEROES.
Lance-Dafadar Gobind Singh, V.C., who won the great decoration "For Valour" by his heroism at Cambrai. He is seen riding in the procession when King George opened Parliament on February 12th, 1918.

African. Of the remaining one hundred and twenty-two, six were won by the Artillery, two by the Cavalry, two by Indian soldiers, two by the Engineers, two by the R.A.M.C., three by the Machine Gun Corps, two by the Tank Corps, one by the Army Service Corps, and one by a chaplain. Of the remainder eight fell to the Guards, and the rest to the line.

Three regiments head the roll with five each to their credit—the Lancashire Fusiliers, the London Regiment, and the Royal Fusiliers. The Rifle Brigade, the Royal Lancaster, and the Worcester carried off four each. The Notts and Derby won three. Two crosses were awarded to men of each of the following twenty-one regiments : King's Royal Rifles, Warwicks, Yorkshires, West Yorkshires, Gloucesters, Northamptons, Hampshires, West Ridings, Manchesters, North Staffordshires, Durham Light Infantry, and Yorkshire Light Infantry, as well as to the Border and Middlesex Regiments among English units ; the Scottish were the Argyll and Sutherland Highlanders, Seaforth Highlanders, Black Watch, Highland Light Infantry, and King's Own Scottish Borderers ; and the remaining two were the Inniskilling and Welsh Fusiliers. Twenty-one other regiments added one each to their battle honours.

A few words of explanation are necessary. As a man cannot be enumerated twice, some rule must be applied to determine the exact section in which to place a V.C. For example, Captain Bishop was a member of the Canadian Cavalry, but as his V.C. was won while he was serving as an airman, he is included among the air heroes. Again, Captain Bishop, Lieutenants Flowerdew and Strachan, and Lance-Dafadar Gobind Singh might have been added to the cavalry. But for greater clearness we have included Flowerdew and Strachan with their countrymen the Canadians, and described Gobind Singh and his comrade Rifleman Rana Karanbahadur as representatives of the Indian Army. Finally, Second-Lieutenant Clement Robertson was officially described as of the Royal West Surreys (S.R.). He is included here with the Tank Corps, for he gained his distinction when serving with that unit.

[*Barnett.*

MAJOR W. H. ANDERSON,
H.L.I.

Skipper T. Crisp, R.N.R. On an August afternoon the smack Nelson was attacked by a submarine. Crisp was below packing fish ; one man was cleaning the deck. Coming up, Crisp saw an object on the horizon, examined it closely, and sang out : "Clear for action. Submarine !" Scarcely had he uttered the words when a shot fell about a hundred yards away. Others followed, and the fourth went through the port bow just below the water-line. The skipper was hit by a shell which took off both his legs. Most of his crew were killed or injured ; but refusing to haul down the flag, he gave the order : "Throw the confidential books overboard, and me after them !" He was too badly wounded to be moved, and the survivors left him on deck and took to the small

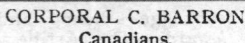

CORPORAL C. BARRON,
Canadians.

SEC.-LT. E. F. BEAL,
Yorks Regt.

LT.-COL. B. BEST-DUNKLEY,
Lancashire Fusiliers.

SEC.-LT. F. BIRKS,
A.I.F.

CAPT. W. A. BISHOP,
R.F.C.

The first naval V.C. to be awarded in the fourth year was won by Skipper Joseph Watt, R.N.R. Watt's V.C. was for gallantry when the allied drifters in the Strait of Otranto were attacked by Austrian light cruisers on May 15th, 1917. Hailed by a cruiser at about one hundred yards range and ordered to stop and abandon his drifter, the Gowan Lea, he replied by ordering full speed ahead and calling upon his crew to fight to a finish. The cruiser was engaged, but after one round had been fired a shot disabled the drifter's gun. The crew, however, stuck to it and endeavoured to make it work. After the cruiser had passed on, Watt took the Gowan Lea alongside the damaged drifter Floandi, and assisted to remove the dead and wounded.

On November 3rd, 1917, three V.C.'s were awarded to seamen for services in action with enemy submarines. Two of the recipients were Lieutenant C. G. Bonner, D.S.C., R.N.R. and Petty-Officer E. Pitcher. Their thrilling story was not made public until just about a year later. It seems that on August 8th, 1917, H.M.S. Dunraven, under Captain Gordon Campbell, V.C., sighted a German submarine. The British ship was disguised as a merchantman, and fulfilling her rôle, allowed the enemy to come close and sent out signals of distress. As arranged, some of the crew, apparently panic-stricken, left the vessel, but a terrible explosion killed some of those who remained on board. The survivors, however, kept to their task of deceiving the Germans until the submarine was near enough to be torpedoed. They did this amid constant explosions of cordite and shells, with a fire burning furiously and with the submarine firing steadily. At last, when the Dunraven was almost a wreck, destroyers arrived and rescued the crew. Among those who assisted Campbell in this most perilous work were the two, an officer and a man, who received the Victoria Cross.

The third V.C. was posthumously granted to

LT.-COL. A. D. BORTON,
London Regt.

SEC.-LT. J. C. BUCHAN,
A. and S. Highlanders.

SERGT. W. F. BURMAN,
Rifle Brigade.

boat. A quarter of an hour afterwards the Nelson went down.

To Ordinary Seaman John Henry Carless the cross was granted for an act of conspicuous bravery in the action in the Heligoland Bight on November 17th, 1917. Carless was mortally wounded, but went on serving the gun at which he was acting as rammer, and helping to clear away the other casualties. He collapsed once, but got up, cheered on the gun's new crew, fell down again, and died. "He not only set a very inspiring and memorable example," said the official account, "but he also, while mortally wounded, continued to do effective work against the King's enemies."

The four remaining naval heroes were awarded the cross on July 24th, 1918, for services against Zeebrugge and Ostend on the night of April 22nd-23rd. In all, six crosses were given for these feats—two to the Royal Marine forces, whose deeds are described later. The storming of Zeebrugge and the operations against Ostend were dealt with in Chapter CCXLIV. (Vol. 11, page 346), so that it is only necessary to indicate briefly the part taken by the four V.C.'s. Commander (later Captain) Alfred Francis Blakeney Carpenter was in command of the Vindictive. He set a magnificent example to all under his command by his calm composure when navigating mined waters, supervising the landing, walking round the decks directing operations and encouraging the men, although his ship was under a murderous fire throughout. He was selected by his officer colleagues to receive the cross. Lieutenant Richard Douglas Sandford, R.N., was in command of submarine C3, and skilfully placed that vessel between the piles of the viaduct before lighting his fuse and abandoning her.

Lieutenant Percy Thompson Dean, R.N.V.R., was in command of the motor-launch 282, and handled her in a magnificent manner when embarking the officers and men from the blockships. He followed them in, and closed

Intrepid and Iphigenia under a constant and deadly fire, taking off over one hundred officers and men. Able-Seaman Albert Edward McKenzie belonged to B Company of the storming-party. He landed on the Mole with his machine-gun and did very good work, using his gun to the utmost advantage and accounting for several of the enemy who were running from a shelter to a destroyer alongside the Mole. McKenzie was severely wounded, and died in the following November. He was selected by the men of the Vindictive and other boats to receive the cross.

Four airmen received the cross in the fourth year of the war, as compared with five in the third. Captain William Avery Bishop, D.S.O., M.C., Canadian Cavalry and R.F.C., ranks with

LT.-COL. C. BUSHELL,
R.W. Surrey Regt.

closed with a tribute to his "utmost gallantry and skill," and said that McCudden, by the great service which he had rendered to his country, was deserving of the very highest honour.

The award of the cross to Lieutenant Alan Jerrard and Second-Lieutenant Alan Arnett McLeod, both of the Royal Air Force, was announced on May 2nd, 1918. The former attacked five enemy aeroplanes and shot one down in flames. He then proceeded to attack an aerodrome from a height of only fifty feet, engaged single-handed some nineteen machines and destroyed one. While attacked by a large number of the enemy, Jerrard observed that one of the pilots of his patrol was in difficulties. He went to his assistance and destroyed another

PTE. W. B. BUTLER,
W. Yorks Regt., attd. T.M.B.

SERGT. R. BYE,
Welsh Guards.

SEAMAN J. H. CARLESS,
R.N.

SEC.-LT. B. M. CASSIDY,
Lancs Fusiliers.

L.-CORPL. J. A. CHRISTIE,
London Regt.

Captains Ball and McCudden as among the most brilliant airmen produced by the war, and the particular deed for which he was awarded the honour stands high in aerial heroism. He was working independently, and flew first of all to an enemy aerodrome. Finding it empty, he flew to another, twelve miles the other side of the line. He attacked seven machines from about fifty feet, and a mechanic, who was starting one of the engines, was seen to fall. One of the enemy machines got off the ground, but Bishop fired fifteen rounds into it at close range and it crashed. He then sent down a second machine, but two more rose from the aerodrome, one of which he engaged at the height of 1,000 feet. This machine crashed three hundred yards from the aerodrome, after which he emptied a drum of ammunition into the fourth.

Lieutenant James Byford McCudden, D.S.O., M.C., M.M., was awarded the V.C. on March 30th, 1918. His record was probably unique. Starting as a private in the R.F.C., he had accompanied that arm of the British Expeditionary Force to France in August, 1914. He went through the retreat and shared in practically every important battle, so that among airmen he could justly claim an unusual wealth of practical experience. The official announcement of McCudden's V.C. award gave a number of instances of his "conspicuous bravery, exceptional perseverance, keenness, and very high devotion to duty." At that time he had accounted for fifty-four enemy aeroplanes. "While in his present squadron he has participated in seventy-eight offensive patrols, and in nearly every case has been the leader. On at least thirty other occasions, while with the same squadron, he has crossed the line alone, either in pursuit or in quest of enemy aeroplanes." Then followed a number of typical examples of particularly fine work. On January 30th, 1918, single-handed, he attacked five enemy scouts, as a result of which two were destroyed. The official account

CORPL. W. CLAMP,
Yorks Regt.

SEC.-LT. J. H. COLLIN,
R. Lanc. Regt.

A.-CPL. J. COLLINS,
Royal Welsh Fus.

machine. He was continually attacked, and only retreated when ordered to do so by his patrol leader. Although wounded, he turned repeatedly and attacked the pursuing machines until he was overwhelmed by numbers and driven to the ground.

While flying with his observer attacking hostile formations, McLeod was assailed at a height of 5,000 feet by eight enemy triplanes. By skilful manœuvring he enabled his observer to fire bursts at each machine in turn, three of them being thus shot down. By this time McLeod had received five wounds and his machine was set on fire. Nothing daunted, he climbed out on to the left bottom plane where, controlling his machine from the fuselage side and side-slipping steeply, he kept the flames to one side and enabled the observer to continue firing until the ground was reached. The observer had been wounded six times when the machine crashed in No Man's Land, and McLeod, notwithstanding his own wounds, dragged him away from the burning wreckage. He was again wounded by a bomb, but succeeded in placing his companion in safety before falling from exhaustion.

Canada carried off eighteen crosses, or, if we include Captain Bishop, nineteen. First in point of time were Sergeant Frederick Hobson and Private Harry Brown, of the infantry. Both made the great sacrifice in winning the distinction. The former rescued a Lewis gun that was buried by a shell, and, though not a gunner, got it into action against the enemy. Then the gun jammed. Realising the importance of the post the enemy was endeavouring to capture, Hobson, though wounded, rushed forward and with bayonet and clubbed rifle held them back until he was killed.

Brown's bravery was equally marked. On a critical occasion it was of the utmost importance to get a message to Headquarters, and he and one other were sent with it with orders to deliver it "at all costs." The other messenger

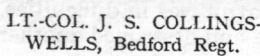

LT.-COL. J. S. COLLINGS-
WELLS, Bedford Regt.

SEC.-LT. H. COLVIN,
Cheshire Regt.

CAPT. T. R. COLYER-
FERGUSSON, Northamptons.

was killed and Brown had his arm shattered, but he fared on through an intense barrage until he arrived at the support lines. He was so spent that he fell down the dug-out steps, but retained consciousness long enough to discharge his mission with the words: "Important message." He then became unconscious and died a few hours later.

In November, 1917, in a list of nine V.C.'s, not less than one-third went to Canada. Captain (Acting Major) Okill Massey Learmouth, M.C., when his company was surprised, charged and personally disposed of the attackers. Later on he carried out a tremendous fight with the advancing enemy. Although under intense barrage fire and mortally wounded, he stood on the parapet of the trench, bombed the enemy continuously, and directed the defence in such a manner as to infuse a spirit of the utmost resistance into his men.

Company Sergeant-Major Robert Hanna showed conspicuous bravery when his attacking company met with most severe resistance and all the officers had become casualties. He led a party of men against a strong point, rushed through the wire, bayoneted three of the enemy, killed a fourth, and finally captured the position and silenced the machine-gun. But for his daring action the attack would not have succeeded.

Equally brave, though somewhat different in character, was the V.C. deed of Private Michael James O'Rourke. For three days and nights this stretcher-bearer worked unceasingly at bringing in the wounded. He was under intense fire, and on several occasions was knocked down and partially buried by shells. Seeing a comrade, who had been blinded, stumbling around ahead of the British trench, in full view of the enemy who were sniping at him, O'Rourke jumped out of his trench and brought the man back. On other occasions he succoured wounded men, richly deserving the official tribute to his "magnificent courage and devotion."

SERGT. E. COOPER,
K.R.R.C.

PTE. J. T. COUNTER,
King's (Liverpool) Regt.

Acting Corporal Filip Konowal took an active share in directing the difficult task of "mopping up" cellars, craters, and machine-gun emplacements. In one cellar he bayoneted three Germans and attacked single-handed seven others in a crater, killing them all. On reaching the objective, Konowal rushed a machine-gun emplacement and brought the gun back to his own lines. The next day he again attacked single-handed another gun emplacement, killed three of the crew, and destroyed the gun and emplacement with explosives.

Two Canadian officers were awarded the cross on December 19th, 1917—Lieutenants Robert Shankland, of the infantry, and Henry Strachan, M.C., of the cavalry. The latter was a member of the Fort Garry Horse, which took part in a magnificent charge at the Battle of Cambrai, November, 1917. Having gained a position, he rallied the remainder of his own platoon **Strachan of the** and men of other companies, disposed them **Fort Garry Horse** to command the ground in front, and inflicted heavy casualties on the retreating enemy. Later, he dispersed a counter-attack, and then personally communicated to battalion headquarters a valuable report about the position.

Strachan took command of the squadron of his regiment when the leader, as they approached the enemy's front line at a gallop, was killed. He led the men through the enemy line of machine-gun posts, and then in the charge on the enemy battery. All the gunners were killed and the battery silenced. Strachan rallied his men and fought his way back at night through the enemy's line, bringing all the unwounded men safely in, together with fifteen prisoners.

On January 12th, 1918, a list of eighteen V.C.'s contained seven Canadian names. Captain (Acting Major) George Randolph Pearkes, M.C., of the Mounted Rifles, led his men to the capture and consolidation of considerably more than the objectives allotted to him in an attack. He took and held a strong point which constituted a danger, and, although wounded, maintained his objective with a small number of men. The official report stated that "his appreciation of the situation throughout and the reports rendered by him were invaluable to his commanding officer in making dispositions of troops to hold the position captured."

Lieutenant (Acting Captain) Christopher Patrick John O'Kelly, M.C., of the infantry, when the enemy position on the crest of a hill had been stormed, personally organised and led a series of attacks against "pill-boxes," his company alone capturing six of them. Later, under his leadership, his men repelled a strong counter-attack and during the night captured a hostile raiding-party.

SERGT. H. COVERDALE,
Manchester Regt.

L.-CPL. A. H. CROSS,
Machine Gun Corps.

SEC.-LT. J. CROWE,
Worcester Regt.

PTE. R. E. CRUICKSHANK,
London Regt.

PTE. F. G. DANCOX,
Worcester Regt.

Sergeant George Harry Mullin, M.M., single-handed captured a "pill-box." He rushed the sniper's post in front, destroyed the garrison with bombs, and, crawling into the top of the "pill-box," shot the machine-gunners. He then rushed to another entrance and compelled the garrison of ten to surrender. Presumably the two "pill-box" heroes just described were engaged in the Third Battle of Ypres, for, taking into account the date of the award, the knowledge that the Canadians had a glorious share in that encounter, and the fact that the Germans trusted much to the "pill-box" in that area, the evidence is fairly clear. Corporal Colin Barron rushed three machine-guns single-handed, killed four of the crew, and captured the remainder. He then turned one of the captured guns on the retiring enemy, and his dash and determination enabled the advance to be continued.

CPL. J. L. DAVIES,
Royal Welsh Fusiliers.

[Bassano.

CPL. S. J. DAY,
Suffolk Regt.

LT. P. T. DEAN,
R.N.V.R.

Private Thomas William Holmes, of the Mounted Rifles, was another "pill-box" hero, for, among other daring deeds, he threw bombs into the entrance of one of these forts, causing the nineteen occupants to surrender. Private Cecil John Kinross, of the infantry, won his cross for an attack on an enemy machine-gun that was holding up the advance. He killed the crew of six and destroyed the gun. His example and courage enabled a further advance of three hundred yards to be made, and a highly important position to be established. Very similar was the deed performed by Private James Peter Robertson. Carrying a captured machine-gun, he led his platoon to the final objective and, selecting an excellent position, got the gun into action on the retreating enemy.

Daring capture of "pill-boxes"

During an attack Lieutenant Hugh Mackenzie, D.C.M., of the Canadian Machine Gun Corps, saw that the men were hesitating before a nest of enemy machine-guns, which on commanding ground were causing severe casualties. He handed over command of his section of machine-guns to an N.C.O., rallied the infantry, organised an attack, and captured the strong point. He was killed while leading a frontal attack on a "pill-box."

CAPT. E. S. DOUGALL,
R.F.A.

SGT. J. J. DWYER,
Australian M.G.C.

Lieutenant Gordon Muriel Flowerdew, of the cavalry, won his cross when in command of a squadron detailed for special service. On reaching the first objective he saw two lines of the enemy, each about sixty strong, with machine-guns in the centre and on the flanks. Realising the critical nature of the operation, he ordered one troop to dismount and carry out a special movement, while he led the remaining three troops to the charge. The squadron, less one troop, passed over both lines, killed many of the enemy, and wheeling about galloped at them again. The enemy broke and retired. Flowerdew was dangerously wounded in both thighs.

The last V.C. gained by Canada in the fourth year fell to Lieutenant George Burdon McKean. Finding his party held up at a block in the communication trench by intense fire, he ran into the open, leaped over the block, and landed on top of the enemy. While lying on the ground a German rushed at him with a bayonet, but McKean shot him. It was owing to his heroism that the enemy's position was captured.

Eleven crosses went to the Australians, the first being awarded to Second-Lieutenant Frederick Birks, who rushed a strong point which was holding up the advance. He organised a small party and attacked another strong point which was occupied by twenty-five of the enemy, of whom many were killed and the others captured. He was killed at his post while endeavouring to extricate some of his men who had been buried by a shell.

Five Australian V.C.'s were gazetted on November 26th, 1917, of whom Sergeant John James Dwyer, of the Machine Gun Corps, comes first. He rushed his machine-gun forward in advance of a captured position in order to obtain a commanding spot. While so doing he noticed an enemy machine-gun firing on the troops on the right flank. Unhesitatingly he dashed with his gun to within thirty yards of the enemy gun and fired point-blank at it, putting it out of action and killing the crew. Dwyer rendered equally valuable service on the following day. On another occasion his gun was blown up by shell fire, but he went through the enemy barrage to headquarters, and brought back another.

Another Australian non-commissioned officer to win the cross was Sergeant Lewis McGee, who led his platoon to the final objective. When they were stopped by machine-gun fire from a "pill-box," he rushed the post single-handed. He reorganised the remnants of his platoon, and was foremost in the remainder of the advance. Lance-Corporal Walter

[Speaight.

SGT. A. EDWARDS,
Seaforth Highlanders.

PTE. W. EDWARDS,
K.O.Y.L.I.

CPL. E. A. EGERTON,
Sherwood Foresters.

LT.-COL. N. B. ELLIOTT-COOPER, Royal Fusiliers.

SEC.-LT. J. S. EMERSON,
R. Inniskilling Fusiliers.

SGT. N. A. FINCH,
R.M.A.

[*Bassano.*

CAPT. R. GEE,
Royal Fusiliers.

[*Bassano.*

SGT. C. E. GOURLEY,
R.F.A.

Peeler rushed a shell-hole where Germans were sniping the first wave of assault, accounted for nine of them, and cleared the way for the advance. During subsequent operations he located and killed the gunner of a machine-gun position and disposed of ten of the enemy who had been dislodged by a bomb from a shelter.

Private Patrick Bugden led small parties to attack "pill-boxes," successfully silenced the machine-guns with bombs, and captured the garrisons. On no less than five occasions he rescued wounded men under intense fire. Private Reginald Roy Inwood, during the advance to the second objective, moved forward through the barrage alone to an enemy strong post and captured it, together with nine prisoners. During the evening he volunteered for a special all-night patrol, and by his coolness and judgment obtained and sent back very valuable information. Later he located a troublesome machine-gun and, going out alone, captured it.

Another machine-gun exploit was performed by Captain Clarence Smith Jeffries, who rushed a concrete emplacement, capturing four machine-guns and thirty-five prisoners. He then led his company forward under heavy artillery barrage to the objective. Later, he captured two machine-guns and thirty more prisoners. He was killed during the attack, but it was entirely due to him that the centre was not held up for a lengthy period.

Captain Jeffries' great exploit

Sergeant Stanley Robert McDougall's prompt action saved the line and enabled the enemy's advance to be stopped. The first German wave broke the line, but he at once charged the second wave, single-handed, with rifle and bayonet, killed seven, and captured a machine-gun. This he turned on to the enemy, thus causing many casualties and checking the advance.

A particularly daring deed won the V.C. for Lieutenant Percy Valentine Storkey, who had been wounded twice. When, after emerging from a wood, the enemy trench line was encountered, Storkey found himself with six men. Moving forward, he noticed that a large enemy party was holding up the advance of the troops to the right. He decided to attack this group from the flank and rear, and while going forward was joined by another officer and four men. The two small bodies charged the enemy position with fixed bayonets; they drove the enemy out, killed or wounded thirty, and captured three officers and fifty men with a machine-gun.

LT. J. R. N. GRAHAM,
A. and S. H., attd. M.G.C.

CPL. F. GREAVES,
Sherwood Foresters.

SGT. W. GREGG,
Rifle Brigade.

One other officer and one man complete the Australian tale. They were Lieutenant Clifford William King Sadlier and Sergeant William Ruthven. The former led his bombing section against a strong enemy machine-gun post which was holding up the advance, killed the crews, and captured two of the guns. By this time his party were all casualties, but alone he attacked a third gun, killing the crew of four and taking the gun. His conduct was the means of clearing the flank and allowing the battalion to move forward. Ruthven showed amazing initiative in action. When his company commander had been severely wounded he assumed command of a portion of the assault, took charge of the company headquarters, and rallied the section in his vicinity. As the leading wave approached its objective it was subjected to heavy fire from a machine-gun. Ruthven sprang out, threw a bomb which landed beside the post, and rushed the position. He then reorganised the men and established a point in the second objective. Soon he observed enemy movements in a sunken road near by. Without hesitation, and armed only with a revolver, he went over the open alone and rushed the position. Single-handed he "mopped up" this post and captured the garrison, thirty-two strong. The official account of these exploits referred to Ruthven's "magnificent courage and determination, his fine fighting spirit, his remarkable courage, and his dashing action."

New Zealand's two V.C. heroes

New Zealand's two heroes in the fourth year were Corporal Leslie William Andrew and Private Henry James Nicholas. The former attacked and captured a machine-gun under circumstances of very great danger, and also reduced a machine-gun post which was holding up the advance. Nicholas, one of a Lewis-gun section, had orders to form a defensive flank to the right of the advance, which was subsequently checked by heavy rifle fire from a strong point. He rushed forward alone, shot the officer in command, and overcame the remainder of the garrison of sixteen.

South Africa's V.C. was Lance-Corporal William Henry Hewitt, who attacked a "pill-box" with his section and tried to rush the doorway. The garrison proved very stubborn, and he was severely wounded. Nevertheless, he proceeded to the loophole where, in his attempts to put a bomb into it, he was again wounded. Undeterred, however, he managed to get a bomb inside which caused the occupants to surrender.

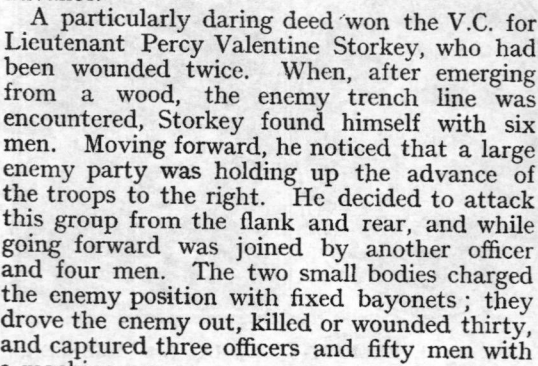

SGT. W. H. GRIMBALDESTON, K.O.S.B.

L.-CPL. J. HALLIWELL,
Lancs Fusiliers.

PTE. A. HALTON,
Royal Lanc. Regt.

Lance-Dafadar Gobind Singh, of the cavalry, was one of the two Indians who won the cross. He showed great bravery in thrice volunteering to carry messages between the battalion and brigade headquarters, a distance of one and a half miles over open ground. He succeeded each time in delivering his message, although on both occasions his horse was shot. Rifleman Rana Karanbahadur, of the Gurkha Rifles, proved as brave as his countryman. During an attack he, with a few other men, succeeded in creeping forward with a Lewis gun to engage a machine-gun that had caused severe casualties. No. 1 of the Lewis gun opened fire and was shot immediately. Karanbahadur at once pushed the dead man off the gun, and, in spite of the bombs thrown at him and heavy fire from both flanks, opened fire and knocked out the machine-gun crew; then, switching his fire on to the bombers and riflemen in front, he silenced their fire also. His work throughout the day was characterised as magnificent.

Five members of the artillery were included in the fourth year's list of Victoria Crosses. Among awards published on February 14th, 1918, were two members of the Royal Field Artillery. Lieutenant Samuel Thomas Dickson Wallace won the cross for amazing bravery when in command of a section.

Artilleryman's amazing bravery When his battery was reduced to five by casualties, and was surrounded on the right flank and in the rear, he maintained the fire of the guns by swinging the trails round close together, the men running and loading from gun to gun. Thus he not only covered other battery positions, but also materially assisted some small infantry detachments to maintain a position against great odds. He was in action for eight hours, firing the whole time, and when compelled to withdraw took with him the essential gun parts and all the wounded men.

Sergeant Cyril Edward Gourley, M.M., kept a gun in action practically throughout the day, although the enemy was almost all round his section of howitzers. When the Germans advanced he pulled his gun out of the pit and engaged a machine-gun at 500 yards, knocking it out with a direct hit. Gunner Charles Edwin Stone, M.M., after working hard at his gun for six hours under heavy gas and shell fire, went to the rear section with an order which he delivered. At dusk he helped to capture a machine-gun and four prisoners—a gallant act, which undoubtedly saved the detachment serving the guns.

Lieutenant (Acting Captain) Eric Stuart Dougall, M.C., R.F.A., maintained his battery

C.-S.-M. R. HANNA, Canadians.

[*Elliott & Fry.*
REV. T. B. HARDY, C.F.

CAPT. R. F. J. HAYWARD, Wiltshire Regt.

SEC.-LT. D. G. W. HEWITT, Hampshire Regt.

[*Bassano.*
L.-CPL. W. H. HEWITT, South African Infantry.

PTE. T. W. HOLMES, Canadian M.R.

in action under heavy gas and shell fire. Finding that he could not clear the crest owing to the withdrawal of the British line, he ran his guns on to the top of the ridge. By this time the infantry had been pressed back in line with the guns, but this resourceful officer assumed command of the situation and rallied and organised the men. With them he formed a line in front of his battery, and, although exposed to both rifle and machine-gun fire, fearlessly walked about as though on parade. He inspired the infantry with his assurance that "so long as you stick to your trenches I will keep my guns here." By this means the line was maintained throughout the day, thereby delaying the enemy's advance for over twelve hours and eventually averting a serious breach. He was killed four days later while directing the fire of his battery.

Sergeant Norman Augustus Finch, Royal Marine Artillery, was one of the heroes of Zeebrugge. He was second in command of the pom-poms and Lewis guns in the foretop of the Vindictive. When it was difficult to locate the enemy's guns, which were causing heavy damage, those in the foretop kept up a continuous fire, changing rapidly from one target to another and thus keeping the enemy's fire down. Then, when all in the top except Finch had been killed or disabled, and he had been severely wounded, he got his Lewis gun into action **One of the heroes of Zeebrugge** and kept up a continuous fire, harassing the enemy on the Mole, until the foretop received another direct hit and the remainder of the armament was completely put out of action. He was selected by the 4th Battalion Royal Marines to receive the V.C.

During the fourth year the war in the west was still mainly stationary, and consequently the cavalry had few chances; but, nevertheless, in one way or another, five members of this arm won the cross. The deeds of three of these— two Canadians and an Indian — have been recorded; the remaining two are Major Alexander Malius Lafone, of the Yeomanry, and Private George William Clare, of the Lancers. Lafone received his cross for bravery, leadership, and self-sacrifice when holding a position for over seven hours against vastly superior forces. When all his men save three had been hit and his trench was full of wounded, he ordered those who could walk to move to a trench slightly in the rear, and from his own position he maintained an heroic resistance. When finally surrounded by the enemy he stepped into the open and

[*Elliott & Fry.*
LT.-COL. C. E. HUDSON, Sherwood Foresters.

[*Bassano.*
CPL. A. HUTT, R. Warwick Regt.

SERGT. H. JACKSON, E. Yorks Regt.

continued the fight until mortally wounded. Clare was a stretcher-bearer, who showed wonderful heroism in dressing and conducting wounded over the open to the dressing-station. At one period he went to a detached post under heavy fire, dressed all the cases, and manned the post single-handed till a relief was sent. Later he warned every company post of an impending gas attack, the whole time under fire, and was himself killed by a shell.

Eight Guardsmen carried off the soldier's highest honour. First in point of date were Sergeant Robert Bye, of the Welsh, and Private Thomas Witham, of the Coldstream Guards. The former rushed a block-house which was troubling the leading wave of an attack, put the garrison out of action and took charge of a party detailed to clear up a line of block-houses which had been passed. Witham per-

Eight heroic Guardsmen

formed a bold action in working his way from shell-hole to shell-hole through the barrage to rush a machine-gun which was enfilading a battalion on the right. He was able to capture the gun, together with an officer and two others.

Private Thomas Woodcock, Irish Guards, a Wigan collier, was one of a post commanded by Lance-Sergeant Moyney, and, in defending it, both won the cross. It had held out for ninety-six hours, when it was attacked from all sides in overwhelming numbers and its garrison forced to retire. Woodcock covered the retirement with a Lewis gun, and then crossed the river ; but, hearing cries for help from behind him, he returned. Wading into the stream amid a shower of bombs, he rescued a comrade, and carried him across the open ground in broad daylight, regardless of bullets. He was killed in action on March 27th, 1918. As for Moyney, he, with Woodcock, covered the retirement of his party across the stream, and did not himself cross till the whole of his force had gained the farther bank. It was due to his endurance, skill, and devotion that his entire force was brought safely out of action.

Lance-Sergeant John Harold Rhodes, Grenadier Guards, when in charge of a Lewis-gun section, went single-handed through his own barrage and effected an entry into a " pillbox," capturing nine of the enemy and securing valuable information. Sergeant John McAulay, D.C.M., Scots Guards, assumed command of his company when all his officers had become casualties, and successfully held and consolidated the objective gained, in addition to repulsing a counter-attack. He carried his company commander, who was mortally wounded, into safety under very heavy fire, being twice knocked down by the concussion of bursting shells.

Lieutenant (Acting Captain) George Henry Tatham Paton, M.C., Grenadier Guards, fearlessly exposed himself in order to readjust the line by walking up and down within fifty yards of the enemy under a withering fire. When the enemy had broken through on his left, he mounted the parapet and, with a few men, forced them once more to withdraw. He was mortally wounded, but saved the left flank.

Lieutenant (Acting Captain) Thomas Tannatt Pryce, M.C., of the Grenadier Guards, was the first member of the Stock Exchange to win the cross in the war. He led two platoons to the capture of a village, and the next day was occupying a position with a handful of men when he was almost surrounded. He was attacked four times, but

Forty men defy a battalion

each time beat off the enemy. The latter then brought up three guns to within three hundred yards and knocked in his trench ; so Pryce called on his men to fight to the last. With him leading, they left their trench and drove back the enemy, and he was last seen engaged in a fierce hand-to-hand struggle with overwhelming numbers. With forty odd men he defied an enemy battalion for over ten hours, and " stopped the advance through the British line."

Two members of the Royal Engineers are among our list of heroes : Lieutenant-Colonel (Temporary Brigadier-General) Clifford Coffin, D.S.O., and Temporary Second-Lieutenant Cecil Leonard Knox. Of the former it is interesting to note that he was fifty-four years old at the time, and was probably the only officer in the British Army up to that date (September, 1917) who had received the V.C. while holding general's rank. When his command was held up in attack and was establishing itself along a forward shell-hole line, he went forward and inspected the front posts, showing an utter disregard of personal danger, giving advice generally, and cheering the men by his presence. His splendid example " saved the situation," said the official report. Knox had twelve bridges entrusted to him for demolition, all of which he successfully destroyed. In the case of one steel girder bridge the time-fuse failed to act. Without hesitation he ran to it under heavy fire and, when the enemy were actually on the bridge, tore away the time-fuse and lit the instantaneous one.

Greater space than that available could be easily devoted to the magnificent services of the Royal Army Medical Corps. Its first member to receive a V.C. in the fourth year was Temporary Captain Harold Ackroyd, M.C., M.D., attached to the Berkshire Regiment. Utterly regardless of danger, he worked continuously for many hours, tending the wounded and saving the lives of officers and men. His duties took him under heavy fire, and on one occasion he carried a wounded officer to a place of safety, regardless of shells and bullets. Later he was killed in action. Captain John Fox Russell, M.C., displayed most conspicuous bravery until he was killed. He repeatedly went out to attend to the wounded under continuous fire from snipers and machine-guns, and, in many cases, where no other means were at hand, carried them in himself.

The third medical V.C. of the fourth year is perhaps the most notable of all. Captain Noel Godfrey Chavasse, a twin son of the Bishop of Liverpool, earned the coveted cross in the third year, and on September 15th, 1917, it was announced that he had been awarded a bar thereto—a most unusual distinction. In the official report of his second honour it was stated that, though most severely wounded early in the action, Captain Chavasse refused to leave his post, and for two days not only continued to perform his duties but, in addition, went out repeatedly under heavy fire to search for and attend to the wounded who were lying out. " By his extraordinary energy

Great heroism of the R.A.M.C.

and inspiring example," it continued, " he was instrumental in rescuing many wounded who would have otherwise undoubtedly succumbed under the weather conditions." He subsequently died of wounds.

Many infantry soldiers were granted the Victoria Cross for conspicuous bravery and skill with machine-guns ; but in the fourth year mention was made of a separate Machine Gun Corps, and three members of this won the cross. In a long list of V.C. awards published on November 27th, 1917, appeared the name of Lance-Corporal Harold Mugford, Machine Gun Corps. Under heavy fire he succeeded in getting his machine-gun into a forward and exposed position, where he dealt very effectively with the enemy, who were massing for a counter-attack. He was ordered to a new position, and, although wounded, refused to go to the dressing-station, but continued on duty with his gun, inflicting severe loss on the enemy. His valour and initiative were instrumental in breaking up an impending counter-attack.

Private Herbert George Columbine took over the command of a gun, and kept it firing from 9 a.m. till 1 p.m. in an isolated position with no wire in front. During this time wave after wave of the enemy failed to get up to him ; but when he was attacked by an aeroplane they gained a footing in the trench on either side. The position was then untenable, so Columbine ordered the two remaining men to get away, and, though bombed from either side, kept his gun in action and inflicted " tremendous losses." He was eventually killed by a bomb.

One of London's many V.C. heroes was Lance-Corporal Arthur Henry Cross, a Camberwell man. Entering the 21st London, he was later transferred to the Machine Gun Corps. He volunteered to make a reconnaissance of the position of two machine-guns, which had been captured by the Germans. He advanced single-handed to the enemy trench and, with his revolver, forced seven of them to surrender and carry the machine-guns, with their tripods and ammunition, to the British lines. He then handed over his prisoners and collected teams for his guns, which he brought into action with exceptional dash and skill. " It is impossible," was the official phrasing, " to speak too highly of the extreme gallantry, initiative, and dash displayed by this N.C.O."

Scenes of tremendous enthusiasm marked the triumphant entry of the British Fifth Army into Lille, on October 17th, 1918. General Birdwood, here seen passing through the square, presented to the town the flag of the army under his command.

As the British drums went throbbing through the city, flags, long concealed during the enemy occupation, appeared at the windows, and the thoroughfares through which the troops marched were thronged by joyous and cheering crowds.

Triumphant entry of the British Fifth Army under General Birdwood into Lille.

Canadian Black Watch marching past the saluting base on the entry of General Horne into Mons. The Imperial Black Watch were the last to leave Mons in 1914, their Canadian comrades were the first to enter in 1918.

Canadian troops recaptured Mons just before dawn on November 11th, 1918. This illustration gives a vivid impression of the scene outside one of the principal buildings as General Horne, commanding the British First Army, entered the town.

Dramatic re-entry of the British into Mons of ever glorious renown:

Canadian Field Artillery passing through the square of Mons on November 11th, 1918. The Mayor of Mons on this occasion said: "We witnessed the wonderful retreat of the British Army from here; we knew it would return."

General Sir Henry Horne, accompanied by the Mayor of Mons, inspecting Princess Patricia's Canadian Light Infantry. The Mayor presented the Canadian 7th Infantry Brigade with the keys of Mons, and General Currie presented the Canadian Corps' flag to the town.

Victorious troops and liberated civilians celebrate the day of Germany's surrender.

General Birdwood inspecting a Guard of Honour outside Tournai Cathedral prior to the Thanksgiving Service there on November 10th. The magnificent structure contains the tomb of King Childeric, and here Henry VIII. attended service in September, 1513.

British troops entering the picturesque old Flemish town of Tournai which, after occupying it for four years, the Germans evacuated on the night of November 8th, 1918. Save for random shell-marks the buildings were undamaged.

Scenes of public rejoicing and thanksgiving in liberated Tournai.

The splendid work of the Tanks has been referred to in many chapters of this history, and it is not surprising that two of the intrepid men who handled them received the Victoria Cross, these being Second-Lieutenant Clement Robertson, formerly Royal West Surrey Regiment, then Temporary Lieutenant (Acting Captain) Tank Corps, and Temporary Lieutenant (Acting Captain) Richard William Leslie Wain. Robertson led his landships to attack under heavy fire of all kinds over ground which had been heavily ploughed by shells. Knowing the risk of the Tanks missing the way, he continued to lead them on foot, guiding them towards their objective, although he must have known that his action would inevitably cost him his life, as it did a few minutes later. Wain was in a Tank which became disabled by a direct hit near a strong point that was holding up the attack. He and one man, both seriously wounded, were the only survivors. Though bleeding profusely, he refused the attention of stretcher-bearers, rushed from behind the Tank with a Lewis gun and captured the strong point, taking about half the garrison prisoners. He then fired at the retiring enemy until he received a fatal wound in the head.

Private Richard George Masters won the cross for the Army Service Corps. When communications were cut off, and wounded could not be evacuated, he volunteered to get through an almost impassable road, and after great difficulty succeeded. He made journey after journey over it when it was swept by shell fire and bombed by an aeroplane. The greater part of the wounded cleared from this area were evacuated by Masters.

Captain Edward Bamford, D.S.O., Royal Marine Light Infantry, was one of the heroes of Zeebrugge. He landed on the Mole from the Vindictive with a storming force. He displayed the greatest initiative and set a magnificent example to his men. He first established a strong point and, when satisfied that it was secure, led an assault on a battery with the utmost coolness. Bamford was selected by his fellow-officers to receive the cross.

The Rev. T. B. Hardy, V.C., D.S.O., M.C.

The third chaplain to win the V.C. in the war, the Rev. Theodore Bayley Hardy, D.S.O., M.C., attached Lincolnshire Regiment, was over fifty years old at the time. The vicar of Hutton Roof, Kirkby Lonsdale, he joined the forces as a chaplain in August, 1916. An infantry patrol had gone out to attack a post in the ruins of a village. Hearing the firing, Hardy followed the patrol, and about 400 yards beyond the British front line of posts found an officer dangerously wounded. He remained with him until he was able to get assistance to bring him in. On a second occasion, when an enemy shell exploded in the middle of the British posts, he at once made his way to the spot, despite heavy shelling, and set to work to extricate the buried men. During the whole of the time he was digging out the men he was in great danger, not only from shell fire, but also because of the dangerous condition of the wall of the building. His services on many occasions justified the lengthy and glowing official story of his V.C. award, published on July 12th, 1918. In October, 1918, this model padre was killed.

We must now tell the story of the V.C. deeds of the ninety-three members of regiments of the line. The Lancashire Fusiliers, with five of these distinctions in the year, proved again their magnificent qualities. Captain (Temporary Lieutenant-Colonel) Bertram Best-Dunkley saw that the leading waves of an attack had become disorganised by reason of heavy fire. He dashed forward, rallied the men, and led them to the assault of the positions, continuing to lead his battalion until all their objectives had been gained. Later, when the British positions were threatened, he collected his battalion headquarters and beat off the advancing enemy, afterwards dying of his wounds.

Sergeant Joseph Lister assaulted a "pill-box" which was holding up an advance. He called to the occupants to surrender, which they did—all but one man, whom he shot dead; whereupon about a hundred Germans emerged from shell-holes farther to the rear and surrendered. Second-Lieutenant Bernard Matthew Cassidy was in command of a company, and was given orders that he must hold on to his position to the

last. He carried this out to the letter. The enemy came on in overwhelming numbers, but Cassidy continually rallied his men under a terrific bombardment. His company was eventually surrounded, but he still fought on until killed.

Second-Lieutenant John Schofield climbed out on the parapet under machine-gun fire, and by his fearless demeanour forced the enemy, one hundred and twenty-three in number, to surrender. He was killed a few minutes later. The fifth hero of the Lancashire Fusiliers was Lance-Corporal Joel Halliwell, a native of Middleton. He gained his cross for "magnificent conduct" during the withdrawal of the remnants of a battalion when closely engaged with the enemy. Having captured a stray enemy horse, Halliwell rode out under heavy fire and rescued a wounded man from No Man's Land. He repeated this performance several times and succeeded in rescuing one officer and nine other ranks.

In chronological order the first of the five V.C. heroes of the London Regiment was Sergeant Alfred Joseph Knight. When his platoon was attacking an enemy strong point he rushed through the British barrage, bayoneted the enemy gunners, and, single-handed, captured the position. **Five heroic Londoners** Later twelve of the enemy with a machine-gun were encountered in a shell-hole, when Knight again rushed forward by himself, bayoneted two, and shot a third.

Lieutenant-Colonel Arthur Drummond Borton, D.S.O., showed splendid leadership. Under difficult conditions, in darkness and in an unknown country, he deployed his battalion for attack, and at dawn led his attacking companies against a strongly-held position. When the leading waves were checked by a withering fire he showed an utter contempt of danger, reorganised his command, and led his men forward and captured the position.

Two more Londoners were honoured on February 28th, 1918: Corporal Charles William Train and Rifleman (Lance-Corporal) John Alexander Christie. As a member of the London Scottish, Train took part in the charge of that regiment at Messines in 1914. His V.C. was earned for remarkable bravery under heavy fire. His company being held up by two machine-guns, Train, on his own initiative, engaged the enemy with rifle-grenades and put some of the team out of action. Christie was a clerk at Euston Station before joining up in September, 1914. His distinction was gained in helping to capture one of the hills before Jerusalem. At a critical time in the darkness and confusion he filled his pockets with bombs. Quite alone he got out of the trenches, and, following the Turkish trench in the open, rained bombs on the hostile bombers. "By his prompt and effective action," it was officially stated, "he undoubtedly cleared a difficult position at a most critical time and saved many lives."

The fifth member of the London Regiment was Private R. E. Cruickshank, of the London Scottish, whose distinction was also earned in the East, if we may judge from the official wording. His platoon came under heavy fire at short range, and was led down a steep bank into a wady, most of the men being hit before they reached the bottom. A runner sent **Royal Fusiliers' five crosses** back for support was wounded and a volunteer to take a second message was called for. Cruickshank responded and rushed up the slope, but was hit and rolled back into the wady bottom. The same thing happened after his wounds had been dressed, and he rushed a third time up the slope and fell badly wounded.

Sergeant John Molyneux won the first of the five crosses that fell to the Royal Fusiliers. A native of St. Helens and a miner, he cleared the enemy from a trench in front of a house and proceeded to the latter, where he engaged in a desperate hand-to-hand fight. With assistance the enemy was beaten and nearly thirty prisoners were captured. His initiative and dash prevented a slight check from becoming a serious block in the advance.

Lieutenant (Temporary Captain) Robert Gee, M.C., was captured when a strong enemy force pierced the British line, but had no intention of accepting his lot. He killed one of his captors with his spiked stick, and succeeded in escaping. He then organised a party of the brigade staff with which,

CAPT. M. A. JAMES,
Gloucester Regt.
[*Elliott & Fry.*

LT. A. JERRARD,
R.A.F.

PTE. C. J. KINROSS,
Canadian Infantry.

SERGT. A. J. KNIGHT,
London Regt.

closely followed and supported by two companies of infantry, he attacked the enemy. Gee established a defensive flank, but finding that an enemy machine-gun was still in action, with a revolver in each hand and followed by one man, he rushed out and captured the gun, killing eight of the crew.

Two more officers of this regiment appeared in the list of V.C.'s dated February 14th, 1918. Captain (Temporary Lieutenant-Colonel) Neville Bowes Elliott-Cooper, D.S.O., M.C., hearing that the enemy had broken through the line, rushed out of his dug-out. Seeing them advancing across the open, he mounted the parapet and dashed forward, calling upon the reserve company and details of battalion headquarters to follow. Absolutely unarmed, he made straight for the advancing enemy, and the men under his direction forced them back six hundred yards. He himself was severely wounded. Lieutenant (Acting Captain) Walter Napleton Stone was ordered to withdraw his company, leaving a rearguard to cover the operation. But the enemy's attack developed with unexpected speed, so he sent back three platoons and remained himself with the rearguard. He stood on the parapet under a tremendous bombardment, observing the enemy, and continued to report valuable information until the telephone wire was cut by his orders. The rearguard was eventually surrounded, and Stone was seen fighting until shot through the head.

The fifth member of the Royal Fusiliers was Lance-Corporal Charles Graham Robertson, M.M. Realising that he was being cut off, he sent back two men to get reinforcements, and remained at his post, with only one other man, firing his Lewis gun and killing large numbers of the enemy. No reinforcements came up, so he withdrew with the only other

survivor, to a point about ten yards farther back, where he successfully held his position. After further deeds of valour, Robertson managed to crawl back, bringing his gun with him.

Of the three regiments with four crosses to their credit the Royal Lancaster is noted first. The award to Corporal (Lance-Sergeant) Tom Fletcher Mayson was announced on September 15th, 1917, and he was one of many who gained the cross by putting out of action a machine-gun. In addition he pursued the team to a dug-out, into which he followed them and disposed of them with his bayonet. Later, when clearing up a strong point, he again tackled a machine-gun single-handed. Private Albert **Royal Lancasters'** Halton, after an objective had been reached, **roll of glory** rushed forward about three hundred yards under heavy fire and captured a machine-gun and its crew. He then went out again and brought in about twelve prisoners.

On June 29th, 1918, Second-Lieutenant Joseph Henry Collin and Lance-Corporal James Hewitson were announced as having been awarded the cross. The former fought against heavy odds in the keep held by his platoon, slowly withdrawing in the face of superior numbers, and contesting every inch of the ground. When the enemy was pressing him hard he attacked the gun and team single-handed, and kept the enemy at bay until he fell mortally wounded. In a daylight attack on a series of crater posts Hewitson led his party to their objective, clearing the enemy from both trench and dug-out. Just afterwards he observed a hostile machine-gun team coming into action. He therefore worked his way round to the edge of the crater and attacked the team, killing four and capturing one.

[*Bassano.*
SERGT. J. LISTER,
Lancs. Fusiliers.

The first of the four Rifle Brigade heroes was Sergeant William Francis Burman. Under grave difficulties he attacked a machine-gun, killed the gunner, and carried the gun to the company's objective, where he subsequently used it with great effect. Later he got behind the enemy, who was impeding the battalion on his right, killing six and capturing thirty-one Germans. The other three crosses of the Rifle Brigade were in the list published on June 29th, 1918. Sergeant William Gregg, D.C.M., M.M., "saved the situation at a critical time" by rushing an enemy post, killing a machine-gun team, and capturing the gun and four men in a dug-out near by.

Corporal (Lance-Sergeant) Joseph Edward Woodall captured a machine-gun and eight men single-handed. After the objective had been gained, heavy fire was encountered from a neighbouring farmhouse, so Woodall collected some men and rushed the farm, taking thirty prisoners. Private William Beesley, single-handed, rushed a post and with his revolver killed two of the enemy. He took four more prisoners from a dug-out and two others from a shelter.

The Worcestershire Regiment also earned four crosses in the fourth year. In a list of twenty awards, dated November

SEC.-LT. C. L. KNOX,
R.E.

CPL. F. KONOWAL,
Canadians.

MAJ. A. M. LAFONE,
Yeomanry.

CAPT. A. M. LASCELLES,
Durham Light Infantry.

MAJ. O. M. LEARMOUTH,
Canadian Infantry.

27th, 1917, appeared the name of Private Frederick George Dancox, who was one of a party of ten detached as "moppers-up." One of their objects was the silencing of a troublesome machine-gun. He worked his way through the barrage and entered the emplacement from the rear, threatening the garrison with a bomb. Shortly afterwards he reappeared with a machine-gun under his arm, followed by forty of the enemy, and the gun was kept in action by him throughout the day. On December 19th, 1917, it was reported that he had been killed in action.

The second cross gained by the Worcesters was that of Captain (Acting Lieutenant-Colonel) Frank Crowther Roberts, D.S.O., M.C. He showed conspicuous bravery during operations covering twelve days. He exhibited "exceptional military skill in dealing with the many very difficult situations of the retirement, and amazing endurance and energy in encouraging and inspiring all ranks under his command." An example was given. The enemy had attacked a village, and had practically cleared it of British troops, when Roberts got together an improvised party and led a counter-attack which temporarily drove them out, thus covering the retirement of some British troops who would otherwise have been cut off. Second-Lieutenant John Crowe twice went forward with nine men to engage the enemy, both times in face of active machine-gun fire and sniping. His action was so daring that on each occasion the enemy withdrew from the high ground into the village, where he followed them and himself opened fire on them as they collected in the doorways.

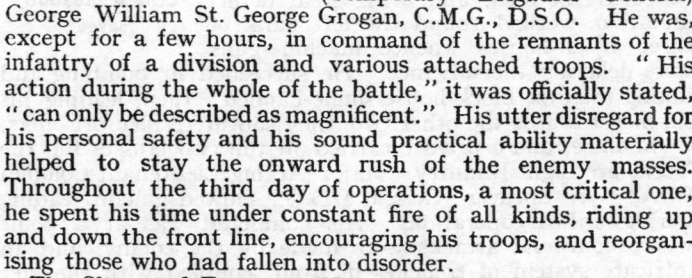

PTE. A. LOOSEMORE,
West Riding Regt.

Particularly conspicuous was the leadership throughout three days of intense fighting of Major and Brevet Lieutenant-Colonel (Temporary Brigadier-General) George William St. George Grogan, C.M.G., D.S.O. He was, except for a few hours, in command of the remnants of the infantry of a division and various attached troops. "His action during the whole of the battle," it was officially stated, "can only be described as magnificent." His utter disregard for his personal safety and his sound practical ability materially helped to stay the onward rush of the enemy masses. Throughout the third day of operations, a most critical one, he spent his time under constant fire of all kinds, riding up and down the front line, encouraging his troops, and reorganising those who had fallen into disorder.

The Sherwood Foresters (Notts and Derbyshire Regiment) carried off three crosses, two of which were announced on November 27th, 1917. When during an attack visibility was obscured owing to fog and smoke, the two leading waves passed over certain hostile dug-outs without clearing them. Thus severe casualties were inflicted on the advancing troops, and volunteers were called for to clear up the situation. Corporal Ernest Albert Egerton at once jumped up and dashed for the dug-outs under heavy fire. He shot in succession three Germans, and then twenty-nine of them surrendered. According to the official report, his "reckless bravery relieved in less than thirty seconds an extremely difficult situation."

His colleague, Acting Corporal Fred Greaves, showed initiative when his platoon was held up by machine-gun fire from a concrete stronghold. Realising that unless this post was taken quickly the men would lose the protection of the barrage, Greaves, followed by another non-commissioned officer, rushed forward and reached the rear of the building; there he bombed the occupants, killing and capturing the garrison and taking four machine-guns. Later in the day, when the troops of a flank brigade had given way, he collected his men and enfiladed the enemy's advance.

The third Sherwood Forester was Captain (Temporary Lieutenant-Colonel) Charles Edward Hudson, D.S.O., M.C. When the enemy had penetrated the front line he collected various head-quarter details and drove the enemy towards the British front line. He then, with two men, rushed the German position, shouting to the enemy to surrender, which some of them did. Although severely wounded he directed the counter-attack, which was successful.

As briefly as possible may now be related the story of the men in the twenty-one regiments which have each two crosses to their credit. Second-Lieutenant (Acting Captain) Thomas Riversdale Colyer-Fergusson won the first of the two for the Northamptons. Finding himself with a sergeant and only five men in a difficult position, he carried out the attack as originally planned, and succeeded in capturing the enemy trench and disposing of the garrison. He successfully resisted a counter-attack, during which, assisted by his orderly only, he

SGT. J. MOLYNEUX,
Royal Fusiliers.

PTE. W. MILLS,
Manchester Regt.

PTE. C. MELVIN,
Black Watch.

SEC.-LT. A. A. McLEOD,
R.A.F.

Captain Roberts of the Worcesters

PTE. R. G. MASTERS,
A.S.C.

L.-CPL. R. McBEATH,
Seaforth Highlanders.

PTE. G. McINTOSH,
Gordon Highlanders.

[*Bassano.*
LT. G. B. McKEAN,
Canadian Infantry.

SEAMAN A. E. McKENZIE,
R.N.

captured a machine-gun and turned it on the assailants. His conduct, said the official account, formed an amazing record of dash, gallantry, and skill " for which no reward can be too great, having regard to the importance of the position won."

Temporary Second-Lieutenant Alfred Cecil Herring saw his post cut off from the troops on both flanks and surrounded. He immediately counter-attacked and recaptured a position the enemy had gained. During the night he was continually attacked, but beat off all assaults.

The first V.C. of the Royal Welsh Fusiliers was Corporal James Llewellyn Davies, who, during an assault, pushed through the British barrage, and, single-handed, attacked

"No-Surrender Buchan"

a machine-gun emplacement after several men had been killed in attempting to take it. This he took; and then, although wounded, led a bombing-party to the assault of a defended house. He died later of wounds

His companion, Acting Corporal John Collins, whose award was announced on December 19th, 1917, repeatedly went out under heavy fire and brought wounded back to cover, thus saving many lives. In subsequent operations on the same day he was conspicuous in rallying and leading his command, and he led the final assault with the utmost skill.

The two Argyll and Sutherland Highlanders were Lieutenant John Reginald Noble Graham, attached Machine Gun Corps, and Second-Lieutenant John Crawford Buchan. Graham accompanied his guns across open ground, under very heavy fire, and when his men had become casualties he assisted in carrying the ammunition. Twice wounded, he continued during the advance to control his guns, and was able to open an accurate fire on the enemy.

"No-Surrender Buchan," as he was afterwards called, was the son of a Scottish journalist—Mr. David Buchan, editor of the "Alloa Advertiser." When fighting with his platoon in a forward position of the battle zone Buchan, although wounded, insisted on remaining with his men, and later, when heavy fire was raking his position, he continued to visit his posts. When his command was surrounded he collected his platoon and prepared to fight his way back to the supporting line. At this point the enemy, who had crept round his right flank, rushed towards him, shouting out "Surrender!" He gave the reply "To hell with surrender!" and, shooting the foremost assailant, finally repelled this advance. He then fought his way back to the supporting line, where he held out till dusk, when he fell back as ordered, but was soon cut off, and was last seen holding out against overwhelming odds.

Second-Lieutenants Denis George Wyldbore Hewitt and Montague Shadworth Seymour Moore were the two members of the Hampshire Regiment to earn the distinction in the fourth year. The former set a magnificent example of coolness and contempt of danger by leading forward the remains of his company under heavy fire. He had been hit by a piece of shell, which exploded the signal lights in his haversack and set fire to his equipment and clothes. Having extinguished the flames, in spite of his severe wound, he continued at the post of duty. He was killed by a sniper.

Moore showed amazing gallantry during a second attack on an objective which had not been captured. He arrived

Post held for thirty-six hours

there with only a sergeant and four men, but, nothing daunted, he at once bombed a large dug-out and took twenty-eight prisoners and three guns. Soon he was reinforced, but his position was entirely isolated, so he dug a trench and repelled bombing attacks throughout the night. In the morning he retired, having held his post for thirty-six hours.

The two King's Royal Rifles were Sergeant Edward Cooper and Rifleman Albert Edward Shepherd. Cooper was Stockton's first V.C. When machine-guns were holding up an advance, with four men he immediately rushed forward to the block-house. About one hundred yards distant he ordered his men to lie down and fire, but finding this did not silence the guns, he rushed forward and fired his revolver into an opening in the block-house. The guns ceased firing and the garrison surrendered, seven machine-guns and forty-five prisoners being

captured. When Shepherd's company was held up by a machine-gun he volunteered to rush it, which he did, killing two gunners and capturing the gun. The company, on continuing its advance, came under heavy enfilade fire, and when the last officer had become a casualty, Shepherd took command, ordered the men to lie down, and himself went back to obtain the help of a Tank. He returned to his company and led them to their last objective.

The two Seaforth Highlanders were Sergeant Alexander Edwards and Lance-Corporal Robert McBeath. The former led several men against a hostile machine-gun, killed all the team, and captured the gun. Later, when a sniper was causing casualties, he crawled out to stalk him, and although badly wounded in the arm, managed to kill him. As only one officer was now left with the company, Edwards, realising that the success of the attack depended on the capture of the farthest objective, led his men on till this had been taken.

Lance-Corporal R. McBeath went out alone and located a hostile machine-gun that was checking the advance; working his way towards it, he shot the gunner with his revolver. Finding other guns in action, he attacked them with the assistance of a Tank, and drove the gunners into a deep dug-out. He rushed in after them, shot one who opposed him on the steps, and captured three officers and thirty men.

Two non-commissioned officers earned the distinction for the King's Own Scottish Borderers: Sergeant (Acting Company Quartermaster-Sergeant) William H. Grimbaldeston and Sergeant (Acting Company Sergeant-Major) John Skinner. Their heroism had much in common. Grimbaldeston collected a small party to fire rifle-grenades on a block-house that was holding up the left of an attack. He then obtained a volunteer to assist him, and, in spite of very heavy fire from the block-house, the two pushed on towards it and made for the entrance. Grimbaldeston threatened with a hand-grenade the men inside, and forced them to surrender, a deed that resulted in a bag of thirty-six prisoners and six machine-guns.

Skinner, although wounded in the head, collected six men, and, with great deter-

Critical situation saved

mination, worked round the left flank of three block-houses whence machine-guns were delaying the advance. He succeeded in bombing and taking the first block-house single-handed; then, leading his six men towards the other two, they captured sixty prisoners.

An officer and a private carried off the two crosses for the Yorkshire Light Infantry. Major (Acting Lieutenant-Colonel) Oliver Cyril Spencer Watson, D.S.O., showed gallant leading during critical operations. His command was at a point where continual attacks were made by the enemy, and an intricate system of trenches in front, coupled with the fact that the position was under constant fire, rendered the situation still more dangerous. A counter-attack had at first achieved its object, but as the enemy were holding out in two improvised strong points, Watson led his remaining reserve to the attack. But he was outnumbered; so finally he ordered his men to retire, remaining himself in a communication trench until killed.

Private Wilfred Edwards, of the same regiment, showed amazing bravery when under heavy fire from a concrete fort. Having lost all his company officers, he dashed forward without hesitation, bombed through the loopholes, surmounted the fort, and motioned to his company to advance. By his splendid example he saved a very critical situation at a time when the whole battalion was held up. Later he performed valuable work as a runner.

Two men in the ranks earned the two crosses credited to the West Riding Regiment. Private Arnold Loosemore crawled through partially cut wire, dragging his Lewis gun with him, and then dealt with a strong party of the enemy who were checking his platoon. He killed about twenty of them. Immediately his Lewis gun was blown up by a bomb, but three of the enemy who rushed for him were shot. Private Arthur Poulter on ten occasions carried badly wounded men to a safer locality through a particularly heavy barrage. Two of these were hit a second time while on his back.

GENERAL THE HON. SIR JULIAN HEDWORTH GEORGE BYNG, G.C.B., K.C.M.G., M.V.O.
Commanding the British Third Army in France

Private William Boynton Butler, of the West Yorkshire Regiment, was in charge of a Stokes gun in trenches which were being heavily shelled. Suddenly one of the fly-off levers of a Stokes shell came off and fired it. Butler picked up the shell and jumped to the entrance of the emplacement, where he yelled out to some infantry who were passing, urging them to hurry on as the shell was exploding. Then, turning round, he placed himself between the men and the live shell, afterwards throwing it on to the parados and taking cover in the bottom of the trench.

Sergeant Albert Mountain was the other West Yorkshireman. His company had dug themselves in, but the position on a sunken road was exposed, and from it they were forced to retire. The enemy was advancing in mass, preceded by an advanced patrol about two hundred strong. Volunteers for a counter-attack were called for, and Mountain immediately stepped forward and his party of ten men followed him. They advanced on the flank with a Lewis gun and brought enfilade fire to bear on

SEC.-LT. M. S. S. MOORE,
Hampshire Regt.

SGT. A. MOUNTAIN,
W. Yorks Regt.

L.-SGT. J. MOYNEY,
Irish Guards.

L.-CPL. H. MUGFORD,
M.G.C.

SGT. J. OCKENDEN,
Royal Dublin Fusiliers.

CAPT. C. P. J. O'KELLY,
Canadian Infantry.

PTE. M. J. O'ROURKE,
Canadian Infantry.

SEC.-LT. H. F. PARSONS,
Gloucester Regt.

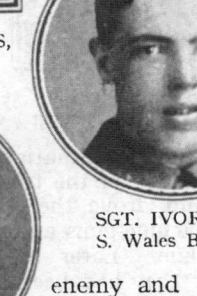

SGT. IVOR REES,
S. Wales Borderers.

MAJOR G. R. PEARKES,
Canadian M.R.

P.-O. E. PITCHER,
R.N.

PTE. A. POULTER,
W. Riding Regt.

CAPT. T. T. PRYCE,
Grenadier Guards.

the enemy patrol, killing about a hundred. Soon the enemy's main body appeared, and Mountain's men began to waver, but he rallied them and formed a defensive position from which to cover the retirement of the rest of the company. He then took command of the flank post, which was "in the air," and held on for twenty-seven hours until finally surrounded by the enemy. Mountain was one of the few who managed to fight their way back.

The two North Staffordshire heroes were Sergeant John Carmichael and Private (Lance-Corporal) John Thomas. When excavating a trench the sergeant saw that a grenade had been unearthed and had started to burn. He immediately rushed to the spot and, shouting to his men to get clear, placed his steel helmet over it. He stood thereon until the grenade exploded and blew him out of the trench. He thus saved many from death, but was himself seriously injured.

When war broke out Thomas was working on the Lusitania, and he was in that liner on her last journey, being one of the survivors. He joined the North Staffords and earned his V.C. thus : Observing the enemy making preparations for a counter-attack, he and a comrade decided to make a close reconnaissance. They went out in broad daylight under heavy fire. The other man was hit, so Thomas went on alone. Walking round a small copse he shot three snipers, and then pushed on to a building used by the enemy as a night post, where he saw whence the Germans were bringing up their troops, returning with information of such value that the hostile attack was broken up.

The two Gloucesters were both young officers. Second-Lieutenant Hardy Falconer Parsons won the V.C. during a night attack on a bombing-post held by his command. The bombers holding the block were forced back, but Parsons remained, and single-handed, although severely scorched and burnt by liquid fire, continued to hold up the enemy by bombs. He delayed the enemy long enough, but as a consequence succumbed to his wounds.

Temporary Captain Mauley Angell James, M.C., led his company forward with "magnificent determination and courage," inflicting severe losses on the enemy and capturing twenty-seven prisoners and two machine-guns. When two days later the enemy had broken through on his right flank he refused to withdraw, and made a most determined stand, gaining valuable time for the withdrawal of the guns. He was ordered by the senior officer on the spot to hold on "to the last" in order to enable the brigade to be extricated. Leading his company forward in a local counter-attack, he was last seen working a machine-gun single-handed.

The two crosses earned by the Black Watch (Royal Highlanders) were announced on November 27th, 1917. Major (Acting Lieutenant-Colonel) Lewis Pugh Evans, D.S.O., was commanding the Lincolns when he performed the services for which he was thus honoured. He took his battalion in perfect order through a terrific enemy barrage, personally formed up all units and led them to the assault. While machine-guns in an emplacement were causing casualties and troops were working round the flank, he rushed at it himself and, firing his revolver through the loophole, forced the garrison to capitulate. After capturing the first objective he was severely wounded, but he re-formed his battalion and again led the men forward.

Humbler in rank but every bit as heroic was Private Charles Melvin. His company had advanced to within fifty yards of the front-line trench of a redoubt, where, owing to the intensity of the fire, the men were obliged to lie down and wait for reinforcements. Melvin, however, rushed on over the ground swept from end to end by bullets. On reaching the enemy trench he halted and fired two or three shots, killing one of the enemy; then he jumped into it and attacked the Germans with his bayonet. Attacked in this resolute manner most of the enemy fled to their second line.

An officer and a private appear together as winners of the Victoria Cross for the Highland Light Infantry. Private (Acting Lance-Corporal) John Brown Hamilton showed conspicuous bravery at a time when the ammunition supply had reached a low ebb. On several occa-

Carrying supplies through fire sions, on his own initiative, he carried supplies of it through the enemy's belts of fire to the front and support lines, and then, passing along these lines in full view of snipers and machine-guns, he distributed the ammunition.

Major (Acting Lieutenant-Colonel) William Herbert Anderson showed great qualities of leadership. The enemy had penetrated a wood held by the British, and the flank of the whole position was in danger of being turned. Grasping the

CAPT. H. REYNOLDS, Royal Scots.   *[Elliott & Fry.* LT.-COL. F. C. ROBERTS, Worcestershire Regt.   LCE.-CPL. C. G. ROBERTSON, Royal Fusiliers.

others to surrender. Later, realising that he had pushed too far, he withdrew his party, personally covering the withdrawal by sniping the enemy.

Gribble was in command of the right company of the battalion when the enemy attacked, and his orders were to " hold on to the last." His company was eventually entirely isolated and his right flank was " in the air." But he intimated his determination to hold on until other orders were received, and this he inspired his company to accomplish. They were eventually surrounded by the enemy, and Gribble was seen fighting to the last.

The Manchester Regiment is represented by Sergeant Harry Coverdale and Private Walter Mills. The former showed the utmost gallantry in approaching an enemy strong post, and

LT.-COL. J. FORBES-ROBERTSON, Border Regt.   *[Speaight.* CAPT. J. F. RUSSELL, R.A.M.C., attd. R.W. Fus.   LT. C. W. K. SADLIER, Australian Imperial Force.   LT. R. D. SANDFORD, R.N.   SEC.-LT. J. SCHOFIELD, Lancs Fusiliers.

seriousness of the situation, Anderson succeeded in gathering the remainder of the two right companies, led the counterattack, and drove the enemy from the wood, capturing twelve machine-guns and seventy prisoners and restoring the original line. Later on the same day he reorganised his men after they had been driven in and made them ready for a counter-attack. This attack, which drove the enemy from his position, he led in person, but at the price of his life.

The Royal Warwicks had for their two V.C.'s Private Arthur Hutt and Lieutenant (Acting Captain) Julian Royds Gribble. Hutt, when all the officers and non-commissioned officers of his platoon had become casualties, took command and led them on. Held up by a strong post on his right, he immediately ran forward alone and shot the officer and three men in the post, causing between forty and fifty

close to it disposed of an officer and two men who were sniping. He rushed two machine-guns, killing or surrounding the teams, and subsequently reorganised his platoon.

Mills set an example of dauntless courage. When after an intense gas attack a strong enemy patrol endeavoured to rush the British posts, the garrisons of which had been overcome, Mills, though badly gassed, met the attack single-handed and continued to throw bombs until the arrival of reinforcements. Almost at once he died from gas poisoning. **Examples of the great sacrifice**

Corporal William Clamp gained the first of the two crosses for the Yorkshire Regiment. He dashed forward with two men and attempted to rush a block-house whence machine-gun fire was checking the British advance. His first attempt failed, but he at once collected some bombs and, calling upon two men to follow him, again dashed forward. He was the first to reach the block-house, hurled in bombs, killing many of the occupants, and then entered and brought out a machine-gun and about twenty prisoners. He then went forward again, encouraging the men until killed.

Second-Lieutenant Ernest Frederick Beal also made the great sacrifice after earning the V.C. When his company was established in a certain section of the trench it was found that a gap between its left flank and the neighbouring unit was strongly held by the enemy. It was vital to clear it, but no troops were available. So organising a small party, Beal led them against the enemy.

PTE. A. E. SHEPHERD, K.R.R.C.   LT.-COL. J. SHERWOOD-KELLY, Norfolk Regt.   C. S.-M. J. SKINNER, K.O.S.B.

GUNNER C. E. STONE, R.F.A.   CAPT. W. N. STONE, Royal Fusiliers.   L.-CPL. J. THOMAS, N. Staffs Regt.

Second-Lieutenant James Samuel Emerson and Private James Duffy won V.C.'s for the Inniskilling Fusiliers. The officer led his company in an attack and cleared four hundred yards of trench. Though wounded, when the enemy attacked in superior numbers, he sprang out of the trench with eight men and met them in the open, killing many and taking six prisoners. For three hours after this, all other officers having become casualties, he remained with his company, refusing to go to the dressing-station, and repeatedly repelled bombing attacks. Later, when the enemy again attacked, he led his men forward and was mortally wounded.

Duffy, a stretcher-bearer, went out, accompanied by another bearer, to bring in a seriously wounded comrade. When the other was wounded Duffy returned to get another; immediately this man was killed. He then went forward alone, **Stretcher-bearer's great gallantry** and under heavy fire succeeded in getting the two wounded men under cover.

With a brief account of how Second-Lieutenant (Acting Captain) Alfred Maurice Toye, M.C., and Lieutenant (Acting Captain) Allastair Malcolm Cluny McReady-Diarmid, of the Middlesex, earned the honour, the narrative of the twenty-one regiments with two crosses each to their credit is concluded. Toye, when the enemy had captured the trench at a bridge-head, three times re-established the post, which was eventually recaptured by fresh hostile attacks.

On reaching a machine-gun he immediately sprang forward, killed the team, and captured the gun. He continued along the trench, where he dealt with another machine-gun in the same manner.

Second-Lieutenant (Acting Captain) Arthur Moore Lascelles and Private Thomas Young were the two Durham Light Infantrymen V.C.'s. The former showed bravery and initiative when in command of his company in a very exposed position. After a heavy bombardment, during which he was wounded, the enemy attacked in very strong force but was driven off, the British success being due in great degree to the fine example set by this officer, who, refusing to allow his wounds to be dressed, continued to organise the defence. The enemy again attacked and captured the trench, whereupon

 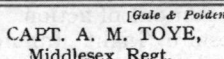    

CAPT. A. M. TOYE, Middlesex Regt.   CPL. C. W. TRAIN, London Regt.   LT. S. T. D. WALLACE, R.F.A.   LT.-COL. O. C. S. WATSON, K.O.Y.L.I.   PTE. T. WITHAM, Coldstream Guards.

Lascelles jumped on the parapet and, followed by the remainder of his company, rushed out and drove over sixty of them back.

Young showed conspicuous courage when acting as stretcher-bearer. On nine occasions he went out in front of the line in broad daylight under heavy fire and brought back wounded men. Under fire he attended to those too badly wounded to be moved before dressing and carried them unaided to safety. For five days, we are told, he worked unceasingly.

The Border Regiment's two V.C.'s were gained by Captain (Acting Lieutenant-Colonel) James Forbes-Robertson, D.S.O., M.C., and Sergeant Charles Edward Spack- **Officer who saved the line** man. The officer, through his judgment, resource, energy, and example, on four different occasions saved the line and averted a danger that might have had far-reaching results. An example or so will suffice to indicate these services. When troops in front were falling back he made a rapid reconnaissance on horse-back, in full view of the enemy and under heavy fire. He organised and, still mounted, led a counter-attack which was completely successful in re-establishing the line. On a subsequent occasion, when troops were retiring on his left and the positions on his right were obscure, he again saved the situation. Spackman went through heavy fire to attack a machine-gun which was checking the leading company. He rushed the gun, thereby enabling the company to advance.

McReady-Diarmid also maintained the tradition of the "Die Hards." When the enemy had penetrated some distance into the British position and the situation was critical, he at once led his company forward through a heavy barrage and engaged the enemy with such success that they were driven back three hundred yards. The next day the enemy drove back another company. At once he called for volunteers. Throughout the ensuing attack he led the way, and it was entirely due to his marvellous throwing of bombs that the ground was regained. He was eventually killed.

As stated at the beginning of the chapter, twenty-one regiments of the line were credited with one Victoria Cross each during the year under consideration.

In the "London Gazette" dated September 6th, 1917, appeared the name of Private Thomas Barratt, South

LCE.-SGT. J. E. WOODALL, Rifle Brigade.   PTE. T. WOODCOCK, Irish Guards.   SEC.-LT. J. S. YOULL, Northumberland Fus.

Staffordshire Regiment. As scout to a patrol he worked his way towards the enemy line with the greatest determination, in spite of fire from hostile snipers, whom he stalked and killed. He covered the retirement of his patrol, caused many casualties to the enemy, and prevented their advance.

For the Gordon Highlanders a V.C. was earned by Private George McIntosh. He rushed forward under heavy fire and threw a grenade into a machine-gun emplacement, killing two of the enemy. Entering, he found two machine-guns, which he carried back with him. His grasp of the situation and the fearlessness and rapidity with which he acted saved many of his comrades.

Sergeant Ivor Rees, of the South Wales Borderers, led his platoon forward by short rushes to a hostile machine-gun, and then worked his way round to the rear **Thrilling moment** of the gun position. When he was about **in a trench** twenty yards from the gun he rushed forward, shot one man, and bayoneted another. He bombed the concrete emplacement, killing five and capturing thirty prisoners, in addition to the machine-gun.

Corporal Sidney James Day, of the Suffolks, was in command of a bombing section detailed to clear a maze of trenches held by the enemy. On reaching a point where the trench had been levelled he went alone and bombed his way through in order to gain touch with the neighbouring troops. On his return to his section a stink-bomb fell into a trench occupied by two officers and three men. Day seized the bomb and threw it over the trench, where it immediately exploded—an act of heroism that saved the lives of those in the trench.

Private (Acting Lance-Corporal) Frederick R. Room, Royal Irish Regiment, showed conspicuous bravery when in charge of some stretcher-bearers. He worked continuously under intense fire, dressing the wounded with entire devotion.

The V.C. of the Royal Scots was earned by Captain Henry Reynolds. His company was attacking, and when approaching their final objective suffered heavily from a " pill-box " which had been passed by the first wave. He reorganised his men and then proceeded alone towards it. When near the " pill-box " he crawled to the entrance and forced a phosphorus grenade inside. This set the place on fire and caused the death of three of the enemy, while the remainder surrendered.

Second-Lieutenant Hugh Colvin, of the Cheshires, assumed command of two companies and led them forward under heavy fire with great dash and success. Seeing the battalion on his right held up, he led a platoon to their assistance. He next went out with only two men to a dug-out, which he entered alone, and brought up fourteen prisoners. He proceeded with his two men to another dug-out which had been holding up the attack. This he reached, and killing or making prisoners of the crew, captured the machine-gun.

On the same date as the last two awards there was announced that of Sergeant James Ockenden, of the Dublin Fusiliers. When acting as company sergeant-major he saw the platoon on the right held up by machine-gun fire. Immediately he rushed the machine-gun and captured it, killing the crew save one man. He then led a section to the attack on a farm, where sixteen men surrendered to him.

The V.C. credited to the West Surrey Regiment was earned by Captain (Temporary Lieutenant-Colonel) Christopher Bushell, D.S.O. He led in person C **" Come on,** Company of his battalion when they were **the Tigers ! "** co-operating with an allied regiment in a counter-attack. He was severely wounded, but he placed the whole line in a sound position.

The cross awarded to Private Thomas Henry Sage, of the Somerset Light Infantry, was for conspicuous bravery during an attack on a strong point. He was in a shell-hole with eight men, one of whom was shot while throwing a bomb. The live bomb fell into the shell-hole, so Sage, with great presence of mind, immediately threw himself on it, thereby saving the lives of several of his comrades.

The crosses gained by the Norfolk and Leicestershire Regiments were announced on January 1st, 1918. Major (Acting Lieutenant-Colonel) John Sherwood-Kelly, C.M.G., D.S.O., of the Norfolks, was commanding a battalion of the Royal Inniskilling Fusiliers when a party of another unit, detailed to cover the passage of a canal by his battalion, was held up. Sherwood-Kelly at once ordered covering fire, personally led the leading company of his battalion across the canal, and then reconnoitred the high ground held by the enemy. The left flank of his battalion, advancing to the assault of this objective, was held up by wire. Thereupon, with a Lewis-gun team he forced his way through obstacles, got the gun in position, and covered the advance through the wire, enabling the position to be captured.

Second-Lieutenant (Temporary Lieutenant-Colonel) Philip Eric Bent, D.S.O., of the Leicestershires, collected a platoon that was in reserve, and together with men from other companies and various details, organised and led them to a counter-attack at a time when the enemy had forced back the line. He was killed while leading a charge which he inspired with the cry, " Come on, the Tigers ! "

Second-Lieutenant Stanley Henry Parry Boughey, of the Royal Scots Fusiliers, rushed forward alone with bombs right up to the enemy, who had crawled to within thirty yards of the firing-line. He did great execution and caused the surrender of a party of thirty, but was mortally wounded.

The V.C.'s credited to the Bedfordshire and Wiltshire Regiments were announced on April 25th, 1918. For the former, Lieutenant-Colonel John Stanhope Collings-Wells, D.S.O., gained it for conduct in very critical situations during a withdrawal. When the rearguard was almost surrounded, he called for volunteers to stay behind and hold up the enemy, while the remainder withdrew. With his small body he kept back the Germans for one and a half hours. On a subsequent occasion he led the assault until killed.

Captain Reginald Frederick Johnson Hayward, M.C., of the Wiltshires, " displayed almost superhuman powers of endurance and consistent courage of the rarest nature." In spite of the fact that he was not only buried, wounded in the head, and rendered deaf on the first day of operations, and had his arm shattered **More machine-gun** two days later, he refused to leave his men, **heroes** until he collapsed from sheer exhaustion.

Sergeant Harold Jackson, of the East Yorkshire Regiment, went through a hostile barrage and brought back valuable information regarding the enemy's movements. Later, when the Germans had established themselves in the British lines, he rushed at them, and single-handed bombed them out into the open. He stalked an enemy machine-gun, threw Mills bombs at the detachment, and put the gun out of action.

Private Harold Whitefield, Shropshire Light Infantry, single-handed, charged and captured a Lewis gun which was harassing his company at short range.

The next three were awarded their crosses on the same date, May 23rd, 1918. Second-Lieutenant Basil Arthur Horsfall, of the East Lancashire Regiment, was in command of the centre platoon during a German attack. When the enemy first attacked, three forward sections were driven back, and he was wounded in the head. Nevertheless, he immediately organised the remainder of his men and made a counter-attack which recovered the positions, but was killed.

Corporal John Thomas Davies, who won the cross for the South Lancashires, mounted a parapet, thus fully exposing himself, in order to get a more effective field of fire. He kept his Lewis gun in action to the last, causing many casualties and checking the advance.

Private Jack Thomas Counter, of the King's (Liverpool) Regiment, volunteered to fetch information which proved of the utmost value. Five runners had attempted to reach the front line, and had all been killed. Counter went out under terrific fire and succeeded in getting through. He returned, carrying with him some vital information, and subsequently carried back five messages across the open.

The last name to be recorded is John Scott Youll, a second-lieutenant in the Northumberland Fusiliers, to whom the cross was awarded on July 26th, 1918. He was in command of a patrol which came under the hostile barrage. Sending his men back to safety, he remained to observe the situation, but unable to rejoin his company, he reported to a neighbouring unit. When the enemy attacked he maintained his position, then rushed a gun and turned it on the enemy.

CHAPTER CCLXXVI.

THE DOWNFALL OF THE AUSTRIAN EMPIRE AND THE FINAL TRIUMPH OF ITALY.

By Robert Machray.

Austria's Strength and Weakness—Insoluble Racial, Political, and Economic Questions—The New Emperor—Pressure of the Czecho-Slovaks and Jugo-Slavs—How They Helped the Allies—Famine Stalks Through the Land—Resignation of Count Czernin Over the Emperor's Letter to Prince Sixte of Bourbon-Parma—Austro-Hungarian Army Still Formidable—The Defeat on the Piave—Increasing Effect of Foch's Blows in the West—German Peace Offensive—Austria's Part—Note to President Wilson—Its Failure—Bulgaria's Surrender a Disaster for Austria—The Collapse of Turkey—More German and Austrian Peace Manœuvres—Entente and America Recognise the Czecho-Slovaks as Belligerents—The Handwriting on the Wall—Federalism No Longer Possible—Growing Disorganisation—Italy Strikes—Austrian Army Shattered—Magnificent British Co-operation—Lord Cavan's Great Story—Austria Seeks an Armistice—Unconditional Surrender—Abdication of the Emperor—" Finis " Written Over the Dual Monarchy.

ALTHOUGH Austria was much the weaker of the Central Powers, and the part she played in the war was systematically belittled by Germany, yet her military contribution to the joint effort of the Germanic Alliance was very considerable in Serbia, Russia, Rumania, and more especially in Italy. It would have been still more considerable but for the defection of her own Slavs—the Czecho-Slovaks in the north and the Jugo-Slavs in the south—who were bitterly opposed to the Austrian Germans and to the Hungarian Magyars, the two dominant races of the country.

As a rule both Austrian Germans and Hungarian Magyars fought well. Austria's lack of strength lay in the political conditions of what Mr. Lloyd George rightly called her "ramshackle Empire," and of which the hostility of the large Slav element of her population was an indication. A striking picture of her internal state was presented in Chapter CXCIV. (Vol. 10, page 43), "Life in Austria - Hungary during the First Three Years of the War."

That chapter shows that the Dual Monarchy was troubled by serious racial, political, and economic questions which were impossible of any satisfactory solution.

Austria was, in fact, a house divided against itself, and was bound sooner or later to meet with the fate inevitably inherent in such a situation. Germany did her utmost to strengthen her, and to a certain extent succeeded in the attempt ; but the time came when her own increasing necessities compelled her to concentrate all her forces

for her own support, and Austria was left to herself, with the result—which was a foregone conclusion in the circumstances—that she went to pieces. The long reign of the Emperor Francis Joseph, and a certain veneration that was felt for him throughout the Austro - Hungarian Empire, had held its uneasy peoples more or less together ; but his death, which occurred towards the end of 1916, saw the instant renewal, in more aggravated form, of those sharp domestic differences that he had been able sufficiently to control. The Archduke Charles, the grand-nephew who followed him on the throne, was a young man untrained in statecraft, and therefore unlikely, even had the times been normal, to be equal to what, it must be admitted, was about as difficult a position as any in the world. And the times were not normal.

Old Francis Joseph had gone into the war without consulting the Parliaments of either Austria or Hungary, and had ruled in reality as an autocrat through his Ministers. As soon as Charles became Emperor there were changes among these Ministers, and the first months of his reign were marked by a succession of political crises which led to his summoning the Reichsrath for May 30th, 1917. In his speech from the throne Charles spoke of a time, which he hoped was not far distant, "when the foundations of a new, strong, and happy Austria will again for generations to come be firmly consolidated internally and externally." He declared that he should always be a ruler " in the sense of the Constitutional idea " and in the spirit of " true democracy." At that time

THE KING OF ITALY AND HIS HEIR.
King Victor Emmanuel III. and Queen Elena with their son, Prince Humbert of Piedmont, visiting a part of " redeemed " Italian territory in 1918.

ON THE LOWER PIAVE.
Two British soldiers at an Italian aid-post by the bank of the Piave. A wounded Italian soldier had just been brought in on a stretcher. It was on the Piave that the Allies' shattering attack on the Austrians began in October, 1918.

there were two chief questions agitating the Dual Monarchy, and their influence was felt up to the end of its participation in the war. One was political, the other economic. The first was embodied in the phrase Czecho-Slovak, the second was hunger—Austria, if not Hungary, was starving.

Slavs of various kinds—Czechs, Slovaks, Poles, Ruthenes, Croats, Serbs, and Slovenes—formed the majority of the entire population, and Bohemia, whose Czechs were Slavs at their cultural best, was demanding independence of the same sort as that enjoyed by German Austria and Magyar Hungary, both of whom, however, were resolutely opposed to its being given, and denounced the Czechs and their kinsmen the Slovaks as traitors. Further, the Czechs upheld the right of the Jugo-Slavs to a similar independence. Under this pressure the young Emperor issued an amnesty to all civilians who had been sentenced to imprisonment for high treason, but this favour was not shown to Professor Masaryk, the Bohemian patriot, and other leaders of the oppressed races who had fled the country. The Emperor's

Political and economic factors

action enraged his German and Magyar subjects. Politically the Dual Monarchy was like a boiling cauldron all through the winter of 1917-18, but for a while the success of the German offensive in the spring of 1918, coming on top, as it did, of the Italian defeat at Caporetto, imparted some semblance of quiet and order to the distracted Empire.

In Chapter CXCIV., and in other chapters incidentally, references were made to the action of those Czecho-Slovak forces who in Russia and elsewhere fought on the side of the Allies. These forces, taken altogether, were much more numerous than was generally understood, the total number of men supporting the Entente being nearly 400,000. Of these, 300,000 left the Austro-Hungarian armies, and voluntarily surrendered to Russia. Out of the 70,000 prisoners taken by the Serbs in the campaigns of 1914-15 rather more than one-half were Czecho-Slovaks, who gave their Serbian friends very little trouble in the field. One of the sorrowful things about the terrible Serbian retreat was that almost all these Czecho-Slovaks perished in the Albanian mountains.

More than 20,000 Czecho-Slovaks, and a large number of Jugo-Slavs, once they were satisfied of sympathy with their national aspirations, surrendered to Italy, and fought shoulder to shoulder with the Italian troops. It was with Austria that, practically entirely, these men were in conflict, and the Austrian Germans and the Magyars, knowing all these facts

perfectly well, hated the Slavs of the Dual Monarchy—with a hatred that, to say the truth, was fully returned.

The second thing that made tension severe throughout Austria was elemental —it was hunger. As regards food, Hungary was much better off than Austria, but she would do little or nothing to supply the needs of her partner, alleging as the reason that it was she who fed the joint Army, and that she could do no more. The Austrians, however, did not believe her, and reviled her accordingly. In January, 1918, as well as later in the year, there were strikes and food riots in Vienna and in other parts of the country. Prices for all commodities rose to such

"PONTOON PARK" ON THE ITALIAN FRONT.
Neat arrangement at one of the camps of the British forces in Italy, where notices were affixed, signal bells hung, fire extinguishers kept handy, a clock was fixed, and letters could be posted.

WATER FROM A HILLSIDE SPRING.
British soldiers filling their water-bottles from a spring issuing from a rocky hill in Italy, the sanitary or other medical authority having satisfied himself of the fitness of the water for use.

an unimaginable height that they found a parallel only in Petrograd under the Bolshevist regime. The nobility and the rich bought what small supplies came on the market ; the poor got hardly anything, and many of them died of famine.

This contrast was heightened by the fact that the nobles and the rich for the most part kept out of the war ; they went on with their usual life, as far as it was possible—a life of frivolity, of feasting, of horse-racing, of gambling. It was a case of Nero fiddling while Rome was burning. The authorities did something for the poor, but it was utterly inadequate. A small amount of food was obtained from Germany, who

UPSTREAM TO THE FINAL VICTORY.
Italian Marines landing from barges on the Piave while on their way up to the front line. The transport of troops up this treacherous river was a triumph of organisation.

NAVAL GUNNERS IN LAND FIGHTING.
Clearing for action on an Italian armoured train during the tremendous bombardment which preceded the final expulsion of the Austro-Hungarian invaders from Italian territory in November, 1918.

WHEN THE TIDE TURNED ON THE PIAVE.
Fifteen-inch gun on a monitor assisting in the operations in the region of the Lower Piave, where some extraordinarily fine shooting was made by the Italian naval gunners.

declared she had not enough for herself, and the immense quantities of provisions that had been expected from conquered Rumania failed to materialise. The general state of the Austrians as regarded food was desperate. Besides, the country was getting deeper and deeper into debt—to all intents Austria was bankrupt.

If ever a country needed peace that country was Austria-Hungary, but her politicians, during the winter of 1917-18, dissembled and played the German game. To make plain its sympathy with Italy after the disaster of Caporetto, the United States declared war on the Dual Monarchy, and sent some of its troops to the Italian front. In carrying out her share of the enemy peace offensive that winter it was to the American President that Austria, as well as Germany, appealed. In this campaign it was the policy of Germany to permit Austria to speak in terms much milder than those she herself employed. On January 8th, 1918, President Wilson made his famous speech in Congress, outlining America's peace terms—the " fourteen points. "

On the last day of the month Count Hertling, the Imperial German Chancellor, delivered a long address in the Reichstag, in which he endorsed some of the President's points, including the " freedom of the seas," and stated the German attitude with regard to the others—an arrogant and insolent **Hapsburg and Hohenzollern** attitude. On the same day Count Czernin, the Foreign Minister of the Dual Monarchy, made a speech in the Reichsrath in which the arrogance and insolence were somewhat toned down for Mr. Wilson's special benefit. When the President replied to them on February 11th, he declared that Czernin's observations were " uttered in a very friendly tone." On the other hand, he stated that Hertling's reply was vague, confusing, and very different from that of Czernin. Mr. Wilson saw well enough, of course, which of the two was the real voice of the enemy, and on April 6th he pronounced for " force to the utmost," to bring about a peace which would be a real peace.

About ten days later there was one more of the many political crises that constantly developed in Austria. On April 15th it was announced that Czernin had resigned over what must be called a very strange and mysterious affair. M. Clemenceau, the French Prime Minister, had made public a letter which purported to be written by the Emperor Charles to his brother-in-law, Prince Sixte of Bourbon-Parma. In this letter the Emperor spoke of the " just claims of France to Alsace." As soon as this document was published there

GOING ON LEAVE.
Railway Transport officer with the British forces in Italy examining the passes of leave men to see that they were all in order.

was far from being a negligible military Power, as was manifested when on June 15th, 1918, she began a powerful offensive on the Italian front, from Asiago to the sea, with a force of about 600,000 men. How disastrous was its issue for herself was recorded in Chapter CCLXVI. (Vol. 12, page 221). By July 6th the Austrians were completely cleared out of the delta of the Piave, while the Italians had made about 25,000 of them prisoners in the course of the operations. And about the same time the Austrians were losing men and ground to the Italians in Albania. The influence of these defeats was felt deeply in every part of the Dual Monarchy, save where the Slav element was strong.

Field-Marshal von Hötzendorff, the Commander-in-Chief, was retired, just two days, as it happened, before

was a tremendous outcry and uproar in Berlin, and Charles was doubtless asked for an explanation. The genuineness and authenticity of the letter were denied, and the Austrian Emperor had to go to Germany to make his peace. Czernin disappeared from office. The bonds of iron which bound Austria to Germany were made stronger and heavier, and the Hapsburg was taught how much lower a place he held in the general scheme of things than the Hohenzollern. This was at the moment when the German offensive of 1918 was in the full flush of success on the western front, and Austria would have very little to do or say except what she was told. In any case the intrigues of Germany for a negotiated peace that would have given her almost everything for which she had made the war resulted in failure.

Early in May, 1918, there occurred in Vienna another of these incessant political crises. The situation, in spite of German victories in the west, had not improved at all in Austria, but on the contrary it had become worse and worse. One observer reported that the whole country was seething with revolt, which was only restrained by fear of the Germans and the absence of leaders. He said that the common people

Allies recognise Czecho-Slovaks

were living on scraps of potatoes, mangelwurzels, and anything they could pick up; and that when a chicken was killed, or a bit of meat was somehow obtained, it was shared in tiny fragments, as if among wrecked men on a raft. All over the land there were ferment, strife, confusion.

In the political world Bohemia was more urgent than ever in her demand for independence. Developments in the Ukraine and in Russia generally were reacting unfavourably on Austria, nor did the " peace " which was being wrung from Rumania make her position more favourable. In the midst of indescribable confusion the Reichsrath was adjourned on May 3rd, Dr. von Seidler, the Premier, announcing that Parliamentary government was impossible, and that a revision of the Constitution was in contemplation by which Bohemia in particular was to be divided into national districts.

Notwithstanding her serious internal troubles, Austria still

DOCUMENTARY EVIDENCE FROM THE ENEMY.
Officers and men attached to the British Intelligence Staff in Italy, with some Italian helpers, engaged in examining sacks full of captured Austrian documents in the courtyard of an Italian palazzo.

Marshal Foch delivered his great counter-attack between Soissons and Château-Thierry which changed the whole face of the world-war. Austria, thinking that Germany was to be victorious in the west, struck her blow at Italy, and it failed and recoiled upon herself.

Little did she realise that Foch's counter-attack, which her defeat on the Italian front materially helped, was the definite turn of the tide, yet in August occurred an event of the utmost significance to herself, and one which was nothing less than a plain intimation that " passing away " was being inscribed by fate on the closing pages of her history. This was the formal recognition by Great Britain of the Czecho-Slovaks as Allies. On August 13th the British Government issued the following declaration :

Since the beginning of the war the Czecho-Slovak nation has resisted the common enemy by every means in its power. The Czecho-Slovaks have constituted a considerable army, fighting on three different battlefields, and attempting, in Russia and Siberia, to arrest the Germanic invasion. In consideration of its efforts to achieve independence, Great Britain regards the Czecho-Slovaks as an allied nation, and recognises the unity of the three Czecho-Slovak armies as an allied and belligerent army, waging regular warfare against Austria-Hungary and Germany. Great Britain also recognises the right of the Czecho-Slovak National Council, as the supreme organ of the Czecho-Slovak national interests, and as the present trustee of the future Czecho-Slovak Government, to exercise supreme authority over this allied and belligerent army.

Before this declaration the French and Italian Governments had concluded special military conventions with the Czecho-Slovak National Council with respect to sections of the Czecho-Slovak forces which had been constituted in France and Italy. With its headquarters at Paris, this Council, composed of patriotic Bohemians, Moravians, and Slovaks, had at its head Professor Masaryk, and was already an embodiment of Czecho-Slovak independence. Of particular interest, then, in the statement of the British Government was the passage which definitely recognised this Council as the " present trustee " of the future State, the inference being that the Allies—all the Allies quickly afterwards recognised the Czecho - Slovak National Council—were to make the institution of a free and independent Government of the Czecho-Slovak nation one of the things that would emerge from the final peace settlement. For Austria this recognition of the Czecho-Slovaks was the handwriting on the wall that foretold the dissolution of her Empire. It was an irony of history that it was Great Britain, traditionally the friend of Austria-Hungary, who wrote the fateful words.

The latter half of August saw the continuation of the great attacks on the Germans, with whom were some Austrian troops and guns, by the Allies under Foch on the western front, and the beginning of the German retreat. Early in September the Wotan line crashed under the blows of the British and Canadians ; by the 8th of that month the French and the British were up, or close, to the Hindenburg line of 1917, and a few days later the Americans were cutting off the St. Mihiel salient. The Germans did not like the look of things, and accordingly they launched a fresh peace offensive. It had three aspects. The first was disclosed in an offer to Belgium, which suggested that on certain conditions her political and economic independence should be restored after the war. In effect the German proposal was that Belgium should again be neutralised — thus barring allied operations in her territory against Germany— that she should try to secure the return to Germany of the colonies the Allies had conquered, that she should agree to maintain the commercial treaties with Germany as they had existed before the war, and, most significant of all, that she should seek neither indemnity nor reparation. In addition to the offer of this peace to Belgium, Germany made an offer, which was communicated through the German Minister at Helsingfors, to the Allies regarding Northern Russia. Germany promised not to attack Eastern Karelia, provided the allied troops were withdrawn from that district

RACIAL DIVISIONS OF AUSTRIA-HUNGARY.
Sketch plan indicating the congeries of races held together by the Hapsburg yoke prior to the Austrian debacle of 1918.

FLIMSY BUT EFFECTIVE SHELTER ON AN ITALIAN HIGHWAY.
British Army motor-car with officers on the Italian front halted at a camouflage curtain dropped across the thoroughfare, and awaiting information as to the road being clear for the next stage of their journey. Such screens of canvas, spotted and streaked with coloured stuffs and placed at irregular intervals across the way, served effectually to break the line of a road and make it indistinguishable to enemy observers flying high overhead.

GREAT COMMANDERS WHO ACHIEVED VICTORY.
Marshal Foch (on left) with General Armando Diaz, Commander-in-Chief of the Italian Army,
at the General Headquarters of the Inter-Allied Command. General Diaz was appointed to
the chief command of the Italian Army in November, 1917, in succession to General Cadorna.

Allies in a peace discussion. Neither Germany nor Austria expected, as a result of their overtures, a negotiated peace, but they hoped that pacifist and defeatist efforts would be stimulated, to the embarrassment of the Allies, and they thought that the rejection of their offers could be used among their own peoples to strengthen their determination to resist the Allies, who would be represented as resolved on their utter destruction.

Within half an hour of his receipt of the message giving the text of the Austrian Note, Mr. Lansing, the American Secretary of State, speaking as the mouthpiece of President Wilson, replied that the Government of the United States had but one answer to make. And that was that it had repeatedly and with entire candour already announced the terms upon which the United States would consider peace, and could not and would not "entertain any proposal for a conference on a matter concerning which it had made its position and purpose so plain." America spoke for the Allies as well as for herself.

In a speech Mr. Balfour referred to the Austrian Note, and, observing that it followed hard on a statement made by the German Vice-Chancellor in which there was to be found little or no modification of the attitude of Germany with respect to her war aims, said there was something cynical in the way in which the Austrians had made their proposals within a few hours of the utterance of that speech. "I suppose," he added, "it is that they count upon the illimitable gullibility of the public in the Entente countries." But that public, he went on, was not so dense as the Central Powers believed, and it knew that until there was a very different feeling in Germany, conversations about peace must be useless. The time was not yet ripe.

As designed, the Austrian Note did have its effect on the pacifists, who made great play with the idea that Austria was breaking away, or on the point of breaking away, from her alliance with Germany. They pointed out how advantageous it would be to the Allies if they helped on the process by accepting the Austrian proposal for a conference. But the American reply and Mr. Balfour's speech gave the views of the overwhelming majority of the peoples of the United States and of the Entente. Commenting on the Note, the "Times," in an editorial, remarked that among the things sought to be gained by it was to extract from one or other of the Allies some declaration to Austria which could be employed to create suspicion in Italy, or to throw doubt on the allied pledges to the Czecho-Slovaks and the sympathies of the Allies with oppressed nationalities. "A declaration of the kind, however vague and guarded, would help to relieve Germany's 'brilliant second' from the discontent, seething to revolution point, in several of her provinces, and such relief to her would naturally increase her usefulness to her German overlords." None of the Allies walked into the trap. As a war manœuvre Austria's Peace Note was an utter failure.

Meanwhile the stupendous drama of the world-war, unfolding in a series of great scenes, was approaching its climax. Three days after the Americans had cleared the St. Mihiel salient, on September 13th, the Allies in Macedonia, with the Serbians in the van, were breaking in the Bulgarian front, and three days after that the British, under Allenby, were smashing the Turkish front in Palestine. The triumphant issue of these operations has already been recorded in this history. By September 22nd the Bulgarians had been routed beyond hope of recovery, and the Turks had two

Austrian conference trap

and the whole Murman coast. This was the second aspect of the peace offensive, but the third, in which Austria once more appeared holding out the olive branch, was the most important of the series. This took the shape of a Note addressed by the Austro-Hungarian Government to all belligerent and neutral Governments, and communicated in a special form to Pope Benedict XV. It invited the Allies and the United States to confidential, non-binding discussions at a neutral centre, and expressed the opinion that all the belligerents owed it to humanity jointly to examine whether, after so many years of a costly but undecided struggle, the course of which pointed to an understanding, it was not possible to make an end of the terrible war.

For some weeks before the issue of this Note the Austrian Government, seriously perturbed, as well it might be, by the increasing disorganisation of the Dual Monarchy, had been endeavouring to get into touch with the Allied Governments, but to no purpose. It had tried to induce neutrals to act as mediators, and these attempts, too, had come to nothing. Though the Note purported to be a spontaneous expression of its individual views, there was not the least doubt that it was prompted by Germany, whose strongest desire at that juncture was to gain time for the reorganisation of her armies, and the reconstruction of lines of defence, by involving the

armies annihilated. On September 28th Bulgaria threw up the sponge, asked for an armistice, and two days later surrendered unconditionally. By that date Allenby had demolished another Turkish army, had conquered Palestine, and was surrounding Damascus, the capital of Syria. The whole world reverberated with the shock of these blows to the Germanic Alliance. Germany confessed herself bewildered. There was something like panic in Austria. And with good reason.

With what was happening to Turkey, Austria was not so intimately concerned as was Germany, who it was that virtually held Constantinople and the Bagdad Railway, and practically ruled the Turks. Yet there had been a not distant time in the war when Turkish divisions had strengthened the Austrian armies in Galicia, and had fought side by side with Austrians, as well as Germans and

Effect of Bulgaria's surrender Bulgarians, in Rumania. Needed in the Middle East, these Turkish forces had gone home. Still Austria was anything but indifferent to the crushing defeats Turkey suffered. Her interest in Bulgaria, however, was much more direct. The connections of Bulgaria with the Central Powers were much more Austrian than German. It was to Austria, much more than to Germany, that Tsar Ferdinand looked for inspiration and help. Throughout the Balkans, Austria had contended with Russia for the mastery, and to a large extent—certainly in Bulgaria — had prevailed, thanks to the backing of Germany, who developed through her the *Drang nach Osten* policy. Bulgaria had been almost the vassal of Austria. And now Bulgaria was gone from her side. Bulgaria surrendered to the Allies—a thing inconceivable to Austria.

Not only had Bulgaria fallen out—or, rather, been struck out—of the war, but her surrender to the Allies had opened up the way to Austria through Serbia, and the Serbs and the Jugo-Slavs, with others of the Allies, were swiftly beating down all resistance and pressing on to the Danube. That river, to use a true if unpoetic metaphor, was the back door of Austria.

In the early days of October the Serbians, whose breasts burned with the fire of intolerable wrongs, were advancing rapidly towards it, and the Jugo-Slavs were drawing near their own country. Not a week before, Count Burian, the successor of Czernin as Austro-Hungarian Foreign Secretary, had assured the German National Deputies that all the measures that were requisite for the security of Austria and Germany in the Balkans had been taken. After the surrender of Bulgaria it was authoritatively declared in Vienna that, though that event had placed the Dual Monarchy in an extraordinarily difficult position, there was no reason for faint-heartedness or despondency, and that Austria's defensive strength would confront the enemy in the south with fresh walls of steel.

This was mere subterfuge. The new walls of steel were never built ; the old were broken in pieces.

Mackensen, brooding darkly in the Royal palace in Bukarest, in which he sat as dictator of Rumania, over the astounding upturn of affairs, was, it was said, to bring into the Balkans Austro-German armies which would speedily change the situation. He did nothing of the kind, for he did not dare to move, knowing, as he did, how the skies were darkening over Germany on the western front, and that not a man could be spared from it for the Balkans or anywhere else. Neither Austria nor Germany offered any effective opposition to the

allied advance in Serbia ; they lost the great trunk railway from Belgrade through Sofia to Constantinople. Further, Austria was compelled to retreat in Albania, her evacuation of that little country and Montenegro being only a question of a very short time.

Towards the end of September, Count Burian stated to the German Austrians that negotiations were proceeding with a view to the joining of Bosnia and Herzegovina to Hungary as autonomous lands. He also remarked that the foreign political situation appeared to necessitate certain internal changes in the nature of federalism in the Monarchy in order to create the prerequisites for peace, just as Germany was about to change her policy in the direction of a Parliamentary form of government, such a change being needed to promote peace. What this really meant was that the peace offensive was being renewed in the most urgent manner by Germany and Austria because of the military situation.

Prince Max of Baden, a supposed " Liberal," suddenly became German Chancellor in place of Hertling, and his first act of importance was to despatch a Note on October 4th to President Wilson requesting him to take steps for the restoration of peace, to notify all belligerents of that request and to invite them to delegate plenipotentiaries for the purpose

HOMEWARD BOUND BY SUNNY WAYS.
Italian troops, elated with victory, halting by the wayside near a pleasant corner on their homeward march, after the collapse of Austria had brought the fighting on the Italian front to an end in the autumn of 1918.

of taking measures to avoid further bloodshed. The German Government then asked the President to bring about the immediate conclusion of a general armistice on land, on water, and in the air. In a Note of its own, the Dual Monarchy followed suit, adding on its own behalf that it desired to enter into negotiations for peace on the basis of the President's " fourteen points " of January 8th, 1918, and the " four points " of February 12th, 1918.

President Wilson did not reply at once to the Austrian Note, but in his answer to the German Note he asked certain questions concerning the exact meaning of Prince Max's words. He inquired if the German Government accepted the terms he had laid down in the " fourteen points " and in his subsequent addresses, and whether all that was left for discussion was an agreement as to their practical application. He suggested that the Central Powers should show their good faith by consenting to withdraw their forces immediately from invaded territory. And he very definitely demanded whether Prince Max was speaking merely for the constituted authorities who had so far conducted the war. This referred to a message of the German Emperor, addressed to Count Hertling on September 30th, in which he expressed his desire that the German people should take part more effectively than hitherto in deciding the fate of the Fatherland, and said that it was his will that men sustained by the people's trust should to a wide extent co-operate in the rights and duties of government. It was to this that Burian alluded in his observations to the German Austrians. On October 12th Germany replied by Herr Solf, the State Secretary of the Foreign Office, apparently accepting the President's conditions, and stating that the German Government then acting had been " conformed " by conference and agreement with the great majority of the Reichstag. To this Mr. Wilson returned answer that the military situation must be dealt with by the military advisers of the Allies and America, that Germany's good faith was in doubt, as the inhuman submarine campaign continued, and that he was committed to the " destruction of every arbitrary power." Germany had been controlled by arbitrary power, but, said the President, it was within the choice of the German nation to alter it ; indeed, the change, he maintained, constituted a condition precedent to peace.

There had been no such change ; there had been an attempt to deceive—subterfuge again. The political gerrymandering that was being made to do duty for real political reform in Germany was a device so transparent that it could take in no one except the man who was willing to be taken in. Neither President Wilson nor the Allies regarded it as anything but what it was—a sham. Solf replied to the President on October 21st, saying, among other things, that whereas the Parliament of the German Empire had had no influence in the past on the formation of the German Government, and under the Constitution had had no voice in the decisions on peace and war, a fundamental change had in truth been made, and that the new Government had been formed in complete accord with the desires of a Parliament based on " equal, general, secret, and direct suffrage." Two days later the President in another Note took cognisance of Solf's statement, but went straight to the heart of the matter by

The Wilson-Solf correspondence

saying that the " determining initiative " in Germany still remained with those who had hitherto been the masters of Germany. He concluded with the words :

Feeling that the whole peace of the world depends now on plain speaking and straightforward action, the President deems it his duty to say, without any attempt to soften what may seem harsh words, that the nations of the world do not and cannot trust the word of those who have hitherto been the masters of German policy, and to point out once more that in concluding peace and attempting to undo the infinite injuries and injustices of this war, the Government of the United States cannot deal with any but veritable representatives of the German people, who have been assured of a genuine constitutional standing, as the real rulers of Germany. If it must deal with the military masters and monarchical autocrats of Germany now, or if it is likely to have to deal with them later in regard to the international obligations of the German Empire, it must demand, not peace negotiations, but surrender.

While this correspondence was going on, President Wilson replied on October 18th to the Austrian Note of October 4th. In spite of their own troubles, the Austrians had watched that correspondence with anxious eyes, and had looked into it closely to see if it gave any sign of what his answer would be to them. In the Dual Monarchy there was no improvement, but the reverse. One well-informed correspondent went so far as to say boldly that the process of internal disintegration in Austria was speeding to its ultimate stage. He reported that in the Reichsrath discussions had made it plain that the domestic political differences were incapable of adjustment. The Socialists demanded autonomous reconstruction of the various constituents of the Empire. The Czechs and Jugo-Slavs would not be satisfied with less than the sovereignty of their national States. In Hungary Count Tisza, the ex-Premier and one of the authors of the war, pointedly referred to the fear that the course the war was taking would so materially affect the Dual Monarchy that it would be incumbent on all Hungarian patriots to think only of preserving the " thousand-year-old independence of Hungary " and to let Austria go. Dr. Wekerle, the Premier, tendered his resignation to the Emperor Charles. The Dual Monarchy was crumbling visibly.

Tisza, in a speech in the Lower House of the Hungarian Diet, frankly admitted that the war was lost. This was on October 18th, and it was on that very day that President Wilson said in his reply to the Austrian Note that he **Count Tisza admits defeat** could not entertain its suggestions, because events had altered the attitude of the United States to the Dual Monarchy since the delivery of his address giving the " fourteen points." The tenth of these points was that the peoples of Austria-Hungary, whose place among the nations America wished to see safeguarded and assured, should be accorded the freest opportunity of autonomous development.

Since that was uttered, the President reminded Austria, the United States had recognised the Czecho-Slovaks as belligerents and the Czecho-Slovak National Council as a Government. America, moreover, also recognised in the fullest manner the justice of the nationalistic aspirations of the Jugo-Slavs for freedom. Such being the case, Mr. Wilson declared that he was no longer at liberty to accept the mere autonomy of these peoples as a basis of peace, but was obliged to insist that they, and not he, should be the judges of what action on the part of the Austro-Hungarian Government would

FIRST PRESIDENT OF THE CZECHO-SLOVAKS.
Professor Masaryk, who on December 22nd, 1918, returned to Prague, after more than four years of exile. He was on the same day sworn in as first President of the Czecho-Slovak Republic, the establishment of which marked the end of nearly three centuries of Bohemia's national martyrdom.

THE DOOM OF GERMANY'S PIRATE FLEET

U boat 48 at Harwich, Nov. 24th, 1918, with the White Ensign flying above the German flag.

"*U boat Avenue, Harwich*": *Interned German submarines moored three abreast in the Sto*

...us of pirate ships surrendered to Admiral Sir Reginald Tyrwhitt, November 20-27th, 1918.

391

Crews of three German submarines leaving their vessels at Harwich after completing the surrender

German U boat crew awaiting return to their own country after hauling down the black flag.

satisfy their conception of their rights and destiny as members of the family of nations.

It was a curious coincidence that on that very day of October, too, the Czecho-Slovak Provisional Government, which had been formed by the National Council at Paris, with Masaryk as Prime Minister, issued a declaration of the independence of their nation. On the previous day the streets of Prague were placarded with posters announcing—

The time has arrived. We already have thrown off the fetters of subjugated Slavs. We have risen to independence by our unshakable will and with the sanction of the whole democratic world. We declare that we stand here to-day as representatives of a new State, as citizens of a free Czecho-Slovak Republic.

As against this, however, in Bohemia the German National Council, which represented the German element in that country, proclaimed its union with the German Empire, thus utterly rejecting the ideas of federation held at the moment by the Austrian Government. And about this time, to make confusion worse confounded in the Dual Monarchy, the Rumanian Deputies of Hungary constituted themselves into a Rumanian National Assembly. In Vienna it was stated that the " German-Austrian State " (Austria proper) would number about ten million German inhabitants, while the Czecho-Slovak State would include upwards of six million people, of whom four millions were in Bohemia, about two millions in Moravia, and a hundred thousand in Silesia.

It was in vain that the Emperor Charles—who, to do him justice, could scarcely be held personally responsible for the condition of his Empire—tried to pour oil on the troubled waters by issuing a manifesto in which he spoke of beginning the reconstruction of the Fatherland on a national basis, and said that Austria, in accordance with the will of her peoples, would become a Federal State, each race within its own domain forming a National State. He concluded with the hope that through the unanimity of the nations it embraced the Fatherland would emerge from the storms of the war fortified as a federation of free peoples. This manifesto was not addressed to Hungary; a message, however, was sent to the Austrian Army and Navy in which the Emperor again said that all the peoples of Austria, in accordance with their wishes, were being united in National States, together making one Federal State.

But the day had gone past in which there was any chance of saving Austria through federalism. And as for Hungary, the party which was led by Count Karolyi in **The " Liquidation** opposition to that headed by Wekerle, took **Ministry "** as its battle-cry in the Diet, " Long live an autonomous and independent Hungary !" At the peace negotiations, Karolyi declared, Hungary must be represented by her own delegates. Violently attacking Tisza and the pro-German party, he demanded that the authors of the war should be brought to the strictest account. Amid a perfect pandemonium one of Karolyi's followers shouted, " We are friends of the Entente !" A few days afterwards Karolyi read a telegram in the Diet announcing that a Croat infantry regiment at Fiume had disarmed the militia, occupied the principal buildings of the town, and seized the railway-station. Fiume, on the Gulf of Quarnero, was the Hungarian naval base on the Adriatic, but geographically it was part of Croatia. Though the mutiny was said to be quelled by three regiments brought from Albania, it was not the less an infallible sign of the times. Germany wirelessed that the fate of Fiume would be " settled at the

Peace Conference." Meanwhile, Croatia was falling away from the Dual Monarchy. In Agram, her capital, her leaders were making straight for independence.

Count Burian resigned as Foreign Secretary, and the Emperor Charles replaced him by Count Julius Andrassy on October 25th. Wekerle, the Hungarian Premier, again pressed his resignation, and Charles accepted it—but on the understanding that Wekerle and his Cabinet were to carry on the Government until the nomination of a new one. A little later the Austrian Cabinet, presided over by Hussarek, resigned, and the Emperor, for whom it was impossible not to feel some sympathy in a situation with which he was so ill-fitted to cope, made Professor Lammasch Premier of Austria. Lammasch's programme comprised the speedy

ITALY'S AIRMAN POET'S GREAT EXPLOIT.
Major Gabriele D'Annunzio, the famous Italian poet, telling of the success of a remarkable air raid to General Bongiovanni, commander of the Italian Flying Corps. On August 9th, 1918, Major D'Annunzio, in command of a squadron of eight aeroplanes, flew over Vienna, and dropped 200,000 manifestos, in German and Italian, urging the people to throw off their servitude to Prussia.

conclusion of peace, the transfer of affairs from the Central Government to National Governments, and the safeguarding of common interests in a Reconstruction Government. Lammasch and his Cabinet were known as the " Liquidation Ministry," and the justness of the phrase—though in a far wider sense than its authors intended—was to be quickly proved by events.

In the midst of the political maelstrom, that other chief factor in the general situation of the Dual Monarchy which was alluded to at the beginning of this chapter—hunger— was making itself felt in the most terrible manner. The gravity of the food question **Gravity of the** had been sharply accentuated by the action **food question** of the Czechs, who held up all supplies from German Austria, and of the Magyars, who insisted that Austria must fulfil her obligations to supply coal and oil in return for the feeding of the Army by Hungary. Austria had no coal to spare—had not enough for her own wants ; even Vienna, ravaged by influenza, was almost destitute of house coal.

The Czechs enforced a rigid boycott of food with respect to Austria, and the German and Austrian papers were full of articles on " The Starving Out of Austria," and " The National War of Starvation." The " Arbeiter Zeitung," of Vienna, said on October 20th that the supply of food from Bohemia and Moravia, from Hungary and Galicia, was at a standstill, and that there was no chance of restoring the flour ration or of meeting the demand for bread. It predicted a catastrophe unless relief came, and of that it saw no prospect whatever. "Hungary," cried this important Austrian journal, "declares her independence; without asking Austria she cuts all ties with us, and shows us her power to enforce her will by blocking our food supply."

On October 27th, amid these increasing portents of the dissolution of his Empire, the Emperor Charles issued an Order to his Army and Navy, in which he said: "The times are full of grave confusion, which must not spread to the Army and Navy." In spite of the grave confusion his armed forces, speaking broadly, still held together. They were strong in Galicia and formidable on the Italian front, though they were retreating as fast as they could in Serbia, Albania, and Montenegro. They continued to be loyal to the monarchy, and at least they were fed. They certainly constituted armies in being, and perhaps the Emperor Charles saw in them some hope of saving the Empire and his dynasty. If this were the case, a great Italian offensive, which began on October 27th, for ever dispelled any prospect of the sort.

By that date the general military situation had become most serious for Germany on the western **The great** front. Under the shattering strokes of the **Italian offensive** British, French, American, and Belgian Armies the Germans were in retreat eastward on much the greater part of the line, and were being given no respite. In the Balkans the Serbs were nearing Belgrade, and the Italians were on the confines of Montenegro. In the Palestine-Syria area Allenby had practically added the conquest of Syria to that of Palestine, while in Mesopotamia Marshall was marching on Mosul. Turkey was known to be at her last gasp—did, in point of fact, open negotiations with

a view to obtaining an armistice next day—October 28th. It was small wonder that Austria—or Germany, for that matter—was extremely anxious for peace, because of the military situation alone. But, as has been seen, Austria had other causes for the deepest anxiety. On top of all these came the Italian offensive, which resulted in the rout of her best armies. In that offensive British troops, under the command of General the Earl of Cavan, K.P., K.C.B., M.V.O., bore a distinguished part.

In a despatch, dated November 15th, 1918, Lord Cavan submitted a report on what the British forces in Italy did from the previous September 15th to the final defeat of the Austrian Army, and at the same time **Lord Cavan's** gave much information respecting General **Italian-British** Diaz's general plan of campaign, and the **command** way in which it worked out in action in the field. After the repulse of the Austrians on the Piave in the preceding June-July operations, little of importance occurred on the Italian front for some weeks, and early in September, as it appeared improbable that offensive operations would be undertaken in Italy in the near future, it was decided to assist France with some or all of the British troops who were then on Italian soil. Accordingly the 7th, 23rd, and 48th Divisions were reduced by three battalions each, and the nine battalions thus released were sent to France on September 13th and 14th. It was intended to despatch the 7th Division almost at once to the western front, its place being taken by a battle-worn division from France; then similarly the 23rd was to go next. But as a result of the tactical situation in France, and the consequent demands on rolling-stock, these exchanges were postponed from day to day. The situation in Italy also was changing, and finally the three divisions remained in that country.

ITALIAN AIRMEN "SNOW" LEAFLETS OVER THE AUSTRIAN CAPITAL.

Photograph showing a shower of leaflets falling over Central Vienna during the wonderful raid made by a squadron of Italian aeroplanes under Major Gabriele D'Annunzio, the famous poet, on August 9th, 1918. This striking photograph, which was taken by one of the raiding airmen, shows St. Stephen's Cathedral in the top right-hand corner, and even reveals the lines of the coloured tiles with which the roof is covered.

BRITISH TORPEDO-BOAT HAILED BY WELCOMING CROWDS AT A HUNGARIAN PORT.

Arrival at Fiume of H.M.S. Martin (No. 19), one of the British torpedo-boats which reached that port in November, 1918, shortly after the signing of the armistice. The streets were beflagged, and vast crowds of the mixed population enthusiastically cheered the visitors, whose arrival was recognised as showing that the long nightmare of war was ending. Fiume is at the head of the Gulf of Quarnero, seventy miles south-east of Trieste.

General Diaz had decided on an offensive, and on October 6th Lord Cavan was offered the command of a mixed Italian-British army, with a view to attacking the Austrians at an early date. Secrecy being vital to success, as little change as possible in the dispositions of the troops was made, and, also to mislead the enemy, the 48th Division remained in position on the Asiago plateau, passing temporarily under the command of General Pennella, the head of the Twelfth Italian Corps. A week later Diaz explained his plans at a conference of his army commanders. Lord Cavan detailed them thus in his despatch :

The general plan for the main attack was to advance across the Piave with the Tenth, Eighth, and Twelfth Italian Armies—to drive a wedge between the Fifth and Sixth Austrian Armies—forcing the Fifth Army eastwards and threatening the communications of the Sixth Army running through the Valmarino Valley. The Fourth Italian Army was simultaneously to take the offensive in the Grappa Valley. The task allotted to the Tenth Army was to reach the Livenza between Portobuffole and Sacile, and thus protect the flank of the Eighth and Twelfth Armies in their move northwards. The co-ordination of the attacks of the Tenth, Eighth, and Twelfth Armies was entrusted to General Caviglia, the commander of the Eighth Army.

It was the Tenth Army that Lord Cavan commanded, and on October 11th its Headquarters were established at Treviso. At first it consisted of the Eleventh Italian Corps, under General Paolini, and the Fourteenth British Corps, commanded by Lieut.-General Sir J. M. Babington, K.C.M.G., C.B. The Italian corps already held a sector on the Piave stretching from Ponte di Piave to Palazzon ; the British were rushed down from the mountains and concentrated in the Treviso area on October 16th. Cavan's forces had to cross the Piave, and how this was to be accomplished was a difficult problem. The breadth of the river on the front of attack was about a mile and a half, in a series of channels interspersed with islands. The main island, which was held by the Austrians as an advanced post, was the Grave di Papadopoli, some three miles long by one mile broad. The current varied according to the channels, running in the principal channel at the rate of more than ten miles an hour in time of flood, and never dropping below three and a half miles an hour at summer level.

Dispositions of Italian armies

On October 21st the British came into line by taking over from the Italians the northern part of the front the latter had held, extending from Salettuol to Palazzon. To conceal this change from the Austrians all troops visible to the enemy wore Italian caps and cloaks, and orders were given that no British gun was to fire a shot before the general bombardment.

On the suggestion of General Babington, Lord Cavan decided to occupy the island of Grave di Papadopoli previous to the general advance on the front. The Piave was in full flood, which not only made reconnaissances of the river-bed impossible, but also suggested the probability of changes in the main channels ; yet on the night of October 23rd-24th, men of the Honourable Artillery Company and of the Welsh Fusiliers, without any previous artillery preparation, crossed the main channel, which was like a torrent, surprised the Austrian garrison, and occupied the northern half of the island. It was a wonderful feat. How it was done was told by a correspondent :

H.A.C. and Welsh cross the Piave

A special fleet, full fifty of them, of a particular type of small, flat-bottomed boat was constituted under an " admiral," an Italian officer named Odini. Sailors and engineers who knew all the treacherous and dangerous currents of the river, which is always shifting and changing, were put in charge of these boats, which held half a dozen men in each. At some points several streams had to be crossed from islet to islet, so that a relay system had to be adopted, ten boats going over and back, while others filled up the gaps. The crossing was made in the night, and the surprise was so complete that part of the garrison were caught in their sleep, and the Welshmen were well entrenched before the Austrians on the farther bank were alive to the situation. They attacked then, however, with undeniable vigour and courage, sending reinforcements over promptly, but were firmly held, and by mid-day the whole north of the island was in our hands, and 700 prisoners had been taken.

In his despatch Lord Cavan reported that the movement owed its success to the careful arrangements made by the 7th Division, the untiring energy of Captain Odini, of the Italian Engineers, and of the Italian pontiere under his command, and to the fine leading of Lieut.-Colonel R. N. O'Connor, D.S.O., M.C., commanding the 2/1st Honourable Artillery Company. The Commander-in-Chief, in particular, spoke very highly of the services rendered by the pontiere,

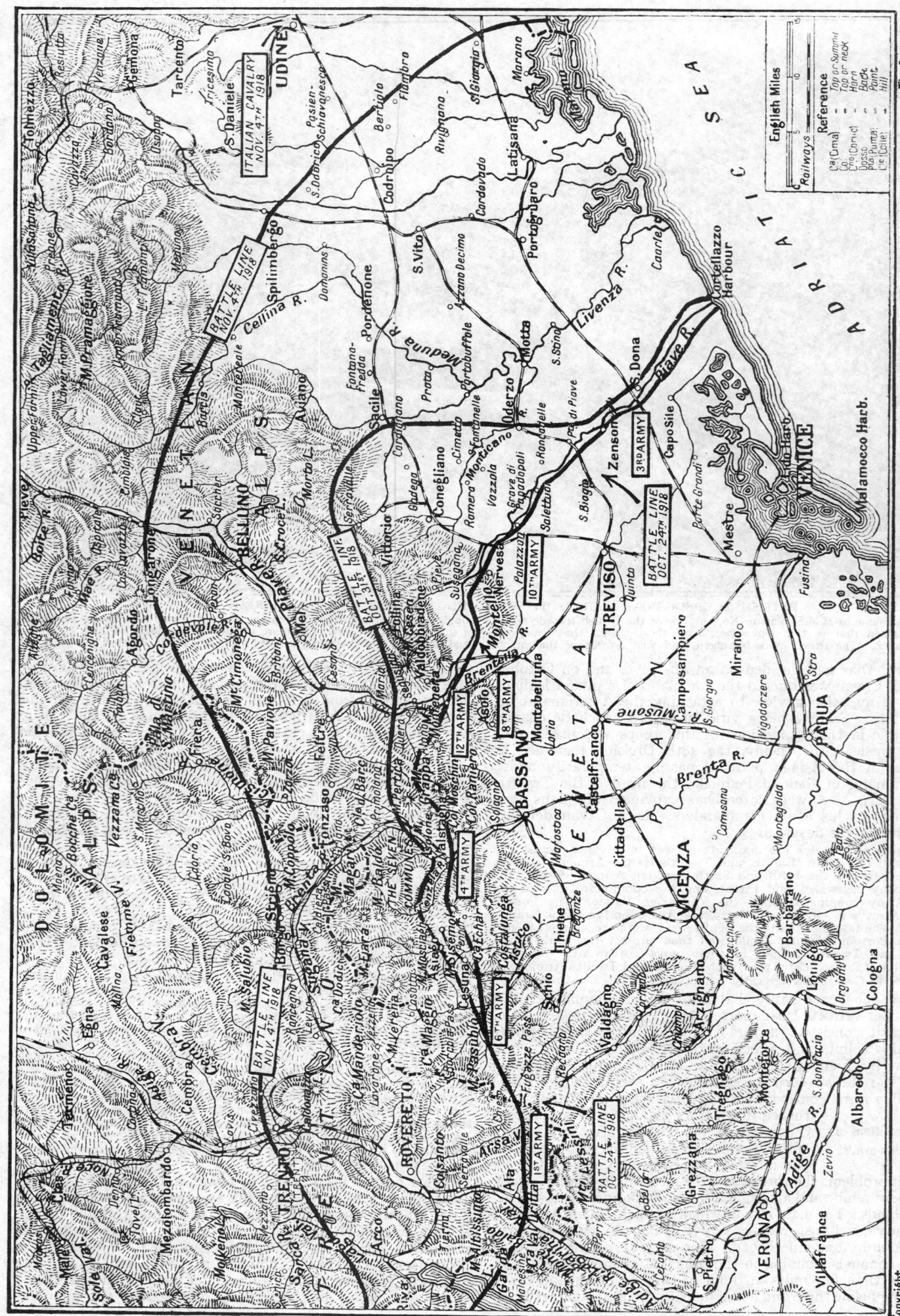

Copyright   The Great War

AREA COVERED BY THE GREAT ITALIAN OFFENSIVE OF OCTOBER, 1918, WHICH RESULTED IN AUSTRIA'S FINAL DEFEAT AND COLLAPSE.

On October 24th the Fourth Italian Army, commanded by General Giardino, launched its attack in the Monte
Grappa sector. On October 27th the Tenth Army, commanded by Lord Cavan, with the Twelfth and Eighth

Armies, crossed the Piave, bridging the Livenza on November 1st and reaching the Tagliamento on November 3rd,
while farther west Trent had passed into the possession of the Italians. Next day Austria was out of the war,

both in the transport of the troops by boat and in the subsequent bridging of the river, and declared that it was impossible to overestimate the value of their help. On the night of October 25-26th the conquest of the island was completed by a combined movement of the 7th British Division from the north and the 37th Italian Division from the south. The Austrians put up a fight, but they withered away under the sustained machine-gun and rifle fire of the British. This thoroughly successful operation placed the main channel of the Piave *behind* the British, and enabled them to begin their bridges and preparations for the main attack in comparative security, although on the island they were subjected to very heavy shelling during the whole of October 26th.

General Diaz began his offensive on the Piave with a

LOST TO THE HUN.
The Austrian battleship Prinz Rupert and destroyers lying in Cattaro Harbour after their seizure by the Jugo-Slavs.

tremendous bombardment of the Austrian front at 11.30 on the night of October 26th. Up to that moment not a single British gun had opened fire on the enemy. Both heavy and field artillery were registered by the 6th Field Service Company, R.E., and they did their work well, for the bombardment and the subsequent barrage were excellent. In the Monte Grappa sector a change in the original plan of Diaz had been shown by the Fourth Italian Army, which was commanded by General Giardino, beginning a vigorous attack on the Austrians on October 24th, which, notwithstanding very bad weather, resulted in a considerable gain of ground and the taking of 4,000 prisoners. In mist and rain, which prevented a barrage, the Italians did not hesitate to assault a line of fifteen miles of mountain heights between the Brenta and the Piave. In this way did they commemorate the first anniversary of Caporetto and pay back some of the debt then incurred. On the 26th the action, to which the continued bad weather

Anniversary of Caporetto had put a stop temporarily, was renewed by the Italians, who after very bitter fighting, with the repulse of incessant counter-attacks, succeeded in capturing Monte Pertica, and later extended their occupation beyond that dominating height.

At 6.45 a.m. on October 27th Cavan launched the attack of the Tenth Army against the enemy defences east of the Piave. On the right the Eleventh Italian Corps, under Paolini, attacked with the 23rd Bersagliere Division, commanded by General Fara, on its right, and the 37th Italian Division on its left. On the left the Fourteenth British Corps attacked with the 7th Division, under Major-General T. H. Shoubridge, C.B., C.M.G., D.S.O., on its right, and the 23rd British Division, under Major-General H. F. Thuillier, C.B., C.M.G., on its left. The British attacking troops moved up from the western

side of the island of Papadopoli, in the midst of a deluge of rain, and reached the eastern bank by half-past five in the morning. When the signal to advance came off they plunged into the river, and struggled forward in the bitterly cold and furious current. The men joined hands in the black darkness of the night and together strove against the swirling waters, but some were swept away and were drowned. Pitilessly the rain beat down on the gallant troops, who had more than a quarter of a mile to swim, wade, and trudge before coming under the protection of their artillery barrage. Those who first reached the east bank of the Piave clung to it, and stretched out an arm to those nearest them; they in their turn held out a hand to those behind them, and so chains **Tenth Army's rapid progress** were formed until all were across. Then they had to force their way through scrub, brush, and hedges up to a line of thick-growing acacia trees, which the Austrians had joined up with wire to make a barricade. Having successfully dealt with this, they stormed an embankment filled with machine-guns, and then carried a series of entrenched block-houses which had been fortified with every conceivable device. In many cases the defenders fought courageously, in others they yielded after a short struggle. For the most part they proved to be Hungarian soldiers. The advance of the British was pushed forward with the utmost

ENEMY MEN-OF-WAR IN THE HANDS OF THE ALLIES.
Austria's battleship Erzherzog Friedrich Karl and her light cruiser Novara in Cattaro Harbour. At the beginning of November, 1918, the Jugo-Slavs, revolting from Austria's rule, seized the whole of the existing Austro-Hungarian Fleet and held it at the disposal of the Allies.

determination. Before the night fell a large bridge-head had been gained and consolidated, and half a dozen villages were in their hands.

In this attack the Honourable Artillery Company and the Welshmen, who were the first to reach the farther side of the river, showed conspicuous coolness while crossing under fire and great bravery in meeting the counter-attacks of the enemy on the bank. Later they gave place to larger and stronger formations, which included Northumberland Fusiliers, Yorkshires, Lancashires, Durham Light Infantry, Queen's, South Staffordshires, Manchesters, Borderers, men of Devon, and Gordons. Lord Cavan specially commended the action of the 22nd Battalion Manchester Regiment and the 11th Battalion Northumberland Fusiliers. During the day the bridging of the Piave went on apace, though the Engineers were incessantly assailed by enemy aircraft, and in any case were hard put to it to contend with the current, but they threw two bridges across the river. Six miles away the Eighth Italian Army had also effected a landing, but was less fortunate with its bridging operations, particularly at the point of junction with Cavan's forces. Thereupon General Diaz allotted the Eighteenth Italian Corps, under General Basso, to Cavan, with a view to passing it across the Piave

ITALY AND HER "REDEEMED" TERRITORIES.
Those portions of Italy of which Austria had possessed herself in the past, "Italia Irredenta," or "un-redeemed" Italy—Trentino, Istria, and part of the Dalmatian coast—were vacated by Austria in accordance with the terms of the armistice of November 3rd, 1918.

With a view to clearing the front of the Third Italian Army the Bersaglieri, who had been with the British, joined that army and were replaced by another Italian regiment. At the same time the 31st Italian Division, which included the 332nd American Regiment, was added to Cavan's command. In face of very considerable resistance—the last serious stand east of the Piave made by the Austrians—passages of the Monticano were forced on the night of October 29-30th. Chiefly by "very gallant work," to quote Lord Cavan, "on the part of the 8th Battalion Yorkshire Regiment," the enemy was skilfully manœuvred out of the rest of his defences on the river. "From that moment the defeat became a rout." On the 30th the British reached the Livenza, and crossed it next day. Part of the Italian forces crossed the Lower Piave, and on October 31st was advancing rapidly to the same river, which was bridged by the British on November 1st, while Italian cavalry went in hot pursuit of the retreating Austrians. On the 3rd, Cavan was on the Tagliamento, and on the following day all was over—Austria, utterly defeated, was out of the war. Inside a week the British, in their victorious advance, took 28,000 prisoners and 219 guns.

While this magnificent movement of Cavan's had been proceeding, the 48th British Division, commanded by Major-General Sir H. H. Walker, K.C.B., D.S.O., had remained on the Asiago plateau, and formed part of the Sixth Italian Army. During October it had carried out several successful raids, in the course of which it captured 445 prisoners and a number of machine-guns. On the 30th of that month, it having been discovered that the Austrians had withdrawn from their positions, Walker's patrols pushed beyond Asiago, and found the enemy entrenched about Monte Catz. On November 1st the Royal Berkshires took that height, and early next morning Walker was in possession also of Monte Mosciagh, rapidly advancing thereafter. By dark his forward troops had reached Vezzena, on Austrian soil. In his comment on this, Lord Cavan stated that by this success the 48th was the first British division to enter enemy territory on the western front. On November 4th the leading companies of this British force were on the outskirts of Trent. In the advance the division attacked most formidable mountain positions, climbing up to heights of 5,000 feet, and it took more than 20,000 prisoners and over 500 guns.

An Italian official communiqué, dated November 4th, gave a condensed account of the tremendous victory brought about by the general offensive of Diaz—in which the British had so brilliant a share. It **Caporetto amply avenged** stated that there were engaged on the side of the Allies fifty-one Italian divisions, three British, two French, one Czecho-Slovak division, and one American regiment. It said, with respect to the operations in the Trentino, that the daring and very rapid advance of the Twenty-ninth Italian Corps on Trent, closing up the way of the enemy's armies in the Trentino, who were overcome to the west by troops of the Seventh Army and to the east by those of the First, Sixth, and Fourth Armies, determined the total collapse of the enemy's front. It spoke of the advance

by the British bridges, whence it was to attack northwards and clear the front of the Eighth Italian Army.

In the morning of October 28th Cavan renewed his attack on the Austrians, and by dark his army had made a considerable advance, his patrols pushing towards and up to the Monticano. The success of these operations brought about the result which had been aimed at. The hold of the enemy on the high ground about Susegana weakened, and during the ensuing night the right wing of the Eighth Italian Army crossed the river about Nervesa, the Eighteenth Corps rejoining it, after having contributed materially to Cavan's rapid forward move, which was resumed next day, his whole army reaching the Monticano from Fontanelle to Ramera.

Much of this quick advance was due to the vigorous action of the Fourteenth Corps Mounted Troops, under Lieut.-Colonel Sir C. B. Lowther, D.S.O., who rode on in front of the infantry and secured the bridge over the Monticano between Vazzola and Cimetta intact, though it had been prepared for demolition. By the evening of the 29th, Lord Cavan noted, the Austrian defence showed manifest signs of crumbling, and numerous fires in rear of the enemy lines suggested that a far-reaching withdrawal was contemplated.

of the Third Army in the plains, and then summed up the whole situation:

The Austro-Hungarian Army is destroyed. It suffered very heavy losses in the fierce resistance of the first days of the struggle and in the pursuit. It has lost an immense quantity of material of all kinds, and nearly all its stores and depots. It has left in our hands about 300,000 prisoners with commands complete, and not less than 5,000 guns. Those left of that which was one of the most powerful armies in the world are in disorder and without hope, returning along the valleys from which they had descended with haughty assurance.

Up till the afternoon of November 4th the pursuit continued, and before three o'clock Trent itself, as well as Udine, on the east, had passed into the possession of the Italians. In the north the remnants of the Austrian forces were driven far into the mountains. In the plains the cavalry threw into panic large units that were still on the march backward, encircled them, and compelled them to surrender. Very little of the once great Austrian Army remained in existence. Caporetto was amply avenged. At three o'clock that afternoon hostilities ceased. An armistice had been arranged. So far as the Dual Monarchy was concerned the war was over.

As early as the evening of October 29th an overture was made with a view to obtaining an armistice. Under a white flag an Austrian officer came into the Italian trenches in the Adige Valley; but it was ascertained that he was without the authoritative documents required in the circumstances, and he was sent back to the enemy lines. Next morning the Austrian General von Weber, a corps commander, accompanied by other officers and some highly-

AMMUNITION BY AIR.
Italian artillerymen receiving a heavy shell lowered to their isolated emplacement by hand "teleferica."

placed civilians, and bearing the proper credentials, was received under a white flag by the Italians and taken to a villa close to the Headquarters of General Diaz, where they were courteously treated. On November 3rd General Badoglio, the Italian Chief of Staff, met them in this villa, and after a time gave them a written draft of the terms of an armistice. Meanwhile Diaz had exchanged telegrams with the Supreme War Council at Versailles, and in the afternoon the precise details under which the armistice would be granted were sent to him by Signor Orlando, the Italian Prime Minister—it was these that were handed to Weber by Badoglio. One of the Austrians took, by motor-car, the draft for communication to the Austrian Government.

While the great battle was being fought from the Brenta to the sea, things were not exactly standing still within the Monarchy itself, or elsewhere. Vienna was in a ferment, and revolutionary outbreaks were imminent. Troops made demonstrations in the streets of Budapest, where Soviets of Soldiers and Workmen were formed on the Bolshevist model. In both cities the cry was raised of "Down with the Hapsburgs!" All the archdukes were said to have fled from the capitals to their estates. Neither Andrassy nor even Karolyi appeared to be able to ride the storm. On November 1st news came that Count Tisza, while walking with a relative, was killed by a soldier with a shot from a revolver. His great aim in life had been the complete Magyarisation of Hungary, whom he

BRIDGING THE CHASMS IN MOUNTAIN RANGES.
The "teleferica," or cable railway, was one of the most useful devices of the Italian engineers. These photographs show ammunition arriving at the landing-station of a hand "teleferica" on a mountain road, and (in circle) lowering wounded to an aid-post.

wished to be the predominant partner in the Empire, and he was the determined opponent of the Slavs, Italians, and Rumanians who lived within it.

The Austro-Hungarian Government sent a Note to President Wilson in reply to his of October 18th. Dated October 29th, it announced that Austria-Hungary " adhered to the previous declarations of the President and his views with respect to the peoples of the Empire, notably the Czecho-Slovaks and the Jugo-Slavs, contained in his last Note. " This being the case," the Note continued, " nothing stood in the way of opening negotiations for an armistice and for peace, and the Austro-Hungarian Government therefore was **Unconditional** ready, without waiting for the outcome of **surrender of Austria** other negotiations, to enter into negotiations for a separate peace with the Entente Powers and for an immediate armistice on all the fronts of the Dual Monarchy. Finally, it begged Mr. Wilson to take such measures as were required in the circumstances.

As Austria now accepted all the President's conditions and sought for a separate armistice immediately, the very great importance of this action of her Government was at once perceived by the Allies. It was plain that Austria had thrown Germany over and had resolved to act alone. By this time it was known in the allied countries that Turkey was seeking an armistice. Probably Austria also was aware of this, and was influenced by it. It looked as if Germany would be absolutely isolated, and there was no possibility of minimising what that meant. Assuredly the end was drawing near. On October 30th Turkey surrendered unconditionally, and was granted an armistice, which came into operation at noon next day. Doubtless this capitulation, expected though it must have been, had its due effect on Austria. Germany herself was being relentlessly pressed and driven back, with enormous losses, in the west, and her military prestige was in eclipse.

Accepting the terms which had been communicated by General Diaz, on behalf of the Associated Powers, the High Command of the Dual Monarchy signed the armistice, which was equivalent to an unconditional surrender, on November 3rd, and it went into effect at 3 p.m. on the following day. Summarised, the terms were :

The total demobilisation of the Austro-Hungarian Army, and the immediate withdrawal of all Austro-Hungarian forces operating on the front from the North Sea to Switzerland. Twenty divisions, but of pre-war strength, were allowed to be kept within Austro-Hungarian territory. Half the divisional corps and army artillery with equipment was to be delivered, at stated points, to the victors.

The evacuation of all invaded territories, and the withdrawal of the Austro-Hungarian Armies on each front behind a line, which, according to a statement made by Mr. Lloyd George in Parliament on November 5th, afforded strategic safeguards for Italy's Alpine frontier. " From the Swiss frontier," said the Prime Minister, " this line follows the watershed of the Rhaetian, Carnic, and Julian Alps to the Gulf of Fiume, excluding the port of that name. It compels Austria-Hungary to evacuate all Tyrol south of the Brenner Pass, and also to evacuate the Carso plateau and the Istrian peninsula, which, of course, includes Trieste. (The Italians had entered that town, the port of which was the best on the Adriatic, on the morning of November 3rd.) Farther south the Austro-Hungarian forces have to evacuate the province of Dalmatia and the Dalmatian islands with the exception of the islands in the Gulf of Spalato." All military and railway equipment, including coal, in the territories to be evacuated had to be surrendered.

The Allies were to have the right to move freely over all Austro-Hungarian roads, railways, and waterways, and to use the necessary Austrian and Hungarian means of transportation. The armies of the Associated Powers were to occupy such strategic points as they deemed necessary to enable them to conduct military operations or maintain order, and were to have the right of requisition, on payment, for the troops.

The complete evacuation of all German troops within fifteen days, not only from the Italian and Balkan fronts, but from all Austro-Hungarian territory. All German troops not so evacuated were to be interned.

The immediate repatriation, without reciprocity, of all allied prisoners of war and interned subjects, and of civil populations which had been removed from their homes. Sick and wounded, who were unable to be moved from the evacuated territory, were to be cared for by Austrian and Hungarian personnel.

The naval terms of the armistice were not less onerous :

Definite information regarding the location and movements of all Austro-Hungarian ships was to be given, and neutrals were to be notified that the naval and merchant marines of the Associated Powers could freely navigate all Austro-Hungarian territorial waters.

Three battleships, three light cruisers, nine destroyers, twelve torpedo-boats, one mine-layer, and six Danube monitors, to be designated with their complete armament and equipment, were to be surrendered. All other surface warships were to be concentrated, paid off and disarmed, and then placed under the supervision of the Associated Powers. Fifteen submarines, completed between the years 1910 and 1918, and all the German submarines in, or which might come into, Austro-Hungarian waters, also had to be surrendered. All other Austro-Hungarian submarines had to be paid off, disarmed, and placed under the supervision of the Associated Powers.

The free navigation by all warships and merchant vessels of the Associated Powers of the Adriatic and the Danube and its tributaries, to ensure which power was given to occupy or dismantle all fortifications or defence works. On the other hand, the blockade was to remain unchanged, and all Austro-Hungarian merchant ships found at sea were still liable to capture.

All naval aircraft were to be concentrated and immobilised.

The evacuation of all the Italian coasts and of all ports occupied by Austria-Hungary outside their national territory, and the abandonment of all floating craft, naval materials, equipment, and materials for inland navigation. The occupation by the Associated Powers of the land and sea fortifications and the islands forming the defences of the dockyards and arsenal of Pola.

All naval and merchant marine prisoners of war were to be returned without reciprocity, and all merchant vessels of the Associated Powers were to be restored.

Without an Army and without a Fleet—for such was the effect of the armistice—Austria was reduced to utter impotency ; whereas Italy, whom both Germany and Austria had derided, was triumphant, and at last was mistress in her own house, after a moral recovery—as one writer finely phrased it —from a crushing disaster scarce paralleled in history. The Czecho-Slovaks and the Jugo-Slavs, already freeing themselves by their own efforts, had their independence now doubly assured. The Serbs were back in Belgrade, on November 1st, and across the Drina and the Save were marching on Sarajevo. And as for Mackensen, still sitting in Bukarest, nothing was left, if he were to save himself, but retreat.

On the military debacle of the Dual Monarchy, the internal political debacle was equally manifest. In the north, Bohemia, Moravia, and the Slovak districts formed one republic, while German Austria was another ; Galicia was split up between the Poles and the Ruthenes. Hungary, as regarded its predominantly Magyar part, was under a National Council, which the Archduke Joseph, who earlier had represented the Emperor in Budapest, and his son the Archduke Franz Joseph, had promised on oath to obey ; it virtually also was a republic. In Transylvania the Rumanians, who had endured so much at the hands of the Magyars, were joining Rumania, who was once more raising her head. National Councils of the Jugo-Slavs were meeting in Agram and Laibach, and Bosnia and Herzegovina were in process of becoming part of a great New Serbia under King Peter. The wonderful thing was that all this really gigantic revolution was accomplished with hardly any bloodshed. Finally, there no longer existed Italia Irredenta, for redeemed Italy was being occupied by Italians.

On November 12th the Emperor Charles announced his abdication in a proclamation that, at least, was not lacking in dignity. He said :

Ever since my accession to the throne I have unceasingly tried to deliver my peoples from the tremendous war, for which I bear no responsibility. I have not retarded the re-establishment of constitutional life, and I have reopened to my people the way to solid national development. Filled with unalterable love for all my peoples, I will not in my person be a hindrance to their free development. I acknowledge the decision of German Austria to take for the future the form of a separate State. The people have by their Deputies taken charge of the Government. I **Abdication of** relinquish all participation in the administration of the State. I likewise release my Austrian **the Emperor** Ministers from their office. May the German-Austrian people harmoniously and peacefully adjust themselves to the new conditions. The happiness of my peoples has from the beginning been the object of my warmest wishes. Internal peace alone will be able to heal the wounds which this war has caused.

This document was countersigned by Lammasch, the head of the " Liquidation Ministry." A day or two later it was announced from Budapest that the Emperor Charles had also relinquished the throne of Hungary. The disintegration of the Austrian Empire was complete. It was more than disintegration : it was dissolution. But mankind had little to thank Austria for ; she had been art and part with Germany in this war. She was guilty. And the Muse of History had few tears to shed when she inscribed " Finis ! " over Austria.

PRISONERS GOING TO WORK

CHAPTER CCLXXVII.

UNDER AN ARMED GUARD.

GREAT BRITAIN'S HUMANE TREATMENT OF GERMAN PRISONERS OF WAR.

By Robert Machray.

False Statements of German Leaders—Hindenburg's Allegations Refuted—Disinterested Evidence—Reports of Americans when the United States was a Neutral—Statement of International Red Cross—Great Britain without Machinery at First for Dealing With Prisoners of War—Steps Taken Promptly—Prison Camps and Ships—Magnificent Work of Prisoners of War Information Bureau—Organisation of Prisoners of War Department of the War Office—Extension of the Camps—Prisoners Well-Fed and Cheerful—Just Treatment as Regards their Labour—What they Did and How they Were Paid—Their Fair Rations in the Time of Straitness—Their Guards—Only Four Escapes from the United Kingdom in the Whole War—Testimony of Prisoners Themselves of Good Treatment—Undeniable Witness to the Humanity of the British.

N O one who knew the British people at all well would believe that their treatment of prisoners of war, German or otherwise, was cruel and barbarous, or was in any way like that which British prisoners of war suffered at the hands of the Germans, as recorded in Chapter XCII. (Vol. 5, page 250), Chapter CLXVII. (Vol. 8, page 453), and Chapter CCXLI. (Vol. 11, page 293). Those chapters show conclusively that the Germans, with a few marked exceptions, regarded and treated their British prisoners as criminals to be punished with the most savage brutality, in spite of the fact that The Hague Convention, to which they themselves were a party, specially guarded as honourable the status of all prisoners of war, and protected them accordingly. As with other compacts, this agreement was in German eyes a mere scrap of paper, to be torn up or thrown aside at convenience. Furthermore, German culpability in this grave matter was distinctly aggravated by assertions, made by their military chiefs, as well as in the Reichstag, that the British treatment of German prisoners was horrible and vile beyond expression.

These assertions of the military and political leaders of Germany were clearly against the light, for they knew perfectly well that there was no truth in them. To suit a special occasion they admitted as much. Thus, in the Reichstag in 1917, Dr. Kriege, of the German

LIEUT.-GENERAL SIR HERBERT BELFIELD, K.C.B., D.S.O.
Having been in charge of the arrangements for enemy prisoners from the outset of the war, Sir Herbert Belfield was, in February, 1915, appointed Director of the then newly-established Directorate of Prisoners of War.

Foreign Office, stated that the treatment of prisoners of war was better in England than anywhere else, but the circumstances in which he spoke were significant. He was explaining why certain exchanges of prisoners, under specific agreements between Great Britain and Germany, were not being carried out by Germany, and said it was for "naval reasons," a specious phrase which covered the malign activities of the U boats. Germany was much more eager to sink British ships than to facilitate the release from captivity even of her own nationals. To quiet the fears, however, of the relatives and friends of these German prisoners, he assured them that there was no need for anxiety, as prisoners of war were not maltreated by the British. This was not the view usually presented to the Germans, whose "hate" of the British was stimulated by terrible pictures of the ruthless manner in which their fellow-countrymen were dealt with in the United Kingdom.

An instance of this was noted in Chapter CCXLI. (page 299). When visiting a hospital behind the western front, Hindenburg sharply rated, and then discharged, an English-speaking German woman who had been nursing some British officers captured on the field of battle in the neighbourhood. The Field-Marshal declared that he would not permit them to be treated better than were "his brave soldiers who were so unfortunate as to be prisoners of war in England." His words were widely quoted throughout Germany as indicating the harsh treatment of German prisoners by Great Britain. That must have been the impression which he intended to give, and it was a deliberate misrepresentation, for from his position he could not but be well aware that German prisoners were treated in hospital precisely the same as British soldiers, no difference being made between them by the doctors and nurses.

Wherever it was practicable, German-speaking nurses were provided for these prisoners; besides, official interpreters were in attendance, and when these were unavailable the orderlies made use of small conversation books, furnished for the express purpose, in order that they might understand and minister to the requirements of these Germans. Such were the facts, and it was impossible to believe that Hindenburg was not familiar with them, particularly as the war had been going on for more than two years when he made his statement.

Hindenburg's calumniating remark was published in January, 1917. Long before that the German Government, through the medium of the American Embassy in Berlin and from other disinterested sources, had obtained unimpeachable evidence with respect to the British treatment of German prisoners of war. In his famous book, "My Four Years in Germany," Mr. James W. Gerard stated that, when he was American Ambassador, so many reports came to Germany about the "bad treatment in England of German prisoners of war" that he arranged to send a member of his staff to Great Britain to investigate and say what really was the case. This gentleman was the **American inquiry** Hon. John B. Jackson, formerly American **into the facts** Minister to the Balkan States, who had volunteered to assist Mr. Gerard at the beginning of the war. He had been Secretary of the Embassy in Berlin for twelve years in a previous period of his career, and therefore was well acquainted not only with Germany but with German official life and customs. He also was the personal choice of the German authorities for this particular inquiry.

The British Government, before whom the matter was brought by Mr. Page, then American Ambassador in London, gave permission to Mr. Jackson to inspect all the prison camps in the United Kingdom, a task for which he was peculiarly well qualified, inasmuch as he had conducted similar investigations with regard to the prison camps in Germany a short time before.

Mr. Jackson arrived in England in the course of the winter of 1914-15, and he was authorised by the British Government to visit all the prison camps in the country without any previous intimation of his coming, and to talk freely with any of the German prisoners without any third party being present. He issued his report in April, 1915, having gone over thirteen places and nine ships in which were interned Germans, of whom there were then about 26,000, the great majority being civilians, including ordinary seamen. At that time there were more than 70,000 German subjects or persons of German birth in the United Kingdom, and the number of those interned was under 20,000. Mr. Jackson heard of no woman being interned. He was given every opportunity of seeing everything, and of finding out anything if there was anything to find out.

He conversed with the prisoners, and listened to all they had to tell him; there was no supervision, dictation, or interference of any sort by the British authorities during these talks; Mr. Jackson and the prisoners were left absolutely to themselves, and he got at what really was in their minds. Twice he had luncheon with German officer prisoners, no British officer or soldier being present. Without exception the German officers assured him that they had always been treated as "officers and gentlemen" by the British. He discovered that while in their camps these officers did practically what they pleased, and that there was no direct contact between them and the British officers and soldiers on guard, except when they were outside the wire enclosure.

Speaking of the camps generally, Mr. Jackson noted that the German prisoners did their own police and fatigue work. He observed that at Frith Hill Camp, at Frimley, near Aldershot, the prisoners ran their "own

"NOT SINGLE SPIES, BUT IN BATTALIONS."
Batch of German prisoners taken by the British in France. The men, assembled at one of the clearing depots, represented a single day's capture on one sector of the front. On each successive day during the closing months of the war the depot was thronged by a similar crowd of captives.

PRISONERS ON LAND WORK.
German prisoners of war, under an armed escort, setting out with their digging implements to get land ready for planting fruit trees.

Mr. Jackson's report dealt with part of the first year of the war, when Great Britain, caught utterly unprepared, had to improvise accommodation for prisoners of war while, at the same time, she had to improvise a thousand other things—armies, munitions, and pretty nearly everything else. These were the circumstances to which Mr. Jackson alluded in the foregoing quotation. But his report was by no means the only one issued by representatives of the American Government. For instance, in a White Paper which was presented to Parliament in September, 1916, there were published reports by officials of the United States Embassy in London giving particulars of visits they had paid to a considerable number of places of internment during the preceding months of that year.

RUTHLESS DESTROYERS SET TO CONSTRUCTIVE LABOUR.
Digging and preparing the ground in readiness for planting young trees on a large English fruit farm. German prisoners of war employed on work which contrasted greatly with the hideous destruction in which they indulged as invaders of Belgium and France.

little republic under their non-commissioned officers," who were responsible to the British military authorities, and that they had their own police, "even their secret police." At all camps opportunities were given for exercise, which, however, was not obligatory, though prisoners had to spend so many hours daily outside their sleeping quarters. Employment or work apart from what was necessary in the camps had not at that time been provided for any of the interned.

Soldiers who had no uniforms were permitted to wear civilian clothes, and when civilians had not the means to buy such things as blankets, shoes, and clothing they got them from the British Government. Books published before the war in English and other languages were allowed, as were British newspapers after January, 1915. The prisoners were under the same regulations as in Germany with respect to the receipt and the despatch of letters; the rules regarding receiving or sending money were the same. The food was practically the ration of the British soldier, and the prisoners thought it satisfactory. The free use of tobacco was permitted, as, in most camps, also were visitors.

There were no complaints, except from some of the civilians who had been taken from neutral ships or had been arrested in the Colonies, but their complaints were **Hon. J. B. Jackson's** concerned with the manner of their arrest **impartial report** and their treatment before being brought to the internment camps—not with their treatment in them. As the result of his independent and impartial survey, Mr. Jackson concluded his report with the following statement:

On the whole, the present treatment seems to be as good as could be expected in the circumstances. The new camps are all better than the old ones, and everywhere there seemed to be an intention to improve on existing conditions. Lack of organisation and preparation would account for most of the hardships which prevailed at first. Absolutely nowhere did there seem to be any wish to make the conditions any harder or more disagreeable for the prisoners than was necessary, and I saw no instance, and heard of none, where any prisoners had been subjected either to intentional personal annoyance or undeserved discipline.

Among the camps inspected were the large civilian camp at Knockaloe, in the Isle of Man, and the camps at Stobbs, in Scotland; the Alexandra Palace; Handforth, in Cheshire; Eastcote, in Northants; Dorchester; Lofthouse, near Wakefield; Oldcastle, in County Meath; and Douglas, in the Isle of Man; as well as many others. All these reports have one feature in common—no complaints; considering their position, the prisoners were uniformly well satisfied. Certainly there was no harshness of any sort in their treatment; on the contrary, everything that was possible was done for them.

All these American reports were transmitted through the United States Embassy in Berlin to the German Government, and the tenor of them, if not their very words, must have been known to Hindenburg, as to many other, if not to all, German leaders. In addition to these reports, there were others giving as independent and impartial accounts of the British treatment of prisoners of war. Thus, as far back as February, 1915, the International Red Cross in Geneva, by its representatives, Professor Edouard Naville and M. Victor van Berchem, who visited and inspected the various prison camps in Great Britain, reported that out of 10,000 German officers and men who were prisoners in the United Kingdom

RECREATION TIME.
German prisoners playing football under the interested eyes of a British officer and N.C.O.

not one was dissatisfied with his food or treatment, and it made a note of the fact that German prisoners who showed that their clothes or boots were in a bad state were given what they required by the British Government, whereas in Germany British prisoners of war were dependent for clothing on supplies provided from their own country.

One of the most striking tributes to the good treatment of German prisoners by the British was that published early in 1915 by Mr. Steen, a Norwegian, in the "Temps" of Paris. He had gone through the camp at Holyport, and had found the prisoners cheerful and contented. On leaving he asked a German colonel whether he had any complaint to make, and was told that he had none. This German officer added: "The English are very kind. I tell my people in Germany of their kindness in every letter I write. . . . The English seem intent on providing their prisoners with comfortable and healthy accommodation." Speaking of the food, he said it was the same as that for the British soldiers, and that it was well known that no soldiers were "better fed than those of the King of England."

Notwithstanding these reports, and others to the same effect, the German leaders persisted in their misrepresentations of the treatment of German prisoners by the British. In a manifesto issued at the beginning of September, 1918, to the German people, Hindenburg, commenting on propaganda leaflets which had been distributed in Germany by the Allies, and which he maintained "decoyed the fighters at the front," said: "There are still some decent and humane

commandants of prisoners' camps in England and France, but these are the exception." In the same month there was found an order signed by Ludendorff, which fell into British hands, as recorded in the "Morning Post" of September 11th, 1918, that illustrated this characteristic German point of view. It read: "Capture at the hands of our inhuman foes, in view of their unexampled brutality of treatment, which is now proved beyond question in so large a number of cases, merely means being slowly tortured to death."

Such statements were false, as this chapter will show by extracts from letters written by German prisoners to their homes in Germany, which were despatched to their destination at the very time these statements were being circulated among the German rank and file on the battlefields. So far as the point of accuracy was concerned, it did not matter that the purpose with which these statements were made was to nerve the German soldiers to fight strenuously to the last—to die rather than be taken prisoner. Many German soldiers who were made prisoners were found to be in absolute terror as to what would happen to them in captivity. Knowing how vilely British and other allied prisoners of war had been treated in Germany, they probably reasoned that they themselves could expect no better fate at the hands of their captors, and thus thought that Hindenburg and Ludendorff were justified in making these assertions.

It must be admitted that when Great Britain entered the war she had no machinery for

PRISONERS AT PLAY WHILE INTERNED IN ENGLAND.
A game of "tag" and (in circle) one of fist ball being played by Germans interned at an English fruit farm. At all camps opportunities were given for exercise which, however, was not compulsory, though prisoners had to spend so many hours daily outside their sleeping quarters.

dealing with prisoners of war. This, of course, was because, not anticipating war, she had not prepared for war. The sole guide for the reception and treatment of such prisoners was a Royal Warrant for the Maintenance of Discipline, dated August 3rd, 1914, which gave a scale of punishments for refractory men. Its rules and regulations had been in course of preparation and amendment for several years, the nucleus being derived from similar rules and regulations at the time of the South African War. Prisoners of war arriving in the United Kingdom were dealt with by a branch of the Department of the Adjutant-General, later compendiously known as "A.G.3," under the War Office.

At the start there were no prison camps, no places set apart for internment, and these had to be improvised as was most feasible in the circumstances. Use was made of the ordinary barracks and camps where possible; in some cases civilians were temporarily detained in prisons, though they were not put under the usual prison regime. As Great Britain was suddenly called on to make provision for a vastly increased Army, it was evident that she would quickly require far larger accommodation for her own soldiers than existed at the time, and that this pressure must have the effect of increasing proportionately the difficulty of arranging adequately for prisoners of war, whether military or civilian.

Civilian prisoners were dealt with by both the Home Office and the War Office, the latter having exclusive charge of the

HARMONIOUS HUNS.
"Music has charms to soothe a savage breast." German prisoners' orchestra on a Gloucestershire fruit farm.

military and naval prisoners. The first German prisoners were received in the Dorchester Camp in August, 1914, and this camp became what may be called a "permanent" camp—that is, a camp for the duration of the war and such longer time as was necessary according to the final settlement at the peace. Other similar permanent prison camps were established during that month at Queen's Ferry and Lancaster, and temporary camps were set up or provided at Horsham, York Castle, Bradford Moor, Olympia (London), Edinburgh, and Fort George. Some of these were merely makeshifts, and were closed before the end of August.

In September the number of camps was increased. Describing one of these camps—that at Frith Hill, Frimley—a representative of the "Times," who paid it a visit, spoke of the prisoners as consisting of Uhlans wearing riding-breeches and spiked helmets, infantry-men in uniforms of blue-green, sailors in navy blue, and civilians in the garb in which they had been arrested—one with a white waistcoat which he had been wearing at a wedding-party when taken. The prisoners solaced themselves with games and music, and were as contented-looking as was to be expected in their position. In another part of the same camp sixty wounded Germans, belonging to the 35th Infantry, were being given the same care as was given to the British wounded.

As accommodation for prisoners throughout the country was very scanty, and far beneath what was required, use was made of some ships for their internment. These vessels, nine in number

LIGHTER MOMENTS DURING LABOUR ON THE LAND.
Some of the German prisoners of war employed on a Gloucestershire fruit farm indulging in a game of "tip-stick" during a rest interval, and (above) others enjoying a smoke during a break in the day's digging of a hillside field, which they were preparing for conversion into an orchard.

in all when Mr. John B. Jackson inspected them, as previously stated, were mostly large ships, of 4,000 to 5,000 tons, of the type of the Canada, the Ascania, and the Ivernia. They were not intended to be permanent "prison camps," but only served as such while established camps were being got ready, and they ceased to be employed for this purpose before the end of June, 1915. They were moored in the Thames, off Ryde, and at Southampton. In Germany objections were raised to these ships being used in this way, but as a matter of fact they were perfectly habitable. The idea at first was to put prisoners into them for the winter, as they could easily be lighted and warmed. Their chief defect was their limited facilities for exercise, but it was one that was overcome to a large extent by method. If they so desired, civilians interned in these vessels could obtain a cabin for a small extra payment.

Ships as prison camps

In August, 1914, within a week of the outbreak of the war, a Prisoners of War Information Bureau was constituted by the Government in compliance with the provisions of The Hague Convention. It took up its quarters at 49, Wellington Street, Strand, London—in the near neighbourhood of Covent Garden. Under the direction of Sir Paul Harvey, an expert staff was recruited from other departments of the Civil Service. Mr. H. S. Hunter resigned his position on the National Health Insurance Commission to become Assistant Director. In 1915 Sir J. D. Rees, K.C.I.E., and M.P. for Nottingham East, succeeded Sir Paul Harvey.

Naturally, as the number of the prisoners increased, the work of the bureau became very heavy, and in 1918 it had a staff of upwards of three hundred. As its first business the bureau kept a complete register of all alien enemies, combatant and civilian, who were interned in any part of the British Empire. The officers in command of prison camps were required to furnish a list of all new prisoners received by them as soon as possible after their arrival, the preliminary list being supplemented later by full individual returns. This register, therefore, contained all relevant particulars of every soldier captured in the field, every sailor taken at sea, and every civilian, man or woman, passing the gates of the camps, not only of German, but of Austrian, Bulgarian, and Turkish

prisoners. This record enabled the British Government to supply the enemy Governments with full lists of their prisoner nationals. The bureau further sent copies of the lists to the German, Austrian, and Bulgarian Red Cross Societies, and to the Ottoman Red Crescent Society.

In the second place the bureau fulfilled a special function with respect to sick and wounded prisoners. The officers commanding the camps part of which was used as hospitals, or which were hospital camps pure and simple, forwarded to the bureau a return of all admissions to and discharges from hospital, and this information was despatched regularly to the enemy Governments, in order that the relatives and friends of these sick or wounded prisoners might know their state of health. With regard to the "enemy dead" the bureau received from General Headquarters as complete returns as were possible, particulars frequently being accompanied by the actual identification disks, and any personal belongings which had been found on the bodies.

Prisoners of War Information Bureau

Information with respect to these dead enemies was forwarded in due course to the enemy Governments by the bureau, which besides was at great pains to make sure of its statements, verifying them, where that could be done, by interrogating prisoners of war who were in a position to give testimony. In this connection it is also to be noted that the bureau did good work by interrogating prisoners concerning the fate of those whose names did not appear in the official lists of dead prepared either in Great Britain or Germany. Prisoners were interviewed in the camps, and where they were able to furnish the necessary particulars as to their fallen comrades, death certificates were issued by the German Government, on the strength of their written statements, to the next of kin. When these relatives made inquiries the bureau gave them any further information it possessed, and stated, wherever it was possible, the burial-place of those who had been killed or had died of wounds—for example, if a cross had been placed above the grave it said so.

Answering inquiries of all kinds formed a very large part of the service rendered by the bureau. These often amounted to as many as four hundred a day from Germany alone; they came by telegrams, by letters, and from people in person. The bureau took charge of the personal belongings of prisoners which came into its possession. It forwarded the personal effects of enemy dead to relatives through diplomatic channels; in all cases, where the thing could be done, it traced out the owners of other articles put in its custody, and, with the exception of arms and military papers, sent them to the proper quarters. It transmitted to prisoners all letters and parcels which came for them under cover of its address.

With respect to correspondence, relatives and friends were advised to address letters, parcels, and money-orders direct to the camps, but where the address was unknown, or where letters were returned as undelivered, it undertook the duty of a post-office. Under The Hague Convention prisoners were permitted to receive and transmit letters and parcels free of charge, and this provision was scrupulously observed by the British authorities. The British did everything that was prescribed by that Convention—and a good deal more—through this bureau, in its widespread and most humane activities, which began, it may well be repeated, in the very first days of the war, and were in marked contrast with the scant respect paid by enemy belligerents to the Convention, by which they were every whit as much bound as was Great Britain.

MAKING GOOD THE WOOD SHORTAGE.
German captives in Britain felling pine trees for the Army's multitudinous needs—for well-nourished men healthy, invigorating, and agreeable work.
Above : Laying the axe to the root of a tree.

Although a large number of civilians were interned, there were still comparatively few military and naval prisoners at the close of 1914. In a letter addressed to Mr. Page, the American Ambassador to Great Britain, and dated December 2nd, 1914, Sir Edward Grey, then Foreign Secretary, gave an account of the provision that had been made for these captives up to that time. The German officers lived in comfortably but not luxuriously furnished quarters, away from the German rank and file, except such as they had as servants; they were given half the pay of the corresponding ranks of infantry officers in the British Army, and they were messed free of charge. Medical attendance and medicine also were gratis. They were expected to clothe themselves, and that was their only necessary expenditure, but they could buy wines and other extras. The rank and file were provided with rations, clothing, and medical attendance free, and also received pay for work done apart from the camp work. They were permitted to purchase fruit, tobacco, and the like in the canteens at the same prices as those paid by the British soldiers.

The ration for each of these prisoners was: Bread, 1 lb. 8 oz., or biscuit, 1 lb.; meat, fresh or frozen, 8 oz., or pressed, 4 oz.; tea, ½ oz., or coffee, 1 oz.; salt, ½ oz.; sugar, 2 oz.; pepper, 1-36th oz.; milk, condensed, 1-20th lb.; fresh vegetables, 8 oz.; and butter or margarine, 1 oz. Later in 1914 2 oz. of cheese was allowed as an alternative to the 1 oz. of butter or margarine, and the pepper ration was reduced by one half. No further change was made till January, 1916, when a slightly reduced bread ration came into force, nor was there any alteration of importance till February, 1917, when the general food situation in the United Kingdom necessitated it.

With respect to the internal government of the camps, it was the policy of the British authorities from the

PRISONER PLOUGHMEN AT WORK ON AN ENGLISH FARM.
From 1917 onwards large numbers of German prisoners were employed on agricultural work, the Government distributing groups of skilled ploughmen and others over the country to work at the disposal of the County Agricultural Committees, under the supervision of the Ministry of National Service.

beginning to get the prisoners to co-operate in the conduct of the various places of internment. In officer camps the senior officer took the lead, and in other camps non-commissioned officers were in charge, these "camp-captains," or "camp-sergeants," being assisted by various committees, which saw to the mess, to recreation and amusements, and other phases of the camp life. In the civilian camps the process of self-government developed amazingly; in one of these there were, under a captain and a general committee of control elected by the prisoners, a canteen committee, a kitchen committee, a worship committee, a bed-room committee, a wages committee, and a relief committee. The relief committee was a feature of most camps; its business was to provide money for those who had none from those who had. Most of the prisoners of all classes devoted much of their time to reading and study, and an education committee was found in

SOME OF THE OPEN-AIR LABOUR IN WHICH GERMAN PRISONERS WERE EMPLOYED.
Agricultural captives preparing a golf-course for tillage. Right: The noon-day rest in a farmyard. Above: A German ploughman whom the camera proved to be able to drive a straight furrow. The prisoner labour army numbered seventy thousand men by the autumn of 1918, thirty thousand of these working as harvesters in roving gangs. Not one was employed in mines or in any class of underground work.

every camp. At the outset the British authorities provided the prisoners with the means of recreation, and most camps had a sports committee. It was not until 1917 that prisoners, in any numbers, were employed on outside work.

Considerable developments with respect to prisoners of war took place in 1915. As it was certain that the war would continue for some time, and that the number of these prisoners would materially increase, steps were taken by the War Office to multiply the camps. In February, 1915, a decided move forward was made by the formation of the Directorate of Prisoners of War as a distinct and separate organisation in the Department of the Adjutant-General to the Forces, who at that time was Lieut.-General Sir. H. C. Sclater, K.C.B. The Director was Lieut.-General Sir Herbert E. Belfield, K.C.B., D.S.O., who had been in charge at the War Office of the arrangements for enemy prisoners from the first. Under him, as D.A.A.G., was Captain (Temporary Major) R. N. W. Larking.

Directorate of Prisoners of War

The Directorate began with a very small staff, which, however, grew as prisoners kept coming in larger quantities into the United Kingdom. By December 31st, 1915, there were interned 12,349 military, 1,147 naval, and 32,272 civilians, the vast majority—practically all—of whom were Germans. At that date the number of camps was twenty-one in England, two in Scotland, one in Ireland, and one in the Channel Islands. There were also forty-two detention barracks—eight for military, six for naval, and twenty-eight for civilian prisoners. These detention barracks were for men found guilty of breaches of discipline in the camps by properly constituted courts, and duly sentenced to shorter or longer terms of imprisonment—real imprisonment—according to the nature of the offence.

During 1915 controversy occurred between the British and German Governments as to what was to be done with the captured officers and crews of U boats. The point to be noted here is that the British Government, having stated that such officers and crews could not be regarded as honourable prisoners of war, put the men of three captured submarines in the Naval Detention Barracks at Chatham Dockyard. In reprisal, Germany imprisoned a corresponding number of British officers. The British Government thereupon made it known that the submarine crews were not "ordinary prisoners." In confirmation of this, Mr. Page, the American Ambassador, said in a telegram to his colleague in Berlin :

Officers and men at Chatham in good health, and supplied with money. Officers receive 2s. 6d. per day from British Government. None in solitary confinement, but are kept in separate rooms at night. Size of room, eight feet by twelve feet. Men eat together in one mess, and officers together in one mess. Officers and men have same food. Dietary composed of bread, cocoa and tea, sugar, potatoes, suet pudding, pork and pea-soup, cheese, beef, mutton, and milk. Officers may have butter. Men supplied with margarine. All supplied with books and tobacco. Officers are allowed servants from among the crew. All have use of well-equipped gymnasium daily at stated periods.

Detention of submarine crews

Permitted to write letters once a week, and to receive money, parcels, and letters. Both men and officers exercise in association, but at different times. Recreation quarters indoors as well as out of doors. Officers complained of being held in detention barracks rather than in officers' camps, but no complaint as to quantity or quality of food. No complaint as to treatment, or as to character of accommodation. Hygiene and sanitary requirements excellent. Rooms and all surroundings specklessly clean.

These submarine officers and crews were, in point of fact, not treated with any degree of harshness, but were well and humanely dealt with ; they were merely separated from other prisoners of war. In June, 1915, the British Government decided to abandon the policy of differential treatment for this class of prisoners, who were afterwards sent to the naval prison camps. Yet it might be asked whether our unfortunate men in German prison camps were ever treated so well as were these German " submariners " in the Chatham Naval Detention Barracks.

During 1916 the number of civilians interned in the United Kingdom slightly decreased, while that of the military and naval prisoners grew considerably, and entailed the provision

of more camps. On the last day of that year there were rather more than 31,000 civilians in the camps, as compared with 48,572 military, and 1,316 naval prisoners. The camps had increased to thirty-eight in England, and to eight in Scotland, with one in Ireland and one in the Channel Islands, as before ; there were two temporary camps in France, but they disappeared before the end of 1917 ; in all there were fifty of these prison camps. The number of detention barracks was fifty-nine—twenty-four for military, fifteen for naval, and twenty for civilian prisoners.

Early in 1917 the Directorate of Prisoners of War, owing to the great increase of its work, and with a view to expediting and simplifying its labours, was divided into three sub-sections. Colonel (Temporary Brig.-General) T. E. O'Leary, C.B., C.M.G., was appointed Deputy-Director ; Brevet Major (Temporary Lieut.-Colonel) Larking became A.A.G., and two D.A.A.G.'s were added, the whole personnel being otherwise much augmented. At the same time, work in connection with British prisoners of war was separated from that which referred to enemy prisoners in British hands. The same arrangement allocated to one branch all questions of policy concerning prisoners, whether British or enemy.

About the same time changes were made in the rations of prisoners, because of the shortage of food in Great Britain, both actual and prospective, due largely to the German submarine campaign. On and after February 19th, 1917, meat, game, and poultry, articles containing sugar, jam and syrup, and articles containing flour were no longer permitted to be sold in canteens, or purchased elsewhere by prisoners, whether combatant or civilian, except in the case of officers and such other prisoners as drew no rations—and they were limited in the purchase of meat, sugar, and flour to the amounts advocated by the Food Controller for the civilian population of the country : $2\frac{1}{2}$ lb. meat, $\frac{3}{4}$ lb. sugar, and 4 lb. bread a week. Also it was announced that parcels sent to prisoners from within the United Kingdom or the Channel Islands after February 25th would not be delivered unless the articles in them were in conformity with the suggestions of the Food Controller.

Rations during food shortage

By the end of 1917 the number of prisoners of war had risen to upwards of 150,000. Of these, 118,864 were German, and nine were Austrian military prisoners ; 1,635 were German naval prisoners, and one Turk was a naval prisoner ; while the civilian prisoners comprised 25,120 Germans, 4,065 Austrians, 108 Turks, and 223 others. England, where there were no fewer than 142 camps, became familiar with the sight of them ; Scotland had fourteen, and Ireland one. The number of detention barracks for civilian prisoners had gone down to nine, while that for military prisoners had only increased to thirty-three, and that for naval prisoners had decreased to five. The disciplined and obedient German military or naval prisoner gave, as a rule, very little trouble. He submitted willingly to the orders of the " camp captain," and finding himself far better off than ever he had imagined possible, cheerfully did what he was told. His lot, he knew well, was infinitely preferable to that of his comrades in Germany. When he was employed outside the camps on work, for which to his unutterable surprise he was paid good wages, he proved himself a steady and reliable worker.

Besides the increase in the number of prisoners, the chief feature of 1917 with respect to them was their employment on work of various kinds outside the camps. The shortage of labour, as well as the shortage of food, made itself felt in the United Kingdom, and it was not unreasonable to call on prisoners of war to work. Within a few months after the war broke out the labour of prisoners had been utilised in Germany, France, and Russia. Under The Hague Convention it was permissible to use the labour of all prisoners of war, except officers, according to their capacity. It was laid down that the work must not be excessive, and that it should have no connection with the operations of the war. Germany paid no respect whatever to these regulations, and many a British soldier was cruelly punished, and even tortured, because he would not do any sort of work that plainly

Two glimpses of Bourlon village seen through gaps in the walls of its damaged church.

Outlook from Bourlon's ruined fane, and (right) the Chateau of Bourlon when wrested from the Hun.

Grand' Place of St. Quentin and the thirteenth-century Hôtel de Ville, as left by the Hun.

Monument to German barbarism : The Gothic Church of St. Quentin towering over the shattered town.

British column on the move amid the ruins of Bellicourt on the St. Quentin Canal.

Canadian engineers bridging the Canal du Nord.   They built the right-hand bridge under shell fire.

One of the many devastated villages of France: A corner of Quéant, Pas de Calais.

British troops marching through Quéant, past a demolished barricade erected by the defeated enemy.

militated against the success of his country in the war, and as plainly aided Germany in the struggle. There was absolutely nothing of that kind in Great Britain. Indeed, there was for a long while a distinct prejudice shown by the people against employing German prisoners at all, a prejudice that died out slowly, particularly in Scotland and Wales.

In 1916 German prisoners were employed to some extent, but it was 1917 that saw them at work on a fairly large scale. In 1918 all military and naval prisoners were working, except officers, some classes of non-commissioned officers, and the physically unfit. This labour army numbered 70,000 men by the autumn, and included about 2,000 non-coms., who got a little extra pay. Not one was employed in mines or in any class of underground work, the nearest approach to anything of the kind being digging in an excavation in the side of a hill in the Isle of Raasay, in the Western Hebrides, and elsewhere in quarrying, but in the open air, limestone and surface ores. Not a few were employed in building operations, in constructing huts, and in timber-cutting. Others made and repaired roads, while others again were engaged in reclaiming waste land. One party of them did good work on the reservoirs at Glendevon, in Scotland. Later the German prisoners were employed in almost every kind of labour. In the autumn 30,000 of them were harvesters, moving about in gangs as required; then they dug up potatoes and took a hand at the threshing of the corn.

These migratory bands of workers, ten or more in number, were a great success, under the direction of about 350 agricultural committees, supervised by the Ministry of National Service. After July, 1918, consequent on the triumphant counter-offensive of Marshal Foch, the number of prisoners went up by leaps and bounds; on October 25th it was well over a quarter of a million; but the new arrivals took some time to settle down, and were not put to work at once. At that date there were 492 camps in England, where the whole country was dotted over with them, twenty-five in Scotland, and one in the Channel Islands; there was none in Ireland. German sick and **Number of camps** wounded prisoners were being treated **in October, 1918** to the number of several thousand in thirty-five hospitals.

In acknowledging the excellent work done by the German prisoners account had to be taken of the fact that, in common with the population of England and Scotland, they had had their rations again reduced. In June, 1918, the ration was: Daily, bread, 9 oz.; broken biscuit, 4 oz.; meat, beef or horseflesh, on three days a week; bacon (Chinese), 1 3-5th oz., on two days a week; salt-cured, smoked, or pickled herrings, 10 oz., on two days a week. Daily, tea, ¼ oz., or coffee, ½ oz.; sugar, 1 oz.; salt, ¾ oz.; potatoes, 20 oz.; other fresh vegetables, 4 oz.; split peas or beans, or rice, 1 oz.; oatmeal, 1 oz.; jam, 1 oz.; cheese, 1 oz.; maize meal, ½ oz.; and pepper 1-100th oz. Weekly, either 8 oz. salt-cured, smoked, or pickled herrings and 2 oz. oatmeal, or 4 oz. salt-cured, smoked, or pickled herrings, 2 oz. oatmeal, and 2½ oz. broken biscuit.

Such was the ration of the rank and file from that time up to the end of October 1918, when jam was stopped, the rest remaining unchanged. In March of that year officers and such other prisoners as drew no rations were limited in the purchase of foodstuffs to 20 oz. of meat, 20 oz. of fish, and 56 oz. of bread a week, with the amount of other necessaries reduced in a similar manner. The system of messing officers free had long before been altered; a daily sum was fixed—early in the war it was 2s. 2d.—and the amount was deducted from the pay allowed to each officer by the British Government.

In Germany there was supposed to be officially an allowance for food in what were styled "working camps" of ten per cent. above what prisoners were given in the ordinary prison camps, but it was a matter of grave doubt in many cases whether the extra amount ever reached these workers. Nor were they paid in proportion to their labour—when they were paid anything at all. In Great Britain prisoners were paid for what they did at the same rates as British soldiers doing similar work. Under the Royal Warrant which governed these rates this pay varied from ½d. to 2d. an hour, according to the nature of the work. In agricultural work, such as harvesting, prisoners earned about a shilling a day. This money was entirely their own.

According to an American official report, the average prisoner worker received about 3d. a day in Germany when engaged in farm labour; this report noted, however, that British prisoners did not accept any payment for the work they did, the reason they gave for this being that the British Government paid them while they were prisoners of war, and they thought that if they accepted anything from any German individual their pay from their Government would be forfeited. By The Hague Convention wages earned by prisoners were to be used for improving their position, and the balance handed over to them on their release, but this was conditioned by the exception of " deductions on account of the cost of maintenance." In the United Kingdom employers were charged for the **Prisoners' wages** services of prisoners the customary local **and maintenance** rates for labour; they paid the full amount to the British authorities, who gave the prisoners the allowance under the Royal Warrant, and credited the remainder against cost of maintenance.

Prisoners working outside the camps gave little or no trouble with respect to guarding them. Nor did prisoners in the camps themselves occasion much anxiety to the guards —who were supplied from the ranks of the Royal Defence Corps, Home Forces. There were not a few escapes from the camps, but in comparison with the large number of prisoners they were in reality not numerous. In only four cases—one for each of the four years 1914-18—did prisoners escape from the United Kingdom; all the rest were caught after a longer or shorter period of freedom. As all the ports were closely watched, and the coasts strictly patrolled day and night, it was an extremely difficult thing for a prisoner, if he contrived to get as far as any place on the sea, to get out of the country.

Of the four who succeeded, two, who had seized an open boat at a point on the North-East Coast, were believed to have perished in the North Sea. Of the two known to have reached Germany, one of them, Kapitänleutnant Gunther Plueschow, published an account of his escape in a highly-interesting book, entitled " The Airman of Tsingtau," a copy of which he sent, with ironic compliments, to General Belfield, the Director of Prisoners of War, at the War Office. It appeared that he had told the authorities that he would escape.

In his earlier years Plueschow had been in London, and acquired a knowledge of it which served him well afterwards. Trained as an airman at Johannisthal, Berlin, he was sent by the German Government to Tsingtau, went through the siege, and, ordered by his commander to leave that town a few hours before its fall, went by aeroplane into China, whence by way of Shanghai and San Francisco he made his way to New York. Passing himself off as a Swiss, he reached Gibraltar, where he was detected, taken to Portsmouth, and put on board the Andania, one of the prison ships, and then despatched to the **Escape of** camp at Dorchester, but having made good **Gunther Plueschow** his claim to be treated as an officer he went on to the officers camp at Holyport, and later was transferred to Donington Hall.

In his book he criticised the management of the Andania, and found fault with the accommodation, but he and another prisoner had a small cabin to themselves, and they made no complaint about the food. Of Dorchester he said that the people always behaved perfectly; " there was not a single contemptuous gesture, and never a word of abuse." He stated that the prisoners were " very contented, the food was good and plentiful, the treatment could not be complained of, and there were plenty of opportunities for games." At Holyport he evidently had a " good time," the only drawback being the lack of liberty:

A number of good books (he wrote), our string quartet, and a choir, which we had got up ourselves, contributed materially to our social life. We used to rag a good deal, too, and sometimes, when we had had a really good laugh once in a way, we seemed to breathe more freely, and for a short time the dreadful weight of captivity seemed to lift from our shoulders.

Of Donington Hall Plueschow said :

Donington Hall was supposed to be the model camp for the whole of England. According to the accounts we had been reading for weeks in the English papers it would seem to be a paradise on earth. Every day you might read columns on the subject, attacking the Government for housing the prisoners too luxuriously. As usual, the women were the most violent, and had gone the length of making the compulsory evacuation of Donington Hall a question for the women of England. Even in Parliament the subject was brought forward more than once. It was said the place was furnished like a palace, with card-rooms and several billiard-rooms, that the game in the park was strictly preserved for the prisoners, and that even hunting was arranged for them. None of this was true. Donington Hall was a fine old seventeenth-century castle, certainly, and surrounded by a magnificent park ; but the rooms were entirely bare of ornament, and the furnishing the scantiest and most primitive imaginable. Not a trace of billiards or card-room or hunting. But everything was spotlessly clean, and the commandant took admirable care that it should be . . . . . Life at Donington Hall was almost the same as at Holyport, except that here we had much more opportunity for exercise on account of the park, and that we played games even harder, if possible, as here we had three very good tennis-courts. . . . The commandant did everything he could to alleviate our hard lot and took particular interest in our games.

Such was Plueschow's testimony to the British treatment of German prisoners. He escaped from Donington Hall, got to London, and, disguised as a dock labourer, eventually succeeded, after many adventures and some narrow squeaks, in boarding a Dutch steamer, which conveyed him, stowed away unknown to anybody in one of the ship's boats, to Holland, whence he travelled into Germany. As evidence of the good treatment by the British of German prisoners his book is most convincing, for throughout it the author is at pains to express his hate of " England and the English."

German prisoners in their letters home constantly referred to the good treatment they received in the United Kingdom. The subjoined extracts are from such correspondence, and are of the same date as Field-Marshal Hindenburg's manifesto to the German people, which was alluded to in a previous paragraph :

If the postcard which I wrote has not relieved your deep anxiety, this letter shall do so. There is not the remotest cause for complaint regarding our treatment. We are respected as befits officers. The accommodation is good, the food supply adequate. . . .

The above was from an officer in Colsterdale Camp. From one of the hospitals a prisoner wrote to a friend in Berlin :

One thing I must say—I always underestimated England. The treatment is excellent. From the first moment of my captivity I have been treated splendidly, and was most carefully transported. Food is plentiful and nourishing. You need not worry. As I write, so it is.

PROFESSOR EDOUARD NAVILLE.
As representative of the Geneva International Committee of the Red Cross, Professor Naville inspected the various prisoner of war camps in Great Britain.

From Dorchester Camp a prisoner wrote to a friend in the United States :

You would like to know something of the life of a prisoner of war, and also whether we may write about it. Of course we may. I live in a well-built room in old artillery barracks, together with four comrades—sergeants. We each have a straw mattress and three woollen blankets. Our quarters are perfect, and our food, with the addition of my working allowance, to a certain extent satisfactory. The quality of the food is beyond reproach, though the amount is small for such a big eater as I am. Herrings and potatoes in limited quantities can be bought at the canteen. On week-days I go to work and earn five to seven shillings a week. In the camp, inside the barb-wire, the greatest freedom reigns.

A German prisoner engaged on farm work wrote to his people in West Prussia :

I am working now with a landowner on a farm. My pay in the week amounts to 6s. 4d. —seven marks in German money. The treatment and living are good. We have fresh meat three times a week, bacon twice, and smoked herrings twice, so I do quite well.

From Shrewsbury Camp was sent to a town near Kiel as striking testimony to the good treatment of German prisoners as could be desired ; the writer of the letter had been getting parcels from his home, and this is what he said :

Send me nothing more, for I live ten times better than you do.

Each prisoner was permitted to write and send two letters a week. In the period referred to immediately above, German prisoners wrote and despatched letters at the rate of 350,000 each week, and it is a perfectly safe thing to say that not one in ten thousand contained a word of complaint. Besides the proof given by the vast mass of correspondence of the humane treatment of German prisoners by Great Britain, there was the further proof from the appearance of the prisoners themselves. How different was their aspect from that of the British prisoners who returned from Germany ! But the British treatment of German prisoners was not merely humane as compared with Germany's treatment of British prisoners—it was humane no matter by what standard it was judged. That is the simple truth. By none was this fact realised more distinctly than by the German prisoners themselves. After the armistice was signed by Germany with the victorious Allies, these prisoners, far from showing disappointment because, under its terms, they were not to be released till after the peace settlement, said they were well content to remain in the United Kingdom. Indeed, not a few of them expressed the hope that, in view of the disturbed conditions prevailing in the Fatherland, as well as the great scarcity of food, it might not be necessary for them to return to their own country for an indefinite time.

PRISONERS AT DONINGTON HALL.
Officer prisoners at an arbour in the grounds of Donington Hall—described by a prisoner as " a fine old seventeenth-century castle, certainly, and surrounded by a magnificent park ; but the rooms were entirely bare of ornament, and the furnishing the scantiest and most primitive imaginable."

THE FLOODTIDE OF VICTORY IN THE WEST.

By Edward Wright.

I.—The Opening of the General Offensive.

Secret Movement by First American Army—General Pershing Opens Meuse and Argonne Offensive—Magnificent Advance by Chicago Brigade—Check in Montfaucon Wood—Breaking of Volker Line and Storming of Montfaucon Crest—How General Gouraud Attacked against the Gouraud System of Defence—Hindenburg again Outplayed by Marshal Foch—First and Third British Armies Close Upon Cambrai—Four Thousand Two Hundred British Guns in Action Round the City—Fanwise Movement through the Bottle-Neck—Smoking of Bourlon Hill—Splendid Success of Canadians and Englishmen—Lancashires Break German Line by the Scheldt—Guards Make a Surprise Rear Attack behind Flesquières Ridge—Magnificent Achievement of British Iron Division—German Withdrawal from the Aisne Plateau—Admiral Keyes Attacks the Flemish Coast—Swift and Fierce Offensive by Belgian Army—Houthulst Forest and Passchendaele Ridge Conquered in Forty-Eight Hours—9th, 29th, and 35th British Divisions Advance on Menin—Incomparable Achievement of Midland Division in Forcing the Scheldt Canal—Gallant Corporal Turns the Tide of War by Capturing a Bridge Single-handed—The Problem of the Tunnel and the Howitzer Solution—Gallant American Division Trapped in Hindenburg Tunnel Defences—Strangest of All Recruiting Campaigns—Australians Make Rescuing Charge—Ludendorff Collapses in Despair and Wants Peace on Any Terms—Prince Max of Baden Arranges to Open Negotiations for Armistice.

FTER the British victories by the North Canal and Scheldt Canal, related in Chapter CCLXXII. (Vol. 12, page 305), Marshal Foch opened a general offensive on a front of more than one hundred miles. He moved first the First American Army and the Fourth French Army into action. It had taken General Pershing only a fortnight to bring his First Army from the Metz sector across the river to the Argonne and Western Meuse front. The Second American Army took over the ground won at St. Mihiel, and continued the bombardment of the defences of the old capital of Lorraine. This secret operation was one of great difficulty, even to forces fully acquainted with the ground. The success with which it was conducted by the officers of the last Great Power to enter the war was high testimony to the abilities of the American commander and his Staff.

The attack which General Pershing intended to open down the Meuse was of grand importance. It was directed against the neck of the enemy's main direct railway and road communications between Metz and Sedan. This was the movement that General Joffre had attempted in August, 1914, and that failed through a check in front and a counter-thrust behind. Always it remained the best opening in theory against the enemy's far-stretched line, but in practice it could not be resumed until the Germans were prevented from making an answering movement from the side of Metz. The victorious armies of the United States were able, in the last week of September, 1918, to

threaten the Metz defences while striking down the Meuse. Their position was, therefore, the strongest that any attacking force had occupied since August, 1914.

Under Lieutenant-General Hunter Liggett, commanding the First Army, were ten divisions—the 4th, 26th, 28th, 33rd, 35th, 37th, 77th, 79th, 80th, and 91st. Further in support were most of the troops who had borne the burden of the St. Mihiel battle, including the 1st, 2nd, 3rd, 5th, 29th, 32nd, 82nd, and 92nd divisions. Behind these were other veteran troops—the 42nd, 78th, 89th, and 90th divisions. Altogether, therefore, the First United States Army employed in its supreme task twenty-two divisions, containing more than six hundred thousand men. They occupied the western part of the old battlefield of Verdun, with Dead Man Hill as their central forward position. Farther westward they took over the labyrinthine jungle of the southern part of the Argonne Forest, on the western outskirts of which they connected with the gallant Fourth French Army, under General Gouraud.

The French gunners had been ready to open battle since the middle of July. They had gone on accumulating shell and increasing the number of their heavy guns, until they were certain of being able to overwhelm all the enemy forces occupying the positions from which their infantry had retired during the last German offensive. The American gunners, suddenly moving to ground with which they were not acquainted, were less happily placed. But the masterly Staff of General Pétain had worked out every detail of

GENERAL HENRI GOURAUD.

In command of the Fourth French Army, which bore a great part in the final allied offensive on the western front, that brought about the German collapse.

both artillery and infantry work on the field where the master-gunner of France had won his first decisive success. The American Staff fully profited by all information furnished to it, and when, in the evening of September 25th, 1918, there opened a bombardment heralding the general offensive of the Associated Powers, the precision as well as the volume of the gun fire was incomparable.

From the forts of Rheims to the forts of Metz the gun fire extended. For eleven hours the armies under the Crown Prince of Prussia and under General von Gallwitz were hammered

and behind that was the third Volker line and the fourth Kriemhilde position. At half-past five o'clock in the morning of September 26th, 1918, the American infantry went out under their barrage in their first grand battle. A dense mist covered the country and made the dark autumnal morning blacker, so that it was a matter of great difficulty for troops inexperienced in groping actions of the latest kind to keep all their intricate directions. Their principal immediate danger was that they might be caught by flanking artillery fire across the Meuse, by a reversion of the tactics with which General

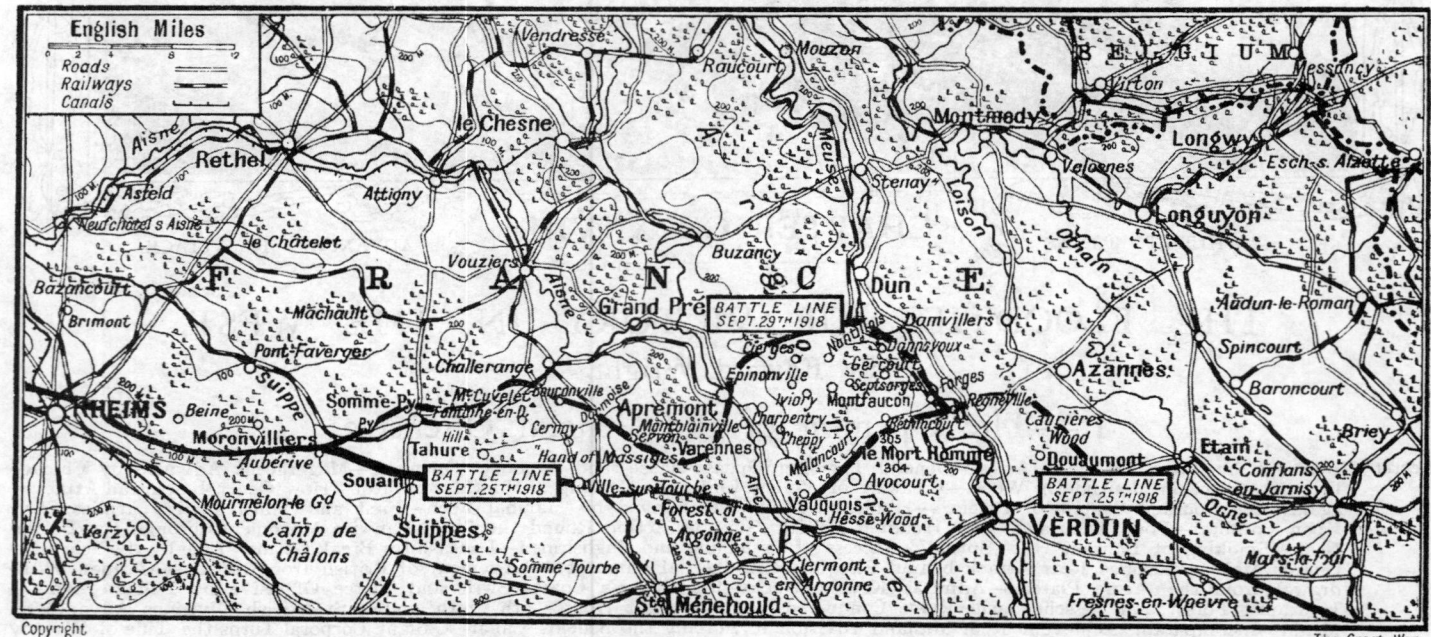

AREA OF THE FRANCO-AMERICAN OPERATIONS ON THE ARGONNE FRONT TOWARDS THE MEUSE.
The First American Army occupied the old battlefield of Verdun, extending thence to the southern portion of the Argonne Forest, where it linked up with Gouraud's army. The attack was directed upon the enemy's railway communications between Metz and Sedan, the main objective being Montfaucon Hill.

by guns and howitzers of every known calibre, the intensest fire being at first thrown on the enemy's flanks. The Second American Army, under Lieutenant-General Bullard, played an important part in the affair by bombarding all the approaches to Briey and Metz in a manner indicating that infantry operations were about to begin. Consequently, the enemy Staff could only guess at the sections between the Aisne and the Moselle where the infantry thrust would be made. While preparing against an attack by Gouraud's men, the German High Command miscalculated the direction of the American assault, and, apparently thinking that General Pershing would try to develop his first victory and drive at the Hindenburg defences in front of Metz, it neglected strongly to reinforce the more critical Meuse sector.

Twenty-three German divisions were in support or reserve, but most of them were used around the Briey mine-fields, where no attack took place, and some of the Prussian Guard were sent towards the Argonne Forest, which was not directly assailed. The main American objective was Montfaucon Hill, rising some twelve hundred feet, between the Meuse River and the Aire torrent, and completely dominating the rolling ground west of Verdun. The enemy possessed some five miles of fortified territory south of Montfaucon, his line running above Regnéville, and along the Forges brook by Dead Man Hill and Hill 305, and enclosing Bethincourt and Malancourt. It then stretched across the Argonne Forest, which was a hog's back, from eight to nine hundred feet high, running for twenty-five miles north to south and forming a battle breakwater of mined, wired, and pitted brushwood, four miles broad, dividing the American and French forces of attack. The Prussian Guard was entrenched in the forest at Varennes and by Vauquois, on the side where the wooded upland broke into numerous low spurs commanded by machine-guns.

Four zones of defensive works faced the American divisions. First was the front Hindenburg line, then came the Hagen line,

American Army's main objective

Pétain had saved Verdun in the spring of 1916. This peril, however, was swiftly overcome. All known or suspected German gun positions on the eastern side of the Meuse were flooded with a special poison gas. The enemy's attempt at a counter-battery duel was of short duration, and while his artillery was temporarily put out of action by the Verdun batteries, the way was cleared for the infantry advance on the other side of the river.

Here, also, the American gunners used an enormous number of gas-shell in counter-battery work, and the infantry advance opened in favouring circumstances. On a front of some twenty miles the Americans worked forward. The natural mist served the same purpose as an artificial smoke-screen, and the sappers were able in the foggy darkness to throw some light bridges over the Forges marshes, enabling a Chicago brigade to emerge with surprising effect against the weakly-held part of the hostile line. By the Meuse the men of Chicago turned Forges by a surprise movement, overcame the machine-gun redoubts in the wood behind the stream, swept through Gercourt, and, after fierce fighting, captured Dannevoux, six miles above their own assembly trenches.

Fine feat by a Chicago brigade

West of this scene of action Bethincourt and Malancourt were overrun in half an hour, but when these forward positions were captured the difficulties of attack greatly increased. On the left was Montfaucon Wood, filled with machine-guns, with Montfaucon crest rising above through the sea of mist, and girdled by a fourfold series of entrenchments. From the right, at Dannevoux and Septsarges, Montfaucon was outflanked, but the encircling movement could not be completed from the left. The American field-guns could not follow the infantry as the ground had been ploughed into chaos by years of artillery and trench-mortar fire between Hesse and Montfaucon Woods. Only the long-range American guns could immediately assist in the struggle for the high pivot point in the German front.

FIELD-MARSHAL SIR DOUGLAS HAIG, K.T., G.C.B., G.C.V.O., K.C.I.E.
Commander-in-Chief of the British Armies in France

Although these guns blew Montfaucon village to pieces and excavated the rocky hillside, they could not reach the numerous machine-guns placed under concrete cover on the slopes. The principal American attack was made from the south-east, and it was held up until the field-guns laboriously worked forward in the morning of September 27th. Then, when the 75's were able to get into action, the infantry quickly worked half round the great hill, carried all the position in a magnificent rush, and at once prepared with the utmost energy to meet a counter-attack from the direction of Cierges.

On the outskirts of the Argonne Forest the enemy held his first positions lightly, and the old horrible field of struggle by Vauquois was easily wrested from the **Americans break the** Prussian Guardsmen. Varennes was also **Volker line** captured early in the morning, when the enemy's artillery fire slackened as he moved his pieces back. The Prussian Guardsmen were workmanlike in their retreat, and by blowing up the bridges at Varennes and Cheppy they prevented the American field-artillery from following in support of the infantry of assault. Meanwhile, in the valley of the Aire, they held the American troops up at Montblainville in a machine-gun duel lasting through the day. By Montblainville the Volker line ran to Montfaucon, and at first it was thought that all this important position had been broken by the American troops on the first day of the battle.

On the morning of September 27th, however, it was found the Germans were still holding, by cross-firing machine-guns, to the Volker line. Yet they did not hold it for long. In the night American engineers built trestle bridges over the Aire and its tributary stream, and by desperate work under shell fire and aerial bombardment got the guns over the following morning. In the afternoon of September 27th Charpentry town was taken, and, with the

ANTI-GAS PIGEON LOFT.
Examining a captured German pigeon loft, with arrangements for fixing messages during a gas attack.

fog still acting as a smoke-screen, the many-caverned and double-trenched Volker line was carried at the point of the bayonet, with the villages of Eclisfontaine, Epinonville, and Ivoiry beyond it. At Nantillois, two miles north of Montfaucon Hill, the vehement, victorious Americans were more than seven and a half miles from their starting-point. When the weather cleared they had, from the peak they had won, a telescopic outlook of twenty-five miles over all the enemy's country northward, eastward, and westward. Meanwhile, close, savage jungle fighting went obscurely on in the secret recesses of the Argonne Forest.

In the simultaneous French offensive General Gouraud was faced by grave difficulties. The German High Command was prepared for strong resistance, and had adapted the attacking commander's method of defence. The main German forces were drawn back for some miles to the Py and Dormoise streams, and forlorn hopes of machine-gunners were placed in concreted works on the slopes of all intervening downs, so as to bring crossing fires to bear upon every way of approach.

Happily, General Gouraud was exactly acquainted with the enemy's new disposi- **General Gouraud's** tions, and he skilfully used a new method **method of attack** of attack. His terrific opening bombardment in the foggy night of September 25th was directed almost entirely upon the German reserve lines. Far from the enemy escaping gun fire, as the French army in Champagne had done in the middle of July, he was devastated by massed heavy artillery and high-velocity guns, his trenches and gun-pits by the Py and Dormoise being inundated with poison gas on a front of some twenty-two miles.

Then, in the darkness of early morning, with fog hanging thick on the rolling, broken wastes of chalk and splintered pine woods, the French infantry worked forward unseen and in scattered groups, with little or no help from the light, storming cars. These the French commander reserved for the

IN CASE OF NECESSITY.
British soldier inspecting the supply of petrol and other combustibles kept handy in case it should become necessary to destroy a bridge near by. In circle: The resourceful engineers: Canadians improvising a field-telephone post from a derelict German rifle which they had picked up.

U.S.A. GUNS ON THEIR WAY TO THE MEUSE.
American light artillery passing through a French village. In the offensive which General Pershing opened on the Meuse in September, 1918, the First United States Army occupied the western part of the old battlefield of Verdun and the southern part of the Argonne Forest.

struggle in the enemy's battle positions, when the foreground was cleared of anti-Tank mines. One by one, in quick, skilful siege operations, the hostile redoubts were reduced between the Suippe River and the western edge of the Argonne Forest, by Servon. The historic line of the " buttes," or downs, over which the war had continually rolled since September, 1914, was finally reduced, Tahure Hill, maintaining the longest, fiercest resistance, being taken, lost, and retaken.

In theory the German front had been made impregnable. The lie of the land had always favoured the defence on either side, and German engineers had dug large new works in the chalk slopes, seamed with the extraordinary number of thirty lines of trenches. They had constructed mine-fields out of 5·9 in. shells against Tanks of all kinds, in addition to anti-Tank pits and other devices. But the skill, alertness, and initiative of the French infantrymen and subalterns enabled them steadily and patiently to overcome the enemy's supreme effort in fortification. There was scarcely a position that could be taken by direct, frontal attack ; yet all were turned.

By nightfall General Gouraud recovered the heights west of the Suippe stream, which he had abandoned three months before, and also won important ground where no free French soldier had trodden since August, 1914. By the Argonne a fine division of dismounted cavalry took Servon—a village on the Upper Aisne, that had been unconquerable in all other French offensives, owing to the marshes that surrounded it. The battered Hand of Massiges was carried, with Naverin Hill, by the Suippe stream.

Against the difficult tangle of the Moronvilliers Hills, which the enemy expected to be the principal object of attack by reason of the observation value of the dominating heights, General Gouraud made only a demonstration. The real direction of his attack, together with the line of advance of the American Army, seems to have been a complete surprise to both German army group commanders and the German High Command. Marshal Foch's aim was to transform the formidable ridge of the Argonne Forest from an obstacle to the Allies into a grand embarrassment for the enemy.

Some ten miles north of the Franco-American assembly trenches the great wooded backbone of the Argonne was cut into a defile by the swerving water of the Aire River, as it made a sudden turn westward to join the Aisne above Vouzièrs. Through the defile at Grandpré there ran a good road and a railway, which branched westward and fed the German line from the western side of the Argonne to Craonne. This line, with its connections with Vouzièrs and the Upper Aisne valley, was the shuttle by which strong German forces had moved eastward and westward for four years.

The enemy's artillery prevented traffic along the Verdun road running across the Argonne Forest, with the result that the long, high hog's-back divided the allied forces while uniting the German armies. If, however, the Aire cutting were reached at Grandpré, the army groups of the Prussian Crown Prince and General von Gallwitz would in turn be divided by the northern prolongation of the wooded ridge, while the Allies would have free connection along the Verdun and Ste. Ménehould highway. This highway was, indeed, completely liberated by nightfall of September 26th, largely as the result of the furious American drive along the Upper Aire valley.

General Gouraud's men were then working from three to four miles beyond their assembly trenches and threatening the Hindenburg line that ran westward to St. Gobain. Behind this old system of defence the American forces were already approaching the Kriemhilde line, that connected with the interior system of defence based on the Serre River. The Serre River line was constructed as a last defence before a general retreat to the Meuse River. It will thus be seen that the combined operations of General Pershing and General Gouraud were directly and immediately aimed at the very heart of the enemy's manifold systems of fortification. While the Belgian and British Armies, and the First, Tenth, and Fifth French Armies were battering down the western and

Advance to the central keep

COMING INTO ACTION IN THE GRAND OFFENSIVE.
United States artillerymen bringing up ammunition. The American Staff mastered every detail of the task entrusted to it, and when, on September 25th, 1918, the bombardment opened, heralding the general offensive of the Associated Powers, the precision and volume of the American gun fire were remarkable.

southern curtain walls of the vast German castle, the forces of General Pershing and General Gouraud were striking at the central keep.

The importance of the Franco-American offensive of September 26th was not to be measured by the ground won and by the number of prisoners and guns taken, although these were considerable. Some 18,000 prisoners and about two hundred guns were captured by the French and Americans in the course of two days; but the first great fact was that the enemy High Command was not able to react strongly against the movement imperilling its main line of communications. Once more Hindenburg, Lossberg, and Ludendorff had been completely outplayed in the art of strategy by Marshal Foch and his lieutenants.

The German masses of reserves had been gathered near Briey and near Rheims, far on the flanks of the new front of battle, and could not be moved forward with sufficient speed to undertake any serious counter-attack. The second great fact was that, as soon as the German High Command recovered some control of the situation, a total of nearly fifty divisions was collected on either side of the Grandpré ravine for the defence of the Argonne Forest and the prolongation of the Serre line of works. That is to say, one-quarter of all the German and Austro-Hungarian forces in the western theatre of war had then **Germans outplayed** to be diverted to a new and extremely **in strategy** difficult task on which the course of the war immediately depended.

In the night of September 26th, while the Germans were left weak and staggering under the unexpected blow to their line around the Argonne, General Gouraud and General Pershing pressed upon the reeling enemy with the utmost speed and energy. The covering fog still remained dense, and although it impeded aeroplane work by the attacking forces, it happily screened the arduous, intense work of reorganising

AMID THE RUIN THEY HAD COME TO AVENGE.
American soldiers, with two British comrades and a French one in the background, at the pump in a village which the enemy had reduced to fragmentary walls. It was such sights as this that strengthened the soldiers from the Western world in their resolve to make an end of German militarism.

the old broken battle zone. Sappers, pioneers, and labour companies worked in the thick gloom in a wonderful way, with the result that the battle went on practically without interruption. While the Americans made good their hold upon the Volker line as far as Montfaucon, the French divisions enlarged their front of attack by Auberive on their western flank, and in the centre, by Somme-Py, broke across the Challerange railway and advanced a mile and a quarter beyond this hostile line of communication and supplies.

The French thrust then reached five miles into the most vital part of the enemy's defences. By the upper course of the Aisne the village and wood of Cernay were taken by the French dismounted cavalry, giving a line of approach to Bouconville and the heights dominating the upper course of the Aisne and the enemy's railway junction at Challerange, near the Grandpré defile. The great fortress systems excavated on the hillsides by Gratreuil and Fontaine-en-Dormois were carried, in very bitter but loose fighting. General Gouraud trickled his men forward, with storming cars and field-gun support, during the attack upon the German main battle positions, and though the work of the troops was of the utmost severity, their total losses were remarkably light, especially in comparison with those in former Champagne offensives. One fine French division broke six German divisions in succession in three days. The dismounted cavalry that began by manoeuvring into the Servon swamps continued, day and night, to work down the Aisne, now dodging forward, now enticing the enemy to collect, and breaking him with light artillery when he did so, and then resuming, on the way to Mont Cuvelet and Bellevue Hill, the method of numerous little local penetrations. While the heavy French guns were being hauled forward slowly over the broken, muddy, slippery chalk wastes, a swarm of bombing aeroplanes served directly as aerial artillery, dropping in a single day

AMERICAN TROOPS MARCHING FORWARD IN FRANCE.
The United States armies played a great and distinguished part in the final attack of the Allies before which Germany finally collapsed. Following on their success at St. Mihiel, they fought magnificently down the valley of the Meuse and through the Argonne.

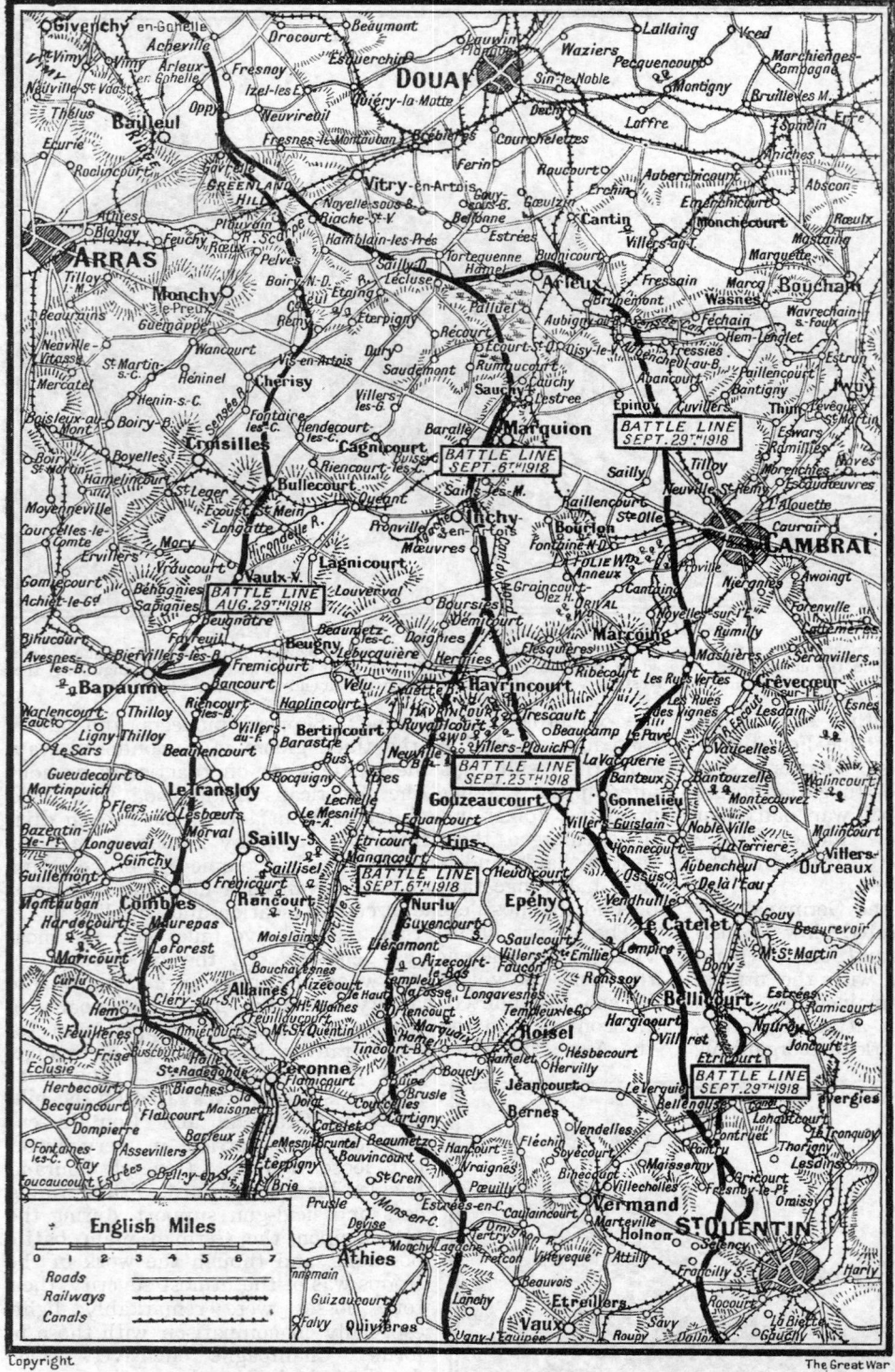

A MONTH OF BATTLE FROM DOUAI TO ST. QUENTIN.

Four successive battle-lines from August 29th to September 29th, 1918. It was on September 27th, after a marvellous feat of concentrated preparation, that the British armies under Generals Horne, Byng, and Rawlinson began their great attack which threatened to pierce the enemy line.

1918, when the enemy's new concentration of one-quarter of all his forces between the Meuse and Upper Aisne was very incomplete, he was called in another direction instantly to find more reserves to save his front from being pierced.

Between the marshes by Douai and the Scheldt Canal, near St. Quentin, the First, Third, and Fourth British Armies had accomplished a marvellous feat of preparation during the deluges of rain of the third week of September. On a front of some thirty miles, over a wide field of old and new battles, where the ground for an incomparable depth seemed impassably broken, Sir Henry Horne, Sir Julian Byng, and Sir Henry Rawlinson got forward guns by the ten thousand, shells by the million, and some sixty Tanks. It was the greatest piece of staff-work in the war. In the middle section, by Gouzeaucourt, there was only a few days' interval between the ending of the first attack and the beginning of the second and far more powerful offensive.

Immediately against the Cambrai defences four thousand two hundred guns, varying from 3 to 15 inches in calibre, were hauled over the indescribable chaos of the old British battle and forefield positions and the main Hindenburg and Wotan switch systems. Moreover, shell was so enormously supplied to the six hundred British batteries that some of the field-guns at last became too hot to fire.

The Germans under General Otto von Below had made a grave tactical mistake. In stupid imitation of Gouraud's trick in Champagne in July, they had withdrawn in force from their magnificent moat of the North Canal, leaving only a rearguard of machine-gunners to impede the attack. For the most part the high, wide canal cutting, with its new, brick-faced walls, was deep in slush at the bottom. Only in an unfinished stretch of three thousand yards, between Inchy and Mœuvres, was it dry enough for troops to work across by scaling-ladders. A few thousand skilled, resolute men, under good cover on the opposite side of the cutting, could have held up two armies.

Owing, however, directly to Ludendorff's insistent order that the Gouraud defensive was generally to be adopted, the most difficult of all obstacles on the western front was feebly held.

Unexpectedly upon the weak garrison there crashed the tremendous barrage of the guns of General Horne's and General Byng's armies, and close on the barrage, scorning all short-pitched shells, came the Canadians of Sir Arthur Currie's corps, and Scotsmen, naval men, Lancashires, with Britons of all breeds, including the Guards and their constant comrades in action the men of the Iron Division, known officially as the 3rd Division.

The first forces of assault entered the bottle-neck of the dry patch of the canal, climbed down and up the sides by ladders and ropes, bombed the enemy machine-gunners from the dug-outs to which they had withdrawn, and then spread out fanwise, northward, eastward, and southward.

some twenty-five tons of shattering missiles upon the German reserve positions by the half-broken railway. Lieutenant Fonck and other young "eagles" of France held the air, clearing it of enemy machines and balloons, while the bombers assailed the German infantry and artillery positions.

In circumstances of great difficulty, with broken local railway communications and ravaged main lines, the German High Command gathered men from Alsace to Malmedy, on the farther edge of the Ardennes, in order to fill the large breach by the inner Serre line which the American and French forces had made. One division on its way to Flanders was diverted to the defence of the Argonne, with results that were soon apparent. For at dawn on Friday, September 27th,

The enemy had one hundred and five batteries ranged about the dry gap; but these had been discovered by the aeroplanes of the attack and were abruptly overwhelmed by massed fire. The 4th Canadian Division turned towards Bourlon Hill, the famous key position in the former Battle of Cambrai. The great, high, forested mass was full of machine-gunners; but General Horne gave the hostile observers little opportunity of directing either artillery or machine-gun fire upon his men.

Hundreds of 60-pounders shelled the high wood and its approaches north, west, and south. The missiles contained only smoke, but in huge quantities, steaming up white and thick until the forces of the defence were entirely blinded. They maintained a sweep of bullets down the slopes, but this was expected. The leading Canadians did not attempt to climb the hill, but worked around it. At the same time the 1st Canadian Division broke across the German line above Bourlon Hill, and linking with the southern encircling brigades, helped in driving a broad wedge up the Arras-Cambrai road, reaching close to Raillencourt and Haynecourt, almost within rifleshot of the north-western suburb of the city.

Canadians at Bourlon Hill

By the afternoon the Dominion troops had overrun the enemy's works for a depth of five miles, capturing 4,000 prisoners and one hundred guns. Their magnificent advance, however, left them with a long exposed northern flank, and Below made a sound, routine counter-move by speeding fresh forces from the south of Douai for a strong attempt to break the adventurous Canadians before they could dig themselves in or obtain full support from their guns. Again the move of the enemy commander had been foreseen. On the left of the Canadians were the Englishmen of the 11th Division. They stormed the rest of the canal, passed through the Dominion line, carried the strong point of Oisy-le-Verger, and gallantly and skilfully prolonged the new Cambrai salient to Epinoy. Also the Londoners of the 56th Division advanced along the Palluel marshes, while on the northern side of the swamp defence of Douai, English and Scottish troops conquered Arleux-en-Gohelle.

This extension of the advance, by providing new tasks for the fresh enemy forces, saved the Canadians from a rending side-thrust. In the evening the Germans made violent counter-attacks, only to be weakened down to the point of surrendering in large numbers. As at night all strength went from them, the 1st Canadian Division made another decisive leap forward across the Douai-Cambrai road. In this grand achievement of cutting communications between the enemy's city centres, the sappers played a high part. They were truly the organisers of victory. Within four hours of the opening of battle they constructed a number of bridges over the North Canal, enabling the guns that had galloped to the cutting to pass over, with trains of motor supplies, and come surprisingly into action close to Cambrai. Tanks also crossed by the bridges and completed the rout of the enemy by climbing Bourlon Hill and breaking machine-gun posts in Raillencourt and along the Douai-Cambrai road.

Sappers play a high part

While the city was thus being enveloped from the north-west and west, the Seventeenth Corps, under Sir Charles Fergusson, which had broken through the Wotan line alongside the Canadians early in the month, also went through the dry gap in the North Canal and spread outward. After carrying the canal works by Mœuvres, the Scots and men of the Naval Division worked towards Cambrai from the south-west by the Bapaume road. Checked south of the ruined highway at Graincourt, they outflanked this village from the

BRITISH TROOPS IN THE CANAL DU NORD WAITING TO GO FORWARD.

In the autumn of 1918, when the great allied attack was developing, the Germans withdrew strong forces from their magnificent moat of the North Canal, leaving only a rearguard of machine-gunners for its defence. Though for the greater part of its course the uncompleted canal was deep in slush, there was a stretch of three thousand yards between Inchy and Mœuvres where it remained dry enough for troops to work across easily.

north, and passed onward to Anneux. The splendid Lancashires of the 57th Division then went through the line reached by the Scots and naval men, and, breaking the enemy's resistance, enabled all the front of advance of the Seventeenth Corps to move towards the seven-spired city on the Scheldt.

Except for the volcanic smoke-screens employed to cover infantry and Tank manœuvres and attacks, the rain-washed autumnal air was brilliantly clear in the latter part of the morning. Forty-three enemy machines and many enemy balloons were brought down, enabling the Royal Air Force to exercise a dominating sway on the course of the battle. The remnants of the hostile artillery, that retired very hastily across the Scheldt Canal, could scarcely come into action

with themselves were the troops of the Iron Division; they wanted to go on, but had to allow other forces that had fought with them since August 21st to leap-frog through them and continue the drive towards the Scheldt Canal when they had gained the spur running towards Marcoing.

The renowned Yorkshiremen of the 62nd Division took up the attack on Marcoing, and on the right the 5th and 42nd Divisions engaged in heavy fighting on Beauchamp Ridge, where all night there was a swaying struggle with counter-attacking German forces who were worn down by the morning, when a farther advance of two miles was made to the Highland and Welsh Ridges. South-west of Cambrai the Lancashires of the 57th Division, who had cleared the way

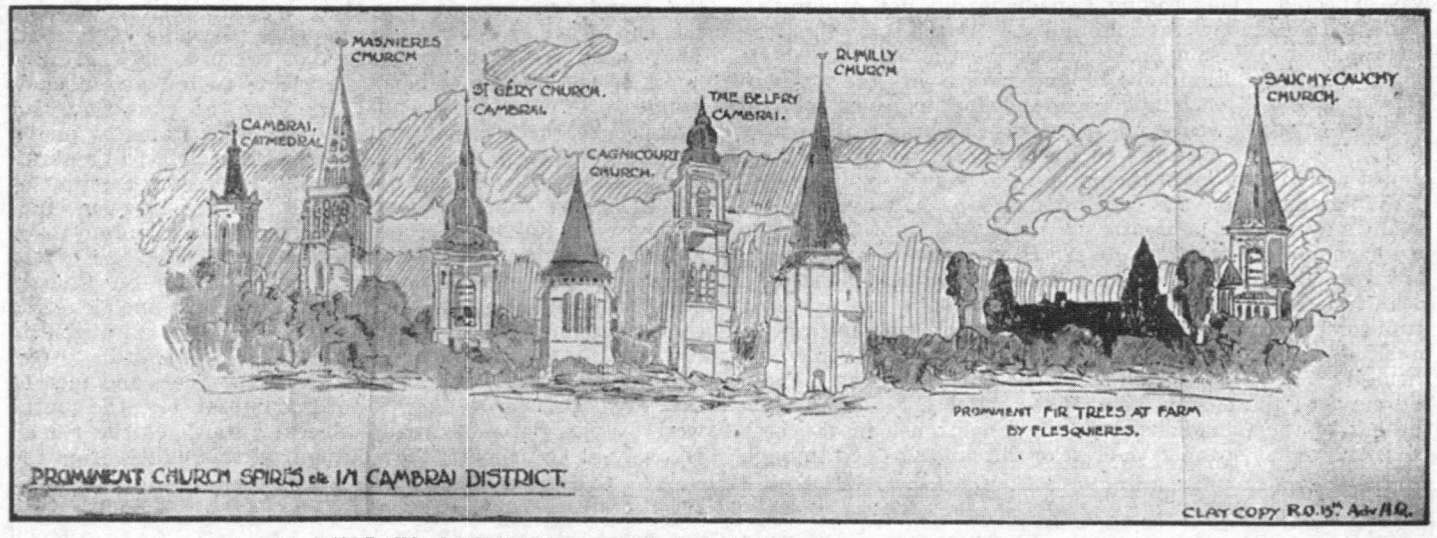

GUIDE TO LANDMARKS FOR TANK OFFICERS IN THE CAMBRAI AREA.

This very interesting sketch, reproduced from a copy printed in blue and red, actually used in the field by an officer in command of a British Tank, was designed to assist in the picking up of landmarks during an advance. It is a notable example of the excellence with which the British staff-work was carried out in providing front-line men with valuable data, including amazingly detailed barrage and other maps, photographs taken from low-flying aeroplanes, of the tract of country in which operations were taking place, and similar aids to men penetrating into territory held by the enemy.

without being again marked down and counter-batteried, and for the most part the German commander had to rely on blind firing by his high-velocity guns, aimed only from the map. British troops moving into action largely avoided this fumbling, long-distance barrage by going forward in Indian file on new duck-board tracks untraced on the enemy gunners' diagrams. Bodies of German infantry, on the other hand, were visible targets both for gunner observers in aeroplanes and on hillsides, and for flying machine-gunners.

On Flesquières Ridge was a strong German garrison, well prepared along the front for any attack by Sir Julian Byng's Third Army. Sir Julian, however, had made one frontal attack on the Flesquières line, and by reason of the extreme difficulty of the ground had been checked there, though enjoying all the benefits of a complete surprise. Fertile in invention, the originator of the Tank offensive thought out another novel method of attack, which caught the Teuton in a trap. The Guards broke into the enemy's rear at Orival Wood, working round the corner of the ridge, with the powerful new Tanks, and cleared the Bapaume-Cambrai road. The Ironsides of the 3rd Division nobly distinguished themselves by sweeping over the long rise from Havrincourt. In particular, the Royal Fusiliers and North Countrymen were not to be stopped. Though the opposing enemy forces were in deep strength, they went through them as far as Ribécourt, killing large numbers, and never submitting even to a temporary stay in their course.

3rd Division's unstayed course

They met at Ribécourt the best force in the Second German Army, the 20th Division, together with part of the 6th Brandenburg Division, fought them and beat them, and continued their career. On their left were Scots and Shropshires; these the North Countrymen passed, stormed into Flesquières with the Tanks, and captured three enemy commandants and a large number of men. Uncommonly pleased

for their corps, fought in the night towards the canal, and with the naval men and troops of the 2nd Division, veterans of the early Cambrai battle, closed upon La Folie Wood, Cantaing, Fontaine-Notre-Dame, and Noyelles. At the end of the first day of the resumed offensive the First and Third British Armies had 10,000 prisoners and 200 guns, with Cambrai in their grip.

In the night of the same day, Friday, September 27th, the enemy High Command endeavoured to increase its reserves in the centre by retiring the army of Carlowitz from the Chemin des Dames. To avoid another wasting struggle with General Mangin's Tenth Army, the overborne, outmanœuvred German commander, who had seemed a few months before the most brilliant of Ludendorff's new men, retreated through Pinon Forest, abandoning Malmaison Fort and a considerable stretch of the Laon road. But the withdrawal came too late. General Mangin's long grind forward had produced its full effect, by both weakening the enemy at one of his strongest gathering points and by leading him so to thin out his forces eastward as to enable General Gouraud and General Pershing to break into the vitals of the Hindenburg system.

Lossberg pressed to desperation

With the vast German salient flattening at its centre by Laon, giving on its southern side round the Argonne, and yielding along its western face at Cambrai, General von Lossberg, managing the whole withdrawal from the salient, was pressed to desperate measures. He was clean outnumbered and outgunned, and also outclassed in those qualities of company and battalion leadership, which, as was widely supposed only six months before, improvised armies like the British and American could never attain. His own special system of myriad machine-gun defence from highly-fortified lines—that is to say the Hindenburg system—in devising which he had played a large part during the First

Battle of the Somme, was clearly defeated by the British method of increased gun fire, dense smoke-screens, rapid Tank movements, and improvements in infantry tactics of assault.

With reserves intended for a surprise offensive in Lorraine, Lossberg was able to slow down the American advance and impede the progress of the French to the Serre line. He had to surrender all hope of recovering the initiative, in order to keep open the main line of retreat by which the German Army might be able to survive through the winter. But he could not hold all his line in fierce strength, and against the incessant hammer-blows of the British Army he could not react. Passive resistance was of no avail ; it would end by the Germans being crowded in increasing disorder into the Ardennes Forest.

Attack had at all cost to be strongly met by counter-attack. Fresh divisions were continually needed, and as there was no longer time to rest and retrain shattered forces coming out of action at the rate of a quarter of a million a week, troops had to be taken from quiet sectors. The enemy commander then had to study the same problem as had perplexed Sir Douglas Haig in the spring of the year. He had to find secure sectors that he could weaken, in order to concentrate anew at endangered points. He selected the Belgian front—a similar choice that Sir Douglas Haig made for somewhat similar reasons. It was a **Enemy's arrogant** notorious region of mud, already stream-**folly** ing in a rainy season, and after his defence of the Flanders Ridge, in 1917, General von Lossberg reckoned that Flemish marsh mud was the safest thing to be behind.

Lossberg, when Chief of Staff to the Bavarian Crown Prince, had controlled operations also against the Belgian Army, and as this Army had no experience in a great offensive with the latest machinery and methods, the German contemned it. The very scientific military Teutons acted only on verified facts. Among the oldest of verified facts was the weakness of the Fleming and Walloon when left with outworn field-guns and small numbers against German siege artillery and huge,

fresh forces. At intervals since the autumn of 1914 the Belgians had shown vigour and skill in local actions, but principally when co-operating with French and British veteran troops. The fact that no Allied Commander-in-Chief —Marshal Joffre, General Nivelle, or Marshal Foch—had entrusted any operation of large scope to the Belgians for four years confirmed the enemy in his view of the matter.

He overlooked the real explanation of the general attitude of the Belgian forces, because there was a generosity underlying it. The Belgians had long fretted with eagerness for a great action. Their passion against the invader, fed continually by new wrongs done **Battle of Flanders** to their countrymen, consumed them. At **opens** times it was not easy to get on with some of them, yet their Allies could not unleash them for a grand battle until the odds against them were definitely reduced by the exhaustion of the hostile reserves. Whenever the tide of war resurged towards the Yser front, as in the Messines and Passchendaele actions, the Belgians hoped that the time for their stroke had come, but though they displayed both skill and bravery in the local attacks they undertook to help at Ypres, the decisive opening was long delayed.

It came at last. The British successes between Douai and St. Quentin, combined with the French and American successes between the Aisne and the Moselle, evened the odds between the Belgian and the Teuton. As was shown by his remarkable offer to evacuate Belgium, the enemy admitted his weakness in the sectors farthest removed from his Rhineland bases, yet it was in these sectors that he most invited attack by reducing the garrison to feed the Cambrai and Champagne furnaces of battle. Marshal Foch arranged to take full advantage of the Germans' last display of arrogant folly.

Under King Albert, the Belgian Army and the Second British Army, with the monitor divisions under Admiral Keyes, opened the Battle of Flanders on a front of twenty miles, from Dixmude to Ploegsteert. Operations began at midnight on Friday, September 27th, 1918, by the monitors

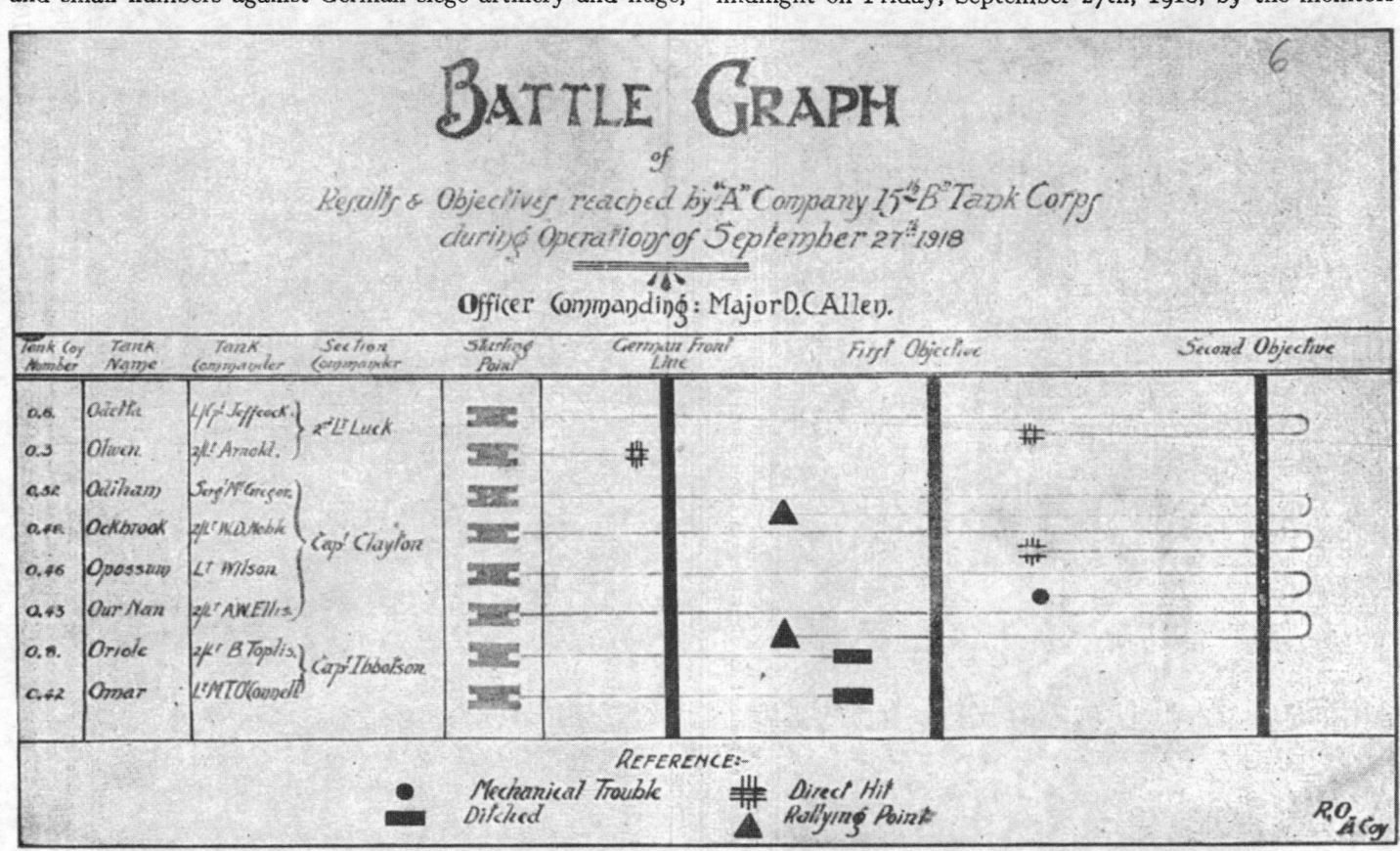

ACTUAL BATTLE GRAPH OF TANK OPERATIONS ON FLESQUIÈRES RIDGE, SEPTEMBER 27TH; 1918.

Eight Tanks, of the powerful Mark V type, each carrying eight men, and travelling eight miles an hour on easy ground and five on bad, attacked the German lines near Flesquières during the course of September 27th, 1918.

One was hit in the approach march, two were bogged, five reached their final objective, but only two came back intact. Three of the eight received direct hits. Our illustration is reproduced from an official record.

Belgian snipers occupying a post from which they could render enemy positions extremely costly to hold. With grim patience the Belgians practised every technique of attack while waiting for their "day" to dawn.

Belgian patrols, on a raft screened by brushwood, waiting for their artillery to open fire before an attack. The Belgian Army joined in the general offensive on September 27th, 1918.

Belgian gun-team, established in country laid absolutely waste by four years of continual fighting, taking part in its final reconquest. The last, victorious, Battle of Flanders began on September 27th, 1918.

Constructing roads on reconquered land to enable transport to be brought up. The Belgians became expert in dealing with the mud and flood that made their country a nightmare to the defeated enemy.

AVENGING BELGIAN SOLDIERS TAKING PART IN THE VICTORIOUS OFFENSIVE WHICH SET THEIR LONG-SUFFERING COUNTRY FREE.

starting a heavy and deep bombardment off the coast. Admiral von Schröder and General Sixt von Armin retained a local reserve of some three divisions between Ostend, Bruges, and Thourout, and it was the aim of Admiral Keyes to attract and fix these forces near the shore, so that they should not be able to enter the first critical phase of the land battle.

In spite of rough weather and rain the naval gunners with their big guns swept the German heavy batteries at Knocke, and then massed upon Zeebrugge, the Bruges Canal, and other enemy centres. One hundred naval aeroplanes dropped from very low swooping positions bombs that wrecked or damaged the network of railways in the battle area and, joined with British and Belgian land machines, attacked gun-pits and troops. The naval demonstration was so intensified that the German admiral, with lively memories of the skill of Admiral Keyes in a landing action, began to prepare for the worst.

Intense naval demonstration

The Belgian Army appeared to be again the demonstrating force, and with sweeps of gun fire and raids harried the enemy. In one raid into Houthulst it was found that the 100th Saxon Regiment had just arrived there. This was the infamous force engaged in the massacres of Dinant in August, 1914, and its presence in the main line of action roused the fighting men of Belgium to supreme fury. When they entered the undulating forest at daybreak on Saturday, September 28th, they were in a mood of avenging anger. The ground through which they fought was as difficult as that of the Argonne, being a rolling woodland full of concealed strong points, with mazes of entrenchments behind brushwood, and overgrown belts of wire, and hundreds of guns. "The master of Houthulst Forest is master of Belgium," remarked one of the greatest of strategists, Turenne. Remembering this saying and acting strongly upon it, the enemy had made the large, marsh-girt wood apparently impregnable by any force. Sir

OVER THE GREAT CANAL BARRIER.
Canadian soldiers inspecting the massive walls of an unfinished lock on the French North Canal. The Germans, strongly posted here with machine-guns, were overcome by the Canadians at the end of September, 1918.

Douglas Haig had preferred to attempt to turn it rather than try to take it.

But King Albert sent his men through it in one swift movement. The Belgians set out in heavy rain, in some places wading up to their arm-pits in mud or swimming deep inundations, in other places crowding in solid columns through bridges of fairly dry land between impassable swamps. But for the screening rain and the dominating power of the Belgian, British, and French artillery, the preliminary losses of the attacking forces might have been crippling. The Belgians, however, were expert in dealing with Belgian mud and flood. At extraordinary speed in the circumstances they followed the grand barrage, and then in a wide movement above and through and below the fortressed forest they carried everything before them.

By thousands they fell, but allowed no losses to check them. In them was the spirit of an infuriated swarm, and the survivors continued without a pause, wading, bombing, and slashing through and around the forest. One small group, using only the knife, stormed a battery in action, some of the men getting blown and scorched by the gun flames while closing upon and killing the crew. On the north they neared Zarren, in the centre they took Houthulst and approached Staden after breaking several counter-attacks. On the south, amid the wilderness of mud by Passchendaele Ridge, they stormed Broodseinde, the point the Australians reached only after a long, terrible struggle.

Belgians take Houthulst Forest

They were not veterans of many great battles, but very grim, patient men, who had constantly practised every new technique of attack worked out by friend or foe, while remaining themselves untried, until they burst upon the invader and broke him. They lost heavily and they killed heavily, yet in spite of their long brooding on things done to children and women of their race, they accepted surrenders

MASSIVE BOMB-PROOF ON THE FRENCH FRONT.
Underground sleeping quarters of French gunners, established in a sector of the western front much visited by bomb-dropping German aeroplanes. It was strongly protected with "head cover" of timber, concrete, and sand-bags.

IN BOURLON VILLAGE AS IT FINALLY FELL INTO THE HANDS OF THE ALLIES.
It was at the beginning of the triumphant allied general offensive that Bourlon—which had proved so obstinate a centre of resistance during Sir Julian Byng's earlier surprise attack towards Cambrai—was at last secured by the British forces. On September 27th, 1918, the Canadians captured the wooded hill of Bourlon and the village, reduced to shattered shells of houses, at the foot of its northern slope, from which it took its name.

somewhat too readily at times. They had to slaughter hundreds of treacherous Germans, yet at the end of the day, after an advance of four miles, they had five thousand prisoners and three hundred German guns, many of which were in action against the Germans before the evening.

Moorslede was appointed the grand common objective of the Belgians and the Scots forming the wings of the two co-operating armies. Sir Herbert Plumer's men of the Second Army were, at the time, too small in number to open battle in the difficult country between the Menin road and the Lys River. General Plumer had given so many divisions to the central and southern British forces that he was not in a position to attack. Yet attack he did, relying on the effect of the Cambrai operations and his long, intimate knowledge of the ground. While the allied artillery thundered in the rain and mist above Ypres, the smallest of British armies, with a strength in attacking infantry less than that of a single American division, went out without an artillery barrage or Tank support. Not only was the ground too muddy for Tanks, but it was thoroughly mined against them, there being, for instance, more than a hundred and fifty mines laid along the Menin road. On the other hand, there was but little wire entanglement facing the Scottish, English, and Irish infantry, so that they did not need the long artillery preparation which the Belgians required.

The Germans were in small numbers as well as the British. The strength had been drawn out of them by the intense

426

conflict between Cambrai and St. Quentin, and they had only five divisions in line. Against them moved through the mud, in rainy darkness, the 9th Division of Scotsmen and South Africans, renowned in many battles, the 29th Division of Gallipoli and Cambrai fame, and the 35th Division that had done much useful work, now gloriously to be crowned. The 14th Division was also in action. At little cost to themselves they broke and pursued the enemy on a front of four and a half miles on either side of the Menin road. The Scotsmen and their comrades stormed Becelaere, in an advance of five miles; the British of the 29th fought through Gheluvelt, with one of their brigadiers riding down the long-inaccessible village road on a captured German pony, and swept over Kruiseecke Hill; while the 35th Division carried Zandvoorde, and thence continued to a depth of nine miles. The Wytschaete-Messines Ridge was turned, and though held strongly, was taken without a formal battle by other divisions of the Second Army. It was the greatest of little battles, illustrating yet again the genius of Sir Herbert Plumer and the remarkable qualities of his Staff and commanders.

At the close of the first day of the last Flanders battle General Plumer's men stood close to Menin, on the line occupied by the 1st and 7th Divisions under Sir John French at the opening of the First Battle of Ypres. The successors of the "Old Contemptibles" then had three thousand six hundred prisoners and a hundred captured guns. The Anglo-Belgian victory was one of

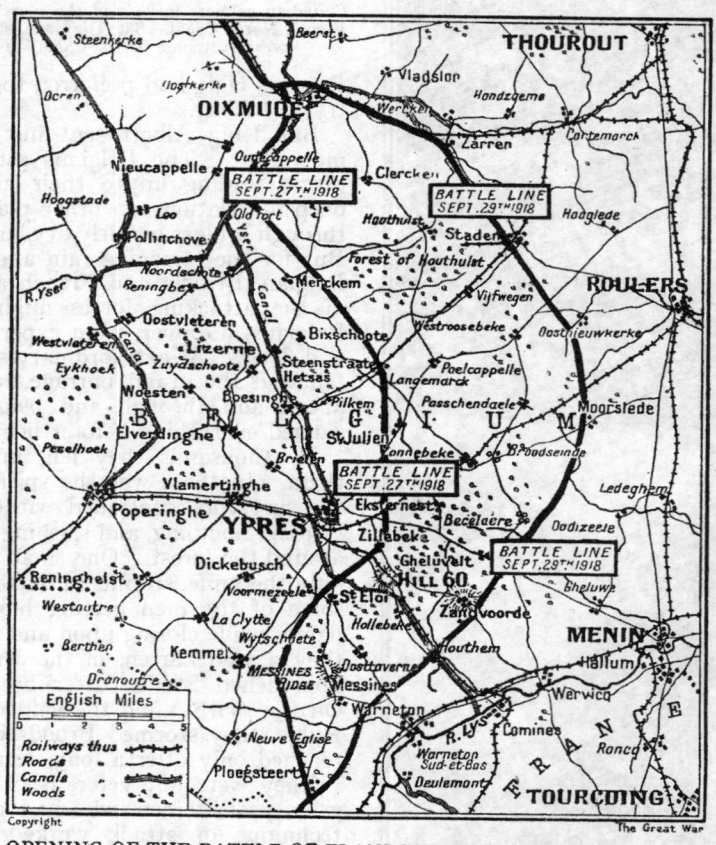

OPENING OF THE BATTLE OF FLANDERS, SEPTEMBER 27-29TH, 1918.
At midnight on September 27th, under King Albert, the Belgian Army and the Second British Army, with the monitor divisions under Admiral Keyes, opened, on a front of twenty miles from Dixmude to Ploegsteert, the last battle of Flanders of the war, and definitely set the Belgian coast free.

the most immediately decisive of all allied successes on the western front. It liberated the Flemish coast, which the enemy began in extreme haste to evacuate ; it imposed a breaking strain upon the last reserves of Hindenburg, who had only one hundred and eighty-seven German divisions and eight Austro-Hungarian divisions remaining in action; and it greatly added to the confusion of the movements of the dispirited and tired German troops.

Throughout Saturday night the army group under King Albert continued to press the broken enemy and work towards the complete conquest of the Flanders Ridge, on which depended the enemy's hold on the Lille and Lens district as well as his control of the Flemish coast. While the German High Command was devising desperate expedients to enable its northern wing to retire in good order, Sir Douglas Haig struck another of his terrible hammer-blows. At dawn on Sunday, September 29th, 1918, the Fourth British Army, under Sir Henry Rawlinson, strengthened by two United States divisions, under Major-General G. W. Read, and assisted by the First French Army, under General Debeney, swung into the battle opened by the First and Third British Armies.

For two days, since the morning of September 27th, General Rawlinson's gunners had maintained heavy incessant gun fire upon the hostile forces in front of them. In its early stage the bombardment had distracted the German **A staggering** army group commander, General von Böhn, **hammer-blow** by keeping him uncertain where the blow would fall. In its late period the hurricane of shell, while warning the enemy that new infantry movements would follow, left the hour of attack still uncertain, and beat down part at least of the formidable works of the defence, which were of a depth varying from 7,000 yards to 10,000 yards. The German infantry was driven into its concreted caverns and tunnel shelters and deprived of food and ammunition.

The main weight of the new attack fell upon the German forces holding the old Hindenburg line by the Scheldt Canal

between Bellenglise and Le Catelet. A brilliant success was won by the North Midlanders of the 46th Division by Bellenglise. The men were largely bootmakers from Leicester, lacemakers from Nottingham, and potters from the Five Towns ; but they were trained in the water of the Somme by an athletic Guards officer, who taught them how to swim while keeping their rifles dry, or get over a stream by ropes if they were not of the swimming kind. Major-General G. F. Boyd directed the attack.

Screened by a thick fog, the leading Midlander brigade crept to the Scheldt Canal carrying lifebelts, scaling-ladders, lead lines, and ropes, with rifles, ammunition, bombs, and entrenching tools. Against **Crossing the** a machine-gun barrage and curtain shell **Scheldt Canal** fire the men swam the canal or hauled themselves across on ropes, and made good the German bank. They then formed up in line in the valley between the ridge on which the Hindenburg system rested and the line of heights from which their guns were thundering. The Germans had an intact bridge across the canal, which both forces refrained from destroying—the British because they hoped to use it, and the Germans because they hoped to trap some of their foes upon it.

Naturally, the bridge was mined, and men were stationed by it ready to fire the charges. The Germans did not use the bridge, having an extraordinary tunnel running for three thousand yards from the canal to their main line of works on the ridge. The enemy's tunnel system extended far northward and connected with the long tunnel through which the Scheldt Canal ran. The existence of many of the Hindenburg galleries was unknown to the British, Australian, and American troops, and this lack of knowledge resulted in at least one heroic reverse after an apparently great and victorious advance.

In the Midlanders' sector the enemy had constructed a tunnel under the canal that could shelter a brigade during a bombardment, and serve also as a safe communication in place of the mined bridge. While the volunteers for the

BRITISH TROOPS SCALING THE WALL OF THE CANAL DU NORD IN THE BATTLE OF CAMBRAI.
Where the canal was dry the British scaled the wall by ladders, placed usually where breaches had been made in the concrete by shell fire, and gained the tow-path above, just beyond which the old German positions can be seen. They advanced over these, using many Lewis guns, and made for Quarry Wood, shown in the background with British shells bursting over it. Bourlon Wood and the village of Bourlon were farther to the left.

canal crossing were swimming or hauling themselves across the waterway, one corporal with a small party worked from house to house in Bellenglise and arrived at the western end of the intact bridge, which was held by two machine-gunners. These he killed. Then he sprinted to the other side of the bridge under a hail of bullets—none of which touched him—and engaged the three German sappers who were preparing to blow up the structure. Two of them he killed and the other surrendered. He asked his prisoner to show him the wires which had been fixed for firing the mine, and having been shown these he cut them, and so transformed the bridge

How the bridge was captured from a trap into a passage by which the main forces of the division crossed with guns and supply trains, with the fog still serving as a smoke barrage.

Then followed the operation of the German tunnel. Both ends were seized, but exploration was impossible, as every adventurer was greeted with a burst of machine-gun fire. The Englishmen, however, captured a howitzer, fired it down one end, and received an offer of surrender. They expected a few Germans to come out, and were amazed at the force concealed under the ground behind their advance. There were almost a thousand Germans waiting to emerge, after their fashion in the first Somme battle, and cut off the advanced bodies of Englishmen and stop reinforcements. They went to swell the total of 4,000 prisoners, with seventy guns, which the Midlanders took at a total cost to themselves of less than nine hundred casualties, many of them light, in their division.

Half a dozen light Tanks crossed the canal and tried to come to the help of the infantry, but they were taken under flanking fire from a hill. It was the infantry who had to come to the help of the Tanks. They made a straightforward, uphill charge with the bayonet, and, while falling under point-blank fire, reached the guns and stabbed the gunners. The effect of their deep advance across the seemingly impassable canal was felt all along the line and opened the way for the capture of St. Quentin and a great advance eastward.

The Americans from New York, Tennessee, and Carolina stormed forward in a most gallant way over the sunken Scheldt Canal, breaking by Bony through two zones of the Hindenburg line and reaching to a great depth at Gouy. Below this point they also passed far beyond their objectives, and after seizing Bellicourt and Nauroy reached out to Joncourt.

Young in experience, they were yet among the keenest, bravest of soldiers, and over a land of traps, with tunnels and dug-outs in every nook and cranny filled with veteran enemies using machine-guns in tens of thousands, they fought forward indomitably.

They struck the Germans a blow which attracted most of the local reserve against them, enabling the line to be completely broken elsewhere, and finally, when cut off in their advanced positions, miles in enemy territory, by thousands of Germans in their rear from unknown galleries, they fought in islands of resistance until they were killed or rescued.

Australians found them still fighting at Joncourt on Monday, and on Tuesday, Englishmen, forcing the canal by Vendhuille, released more of them who had been deeply encircled by Le

Heroism of U.S. troops Catelet for three days, holding off continual attacks, under artillery fire, all that time. The Australians were in immediate support to the Americans, and they had an extraordinary experience while their engineers were working on the tracks by which they were to advance and pass through the United States troops.

From some American assembly trenches, which had been won from the enemy in a local action two days previous to the general battle heavy machine-gun fire swept the leading men in the supporting divisions. Fortunately, in the southern half of the front, where the Americans had attacked Bellicourt, the enemy had not returned underground to his original outpost line. On Sunday afternoon the men of the Commonwealth spread out fanwise from Bellicourt and Nauroy, and

seized part of the second Hindenburg system by Cabaret Farm.

During the temporary disorganisation of some American units, when men who had fought their way out of the German tunnel traps were coming back to the lines without officers to direct them, the Australians started a brilliant recruiting system. Standing up like bookmakers crying the odds at a race meeting, they vociferously advertised the merits of their various battalions and brigades. "This way to the best fighting force!" "Come with us and give them hell!" These were some of the less violently coloured recruiting appeals. The United States troops responded to the wild humour of this extraordinary advertising campaign, conducted amid the rattle of machine-guns, the screech and burst of shell, and the thunder of the artillery. Instantly joining up with the Australians, they went back into action as temporary soldiers of the British Empire, fighting with a furious vehemence that commanded the admiration of their new comrades.

By nightfall, though part of the advance was held up by the mysterious tunnels, the Americans and Australians had given the enemy a terrible shaking, and had captured some 2,000 prisoners. Very many more Germans had been taken by the United States troops, only to be liberated by fellow-countrymen who emerged from under the ground when the captives were trooping towards the wire cages. Four German divisions were shattered and disorganised by the American advance, and three other enemy divisions, including one of the Prussian Guard, were rushed up to save the situation and hinder the following attack by the Australians. The enemy, however, only fought to save his guns and withdraw in good order, the struggle for the Scheldt Canal having been won by the Allies on Sunday.

While the Fourth Army was turning St. Quentin, and breaking through the three zones of the Hindenburg system, the Third Army con- **Canadians enter Cambrai** tinued the encircling movement south of Cambrai. The Yorkshiremen of the 62nd Division, having forced the Scheldt Canal at Marcoing, enlarged their bridge-head, fought through Masnières and Les Rues Vertes, and made a daring advance towards Crèvecœur and Rumilly. On their right the New Zealand Division worked towards the canal, while the struggle for Rumilly continued. Above the Yorkshiremen, the Naval Division, helped by the 2nd Division, made a magnificent advance from Folie Wood to the southern outskirts of Cambrai, while the Canadians, continuing the greatest and costliest of all their actions, forced an entrance into the northerly suburbs of the city. Southward the 12th and 18th Divisions cleared the approaches to Vendhuille.

At German Headquarters, Hindenburg, Ludendorff, and Lossberg were left utterly without hope of being able to avoid complete and rapid disaster. So far as their calculations went at the time, it seemed quite impossible for them to retire their troops in good order or strengthen them for a few weeks longer. Only by means of a general surrender, the startled Kaiser was informed, could the dreadful, unparalleled rout of millions of men be avoided. Prince Max of Baden, heir presumptive to the Grand Duchy, was summoned to Headquarters, and by reason of his false prestige as a generous democrat was entrusted with the task of obtaining from the Associated Powers the best possible terms of peace.

For this purpose he was appointed Imperial Chancellor in the place of the more honest reactionary Count von Hertling. According to the statement afterwards made by him, Ludendorff, on Sunday, September 29th, 1918, was in a condition of blank despair, and wanted nothing but any kind of peace, if it could be immediately obtained. Hindenburg agreed with this view, but Lossberg, Böhn, and other actual managers of operations, although at the time almost as apprehensive as Ludendorff, did not, like the fallen dictator, suffer from hysteria and physical collapse. Keeping their heads and working steadily they saved for a time the German armies, and while Prince Max was opening negotiations with President Woodrow Wilson, the tremendous struggle went on with increasing fury.

Section of the debris-strewn canal in La Bassée, evacuated by the Germans, October 3rd, 1918.

Desolated, but cleared of the invader: Destroyed bridge over the canal at La Bassée.

Bridge-builders along broken ways: British engineers at work in rear of the Somme advance, 1918.

Royal Engineers make a destroyed bridge in the Somme area temporarily serviceable.

Within range of enemy artillery : A roadside shell-crater in the Somme area.

Enemy trick discovered at La Bassée : Mine-crater covered over for entrapping allied transport.

Transport of the British road repairing service in a recovered town on the western front.

French regiment returning through a woodland roadway from the battle=front.

DEBRIS-STREWN WASTE

CHAPTER CCLXXIX.

THAT HAD BEEN LENS.

THE FLOODTIDE OF VICTORY IN THE WEST.
By Edward Wright.
II.—The Bending of the German Wings.

Drenching Rain and Clogging Mud in Wettest September for Sixty-one Years—Speed of King Albert's Attack Saves Situation—Germans Abandon Elastic Defence and Fight Yard by Yard—Second British Army Makes Further Advance—Wild Adventures of Belgian Motor-Car—British Enveloping Movement Round Lille—Albrecht's Stubborn Defence of Cambrai—Canadian Attack of September 30th Taken in Flank—Fine Bridge-head Work by British Naval Division—Check to Progress of Seventeenth and Sixth British Army Corps—Australians Fight Through Labyrinth to Bony—Ghastly Kitchen Scene in Scheldt Tunnel—32nd Division Brilliantly Conquers Le Tronquoy Tunnel—Fifth French Army Opens Offensive on Vesle—Foch's Roaring Battle-Line of Two Hundred Miles—First American Army Checked by Kriemhilde Line—Terrible Jungle Fighting in Argonne Forest—Extraordinary System of Aerial Supply Squadrons Prevents Allied Withdrawal in Flanders—British 9th Division Takes Ledeghem—Canadians Again Checked North of Cambrai—Albrecht Wins a Local Action and Loses the Battle—Cambrai Outflanked on the South—German Retirement in Front of Lille—Beaurevoir Line Broken by 2nd Australian Division—American 20th Division Achieves Great Success in Champagne—Heroic Stand by Encircled Force in Argonne Forest.

THE year 1918 saw the wettest September for sixty-one years. The operations related in the last chapter were impeded by the exceptional weather, and although the Allies managed, by magnificent organisation, to maintain their general offensive, the clogging mud interfered with the speed of their enveloping movements. The First American Army, in particular, was hindered in its progress down the Meuse and along the Argonne.

On the western side of the Argonne Forest the co-operating Fourth French Army, under General Gouraud, was likewise checked by deluges of rain, which turned the broken chalk surfaces of the Champagne downs and valleys into slides and glue-like morasses. In watery Flanders, where the enemy's wing was also being bent back in a threatening manner, the abnormal rains of September made the task of King Albert's group of armies almost as difficult as that of the British forces in the heavy rains of the Passchendaele campaign.

Only the speed with which the Flanders Ridge had been won in the first day of battle, together with Houthulst Forest, saved the Allies another long, weary wrestle in the mud. Even when all the high ground between the Lys River and Dixmude

ENEMY OBSERVATION-POST AT LA BASSÉE.
British soldiers passing a concrete observation-post among the ruins of La Bassée. On October 3rd, 1918, the Germans were retiring along the whole of this sector, and the British had reached a point over three thousand yards to the east.

was gained, and the Germans were thrown into the wet, low-lying ground eastward, the work of getting the guns of attack forward, repairing roads, and building new faggot and duck-board tracks across the swamps involved immense labour.

The Germans were well served by their high-velocity guns. Most of the 5·9 in. howitzers taken by the Belgians and British were fitted with a great screw breech-block, by means of which shells could be thrown more than eleven miles

The Allies had been loath to make guns of a similar kind, because they could not fire deep into the enemy's lines without injuring the French and Belgian villagers. Combined with the employment of light machine-guns as a common infantry weapon, the enemy's long-distance artillery was a terrible scourge to the armies of the Associated Powers. One machine-gun to every ten yards of front was a new standard of defence adopted by the enemy commander in his most important battles, and the state of the ground usually prevented light Tanks from operating in any numbers against the machine-gun line.

General von Lossberg, at the end of September, 1918, abolished both the elastic scheme of defence of Ludendorff and Ludendorff's latest imitation of General Gouraud's trick in withdrawing from an assault. He pointed out to

29th, 14th, and 35th—continued their miraculous progress against an enemy in superior force. The Scotsmen and other troops of the 9th Division worked fiercely and skilfully towards Ledeghem across the road and railway between Menin and Roulers, while the 29th Division advanced with heavy fighting down the Ypres-Menin road towards Gheluwe, in a frontal attack on Menin in which the 35th Division co-operated. In the later stages of the battle the 41st Division and 36th Division supported the leading forces of assault, and the 31st, 30th, and 34th Divisions undertook a series of minor operations by Wytschaete, and then drove the enemy from the ridge and Ploegsteert Wood. In spite of the rain and lack of good roads the British troops won the left bank of the Lys River as far as

all officers and men that his own method of defending the Flanders Ridge in 1917 had proved most successful, and had prepared the way for the German offensives in the winter of 1917 and the spring of 1918. He therefore insisted that every yard of ground should be fiercely contested, not only because continual strategic withdrawals undermined the moral of the ordinary soldier, but also because the Hindenburg system provided the only safe winter quarters the German armies possessed.

The appeal of the new German commander did not fail of effect. Ludendorff was demoralised, after having been overwhelmingly outmanœuvred by Marshal Foch in battle after battle. Yet many German soldiers in the field continued to fight with desperate courage under adverse conditions. They knew at last, clearly and thoroughly, that they were fighting to save themselves from perishing in the greatest rout in history, and they set themselves grimly to the job of holding out until an armistice was arranged. Their main task was to hold on to the Hindenburg defences between St. Quentin and Douai while their broken northern wing retired in good order from the Flemish coast towards Ghent and the line of the Scheldt. As long as the Franco-American forces were prevented from closing the southern line of retreat to Metz, and the lower part of the Hindenburg system was held against General Horne, General Byng, and General Rawlinson, there appeared to be no immediate danger of a general disaster.

German obstinacy under adversity

In the north the Belgian and Second British Armies, after securing the whole of the Flanders Ridge in an attack lasting forty-eight hours, settled down to local operations in unfavourable weather on September 30th. The immediate aim of King Albert was to win the command of all the eastern approaches to the ridge, where the Belgians and British had arrived at points nine miles from their assembly trenches. The fine French army under General Degoutte, which had secretly moved northward in the general reserve, after helping to win the Second Battle of the Marne, came strongly into action as a reinforcement to the Belgians.

General Plumer's renowned divisions of attack—the 9th,

DEVASTATION AND DESOLATION IN LENS.
General view of Lens, taken after the Germans had been driven from that ruined centre of the Pas de Calais coalfield. The mound in the middle was all that was left of Lens Church. The upper photograph shows part of the same town as seen from a British outpost before the final advance.

Comines, and closed upon Werwicq, Gheluwe, and Ledeghem. With their right they threatened the southern approaches to Roulers.

Immediately round Roulers the Belgian and French forces laboured forward against machine-gun barrages and high-velocity gun fire with such success that one Belgian armoured motor-car drove into the city, and after a series of wild adventures safely returned to the allied line. The French forces, coming into action on September 30th, spread out from Staden, and the Belgians made gradual progress north of Roulers in the direction of Thourout. In this sector the enemy counter-attacked with continuing violence by means of the troops he was withdrawing from the coast. While General Sixt von Armin was thus endeavouring to repair his broken front of battle in Belgium, General von Quast began to prepare the evacuation of the Lille region by a retirement from the Lys River at Armentières, in order also to collect troops for the new battle that would take place as soon as the Allies could drag their guns and supply columns over the nine miles of conquered marshland.

It took a fortnight for the three armies under King Albert to accomplish all the engineering work required for a resumption of their deadly offensive, but during this period the

German forces remained in a condition of impotence ; the only grand counter-attack they attempted against the Belgian-French front was completely broken by gun fire before the infantry was engaged.

The capture of nearly six hundred German guns, mostly intact and largely of heavy calibre, was a decisive factor in the conquerors' defence of the Flanders Ridge. It enabled them to beat the enemy with his own high-velocity guns and shell, while the greater part of the allied artillery was still struggling forward through mud even deeper than that which upset the barrage of the Australians on the same ground in October, 1917.

On September 30th, as the Sixth German Army, under General von Quast, reeled under the indirect effect of the blow that had broken the Fourth Army, under General von Armin, the resurrected Fifth British Army, arrayed around Lille under Sir William R. Birdwood, took instant advantage of the enemy's weakness and confusion. The left British wing began to envelop Armentières from Fleurbaix between the Lys River and Lille, while the right wing made a leap towards the dominating Aubers Ridge by **On to Armentières** the historic and almost vanished ruins **and Aubers Ridge** of Neuve Chapelle village. This movement, however, was in the nature of a pursuit rather than of an attack. Everything that happened between the North Sea and the Vimy Ridge was conditioned by the struggle north and south of Cambrai between the main forces of the British Commonwealth and the main armies of Germany.

The reason why Sir Herbert Plumer could attack from Ypres with only four reduced divisions, and why Sir William Birdwood could only wait on events with another reduced force round Lille, was that Sir Douglas Haig was concentrating all his striking force against the half-broken Hindenburg system between Douai and St. Quentin. The main British forces were terribly worn. They had been engaged in battle since August, practically every army corps maintaining incessant action against the enemy.

The losses were very heavy. The four Canadian divisions, for example, lost more men in the struggle round Cambrai than they had suffered in any action in their entire career of victories. English divisions had to be placed under the command of the Canadian Corps commander, Sir Arthur Currie, to enable him to persist in his attack upon the city. Then, in the section south of Cambrai, where the left wing of the Third Army was fighting against hostile positions of enormous natural and artificial strength, the Seventeenth Corps, under General Fergusson, and the Sixth Corps, under General Haldane, wasted **"Cambrai must** down to ordinary divisional strength in one **not fall ! "** of the most desperate battles in history.

"Cambrai must not fall !" ran the order from German Headquarters on the day when Ludendorff was preparing for a general surrender by an armistice. In local command at Cambrai was General von Albrecht, whose corps organisation was fed from Below's Seventeenth Army and Marwitz's former command, the Second Army. General von der Marwitz, as we have seen, had gone to the Meuse and Argonne to conduct operations against the United States forces. His change of command occurred just in time to save him from complete loss of reputation, as his Second Army, after being broken successively between Villers-Bretonneux and the Scheldt Canal, was nearing its final overthrow. In the meantime General von Albrecht, with his corps swelling into a great army, and reinforced by the special corps of machine-gun marksmen under General Headquarters, made a tremendous attempt to save Cambrai.

The German machine-gunners, in particular, were disposed in positions by a commander of remarkable talent. They were concealed on the roofs of the city, with the buildings mined beneath them ; they were placed on the great plateau of La Terrière, extending south of Cambrai between Crèvecœur

LANDSHIPS WRECKED ON THE ROAD TO VICTORY.
Desolate scene of the Flanders fighting in the closing days of September, 1918, depicted by a French artist. Derelict British Tanks on the crest of Passchendaele, near to which was the linking point of the Belgian Army and the Second British Army—the forces that, under the command of King Albert, triumphantly carried out the most northerly part of the great allied offensive which finally brought about the German downfall.

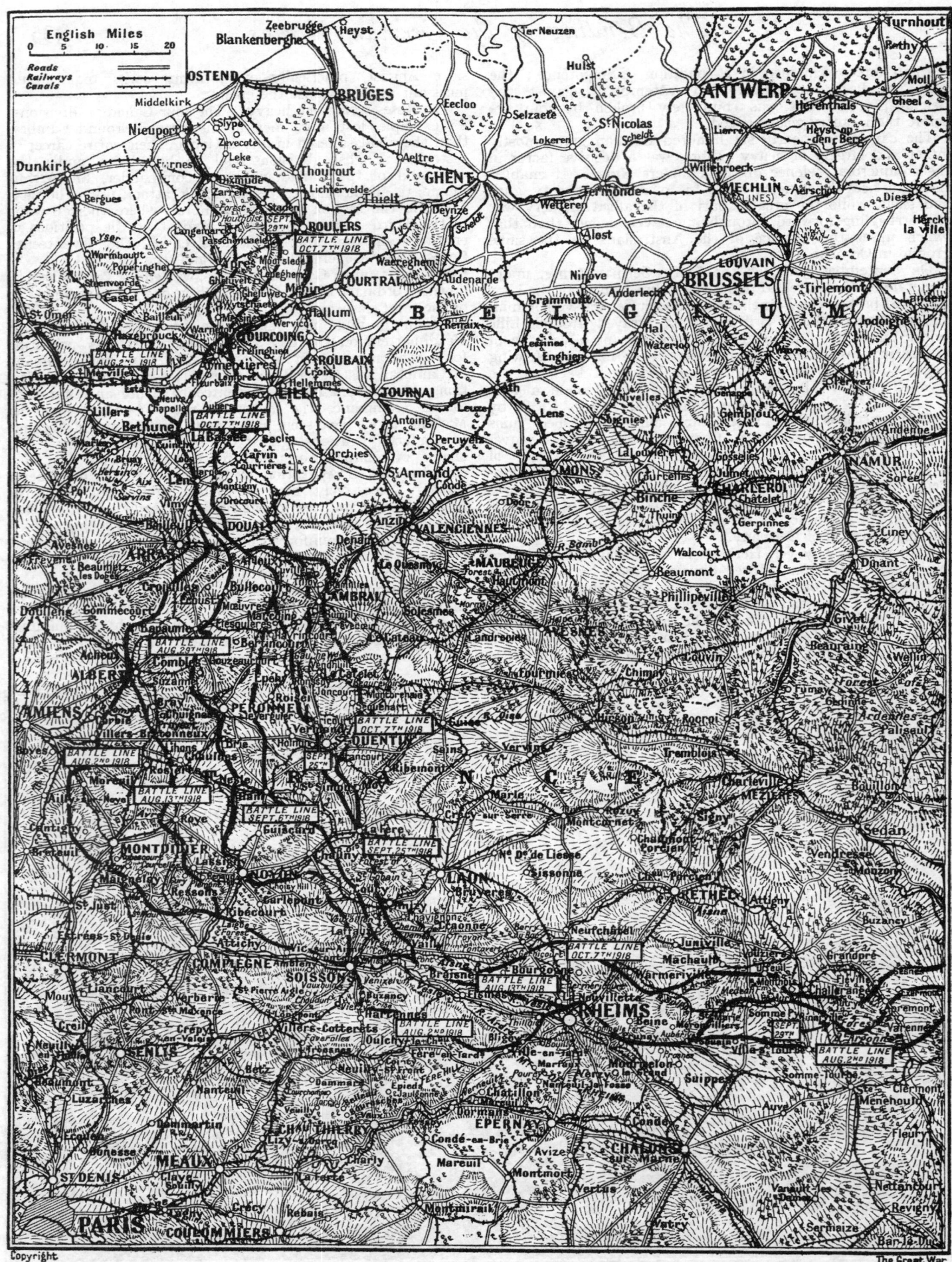

THE MOVING LINE IN THE FINAL OFFENSIVE FROM THE COAST TO THE ARGONNE.

Here are shown the successive battle lines from the beginning of August, 1918, up to the end of the first week in October. By that time the salient towards Paris and Amiens had been reduced by the British and French by as much as fifty miles, while the Belgians and British had reached Roulers at the northern part of the line and the French and Americans at the southern end of the offensive were pressing towards Sedan.

and Le Catelet ; they were arrayed along the Cambrai-Douai railway northward, among the low undulations running towards the Selle River.

Hills and high ridges, which had lost a great deal of their military value after the First Battle of the Somme, had become of little importance. For observation purposes, in the misty autumnal weather, kite-balloons and aeroplanes, even when the latter did not cross the British lines, enabled the high-velocity guns to be used with good defensive effect. As for the German machine-gunners, fighting at only ten yards distance from each other, like riflemen in very open order, long stretches of almost level ground were found to be their best terrain. The more level the country was the deeper was the effect of their barrage of bullets and the clearer their field of fire. There had been strong advocates of this tactical view in the British Army from the opening of the struggle, but they were mainly infantry men, and it took long for the hill worshippers to disappear on both sides.

British and Teutons attacked and counter-attacked by means of travelling screens of dense smoke, formed by guns firing at long range behind the light and medium artillery that barraged the ground in front of the moving infantry. Battles once more became tragically spectacular, although the apparently old-fashioned clouds of battle smoke were revived as the last refinement in tactics of slaughter in the age of smokeless gunpowder.

Forlorn hopes, another old-fashioned device, once used so exceptionally as to illustrate for centuries the heroism of the men engaged in them, became a general, daily affair of routine in attack and defence. Troops holding or attacking from the firing-line in struggles of such intensity as that which raged round Cambrai were often the most desperate of forlorn hopes. Either they had to die in order to win time for the men behind them to save the line or they had to fall in a gallant charge in order to break a path through which an assault could develop.

The Canadians attacked at dawn on September 30th, after spending a bitterly cold and rainy night along the Cambrai-Douai road. The German line ran by the railway between the two cities, at a distance from the road varying from two hundred to fifteen hundred yards. The spurs of Cuvillers and Ramillies were held as redoubts to the Scheldt Canal line. In a most gallant endeavour the 3rd and 4th Divisions of Dominion troops broke across the railway and pressed into the villages of Blécourt and Tilloy, swinging their front forward against the murderous fire of machine-guns. The enemy commander, however, had concentrated a great number of batteries by the Sensée River, and with these he broke into the northern Canadian flank, winning back the high ground by the railway.

General Currie accepted the reverse quickly, and, without allowing it to develop into a serious disaster, withdrew his men, and spent the evening and the night in **Withdrawal for renewed attack** getting more guns forward for a heavier barrage to match the great new hostile parks of guns on his flank. On an arc of some five and a half miles and round the northern suburbs of Cambrai there were eleven German divisions against the Canadian Corps, and the 11th English Division and the 56th London Division came up to support the Dominion troops in the dreadful wrestle for the town.

Below the Canadians the naval men, Lancashires, and Scots, under Sir Charles Fergusson, fought through Proville village to the southern Cambrai suburbs such as the Faubourg de Paris. The Hawke, Hood, and Drake Battalions led the

storming attack across the moat of the canal, crossing the water by single planks, or wading through it, always under an apparently impassable barrage of machine-gun fire.

Day and night the struggle for the bridge-head went on, and, desperately strong as the enemy's resistance was, it was borne down by noon on Monday, September 30th. The naval men then formed up on the eastern side of the canal and, joined by other English troops, nobly endeavoured to break the enemy, who was resting on the knolls and crests by the Masnières road. Again, however, the Germans held the approaches to the city with great determination, and the British Seventeenth Corps was checked south of the city

REPRESENTATIVES OF THE SOLIDARITY OF THE GRAND ALLIANCE.
Italian soldiers at one of the camps established in the back areas of the western front for the Italian division that was sent to participate in the fighting in France against the common foe whom British and French divisions assisted Italy to repel from the Venetian Plain.

at the same time as the Canadian Corps was thrown back on the north.

The British Sixth Corps also failed to take its main objectives. At Rumilly village the Yorkshires of the 62nd Division, who had made a splendid advance across the Scheldt Canal at Marcoing, were held up by flanking machine-gun fire from rising ground near Cambrai. On their left the New Zealand Division also forced the Scheldt Canal, and made heroic but unavailing efforts to get into Crêvecœur. The ground in front of them was so lashed by bullets that every attempt at covering it in the widest skirmishing order failed.

Thus, on the entire front of the Cambrai battle of September 30th, the Germans were able to claim that their defence had succeeded. But it cost them very dear.

They had to hold their lines in strength, **4,200 British guns** with the finest troops of the German Empire **in action** exposed in the forefield of the struggle, and Sir Henry Horne and Sir Julian Byng, discovering the density of the opposing forces, once more laid a tremendous shell curtain around the doomed city.

In general strength of artillery the British were still superior to the enemy, and they worked their four thousand two hundred guns all day until the barrels of many of the quick-firers grew too hot to fire. The German naval division that held part of the line south of Cambrai had to be withdrawn in the night, owing to its hopelessly shattered condition, and fresh enemy divisions were also hurried into the northern line from Valenciennes with a serious weakening effect upon the Lille and Courtrai defences. To a very considerable extent the Flemish coast and the coalfields of France were being reconquered at Cambrai.

CAPTORS AND CAPTURED NEAR ST. QUENTIN.
At an advanced British dressing-station north of St. Quentin during one of the preliminary "pushes" which preceded the developing of the great allied offensive along the whole western front.

Even at Cambrai the Germans could not hold all their line against the sustained, grim strength of the British attack. English troops recovered the difficult ground at Villers-Guislain, over which a struggle had swayed for weeks, and captured Gonnelieu on the left, and made a splendid advance on the right to Vendhuille. This removed the last hostile salient bridge-head, and brought the British front everywhere down to the Scheldt Canal. The success of the southern wing of the Third British Army had the effect of enabling all the Fourth British Army to develop the advantages gained above St. Quentin.

Over the hidden water-way, in the gap of three and a half miles between the moat of the German system, the Australians, with their American recruits, attacked up the Hindenburg system towards Bony, and bombed up the enemy's second line towards Le Catelet. Three rested German divisions had been hurried forward, including the 2nd Division of the Prussian Guard and the 21st Division, both of which had been smashed by the Commonwealth troops at Mont St. Quentin.

Their fortnight's rest had not restored their strength, and the Australians and Americans broke through them and reached the outskirts of Bony, the village at which the northern part of the advance had been held up for two days. There was very stiff fighting in the labyrinth of surface trenches and underground workings, and the attackers continually found machine-gun fire coming from the railway track and sunken road marking the course of the canal tunnel.

The canal was led through a huge cutting to a depth of eighty feet below the hill-side, where the tunnel began. Over the entrance the Germans had built a concrete partition, extending on a bridge from tow-path to tow-path and leaving only an open space a few feet above the water-line. Within the great underground waterway, finished under Napoleon in 1810, the Germans had collected barges, which served as bunks in the long, unwholesome underground barracks. At intervals shafts ran up to the surface, enabling the garrison to slip into the trenches above, and there were new branching galleries on which thousands of Russian and Rumanian prisoners of war had been kept working.

Nevertheless, all the forces in the great tunnel outwork to the Hindenburg line were not secure from the guns of the attack. In one chamber, near the southern entrance, reached by a stone stairway from the towing-path, the Germans had built a kitchen with boilers and bunks for some fifteen men. A shell broke through the roof, exploded inside, and mangled some of the men, tossing one in pieces into a boiler and wounding thirteen others. After this ghastly event the garrison seems to have resolved that it was better to die fighting in the open than remain trapped some eighty or a hundred feet below ground. **Ghastly incident inside the tunnel** They swarmed up into the surface machine-gun positions, where they were broken by the vehement charge of the American infantry and by the following attack of the Australians.

When, on September 30th, the Commonwealth troops captured the commander of the 2nd Battalion of the 2nd Prussian Guard, together with battalion headquarter records, they found that the battalion had been wasted in fighting down to the extraordinary total of ninety men. At the end of the day the Australians emerged from the wide, shell-shattered zone of ancient battles into a green, unbroken country. On their right the 46th Division, after winning one of the supreme actions of the war, had worked against bitter opposition into the bend of the railway between Joncourt and Le Vergies.

They were relieved by the Lancashire Fusiliers, King's Own Yorkshire Light Infantry, Highland Light Infantry, and Argyll and Sutherlands of the 32nd Division, who rapidly developed their decisive

LIGHT RAILWAYS IN THE SERVICE OF THE WOUNDED.
Canadian casualties during the great final advance being carried back along one of the light railways which the Dominion troops developed greatly on their sector of the front, and (in oval) British wounded getting into light-railway trucks for speedy removal to a hospital behind the lines.

success by a brilliant advance into Le Tronquoy. This was another underground fortress, where Napoleon's canal burrowed again under a hill for nearly a mile before flowing into St. Quentin. Some of the ground on the left was recovered by a strong hostile force, but the Englishmen and Scottish Highlanders reconquered it, and then broke another counter-attack on their right.

Here the Lancashires, Welshmen, and Scotsmen of the veteran 1st Division, forming the linking force between the Fourth British Army and the First French Army, actively protected the flank of the grand advance by storming the hill and village of Thorigny. As the British went forward,

the Chemin des Dames, above the Aisne. The gallant Italian contingent carried Soupir, working in the rear of the German forces along the Vesle River and driving the troops of Carlowitz back towards Laon in swift rushes. The enemy army commander refused to withdraw directly northward, because of the danger of the British attack on his communications, and, with Eberhardt's forces, held on fiercely to the block of heights between Rheims and the Aisne, so as to maintain a road of retirement north-eastward on the way to the Meuse.

The enemy, however, was left in a deepening salient between the wedge made by the forces of General Gouraud in

OPEN-AIR SURGERY.
At a Canadian casualty clearing-station near Arras, where the patients, sitting and lying outside the temporary building, received open-air attention from the surgical staff.

AT A FIELD DRESSING-STATION.
German prisoners acting as stretcher-bearers at a field dressing-station on the British western front, and placing the wounded men in readiness for removal by the ambulances.

General Debeney's troops worked through Omissy, a canal village about one mile north-north-east of St. Quentin, thus completely turning the city on the northern side. But though St. Quentin town was theirs to take they did not take it.

Above the tragic, mined ruins, including one of the finest Gothic cathedrals in Northern France, and an admirable town-hall in the Flemish-Gothic manner, there rose the entrenchments of the Hindenburg line, on the farther side of the Scheldt Canal, from which enemy guns completely dominated the city. In the vain hope of saving St. Quentin from any further general destruction, the French commander refrained from battling in strength through the streets, and went on with the thrusts through the hostile main lines which the encircling British armies had begun, giving good aid to the British divisions by Thorigny and Le Tronquoy.

Below St. Quentin the First Army of France made an advance towards Urvillers and Vendeuil—the former outpost line of General Gough's divisions—while the Tenth Army, under General Mangin, strongly increased its pressure along

Champagne and the prolonging thrust of General Mangin. German Headquarters ordered an immediate retreat from the Vesle hills, and the movement was arranged to take place on October 1st.

General Berthelot, who had returned to the command of the Fifth French Army, divined the enemy's plan, and upset it by opening an offensive at half-past five in the morning of September 30th. On a front of nine miles the infantry went forward without artillery preparation, stealing across footbridges over the Vesle almost without loss. By the time the Germans opened fire from their closely-placed machine-gun posts the Frenchmen were well over the water and storming the hill-sides. There was savage fighting on the left, in the villages of Revillon and Clennes, but the enemy was generally caught in a state of confusion, with his artillery moving back, and at least one of his supporting divisions on the march.

This division of Bavarians was brought back in haste to make a counter-attack, but it was only wasted. So weak was the enemy's attempted stand on his second position that in the evening of September 30th **Entire western front ablaze** General Berthelot allowed his men to continue their sweep forward on the right to the objectives fixed for October 1st.

In the night the enemy precipitated his retreat from the St. Thierry heights, west of Rheims, and the Fifth French Army rolled onward towards the Aisne-Marne Canal, with a far-reaching effect upon all the German front. Once more Marshal Foch had succeeded in striking the enemy unexpectedly in a weakened sector, inflicting heavy losses upon him and also extending the line of incessant strain. The combined fronts of battle from the Yser in Flanders to the Moselle in Lorraine, on which twelve armies of the Associated Powers were engaged in intense attack, formed a single conflict between millions of men on a front of two hundred miles.

From the approaches to Thourout to the neighbourhood of Verdun only the Fifth British Army remained for the time

DESTRUCTION WROUGHT AT ST. QUENTIN.
The Market Hall at St. Quentin, as it was found when the French troops recovered that town on October 2nd, 1918. In circle : The Church of St. Martin, or Cathedral of St. Quentin, " so battered as to be hardly recognisable " ; and (above) a bridge at St. Quentin which had been destroyed by the retreating Germans.

deadly leap towards the end of the high forest and the Grandpré defile. His men worked behind Aure, by a cross ravine, pressed on in little groups that rushed or turned each machine-gun point, and widened and deepened their front for some three miles. By nightfall they were by Monthois, on a level with the critical railway junction of Challerange and the Aire valley.

On the eastern side of the forested ridge of the Argonne the American army struggled forward more slowly, along the Meuse by Briculles and by Exermont Hill. More Prussian Guards and other fresh forces arrived towards the end of September, and made heavy counter-thrusts along the Kriemhilde line. After sweeping the charging waves with artillery, machine-guns, and rifle fire, the Americans were compelled to give way at some points ; but they regained most of the ground at nightfall, fighting a pitched battle amid the ravines, woods, and hills between the ridge and the river.

In the high forest, where every clear path or open patch was a trap, and where the enemy had secret ways of emerging behind adventurous and apparently victorious groups, the wire entanglements thickened and spread until they at last became impassable by any known method. Even the pipe of high explosive, pushed stealthily through the wire and fired as the attack opened, was useless. An engineer colonel, however, invented a way of stealing over the wire-fields. He used rolls of wire-netting, strengthened by iron bars, to form a bridge over which the troops crawled, dropping on the garrisons with surprise effect.

Camouflaged machine-gun works were the most difficult of the Argonne Forest defences, and it was almost a relief when a zone of ambushes was explored and cleared, and an organised regular German line was reached, where the enemy could be fought in a downright trial of strength with bombs, trench-guns, bayonets and light Tanks. Here, however, the German commander allowed none of his lieutenants to accept a local defeat. Every attack was followed by a strong counter-attack, launched under a storm of shell fire, poison gas, and tear gas from the high-velocity guns, in the use of which the enemy army chief was a master. There was no elastic defence of the Argonne Ridge and of the

out of the general offensive. The Army of Belgium and the armies under Degoutte, Plumer, Horne, Byng, Rawlinson, Debeney, Mangin, Berthelot, Gouraud, Liggett, and Bullard were all in violent action in the greatest struggle on earth. This effort did not exhaust the resources of Marshal Foch. Although he had nearly twice as many armies in operation as Marshal Joffre had commanded in the first action by the Meuse, he still had men, guns, shell, and trains to spare for an organisation of battle in another direction. As the United States divisions continued to pour across the Atlantic Ocean at the rate of more than three hundred thousand men a month, a supreme force of some 600,000 men, with 3,000 guns and hundreds of light storming cars, was being gathered under General de Castelnau for the final attack through Lorraine into Rhenish Prussia.

Meanwhile, Marshal Foch subjected the enemy's principal body of power to a strain that often came near to breaking-point, and reserved the decisive blow for the day when the strain should have become absolutely unbearable. General Gouraud immediately profited by the success won by his countrymen near Rheims. On his left he thrust over the Py stream against the fortified plateau of Ste. Marie des Champs, where the reinforced Germans were resisting behind wire entanglements and tiers of machine-gun redoubts. With his right wing of tireless divisions, fighting from Binarville, in the Argonne, to the fortress position of Aure, he made a

approaches to the Grandpré defile. The Germans fought stubbornly for every patch of ground with a view to preventing the American and French armies from making a junction above the forest.

GENERAL SIR HENRY SINCLAIR HORNE, K.C.B., K.C.M.G.
Commanding the British First Army

Like Sir Douglas Haig in the action against the Passchendaele Ridge, General John Pershing did not secure a decisive result. This could have been obtained only by a rapid break through the Kriemhilde line by the Aire valley. When the Germans rallied by their last prepared line, and won time to make more entrenchments in the rear and collect another army, with a large mass of additional guns, the situation of the United States forces resembled that of the British forces under General Gough in the Ypres swamps. The mud, in the rainiest September that men could remember, conquered them.

In spite of the strenuous way in which sappers and labour battalions built corduroy tracks of tree-trunks through the morasses of the old battlefields of Verdun, the guns could not be hauled forward quickly in sufficient numbers to shatter the enemy's Hindenburg system. Indeed, it was for some days as much as the tenacious American infantry could do to hold on to their gains until their artillery support was sufficient for defence.

General Pershing's tactical success was important in that he compelled the enemy to concentrate against him in great force, and thus weakened the hostile reserve power in other directions. At the time, however, the enemy High Command reckoned it had survived the grand crisis in the war. On October 1st both wings of attack were floundering in the mud. In Flanders some of the forward divisions of assault could not be fed, owing to the extreme difficulty of communications, and as the enemy was multiplying his machine-guns and his artillery, bombarding all the ground as far back as Ypres, and probing the Allies' advanced line in quest of an opening for a counter-offensive, it seemed at first safest to draw the troops back to the point at which supplies could reach them. This would have seriously interfered with the plan of King Albert, whose aim it was to press the Germans out of Western

Air Service and food supplies

Flanders and the Lille district by continuous local attacks between the general battles.

The airmen solved the problem of getting supplies over the sea of mud. The Air Service had been used for succouring encircled detachments on the western front, and for partly helping a large garrison at Kut. It was now employed for feeding an army. Two hundred pound parcels of biscuit, chocolate, and preserved food were made up in large numbers, carried by bombing machines at night to the front line, and there lowered to the troops by parachute. Much as the hungry troops appreciated this exhibition of aerial transport, they regretted that the aeroplane had arrived in the age when the leather bottle had vanished from common use. For drink they had to catch rainwater.

German retreat from Lille

While waiting for roads to be built behind them, they cut the enemy's communications between Roulers and Thourout. The British 9th Division completed the conquest of Ledeghem, on October 1st, while other troops under General Plumer forced the Lys, quickening General von Quast's retreat from Lille. In the night this retreat began, by a wide withdrawal from Armentières, the La Bassée salient, and Lens. The Germans had prepared dummy figures to place in their evacuated trenches, in addition to mine-traps of every kind : but the soldiers of the southern wing of the Second Army and all the troops of the Fifth Army, discovering the movement before them, stayed not for dummy Germans but pursued the real, and, sending out cavalry patrols, caught up with some of them.

South of the endangered German Sixth Army, swinging back to safety, the Seventeenth Army and Second Army, directed by General von Böhn, again rocked in battle all along the Scheldt Canal line, as the angry Canadians came out to avenge their reverse of the previous day. Again the troops of the Dominion were unable to capture Cambrai, but they

OVER THE BROKEN WAYS THAT LED TO THE REDEMPTION OF BELGIUM.

Belgian ammunition column pressing on towards Roulers, on the heels of their advancing front line, during the wonderful days that followed on the opening of the Flanders battle at the end of September, 1918. It was on October 14th that the important railway centre of Roulers was retaken practically intact. Some 1,200 civilians, who had remained hidden in the town, emerged from their hiding-places to welcome their deliverers.

GERMAN ABUSE OF THE RED CROSS.
British soldier removing grenades from an enemy Red Cross train on the western front. The train had been employed, against all international usage, for the conveyance of munitions of war.

loosened the enemy's hold upon it by the terrible losses inflicted upon him in one of the great massacres of the war. General Currie had brought up his guns to balance the artillery of some eleven divisions which General von Albrecht had massed for the defence. The Yorks and Lancasters of the 11th Division fought over the Epinoy spur, while with a tremendous barrage the Canadians returned to the Cuvillers and Ramillies hills. The Germans had more heavy guns ready and fresh infantry forces in reserve. Their defensive curtain fire fell five minutes after the barrage of attack opened, and their thrashing sweep of machine-gun fire, with gunners four yards apart instead of ten yards, as in the last action, immediately met the Canadians.

The British artillery, however, was the stronger. It hammered and blasted a broad path for the attackers, and by nine o'clock in the morning they broke through line after line of machine-gunners and riflemen, and reached the northern stretch of the Scheldt Canal at Morenchies and Eswars, outflanking the city, while climbing the Bantigny spur on the left. Above them their English comrades made an advance of equal vehemence to the high ground at Fressies, by the Sensée River.

Thereupon a great pillar of smoke arose from Cambrai. The incurable barbarians, having pillaged the famous city, were setting it on fire, and this at the time they were appealing for an armistice! Clouds of smoke also hung over Douai, and in all towns and villages which the enemy was compelled to surrender there were innumerable mines, often concealed beneath unfired bags of explosive, and fitted with a delaying steel spring through which acid was eating.

Apparently Ludendorff was not only recovering confidence, but partly directing the policy of the German High Command. He was now careless whether he blackmailed France and Belgium into negotiations by his measures of complete destructiveness or whether he angered them into fighting to a finish on the field. His extreme, sudden alternations of mood were but another symptom of hysteria. He was still panic-stricken, sometimes to desperation, sometimes to despair.

Desperate were the measures taken by his lieutenant to hold Cambrai for a few days longer. General von Albrecht resorted to the method of mass attack in order to press the Canadians from the Scheldt line. The German troops were told that the existence of their country was at stake, and they poured along the valleys by Bantigny in such dense formations that the Canadian and British artillery shot them down at short range, through open sights, while machine-gunners and riflemen fired until their weapons grew too hot. There occurred a slaughter like that in the first struggle for Ypres and at the close of the first action on Bourlon Hill. The men who wrought the massacre doubted if there had ever been so many Germans killed before in a single fight.

The columns came on at last faster than shell or bullet could kill, and the Canadians had to fall back by Blécourt, half the distance of the total advance made earlier in the day. A Toronto battalion, **Albrecht's costly** however, held on by Cuvillers for four **local success** hours, while encircled, and after covering the withdrawal on either side cut its way back. Against the midway Canadian line the massed rushes continued until nightfall without any compensation for the losses.

According to prisoners, of whom the Canadians took thousands, the explanation of the vain fury of these counter-assaults was that General von Albrecht had been given special forces for saving Cambrai by a grand return offensive. But he was anticipated by half an hour, with the effect that his plan was entirely annulled, and he could only use his unusual number of men in preventing a break-through. In the night of October 1st Albrecht had won a local action and lost the main battle. He had stood his ground in Cambrai at a cost in life which left the German forces between that city and St. Quentin so weak that they could not hold the remainder of the Hindenburg defences. The Canadians also had heavy losses, but they were not fruitless.

In places the Hindenburg system was already passed, leaving the Germans with only the practice trenches, in which the shock troops of the Second Army used to train for their assaults. South of Cambrai there was even an artificial shell-crater area in front of the drill positions, but the British gunners soon transformed it into a real crater-land. After the

RANGE-FINDING AND SIGNALLING.
American and British officers and a padre interested in inspecting a German artillery range-table on a captured position in France. In oval: British soldiers engaged in daylight signalling during the great closing offensive.

Lancashires and Scotsmen had cleared the ground by Proville, while the Naval Division tried to turn the city from the south, English and Irish troops fought forward to the suburbs, reaching somewhat nearer to the centre of the town than the Canadians were on the other side.

A deadly obstacle was the rise of Mont-sur-l'Œuvre, by the city, from which a raking fire held the Yorkshires in their gallant attempts to take Rumilly. The 2nd and 3rd Divisions resumed the Rumilly action, and, after another long tussle on October 1st, the rise was carried by troops of the 2nd Division, enabling the Scottish Fusiliers and Shropshire Light Infantry to work round the eastern side of Rumilly, while the Suffolks outflanked it on the west. The Iron Division of Britain advanced into open country towards Séranvillers, outflanking Cambrai to the distance of a mile. The New Zealand Division, on the right of the 3rd Division, grimly finished their work in Crêvecœur, and worked beyond it to the upland from which they had been swept with fire.

Farther south the Australians methodically cleared the ground for another attack in force in the last system of the Hindenburg line. They worked up to the hill by Gouy, and, with an artillery barrage and a line of light Tanks, stormed beyond Joncourt, captured part of Estrées, and arrived in front of the Beaurevoir line, a prolongation of the Masnières system which had checked Sir Julian Byng in his first thrust towards Cambrai in November, 1917.

On the right of the Australians the leading divisions of the Ninth British Corps were engaged in a continuous struggle for Sequehart, in which they twice captured a remnant of the garrison, numbering some hundreds, but yielded the village back to other strong counter-attacking forces.

Meanwhile, General Debeney's northernmost division captured Lesdins, by the source of the Somme River, and a company entered St. Quentin, arresting a German officer who had returned in a motor-waggon hoping that there was

BURNT OUT.
A couple of British soldiers interested in looking over a train which had been burnt to a mere framework.

time to carry away one more load of plunder. The canal was crossed in the doomed, mined town, and Moy village taken by the Oise.

By the Oise-Aisne Canal the Italian Corps of General Mangin's army continued to fight forward against a strong rearguard, while General Berthelot's troops conquered all the heights west of Rheims, taking some three thousand prisoners and twenty guns. The army of General Gouraud reached the outskirts of Challerange railway-station, and the United States troops battled forward in the Argonne.

October 2nd was a day of preparation along the main fronts of conflict. In Flanders the 29th Division of General Plumer's army captured Gheluwe, the village bastion of the Menin gateway, while Bizet and other outworks of Lille were taken by other men of the Second Army. The Fifth British Army began to work forward all along its front at eight o'clock in the morning, four hours after the Germans left their front line.

Patrols of Lancashire, Scottish, and Irish troops overtook small stray enemy parties, in the deserted positions, and gradually gained the Aubers Ridge, from which they could gaze for the first time on the silent city of Lille, with the smokeless chimneys of the sister towns of Roubaix and Tourcoing pencilled against the dark rainclouds eastward.

Occupation of Lens

The underground city of La Bassée was explored, and the new German line reached by the Haute Deule Canal, extending between Lille and Douai. Lens, with its wrecked, flooded coalmines, was occupied, together with a large stretch of country that had been reduced to a wilderness of terrors. There was a little brisk engagement in the colliers' village of Cité St. Auguste, which the gallant Gordons had reached in the Battle of Loos, and Uhlans were seen acting as a rearguard by the suburbs of Lille.

For the most part, however, this great British advance of liberation, produced by fierce pressure on either side of the most important manufacturing districts in France, was conducted by military detectives. General Birdwood was an expert in trapping large forces on mined ground, as he had shown when he left the Gallipoli Peninsula, and he kept

WON BACK FOR ITS MAKERS.
Powerful railway armoured car—which had been made in England—part of the booty that was captured from the Germans by the Irish Guards during the closing stages of the war on the western front.

ENEMY TRAP FOR INTERCEPTING TANKS.
Ferro-concrete wall at Pronville, with a gap large enough for a lorry, but too small for a Tank—one of the German methods employed in their fruitless attempt to delay the advancing Allies in the autumn of 1918.

IN FLANDERS REWON.
British soldiers, and some of the civilians whom
they had relieved, in one of the towns in the
Courtrai district.

infantry went to it with the bayonet,
and broke counter-attack after counter-
attack. They fought for six hours
around Beaurevoir, in a fog of horrible
gas, blinding the eyes and corroding the
flesh. The strain of bayonet fighting in
gas-masks was great : but the men of
the Commonwealth never slackened
their efforts, and in the afternoon they
firmly established themselves in the
last zone of the Hindenburg defences
by carrying the fortress of concrete at
the eastern end of Estrées, which was a
local Gibraltar, commanding both the
front and the support trenches running
by it.

In the evening the tired conquerors
made another fine effort and stormed
over the high ground between Beaurevoir and Montbrehain villages, taking
a ruined windmill and farmstead from

his troops back while his engineers
carefully and patiently cleared the land.

By Rheims, where the enemy had
not had time to lay many mines, the
Fifth French Army rapidly worked
towards Brimont Fort, while the army
of Champagne closed on the flank of
the Moronvilliers Hills and continued
the fight for the Grandpré defile.

Everything depended on the weather.
Happily, October 3rd was a day of clear
sky and bright air, and the ground
rapidly became good for ordinary
traffic and for Tanks.

General Rawlinson resumed his
offensive immediately. On October 3rd
he attacked with the Australian Corps
and the Ninth Corps on a front of some
ten miles between Le Catelet and
Sequehart. The enemy's last strong
line of works formed a curve resting
on the Scheldt Canal at either end.

DESOLATION IN THE WAKE OF WAR.
Debris and fragmentary walls—all that remained of a once prosperous town on the western front after
the enemy had been finally driven eastward. British soldiers were surveying the wreckage, which they were
about to "tidy up" in order to make a thoroughfare through the town.

By Le Catelet and Gouy, where the enemy still held the
northern entrance to the canal tunnel, English and Irish
troops stormed the bulwark which had resisted all attacks
during a week of battle. Early in the morning the first
British advance swept beyond the underground waterway, and
the garrison held out with their machine-guns, trusting in
their moat to save them from defeat. But they were
attacked directly in front by Englishmen and Irishmen, who
crossed the canal and stormed the fortress.

The 2nd Australian Division, which had fought all the way
from the valleys by Amiens, was faced by
much superior numbers of Germans holding
the Beaurevoir line that bristled with
machine-guns. It was a system of concrete
redoubts, with front and support trenches deeply wired,
extending round the rim of a saucer-shaped position, which
was reckoned impregnable when constructed in the latter
part of 1916. All the Australians worried about was the
branch canal, running between Mont St. Martin and Estrées,
which was reckoned to contain nine feet of water.

When all the ground to be attacked was covered with a
British smoke barrage, through which the barrage of attack
travelled with Tanks and Australians closely following it, the
Torrens Canal was fortunately found to be passable. The

Six hours in a fog of gas

which they could sweep the houses and streets with machine-
gun fire. Montbrehain was captured early in the day by
Midlanders, who took prisoners from thirty-eight German
battalions, representing eight divisions, in their sweep from
the right.

For eight hours the advanced force, the famous 46th
Division, held Montbrehain, inflicting extraordinary losses
on the German masses continually trying to recover the village.
At last sheer weight of numbers told, and with forces hurried
up from St. Quentin and Cambrai, the Englishmen were driven
back. But they held to Ramicourt and Wiancourt, and ended
the day with another two thousand prisoners added to their
capture of four thousand men a few days previously.

Scotsmen and Englishmen of the 32nd Division once more
captured Sequehart village, and broke every counter-
attack. The First French Army joined furiously in the
combat between Sequehart and Lesdins, and also made a
strong demonstration from the eastern side of St. Quentin and
round the southern heights by Itancourt.

There was another fierce battle in Champagne, where the fine
U.S. 2nd Division, serving with the Fourth French Army
under General Gouraud, broke the enemy's line above
Somme-Py, and in an advance of two and a half miles through
strongly fortressed ground, stormed the height known as

Mont Blanc and the hill crowned by Medéah Farm. Six hundred feet high, the positions gave in the bright weather an uninterrupted view over a great stretch of country to the north, and threatened an enveloping movement against the Moronvilliers system eastward. The speed and power of the attack of the American division was the admiration of the Frenchmen. One company, with the help of French volunteers, stormed a machine-gun fort on Mont Blanc, taking nearly three hundred Germans, with seventy-five machine-guns and trench-mortars, without a single casualty to themselves. The troops who first came into action by Belleau Wood carried Mont Blanc. On their right the Frenchmen stormed through Orfeuil and the second grand battle position of General von Einem,

STRONG, BUT NOT IMPREGNABLE.
German machine-gun post, of reinforced concrete, captured by the Canadians when they stormed through the Quéant-Drocourt line.

WHEN QUIET REIGNED IN QUÉANT.
Quéant after the Canadian and English troops of the First British Army, under General Horne, broke through the Quéant-Drocourt, or "switch," line of the famous Hindenburg defences.

making the conquest of the Grandpré defile assured. The German commander replied by massing a park of guns on the railway junction; but it was sufficient for the purpose of Marshal Foch that the entrance to the large gap of the Argonne Forest was completely commanded.

In the night of October 3rd the effect of the American thrust to Mont Blanc and the pressure which the Fifth French Army was exercising above Rheims produced another broad and deep retirement on the part of the enemy. The German army under General von Mudra began to withdraw between the Aisne and the Suippe Rivers on a front of some twenty miles.

General Gouraud and General Pershing answered this movement by a resumption of their great combined offensive between the Suippe and the Meuse. On the left, by Ste. Marie on the Py stream, the upland of Notre Dame des Champs with its successive roads of concrete works was turned from the north on the line the Americans had reached. As the Germans began to waver under this attack from their rear, a thrust was made through them to a depth of five miles to the valley of the Arnes River, where Ste. Etienne and Autry were taken after a fierce struggle, and other villages by the Moronvilliers system. In the night the sentinels of the Fourth and Fifth French Armies watched the great fires of evacuation

burst from the hill forts round Rheims and the crests above the Suippe stream.

Between the Aire and the Meuse fresh American forces made an attack on the Kriemhilde line from Apremont in the Argonne to Brieulles on the Meuse. The resistance of the enemy grew fiercer and greater as the Americans approached the last finished system of defence. The Tanks that preceded the infantry were met by the fire of mobile field-guns and special rifles, and were smothered with poison gas. They climbed up Exermont Hill and into Gesnes, Fléville, and other fortified villages, but were held up in the woods through which the enemy's main battle position ran.

When the American smoke-screen thinned out, the German artillery threw a fog of poison over the positions they had lost, and the infantry of the defence made a series of strong counter-attacks, in which they also used Tanks. This counter-offensive was shattered, leaving the Americans masters of ground to the depth of three miles. By Exermont Hill the Prussian Guard debouched from a wood in an attempt to recover the height. There was another wood on their flank full of Americans, and the commander shrewdly withdrew his men, so that they should not be seen during the enemy's advance, and then sent them forward in a surprise charge against the rear of the Guardsmen. The Germans that survived fled in a panic, even their officers, after an attempted stand, joining in the flight.

Americans' great attack

In the Argonne Forest an American force was enveloped by Charlevaux Mill, on the road from Binarville. Under the command of a New York lawyer, Major Charles Whittlesy, in a great fight lasting for four days and nights they beat off every attack, being resolutely determined to die in the attack rather than to surrender. They were at last relieved by a general advance of the American line in the evening of October 7th.

On the day in which they were surrounded, Prince Max of Baden, the new Imperial Chancellor of Germany, requested President Wilson to arrange the terms of an armistice.

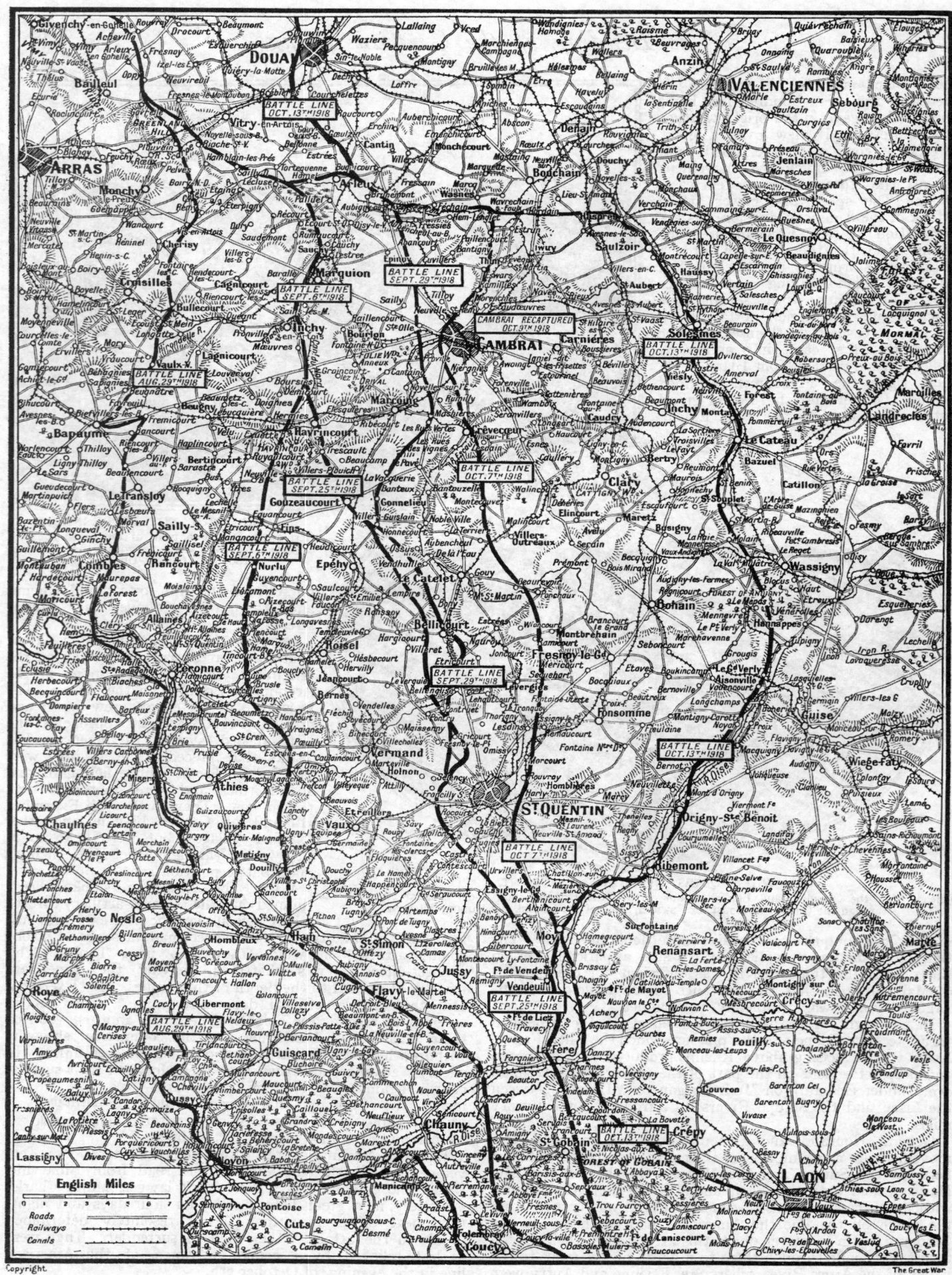

AREA OF FRANCE INVOLVED IN THE DECISIVE SECOND BATTLE OF LE CATEAU.

After the rupture of the Hindenburg line the enemy stood to battle in front of Le Cateau. For this decisive action Sir Douglas Haig's operations extended from Douai to Laon. Cambrai fell to him October 9th, 1918, and by the 13th the British line had been carried from Douai to Solesmes, southwards through Le Cateau, along the Oise River and Canal to La Fère, and south-eastwards to Laon.

446

CHAPTER CCLXXX

THE FLOODTIDE OF VICTORY IN THE WEST.

By Edward Wright.

III.—The Decisive Second Battle of Le Cateau.

Haig's Plan for Turning Entire Hindenburg System—Problem of Reaching Maubeuge before Winter—Ludendorff Revives Ghastly Method of Terrorisation—Clemenceau Proclaims Policy of National Reprisals—Australians Take Montbrehain-Beaurevoir Works—Germans Pinched Out of the Terrère—The Line of Battle on October 8th, 1918—Welsh Division Opens Attacks in Darkness—Enemy Swings His Last Reserves Into Wrong Position—Naval Division's Strange Adventure with British Tanks—How the German Counter-attack was Broken—Conquest of Cambrai—Advance of 2nd and 3rd Divisions—A Flourishing Prize of War—New Zealanders' Fast Fight through Esnes—Malincourt Taken by 21st Division—How the Irish and Lancashiremen Fought Along the Road to Le Cateau —25th Division's Decisive Achievement—Men of Tennessee and Carolina Drive to Bohain—General Debeney's Men Break Line near St. Quentin—Sir Douglas Haig Cuts Off St. Gobain and Laon—British and Canadian Cavalry in Pursuit—66th Division and 25th Division at Le Cateau—Canadians and Lancashires Meet in Cambrai—English and Scots Force Selle River—New Zealanders Carry Briastre—Tales of Sufferings of Smith-Dorrien's Rearguard—New Army Completes the Decisive Action of the War.

WHEN, as related in the previous chapter, Prince Max of Baden sent his request for an armistice to the President of the United States the decisive struggle in the war had reached its last critical phase. Between September 27th and October 4th, 1918, the main forces of the British armies had broken through the German lines and reached open country. The Hindenburg system was described very fully at the time by a German military writer, General von Ardenne, who still firmly believed that the defensive position was impregnable. He remarked :

Englishmen call our defensive front the Hindenburg line, and thereby show they fail to grasp the real character of our defences. We have no line, but a complicated, four-sided system of redoubts and fortifications extending from Cambrai to La Fère, a distance of nearly forty miles. The system, however, has a depth of twenty-five miles, so that, instead of having to penetrate a line, the enemy has to destroy a granite block with an area of one thousand square miles before he arrives at a position to deploy his forces in complete freedom and direct his attacks to high strategic ends. The conquest of the Siegfried works and its collateral positions would only form the overture to further developments, removing the objectives of the Entente armies into the twilight distance. Time is an ally of the German High Command. At rapid pace winter is approaching, and by robbing Marshal Foch of his African troops it will reduce the French armies by from one to two-thirds of their active strength.

The writer went on to remark that, after the check to the American Army's dangerous advance along the Meuse, the German High Command, having solved its railway transport difficulties, intended to wear its enemies down in the struggle for the extensive Hindenburg system and deprive the Entente of its renewed offensive energy.

The Hindenburg system, however, was not so solid a block of fortifications as General von Ardenne described. Its characteristic was length rather than depth. It originally extended from the neighbourhood of Lens to the neighbourhood of Metz, and after being strengthened westward by the Drocourt-Quéant switch-line and the Masnières-Beaurevoir secondary line, it was further supported by southern lines running along the Serre and Sissonne, and connecting by the Hunding line with the Upper Aisne defences and the Argonne works.

The grand British victories in the Siegfried line and Wotan line, between Arras and Cambrai, followed by the rapid conquest of part of the middle Siegfried line and its Masnières switch between Cambrai and St. Quentin, threatened to turn the enemy's lines of defence southward between the Aisne, Serre, and Sissonne Rivers. Although Hindenburg and his lieutenants had temporarily succeeded in

FRENCH AND BRITISH LEADERS IN CAMBRAI.
M. Clemenceau (second from right) and Sir Douglas Haig (in the foreground), with officers and war correspondents, before the Hôtel de Ville of Cambrai, in October, 1918. Cambrai had been recaptured by the Allies a few days before.

making a strong stand along the southern Hindenburg works against the American and French Armies, there remained to them on the western face of their fortifications only a few miles of intact works, extending from Beaurevoir village to Fonsomme village by the Scheldt Canal.

Behind this last fragment of the western Hindenburg works was rolling, open, well-watered country, already partly reached by the Australians and Midlanders. Through it ran, by Le Cateau, the railway supplying the German front from St. Quentin to Laon. There was the Maubeuge railway, in particular, which was the enemy's chief lateral line of communication with Cologne, connecting by Le Cateau with the Brussels and Valenciennes lines, and by Busigny and Bohain branching toward Guise, Hirson, and other bases for the Serre and Hunding line and Champagne front.

Le Cateau, Busigny, and Bohain were only a few miles behind the Hindenburg works at Beaurevoir, which had been con-

Haig's thrust at Maubeuge

structed to protect them. Relying on the moat of the Scheldt Canal, with its old and new tunnel refuges, and the maze of fortifications broadening over six miles of ridges, cuttings, and hollows, the enemy command had not excavated and concreted any further support system immediately in front of the Le Cateau-Bohain railway lines and junctions. Sir Douglas Haig had refrained from attacking this section of the German system in 1917 because of its incomparable strength, due in part to the skill with which the enemy had so sited his lines as to allow no good artillery positions to the attacking forces.

Confirmed in his view of his strength by long freedom from attack, the enemy had only a few practice trenches behind his Hindenburg system, and in order to win time to dig new entrenchments he stood to pitched battle in front of Le Cateau. Under General von Böhn the Seventeenth and Second German Armies combined for the last stand along a well-fortified line against the Third and Fourth British Armies.

Sir Douglas Haig's grand objective was Maubeuge and the line to Hirson. His thrust was made along the rear of the army groups of General von Böhn and the Prussian Crown Prince, and while he aimed at forcing the enemy masses back to the Ardennes Forest, they were to be broken also by the Franco-American thrust along the Meuse towards Sedan.

The problem was whether this great converging movement could be completed in the early winter of 1918, or whether rain, mud, and incessant fighting would tire out the armies of the Allied and Associated Powers and compel them to allow the enemy to rest and reorganise in the middle of winter. There were grounds for supposing that if Hindenburg were able to move his forces slowly back in good order Germany would not be disastrously dismayed by the loss of her allies.

The Germans considered they had given too much of their strength to Austria-Hungary, Bulgaria, and Turkey, and as Russia was overthrown and little help was obtained by the Germans from their allies against the fresh armies of the

German Command's misjudgment

United States, the fall of Bulgaria, the Ottoman reverses, and the unsteady position of Austria-Hungary did not end all hope for the Teutons. They trusted they would be able to stand out through the winter.

Strange as it may seem, the German High Command recovered more confidence when Bulgaria went out of the war and Turkey followed the same course. The men of Ludendorff's party became averse from the negotiations for an armistice for which Ludendorff himself had directly asked. As when they had decided on the invasion of Belgium and the criminal submarine campaign, so now they fatally misjudged the situation.

The Kaiser also recovered hope, and proclaimed that only a peace with honour would satisfy his armies. At first there was a tendency on the part of the Allies to regard this statement as an ordinary piece of bluff, designed to cover the confession of weakness made by the request for an armistice.

This was not so. The armistice proposal, made at first in a sincere but passing mood of despair, was being transformed into the last grand act of camouflage by the military party. While Prince Max of Baden was moving for a peace by

surrender, and parading the democratic and humanitarian sentiments suiting with the occasion, the German High Command was reviving and developing the old Prussian method of terrorisation. It was preparing to mine and fire every town and hamlet in Flanders and France which it was forced to evacuate. Clouds of smoke above Douai and Cambrai, and a trail of wrecked and mined villages behind Lille, advertised the dreadful purpose.

Their plan was an enlargement of the scheme of devastation carried out during the first withdrawal to the Hindenburg line. An arrangement was made to hold sufficient of Belgium and North-Western France to form a covering defensive ground to the Rhineland, while the evacuated territory was to be transformed into a waste of charred and blasted cities, unroofed and wrecked villages, and polluted wells, like the wilderness belt between Albert and Cambrai, but on a vaster scale.

Prince Max of Baden seems to have been genuinely upset when he learnt that the military party was bent on the scheme of general destruction. He pointed out that all the opposing nations would be so infuriated that no armistice could be arranged. Thereupon he discovered that no armistice was any longer desired, and that the horrible method of wholesale devastation was intended partly to blackmail the French and Belgian peoples into a negotiated peace, and partly to make it practically impossible for the German people to refuse a fight to the death.

The men around Ludendorff, representing the landowning nobility and some of the more desperate industrial magnates, calculated they would lose as much in a Socialistic revolution if they were defeated waging war in a civilised way as they would if their country were utterly broken in a struggle increasing in intense savagery as it neared its close.

Happily, there was a way by which the Allies could appeal directly to the fear of punishment stirring in the German people before Germany was so completely loaded with crime as to have lost all fear of consequences. There was a strong agitation in the public Press of France and Great Britain in favour of the course of naming the German cities appointed as hostages for French and Belgian towns. Stern

Savage scheme of destruction

American feeling in the matter was also expressed. But it was M. Georges Clemenceau, the energetic head of the French Government, who actively moved against the eternal barbarians and saved the world from the last foul horrors of German warfare.

On October 5th, 1918, M. Clemenceau proclaimed that, as the German Government was carrying out its savage threat to devastate and desolate completely the territories it was obliged to abandon, the German people would have to bear the consequences as accomplices in the crime. France, it was stated, had opened up negotiations with her Allies in regard to both the individual punishment of the authors and directors of the scheme of destruction, and the national reprisals which would be inexorably executed when the war was carried into German land.

"Never has there been opened such a terrible account between two nations," thundered M. Clemenceau, "and it shall be settled." He succeeded in thoroughly alarming the German Emperor, and orders came from General Headquarters to the fighting-line that the plan for blowing up Lille and Ostend was to be abandoned, and that only buildings of military value, such as those giving observation over the retiring German works, should be destroyed, together with railway lines, roads, and canals.

The order was not carried out by all enemy commanders, some of whom continued in mad spite the work of destruction for which their country would have to pay. In Cambrai and other places, where the delayed mines were already set and the fires lighted, it was too late to prevent a considerable amount of wrecking being done; but Lille, which prisoners at first reported to be full of high explosive, was saved from being burnt and gutted, and the population was not removed.

It was not, however, merely the threat made by M. Clemenceau that daunted the German War Lord and his ruling lieutenants. While the enemy High Command was hesitating between the fear of the consequences of defeat and

Fired by the retreating Germans : One of the streets of Cambrai when British troops reached the town on October 9th, 1918.

Explosion of a mine which had been left by the enemy. It went up immediately after the British troops entered Cambrai.

British infantry advancing over shell-swept ground in the Battle of Cambrai, October, 1918. Vivid photographic impression of a portion of the extensive battlefield during the course of the great allied offensive which brought about the sudden collapse of Germany.

Terrific battle that culminated in the capture of Cambrai.

Canadians entering the great square of Cambrai, when they retook that town on October 9th, 1918. Three sides of the square were on fire, throug[h] smoke of which, to the left, can dimly be seen the Hôtel de Ville. As the Allies had refrained from shelling it, all the damage to Cambrai was done by the Ger[mans]

One of the gates of Cambrai and some of the ruined buildings near to it. The German notice, "Unterstand," was probably meant as an indication [that] when allied airmen were flying about, shelter from bombs might be sought beneath the substantial structure.

Devastation in Cambrai by conflagration and explos[ion]

by means of fires started and mines prepared when they found themselves compelled to evacuate it. On the afternoon of the day on which they left it the ...ated enemy started shelling the town, adding thus to the earlier destruction which they had wantonly wrought.

...le the railway-station at Cambrai after the town had been retaken for France by Canadian and British troops, showing something of the damage wrought to the station building and in its immediate neighbourhood by the enemy when compelled to retire.

...ples of destruction caused by the retreating enemy.

Field-Marshal Sir Douglas Haig, with M. Clemenceau and other notables, standing on the steps of the former German Headquarters at Cambrai.

One of the churches in Cambrai, seen from the only side which was not on fire, with Canadian troops passing through on their advance.

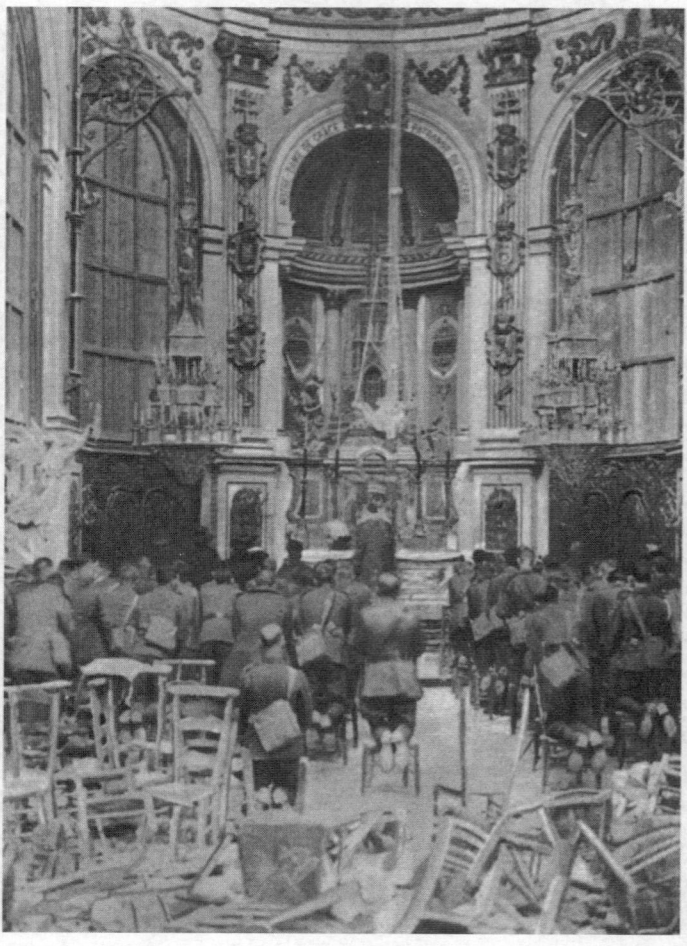

Interior of Cambrai Cathedral after the German retreat in October, 1918. This building was erected in 1825 to replace the one destroyed in 1793.

Thanksgiving Service for the deliverance of the town, and prayers for those fallen in the battle, held in Cambrai Cathedral, October 13th, 1918.

Praise and prayer arising from the ruins of liberated Cambrai.

their renewed faith in their power to avoid complete disaster, they found themselves overwhelmed, overrun, and broken in the most critical part of their line of defences. It was the British soldier who utterly convinced the Teuton that methods of barbarism were unsuitable in wars between highly industrialised peoples. With the breaking of the Hindenburg line in front of Le Cateau the lovely old cities of Flanders, the mines of Belgium, and the towns of North-Eastern France were generally redeemed from destruction.

On October 5th, 1918, Sir Henry Rawlinson's Australian and British corps made good their hold upon the Montbrehain and Beaurevoir works in a preliminary operation for the decisive battle. On the left the Victorians set out from Ramicourt village, at the foot of the hill on which the Montbrehain works were constructed. The Australians had some six hundred yards to climb before reaching the outskirts of the hill fortress, and the enemy, who expected the attack, met the advance with an intense machine-gun barrage and heavy shell fire. As the British barrage lengthened the German barrage shortened, until the two fell almost together ; but the attackers went through the enemy's curtain of shell and sleet of bullets, and when they reached Montbrehain the German garrison ran.

On reaching the hill-top just above the village the Germans were able to see how small were the numbers of the Victorians, and gathered and made a counter-attack on the thin khaki line, but failed to win back the village on the high slope. A battalion of pioneers of the 2nd Australian Division gallantly helped the conquerors of the village, and carrying out one of the most difficult of movements in the furnace of battle, altered their front and swung round southward, forming a defensive flank to protect the men who had fought through the houses and gardens. One of their companies also went through the village and completed the clearing of the cellars, preventing enemy machine-gunners and snipers from emerging in the rear of the Victorians.

New South Wales men and South Australians came up and filled the gaps in the line, after two posts had been driven in, and signallers secured the conquered village **Montbrehain and** by maintaining, under continual damage, a **Beaurevoir** telephone line connecting an observation outpost with the field batteries. A German division made repeated attempts to concentrate in the sunken roads about the hill-top for a counter-attack, but the Australian forward observation officer brought his guns upon them in sweeps of shrapnel and spreading high-explosive, compelling all hostile movements to cease.

On the right, by Beaurevoir, the attackers had a more arduous task. Ever since the Midlanders broke the enemy's line there had been constant in-and-out fighting in this key position, and after the Australians regained it the Germans counter-attacked, recovered the village, and fiercely held it. It was not until nightfall, after Tanks had crawled up the spur with the infantry of attack, that Beaurevoir was definitely conquered at the point of the bayonet. The enemy still made furious attempts to hold this point in the Hindenburg line, but ended with the loss of a thousand prisoners from the two villages and the weakening of his entire position.

All the Terrière upland, in the bend of the Scheldt Canal between Crêvecœur and Le Catelet, was abandoned by the enemy. While the struggle was raging round Beaurevoir Hill the New Zealand Division, the 21st Division, and 38th Division worked over La Terrière plateau and occupied the main Hindenburg line in preparation for a closing attack upon the last fragment of the Masnières switch that originally extended from the neighbourhood of Marquion, behind the Wotan line, through Masnières and Rumilly and Beaurevoir.

The capture of the unbroken outpost positions of the Hindenburg line by La Terrière was the result of the thrusts north and south, but the enemy only precipitated a general attack by refusing to stand for a while in his works on the high Terrière positions. His idea was to avoid another local defeat, and in avoiding it he greatly simplified the arrangements which the Third British Army, under Sir Julian Byng, was making to co-operate in the Battle of Le Cateau. Many guns and Tanks were enabled to be brought over rapidly erected bridges on the canal and placed on the hilly land in the bend of the waterway, where there were heights of 478 feet overlooking the highest points occupied by the enemy on the opposite ridge.

This line stretched from Niergnies Hill, south-east of Cambrai, to Esnes, Walincourt, and Villers-Outréaux. The last point was a small town by a hill dominating the captured Beaurevoir position. From Villers-Outréaux northward to Lesdain remained some five miles of unbroken line, running on low ground behind formidable belts of wire and covered by positions on the eastward slopes. The enemy also occupied some foreground posts on the westward slopes of La Terrière plateau, but these were won from him at the end of the first week in October by small fierce actions, such as that at Mortho Farm. At the southern end of the line the First French Army made a **Oppy and Fresnoy** determined local advance to Remaucourt, **recovered** two miles beyond the Scheldt Canal, bringing its line up to a level with that of the Fourth, Third, and First British Armies.

At the same time the northern divisions of the First British Army evicted the wing of the Seventeenth German Army from the old Hindenburg line north of the Scarpe, recovering the old battle places of Oppy and Fresnoy and prodding the enemy from the Fresnes-Rouvroy trench system. Douai was approached from the south-west at Biache, and menaced directly southwards by revived British activity on the Epinoy spur.

Meanwhile, behind the forefield actions between Lens and St. Quentin there went on a high-speed organisation for battle. Upon Sir Julian Byng, Sir Henry Rawlinson, and their Staffs fell the main work. They brought their Tanks and guns forward upon the newly-conquered uplands and ridges between Crêvecœur and Montbrehain, arranged supply tracks across the canal, piled up shell and charges for the big guns, and brought into line the freshest divisions in their worn yet tireless army corps.

In the southern suburbs of Cambrai were the fighting men of the 57th Division, and on their right the naval men of the 63rd Division. The 2nd Division worked alongside the 3rd Division, and on their right were the New Zealand Division and the 37th and 21st Divisions. Next came the 30th Division, the Irish and Englishmen of the 66th Division, and the Englishmen and Scotsmen of the 25th Division, the 30th U.S.A. Division, and the 6th Division. Supporting these twelve divisions of assault were eight other infantry divisions, with two cavalry divisions ready to exploit a break-through. General von Böhn had twenty-four infantry divisions in line, together with a special force of machine-gunners sent from General Headquarters. The enemy army group commander did not expect to be assailed in strength for some days, and was completely surprised by the speed and force of the supreme offensive movement of the war.

There was likewise a tactical element of surprise in the way in which the artillery of the attack was handled. The weather was very unpromising in the night of October 7th, and storms made the assembling of the troops an affair of great difficulty ; but as both regimental and Staff officers in the German lines were certain no attack could successfully be launched **Battle of Le Cateau** against them in the deluges, the great **opens** troubles which the British, American, and French met and mastered were among the factors of victory.

The heavy downpours screened the final activity of preparation from the enemy, as none of his machines could carry out nocturnal reconnaissance with flares in the tempest. When the Battle of Le Cateau opened at 1 a.m. on Tuesday, October 8th, 1918, German officers at Villers-Outréaux told their men it was only an artillery demonstration, likely to last two hours, and that they would be safe in the cellars and dug-outs. The previous afternoon the troops in the front line had been informed for the first time that their Kaiser had asked for peace, and the news had not improved their fighting quality

Huddling in their underground shelters, with the drum-fire thumping above them, they talked the matter over, and many of them came to the conclusion it was no use dying if the war was about to end. Few of them died. At the close of two hours, as their officers had foretold, the bombardment stopped, but as the garrison began to brighten, with the feeling they were at least secure until daybreak, they heard English voices shouting above them. They surrendered.

The Welsh of the 38th Division, under Major-General Ramsay, led this assault, in tempestuous darkness, on the commanding Villers-Outréaux position. With the 124-Metre and 147-Metre Hills beside it, this small town formed an important outer fortress to the enemy's general line, with enfilading fields of fire against an attacking army. The position was so strong that a frontal assault in daylight was impracticable, so the Welsh troops went out in the storm at night and slowly worked forward over the slippery ground and through deep wire entanglements, where they had to grope for the lanes made by their guns.

German outposts gave the alarm, and from the edge of the town issued a machine-gun barrage sweeping every way of approach and checking the advance, but nothing could check the landships used with the British forces. Up and down the slimy slopes of chalk, streaming with rain, the fast British Tanks drove into Villers-Outréaux, and the Welshmen, with a supporting English force, broke yelling into the town, apprising the garrison, still largely sheltering beneath the houses, that they were surrounded. By the early morning a large number of prisoners had been taken, and with the removal of the barbican work to the defences of Le Cateau the grand struggle began.

For the confusion of the enemy commander it was divided into two separately timed movements. At half-past four in the morning the forces of the Third Army came out in the darkness, in a fine interval between the rainstorms. Sir Julian Byng's divisions attacked from the south of Cambrai to the ridge opposite La Terrière, where the action at Villers-Outréaux was now seen to be a preliminary to a pitched battle. It seemed the British intention was to turn Cambrai by a great movement from the south, and as the defending forces on either side of the city were much worn by the intense, prolonged struggle with the Canadian Corps, and the Seventeenth and Sixth British Corps, the German commander hurried his last reserves towards the road running south from Cambrai.

By this time all the front between Cambrai and St. Quentin was blazing with gun fire, but the enemy reckoned that the artillery action of the Fourth British Army and the First French Army was but a feint. Both these armies had been strongly in action up to October 5th and 6th, and, as the German Staff probably knew, the Australian Corps, the Northern American Division, and most of the Ninth British Corps had been relieved in the line. With these excellent troops of attack withdrawn, the enemy commander felt relieved on the southern part of his front, and decided the gun fire there was a demonstration to prevent defending forces being shifted towards Cambrai. From the beginning of the summer campaign Sir Douglas Haig had hit with one

Major-General Edward M. Lewis, in command of the 30th American Division.

[Elliott & Fry. Major-General C. J. Deverell, in command of the 3rd British Division.
[Elliott & Fry. Major-General Sir A. H. Russell, in command of the New Zealand Division.

[Elliott & Fry. Major-General C. A. Blacklock, C.M.G., D.S.O., in command of the Naval Division.
LEADERS IN LE CATEAU BATTLE.

army or army group, while his other forces were organising their conquered ground for an alternate attack.

But it was not so in this case. Sir Henry Rawlinson had been strenuously preparing while fighting, and with the reinforcement of two United States divisions he had been able to keep a strong army reserve ready to develop at once the advantages won in the opening offensive against the Hindenburg works. About forty minutes after the Third British Army attacked, the Fourth British Army came into action, lengthening the front of battle to seventeen miles. Then the First French Army further extended the line of conflict for another six miles. The result was that General von Böhn used his reserves too quickly, concentrating them northward, and before he could redistribute the troops his last entrenchments were overrun, and British and Canadian cavalry were riding through open country, capturing intact railways.

South of Cambrai the enemy's resistance was, in the circumstances, very strong. The gallant troops of the 57th Division, under Major-General R. W. R. Barnes, who had battled for ten days into the suburbs, made another determined attempt to enter the city by the Faubourg de Paris, and there formed a defensive flank protecting the advance of the Naval Division.

It was the Anson, Hood, and other battalions of naval men, under Major-General C. A. Blacklock, that opened the main operations. In a striding assault, right across the southern defences of the city, they took the village of Niergnies, on the Cambrai-Bohain road, and thereby instantly and directly threatened the large enemy garrison between them and the Canadians with envelopment.

By eight o'clock in the morning General von Albrecht, commanding in and around Cambrai, was in a position of extreme danger, and once more there was despatched to his line a large portion of the German reserve. The Naval Division was counter-attacked in overwhelming strength, but was not overwhelmed. Its corps commander, Sir Charles Fergusson, had a powerful mass of guns, admirably directed by low-flying aeroplanes, darting below the rainclouds and dropping messages by parachute for gunners and Staff. Two hostile divisions, deploying for a counter-offensive, were marked down and shattered by the guns of the Seventeenth Corps.

Though the naval men lost Niergnies for a time, it was more by an accident than by any weakness against superior numbers. In the course of the morning the Germans gathered from the railway line at Awoingt and the Le Cateau highway and, collecting in a sunken road, stormed back to the key village. With them came some seven Tanks. The naval men thought the leading storming cars were British. In this they were correct. They naturally concluded that British Tanks would help them. In this they were wrong. The chariots of war had been captured by the enemy, repaired by his engineers, and provided with trained German crews.

They were reserved for a great surprise on an important occasion, and sent out to save Cambrai. There was only one

British-manned Tank in Niergnies, and it had exhausted its ammunition in breaking into hostile machine-gun positions in the advance, so could do nothing against the perverted landships. The naval men had to fall back from the village, but by this time they understood the character of the new Tanks, and replied to the enemy's trick by using captured German weapons against the lost British landships. Two of their officers employed long anti-Tank rifles, and proved their efficacy by putting out of action four Tanks in succession. Then another officer, with some men, brought German field-guns to bear at short range and destroyed another Tank. The remaining two fled.

Once more the British creeping barrage travelled up to Niergnies, and the naval men returned close behind

LEGITIMATE DESTRUCTION.
Bridge across the St. Quentin Canal, on the Arras-Cambrai road, blown up by the departing foe.

ALL IN THE DAY'S WORK FOR THE ENGINEERS.
Bridge destroyed by the Germans during their retreat from the Cambrai front. Canadians, engaged on its repair, were having a meal under the shadow of the broken structure. The engineers won the Commander-in-Chief's particular praise for their skill and energy in bridge construction and repair.

it, recovered the village, advanced towards the railway, and took more than a thousand prisoners from the broken enemy forces. This great infantry success on the southern rear flank of Cambrai, together with the reach and marksmanship of the gunners following the Naval Division and the strength with which the 57th Division held back any flank movement, decided immediately the fall of the famous city. On the north the Canadians, who had done most to wear down the strength of the garrisoning army, were alert for any sign of weakness. In the night they closed with the rearguard on their side, broke through it, capturing hundreds of prisoners, entered the city, and there met, in the early morning of October 9th, a patrol of the 57th Division that had worked from the southern side.

The 2nd Division, under Major-General Pereira, attacked the village of Forenville, alongside the 3rd Division, under Major-General C. J. Deverell, that advanced on Seranvillers. Both of these forces belonged to the Sixth Corps, commanded by Sir J. A. L. Haldane, who had the Guards Division in support and prepared to extend the thrust. The leading battalions of the 2nd Division, after taking Forenville, shared in the struggle against the great counter-attacking force that pushed the naval men back for a time. A fresh German

division—the 208th—brought from the St. Quentin sector, was launched against them, with the effect of delaying their progress to the Cambrai-Bohain road, but the slight, temporary strengthening of the enemy was of mortal cost to him.

The English troops and their Scottish comrades probably thought they were unlucky when they found the struggle grow more intense as they advanced. From the point of view of Sir Douglas Haig, however, they were meeting with the supreme luck of the whole battle-front. They were doing something far more decisive than gaining a remarkable depth of ground. They were attracting, engaging, and nullifying a considerable German force which had been wrongly moved northward, and which would have been worth an army corps to its commander had it been in its original, proper position by the southern part of the line.

The brigades of the 3rd Division, that equalled the British Guards in the power of withstanding attack, and approached very close to the oversea corps in vehemence in assault, took Seranvillers with the brilliancy they had recently displayed in their drive over the Flesquières Ridge. They met the misdirected counter-attack from the Le Cateau-Cambrai railway line, with the 2nd Division and Naval Division, let some of their daring light Tanks through to Wambaix about mid-day, and with the forces on their left advanced towards the railway at nightfall.

At daylight on October 9th the three divisions were moving on the main road to Le Cateau, by Igniel and Estourmel, having crossed the road to Bohain and the railway to Busigny. Beyond the Le Cateau road they met with a flourishing reward. It was a German military garden, a thousand acres in extent, admirably tended and filled with fine vegetables by the soldier market-gardeners of Albrecht's corps.

Assault of Seranvillers

This revived one of the lost delights of conquest. There was a time when a good German breakfast, with cigars to follow, was a common prize of a morning's victory in enemy entrenchments. But the wily, foul-fighting Teuton had destroyed this simple pleasure by the trick of leaving behind tempting, poisoned food when preparing to evacuate dug-outs at short notice. This was one of the little things that greatly embittered the Briton, and the angry memory of it cost the poisoners something. But the vast military garden at Boussières was a pure delight, though the things that grew in it were not cooked and ready to eat.

On the right of the Iron Division the magnificent New Zealanders, under Major-General Sir A. H. Russell, had a difficult task between Lesdain and Esnes. They had first a bout of fierce fighting in the fortressed village on which the unbroken part of the Hindenburg line rested. Behind it ran the deep bed of a torrent, usually a strong swirl of waters in rainy weather. In spite of the October storm, the rain had washed away, leaving only a small stream.

The Germans, however, were in force in the numerous concrete works built in the sides of the winding hollow. In swift, continuous action the New Zealanders took some seven hundred prisoners before nine o'clock in the morning, killing many more men who fought desperately. Tanks of the heavy sort cruised on either side of the torrent, while the lighter storming cars noisily rattled ahead, crushing down the belts of wire and spreading dismay among the Teutonic soldiery.

The New Zealand Division, with the Island Brigade on the right and the Rifles on the left, and Wellington and Auckland machine-gun companies supporting with covering fire, went forward so fast through all their difficulties that they had to stop to get in touch with the troops on both flanks. Using a smoke barrage, to screen themselves and their Tanks, the men from the happy isles carried Esnes village and rested at night before Wambaix.

New Zealanders carry Esnes

Near them was the 21st Division, which, under Major-General D. G. M. Campbell, had crowned itself with glory by Rheims in May, after doing much to save the flank of the Third Army between Epéhy and Bray-sur-Somme in March, and holding the Lys line in April. Most of its veterans

IMPROVISED SUBSTITUTE FOR A STRETCHER.
German prisoners, taken by the Canadians during the fighting forward towards the capture of Cambrai, passing a wayside British howitzer post. They were bringing in one of their wounded comrades in a blanket slung hammock-wise from a pole.

were gone, and the young troops, though already hardened in battle, were set a stiff job against the intact stretch of the Hindenburg system between Esnes and Villers-Outréaux. The trenches at the foot of the ridge were full of Germans who escaped the bombardment, and when pressed they fell back to a labyrinth of works in orchards, cottages, farm-buildings, and woods.

One brickyard that withstood all infantry attack was cleared from the air by contact pilots, who first dropped bombs and then swooped low with machine-guns in action, driving the garrison to earth and allowing the attacking force to close. At the end of the day Malincourt was won, but the village of Walincourt, northward on the Cambrai-Bohain road, was still fiercely defended. The garrison, however, withdrew in the night; they found the net closing round them.

Beyond Villers-Outréaux, where the Welsh division preceded the general movement by an impetuous local attack on the enemy's centre, Englishmen and Irishmen of the 66th Division, under Major-General H. K. Bethell, and Englishmen and Scots of the 25th Division, under Major-General J. R. E. Charles, fought towards Le Cateau with superb gallantry.

The Connaught Rangers, Dublins, and Inniskillings of the 66th Division drove down the Roman road leading past Le Cateau to Mons, with Lancashires, Manchesters, and three battalions of Fusiliers on their flanks, and carried Serain at unexpected speed, reaching past the German field-artillery to a battery of 8 in. howitzers and releasing the remaining inhabitants, old men, women, and children.

As the people came out to greet their liberators the enemy's barrage crashed on the village, and the counter-attack opened. Fiercely the Germans strove to recover their heavy guns. They pushed the Rangers back from the houses, but the Irishmen returned to the assault and regained Serain, while other British troops and Americans were fighting for the villages on either side.

This action, along the historic path of the retreat of the 5th and 3rd Divisions after the First Battle of Le

ADVANCING OVER GROUND WHERE SNIPERS STILL LURKED.
Canadian machine-gunner who had reached the outskirts of Cambrai. Having become aware that a sniper still remained hidden in some coign of vantage ahead of him, the soldier had taken cover behind a sturdy tree-trunk.

Cateau, on August 26th, 1914, was the decisive event of the struggle. Indeed, it was the decisive event of the war on land. In the afternoon five broken German divisions fell back from the Serain crossway, where the highways to Le Cateau and Bohain met. So weakened was the enemy in strength and so demoralised in spirit that he could not stand on the rising ground to which he had retired on the left, and he abandoned it at nightfall.

He had prepared a scheme of general destruction, but most of the explosives he had placed were not fired. He had no time to think of ruining the countryside. Even at the cross-roads the mining had not been steadily carried out. Three Germans were stretched dead by the roadside, having in their perturbation been blown up by their explosive. East of Serain the villages were picturesque clusters of red-roofed, white-walled houses shining under the church spire.

A decisive achievement The rolling countryside, save for a scattering rearguard shell fire, was less damaged by war than it had been in August, 1914.

Inside the houses, however, from which some ten thousand country-folk were rescued, there was cruel wreckage. Not only had the German soldiers plundered the furniture, but they had started the savage campaign for crippling the French people for a generation by wantonly destroying the industry of fine lace-making around Le Cateau and Bohain. In all the farmsteads and many cottages was the family heirloom by which the people lived, consisting of a delicate piece of machinery, running up to a cost of two thousand pounds.

These machines the Germans had broken, and there can be no doubt that they would have burnt and blasted farms, cottages, and churches had not the decisive break-through along the Le Cateau road been carried out with such overwhelming swiftness. French parish priests saved some of their churches by cutting the wires to the mines. German prisoners were tearful at the suddenness of the disaster, pleading that the offensive was unfairly delivered, as the Kaiser had opened negotiations for a peace with honour. Among the men who **American drive to Bohain** talked in this manner were those who had broken the peasants' lace-making machines, carried off men, women, and girls into slavery, and slowly starved the children in a land of good harvests.

These men broke under the attack of the 30th United States Division, under Major-General E. M. Lewis, as completely as under the assault of the 66th and 25th British Divisions. The Americans were the men from North and South Carolina and Tennessee, who had made the more successful part of the earlier advance across the Scheldt Canal to Nauroy. They formed up in the night between Ponchaux and Montbrehain, facing the enemy who was on Faicourt Hill. The Germans were in superior strength, holding the uncompleted bits of trench behind their lost Hindenburg line and using the sunken roads as fresh entrenchments for their thousands of machine-gunners.

Setting out in black darkness, the Americans surprised the hostile outpost line, and then in a steady, workmanlike manner bore down the increasing resistance from the flanking

BRITISH TRANSPORT GOING FORWARD DURING THE FINALLY VICTORIOUS OFFENSIVE.

Very heavy work was thrown upon the Army Transport Service as the offensive progressed, and especially in its last stages. Every advance made supply more difficult, and the greatest testimony to the efficiency of the supply services, Sir Douglas Haig said in his despatch of December 21st, 1918, was the rapidity of the advances, which otherwise would have been impossible. Their work was unostentatious, but its effect was far-reaching.

position at Brancourt, while their left wing fought onward alongside the English and Irish troops on the right of the Le Cateau road to Prémont village. Here, in line with the Connaught Rangers at Serain, along the Cambrai-Bohain highway, they had heavy fighting against a strong counter-attacking force. Again they broke the enemy, and after rescuing some civilians they extended from Prémont and from Brancourt in an arc forming the first part of the enveloping movement round Bohain.

On the right of the United States Division the 6th Division and other English troops made a sharp advance to Beauregard, by the Bohain-St. Quentin road, and there formed, by nine o'clock in the morning, a defensive flank to the main thrust towards Le Cateau. Then on their right the First French Army skilfully attacked on a front of some six miles against the Fonsommes end of the Beaurevoir line to the neighbourhood of Ribémont, on the Oise River. In their first advance the French carried the maze of strong works near the sources of the River Somme, and against continual counter-attacks worked over the fortress ground extending about the sunken roads by the St. Quentin-Le Cateau railway line.

It was one of the strongest knots in the old Hindenburg system through which General Debeney's divisions had to struggle. There were, for instance, caverns made to shelter three thousand men, and containing t u n n e l s from which sorties could be made against the rear of the small forces, bombing their way under the cover of shell fire through the works. In the course of the day five hundred

prisoners were captured beneath a single farm, and another fifteen hundred Germans were collected, usually in small groups, during the progress beyond the railway line.

The British troops and the American division took ten thousand prisoners and some two hundred guns in the course of the day, and the Royal Air Force, skirmishing far in advance of the infantry and swooping upon all the enemy's roads of retreat, added greatly to the German losses in men and artillery. The airmen again exercised their extraordinary power of aerial blockade, and, in spite of the sagging clouds and curtains of rain, swooped upon the columns of troops and transport that blocked the roads converging on Le Cateau, and captured a considerable number of guns by killing the horses and scattering the gunners, so that when the British infantry came along they found the abandoned pieces, limbers, waggons, and lorries. Fifty additional guns and two thousand more prisoners were obtained by the British armies.

In the night of October 8th, 1918, the Second German Army was thoroughly disorganised. In the Battle of Amiens, on August 8th, only its southern wing had been shattered and demoralised, t w o a r m y corps breaking in panic right towards the bend of the Somme. The breach in the line had then been repaired, owing to the strength with which the centre and northern wing held north of the river.

On October 8th, however, the force and spirit of all the Second Army were broken, and a considerable portion of the troops of the Seventeenth Army also. There was no reserve available to pour up in the night of October 8-9th, and

HONOUR AND THANKS IN CAMBRAI TO THE REPRESENTATIVES OF VICTORY.
Sir Douglas Haig and M. Clemenceau visiting Cambrai, in October, 1918, immediately after the recapture of the town. They inspected the French Guard of Honour drawn up to receive them, and—as shown in the oval— conversed with a priest and several of the inhabitants who had remained in Cambrai till its deliverance, despite the Germans' orders for its complete evacuation by all civilians as long before as September 8th.

General von Böhn could do nothing more than order a fighting retreat to the Selle River, by Le Cateau, and arrange with Headquarters for some fresh troops to be speeded to the new river line to stiffen the broken army.

But Sir Douglas Haig and his lieutenants, with General Fayolle directing the French army group between the Oise and the Middle Aisne, pressed the advantage won on and round the Le Cateau road with such speed and striking power that no stiffening of the limp fragments of the Second German Army could be effected in time to prevent the reverse from developing into a tremendous disaster. Early in the morning of October 9th the First, Third, and Fourth British Armies and the First French Army leaped forward to exploit to the uttermost the decision achieved the previous day.

All the great German salient of St. Gobain and Laon was cut by Sir

CARRYING FORWARD THE IRON ROAD.
British railway troops pushing forward the reconstruction of one of the lines close on the heels of their advancing combatant comrades on the western front in France.

LAYING THE RAILS OF A LINE RENEWED.
Men of the British military railway service carrying on the work of rapid reconstruction necessary for maintaining the supplies required by the forces in the field.

Douglas Haig from the north. To a considerable extent General Fayolle's army group of the First, Fifth, and Tenth French Armies had its work taken away from it by the British victory. General Mangin, in particular, who had steadily ground down the strength of General von Carlowitz's forces, had but to gather a last harvest by pressing his old enemy in front, while the British troops were cutting the German communications far in the rear.

There was thus a double problem for the German High Command and General von Böhn to solve. They had to withdraw the armies of General von Hutier and General von Carlowitz from the St. Gobain and Laon sectors, along the routes from the Serre line, below Hirson. Some of these routes were already crowded with the troops and transport of General von Eberhardt and General von Mudra's army, withdrawing from the Craonne and Rheims front under severe pressure from the Fifth and Fourth French Armies.

In these circumstances it was not easy for General von Böhn to follow his usual course of feeding his weakened flank

with the force moving from his endangered front. The Allies' mastery in the air exposed his rail and road communications to disorganising raids by the new machines carrying large cargoes of devastating bombs, loosed from a deadly sighting apparatus.

The German forces, streaming upward from St. Gobain, between the Oise and the Peron Rivers, succeeded in gathering strongly by Guise, where the Oise bends westward towards Hirson. This movement saved for a time the outflanked Serre line of the great Hindenburg system from being enveloped by the First French Army, but it could not be extended far enough to cover the middle part of the Maubeuge railway lines, which the Third and Fourth British Armies instantly menaced.

On Wednesday, October 9th, Sir Julian Byng and Sir Henry Rawlinson moved infantry, cavalry, Tanks, and guns forward over the rolling open country towards the Selle River. At the critical point of Serain the Connaught Rangers, with other Irishmen and Lancashiremen, went forward along the road to Mons and took Maretz. Then the Dragoon Guards and Canadian Horse rode through them, and carried the old battle positions of General **Cavalry carry old positions** Smith-Dorrien's corps at Troisvilles and Reumont, and the Fort Garry Horse took Cattigny Wood at a gallop, opening the way for the Scots and Surreys to Clary.

The cavalry then reconnoitred Le Cateau, but found it too strongly held by machine-gunners to make a sweeping charge practicable. So the Rangers, Manchesters, and Fusiliers of the 66th Division, with the English and Scotsmen of the famous 25th Division, came up in the evening and began working towards the suburbs of the town in an enveloping movement. South of Le Cateau German machine-gunners held strongly to positions by the village of St. Benin, and northward they had a half-made but very useful trench line running to Solesmes. After fighting into the western side of the town the British infantry had to wait for artillery support. They could well afford to do this by the Selle. This upper course of a small stream, with the railway line by it, and the enemy's incompleted trenches, formed a position that was little better than an open field warfare obstacle, against which the new method of attack with smoke-clouds, fast storming cars, and intricate barrages by light and heavy guns, was likely to prevail. The Germans were busy putting up wires and digging machine-gun shelters, but their works did not enable them to stand for long.

The great success of the second day was the capture of Bohain by the American and British wing of the Fourth Army, which had closely approached the town the previous night. About the same time Busigny Junction was also stormed, and the railways feeding the enemy's St. Gobain and Laon sectors were thereby cut some thirty miles in the rear. Along the northern branch line running to Cambrai, which the enemy had used for his grand counter-attack the previous day, the British cavalry were so quick in action that the line was conquered in a very useful condition. The important manufacturing town of Caudry was attacked from the south, in a movement against the long flank which the

St. Gobain and Laon cut off
Seventeenth German Army formed, while drawing off behind Douai and retiring its forces from the Wotan line in front of the city, under strong pressure from the 11th English Division and other northerly forces of General Horne's First Army.

While General von Below was withdrawing to the Haute Deule at Douai, to keep in line with General von Quast's retreat to the same canal line against the Fifth British Army, he used the men he obtained by shortening his front to strengthen his southern flank covering Solesmes, Le Quesnoy, and the approaches to Valenciennes. As far as Lille and Tourcoing in the north, and Gobain and Laon in the south, the victory of General Byng's and General Rawlinson's forces told with instantaneous effect.

The enemy had to withdraw with the utmost speed from the ends of his broken line, both to prevent complete disaster and to save divisions to reinforce the broken centre. The end of the Wotan line, by Drocourt, was thus conquered in a walking exploration.

Below Douai the vigorous attack by the Canadian Corps, through the German rearguard in Cambrai, led to another large result. Breaking through the city, with the 57th Division on the right and the 11th Division on their left, the Dominion troops upset the plan of the enemy commander, and struck into his flank along the Ereclin stream, between the roads leading towards Valenciennes and Solesmes.

While Sir A. W. Currie's men drove in the enemy's front, the divisions of Sir Charles Fergusson's Seventeenth Corps, Sir J. A. L. Haldane's Sixth Corps, and Sir G. M. Harper's Fourth Corps furiously assailed the new German flank between Le Cateau and Solesmes road. The Guards Division and the 24th Division closed on Solesmes westward, along the road from Cambrai, and this important centre of communications, with its suburb of St. Python, was further encircled from the south at Viesly. All the western bank of the Selle River below Viesly was reached in a resumption of the general offensive which began at dawn on October 10th, 1918.

Le Cateau was then partly carried by the tireless 66th and

Passage of Selle River forced
25th Divisions, who forced the enemy out of the city back to the railway embankments and Landrecies suburb. The enemy made a violent attempt to recover the town, but the rush of his infantry was checked, and the counter-attacking forces were thrown back to the railway. South of the town the American troops made a magnificent advance across the railway to St. Souplet and to the village of Vaux, above the large Forest of Andigny protecting the secondary railway junction of Wassigny. The large tract of woodland was entered by the English troops forming the right wing of the Fourth Army, and the French forces connecting with them continued their advance up the Oise towards Guise.

Above Le Cateau the passage of the Selle River was forced by the Highlanders, Yorkshiremen, Lancashires, Worcesters, and Riflemen. The Scotsmen first arrived at Neuvilly, after marching sixteen miles and fighting for twelve miles in the evening of October 9th. The Selle stream was only neck deep or chest deep in places, but it ran between steep banks. On the eastern side a strong front of German machine-

gunners was hidden in orchards, concealed positions, and half-finished trenches, with some eight feet of wire entanglement hastily erected.

In the night of October 11th East Yorkshires waded the stream, rushed a trench full of Germans, and made an advance to the railway; but after trying to form a bridge-head they found their flanks were exposed and returned across the stream, having suffered much smaller losses than they had inflicted on the enemy.

On Saturday morning, October 12th, the Manchesters resolved to force the river. Carrying planks, and accompanied by sappers with light bridges, the troops went through a barrage of heavy gun fire. While the sappers stood in the water holding up their bridges, which were not quite long enough to reach the opposite bank, the Manchesters either went over in single file or forded the stream in their heavy kit.

There followed a fierce struggle with the bayonet in Neuvilly, and while the combat was still raging amid the houses, other English troops crossed the Selle to the north, where they had gained a footing on Friday night, and cleared the enemy out of his riverside positions. The New Zealanders stormed Briastre and fought up the heights of Bellevue, while the Guards advanced on their left on Solesmes and took some of the buildings on the outskirts.

All this scene of conflict was sacred ground to the men of the New Army. For it was in the valley running by Briastre, from Le Cateau to Solesmes, that the 4th and 5th Divisions had stood against the overwhelming enveloping army corps of General von Kluck when that German commander boasted that he had the British Expeditionary Force in a ring of iron. Brigadiers in the First Battle of Le Cateau were army corps commanders in the second engagement; battalion officers were commanding brigades and divisions. They all were in grim mood, and so were the new veterans whom they directed in action.

From parish priests and farmers, in the newly-conquered country between the Scheldt Canal and the Selle River, news was at last obtained regarding the men of the old British Regular rearguard, who fought to the end to enable the rest of General Smith-Dorrien's troops to retreat towards St. Quentin. Some **A new Battle of Waterloo** of the soldiers had taken refuge in the farmhouses, and when discovered had been made to dig their own graves, and were then shot. Eye-witnesses described the scenes to the officers and men of the Third and Fourth Armies.

The British troops who listened to the story were in grave danger of becoming worn out. They had been conducting practically a continuous battle for nearly three months, some of them indeed having fought from Amiens to Le Cateau and Solesmes in a series of terrific actions lasting more than three months. They had shattered half of the entire German Army in the west, having attacked all the way at the odds of one against two. They were very tired men at the beginning of the second week in October, and only the strength of the spirit in them kept them moving with the old majestic pace and skill against the last rested divisions which the enemy brought against them in the last of the quiet sectors between Douai and Lille.

The tale of the end of some of the bravest of their countrymen in the great defensive action of Le Cateau in the summer of 1914 whipped up their passion for a supreme effort before they were relieved by the troops they had relieved about a week before. They completed the conquest of Le Cateau, broke over the Selle River at various points between that town and Solesmes, and in the afternoon of October 13th held and repulsed a great counter-attack which the enemy made along the new river line.

This completed one of the most decisive actions in history. The British armies, with their assistant American force, had fought their new Battle of Waterloo, and for the rest of the campaign were in pursuit of a crushed, disorganised, dispirited enemy, whom they were shepherding towards the scene of supreme disaster. Henceforward it was a race between the armistice-makers and the forces of Sir Douglas Haig.

THE FLOODTIDE OF VICTORY IN THE WEST.

By Edward Wright.

IV.—The Beginning of the Pursuit.

French Enveloping Movement Round Laon—Mudra and the Wine of Rheims—Enthusiasm of Advancing French Armies—Germans Fall Back on Pine Woods of the Retourne—Germans Fight with Renewed Courage for Armistice—American Success at Chatel Chéhéry—Hirschauer Attacks from Verdun—Gouraud Breaks Across the Arne Stream—Complete American Conquest of Argonne Forest—Great Withdrawal by Einem's and Mudra's Armies—Difficulties in German Railway Transport—Mangin Attacks Along Chemin des Dames—Böhn Escapes from Encircling Movement—Recovery of St. Gobain and Laon—Heroic American Advance at Chatillon Crest—Hindenburg's Problem of the Shortened Front.

WHILE Sir Douglas Haig was making his decisive attack through the western face of the Hindenburg system, and arriving behind the southern lines of the enemy's immense stretch of works, General Pétain was using the main French forces in an encircling movement round uplands and ridges by Laon. There was, of course, intimate connection between the British and French operations, with General Fayolle as French army group commander keeping in personal touch with Sir Douglas Haig, and Marshal Foch approving and co-ordinating every movement.

As has already been shown, the Franco-American forces of the Fourth French Army delivered the first blow on the southern line that broke the enemy's front. From the Oise at Tergnier to the Meuse at Brieulles there were six German armies gathered in the shelter of the lower Siegfried line, with its Hunding, Brunnhilde, and Kriemhilde prolongations and switches. The army of General von Hutier was still clinging to La Fère, with a bridge-head at Tergnier. and fighting up the Oise east of St. Quentin. The army of General von Carlowitz stretched from the high St. Gobain Forest to the Aisne. The army of General von Eberhardt held the eastern part of the Aisne plateau and Berry-au-Bac. General von Mudra's army, after getting Rheims almost within its grip, was falling back between Berry-au-Bac and the Suippe River. The army of General von Einem extended from the Arne stream, by Béthenville, to the Argonne Forest.

From the Argonne to the Meuse was the new army under General von der Marwitz, forming part of General von Gallwitz's army group, with the army of General von Fuchs arrayed around Verdun.

The blow struck by General Gouraud

A GREAT FRENCH ARMY LEADER.
General Humbert, in command of the Third French Army during the attack on the St. Quentin front and the subsequent pursuit of the retreating foe.

on October 3rd shattered the left battle position of General von Einem between Béthenville and St. Etienne, on the Arne River. As the old German army of Champagne rolled back it left nearly seven miles of the right flank of General von Mudra's army exposed. At the same time the left flank of Mudra's forces was seriously endangered by the thrust which General Berthelot had made with French and American divisions of the Fifth French Army against Eberhardt's advanced positions along the Vesle River. General von Mudra was beaten without a struggle, and on a front of nearly thirty miles he retired from the salient which had been formed around him at Rheims. The ground from which he retired was of enormous strength. Much of it had been held by the enemy since the summer of 1914. It included the hill forts of Brimont and Nogent l'Abbesse, which, with the neighbouring highland north-eastward, had given the Germans for four years dominating points of attack upon Rheims.

Forty million pounds' worth of wine lay in the cellars beneath that city, and Mudra's officers and men coveting this treasure in July, 1918, with the help of Eberhardt's army had come near to capturing it. Without a battle they had to abandon not only their old hill forts, but the great block of white Moronvilliers Hills, in wrestling for which they had spent lives by tens of thousands throughout 1917 and the spring and summer of 1918. The natural colour of the great downs was green, but the earth had been bleached by hurricanes of shell from both sides until the heights were nothing but ghastly lumps of rough chalk.

On recovering the downs at fearful cost in July, 1918, Mudra, who was a sapper general, had determined that no force should make him again loosen his hold. He had tunnelled and caverned below and around the system which

General Gouraud had constructed the previous May, and made the Moronvilliers system one of the supreme wonders of modern fortification. His men were still busily engaged upon this Gibraltar of Champagne when the famous 2nd United States Division broke across its eastern flank and stormed the more northern higher point of Mont Blanc.

Mudra was an energetic and skilful sapper, but no great strategist, as indeed he had shown when succeeding to the command of the Crown Prince's armies by Verdun in the late spring of 1916. All his work went for nothing, and, angrily setting fire to Brimont, Nogent, and the hamlets in the valley of the Suippe, he drew his army back on October 5th, with French cavalry patrols pressing and rounding up his rearguards and taking some of his fortifications at the gallop.

The enthusiasm of the advancing French troops was unlike anything seen in them throughout the war. The tide of victory ran in their blood. Confidence was a thing of the past. What they possessed was certainty. The sudden revelation of the enemy's complete weakness came after the period of incessant desperate fighting. After the opening of their last Champagne offensive the French soldiers had always advanced, but always each step forward had been met by a renewed resistance of the most stubborn kind. They had swung on the right to the railway junction of the Grandpré defile, and reached it only to be hammered out of it across the Argonne Forest. The American Army, checked in the foreground of the Kriemhilde line, had been unable to keep pace with the French forces in t h e enveloping manœuvre round the forest ridge. There had thus been no scope for the genius in manœuvre of their commander. The men had had to fight forward in continual, downright, frontal attack, discovering most of the enemy's camouflaged strong points by first trying to work over the apparently empty ground, and then smashing sideway approaches with massed gun fire, smoke barrages, and light Tank charges.

General Gouraud, however, still retained his gift for fencing with the enemy, and, when he had bunched

French certainty of victory

General von Einem's main forces on the western side of the Argonne Forest, he moved his own point of attack quickly and stealthily in the night towards the flank of the Moronvilliers system, and there achieved one of those fine, strategic strokes that altered the complexion of the war. It was because his men suddenly perceived the large idea underlying all their hard, slow, slogging work that they went wild with excitement while sweeping in pursuit of the outplayed as well as outfought enemy.

There was a similar high mood among the troops of the rapidly advancing Fifth French Army, under General Berthelot. This distinguished commander, however, disappeared from the scene of his victory between the Vesle River and the Lower Suippe, being once more replaced by General Guillaumat, who was largely responsible for the decisive campaign against Bulgaria. The Third French Army, under General Humbert, which had retired from the fighting-line during the closing struggle on St. Quentin, and became again part of Marshal Foch's reserve army, prepared to appear in its old position alongside the First French Army.

Marshal Foch's new dispositions

The Tenth French Army, under General Mangin, seemed also to be losing some of its established strength, while the Second French Army, under the Alsatian commander,

General Hirschauer, appeared again somewhat shorn of force at Verdun, but soon afterwards disappeared. The American divisions, which had fought under Major-General Bullard along the Vesle, grew into a great force — the Second Army of the United States — to the command of which General Bullard was appointed. Other strong forces were being organised. The explanation of all these new dispositions was that Marshal Foch was preparing his own battle, which was to be distinct from the operations conducted by the British, French, and American Commanders-in-Chief, but greatly assistant to them.

The enemy commander also obtained more forces for the final battle by shortening his line round Rheims. Fiercely holding on to the Aisne River line by the promontory of Craonne, he swung back on either side of the highway from Rheims to Rethel. This brought him along the lower course

TO SAFETY FROM THE SHIFTING BATTLE-LINE.
Canadian soldier held up by a comrade while helping some women to remove a portion of their belongings to safety in a village under enemy shell fire. In oval: French villagers, moving westward from a threatened area, passing one of the big guns going forward.

of the Suippe River, where he had four miles of dense pine woods covering the ground to the Retourne stream, a smaller tributary of the Aisne. Behind the Retourne was another eight miles of difficult country formed by the great bend of the Upper Aisne at Château Porcien and Rethel. This Upper Aisne line was the last of the Hindenburg works on the Champagne front, and it connected by the Hunding line with the Serre River defences above La Fère.

The Germans thus had a series of fortifications on which to fall back when they withdrew across the Lower Suippe River. With their high-velocity guns they maintained a gas-shell bombardment upon the southern bank of the Suippe, in order to win time for another orderly withdrawal. The Fifth French Army forced the Suippe by its junction with the Aisne, crossing the Aisne - Marne Canal, which had been the dividing-line between the opposing forces in the French offensive in the spring of 1917. The Fourth French Army also broke the Suippe line at Bétheniville, and by October 6th, 1918, the French advance guards were beginning to trickle through the mass of pine woods towards the Retourne.

Then, however, the elastic scheme of defence, which General von Mudra and General von Einem were following, was abruptly changed to a continuous desperate struggle for every yard of ground. Someone in the German High Command had intervened at the moment when the Prussian Crown Prince was abandoning Mezières as army group headquarters and moving to Spa. The intention, apparently, had been to withdraw to the last Hindenburg line along the Upper Aisne, but the new enemy battle director could not allow any more strategic retirements.

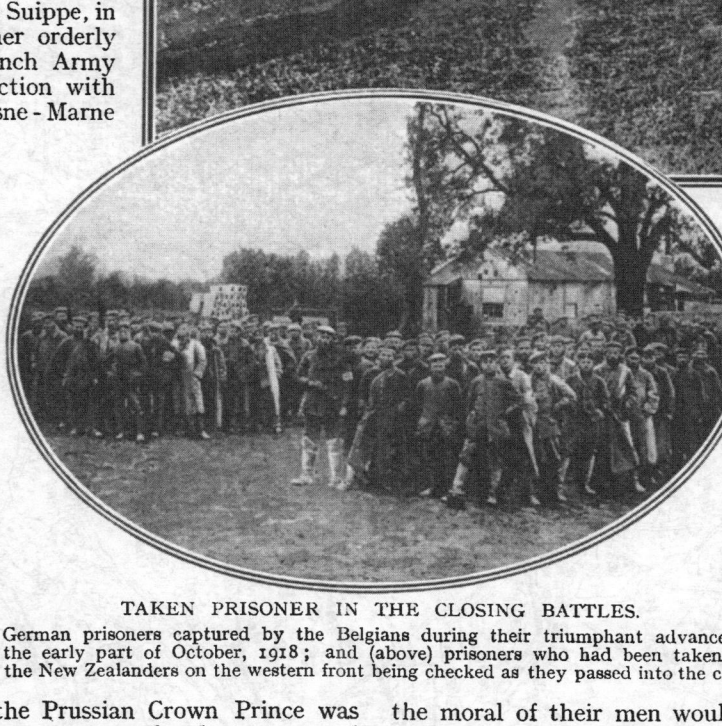

TAKEN PRISONER IN THE CLOSING BATTLES.
German prisoners captured by the Belgians during their triumphant advance in the early part of October, 1918; and (above) prisoners who had been taken by the New Zealanders on the western front being checked as they passed into the cage.

CAPTIVE BUT NOT ILL-CONTENT.
Batch of prisoners captured by the French making themselves comfortable at the pleasant place in which they passed part of the period of their captivity. They were seemingly glad to be safely out of the fighting.

The spirit of the German soldiers, already badly worn by four years of bitter conflict, was deeply troubled by light Tank attacks, and by increasing inferiority in gun power and aerial power. All along the front regimental officers found it continually more difficult to keep their men in action. The machine-like power of Prussian discipline had been losing its efficacy since the Battle for Amiens, and, as was revealed when the war came to an end, the German leaders were under a constant apprehension that the moral of their men would give. The Prussain machine was still strong, but the material it used was wearing out.

To keep the men well in hand they were informed that the Kaiser had opened negotiations for an armistice to treat for peace. They were told that if they only succeeded in checking the enemy during the conduct of negotiations, and thus saving their country from the immediate perils of invasion, the war could be brought to a good conclusion. Picked forces were used for the counter-attacks against the Fifth and Fourth French Armies to win time for the retreating columns to deploy in the new positions. Had the Crown Prince's group of armies been subjected to a tremendous general attack as soon as they learnt that their Emperor was **Germans fight for time** suing for peace, they would probably have been caught in the same despondent and yielding frame of mind as that in which the men of the Second German Army were caught.

However, during the interval between the enemy's withdrawal from Champagne to the Upper Aisne line in the French Ardennes, his troops acquired a fresh fund of courage from the thought that they were fighting the last, short battle of defence, on their efforts in which a quick and good peace depended. Even when, on October 8th, the British armies completely shattered and turned the entire Hindenburg system and destroyed the main railway communications between Berlin, Cologne, and the Lower Oise and Middle Aisne sectors, the renewed courage of the German soldier did not vanish, at least on the French and American fronts of attack. Prisoners and guns were taken in large numbers, yet the German machine-gun defence and covering fire of artillery remained very strong along and round the Upper Aisne.

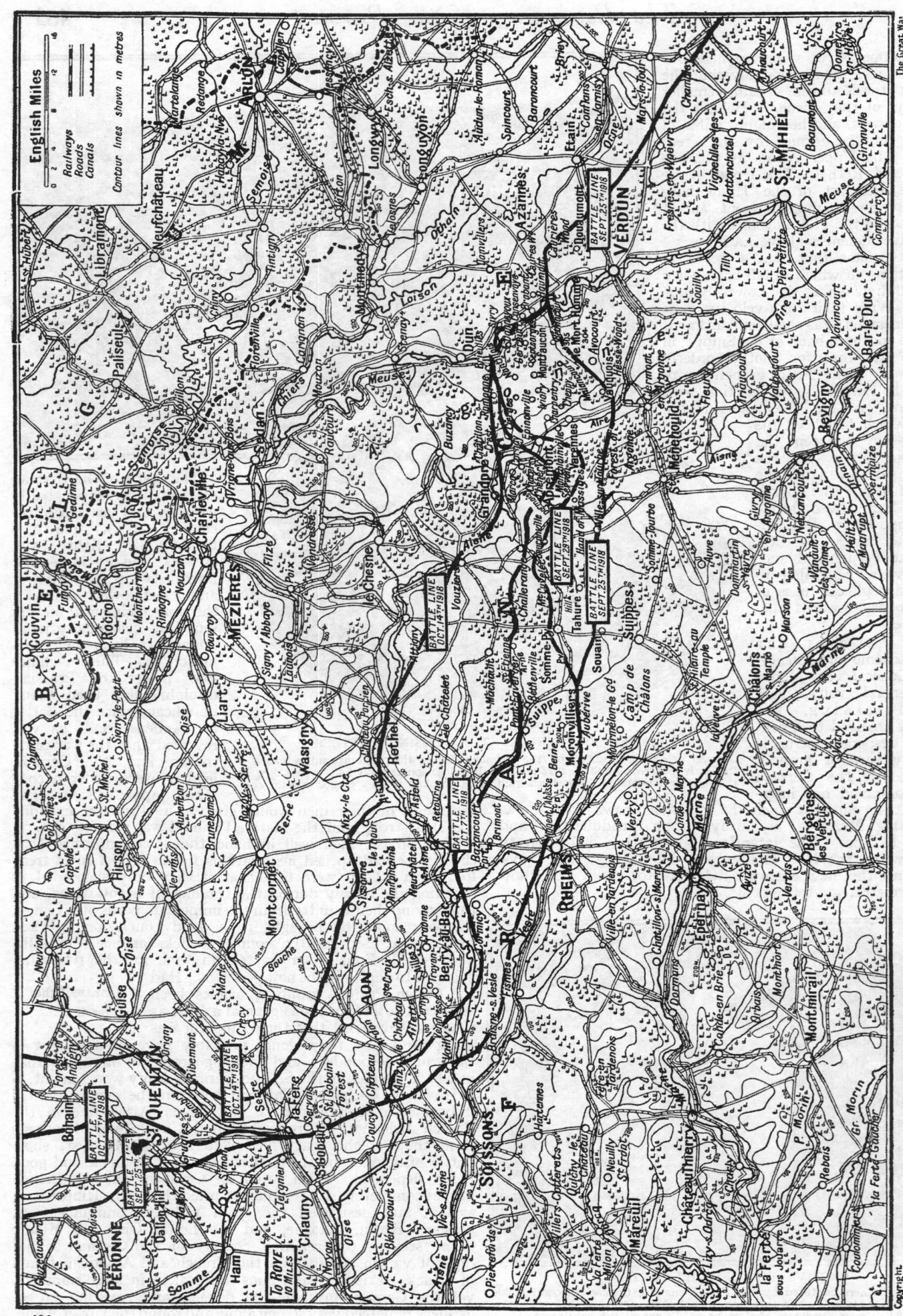

HASTENING THE RETREAT OF THE ENEMY ON THE CHAMPAGNE FRONT IN OCTOBER, 1918.

Important progress was made by the allied armies along the southern part of the battle-front during the first week of October, 1918. At the beginning of that week the German forces still occupied the greater part of the heights of the Argonne and St. Gobain Forest. By the end of that week they had been forced from both strongholds, while Laon had been recaptured by the French, and the enemy's railway lines threatened.

464

The American Army also continued to meet with stubborn and skilful opposition, being practically brought to a strategic standstill between the Meuse and the upper end of the Argonne Forest. In spite of the great number of men and guns that General Pershing employed, he was for some time unable to achieve a success comparable with that of General Gouraud's army on his left. He was attacking the main artery of the enemy's communications, and therefore met the strongest resistance. Gradually, however, his men pushed the enemy back.

On October 7th they won an important success along the eastern edge of the Argonne by Chatel Chéhéry, where there were three dominating heights commanding all the Aire valley alongside the forest. Under cover of a mist the United States troops crossed the Aire at dawn, and against heavy machine-gun fire re-formed on the opposite side of the river and charged up the three hills, on the crest of which the Germans made a desperate struggle in a series of strongly-built defences. There were long and bitter, but successful, actions on the hill-tops, and at the end of the day the American forces had made an important step towards the complete envelopment of the great wooded ridge by reaching almost to the north-eastern corner of the Argonne Forest at Cornay.

On October 8th some of the divisions of the First American Army joined with part of the Second French Army of Verdun, under General Hirschauer, in an offensive along the eastern side of the Meuse. Here the Germans still held some of the line lost by the French in February, 1916, As the ground which they occupied was higher than that which the Americans had won on the western bank, they exercised considerable artillery pressure upon the flank of advance of the First American Army.

The German commander was either lacking in a sense of the realities of his position, or more likely ready to take desperate odds in order to check the main advance. Although his forces round Verdun outflanked the Americans above Montfaucon, the Americans at the same time also outflanked his troops across the river. General Hirschauer prepared a local offensive at the end of September, and only waited for a favouring mist and for the enemy to be lulled to a sense of security and use considerable forces in the operations against the American flank.

When the Franco-American attack was delivered under combined frontal and flanking hurricanes of fire, the Austrian and German divisions holding Caures Wood, **Franco-American** Haumont Wood, and Consenvoye, Brabant, **offensive** Haumont, and Beaumont villages were rapidly overrun and surrounded with a loss, in prisoners alone, of three thousand men. The French attacked in front and the Americans in the flank; everything went like clockwork, and, in spite of the strength with which the enemy had organised his endangered positions, each objective was reached with comparative ease according to time-table.

Great was the contrast between the beginning of the struggle round Verdun in Caures Wood in February, 1917, and the end of it in October, 1918. All the terrible confusion and strain of the opening battle were replaced by ease and orderly arrangement in the last assault. Under the methodical genius of General Pétain the French had become better at organisation than the Teutons, while retaining all the vehement daring of character which was a matter of race.

General von Gallwitz had concentrated his reserves on the western side of the river for fear the Americans should attempt to break through there. Before he was able to send reinforcements across the Meuse to General von Fuchs, the

Austrians, who were suffering most under the attack, gave up hope of being supported and surrendered. The attacking troops reached the German lines of 1916, but did not go beyond their objectives, by reason of the strength of the hostile barrage.

Their success, however, compelled the enemy commander to detach considerable forces for defensive purposes north of Verdun. Thereupon, General Hunter Liggett and General Gouraud combined once more in a central action in and around the Argonne Forest. General Gouraud made a thrust of some two miles across the Arne stream, and, again helped by United States troops, carried the high hill by Machault, with Lancon village and some important heights on the western side of the Argonne.

In the heart of the high forest and along the Aire River

PRIDE AND HAPPINESS IN LIBERATED LAON.
At mid-day on October 13th, 1918, the French entered Laon, which for four years had been in German hands, and shortly afterwards General Mangin, whose Tenth Army had won the city after three months' hard fighting, proudly delivered the town to the French President in the presence of the municipal authorities.

the First American Army made a magnificent final leap forward to the railway line at Marcq, driving the enemy from the northern end of the great upland, and arriving on the slope of the defile opposite Grandpré. The forest of the Argonne was definitely conquered on October 10th, fourteen days after the opening of the great Franco-American offensive.

The campaign was a matter of thousands of obscure adventures of strangely picturesque heroism, but lacking in the broad outlines of the more rapid movements in clearer sections. It was jungle fighting, complicated by all the ghastly defences of ambushes and traps that modern science could devise— stagnant pools of poison gas, trip and pressure mines, log barricades and fields of wire entanglements, wolf-pits, aerial torpedoes, tunnels, and the ubiquitous machine-gun redoubt. The high, foliaged, screened land, with its poor roads and blind terrain, did not permit **Jungle fighting in** the use of artillery with aerial fire control. **the Argonne** Tanks, also, were of less value than elsewhere, and for the most part the infantry had to work forward with its own power, exploring, skirmishing, and continually inventing on the spot novel ways of circumventing the innumerable works on which the enemy had spent the labour and thought of four years.

The Argonne fighting suited with the American temperament. It was a combination of pioneer work and Red Indian warfare, and there were Red Indians engaged in it, who could worm their way through brushwood almost as silently as a snake. Individual initiative on the part of a patrol or a platoon commander was a priceless thing in the dog-fights in the forest.

R.A.F. PATROL SETTING OUT FOR THE ENEMY LINES.
Sir Douglas Haig, in his despatch on the closing months of the war, said that the ever-increasing size of the Royal Air Force, and the constant improvement in the power and performance of machines, enabled intense activity to be maintained at all times.

In spite of the fact that the Germans, always retiring on undamaged country, were able to keep their line under delicate, flexible control by means of an intact signalling system and concealed communications, the American divisions steadily won forward, and with the help of the French on the western side conquered the greatest hostile barrier on the western front, and thereby greatly added to the enemy's difficulties in the decisive weeks of the war.

Over the conquered ground the First American Army and the Fourth French Army united into practically a single, grand, manœuvring force. General Hunter Liggett could at last despatch a division or more to reinforce the French in the course of a few hours when motor-lorries were available. On the other hand, the army group of the Prussian Crown Prince and the army group of General von Gallwitz were divided by the large block of the Upper Argonne between Vouziers, and the neighbourhood of Sedan. Their railway communications ran in a large northern swerve to a point just below Sedan, and the section of railway east of the Meuse had to carry the traffic through Luxemburg, Northern Lorraine, the Rhineland bases of Coblenz, and the neighbourhood of Mayence.

To keep the enemy apprehensive in regard to this most vital section of his line, east of the Meuse, and compel him to concentrate strongly for its protection. General Hirschauer resumed his attack from Verdun on October 10th. The German commander had been making strong but belated counter-attacks upon his lost positions, while the French and American gunners were hauling their pieces forward. At the end of two days, when the enemy's fresh forces were densely assembled and appointed to attempt a stronger assault, the guns of France and America again broke upon them without any warning bombardment of preparation. On the eastern side of the river the downs by Sivry were taken.

On the western bank of the Meuse, General Hunter Liggett, employing a tremendous sweep of gun fire for sixteen hours against the enemy's Kriemhilde line, broke into the northern part of Cunel Wood and battled towards Dun, on the Meuse.

On the same day, October 10th, 1918, the Fourth French Army, under General Gouraud, completed another period of heavy, close fighting with General von Einem's army and the wing of General von Mudra's army by a wide, deep advance to the last Hindenburg line along the bend of the Upper Aisne. On a front of some thirty-seven and a half miles, from the outskirts of the Argonne Forest by Vouziers to the junction of the Suippe and Middle Aisne by Berry-au-Bac, the German armies abandoned their attempts to hold the Aisne tributaries, and withdrew against both the Fourth and Fifth French Armies to Rethel and the Hunding line.

On captured Germans was found an order commanding them to hold the Suippe line until October 13th at least, to enable the material to be removed and methodical operations of retirement to be carried out by neighbouring armies. The vigour with which the leading French brigades fought forward along the streams in the great thrust by the Franco-American force on Machault, a few miles west of Vouziers, brought about the new retreat. In an extraordinary communiqué the successor to Ludendorff claimed the strategic movement to the rear as a victory for General von Einem. "The victorious issue of the great battle in Champagne, won with relatively weak forces by the army of General von Einem over the immensely **German perversion** superior strength of French and American **of the truth** armies in a fortnight's struggle, with the exhaustion of the enemy owing to his remarkably heavy losses, made it possible for us smoothly to execute our difficult movements." Thus ran the most remarkable statement published by the German High Command since Helmuth von Moltke's report on the issue of the First Battle of the Marne.

As a matter of fact, General von Einem alone commanded twenty-five divisions, ten of which were composed of rested

SQUADRON OF SCOUTS OF THE R.A.F.
Some of the men and machines of the Royal Air Force that took part in the splendid air work during the closing months of the struggle on the western front. The Commander-in-Chief paid special tribute to the unfailing keenness of the pilots and observers.

troops. He had a quarter of a million men in line against the Fourth French Army and a few American divisions, and he lost twenty-three thousand officers and men as prisoners, and six hundred guns.

The neighbouring armies involved in General von Einem's unexpected, sudden defeat were those of General von Mudra, General von Eberhardt, and General von Carlowitz. The British victory at Le Cateau had a governing influence along the entire front of conflict. A rapid retreat was necessary for all enemy forces west, south-west, and south of the Serre-Hunding-Upper Aisne line fortifications.

To guard against any confusion, with weakening gaps along the front of five outmanœuvred armies in hasty retreat and under hot pursuit, the timing of the various processes of withdrawal had to be carefully observed. The entire German armies in France and Flanders had lost, in fifteen days, a total of sixty thousand prisoners and one thousand five hundred guns. But far greater losses in men and material were probable unless extreme care were taken.

BRITISH TRANSPORT FOLLOWING THE EASTWARD ADVANCE.
As they retreated the Germans, quite legitimately, destroyed and mined the roads behind them, but the oncoming British easily skirted the craters until these were filled up, and meantime light railways, spun alongside the old highway greatly expedited the forwarding of supplies.

The enemy's line had been resolved into a series of gigantic salients, with the St. Gobain upland in the extreme angle. The army of General von Hutier had to travel by road to Guise, and thence to Hirson. The army of General von Carlowitz was happier in having direct railway communication from Laon, by Marle and Vervins to Hirson, and was able also to send reinforcements by rail towards Guise and the British line by Wassigny. General von Carlowitz further possessed short, direct railway communication with Rozoy and the Namur line at Mezières.

Critical position of the enemy

So long as he retained an effective hold upon Laon, from which six railway lines radiated, he had many routes of retreat ; but his friend General von Eberhardt, who had been army corps commander with him in the Lys battle and received promotion to army command at the same time as he

did, was in a desperate condition in regard to facilities for withdrawal. From his Middle Aisne sector there was no line of retirement except one light railway, in the centre by Sissonne, which ran within four miles of Rozoy and then swerved southward.

General von Mudra had a railway to Rethel, but he had to share this with the left divisions of General von Einem's army. Einem's forces on the right, having the remaining part of the Vouziers railway, and being covered by large tracks of pine wood, was expected by the High Command to resist along the Arne and the Suippe while the forces of General von Mudra and General von Eberhardt conducted their most difficult operations of withdrawal. When, therefore, Einem's troops were compelled to retreat on October 10th, three days before the earliest date fixed by the German High Command, the movements of the other enemy armies were seriously disarranged.

General von Mudra's men were fiercely pressed between the Lower Suippe and the Aisne, where the Fifth French Army began another great advance, reaching some twenty-four miles north of Rheims. Even severer was the pressure exerted upon the armies of Eberhardt and Carlowitz on the Craonne height, the Chemin des Dames, and the ground about the St. Gobain Forest. The enemy wished to disengage in the centre and hold on at the side, and came near to disaster.

North of St. Gobain the wing of General Debeney's First Army drove into Servais, between La Fère and the forested height, while all General Mangin's Tenth Army stormed forward from the south of St. Gobain to the California plateau, where the Italian divisions displayed magnificent staying-power in their continuous assault on difficult hill positions. Here the forces of Eberhardt held on to the middle course of the Aisne, directly above Fismes, protecting and being protected by the promontory of Craonne. They were attacked on October 10th at Vendresse, Troyon, and Cerny, places at

THE ACTIVITY OF THE PURSUING FRENCH.
Light transport passing over a bridge still in process of completion by French engineers. Quite remarkable quickness of execution distinguished the work of the French engineers during the rapid last advance of the war. The construction of this particular bridge constituted a record in point of time.

which Sir Douglas Haig won his first grand success in the war, when with two divisions he forced the Aisne in September, 1914, and reached the Chemin des Dames.

The Franco-Italian attack, however, was made in circumstances happier than those following the First Battle of the Marne. It was delivered against the enemy's flank, instead of upon his front, and only as he weakened on the ridge and spurs did the left wing of the Fifth French Army strike along the low land by the river. Day and night the last wrestle for the most famous ridge in France went on under strangely paradoxical conditions. The Germans wanted to be allowed to retire; the French and Italians strove to make them stand their ground, and provoked counter-attacks by insistent, imperilling thrusts toward Anizy, Laon, Ailles, and Craonne.

There was high hope that if the large enemy forces could be kept in action on the semicircle of **General von Böhn's** heights south of Laon they could be en- **skilful retreat** veloped by the Fifth and First French Armies. Once more, however, General von Böhn managed a hasty, intricate retirement with successful skill. With the men and guns that he withdrew he continually strengthened the forces standing along the Oise River, so that the line there held for more than a week, by Guise, Ribemont, and the western forts of La Fère. He also found troops and artillery to pour above Guise into the Forest of Andigny and along the Sambre Canal, while meeting the gallant French attempts to break over the Oise by Origny.

This he achieved by sacrificing his stocks of war material round Laon. His lieutenants, Carlowitz and Eberhardt, fled from General Mangin in the night of October 11th, when the Chemin des Dames was evacuated; but German rearguards were still holding out at Tergnier, directly south of St. Quentin. On October 12th Tergnier was at last recovered, after being outflanked for some days, and La Fère, in spite of its marshland defences, was turned from the south by a knife-like movement through St. Gobain. At the same time the hill forest, with its tangle of fortifications, was encircled by the northern wing and centre of the Tenth French Army, marching on Laon down the Ardon valley, while the southern wing spread above Craonne over the Croix heights.

There was only one gap of weakness in the retiring lines of the Teutons. The Army of General von Mudra, upset on its right by the premature withdrawal of Einem's forces, and disarranged on its left by the sudden retreat of Eberhardt from the Aisne plateau and the upper part of the Laon-Rheims railway, gave an opportunity to General Guillaumat and his Fifth Army. On October 12th the French troops fought across the Aisne at Neufchatel and, farther up the river, stormed into Asfeld and neighbouring villages.

Above the Aisne the railway was cut at Amifontaine, and a rapid advance made to Sissonne Camp, the marshes of Marchais, Le Thour, and Nizy-le-Comte. Thousands of people were liberated, and for a brief while it looked as though a decisive movement would be effected. But General Guillaumat and his men were arrested by the Hunding line, just above **General Mangin** Sissonne and the marshes. The German **recovers Laon** commander succeeded in shortening his front and releasing divisions for the general reserve without any local disaster.

On the same day, October 12th, General Mangin made a rapid leap forward, also without overtaking the enemy. In thirty-six hours he advanced more than eleven miles, taking his guns with him across the Ailette stream and up the Ardon, and arriving at nightfall by the outskirts of Laon. The city was entered the next morning, and happily found to be intact, with its magnificent cathedral that crowns the hill.

The menace of reprisals by M. Clemenceau was having effect, and so were the speed and power of the British movement across the enemy's communications with Cologne and Berlin. The Germans had not had time to fire much of the immense stores they left, or to mine roads sufficiently to impede the progress of General Mangin's supply columns. The invaders were not entirely reformed. They took with them as hostages the Mayor of Laon and some five hundred male citizens, after vainly calling upon all men and lads of military age to tramp with them into further captivity. Having no leisure to search for those who hid themselves, they went off with their hostages, leaving Laon with a free population of 6,500. There was a stretch of some ten miles of devastated ground between Soissons and Laon; but the French Army worked forward quickly, capturing not only a great amount of the enemy's shell supply, but many miles of his light-railway system.

From July 15th to October 13th the enemy had lost by capture four thousand five hundred guns, and by destruction at least five thousand more. His artillery units had to be reduced through lack of material, with the result that his general strength was doubly decayed, his weakness in artillery increasing the dispiritedness of his infantry. General Mangin pressed the Germans from all the heights south of Laon, and with the wing of General Debeney's army and with General Guillaumat's forces established a line running below the Serre River, the Souche stream, and along the Hunding line to the bend of the Upper Aisne by Château Porcien.

For some days the Germans kept strong rearguards posted two or three miles in front of their Hindenburg system of defence. As soon as the pursuers brought their heavy artillery forward, with ample shell supplies, the covering German forces fell back to the entrenched lines, with the usual concreted machine-gun positions and belts of wire. The rivers, flooded canals, and marshes between Guise and Rethel were the greatest obstacles to a continuation of the French pursuit.

Hindenburg sappers had chosen the line of water defences at the time when the primitive heavy British Tank was shaking the German infantry around Bapaume, in the latter part of 1916. Under the deluges of September the river valleys had become inundated, and the enemy had done all he could to collect as much water as possible. The rainfall in October, however, was little more than one-fourth that of the previous month, and it became possible, when the light Tank **Floods delay French** brigades were organised within attacking distance **pursuit** of the moated Hindenburg works, to repeat the tactics employed along the Scheldt Canal. There was, however, a pause in the action along the Serre, Hunding, and Rethel line, while the principal French armies were rebuilding railways and remaking roads for bringing forward all their battle machinery. General Gouraud captured Vouziers, seven miles above the Grandpré defile, and some of his cavalry approached Attigny, from which the northern extension of the Argonne Forest might have been turned.

The German commander, however, fought in strength for the wooded ridge above Grandpré. Still keeping the American Army back along the Kriemhilde line (which was roughly on a level with Grandpré), he strongly garrisoned the Grandpré Hills so as to form them into an upland salient along the right flank of the Fourth American Army. Thereupon, General Gouraud opened another struggle against the flank of the German forces that held up the First American Army.

The Americans were still bogged in the clay between the Meuse River and the forested ridge. Here the September rain did not drain away as it did in the Scheldt country, and the Germans, standing for the most part on high ground, made continual sorties with a view to upsetting the organisation of the attack. They drenched all the American line from Montfaucon to the Aire stream with poison gas that clung horribly about the wet ground; yet, in the most depressing conditions, the spirit of the American infantry remained high, and on October 14th they resumed the offensive by Châtillon Crest, a steep hill 280 feet high, thickly covered with trees.

The Americans went up and found themselves in an arc of machine-gun forts, with showers of shrapnel playing upon them in addition to a sleet of bullets. The trees were all wired together, and for forty hours volunteers gallantly yet fruitlessly endeavoured to make paths through the belt of wire. At last Stokes guns were brought up. The little English gun smashed the wire and broke into the enemy's works, from which hundreds of dazed prisoners were taken. When the ground was cleared the Americans went up with the bayonet. Most of the Germans fought their guns to the death.

In the meantime other American divisions worked round

SEA WONDERS REVEALED FROM THE SKY

H.M. Airship C*5 entering her hangar in a thirty=mile=an=hour wind.

On board a British airship used for convoy purposes over the North Sea.

Convoyed: Wonderful view from H.M.A. C*2 of the vessels under her protecting guidance.

Scandinavian convoy under full steam: Photographed from a convoying British airship.

Motor=boats off Dover travelling at top speed: Photographed from the air.

Air view of coastal motor=boat: Showing the great wash of the swift little craft.

Torpedoed by the enemy and set on fire: Air photograph of the steamer Audex.

Through defensive clouds: View from the air of H.M.S. Onslaught passing through a smoke screen

Romagne Wood through valleys covered by machine-guns and artillery, and in spite of heavy losses stormed the village, lost it under a hostile whirlwind bombardment covering a counter-attack, and reconquered it. Westward there was another long, terrible struggle for the town of Grandpré and the heights above it. The general gain in territory was small, and the enemy commander won time to make a new line of trenches and linked shell-holes, known as the Freya line. It ran near the northern part of the Argonne Forest, above Grandpré to the Meuse, at a distance varying from two to six miles behind the Kriemhilde line. The original Hindenburg system having been partially breached, was employed as an outpost machine-gun screen, and the grinding battle went on with little immediate result except the containing of a large German army and the wastage of all its front-line divisions.

The new men in the German High Command, however, were building up a considerable general reserve that appeared to vary from thirty to forty divisions. It was estimated that the Germans were in the course of saving about a hundred and fifty divisions by the shortening of their line. They had also about a hundred thousand lightly wounded soldiers coming back from hospital, and most of the lads of the 1920 class were practically ready for service.

The condition of the German forces in the field was confusing to the judgment. While some officers thought their men were hopeless, others were so confident that they were inclined to agitate against the armistice proposal. No doubt it was in the sectors where a successful resistance had been maintained that the feeling obtained that the war might still be won. General von Lossberg did not succeed Ludendorff, but went to Lorraine as Chief of Staff to the Duke of Würtemberg. His task was to withstand the attack by the special army which Foch was building up out of French troops withdrawn both from the shortening front and from sectors taken over by the Second American Army. Some twenty French divisions with six United States divisions were obtained for the stroke through Lorraine, and General von Lossberg had to make demands upon the

German need of fresh divisions German divisions in reserve, which left the enemy forces between the North Sea and Guise in a condition of permanent weakness.

These forces were still strong in numbers, forming indeed half the entire enemy effectives, but they were growing demoralised, and badly needed relief by fresh divisions and a long rest. Only by an orderly withdrawal to the Meuse and the eastern part of Belgium could the Germans obtain the additional fifty divisions required to counter the blow that Marshal Foch in person was preparing in Lorraine. The enemy would have to meet the Second American Army as well as the French army group under General de Castelnau, and the strain on his resources increased not only with every action but with every troopship that crossed the Atlantic.

Field-Marshal von Hindenburg appears to have been both clearer-minded and steadier in influence than Ludendorff. He published an appeal to German officers to refrain from agitating against the armistice proposal and to obey the Emperor in his political policy. This was the time when the extraordinary legend of an undefeated Germany began to take shape. It was partly a device for maintaining the spirit of the German soldier, but largely a reflection of the policy of a fight to the death which Ludendorff's lieutenants tried to force on Hindenburg when they found that they could master the railway and other difficulties caused by the various withdrawals and by the British break-through at Le Cateau.

According to revelations afterwards made by a German

officer in the fighting-line, Ludendorff and Hindenburg, in the supreme crisis, reversed their rôles. Ludendorff was the man with the iron will and the blind brain ; Hindenburg was the man who summed up things with intelligence, and came to the conclusion that it was better to lose the war than to let the nation be destroyed. As a member of the Prussian nobility the old Field-Marshal wanted to save what he could from the wreck.

Hindenburg's victories in Russia were becoming disasters. The fire he had lighted, directly at the instigation of Ludendorff, was sending sparks into Germany, and all the infinite care and intrigue spent by the German Government in the

PITIFUL HAVOC IN A STATELY HOME OF FRANCE.
Ruins of an old château on the western front. French soldiers who had reached the neighbourhood were taking the opportunity of having a swim in the moat, the bridge over which had been destroyed.

course of a generation in taming and seducing the German Socialist leaders were likely to be lost in a genuine, popular insurrection. Hindenburg had, perhaps, less knowledge than Ludendorff, but more wisdom, and his aim was to withdraw his army in a condition for use in Germany if needed.

Hindenburg, however, was not dictator. The enemy's direction of the High Command seems to have been in commission, with two parties alternating in actual power, according to the complexion of affairs in the field. No doubt the personality of the German Emperor told in the matter, and he was a gambler like Ludendorff, whom he had continually supported. By losing the war he personally was likely to lose everything, and he would have ridden his people to the death. But the old Prussian nobility had much that they hoped to save, and they had never liked their Emperor or his heir. They foresaw that if their armies were routed Bolshevism would follow. Hindenburg was their true representative.

Although the old Field-Marshal gradually returned to power the work of keeping the troops actively resisting was carried out by officers of subordinate rank. Staff officers **Position of Hindenburg** of the rank of major—like the gunnery instructor, Major Bruchmüller—travelled from unit to unit arranging in detail the work of the defence. The looser grew the fibre of the ordinary German soldier the stronger became the staff-work. There were some travelling machine-gun instructors as capable and laborious as Bruchmüller was with trench-mortar and artillery direction. These military commercial travellers, as the tired German troops sometimes called them, were the last expression of the Prussian gift of method. Employed first in arranging the spring offensive, they often saved the situation in the autumn defensive. They it was who prevented for the time the British decision at Le Cateau from producing any subsidiary disasters round Laon.

Scene of long and bitter contest—all that was left of one of the roads at Lens, in the centre of the coal-mining district of the Pas de Calais. Although the British front line was long within sight of the ruined town, the enemy clung obstinately to its subterranean defences until their final breaking in the autumn of 1918.

British troops who had fought in Champagne marching past General Berthelot and British and Italian commanders. General Berthelot, on behalf of the French Army, said : " Your French comrades will always remember with devotion your splendid gallantry and your perfect fellowship in the fight."

BRITISH TROOPS WHO FOUGHT WITH SPLENDID GALLANTRY FROM LENS TO CHAMPAGNE.

CHAPTER CCLXXXII.

THE FLOODTIDE OF VICTORY IN THE WEST.

By Edward Wright.

V.—The Reconquest of Western Flanders and the Battle of the Sambre Canal.

British Admiralty Hoodwinks the German Secret Service with Bogus Reports of a Contemplated Landing Battle in Flanders—Armies Under King Albert's Command Resume Their Advance—General von Armin's Mass Tactics of Defence on Flanders Ridge—British Smoke-Screen Method of Attack—General Jacob's Advance Through Moorseele and Heule Startles the German Officers at a Ball in Courtrai—Extraordinary Situation at Courtrai—General Degoutte's Fierce Struggle for Roulers—Infuriated Belgians Capture Iseghem and Lendelede—Double Turning Movement Round Thielt and Thourout Compels the Germans to Retreat towards Bruges and Ghent—Sir Roger Keyes Lands at Ostend, Followed by the King and Queen of the Belgians—Fifth British Army Liberates Lille—Turcoing and Roubaix Set Free—Sufferings of the Population of the Occupied Districts—Strain Imposed on the British Army in Feeding the Liberated People—Tragedy of Douai—Marshal Foch " Castling His Forces " Outplays the German High Command—Military Situation on October 19th, 1918.

THE British Admiralty had a kind way with German spies. Several years before the war it treated them tenderly and carefully, and during the struggle was repaid a thousandfold for its benevolence.

Germany was always able to obtain information, some of which was undoubtedly correct. When, for example, plans were made for a great landing battle on the Flemish coast, in which flat-bottomed boats carrying Tanks were designed to play a leading part, the details of the scheme reached the German Staff, not without some complicity on the part of a certain British admiral who had fought under the leadership of Sir David Beatty.

The remarkable thing about the strange affair was that the German Staff received the information about six months after the idea of a landing on the Flemish coast was abandoned by the British authorities. This, however, did not at the time interfere with the Teutons' joy in the great achievement of their Secret Service men.

The German Marine Corps and coastal engineers had a long period of exciting activity in designing and constructing the great works which were to break and shatter hundreds of thousands of Britons. The Ostend Esplanade was honey-combed into shell-proof machine-gun positions; the long line of sand-dunes was more strongly fortified than the cliffs at Gallipoli had been; and on the sands, over which the Tanks were expected to charge, various kinds of steel obstacles and traps were built.

From apparently the same authentic source as that from which the original British plan had been received, information was obtained by the enemy, in the second week of October, 1918, that the great landing battle would be opened on the fourteenth of the month. Admiral von Schröder had been preparing to evacuate the shore since King Albert opened the Flanders offensive towards the end of September, but the work of removing the heavy guns and huge stores and getting the ships in port away was exceedingly difficult.

General Sixt von Armin, with twenty divisions of the Fourth German Army and many divisions borrowed from the Sixth German Army, under General von Quast, at Lille, was making a prolonged and determined stand by Dixmude, Roulers, and Menin in order to win time for the transport of material and the strengthening of a series of new lines by Ghent and Antwerp.

The news that the British intended to force a decision in Flanders by means of a landing battle was, therefore, disconcerting. The German High Command had not allocated to its northern wing sufficient reserve forces for a stand in strength along the coast in addition to a covering battle between Lille and Bruges.

There was a panic retreat

EMBLEM OF A CITY'S GRATITUDE.
General Sir William Birdwood, Commander of the Fifth British Army, holding aloft the flag presented to him by the Mayor of Lille and embroidered with words of gratitude from the city to its liberators.

in Western Flanders. As far back as Bruges German officials and civilians fled. In Ostend no enemy remained save some gunners left to cover the withdrawal. For nearly two days the Flemish people were free of the invaders, who, however, returned for a very brief time on finding no British force attempting to storm the coast.

When the bombarding ships opened fire in superb gunnery weather in the early morning of October 14th no reply came from the hostile coastal batteries. It was not until some British ships made a reconnaissance by West Deep, under cover of a smoke screen from motor-launches, that mile after mile of big German guns awoke and blazed into the bank of artificial fog.

In the evening a flotilla of motor-boats made a dash inside the Mole of Zeebrugge towards the Heyst beach and loosed torpedoes at various targets, while a strong group of British aeroplanes first lighted the scene with flares and then bombed the enemy. These operations kept the German rearguard busy, and in the night some of the gun positions at Zeebrugge were blown up by the Germans as a signal of defeat.

On the whole, however, the great trick of the British Navy in warning the enemy of something that was not to happen did not produce its full effect. What was **King Albert's** vainly required was that General Sixt von **army advances** Armin should lend some of his divisions to Admiral von Schröder for the shore battle against non-existing Tanks, phantom flat-bottomed boats, and spectral swarms of innumerable British soldiers.

By practically evacuating the coast and concentrating against the Flanders group of armies General von Armin unwittingly did the best thing in the circumstances. Admiral Hall's supreme masterpiece in the art of counter-espionage ended merely in a display of artillery fireworks. By, however, inducing the enemy to keep his coastal batteries in action until the last minute, the great plan that did not come off provided the Belgian nation with a large and valuable assortment of heavy German guns, including a piece used to the last minute in long-distance shooting at Dunkirk.

While the demonstration along the coast was proceeding,

the three Belgian, British, and French armies, under the direction of King Albert, resumed their advance between the Lys River at Comines and the Yser at Dixmude. Upon the British divisions, under Sir Herbert Plumer, there fell the most important part of the work.

The magnificent Belgian forces, which had done most in carrying the Flanders Ridge at the end of September, still retained a masterly part in the operations, but the veterans of the former Ypres battles now struck the heaviest blow. Their task was a double one. They had to prolong their defensive flank down the Lys River so as to guard all the attacking forces from a grand counter-thrust by the Sixth German Army round Lille. **British part in** Then they had to inflict a great strategic **the scheme** defeat upon this German army on their right flank by driving with their left through the Fourth German Army to the middle reach of the Lys River above the Flemish town of Courtrai.

There, on a position behind Lille, Roubaix, and Tourcoing, they could cut General von Quast's northern railway communications running through Courtrai and clean outflank him. Covered by this great British advance, one Belgian force was to strike south of Roulers towards the Middle Lys, while the French army under General Degoutte carried Roulers and advanced on Thielt, and the main Belgian force attacked Thourout and swept towards Bruges and the Dutch frontier.

Everything thus depended on the pace and power of the southern British movement. This was conducted by the brilliant Second Corps, under Lieut.-General Sir C. W. Jacob, comprising the 9th Division, the 29th Division, and the 36th Division. The Nineteenth Corps, under General Sir H. E. Watts, employing the 41st Division and the 35th Division, each of which had assisted in the first operations, took part in the great drive. Also the Tenth Corps, under Lieut.-General R. B. Stephens, employing the 30th Division and the 34th Division, which had been in reserve at the first battle, joined in the struggle.

Once more Sir C. W. Jacob and his men proved the

GALLANT ATTACK BY NEW ZEALANDERS ADVANCING TOWARDS LE CATEAU.

On October 11th, 1918, New Zealanders, attacking the German positions indicated on the left in the sky-line, had to cross a forty-feet-wide stream by a footbridge under machine-gun fire from the house on the right. Rushing across the bridge in little groups some stayed under the cover of a mound on the opposite bank to engage the machine-gun post, while the rest deployed in open order and won their objective.

irresistible spear-head of the advance. The German Emperor had stopped and congratulated some officers and men of the Scottish and South African 9th Division, captured the previous April in the struggle for Messines Ridge, on the fact that there were not two 9th Divisions in the British Army. He said he could not have made headway had this been so.

The immortal force of veterans and youngsters had not lost any of its edge and speed in battling over the Passchendaele Ridge, and with the equally renowned battalions of the 29th Division and the gallant men of the 36th Division they met and broke a large part of the combined forces of the Fourth and Sixth German Armies.

General von Armin, who had fought the British from the Somme Downs to Passchendaele Ridge and Kemmel Hill, stood in manful fashion for the decisive struggle. He changed the disposition of defence he had used for more than two years and placed his troops densely in the fighting-line, with hundreds of guns closely supporting them. There were two German battalions deployed to take the shock, with only one battalion in support. It was mass tactics applied to defence in the age of the hurricane bombardment. The enemy commander intended a quick decision and obtained one.

He had the desperate hope of balancing the defeat at Le Cateau by a defensive victory in Flanders that would relieve pressure all along the line. Moreover, some of the German troops were half-demoralised by the opening of peace negotiations, and disinclined further to risk their lives when the end of the war seemed in sight. If these troops had been deployed widely and in great depth there would have been a weakening of control over them, with obvious consequences.

Mass tactics in defence

Everything, therefore, concurred in inducing General von Armin to mass for battle with a nominal establishment strength of nearly a quarter of a million men. As a matter of fact, the divisions he borrowed from General von Quast did not balance his losses in the action for the Flanders Ridge. Yet the total number of German troops in line was very great, and the allied troops had a severe struggle against the closely-packed invaders.

TRAFFIC CONTROL IN THE WAR ZONE.
A military motor-car halted by a British soldier on traffic-control duty on the western front. The man is pointing out to the driver an important notice emphasising the necessity of avoiding any such movement as should draw the attention of distant German artillery observers.

The Second British Army was at a disadvantage in comparison with the Belgian and French forces. While some of the ground on the northern front of attack was firm enough to allow Renault storming cars and "whippet" Tanks to charge with dismaying effect upon the enemy, no chariots of war could be employed in the southern waste of mud round Menin. The Second British Corps had to make its thrust without its special machine of victory and bring all its material over the worst piece of ground on the western front.

The leading British divisions struck the enemy north of Menin and drove him from Moorseele and Heule towards Harlebeke, on the Lys, north of Courtrai, some eleven miles above Lille. While the great centres of manufacture in North-Western France were thus being turned by a movement through the Flanders lowland, the Tenth and Nineteenth British Corps fought towards the rising ground by Comines, Wervicq, and Menin. Along this line divisions of the Sixth German Army protected themselves to some extent by making walls of flame out of the outer buildings of the menaced towns.

Many German machine-gunners still fought with the old determination, but bodies of ordinary infantry showed considerable flabbiness of character. One British battalion for example, captured an entire German battalion at a cost of twelve casualties, mostly light. The army corps of General von Bernhardi garrisoned the outskirts of Lille, and it is certain that Bernhardi had to fine himself as well as many of his officers in the course of the day. He had made it a custom that Britons should always be called "Baralongers," and that a fine should be paid if any other term were used to denote the most hated of enemies. Every message that arrived told of the enveloping progress of the "Engländer."

The German line along the Middle Lys by Wervicq gave easily, although it was covered by "pill-boxes," with a fortified railway embankment and a canalised stream overlooked by enemy gunner observers in church towers and high-roofed buildings. No town or hamlet on the Lille side was carried by storm, as the operations were merely intended to occupy the enemy and prevent him from making a counter-offensive against the base of the enlarging salient of the allied advance. Also

SENTRY ON ROAD DUTY IN FRANCE.
At a traffic examining post in a forward area on the western front. British sentry looking at the papers of a motorist entering a district where special care was needed in traffic control. The "pill-box" served as shelter for the sentry on duty when the enemy started shell firing.

WHEN ZEEBRUGGE WAS SEALED.
One of the vessels sunk near the Zeebrugge
Mole by the British naval forces during their
historic raid in April, 1918.

frontal attacks were avoided on towns, because they would have drawn the enemy's gun fire on the buildings and any people sheltering in the houses.

The method adopted was for the British 60-pounders to cover the objective with a vast cloud of smoke, through which two infantry forces made flanking thrusts and connected in the rear. The crews of the "pill-boxes," when blinded by the artificial fog, could either warn the invisible British troops of their whereabouts by working their guns aimlessly, or wait without fighting until they were encircled, and bombs could be thrown into them from their weakly-built rear side. Had the great smoke-screen method of attack been worked out by July, 1917, the Flanders Ridge might have been won that summer, together with the Flemish coast.

The smoke barrage was indeed a device as important as the use of storming cars. This was seen in the main field of battle north of Menin, where the enemy had a great advantage in ground and fought with remarkable heroism. It was a land of hedges and ditches, and the Germans were stretched in the mud behind low bushes in which were hidden new wire entanglements. Canals and irrigation ditches made the marshy ground look like a silver riddle in the sunlight. All the ruined villages had been fortified in 1917, and the "pill-box" system that began near Ypres had been gradually extended beyond Menin.

Bavarians, who had been resting for months and were full of fight, held the ground, together with a famous German cavalry division. Their gunners drenched the British positions

THE "NEST" OF WHICH THE "HORNETS" WERE DISPOSSESSED.
Lock gates at Zeebrugge after the British occupation. The massive structure on the right was used by the Germans as a shelter for submarines from shells and aerial bombs.

with gas during the night, being aware an attack was impending, and when the British barrage crashed over their line the Bavarians most gallantly rose and came forward in the Gommecourt fashion of 1916.

Stout-hearted, however, as these men were, they could not stay the Scotsmen, Englishmen, and Irishmen under General Jacob. **The 9th Division's** The 9th Division went through two **fierce onslaught** deep lines of wire heavily defended, rushed the rows of concrete forts, reaching the river with their front line, and counter-attacked on three sides. From Winkle St. Eloi, the point of contact with the Belgians, the troops fought hard and bitterly along the canalised Heule stream towards Gulleghem. Irish troops captured Moorseele about noon, and with their comrades reached the wire entanglements by Heule village and wood at five o'clock in the afternoon. There they waited for guns to break the wire.

In the meantime English troops stormed into the German line immediately above Menin, scattered the defending infantry, and by Roesthoek Farm charged a battery of 5·9 in. howitzers, capturing every officer and man unhurt, before these could even start to run.

Some German gunners fought their pieces with open sights when their infantry had fled. Others abandoned guns and ammunition

IN BRITISH HANDS ONCE MORE.
The s.s. Brussels, Captain Fryatt's old ship, torpedoed off Zeebrugge to prevent the enemy using her as a supply ship. In circle: H.M.S. Thetis, sunk in the Zeebrugge raid, flying the White Ensign again.

and sights, and were shelled with their own stuff as they ran. Some of the fiercest combats took place along the Heule stream, which was a waterway about twelve feet wide, with the banks lined with machine-guns firing from "pill-boxes" and concrete-strengthened cellars. There were no connecting trenches, yet the separated little forts held out stubbornly but unavailingly. By dusk the British had a straight line near the Lys above Courtrai, and bringing forward some of the captured guns they shelled the enemy machine-gunners out of Heule village and sent them scurrying in a disorderly mob into Courtrai.

In the pleasant old Flemish city, famous alike for its architecture and the courage of its burghers in the Battle of the Spurs, German cavalry officers in the night of Monday, October 14th, were holding a dance in celebration of peace with honour. The town folk were moving joyfully along both banks of the Lys, glorying in the near liberation of their country, when the routed enemy force from Heule tumbled into the northern part of the town and scampered for shelter into the cellars.

The thunder of the British guns changed from a dull thudding into shaking explosions. In the early morning of October 15th the artillery of attack swept the last wire entanglements away, and the Irish troops, leading the pursuit, closed with the German rearguard in the northern part of Courtrai and carried the buildings as far as the Lys.

The enemy then lined the farther bank with covered machine-guns, while most of the Flemish population of some thirty thousand people had to take refuge in their cellars alongside their persecutors. Peering through the chinks of the shutters of the upper windows of the buildings they had conquered, Irishmen and Englishmen could see across the canal down the empty streets to the old town-hall and to the magnificent church which had survived the Battle of the Spurs in the fourteenth century and all later actions. Beyond the town the road ran to Oudenarde, the scene of one of the most remarkable of Marlborough's victories.

For some days the situation at Courtrai remained extraordinary. On one side of the canal the German garrison ate and slept in indescribable conditions within the same walls as the Flemish women and children. On the other side fought the British soldiers, in equally close but more decent company with that part of the population which they had freed.

One attempt was made to force the canal by a surprise stroke, and some sixty men of the Middlesex and Queen's Regiments, who arrived from the south, by Menin, poled themselves over the water in pontoons, and, under point-blank fire, stormed some of the houses and held them until nightfall. Men whose pontoons were sunk swam the water, and took a gallant share in the fighting; but the party of dashing attackers was not large enough to overawe the enemy, who blew one English officer from room to room with trench-mortar bombs. In order to prevent the city being destroyed

Odd situation in Courtrai

CHANGE OF OWNERS.
British soldiers by one of the German heavy guns sited for the defence of the Mole at Zeebrugge.

GERMAN GUN EMPLACEMENT ON THE BELGIAN COAST.
The defensive power of the land fortifications on the coastal sector of the western front was immense, and gave the Germans a sense of security which the British naval raids rudely dispelled.

by the German guns, Sir Herbert Plumer ordered that the enemy should merely be contained along the waterway.

By this time all the Courtrai position was turned, some miles northward, by Harlebeke, which the left wing of the Second Army reached immediately the Germans broke around Heule. While resting in and above Courtrai the British commander cleared the middle course of the Lys, and through Menin and Wervicq began to encircle Courtrai on the south, and turn Tourcoing, Roubaix, and Lille from the north.

There was a panic among the Germans who were covering the withdrawal from the French towns. When the smoke screen rolled over them they fled—not only from positions that were being attacked, but from the dominating rising ground eastward. In the night of October 15th, finding that the British did not attempt a further advance, some German officers induced their men to return and hold the high positions on the extreme right by Halluin.

When daylight came, with a thicker, wider British smoke

BREACH BLOWN IN ZEEBRUGGE MOLE BY A BRITISH SUBMARINE.
The concrete mass of the Mole was connected with the shore by a jetty, and to prevent reinforcements reaching the Germans fighting the storming-parties from Vindictive, Iris, and Daffodil, in the course of the raid on St. George's Day, 1918, Lieutenant R. D. Sandford, R.N., ran an old submarine into the piles and touched off the explosives with which she was loaded for the purpose, tearing the jetty in half and leaving a gap over 100 feet wide.

barrage and a heavier shower of shell, the Germans again broke, with little infantry action, and the attacking troops sent back an urgent message asking to be allowed to spread beyond their objectives. They had, however, to wait for some time, for the reason that their thrust had definitely liberated all the manufacturing districts round Lille. It was necessary for the Fifth British Army to pass round Lille, and come into line with the Second British Army before the next grand advance could be made.

Meanwhile, the Belgian and French forces, composing the rest of the command of King Albert, had a similar experience to the British forces. The Germans met them in massive strength immediately action opened. As soon, however, as General von Armin's line was broken, many of his remaining troops, as a rule, could not be induced to make a long stand. The French had a fierce struggle round Roulers. Some of their men marched twenty miles in order to fight, yet went into it grandly. So fierce was the struggle that only a series of happy strokes by sympathisers with the Allies among the hostile forces saved Roulers from becoming one of the last theatres of Prussian savagery.

General Degoutte closed round the town from three sides, his men meeting immediately behind the barrage, counter-charging the Germans and bearing them **Alsatians save** down with the bayonet and the fire of storm-**Roulers from ruin** ing cars. The French fought round the town, and one battalion then broke into the streets and swept towards the market-square, pushing back enemy machine-gunners, until a German gunner-officer, whose field-gun was trained upon the open space, gave the order to fire. Among his men, however, was an Alsatian, and he shouted: " Don't fire ! Surrender ! " He covered the German officer with a revolver, and the battery surrendered instead of shattering the peopled town with its shells.

At the same time another German officer gave orders for all mines to be exploded as the victorious French swept into the streets. It was intended to transform Roulers into another Louvain ; but the engineer left in charge of the mines in the belfry and other picturesque old buildings was also an Alsatian, and he saw to it that Roulers was not blown up. He could not prevent all the mines exploding, but he stopped many of them.

Between Roulers and the British forces working above Menin was an admirable Belgian division, provided with light British Tanks. They made the same kind of infuriated attack as their countrymen had done in Houthulst Forest. By their valorous vehemence they greatly helped the British thrust into Courtrai, and arrived, themselves, at Iseghem, close to the important railway **Avenging Belgians** junction of Ingelmunster. Here the enemy **in Iseghem** had another tributary of the Lys as a defensive moat, with a range of low hills immediately behind it. Down the three railway lines meeting near Iseghem the enemy commander sent a succession of strong counter-attacking forces. Three times the Belgians were obliged to draw back ; but every time they did so they returned and crushed the Germans who had advanced beyond the cover of the hills and stream.

It was the last incident that occurred in Iseghem that made the Belgians fight like avenging angels. As the Germans retired from the town for the last time they threw hand-bombs down the cellars, among the people whose shelters they had shared. It was a way some Teutons had of assuaging their anger, Bavarians being as bad losers as Prussians. As a consequence of this the Belgians took fewer prisoners ; they fought into Lendelede, by the railway, running between Courtrai and Iseghem, and gradually worked across another railway line to the high ground by the Lys.

As the Germans had a gridiron of railways in this sector, the embankments of which they had fortified and screened with a system of " pill-boxes " ever since they anticipated an advance from the Passchendaele Ridge, the task of the Belgians was one that required the highest technical skill, in addition to valiant courage.

GERMAN JETSAM ON THE COAST OF FLANDERS : WIRE ENTANGLEMENTS AT ZEEBRUGGE.

On the morning of October 17th, 1918, a division of British destroyers, assisted by aircraft, reconnoitred the coast between Nieuport and Ostend, Vice-Admiral Sir Roger Keyes landing at the latter town. The enemy was then evacuating the whole coast of Belgium, and allied troops, advancing from the south and along the beach, occupied Ostend, whither the King and Queen of the Belgians proceeded on H.M. destroyer Termagant in the evening of that day.

Once more, however, the Belgians showed that their training had not slackened during their long standstill along the Yser. They used all the devices and machinery of the British Army, blanketing the enemy's works with smoke, thrusting through him and round him with Tanks and with following companies of bombers, riflemen, and trench-mortar men, while dominating the Germans completely from the air and ranging massed artillery upon hostile trains, supply columns, and bodies of troops.

Above Roulers the main Belgian forces of attack fought across the Dixmude-Thielt railway, towards the centre of West Flanders, at Thourout. They stormed Cortemarck and Handzaeme. This movement threatened to turn the enemy positions on the coast. The German rearguard at Westende, for example, was fifteen miles behind the victorious forces. A retreat towards Bruges and Ghent was imposed on the enemy, who drew his troops from the Yser to strengthen himself temporarily at Thourout. The French Army, however, severed direct communications between Thourout and Ghent by carrying the Hooglede upland and cutting the railway line above Beveren, from which point General Degoutte began a double turning movement round Thielt and Thourout.

On October 15th the main Belgian forces closed directly on Thourout, enveloping it, while the French converged on the town by Lichtervelde. It was then exactly four years to the day that Western Flanders had fallen to the invader, and in the night he prepared to retire, being considerably harried by the Belgian forces remaining along the Yser, between Dixmude and Nieuport, who could not bear to be out of the fighting.

Their proper task was merely to watch the enemy quietly, as he was being turned from the east; but they became so restless that King Albert allowed them to take part in the advance. Springing over the flooded wilderness, they caught and broke the enemy at Keyem, Schoore, and other vanished villages, where they had been overwhelmed by superior strength in 1914, and they chased his rearguards, from polder to polder and dune to dune, for three days until they reached the Dutch frontier.

Speeding the retreating foe

Zeebrugge began to smoke like a volcano, the Germans setting their oil fuel and other stores on fire and sinking the vessels they were unable to remove. By October 16th the Belgians on the right had reached the Lys, after taking Ingelmunster railway-station, and on the left they were working along the coast towards Ostend. That night the German retreat quickened throughout Western Flanders, beginning with a retirement on a thirty-two-mile front to a depth of twelve and a half miles. Soon after daybreak on October 17th the infantry of the attack found so little resistance in front of them that Belgian and French cavalry were employed to reconnoitre the country.

In spite of the difficulty of making speedy progress through the closed and diked lowlands and over the embanked, cobbled roads, the outskirts of Bruges were attained at

AT THE GATE OF LILLE.
M. Poincaré, President of the French Republic, received by a British Guard of Honour on his arrival at Lille, which he visited shortly after the recapture of the city by the Fifth British Army, under General Birdwood, October 17th, 1918.

nightfall. Ostend was reached still more quickly by aircraft and naval forces under Vice-Admiral Sir Roger Keyes. Destroyers and seaplanes approached the coast, and at eleven o'clock in the morning a British airman landed on the beach, where he was greeted by thousands of the townspeople. Half an hour afterwards Sir Roger Keyes entered the harbour in a ship's whaler and proceeded ashore.

The enemy at the time was not clear of the town. With a light battery in the neighbourhood he opened fire on the ships, sending shells upon the beach crowded with people. Four German heavy guns at Zeebrugge fired on the British destroyers, and as it seemed likely that the enemy was waiting for an excuse to shell the town, which in places he had mined with very long-delayed action fuses, the British admiral withdrew his forces, leaving merely four motor-launches inshore as a patrol. In the evening, when all had been quiet for some hours, the King and Queen of the Belgians landed in Ostend from the destroyer Termagant, and, in a scene of popular ecstasy, went to the town-hall, returning to Dunkirk by sea late at night.

The Belgian cavalry arrived in a gallop along the shore. Except for the secret mines, some of which did not explode for weeks, the historic seaport was not seriously damaged by the enemy. The Germans wrecked the plants and broke the connections of gas, electricity, and water services, and, after dragging the Vindictive to the piling of the pier, they again blocked the fairway with sunken vessels, so that food could not be brought by sea to the people. But the British bombing aeroplanes, that had fed the allied army on the Flanders Ridge at the beginning of the month, lowered supplies by parachute until the way was clear for food to be sent by ordinary methods.

At any time the recovery of Ostend would have been an event of high significance. No reconquered French town compared with it in strategic importance. By losing it the enemy lost his partial hold upon the narrow waters of England and his means of making short-distance bombing raids upon London, Dover, Sheerness, and Woolwich. The German Marine Office had **Strategic value of Ostend** at once to prepare to send out its naval forces for desperate action between Harwich and Dover, in the forlorn hope of being able to deal a stroke counter-balancing the loss of the command of the Flemish coast. The increased facility in traffic won by the Associated Powers aggravated the enemy's peril. As soon as the Flemish fairways were cleared and the connecting railway lines freed of mines and repaired, there would come a new flexibility in manœuvring great masses of men and guns which was likely to end the war suddenly before winter set in.

The German High Command appreciated fully the scope of sea-power—when it was too late. It had been wasted effort and false economy on its part to concentrate for a counter-offensive, under General von Lossberg, in Lorraine, and to refrain from using the lads of the youngest class in the field. The Flemish coast should have been held against King Albert's group of armies with the help of the 1920 class. As this was not done, the High Sea Fleet had, so Admiral von Scheer decided, to be risked to prevent the consequences of the grave mistake of the perturbed military leaders. As by attempting to risk his fleet Admiral von Scheer provoked a general revolution, we may fairly attribute decisive importance to the recovery· of Ostend and the march along the Flanders shore.

It may also be remarked that the event showed how far-sighted Sir Douglas Haig was in the strategic aim with which he tried to conquer the Flanders Ridge in 1917. He had to open his campaign late in a rainy year, and he was further delayed by the need for pressing the enemy elsewhere at the time when the French front was weakened by outbreaks of unrest and the Russian front dissolving through treachery. He failed in his grand design, though it was sound. His men who fell between Ypres and Passchendaele did not fall in vain.

Though the Germans returned over their bodies, their tragic heroism purchased the means of victory for their comrades of the Second and Fifth British Armies and for the Belgians and French. They won the knowledge that others triumphantly used; indeed, if they had not come so close to a grand decision against the concentrated main forces of the enemy in the

REWON FOR FRANCE.
General Birdwood and the Mayor of Lille at the saluting base during the formal entry of the British army of deliverance, October 28th, 1918.

was landing at Ostend, a patrol of the Liverpool Regiment, working down the road from Armentières, entered Lille. From the singing, cheering, sobbing multitudes of liberated citizens, girls came forward with flowers for the army of saviours, which, however, did not take the grateful greeting, but swung round the city north and south in pursuit of the out-manœuvred enemy.

This was partly courtesy and partly precaution on the part of Sir William Birdwood, commanding the Fifth Army. He took much trouble and lost some time in keeping his forces out of the streets, in order to allow the enemy no shadow of any military excuse for turning guns on the thronged ways of the city, or sending bombing aeroplanes by night to wreck the buildings and murder the people.

With happy thoughtfulness a French regiment, which had been fighting alongside the British, was sent first into the centre of Lille, and Lieut.-General Sir R. C. B. Haking, whose Eleventh Corps had held the sector by the city for three years, despatched the flag of his army corps to Paris, to be **Lille's day of liberation** placed on the Lille Statue in the Place de la Concorde, when he entered the Manchester of France on the evening of October 17th.

The Mayor of Lille did not have to wait, either, for French or British infantry to learn that his city was free. At dawn of the day of liberation, while General von Bernhardi's men were marching away eastward to escape envelopment by the Second British Army on the Lys and the First British Army on the Sensée River, friendly pilots came flying low over the houses. One of them, flying the Tricolour, landed by the public gardens. He was Captain Delesalle, the son of the Mayor. After giving the news he flew away—also with a view to giving the enemy no provocation. Lille was undamaged except for the effects of the early enemy bombardment in the autumn of 1914.

The suburbs were looted, there having been a plan to despoil every house and then burn down the city; and the factories were not in working order, as the Germans had taken the

THE PRESIDENT RECEIVES LILLE FROM THE VICTORS.
M. Poincaré, with General Birdwood, inspecting the Guard of Honour when he received Lille from the victorious Fifth British Army in October, 1918; and (in oval) the French President near one of the gates of the city.

year of his renewed strength, the final victorious offensive in Flanders might not have been undertaken even when the enemy was permanently weakened.

The Fifth British Army, which had shared fully in the earlier Flemish campaign, was again joined with the Second British Army in the glory of the decisive advance. In the morning of October 17th, about the time Sir Roger Keyes

RIBBONS WORN BY HEROES OF THE WAR

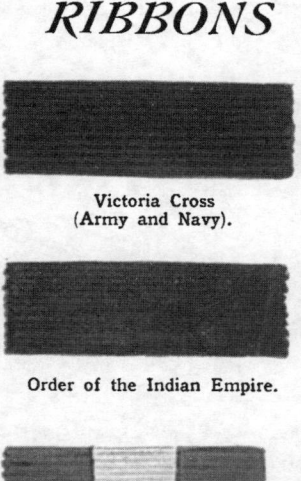

Victoria Cross
(Army and Navy).

Order of the Bath.

Order of the Star of India.

Order of St. Michael and
St. George.

Order of the Indian Empire.

Royal Victorian Order.

Order of the British Empire.

Distinguished Service
Order.

Distinguished Service Cross and
Conspicuous Gallantry Medal.

Military Cross.

Distinguished Flying Cross.

Air Force Cross.

Royal Red Cross.

Albert Medal
(1st Class, Sea).

Albert Medal
(2nd Class, Sea).

Albert Medal
(1st Class, Land).

Albert Medal
(2nd Class, Land).

Medal for Distinguished
Conduct in the Field.

Distinguished Service Medal.

Military Medal.

Distinguished Flying Medal.

Air Force Medal.

Indian Distinguished Service
Medal.

Long Service and Good
Conduct (Navy).

Long Service and Good Conduct
(Army).

The 1914 (Mons) Star.

Order of the Nile (Egypt).

Order of St. John of Jerusalem.

Legion of Honour (France).

Medaille Militaire (France).

Croix de Guerre (France).

Order of Leopold (Belgium).

Order of the Crown (Belgium).

Croix de Guerre (Belgium).

Order of the Crown (Italy).

SS. Maurice and Lazarus (Italy).

Croce de Guerre (Italy).

Order of Karageorge (Serbia).

Order of the Sacred Treasure
(Japan).

Order of the Rising Sun
(Japan).

A GREAT MOMENT.
General Birdwood and other officers, French and British, on the steps of the Prefecture of Lille after they had made their formal entry into the city.

machinery, or destroyed it, when intending to shatter the manufacturing power of France. But M. Clemenceau's stern threat of national reprisals, and the speed and vigour of the British encircling movements, had prevented the Germans from laying waste the city.

General von Bernhardi showed a considerable amount of foul cunning in the last phase of the struggle round Lille. After being driven back from Merville to his original line, and then forced to abandon the Aubers Ridge, the spokesman of Prussianism placed his 8 in. batteries in Vauban Park, inside the city, and there fired them furiously, to use up ammunition he could not take away, and to incite the heavy British guns to counter-battery work upon Lille.

Naturally, General Haking and his men suffered in silence, and when, on October 14th, Bernhardi found he had failed to provoke either a frontal attack or a bombardment, but was being turned from the north, he hauled his guns away from Lille and, with cynical humour, placarded Lille with the statement that the townspeople had nothing to fear, as he had persuaded the British not to damage the city.

Turcoing and Roubaix freed

On the same day of liberation a force of Yorkshire cyclists, coming from the north in search of enemy rearguards, reached the edge of the weaving town of Tourcoing. The Yorkshiremen were told not to enter the streets, but circumstances were too strong for them. Tens of thousands of women and girls and boys surrounded the soldiers, captured them, and carried them to the town-hall. When there arrived the British general, who had wished to keep his men out of the town, also for fear of provoking German gun fire, he was carried to the town-hall.

At the same time similar scenes of wild, deeply-touching rejoicing occurred in the connecting town of Roubaix, entered by Lancashires and Yorkshiremen, so that parts of the former great hive of industry centring at Lille were filled with strange, weeping gladness. There were many English factories, with colonies of Lancashire men and women in the three

towns, and still many more Flemish workers. Thus the people of the three most closely-blent Allies struggled together to touch the soldiers and kiss their faces or their uniforms.

Terrible had been the sufferings of the townsfolk, the women having lost sons and husbands in the final deportation of males of military age that took place as the invaders retired. Many of their daughters had previously been torn away from them, together with young and comely married women, for a horrible usage, and hundreds of hostages had been sent in the early part of 1918 to perish along the Baltic coast in winter on some pretext of barbaric reprisals in respect of the Alsace potash mines or the bombardment of Turkish territory by a French warship.

The people had seen captured British soldiers fall dead in the streets from prolonged ill-treatment, and the graves of hundreds of them who had been done to death were pointed out to the liberators. All British prisoners were kept three days and three nights without food, to break their spirit. When brought out to dig trenches and do other labour they would rake through piles of refuse in the Lille streets, and devour bits of cabbage leaf and other scanty edible waste, being so weak from want of nourishment they could not walk properly.

In spite of arrangements made to supply the population of occupied territories with food, there were many

REJOICINGS IN A CITY RECOVERED FROM THE FOE.
General Haking, standing by the Mayor of Lille, while the British National Anthem was played on the entry into the recovered city; and (in oval) animated scene in a street of the city set free from the invader.

deaths from famine, especially among poor children and aged persons. In Roubaix the mortality from gradual starvation was heavy. Through the organisation of the International Relief Committee food was supplied to keep the people in health, but the Teuton appears to have intervened, in the design to undermine the living strength of the great French manufacturing centre.

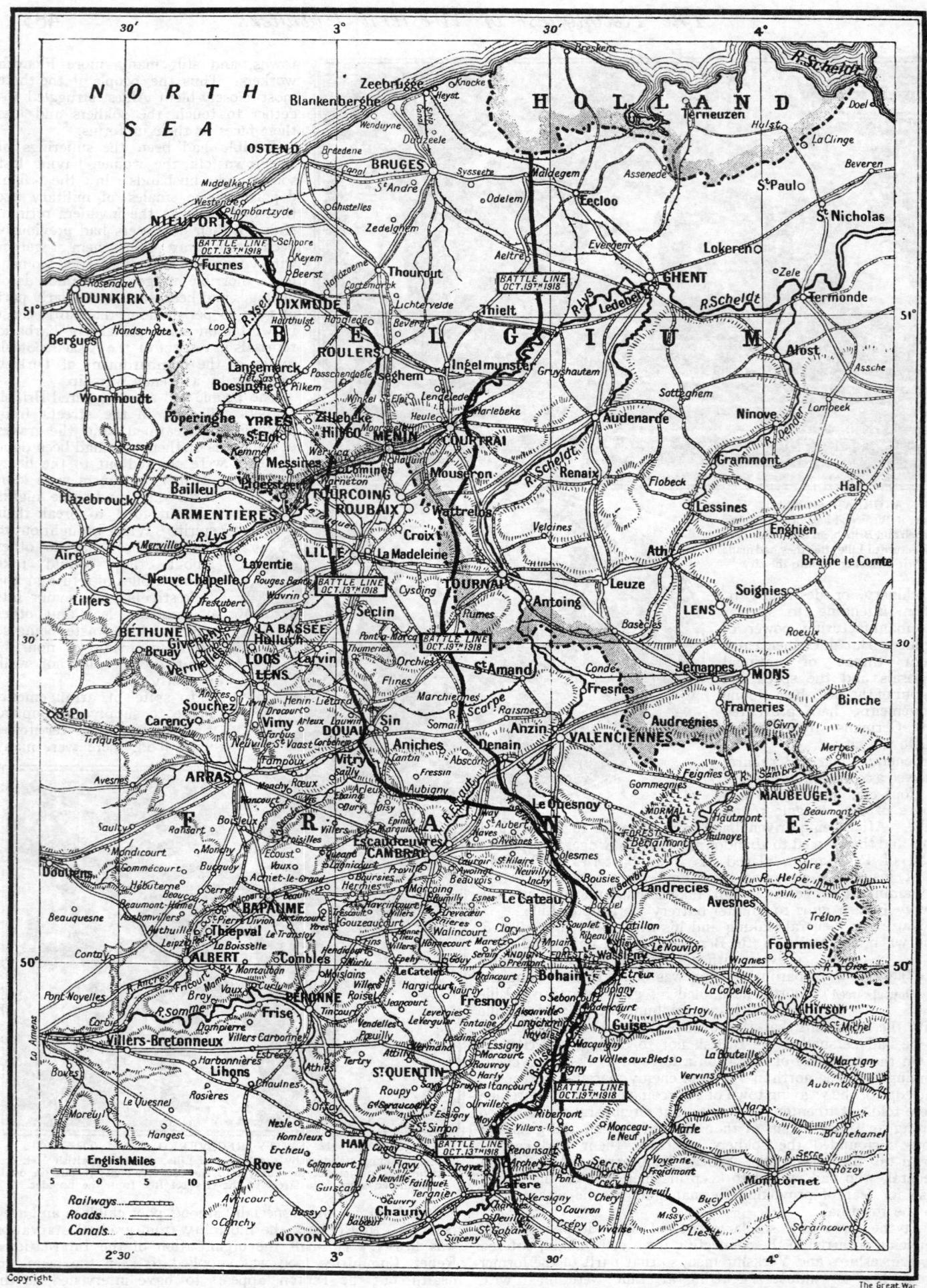

FOUR DAYS OF FIGHTING FORWARD IN THE EVENTFUL CLOSING WEEKS OF THE WAR.

But all the hardships of the people remained to them insignificant in comparison with the wrong done to women and girls deported, as part of the levy of fifty thousand slaves made on the three towns at Easter, 1916. "We demand vengeance!" cried the old men, weeping still in the streets, and representing chiefly all that remained of French manhood. Maids of seventeen and eighteen were torn by night from their beds and carried off screaming. Unspeakable things happened. Of those who returned, aged with misery, a large proportion were in such a condition they could never bear children. In this manner the Teuton sapped the vitality of the French race.

These facts were only clearly known when the towns were recovered. They spurred the angry British troops to further efforts against the enemy, and inspired the British railway and road repairers to great achievements, not fully equalled, perhaps, by the civil administration of France, though M. Clemenceau in person closely followed the British patrols in visiting the recovered cities. The poor people of the liberated towns soon lost their rapture, and continued to weaken and die of cold. Some French authorities stated they could not manage to get supplies through the zone of communications of the British forces in action.

It was not until the latter part of January, 1919, that some man of intelligence in the French department of aviation thought of using large bombing aeroplanes, **Supplies for the freed** with parachuted cargoes of supplies, such **population** as had been employed in Flanders in September, 1918.

Yet British railway construction troops worked into the Lille area with wonderful speed. They benefited by the great organisation for a campaign against the Channel ports, which the Germans had undertaken in the spring and summer of the year when the Emperor came to Lille aflame with excitement. By July, 1918, enemy engineers had carried new roads and tracks on embankments over the Lys marshland, created new water supplies, towns of hutments, distribution centres, and other works. When the armies of attack had to withdraw southward hurriedly and spend themselves in defensive actions, much of the solid part of the works was captured by the Fifth British Army. Before Lille was recovered the greater part of the enemy's constructions was repaired and connected with the Hazebrouck and Aire systems, and material was accumulated in scientific order for rapid work.

In less than eight days after General Haking's army corps passed round Lille the first train of supplies for the civil population ran into the city, the railway being carried across the Lys River at Armentières by a bridge erected in four days. By the end of October the British railway construction troops had brought into service one thousand and fifty miles more of line than had been available in August, 1918. Of this nearly a half consisted of new track, and the rest was line destroyed by the retreating enemy in a way he vainly hoped would prevent pursuit.

The British Army thus worked hard to bring food to the populations it redeemed. British soldiers often fed the people as they passed, and went hungry into battle themselves. Yet there was little relief for multitudes of townfolk. For weeks they lived as they had done under the Germans, or rather existed, under worse conditions, as the weather grew colder. Silent, white, thin children envied the British soldier his bread, but did not like to beg for a piece. The death-rate increased among the very young and aged, especially by the time the armistice was signed and the Germans were trying to work on the sympathies of the Americans by crying that they were starving. It was the liberated French and Belgians who were dying of hunger, but even from England comforts were sent for German babies by the Women's International League, while infants of France and Belgium, whose food the Teutons had stolen, were still dying of want.

British journalists acquainted with the tragic condition of affairs did not like to appeal direct to their own public for the despatch of food-ships for the northern French ports, the matter being one peculiarly affecting the civil authorities of France. When the bitter feeling of the liberated populations

MOURNING REPLACED BY EMBLEMS OF JOY.
On the news of the recovery of Lille, the Lillois living in Paris marched to the Place de la Concorde, removed the crape which had been hung on the Statue of Lille since the German occupation of the city, and replaced that emblem of mourning with garlands and flags.

became generally known in Paris, M. Clemenceau might have fallen from power had he been an ordinary politician.

Deep and intense was the indignation of the country. On consideration, however, it was admitted that the new French leader could not be held responsible for the defects in the system of administration which he had had no time to reform. Only with difficulty had he succeeded in making some improvement in the Department of Police, where there had obtained something worse than eloquent incompetence.

Thus the honeymoon of the liberation quickly and sadly passed. Only in Douai, **Organised havoc** which was also liberated on the memorable **in Douai** day that Ostend, Lille, Roubaix, Tourcoing, and part of Courtrai were freed, were there no complaints of continued famine.

Douai, old, picturesque city of scholars and weavers, with its gabled and carved fronts and venerable buildings, was first selected by the invader for the display of his early policy of a terrorisation retreat. The entire population was removed, the strongest persons being set to help in making new entrenchments, and the others being left to tramp into Belgium, unless they fell by the wayside.

Into the empty houses poured an army of plunderers. Every room was stripped of furniture, and the lovely, ancient town-hall was piled with rubbish left by the looters when they had finished their work. In the principal church, even the remains of the organ were strewn on the nave, after every

GERMAN GRATITUDE FOR HOSPITALITY.
This house was placed at the disposal of the Red Cross when the Germans occupied Douai. When they evacuated the town in October, 1918, they responded by wrecking every room.

bit of brass had been taken away, while torn vestments and sacred ornaments were scattered about, either as being too bulky or regarded as worthless as a cargo for the plunder waggons.

The wildest of Bolshevists had little to learn from the disciplined German soldiery in the matter of destructiveness. Even the old archives were ransacked by the Teutons, who left disordered stacks of valuable papers to make a great bonfire. The Grand' Place was partially burnt, and fires lighted in other parts of the city went on smouldering until the fourth week of October. But the 8th British Division, who had completed the envelopment of Douai before the enemy could completely burn the record of his organised national crimes, saved the town from entire destruction.

Throughout the territory from which the Germans retired, their destructiveness was largely in proportion to the length of time they had to prepare for evacuation before recognising that retreat was inevitable. Though at Douai they had opportunity to turn the city into a solitude and to attempt to lay it waste, they were not rapid enough in their withdrawal to carry all their civilian captives with them.

One British army corps, moving beyond the town towards Valenciennes, gathered in half a week's advance some forty-two thousand French people, including many children, all destitute and in very grave peril of death from hunger.

A.S.C. help for the destitute

Thousands of rations were brought up by Army Service Corps men, driving all night without sleep, to save the women and children and helpless aged persons. Also ambulance drivers, after long hours at the casualty clearing-stations, volunteered to work overtime in order to get up supplies to the starving souls.

The British Quartermaster-General's department saved the situation for the time being, in spite of the fact that the grand battle was proceeding along all the British front. Energetic young officers accomplished the seemingly impossible by feeding the guns, supplying the troops, bringing construction material for engineers, and also filling many of the roads with the vast movements of marching divisions of infantry. When the British Army had to feed the liberated peoples it did so in spite of all difficulties, and won great victories at the same time.

On the same great day of liberation, October 17th, 1918, when the first harvest of the decisive victory of Le Cateau was gathered between the Sensée River and the sea, the Fourth British Army, under Sir Henry Rawlinson, resumed the offensive, in conjunction with the First French Army.

Only five days had passed since the breaking of the enemy's last fortified line and the skirmishing along the Selle River.

Short as the time was, it was sufficient to enable the Royal Engineers and pioneer forces to prolong communications through the Le Cateau front and organise the means of another general assault. General Debeney's sappers and road-makers were equally quick at their work. The enemy was surprised at the speed with which the great movement against him was renewed in strength, and one of the leading German military writers, General Baron von Ardenne, complained that Marshal Foch had invented a way of castling his forces.

By this metaphor from chess he meant that the Allied Command had a disconcerting method of moving

A POSSIBLE TRAP FOR THE UNWARY.
Front door of the house used as headquarters of the German Red Cross in Douai. Royal Engineers, suspicious of the notice, searched the house for booby-traps and then marked it safe for entrance.

masses of men suddenly from point to point. This was an affair of facilities in lateral communication, employed without discovery by the Germans. Night marches by foot, guns, motor-lorry columns, steam tractors, and Tanks, combined with superb staff-work in placing the troops and ranging the artillery, were the essence of the castling tactics.

Sir Douglas Haig and his lieutenants were the great masters of this method, which enabled them to burst upon the enemy in multitudinous force from ground that seemed the evening before to be occupied only by covering outposts. The British mechanism for castling partly dated from 1917, before Marshal Foch assumed supreme command. It left an enemy commander uncertain whether he would have a thousand guns opening against him or five thousand.

General Rawlinson attacked on a front of ten miles from the south of Le Cateau to the neighbourhood of Wassigny, along the Selle River, and the difficult wooded country of Andigny Forest. General Debeney also attacked on a line of ten miles from Andigny Forest to Ribemont, on the Oise River, pressing with most force towards Guise. In the British Army the Ninth Army Corps, the Thirteenth Army Corps, and the Second American Army Corps came into action, employing the famous Midlanders of the 46th Division, the veteran 1st, the 6th, 50th, and 66th Divisions, with the 30th and 27th American Divisions that had taken a notable part in the fighting by Nauroy and Bohain.

The Germans were gathered in strength, having been greatly reinforced by the armies withdrawing to a shorter front north and south of them, and by the general reserve of their High Command. Scarcely more than four fresh divisions appear to have been left in the enemy's general reserve at the time, and although there were some thirty-six weary and wasted divisions drawn from his fighting-line, they were not of much use until rested and filled out with drafts.

Some of these wasted divisions had been sent to Flanders to recuperate and had completely broken there. But the men who took their place along the Selle River, in Andigny Forest, and along the canalised Oise, were of a kind which seemed to justify the hope of their High Command that the war could be prolonged over winter.

There were some ninety German divisions between the Dutch frontier and the Oise, and most of them were massed against the British forces.

All along the front of battle at dawn on October 17th the enemy made a stubborn resistance, fiercely counter-attacking and bringing a heavy artillery

CAPTURED AND PUT TO A NEW USE.
One of a series of concrete " pill-boxes "—quite unlike the original from which the name derived—which formed part of the Hindenburg line near St. Quentin. On being taken by the British it was converted into a signal-post.

ARCHITECTURAL CAMOUFLAGE.
Concrete German machine-gun position and observation-post on the western front. It was so constructed as to appear from a distance like an inoffensive deserted cottage.

fire to bear, in spite of the loss of much of his gun-power. Le Cateau was cleared as far as the railway embankment and below this famous town of battles, the Selle River was most gallantly forced, and ground won in bitter struggle in the direction of the Oise-Sambre Canal, by Bazeul.

The American troops were in excellent form, fighting their way forward from St. Souplet by Molain to the hills by the canal, while the Thirteenth British Corps drove towards Wassigny railway junction.

The veteran Chasseurs, infantry of the line, and dismounted cavalry under General Debeney were faced by two serious obstacles, consisting of a block of hills in the Guise sector and the mass of Andigny Forest, north of the town. They shook the enemy by storming Origny Hill on the Oise, from which they threatened to turn the Serre line which General Mangin pressed above Laon. Then they settled down alongside the British and American troops for the main wrestle for the approaches to the Sambre Canal.

As was his wont, General Debeney employed light forces of infantry, under a heavy barrage, in which masses of 75's were used with intense effect.

All the allied line went slowly forward on a length of some twenty miles, bending in places under a fierce counter-attack, but more often withstanding and breaking the enemy's violent attempts at reaction. The charges delivered by the British troops across the Selle were magnificent in driving power and valorous endurance.

As in Flanders, the Germans began to resemble armour-plated wood. In front of their masses of men was a dense line of picked troops, with both courage and skill. A great and prolonged effort was required to bear down the fighting

spirit of these ably-handled forces, who counter-charged as the Bavarians did in the north. All through the night the struggle went on, General von Böhn and his army commanders bringing into action reserves hidden in the woods and folds of the woods, when the line broke, and continuing the contest.

At dawn on October 18th the battle went on, and although the enemy was in superior numbers, as was almost always the case when the British Empire was fighting the German Empire, the quality of the Briton proved better than the quality of the German.

The ordinary German soldier was beaten, and he knew it. His officers could pretend to mutiny against the armistice, and Hindenburg could pretend to rebuke the officers for not subordinating their military fervour to political considerations. The spirit of the German nation was broken, and it was the Briton who directly had broken it, so that the Teuton could not stand against a British attack with the same self-confidence as he was then standing against the French and American armies along the Hunding, Brunnhilde, and Kriemhilde lines.

In the morning of October 18th, when the veritable German rearguard was broken, some hundred thousand troops, who were in danger of degenerating into a routed mob, gave ground and allowed the **German national** advance to the Sambre Canal to proceed at **spirit broken** a quickened pace. Wassigny was taken and Ribeauville, and in fierce flanking action at Bazeul the German positions east of Le Cateau were threatened.

Below Wassigny General Debeney's troops stormed through Andigny Forest over a distance of three miles, working through wired woodland and various kinds of forest ambushes, which the enemy had expected to be impassable. The block of hills by the Oise was carried with the same talent in tricky manœuvre, and the Sambre Canal was reached at Tupigny and other places.

On October 19th the tireless divisions of British, Americans, and French continued to fight onward, and after having worn the enemy down in mind as well as in body by a struggle lasting more than sixty hours, they attained the objective desired by Sir Douglas Haig, which was the west bank of the Sambre and Oise Canal, between Catillon and Oisy, Etreux and Noyelles.

General Debeney also carried beyond Ribemont the commanding position of Villers-le-Sec, the loss of which compelled the enemy to withdraw between the southern part of the Oise and Serre.

The aim of Sir Douglas Haig in this advance to the Sambre Canal was to reach a strategic artillery position. From the high ground by Catillon there was a range of some twelve miles to the village of Aulnoye, by the eastern edge of Mormal Forest. At Aulnoye the railway from Valenciennes to Hirson crossed the great trunk line from Cologne and Maubeuge to Landrecies. By winning a position along the Sambre Canal, from which he could in the next advance bring a mass of big guns to bear upon Aulnoye junction, the British Commander-in-Chief began to threaten the enemy's communications between Le Cateau, Guise, the Serre front, and the Hunding line. He left only one branch railway, running from Maubeuge to Hirson, Vervins, and Marle, safe for some weeks longer for supplying the forces facing General Rawlinson, General Debeney, General Mangin, and General Guillaumat.

Menace to enemy lines

Moreover, with the terrifying increase in the number and carrying capacity of British and French bombing aeroplanes, the branch line between Maubeuge and Hirson could be continually put out of working order, while the roads, with their columns of motor-vehicles, carts, and the narrow-gauge military railways, serving the remaining part of the southern Hindenburg defences, also came under attack by the nations who were dominant in the air.

The enemy High Command saw what was impending. It placed about half its forces between the North Sea and the Serre River, held the French armies as economically as possible by the Hindenburg works, threw in two more divisions to press the Americans back, withdrew in Western Flanders behind a strong canal line at Ghent, and concentrated against the main British armies to prevent a rout through the Ardennes.

In Paris the situation at this period was not regarded in a very hopeful light. Measures were taken to prepare the public for a return of winter warfare. Writers, inspired by the French Staff, began to point out that the German armies were holding together remarkably well, under a succession of heavy blows, making rapid retreat where necessary, as in Western Flanders and the Laon corner, and fighting with great firmness on either side of the gap of Grandpré.

The enemy's front was being constantly shortened, the army of General von der Marwitz having been taken out of line, and another army—that of General von Carlowitz on the Hunding line—being in course of removal to reserve. The weather, after favouring the Allies, was turning against them, with bitterly cold nights and continued rain, that tested the endurance of moving troops, who carried but slight covering, only less than did the ordeal of battle. The marshy valleys of the Aisne and Oise and many lesser streams were flooding; the swamps by Sissonne, at the French centre, were impossible to cross, and universal mud made dragging work for the supply carts, artillery, and ambulances.

It was observed that from the Oise to the Meuse the Germans continued not only to hold with great tenacity, but brought stronger artillery and machine-gun fire to bear upon the French and American troops. The floods left only small gaps through which storming cars could attempt to work along the southern line, and these gaps were covered by special artillery and mine-fields.

French view of the outlook

There was indeed a current of opinion spreading from France to Great Britain and the United States which, by the critical date of October 19th, 1918, was inclined to see in the new Hindenburg retreat a movement likely to succeed, as a large measure of strategy, even as the enemy's backward ingenious stroke did in the spring of 1917. The German High Command was striving to shorten its front from five hundred and sixty miles to a little over three hundred miles, leaving delayed-action mines along all abandoned routes of supply, in order definitely to win a practical winter armistice.

The armistice negotiations, it was remarked, were no longer a symptom that the enemy was exhausted and ready to surrender, but that the Germans were desperately anxious to secure breathing time, to put their frontier in a state of defence, to rest their troops, and provoke a resurgence of patriotic spirit in a struggle against invasion.

This was, to a considerable extent, the view of Marshal Foch. He accelerated the formation of his grand army of Lorraine by withdrawing the French divisions from the floods and marshes of the southern Hindenburg systems, and giving them about a month's rest before the battle against General von Lossberg.

The British point of view, however, was different. Officers and men had the sense of victory. It was something hard to describe and impossible to analyse. It was an emotion, but born and developed by continual experience and directed by a reasoned outlook. As Sir Douglas Haig afterwards explained in his classic despatch, his armies were no longer conducting a battle, they were pursuing an enemy whom they had broken.

The enemy, having millions of men still available, could at first find sufficient fresh divisions to form strong rearguards capable of offering resistance to an initial assault. But neither the ordinary German machine-gunner nor the German rifleman was any longer reliable. There were cases, mentioned by the British commander, when his artillery barrage alone led large bodies of Germans to run away. There were other instances on a smaller scale when the smoke screen, indicating a Tank attack with infantry thrusts, caused the German line to break, though it might have remained firm under shell fire.

The British armies were not stronger than the Germans on their front. They were very much inferior in number of men, and, as has been already observed, Britons had to struggle continuously against the odds of two to one, in order to perform their leading part in both the defensive and offensive campaigns of 1917 and 1918.

The man of destiny

The French forces had been eased of the main burden of the western conflict after Verdun, and had definitely taken the position of brilliant second after General Nivelle's attempt to break through to Laon in April, 1917.

The American forces were as rich in promise as the new British armies had been at the opening of the First Battle of the Somme, with an extending list of divisions of veteran craft and power, but their principal value at the time was that of forming the reservoir of strength of the attack. Upon them would have fallen the leading part in the spring of 1919, if the British armies had proved unable to exploit the decision of Le Cateau and if the new French army of Lorraine had come into action and failed to break through.

Marshal Foch had so arranged things that the Associated Powers were in immediate possession of means of victory on the British front, and also reinsured for a definite success on the French Lorraine front, and finally insured again of triumph by the increasing strength and experience of the American forces. In case of future need there were also opening other lines of advance into Germany, owing to the capitulation of Turkey and Bulgaria and the imminent collapse of Austria-Hungary.

Nevertheless, in the month which was the grand turning point in the history of the modern world, the Briton was the man of destiny. While French opinion began to incline against the probability of an early, easy strategic victory, brought about by manœuvring actions rather than by a grand offensive in a new direction, the British soldier, by the union of incomparable endurance and irresistible fighting power, brought his guns nearer Aulnoye junction preparatory to breaking the railway line to Cologne at another junction a few miles above Aulnoye.

British airmen reconnoitring over Ostend to verify the German evacuation of the Belgian coast.

Pier and esplanade of Ostend viewed from the deck of H.M.S. Vindictive blocking the waterway.

Formal entry of the victorious British Fifth Army into liberated Lille, October 28th, 19

s marching into the thronged and beflagged Grand' Place for review by General Sir William Birdwood.

491

Trenches and wire entanglements left on the sea-front at Blankenberghe by the retreating Germans.

Wreckage of Zeebrugge Mole as it passed into British and Belgian hands in October, 1918.

THE FLOODTIDE OF VICTORY IN THE WEST.
By Edward Wright.
VI.—The British Victories on the Selle and Ecaillon Rivers.

Joy in Bruges when Freed from the Invader—Failure of the German Intrigue to Seduce the Flemings from their Allegiance—Allies Advance to the Dutch Frontier and Join Hands above Courtrai—Difficulties Attending the Communications of the Flanders Group of Armies—Fine Work of the British Railway Construction Troops—Successful Withdrawal of General Sixt von Armin—British Troops Enter Courtrai—Dastardly German Bombardment of Courtrai and St. Amand after Evacuation—Canadians Recover Denain—Spectacular Battle on the Bossuyt Canal—Bridge-building Extraordinary in the Sappers' Battle of the River Selle—German Recovery in Resoluteness of Spirit and Military Science—Construction of the Hermann Line from Origny to Marle—Obstinate Resistance to the French Armies between Ribemont and Asfeld and to the American Army above Grandpré—Optimism of the British Army a Definite Factor in the Ultimate Triumph—Sir Douglas Haig's Attack in the Landrecies Sector Launched on October 23rd—New Zealanders Inflamed by a Ghastly Tragedy Discovered at Solesmes—Capture of Escarmais and the Forest of Raismes—Turning Movement Round Valenciennes Begun—Vendegies Secured and the Battle of the Selle River Won.

HILE Sir Douglas Haig was driving deeper into the most delicate part of the enemy's front along the Oise and Sambre Canal, King Albert's forces completed, on October 19th, 1918, the recovery of Western Flanders. Bruges was still held by the enemy on October 18th, when a British officer and some Belgian officers endeavoured to penetrate into the town and were met by machine-gun fire. The exodus had then, however, been going on for two days, and the artillery behind the Belgian lancers and infantry shelled the retreating columns winding down the road to Aeltre and Ghent. Some great explosions were heard from the town, announcing the destruction of plant worth one million pounds sterling in the Brugeois Works, which was a waggon-making establishment that the enemy had transformed into a munition factory. In the night of October 18th members of the German rearguard forced their way, by threats with revolvers, into shops and private houses, and looted like common burglars. This seems to have been more an outburst of indiscipline than an official action such as had occurred at Cambrai, St. Quentin, and Douai.

Bruges the Beautiful was intact, with her famous belfry

ROYAL RE-ENTRY INTO BELGIUM'S CAPITAL.
King Albert, with Prince Albert of Great Britain, passing along a Brussels street on his formal return, amid scenes of indescribable enthusiasm, to his capital on November 22nd, 1918.

and other buildings of old romance undamaged. Most of the pictures were left in the galleries, and when the Belgian Army entered on Saturday, October 19th, the loveliest city in Northern Europe was seen to have weathered the war in a happy manner. A few bombs aimed by British airmen at the German submarine base in the inland port at the end of the sea canal had gone wide of the mark, but the townspeople retained great admiration for the courage and skill of the attacking airmen.

The scene of enthusiasm when the army of liberation entered the town had a wilder joy in it than even the spectacle at Lille. The people packed the streets, and some of them sang "Tipperary," with flourishes and special effects, showing they had long been practising in secret the famous music-hall song of the First Expeditionary Force. Forty thousand towns-people had lived for four years under the rule of the invader, who—while ruining their industries, setting them to forced labour, and taking their provisions — endeavoured with strange impudence to seduce them from their allegiance to their King.

The Flemings were told that they were the western branch of the great Teutonic family, and Dutchmen of a base order of mind, with some renegade Belgians, were given power and

493

opportunity of converting the people to the Germanic doctrine. This German party fled before the German rearguard left, and any person who had shown any sympathy with the curious movement had a bad time of it when the town was liberated.

There had been a considerable amount of trouble between Flemings and Walloons in the years before the war, owing to the language question and to the fear which the clergy had of the anti-clerical element in French influence. There was, however, a good deal of artificial intrigue in this Flemish movement, the intrigues being, of course, Teutonic in origin. The Germans took up the Fleming movement as they took up the Sinn Fein movement; but although, during the period of preparation for hostilities, they devoted far more attention to the Flamingants than they did to the Sinn Feiners, they were not so successful in Belgium as they were in Ireland. This may have been partly due to the fact that the Flemings had a larger amount of personal knowledge of the Germans.

Flemish hatred of the Hun Their feelings towards them, indeed, seemed to be more intense than were the feelings of the French, and when King Albert entered Bruges by aeroplane he was received in an ecstasy of emotion by one of the most united races in Europe. The Fleming and the Walloon were both Belgians, and of the two, probably the fair-haired, tallish, blue-eyed people by the sea-board was the more deadly in the operations in the pursuit against the withdrawing foe.

The Dutch frontier was reached without any opposition. The German guard marched away in the moonlight at three o'clock in the morning. Watchers by the border could see little of their movements, but heard through the still air the rumble of endless wheels and the measured footfall of apparently interminable columns of infantry. At Knocke and elsewhere large ammunition dumps were fired, but most of the heavy artillery was not removed, and fell, more or less damaged, into the hands of the Belgians. More than 12,000 prisoners were taken in roughly equal proportions by the Belgian, French, and British forces between October 14th and October 19th, and the guns captured numbered more than five hundred and fifty.

When the Netherlands frontier was reached by Eede, the enemy fell back across the Schipdonck Canal, which connected with the Lys River and covered Eecloo and Ghent. With rearguards and machine-gunners he tried to delay the advanced **Netherlands frontier reached** Belgian forces on the low hills in front of the canal, but the pursuers worked directly along the Ghent Canal and the highway by Aeltre, turning the positions on the rising ground, where the Germans were forced to abandon a great supply train in the haste of retreat.

General Degoutte's army, which had been checked by the hostile force at Thielt, did not get out of step with its Allies by waiting for its guns to come forward and for its cavalry to move against the enemy's flank.

The Germans had wired the country very deeply during the 1917 campaign, and had then also extended their concreted fortifications to Audenarde and Renaix, some forty-five miles from the coast. But the wire round the rising ground and railway junction of Thielt, from which five lines branched, led the Germans to stay a little too long. On October 19th the French utterly crushed all resistance and made a rapid advance to the Lys River, where they came in line with the British and Belgian forces above Courtrai.

SCENE OF ENTHUSIASM AT THE ROYAL RETURN TO BRUGES.
The King and the Queen of the Belgians on the steps of one of the public buildings of Bruges receive an ovation from their delighted subjects. It was in the "wonderful days" of the second half of October, 1918, that the city of bridges was retaken. On October 19th a Belgian cavalry officer was able to say, "Bruges is ours to-day." A week later King Albert and his Queen made their triumphal entry into the recovered city.

There was, however, a great technical difficulty in the Belgian and French movement in Western Flanders. The two allied armies, having occupied all the land up to the Dutch frontier, had to make a general change of direction and wheel into a new front of attack eastward. The northern movement between Roulers and the coast was finished, and its success strained the old system of communications of the Flanders group of armies.

Sir Herbert Plumer was the most fortunate of the three commanders in respect to supplies, as he was able to move while suffering from broken communications in the newly-recovered territory, had to feed hundreds of thousands of hungry civilians, as well as bring up their own supplies, haul their heavy artillery forward, repair old roads, and make new corduroy tracks for their lorries, carts, Tanks, and other vehicles.

King Albert's own men and General Degoutte's forces found that they could not get forward in strength for a resumption of their general offensive until they were based upon the Flemish coast. The battered, flooded wilderness of swamp along the old Yser line could not be embanked and bridged

HUN DESECRATION OF SHRINES OF CULTURE AND RELIGION IN DOUAI.
School of Fine Arts, Industry, and Commerce at Douai as it was when the British entered the town. The building had been used by the Germans as "Rupprecht Barracks." Right: Organ pipes of Douai Cathedral stacked on the floor for removal to Germany to be converted into munitions. The Huns left them there when hurriedly evacuating the city on October 17th, 1918. The structure of the great church was not seriously damaged.

in a south-easterly direction and help once more in the general British offensive, receiving food and munitions by the old routes running through Ypres and Lille. The British railway construction troops designed to extend their track to Mons, and by rapidly bridging the Lys and lightening the traffic on the new roads that were also flung across the river and through the old wilderness of battle they admirably maintained all the British strength in action.

A week of rain made both work and movement arduous, but the British steadily and powerfully laboured on. The Belgian and French forces, however, could not continue to put forth their strength merely by continuing to work on their old communications. Having entirely changed their direction from the north to the east, after an advance of some thirty-two miles on a front of nearly thirty-eight miles, the northernmost armies had to create new and direct lines of supply running to the Flemish coast. Here it was that the destruction wrought by the enemy in the harbours, basins, docks, canals, highway embankments, and railways told heavily against the Allies.

On the whole the Germans took only legitimate military measures in this sector of their retreat, and the effectiveness of their work showed how unnecessary all their purely barbaric vandalism had been. They increased their own security and augmented the troubles of the Allies by leaving behind them a series of undamaged cities filled with large populations. The advancing forces, quickly enough. Moreover, extensions of these roads and lines would give only lateral communications to the new front, and if the enemy succeeded in getting enough rested divisions into reserve for a counter-movement, the weak communications of the Western Flanders front might provoke him to strike there.

King Albert was asked by his enthusiastic liberated people when he would ride into Brussels, and he remarked that Brussels was still very far off. The distance was not great, but the work required to arrive there was tremendous. This was the reason why the Belgian Army, which had shown itself one of the most vehement in attack, was compelled to remain inactive while the British movement continued. King Albert desired to recover his kingdom undamaged as far as possible, and naturally refrained from assailing Ghent. As the enemy had used a very considerable number of concealed mines with delayed action in and around the Flemish seaports, some time passed before regular communications could be established between the armies and the coast.

The immediate, practical result was that General Sixt von Armin effected his withdrawal in a very successful manner, considering the heavy losses in men and material which he had incurred between the end of September and the middle of October.

His line was greatly shortened by the abolition of the wide angle from Knocke and Lombartzyde to Dixmude and Menin. With the Terneuzen Canal and the Dender

ON THE CONGESTED WAYS OF RETREAT AND ADVANCE.
Defeated German soldiers and transport column passing through Belgium on their way back to their country.

River lines as steps in a fighting retreat on Antwerp, he was able to make the Fourth German Army and the German Marine Corps a strong pivot on which the rest of the front, between the Scheldt and the Meuse, could turn.

The German lines by the Lys, Scheldt, and Dender were, however, lessened in value by the British advance southward. They were, in fact, being turned by Sir Douglas Haig in his thrust towards Maubeuge, so that the invader, while lingering in North-Western Belgium, was once more exposed to a flanking movement. The French army under General Degoutte began to turn General von Armin's line immediately after the action at Thielt. In a dashing fight for bridge-heads the French horse forced the passage of the inundated Lys at two places below Deynze, and advanced on a front of two and a half miles towards the south-east approach to Ghent, taking eleven hundred prisoners. With more hard fighting, Degoutte's men gradually reached the railway junction of Waereghem, and extended by the hills in front of Audenarde.

Revival of terrorisation

During this action the enemy stated, in his daily report, that the inhabitants of the country took part in the fighting against the German troops. This meant that the Germans, in their anger at continual defeats, were resorting to the method of vengeance that they had practised in the cellars of Iseghem, and turning upon the unarmed countrymen of the victors and murdering them. Almost to the last day of the war the fluctuations of hope and despair in the Teuton were shown by his vacillations between decency and savagery. Whenever the situation seemed to promise that the great withdrawal towards the shortened Meuse line could be successfully conducted, some German commander would revive the old methods of terrorisation of non-combatants. The action at Courtrai was a shocking instance of the way of fighting the Teuton was eager to adopt when he felt it safe to do so.

As explained in the previous chapter, the advance of the

BELGIAN HOMAGE TO THE MEMORY OF BRITAIN'S MARTYRED NURSE.
The Belgian Army Rifle Range in Brussels, Miss Edith Cavell's prison on the night before her execution. Above: Statue to Miss Cavell and "homage to England," the finest spirit of which she so finely represented. This was part of the statuary with which Brussels was decorated to celebrate King Albert's entry on November 22nd, 1918. The statue was the work of the distinguished Belgian scupltor, M. Marin.

Second British Army ended for the time in the British troops occupying part of the town, being divided by the canalised Lys from the market-square and the main buildings which the enemy held. All along the new German water-line a new instrument of defence was adopted in the form of a trench-mortar barrage, additional to the ordinary machine-gun protection. An intense shattering barrage of aerial torpedoes and smaller mortar-bombs was employed, apparently under the direction of Major Bruchmüller, as a means of breaking up small attacking forces collected for bridge-head operations. The device was undoubtedly effective in checking pursuit across the canal by skirmishing bodies of infantry without strong artillery support. Especially where the trench-mortar forces worked under the cover of houses by the water-side, and pitched their heavy projectiles into buildings which the British infantrymen were using as secure covering against machine-gun fire, the enemy's trick was hard to counter.

In Courtrai, where the Germans used their trench-guns,

the Englishmen and Irishmen could not answer with their 3 in. Stokes or their 6 in. Newtons, because the Germans were fighting and living alongside some thirty thousand children, women, and other non-combatants. The town had to be freed by a battle amid the hills southward and across the flatter country through which the Fifth British Army was fighting towards Tournai. By October 19th the wing of General von Quast's army was so outflanked on the south and pressed on the north that Courtrai was evacuated without a serious struggle.

It was the Lancashire and Yorkshire troops, who had cleared Roubaix, that pushed on through Estaimpuis and reached the Scheldt, some two and a half miles from Tournai. Baron von Richthofen, the father of the dead German champion of the air, was commandant of the town, and a bitterly hard ruler of it. But he left on Friday night, and on Saturday morning a party of seven English troops crossed the canal, and were met by some of the Flemings, who told them that the enemy had gone. **English troops enter Courtrai**

In spite of the ordeal they had undergone, the townspeople were at first as joyfully excited as their countrymen at Bruges and Ostend had been. Some of them had been killed and more had been wounded during the action in the streets, when gun fire roared from gardens, courtyards, and neighbouring fields, and a sleet of lead poured down all ways to the canal side. Emerging from the black cellars, where men, women, and children had been huddled together with their invading foes for days in horrible squalor, the people overwhelmed with

"THE SPIRIT OF BELGIUM."
Emblematic figure representing the Spirit of Belgium holding up the hordes
of German invaders. One of the many statuary decorations of Brussels
when King Albert returned to his own.

their greeting the Kent, Surrey, and Rifle men, carried them
to the old town-hall in the market-place, and then marched
in a cheering procession from end to end of the old city.

Many of the women and children were without shoes and
stockings, and their clothes were rags, in spite of the fact
that they were one of the great weaving peoples of Europe,
famous throughout the centuries for their work in wool and
linen. The enemy had stripped all their factories and stolen
the food supplied for them by the International Relief Commission. As many Germans in position of authority stole
food intended for their own troops, sending it to their families
at home when they did not eat it themselves, naturally supplies
for civilians in occupied territories were subjected to serious
diminution. In Courtrai, as elsewhere, many of the children
died for want of food, and of those who palely

Courtrai stripped survived, a half were stricken with disease.
and starving A cousin of President Woodrow Wilson was
discovered in Courtrai by the liberators.
She was a lady of more than seventy years of age, who had
fallen from comfort into misery under the German rule.

The British fired only one shell into the town. One of
their observers spied through his field-glasses a German
crouching in the small chamber at the top of the belfry
of St. Martin's Church and ranging the guns that were
shelling the infantry of attack on the roads outside the town.
With a single shell a British gunner punched out the observation chamber and the observer, and fired no more. The
Germans, however, turned their high-velocity guns on to
the city with malignant intensity as soon as they knew
their rearguards were clear of it. They promised the townspeople there would be no bombardment, and having thus

led them to stay and walk in the open, they turned the guns
upon them.

The scene of general rejoicing was broken by a fierce,
dastardly bombardment that lasted until late in the night
and started again in the morning of Sunday, October 20th.
Carrying their dead and wounded, the unhappy people
went back to their noisome cellars, while the great shells
crashed in frightful explosions above them. When the
townsfolk were at last able to emerge in security, owing to
the British reaching the Scheldt and forcing the enemy to
withdraw his guns again, they were dazed by their sufferings
and full of a bitterness towards the Teuton that was not
likely to be quenched for a generation. Their women had been
treated abominably, their children starved
to death, and, finally, when the German was   **Hun outrage**
appealing in the name of humanity to   **on St. Amand**
President Woodrow Wilson, he had turned
his guns on the city of some thirty thousand non-combatants.

About the same time there was a worse scene in the smaller
French town of St. Amand, between Tournai and Valenciennes.
A cyclist patrol of the First British Army worked down
the Scarpe River towards its junction with the Scheldt,
and after a skirmish with enemy forces entered St. Amand,
and found that the town was in a woeful condition, some
fifteen hundred of the people being stricken with pneumonic
influenza. Most of the cases were so acute that the patients
could not be removed. The Germans were well aware of
the situation, having created it by collecting patients from the
countryside and making St. Amand an isolation epidemic
centre to save their troops from infection. And they had decided
not to attempt a delaying stand at the waterlogged position
of St. Amand, because of the danger of having the garrison
infected with lung trouble. Yet as soon as the enemy left
the town he began shelling it. After some rounds of ordinary
ammunition, he used only mustard-gas shell in large quantities.

' KING OF THE BELGIANS."
One of the impromptu " stucco works of art that would deceive even the elect,"
which were used to decorate Brussels set free. Statue to King Albert. Note
the Belgian lion over the dead German eagle.

BRITAIN'S HOMAGE TO BELGIUM.
British battalion saluting the King of the Belgians on the occasion of his formal re-entry into his capital, November 22nd, 1918.

The place was drenched with the horrible poison, and hundreds of children, women, and old men, struggling for life on beds of sickness, were killed in the night.

The overcrowded hospital, which German authorities themselves h a d filled with patients, was selected as a special target during the gas bombardment. When British ambulances came through the poison flood and the shell fire, with gallant nurses, to rescue the sufferers, many of them were dead. The crime of St. Amand was one of the foulest things the Teuton did in the whole course of the war. The Staff of the Seventeenth German Army, under General Otto von Below, was responsible, and the army corps commanded by General von Albrecht, which had been broken at Cambrai, appears to have been concerned in the matter.

Punishment followed swiftly. The enemy was becoming arrogantly vicious by reason of the general success in withdrawing and reconcentrating his forces. He had between eighty and ninety divisions arrayed between Ghent and the Serre River, and being protected northward by a series of canals, and southward by the remaining part of the Hindenburg works, he was able to mass an extraordinary number of men against the British armies along the Scheldt and Sambre-Oise

Germans massed on river-line

water-line. In spite of the loss of the hills in the centre of the battle-line by Catillon, the Germans were confident at last of their ability to stop the British pursuit.

Above Le Cateau, where the Selle River ran by Solesmes into the Scheldt below Valenciennes, the British line had scarcely moved since the Third Army arrived there on October 10th, after the Battle of Le Cateau. There had been fierce fighting at the bridge-head villages, such as St. Python and Haussy, but the enemy, with his trench-mortar barrage, machine-gun fire, and curtains of shell from high-velocity guns, maintained his hold on the river-line and went on strengthening his positions for a week.

Over the ground occupied by Sir Julian Byng's and Sir Henry Horne's men the German gunners constantly poured poison gas from positions round the outskirts of the Forest

of Mormal that could not be reached by the shorter-ranged British artillery. Moreover, the great parks of British "heavies" could only creep forward slowly, as roads and tracks were made from the old Hindenburg line to the new positions along the tributary of the Scheldt. As has been shown in Chapter CCLXXXI., the Fourth British Army, under Sir Henry Rawlinson, was the first to get its guns and supply columns well over the Scheldt Canal for a renewal of the offensive on October 17th, when, in a struggle lasting three days, the Germans were driven across the Sambre and Oise Canals in the sector below Le Cateau.

While this battle was proceeding, the Third British Army remained along the Lower Selle with the left wing of the First British Army, while the rest of

RIGHT VINDICATED AND MIGHT DISPOSSESSED.
Reception of King Albert by the members of the Belgian Judicature at the Law Courts, Brussels, in November, 1918, when the dispensation was resumed of that justice which had been unknown in the capital ever since the Germans occupied the city four years before.

Sir Henry Horne's divisions advanced from Douai towards Valenciennes, to get in line with the sweeping eastern movement of the Fifth and Second Armies through Lille, Roubaix, Tourcoing, and Courtrai.

The victories of the northern and southern British armies had created a great German salient in front of Tournai some forty miles wide and thirty miles deep. This salient was rapidly evacuated by the enemy between October 16th and October 19th, when General Plumer was fiercely pressing on its northern corner at Pecq, on the Scheldt above Tournai, and General Horne was continually thrusting into its southern corner by Denain, where the Selle stream flowed into the larger river. During this operation there was no opportunity of enveloping the enemy's forces in the great salient, as the advanced divisions of General Plumer and General Horne were not strong enough for the purpose. They were used only to threaten the enemy and quicken his withdrawal from the great French industrial region. In the southern operations there was a fine achievement by the 8th Division, which, after having been in line continually for a long period, broke into Douai and then on a wide front violently pursued the enemy along the Scarpe River towards St. Amand, forcing him to give ground so hastily that all his operations of withdrawal had to be quickened. He lacked the time to mine thoroughly the traffic routes he abandoned.

The Canadian Corps changed direction after its success at Cambrai and turned north-eastward towards Denain, the lower base of the new enemy salient. In the space of a week the Dominion forces drove into the enemy's territory to a depth of twenty-three miles, recovering twenty-eight towns and villages, and liberating multitudes of French civilians. Denain was reached on the heels of the retreating enemy on October 19th, and its capture completed the following day in circumstances of considerable difficulty. The Canadians fought the Germans from street to street, in the Grand' Place and round St. Martin's Church, amid twenty thousand French people, who refused to wait until the action was over before welcoming their redeemers. The townsfolk made coffee for the troops, who paused to drink and then went on with their fighting. Even when enemy shells began to fall the people would not cease tending the soldiers, and women were hit by German snipers and by shell fragments.

In the Le Cateau battle the Fort Garry Horse had swept into towns and villages, meeting a barrage of kisses and embraces that made them carry themselves afterwards with a certain romantic swagger. For more than a week, in fact, they boasted that theirs was the most romantic experience in the war. But the foot caught up with the horse at Denain, and the Canadian Corps found itself faced with the hardest problem in commissariat after the victory in Denain market-place. Twenty thousand French people were rescued in the town, bringing the number of children, women, and old men attached to the command of Sir Arthur Currie to the extraordinary number of seventy-three thousand. All this huge family required food, comfort, shelter, and transport, which had to be provided during one of the most important and intricate manœuvres of the war. Yet the Canadian genius for organisation was equal to the strain. A special department was established for looking after the women and children, most of whom were starving; the sick were sorted

Canadian Corps recaptures Denain

STRAINS OF PRAISE AND TRIUMPH.
One of the military bands accompanying the troops that escorted King Albert back to his capital in triumph. Two divisions of the Belgian Army, accompanied by British, French, and American battalions with their artillery, provided a military pageant that occupied fifteen miles of road.

out and attended to, and new homes were found for those who were too near the German guns. With a French-Canadian acting as commandant of Denain, the work of rescuing and fighting went on with admirable efficiency.

The ground the Canadians covered was classic in British military history. Over it the Duke of Marlborough had fought his last campaign with Marshal Villars, through the dammed and inundated streams of the Sensée and the Scarpe to the Scheldt, which for eighteen months had been obstacles to the First Army's advance. Denain was the scene of one of Villars' successes after Marlborough was retired from his command and betrayed by the British Government of his day when moving on Le Quesnoy. The Germans had overthrown the monument to Villars, but they fell back before Haig's men, who proceeded against the enemy along the very road Marlborough had designed to take before the British home front was broken by Louis XIV. Why the Teutons should have expended their wrath upon the statue of Marshal Villars is a thing no civilised man can understand.

They were, however, unable to continue shelling the famous old battle town, as the Highland Territorials of the 51st Division were in action alongside the Dominion troops, and with the kilties of Scotland and Canada both in pursuit of the enemy, and the large force of English, Irish and Welsh stock vying, under General Currie, with the Highlanders, the pace of the action in the southern corner of the salient quickened. The Scotsmen stormed into Thiant, a village below Valenciennes, and had a fierce struggle with Germans shooting from the houses, while the villagers sheltered in the cellars. The enemy commander could not let his flank be driven in at Thiant, and sent strong reinforcements, who succeeded in pressing the Scotsmen partly out of the place, but the Highlanders hung on grimly and then renewed the attack, clearing all the village and releasing the people.

While the struggle was going on in and around Denain there was another fiercer conflict in the northern corner of the Tournai salient. Sir Herbert Plumer's divisions combined above and below Courtrai in a magnificent sweeping advance down to the Scheldt. The Second British Army was then practically detached from King Albert's group of forces, and once more employed as one of the spear-heads of Sir Douglas Haig's operations. The Yorkshiremen and

BELGIUM'S KING SALUTING THE STARS AND STRIPES.
American infantry marching past the King and Queen of the Belgians in the great square before the Town Hall, Brussels, on November 22nd, 1918. The American troops followed immediately after the British battalion and evoked enthusiastic admiration for their fine military bearing and splendid marching.

Lancashiremen who had carried Roubaix and fought down to the Scheldt near Tournai, opened another line of attack against the enemy between the two towns. The Kents, Surreys, Rifles, and other English battalions, who had conducted the canal battle in Courtrai, advanced along the road to Courtrai, while the division that had carried Harlebeke fought across the Lys and along the Bossuyt Canal that connected the two villages and entered the Scheldt at the village of that name.

The Germans were very strongly placed between the two rivers. Their infantry was dug in along the canal and the neighbouring railway embankment and protected by the ubiquitous wire-field, with both field-guns and heavy guns in immediate support. The main German artillery poured a flanking fire against the northern British wing from the hills in front of Audenarde, sent out a frontal barrage from the heights round Renaix, and directed another cross-fire south-wards from the hills dominating Tournai.

Gun duel on the Bossuyt Canal In spite, however, of the enemy's shell fire and his trick of flooding the ground with poison gas, the gunners of the Second British Army were well forward, and the result was one of the most spectacular battles of the campaign, resembling rather one of Marlborough's conflicts than the ordinary camouflaged struggles at the end of the Great War. The guns on both sides came into action at close range, shelling each other without cover from either bank of the Bossuyt Canal. It was a supreme test of nerve, marksmanship, and speedy firing and the British artillery completely won. As the gunners beat down the enemy's pieces the British infantry charged, breaking through the German line, reaching the German guns with the bayonet and capturing a score of field-pieces and howitzers, with one of the naval guns that had been bombarding Courtrai, and two undamaged trains loaded with material.

The victors then worked down both banks of the canal to the river, and extended over the northern hills to the Audenarde railway at Vichte, thus preparing the way for a French move-ment alongside them against the enemy's last line of concrete fortifications between Audenarde and Renaix, constructed to cover a turning movement round Ghent and prevent a direct thrust towards Brussels. Meanwhile, the ground above Tournai was the next objective of General Plumer's finely-handled divisions, but they could not at once resume operations. Their period of fast and furious manœuvring was for the time ended. In three weeks they had advanced, often by roundabout ways, through forty miles of the worst ground on the western front, breaking the enemy and turning him whenever he tried to stand. They had, however, to pause by the Scheldt, as also did the forces of the Fifth Army that came alongside them, directly in front of Tournai, with some stiff fighting at Froyennes and St. Maur.

Round Tournai the German positions were very strong. Immediately north of the city St. Aubert Hill overlooked the new British lines, and miles of undulating ground stretched eastward, giving the enemy cover from direct fire and screened gun positions. His losses were compensated by the shortening of his line, as he had intact, excellent com-

Third Army's renewed effort munications, while General Plumer and General Birdwood were in a country of ruined railways and damaged roads. The impetus of the northern offensive was temporarily spent by October 20th. Forty miles from the old British bases, over stretches of mud and swamp in the filthiest condition, there had to be moved aerodromes and hospitals, water supply, store places, telegraphs and transport, and all the rest of the immense mechanism and population required behind modern fighting men.

But Sir Douglas Haig's main forces of the Fourth, Third, and First Armies had been gathering power for another spring during the week of operations against the enemy's left wing. As already related, the traffic lines from Péronne were so quickly extended that the British Commander-in-Chief was able to resume his general pursuit on October 17th, with an advance by the Fourth Army to the Oise and Sambre Canal. As this movement slowed down, in the night of October 19th, to allow the heavy guns and supply columns to catch up with the tireless infantry and field-artillery, the Third Army came into action from its new base around Cambrai.

The 19th Division marched from Sir William Birdwood's command at Lille down to the Third Army on the Selle River. The 4th Division, belonging to the First Army, was also engaged in Sir Julian Byng's attack, in which the Guards, the 62nd, 42nd, 5th, 17th, and the 38th Divisions were concerned. Many of these forces had been fighting along the Selle River for a week, reaching some of the eastern villages by feats of dashing valour, only to fall back against over-whelming artillery and infantry counter-attacks. The supreme difficulty was to make and maintain bridges across the stream with the enemy above the water pitching trench-mortar bombs over in a barrage, as well as sweeping the ground with heavy shell fire and machine-gun bursts. Owing to the rainy weather it was impossible for aerial observers to locate the hostile batteries, and although the British Staff had devices for discovering enemy gun positions by microphone measure-ments of sounds of firing and shell noises, these were useless against batteries reserving their fire until a great battle.

Sir Julian Byng met the circumstances by opening the Selle River action at two o'clock in the morning, when rain was falling. The rain was heavy and continuous, and greatly impeded the infantry and Tank forces, but it helped to screen the storming rushes of the leading infantry. From the neighbourhood of Denain to the vicinity of Le Cateau the British troops charged in darkness and rain across the valley where General Smith-Dorrien's line had run early in the war. Instead of the poor, shallow trench made hastily by French peasants, the enemy had begun to construct, while preparing to retire from Cambrai, deep, wired, and hidden earthworks, from which he could command the stream and its approaches. These works he had completed after the first skirmishes along the riverside. With guns of every calibre he curtained all the western bank to a considerable depth and swept the roads, so that it was largely a matter of luck if the first forces of assault found their bridges intact and them-selves survived the shells and bullets poured upon them.

Their own batteries, having few targets for counter-battery work, could only drench with gas all likely German gun-pits, while making as dense a **Bridge-building** travelling barrage as possible, to keep down **extraordinary** the machine-guns and rifles of the defence. The opposing artillery forces, instead of engaging each other as usual, hammered the hostile infantries, making the battle one of the most dreadful ordeals for the foot soldiers on both sides. The Briton won by downright gallantry, under conditions as grave as those obtaining round the Serre plateau in the First Battle of the Somme. Moving out in the open against forces in much superior numbers, sheltered in earth-works and cellars, the British troops forced the Selle River at Haspres, St. Python, Solesmes, Neuvilly, and Amerval.

As soon as the river-line was secured, by wading, floating, or footbridge transit, there came the operation on the success of which everything in Sir Douglas Haig's scheme depended. The troops of the Third Army had forced the river on many occasions in many places since reaching it on October 10th, but they had been unable to throw strong bridges over the water by which guns and Tanks could follow immediately in support. When the artillery and storming cars were ready to advance the task of getting them over the water had become ten times more difficult. Yet the bridge-building was accomplished, in the rain and gloom of October 20th, under heavy fire from both artillery and machine-guns. One field company of the Welsh (38th) Division lost half of its effectives in the terrible work, but completed its bridge with such steady skill that the British Commander-in-Chief singled out the feat as one of the finest instances of pluck and determination in the campaign.

It was indeed a sappers' battle. The foot did all that men could do, working with deathless stubbornness along the roads and railways towards Landrecies and Le Quesnoy, and getting footholds on the slopes between the Selle stream and the tributary rivulets of the Ecaillon. But without the heroic bridge work of the engineers the attack would have been held, and probably broken.

After a long, desperate struggle in St. Python and Solesmes the German front-line troops were broken; but General von Below had about five divisions more than the British commander, and with them he made a great counter-attack from the direction of Le Quesnoy.

By this time the British guns had been brought across the river, and in front of them were some of the light storming cars. At short range the enemy was again engaged, the counter-attack was shattered, and, in a fierce, swaying struggle lasting for twenty-four hours, Amerval was retained, and the hills above the tributary of the Ecaillon won, with some three thousand prisoners and a number of guns. Like the advance of the Fourth Army, which immediately preceded it, the forward sweep of the Third Army led to one of the hardest fought actions of the campaign.

In both resoluteness of spirit and military science the Teutonic forces seemed to have recovered from the Le Cateau disaster. Their resistance gave some colour to the French view that they would be able to stand until the winter, and conduct their retirement to the Meuse in fighting order, in time for their last reinforcement of half a million young recruits and recovered light casualties to take part in the final struggle. General Debeney, whose First Army had for a long period been acting close alongside General Rawlinson's Fourth Army, found that the inundated valley of the Oise by Guise prevented him from working forward. His bridge-

HUN DISHONOUR TO A SOLDIER'S MEMORY.
Plinth of the monument to Marshal Villars, in Denain, from which the Germans removed the colossal bronze horse and rider and the inscription plates, either from malice or for use in the manufacture of munitions.

head at Mont d'Origny, taken by a splendid regiment, was not capable of being developed into a route of advance. Only by heroic endurance were the conquerors able merely to hold on to the height against continual counter-attacks. It was impossible for them to debouch from it.

The fact was that the careful Teutons were not relying wholly on their Serre-Hunding works southward. They had constructed a new inner system, the Hermann line, extending from the neighbourhood of Origny to the hills above Marle. General Debeney decided that it would be better to shift his point of attack to the Hermann line, and on October 19, 1918, General Pétain came to take direction of a combined attack by the forces of General Debeney, General Mangin, and General Guillaumat upon the Guise plateau and the enemy's communications at Hirson. It was at Hirson that Sir Douglas Haig was aiming in his thrust towards the Aulnoye and Maubeuge railway junctions, so there were six allied armies moving against the German centre.

Yet again the desperate character of the enemy's resistance and the sustained violence of his counter-attacks appeared to make an early end of the war very uncertain. From the Oise by Ribemont to the Aisne by Asfeld the First, Tenth, and Fifth French Armies could only win forward by slow degrees. Every step they made through the lines of caverns, concrete works, and entanglements provoked reactions in strength by the enemy. Debeney's main forces, secretly

TRIBUTE OF GRATITUDE FROM DENAIN TO THE CANADIANS WHO SET IT FREE.
Presentation of a flag by the Mayor of Denain to the Commander of the 4th Canadian Division, to be preserved in Canada as a memorial of their liberation of the town in October, 1918. The ceremony, which took place on October 27th, was attended by the Prince of Wales, General Currie, and the Canadian Divisional Commander and Staff, and was followed by a most impressive Thanksgiving Service in the Church of St. Martin.

KEEPING IN CLOSE TOUCH.
Canadian patrol dashing across the railway line at Valenciennes while the place was still being subjected to heavy machine-gun fire from the rear-guarding forces of the retreating Germans.

moved southward, drove between the Oise and Serre Rivers on the left rear of the Hunding line, which General Mangin attacked in front, while General Guillaumat assailed it for fifteen miles on the right.

General von Hutier acknowledged the skill with which the First French Army had suddenly been manœuvred by withdrawing from the angle of the Oise and Serre and massing along the Hermann line ; while General von Eberhardt counter-attacked Mangin by the Laon railway, also in the design of freeing himself for a short retirement. General von Mudra likewise counter-attacked furiously, and in the Upper Argonne hills, where a Czecho-Slovak contingent was fighting under General Gouraud, some seventy enemy divisions were employed to recover the heights above Vouziers. The First American Army was also fiercely countered on the ridge above Grandpré and in the woods by Bantheville.

Moral as the deciding factor

The decision turned almost entirely upon the question of moral. The doctrine of Marshal Foch—that a battle is never lost unless an army thinks it is lost—applied with remarkable point to the general situation. Both sides were drenched, cold, and miserable, with the prospect of a bitter winter struggle against epidemic sickness as well as the

enemy. The allied soldiers had the disadvantage of drawing little hope from the armistice proposals, as they did not believe the Germans intended to surrender. The German troops, on the other hand, having recovered somewhat from their view that it was better to be captured than to die if the war was about to be finished, were fighting with renewed energy, in the inculcated belief that the more steadily they held out the sooner peace would be settled. The French soldiers, having been rather too enthusiastic when pursuing the enemy across large tracts of recovered territory, were somewhat dashed when they arrived at the inner Hindenburg systems, tested the great strength of them, and found how cunningly the flooded streams had

IN VALENCIENNES REGAINED.
The French commandant welcomed in Valenciennes immediately after its recapture. It was early on November 3rd, 1918, that Canadian troops entered the town, and at about 10 o'clock the French flag was hoisted over the town-hall.

been used as anti-Tank moats. But the British forces, which had done by far the hardest part of all the fighting for three months, though ranking in strength of numbers below both the French and American forces, were not to be argued into despondency. They had acquired the habit of victory, and were not to be cheated out of it by any revival of confidence on the part of the enemy. Their commanders were supremely confident, and Sir Douglas Haig himself communicated some of his grim optimism to General Pétain.

The British Staff knew that the masses of Germans opposed to them had lost heart. The resistance offered along the Selle River had definitely exhausted the fresh forces obtained by the withdrawals between Douai and the Flemish coast. All that was needed was to maintain the utmost pressure upon the yielding Germans, numbering some thirty-one divisions, and collected between the Forest of Mormal and Condé, until they again lost faith in themselves and fled.

As General Debeney had moved his main forces of attack from the Sambre and Oise Canal, Sir Henry Rawlinson did not continue his offensive above Guise, but swung on the left by Bazeul

CANADIANS WIN A FAMOUS TOWN BACK FOR FRANCE.
Men of the first Canadian patrols advancing across a barricaded street in the western suburbs of Valenciennes. Though the Germans left the town early on that day, they covered their retirement by such strong machine-gun fire as made it necessary for the relieving troops to push forward with great care.

so as to make a side thrust between Le Cateau and Landrecies, while Sir Julian Byng and Sir Henry Horne resumed their attack over the Selle River line. The 1st, 6th, 26th, and 18th Divisions of the Fourth Army were deployed on the night of October 22nd alongside the 33rd, 21st, 5th, 42nd, 37th, the New Zealand Division, and the 3rd, 2nd, and 19th Divisions. On the left were the 61st Division, 4th Division, and 51st Division, mainly of First Army troops, who waited to exploit the advantages gained by the Third Army.

In spite of the screen of bad weather the German Staff knew that the supreme crisis in the British campaign was at hand, and by means of enormous dispositions, alike in the grouping of

GREAT JOY AFTER MUCH TRIBULATION.
Sisters of the Hôtel Dieu, Valenciennes, welcoming the first Canadians to enter the city. These good women attended the Canadians who were wounded during the early part of the fierce fighting for possession of the town.

STATE CONGRATULATIONS TO A RECOVERED TOWN.
M. Raymond Poincaré walking through the streets of Valenciennes on the occasion of his first visit to the town after its deliverance in his official capacity of President of the French Republic.

forces and the rate of artillery firing, endeavoured to bring the pursuit to a standstill. At midnight on October 22nd the enemy began a very violent bombardment of the British assembly places, inflicting considerable losses on one British division and injuring men in other units. Nearly everything was in favour of the enemy. The weather continued bad, allowing him to escape again from counter-battery work, and the ground he occupied between the Scheldt and the Sambre was as though marked out by nature for an obstinate defence. It was crossed by a succession of tributary streams, beginning with the brooks in the cloughs by Cambrai and continuing farther north with wider, deeper, water-courses — first the Selle, then the Ecaillon, with a number of branching brooks, and the Harpies and the Rhonelle.

Between these rivers rose the foothills of the Ardennes, many of which were covered by the outpost copses of the great Forest of Mormal. All the slopes were trenched, and many wired and excavated, for the Germans had worked with tremendous energy after their defeat at Le Cateau.

The Mormal woodland was the last hope of the German Staff. If the course of battle could be kept in the forest

sector there would follow a long wrestle like that in the Argonne. Sir Douglas Haig wanted room to swing round the forest, and before the enemy could recover from the defeats of October 19th and October 20th the British commander launched against him a hundred and fifty thousand troops.

The action opened in a fog at night, with a difference in timing the two parts of the operations similar to that successfully adopted in the Battle of Le Cateau.

The Fourth Army started its whirlwind bombardment and infantry movements at twenty past one in the morning of October 23rd. Then at three o'clock, when the German commander was marching his last reserves from the cover of the Mormal Forest towards the Landrecies sector, the Third Army, which from the enemy's point of view was temporarily exhausted in the struggle along the Selle River, also attacked as far north as the hills above Haussy, prolonging the line of battle to a total length of fifteen miles.

In front of Catillon and the hills above it the 1st and 6th Divisions won ground all along the waterway preparatory to an action for forcing the passage. On their right some of the forces of the First French Army demonstrated violently

Supreme crisis at hand

MUSIC MADE BY CONQUERING HEROES.
Canadian band playing outside the Hôtel de Ville, Valenciennes. A pitched battle, lasting two days, was needed to rescue the town from the enemy, and much of the credit for its capture went to the Canadians. some of whom were the first British troops to enter it—just a week before the armistice stopped hostilities

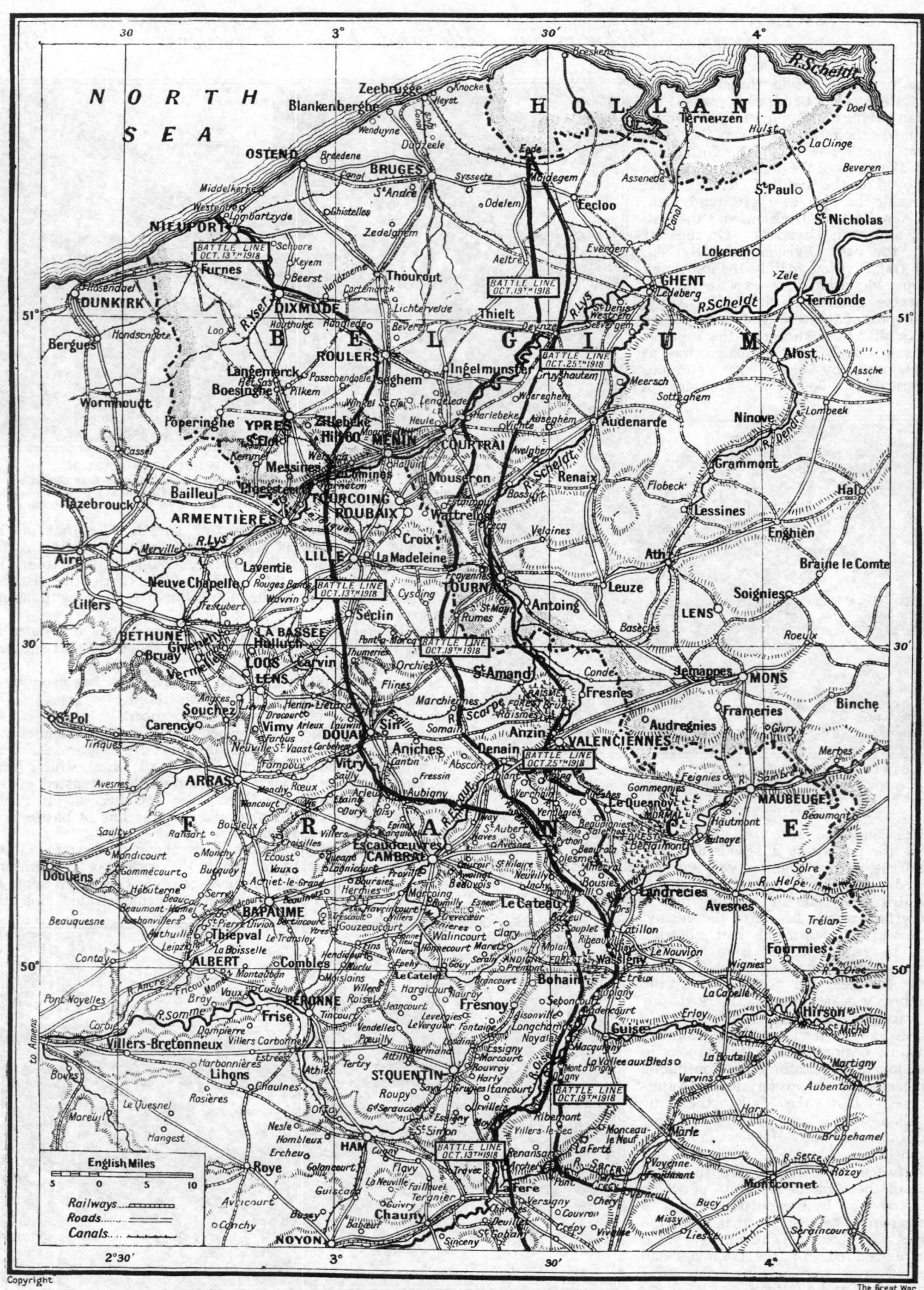

FORWARD MOVEMENT OF THE ALLIES IN THE SECOND HALF OF OCTOBER, 1918.

Mormal Forest was the last hope of the German High Command trying to stem the Allies' pursuit. To avoid a long struggle in that forest sector Sir Douglas Haig desired to swing round it on his way to Maubeuge and to the enemy's communications at Hirson. The Battles of the Selle and Ecaillon Rivers were the result of this plan, ending in complete victory for the British arms.

with tempestuous gun fire and skirmishing infantry movements along the approaches to Guise, with a view to assisting the British offensive and also veiling the transfer of force against the Hermann line. All this movement for holding the enemy along the canal, where he was not menaced, was so successful that the Germans claimed a victorious defence there.

Meanwhile, the renowned 25th Division of English County troops broke through the German flank by Pommereuil and stormed into the large maze of Bishop's Wood, stretching midway between Le Cateau and Landrecies. Here the fighting was swift and savage at the beginning, as the Cheshires and other battalions, distinguished since the Battle of Vimy Ridge for vehemence and endurance, strove to pass in a bound through the wired and pitted barbican of the great forest. Mormal Forest was not the cover it had been in 1914, owing to the great clearings that enemy woodcutters had made, while Bishop's Wood, having a railway running by it, was partly destroyed. When, however, the enemy commander recovered from the distracting demonstration along the Sambre and Oise Canal he brought forces into Landrecies and sent them into the eastern end of the wood and down the road to Bousies village above the forest combat. Throughout all the afternoon and far into the night the 25th Division continued to wrestle for the Bishop's Wood, being greatly helped by a magnificent advance made on their left flank by the Surreys, East County troops, and other battalions of the 18th Division.

IN A MUSEUM LOOTED BY THE HUN.
Hall of the museum at Valenciennes as it was found when the Canadian troops reached the town early in November, 1918; and (above) a cleared picture gallery in the same museum. The Germans had carried off most of the tapestries, bronzes, statues, pictures, and other removable objects.

This northernmost force of Sir Henry Rawlinson's command worked quickly forward over four miles of hills and valleys before reaching Bousies village. Then, in fierce street fighting, they broke the German supporting force, and holding on to the houses against all counter-attacks, completely covered the principal operations in Bishop's Wood.

All the way there was downright, dogged, slogging fighting against more numerous forces. Only the spirit of the attackers enabled them to outlast and wear down the divisions of the defence. When the Surreys, with the help of a Tank, broke through the copse and farmstead in front of

Bousies, while the leading companies of the 25th Division were reaching open ground beyond Bishop's Wood, the moral of the German divisions in this sector was broken. The rapid, unexpected turning movement behind Le Cateau, together with the appearance of "whippet" Tanks five miles beyond the Selle River, convinced some tens of thousands of Teutons that the war was lost.

Only a few of them stood to defend Bousies, and most of these fled when the Tank, accompanied by less than one hundred Surreys, entered the village. British aerial observers reported that the road running along the edge of Mormal Forest was grey with fugitives, who were crowding in utter confusion into the cover of the trees. Thereupon the heavy British artillery swept the fleeing masses with poison gas and the vulcanite fuse shell. As previously explained, this delicate fuse mechanism caused the shell to explode at the slightest touch, and spread its force above the ground, instead of spending much of it in making a crater. .

A strong, fresh German force had been collected in the great

DESTRUCTION WROUGHT BY THE RETREATING FOE AT VALENCIENNES RAILWAY STATION.
It was in the semi-darkness of the early morning of November 3rd, 1918, that the British troops began to percolate into the town in small parties, which worked systematically up the streets, searching every nook for remaining Germans. Though they found the station destroyed, on the whole Valenciennes was comparatively little damaged structurally until the Germans, in wrath at the humiliation of being driven out, began a systematic bombardment.

forest for the special purpose of preventing a break-through in the Le Cateau manner. As it came forward, according to plan, to assail the small English advance guard, the beaten troops mingled with it in such numbers that they could not be re-formed. They checked the great counter-attack and communicated some of their panic feeling in regard to the British storming cars to the new force, thus causing more confusion. Some four divisions were overthrown round Mormal Forest, and when, in the latter part of the morning the fog lifted to enhance the British victory, the first stage of which it had promoted, the mastery of the air exercised by British pilots served to complete the German disaster.

The light Tanks also played an important part in the capture of Beaurain village, where Kent, Devon, and Cornish men of the 5th Division, who had fought alongside the New Zealanders on the Ancre, added another victory to their list. The New Zealanders, assembling by Solesmes, pressed forward quickly through Vertain, found the bridges over the neighbouring brook blown up, and waded across under machine-gun and shell fire, with few casualties, and with continuous streams of traffic behind them and regimental bands playing the supports into action under the enemy's high-velocity barrage, the gallant islanders reached their objectives in such strength and spirit that they formed for another attack in the evening, won bridge-head after bridge-head along the Ecaillon River and advanced from Beaudignies over the hills eastward within rifle range of Le Quesnoy.

Behind them, in Solesmes, had occurred, just as they finished their first superb advance, a tragedy of the war that fired them with fury. After they had passed through the plundered and wrecked town, releasing the population who had been sheltering in the cellars, some of the prisoners they made were madly assailed by the Frenchwomen. A gendarme had followed the New Zealanders into Solesmes in order to rescue at once his wife and two children, from whom he had had no news for four years. He found his two children locked in a room and his wife **Ghastly outrage in Solesmes** gagged, outraged, and dead in another chamber. The crime had only been committed when the Germans were leaving the town. It was the discovery of it by the husband that caused the people to attempt to kill every German prisoner. The New Zealanders prevented this act of vengeance, but they went forward themselves in the evening against the forces along the Ecaillon River like avenging angels.

The Home County and Highland troops of the 33rd Division, with the Northumberlands, Yorks, and other battalions of the 21st Division, stormed forward south of Solesmes to Vendegies Wood, but could not carry the village. Amid the houses fighting went on fiercely till the close of the day, when the enemy made a counter-attack, strongly supported by artillery fire, and, after being repulsed, renewed the struggle in the night and recovered the village.

Farther north the Iron Division, with its Lancashire and other Northern troops fighting alongside its old companions of the 2nd Division of Londoners, Scotsmen, and English County troops, took Escarmais, and there opened the way for a turning movement round Valenciennes by the First Army. While the main battle was developing into one of the decisive actions in the war, Sir Henry Horne further cleared the ground for his strong intervention in the struggle by turning and taking, with light Canadian skirmishers, the large Forest of Raismes that covered the approaches to Condé. Fifteen hundred Germans were caught in this brilliant movement of envelopment.

The western suburbs of Valenciennes were reached at the mining centres of Anzin and Bruay, the Scheldt becoming, as at Cambrai, the temporary dividing line between the Canadian Corps with its British comrades and the German forces. As at Cambrai, General Horne and General Byng combined in flanking thrusts above and below the city, while menacing the garrison on the outskirts. The Germans for a time retained bridge-heads on the western bank of the Scheldt, which they had fenced with a double line of entanglements, but they were merely occupied in the front, while the British forces poured in two streams round the historic, peopled city.

After the nocturnal fighting on October 23rd the battle increased in intensity and scope between Valenciennes and Landrecies before break of day on October 24th. The British armies were west of **Enemy routed along the Selle** Catillon and Ors, by the Sambre and Oise Canal, on the eastern edge of Bishop's Wood, in Bousies and Vendegies Wood, Saleches, Beaudignies, and Verchain. Some fifteen villages were captured, three streams forced, two plateaux completely conquered and passed, and guns captured in hundreds. From all the positions named, the Fourth, Third, and First Armies continued to storm forward with practically no pause on October 24th. The Germans were becoming physically exhausted, as was shown by the grave weakness of their counter-attacks; nevertheless, they clung to many of their strong points with desperate courage. Only towards nightfall on the second day of the great battle was it patent that the strength of their reserves was exhausted.

Beaudignies, the New Zealand bridge-head, was the main starting-point for the renewal of the attack in the darkness of October 24th. The New Zealanders went forward, with British troops on either side, and fought up the ridge leading to Le Quesnoy. When the German infantry broke, the enemy gunners bravely tried to cover the retreat, but they were unaccustomed to the speed of the New Zealand attack. As the crews were limbering up, the overseas troops rushed them and captured field-guns and a heavy howitzer, all intact with ammunition. This stroke had a general effect upon the enemy. He withdrew all his other batteries from their positions south of the Valenciennes railway, with the result that the garrisons of positions on either side of Beaudignies were left without artillery support. Thereupon, the leading brigade of the 37th Division made a rushing advance on Chissignies, a village one mile away on the valley road to Mormal Forest. The men worked through severe machine-gun fire when crossing the river, and then fought down barricaded streets with victorious skill. North of Beaudignies other British battalions pushed from the Ecaillon River up the hill and over a lesser stream, and took Ruesnes village.

Northward, Thiant was definitely secured, and the 4th Division took Verchain and Moncheaux, while the Highland Territorials cleared the riverbank to Maing. Vendegies, that much-contested point, was finally secured by envelopment in the afternoon, and found to be honeycombed with camouflaged works and wired and barricaded into one of the most remarkable of improvised strongholds. Only when the Germans were dropping from fatigue were they finally overcome and all the ground cleared for the closing operations of the war. The action along the Selle River ended with the total capture of some twenty thousand prisoners and four hundred and seventy-five guns and the collapse of the German moral. It decided the question whether the war was likely to be prolonged until the spring of 1919.

ARROGANCE CHASTENED BY REVERSE.
German officers being escorted into the British lines as prisoners of war. No fewer than 2,472 were captured by the Allies in the month of October, 1918, alone.

CANADIANS PRACTISING **CHAPTER CCLXXXIV.** ADVANCE WITH A TANK.

THE FLOODTIDE OF VICTORY IN THE WEST.
By Edward Wright.
VII.—The Breaking of the German Wings.

Pétain with Three Armies Attacks German Centre—Hutier's Fierce Counter-thrusts by Oise—Twentieth Siege of Guise Castle—First French Army's Struggle in Hunding Line—Eberhardt and Mudra Combine to Check French Progress—Guillaumat's Men Win Footing above Château Porcien—Quast Breaks the Scheldt Sluices and Floods Condé and Valenciennes—Gordon Highlanders Recover Famars by the Bayonet—Fierce Struggle for Valenciennes—German Retreat Blocked by Deported Townsfolk—Horne and Byng Encircle City with Gun Fire—Terrible Scene of Slaughter by Rhonelle River—Hopeless Condition of Liberated French People—Plumer and Degoutte Advance on Audenarde—Gallantry of American Contingent in Flanders—Strange Scenes on Outskirts of Ghent—Grand Attack between Meuse and Aire by First U.S.A. Army—How General Liggett Motored the Shock Troops through Buzancy—Capture of Von Der Marwitz's Headquarters—General Gouraud Strikes Across Upper Argonne—Germans Encircled in the Wooded Hills—Junction of French and Americans at Châtillon—The Opening of the Road to Sedan.

I T was the design of the German High Command to withdraw on Antwerp, Brussels, and Namur, hold the line of the Meuse to the end of the Ardennes Forest, and connect with the Moselle at Thionville and Metz, while retaining the southern mountain line to Mulhouse. This plan had been formed by Ludendorff at the end of September, 1918, when he asked Prince Max of Baden to arrange an armistice, and he and his lieutenants steadily worked at the great retirement during the following month. Guns were lost by the thousand and men captured by the tens of thousand ; but the movement of retreat was generally successful, with the exception of the operations in the sectors of the persistent British attack. Sir Douglas Haig continually moved forward in irresistible strength at a pace that interfered with the German plan of retirement.

The British thrust across the tributaries of the Scheldt, described in the preceding chapter, had disconcerting consequences for the enemy armies under the nominal command of the Prussian Crown Prince. Orders were issued to General von Hutier, commanding along the Oise line, that he must stand firm at any cost against General Debeney, in order to gain time for the accelerated withdrawals of all the forces depending upon the Maubeuge and Hirson lines of railway communication. General von Hutier repeated the command to all his commanders down to the commandants of battalions, and some

GERMAN ANTI-TANK DEVICE.
Trench fitted with explosives and mines connected with electric wires—one of the "Tank destroyers" arranged by the enemy in their Hindenburg line.

of the last were captured on October 19th with copies of the order on them. Then it was that Marshal Foch sent General Pétain to the Serre-Hunding line to arrange a converging attack by the First, Tenth, and Fifth French Armies in the direction of Hirson. General Pétain's task was one of tremendous difficulty. His line of attack from the Oise to the Aisne formed a rough crescent some forty miles in length, and his ultimate objective—the five branching railway tracks at Hirson junction—was about twenty-five miles distant from each of his three armies.

There was a double Hindenburg system to overcome, consisting of separated zones, each with five trenches and five wire-fields, with an abundance of the usual concrete works, flooded streams, and anti-Tank mine-fields. Behind the Hindenburg works was the wooded, broken, wet countryside of the region known as the Thierache, which by reason of the nature of its ground was a perfect field for machine-gun and trench-mortar defence.

On their trench-mortars the Germans continued to place great reliance. They were used in more abundance than machine-guns had been at the opening of the war, the construction being changed so that, instead of firing at a high angle with howitzer effect, they were employed like cannon, for direct, short-range shooting. These trench-mortars saved many of the bridge-heads of the Scheldt and Oise from being quickly carried by the Allies, and also caused considerable damage to the light, fast storming cars.

507

After the operations of the First French Army, on October 19th, described in the preceding chapter, General von Hutier obeyed the order given to him. With every man that could be thrown into battle he made a successful counter-attack along the Hermann line, between the Oise and Serre Rivers. He recovered the high flanking position of Mont d'Origny and the dominating point of Villers-le-Sec, with the ground along the railway line to La Ferté. Along the Serre and Souche swamps the German commander retired from his bridge-head positions, allowing the Tenth French Army to advance a short distance ; but the ground by the streams was so flooded that General Mangin was brought to a standstill.

Then it was that General Pétain opened his main operations. On October 25th, as the British offensive between Valenciennes and Landrecies came victoriously to a pause, for the forward movement of guns and supplies, General Debeney, General Mangin, and General Guillaumat made a **Pétain's main** combined attack, on a front of some forty **operations begun** miles, between the Oise above Ribecourt and the Aisne below Château Porcien. General Debeney first struck at Guise to draw General von Hutier's last reserves northward, and then assailed Villers-le-Sec and all its connected works covering a depth of nearly two miles. A multitude of Renault cars was employed, together with a tremendous travelling barrage and long-distance fire upon all the enemy's railway centres between Guise and Montcornet. The German line was broken to a depth of some three miles ; but General von Hutier again succeeded in rallying his forces, and in a fine counter-attack recovered most of the Hermann line from Mont d'Origny to the Ribemont and La Ferté railway.

This, however, was the last effort of Ludendorff's brother-in-law, who in the prime of his power had broken into the Fifth British Army round St. Quentin and pursued it to Amiens. Hutier had owed most of his success to capable but obscure Staff officers, like Major Bruchmüller, and to the possession of overwhelming numbers. General Debeney attacked again in the night, and continued to press the enemy throughout October 26th, striking him in the flank by the Origny position, as well as working gradually forward with Tanks and infantry and hurricane bombardments through the Hermann system. He recaptured the villages along the railway between the two rivers, and pushed through the breaches in the fortified line towards the tableland round Guise. In the evening of October 26th General von Hutier prepared to retreat, and the First French Army, feeling the enemy give, redoubled its efforts, breaking in on the flank across the flooded Oise valley and thrusting into the centre, capturing nearly four thousand prisoners and some twenty guns.

General von Hutier saved his artillery at heavy cost in men, and General Debeney pressed onward to the high land about Guise, on an advancing front of some twenty miles, from the outskirts of the famous old town on the Oise to Mesbrecourt, above the Serre. In the sweep of his right wing General Debeney struck the forces of General von Eberhardt, on the Serre, compelling this enemy commander to uncover the town of Crécy, into which General Mangin's **Struggle for** men poured on October 27th. On the **historic Guise** same day General Debeney's left wing, in an advance of some five miles, closed in on Guise town, fighting through the hospital barracks and sidings and branch lines of the railway.

The old Castle of Guise proved, however, a serious obstacle, and for the twentieth time in its romantic history had to stand a siege. It was the kind of building that Richelieu or Cromwell could have taken with a few old-fashioned cannon, firing almost point-blank into the walls. The picturesque old building could not be so easily reached and stormed under modern conditions of defence. It stood on a cliff, above the looping waters of the Oise running through a deep, narrow gap in the Guise plateau. The large underground passages of the ruined fortress made it a magnificent machine-gun position, especially when the Germans dug a new entrenchment round the place and registered their guns upon all the approaches.

With its cliffs towering five hundred and thirty feet above the Oise, and extending in a series of ridges in the bend of the river, Guise was a place of great military importance. It was the gate to Hirson and the Meuse during the last campaign of the war, as it had been the gate to St. Quentin and Laon during the first campaign. It had been the decisive rallying-point of the Fifth French Army in August, 1914, and ranked with Le Cateau in British and French military history. There the Tenth Prussian Army Corps and the Prussian Guard, while making a great turning movement towards St. Quentin in pursuit of Sir Douglas Haig's two weary divisions, had been checked by the wing of the Fifth French Army rallying on the Guise plateau.

The First Battle of Guise had saved both General Lanrezac's forces and Sir John French's troops. The town had, therefore, become to the French soldier what Le Cateau was to the British soldier, and Debeney's men fought their way into the trenches round the old castle with the same vehemence that the British displayed against the railway embankment by the Selle River. Guise, however, could not be carried by even the most spirited of advanced forces, and after winning the entrenchment round the castle the French troops had to wait for their heavy artillery to cross the large stretch of recovered country between the two rivers and accumulate shell for another grand barrage of assault.

While the First French Army was making its great advance, General Mangin's men increased the number of their bridge-heads across the Serre, where the enemy was shaken by the northward thrust, and also won a road of approach at the end of the Sissonne marshlands. The effect of these two movements of the Tenth Army was to threaten with envelopment the railway junction of Marle, where the lines from Maubeuge and Metz met. General Mangin, however, did not employ much force in his central operations along the river swamps, and only engaged and worried the enemy during the stronger movements on either side of Eberhardt's forces.

It was upon the men of the Fifth French Army, under General Guillaumat, that the hardest task fell. They had to assail the original Hunding line between Sissonne and Château Porcien, on a front of some fifteen miles of hilly country furnished **Assault on the** with every means of defence, old and new, **Hunding line** that the Teutons could assemble. More important than all the mechanical obstacles were the hostile effectives available. There were thirty-nine German divisions arrayed between the Oise and the Aisne.

General von Hutier, holding the line south-east of Le Cateau to the Serre River, had eighteen divisions in action and five more in immediate reserve. He was occupied by the wing of the Fourth British Army, under General Rawlinson, by all the forces under General Debeney, and by some of the divisions of the Tenth French Army working across the Serre on to his flank. General von Eberhardt, commanding the Seventh German Army, had only ten divisions in action between the Serre and the road to Montcornet junction, as a considerable part of his front was covered by the marshlands. On his left was the First German Army, under General von Mudra, stretching along the Aisne to Rethel, and co-operating with six or more divisions in the defence of the Hunding line.

When the Fifth French Army attacked on October 25th, Eberhardt and Mudra combined in massing against the French forces. After a tremendous artillery preparation directed against the new anti-Tank pillars of armoured concrete, as well as upon the caves and forts of the Hindenburg system, General Guillaumat sent out his storming cars and low-flying aeroplanes, and launched his veteran infantry in a desperate struggle against the wings of the fortified zone between the Sissonne marshes and the Aisne River. Then, in main force, the French commander struck the enemy's centre where Eberhardt and Mudra's divisions connected.

The first zone of manifold works was overrun, but on the thickly-wooded hills covering the second Hindenburg line the Germans rallied and, receiving strong reinforcements, made a great counter-attack and recovered a considerable stretch of the southern part of the Hunding line. In the centre, by the road to Montcornet, the French troops held strongly against the enemy's whirlwind barrages and

King Albert, with the Prince of Wales and Prince Albert, reviewing British troops in Brussels.

Ovation to the King and Queen of the Belgians in the great square of Bruges, Oct. 25th, 1918.

Military pageant celebrating the State re=entry of King Albert into Brussels, November 22nd,

...ntry of the contingent representing the French Army marching past the King and Queen.

Belgium's triumphant Army re=enters Liège, where it had stayed the first onrush of invading Huns.

Flowers for Queen Elizabeth re=entering Ghent with victorious King Albert, Nov. 13th, 1918.

continuous counter-attacks, and in a contest of extreme violence reached the village of St. Quentin-le-Petit and the hamlet of Recouvrance.

Again the enemy commanders poured in fresh divisions, and the battle continued all night and through October 26th. The advanced French forces formed a blunt wedge on a front of four and a half miles and a depth of about two miles, between the Montcornet road and the stream-moated table-land at St. Fergeux, below Château Porcien. The new salient was a difficult one to hold, as the enemy could sweep it completely with fire from three sides, even his trench-mortar barrages being able almost to cover the lost portion of the Hunding defences. Yet the lot of the German counter-attacking troops was not easy, as the massed French guns commanded all the ground, and throughout October 26th crashed with murderous effect upon every hostile force. Every time the Teutons reeled back the French went forward, and by October 27th they had extended their gains along the road between Château Porcien and Banogne, and con-solidated their conquest of the larger part of the first Hunding system, taking two thousand five hundred prisoners. Fierce local bursts of trench warfare went on in the maze of the Hunding system until October 29th, when the tireless troops of the Fifth Army, having brought their guns forward, made another thrust across the ten miles of front between the Montcornet road and the Aisne.

Again the enemy countered in great strength, General von Below appearing alongside General von Eberhardt and General von Mudra in the swaying battle. The French were again checked along the Montcornet road, but they broke the enemy on the hills by the Aisne and won a footing on the western slopes of the St. Fergeux upland, on the flank of the enemy's riverside fortress of Château Porcien. Here the struggle went on day and night until the end of the month. With admirable gallantry a French division stormed the heights above Château Porcien, fell back under the full weight of General von Mudra's forces, and **Swaying fight for Château Porcien** once more surged over the plateau, only to be compelled to retire to the shelter of the western slopes by November 1st. These attacks, which were supported by a thrust across the Aisne made by the Fourth French Army, were the most thankless operations in which an army could engage. No decisive result was expected by General Pétain and Marshal Foch when they ordered General Guillaumat to maintain with the utmost vigour the struggle in the Hunding line.

The Fourth French Army, under General Gouraud, and the First American Army, under General Hunter Liggett, were then completing their preparations for a combined offensive round the northern prolongation of the Argonne Forest. It was necessary to keep the enemy at an extreme tension in his salient position on the Upper Aisne River in order to weaken his reserve power between the Aisne and the Meuse. So the Fifth French Army, having failed to break through the Hunding line in the first period of its offensive, had to continue fighting amid its wrecked Tanks, in hollows and river-courses flooded with poison gas, against an enemy sheltering on the hillsides and screened by innumerable patches of woodland.

On the whole the converging operations of the First, Tenth, and Fifth French Armies during the last week in October, 1918, were not so successful as had been anticipated. Although the new Hermann line, begun in the middle of August, was pierced, the main old Hindenburg defences from Guise to Rethel were not broken through. The enemy held strongly to his second zone of works, and in places retained con-siderable fragments of his first zone.

From the French standpoint the result confirmed the view of the skill and strength with which the German with-drawal was being effected that had led Marshal Foch to place his chief hope upon the Army of Lorraine, under General de Castelnau. The German Staff required the Hunding fence and the Guise gateway as a central pivot for wheeling slowly back from the British armies towards Namur. Although they were able to hold to their hinge on the Serre by Marle, this did not save them from the danger of being driven in confusion from the Ardennes Forest before they could withdraw in strong order to the Meuse line.

Sir Douglas Haig immediately followed up the advantages won by his Fourth and Third Armies in the struggle over the Selle and Ecaillon Rivers by an enveloping movement round Valenciennes. From October 25th to October 31st there was a continuous battle for Valenciennes and the approaches to Mons behind it. The Canadian Corps and the Twenty-second Corps of the First Army and the Seventeenth Corps of the Third Army were employed in the struggle for the city, the Fourth Canadian Division, the 51st Highland Division, the 61st Division, the 49th Division, and 4th British Division being principally engaged in the action. The Germans protected themselves by destroying the sluices of the Scheldt Canal between Valenciennes and Tournai.

Along this stretch of some twenty-two miles there was some fifteen miles of lake water. By Condé the valley was a lagoon, from three to four miles wide, and although the water in places came scarcely up to the knees of the wading infantry, it made the ground impossible for general movements. **The Battle of Valenciennes** Enemy snipers and machine-gunners occupied the buildings in the flood, and transformed them into little island forts and observation-posts. Only three German divisions were required along the lake-land by the Franco-Belgian frontier, and the German commander was able to concentrate six divisions on a four-mile strip of ground in the Rhonelle valley, south of Valenciennes.

This strip of dry ground was the only gate of attack against the city, and along it the Battle of Valenciennes was fought. In an exploring skirmish on October 25th the Highland Territorials took Maing, some four and a half miles below Valenciennes, while a dashing cyclist patrol entered the village of Artres by the Rhonelle stream. The cyclists were driven back by strong forces, and the Highlanders, while engaged in close fighting with an enemy garrison in the manor-house of Maing, were attacked on October 26th by wave after wave of fresh enemies. The last wave of assault was met by the Argyll and Sutherland Highlanders, who counter-charged with the bayonet, killed all the Germans who had any fight in them, and chased the rest for two miles down the Valenciennes road to Famars village. About the same time the Artres bridge-head of the Rhonelle stream was stormed, and the passage of the river forced, producing panic among the German troops, who fled along the road to Maresches in complete confusion, dropping as they ran machine-guns, rifles, and equipment.

On the line of the next ridge between the Rhonelle and the old fortress town of Le Quesnoy a strong German reserve force, comprising some two divisions additional to the six divisions holding the gate to Valenciennes, stood steady, and, after their artillery swept the river, the fresh troops charged down from the ridge, and tried to turn the Artres bridge-head by breaking through on the left across the Le Quesnoy and Valenciennes railway. The counter-thrust was delivered in large masses of men; but the British troops were unshakable, and with machine-gun and rifle fire covered the slopes by the river with grey figures until the dis-pirited Teutons drew back over the crest. **Famars won with the bayonet**

Meanwhile, the Argyll and Sutherlands and Gordons worked through Famars, after their remarkable running match with the bayonet; and, when they had established themselves in the village and reached Mont Houy, a fortressed, wooded rise close to the city, another enemy force made a nocturnal counter-attack on October 27th, and won back the northern part of Famars. From the southern streets the Gordon High-landers advanced with the bayonet and, rushing machine-guns and riflemen, recaptured the houses. Mont Houy, however, remained in part in the enemy's hands, as his machine-gunners on the wooded slope were resolute and alert and less frightened by a distant bayonet than the infantry of the line had been. The advantage won and retained on the high-road at Famars was extended in the morning of October 28th by an attack on the right against the village of Aulnoye. At this point Valenciennes was definitely outflanked, and as the Canadians were behind the city northward, having fought their way along the railway embankment to the outskirts of Condé at Fresnes, Valenciennes was encircled for three-quarters of its circuit.

Again the German commander reacted with all the strength of his wasted eight divisions. He recovered Aulnoye and the fortressed height of Mont Houy, and pressed hard but vainly along the strip of ground between the Scheldt and the Rhonelle. Upon the failure of this counter-attack the enemy began quickly to withdraw from the city. He endeavoured to cover his movements by a continual rattle of machine-guns along his endangered southern flank.

This line of outposts could have been driven in by local operations in the course of a few days ; but Sir Douglas Haig intervened, and asked General Horne and General Byng to carry Valenciennes at once by storm. The British commander was aware of the fact that the German Command designed to profit by its strong stand on the Serre River

Enemy in Haig's power

by making a large, quiet, undisturbed withdrawal from the British armies. The Germans, being pursued, wanted breathing-space ; but they were too weak and too unsteady to be able to break off action when it pleased them. Sir Douglas Haig had won complete power over them, and at any point and time he selected he could compel the Germans to turn and mass together, like a grand rearguard, to prevent the British forces breaking through and spreading out along their communications in the rear.

The immediate German plan was to retreat into the Mormal Forest, on the outskirts of which the magnificent divisions of the Fourth British Army had already arrived, by Fontaine and Robersart, while the wing of the Third Army was driving against the north-western flank of the great woodland along the road to Bavai. The enemy's scheme, however, was completely upset by a combined movement by King Albert and Sir Douglas Haig and by certain difficulties which the enemy caused himself by his cruelty to the townspeople. On October 31st the Flanders group of armies broke over the Scheldt into Audenarde, while the Canadian and British Corps of the First

GERMANS' WANTON INCENDIARISM.
British officer watches one of the fires which were started by the Germans in Valenciennes when they found the allied pressure so great that their retirement was rendered inevitable.

and Third Armies began to complete their encircling operations round Valenciennes.

The Germans were then engaged in emptying the city of its remaining population of some twenty thousand persons. The last batch of lads and men between the ages of sixteen and fifty years came to the town-hall for deportation to some place of slavery across the Rhine. They found that the German commandant had become a man of extraordinarily humane feeling. He patted some of them on the head and told them they could go home. " The enemy," said one German officer, " is already in Famars Avenue, and we shall only make a little show of resistance and depart in the night. By to-morrow morning you will all be English."

The Germans, however, found they could not retreat in the night of October 31st. Between them and Mons, blocking the road to their congested columns of troops and transport, were the fifteen thousand people who had been deported during the Battle of the Selle River, when the German High Command had still hoped to make a long stand round Valenciennes, fight there until the city was destroyed, and carry the population into captivity. The sufferings of the great homeless multitude on the way to Mons were terrible, and many of them died ;   **German crime proved a blunder** but they avenged themselves upon the cruel invaders by passively blocking his only route of retreat and endangering most of his war material. The German commander tried to undo his crime on discovering it was also a blunder. He proclaimed that he had only removed the townspeople to save them from British gun fire, and that, as he had received assurance that Sir Douglas Haig would not bombard the city, all the people could return.

This hypocritical permission was given too late. The British barrage was already settling on the only road leading back to Valenciennes, and although some of the hapless folk made the terrible return journey to their homes, most of them did not dare to undertake it. The German garrison also spent too much time in looting the emptied city, carrying off the

SMOKE AND FLAME FROM HATE-LIT FIRES.
Dense column of smoke and flame arising from some of Valenciennes' burning buildings. These had been fired in accordance with the German spirit which dictated destruction of that which they failed to hold.

stocks of valuable lace, breaking into shops of every kind, and pillaging private houses. It is clear that the intention was to deal with Valenciennes as Cambrai and Douai had been dealt with, and to fire the empty city after stripping it.

The German High Command was again confident in the middle of October of being able to carry out its withdrawal to the Antwerp-Namur-Meuse line and revive Ludendorff's plan of devastation, in spite of the policy of national reprisal proclaimed by M. Clemenceau.

Once more the speed and strength of the British attack had prevented the enemy from carrying out his work of complete destruction. He was caught with **Great rearguard** his only eastward traffic route blocked by **action joined** fifteen thousand homeless French women, children, and old men, and with some six or eight divisions of infantry, with their guns and stores, unable to retire without abandoning their means of making another stand by Mons. Such were the circumstances, known to Sir Douglas Haig and his lieutenants from aerial observation and other sources of knowledge, in which the Germans were forced into one of the most critical of general engagements.

Both Sir Henry Horne and Sir Julian Byng had massed a tremendous force of artillery round the city. The guns employed were almost as numerous as those used by the same leaders in ringing Cambrai with blasting fire. When, at dawn on November 1st, the grand barrage of two British armies fell on the enemy's outpost line by the Scheldt, and across the Famars Avenue, and along the ridge of the Rhonelle valley, the

German commander had to answer force by force. He threw every available man into a great rearguard action in order to save his own army from being broken and enveloped and to prevent an outflanking movement against the other German forces fighting northward by Renaix and Audenarde.

The 4th Division of Canadians carried Mont Houy under a smoke screen and travelling curtain of shell fire, and stormed towards the southern part of the city. Enemy gunners tried to stop them by a defensive barrage, but the British artillery fire was of unparalleled intensity, and it beat down the hostile pieces, leaving the infantry of attack only to face machine-gun fire from ruined buildings and embanked ditches by the railway **Terrific British** line. Some of the Germans fought hard, but **artillery fire** more than two thousand of them surrendered. On the western side of the city a single brigade of Canadians forced the passage of the canalised Scheldt and established posts among the houses.

The German commander did not attempt to react against the Canadians. Their barrage was too overwhelming and their positions at the extreme corner of the battlefield were in the nature of a trap.

Had he massed there he would have been outflanked some miles eastward. Instead of a direct counter-attack, he struck on the British flank by the Rhonelle River, from which, if successful, he could have turned the Dominion forces. From the heights just covering the road and railway to Bavai and Maubeuge, remnants of General Otto von Below's armies of the Mars and Michael groups, with reinforcements from General von

HUMILIATION OF THE GERMAN FLAG REMOVED FROM VALENCIENNES.
Valenciennes viewed from above. The centre building is the Hôtel de Ville, which the enemy shelled when the Canadians hauled down the German flag and hoisted the French Tricolour. Two shells can be seen bursting to the left of the Hôtel de Ville. Above : The German flag taken from the Hôtel de Ville by Canadian artillery officers and a helmet belonging to the German town commandment, interesting trophies of a crowning victory.

Quast, poured in grey masses down to the riverside. There was little change in the Prussian tactics of infantry attack between Mons and Valenciennes in 1914 and between Valenciennes and Mons in 1918. In his death agony the enemy returned to his old method of the swarm assault, but he no longer had four or five guns to one.

The artillery odds were against him at last, and the 61st, 49th, and 4th British Divisions, with part of the 4th Canadian Division at Aulnoye village, were at least equal in effectives to the six worn German divisions that charged them. There was a terrible scene of slaughter on a front of barely six miles.

Five German Tanks were employed; three were broken and captured and two turned tail. Only at the village of Maresches did the charging swarms survive the barrage of shell and bullets in sufficient force to break into the river-line, and before night fell the English troops recovered all the ground and began to press over the Rhonelle, driving the shattered Germans from the ridge, taking Préseau village in an advance of two miles, and making some five thousand prisoners. This was the decisive movement **Capture of** in the Battle of Valenciennes, and although **Valenciennes** the city was formally taken by Canadian patrols on Saturday morning, November 2nd, 1918, it was in large measure the English divisions that broke the enemy's heavy counter-attacks and crushed his last attempt to hold the place.

Snipers and machine-gunners behind barricades and in the upper windows of houses endeavoured to delay the occupation of the city, but the Canadians were practised in cleaning-up work. Soon after they started their deadly work of exploration the last German battalion withdrew from Valenciennes and German guns poured a farewell bombardment of poison-gas, high-explosive, and incendiary shell into the partly-peopled frontier city of France, with its ruined foundries, glass works, and despoiled lace shops.

The remaining five thousand townspeople had crept into cellars when the great noise of battle broke over the town. In the northern quarter the waters of the Scheldt, loosened by the breaking of the sluices, flowed into the underground retreats, where families were crowded together in darkness, and compelled them to stay upstairs in constant danger of shell fire.

In the higher part of the town the people escaped the flood, but those near the canal-bed suffered extreme misery, flood and siege coming as crowning horrors to four years of terrible hardship. As in other occupied towns, the vital strength of the race was sapped by disease brought on by under-nourishment and ill-treatment. The babies were the healthiest, noticeably better, indeed, than they had been in peace time, because, owing to the lack of cow's milk and artificial foods, they had been kept entirely at their mother's breast, and thereby escaped the intestinal complaints that

AFTER TWO CENTURIES.
Advancing British soldiers, in November, 1918, on the field of one of Marlborough's victories. They were inspecting the monument erected to commemorate the Battle of Malplaquet, fought in 1709.

kill the infants of over-civilised women. On the other hand, children and youths were dreadfully undersized and stricken with maladies, considerably more than half of them being diseased.

The general fact may here be placed on record that under Dutch and Spanish authorities the International Relief Commission did not succeed in defeating the ghastly Teutonic plot for slowly depopulating, with the infinite torture of slow hunger, the territories of France lost in 1914. Had the German people won the war as they hoped, they would have found room for settling in the naturally rich region of coal-fields between Maubeuge and Lens, where the tuberculous, dying French race would quickly have perished, whether it migrated or not.

The German private soldier, representing the common German people who afterwards voted largely for Socialist members of the Weimar National Assembly, was generally as merciless a plunderer of the food and goods of the starving, broken French people as were the German officers and administrators of the landowning, manufacturing, and merchant classes.

All the German tribes were bent on killing that part of the French people that was in their power, and the material ruins that marked the returning trail of the defeated invaders were not such ghastly evidence of the qualities of the German character as were the hundreds of thousands of human wrecks they reluctantly left behind them.

RETURNING FROM THE CHASE.
British cavalry going back after taking part in the incessant pressure maintained upon the retreating enemy on the western front. It was the relentless pressure of the allied forces which, if it did not break the German line in spectacular fashion, effectively destroyed the German Army's moral.

There was no hope for the larger part of the liberated French people. They could neither recover their health nor produce children likely to live to strong manhood and womanhood. The Huns under Attila did not so enfeeble the races they conquered as did the Germans under William of Hohenzollern. The ancient conqueror wanted healthy serfs, and after carrying off the vanquished people he allowed subject races to win food for themselves so that they might be strong in body to serve him. At Valenciennes the women, girls, and old men were set to work in allotment gardens, and when the crops matured the Germans took everything, and the food received through neutral countries did not keep the people from gradually dying of hunger.

Audenarde was liberated a day earlier than Valenciennes, in spite of the fact that the resumed offensive in Flanders began later than the **Turning movement** encircling movement **above Tournai** round the French frontier city. On October 31st the Second British Army and the French army of General Degoutte, reinforced by a gallant American contingent, opened a turning movement above Tournai, on a front of some fourteen miles between the Lys River by Deynst and the Scheldt by Avelghem. The movement had a double design. On the north it threatened to turn the enemy's defences in front of Ghent, where the German Marine Corps was still holding to the Schipdonck (or Derivation) Canal at Eecloo, some ten miles in front of the Terneuzen Canal, that .ran through Ghent and connected there with the Scheldt waterway.

On the south it threatened to turn the water defences of Tournai at the time when the Tournai garrison was also menaced by an outflanking advance by the First and Third British Armies striking upward from Valenciennes. Sir Douglas Haig and King Albert assisted each other by their operations at the end of October, and imposed so violent a strain upon all the German line between the Dutch frontier and the northern outskirts of the Forest of Mormal that the enemy High Command could not provide a single fresh division for the closing battle of the war in Mormal Forest, final preparations for which the British Commander-in-Chief was making while his Second, First, and Third Armies were fighting forward.

Marshal Foch also took a leading part in the general direction of the last battle in Flanders. He it was who sent from general reserve the fine United States force to act as a spearhead in the northern thrust across the Scheldt to Audenarde. At the same time the Generalissimo of the Associated Powers arranged and timed an overpowering sweeping advance by the First American Army and the Fourth French Army between the Meuse and the Upper Aisne Rivers, that broke the resistance of the armies of General von der Marwitz and General von Einem. Thus the Flanders group of armies once more acted as the northern claw in a great pincer movement by Marshal Foch, and between the claws of the pincers Sir Douglas Haig's men held the sword for the last mortal stroke into the vitals of the enemy.

Owing mainly to the uninterrupted succession of victorious advances made by the Fourth and Third Armies of the British Commonwealth, Marshal Foch was at last in a position to punish the enemy for his long and obstinate stand along the Serre-Hunding line. Too long had the armies of General von Hutier, General von Eberhardt, and General Mudra delayed their withdrawal from the corner of the large salient between Rethel and Guise. Their forces were to be driven suddenly towards the Ardennes Forest, there confusing and overcrowding the other German armies that Sir Douglas Haig was grimly shepherding in the same direction.

The new Flanders operation likewise was calculated to loosen the enemy's hold upon the ground north of the road to Mons, so that all the British armies would be able to close around the Maubeuge-Cologne trunk railway and there prevent the central German forces from escaping

A MINED ROAD JUNCTION.
Civilians from Mons filling in a crater made by the enemy. They were watching Canadian transport passing.

WOUNDED AND CAPTIVE, BUT SAFE.
German Red Cross men wheeling wounded comrades to an aid-post in Valenciennes halt for a moment's rest in the fatiguing journey over the rough-paved roadway.

from supreme and complete disaster.

On October 31st Sir Herbert Plumer's troops took only a secondary part in the attack, having already won a line well in advance of the other forces of the Flanders group. Their immediate work consisted in clearing a triangle of rising ground along the western side of the Scheldt, from Avelghem to Meersche, from which the main Franco-American advance would have been enfiladed. On a line of some six miles the British troops.fought over the riverside sector of the railway from Courtrai to Audenarde. Scottish and Welsh troops carried Anseghem, while the French struggled, in the manor-house of the village, against an enemy garrison who held out long after the Welsh Fusiliers, Scottish Borderers, and Scottish Rifles had taken the street and wood. It was not until the second day of battle, November 1st, that the French carried the manor-house. In the mean- **Germans driven** time Lancashire Fusiliers, Durhams, and **over the Scheldt** other battalions stormed over the hills and water-courses southward, taking a thousand prisoners in the course of the day, and driving the Germans over the Scheldt to the hills covering Renaix.

While the French were fighting in the manor-house alongside the Welsh and Scots, the Americans in the centre stormed into Waereghem and made a remarkable advance through wired woods and flaming farms where the Germans fought among the Flemish peasantry so that the guns of the attack could not intervene. British, French, and American infantry

HELP FOR MONS CIVILIANS.
Canadian transport arrives in Valenciennes with civilians rescued from the area of battle in the Mons district. The girls standing in the doorway had returned to find the interior of their house shattered.

Air Force squadrons working with General Plumer's forces. One British formation destroyed twenty-two German machines and an observation balloon in a single day, and defeated every attempt made by the enemy to reconnoitre the allied lines.

During the great and rapid advance of the armies of Sir Douglas Haig and King Albert the Allies had been seriously inconvenienced by the lack of new aerodromes. The shed-builders could not keep pace with the movement of foot and guns. German airmen quickly seized their advantage and specialised in low-flying attacks upon infantry and road traffic. In the last week of October, however, the new forward British aerodromes were ready, and swarms of British pilots, aerial machine-gunners, and bomb-droppers descended

had to work forward without artillery and carry farmsteads and hamlets with rifle and bayonet in order to save the civilians. Then, as the Germans fell back, their high-velocity guns across the Scheldt poured gas-shell upon the country people. To meet this outrage the allied soldiers took gas-masks from German prisoners and gave them to the Flemings.

Being, however, unskilled in the use of the masks, many of the country people were overcome with the mustard gas and required most of the ambulances of the attacking armies. The German gunners fought from the upper stories of cottages, while women and children sheltered in the cellars. In some of the captured villages the inhabitants were so wild with joy over their liberation and the German defeat that they stopped for a time the pursuit of the enemy and even tried to follow the victors over the bullet-swept fields.

In the night of October 31st the Germans fired many farms, which served to illuminate the closing struggle of the American and French forces who drove the enemy across the Scheldt. The Americans entered the western part of Audenarde on November 2nd, after an advance of ten miles in two days, and found an intact bridge over the Scheldt. The French made a similar sweeping advance, and, on **Strange scenes outside Ghent** reaching the river, wheeled on their left between the Lys and the Scheldt, stormed into St. Denis Westrem, the south-western suburb of Ghent, by the Lys, and approached within three miles of the city directly southward by Seevergem, on the Scheldt.

As a result of this outflanking movement the northern wing of the German Army withdrew hastily from the Schipdonck Canal, pursued for some ten miles by Belgian machine-gunners in light Tanks. Then was seen one of the strangest scenes of the war on the outskirts of Ghent. The Queen of the Belgians travelled close to the front line, and in the western suburbs the Flemish townspeople came out to greet the Belgian and French troops, mingling with them on the road and rowing up and down the canal in pleasure-boats, while German machine-gun bullets from upper stories of outlying houses sang over their heads.

Ghent, however, did not fall as quickly as its citizens expected. The German Marine Corps, with the Fourth and Sixth German Armies, still held in a general way to the Scheldt Canal and the Terneuzen waterway, from the Dutch frontier by Selzaete to the floods by Condé above the road to Mons. A remarkable feature of these operations by the Flanders group of armies was the power and skill of the Royal

FOOD FOR RESCUED TOWNSPEOPLE.
Before the Mairie in Valenciennes. Canadian lorry arriving with food supplies for the suffering civilians immediately after the town had been retaken. The two deputy mayors, bareheaded, are receiving the gift.

upon the German front. After clearing the sky of hostile fighting aeroplanes, they acted as the advance guard of the pursuit in such large numbers and with such deadly skill as completed the demoralisation of the German infantry of the line.

On the same day as the enemy was breaking round Valenciennes and Audenarde, the First American Army passed in a bound from its period of apprenticeship to a position of highly-effective mastery. There had been considerable disappointment among both the American troops and the American people over the apparently small results of the great offensive that General Pershing opened between the Meuse and the Argonne on September 26th, 1918. In the United States the lack of success was in some quarters attributed to President Woodrow Wilson in person.

There had been some extraordinary dilatoriness in American munition-making, and the American forces were provided with French artillery because their own guns were not ready. They had no poison-gas shells of their own with which to reply to the enemy's severe gas bombardments, the stocks of this kind of munition accumulating in America for transport just as the war closed. In other ways the American forces in the field had suffered from lack of preparation.

The consequence was that the troops entered upon their main task in the war with a considerable want of experience. There were a few divisions, such as the 2nd, which had fought in great battles during the trying period of the British and French retreats, and had thereby won at serious yet inevitable cost the skilled precision and varied, practical knowledge that distinguished the veteran force.

The admirable local assault against the St. Mihiel salient was not sufficient to transform the learning of the American divisions engaged into living knowledge. The position was one which the Germans had been prepared to evacuate under a heavy attack, and although they were trapped in consider-

HOME FROM HOME IN VALENCIENNES.
Canadian Sisters talking to Canadian soldiers in Valenciennes outside a Y.M.C.A. centre that was established and put in running order a week after the liberators' entry into the town.

A "PARFAIT GENTIL KNIGHT."
Canadian soldiers helping a French mother and her children through a destroyed railway bridge outside Valenciennes. The Germans began systematic destruction in and round the town three weeks before they retreated.

able numbers, the stroke was not quite the success which the French Staff expected. In the grand offensive between the Argonne and the Meuse the Americans had still to fight not only the enemy but also their own inexperience. Their Staff failed to appreciate the difficulties of transport and signalling in a region of clay, flooded by the rain of the wettest September ever known. The French and British had purchased their knowledge of autumnal mud, as had also the Belgians, after living in swamps for four years. They knew what massed modern shell fire could accomplish in blasting earth into powder and tumbling ground into a chaos of disintegrated soil that even a little rain could turn into an impassable marsh.

The American Staff hustled rather too much and prepared too little when swinging the First Army swiftly across the Meuse from the Hindenburg line by Metz towards the Kriemhilde line below Buzancy. As in the St. Mihiel operations, the enemy somehow learnt what to expect, and he adopted General Gouraud's ruse of drawing his main forces back for several miles and leaving only strong machine-gun rearguards in partly evacuated territory. When his rearguards were broken or captured, the German

commander covered the abandoned ground with an enormous barrage of shrapnel, high-explosive, and gas shell, against which the American divisions most gallantly struggled for a month. By high personal bravery they gradually fought their way, in innumerable soldiers' battles, into and through the Kriemhilde line, but the Germans gained time to construct another line of trenches on the wooded ridges between the Grandpré Hills and the Meuse by Brieulles.

Already, in the second day of battle, September 28th, a finely-handled Chicago brigade won ground from which long-range guns could have shelled the main German line of railway transport by Longuyon and Montmédy, but the American Army had no American guns of the required range, and it was not until the last days in October that the German line of communications between Thionville and Sedan was brought under constant heavy gun fire directly by aeroplane observation. By this time, however, General Pershing had both an abundance of men and improved traffic ways between the Aire stream and the Meuse. On the east of the Meuse he was able to take over the Metz sector with **Growing American man-power** his Second Army, under General Bullard, while strongly reinforcing west of the river his First Army, under General Hunter Liggett.

Owing in large part to the speed with which American troops had been trained and transported across the Atlantic Ocean, since Mr. Lloyd George's appeal to President Woodrow Wilson, the Associated Powers had changed the proportion in rifle strength between themselves and the enemy from an equality in June, 1918, to an advantage of two to one at the beginning of November, 1918. The enormous multitudes of prisoners taken by the British armies, and the great number of enemies they killed or maimed, together with the heavy losses inflicted on the enemy by the French armies between the spring and autumn of the year, were the main factors in the process of German demoralisation. Yet the tremendous flow of American man-power into France had a large influence upon the issue of the struggle.

The American forces not only grew at last more numerous than the British forces, but also exceeded in number the French forces when the native African regiments were excluded. As the Africans wasted with rapidity when retained in action in cold, wet weather, French commanders usually withdrew them at the close of autumn. The winter withdrawal of French African troops had been an important factor in the enemy's calculations for escaping complete disaster.

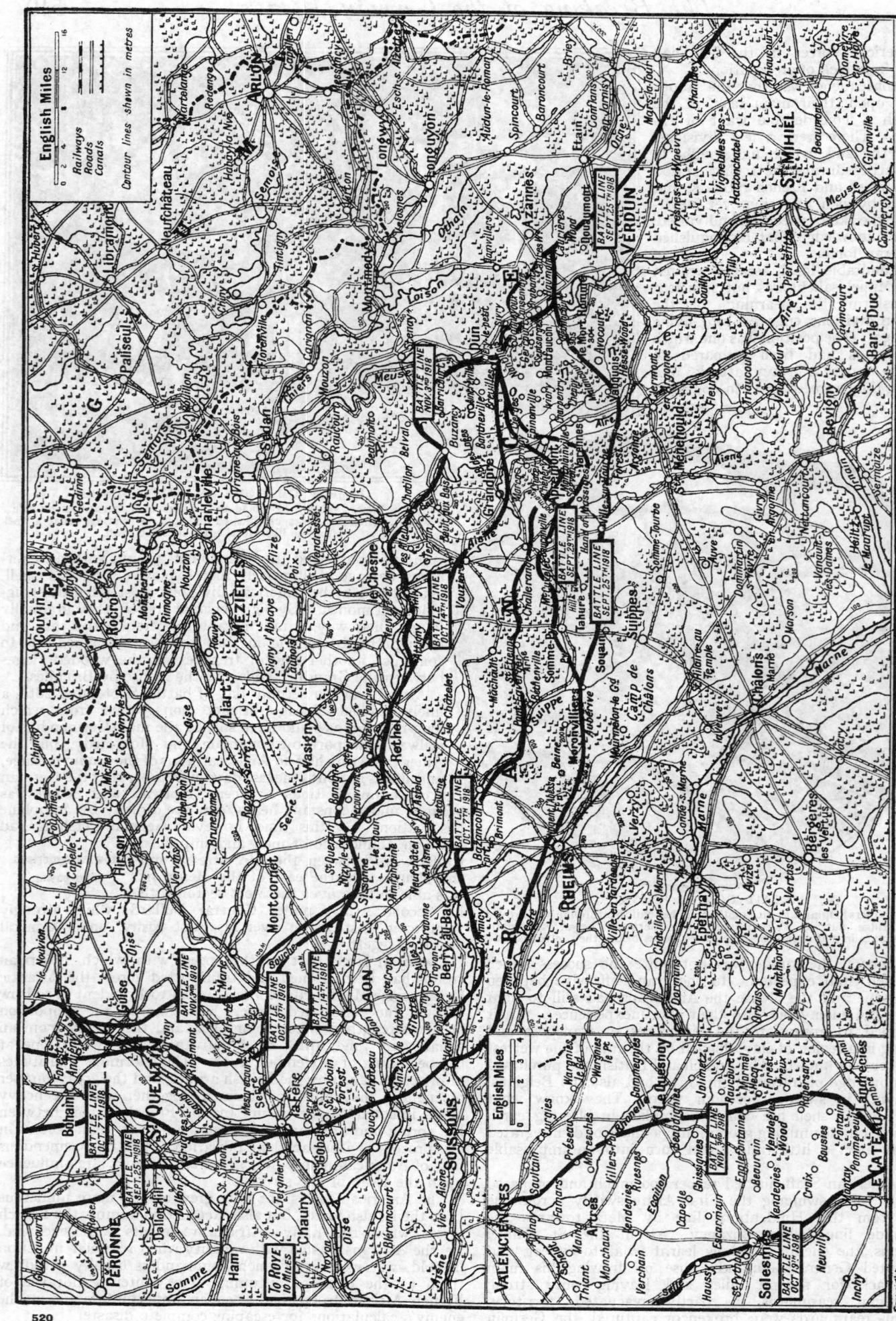

RETREAT OF THE GERMAN LEFT WING UP TO NOVEMBER 3RD, 1918. INSET: THE BATTLEFIELD OF VALENCIENNES.

The Great War

Copyright

GENERAL SIR HERBERT CHARLES ONSLOW PLUMER, G.C.B., G.C.M.G., G.C.V.O., A.D.C.
Commanding the British Second Army

The achievement of the British Controller of Shipping, Sir Joseph Maclay, in providing transport for American troops, while feeding and supplying the British people, in spite of the effect of the enemy submarine campaign, brought the United States armies into a position of predominant strength in France. Being aware of their own great numbers, the Americans had hoped in September to deal the stroke by which the war should be ended, and profound was their disappointment when they found themselves held by an inferior number of foes using a skilful combination of machine-gun fire and high-velocity gun fire to check the intended advance to the hostile main line of communications.

General Pershing, however, was not at the end of his resources. He reinforced his First Army with a large number of divisions, amounting to another grand army, brought up long-range guns, bridged the marshes in the clay bottoms between the Aire and the Meuse, and notably reorganised and extended the means of maintaining quick and thorough communication between all forces in action.

In the last week of October there were fierce local actions in the woods by Bantheville, where the American centre had been slowly pushed forward until the enemy's new Freya line became visible. In the Verdun sector there was a strong American advance on October 23rd along the wooded heights by the Damvillers road, against which the enemy violently reacted, counter-attacking day and night until October 28th, winning back some of the high ground, and losing it again by a fresh local American advance. Towards the end of the month there were also fierce counter-charges against the Bantheville positions, but in the night of October 29th General von der Marwitz suddenly abandoned Aincreville, Brieulles, and Cléry-le-Petit, by the western bank of the Meuse near Dun. The next morning aerial observers saw large bodies of German troops and transport moving backward, and great explosions proclaimed that ammunition dumps were being sacrificed.

The German commander clearly knew what was impending, having purchased his knowledge of the great preparations behind General Liggett's and General Gouraud's front by continual aerial fighting that crippled his flying power. Against the Americans alone the Germans lost a hundred and twenty-four machines, while the missing American machines numbered only twenty-nine. Being blinded in the air, the enemy resorted to his old trick of withdrawing his main forces and concealing them in woods, leaving only a line of cross-firing machine-guns in the Freya system and upon the remaining high ground that covered this new line.

Freya line broken through When the French and American guns opened fire at dawn on November 1st, 1918, the disposition of forces which the enemy adopted did not avail him. On a front of some thirty miles, from Attigny on the Aisne to the Dun bridge-head on the Meuse, an enormous number of shells fell upon the Germans. General Gouraud gave his gunners only half an hour in which to smash a path for his infantry, but General Liggett, having less expert artillerymen, relied more upon length of bombardment, and maintained his terrific barrage for two hours. Then, as the heaviest guns concentrated on counter-battery work and the blockade of roads of communication, the other pieces formed the travelling barrage for the infantry.

On the left above the Grandpré defile the artillery work was not decisive. From their dug-outs in the Bois des Loges the undaunted German machine-gunners emerged and kept the American troops in check all day long, amid the wired, dense thickets and innumerable traps of the forest. This operation, however, was of small importance. In the centre and on the right wing, in spite of the flanking fire the enemy attempted to throw over the Meuse, decisive victory was achieved by the corps under Major-General Dickmann, Major-General Summerall, and Major-General Hine. Hundreds of Tanks went out with the infantry, and above the Tanks and troops were swarms of low-flying aeroplanes, from which pilots and observers watched every movement and sent by wireless a continual stream of information to all Staff centres and artillery directors. Many of the German machine-gunners, hiding in pits covered with brush-wood, were killed or crippled by the preliminary bombardment; and hundreds of the supporting groups of hostile infantry, concealed in the wooded slopes behind the Freya line, were also caught in the bombardment. When the remnants re-formed for the customary grand counter-attack a travelling barrage fell upon them, and the light storming cars and waves of masked riflemen surged over them.

On this occasion the American staff-work was magnificent. It was by generalship that the German front was completely broken. Unlike Sir Douglas Haig and General Pétain, General Pershing adopted the Teutonic device of employing picked officers and men for special shock tactics. From divisions that had distinguished themselves in action storming forces were selected and given an intense training, and finally brought close to the battle in long columns of motor-lorries.

As soon as the infantry of the line worked through the Freya system the fleet of motor-lorries carrying the shock forces swept over the battlefield and through the clouds of mustard gas and arsenic **Rail-head at Buzancy carried** fume poured out from the long-range high-velocity guns of the Germans. Owing to the finely organised work of the American sappers working gallantly behind the first waves of infantry most of the obstacles had been bridged over, enabling the shock troops to be carried within a couple of miles of the fleeing enemy batteries.

Here and there a few dauntless Germans holding isolated points made gallant attempts to check the sweeping American movement, but they were foiled by the unexpected rapidity with which the offensive was conducted and by the deadly precision of the American staff-work. There were one or two brilliant bayonet charges by the Americans, but along most of the broken line the Germans found themselves being quickly enveloped and fled in disorder, enabling all the main objectives of the day to be passed. Buzancy, the enemy's rail-head for the Kriemhilde and Freya lines, was carried by some of the shock troops, enabling the motor-lorry column to pass through the town. There was a fierce fight at Barri-court, by the large wood on the right of Buzancy, and the headquarters of General von der Marwitz, in a château at Buzancy, was captured.

At the close of the day Lieutenant-General Liggett and his corps commanders had created a wedge of some eighty square miles in the German front between the Bois des Loges and

PREPARING FOR THE PURSUIT.
Taking weapons for offence and defence aboard a British "whippet" Tank preparatory to its advance. One soldier was handing in a machine-gun while the other was holding in readiness its belt of cartridges.

BRITISH TROOPS ENTERING TOURNAI.
Though British soldiers reached the western outskirts of Tournai during the last week in October, 1918, it was not until November 11th that it was definitely announced that the Fifth Army had fully captured the town.

Dun, and at one spot by Buzancy the shock troops lost contact with the enemy by reason of the Germans' running powers. Some four thousand prisoners were taken, with sixty-three guns and large quantities of war material.

At Buzancy the Americans were practically on a level with the French position at Vouziers which General Gouraud's men had reached on October 12th. The French commander had rapidly extended his line to Attigny, some nine miles above Vouziers, and by continual local actions had won a series of footholds along the western side of the Upper Ardennes hills. To a very considerable extent it was the fierce constant pressure exercised by General Gouraud upon the rear of General von der Marwitz's army that opened the way for the American victory.

On October 20th the Czecho-Slovak contingent of the Fourth French Army had stormed across the Aisne to Terron and extended towards Les Alleux. The **Czecho-Slovaks capture Terron** Germans counter-attacked in great strength, employing some seven divisions, and although the Bohemians were forced back they returned to the attack and recovered Terron. From that point they were only five miles from the town of Le Chesne, on the Ardennes Canal.

Le Chesne was nearly twelve miles in the rear of Buzancy, and at Châtillon, between Buzancy and Le Chesne, the Upper Argonne Forest ended in another defile through which ran a railway connecting with Buzancy southward and with Le Chesne and Sedan and Mézières northward. Thus, for nearly a fortnight before the resumption of the combined Franco-American offensive, General Gouraud had broken General von der Marwitz's railway communications by medium-range bombardment of Le Chesne. When the Americans in turn were able to train long-range guns upon the Mézières-Sedan-Montmedy railway line, on the eastern side of the Meuse, the difficulties of General von der Marwitz became very serious. This, no doubt, was the reason why he began retiring before the grand attack opened.

Against the French army of Champagne, General von Mudra and General von Einem combined with General von der Marwitz in resisting the attack. But the French forces were irresistible. In a hurricane bombardment of appalling power, sweeping all the Upper Argonne Woods and the approaches to Le Chesne, on a front of twelve and a half miles, the French and Bohemian (Czecho-Slovak) divisions assailed the enemy all along the forest-line while making drives at special points. On the wooded ridges east of Vouziers the

French operations were only in the nature of violent demonstrations designed to help the American advance, and met with severe resistance from the garrisons of the hills above the flooded river, where the water defences were two miles wide. The main force of General Gouraud was directed along the two ways of approach to Le Chesne—across the Aisne and along the Ardennes Canal by Rilly and over the Les Alleux upland.

The Germans fought skilfully and stubbornly, collecting in the wooded hollows and counter-charging every wave of attack. General von Mudra took over most of the defences along the Upper Aisne and enabled General von Einem to pour his divisions along the Ardennes Canal, while General von der Marwitz helped in the conflict in the Argonne Woods. The veteran French

DESTRUCTION IN A RETAKEN TOWN.
Heavy bridge across the railway at Tournai destroyed by the Germans. It was found thus when the British recaptured the town and released the twenty thousand civil inhabitants who still remained there.

gunners, however, allowed no force to live long in front of their own infantry. With great gusts of fire they cleared the ground by Neuville-et-Day, on the outskirts of the wood west of Le Chesne, and south of the town they curtained the edge of the Les Alleux tableland, while in wave after wave the troops of the assault manœuvred forward. By the evening an advance of two miles was achieved, and after spending the night in prolonging their roads and throwing more bridges over the Aisne River and Aire stream, the French and American armies at dawn on November 2nd began to exploit their victories.

General Gouraud resumed his double thrust towards Le Chesne, throwing the Germans back by the Ardennes Canal, progressing on the Les Alleux plateau, and seizing the pass of Croix-aux-Bois. Then in the Châtillon defile, after a prolonged, savage struggle by the **Franco-American** gateway at Quatre Champs, his troops **encircling movement** worked round the Argonne while co-operating with the Americans in the great stretch of hills below. The German forces that had stood stubbornly to battle on the Grandpré hills found themselves in a large salient which was being closed some twelve miles in their rear. They fell back in haste, losing thousands of men as they did so, and in spite of the fact that the retreating forces were diverted mainly against the French Army, General Gouraud's men steadily worked onward.

The weather took an unfavourable turn. After the mist of the first day of battle heavy rain fell, making aeroplane observation practically impossible and disarranging the connection between infantry and artillery on which success largely depended. The enemy, however, was declining into such a condition of disorganisation and dispiritedness that the Franco-American encircling movement continued to increase in scope in spite of the bad weather and the difficulties of traffic. French and Americans fought on through the night, and General Gouraud pressed with his centre into the Le Chesne Woods, while his left stood ready along the Aisne to break any German counter-offensive, and his right divisions fought with increasing fury towards Châtillon.

Châtillon was also the supreme objective of many of the American shock troops who had come in motor-lorries to Buzancy. They pressed upon the hostile forces in the Argonne Forest at the end of the valley of the pass of Croix-aux-Bois and outflanked them. As the French had arrived victoriously at the other stretch of the pass, the two armies closed the greater part of the Upper Argonne to the enemy. Then from Boult-aux-Bois the troops of Major-General Dickmann's corps worked up both banks of the Bar stream, encircled Châtillon from the north, and on November 3rd linked with the French in Châtillon, completing the grand enveloping movement, that had begun three days before on a front of over thirty miles. The entire obstacle of the Argonne Forest with its outside railway system and its two valley tracks was completely conquered, leaving the enemy broken in power and crippled in communication facilities. On their left the Americans pursued the Germans to within four miles of the Stenay gap, which was one of the two gates of retreat that the enemy possessed along the Meuse. By closing the Stenay gap the Americans could deny to their foes any line of withdrawal south of the Ardennes. The Germans endeavoured to retain a bridge-head at Stenay by flooding the ground and erecting new defences on the neighbouring heights. All along the river from Dun to Stenay they fought hard. Only by very fierce fighting were the

Argonne Forest wholly conquered

Americans able to advance by the riverside, as the Germans held across the water the upper stretch of the famous Heights of the Meuse, rising to thirteen hundred feet by Dun and subsiding in hilly country by the bend of the river below Sedan.

Nevertheless, the American forces worked onward quickly and generally. From their advanced centre in the Belval Woods above Buzancy, and twelve miles north of their starting-point, the troops of Major-General Summerall were able to begin suddenly to turn all the Heights of the Meuse on November 3rd by an advance towards Beaumont. This position was so far in the rear of the Dun hills that, as soon as it was imperilled, General von Fuchs began to retire along the eastern bank of the river, violently pressed by the American army corps under General Hine. By the evening of November 3rd seventeen German divisions had been shattered by the Americans, with a loss of five thousand prisoners and one hundred guns, and the road to Sedan was opening.

FURY OF FIRE IN WHICH BELGIUM WAS PURGED OF THE PRESENCE OF THE HUN.
British soldiers helping firemen to quell the fires set burning in Tournai by incendiary shells hurled into the town by the Germans when evacuating the position to which they clung almost to the last minute. Above : Soldiers laying wires through the flames and smoke of the burning town.

Observing officers in the crow's-nest of a great Zeppelin shed captured at Maubeuge watching the enemy retiring over the Belgian frontier. British infantry are shown on the left advancing, with field-artillery galloping into action nearer in the foreground.

British Guardsmen at the bridge across the Sambre at Maubeuge which the retreating Germans had destroyed. One of the men was hailing with a hearty cheer the raising of the Tricolour by one of the relieved inhabitants on the farther side of the river.

BRITISH TROOPS RECAPTURE FOR FRANCE THE FAMOUS FORTRESS TOWN OF MAUBEUGE.

THE FLOODTIDE OF VICTORY IN THE WEST.
By Edward Wright.

VIII.—The Battle of Mormal Forest and the Final Rout of the Germans.

Germans Prepare Great Retreat—Haig Compels Them to Stand to Battle—Glorious Achievement of 1st Division by Sambre Canal—Colonel Marshall and Lancashire Fusiliers—How Major Waters Got the 32nd Division Over the Water at Ors—Storming of Landrecies by English Troops—Magnificent Progress by Third Army Towards Aulnoye Railway Line—New Zealanders Breach and Scale Outer Ramparts of Le Quesnoy—New Zealand and 37th Break Past German Artillery Positions—Bitter Struggle by Guards and 62nd Division—Swaying Struggle on Aunelle River—Incomparable Aerial Exploit of Major Barker—Final Grand Victory of All British Arms—Ninety-nine Enemy Divisions Beaten and Broken by Fifty-Nine British Divisions—Gallant Co-operation of First French Army—Fresh French and Italian Divisions under General Humbert Smash Into German Centre—Italians Cut Railway Line at Rozoy—Grenadier Guards Carry Maubeuge—Gouraud Races for Sedan Against Liggett—Rainbow Division and 1st Division Contend for Capture of Sedan Suburbs—Two Million Germans Broken Upon Rocky Mass of the Ardennes—East Lancashires in Ath—Canadian Highlanders in Mons—Line Occupied on November 11th, 1918, by Allied Armies.

THE successes of the Belgian, French, and American forces, described in the last chapter, were mainly due to the exhaustion of the enemy under the continuous attacks of the British armies. For twelve weeks Sir Douglas Haig had struck the enemy a rapid succession of heavy blows, which had a cumulative effect upon both the material strength and the spirit of the German forces. After every defeat there was an increase in Hindenburg's difficulty in replacing lost guns, machine-guns, and ammunition, and at the beginning of November, 1918, his reserves in men were exhausted. The British victories had also so weakened the general power of the Germans that they were unable to send help to Turkey, Bulgaria, and Austria-Hungary, with the result that their desperate situation on the western front was complicated by the opening of new lines of attack against them across the Danube and through and along the Alps.

General Pershing's and General Gouraud's advance towards Sedan had blocked the only path of retreat south of the Ardennes Forest. The German High Command immediately prepared to evacuate its central forces by way of Namur. General von Gröner, who had the reputation of being the enemy's greatest expert in railway management and supply, came to Spa to conduct the grand withdrawal. General von Lossberg's

CIVIL HOMAGE TO MILITARY PROWESS.
M. Jules Walrand, Mayor of Maubeuge, expressing the gratitude of the municipality to the British troops who liberated the town, and welcoming them in the person of their commander.

army of Lorraine, with which he had hoped to recover the initiative by a stroke through Eastern France, was reduced to eleven divisions, owing to the need of reinforcing the troops along the Meuse. Against this enfeebled army General de Castelnau was accumulating some twenty French divisions and from four to six American divisions. And there were other French forces in reserve.

In these circumstances the German High Command prepared a rapid retreat northward from the line of the Scheldt and Mormal Forest. On November 3rd Tournai was about to be abandoned, together with the Guise gap and the Oise and Sambre Canal. Hindenburg still hoped to prolong the war through the winter, if only he could withdraw his main armies back to Antwerp and Namur. Sir Douglas Haig, however, had mounted a grand attack upon a vital centre in prevision of the enemy's movements. He intended to anticipate the German withdrawal, and by a final battle bring the entire struggle to an immediate conclusion.

While the Battle of Valenciennes was going on between some eight German divisions and the Twenty-Second, the Canadian, and the Seventeenth Army Corps of the First and Third British Armies, other British forces prepared for the last great general action of a decisive nature. The Ninth Corps, under Sir W. P. Braithwaite, arranged to force the Sambre and Oise Canal;

the Thirteenth Corps, under Sir T. L. N. Morland, deployed most of its strength in an attack on Landrecies and the southern part of Mormal Forest. This was the main work of the Fourth Army, employing the 25th, 50th, 18th, 32nd, and 1st Divisions.

On their left the Third Army used the Fifth Corps, under the command of Lieutenant-General C. D. Shute; the Fourth Corps, under Sir G. M. Harper; the Sixth Corps, under Sir J. A. L. Haldane; and the Seventeenth Corps, under Sir Charles Fergusson. The First Army again employed the Twenty-second Corps and the Canadian Corps, which were concluding the struggle round Valenciennes. The 38th, 17th, 37th, New Zealand, 62nd, Guards, and 34th Divisions, and the 11th, 56th, 3rd, and 4th Canadian Divisions were engaged. Including British and German divisions just drawn out of action there were twenty divisions of assault against thirty-two divisions of defence.

The enemy troops, however, were so despondent, dispirited, and ready to scatter when their front was driven in, that the weary, wasted British were once more rather **Reluctant enemy** a pursuing force than men fighting a pitched **forced to fight** battle. As both the Teutonic soldier and his commanders wished only to disengage and retire rapidly, it is indeed somewhat strange to describe the action as a pitched battle. Nevertheless, it was one, for the old reason that the enemy was no longer master of his movements, but had to stand and fight where and whenever Sir Douglas Haig decided.

The First French Army, under General Debeney, again moved its point of attack, and its principal divisions of assault came alongside the Fourth British Army north of Guise, making a battle front of nearly forty miles between the Scheldt and the Oise. On the right of the First French Army other French and Italians divisions maintained their pressure

against the last of the Hunding defences, thus prolonging the line of battle another sixty miles to the Aisne at Château Porcien. Farther up the Aisne, by Attigny, General Gouraud and General Liggett continued fiercely to drive into the armies of General von Einem and General von der Marwitz. So that on a line of more than a hundred and thirty miles the German forces had to stand to battle at the time when an undisturbed withdrawal was their only means of escape from general disaster.

Sir Henry Rawlinson opened the battle with a whirlwind bombardment in the moonless night before dawn, and sent the men of his 1st Division out under a tremen- dous barrage at a quarter to six, an hour **Battlefield of** before sunrise. They attacked along the **tragic memories** Sambre Canal by Catillon village and the canal lock, some two miles to the south. Some men remaining in the 1st Division had tragic memories of the ground about the Sambre Canal. Over it the old force had retreated from Landrecies on August 26th, 1914, losing heavily in a rearguard action between Fesmy and the canal, where the 2nd Munsters were cut off. The division had changed in composition between its retreat from and return to Mons; but the 1st Northamptons were a veteran unit, and with the 1st Cameron Highlanders, which had immediately taken the place of the brave but un- happy Munsters, the 16th Lancashire Fusiliers, and other fine battalions, the renowned 1st Division, under Major-General F. P. Strickland, resolved to make the return across the Sambre an historic event.

The troops had fought across the tunnels of the Scheldt Canal with the Midlanders of the 46th Division, and they employed many of the devices of their comrades. Some of the officers and men swam the thirty yards of open water, others floated across on lifebelts, or rowed across in canvas canoes, while their daring sappers erected light plank bridges,

ONE OF THE CROWNING ACHIEVEMENTS OF THE LAST DAYS OF THE WAR.
First British troops entering Maubeuge in the early morning of November 9th, 1918. Scene of a tragic blow to France in 1914, when the Germans captured the town with 35,000 French troops, Maubeuge shared with Mons the distinction of being one of the places avenged in the closing hours of the war. It was recaptured by the British Guards Division and 62nd Division men of the Grenadiers being the first to break through the enemy rearguard.

BRITISH TROOPS IN MONS OF TRAGIC BUT GLORIOUS MEMORY.

Canadian soldiers marching past General Horne in Mons—scene of the glorious stand of the "Old Contemptibles" in 1914, and by a dramatic coincidence the last place of importance to be captured before the war lapsed into armistice. It was shortly before dawn on November 11th, 1918, that Canadians took Mons a few hours before hostilities ceased. At the time fixed for the cessation of hostilities there was a solemn parade of British troops in Mons.

over which the rest of the Scotsmen and Englishmen poured. The opposite bank was lined with an extraordinary number of machine-gunners with assistant snipers and trench-mortar crews, and a dense curtain of shell fire was thrown, almost at point-blank range, over the western side of the waterway. Sir Henry Rawlinson was, however, the supreme master in the art of forcing a passage, having done more to break the enemy than any other army commander among the Allies.

His whirlwind bombardment did not completely clear the way for the gallant Englishmen and Scotsmen who led the attack, but it reduced their task from an impossibility into a feat that dauntless and highly-skilled men might accomplish. The new Hermann system, begun between the Oise and Serre, where the First French Army had partly broken it, was prolonged upward by the Oise and Sambre Canal, in a series of three widely-spaced zones. The first zone of works by the canal was completed; the second at some distance behind was very strong, but the third and main line was unfinished. To make all possible use of the cover of the two completed lines the enemy commander pushed practically all his men forward fighting at close quarters.

Catillon village was rapidly carried, and a bridge-head formed. Then for two hours there was a furious struggle in the morning mist, with the opposing guns **Bridge-building** smashing down upon the contending infantry **under massed fire** and machine-gunners, trench-mortar teams and riflemen firing at opponents within a stone's throw. Shattered though the German Army was, it yet contained tens of thousands of men ready to fall rather than see their country invaded; but these sons of Blücher were not numerous enough to alter the stream of events.

The British were still braver. Eminent among them was a former lieutenant of the Irish Guards, acting as lieutenant-colonel of the 16th Lancashire Fusiliers. He was Lieutenant Colonel J. N. Marshall. Before his advanced troops could cross the canal the sapper's bridge was broken by the enemy's massed fire. He gathered a repairing party, all of whom were killed or wounded. Standing on the bank, under intense fire, the commandant called for volunteers, and with instant

assistance repaired the bridge and led his battalion charging over the water, falling dead, but living in spirit; for his men avenged his death by their victory.

Bridge-heads were formed opposite Catillon and the canal lock, and wonderful bridges made, light yet strong, so that storming cars and guns could cross in scores and help the infantry in working through the Hermann defences. The 1st Division spread out in a great fighting advance past Bois l'Abbaye and Hautreve villages. At Fesmy, the ancient scene of misfortune in 1914, where the Munsters fell valiantly through failing to receive the order to retire, fate again seemed, in 1918, to be against the **On through Fesmy** division. For progress was checked from **and La Groise** the fortified houses and cellar refuges by a stubborn and strong force of Germans. The attack on Fesmy, however, was renewed in the afternoon, and executed with such determination that the place was taken and an advance made far to the east of it. In the meantime the main objective, La Groise, was captured and passed, bringing General Strickland's men directly south of their old battle-place, Landrecies.

On the left of the 1st Division, the 32nd Division made as glorious a passage over the bending waterway at Ors, using also portable bridges, canvas canoes, lifebelts, and cork floats, while some men swam against death. Here, as elsewhere, German staff-work was excellent, and the picked enemy troops given the dangerous line of the canal were worthy of the men they met in the matter of resolution and expertness. There was a time when failure in the attack seemed likely. With artillery and machine-gun fire at close range the Germans destroyed the light bridge which the sappers erected, killing or wounding most of the officers and men.

Major A. M. S. Waters came forward, and with another building party worked on cork floats repairing the bridge over the canal. The dauntless sapper officer was under point-blank fire, and it seemed impossible for him to escape being killed. Yet the enemy could not hit him, and inspired by his imperturbability his assistants made the passage, over which the division attacked and won a bridge-head. The success of the operation was entirely due to Major Waters, who was awarded the Victoria Cross.

This, however, did not end the struggle by Ors. The Germans collected on both sides of the bridge-head, which the leading battalions of the 32nd Division gained, and at Rue le Haut and Happegarbes met the attackers with more hard fighting. The British, however, were the harder fighters, and in spite of the difficult ground in the undulating, wood-dappled bend of the Sambre, they drove the enemy back to La Folie. There other troops of the division forced another passage over the river, south of Landrecies, closing down on La Folie from the north, while their comrades extended round it on the other side. The village was carried, opening another line of advance across the Sambre tributaries towards Avesnes.

The 25th Division, which had done such fine work on October 23rd in turning Bishop's Wood, battled from the ground it had won into Landrecies, against **25th Division capture Landrecies** a division of the Prussian Guard reinforced by other special troops. The County battalions and other men of the 25th were not special troops, but only ordinary British soldiers, with a glorious tradition of achievements from Vimy Ridge to the slopes by Kemmel Hill. They fought round the town for some hours, destroying machine-gun posts and breaking counter-attacks, and, having overcome the Prussian Guard and other troops, they forced the passage of the Sambre both north and south of Landrecies, crossing the bullet-swept water on rafts, linked their bridge-heads together in another hard bout of fighting, and so captured the historic, picturesque place that Robert Louis Stevenson, visiting it in his younger days, once dreamt would be ringed with the flame of guns. It was in Landrecies that the Coldstream Guards choked the street with German dead on August 25th, 1914, leaving behind some of their wounded, who were inhumanly treated by both the German Army and the German people. A brigade of British Guards had been sufficient to shatter the German mass formations brought up by motor-lorries through Mormal Forest, but an entire division of the Prussian Guard, with at least another division of German troops, was not strong enough to hold the town against the 25th Division.

The Germans, however, put up a harder fight on the western face of Mormal Forest, where the 18th Division and 50th Division of the Thirteenth Corps attacked. At Preux-au-Bois the German garrison held out until the village was completely surrounded by the British infantry with their storming cars. When, at last, this front-line opposition was overcome, the advance of the wing of the Fourth Army proceeded at a remarkable pace. In all there were some twelve German divisions opposed to the five British divisions deployed by Sir Henry Rawlinson. The enemy regarded his defences in Mormal Forest as impregnable to everything except an immense and sustained gas bombardment.

As already explained, the enemy had cut a great deal of the timber in the forest, making large new clearings, in addition to the old open spaces and wide **Light Tanks in forest fighting** glades in the centre. Where the trees were thinned he endeavoured to create new obstacles by means of wire entanglements, log barricades, pits and other traps, and in addition to packing his line with machine-gunners, he employed a first-rate fighting force of cycling machine-gunners and marksmen to strengthen endangered points. The British infantrymen, however, had become masters in the art of forest fighting, and they did not give the enemy any opportunity of rallying, even in the old parts of the great tract of woodland, where the brushwood had grown with jungle-like luxuriance.

The travelling barrage had a weight and precision unlike that used in Delville Wood and other early woodland combats. Heavy guns were employed in masses like machine-guns, and directed by aeroplane control in a far-reaching sweep of thunder and flame, while the dense, white mist of early morning blinded enemy gunners and machine-gunners. Mainly, however, it was the light, fast British Tank that transformed the conditions of forest fighting, and made the smaller forces of attack greatly superior to the defending corps.

In thick fog the Tank pilots had to steer by compass, yet skilfully they broke through the thick-set hedges and searched out machine-gun nests in front of the British infantry. When the sun came up, the day of the last great British battle was wonderfully fine, with a blue dome of sky and sunshine sparkling on every russet leaf. The bright and lucid air was a godsend to the victors, enabling them to distinguish obstacles, and work together like an immense football team.

The adventurous Tankmen entered with increased zest into the business of hunting out machine-gun nests, crashing at them through brushwood, log works, and wire entanglements, and generally avoiding easy and open ways of approach likely to be sown with anti-Tank mines. Some German machine-gun parties, in finely camouflaged positions, did not fire a shot. Many marksmen, in rifle pits and behind hedges, were equally ready to surrender without using their rifles. From one village fifty Germans came out of cellars, where they had been hiding with the inhabitants, and gave themselves up.

As in other forest combats, there were Germans hidden in tree-tops—good men, most of them, ready to fight to the death. But the trick that had been played in Oppy Wood in 1917 was of little service in Mormal Forest in the autumn of 1918. The British Staff had expected that the Teuton would again resort to the habit of his arboreal ancestor, and field-guns were pushed forward with rounds of case-shot, to make life uncertain to the latest species of tree-dwellers. As a rule the men on concealed platforms up the big trees were able to escape notice from the mechanical cavalry of the Tank brigades, and the fire from their machine-guns and magazine rifles was disconcerting to British infantry parties exploring the ground beneath. Well-spread bursts of case-shot, however, cleared the trees, while the ordinary travelling barrage swept the earth.

Very fast through Mormal Forest went the men of the 18th Division, who had been responsible for the finest achievement in the previous action along the outskirts of the great woodland. With their corps companions of the 50th Division they practically cleared the southern part of the forest in the night, and when dawn came were looking out over open country towards Berlaimont. **Mormal Forest left behind** Equally rapid was the progress of the southern wing of the Third Army, represented by the 38th and 17th Divisions. In the morning fog these two gallant forces began by driving forward for some four miles through thickly-timbered ground by the old Roman road connecting Le Cateau with Bavai.

The German defence was patchy, some regiments fighting manfully and adroitly in the last pitch of despair, others yielding without much show of fighting. This was largely a matter of the freshness or staleness of General von Below's divisions. Some that he had used since the opening of Sir Julian Byng's offensive were wasted down to less than a skeleton. The whole of the 111th German Division was reported by prisoners to have been reduced to two hundred and fifty men—the establishment of an ordinary company. On the other hand the forces brought from the eastern front were strong in both numbers and spirit, and fought far better than the Prussian Guard.

The German High Command was probably correct in assuming that it could generally restore the moral of its men by a winter rest and large drafts of the youngest recruits. The Germans had been great soldiers, and where they were under able officers and not completely worn out by lost battle after lost battle, they still struggled with the old determination. They were, however, overwhelmed by the tremendous machinery of the British attack, as well as overborne by the indefatigable vigour of the British "thrusting" troops. With a devastating barrage in front of them and the ubiquitous light Tanks as scouts and supports, the leading brigade of the 38th Division reached by mid-day the wide, open glades of Les Grandes Pâtures. At the neighbouring hamlet and clearing of Locquignol the 17th Division had some hard fighting against a strong garrison with machine-guns sweeping the open ground. As was remarked in connection with the Cambrai action, clear, level spaces had become harder to cross

Liberated inhabitants of Tournai inspecting one of the broken bridges over the canalised Scheldt.

British sentry guarding a bridge across the Scheldt on the pleasant embankment at Tournai.

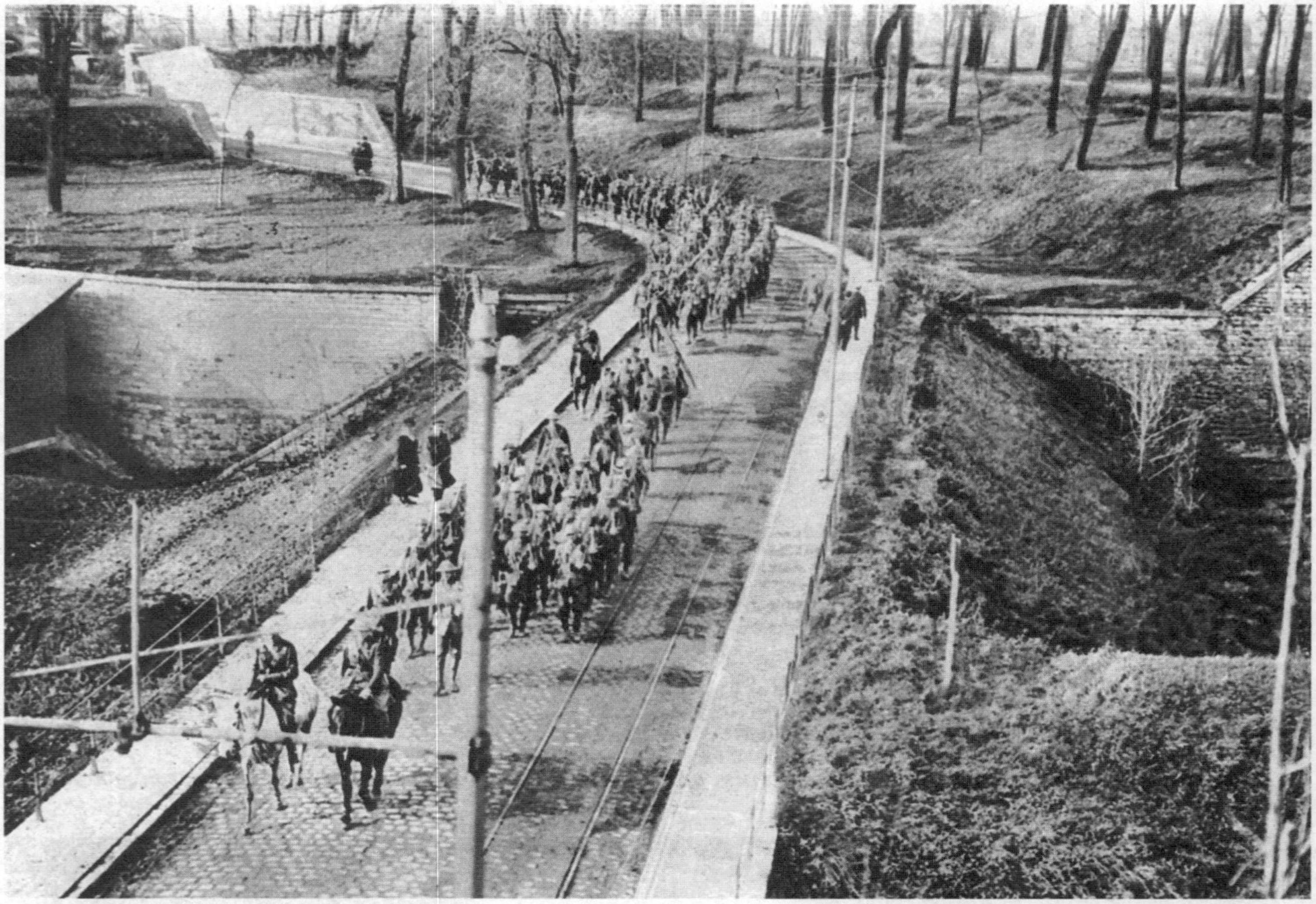

Grenadier Guards marching into Maubeuge, whence they cleared the enemy two days before the armistice.

Kraftfahrzeuge
Höchstgeschwindigkeit in der Stadt:
Personenkraftwagen 10 km.
Lastkraftwagen 8 km.
Krankenkraftwagen 8 km.
Krafträder 10 km.
Überschreitung wird streng bestraft
der Etappenkommandant

British Grenadiers entering Maubeuge over a bridge disfigured with a notice posted by the Hun.

Irish Guards at the Mons Gate of Maubeuge, which had been held by the Germans for fifty months.

British soldiers patching up for temporary use a destroyed bridge over the canal near Maubeuge.

The Condé road from Valenciennes, just after the Canadians had driven the enemy from the town on the Scheldt in the morning of November 3rd.

Canadian signallers mending wires in inundated Valenciennes. German notices of things "forbidden" and of shell-proof dug-outs still plastered the walls of the long-suffering town.

Crater of a mine blown in a thoroughfare in Dénain by the Germans to delay pursuit when retreating before the Canadians at the end of October, 1918.

Happy civilians being driven by some of the Canadians who had set them free back to their homes in Valenciennes through streets flooded by the retreating foes.

Damage in Dénain and floods in Valenciennes—towns wrested from the Germans during the closing weeks of the war.

than hills or forests, by reason of the enormous number of machine-guns employed by the enemy. Locquignol, however, surrendered in the afternoon when the British guns were rapidly hauled forward. The struggle went on during the night, when the enemy completely broke and retired, and before dawn the 38th Division reached beyond the eastern edge of the forest towards the railway running to Aulnoye junction, thereby achieving the deepest advance in the battle, while the leading troops of the 17th Division were one mile beyond Locquignol.

Above the Roman road to Bavai the 37th Division and the New Zealand Division had the severest struggle in the action. They had to advance by Chissignies and the hills above the Ecaillon stream towards the old fortress town of Le Quesnoy. By this picturesque old walled city Englishmen first came under the fire of cannon in the year of Crécy, and in 1711 the Duke of Marlborough ended his last campaign by its walls.

As in the case of Guise Castle, the old ramparts and bastions acquired renewed importance in the age of the machine-gun and trench-mortar, and by allowing observation over the ground of approach made excellent telephone positions for gunnery observation officers. General Harper, commanding the Fourth Corps and using only two of his divisions, arranged to take Le Quesnoy by envelopment; but his lieutenant, General Russell, provided the New Zealanders with mediæval devices of attack for an assault upon the old-world walled town, so as to make a frontal stroke as well as a turning movement.

In the opening phase of the action the German forces were full of fight. Strengthened by troops withdrawing from the Tournai salient and the flooded land south of it, they met the attack with a fierce massed counter-charge. The 37th and New Zealand Divisions opened with a mighty bombardment with guns and trench-mortars; but formidable as the barrage was it did not shatter the German works. The two divisions were held up along the railway embankment by Chissignies, between the Bavai road and Le Quesnoy,

New Zealanders besiege Le Quesnoy the chapel at the edge of Chissignies village being one of the concealed strong points held by enemy machine-gunners.

As soon as the German commander learnt that his front-line troops had checked the advance on the outskirts of the northern part of Mormal Forest, he launched the great counter-attack in mass, hoping to retrieve in his centre the critical reverse on his southern wing. But as had been proved in the Battle of Valenciennes, the old-fashioned swarm attack was useless against British troops, who had been taught in March and April of the year that intense rifle fire remained the grandest of infantry tactics.

The Germans were completely shattered, with losses so heavy that they demoralised the survivors. The British travelling barrage was resumed, and five Tanks charged along the embankment. Though only two of the storming cars got across, they were very helpful in the wrestling round the fortress chapel. When their new line went, the Germans broke above the Roman road. The 37th Division stormed into Louvignies, on the highway to Le Quesnoy, and then swept through all the upper forest defences to the village of Jolimetz, and there worked through the last ambushes towards the railway running to Aulnoye junction.

In the meantime some of the New Zealanders were engaged in the most picturesque struggle in the war. In ancient fashion, with scaling-ladders, they carried the outer ramparts of Le Quesnoy as soon as Chissignies fell, and with their artillery breached the curtain wall. Under fierce gusts of raking fire from the garrison of some two thousand men the outer fortifications were stormed; but, as at Guise Castle, the machine-gun checked the assailants in the main works. Thereupon General Russell picketed the town, and poured his troops round it north and south, meeting again with fierce resistance at the village of Herbignies, where in a swaying contest the Germans held out until the evening.

There were many enemy batteries assisting in the defence of Le Quesnoy, from the cover of houses, trees, and hedges in Mormal Forest. They stayed too long in action. Before any of them could be withdrawn the New Zealanders charged

with the bayonet among the gun crews. Without stopping to count their captures the vehement islanders continued their long thrust behind Le Quesnoy, breaking through the German artillery line, and reaching the waggon-line and cutting off the transport as the drivers were on the point of galloping off.

One hundred guns were captured by the New Zealanders and the 37th Division, leaving the garrison of Le Quesnoy perplexed over the disappearance of their protective barrage. Yet the Germans in the old fortressed town remained defiant behind its breached outer wall. So parley was opened after the manner of the Middle Ages, but with very modern means. British aeroplanes flying low over the town dropped messages reading: "You are completely surrounded, and our troops are far to the east of you. If you will surrender, you will be treated as honourable prisoners of war."

The Germans read the message, but their commandant would not surrender. Then two treating parties were sent in, each consisting of a New Zealand officer and a couple of German officer prisoners. **Romantic siege ends in victory** Entering by the breach in the outer ramparts, they shouted the summons to surrender, and the promise of honourable treatment. A few men accepted the offer and came out, but the German commandant and many of his officers resolved to stand in Le Quesnoy to the last moment, hoping thereby to win more time for the withdrawal of the main German forces. The fortress town controlled the railway between Valenciennes and Aulnoye, and the longer the line could be held and the more destruction done to it the greater would be the difficulties under which the British railway construction troops would labour in lengthening the British lines of communication.

In the afternoon Sir A. H. Russell determined to carry the great fortress by storm. Under another fierce bombardment the New Zealanders scaled the high sheer inner walls, and while their guns blasted more breaches in the ramparts, the leading troops of the attack rushed hostile machine-gun nests with the bayonet, and fought from barricade to barricade through the streets. About four o'clock in the afternoon a thousand Germans, surviving from the original garrison force, found that all exits from the town were stopped, and surrendered in batches from cellars and chambers in the old fortifications. Altogether, the Battle of Le Quesnoy, in which for the first time in the war a besieged town was formally called upon to submit to British troops, was like an episode of the age of Agincourt interpolated in the scientific, mechanical, chemical warfare of the twentieth century.

The New Zealanders well deserved the romantic distinction they won towards the close of the campaign. They were a force small in numbers when compared with the army corps maintained by the larger and more populous dominions of Canada and Australia, but in quality they were excelled by no other troops on the continent of Europe. In their ranks served more than half of all the men of military age in their lovely islands.

After closing the line above Albert in the enemy's spring offensive they had fought from August 21st to November 4th from the Serre plateau to the eastern edge of Mormal Forest, with a sustained magni- **New Zealanders' splendid service** ficence of spirit and body revealing, as nothing else could, what kind of men they were. They were of the same blood as the other British forces that battled forward for three months of successive triumphs over enemies nearly twice as numerous as themselves.

Above the New Zealand Division, by Orsinval and the sources of the Rhonelle stream, the 62nd Division of naval men opened the attack under General Haldane, while the British Guards waited on their left to develop their action as soon as Orsinval was taken. Again there was a hard struggle against the massed front line of defending forces, and after the naval men breached the German front and the Guards swung alongside them on the left, there was much desperate fighting among the marshes and artificial floods.

Although the Guards and the 62nd Division had difficult work before them, they were never checked in their large sweep through Fresnoy and Preux-au-Sart to the outskirts of Commegnies. Indeed, like the New Zealanders, they went

IN MONS REWON.
The Mayor of Mons addressing General Horne, Commander of the First British Army, which had recaptured the town on November 11th, 1918.

was maintaining round Tournai. Again the German commander collected strong forces from his withdrawing northern armies, in order to save the position on his left flank rear. When the 11th and 56th Divisions pressed forward on November 5th from the hills by the Aunelle to the Honnelle River, they met another great counter-attack, but they shattered it, and the British and Canadian troops worked still more deeply into the German flank, until at night all the ground before them flamed and thundered with the ammunition dumps which the Germans were busily exploding because they could not remove them.

The principal reason why the enemy had to destroy his material of war was the power exercised by the Royal Air Force. The pilots and aerial observers

so quickly that they ran into a battery of large howitzers, capturing them as the drivers were beginning to limber up. Field-guns were taken in considerable number, and ground won by Wargnies. On the left of the Guards the 24th Division, under General Daly, stormed forward quickly towards the two villages of Wargnies, meeting with little determined resistance, save from machine-gunners in Wargnies-le-Petit. The 19th Division also, which was in excellent form, advanced with comparative ease on Bry and Eth.

Behind Valenciennes the enemy had not recovered from the slaughter of the previous action, and it was more difficult to get him to stand to fight than to take ground from him.

On the front of the First Army Sir Henry Horne employed the 11th Division, the 56th Division, with the 3rd and 4th Canadian Divisions, reaching to the eastern side of the marshes north of Valenciennes. The Germans had fallen back after their defeat on November 2nd to the line of the Aunelle River, five miles from the city. The English and Scottish troops forced the stream, and won the high ground beyond where the German commander tried to check them by a counter-attack on the hamlet of Sebourg.

German resistance weakening

There was, however, little force behind this last attempt at holding an elastic front. One Baden regiment, launched in the direction of Preseau, surrendered with its three commandants merely as a protest against its Prussian commander. A German major, leading another regiment, deliberately surrendered with his men at the earliest opportunity out of hatred for Ludendorff. Other forces that did not counter-attack with any vehemence were so reduced in strength that one had a total of only fifty rifles, and another, the 73rd Fusilier Regiment, once consisting of three thousand men, mustered scarcely a platoon, of which a few stragglers survived in the prisoners' cage.

The British line was pressed back slightly on the high ground above the stream, and after recovering the lost ridge by the Aunelle the attackers went forward again towards the Mons road into the flank of the great salient the enemy

MUTUAL CONGRATULATIONS ON FREEDOM REGAINED.
At the civic rejoicings in Mons which followed close upon the recapture of the town from the Germans in the early hours of Armistice Day. The Mayor of Mons (left) shaking hands with the Mayor of Valenciennes.

were masters of the situation in the gloriously clear weather of November 4th. Under their direction the massed batteries of British heavy guns punctured every road of retreat.

The British airmen chased fugitive columns of guns, and by killing the horses, scattering the men, and bombing the roads, left scores of pieces by the roadside for the infantry to collect. One British battalion collected thirty German guns abandoned under aerial assaults. In all more than 450 guns were captured, together with 19,000 Germans, during the action in and around Mormal Forest.

The hero of the battle was an airman, Major W. G. Barker. He was a Canadian officer who had been recalled to England for training duties, but he resolved to have one last day's fighting before he left. He went out alone and, in view of the attacking British troops, chased an enemy machine and broke it into bits in the air. The German, however, had been only a decoy, and some fifteen Fokkers swooped upon Major Barker. He was wounded in the thigh, and stunned for a moment, losing control of his machine. But recovering his senses, he shot down two of the German machines in a marvellous display of skill, and set a third on fire.

In this combat of one against fifteen the major had his

other thigh shattered by a bullet, and once more he fainted, leaving his machine to spin down apparently to destruction. But before reaching ground he again recovered control, only to find himself surrounded by a fresh formation of Germans, numbering at least a dozen machines. He was dazed and giddy, and with both legs useless, but he made up his mind to die gloriously. He charged the nearest machine, intending to ram it, but firing as he went he sent it down in flames, the fiery wreck just clearing his propeller.

He turned and made another attack and had his left elbow broken by a bullet. Happily, on this occasion, the shock did not cause him to faint, in spite of the continuing loss of blood from his broken thighs and his agony and dreadful weakness. With only one hand to work his levers and his gun, Major Barker charged again in an endeavour to ram. Once more his shots told before he reached his desperate goal, and another German went down burning.

Major Barker turned for the British lines, flying at a low altitude, and for the third time a large enemy formation darted between him and the hospital. Then the British troops close below saw the most wonderful of air combats, though those that cheered the single fighter **Major Barker's** did not know he was a very badly wounded **amazing feat** man. Whirling first against one and then against another and making disconcerting movements, Major Barker crashed two more German machines, broke through the circle of enemies, and dived for the ground. Having only one hand and being very near to swooning, he could no longer properly control his machine and landed at great speed, crashing into a hedge, ripping off the undercarriage, and fainting.

The total number of German machines that assailed Major Barker over Mormal Forest was sixty, and at least ten of them he either crashed or sent down out of control. On his own estimate this brought his record of enemy aeroplanes shot down in the war to the number of fifty-one, but many airmen who fought with him reckoned he was far too modest in numbering

his victories, because he never included any crashed enemy who had not been seen to fall by British troops or companion airmen. In spite of his bone-shattering wounds, Major Barker gradually recovered in hospital, and although Captain Fonck, of the French Air Service, had a longer record of victories entitling him to rank as king of the air, the Canadian officer was at least the most gallant of all the princes, of the skies, dead or living. His unparalleled achievement crowned with an heroic romance the final grand victory of all British arms.

When Napoleon saw his last reserves break at Waterloo he is said to have remarked that the action had gone as it did at Crécy. Gröner, or Hindenburg, or whoever actually was directing movements on the German side in the first week of November, 1918, might have **One Briton worth** said the same thing as Napoleon. Between **four Germans** August and November, 1918, fifty-nine British divisions engaged and defeated ninety-nine separate German divisions, taking from the enemy 187,000 prisoners, 2,850 guns, 29,000 machine-guns, and 3,000 trench-mortars. The strongest and most vital parts of the enemy's fronts were attacked by the British troops, who were always inferior in force. In defence of his lateral communications the German Commander-in-Chief employed his best divisions, but they could not prevent his railways and roads from being decisively cut.

As Sir Douglas Haig pointed out in his classic despatch of December 21st, 1918, it was a generally accepted military doctrine that, in good defensive positions, a resisting force could defeat an attacking army of much greater numbers. The truth of this often-proved doctrine seemed to be finally confirmed in the Anglo-Teutonic campaigns of March and April, 1918. Then, in spite of the enormous superiority in number of both men and guns with which General von Ludendorff massed against the wings of the British Army, his efforts to break through towards the coast were so completely defeated that he himself was too dispirited to continue operations.

ONE OF THE PROUDEST MOMENTS IN THE WAR FOR CANADA'S HEROIC TROOPS.

General Sir Arthur Currie, Commander of the Canadian Corps, taking the salute of the troops at the solemn parade held in the main square of Mons on November 11th, 1918, at the hour when by the terms of the armistice the "Cease fire" put an end to hostilities on all fronts. On his left is the general commanding the division of Canadians that recaptured the town. Bands played the "Brabançonne" and "God Save the King" amid enthusiastic scenes.

Yet, what the Teuton could not do when he outnumbered the Briton by more than two to one, the Briton accomplished with almost the same odds in men against him. Indeed, when we consider the material elements against the attackers of the great Hindenburg works and add these disadvantages to the personal odds of nearly two to one, we must conclude that from August to November, 1918, each British soldier practically fought forward against four Germans.

The strength of each German was at least doubled by the cover and fields of fire he enjoyed in line after line of old French and British fortifications, zone after zone of the original Hindenburg defences, and the new works of the Hermann system extending to Mormal Forest. From Villers-Bretonneux to Maubeuge there was a tract of highly fortified ground some sixty-five miles in depth. Through this enormous fortress the soldiers of the British Commonwealth victoriously struggled for three **Briton and** months against every device which the **Teuton compared** talent and experience of the largest of military Powers could devise.

When the war broke out there was a sense of competition between the Briton and the Teuton in regard to personal fighting power. The British had an advantage over the enemy in having a better cause, yet the fanatic, semi-religious patriotism of aggression of the German long upheld him against any weakening of spirit. In actual battle the issue was simplified into the personal problem whether the Briton or the Teuton was the better fighting man.

Both fought with their heads as well as with their hands and feet. The Germans, having excelled the French and Russians in foresight and the theory on which preparations were made, brought the British Expeditionary Force to a ghastly ordeal round Ypres. There were no French siege-guns to counter-battery the armament employed by the enemy. Two years passed before France recovered from the effects of the miscalculations of her politicians, who refused to grant funds for heavy artillery. Russia never recovered from a

similar early mistake, and the main burden of the land war, as well as practically the entire burden of sea warfare, fell upon the British people.

The British fighting soldier in the field on the western front was not altogether well served by his political leaders of any party, but with the help of British inventors he played on land, on sea, and in the air a decisive part out of all proportion to his numbers. In both battle achievements and the invention of new mechanisms he greatly assisted the Frenchman and the American, who, in larger numbers than his own, splendidly seconded the grand achievements by which he routed the enemy.

It was the Briton who saw the Russian turn tail and sell his guns to the Teutons for a bottle of brandy, and watched some of the French troops grow despondent and inclined to insubordination, yet he went on attacking against apparently impregnable posi-

CROWNING TRIUMPH OF THE CANADIANS.
Canadian Scottish troops resting in the Grand' Place at Mons on November 11th, 1918, just after they had crowned their final triumphant advance with the recapture of the town in the closing hours of the war. Above: Mons townsfolk with some of their deliverers.

tions held by superior numbers. When seemingly exhausted, he took the full shock of the renewed power of the Teuton, wore it down in one of the greatest defensive campaigns in history, and then with tired, wasted armies attacked and drove the enemy before him until that enemy sued for peace. As Hindenburg frankly admitted to members of the Reichstag, his "men were beginning to run."

It is doubtful whether anything in the past history of the English and Celtic stocks of the people of the British Isles can compare with the enduring valour and blaze of mind and spirit of the modern fighting Briton. In spite of the loss of much of the young **Renaissance of the** flower of the race, the British people won **British people** something more than the war. They gained all the elements of a renaissance of universal scope, likely to issue in influences shaping the destiny of man. Of this achievement of theirs the battlefield of Mormal Forest became a monument infinitely more significant than the ridge of Waterloo, the hill of Malplaquet, the rolling plain of Agincourt, or the swell of ground at Crécy.

In Mormal Forest the armies of Sir Douglas Haig prevented the Teuton from gaining time to rest and reorganise, while his agents endeavoured to wreck the social foundations of

Great Britain as they had wrecked the half-grown structure of Russian society. It is in the light of later events in the industries of the British Isles and the United States that we must interpret the significance of the swift, final victory of British arms. At the time the Teutons were already engaged in transforming the genuine mutiny of their seamen into a pseudo-revolution, under cover of which they began strongly to promote anarchical disorder among the British working classes. This later " campaign of rat warfare," which the Teutons named, and of which they openly boasted they were the authors, would have had in all probability serious consequences, military as well as political and social, if the British commander and his men had not succeeded in forcing a decision on November 4th.

France was immediately beside Great Britain, Canada, and New Zealand in the action that changed the principal German armies from a desperate rearguard into a routed mob. On the right of the Fourth British Army, General Debeney's men, who had fought alongside General Rawlinson's troops from the Avre to the Sambre and Oise waterway, launched a knife-like attack some time after the 1st Division had forced the canal. Once more General Debeney had changed his concentration of assault, moving his main strength above Guise, and turning the upland town by a thrust on an eight-mile front between Oisy and Grand Verly. He assisted General Rawlinson by attracting some eight divisions of General von Hutier's weakened forces, and General Rawlinson helped him by first breaking the enemy's lines and thereby endangering all the front.

FARTHEST EAST.
The most eastern outpost on the British western front when hostilities ended. It was beyond Mons and was held by Canadians.

SOURCES OF RELIABLE INTELLIGENCE.
Sentry at a Canadian outpost stopping for interrogation four British soldiers escaped from German hands and proceeding to Mons to give information about the rapidly retreating enemy.

collected after the retreat from Mons. At Venerolles and other villages of historic memory there was a continuation of the Hermann system, erected in August after the break along the Somme. While the British troops, by bridging the canal for Tanks, managed quickly to shatter all the system, the French infantry had a more arduous task and did not capture so large a number of guns. Yet they took some five thousand prisoners, which was more in proportion to the numbers engaged southwards than were those taken northward. The German divisions between Oisy and Guise were utterly destroyed when

Nevertheless, the Germans fought hard and long against the French, using the large screen of Nouvion and Regneval Forests for collecting counter-attacking masses that kept Debeney's troops by the canal-side until mid-day. The enemy however, gained little by delaying the movement of the First French Army, while breaking before the Fourth British Army. He was completely exhausted when General Debeney's divisions deployed across the wide waterway, exactly by the villages where the First British Army Corps, under Sir Douglas Haig,

Debeney's men had finished rolling barrages over them, charging them, and shattering counter-attacks. Guise then fell without a struggle, and Nouvion Forest and other tracts of woodland were overrun with practically no resistance.

This immediately led Marshal Foch to prolong the front of battle another forty miles to Château Porcien, making, as General Debeney's centre and southern **100 miles of moving fire** wing came into action, a line of moving fire stretching for a hundred miles from the Scheldt near Condé to the Aisne.

General Mangin and the Tenth French Army vanished ; General Guillaumat and the Fifth French Army were departing ; their common direction was the Lorraine front. In their stead appeared the rested famous Third French Army, under General Humbert, that had filled the gap by Noyon in March, when Sir Hubert Gough's divisions were overwhelmed by immense numbers. The Second Italian Army Corps of remarkably good fighting men also came into action along the Hunding line, and with the strong mass of fresh French troops swiftly broke any further attempts at resistance by General von Eberhardt and General von Mudra.

Instant retreat had been imposed upon the enemy's centre armies by the British advance along the Maubeuge railway. Lines of supply and reinforcement

ALMOST AT THE END OF THEIR SUFFERINGS.
Civilians from the outskirts of Mons passing Canadian kilted troops on their way up to the town, on the day before it was recaptured, and they were delivered from their long-drawn-out suffering under the heel of the tyrannical invader.

MARCHING THROUGH MONS TO THE MUSIC OF THE PIPES.

Familiar scene in the streets on the great day of the deliverance of Mons, after the town had been for more than four years in the occupation of the invading Germans. The fact that the day of deliverance, November 11th, 1918, was also the day on which the enemy submitted to the drastic terms of armistice dictated by the Allies made the occasion doubly memorable, and the inhabitants crowded the ways to hail with joy the men who had freed them.

were being cut in the rear of the Seventeenth, Eighteenth, and Seventh German Armies, and to a considerable extent the traffic of the First German Army was disorganised. Above these broken or breaking forces the Sixth German Army was in increasing difficulties in the deep Tournai salient and crowding back along the bombed, round-about cross-country railways running to Nivelles and the region south of Brussels. One branch railway, running from Hirson to Chimay over the Belgian frontier and into the Ardennes, remained for the time unimperilled, except by aeroplane raids, but this could not carry the material of a single army.

Valuable Italian co-operation Thus, though the centre German forces had instantly to [retreat, they also had vehemently to fight great rearguard actions in the centre in order to win a few days for getting guns and other vitally important material away. This was the reason why Marshal Foch brought fresh French and Italian troops into action between the Serre and the Upper Aisne. He would not give the enemy the grace of an hour.

Attacking on November 4th, from the Sissonne sector, the Italian divisions gallantly and swiftly stormed through the Hindenburg defences round Montcornet, and made a fine advance to Le Thuel. Thence, in a fierce action along the Hurtaut torrent, the victorious Latins, greatly inspired by their complete trumph over Austrian and Magyar, broke over the highway between Rozoy and Rethel, and closed on Rozoy, carrying it on November 6th. This advance, continued northward toward the ancient battlefield of Rocroy, was of high importance. It cut across the centre railways

connecting at Mézières and Charleville with the Namur and Metz lines of retreat, and hurried into choking, jammed confusion the German movements over the Meuse into the forest maze of the Ardennes.

On either side of the Italian divisions the French under General Debeney and General Humbert were of equally impetuous power in exploiting the collapse of the invader. The weather, after the spell of clearness and sunshine in which the British delivered the last matador stroke of the war, turned cold and very rainy, making life miserable for the foot-soldier, and straining to the uttermost gun-teams, supply columns, tractor drivers, Tankmen, and airmen. Yet the exhilaration of an almost general pursuit between Mons and Sedan kept the allied troops in a condition of almost tireless cheerfulness.

It was upon the Teuton that the weather, with everything else, broke. Mutiny was spreading, like flame through stubble, from the Navy to the Army. As we shall see in detail, when recording the events leading up to the practical surrender of Germany in **Spreading contagion** negotiations for the armistice, the outbreak **of insurrection** of rebellion among the sailors and Marines of the enemy High Sea Fleet, when called upon to steam out and make a strong diversion to help the unnerved, confused, and breaking troops, was a factor of decision in the final issue. At present we can only note the effect of the naval demoralisation and revolutionary movement upon the fugitive armies.

The military authorities endeavoured to keep their forces from the contagion of insurrection spreading from Wilhelmshaven and Kiel to Berlin and the Rhineland. Even when at Brussels and other places soldiers began to mutiny as sailors had done, the memorable legend was intensely propagated that the Army was undefeated and still capable of saving the Fatherland from invasion. This essay in fiction was of more importance in its later developments; it had some effect as a salve for troubled minds in sections where there had been no definite rupture, but it could not at the time convince masses breaking into mobs, as their rearguards weakened, that there was hope in anything but an armistice on any terms.

Officers of the regular class, who had been held from the fighting-line since the opening of the British offensive, and replaced in many battalions by former civilians, were brought forward, the grand crisis having arisen, though not the one for which they had been saved. They tried either to persuade or terrorise troops back into discipline. Some of them were killed by the men; some found the task hopeless, and let the troops plunder as they fled; others were successful in forming new rearguard forces that struggled desperately at certain points. But these local stands had little influence

CANCELLED ANNOUNCEMENTS.
British soldiers scrutinising an indicator outside Mons Station. The Germans had already erased Aulnoye, Tournai, and Valenciennes, captured by the Allies, from their list.

upon the course of the final disaster. Along the line of the British thrust the only serious resistance encountered was that which checked the Twenty-second Corps of the First Army by the Honnelle River between Valenciennes and Mons. At this point the German garrison at the end of the Tournai salient was some twenty miles in the rear of the forces of attack advancing towards Bavai and the Mons Canal. General von Quast had to hold the ground by the Honnelle River until his troops retired from the Tournai region, where the floods they had created in the Scheldt valley, by saving them from direct attack, had induced them to stay too long. For the fourth time the great mass of rested troops was directed across the Mons Canal upon the northern flank of the great British wedge driving at Maubeuge. The ensuing Battle of the Honnelle River

resembled the action along the Aunelle stream. The British forces first broke through the ordinary rearguards and climbed the heights leading through brook valleys towards Dour and Malplaquet. A strong, new German force arrived and gave battle, and the advanced British forces withdrew over the stream. Reinforced in turn, they renewed the attack, once more forced the passage, and charged up the hills; then the German commander used all his available strength, and, drawing on the troops as far as the Dutch frontier and with a great mass of guns, attempted a counter-offensive to save Maubeuge.

As on previous occasions of a similar kind, Sir Henry Horne and Sir Julian Byng combined in mass to defeat the enemy. In spite of the streaming ground, guns were hauled forward with an abundance of shell, and on November 6th, while the Canadians stormed **Guards Division** into Baisieux and Quivrechain, the British **storm Bavai** troops carried Ancre, and forced the Honnelle River for the third time; and the Guards, after breaking enemy counter-attacks, closed upon the cross-roads of Bavai.

In the night the northern German armies accepted defeat. The thick, wet weather had not saved their moving columns of men and vehicles from the British airmen in daylight and darkness. They descended in the rain over the packed roads, and completed the demoralisation of the German forces by incessant machine-gun and bomb attacks. The German hold upon the Mons line weakened. In the early morning of November 7th the Guards Division stormed into Bavai, and with the 62nd Division closed upon Maubeuge.

Thereupon, General von Quast evacuated Tournai and all the line of the Scheldt after pouring into Audenarde a great number of gas-shells, causing death and suffering to some four thousand starving women, children, and old men.

Apparently, some German generals were seized with homicidal frenzy, and wished to kill non-combatants because armed foes were beyond their power of vengeance, clearly foreshadowing that the leading military men in Germany, who remained in command under the Socialistic and Democratic National Assembly, were as complete incarnations of the spirit of evil as were known in recorded history. They and their armies and their country were absolutely beaten.

AVENGERS OF THE "OLD CONTEMPTIBLES."
Pipers playing Canadian troops into the temporary barracks allotted to them on their arrival in Mons on the great morning of November 11th, 1918. It was the first time since the famous retreat in 1914 that the inhabitants had seen British troops other than prisoners of war

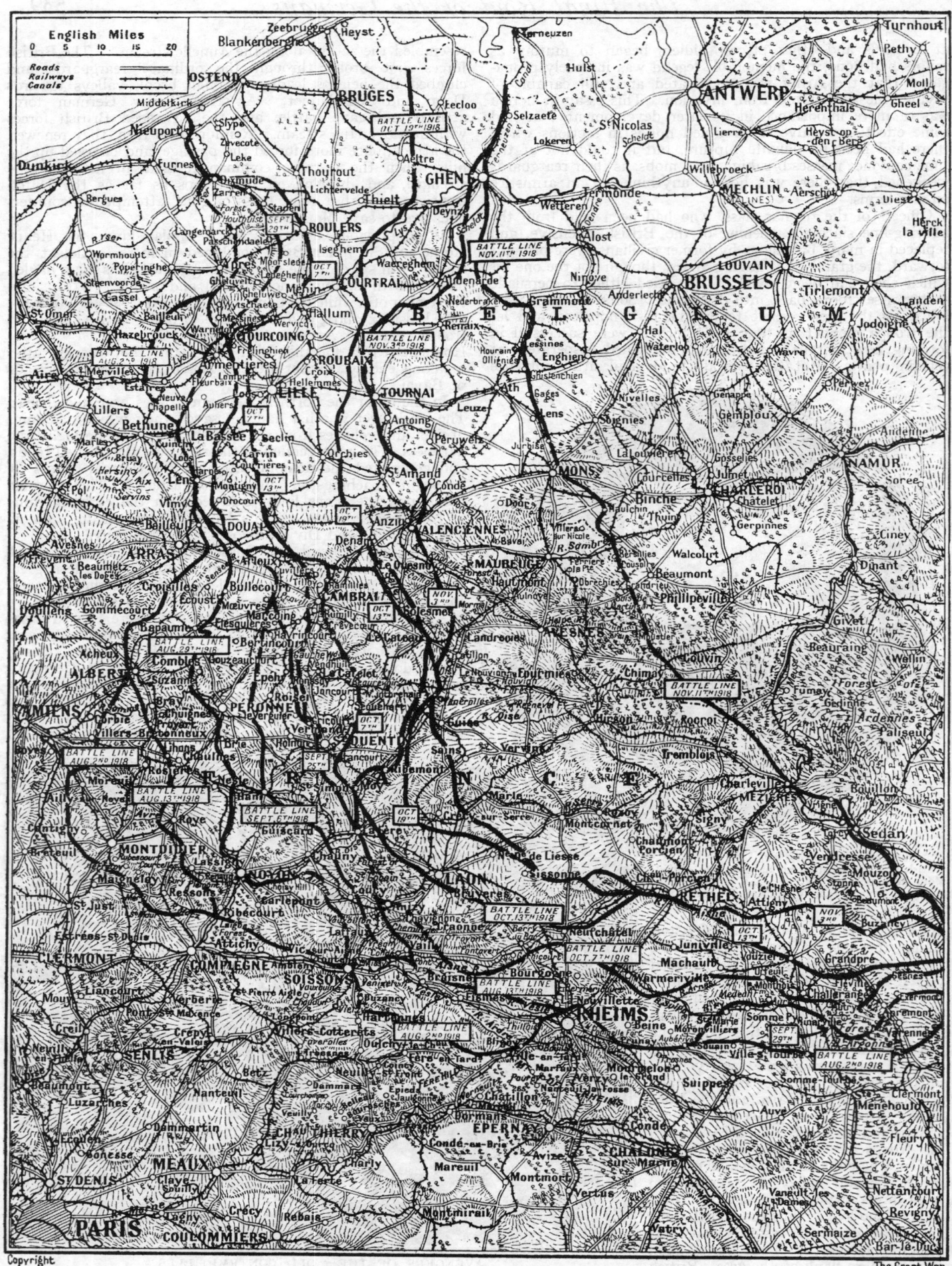

LAST STAGES OF THE ALLIES' ADVANCE TO THE VICTORY LINE ON THE WESTERN FRONT.

The Great War

Some of the men were in mutiny, others were fleeing in disorder, and it was patent that every wrong done would aggravate the victors' terms of peace; yet the maddened miscreants, in their final agony of despair, made their first atrocities in Dinant and Louvain seem like accidents when compared with their last displays of irrational devilry. They did not even commit suicide after the last explosions of murderous feeling. There was a strong streak of cowardice in these Prussian bullies, who made soldiers feel as sailors felt towards German seamen—that it was almost a disgrace to belong to the same profession of arms.

During the night of November 7th the old fortress of Condé was evacuated by the enemy, and the First Corps of the Fifth British Army, and the Eighth Corps of the First Army, under Sir Arthur Holland and Sir A. Hunter-Weston respectively, crossed the Scheldt on a wide front below Antoing. Farther north the enemy began a movement of withdrawal by Renaix, and abandoned the western part of Tournai in immediate preparation for an enforced rapid retreat from the city, which was completed the following day, when the Black Watch swung through the picturesque cathedral city to the music of their bagpipes, followed by English troops with bands and the flourish of trumpets.

The fortified town of Maubeuge was carried by the Grenadier Guards before dawn on November 9th, after some fierce fighting by the outer fortifications of the

A LEADER IN THE FINAL FIGHTING.
Lieut.-General Sir Cameron D. Shute, K.C.B., C.M.G., who commanded the Fifth Corps of the British Third Army in the attack on Mormal Forest at the beginning of November, 1918.

CORPS COMMANDER AT MORMAL FOREST.
Lieut.-General Sir George M. Harper, K.C.B., D.S.O., who commanded the Fourth Corps of the British Third Army in the great battle of early November, 1918, for the possession of Mormal Forest.

British commander saved his troops, and also saved France. There was something very appropriate in the fact that the war practically ended with the Grenadier Guards, representing Sir Douglas Haig's original forces that had fought by the fortress in August, 1914, storming into the strategic railway centre on which all the enemy's fugitive centre armies had depended for food and munitions.

While the Third British Army conquered Maubeuge, the Fourth Army, having taken Avesnes, marched towards the Belgian frontier above Trelon Forest towards Sivry. Cavalry, cyclists, and tunnellers, expert in the discovery of road mines, scouted in front of foot and guns. On the right of General Rawlinson's troops their old companions of the First French Army, after making a swift advance to Nouvion on November 6th, and sweeping through Vervins on the same day, sent out their cavalry and armoured motor-cars to maintain contact with the vanishing Teutons, reaching the railway junction of Hirson on November 8th.

On the same day the more southerly railway junction of Liart, connecting the old Aisne lines with the Namur and Metz communications, was taken by the Third French Army.

In front of the heroic Fourth French Army, under General Gouraud, the Germans broke and ran behind the protecting water of the Meuse. Le Chesne was taken on November 4th. The next day the thrust made by General Humbert's French and Italian divisions

HERO OF EPIC AIR FIGHTS.
Major W. G. Barker, V.C., hero of the air fighting in the Mormal Forest Battle of November 4th, 1918. Though badly wounded, he fought sixty enemy aeroplanes, destroying ten of them.

great entrenched camp in which a large French force had been captured in September, 1914. Maubeuge was a memorable place from many points of view. The failure of its forts against the German siege artillery made the First Battle of the Marne indecisive by allowing the enemy to stand along the Aisne with his heavy artillery, race to the Flemish coast, and threaten the Channel ports.

Old memories of Maubeuge, however, were not altogether tragic. Into this doomed entrenched camp General von Kluck had designed to drive Sir John French's forces after encircling them in his famous ring of iron. By refusing the shelter of the frontier fortress the

into the enemy's flank above Rethel brought about a deep and quick withdrawal from the fortifications along the Upper Aisne. General Gouraud joined in the pursuit with his left wing, but did not press on that side. His tactics were larger, more practical, and more romantic. He kept his main forces on the right, by the road he had won through Le Chesne, and struck out towards the Meuse at the town of glorious and tragic fame, Sedan, where Turenne was born and the Second Empire buried.

The military importance of Sedan was restored by the invader's occupation of Luxemburg. For the town, with Mézières and Charleville,

REWARDED AFTER DEATH.
Lieut.-Colonel John N. Marshall, V.C., M.C., who was awarded the Victoria Cross posthumously for his great heroism at the fighting across the Oise and Sambre Canal, beyond Catillon.

LLL

TERRAIN OF THE BATTLE OF MAUBEUGE.
On November 9th the Third British Army captured Maubeuge, the enemy's main strategic railway centre. This victory cut the last of his important lateral communications, and in effect split the German forces into two parts, one on each side of the Ardennes barrier.

commanded the way from France into the Ardennes, through the rugged gap of the Semois River and the old border territory of the Dukes of Bouillon. General Gouraud worked towards the frontier towns on the Meuse, down the Bar stream, and over the ridges of the Vence tributary, with his cavalry riding after the enemy. In the meantime the American forces quickened their pace over the high wooded land between the Bar and the Meuse, storming the great 338-metre height by Stonne, an outlying eminence of the Argonne Forest ridges, and the road centre of Beaumont, by the Meuse, on November 5th.

At the same time the passage of the river was forced southward at Dun, where the Heights of the Meuse were gallantly carried. Here the 5th Division and the National Guard, recruited from Wisconsin and Michigan, steadily fought onward and upward for three days, taking Lion-devant-Dun and the hills by Brandeville. Other American and French forces, operating from Verdun, assailed the enemy from the south, while he was being fiercely pressed from the west, with

Heights of the Meuse carried

the result that all the Heights of the Meuse were wrested from the stricken invader by the afternoon of November 8th. The German troops under General von Fuchs were thrown back nearly four miles on a front of some nine miles, by Damvillers, into the bog of the Woevre plain. There the Second American Army began to enter into action in the direction of Metz, winning ways of approach by the old Hindenburg line extending from behind St. Mihiel.

This, however, was in preparation for the stroke through Lorraine arranged for November 14th. Of more historic interest was the race to Sedan between the Americans and French. The French made a wider sweep northward to Mézières, reaching it on November 7th. The Americans drove straight northward at Sedan, the 42nd (or Rainbow) Division working forward with a French force on its left,

and the 1st Division fighting along the Meuse and looking for a crossing. The weather was continuously wet and misty, but the troops were tense with excitement. The thought of executing one of the most remarkable of ironic strokes animated them. They quickened their advance, and where the ground was clogging their field-artillery they reduced the batteries from four to two guns, and used double teams of horses to precipitate the rush of the pursuit.

In the afternoon of November 6th, as the 1st American Division came round the bend of the Meuse, it ran into the Rainbow Division, and the patrols of the two forces gallantly competed for the honour of the first entry into the western suburb of Sedan. Which won is a matter of dispute that later history will have to decide. Only the Torcy suburb was reached, marking an advance of twenty-five miles since November 1st by the First American Army. As the bridges were broken, and the enemy was standing on the heights on the other edge of the town, the Meuse could not be crossed. But the German communications between Lorraine and Belgium were cut.

The invading host was visibly broken into two pieces. The part trying to defend itself between Ghent and Rocroi had lines of retreat converging on Namur and Liège. A mass of cavalry, preceded by light storming cars, might cut the ways of withdrawal in Belgium by a terrifying raid. The part struggling south of Rocroi was cornered by the Ardennes course of the Meuse, in front of a great rugged highland, almost without practicable traffic way, and cross-cut by gorges of the Semois River. The Allies, on the other hand, had several means of taking fiercely in the flank, from the Longwy gap and Arlon, the disrupted hostile columns mazed in the narrow, roundabout byways of the Ardennes. And there was the larger envelopment moving through Lorraine which Marshal Foch in person had prepared.

The situation which the elder Moltke arranged by Sedan in September, 1870, bore no comparison with that obtaining by the same town in November, 1918. Where a hundred thousand Frenchmen had been trapped, two million **Huns' war-machine falling to pieces** Germans were broken into hopeless fragments. From Villers-Bretonneux to the Meuse their centre had been driven straight for a hundred miles upon the rocky mass of the Ardennes and there smashed, and their wings were failing from exhaustion.

On the British front all the German war-machine was falling to pieces. The beaten rearguards were composed of ragged, despairing men, lost to all sense of discipline, unwilling to fight any more, and full of bitterness against their ruler and their officers. Their horses were bare-ribbed through starvation and their transport rotting beyond repair. As they fled they plundered farms of live-stock to feed themselves until they reached Germany. Very quickly they moved, destroying less of their own abandoned war material as they went.

When Tournai was recovered on November 8th the British cavalry had to gallop to find the enemy, and only after a ride of ten miles to the outskirts of the town of Ath, on the turned line of the Dendre, was contact resumed with the northern German forces on November 10th. The weather had cleared two days previously, which did not improve matters from the enemy's point of view. All his movements were more easily and minutely traced day and night, and pursuing attack from the air broke what moral remained generally among his troops.

Belgian and French forces, having won bridge-heads along the Scheldt between Ghent and Audenarde, began an advance towards Brussels, where the German troops were mutinying. In this movement the Second British Army took a leading part, sweeping through Renaix on November 9th, and reaching the edge of Grammont the following day. Below Grammont the old moat of the Dendre, famous in Marlborough's campaign, was carried in a leap. The East Lancashires of the 55th Division, who held Givenchy in the last struggle for the Channel ports, carried the barricades of Ath, under cover of Lewis-gun fire from the upper part of a house, won the bridge intact, and shot the men trying to blow it up ; then, as King Edward's Horse encircled the town, the Germans fled in an utter mob. There is reason to suppose they were starving in this sector, transport and ration services having completely broken down for some days, in regard to the rearguard troops especially.

Only round Mons was there any resistance of importance by the enemy as the Canadians of the First Army worked round it from the north, west, and south. The picked German garrison, being based on a railway junction, were well supplied and fed, their task being to save the flank of the retiring, half-demoralised northern armies. There was no military need to accelerate the attack on them, as Mons was being deeply outflanked southward, where the divisions of Sir Henry Rawlinson and Sir Julian Byng had still to move swiftly to keep in touch with the completely shattered enemy.

The Canadians, however, were resolved that the war should not end for the British before the town was reached where it began. They swore to have Mons even at the cost of their lives. They closed upon the town in the evening of November 10th, and in early darkness of the day of the armistice the Montreal Highland battalion of the 7th Canadian Brigade recovered Mons.

East of Ath, in the morning of November 11th, 1918, the East Lancashires and King Edward's Horse were standing for battle along the road to Brussels, with their 60-pounders, 6 in. howitzers, and field-artillery ranged for the barrage. When the armistice order reached divisional headquarters only an hour and twenty-six minutes of war remained. So the battle was not fought. Yet just before eleven o'clock in the morning—the time fixed for cessation of action—a German gun was firing on a patrol of King Edward's Horse, and the troopers resolved to capture it against time. Their commander stood with watch in hand during this deed of retribution. As the troopers reached the piece and killed two of the crew the officer called " Eleven o'clock ! " and the remaining Teutons were allowed to escape.

Dramatic race against time

In the Verdun sector there was an American offensive strongly mounted from the direction of Douaumont Fort. Orders were given the previous night for the action to continue until armistice was proclaimed. In the darkness there was a heavy bombardment by the artillery on both sides, at daybreak the shell fire increased, and at half-past nine the American troops advanced and covered a mile and a half of ground. At last a minute separated many men from a grave or the hospital. Then silence fell upon the shell-swept hills, and Verdun held festival.

The Belgians recaptured Ghent four hours before the armistice, the enemy having evacuated the city at two o'clock in the morning. The French recovered Mézières entirely the evening before the fighting ended, but in tragic circumstances that made General Gouraud's veterans sorry they could not continue the attack across the Meuse which they had opened between Sedan and Mézières. After the hour at which German representatives signed the armistice agreement, and just before the time for ceasing hostilities, a tempest of poison-gas shell and incendiary shell fell upon the twenty thousand townspeople whom the assassins had pillaged, oppressed, and starved. In the early morning of November 11th the hospital, of which the wretches knew the exact position, was completely burnt by incendiary shell.

That a vanquished army asking for mercy should be capable of such an action seems inexplicable. Up to the last minute brutes the Germans were and brutes they remained.

The day of the armistice burnt into the mind of the French soldier along the Meuse. While the French people rejoiced in villages and cities, he was quiet. His thoughts were interpreted by M. Georges Clemenceau when President Woodrow Wilson arrived in France, keen to establish a working distinction between the Imperial Government of Germany and the German people. The Teutons' last outburst of atrocity cost them dear ; it was one of the things that prevented them from winning the peace after losing the war.

At eleven o'clock on Monday, November 11th, 1918, the allied line ran along the Terneuzen Canal and beyond Ghent towards Nederbrakel, on the Ninove road. It passed beyond Nederbrakel, held by Sir Herbert Plumer's troops, to Grammont, and along the Dendre to Lessines and east of Hourain, where the British had forced the river. The Fifth Army, under Sir William Birdwood, had its line through Ollignies, Ghisenglise, and Gages.

Victorious Allies' final positions

The First British Army was beyond Jurbise and stretching past Mons to the Binche road by Haulchin. The front of the Third Army ran by Villers-sire-Nicole, beyond Bersillies and Ferrière-la-Petite and Obrechies. The Fourth Army stood on a line by Cousoire, Grandrieu, the Bois de Martinsart, Sivry, and Grande Helpe river to Moustier, the junction with the First French Army. Cavalry patrols, however, were much farther east, and a great depth of ground was unoccupied by the enemy.

The French were well across the Belgian frontier beyond Chimay, and above Rocroi were the Italians, and along the Meuse the French, and across it at Vrigne and in the western suburb of Sedan. A little southward the Americans held the Meuse line, reaching with French units the outskirts of Stenay, crossing the river above the Heights of the Meuse, stretching across the Woevre to Marcheville and St. Hilaire and Dommartin Wood to the Moselle west of the Metz forts. Thence the front ran without change to Thann, in Alsace.

PILLAGE ON THE WHOLESALE SCALE.

Railway waggons loaded with stolen property of every conceivable kind which the Allies' rapid pursuit prevented the Huns from despatching to Germany. Nearly three thousand of these trucks were abandoned at Auer.

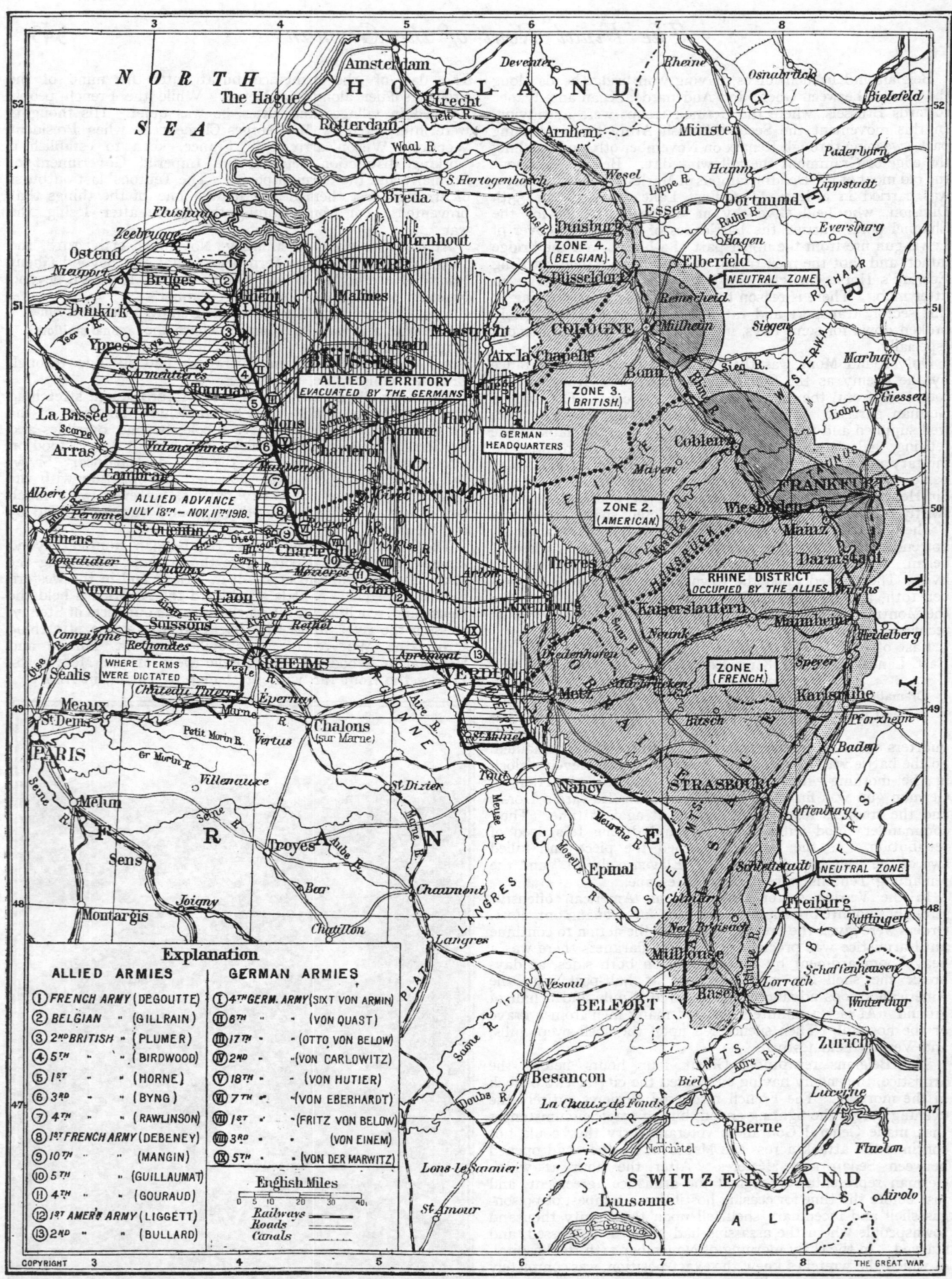

SURVEY OF THE RESULTS ACHIEVED BY THE ALLIES' OFFENSIVE, JULY TO NOVEMBER, 1918.

The Arabic figures in circles indicate the approximate positions reached by the Allied Armies, after four months' continuous fighting, on the day the armistice took effect: the Roman numerals indicate those of the German

Armies. Along the Rhine are shown the zones and bridgeheads occupied under the terms of the armistice by the several armies of the Allies, and, beyond, the neutral zones on the east bank of the river.

ALLIED COMMISSIONERS

CHAPTER CCLXXXVI.

ARRIVING AT SPA.

THE SURRENDER OF GERMANY.

By Edward Wright.

German Attempts at Peace of Compromise—Lure to Western Allies to Betray Russia—Austrian Emperor Tries to Win Over France—Pope Benedict Proposes Peace—Erzberger and Reichstag Peace Resolution—Kaiser Brings Majority Socialists Over to Aggressive Action—Grand Political Comedy of Brest Litovsk Negotiations—Lloyd George and President Wilson Vainly Try to Save Russia—British Premier's Trade Unionist Speech on War Aims—President Wilson's Famous Fourteen Points—American Design to Separate German Liberals from German Reactionaries—The Mount Vernon Declaration on Fourth of July—President Wilson's Promise of September 27th to Prevent Economic Boycott—Ludendorff Ready for Unconditional Surrender—Max of Baden Constructs a Democratic Party for Armistice Proposal—Why President Wilson Played for Time—Failure of German Propaganda of Desperation—Outbreak of Revolution in Navy—Allies Consent to Treat—Meeting in Compiègne Forest—Full Terms of the Armistice Treaty—Concessions Made to the Enemy over Rhineland—Cunning Trick by Erzberger in the Polish Conditions—Strong German Party Try to Denounce Armistice—Hindenburg Concentrates Against Poland—Marshal Foch Prepares for Battle—Germans Sign New and Severer Terms.

I N the course of the struggle Germany made many attempts to negotiate a peace of compromise, either through some neutral representative or through Austria-Hungary. All she practically offered in the first period of the war was to return to the state of affairs before the outbreak of hostilities, evacuating the occupied territory in Belgium and France in return for the restitution of her overseas possessions. In December, 1916, the Central Empires seemed inclined to make some concessions to France and Italy, but required the Western Allies to betray Russia.

There was a profound difference in the tone of the negotiations opened through Austria-Hungary with France in March, 1917, when the first effects of the Russian Revolution were felt in Middle Europe. The Teutonic and Magyar nobility were then genuinely alarmed in respect to their own estates and political power, as they could no longer pretend to their Socialistic parties that they were fighting against Russian autocracy. The entrance of the United States into the struggle further perturbed the spirit of the governing classes of the Central Empires.

The young Austrian Emperor Charles addressed a letter to the President of the French Republic, through Prince Sixte of Parma, a relative of the Austrian Empress, pleading for peace, and stating that he would promote the just French claims to Alsace and Lorraine.

L. Russell.
VICE-ADMIRAL SIR ROSSLYN WEMYSS, G.C.B.
Sir Rosslyn Wemyss represented the British Navy at the Conferences when the Allies settled the armistice terms, and was present when Marshal Foch handed them to the Germans.

The claims of Italy were not mentioned in the letter, and nothing was said regarding Poland, the Baltic provinces, and Russia generally. The letter appears to have been written with the knowledge of Count Czernin, the then new Austro-Hungarian Minister for Foreign Affairs, who in turn had an understanding in the matter with Baron von Kühlmann, the German Minister representing the enlightened selfishness of German business circles against the bull-necked Prussian caste.

The Allies did not pursue the negotiations with Austria-Hungary, after discovering that the offer to the Western Powers was not made in the desire for a genuine settlement of European affairs, but to profit by the weakness of Russia. A considerable time afterwards General Smuts went to Switzerland for a discussion with Count Mensdorff, the former Austro-Hungarian Ambassador in London, but found that the Hapsburg Government was still acting merely as the agent for a Germanic policy of political and economic conquests in the East.

In the meantime the Austrians, who desired to save their polity and escape from the rigorous overlordship of the Hohenzollerns, engineered a widespread movement for a general settlement on the basis of peace without annexations and indemnities. The Polish Superior of the Jesuit Order came to Switzerland, being greatly concerned in the interests of the Church at home, where rich ecclesiastical estates were threatened by the contagious growth of Socialism of the Russian

545

sort, and much perturbed by the power which the Orthodox Churches might win if the democratic Slav movements were successful. There was also the menace of the murderous, confiscating anti-religious movement among some powerful parties of Russian Revolutionists, which might lead to violent anti-clerical outbreaks in Poland and Austria-Hungary.

Pope Benedict took up the movement for peace, and the Roman Catholic party in Germany, representing the rich industrial and wine-growing regions of the Rhine basin and the peasantry and landowners of Bavaria and other southern States, were engaged in the interests of the general peace. Herr Erzberger, a bustling, intriguing politician of the second order in the Roman Catholic party, who worked among the Catholic Trade Unions at home and conducted clerical plots with reactionary Italians from Switzerland, was appointed promoter of the Catholic peace, together with Herr Sudeküm, a Socialist of the Imperial school.

Erzberger had to attack the Protestant Junker party, the military dictator, General von Ludendorff, and the men of Grand-Admiral von Tirpitz's school. After some negotiations with the Socialists, Radicals, and Liberals, he opened his campaign in a secret sitting of the Grand Committee of the Reichstag on July 8th, 1917. By a very effective and damaging criticism of the submarine policy of the German High Command he shook the confidence of the Reichstag in the entire conduct of the war.

Erzberger opens peace campaign

The effect of his speech was tremendous. Not only did it produce a panic in the Reichstag, but it extended the panic outside to business circles and, what was worse, to the Prussian bureaucracy. The large majority of the three great parties—

Socialists, Catholics, and Radicals—agreed together on a resolution of peace and the lasting conciliation of nations, without "annexations or political, economic, and financial oppression."

The German Emperor returned to Berlin, summoned the Crown Prince, Hindenburg, and Ludendorff to a Council of State, and for some ten days the continuance of the war hung in the balance against the project of peace. The matter, however, was not to be decided by the majority vote of the Reichstag, who succeeded in passing their resolution on July 19th, 1917. It was to be decided by events in the field.

Conciliation by reform policy

There can be no doubt that the German Emperor and his Chancellor, Dr. Bethmann-Hollweg, with General Ludendorff and Field-Marshal von Hindenburg, favoured the course which Herr Erzberger adopted in the first week of July. Instead of being their opponent, he was their spokesman and agent. The Kaiser published a demand that the democratisation of Prussia should be at once undertaken. The scheme was to appease the Western Powers and the United States by hastily constructing a façade of free government in order to facilitate peace negotiations.

When, however, these preparations for practical surrender, under conditions, were being made, the German High Command was in doubt how to meet the double offensive from the east and from the west. In the east General Brussiloff was attacking with a great force which had been re-armed by the Western Allies with machinery of battle much superior to that which the Russians had provided for themselves in other actions. In the west the Fifth

THE LITTLE WOOD WHEREIN THE ALLIES' ARMISTICE TERMS WERE DICTATED TO GERMANY
Sentry on guard in the Forest of Compiègne, between Choisy-au-Bac and Rethondes, where Marshal Foch presented to the enemy parlementaires the terms on which he was prepared to grant an armistice. The fateful meeting took place in one of the coaches of the train that had brought the Marshal. That train and the train in which the enemy representatives had journeyed are to be seen in the background through the trees.

WHERE FATEFUL CONFERENCE TOOK PLACE.
The Grand Hotel Britannique at Spa, where the International Armistice Commission sat to settle the details of execution of the terms dictated by Marshal Foch on November 8th, 1918.

British Army, under Sir Hubert Gough, had opened a campaign against the Flanders Ridge, threatening to turn all the Flemish coast and the submarine and destroyer bases there.

These were the reasons why Herr Erzberger, with a false show of political independence, promoted the peace resolution in the Reichstag. As soon as the Russian offensive ended by the Russian soldiers walking away and selling their guns, while the British campaign in Flanders was checked by bad weather and unsuccessful generalship, the peace resolution of the Majority Party vanished like rags of camouflage in a hurricane of fire.

The German Emperor had a public interview with Scheidemann, David, Sudeküm, and other Majority Socialists. He convinced them that the piratical submarine operations would succeed while the war was being won on land. In more private meetings the leaders of the Roman Catholic and Radical parties were also convinced that the war was still going well for the German people. General von Ludendorff again became practical dictator, governing foreign policy through his political department, and after appointing a nominee to the Chancellorship in the person of a bureaucrat, Michaelis, he found a better figurehead in Count Hertling, one of the chiefs of the Roman Catholic Party.

Germany's desire for peace on terms in the first week of July, 1917, had

undoubtedly been genuine at the time it was expressed. When, however, the new Russian armies broke in the wildest and most complete of moral disasters, no responsible body of Germans had the slightest idea of abandoning the struggle. Peace negotiations were indeed continued. According to the Russian Attaché at Berne, there was a meeting of friendly and hostile financiers in Switzerland, at which the Teutonic representatives proposed that France, Italy, and Great Britain should be placated at the expense of Russia.

On August 1st, 1917, Pope Benedict XV. made peace proposals, condemning the war as a useless massacre, and suggesting that Germany should give Belgium another scrap of paper, guaranteeing her political and economic independence. In September, 1917, the German Government sent, through a neutral diplomatic channel, a message that they would be glad to open negotiations for peace with Great Britain. Mr. Arthur Balfour, as Foreign Secretary of State, informed the Allied and Associated Powers of the communication received, and replied to the enemy that he would be prepared to receive any communications, so that the British Cabinet could discuss it with its Allies. Nothing further was heard from Germany, and although negotiations were continued by Austria-Hungary they did not come to anything.

Brest Litovsk political farce

When on November 28th, 1917, the Bolshevist leaders of Russia opened parley with the Central Powers for an armistice and a treaty of peace, there followed a grand political comedy, in the course of which the British and American Governments were to some extent duped. The German and Austrian Foreign Secretaries, Baron von Kühlmann and Count Czernin, were bent on making the negotiations with the Bolshevists, South Russians, and Poles a trap for snaring the Allies. They professed to be ready to agree to a general peace, without annexations or indemnities, and the Russian delegates interrupted negotiations for ten days, from December 25th, 1917, to January 4th, 1918, in order that all belligerent nations should have an opportunity of taking part in the Brest Litovsk proceedings for ending the war.

One of the results of this remarkable intrigue on the part of the Germanic Powers and their Bolshevist agents in Russia was to alarm the former leader of the British House of Lords, Lord Lansdowne, and induce him to write and agitate for a peace by compromise with Germany.

As a former Secretary for Foreign Affairs, Leader of the Second Chamber, and chief of the Unionist Party, Lord

WHERE GERMAN MILITARY PRIDE WAS LAID LOW.
Headquarters at Spa of the German delegates to the Armistice Commission, with a German sentry on duty and a German car, flying the white flag, coming out of the gateway. The town had long been the site of the German General Headquarters, and it was thence that the Kaiser fled to Holland.

Lansdowne was a man of some influence. His action, however, was so contrary to the general policy of the nation that it lost him all power and authority, and he fell into insignificance. He was moved by the fear of the general spread of Bolshevism, which was one of the principal weapons of secret intrigue used by the Teutons and Magyars. Having promoted, financed, and directed the Bolshevist movement, the governors of the Central Empires employed this engine of intrigue directly in conquering Russia and indirectly in attempting to dismay the leading men of the allied nations. Lord Lansdowne earned the peculiar distinction of being practically the only man of importance in the Grand Alliance who fell before the class intrigues of the enemy.

Yet the Prime Minister of Great Britain and the President of the United States were not uninfluenced by the Brest Litovsk comedy. Both Mr. Lloyd George and President Wilson thought that Lenin, Trotsky, Radek, **Disintegration** and scores of persons with German names **of Russia** and Russian aliases were genuinely perturbed by the heavy terms imposed by the German and Austrian Governments. When all pretence of a peace in accordance with the Reichstag resolution was lifted, and the creatures in German pay were called to account by their masters, it was seen that Russia was being dissolved into warring chaos.

From her were detached Finland, Esthonia, Courland, and Lithuania, part of White Russia, and the rich wheatlands and coalfields of Southern Russia. Poland was robbed of settled Polish territory, and the Baltic peasantry were placed under the reinforced tyranny of their German barons. A population of 66,000,000 persons, with territory amounting to 600,000 square miles, was detached from Russia in the peace without annexations and indemnities.

All available food supplies in Southern Russia were designed to be taken by force from the peasantry, great raiding parties of German and Austrian cavalry being used for the purpose. Furthermore, measures were taken, by Bolshevists acting under German orders, to destroy the machinery in Russian factories, so as to place Russia in absolute dependence upon German manufacturers, thus ensuring the Teutonic exploitation of all territories of the old Russian Empire. Such were the circumstances in which Mr. Lloyd George and President Wilson began vain endeavours to convince the Bolshevists of Russia and the German and Austro-Hungarian peoples that a lasting general peace could be made on fair terms.

On January 5th, 1918, in an address to Trade Unionists, Mr. Lloyd George published his peace terms. Among them were the independence of Belgium, Serbia, and Montenegro; the restoration of Alsace and Lorraine to France; the independence of Poland; Home Rule for the Slav races of Austria-Hungary; the restoration of Italian and Rumanian territory to Italy and Rumania; Turkish possession of Constantinople and internationalisation of the Dardanelles; recognition of the nationality of Arabia, **President Wilson's** Armenia, Mesopotamia, Syria, and Pales- **Fourteen Points** tine; the placing of German colonies under administrations acceptable to the natives; reparation for injuries done in violation of international law, and establishment of a League of Nations.

Directly inspired by the programme of Mr. Lloyd George, President Wilson on January 8th, 1918, delivered a message to Congress, in which he reduced the programme of the world's peace to the following fourteen points:

1. Open covenants of peace openly arrived at after which there shall be no private international understandings of any kind, but diplomacy shall proceed always frankly and in the public view.

2. Absolute freedom of navigation upon the seas outside territorial waters, alike in peace and in war, except as the seas may be closed in whole or in part by international action for the enforcement of international covenants.

3. The removal so far as possible of all economic barriers, and the establishment of an equality of trade conditions among all the nations consenting to the peace, and associating themselves for its maintenance.

4. Adequate guarantees given and taken that national armaments will be reduced to the lowest point consistent with domestic safety.

5. A free, open-minded, and absolutely impartial adjustment of all Colonial claims based upon a strict observance of the principle that in determining all such questions of sovereignty the interests of the populations concerned must have equal weight with the equitable claims of the Government whose title is to be determined.

6. The evacuation of all Russian territory and such a settlement of all questions affecting Russia as will secure the best and freest cooperation of the other nations of the world in obtaining for her an unhampered and unembarrassed opportunity for the independent determination of her own political development and national policy, and assure her of a sincere welcome into the society of free nations under institutions of her own choosing; and more than a welcome assistance also of every kind that she may need and may herself desire. The treatment accorded Russia by her sister nations in the months to come will be the acid test of their good will, of their comprehension of her needs, as distinguished from their own interests, and of their intelligent and unselfish sympathy.

7. Belgium, the whole world will agree, must be evacuated and restored without any attempt to limit the sovereignty which she enjoys in common with all other free nations. No other single act will serve as this will serve to restore confidence among the nations in the laws which they have themselves set and determined for the government of their relations with one another. Without this healing act the whole structure and validity of international law is for ever impaired.

8. All French territory should be freed and the invaded portions restored, and the wrong done to France by Prussia in 1871 in the matter of Alsace-Lorraine, which has unsettled the peace of the world for nearly fifty years, should be righted, in order that peace may once more be made secure in the interest of all.

9. A readjustment of the frontiers of Italy should be effected along clearly recognisable lines of nationality.

10. The peoples of Austria-Hungary, whose place among the nations we wish to see safeguarded and assured, should be accorded the first opportunity of autonomous development.

11. Rumania, Serbia, and Montenegro should be evacuated, occupied territories restored, Serbia accorded free and secure access to the sea, and the relations of the several Balkan States to one another determined by friendly counsel along historically-established lines of allegiance and nationality, and international guarantees of the political and economic independence and territorial integrity of the several Balkan States should be entered into.

12. The Turkish portions of the present Ottoman Empire should be assured a secure sovereignty, but the other nationalities which are now under Turkish rule should be assured an undoubted security of life and an absolutely unmolested opportunity of autonomous development, and the Dardanelles should be permanently opened as a free passage to the ships and com- **Design behind** merce of all nations under international guarantees. **the programme**

13. An independent Polish State should be erected which should include the territories inhabited by indisputably Polish populations, which should be assured a free and secure access to the sea, and whose political and economic independence and territorial integrity should be guaranteed by international covenant.

14. A general association of nations must be formed under specific covenants for the purpose of affording mutual guarantees of political and territorial independence for great and small States alike.

These famous fourteen points were not drawn up as terms of surrender for an utterly defeated enemy. They were chosen, as President Wilson explained in the course of his speech, with a view to appealing to the prostrate Russian people and inspiring them to withstand the dreadful exactions of the Governments of the Central Empires. Even more particularly and directly was the programme of fourteen points devised by its author in the design to drive a wedge into the political structure of Germany by encouraging Socialists and Liberal elements to maintain in practice the peace resolution of the Reichstag, and exhibit the military party as the only obstacle to universal democracy and lasting peace.

It will be remarked that the French Premier, M. Clemenceau, took no part whatever in these attempts to influence the course of events in Russia, Germany, and Austria-Hungary. M. Clemenceau, while delighting that the British Government publicly proclaimed the war could not end without Alsace and Lorraine returning to France, considered that the President of the United States went dangerously far in trying to obtain by oratory what could only be achieved by fighting. The French point of view was that for all immediate practical purposes the German Government and the German people were one.

The soundness of this view was proved by the way in which the majority parties of the Reichstag received the accomplished fact of the subjugation, disruption, and exploitation of Russia when the Brest Litovsk treaty was signed on March 3rd, 1918. Except by a few German Socialists of the Independent Party, the conquest and partial digestion of Russia, with the total digestion of all the enormous realm of

On the night of November 11th, 1918, the Grand Fleet, so long veiled in mist and silence, burst into triumphant splendour. All the ships lighted up, and for an hour flares, star-shells, and fireworks illuminated the gloom, countless searchlights pierced the skies, and sirens shattered the silence.

How the British Navy, mainstay of the Allied Armies, celebrated the signing of the armistice.

Left to right : Col. Nagai (Japan), Gen. di Robilant, Baron Sonnino, and Sig. Orlando (Italy), Col. House, Gen. Bliss and Mr. Auchincloss (U.S.A.), M. Venizelos (Greece), and M. Vesnitch (Serbia). Sir Douglas Haig sits opposite, leaning back in his chair, with Lord Milner on his right.

Nearing the end. Sessions of the Inter=Allied Conference at Versailles to settle the terms of armistice:

Revolution in Berlin. It was on November 9th, 1918, the day when the flight of the Kaiser made it plain to the whole German proletariat that the military system had broken down, that Germany was declared a Republic.

Herr Scheidemann proclaiming the German Republic to a Berlin crowd outside the Reichstag.

Sitting on the right-hand side of the table (reading from left to right) are General Belin (France), Marshal Foch, Commander-in-Chief of the Allied Armies, M. Pichon, M. Clemenceau, Mr. Lloyd George, Mr. Bonar Law, Lord Milner, and Field-Marshal Sir Douglas Haig.

Ministers and military representatives of the Allied Powers that brought German Imperialism to the dust.

The next day, Sunday, November 10th, the first meeting of the Berlin Workers' and Sokliers' Council was opened by Herr Barth as President. He greeted the victorious revolt of the Berlin populace, and paid a tribute to the garrison, which had sided with the people in an almost bloodless victory.

The President addressing the Workers' and Soldiers' Council in session inside the Reichstag.

Germans retreating through Brussels, already decked with flags of the victorious Allies.

British cavalry entering Spa, late German H.Q., where the Armistice Commission was sitting.

the Tsar in prospect, was received generally in Germany with a placid satisfaction.

From the Teutonic point of view the war was won. Among the Reichstag parties, General von Ludendorff afterwards received the consent of a majority to the large sacrifice of life required, in the estimate of his Staff, to bring the struggle to an end in Italy, France, and Flanders before the American armies could intervene in strength. The British and American Governments were mistaken in their judgments of the efficacy of their peace offensive against the enemy. Far from their self-denying proposals having any effect upon the course of events, they did not alter in any way the plans of Germany and Austria-Hungary, who took advantage of the dispersal of the allied forces to make tremendous attempts to force a decision at Caporetto, along the Piave, at St. Quentin, along the Lys, and by the Marne.

Thereupon President Woodrow Wilson withdrew his peace programme of the fourteen points. At the Fourth of July celebration at Mount Vernon, the burial-place of Washington, he laid a new and more rigorous policy of peace before the Diplomatic Corps and an American audience. After stating that the enemy's plot was written plain upon every scene and every act of the supreme tragedy, he renounced all negotiations for a compromise with "the blinded rulers of Prussia." Reducing his programme from fourteen to four points, he definitely fixed, with the approval of the American nation, the following ends of the war:

First, the destruction of every arbitrary power anywhere that can separately, secretly, and of its single choice disturb the peace of the world, or, if it cannot be presently destroyed, at the least its reduction to virtual impotence.

Second, the settlement of every question, whether of territory, of sovereignty, of economic arrangement, or of political relationship, upon the basis of the free acceptance of that settlement by the people immediately concerned, and not upon the basis of the material interest or advantage of any other nation or people which may desire a different settlement for the sake of its own exterior influence or mastery.

Third, the consent of all nations to be governed in their conduct towards each other by the same principles of honour and of respect for the common law of civilised society that govern **President Wilson's amended programme** the individual citizens of all modern States, and in their relations with one another, to the end that all promises and covenants may be sacredly observed, no private plots or conspiracies hatched, no selfish injuries wrought with impunity, and a mutual trust established upon the handsome foundation of a mutual respect for right.

Fourth, the establishment of an organisation of peace which shall make it certain that the combined power of free nations will check every invasion of right and serve to make peace and justice the more secure by affording a definite tribunal of opinion to which all must submit, and by which every international readjustment that cannot be amicably agreed upon by the peoples directly concerned shall be sanctioned.

All lures to the supposed Liberal elements in the hostile camp were dropped. They were no longer offered, by the United States alone, freedom of navigation in war, adjustment of colonial claims, and escape from general war indemnities. All that President Wilson offered the enemy in another remarkable speech was force without stint and without limit. He rightly felt he had been betrayed by the German majority parties, which had first resolved on a peace without conquest, when their country was in danger, and then had consented to an enormous scheme of political and economic subjugation when the danger seemed to have passed.

In a final historic speech, made in New York on September 27th, 1918, when Bulgaria was surrendering unconditionally and Turkey preparing to follow course, while the western German front was bending at the wings and breaking in the centre, the President of the United States resumed his oratorical offensive against the governing classes of the Central Empires. His clear object on this occasion was to provoke a German revolution, or at least a thorough political transformation. He came forward with a five-point programme, introduced by an attack upon the Imperial German Government. The following is the part of his speech of which the enemy afterwards tried to make use to escape the consequences of defeat:

We are all agreed that there can be no peace obtained by any kind of bargain or compromise with the Governments of the Central Empires, because we have dealt with them already, and have seen them deal with other Governments that were parties to this struggle at Brest Litovsk and Bukarest.

They have convinced us that they are without honour, and do not intend justice. They observe no covenants, accept no principle, but force their own interest. We cannot come to terms with them. They have made it impossible. The German people must by this time be fully aware that we cannot accept the word of those who forced this war upon us. We do not think the same thoughts or speak the same language of agreement. It is of capital importance that we should also be explicitly agreed that no peace shall be obtained by any kind of compromise or abatement of the principles we have avowed as the principles for which we are fighting. There should exist no doubt about that. I am, therefore, going to take the liberty of speaking wth the utmost frankness about the tacit implications that are involved in it.

1. The impartial justice meted out must involve no discrimination between those to whom we wish to be just and those to whom we do not wish to be just. It must be a justice that knows no favourites and knows no standards but the equal rights of the several peoples concerned.

2. No special or separate interest of any single nation or any group of nations can be made the basis of any part of the settlement which is not consistent with the common interest of all.

3. There can be no leagues or alliances or special covenants and understandings within the general and common family of the League of Nations. **No peace with the Hohenzollerns**

4. And, more specifically, there can be no special selfish economic combinations within the League, and no employment of anyform of economic boycott or exclusion except as the power of economic penalty by exclusion from the markets of the world may be vested in the League of Nations itself as a means of discipline and control.

5. All international agreements and treaties of every kind must be made known in their entirety to the rest of the world. Special alliances and economic rivalries and hostilities have been the prolific source in the modern world of the plans and passions that produce war. It would be an insincere as well as an insecure peace that did not exclude them in definite and binding terms.

The confidence with which I venture to speak for our people in these matters does not spring from our traditions merely and the well-known principles of international action which we have always professed and followed.

This last speech by the President was too late to influence the course of the war. On September 29th, as the result of the collapse of Bulgaria, Ludendorff secretly informed the Grand Committee of the Reichstag that the war was lost. Some days before there had begun a panic run on German banks, and extreme agitation throughout the country, indicating that the attacks of the British armies were demoralising the enemy forces and population even before the American and Belgian offensives opened. On the 27th, in a fierce and terrible battle, the British troops broke right through the main Hindenburg line and inflicted a great defeat on the Germans. In the Near East the lightning advance of General Allenby rendered it certain that Turkey would speedily surrender. The failure of the German harvest was known, and indicated the impossibility of enduring the blockade for another year. After several consultations, Prince Max, heir to the Grand Duchy of Baden, was appointed Chancellor for the purpose of negotiating peace, the Majority Party supporting him.

Prince Max was a fierce reactionary, who at times pretended to be a democrat, and laughed at the people he deceived. He was a violent opponent of the peace resolution of July, 1917, but was supposed to be a favourite of the former American Ambassador in Berlin. This was the reason why he was appointed negotiator. He came to Berlin with the scheme for **Max of Baden made Chancellor** making such a statement of German war aims as would be likely to attract the attention of President Wilson. To his dismay he was informed by Ludendorff that there was no time for any further intrigues, as the Army was breaking up, and an armistice must be arranged within forty-eight hours. This panic statement entirely upset the prince's peace policy. After trying to struggle against the views of Ludendorff and Hindenburg, he accepted the situation. He became political chief of the German Empire on October 1st, bringing some of the leading Socialists of the Majority Party into the Government, according to the plan proposed by Ludendorff. On his own initiative Prince Max then endeavoured to induce the Emperor to abdicate, in the hope of saving the country from serious disturbances. The military authorities, however, would not agree to this measure, arguing that, if it were carried out, the armies would break up.

In the night of October 4th the new German Chancellor

KING GEORGE'S "VICTORY" ADDRESS TO THE LORDS AND COMMONS.
On November 19th, 1918, little more than a week after the signing of the armistice, King George and Queen Mary, accompanied by the Prince of Wales and Princess Mary, met the members of the Houses of Lords and Commons in the Royal Gallery at Westminster. In his address his Majesty said : " During the past four years of national stress and anxiety my support has been faith in God and confidence in my people. In the days to come, days of uncertainty and of trial, strengthened by the same help, I shall strive to the utmost of my power to discharge the responsibilities laid upon me to uphold the honour of the Empire and to promote the well-being of the peoples."

Minister, answered that the Majority Party of the Reichstag supported the actions of the new Chancellor, who spoke in the name of the German people. The President's proposal with regard to the invaded territory was agreed to in principle, with the suggestion that a mixed Commission should be appointed to arrange the withdrawal.

Further protracting the preliminaries of negotiation, President Wilson, on October 14th, sent a note to the German Government raising doubts in regard to the democratic character of the new German Government. He insisted that the arbitrary power of the German Emperor should be abolished, and remarked that the sinking of passenger ships at sea and the wanton destruction of cities and villages in France and Flanders were not consonant with the peace proposals being made.

As a matter of fact Ludendorff had recovered from his panic within a week of the opening of the parley. Prince Max was informed by the German military authorities that they had been mistaken in the judgment which they had formed with regard to the situation at the front.

Yet the German Staff must have known perfectly well that the submission of Bulgaria, the imminent surrender of Turkey, and the collapse of Austria, which all of them knew could not be averted, must leave Germany isolated, and in an utterly desperate position.

This extraordinary change of mind on the part of the German Army Command was known to President Wilson and the chief Ministers of the Associated Powers. It was announced by the torpedoing, in the morning of October 10th, of the mail steamer running between Kingston and Holyhead, and by the resumption of horrible gas and high-explosive bombardments of the newly-liberated Flemish and French towns and villages. The deportation of people in occupied territory was resumed, together with the general destruction of buildings, with a view to creating the last trail of desolation behind the retreating invaders. Definite news was also received by the Allied Governments of the restored confidence of the enemy High Command.

As was afterwards explained in the German Constituent Assembly, Ludendorff had been completely overcome by the fact that his armies were beginning to run away from the British forces. When, however, he found that his troops were standing firm against the American attack, and withdrawing in order in Flanders, while **Propaganda of** showing some signs of stiffening along the **desperation** Selle River against Sir Henry Rawlinson's and Sir Julian Byng's armies on October 13th, he determined to fight to the bitter end. Hindenburg remained more doubtful of the German power of resistance, yet he, too, proclaimed that the German Army and the German Fleet would never surrender. The old Field-Marshal, however, had the wisdom to order that all unnecessary destruction should cease, and while refraining for a time from interfering with his more energetic collaborator, he showed some sympathy with the apprehensions of the German Majority Socialists, and gradually became an advocate of their views. It was well that he did so. For something had suddenly been broken that could not be repaired.

sent, through the Swiss Government, a request to President Wilson to open negotiations for peace with belligerent States on the basis of the fourteen points' programme stated in the address to Congress of January 8th, 1918. The Austro-Hungarian Government and the Ottoman Government also forwarded about the same time a similar request to the President of the United States, mentioning the programme of September 27th as well as the fourteen points of January 8th. Prince Max also referred to the September 27th programme in his speech on peace negotiations.

President Wilson did not reply to the Ottoman proposal. He informed the Austro-Hungarian Government he could not adhere to his early programme of peace, because the national independence of Bohemia and Slovakia had been recognised by the United States, thus annulling one of the fourteen points. To the new German Chancellor there was despatched a delaying reply, asking whether Prince Max was speaking merely for the Imperial authorities who had conducted the war, and whether all hostile forces would be withdrawn from occupied territory before the cessation of arms.

On October 12th Dr. Solf, the New German Foreign

Ludendorff could not restore the spirit of either the German Army or the German people. Having terrified his nation by his first urgent appeal for an armistice at any price, he could not prevail against the feelings he had excited. He started a frenzied propaganda among the troops and the public, the most remarkable item of which was the " Durchhalten oder Untergehen " number of the popular weekly paper the " Illustrirte Zeitung." In its " Hold On or Go Under " issue, prepared, under military control, in the second week of October for publication towards the end of the month, an attempt was made to scare the people into a determination to fight to the death.

There were pictures of German workmen being driven by whips to enforced labour in France and Flanders, of flaming German towns and ravaged farms, by which the God of War, no longer Teutonic, was striding, of German Michael being crushed by the heel of Britannia. On the front page was a drawing of a crowd of unarmed wounded soldiers, working women, and aged men, gathered by night under a street lamp, listening to an excited popular orator crying " The fate of Germany is in the hands of all of us ! "

In the articles the working classes were told that the defeat of their country would end all the great schemes for social progress. The peasants were informed that famine and disease would follow military disaster. Clerks were reminded that work and food would be lacking, while merchants and manufacturers were told they would be bankrupt. Appeal was made to the self-interest of every class in the design to evoke a general resolution of spirit.

Far from reviving the courage of the forces and populace, the propaganda of desperation completed the demoralisation of the country. In action the tendency to run or surrender increased, the troops arguing that it was useless to get killed when peace was coming. Yet the negotiations for an armistice had to be maintained, as they had become the only means of preventing an absolute collapse.

The aim of the Government of Prince Max was then to prolong the preliminaries until the military situation was clarified by the successful retreat which the military authorities promised to accomplish. So on both sides there was a diplomatic slowness in exchanging views. On October 20th Dr. Solf, the German Foreign Minister, blandly proposed that the actual standard of power on both sides of the field should form the ground of the armistice arrangements. He, how-

Herr Scheidemann became Minister of Finance immediately after the Revolution.

Herr Ebert, appointed Imperial Chancellor in succession to Prince Max of Baden.

Dr. Solf, Foreign Minister, who had earlier been Secretary for the Colonies.

Dr. David, one of the Majority Socialists in the Reichstag.

Dr. Südekům, Majority Socialist leader in the Reichstag.

Prince Max of Baden, appointed Imperial Chancellor a few weeks before Germany's debacle in the hope that he would be able to negotiate a peace.
GERMAN LEADERS IN TIME OF DEFEAT.

ever, condescended to the assertion that responsible Parliamentary government had definitely replaced the old military policy of Germany.

President Wilson changed his tactics, and gave a quick reply. He accepted the assurance that the Germans had adopted a representative system of government, and, while claiming for the victors unrestricted power to safeguard and enforce the details of the peace, he communicated to the Allies the request for the opening of negotiations on the terms of his address to Congress of January 8th, 1918. On October 24th the Supreme Council of War at Versailles began to consider the American fourteen points in connection with the terms of the armistice to be imposed upon the enemy.

The proceedings, prolonged for a fortnight, were partly a solemn farce and partly an anxious debate. The farce arose from the fact that the German High Command no longer admitted defeat, and did not intend to submit to the conditions of surrender which at first it had implored. The anxiety was due to the clash of views between the Franco-British representatives and the American representatives over the question of the freedom of the seas and claims to indemnification.

While these points were being debated, the military authorities of Germany brought complete disaster upon their country by trying to use the Fleet to save the Army. Amid violent demonstrations at Kiel, submarine flotillas were sent out to wait in ambush for the British Fleet. Then the order was given for all the German High Sea Fleet to put out to sea on October 31st. The practising of manœuvres in the Bight of Heligoland was all that was intended, so the seamen were informed.

No one was deceived by this absurd explanation. Suspicion was further aroused by the fact that most of the older married officers were given leave. Stewards overheard talk by commanders of the coming battle to the death. Far more coal was taken in than was required for manœuvres. To calm the men they were then told that no desperate fleet engagement was intended, but that the ships of the line were steaming out to cover a raid by light cruisers and destroyers upon the British sea communications in the English Channel.

The immediate result was mutiny among the seamen, who saw what was intended and flatly refused to fight. The number of naval officers who sympathised with the mutineers was considerable. They did not see why they should perish unavailingly to save an Army that could not even retreat in good order. When an attempt was made to reduce the men to discipline at Kiel the Revolution broke out.

By November 4th Kiel was the centre of a Soviet movement, despatching missionaries of revolt through Germany. Infantry brought to Kiel were either won over or disarmed, and cavalry forces approaching the port were met with machine-gun fire and defeated and converted. A few officers died defending the Imperial flag, but most of them quietly submitted, some joining the Soviet, and the movement of Revolution spread with extraordinary rapidity to all the ports, and then expanded inland.

In these circumstances, with the German Fleet put out of action by its own men, and the German Army broken into two pieces by the Ardennes Forest and beginning to flee in disordered fragments towards the Rhineland, the Western Allies opened negotiations with the enemy. On November 5th, 1918, Mr. Robert Lansing, the American Secretary of State, communicated to the German Government the following memorandum of observations received from the Allies :

Allies consent to negotiate

The Allied Governments have given careful consideration to the correspondence which has passed between the President of the United States and the German Government.

Subject to the qualifications which follow, they declare their willingness to make peace with the Government of Germany on the terms of peace laid down in the President's address to Congress of January 8th, 1918, and the principles of settlement enunciated in his subsequent addresses.

They must point out, however, that Clause II., relating to what is usually described as the freedom of the seas, is open to various interpretations, some of which they could not accept. They must therefore reserve to themselves complete freedom on this subject when they enter the Peace Conference.

Further, in the conditions of peace laid down in his address to Congress of January 8th, 1918, the President declared that invaded territories must be restored as well as evacuated and freed.

The Allied Governments feel that no doubt ought to be allowed to exist as to what this provision implies. By it they understand that compensation will be made by Germany for all damage done to the civilian population of the Allies and their property by the aggression of Germany by land, by sea, and from air.

[In the 19th clause of the armistice "future claims and demands" were expressly "reserved"—i.e., the Germans were warned that they would have to meet such claims.]

I am instructed by the President, said Mr. Lansing when forwarding the memorandum, to say that he is in agreement with the interpretation set forth in the last paragraph of the memorandum above quoted.

I am further instructed by the President to request you to notify the German Government that Marshal Foch has been authorised by the Government of the United States and the Allied Governments to receive properly accredited representatives of the German Government and to communicate to them the terms of an armistice.

As a matter of fact there was no further need to offer Germany any terms except unconditional surrender. It was unconditional surrender that Ludendorff would have made, if pressed, at the end of September, and although he had fled by Sässnitz to Sweden, leaving Hindenburg the task of bringing the defeated forces back to Germany, his successor candidly admitted at the time that he could not manage the withdrawal, except at the mercy of the victors. It was no longer possible to get men to stand in sufficient numbers, even for fighting rearguard actions at the most critical points.

Germany at the Allies' mercy

The Crown Prince of Prussia started the legend of Germany surrendering without being defeated, in his address of farewell to his army group, when preparing to escape to Holland. According to the view he spread, which was immediately adopted by the Socialists of the Majority Party, as well as by Radical, Liberal, Catholic, and Conservative politicians,

DEFEATED AND DEJECTED GERMANS HOMEWARD BOUND THROUGH BELGIUM.

German troops marching through Liège on their way back to Germany after the final collapse of their front and home lines. As they passed laden through the streets they were almost ignored by the people of the town, whose house fronts were already decked with the flags of the Allies, the arrival of whom the inhabitants were joyously anticipating. Inset : Column of retreating German soldiers marching in disorderly fashion through a Belgian village.

only the pressure of hunger, due to Britain's disregard of the American doctrine of the freedom of the seas, had brought about the downfall of the nation. Thus the Teuton opened the new war of words when utterly broken in military power, trying to create by intrigue a breach between the Franco-British Governments and the American Government, so as to obtain an easy peace and prepare a war of revenge.

Against the British and French Governments the Revolutionary movement was skilfully employed to enforce a mitigation of the terms of surrender. While the leaders of the Imperial Socialist Party energetically worked at stifling the Communist and leveller elements in the Sailors', Soldiers' and

CAPTIVES HOMEWARD BOUND.
French civilians who had been deported to Germany for enforced labour meeting the British troops to whom they owed their return to civilisation.

ROBBERS RETREATING, DRAWN BY STOLEN OXEN.
True to their predatory tradition, the Huns when forced to retire to their own land took away with them all the loot they could carry, and the inhabitants of the invaded countries had the exasperation of seeing their own cattle being used as draught animals.

Workmen's Councils, by taking the lead in the debates and in the re-ordering of things, and keeping all the old bureaucracy in actual power, they pretended it was only with extreme difficulty that they were preventing all the German people from turning Bolshevist. Hard terms, outside the programme of the fourteen points of President Wilson, would, they clamoured, dissolve Germany into as wild an anarchy as that obtaining in Russia. If Germany were to remain solvent enough to make reparation to Belgium and France, it was contended, her Revolutionary mobs must not be driven into frantic desperation by rigorous demands.

The use of the menace of a Bolshevist Germany, united with Russia in destroying civilisation throughout the world, was a stroke of genius on the part of the new German Government. It dismayed some British statesmen, and until the pressure of public opinion told strongly upon Mr. Lloyd George, there seemed a possibility that the claim for a proper war indemnity would be forgone by the British Government. The Communist threat was also remarkably effective in inducing the Supreme Council of War to refrain from continuing operations until the German armies were patently broken and thrown in famished, fugitive remnants into the Rhineland. It was thought that if the Rhineland

were overcrowded by hungry, despairing soldiers bent on pillage Germany would be wrecked.

The condition of the German forces was already such that Hindenburg wanted an armistice at the earliest possible moment. He had to keep his demoralised men in hand and feed them, so that they might be used, if necessary, in putting down Communists at home. One of the reasons why the troops were told they were undefeated in battle was the hope that the legend would maintain their self-respect and their sense of discipline, so that they could, if needed, be employed against the sailors. The earlier the armistice came the more useful the troops would prove to be.

On November 6th the enemy delegation for the conclusion of an armistice left Berlin. It was headed by the notorious Herr Erzberger, who, after being a violent Pan-German for the first three years of the war and acting as Bethmann-Hollweg's confidential agent, overthrew his master, promoted the Reichstag's peace resolution, and then rejoiced in the plundering of Russia and Rumania.

With this impossible person came a German general, wearing the order of the French Legion of Honour. He was General von Winterfeld, who, while attending the last French Army manœuvres before the war and playing the part of a friend of France, had been injured **German delegates** in a motor-car accident and given the **meet Marshal Foch** famous decoration as a solace. The extraordinary Teutons thought that this man would receive a friendly welcome from Marshal Foch. They were mistaken. When Marshal Foch met General von Winterfeld he grimly eyed the Order of the Legion of Honour, and said : " You have my permission not to wear that ! " General von Gündell, Count Oberndorff, and other persons of slight distinction made up the delegation.

Directed from German Headquarters into the lines of the First French Army on the Hirson-Guise road, the enemy envoys arrived by La Capelle in the evening of November 8th, under the customary white flag. The Germans were motored to a château by the Aisne, where they rested for the

このは

night. In the morning of November 9th they were taken by train to the Forest of Compiègne, where there was another train awaiting them containing Marshal Foch, the military representative of the Allies, and Sir Rosslyn Wemyss, the naval representative, with Staff officers and other personages.

In the saloon of Marshal Foch's train the meeting took place. Herr Erzberger, as the head of the envoys, asked for an immediate cessation of hostilities. Marshal Foch said the terms of the armistice were drawn up and dealt with the point in question to the effect that the war must continue until the agreement was signed. The Generalissimo then read out the terms of armistice fixed by the Supreme Council of War at Versailles.

Vain attempts to procrastinate The Teutons were tricky to the last. On hearing the conditions they stated they were not empowered to sign everything unconditionally, and that as the German Government had changed in character since their appointment, they requested means of communicating the terms to German Headquarters. By this time the German Emperor had fled, like his heir, to Holland, being compelled to practical abdication by the Socialist Majority Party, who at last found that they could neither negotiate a peace nor assuage the rising temper of the people while William of Hohenzollern remained in power. Most of the enemy military authorities tried to the end to save the Emperor from disgraceful flight, in order to make him the centre of a constitutional monarchy, but Hindenburg, in person, finally informed the fallen autocrat that a stay in Holland was advisable.

For, in order to bring under control the Revolutionary movements in Berlin and other cities, the Socialists of the Imperial school had to abandon their scheme of a reformed monarchy and, sacrificing Emperor, Kings, Grand Dukes, and Princes, proclaim a republic. Little, however, was actually changed in Germany, except the appearance of things, all rearrangements being made by the Socialist leaders, Scheidemann and Ebert, in consultation with other party chiefs and military authorities.

Prince Max of Baden resigned in favour of a Socialist Chancellor, Herr Ebert, once a saddler, on the day when the German delegates motored into the French lines. Undoubtedly Erzberger and his party knew what was occurring, and took part in the shaping of the new Government, along with Hindenburg. But in Compiègne Forest they turned to profit the new misfortune of their country, and, by pleading they were unauthorised to sign conditions, obtained an extension of the time given by Marshal Foch for acceptance or refusal.

Herr Matthias Erzberger, Reichstag representative and Secretary of State, one of the civilian members of the German Delegation.

Count von Oberndorff, who had at one time been the German Ambassador in Sofia, the second civilian delegate.

General von Winterfeldt, former German Military Attaché in Paris, and (right) General von Gündell, Germany's military delegate at The Hague Peace Conference, who were the military members of the German Armistice Delegation that accepted the Allies' severe terms of November 11th, 1918.

GERMANY'S ARMISTICE PLENIPOTENTIARIES.

Seventy-two hours was the time fixed, but the German courier taking the armistice conditions to enemy Headquarters was held up on the La Capelle road by German gun fire, and did not reach Spa until November 10th. Hindenburg at once telegraphed the Allies' terms to the Chancellor's palace in Berlin, where Ebert, Scheidemann, and most of the members of old and new Ministries listened to the communication. There was some strong opposition to the conditions, but Hindenburg bore it completely down by telegraphing that all terms must be accepted without any delay whatever, as his forces were running away and he would be compelled to capitulate unconditionally.

Much trouble would have been saved if the Supreme Council of War at Versailles had been more confident in the immediate efficacy of their forces. As a matter of fact, even **Terms of the armistice** Marshal Foch did not suspect the utter weakness of the enemy, and thought he was saving considerable casualties in the reserve army in Lorraine by permitting the Teutons to make terms. Only Sir Douglas Haig and his troops were to the last as well informed about the complete helplessness of Hindenburg as was Hindenburg himself.

The German delegates played their comedy of resistance to the end. They made verbal and written protests against the "inhuman conditions" on which the armistice was granted, and obtained some alterations in regard to the depth of the allied bridge-heads to be established across the Rhine and other technical points. Then, still protesting, they signed, at five o'clock on Monday morning, November 11th, 1918, the conditions for the cessation of hostilities.

This was the historic document:

THE WESTERN FRONT.

I. Cessation of operations by land and in the air six hours after the signature of the armistice.

II. Immediate evacuation of invaded countries—Belgium, France, Alsace-Lorraine, Luxemburg—so ordered as to be completed within fourteen days from the signature of the armistice.

German troops which have not left the above-mentioned territories within the period fixed will become prisoners of war.

Occupation by the Allied and United States forces jointly will keep pace with evacuation in these areas.

All movements of evacuation and occupation will be regulated in accordance with a Note. [Which was served on the German Commander-in-Chief.]

III. Repatriation, beginning at once, to be completed within fourteen days of all inhabitants of the countries above enumerated (including hostages, persons under trial or convicted).

IV. Surrender in good condition by the German armies of the following equipment:

5,000 guns (2,500 heavy, 2,500 field);
30,000 machine-guns;
3,000 minenwerfer;
2,000 aeroplanes (fighters, bombers—firstly D.7's and night-bombing machines).

The above to be delivered *in situ* to the Allied and United States troops in accordance with the detailed conditions laid down.

V. Evacuation by the German armies of the countries on the left bank of the Rhine. These countries on the left bank of the Rhine shall be administered by the local authorities under the control of the Allied and United States Armies of Occupation.

The occupation of these territories will be carried out by Allied and United States garrisons holding the principal crossings of the Rhine (Mayence, Coblenz, Cologne), together with bridge-heads at these points of a 30-kilometre (18·63 miles) radius on the right bank, and by garrisons similarly holding the strategic points of the regions.

A neutral zone to be set up on the right bank of the Rhine between the river and a line drawn ten kilometres (6·21 miles) distant, starting from the Dutch frontier to the Swiss frontier. In the case of inhabitants, no person shall be prosecuted for having taken part in any military measures previous to the signing of the armistice.

No measure of a general or official character shall be taken which would have, as a consequence, the depreciation of industrial establishments or a reduction of their personnel.

Evacuation by the enemy of the Rhinelands shall be so ordered as to be completed within a further period of sixteen days—in all, thirty-one days after the signature of the armistice.

All movements of evacuation and occupation will be regulated according to the Note.

VI. In all territory evacuated by the enemy there shall be no evacuation of inhabitants ; no damage or harm shall be done to the persons or property of the inhabitants.

No destruction of any kind to be committed.

Military establishments of all kinds shall be delivered intact, as well

WORDS AND DEEDS IN REVOLUTIONARY BERLIN.
Workman addressing a Berlin crowd from the top of an ambulance car shortly after the declaration of a German Republic on November 9th, 1918. Inset above : Revolutionary scene in the Prussian capital— members of the Workmen's and Soldiers' Council handing out arms and ammunition to workmen.

as military stores of food, munitions, equipment not removed during the period of evacuation.

Stores of food of all kinds for the civil population, cattle, etc., shall be left *in situ*.

Industrial establishments shall not be impaired in any way, and their personnel shall not be moved.

VII. Roads and means of communication of every kind, railroads, waterways, main roads, bridges, telegraphs, telephones, shall be in no manner impaired.

All civil and military personnel at present employed on them shall remain.

Five thousand locomotives, 150,000 waggons, and 5,000 motor-lorries, in good working order, with all necessary spare parts and fittings, shall be delivered to the Associated Powers within the period fixed for the evacuation of Belgium and Luxemburg.

The railways of Alsace-Lorraine shall be handed over within the same period, together with all pre-war personnel and material.

Further, material necessary for the working of railways in the country on the left bank of the Rhine shall be left *in situ*.

All stores of coal and material for upkeep of permanent way, signals, and repair shops, shall be left *in situ*, and kept in an efficient state by Germany as far as the means of communication are concerned during the whole period of the armistice.

All barges taken from the Allies shall be restored to them ; the Note appended as Annexure 2 regulates the details of these measures.

VIII. The German Command shall be responsible for revealing all mines or delay-action fuses disposed on territory evacuated by the German troops, and shall assist in their discovery and destruction.

The German Command shall also reveal all destructive measures that may have been taken (such as poisoning or pollution of springs, wells, etc.), under penalty of reprisals.

IX. The right of requisition shall be exercised by the Allied and United States Armies in all occupied territory, save for settlement of accounts with authorised persons.

The upkeep of the troops of occupation in the Rhineland (excluding Alsace - Lorraine) shall be charged to the German Government.

X. The immediate repatriation, without reciprocity, according to detailed conditions which shall be fixed, of all Allied and United States prisoners of war ; the Allied Powers and the United States of America shall be able to dispose of these prisoners as they wish. However, the return of German prisoners of war interned in Holland and Switzerland shall continue as heretofore. The return of German prisoners of war shall be settled at peace preliminaries.

XI. Sick and wounded who cannot be removed from evacuated territory will be cared for by German personnel, who will be left on the spot, with the medical material required.

EASTERN FRONTIERS OF GERMANY.

XII. All German troops at present in any territory which before the war belonged to Russia, Rumania, or Turkey shall withdraw within the frontiers of Germany as they existed on August 1st, 1914, and all German troops at present in territories which before the war formed part of Russia must likewise return to within the frontiers of Germany as above defined as soon as the Allies shall think the moment suitable, having regard to the internal situation of these territories.

XIII. Evacuation by German troops to begin at once ; and all German instructors, prisoners, and civilian as well as military agents now on the territory of Russia (as defined on August 1st, 1914) to be recalled.

XIV. German troops to cease at once all requisitions and seizures, and any other undertaking with a view to obtaining supplies intended for Germany, in Rumania and Russia, as defined on August 1st, 1914.

XV. Abandonment of the treaties of Bukarest and Brest Litovsk and of the supplementary treaties. **Germany's previous treaties cancelled**

XVI. The Allies shall have free access to the territories evacuated by the Germans on their eastern frontier, either through Danzig or by the Vistula, in order to convey supplies to the population of these territories or for the purpose of maintaining order.

EAST AFRICA.

XVII. Unconditional evacuation of all German forces operating in East Africa within one month.

GENERAL CLAUSES.

XVIII. Repatriation, without reciprocity, within a maximum period of one month, in accordance with detailed conditions hereafter to be fixed, of all civilians, interned or deported, who may be citizens of other Allied or Associated States than those mentioned in Clause III.

XIX. With the reservation that any future claims and demands of the Allies and United States of America remain unaffected, the following financial conditions are required :—

Reparation for damage done.

While the armistice lasts no public securities shall be removed by the enemy which can serve as a pledge to the Allies for the recovery or reparation for war losses.

Immediate restitution of the cash deposit in the National Bank of Belgium and, in general, immediate return of all documents, specie, stock, shares, paper money, together with plant for the issue thereof, touching public or private interests in the invaded countries.

Restitution of the Russian and Rumanian gold yielded to Germany or taken by that Power.

This gold to be delivered in trust to the Allies until the signature of peace.

NAVAL CONDITIONS.

XX. Immediate cessation of all hostilities at sea, and definite information to be given as to the location and movements of all German ships.

Notification to be given to neutrals that freedom of navigation in all territorial waters is given to the naval and mercantile marines of the Allied and Associated Powers, all questions of neutrality being waived.

Surrender of the German Fleet

XXI. All naval and mercantile marine prisoners of war of the Allied and Associated Powers in German hands to be returned without reciprocity.

XXII. Handing over to the Allies and the United States of all submarines (including all submarine cruisers and mine-layers) which are present at the moment with full complement in the ports specified by the Allies and the United States. Those that cannot put to sea to be deprived of crews and supplies, and shall remain under the supervision of the Allies and the United States. Submarines ready to put to sea shall be prepared to leave German ports immediately on receipt of wireless order to sail to the port of surrender, the remainder to follow as early as possible. The conditions of this article shall be carried out within fourteen days after the signing of the armistice.

XXIII. The following German surface warships, which shall be designated by the Allies and the United States of America, shall forthwith be disarmed and thereafter interned in neutral ports, or, failing them, Allied ports, to be designated by the Allies and the United States of America, and placed under the surveillance of the Allies and the United States of America, only caretakers being left on board, namely :

6 Battle-cruisers.
10 Battleships.
8 Light cruisers, including two mine-layers.
50 Destroyers of the most modern types.

All other surface warships (including river craft) are to be concentrated in German naval bases to be designated by the Allies and the United States of America, and are to be paid-off and completely disarmed and placed under the supervision of the Allies and the United States of America. All vessels of the auxiliary fleet (trawlers, motor-vessels, etc.) are to be disarmed. All vessels specified for internment shall be ready to leave German ports seven days after the signing of the armistice. Directions of the voyage will be given by wireless.

Note—A declaration has been signed by the Allied delegates and handed to the German delegates to the effect that in the event of ships not being handed over owing to the mutinous state of the Fleet, the Allies reserve the right to occupy Heligoland as an advanced base to enable them to enforce the terms of the armistice. The German delegates have, on their part, signed a declaration that they will recommend the Chancellor to accept this.

XXIV. The Allies and the United States of America shall have the right to sweep up all mine-fields and obstructions laid by Germany outside German territorial waters, and the positions of these are to be indicated.

XXV. Freedom of access to and from the Baltic to be given to the naval and mercantile marines of the Allied and Associated Powers.

Continuation of the blockade

To secure this the Allies and the United States of America shall be empowered to occupy all German forts, fortifications, batteries, and defence works of all kinds in all the entrances from the Kattegat into the Baltic, and to sweep up all mines and obstructions within and without German territorial waters without any questions of neutrality being raised and the positions of all such mines and obstructions are to be indicated.

XXVI. The existing blockade conditions set up by the Allied and Associated Powers are to remain unchanged, and all German merchant ships found at sea are to remain liable to capture. The Allies and United States contemplate the provisioning of Germany during the armistice as shall be found necessary.

XXVII. All naval aircraft are to be concentrated and immobilised in German bases to be specified by the Allies and the United States of America.

XXVIII. In evacuating the Belgian coasts and ports Germany shall abandon all merchant ships, tugs, lighters, cranes, and all other harbour materials, all materials for inland navigation, all aircraft and air materials and stores, all arms and armaments, and all stores and apparatus of all kinds.

XXIX. All Black Sea ports are to be evacuated by Germany ; all Russian warships of all descriptions seized by Germany in the Black Sea are to be handed over to the Allies and the United States of America ; all neutral merchant ships seized are to be released ; all warlike and other materials of all kinds seized in those ports are to be returned, and German materials as specified in Clause XXVIII. are to be abandoned.

XXX. All merchant ships in German hands belonging to the Allied and Associated Powers are to be restored in ports to be specified by the Allies and the United States of America without reciprocity.

XXXI. No destruction of ships or of materials to be permitted before evacuation, surrender, or restoration.

XXXII. The German Government shall formally notify the neutral Governments of the world—and particularly the Governments of Norway, Sweden, Denmark, and Holland—that all restrictions placed on the trading of their vessels with the Allied and Associated Countries, whether by the German Government or by private German interests, and, whether in return for specific concessions, such as the export of ship-building materials or not, are immediately cancelled.

XXXIII. No transfers of German merchant shipping of any description to any neutral flag are to take place after signature of the armistice.

DURATION OF ARMISTICE.

XXXIV. The duration of the armistice is to be thirty-six days, with option to extend. During this period, on failure of execution of any of the above clauses, the armistice may be denounced by one of the contracting parties on forty-eight hours' previous notice.

TIME-LIMIT FOR REPLY.

XXXV. This armistice to be accepted or refused by Germany within seventy-two hours of notification.

When, on December 13th, the armistice was renewed, Marshal Foch had to obtain further guarantees, and reserve the right to occupy the neutral zone from the Dutch frontier to Cologne on giving six days' notice. The Germans had to furnish two and a half million tons of shipping for general use in the transport of foodstuffs, and the Baden battleship was to be handed over instead of the unfinished Mackensen.

There had arisen in Germany a strong party which held that the armistice could safely be disowned. General von Winterfeldt became the representative of this party on the Armistice Commission, and at the conference at Treves on January 16th, 1919, he made a determined effort to induce his fellow-delegates to denounce the agreement for cessation of hostilities.

When Herr Erzberger refused to do so, General von Winterfeldt resigned, nominally over the question of extending the zone of French occupation from Strasbourg to a strip of territory on the eastern bank of the Rhine. New clauses were then signed by the rest of the enemy envoys, concerning **Germany finally brought to heel** the surrender of the hidden U boats which Sir Montague Browning had discovered, the placing of the German merchant fleet at the disposal of the Allies, the replacement of farming machinery in the invaded territories, and of industrial stocks and factory equipment stolen from the French and Belgians. The punishment of persons guilty of illegal treatment of prisoners of war was also demanded.

The mildness of these new terms encouraged the Teutons in their belief that the Allies had become so weakened by demobilisation troubles that their troops would not fight. Hindenburg concentrated a strong army round Danzig, and opened skirmishing actions against the Poles along the lake and marshland defences of Posen. This attack on Poland was a direct test of the strength and stability of the Associated Powers. The Supreme Council of War was at last aroused. Marshal Foch was empowered to resume the offensive if the enemy did not at once agree to new conditions being imposed upon him. There was another meeting of the Armistice Commission at Treves on Friday, February 14th, 1919. The Germans were ordered to cease all attacks upon the Poles, and to keep outside the purely Polish district of Posen.

While the Teutons were hesitating between peace and war, hundreds of new guns, with fresh shell supplies, rolled past the train in which Erzberger and his associates sat by Treves Station. They were a strong hint, and the enemy delegates signed the new treaty in the evening of February 16th, 1919.

A means being found of quelling the stubborn, intriguing spirit of the enemy, the scope of the convention at Treves was thereupon enlarged. The armistice was employed as the implement of peace. The Allies felt they could regulate with most speed many important matters of final settlement by introducing them as terms enforceable at three days' notice. At Treves the victors had immediate force to make their just decisions effective, so they resolved to merge the general peace negotiations into the armistice. Treves was to be the gateway to the Palace of Peace at Versailles.

THE SURPASSING TRIUMPH OF THE BRITISH NAVY.

Failure of Germany's Submarine War and Surrender of her High Sea Fleet.

By H. W. Wilson.

Difficulties Confronting the Admiralty at the Beginning of Germany's Submarine Campaign—Development and Increased Provision of Depth Charges and Mines—Two Varieties of Mine-Fields—The Dover Barrage—Vigorous Offensive Against Germany's Naval Bases on the Flanders Coast — Percentage of Shipping Losses Reduced by Employment of Convoy — Aggressive Operations Against U Boats : Q Ships, Aircraft Patrol, and Counter-Mining—The Paravane—Barrage Across the Strait of Otranto—Austrian Naval Losses—Captain Luigi Rizzo's Daring Motor-Boat Attack on Austrian Battleships—Official Statement of Germany's Submarine Losses—Moral Effect on the Central Powers of the Failure of the Submarine Campaign—Intensification of the Blockade—German Land-Power at Its Maximum—Allies' Position in the East Dependent on Britain's Sea-Power—Food Condition in Enemy and Neutral States—Lieutenant Raffaele Paolucci's and Major Rossetti's Astounding Feat in Pola Harbour—Austria and Turkey Out of the War—Allied Fleet Passes up the Dardanelles—Mutiny in the German Navy—Surrender of the High Sea Fleet—Disarmament of the German Ships Remaining in Germany—Vice-Admiral Browning Proceeds to the Kiel Canal in H.M.S. Hercules, with the International Naval Commission, to Inspect all Germany's Naval Bases and Airship and Aeroplane Stations.

IN Chapter CCXLIV. (Vol. II, p. 347) the history of the war at sea was brought down to the end of May, 1918, when the creation of an efficient War Staff at the Admiralty was beginning to influence the conduct of operations, and new methods of combating the submarines were being introduced with great success. The British Navy, so far as the strain imposed on it by the provision of convoy for the American troopships permitted, was everywhere taking the offensive against the U boats. In the remaining months of the war three features are of paramount interest — the conflict with the submarines, the severance of German land communications with the Near East (restoring the pressure of sea-power upon the German nation), and the unceasing watch on the High Sea Fleet maintained by the Grand Fleet.

Of all the dangers which the British Empire had to face in the war the submarine campaign was far the most formidable. The submarine attacked the unity, the very existence, of that Empire. Had it prevailed, the people of Great Britain must have starved, the allied armies have been deprived of supplies and munitions, and the whole world have passed under German domination. The difficulty

ADMIRAL SIR REGINALD TYRWHITT, K.C.B., D.S.O.
Admiral Tyrwhitt on board his flagship H.M.S. Curaçao, at the time of the surrender of the first batch of German submarines off Harwich on November 20th, 1918.

of defeating the submarine as it was used by the Germans was great. It was a new weapon, and owing to the absence of an efficient Naval Staff in Great Britain before the war to study war problems, the methods of fighting it had not been ascertained before the war began. They had to be worked out and tested during the actual conflict. In the earlier period of the war, strange as it may sound, the Navy, on which so much depended, was hampered by want of funds. For example, the Admiralty could not obtain the money required for the provision of depth charges on a sufficient scale or for the improvement of the patterns supplied. It experienced similar difficulty in securing aircraft. The needs of the Army were so great, the supply of explosives, steel, and other munitions was so limited, that the British sea forces were imperfectly equipped for this new and extraordinary kind of war. Gradually this state of affairs passed. With the vast development of the munition industry in Great Britain, which accompanied and followed Mr. Lloyd George's campaign in 1915, the position improved, though not until 1917—late in that year— were the most urgent needs of the Navy met. The new Admiralty recognised that mines and depth charges in large quantities were as vital for success at sea as abundance of shells on land. The output of both was enormously increased; the efficiency of depth charges was singularly improved. These underwater bombs at first were dropped in waters where submarines were located, and then afterwards were fired by a species of gun, like a trench-mortar, from destroyers, armed trawlers, or merchantmen. They were steadily increased in power, until towards the end of the war they carried charges of 300 lb. of high explosive, and could be set by a hydrostatic valve, worked by the pressure of the water, to explode at various depths. The detonation of a depth charge within fifty feet of a submarine was fatal; cases were known of U boats being sunk at distance of seventy-five feet, and even at one hundred feet a depth charge was apt to cause leaks, damage the machinery, or demoralise the crew.

As with depth charges, so with mines. In the earlier period of the war the British type of mine was too weak and too uncertain in its action. The Navy complained that it failed to blow up German vessels, but by some odd freak of chance was usually effective against British vessels if by any accident they happened to enter a British mine-field. All these defects were removed with time. The **British mines and mine-fields** British mine was perfected, the charge carried in it was increased, the supply was enormously augmented. Two distinct varieties of mine-field were employed against the Germans. The first variety had mines anchored near the surface—usually at a depth of eight to fifteen feet—so as to render the area comprised in it dangerous both to surface ships and to submarines. This kind of mine-field was publicly notified to neutrals and belligerents alike, in order that neutral shipping might not be destroyed. A second kind of mine-field was laid below the surface at such depths that there would be no danger to neutral shipping or surface vessels, but only to submarines navigated below the surface. This was not publicly announced. The mines in such fields were placed at a depth of thirty feet or more, so that the largest surface ship, with an extreme draught of water of about twenty-seven feet, would be safe. The German Admiralty, with characteristic disregard for truth and for the safety of shipping, laid surface mine-fields in all directions without any notice, and attempted to place the odium of this practice on the British Government by pretending that the British Navy had created these mine-fields. Thus in the summer of 1918 German vessels laid a surface mine-field in the Cattegat, in which various Swedish

merchant vessels or fishing craft and one Swedish warship were destroyed, and then, when complaint was made, denied that the mines were German. Towards the close of the war the British Navy was laying mines at the rate of 10,000 a month, and that rate would have been rapidly increased but for the German collapse.

Another method of defence adopted by the British Navy and carried out with great success was the construction of barrages, or surface barriers, supplemented by mines at some depth. Such a barrage was constructed across the Strait of Dover early in the year. A similar barrage in the summer of 1918 was carried across the Strait of Otranto, closing it to submarines. The Dover barrage was of immense importance, because it prevented German surface craft or submarines from reaching by the shortest and easiest route the Channel, or the waters across which lay the main lines of communication with the British armies in France. It was composed of a double series of obstructions. One series consisted of specially-built vessels, which could ride out the heaviest gale at anchor. It ran from Folkestone to Cape

EARLY AND LATE IN THE WAR: TWO BRITISH WARSHIPS LOST BY MINE AND TORPEDO.
Sinking of H.M.S. Audacious after striking a mine off the North Coast of Ireland on October 27th, 1914, with boats engaged in rescue work. The loss of this Dreadnought (only made public four years later) was the heaviest blow which the Germans succeeded in inflicting upon the British Navy by means of the mine. In circle: H.M.S. Britannia sinking after being torpedoed off Gibraltar, November 9th, 1918, two days before the armistice.

were specially favourable, and at those times the entrances were closely watched. This naval offensive was supplemented by an equally violent air offensive, carried out by the Royal Naval Air Service in the earlier months of 1918, and later by contingents from the Royal Air Force, with the greatest heroism and persistence. The frontier was moved to the enemy's coast. The continual bombing of Zeebrugge and Ostend deprived the German crews of rest, and inflicted so much material damage upon the German vessels and naval establishments that their efficiency was markedly reduced. The operations as conceived and carried out were a model in war, and reflected the utmost honour on all concerned in them. Towards the close of the summer bombs weighing 1,600 lb. were employed with terrible effect, and still more powerful bombs, to be dropped from gigantic machines, were under construction when the war ended.

Germany's naval bases bombarded

Yet another method of defence against submarines was the employment of convoy. Merchantmen, when they neared the danger zone, were met by destroyers or other naval craft; sometimes they were escorted by special British convoy submarines. This was not a complete guarantee against submarine attack. In one case the Justitia, a large vessel, was sunk in the presence of numerous destroyers—but only after she had been badly damaged by an attack delivered just after the escort had left her and after she had passed through the zone of maximum danger. Four German submarines were in the neighbourhood, and the vessel which fired the torpedoes, U124, was destroyed. No fewer than twenty-five depth charges were exploded near U124, and she was forced to a great depth, where her hull began to leak. Finally she surrendered to the British destroyer Marne.

This episode showed that where attacks were made on convoyed ships or ships in the neighbourhood of a destroyer force the submarine crew had to be prepared for death. The game, in fact, was no longer worth the candle. The losses fell, as the result of the convoy system, from a percentage of

Griz Nez. West of this, at an interval of seven miles, was another line of similar vessels. The barrage vessels were equipped with special searchlights of great power which swept the surface of the water and prevented the German submarines from carrying out their old plan of making a dash in surface trim through the Strait of Dover during the dark hours. Between the two barrages were scores of drifters (armed fishing vessels with depth charges and light guns) constantly patrolling. Below the surface were deep mines, nets, and other devices. The object of the patrol was to force submarines below the surface, when they struck the mines or fouled obstructions. This system of defence was installed under Vice-Admiral Sir Roger Keyes, and it proved most effective. Between January 1st and the end of August, 1918, no fewer than thirty German submarines were destroyed in the attempt to pass the barrages, of which fifteen were definitely identified, lying under the patrolled area. The work done was the more remarkable because the barrage and the patrol craft were exposed to attack from the German surface craft at Zeebrugge and Ostend, and because this whole system of war was entirely new and demanded special appliances of every kind.

The Dover barrage was supplemented by a most vigorous and violent offensive against the German bases on the Flanders coast. By sinking blockships in the entrances to these bases the British Navy made it difficult for the Germans to come in or go out, except when the conditions of tide or light

DEPTH CHARGES—DEADLIEST PERIL TO THE SUBMARINE.
Crew of an American destroyer watching the explosion of a depth charge which they had just dropped. In circle: The apparatus by which the depth charge was brought into position, photographed on one of the famous British "mystery ships." In top picture: Loading up depth charges on a U.S. transport.

5.41 British steamers sunk in April-June, 1917, to .59 per cent. in the last twelve months of the war. German submarine commanders, with rare exceptions where their courage or skill was much above the common, decided to leave convoys alone, and concentrated their attacks on stray ships or occasional stragglers. Fast ships were not convoyed, because the destroyers needed for such duty were not available, and this fact explains the loss of the Irish mail-boat Leinster with five hundred and ten lives. She was twice torpedoed on October 10th, 1918, and sank almost instantly. The Japanese liner Hiramo Maru was sunk off the Irish coast on October 4th, with the loss of three hundred and ten souls.

Complete security could not be given, nor the whole voyage of merchantmen protected, because of the lack of destroyers, which were wanted in every direction. The Grand Fleet required a very large force which had to be held in constant readiness for sea. It had always to be prepared to meet a sortie of the High Sea Fleet, for which it was certain that all the available German destroyers and submarines would be concentrated, and as it was the mainstay of the whole Alliance its needs had to be considered first, and provision made for screening and protecting any of its large ships that might be damaged in action.

Apart from the defensive war against the submarine, aggressive operations were carried out by all available vessels, on the principle that the best defence is to attack the enemy. But when large American forces were being moved to Europe to meet the German offensive on land, the attack at sea on the submarines had to be weakened because there were not ships to spare for it. The energy with which the German boats were hunted was revealed by the statements of survivors from their crews and by the daily reports of the British squadrons and flotillas. In one typical instance the crew of a German submarine which was sunk by the British Navy reported that no fewer than eighty-eight depth charges had been exploded near her in the space of three days before she was destroyed.

The use of "decoy-ships," or Q ships, was extended with considerable success. They were vessels rigged like merchantmen, with a powerful armament well concealed. When the submarine approached to destroy them with gun fire or with explosive charges placed in the hull—which was a regular practice of the U boats to avoid expending torpedoes —canvas screens or other devices hiding the guns were dropped, the guns opened, and the submarine was sunk. Each side employed such vessels in the war, though the British Navy never sank merchant vessels, even when these flew the German flag, without proper warning.

So effective were the British measures for closing the Strait of Dover that by the end of June Ostend and Zeebrugge had lost their value as submarine bases. The Flanders coast became a liability instead of an asset to the German Staff. All submarines had to pass round the North of Scotland to reach the cruising grounds where traffic was most easily attacked, and if they used the Flanders coast as their base the voyage had to be made up the East Coast of Great Britain through waters which were generally shallow and always closely watched. The larger U boats therefore avoided Flanders, and the vessels operating from that coast were principally small submarines which hovered off the East Coast, attacking trawlers and fishing craft. As it was impossible to give protection everywhere, the damage which they caused had to be endured. It was not serious, and a very heavy toll was taken of these small submarines. In the North Sea the British Navy employed with considerable success the hydrophone, an instrument by which—it has already been mentioned—the sound waves caused by the submarine's propellers could be detected. Flotillas trained in its use hunted the U boats, and were often able to locate them by its means. Elsewhere it did not give such satisfactory results. The problem of the U boat war changed with every sea.

The use of aircraft in anti-submarine work constantly extended, and one reason why the losses of shipping rose in bad weather was that then aeroplanes and airships could not always operate. Many types of aircraft were employed. Large "flying boats" were among them. These were fitted with two engines developing 350 h.p. each, and they could alight on the surface of the water. They were employed on patrol work at some distance from the coast. To protect convoys moving along the coast

ONE OF SIR PERCY SCOTT'S INVENTIONS.
Naval officer showing one of the bomb-lances invented by Admiral Sir Percy Scott for coping with the submarine menace.

LISTENING FOR APPROACHING U BOATS AND INTERCEPTING THEM WITH NETS.
The hydrophone, one of the many wonderful inventions which were called into existence by the war. It was devised by British ingenuity as one of the means of fighting the German submarine. By the use of this, and other mechanism for gathering sounds, it was possible not only to hear submarines at a distance but also to judge the direction of their approach. Right : Hauling in submarine nets on a British warship in the Mediterranean.

aeroplanes patrolled to a distance of ten miles the channel by which traffic proceeded. These machines were in some cases supplied with depth charges, but more commonly carried only bombs. They either attacked submarines with their bombs, or notified the whereabouts of the hostile craft to the surface vessels engaged in patrol work. So efficient did they become that in the closing period of the war few attacks were made by the Germans in the patrolled area during flying hours. The Germans in 1918 found the British aircraft such a danger to their submarines that they attempted counter-measures. They sent out from the Flanders coast very fast and powerfully armed monoplanes. The British reply to this move was to escort the patrol aircraft with powerful fighting machines such as the famous " Camel " type. Between April 1st and October 31st, 1918, marvellous results were obtained by the Royal Air Force in this peculiar branch of air work. In 39,000 flying hours there were 216 cases in which submarines were sighted, and 189 in which they were attacked. There were 351 encounters with hostile aircraft, of which 184 were destroyed and 151 damaged. No fewer than 15,313 bombs were dropped. Thus, concomitantly with the submarine war, air war at sea developed to an extent of which only the most far-sighted had dreamed early in the war. More and more, with their ever-widening radius of action and ever-increasing armament, aircraft proved themselves the deadliest enemies of the submarine. American airmen rendered the greatest aid in the summer of 1918, and distinguished themselves by splendid work on the East Coast and Irish coast.

The heavy German submarine losses in the spring of 1918 led the Emperor William to visit the Flanders ports in June and do what he could to encourage the crews. The grim fact remained that one-half of the small U boats based on this coast had disappeared at sea, sunk by British mines or depth charges. So useless had the Flanders coast become that its abandonment by the Germans was expected at any moment when their final offensive collapsed in July, 1918. Large numbers of men and guns were required to guard it, to prevent a British landing behind the German lines. Ludendorff's strength at the decisive point was correspondingly

THE LISTENERS.
Instruments for detecting the sound waves caused by submarines' propellers were inventions developed to a high pitch of perfection during the war.

weakened. Attempting to hold everything, he lost everything, and by dispersing his forces prepared the way for the final catastrophe.

The larger German submarines, towards the close of the war, found it dangerous to venture through the British mine-fields, the laying of which has been mentioned in Chapter CCXLIV. These were at first treated with some contempt ; but, as the number of mines constantly increased, the risks of crossing the mine-fields became too great to be taken. Over one hundred German surface craft are known to have perished in the mine-fields in the Bight of Heligoland. Most of them were small craft, as the larger German vessels no longer ventured into the North Sea, but kept within the Baltic or their protected anchorages. Among the German submarines which were destroyed in the mine-fields was U88, commanded by Lieut.-Commander Schwieger, the officer who in U20 had sunk the Lusitania in 1915. In September, 1917, he was proceeding to sea in company with another submarine, which was subsequently sunk by the British. The survivors of her crew gave this account of Schwieger's end. Off the Danish coast their vessel struck a chain, and the crew at once realised that they were in the midst of a number of British mines. A few minutes later a heavy explosion at no great distance shook them violently. Their boat rose to the surface and attempted to communicate with U88 by wireless signals, but to these signals there was no reply. U88 with all on board had perished, and thus in the waters of the North Sea justice was done at last. Schwieger before his death seemed to feel the ignominy of his deed.

One of the reasons why the German losses in the mine-fields were so heavy was that in the closing period of the war the British submarines and mine-layers night after night entered the German mine-fields off Heligoland and carefully laid mines in the channels which German craft had cleared and used to put to sea. Thus, returning to harbour through passages which they supposed to be safe, the German vessels were sunk. The mine was turned against the Germans with a vengeance, and they had good cause to regret ever introducing the practice of promiscuous mine-laying at sea. This work of offensive mine-laying was for the most part carried

MECHANICAL CONTRIVANCES WHICH DEPRIVED MINE-FIELDS OF THEIR MENACE.
Two views of the paravane on the crane which lowered it over the ship's side, with men standing by awaiting the order to launch it. These valuable contrivances, invented by Lieutenant Burney, were torpedo-shaped vessels devised either to cut the wires of anchored mines or to explode a charge of T.N.T. on contact with submarines. Towed at any depth up to two hundred feet they could sweep almost any waters used by submarines.

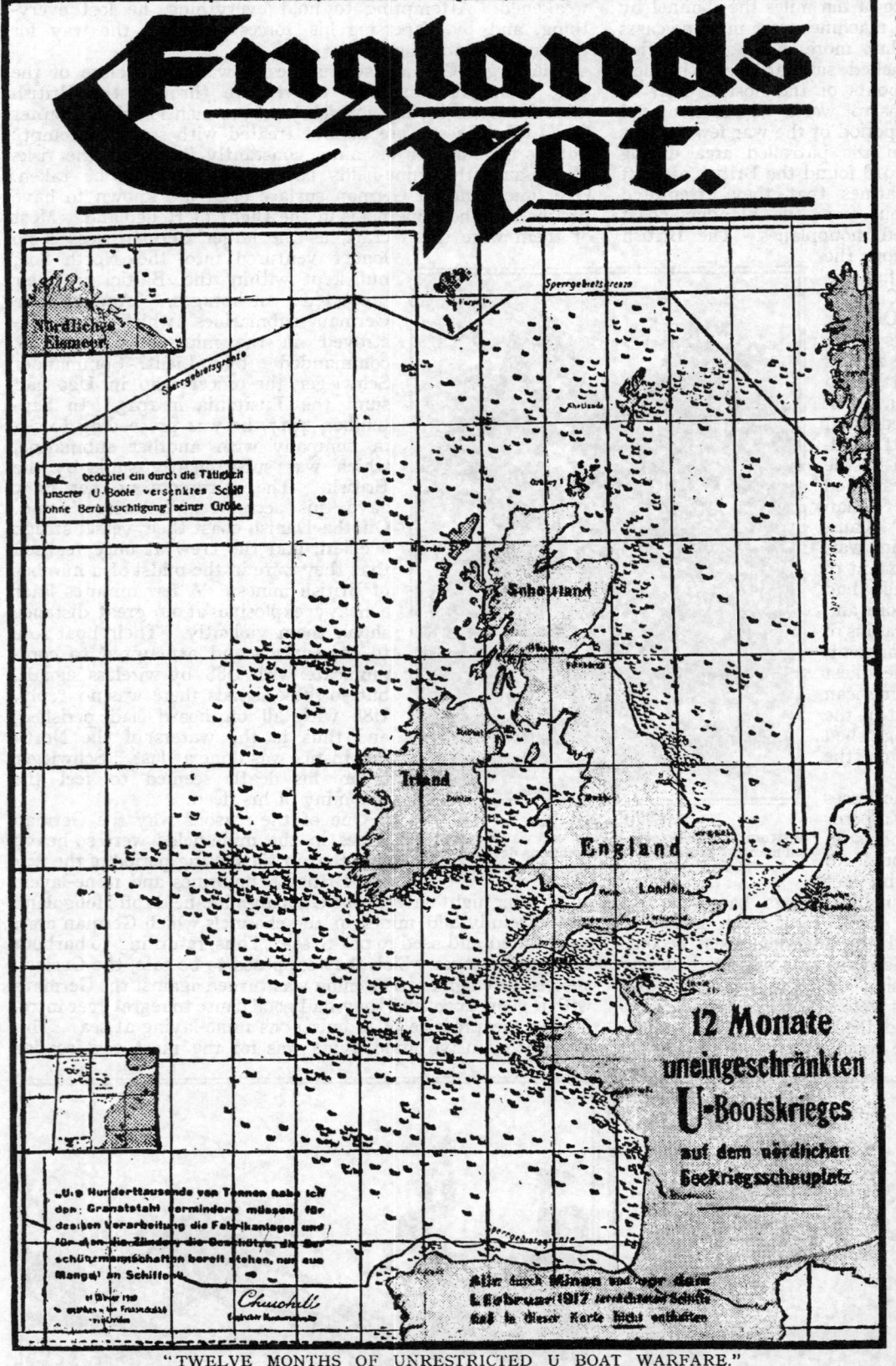

Englands Not.

12 Monate uneingeschränkten U-Bootskrieges auf dem nördlichen Seekriegsschauplatz

"TWELVE MONTHS OF UNRESTRICTED U BOAT WARFARE."

Germany's own statement of her U boat outrages issued in map form. This German map shows, by the little black specks, the vessels which the enemy claimed to have sunk by submarines only around the shores of the British islands during twelve months from February, 1917. The map is headed "England's Misery," and in the left bottom corner is an extract signed "Churchill": "It is entirely for lack of ships that I have had to reduce by hundreds of thousands of tons the steel for shells, for the making of which the factories, fuses, guns, and gun crews are all waiting."

Germans to abandon the Bight of Heligoland, and when they put to sea to come out by the Cattegat and the strip of territorial water on the Norwegian coast. The constant use of this Norwegian "corridor" by the U boats was a gross abuse of Norwegian neutrality, but it was closed at last by the Norwegian Government in October, 1918, with a special mine-field.

British skill and ingenuity by 1918 had overcome the menace of the submarine so far as well-equipped warships were concerned, though the danger to merchant steamers continued. In the closing months of the war the British losses in warships, whether from torpedoes or mines, were very small. This was in part due to increased experience, in part to the wider use of aircraft of all kinds by the British Fleet, in part to a new and important mechanical contrivance, the paravane, invented by Lieutenant Burney, son of the admiral of that name. It was supplied to warships as fast as it could be made, and, as soon as the Fleet had been provided with it, it was issued to merchantmen.

In appearance the paravane was like a torpedo. It was a cigar-shaped metal vessel, so constructed as to be buoyant. To force it below the water when it was towed from the ship it was fitted with a plane or kite, like that employed in the trawl used by fishermen. That is to say, it had a metal surface, sloping downwards, which made it dive when the pull came on the wire by which it was towed, just as a kite rises in the air from the pull on the string attached to it. It was equipped with an ingenious rudder for maintaining a fixed depth. When this rudder had been set any increase in the pressure of the water from the paravane diving to greater depth than had been intended, turned the rudder upward and sent the paravane nearer the surface. In the same way, if it rose, the lessened pressure turned the rudder down and forced the head of the paravane down.

One kind of paravane fitted with a large explosive charge of 400 lb. of T.N.T. was used chiefly against submarines. If the wire by which the paravane was towed touched a submarine's hull it slipped along it till the paravane itself touched the hull and exploded in contact with it. The effect was usually deadly. This paravane could be set to run at any depth up to two hundred feet, so that it could sweep almost any waters used by the submarine. There

out by the British Twentieth Destroyer Flotilla, with special submarines attached to it, under the flotilla-leader Abdiel, a vessel of extraordinary speed. The Twentieth Flotilla was constituted in March, 1918, and remained at work until the end of the war. So successful was it that it compelled the

was a second type of paravane, provided in pairs for use in ships against mines. This was like the explosive pattern in appearance, but smaller, and the planes were so arranged as to make the paravane tow obliquely outwards from the ship and not directly in her wake. One pair in large ships was towed from the bows on either side, and a second pair from amidships on a strong flexible steel wire, one and a half inches thick. If this wire touched a mine mooring it forced the mooring away from the hull of the ship to the paravane, where the mooring was caught in a slot and cut through by a saw fixed in the paravane. The mine then came to the surface and was destroyed.

The speed which could be maintained with paravanes was high, reaching twenty-eight knots, **Complete success** and the effect on the **of the paravane** ship which t o w e d them was not serious, only reducing her pace by half a knot to a knot. So successful was this device that British squadrons towards the close of the war could steam with perfect impunity through the German mine-fields, which entirely lost their menace. The Germans did not know the secret, as it was jealously guarded, but they must have suspected something, as they practically ceased mine-laying in the closing months of the war.

In the last three months of the war only two light cruisers were sunk by mines, one of them in the Baltic after the armistice. Earlier in the war large numbers of warships were thus destroyed. T h e

heaviest blow which the Germans succeeded in inflicting with the mine was the destruction of the British Dreadnought Audacious. This took place on October 27th, 1914, but it was kept secret by the Admiralty, in pursuance of the policy which it laid down in a secret circular to the Press, urging " the importance of shrouding in mystery and secrecy at all times and by every means the number of Dreadnoughts available with the flag of the Commander-in-Chief at any particular period." This was a very sound policy, and it enabled the Admiralty in the autumn of 1914 to despatch the battle-cruisers Invincible and Inflexible to the Falkland Islands and thus defeat and destroy Admiral von Spee's squadron.

The Audacious, of course, was not equipped with the paravane, and on the date stated, while preparing for target **H.M.S. Audacious** practice off the North **mined and lost** Coast of Ireland, she struck a mine and sank slowly in a heavy sea. Just after she had been abandoned there was a violent explosion on board, possibly due to shells falling in the magazine. There was no loss of life in her (though one man in another ship was killed by the explosion), but she was a very powerful ship, and at that moment she could not easily be spared. The catastrophe was witnessed by a large number of neutrals, and accounts of it appeared in neutral newspapers at the time. But it always remained uncertain whether she might not have been raised and repaired, as those neutrals did not see her end.

In the Mediterranean a visit of the heads of the Admiralty to Italy in May, 1918, brought valuable results. In

SEAPLANE FLIGHT FROM A BRITISH CRUISER.
Seaplane on board a British cruiser ready to set out on a flight. The platform was carried across the pair of foreground guns to afford the aeroplane sufficient " way " to take off. In circle : The machine takes the air, and (above) goes forth on a flight from the parent ship.

co-operation with the Italian Navy a barrage similar to that at Dover was gradually carried across the Strait of Otranto. Mention has already been made of this in an earlier chapter, but it was then impossible, for military reasons, to give any details of the work. This was of special interest in view of the peculiar difficulties that had to be overcome. In the

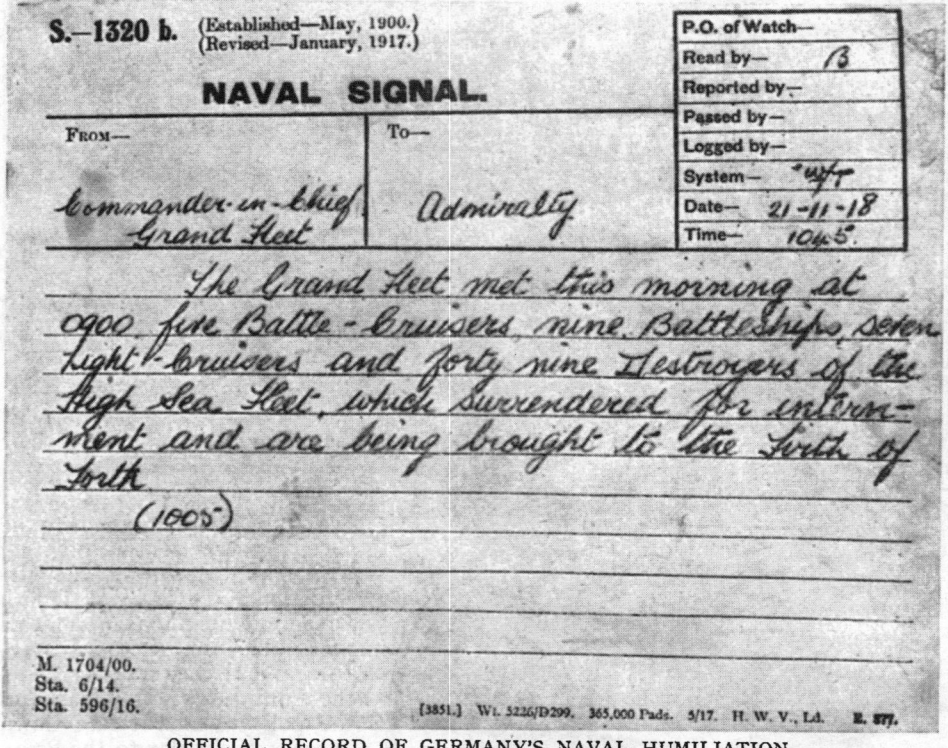

S.—1320 b. (Established—May, 1900.)
            (Revised—January, 1917.)

NAVAL SIGNAL.

From—	To—
Commander-in-Chief Grand Fleet	Admiralty

P.O. of Watch—
Read by— *13*
Reported by—
Passed by—
Logged by—
System— *w/t*
Date— 21-11-18
Time— 1045.

The Grand Fleet met this morning at 0900 five Battle-Cruisers, nine Battleships, seven Light-Cruisers and forty nine Destroyers of the High Sea Fleet, which surrendered for internment and are being brought to the Firth of Forth.

(1005)

M. 1704/00.
Sta. 6/14.
Sta. 596/16.

[3851.] Wt. 5226/D299. 365,000 Pads. 5/17. H. W. V., Ld. **E. 877.**

OFFICIAL RECORD OF GERMANY'S NAVAL HUMILIATION.
Admiral Sir David Beatty's historic message to the Admiralty announcing the bloodless, most glorious triumph of the British Navy, the surrender of the seventy units of the German High Sea Fleet at the appointed rendezvous in the North Sea on November 21st, 1918, in obedience to the armistice terms.

first place, the width of the Strait of Otranto is about forty-five miles, nearly double that of the Strait of Dover. In the second place, whereas the water at Dover is shallow and therefore favourable to mining, at Otranto it is exceedingly deep, and there is a depth of 1,800 feet only a short distance from the coast. Many ingenious devices were therefore employed. There was a movable barrier on the surface attached to special vessels. In order to increase the effectiveness of the watch numerous kite or "sausage" balloons were used. Precautions had to be taken against an attack by the Austrian Fleet, which had an excellent base at Bocche di Cattaro, only one hundred and forty miles from the strait. No such menace had existed near the Strait of Dover, from which the German battleships and main bases were four hundred miles distant. Unfortunately the Italian coast had no good harbour north of the Strait of Otranto from which the Austrians could be blockaded by the Italian Fleet, so that there was always risk that the Austrians might steam up to the barrage before the main Italian

Barrage across the Adriatic

Fleet could arrive. To give what protection was possible a number of British monitors were allotted to the barrage. Luckily, the Austrians showed little energy or enterprise, and the barrage vessels were not molested in 1918.

One cause of the Austrian inactivity was the heavy losses which the Austrian Battle Fleet had suffered from the energetic enterprises of Italian torpedo craft. The destruction of a Dreadnought of the Viribus Unitis type in May, 1918, has been recorded in Chapter CCXLIV. It was one of the most daring deeds of the war, and reflected the greatest honour on Captain Pellegrini, of the Italian Navy, who was responsible for it. It was followed a few weeks later by an achievement as brilliant which stands to the credit of Captain Luigi Rizzo. He had already won distinction by forcing his way into Trieste Harbour in December, 1917, and torpedoing the small battleships Monarch and Wien, of which the Wien

was sunk. At 3.15 a.m. of June 10th he was cruising off the Dalmatian coast with two tiny motor-boats, each of which carried two torpedoes and a few depth charges, when he sighted smoke to the north in the first faint light of dawn. He proceeded cautiously towards this smoke, expecting to find that it came from Austrian destroyers on patrol, but was startled as he drew nearer to discover that an Austrian squadron was at sea. It consisted of two Dreadnoughts (probably the Szent Istvan and Prinz Eugen), which were steaming in line with an interval of four hundred yards between them. Ten destroyers were screening them from torpedo attack, moving at some distance from them in two lines. Captain Rizzo at once determined to attack. His bravery was famous in the Italian Navy, and it was allied to a shrewd insight and judgment which made him a great leader. He signalled to the other motor-boat to act independently, and with his own boat he ran very cautiously at reduced speed—so as to make little or no noise—for the gap between the second and third destroyers on the starboard (right) side of the Austrian squadron. He had reached a point almost ahead of the third destroyer in the gap when the Austrians in that vessel saw him, and whistles sounded calling the crews to action-stations. No alarm, however, was given to the battleships. They did not go to quarters or open fire, and Rizzo was able to run in to a distance of only two hundred yards from the leading battleship, when he fired his two torpedoes in quick succession. The first struck her between the two funnels, the second astern of the after-funnel. The second motor-boat, at almost the same moment, reached the gap between the fourth and fifth destroyers and fired at the second Austrian Dreadnought. One of the torpedoes ran badly and missed; the second struck the Austrian ship astern and exploded.

Rizzo had still to make his escape. He was now running on a course parallel to that which the Austrians had been steering, right in among the Austrian squadron. In the confusion an Austrian destroyer sighted him and steamed at him. His only chance of escape was to use his depth charges. The first was dropped in the course which the destroyer was steering as she approached him to run him down. It failed to explode. A second was discharged, and this went off under the very bows of the Austrian vessel, shattering her and perhaps sinking her. Captain Rizzo did not stop to ascertain her fate. He made good his retreat with the other motor-boat, and a few hours later Italian seaplanes searched the waters where the attack had taken place. They found an area of sea twenty miles north of the point of encounter covered for a square mile with wreckage, but of the Austrian squadron there was no sign. An Austrian report two days later admitted the loss of the Szent Istvan. The Italian naval authorities believed that the Prinz Eugen also sank when attempting to reach port. The loss of life in the Szent Istvan was about ninety officers and men drowned or killed by the explosion.

The effect of the Adriatic barrage showed itself by degrees. The loss of the Allies from submarine attacks in the Mediterranean had been very heavy in 1917 and early 1918. It now rapidly diminished. From June, 1918, onwards the German submarines operating in the Mediterranean had to return to the German coast for their rest and refit, and their activity was greatly reduced. They still caused some trouble near the Strait of Gibraltar, where they were aided

Luigi Rizzo's daring feat

Admiral Beatty, with Flag=Captain Chatfield, watching the surrender of the German Fleet.

Without firing a shot, seventy ships of the German High Sea Fleet surrendered to Admiral Sir David Beatty on November 21st, 1918, as required by the te
armistice granted to the German High Command after its final defeat upon the western front. After the main bulk of the enemy forces had been yielde

On November 20th, 1918, the day before that fixed for the surrender of her surface ships, Germany began the delivery of her submarine fleet to Admiral
at Harwich, and a procession of dejected pirates filed between British ships into internment.

Sunset on Germany's naval hopes: U boats proceeding to internment in the Stour.

per-Dreadnought Baden (left), surrendered on completion as substitute for another capital ship and accompanied by the three-funnelled cruiser Regensburg
atriate her surplus crew, steamed into Scapa Flow in custody of the British battleship Monarch and the light cruiser Champion.

German battle-cruisers Hindenburg (left) and Moltke (centre) and the light cruiser Karlsruhe (right) lowering their colours in obedience to Admiral Beatty's
signal : "The German flag will be hauled down at sunset to-day, and will not be hoisted again without permission."

Germany's High Sea Fleet striking its colours at the ignominious end of " The Day."

On December 4th, 1918, Vice-Admiral Browning arrived at Kiel in H.M.S. Hercules to enforce the naval terms of the armistice. Near the high bridge at Rendsburg a trainload of returning British prisoners frantically cheered the White Ensign floating on German waters.

Triumphant proof of Britain's naval supremacy: H.M.S. Hercules passing through Kiel Canal.

by a very complete intelligence system installed in Spanish territory near Gibraltar on both sides of the strait there, in entire defiance of Spanish neutrality. But there also, a little before the close of the war, special measures were taken which would have borne fruit had the struggle continued. The last important ship to be torpedoed was the British pre-Dreadnought battleship Britannia, sunk off Gibraltar on November 9th, a sister ship of the King Edward, which was destroyed by a German mine in January, 1916, off the Scottish coast. On the eve of the armistice the losses of shipping in the Mediterranean had sunk to insignificant proportions.

In September, 1918, the British Admiralty published a list of one hundred and fifty German submarine commanders killed, taken prisoner, or interned. This was its effective reply to German assertions that the British Government exaggerated the German submarine losses. In actual fact this list was not exhaustive or complete. The Germans were known to have lost about one hundred and seventy-eight submarines before it appeared, but the British Admiralty exercised the greatest caution in claiming vessels as sunk, and never put forward claims unless survivors or wreckage sufficient for identification had been obtained from the boats destroyed, or unless there was evidence from the statements of the German officers and seamen taken in other boats to establish the loss conclusively. In an appendix to the list of German submarine officers

SURRENDERED U BOATS IN THE THAMES.
U155 (the Deutschland) moored off the Tower Bridge and (above) U64 lying off the Houses of Parliament. After the surrender of the German submarines to the British Navy in November, 1918, some of the sinister vessels which had been yielded up by the defeated enemy were exhibited in the Thames to Londoners.

whose boats were out of action a brief account was given of a few of the worst German submarine criminals, and it was announced that special efforts were made to destroy them. The chief on the list was Lieutenant-Commander Schwieger, whose fate has already been mentioned. Lieutenant Paul

German pirates accounted for

Wagenfuhr, of U44, was stated to have been guilty of the crime of killing the crew of the Belgian Prince in July, 1917. He lined up some forty officers and men on the deck of his submarine, smashed their boats, deprived them of lifebelts and clothing, and then sent his crew below and closed down his submarine, ordering the British to remain on deck. After a short interval he submerged, leaving his hapless victims to drown. He was shortly afterwards killed with most of his crew by a depth charge. Lieutenant Schneider was the officer who sank the Arabic in August, 1915, causing a loss of thirty-nine civilian lives. Admiral Tirpitz, in response to representations by the United States, made a promise to punish him, but before he could return he was destroyed by the British Navy. Three of the worst offenders remained alive at the date when the list was prepared. The first was Commander von Forstner, who torpedoed the Falaba and jeered at the women and seamen on board her when they drowned. The second was Lieutenant Wilhelm Werner, whose speciality was the sinking of hospital-ships. The last was Lieutenant-Commander Valentiner, who sank the Persia, and behaved with extreme

brutality to the crews of certain neutral ships which he lawlessly sank.

The total German submarine losses in the war were proved at the armistice to have been two hundred and three boats out of a total of three hundred and eighty-eight completed from the date some years before the war when Germany began to build these vessels. Of this enormous loss one hundred and eighty-two boats were sunk by the Allies, nearly all by the British Navy, which from the first bore the brunt of the submarine war. The German people were grossly deceived by the German Admiralty and the German Government as to the progress of this struggle. German officials consistently exaggerated the tonnage of allied ships sunk and concealed the losses of U boats. Having in the submarine campaign repeated the terrible crime and blunder of the attack on Belgium, they endeavoured to justify it by claiming a success which they never gained. After the armistice negotiations figures were published by Captain Persius, a German naval writer, which showed that in 1917 the Germans had completed eighty-three submarines against sixty-six lost. The submarines available for work at sea rose from one hundred and twenty-six in April, 1917, to one hundred and forty-six in October of that year, and this was the **Germany's total** highest figure attained. From that date the **submarine losses** total fell with some fluctuations to one hundred and thirteen in June, 1918. Of these boats, at any given time, only a small number were at sea. Thus he asserted that in January, 1917, though the conditions were then generally favourable to Germany, only twelve per cent. of the submarines were on active service, while thirty per cent. were resting in port, thirty-eight per cent. were doing trials and training, and twenty per cent. were refitting. These figures were violently assailed by an official German writer, Captain Pustau, who stated that the conditions of January, 1917, were quite abnormal, and that in 1917 there were usually from forty-five to fifty boats operating. If so, the success

AN ANIMATED AUDIENCE.
Lower-deck gun crew of a British battleship, in their flash-masks, eagerly watching the historic spectacle of the surrender of the German High Sea Fleet.

with which the British Navy combated their attacks was the more remarkable. Captain Pustau added that no fewer than three hundred and fifty-nine submarines were ordered for the German Navy between March, 1916, and the close of 1917, and that a total of one hundred and eighty boats was complete and effective in August, 1918. In December, 1918, the Allies found one hundred and seventy unfinished U boats in German yards, making a grand total of five hundred and fifty-three built from start to finish.

To build these submarines labour and material were diverted from the construction of large ships and of other war material such as Tanks. The smallest submarines, of two hundred and sixty-seven tons, took thirteen months or more to build. The medium submarines of eight hundred tons required twenty-four to thirty months to complete, and the powerful submarine cruisers of 1,800 to 3,000 tons, of which several were completed, took even longer. The demand which they

A WISE PRECAUTION.
Sailors in H.M.S. Hercules, the flagship of the Fourth Battle Squadron, wearing gas-masks while on their way out to meet the enemy fleet in case a fight should be put up.

made on the personnel of the German Navy was so serious that all the older battleships of pre-Dreadnought type and the surviving armoured cruisers had to be paid off and placed in reserve to provide crews.

The submarine losses reached the highest level in the second quarter of 1917, in which 2,236,000 tons of shipping (1,361,000 of it British) was destroyed. From that they fell each succeeding quarter until the third quarter of 1918, when only 915,000 tons (512,000 of it British) was destroyed. The output of new shipping rose as steadily, until in the second quarter of 1918, for the first time, it considerably exceeded the loss, as has already been stated. In the third quarter of 1918 it was 1,384,000 tons, or more than fifty per cent. in excess of the tonnage destroyed. This rapid increase in the output rendered the submarine campaign futile. In Captain Persius's words, " our [German] experienced seamen saw clearly and recognised how vain was all their sacrifice," and therefore they displayed in the later months of the war " little inclination for this dangerous service."

The total loss of shipping during the war reached the stupendous figure of 15,053,000 tons, against which, however, 10,849,000 tons of new shipping was constructed and 2,392,000 tons captured from the Germans, leaving a net loss of only 1,811,000 tons. But on British shipping the German campaign left its mark. The British loss was 9,031,000 tons, against which 5,588,000 tons of shipping was built, purchased, or captured. The net loss was thus 3,443,000 tons, or about one-sixth of British shipping as it stood before the war. There were two reasons why the British merchant service suffered so severely. The first was that it was the largest in the world, and that throughout the war its officers and men defied the submarine with singular heroism. It travelled through the most dangerous waters; it was the special target of attack. The second reason was that the British ship-

READY TO ADMINISTER A KNOCK-OUT BLOW IN THE EVENT OF RESISTANCE.
Up to the last moment it was deemed not impossible that at least some of the German sailors might prefer to be sunk in action rather than to surrender without firing a shot. Therefore every precaution was taken, and when the British Grand Fleet went out to take the surrender, all hands were at action-stations with guns trained, as shown in these photographs. Men of the lower deck were allowed to come up in relays to witness the triumph.

building yards were hampered by war demands and necessities. Much of their best labour was taken for the fighting ranks. Maintaining, as Great Britain did, some 5,000,000 men in her armies and fleets, and having to meet, as she had, the drain of 3,000,000 casualties in the four and a quarter years of war, she had not the workers left who were needed for an immense programme. Her yards had also to build every kind of warship to meet the submarine. Tens of thousands of men were employed in the construction of light cruisers, destroyers, and patrol craft, while in the United States the yards were comparatively free from the **British shipyards'** pressure of such requirements, and could **heavy handicap** concentrate on the building of merchant tonnage. Thus in the third quarter of 1918 only 411,000 tons was completed in the United Kingdom against 972,000 completed abroad, most of it in the United States. British shipbuilding was also delayed by the constant strikes fomented by pacifists, defeatists, and Bolshevists, who rendered the U boats notable aid and were permitted to exploit the difficulties of the nation for their own shameful ends.

The moral effect of the failure of the submarine campaign on the German people and their allies was far-reaching. They had placed the brightest hopes in the success of this campaign ; for its prosecution they had condoned the violation

This terrible disillusionment came at a time when the German offensives in France had collapsed, and when the allied armies were inflicting blow after blow upon Ludendorff, so that the whole German west front tottered. So alarming was the truth that when Professor Delbrück wished to publish the facts as to the number of American troops transported to France down to the end of June, 1918 (totalling 500,000 men for the two months of May and June), he was forbidden by the German censorship, on the ground that they were " nothing but American bluff intended to deceive the Germans." A bitter awakening was in store for Germany when, as the result of brilliant naval work and President Wilson's efforts, in the autumn of 1918 the American First and Second Armies entered the battlefield on the western front with their splendid troops. The effect of the submarine failure on the German allies—on Austria, Bulgaria, and Turkey—was disastrous. They had been led to believe that the submarine would quickly end the war. When **Moral effect of** the German Staff was proved so gravely **the U boat failure** at fault in its calculations on this head, all faith in its other judgments was shattered. The German allies watched the German armies retiring in France, and began to doubt the German tale that these retirements were "according to plan." They saw more clearly than ever that,

the collapse of the German land attacks accompanied by the failure of the German submarine campaign, rendered a German victory out of the question. Their surrender under the steady pressure of British and allied sea-power, reinforced by the violent attacks of the allied armies, was therefore only a question of time. The defeat of the submarine campaign was one of the dominating events of the war and of all history—one of the decisive causes of peace. In the winter of 1917 it had been predicted that a change in British naval policy and in the British Admiralty would determine the fate of the war. Within twelve months that prediction was verified by events. The change rendered possible the transport of immense American forces to Europe ; and the arrival of those forces on the front turned the scale.

of every law of God and man ; almost to the very last deceived, as Captain Persius wrote, " by lies— lies which were one of the chief weapons of our leaders on land and sea," and by " orgies of bluff," they had believed that it would destroy Great Britain, whom they rightly regarded as the pivot and mainspring of the whole Alliance. They were told in early 1917 that Great Britain must collapse by July of that year ; then the date was shifted to October ; then it was placed in early 1918. The first clear hint of failure was given by a German naval officer and official, Captain Kühlwetter, who stated in August, 1918, in the " Lokalanzeiger," " we have been deceived regarding the enemy's tenacity. We did not expect that Great Britain and her Allies would be so disinclined for peace after one and a half year's unrestricted submarine war. We have also been deceived regarding the ability of our enemies to hold out for so long."

BRITISH NAVAL OFFICER TAKING OVER A U BOAT.
Examining the papers of a U boat commander at the surrender of the German submarines to the British Navy, and (in oval) part of Rear-Admiral Sir Reginald Tyrwhitt's force escorting the surrendered U boats to their place of internment at Harwich in November, 1918.

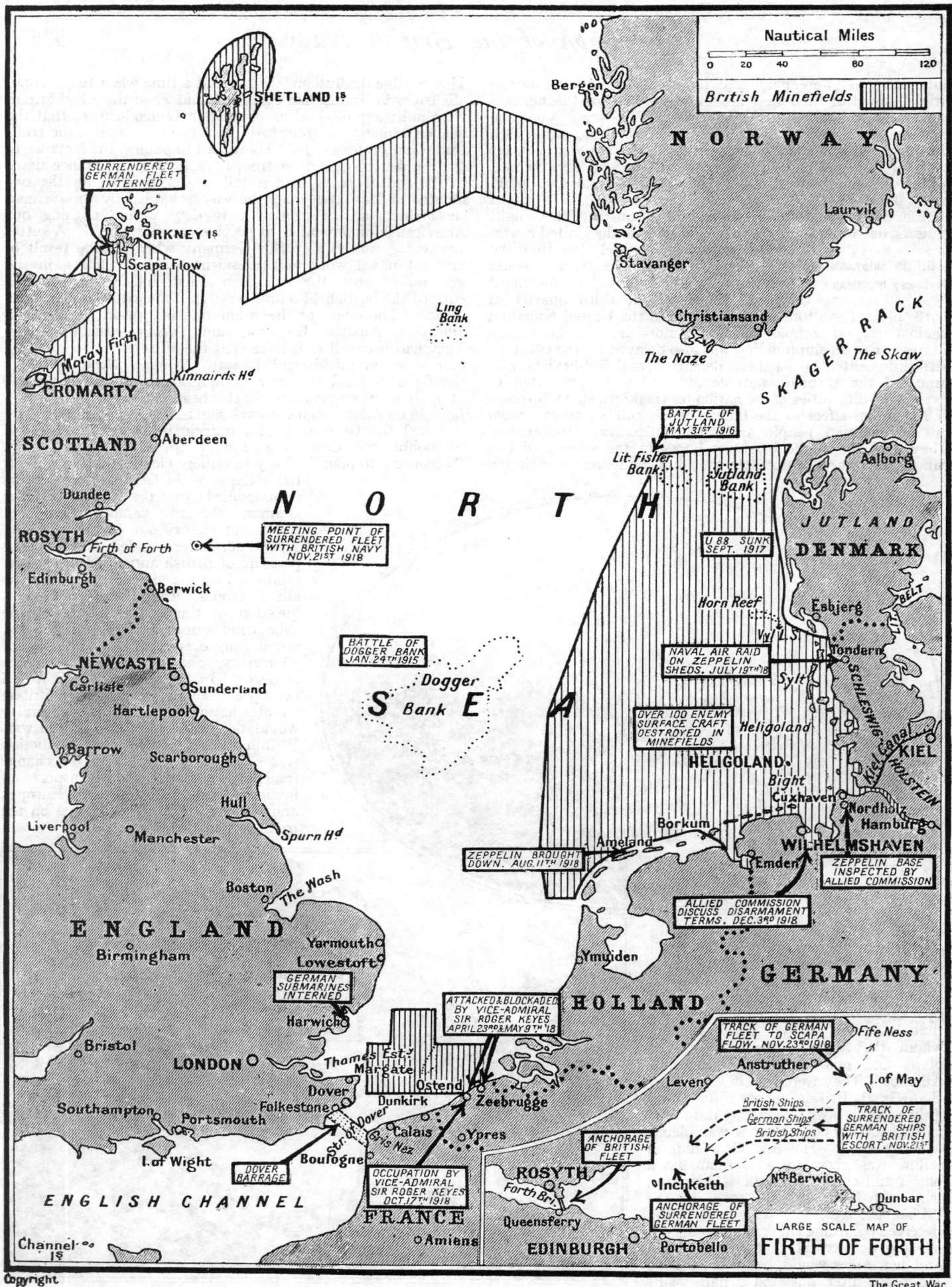

Nautical Miles

0   20   40   80   120

British Minefields

NORWAY

Bergen

Laurvik

Stavanger

Christiansand

The Naze

SKAGER RACK

The Skaw

SHETLAND IS

SURRENDERED
GERMAN FLEET
INTERNED

ORKNEY IS

Scapa Flow

Moray Firth

Kinnairds Hd

CROMARTY

SCOTLAND

Aberdeen

Dundee

ROSYTH

Firth of Forth

Edinburgh

Berwick

MEETING POINT OF
SURRENDERED FLEET
WITH BRITISH NAVY
NOV. 21ST 1918

BATTLE OF
JUTLAND
MAY 31ST 1916

Lit. Fisher
Bank

Ling
Bank

Jutland
Bank

JUTLAND

DENMARK

Aalborg

U 88 SUNK
SEPT. 1917

Esbjerg

Horn Reef

Tondern

NAVAL AIR RAID
ON ZEPPELIN
SHEDS. JULY 19TH 18

Sylt

KIEL

BELT

N O R T H

S E A

Dogger
Bank

BATTLE OF
DOGGER BANK
JAN. 24TH 1915

OVER 100 ENEMY
SURFACE CRAFT
DESTROYED IN
MINEFIELDS

Heligoland

HELIGOLAND

Bight

Cuxhaven

Nordholz

Hamburg

Kiel Canal

HOLSTEIN

SCHLESWIG

NEWCASTLE

Carlisle

Sunderland

Hartlepool

Barrow

Scarborough

Hull

Liverpool

Manchester

Spurn Hd

Boston

The Wash

ENGLAND

Birmingham

Yarmouth

Lowestoft

GERMAN
SUBMARINES
INTERNED

Harwich

ZEPPELIN BROUGHT
DOWN. AUG. 11TH 1918

Ameland

Borkum

WILHELMSHAVEN

Emden

ZEPPELIN BASE
INSPECTED BY
ALLIED COMMISSION

ALLIED COMMISSION
DISCUSS DISARMAMENT
TERMS. DEC. 3RD 1918

GERMANY

Bristol

LONDON

Thames Est.

Margate

ATTACKED & BLOCKADED
BY VICE-ADMIRAL
SIR ROGER KEYES
APRIL 23RD & MAY 9TH 18

Ymuiden

HOLLAND

TRACK OF GERMAN
FLEET TO SCAPA
FLOW. NOV. 23RD 1918

Fife Ness

Anstruther

I. of May

Southampton

Portsmouth

Dover

Folkestone

Calais

Gris Nez

Boulogne

Dunkirk

Ostend

Zeebrugge

Ypres

Leven

British Ships

German Ships

British Ships

TRACK OF
SURRENDERED
GERMAN SHIPS
WITH BRITISH
ESCORT. NOV. 21ST

I. of Wight

DOVER
BARRAGE

Str. of Dover

OCCUPATION BY
VICE-ADMIRAL
SIR ROGER KEYES
OCT. 17TH 1918

ANCHORAGE
OF BRITISH
FLEET

ROSYTH

Forth Bri.

Inchkeith

Nth Berwick

Dunbar

ENGLISH CHANNEL

Channel Is

FRANCE

Amiens

Queensferry

EDINBURGH

Portobello

ANCHORAGE OF
SURRENDERED
GERMAN FLEET

LARGE SCALE MAP OF

FIRTH OF FORTH

Copyright

The Great War

HOW THE BRITISH NAVY DEFENDED BRITAIN AND PINNED THE GERMAN NAVY TO ITS BASES.

In this admirable, self-explanatory outline map are shown the localities of the most notable naval events in the North Sea and the British mine-fields which practically closed egress to enemy ships. The inset plan shows in detail the course of the German ships from the rendezvous for surrender to their temporary anchorage at Inchkeith and thence to internment in Scapa Flow.

The second great feature of this period of the naval war was the intensification of the blockade through the severance of the German communications with the Near East. This was only possible because sea-power enabled the Allies to choose their theatre of attack, and because the naval offensive held the submarines in check and permitted the movement of transport and supplies by sea. In the early weeks of the summer of 1918 German land-power reached its fullest development. German armies had overrun all Western Russia. Finland, Poland, Lithuania, the Ukraine, most of Southern Russia (to within a few miles of the Volga), the Caucasus, and Northern Persia—all these were in German hands or under German influence. The tunnels through the Taurus range were finished; the gaps which had long impeded traffic on the Bagdad Railway were bridged, and trains could run from Berlin, with only the brief interruption at the Bosphorus, to Nisibin, in Western Mesopotamia. The Damascus Railway connected the Bagdad line with Syria and Palestine, and the Hedjaz line, which was still in the hands of the Turks, gave a connection with Arabia. Thus a solid block of nearly 2,000,000 square miles under German control extended from the North Sea and Channel to points well within the confines of Asia. Mittel-Europa, the vast land confederation of which the Pan-Germans had dreamed, seemed a reality accomplished. Russia, Germany's former rival in the East, had perished, committing suicide. The two great inland seas, the Baltic and Black Sea, had both become German lakes, thus supplementing German land-power, and bringing Germany nearer to the rich territories of the Caucasus and Asia Minor, where crops ripened early in the summer. Steps were being taken to organise the production of food in the Ukraine and Rumania, so that it might

German land-power at its maximum suffice in a not distant future for German needs. Germany appeared, in fact, to have counteracted the British blockade by a land expansion which opened to her every climate, and would give her command—so soon as she could perfect her measures—of every kind of product. She had come within sight of realising her most dazzling dreams. The French Empire at the moment of its greatest extent under Napoleon I. never held such control of the fertile territories of Europe; it never reached Western Asia, and never succeeded, as did Germany, in opening communication with tropical and sub-tropical climates.

The Allies' position in the East against this colossal power appeared most precarious. From Salonika to the Adriatic an allied army watched the Bulgarians, but down to the end of summer could make no progress against them. In Palestine, north of Jerusalem, was General Allenby with a force which was greatly underestimated by the German High Command, and which seemed to the allied nations to have been brought to a standstill. Its white troops had been greatly depleted to reinforce the army in France. In Mesopotamia was another British force which had to overcome serious transport difficulties before it could move northward from Bagdad. It had also to cover its right flank against the Turkish and German forces which were appearing in Persia, while other British detachments had to watch so-called Bolshevist forces that, under German direction, were attempting to move down the Transcaspian Railway towards the north-west frontier of India.

Yet other allied detachments were in Northern Russia, holding the bases on the Arctic coast and preventing the advance to them of the Germans from Finland. In Siberia, too, small allied forces were guarding the Siberian Railway,

and doing their best to prevent the seizure of the military stores and supplies of provisions scattered at its eastern stations and junctions. The Germans, holding the central position, with the numerous and excellent railway routes which they possessed, could throw their forces against any point if those forces were not pinned down by constant attacks. But if the German main forces were held in any field, then the British sea-power could make its influence felt in the subsidiary fields by covering the movement to them of troops. In this period of the war the enormous resources of India were much more freely and intelligently

OUTWARD BOUND ON THE GREATEST MISSION IN HISTORY.
The British Grand Fleet steaming under the Forth Bridge when putting to sea to take the surrender of the German High Sea Fleet on November 21st, 1918. Human records contained no precedent for such a tribute by one Power to the naval supremacy of another

used. New units were raised there, and moved by sea to Mesopotamia and Palestine, under cover of the far-off Grand Fleet and the anti-submarine flotillas guarding the Atlantic and North Sea. They replaced the troops that had been diverted to the western front to meet the main German offensive of 1918. The strength of General Allenby's army steadily rose; the British force in Mesopotamia increased, while the strictest silence was maintained and nothing was said or done that could prematurely alarm the enemy. At the appointed hour, when the allied offensive on the western front developed in all its violence, each of these secondary fronts was to burst into flame.

Previous chapters of this volume have told how the Salonika armies dealt the first great blow by reaching the vital Berlin-Bagdad line in Serbian territory and compelling the surrender of Bulgaria. The land communications of Mittel-Europa were **British sea-power emerges supreme** destroyed by this stroke, though the sea route from Odessa to Constantinople still remained open for the Germans. This, too, was speedily cut. General Allenby's troops, three days after the break-through on the Salonika front, burst in greatly superior force through the Turkish line in Palestine, and advanced with extraordinary speed and energy through Syria. Finally the Mesopotamian army, as soon as climatic conditions and the progress of General Allenby's army permitted, put itself in movement and drove the Turks out of the last shred of Mesopotamia. Jointly these two armies compelled the surrender of Turkey, and by brilliant generalship, which attracted regretful praise even from German critics, wiped out the defeats of Gallipoli and Kut, and forced the opening of the Dardanelles and Bosphorus to the allied fleet. The effect of this on Germany's position was catastrophic, because it gave sea-power means of striking at the Germans in the Ukraine and Southern Russia, and cut off all hope of large future supplies from that quarter. On the day on which the armistice with Turkey took effect, Austria asked for an armistice, and Germany's last ally deserted.

Though the food position in Germany never became utterly desperate it slowly deteriorated under the steady pressure of the blockade. In 1918 some small supplies of meat and wheat were obtained from the Ukraine, but the break-down of transport on the Russian railways had been so complete, and friction with the Ukraine peasants was so continuous, that the task of revictualling Germany and Austria from this quarter was greatly hindered. Germany, after conquering Russia with the aid of Karl Marx and of a little gang of international criminals, paid a bitter penalty for her treason to mankind. The Bolshevist system so entirely destroyed production and transport in Russia that it made of fertile territory a desert from which nothing could be drawn. Fats and meat became increasingly scarce in Germany and Austria, especially in the towns. The scarcity of fodder, due to a bad hay harvest in 1917, compelled the slaughter of cattle and pigs in miserable condition. Official figures showed that whereas in 1914 the German ox on an average had yielded six to seven and a half hundredweight of meat, in the summer of 1918 it gave only three hundredweight.

Steady pressure of the blockade Meatless weeks were enforced in most parts of Germany between August and November, 1918. Though the official regulations were evaded by a system of wholesale fraud, the effect was to strengthen the desire for peace at any price. Even bread was scarce, though here again fraudulent trading had to be taken into account. The official ration was in many cases not more than six ounces a day. In Austria conditions were worse. In the suburbs of Vienna, in Tyrol, in Carinthia, Styria, and Carniola, and in German Bohemia the shortage of food was such that many cases of hunger typhus were reported, and the German Government was compelled to promise aid.

The blockade cut off the supply of wool and cotton, and compelled the Germans to fall back on thread made from cellulose or wood-pulp, which was used for such purposes as making sand-bags, and even for clothes, though the wearing qualities of this fabric were wretched. Leather and rubber grew scarcer every month, though up to the last the German soldiers were supplied with good boots. The want of such metals as nickel and tungsten, used in making the finer qualities of steel, affected the output of munitions and the efficiency of such weapons as the German Tanks, which for lack of high-quality armour had to be plated thickly, and were consequently lacking in **Germany on the** mobility. When the Germans surrendered **verge of breakdown** they were on the verge of a general break-down for want of these and other indispensable requisites of war. The blockade had cut off the oversea supplies, and the progress of the allied armies in the Near and Middle East had destroyed the last hope of obtaining what was needed from those regions of the world. Had the blockade been vigorously enforced at the outset, in 1914 and 1915, the agony of Europe might have been shortened by two years.

In this last period neutral States were strictly rationed, and the growing shortage of transport—caused in large part by the submarine campaign—and scarcity of food throughout the world—caused by the diversion of man-power from food production to the fighting-line and the supply of munitions—left no margin available for the trade which they had conducted with such profit to themselves in the earlier period of the war. All foodstuffs and all shipping were controlled by the Allies, and except for some small leakage through Holland, Denmark, and Sweden, where the "goulash millionaires," or men who had made fortunes by supplying Germany, still snatched at every opportunity for gain, even at the price of suffering in their own countries, the blockade was "watertight." Neutrals felt the food scarcity severely, and in Holland in 1917-18 there was real distress, though for this not the Allies but the Dutch exporters were to blame.

THE PASSING OF THE GERMAN NAVY INTO BRITISH CUSTODY, NOVEMBER 21st, 1918.

As the German ships, steaming slowly down the centre of the British lines, came abreast the 1st Battle Squadron, every squadron of the Grand Fleet made a half circle and, led by its flagship, steamed back on the course it had come, with the German vessels between the two columns. The 1st and 4th Battle Squadrons steamed on the south side of the enemy capital ships, and on the north side Admiral Beatty's flagship led the 2nd and 6th Battle Squadrons.

GERMAN DESTROYERS STEAMING TO SURRENDER.
Fifty German destroyers were to have been handed over when Admiral Beatty took the surrender of the German High Sea Fleet, but one was mined on its way to the rendezvous. Thus forty-nine, surrounded by nearly one hundred and fifty British destroyers, were led by H.M.S. Castor to the point of surrender.

In the last months of the war the German High Sea Fleet remained inactive in its ports, or cruised only in the Baltic, where it had not to fear attack by the British Navy. The British Grand Fleet was strengthened by the accession of six American Dreadnoughts, which formed the Sixth Battle Squadron, and raised the total of Dreadnought battleships available in the North Sea to forty-one. The battle-cruiser force, which had been weakened by the heavy losses in the Battle of Jutland, was raised by the completion of the Renown, Repulse, Courageous, and Glorious to ten. The Grand Fleet had therefore an overwhelming superiority, as the German Dreadnought battleships only numbered eighteen completed in the summer of 1918, and the German battle-cruisers five. Yet so long as this German force remained in existence it acted as a check on the Grand Fleet. It had prevented the British Fleet from entering the Baltic in the critical weeks of 1917, when the Germans were attacking Riga and threatening Petrograd, and it prevented the Allies from operating in that sea in 1918, when a close blockade of the German Baltic coast would have greatly added to German transport difficulties. It protected the German North Sea bases and kept them open for the submarines until the British mine-fields stopped U boat movements. It was thus an important factor in the naval war.

Had it been destroyed in the Battle of Jutland, when it was caught at sea by British forces of far greater strength, the submarine campaign could never have been attempted, and some ten million tons of merchant shipping would have been saved from destruction. As the battle ended, the Germans returned to port with shattered ships and weakened moral. Though a few weeks after Jutland the High Sea Fleet again put to sea, and was seen off the Dutch coast, it never risked an encounter with the British. Among the seamen inactivity bred discontent, which was intensified by bad food. In the summer of 1917, as was known from statements in the Reichstag, a mutiny was planned. The discontented seamen intended to seize some of the most unpopular officers and force the others to take the ships to a neutral port, where they would be interned. The German Admiralty discovered what was brewing, and struck before the men's plans were ripe. It arrested a number of ringleaders, though not without difficulty. In several ships there were disturbances, and one captain of a battleship was killed. It was impossible at the time for the Allies to determine whether the mutiny was serious. Information obtained after the surrender of the fleet showed that it was. A few of the ringleaders were shot ; others were sent to Flanders and put to dangerous work in the trenches. One of the men's chief grievances was the badness of the food, and this was improved by the German naval authorities. Steps were taken to give the men more leave and better opportunities of recreation, but not with entire success. A small minority of extremists remained in the ships and worked in combination with Anarchists of the Liebknecht type in the Reichstag.

This internal discontent further reduced the fighting power of the High Sea Fleet. It does not seem to have so seriously infected the submarine flotillas or the destroyers, and no case was known of a submarine crew mutinying and surrendering, notwithstanding rumours to **Discontent in the** that effect which from time to time circu- **German Navy** lated in Britain. The crews, however, were determined on one thing—that they would not fight another great battle, and this determination seems to have been shared by some of the officers. The consequence was that all through 1918 the High Sea Fleet was little more than a make-believe. Its efficiency had departed, and it could not be used for any difficult or dangerous work. Even the German destroyer flotillas showed less enterprise than earlier in the war—perhaps as the result of the terrible lessons which they had received from the British Navy. At short intervals Admiral Beatty, with his light and fast ships, swept the Bight

SEVEN LIGHT CRUISERS LED TO INTERNMENT.
H.M.S. Phaeton leading the German light cruisers, which formed a portion of the fleet handed over to Admiral Beatty in the North Sea on November 21st, 1918. In the rear of the cruisers came a crowded mass of the enemy's torpedo-boat destroyers.

of Heligoland. On these occasions the heavy ships were always ready to give support. On June 19th British light craft searched the waters off the German coast and encountered nothing more formidable than seaplanes, one of which was brought down.

Exactly a month later, on July 19th, the Grand Fleet conducted another sweep. On this occasion it was off the Schleswig coast for the best part of two days, and it effected with naval aircraft a very successful raid against the Zeppelin sheds at Tondern. Aeroplanes were now carried in all the British battleships and battle-cruisers of the Dreadnought class, and used for " spotting " and assisting the gunnery officers in battle, or for attack on Zeppelins and enemy aircraft and for bombing. They were the light fast type of fighting machine, so that the weight of bombs which

Naval aeroplane raid on Tondern they could carry was not large. In a few ships two aeroplanes were supplied, the additional machine for protecting the aeroplane used in scouting.

In the attack on Tondern a number of machines were engaged, making their ascent from the huge aeroplane-carrying ship Furious, which was so fitted that machines could rise from her at sea and even alight on her in fair weather conditions. The aeroplanes left in two flights, timing their movements so as to arrive at Tondern just before dawn. One machine was compelled to return owing to engine trouble, but the others proceeded to Tondern and carried out their orders. Captain Dickson, of the Royal Air Force, was the first to arrive. He flew down the main street at a height of only fifty feet, and was apparently mistaken for a German airman, as the anti-aircraft guns did not open fire and a welcome was waved to him by a stray milkman in the sleeping town below. He found what he supposed to be a Zeppelin shed and dropped a bomb on it, when there was a terrific explosion, showing that he had hit an ammunition store. He then steered for the Zeppelin shed, as it was clear that the building he had attacked was not his objective. He discovered the shed, came down low, and bombed it, when it burst into flames. The gas in the two Zeppelins which were known to be inside must have caught fire, as a blaze shot up from it to a height of a thousand feet. Meanwhile, the German guns opened fire, but through their barrage came the other British aircraft, guided by the glare of the fires, and completed the work. Yet another large shed was bombed and wrecked. Of the British airmen, three were compelled to alight on Danish territory, where they were interned, but one of the three almost immediately made his escape.

This operation destroyed two of the best Zeppelins, and was an example of the work which aircraft could accomplish when skilfully used in conjunction with a naval force. The whole of North Germany was exposed to the raids of machines carried by such vessels as the Furious. A few weeks later, on August 11th, yet another sweep of the Bight of Heligoland was carried out, and again the German Navy declined battle. On this occasion one of the latest and most powerful Zeppelins was encountered and destroyed north of the island of Ameland. It was flying at 19,000 feet when it was attacked by a British aeroplane and its crew perished, with the exception of a single survivor who was picked up by a Dutch fishing vessel. The British light craft working inshore were

Heligoland Bight swept again violently attacked by German aircraft, and six British motor-boats were forced into Dutch waters, where the German aircraft followed them and destroyed or disabled them. They had no weapon more powerful than a Lewis gun, and their ammunition was exhausted. All the crews escaped, with a loss of four men wounded. Several German destroyers and one German battleship were seen, but they kept at such a distance that they could not be cut off and brought to action.

In August a complete change in the higher personnel of the German Admiralty was carried out, apparently because General Ludendorff and the German Staff wished to send the High Sea Fleet out to battle in a last desperate effort to break British communications with France and the United States. Vice-Admiral Behnke succeeded Admiral Capelle as Secretary of State for the Admiralty. Admiral Scheer, who had

commanded the High Sea Fleet in the Battle of Jutland, became Chief of the Admiralty Staff, and was succeeded in command by Admiral Hipper. This officer had previously commanded the German battle-cruisers and carried out the raids on British open towns which ended so ignominiously in the Battle of the Dogger Bank, where his force had a very narrow escape from total destruction. Admiral Holtzendorff, whom Scheer superseded, was regarded as an advocate of brutal submarine war and an opponent of any strategy which would have risked the High Sea Fleet. He was one of the officers responsible for the comparatively feeble armament of the German battleships, for the failure to meet the British advance in calibre, and for the retention of the 12 in. gun in new designs at a date when Great Britain was building vessels armed with the 15 in. weapon. From statements in the German Press there was clear evidence of dissatisfaction with the armament and performance of the Germany Navy, and in particular with the failure of its submarines to stop the movement of American troops to Europe in British and American transports. Scheer was known to have protested against military interference with German naval strategy during his command of the High Sea Fleet. There may have been hopes that he would be more amenable to pressure if he were brought to Berlin. A few weeks later, as the German position on land was rapidly becoming desperate, preparations were made for a naval battle.

Meanwhile, complete disaster befell the German and Austrian naval forces in the Mediterranean and Black Sea. In late 1917 a mutinous feeling had shown itself in the Austrian Fleet, and had led in February, 1918, to a serious outbreak among the Jugo-Slav seamen, who formed the bulk of the crews. Two of the smaller ships, the St. George and Erzherzog Rudolf, hoisted the Red Flag, and were joined by some other vessels, but not by the bulk of the Fleet. The outbreak was speedily suppressed, and many of those concerned in it were executed. After the great defeat of the Austrian armies on the Piave in October, **Italian officers'** 1918, the Jugo-Slavs declared their independ- **feat at Pola** ence, and thus the Austrian naval bases were cut off from Austria proper and left isolated in Jugo-Slav territory. On October 31st the crews of the Austrian Fleet at Pola mutinied and seized all the remaining vessels of the Fleet. The same day the Austrian Government announced that " the Fleet, naval works, and other naval property shall be handed over to the South Slav National Council, sitting at Pola." Doubt remained as to whether this was not a trick designed to embarrass the Allies. At the same time Fiume was seized by Croat troops for the Jugo-Slavs, and to complete the confusion the people of the town declared its union with Italy.

Accurate news of the situation had not reached the Allies when a very daring and successful attack was made by an Italian officer, Lieutenant Raffaele Paolucci, on the Austrian Dreadnought Viribus Unitis in the port of Pola. He had devised a type of mine which could be propelled by a compressed air-motor and guided by a swimmer. With two of these, one of them in charge of Major Rossetti, he arrived in a motor-boat off Pola at nightfall of November 1st. Paolucci and Rossetti each guided one of the mines and made their way quietly into the harbour. They passed a wooden pier, along which Austrian sentries were patrolling, escaping detection by wearing hats which looked like bottles floating in the water. They then worked past a boom, carrying an electric alarm wire, and reached three rows of steel nets, through which they had to cut. They got through these only to find yet another series of three nets, and they were so long in breaking through them that it became clear to them that they could not escape from the harbour before day broke. They determined therefore to abandon one of their mines and with the other to go right into the harbour and sink the flagship. She was the huge Viribus Unitis, and undiscovered they made their way to her and placed their mine under her, timing it to explode at 6.30. They had now been nine hours in the water, and were completely exhausted. As they were attempting to escape they were discovered and seized. Taken on board the Viribus Unitis, they were brought to Admiral Voucovich, who commanded the squadron.

ADMIRAL SIR DAVID BEATTY, G.C.B., G.C.V.O., D.S.O..
Commander-in-Chief of the Grand Fleet.

ADMIRAL SIR DAVID BEATTY, G.C.B., G.C.V.O., D.S.O.
Commander-in-Chief of the Grand Fleet

It was now so near the time when the mine was to explode that there was no possibility of the Austrians removing it, and the two Italian officers informed the admiral of what they had done, so that he might abandon ship and take measures to save life. He treated them with chivalry, told them that they were brave men and deserved to live, and gave orders to abandon ship, permitting them to save themselves. But then, suspecting that they had tricked him, he ordered them to be brought back, and they came up the side just two minutes before the mine was to explode. On deck they ran for the stern as fast as they could when the explosion took place. Both escaped by swimming, but the ship went down with Admiral Voucovich, who remained gallantly on board to the last. The two Italian officers were picked up in the water by the Austrians and were liberated at the armistice. The other mine was carried by the current under a large Austrian steamer and there exploded, causing great damage.

As the result of these incidents and of the earlier losses which the Austrian Navy had sustained, its fighting value had vanished. By the armistice terms, which came into force on November 4th, Austria was required to surrender to the Allies three battleships, three light cruisers, nine destroyers, twelve torpedo-boats, one mine-layer, six Danube monitors, and fifteen Austrian submarines, in addition to all the German submarines then in Austrian waters. All other **Austrian Navy out** warships were to be disarmed under allied **of the war** supervision, as also were all naval aircraft. The Allies were to have the right of occupying Pola, Istria (including Trieste), and a part of Dalmatia. All allied prisoners in Austrian hands were to be surrendered. These conditions were carried out, though not without some little difficulty. The Jugo-Slavs, into whose hands the Fleet had been given by the Government as being allies, claimed the warships, and considerable friction arose between them and the Italian Government. This friction, however, concerns political rather than naval history. From the opening of November the Austrian Navy was out of the war and the Austrian naval bases irrevocably lost to Germany, with the great port of Trieste, which Bismarck and his successors had

regarded as German and to be preserved in German hands at whatever sacrifice.

As in Austria, so in Turkey, utter catastrophe befell the German plans. On October 30th the announcement was made that that day an armistice with Turkey came into force, the result of the magnificent victories gained by General Allenby in the most astounding campaign which figures in British military records. The influence of this campaign on the war was vast, and it was one of the direct and immediate causes of the German collapse. By the armistice conditions the Dardanelles and Bosphorus were opened to the Allies, who were given the right to occupy strategic points in Turkey, such as the forts on these passages, and to use Turkish ports, bases, and anchorages. All Turkish **Allies pass up the** ships were to be surrendered for dis- **Dardanelles** armament and internment at Turkish ports, under the supervision of the Allies. In these ships was necessarily included the German battle-cruiser Goeben, which had remained in Turkish waters with a largely German crew.

One problem remained after this surrender—whether the Goeben and the other German forces in Turkey and the Black Sea would resist. Not for some days was it possible for the Allies to pass up the Dardanelles, though a very powerful fleet had been collected at Mudros in preparation for any resistance on the German part. It was under the command of Vice-Admiral Gough-Calthorpe, and it included two British Dreadnoughts, the Temeraire and Superb ; two of the most powerful pre-Dreadnoughts, Lord Nelson and Agamemnon ; and a number of French, Italian, and Greek battleships, so that it was amply sufficient for any work that might have to be done. The Germans had no inconsiderable number of ships available, but their fighting quality was not high. Owing to the treachery of the Bolshevists they had in their control the following Russian ships :

Volia, Dreadnought, 23,000 tons, 21 knots, twelve 12 in. guns.
Evstafi, Zlatoust, Svobodnaia Rossiya, Sinope, Tri Sviatitelya, Rostislav, Georghi Pobiedonosetz, pre-Dreadnoughts.
Pamyat, Merkurya, Ochakoff, Nakhimoff, light cruisers.
Almaz, aeroplane carrier.
Twenty-one destroyers, eleven submarines, one submarine mine-layer.

AFTER THE COLLAPSE OF TURKEY: BRITISH SHIPS ANCHORED OFF CONSTANTINOPLE.
British cruiser, in the foreground to the right, and other British vessels moored alongside at Constantinople. It was on November 13th, 1918, that the Allied Fleet steamed up the Dardanelles to the Turkish capital—the first time in history since the coming of the Turk into Europe that a victorious navy had made its way to Constantinople. On the following day the British flag was rehoisted over the British Embassy.

ONE OF BRITAIN'S NAVAL SECRETS REVEALED AFTER THE CLOSE OF THE WAR.

The monitor-submarine M1, one of the many remarkable additions to the naval strength of Britain armed submersible vessel that had ever been constructed. Though the M1 was laid down in 1914, the which were made during the course of the war. The long and powerful craft was a submersible type was kept secret until after the armistice, when photographs were allowed to be made public and monitor, and as she carried a 12 in. gun, which fired a shell of 850 lb., she was the most powerfully some details of the wonderful vessel were made known.

These vessels might be supported by the Goeben, and were based on the great ports and dockyards of Odessa, Nikolaieff, and Sebastopol, where they were in more or less direct railway communication with Germany through Southern Russia. Over 100,000 tons of British shipping was in German hands in the Black Sea, and some of these vessels might have been armed. The Russian warships had been carefully overhauled and were understood to have been put into good condition after they had been taken over from the Bolshevists. German crews had been despatched to them. There was one difficulty in the way of operations on their part. All the ships burned oil fuel, and there was a great scarcity of this, since Baku, the great oil centre of Russia, remained, except for a short interval, in the hands of Russians loyal to the Allies and of a small British expeditionary force despatched there.

Some days passed before a passage through the Dardanelles could be cleared by the British mine-sweepers. The weather was bad, and this greatly interfered with their work. On November 5th, for the first time since the tragic days when the Allies withdrew from Gallipoli, British fighting **British flag on Gallipoli** men landed on that terrible Peninsula. They came from aircraft, half a dozen of which descended at Galata, where was a German aerodrome. They flew low, at a height of only about 400 feet above the ground, and carried white streamers. It was lucky that they took this precaution. The Turks, it afterwards appeared, had not been warned, and were greatly surprised. On November 9th British troops landed at Gallipoli to occupy the Peninsula and forts. There was something strangely dramatic in this victorious return of the British flag after so many months to the scene of the greatest tragedy in the war. The works and trenches which in 1915 had seethed with activity and crackled with rifle fire were still and desolate. Thorn bush was spreading over the thousands of graves. In the channel below the heights of the Peninsula lay the wrecks of the allied battleships, and the rusty hull of the Messudiyeh, sunk by a British submarine, could be made out. The British troops peacefully tramped ashore where years before they had had to fight every inch of the way with fearful losses through the hail of lead from machine-guns ; and with no ado or display, as is the fashion of the race, famous battalions from Salonika took possession of the forts.

A little later the Allied Fleet passed up the Dardanelles. This was the first time in history—since the coming of the Turk—that a victorious navy had made its way to Constantinople. In 1878 Sir Geoffrey Hornby had passed the Dardanelles with the connivance if not the actual consent of the Turks ; in 1807 Sir John Duckworth had fought his way up and narrowly escaped disaster on his return. Now the Allies steamed by the Plains of Troy and the lands which through all the generations of man have been the theatre of world-encounters. It was a signal demonstration of the tenacity of the British spirit that after such vicissitudes and so much suffered and endured, the goal of 1915 should at last have been reached and the fearful sacrifices of 1915 at Gallipoli redeemed. The imposing force without misadventure threaded the narrow **Allied Fleet at** strait and debouched in the Sea of Marmora. **Constantinople** On November 13th the Allied Fleet was off Constantinople. The flagship Superb led the array, with the Temeraire, Lord Nelson, and Agamemnon following her, and the other cruisers, destroyers, and mine-sweepers of the British squadron. Then at an interval of half an hour came the French squadron, and after that again the Italian and Greek squadrons. The two British Dreadnoughts, with two French battleships, anchored close to the European side of the Bosphorus, in sight of the Sultan's Palace and the Chamber of Deputies, while from the ships the minarets and domes of the Turkish capital were in full view. On the following day, November 14th, after four years of absence the British flag was hoisted over the British Embassy on the arrival of Sir Somerset Gough-Calthorpe, Admiral and British High Commissioner, to take up residence there. The ceremony was carried out in presence of vast crowds, among which were many hundred German soldiers and seamen watching curiously and sullenly.

All this time there was no sign of the German ships in the Black Sea. They remained inert while the Goeben was surrendered and interned, after her disarmament, under British supervision. The armistice with Germany was signed before the Allied Fleet was ready to proceed into the Black Sea. By a clause in this the German Navy was required to evacuate the Black Sea ports, surrender British merchant shipping, and hand over to the Allies, for ultimate return to Russia, the Russian warships which had temporarily fallen into Germany's power. Shortly after the signing of the armistice the Allied Fleet entered the Black Sea and visited

Sachsen, and Württemberg, and the new battle-cruisers Mackensen and Von Spee, were still incomplete, though they had all been laid down four years before, in 1914. Their construction had been delayed by the submarine programme. There were only eighteen battleships and five battle-cruisers of the Dreadnought type available. Not only was the British-American force superior in ships of this type, of which it had fifty-one to the German twenty-three—an overwhelming superiority in numbers; it was also far more powerfully armed, as the British had adopted the 13·5 in. and 15 in. gun, while the Germans were still clinging to the 11 in. and 12 in.

CENTRES OF NAVAL ACTIVITY IN THE MEDITERRANEAN AND THE NEAR EAST.

During the early days of November, 1918, which preceded the final collapse of Germany on the western front, events moved rapidly in the south-eastern theatre of the war. The successive surrenders of Bulgaria, Turkey, and Austria were followed by the allied occupation of such important centres as Trieste and Constantinople. In this map are indicated some outstanding events of the last month of the Great War from the Adriatic to the Black Sea.

the bases where the Russian warships had been collected. On November 26th it arrived at Sebastopol, and found that the ships there had been greatly neglected since the German collapse. No resistance was offered; the Russian vessels were quietly handed over, and the Allies left detachments of troops for the protection of Odessa and Sebastopol, and sent aid to the Cossacks under Generals Denikin and Krasnoff, who were in arms against the Bolshevists.

Germany's one remaining hope The collapse of her allies rendered the naval position of Germany more and more difficult, while the rapid advance of Marshal Foch's armies menaced the Fatherland with invasion. Only one hope remained, and that an elusive and desperate one. The German Naval Staff determined to make a last attempt to meet the British Fleet at sea. There were clear signs of such an intention which did not escape the British Admiralty. In the week ending October 23rd the submarines did not sink a single vessel except for one ship torpedoed in the Mediterranean. The fact was that they were concentrating in the North Sea with a battle in view. At the end of October orders were issued to the captains of the various German ships to prepare for sea, and the submarine flotillas which returned to Heligoland found the whole German Fleet there lying ready. On October 30th instructions were given for the Fleet to get ready for a cruise, and go out on the following day, October 31st. It was reported that the Commander-in-Chief wished to "manœuvre in the Bight." The men at once suspected that Admiral Hipper meant to meet the British in battle.

They considered the chances. The new battleships Baden,

weapon. Thus the vessels of Dreadnought type in the two fleets mounted the following guns:

Guns.	British-American Shells. lb.	Grand Fleet. Guns.	German Shells. lb.	High Sea Fleet. Guns.
15 in.	1,720	100	1,675	8
14 in.	1,400	30	—	—
13·5 in.	1,250	144	—	—
12 in.	850	198	860	106
11 in.	—	—	660	124
		472		238

In numbers the artillery preponderance of the Grand Fleet was two to one; in smashing power and weight of metal it was three to one. Moreover, many of the German vessels were in poor order. The older ships, including the battleships of the Deutschland class, some of which had fought at Jutland, were there found such an embarrassment that they had been paid off and their crews used to man submarines. On paper the German Navy had not the remotest chance of victory; at the best it could only hope to sink with honour, as did Admiral **The Grand Fleet's** Rojdestvensky's fleet in the Battle of **vast preponderance** Tsushima in 1905, and Admiral Cervera's little Spanish squadron off Santiago in 1898. It might go down firing for the honour of the flag, and thus wipe out something of the infamy which attached to it for its conduct in the lawless submarine campaign.

Jutland had demonstrated to the German seaman the sad deficiencies of the German Fleet. Before the battle he had been led to believe that the German artillery was greatly superior to the British, and that the 12 in. Krupp was a full match for the British 15 in. weapon. He had been taught that the German Navy was invincible. But though at Jutland the German Fleet had met the British and, after inflicting very heavy losses on the Grand Fleet, had itself got away with comparatively small sacrifice of ships, no doubt remained as to the relative position of the two forces. As the German naval writer Captain Persius stated, " had the weather been clear, and had the British commander been resolute, the result **German seamen** would have been **refuse to fight** annihilation for us. The long-ranged British guns would soon have sent our weakly armoured ships to the bottom. In spite of fortune which smiled upon us, our Fleet's losses were severe, and on June 1st, 1916, it was clear to every reasoning person that this battle must and would be the only one. That was openly stated in authoritative circles." The Germans did not believe that the series of events by which a completely beaten fleet was allowed to get away from a force greatly its superior would ever be repeated, and they knew that the command of the British Grand Fleet had been changed. The German seamen were determined on one

land the crews barricaded themselves in the fore-parts of the ship, and took possession of certain guns. Orders were then given by the admiral for German destroyers to approach the two mutinous ships, with guns loaded and torpedoes ready, while Marines were brought on board to take off the mutineers. There was no fighting, however. After an hour's parley the mutineers hoisted the Red Cross flag and submitted. Some six hundred of them were sent ashore. But their act had prevented any sortie. It had shown the temper of the Fleet, and had elicited so much sympathy in the other ships that the crews could not be trusted to fight. In the words of a German seaman, writing about November 2nd: " The Fleet will not put to sea in the near future, and peace must come soon, or we shall make it ourselves. The Navy will take no further hand; if only the Army and the people would follow soon!" Immediately after, the crews took charge and set up Seamen's Councils in control.

The alternative to a final battle, in which the German Navy should perish with honour, was the ignominious surrender of that Navy. It had proved too grave a danger to the peace of the world and to the safety of neutrals to be left in German hands; and the deadliness of the submarine was such that the German U boat had to be placed in sure keeping. The collapse of the German Navy led directly up to the conclusion of the armistice, when terms were dictated by Marshal Foch and Admiral Sir Rosslyn Wemyss, representing respectively the land forces and the sea forces of the Alliance. By the

SHIPS OF THE ALLIES IN THE SEA OF MARMORA.
Greek and French warships anchored off Constantinople in November, 1918. In circle : The German warship **Goeben** after it had been handed over to the Allies on the surrender of Turkey. The top photograph shows ships of the Allied Fleet on their way to Constantinople.

thing—they would not go out and fight. They speedily manifested their determination, and according to Captain Persius, " every German who is not deluded by inflated phrases will be glad that they did this ; by their action they rendered the German Navy an incalculable service."

In many of the ships the crews quietly acted and refused to obey the orders to prepare for sea. They used the fire-extinguishing appliances to put out the fires which had been lighted in the boilers. In the Thüringen the captain addressed the crew and told them : " We will fire off our two thousand rounds (of big-gun ammunition), and will go down with colours flying." The crew at once shouted that, if so, he would have to go out and go down alone. In the Thüringen and Helgo-

naval terms all the effective German submarines were to proceed to an allied port for internment there. The Germans were to surrender for internment at a neutral port, or allied port, all their newest Dreadnoughts (sixteen in number), eight light cruisers, and fifty of their latest destroyers. All their other surface warships and naval aircraft were to be disarmed and interned under allied supervision in German ports. The task of settling the details of this surrender was given to Admiral Sir David Beatty, Commander-in-Chief of the Grand Fleet. He fixed upon Harwich as the place of internment for the submarines. As no neutral would undertake the dangerous business of guarding the German Fleet, he finally directed that the German ships should proceed to Rosyth and there be met by the Grand Fleet and inspected, after which they would be sent north to Scapa Flow.

There was some resistance to the allied order for the surrender of this enormous force, an event without parallel in the whole history of naval war. At the armistice discussions the German naval representative protested. "Is it admissible," he said, "that we should surrender our Fleet though it has not been beaten?" Sir Rosslyn Wemyss answered at once, "It has only to come out," and the Germans protested no more. On November 16th a force of British light cruisers left Rosyth to escort the German cruiser Königsberg, which brought with her Rear-Admiral Meurer,

who had commanded the German Dreadnought König at Jutland, and was appointed to arrange the final details of the surrender with Admiral Beatty. He was accompanied by three other naval officers and a number of delegates from the Seamen's and Workmen's Councils. The Königsberg was late at her rendezvous, but at 2.20 p.m. she came into sight in misty weather, received orders by searchlight flashes from the British light cruiser flagship Cardiff, and fell in astern of that vessel, following her through the gates of the various booms which protected the vast anchorage of Rosyth, till in the dusk she was berthed off Inch-keith, showing brilliant riding lights, **Admiral Meurer's** according to Admiral Beatty's orders. **humiliating errand** Admiral Meurer and his officers were then escorted on board the British destroyer Oak, and taken to the Queen Elizabeth, when they went below.

Certain members of the German Seamen's Soviet had intended to accompany them; they were told that in no circumstances would Admiral Beatty meet them, and they had to stop behind. The interview was of a most tragic character. As Grant's heart melted when at Appomattox he received the surrender of Lee, so British officers felt it hard to resist sympathy for the fallen. Meurer insisted that if the Allies did not feed Germany she would starve. He said that the armistice conditions were cruel, and were only accepted because otherwise not a child would be left alive in Germany under five years of age. One of the German officers added that he expected on his return to be selling newspapers in Berlin. All of them showed every sign of depression. On November 16th the conference ended, and on the following day the Königsberg left.

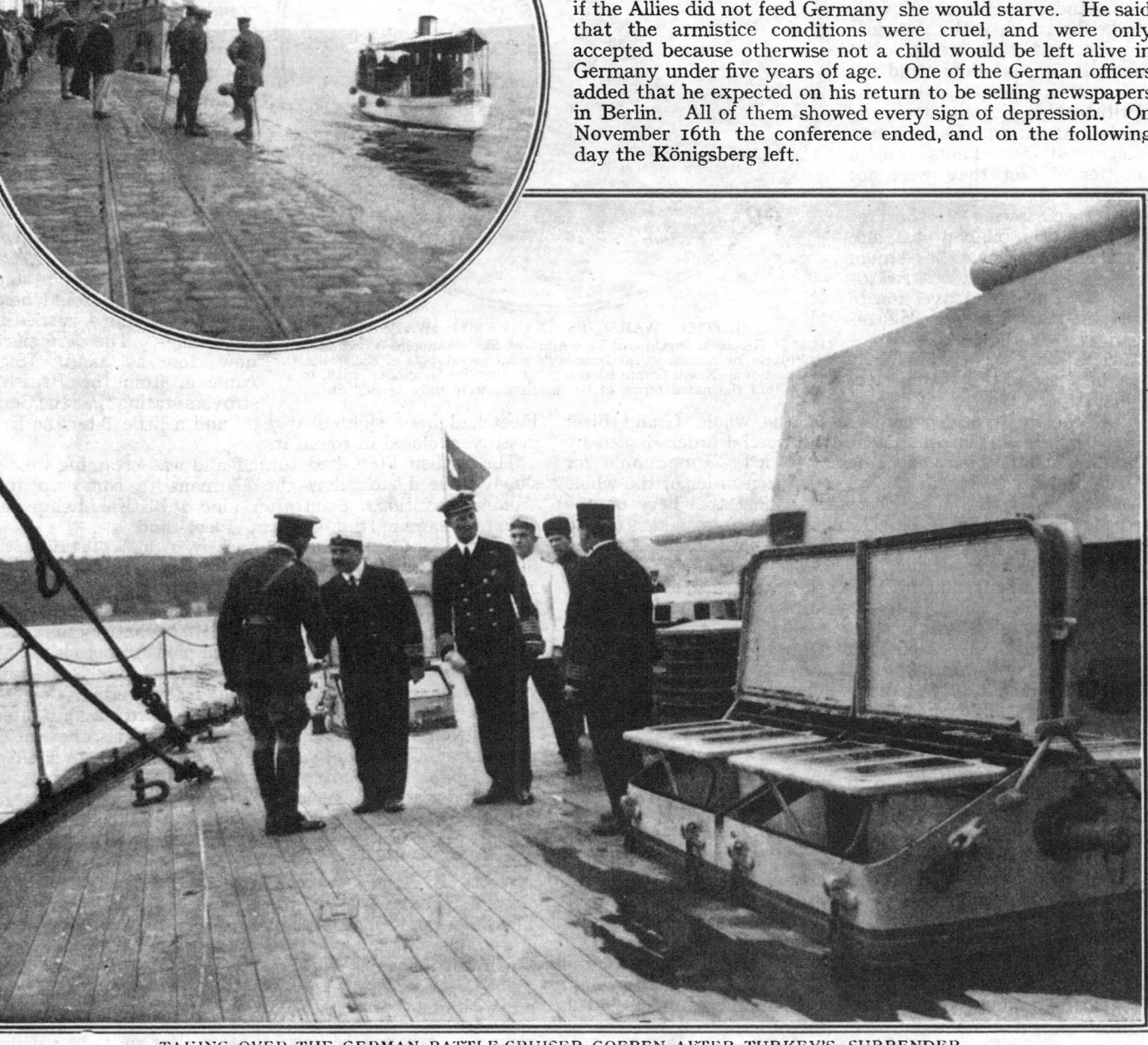

TAKING OVER THE GERMAN BATTLE-CRUISER GOEBEN AFTER TURKEY'S SURRENDER.
The first British officers to set foot on the Goeben: The Chief of Staff at Salonika and a naval captain being received aboard the ex-German battle-cruiser by the Turkish Admiral Aziz Pasha, November 12th, 1918. In circle: Lieut.-General Sir Henry F. M. Wilson, Commander-in-Chief of the Allied Forces occupying Turkish territory under the armistice terms, landing at Constantinople, November 13th, 1918.

Admiral Beatty required the surrender of the following ships:

Dreadnought Battleships.—Bayern, König, Markgraf, Grosser Kurfürst, Kronprinz, Kaiser, Kaiserin, König Albert, Friedrich der Grosse, Prinzregent Luitpold.
Battle-Cruisers.—Hindenburg, Derfflinger, Seydlitz, Moltke, Von der Tann.
Light Cruisers.—Emden, Frankfurt, Bremen, Köln, Dresden, Strassburg, Brummer, Bremse,

with fifty of the latest destroyers. The battle-cruiser Mackensen was originally named for surrender, but as she was not in a condition to put to sea, it was agreed that the new Dreadnought battleship Baden, when completed, should be substituted for her. The German ships were given a rendezvous at which they were to meet the British Fleet on November 21st. This point was at north latitude 56 deg. 11, west longitude 1 deg. 20, or about seventy miles from Rosyth. Elaborate directions were issued to the German commander. His ships were to be disarmed, with magazines empty, and guns trained fore and aft, so that they could not turn their weapons on the British ships without attracting instant attention. They were to steam at ten knots — as a matter of fact they were not capable of greatly exceeding that speed, owing to shortage of lubricating oil, bad coal, and indifferent stoking. The German crews then and afterwards showed a profound aversion to any kind of work; the officers had no authority, and the Soviets in the ship were unable to make themselves obeyed.

BRITISH WARSHIPS IN GERMAN WATERS.
H.M.S. Hercules, flagship of Vice-Admiral Sir Montague Browning, with destroyers of her escort in Germany's great naval port of Kiel, when the International Naval Commission went thither in December, 1918, to see that the naval terms of the armistice were duly carried out.

On the night of November 20th the whole Grand Fleet prepared for sea, in accordance with special orders issued by Admiral Beatty in a document headed "Programme for Operation ZZ." It was the last operation order of the whole war. It made thorough provision against treachery on the part of the Germans. The Grand Fleet was to steam out to the rendezvous, preceded by its torpedo flotillas, one hundred and fifty destroyers strong. It was to form in two immense lines, six miles apart, and between them the German ships were to proceed, three miles from each of the British lines, exactly as a malefactor is conducted to the police-station between two constables. The hour for meeting the Germans was fixed at 9.10 a.m. The British ships were to tow paravanes, but not to tow their captive balloons (one of which was allotted in ordinary conditions to each battleship, to regulate firing). The light cruiser Cardiff alone, flagship of the commodore charged with guiding the Germans, would tow her balloon. Her business was to direct the movements of the Germans, and lead them in, if possible, at a speed of twelve knots. Aircraft from the local stations on the Firth of Forth were to fly over the Fleet. In all the ships, before meeting the Germans, and until the negative signal was made, the crews were to be at action-stations. Turrets and guns were to be kept in the securing position (trained fore and aft), but free. The guns were to be empty, but the cages in the great lifts which bring up the shell and the cordite charge to the breech of the weapons in the turrets were to be up and loaded, ready for ramming home with the hydraulic rammers. The directors and armoured towers (for fire control) were to be trained on the Germans, and correct range and deflection were to be kept set continuously on the sights. With these orders, in a few seconds fire could be opened, if necessary, while the

"Programme for Operation ZZ"

considerable distance at which the British lines steamed from the Germans rendered any sudden attack by the ram or torpedo difficult.

Throughout the 20th signals had been coming in from the Germans as they steamed towards the rendezvous, and orders had been issued to them. It was learnt that the König had been unable to come, but would arrive later, that the light cruiser Dresden was not yet ready for sea, and that one of the fifty destroyers had struck a mine and sunk. Between 3 and 4 a.m. the Grand Fleet weighed anchor, and with navigation lights (the red, white, and green lamps carried by steamers at sea), which it employed for the first time in a cruise at sea during the war, its squadrons passed, one after another, the blazing lights of Rosyth dockyard, under the immense structure of the Forth Bridge, through the various booms, to sea. The night was still and cloudy. In the ships there was perfect silence. On the upper bridges of the Dreadnoughts, eighty feet or so above the black water, were little groups of officers working the ship and controlling the night defence system. Quiet orders from time to time broke the stillness. Towards dawn the moon showed over the interminable lines of black hulls, moving like so many enormous hearses through the water, and about 8.30 the sun showed through the clouds. At that hour the crews went to action-stations, and it could be seen that all the ships carried their battle-flags. The Germans were now close at hand. Signals came in from the British destroyers stating that the German Fleet had been sighted at 7.40, and a little later the British destroyers closed in round it.

The British Fleet had turned and was steaming west very slowly indeed, to allow the Germans to come up to the ordained position. Soon after nine a British airship passed out to examine the German Fleet and report; about 9.30 the Germans were in full view from the British battleships. In front of them steamed the Cardiff with her balloon. Then came the Seydlitz, flying the broad pennant of Commodore Taegert in command of the battle-cruisers, with astern of her the four other German ships of her class. After them came the Friedrich der Grosse, flagship of Rear-Admiral von Reuter, who commanded the whole German force, and eight other German battleships. Then, after a long interval, came seven light cruisers, led by the Karlsruhe with the pennant of Commodore Harder, and behind them again were the German destroyers.

The High Sea Fleet comes out

The critical moment had arrived if resistance was to be offered. The Germans in the morning haze looked in good order and well-painted; they kept excellent station and seemed to manœuvre well. Over them hovered a British airship. But there was no sign of hostility. The German crews laughed and waved their hands to the British destroyers when these passed near, though to this the British crews made no response. They acted on orders given by Admiral Beatty, which ran thus:

1. It is to be impressed on all officers and men that a state of war exists during the armistice.

2. Their relations with officers and men of the German Navy with whom they may now be brought into contact are to be strictly of a formal character.

3. In dealing with the late enemy, while courtesy is obligatory, the methods with which they have waged the war must not be forgotten.

4. No international compliments are to be paid, and all conversation is forbidden except in regard to the immediate business to be transacted.

5. If it is necessary to provide food for German officers and men, they should not be entertained, but it should be served to them in a place specially set apart. If it is necessary to accept food from the Germans, a request is to be made that it is to be similarly served.

Over the German vessels flew for the last time the German flag. It stood out, red, white, and black, against the faint mist in the sunlight. In the British ships officers and men, in the peculiar battle dress worn by the Navy, with protection for head and hands against the flash of explosives, and with gas-masks at the ready, watched the strangest spectacle that has ever been beheld by seamen. The Germans did not mean fighting. There was a sigh of disappointment in the Grand Fleet that the war had ended thus tamely.

As the vast procession moved at a funereal pace—some ten to eleven knots, the best that the Germans could do—towards Rosyth, it seemed as though the German Navy of the past was being escorted to its grave. The rivalry of twenty years —for in 1898 came the first of the great **Beatty's historic** German Naval Acts which openly challenged **signal** Great Britain—was over at last. It had closed in shame for the German Fleet. At 11.4 a.m. Admiral Beatty made an historic signal :

The German flag will be hauled down at sunset to-day, and will not be hoisted again without permission.

It was as at the burial of the dead—no manning of ships, no display of bunting, no exchange of salutes. Slowly and solemnly moved the great ships, like painted toys, on the still sea ; from the British line to the south of the Germans the line to the north was invisible except at rare moments when the mist lifted. Then came the end. The last war signal fluttered out from the flagship or was flashed from the search-lights, " Negative man action-stations." The crews left their battle places and streamed aft. The Germans anchored about Inchkeith. The Queen Elizabeth, the British flagship, anchored by them, and past her steamed the battleships of the Grand Fleet, each as it came abeam of her giving three cheers for Admiral Beatty. Standing on the bridge he waved his cap in recognition. At 4 p.m., as the bugle in the Queen Elizabeth rang out " making sunset " after the old naval fashion, the German flags came down. To the crew of the Queen Elizabeth, who had been piped aft, Admiral Beatty delivered this brief speech : " I always told you they would have to come out."

A special message was issued by him to every ship of the Fleet. In it he said :

It is my intention to hold a service of thanksgiving at 18.00 (6 p.m.) to-day, for the victory which Almighty God has vouchsafed to H.M. arms, and every ship is recommended to do the same.

I wish to express to the flag - officers, captains, officers, and men of the Grand Fleet my congratulations on the victory which has been gained over the sea-power of our enemy. The greatness of this achievement is is no way lessened by the fact that the final episode did not take the form of a fleet action. Although deprived of this opportunity which we had so long and eagerly awaited, and of striking the final blow for the freedom of the world, we may derive satisfaction from the singular tribute which the enemy has accorded to the Grand Fleet.

Without joining us in action, he has given testimony to the prestige and efficiency of the Fleet without parallel in history, and it has to be remembered that this testimony has been accorded to us by those who were in the best position to judge. I desire to express my thanks and appreciation to all who have assisted me in maintaining the Fleet in instant readiness for action, and who have borne the arduous and exacting labours which have been necessary for the perfecting of the efficiency which has accomplished so much.

The sun sank scarlet into the sea and the mist closed down. That day marked the close of an era. The Grand Fleet had

escorted the fourteen best armoured ships that Germany possessed into a British port, whole and intact, not battered wrecks, as the guerdon of its surpassing victory. It had eclipsed all the achievements of the past. And yet there was a double feeling of regret in the British ships—regret that the war had ended without such a vindication of British fighting power as Trafalgar ; regret, too, that four years of loyal comradeship, devoted service, and steadfastness in the face of danger and death were past ; that the heroic days were gone, leaving, none the less, a glorious memory, a tradition that should be the noblest inheritance of the British race.

In the dusk boats put off to the German ships, which, on close examination were found to be shabbily painted and in poor condition, exceedingly **Dirty German** dirty below—though this was probably to be **warships** explained by the fact that they had just come out of dockyard hands after having their gun-fittings removed. The British officers who inspected them found that large crews were on board, that discipline was non-existent, but that Admiral Beatty's orders had been obeyed. A further and more detailed examination took place on the following day, which proved that all was in order. Most of the copper and brass work had been removed where this could be done without serious injury to the ship. There were no surprises in the vessels. They were in no respect superior to British ships, except that they were more thoroughly divided into compartments and that there were few or no openings and doors below the armoured deck. The result of this, however was to interfere with their habitability. The British ships were built for cruising as well as fighting. The German ships were designed to remain in harbour while the crews lived on shore. The gunnery appliances had been removed, but there was no reason to suppose that they were in any respect superior to the British, except possibly in the quality of their optical glass. The good shooting of the German Fleet at Jutland and its quickness in picking up the range were to be ascribed to the extreme care with which the

BRITISH WAR VESSEL IN KIEL HARBOUR.
H.M.S. Verdun at Kiel with the International Naval Commission in December, 1918, showing, to the left, a huge floating dock that had been used by the Germans for the repairing of their U boats.

German Staff had made its preparations, selecting men with specially good eyesight and rapid judgment for work at the range-finders.

After the great ceremony of the surrender the German ships were taken north under escort to Scapa Flow, where they were left under guard with small care-and-maintenance parties of German seamen on board, until their final disposal was settled by the Peace Conference. The other officers and men returned to Germany in German transports, which were given safe-conducts. The missing ships were sent on or replaced. The full total of Dreadnoughts surrendered was brought up to sixteen, of light cruisers to eight, and of destroyers to fifty.

All the great Allied Navies and the Dominions were represented at the surrender. The Dominion battle-cruisers Australia and New Zealand were there; the battleship Canada was in the Grand Fleet. The American flag was flown by the Dreadnoughts of the Sixth Battle Squadron, under Admiral Rodman. Rear-Admiral Grasset, in the Amiral Aube, with two destroyers, represented the French Navy. The Italian Navy had not had time to send ships, but Admiral Lorenzi, in the British battleship Hercules, was present on Italy's behalf.

It was right that the Grand Fleet should have received this unparalleled surrender, for the Grand Fleet and the blockade it maintained were the prime causes of victory in the war. This fact was generously acknowledged by the Allies. " Where should we have been but for the immense help—immense beyond all computation — of the British Fleet?" asked a distinguished French naval officer. At the close of the war, by the unanimous judgment of competent witnesses, the efficiency of the Grand Fleet had reached a point never approached before. The advance between 1916 and 1918 was immense. In fighting quality the Grand Fleet was, man for man, greatly superior to the Germans. In material the figures already given have proved its overwhelming superiority—a superiority which had in large measure been gained by British constructors and designers in the war. In every respect—ingenuity, new appliances, tactical handling, strategical control—it had advanced far beyond the Germans. The weakness in the High Command and in staff-work had been removed. It was such a force as Nelson never commanded, under officers who were determined that if the enemy came out the issue this time should be "not victory but annihilation."

While the large German ships were being interned, the German submarines were surrendering at Harwich. The first twenty arrived on November 20th; another twenty on the 21st. and yet another twenty on the 22nd. Each detachment was met at a point off that base by British light cruisers and destroyers and then was shepherded into port. The crews of the German boats were, by British orders, lined up on deck, and the guns in the submarines were trained fore and aft. At first the German authorities had difficulty in obtaining men to navigate these vessels across the North Sea. In view of the terrible record of the German submarine flotilla the seamen were afraid that their lives would be taken. But gradually this fear passed On surrendering, every boat was inspected as a precaution against treachery. There was none. The Germans submitted with an obsequious air. Week after week additional submarines were given up, usually under pressure, till on January 15th, 1919, one hundred and thirty-six were in British hands; forty-nine had still to come, making a total of one hundred and eighty-five given up. When the crews had been sent home these boats were distributed between various British ports for exhibition, and a number of them were handed over to the Allies.

The last detail of the surrender—the disarmament of the German ships which remained in Germany—had still to be carried out. An International Naval Commission had been formed under the presidency of Vice-Admiral Sir Montague Browning, with whom were Rear-Admiral Robinson, United States Navy, Rear-Admiral Grasset, French Navy, Captain Nakamura, Japanese Navy, and Commander Gulli, Italian Navy, besides a number of other British and allied experts. It was decided that they should go by sea to the German ports in the battleship Hercules, accompanied by the destroyers Verdun, Viceroy, Vidette, and Venetia. The squadron left Rosyth on December 3rd, and, passing many floating mines, anchored near Heligoland in dense fog until German pilots came on board and took the British ships into Wilhelmshaven. On the entry into that port various German vessels dipped their flags to the Hercules, which returned this courtesy by dipping her flag—the first such interchange with the Germans since the outbreak of war. The Allied Commission was met by a German Commission consisting of Rear-Admiral Goette

with Captain Müller (who had commanded the Emden) as his assistant. The practical work of disarmament was then discussed. The allied conditions were received by the Germans with cries of protest, and assertions that they could not be carried out. What was required was that the warships remaining in Germany should be stripped of their fighting fittings, land their guns, ammunition, and torpedoes, and be laid up under allied supervision. Through Admiral Browning's firmness this was secured.

The effective ships remaining to the German Navy were four incomplete Dreadnoughts—Von Spee, Mackensen, Sachsen, and Württemberg—all of great fighting power; eight older Dreadnoughts of the Nassau and Helgoland classes, which were comparatively weak ships; a dozen good light cruisers; and about a hundred older destroyers, with many submarines in every stage of construction and completion. The German ships were found to be in an extraordinary condition of filth, and could not be kept clean because the German crews obeyed no one. As it was stipulated that all naval and air stations were to be clear of men, as the presence of lounging, dirty German seamen was an infraction of the armistice. A British officer inspecting one of the first German ships to be examined had to state that unless all these men were cleared out of the way forthwith, he would cease his inspection and report that he had been obstructed—whereupon the men hurriedly disappeared. One by one all the naval bases and all the airship and naval aeroplane stations were examined, including Nordholz, which the Germans only showed with extreme reluctance. It was the base from which their Zeppelins usually started to raid Great Britain. Here was found L14 still in existence, in use as a school ship, with twenty-four raids over British soil to its credit. All the other ships which had accompanied it in the early raids had perished. Near it was L71, the latest monster Zeppelin, a sister ship of L70 brought down by the British in the North Sea in August, 1918.

Passing through the Kiel Canal the Hercules was cheered by a trainload of British prisoners on their way to release, until the air rang. At Warnemunde the experimental aeroplane station, where all the newest types were assembled for trial, was inspected, despite a good deal of resistance by the Germans, and on December 18th the Hercules began her home voyage. The submarines building in the German yards had been examined previously. These were tools too dangerous to be left in German hands after past experience, and when the armistice terms were modified on January 16th, the Allies required the destruction of all incomplete U boats and the stoppage of further building.

The service rendered by the British Navy in destroying German sea-power was the more remarkable when it is remembered that throughout the closing period of the war Great Britain maintained enormous armies on many fronts where her troops continuously attacked. Her naval activity was, therefore, only a part of the colossal work which she accomplished. Yet, despite all her efforts on land, the strength of her Fleet was immense at the close of the war. It was manned by nearly 400,000 officers and men. It comprised about 5,000 vessels of all kinds. From a peace establishment of about 600 ships and 150,000 officers and men it had thus expanded to gigantic proportions. Nor was this the only contribution which Great Britain made at sea. Her merchant service required some 200,000 seamen, and it was used not to steal the trade of competitors but to serve and supply the Allies or to convey American troops to Europe. Generations may pass before any people achieves so much or puts forth such energy as the British manifested in the war. There was nothing to approach it in earlier history. Nor could any other of the Allies, great though the work of all was, show such a record of accomplishment. From first to last Great Britain was the soul and mainspring of the alliance against German lawlessness, and with her rests the surpassing glory of the final victory. Once again, as in the Napoleonic Wars she led a coalition. Once more she "was made glorious in the midst of the sea"; but, whereas in the Napoleonic Wars her military effort—though important—was of a secondary character, in this war she fought with all her strength.

Releasing the torpedo from a British torpedo aeroplane, one of the many promising ventures which the surrender of Germany prevented from being put into use.   It was a development of the seaplane torpedo-carrier which had been effectively employed earlier in the war.

Torpedo fired from the special torpedo aeroplane striking the water. The torpedo fired weighed about half a ton, and proved more efficient than when employed in any other way.   The invention was regarded as of even greater potential value than the submarine.

Wonderful torpedo=firing aeroplane of the Royal Air Force.

" Attack, the best defence." Aeroplane convoy that proved successful against the German submarine.

Activity in a British shipbuilding yard to counter the U boat menace by construction.

Great Britain's masterpiece in underwater craft construction: K17 dazzle=painted for surface work.

War=time shipbuilding in a Scottish yard: An impression by M. Albert Sebille.

One of Britain's giant submarines of the K class, the centre part showing funnels about to close in readiness for submerging.

K22 preparing to submerge, the funnels—employed when the vessel travelled on the surface by steam-power—being lowered.

The super-submarine going under. The K boats, 350 feet in length, were first commissioned in August, 1916, and were practically submersible cruisers.

With her hull well under, the great boat was about to disappear below the surface of the water.

Cruisers by night and submarines by day: Britain's giant K class boats.

CHAPTER CCLXXXVIII.

THE ROLL OF HONOUR : CONCLUDING SURVEY.

Previous Chapters—A Final Survey—Difficulties of the Censorship Overcome—Full Return of British Military Casualties—Losses in the Various Theatres of War—The Western Front and Others—A Corrected Return—The Final Figures—Canadian and Australian Losses : A Comparison—India's Share in the Total—New Zealand and South Africa—Naval Casualties—The Mercantile Marine's Share—Losses in the Air Force—The Grand Total and the Number of the Dead—Civilians Killed by the Enemy—The Burden of England and Scotland—Losses of the Guards and the 7th Division—Losses in the Artillery and the Army Service Corps—Killed and Wounded—The Numbers in the Field—The Losses of France—Officers Killed and Missing—Italy and the United States—Russia's Huge Total—Serbian Casualties—The German Losses Analysed—Some Returns about Würtemberg—The Figures for Austria-Hungary—Turkey and Other Belligerents—Estimate of the Total Casualties—Britain's Losses in 1918—Some Considerations Noted—Figures for Six Months—The Year's Fighting—Cost of the March Reverse—Individual Casualties—Peers and their Relatives—M.P.'s and Other Prominent Men—Winners of the V.C.—Scholars and Athletes—Casualties Among the Clergy—Universities and Public Schools—Losses of the Lawyers and the Press—A Final Word.

O N three previous occasions THE GREAT WAR has devoted a chapter to a detailed consideration of the British losses in the tremendous struggle that ended on November 11th, 1918, and the time for a fourth and final survey has now arrived. The first chapter was written when most of the relevant facts and figures were made public without delay or deletion, but it was quite otherwise with the second and third.

These were written under grave disadvantages, for from early in 1916 to the end of the war the authorities gave no information about the British losses beyond publicly recording the names. However, the wheel at length came full circle, and most of the information given and analysed in this chapter is based on official returns.

Another word of retrospect before coming to grips with the subject. The second and third of these four chapters, in spite of the obvious disadvantages mentioned above, were far from superfluous, far from being devoid of interest or even of authority.

Quite the reverse. They appeared at a time when little or nothing was known about the extent of Britain's sacrifices, when the most absurd guesses were given to the public as if they were the truth, and when alarmists of all kinds were using the darkness in which this subject was veiled for their own ends. THE GREAT WAR supplied the public with a wholesome corrective to the twin dangers of unreasoning pessimism and absurd optimism, and that publication was, moreover, the only one to do so on any considerable scale.

The publication of the official figures at the end of the war left the conclusions of the two chapters in question intact. They were reached in that particular kind of darkness created by the censor ; but a searching examination of the figures supplied by the military authorities after November, 1918, shows that light was obtained from some other source.

The most exhaustive statement made on this subject was that of Mr. Ian Macpherson in the House of Commons in November, 1918. Prefacing the figures with the remark that they were necessarily incomplete, he gave them for the period of the war to November 10th, 1918, the day before the armistice was signed. The main results were :

		OFFICERS.
Killed ..	..	37,876
Wounded	..	92,664
Missing..	..	12,094
		142,634
		OTHER RANKS.
Killed ..	..	620,828
Wounded	..	1,939,478
Missing..	..	347,051
		2,907,357
		TOTAL.
Killed ..	..	658,704
Wounded	..	2,032,142
Missing..	..	359,145
		3,049,991

In addition to this vast total there were 19,000 deaths from various causes among troops who did not form part of any expeditionary force. The missing included, as is usual, the prisoners, who are known

FALLEN HEROES OF THE R.A.F.
British airmen tending the graves of fallen comrades of the Royal Air Force. Damaged propellers were set at the head of many graves instead of the usual wooden cross.

to have numbered 6,741 officers and 164,767 men, and may possibly have been more than that.

The return, moreover, divided the casualties according to the various theatres of war, and these totals are as follows, placing the eight theatres in order of importance :

	OFFICERS.	OTHER RANKS.	TOTAL.
France.. ..	126,757	2,592,895	2,719,652
Dardanelles ..	5,053	114,676	119,729
Mesopotamia ..	4,335	93,244	97,579
Egypt	3,592	54,261	57,853
Salonika ..	1,217	26,101	27,318
East Africa ..	896	16,929	17,825
Italy	458	6,280	6,738
Miscellaneous ..	326	2,971	3,297

This classification calls for little comment. The western front was ever the decisive theatre, and there nearly ninety per cent. of the total casualties were incurred. For 1917 we estimated its proportion at 95·82 per cent. ; but in that year there was no fighting in Gallipoli to take part of the burden, so that proportion was almost certainly correct.

The Gallipoli enterprise was generally regarded as second in order of cost, and so it proved. Rather less than 100,000 is not, perhaps, excessive for Mesopotamia, especially when one reflects that the figure includes the disasters in and around Kut in 1916. The casualties incurred in Egypt were high, but there was much heavier and more obstinate fighting in Palestine in 1917 than the public were allowed to know at the time. The other figures are also worthy of record, when we are considering what was achieved, or what was not achieved, by British arms in East Africa, the Balkans, and Italy.

In the following February, in reply to a questioner, Mr. Bonar Law issued some figures which corrected, but in totals only, those just examined, and were at first sight somewhat perplexing. The total of 2,882,954 for the military casualties is rather less than the one we have been considering ; but the main reason is clearly that the returned prisoners have been crossed off. The dead and the wounded have larger figures, but the missing is a much smaller one.

This return may be regarded as the final estimate of the British War Office, and it is as follows :

	OFFICERS.	OTHER RANKS.	TOTAL.
Killed	38,409	635,534	673,943
Wounded	93,257	1,953,954	2,047,211
Total	131,666	2,589,488	2,721,154

In addition 97,000 were added to the dead, for although there was no certain information about these men, they were presumed dead on account of the lapse of time. A further 64,800 were unaccounted for, and must be regarded therefore as missing, probably dead. Thus the final figures for the Army are :

Killed or died ..	..	..	770,943
Wounded	..	..	2,047,211
Missing ..	..	..	64,800
			2,882,954

Between this return and the earlier one already discussed the main difference is accounted for by a transfer from the category of the missing to that of the dead ; the latter had increased by 110,000, mainly the 97,000 whose deaths were of necessity presumed after long absence ; the former had decreased by nearly 300,000, of whom 150,000 were accounted for by returned prisoners of war. The wounded had gone up a little, just about 15,000, mainly the casualties in the last few days of the fighting.

This return did not, as did the earlier one, divide the casualties among the various theatres of war, but it did make a distinction between troops from the homeland, the British, strictly speaking, and those from the Dominions and India. For the former the total was 2,106,322, and for the latter it may be set out more fully :

			OFFICERS.
Killed ..	..	..	7,602
Wounded	..	..	17,125
Total ..		..	24,727
			OTHER RANKS.
Killed ..	..	..	168,703
Wounded	..	..	421,402
Total ..		..	590,105
			TOTAL.
Killed ..	..	..	176,305
Wounded	..	..	438,527
Total ..		..	614,832

The return did not separate the number of those presumed dead or still missing, nor did it say anything about the losses of any particular dependency. On this subject, however, there is certain information available.

The losses of Canada and Australia were as follows :

	CANADA.	AUSTRALIA.
Killed or died of wounds or disease	50,585	54,431
Wounded	154,361	156,173
Missing and prisoners ..	8,322	3,494
Total	213,268	214,098

There is a remarkable resemblance in the set figures of the sacrifice made by the two strongest of Britain's daughter States ; only in the case of the missing is there any serious disparity, and it is not easy to say what is the real reason for this. It may be merely a difference in methods of reckoning, as the Canadian total of missing includes 4,620 who were "presumed dead." If this figure is taken from that of the

[Elliott & Fry.
MAJ.-GEN. R. H. DAVIES, C.B., N.Z. Force.

MAJ.-GEN. LIPSETT, C.B., C.M.G.

[Elliott & Fry.
BRIG.-GEN. S. C. TAYLOR, D.S.O.

[Bassano.
BRIG.-GEN. R. C. GORE, C.B.

[Swaine.
BRIG.-GEN. R. H. HUSEY, D.S.O., M.C.

[Elliott & Fry.
BRIG.-GEN. G. B. S. FOLLETT, D.S.O.

[Elliott & Fry.
BRIG.-GEN. C. L. MACNAB, C.M.G.

LT.-CL. B. W. VANN, V.C., M.C., Notts and Derby.

[Lafayette.
LT.-CL. A. L. WREN-FORD, Worcesters.

LT.-CL. P. A. CLIVE, M.P., Grenadiers.

[Lafayette.
LT.-CL. S. ACKLOM, D.S.O., M.C., H.L.I.

[Lafayette.
LT.-CL. C. K. JAMES, D.S.O., Border Regt.

[Elliott & Fry.
LT.-CL. F. B. DENNIS, D.S.O., K.O.S.B.

[Elliott & Fry.
LT.-CL. ROBINSON, D.S.O., R. Sussex.

[Swaine.
LT.-CL. O'DONAHOE, D.S.O., Canadians.

missing and prisoners, the remainder would approximate very closely to Australia's total. As regards the Canadian figures, they only go down to November 5th, six days before the signing of the armistice, and the official warning was added that " as the Canadian Corps was actively engaged up to the morning of the armistice, on which this force captured Mons, the casualty reports yet to be estimated will considerably increase the total losses." The Australian figures covered a still shorter period—that to October 28th only—so that something of the same kind will doubtless be added to them. In addition to the total of 214,098, the Australians gave a further figure—75,877 for the sick.

India's share in the total comes next in point of magnitude. Altogether that Empire sent 1,172,908 men to eight theatres of war—well over half of them to Mesopotamia; 953,374 of these were Indians, the rest being British soldiers sent out from India. The total of India's casualties down to September 30th, 1918, was 101,439, of which nearly half were incurred in Mesopotamia, where 14,742 were killed and 30,589 wounded. Casualties incurred in France were 6,900 killed and 16,380 wounded. The New Zealand losses totalled 57,932. Of these 16,456 were killed, 41,404 were wounded, and only 75 were missing or prisoners. The total was divided into 2,588 officers and 55,344 men. The South African losses came to 19,931—6,633 killed, 11,661 wounded, and 1,637 missing and prisoners. The bulk of these were incurred in Europe, but East Africa was responsible for 1,800, of whom 1,200 died of disease.

The serious participation of all parts of the Empire, which these figures so eloquently prove, was only possible because behind all the mighty movements which these suggest was the sure shield of the Imperial Navy keeping watch, as Themistocles said of that of Athens, "over the city and the sea." Its work, too, was not accomplished without price. At the end of November the Admiralty issued a statement of the total number of casualties suffered by officers and men of the Royal Navy and Royal Marines, and in February revised totals appeared. The period covered is from the outbreak of the war to November 11th, 1918; but the total does not include the losses suffered by the Royal Naval Division, as these were in the figures issued by the War Office. The revised figures are as follows:

	OFFICERS.	MEN.	TOTAL.
Killed	2,061	20,197	22,258
Wounded	813	4,081	4,894
Missing	15	8	23
	2,889	24,286	27,175

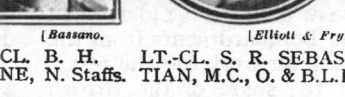

LT.-CL. LORD FARN-HAM, Inniskillings. *[Lafayette.*

LT.-CL. E. S. CHANCE, Leicestershire. *[Lafayette.*
LT.-CL. B. H. THORNE, N. Staffs. *[Bassano.*
LT.-CL. S. R. SEBAS-TIAN, M.C., O. & B.L.I. *[Elliott & Fry.*

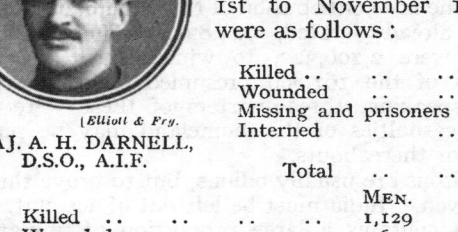

MAJ. N. S. THORNTON, Rifle Brigade. *[Bassano.*
LT.-CL. R. T. F. HOOD, D.S.O., R.A.F. *[Elliott & Fry.*
MAJ. A. H. DARNELL, D.S.O., A.I.F. *[Elliott & Fry.*

MAJ. E. H. H. CARLILE, Yeomanry.

This is a most satisfactory return, especially when compared with the November one. Only twenty-three officers and men remained untraced; but still more striking, if somewhat inexplicable, was it to learn that in November the Admiralty overestimated the number of dead by 401 officers and 10,698 men. The interned and the prisoners, 1,175 in November, had apparently all returned home by February, another satisfactory feature.

This is not the full tale of the sea losses, however. In addition, while pursuing their ordinary vocations, 14,661 officers and men of British merchant ships and fishing vessels lost their lives through enemy action, and a further 3,295 were captured and detained in enemy countries as prisoners of war.

In all past wars this story would have been complete with the losses in the Army and the Navy, but in the Great War there was a third Service. Up to April 1st, 1918, the Air Force was partly under naval and partly under military control, and the casualties of the flying men were returned accordingly with those of the other sailors or soldiers, and the Admiralty return already mentioned states distinctly that its figures include the losses of the Royal Naval Air Service to March 31st, 1918. On April 1st, 1918, the Royal Air Force came into existence, taking both naval and military airmen under its control, and after that date its casualties were recorded separately. From April 1st to November 11th they were as follows:

	OFFICERS
Killed	1,551
Wounded	2,357
Missing and prisoners	1,612
Interned	45
Total	5,565

	MEN.	TOTAL.
Killed	1,129	2,680
Wounded	631	2,988
Missing and prisoners	225	1,837
Interned	39	84
	2,024	7,589

For the whole period of the war the casualties among airmen were as follows, the figures being arrived at by adding the above totals to those suffered by the Royal Naval Air Service and the Royal Flying Corps before April 1st, 1918.

	OFFICERS.	MEN.	TOTAL.
Killed	4,579	1,587	6,166
Wounded	5,369	1,876	7,245
Missing and prisoners	2,794	334	3,128
Interned	45	39	84
	12,787	3,836	16,623

The conditions of this Service were so different from those of the Navy and Army that it is useless to compare the

MAJ. QUARRY, R. Berks. Regt.
MAJ. BOOKER, D.S.C., R.A.F. *[Russell.*
MAJ. S. RIGG, Border Regt. *[Elliott & Fry.*
CPT. P. SPUR-GEON, Queens.
CPT. W. H. GLAD-STONE, M.C., C.Gds.
CPT. G. B. TATHAM, M.C., Rifle Brigade. *[Swaine.*
CPT. O. CAWLEY, M.P., Shropshire Y. *[Lafayette.*

proportions between officers and men and between killed and wounded with those of the other Services. The foregoing figures, however, are worth more than a passing glance; they merit some reflection.

We can now obtain some idea of the grand total of Britain's losses in the Great War:

	TOTAL CASUALTIES.	NUMBER KILLED.
Army	2,882,954	770,943
Navy (including Mercantile Marine)..	41,836	36,919
Air Force	7,589	2,680
	2,932,379	810,542

In addition there were about 19,000 deaths from various causes among troops not forming any part of the various expeditionary forces. The total of the dead is therefore raised to 830,000 or thereabouts. The

British casualties 2,000 a day

struggle lasted four years and three months, or 1,560 days. The killed were therefore on an average rather more than 500 a day, and the total casualties something like 2,000 a day.

This is not quite all, and, although numerically the addition makes little difference to the total, it is an important item in humanity's count against Germany. In air raids over Great Britain and in bombardments of unfortified coast towns 5,611 casualties were inflicted. Of these 861 were suffered by sailors and soldiers, the rest by civilians; 1,570 were killed and 4,041 injured. Of the 1,260 civilians killed, 554 were men, 411 were women, and 295 were children; 140 women and 771 children were injured. The bombardments from the sea accounted for 791 of the casualties, air work did the rest.

A word may be said here about the share of the British Isles in this gigantic total of casualties, for, as ever, the Motherland bore the heavier part of the burden. Some idea of the magnitude of this can best be reached by a process of exclusion. The total losses suffered by Canada, Australia, New Zealand, India, and South Africa, and other parts of the Empire—the fine contribution of Newfoundland, for instance—were, as already stated, 614,832. Those of the United Kingdom were 2,106,322, to which must be added some proportion of the 161,800 presumed dead or still missing. Roughly speaking, three-quarters of these were British, so the total casualties of the homeland may be put down at 2,250,000 or thereabouts.

Comparisons are usually odious, but to prove this point one may be given. India must be left out of account, because its population contains a large proportion of unmartial races; South Africa, too, cannot be judged by standards applicable to countries solely inhabited by whites. Canada and Australia remain, and the deeds of each are so shining that there can be no detraction in our comparison. The following table gives the population in 1911, the number of casualties suffered, and the percentage of the one to the other:

	POPULATION. 1911.	CASUALTIES.	PERCENTAGE.
United Kingdom ..	45,370,530	2,250,000	5·0
Canada	7,206,643	213,268	3·0
Australia	4,455,005	214,098	4·8

If this conclusion is true, or anything like true, then the British Isles suffered, not only the greatest number, but the greatest proportion of casualties, and,

Scotland's supreme sacrifice of men

moreover, did this with the handicap of Ireland's partial abstinence from the struggle. England's share was thus even better than the figures show. And what of Scotland's? It is notorious that the northern kingdom denuded itself of men to an extraordinary extent, and its losses may well constitute a new record in the long history of war. "Many have done excellently, but thou excellest them all."

It is not possible to go into detail about the losses of the various units, regiments, brigades, or divisions, but some figures about the Guards may be of interest. The losses of their division during the struggle were as follows:

	OFFICERS.	OTHER RANKS.	TOTAL.
Killed or died of wounds	628	12,922	13,550
Wounded	969	28,986	29,955
Total	1,597	41,908	43,505

In the ordinary way the division consisted of thirteen battalions, one of pioneers, and three brigades of four each, but its composition was altered in 1917. Its strength, however, would never be more than fifteen thousand, and its actual fighting strength not more than ten thousand. This will give some idea of the losses incurred. The whole division was destroyed four times; it seems almost a miracle that a single Guardsman should have survived. But the tabulated figures reveal one fact still more significant. It is the proportion between the number of officers killed and the number wounded. Not the usual ratio of three or four wounded to every one killed; but, instead, one killed for every one and a half wounded. What a world of daring these figures suggest.

Equally instructive are the losses of that fine division, the 7th, the one that landed on the Belgian coast under Sir Henry Rawlinson in the early days of the war, and fought steadily through some of the fiercest engagements of four and a half years, finishing up in Italy. It will be remembered by many that the losses of this division were made public towards the end of 1914. We were then told that when it landed it was 12,000 strong, but when, early in November, less than two months later, after having been in the thick of the first terrible struggle for Ypres, it was withdrawn from the line it consisted only of 2,333 officers and men. Losses on this scale were repeated again and again, until for the war its total casualties reached the appalling figure of 61,000. In other words, it had in effect been five times destroyed.

The losses of the British Army fell most heavily, it is again safe to say, on the infantry of the line, and the record of the 7th Division is but further testimony to an accepted fact. The material is not yet available by the aid of which one may estimate the exact proportion of the losses of each arm of the Service, but as regards the Artillery some useful figures have been made public. It is recorded that in 1918 this service totalled 30,960 officers and 501,030 other ranks. Its casualties during the war were 34,844 killed, 129,156 wounded, and 6,689 missing and prisoners,

Losses of the Royal Artillery

a total of 170,689. Rather less than one in three, therefore, became a casualty, but among the fighters the ratio was certainly higher, for the 531,990 included presumably those who served at home as well as those who went abroad. The Army Service Corps had 95 officers and 1,933 men killed in action or died of wounds, and 193 officers and 5,083 men who died of accident or disease.

The proportion of killed to wounded, so far as the Army is concerned, was very much the same in the aggregate as it had been in the yearly totals. Out of four soldiers hit three, on an average, will recover, at least in armies where the medical services are as prompt and efficient as in the British. As a matter of fact, the actual proportion was even better than that, and as such may be taken as a tribute to the nurses, doctors, and their assistants; 2,690,846 soldiers were hit, but the death-roll, instead of being 672,711, exactly a quarter, was 658,704. In the Naval and Air Services, owing to the different conditions under which the men fight, the proportion killed is much higher. In the Navy, in fact, the proportions are reversed. The chances of escape are not three, but rather less than one, in four. Artillerymen are in this respect more fortunate, apparently, than other soldiers; 164,000 of them were hit, and 34,844, not 41,000, were killed.

On this occasion there is no space available for an inquiry into the relation of the war's losses to the vital welfare of the country and the Empire, nor is there any great need for such, as the essential considerations have already been laid before the readers of THE GREAT WAR, and the figures now available do not materially alter any of the conclusions reached. A statement made, however, by General Peyton March, Chief of the Staff of the American Army, may be mentioned, as it goes to prove a theory several times advanced in these pages—namely, that the actual number of British soldiers on the various fronts was much less than was commonly supposed. General March said that on Armistice Day the

CPT. G. A. HUGHES,
M.C.,
Duke of Wellington's.

CPT. W. HUGHES,
M.C.,
R.F.A. attd. R.A.F.

CPT. F. SCOTT,
M.C.,
Leicesters.

CPT. A. WALSH,
M.C.,
South Lancs.

CPT. C. F. W. NASH,
M.C.,
Norfolk Regt.

CPT. K. N. BION,
M.C.,
Sherwood Foresters.

CPT. K. C. GILL,
M.C.,
R.A.F.

CPT. C. E. H. TEM-
PEST-HICKS, M.C.,
Lancers.

CPT. G. E. CARDEW,
Devonshire Regt.,
attd. D.L.I.

CPT. J. E. TREVOR-
JONES, M.C.,
Rifle Brigade.

CPT. R. C. MAC-
PHERSON,
R.F.A.

CPT. R. S.
KENNEDY, M.C.,
R.A.M.C.

CPT. C. Y. PEASE,
Yeo., attd. W. Yorks.
Regt.

CPT. J. H. E. DEAN,
M.C.,
Cheshire.

CPT. E. BUDD,
M.C.,
Irish Guards.

CPT. PULTENEY
MALCOLM,
Grenadier Guards.

CPT. H. J. WEST,
M.C.,
Bedfords.

CPT. G. W.
TOWELL, M.C.,
R.H.A.

CPT. JOHN KEITH
MEWS,
London.

LT. W. H.
REBBECK, M.C.,
R.E.

LT. W. E. SMITH,
M.C.,
London.

LT. HON. H. F. P.
LUBBOCK,
Grenadier Guards.

LT. EBENEZER
MACLAY,
Scots Guards.

LT. ALAN SCOTT
BALFOUR,
R.F.A., attd. R.F.C.

LT. FELIX NOEL
PERRIS,
R.A.F.

LT. T. H. L. ADDIS,
M.C.,
R. Dublin Fusiliers.

LT. FRANCIS L.
MOND,
R.F.A. and R.A.F.

LT. A. W. FORBES,
D.S.O.,
R.N.

LT. P. M.
CHADWICK,
R.E.

LT. H. W. JONES,
M.G. Squadron,
Cavalry Div.

LT. FRANK
WILLIAM SYKES,
R.F.A.

LT. W. K.
ANDERSON,
Black Watch.

LT. J. H. MORRIS,
R.H.A.,
attd. R.F.C.

LT. CHARLES F. G.
HOLLIS, M.C.,
Buffs.

LT. W. P.
CLOWES,
Hussars.

LT. N. G. SHEPPEY-
GREENE,
R.W. Kent Regt.

LT. H. F. A.
KEATING,
R.E.

LT. G. W. E.
WHITEHEAD,
R.F.A., attd. R.A.F.

LT. A. J. MAXWELL
STUART,
Coldstream Guards.

LT. P. De M. W.
GREY-EGERTON,
Hussars.

S.-LT. ARTHUR C.
TURNER,
Rifle Brigade.

VISCT. IPSWICH,
Coldstream Guards,
attd. R.A.F.

THE ROLL OF HONOUR, 1918-19.

Photos by Lafayette, Elliott & Fry, Bassano, Walter Barnett, Russell and Chancellor.

strength of the British Army in France, including some Portuguese serving with it, was only 1,710,000, and many expressed surprise at so meagre a total. Their minds had imagined millions.

In a previous chapter the estimate was made that the total of Britain's fighting men, using the word only for those actually at the front somewhere or other, was not more than 3,000,000, and in France it was perhaps 2,000,000. This is borne out by the American statement and it affects the subject in hand because it is upon these men, not upon the 5,000,000 or 6,000,000 under arms, as the phrase is, that the losses fall. Heavy indeed on them they were, and slight was the chance of escape for one in the forefront of the battle. It gives some idea of the extent of Britain's contribution to say that the casualties were equal to the number of fighting men. The whole force was put out of action and was remade.

We may turn now for a moment to the losses suffered by the other belligerents, both friend and foe. In December, 1918, France issued some figures, although these made no mention of the wounded. Down to November 1st, 1918, the losses were as follows :

	OFFICERS.
Killed or died	31,300
Missing	3,000
Prisoners	8,300
Total	42,600
	MEN.
Killed or died ..	1,040,000
Missing	311,000
Prisoners	438,000
Total	1,789,000

	TOTAL.
Killed or died	1,071,300
Missing	314,000
Prisoners	446,300
	1,831,600

As was expected, the French losses were heavier than the British. The majority of the missing were certainly dead, and so a population of 40,000,000 or thereabouts suffered a loss in killed alone of 1,400,000.

Awful drain on French man-power If we reckon the number of wounded as three times that of the killed, that being roughly the British proportion, the total of France's casualties would be in the neighbourhood of 5,000,000, one in eight of her population and one in four of her males, boys and old men included. It seems almost incredible that any nation could survive such a loss, but truly the spirit of France is immortal. It is only just to say, however, that the total certainly includes a considerable number of coloured troops, Algerians and the like, but even giving this consideration full weight detracts little from the marvel.

Two facts in the above table invite comment. One is the large number of prisoners. From time to time the Germans said they had made great captures of French troops, in the early days of the war and at Verdun in 1916 for instance, and these figures certainly show that they did not speak without the book—446,000 is no meagre figure, even for the Great War.

The second point is an extraordinary fact which almost baffles explanation. Although in killed, missing, and prisoners France lost nearly twice as many as did Britain, yet her

"HERE LIES A BRITISH SOLDIER. R.I.P."
Graveyard in which lie buried some of those who died that England might live. It is at Vlamerting, in Belgium, and on each, besides the soldier's name, was placed the above simple epitaph.

losses in officers were actually less—only 31,300 dead against her ally's 37,876. Including the missing and the prisoners the comparison is : France 42,600, and Britain 49,970.

Italy may be taken next, and here again the figures are not as complete as they might be. The killed were given as 460,000 and the wounded as 947,000 ; 16,362 of the killed and 33,347 of the wounded were officers, so that in this matter the Italian proportion approximates more to the French than to the British. These Italian totals say nothing about the missing and prisoners ; for these a very high figure is unfortunately necessary. A whole army does not break, as one Italian force did at Caporetto, without heavy losses in missing and prisoners, and beyond this there is the usual toll of warfare carried on for over three years with fortune swaying from side to side. Half a million would not perhaps be excessive for this heading, and we may safely estimate the total of Italy's casualties at 2,000,000.

As regards the United States the total was 262,763, exclusive of prisoners, and this certainly shows that the Americans were in some very heavy fighting during the few months they were in the field. The figure was divided thus :

Killed or died ..	58,478
Wounded	189,995
Missing	14,290

As regards Russia the figures published in the British papers can be little more than guesswork. It is probably true that the fallen Empire of the Tsar lost more men than any other belligerent, for it is certain that from time to time Germany gathered in Russian prisoners on an enormous and sometimes embarrassing scale. A report from Copenhagen, purporting to be from Petrograd, placed the total at 9,150,000, divided thus :

Killed	1,700,000
Wounded	4,950,000
Prisoners	2,500,000

The returns may or may not be based upon official information, but there is good reason for believing that they were not very wide of the mark.

More reliable, perhaps, were the figures issued in 1919 by the Serbian War Office. The total of effectives mobilised by Serbia was 757,343 men ; soldiers killed on the field of battle or dead as the result of wounds or illness before the last offensive in the Balkans were 320,925. The losses suffered during the last offensive, which had for its result the capitulation of Bulgaria and the liberation of national soil, increased the Serbian casualties by some tens of thousands, so that the total figure would be from 335,000 to **Serbian male population halved** 340,000 men, which represents one-half of the male population of the old kingdom. In this number there are not included the losses of troops of voluntary Jugo-Slavs, which were also severely tried, their losses having exceeded 70,000 men.

Turning to the Central Powers, as regards Germany there is little need to do anything more than to bring down the estimates already given in these pages to the end of the struggle. In discussing the German losses down to the end of 1917 we dismissed as exaggerated an estimate that the German losses by then had totalled 8,000,000. To the end of 1917 our opinion was that the German losses totalled at least 5,000,000. For the whole course of the war they are stated to have reached 6,385,000, which includes, of course, those suffered in 1918. Seeing that 1,385,000 would be about a fair estimate for nearly a year's hard fighting, the previous estimate given in THE GREAT WAR was not far from the truth. We should perhaps say that it is not certain how far these figures are official. However, taking them for what they are worth, and there is some independent evidence that they are not far from the mark, the classification is as follows:

Killed	..	..	..	1,600,000
Wounded	..	..	..	4,064,000
Missing	..	..	..	103,000
Prisoners	..	..	..	618,000
				6,385,000

Of the Germans who were taken prisoners the British were responsible for 264,242.

One slight piece of that independent evidence just referred to may be given. From Stuttgart, in January, 1919, there came returns of the losses suffered by the little **Losses suffered** German State of Würtemberg during the **by Würtemberg** Great War. They were altogether 234,000, of whom 59,000 were killed, 158,000 wounded, and 17,000 prisoners and missing. Now for a moment let us assume that these figures were typical of Germany as a whole. In 1910 the whole Empire had a population of 65,000,000— the exact figure was 64,925,993—and Würtemberg had one of 2,437,574, say 2,500,000. In other words, one German out of every 26 lived in that State. The rest is simple multiplication. On the Würtemberg basis Germany's casualties would be:

Killed	..	..	..	1,534,000
Wounded	..	..	..	4,108,000
Prisoners and missing		..	..	454,000
				6,096,000

The total is extraordinarily near the one of 6,385,000 already given, and, moreover, it is extraordinarily near it in each of the three classes, not in the aggregate only. It is very strong evidence in favour of accepting the figures given here as the correct official returns, and such they may well be.

For Austria-Hungary the figures are as vague as, perhaps more so than, those of Russia. One estimate gave the total as 4,000,000, of whom 800,000 were dead, and later some returns about Hungary went into more detail. They are as follows:

				OFFICERS.	MEN.
Killed	..	..	..	24,000	815,000
Wounded	..	..	..	41,000	1,900,000
Missing and prisoners		..	22,000	150,000
Total	..	..	..	87,000	2,865,000

These figures should be taken with considerable reserve, but if they are anything like true they are far from creditable to the Hungarian officers. When it was a question of being killed there was only one of them to about 34 men; when it was a question of being wounded, only one to about 46; but what a difference when it came to surrendering. In that case there was one officer to every seven men. These proportions should be compared with corresponding ones in the British Army to realise their full significance.

This, however, is only a digression. If the Hungarian losses were anything like the above figures, the total for the Dual Monarchy must have been much more than 4,000,000. Probably the explanation is that the 4,000,000 refers to Austria alone, making nearly 7,000,000 for the whole of the "ramshackle Empire" as it then was. There is nothing very improbable in this total, although it is very heavy for a population of under 50,000,000. But then Austria-Hungary did suffer heavily, as the whole story of her collapse shows. In the early days of the war Russia took from her prisoners on the grand scale, and the campaigns in the Balkans were far from bloodless, even to the victor. The German High Command, as we know, was particularly prodigal with Austrian lives when a thrust was to be made. The official returns of the Turkish losses were given as 436,974 killed, 407,772 wounded, and 103,731 prisoners and missing, a total of 948,477, but the number lost as prisoners was far greater than 103,000.

About the total losses incurred by all the belligerents no exact statement is possible. The following, however, may be given as probably not far from the truth.

ALLIES.				CENTRAL POWERS.			
Russia	..	..	9,000,000	Germany	..	..	6,500,000
France	..	..	5,000,000	Austria-Hungary	..	7,000,000
Great Britain	..	..	3,250,000	Turkey	..	..	1,000,000
Italy	..	..	2,000,000				
Serbia	..	..	350,000				14,500,000
United States	..	..	300,000				
			19,900,000				

Something must be added for Rumania, Greece, Belgium, Bulgaria, which reported 201,224 dead, and the other belligerents, and for this 4,000,000 would not be an excessive estimate. This makes a grand total of 38,400,000, so we can say it is something between 35,000,000 and 40,000,000. Arguing from the known to the unknown it may be assumed that about a quarter—9,000,000 or 10,000,000—were dead, killed or died of wounds or disease. The proportion of dead may have been somewhat less than this in the well-organised, well-served armies of Britain, France, Germany, and Italy; and it may have been less in those of Russia and Austria-Hungary, owing to the high proportion of prisoners in the totals. On the other hand, the proportion was certainly greater than one in four among the belligerents in the Balkans, where medical aid was so lacking and racial hatreds added a sharper edge to the fighter's sword. Moreover, the death-rate among all the prisoners of war, except those **Unimaginable sum** in the hands of the Western Allies, must have **of suffering** been very high, and ten millions may well be nearer the truth than nine. But whether nine or ten, somewhat more or somewhat less, the imagination is fortunately powerless before it. Happily for the reason of mortal man, he cannot faintly picture the amount of suffering it represents.

These issues are fully relevant to our subject, and THE GREAT WAR cannot well be without them, but Britain's own Roll of Honour in 1918 is still before us. Happily in these pages the foundations have been carefully laid. There is no need to explain away past errors, but only to complete the story.

To the end of 1917 our estimate of Britain's total casualties was 2,080,000 and now we learn officially that the figure for the whole war was 3,120,000 or thereabouts, including those prisoners who had returned home when the final figures were compiled. This meant rather more than a million for the ten months of 1918, a figure which is certainly excessive, even allowing for the costly reverse in March. But there are one or two deductions to be made. Our estimate did not

S.-LT. J. H. LAW-   S.-LT. P. A. WARD,   S.-LT. S. B. YATES,   S.-LT. J. B. FRIEND,   S.-LT. W. RUSSELL,   S.-LT. B. G. A.   S.-LT. R. VAN T.
RENCE, D.C.L.I.   R.F.A.   Manchester.   King's (Liverpool).   Tank Corps.   BELL, R.A.F.   RANNEY, Grenadiers.

include, so far at least as 1916 and 1917 were concerned, the Indian casualties, and these were in the neighbourhood of 100,000. No allowance, moreover, was made for deaths among the troops at home, and for this the authorities give 19,000. Again, our figures were based on the casualties reported, not necessarily incurred during the periods under consideration, and this probably meant that, at the end of 1917, something like 100,000 men had been killed or wounded in addition to those reported to December 31st. For 1918, therefore, it will not be very rash to assume 800,000 as the total of Britain's casualties. In 1917 the figure was 839,123 and in 1916 it was 660,071, with a small addition in each case for naval losses.

Britain's losses during 1918 For the first six months of the year we will take the totals recorded in the "Daily Telegraph" and see what light they throw on the subject. The figures are as follows :

					OFFICERS.	MEN.
January	..	..	..	..	1,481	72,912
February	..	..	..	..	657	18,412
March	..	..	..	..	1,043	11,074
April	..	..	..	..	8,996	47,250
May	..	..	..	..	7,695	154,939
June	..	..	..	..	4,406	135,729
					24,278	440,316

The history of the fighting is revealed in these figures. As in previous years, January and February were quiet months, for the casualties recorded in January were mainly suffered in December. So also was March of 1918 quiet, at least until the 21st, when the storm broke. The April and May figures tell something of its severity, and their returns should be looked at more closely. The following gives approximately an idea of the British losses in the last German throw of the dice. Both officers and men are included :

	MAY.	JUNE.	TOTAL.
Killed	21,826	18,532	40,358
Wounded ..	100,448	80,228	180,676
Missing and prisoners ..	40,692	41,475	82,167
	162,966	140,235	303,201

For six months, or more correctly, for the six months between December 1st, 1917, and May 30th, 1918, the British losses were 464,594, of which 303,201 were incurred in resisting the German onslaught. The large number of missing bears witness to the severity of the calamity, for 82,167 British soldiers do not surrender without good cause.

For the remainder of the year and of the struggle—*i.e.*, the period between June 1st and November 11th—the British losses may be put down at 350,000, and for this there was, to an extent never realised before, almost adequate compensation. The bulk of them were incurred on the western front, but some were suffered in defending Italy from the Austrian invader and in giving a final blow to the tottering power of the Turk. The exact figures for that year are not, however, a matter of much moment, as for the whole campaign they have already been stated and analysed.

As before, many pages could be devoted to an enumeration of those who during the year gave their lives for their country ; but more even than in past chapters the space allotted to them must be scant. The number of peers and sons of peers who fell was less than in former years, but **Some prominent men bereaved** Lord Farnham and Viscount Ipswich, the latter the grandson and ultimate heir of the aged Duke of Grafton, were killed. One of the Cecils, the Bishop of Exeter, lost another son, as did Lord Tennyson and Lord Ashcombe. Of the House of Commons two members fell. The death of Captain Oswald Cawley was especially sad. Not only was he the third son of his father, Lord Cawley, to be killed in the war, but he had succeeded his fallen brother as M.P., and had never been home to take his seat. The other was Captain P. A. Clive, a Guardsman and a popular figure in his own county of Hereford. Lord Ernle— then Mr. R. E. Prothero, the Minister for Agriculture—lost his only son in 1918, and among other members who suffered loss were Sir E. Hildred Carlile, Sir Robert Balfour, Sir E. M.

Pollock, the new Solicitor-General, Mr. Stephen Walsh, and Mr. C. K. Murchison. The Hon. Harold Ritchie, killed towards the close of the year, was a son of the late Lord Ritchie.

Other prominent men who lost sons included the Bishops of Llandaff and Islington and the Rev. Stephen Gladstone. Dr. Scott Lidgett was another. Sir David Semple, Sir Alex. Bethell, Sir W. Gibbons, Sir John Bell, Town Clerk of London, Sir Charles Parsons, and Sir Arthur Spurgeon may be added, as may Mr. G. Saunders, of the "Times," and Mr. G. H. Perris, of the "Daily Chronicle."

As for the fallen themselves the roll includes, as before, a great number who, young as they were, had already won distinction in some walk of life, perhaps by brain, perhaps by muscle, perhaps by both. Several who had previously won the V.C. were on the list, these including Lieut.-Colonel W. L. Brodie, Lieut.-Colonel Dimmer, and Major David Nelson, and there were, as usual, a large number killed in the act that won for each that coveted honour.

Scholars and athletes are mingled in the list. A few only can be named, and they but at random and as types of the others. Captain E. G. Colbeck, of the Artillery, was a cricket blue at Cambridge ; Captain C. E. Hatfeild, of the Yeomanry, was one at Oxford, having also played for Eton and Kent, and Captain W. G. Gobain was a Cambridge boxer. H. C. Boycott was an international hockey player, and Gerald B. Brown an Oxford player at the same game. A. F. Dickson and D. Dewar were Cambridge oarsmen, and D. W. Jennings a professional cricketer. Captain G. B. Tatham, of the Rifle Brigade, was a Fellow of Trinity College, Cambridge, and Captain W. H. Lister a Fellow of University College, London. Bertram Hopkinson, killed while flying, was a Cambridge scholar who had won the F.R.S. **From schools and** The names of Brock and Halahan remind **playing fields** one of the Zeebrugge enterprise, and that of McCudden of the many heroes of the air who died for the cause. Lieut.-Colonel B. W. Vann, like McCudden, a V.C., is an instance of a clergyman who rose to command a battalion.

Passing to the losses of institutions and societies of all kinds during the course of the war there are abundant evidences of the greatness and variety of the losses suffered by Britain. Cambridge University reported 8,407 casualties—2,382 killed, 3,154 wounded and 2,671 missing or prisoners. "This," we were told, "means nearly, but not quite, that out of every three Cambridge men serving two were either killed, wounded, missing, or prisoners." The figures were issued in September, 1918, so a certain addition is necessary. Oxford reported that out of 12,000 serving, one in six, or 2,000 had given their lives ; 584 men who had passed through the O.T.C. at London University had made the same last sacrifice. The Artists Rifles suffered 5,446 casualties out of 14,291 who had enlisted in that unit. Of these 1,549 had been killed and 3,079 wounded.

The schools, every one of them, had long rolls of honour. Eton returned her losses at 1,124 killed, and, taking a few others at random, we find Christ's Hospital, 325 killed ; Rugby, 635 killed and missing ; Rossall, 265 killed and 380 wounded ; Tonbridge, 377, including three masters, killed ; the City of London, 316 killed ; Cheltenham, 637 ; Radley, 189 ; Berkhamsted, 208 ; Bradfield, 237 ; and Stonyhurst, 155.

The legal profession sent a large number to the war and many, too, did not return. It was stated that 569 solicitors and 341 articled clerks had lost their lives ; while 190 barristers and a large number of bar students also made the supreme sacrifice. The Amalgamated Press lost 101 of its employees, and when a service for fallen Press men was held in St. Paul's Cathedral on February 22nd, 1919, it was stated that between 5,000 and 6,000 men connected with newspapers had fallen.

To praise those who gave their lives for their country would be an impertinence, but they cannot be left entirely without a tribute of respect and thanks. Literature is full of passages which express in stately prose or haunting verse sorrow for the great dead ; and in the words of Ecclesiasticus, chosen by Rudyard Kipling for the graves of the fallen, "their name liveth for evermore."

END OF VOLUME 12.

THE GREAT WAR

VOLUME XIII

"The Glorious Dead"

Laying Wreaths at the Foot of the Cenotaph in Whitehall.

THE GREAT WAR

THE STANDARD HISTORY OF
THE WORLD-WIDE CONFLICT

EDITED BY

H. W. WILSON

Author of "With the Flag to Pretoria"
"Japan's Fight for Freedom" etc.

and

J. A. HAMMERTON

Editor "Harmsworth History of the World"

VOLUME XIII

WITH GENERAL INDEX

LONDON
THE AMALGAMATED PRESS LIMITED
1919

CONTENTS OF VOLUME XIII

COLOURED PLATES, MAPS, AND PORTRAITS

PHOTOGRAVURE PLATE

GENERAL INDEX TO "THE GREAT WAR"

Complete Table of Reference to the Contents of the Thirteen Volumes: Text, Pictures, Plates, and Maps

THE index to THE GREAT WAR, comprising approximately 27,000 entries, has been compiled with the primary object of enabling readers to locate with a minimum of effort the thousands of incidents and illustrations contained in its thirteen volumes. In a work of so great a length and covering such a diversity of subjects it has been no light task to effect this object, but it has been achieved by the classification of many of the references under general headings. When readers have become accustomed to the arrangement of the index they should experience no trouble in turning up any incident or illustration to which they may desire to refer.

As examples, two of the general headings may be cited—namely, AIR RAIDS and WARSHIPS. Under the former will be found a list

of the principal British and foreign places which were subjected to bombardment from the air, and under the latter appear the names of warships of the belligerent nations which played a prominent part in the naval operations. This arrangement is deemed preferable to the alternative of spreading the references throughout the index under the specific names of the places or warships concerned. Similarly the valuable collection of maps, including those reproduced in full colours, specially prepared for THE GREAT WAR, will be found alphabetically arranged under the heading MAPS.

To distinguish pictures from text, all references to illustrations have the page numbers printed in blacker type, the ordinary light figures being used for page numbers of references to reading matter.

7 GENERAL INDEX TO "THE GREAT WAR" BRITISH-CANADIAN

British Navy (cont.)
preparedness for war I 62; 219
prize bounties X 114, 116
promotion grievances X 111
—innovations IX 363
provisioning vessel X 116
quick-firing gun in action I 223
repair ship XI 346
reserve forces X 106
routine aboard X 110
sailor's funeral at Reval XI 173
sailors inspected by King XI 354
—lying by gun I 223
scenes on deck VII 136, 137
Schleswig coast swept XII 580
sea patrol incidents IV 202, 203
shells taken aboard IX 371
ships in Kola Inlet XI 352
sickness X 119
silent activity I 225; VI 9
special flag VII 197
speed of vessels IX 366
Spithead review I 29, 221; X 3
stokers' branch IX 360
—of the Kent IX 364
—at work VI 240
storing munitions VI 10
suspect ship searched VI 11
tailoring X 115
tank-steamers convoyed X 597
targets after gun practice I 30
Third Destroyer Flotilla I 248
torpedo-boats VIII 531
—practice IX 240, 241, 367
tribute by Admiral Jellicoe X 123
triumph XII 561
two schools of thought I 226
U boat engaged VI 68
victualling X 113
vote for 1914-15 I 230
warrant-officers IX 358
warship, armour plate in belt I 33
—cleaning I 13
—provisioning I 51
—ready for action XII 4
—steaming to her base X 590
washing day VI 74; XI 361
wheeling coal from bunkers X 598
wounded, stretcher-cases X 119
see also Naval Engagements; Submarines; Warships, etc.
British Red Cross Soc. XIII 136
see also Red Cross, British
British retreat: see Mons, retreat from
British Salonika Force, Army Service Corps VIII 399
artillery VIII 398
—telephone operators XIII 581
camp V 438
—conflagration VIII 415
—in Macedonia IX 431; XII 331
convoy VI 132
—crossing plains XIII 581
engineers laying tracks V 443
fortification VII 470
fortified post 3000 ft. above sea-level XII 322
General Staff VII 467
gun VII 470
Highlanders marching VII 477
kit inspection V 271
military band VII 463
monastery used as canteen XII 331
motor-convoy assembling XII 330
mountain battery VIII 401
—road made by XII 332
patrol V 438
patrols nearing village in Macedonia XII 327
record IX 445
repairing trench parapet V 428
sailors with Greeks V 26
Scottish sentry VII 473; XI 67
—soldier on guard duty XI 53
—soldiers in trenches XI 53
— —leaving dressing station XI 54
— —with trench props XI 52
sentry V 281
signallers VI 509
soldiers crossing river V 281
—disembarking V 3
—going to trenches V 439
—marching along railway IX 429
—on quay V 283
—reviewed in Macedonia XII 321
—in trenches VIII 400
stretcher bearers V 4
transport arriving V 3
unloading transport cart V 283
watering horses X 344
Brits, General C. III 147; IX 222
Piet de Wet with III 145
Brlog, General P. von VII 326
Broadstairs, bombardment IX 237
Broadwood, General VII 51
Broadwood, Lt.-Gen. R. G. XI 550
Brobrinsky, Gen. Count II 147
Brock, Wing-Com. XI 369, 374
killed XI 376
Brock, Admiral O. de B. III 12; VII 419, 434
Brockdorff-Rantzau, Count von XIII 464, 499, 536, 547
Brocklebank, Miss S. XIII 26, 26
Brod IX 431
capture VIII 416
Brodie, Lieut.-Com. T. S. VI 46
Brodie, Lieut. W. L. IV 367, 381
Brody, capture V 52; VII 339
Bromley, Major C. X 603, 616
Broodseinde, capture XII 425
operations X 513
plateau, capture X 519
Brook, Lieut.-Col. A., killed IV 88
Brooke, Lieut.-Col. Lord I 351
Brooke, Lieutenant J. A. O. IV 381
Brooke, Lieut. J. W. X 427, 428
Brooke, R. XII 238; XIII 591
grave XII 237
war poem XII 242
Brooking, Maj.-Gen. Sir H. T. XI 427; XIII 174
Brooklyn, Lafayette memorial X 277
Brooks, Lieut. E. X 427, 428
Brooks, Sgt.-Maj. E. X 603, 624
Brooks, Sgt. O. VII 494, 501; X 24
Broqueville, Baron C. de I 404
Broughton, Capt. H. D. VIII 543
Brown, Sergt. D. F. X 608
Brown, Private H. XII 363
Brown, Mr. J. IX 456
Brown, Cpl. W. E. XIII 567
Brown Hill, capture XI 18
Browning, Vice-Ad. Sir M. XII 588
Bruce, Sir D. XIII 214
Bruce, Lt. W. A. McC. XIII 565
Bruges, capture XII 493
fined VIII 199
fortification II 404
Ghent Gate II 345
inhabitants, German food for I 443
liberation scenes XIII 44, 49
outskirts reached XII 481
Bruges (cont.)
royal entry XII 210, 494, 494; XIII 46
Bruges Canal, bombardment XII 425
Brulard, General VI 172
Lord Kitchener and V 321, 323
Brunswick, Soviet XIII 496, 498
Brunswick, Duke of VI 444; XIII 466
Brussels, King Albert's re-entry XII 493
army rifle range XII 496
barricades I 86, 92
Belgian Army enters XIII 74
—occupation XIII 64
—soldiers guarding I 57
— —march past King Albert XII 493
Civic Guard I 75, 93
closing events XIII 47
early scenes I 398
Ecole Militaire, apparatus XIII 45
final German outrages XIII 68
fined VIII 192
French troops entering XIII 41
German advance I 397
—authority I 404
—cavalry I 160
—commissariat I 145
—entry I 217, 403
—field kitchen I 394
—hussar officers I 161
—military commandant I 393
—mounted palace guard XI 203
—occupation I 392
—rioting XIII 48
—troops I 87, 145, 159
— —confiscate cattle I 394
— —mutiny XII 539; XIII 62
— —parading XI 203
— —retreating through XII 553
goose-step I 403
Grande Place, Germans in I 272
indemnity imposed I 404
inhabitants, exodus I 400
liberation XIII 48, 74
—scenes XIII 67
life during war XI 210
"Little Bees" XI 210
march of British Third Corps XIII 51
military pageant XII 510
newspaper censorship I 398
Palais de Justice I 87, 397
— — —German defences I 395
— — —Germans quartered in I 272
Palais de Academies, damage done by Germans XIII 56
people outside communal kitchen XI 195
—waiting for food XI 194
proclamation I 401
refugees, arrival I 399
royal family leave I 399
—palace, hospital I 78
royal re-entry XIII 53, 74
Royal Palace Hotel, hospital I 176
shop as hospital I 78
statue, the Spirit of Belgium XII 497
surrender demanded I 402
Town Guards I 63
War Office I 93
war statuary XII 497, 498
wounded in hospital I 167
Brussels, The, capture VII 203; IX 11
torpedoed off Zeebrugge XII 478
Brussiloff, General A. I 301; II 85, 97, 98, 100, 106, 115; III 81, 220, 223, 246, 418, 426, 432, 437, 446; IV 260, 277; V 52; VII 319, 320, 325
Galicia invaded II 92
Brussiloff M. IX 133
Bry, advance on XII 534
Bryan, Professor G. H. V 357
Bryan, Lce.-Corpl. T. X 603, 623.
Bryan, Mr. W. III 114, 131; IX 77
attitude VI 64
resignation VI 87
Brzezany, battles XI 168
fighting IX 45
Buchan, Mr. J., propaganda XIII 394
Buchan, Sec.-Lt. J. C. XII 362, 376
Buchanan, Captain A. X 620
Buchanan, Sir G. VI 235; IX 56, 117, 117
Buchanan, Miss M. III 412
Buckingham, Pte. W. IV 367, 387
Buckingham Palace, posting sentry XIII 241
soldiers rest VI 558
Buckley, Cpl. A. H. XIII 568
Buckley, Sgt. M. XIII 558, 568
Buckmaster, Sir S., Press Bureau director X 417
Bucquoy, British retirement XII 68
fighting XII 73
Buczacz, occupation VII 342
Budapest X 53
complete dislocation XIII 474
demonstrations XII 399
insurrection XIII 475
Liberty Square XIII 476
National Council XIII 473
parliament house X 52; XIII 476
royal palace X 53
Rumanian advance forbidden XIII 477
Budd, Captain E. XII 597
Buenos Aires, Congress building X 377
offices of "La Prensa" X 378
welcome to British Mission XIII 284
Bufta, peace declaration XII 327
Bug River, fighting V 30
passage forced IV 301
Bugden, Private P. XII 366
Buissy, capture XII 287
Bukarest, advance on VIII 272
air raids VII 521, 528
apprehension III 114
British attaché's house VIII 271
capture VIII 274
citizens' war demonstration XIII 196
flight from XIII 203
German motor-vans in XIII 203
—troops in IX 430; XIII 202
Ministry of Foreign Affairs VII 509
peace of XII 328; XIII 327, 514
petrol tanks XIII 198
royal palace VII 509
Treaty of III 34
troops guarding street XIII 196
view II 309
Bukoba, action VII 178
capture IX 212
Bukovina, Germans recover XI 169
operations III 246, 446; IV 273, 277; VII 329, 343; IX 435
Russian advance II 12
scenes VII 327
Bukovitch, General X 353
Bulair, view III 338
Bulak, fighting V 394
Bulfin, Maj-Gen. E. S. II 230, 246, 385; V 348
made K.C.B. XII 345
Bulgaria, agreement with Austria I 357
— —Turkey IV 437
armistice request XII 340; XIII 435
attitude II 309; III 110, 116; IV 172
—towards Rumania VII 516
Balkan peace I 354
—war sequel I 357
British enter XII 339
cession by Turkey V 21
German loan III 122; V 12
relations with Russia I 356
significant act III 122
State Treasury I 355
surrender XII 340
—effect XII 387
treaty with Central Powers V 10, 28
war declaration V 278
— —on Rumania VII 488
—disinclination I 355
warning by Sir E. Grey V 26
Bulgarian Army V 423
artillery in Serbian town XII 323
bomb-proof shelter V 11
losses VIII 403
mobilisation V 24, 273
patrol in Krushevo XII 323
retreat XII 337
strength at armistice XIII 586
troops in Serbian village VIII 467
Bulgarian Campaign: see Serbian Campaign, etc.
Bulgaroff, Gen. von III 232, 249
Bulkeley-Johnson, Brig.-Gen. C. B. XI 550
Bullard, General XII 305, 462, 519
Bullecourt, battles IX 409
British artillery success IX 423
—retirement XII 58
capture IX 428; XII 280
enemy surrounded IX 421
fighting IX 345; XI 226, 253; XII 284
German counter-attack IX 427
—losses IX 426
Londoners isolated IX 414
tunnel system IX 420
Buller, Colonel H. C. III 176; VIII 535
Buller, Captain H. T. I 284
Bullitt, Mr. W. C. XIII 546
Bullocks, siege-train IX 142
Bulow, Captain von IX 277
Bulow, General von II 30, 34, 39, 50, 67, 79, 178, 250; III 232, 415
Bulow, Prince von III 110
intrigues in Italy III 111, 112
in Rome IV 106
Bumpus, L. R. XII 238
Bunbury, Colonel V. T. I 351
Bunning, Mr. S. XIII 438
Bunsen, Sir M. de I 46; X 64; XIII 284, 285
speech at Santiago XIII 286
Buole Pass, battle VII 271
Burchill, Lieut.-Col. VII 7; IV 17
Burges, Lt.-Col. D. XIII 558, 564
Burial service III 332; VII 227, 231
Burian, Count S. de III 114
appointed foreign minister III 120
resignation XII 393
Burj, El, capture XII 344
fighting XI 23
Burj el Lisaneh, fighting XII 353
Burkah, capture XI 18; XII 344
Burkhart, Major, decorated X 437
Burleson, Mr. A. S. X 261
Burman, Sgt. W. F. XII 362, 374
Burney, Admiral Sir C. VII 408, 440; IX 20; X 83
Burt, Corporal A. A. VII 494, 504
Burt, Lieut.-Col. A. G. VI 391
Burtchaell, Sir C. H. XIII 205, 222
Burton, Corporal A. S. VII 497
Bushell, Lieut.-Col. C. XII 363, 380
Bushire, view V 297
Busigny, Junction, capture XII 460
Busk, fighting XI 168
Bussell, Captain Rev. J. G. VI 395
Bussus, capture VII 550
Butler, Mr. G., propaganda XIII 396
Butler, Captain J. F. P. VII 499
Butler, Dr. N. M. X 283
Butler, Private W. B. XII 363, 377
Buxton, Mr. N. II 309
Buzancy, enemy line broken XII 128
railhead captured XII 521
Buzau, capture IX 434
fighting IX 433
Buzau Pass VII 516
fighting VII 528
Buzau River, fighting IX 433
Bychava, capture IV 292
Byng, Gen. Hon. Sir J. H. G. II 378; V 347; VIII 137, 240; IX 191, 266, 269, 311; XI 224; XII 35, 253 261, facing 376, 420, 454, 499, 515
Army command XI 143
command of Third Army X 432
King and Army leaders with XIII 405
By-products VII 77
Byron, Lady IX 397; X 516
Byron, Lieut.-Col. VII 188
Bye, Sergt. R. XII 363, 368
Bzura River, action III 208
bayonet fighting III 215
defence III 218
German casualties III 219
Germans trapped III 213
Russians forced back III 248
Würtembergers annihilated III 218

C

Cabaret Farm, fighting XII 428
Cable, Mr. A. G. X 268
Cable, Mr. B. XII 241
Cables, British service XI 213
— —to Holland suspended XI 222
—ships at Gallipoli XI 222
Cameroon stations XI 221
Cocos Island XI 217
—Batavian, laying line XI 213
German espionage XI 222
—service XI 214
Cable-ship, Levant II. XI 220
Cadbury, Lieut. E. VIII 225, 231
Cadet Corps, London Scottish XI 340
Cadets, naval, compass instruction XI 345
—heaving the lead XI 345
—taking sun sights XI 345
Cadiz, U 293 at XI 360
Cadogan, Lt.-Col. H. O. S. VI 389
Cadorna, General Count L. III 112; IV 100, V 207, 207; VI 501; VII 264, 272, 284; IX 103, 474, 482; XI 73
British batteries visited XI 69
early operations VI 487
Cadorna, General (cont.)
inspecting Alpini VII 299
General Joffre with V 215
strategy VII 284
visit to western front VI 420
Caffrey, Private J. VII 494, 504
Cagnicourt, capture XII 284
Caillaux, M. J. I 102
German peace inclination X 221
Caillaux trial I 102
Caillette Wood VII 385, 390, 394, 400; VIII 358
capture VIII 346
Cairns, Sgt. H. XIII 567
Cairo, Ghezireh Palace Hotel III 384
Heliopolis Grand Hotel III 384
hospital scenes IV 131
hotels as hospitals III 384
new Sultan, proclamation III 33
Calais, apprehension II 351
bombardment IX 240
coast road to VI 400
struggle for II 347
Caldwell, Sgt. T. XIII 558, 565
Caledonia, The, sunk IX 25
California Plateau, capture X 216
fighting X 234, 238, 242; XII 115
Callaghan, Admrl. Sir G. I 35, 221
Callao X 384
Calonne, Grand Tranchee, fighting XII 300
Calvario, attack VII 288
Calvert, Sgt. L. XIII 558, 563
Cambrai, battle (1917) XI 223
—captured rifles XI 233
—individual heroism XI 258
—Irish troops resting XI 233
—official report XI 260
—underground dressing-station XI 243
—(1918) XII 420
— —British infantry advancing XII 449
— — —scaling North Canal wall XII 427
— —landmark guide to Tank officers XII 422
British attack from south XII 454
—guns going forward XII 309
—infantry advancing XII 152, 309
—progress XII 306
—retreat to the Somme XII 35
Canadians enter XII 310, 428
—entering the square XII 450
—putting out fire XII 311
—reach suburbs XII 437
capture II 37
cathedral, interior damage XII 452
—Thanksgiving Service XII 452
church ruins XII 452
destruction XII 448
explosion of German mine XII 311
fighting XII 36
fired by Germans XII 442, 449
German counter-attack XI 253
—defence XII 435
—headquarters XII 452
Germans trapped near II 32
Highland Territorials attack X 470
mine explosion after capture XII 449
North Lancashire patrol in XII 312
Place de Sépulcre II 38
railway-station XII 451
rearguard action XII 460
ruins XII 310, 449, 450, 451, 452
Tank offensive XI 226
Cambrai—Le Cateau, battle II 63
—British surrounded II 66
—German rifle fire II 65
— —guns ineffective II 65
—Gordons trapped by enemy II 70
Cambridge, allied leaders honoured XIII 415
Cambridge, Lieut.-Col. Marquis of X 30
Camels, commissariat XI 315
employment in Egypt X 71
farm work VI 550
supply train IX 153
transport laden with bags of bread XI 329
unloading VI 371
Cameron, Captain A. G. XI 53
Cameron, Mr. D. Y., war picture XII 179
Cameron, Lieutenant N. XI 53
Cameron House, fighting X 509
Cameronian, The, sunk IX 257
Cameroon V 80
cable-stations XI 221
river scene XII 205
views VII 94, 95
Cameroon Campaign V 82; VII 95
advance along railway V 85
allied officers V 89
armistice accepted VII 110
armoured barge VII 106
barbed-wire defences V 81
block-house ruins VII 107
British disaster V 82
captured weapons VII 111
French commissariat V 87
—successes V 84, 85
German cruelty VII 102
—machine-guns VII 101
—mutiny VII 105
—posts captured V 85
—retreat VII 114
Gold Coast troops VII 113
heroic incident VII 101
material captured V 82
native carriers VII 113, 114
—encampment VII 103
—soldiers V 87; VII 115
naval artillery V 87
Nigerian artillery's attack V 90
—camp VII 104
—officers VII 102
—soldiers V 79, 83, 84; VII 96
— —guard prisoners VII 111
Nlohe Bridge V 88
officers' baggage V 83
—tent VII 102
Senegalese troops V 89; VII 115
train captured VII 95
wounded natives VII 105
Cameroon River, naval action II 301
Camouflage XI 448
heavy gun XI 448
Camp Dix, New Jersey X 281
Campbell, Lieut. D. VIII 551
Campbell, Colonel D. F. VIII 535
Campbell, Maj.-Gen. D. G. M. XII 456
Campbell, Lieut. F. W. VII 14, 501
Campbell, Commander G. X 603, 604; XIII 559
Campbell, Mr. G. X 427, 428
Campbell, Lieutenant H. XI 376
Campbell, Captain Hon. J. B. VIII 541
Campbell, Colonel J. V. VIII 142; X 603, 615
Campbell, General P. VIII 367
Campion, Major E. VIII 537
Campu Lung VIII 257
capture VIII 269
fighting VIII 271
Canada, aliens interned VII 4
Conscription Law XIII 355
co-operation III 162
development XIII 356
general election XI 159
German population XIII 353
gifts II 8; III 163
internal conditions XI 153
Military Service Bill XI 154
Parliament House fire VI 75, 112
presentation of aeroplanes to XIII 358
recruiting III 163
Red Cross campaign XI 159
Union Ministry XI 154
war loan XI 159
—material contribution XIII 353
—museum trophies XIII 357
—preparedness XIII 347
—response XIII 348
Canadian Army II 133
advance under shell fire VII 503
General Alderson's message III 171
— —tribute VII 13
ammunition column X 479
—dump XI 134
— —preparing XI 143
—lorries VII 23
Arleux operations XI 142
artillery awaiting inspection X 185
—with 4.7 gun I 238
barricade, ruins of captured XI 131
bayonet charge, Ypres VII 30, 31
bomb-proof station VII 21
Bourlon Hill XII 421
brushwood for billets XI 153
Cambrai, advance on XII 421
—losses XII 435
—operations XI 148
camp-cookers VII 23
campaign of 1916-17 XI 127
cavalry exercising I 239
—in hoods V 417
—machine-gun section XI 133
—machine-gunners XII 53
—test VII 22
—training in France XI 145
colours deposited in Belfast Cathedral XIII 282
composition in 1917 XI 152
Courcelette fighting VIII 118
—return from VIII 117
—wounded at VIII 129
Denain captured XII 499
England, arrival III 167
—landing III 166
entry into Mons XII 370, 371
expeditionary force III 163
field-kitchen near Hill 70 XI 144
Festubert battle IV 79, 85, 91
field-ambulance ward VII 21
—operations in Wilts III 177
first contingent III 164; VII 33
— —composition VII 33
— —in France III 171; VII 1
— —group III 162
— —officers III 162
Forestry Corps XI 150
French Canadians XIII 354
General French's tribute III 172
Fresnoy operations XI 143
game of cards VII 23
gas-attack practice VIII 501
getting guns into action XIII 417
Givenchy operations VII 18
gun emplacement at Lens XI 150
gunners drawing ammunition IX 379
Hill 70 operations XI 144
honours list VII 23
Hooge, losses at VII 27
horse ambulance VII 32
hut kitchen II 242
incidents in France VII 6, 7
individual heroism VII 22; XI 130
infantry covered by armoured car XII 151
—passing Stonehenge II 137
—ready for inspection I 238, 239
inspection by Duke of Connaught III 154, 155
—by General Hughes VII 5
issue of rations VII 25
lance-corporal decorated VII 1
Lens attack X 463
—fighting near X 481
light railway building XI 142, 149
limbers passing motor-lorries XII 249
loading ammunition XI 126
—15-in. gun X 348
London procession XIII 351
lumbering at Windsor VII 27
machine-gunner in Cambrai XII 456
machine-gunners in shell-holes IX 350
march to the Rhine XIII 64
marching to trenches IX 380
meal-time in trenches VII 29
memorial to Vimy Ridge victims XI 127
—service to Vimy Ridge victims XI 549
men from Calgary VII 9, 24
motor machine-gun section XII 312
—machine-gunner XII 44
narrow-gauge ammunition train XI 134
numerical strength I 168; XIII 356, 584, 585
officer instructing men VIII 44
—with grenades V 123
officers I 237; VII 19
—and men II 242, 243
—leaving Liverpool for home XIII 355
Officers Training Corps VII 9
Oppy line operations IX 373
organisation VII 31
—in England XI 138
"Over the top" IX 201
Passchendaele Ridge operations X 546; XI 145
pay-parade in captured village XI 151
— —in snow XI 143
Pioneers felling shattered trees XI 152
—returning to billets XII 55
—splitting logs XI 153
platoon system XI 140
poison gas experience VII 4
post-office VII 25
practising advance with Tank XII 507
Prince of Wales presenting colours XIII 349
quarters in a barn XI 129
Quebec men in training VII 26
Quinque Rue, La VII 17

GUNS-HOSPITALS GENERAL INDEX TO "THE GREAT WAR" 14

Guns (cont.)
machine, British explaining to Cossacks XI 192
— —officers' practice V 101
— —transport XII 45
—Canadians repairing XII 137
—emplacement X 453
— —German X 459
— — —camouflaged XII 487
— — —reinforced concrete XII 445
— —at Thelus IX 339
—French, in action IV 66
— —in trench IV 31
—German VIII 30
— —in action VI 410
— —captured VI 537; VII 89; VIII 49
— — —at Beaucourt VIII 161
— —in graveyard II 406
— —heavy type VI 538
—Italian XI 81
—Montenegrin V 19
—motor, fixing ammunition belt XII 44
—motor-battery VIII 46
—Nigerian V 83
—Russian V 370
— —in action IV 264
—South African IV 58
—Zouaves working V 148
Madsen XI 444, 460
naval, American XI 537
— —spray shields XI 537
—British 15-in. IX 1, 259; XII 5
—Canadians firing IX 274
—French, and gunners VIII 28
— —in Oise sector XII 86
—Italian battery in action XI 68
— —heavy gun on pontoon XI 99
—lifting 14 in. gun on board XI 347
—loading IX 278
platform, Austrians erecting XI 99
Stokes IX 309; XI 443
—fitting fuses XI 441
—Portuguese in trench with XI 451
trench VI 528
—howitzer VI 527
—loading XI 443
see also Artillery
Gurkhas: see Indian troops
Gurnsey, Captain Lord VI 395
Gury Hill, fighting XII 121
Gustav, crown prince of Sweden IX 187
Gustav V. king of Sweden IX 172, 182, 187
Gutchkoff, M. A. IX 121, 130, 131
Gutor, General, relieved of command XI 169
Guynemer, Captain VIII 289; XI 395
killed XI 393
Gwalior, Maharaja of III 349, 358
Gwynne, Bishop VII 222
Gyergyoszentmiklos VII 522
Gyimes Pass VII 516
fighting VII 528, 530
Gyles, Midshipman D. IX 242, 244, 247; XI 39, 40

H

Haakon VII, king of Norway IX 182, 183
Haase, Herr H. XIII 453, 456
Habibullah Khan XIII 520
Habarovsk, capture XIII 517
Hackett, Sapper W. X 608, 615
Haddock, Captain H. J. XI 47
Haditha, capture XI 437
Hadjimischeff, M. P. V 5
Haelen, battle I 213
—German equipment taken I 148
—individual bravery I 214
—scene I 96
church damaged I 65
house destroyed by shell I 79
Haeseler, Field-Marshal von VI 320, 325
Hafiz Kor, operations VII 167
Haggard, Captain, "Stick it Welsh" XIII 272
Hague, The, Binnenhof IX 173
British soldiers interned XI 297
Hague Conferences I 60, 241; VI 243
Hague Conventions, violation 1 439
Hai River, feint attack IX 149
Haifa, British cavalry XIII 584
capture XII 359
Indian Lancers in XII 349
Haig, Field-Marshal Sir D. I 349; II 20, 22, 28, 49, 58, 166, 229, 231, 349, 367, 374, 388; III 275, facing 280, 286, 301; IV 67, 226, 329; V 107, 141; VI 200, 201; VII 48, 397; VIII 1, 5, 29, 38, 41, 85, 162; IX 264, 475; XI 49; XII fac. 416, 435
arrival at Dover XIII 508
"backs to the wall" order XII 102
biographical sketch V 343
Commander-in-Chief XI 56; XIII 408
congratulating Canadians XII 249
Sir A. Currie with XI 136
Gen. French and Gen. Joffre with IV 41, 42
King George with VII 322
— —and Army leaders with XIII 405
greeting Canadian officers XIII 68
inspecting Canadians XII 49
—French troops V 327
—guard of honour in Cambrai XII 458
General Joffre and V 327; VII 67
in liberated Cambrai XII 447, 452
London procession XIII 404
—welcome XIII 403
Messines Ridge battle X 343
Sir Pertab Singh with VII 152
Sambre Canal battle XII 488
succeeds General French VI 418
talking with priest in Cambrai XII 458
tribute by Sir J. French II 58
victory march XIII 550
"Hail, Columbia!" XI 531
Haine, Sec.-Lieut. R. L. X 623
Haines, Colonel XI 420
Haines, Mr. W. XI 406
Haiti, disturbance IX 58
Haking, Lieut.-Gen. Sir R. C. B. II 41, 63; V 348; XII 482
Lille liberation ceremonies XII 483
Halahan, Captain H. C. XI 369
killed XI 375
Haldane, Lieut.-General J. A. L. I 351; II 60; V 348; X 85; XI 55; XII 435, 455, 526
Hales, Captain A. H. VIII 551
Halicz, battles II 99, 109; IX 45
capture II 99; XI 168
fighting IX 40
Halicz (cont.)
retreat on IV 275
view II 97
Hali Bey, Colonel III 35
Halki, sanatorium III 316
Hall, Corpl. A. C. XIII 568
Hall, Colour-Sergeant F. W. IV 388; VII 17
Hall, Captain W. R. IX 357
Halle, stormed XIII 498
Haller, Gen. XIII 297, 495, 499
Halliwell, Lance-Corporal J. XII 366, 373
Hallowes, Sec.-Lieut. R. P. V 122; VII 495, 504
Halsey, Captain L. I 295; III 12
Halsey, Rear-Admiral L. XI 349
Halswelle, Captain W. VI 395
Halton, Private A. XII 366, 374
Ham, capture X 199; XII 28, 288
destruction XII 288
fighting XII 33, 77
Hamadan, railway to XIII 185
Hamann, Dr. II 318
Hamburg, republic capital XIII 461
revolution XIII 453
shipbuilding yard I 254
Hamburg, The, interned IX 60
Hamel, Australians' action XII 124
shock tactics XII 253
Hamelincourt, fighting XII 267
Hamilton, General Sir B. M. III 285; IV 237
Hamilton, Maj.-Gen. H. I. W. I 350; II 28, 39, 41, 223
killed II 363; V 348
Hamilton, Gen. Sir I. III 315, 336, 371; IV 153, 409; V 326; VI 165
addressing French officers VI 190
biographical sketch V 341
going ashore IV 413
General Gouraud and IV 409
inspecting Anzacs III 175; VII 359
—Royal Naval Division IV 413
recalled VI 171
Staff officers with VI 181
at Suvla Bay VI 167
Hamilton, Capt. Lord J. VI 395
Hamilton, Pte. J. VII 496, 498
Hamilton, Private J. B. XII 378
Hamilton, Mr. J. P. XI 414
Hammarskjold, M. IX 169, 186
Hamme, Belgian infantry I 179
Hammersley, Maj.-Gen. F. VI 165, 188
Hamont, fined VIII 192
Hamrin, Jebel, fighting XIII 193
Hanafish, Wady, fighting XI 7
Handeni, occupation VII 192
Handzaeme, stormed XII 481
Hangard, fighting XII 88, 93
woods, fighting XII 258
Hango, ruins I 306
Hankey, D. XII 239
war literature XII 241
Hanna, Coy.-Sgt.-Maj. R. XII 364, 367
Hannan, Lt.-Col. H. M. VI 389
Hannebeek, fighting X 519
Hannyngton, Brig. Gen. VII 191; IX 219, 219
interrogating native prisoner X 588
Hanover, rabbit breeding VIII 385
Hanrys, General XII 338
Hansen, Captain P. H. IV 439; VII 495; 499
Hanskerke, damage XIII 47
Haplincourt, advance on XII 280
Hapsburgs, imperial rule II 116
Haram, El, capture XII 342
Harbin, rioting XI 520
Hardaumont, promontory carried VIII 357
quarries VIII 344
Hardaumont Wood VII 397
Hardecourt, capture VIII 12
Hardinge, Viscount III 348, 353
Arab chiefs with V 320
Hardy, Mr. T., war poem XII 238
Hardy, Rev. T. B. XII 367, 373
Hareira Redoubt, capture XI 15
Hargicourt, capture XII 315
enemy break through XII 37
—front broken XII 259
Haricot Redoubt, attack IV 418
Harington, Col. H. H. VIII 535
Harley, Mrs., funeral VIII 560
killed IX 449
with wounded IV 133
Harlock, Bomb. E. G. IV 373, 376
Harmsworth, Captain Hon. H. A. V. XI 543
Harmsworth, Lieutenant Hon. V. S. T. VIII 551
Harper, Lieut. A. G. XI 555
Harper, Lieut.-Gen. G. M. XII 526, 541
Harrington, Lieut. H. N. XI 295
Harris, Captain J. H. XIII 245
Harris, Mr. P. XI 494
Harris, Sgt. T. J. XIII 559, 563
Harrison, Lt.-Com. A. XIII 559, 559
Harrison, Sec.-Lt. J. X 609, 619
Harsova, occupation VIII 262
Hartlepools, bombardment III 6, 7, 13
—Baptist Chapel wrecked III 9
views III 10
Hartmannsweilerkopf III 269
battles IV 179
Harvey, Pte. J. XIII 559, 564
Harvey, Major F. J. W. VII 455, 460; X 603, 609; XIII 6
Harvey, Lt. F. M. W. X 609, 610
Harvey, Corpl. N. XIII 559, 564
Harvey, Private S. VII 498, 503
Harvey, General W. J. St. J. VII 534
Harvey Pasha III 371
Harwich, surrendered U boats XII 390, 391, 392, 561, 588
Hasler, Brig.-Gen. J. VI 384
killed V 348
Haspres, fighting XII 500
Hassana, action VI 458
capture X 81, 82
Hassana Well, air attack VI 457
Hassankale, capture VI 229
Hasselt, German raid I 208
Hatfield, Mrs. A. S. L. X 518
Hatszeg, fighting VII 523, 525
Haut, Mont, fighting X 231
Haucourt VII 385
Haumont, capture XII 465
destroyed VI 318
Haumont Wood, capture XII 465
Hausen, General von II 34, 39, 67, 79, 152, 183, 191
Haverfield, Hon. Mrs. XIII 21, 140
Havre, Allies' base VI 398, 399
R.A.M.C. kit inspection I 170
Havrincourt, capture XI 232
fighting XI 226, 231; XII 43, 306, 320
German air attack XII 306
Havrincourt Wood, fighting IX 304; XII 295
Hawarden, Viscount VI 397
killed XIII 228
Hawker, Major L. G. III 278; VII 495, 498
Hawkins, Lieut. C. E. V. XI 376
Hawksley, Com. VII 446; X 86
Hawthorn, Colonel X 579
Hay, Russian supply VII 333
Hay, Lord A. VI 395
killed XIII 233
Hayes, Private XIII 281
Hayward, Capt. R. XII 367, 380
Haywood, Lt.-Col. A. VII 106, 114
Hazalin, battle VI 474
Hazebrouck II 359, 360
German objective XII 100
Hazy Trench VIII 162
Headfort, Lady XIII 26
Headlam, Brig.-Gen. J. E. W. V 348
Headlam, Brig.-Gen. J. G. I 351; II 43
Headlam-Morley, Dr. XIII 400
Heath, Vice-Admiral H. L. VII 434, 440, 448; XI 349
Heaviside, Pte. M. X 609, 620
Hebron XII 349
capture XI 24
Hebuterne VIII 46
British retire to XII 73
fighting XII 76
Hedges, Lieut. F. W. XIII 559, 563
Hedin, Dr. S. II 317
visit to the Kaiser X 569
Hedjaz, Arab camp at Kalat el Akaba XII 342
king of: see Hussein
operations X 88; XII 347, 360
railway, advance on XII 348
—raids XII 360
Heeringen, General J. von II 173, 184, 219, 224, 226, 240, 249, 274; III 262
Heidelberg Camp VIII 389
Heintz, Capt., wearing gas-mask X 282
Helena, princess of Serbia V 180
Helfferich, Dr. IX 57, 58
Heligoland I 409
revolution XIII 453
torpedo-boat harbours II 308
Heligoland Bight, British Navy sweeps XII 580
Heligoland Bight, Battle of I 128, 409
British rescue German crews I 407
—ships, disposition I 410
— —in action I 405
— —return to Harwich I 406
—squadrons engaged I 410
decoy manœuvre I 411
diagram I 412, 413
First Light Cruiser Squadron I 406
German casualties I 417
—cruisers in action I 412
—destroyer sunk I 413
—gunnery defective I 414
sailors rescued by submarine I 382
submarine reconnaissance I 409
trap for German Navy I 409
Heliograph, optic VI 309
Hell Wood, fighting X 338
Helles, attack VI 188
battery at III 381
day of crisis VI 194
struggle III 375
Helmets, German V 160
poison gas V 95
steel IV 216, 329; VI 415; IX 194, 491
—French wearing V 125, 159
Helsingfors, harbour XIII 375
Helyar, Lt.-Com. K. C. XI 377
Hem, capture VIII 9
Hemy, Mr. N., war picture XII 173
Hendecourt, capture XII 280
fighting IX 412; XII 282
Henderson, Captain VIII 316
Henderson, Lieutenant XI 376
Henderson, Capt. A. X 609, 624
Henderson, Rt. Hon. A. VIII 349, 360, 372
Cabinet Minister XIII 437
Peace Conference XIII 438
visit to Russia XIII 438
Henderson, Brig.-Gen. Sir D. I 321, 337; V 348; VIII 288, 291
Henderson, Capt. D. VIII 542
Henderson, Lieut.-Col. E. E. D. X 609, 624
Henin, capture IX 302
fighting XII 76
—around XII 57
Henin Hill, capture XII 275
defence XII 62
fighting XII 57, 60, 74
Heninel, Tank in action IX 332, 376
Hennocque, General XIII 482
Henry, Prince (of England) X 4
Henry, Prince (of Holland) IX 172
Henry, Prince (of Mecklenburg-Schwerin) III 113
Henry, Prince (of Prussia) III 289; IV 257, 286; X 575
espionage X 386
interview with King George X 4
leaving for the front IV 158
Henry, Princess (of Pless) IV 142
Henry, Lieut. C. C. VIII 557
Henry, Sir E. X 358
Henty, Captain A. F. VIII 542
Herbebois VI 318
Herbecourt, capture VII 551
Herbert, Lieutenant G. XI 33
Herbert, Lieut.-Com. G. III 2
Herbertshohe, bungalow II 290
capture II 306
Herbignies, capture XII 533
Hereford, Lieut. F. R. XI 39
Herenthage Chateau X 487
Herenthage Park, fighting X 507
Heresco, General VII 526
Hermada, Mount, attack XI 73
fighting XI 75
naval guns bombarding XI 68
Hermann line XII 501
German counter-attack XII 508
pierced XII 513
Hermannstadt, battle VII 526
Rumanian retreat VII 524
Hermies, fighting XII 42, 43
Herr, General VI 313
Herring, Sec-Lieut. A. C. XII 376
Hersee, Lieut. C. P. A. VIII 559
Hersing, Lieut. von VI 10, 29
Hertzog, General III 136, 149; XIII 363
policy III 137
Herve, destruction I 200
Hervey, Mdshpmn. W. VII 450
Hervilly, Tank counter-attack XII 38
Herzegovina, annexation I 26
disaffection I 22
Landsturm in stone quarry III 425
religion I 24
Hesse, Grand Duke of XIII 466
Hessian Trench VIII 151
Hetsas, Belgian success IV 363
Heudicourt, action IX 343
Heule, Germans evacuate XII 478
Heurteaux, Capt., decorated X 437
Hewitson, Lce.-Corpl. J. XII 374
Hewitt, Sec.-Lieut. D. G. W. XII 367, 376
Hewitt, Lce.-Corpl. W. H. XII 366, 367
Hewlett, Flight-Com. III 186
rescue III 201
Hewlett, Mr. M., war poem XII 240
Heyn, Major XIII 87
Heyworth, Gen. F. J. VIII 534
Hibiki, General N. XI 505
Hickman, Lieut. G. V. IX 247
Hicks, Lieutenant B. B. VIII 555
"Hidden Hand" X 390
High explosives VII 78
High Wood VIII 236
counter-attack VIII 122
fighting VIII 95, 101, 110; XII 276
German gun taken VIII 95
Londoners' ordeal VIII 138
Highbury, hospital at VIII 328
Hilder, Captain M. L. XI 547
Hill, Private A. X 609, 621
Hill, Brig.-General F. F. VI 179
Hill, Mr. J. XIII 444
Hill Q, attack IV 442
Hill 35, fighting X 473, 486
Hill 37, fighting X 497
Hill 40, fighting X 510
Hill 60 (Belgium) III 269
battles IV 7, 33
capture X 487
fighting X 502
mined X 331
raids IX 196
recapture IV 337
Hill 60 (Gallipoli), attack IV 448
capture VI 170
Hill 63, capture XII 287
fighting XII 102
Hill 65, capture X 433
Hill 70, attack IV 446
battle V 121, 123
capture V 116; X 463
Canadians return from X frontis., 454
fighting X 480, 482
Guards attack V 139
individual heroism V 139, 146
Hill 85, capture VII 286
Hill 109, fighting VIII 23
Hill 112, attack IV 446
Hill 121, capture VII 286
fighting VIII 25
Hill 144 IX 93
capture IX 96
strategic importance IX 94
Hill 145, fighting IX 313
Hill 208, capture IX 106
Hill 218, battle IV 297
Hill 219, fighting XI 74
Hill 265, capture XII 127
Hill 287 VII 390
Hill 304, capture XI 281
fighting VII 385, 397; XI 279, 280
outflanked X 242
Hill 413, fighting IX 40
Hill 1070, fighting XI 8
Hill 1212, fighting X 353
Hill 1248, capture IX 449
Hindenburg, Field-Marshal von I 419, 424; III 60, 67, 75, 207, 213, 246, 416; IV 286; V 30, 48, 375; VII 325; VIII 256, 389, 393, 472
counter-attack III 220
dismissal III 432
German Emperor and IV 145
headquarters near Cassel XIII 81
reinstatement IV 257
remains chief of Army XIII 508
resumes western command XII 247
return to power XII 473
Russian advance checked I 425
Staff I 419; XIII 422
studying war map VIII 393
Hindenburg line IX 263, 307; XI 243; XII 288, 308
advance to IX 285
attack XII 306
Australians attack XII 284
—storm IX 412
bastion, captured IX 342
Cambrai offensive XI 226
description XII 447
fighting XII 438, 453, 466
French attack X 200
importance of storming XIII 588
pierced XII 278
snow-covered trenches XIII 417
threatened IX 385
tunnel entrance XII 319
—system IX 412; XII 427
turned XII 463
Hindlip, Lady XIII 26
Hinges, fighting XII 107
Hipper, Admiral III 10, 18, 28; VII 410, 413; XII 580; XIII 5
Hirondelle River, fighting XII 60
Hirsch, Captain D. P. X 609, 618
Hirschauer, General XII 462; XIII 65
Kehl bridge-head ceremony XIII 89
Hirson, advance on XII 507
attack XII 501
railway junction reached XII 541
Hitchins, Lieut.-Colonel, killed in second battle of Ypres VI 389
Hizmeh, capture XII 344
Ho Sue, Major X 499
Hobbs, General Sir J. T. XI 336
Hoboken, Stevens Institute IX 65
Hobson, Sergeant F. XII 363
Hodge, Rt. Hon. J. VIII 351, 371; IX 473; XIII 437
Cabinet Minister XIII 437
Hodson, Brig.-Gen. G. VI 384
Hofer, General von V 213
Hoffmann, Gen. XI 188; XIII 493
Hoffmann, Herr A. XIII 455, 496
Hogan, Sergeant J. IV 378, 381
Hog's Back, fighting X 233
Hogsheads, Italian officers' quarters XI 72
Hohenberg, Duchess of, assassination I 3, 10
Hohenzollern, yacht I 100
Hohenzollern Redoubt V 133, 140; VI 432
gas attack V 97
Hoidge, Lieutenant T. C. XI 399
Holbrook, Lieutenant N. D. IV 368, 373
crew of the B11 and III 400
exploit VI 46
on H.M.S. Adamant IV 413
"Iron Cross" incident III 44
how V.C. was won III 389
Holden, Sir E. VI 64
Holder, Sec.-Lieut. F. D. X 145
Holland, Army mobilised IX 166
—waggon II 320
attitude II 315; IX 165
Binnenhof IX 173
exports VII 137
frontier guards II 343; IX 173
Navy, gun practice IX 174
neutrality, breach XIII 63
queen: see Wilhelmina
Socialist scheming XIII 458
Holland, General Sir A. XII 547
Holland, Lieut. J. V. X 609, 622
Hollebeke, capture X 455
fighting X 457; XII 101
sector fighting X 504
Hollis, Lieut. C. F. G. XII 597
Holmes, Lce.-Corpl. F. W. II 45; IV 369, 373, 374
Holmes, Pte. T. W. XII 365, 367
Holmes, Pte. W. E. XIII 561
Holnon, fighting XII 320
Holnon Wood, fighting IX 304; XII 295, 315, 316
Holt, Deckhand A. XI 355
Holt, Captain F. V. III 194
Holy Communion, in chalk cave XI 411
Home Defence XI 493
Homorod Almas, capture VII 525
Homs, occupation XII 360
Honey, Lieut. S. L. XIII 567
Honnelle River, fighting XII 539
Hood, Lt.-Col. E. T. F. XII 595
Hood, Admiral Hon. H. I 385; II 422; VII fac. 421, 431, 432, 436
death VII 437; XIII 8
Jutland battle XIII 7
Hooge, battle IV 68, 336
—British charge IV 328
capture X 452
fighting VI 423
Hoosac tunnel, guarding IX 88
Hoover, Mr. H. C. VIII 202, 217; X 260
food administrator X 273, 306
—distribution XIII 542
Hope, Adml. G. XI 349; XIII 501
Hope, Lieut.-Col. G. E. XI 550
Hopley, Sec.-Lt. G. W. V. VI 396
Hoppner, Gen. von X 127; XI 387, 398
Hopwood, R. A. XII 241
war poems XII 243
Horan, Lieutenant H. E. I 385
Hore, Eng.-Captain F. IX 371
Horn, Major G. M. XIII 138
Horne, General H. S. VI 41; VIII 40, 75; IX 190, 262, 266, 309, 336, 373; X 29, 429, 432; XI 58; XII 74, 113, 253, 420, fac. 440, 499, 515; XIII 325, 326
addressing troops X 469
Lord Allenby at Dover with XIII 569
Canadians march past at Mons XII 527
inspecting Canadians XI 127
—machine-gun battalion XII 9
King and Army leaders with XIII 405
scenes during entry into Mons XII 370, 371
Horne, Rt. Hon. Sir R., Minister of Labour XIII 334
Horse Guards Parade, trophies VI 2, 3
Horses VI 347; IX 453, 454
ambulance IX 461
American depots IX 458, 459
ammunition carriers IX 460
army division, number in IX 454
artillery, destruction II 275
awaiting shipment in pen IX 457
born on battlefield IX 470
bringing up Canadian guns IX 468
capture of German II 148
crossing river IV 154
demobilisation XIII 319
forage distribution VI 343
foreign supply IX 456
graves near Compiègne II 140
hospital treatment IX 467
inoculation IX 457
mare and foal in hospital IX 453
mortality IX 470
in mudbank V 372
operation IX 469
remounts, commissioners IX 456
—under supervision IX 457
round up near Compiègne II 134
sale XIII 319
shell pack XII fac. 201
sheltered near church ruins XI 247
shipment VI 203
sketches II 365; IV 27
supply VI 348
—methods IX 454
teeth extracted IV 315
under shell fire IX 464
veterinary camp II 268
war training IX 462
—use IX 453
watering VI 342; VII 321; IX 455
—in Tigris IX 143
wounded II 275; IX 463
—care on battlefield IX 465
Horse-shoe Hill, capture VII 478
Horse-shoe Marsh V 313
Horse-waggon, wounded in III 286
Horsey, Rear-Adml. S. de XI 47
Horsfall, Sec.-Lt. B. A. XII 380
Horsing, Herr XIII 495
Horsley, Sir V. IX 144
Horton, Commander M. K. I 373, 393; II 286; IV 286; VI 13, 33, 49; VIII 521
Hoskins, Lieut.-Gen. A. R. VII 191; IX 219; X 577
command in East Africa X 584
Hospital Farm VIII 26
Hospital Motor Squadron XIII 138
Hospital-barges VIII 303
scenes XIII 24
Hospitals, Abbaye de Royaumont V 189
base, nurses in XIII 25
Belgian, women workers V 189
boot-making at Southall XIII 216
British, hut in France XIII 211
Cairo, grass-matting ward XIII 211
Canadian, X-ray treatment XIII 221
carpentry at Southall XIII 216
concert X 540
curative workshops XIII 218
destruction by German airmen XIII 127
education of patients XIII 220
field, British, in Italy XII 225
—wounded arriving IV 186
French abbey IV 133
German electric treatment IV 135
—raids on XIII 127
gifts, Queen Mary's IV 140
Japanese in Paris IV 141
kitchen IV 132

U

V

W

Y

Z

ERRATA AND ADDENDA

MANY of the corrections in the following list apply only to portions of the issue of THE GREAT WAR, as the necessary alterations were frequently made while the work was on the press.

Certain instances of the slight misprinting of proper names—such, for example, as " Silistra " for " Silistria "—are correctly rendered in the Index, so do not call for special notice here.

p.	col.	line.	
			VOL. I.
127			Top portrait should be that of Rear-Admiral Sir A. G. W. Moore ; it is given on p. 384.
170			Under top illus. for " Infantry " read " R.A.M.C." ; for " Inspection " read " Kit inspection."
377			Under illus. for " at thirty-three " read " in 1882."
378			Under illus. for " Commander " in each case read " Captain."
429			Under illus. for " Luck " read " Lyck."
			VOL. II.
45			Under fifth portrait, for " Deace " read " Dease."
60	2	24	for " 18th Brigade " read " 10th Brigade."
60	2	32	for " 1st Lancashire Fusiliers " read " 2nd Lancashire Fusiliers."
72	2	61	for " the previous day " read " on August 15th."
228	1	18	for " 1st Worcesters " read " 1st Warwicks."
246	2	26	for " east of Soissons " read " west of Soissons."
322			Under illus. for " Antwerp " read " Ostend."
398			Under bottom illus., 2nd line, for " French " read " Belgian."
399			Under illus. for " the French " read " his Belgian."
450			An obvious error of season is made in describing the Battle off the Falkland Islands, which lie on the 52nd degree of south latitude, as having taken place on a " winter " day. Though all the actual conditions were those of mid-winter, the seasons being reversed south of the Equator, the time was nominally " summer " there.
			VOL. III.
149	1	last	For " both General Botha and Mr. Steyn " read " both General Hertzog and Mr. Steyn."
166			Under first illus. should read, " The Coming of the Australians. Arrival of Australian reservists at Plymouth."
202	1	2, 10	for " Lieut.-Commander Nasmyth " read " Lieut.-Commander M. E. Nasmith."
260	2	10	for " twenty hours " read " thirty hours."
289			Under top illus. for " King " read " Prince."
320	2	43	for " from " read " for."

p.	col.	line.	
			VOL. IV.
1 et seq.			Among the regiments that especially distinguished themselves at the Second Battle of Ypres mention should have been included of the 1st Battalion of the Manchester Regiment, who was singled out by the General Officer Commanding the Second Army for commendation for the great services it performed on those two eventful days, April 26-27th, 1915.
257	2		Side heading, for " Recall of Von Hindenburg " read " Return of Von Hindenburg."
363	1	7	for " Ypres Canal " read " Yser Canal."
409	1	27	for " Mudros " read " Lemnos."
438	1	39	for " April " read " August."
			VOL. V.
9	1	38	for " only sister " read " third sister."
115	1	3	for " unable " read " able."
137	2		In last two lines for " Lieutenant Ayres " and " Lieutenant Ritchie " in each case read " Lieutenant A. T. Ayres Ritchie."
185			Under illus. for " Lady Ralph Paget bidding good-bye," etc., read " Lady Ralph Paget at Uskub after being decorated by King Peter of Serbia."
188			Under illus. This should read " Interior scene in the Streatham Common War Supply Depot," etc.; and at the end, " The smaller portrait is of Lady Parsons, one of the heads of the Pine Dressing Room of the Streatham Common War Supply Depot."
343			Under top illus. for " on the western front " read " at Suvla Bay and Salonika."
363			Under portrait of Flight-Lieut. Viney, read " who was awarded the D.S.O."
394			Sidehead, for " Russian successes in Asia Minor " read " Russian successes in Persia."
			VOL. VI.
18	1	14	for " September 14th " read " August 14th."
32 et seq.			With reference to the current account of the Baralong case given, Mr. C. H. Manning, master of the Nicosian, wrote correcting this, saying : " I was the last person to leave the Nicosian, one of my

p.	col.	line.	
32 et seq.			officers and one engineer remaining with me to the last, and until I ordered them into their respective boats. There was then no one on board but myself ; even the ship's cat had been cared for. It was not possible to do anything for the mules ; they had already begun to suffer from the brutal fire of the submarine. I might add that Americans and British were most obedient to all orders ; in fact, either muleteer or seaman refusing to obey orders at that particular time took a very grave risk of being instantly shot."
74	2	23	for " torpedoed and sunk by a German submarine " read " sunk by the Prinz Eitel Friedrich on January 27th, 1915."
177			Under lower illus. for " Colonel Kisham Singh Sardar Bahardur " read " Colonel Kishan Singh Sardar Bahadur."
389			Under portrait of Lt.-Col. Hitchins should read " Killed at Second Battle of Ypres."
396	1	73	The name of Lt.-Col. H. W. E. Hitchins should be among the colonels killed at the Second Battle of Ypres, not among those killed at Neuve Chapelle.
			VOL. VII.
17	1	25	for " Captain Francis Scrymgeour " read " Captain Francis Scrimger."
103			Lines under middle illus. should read " Lieut.-Colonel W. C. Wright (left)—Chief of Staff to Brigadier-General Cunliffe — with a French officer outside his tent."
135	2	6	for " March 15th " read " March 11th."
176	2	5	for " 1st Loyal North Lancashires " read " 2nd Loyal North Lancashires."
233	2	14	omit the words " attached to the Highland Brigade."
273	1	last	for " Hill 1,859 " read " Height 1,869."
312			First portrait is not that of Capt. Eric S. Ayre.
482	2	56	for " Colonel " read " General."
494	1	19	Delete, " Only once before has the V.C. been won by a midshipman—at Tientsin."
494	1	33	for " there is only one instance," etc., read " there are but few instances of a seaman winning the V.C."

p.	col.	line.	
			VOL. VIII.
225			Under portrait of Flight-Lieut. Cadbury, for " D.S.O." read " D.S.C."
271	2	1	Delete " unattended."
			VOL. X.
43			Under bottom illus. for " He is here seen," etc., read " From a portrait taken before his accession."
380			Under first illus. for " cities " read " centres."
387	1	72	for " About 1909 he opened " read " In 1907 he opened."
518			Under second portrait, for " Marchioness of Londonderry," D.B.E.," read " Marchioness of Lansdowne, C.H."
			VOL. XI.
98	2	43	for " General Pecori " read " General Pecori-Giraldi."
226			Under illus. for " Mr. C. W. R. Nevison " read " Mr. C. R. W. Nevinson."
			VOL. XII.
7 opposite			Coloured map. With regard to the northern part of the 1914 battle-line, it may be pointed out that though Ypres was never in the enemy's hands, it was for a time in October, 1914, enveloped by German cavalry patrols which penetrated considerably to the west of the town.
533	2	65 & 73	for " 62nd Division " read " 63rd Division."
			VOL. XIII.
100 opposite			This map, showing the places in England and Scotland that suffered from hostile air raids, was based on the fullest available official information. After its appearance some correspondents stated that bombs were also dropped on or in the neighbourhood of Walsall, Wednesbury, Tipton, and Sunderland.
94			Under top illus. for " December 18th " read " September 4th."
275			Under upper illus. first sentence should read, " Colours of the 6th Welsh Regiment being taken from Christ Church, Swansea, where they had been deposited in 1914." Under lower illus. for " Christchurch," read " Swansea."
420	2	20	for " Mézières " read " Tournai."
505			Under lower illus. for " November 21st " read " November 16th."

THE GREAT WAR

THE STANDARD HISTORY OF THE WORLD-WIDE CONFLICT

VOLUME 13

THE SECRET OF JUTLAND.
By H. W. Wilson.

British Forces in the Mediterranean under Sir Berkeley Milne in August, 1914—Goeben and Breslau Bombard Bona and are Chased to Messina—Alternative Ways of Escape Open to Admiral Souchon—German Squadron Puts to Sea, August 6th, followed by H.M.S. Gloucester—German Squadron Foils British Battle-Cruisers, Enters the Dardanelles, and Proceeds Towards the Sea of Marmora Unmolested—Admiral Sir Berkeley Milne's Conduct and Dispositions Examined and Approved by the Board of Admiralty—Rear-Admiral Troubridge Exonerated—Comparison of the British and German Naval Forces Engaged at Jutland—Explanation of the Heavy British Losses in Battle-Cruisers—Narrow Escapes of Other British Ships—The Position at 6.14 p.m.—Three Courses Open to Admiral Jellicoe—Chance of Immediate Victory Lost by Decision to Avoid Risk—German Surprise at British Omission to Close—Beatty's Signal to Jellicoe—End of the Daylight Engagement—Jellicoe's Reason for Refusing a Night Action—Gallant Night Work by British Destroyers—Escape of the High Sea Fleet—Tabulated Statements of the British and German Fleets Engaged at Jutland.

ITH the removal of the naval censorship it has become possible to investigate the two greatest mysteries of the naval war. These are the escape of the German cruisers Goeben and Breslau in the Mediterranean, in August, 1914, and the escape of the German Fleet at Jutland. Both these events were fraught with the gravest consequences and had a far-reaching influence on the struggle.

The Goeben and Breslau, as stated in Chapter XLVIII., (Vol. 3, page 29) were in the Mediterranean. The Goeben was a battle-cruiser with a nominal speed of 25½ knots and an actual speed of about 27 knots, carrying a main armament of ten 11 in. guns. The Breslau was a light cruiser of 27 knots with an armament of twelve 4·1 in. guns. The two ships were commanded by Rear - Admiral Souchon. Great Britain at that date had in the Mediterranean a force which should have been amply sufficient to deal with them, under Admiral Sir A. Berkeley Milne. He had, first, the Second Battle - Cruiser Squadron, composed of the Inflexible (his flagship), Indefatigable, and Indomitable. All three had

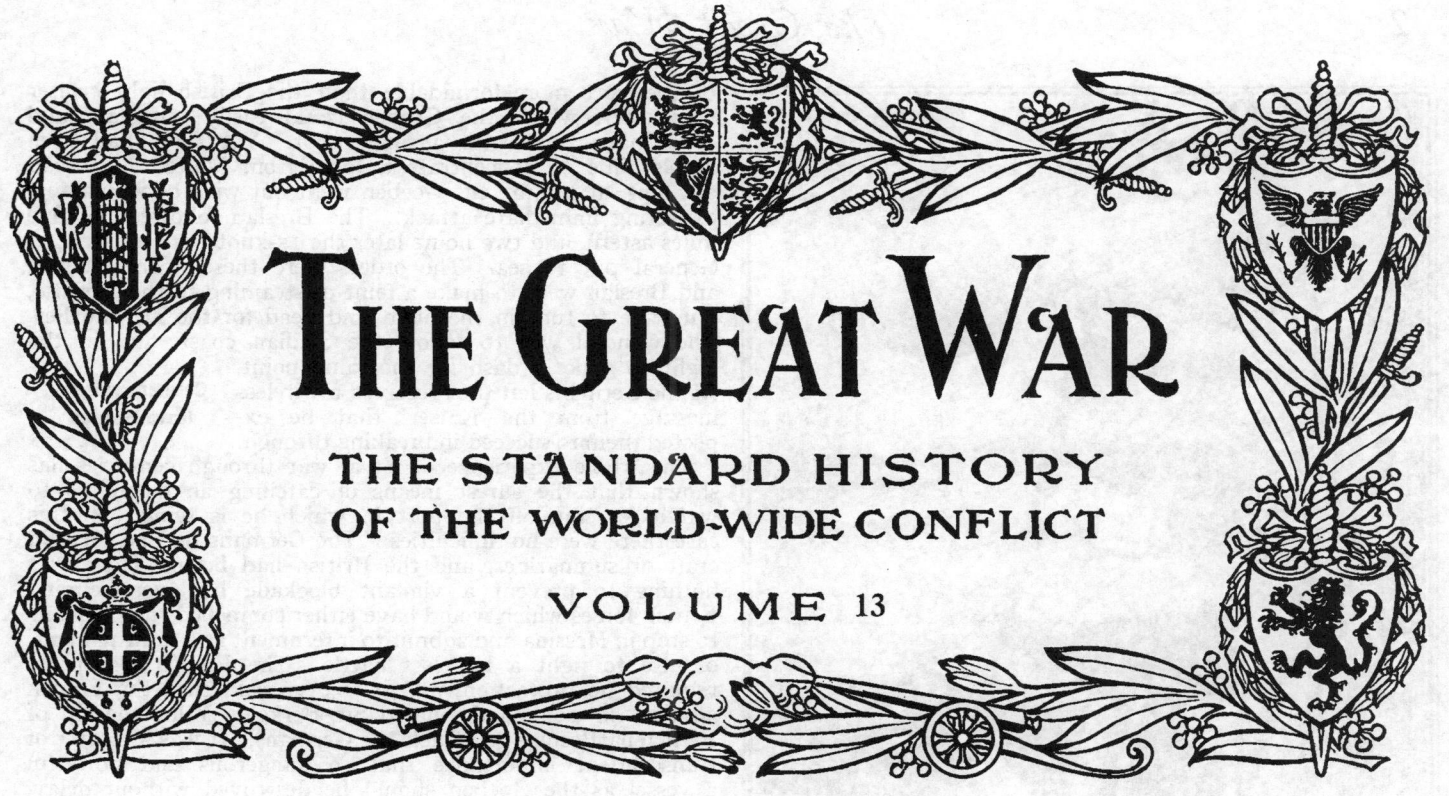

HIGH SPEED AND GREAT GUNS.
H.M.S. battle-cruisers Princess Royal and New Zealand going full speed ahead and cleared for action—as seen from another British warship, a pair of whose 13·5 in. guns are shown strikingly in the immediate foreground.

nominal speeds of 25 knots, but had in actual service attained 27 knots. They were armed with eight 12 in. guns apiece. In speed they were very slightly slower than the Goeben ; in gun-power each of them was about equal to her (broadside 6,800 lb. from big guns against her 6,600) ; but she was slightly more modern and had thicker armour. In addition to these three very powerful vessels there were four armoured cruisers of older type under Rear-Admiral E. C. T. Troubridge, second in command on the station. These were the Defence (flagship), Black Prince, Duke of Edinburgh, and Warrior, with speeds of 22 to 23 knots and batteries of 9·2 in., 7·5 in., and 6 in. guns. A light - cruiser squadron was attached to the fleet, consisting of the Gloucester, Weymouth, Chatham, and Dublin, steaming 25 or 26 knots, with batteries in the last three of eight 6 in. guns, and in the first of two 6 in. and ten 4 in. Finally there were sixteen modern but somewhat slow destroyers, sixteen old torpedo-boats, and six small submarines.

The Goeben and Breslau, on August 4th, 1914, appeared off Bona and Philippeville, on the coast of Algiers, and fired sixty shells into Bona, killing

BRIDGES OF A BATTLESHIP.
End view of the tiered bridges of H.M.S. Marlborough, with part of the signal deck showing below.

of the port more formidable than the British light cruiser Gloucester, which the Goeben could easily outsteam and could have sunk with a single shot. Yet there had been ample time to concentrate a force from Malta. In broad daylight, at 5 p.m., the Goeben went out with band playing, expecting immediate attack. The Breslau followed her five miles astern, and two hours later the 15-knot German steamer General put to sea. The orders were these: The Goeben and Breslau were to make a feint of steaming to the Adriatic, but were to turn in the night and head for the Dardanelles. The General was to follow the Sicilian coast, and in the night to make a dash for the same point.

As the Germans left they received a wireless message from the Kaiser that he expected them to succeed in breaking through.   **German cruisers leave Messina**

The whole experience of naval war through centuries has shown that the surest means of catching an enemy is to watch for him off the port in which he is lying. In this case there were no difficulties. The Germans had no torpedo craft or submarines, and the British had both. There was nothing to prevent a vigilant blockade by overwhelming British forces which would have either compelled the Germans to stop in Messina and submit to internment and disarmament, or else to fight a hopeless battle. The French transports required no protection, and it is even said that the French admiral in command offered Sir Berkeley Milne the aid of French battleships to attack the Germans. It was a matter of transcendent importance that so dangerous and powerful a vessel as the Goeben should be destroyed without delay. What happened is one of the most extraordinary chapters of the war. As the Goeben and Breslau steamed off, the

one person and wounding six. The object of this raid was to interfere with the embarkation of French troops in Algeria for service in France. There never was any serious risk of injury to the French transports, as the French Mediterranean Fleet was mobilised and was available to cover them with eight powerful battleships, any one of which could have engaged the Goeben with every chance of success. All the world expected that the two cruisers would be promptly caught and sunk by the British squadron in the Mediterranean, which, as has been said, was of ample strength and must have received instructions to hold itself in readiness, as on August 3rd the Admiralty announced that "the entire Navy" was then "on a war footing." A few hours later two of the British battle-cruisers were in chase, but late on August 5th the German ships entered the harbour of Messina, on the Sicilian coast, which at that date was neutral. From this port

"COFFEE-BOXES" OF H.M.S. MARLBOROUGH.
Part of the superstructure of H.M.S. Marlborough, showing to the right and left of the tunnel the circular protectors into which the searchlights descended on the ship going into action. These protectors came to be known in the Navy as "coffee-boxes."

they had two different lines of escape. They could go north through the Strait of Messina, or east towards the Adriatic or Levant. If they went north, however, they would sooner or later be rounded up in the Western Mediterranean, and either be sunk or be driven into some neutral port where they would be interned. This was not, therefore, a route that was likely to appeal to Admiral Souchon. If they went east they could steer for the Adriatic, to join the Austrian Fleet—though Austria was not yet nominally at war with France and Britain—or for the neutral Turkish coast

The Germans coaled at Messina, from German steamers. When they put to sea, on August 6th the British dispositions were such that there was nothing in the immediate vicinity

Gloucester most gallantly fell in astern, emitting, as the German accounts state, wireless signals, which were deciphered in the Goeben, and read to mean: "Goeben making for Adriatic." The German wireless operators were ordered not to "jam" the message because the real aim of Admiral Souchon was to reach the Dardanelles, and he hoped to mislead the British. He did not fire at the Gloucester, probably because he was anxious to reserve his ammunition for the action with the British battle-cruisers which he expected. These did not appear. At night the Germans duly altered course, and then the order was given to "jam" the Gloucester's wireless.

Instead of watching for the Germans outside their refuge the British battle-cruisers had taken up "a defensive line from Bizerta to Sardinia," guarding the outlet to the Western Mediterranean, and the British armoured cruisers had proceeded to the Strait of Otranto at the entrance to the Adriatic, and there they waited for the Germans in vain. They had been foiled by Admiral Souchon, who showed them a clean pair of heels. That no close watch was kept over the Germans at Messina was shown by the escape of the slow steamer *General*, which, by a quite different route, succeeded in reaching the Dardanelles. On August 10th all the three German ships entered the Dardanelles and proceeded towards the Sea of Marmora. This was a clear breach of international law, by which the Dardanelles were closed to all but Turkish warships. Yet no steps were taken to follow and destroy the German squadron. A second time it was allowed to escape, though the French admiral is stated to have been eager to pursue and attack. Possibly the British commander was held back by orders from the British Foreign Office, which seems at that date to have been under the delusion that Turkey would remain neutral. The immediate consequences were surpassingly grave. Owing to the pressure

Escape of the German squadron which Admiral Souchon exercised, and owing to the shaken prestige of the Allies, Turkey entered the war. Some 500,000 allied troops were ultimately withdrawn from the western front to meet this new peril.

Universal and not unreasonable surprise was expressed in Great Britain at the escape of the German squadron. The Admiralty, however, gave no sign of dissatisfaction. It announced on August 11th "with the dismantling and internment of these ships the safety of trade will have been almost entirely secured." As a matter of fact, the "dismantling

and internment" of these ships had not been secured, nor was there any prospect of obtaining it. They remained in German hands, powerful for mischief, and the Goeben was still in being when Turkey surrendered.

Of the two British admirals in the Mediterranean, Admiral Sir A. Berkeley Milne shortly afterwards returned home when the Admiralty issued a statement to the effect that his conduct and dispositions "have been subject to careful examination of the Board of Admiralty, with the result that their lordships have approved of the measures taken in all respects." **British Admirals exonerated** That is to say, their lordships approved of dispositions which, with a total British force of seven armoured cruisers (three of power as great as the Goeben's), four light cruisers, and sixteen destroyers, allowed three German vessels to escape. Subsequently Rear-Admiral Troubridge asked for a court-martial on his conduct, and was completely exonerated.

The real test of leadership in war is success. There is no other. On this occasion it was present on the German side and wanting on the British side. If so, the fault must lie either in the Admiralty's instructions, which possibly did not sufficiently emphasise the importance of bringing the Germans to battle, or else in the manner in which the instructions were carried out. In any case there was a departure from the historic strategy and tactics of the British Navy with most unfortunate results. Never had so small a force eluded so easily a large squadron. Here, as afterwards at Jutland, the swift destruction of the German ships would have had important moral effects. It would have freed the Allies from the necessity of constantly watching the Goeben. That

BRITISH BATTLE FLEET COMING INTO ACTION AT THE BATTLE OF JUTLAND.

This striking picture gives the impression of an eye-witness of the Battle Fleet forming into line and firing at the Germans away on the left. The picture—which is fittingly preserved in the Imperial War Museum—was painted by Lieutenant Robert H. Smith, R.N.V.R., of H.M.S. Conqueror. It shows first the Thunderer and then the Iron Duke with, beyond them, the ships of the Fourth Battle Squadron coming into action.

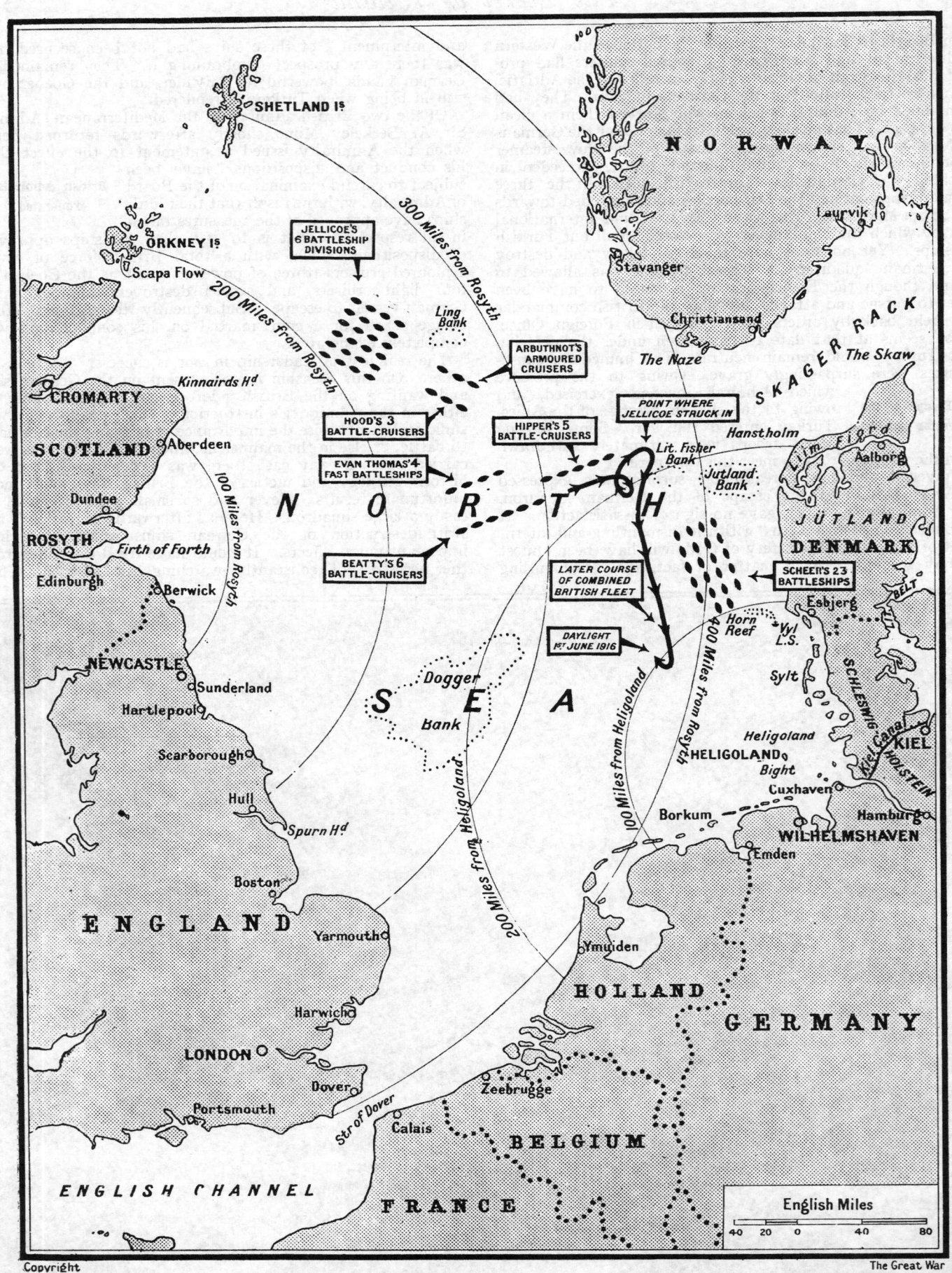

POSITIONS OF BRITISH AND GERMAN NAVAL FORCES AT OPENING OF THE ACTION.

This diagram roughly shows the numbers and positions of the separated British squadrons which were steaming towards the point at which they could combine in overwhelming force against Admiral Hipper's Battle-Cruiser Squadron and Admiral von Scheer's Battle Divisions. Scheer, at Horn Reef, was closer to the scene of action than Sir John Jellicoe was at Ling Bank; so Sir David Beatty had afterwards to make a running fight northward, back to Little Fisher Bank, to enable our Battle Squadrons and our Third Battle-Cruiser Squadron to get within reach of the enemy.

Turkey would have entered the war if the Goeben and Breslau had been sunk is distinctly improbable.

All accounts of the Battle of Jutland (May 31st, 1916) published during the war were naturally subjected to a severe censorship. Though every effort was made to avoid controversial questions, the narrative prepared for this history dealing with the battle suffered important excisions, and the maps and diagrams which were submitted to the censor were suppressed. After the lapse of nearly three years it is now at last possible to publish these diagrams with additions and corrections. For want of such information the battle remained a puzzle to the public, which did not understand how a German force, so greatly inferior in strength and speed to the British Fleet, had been able to return to port with losses less than those which it had inflicted on the British, who had the three battle-cruisers Indefatigable, Queen Mary, and Invincible sunk, in addition to three armoured cruisers and eight destroyers.

The names of the ships present are no longer secret, and they will be found in the appendix to this chapter. The names of the German admirals in command.

SUNSET AT SCAPA FLOW.
H.M.S. Tiger lying in Scapa Flow. This fine battle-cruiser sustained four hits in the Battle of Jutland.

shells struck turrets, pierced the plating, and burst within. The flash of the explosion probably lighted the cordite charges at the breeches of the guns, causing a violent rush of flame. This, again, probably travelled down the ammunition hoists to the open magazines. "It is," said a survivor of the Invincible, which sank at 6.33 p.m., the last of the three to be destroyed, "just as if a great fire burst out at the top of a lift; the flames dash down the lift-shaft, and, if there were explosives at the bottom the building would collapse. Battering at the armour does not produce great effect, but with a hit on the top of a turret the end comes suddenly. There is a terrific explosion, a vast upheaval of water, a tremendous discharge of smoke and steam, and down goes the ship, split in two by the blowing up of the magazine."

In the case of the Queen Mary, which was sunk at 4.26 p.m., the Germans hit her near "Q" turret (the turret between the funnels), causing a great fire. A midshipman in another turret who survived stated that his turret seemed to have been lifted off its rollers by the blow, and immediately afterwards a "terrific explosion occurred in the second magazine." The ship turned over on her side, when he saw that the stern was on fire and red-hot. Two other great explosions followed in quick succession, and she sank in a minute, taking with her one thousand most gallant and devoted officers and men. The same cause may have accounted for the loss of the Indefatigable, which was the first to sink, at 4.6 p.m., after a salvo of German shells struck her close to the after-turret. A great explosion was seen in her and she began to sink, when another German salvo struck her forward and sent her to the bottom.

It is probable that in her case the ammunition in the turret, or below it, was ignited, and that the flash passed down to the magazine, but definite evidence on that point is wanting. **Battle-cruiser loss explained**

GREAT BRITISH BATTLESHIPS CHALLENGING THE ENEMY.
H.M.S. Benbow and Marlborough, cleared for action, steaming out from their base on one of the periodical sweeps through the North Sea which were part of the general policy pursued by the Grand Fleet. Battle-cruisers, cruisers, light cruisers, and destroyers accompanied the Battle Fleet on these occasions.

other than Admiral Scheer, who commanded the High Sea Fleet, Vice-Admiral Hipper, who commanded the battle-cruisers, and Rear-Admiral Behncke, who commanded the Third German Battle Squadron, are not vital to the story. The authoritative figures, which appear in the appendix, show that the Grand Fleet brought into action 37 Dreadnoughts and battle-cruisers, against 21 in the High Sea Fleet, and that, in weight of broadside from battleships of all classes and battle-cruisers, the British had a superiority of 386,000 lb. to 165,520 lb., or more than one hundred per cent. As against this, however, the German ships were better protected by armour. The truest basis of comparison is that of displacement. Here the British had in these classes of ships a tonnage of 840,450 to a German tonnage of 561,270.

The heavy British losses in battle-cruisers were explained by two defects which could not be disclosed earlier in the war. These ships were imperfectly armoured, and insufficient provision was made in them against the ignition of their magazines by the flash from exploding shells which entered their turrets, and in particular against the risk of shells falling almost vertically, at extreme range, and piercing the turret roofs. In the Queen Mary and Invincible, German

One reason why the Germans inflicted these losses was that their armour-piercing shell was then better than the British, and was supplied with a better fuse; so that while the British heavy shells for the most part burst outside the German armour, the German shells came through the British armour and burst inside, with deplorable results. After the battle this grave defect in the British ammunition was remedied. With a proper War Staff before the war it ought never to have existed. But, as has been explained in an earlier chapter, a real War Staff was not created until 1918. Nevertheless, the large amount of ammunition required to put the Scharnhorst and Gneisenau out of action in the Battle of the Falkland Islands (December 8th, 1914) and to sink the Blücher in the Battle of the Dogger Bank (January 24th, 1915) indicated that something was wrong, though for obvious reasons nothing was said in public about this at the time. All those three German ships were armoured vessels of the pre-Dreadnought cruiser type, and were attacked by battle-cruisers. Had the British ammunition been as good as the German ammunition proved to be in the Battle of Jutland, it is certain that they must have succumbed much earlier. As it was, the Blücher seems in the end to have been sent to the bottom by the Aurora's torpedoes.

The Germans may have profited by the experience they gained at the Dogger Bank, and may have taken precautions against the danger of fire in the magazines and turrets, as the British did after Jutland. It is known that at the Dogger Bank the German battle-cruisers had many bad fires. In the British ships ammunition was contained in silk cases, which were easily set on fire. In the German ships the charge was in a brass case, which would offer better resistance to the flash of an explosion. Immediately after Jutland, measures were carried out in the British Fleet which gave comparative security against this risk, and had the High Sea Fleet been encountered again there would in all probability have been no repetition of these terrible explosions. Steps were also taken to protect the gun-crews against the flash of shells and flame of cordite by covering the face and hands. With a good War Staff, all these measures might have been adopted before the war.

Other warships' narrow escape

One or two of the other British ships had narrow escapes. Admiral Beatty's flagship, the Lion, was struck in a turret by a heavy German shell, which tore off the roof and caused a bad fire. The ship herself was probably only saved from disaster by the heroic conduct of Major Harvey, of the Marines, who, mortally wounded himself, and with all the crew of the turret but one killed or mortally wounded, had the presence of mind to order the magazine doors to be closed. For this act of sublime devotion, so glorious to the great Service of which he was an ornament, the Victoria Cross was posthumously awarded, and never was it more splendidly earned. The Lion had eleven other hits from heavy guns, two of which caused serious loss of life ; but the injuries to the ship, except in the case of her turret, were trifling. The Princess Royal had been hit on three different turrets ; one turret was jammed and all the crew of its left gun killed ; one other gun was damaged on the muzzle. There were nine hits in all. The Tiger had been struck on two of her turrets, and had one gun put out of action in each, and she was also damaged forward. The New Zealand was hit on one of her turrets, but no damage was done.

The real mystery of Jutland was as to what happened after the British Battle Fleet appeared about 6.14 p.m. At this moment Admiral Beatty, after leading the German Fleet northwards towards the British Battle Fleet, had gradually worked round until he was steering eastward and south-eastward, to cross the head of the German line. He had with him his four battle-cruisers. A little over two miles astern of him was Rear-Admiral Evan-Thomas with four magnificent battleships of the Queen Elizabeth class (though the Queen Elizabeth was absent), mounting eight 15 in. guns apiece. The leading German cruisers were about 8,000 yards distant from Admiral Beatty, and after steering north they were beginning to edge away north-eastward to avoid his attack on the head of their line. Two of the German battle-cruisers had been driven out of the line by the British fire, leaving only three in it, and it is known from the statements of their crews that the others had been much battered. The German battleships near the head of the line had been severely pounded, and either the Markgraf or the Grosser Kurfürst had been hit by a torpedo and was seen emitting clouds of steam. The extreme speed of the German Fleet, unless it abandoned its six old and comparatively slow ships and its damaged vessel to destruction,

IN THE FINAL STAGES : SINKING OF A GERMAN BATTLESHIP.
At about midnight, in the Battle of Jutland, the German battleship Pommern was torpedoed and sunk, while as dawn approached the battle-cruiser Lützow was abandoned by her crew near Horn Reef ; she was sinking fast, having been hit by two torpedoes as well as many British shells.

A Suspect: British Patrols Examining a Merchantman

Specially Painted for "The Great War" by C. M. Padday

was something under 18 knots. Admiral Beatty's ships were actually steaming at 25. Admiral Evan-Thomas's ships were steaming in excess of 23 knots. and engaging the Germans at about 10,000 yards with their huge guns. The British Battle Fleet was good for 20 knots. The British losses up to this moment had been severe. Two battle-cruisers and three destroyers had gone. But the Germans in greatly inferior force had been held, pounded, and led to the much superior British Battle Fleet, and the German fire was beginning to lose its sting.

Such was the situation at the crisis of the battle, shortly after the point shown in Diagram V. (p. 15), giving the position from 5.56 to 6.10. The British Battle Fleet, twenty-four ships strong, intact and mounting powerful batteries behind better armour than the battle-cruisers possessed, was fast coming up from the north-west at a speed of 20 knots. From the east a squadron of battle-cruisers, under Admiral Hood (Invincible, Inflexible, Indomitable), was moving swiftly to take station at the head of Admiral Beatty's line and prolong it as it steamed across the head of the Germans. Admiral Hood had previously proceeded some distance to the south to get touch of the Germans. The exact positions of the German Battle Fleet and the British battle-cruisers had not been given quite correctly to the British Battle Fleet by the signals from the battle-cruisers which were in action. This was natural, and indeed inevitable under the conditions. The error was about twelve miles, according to Lord Jellicoe, and it led him to think that he would sight the Germans later than he did, and at a point directly ahead of his Battle Fleet, which was approaching, formed in six divisions, each of four battleships in line. The divisions were abreast of one another, a little over a mile apart, and a line drawn through the leading ships of the six divisions would have been about five and a half miles long and would have run north-eastward, roughly parallel to the direction of the German advance. A quarter turn either to left (port) or right (starboard) by the leader of each division, followed by the ships astern in succession, would bring the whole twenty-four battleships into line. The Germans, however, proved to be not directly in front of this mass of ships but to its right (or starboard).

There were three possible courses. The first was to disregard the accepted plan of forming a long single line, a process which occupied over twenty minutes. In the **Three courses** old wars, before the introduction of long-**open to Jellicoe** range artillery and torpedoes, Nelson had deliberately rejected the formation of a line of battle because it took too much time, and in thick weather, such as prevailed in the Battle of Jutland, usually, ended in the enemy's escape without decisive action. Nelson brought his fleet close to the enemy and then hurled it on the hostile forces with such violence and determination that either his ships must be overwhelmed or the enemy's. He sought the closest possible quarters, because his gunners could fire three times as fast as his enemy's, a condition which did not exist at Jutland, though against that the British there had twice the weight of metal in the German Fleet, and because

AN ENEMY BATTLESHIP BEING ATTACKED BY H.M.S. WARSPITE.
German battleship, in the foreground, which was directly attacked by H.M.S. Warspite in the Battle of Jutland. The Warspite, which had gone to the rescue of the sinking Warrior, smashed up one of the leading German battleships, knocking over two of her gun-turrets, and setting her on fire fore and aft.

a close and determined attack cowed the enemy and had an important moral effect. Such a method of attack at Jutland does not seem to have been contemplated at any time. It would have been rendered more dangerous by the great range of modern guns, which enables an enemy to concentrate a violent fire on a force closing in this fashion, and by the existence of torpedoes—but these were peculiarly deadly to a fleet formed in a long single line. The second course was to turn to the right (starboard), and then afterwards make a further turn and form in line astern of the British battle-cruisers, or else to steam past the German Fleet in the opposite direction, when the Germans might have been taken between the battle-cruisers and the Battle Fleet. A turn in this direction would have brought the Fleet quickly into action, but Admiral Jellicoe argued that the weaker British ships were on the right, and they might have been exposed, in turning, to the fire of the German battleships, whose van was 13,000 yards from the nearest British battle-ship. The risk of a torpedo attack had also to be faced if the turn was made in this direction. The third course was to turn to the left (port), but this, though it gave safety from torpedo attack, would take the battleships right away from the German Fleet and leave the British battle-cruisers between them and it.

It was this third course that Admiral Jellicoe decided to adopt. He had two minutes in which to make his choice. Stendhal, one of Napoleon's best critics, has noted that the real difficulty of war lies in this: that the vital decisions must usually be made in two minutes. At 6.16 he issued the signal to the Battle Fleet to turn to port, away from the enemy, and form line of battle, and he reduced speed from 20 knots to 14. The signal did not get through quickly, and the great reduction in speed caused some con-

Jellicoe decides to avoid risk

fusion in the Fleet, the ships which first received the signal dropping back on those which had not received it. The result of this signal and of this turn was to place the Battle Fleet, containing the ships with the heaviest armour and most powerful batteries, from 3,000 to 5,000 yards farther from the Germans than were the British battle-cruisers, and most serious of all, to postpone all possibility of closing with the Germans for half an hour, at a time when the weather was thickening and the day was drawing to evening even in the high latitude where the battle was fought. It avoided risk, but it also lost any chance of immediate victory. As the Battle Fleet was forming in this direction the Fifth Battle

BEATTY FORMS LINE OF BATTLE.

3.30-3.48 p.m.—Beatty forms line of battle at 3.30 p.m., and turns E.S.E. At 3.48 p.m. the battle begins, when he turns S.S.E. and closes a little. Jellicoe is far to the north. Scheer is out of sight in the direction in which Hipper is moving. Hipper has turned on seeing Beatty, and is retiring. Evan-Thomas, with the Fifth Battle Squadron, is 10,000 yards from Beatty when the battle opens. Many of the light craft are omitted for clearness.

Squadron, which was awkwardly placed, had to execute a turn under the German fire in order not to get in the way of the other British battleships. In that turn the Warspite's helm jammed and she circled alone near the Germans, passing apparently not much more than 6,000 yards from them. She was damaged and forced to leave the line, but none of the other three ships of the Fifth Battle Squadron suffered any disabling injury, which suggests again that the German fire had lost much of its vehemence. At 6.17 the first shots were fired by the British Battle Fleet. The Marlborough, leading the extreme starboard (or right) column, opened at 13,000 yards on a German battleship.

At St. Vincent Nelson disobeyed orders when his commander-in-chief was forming a line of battle, and closed with the enemy. At Jutland no officer acted on such an initiative, as a turn-away from the enemy had been prescribed by standing orders and formed part of the Grand Fleet battle instruction for meeting torpedo attack. This manœuvre had apparently received the sanction of the Admiralty, which had been consulted as to the best method of combating torpedo attack, so that the Admiralty shares the responsibility for it.

As the British battleships turned away so did the battle-cruisers, under Admiral Beatty, though not to such an extent, for it now became necessary for them, failing immediate support, to increase their distance from the Germans and avoid the risk of being crushed by the German battleship fire.

They were in an admirable position to cover the British Battleship Fleet had it closed, and to crush any attempt by the German battle-cruisers to interfere with it.

At 6.38 the British battleships were at last in line; eight minutes earlier Admiral Jellicoe's flagship the Iron Duke had opened fire on a German ship 12,000 yards distant, and almost immediately a German battleship was seen badly hit, on fire, and down by the stern. At 6.33 the last great British catastrophe of the day had occurred while the Battle Fleet was turning, and virtually out of action. The Invincible, leading her division of battle-cruisers, had steamed in magnificently to take station at the head of Admiral Beatty's line. Rear-Admiral Hood in these last moments of his life set a most gallant example. His ship, according to some accounts, closed the enemy to within 7,000 yards; according to other accounts she was just inside 8,000 yards and was hitting with every shot, when a German salvo caught one of her turrets and she blew up. She was one of the weakest vessels in the British line.

The German Fleet was now turning slowly inside the British Fleet, which had essayed no decisive manœuvre, but had formed in an enormous line and was turning outside the Germans on a longer radius. By keeping inside on the turn the Germans neutralised the British advantage in speed. They did this, however, with the disadvantage that the British battle-cruisers, if well supported and if mist and darkness had not intervened, could have kept them revolving in a circle and have prevented them from regaining port, thus ensuring their destruction. The British battle-cruisers had worked to the east of the Germans and cut them off from any direct retreat to their bases. The Germans were surprised that the British did not close, and after the battle they frequently asked British naval prisoners for an explanation of this decision to fight at long range, saying that if the British Fleet had closed the fate of the German ships was sealed. The Germans were certainly in a most dangerous position. Their battle-cruisers were severely hit, and one of them was giving great trouble. Their shooting had gone to pieces after the last effort, which issued in the destruction of the Invincible. "From steady and accurate fire," says a British officer present, "the German changed to wild and irregular shooting within a few minutes; we watched with interest the splashes of shells falling a mile or more from their intended target." The Germans were hampered by a number of slow old battleships which could not have withstood a close attack, and, by several damaged vessels, some of which were well on fire. Their tactics of turning in a circle were not novel, but had been carried by the Russians at Tsushima in 1905. But at Tsushima, as the Russian Fleet began to show signs of distress, Admiral Togo closed on it until his fire became anni-

German Fleet's perilous position

hilating. In war, to achieve decisive results, risks must always be taken. They were taken unhesitatingly by Nelson at the Nile and at Trafalgar, by Togo at Tsushima. As M. Clemenceau told France in 1918, when a purely defensive policy was proposed, " to conquer you must fight."

The British Battle Fleet only continued a few minutes in line. About 6.50 it altered course to get nearer the Germans, and re-formed into divisions steering south-east, but at only 17 knots. At 6.54 the Marlborough was struck by a German torpedo; she was skilfully handled and she remained in station. Torpedoes crossing the course of the British Fleet were seen from other ships, but were dexterously avoided. At 7.12, for the second time, Admiral Jellicoe began to form his battleships into line of battle. The British battle-cruisers were now moving in on the German Fleet (which had worked

H.M.S. Iron Duke, flagship of Admiral Jellicoe, Commander-in-Chief of the Grand Fleet, Jutland.

H.M.S. Lion, flagship of Vice-Admiral Beatty, Commander of the Battle-Cruiser Force, Jutland.

H.M.S. Indomitable under full steam. This 41,000=h.p. battle=cruiser's speed was 25 knots.

H.M.S. Monarch, battleship of 22,500 tons, firing her 13·5 in. guns, of which she carried ten.

H.M.S. Emperor of India, Benbow, and Agincourt steaming full speed, cleared for action.

H.M.S. Colossus firing a salvo. Her principal armament consisted of ten 12 in. guns.

H.M.S. Orion, flagship of Rear-Admiral A. C. Leveson, Second-in-Command of the Second Battle Squadron.

H.M.S. King George V., flagship of Vice-Admiral Sir Thomas Jerram, Commander of the Second Battle Squadron.

H.M.S. Princess Royal, flagship of Rear-Admiral Brock, Second-in-Command of the First Battle-Cruiser Squadron.

H.M.S. New Zealand, flagship of Rear-Admiral Pakenham, Commander of the Second Battle-Cruiser Squadron.

H.M.S. Invincible, flagship of Rear-Admiral the Hon. Horace Hood, Commander of the Third Battle-Cruiser Squadron (sunk).

H.M.S. Superb, flagship of Rear-Admiral Duff, Second-in-Command of the Fourth Battle Squadron.

H.M.S. Defence, flagship of Rear-Admiral Sir Robert Arbuthnot, Commander of the First Cruiser Squadron (sunk).

H.M.S. Southampton, flagship of Commodore Goodenough, Commander of the Second Light Cruiser Squadron.

Ships that flew the flags of Great Britain's great admirals at the Battle of Jutland.

to the west), in order to close, when at 7.15 the British battle-ships made a second turn away from the enemy, to avoid a torpedo attack from a number of destroyers, and steamed about 1,750 yards farther from the Germans and about 3,000 yards away from the Lion and the British battle-cruisers.

It was at this juncture that the famous signal was made by Sir David Beatty to Admiral Jerram, commanding the leading battle-ship division, and was taken in by the whole Battle Fleet. Its exact wording is uncertain, as it has never been officially published. There are three unofficial versions, which differ as to words but not as to meaning :

" If you will follow me, we can annihilate the enemy."

" Follow me, and we can cut off the enemy."

" If you will follow me, we can defeat them."

The British Battle Fleet did not follow Admiral Beatty after this appeal. In justification it is stated that twenty torpedoes passed without effect through the British line. But the result was that, while the British battle-ships turned south-eastwards, the German turned westwards, and contact was never again recovered by the battleships. After this outward turn the Lion and the British battle-cruisers were fully 6,000 yards nearer to the Germans than was the British Battle Fleet, if the Lion's track chart is correct, and about 4,000 yards if the track chart of an independent observer is accepted.

Critics of this turn have pointed out that there was another way of meeting torpedo attack, by turning toward the enemy and placing the ship bow-on to the attack. The bow is the least vulnerable part of a modern ship, and by turning four points (or a right angle) the breadth of ship and not its whole length is exposed. Such a turn, they contend, would not have so greatly increased the distance from the German battleships as to lose them in the smoke and mist. " We were utterly crushed from the moment your Battle Fleet came into action," said a German officer afterwards. But the strange fact of the battle is that the main British Battle Fleet, as distinguished from the Fifth Battle Squadron, never really came into action at all. Only one of its ships, the Colossus, was hit, and that very slightly, by three big shells, and it seems to be the case that only eleven ships out of a total of twenty-four claimed to have hit the Germans.

It is now known that Admiral Jellicoe had determined not to fight a night action, so that this was the last moment of the day when it was possible to have attacked effectively. The superiority of the British Fleet was overwhelming. It had more ships, more guns, and much heavier guns. It may have had fewer torpedo-tubes, and inferior armour and worse ammunition, but at close quarters these defects would have been less felt and the British

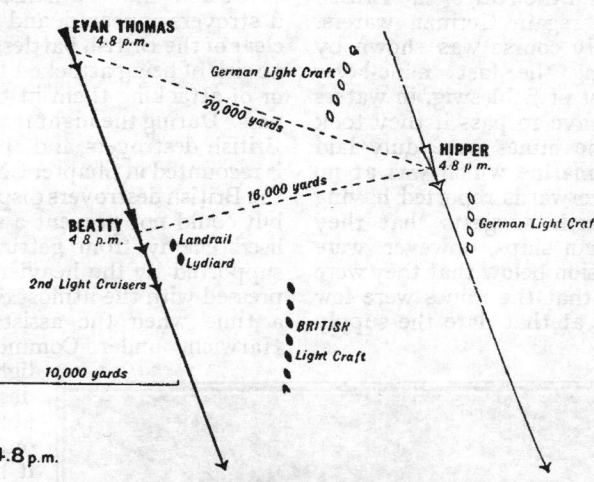

BATTLE SQUADRON OPENS FIRE.

4.8 p.m.—Evan-Thomas, with the Fifth Battle Squadron, has just opened fire at 20,000 yards. Beatty is firing at 16,000 yards, and slowly closing the Germans, who are still steaming south to join their Battle Fleet. The British light craft are preparing for a destroyer attack on Hipper, and the Germans are preparing for a similar attack on the British. About this time the Indefatigable and Queen Mary were sunk, and a German ship was seen on fire.

BEATTY SIGHTS SCHEER.

4.42-4.57 p.m.—Beatty sights Scheer with the German Battle Fleet to the south-east, and swiftly turns and retraces his course. Evan-Thomas, with the Fifth Battle Squadron, does not turn at once, but keeps on upon the opposite course and falls in astern of Beatty when he turns. The Second Light Cruisers close the German Battle Fleet to reconnoitre before turning. Hipper, when he sees the German Battle Fleet, turns and forms its van. The battle now moves northwards towards the British Grand Fleet, which is far away to the north.

numerical superiority would have been irresistible. But the Germans very severely criticised the construction of their own vessels, and Captain Persius, after the armistice, indulged in some very plain speaking as to the German inferiority in calibre. One of the tragedies of the battle was that the weaker British ships so often tried to close, and suffered heavily in doing so, while the more powerful British ships were kept away by the danger from torpedoes. The secret of Jutland was that the British Battle Fleet never entered battle.

In this narrative no allusion has been made to the end of the Defence, which, with the Warrior, passed between the British and German Battle Fleets under a violent fire about 6.16 p.m. It was an episode which had no connection with the main story, and was due to Rear-Admiral Sir Robert Arbuthnot's determination to destroy a German cruiser squadron he had encountered. The Defence was caught by the heavy German ships at a range of about 6,000 yards and was repeatedly hit, when she blew up. The Warrior was badly damaged but was extricated, though she sank after the battle.

A third ship of this squadron, the Black Prince, was badly damaged and blew up about 8.40.

The turn of the British Battle Fleet away from the Germans and of the Germans away from the British Battle Fleet thus virtually ended the daylight engagement, though the battle-cruisers gallantly kept touch and fought a sharp action with the Germans at 10,000 yards soon after 8.20, inflicting serious damage on them. A little later the High Sea Fleet vanished in the mist and darkness. Sir David Beatty did not consider it wise to close upon the German Battle Fleet with his battle-cruisers (most of which had been for several hours in almost continuous action, and some of which had suffered heavy casualties). To fight battleships at close quarters is the work of battleships and not of such fast and delicate vessels as battle-cruisers. He also thought that the British position was such as to render it certain that the Germans would be located at daylight in favourable conditions for attack.

Admiral Jellicoe has told the world that for various reasons he considered a night action inexpedient. The German searchlights, he states, were better than the British. The German ships were supplied with star-shells, which enabled them to light up the water without disclosing their own position, as a searchlight does, and the British ships were without these projectiles, though star-shells had been used on land since the outbreak of the war. The control and director gear for the lighter guns of the British Battle Fleet was inferior. The Germans were fitted with more torpedo-tubes per ship than the British carried, and in the mist it would be difficult to see the German destroyers. Very similar risks, allowing for the different era, were faced by Nelson when he deliberately determined to attack the French Fleet at the Nile in 1798 and destroyed it.

When the decision not to attack at night had been taken, touch with the Germans was not maintained. The real danger always was that they would pass round the rear of the British Fleet, as they actually did, and so regain German waters. That this was regarded as their likely course was shown by Admiral Jellicoe's action in sending the fast mine-layer Abdiel to lay mines off the west coast of Schleswig, in waters through which the Germans would have to pass if they took that route back to their ports. The mines were duly laid during the night, and a British submarine which was at no great distance from the mine-field afterwards reported having heard several heavy explosions, which suggests that they were not without effect. The German ships, however, were so constructed with complete subdivision below that they were not easy to sink, and it is probable that the mines were few or of a comparatively weak type, as at that date the supply was limited.

There was no pursuit. The British Battle Fleet formed for the night in columns one mile apart, with the destroyers astern of it, and it steamed south at a speed of 17 knots. The object in stationing the destroyers astern was, according to Admiral Jellicoe, that they might be in a favourable position to attack the Germans, whether their main Fleet or their destroyers appeared, and that they might be clear of the British battleships and might run no risk of being attacked by these in mistake or of attacking them in the mist and dark- **British destroyers' gallant night work** ness. During the night many encounters took place between the British destroyers and the German Fleet or light cruisers, as is recounted in Chapter CXLII. (Vol. 7, p. 441). In these actions the British destroyers displayed magnificent dash and gallantry, but could not prevent a shaken, badly damaged, and demoralised enemy from getting away. Nor were the destroyers supported by the heavier ships, whence their attacks, though pressed with the utmost determination, were costly. This was a time when the assistance of the powerful squadron at Harwich, under Commodore Tyrwhitt, containing several light cruisers and a number of destroyers, would have been of inestimable value, but owing to an unfortunate omission on the part of the Admiralty it had not been ordered to take part in the operations. It was, however, able to assist in escorting the Marlborough, which battleship was detached late in the night of the battle to a British port for repair, as she could no longer steam at 17 knots.

During the night many of the German battleships and battle-cruisers were seen crossing the British rear and were attacked by British destroyers. They first went north and then turned south-east, when they got behind the British heavy ships. About midnight the Second German Battle Squadron was discovered, and the battleship Pommern was torpedoed and sunk. In the confusion the battleship Schlesien collided with another vessel and was much damaged. At 1.45 a.m. of June 1st six German Dreadnoughts of the Kaiser class were seen steaming south-east, and one at least of them was torpedoed, suffering serious damage. The position of the Germans was reported to Admiral Jellicoe by wireless, but the message was not received by the British Battle Fleet, then about ten miles distant, "owing," Admiral Jellicoe states, "presumably to the strong interference caused by German wireless signalling at the time." At 2.35 four old German battleships of the pre-Dreadnought type were sighted. Thus everything during the night indicated that the German Fleet, while the British Fleet steamed south, had moved behind it to the nearest German ports.

As dawn approached the condition of the German ships was something as follows : About daylight the battle-cruiser Lützow was abandoned by her crew near Horn Reef. She was sinking fast, and had been hit by two torpedoes as well as by many British shells. When the men had been removed from her she was finished off by firing two German torpedoes at her, and these sent her to the bottom. The battle-cruiser Seydlitz was hardly capable of steaming, and in the morning was taken in tow by a light cruiser. She was slowly sinking, and the whole forward part of

H.M.S AGINCOURT FIRING A BROADSIDE FROM HER HEAVY GUNS.
An awe-inspiring spectacle was furnished by H.M.S. Agincourt during the Battle of Jutland. Coming into action in the later stages of the battle, she was observed to be firing all her fourteen 12 in. guns at once. The weight of the projectiles thus discharged in a single broadside was 11,900 lb.

the ship was flooded. Her fore superimposed turret had been hit by a heavy British shell, which put it out of action, and set the magazine on fire. A great disaster was only averted by the instant flooding of the magazine, but between 100 and 120 men are believed to have perished

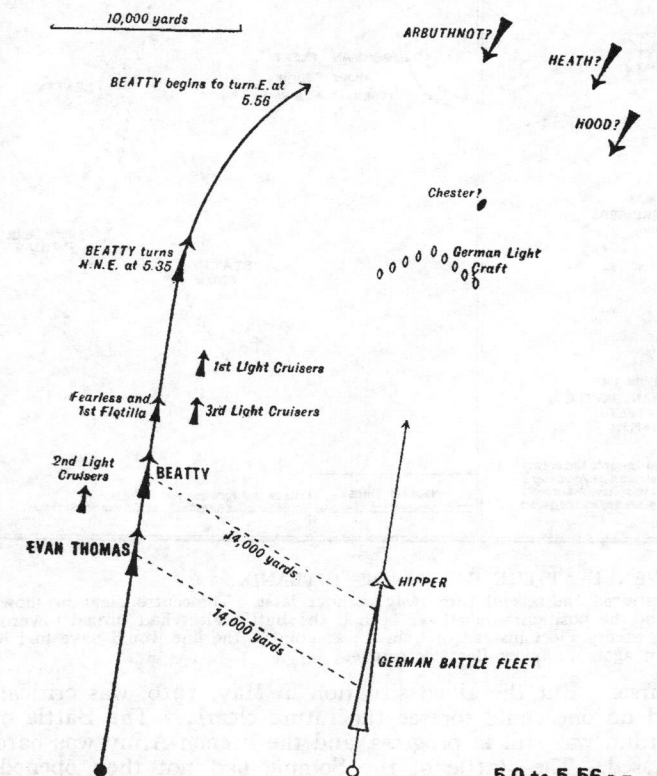

5.0 to 5.56 p.m.

BEATTY MOVES TO HEAD THE GERMANS OFF.

5.0–5.56 p.m.—Just before the junction with Jellicoe. Beatty is steaming northward and begins to work east, to join Jellicoe and head the Germans off. He has gained on the head of the German line. The positions of the Chester, Arbuthnot (with the First Cruiser Squadron), Heath (Second Cruiser Squadron), and Hood (Third Battle-Cruiser Squadron) are inserted from conjecture. The enemy at this stage is being severely punished and slowly forced east away from his bases. According to German accounts, only eight German battleships were able to fire, the others being too far astern.

from this single hit. Three of her five turrets were either partially or completely out of action. She was ultimately beached near Wilhelmshaven, but was afterwards floated off. The Derfflinger had been very severely damaged and had been knocked about in every part of her structure, so that she, too, was in difficulties. The battleship König had had her bows torn open as the result of two hits by heavy British shells, and she gradually sank by the head until her forecastle was only six and a half feet above water. The injury to her could not be repaired nor the water be pumped out, and the crew of her forward torpedo-tube was imprisoned below and so remained for five days, till the ship was docked; they were fed in the meantime through a voice-pipe. The foremost turret had been hit and put out of action. The foremost superimposed turret had been damaged. She had in all 14 hits on her port (left) side, and the consequent damage gave her such a list to port that water had to be admitted to some of her starboard (right) compartments to trim the ship. She had lost 65 killed and from 30 to 35 wounded, and Rear-Admiral Behncke, who commanded the Third Battle Squadron, had been wounded on the back of the head by a shell splinter as he stood on her fore-bridge. She was thus in no posture for action. The Grosser Kurfürst had been hit by four heavy shells and by a torpedo, and had sustained serious damage to one of her engines. She was probably the battleship from which clouds of steam were seen rising after a British torpedo attack, comparatively early in the battle. The Markgraf had also been badly damaged and had been hit by a torpedo. The other German Dreadnought battleships had suffered little or no serious injury, with the exception of the Ostfriesland,

Damage to German ships

which struck a mine, apparently one of those laid by the Abdiel, and had a large hole in her starboard side. Of the five surviving pre-Dreadnoughts only one had suffered any serious hits. Apart from the Lützow there were thus six badly-damaged vessels among the twenty surviving German Dreadnoughts.

The British force available to attack the 14 intact German Dreadnoughts consisted of 26 battleships, all of Dreadnought class, and 6 battle-cruisers, with about 20 intact British light cruisers and probably 60 intact destroyers. The damaged German Fleet could scarcely have steamed 15 knots; the undamaged or slighty damaged part of the British Fleet should have been good for at least 19 or 20 knots. The weather was misty and much difficulty was experienced in collecting the British ships; indeed, the destroyers did not join the flag until 9 a.m. So much time was occupied in effecting this concentration that the Germans were able to move with their disabled ships past Horn Reef and to reach the shelter of their mine-fields before any British force sighted them. Information from the British directional wireless stations (which took in the German wireless signals and were able to calculate from them the positions of the ships signalling) showed that the bulk of the German Fleet must have passed Horn Reef soon after daylight, which in that latitude and at that time of year came a little before 3 a.m. A Zeppelin was sighted and fired at about 3.30 a.m., but other indication of the High Sea Fleet's presence there was none, apart from wreckage of sunken ships. No disabled vessels were discovered. Admiral Scheer had escaped from a situation of desperate danger. The British Battle Fleet had not been able to make its strength felt, and as the morning advanced it returned to port.

Escape of the High Sea Fleet

The tactics pursued in the battle met with the commendation of the British Admiralty. The dominating feature of the

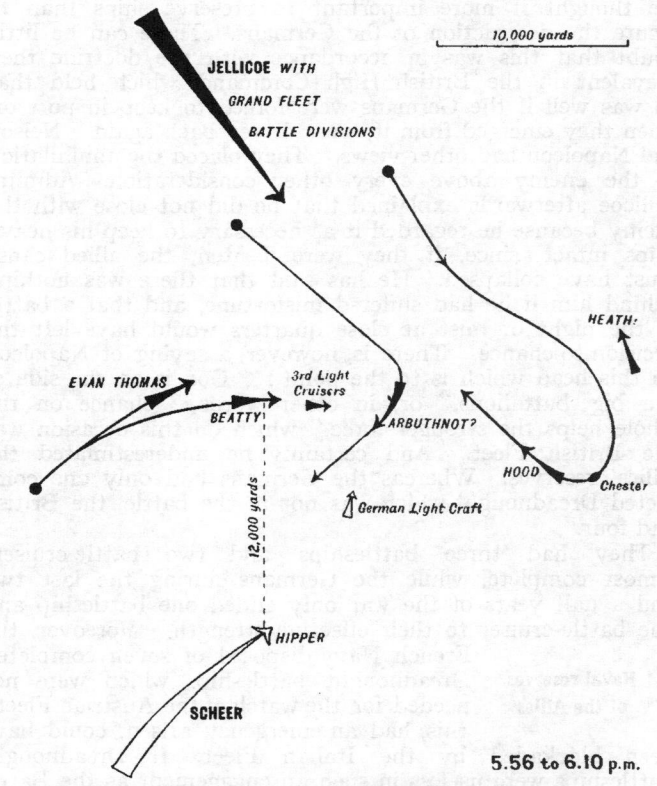

5.56 to 6.10 p.m.

BEATTY FORCES THE GERMANS TO TURN.

5.56–6.10 p.m.—The junction of Beatty and Jellicoe, illustrating the extraordinarily complicated situation (though most of the light-cruiser squadrons and all the flotillas are omitted for clearness). Beatty sees Jellicoe and turns east to clear him and get across the head of the German line, increasing to his highest speed. Hood sees Beatty, and turns north-west to join him and take station at the head of his line. Evan-Thomas, with the Fifth Battle Squadron, is endeavouring to form up with the Grand Fleet as its van. Beatty's turn forces the Germans to turn or have their head crossed. At 6.16 Admiral Jellicoe turned to the left to form his Fleet in line, instead of prolonging the line in which Admiral Beatty's ships were formed, draws up farther away from the Germans. The Invincible was sunk at 6.33 p.m.

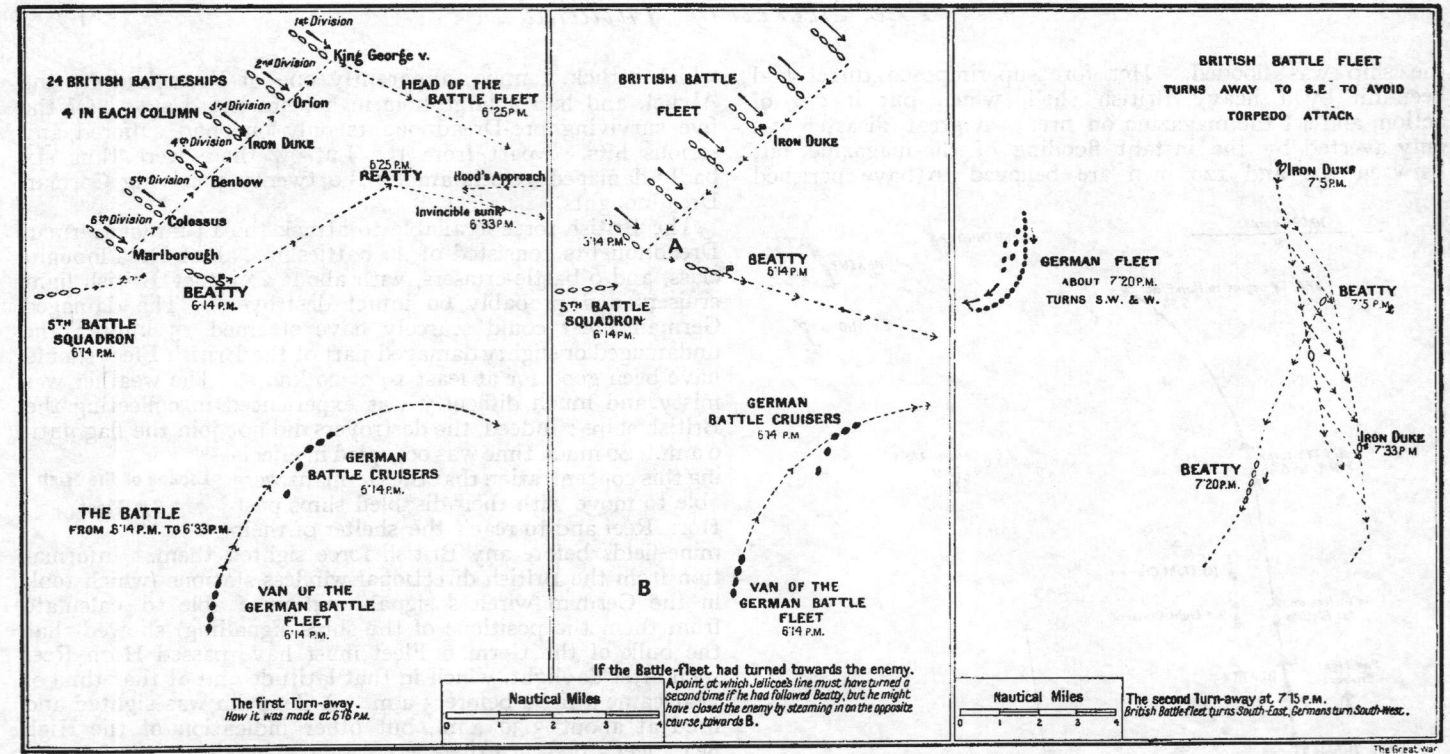

WHAT HAPPENED AND WHAT MIGHT HAVE HAPPENED AT THE BATTLE OF JUTLAND.

In the first of these diagrams is indicated the way in which, when the enemy Fleet was curving round to the east and south-east, and Admiral Beatty's force was steering a more or less-parallel course, the British Battle Fleet turned, at 6.16 p.m., to the north-eastward; while in the third diagram is illustrated the second turn away an hour later. The centre diagram shows what the position would have been if the Battle Fleet had turned towards the enemy Fleet instead of from it; at point A the line would have had to turn again to follow Beatty's course.

engagement was the avoidance of risk by the Commander-in-Chief and his refusal to close and fight a decisive action. He thought it more important to preserve ships than to secure the destruction of the Germans. There can be little doubt that this was in accordance with the doctrine then prevalent in the British High Command, which held that all was well if the Germans were forced to keep in port or, when they emerged from it, were driven back again. Nelson and Napoleon had other views. They placed the annihilation of the enemy above every other consideration. Admiral Jellicoe afterwards explained that he did not close with the enemy because he regarded it as necessary to keep his heavy ships intact, since, if they were beaten, the allied cause must have collapsed. He has said that there was nothing behind him if he had suffered misfortune, and that a battle in the night or mist at close quarters would have left the decision to chance. There is, however, a saying of Napoleon on this head which is to the point: "God is on the side of the big battalions," or, in other words, "chance on the whole helps the stronger force," which on this occasion was the British Fleet. And certainly he underestimated the Allies' reserves. Whereas the Germans had only one completed Dreadnought which was not in the battle, the British had four.

They had three battleships and two battle-cruisers almost complete, while the Germans during the last two and a half years of the war only added one battleship and one battle-cruiser to their effective strength. Moreover, the French Navy disposed of seven completed Dreadnought battleships which were not needed for the watch of the Austrian Fleet; this, had an emergency arisen, could have been blockaded by the Italian Fleet. If Dreadnought battleships were useless in such an engagement as the Battle of Jutland, if they could not withstand destroyer and submarine attack, then did they possess any real value for war? If they could not be employed for the destruction of the German Fleet when it was caught at sea in very inferior force, there were few occasions on which they could serve. And if so there was no obvious motive for sparing them.

The unwillingness of the German Fleet to fight a second time after the handling it received at Jutland and its eventual end have been invoked as fully justifying Admiral Jellicoe's

Naval reserves of the Allies

course. But the allied situation in May, 1916, was critical, and no one could foresee the future clearly. The Battle of Verdun was still in progress, and the French Army was hard pressed. The Battle of the Somme had not then opened. The Russians were known to be in sore straits for want of munitions. Had such a blow been dealt to the Germans as Nelson, with a relatively much inferior force, inflicted at the Nile or Trafalgar, had the battle issued in "not victory but annihilation," the effect would have been instant and far-reaching. The destruction of the German Fleet would have enabled British cruiser squadrons to maintain a far closer

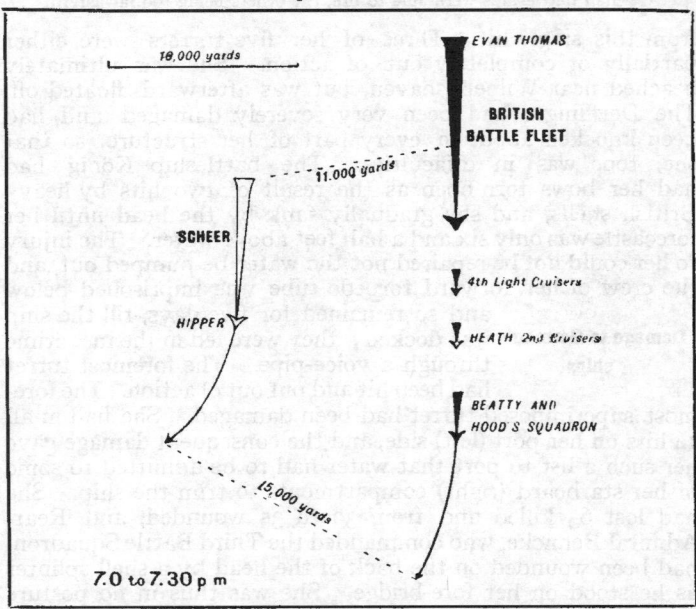

ENEMY CUT OFF FROM HIS BASES.

7.0–7.30 p.m.—The Germans have been forced out against the sunset sky. The British, after effecting their junction, steam south about 7 p.m., and haul westwards in their endeavour to close the Germans; the enemy constantly turns away, allowing the British to cut him off from his bases. At 7.15 the British Battle Fleet, but not the battle-cruisers, makes a turn away from the Germans, when Admiral Beatty makes his famous signal. After that Beatty, with what remains of Hood's squadron, leads the Fleet, and at 7.22 p.m. increases to twenty-two knots. The German destroyers (not shown) at the head of the enemy's line are emitting smoke.

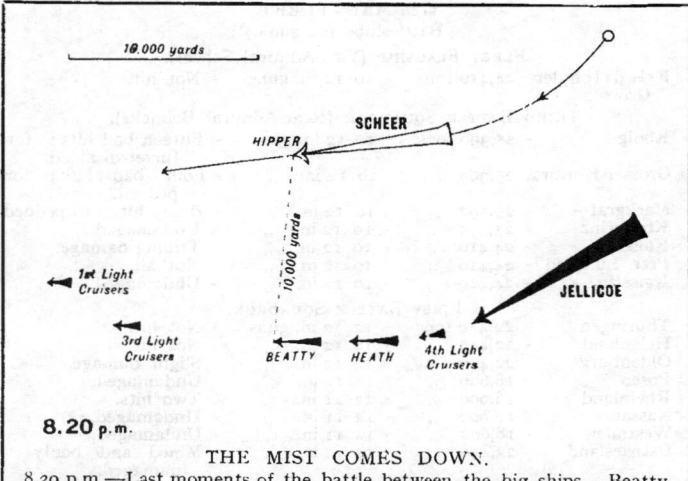

8.20 p.m.

THE MIST COMES DOWN.

8.20 p.m.—Last moments of the battle between the big ships. Beatty alters course west to support his light cruisers and attack the head of the German Fleet; just after this he is heavily engaged at 10,000 yards with two battle-cruisers and battleships. Then the mist comes down, and at 8.28 p.m. the German Fleet is last seen from the big ships steaming west.

watch on the German coast, and would correspondingly have hampered the submarine campaign when it was begun in 1917. It would have enabled the British Fleet to enter the Baltic and to act against Germany at her most vulnerable points in conjunction with Russia, whose Army was then intact. The moral influence would have been felt everywhere. In short, it is probable that an annihilating defeat of the Germans at Jutland would have shattered the German Alliance, have protected Russia from the Bolshevist movement, have brought peace a year or eighteen months earlier, and have saved thousands of millions of money and hundreds of thousands of lives. Risks must undoubtedly have been run, but when the controversies of the present have died away the historians of the future will probably decide that they ought to have been run, and will echo Nelson's great saying: "Nothing great can be achieved without risk."

THE FLEETS AND ADMIRALS AT JUTLAND.
I.—BRITISH.
(Admirals and flagships in parentheses.)

Commander-in-Chief of Grand Fleet—Admiral Sir J. R. Jellicoe (Iron Duke).
Second-in-Command of Grand Fleet and Commander of First Battle Squadron—Vice-Admiral Sir C. Burney (Marlborough).
Commander of Battle-Cruiser Force—Vice-Admiral Sir D. Beatty (Lion).
First Battle Squadron—Vice-Admiral Sir C. Burney (Marlborough).
Rear-Admiral E. F. A. Gaunt (Colossus).
Second Battle Squadron—Vice-Admiral Sir T. M. Jerram (King George V.).
Rear-Admiral A. C. Leveson (Orion).
Fourth Battle Squadron—Vice-Admiral Sir D. Sturdee (Benbow).
Rear-Admiral A. L. Duff (Superb).
Fifth Battle Squadron—Rear-Admiral H. Evan-Thomas (Barham).
First Battle-Cruiser Squadron—Rear-Admiral O. de B. Brock (Princess Royal.)
Second Battle-Cruiser Squadron—Rear-Admiral W. Pakenham (New Zealand.)
Third Battle-Cruiser Squadron—Rear-Admiral H. Hood (Invincible).
First Cruiser Squadron—Rear-Admiral Sir R. Arbuthnot (Defence).
Second Cruiser Squadron—Rear-Admiral H. L. Heath (Minotaur).
First Light Cruiser Squadron—Commodore E. S. Alexander-Sinclair (Galatea).
Second Light Cruiser Squadron—Commodore W. E. Goodenough (Southampton).
Third Light Cruiser Squadron—Rear-Admiral T. D. W. Napier (Falmouth).
Fourth Light Cruiser Squadron—Commodore C. E. Le Mesurier (Calliope).

SHIPS AND ARMAMENT.
(Flagships, in italics; Fleet flagship, in capitals; Dreadnought, *; super-Dreadnought, †; ships sunk, s.)
When approaching, the division was disposed from right to left in the order given, flagship leading each division.

FIRST BATTLE SQUADRON.
SIXTH DIVISION.
1. †*Marlborough* - 25,000 tons - 10 13·5 in. guns - Torpedoed. Steamed
2. †Revenge - 25,750 „ - 8 15 in. „ - 17 knots for some
3. *Hercules - 20,000 „ - 10 12 in. „ - time afterwards, and
4. *Agincourt - 27,500 „ - 14 12 in. „ - reached port safely.

FIFTH DIVISION.
5. *Colossus - 20,000 tons - 10 12 in. guns - Only battleship hit by
6. *Collingwood - 19,250 „ - 10 12 in. „ - shell in Battle Fleet.
7. *Neptune - 20,000 „ - 10 12 in. „ - Three hits; slight
8. *St. Vincent - 19,250 „ - 10 12 in. „ - damage.

FOURTH BATTLE SQUADRON.
FOURTH DIVISION.
9. †*Benbow* - 25,000 tons - 10 13·5 in. guns - —
10. *Bellerophon - 18,600 „ - 10 12 in. „ - —
11. *Temeraire - 18,600 „ - 10 12 in. „ - —
12. *Vanguard - 19,250 „ - 10 12 in. „ - —

THIRD DIVISION.
13. †IRON DUKE 25,000 tons - 10 13·5 in. guns - —
14. †Royal Oak - 25,750 „ - 8 15 in. „ - —
15. *Superb - 19,250 „ - 10 12 in. „ - —
16. †Canada - 28,000 „ - 10 14 in. „ - —

SECOND BATTLE SQUADRON.
SECOND DIVISION.
17. †Orion - 22,500 tons - 10 13·5 in. guns - —
18. †Monarch - 22,500 „ - 10 13·5 in. „ - —
19. †Conqueror - 22,500 „ - 10 13·5 in. „ - —
20. †Thunderer - 22,500 „ - 10 13·5 in. „ - —

FIRST DIVISION.
21. †*King George V.* - 23,000 tons - 10 13·5 in. guns - —
22. †Ajax - 23,000 „ - 10 13·5 in. „ - —
23. †Centurion - 23,000 „ - 10 13·5 in. „ - —
24. †Erin - 23,000 „ - 10 13·5 in. „ - —

FIFTH BATTLE SQUADRON.
(Attached to Sir D. Beatty's Force.)
25. †*Barham* - 27,500 tons - 8 15 in. guns - Six big hits; slight damage.
26. †Valiant - 27,500 „ - 8 15 in. „ - No hits.
27. †Malaya - 27,500 „ - 8 15 in. „ - Eight hits; one turret out of action through hoist jamming.
28. †Warspite - 27,500 „ - 8 15 in. „ - Eighteen big hits; one turret gun out of action; considerable damage.

648,200

FIRST BATTLE-CRUISER SQUADRON.
1. †LION - 26,350 tons - 8 13·5 in. guns - Twelve big hits; one turret disabled; damage not serious.
2. †*Princess Royal* 26,350 „ - 8 13·5 in. „ - Nine hits; one turret jammed; two other turrets hit slightly.
3. s†Queen Mary - 26,350 „ - 8 13·5 in. „ - Sunk.
4. †Tiger - 28,500 „ - 8 13·5 in. „ - Four hits; two heavy guns disabled.

SECOND BATTLE-CRUISER SQUADRON.
5. *New Zealand- 18,800 tons - 8 12 in. guns - One hit on a turret.
6. s*Indefatigable- 18,800 „ - 8 12 in. „ - Sunk.

THIRD BATTLE-CRUISER SQUADRON.
7. s*Invincible - 17,250 tons - 8 12 in. guns - Sunk.
8. *Indomitable - 17,250 „ - 8 12 in. „ - Trivial damage.
9. *Inflexible - 17,250 „ - 8 12 in. „ - Not hit.

196,900

FIRST CRUISER SQUADRON.
1. sDefence.
2. Warrior.
3. sDuke of Edinburgh.
4. sBlack Prince.

SECOND CRUISER SQUADRON.
5. Minotaur.
6. Shannon.
7. Cochrane.
8. Hampshire.

FIRST LIGHT CRUISER SQUADRON.
1. Galatea.
2. Inconstant.
3. Cordelia.
4. Phaeton.

SECOND LIGHT CRUISER SQUADRON.
5. Southampton.
6. Nottingham.
7. Birmingham.
8. Dublin.

THIRD LIGHT CRUISER SQUADRON.
9. Falmouth.
10. Birkenhead.
11. Gloucester.
12. Yarmouth.

FOURTH LIGHT CRUISER SQUADRON.
13. Calliope.
14. Constance.
15. Comus.
16. Caroline.
17. Royalist.

OTHER LIGHT CRUISERS.
(Some attached to Battle Fleet.)
18. Boadicea.
19. Blanche.
20. Bellona.
21. Active.
22. Canterbury.

LIGHT CRUISERS, ACTING AS DESTROYER-FLOTILLA LEADERS.
23. Fearless (First Flotilla).
24. Champion (Thirteenth Flotilla).
25. Castor (Eleventh Flotilla).

SPECIAL SERVICE DESTROYERS.
Oak (attached to Iron Duke). Abdiel (mine-layer).

DESTROYER FLOTILLAS.
Twelfth Flotilla.
Faulknor. Marksman. Obedient. Maenad.
Opal. Mary Rose. Marvel. Nessus.
Narwhal. Mindful. Onslaught. Munster.
Nonsuch. Noble. Mischief.

Eleventh Flotilla.
Kempenfelt. Ossory. Mystic. Moon.
Morning Star. Magic. Mandate. Marne.
Minion. Manners. Michael. Mons.
Martial. Milbrook.

Fourth Flotilla.
sTipperary. Broke. Achates. Porpoise.
Spitfire. Unity. Garland. sArdent.
sFortune. sSparrowhawk. Contest. sShark.
Acasta. Ophelia. Christopher. Owl.
Hardy. Midge.

BRITISH FLEET (continued).
DESTROYER FLOTILLAS (continued).
First Flotilla.

Acheron.	Ariel.	Attack.	Hydra.
Badger.	Goshawk.	Defender.	Lizard.
Lapwing.			

Thirteenth Flotilla.

sNestor.	sNomad.	Narborough.	Obdurate.
Petard.	Pelican.	Nerissa.	Onslow.
Moresby.	Nicator.		

Harwich Destroyers.

Lydiard.	Liberty.	Landrail.	Laurel.
Moorsom.	Morris.	sTurbulent.	Termagant.

Seaplane-Carrier : Engadine.

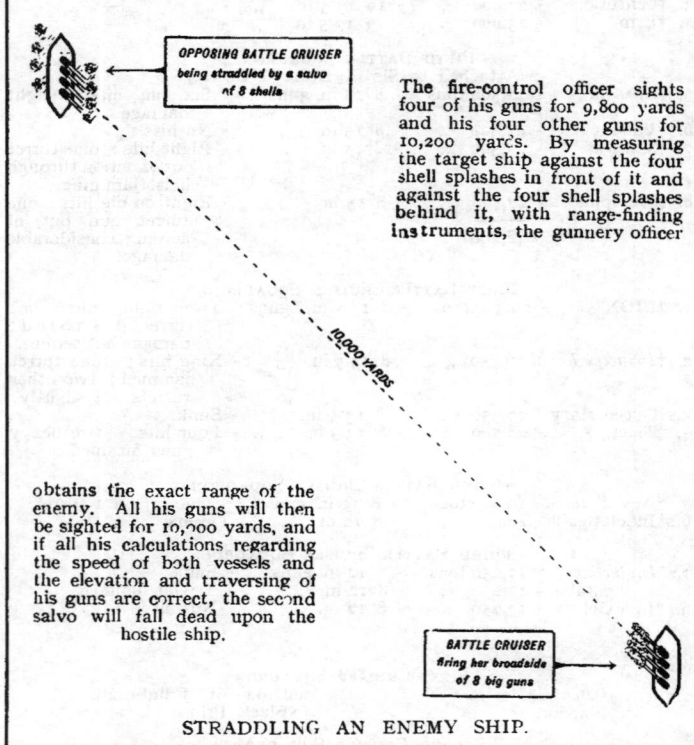

OPPOSING BATTLE CRUISER *being straddled by a salvo of 8 shells*

10,000 YARDS

The fire-control officer sights four of his guns for 9,800 yards and his four other guns for 10,200 yards. By measuring the target ship against the four shell splashes in front of it and against the four shell splashes behind it, with range-finding instruments, the gunnery officer

obtains the exact range of the enemy. All his guns will then be sighted for 10,000 yards, and if all his calculations regarding the speed of both vessels and the elevation and traversing of his guns are correct, the second salvo will fall dead upon the hostile ship.

BATTLE CRUISER *firing her broadside of 8 big guns*

STRADDLING AN ENEMY SHIP.

GERMAN FLEET.
Battleships (s=sunk.)
FLEET FLAGSHIP (Vice-Admiral Scheer).

Friedrich der Grosse.	24,410 tons	- 10 12 in. guns	- Not hit.

THIRD BATTLE SQUADRON (Rear-Admiral Behncke).

König -	25,390 tons	- 10 12 in. guns	- Fifteen bad hits; fore turret disabled.
Grosser Kurfürst	25,390 ,,	- 10 12 in. ,,	- Four bad hits; torpedoed.
Markgraf -	25,390 ,,	- 10 12 in. ,,	- Badly hit; torpedoed.
Kronprinz -	25,390 ,,	- 10 12 in. ,,	- Undamaged.
Kaiser -	24,410 ,,	- 10 12 in. ,,	- Trifling damage.
Przr. Luitpold -	24,410 ,,	- 10 12 in. ,,	- Not hit.
Kaiserin -	24,410 ,,	- 10 12 in. ,,	- Undamaged.

FIRST BATTLE SQUADRON.

Thüringen -	22,440 tons	- 12 12 in. guns	- Not hit.
Helgoland -	22,440 ,,	- 12 12 in. ,,	- Not hit.
Oldenburg -	22,440 ,,	- 12 12 in. ,,	- Slight damage.
Posen -	18,600 ,,	- 12 11 in. ,,	- Undamaged.
Rheinland -	18,600 ,,	- 12 11 in. ,,	- Two hits.
Nassau -	18,600 ,,	- 12 11 in. ,,	- Undamaged.
Westfalen -	18,600 ,,	- 12 11 in. ,,	- Undamaged.
Ostfriesland -	22,440 ,,	- 12 12 in. ,,	- Mined and badly damaged.

SECOND BATTLE SQUADRON (pre-Dreadnoughts).

Schlesien -	13,200 tons	- 4 11 in. guns	- Damaged by collision.
Hessen -	13,200 ,,	- 4 11 in. ,,	- Untouched.
Hannover -	13,200 ,,	- 4 11 in. ,,	- No report.
Schleswig - Holstein -	13,200 ,,	- 4 11 in. ,,	- Two hits.
Pommern -	13,200 ,,	- 4 11 in. ,,	- Torpedoed and sunk.
Deutschland -	13,200 ,,	- 4 11 in. ,,	- Not hit.

442,560

BATTLE-CRUISERS (Vice-Admiral Hipper).

sLützow -	26,180 tons	- 8 12 in. guns	- Forty hits; twice torpedoed; sunk.
Derfflinger -	26,180 ,,	- 8 12 in. ,,	- Seven bad hits; great damage.
Seydlitz -	26,180 ,,	- 10 11 in. ,,	- Twenty - eight hits; torpedoed; two turrets disabled.
Moltke -	22,640 ,,	- 10 11 in. ,,	- Three bad hits; six less serious.
Von der Tann -	19,100 ,,	- 8 11 in. ,,	- One turret completely and another partially disabled.

120,280

LIGHT CRUISERS.
SECOND SCOUTING GROUP.

Regensburg.	sRostock.	Pillau.
Frankfurt.	sWiesbaden.	sElbing.

FOURTH SCOUTING GROUP.

Stettin.	Stuttgart.	München.
Berlin.	sFrauenlob.	

BRITISH LIGHT CRUISERS.
H.M.S. Falmouth, flagship of the Third Light Cruiser Squadron at the Battle of Jutland, and (above) H.M.S. Fearless, which acted as leader of the First Destroyer Flotilla.

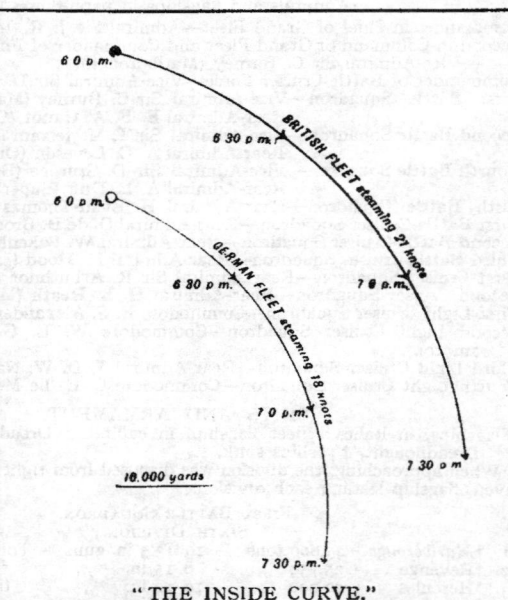

6 0 p.m.
6 30 p.m.
BRITISH FLEET *steaming 21 knots*
6 0 p.m.
6 30 p.m.
GERMAN FLEET *steaming 18 knots*
7 0 p.m.
7 0 p.m.
7 30 p.m.
7 30 p.m.
10,000 yards

"THE INSIDE CURVE."
The "inside curve" atones for want of speed. The German Fleet is here assumed to be steaming 18 knots, and the British 21 knots, but the Germans, by turning constantly away from the British, avoid being "crossed." On the other hand, the fast fleet on the outside curve controls the enemy's movements. The position shown was roughly that between 6 p.m. and 7.30 p.m. in the actual battle, though in reality the Germans turned rather more to the west and were followed by the British battle-cruisers.

H.M.S. Birkenhead, a unit of the Third Light Cruiser Squadron, showing an aeroplane in the fore turret, which forms the base for the launching platform.

H.M.S. Shannon, armoured cruiser attached to the Second Cruiser Squadron. Her armament was four 9·2 in. and ten 7·5 in. guns.

H.M.S. Neptune, Dreadnought of 19,250 tons, carrying ten 12 in. guns. She was in the Fifth Division of the First Battle Squadron.

H.M.S. Indefatigable, 18,800-ton battle-cruiser, carrying eight 12 in. guns. Hit by a salvo, she blew up and sank.

H.M.S. Shark, destroyer in the Fourth Flotilla. Sunk after an heroic action, for which Commander Loftus Jones was awarded the V.C.

H.M.S. Birmingham, light cruiser carrying eight 6 in. guns, completed in 1914. She was a unit of the Second Light-Cruiser Squadron.

H.M.S. Erin, super-Dreadnought of 23,000 tons, armed with ten 13·5 in. and sixteen 6 in. guns. She was built at Barrow for the Turkish Government. and appropriated for the British Navy on her completion in 1914, at the outbreak of the war.

SEVEN OF THE BRITISH WARSHIPS THAT WON GLORY IN THE BATTLE OF JUTLAND.

[*The Autotype Co.*

H.M.S. LION AND TIGER : PART OF THE FIRST BATTLE-CRUISER SQUADRON.

The Lion was the flagship of Vice-Admiral Sir David Beatty, who was in chief command of the battle-cruiser force at the Battle of Jutland, while the Tiger belonged to the same squadron. The flagship received a dozen hits during the battle. One shell struck a turret and caused a bad fire, and the ship was probably only saved by the heroism of Major Harvey, of the Marines, who, though mortally wounded, ordered the magazine doors to be closed.

GERMAN FLEET (continued).
DESTROYERS.

First, Second, Third, Fifth, Sixth, Seventh, and Ninth Flotillas, each of eleven boats maximum strength. It is not certain whether the second half of the First Flotilla was present. Maximum force, 77 destroyers.

The German destroyers known to have been sunk were V4, V27, V29, S35, V48.

COMPARISON OF FORCE.

	British.	Germans.
Dreadnought Battleships	28	16
Battle-Cruisers	9	5
Pre-Dreadnought Battleships	0	6
Armoured Cruisers	8	0
Light Cruisers	25	11
Destroyers	**77**	77 or 72

Comparison of—A, guns mounted ; B, firing on broadside ; c, weight of broadside (all weapons of 11 in. and over in Battle Fleets and battle-cruisers). In armour the Germans had a distinct advantage.

		Number of ships with that gun.	A Total number of that gun mounted.	B Total number of that gun firing on broadside.	C Total weight of broadside. lb.
BRITISH :					
15 in.	.. .. ..	6	48	48	82,560
14 in.	.. .. ..	1	10	10	14,000
13·5 in.	.. .. ..	15	142	142	177,550
12 in.	.. .. ..	15	144	132	112,200
	Totals	37	344	332	386,310
GERMAN :					
12 in.	.. .. ..	14	144	128	110,080
11 in.	.. .. ..	13	100	84	55,440
	Totals	27	244	212	165,520

Displacement of the two Fleets (Battleships and Battle-Cruisers) :

		Dreadnoughts.	Pre-Dreadnoughts.	Battle-Cruisers.	Total.
British	.. .. ..	648,200	—	196,900	845,100
German	.. .. ..	363,360	79,200	120,280	562,840

The completed ships absent from the British Fleet, owing to refits, or other causes, and the ships approaching completion, were :

BATTLESHIPS.
(R, refitting ; c, completing.)

R	Queen Elizabeth	..	..	..	27,500 tons	..	8	15 in. guns.
R	Emperor of India	..	..	..	25,000 ,,	..	10	13.5in. ,,
R	Dreadnought	..	..	..	17,900 ,,	..	10	12 in. ,,
c	Ramillies	..	..	..	25,750 ,,	..	8	15 in. ,,
c	Resolution	..	..	..	25,750 ,,	..	8	15 in. ,,
c	Royal Sovereign	..	..	..	25,750 ,,	..	8	15 in. ,,

BATTLE-CRUISERS.

c	Renown	..	..	..	27,000 (?)	..	6	15 in. ,,
c	Repulse ..	..	..	..	27,000 (?)	..	6	15 in. ,,
R	Australia	..	..	..	19,200 tons	..	8	12 in. ,,

German ships refitting or approaching completion, and not present, were :

BATTLESHIPS.

R	König Albert	..	..	..	24,410 tons	..	10	12 in. guns.
c	Baden	..	..	..	28,000 (?)	..	8	15 in. ,,
c	Bayern	..	..	..	28,000 (?)	..	8	15 in. ,,
c	Sachsen	..	..	..	28,000 (?)	..	8	15 in. ,,
c	Württemberg	..	..	..	28,000 (?)	..	8	15 in. ,,

BATTLE-CRUISERS.

c	Mackensen	..	..	..	30,000 (?)	..	8	15 in. guns.
c	Hindenburg	..	..	..	28,000 (?)	..	8	12 in. ,,

THE CAMOUFLAGED INFLEXIBLE.

H.M.S Inflexible, one of the ships of the Third Battle-Cruiser Squadron, camouflaged at the bows. She was built at Clydebank in 1908, was of 17,250 tons, and her armament included eight 12 in. guns.

WOMEN'S WORK IN THE GREAT WAR.

Introduction by the Marchioness of Londonderry.

Response of Women to the Nation's Call—Birth of the Women's Legion—Its Various Offshoots—Work of the Land Army—Women's Share in Munition Making—The V.A.D. at the Outbreak of the War—Their Early Activities in France—They Undertake the Actual Work of Nursing—V.A.D. General Service Section—V.A.D. Workers Sent to the East—Care of the Workers Themselves—Arrangements for their Future Training—Women Doctors—A Hospital Staffed Entirely by Women—Women in the Medical Profession—The War Service Legion—Its Several Sections—Its Work for Agriculture—Soldiers' and Sailors' Work Section—Disabled Men Trained to Make Embroidery—Keen and Successful Workers Come Forward—The Q.M.A.A.C. Originates as the W.A.A.C.—Heroism of Its Members in France in 1918—The Land Army—Its Inception—Farmers and the Lasses—Value of their Work—Successes and Failures—W.R.N.S., or "Wrens"—Nature of their Work—Uniform and Payment—Women Police—First a Voluntary Organisation—The Work Develops—Women Patrols Given Official Status—Women in Industrial Life—Figures Showing How they Took the Place of Men—Munition Workers—Varieties of Occupation—Measures for Health and Protection—Aeroplane Workers—Wireless Workers—Transport Workers—Women Drive the Mails—The Mothers at Work—Their Difficulties, Especially Financial Ones.

THE influence of the Great War on the sphere of women's activities is a subject so far-reaching, and so vast in its scope, that the limits of this chapter will not allow of more than a general review of the admirable way in which women of all classes responded to the national need for their services. It will thus form a continuation of the earlier account given in Chapter XC.

This response may be divided into two main categories. First, the magnificent work of the nursing services and the V.A.D., and of all those who undertook the care and welfare of the wounded, the prisoners and refugees, and the suffering populations of the invaded countries. The organisation, courage, and devotion with which these self-imposed duties were carried out, often in the most trying circumstances, cannot be praised too highly, and the long Roll of Honour among these women is a fitting testimony to their willing self-sacrifice. This admirable work, however, did not constitute so great a departure from the preconceived ideas of women's capabilities as did another field of activity, for throughout history they have given ample proof of their ability for such sacrifices.

It is in the sphere of the substitution of women for men that the outstanding feature of women's work during the war may be looked for. There was hardly an essential occupation in which they

THE MARCHIONESS OF LONDONDERRY.
When the Women's Emergency Corps came into existence in 1914, Lady Londonderry accepted the position of Colonel-in-Chief, and later that of Commandant of the Women's Legion.

did not come forward to take the place of the men called to the Colours. This idea—that women would be needed to take the place of men fit for combatant service—became evident to me as early as 1914, and although the suggestion that they could do so, both with the Army and on the land, was at first considered utterly fantastic by the great majority, I was encouraged to persevere by the belief and enthusiasm of the few.

The Women's Emergency Corps first came into existence in 1914, at the old Bedford College for Women in Baker Street; affiliated to it and with its energies directed from under the same roof, the Women's Volunteer Reserve was formed, with the Hon. Mrs. Haverfield as honorary colonel and Mrs. Charlesworth as commanding officer. I was asked to become the colonel-in-chief of the reserve, and accepted the honorary position. The spirit of the movement found its expression in voluntary service and discipline, and the cry of all was "organise us, so that we may be efficient, and may give of our best to our country." In December, 1914, a large meeting was held at the Mansion House, followed shortly after by one at Londonderry House, which saw the birth of the Women's Legion.

Our first organised activities consisted in the formation of a Military Cookery Section, working under the War Office to replace male cooks with the Army, and an Agricultural Section for the furthering of the employment of women in agriculture.

I think that I may justly say that it was from these beginnings that the vast organisations of women serving with the forces and on the land sprang, for it was the Legion's Military Cookery Section, numbering over 30,000 members, and the Motor Transport Section which, after two years of successful work under the War Office, formed the nucleus of the Women's Army Auxiliary Corps on its inauguration in March, 1917. The formation of a Women's Royal Naval Service followed shortly after ; and later that of a Women's Royal Air Force. Then it was that, in recognition of the gallant behaviour of the W.A.A.C.'s during the terrible days of the German offensive in the spring of 1918, her Majesty the Queen signified her desire to become the Commander-in-Chief. The final seal of the Royal approval was thus given to the corps, which was renamed Queen Mary's Army Auxiliary Corps.

It is an unquestionable fact that the efforts of the 15,000 women of the Land Army contributed greatly to the keeping of our food supplies at a high level despite the U boat campaign. Cheerfully and energetically they undertook even the heaviest work, in spite of wind, weather, difficulties of housing, and many other adversities, and their success as a war emergency measure was undeniable. The continued employment of women for the heavier forms of agricultural labour may be doubted, as they cannot be said to be really fitted for it, nor would they be willing to undertake it except for patriotic motives. Nevertheless, in all the lighter forms of work, and particularly in the branches of stock feeding and management, poultry-keeping, and fruit and market gardening, they amply proved their economic value.

One of the most interesting developments of the war was the employment of women on many of the semi-skilled and skilled processes of munition making and aircraft production, hitherto entirely carried out by men, and in these trades they achieved the most marked successes. They came forward in their hundreds of thousands to release those called up for military service. Indeed, some of the more recent and delicate forms of work connected with wireless apparatus and aircraft instruments were undertaken directly by the women, who thus proved their aptitude for this class of technical work. The same may be said of the women who stepped into the clerical posts vacated by the men, both in the Government departments and in the countless banks and

offices which employed them. Their attention to detail and ability to organise the necessary routine of duties made them conspicuously successful in all branches of clerical labour, and in view of the marked disinclination of a great number of the men serving with the Army to return to such sedentary work, the continued employment of women in these posts appears certain.

It is through the very wide field of their war activities, and the strong desire manifested by so large a majority to undertake national service, that the women proved their fitness for a share in public life, and it is a fitting recognition of this desire that the power to vote and the possibility of entering Parliament are now theirs.

The Work of the V.A.D.

By LADY AMPTHILL.

[*Bassano.*

LADY AMPTHILL, G.B.E.
Representative of the Voluntary Aid Detachment and member of the Queen Alexandra Army Nursing Board.

Voluntary Aid Detachments first came into existence in 1909, their original purpose being to have in readiness bands of trained voluntary workers to assist the regular nurses if Britain were invaded. As the name suggests, they were voluntary workers and were organised locally in detachments.

When the war broke out in August, 1914, there were no fewer than 40,018 women enrolled as members of the 1,582 detachments scattered all over the country. These were at once mobilised as need arose for the numerous auxiliary hospitals—that is, hospitals controlled by the Joint War Committee of the British Red Cross Society and the Order of St. John of Jerusalem, as distinct from those owned by the Admiralty or War Office—which sprang into existence.

All kinds of buildings were placed at the disposal of the authorities ; the residences of the wealthy, school buildings, town-halls, and other public and private establishments were amongst those offered and utilised. The extent to which these auxiliary hospitals grew as the need increased may be gathered from the fact that at the time of the signing of the armistice there were about 1,450 of them. These were mainly staffed by voluntary part-time members with usually a few resident workers.

Before two months of war had elapsed, however, it was seen that work awaited the V.A.D. abroad, and in October, 1914, immediately after the Joint War Committee of the British Red Cross Society and the Order of St. John of Jerusalem had been established, the first V.A.D. unit left for

ROYAL INSPECTION OF V.A.D. MOTOR-AMBULANCE DRIVERS ON ACTIVE SERVICE.
Princess Mary's V.A.D. chauffeur, and (right) motor-ambulance drivers of the Voluntary Aid Detachment on service in France being inspected by Princess Mary, herself a V.A.D. commandant. These drivers proved triumphantly successful, displaying the greatest skill, courage, and endurance. Their wonderful gallantry during the iniquitous German raid on Etaples, when two sections were driving all night, won four Military Medals.

Boulogne. Here they formed a rest station, and very rapidly other units were launched from Boulogne, thus establishing that town as the headquarters of the V.A.D. in France. Early in 1915, Devonshire House, the London residence of the Duke of Devonshire, was put at the disposal of the authorities, and was opened as the general headquarters of the V.A.D.

The work of the Joint Committee in France grew rapidly. The first hospital to be established by the committee and to be staffed by V.A.D.'s was a small one in Normandy for men working at the convalescent horse camp depots. The nearest military hospital was a considerable distance away, and this one, installed in a charming French villa, was therefore established for the

MARCH OF V.A.D. WORKERS.
Part of the procession of 3,000 women war workers who, in the summer of 1918, presented an address of homage at Buckingham Palace to King George and Queen Mary on the occasion of their silver wedding.

V.A.D.'s SALONIKA BOUND.
A party of V.A.D. workers, who were bound for Salonika, at the rooms in the Royal Mews at Buckingham Palace which, by King George's desire, had been set apart for them during their stay in London.

treatment of pneumonia and of minor complaints, chiefly kicks. After the opening of this, two others were established at convalescent horse camp depots, making three in all.

Still another opening for the activities of the V.A.D.'s occurred in the institution, also under the Joint Committee, of hostels for the relatives of the wounded. The first of these hostels was established at Rouen, and at the time of the signing of the armistice four others had been opened at other bases, where relatives were accommodated from the moment of their arrival at the hospital to the time of their departure. One other form of service performed by the V.A.D. abroad at this period must be mentioned, and that was the staffing of the Princess Victoria Rest Clubs for nurses and V.A.D.'s which, under the direction of Lady Algernon Gordon-Lennox, were established in all military hospital bases and were a great boon to the hospital workers.

Meanwhile a very important decision was being arrived at in London by the military authorities in regard to the further utilisation of the services of the ever-growing army of women V.A.D.'s. It was becoming increasingly difficult to staff the military hospitals with fully-trained hospital nurses, and it was decided to make the experiment of admitting to the hospitals in Britain a certain number of V.A.D.'s to serve under the trained nurses.

The first of these requisitions came

from London, eight V.A.D. nursing members being asked for in March, 1915, by the Hampstead Military Hospital. This requisition was immediately followed by demands from military hospitals all over the country, and members were posted as rapidly as possible. In August of the same year the military authorities discovered yet another capacity in which the V.A.D. could serve, and requisitions for cooks and clerks, to release for active service the male orderlies in the hospitals, were received at Devonshire House. Thus sprang into existence the general service section of V.A.D. effort, through which were supplied, not only cooks and clerks, but afterwards housemaids, waitresses, ward-orderlies, laundresses, dispensers, X-ray and dental assistants, **V.A.D. general** accountants and telephonists. These workers **service section** were paid at varying rates according to the class of work done and to their qualifications, and those responding were drawn from all grades of society. The general service section offered, indeed, an opportunity to the woman who was not fitted for nursing, but who yet was able and qualified to undertake some other form of work. The general service member merits special mention in that her work had not the glamour of nursing, while the spirit in which it was carried out made her a credit to the organisation.

In the following April another new departure was made in the appointment of women motor-ambulance drivers in

CLEANING UP THEIR AMBULANCE CARS.
Women motor-drivers of the V.A.D. on active service in France. It was in April, 1916, that women motor-ambulance drivers were first sent to France under the Joint Committee, and though nearly everybody prophesied failure, they proved a triumphant success.

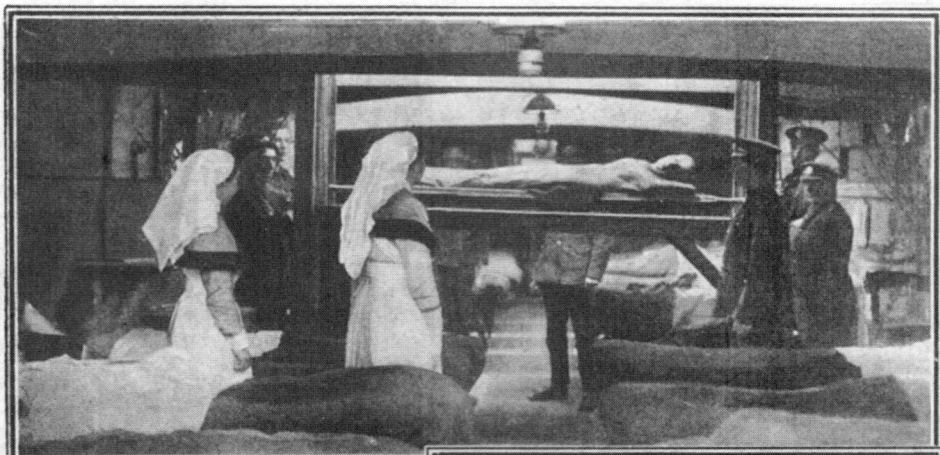

IN A RED CROSS BARGE.
Lowering a patient by a lift from the deck into the ward on a hospital barge in France.

France under the Joint Committee. Nearly everybody prophesied failure to the enterprise. Despite these forebodings, twelve qualified drivers were sent to France, and so far from their proving failures, more were demanded, and exactly treble the number were sent out later, while the biggest unit of all, consisting of one hundred and ten drivers, was sent out in March, 1917.

These women were splendid. They took over the entire work hitherto done by men, with the exception of heavy mechanical work. They kept the cars on the road, did all the ordinary running repairs, all the tyre and wheel changing when out, and a good deal of their own tyre mending, as well as the ordinary washing and greasing. The work involved driving by night as well as by day, and in all kinds of weather, and as the convoys nearly always came in at night, the women ambulance drivers had to be prepared to be called out at a moment's notice at any hour of the day or night.

Military Medals for brave women Their wonderful gallantry during the Etaples raid, when two sections were driving during the whole of that night, won for them four Military Medals.

The summer of 1917 saw the introduction of a very interesting development of the work of the department in the employment of women in the military hospitals in the East. This was to supply cooks for the invalid-diet kitchens which were set up under the direction of Sir Courtauld Thomson in all the military hospitals in Italy and the East. The first unit was sent to Malta, other units proceeding shortly afterwards to Italy, Salonika, and Egypt. These kitchens were extraordinarily successful, proving a great boon to the sick man who could not relish an ordinary solid diet. About the same time the first V.A.D. nursing members to serve at Salonika left Britain, and also a unit of shorthand typists.

Something must be said about the co-operation of the Dominions with the work of the department. At the invitation of the Joint Committee, units of V.A.D. members were selected, and at the call of the Mother Country came most patriotically from Australia, Canada, South Africa, and Newfoundland. It will be remembered that they ran an additional risk in crossing the ocean in time of war—some, alas! lost their lives on the journey, as was the case with the unit from South Africa, when two nurses in the Kenilworth Castle were drowned as a result of the collision between that vessel and one of the convoy.

But owing to transport difficulties it was not possible to bring over sufficient workers to staff the Dominion hospitals, and Devonshire House was therefore asked to supply general service members to the Canadian and Australian hospitals, while Britain staffed the South African and New Zealand hospitals with both nursing and general service members. Later on similar requests came from the American Army, and a motor unit was also supplied for service with the American Army in England.

In the midst of these growing demands from Oversea Forces, and with the increasing claims of the hospitals on the western front and in the East during the final phases of the great struggle, a great request from the Admiralty was received. Already the V.A.D. had posted the first nursing members in response to demands from the Admiralty in 1917, and now, in the early autumn of 1918, it was asked to send 300 nursing members to the various naval hospitals. It says much for the spirit of the British women that the organisation was never without a steady stream of recruits.

The opening of 1918 saw developments of the work which was being carried out for the welfare of the V.A.D. herself. Two beautiful convalescent and rest homes, one at Ardington, in Berkshire, kindly lent by Lady Wantage, and the other at Fulbrook, near Stratford-on-Avon, were opened in February, 1918, for V.A.D.'s recovering from illness or needing a rest. A considerable number passed through these homes, and the overseas members, who had no friends in Britain with whom they could stay, especially appreciated these opportunities of rest at Ardington and

TRANSPORT OF THE WOUNDED IN FRANCE.
Wounded British soldiers in the hospital ward on a Red Cross barge in France, and (above) a nurse attending to one of her patients in a British ambulance train in France.

Fulbrook. The club for V.A.D.'s opened at Devonshire House on May 23rd of the same year met another real want, more especially of the V.A.D. passing through or working in Central London. There was no subscription, and the large, tastefully decorated rooms, opening out on to the beautiful garden of Devonshire House, made a delightful rendezvous for V.A.D.'s of all ranks. Her Majesty the Queen, and H.R.H

Princess Mary, herself a V.A.D. commandant, visited the club on July 25th, 1918, and expressed their approval of the arrangements. The canteen, where well-cooked lunches and teas at very reasonable prices could be had, was also much appreciated.

What, it was asked in 1919, is to be the future of the V.A.D. when demobilisation is completed? It had been felt strongly by the Joint War Committee that it would be a real national loss if in the years of peace no use were made of the training and experience gained by such a large and devoted body of women. It was, therefore, decided to offer scholarships for special training in the various forms of health work open to women. Under this scheme, which is a tribute to the magnificent work so generously given by V.A.D. members during the war, a limited number of scholarships, to cover the fee and the cost of living, were given to those who passed the qualifying examinations with special proficiency; but in other cases it was hoped to assist materially those members who wished to be trained for their various professions in centres all over the country. The list of positions from which candidates might make their choice was a long one, and included medicine, nursing, physical culture, pharmacy, dentistry, domestic science, health visitors, hospital almoners, and infant welfare work. The scholarships were open to all V.A.D. members from twenty to forty years of age who had

Scholarships for special training worked officially in a recognised British unit prior to January, 1917, and had continued working until their services were no longer required. Applications were to be made before March 31st, 1919; but if a scholarship was allotted to a member who was still working it would be kept open for her until her services were no longer required.

Women Doctors.

The work done by the woman doctor after the outbreak of war was very fine, and practically broke down any prejudice that might have existed against her. She came forward and gave her services, both for Britain's own wounded and for those of her Allies. Especially notable was the work

A BRIGHT MOMENT IN A HOUSE OF HEALING.
Nurses awaiting the arrival of the King at a base hospital visited by his Majesty during one of his many visits to the Army in France. The white-garbed women were pleasantly conscious of the charming picture their ward presented, with sunshine streaming on polished furniture and gleaming lilies.

undertaken by the Scottish Women's Hospitals. When the retreat came they had established five hospitals in Serbia, and during it they suffered untold hardships, including being made prisoners of war. They also undertook work in Rumania, Salonika, Russia, and France, and for a short while were at Malta attending to British wounded.

Of special interest to English people was the military hospital, Endell Street, London, where the entire medical and surgical staff were women. This hospital was started by two women doctors, who were asked by the War Office to undertake the entire management. It was a great success in every way. The soldiers who were patients were all well satisfied with their treatment; none objected in any way that their "surgeon" was a woman; rather they were loud in their praise of the care and attention bestowed upon them, and all felt their women surgeons did everything for them that skill and devotion could. In London, the one city of the world where the woman doctor had a hard fight to obtain recognition, the highest that could be **Praise for women** bestowed upon her in the eyes of the nation **surgeons** was given to her—she was asked to run a military hospital. Besides the actual war work, covering too large a field to mention, the woman doctor came forward and, by filling a man's place, released numbers of doctors for active service. We found them filling important positions at hospitals, holding appointments as house surgeons and house physicians, where previously only men were. Soon they were appointed as medical officers in prisons, and were found as the medical officers in munition works. They were included on nearly all Government committees and commissions dealing with such matters as housing and health. A woman doctor for the first time was appointed as a (temporary) county medical officer of health. In general practice there was a great demand for medical women. In many instances, where medical men were called up, women were acting as their locum-tenens, and the fact of the locum-tenens being a woman made, as a rule, but little difference to the practice.

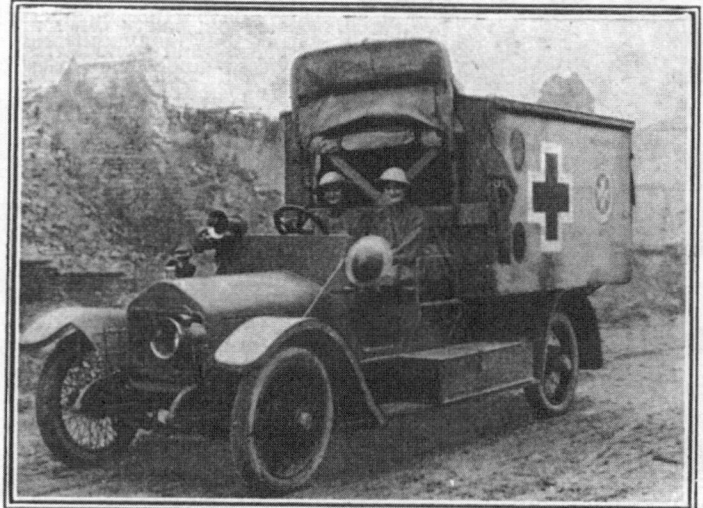

ON ACTIVE SERVICE IN FRANCE.
Women ambulance drivers passing through a shattered village on the western front. They took over the entire work previously done by men, with the exception of the heaviest mechanical jobs.

The War Service Legion.

BY THE MARCHIONESS OF LONDONDERRY.

Early in 1918 the promoters of the Women's Legion decided that the name should be changed to that of War

Service Legion, as the scope of its work had been extended by adding a Sailors' and Soldiers' Work Section, with the Marchioness of Titchfield as director and Mrs. Antrobus as commandant. Moreover, the legion as a whole was no longer confined to women, for many farmers who had employed the girls on the land had asked to become members. The Military Sections—viz., the motorists and cooks—had the distinction of forming the nucleus of the Q.M.A.A.C., in February, 1917; but the women drivers in the Army Service Corps returned some months later to form part of the Women's Legion, with Miss Christobel Ellis, O.B.E., as commandant. All members who were afterwards enrolled in the Q.M.A.A.C. were permitted to continue to wear the legion badge on the lapel of the coat. The words "War Service" were dropped and the original name of Women's Legion was reverted to in 1919.

The Canteen Section supplied paid staffs for running canteens for factories. These were conducted on a strictly business basis. After deducting salaries of the staff and other expenses incidental to the work, all profits were to be returned to the firm and allocated for the betterment of the employees. A Mechanics Section formed part of the legion. In this were enrolled a large number of women who had been trained in certain partly-skilled branches of munition work, aeroplane production, wireless telegraphy, and so on, in connection with the Training Section of the Ministry of Munitions.

Regarding the Agricultural Section, by the early part of 1918 the Board of Agriculture had so substantially covered the ground in relation to women workers on the land that the legion decided to specialise in dairy-farming and market-gardening. The leaders sought specially to persuade women of independent means, whose services would not otherwise come into the labour market, to come forward and undergo a thorough training in order to qualify them to manage their own dairies and gardens, and to be able to give instruction to others in their neighbourhood. The Cottesmore Hunt Kennels were lent by Lord Lonsdale as a hostel, and in the gardens of Burley-on-the-Hill, lent by the Hon. Mrs. Frederick Guest to the legion at the same time that she lent the house to the War Office as a hospital for officers, pupils were trained in market-gardening and horticulture. In 1915 Miss Sylvia Brocklebank, the well-known whip, became the commandant of this section. It was thanks to the generosity of her sister and brother-in-law, Mr. and Mrs. Westinghouse, who sent donations of over £7,000 from America, that in the early days of the

war it was possible to purchase a large number of tractors and hire them out to farmers in Rutlandshire and Northamptonshire.

In the spring of 1917 the Agricultural Committee suggested that, as there would be a great shortage of preserving sugar for jam-making, something should be done to save the fruit which would otherwise be wasted. I therefore made inquiries of the Navy and Army Canteen Board, and found that the Board would be glad to purchase any quantity of bottled fruit for the use of the troops. A committee was formed, consisting of the Marchioness of Titchfield, Lady Hindlip, Mr. and Mrs. Drysdale Bowden, and myself.

Thirty-five centres for fruit-bottling were started in various parts of the country, each in charge of a responsible organiser. Then ten thousand seven-pound bottles were distributed among the centres, and were filled with sterilised fruit.

A further consignment of three thousand three-pound bottles was also supplied to a fruit-bottling centre in Southampton, and the bottles were all very satisfactorily filled.

In conclusion, I would emphasise the fact that, whereas in the past the members of the Women's Legion came forward to fill the places, to the best of their ability, of the men who went out to fight, so, when these same warriors were returning wounded and disabled, the women of the War Service Legion felt that nothing they could do or give was too much for those who had sacrificed all but their lives.

[Lafayette.
THE MARCHIONESS OF HEADFORT.
Lady Headfort took an active part in many manifestations of women's war work, and was Director of Motor Drivers of the Women's Legion and Commandant of the Women's Legion Household Service Section.

The Sailors' and Soldiers' Work Section of the Women's Legion.
BY THE MARCHIONESS OF TITCHFIELD.

At the beginning of the war the Women's Legion was raised as a body of women willing to fill the places of men joining the Army, and after those early days its members carried out many different services and industries. One of the schemes undertaken later was the employment of disabled sailors and soldiers, and it was partly on this account that it was decided to change the name to War Service Legion, the members being no longer exclusively women.

In 1918 a special section was formed known as the Sailors' and Soldiers' Work Section, for the training of disabled sailors and soldiers in making gold embroidery for naval and military purposes. I was appointed director of this section, and received valuable assistance from Mrs. Antrobus, the

LEADERS OF THE WOMEN'S LEGION.
In the front row (right to left): Lady Titchfield, Chairman Sailors' and Soldiers' Work Section; Lady Londonderry, President of the Legion; Miss Christobel Ellis, Commandant Motor Transport Section. Back row: Miss Replin, Commandant Munitions Section; Miss Brocklebank, Commandant Agricultural Section; Lady Massereene and Ferrard; Mrs. Nugent Allfrey; and Mrs. Antrobus, Commandant Borderers' Section.

authority on embroidery who, as commandant, superintended the Embroidery Training School, and from the Hon. Mrs. Eric Chaplin and Mrs. Nugent Allfrey as joint secretaries.

The scheme received the sanction of the Ministry of Pensions, who paid the men the usual allowances during the training. The Company of Broiderers gave their generous support by equipping some light and airy work-rooms, which they placed at our disposal for a period of three years, while the Queen visited the school and showed much interest in the scheme. We did not anticipate any lack of work even when the war was over as, should the demand for naval and military badges abate, there would be other forms of gold embroidery always required.

The training was to last nine months, which was found to be the shortest period possible—the usual time of training in gold embroidery being of a much greater length—but our object was to fit the men to earn good pay as soon as possible. We found that many took to the work very quickly, and it was remarkable how soon they became accurate, when to attain speed is only a question of time and practice.

So many men had taken up embroidery in hospital, and were already accustomed to using a needle, that they did not all come to us as complete novices. It did not seem to matter what trade a man had followed before the war; we had market-gardeners, colliers, printers, motor-drivers, and so on. Any man who has one good eye and the use of his hands can learn to embroider properly; the only essential attribute is patience, and nearly all mastered this great lesson during the long hours in hospital, and with patience much can be attained.

One of our men who had nine months' training was soon instructing a class for the blind at St. Dunstan's, and was doing remarkably well. He realised the difficulties of his pupils, having so recently experienced them himself, although not handicapped by lack of sight; another man who had seven months' training went as instructor to Belfast, where a school was started. We were anxious to develop the work for the **Women capture** reason that this trade was **embroidery trade** largely in the hands of aliens before the war, and by capturing it for our sailors and soldiers we should be doing a double service to them and to the country.

[Bassano.

MISS CHRISTOBEL
ELLIS, O.B.E.
Commandant Motor-
Transport Section of the
Women's Legion.

[Bassano.

MRS. SYBIL THATCHER.
Assistant Commandant of the
Women's Legion.

Queen Mary's Army Auxiliary Corps.

The Q.M.A.A.C., or the W.A.A.C., the name by which the corps was first known, came into being in the early part of 1917. It was part of the programme of the Women's Branch of National Service. Mrs. Chalmers Watson, M.D., the first Controller-in-Chief, a sister of Sir Eric and Sir Auckland Geddes,

was succeeded in 1918 by Mrs. Burleigh Leach, while Mrs. V. A. Long was Deputy Chief Controller. As may be recalled, the latter was a victim to the brutality of the U boats in 1918.

The aim of the corps was to effect the substitution of women for soldiers in certain employments throughout the units, formations, and offices administered by the Army Council, but they were not to take the place of batmen.

Except in certain specified cases no woman of the corps was employed unless a soldier was relieved for other purposes. The main employments for the women at home and abroad, at the base and on the lines of communication overseas, were as **Posts filled** follows : (*a*) Clerks, librarians, **by women** accountants, etc. ; (*b*) cooks, waitresses, butlers, laundresses, pantrymaids, etc. ; (*c*) motor-transport service ; (*d*) storehouse women, checkers, etc. ; (*e*) telephone and postal service ; (*f*) miscellaneous services ; (*g*) technical women employed with the R.A.F. and the A.S.C. motor transport.

The excellent work that was done by this corps at home and abroad is so well known that it would be superfluous to dwell on its details here. There was never any difficulty in obtaining recruits ; as a matter of fact, from all parts of the kingdom came continuous appeals to aid in this work of substitution.

It should, however, be put on record that an official announcement was made on April 7th, 1918, saying that excellent reports had been received by the Army Council on the behaviour of members of the corps during the heavy fighting in France. One party employed at an Army school within the area of operations was offered transport to convey them to a safer locality farther back. The women refused to avail themselves of it, on the ground that it would probably be wanted for something more important, and they marched fifteen miles back to the place to which they had been ordered. During this terrible crisis of the war they justified their existence and well maintained the credit of their sex and the Army to which they belonged.

On April 9th, 1918, as a mark of her appreciation of the good services rendered by the W.A.A.C. both at home and abroad since its inauguration, and especially of the distinction it had earned in France by its work for the armies during the fighting on the western front, the Queen was graciously pleased to assume the position and title of Commander-in-Chief of the corps, which thereafter bore the name of Queen Mary's Army Auxiliary Corps.

The Land Army.
By the Hon. Mrs. Alfred Lyttelton.

In the summer of 1916 the Minister of Agriculture, Lord Selborne, foresaw that a serious shortage of agricultural

MISS I. STEPHENS.
Driver-mechanic, who was the first lady driver to drive the King.

MRS. N. ALLFREY.
Secretary Soldiers' and Sailors' Embroidery Section, War Service Legion.

MISS WARD, M.B.E.
Deputy Commandant of the Women's War Service Legion.

MRS. COOK,
M.B.E.
Assistant Commandant of the Women's Legion.

MISS A. LEVEY.
Superintendent of the Motor-Transport Training Section, Osterley Park.

MISS PATTERSON.
Officer-in-Charge of the Recruiting Staff of the Women's Legion.

[Photos: Bassano.

labour was inevitable, and that an organisation must be put in readiness to meet it which should be capable of expansion as the need arose. In the following January, when Mr. Prothero had succeeded to the Ministry, the organisation known as the Women's Land Army was born, and under the shadow of what scepticism and prejudice it increased and multiplied only those know who toiled for its growth and are responsible for its maturity.

The general organisation and administration was as follows : The Women's Branch of the Board of Agriculture, under the directorship of Miss Meriel Talbot, with Mrs. Alfred Lyttelton as deputy director, and Mrs. Bayne as chief inspector, came into being. An organising secretary was appointed for each county, and a travelling inspector for each group of counties. The Board then proceeded to take over the already existing war institutions — the Women's Farm Labour Committees, later known as the Women's War Agricultural Committees, which had hitherto been working under the Board of Trade. They asked that the Men's War Agricultural Committees should continue to act in close co-operation with these, and the staff at London headquarters was adequately provided with technical advisers. It could not be said then that the agricultural interests of the country were in the hands—as one farmer bluntly put it—of "poor, ignorant women."

So much for the framework of the organisation. The next step was to convince the farmers of the fact that the labour shortage must come even to them who had been justly spared, and to overcome their characteristic fear of employing female labour and, worse still, female labour in breeches !

"Puttin' an ordinary female into trews," a farm labourer complained bitterly to one county secretary, "and tryin' to pass her off as a farm-hand ! Might just as well tell us that that there scarecrow could clean out my byre 'cause he's dressed up in t' measter's breeks !" It is, however, satisfactory to note that the farmers' appreciation of the workmanlike breeches and overalls grew with their appreciation of the women themselves.

Then came a technical problem. The Board was faced with the difficult question of the training of the women with the following all-important considerations :

Farmers' approval As high a standard of efficiency to be
of the Land Girls attained as possible, as great an economy, and as much saving of valuable time as was consistent with these.

The Board's own attitude on this subject has been frequently misunderstood. It should be urged again and again that the scheme was framed as an emergency measure, and that no one realised the practical significance of this, nor of the harassing difficulties attending it, more keenly than the headquarters staff itself. The labour was sent out to meet a crisis, and with the full knowledge of its limitations in the matter of intrinsic value. It cannot be denied, however, that those farmers who were long-sighted enough and patient enough to "give the lassies a chance" soon found out that this new labour was full of unexpected promise.

The farmers were not asked to run a serious financial risk. The Board of Agriculture only insisted upon a minimum wage of 18s. a week, without board and lodging, to start with ; and later on, when the new labour had established itself, of 22s. per week for the woman who had successfully passed

the test of her efficiency at the training centre, or at an efficiency test examination later on.

But the British farmer, canny as he is until he knows his ground, is open-handed enough when he has found the thing that suits him. "What's worth keeping is worth paying for" is a common saying amongst farmers, and a county organiser in the North of England received the following letter from one of her most diffident employers of women :

If you please, madam (it ran), have I the free hand to raise my new Land Army female (sic.) to 30s. a week ? She has now been with me for three months, and is shaping that promising, I would gladly have the free hand to raise her to 30s., so as to be sure and keep so promising a female.

Is the fact, however, that the farmers were raising her wages in many parts of the country to be taken as proof that the Land Army "female" was so universally successful that they willingly and spontaneously offered 30s. a week to their women employees ? It is not. The Land Army girl was human, and very human. She no more gave universal satisfaction than did her male predecessor. What, then, do the organisers of the scheme actually claim for the Land Army girl ? She had youth, and the adaptability of youth. She had a very good measure of health and strength, both capable of still greater development, she had a twentieth-century education, and, finally, she had the deftness and quick intuition which are her native inheritance. These were in themselves no mean assets. What, then, did she actually achieve in the matter of solid usefulness ?

She milked, and she cleaned out her byres with the best of them. She groomed and carted. She planted and lifted potatoes, and singled and hoed in season. She played her part in the hay and harvest fields. Some of her kind could plough with horses, and the

[Bassano.
HON. MRS. ALFRED LYTTELTON, D.B.E.
Deputy Director of the Women's Branch of the Board of Agriculture, and one of the foundresses of the Women's Land Army in January, 1917.

success of the motor-tractor drivers was the subject of great approval amongst even the more critical of the farmers. She threshed and she thatched. She was especially good with young stock, and perhaps no part of her work appealed more to the girl of town traditions, whose lot it had been, ever since she grew a pigtail and the germ of an individuality, to take motherly care of those even younger and smaller than herself. The Land Army girl was generally good at odd jobs and liked them, lending a willing hand in the house and dairy. She was, moreover, proving herself an adept forester.

Her work frequently showed forethought and judgment, and sometimes it did not. Sometimes she failed altogether; but even then she was no scarecrow in breeches to deceive the unwary, for if she could not **Final verdict on** achieve at any rate some of these things, **the Land Women** she proved her failure as an individual and was seen on the farm no more. If no greater thing could be said of the Land Army girl than that she had served her purpose in a crisis, she would have deserved her country's praise. But those responsible for her claimed more than that, and because they considered her work so full of promise as to be worthy of future development, two objects were specially dear to their hearts. One was that her mental and moral and physical welfare should be cared for in every possible way so that she might in this respect prove to be the gainer by an experience which she would never forget ; and, secondly, that every woman who had proved herself a worthy pioneer in an enterprise so beset with difficulties, and who had shown

Officers of the Women's Royal Naval Service marching past the Director at the Crystal Palace.

"Wrens" semaphore signalling. Right: Dame Katharine Furse, G.B.E., inspecting officers.

Dame Katharine Furse, G.B.E., the Director, addressing ratings of the Women's Royal Naval Service.

Land Army women taking part in a tractor ploughing competition near Maidstone.

Munition girls twisting haybands during their dinner-hour to help a farmer.

A lesson in the handling of motor ploughs and tractors at one of the schools of instruction for women giving their services in land cultivation.

Women students, working under the ægis of the Nottingham Education Committee on the Duke ot Portland's estate at Welbeck Abbey, bringing in Alderney cows from pasture at milking-time.

Woman's part in defeating the German threat to starve out Britain by the submarine campaign:

Farm pupils feeding young pigs at the Women's Farm Colony near Heathfield, Sussex.

Girls, undergoing the eight weeks' course of instruction in land work at an agricultural school in Buckinghamshire, bringing in a sack of corn from the thresher.

A splendid specimen of the Women's Land Army harrowing with four horses in Oxfordshire.

General view of Land Girls at work upon a rick in Buckinghamshire. After two months' training at the centres run by the County Education Committees, the women had acquired sufficient practical knowledge to be detached for service on farms.

Training the Women's Land Army in the theory and practice of all branches of agriculture.

Painting the wing of an aeroplane, and (right) constructing the ribs of the wings.

Making the lining for R.N. non=rigid airships, and (right) testing balance of an airship propeller.

Women workers in the R.N. Air Service: Preparing wire for the external rigging of an airship.

herself capable and possessed of real interest, should be given an opportunity in the future to develop her powers, either in the less trodden field of the Colonies, or, if she were so inclined, in the home country to whom she gave her untried energies in the hour of need.

The Women's Royal Naval Service.

The Women's Royal Naval Service, whose popular name was the "Wrens," was one of the later Women's War Services. It was started towards the end of 1917 with the intention of organising women workers in connection with the Navy, the object being to do as much non-combatant work as possible, and thus release a number of men for more strenuous duties. Since the outbreak of war women had had so many opportunities of working for soldiers that it was a happy as well as a useful idea to raise this service and thus give them an opportunity of doing something for the Navy. A number of women responded directly recruiting started.

Working for the Senior Service

They enrolled for the duration of war ; but if the war should be over in less than a year from the time of their enrolment they must serve for one year. There were two branches of service, mobile and immobile. The former could be sent to work anywhere in the United Kingdom ; the latter were those who, still living at home, were engaged locally. This plan, which was also followed out in other corps, enabled women to join, who otherwise could not do so, and also helped to solve the housing difficulty, which in the early stages of the war was very acute. The members not living at home had hostels provided for them when possible, or else resided in approved lodgings.

They wore a serviceable but smart blue uniform, and, when their work required it, overalls. The motor-drivers had special additions to their uniform suitable to their work.

DAME KATHARINE FURSE, G.B.E.
Appointed Director of the Women's Royal Naval Service, 1917.

DAME FLORENCE LEACH, D.B.E.
Appointed Chief Controller of Queen Mary's Army Auxiliary Corps, 1918.

[Photos: Hoppe.

The officers were trained at the Crystal Palace, and from there were sent off to their allotted appointments.

The actual work done by the service covered a wide range. The women were divided up into chief section leaders and ratings, and the work was classified into different categories. There was a clerical branch, and a household one chiefly composed of cooks and laundresses. There was a section composed of garage workers and a general unskilled branch. The postal workers had a section to themselves. There was a miscellaneous branch, a signal branch, and a very large technical branch. The cookery at Greenwich Hospital was done by a staff of "Wrens."

In the technical branch there were women engaged in what before the war was a man's world. Many trades were classified in the engineering groups ; they included copper-smiths, tinsmiths, plumbers, fitters, and practically every branch of work undertaken in an engineering shed. A good deal of electrical work was also done. There were sail-makers, armourers, and gun cleaners ; photographers were another group of workers ; tracers and draughtswomen another.

Women who were skilled received a higher salary than the unskilled, but new members were taught a skilled trade, and then received pay equal to that of their sisters. The pay of the "Wrens" was a fair wage without being a fancy one, and the women who joined felt that they were doing a real share of war work and, although in many instances skilled workers could obtain a far higher salary if working for private firms, they were content to join up and work for a higher motive than money.

The uniform had always to be worn, and no mufti was allowed to officers and ratings of the mobile branch, but the immobile could wear mufti in their homes. A fortnight's leave was allowed to officers and ratings for each year's service. In exceptional circumstances extra leave was allowed, but no pay was given for the extra time. The women had a fixed amount deducted from their pay to cover their expenses at the hostels or lodgings where they were. The immobile women who lived at home had no reduction made from their pay. If a woman was absent without leave or in excess of paid leave, part of her pay was deducted, the reduction made being one day's pay for each day's or part of a day's absence. The "Wrens" came directly under the Admiralty. On enrolment applicants had to fill up a special form, and among other things agreed that, in matters of discipline, the decision of a naval or W.R.N.S. officer was final ; indeed, the form went on to say "in all matters relating to your service," so that the "Wrens" really felt they were in the Navy.

The Women Police.

By Mrs. Carden.

Women patrols came into existence as early as October, 1914, only a few months after the outbreak of war. The pressing need of some organisation to meet the abnormal social condition was then brought to the notice of Mrs. James Gow, of the Rescue-Preventive Committee of the National Union of Women Workers. It was realised that in those early stages of the war an unusual excitement and unrest prevailed which made the streets a source of danger to the younger and less experienced women. There was no time to be lost. A special committee was at once appointed to deal with the problem, and within a month of the formation of this committee the patrols were actually at work.

To understand the spirit in which this movement began its work, it is necessary to remember that the scheme for placing patrols in the streets for the protection and control of women was inaugurated at the start on a purely voluntary basis. That the organisation came to meet a need was seen at the outset in the keen interest shown in the scheme by those who came forward to offer their services and by the general public. Large numbers of volunteers were forthcoming, and a ready response was made to appeals for funds at a time when general financial anxiety made such a response the more remarkable.

The work was frequently rough and thankless, but the workers were in dead earnest, and, not contented with merely accomplishing their daily round of duty, deterring, warning, and advising, they began at the outset to take a keen personal interest in the women with whom they dealt and to use initiative and forethought on their behalf. They **Work and methods of the Force** realised, as all good social workers realise, that preventive measures were of little use unless accompanied by practical help and encouragement.

As early as November, 1914, mixed clubs were started in various parts of the country. These clubs provided shelter and entertainment for the women, and were largely used and cordially welcomed, not only as a refuge from the darkness and the dangers of the streets but also as places of good cheer. They were the more warmly appreciated for the fact that every girl was not only allowed but encouraged to bring her "boy," and the wisdom of this step is obvious to anyone who knows the girl of the working classes.

The methods on which the new organisation worked were as follows : A body of organisers was appointed and carefully trained in London. These women were sent out into the

BUILDERS OF THE AIRSHIPS.
Women at work on the great British airships of the R class, that surpassed Germany's best Zeppelins in size and power.

fact is significant that within six months of her first occupation of the post the new officer had dealt with over two hundred cases of women in need of personal help and advice.

The work of the women patrols was by no means at an end with the signing of the armistice. Conditions immediately following the war made an even greater call on their activities. To crown the efforts of the patrols, came the demand on the part of the Commissioner of Police for a body of women to work under the regular police and to be salaried out of the Police Fund. It was to the women patrols that the Commissioner looked to form the nucleus of the new force, and the women were carefully selected. **1,500,000 women replacing men** Even more satisfactory was his own statement that it was the success of these women as war workers which induced him to consider their employment in an official and permanent capacity.

Women in Industrial Life.

The war work of a large number of women falls into the sections which have just been described, but that of a still larger number yet remains untold. Of the 1,500,000 women who, it is estimated, were added to the nation's workers as a result of the Great War, the vast majority entered industrial life, in which the demand for them was insatiable, especially when it was realised, as it began to be early in 1915, that Britain would have to take upon herself the lion's share of the allied task. The subject is a big one, so we can only touch here on one or two of its aspects. Munition workers is a designation that covered a vast army of workers at multifarious tasks; they supplied modern warfare with an immense variety of weapons, both of offence and defence, and these, too, in unprecedented quantities. In addition, the work on aeroplanes and on wireless telegraphy deserves a word on account of its novelty; while transport workers became of increasing importance to the community every day.

Early in 1919, to show the extent to which women had displaced men in industrial and commercial life, the authorities issued some instructive figures. An official return said that there were employed in July, 1914, 3,276,000 females, equal to a percentage of 24 of the total number of workpeople in the United Kingdom. By the end of April, 1918, these numbers had increased by 1,532,000, or 37 per cent. The approximate increases, together with the number of females directly replacing males, are shown by the following table:

Occupation.	Estimated Number of Females employed, July, 1914.	Approximate Increase in Numbers.	Number of Females stated by Employers to be directly replacing Males.
Industries	2,176,000	537,000	531,000
Government Establishments ..	2,000	197,000	187,000
Gas, Water, and Electricity (under Local Authorities) ..	600	4,000	4,000
Agriculture in Great Britain (Permanent Labour).. ..	80,000	9,000	40,000
Transport (excluding Tramways under Local Authorities) ..	17,000	78,000	79,500
Tramways (under Local Authorities)	1,200	18,000	17,000
Finance and Banking	9,500	63,000	59,500
Commerce	496,000	354,000	352,000
Professions (employed persons—i.e., except in the case of Hospitals, mainly Clerks	50,500	57,000	22,500
Hotels, Public-houses, Cinemas, Theatres, etc.	181,000	25,000	44,500
Civil Service, Post Office ..	60,500	59,500	64,000
Other Civil Service	5,500	99,500	89,000
Other Services under Local Authorities	196,200	31,000	26,000
Total	3,276,000	1,532,000	1,516,000

country towns to select and train other women as patrols, and before leaving they selected one of their number to act as patrol leader. Full official recognition was given to the work of the patrols by the heads of nearly every Government department, and in July, 1916, a warm tribute was paid to the success of the undertaking by Sir Edward Henry, Commissioner of Police, who, after expressing his cordial appreciation of the work, which he had been watching with keen interest for some time, decided to employ some of the women patrols as auxiliaries to the police. They started in this capacity in Hyde Park. These special women patrols were paid out of the Police Fund. The experiment proved so successful that Sir Edward asked for a further supply of women patrols to work in those streets **Police engage women patrols** where their services were most likely to be specially useful—such as the Strand and Leicester Square—and a little later on, on his recommendation, two women park-keepers were appointed from the ranks of the N.U.W.W. These women had the right to arrest.

Meanwhile the work in the country towns developed rapidly. By June, 1916, salaried working-policewomen were appointed as the result of the excellent work done by the patrols in Bath, Cheltenham, Carlisle, Sheffield, and many other large towns, and their services proved invaluable in the rough manufacturing towns. The policewomen received salaries of from thirty shillings to forty shillings per week with uniform.

So warmly indeed did the women they dealt with respond to the interest of the patrols, that in 1916 Sir Edward Henry was approached on the subject of the appointment of a special woman patrol to deal with the more personal side of the work. Ready consent to this appointment was given; one of the special patrols was detailed for the work, and the

Munition Workers.

Of the various fields of labour open to women after the outbreak of war that of "munitions" occupied the very great majority. The term covered many classes of work, and altogether there were over seven hundred and fifty thousand women employed under this heading. Four hundred thousand of these were engaged on work that women had never done before. The Parliamentary Secretary of the Ministry of Munitions openly stated that "without their help the Germans would have won the war." Women in large numbers were engaged in making shells, bullets, and cartridges.

The Ministry of Munitions started a large number of training centres in London and the provinces, where in a few weeks women were taught a special branch of munition work; it might be lens grinding, or it might be an engineering job, so varied was the work. They were engaged on the most delicate tasks in the manufacture of ammunition. Here they were most skilful, as their

LAST SERVICE OF LOVE.
Members of Queen Mary's Army Auxiliary Corps serving in France tending the graves in a military cemetery.

light touch and small hands made them very suitable workers. Women were employed in very many thousands in filling factories, and they were to be found working among high explosives, handling cordite, and doing the most dangerous forms of work. Not only did they show their disregard of danger by working in a danger zone, but when, unfortunately, an accident happened, they behaved splendidly and showed pluck of which the nation might well be proud. One factory, where all the work carried on was of a dangerous nature, had a woman works manager, and the entire factory was "manned" by women with the exception of a few skilled men.

The delicately nurtured girl was suddenly plunged into factory life, and spent months—in many cases years—in an atmosphere of noise. She stood for long hours, sometimes in uncongenial surroundings, with fellow-workers drawn from all classes. For these things she cared nothing; the one sound she heard from across the sea was "Send us more shells!" One great achievement of the women was the fact that some of them could soon set up their own machines, and set tools as well. In the early days of women's advent in the engineering world this work was supposed to be absolutely outside a woman's sphere, a thing she could never do, but a certain number proved their ability to master it, difficult though it was.

One very satisfactory point in connection with the munition workers was that the health of the women was well maintained, in spite of long hours of hard work and many night shifts. This was certainly due to the care and thought that was devoted to everything connected with their welfare. Many of the factories where they worked had as good an atmosphere as possible; the best systems of ventilation were employed. The girls who worked with any dangerous materials wore special protective clothing as a safeguard against accidents; those, for example, working with acids wore clogs instead of ordinary shoes. Food and recreation, two very important points, were also thoroughly well managed. Good, well-cooked food was provided at little above cost price, and quite an army of workers were engaged in this department.

QUEEN MARY'S ARMY AUXILIARY CORPS REVIEWED BY THE KING AND QUEEN AT ALDERSHOT.
An Army Council instruction published in 1917 approved the formation of this corps to effect the substitution of women for soldiers in certain employments. The corps speedily justified its existence, and the Queen gave her name to it in 1918.

labour, even such work as shoemaking and carpentry, with which women generally were not previously familiar, was very speedily proved, and won highest encomiums from the Army Council.

as cooks in military hospitals and camps were recognised early in the war, and the Marchioness of Londonderry supplied great numbers through the Women's Legion to meet the constant demands of the War Office.

Company of Queen Mary's Army Auxiliary Corps marching back to billets in France, and (right) women carpenters building an extension to their workshops. The practical usefulness of the force in all branches of

Cooks "assembling" the materials for apple-puddings for soldiers' dinners, and (right) at work in an Army camp kitchen at Dartford, in Kent. The advantages to be derived from employing women instead of men

WOMEN SUBSTITUTES FOR SOLDIERS: ONE OF BRITAIN'S SUCCESSFUL INNOVATIONS IN ARMY ORGANISATION FOR ACTIVE SERVICE.

Recreation also required a large amount of labour on the part of those who undertook welfare work. The welfare superintendent had many things to do. It was to her the girls went for advice and help—for one it might be a matter of health, for another some personal grievance, very real perhaps to the girl away from home for the first time; to another a question of meals; to one and all the lady superintendent was mother for the time being. Then the hostels—these had to be run—and their supervision also came under the welfare workers. The heads of the department were never satisfied with their work, but were always on the watch for improvements, and in consequence fresh schemes were continually forthcoming.

Aeroplane Workers.

In the early days of the war it was quite a novelty when women were first employed in the construction of aeroplanes. They were put on wood-work and fabrics, but soon, it is safe to say, there was hardly a part of the manufacture of these machines in which a woman's hand could not be traced.

The wood-work of an aeroplane has to be most carefully made, each piece has to fit exactly into its place; nothing, not even the smallest portion, is used until it **Doping, welding, and** is officially passed. Although when finished **engineering** the wood-work of an aeroplane is very strong, each separate piece is most delicate. This fact makes women very suitable workers, and it is comparatively light work. Women were engaged in doping; and here, although all possible care was taken with reference to ventilation, it was certainly "war work." Many women were engaged as acetylene welders. This was skilled work for which the Ministry of Munitions had special training centres. The women welders were a great success, and theirs was a most important work. In the machinery rooms of aeroplane factories numbers of girls were to be found engaged on various forms of engineering work, and they had mostly been trained in one of the special training centres. While training they learnt to make screws, bolts, and the various metal parts of an aeroplane, including the engine.

The manufacture of the engine is one of the most important parts of an aeroplane. Special factories existed for engines alone. There one saw girls operating milling machines and

AT THE AUTO-MACHINE.
One of the women workers engaged in aircraft construction at a Royal Naval Airship Station; she was the machinist in charge of one of the intricate pieces of machinery employed.

grinding machines, working on valves and other parts of what may be called the heart of the aeroplane.

The life in an engineering shop was quite a new experience for women, and it was wonderful how soon they settled down; and even the noise did not trouble them. The aeroplane workers all wore a suitable dress according to what they were engaged on. The oxy-acetylene welders wore goggles to protect their eyes. All wore overalls best suited to their special work.

The fabric workers had quite dainty work. Here the classes of work are so many and of such completely different character that practically in no other form of war work was such a variety of women workers found. There were skilled, partly skilled, and un- **Fabric workers and** skilled ones. There were jobs that could only **draughtswomen** be undertaken by those who were physically fit, and others that could be done by the women who had not such a good physique. As with shell-making and all other forms of war work, the women were drawn from all classes of society; highly-educated ones, who previously had used their heads and not their hands, came forward as well as those from humbler homes. In one large department, where all the tracing and draughtsmanship was done, women were engaged, and for this department those who had a special aptitude for the work were chosen.

The welfare supervisors did all that was possible to make the workers comfortable and happy, both when off duty and on. In many factories canteens were provided for them where they got their meals, and, when necessary, hostels for those who came from a distance. Various forms of recreation to suit all tastes and classes were not forgotten.

Wireless Workers.

One branch of war work that was undertaken by women who had previously received a scientific training, or who had at least a taste for it, was "wireless work." Their duty was not to operate the wireless apparatus, but to keep it in perfect order. To them fell the task of cleaning and repairing what certainly is one of the most important features in modern warfare.

The more highly skilled the woman the more valuable

WIRE WELDING FOR AIRCRAFT.
Acetylene welding at a Royal Naval Airship Station. The many women who engaged in this important branch of skilled work had to wear goggles for the protection of their eyes.

her work. A course of from six weeks' to two months' training was given to the wireless workers, and then they were appointed to their posts. The majority worked in London, but some in the provinces. Those who were the most highly trained were able, not only to keep the apparatus in order, but to take to pieces, do any necessary repairs, and then put the apparatus together again. At Woolwich the women were able to give valuable assistance to the Royal Engineer officers who were responsible for supplying wireless apparatus to the fighting forces at home and abroad. The hours were rather shorter than those of the ordinary war workers in factories, for this was thought desirable, as the handling of such delicate instruments is a considerable mental strain.

The women wireless workers first started their work in June, 1917. They were civilians, they belonged to no special corps, and consequently wore no uniform, their work being done in overalls. The work was found to be very suitable for women; their hands being smaller than men's hands, they were just right for handling delicate apparatus. Few people realised the enormous amount of wireless apparatus in daily use in war time, and, as it was by its very nature not always before the public eye, it was apt to be overlooked, the women workers being practically unknown outside scientific circles, who realised how valuable their work was. They might almost be looked upon as the V.A.D.'s of the wireless world, as their time was devoted to tending the sick and injured apparatus, in the special centre where all apparatus found its way to be overhauled and then sent off again to active service.

Transport Workers.

During the Great War the traveller by train, tram, or omnibus became quite familiar with the women workers, especially in London. They were employed in thousands, and on the Underground, District, and Tube railways, acted as

SAFEGUARDING THE KENTISH FRUIT CROP.
Women of the Land Army engaged in spraying fruit trees in the Maidstone district to free them from insect pests. Women entered largely into all kinds of work connected with increasing and protecting all home-grown supplies of food.

lift operators, ticket collectors, and gate-women on the trains. Some were porters, others travelling ticket inspectors, and clerks in the booking-office. The London General Omnibus Company employed about 2,100 women on omnibuses as conductors and time-keepers at points, and the Underground railways of London a large number.

Women were also largely employed by other railway companies, and proved themselves capable workers. During the air raids those employed on omnibuses behaved splendidly in the face of danger, and the same may be said of those who worked on the Tubes, where the dense crowds that assembled made their work very trying. A large number of women were engaged on the trams as conductors. They had to undergo a special course of training before taking up any branch of the work, for to "conduct" an omnibus or tram requires a good deal more head-work than many people think. A good many of the women engaged as conductors on omnibuses and trams were women whose husbands had been called up.

Women's courage during air-raids

There was one branch of war work undertaken by women that is practically unknown, but that was one of vital importance to everybody. This was the work done by them at Messrs. McNamara's in connection with the Royal Mails. In this employment women who had had experience with horses found plenty of scope for their services. As soon as it was known that they were wanted, first-rate whips came forward, and instead of coach-and-tandem driving took the reins of the Royal Mails. But the work was no pastime, driving in the early hours of a winter morning, or the heat of a noonday sun, month after month. None were taken on but those who were willing to work hard.

Besides the drivers there was another class of worker—lady grooms. The majority of these were girls who had plenty of previous experience with horses, and were anxious to turn their knowledge to national use. The innovation was at first looked upon with great distrust by the men workers, but in a short while the women not only proved

WOMEN FORESTERS AT WORK.
Members of the Women's Forestry Corps engaged in tree-felling. In all parts of the country where timber was obtainable camps of the W.F.C. were established, and the women proved themselves thoroughly capable in all branches of woodcraft.

themselves capable workers, but by their grit and hard work won the respect and esteem of all in the employ of Messrs. McNamara & Co. Not only did women drive and groom the horses, but there was a woman supervisor who was head of what might be called the welfare section. In her office each horse had his "card," and she could tell you in one moment all about him. The horses had the greatest care taken of them, and the stable-women had all up-to-date appliances, such as electric brushes, to groom them with.

The Wives and Mothers at Home.

In conclusion, one large body of women workers, too often forgotten, and yet perhaps the largest of all, should be mentioned. Undistinguished by any attractive uniform, with no prospect of high wages, or bonuses, or extra pay of any kind, with no material reward before them, and without, in many instances, a day's rest or relaxation, the housewives and mothers of Britain carried on bravely during the weary months of war.

It does not sound much. It was the obvious thing for any woman to do, one might have said, but there were countless heroines among these women, who cleaned and sewed and mended, fed hungry little mouths, practised rigorous and unwonted economies, disguised their anxieties, and suffered deprivations cheerfully to keep things going till their "man" came home.

It was not one class alone, either. High and low alike felt the burden of living under war conditions; but the daily problems of food shortage, the cost of clothing and fuel, and the scarcity of every kind of domestic help made life increasingly and especially difficult for the women with little children.

The rationing system

Before the rationing of meat and butter was introduced, the food queues all over the kingdom witnessed to the crying need for a drastic change in methods of distribution. Hours were spent daily in all weathers, waiting and then struggling at different shops for necessaries, and it was on the shoulders of the housewives that the chief weight of this anxiety and weariness fell. Happily, with the rationing system, things became somewhat better, and supplies were more fairly allotted and distributed, but at various times the milk shortage was acute, and this, with the augmented cost of all infants'

foods, and in many cases shortage of these also, added to the mothers' anxieties.

Gradually the question of cost became an increasingly serious problem to the wife who had to provide for her household on a limited income. In 1918, especially, prices, already high, seemed to rise almost daily, and with many it was not a question of what one could have, but what could one do without. Compare, for instance, the following prices taken from the books of an ordinary middle-class household for 1914 and 1918 respectively to see what housekeeping meant, even when circumstances allowed some addition to the pre-war weekly allowance.

Butter was 2s. 6d. a pound, instead of 1s. 3d. Golden syrup, formerly 6½d., was then 1s. 10½d. for a two-pound tin. Matches had jumped from 1½d. a dozen to 1½d. a box; and new-laid eggs from 1s. 6d. per dozen to prices as high as 8d. and 9d. each. Bacon had risen from 10d. to 2s. 4d. and 2s. 6d. per pound; meat had doubled and more than doubled in price. Marmalade had gone up from 10½d. to 2s. 10½d. for a three-pound jar, and tea had doubled in price. Instances could be multipled, but those quoted, added to the increased cost of bread and milk, gave the mothers exercise enough for their wits. Soap, brushes, kitchen utensils, chinaware, everything went up in the same ratio, and a breakage, once a misfortune, now often resembled a calamity. Children's clothing was especially difficult. Many articles were almost unobtainable, and woollen goods in particular attained a price prohibitive to those with slender incomes. Coal, and consequently gas, became scarcer and dearer; household help of any kind was almost impossible to get, and fresh difficulties seemed to crop up daily. Taken altogether, food was certainly doubled in price, and at such prices, moreover, was usually hard to get.

Comparison of prices

All honour to the wives and mothers of Britain, the "woman who stayed at home," who fought for the home and the children in these circumstances. More than ever before, in view of the serious fall in the birth-rate, the lives of the children were precious, and the nation as a whole began to realise this fact. The care which the mothers, and the mothers alone, can give them, is one of the nation's assets. How unselfishly it was given during the four years of war few fully realise, but its reward was certain.

BOUND FOR THE EASTERN EUROPEAN FRONT WITH TRAINED HELP FOR THE WOUNDED.
Section of the Women's Reserve Ambulance Corps serving with the Scottish Women's Hospitals paraded in London with their cars and equipment before driving to Liverpool, whence they embarked for Russia where, as in Serbia, Rumania, and elsewhere abroad, they did notably good work.

Happy Belgian civilians laden with bundles and boxes hurrying back to Antwerp immediately the retreat of the Germans made their return home possible.

Directly the Dover-Ostend Channel service was resumed, Belgian refugees in Britain streamed home in thousands, and busy scenes like this were witnessed daily in Ostend Harbour. In circle. A repatriated family enjoying the coffee and the milk waiting ready for them on their own shore.

HOMEWARD RUSH OF BELGIAN REFUGEES AFTER THEIR LONG SUFFERING AND EXILE.

THE DELIVERANCE OF BELGIUM.

By Emile Cammaerts.

Complete Devastation of West Flanders and Comparative Immunity of the Countryside beyond Roulers and Menin—Meeting near Roulers with the First of the Liberated Population—Belgian's Thrilling Moments in Hulste—Reception of the British at Menin and of the French at Roulers—Dramatic Liberation of Ostend—Visit of King Albert and Queen Elizabeth—Bitter Sufferings of the Ostendais during the Occupation—Burgomaster Visart's Description of the Liberation of Bruges—King Albert's Re-entry into Bruges—Agony of the People of Courtrai up to the Very Moment of Deliverance—Memorable Scenes Attending the Liberation of Tournai—German Preparations to Evacuate Brussels—Collapse of Discipline among the German Troops—Day of Reckoning for the Activists in Ghent—Solemnity of the Belgian Army's March through Flanders—Joy and Illumination in Antwerp—King Albert's State Re-entry into Brussels—Urgent Problems Confronting the Belgian Government on the Morrow of Liberation—Unavoidable Delay in Beginning the Work of Reconstruction—Its Effect on the Moral of the People—Territorial Claims Presented by the Commission for Belgian Affairs in Paris—Historical Review of the Treaties Settling the Frontiers, Neutrality, and Inviolability of Belgium—The Question of Limburg and Luxemburg.

T HE story of the home-coming of the Belgian Army and of the liberation of Flanders and Hainault up to the armistice follows closely the operations of the allied armies under the supreme command of King Albert.

Owing chiefly to the bad weather, which caused transport difficulties, and also to the strong resistance put up in certain strategical positions by the rearguards of the retreating German armies, the allied advance was not continuous. The first attack, begun on September 28th, 1918, carried the Belgian and French troops beyond the Houthulst Wood as far as Roulers, and the British close to Wervicq and Menin. The second (October 14th) swept through the greater part of Flanders, as far as the Lys Canal between Bruges and Ghent; Thielt, Thourout, Ostend, Bruges, and Courtrai being evacuated by the enemy. The third move, early in November, which liberated Audenarde and Tournai and brought the Belgians to the gates of Ghent, was interrupted by the armistice.

Very little was seen of the civil population during the first stage of the advance. It took place on shell-shattered ground from which four years of artillery fire had obliterated every vestige of human habitation. The former emplacements of small towns, like Dixmude, and large villages like Langemarck, Poelcappelle, Passchendaele, and many others were scarcely distinguishable. The spots where thousands of people had dwelt for many generations had been wiped out, and in many places signposts were the only landmarks available. The very features of the

AN HONOURED GUEST.
Admiral Sir David Beatty, Commander-in-Chief of the British Grand Fleet, with King Albert, whose guest at Brussels he was after the victory of the Allies.

country had been changed, so that maps could be of very little use. New roads, new railway lines, had replaced the old ones, and even the streams had changed their course. Mile after mile the Allies, after crushing the enemy's first lines of defence, advanced through a desert of shell-pocked mud where the black outlines of a few mangled trees showed against the grey sky. The few ruins that remained were subjected to enemy fire, so that some of the Belgian soldiers wondered for a time if all their efforts had not been in vain and if the greater part of their martyred country would not be laid waste before the end of hostilities. Those who had come from this part of West Flanders could not recognise the place where they had spent their youth.

When, after a few days, the offensive was resumed, the aspect of the country changed suddenly. Beyond Roulers and Menin the Flemish countryside revealed itself as the promised land for which Belgian hearts had hungered during so many years and of which many a soldier had dreamt during his restless sleep in the Yser trenches. When the sun showed itself between the autumn clouds it shone on quiet fields, red-tiled roofs, whitewashed walls, rows of high poplars, and stumpy pollard willows bending over the rushing brooks. Those who had taken part in the Antwerp retreat and the Battle of the Yser remembered. It was almost four years since, through the same autumn landscape, they were struggling desperately, one against five, in their last defences in the last strip of free Belgium. They could scarcely believe then in victory; they fought doggedly to fulfil their duty, to avenge their wrongs.

IMPERIAL GUILE EXPOSED BY THE CAMERA.
Kaiser Wilhelm awaiting the Emperor of Austria's arrival at Spa, August 14th, 1918, giving one of his Staff a final injunction to be circumspect and wary.

And now, after the long wait and many disappointments, they had come at last into their own. From one day to another the mirage had become a living picture, the dream had materialised, the Flemish plains, glowing with Flemish light, lay once more before them.

The transition between the devastated war zone and normal life was not nearly so sudden on the allied side. Furnes had been badly shelled and bombed; there was scarcely a street in Dunkirk which had not suffered. The Germans had carried war against the civilians as far as Boulogne and Calais. The Allies, on the other hand, had refrained from bombarding places situated behind the war zone unless this was absolutely necessary. Their airmen succeeded in inflicting as little damage as possible on the civil population. Ghistelles aerodrome showed evident **Country found** traces of their visitations, but Ghistelles **little damaged** village, just beside it, was practically untouched. The port of Bruges was wrecked, but the town had been spared. The German motto " It is war " did not explain everything.

Thus the vision of his land, apparently unspoiled, came as a surprise to the Belgian soldier. It needs a good deal to alter a landscape, and if the enemy had left his mark on many towns, if the people had been reduced to a state of semi-starvation, the country was still, in its broad outlines, what it had been four years before. This revelation came as a relief after the depressing scenery of No Man's Land. Nature, which seemed so indifferent during the dark days of defeat, smiled once more on the conquerors.

All this the soldiers felt dimly, but the climax must have come for them when they met for the first time their liberated compatriots. During the fighting round Roulers some peasants were seen driving their cattle before them to the allied lines. They often came under fire, but they preferred taking the risks of this perilous journey to remaining any longer in the German lines exposed to violence and deportation. Their fears most of the time proved groundless, because the enemy had not time to carry into effect his intention of taking away with him the civil population of the evacuated territory. The men from seventeen to forty-five years of age had been summoned a fortnight or a month before, and a certain number had been taken away to be forced to work behind the lines. But many, and in several places most of them, had succeeded in hiding themselves in cellars, in barns, in the crypts of churches, even in the chimneys of abandoned factories. The **Greetings from** Germans were kept too busy to organise **the population** search-parties, as they had done before, and as soon as their liberators entered towns and villages the unshaven and bedraggled men emerged from their hiding-places to greet them.

As for the old men, the women, and children, they simply refused to go when ordered to do so, and, most of the time the officers were not in a position to compel them, owing to the slackness of discipline among their soldiers and the hurried character of the retreat. The people took to their cellars when the battle-front reached them, and did not wait until the end of the bombardment of the retreating German batteries to rush towards their friends and warn them of the movements of the enemy.

The following extract from a letter written by a Belgian officer who entered Hulste affords a good example of the scenes

PROUD IN ADVERSITY.
A captain of the R.M.L.I., captured during the naval raid on Zeebrugge in 1918, was brought before the Kaiser, who offered him his hand. The attention was ignored.

which took place at the time in almost every town and village of West Flanders :

On the Lys,
October 17th, 1918.
Yesterday I passed one of the most thrilling days of my existence. Early in the morning, having spent the day and night before in the second line, I went with my battalion to the first line so as to continue our advance towards the Lys. And so it happened that I was one of the first to enter the village of Hulste, one of the first places of any importance anything like intact that we have found in reconquered Belgium.

I can only give you a feeble idea of this spectacle. My companies advanced with caution south of the place, and were fighting step by

VON BISSING'S SUCCESSOR.
General von Swehl, who was appointed German Governor-General of Belgium in succession to the notorious Von Bissing.

step to the north with groups of enemy machine-gunners who tried to check us, pushing them back, killing them, and taking them prisoner; then in the centre the advance with the Staff took place, and our entry into the main road of the village.

Windows and doors opened one after another, heads appeared and looked at us anxiously. Questions were thrown at us: "Are you English?" (This because of our khaki uniforms and the stories by the Germans, who had announced an attack by "Tommies" because the Belgians were incapable of one!)

Then a regular delirium. Cries all round: "'T Zijn Belgen! 'T Zijn Belgen!" (They are Belgians!). Hundreds of persons rushed out of cellars and filled up the street. Women, men, old men, children, shrieked and shouted, laughed, wept, and embraced the soldiers; never stopped shaking hands with all who passed, their eyes shining with joy.

Little girls, boys of four or five, ran by our sides shouting "Welkom! Welkom!" Women called to us, their eyes full of tears: "We have been waiting for you for four years."

When I had got over my first excitement, I asked, "Well, aren't you going to hang out the Belgian flag?"

Immediately, as if I had fired a train of powder, the cry ran through the crowd: "Flags, flags!" And by some extraordinary phenomenon they appeared from all corners. My adjutant saw **Hulste re-hoists the Belgian flag** an old woman go into her garden and dig up a little box out of which she took an enormous Belgian flag, which a few minutes later fluttered joyously from the front of her house.

Then came our entry into the main square in front of the church, where we were received by the old priest in tears, supported by the local policeman in a brand-new uniform. Accompanied by violent bell-ringing the good man read out a proclamation announcing to the civil population the victorious entry of the Belgian Army on October 16th, 1918, into the village of Hulste, which the Germans had seized on October 17th, 1914.

The reception of the British at Menin and of the French at Roulers was not less cordial. The last German had scarcely left those places when flags were hoisted in every house, and the liberated population came out of their cellars to greet their friends, bringing them the few tokens of welcome which they could still extract from their depleted larders and plundered wine-cellars. While ammunition dumps exploded in the neighbourhood, and German shells burst in the market-place, the people fraternised happily with the soldiers. It seemed as if all the enemy's frightfulness could not overshadow their happiness. The explosion of delay-action mines sounded like the salute of many guns proclaiming victory.

The liberation of Ostend, on October 17th, was particularly dramatic owing to the emulation between the Allies to reach the town, and to the presence of the King and Queen of the

IN THE LAST DAYS OF BELGIUM'S AGONY.
French troops advancing into Audenarde in the opening days of November, 1918, had to exercise great caution, and their machine-gunners were still crawling along the streets when a priest emerged from a building and announced that the Germans had evacuated the town.

Belgians, who landed in the port while the firing was still taking place in the outskirts.

A French airman, in the early morning, noticing that the German guns remained silent, ventured to fly at a low altitude and landed ultimately near the town. He brought back the news that the Germans had left during the night. A little later, at 11 a.m. a British airman, after landing on the beach, was able to communicate with Vice-Admiral Keyes' flotilla, which was approaching the coast. The vice-admiral succeeded in landing in a whaler, and was enthusiastically received, but, as a German battery had opened fire on the beach, he decided to re-embark in order not to give any pretext to the enemy for shelling the town.

Meanwhile, King Albert and Queen Elizabeth had expressed a desire to visit Ostend. Vice-Admiral Keyes placed at their disposal the destroyer Termagant, which reached the port in the afternoon, the party being cheered by Ostend boys perched on the hull of the old Vindictive. The daring of this action of the Belgian sovereigns could not surprise those who had witnessed the risks taken every day by them at La Panne and on the Yser. But the Ostendais, who had only heard of them, did not expect such an early visit.

Their enthusiasm was indescribable. As **Ostend welcomes** soon as the shrill voice of a few urchins **King and Queen** on the quays announced "They have come," all the inhabitants left in the town rushed towards the port and the town-hall, where they knew the sovereigns would be greeted by the burgomaster and aldermen. It was with great difficulty that King Albert reached the centre of the town, and for a time the Queen was separated from him by the women and children crowding around her and cheering themselves hoarse. In the town-hall King Albert congratulated the people of Ostend, and thanked them for their patriotic attitude during the occupation. The burgomaster was so deeply moved that he only managed to say a few words of thanks. The circumstances did not lend themselves to long speeches. Booby-traps, carefully laid by the enemy before leaving the town, were exploding from time to time, and it was well known—as subsequently discovered—that the Germans had left behind them some of their agents, who only awaited their opportunity to avenge the Fatherland. The return to the port was more orderly, the people lining the pavement and bursting spontaneously into patriotic songs. When

LITTER OF WAR ON THE VICTORS' ROAD TO ROULERS.
Field-kitchen and ammunition lorries on the march towards Roulers in the great advance which the allied forces under King Albert's command began on October 14th, while the British Fleet co-operated off the Belgian coast. Roulers was recovered that day and a line established south-east towards Courtrai.

King Albert reached the Termagant the emotion again was intense : " You must not go. You must come back to-morrow." They came back next day in a Handley Page piloted by a British officer, and circled six times at a low altitude over the town. The explosions had not yet ceased and some firing was taking place in the outskirts.

Early in the afternoon of the 17th the Belgian infantry, coming from Nieuport and across the Yser floods, reached Ostend on their way to Bruges and the Dutch frontier. The soldiers had passed through Lombaertzyde, Westende, Middelkerke, and Mariakerke without meeting any resistance. Those who had come from Antwerp in 1914 recognised the road. They had passed then with a

Sufferings of the Ostendais heavy heart through these cheery Belgian seaside places. The havoc wrought along the coast during four years did not, however, damp their enthusiasm. Was it not understood that Germany would foot the bill ?

If the buildings of Ostend had been comparatively spared, the people had a terrible story to tell. Out of 45,000 inhabitants only 25,000 remained in the town. Some had sought refuge abroad. Others had been deported to work behind the German lines, even the work of women being requisitioned. If the mass deportations to Germany had practically ceased in April, 1917, forcible work had never stopped in the army zone (Etappengebiet). Flanders and Hainault had been subjected to such levies from time to time up to the eve of liberation. Since the recent allied offensive the deportees had again been sent towards Germany. At the beginning of the month one thousand two hundred citizens from Ostend had been seized. A fortnight later a second raid yielded three hundred men, and the rapid and unexpected progress of the Allies had alone prevented the authorities from taking away those who escaped. During the last months all the copper and bronze had been requisitioned, even the peal of bells of the town-hall, and all the wool, even the mattresses of sick people. Under the iron rule of Admiral Fischer the people had been watched narrowly, and fines and imprisonment inflicted for the most trivial offences. But the traitors who had helped the enemy in his evil work were still much more to blame. In every town, every village, on the day of liberation popular reprisals took place. Activists were hunted down, and had the Belgian gendarmes and police not been on the alert those who had not escaped to Holland or Germany would have been lynched. Any man suspected of trading with the enemy was promptly denounced, and a certain number of women were roughly handled, their heads being shorn as a distinctive mark of shame. Forbearance is no Flemish quality.

Burgomaster Visart, who in spite of his great age—eighty-two years—had so energetically opposed German policy and consequently been dismissed by the occupying authorities, gave a vivid description of the liberation of Bruges. News of the allied progress had reached the town, and the intense traffic, directed mostly towards Ghent, was an evident sign that a change would soon occur. For several days and nights people were watching. They were not allowed to keep any light burning, but they were too anxious to go to sleep. " Would Bruges come in the fighting zone ? " they asked themselves. " Would they be obliged to leave their town and take to the road or to shelter in their cellars ? " Gradually, during the night of the 18th, the noise of heavy traffic upon the cobble-stones diminished. At 2 a.m. complete silence ; two hours later a solitary cry : " They have gone ! " A fisherman, who had watched the comings and goings of the Germans, was shouting in the market-place. He was soon joined by a few men who, after hearing from him that the

"THE TUBE" AT NIEUPORT.
In order to revictual the Belgian firing-line in front of Nieuport without exposing the fatigue-parties to enemy fire, miles of tunnel like this were constructed under Nieuport.

last German convoy had disappeared through the " Porte de Gand," ran along the main streets shouting the good news. People opened their doors and windows, lit their lamps, hoisted their flags—preserved so long for this memorable occasion. At dawn the town was ready to receive her guests.

But Bruges hospitality was no longer what it had been. A Cabinet Minister came to spend the night at the burgomaster's house. He was obliged to sleep on a sack filled with straw and newspapers. The bishop himself had nothing else to offer. A few days later, partly with the help of material and food provided by the Army, the hotels frequented by officers and war correspondents were able to provide their guests with a comfortable bed and decent food—at a price.

But anybody acquainted with the country must have been painfully shocked at the situation brought about by the enemy's seizures and requisitions. The latter amounted to no less than £1,000,000 for Bruges alone. The principal factory, " La Brugeoise," employing before the war 2,500 workmen, had been ruined, all the machinery being taken away. Elsewhere, in Brussels and in certain parts of the country under civil government, the situation may have been better, the people there having succeeded in hiding many requisitioned articles and in avoiding some of the German regulations. But in Ostend, Bruges, Ghent, Tournai, Mons—in all the region liberated on the eve of the armistice—the pressure of the military, sole master in the army zone, had been relentless.

British visitors who reached Bruges on the morrow of the evacuation were afforded many opportunities of realising the true character of German oppression. After visiting the small cemetery outside the town, where they found Captain Fryatt's grave surrounded by thirteen crosses bearing the names of Belgian martyrs executed for some " political crime," they were shown the prison in which the captain had spent his last days on his return from Germany. There, in her neat parlour, the Mother Superior in charge of the women's quarters was able to relate some of her experiences. She had been the only person in Bruges allowed to bring to the prisoners a few comforts before their execution, and the little parlour had witnessed terrible scenes when mothers and wives bade a last farewell to the noble men who had given their life in order to serve their country. Sometimes many days passed between the condemnation and the execution, and at the last moment orders were altered so that the family went away comforted, trusting that the death sentence would be reprieved. The execution of four men accused of espionage had been thus postponed twice—and finally carried out.

The Mother Superior had also a very touching story to tell about a little boy of fourteen sentenced to a fortnight's imprisonment for having played the " Brabançonne " on his fiddle. The mother, who was condemned " for listening to the tune," was confined in an adjoining cell, and, when the German sentry retired to take his meal, the good Sisters contrived to extract the boy from his cell **Poignant stories of Bruges** through the peep-hole—he was so slight that he slipped through easily—so that he could see his mother.

According to Admiral Schröder's orders, an alderman of Bruges had to be present at every execution. Thus Captain Fryatt's hasty execution was witnessed at least by one friend. The firing-squad arrived at the barracks preceded by a military band, and the military commandant of Bruges, Von Buttlar, strode about the courtyard smoking his cigar as the order to fire was given. A few grim touches suggested what life must have been for the peaceful Brugeois under the iron heel of the enemy. A girl who tried to take a parcel to a British prisoner before her door was struck in the face by

Instruments and apparatus belonging to the Ecole Militaire, Brussels, which the Germans had packed up, but had no opportunity to remove.

Packing-cases left in the Ecole Militaire by the Huns, filled with apparatus which they had intended to carry away as loot.

Movable electric cranes in Ostend Harbour destroyed by the Germans just before they evacuated the Belgian naval bases on October 16th, 1918.

Swing-bridge of the Outer Port, Ostend, broken by the discomfited Huns. Before leaving they also tried to bottle up the harbour completely.

"Tirpitz" Battery, Ostend, in which, though they removed the breech-blocks and dismantled the pieces, the Germans had to leave the guns.

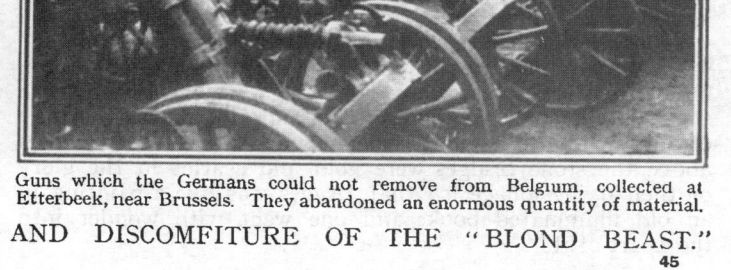

Guns which the Germans could not remove from Belgium, collected at Etterbeek, near Brussels. They abandoned an enormous quantity of material.

PROOFS OF THE CUPIDITY, DESTRUCTIVENESS, AND DISCOMFITURE OF THE "BLOND BEAST."

the sentry, and the scar was still visible. A little farther on in the street Von Schröder had shot a dog with his revolver, because the animal, no doubt of Flemish breed, had dared to show fight when provoked by the admiral's huge Dane.

King Albert and Queen Elizabeth reached Bruges on the 20th. They stayed only a short time, and returned the next day with Prince Leopold, when they were received by Burgomaster Visart, reinstated in his office, and the Communal Council. This time they were recognised, and their car, surrounded by a delirious crowd, progressed slowly through the narrow streets. The formal entry took place on the 25th, when King Albert, surrounded by Belgian and Allied Staffs, reviewed his troops in the large market-place under the great tower of the belfry.

Ostend had only been the prelude of the Royal progress. Bruges was the first act. Those last days of autumn were wonderful, with the soft glowing October light, the crisp air,

AT THE JOURNEY'S END.
The Belgian ship Ville de Liège, used as a hospital-ship during the war, arriving at Ostend Harbour with refugees repatriated from England.

the mellow autumnal haze, the perfect stillness of the air—most wonderful in liberated Bruges amidst the radiance of colours and the constant peal of bells. The "dead city" was strangely alive. Helmeted warriors passed through the great square and the narrow streets amidst the happy citizens dressed in their Sunday best, and the old houses, the great towers, the lofty churches which had witnessed the intense life of the Communes, the gorgeous pageants of the Burgundian period, and the bitter ordeal of recent years, seemed to awaken from their dream amidst the flourish of trumpets and the blaze of a thousand flags.

"For a time, when King Albert reviewed his troops," wrote Philip Gibbs, "the people of Bruges held back in a hollow square, but afterwards, when he went up the steps of the Governor's house, they broke bounds, and tens of thousands of them surged round him cheering that tall figure—who looked down at them with his hand at the salute—with most joyous and wonderful emotion. From hundreds of old houses in Bruges long banners floated, with the rich colours of the Belgian flag, and on this splendid day of autumn the trees along the canals and the walls of houses above the stone bridges were gold and scarlet in the glory of their dying foliage, so that Bruges was like a painting in an old illuminated book, and one went with wonder into the heart of it.

"The belfry rang out a joyous carillon, and from other tall towers of churches, built high, like dream castles, above the gabled roofs, there was the booming of deep-toned bells, very solemn below the singing notes of the belfry chimes. Voices of many centuries seemed to mingle with shouts of living people, and four years of agony were drawn into the past history of Bruges when there were other wars and other servitudes, and the music of the bells was full of the old sadness of life, mingled with that dancing carillon, like the laughter of children who forget."

Meanwhile the Belgian vanguard, **Courtrai shelled** pursuing the enemy towards Ghent, had **to the very last** been stopped along the Lys Canal, where the enemy put up a strong defence. Bruges had had a wonderful escape.

The position of other towns, like Courtrai, was far less favourable. They remained many days in the front line, and paid so heavily for liberation that when it came at last the inhabitants were too worn out to rejoice. In Courtrai the British held one bank of the canal, while the greatest part of the town, in which 30,000 civilians remained, was still in German hands. Here, also, soldiers witnessed a constant procession of men, women, and children, some of them pushing perambulators, passing through the lines, often exposed to shell fire. The troops worked round the town in order to spare the people the horrors of street fighting. At last, on October 19th, the Germans began to evacuate the place. But no sooner had they left it than their batteries, established east of Courtrai, bombarded the centre of the town with high-velocity and gas shells. The Gothic town-hall and the old Church of St. Martin were badly scarred, and many civilians were killed and gassed. In one day, the 20th, five hundred shells fell on the market-place. Courtrai was not the only

WHEN OVERCROWDING WAS CHEERFULLY ENDURED.
Belgian officials examining the papers of returned refugees on their arrival at Ghent Station. In circle All the available rolling-stock in Belgium, including much left by the Germans, was crowded when the refugees began to return, passengers standing on the footboards with bicycles and bundles.

place where people died on the threshold of liberty and peace. Many villages on the Belgian front suffered the same fate, and more than once soldiers rushed to their homes only to discover the dead bodies of their wives and children, who had refused to leave in order to meet them sooner. Most of these bombardments were useless, since no allied soldiers passed through these places, but German methods of frightfulness were to be pursued to the very end, and the Belgian civilians had to suffer for their friends' victories in 1918 as they had had to suffer for their defeats in 1914.

When the advance was resumed all along the line on November 3rd, Hanskerke, Landeghem, and Tronchiennes were badly damaged. The wonderful little Gothic town-hall at Audenarde was not spared, and the great Cathedral of Tournai received its due share of Germany's parting gifts.

This historical town of Wallonie was, nevertheless, the scene of a great British pageant of liberation. Severe deportations had taken place there a month before, 10,000 men being taken away. For a fortnight the 25,000 people who had remained had lived in their cellars, awaiting patiently the end of their last trial. Placards announcing the forthcoming armistice had greatly excited the troops.

Thanksgiving at Tournai

Houses had been looted, and during the last days soldiers had been seen going to their trenches in fancy uniforms, some of them substituting stolen top-hats for their steel helmets. On the night of November 8th officers had been seen indulging in a last orgy at the local hotel. When the next day, at dawn, a British sergeant crept over a bridge on the canal in order to reconnoitre, he was met by a joyful crowd who told him that the last German machine-gunners had left their post. Flags were hoisted, and, while shells were bursting on the Grand' Place, the cathedral bells rang merrily and bunting appeared at every window. The British Staff arrived at noon, and the next day, as soon as the enemy bombardment allowed it, the people congregated in the vast nave of the cathedral to join in a solemn Thanksgiving Service.

The *Te Deum*, which was sung at eleven o'clock (wrote the correspondent of the "Morning Post"), brought to the cathedral a congregation which filled the nave, the aisles, the transepts, and the triforium, and overflowed into the streets. When the stately figure of the bishop, in cloth of gold, mitre, and brocaded cope, turned from the altar towards his expectant flock a flood of emotion swept over the crowded cathedral and shook our very hearts. A priest at the great organ in the west gallery put all his soul into the strains of the "Brabançonne." The ancient nave vibrated with it as the bishop came slowly towards the west door, his hand uplifted in benediction. I do not think the people saw him till he was at their side, for all eyes were fixed on the flag of red and yellow and black borne aloft at the head of the procession by an old man, down whose thin cheeks the tears coursed as he tried to keep erect and hold aloft the emblem of freed Belgium.

So completely did the people abandon themselves to their rejoicing that they brought this memorable ceremony to an unheard-of, almost an astounding climax. At the west door the bishop halted for a moment, the organ paused, and mighty cheers swept the congregation—cheers for the King, for Belgium brought out of her bondage, for the Allies who had set her free.

The streets of Tournai were like a carnival when the canons went out into the sunshine. Scottish troops in kilts were marching behind their pipes escorted by a glad throng, and after them came Devons and other English County battalions, each with its attendant throng, winding through the narrow streets between the tall Flemish houses, from which innumerable flags fluttered in the crisp autumn breeze. The President of the tribunal of Tournai, in his cocked hat of ceremony

RECONSTRUCTION FOLLOWING HARD ON DESTRUCTION.
Engineers of the Belgian Army laying a new railway track at Ghent Station. Evacuated by the invader on November 10th, Ghent was comparatively little damaged structurally, and repairs were begun at once.

REMOVING THE MARK OF THE BEAST.
Belgian workmen taking down the iron-work of Ghent Railway Station, which the Germans destroyed when evacuating the town on November 10th, the night before the armistice took effect.

and snowy shirt-front, pressed through the crowd to shake our officers by the hand as they passed, and the remaining magistrates kept darting eagerly into the maze of traffic to greet their deliverers. Nuns in white and grey habits gathered at street corners and smiled benignantly on the soldiers, houses were thrown open, and all that Tournai had was at the bidding of the British.

Then came the wonderful news, expected by the allied troops and by all those who had been able to follow closely the developments of military operations during the last month, a welcome surprise to the majority of the Belgian people, who did not realise how close they were to the long-delayed final liberation. For the first time after four years, on November 11th, in the morning, the guns were silent. The armistice had been signed. British troops marched towards Mons with bands playing, officers fired rockets, airmen indulged in joy-rides over the heads of amazed cottagers, and the soldiers, as they passed, cried "Guerre finie! Boche napoo!" The news spread like wildfire. Children and women rushed from their homes with flowers in their hands and laughter on their lips. The war was ended. It had ended where it had begun for Britain—on the edge of Hainault, in view of Mons' towers.

Meanwhile in Brussels extraordinary events were taking place. For a month the capital had lived in a state of suppressed excitement caused less by the news that could be read between the lines of the censored papers than by the preparations made by the enemy to evacuate the town. The archives had been removed from the sixty offices occupied by German bureaucracy. Hundreds of boxes filled with documents were being constantly loaded on military vans stationed before the Kommandantur and its countless dependencies. Then the German women had departed, the "Amazons" employed in the General Government's offices. The civilian employees had followed suit, and the Red Cross ambulances were removed to Germany. The Bruxellois watched these signs intently, and, on the morrow of the first German reply to President Wilson, a "general rehearsal" took place in the suburbs. Flags were hoisted in many houses, and the national cockade displayed. The local police were obliged to warn the people that they had better postpone the festival, and the flags were removed.

Shadows of coming events

But when the news of the Kaiser's abdication reached the town, on the 10th, the last shreds of discipline in the Army gave way, and the people witnessed an extraordinary demonstration. Thousands of soldiers formed a cortège, which wandered through the town. They carried red flags, and even the French Tricolour, and sang Revolutionary songs. They passed through the Place de Brouckère, and called at the Maison du Peuple—the Belgian Socialist headquarters. Before the Palais de Justice and in the old market-place fiery speeches were made condemning the Kaiser and praising

King Albert. Whenever officers were met they were compelled to join in or were molested by the crowd, which tore off their epaulettes and regimental badges. Meanwhile the Council of Soldiers, through its chief representative, Dr. Freund, was negotiating with the Kommandantur, and Governor von Falkenhausen was obliged to acknowledge its authority. The news spread that similar councils had been constituted in Antwerp, Louvain, Tirlemont, Liège, and Namur, after the arrival in these towns of delegates coming from Germany. Prince Rupprecht sought refuge at the Spanish Embassy. For two days, November 10th and 11th, the town was plunged in a state of anarchy as far as the Germans were concerned.

Alarming rumours appeared at the time stating that the Belgian population had joined in these demonstrations. It was soon shown that they were groundless. At **German rioting in Brussels** first Bruxellois looked on, wondering what it all meant. They had not forgotten the entry of the German troops into their town, and, though many symptoms of slackness and crumbling discipline had shown themselves lately, they were not prepared for this sudden outburst. It is true that, blinded by appearances, realising all that the change meant to them, a small number of Bruxellois could not refrain from joining in when the "Reds" passed before them singing the "Marseillaise" and the "Brabançonne." But, warned by their companions, they soon left the cortège and watched impending developments with a keen and somewhat ironic interest. As one of them put it to the present writer when he reached Brussels a few days later: "The Boche may paint himself red or white. I do not care. He will always remain a Boche."

This was soon made plain during the following day, when street fighting took place between some officers and men who had remained faithful to the old regime and the Red Guards of the Soldiers' Council. Machine-guns were trained on the Palace Hotel, near the North Station, and the surrounding houses were guarded and searched by the Revolutionists. The latter, firing indiscriminately, managed to kill fifteen civilians and to wound a hundred. Several houses were looted, and it looked for a moment as if the partisans of the new order were going to repeat the exploits of Louvain and Dinant. At the Hotel Regent the Guards placed in the house by the Council plundered the cellar, murdered the hotel-keeper, and tortured his sister in order to obtain from them the key of the safe. Some soldiers, unable to carry away with them the fruit of their robberies, set up small stalls in the streets and endeavoured to sell them. When, however, the news of the armistice reached Brussels, and it was made clear that the authorities intended to comply with the conditions imposed by the Allies, calm was more or less restored. The evacuation took place without further disorder; some troops were even seen leaving the town as on parade, goose-stepping and cheering their officers.

Echoes of the Brussels riot reached King Albert and the members of his Government on the day of the King's entry into Ghent. Ghent and Tournai were the two last important towns reconquered before the armistice. The enemy was compelled to evacuate the suburbs before daybreak on the 11th. At 7 a.m. twelve Belgian soldiers led by **Ghent Activists brought to book** a lieutenant, entering the town, were surrounded by a crowd of cheering civilians. The enthusiasm of the citizens was overwhelming, and all the more touching because it was known that Ghent, the largest industrial town situated in the army zone, had been sorely tried. It had not only suffered through severe requisitions and the wreckage of its industry, but through the manœuvres of a few traitors who had persecuted the patriots under the pretext of furthering their separatist scheme. It was in Ghent that Von Bissing, the second Governor-General, had opened in 1916 the German Flemish University, and nowhere else in Flanders was the arrogance of the so-called Activists, who had helped in the reform, more bitterly resented.

For the Gantois the hour of liberation was also the hour of revenge. Most of the traitors had gone to Germany or sought refuge in Holland. Those who remained were promptly

arrested; they must have been thankful to the gendarmes who, by taking charge of them, preserved them from a worse ordeal at the hands of the crowd. While soldiers, men, and women were dancing on the night of the 11th, with linked arms, in the squares of Ghent, some fires broke out in the town. About twenty houses were sacked, all the furniture and even the window-frames being burnt in huge bonfires in the middle of the street. The Activist café was the first to suffer, then the houses of the professors selected by the German authorities. The festival would not have been complete if the people had not been able to show their hatred for the traitors who had dishonoured the proud name of their town.

On the 12th, at night, the Spanish Ambassador, Marquis de Villalobar, arrived in Ghent in a German motor-car. King Albert received him the next day, after his triumphal entry between the Queen and Prince Leopold. A little later, on the 13th, a Belgian deputation, including prominent members of the three political parties, came to report on the situation in Brussels. Some of their members advised a change in the constitution of the Government. The principle of coalition should be preserved, but those who had lived in close contact with the people under German occupation should be given a large share in the direction of affairs. The Socialists and Radicals urged that the principle of universal suffrage should be granted without further delay. These wishes were in complete harmony with the views of the Government coming from Le Havre. It had always been understood that a certain number of Ministers "from outside" would make room for the men "from inside" the country. With regard to universal suffrage—instead of plural suffrage giving extra votes to fathers of families, taxpayers, and educated men—the justice of the reform had been recognised by King Albert as early as 1914, his idea being that equal risks implied equal rights, and that the soldiers who had fought for their country should be the first entitled to exercise the franchise.

An agreement was therefore easily reached **Revision of** and the Ministry was soon remodelled, three **the Constitution** only of the old Ministers remaining in power. Owing to the riots and the consequent delay in the evacuation it was decided to postpone the entry of King Albert into Brussels.

For a week the Bruxellois witnessed an unprecedented situation. The Germans had not gone yet, and officially no allied soldiers were supposed to enter the town. This did not prevent some war correspondents, and even some soldiers in uniform, from slipping through the lines without being stopped by the enemy. Owing to their khaki uniform the first Belgians who reached Brussels were at first taken for American or British troops. Only when they burst out laughing and chaffed the crowd surrounding them in the local patois were they recognised and greeted with cheers and laughter under the very eyes of German soldiers and officers, who did not dare or did not care to interfere.

At Antwerp on November 15th, a few hours after the evacuation and the arrival of the Belgian vanguard, a glimpse was afforded of the scenes of welcome given the victorious armies wherever they passed. Something was certainly changed in Belgium. In this far-away corner of Flanders, separated from Antwerp by the Scheldt, in Lokeren, St. Nicolas, and the smallest villages there was not a house without a flag, not a window without a portrait of the King, and the cheering went on for hours and hours while the infantry, artillery, and transport columns went forward in monotonous and noisy succession on the paved road, shaking the windows of the low Flemish houses. This was the country where "Not a penny, not a soldier" had stood as a political watchword for many years, where narrow-mindedness and provincialism had blinded the peasantry to the larger issues of national politics. And now in towns and villages the Army passed as a solemn procession, and the people stood in awe and admiration before the once despised guns which had knocked down the gates of their prison. They uncovered their heads with tears of joy before the regimental flag as though it had been the Holy Sacrament

From the Belfry of Bruges six centuries look down on Belgium's triumph in the Grand' Place.

King Albert and his Queen entering Liège with General Leman, the town's heroic defender in 1914

Jubilation after long distress: Triumphal march of Belgium's King and Army into Liège in 1918.

King Albert of Belgium, with the Prince of Wales, reviewing the British troops in Brussels.

British Third Corps passing the Royal Palace, Brussels, during Belgium's celebration of the Allies' victory.

King George amidst the ruins of Ypres: Monument of Belgium's glory and Germany's eternal shame.

On Zeebrugge Mole: King George hearing details of the naval raid from Vice=Admiral Keyes.

Photo: Russell.

GENERAL SIR HENRY RAWLINSON BART., G.C.B., K.C.M.G., G.C.V.O.
Commander of the British Fourth Army

Great pageants are no doubt impressive, but for those who know the country they do not convey so much. A big crowd can always be moved before a dramatic situation. More than the entry into Antwerp and into Brussels the scenes witnessed in Lokeren and St. Nicolas were proof that the spirit of the people had undergone a complete transformation, that Belgium was no longer what it had been, and that the ordeal of the war had not been suffered in vain.

At the " Tête de Flandre," the pontoon bridge having been destroyed, the Scheldt had to be crossed in a small tug-boat. A few soldiers on leave were expected on the other bank by their mothers, wives, and children. Flemish seems a rough tongue to the foreigner, but it may become wonderfully soft when spoken by women who recover their loved ones after a long and anxious separation. These happy family groups— women hanging on the soldiers' arms, boys and girls carrying rifles and knapsacks—were lost sight of as one merged into the dense crowd which flooded Place Verte, Place de Meir, and the adjoining streets. People were wonderfully silent, as if they did not dare yet to believe in their liberation, as if they feared some new disillusion. It had been so sudden, they explained. The Revolutionary movement had not met with any serious resistance. They scarcely had realised the change when the Boche began to evacuate the town. Here also a few Activists had been arrested, but Antwerp remained apparently much calmer than Ghent.

Only when the electric lights were lit in the large square did the people begin to cry out. This was a visible sign of triumph. The lights had not been seen for a very long time. It was the signal for shouts and laughter and merry-making. The first flags were hoisted. After the expectant and awful silence of dawn the sun of liberty had risen at last.

The weather, which had kept wonderfully clear and bright since the armistice, broke on the 19th, to the great disappointment of the Anversois, since all preparations had been made for the entry of King Albert into his "second capital." The autumn rain did not, however, damp their feelings, and they had no difficulty in giving their sovereign strong and loud proofs of their deep attachment.

Brussels prepares for the triumph

Meanwhile, Brussels was anxiously waiting for the great day, and the decoration scheme of the town was being completed. Symbolic monuments representing the " Brabançonne," the " Triumph of Right," and the " Soul of Liberty " were hastily erected in various spots of the old town. The wonderful green-and-gold corporation flags were made ready, and the whole city was draped in the national and allied colours—a blaze of red, yellow, black, white, and blue. From the spire of the town-hall streams of small flags floated in the breeze, and a huge banner was twisted round the " Colonne du Congrès " in the Rue Royale. The Bruxellois took great pains to show that they associated their liberators of 1830 with those of 1918, and special care was taken to decorate the " Place des Martyrs " and various monuments commemorating the first fight for independence.

All this work and the crowds of people massed in the narrow streets gave to the popular quarters of the city a cheerful appearance, contrasting with the mournful aspect of the Quartier Léopold and Avenue Louise. There, in spite of flags and banners, the contrast between past and present was too vivid to remain unnoticed. There was scarcely any traffic, with the exception of a few crowded trams, and an occasional cart slowly drawn by a pair of oxen. The grass was growing between the cobble-stones, and from the doors of big houses and mansions every trace of brass had disappeared. A piece of wire hung where the bell had been, and the letter-box was a mere slit in the wood. Some of these houses, deserted by their owners, had a dismal and abandoned appearance, and traces of looting could be seen through the broken windows. Arriving in Brussels at that time was like coming back to a dream-city not yet awakened from her deadly sleep.

Life, however, was running fast round the town-hall, where, on November 17th, Burgomaster Max was solemnly reinstated in his office by his colleagues on his return from Germany. " I am almost tempted to say," declared the burgomaster on this occasion, " that I do not regret the aggression from which the country has suffered, for it permitted her to safeguard her honour and acquire immortal glory." The last Germans had left before dawn, taking the direction of Louvain, and leaving behind them an enormous amount of war material and munitions. Soon after noon the whole town was shaken by a series of explosions. It was rumoured that the Germans had blown up all the stations by means of delay-action mines ; that hundreds of people had perished, and that all the adjoining houses were aflame. The first news conveyed by the Brussels papers, which reappeared a few hours after the evacuation, reassured the excited crowds to a certain extent. The explosions had occurred at the Stations du Nord, du Midi, Schaerbeek, Etterbeek, and in some villages of the neighbourhood, where ammunition trains had been left on the sidings. About twenty people had been killed in Brussels, and the damage caused to the houses in the vicinity was considerable. In one or two cases, at least, the responsibility of the Germans was clearly established. If anything had been wanted to confirm the Belgians in their distrust of German methods, whether militarist or Revolutionary, this last cowardly crime would have been enough. The enemy left Belgium as he had entered it, and if he was not able to perform the same crimes it was only because the drastic conditions of the armistice prevented him from doing so.

Beaten Huns' parting crimes

A few hours later the Belgian cavalry entered the town, and a continuous stream of soldiers, column after column, passed along the boulevards. Some units went straight to their quarters, others passed through the capital, following the retreat, on their way to Germany. They received a glorious welcome. As far as Assche the people lined the Ghent road, and for hours and hours, from dawn to night, day after day, the tireless cheering went on.

There are moments in life when the millennium of brotherhood and good-will between men seems almost realised—when people of all classes, of all standing, forget their prejudices and differences, when a common faith, a common enthusiasm animates all members of the same nation, so that all barriers are removed as if by magic and unity is at last achieved. Such moments were lived through in 1914 in all allied countries. The Belgians lived through them, for a second time, in November, 1918, and especially on the great day of King Albert's entry into Brussels. The crowd which lined the appointed course of the procession was most interesting to watch. It was very eager and remained very calm ; it filled every available space up to the roofs of the houses, but it was so benevolent and kind-hearted that a cordon of Boy Scouts and school-children was able to master it. The sun was shining, but the wind was sharp, and, to keep themselves warm during the long waiting, the people stamped, keeping time and singing the " Brabançonne." They had waited four years for this day, and nothing should deprive them of its glory. They were determined to enjoy themselves, and the least incident—an allied officer passing, a band of school-children with their banner going to their meeting-place, a lost dog running in the middle of the thoroughfare—became a pretext for shouts, laughter, and merriment. To the accompaniment of the stamping of thousands of feet, patriotic songs burst from every lip, the voices of the children shrilling in the keen air, while flowers were thrown to passing soldiers and joyful greetings exchanged from roof to roof.

King Albert enters Brussels

A sudden hush—then a great clamour came rolling along. Before realising what had happened, people were waving hats and handkerchiefs, and screaming themselves hoarse, while the King passed quickly—much too quickly—on his white steed, followed by the Allied Staff. The tall figure in khaki, hand raised to the steel helmet, had already disappeared when the allied contingents were heralded by a fresh outburst of enthusiasm—the Americans and the French with crashing bands and the British led by a hundred pipers. A Belgian division followed. The whole pageant lasted over an hour and the cheers never ceased. There was something almost painful in their sound. It was a cry of deliverance telling of past suffering as much as of present relief. From time

WHERE EVERYTHING FROM GERMANY WAS SUSPECT.
Belgian sentries on the bridge at Düsseldorf searching the cart of a homing refugee in case he should have been induced to try to smuggle goods or business communications from Germans out of their country.

to time Red Cross volunteers hurried along, carrying fainting women and children on stretchers. Their number was extraordinarily high, and showed that many of those who had come felt the strain of four years' privations and anxiety. What about those who were obliged to stay at home and who filled to overflowing the capital's hospitals ?

The march-past took place in front of the " Palais de la Nation." As soon as it was over the King, at the opening of Parliament, addressed the Belgian deputies : "I bring you the greeting of the Army. We come from the Yser, my soldiers and myself, through our liberated towns and fields, and here I find myself again before the representatives of the country. Four years ago you entrusted the national Army to me and the defence of our threatened country. I have come to give an account of my actions." It was a simple, modest, and dignified speech ; not a word was uttered which did not ring true. It was a striking example of what modern democratic kingship could do for a country in case of emergency. Had not the King been there in 1914, and during the following years, to take charge of the interests of the nation, to assume all the necessary responsibilities, matters might have been very different. All the prestige, all the popularity, of a king was needed to weather the storm and to rule the country, as it were, from outside without any further mandate from the people. But, far from taking advantage of the situation, King Albert was seizing the first opportunity afforded to him of resuming his former position in the State—as a constitutional sovereign. After doing and enduring so much, any Minister, any President might have expected some reward. It is the privilege of Kings to devote themselves to their people without any afterthought. From the lofty and disinterested position they occupy they have nothing to expect and nothing to claim.

Later in the day a great reception took place in the town-hall, while in the adjoining streets popular **Facing the problems of life** enthusiasm reached its climax, stimulated by the presence of men of the allied contingents. All the lights were burning, and dancing and singing went on late into the night. There was very little left to drink, but the new, exhilarating sense of freedom made up for the lack of good beer, so that Brussels had a regular " Kermesse " after all, as in the good old time of peace.

We must now abandon the track of the allied armies, working their way towards the left bank of the Rhine, to turn our attention towards the urgent problems confronting the Belgian Government on the morrow of liberation. As soon as the Government was settled in Brussels the work of reconstruction began. It soon became plain that political freedom, so dearly bought by the devotion of the Army and the heroic resistance of the civil population, would bear no

fruit unless the economic situation were made secure, and the Belgian representatives at the Peace Conference obtained the revision of the treaty of 1839, which deprived the country of its natural and strategic frontiers and left it defenceless against future aggression.

The plans of the new Government were outlined in King Albert's speech. Political union was to be maintained under a Coalition Ministry (including six Catholics, three Liberals, and three Socialists). As soon as the Army could be demobilised new elections would take place under the regime of general suffrage. Meanwhile the present Parliament would take the necessary measures required by the situation. Ministers would be helped in their work by committees of experts drawn from industrial, financial, and labour circles. The revictualling of the population would be carried on for the time being by the " Comité d'Alimentation," as in the days of German occupation. In order to favour a close co-operation between Capital and Labour, full civil rights would be granted to trade unions. While the small band of traitors who took advantage of the language problem to help the enemy would be severely punished, the claims of the loyal Flemings would be favourably considered as well as the creation of a Flemish University at Ghent. The King's reference to external policy was short : " Victorious Belgium, freed from a neutrality imposed upon her by treaties whose foundations have been shaken by the war, will enjoy complete independence. These treaties which determined her status in Europe did not protect her against a criminal aggression. They cannot survive the crisis of which she has been a victim."

Policy internal and external

The King declared that the restoration of the country was a gigantic task requiring all the strength of the nation, and that it needed no less devotion and self-sacrifice to achieve than its liberation. The people who had been carried away by the glamour of festivals and rejoicing soon realised the soundness of their leader's warning.

Belgium was free at last. But how was she to live ? Her industry was wrecked. A great number of spinning mills in Flanders had been destroyed. When machinery was available or could promptly be set in order, raw material was lacking through the enemy's systematic seizures and requisitions, so that 800,000 industrial workers remained unemployed. The situation with regard to commerce was equally critical. More than a third of the country's railway lines, bridges, and roads was in a state of complete destruction. Lines were blocked with hundreds of waggons which the Germans had not been able to take away with them. Almost all the rolling-stock had disappeared, and the rails and material of the light railways, which render such great service in the countryside, had for a long time been requisitioned. In many places the canals were blocked with sunken barges. Agriculture, though still alive, suffered a great deal through lack of manure and, especially in Flanders, through want of cattle and horses. All over the country 50,000 houses and buildings were in ruin, and whole provinces had been actually converted into deserts. In spite of all efforts living was still three—and in some parts four—times as expensive as in England, and more than half the population—3,500,000 people—were still dependent on relief. Owing to the fact that she was invaded at the beginning of the war and that the Germans had succeeded in preventing most of the young men from joining the Army, Belgium could draw on her reserve of man-power. But ill-treatment, deportations, and short rations had done their work ; the vitality and energy of the working classes had greatly diminished, and tuberculosis was threatening the younger generation.

Not a week, not a day, was to be lost ; but, owing to the transfer of the Government from Le Havre and to the change in its personnel, delays became unavoidable. Besides, Belgium had to adapt herself to fresh economic conditions created by the war. For better or for worse the world had undergone tremendous changes during the preceding four years, and the Belgians, isolated in their German prison, were not prepared at first to realise the importance of these. The country was clamouring for imports, while restrictions had to be maintained until financial credits were opened abroad in order to prevent the depreciation of Belgian money. She was in sore need of financial help at a time when her Allies, obsessed by their own internal difficulties, could not afford to make the necessary sacrifices. And, while the workers were ready enough to begin work, they would not accept the wages and hours of pre-war time. When at last financial arrangements could be made abroad, —various credits, ranging from £9,000,000 to £12,000,000, being granted by Great Britain, America, and France—another difficulty stood in the way. While the Allies were prepared to export manufactured articles, some of the raw materials most needed in Belgium could not be sent without an export licence, so that the restarting of some of the corresponding industries suffered new delays, and many workmen remained idle who might have begun work at once.

It is true that most of the lands which suffered from enemy invasion were faced at the same time with the same problems, but the situation

Some necessary disillusionment was rendered more painful in Belgium owing to the fact that all the provinces had been occupied—while in France the northern districts had alone been affected—and that industry was the main resource of the country, while Serbia, for instance, is agricultural and thinly populated.

The people's moral had also to be considered. During the long years of oppression they had been led to believe that their sufferings would end with the liberation of Belgian territory. They trusted that, as soon as the enemy had evacuated the country, they would be able to take up the thread of their daily occupations. Life would be again what it was in 1914, industry would revive, prosperity would be restored. The world had been so moved by the Belgian tragedy that nations would rush with one accord to their help. If the work of relief had not always been as efficient as it might have been, Germany alone was to be made responsible. She was the only obstacle to their happiness. This obstacle once removed, the country would be restored to its former state as by the touch of a magic wand.

Such illusions, fostered by the emphatic declarations of allied statesmen which had reached occupied Belgium, were only too natural; they were necessary. Without them the population would not have been able to stand the strain.

FORTIFYING THE ALLIES' RHINE FRONTIER.
Belgian engineers making trenches on the western bank of the Rhine. The Belgian zone of occupation was the area between the Dutch frontier and a line drawn from Liège through Aix-la-Chapelle to Düsseldorf, the Rhine forming the base of a rough triangle.

When weeks and months passed without bringing about any important change, a reaction was inevitable. The cost of living diminished slightly, but the chimneys of the factories remained smokeless, the workshops remained idle, and trade was still paralysed. The Belgians began slowly to realise that they were only one factor in the great problem. They saw that the attention of the Powers was divided between them and new nations whose names were scarcely known to them before the war. They understood more and more that the Allies had their own internal difficulties, which must be solved before attending to Belgium's need. They were not embittered, but for a few weeks their splendid energy, their obstinate optimism, were shaken. They had kept up the fight too long, and the longed-for miracle had not taken place. They had not yet reaped the expected reward.

This feeling was partly caused by the news from the Conference sitting in Paris with regard to the restoration of the machinery stolen by the enemy and the payment of the German war indemnity. While the enemy had wantonly destroyed their factories, not only in order to help his own war industries but for the deliberate purpose of stealing a march on his rivals and capturing their markets, the Allied Powers did not allow the French and Belgian manufacturers **Effect upon Belgium's moral** to requisition machinery similar to their own in order to start work at once. The actual machines which had been taken away must be traced in Germany, and so much time was lost in the process that in many cases the restoration of the stolen goods came too late. Often, also, the machinery when discovered was useless. One of the conditions of the armistice was the delivery by Germany of a certain number of engines and waggons. But when these were delivered it was found that about thirty per cent. had to be scrapped, so that in January, 1919, there were only six hundred locomotives in the whole of Belgium, as against four thousand in 1914. The result was that, so far as industry was concerned, the Germans in the Rhine country were far better off than the Belgians, and that the conquerors envied the situation of the conquered.

With regard to the war indemnity, the Belgians had all along expected privileged treatment. It had been declared again and again in allied quarters during the war that the reparation due to Belgium would be the first condition imposed on Germany. The unstable political situation beyond the Rhine on the one hand, and

DETERMINED TO RUN NO RISKS.
Machine-gun emplacement on Düsseldorf Bridge, with Belgian gunners and an armed guard standing by ready for all emergencies. Major Dillemont, temporarily commanding at Obercassel, was in charge of the post at the time.

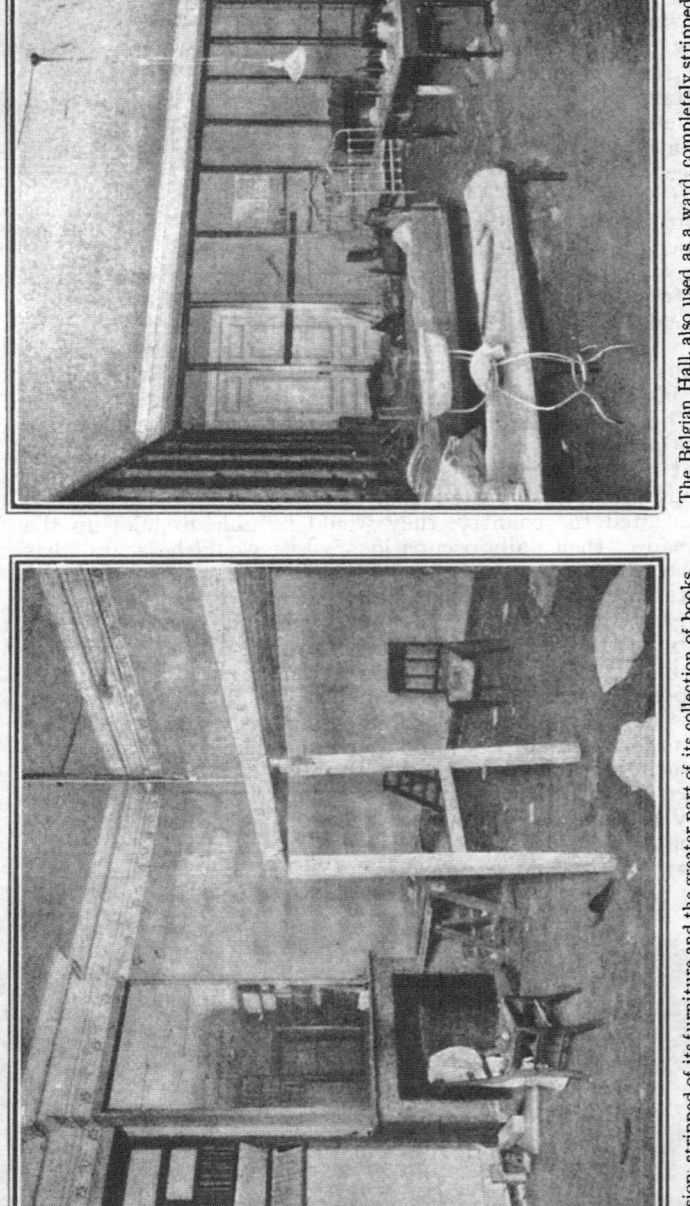

The Great Hall, used as a hospital ward, and containing a number of machine-guns. Portraits of Leopold I. had had the Iron Cross painted on them. Here, too, mouldering food and filth fouled the air.

The Belgian Hall, also used as a ward, completely stripped of its collection of Transactions of Belgian Learned Societies. Some of these were found in a loft, badly damaged by damp and rats.

One end of the Marble Hall. A huge heap of filthy linen, alive with vermin, occupied all the floor space, and plates and dishes with scraps of decomposing food littered the tables and shelves.

Hall of the Royal Historical Commission, stripped of its furniture and the greater part of its collection of books. A frame had been erected on which to hang hams obtained from the piggery established in the grounds.

CONDITION OF THE PALAIS DES ACADEMIES AS LEFT BY THE GERMANS WHEN EVACUATING BRUSSELS. OCTOBER 17TH. 1918.

KING ALBERT REVIEWS A BRITISH DIVISION IN BRUSSELS.
Men of the British 55th Division marching past the King of the Belgians after the recovery of his capital from the invader. This division, under Major-General Sir H. S. Jeudwine, gained the high commendation of the Commander-in-Chief for its fine work in the fighting forward in the Lens-Armentières area at the beginning of September, 1918, when it helped in the carrying of the line to the outskirts of La Bassée.

some rival claims put forward at the Peace Conference on the other, rendered the fulfilment of this promise more and more difficult. Belgium's bill presented to the Reparation Committee amounted to anything between £1,400,000,000 and £1,600,000,000. How soon could it be paid ? "If Belgium has to wait until Germany is made to pay her debt, she will be dead before the payment of the first instalment," stated the Belgian Minister of Economic Affairs, who expressed the anxiety of the people when he further declared that "Belgium was wondering whether she was going to live or to die."

In spite of these misgivings, however, and thanks to the tireless energy of the whole people, the **Beginning to turn the corner** work of reconstruction was already started. Slowly, very slowly, life was beginning to flow again in the country's arteries, along the railways which were being repaired by the military authorities (at the end of January, 1919, the number of travellers was forty per cent. of pre-war times) in Antwerp, which had become the base of the Allied Army of Occupation on the Rhine, and even in a few industries for which raw material could be provided. The financial difficulties would no doubt be solved by a grant from the Allies on the German indemnity. The price of food had fallen considerably by March owing to imports, and great stocks of boots and clothing had been purchased abroad. With the spring the situation improved considerably, and, though the crisis was not yet mastered, the Belgians realised that the worst was already over for them.

Belgium's territorial claims, however, were yet unsettled, though the Commission for Belgian Affairs in Paris had reported favourably on the principle of the revision of the 1839 treaties.

Some people may have been surprised to see the Belgian delegates in Paris making territorial claims. The right of the country to an economic indemnity had been recognised by all. But there still existed in some minds a doubt concerning the legitimate claim to territorial compensation. Belgium, having been the victim of brutal aggression, and having throughout the war remained scrupulously disinterested, it seemed to them that an indemnity was all that she ought to ask for, and that the *status quo ante* ought to be established from the territorial point of view.

There was a misapprehension here. The frontiers of modern Belgium were fixed by the treaty of 1839, imposed

A FINE RECORD
Lieutenant-General Gillain, who was appointed Chief of Staff of the Belgian Army in the early spring of 1918, he having risen by sheer military merit from his original status of private in the ranks.

by the Powers in spite of energetic protests. This same treaty established the neutrality and inviolability of Belgian territory. It was by reason of this moral guarantee that the Powers thought well to weaken the country by taking from her Luxemburg, half of Limburg, and Dutch Flanders, and in maintaining the eastern frontier as it had been fixed by the treaties of 1814-16. It is evident that, neutrality having disappeared, a rectification of the frontiers became necessary in order to allow the country to defend herself. It was not to 1814 that reference should be made when determining the new frontiers of the country, but to 1830 and 1839, at which time the legitimate claims of the **Belgium's claims to territory** Belgian people suffered a check unjustifiable in the light of more recent events.

The Treaty of Munster closed the mouths of the Scheldt and ruined the trade of Antwerp for the benefit of Dutch ports. This clause was maintained during the eighteenth century, in spite of the efforts of Joseph II. of Austria, under whose suzerainty the Belgian provinces had been placed, and it was not until 1795, at the time of the French conquest, that Antwerp was liberated and the left bank of the Scheldt restored to Belgium. The Congress of Vienna, having united Holland and Belgium, the question of the Scheldt gave rise to no discussion, but when in 1830 the Belgians revolted against Dutch domination, King William claimed Dutch Flanders and the right to close the mouth of the Scheldt, thus ruining the activity of Antwerp. The London Conference at first decided that the belligerents must retire behind the respective frontiers of the two countries before their union, that is in 1814. But under pressure from the Dutch this date was changed to 1790, the change giving Dutch Flanders to Holland. The Belgians were promised free navigation on the river, but the treaty of 1839 gave to Holland a right to levy a tax on the trade of Antwerp. This right was redeemed by Belgium in 1863, and it was after this date that the great port retrieved its former prosperity. The piloting and buoying of the river were under the control of both countries, and Holland announced her right to neutralise the waters in time of war.

The disastrous consequences of this state of things were seen in the impossibility for Great Britain to land necessary reinforcements at Antwerp, and in the internment of 30,000 combatants driven into Holland during the retreat.

The intention of the Powers in 1815, when creating the Kingdom of the Netherlands, was obviously to place on the north of France a State strong enough to bar French Imperial aggression. But Prussia seems to have pursued a more selfish aim even then. She got the frontiers of the provinces of Limburg, Liège, and Luxemburg rectified for her benefit, thus obtaining some Belgian districts where Walloon is spoken to this day. She also took Luxemburg from Belgium and converted it into a Grand Duchy depending on the German confederation (with the right to maintain a garrison in the capital), and gave it in this new form to King William in exchange for his German provinces. This arrangement, to which the other Powers were party, was very advantageous to Prussia from more than one point of view. It is interesting to note that a century before the invasion of Belgium and Luxemburg, Prussia had already acquired the high ground commanding the approaches to Liège, and had established her rights to a suzerainty over the Grand Duchy which opened a direct route to France.

Except as regards the Eifel, Belgium did not suffer by

IN GHENT REGAINED.
So thoroughly had the Germans wrecked the railway and the railway station at Ghent that a fresh track had to be laid along the street, and a new station to be established outside the old one.

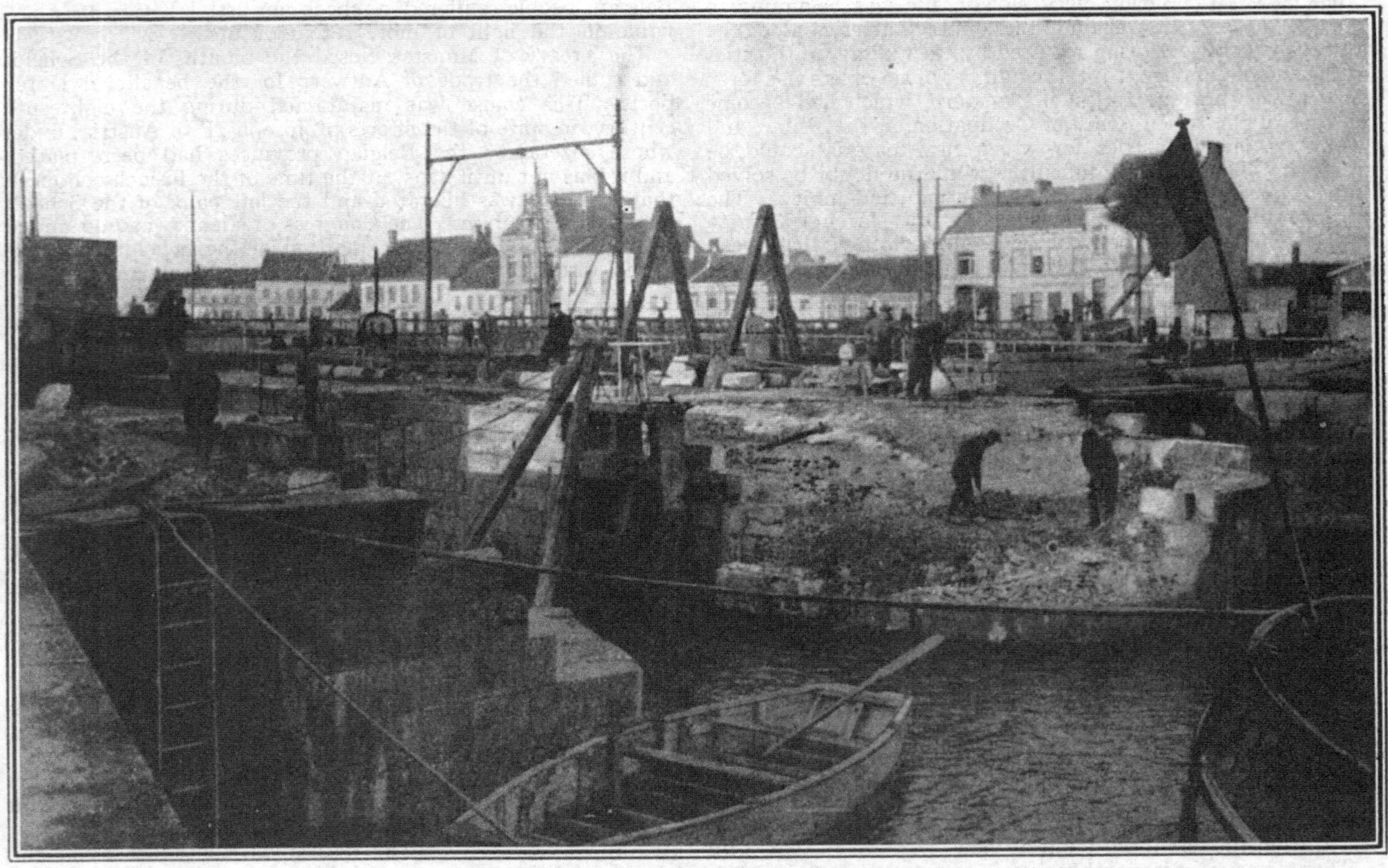

this arrangement as long as the union lasted. It was, in fact, to the interest of King William to treat the Grand Duchy as an integral part of his kingdom, and Luxemburg remained Belgian from every point of view, and sent its representatives to the National Congress. But when, in 1830, the terms of separation were discussed, the policy of the King of Holland changed completely. He claimed possession of the Grand Duchy as a personal right, and his demands were vigorously upheld by Prussia at the London Conference.

After long and laborious discussions the Belgian delegates obtained from the Powers the right to treat direct with the King of Holland with a view to buying back his rights over Luxemburg. But the King broke the armistice and inflicted a defeat on the Belgians, who were obliged to accept help from Britain and France. He thus obtained half of Luxemburg and half of Limburg, with Maestricht, in spite of the protests of the Belgian delegates and the representatives of these provinces at the congress at Brussels. Threatened with invasion, the Belgians were obliged to give way. They were too weak to claim their rights by arms, and France and Britain were determined to have the matter settled quickly. According to the

REPAIRING A DAMAGED LOCK AT OSTEND.
Belgians at work in Ostend, rewon after four years in German occupation; they were clearing away debris preparatory to the repair of the small Stykens Lock at Ostend Harbour, which had been destroyed by the enemy before they left the town in the early hours of October 17th, 1918. As soon as Ostend was regained the work of reparation was begun, for though the town itself had suffered little the harbour had been considerably damaged.

MODERN HEROES PASSING ACROSS ONE OF HISTORY'S GREAT BATTLEFIELDS.
British troops passing over part of the battlefield of Waterloo on their way to the Rhine towards the end of November, 1918. The pyramidal mound in the background, known as the Mound of the Belgian Lion, was raised over the spot where the Prince of Orange was wounded in the Battle of Waterloo.

Minister, Nothomb, "Belgium had not yet rendered any service to Europe, and had not won the right to make herself heard."

Limburg and Luxemburg are for the Belgians what Alsace and Lorraine are for the French. But there is a distinction to make. The comparative independence enjoyed by Luxemburg since 1839, and the Dutch regime to which Limburg was subjected, created scarcely any opposition in these provinces, and did not hamper their development. Therefore, as regards these two questions, the Belgian delegates at the Paris Conference, while declaring their rights, did not in any way stipulate whether the rapprochement they wished for was to be political, economic, or merely strategic.

Whatever measures may be taken for the maintenance of European peace, it must remain Great Britain's policy to see that Belgium and the Belgian coast remain free and independent. European and American statesmen may alter the course of foreign politics, but they cannot alter physical features of the map, and the maintenance of Belgium as a strong nation, able to defend herself in case of need and to receive prompt reinforcements if necessary, remains the best safeguard of Great Britain's security. The war brought the two nations closer together. It was on Belgian soil that the Empire's new armies fought their most heroic battles. It was to fulfil her duty towards Britain and France that Belgium made her stand at Liège and on the Yser. Common sacrifices, common sufferings, created bonds of sympathy between the two nations. Common victory ought to strengthen them. The time when men could love their country while ignoring that of their neighbours is past. The security of every nation depends henceforth on a clear knowledge of events abroad. A League of Nations, to be a sound reality, must be based even more on the confidence than on the apprehensions born of the World War.

IN THE GRAND' PLACE, TERMONDE, 1918.
Termonde, near Antwerp, was the scene of fierce fighting in October, 1914, when the Belgians inflicted tremendous losses on the German Army commanded by Von Beseler. In revenge the Huns burned the town almost to the ground, the German general and his aides watching the wanton destruction.

KING ALBERT'S BAND AT THE ALBERT HALL.
When, during the war, King Albert of Belgium sent his private band to England to give performances, he himself and Queen Elizabeth flew over from Belgium to attend a grand concert in the Albert Hall and were given a deliriously enthusiastic welcome in London.

A scene on the ice by the Rhine-side at Cologne during the winter of 1918-19, when the city was the Headquarters of the British Army of Occupation. A number of the British soldiers stationed there took the opportunity of getting some skating amid their novel surroundings.

British soldiers watching the ice floating down the Rhine. The spectacle, interesting to them, was one to add to the depression of the German people still suffering from shortage of foodstuffs and warm clothing as a result of the blockade.

WITH THE BRITISH ARMY OF OCCUPATION ON THE WINTRY RHINE.

CHAPTER CCXCII.

THE MARCH TO THE RHINE.
By Edward Wright.

Armistice Terms Facilitate German Retreat—Loosing Anarchy in Alsace-Lorraine—Attempt to Spread Revolution among Belgians—Last Convulsions of Imperial Socialists of Germany—Looters Sell Loot to Looted—Hindenburg Recovers Control of his Armies—Trooper Fitzgerald Captures Enghien—Great March Opens on Four Hundred Mile Front—Dutch Government Allows Enemy Passage through Limburg—Belgians Enter Ruined Termonde—Plumer's Men Advance towards Spa—Mangin's Army Appears in Lorraine—Hirschauer in his Native City of Mulhouse—Frenzied Joy of Alsatians—Max Returns Triumphantly to Brussels—Germans Start Terrible Explosions—Tragedy of Returning British Prisoners—Charleroi Miners Arm against Enemy—King Albert in Happy Antwerp—Great Allied Festival in Brussels—Strange Silence of Liberated Metz—Americans Tumble into Political Comedy at Luxemburg—Foch's Dramatic Action in Kléber Square, Strasbourg—Germans Dreaming Revenge in Five Years—Hindenburg in Napoleon the Third's Palace—British Army of Occupation Crosses the Red Water of Germany—Happy Surprises in Belgian Prussia—Britons Become the Saviours of Germany—New Enemy Intrigues among Forces of Occupation—Grand Spectacle on Hohenzollern Bridge of Cologne—Rhinelanders at Last Convinced of Utter Defeat—General Fayolle's Remarkable Speech at Mayence—Why Mangin Brought the Moors to the Rhine—Armies of Victory Established in their Three Bridge-heads.

FTER the signing of the armistice on November 11th, 1918, described in Chapter CCLXXXVI. (Vol 12, page 545), the enemy had a week in which to prepare his movement of withdrawal across the Rhine and beyond the allied bridge-heads. In 1914 he had taken barely three weeks to throw a million and a half men across the frontier, and his enlarged armies had to retire at least as fast as they came, in five stages, marked by Charleroi, Huy, Aix-la-Chapelle, Düren, and Cologne. This was no matter of great difficulty. In the rear the older troops had begun to return to their country by the simple process of deserting in masses along with Austrian and Hungarian forces. Divisions in support were electing Soldiers' Councils, and arranging to tramp back to the Rhine and establish Soviet government in Germany. The Germans were able to save transport by the surrender of the appointed quantities of war material and by leaving behind them food for the civil population and coal and working staffs for the railways. They were thus able to travel very light, and all the conditions of the armistice made for a quick retreat. Hindenburg succeeded in maintaining discipline by changing the character of the Soldiers' Councils, and promoting them throughout the armies. Trustworthy non-commissioned officers, working under Headquarters' direction, came

forth as champions of the rank and file, and transformed the centres of Communism into military establishments. Most of the battle-line fighting troops were reorganised in this way and set against the purely Revolutionary elements in the bases and along the lines of communication. With remarkable speed the men were brought again under control, and inspired with the idea that they could only save their country by maintaining order and working for the election of a National Assembly.

Hindenburg's first plan was to create anarchy in the occupied part of Belgium and in Alsace-Lorraine, so as to win breathing time for his own demoralised forces. On November 13th a special train ran from Wilhelmshaven to Strasbourg carrying a band of Alsatian sailors who had led the rebellion at Kiel. Twenty-four thousand men from Alsace and Lorraine had been employed in the German Fleet and naval ports, and it had been largely owing to their rebellious spirit that the Imperial system of government had been broken. After they had carried out their work of disruption, in a manner that completely avenged the wrongs done to their country, the German Socialists of the Majority school, in alliance with the representatives of the old Government, skilfully endeavoured to turn to profit the Revolutionary spirit of the Alsace and Lorraine sailors. An attempt to stir up Bolshevist outbreaks in Strasbourg and Metz, however, failed completely.

SIR HERBERT PLUMER IN COLOGNE.
General Plumer, who was in command of the British Second Army, inspecting one of the vessels of the Rhine gunboat patrol at Cologne.

THE DURHAMS ON GUARD IN COLOGNE.
Changing the guard outside the house of the British Military Governor of Cologne, the 20th Battalion of the Durham Light Infantry providing the troops for this duty.

Hindenburg, after confessing to the Reichstag that his troops were running away, so that he would have to capitulate if an armistice were not immediately arranged, changed his tone when his armies were reduced to order. In an Order of the Day to his troops he gave his authority to the legend that Germany was still undefeated, by proclaiming that only famine had forced him to submit to the hard terms of the Associated Powers. All the old Prussian machinery of administration took the note from Hindenburg, and as the German columns tramped over the frontier into their own country some of them were received with garlands of the last flowers of autumn, and all were greeted with flowery speeches as men who had been invincible by arms but had been starved into retreat through their country weakening under pressure of the British Navy. In the Cathedral of

Brussels and Charleroi were the chief places in Belgium in which the creatures of the fugitive Hohenzollern vainly tried to spoil the home-coming of King Albert and his troops. At Brussels there was at first a genuine mutiny the day before the armistice was signed, and some officers were killed in an attempt to maintain discipline. Then, under an official German agitator, there followed a sham movement of Revolution. Five thousand German soldiers, parading with red flags, tried to bring the Belgian people into an anarchic mood so that they might form part of the new Middle Europe Republic. The Belgians, however, were even more averse to the new sinister influences of the enemy than were the Alsatians, and all possible trouble was soon quietened by the arrival of British and Belgian columns.

German intrigue fails in Belgium At Charleroi the oppressed, overworked miners were subjected to the intrigues of the false school of German Bolshevists, but their joy in their rapid liberation saved them from the contagion of the Soviets. The national spirit of patriotism, strengthened and purified by years of suffering, prevented the people in all the occupied territories from taking any serious part in the last vile game of the enemy.

All these improvised plans, carried out in wild, spasmodic efforts, failed of effect. The last convulsions of Imperial Socialism in Germany merely taught the rest of Europe what saving virtue there was in old-fashioned patriotism. By employing, as a final desperate resource, all that remained of the forces of International Socialism, in the hope of drawing out the war with larger territory, the Teutons so discredited themselves and their agents that the rest of Western Europe was, for the time at least, proof against their intrigues.

In the meantime Hindenburg and Gröner recovered control of their armies. The looters of Belgium and Northern France began to sell some of their loot back to the looted, finding that there was no longer any means of sending all the plunder to Germany. The sales in Brussels especially were a strange comedy. The German soldiers set up a market in which they sold things that did not belong to them to the people whom they had robbed, receiving in exchange their own paper money, the value of which was rapidly falling. Some of the invaders kept barrows and small carts on which to transport their last stocks of plundered food. As they trailed away eastward, grimy of feature, ragged, and straggling, like an army of broken mendicants, there was no resemblance between them and the fierce, proud, mightily-organised forces of invasion that had crossed the frontier in August, 1914.

BRITISH SENTRIES IN A GERMAN CITY.
The house taken over as a residence for the British Army Commander in occupied Cologne, showing two British soldiers on sentry duty at the entrance.

Aix-la-Chapelle a service of penitence was held when the Fourth German Army, under General von Armin, passed through the city of Charlemagne. The service of penitence had no relation whatever to the deeds done by Germans on the Belgian people, but referred merely to the sufferings of the innocent Teutons under the armistice imposed by the Allies.

The German people, however, were soon able to appreciate the difference between their broken, dispirited, gloomy soldiers and the bearing of the hosts of victory. During the short interval between the cessation of hostilities and the opening of the march across the Rhine all the conquering armies reflected the temper of their minds in their outward appearance. The infantry spent a week in smartening themselves up and cleaning their arms and putting on new uniforms. The gunners in the forces of occu- **Conquering armies' splendid bearing** pation groomed their horses and made their guns and limbers look bright and fresh, receiving often new guns from the material prepared for a winter war, while the cavalry, on well-fed and well-kept mounts, with arms and equipment in brilliant parade order, rode out in dazzling form as a scouting screen.

Although the general advance did not open until Sunday morning, November 17th, 1918, it began in a very irregular and extraordinary manner the previous week. One of the troopers of King Edward's Horse, in action beyond Ath, did not hear of the armistice while on reconnaissance work. On November 12th Trooper Gerald Fitzgerald was still trotting along the Enghien road, having lost touch with his regiment, but being full of determination to get in contact with the enemy. On the way he was stopped by a German gunner officer, who inquired whether he had come to take over the guns. Fitzgerald answered that he did not want guns, and rode onward into Enghien, where he was met by excited civilians and released prisoners of war, who told him to go back as the town was full of German troops.

The trooper, however, considered that he had gone too far to turn back, and in the market-place he rode into a company of Germans drawn up on parade. Stopped by a sentry, he lighted a cigarette, and was approached by an angry officer, who informed him he would be shot if he crossed a line in the market-place. With staggering impudence the trooper met the German attack by giving the enemy commander two hours to evacuate Enghien. At the end of two hours two thousand Germans were hastily retreating towards Brussels, leaving Fitzgerald master of the town. This conquest was insufficient to still the adventurous spirit of the solitary cavalryman. He continued his advance, after a great reception by the freed townspeople, and, pursuing the bluffed and perturbed enemy,

Trooper Fitzgerald's great adventure rode in conquering style into Brussels on November 15th. Happily, General Jeudwine, commanding the Lancashire Division with which King Edward's Horse were working, regarded the affair as a glorious joke, and Trooper Fitzgerald ended his career rather as a popular hero than as the culprit in a court-martial.

On the day when the first of the British reached Brussels, King Albert was compelled to despatch cavalry and cyclists to his capital and to Antwerp. The rioting, plundering Germans seemed at the time likely to get out of hand, and terrifying explosions of ammunition and mines were perturbing the people. The menace of an allied advance in strength was sufficient to make the German commanders abandon the method of trying to frighten the Belgians into Revolution, and the enemy's retreat went on in a more orderly manner. Farmers were robbed of cattle, sheep, goats, and poultry wherever the Germans passed, and delay-action mines were

left working in towns, but the chief trouble ceased as soon as the light Belgian forces approached the capital. In Southern Belgium the Seventh German Army began to surrender its war material to the First French Army, under General Debeney, on November 15th, and two days afterwards, when the enemy was practically a day's march distant from the line of the armistice, the forces appointed for the occupation of Germany began to march between the Dutch frontier near Salzaele and the Swiss frontier near Basle. With all its bends the line was about four hundred miles in length.

To a considerable extent the composition of the allied troops moving towards the Rhine was governed by the plan of the closing battle arranged by Marshal Foch for November 14th. The Belgian Army, under General Michel, started to march by **Dutch breach of neutrality** Antwerp, Brussels, and Liège and spread out by Aix-la-Chapelle north-westward along the Rhine from Düsseldorf to Emmerich. There was a great obstacle in the way of the Belgian troops, formed by the lost Belgian province of Eastern Limburg, which had been given to the Dutch in the period when Belgium was suspected of sympathising with the French, and when Prussia and Great Britain were united in repressing France. During the German retreat the Dutch Government allowed seventy thousand German troops to pass through the Limburg province without being interned. At the same time as extraordinary facilities to escape were given to the enemy, without any consultation with the Associated Powers, the Dutch Foreign Minister informed the Belgian Ambassador at The Hague that no Belgians interned since the fall of Antwerp could be liberated without the consent of Germany.

The attitude of the Dutch Government was a grave prejudice to Belgian interests. Not only was one of the best German armies able to avoid capture, but it was able to carry back to Germany a mass of war material of extreme importance, and abundant plunder, which could not have been transported through the overcrowded funnel of Liège. The stores of food, the magazines of machine-guns, and most of the

BRITISH ARTILLERY BATTERY THAT PASSED FAR BEYOND THE RHINE.

Battery of the Royal Field Artillery photographed thirteen miles to the east of the Rhine at a time when no other British troops had penetrated so far into occupied Germany. Men who had fought so long in the devastated war zone could not fail to be struck on their march into Germany by the way in which the country that had willed the war was spared all the worst of war's horrors by the collapse of its own armies.

POINT DUTY ON THE RHINE.
British soldiers on guard at the eastern end of one of Cologne's bridges.

by favour of a nation that had for centuries strangled Belgian commerce through the Scheldt and played a main part in separating Luxemburg from Belgium, had a very profound effect upon the Belgians. The Belgians had won their independence by an insurrection against the Dutch in 1830, and they were far from pleased at the actions of their old oppressors when the war was ending.

The French commander General Degoutte was acting at the time as Chief of Staff to King Albert, while General Michel commanded the Belgian forces chosen for crossing the frontier. After the disappointment with regard to the result of the difficulties in which the Fourth German Army was placed, the Belgians moved rapidly into Malines, Antwerp, and Brussels. The gaunt ruins of the town of Termonde, destroyed by the enemy in 1914, were occupied in the first day's march.

The Second British Army, under Sir Herbert Plumer, began to move below Brussels towards Liège, where it would swerve across the Meuse by Spa, on the road to Cologne. From the First British Army the Canadian Corps, under Sir Arthur Currie, was appointed to continue the march from Mons and proceed towards Huy, on the Meuse, towards Bonn. From the Third British Army the brilliant corps commander Sir Charles Fergusson was selected as Governor of Cologne. Divisions of the most gallant Fourth British Army, under Sir Henry Rawlinson, moved across the Belgian frontier towards the Ardennes Forest.

ammunition of the Fourth German Army and the German Marine Corps had been concentrated round Antwerp. Under the conditions of the armistice the Allies expected there would be such a confusion when the Fourth, Sixth, and Seventh German Armies retreated along the Lower Meuse that General von Armin's forces would be dissolved and captured.

Owing, however, to the breach of neutrality by the Dutch Government, which had received the German Emperor as an honoured guest long

OUTSIDE AN ARMY BANK.
One of the Guards on sentry duty at the entrance to an Army bank at Cologne. In the office hours' notice Army time was employed, the afternoon time being shown as 14.30 to 16.30, otherwise 2.30 to 4.30

before he abdicated, and also had welcomed his heir, the Fourth German Army was not only enabled to escape but was permitted to transport over Dutch territory the cattle, horses, sheep, carts, furniture, and other product of robbery of the Belgian people. The fact that this action occurred in the unredeemed part of the Belgian province of Limburg,

Debeney, advanced from the armistice line across the Meuse towards the southern part of the Belgian Ardennes. All this movement took place with little alteration in the main forces. Large masses of troops remained for a time on the ground they had won, acting as an immediate reserve to the forces in progress. It had been Marshal Foch's intention to

Cavalry, cyclists, and some of the infantry of the First French Army, under General

BRITISH SENTRIES ON GUARD IN OCCUPIED GERMANY.
A sentry of the Notts and Derby Regiment, the Sherwood Foresters, on duty in one of the streets of Cologne, and (right) the entrance to a Royal Palace guarded by Canadian sentries. The palace was that of the Princess Victoria, sister of the German Emperor, and was used as the residence of Sir Arthur Currie, the Canadians' G.O.C.; hence the Maple Leaf over the sentry-boxes, and over the board indicating that it was the G.O.C.'s headquarters.

launch the Flanders Army Group, with all the British Armies and the First French Army, directly against the enemy on November 14th. When the enemy surrendered the intended movement was made peacefully, with only a fraction of the forces of assault.

There was, however, great change in the disposition of troops on the line below the Belgian frontier. The Fourth French Army, under General Gouraud, which had been appointed to attack across the Meuse, by Sedan, made a long march southward between November 11th and November 17th, and

points of view it was to be regretted that the politicians of the Grand Alliance did not allow their commanders to finish the struggle with the sword, and compel the stricken enemy to cease all his intrigues and pretences, and capitulate in mass on the field of battle.

As it was, General Mangin prepared to march peacefully through Morhange and Sarrelouis into Metz, on the road to Mayence. Unfortunately the famous commander, whose face was scorched and lined by service in the desert of Africa long before he rose to fame by the Meuse and the Aisne, had

WHERE THE AMERICANS LINKED WITH THE BRITISH.
Military police of the 42nd Division of the U.S. Army paraded for duty at Rolandseck, site of the last relic of the castle built by the Knight Roland, paladin of Charlemagne, on a rock towering above the Rhine.

MOUNTED MILITARY POLICEMAN IN COLOGNE.
Some fifty of these men, all experienced members of the Police Force at home before being called up to the Army, sufficed to police Cologne during the British occupation.

reappeared by the high wall of the Vosges Mountains in the neighbourhood of Strasbourg. A new American army, the Third, under General Dickmann, who had led divisions and army corps to victory by the Marne and along the Upper Argonne, was ready to march across the Meuse into Luxemburg, and thence travel through the wildly picturesque Eifel region along the Moselle to Coblenz.

On the right of the Americans were the French forces with which Marshal Foch had hoped to fight his own grand battle. Pre-eminent among these was the Tenth French Army, under General Mangin, which had suddenly vanished from the centre of the battlefield in October. General Mangin's men were arrayed round the hills of Nancy and Parroy Forest. They had prepared to attack the enemy on November 14th, as the spearhead of the large new Army of Lorraine, under General de Castelnau. Castelnau had arranged to fight once more the Battle of Morhange, where he had been defeated at the opening of the war, but saved from complete disaster by his Twentieth Corps, then commanded by Foch. Both Foch and Castelnau had been looking forward with passionate anticipation to their return match at Morhange, where Mangin designed to fight to St. Avold and Sarrelouis, isolating Metz on one side and Alsace on the other side, and cutting the enemy's communications, while his western wing and centre were smashed by Belgian, British, French, and American forces.

There can be no possible doubt whatever, that had the new Battle of Lorraine been fought on November 14th, few German divisions would have reached the Rhine intact. It would have ended either in the greatest slaughter or the greatest surrender in history. The Germans, who were already breaking and partly in flight, would have been outflanked in the Ardennes and surrounded in Lorraine. From many

The battle that was not fought

a serious accident just as his army was beginning to march. A splendid horseman, he selected a pure-blooded Arab as his mount for taking the salute at Metz, but the horse, being fresh after a long stay in stable, threw him and hurt him badly. General Pétain, with General Fayolle, took for a time the place of General Mangin.

Alongside Mangin's men was the Eighth French Army, under General Gérard, which had fought many actions amid the Vosges Mountains of Alsace. After forming part of the Army of Lorraine it was appointed to march to the Rhine by way of the historic town of Saverne, which had become notorious in the annals of Prussian militarism under its German name of Zabern. Below the Eighth Army was the Alsatian commander General Hirschauer, with the Second Army of Verdun fame, directed towards Mulhouse and the Lower Rhine. Coloured American forces were also arrayed along the Vosges.

A RHINE CONTRAST.
German officer crossing one of the Rhine bridges, and passing French sentries who watched him in sardonic silence from the box, still striped in the German colours.

At eleven o'clock in the morning of Sunday, November 17th, 1918, all the allied armies of occupation began to move forward in strict battle order. Mounted patrols went out, followed by cavalry screens with horse artillery, behind which foot and guns travelled on a carefully arranged schedule. As the advanced troops occupied towns and villages, preparations were made for the arrival of the main forces. The men carried their helmets, gas-masks, and full equipment, for an armistice was not peace, and orders were given to be ready for all emergencies. It was a day of hard frost with an icy wind, but the bronzed, shining faces of the troopers were full of grim satisfaction.

The Second French Army was the first to enter an important town. At noon the cavalry galloped into Mulhouse, amid a moving scene of rejoicing. By villages on the way they rode through arches of triumph made of woven boughs, by houses all flagged and decorated, coloured paper being flown from humble dwellings that could find no bunting of the proper hue. Young children, women, and old men shouted greetings, taking a pride in showing the army of deliverance that they had not forgotten the French language, which they had long been forbidden to speak.

Even the cattle in the fields had their horns festooned with the colours of France. Many farmsteads were **Carnival of joy in Mulhouse** hung with religious banners of the time of the Second Empire, which for half a century had been piously preserved at the bottom of ancient chests, along with bridal costumes and other family relics. Girls, with Tricolour ribbons in their hair, and shouting and laughing boys ran forward, seized the reins of the horses and jumped on the gun-carriages of the 168th Division, at the head of which General Hirschauer rode into his native town of Mulhouse. Forty thousand people thronged the streets and climbed roofs and lamp-posts, while squadrons of French aeroplanes circled above the resonant city, where a pathetic little band of Alsatian veterans of the Franco-Prussian War led the victorious Alsatian commander to the town-hall. In a fine speech General Hirschauer spoke of his father and other old fighting men of France sleeping at last in French soil. The old priest of the town, who was among the leading citizens welcoming the army of liberation, died from sheer excess of joy while the general was speaking. His aged heart could not carry the tide of blood created by his strong emotions. Yet his sudden death cast no sadness

over the carnival of victory. Rather did it testify to the strength of joyful feeling that swept through every spectator belonging to the old true stock.

There were Germans in civil employments remaining in Mulhouse—administrators, important business men, and other persons of the governing class, who had won or purchased interests in the country. Some of them were eager to become French subjects, and so save their property from taxation or war indemnity, and from possible confiscation under the revolutionary government in Germany. Others, in spite of all their professions of loyalty, remained hostile to France, and in the later stage of the rearrangement of government worked bitterly against the French nation and its recovered province.

After a century of blundering crimes

GUARDING A BRIDGE OF BOATS.
French soldiers with a machine-gun posted at the end of a bridge of boats across the Rhine when the allied forces first passed into occupation of the Rhine territories.

the Teutons could not leave in friendly fashion their kindred but more liberal-minded neighbours. Almost to the last they vented their spite upon the Alsatians, pillaging them, selling back looted goods to them, and finally, at Mulhouse, taking considerable sums of money for stacks of timber cut for strengthening entrenchments, and then setting fire to the material when retreating. Compared with all that occurred during the Prussian period of rule, the little episode of selling and burning of firewood did not seem of importance. But it was biting cold weather in the middle of November, 1918, and the last act of the retreating Germans became a memorable symbol of the character of their broken tyranny.

At Gebweiler, above Mulhouse, the French forces were greeted in a most graceful, thoughtful manner. In the brief interval between the departure of the gaolers and the arrival of the liberators a subscription was opened, and the French commander was given ten thousand francs. " It is our first contribution towards the relief of the towns of Northern France, which have suffered so much in the war of our deliverance," said the spokesman of Gebweiler. The Alsatians were not flourishing. Many of their menfolk had perished in the enforced service of the enemy, and many of their native leaders had been persecuted, and among the lower class in the large towns there was want. A country girl exclaimed as she met the troops by her farm, " Oh, if you had come and stayed with us at the beginning of the war, we should have met you with full hands. Now our hands are empty!" But their hearts were brimming with loyal affection. And Alsace was still rich. Her vast mines of potash were happily intact, promising to fertilise the decaying soil of France, Britain, and America, and, by their almost untouched natural wealth, help the motherland to recover from the material losses and break completely the Teutonic monopoly in one of the most precious of metals.

But the people were the lasting wealth of the country. They were skilled weavers of cotton and silk, splendid farmers, artisans, and chemical workers. From their rich red soil had sprung some of the best military leaders of the French Revolutionary age, and General Hirschauer proved at Verdun that the fighting talent of the race was not exhausted. The commander of the Second Army moved down to the Rhine, near Basle, his troops being the first of the forces of the Allies to attain the river frontier between Gaul and Teuton. Northward he extended his divisions to the pleasant town of Colmar, which was the intellectual centre of the spirit of resistance of the province, and General de Castelnau took part in the happy pageant of redemption.

Alsace reunited to France Above Colmar the French marched through the plain where Turenne broke the Germans and drove them over the Rhine in 1675, in a victory that consummated the union of the province with France. Yet more profound in effect was the victory of Foch. It elicited an instant and general enthusiasm among the Alsatians, on which the German Press could not refrain from remarking. As the enemy then openly confessed, there was no need for a referendum on the question whether the people wished to return to the democracy of France. The matter was carried by acclamation.

At the northern end of the grand line of the advance of the allied armies, Brussels held festival while Mulhouse roared and danced in gladness. M. Max, the heroic burgomaster, having escaped from prison during the Revolution in Germany made his way back to his native city, boarding enemy lorries, cars, and military trains without concealment and against all difficulties. Clad in the clothes in which he had been exiled and imprisoned, worn out, dirty, and exhausted, he forced his way through the last columns of the retreating Germans, and arrived in Brussels just as Belgian cavalry and cyclists were coming in, with British troops under General Bulfin.

The Germans had been marching out of the city at four o'clock in the morning with their bands playing. But not a flag flew in Brussels. During the attempt to spread the Revolution into Belgium the German commander had called the townspeople to put out flags and rejoice at their **Burgomaster Max home in Brussels** liberation. Not a flag appeared and not a cheer was given. The Bruxellois were taking no orders of any kind from the enemy. So they left their city undecorated when their beloved burgomaster returned, after fifty months' captivity, and the first forces of the army of victory appeared in the suburbs.

Flags by the hundred thousand soon appeared. Like a human inundation the people thronged the streets, dancing and singing, and tried to get a glimpse of ragged, bushy-haired Max by the old town-hall in the picturesque square, which was far too small to hold the crowds. M. Max was almost buried in flowers, and open-air speeches from the Lion Staircase were drowned by the thunder of the multitude. M. Max, himself the incarnation of the civic virtues which had kept the Belgians independent in spirit through the ages, had the courage to state that, in spite of all his country had suffered, he no longer regretted it had been invaded, for the enemy had enabled Belgium to safeguard her honour and win spiritual greatness.

GERMANS CAP-IN-HAND TO THE CONQUERING ALLIES.

General Lecomte, on the right, who was in command of the Thirty-third Corps of the French Army, receiving a deputation of leading German officials at Wiesbaden. The officials waited on the commander of the French occupying troops to assure him of the loyal co-operation of the local authorities. The first French troops of the armies of occupation to reach Wiesbaden did so on December 14th, 1918.

THE BRITISH COMMANDER-IN-CHIEF IN GERMANY.
Sir Douglas Haig with officers of the 2nd Canadian Division Headquarters on the east side of the Rhine. The Commander-in-Chief is seen shaking hands with Lieut.-Colonel P. T. Montague, D.S.O., M.C.

But the sufferings of the Bruxellois were not at an end. The incorrigible Teuton, while whining for pity to the American Government, and crying out against the French and British, and pleading for food for his people, could not retreat from Brussels along the road to Louvain without again breaking out murderously against the little nation that had done so much to defeat him. Late in the afternoon, while the people in the city were growing wilder and wilder in their gladness and making a " Kermesse " in every wide thoroughfare and open space, a tremendous explosion occurred in the Northern Railway Station. Soon afterwards the Southern Station flamed and rocked. All night the fires and detonations continued on the railways, and when morning came there was still grave danger of further explosions, as some of the fires were still burning.

Final outrages by the Huns Some Germans, officers as well as privates, whose tongues were loosened by drink, had boasted that they would leave Brussels in a bath of blood. One German cyclist had been seen with a light by the long trains of ammunition waggons which the Germans had abandoned in the stations and along the tracks leading out of the city. Marshal Foch sent a stern warning to the German High Command, and the Germans in reply charged the disasters to the carelessness of some of the townspeople. This pretence at an excuse was however invalidated by discoveries made in the Western Railway Station, where no explosions had taken place. Fuses were found there connected with abandoned high explosives, and either through hurried oversight or humane disobedience of orders, such as saved Bruges Belfry from being blown up by the mines left underneath it, the fuses had not been fired.

The suffering and damage wrought by fires and delay-action mines in and around the Brussels railway-stations were very grave. Hundreds of persons were killed or injured, buildings were wrecked within the radius of a quarter of a mile, engine-sheds and a great number of trucks were lost, and the means of feeding and supplying the capital and conducting the march to the Lower Rhine were seriously interrupted. The crimes put an end for a while to the public rejoicing, and there was some risk of all members of the criminal nation within reach being assailed by the angry people. The mood of the advanced Belgian forces became very grim when, passing by the ruined scenes of early atrocities by the invader, they arrived and witnessed his fiendish new crimes. Happily, civic and military discipline prevailed, and although the German people were, with good reason in their own conscience, apprehensive when the Belgian Army afterwards passed the ruined frontier villages and entered German towns, the victors of the Yser kept themselves in hand.

The British armies also became fiercely bitter against their defeated foe, as they moved forward on a broad front below Brussels and towards Dinant. Nine miles west of Brussels, at Lasquin, the Germans had a vast ammunition dump and food-supply depot for their Fourth Army. Here some eight hundred British prisoners of war were kept working ten hours a day and seven days a week, on a ration of a piece of dark brown bread and watery soup. They died by the hundred of slow starvation and brutal ill-treatment, and when some of the survivors drifted after the armistice towards the British lines their condition wrung the hearts of the men who met them.

All along the four-hundred-mile line of the allied advance, from the neighbourhood of Antwerp to the Vosges Mountains, ghastly wrecks of British manhood straggled towards the cavalry patrols, or were found dying and dead on the roads along which horsemen **British prisoners'** and cyclists were riding. There were multi- **pitiful plight** tudes of other returning prisoners, French, Italians, Belgians, Americans, and some Russians, but the plight of the British was so exceptionally dreadful that every advancing army remarked upon it. The spirit of the Hymn of Hate had not evaporated in November, 1918.

British soldiers had been misused with a special ferocity, to which other allied prisoners of war indignantly testified. They were done to death slowly and deliberately, the Teuton even sacrificing their immediate value to him as labouring slaves in order to subject them to torture. When those who had not been killed were released, after the signing of the armistice, no food was given to them and no transport provided. Men who had enough strength left to walk set out westward, but a considerable proportion of them fell by the way. Those who reached their own countrymen or their allies usually had to be put in ambulances and taken to hospital.

It is difficult to discern the motive of the enemy's conduct in this matter. It is clear that the affair was organised under the orders of the German High Command, for all along the line there was the same method of turning prisoners of war adrift without food. Hindenburg was under no illusion regarding his complete defeat and the power of the Associated Powers to inflict punishment upon the German nation, yet when the German forces were at their weakest, and still liable to break and throw the civilian population into the wildest disorder, the enemy commander and his lieutenants went out of their way to incite an almost speechless passion of vengeance in the victorious pursuing armies.

There is one possible explanation of the extraordinary conduct of the enemy. Perhaps the starving, tottering wrecks of men were sent into the allied lines in the design to convince the Allies that Germany was breaking down through famine, and that if the appeals of Dr. Solf, the new Foreign Minister, were not met by the lifting of the naval blockade and the transport of huge quantities of food, Germany would at once dissolve into Bolshevist anarchy. If this was the plot, which had the advantage of inflicting the last tortures on the British prisoners of war while promoting the intrigue of Dr. Solf, the political effect did not last long. As soon as the Allies arrived in German cities they found confectioners' shops displaying finer delicacies than were to be obtained in France and Great Britain, and saw that the

Grenadier Guards marching up to the Hohenzollern Bridge during their occupation of Cologne.

British sentries detailed to examine barges plying on the Rhine during the blockade of Germany.

Units of the British motor-launch Rhine patrol lying alongside the embankment at Cologne.

Grenadier Guards returning to their barracks after a route march along the Rhine.

British motor=launches on patrol on the Rhine passing under the Hohenzollern Bridge at Cologne.

Changing the Guard at Bonn University: Lancashire Fusiliers relieving the Border Regiment.

Battalion of the 21st Canadians crossing the Rhine at Bonn salute the Canadian Corps Commander.

hostile populace was on the whole fairly well fed and provided with a sufficient store of food to last until the spring of 1919.

The Germans were punished silently in the course of months for their final outburst of inhumanity towards the unhappy men whom they had at their mercy. Instead of the blockade being lifted, it was rigorously continued, and when President Wilson arrived in France he consented to the policy adopted. The American troops were, indeed, most angry over the condition of British soldiers whom they met on their way to Luxemburg. The Americans were still capable of being surprised at the character of the Teuton, not having fought against him so long as the Allies, and being therefore liable, during the stage transformations in the enemy's form of government, to accept things as they seemed on the surface. Altogether, the enemy's amazing treatment of prisoners of war released after the armistice was one of his supreme blunders in crime.

As soon as the tragedy of the prisoners was revealed, the German Government was ordered to adopt civilised methods in the treatment of returning prisoners of war. Meanwhile, Sir Douglas Haig and other allied commanders did all they could to mitigate the sufferings of the men. The warlike order of the advance was altered, travelling kitchens, ambulances with doctors and nurses, and motor transport were sent out along with the skirmishing forces, and cavalry patrols found their main work in scouting for returning prisoners, and also in acting as advanced agents of relief for the multitudes of deported civilians streaming back upon all roads.

A hundred and twenty thousand French refugees passed through the front of the Second British Army at Nivelles. Some had been walking for three weeks, poorly clothed, underfed, and exposed day and night to wind and rain. Many of them had been deported from Valenciennes in October, and used in groups of hundreds to screen the retreating German column from machine-gun fire from British airmen. Influenza ravaged them, and they died in large numbers on their way home. Ambulance stations were arranged along the roads, and Army motor-lorries employed to carry those who were too weak to walk.

Belgian vengeance on Hun miscreants They tramped from the German lines along with the returning prisoners of war, and it was the nurses of the Cavell school who organised places along the road where the sick were fed and tended until the terrible death-rate was brought down.

On November 18th it was the turn of the First British Army to engage in the work of rescue. They had to rescue Germans. The burgomaster with one of the aldermen of Charleroi came to Mons to ask for troops to be sent to their town. The enemy, after abandoning large quantities of rifles and ammunition and leaving trains of high explosive and large munition dumps, was marching eastward, but he left behind some men in uniform and some soldiers who had changed into civilian clothes. Two of these were caught firing the trucks of high explosive and some of the dumps, causing great explosions such as had occurred in Brussels.

The Belgian miners, who had lived and worked like slaves for the enemy, grew mad with anger. They seized rifles and ammunition and began searching for the disguised Germans. Flushed with success, after catching two assassins actually at work and shooting them, the townsfolk began to spread out eastward to catch up with the rear of the Sixth German Army.

The miners were but a mob of men with rifles, entirely without organisation. Fearful lest they should provoke the enemy to turn and massacre them, the burgomaster and

aldermen ran after them and endeavoured to induce the steadier men in the crowd to maintain public order. Unhappily, a German motor-car came along the road, carrying officers to British Headquarters with information about the guns to be delivered up. The miners fired, and when their burgomaster got between them and the car, to prevent the Germans being torn to pieces, the men attacked their own leader and injured him while he was saving the Germans. French and British prisoners of war, who remained strong enough for service, took arms, and with some of the citizens formed a town guard. Then the British troops arrived in advance of the progress of the march, and the miners of Charleroi gave up their rifles and cartridges and their wild plan of vengeance.

As the British were entering Charleroi in the falling

COLOURS FOR THE CANADIANS.
Prince Arthur of Connaught handing regimental colours to an officer of the Victoria Rifles. The presentation took place in Germany when the battalion formed part of the British Army of Occupation.

rain, King Albert drove into Antwerp, the great port of the country which the invaders had bombarded and reduced to a place of desolation. The cold drizzle could not chill the people of the city. They filled the streets, and while the air above rang with the music of the city of bells, the roar of greeting below made the King's words unheard.

There had been a German Revolution in the port, but, starting directly by agents from the naval forces, it had been a genuine affair. The men separated from the officers and yet preserved order, and took special care to avoid all conflict with the Belgian people. **Antwerp veterans salute their King** They sold huge quantities of Army stores to the civilians, and both released prisoners of war coming in from the countryside and interned officers and men arriving from Holland were well supplied with food in Antwerp.

Ragged, grimy Britons, with hollow-cheeked Italians and hairy, fugitive Russians, were fed by the Antwerpers outside pastry shops, the rooms of which were too small to hold the starving crowds. Then, arm in arm, men from every old and new country of the Grand Alliance marched with the Flemish women and girls, dancing and singing in a variety of tongues. The most touching of all groups of men were those who went past the saluting-base where King Albert stood. They could not maintain any formation.

The men walked very slowly, with the help of crutches and sticks, and with a banner flying above them. Many of them wore the old Belgian uniform, others only a coloured armlet.

HONOURING A FRENCH PADRE.
General Mangin at Kreuznach, in Germany, bestowing decorations on his men who had distinguished themselves in the great advance. He was pinning the Legion of Honour on a heroic French chaplain.

British Army approached Brussels by the field of Waterloo, the villagers managed to erect triumphal arches, in spite of the scarcity of timber and materials, and before nearly every house was a row of Christmas-trees with tiny flags and paper flowers. In the inns round Waterloo, British prisoners gathered, being fed by the Belgians from their scanty store while awaiting motor-lorries. Then, by happy chance, some of the French troops in the Army Group of Flanders marched in a misty morning over the scene of conflict between Wellington and Napoleon, alongside British troops, both moving towards the frontier of the land of Blücher. From the mound dominating the old battlefield the British general watched, when the air cleared, his thin, winding trails of forces spreading far out into the distance towards Germany.

Many British troops and returning

They were the remnant of those veterans of the first year of the war, who had fought in the siege of Antwerp. After checking the invader for a little while, alongside the untrained men of the Royal Naval Division, and exposing their bodies to the tremendous fire of the enemy's siege-guns, they had either crawled away crippled or had been carried home and made a slow recovery. They were Antwerp's own heroes, not one man of them needing a medal to show he had fought to the end.

Antwerp was in many respects the happiest centre of Belgium. The people there had seen the best side of the German Revolution, and so lost most of their bitterness against the beaten foe. Only the renegades of Flemish stock, who had tried during the long period of hostile occupation to separate Fleming from Walloon and rend Belgium in two in the interest of the Teuton, excited any popular resentment. Some of these men, who had the impudence to remain in the city when their masters had fled, were savagely handled. Before the war Antwerp had been a hot-bed of pro-Germanism, and the sinister opposition to all measures for strengthening the Belgian Army had been engineered in the great port, which, as an outlet for the commerce of the Rhineland, contained many Germans. The Antwerper no longer minded the Teuton, but he was inclined to lynch men of his own race who had gone over to the enemy and enjoyed for four years the fruits of their treason.

Purging Belgium of treason

Throughout the redeemed territories of the Belgians and French there were several men and women whose souls had been purchased by the invader and degraded at times beyond description. They were pursued by the liberated people in a passion that at times appalled the fighting men who helped to maintain public order. The soldiers, with their active way of purging their anger in battle, were scarcely in a position to appreciate the exasperated, pent-up feelings of the suffering, passive populace, but they managed somehow to keep the outbursts of passion within limits and saved most of the wrong-doers for legal trial. The man alleged to have betrayed Edith Cavell was traced and arrested, and French and Belgian spies who had served the Germans were discovered.

These incidents, however, did not dim the festival brightness of mind of the people through whose hamlets and towns the long columns of the victorious armies passed. As the Second

THE LEGION OF HONOUR FOR FRENCH COLONIALS.
General Mangin, at a review of his forces at Kreuznach, in occupied Germany, fastening the Legion of Honour to the flag of the 22nd Colonial Artillery.

prisoners toured the battlefield with Belgian guides, who related the story of the action in excellent English, and replied with point under the bombardment of questions. The modern Briton was amazed to find his forefathers fought so close to the enemy, and the old breakwater of Hougomont was commonly regarded as a poor position. " I could have finished it in a few minutes with a trench-mortar battery," said an English sergeant, studying the historic farm from Napoleon's point of view.

On November 22nd King Albert entered his capital at the head of two divisions of the Belgian Army and a contingent of French, American, English, Scottish, and Newfoundland troops. General Plumer, of the Second Army, General Birdwood, of the Fifth Army, with Sir Roger Keyes, of the Dover Patrol, took part in the celebration of victory.

King Albert re-enters Brussels

Seldom did a sovereign enter his capital in such impressive circumstances or receive from his people so tumultuous a display of loyalty as did Albert of Belgium. After the tragedy of the German evacuation the people seemed not merely to have recovered the joyous sense of personal freedom, but to have been stimulated into a delightful ecstasy of feeling.

There was sunshine by day and clear moonlight by night. In the golden and silver air Brussels held carnival, down the broad avenues and in the wide squares by the white Palace of Justice crowning the city. Rich and poor, peasants and noblemen, soldiers and high officers, made swirling crowds of revellers. The girls clasped hands and danced round the soldiers, and swept their heroes along with them in a commonalty of joy.

Scottish Highlanders, by reason of their picturesque kilts, were the favourites. In the afternoon, when they marched past, the sound of the pipes was overwhelmed in the clamour of welcome. In the evening every man who wore the kilt was captured by scores of girls, who took turns in holding his arms and dancing round him. Hero-worship did not seem to embarrass many of the " Jocks." It was well they had a good training in Brussels, for they remained inspirers of popular enthusiasm all the way to the German frontier, and ending their career by surprising the Teutons into admiration.

The kilt hailed with acclamation All the merit of eliciting popularity was not theirs, in spite of the romance of their attire. Owing largely to German caricaturists having from the beginning of the war depicted the " Engländer " in the bonnet and kilt of the Scottish Highlander, the Belgian people commonly regarded the Scotsmen as typical Englishmen. The affection shown towards all Britons was very remarkable ; it was a moving testimony to the part that the British peoples had played against the aggressors.

The great event of the day at the Brussels celebration was a speech made by King Albert in Parliament, where a new Coalition Government, including the Socialists, arranged a large programme of reform. After referring to the Revolution of 1830, that freed his people from Dutch rule, but left them shorn of territory and shackled in commerce, King Albert said in a passage of far-reaching importance : " Belgium, victorious and liberated from the neutrality which was imposed upon her by treaties of which the base was shattered

by the war, will enjoy complete independence. These treaties, that determined her position in Europe, have not protected her against the most criminal of outrages. They cannot survive the crisis which overtook our country. There must be no more crises such as those of which our land was a victim. Restored to her rights, Belgium will settle her destinies according to her needs and aspirations in complete sovereignty."

The significance of this speech was only appreciated in Holland. After the Belgians had won their freedom from

FRENCH TROOPS ESTABLISHING A CROSSING OF THE RHINE.

Pontoon bridge in course of construction by French troops over the Rhine at St. Goar. On reaching the Rhine at this pleasant part of the river, some miles above Coblenz, the French forces had to make a bridge to give them access to the territory they were to occupy on the eastern bank. Inset : Two distinguished French leaders, Generals Mangin and Marchand, meeting on the pontoon bridge by which the French troops spanned the Rhine at St. Goar.

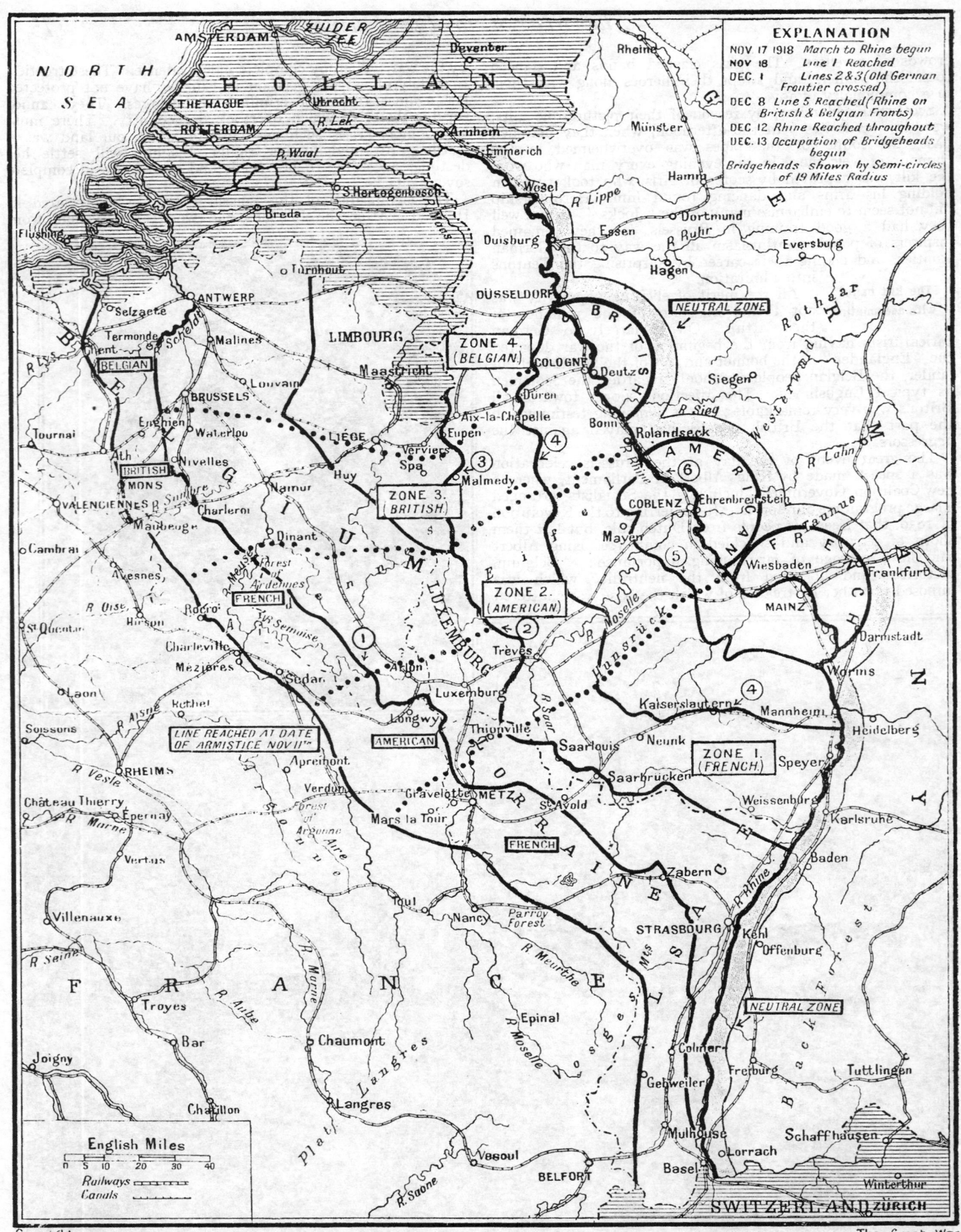

The Great War

ALLIED BRIDGE-HEADS AND NEUTRAL ZONE ALONG THE OCCUPIED RHINE.

From the line reached on November 11th, 1918, the Allies marched to the Rhine along the whole western front in stages shown above. French, American, and British armies occupied zones of the Rhine provinces lying between the pre-war frontier and the bridge-heads at Mainz, Coblenz, and Cologne. The zone north of the British, between the Belgian frontier and the Rhine from Emmerich to Düsseldorf, was held by Belgian forces.

the Dutch, neutrality had been imposed upon them against their will and at crippling cost. They had to surrender to Holland part of the Belgian province of Limburg, in which a Belgian population still existed and longed to return to the motherland. They had to suffer the loss of the Duchy of Luxemburg, which went to the King of Holland and his heirs, and was afterwards drawn into a German connection against the wishes of its people. The Belgians had also to surrender the southern bank of the Scheldt to the Dutch, who for the best part of a century used the power they had acquired to check the development of Antwerp and promote the development of Rotterdam. Far from the loss of power on one of the grand routes of commerce in Europe helping to maintain Belgium as a neutral State, the Dutch had closed the Scheldt at the opening of the war and prevented British warships and troop transports from reaching Antwerp, while providing the enemy with war material along their railways.

None of the peoples of the Great Powers associated with Belgium understood at the time the importance of the speech made by King Albert when he entered his capital. Indeed, scarcely one of the leading statesmen of the Allies grasped the scope of the declaration. Belgium was not given the position in the formative council of the League of Nations to which she was entitled as the keystone in the construction of a new Europe.

Months elapsed before King Albert and his Ministers were enabled to begin to assert the sovereign rights of their country. King Albert, however, was a born fighter, and he at least succeeded in making the governing class in Holland, which to a considerable extent had favoured the Teutons from the opening to the end of the struggle, feel that he would make good the words he had spoken on the day when he returned victorious to his capital.

DRAMATIC CONTRAST AT COLOGNE.
General Sir Herbert Plumer, in command of the British Second Army, watching his troops crossing the Rhine at Cologne on December 12th, 1918. The general and his Staff, with the Union Jack, were strikingly grouped at the base of the colossal statue of the ex-Kaiser.

While Brussels danced and sang and made more liberal laws for the people, and a sounder policy for the State, the fortress city of Metz opened to the forces of freedom after a longer captivity. Metz was entered on November 19th by the army of General Mangin, under the leadership of Pétain, promoted to the glorious rank of Marshal of France. The Lorrainers, who had waited nearly half a century for liberation, accepted their release from Prussian tyranny in a strange way. Their character was colder than that of the people of Alsace. Many of their women were in mourning, and the road from Gravelotte to Mars-la-Tour was a long street of tombs of men fallen in the old battles in which the fortress city was lost to France.

Metz put out flags, largely made from the dresses of its women for lack of proper material. When, however, the French Army appeared not a cheer was raised. Metz, with her tremendous fortifications, magnificent cathedral, assembly place, and the huge German barracks glistening under a quiet blue sky, became an open-air temple filled with a people in prayer. As the regiments passed with their colours there was still no roar of welcome. The Lorrainers gripped each other by the hand, some of the women and men began crying, and, as the intense emotions loosened, persons unknown to each other kissed.

French of the French was Metz. She had no need to speak, and in solemn, religious fashion the procession went on. The crowd broke into the road where the troops marched, while Marshal Pétain took the salute by the statue of Marshal

Metz freed after nearly fifty years

Ney. After the review the French Commander-in-Chief completed the religious character of the ceremony by walking into the cathedral to close the great day in prayer after the chanting of the *Te Deum*. Meanwhile the city at last broke into loud rejoicing. Chasseurs, Spahis, and other troops promenaded the town, arm in arm with the pretty girls, singing the soldier's song of Madelon. The colossal figure of William the First of Germany, mounted on his favourite charger on a point overlooking the whole valley of the Moselle, was overthrown, and sent prone and headless down the slope of the old ramparts. Other German figures were pulled down, with the exception of the statue of William the Second, erected over the door of the cathedral. In the hands of the Imperial criminal there was placed an inscription: "*Sic transit gloria mundi.*"

There were thousands of Germans in Metz. They had been brought in under a policy of colonisation, directed towards making the fortress city gradually but thoroughly Germanic. About one-fourth of the civil population was alien and hostile, and the French themselves had diminished in number through large migrations to France. The natives, in the supreme day of triumph, retained self-control, and the Germans were able to walk about the streets without any fear of personal violence.

Some of them indeed displayed, when they saw they were not in peril, the old arrogance of the Prussian. It took some time for General Maud'huy, the new Governor of Metz, to change the administration and bring in Lorrainers to

Lorrainers replace German officials

BRITISH GUN ON A GERMAN QUAY.
Big British howitzer posted on the Rhine bank at
Cologne in December, 1918, owing to the outbreak
of rioting in that city.

the Americans dvanced so quickly that it hardly appeared worth while to interrupt the festival of liberation by a Revolution. But on November 22nd, when the American troops were far beyond the city and the duties of hospitality were completed, the Luxemburgers gathered in front of the palace and called upon their girl ruler to abdicate. A French regiment entered the city to prevent disorder, and a committee of the people insisted that the Grand Duchess should not be allowed to pass the French troops in review. There was a threat that if the young lady would not voluntarily surrender her position she would be taken and carried out of the country.

A small but fierce Revolutionary party, with French sympathies, wished to establish a republic and unite with

replace the German officials and managers.

Happily, France had an abundance of brilliant, experienced men of Lorraine and Alsace stock, who had been driven into the mother country by the vindictive foreigner and trained in French offices. They came back and amalgamated with many of the subordinates of the official world, who were natives of the place, and after some confusion the French administrative system was established on a better basis than that obtaining under the Second Empire.

The large German element began to make trouble during the trying period when communications with France were weak and slow, and food and material were conveyed with difficulty over the chaos of the battlefields by the Meuse and Moselle. General Maud'huy, a

IN OCCUPIED COLOGNE.
British armoured car, part of the force which reached that city early in December, 1918, beside a German tramcar, the driver and woman conductor of which were both wearing semi-military uniform. The townsfolk manifested something of interested curiosity in the British arrivals.

famous fighting man, was not inclined to allow any scope to the last mass of enemies at large in French territory. He

Maud'huy's firm but gentle hand

put down the movement, and asked the loyal natives to wait in patience until railway and road communications were improved. The men and women of Lorraine had not to walk far from their city in order to see for themselves over what ground supplies had to be brought in order to set industries in full working order while the troops were marching to Mayence. Thus Metz, that had waited so long for the day of victory, abided in patience the return of full life and prosperity.

The Third American Army, after passing through the famous fortress town of Longwy and by the Briey mine-fields, reached the romantic mountain town of Luxemburg, amid the ravines and precipices of the lost duchy of Belgium. It was one of the most picturesque fortresses in Europe, perched on a rocky tableland, moated by Nature with streams cutting deep into the wild upland, and forming an outer ridge, honeycombed with casemates and embrasures, from which the road to Treves might be swept. Impregnable to attack, it menaced the Moselle road between France and the Rhineland.

While the German forces were in occupation of the duchy the people could take no action. After the enemy departed,

France. Most of the people, however, were Catholics and apprehensive of the anti-clericalism of the ruling parties in the French Government. Their aim was either to remain independent and maintain the duchy, or to join again with Belgium, which was largely Catholic in policy and possessed in Cardinal Mercier and other heroic priests with enlightened views a progressive force in religion.

The Grand Duchess retired from Luxemburg, and was succeeded by her sister Charlotte; but the agitation among the people continued, some calling upon France to annex the country, others sending deputations to Brussels to advocate reunion under King Albert.

The position of liberated but uncertain Luxemburg continued to be perplexing. Her great wealth in iron, as well as her natural barrier strength, gave a peculiar importance to the little country newly released from practically a century of German political and industrial overlordship.

While the quarter of a million people of Luxemburg were going through their first distemper of democratic liberty the tide of liberation swept over the high, wild, granite wall of the Vosges Mountains, and flowed by the old, red cathedral and picturesque houses of the city of the "Marseillaise"—Strasbourg. On November 25th the capital of Alsace-Lorraine was entered by the Fourth French Army, led by

Marshal Foch, Marshal Pétain, General Gouraud, and other Army chiefs. The Strasbourgers were as different in temperament from the people of Metz as Northerners are from Southerners. They were Alsatians, with a new German element introduced as a colonising force, and by musical clubs and sporting clubs the natives of the city had secretly maintained and fostered love for the mother country during the forty-eight years of oppression and espionage. Far more emotional than the French-speaking race of Metz, the Strasbourgers streamed out of their city in a delirium of gladness. Foch first took the salute on the esplanade outside the town, where the German Emperor used to review the enemy garrison. After this symbolic military ceremony, festival was held in the old Kléber Square, where the figure of the great commander of the Revolutionary age rose in the centre of his native city, in a framework of old, rose-red gabled houses.

The Germans had left Kléber standing in Strasbourg, as they had left Ney in Metz, as tokens of the forces they had conquered in 1870. Marshal Foch, whose genius was based on a romantic temperament, wished to purify the image of Kléber. In a great dramatic spectacle, with people and troops

ploughlands of France for a century had thirsted. "*Qu' un sang impur abreuve nos sillons!*" Yet it was sung with the solemnity of a hymn, in an enormous volume of sound carrying over the Rhine into the gloomy pinewoods of the Black Forest.

Immediately afterwards Marshal Foch entered the cathedral, where three French officer priests conducted a service of thanksgiving for victory. Foch, a very religious man, who used to retire and pray in the interval between launching an action and receiving reports, wept as he prayed, covering his face to hide his tears. No joy then moved him, but great sorrow. In the Catholic way he was praying for the souls of dead soldiers, and for all whose sufferings had saved the world from degradation and profound tyranny. Like a woman of Metz, who exclaimed she would have disbelieved in God if the Germans had won, Marshal Foch regarded the war as something more than a national or an international struggle. His intense belief was the source of his desperate courage in extreme difficulty and of his flashing inspiration.

Foch's emotion in thanksgiving

He resembled Napoleon only in having a romantic temperament, employing a large fund of classic knowledge of the art of war. For the rest, he was a Christian gentleman. To him the Prussian of the governing class had been an incarnate devil. From his point of view his own country stood for a Divine cause, and its multitudinous dead were its altar sacrifice of the best. So he wept for France's dead.

Outside, in square and streets, under a fine rain, young men and maidens rejoiced, the head-dress of ribbon of the Alsatian girls giving a picturesque character to the carnival, which obtained a peculiar distinction by the presence of a great multitude of men in German uniforms. They were soldiers of Alsace and Lorraine who had been forced to serve the enemy, and were wildest of all in their joy at being free. At Kehl

EXPLOSIVES IN SAFE CUSTODY.
British sentry on guard over a store of shells in a German munition factory near Cologne.

roaring and waving, the victorious leader of the Grand Alliance walked up to the statue, drew his own sword and gravely saluted. Then, with band music and song, the torn, dulled colours of the French forces were placed in front of the statue. Foch laid his sword aside, took an historic sabre of jewelled gold and steel from a silken green scabbard, drew the blade, and cried, "On guard!" Trumpets and drums sounded. "To the colours!" rang the voice of Foch. Then, with the sabre which the city of Strasbourg had presented to Kléber after his triumphs over Germans and Austrians, Foch saluted the flags of the French Army.

The Strasbourgers understood, and sang the "Marseillaise" in a wonderful way. It was the chant of battle of the old Armies of the Rhine, composed in the democratic city against the Imperial Teutons, and ending with the old imprecation against the impure blood of the invaders, for which the

SAVING THE BEATEN FOE FROM HIS OWN FRIENDS.
British machine-gun post in Cologne docks reinforced by armed civilian police recruited from the German Army. Owing to Revolutionary riots in Cologne, that caused many casualties among civilians, an advance detachment of the 18th Hussars arrived there on December 6th, 1918, to restore order.

Bridge, crossing the Rhine a mile and a half from Strasbourg, and separating the French Army from the German Army, there was still a continual movement of returning Alsatians and Lorrainers—old men coming from prison or internment camps, and middle-aged men, young men, and lads from the defeated Army and Fleet. There were also deported family groups released from servitude, and pinched, grey-faced prisoners of war. Penniless, ragged, and exhausted, they trudged into the rejoicing city and, under its canopy of flags and lanterns, caught some warmth from the light-hearted crowds and found food and shelter.

There were, however, some scenes of bitterness in the by-streets of the city, and in many other places in Alsace-Lorraine withdrawn from the celebration of redemption. At one German restaurant, quiet and shuttered, a well-known Frenchman of letters entered in search of food. He found the dining-room lighted, and a dozen persons at the table talking loudly. At the sight of his uniform they all became silent, and a serving-maid called out there was nothing but German cooking in the place. The Frenchman remarked that any cooking would suit him, as he was hungry. Thereupon a man with gold-rimmed glasses, looking like an official, said it was a German gathering and no strangers were wanted.

Indiscretion of angry Germans

"I am a Frenchman in France," was the answer. "I need something to eat."

All the Germans, some women among them, broke out into angry cries. "Our revenge will come! Yes, in five years! You only did it with the help of the Americans! We were alone in the world! All our allies betrayed us! We will settle with them when we have finished you off! It took the entire earth to bring us down after four years of war; but we will rise again, and we know how to wait!"

The Frenchman became interested. He could not answer all his verbal assailants, and selected the official with the gold

ON BRIDGE GUARD IN OCCUPIED GERMANY.
One of the soldiers of the battalions of the young Guards that went to Cologne early in 1919 to relieve the Guards Division there. He was posted as sentry at one end of the great suspension bridge, and was being closely scrutinised by the veteran German ticket collector on his right.

glasses. "Are you sure," he asked, "that your troops think in this way, after being dragged for fifty months from battle to battle?"

"We don't trouble about the cowards and traitors!" was the reply. "The people are the real Germany. Give us only time to recover. The talkers think they are now the masters. Let them talk. We shall act. Our race is broken to discipline, and we know how to make it obey. It will remain German through any disorder. Here last week the Soldiers' Council degraded its officers, but gave them the duty of continuing to command in all matters of military technique. Only the fools among us hope to disarm you by pretending to imitate you. We shall escape by our strength. We shall not breathe freely until we are avenged. The next time we shall not leave France. We shall eat you up like this!" And he swallowed a fruit tart in a mouthful—a striking example of humble, starving Teutondom.

It was an angry, indiscreet explosion on the part of the leaders of the lost colony of Germans in Strasbourg. It cost them something, as the report of the conversation appeared in one of the most popular Paris newspapers, and was reprinted throughout France. One immediate result was an acceleration of the process of removing all German officials from Alsace and Lorraine, and a strong popular agitation for the transport across the Rhine of all German workmen, managers, and business men, even at some cost in the manufacturing power of the provinces. As in Lorraine, so in Alsace, the Germans in civil employment, who were allowed to remain in large numbers, worked at creating labour unrest and apprehensions of permanent loss of trade during the months in which railway connection with France was slow, small, and irregular, making general intercourse very difficult.

The great days of rejoicing in Brussels, Metz, and Strasbourg did not disturb the military precision of the advance towards the Rhineland.

LAW AND ORDER RESTORED BY CONQUEST.
British sentry watching the Rhine. The advance-guard of the Army of Occupation took possession of the great iron suspension bridge at Cologne early in December, and, speaking generally, was welcomed by the civilian population as being a guarantee for the maintenance of order.

Towards the end of November some forty divisions and strong cavalry forces of the Associated Armies were ready to move into German territory and occupy the ground and bridge-heads fixed in the armistice. The German forces in retreat numbered considerably over three millions of men, but a large number of the troops in the interior and on lines of communication went home. The actual fighting forces in the west more or less preserved order and discipline, and usually it was only when they passed beyond a town, leaving disbanded natives behind, that pillaging and other disorders occurred. Hindenburg fixed his Headquarters by Cassel, selecting with some sense of historic irony, the palace of Wilhelmshöhe, in which Napoleon III. was placed as prisoner of war after his surrender at Sedan.

General von Armin's troops were training through Holland and Aix-la-Chapelle. The armies of Quast and Eberhardt, each reported to number four hundred thousand men, were streaming over the river by Bonn. Through Mayence, General von der Marwitz led some hundred thousand men. At Mannheim troops were coming at the rate of one hundred thousand a day from the armies of General von Einem and General von Gallwitz, while Baden received the sadly reduced army group that **Clockwork retreat** General von Lossberg once had hoped to **of the Germans** launch into action. Men from Alsace-Lorraine and the Rhineland were given leave to go home, with the exception of two classes of Germans, but the rest of the troops were held together.

The broad front of retreat, the general preservation of order, and the numerous permanent or boat bridges over the Rhine made the withdrawal a fairly easy Staff operation so far as marching troops were concerned. And having a network of unbroken railways before them, the organisers of the retreat got most of their allowed material away in due time. Through Frankfort, for example, one hundred military trains ran daily, keeping to scheduled time.

Owing to the fact that demobilisation had not been imposed upon Germany, out of the Allies' fear of a contagious Bolshevist movement, the general situation was not entirely safe for the Associated Powers. Most of their men expected to be released from service quickly after the victory in the field; but as the Germans conducted their retreat with great skill, tact, and precision, and did not demobilise, it was dangerous for the victors seriously to weaken their armies. The use the Teuton made of the menace of Bolshevism to avoid being reduced to **Crafty Teutons'** impotence, after narrowly escaping annihila- **use of Bolshevism** tion, deserves to rank as one of the most famous tricks of war, alongside the device by which the Prussians trained and raised a large army under the eyes of their French conquerors in the age of Napoleon.

At the end of November the British forces of occupation had marched from Ath, Mons, and Avesnes to the German frontier near Malmédy. Many of the leading troops had sung, danced, cheered, and revelled from Namur to Liège, Spa, and Verviers. By thousands returning prisoners of war still entered the British lines, and, as most of them were in prison-camp uniforms with long black coats and round black caps, while others were in odd garments of all nations, their nationality was not known until they spoke. They were homing birds on far journeys, such as Glasgow or Sicily, Rouen or some Berkshire village, and occasionally Russia, Poland, the United States, or British Dominions overseas. Some came down the Meuse in boats, happy at last to rest their feet, but thousands of their comrades in misery continued to tramp along roads, straggling along in small groups in a fellowship of the wayside, helping each other, sharing bits of bread, yet often unable to converse. There were women among the groups. As bravely as the men they walked home, with packs strapped over their shoulders, skirts torn and muddy, and rough hair, yet with eyes lighted with eagerness.

PÉTAIN, MARSHAL OF FRANCE, RECEIVES HIS BATON IN METZ.

M. Poincaré, President of the French Republic, presenting General Pétain with his baton as a Marshal of France. The historic scene took place at Metz on December 8th, 1918. Behind the new Marshal were the chief leaders of the armies of the Allies—Marshal Joffre, Marshal Foch, Field-Marshal Sir Douglas Haig, General Pershing, General Gillian (Belgium), General Haller (Portugal), General Albricci (Italy), and General Weygand.

Happily there was plenty of food in the territory from which the enemy had retired. At Namur and Huy were many butchers' shops hung with meat, and Liège was far from starving. Over the German frontier was a similar abundance, and, although prices were high, the food conditions of the country were very different from those which had obtained round Lille and Douai. The Germans could feed themselves and also allow the Belgians to feed, when they thought it policy to do so, yet the French had been allowed to starve in the coal-mining region in a slow process of extermination.

At Liège the townspeople carried out magnificent work in looking after returning British prisoners of war. Belgian business men took charge of all wanderers entering the city; a fine mansion was made into a rest and recreation centre, and thousands of families in every walk of life asked as a privilege to have British soldiers billeted upon them as guests. Pocket-money was provided, and the receiving families took pride in walking out with their prisoners arm in arm, and many of the returned soldiers soon became strong enough to promenade, carrying the little children with whom they lived. It was a delightful, memorable ending to the first phase of the great march over friendly territory into hostile country.

British cavalry on German soil

On the last day of November, Hussars, Lancers, and Dragoons of the Second British Army picketed for the night at the frontier of Germany. Between them and the Germans was a brook running down a green and pleasant valley, and the brook was named Red Water. Over the Red Water, by the stone bridge, the invaders had come in the first week of August, 1914; over the Red Water they returned in the last week of November, 1918. Above the Red Water in the morning of December 1st, as the mist thinned away, the hill-side seemed streaming with blood. It was only the scarlet of dead bracken and the reddish leaves of saplings, yet there seemed something significant in the gate to Germany opening in blood-red beauty.

There was a surprise awaiting the cavalry as, at the sound of the bugle, they rode into Germany, along the

READY TO HAND OVER TO THE NEW GUARD.
Changing the guard at Bonn University. The old guard—consisting of men of the Border Regiment —formed up preparatory to handing over the guard duties to the men of the regiment that was to relieve them. Crowds of Bonn folks assembled to witness the ceremony.

frozen road leading to Malmédy through the lovely Ardennes country of ravines, fir forests, and green steppes. Some girls on a hillside waved and cheered, and although the land was lonely in the peace of the Sabbath, it did not seem hostile. Children watched from cottage windows

with friendly faces, and farmers lifted their hats.

The leading young cavalry officer was in an anxious frame of mind. He swore he did not know a word of German, and could not pronounce a single name, and it would be no fault of his if he took a wrong turning. When he rode into Malmédy he had a surprise, which was one that should not have taken him if he had studied Belgian history. The people were going to church and speaking French as they walked. They were Walloons, Belgians of the Belgians, torn from their country and Prussianised after the Battle of Waterloo. The French the people spoke among themselves was not the French of Paris, but the Walloon dialect, yet many of them spoke also classic French.

LANCASHIRE MEN ON DUTY IN BONN.
Relief guard of Lancashire Fusiliers marching through Bonn to take over the guard duties at the University, and (in oval) clothing parade of the 13th Battalion of the King's Liverpool Regiment on the Rhine bank by Bonn bridge.

NAVAL SUPREMACY DEMONSTRATED UP THE RHINE.
Some of the crews of Britain's Rhine Naval Patrol at drill on the bank of the Rhine at Cologne. The building on the right was the German "Water Sport Club." Youthful Cologners seemed particularly interested in the drill of the British sailor lads.

of liberty. At Eupen, a more northerly frontier town, the reception of the British troops was very different. The people were of Germanic stock; they showed no interest in the arrival of their conquerors, and for a time pretended they were on famine rations. Many men and women had scowling faces, but they lost their appearance of being living expressions of the Hymn of Hate when the novelty of the British occupation wore away and commerce with the British soldier was seen to be profitable.

The strip of lost Belgian territory was passed quickly by the cavalry patrols, while the infantry in depth behind them were still holding festival at Verviers and other Belgian towns, and making dancing streams of merriment down the streets with the girls. The British forces continued through the German Ardennes to Düren, and completely lost all appreciation of the scenery of one of the fairest holiday places on the Continent. The roads crawled up steep mountains, and slid dizzily into profound valleys, and, under the steady downpour of rain, horse, foot, and guns vied with motor-lorry drivers in the art of execration.

The beautiful look of the British horses and the smart appearance of the cavalrymen roused the astonishment of the redeemed Walloons, who quickly became friendly. Their preliminary attitude of reserve appeared to be due to fears raised by the German authorities, who had printed in imposing

Saving the Huns from themselves

When, however, the sun shone over the panorama of pine forests and mountaintops, and the troops marched out in the morning, dried and rested, and met the invigorating wind, and wound from village to village in a triumphal procession, they began to enjoy the march to the Rhine. Cologne was reached by special machine-gun brigades on December 7th, British troops being summoned by the burgomaster and sent by special train to put down rioting groups of disbanded troops who were plundering the shops and endeavouring to overwhelm the city in Bolshevist anarchy. There had been a similar outbreak at Düren, where the 1st Cavalry Division sent out strong patrols in advance of the programme to help in maintaining order

The riots greatly facilitated the work of the forces of occupation. By an extraordinary transformation the British soldier, after defeating the German soldier, became the saviour of Germany. He saved the wealthiest and most populous part of the Rhineland from devastating experiments by Soviets, who were

type and placarded in all prominent places appeals imploring the people to be careful and courteous and avoid outrages that would have terrifying consequences. It was a characteristic piece of Prussian impertinence to address in this manner redeemed Belgians, whose sons and husbands had been used for a century as cannon fodder by the enemy of Belgium. Great Britain was not entirely free from blame for the sufferings of the outer Walloons, who had been unfairly punished for generations because the Belgian people in 1814 sympathised with the French and were not at all keen on helping to defeat Napoleon. However, this old wrong was in course of being righted when the British formed in the marketplace of Malmédy and the inns opened with abundant provisions for the forces

WITH THE BRITISH FORCES IN COLOGNE.
Detachment of the 18th Hussars patrolling the Rhine bank at Cologne early in December, 1918. They formed part of the force that went ahead of the main body of occupying troops to maintain order in the city. In oval: British nurses paying a visit to the Rhine Naval Patrol.

THE FRENCH FLAG IN STRASBOURG.
March-past of French troops by the Cathedral of Strasbourg on the occasion of the solemn entry of the victorious French Army, led by Marshal Foch and Marshal Pétain, on November 25th, 1918.

bent upon following the example of Lenin's Communists. The Belgians who entered Aix-la-Chapelle and the Americans who marched into Treves had a similar variety of experience. They met at first a sullen, moody people who gradually changed into a grateful race when they appreciated the danger of the Communist agitation, to which the Socialist leader Karl Liebknecht, writing under the name of Spartacus, had given the name of the Spartacist movement.

Even the Belgians, whom the vanquished Teutons at first regarded with especial dislike, which was a form of fear, were invited to cross the Rhine and take over Düsseldorf against the terms of the armistice. The Spartacists had won ruling power in this great steel-making centre, and the main body of townspeople openly preferred to live under Belgian martial law rather than to organise themselves for a struggle with the Red Revolutionists. It was a sad day for the Germans when they learnt that the troops of

the little nation they had wronged could not cross the river and establish law and order for them, as this measure would have been a serious infringement of armistice conditions.

In consequence of a general and complete change of mind among the Rhinelanders a new difficulty arose. The vanquished people, whose tremendous power in steel-making, in the manufacture of chemicals and general industry, based on the vast coal resources of the Rhine basin, had formed the grand source of aggressive strength of the Hohenzollern Empire, became too friendly disposed, especially towards British, Canadian, and American troops. The prevention of fraternisation was then the perplexing problem of allied commanders and their Staffs.

Approaches were first made by swarms of German children, who were usually allowed to make friends. They were indeed irresistible. Then girls and women began to smile, and men became eager to talk over the origin of the war and branch into discussions over Socialism. Finally, if permitted, **Perplexing problem of fraternisation** they would talk to troops in good English, French, and even Flemish, concerning supposed difficulties which the listener's country would encounter, owing to the greed for power of other countries in the Grand Alliance. The Briton was informed that the French were ruining the peace by their claim to the Saar coal-fields, or that the Americans were bent on ruling the European Powers and obtaining complete economic mastery over friend and foe.

The Americans were instructed, by subtle gradations in suggestion, that they were the mere tools of the British, who were making themselves practically masters of the whole world, while the French were, of course ruining all prospect of peace by carrying their passion for revenge beyond tolerable bounds. Women as well as men were used in this remarkable scheme for creating divisions between the troops of the Associated Powers, and considerable talent was displayed by many of the agents of the last great German intrigue.

The way in which the French were approached was masterly. The campaign was not directed upon the rank and file, but upon leading Frenchmen in the Army, administration, on the Press, and in business circles. France was offered an alliance with the Rhineland and Westphalia, which, as centres of Catholicism, were alleged to be ready to break away from both Prussianism and Bolshevism and perhaps unite with Bavaria and Austria in forming a French connection. Something like a Germanic party was apparently formed to advocate and organise this movement. Then when the plan was made public and discussed under reserve by the French Press, it was adduced in propaganda among British and American forces as an example of the intolerable ambition of the Gaul. There can be little doubt that the scheme for dividing the Allies by furtive talk, aptly addressed to men of each allied nation, was conducted by some Germans of high authority and considerable intelligence. When the men began to wonder at the delay in demobilisation, the unseen army of German agents turned this difficulty into a means of weakening the new Watch on the Rhine.

The Teutons ended by arriving at the extraordinary conclusion that their minute, persistent work of intrigue was successful. Ministers openly boasted that the British forces had become too discontented to execute any military movements,

Subtle scheme to sow dissension

and endeavoured at last to get the armistice denounced, and put the matter of forcing terms of peace to an actual trial of strength.

Once more, therefore, there was an amazing transformation in the enemy's mood towards the victorious forces arrayed along the Rhine. He first met them with glowering, brooding hate, then welcomed them exuberantly as saviours of civilisation, and finally regarded them as " contemptible little armies " too dispirited and slack in discipline ever to make good their menace of a sweep towards Essen and over Frankfort. A considerable time, however, passed before the wheel of German moods thus came full circle.

When, at mid-day, December 6th, 1918, the first British cavalry patrol entered Cologne, and rode to the great bridge, the fantastic vision at which men had grimly jested in dugouts between the Yser and the Somme was realised as a sober routine fact. Hussars were posted as sentries both on

HAPPY PAGEANT OF REDEMPTION IN COLMAR, CAPITAL OF UPPER ALSACE.
French troops defiling past General Castelnau in the Rue de la Clef, Colmar, after he had formally re-entered the town in December, 1918. Above : The troops assembling for the triumphal march, which was led by General Castelnau in person.

the town side of the bridge and on the eastern side by the village of Deutz. Germans passing over the bridge even stopped to speak and make jokes with young cavalrymen. "So you have wound up the Watch on the Rhine!" was one of the remarkable sayings. Waiters in the hotels were practised in both English song and slang. They had served the British in English and Scottish hotels, fought them from Ypres to Maubeuge, and were again ready to wait upon them in the Domhof and other well-stored hotels and restaurants in the shadow of Cologne Cathedral.

In the first week of occupation, when a general studied reserve prevailed, the Scottish Highlanders arrived. As always, they were a conquering attraction. Men and women rushed from trams when the music of the pipes sounded, and, led by girls and boys, the Scots had to make their way through a dense throng to the approaches of the **Formal occupation** Hohenzollern Bridge. On German country **of Cologne** roads boys marched for miles away from their homes in rain, fascinated by the kilts and bonnets and the strange melody of the pipes. The khaki pipers were almost as magical as the Pied Piper of German legend and English poetry.

Bonn was occupied by the Canadians on December 8th, when a small force of cavalry entered the town and held the Rhine bridge. Then, on December 12th, Sir Arthur Currie took the salute at the end of the great iron bridge, and troopers rode eastward to take up the outpost line beyond the river.

The grand ceremony of the occupation took place the same day on the immense, spectacular bridge of Cologne, with its massive, towered gateways and statues of the Hohenzollern Emperors. William the Second had but recently erected a great image of himself, seated on a prancing steed, and gazing in warlike pose at the majestic cathedral from under a spiked helmet. The Union Jack was raised beside this statue. Below, in an enclosure, stood Sir Herbert Plumer, with the Staff of the Army of Occupation, and an escort of Lancers on the approach to the bridge.

It was raining slightly, but the Germans gathered in a

NEW HISTORY ADDED TO STORIED STONES.
French guard posted below the ruin of Limburg, birthplace of Rudolph of Hapsburg in 1218. Near Riegel, on the right bank of the Rhine, this was the limit of the French zone of occupation in Baden.

vast multitude to watch the procession of victory. It was worth seeing, for the British cavalry in mass rode through the avenues of sombre crowds, and the effect left the people astonished and incredulous. Germans were heard to remark that parade troopers, kept in England throughout the war, had been sent out to impress the Rhine Provinces. They could not believe that the force they saw was the working vanguard of the Army which had pursued their men relentlessly from the Ridge of Flanders.

The squadrons were played through the archway by musicians as they went with eyes fixed on the army commander. Spaced and timed by expert hands they followed each other without pause, splendid men on splendid horses, and terrible in their beauty. General Plumer saluted them all. His hand was never away from the peak of his cap. Every soldier he saluted, as thanking every man personally. Then the tense, silent multitude could not help laughing and cheering when the armoured cars followed in procession. They answered to the command, "Eyes right!" like living creatures, turning their conning-towers about and dipping their guns with comical effect. By the evening the Lancers, Dragoon Guards, and **British infantry** Hussars had extended some nineteen **cross the Rhine** miles from the Rhine bridge-head to the limit of the zone of occupation by the cutlers' town of Solingen, where German bayonets had been made.

The next day the infantry, the 9th and 29th British Divisions, and the 2nd Canadian Division crossed the river in the heavy rain, Sir Herbert Plumer again taking the salute, with General Fergusson, General Jacob, and Sir Arthur Currie. Again, in spite of the weather, a large crowd collected, and was affected by the sight of the magnificence of the men in fitness and marching power and smartness, and by the superb condition of horses and transport. For seven hours the troops flowed over the river by which the ancient Romans held back the Teutons for centuries from the city that won its name from a Roman colony forming the garrison force of the very bridge-head the British held.

SYMBOLIC BAPTISM IN THE RHINE.
Reaching the Rhine at Huningue, in Alsace, on November 20th, French troops of the 2nd Moroccan Division, commanded by General Modelon, celebrated the occasion by dipping their colours in the waters of the river.

The spectacle conquered the Rhinelanders as nothing else probably could have done. They had been convinced by their Government Press that the British forces had been reduced to a skeleton, with outworn material of war, resembling the grey army of tramps lately streaming through the city. They considered the struggle had not been fought out rigorously in the field, but that their men had been weakened in the crisis by the defection of the Fleet and the slow pressure of the blockade, so that the sword had not given the decision on either side.

By taking the British cavalry as parade troops fresh from England they maintained their self-flattering illusion. When, however, they saw the infantry that had broken their line at Menin, and fought from Gallipoli to Cambrai, Tournai, and Valenciennes, and were about to break through to Brussels when the white flag went up, they recognised that they had been beaten on the battlefield. The evidence of their own eyes destroyed the legend regarding their own unvanquished Army. So the material victory over the German soldiers was followed by a moral victory over the German people.

It was at Cologne Station that wounded, hungry, thirsty British prisoners of war had been offered glasses of water by German Red Cross nurses, who had smiled **Hun servility** like daughters of Satan and poured the water **towards success** on the ground when the suffering men stretched out their hands for it. They were proud then, the Rhinelanders, of being Prussian by annexation, but as their pride had come from the worship of success rather than from any native fund of character, they began to admire the British Army and mounted "The Taming of the Shrew" at one of their theatres. Some of the British in Cologne, thinking of the German Red Cross nurses and the glass of water, regarded the title of Shakespeare's play as appropriate to the situation. Many German women became at last too kindly disposed towards the British forces. They were, indeed, the plague of the Army.

Higher up the river, by Coblenz and the picturesque fortress of Ehrenbreitstein, the Third American Army passed over to their bridge-head, with colours flying in a magnificent spectacle of power. The 1st, 2nd, and 23rd Divisions were selected as occupation forces in General Dickmann's army, and held the Rhine between Rolandseck and Brey. Of all the allied garrisons the Americans had the hardest job, because it was the softest. The Germans were curious to see them, and became remarkably gay when they arrived. They were accepted as the supreme hope of Germany, and as representatives of all that was promising in President Wilson's old programme of the fourteen points of peace.

Flattery and cajolement were poured out like Rhine wine, and poison for the mind was then introduced into the draught in the vain endeavour to separate the soldiers of the United States from their French and British comrades. The forces of occupation were accepted in Coblenz as gratefully as French policemen would be **Flattering welcome** welcomed in a disturbance in Paris. **to the Americans** Secure from riots by their own disbanded soldiers, the people turned their city into a bright festival town. The streets were crowded, the cafés filled, and the brilliant shops attractively stored. The war was forgotten in the Christmas mood prevailing in the American section.

Into Mayence and the French bridge-head round the pleasant health resort of Wiesbaden, General Mangin, recovered from his injuries, led the gallant Tenth Army. His troops were in a state of quiet excitement, and as many of them had had their women ill-treated, there was some apprehension regarding their conduct to any Germans who made them angry. But in a fine address to his men the general said:

You are about to mingle with new populations that have forgotten the past benefits they received from a French administration. No one can ask you to forget the abominations committed by your foes during four years of war—the violation of sworn faith, murders of women and children, systematic devastations without any military necessity.

But you cannot compete with your savage enemies in barbarity; you would be overcome in advance. Therefore, everywhere you will remain worthy of your great mission and of your victories. Remember that on the left bank of the Rhine the armies of the French Republic at the opening of the great wars of the Revolution conducted themselves in such a manner that the Rhineland people voted by acclamation to be incorporated with France.

For twenty-three years the forefathers of the people whom you are

ALLIED MILITARY ATTACHÉS AT THE BRITISH SECOND ARMY HEADQUARTERS, COLOGNE, FEBRUARY, 1919.
Standing (left to right): Lt.-Col. Prince Amozadhat, Siam; Lt.-Col. Arion, Rumania; Maj. Heyn, Belgian Mission (fourth figure); Maj. Verdet, French Mission; Lt.-Col. Slocum, United States (seventh figure); Maj. Casquiero, Portugal; Maj. Morita, Japan (extreme right). Seated: The second, fourth, sixth, and eighth figures, read from the left are: Lt.-Col. Fagalde, France; Brig.-Gen. Mola, Italy; Col. Perantzes, Greece; Col. Biddle, United States.

about to meet, fought side by side with ours on all the fields of battle of Europe. Be worthy of your forefathers and think of your children whose future you are preparing. No stain on the laurels of the Tenth Army !

It was eloquent and moving, but it is to be doubted if the French privates required the exhortation. Some days after they reached the Rhine there was trouble in getting food, and General Mangin was afraid that hunger would make his men irritable. So he went among them and talked to them. He found one sentry dreamily watching the swirling river. When asked how he was feeling, the man said he believed he could starve for a week if he were allowed to keep looking at the Rhine. "We have done more than go without food to reach the Rhine, my general," he said, "and it is worth it all."

The march-past at Mayence took place on December 14th. General Fayolle took the salute, and General Mangin and General Gouraud were with him. There were no large crowds, flags, or cheers, but only the tramp of men and horses in the great silent city. Yet the silence of the people was eloquent of triumph to the conquerors.

French troops reach the Rhine After the march was ended General Fayolle, General Mangin, and General Gouraud rode to the palace of the Duke of Hesse to receive a deputation of the leading citizens. After the Germans had spoken of the interests of the people, General Fayolle replied. It was an historic scene. It was the first time since the war began that a Frenchman in a position of power, standing face to face with Germans of authority, was able to inform the enemy of the opinion of France and the civilised world. No one in the great hall of the palace stirred while Fayolle spoke, and the black row of burghers, standing bareheaded three paces in front of him, was as motionless as criminals in the dock when the judge was pronouncing sentence.

The famous commander said that the war which had been forced on France was the most unjust and cruel that mankind had known, and marked by refinements of barbarity which the whole world condemned. He described in some detail the misery and destruction wrought in Flanders and the northern French provinces, and the plunder carried into Germany, saying :

You made terrorism a system of war. You succeeded only in hardening our strength of resistance and quickening our victory. Since July, 1918, your armies, after being everywhere repulsed, have undergone an uninterrupted series of defeats, losing hundreds of thousands of prisoners and thousands of guns, until the day when, standing on the brink of complete disaster, you asked for mercy. Now we are on the Rhine !

General Fayolle then told the Germans that he knew they were fearing reprisals for all their crimes, but they could rely on the traditions of France. He reminded them that their grandfathers had fought by the side of the French, and had recognised the spiritual greatness of the French soldiers. The French, he said, would hurt nobody and destroy nothing, and the Germans must think themselves happy to have among them a people faithful to the principles of justice. Not a single complaint on the conduct of the French troops had been made since the first patrols entered the town.

General Fayolle's plain speaking It was after this speech that some of the magnates of the Rhineland and Westphalia started a movement for incorporation with France. The movement, however, stopped when the National Assembly was elected and the German Catholic authorities were freed to some extent from the control of Jewish and other anti-clerical Socialists who had climbed to power in Prussia. The Catholics of the Rhine then sought political salvation by union with the Catholics of Southern Germany and Austria. The governing anti-clerical circles in Republican France lost their country some grand opportunities.

As the military chiefs of France were Catholics, happy to facilitate easy relations, and paying graceful little attentions, such as Mangin's visit to the tombs of men of Mayence who had fought for Napoleon, the arrangements of the occupation went on smoothly. General Mangin, however, could not help introducing just one sharp note. He was a soldier of Africa, mainly responsible for the great extension of the native forces of French Africa, which had saved France from exhaustion of man-power. With a view both to honouring the native forces and promoting French prestige in the troubled land of Morocco, the Moroccan Division was employed as part of the occupation forces. The German Government at once protested that the use of coloured troops in the Palatinate was an insult to the sentiments of community of all white races. In Mayence a demobilised German officer exclaimed : " Look at the savages the French use to impose their culture on Germany ! "

" Salute them ! " cried a French officer. " Our African soldiers have fought like men. They are more civilised than your Guardsmen, who came into Belgium and France and conducted themselves like bandits and assassins. Salute them, I say ! "

The German was wearing a little green hat with a feather in it. He lifted it.

The Moroccan regiments were those among whom German agents had spread appeals to massacre their French officers and declare a holy war on France. The appeals were printed in Arabic in the name of " The Mohammedan Emperor Hadji Wilhelm," and were scattered broadcast in Morocco before the regiments departed. It was partly owing to this remarkable exhibition of the German view of the sentiments of community of white races that the tribesmen from the interior of Morocco, who had had some of the hardest fighting by the Chemin des Dames, were brought forward to help in occupying the Rhineland bridge-heads, and give the Teutons the privilege of seeing the bravest of African troops, whose loyalty had never swerved and who looked with horror upon the atrocities committed by order of Hadji Wilhelm.

The French forces, like their allies, threw numerous new bridges across the Rhine, and became at last welcome to the German population as guaranteeing them against the disorders shaking the rest of Germany. The Frenchmen filled the cafés and shops, having leisure and money to spend, and were met with increasing friendliness. Yet they never fraternised. The contrast **Hun and Gaul** between their desolate regions of famine in **irreconcilable** France, where food was still lacking months after the signing of the armistice, and the placid felicity of the occupied German country, where the beer-halls rang with music and the shops contained good provisions and costly silken clothes, inspired them with a silent, lasting anger. The Germans conducted themselves well, and the French maintained their self-control, but there was no sign of reconciliation between the peoples.

Altogether the march of the conquering armies to the Rhine was conducted in an easy manner. The Rhinelanders were naturally pliant to Western and Southern influences. As their Romanesque and Gothic cathedrals and other monuments showed, they were bred in the main stream of civilisation, and open largely to Italian, Flemish, French, and English inspiration. They had as little in common with the Prussians who annexed them as had the Germanic Swiss. Some Prussian colour they had acquired in the course of a century, but it was such as could be washed off, leaving the Cologner as Western in character as the Strasbourger. Their greater writers had celebrated the genius of Napoleon long before their men of talent found an object of hero-worship in Bismarck. Beethoven, of Bonn, had composed a Napoleonic symphony ; Heine, at Düsseldorf, had written the finest of poems on Napoleon's Grenadiers ; Goethe, of Frankfort, had seen something god-like in the Corsican of France.

Like many of the German Swiss, the Rhinelanders had become proud of the Hohenzollern Empire in its period of resplendent success. Pride of race had then made them at times vie with the worst of Prussians. Some of their industrial magnates, growing up under Bismarck, were far worse than Bismarck. Having a kind of theatrical quality in their wickedness, they were the worst of the megalomaniacs of economic power. But the general people were docile. Perhaps their greatest fundamental fault was their docility. But, at least, they were docile enough when the armies of victory held their river and formed three great bridge-heads beyond it, each running to a distance of some nineteen miles.

It was on January 30th, 1919, that General Hirschauer crossed the Rhine and took possession of the bridge-head on the right bank.   Accompanied by an imposing military cavalcade he rode into Kehl, where he read a stern proclamation to the German notables standing at attention before him.

General Hirschauer, French Military Governor of Strasbourg, taking possession of Kehl bridge=head.

France keeping night=watch on the Rhine: A giant searchlight stationed near St. Goar.

General Lecomte reviewing French troops at Wiesbaden, Dec. 15th, 1918, when taking over the bridge-head.

Great welcome for the victors in the capital of Alsace-Lorraine : French cavalry passing along the Pont National, Strasbourg.

INSPECTION OF MOBILE

CHAPTER CCXCIII.

ANTI-AIRCRAFT GUNS.

FINAL PHASES OF THE WAR IN THE AIR.
I.—The Air Battles Over London : How the Gothas were Defeated.
By H. W. Wilson.

German Raiders' Perpetually Improving Weapons—Large-scale Reconnaissances in Preparation for the Actual Destruction of London—Preparatory Measures Taken in Britain: Mobilisation of Ambulances and Special Constables and Issue of Air Raid Warnings—Enlarged Organisation of the London Fire Brigade—Darkening of the Country—Artillery Defences of the Large Towns—Counter-work of the British Air Forces—Triumph of the Pomeroy Incendiary Bullet—Introduction of the "Apron" Defence—Four Raids in the Last Six Nights of September 1917—Fierce Attack of October 1st—Amazing Raid by and Rout of an Armada of Zeppelins, October 19th—Capture of L39 Intact—Dangerous Aeroplane Raid with Many Incendiary Bombs, December 6th—Lord Rothermere Appointed Air Minister—Raid in Force, December 18th—Prolonged and Serious Raid, January 28th, 1918—Exodus of Aliens from London—Violent Air Battle, February 17th—Raid of March 7th during Brilliant Aurora Borealis—Raiders Heavily Punished in their Final Raid of May 19th—Minor Zeppelin Raids during Spring of 1918—Summary of Casualties—Enemy Raids on Paris—Strategic Effect of Air Raids.

IN Chapter CXCVIII. (Vol. 10, page 125) the history of the German air raids upon Great Britain was brought down to September 24th, 1917, the date of the second night raid upon London, which was of great importance, as then for the first time a barrage of artillery fire was used to protect the capital. It was clear that the Germans had introduced a new and formidable means of attack. It was not clear whether any effective means of defence against that attack had been devised, and this question, of agonising importance for the women and children of the great cities in Southern England, remained to be answered. In this chapter it will be shown how the air menace, as it constantly grew, was met by a constant development of the air defences, and finally was overcome by a combined system of defence and attack. The soundest policy was always to protect the non-combatants of Great Britain by relentlessly attacking the German cities, by pushing the air war home into the heart of Germany, and giving the German airmen work to do in their own country. In carrying out this policy, when it was at last adopted late in 1917, British airmen were greatly handicapped by strikes in munition factories—always at critical moments—by the routine,

R.N.A.S.A.A.C. GETTING TO WORK.
Gun team of the Royal Naval Air Service Anti-Aircraft Corps bringing their weapon into action. Much of the work of defending Britain against aerial attack devolved on this fine corps.

dilatoriness, and want of initiative of British officialdom, and by the inferior machines and engines with which they were too often supplied. But even these handicaps were overcome at last, and this chapter will be a record of patience, of persistence, and, with some vicissitudes, of triumph on the part of the British fighting man. As British ingenuity and courage had destroyed the menace of the Zeppelins, and rendered those huge vessels useless for land war, so in the end they overcame the Gothas and even more powerful and terrible German aircraft.

Great stakes depended on the victory in this air struggle. The German blows were aimed at the very heart and centre of British resistance. They were meant to paralyse economic life, to hamper the manufacture of munitions, to retard transport, to terrorise the civilian population of Great Britain.

The German airmen operated with perpetually improving weapons. From the small bombs with which they made their earlier attacks they advanced to bombs of 660 lb., the heaviest, it is believed, that were dropped from an aeroplane on British soil, and they had bombs of 1,300, 1,600, 2,400 lb., and even of a ton and a half (about 3,300 lb.) under construction or available for use in France. A single one of these enormous bombs would wreck a whole neighbourhood.

BOMB DAMAGE ON THE EMBANKMENT.
Hole in the pavement caused by one of the fifty-three bombs dropped during the raid on the evening of December 18th, 1917. It fell on the Thames Embankment near Cleopatra's Needle, which was damaged by splinters, while the base of one of the Sphinxes was also somewhat damaged.

They were also planning the use of gas-bombs about the date when the British Government at last reluctantly and slowly decided to strike back, and they were probably only deterred from the employment of them by the certainty that for every gas-bomb dropped in London one would be delivered in Cologne or Frankfort. Thus reprisals became a means of protection, but the account of the raids into Germany falls to the chapter dealing with the offensive air war.

The German aim was to attack in great force with heavy bombs and incendiary bombs intermingled, so soon as the necessary machines and the necessary bombs could be manufactured, and the raids with which this chapter is concerned were really large-scale reconnaissances, preparing the way for such a blow as, it was hoped, would leave London a heap of ruins and ashes, and training airmen for it. Fortunately, the measures taken in Great Britain, the activity of the British air forces on the front in France, and the terrific fighting of 1918 prevented the Germans from accomplishing their aim. But the danger was great and real. It was faced unflinchingly by the British people, and the only cry of surrender, raised by Mr. Lansbury in the "Herald," was indignantly spurned. There was no fine moonlit night — for the German airmen avoided dark nights, because then they could not see so clearly, and were apt to be caught by the searchlights and shown up — that a raid was not to be feared. Night after night the tide of battle rolled over London, with the crashing and hammering of the guns of the defence, with the dull, thudding boom of the bombs, with the beams of the searchlights stabbing the air and searching for the assailants, with the buzzing of machines, British and German, overhead, and with the blaze of fires at intervals. The map showing the points where bombs fell indicates that almost every part of London, except certain areas in the west and south-west, was attacked with indiscriminating savagery; but East and Central London suffered most.

From Central London to the German raiding bases in Flanders was a distance of about one hundred and fifty or one hundred and sixty miles, which would be covered by heavily loaded bombing machines in between two and three hours, and by lightly laden machines in much less. The distance from the coast to London was about seventy miles, so that there was usually about an hour's warning when an attack was imminent. In that time all the preparations had to be made. The searchlights and guns in London and on the coast were manned nightly and always held ready; but when a raid was expected the ambulances had to be mobilised for their work, the Fire Brigade to have all its strength available, the engineer troops attached to it for rescue and demolition work in the ruins to stand to, the airmen to go up, the "Specials" to be summoned and the hospitals warned. As the raiders drew nearer, and it became certain that they were making for London, the public warning was issued, at first by the ineffective and slow method of sending police and "Specials" with whistles and motor-cars through the streets, but afterwards by the far simpler, quicker, and more effective one of signals with bomb rockets, which were fired from the fire-stations. This latter means of giving the alarm for late night raids was not introduced till 1918, under strong public pressure. There is no doubt that the system of air-raid alarms, which enabled those living in small houses to seek comparative security, saved hundreds of lives and greatly reduced the danger.

The first necessity in fighting the raiders was to see them. The searchlight crews were supplied with lights of constantly increasing power, and were directed at their work by a master searchlight, which flashed the orders to them. They did their difficult duty with great coolness and courage; they were obvious targets, and many bombs were directed at them by the assailants. On one occasion a Zeppelin aimed twenty

(marginal note: Preparing for raid action)

THE WORST HIT OF THE WORST RAID.
Printing works in Long Acre destroyed by a bomb dropped from a Gotha during the raid of January 28th, 1918, which was the worst raid that London experienced, in that it was the most prolonged. The building was used as an air-raid shelter, and twenty-eight people were killed and ninety-seven injured there.

bombs at one most pertinacious search-light, all without effect. Very seldom did they fail to locate the attacking aeroplanes and to hold them in the glare of their beams, after which the fire of the guns was brought to bear, and the British aeroplanes got ready to enter action. A system of combined attack was worked out, and when the defending aeroplanes attacked, the gun fire was switched off or turned in other directions.

Elaborate instruments were introduced and steadily improved for detecting the position of the German aeroplanes by the sound they made. Range-finders were also improved out of recognition. Round London a circle of searchlights was gradually drawn, so that towards the close of the war there were over two hundred,

HAVOC IN WARRINGTON CRESCENT, MAIDA VALE.
On the night of March 7th, 1918, when a brilliant aurora facilitated their flight, two of seven or eight enemy aeroplanes penetrated over London. The four houses shown above were demolished by a single bomb weighing 660 lb.

In the later stages of the struggle the London Fire Brigade had to be greatly strengthened to meet the grave peril of enormous fires. In the summer of 1917 ninety fire brigades, in an area of seven hundred and fifty square miles, were organised to give aid in London in any emergency. All the reservists in them were recalled from the front, the Royal Engineer detachments attached to the firemen were doubled, and arrangements were made for bringing up additional men in motor-lorries in the event of any grave fire. When the first warning reached the Fire Brigade its supports closed in from the outlying area towards the most dangerous points, and thus on December 16th, 1917, when two hundred and seventy-six incendiary bombs were dropped in London, motor-engines

IN CHELSEA HOSPITAL.
Occupied residential quarters in Chelsea Hospital pulverised by a bomb of great size on the night of February 16th, 1918.

many of immense power. The moral effect of these searchlights on the Germans was great. The raiders were often kept out of the areas where they sought to bomb by the blades of light sweeping the sky. When held in a searchlight beam German machines would sometimes drop their bombs at random in open country in order to rise and escape. The British aeroplanes were greatly helped in their search for their enemies by the lights, which pointed to the quarter of the sky where the Germans were to be found, and handed them on from one district to another. At first the Germans were able to see the British machines because of the red flame from the exhausts, and thus could avoid them; but as the air war progressed this defect was removed; and invisible, the British airman swooped upon his prey.

RUIN IN A NORTH LONDON THOROUGHFARE.
The Eaglet public-house, at the corner of Hornsey Road and Seven Sisters Road, in North London, shattered in an aeroplane raid on the night of September 29th, 1917. This was the third of four enemy raids made on London in the last six nights of that month.

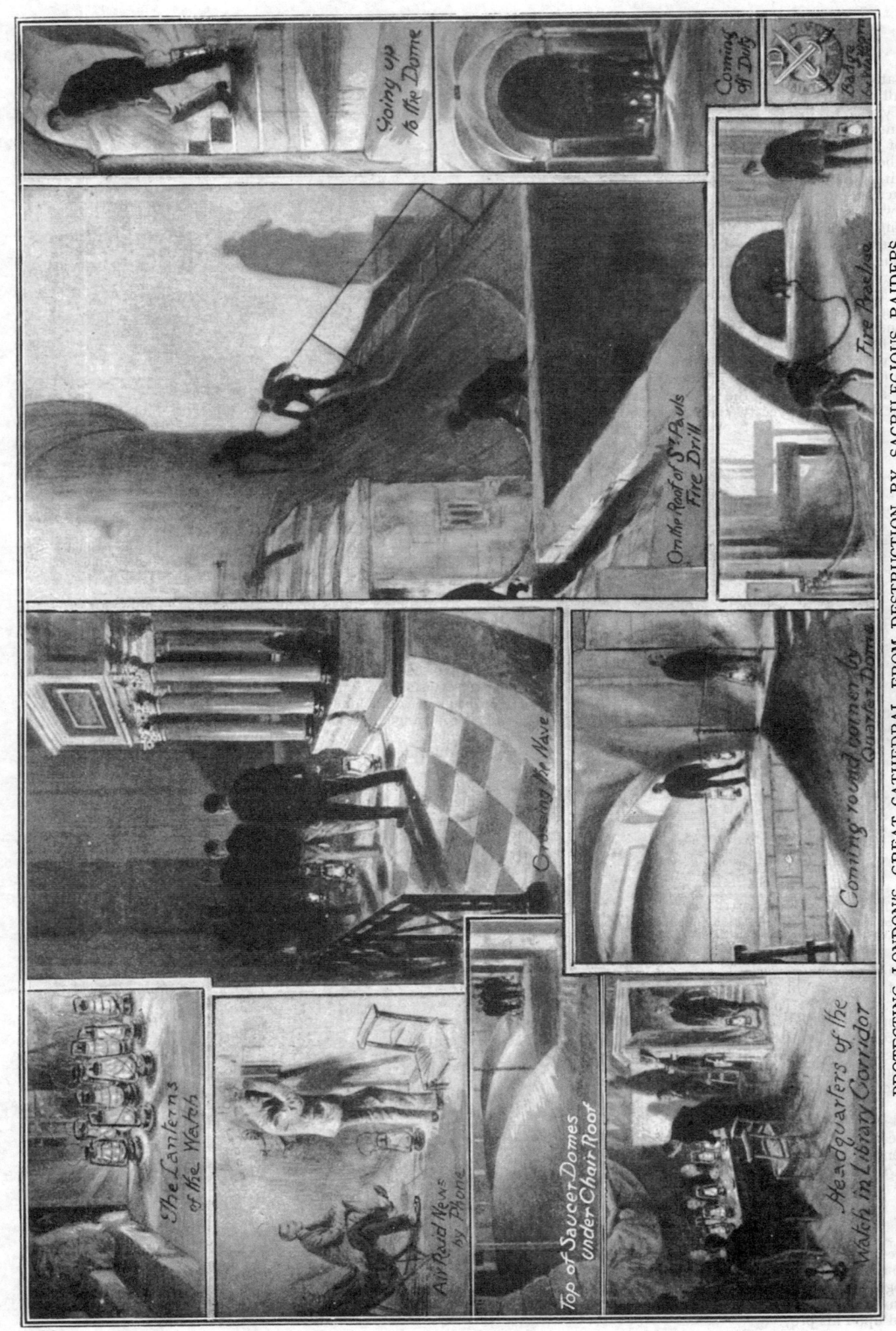

PROTECTING LONDON'S GREAT CATHEDRAL FROM DESTRUCTION BY SACRILEGIOUS RAIDERS.

In June, 1915, Canon Alexander, Treasurer of St. Paul's Cathedral, organised a band of volunteers to keep constant watch in the church to check any fires that might be caused by German bombs dropped during air raids. The members of the watch were trained by the London Fire Brigade. narrow escapes, but the only mark made on it by German airmen was caused by a fragment of an explosive bomb which fell close to the north side and was thrown up on to the Stone Gallery, slightly denting the asphalt. It was twice struck by anti-aircraft shells, one ot which penetrated the roof of the south transept. The cathedral had several

from Twickenham and Wembley were used in Shoreditch. Night after night when the barrage was violent in London the firemen could be seen and heard turning out. The spirit of the force was inimitable. "The sick and injured," says Lieut.-Commander Sladen, the Chief of the London Fire Brigade, "booked on duty as far as possible when air-raid action was taken, and men on leave reported for duty at the nearest fire-stations, so as to swell the numbers of men manning the engines. No fewer than fifty members of the various forces were cited in brigade orders for saving life during raids."

There had been a persistent call for "darkness and composure" as the surest defence against Zeppelin raids—or, in fact, for complete passivity. Darkness was in actual fact a valuable protection. Outside London the country was darkened with great success when notice was given of air raids. Captain Buttlaer-Brandenfels, of the German Zeppelin service, admitted in a lecture he gave at Berlin on the work of the German airships that "the English have learnt in the course of the war how to darken the country perfectly." But London could not be hidden completely by such a darkening. The authorities decided that it was impossible to extinguish all the lights, though a good many people in touch with London problems believed that this was feasible. If all the artificial lights had been extinguished the Thames would still have shown up the position of the great city. It was found impracticable to mask a great river. Just as British airmen flying in the Ypres district at night took their bearings from Zillebeke Lake, so the Germans took their bearings from the Thames, and perhaps from the Brent Reservoir, which threw up a shimmer of light under the rays of the moon. The lighting of the London streets was steadily reduced under military supervision until the glow could no longer be seen forty or fifty miles away. It was also altered from day to day, various districts being darkened and modifications introduced in the lighting scheme. Thus the Germans were prevented from getting their bearings with ease, though the river remained, and down to the close of the war no one had devised any means of dealing with it.

The darkening of the capital and of the country involved some interference with railway traffic, though far less than Germans supposed. Captain Buttlaer-Brandenfels was under the delusion that all railway traffic ceased when a raid was imminent. This was not the case. In many raids trains ran, though always with some danger. The tell-tale glare from the locomotive fires was screened and the lamps were put out at stations. The signal-lights were either extinguished or masked. All lights in the trains were in theory masked by drawing the blinds, or else were extinguished, though in the Zeppelin raid of October 19-20th, 1917, one train at least was caught with unscreened lights, and was the target of several bombs, one of which broke the glass of some carriages and considerably frightened the passengers.

Trains as targets for raiders' bombs There were other experiences of a similar nature. On one occasion the driver of a luggage train in the Eastern Counties, while running in misty weather, heard above him a strange noise, and, looking up, saw that a Zeppelin was immediately overhead, low down. The night was dark, and the mist had only lifted for a moment; to that he probably owed his escape. He was in a lonely stretch of country, and had he been attacked there was no help at hand.

The artillery protecting London and the great towns was steadily strengthened. There were many guns in fixed positions, and other guns on motor-lorries capable of moving at high speed. In the early days of air raids London had no more powerful weapon to protect it than the old "Pom-pom" and naval 6-pounder, very clumsily mounted. After the barrage was established it was gradually improved. More guns were supplied and heavier guns, and the main defence was continually moved farther out. There was one system of defence on the coast and a second on the outskirts of London, while inside London a number of guns in fixed positions and many motor-guns were brought into play when the Germans succeeded in passing the outer barrage. Weapons of great power were used, though there was always the danger that if large shells were fired their fragments might do damage

RAILWAY RED CROSS STAFF AT WORK.
Attending to cases in a subterranean passage, used as a first-aid hospital during air raids, at Waterloo Station. The vaults and underground passages at the great station were thrown open for the use of the railway staff and the public, and a special Red Cross unit was formed amongst the staff.

in falling. In one case the base of a 60 lb. shell came through the roof of a building in the City of London, and there were many other examples of injury from the British protective fire. In the later periods of the raids precautions had to be taken against the possibility of the Germans flying low and using their machine-guns on the streets. To meet that a number of machine-guns were mounted on buildings and manned by volunteers.

The German airmen preferred to attack with a westerly wind, which was against them coming, but helped them on their way back; and when they found their easiest line of approach barred by gun fire they tried **Girdle of guns and searchlights** to work round into London by the north, south, or west, skirting the capital before delivering their attack. A girdle of searchlights and guns had therefore to be carried round the great city. Apart from London, according to an account by Captain Buttlaer-Brandenfels, "places like Hull and the inland industrial centres such as Liverpool, Manchester, Sheffield, and Leeds, were provided with a quite respectable system of defence, in many cases not inferior to that of London." Other areas were protected by motor-guns and searchlights carried in motors, which could be moved from place to place, and which patrolled the roads when Zeppelins or other aircraft were expected. When the general direction of the raiders' movement had been ascertained it was possible to effect rapid concentrations of these mobile forces.

The main defence, however, was in the activity and courage of the British air forces which were organised to attack raiders and hamper them in every possible way. In the case of raiding aeroplanes these invariably came from the Flanders coast. They were watched by British aircraft at Dunkirk and Dover, forming the 5th Group, R.A.F. So soon as the Gothas left their aerodromes to attack Great Britain, British bombing machines proceeded toward those aerodromes and bombed them heavily. The object of this was to render the raiders' landing on their return difficult and dangerous. The smooth landing grounds were pitted with craters; blocks of cement were torn up and thrown about; and the result of these operations was that many German machines were badly damaged or completely wrecked on their return. An additional and very serious nerve strain was imposed on the hostile pilots, who never knew what they would find when they approached their aerodromes. Other British aircraft, if touch could be obtained with the raiders, attacked them on their outward journey across the Channel. On the British side of the Channel yet other aircraft were waiting and watching, and joined in the air battle. For the defence of London there were, towards the close of the war, over two hundred aeroplanes, stationed at a series of aerodromes which were placed in favourable strategic positions. Many of these machines were handled by pilots of quite exceptional skill, and they rendered magnificent service. On the Norfolk coast was a squadron of "Zepp-strafers," who hunted Zeppelins as an English squire hunts the fox. It was a terrible pastime, involving great risk and making the highest demands on nerve and skill. In one case an Anzac pilot chased a Zeppelin to the very outskirts of Birmingham in misty weather. He was never able to see the airship,

Counter-offence as a defence

though it fired at him and he at it, and he only kept touch with it by following in the wake of disturbed air, knowing by the rolling of his machine that he was near his enemy. He was shot down without being able to destroy the Zeppelin, but he landed alive and recovered. There were many such encounters of which nothing was heard, but generally, in the later period of the war, if the weather gave the British airmen the slightest chance, a Zeppelin which was sighted was a Zeppelin destroyed.

The armament of the British aeroplanes had been greatly improved. At the outset British pilots were left to fight airships with nothing more formidable than hand bombs or pistols. Lieut. Warneford's attack on a Zeppelin—the first occasion on which one of these airships was destroyed by an airman—was the more astonishing in its superlative bravery because it was carried out with bombs. Many devices were suggested and tried for destroying Zeppelins, until the great discovery was made by Mr. Pomeroy of an incendiary bullet which would infallibly set them on fire. The secret of its construction and of the composition used in it was most strictly and wisely guarded. A small number of these bullets were made experimentally, and the charge for them was prepared by the inventor's wife—a work of real danger. They were first tried in action by Lieut. Robinson, who went up with only a few of them on September 2nd, 1916, as is recounted in Chapter CLVII. (Vol. 8, page 219), though there the details of his exploit could not for reasons of national safety be disclosed. From Lieut. Robinson himself the writer afterwards heard the full account of his attack; how the first shots appeared to produce little effect, and it seemed to him that the invention —on which so much depended—had failed, till he suddenly saw dull red patches appear, and these burst into flame, when he knew that he had performed one of the greatest feats of the war, and that the women and children of England had been saved by the new device. The airship he assailed fell in a blaze of fire at Cuffley and all its crew perished. The manufacture of the new bullet was then pressed, and in the two following months four Zeppelins were destroyed by it, killing all their crews.

Triumph of the Pomeroy bullet

Many improvements were made in the Pomeroy bullet as the war advanced, and it was made a serviceable instrument for the attack upon aeroplanes, but, to prevent the Germans from acquiring its secret, it was never used in British machines that crossed the German lines. In the attack on Zeppelins British machines usually worked as near as possible to the airship. Thus in the destruction of L34 off the Durham coast on November, 27-28th, 1916, Lieut. I. V. Pyott, after chasing the Zeppelin for five miles, got near her, put into her a number of Pomeroy bullets, and then swerved, but though he was 300 yards away when she burst into flames his face was scorched. In the attack on another Zeppelin that same night Lieut. Pulling closed almost within touch of the airship's hull, and fired into it till it burst into flame, and he was fired at by the raiders on board it as it fell blazing into the sea. He only escaped the debris of it by diving swiftly.

While the British improved their methods of defence the Germans also improved their weapons and aircraft.

AIR TRAPS FOR NIGHT RAIDERS.

[R.A.F. official photograph.

The "balloon apron," introduced by Major-General E. B. Ashmore, who was appointed to command the London Air Defence Area in August, 1917, was a movable defence which had considerable effect on the moral of the enemy airmen. The "apron" consisted of series of slender steel wires hanging from cross cables connecting the mooring-cables of observation balloons.

Their earlier bombs often failed to explode. This fact was disclosed—as the censorship at that date was not sufficiently strict—and they at once improved their fuses. In the later raids they employed many delay-action bombs, designed to burst after passing through the roofs of houses or buildings, and one such produced great loss of life among a number of women and children assembled in a shelter in the raid of January 28-29th, 1918, which was marked by the heaviest casualties that occurred in any air attack of the war in this country. The Zeppelins were lightened and rendered better able to navigate at great heights, to avoid —as the Germans hoped—the attack of aeroplanes and artillery. During the early Zeppelin flights a level of 4,000 feet was rarely exceeded, but in the last attacks of the war the Germans constantly flew at 18,000 or even 20,000 feet. But then they were faced with new difficulties. Compressed oxygen had to be inhaled by the crew to prevent their suffocation in the tenuous air. The water froze in the ballast tanks, though glycerine was mixed with it to prevent it from freezing. The intense cold of those high altitudes turned all food into a substance hard as rock, and affected the men and the engines. Another danger was discovered. At immense heights, when the weather was relatively calm below, great atmospheric disturbances were encountered.

For their aeroplane raids the Germans were unable to spare the best pilots or the best machines. The service was unpopular among the pick of the German airmen, as there were some men who were revolted by the cruel and unnecessary murder of civilians, and who realised that sooner or later it would bring stern retribution. A couple of hours before the Gothas started their crews were summoned from the brothels in which they spent most of their time, and **Raiders' nerve- testing adventure** one after another the machines were made ready and rose. They left in detachments, usually with an interval of five or ten minutes between each, and headed for London, at a level of about 10,000 feet in the earlier raids, though this was afterwards raised to 17,000 feet. They steered for the North Foreland, and there their trial began. When they passed the barrage—if they were bold enough to run through it—their machines rocked and rolled in the disturbed air. Often they turned back from the encounter. In many cases they received more or less serious hits. The number of machines brought down by British fire from the ground was small at first, yet it steadily rose. The artillery fire had a very important influence on the raiders' action. It forced them to fly at a great height, and this meant that they could not see their targets clearly and bombed at random, hurling down their explosives upon the people beneath.

Their machines were roughly constructed though effective for their purpose. The wreckage showed that no labour was wasted upon them; they were built of thick wood, and in some cases the linen on their frames was tacked to the wood. The engines were good. In 1918 a very powerful type of bombing machine was introduced—the Riesen, or giant—

RAIDERS READY TO LEAVE THEIR LAIR.
German aeroplanes used for attacks on Britain photographed from an aeroplane flying at a low altitude above them. The aerodromes on the Flanders coast from which the raiders started were constantly bombed by British airmen.

MR. J. POMEROY.
Inventor of the Pomeroy incendiary bullet, one of the most effective instruments devised for aerial combat. It finally disposed of the Zeppelin menace.

driven by five engines, each of about 300 horse-power, and carrying a crew of eight or nine men. These machines, like most of the German aeroplanes about that date, were supplied with parachutes, so that in the event of a disaster the men on board them had some chance of escape. From one of these giants shot down in France two men landed, though one was killed by the troops, whom a few seconds before he had been bombing, before the officers could protect him. The giants were over London on one or two occasions and the peculiar buzz of their numerous engines could be heard from the ground.

In the later raids a new means of defence was brought into play by the British. This consisted of "aprons" of thin high-tensile steel wire, suspended from a transverse cord which was held in the air by captive balloons. They were modelled upon a design which had been introduced by the Italian Government for the defence of Venice, where they were found highly effective. One accident occurred when they were being tried. An apron of five balloons was up in a light wind, when three balloons broke adrift carrying two men with them. One of the men was holding on to a cord and released his hold, falling **Efficacy of the** about a thousand feet into Richmond Park, **"apron" device** where he was instantly killed. The second man attempted to climb into the rigging of one of the balloons, but could not maintain his hold and fell from a great height, meeting the same sad fate. The balloons were finally shot down by the coast batteries at Dover. But after this misadventure the aprons were adopted and improved, and a special force of men was trained in handling them. They were stationed to the east of London, though their position and the height at which they were moored was constantly changed, so that the Germans could never be certain where they were to be encountered. They were so arranged as to keep the raiders at a certain height where the British airmen would be able to swoop down on them. They prevented the Germans from diving low upon points to be attacked, because an aeroplane which did this would have to climb to get over the aprons, and in the process it was liable to be attacked from above by the British machines. In one case the wing-tip of a German machine touched the anchor-rope of a British balloon. The machine spun round in the air, and dropped 600 feet before control of it could be recovered. Several of the German machines had narrow escapes, passing slightly above the aprons as they fled from British aircraft.

Of this fierce struggle and contest of ingenuity in the upper air the public during the war knew little. As the aprons multiplied the Germans became more and more reluctant to raid and more fearful of the danger. After the raid of March 7-8th the raiders reported that the aprons had become so numerous that any further increase or improvement in them would render raiding almost impossible.

German raiding squadron leaders The commanders of the German raiding squadrons of aeroplanes in 1917-18 were Captain Brandenburg, Captain Kleine, and Lieut. Walter. Brandenburg was in charge in the earliest and latest raids, but for some months was absent with a broken leg, due to a fall while on his way to receive a decoration from the Kaiser. Kleine was the most energetic of the three, but he was killed at the end of 1917 over Ypres. Walter, who next took charge, was less enthusiastic and determined as a raider, and gave his pilots a much less strenuous life. Despite the strictness of German discipline only three-fourths of the machines that started on these raids reached the British coast, and only half pushed as far as the outer London defences.

On September 25th, 1917, a comparatively small force of aeroplanes attacked London. Probably not more than ten machines reached the outer defences, and they showed some shyness in passing through the barrage. Fire was opened by the British guns some minutes before 8 p.m., and a little later the first bomb was dropped. By 9 p.m. the attack was over. Twenty-two bombs were dropped in South London, doing comparatively little damage. There was, however, much damage to roofs from the British anti-aircraft fire. From the roof of a high building in Central London, when the barrage was firing its hardest, it looked as though a great electric storm was raging on the horizon. Two days of overcast and cloudy weather interfered with the Germans and gave London a respite; but on the night of September 28th the attack was renewed with even less success, as the raiders never reached the London area. They were caught by the outer defences and driven back. Two German machines were shot down, either by the British aeroplanes or by the British artillery. There were no British casualties. The following night, September 29th, came a much more determined attack, which lasted about an hour, from 9.15 to 10.15, with six very heavy bursts of firing from the guns of the inner defences. The raiders seemingly entered London by the north and passed right across it, dropping twenty-two bombs in the London area, and going as far out to the south-west as Putney Common, where two persons were killed in an allotment garden. One bomb fell on the London and South-Western Railway in Waterloo Road, but **Five raids in seven nights** only caused slight damage. Twenty German machines were engaged; few of them can have reached the London area. One of the more destructive hits was in Seven Sisters Road, where a public-house was shattered.

On the night of September 30th, about eight, a fresh attack was delivered; but all the German machines save four were driven back by the fire of the outer defences. It was strange during the bursts of firing to feel the concussion in the autumn air and to note the fall of leaves from the trees. Between the bursts the streets were silent and empty; the Tube railways and shelters were crowded. The patter of fragments from the British anti-aircraft projectiles was plainly noticeable. About 8.30 two blazing objects were seen to fall; they were taken at first for German aeroplanes, but they were really flares dropped by them. The raiders attacked North and East London, and penetrated to Woolwich. They did no damage to the Arsenal, but with the thirteen bombs which they dropped they inflicted considerable damage upon small shops and houses. The loss of life in London was small, only one person being killed; but outside London there were many casualties. One German machine was shot down.

On the night of October 1st there was another and fiercer attack, lasting from eight to ten. Twenty-five bombs in all were dropped. The raiders penetrated to West London and attacked Victoria Station. One bomb struck Grosvenor Bridge, across the Thames, and set fire to the gas main on it, which burnt, emitting a brilliant light. Other bombs dropped in Pimlico and in Hyde Park, but the casualties were small. On the following morning Mr. Lloyd George visited the districts which had suffered most, and gave a definite pledge that reprisals should be carried out against Germany. After this raid continued bad weather and cloudy nights prevented a repetition of the attacks for several days.

The next raid was one of the most extraordinary of the series. It was the last on a large scale carried out by Zeppelins. No fewer than thirteen of these, all of the latest patterns available, took part in it, under Captain Buttlaer-Brandenfels, and their objectives were London and the Midland towns. They flew at a height of 16,000 feet across the North Sea, but when they reached English soil were much annoyed by anti-aircraft fire. One or two of them sustained slight injury, and some wreckage was afterwards picked up. Under fire the Zeppelins dropped many of their bombs without any attempt to hit any target. Moving inland, they encountered fog and ground mist and lost their way.

The usual Zeppelin practice was to rely on directional wireless in cloudy and foggy weather. By this system the German wireless stations ashore were able, from the direction of the messages received, to determine the position of a vessel and to signal it back to her. The number of airships, however, was so large on this occasion that the stations became confused and could not make their calculations. Thus the Germans did not know where they were, but wandered in the darkness, occasionally descending to bomb some place at random. In this fashion they attacked several towns in the Midlands, among them Bedford and Hitchin. At the latter place the **Rout of the Zeppelin armada** attack was typical of their methods. They sighted and assailed a train which was approaching the station with lights showing, and dropped several bombs in the attempt to hit it. They did no damage beyond causing some slight alarm and breaking a little glass, though in all they discharged a ton or more of bombs.

The British aircraft could not attack the raiders because of mist or the height at which the Zeppelins flew. Three of the German airships during the evening moved south with engines stopped and passed over London about 11.45. An air warning had been given much earlier in the evening, but as nothing happened, as the searchlights were not working and no guns had been heard, many people were in the streets when several reports in quick succession shook the air. The Germans, flying at a great height, had dropped two or three bombs just outside the London area and three inside it. One fell in the centre of Piccadilly, killing seven persons and wounding eighteen; a second dropped in Camberwell, killing ten people and injuring twenty-two; a third fell at Lewisham, where it killed fourteen persons and injured nine. The guns of the defences did not open fire as the night was so dark that nothing could be seen, and the Zeppelins were obviously above the clouds.

The Germans did not escape scot-free. Most of the Zeppelins had risen to enormous heights; instruments afterwards captured showed that one had reached 20,000 feet. At this extreme level they encountered a violent north-east wind and the most intense cold. The cold for some hours interfered with the running of their engines; the wind swept them away south-eastward, and they entirely lost their bearings, drifting over to France. The Zeppelin crews probably never had a more terrifying experience than thus to be carried off towards hostile territory where at daylight they must be discovered. Nine Zeppelins in all were sighted by the French and were pursued.

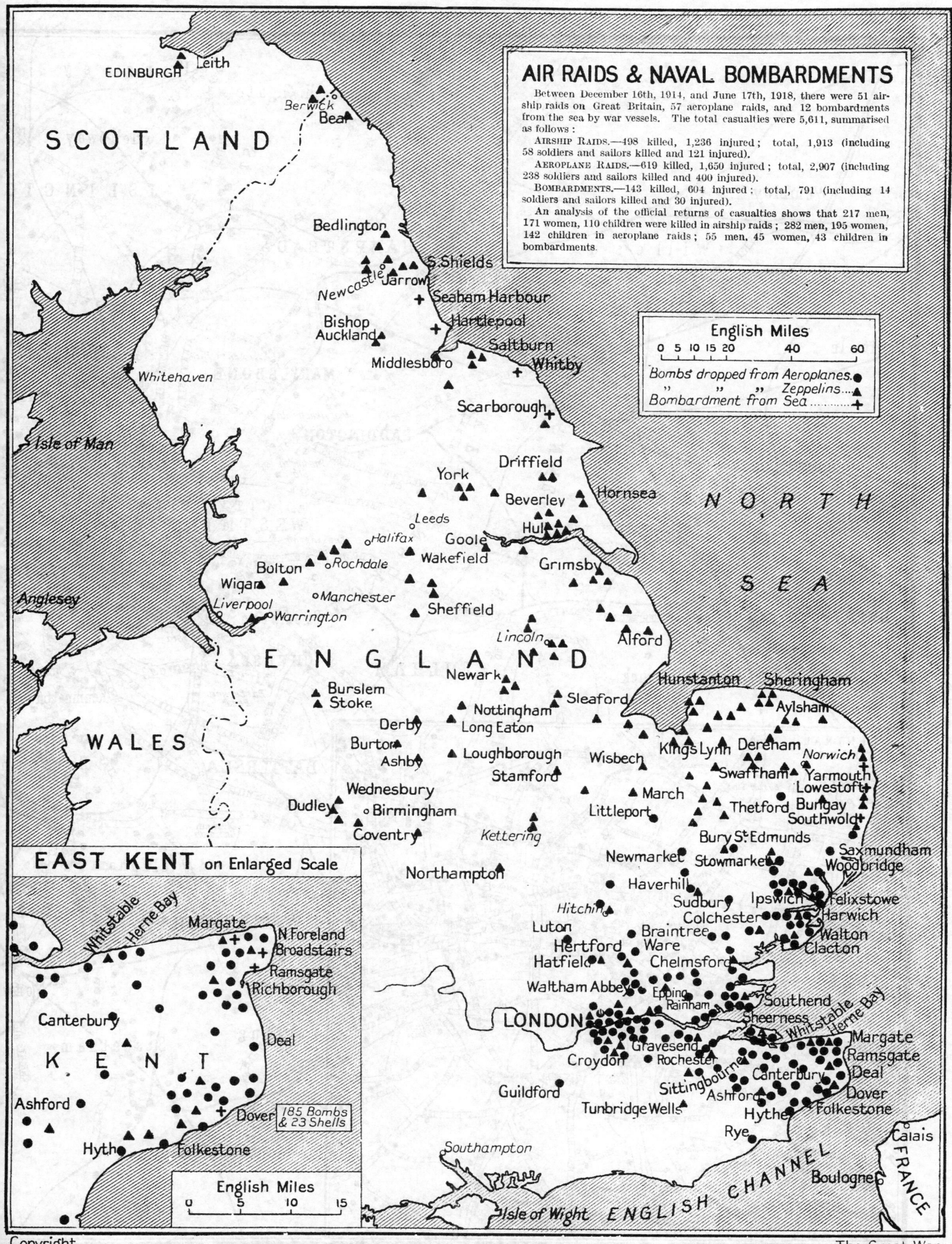

AIR RAIDS & NAVAL BOMBARDMENTS

Between December 16th, 1914, and June 17th, 1918, there were 51 airship raids on Great Britain, 57 aeroplane raids, and 12 bombardments from the sea by war vessels. The total casualties were 5,611, summarised as follows :

AIRSHIP RAIDS.—498 killed, 1,236 injured ; total, 1,913 (including 58 soldiers and sailors killed and 121 injured).

AEROPLANE RAIDS.—619 killed, 1,650 injured ; total, 2,907 (including 238 soldiers and sailors killed and 400 injured).

BOMBARDMENTS.—143 killed, 604 injured : total, 791 (including 14 soldiers and sailors killed and 30 injured).

An analysis of the official returns of casualties shows that 217 men, 171 women, 110 children were killed in airship raids ; 282 men, 195 women, 142 children in aeroplane raids ; 55 men, 45 women, 43 children in bombardments.

English Miles

0 5 10 15 20   40   60

Bombs dropped from Aeroplanes........●
  "   "   " Zeppelins.......▲
Bombardment from Sea............+

SCOTLAND

EDINBURGH Leith
Berwick Beal

Bedlington
Newcastle Jarrow S.Shields
Seaham Harbour
Bishop Auckland Hartlepool
Middlesboro Saltburn Whitby

Scarborough

Whitehaven

Isle of Man

Driffield
York Beverley Hornsea
Leeds Hull
Halifax Goole
Bolton Rochdale Wakefield Grimsby
Wigan Manchester
Anglesey Liverpool Warrington Sheffield
Lincoln Alford

NORTH SEA

ENGLAND

Newark
Burslem Sleaford Hunstanton Sheringham
Stoke Nottingham Aylsham
WALES Derby Long Eaton
Burton Loughborough Wisbech Kings Lynn Dereham Norwich
Ashby Stamford March Swaffham Yarmouth
Dudley Wednesbury Littleport Thetford Lowestoft
Birmingham Bungay
Coventry Southwold
Kettering Bury St Edmunds Saxmundham
Northampton Newmarket Stowmarket Woodbridge
Haverhill Ipswich Felixstowe
Sudbury Colchester Harwich
Hitchin Braintree Walton
Luton Ware Clacton
Hertford Chelmsford
Hatfield
Waltham Abbey Epping Southend
LONDON Rainham Sheerness
Gravesend Whitstable Bay Margate
Croydon Rochester Ramsgate
Sittingbourne Canterbury Deal
Guildford Ashford Dover
Tunbridge Wells Hythe Folkestone
Rye
Southampton Calais
Isle of Wight ENGLISH CHANNEL Boulogne FRANCE

EAST KENT on Enlarged Scale

Whitstable Herne Bay Margate
N.Foreland Broadstairs
Ramsgate
Richborough
Canterbury
KENT Deal
Ashford
Hythe Folkestone Dover

185 Bombs & 23 Shells

English Miles

0   5   10   15

Copyright   The Great War

CHART SHOWING THE EXACT LOCALITIES IN ENGLAND AND SCOTLAND THAT SUFFERED FROM HOSTILE AIR RAIDS AND BOMBARDMENTS FROM DECEMBER 16TH, 1914, TO JUNE 17TH, 1918.

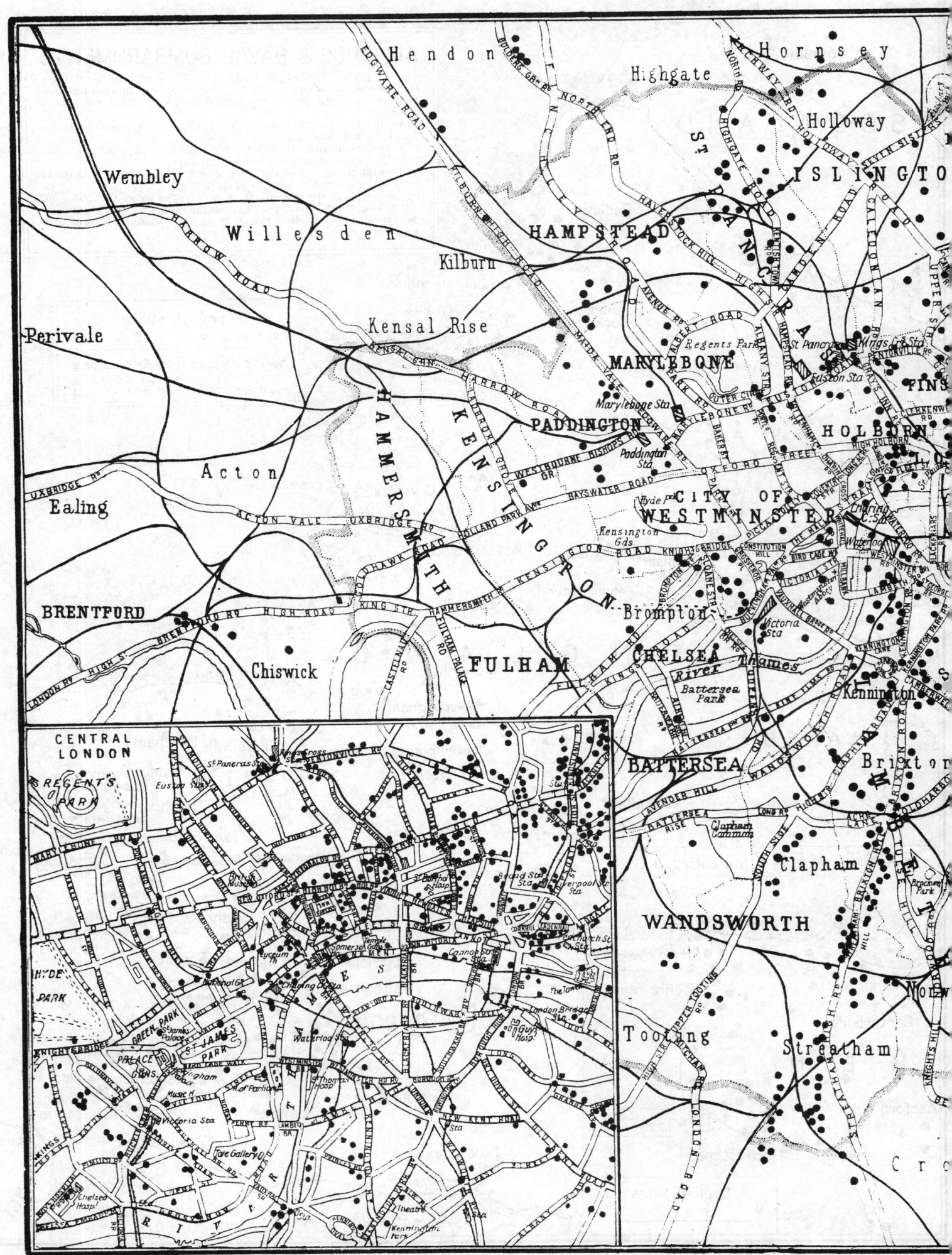

WHAT LONDON SUFFERED FROM ZEPPELINS AND GOTHAS:

The above map of the London area, with its larger-scale inset of Central London, has been carefully compiled by our cartographic department to show with approximate accuracy
bombs fell in the many air raids which the metropolis endured throughout the war. It is based upon official information, withheld until after the cessation of hostilities, and
supplied by the Fire Brigades of the London area. It will be noticed that all parts of London suffered, though some districts received a worse visitation than others, particularly

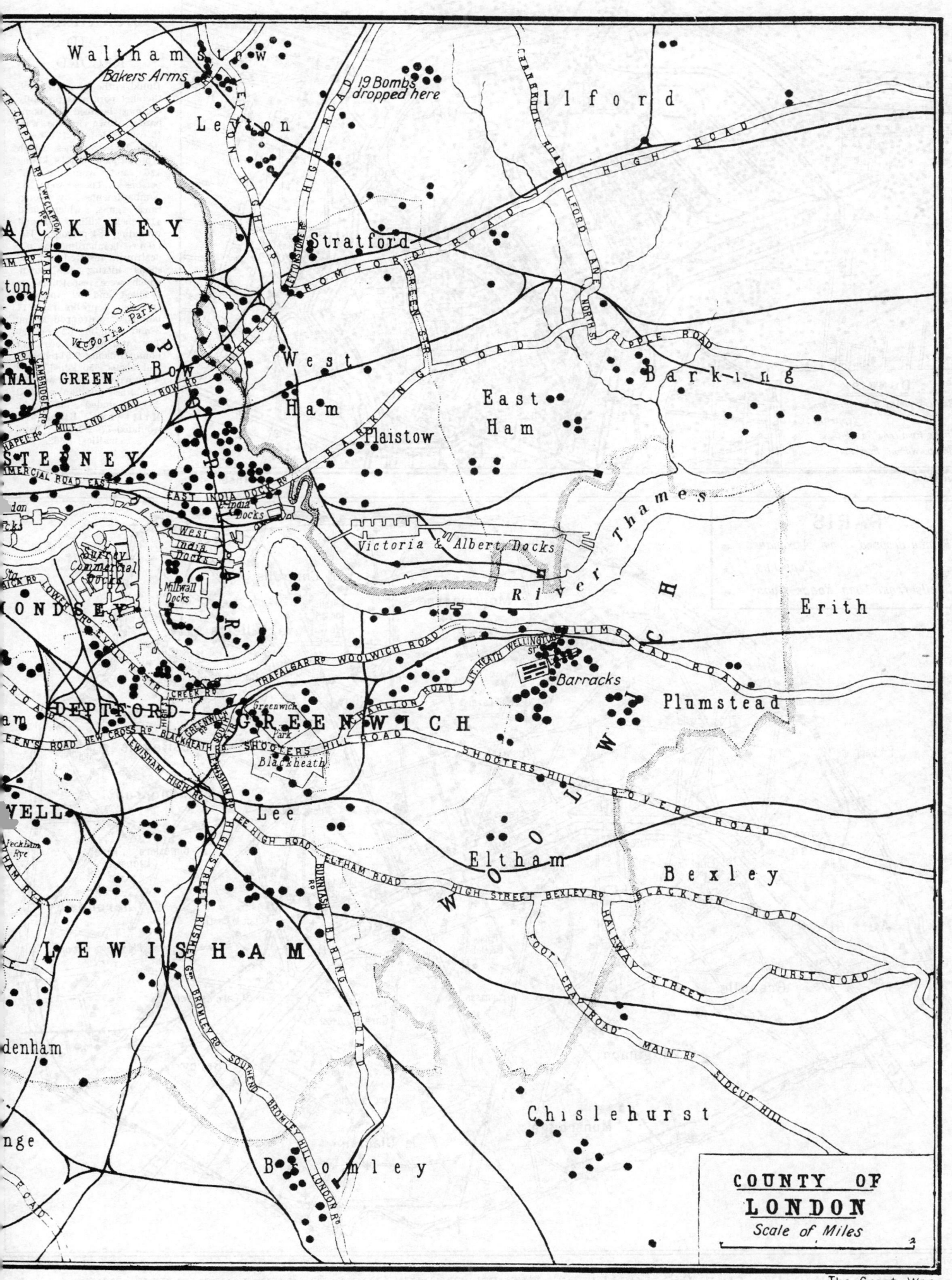

Waltham Stow
Bakers Arms
Leyton
Ilford
19 Bombs dropped here
ACKNEY
Stratford
ton
NAL GREEN
Bow
West Ham
Bark-ing
STEPNEY
Plaistow
East Ham
River Thames
East India Docks
Victoria & Albert Docks
West India Docks
Erith
Surrey Commercial Dock
Millwall Docks
MONDSEY
Woolwich Road
Barracks
Plumstead
DEPTFORD
GREENWICH
Greenwich Park
SHOOTERS HILL
Blackheath
Lee
Eltham
Bexley
WELL
LEWISHAM
SHOOTERS HILL
DOVER ROAD
Chislehurst
denham
Bromley
COUNTY OF
LONDON
Scale of Miles

The Great War

WHERE THE BOMBS FELL THROUGHOUT THE METROPOLIS.
t. Many public buildings were hit, including the Central Telegraph Office, Charing Cross Hospital, Benchers' Buildings of Gray's Inn, Examination Hall of the Royal College of
and Surgeons, Hall and Chapel of Lincoln's Inn, Ministry of Munitions, Embankment Gardens, Royal Academy Buildings, Somerset House. From the map it will be seen
ow escapes were experienced by both Westminster Abbey and St. Paul's Cathedral. Each red dot in the map indicates where a bomb fell.

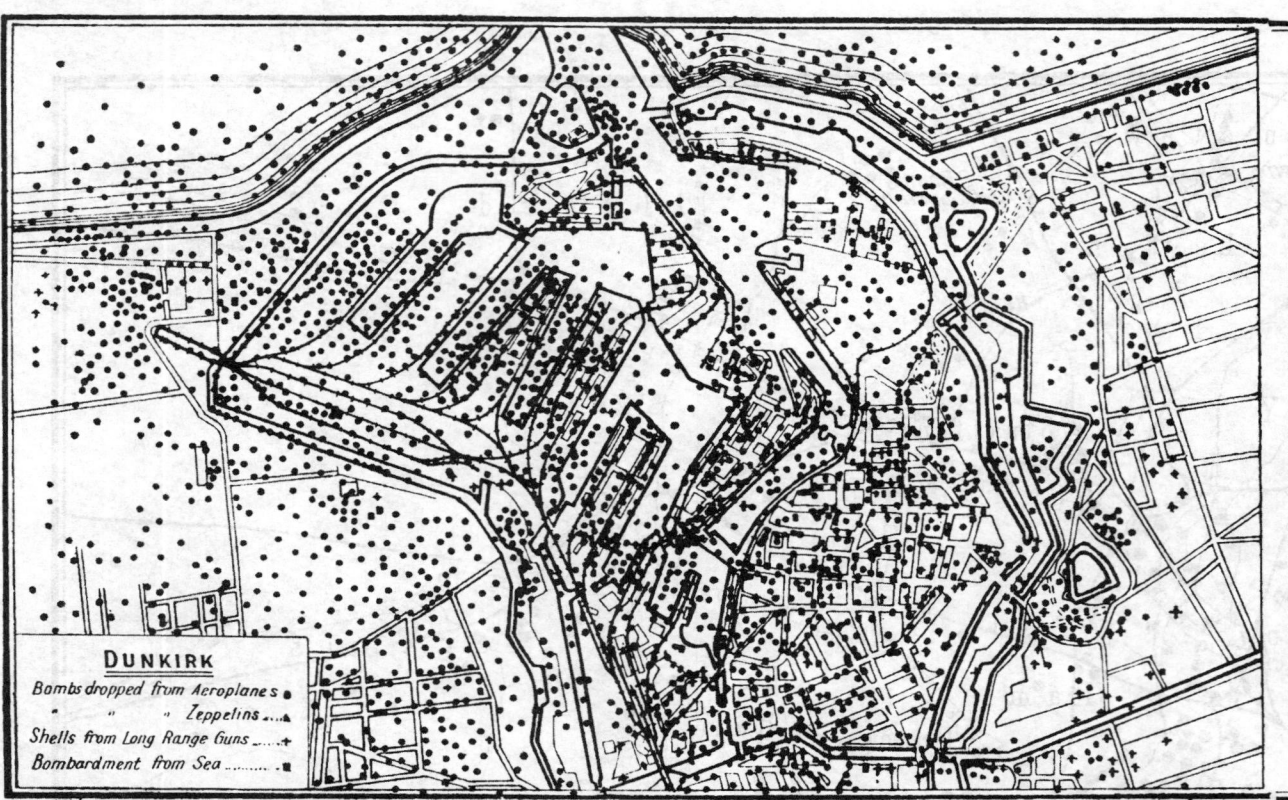

DUNKIRK
Bombs dropped from Aeroplanes •
" " Zeppelins .....
Shells from Long Range Guns ......+
Bombardment from Sea ....▪

DUNKIRK'S RAID RECORD.

Dunkirk, the famous French Channel port, was probably the most bombed and bombarded town in the war. It was raided on 177 occasions by aeroplanes, which dropped 5,092 bombs, killing 426 and wounding 887 persons. There were 32 bombardments by long-range guns, which fired 411 shells, killing 114 and wounding 184 persons. The four bombardments by destroyers resulted in 2,000 shells hitting the town, which were responsible for 7 killed and 32 wounded. In one Zeppelin raid 11 bombs were dropped, killing 3 and wounding 32 persons. The total figures were : 214 bombardments 7,514 bombs and shells, 550 killed, 1,112 wounded. Summary of casualties—Civilians : Killed 233, wounded 336 — 569. Military : Killed 317, wounded 776—1,093. Total casualties, 1.662.

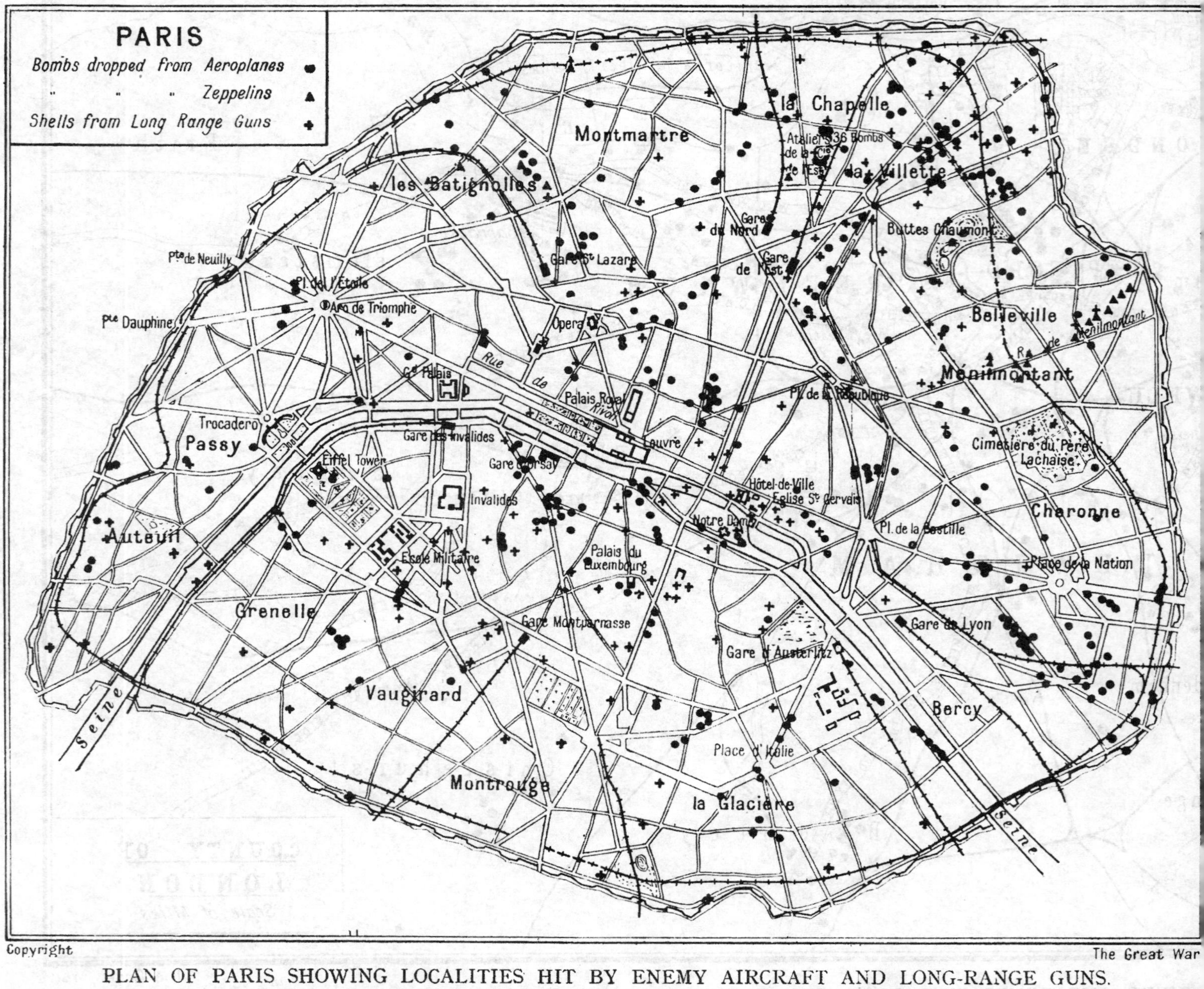

PARIS
Bombs dropped from Aeroplanes •
" " " Zeppelins ▲
Shells from Long Range Guns +

PLAN OF PARIS SHOWING LOCALITIES HIT BY ENEMY AIRCRAFT AND LONG-RANGE GUNS.

In the above plan of Paris are marked the exact spots which suffered from bombs dropped from aeroplanes and Zeppelins and from shells from long-range guns. There were 746 aerial bombs traced, which killed 266 and wounded 603 persons. The city was bombarded for 44 days by " Big Bertha," and 303 shells which fell on Paris killed 256 and wounded 620 persons.

The first batch, three in number, had nearly reached German territory, close to Lunéville, travelling at a rate of fifty-five miles an hour against a wind of eleven or twelve miles an hour, when at 6.20 a.m. of October 20th the French anti-aircraft artillery opened on them at a range of 13,000 feet. At the seventh shot one of the three was hit; one of its gondolas dropped and the airship was set on fire. At 6.45 she crashed in a mass of flames to the ground and all in her were killed. Several mangled bodies were found near the wreck. Another Zeppelin, L49, was pursued by a strong force of French aeroplanes, and was overtaken west of Belfort

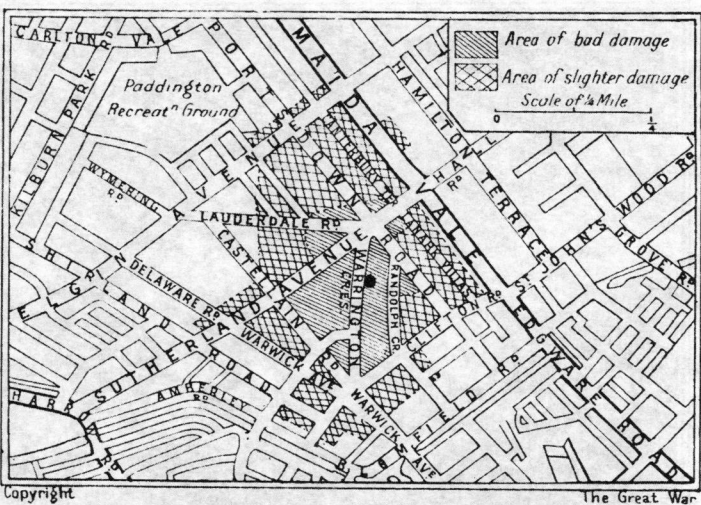

THE HUNS' MOST DESTRUCTIVE BOMB.
District affected by the single 660 lb. bomb dropped from an aeroplane in Warrington Crescent, London, W., March 7th, 1918. It pulverised four houses and broke the glass of almost a thousand others.

prisoner. This was the only Zeppelin captured during the war complete, with all appliances, and the examination of her secrets yielded excellent information to the Allies. Yet another airship, L50, passed close to L49 and was also compelled to land. The crew, finding they were in France, lightened her by cutting away one of the gondolas and leaving behind sixteen officers and men, two of whom were slightly wounded. The vessel then rose and went off in the direction of German territory, though it is possible that she was one of the four which were afterwards seen in the Rhone Valley. She was chased by French aeroplanes, but was so light that she eventually shook them off.

A group of four Zeppelins was driven southwards towards the Rhone and the Italian frontier. Two of them were seen drifting north-west of Gap, over the Rhone Valley, but

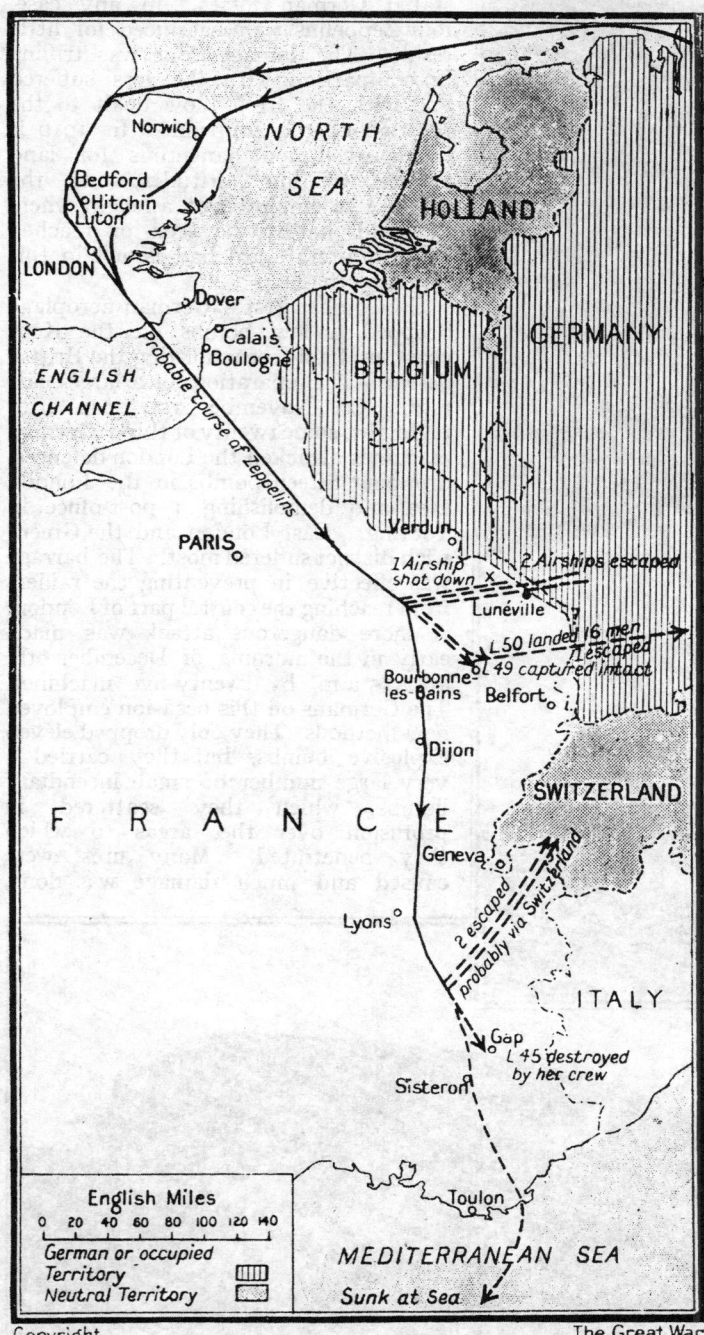

COURSE OF THE ZEPPELIN ARMADA.
Entering England by Norfolk on the night of October 19-20th, 1917, thirteen Zeppelins dropped bombs in several Midland towns and in London before being caught in a gale and swept south-eastwards over France to disaster.

after a prolonged chase. Her officers apparently supposed they were over Westphalia or Holland, and had been flying low. The airship was forced down and landed at 9.20 near Bourbonne-les-Bains, where she was captured intact through the energy of a French civilian armed with a sporting gun, who rushed up and threatened to shoot any German that attempted to set fire to her. Nineteen officers and men were taken

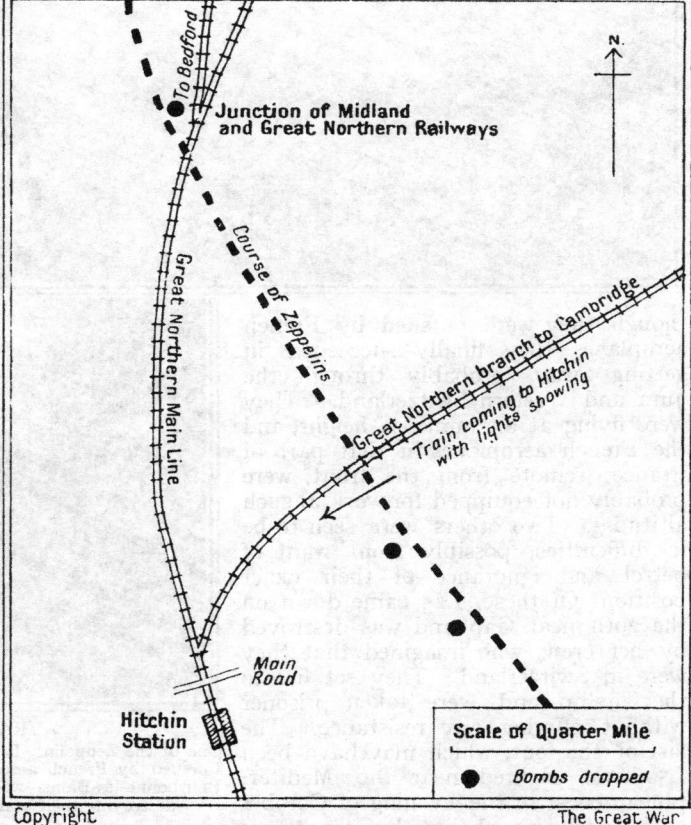

RAILWAY SYSTEMS' NARROW ESCAPE.
Attacking a train that was approaching Hitchin with lights showing, some of the thirteen Zeppelins that raided the Midlands on October 19-20th, 1917, narrowly missed the railway lines north of that town.

L.

No further news of her was received, and as the weather was stormy it is certain that she was destroyed. The Germans admitted a loss of four airships under Commanders Habbert, Koolle, Geyer, and Schwander. There were reports that a fifth airship was lost in the Alps, but as no trace of her wreck was afterwards discovered these were probably untrue, though the German bulletins systematically understated German losses. In any case, four Zeppelins were sacrificed for little result. The damage done was trifling in comparison with the loss suffered and with the fresh blow dealt to the prestige of the Zeppelin. In 1916 it had proved too dangerous for land attacks at low altitudes, and the attempt to employ it at a height where it could hardly be seen or reached by anti-aircraft fire had issued in this miserable fiasco.

On October 31st a German aeroplane dropped a few bombs on the Kent coast, probably reconnoitring the British defences in preparation for a large-scale raid. On November 1st, soon after midnight, some twenty or thirty German machines attacked the London defences, dropping fifteen bombs in the London area and demolishing a post-office in Tooting. East London and the Greenwich district suffered most. The barrage was effective in preventing the raiders from reaching the central part of London. A more dangerous attack was made early in the morning of December 6th, at 4.35 a.m., by twenty-five machines. The Germans on this occasion employed new methods. They only dropped eleven explosive bombs, but they carried a very large number of small incendiary bombs, which they scattered in profusion over the areas to which they penetrated. Many fires were caused and much damage was done,

though they were pursued by French aeroplanes they finally succeeded in getting away, probably through the Jura and Western Switzerland. They were flying at an immense height, and the French aeroplanes in that part of France, remote from the front, were probably not equipped for work at such altitudes. Two others were seen to be in difficulties, possibly from want of petrol and ignorance of their exact position. Of these, L25 came down on the 20th near Gap and was destroyed by her crew, who imagined that they were in Switzerland. They set fire to the airship, and were taken prisoner without offering any resistance. The last of the four, which may have been L50, was sighted near the Mediterranean coast in the evening of October 20th, and was chased by aeroplanes and driven out to sea. Later in the evening she was seen off Toulon, apparently out of control and almost standing on her end; she was then drifting southwards to sea.

A RAIDING ZEPPELIN THAT WAS CAPTURED INTACT.
One of the Zeppelins, L49, that raided England on October 19th, 1917, and drifted across the Channel. Pursued by French aeroplanes in the early hours of the following morning, it was forced to land at Bourbonne-les-Bains, where a French civilian armed with a sporting gun prevented the crew from destroying their craft. Above: A French officer climbed into L49 and secured the German flag.

but the loss of life was not heavy. The aim of the Germans was evidently to test methods of setting the whole of London on fire. This was another of their experimental attacks. In some instances their incendiary bombs proved singularly harmless. People boldly seized them with tongs and put them in buckets of water. Two machines were forced down either by engine trouble or by the British fire, and in one of them there were about sixty bombs which had not been used, all of the size of a champagne bottle and all of the incendiary type. Among the buildings hit were Scotland Yard, where a coal dump was set on fire and quickly put out, and Somerset House, but nearly every part of Central and Western London suffered.

On November 26th the appointment of the first British Air Minister was announced, and Lord Rothermere was offered and accepted the post. An independent organisation of the Air Force had already been carried out in Germany and to some extent in France. One result of the creation of a new Ministry was a rapid expansion in the British Air Force, which in the face of many difficulties Lord Rothermere effected.

On the evening of December 18th the Germans raided in some force with from sixteen to twenty machines, and succeeded in penetrating the London defences with at least six machines. The following notes of this raid, taken in Central London while it was in progress, will illustrate the methods and conditions of a typical air raid :

First warning, 6.35 p.m.; whistles from police to take cover, 6.50 ; first gun, 6.55, followed by five detonations, all heavy and probably all from largish guns, but one may have been a bomb. Then distant firing only. At 7.5 distant firing after a lull ; heavy detonation ; sharp firing at 7.9 ; guns ceased, 7.11. Vigorous firing at 7.15 ; large fire reported near King's Cross, Fire Brigade turned out in the midst of the gun fire. Fresh burst of heavy firing at 7.20 ; 7.25, two very heavy bangs, probably bombs ; sound of machine-guns ; violent fire from guns near. Lull, and then distant firing at 7.30 ; noise of a bomb at 7.33 ; reports that Woolwich and North-Eastern London are being bombed ; 7.35, bomb fell ; hum of aeroplanes plainly heard ; machine-gun fire overhead ; then a lull ; at 8 very sharp firing ; 8.5, heavy explosions ; 8.6, very loud explosion ; heavy and rapid firing ; bomb shook the building, not far off, at 8.10. Lull, and distant firing at 8.14. Lull till 9, when distant firing, drawing near at 9.5, and then receding. All clear at 9.35.

In this raid fifty-three bombs were dropped, and the Fire Brigade reported "great damage." Two large factories were burnt ; one of them was engaged in making aeroplanes.

Two of the German machines were destroyed ; one of these came down with two men on board alive, while the other fell in the Channel. Nearly all parts of inner London were "peppered," from Eaton Square to Clerkenwell. Three days later, on December 22nd, a German force attempted another raid, but was severely handled before getting clear of the English coast. One machine was set on fire and compelled to land, when the crew of three were taken prisoner. A few bombs were dropped at random in Thanet, without inflicting casualties or causing damage to property.

London's worst Gotha raid On the night of January 28th, 1918, London experienced the worst raid in the whole series. It was also the most prolonged, as firing opened at 8.34 and the last attack came after 12.30. The barrage firing was the heaviest that had been known up to that date. The worst hit was on a large building, Messrs. Odhams' Printing Works, used as an air-raid shelter, in Long Acre. The bomb penetrated the building ; it was probably fitted with a delay-action fuse, and it burst in the lower part of the structure, setting fire to it. The greatest difficulty was experienced in rescuing those who remained alive. In all twenty-eight persons were killed and ninety-seven injured, and it is possible that others, who were

reported at the time as missing, perished in the ruins. This incident showed that even the strongest building was not safe from a direct hit. As a matter of fact, the only places which were really secure in a raid were the London Tubes, and these were to a great extent monopolised by crowds of aliens, many of them young men of military age, who set a disgraceful example. Other points where hits were made were Covent Garden and the City. The Floral Hall was struck and the interior much **Attacks on Kew** damaged. Two large bombs fell into the **Bridge and Brentford** river. One of them was probably aimed at Waterloo Bridge, and caused an explosion in the river-bed which was felt to a great distance. St. John's Wood and Kilburn were also attacked, and two bombs in that quarter narrowly missed the London and North-Western main line, causing serious damage to buildings. At Sheerness the raiders bombed a dump, which blew up, destroying much material.

IN THE COMMANDER'S CABIN OF L49.

Looking forward in the cabin of the commander of the Zeppelin L49, captured intact in France after the raid on England of October 19th, 1917. In the cabin, which was furnished with plate-glass windows, may be observed the steering-wheel, eye-piece, bomb-sight, and oxygen bottle for assisting respiration at great heights. To the left is a folded parachute for the use of the commander in case of emergency.

The Germans employed about ten machines, of which only one was shot down.

On the following night a much less dangerous attack was made. The raiders again numbered fifteen, and were caught by the barrage and prevented from entering the London area. They skirted it to the north and worked as far west as Kew and Brentford, the most westerly points reached in any of their aeroplane raids. They attacked Kew Bridge, but did it no damage whatever.

The raids affected the moral of the alien inhabitants of London and led many thousands of them to take refuge in towns and villages where they thought themselves safe. This exodus raised new problems. These undesirables congested the already overtaxed railways, and became such a nuisance that in the spring of 1918 special restrictions on the issue of season tickets had to be enforced. The proper course to have taken would have been to deport this foreign population or to require the able-bodied young men in it to enter the Army, but the Government hesitated, and did not act promptly and effectively. In many London houses shelters were improvised, so as to give comparative safety from anything but a direct hit, but elaborate concrete works, for which both the labour and material were lacking, would have been required to provide adequate shelter for any large

Germans encountered the full strength of the London defences, and received such treatment that they never repeated their attacks. They came in considerable force ; no estimate placed their strength at less than twenty machines, and they may have had more, as observers on the coast believed. The fighting lasted three hours, with some intervals, and was of extraordinary violence. The barrage was active, having been greatly strengthened ; the aprons were in play ; and a very powerful force of British airmen was engaged with the Germans. About 11.30 p.m. a German machine was set on fire by a British airman, and a little later fell a blazing wreck. Another was brought down by gun fire shortly afterwards. Three were destroyed between London and the coast on their retreat, and two more fell into the sea, one of them in flames. In addition it is believed that some of the machines crashed on returning to their aerodromes as the result of the attentions of British aeroplanes. The lowest estimate of the German loss is seven ; the highest eleven machines. As against this, twenty-nine bombs were dropped in the London area, and " great damage " was reported in many quarters. Some of the largest bombs did not explode, whence the casualties were not so heavy as might

part of the population. The large majority of Londoners faced the peril calmly in their own houses ; where these were strongly built the risk was not extreme, though it was one which told upon women and young children, and the strain became greater with each attack, especially when raids followed in quick succession.

On February 16th a small force of raiders, six strong, reached the outer London defences, and only one machine is believed to have penetrated them. This was probably of the giant type. It dropped three bombs of very great size, one on Chelsea Hospital, which completely destroyed a house, and broke much glass, but otherwise did little damage, and two others at Woolwich.

The following night the Germans renewed the assault on London with six machines, and for about an hour there was a violent engagement, the barrage firing with great energy. Sixteen bombs were dropped by the few machines which got through the defences, and St. Pancras Station was hit ; the two eastern pinnacles were blown off the tower, and other damage was caused ; one **The destructive** of the bombs fell in the booking-office, **Maida Vale bomb** wrecking it, and the casualties were comparatively heavy—20 killed, and 22 injured, among whom were several soldiers on leave from the front. On March 7th the Germans were over London again. On this occasion they attacked with seven or eight machines on a moonless night, when there was an extraordinarily bright aurora borealis, producing the appearance of a fire to the north of London. They passed north of London, investigating this light, and were sighted near Hatfield, and then, turning south, two or three of their machines penetrated the barrage, dropping several bombs in Hampstead and one in Maida Vale. This last bomb, of 660 lb., fell in Warrington Crescent ; it demolished in all four houses (Nos. 61, 63, 65, 67), and badly damaged the houses opposite. In about a thousand houses glass was more or less broken ; and more damage was probably done to house property than by any other single bomb. The casualties were, however, small at this point in comparison with destruction of property. Ten persons were killed and 29 injured, while two were rescued unhurt from the debris after some hours work by the firemen. Seven bombs were dropped in this raid.

The last raid took place on Sunday, May 19th, when the

GOTHAS BROUGHT DOWN IN THE RAID OF MAY 19TH, 1918.
One of the Gothas which paid the full penalty during the aeroplane raid on England of May 19th, 1918. On that occasion the Germans encountered the full strength of the London defences, and were so punished that no further air attack followed. Above : All that was left of another of the same party of raiders.

have been expected from so formidable an attack, in which at least one and possibly more of the giants took part. The Germans at times were seen low ; the heavy and constant machine-gun firing indicated the vehemence with which they were attacked by the British.

The German losses in this raid may have reached 50 per cent. of the machines engaged, and were certainly in excess of 25 per cent. Much larger bombing machines were in course of construction in the German works, and a pattern was reported to be in hand, in which no fewer than eleven engines were employed, giving a total output of nearly 3,000 horse-power. As British machines of 2,500 horse-power were under construction it is possible that the Germans had such designs, and the effect of bombs of a ton weight dropped by these monster aircraft would certainly have been disastrous. It was therefore well that the May attack met with such punishment. Besides the steady development **End of the** of the London defences there were other **Gotha raids** factors which towards the close of the war hampered raiding. The British Navy and the aircraft co-operating with it now maintained a far closer watch on the Flanders coast ; and in September, 1918, the allied advance from Ypres endangered the raiders' aerodromes and compelled their removal to safer sites. With the fall of Zeebrugge and Ostend all danger passed. Thenceforth raiders were liable to attack before they reached the sea on their journey out, and they would have had to pass a strip of allied territory on their return. Much earlier warning could have been given to the London defences and fuller preparations could have been made to meet the raid.

Three minor Zeppelin raids were carried out during the spring of 1918, probably with the object of compelling the British Command to keep a large force of aeroplanes in Great Britain during the great German offensive. On March 12-13th German airships appeared at Hull and dropped several bombs there, but caused little damage beyond breakage of glass. On

Three minor Zeppelin raids

March 13-14th they attacked the Durham coast, and inflicted somewhat heavy casualties there. On April 12-13th four Zeppelins crossed the coast, and in cloudy weather pushed as far inland as Warwickshire in the south and Lancashire in the north. Among the places bombed were the outskirts of Birmingham, Wigan, and Yarmouth. This was the last Zeppelin raid in which a German airship dropped bombs on British soil, but on August 5th a squadron of four of the latest and most powerful Zeppelins, commanded by Captain Strasser, the chief of the German airship staff, was sighted on the East Coast before it was dark. British aeroplanes at once attacked. The Germans rose to 19,000 feet, and

AIR RAIDERS REDUCED TO WRECKAGE.
One of the two Gothas that were brought down in the raid of December 6th, 1917, when not far short of three hundred incendiary bombs were dropped in the London area. Above: Wreckage of one of the destroyed raiders of May 19th, 1918. The arrow at the bottom of the picture indicates the position of an unused bomb.

trouble with its machine-gun; the other two attacked L70 on opposite sides at the same moment, and saw her burst into flame and plunge hissing into the sea. In her perished the planner of these cruel raids, Captain Strasser, with all her crew.

Throughout the raids a careful watch was maintained on historic buildings, and art treasures were as far as possible removed to safe places. The most thrilling work was done by the volunteer staff which protected St. Paul's, where sentinels high up above the dome looked out into the night. Twice the cathedral was struck at night by British anti-aircraft shells, and in June, 1917, during the day raid, a fragment of a bomb dented the asphalt of the Stone Gallery.

The total casualties inflicted by the Germans in their airship raids were 498 civilians killed and 1,236 wounded, while 58 soldiers were killed and 121 wounded. In the aeroplane raids 619 civilians were killed and 1,650 wounded, while 238 soldiers or seamen were killed and 400 wounded. In addition there were probably a few missing, so that the casualties were not far from 5,000 in all, a very serious figure indeed.

retreated with all possible speed, but about 40 miles from the coast, L70, then the newest and most powerful German airship, was overtaken by four machines of the D.H.9 type. One was hit by the Germans and fell into the sea; a second had

CROWDS OF SIGHTSEERS VISIT THE SCENE OF A GOTHA'S DESTRUCTION.
Wreckage of one of the Gothas brought down on May 19th, 1918, with some of the Whitsun holiday crowds that gathered to have ocular evidence of the destruction of the raider. Of the machines taking part in that raid, seven were known to be destroyed, and some estimates placed the number at eleven.

The great strength of the London defences was probably the reason why the Germans in 1918 made a number of violent air attacks on Paris, thirteen in all, dropping 664 bombs. The first raid on January 30th-31st, was most terrible; the barrage was feeble; apron defences do not seem to have existed; and the French aeroplanes were not able to inflict serious casualties on the assailants. In this raid bombs of 660 lb., such as were dropped in London, were employed by the Germans, and another which was recovered intact was found to measure nine feet in height, and to contain a charge of 350 lb. of explosive. Other raids followed on March 8th and 11th, April 2nd and 12th, May 21st, 22nd, and 30th; June 2nd, 6th, 15th, 26th, and 27th; and then, after a long pause, due to the disorganisation caused by the German retreat, the last took place on September 14-15th. The total of killed was 208 and of wounded 392 in all the air raids. The Germans shortly before the close of the war intended to attack Paris with an advance squadron of thirty-five machines, dropping special incendiary bombs to the number of 5,000. These were to be followed by a second relay of thirty-five machines, which was to use the glare of the fires to bomb the firemen and troops engaged in dealing with the conflagration. One of the large German incendiary bombs was captured and preserved; it contained 200 small incendiary grenades, which could not be extinguished with water.

Violent attacks on Paris

If attempts of this kind had been made they would have been followed by a terrible retaliation, as by September 15th the Allies were in a position to bomb any town in Western Germany and destroy it. Considerations of prudence may have curbed the savagery of the German High Command, for as the war was manifestly going against the Germans, it became certain that they would be called to account sooner or later and made to pay for their atrocities.

The strategic effect of the German raids so long as the Allies failed to hit back was great. They diverted large forces of men, machines, and guns from active work to passive defence, and gave the German Army opportunities which it failed completely to seize. But, so soon as the Allies began systematic retaliatory raids, all the advantage passed; indeed Germany, from the large number of her towns exposed to air attack, had to draw more heavily than Great Britain upon her active forces for defence. The Germans in the end profited nothing by their air crimes. They aroused against themselves the detestation of humanity and increased the determination of the Allies to rest satisfied with no peace which did not give effective protection against this newest and most barbarous form of war. The defensive air struggle brought all the best British qualities into relief. British brains and British courage overcame the menace of the Zeppelin and practically paralysed the aeroplane. Yet not without grievous suffering and loss, and at times almost unendurable tension, was this great victory gained. In the rush of tremendous events it passed almost unnoticed, yet posterity will account it one of the most notable achievements of the war.

Strategic effect of air raids

AIRSHIP AND AEROPLANE RAIDS OVER GREAT BRITAIN, 1914-18.

The following figures are taken from the official return of airship and aeroplane raids over Great Britain, with the resulting casualties. Between December 24th, 1914, and June 17th, 1918, there were 51 airship raids and 57 aeroplane raids:

AIRSHIP RAIDS, JANUARY 19th, 1915, TO APRIL 13th, 1918. — AEROPLANE RAIDS, DECEMBER 24th, 1914, TO JUNE 17th, 1918.

Date and Locality.	Civilian Casualties. Killed.	Injured.	Sailors and Soldiers. Killed.	Injured.	Date and Locality.	Civilian Casualties. Killed.	Injured.	Sailors and Soldiers. Killed.	Injured.
1915.—Jan. 19-20, Norfolk	4	15	—	1	**1914.**—Dec. 24, Dover	—	—	—	—
April 14-15, Northumberland	—	2	—	—	Dec. 25, Kent	—	—	—	—
April 15-16, Essex and Suffolk	—	—	—	—					
April 29-30, Suffolk	—	—	—	—	**1915.**—Feb. 21, Essex	—	—	—	—
May 9-10, Southend	1	1	—	1	April 16, Kent	—	—	—	—
May 16-17, Ramsgate	2	1	—	—	July 3, East Suffolk	—	—	—	—
May 26-27, Southend	3	3	—	—	Sept. 13, Margate	2	6	—	—
May 31st-June 1st, East London	7	33	—	2					
June 4-5, Kent, Essex, and East Riding	—	8	—	—	**1916.**—Jan. 22-23, Dover	1	6	—	—
June 6-7, Hull, Grimsby, and East Riding	24	38	—	2	Jan. 23, Kent	—	—	—	—
June 15-16, Northumberland and Durham	18	72	—	—	Feb. 9, Kent	—	3	—	—
Aug. 9-10, Goole, East Riding, Suffolk, & Dover	17	18	—	3	Feb. 20, Kent and East Suffolk	1	1	—	—
Aug. 12-13, East Suffolk and Essex	6	24	—	—	March 1, Broadstairs and Margate	1	—	—	—
Aug. 17-18, Kent, Essex, and London	10	48	—	—	March 19, Deal, Dover, Margate, and Ramsgate	10	15	4	11
Sept. 7-8, East Suffolk and London	18	37	—	1	April 24, Dover	—	—	—	—
Sept. 8-9, North Riding, Norfolk, and London	24	92	2	2	May 3, Deal	—	4	—	—
Sept. 11-12, Essex	—	—	—	—	May 19-20, Kent and Dover	—	1	1	1
Sept. 12-13, Essex and East Suffolk	—	—	—	—	July 9, Kent (North Foreland)	—	—	—	—
Sept. 13-14, East Suffolk	—	—	—	—	July 9-10, Dover	—	—	—	—
Oct. 13-14, Norfolk, Suffolk, Home Counties, and London	54	107	17	21	Aug. 12, Dover	—	—	—	7
1916.—Jan. 31-Feb. 1, West Suffolk and Midland Counties	70	112	—	1	Sept. 22, Kent and Dover	—	—	—	—
March 5-6, Hull and East Riding, Lincolnshire, Leicestershire, Rutland, and Kent	18	52	—	—	Oct. 22, Sheerness	—	—	—	—
March 31-April 1, Lincs, Essex, and Suffolk	17	9	31	55	Oct. 23, Margate	—	2	—	—
April 1-2, Co. Durham and North Riding*	22	128	—	2	Nov. 28, London	—	10	—	—
April 2-3, E. Suffolk, Northumberland, London, and Scotland	13	24	—	—					
April 3-4, Norfolk	—	—	—	—	**1917.**—March 1, Kent	—	6	—	—
April 5-6, Yorkshire and Co. Durham	1	9	—	—	March 16, Kent and Margate	—	—	—	—
April 24-25, Norfolk, Lincs, Cambs, and Suffolk	1	1	—	—	March 17, Kent	—	—	—	—
April 25-26, E. Suffolk, Essex, Kent, & London	—	1	—	—	April 5, Kent and Ramsgate	—	—	—	—
April 26-27, Kent	—	—	—	—	May 6-7, London	1	2	—	—
May 2-3, Yorks, Northumberland, & Scotland	7	25	2	5	May 25, Kent and Folkestone	77	94	18	98
July 28-29, Lincolnshire and Norfolk	—	—	—	—	June 5, Essex and Kent	3	8	10	26
July 31-Aug. 1, Norfolk, Suffolk, Cambs, Lincs, Notts, and Kent	—	—	—	—	June 13, Margate, Essex, and London	158	425	4	7
Aug. 2-3, Norfolk, East Suffolk, and Kent	—	—	—	—	July 4, Essex and Suffolk	3	1	14	29
Aug. 8-9, Northumberland, Durham, East Riding, North Riding, Hull, and Norfolk	10	15	—	1	July 7, Margate and London	55	190	2	3
Aug. 23-24, East Suffolk	—	—	—	—	July 22, Essex and Suffolk	1	3	12	23
Aug. 24-25, E. Suffolk, Essex, Kent, & London	9	25	—	15	Aug. 12, Essex and Margate	32	44	—	2
Sept. 2-3, East Riding, Lincolnshire, Nottinghamshire, Norfolk, Suffolk, Cambridgeshire, Huntingdonshire, Essex, Hertfordshire, Beds, Kent, and London	4	12	—	—	Aug. 22, Kent	8	13	4	12
Sept. 23-24, Lincs, Notts, Norf., Kent, & London	40	126	—	4	Sept. 2-3, Dover	—	6	1	—
Sept. 25-26, Lancs, Yorks, and Lincolnshire	43	31	—	—	Sept. 3-4, Kent	1	6	131	90
Oct. 1-2, Lincs, Norfolk, Cambs, Northants, Herts, and London	—	1	1	—	Sept. 4-5, Home Counties and London	16	59	3	12
Nov. 27-28, Durham, Yorks, Staffs, & Cheshire	4	37	—	—	Sept. 24-25, Kent, Essex, and London	11	50	10	20
1917.—March 16-17, Kent and Sussex	—	—	—	—	Sept. 25-26, Kent and London	8	21	1	2
May 23-24, Essex, Norfolk, and Suffolk	1	—	—	—	Sept. 28-29, Home Counties	—	6	—	—
June 16-17, Kent and Suffolk	3	14	—	2	Sept. 29-30, Kent and London	13	82	1	5
Aug. 21-22, East Riding	—	1	—	—	Sept. 30-Oct. 1, Kent, Essex, and London	9	33	5	5
Sept. 24-25, Lincolnshire and Yorkshire	—	3	—	—	Oct. 1-2, Kent, Essex, and London	11	41	—	—
Oct. 19-20, Midlands, E. Counties, and London	31	52	5	3	Oct. 29-30, Essex	—	—	—	—
1918.—March 12-13, East Riding	1	—	—	—	Oct. 31, Kent and Dover	—	—	—	—
March 13-14, Durham	8	39	—	—	Oct. 31-Nov. 1, Kent, Essex, and London	8	21	2	1
April 12-13, Lincs, Lancs, & Warwickshire	7	20	—	—	Dec. 6, Kent, Essex, and London	7	27	1	1
					Dec. 18, Kent, Essex, and London	14	79	—	6
					1918.—Jan. 28-29, Kent, Essex, and London	65	160	2	6
					Jan. 29-30, Kent, Essex, and London	10	10	—	—
					Feb. 16-17, Kent, Essex, and London	9	6	3	—
					Feb. 17-18, Kent, Essex, and London	20	26	1	6
					Feb. 18-19, Kent, Essex, and London	—	—	—	—
					March 7-8, Kent, Essex, Herts, Beds, London	21	39	2	—
					May 19-20, Kent, Essex, and London	43	150	6	27
					June 17, Kent	—	—	—	—
Totals for airship raids	498	1,236	58	121	Totals for aeroplane raids	619	1,650	238	400

* The relative proportions of men, women, and children injured in this raid are not known exactly.

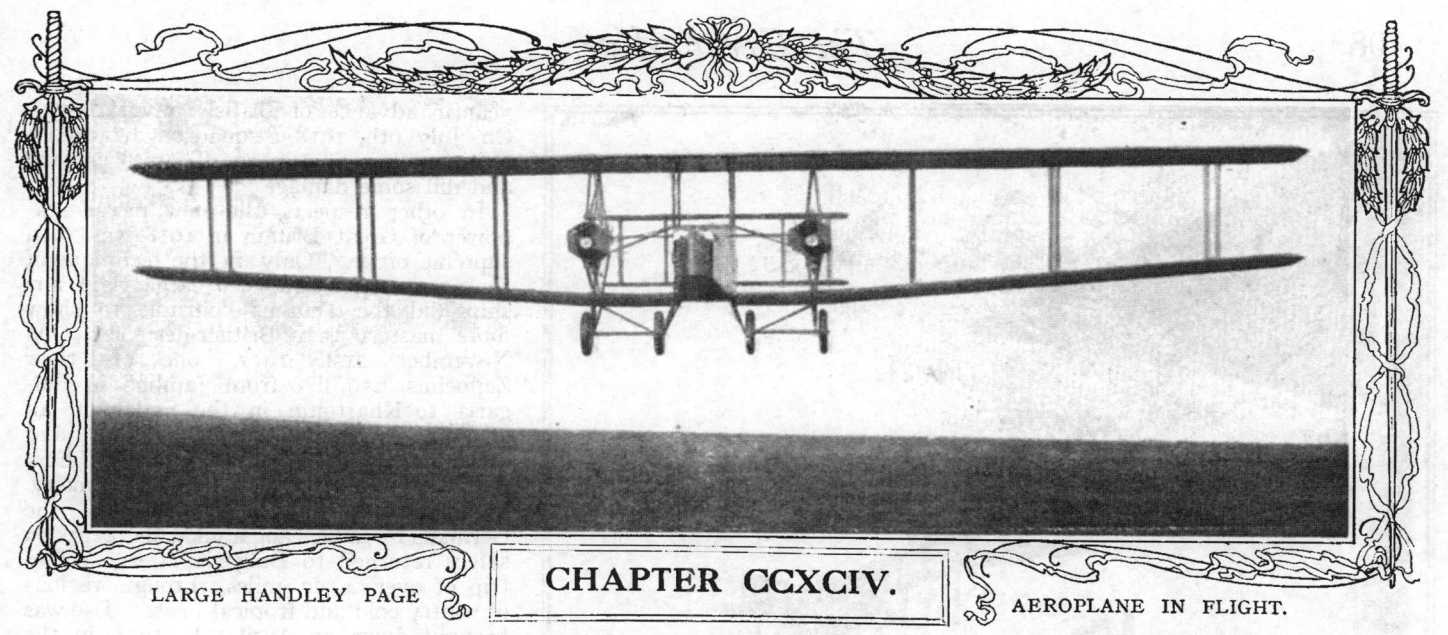

CHAPTER CCXCIV.

FINAL PHASES OF THE WAR IN THE AIR.
II.—The Decisive Supremacy of the British Air Force.
By Edward Wright.

Victorious Expansion of British Aircraft—Remarkable Success of Porte Flying - Boat—German Brandenburg Fighter in Action in Thames Estuary—Zeppelin Over Khartoum—Grand Reorganisation of British Naval Aircraft—Kite-Balloon Victory over U Boats—British Success in Non-Inflammable Airships—Germans Out-numbered in Men and Material—French Surprised in the Air by the Marne—Foch Recovers a Working Equality in Aerial Power—How British Aircraft Saved the Italian Front—Strange Story of the Albatros and the Martinsydes—Sir Hugh Trenchard Begins Operations Against Rhineland—Marvellous Determination of British Airmen—Adventures of Handley Page Machines Over Mannheim—How British Bombers Demoralised German Nation—Rise of New British Champions of the Air—How Sir Douglas Haig Made Strength Out of Weakness—Immense Achievement of British Aerial Photographers—New Uses for Aircraft During Grand Offensive—As Germany Weakens, Britain Grows Stronger—Aerial Blockade of the Jordan that Crowned Allenby's Victory—Aerial Rear Attack on Bulgars Completes their Overthrow—The Decisive Aerial Battle of October 30th, 1918—Some Remarkable Figures of British Aerial Power—Greatest British Achievement Since the Destruction of the Armada.

AFTER the establishment of the Royal Air Force on April 1st, 1918, as described in Chapter CCXLV. (Vol. 11, page 381) Great Britain became the dominant Power in the air. Sir William Weir, who succeeded Lord Rothermere as Minister of the Air, enjoyed the results of the great construction programme which he had carried through in the summer of 1917 when directing aircraft production. An average of four thousand machines and engines were built every month, until there were more machines than there were men to fly them. With one exception, the British machines were generally superior in quality to German machines, with the result that the enemy pilots were not merely out-fought by better men than themselves, but were dispirited by their inferior material, and made as angry with their construction authorities as British pilots had been with the Royal Aircraft Factory regime.

Only at sea was there any serious deficiency in the quality of British aircraft production in the spring of 1918. The remarkable success of Wing-Commander (afterwards Colonel) J. C. Porte had not been supported by foresightful development in seaplane design. Colonel Porte's flying-boat was produced in an experimental manner in 1914, and during the years in which the admirals of Great Britain had little appreciation of the possibilities of

COLONEL J. C. PORTE,
inventor of the flying-boat that bore his name, one of the remarkable triumphs of the war.

aerial power the Porte boat increased in weight, wing span, and engine-power until 1917. It was then the terror of the seas. Although there was an average of only ten boats in service each month at Felixstowe, they made the waters between Western Holland and the English coast a death-trap for the enemy, and the use of the flying - boats extended down the English Channel to the Mediterranean. Small as was the number of Porte boats, they destroyed in the year forty-four German sub-marines, as against forty - one bombed by seaplanes, sixteen by airships, and four by land machines. The flying-boats were about fifteen times less numerous than the seaplanes and land aeroplanes engaged in U boat hunting, yet did practically equal work. Zeppelins were brought down by the flying-boats, enemy destroyers were watched and sometimes bombed, and the traffic between England and Holland was guarded by flying-boats assistant to the protecting surface craft.

In 1918 the Porte boat increased to a weight of fifteen tons, with 1,800 horse-power, and seemed to be the mistress of the southern part of the North Sea. Here it was that the splendid work of Colonel Porte was not fully supported by the authorities responsible for the design of naval aircraft. The Germans, quickened by their sufferings in 1917, built a fast fighting seaplane, the Brandenburg, with all its guns on the top line,

FLYING-BOAT ON PATROL OFF FELIXSTOWE.
Colonel Porte's flying boats, which had been produced in an experimental manner in 1914, came to be a terror of the seas to enemy submarines before the end of the war. In one year they destroyed forty-four U boats, though greatly outnumbered by other aircraft engaged on anti-submarine work.

year in advance of British naval design. On July 6th, 1918, a squadron attacked a British submarine in the Thames estuary and did some damage.

In other respects the new naval sea-power of Great Britain in 1918 was of a supreme order. Only in the technique of the construction of very large rigid airships did the Teutons continue to show more mastery than British designers. On November 21st, 1917, one of their Zeppelins, L59, flew from Jamboli in Bulgaria to Khartoum in the Sudan, in an attempt to carry tons of stores and medicines to the German forces in East Africa. Recalled by wireless from Germany, immediately after the surrender of the Germans by Lake Tanganyika, the Zeppelin safely returned to Bulgaria after a round trip of over 4,500 miles, through regions of wintry cold and tropical heat. L59 was brought down on April 7th, 1918, in the channel by Otranto. British rigid airships, based on the Zeppelin design, were not very successful. Some of them lacked the power to rise properly above anti-aircraft guns, and at least one was reported to require, some months after the cessation of hostilities, more powerful engines. All the practical work of airship reconnaissance on the British side was generally carried out with small non-rigid craft, whose lack of framework enabled them to operate with small engine-power and a small quantity of fuel.

For the task of convoying a group of merchant ships against submarine attack, the airship, the flying-boat, and the sea-plane proved excellent instruments. Indeed, so generally successful were the anti-submarine operations of the various kinds of British naval aircraft that we must attribute in large measure the enemy's first great victorious campaign of piracy to the early lack of interest in aircraft shown by the administrators and leaders of the British Navy. Many of the admirals of Great Britain were men of a conservative nature. As their predecessors were averse to using steam-power instead of wind-power, so they were perhaps unconsciously loath to adapt themselves to the new conditions of aerial power at sea. **Aircraft bases on battleships** The experimental use of a single low-engined British seaplane in the early part of the action off Jutland Bank was a measure of the power of fore-thoughtful preparation on the part of the chief men then at Whitehall and Scapa Flow.

Afterwards, the sailor recognised that the airman was his best friend. When the British Navy did move in aerial organisation a high degree of energy and originality was displayed. By the summer of 1918 the naval aerial offensive power of Great Britain was enormously developed. Some of Lord Fisher's early improvisations in swift, long, big-gunned vessels, such as H.M.S. Furious, were transformed into incomparable aeroplane carriers, on which Sopwith Camels and other machines were able to land, and special large, fast ships, like the new Vindictive and the Argus, were built as machine carriers. Modern battleships, battle-cruisers, and light cruisers were also transformed into their own aircraft bases. In the capital ships, turrets were made into aeroplane platforms, the flat surface being extended by means of a folding flap that could rest on the barrels of the big guns. In the light cruisers there was a revolving platform.

Owing to the remarkable improvements in design and engine-power of British machines, the Camels and other land craft were fitted at times with flotation gear, and could launch

and designed for fighting the Porte boat near the water. It should have been clear from the beginning that the big British boat was like a battle-cruiser of the skies and required attendant lighter craft. None, however, was provided until late in the year the Fairey seaplane, with remarkable climbing power and speed, and variable angle of supporting surface, was produced as an aerial destroyer accompanying the aerial battle-cruiser. The ruling British opinion in 1917 had been that the seaplane was obsolete, and, although superb new British designs were available, they were contemned.

In the meantime the Porte flying-boats were often completely outnumbered. The Teutons had seaplane stations on Borkum Island, in the Bight of Heligoland, and at Zeebrugge, and established a combined system of patrolling flights round the coast of Holland. A **Brandenburgs v. Porte boats** squadron of the Brandenburgers would float on the waves like sea-gulls, and fly up from unexpected spots in an attack on flying-boats, when these were carrying out their ordinary work of hunting down the U boat.

A complete record of all encounters showed that the honours of battle were even, in addition to which the Porte boats went on with their special work. Yet when one of the great British craft was destroyed, after destroying one of its opponents, the Germans had the advantage of having sacrificed only a little monoplane to bring down a giant flying machine, with its crew of pilot, navigator, engineer, and wireless operator.

In the course of the year the Brandenburgers became more daring, their designer having gained practically a

Front view of a British triplane flying=boat, showing its wing span of 123 feet.

Side view of the same aeroplane.   Its height was 27 feet. its fuselage 60 feet long.

First landing of an aeroplane on the deck of a warship steaming at full speed.

Aeroplanes aboard H.M.S. Furious off to bomb the Zeppelin sheds at Tondern, in Schleswig-Holstein.

H.M.S. Furious, the British Navy's floating aerodrome, with an aeroplane forward and an airship aft.

Naval airship coming down to her moorings on the after deck of H.M.S. Furious.

Commandant and Staff of the French Department of Aviation marking the progress of a Gotha raid on Paris.

Models of aeroplanes were figured on the map at the spots where they were first detected, and their subsequent course as reported by telephone from the observation stations was marked by arrows. Small circles indicated the observation stations, triangles the firing points, spades the points where raiders were turned back. Officers stood by awaiting the commandant's orders to warn the population.

themselves from the turret and fly far out in front of the fleet, searching for enemy surface vessels, underwater craft, and new mine-fields. There was also considerable practice in extending the range of observed and controlled gun fire by means of aerial observers. This interesting development, however, was not tested in another fleet action. The great increase in the British power of aerial reconnaissance and aerial power of attack told upon the course of operations in the great British mine-field between Denmark and Holland. The hundred or more enemy surface craft destroyed in the great British mine-field, as mentioned in Chapter CCLXXXVII. (Vol. 12, page 576), were usually tracked down by British aircraft.

Even the humble kite-balloon, the design of which was originally due to the Royal Naval Air Wing in France, which gave the Army the Tank, played a remarkable part in countering German submarine piracy. On June 8th, 1918, for example, one British kite-balloon first discovered a U boat working at a considerable depth under water, and directed the throwing of depth bombs that destroyed the enemy. Then it sighted at a distance another German submarine just breaking surface, and called up and guided British warships which sank the hostile vessel. Such operations as this could have been carried out in 1915, 1916, and 1917 as easily and as effectively as in 1918.

The kite-balloon was fitted with wireless and towed by one of the ships in a merchantmen convoy. The observers, from their commanding position, watched the water for the shadow of a submerged enemy or the broken surface indicating where he was emerging. In the latter part of the struggle for unimpeded sea traffic scarcely one group of cargo boats protected by a kite-balloon was attacked by German underwater craft. Certain German naval officers had returned to their base and reported such miraculous escapes from operations with kite-balloon convoyed shipping that the British kite-balloon had become a danger signal to the enemy when he glimpsed one through a periscope.

Airships best for naval patrols The Germans made no attempt whatever to carry their flying machines out to sea. In their designs, as in their strategy, they were entirely on the defensive. They protected their coasts with large numbers of light, fast machines, which sallied out against British light surface craft in the Bight of Heligoland, as well as against the Porte flying-boats and British seaplanes and land machines carried across the North Sea. Being, however, unable to travel in strength for a great distance, as German airships had done in their period of supremacy, the enemy machines could not act as reconnoitring escort for their submarines.

With the possible exception of the proved Porte flying-boat, which could stand bad weather, move on the surface of the sea, and make voyages of two thousand miles, the airship remained the best instrument of naval patrol in clear weather. German airships, however, were reduced to a condition of defeat by progress in the speed and climbing power of machines and the invention of the incendiary bullet for machine-guns. The Germans in airships could do practically nothing against aeroplane attack, and they eagerly adopted the idea of the Porte flying-boat with a view to regaining the power of long-distance aerial reconnaissance. Count Zeppelin, before his death, designed a giant machine to carry out the work which had become increasingly difficult for his hydrogen-filled airships.

The British, on the other hand, proceeded to make their airships non-inflammable. There was a rare gas, helium, originally discovered in the sun, and afterwards found by Sir William Crookes and Sir William Ramsay, in certain minerals. This gas was light enough to use and, unlike hydrogen, could not be set on fire. The price of helium was utterly impracticable,

"DAZZLE" PAINTING APPLIED TO AIRCRAFT.
One of the largest of the British flying-boats which were effectively employed against enemy submarines. The Porte flying-boat had by 1918 increased to a weight of about fifteen tons, with engines of 1,800 horse-power, and for a time seemed to be mistress of the southern part of the North Sea.

but this small detail did not daunt British experts in naval aviation. They despatched some men of science to some natural gas wells in Canada, where a cheap process of extraction was devised. Then the United States Government was approached in regard to the richer sources of natural gas in the country, and helium gas was at last produced at a fairly cheap price and compressed into steel cylinders for filling British airships.

The affair was a remarkable example of Teutonic boastfulness and British performance. Throughout the war the Germans spread the report that their nation possessed a secret, non-inflammable light gas that would make Zeppelins impregnable. Yet every German airship brought within close range of fire came down in flames. It was the Briton, slow to move but rapid when in action, who achieved the crowning triumph in airship technique.

As the war was drawing to a close, British **Non-inflammable** rigid air vessels began to appear, which **British airships** were larger and more powerful than any existing German craft. British inventiveness, moreover, solved a difficult problem by dispensing with sheds, and tethering vessels in the open by means of mooring-masts.

The Germans had only one turn-table airship shed at their great station of Nordholz, in the corner of the Bight of Heligoland. They found the expense of building the turntable shed so great that they constructed no more, and relied upon immovable sheds, which airships could leave or enter safely only when the wind was in the right direction. With all its patient, plodding, craftsmanlike qualities the Teutonic mind lacked the surprising virtue of genius.

The Briton accomplished more in flashes of creative imagination than his enemy did in years of creative work.

It was far from easy for the British creative minds in aircraft affairs to break through the crust of dull officialism and arrive at positions of directing importance. Yet this was done so soon as a Scottish man of business and engineering knowledge, Sir William Weir, was placed in commanding authority. Lord Weir, as he became in 1918, gave free scope to some of the best machine and engine designers and makers, and obtained some at least of the best aero-motors in the world and many of the best machines.

Even this brilliant, energetic, enlightened engineer was, however, unable to bring out the full capacity of British inventiveness and production in aircraft. When Lord Weir became Minister of the Air, and appointed **Inadequate output of new machines** other apparently able men to direct manufacture, there was a serious slackening in the output of machines of new and more powerful type and engines with new and valuable features. The Napier Lion engine which, after the cessation of hostilities, carried a De Havilland aeroplane to an altitude of 30,500 feet, was not rightly developed in regard to amount of production. It could have been produced in quantity in the spring of 1918 so far as the makers were concerned. Other very promising engines were also apparently neglected, so that machines of high quality, like the Bristol fighter, were not given full power and produced in required numbers.

In regard to new British machines of very superior design, few were likely to be ready for active service until the summer of 1919. The new Handley Page and the new Harland Wolff machines were among the neglected opportunities of British aerial power. During 1918 the Royal Air Force lived in the matter of material on the capital of new inventions gathered during the crisis of 1917. Very old and inadequate machines were employed until the end of the war for artillery spotting and other purposes. Huge as was the production of British factories, the directing intelligence at work was not always of the highest order.

Sufficient, however, was done to mount most of the British fighting airmen in such fashion that they could overwhelm the outnumbered forces of Germany. It was mainly the Royal Independent Air Force, engaged in bombing enemy

territory, that was inadequately supplied with fully available material.

The Germans were outnumbered in aircraft and aero-motor workmen as well as in aerial fighting men. The engineering men and mechanics of Great Britain, France, Italy, and the United States were in a position to overwhelm Teutonic designers and working men. Great Britain led the way in the struggle for superiority of material, and with Sopwith, Bristol, Martinsyde, British Nieuport, Fairey, and other splendid fighting machines, Porte flying-boats, Handley Page and De Havilland machines, most of them produced in large quantities, dominated the air wherever British pilots worked over land. Among the engines used were the finely-improved Hispano-Suiza, which owed a good deal to Italian refinement, the Rolls-Royce of various types, the Siddeley-Deasy and other British designs, with French air-cooled motors, such as Le Rhône, which the Germans also adopted for fighting aeroplanes working in high altitudes. Very high compression, produced by alterations in design, was employed to give greater power. The difficulty of getting enough air in the thin atmosphere at great heights was usually overcome by providing additional slots in the carburetter and fixing an altitude control for opening these slots when the engine was failing through lack of air. These improvements were adopted by friend and foe, the Germans being quick in picking up ideas from all machines that fell in their lines.

France, the pioneer in fine engine design, and for long the peer of Great Britain in light and handy fighting machines, suffered from the misfortune of having had no public scandal over her crisis in the production of material. Her bureaucracy was not shaken from its complacency, or stimulated by criticism as the officialism of the Hotel Cecil and the Royal Aircraft Factory partly was. Consequently, the material power of French aviation declined, and in spite of the successes of Lieutenant Fonck and other French champions, France remained inferior to Germany in general strength in the air.

WITH BRITISH BOMBERS IN FRANCE.
Taking petrol supplies on board a British machine in readiness for starting on a bombing raid over the German lines. Above: Diminutive motor-tractor drawing a huge British bombing machine into position on an aerodrome in France. Above in circle: Forepart of a British bombing machine ready to start.

She was largely assisted by the American flying corps, which obtained at last some examples of that much-advertised combination of all the talents of American engineering—the Liberty motor. This production of the united genius of Ford, Packard, and other American builders of standardised motor-vehicles was eventually made into something practical, under the organising power of an American copper magnate, Mr. John Ryan, who was appointed to a position somewhat similar to that occupied in Great Britain by the Scottish engineer, Lord Weir.

The Liberty motor was not so good as the best British, French, and Italian engines. After being advertised like a patent medicine it turned out a failure, but was improved into something like an obsolescent Rolls-Royce or Napier. British firms were generally about a year in advance of American design. The Liberty engine possessed the virtue of cheapness and large output, and was serviceable in machines that did not need great speed and climbing power.

The American flying corps continued to use foreign engines and foreign machines for fighting purposes, and to a

HANDLEY PAGE BOMBING MACHINE TAKING FLIGHT.
In the rivalry among designers and manufacturers of aeroplanes that was fostered by the stress of the war the Handley Page great weight-carrying machines emerged as perhaps the most notable successes in aircraft construction, and had the greatest effect on the moral of the German people.

of which he seriously delayed any decisive victory by the main forces under Marshal Foch.

Italy was saved from weakness by two forces of British machines that helped her decisively to dominate the Austro-Hungarians. One British group operated in Italy from the Asiago upland to the Piave River, while the other worked across the Southern Adriatic against Durazzo and Cattaro, the pilots using land aeroplanes and continually making the journey of two hundred and forty miles without any means of floating on the sea.

Italian engineers and fitters were thoroughly competent, and Italian designers notably inventive, but they lacked the abundance of coal and metal needed for huge-quantity production of machines. Their comparative failure in air material was due to the same cause as their deficiency in land armament, which was want of coal and shipping. They had to rely to some extent on their Allies, who had been more amply provided with natural resources. They furnished in return inspiring ideas and admirable designs, so that Mr. Handley Page and Signor Caproni vied with each other and with Mr. Holt Thomas in the construction of great cargo-carrying machines. Engines of Italian design were used in American fighter aeroplanes, and an interesting semi-rigid airship was sent from Italy to England.

Italian genius in invention

The French aviation service was completely surprised by the German offensive across the Ailette, Aisne, and Vesle on May 27th, 1918. Most of the crack German pilots were then concentrated about Laon. Among them were Captain Berthold and Captain Meckhoff, each with some thirty victories, and Lieutenants Udet, Lowenhardt, Kirsten, Kroll, Peutten, and the brother of Manfred von Richthofen.

They completely held the air beyond the Marne River for at least twenty-four hours, destroying or forcing down the

considerable extent remained a charge upon the manufacturing power of the French, instead of relieving the strain upon the French war factories.

But for the early failure of the Americans in the manufacture of engines and machines Germany might have been chased completely from the air by the summer of 1918. Only on the British and Belgian fronts, however, was the industrious and able Teuton completely vanquished in invention and productive energy. Over the French and American fronts he maintained for months a power of asserting a local working superiority in the air by means

AEROPLANES THAT EFFECTED THE ECLIPSE OF GERMAN AIR-POWER.
Handley Page bombing machine used by the Royal Air Force in long-distance raids on enemy towns in the spring of 1918. Above: One of the Handley Page super-aeroplanes that were prepared for the raiding of Berlin just at the time when the armistice ended hostilities.

PREPARATION FOR EMERGENCY.
Observers adjusting the harness to which their parachutes were attached before going up on duty in a kite-balloon.

aerial forces of the Sixth French Army and overcoming many of the machines working with the British divisions of the Ninth Corps. Hundreds of low-flying German machines swept the ground with fire, and released bombs upon targets of war material and bodies of troops. All that the Germans had been taught by the British in the aerial blockade of roads of advance by Albert and Amiens they put into intensive practice in the night of May 27th and the following morning. The bridge by Château-Thierry, for example, was made almost impassable even for ammunition carriers, and the great loss of guns, shell, and general material was in large measure due to the devastating swoop of the massed forces of the German flying corps.

As in the British retreat in March, aerodromes were lost over a considerable depth of country, leaving the retiring French Army practically without any immediate reserve of air-power. The desperate gallantry of a few outnumbered French and British airmen, often contending singly against combined formations of hostile chaser aeroplanes, did not serve to hinder the enemy's mastery of the air. Marshal Foch, however, had strong forces within call, and he began counter operations in the first night of the battle by concentrating every available bombing machine in attacks upon the bridges and crossings of the Ailette and the Aisne, where twenty-three tons of explosives were dropped.

Bombing operations were continued the next day and the

GOING ALOFT TO "SPOT" FOR THE GUNS.
Parachutes in position outside the car of a kite-balloon. In the event of their balloon being shelled or attacked by aircraft, descent by parachute was the observers' sole way of escape.

following night, some thirty-seven tons of projectiles being released upon railway-stations, roads, and marching columns of troops between Laon and Fismes. For a time there was a period of mutual harrying, during which the German squadrons attacked the French communications as far as the suburbs of Paris. Meanwhile, the principal pilots of France began to wear down the enemy's strength in high-flying fighter machines. Only a few of these were destroyed on May 27th, 28th, 29th, and 30th, but on May 31st the French airmen shot down some thirty-seven machines, which was at least double the number of enemy victories for the day.

Across the main German railway communications between Laon and Maubeuge the British air force began to strike at Busigny and Le Cateau, besides making excursions to Valenciennes. German machines were brought down in great numbers, often in the proportion of five to one lost British machine, and seldom in less proportion than four to one. Lieutenant Bongartz, one of the German champions of the air, was brought down wounded in the eye by a British airman.

On the other hand, the American flying corps lost before the battle its greatest fighting pilot, Major Raoul Lufbery, who had fought on the French front for about two years, bringing down eighteen German aeroplanes. He was shot down in flames by a German triplane carrying two guns. He jumped some two thousand five hundred feet from the ground and perished. In almost exactly similar circumstances one of the new German champions, Lieutenant Udet, descended from his burning machine at a height of about a thousand feet. He had a parachute which, owing to the hasty manner in which it was used, did not open quickly, yet it kept the pilot up sufficiently to enable him to escape with only a hurt ankle.

By the end of the month the French had recovered a working equality in the air round the new front of battle from Soissons to the Marne and Rheims. To assist them in checking reconnoitring enemy forces, Major-General John Salmond, commanding the British air forces on the western front, sent a strong contingent of fighting and bombing machines to the Oise sector of the Third French Army, where General Fayolle, the army group commander, was preparing his first counter-stroke.

The British pilots, machine-gunners, and bombers made a fine attack at the end of the first week in June, breaking over the German lines by Conchy and Lagny, assailing gun teams and columns of motor-lorries, and scattering troops on the ground by the operation known as contour flying, in which a pilot follows the contour of the ground from a low position. Thirty-one German machines were brought down, and only three British machines lost on the entire front of operations from Flanders to the Rhineland.

In Italy in the month of May the success of the British flying contingent was extraordinary. The British brought down eighty-two Austrian machines with a loss of only two of their own machines. The Italians also lost two machines and destroyed fifty-four enemy machines. Two Italian pilots, on June 13th, flew to the Zeppelin works at Friedrichshafen and back, a distance of five hundred miles, one of the longest non-stop machine flights in the war. By this time the Italian front had become the critical part of the battle-line of the Grand Alliance. On June 15th the Austrians opened their last offensive, to which their costly aerial battles in the first part of the month had been a preliminary.

As by the middle of June the Austrians had lost some hundreds of machines, together with their best pilots, in a vain attempt to win free reconnoitring power behind the Piave River and the foot-hills of the Alps, the power of the air was completely against them. They sacrificed another hundred and seven machines in a final endeavour to obtain reconnaissance and artillery observation, but their pilots were shot down by Britons and Italians at the incomparably light allied sacrifice of nine machines. During the fighting between June 15th and June 25th, Italian and British observers discovered three hundred and ninety Austrian artillery positions, directing fire upon them until they were smothered.

Allies' aerial triumph in Italy

While this work of light-machine operations was going on in the high-fighting altitudes, in the lower observation positions the great aeroplanes of Caproni, Handley Page, and De Havilland played a very important part in deciding the issue of the Battle of the Piave. The enemy's bridges, boats, and fords, and his assembly places west of the river were bombed with huge projectiles, aimed by means of improved releases like shots out of a gun.

THE LEAP FOR LIFE.

The observer of a German observation balloon jumping from the basket after his balloon had been set on fire. The man's weight was just releasing the parachute on which his life depended.

before the main action opened. Every aerial offensive they attempted for some weeks before the battle was defeated with crippling losses.

The result was that the defending forces were able to range by day and night far over hostile territory, and study closely the amount of rolling-stock in stations and the movement of transports along all roads. They provoked the enemy to continue his attempts to break through their patrolling lines, and again weakened him disastrously in material and men. When all his concealed batteries opened fire, the allied airmen held the air so completely that they were able to mark down hostile guns by the hundred, and thus leave hundreds of thousands of the infantry attack without protection against the massed Italian guns. At the close of the battle, when the routed Austrian forces were in flight over the river, the allied bombing machines flew in advance of the Italian cavalry, and the fugitives were also machine-gunned by a remarkable number of low-flying aeroplanes. Major Baracca, the Italian champion, was killed on June 19th, after winning his fortieth victory, being brought down in a Nieuport on the Montello by the Austrian champion, Captain Brumowski, who also claimed the same number of victories.

Routed Austrians pursued by airmen

COMING SAFELY TO EARTH.

German observer who had leaped from his blazing balloon nearing the end of his descent. (This photograph was found on a German prisoner who was captured during the closing stages of the war on the western front.)

The enemy was unable to bring any artillery over the river before the flood torrent came down, and when the rain water fell as suddenly as it rose, the terrible demoralising mastery of the air continued to be exercised against the shattered enemy. In many respects the magnificent Italian stand between the Brenta and the Piave was of classic importance as an illustration of the value of air-power. The Austrians were allowed to make no surprise concentration

The effect of improved material of the Royal Air Force was seen on the Salonika front, where Lieutenant Colonel G. W. Dawes and his successor, Lieutenant-Colonel G. E. Todd, maintained the splendidly efficient force. The pilots only needed up-to-date machines in order to gain command of the air. They then brought down an average of eight enemy machines for every one of theirs that was lost, and their bombing raids against Bulgarian communications and hutments, and against the Berlin-Constantinople Railway were a considerable factor in reducing the Bulgarian peasant soldiers into a condition of dispiritedness. In the Eastern Mediterranean the naval patrol carried out terrifying bombing attacks on Constantinople, and with Porte flying-boats, seaplanes, and aeroplanes assisted in the hunt for submarines.

French, Italian, and Greek aviation services naturally carried out a good deal of the work of U boat hunting in the Mediterranean, Adriatic, and Ægean, and there were numerous tales of gallant endurance and skill on the part of pilots and observers whose machines broke down far out at sea. U39, that entered the Spanish harbour of Cartagena in a badly damaged condition, received her injuries from two seaplanes of the Algerian aviation station. At a signal from a convoy that an enemy submarine was attacking, two French seaplanes went out in bad, stormy weather and escorted the merchant ships for some distance, until the enemy boat broke surface five miles away.

Masked by the clouds and with the noise of their coming drowned by the tempest, the two French machines attacked with bombs, and drove the submarine under water. One of the French airmen descended to make sure that the enemy was destroyed, but the submarine rose on an even keel, and the crew came on deck and opened fire. This happened on May 18th, 1918, when the French still had many machines with small fuel capacity. The two attacking seaplanes found that their petrol was low, and were compelled to make for the coast without completing the destruction of the enemy. She got away, but was so injured that she had to seek shelter in Spain.

To Palestine many good British machines went when they died. The Holy Land was indeed the last resting-place of both German and British machines of a serviceable type which had become outclassed in the intense struggle on the western front. Matters were thus fairly equal between the British, Australians, Germans, and Austrians engaged in celestial work on the last crusade. When, however, Sir Edmund Allenby began strongly to press the Ottoman forces, the new enemy commander, Liman von Sanders, had the ingenious idea of bringing a crack German pilot, on a new Albatros of remarkable pace and climb, to

A bright idea anticipated put an end to the British power in the air. It was a simple idea and a cheap one, as one good pilot on a first-class machine would not be missed from the main front.

One morning, before breakfast, the German set out to make his first victims. He espied two British machines and recognised them as old-fashioned Martinsydes, which had done excellent work in the main theatre of war before they were out-built and out-engined. The German prepared to climb above them for a deadly attack. The rate at which he climbed was extraordinary, but he found that the apparently old machines rose quicker than his new Albatros. He endeavoured to break off the action and met with another surprise.

The British machines were much more responsive to handling than his was. They cut him off from his lines, and then in a combined movement forced him to descend, and without firing a shot the German was made a prisoner,

and a perfect Albatros of the newest type was captured. Major-General William Salmond, commanding the air forces in Palestine, had had the same idea as General Liman von Sanders, but instead of ordering a single new machine of the highest power the British commander had ordered two.

In Mesopotamia the reorganisation of the Royal Air Force's material had the same effect as elsewhere. Against the poorly-equipped Turks, British pilots held a far-reaching mastery, limited only by the effects of sandstorms and boiling heat on the delicate mechanism of engines and the cooling capacity of water-jackets. General Marshall employed contour fighting aeroplanes against hostile tribesmen, who were scattered as much by panic as by bullets and bombs.

For policing the wild Bedouin of the desert the aeroplane was a perfect instrument. It created superstitious terror as well as the ordinary demoralisation due to the landsmen's feeling of helplessness against attack from the skies. Nomad Arabs, who had been regarded as hopelessly lawless and amenable to no threat of force when roaming their own sandy wastes, became half-civilised, some of the worst of them entering the Royal Air Force, becoming skilled in kite-balloon work and mightily proud of wearing the British uniform.

IN ACTION ON THE WESTERN FRONT.
The forepart of a Handley Page aeroplane in flight on the British western front in France, with a machine-gun in action. When the photograph was taken another machine, some distance ahead, showed clearly framed in the struts and cross-pieces.

As an instrument of civilising influence the flying machine was used upon the German people with marked effect in the summer of 1918. While directing the British aviation service on the western front, Major-General Sir Hugh Trenchard had strongly maintained that the bombing of enemy territory was a luxury, so long as the pilots along the battle-line were insufficiently equipped. On the other hand he held that destructive raids into Germany were a necessity so soon as the Royal Air Force was well provided with machines of good quality. On June 5th, 1918, Sir Hugh Trenchard went to Nancy to take over the bombing force there, which had been sadly crippled in its development since it was started by the old R.N.A.S.

Independent Air Force organised

Formed into the 8th Brigade of the Royal Air Force, the bombing organisation consisted of four squadrons, two of which were of inferior quality. There were F.E.2b machines, with 160 h.p. Beardmore engines, which could fly only a comparatively short distance, and there were De Havilland 9 machines, excellent in themselves, but fitted with 200 B.H.P. engines, which had defects. A squadron of Handley Page machines, with 375 Rolls-Royce motors, and a squadron of De Havilland 4 machines, with 275 Rolls-Royce engines, constituted the striking power of the Independent Force, of which the greatest of aerial commanders was made director. It was rather like appointing Marshal Foch to the command of a poorly-equipped volunteer brigade.

Sir Hugh Trenchard estimated that it would probably take him four years to develop the Independent Force to a strength sufficient to make one large German centre of industry uninhabitable, and then proceed to disperse other enemy industrial populations. He had to construct aerodromes on land requiring a large amount of draining work, and it was not until November 1st that this task was almost completed. Owing to the official mismanagement of powerful engine production at home the pilots had not the range of action and

Mechanical apparatus for registering the position of enemy aircraft. The orientation of the stucco cap was guided by an observer seated in a pivotal chair, who listened to the sound of the aircraft engines and distinguished enemy machines from the others.

Staff of the central listening-post in Paris at work during a Gotha raid on the capital in 1918. Listeners to the anti-aircraft artillery reported results to the telephone operator, who issued instructions to the gunners on the inner defences.

MECHANICAL DEVICES EMPLOYED IN THE FRENCH SYSTEM OF AIR DEFENCES OF PARIS.

the staying power required for their work. Their engineers increased the air endurance of some machines by adding extra petrol tanks, and gradually replaced the weak B.H.P. engines with Liberty motors in the absence of the Napiers, big Siddeley-Deasy's, and other good British engines, the production of which had not been encouraged.

In the circumstances the commander of the Independent Force resolved rather to aim at moral effect upon the German people than vainly to strive for large destructive action. He sent his squadrons ranging over as many German centres as were within reach, selecting as targets poison-gas factories, aeroplane works, engine factories, and other military objectives. He used more machines on daylight raids than on nocturnal attacks, in order to disturb the spirit of the German people and interrupt their work as well as their sleep.

Operations were begun in June, 1918, by a campaign against German aerodromes. This was designed to **Campaign against German aerodromes** protect the British sheds from night raids and diminish the number of German fighter machines that would counter-attack by day. The Germans were re-equipping for home defence work a large number of squadrons withdrawn from the Russian front in direct preparation against Sir Hugh Trenchard's campaign. This made it more necessary to begin with attacks on enemy aerodromes. Sir Hugh Trenchard needed long-range fighting scouts to attack the German scouts which assailed his slow and heavy bombing machines. But the Handley Page and De Havilland bombers remained throughout the war in somewhat the position of the Porte flying-boat. The long-range scouts needed to protect them did not arrive until the armistice was signed.

There arrived instead more machines with defective engines, which had to be replaced by other motors, and this work was not completed before the cessation of hostilities. A special group of machines, capable of carrying a cargo of bombs as far as Berlin, arrived late, and the machines were only ready to attack three days before the armistice was signed, and did not come into action.

Between June 6th and November 10th, 1918, the Independent Force dropped five hundred and fifty tons of bombs in Alsace-Lorraine and the regions of the Rhine, one hundred and sixty tons being released by day and three hundred and ninety tons by night. Of the total of projectiles used, two hundred and twenty and a quarter tons were launched upon German aerodromes, as a measure of advanced counter-attack upon fast enemy scout machines that could not be met on equal terms in the air. General Trenchard's strategy in this respect was undoubtedly sound and even brilliant ; but he would have saved men, machines, and bombs for more important work if foresight had been shown in ordering long-distance fighter machines to accompany the bombing squadrons.

Moreover, owing to the lack of air endurance that distinguished many machines of the Independent Force, a very large proportion of the projectiles was employed against railway-stations and blast furnaces in the **British pilots' resolution** neighbourhood of Metz, because the pilots were unable to reach German territory. Sometimes their engines were not powerful enough to fight against the strong winds encountered, and squadron leaders had to use nice judgment to determine whether their petrol would last out. This was usually the time when the railways and furnaces of Lorraine received the bombs intended for German war factories.

The losses in British machines were high, probably amounting quite to one machine for every ton of bombs dropped upon objectives in German territory as distinct from targets in the lost provinces of France. The task of Sir Hugh Trenchard and his officers grew at times as desperate as had been the work which the Royal Flying Corps carried out under the same general on the British fighting-front in the days of the Fokker scourge. Once more Sir Hugh Trenchard proved that he could inspire his pilots with the utmost determination.

There were cases in which a squadron lost the greater part of its machines in a raid, yet, instead of the pilots accepting the disaster as a defeat, they turned it into a moral victory by immediately assailing the same targets with gallant resolution. They were inspired with the feeling that their sacrifices would be fruitful if they could shorten the war by one day, and thereby save the lives of thousands of men in the field. When the losses of the Independent Force were heaviest there was no wavering in the desire to get well into Germany.

Bad organisation and lack of foresight on the part of the authorities responsible for the production of material was redeemed by the courage of British airmen and the strategy and personality of their commander. Sir Hugh Trenchard had the same idea as the German commander who directed the airship and aeroplane raids on England. Reckoning that the moral effect of bombing stood to the material effect in a proportion of twenty to one, he struck at the fighting spirit of the enemy by the process of alarming the German population and stirring them to revolt against their military masters.

On the British side the campaign was carried out in soldier-like fashion, by restricting attack to points of military importance. About the time when Sir Hugh Trenchard assumed command, Gotha raiders were both bombing and machine-gunning British military hospitals, one enemy pilot being brought down alive but wounded, and taken into a hospital that he had deliberately attacked. The enemy photographed the hospitals before dropping bombs and machine-gunning nurses and patients, so that it was clear that his savage intention was to attempt to terrorise fighting men whom he could not defeat either on the ground or in the air. The fact was the German Emperor very narrowly escaped in person from the bombs of the Independent Force when travelling by Metz, and this act of lèse-majesté on the part of Sir Hugh Trenchard's pilots seems to have been punished by the assassination of wounded British soldiers and their attendants.

In spite of all temptations to reprisal, the Independent Force confined its attacks to munition works, railway-stations, and the rolling-stock on some of the main rails feeding the German Army, which was already beginning to suffer from an extreme shortage of trucks **Mannheim and** and locomotive engines. Among the most **Coblenz bombed** striking of the British operations was an attack by Handley Page machines on the chemical works at Mannheim in the night of June 29th. Owing to bad weather and tempestuous wind only one machine reached the great dye factory where poison gas was being made. The bombs were dropped on the target, but in the return journey the machine was blown out of its course, landing undamaged a hundred and sixty miles south-west of the aerodrome.

On July 5th twelve De Havilland machines set out to attack the railway sidings at Coblenz. Thick clouds were met at the beginning of the voyage, and the squadron steered by compass, and, reaching the Rhine, found the city covered in clouds. The leader turned to find another and clearer target, but the anti-aircraft gunners of Coblenz heard the machines and guided the pilots to their city by means of a fierce barrage. The Britons whirled into the zone of gun fire and there found a small hole in the carpet of cloud through which part of the railway could be seen. All the bombs were released.

At the end of the same month another squadron of De Havillands went out to attack Mayence. South of Saarbrücken forty German fighting aeroplanes surrounded the little British formation. It was impossible for the British pilots to keep completely in such positions as to protect each other. The Germans concentrated on the rear machines and on the leading machine, and in a fierce fight four of the De Havillands were shot down. The rest reached Saarbrücken and bombed the railway-station, but on their way home they were again attacked in overwhelming force, and three more of their number were brought down.

Immediately the few survivors reached their own aerodrome another squadron of De Havilland machines made another raid upon the factories and sidings at Saarbrücken, and did great damage there with no loss to themselves. Afterwards the same squadron set out in bad weather for Karlsruhe, reaching the station, which was partly blown up after the railway sidings had been badly damaged. Again German chaser machines started in pursuit, but three of them were driven down out of control at the cost of one De Havilland.

A FOG-PRODUCING "BOLT FROM THE BLUE."
Remarkable photograph of a smoke-bomb that had been dropped from an aeroplane of the R.A.F. It was photographed at the very moment of its bursting near the surface of the water, where it was intended to create a thick fog obscuring any vessels.

then glided down and the searchlights and guns turned on their new foe. The two British machines came very low above the poison-gas works, and sent their cargoes of bombs clean into the buildings, against an almost horizontal fire from the German batteries. The Britons replied with their machine-guns, swooping low and raking gun positions, searchlights, roofs, and streets with bullets, and made their return journey through a thunderstorm. The Mannheim factories were attacked once more on September 7th.

By this time the enemy had completed his great scheme of offensive defence along the basin of the Rhine and its tributaries, employing hundreds of machines that would have been serviceable on the battle-front. He strove to inflict a series of decisive defeats upon the inadequately equipped Independent Force. All the **Demoralisation in** Rhineland population was **the Rhineland** becoming demoralised under an ordeal similar to that which the British and French peoples had stoically endured for years. Coinciding with the deep discouragement produced by British and French victories in the field, the operations of the Independent Force had become a far-spreading menace to the stability of the German Government. In the great industrial region, on which the material power of the enemy depended, his working people were becoming ready to accept peace on any terms.

It was to combat this failure in moral that a grand effort was made to overwhelm Sir Hugh Trenchard's squadrons. In the field the German aviation service was in extreme need of fighter machines, marksman pilots, and aerial machine-gunners. On

The important financial nerve centre of Germany, Frankfort, was attacked for the first time by twelve De Havilland machines. Most of the bombs burst by the goods station, east of the town, and except for the loss of one observer, who was killed by machine-gun fire, all the machines returned safely, in spite of a mass attack by forty German scouts, who met the British squadron at Mannheim on the way to Frankfort and pursued it back to France. Two of the German machines were destroyed, and three were driven down, while the twelve De Havillands ran out of petrol and only just cleared the trenches on their return. Five and a half hours they took in this attack on Frankfort.

The Handley Pages had more endurance. Two of them took seven hours in the night of August 21st to carry about a ton of bombs to the railway-station of Cologne. The tremendous projectiles crashed down upon this critical centre of the enemy's communication system, and the pilots and crew made a safe return. The next day **Obstinate raids** twelve De Havillands, with B.H.P. engines, **upon Mannheim** made another raid on Mannheim. The power of travelling at a high altitude with a cargo of bombs was vital to the heavy British aeroplanes in the absence of an escort of long-distance fighting scouts. This high altitude the B.H.P. engines could not then give.

Two of the British machines, attacked by eight Germans, were compelled to land about five miles over the lines. Then, near Mannheim, another fifteen hostile scouts, with great speed, climbing power, and agility, swooped down on the British formation and a fight followed at six thousand feet. The leader was shot down out of control, and three other enemy machines were destroyed, while under resolute and incessant attack by superior numbers the ten De Havillands carried out their operations at Mannheim, making seven bursts on a factory and also wrecking a large new building.

Three days afterwards the same works were attacked by two Handley Page machines. One pilot followed the Rhine, shut off his engine at five thousand feet and softly glided on the factories. He was picked up by German searchlights and a storm of shell was poured at him. The second pilot

SMOKE-CLOUD SETTLING ON THE FACE OF THE WATERS.
The effect of a smoke-bomb dropped from the air on the sea. After the bomb had burst, the smoke-cloud gradually settled down and spread, creating a dense fog over the sea or land on which it had been dropped.

N

the battle-front the Germans were thousands of machines short, yet such was the effect of the moral pressure which the British Independent Force exerted that the enemy High Command had to strengthen its home defence, with disastrous results to its troops on the battlefield. Great Britain had been weakened in the theatre of war by the need of gunners, searchlight men, airmen, and machines required for home defence. Her military power in the air had further been diminished by the need for machines, engines, and highly-trained airmen to fight from the coast against U boats. In the end, however, the Germany Army suffered from at least as much distraction of aerial force from the field of decisive conflict as did the British Army.

From September, 1918, to the close of hostilities the British bombing machines were attacked from their front line to their objective, and from there to their aerodrome. Sometimes they had to fight the whole way out and the whole way back. But for General Trenchard's plan of keeping all German aerodromes within reach under constant photographic survey and devastating bombardment, the operations of his force would probably have had to be suspended. Never were the odds of battle equal, for the British had no machines as quick and handy as the chaser aeroplanes that ever attacked them in much superior numbers.

On the night of September 16th seven Handley Page machines were lost. They set out to bomb Cologne, Mannheim, and Bonn, and reached most of their targets, but in the return journey they were met by a south-westerly gale. One machine landed in Holland with engine trouble, and most of the others seemed to have run out of petrol. On the 25th of the month four De Havilland machines with Liberty motors were brought down during a raid on Frankfort, in which eight tons and a half of bombs were dropped. Then the Independent Force assisted the First American Army in the attack on the St. Mihiel salient, and continued to co-operate with General Pershing's forces by wrecking the German railway communications during the Franco-American thrust along the Argonne towards Sedan.

Last phase of the air struggle

During this last phase of the struggle Sir Hugh Trenchard's improvised squadrons became better equipped for long-distance work and for their main task of wrecking the sources of supply of the German Army. The British bombs were made more destructive in a race of deadly inventiveness with German chemists. The Teutons contrived a special incendiary projectile with which, so they afterwards reported, they had intended to set fire to Paris. This was not possible, as German pilots had lost the command of the air and were exposed to their machines being attacked in overwhelming power in their sheds, in addition to being harassed in their nocturnal voyages. The British Independent Force, on the other hand, was at last given, at the end of October, 1918, a range of action as far as Berlin, when the 27th Group, under Colonel R. H. Mulock, received its special machines. Some inkling of knowledge of the new means of power in the hands of Sir Hugh Trenchard proved a factor of importance in hastening the new and confused German Government to accept the terms of the armistice.

Germany bombed into Revolution

Perhaps the main reason why the movement of Revolution at Kiel spread so quickly to the Rhineland and Palatinate, and affected the troops on lines of communication from Mayence to Cologne, is to be found in the moral effect of the short campaign of the Independent Force. Many of the industrial and financial magnates of Western Germany fled from the range of Sir Hugh Trenchard's operations, leaving behind them embittered, frightened working classes and middle classes who gradually affected the dispirited troops with their feeling of angry hopelessness. Sir Douglas Haig, Sir David Beatty, and Sir Hugh Trenchard may be regarded as collaborating original authors of the first German Revolution. The first broke the spirit of the German soldier, the second took the heart out of the German sailor, and the third filled with explosive panic the most important section of the German working people.

We must, however, observe that the Handley Page machine was flown in 1915 and not ordered in any large number until August, 1917. The number then ordered, though fairly sufficient with other bombing machines for direct military purposes, was not large enough to supply the bombing force in Lorraine with cargo-carrying aeroplanes of long air endurance and high-altitude travelling powers. The best of available types of the Handley Page machine that could have been produced in quantity in 1918 was never brought into service, while arrangements for the production of powerful engines were totally inadequate. It is difficult to avoid the conclusion that no plan was made in the summer of 1917 for the creation of a strong bombing force, with the result

BOMBS FROM BRITISH AEROPLANES DROPPING ON DERAA RAILWAY JUNCTION.

This bombing raid was carried out from a height of seven hundred feet, and resulted in the destruction of sheds, the wireless station, and much rolling-stock. From Deraa, east of the Jordan, several railways radiated, of vital importance to the Turks. On these numerous demolitions were effected by the Arab forces of the King of the Hedjaz, and the British airmen completed the destruction in September, 1918, just before Turkey's final collapse.

that the new director of aircraft supplies was not concerned to discover and foster the production of the machines and engines required.

Happily, the impetus to the organisation of superior material of aerial warfare was sufficient to carry the armies in the field to victory. There was a serious loss on July 9th, 1918, when Major J. B. McCudden was killed by an engine accident when on his way to take over a new command. He had just been promoted squadron commander and was the then British champion on the western front, with a recorded fifty-seven victories. He was returning to battle in an intense eager mood to assist in the grand offensive. On leaving an aerodrome on the last stage of his journey his engine stopped, and while trying to turn he side-slipped. Major McCudden's record was surpassed by another Irishman, Major Edward Mannock, who led Major Bishop's squadron and won seventy-three victories. Major Mannock was brought down in flames over the German lines on July 20th.

But the spirit that had inspired him and Major McCudden and Captain Albert Ball lived in the united corps. From the old naval wing there came Major Raymond Collishaw, who proved a magnificent squadron leader, increasing his record of destroyed enemy machines to the number of fifty-one with remarkable rapidity. Captain D. M. MacLaren was another young pilot of the champion class, and in four and a half months he destroyed thirty-seven German machines and six kite-balloons.

Captain A. H. Cobby, of the Australian Flying Corps, greatly distinguished himself by meeting an attack by Pfaltz fighters, breaking one up in the air and sending another down in flames, and making a record of twenty-one enemy machines and balloons destroyed in the opening of the first part of the offensive.

Captain A. W. Beauchamp Proctor, starting on August 8th, 1918, specialised in attacks upon hostile kite-balloons, which were often more difficult to destroy than aircraft. He fought over the French armies as well as over the British, and by the time he had reached his fifty-fourth victory his work was officially recognised as being almost unsurpassed in its brilliancy.

Captain Beauchamp Proctor was, however, surpassed by a Canadian officer, who first distinguished himself in a Sopwith Camel on the Italian front. He **Some champion** was Major W. G. Barker, whose incom- **British airmen** parable fight, when wounded in both legs and one arm, against successive formations of enemy machines, estimated to number in all sixty, was described in the general account of the Battle of Mormal Forest in Chapter CCLXXXV. (Vol. 12, page 535).

First by scores and then by hundreds the airmen of the British Commonwealth won distinction during the summer and the autumn of 1918. Some of them, as we have seen, assisted the French aviation service in the long struggle by the Oise and the Aisne in June and July, 1918. The series of victories won by General Gouraud, General Berthelot, General Mitry, General Degoutte, and General Mangin in the middle of July, 1918, was to a considerable extent due to the excellence

BIRD'S-EYE VIEW OF THE INN OF THE GOOD SAMARITAN.
Talal Ed Dumm, on the road between Jerusalem and Jericho, seen from the air. Within the upper of the two rectangular enclosures on the left of the road is an ancient inn associated from time immemorial with the story of the Good Samaritan.

of their improved and reinforced aerial organisation. During the last period of the German offensive the enemy tried to conceal his movements, especially on the Marne River, by means of vast barrages of smoke. French and American forward observation officers, though occupying hill positions, could seldom discover the direction of main attacks. Had the German Flying Corps gained the command in the air on July 15th, as on May 27th, Ludendorff might have succeeded in part of his plan.

But the allied airmen swept in strength over the German lines, tracing the movements of the hostile masses, discovering the positions of attacking batteries, and blocking the transport of supplies by concentrated bombing attacks on the railway and roads of the Marne salient. On the Champagne front the outmanœuvred German armies were practically shepherded through the scene of slaughter by the aeroplanes of defence, and all along the battle-line the victorious cavalry of the air harried the enemy when he was broken on the firing-line.

It was partly by reason of the care with which his airmen guarded his lines that General Mangin was then able to take the Germans by surprise on their flank. The French commander had large forests in full foliage to screen the gathering of his French, American, and British forces, but the traffic in his rear areas would probably have made the Germans suspicious had they possessed the power of making long reconnaissances such as British airmen had won.

When Marshal Foch began to press the Germans all round the Marne salient the power he exercised in the air by means of squadrons of French, American, and British machines was of decisive importance. The enemy could not maintain himself in a great stretch of territory, incomparably larger and better suited for defence than the little British Ypres salient. The development of the power and capacity of the bombing aeroplane made his withdrawal a necessity, in spite of his advantage in occupying heavily-wooded country.

VICTOR IN OVER FIFTY FIGHTS.
Major Raymond Collishaw, D.S.O. and bar, M.C. and bar, D.S.C., D.F.C., had destroyed fifty-one enemy machines when awarded the bar to his D.S.O. in September, 1918.

He could not supply his troops or move them freely. The new army he introduced to strengthen his lines merely added to his difficulties when his railway communications from the Belgian frontier to the bridge across the Aisne were interrupted for hours by day and night. In the overcrowded salient the roads were grey with marching men in two streams, one of exhausted forces tramping to their rest-places, the other of relieving divisions going into action. The allied

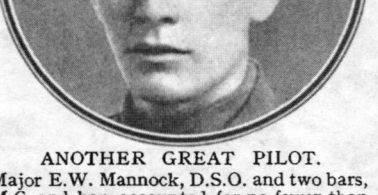

ANOTHER GREAT PILOT.
Major E.W. Mannock, D.S.O. and two bars, M.C. and bar, accounted for no fewer than seventy-three enemy machines.

airmen not only directly attacked these myriad targets but continually ranged upon them the big French guns that carried to the Vesle River. It was only when General von Böhn extracted the remnants of his corps and left mere covering lines of machine-gunners concealed in the woodlands that the victorious work of the allied squadrons lessened in scope.

Meanwhile, Sir Douglas Haig and his Staff were making very skilful use of the weak part of their aerial system of patrol. Owing to the westerly curve of the northern part of the Belgian-British front, fast, high-flying enemy reconnaissance machines were usually able to explore freely the back areas of the forces holding the Ypres and La Bassée sectors. They came over the Yser towards St. Omer, keeping very high and darting back to Flanders if an allied machine started to climb up to them. Anti-aircraft guns at important points could compel these hurried visitors to maintain an altitude at which it was difficult to photograph, and some were occasionally brought down who patiently waited aloft for them. In a general way, however, it was not worth trying to prevent the enemy's observation visits.

Tricking the enemy observers

So he was provided with sights worth studying and photographing. Parks of Tanks, some of painted wood, were set where he could see them, along with other signs of an impending grand attack. General von Armin and General von Quast responded to the use made against them of the aerial power

of vision they enjoyed. They prepared a strong defence, retaining large masses of men that were soon urgently and vainly required along the Somme. Altogether the British trick of using a sector of aerial weakness to cover activities in a sector held in strength was a classic example of the art of adapting new methods to old principles.

As a rule, experienced airmen could foretell the direction of a coming hostile offensive simply by the activity of enemy photographing machines. Fighter formations could easily make feints for breaking a path for reconnaissance on any sector, but the continual work, carried on week after week, and even month after **Work of the aerial photographers** month, by flying photographers at incessant risk was something about which experienced fighting patrols engaged in chasing the camera men could not be mistaken. This was one of the ways in which the attack on the Fifth British Army had been foreseen by February, 1918.

When, however, it was the turn of the British to attempt a surprise offensive, their increased strength in the air enabled them to give no genuine photographic indication of their intentions. All the German front, from the Passchendaele Ridge to the Luce Brook, was mapped minutely by the camera. A pretence of extreme interest in the northern sector was of course made, and fighting and bombing formations were largely used there also, but the British victories were prepared in advance by the general, methodical labours of the photographic airmen who extended their work over some four thousand square miles of territory occupied by the invader, recording this enormous stretch of ground not once but many times. Theirs was the least exhilarating lot of the flying man. They ran more than the usual peril of attack by superior enemy machines. They had not even the second-hand satisfaction of pilots and observers on artillery duty, on those sad legacies of the Royal Aircraft Factory, the slow, unhandy R.E.8's, who could at least watch the shots which they directed strike the target, or relieve their feelings by remarks to the gunners afterwards. Yet the aerial photographers and the originator of their art, Colonel T. T. C. Moore Brabazon, were among the most important makers of victory. Directly on their work was based the intricate movements of attack opening on August 8th, 1918, and continuing until the enemy sued for armistice to make peace.

Sir Douglas Haig and his army commanders and Staffs relied especially upon aerial photographic work. Preferring to launch assaults either in a fog or through clouds of chemical smoke, the British leaders required well-defined enlarged camera records of all enemy positions. While photographic work in the air increased in importance and quickened in reproductive technique, the visual labour of artillery machines somewhat declined in general range. Direct fire-control was intensified, but the detection of hostile batteries grew into a problem too difficult for airmen alone to solve. As they had helped forward observation officers, so in turn they were assisted by a new scientific force.

On the western front Briton, Gaul, and Teuton contended in subtle ingenuity. They began deluding opposing young pilots and observers with dummy guns emitting sham flashes of flame. Then they used small smoke-screens to veil their batteries, or to attract shell fire to empty ground, while noting the positions of the attacking ordnance. Owing to these misleading devices there came into use a method of detection by sound instead of sight. The distant noise of a hostile gun was registered as it travelled to two or more points in the opposite lines, and the sound of its shell was likewise recorded. Then by a method of triangulation the exact position of the gun was discovered.

Visual observation remained of high importance in battles, when the enemy revealed the batteries he had carefully refrained from firing during ordinary operations. Yet as

Armoury of a night-bombing squadron on the British front in France. Pilots and observers took scrupulous care of their guns and pistols, and this squadron took particular pride in its armoury, which it claimed to be the finest in Europe.

An instructive pastime for pilots on the western front, especially those employed on night-bombing work—piecing together a dissected map, a kind of geographical jig-saw puzzle, in order to obtain familiarity with country over which they might have to fly by night.

USEFUL PASTIMES FOR PILOTS OF THE ROYAL AIR FORCE WHEN OFF DUTY.

this usually happened in smoke or fog, and as the firing batteries often screened themselves with clouds from their own chemical ovens, the experts who worked the sound detectors continued to be as serviceable as were the aerial observers. But Major-General John Salmond and his brilliant Staff devised new uses of aircraft, which were practised in the last Battle of the Somme opening on August 8th, 1918.

Machines were sent out carrying cargoes of smoke-bombs, and with these they screened the light British storming cars against artillery fire, while themselves attacking the anti-Tank guns. By this time the wireless telephone had been ably developed by the successors of the Royal Flying Corps, who made it a great instrument of communication and co-operation. Contact machines were not yet able to talk to the signallers in advanced infantry forces, but they could, **Development of wireless telephony** if fitted with the new wireless, listen to questions and change their work to meet an emergency. Formation fighting increased as the leader acquired the power of speaking to his pilots, and with every extension in the radius of call of the operators on machines the power of rapid concentration of the new army of the air was augmented. Machines with the new device were not at first used over enemy territory, for fear the invention should be presented to the Germans before it was fully developed, but the R.F.C. and R.A.F. invention became, with other devices in wireless warfare, a very remarkable contribution to the triumph of British arms.

There is no need to describe in detail the operations of the Royal Air Force during the amazing succession of victories between August and November, 1918. Much of the work of the airmen was of as routine but exciting kind as that of the fighting troops on the ground. The mist, in which both British and German commanders loved to launch an attack, after the development of aerial photography gave them all the knowledge of terrain they needed, caused many accidents to low-flying machines engaged on contact and bombing

at last, and confused the wing of General von Hutier's army, as a consequence of the appalling pressure exerted by the massed British bombing squadrons. Thereupon German fighters collected in hundreds above the Somme to clear a passage for the fresh columns of men and guns streaming down to prevent an utter break-through. As they assailed the British bombers they were in turn attacked by the British fighters. At first the total British air losses were slightly heavier than the German, but most of the British casualties were due to perils run by low-flying contact aeroplanes. On August 10th the Germans began to lose in a proportion of more than two to one, which proportion was rapidly increased, reaching one day to more than six to one. As a rule British losses were greatest in misty weather and German losses heaviest when the air was clear—a striking indication of both the audacity in contact and bombing work of British pilots and of their superior fighting power in light, fast machines.

The German air forces on the western front were estimated at 2,700 machines. These consisted of some 250 bombing aeroplanes, 250 contact machines, 1,100 fighting machines, and 1,100 observation and spotting aeroplanes. Nine hundred

UNDER THE SEARCHLIGHT.
Bombing machine of the R.A.F. about to start on a night raid over the enemy's lines. It was photographed under the beam of a searchlight.

were destroyed by fighting in a month, and about the same number was wrecked through accidents and various troubles. Thus three-fourths of the total strength of machines in the German aviation service needed replacing every four weeks, together with half the personnel. As the German weakened the British grew stronger.

Great Britain was at last profiting by all her advantages in inventiveness, manufacture, and resources to win in the air the power she exercised at sea. She was directly outbuilding Germany in machines, having been aroused, both by the submarine menace and the needs of the Army to exert herself to the utmost. Her dispersal of aerial force outside France and Flanders was balanced by the increasing efforts of the French and American aviation services, and as the Italians and their comrades completely dominated the airmen of Austria-Hungary at a time when Germany could no longer give any proper help to her allies, the struggle between Briton and Teuton was conducted in circumstances highly favourable to the island race and its oversea kinsmen.

The Canadians continued to display a remarkable talent in aviation. They piloted some of the Porte flying-boats that brought down Zeppelins on the Terschelling Bank patrol, and with Colonel Bishop, Major Barker, and Major Collishaw

GETTING READY FOR A NIGHT RAID.
One night's "rations" for a bombing squadron of the Royal Air Force when it was about to set out on a night raid on enemy munition dumps, railways, and other objectives behind the fighting-line on the western front.

duties. But British pilots accepted all risks to help their comrades. In bad weather they flew as low as swallows to make sure of hitting targets, and they were assailed, when the air cleared, by multitudes of enemy fighting aeroplanes.

The principal air battles during the opening of the British offensive took place over the Somme. Here the British bombing machines, that suffered the largest proportion of losses, made the river crossings impracticable to the retreating enemy. General von der Marwitz's broken men turned south

THE LAST POST.
Military funeral of Sister Margaret Lowe, died of wounds received during an air raid by Huns on a Canadian General Hospital.

they produced, in proportion to their population, a notable number of the supreme champions of the air. The Australians also displayed magnificent ability, and both in Palestine and in France gained many high honours. Irishmen made great fighting pilots, but the best of them, Major McCudden, considered that recklessness was often both their defect and their virtue.

The Englishman contended with the Irishmen and Canadians in fighting up to the position of champion, and there were many Scottish and Welsh pilots of distinction. Fame as an air fighter was not, however, a complete test of personal merit. Defects in machines and engines ended or checked the career of hundreds of young men who were acquiring the genius in airmanship and in marksmanship on which victories depended. It was the general work of the Royal Air Force that showed its superiority to the German aviation service and cleared the road for the triumphs of all British arms and of the arms of Allied and Associated Powers.

In about three weeks of battle in August the British had 262 machines missing, while of the German air force in the same sectors of action 465 machines were destroyed and 200 sent down out of control, with 61 kite-balloons set on fire. Practically the whole of the air fighting was conducted over the German lines, where the terrifying quantity of about 912 tons of bombs was dropped by British airmen in less than a month.

At the end of the first week in September rain-storms and high winds interfered with flying work. Few

German machines appeared, but British pilots and observers continued their artillery work and reconnoitring and patrol duties. For a time night flying became impossible, much to the advantage of the enemy, and when, in the middle of September, the weather improved it was found that the Germans had employed their interval of rest in gathering stronger formations of attack. After a short period of clear air the weather again became adverse to flying, and remained so until the last days of the month. This was one of the reasons why the German armies were able to make so strong a stand north and south of Cambrai. Their communications were not broken by the fall of more than nine hundred tons of aeroplane bombs, as in August, and the direction of their columns of reinforcements was not clearly traced. British airmen, however, continued their ordinary work in spite of extreme weather difficulties, and the armies worked forward through rain, mud, and mist, with their contact and spotting aeroplanes droning out in front of them.

It was in the clear air of Palestine in the month of September, 1918, that the Royal Air Force achieved the most striking of successes. The strategy of Sir Edmund Allenby's attack was largely based upon the supremacy in the air won by his pilots. The process of wearing down enemy aircraft had gone on all through the summer. During one week in June, 1918, a hundred hostile aeroplanes crossed the British lines. In the last week of August only eighteen hostile machines passed over. Many

CRIMINAL ATTACKS ON HOSPITALS BY HUN AIRMEN.
Destruction wrought in a British military hospital in France by German bombing pilots. The situation of the hospital was well known, and this photograph from the air proves that its distinguishing marks were unmistakable. In circle: Sisters clearing up a ward in another Canadian hospital bombed by the Huns.

of them were shot down in the first week of September, with the result that during the period of the grand manœuvres of attack the enemy general obtained no knowledge of the British preparations. Only four enemy machines scouted over British territory, keeping at so great a height that their observers failed to detect any alterations whatever in the British dispositions, or distinguish General Allenby's new grand headquarters. Enemy aeroplane reports, afterwards captured, stated that the great camp was only an ordinary infantry camp, containing two battalions of troops.

At the opening of his offensive on September 19th, 1918, General Allenby, inspired by his brilliant director of aerial operations, Major-General William Salmond, sent out a strong air force to bomb all enemy signal stations, headquarters' telephone and telegraph exchanges, and wireless installations.

Airmen's triumph in Palestine This operation was carried out with decisive success. The Germans and Turks were deprived of all means of communication other than visual signalling and despatch-riders, and for some days their commander and Staff were unable to ascertain the scope and details of the disaster that overwhelmed them.

When on September 21st the broken enemy forces were entirely engaged in seeking to escape through the only gap in the Allenby net of cavalry and infantry forces, the British airmen achieved another historic triumph by executing an outflanking movement that closed the crossing of the Jordan against the fugitives. They turned one column of transport so that it fell into the hands of their cavalry, and completely blocked a crowded road at the point where it ran through a gorge ; thence they pursued what remained of the transport until it turned in the required direction for surrendering to the mounted troops.

At the British aerodrome at Ramleh, so soon as the direction of the enemy's intended flight was reported by an aerial scout, two machines left for the gorge every three minutes with a cargo of bombs and a large supply of machine-gun trays of cartridges. Then every half hour an additional formation of six machines whirled into action. For four hours the aerial blockade was maintained, together with the process of shepherding the remnants of Turks by machine-gun fire towards the waiting cavalry.

More than a thousand motor lorries and waggons were destroyed, and the wreckage of some eighty-seven guns was afterwards found on the stopped road. Over a vast stretch of country straggling fragments of three Turkish armies were tracked from the air and worked into the prisoners' camp. The wild, rough, broken country over which the first out-flanking aerial movement was successfully conducted made speedy movements by any land forces impossible. It was entirely owing to the adequate material and the well-trained pilots, bombers, and machine-gunners that Major-General William Salmond obtained and organised that Sir Edmund Allenby's victory was so wonderfully complete and rapid.

The overthrow of the Bulgarian armies, which took place at the time of the envelopment of the Ottoman forces in Palestine, was also partly brought about by the pressure of the air-power of the Allies. Between the eastern **Bulgars routed by allied airmen** and western Bulgar forces was a connecting lateral road, about twenty miles long, between Veles and Ishtip. This road was blocked by the allied airmen, so that the main Bulgarian forces engaged against the British and Greek divisions could not send reinforcements to their stricken and breaking western divisions. When the Bulgarian Army was broken into fragments the allied cavalry of the air turned the retreat into a rout, the Bulgars being so completely demoralised that their commander could do nothing but offer to surrender at mercy.

In the Balkan War the Bulgarians had been among the first to experiment in battle with flying machines, but they had failed completely to keep pace with the intense progress in design, engine-power, and equipment during the European War. It was an age of highly industrialised warfare, with almost a daily stream of improvements and inventions in weapons of attack, and the Slav-speaking peasant race fell

at last with as little resistance as the barbaric agriculturists of Turkey.

By October 1st the Germans, although they had been the most industrious, enterprising, and powerful of manufacturing nations in Europe, were also being borne down by the quicker powers of mind, productive energy, and personal fighting power of the peoples of the Grand Alliance. In a week of cloudy, unsettled weather in France, Major-General John Salmond, the brother of the aerial blockader of the Jordan, concentrated on the Aulnoy railway junction, through which the enemy armies opposing most of the French forces were supplied. British bombers had the good fortune to discover a trainload of ammunition in Aulnoy Station, and by blowing this up, while releasing other bombs on the junction, they wrecked the centre of German communication, and thereby compelled the enemy centre to retire with the utmost speed.

In the action of October 4th there was a new development in British air tactics. After bringing down thirty-two German machines the British fighting squadrons kept the air so free from hostile machines that they were able to take part in attacking troops and transport on the ground. Under their complete protection swarms of British contact machines acted as makers of smoke curtains for the British infantry, and the advanced machine-guns of the attack were supplied with ammunition by aeroplane.

General weather conditions, however, prevented night flying nearly all through the month. Consequently, the enemy was able to bring fresh troops and guns into position and again prevent a complete break-through. Reconnaissance machines had to carry out their work in mist and rain at a very low height, with enemy troops and machine-gunners firing at them at a range of one or two hundred feet. There was little fighting in the air on the British front, and the main work of the Royal Air Force and the allied aviation services associated with it in the fighting in Flanders was the building of sheds and levelling of ground for new aerodromes near the continually withdrawing German front.

During the thick weather in October the commander of the German air forces adopted **Enemy airmen act as rearguards** a desperate method of attempting to save the Army. He sacrificed machines in large numbers by using them as rearguards to cover the retreat of the troops. Especially in Flanders and along the front of the French advance, Fokker patrols and small formations of other types of enemy machines were remarkably aggressive, sweeping under the low clouds and through the drizzle to the ground that had been recently evacuated and machine-gunning both infantry and artillery occupying it. The battle had swung forward, in the centre and on the northern wing, close to the German aerodromes, so that the daring pilots had but a short distance to go in making their dashes upon the advancing forces. The allied aerodromes had been left far behind, and machines could not arrive in time to find and engage the Fokker patrols. Clear weather was required to keep the enemy under control and discover and wreck his sheds, and new aerodromes were needed close to the new fighting-line. The principal British armies, which had been advancing since August, and had organised their means of regular, steady progress, were less subject to the new kind of Fokker surprise raids. They already possessed most of the German aerodromes.

The French relied mainly upon their anti-aircraft gunners, who brought their pieces forward and shot down thirty-five hostile low-flying aeroplanes. There was an extraordinary fight between a section of French auto-cannon and five Fokker machines. The Fokkers charged, releasing bombs as they passed over the battery, and pouring out bullets from their machine-guns while circling round. The Frenchmen stood to their guns, coolly marked down three machines which they wrecked, and a fourth Fokker, trying to escape them, was smashed by the fire of a neighbouring section.

When the weather cleared for a time at the end of October the Germans made a desperate effort to save their armies from air attack. There was a great battle by the British front on October 30th, when large enemy formations came out for action and engaged in heavy, continuous fighting

British airships of differing types that served as guardians of the Fleet.

British fighting aeroplane in pursuit of a German machine over a turbulent sea of clouds.

Over the Alps in aeroplanes: Squadron of British battle=planes crossing Italy's mountain frontier.

Ship's aeroplane about to make a landing on the specially constructed deck of H.M.S. Argus.

H.M.S. Argus, aeroplane carrier to the British Navy: Strange contrast to the battle=cruiser beyond.

R34, Britain's titanic airship, 670 feet long and 1,250 h.p., launched at Inchinnan, near Glasgow, March 14th, 1919.

until sunset. When night fell German power in the air was definitely broken. Sixty-four enemy machines were smashed in the air or sent down in flames; fifteen more were driven down out of control. A large bombing machine was shot down in flames and a kite-balloon was destroyed. In addition a German aerodrome was wrecked, two sheds containing machines being demolished and two machines on the open ground being destroyed. Only eighteen British machines were missing, one of which was lost in the night on a bombing raid. It was a record day in the annals of the Royal Air Force. All the allied airmen began to vie with each other in courage and skill, maintaining complete mastery of the air and spreading disorder in the German armies. On the same day the American airmen shot down twenty-one German machines and two balloons, themselves losing only two machines, and the French destroyed seventeen machines and one balloon.

The American aviation service made good progress, playing probably the most important part in opening wide the gate of victory for General Pershing's artillery and infantry. Foot and guns were kept in quick, flexible communi-

AEROPLANE ATTACK ON ENEMY KITE-BALLOONS.
German observation balloons attacked by allied aeroplanes on the Champagne front. (From a graphic French sketch.) On the left a kite-balloon had been thoroughly destroyed, while the balloon on the right had just taken fire, the observer dropping in his parachute.

machines missing. The Italian airmen destroyed 16 enemies. The figures for a month of continually bad weather, favourable to the foe, were yet eloquent of the growth of British air-power.

At the opening of the final offensive on the Italian front, mist and fog, that served the infantry of attack in forcing the passage of the Piave River, hindered the work of the allied airmen. But during the clear days of the pursuit and rout the combined flying organisations were of magnificent use, carrying supplies to forces over the river, and then acting as the advanced units in the great chase that broke up the

cation, while large forces of bombing machines escorted by fighting aeroplanes ravaged the German back areas in front of the Fourth French Army and the American Army.

Between October 29th and November 4th the Americans brought down 76 German machines and five kite-balloons, at a loss of 14 of their aeroplanes; their record for the whole of October being 94 German machines brought down, and only 18 American machines missing. In the same month the French reported 218 German machines and balloons put out of action, but gave no figures of their own losses. Lieutenant Fonck won his seventy-fifth victory.

The British reported 396 German units destroyed, 128 driven down out of control, and 209 British machines missing. On the Italian front British airmen destroyed 24 Austrian machines and balloons and drove seven machines down out of control, having 13 of their

WHERE GERMANS HOUSED THEIR ZEPPELINS.
Great Zeppelin shed of which the British took possession after the Germans had retreated. It had been employed by the enemy as an aeroplane factory during the later stages of the war. Above: British aeroplanes ranged along a wayside on the western front in France, ready to fly off as ordered and bring in reports of enemy movements during the great German offensive of the spring of 1918.

Austro-Hungarian armies and brought about their practical surrender.

The condition to which the German aviation service was reduced on the British front, immediately before the close of hostilities, was patent when an interval of fine weather occurred on November 9th. A vast number of British machines went out for action, harrying the German columns, disorganising their retreat, and shattering the railway junctions on the line to Aix-la-Chapelle. Only a small number of German machines was seen, and nineteen of them were shot or driven down. Thirteen British machines were missing, many of them being contact aeroplanes shot down from the ground.

November 10th was another day of clear weather, but the Germans remained weak in the air, while the British vigorously continued their successful work of turning a retreat into a rout. German forces, left as rearguards, surrendered because no food reached them, and the main masses, having been exposed for months to aerial attack until they were full of contempt for their own airmen, were hesitating between an avenging mutiny against their officers or a mob flight towards their own frontier.

The accompanying tables, prepared and published by the Air Ministry, give a clear account of the extraordinary development of British aerial power between August, 1914, and November, 1918.

The eclipse of Germanic air-power was one of the most remarkable events in the history of warfare.

The Teutons started in the struggle for air supremacy with almost every advantage, including that of long scientific research and intense craftsmanship. In the field they had a prevailing favouring wind making for a speedy return journey, at home they possessed an enlightened, fostering, comprehensive organisation that used to the full the engineering resources of leading motor-engine makers. Yet they failed.

Before the British exercised the fullness of their improvised new power and struck directly at Berlin, their enemy admitted defeat. His troops flying from the field of battle, and his sailors mutinying rather than put out to sea, were so completely vanquished that there was no occasion to submit the populace of the German capital to the test they had gloried in imposing upon the people of London and Paris. Mastery of the air was then becoming an instrument with such dreadful possibilities that the people who won it, in a fair race with friends as well as with foes, scarcely appreciated the scope of the new national achievement.

PERSONNEL.

—	August, 1914.			December, 1916.		
—	Officers.	Other Ranks.	Total.	Officers.	Other Ranks.	Total.
R.F.C.	147	1,097	1,244	5,982	51,915	57,897
R.N.A.S.	50	550	600	2,764	26,129	28,893
R.A.F.	—	—	—	—	—	—
Total	—	—	1,844	—	—	86,790

—	December, 1917.			October, 1918.		
—	Officers.	Other Ranks.	Total.	Officers.	Other Ranks.	Total.
R.F.C.	15,522	98,738	114,260	—	—	—
R.N.A.S.	4,765	43,050	47,815	—	—	—
R.A.F.	—	—	—	27,906	263,842	291,748
Total	—	—	162,075	—	—	291,748

MACHINES AND ENGINES ON CHARGE—(*continued*.)

—	January, 1918.		October, 1918.	
—	Machines.	Engines.	Machines.	Engines.
R.F.C.	8,350	14,755	—	—
R.N.A.S.	2,741	6,902	—	—
R.A.F.	—	—	22,171	37,702
Total	11,091	21,657	22,171	37,702

OUTPUT OF MACHINES AND ENGINES.

—	August, 1914, to May, 1915 (10 months).		June, 1915, to February, 1917 (21 months).	
—	Machines.	Engines.	Machines.	Engines.
R.F.C.	530	141	7,137	8,917
R.N.A.S.	No record	No record	No record	No record
R.A.F.	—	—	—	—
Total	530	141	7,137	8,917

MACHINES AND ENGINES ON CHARGE.

—	August, 1914.		January, 1917.	
—	Machines.	Engines.	Machines.	Engines.
R.F.C.	179	—	3,929	6,056
R.N.A.S.	93	—	1,567	3,672
R.A.F.	—	—	—	—
Total	272	—	5,496	9,728

—	March, 1917, to December, 1917 (10 months).		January, 1918, to October, 1918 (10 months).	
—	Machines.	Engines.	Machines.	Engines.
R.F.C.	12,275	—	—	—
R.N.A.S.	1,246	—	—	—
R.A.F.	—	—	26,685	29,561
Total	13,521	13,979	26,685	29,561

EXPANSION OF MOTOR TRANSPORT FOR AIRCRAFT.

Motor Transport (All Types.)	R.F.C. Only.				Royal Air Force.
—	August, 1914.	August, 1915.	August, 1916.	August, 1917.	October 31, 1918.
On Charge	320	2,469	5,282	8,584	23,260

SQUADRONS MAINTAINED.

—	Service.		—	Training. (1 Training Depot Station reckoned as 3 Squadrons).	
—	August, 1914.	October 31, 1918.	—	August, 1914.	October 31, 1918.
Western Front	4 (R.F.C.)	84 & 5 flights	Home	1 (R.F.C.) 2 (R.N.A.S.)	174
Independent Force	—	10	Egypt	—	10
5 Group	—	3	Canada	—	15
India	—	2			
Italy	—	4			
Middle East	—	13			
Russia	—	½			
Home Defence	—	18			
Naval units	1 (R.N.A.S.)	64			
Total	5	198½ & 5 flights	—	3	199

RESULTS OF OPERATIONS IN THE AIR.

—	July, 1918, to Nov. 11, 1918.	January 1, 1918, to November 11, 1918.									
—	Western Front.	Independent Force.	Home Forces.	5th Gr'p & Naval Units.	Italy.	Egypt.	Mesopotamia.	Salonika.	Palestine.	India (Aden).	Total.
Enemy aircraft accounted for—*i.e.*, brought down or driven down	6,904	150	8	470	405	25	6	59	81	—	7,908
British machines missing	2,484	111	—	114	44	9	13	8	24	—	2,810
Bombs dropped (tons)	6,402	540	—	662	59	43	25	130	74	30	7,945
Hours flown	889,526	11,784	—	39,102	25,206	7,022	7,862	13,417	21,848	579	1,016,346
Rounds fired at ground targets	10,238,182	353,257	—	—	222,704	50,937	107,563	193,354	735,550	7,527	11,858,137
Photographs taken	401,375	3,682	—	3,440	14,596	8,135	66,720	15,587	27,039	542	501,116
Enemy balloons brought down	258	—	—	—	—	—	—	—	—	—	258

DEVELOPMENT OF BRITISH AERIAL POWER, AUGUST, 1914, TO NOVEMBER, 1918.

GENERAL SIR WILLIAM R. BIRDWOOD, G.C.M.G., K.C.B., K.C.S.I., D.S.O.
Commander of the British Fifth Army, 1918

GENERAL SIR WILLIAM R. BIRDWOOD, G.C.M.G., K.C.B., K.C.S.I., D.S.O.
Commander of the Australian Army, 1915

CHAPTER CCXCV.

VOLUNTARY MOTOR TRANSPORT IN THE WAR.
Magnificent and Varied Work of British Motorists.
By R. P. Hearne.

Pre-War Strength of the British and Backwardness of the German Motor Movement and Industry—Motor Transport of the British Red Cross—Failure of the Authorities to Anticipate the Needs of Casualties Arriving in London—Motor Volunteers Come to the Rescue—Formation of the London Ambulance Column—Gifts of Ambulances from Business Firms and Private Individuals—600,000 Cases Distributed by the London Ambulance Column—The Column's Work in Air Raids—Motor Organisations in Other Great Towns—Evolution of the Hospital Motor Squadron—Help for the Refugees—Outings. for Convalescents—Mr. Arthur Wilson's Fine Record—Work of the Motor Transport Volunteers in Solving the Inter-Station Problem of Soldiers Passing through London—Y.M.C.A. Motor Transport Department—The Irish and the Hampshire Automobile Clubs—Great Work of the Women's Reserve Ambulance, the Green Cross Society—The Scottish Women's Ambulance Corps—Motor Transport Service of the Women's First Aid Nursing Yeomanry Corps in the War Zone—Women's Legion as Recruiting and Training Department for Women Motor Drivers—Drivers of the Women's Royal Air Force and Women's Army Service Corps—Motor Ploughing by the Women's Land Army.

NO finer or more varied voluntary work was accomplished during the Great War than that carried out by motorists and motoring organisations, and by other bodies which availed themselves of Britain's motoring resources. Indeed, so widespread has been the movement and so numerous the activities that it is practically impossible to deal with them all.

The British Isles in 1914 had the largest motoring population in Europe, and when the war came the voluntary response of motorists was as remarkable as it was serviceable. It is certain that the strength of the British motor movement and of the industry which that movement built up were potent factors in the defeat of Germany — i n which country motoring was almost as feebly developed as the voluntary spirit. Official restrictions and lack of sporting instincts account for Germany's backwardness in motoring, and she suffered severely thereby when the test of war came.

From the first the British armies were remarkable for the excellence of their motor transport. Crack drivers instantly volunteered to drive the staff cars of British generals. London motor-omnibus men and skilled mechanics and drivers from all over the country took their places quickly in the transport columns, while other volunteers had undertaken the motor-ambulance work. Not only were British motor volunteers serving with their own Army, but others of them were helping with the French and Belgian Armies in the field at a time when none of the combatants had clearly realised the vast importance of motor transport.

If the German strategists had held advanced views on mechanical transport, and had secretly built up a great system of traffic by road and through the air, the history of 1914 would have been very different, and one shudders to think of the consequences. But by a very fortunate circumstance both Britain and France were considerably ahead of Germany in automobile resources, and the last phase of that superiority came in 1918 when the Allies beat Germany out of the air by their aerial engines, and aided by Tanks and transports completed the victory on land.

This statement of the case is a necessary introduction to the main theme, which essays to give a summary of the work done

INSPECTION OF ESSEX MOTOR VOLUNTEERS.
Major-General Macintyre inspecting the troops of the Essex Motor Volunteers in the grounds of Felix Hall, Kelvedon, the residence of Major H. Wrightson. Major Wrightson, who was commandant of the company, threw open the beautiful grounds of Felix Hall as a camp for his men.

by the numerous motor organisations behind the battle-lines. The major part of this work was not spectacular, nor has it been brought prominently to the public notice. What it may have lacked in actual danger, however, was surely counter-balanced in hardship, drudgery, endurance, and self-sacrifice by men and women who cheerfully did their utmost to help the fighters.

A new spirit was brought into militarism by these voluntary motor workers—the spirit of kindliness, comradeship, and sympathy, and very wisely our military chiefs allowed the work to go forward along almost the same lines to the end of the war. Again and again wounded soldiers and travel-weary men have borne testimony to the revivifying effect of this friendly assistance rendered by kindly men and women motorists who regarded it as their privilege to assist the fighting men.

Taken in the mass, this voluntary motor work had a considerable effect in improving the efficiency and the spirit of the whole British Army. It saved the time of millions of men on many important occasions; it saved them from much unnecessary hardship and weariness, and in hundreds of ways it helped the working of the great war-machine.

Again and again motor transport afforded the solution to the new and unexpected problems which arose during the war. Verdun was saved in the great crisis by motor traffic relieving the broken railway system, and there were British motor volunteers in that dramatic episode.

So great was the volume of work done by voluntary motor organisations all over the Empire that it is impracticable to go into details in every case, and rather than create a sense of weariness by a long list, and the unavoidable repetition of similarities, it is preferable to select a certain number of typical organisations and let them serve as an index to the scope and utility of the whole movement.

First place in our attention is demanded by the British Red Cross Society, although, strictly speaking, this body is outside the scope of this chapter and deserves to be treated separately. The British Red Cross Society was incorporated before the war—in the year 1908—and it was confidently believed that if war came it would rise to expectations. During the war Sir Arthur Stanley, brother of Lord Derby, and a prominent motorist, became chairman of the Joint War Committee of the British Red Cross Society and the Order of St. John, and he rendered inestimable **British Red Cross Society** service. Motor transport is but one of the Red Cross Society's many departments, and it would be most interesting to give figures as to the work done here, but so vast was the undertaking that when this chapter was written the society had not been able to tabulate the information. The work of the Red Cross did not cease with the signing of the armistice, and the society preferred to delay its report until the work was completed.

When we consider the millions of men who have been wounded in the war, and when we bear in mind the many fronts on which the British Red Cross ambulances were at work, we can be prepared to some extent for the remarkable statistics as to the mileage of the Red Cross ambulances and the number of cases handled; but no one will be able fully to appreciate the true nobility of the work, the number of lives

MR. A. J. WILSON.
Commandant of the Hospital Motor Squadron in the London District.

saved, and the extent to which anguish has been assuaged and sufferings allayed by this splendid organisation.

In this chapter, therefore, one must take up the tale of the motor voluntary organisations at the point where the Red Cross ambulance service leaves off. The wounded man in France would require to make various journeys from the point where he fell; and by a succession of stages, in which the Red Cross workers were as ministering angels, he would reach London as the great centre of distribution.

In August, 1914, it was hastily realised that the distribution of the wounded arriving in London by hospital-train required a separate organisation. The first hospital-train steamed in on August 30th, 1914, and by the efforts of Mr. and Mrs. Lionel Dent, at the request of the British Red Cross Society, a supplementary group of private motors and some motor-vans were in readiness to transport the wounded, as the ordinary horse ambulances were found to be insufficient.

A curious sidelight is thrown by this affair on official estimates of the war in 1914. It was computed by the powers in being that the number of British wounded would be such that they could be easily dealt with in France, and if any surplus came to London they could be distributed by the ordinary horsed ambulances! The motor-ambulance was not seriously considered by some of the experts, and little provision had been made for its extensive employment.

[*Lafayette.*
SIR ARTHUR STANLEY.
Chairman Joint War Committee of the British Red Cross Society and the Order of St. John.

The first battle wholly upset all these comfortable calculations, and so overwhelming was the stream of wounded sent to London that the assistance of motor volunteers was urgently sought. Motor-vans and private cars were hastily requisitioned, and but for the assistance thus rendered by volunteers great hardship would have been endured by the wounded. Practically all the **London Ambulance Column formed** available motor-ambulances were urgently needed for the front, and thus it became necessary for private cars to be fitted up for the work in London. In the first moments of confusion the volunteer effort was more quickly available than the official.

From this small scale and hastily got together body was formed the London Ambulance Column, but not until 1917 was the organisation fully developed. By that time it had established headquarters at Gower Street, where in addition to the administrative offices and well-equipped stores, workshops, etc., there was extensive garage accommodation for the cars.

So considerable was the number of vehicles required, however, that many of the cars were housed at private garages. A central telephone system kept in touch with all the units day and night, and whenever a hospital-train was announced on the way to London the ambulance staff was summoned from all parts of the metropolis. At any hour by day and night these devoted volunteers never failed to respond to the call, and they enabled a rapid and comfortable distribution of the wounded to be made to the various hospitals.

As the war wore on, the supply of ambulances approximated more closely to the demand, and great commercial undertakings like Lloyd's and the Baltic Corn Exchange presented the Red Cross Society with splendidly equipped ambulance units. They formed welcome additions to the London Ambulance Column, which worked in unison with the Red Cross; but so great was the volume of traffic that many of the original members of the column found it essential to continue their activities to the very end. A few figures will give an idea of the labours of this organisation, which had sprung into being during the war by reason of an unprepared-for necessity.

Over one hundred hospitals were rapidly equipped in the metropolitan area to deal with the wounded. These hospitals, however, were never planned with an eye to traffic facilities or war requirements. They lay anyhow in the great jumble of London, and but for the swift and ubiquitous motor-car the work of distributing the wounded would have been a veritable and slow torture for the poor fellows after their weary journey from the front.

But, as it was, the society was able to adapt the old system to the new needs by the aid of a splendid motor-transport system, and neither France nor Germany **Varied service** equalled Britain in the task of speedily and **of the staff** comfortably distributing the wounded, considering that British casualties had to be taken by ambulance and train in France, shipped across the Channel, conveyed by train to London, and there distributed to the hospitals by motor-ambulance.

More than 600,000 cases were dealt with by the London Ambulance Column during the war, and in addition to the wounded it provided transport for convalescents moving from one hospital to another, and also for repatriated prisoners passing through London. During big offensives the trains came in with their loads of wounded at all hours of the day and night, and nothing could have been finer than the willingness of the ambulance staff in working for abnormally long hours.

Not content with this duty, they gave assistance also during air raids, and we can measure the devotion of these good men and women when we consider the strain of driving through darkened streets with precious loads of suffering humanity, and taking the risks of traffic, shrapnel, and bombs in this extra labour after perhaps a heavy day spent in the usual ambulance duty. Some eighty ambulances and seventy

cars, suitable for sitting-up cases, were in active service at the close of hostilities, and every one of these vehicles had been provided free of cost to the nation, while many motorists and engineers had given their services continuously from the first call in 1914.

Voluntary motor-ambulance corps on somewhat similar lines were established in Birmingham, Edinburgh, Dublin, and the other great towns, for, as the war progressed, hospital accommodation all over the country was required. In every case private motorists were eager to use their cars and give their own services. It should be mentioned, too, that not a few Britons volunteered for service with the French Red Cross, and in Belgium, Serbia, Russia, and Italy British motor volunteers were to be found, for all the warring countries discovered very soon that the official estimates of wounded and the official arrangements for their transport were wholly inadequate.

Britain led the way in 1914 as having the greatest number of motor-cars and drivers of any nation in Europe, and from this reservoir generous contribution was made to every ally. The Germans were greatly inferior in their motoring resources, and there was a consequent loss of efficiency which was indicated in many phases of the conflict, and told with especial force towards the end, when the German motor transport literally went to pieces owing to lack of tyres and other essentials.

At the very outbreak of war British motorists came forward with the utmost zeal to help the authorities, and if only the locomotive problem of war had been better studied we could have made far better use of our motor strength at the very outset. But, as it was, one new problem after another arose to take the bewildered experts by surprise. The war, instead of being a War Office affair, turned out to be a national affair, which only the nation could grapple with.

Take the case of the French and Belgian refugees, who poured panic-stricken into Britain in the early months of the war. Their coming had never been officially counted upon, and when the trains **Distribution of** dumped them down in London there was no **the refugees** official method of taking them from the stations to the numerous homes where shelter was offered to them. At that time the authorities were overwhelmed by other problems.

Again, the motor-car solved the difficulty. A little band of motorists undertook to convey the poor stranded refugees from the railway-stations to their new homes, and night after night one saw loads of worn-out, dazed, and nerve-racked women and children safely piloted through the maze of London. As if to cheer themselves up in face of the sorrowful scenes they witnessed, these motor volunteers eventually took the name of the Optimist National Corps, Transport Section.

When its scope and work developed the Optimists' Corps changed its name to the Motor Squadron of the London Volunteer Rifles, and it was from the Optimists that the National Motor Volunteers developed, largely owing to the good work of Major-General D. C. F. Macintyre.

It is desirable to trace a little further the history of the Motor Squadron of the L.V.R., as here we have a remarkable example of splendid and unselfish endeavour which is hardly known to the general public.

When the Motor Squadron had distributed the war refugees it cast about for the next good work, and it found in the wounded soldier a case for its full sympathy. In previous wars the problem of the convalescent soldier was doubtless

IN THE SERVICE OF SOLDIERS AND VOLUNTEERS.
Driving a load of wounded soldiers for a day's outing in the country, and (above) lady chauffeurs of the British Service Corps conveying volunteers to the scene of their field-day operations.

very simple. Most probably he did not convalesce to any great extent. If he were of iron constitution he pulled through unaided, otherwise he died or faded away from the scene and had no further military importance. The heavy losses in the Great War made the salvage of the wounded soldier a military necessity.

How to help the soldier through convalescence thus became an important task and one not easily solved. There comes

OFFICERS OF THE MOTOR TRANSPORT VOLUNTEERS.   [*Bassano.*

From left to right : Seated, Capt. the Rt. Hon. the Earl of Cottenham, Hon. Treasurer ; Major G. M. Horn, Acting Adjutant ; Major C. R. Freemantle, O.C. ; Capt. the Rt. Hon. the Earl of Chesterfield, and Capt. the Hon. Harry Stonor. Standing : Capt. C. H. de W. Green, Sec.-Lieut. T. G. Clare, Sec.-Lieut. J. Durham, Sec.-Lieut. the Hon. Claude Yorke, Sec.-Lieut. H. J. S. Cave, Assistant Acting Adjutant ; and Lieut. R. T. Mence, Quartermaster.

a difficult stage, when the wounded or ill man is too well to be cooped up all the time in hospital, and yet is not well enough to leave it altogether. Fresh air, entertainment, and change of scene then help him more than hospital treatment. Neglect these matters and he may relapse, or his cure is much delayed.

The Motor Squadron took up this task by organising motor outings for the wounded soldiers, and at the same time arranging for golf club-houses and London clubs to entertain the men. In August, 1916, as many as 1,031 wounded heroes were taken out to Tagg's Island, on the Thames, for entertainment, and London clubs such as the Devonshire, Eccentric, National Liberal, etc., gave hospitality to the men, the transport being supplied on every occasion by the Hospital Motor Squadron, as it now was named.

The members of the Hospital Motor Squadron were private motorists, paying their own expenses and supplying their cars free of cost. From an early period Mr. Arthur J. Wilson was prominent in this undertaking, and he became commandant of the squadron in the London district. As a case of individual devotion his record is noteworthy. Mr. Wilson was a pioneer motorist, who, despite his physical affliction of total deafness, was a most careful and successful driver. In the early days of the war he converted one of his cars into an ambulance, and, in addition to doing ordinary hospital transport work day and night with this ambulance, he turned out on the occasion of every air raid, standing by at the London Fire Brigade Headquarters until sent out to pick up casualties and take them to hospital. This ambulance and two of his closed cars were still in use in 1919 for hospital work, taking wounded men for operations and also for health rides. We may form some idea of the magnitude of London as a military hospital centre from the official estimate that this hospital voluntary

Mr. A. J. Wilson's fine record

motor-transport work was expected to go on until 1920, as it would take that time before all the badly wounded cases had been evacuated from the hospitals.

Many ladies assisted in the work of the motor services, and in the Hospital Squadron Miss Ethel Sayer, secretary to Mr. A. J. Wilson, was particularly active, as she acted as interpreter for Mr. Wilson, and showed great organising skill. It was no easy task for a busy man, of affairs to keep up the day and night activities of a corps like the Hospital Squadron, more especially when he was handicapped by deafness : but Mr. Wilson made this corps one of the best organised bodies of the war period. More than one hundred thousand wounded men were given healthful and thoroughly enjoyable motor rides by the Hospital Motor Squadron. These outings were officially recognised, and had the support of the British Red Cross Society. The squadron during the last days of the war was attached to the Royal Automobile Club War Service, and the members wore the distinctive war service uniform authorised by the War Office.

In endeavouring to trace the history of voluntary motor transport during the war period one notices, and oft-times is puzzled by, the frequent changes of title of the bodies engaged. This in itself is evidence of the rapid and unexpected evolution which went on, but it also showed that few people in this country had given serious thought to the locomotive side of the war problem. The minor issues of war had not been considered, and we waited for a difficulty to arise ere any attempt was made to solve it. Almost invariably the volunteer filled the breach while official plans were being got ready.

One highly important task was discharged by an organisation which eventually was known as the Motor Transport Volunteers (Group 2, City of London A.S.C. Motor Transport Volunteers), to give it the full ultimately developed official title, and sometimes known as the Motor Volunteer Corps, but more generally styled the M.T.V.

As the war grew in magnitude London became the central clearing-house of the whole British military effort. It was not altogether wise to have had so much centralisation, but it seemed impossible to keep the soldiers, whether wounded or healthy, from gravitating to London. Britain's railways were not planned on strategic lines, and by converging on London from all parts they brought about a congestion in the capital which it was impossible to cope with by ordinary means.

London as a clearing-house

With the ever-growing armies thousands of troops poured into and out of London daily, and in most cases a cross-city journey had to be made in order to establish connection between the various railway termini, the clumsy arangement of which in London is a national scandal.

By day a soldier might find his way easily enough across London by omnibus or Tube, but it seemed the established thing that soldiers should travel by night at hours when the usual inter-station connections had closed down—and, of course, during the war there was a considerable shrinkage in these services. Soldiers, too, by conditions of leave had often to reach London in the small hours of Sunday morning, although this was the " dead " morning on which cross-London traffic was at its lowest ebb.

The authorities did not seem to know what to do with this highly puzzling inter-station problem in London, and they simply left it to the men themselves to find their way. The observer who spent a winter's night at one after another of the main London stations, watching the transfer of troops by voluntary motor organisations, was afforded ample evidence of the dangers and hardships which the soldiers were subjected to in crossing London on foot with their heavy kits until these voluntary organisations came to their aid.

The men arrived dead tired at Euston, for instance, late at night, after a long journey in packed railway carriages. They tumbled out dazed and tired on the platform, with the vague knowledge that they were to convey themselves to another station on the other side of London. After midnight there was nothing for it but to walk through the maze of miles of dark and unknown streets, carrying sixty to ninety-pound kits, and exposed to the risk of being robbed, drugged, or misdirected by the prowling ghouls who lay in wait for them. At one time this waylaying of stranded soldiers had become a serious evil, and many foul crimes were committed.

It was in February, 1916, that Sir John Lister Kaye, realising the hardships of travelling soldiers, formed the Motor Volunteer Corps with the aid of a few motorists ; and, beginning in a very modest way, they established a service between some of the principal stations. The task was by no means simple, for the train arrivals and departures at the various termini did not study the convenience of the cross-city transport service, and with only a limited number of motors available it often meant that many soldiers had

MOTOR GARAGE "MANNED" BY WOMEN.
Staff of the Women's Volunteer Reserve cleaning up and doing running repairs to cars in their garage.

weary waits before they could find accommodation in a vehicle. The observer, however, could not but admit the cheerfulness and uncomplainingness of these soldiers while enduring delays and hardships which no one attempted to relieve until a few devoted motorists and other volunteers took up the task.

At first only one London station could be served, but by degrees, as the good work became known, more volunteers were found. City firms lent their motor-lorries, and private motorists their cars, and in most cases the drivers put in this night work voluntarily after the finish of their usual daily labours. It was no small feat of endurance for

Inter-station transport service

a London motor-driver, after his ordinary hard day's work, to carry on an all night service across the darkened city streets in all weathers, and sometimes during the thick of air raids. Yet from 1916, and long after the armistice, men and women drivers performed that task without reward, and hardly with any recognition from the nation.

During a typical Sunday night in the war period from five thousand to six thousand men, with their kits, were transported free of charge across London by the M.T.V. Expressed in tons, it was no small weight, for with their kits and baggage it only took ten soldiers to weigh a ton on an average, and thus the total Sunday night load came to about

five hundred and fifty tons. The actual carrying cost worked out at threepence a man, so that in point of saving to the nation there was an economy of £75 on one night's work.

But, of course, the real economy was the saving of the soldiers from extra fatigue at the end of a long journey, and also the saving from cruel exposure and grave risks of other kinds. As the motor service progressed it was able to take a man away quickly from the arrival station, and if he had any time to spare before catching the next connection he was taken by motor to a Y.M.C.A. or other hut, where he could obtain refreshment and rest, and at the proper time he would be conveyed by another motor to the station of departure. He was a totally different man from the poor **Helping one and a half million men** fellow who in earlier days had to drag himself wearily across London by his own devices. Everyone who saw this service in operation was particularly impressed by the kindly comradeship which existed between the soldiers and the motor-transport workers. There was no suspicion of patronage on the one side, and the soldiers behaved like gentlemen.

On an average twenty thousand men were conveyed across London weekly during the war by the Motor Transport Volunteers, and the total up to the cessation of hostilities was not far short of one million five hundred thousand men, or a weight of some one hundred and fifty thousand tons.

The usual fleet for a Sunday night's work was sixteen lorries and thirty-five cars, and on one night they carried no fewer than six thousand three hundred and thirty men, and had every station clear by eight-thirty in the morning.

Over three hundred cars and lorries were in this service, with a personnel of six hundred drivers and assistants. Obviously the strain would be too much for any driver to serve every night, and thus the fleet was used in rotation, but nevertheless every helper in the scheme was severely tested, for all-night traffic driving is a tremendous strain.

The Y.M.C.A. instituted a similar transport service of its own in order to cope with the great increase of military traffic during the last two years of the war. In

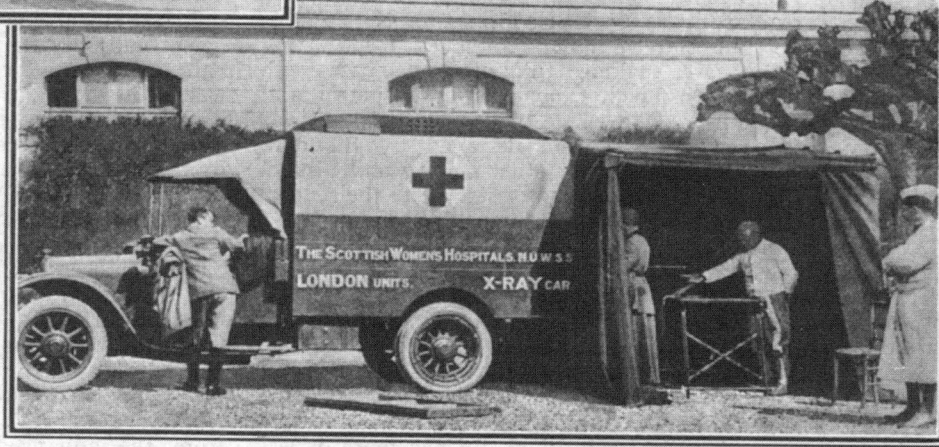

A SERVICE WITH A REMARKABLE RECORD.
X-ray car of the Scottish Women's Hospital having finishing touches put to it before leaving for the front. A detachment of the Women's Reserve Ambulance Corps went to Russia and Rumania as ambulance drivers with this service, and displayed great skill, courage, and endurance.

addition to working several railway-stations on lines similar to the Motor Transport Volunteers, the Y.M.C.A. Motor Transport kept up a constant night service between their numerous rest and refreshment huts. It happened almost every night that weary soldiers would pour into one hut until the place was overcrowded. To send the men out on a search for another hut would have been hard-hearted, to say the least of it, as the buildings were distributed over a wide area, and even the Londoner would not find it easy to locate some of them, tucked away as they were in the most unexpected places.

Accordingly, the Y.M.C.A. Transport Department established a very efficient Volunteer Motor Service in circulation between the London huts, and by telephone each hut kept headquarters acquainted with its accommodation capacity at the moment. The unpleasantly overcrowded hut was promptly visited by a motor fleet, and the surplus soldiers taken away for distribution to other huts where better accommodation offered. It was really a clearing-house system, which might well be adopted by hotels and other institutions in peace time.

Through a whole night the writer watched the working of the Y.M.C.A. motor transport both at the railway-stations and the huts, and he can pay a very high tribute to the self-sacrifice and the courtesy of the men and women volunteers who carried on the work through the war. It was a most arduous occupation, but the gratitude of the soldiers was felt to be the best recompense. As in the **Motor organisation** case of the other transport workers, these **in the provinces** volunteers cheerfully faced the risks of air raids, fogs, and all the other chances of London traffic in war time.

In Birmingham, Edinburgh, and other large cities with any serious amount of troop traffic, local voluntary motor organisations similar to those in London sprang up; and in Ireland the Irish Automobile Club placed all its facilities at the service of the soldiers. Indeed, it can be safely said that throughout the British Isles the vast majority of motorists did their utmost to use their cars in the national interest, and but for the serious shortage of petrol, which at times hampered even the big organisations, every car in the country would have been usefully employed right through the war. As it was, and faced in many instances by official discouragement or apathy, the motorists did an immense volume of useful work, which but for their aid would have remained undone.

An excellent example of the work done by county motorists was that carried out by the Southern Division of the Hampshire Automobile Club, which has three branches in all. The Southern Division maintained a fleet of ambulances from the beginning of the war, and with these they met every hospital-ship arriving at Southampton Docks day and night. They also met hospital-trains arriving in Southampton, Bournemouth, and Brockenhurst districts, and conveyed patients to and from various hospitals in these regions. Further, they maintained a regular bi-weekly service of cars for Netley Hospital. In all, the Hampshire volunteers conveyed 48,000 sitting cases, and 82,000 cot cases, making a total of 130,000 cases. In this work their cars consumed 43,000 gallons of petrol, and travelled 476,000 miles. The whole of this undertaking was voluntary, and the expenses were defrayed by the club members and their friends. Many other county and district motor clubs and groups of motorists met their local requirements during the war in the same willing manner.

A special section must be devoted to the women drivers and their war work. Not only did women take a share in the various organisations already referred to, but they also formed a wonderful series of their own, the very number and variation of which are bewildering. In some cases, it is true, the members received wages or payment, **Women motorists'** and thus might be considered outside the **patriotic work** terms of this chapter; but it is only just to bring them all in, for the more or less nominal wages paid in no instance detracted from the sacrifice made by women in taking up hard and dangerous work from patriotic motives, and accepting for their invaluable services mere pittances which often did not cover the out-of-pocket expenses.

One of the first bodies to take up duty was the Green Cross Society, or Women's Reserve Ambulance. Members drove either their own cars or vehicles lent by other members or owned by the corps. This corps specialised in connecting the ambulance trains arriving in London with certain hospitals, mostly in the suburbs. To the Roehampton Hospital alone they carried tens of thousands of limbless cases, but the corps was trained and equipped to render ambulance service in any direction. On an average from two thousand to three thousand miles a week were travelled by the cars of the W.R.A., which was known as the "Green Cross Corps."

Founded in June, 1915, with a handful of enthusiasts, prominent amongst whom was Mrs. Beatty, the organisation at the close of the war had over six hundred members, after sending large numbers of recruits to other corps.

To the credit of some members of the Green Cross Corps is the record of being earliest on the scene during the first London Zeppelin raid. It was a wholly voluntary and unofficial undertaking, arrived at by some of the women themselves when they heard the bombs. An ambulance was out within a few minutes, and it reached the first fire within ten minutes. The ambulance crew had picked up the casualties and were setting out for hospital before any other ambulance arrived. Considering the nerve-shattering experience of the first raid it was an exceedingly plucky act. In recognition of this feat the W.R.A. was officially attached to the " D " Division of the London Metropolitan Police for air-raid defence duties.

It was a detachment of the Women's Reserve Ambulance Corps which went as ambulance drivers with Dr. Elsie Inglis, of the Scottish Women's Hospital, to Russia and Rumania, and rendered magnificent service there under the most appalling conditions.

The Scottish Women's Ambulance Corps had, perhaps, the most remarkable record of the war by reason of its heroism in the terrible Serbian retreat. Under the leadership of Mrs. Haverfield, it went through privations and horrors which one would have thought no woman could have stood, and in these conditions it rendered priceless service to the sick and wounded soldiers. One may well believe that the calm courage and ceaseless devotion of these women must have put a new heart into the retreating armies. The road conditions during the retreat were indescribably bad.

If other groups of women drivers were spared the supreme agony and dramatic episodes of a disastrous retreat with an army, they nevertheless, within their opportunities, showed equal bravery and devotion **F.A.N.Y. pioneers** to duty. Nothing could be finer than the war **in the war zone** record of the Women's First Aid Nursing Yeomanry Corps, oft-times styled "The Fannys." This organisation existed before the war, but it shows how little the military authorities had foreseen the true place of the motor in war, when we find the F.A.N.Y. Corps trained in horse-riding, and then, under the experience of actual warfare, suddenly discarding the horse and taking up the motor.

Not had only the old school of military expert ignored the value of the motor, he also was doubtful of the utility of woman in the war zone, so that even when the F.A.N.Y. had its motor convoy ready for action, its services in France were not fully accepted until the middle of 1916, though from January of that year some of the Red Cross men drivers in the Calais area had been replaced by women, and the experiment had proved what women could do.

Ambulance service was rendered to the Belgian and French Armies on occasion, as well as to the British, and the F.A.N.Y. was the first women's corps to be officially entrusted with the transport of British wounded in what was really the war zone. On many occasions these convoys were less than five miles from the actual firing-line, and what with air raids and long-range bombardments they were seldom out of danger.

Very varied work fell to this corps. They carried wounded from the advanced dressing-stations to the nearest field hospitals, and in many instances members of the F.A.N.Y. helped the doctors behind the trenches when there had been a heavy influx of wounded. Clothing and comforts for the troops were also brought up by them from the bases, motor-kitchens arranged and worked for the wounded; and in and about Calais there was an immense volume of motor-ambulance traffic done by them in connecting the clearing-stations, hospitals, boats, and trains.

Life in France under war conditions was very hard for members of this corps, and during wet and wintry weather the women motor-drivers had many additional hardships and dangers peculiar to that calling. Cars had to be kept ready for a call at any hour of the day or night, and the task of starting a cold engine on a winter's night, and making a perilous journey over shell-torn roads in the dark was as great a trial of a woman's grit as can well be imagined.

The full story has yet to be written of all the achievements of women motorists in the war, and possibly in the welter of heroism which the war called forth it will never receive the attention it deserves. But when we contrast the normal lives of these women in July, 1914, with what they went through of their own accord in the following four years, we are helped in getting the true perspective of their heroism.

When the woman motor-driver had proved her worth in every theatre of war work there arose no small amount of confusion in arranging recruitment and meeting the increased demands of the authorities. The Women's Legion rendered most useful assistance in removing this confusion by acting as the recruiting headquarters. The demand rapidly grew as the war went on, and not the least of the difficulties was that of securing the right degree of competence in the candidates selected. Not every woman is cut out for being a motor-driver in war time, and the training of otherwise suitable women was not always satisfactory. The life had become more strenuous and driving conditions more severe than in the early days ere any military traffic system had been evolved.

A training school and hostels for the girls were established by the Women's Legion in order to help on matters, and on going through the school the drivers were allotted to the military department in which they were required. In this manner a constant supply of competent **Success of** drivers was made possible at short notice to **women drivers** the Royal Air Force (the "W.R.A.F.'s"), the Royal Naval Air Service (the "Wrens"), and to the Army Service Corps. An enormous number of men drivers was released for military service, and at very critical periods in the war the women drivers, by their presence in ample numbers, tided Britain over serious difficulties in making up losses.

The success of the women drivers in the Army services was remarkable. They showed themselves competent and considerate drivers, and their presence on the roads brought a new amenity into motoring. The Women's Royal Air Force, or W.R.A.F., drivers were the corps d'élite of the movement, one reason being that they were entrusted with fast and powerful cars; for when the flying men came to earth they resented slow travel, and speed was the fetish of the whole Air Service, as befitted a body of young and daring fellows.

High-speed motoring is a distinctly dangerous occupation, and more than one flying man expressed the opinion that he got more thrills when motoring through London than when flying over the enemy trenches. At first it seemed a doubtful policy to entrust very fast cars to women drivers, but the W.R.A.F. dispelled the illusion.

On various official tours motor experts were driven for long distances by W.R.A.F. drivers, and they paid high tribute to the women's skill and good driving. Particularly noteworthy was their courtesy **Women's Army** and fairness to all classes of other drivers on **Service Corps** the road. The W.R.A.F.'s were in strong contrast in this respect to the all too frequent "road hog" of the male sex. The woman driver proved herself to be a lady, while it is the fault of many men who are gentlemen ordinarily that when in charge of a fast car they lose their good manners, and become very objectionable and selfish users of the highway.

If ordinarily more prosaic than the W.R.A.F. duties, those of the Women's Army Service Corps were none the less useful. Motor-cycles, side-cars, light cars, large cars, and even lorries and vans were driven by the women; and though

MOTORS FOR THE SERVICE OF WOUNDED SOLDIERS.
Members and cars of the Southend Section of the National Motor Volunteers lined up at Westcliff for inspection by Major-General MacIntyre. Above: A motor trailer designed for the conveyance of wounded soldiers which was subscribed for by members of the Southend Automobile Club. The trailer, which could be attached to any car, served for the conveyance of two "stretcher cases," while walking cases were taken in the car.

in sundry cases one would have said that the work was too severe for them, they heroically persevered, and in all weathers they were to be seen carrying out their tasks under the most uncongenial conditions. It would hardly be possible to compute accurately the total mileage accomplished by all the women drivers, but the figures must have been stupendous.

Beyond a shadow of doubt the British Army had the finest motor-transport service of any combatant in the war, and though there may have been a large margin of transport waste —as in conveying indolent Staff officers to and from lunch, or in using a huge motor-lorry to convey a tiny parcel—it was far better to have this margin of excess than to be actually short of transport in the vital directions. Germany was beaten hopelessly in motor transport, and she lost tactical opportunities again and again through not having the road facilities to follow up a blow quickly, and through being unable to penetrate deeply enough into the defenders' lines.

Within Germany there was nothing comparable to the magnificent service of volunteer motorists whose efforts have here been sketched; and thus through an enormous range of operations Germany was losing time and wasting energy in every phase of the war.

Of the many auxiliary forces of volunteer motorists yet to be touched upon by reason of their later origin one may select the War Service Corps of the Royal Automobile Club as a good example. Owner-drivers of cars placed their services and their vehicles at the disposal of the Government and the military authorities, and very extensive use was made of these facilities, for the traffic between the innumerable offices, factories, and camps had become colossal. Even after making a liberal allowance for unnecessary travelling by superfluous officials, we still have a big net sum of utility. On an average a car on duty in the London region did fifty miles in the day, and the hardship of this to the driver was small as compared with that of having to wait for hours while some important, or self-important, official was in conference.

At the most intense stage of the war the whole London area to its uttermost confines was honeycombed with offices, factories, stores, and works which required the frequent visits of officials; and so bad were the ordinary traffic arrangements during the war period that an unconscionable amount of time would have been lost if voluntary motor organisations like the R.A.C. War Service Corps had not rendered assistance. The owner-drivers were men over military age or unfit for military service, and in several instances women owner-drivers took up the task, while a considerable number of women drivers volunteered to drive cars owned by members.

It was a far cry from driving a luxurious limousine in Whitehall to handling a motor-plough in the depths of the country, but the whole range of experience between these extremes was gone through by women motorists during the war. As a branch of the Food Production Department there was formed the Women's Land Army, and amongst the duties it took up was working the motor-plough. It is slow work jolting along at three miles an hour up and down an old grass field, and a short experience of motor-ploughing yielded the experimenter no joy in the calling. Yet girls were found to stand the hard and monotonous work during long periods, and their assistance undoubtedly helped to bring a great deal of additional land under cultivation. Many of the motor-ploughs were by no means mechanial successes, and a considerable amount of patient tinkering was necessary at

From limousine to motor-plough

times. And as very few people really knew anything about them at first, it is quite probable that the girls were often as successful with obdurate machines as were the other people who struggled with them. The women showed wonderful patience and perseverance in this as in every other branch of motoring.

For men the war established a wider and more adventurous range of motoring, extending as it did from the dashing volunteer motor-cyclist despatch-rider of the early days of the war to the volunteer motorists who formed a large section of the Tank crews in the later stages. Many thousands of these were young motor-cyclists and engineers, who volunteered for this terribly hard and dangerous work.

There were volunteers manning the first armoured cars in Belgium and France in 1914, others were in the Russian and Asiatic campaigns, and in the African campaigns many brilliant feats were accomplished by motor - cyclists and motorists; here, as in all the other theatres of war, the Germans being beaten hollow by the British motor transport. At home during the air-raid period the motorist played a useful part also in assisting the Special Constabulary and Ambulance Corps after a big air attack. In London and every other raided town the motor volunteer was of great assistance.

Taken altogether the motor effort of Britain in the Great War proved to be one of the most remarkable manifestations of bravery, endurance, technical skill, and voluntary effort brought out by the crisis. In the lifetime of the man of forty the British motor industry had grown up from a few little workshops to a magnificent and widespread organisation which produced hundreds of thousands of engines for aeroplanes, airships, motor-cars, armoured cars, ambulances, military lorries, motor-cycles, and Tanks. That whole development was born of the national love of sport and travel—it came from the love of free effort and a deep affection for revolving wheels.

If it were possible to put a military valuation on the millions of miles travelled by motor-vehicles in the war and to put a national valuation on the whole activity of motor volunteers in every section, we should arrive at astounding calculations. But as it is impossible to measure courage, humaneness, self-sacrifice, and the difference between saving life and losing life, it is out of the question to give precise evaluation of what motorists did in the war.

Birth of a great organisation

Even this brief survey of their work, however, sets it beyond all doubt that they helped the Allies from the very first to avert defeat; and then, through Britain's motor excellence, was gained that final victory more rapidly, more thoroughly, and with far less sacrifice in blood and anguish than if Britain had in 1914 stood at the German level of motor resources. The British military teachers, let us add, were no more conservative than the German or French experts in this matter of the use of motors in warfare; and Britain's first little Army went into battle better equipped in motor material than the two great Continental Powers which had been studying the war problem so intently for years. America was the only other country which was able to emulate to any degree the gigantic voluntary effort which was made by motorists in the British Empire; but the full brunt of the work fell on Britain from that dramatic day in August, 1914, when many a motorist setting out on a pleasure tour turned in his tracks to take up the Great Adventure, which, alas! for great numbers of them was destined to end in grim tragedy.

AMBULANCE DE LUXE FOR SERVICE IN FRANCE.
The "Millicent Sutherland Ambulance," which was presented by Millicent Duchess of Sutherland for service in connection with her Red Cross Work on the western front.

AMERICAN TROOPS WITH TANKS

CHAPTER CCXCVI.

GOING FORWARD TO CANTIGNY.

AMERICA'S SHARE IN THE VICTORY.

By Hamilton Fyfe.

Exaggerated Expectations of American Performances Spread Abroad by Irresponsible Newspapers—Wonders Actually Accomplished—Moral Effect in France and Germany of the United States' Entry Into the War—The Idealism and the Business Instinct of the American People—Inspiration Behind their War Activity—Statesmanship of President and People—War Spirit Fanned by Seditious Attempts to Germanise America—Advantages and Disadvantages of One-Man Rule—National Registration—Astonishing Success of the Liberty Loans—Part Played by the United States Navy—Enrolment of the National Army—German Offensive of July 15th, 1918—42nd American Division at Perthes-les-Hurlus—3rd American Division Hold the Enemy Back in the Mézy-Surmelin Sector on the Marne—Franco-American Forces Pinch Out the German Salient in the Country of the Marne and Vesle—Americans Capture Château-Thierry—First American Army Flattens Out the St. Mihiel Salient—American Offensive through the Argonne Forest to the Sedan-Montmédy Railway and Breach of the Hindenburg and Kriemhilde Lines—Americans Cross the Meuse at Sedan—General Contribution to the Success of the Allied Effort Made by the American People as a Whole.

WHEN the United States declared war exaggerated expectations were formed of what the Americans would be able to do. These were put about by imaginative newspaper writers in New York. In America little attention was paid to them. But in Britain newspapers are not so imaginative, and the wild forecasts trumpeted forth by these writers were accepted as trustworthy. When they proved, as they were bound to prove, illusory, some disappointment was felt. The hundred thousand aeroplanes did not fly across the Atlantic. It was not even found possible to construct a good " Liberty air-motor." The shipping problem was not solved either by wooden or by concrete ships. Yet no disappointment of exaggerated hopes should lead us to underestimate the great part which the United States played in bringing the war to a successful close. They did not perform miracles but they did wonders. They sent their partially trained troops to Europe sooner than good judges believed it to be possible for them to come ; and when they were put into the battle they acquitted themselves like men. Everything that was possible the Americans did. That impossibilities were not achieved was not their fault—it was due to the limitations which are set to human effort by human nature. The quarrels among the earlier shipping controllers before Mr. Hurley took charge ; the tie-up of traffic on the railways which forced the proclamation of five holidays in the month of January, 1918 ; the mismanagement of the " Publicity " side; the slowness of aeroplane construction—these were mere incidents, inevitable in a campaign which to be effective had to be rapid ; unimportant when we figure out results. The entry of America into the war was immensely valuable in the steadying effect it had upon France. The effective blows struck by her troops in the autumn of 1918 had much to do with demoralising the German troops. The most useful, depressing propaganda method employed by us was the repetition of the American numbers. America's share in the victory was a very helpful share indeed.

One feature of it should not be left out of the account. The Americans brought into the struggle a renewal of that moral stimulus which had so powerfully swayed the British peoples in 1914. This made a visit to the United States in 1917 specially interesting. It was the writer's fortune to see much of the war. Not his good fortune, for it can never be good to witness evil happenings. But he saw many vastly interesting events in progress, and in some particulars can compare one country with another. For example, he saw France begin war. He saw Britain begin war. He saw Rumania begin war. He saw Russia in the early stages of the world-upheaval ; saw her failing disastrously to prepare herself for the trials and tribulations ahead of her. He saw Italy after the Italians had made their minds up that they were in for a long struggle, and not for the short campaign which was in the thoughts of most of them when they began. And then he saw the United States beginning war.

When, in some future day, he looks back upon all these memories and sees everything that has happened in its true perspective, it is pretty certain that he will set down his American experiences as the most impressive of all.

AMERICAN AND CANADIAN BROTHERS-IN-ARMS.
General Pershing (in front, fourth from the left), in chief command of the American military forces in Europe, with Sir Arthur Currie (in front, third from left), commander of the Canadian Corps at the Canadian Headquarters in France.

Britain went to war in a hurry, France with a sigh of apprehension. Russia sang marching songs with a melancholy lilt in them, and wondered what it was all about. Rumania light-heartedly fancied that occupying Transylvania would be no harder than the taking of Jericho after its walls had been trumpeted down. Americans were neither up in the air nor down in the depths. They neither sighed nor sang. They had no illusion about the war being quickly finished, nor were they in doubt as to the reasons for their entry into it. They did not hurry too much for safety. They treated war as a matter of business, and they applied the ordinary rules of business to it.

OUTWARD-BOUND FOR VICTORY.
American troops leaving their trenches for the attack on Cantigny, captured May 28th, 1918.

AMERICANS SHARING IN THE SECOND VICTORY OF THE MARNE.
Barricade in the streets of Fismes, where the Germans, retreating from the "pocket" they had created in the Marne sector, tried in vain to stop the advance of the Americans. The U.S. troops captured Fismes on August 4th, 1918, and the next day the Germans withdrew to the north bank of the Vesle.

The Americans are, above all else, a business people. This does not mean that they have no interests beyond business. There is a foolish idea among some who do not know them well that they are intent upon nothing but making money. The Germans thought this, and in their stupid, tactless way, let Americans see it. When Mr. Hoover was distributing food in Belgium, an officer on Governor von Bissing's Staff had the insolence to inquire, "*What do you Americans get out of this business ?*" Another German officer, of general rank, sat down beside one of Mr. Hoover's assistants, a very distinguished University professor, and asked him at once, "*Vell, how is piznis ?*" His notion apparently was that no American could talk about anything else.

In the American mind there are two predominant strains. One is the desire for success and its material fruits. The other is that strong strain of warm-hearted idealism which has prevented the struggle for riches from shifting their social system on to a purely material basis. Their idealism made them hate war and shrink from entering upon it. It was their business instinct which made them see that they could not stand aside, save at the cost of sacrifices which no self-respecting people could endure.

America's warm-hearted idealism

Nothing that happened in the war was more encouraging than the spectacle of a great nation taking up arms, not in sudden anger, not for conquest of territory, neither at the bidding of a despot nor upon the persuasion of a demogogue, but in order to defend itself, its principles, and its ideal. The intervention of the United States added a new feature to history. No parallel to it can be quoted. The world had never seen war undertaken in quite this same spirit before.

The explanation was, no doubt, that nations are growing towards the same stage of development which individual men reached when they ceased to fight because they enjoyed it, or because they had no other means of settling their disputes. Individual men no longer delight in bloodshed, but their instinct teaches them that force must be employed against enemies of law and order. Policemen have clubs and use them when necessary. Breakers of the law may be restrained or apprehended by any means whatever. No one would hesitate to use a rifle or a knife against a wild beast that threatened attack. No man would fail to help a policeman to arrest a criminal, even at the risk of injury. But in performing such acts there is no enjoyment.

We can imagine the members of some primitive tribe sallying forth to chase and kill or capture, and perhaps eat, tribesmen who had offended against the rules and regulations in force. We can fancy their joy in the hunt, in the satisfaction of their fighting instinct. Among individuals in our day such joy and such satisfaction are so rare that we can almost say they have ceased to influence civilised mankind.

Why America entered the war

All the time the writer was on the various battle fronts he never heard any soldier say that he liked killing. Nor shall we henceforth find nations enjoying war. There will be no more open declarations, like those of Moltke and Lord Kitchener, that war is healthy and desirable. Partly this is due to the change in the character of warfare; partly to the change in the motives for making war. Wars cannot now be undertaken, by nations which are really civilised, with exultation, but only as a duty, as an unpleasant necessity, which their instinct tells them they must accept if their ideals are to prevail over the criminal efforts of less civilised communities. It was instinct which drove the American people to make war. They felt, if a phrase may be borrowed from Mr. Franklin Lane, United States Home Secretary, that they must fight " to justify our right to live as we have lived, not as someone else wishes us to live." That right they fought for and that right they won.

They were not enthusiastic, but they were grimly determined. They did not parade the streets singing patriotic songs. They did not throw flowers to the soldiers who marched through their cities, though they threw them more useful things such as cigarettes, chocolate, fruit, and chewing-gum.

There were no thrills to their loyalty. They had to learn—and they did not learn quickly—to take off their hats to their national flag. But there was a spirit in the nation which was of value far above the worth of the spirit which finds its vent in shouting and singing.

One could feel this when one saw the first enrolled units of the National Guard marching to Central Park, New York, to go through their drill and physical exercises. One felt it more than ever watching the stirring march of the men of the New York National Guard down Fifth Avenue on the day they went off to their training camps. The crowd which lined the pavements for five miles did not make a continuous noise.

Nothing wonderful in that to those who remember how silently London crowds used to stand while soldiers passed through the streets in the early days of the new British armies. We knew that for all their silence there were pride and gratitude and stubborn resolution in the hearts of our people. There were just those feelings in American hearts.

It was a new thing in the history of the world, this gathering of a vast army, this enrolment of the youth of a nation essentially peaceful, not under the influence of some passing excitement, some carefully engineered thrill, but in a stern, almost solemn mood to chastise an offender against the common right and the common interest of all peoples. There was an inspiration in it which went far beyond that of any war activity of the past. These armies fought the battle of

German people. They wanted to give them something. The great desire of Americans, taking them in the mass, was to see Germany a free republic. The youth and flower of the United States went forth to war with the determination to free the world from Hohenzollern despotism, just as the British soldiers of the Napoleonic Wars set before themselves the one aim of getting rid of " Boney."

The American people were convinced that the time had come when it was necessary to have done with monarchies which, under pretence of ruling by Divine appointment, gave rein to the most criminal ambitions and kept the world in a state of perpetual unrest. They were convinced that it was time to have done with " militarism," by which they meant the bad old Bismarckian creed that force is the one thing needful, that nations are natural enemies, that every people has a right to what it can seize and keep by force. The Americans, following the lead of their President, who, in the writer's opinion, proved himself the only living statesman of **Statesmanship of the Americans** the first rank in the world, were resolved to establish, in place of this creed, the rule of law and order. They had, it seemed to many observers, a wider conception of the issue at stake than any of the other nations, whether on the allied or on Germany's side. They had had a long time to think it over, and they knew what the war was really about.

This light had come to the people of the Eastern States, especially those on the seaboard, by the month of April, 1917, when the American nation entered the war. It did not illuminate the mind of the Middle West and the Far West until some months had passed. When the people of those vast territories understood, it was because the lofty, yet unmistakably sincere, aims set forth by their President had reached that bedrock of moral fervour which lay beneath their cynical speech and contemptuous disregard of what " old Europe " was fighting about.

Such contempt they had been taught from their childhood. Such disregard, enjoined as the highest wisdom by Washington, seemed to them to be their line of security from profitless entanglements.

Gradually the President made them see that something more was at issue than the dignity of sovereigns

ON VICTORY'S FLOOD-TIDE.
American troops fighting forward from a newly-captured position during their First Army's drive towards the Moselle.

humanity. While they defended the right of Americans to live as they pleased and not as someone else pleased, they upheld that right for everybody. They were even helping the enemy towards it. I am sure that some day the Germans will acknowledge their liberation from Kaiserism to have been due in large part to the United States.

These men of the new American armies knew what they were going to fight for. They were not filled with hatred of the German people, though the approval given by the German people to the savageries of U boats, Zeppelins, and bomb-dropping Gothas did arouse strong feelings of disgust and contempt. The Americans did not want to take anything from the

AMERICAN HEAVY GUNS HURLING DEATH ON THE FOE.
Gunners of the 7th Battery of an American howitzer regiment in action. Splendid support was given by the American artillery to their infantry when these first met the shock of the German offensive in July, 1918, and subsequently in preparing the way for the successful American counter-offensive.

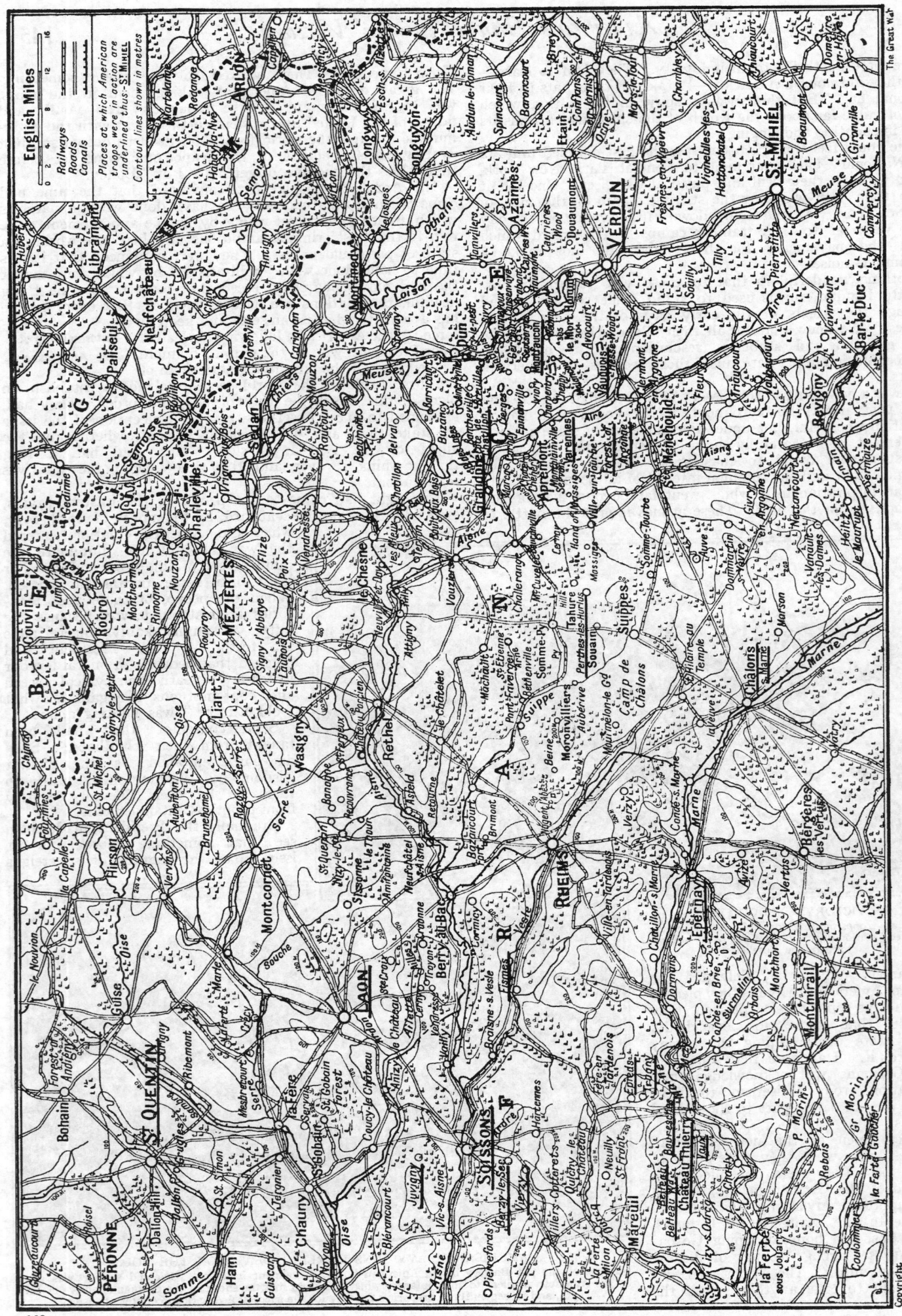

AREA OF THE AMERICAN OFFENSIVES ON THE MARNE, ARGONNE, AND MEUSE FRONTS, TOWARDS SEDAN, JULY-NOVEMBER, 1918.

or the right of this or that greedy kingdom to despoil another. They knew that the Crimean War had arisen out of a shadowy squabble, and the Franco-Prussian War out of Bismarck's criminal ambition, assisted by the folly of the French Empress and by the weakness of her husband and his Ministers. They thought this war had its springs in similar causes.

It took Mr. Wilson a long time to prove to them that they were wrong, and if he had tried to hurry the process of enlightenment it would have taken him longer still. For they are an obstinate folk in the Middle and West. No use attempting with them the tone of the man who said " I'm not a-arguing with yer ; I'm a-telling of yer." They had to be handled tactfully, and by his handling of them the President proved that tact was his strong suit.

One useful impetus in the direction of the President's endeavour was supplied by the German-American newspapers in the United States. Everything that the German-Americans (or it would be fairer to say the German German-Americans) could do to prejudice the case of the country of their birth, and to enrol the United States among the Powers fighting against her, seemed to have been already done. If they had not so persistently backed up the President by providing just the evidence that was needed to drive home his words, it is doubtful whether the United States would have been ready to come in even after two and a half years of war. There is no doubt but that the stupid and traitorous language of the German-American newspapers was of great service in fanning the war spirit after the country had come in.

These newspapers, printed in German, appeared in a great many cities of the Union. There were a large number in New York alone. Their original purpose was to give recent arrivals from German-speaking lands, who did not yet know English, a chance to read the news of the day. By their heated advocacy of the German cause they gave rise little by little to the belief that they were part of the machinery of a deep-laid plot to Germanise America.

Germans of influence had said openly that they looked forward to a day coming when the United States would be
more German than anything else. Many
Hun attempts to Americans were forced to learn some German
Germanise America in order to speak to their German domestic
servants. Germany sent to the United States many of her ablest professors to spread German ideas and a false notion of German Kultur. There was nothing fantastic in the suspicion that the German-language newspapers existed in such large numbers in pursuance of a policy of " peaceful penetration." They themselves promoted this belief. The " Cologne Gazette " called them " Germany's best allies in the United States," and added with the true Teutonic touch, blundering into expressions eminently apt to defeat the object of those who used them, " We may be sure that in this hour they are doing their duty."

Here are some examples of the manner in which they " did their duty," and fanned the righteous flame of American indignation. The " Staats-Zeitung," New York, taunted the young men of the country with seeking safety, when the obligation to fight was put upon them, " behind the petticoats

THE CAPTURE OF VAUX.

Vaux after artillery fire from American batteries had killed or driven out most of the Germans who had occupied it. The American infantry advancing took the town and captured five hundred prisoners who had survived. The crosses mark the graves of Americans who fell in the charge.

of women." It triumphantly added to this the remark that " the youths are so underfed that they cannot be used for real fighting." The chief Cleveland German-language journal announced that it had been " definitely and indubitably proved that the guilt of the war rests not upon the Kaiser but upon the European enemies of Germany." The " Abend-post " (" Evening Post "), of Detroit, called the Allies bluntly " robber States." " England fights because she wants to destroy Germany's commerce, France because she wants to recover Alsace-Lorraine. Italy wants the Trentino, Russia wants Galicia and other Austrian territories." The leading German paper in Illinois, published in Chicago, declared that American participation in the war could not save the Allies from defeat, and put forward as the best American policy " to separate ourselves as quickly as possible from the corpse of the Allies." The leading German paper in San Francisco asserted that " the German Kaiser and Chancellor had left nothing undone to prevent the war." A Brooklyn German-language paper (Brooklyn is a suburb of New York) referred to France as an " enemy country." The chief German newspaper of St. Louis devoted a page to glorifying Hindenburg.

The effect of these seditious expressions, which ignored the state of war between the United States and Germany, or at least claimed to separate the German-Americans from the rest of the population, was to stimulate the war spirit in the East and in the West, to anger the mass of the people who had before this felt no indignation. They lightened the task of the President and those who worked with him at preparing the country for war.

That task presented difficulties enough. It was supposed by many that the United States would be able to learn from British mistakes and those of other nations which had been fighting for two and a half years. But very few individuals ever benefit by the experience of other individuals, and the only nation which has done it in the whole course of history is Japan. The United States had to learn and unlearn just as Britain had done. They had, however, one advantage over the British people. Their initial effort was directed by one brain, not by the confused and indeterminate minds of a Cabinet of twenty-two. The authority, almost without limit, which is exercised by an American President in war time has its drawbacks. There were times when preparations of great pith and moment were at a standstill because some decision had to be **Advantages of** taken. No one could take it but the **one-man rule** President, and the President was occupied with other matters—thinking out a speech for Congress, perhaps, or worrying through some diplomatic difficulty. These delays might have been avoided if the President had formed a Coalition Cabinet, with all the ablest and most experienced men he could induce to join him, disregarding political differences. Then he would have been able to rely upon decisions taken by others. As it was, the Democratic politicians included in his Cabinet were not strong enough or sufficiently versed in great affairs to decide matters involving consequences that might impair the national energy. Nor were the men whom Mr. Wilson drew from the management of industry and from business given the free hand which might have speeded up the production of war necessaries, but which might also have led to confusion through lack of co-ordination of effort and that nice adjustment of personal balances which has always to be thought of in matters of State.

On the whole, however, the one-man rule which obtained from the outset was of value. It put before the nation a clear and comprehensive programme. It left nothing to chance. When mistakes were made they were mistakes of commission not of omission. From the start the country was warned of the tremendous burden it had shouldered, and it was enabled to bear it calmly and confidently because it saw that the Government was working resolutely and with foresight to make success sure.

The President had seen before war was declared that his earliest endeavours must be to provide, firstly, money and, in the second place, men. It would be no use having the men until there was money enough to equip them ; but in the meantime he decided that he would at once order a national registration of citizens available for national service. This was considered by many, even on his own side, as a daring and doubtful experiment. These doubters spoke of it as likely to be resented because it would be an infringement of American liberty. It passed off, in the result, without any disturbances. Nearly ten million men registered in twelve hours. Only one in a thousand refused. This **National alacrity** showed that there was a general readiness **to register** to serve the country, and that compulsory service, upon which the President had decided, would meet with no serious opposition.

This was satisfactory ; but still the first need of the Government after war had been declared was money. A loan was therefore prepared at once for issue. An attractive title had to be found for it, and none better calculated to appeal to American sentiment could have been hit upon. This and the three loans which followed it were known as Liberty Loans. The amount asked for in the late spring of 1917 was £400,000,000, and immense energy was applied to the task of raising this sum. Every kind of advertising method was employed. Meetings were held in every city. At theatres and picture-halls speakers gave ten-minute talks about the uses to which the money would be put. Posters were, of course, made a feature of the campaign, but somehow these did not at any time reach a very persuasive level. The newspapers helped vigorously and with the most valuable effect.

When the lists closed in June it was found that the loan had been over-subscribed by a very large amount. The total exceeded by more than fifty per cent. the sum asked for. The final figures were £607,045,370.

Later in the year the second Liberty Loan was floated to meet the huge expenditure upon America's preparations. This time the amount to be raised was £600,000,000. By now the West and the Middle West were interested in the war. They had been touched by the note of moral appeal in the President's speeches. The efforts which had been made before to stimulate investment were now increased. There were some who gloomily prophesied that the amount called for would not be subscribed. It was too soon, said the croakers, to come before the public again. There was not enough liquid capital in the country to stand such demands.

The figures of the response showed how utterly the makers of these discouraging forecasts had miscalculated. Instead of £600,000,000, the total of the subscriptions was £923,000,000 —again an over-subscription of more than fifty per cent. This time the number of subscribers was announced to be very much larger than before. To the first loan four million persons had contributed. To the second more than twice that number subscribed. The figure was 9,400,000.

By the spring of 1918 the Treasury began to need filling up once more, and a third Liberty Loan was put on the market. Again it was fixed at £600,000,000, and this time it was decided to try to induce people to subscribe who had never invested money before. The rich individuals and corporations had come forward with readiness in the previous year. It was now necessary to appeal to a wider class. The small towns had special attention paid to them. Prospectuses, not couched merely in the usual formal terms, were spread broadcast among the scattered farms of the West, North-West, and Middle West. The country newspapers took up the torch which their big brothers in the great cities had so worthily and compellingly borne, and urged their readers to come forward with their **Success of the** savings in their country's hour of need. **Liberty Loans**

The result of this was seen in a further very large increase in the number of subscribers. They now totalled 17,000,000, nearly double the number of those who contributed to the second, and nearly four times as many as subscribed to the first. The sum subscribed for was £835,303,370, not quite so heavy an excess as the time before, but still very encouraging.

In the autumn of 1918 the fourth Liberty Loan was floated, and this time the good effect of the campaign among small investors was seen even more clearly. The expenditure of the United States Treasury had been steadily rising. As the troops were sent to Europe the cost of the war became heavier. Shipbuilding was a very large item in the bill which had to be met. There was an aeroplane programme which ran into hundreds of millions. It was necessary now to make a bigger call upon the nation than had been made before. The amount of the loan was fixed at £1,200,000,000. That this would be over-subscribed seemed scarcely possible. That so large a sum could be raised, after all that had been poured out earlier, was not altogether certain. Yet when the lists closed it was seen that the scarcely possible had happened.

Once more there had been an enormous over-subscription. Nearly two hundred million pounds in excess of the sum asked for had been willingly lent to the State. The actual figure was £1,397,809,400. This brought the amount of money lent by the nation for war purposes up to the colossal figure of £3,760,000,000 odd.

But that does not cover all that was raised by loan, in addition to taxation, for in May, 1919, another loan, this time the Victory Loan, was before the country. The amount aimed at was £1,000,000,000. Even in the event of this not being over-subscribed, it would bring up the total of sums raised in this way to not far short of £5,000,000,000.

To return now to the first steps taken by the United States on their entry into the war. One was the immediate despatch of an American flotilla to Europe. Admiral Sims was in

Admiral William Sowden Sims, in chief command of the American Fleet in Europe.

Troops of the U.S. Army of Occupation marching through Treves, on the Moselle.

American soldiers look out across the storied Rhine to the Fort of Coblenz.

1st Division, U.S. Army, entering Coblenz, whose bridge-head they occupied December 13th, 1918.

Americans at Die Phalz, the hexagonal castle in the middle of the Rhine, near Caub.

Triumphal march of the 27th Division, U.S. Army, in New York, March 25th, 1919.

England a week after his country declared itself. He acted as Commander-in-Chief of the United States naval forces all through, and won golden opinions from everybody. His first resolve was that there must be a single naval command ; that he and his forces must act under the orders of the British Admiralty. This meant the subordination of personal ambitions, and also of national susceptibilities, to the general interest. The admiral showed that he himself was not out for advancement, and he told his countrymen plainly that they must be content to see Britain play the chief part in the war on the sea.

At the same time it is only just to say that the part played by the men and ships of the United States Navy was both vigorous and valuable. American warships escorted through the war zone sixty-two per cent. of the American troops sent to Europe—that meant about 1,125,000 men. Of the two million soldiers who were in France when the war ended, nearly half crossed the ocean in American transports. Twenty-seven per cent. of all the cargo ships which left United States ports for Britain, France, or Italy during the last eighteen months of war were convoyed by the American Navy.

American submarines and submarine chasers did good work in the Channel. Their base was in Ireland, and for a time Admiral Sims was in command of a British naval station in Ireland, a compliment both to his high ability in his profession and to his charm of personality, which made him popular wherever he went. His forces took an important share in laying a vast North Sea mine barrage extending from the Orkneys to Norway. He employed in this task a squadron of merchant ships converted into mine-layers, and in one operation the entirely American crews established a record by laying a field of five thousand mines in four hours, though the American mines did not explode with the precision of those made in Britain. Finally, a squadron of American Dreadnoughts was under Admiral Beatty's orders during the last year of the war. Thus, the American Navy, though little was heard of it, had every reason to congratulate itself upon the way its work was done.

Enrolment of the National Army Not long after the first naval forces had been despatched, the small regular American Army began to cross the Atlantic. This numbered at the time of the declaration of war not more than 100,000 men. It was raised by voluntary recruiting to 300,000. At the same time the National Guard, a militia force which had never been taken very seriously, was raised to its full strength of 400,000, and then the enrolment and training of the new National Army began. The gigantic effort made by the United States resulted in putting into the field in France a total of nearly a million and a half soldiers within a year of the date on which they were enrolled. What they did in France up to mid-June, 1918, has already been recounted in THE GREAT WAR. Now it remains to relate their share in the final battles which brought the German people to its knees, suing for peace.

The story came down to the capture of Balleau Wood and the village of Bouresches. The only other operation of note by the American divisions before they took part in repelling the German mid-July thrust was the capture at the beginning of the month of the village of Vaux. This lies on the road to Château-Thierry. Before the attack there was some good work by the gunners. The Intelligence Service had discovered which of the houses in the village had big cellars, and gave the artillery commander a plan upon which these were shown. In the cellars it was evident that the Germans must be living. Upon the houses marked the gunners therefore got to work with heavy shells, and, as was proved when the place fell, they made very accurate shooting. The infantry made straight for the cellars when they got into Vaux. They found them greatly damaged, and the men in them not inclined to put up much fight. They captured the village without difficulty and held it firmly against counter-attacks.

Now there came a fiercer ordeal for American troops than they had yet been through. They had to bear the onslaught of German shock troops. The resolution with which they bore it, even those who were thought to be only half trained, proved to the enemy the deceptive nature of the hope they had cherished that " the Yankees would break down."

Thenceforward the German commanders ceased to issue to their men orders in which they were encouraged to believe that the Americans would offer next to no resistance. The tune had to be changed. Henceforth it was the story that the Americans took no prisoners which was used as a means of stiffening the German moral.

The German offensive began on July 15th. At that date the 42nd American Division was on the right flank of the allied positions attacked, in Champagne, near Perthes-les-Hurlus. The artillery preparation for the attempted breakthrough was methodical and searching. Roads were shelled steadily. The "heavies" got to work on villages behind the line. Woods were filled with gas fumes. All this the 42nd disliked exceedingly, but they endured it with set teeth. It was their task to help prevent the Germans from reaching Epernay and Châlons. They had been given a post of honour, and they meant to justify the choice.

They had the consolation, such as it was — and every soldier knows what a consolation it can be in such an hour—of **42nd Division in Champagne** knowing that their guns were giving the enemy as good as he gave. His villages were being pounded, his roads of advance were under fierce fire. As his infantry pushed forward they met intensive barrages which tore holes in their ranks. So when the attack started the American troops were not only ready for it but they were in good fighting spirit. They met the Germans with a deadly rifle and machine-gun fire. They left their trenches to drive them back upon their reserves. Only in a heavily-wooded part of their line did the enemy get even a short-lived footing. Here he dribbled in machine-gunners and got through the first line of the American defences. But he was held at the second line, and when the guns were able to turn their attention to the small area he had captured he was soon driven out and the line restored.

Farther west the 3rd American Division played a vigorous part in delaying the Germans at the crossing of the Marne and in demoralising them wherever they had managed to get over. The weight of the enemy's effort fell on the Mézy-Surmelin sector. To occupy the plateau overlooking the Surmelin valley was his objective. Once in a position commanding the valley the Germans would have had the road to Montmirail open to them, and from Montmirail there was a high road leading through Meaux to Paris. To prevent them from reaching their objective was of the first importance, therefore, and the 3rd Division was ordered to hold them off at all costs.

This was the period when Paris was still considered to be in danger. Looking back upon those days—which saw the breaking of the enemy offensive and the quick strike-back of the allied forces on July 18th, from which date the Germans were kept in retreat until their spirit could endure it no longer—one can appreciate only with difficulty how dark the outlook still seemed. Everything appeared to depend, and no doubt mainly did depend, upon holding the enemy until the beginning of August, when the American troops would be able to take the field in really considerable numbers. The 3rd Division knew what grave decisions hung upon their steadiness. **3rd Division on the Marne** They waited for the blow to fall with the determination that, though it might break them, it should not make them budge.

The beginning was common form, an artillery preparation of furious violence. Then came a smoke barrage to hide the stream, and at the same time a carefully-planned bombardment of the positions above the river, intended to keep the Americans in their rifle-pits, while the Germans crossed. But the precautions failed utterly to make the passage safe. The Americans got out into the open among the bursting shells, and wherever the smoke-screen was a little thin they poured in a well-aimed rifle fire as the boats packed with German soldiers were hurried over. Already the promise made to the Germans that their crossing would meet with very little opposition had been proved illusory by the American gunners. They had searched the ravines along which the Germans advanced towards the river. This had not been expected, and its result was therefore extremely discomposing. Then, when they got on to the boats, with no room to move, let alone take cover, they came under the fire of the riflemen upon the heights. Dead and wounded men fell into the water; others jumped in to save themselves. Boats capsized or had holes shot in them. Where the Marne curves at the point where it receives the little Surmelin not one German could get ashore.

This was particularly useful because here was the point of union between two German divisions, which thus had their connection broken. Twenty boats or so floated down stream or went to the bottom, the German landing plans were disorganised, the German troops had their nerve shaken by a very unpleasant surprise, and all this was due to the confidence which the American soldiers had in their rifles. It gave them courage to come out under the shell fire which the German commanders believed would keep them in their rifle-pits, and the accuracy of their aim fully justified their confidence. Never was the value of musketry training more clearly proved than on this day.

At another point where the Germans did land, a point near the village of Mézy, American stubbornness robbed them of their advantage. One American platoon was annihilated on the river-bank. A German Grenadier regiment (the 6th) got ashore, and made for the railway line which runs parallel with the Marne. This Americans defended, firing into the Germans as they came on, and then meeting them with bayonets and grenades at close quarters. The Germans had

U.S. ENGINES FOR THE A.E.F.
Quintet of huge American locomotives brought across the Atlantic for military use on French railroads.

AMERICAN ENGINEERS BUSY IN FRANCE.
Locomotive engineers putting the finishing touches to a Baldwin engine. In circle: Construction company laying heavy timbers in a new dock at an American base port on the French coast.

to the Surmelin valley were attacked on both flanks. The orders they had were to hold their positions, and they had prepared for flank attack by making trenches. When the Germans came on the fire from these trenches broke their onslaught and, as they faltered, the Americans saw their opportunity and took it. They counter-attacked and drove them back. Thus the American Army did its share well in repulsing the last of the German offensives. Now it was to show what it could do in the way of taking the offensive itself.

Nearly a month earlier General Pershing had argued with Marshal Foch and M. Clemenceau in favour of a swift effort to pinch out the German salient in the country of the Marne and Vesle. The enemy's troops had pushed the point of it a little farther since then, and they were at this moment suffering from the depression caused by their failure to push it farther still. Marshal Foch now gave the word to strike back. Whether he calculated that this was to be the first of a series of blows which would not end until the enemy was obliged to ask for an **Divisions in line** armistice, it is impossible to tell. So it **with French** turned out. From July 18th the allied armies swept on from one success to another. But at that moment any prophecy of such a turning of the tables would have needed more than human foresight.

The 1st and 2nd American Divisions were given places in the line on either side of the French Division of Morocco. They had to get into their places quickly. The operation was planned in a hurry, and must be carried out in a hurry if the enemy was to be surprised. At times it seemed as if there would be a fresh illustration of the adage "More haste, less speed." The two divisions had to make their way through a forest, the Bois de Retz, where there are few roads, and these for the most part narrow and none too hard. In the black night, with a light rain falling, it was the easiest thing possible for units to be broken in pieces, for wrong turnings to be taken, for transport to become an inextricable tangle. Yet somehow, chiefly by doing what they had been taught to do in view of such an emergency, the American troops were all in the line when the "zero" hour came.

There were guides posted all through the forest to pass the traffic on. The 1st Division had arrived in good time. It was the 2nd which had to "step lively" in order not to be late. As each battalion, each ammunition column, each

the advantage in numbers, but as quickly as one lot of Americans was put out of action another took its place. Step by step the Germans were driven off the embankment, and then a fresh body of Americans drove at them in a counter-attack. This was too much for the enemy. There was the river behind him, and in front there seemed to be endless reinforcements of Americans, so he began to surrender. Between that railway embankment and the river four hundred prisoners were rounded up. They were all that remained of the 6th German Grenadiers.

But although the landing-party here was thus wiped out, and although at the outflow of the Surmelin no landing had been possible, yet at other points the enemy had got his troops across, and now the Americans holding the entrance

battery of guns plunged into the dark forest, they were entirely dependent upon the guides for instructions. Some of these were French, and there were hitches now and then because they could not make themselves understood. Commanding officers who had gone ahead returned to bustle their men on. How all the commands got into the line on time no one who was in that dark forest will ever quite understand. But they did it, and the fear that had weighed upon the French officers that there would be a break in the line when the advance began (for it could not be countermanded at that eleventh hour) was lifted. At 4.35 the gunners put down a rolling barrage, and behind it the infantry went forward, some of the 2nd Division still panting from their exertions to get there at the appointed hour.

Large haul of German prisoners The Germans were surprised, as the High Command had hoped they would be. The absence of any preparatory bombardment misled them. Before they realised that they were being attacked in force they had the French and Americans upon them. They surrendered with the new readiness which had come to them since the fibre of their Army had become weaker. Lieut.-Colonel Frederick Palmer told of a German officer prisoner who looked at the Americans swinging past him, and then looked at some of the men who had been captured with him, one a narrow-chested, studious-looking youth in spectacles, another a short, bow-legged man of forty-five. Then he said sadly: " I'd like to have had to-day the men who marched with me through Belgium four years ago. It wouldn't have been so easy for you. We have old men and boys now, and you are as fresh as we were in the beginning. You are too young, too lusty, too swift. We can't do it."

As a commentary upon that opinion, there was marched in that day a whole battalion of Germans who had been found in a quarry. There had been some firing from this quarry, and soldiers were seen rushing into a cave. A message was shouted at them : " Will you surrender, or shall we bomb you ? " In reply came a German carrying a note. It was from the officer commanding the battalion. He agreed to surrender, and out came some five hundred men, an agreeable surprise for the Americans, who had not expected more than a dozen or two.

But it must not be supposed that there was no hard fighting to be done in this drive towards Soissons. The German resistance stiffened, as it always did after an interval. There were some ravines in the way which gave them useful defensive positions. Both American divisions got most of their objectives, but they had some rough work at times, especially in the taking of the villages of Vierzy and Berzy-le-Sec. Some regiments suffered heavy losses. One had only fifteen hundred men left out of three thousand four hundred, and thirty-seven officers out of ninety-nine. For four days they kept at it, until some of them could look down on Soissons, and then, having well earned their rest, they were relieved on July 22nd.

Meanwhile the 3rd, 26th, and 28th American Divisions were engaged farther to the west, and were contributing usefully to the reduction of the Marne salient. Château-Thierry was the first prize which fell to them. Then they found a harder task before them. The villages of Trugny and Epieds had been strongly fortified. The Germans had been allowed four days in which to prepare defensive measures, and no American could appear in the open without attracting

VARIED VEHICLES IN THE ADVANCE.
Tank drawing a truck loaded with "push" bicycles going forward during the first day of the American offensive.

a storm of machine-gun bullets. Unfortunately, it was necessary to cross open ground in places. A few men got through the fire, one here and there, but losses were heavy. Some manœuvre had to be thought out. The solution of the difficulty was notably assisted by a motor machine-gun battalion. At full speed it dashed towards the enemy's " nests," and holding its position it replied to and finally smothered his fire. The two villages were taken on July 24th, and the first stage of the struggle for the salient came to an end.

The best testimonials to an army's fighting quality come from the enemy. A German report on this phase of the war, captured some time later, spoke highly of the " dash and intrepidity " of the American troops. " The moral effect of our fire was not able seriously

CAPTIVES OF AMERICA'S SWORD AND BOW.
German prisoners captured by American troops passing through a village in the St. Mihiel salient. This salient, interrupting French railway communications between Verdun and Nancy, was flattened out by the First American Army, September 12th, 1918, after the Germans had held it for four years.

FREIGHTED WITH JUBILATION.
The Lapland steaming into New York Harbour with the second draft of American troops repatriated after the victory.

By the beginning of August the resistance of the enemy had been for the moment broken. He was in retirement again until he could reshape his battered units and make another stand. In the pursuit the Americans joined with hearty zest. In an Army order issued by the French General Mangin, he wrote:

You went to the battle as to a fête. Your magnificent dash overthrew and startled the enemy; your indomitable tenacity stopped the counter-attack of his fresh divisions. You have shown yourselves worthy sons of your great country and won the admiration of your comrades in arms.

The next German stand began sooner than was expected. They did not attempt to hold the defensive line they had prepared south of the River Vesle. Here were found trenches carefully sited, gun emplacements, and concrete "pill-boxes," all new. The French and American pressure was too urgent to permit of their being used. The Germans crossed the Vesle and prepared to hold out against the pressure upon the wooded high banks of the river, rising steeply from the stream. This feature, coupled with the narrowness of the valley, gave them a marked advantage over the attacking troops. To begin with, they caught the advancing American columns which emerged from the valley of the Ardre in a costly trap. Misled by the speed of the enemy's retirement, these columns had forced the pace, believing themselves secure. Fismes, on the opposite side of the Vesle, gave no sign of life. It was supposed to have been deserted. In fact, it was full of machine-gunners, who were provided for a little while with a splendid target and took deadly advantage of it.

Soon, however, the Americans

to check the advance of their infantry. The nerves of the Americans are not yet shaken. . . . The quality of the men must be characterised as remarkable. They carry themselves well, and are well developed physically. Their spirit is fresh and full of naïve confidence. . . . The prisoners in general make a good impression. Their manner is alert. Their opinions have a certain moral basis." No warmer or more discriminating praise could have been hoped for by the American troops.

The next stage in the fight for the salient, so far as the Americans were concerned, was the taking of the hills above the Ourcq River and the carrying forward of the advance as far as the River Vesle. In these operations four more divisions, the 42nd, the 32nd, the 4th, and the 77th, took part along with those already mentioned. The heights of the Ourcq rise in long ascents from the usually tiny river, and there is very little cover to be found upon them. Every farm was a fortress. Batteries skilfully placed swept the open ground with shells. The only way to reduce the farm-fortresses was patiently to outflank them or to creep up and rush them in the early morning when the defenders' watchfulness was at its lowest. This way was necessarily slow, but it had the advantage of being sure. One by one these obstacles were removed. One by one the woods which barred the advance were cleared of the enemy. In a night attack by the Germans on Grimpettes Wood the young and hitherto untried troops of the 32nd Division showed that their training had been of the right kind. They yielded not a yard of ground.

A TERROR TO U BOATS.
U.S. destroyer Warmington, dazzle-painted for war service as convoy to the great fleet of transports that brought the American troops over the Atlantic.

U.S. WARSHIPS THAT RENDERED VALUABLE SERVICE.
Two American battleships that assisted in escorting to Europe the two million men of the American National Army, who were in France when the war ended. In oval: U.S. destroyer Shaw, dazzle-painted for service with the Grand Fleet in British waters.

were across the river. Their engineers built two double trestle bridges out of wood cut down under fire, and the troops got to the bottom of the hills which slope to the bank. Here they were better off, but not much. Above them, out of sight among the trees, were the Germans with a clear field of fire. The lower hillsides were largely bare, and to storm a way up them meant exposing oneself almost in the open to a storm of shell and the streams of bullets that the concealed machine-gunners poured upon any attempted advance. So for a few weeks the front in this sector was stabilised. The only hope seemed to lie in getting round the impregnable German position.

At times the enemy tried to drive the Americans back across the river. Towards the end of August a tannery west of Fismes was captured. Its

AMERICAN TROPHIES OF THE ALLIES' NAVAL TRIUMPH.
Some of the German submarines that were allotted to the United States as part of her spoils of war awaiting conduct across the Atlantic after being overhauled, cleaned, and repainted.

PIRATE VESSELS IN SAFE CUSTODY.
American sailor giving a coat of paint to the gun on a German submarine. In circle: "Old Glory" flying above the conning-tower of the Hun pirate ship UC97.

activity as a fortress had become too costly to be tolerated. The Germans were driven out. But they came back almost immediately, with a fierce counter-attack in considerable force. Their centre pushed through to the river and halted there, very pleased with itself for having reached its objective. But it discovered in a short time that both its right and its left flank were "in the air." On either side were Americans, also in the rear. The German troops were captured, grumbling loudly about their comrades' failure to get through. On each flank the German thrust had been parried by American steadiness and grit. It was September before the allied forces obliged the Germans to retire once more. There was more heavy fighting for the Americans on the Aisne before the enemy was yet again dislodged **Flattening out the** and pushed back to the Chemin des Dames. **St. Mihiel salient** About the same time other American divisions were doing good service north of Soissons, where, after three days' severe combat, they captured Juvigny, another name which will shine in American military history.

Now the time had come for a fresh unfolding of United States plans. American troops were, for the first time, to take the field as an Army under its own commander with its own army corps, as well as its own divisional Staffs. The assembly of this new force took place in Lorraine, which was henceforth to be the chief scene of American effort. There were American troops with British troops in the north of France and Flanders. There was a battalion on the Italian front that took part in the offensive which crumpled up the last of the Austrian strength. There were still some left to aid in driving the enemy northward through Noyon, Laon, and St. Quentin. But the bulk of the American forces was now in Lorraine.

For nearly a month they enjoyed the repose which they had well earned. It was not until September 12th that they made their reappearance, and by a rapid, well-planned coup flattened out another salient, the salient of St. Mihiel. Ever since the autumn of 1914 this swelling in the German line in Lorraine had stubbornly resisted treatment. It was not now of much practical value, but the Germans held on to it as if it were an integral part of their defensive system. It is true that it interrupted the railway from Verdun to

ARMED U.S. MOTOR-LAUNCH ON PATROL DUTY.
American motor-launch, armed with a machine-gun, on patrol on the section of the Rhine occupied by the U.S. troops. This extended from Bonn upstream to a point below Bingen.

Nancy. In 1916 it had supported the movement against Verdun. It was a difficulty in the way of any allied attack in Lorraine. But the usefulness of it to the enemy at this period was small, and it was improbable that he would think twice about yielding to a vigorous push.

This push General Pershing gave him on September 12th. Seven divisions were lined up for the operation—the 1st, 2nd, 5th, 42nd, 82nd, 89th, and 90th. If there had been resistance they would certainly have overborne it. But the threat alone sufficed. The Germans gave up the salient which they had held so long and fortified so powerfully. They retired without attempting even to delay the attacking force. The first piece of work which the American Army had been given to do, as an Army self-contained, was a complete success. The Germans claimed that they retreated according to plan. But they did not make that plan willingly. They made it because they knew they could not withstand the vigour of the American thrust.

Congratulations from King George King George expressed what the British people felt when he cabled on this occasion to President Wilson, congratulating him upon this "brilliant achievement," and adding :

The far-reaching results secured by these successful operations, which have marked the active intervention of the American Army on a great scale under its own administrations, are the happiest augury for the complete and, I hope, not far distant triumph of the allied cause.

Sir Douglas Haig, at the same time, assured General Pershing that "all ranks of the British armies in France welcome with unbounded admiration and pleasure the victory which has attended the initial offensive of the great American Army under your personal leadership."

After this good beginning there was a pause. Then on September 26th began the main task of the American troops on the western front. When, more than a month earlier it had been announced that the First American Army had been formed, it was known to consist of twenty-one divisions, seven of which had never yet been in an active sector. It numbered, therefore—since the American division is so much larger than the British, or indeed any other—some 750,000 men. What these divisions had now to do was to push through the thick Argonne Forest and then to force the

enemy back steadily, giving him as little time as possible to pull himself together, until they had got to the railway which ran along behind the German front and which was the enemy's main line of communication.

This was an ambitious programme. It was clear that it would test both the generalship and the endurance of the Army. It would have tested an army composed entirely of seasoned troops. If here and there errors were made, if some of the hopes based upon the final operations of the war were not fulfilled, every allowance must be made. That the Americans accomplished so much, and did eventually get to the Sedan-Montmédy line of railway, reflected immense credit upon them. This credit Marshal Foch gave them without stint. They played a great part in bringing the war to an end.

When the offensive began, on September 26th, they were holding a

AT THE CONFLUENCE OF THE RIVERS.
U.S. military policeman with a German policeman guarding the old Moselle Bridge at Coblenz. The bridge was erected in 1344 by the Elector Baldwin, was restored in 1440, and widened in 1884.

line from the Argonne Forest to the Meuse at Verdun. Their first severe fighting was round Montfaucon. This town lies at the junction of six cross-roads, and from it good views are obtained down the neighbouring valleys. By a persevering movement which eventually got round the German flanks the Americans surrounded Montfaucon and so made it theirs.

Their first impetus carried them through the Hindenburg line. Now they were between it and the Kriemhilde line, which the Germans meant to defend with all their might. They put in some of their best troops with orders to fight to the last man. But with "Lusitania" as their battle-cry the Americans pushed steadily on. At Vauquois they encountered a Prussian Guard division. They drove it thence, and it made a further stand at Varennes. But it had to yield that up as well.

The struggle became tougher as the Germans brought up reinforcements, and the conditions were made harder by rain and mud. The German counter-attacks were fierce and stubborn, but the Americans were never in a mood to give up any of the ground they had won. If they lost it for the moment they always returned to the charge and rewon it. By the end of the first week of October they were facing the main German position, which ran just below the crest of the ridge between the Argonne Forest and the Meuse. They looked up to steep hillsides scarred with trenches and defended by masses of barbed-wire hidden cunningly among the undergrowth. Up those steep hills they must fight their way, and then up other hills, all wooded, all bristling with machine-guns, until they could win their way down to the Meuse.

The taking of the Côte de Châtillon may serve to illustrate each and all of these encounters. This height ran up to 820 feet. On the summit was a machine-gun fortress and a field-gun. On the way up the trees were all wired together. It was impossible to cut these barriers without coming under a hot fire. For forty hours American soldiers crawled slowly towards the top, all day and all night. They even dragged up Stokes mortars and bombarded the German position so vigorously that some less stout-hearted men surrendered. But most of the enemy kept up the resistance to the end, which only came when the stormers had broken through all the wire and swarmed up to the fortress with bayonets fixed.

In the wooded country it was easy to lose oneself, as one detachment of five hundred found, which was "lost"

for five days. They had pushed ahead, and when darkness came on were separated from the neighbouring detachments. Instead of trying to grope their way back so as to re-establish connection, they stayed where they were in a half-ruined mill on a high road running east and west. In the morning they saw that they had Germans all round them. They had overrun the enemy's trenches, but he had got back into them, and now cut the five hundred off from the rest of the American forces.

But, surrounded as they were, they had no thought of surrender. The officer in command was a New York lawyer, Major Whittlesey. He said afterwards, "We just stuck. So far as we were concerned the Germans could go to hell." When the Americans ran out of food they chewed leaves. When

the wounded seemed likely to die of cold, those who were whole lent them greatcoats and kept them warm. Many men wrote last letters to their families in anticipation of death. But in the end they neither died nor were captured. They held their mill until their comrades renewed the attack and came sweeping past them, restoring to them the freedom of which nearly all had begun to despair.

In the second week of October a breach was made in the Kriemhilde line, and the Argonne Forest was captured south of Grand Pré. A few days after this Grand Pré itself fell to a dashing attack without artillery preparation, the troops wading the Aire River to get at the town. It took some little time to drive the enemy out of the whole of the Kriemhilde line, and, when this was accomplished, news came of a fresh obstacle being prepared, another defensive line called the Freya. The Germans were now fighting resolutely and seemed to have plenty of troops. They made some heavy counter-attacks towards the end of October. The line swayed to and fro. One day the enemy would gain some ground back, next day it would be won again by the Americans.

On balance the Americans had much the best of it, however, and by the beginning of November they were within five miles of Stenay, one of the gaps **The Second** which had to be closed if the German armies **American Army** were to be treated as they treated the French Army in 1870 at Sedan. This gap was not completely closed, as Marshal Foch meant it to be, and it was only just before the armistice that the Americans entered Sedan and cut the railway, or rather made the Germans cut it themselves by blowing up a bridge as they retired. By this time there had for nearly a month been a Second American Army in the field, but its staff-work was not comparable with that of the First Army. There was some criticism of General Pershing for attempting to form the Second before he had enough trained Staff officers. The transport of the new force was not handled with the same skill and sureness as characterised this branch of the Service under the Staff officers of the First Army. The part assigned to the American troops would have been carried out with even more brilliance if another army like the First could have been organised. But even admitting the defects of the Second, its appearance must be counted as having hastened the end by proving to the Germans, and especially to the German people, that nothing could save them from being swamped by the American flood.

The crossing of the Meuse at Sedan was a very fine piece

PROUD SYMBOLS OF AMERICA'S VICTORIOUS POWER.
The American colours being borne into Coblenz at the head of the troops arriving in that town to take possession of the American zone of occupation in the Rhineland. In circle: American troops on guard on the Ludendorff Bridge across the river.

THE BRIDGE OF BOATS ACROSS THE RHINE AT COBLENZ.
The famous Schiffbrücke, which connects Coblenz with Thal-Ehrenbreitstein on the right bank of the Rhine, opened to allow boats to pass. This bridge, about four hundred yards in length, is a favourite promenade of the townspeople in the morning and evening.

allied effort as a whole. They rose very quickly to the needs of the situation in Europe, especially the food situation, with good will. As soon as it was known that wheat was urgently needed to save people in Britain from discomfort, and people in France and Italy from famine, the most eager readiness was shown to send wheat to them. Wheatless days were at once ordered. Meat was eaten in smaller quantities so that supplies might be shipped for the American troops and the allied populations.

Many men over military age offered their energies to the State and worked in some department of administration for merely nominal pay. Many advanced in years went back to office drudgery in order to release younger men. For the Y.M.C.A., which undertook the supply of food and clothing parcels to the troops as well as the provision of huts in the war zone and wherever the soldiers needed them, the sum of £7,000,000 was raised in a fortnight. The American Red Cross Society secured ten million new members at a dollar apiece, within seven days. Taxes advanced the cost of the necessaries and the pleasures of life. There was a railway-ticket tax, a telephone-call tax, a tax on club subscriptions, a tax on luggage delivered by "express" from railway-stations.

of work, of which the recital may fitly conclude the story of the great battle in which the Americans contributed so large a share to the attainment of the common victory. The river had been dammed by the enemy and spread out hundreds of yards in width. Bridge after bridge was thrown across the deep channel, only to be wrecked by German shell fire. This method was evidently useless, so volunteers were called for to swim the river. Over they went amid bullets flicking the water and shells sending splinters among them. When they got across they had steep banks to climb. They clawed their way up these with grappling-irons, and in the face of a fierce fire held their ground, made some kind of positions, and were so rapidly increased in number by fresh arrivals that the Germans felt resistance was hopeless and retired. Behind these stout pioneers bridges were hastily thrown over the river and the main body of Americans marched across.

"Nothing after this," to quote General Pershing's despatch to the American Government, "nothing but surrender or armistice could save the enemy's army, when we had cut its lines of communication, from complete disaster." A few days later the armistice had been signed. General Pershing paid a warm tribute to the qualities displayed by the officers and soldiers of the line. "When I think of their heroism, their patience under hardships, their unflinching spirit in offensive action, I am filled with emotion which I am unable to express. Their deeds are immortal, and they have earned the eternal gratitude of our country."

Something remains to be said of the way in which the Americans who stayed at home contributed to the success, not alone of the American arms but of the

Stamps cost more as in Britain, so did all drinks, so did tobacco, so did seats at all entertainments. There seemed to be no limit to the amount of money that could be extracted from American pockets. The people at home supported with all their might the troops at the front, and by their united efforts the end was brought nearer. To the entire American people must be given the credit for America's share in the victory.

CLASSIC GROUND IN MILITARY HISTORY.
American troops marching into Coblenz across the Bridge of Boats. Near this point is the Fortress of Ehrenbreitstein, a very important point in the defences of the bridge-head of Coblenz, which the Germans surrendered into the control of the Allies under the terms of the armistice.

PRESIDENT WILSON

CHAPTER CCXCVII.

ARRIVING AT BREST.

PRESIDENT WILSON'S VISIT TO EUROPE.

By Edward Wright.

Triumph of Republicans in New Congress—Americans Refuse to Answer President's Personal Appeal—Wilson Surprises his Opponents by Travelling to Europe and Governing by Cablegram—Welcome of Gratitude in Paris—Clemenceau Explains his Disagreements with Fourteen-Point Peace Programme—American Leader Makes Democratic Appeal in " Times " Interview—Historic Scene in London on Boxing Day—Moral Partnership of English-Speaking Nations—" The Day Our Son Came Home "—President Wilson's Speech in Buckingham Palace—British General Election and Vote for War Indemnity—American Scheme for Overwhelming Navy—American Republicans Veer in Opinion on League of Nations—President's Address to Free Churchmen in the Congregational Chapel at Carlisle—Progress through Manchester—United States Refuses to Form any Balance of Power—Roses and Thorns in Popular Welcome at Rome—Early Difficulties over Fiume and Dalmatia—United States President and Italian Socialists—Peace Conference Opens with Serious and Delicate Problems that Delay Settlement for Months.

IN the first week of November, 1918, when the American Army was making its rapid advance towards Sedan and the British forces were closing on Maubeuge and Mons, a remarkable change occurred in the Government of the United States. The Republican Party was returned to power, with a working majority in the House of Representatives and a light balance in the Senate. The Democratic President was therefore likely to find himself in an awkward position in a Congress of victorious opponents.

The election largely turned upon the policy of making peace with Germany. The enemy Government was at the time proposing a settlement on the early programme of the fourteen points formulated by President Wilson. The American people, however, agitated for the war to be pursued until unconditional surrender was offered by the Germans. During the election the Republicans as a whole made the policy of unconditional surrender the principal feature of their programme, and by an extraordinary change of mind the Western States, which in 1916 had been averse to war, became more bent on reducing Germany to surrender without terms than were the Eastern States.

President Wilson issued a personal appeal to the country to return his own Democratic Party to power. " If you have approved of my leadership," he wrote in his address, " and wish me to continue as your unembarrassed spokesman in affairs at home and abroad, I earnestly beg that you will express yourself unmistakably to that effect by returning a Democratic majority to both the Senate and the House of Representatives."

A SCULPTOR'S IMPRESSION.
Bust of President Wilson, by Mr. John Davidson. This presentment of the Chief Magistrate of the United States was regarded by experts as wonderfully lifelike.

Apparently the American people did not altogether approve of their President's leadership. They made him, rather, their embarrassed spokesman by putting into power some two hundred and thirty-nine Republicans against one hundred and ninety-four Democrats, so that in the course of four months all treaties would have to pass a Congress hostile to the President. The fear that President Wilson, by reason of his idealistic views, might bring American influence to bear upon France, Great Britain, and Italy, and make a lenient settlement with the Teutons, was undoubtedly one of the general motives that led the American nation to begin " swapping horses when crossing the stream." It was against the tradition of the country to weaken a Government conducting a great war. Yet if President Wilson had also been standing for re-election against Colonel Roosevelt, he would probably have gone down too with the majority of his Representatives and Senators. More than a million votes were cast against his party after his strong personal appeal to the electorate.

This deep and widespread change in the Government of the United States had a considerable effect upon the negotiations which the Germans were conducting in the first week of November, 1918. It looked as though their military disasters might be completed by a political disaster, leaving them without any of the fourteen planks of the Wilsonian programme to cling to during the peace settlement. Hundreds of thousands of letters from American troops in action to their people at home had enlightened the Americans as to the character of their foe, so that they had become sterner in their view of all the German

FRANCO-AMERICAN FRIENDSHIP BOUND ANEW.
President Wilson addressing the French Chamber of Deputies on February 3rd, 1919.   The three figures
standing beneath the Tribune are (left to right) M. Dubost (President of the Senate), President Poincaré,
and M. Clemenceau, who are seen applauding the spokesman of the Great Republic of the West.

United States, especially in war time, was a man with many of the powers of a dictator. He was a Prime Minister and also a temporary monarch. The founders of the American Commonwealth had been alert to all the disadvantages of lack of unified control during war, and had therefore made the position of their President stronger than was that of the British King in the eighteenth century.

In the actual exercise of power Mr. Lloyd George, M. Clemenceau, and Signor Orlando could not compare with the President of the United States. He had more resemblance to the Lord Protector of England during the age of Cromwell than to any other modern leader of a democratic State. During the interval between the passing of his Democratic Congress and the session of the hostile Republican Congress, President Wilson was in actual effect a dictator. His Cabinet had been selected by him somewhat in the manner that a Commander-in-Chief chooses his Staff, and most of his secretaries were simply executants of his policy. The makers of the American Constitution had so arranged it that a United States President, with his own party in power, was equal to any potentate and much superior to any Premier.

The personal weight that President Wilson brought to the Peace Conference was thus tremendous. He had behind him also all the fluctuant, uncrystallised, popular sentiment regarding the proposed League of Nations. Pacifists and sentimentalists, who wished to cure the Germans by kindness, found themselves in agreement with Radicals of the commercial school, and Socialists joined with many Conservatives in the endeavour to find in the League a means of preventing future war. As the grand advocate of the League of Nations, Mr. Wilson sailed for Europe, and there received a general welcome that seemed to promise him an increase of prestige more than compensating for his loss of authority in his own country.

tribes, and less inclined to attribute the atrocious quality of the struggle merely to the German Emperor and his military and naval chiefs. The Teutons were acutely aware of the great change in American opinion. They accelerated the negotiations for an armistice in the hope of completing the Peace Treaty before a Republican Congress could win the power of refusing to sanction arrangements made by its Democratic President.

President Wilson did not accept the defeat that had been inflicted upon him. He had always been a most masterful man throughout both his academic and his political career. He rather joyed in fighting than avoided it, as he had shown during his struggles with the "bosses" of his own party. In the second week in November, when everything seemed to be against him, he surprised and disconcerted the triumphant Republicans by arranging to attend in person the Peace Conference in France.

This was contrary to American tradition and inconvenient in practice. Loud was the outcry in America when the President resolved to travel to Europe and to govern his own country by cablegram. Some Senators tried to arrange to send across the Atlantic a special committee to watch developments in the negotiations for peace, but this attempt at interference was defeated. The Chief Magistrate of the

Escorted by ten American battleships and thirty destroyers, with British and French warships in attendance, President Wilson and his suite arrived at Brest in a German steamer named the George Washington. Met by the French Minister for Foreign Affairs, M. Pichon, and the American Commander-in-Chief, President Wilson, with his Secretary of State, Mr. Robert Lansing, entrained for Paris, where he was greeted with multitudinous acclaim. **President Wilson** Waving, roaring crowds filled the avenues **arrives in France** and open spaces on the way to the Murat Hotel, at which the President stayed, and the Elysée, where a banquet was given in his honour. The winning smile of the great American, his fresh-coloured, radiant face, so unlike the ascetic visage represented by photographers, evoked an intense personal cordiality from the Parisian people. There was little special political significance in the triumphing progress of the guest of France.

With the exception of the French Socialists, there was no important French party with any great enthusiasm for a Society of Nations that Germany might enter. It was in simple, passionate gratitude for American help that the French people gave the American President so wonderful a welcome that he said it was a unique and inspiring experience in his life. Amid the popular excitement there was some political manœuvring. When landing at Brest, President Wilson made it understood that he would fight, if necessary, for his fourteen points, and that his view on the question of the freedom of the seas was governed by the idea that the entire world should be the guardian of the ocean routes of commerce. Furthermore, he supported the naval programme for making the American Fleet at least as strong as the British Fleet, and held that all nations would have to make sacrifices to obtain relief from war.

"We must have a secure peace," said M. Poincaré, as he toasted the American President at the Elysée. France, as a whole, was in no mood of idealism. She wanted only guarantees against another attack by the Teutons, with reparation for the wasting of her life and power. M. Clemenceau frankly informed President Wilson that, if the American doctrine regarding the freedom of the seas would restrict the maritime power of the British Empire, France would not agree to the point. British sea-power had become one of the guarantees of peace for France.

President and Premier contrasted Both M. Clemenceau and President Wilson were men of a militant temperament, and they differed considerably in their points of view. The French Premier was a sceptic, who regarded human nature with little trust in its native goodness. The American President was a man of religious principle, educated in a belief in cataclysmal conversions, and inclined at first to place faith in the German Revolutionary Government. In these circumstances M. Clemenceau would readily accept only so much of the plan for a League of

Nations as would serve as the ornamental superstructure for a permanent alliance between the victorious nations. If, in course of time, the superstructure became useful as well as ornamental, so much the better in the French view, but the main foundations had first to be laid by "neither children nor gods, but men in a world of men."

M. Clemenceau's frank account of his first interview with the President of the United States was given in the Chamber of Deputies :

First interview with Clemenceau

I had made up my mind not to question him but to let him talk. President Wilson did talk. He explained his views, his reasons for them, and his plans for applying them. I should not be telling the truth if I said I was in agreement with him on all points. America is far away from Germany, while France is very near, and I have things to think of which do not touch him as they do a man who for four years has seen the Germans in his own country. There are a thousand injustices to be righted. I do not think we shall get them all righted, but we shall try. President Wilson said to me, "I am trying to convince you, but perhaps you will convince me." The question of the freedom of the seas was reserved for future discussion, but President Wilson talked with me on the subject. I said to him that the question was a difficult one, and related to President Wilson a conversation which I had had previously with Mr. Lloyd George. The latter had one day asked me, "Do you realise that without the British Fleet you would have been unable to go on with the war ?" I replied, "Yes." Mr. Lloyd George then asked, "Are you disposed to do something which would make it impossible for us to do the same again ? " and I replied that I was not. Would you have preferred me not to say to President Wilson, "I will not be ungrateful to Great Britain "? In any case, Mr. Wilson replied, "I approve what you said to Mr. Lloyd George. What I have to submit to the Allied Governments will change nothing in your replies to Mr. Lloyd George. Each one will retain his freedom." That

ACCLAIMING CROWDS IN THE PLACE DE LA CONCORDE.

After his arrival in France, on December 13th, 1918, President Wilson, accompanied by Mrs. Wilson, proceeded to Paris, where he was the guest of the President of the Republic. M. Poincaré met him at the railway-station, a procession was formed, and Paris gave its distinguished guest a stirring welcome. The demonstrations of the populace were particularly conspicuous as Presidents Wilson and Poincaré drove along the famous Place de la Concorde.

WITH THE U.S. TROOPS IN FRANCE.
President Wilson watching a march-past of soldiers of the " Liberty " Army in France. This stirring scene took place on Christmas Day, 1918.

is how there began in those conversations the first pourparlers which must now lead to laborious negotiations that may have the most serious consequences, for if we do not arrive at an agreement our victory will have been in vain and terrible disasters will soon be again upon us. It is impossible to build a new edifice with the old stones on the old architectural methods. You want to introduce a new spirit into the old diplomacy. I am with you.

It was, perhaps, when comparing the tremendous reception he received in the streets with the friendly reservations he encountered in political discussions that the President began to think that the people were with him, even when statesmen differed from him. He was certain that he was the complete representative of his own people. " I know what they have thought," he said at the Hôtel de Ville, where the freedom of Paris was conferred upon him. " I know what they have desired, and when I have spoken what I know was in their minds it has been delightful to see how the consciences and purposes of free men everywhere responded. You have made me realise to the utmost the intimate community of thought and ideal which characterises your people and the great nation which I have the honour for the time to represent."

Again, in a speech at the Sorbonne, where he received the degree of doctor, the President advocated his scheme for a League of Nations, operating throughout the world as the organised moral force of men turning the searchlight of conscience upon all wrong and aggression. Amid the firework display of compliments and cheering crowds the American President felt the influence of the realistic spirit in which war-worn, wasted France approached the problem of peace that should allow her to recover strength in security. He decided to visit England at a much earlier date than had been contemplated, and the British Prime Minister cancelled his plan for a meeting in Paris and awaited the President in London, to hold there the conversations preliminary to the Peace Conference.

Mr. Wilson recognised that his scheme for using the money due to his country from Great Britain for construction of an incomparably more powerful Fleet than the British was scarcely regarded as an act of pure friendliness by the British nation. The fact that his naval plan was only intended to be fully carried out if the scheme for a League of Nations failed did not make it appear more amicable. As explained by Mr. Josephus Daniels, the American Secretary of the Navy, and by American publicity agents, the American naval programme at times appeared to be a whip for driving the British Commonwealth the way in which Mr. Wilson

Advocating the League of Nations

wished it to go. In the United States, Colonel Roosevelt denounced the construction of what he called "a spite Navy," and many of the organs of opinion of the Republican Party agitated for the new Congress to refuse funds for the Wilsonian programme "for the creation of the greatest Navy in the world."

President Wilson did not visit the British people with an open threat in one hand and the offer of friendly co-operation in the other. He prepared the way by breaking another Presidential tradition and giving an interview to the Paris correspondent of the "Times," on December 18th, 1918. His admitted aim was to appeal directly to the people through the democratic agency of the Press before working through the formal channels of diplomacy. Maybe his new position in

THE HAPPY WILSON SMILE.
The President of the United States driving in an open carriage with President Poincaré. He was much moved by the warmth of his public reception in the capital of the French Republic.

his own country led him to prefer a popular method of address.

With regard to the problems involved in his view of the freedom of the seas, Mr. Wilson said :

I am glad to say that I am hoping to visit England very shortly. I am the more anxious to go because I have reason to know with what unanimity and with what passionate conviction the people of Great Britain and America have entertained the same conception of liberty and justice. It is essential to the future peace of the world that there should be the frankest possible co-operation and the most generous understanding between the two English-speaking democracies. We comprehend and appreciate, I believe, the grave problems which the war has brought to the British people, and fully understand the special international questions which arise from the fact of your position as an Island Empire.

With reference to the problems of the Peace Conference, the President stated :

There is no master-mind that can settle the problems of to-day. If there is anybody who thinks that he knows what is in the mind of all the peoples, that man is a fool. We've all got to put our heads together and pool everything we've got for the benefit of the ideals that are common to us all. . . . It will be my privilege, I hope, in the near future, not only to confer with the allied statesmen in France but also to visit the allied countries, and there learn by personal contact as much as I can of the general sentiments with regard to the chief problems involved.

WOODROW WILSON, PRESIDENT OF THE UNITED STATES THROUGHOUT THE GREAT WAR

After spending Christmas with some of the American forces in France, Mr. Wilson landed in England on December 26th, 1918, and met with a magnificent popular reception from Dover Pier to Buckingham Palace. Having a general holiday, the English people gathered in such crowds as had not been seen since the crowning of their King. Inspired by genuine affection towards the Chief Magistrate of the great kindred nation, and by the happiness of the first festival since the cessation of hostilities, they marked the historic event of the arrival of an American President at the British Court by a conclamation of thrilling intensity.

There was no doubt that the visit of President Wilson was hailed as the grand symbol of the refraternisation of the English-speaking races. To many it seemed the greatest event of the war, exceeding in importance the defeat of the Central Empires. There were men in the United States, as well as in the British Isles, who took the view that the welding of the English-speaking world in the furnace of battle brought larger promise for man than any occurrence since the birth of Christ.

Welding of English-speaking world

In the expression of general joy there seemed to be little popular thought about the League of Nations or any other machinery of co-operation. There was sufficient in which to rejoice in the mere fact of the coming together of the English-speaking democracies, as represented by the spectacle of the descendant of King George III. and the successor of General Washington driving side by side in a progress of friendship through a London fluttering with colours and thundering with saluting guns and cheering multitudes.

Popular feeling in London was deeper than it had been in Paris. Parisians had to be reminded by their Press of the achievements of the Royal forces of France in the American Revolution. For the French had had so many adventures since the eighteenth century that they were surprised at the long memories of the Americans. They scarcely recollected that their own Revolution had been directly inspired by the American example. The British, on the other hand, had long memories, perhaps for the same reason that their history on the whole had run without a serious break since the disruption of the first English-speaking Commonwealth.

HIS MOTHER'S GIRLHOOD HOME.
The house in Warwick Road, Carlisle, where President Wilson's grandfather, the Rev. Thomas Woodrow, lived, and where the President's mother was born.

ANOTHER LINK WITH THE PAST.
The church at Carlisle where the President's maternal grandfather taught in the Sunday School. A veteran scholar met President Wilson on his visit, December 29th, 1918.

The actual blood relationship between Great Britain and the United States had weakened considerably since the last of their wars. America had become rather a melting-pot for the whole of Europe than an enlarged British plantation. After absorbing a very considerable part of the most adventurous men of Teutonic stock, it had lately taken on a new Latin colour by a great Italian migration. Yet forces more powerful and more permanent than consanguinity united the two branches of the English-speaking peoples. They differed profoundly in social structure, but so did the Mother Country and her more democratic daughter States.

The Canadians were being swayed by American influence in their refusal to allow the creation of a Canadian nobility, and the Australians were of the same way of thinking. The Americans had, indeed, remained moral partners in an English-speaking world by reason of the binding strength which common language, common law, common creeds, and practically common culture acquired by the marvellous development of electric-power and steam-power means of communication.

Their inventors had remedied the mistakes of their statesmen. They had a facility for understanding each other which did not obtain in intercourse with other nations, and their parallel systems of development, continually brought into closer communication by modern inventions, led them to think the same thoughts about the fundamental things in life, and, quickly or slowly, come to similar conclusions. While growing apart, the British had fostered equality and the Americans had fostered freedom, and so to a very considerable extent had completed each other. Hostile elements in the United States, such as the purely German party and the Fenian Sinn-Fein organisations more or less allied with the Teutons, served for a time as a rallying force for every possible kind of criticism of the new understanding, yet lacked sufficient strength to bring about another divorce between the English-speaking peoples.

Equality and freedom fostered

No formal alliance was necessary or practicable. Something finer and more intimate than an alliance had been created in the slow growth of a wonderful century. There was room left for rivalry in all directions, from fiercely competitive trade and concession-hunting down to contests in sports. It was

TANGIBLE EVIDENCE OF VICTORY.
One of the powerful German guns captured by the British and placed in front of Buckingham Palace. The Stars and Stripes and Union Jack flew side by side on the occasion of President Wilson's stay at the Palace.

just possible even for the two great friendly Common-wealths to play against each other with gunpowder in the matter of fleet-building, as President Wilson and Mr. Josephus Daniels apparently intended to do, if the Republican Congress agreed to vote the huge funds demanded. Great Britain had lost her superiority in money-power, and had become the debtor instead of the creditor of the United States, and her Mercantile Marine was temporarily crippled both by great war losses and by diversion of building-yards to purely naval work.

Coming late into the war, with an annual wealth in crops rising in 1918 to the amount of two thousand eight hundred million pounds a year, the Americans generally had more than balanced their military expenditure by their profits in commerce. When the armistice was signed their loss in man-power was less than that of Belgium, and in money, manufacturing, and food power they dominated the world.

Yet there had likewise been a remarkable increase in the general productiveness of the British Empire and its depen-dencies. Although the additional vital strength of the Briton was temporarily veiled by many difficulties which could **Increase in** not be removed until the period of recon-**productiveness** struction, he was, in spite of terrible loss of life, falling birth-rate, impoverishing taxes, and high cost of living, stronger than was his ancestor at the close of the Napoleonic Wars. American and Briton, with Canadian, Australian, New Zealander, and South African, and the vast amount of raw and finished material they handled, could maintain the peace of the world.

This was the one practical reality in the scheme for a League of Nations. In a working agreement with other countries of the Grand Alliance the English-speaking peoples could control a large part of the material of civilised life by a combination of shipping power and export power. The sense of the combination of victorious power, represented by the

persons of the American President and the British King, was one of the things that inspired the people of London in their resonant exultation on Boxing Day, 1918. They rejoiced as the Judeans might have done had the lost tribes of Israel come back to them, clothed in magnificent power and universal glory, to help in establishing the kingdom of God.

President Wilson felt the wonderful influence of spirit about him as he moved within the capital of the kingdom from which his ancestors had sprung. At the banquet at Buckingham Palace, given in his honour, he said:

There is a great tide running in the hearts of men. The hearts of men have never beaten so singularly in unison before. Men have never been before so conscious **Consciousness** of their brotherhood. Men have never before **of brotherhood** realised how little difference there was between right and justice in one latitude and in another, under one sovereignty and under another. And it will be our high privilege, I believe, not only to apply the moral judgment of the world to the particular settlements which we shall attempt, but also to organise the moral force of the world to preserve those settlements, to steady the forces of mankind, and to make the right and the justice, to which great nations like our own have devoted themselves, the predominant and controlling forces of the world. There is something inspiriting in knowing that this is the errand we have come on. Nothing less than this would have justified me in leaving the important tasks which fall upon me on the other side of the sea—nothing but the consciousness that nothing else compares with this in dignity and importance. Therefore, it is the more delightful to find myself in the company of a body of men united in ideal and in purpose, and to feel that I am privileged to unite my thought with yours in carrying forward those standards which we are so proud to hold high and to defend.

There was a long conference between President Wilson and Mr. Lloyd George before the State banquet. It was the first time the leaders of the two nations had met, and it was reported that they found they had many interests and ideas in common, and that their differences of opinion seemed to be few and unimportant. It was partly this confirmation of similarity between British and American

AT BUCKINGHAM PALACE: JUST BEFORE THE PRESIDENT'S DEPARTURE FROM ENGLAND.

After a stay of five days in England, President Wilson left London on December 31st, 1918, for Paris and Rome. On the previous night the King and Queen gave a dinner-party in his honour. Our photograph was taken just before the President's departure from Buckingham Palace, and shows (left to right) Mrs. Wilson, the Queen, President Wilson, the King, and Princess Mary, who accompanied the Presidential party to Victoria railway-station. Prior to the departure it was understood that the most cordial messages were privately exchanged between the King and the President.

views that moved President Wilson to speak of the moral tide in the hearts of men, but largely it was the speaker's feeling of the passionate friendship of the British people towards himself as the representative of the American people that made it appear that the world was entering on a new age. That is to say, there was perhaps more intensity in the general welcome and less of universal scope than the President from his high idealistic standpoint estimated. World politics at the time had little interest for the multitudes of Londoners and for the American soldiers who mingled with them. It was the festival of Atlantic union that they held under the clear winter sky, with the streets a riot of colour and the air vibrant with enthusiasm.

Cheered on his way from Buckingham Palace to the Guildhall on December 28th, 1918, President Wilson refused to take the cheers as a personal welcome. In his speech in the City he said :

I heard the voice of one people speaking to another people. There was the deep gratefulness that fighting was over. There was pride that the fighting had such a culmination, and there was there that thought of gratitude that the nations engaged should have produced such men as the soldiers of Great Britain and of the United States, of France, and of Italy. But there was something more in it—the consciousness that the business is not yet done. There was the consciousness that it now rests upon others to see that those lives were not lost in vain.

I have not yet been to the actual battlefields, but I have been with many of the men who have fought the battles. And as I have conversed with the soldiers I have been more and more aware that they fought for something that not all of them had defined, but which all of them recognised the moment you stated it to them. They fought to do away with an old order and establish a new one. And the centre and characteristic of the old order was that unstable thing

THE PRESIDENT'S VISIT TO THE CITY OF LONDON.
Cheered on the journey by enthusiastic crowds, President Wilson, accompanied by Mrs. Wilson, was on December 28th, 1918, his sixty-second birthday, the guest of the City of London, which paid honour to its distinguished visitor at the historic Guildhall. Our photograph was taken at the moment of his arrival in an open carriage from Buckingham Palace.

which we used to call the balance of power—the thing in which the balance was determined by the sword, which was thrown into one side or the other, the balance which was determined by the unstable equilibrium of competitive interests, the balance which was maintained by jealous watchfulness and antagonism of interests which, though it was generally latent, was always deep-seated. And the men who have fought this war have been the men from free nations who were determined that that sort of thing should end now and for ever. . . . There must now be a single, overwhelming powerful group of nations who shall be the trustees of the peace of the world.

It has been delightful in the conference with the leaders of your Government to find how our minds moved exactly along the same lines, how our thought was always that the key to the peace was the guarantee of a peace, not the items of it, and that the items would be worthless unless there stood at the back of them a permanent consort of power for the maintenance of them. I am particularly happy that the ground is cleared and the foundation laid, for we have already accepted the same body of principles. Those principles are clearly and definitely enough stated to make their application a matter which would afford no fundamental difficulty. The peoples of the world want peace and they want it now, not simply by conquest of arms but by agreement of mind. It was this incomparably great object which brought me overseas. It has never before been deemed excusable for a President of the United States to leave the territory of the United States. But it was my paramount duty to turn away from the imperative tasks at home to lend such counsels and aid as I could to this great—may I not say final ?—enterprise of humanity.

On the day on which this eloquent speech was made the returns of the British General Election came in. As in the United States, the popular vote turned mainly upon the nature of the terms of peace to Germany. Practically every candidate in Great Britain suspected of leniency towards the enemy was rejected, and most of the successful members were specially pledged to obtain a war indemnity.

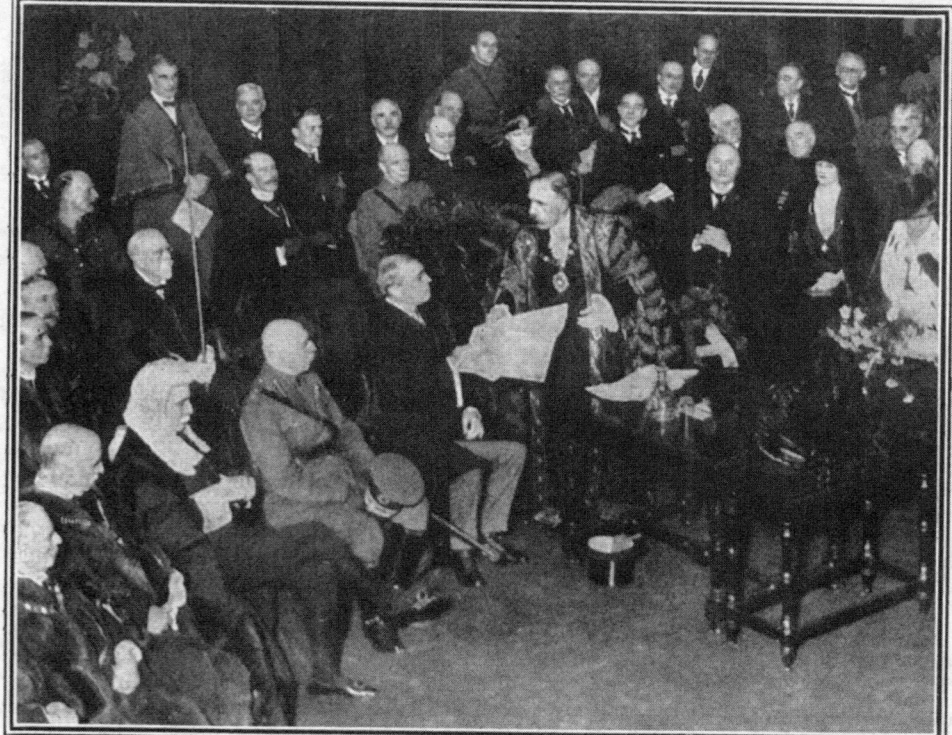

PRESENTATION OF THE ADDRESS OF WELCOME BY THE LORD MAYOR.
Scene in Guildhall, London, December 28th, 1918, when the Lord Mayor, Sir Horace Brooks Marshall, presented President Wilson with an address of welcome. In reply to this address Mr. Wilson used the memorable words : "In the voice of welcome I seem to hear the voice of one people speaking to another people." The Duke of Connaught is seated on President Wilson's right,

Mr. Lloyd George himself undertook to compel the Germans to pay as much as was possible. The United States, on the other hand, was in the happy position of being able to forgo any indemnity. American war expenses were far from threatening either to bankrupt the country or even to reduce it more or less to a condition of economic servitude. France and Italy were in a state of bankruptcy, and Great Britain was bound in debt. Enthusiastically as President Wilson spoke of " peace by agreement of mind," as against " peace by conquest of arms," it was much to be doubted whether he rightly interpreted the wants of the victorious peoples of Europe in the matter.

A suggestion was made that the war expenses of the Associated Powers should be added together and borne in common, the United States taking over a large part in

THE PRESIDENTIAL VISIT TO " COTTONOPOLIS."
Scene outside the Town Hall, Manchester, as the Presidential party was leaving after Mr. Wilson had been presented with the Freedom of the City, December 30th, 1918. The President had a splendid reception as he signed the Burgess Roll. He afterwards drove through the business heart of the city, dense crowds cheering with North-country heartiness.

generous recognition of the greater burden in blood and treasure carried by the nations that had done most from the opening of the struggle to bring about the victory of liberation. This was an unofficial American proposal, but it met with little approval when set before the American people.

The Americans generally remained business-like in regard to European affairs. Their opposition to the extraordinary course adopted by their President was at first very strong. In the Senate on December 21st, 1918, Mr. Lodge, who was regarded as the majority Republican leader in the next
Senator Lodge's opposition session, made a speech condemning five points in the President's programme of fourteen points. He attacked the articles relating to secret treaties, the freedom of the seas, the removal of economic barriers, the reduction of armaments, and any discussion of the League of Nations before peace with Germany was arranged.

I have heard reports (said the Senator) that America's new naval programme is intended to be used in the negotiations to compel Britain to agree to disarmament, under menace of a great naval competition on our part. I mention this rumour only to say that it is unbelievable. Such a motive as that is too entirely unworthy to be entertained by any responsible public man. How it fits in with the policy of reduction of naval and military forces, or with the high objects of the League of Nations, I cannot conceive.

The Senator asked for indemnities and ample guarantees from Germany, and threatened that if an attempt were made

to hurry the Treaty of Peace through Congress for ratification, the Republican Party would amend it and strike out some provisions. On the other hand Mr. Taft, a former Republican President, appeared as an energetic advocate of the League of Nations, and the American people generally were considerably influenced by the instant, extraordinary personal popularity which their President won in Paris and London.

To some extent the Americans accepted the enthusiasm of their European associates as direct evidence of eager adherence to the principle of the League, if not altogether to Mr. Wilson's programme of " peace by agreement of mind." Under pressure of American public opinion the new majority parties in Congress then began skilfully to veer in their standpoint towards the League of Nations.

Senators and Representatives explained that they stood for the League, and aimed only at removing the defects in it and making the great plan for preventing war consonant with the Monroe Doctrine and the full maintenance of the sovereign powers of their own nation. This great change in opinion was a striking personal victory for President Wilson, who was reported to be contemplating another movement against his opponents by so linking the Treaty of Peace with Germany with the treaty establishing the League of Nations as to make it impossible for the Republican Congress to ratify the peace without consenting to the League.

Great and intense was the anger among the Republicans when they learnt of this device of their masterful, militant President as he rode in triumph after triumph through the cities of France, Britain, and Italy. Their combination against the President continued to increase in range, while narrowing in aim, through the long preliminaries of the Peace Conference. Meanwhile President Wilson worked directly upon the mind of the American people by means of an augmented prestige derived from his European successes.

At the American Embassy, on December 28th, he met Viscount Grey of Fallodon, Mr. Asquith, and Viscount Bryce, representing the League of Nations Union, and said to them that he greatly admired the moral principles on which the British Government in 1914 had entered the war. Then, in answer to an address from the English-speaking Union, represented by Major Evelyn Wrench and other gentlemen, the President
happily escaped from any difficulty with **Visit to his** the anti-British element in his country by **mother's homeland** remarking, half in jest and half in earnest,
that one had to be careful in saying anything about the language of the English-speaking peoples as everybody understood it.

Delegates of the British Trade Union Congress and the British Labour Party congratulated the President for standing against secret methods in diplomacy and formulating the principles of a democratic peace. The Society of Friends sent a delegation who made the somewhat remarkable statement that their community was prepared to use force in a last resort to secure permanent peace through a League of Nations. Other addresses were presented by Churchmen and Free Churchmen, and the following day Mr. Wilson broke his rule of not travelling for any other purpose than the cause he had crossed the sea to advocate, and made a long train journey from London to Carlisle.

In this Cumberland town his mother, Jessie Woodrow, had been born, his grandfather, the Rev. Thomas Woodrow, being minister of the Congregational chapel there. Miss

Anglo-Saxon Brotherhood: President Wilson with King George at Buckingham Palace.

North Gate, Teheran: One of the twelve gates of the typically Oriental capital of Persia.

Teheran Gate, Kazvin, the ancient city on the highway between Teheran and the Caspian Sea.

Remains of the great processional wall of a ruined temple in immemorial Mesopotamia.

Old stone bridge near Kangavar, crossed by the British marching through Mesopotamia to Baku.

171

Gurkha Post, Imamzadeh, in Northern Persia, on the road from the Caspian Sea to Teheran.

British infantry before the Turkish headquarters, Kirkuk, captured in the advance from Bagdad.

Woodrow was taken to Canada at the age of seven, where in course of time she moved to Ohio, and married the son of an Ulster man from County Down. President Wilson had made several holiday sojourns among the Cumberland hills, but as an act of filial piety he came at the height of his fame to Carlisle, spoke to the survivors of his grandfather's congregation and delivered an address in the chapel, being himself a Presbyterian elder.

After saying that he was reluctant to speak because the feelings excited in him were too intimate and too deep for public expression, he made an appeal to the religious spirit of the English-speaking peoples :

The memories that have come to me to-day of the mother who was born here are very affecting, and her quiet character, her sense of duty and dislike of ostentation, have come back to me with increasing force as those years of duty have accumulated. Yet perhaps it is appropriate that in a place of worship I should acknowledge my indebtedness to her and to her remarkable father, because, after all, what the world is now seeking to do is to return to the paths of duty, to turn away from the savagery of interest to the dignity of the performance of right. And I believe that as this war has drawn the nations temporarily together in a combination of physical force we shall now be drawn together in a combination of moral force that will be irresistible.

It is moral force that is irresistible. It is moral force as much as physical that has defeated the efforts to subdue the world. Words have cut as deep as the sword. The knowledge that wrong was being attempted has aroused the nations. They have gone out like men upon a crusade. No other cause could have drawn so many nations together. They knew that an outlaw was abroad who purposed unspeakable things. It is from quiet places like this all over the world that the forces accumulate which presently will overbear any attempt to accomplish evil on a large scale. Like the rivulets gathering into the river and the river into the sea, there come from communities like this streams that fertilise the consciences of men, and it is the conscience of the world that we are trying to place upon the throne which others would usurp.

It is clear there was a method in the President's excursion to Carlisle. He wished to speak to the Free Churches, with which he was closely associated both as the **Freedom of** son of a minister and as former head of **Manchester** Princetown University. Even more than Mr. Lloyd George, he seemed likely at the time to become the leader of the Protestant communities among the English-speaking races, and his design was to direct religious feeling into the scheme for the League of Nations. His dramatic sense, to which in large measure he owed his political success, was well displayed in his choice of the small, humble chapel in Carlisle for the delivery of his appeal to the Free Churches.

In the afternoon of December 29th the whirlwind missionary of peace travelled to Manchester, and drove to the town-hall through an embankment of cheering spectators. The next day the President made nine street processions, one boat trip, three speeches, and received the freedom of the city and a lunch all in the space of five and a quarter hours. He was shown a mystery ship, the Hyderabad, and a captured German submarine, and hustled through happy, roaring multitudes of mill girls, lads, and men, passing by wonders in industry that led him to remark that Great Britain was vying with his own country in productive progressiveness.

Once more the Chief Magistrate of the United States stated that his country would take no interest in any attempt to keep the world at a right poise by a balance of power, because she was not concerned in European politics, but only in the partnership of right between America and Europe. In the course of another long and remarkable speech he said :

The United States will join no combination of Powers which is not a combination of all of us. She is not interested merely in the peace of Europe, but in the peace of the world. Therefore it seems to me that in the settlement which is just ahead of us, something more delicate and difficult than was ever attempted before has to be accomplished— a genuine consort of mind and of purpose. I am not hopeful that the individual items of the settlement which we are about to attempt will be altogether satisfactory. One has only to apply his mind to any of the questions of boundary and of altered sovereignty and of racial aspiration to do something more than conjecture that there is no body of men who know just how they ought to be settled. Yet if we are to make unsatisfactory settlements, we must see to it that they are rendered more and more satisfactory by the subsequent adjustments which are made possible. We must provide a machinery of readjustment, in order that we may have a machinery of good-will and friendship. It is the wish to come together that is more than half the process.

President Wilson returned to London, and, after a farewell banquet at Buckingham Palace, set out for France on December 31st, 1918, having been greatly impressed by the warm-hearted welcome given to him and his party from all sides. As he steamed from Dover in mist and drizzling rain his Secretary of the Navy laid before a Committee of the House of Representatives a scheme for spending six hundred million dollars (£120,000,000) in a three-year building programme, likely to end in making the American Navy the greatest in the world. **United States** The scheme, it was explained, had been **naval programme** approved by the President after the signing of the armistice. Mr. Josephus Daniels, Secretary of the Navy, said :

You cannot do anything in the world which would so strengthen this country's position in the Peace Conference as to authorise this enlarged naval programme. If the Conference does not result in a general agreement to put an end to naval building on the part of all nations, the United States must bend her will and bend her energies, must give her men and give her money for the task of the creation of incomparably the greatest Navy in the world. She has no design upon the territory or trade of any other nation or group of nations, but she is pledged to support the Monroe Doctrine, she is pledged to the protection of the weak wherever they may suffer threats, she is incomparably rich, incomparably strong in natural resources. If need be, she must be incomparably strong in defence against aggressors and in offence against evil-doers.

Unperturbed by the criticism of his countrymen, President Wilson continued his progress through the capitals of the Associated Powers, arriving in Italy on January 2nd, 1919, and receiving an enthusiastic welcome in Rome on the following day. In an address to the Italian Parliament he said that the distinguishing fact of the war was that great Empires had gone to pieces through holding different races together by force and intrigue. He intended this remark, of course, to bear upon the coming arrangement of territory and population between the Italians and the Southern Slavs. He spoke at the State dinner given by the King of Italy and in the Municipal Palace, where he received the freedom of Rome. He called upon Pope Benedict XV. and addressed representatives of the Italian Press, visited Milan, Genoa, and Turin, returning to Paris on January 7th, in time for the opening of the Peace Conference. In his last Italian address there could be traced his reliance upon the labouring classes rather than upon the governing classes for the establishment of the principle underlying the League of Nations. He said to the Socialist Town Council of Turin, whose military and patriotic work during the war had not been altogether remarkable :

I am profoundly conscious that the whole social structure of the world is based on the labouring classes. I am convinced also that the labouring classes in every country, through the consciousness of their common ideals, have co-operated, perhaps more than any other influence, towards establishing a world consensus, which is not that of one nation nor of one continent, but a consensus of the whole world.

As a political stroke this was the most telling that Mr. Wilson had ever dealt. He won over to his cause the Italian Socialists, both those of the Teutonic **President and** school and those of the sounder Mazzini **Italian Socialists** school of patriotism, producing also a strong eddy in Italian life of more than passing importance.

The official Italian Socialists, however, were scarcely in the main current of life of the Italian people, who were enjoying a victory such as they had not dreamt of. Neither in Italy nor in France did President Wilson generally discover that agreement of mind on the practical principles of peace settlement for which he was seeking. In these circumstances the Peace Conference opened with so many delicate and serious problems before it that a settlement was delayed for months, and defeated nations drifted into anarchy while the debate went on among the victors concerning the methods of preventing future wars and establishing a confraternity of peoples.

MAJOR-GENERAL W. GILLMAN,
C.B., C.M.G., D.S.O., R.A., Chief of the General Staff.

MAJOR-GENERAL HON. R. STUART-WORTLEY,
C.B., D.S.O., Deputy Q.M.G., General Headquarters.

MAJOR-GENERAL SIR H. T. BROOKING,
K.C.B., K.C.M.G., G.O.C. 15th Division.

MAJOR-GENERAL F. F. READY,
C.B., C.M.G., D.S.O., D.A.G., General Headquarters.

DISTINGUISHED GENERALS OF THE MESOPOTAMIA EXPEDITIONARY FORCE.

CHAPTER CCXCVIII.

THE TRIUMPH OF THE ARMY OF MESOPOTAMIA.
By Edward Wright.

Marshall's Forces Weakened to Strengthen Haig—Battle of Tact and Ingenuity at Tomb of Ali—Ludendorff and Enver Change from B.B.B. Scheme to B.B.B.B. Plan—Far-stretched New Threat to India—Enemy Seizes Rail-heads by Afghan Border—Struggle for Central Asia between Quetta Column and Austrian-Bolshevist Forces—Gallant Punjabi Officer Turns Defeat Into Victory—Russian Railway Bases Conquered—General Dunsterville's "Hush-Hush Push" to Baku—How Stalky Handled the Bolshevists—Rescuing Assyrians and Hammering Jangalis—Gallant British Defence of Baku—Armenians and Russians Betray Dunsterville and his Men—Successful Rearguard Actions Amid Traitors and Withdrawal Over Caspian—How Dunsterville and his Heroic Detachment Helped Allenby—Sir Percy Sykes Finds his Persian Levies Growing Treacherous—The Great Mutiny that Was Arranged Too Late—Traitors and Assassins in Khan-i-Zinian Fort—Saulat and the Kashgais Lay Siege to Shiraz—Nightmare Days in the City of Roses, with Rebellion Within and War Without—Saulat Camouflages a Defeat Into a Success—Sykes' Trick in Making Traitors Loyal—Disillusioned Persians Rally to British—Great Rescue March to Abadeh—Influenza Epidemic Routs the Enemy—Main Mesopotamia Force Gives Battle by Ruins of Assur—Magnificent Endurance of 17th Division—Highland Light Infantry Storm the Key Bridge—West Kents Break Through—7th Cavalry Brigade Block Turks' Road of Retreat—White Flag Goes Up All Along Enemy's Line—Ride of Victory into Mosul—Britons Succeed where Greeks and Romans Failed—India's Glorious Share in the Conquest.

AFTER the British victories in Mesopotamia in April, 1918, described in Chapter CCXLVII. (Vol. 11, page 425), the forces under Sir William Marshall were seriously diminished, by reason of Sir Douglas Haig's urgent need for reinforcements in France and Flanders. To release British troops in Palestine and India the 7th Division was sent to join Sir Edmund Allenby's command, and was followed in May, 1918, by the 3rd Division and three siege batteries. A fresh Indian division was formed out of companies of veteran troops in Mesopotamia, filled out with a small proportion of recruits, and despatched with a brigade formed in the same way, further to relieve white troops in Palestine and India. More siege batteries departed, and although Sir William Marshall was left with five infantry divisions, three cavalry brigades, and a ration strength of 420,000, his forces were largely composed of young Indian troops and Arab labour battalions.

Mesopotamia was won. Little more than strong military police work was required to guard it. The victors reaped the crops on the Kurdistan tableland as far as Kirkuk, and pastured their horses in the vast stretches of blossoming clover and wild oats while waiting for the corn to

ripen. In the southern irrigated plain, by Sir William Willcocks' barrage, an army of Arabs made new canals and cleared old ones, and from the greatest harvest since the days of Nebuchadnezzar the forward army obtained enough grain to feed itself. A large part of the newly irrigated country was Government land, from which the British authorities obtained one-third of the crops; they also took payment for seed, labour, and revenue charges in the form of grain from the wilderness they had made to blossom. Consequently, transport on the lines of communication was reduced by thousands of tons, and rolling-stock and river craft were released for other purposes. Towards the end of the war Mesopotamia, instead of merely feeding its conquerors and enriching its people with wealth beyond their dreams, was exporting grain. With the immense cotton ground in the north and the great corn-land of Babylonia the resources of the enlarged British Empire promised gloriously to be completed. Dependence upon the United States for cotton and corn did not seem likely to last long when the oldest and greatest granary in the world was fully developed.

Development work went on magnificently. Babylon was connected with Bagdad by a broad-gauge railway, that carried most of the corn required by the

TURKS WHO GAVE UP THE FIGHT.
Turkish prisoners surrendering to British troops in Mesopotamia. They adopted the German cry of "Kamerad!" The motor-lorries in the background of the photograph are heavy German cars which had become embedded in the mud.

PERSIAN POLICE AT DRILL.
Persian levies drilling at Resht, the capital of the province of Ghilan. Resht is 150 miles north-west of Teheran, with a port, Enzeli, 14 miles to the north-west, on the Caspian Sea.

In the meantime the guardian of the shrine and his Persian students were treated with consideration by the besieging force, and negotiations were opened for all the holy men and loyal citizens to be given protection if and when the assault was launched. Owing, however, to the tact and firmness with which the operations were conducted, operations ended by the guardian of the shrine leading the loyal inhabitants in rebellion against the rebels, who were captured and handed over to the British on April 13th, 1918. The siege was then raised, and the surrounding tribes, overawed by British power, and charmed by the tactful way in which this power had been used, became friendly and loyal to the new Government.

Sterner measures were required against certain tribes on the Persian

army and its hundred thousand dependents. The port of Basra was prepared for the vast commerce of peace, with twelve permanent berths at which ocean-going steamers could be loaded and unloaded, great electric cranes being fitted for dealing with some six thousand tons of cargo a day. In addition to the railways, two thousand steamers, launches, and barges were employed by the Inland Water Transport Department of the Royal Engineers, and along the Tigris alone there was an average daily traffic of two thousand tons of general cargo and six hundred tons of fuel. Special construction yards were opened for assembling steamers and barges, the parts of which were brought from England, and new roads were made in many directions.

By each border of the redeemed and refertilised waste there were tribes remaining in Ottoman and Teutonic pay, and inclined either to rebel or to attack friendly tribes working with the British forces. At Nedjef, in the lake-land south of Babylon, there was a band of conspirators, provided with German money, who spread unrest up and down the Euphrates valley. The plotters assassinated the British political officer at Nedjef, and when threatened by a punitive column, retired into the city. They were protected not only by a very high, wide wall, which might have made a direct assault costly, but by the presence of the most holy of the shrines of the Shiah, or Persian sect of Islam—the Tomb of Ali.

Emissaries of unrest

There would have been long and serious trouble with the Persians had artillery been employed, and British and Indian losses might have been heavy had an attempt been made to take the town without the use of gun fire. In these circumstances Brigadier-General G. A. F. Sanders, commanding the punitive force, surrounded Nedjef with barbed-wire entanglements and cut off the outside water supply. The rebels made two vain attempts to break through the blockade, and after they were driven back important ground was won from them. Gradually the British lines were drawn in until they included the bastions of the city walls and the entrance gates.

WESTERN METHODS IN AN EASTERN SETTING.
Another view of a drilling centre for Persian levies at Resht. The Persians did not take kindly to military discipline, and prejudice against being drilled by British officers with an Indian Staff was strong. It was neutralised, however, by the spread of confidence in British honesty and fair play.

border. They were under a man in German pay, and, dwelling near the main road between Bagdad and Teheran, they seriously threatened the British lines of communication into Persia. Some of the tribes of Sinjabis round the highway were favourable to the British cause, and they offered to attack the other hillmen. Sir William Marshall sent a small column of all arms to co-operate in the action, and as a squadron of aeroplanes was included the issue was a decisive one. There was a sharp action by Kasr-i-shirin on April 26th, and the hostile tribesmen were defeated. As they were retiring the British airmen swept upon them with bombs and machine-gun fire, and scattered them, panic-stricken, in a wild rout. The fame of the British cavalry of the air spread from the borderland through Persia, making the lines of communication there so safe that a new, far-reaching scheme of operations was developed.

By the summer of 1918 General von Ludendorff had accepted defeat in Mesopotamia, and was directing a new and larger scheme in the direction of Bokhara. In place of the B.B.B. (Berlin, Byzantium, Bagdad) plan, the B.B.B.B. (Berlin, Batum, Baku, Bokhara) scheme was put into execution as far as circumstances allowed. With direct help from the Soviet tyrants of the larger part of Russia, a Bolshevist force, backed by armoured trains and Austrian, Hungarian, and German prisoners of war, began operations round Merv, by the northern frontiers of Persia and Afghanistan. On the other side of the Caspian Sea a strong Turkish force swept into the Tartar territories of Caucasia, while some six German battalions crossed the Black Sea and entered Georgia, and, after supporting the claims of the Georgians, endeavoured to seize Baku, the bridge-head of the Caspian and centre of the petroleum industry.

The design was for Teutons and Turks to act together in seizing the railways which the Russians had built in the old days for the invasion of India, raise all the Mohammedans of Turkestan, Persia, and Afghanistan, and, with the liberated Austrian and German prisoners of war in Siberia and Bolshevists, press down towards the Khyber Pass. The direction of this new attack was well chosen. The Russian railways connecting with Baku and with Oren-berg, and linking Samarkand, Bokhara, and Merv, gave much nearer bases of attack than Bagdad, and enabled the Army of Mesopotamia to be neglected by a direct menace to the British power in India.

Things, however, did not go very well from the German point of view. The Turks became extremely jealous of the new Teutonic power in Georgia, and lost the campaign in Palestine, and with it the whole war, by drawing off great forces for a very ambitious scheme in Central Asia. Enver Pasha resolved to unite the Turco-mans and other kinsmen of the Turks in a grand Turanian movement which would dominate Asia. Seeing himself in a con-quering part like that of a new Genghis Khan, the Ottoman dictator wanted only munitions and equipment from the Teutons.

GAS-MASK PARADE.
Inspection of gas-masks after testing in the gas chamber. In East as well as West the British had to be prepared against the use of German poison-gas.

When the Germans took the old Tartar lands in the Crimea, together with the Russian Black Sea Fleet, and, landing in the Caucasus, settled in Tiflis and, taking the Georgians under their protection, struck out for the oil-wells and Caspian steamers at Baku, Enver and his associates became exceedingly angry. They were ready to negotiate a friendly peace with the British, yielding Persia, Mesopotamia, Arabia, and Palestine, if help were given them against the Teutons, together with a free hand in the Caucasus and in Turkestan.

The British Government and its Allies gave no answer to the Turkish proposal. It was best to allow Turk and Teuton to quarrel with increasing bitterness over the spoil they had not secured, rather than make even the pretence of siding with the angry, disillusioned, weakening Ottoman. Preparations were made by Sir Charles Monro, Commander-in-Chief in India, to despatch from Quetta to Meshed, by the northern frontier of Persia, a small force for watching the new front of attack between the Caspian Sea and the Oxus River.

The enemy had a rail-head at Kushk, on the Afghan border, and another at Askhabad, near the Persian border, with carriage-roads and mule-tracks running towards India. There was no immediate danger of an invasion in force, but of political penetration, with the spread of fanaticism among the Moslems and a loss of British prestige, followed by the organisation of a series of German strategic railway bases in place of the old, slovenly, happy-go-lucky Russian system circling round Khiva.

The question whether the leaders of Bolshevist Russia were in German pay and under German Staff direction was clearly answered in the operations along the Persian and Afghan border. Under

WHITE-ROBED ARABS WHO FOUGHT FOR CIVILISATION.
Arab police being instructed in the use of the modern rifle. When Mesopotamia was won little more than military police work was required to guard it; and from the greatest harvest since the days of Nebuchadnezzar the forward army obtained enough grain to feed itself. Above: Types of mounted police.

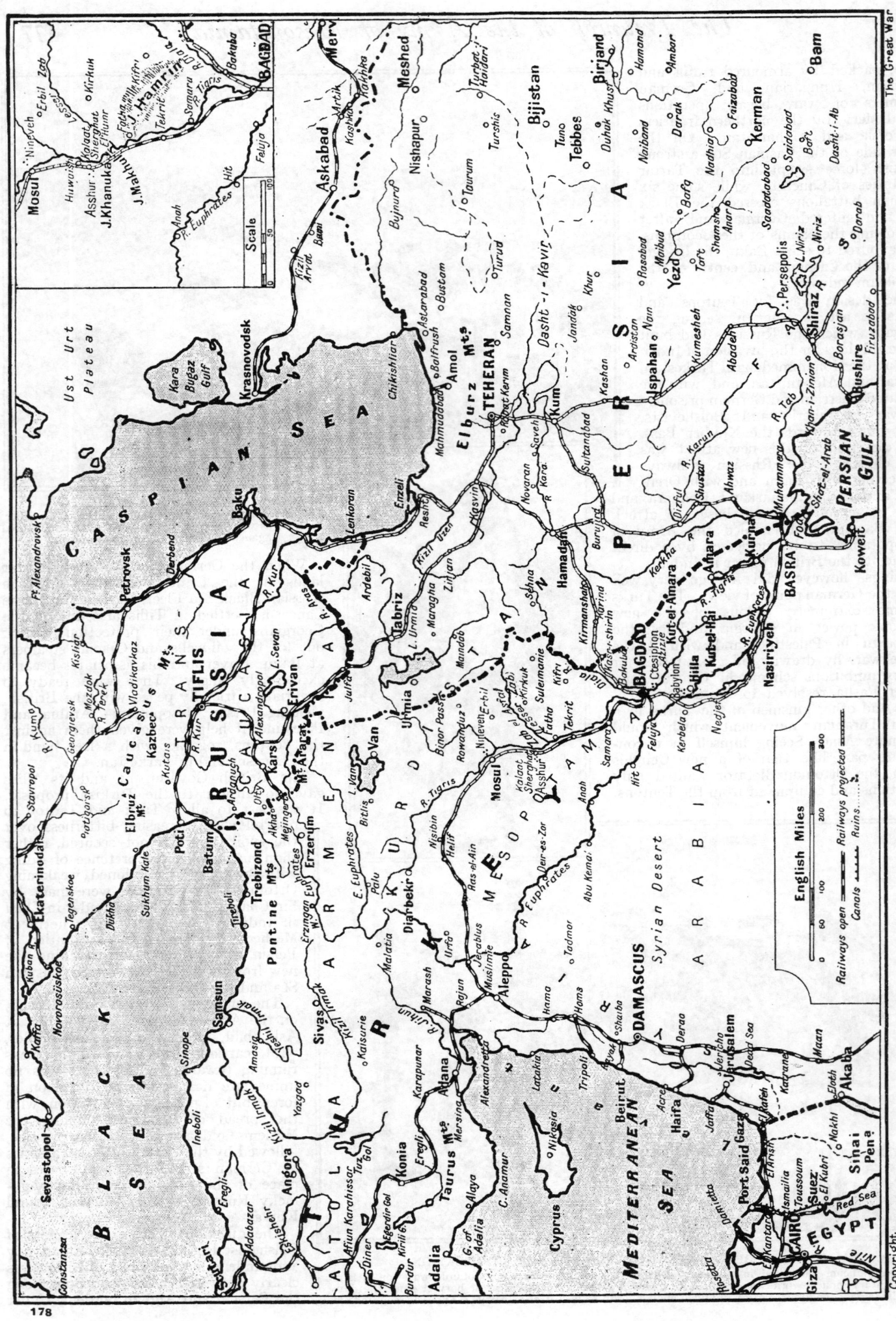

THEATRE OF THE BRITISH MILITARY OPERATIONS IN MESOPOTAMIA, CAUCASIA, PERSIA, AND AROUND THE CASPIAN SEA IN 1918.

The Great War.

the orders of Trotsky the Bolshevists seized the strategic railway and the Russian military bases of Merv and Askhabad, and began to sweep the Turcoman herdsmen into an army for the invasion of India.

Behind the Bolshevist agents were well-drilled bodies of Germanic troops, mainly Austrian and Hungarian, released from internment camps in Siberia and brought in trains from Tashkend, which had become the seat of Asiatic Bolshevism. The Austrians were not at all willing to fight, but they were told that the Germans had reached the eastern shore of the Caspian, so that they had only to cut a path along the railway to the middle of the Caspian in order to be able to travel home.

Their fighting quality was not sufficient to overawe the Turcomans. Thereupon, Ottoman missionaries and Bolshevist gospellers endeavoured by a combination of religious and communist doctrine to convert the tribesmen into active allies. At the beginning of August, 1918, there seemed a prospect of success for the strange trio of Ludendorff, Enver, and Trotsky. By the middle of the month, however, the enemy was overthrown in the great military base of Askhabad, which had been the Russian equivalent of the British military centre of Peshawar.

The Turcoman herdsman saw nothing to his profit either in the Turkish alliance or in a Jewish communism. He was already a free man under a chief of his own race, and as he had just escaped from the Imperial bureaucracy of old Russia, he was inclined to remain free, tending his cattle and obeying his tribal chief. He had no love for any Russian, but began to sympathise with the Menshevists, or Minority Socialists, when an extraordinary agent of Trotsky arrived on the frontier to preach Bolshevism. The agent was a man named Frolov. He was a strong and remarkably handsome man, with the soul of a savage and as devilish joy in slaughter as Carrier displayed in the Terror at Nantes. Not content with ordering wholesale executions, Frolov took to shooting men himself for sport. But when he shot five friendly railwaymen, who came to him with a petition, other men on the railway killed him and his wife and associates.

The Bolshevists were overthrown all along the frontier railway between the Caspian Sea and the Oxus River. Reinforced at the end of July with more released Germanic prisoners, they battled back to Merv and again threatened to conquer all the border country. Then it was that from both Russians and Turcomans an urgent message for help was sent to the little Indo-British force at Meshed, some ninety miles distant from the contested railway line.

Overthrow of the Bolshevists Down a mule-track the Punjabis and their comrades marched to the nearest railway-station of Artik. There they entrained, and were carried some two stations up the line to Kakhka, after sending a single machine-gun section into a skirmish.

The Turcomans and Russians had determined to make a stand at Kakhka, and well for them it was that the Indian troops arrived. After the skirmish in the middle of the month the Austrians, either under their own officers or under Germans, opened their main attack in the last week of August. Helped by some Bolshevist soldiers, who were little more than an irregular force, they turned the flank of the Turcomans by

SIKH FESTIVAL IN MESOPOTAMIA.
Sikhs serving with the British forces along the Tigris on their way to a festival of their race, a punkah-wallah warding the flies off the holy book borne on the head of the man in the foreground.

the railway and captured the railway-station. By a brilliant counter-attack the Punjabis recovered the station and drove the broken enemy to the corner of the Persian frontier, close to the branch railway leading to Afghanistan.

This gallant and most timely intervention by the far-travelled little column from Quetta had a decisive effect upon the general situation in Central Asia. The British and their Allies retained control of most of the country between the Caspian Sea and Merv, and with the help of British officers and non-commissioned officers, and some Russian officers who served in the ranks with the Menshevist artillery, a Turcoman army was improvised.

The Turcomans were fine-looking men with splendid physique, but impossible to discipline. Neither for attack nor defence could they be relied on; but when the Austrians were defeated they would pursue on their ponies and cut off stragglers. Happily, the British officer in command managed to obtain a Russian armoured train to balance the armoured trains the Bolshevists possessed, and with his dauntless band of Russian officers, who were ready to serve their guns to the death, and the dashing Punjabis he arranged an attack on October 14th. Mounted Turcomans were sent in a wide circle against the enemy's rear to cut the railway line, while the Punjabis made a flanking attack on the left of the railway line after a two days' march. The attack was completely successful. Dunshak was carried, and one of the enemy's armoured trains was set on fire by a shell and the crew pursued and overtaken by the Turcomans.

The Punjabis, however, lost all their British officers in the assault, and the scheme of operations then went to pieces. The Russian Socialists and the Turcomans, instead of preparing to resist a counter-attack, left the line and took to looting. A strong Austrian reinforcement arrived, and its officers rallied the survivors of the first action and closed down on three sides on the little force of Indian infantry. At the same time another hostile armoured train, which should have been cut off had the Turcoman cavalry played its part, came into action against the Punjabis.

In these desperate circumstances the Indian officer left in command conducted an heroic resistance. All his superior officers were out of action, but he refused to retire unless he received an **Punjabi who emulated Clive** order to do so, and there was nobody left to give him such an order. Keeping his men finely in hand, and admirably supported by them, he fought the enemy off until the British cavalry that had been operating far across the right of the railway, crossed the line and continued the struggle. Their officer gave the Punjabi leader the order to retire, and as the Indian infantry fell back, the cavalry got home with the lance upon the Austro-Hungarians, who were so completely demoralised that they fled for three hundred miles to Chargui, on the Oxus, abandoning Merv, the railway to Afghanistan, and all the Transcaspian region.

But for the lack of a final ounce of courage the Austro-Hungarians and their Bolshevist friends might have been the victors in Central Asia. The Turcomans were in disorder, and the heroic Punjabis were withdrawing to avoid complete destruction, with the cavalry acting as the rearguard. The released Germanic prisoners of war, however, had lost about a thousand men around the railway-station, and largely owing to the devoted resistance of the Punjabis they made quite a wrong calculation of the number of men in action against them and fled for hundreds of miles to avoid any possible risk of another battle.

The British conquest of Merv, Penjdeh, and other Russian railway bases, the establishment of which had almost brought Great Britain and Russia to war in the latter part of the nineteenth century, was accomplished by as striking a feat as that by which Clive had saved the British power in India.

to reach them and help them to organise themselves into a modern army.

On January 27th, 1918, General Dunsterville left Bagdad with a party less than a battalion strong and a transport of seven hundred and fifty Ford vans. He took the old road of adventure from Bagdad through Kirmanshah to the Caspian Sea, which had been trodden by the armies of Cyrus and Darius and the later Mongol invaders. It was a marvel how any large armed forces could use such a road. It was unmetalled and worn down in a soil of black dust,

BRITISH CAVALRY OF THE AIR TAKE PART IN THE DEFENCE OF THE BAGDAD-CASPIAN ROAD.
Before the conclusion of the struggle with the Turk there were many skirmishes with him in the great mountain region between the Caspian Sea and the Kurdistan highlands. The British attacked in order to defend the Bagdad-Caspian road, and mainly with aeroplanes and light armoured motor-cars and cavalry retained the enemy. By these and similar operations the fame of the British airmen resounded throughout Persia.

But the new Clive was a Punjabi, one of the members of the great fighting races of North-Western India who came forward in hundreds of thousands to battle.

There were Hindus of high gallantry in the Indian forces, but none of them came from the people who made most noise in India and used a veneer of European democratic ideas in an attempt to extend and aggravate the old tyranny of their caste system. The warrior races of India stood by the British Raj, and proved their own title to a larger measure of self-government, clear of all Bengali Babu interference, by the glorious strength of soul they showed in battle.

After the railway victory in Transcaspia the main interest in the new operations against Ludendorff and Enver's scheme shifted directly to Baku. Sir William Marshall had not been idle while the enemy was preparing the new movement towards India. At the end of 1917 volunteers were called for in the Army of Mesopotamia, and some officers and non-commissioned officers, with a small number of recruits, were mysteriously collected in a camp near Bagdad. There they forsook the study of Arabic and displayed an interest in the Persian language, the Armenian tongue,
Stalky and the and other strange ways of speech. To add
"Hush-hush Push" to the mystery they took to dressing themselves up like Arctic explorers. About the middle of January, 1918, Major-General E. L. Dunsterville, who in boyhood had stood for the model of Stalky in Mr. Kipling's tale, arrived in Bagdad to lead the band of adventurers in the "Hush-hush Push."

Armenia was originally Stalky's goal, and merchants of romance spread the rumour that he was about to found a kingdom in the Caucasus. Here the Armenians had been making a long, heroic stand against the Turk and upsetting Enver Pasha's Turanian scheme. They fell, however, against the renewed pressure of Turk and Teuton long before it became possible for General Dunsterville even to attempt

famous for its fertility, but dreadful to march or drive through after rain. One heavy shower made it impassable for wheeled traffic.

In the highlands, where the passes rose more than seven thousand feet, the sharp rock surface added a modern difficulty to transport problems by cutting up the tyres of the motor-vans with delaying rapidity. There were many swift-running streams which had to be bridged, the enemy having blown up the old bridges. Then, far from being able to live in the fertile plains, during his **Fighting against** journey of seven hundred miles to the **famine and drought** Caspian Sea, General Dunsterville had to rescue the dying population of North-Western Persia. Through the unhappy land five armies had passed in eighteen months, both Turk and Cossack living on the country, and leaving desolation behind them. Standing crops had been burnt and granaries seized or destroyed, so that no grain was left for a new harvest. Crowning all the misery came a great drought. The Persians were as hostile as their strength permitted, their natural aversion to allowing another army to pass over their land being fostered by Ottoman and German missionaries of disorder.

But the Briton did not take; he gave. He found dead and dying stretched by the roadside, and could not bear to leave them and speed on towards the Caspian and join in the Turkish and Teutonic race for Baku. Relief works were opened at Karind, Hamadan, Kirmanshah, and other places, and, with the help of Mr. and Mrs. Stead, American missionaries, tens of thousands were saved from death by hunger.

In the meantime British engineers blasted and levelled easier gradients on the series of mountain passes between Bagdad and Kirmanshah, and the systematic metalling of the road was begun. Even then it took the entire convoy of seven hundred and fifty motor-vans, plying daily in stages from the frontier, to feed less than a thousand men at Hamadan.

In spite of all difficulties General Dunsterville arrived at Kasvin, west of Teheran, on June 1st, 1918, and met the volunteer Russian force, twelve hundred strong, under General Bicherakhoff. With a small British detachment the Russian volunteers set out for Enzeli, on the southern shore of the Caspian, but were held up by a tribe, the Jangalis who were led by German officers. Assisted by the light-armoured cars of the British force the Russians attacked, won the bridge, and reached Enzeli.

The Jangalis lived in dense forests by the town of Resht, and, by reason of their cover, were able to raid the new line of communications of the Mesopotamian force outstretched seven hundred miles from its base. The chiefs had lost a considerable amount of prestige in their defeat by the bridge, and the tribesmen no longer believed all that the Germans told them. For some weeks they continued casually to snipe at the British convoy, but on July 20th they descended on Resht, which was held by a small detachment of Hampshires and Gurkhas.

The garrison was not large enough to man a line round the town, and the enemy drove in and assailed the British Consulate and bank, only to be swept out in fierce hand-to-hand fighting by the little British and Indian force, who killed more than a hundred of the tribesmen. This finally convinced the Jangalis that the tales told them by Turk and Teuton were fictions. They agreed to break with the Ottoman, and gave no more trouble to General Dunsterville's small force. The forest tribe could have completely defeated the little daring expedition before the real British operations began, but, like

all the undisciplined, barbaric fighting men, to whom war was a lifelong profession, the Jangalis could not stand heavy losses in a balked offensive. Handled in friendly fashion, after a sound thrashing, in the best Stalky manner of diplomacy, they became the western rampart to the new British line.

Eastward, the Caspian road was menaced by another tribe in German pay, the Kuhgalus. These began operations by raids against the Bakhtiari Khans, a friendly race of hillmen, who, through the war, guarded the British oil-fields near Ahwaz, on which the British Navy largely depended for fuel. Small detachments of Indian troops were sent eastward to secure the Ahwaz-Ispahan road and generally protect communications. One section of an Indian mountain battery marched three hundred and ninety-five miles in twenty-eight days in the hottest part of the year, and, after reducing to order the German-paid tribesmen, returned to its base all in excellent condition.

With the road secure on either side, General Dunsterville completed his journey of seven hundred miles and arrived at Enzeli. General Bicherakhoff had then sailed away and accepted the post of commander of the Red Army of the Caucasus. At this time the Bolshevists held almost complete sway round the Caspian, and were naturally strongly opposed to British intervention and subtly favourable to Germanic interests. General Dunsterville arrived at Enzeli, with a small party of officers and no escort except the drivers of the motor-vans in which he and his Staff had come from Hamadan. The Bolshevist tribunal summoned the

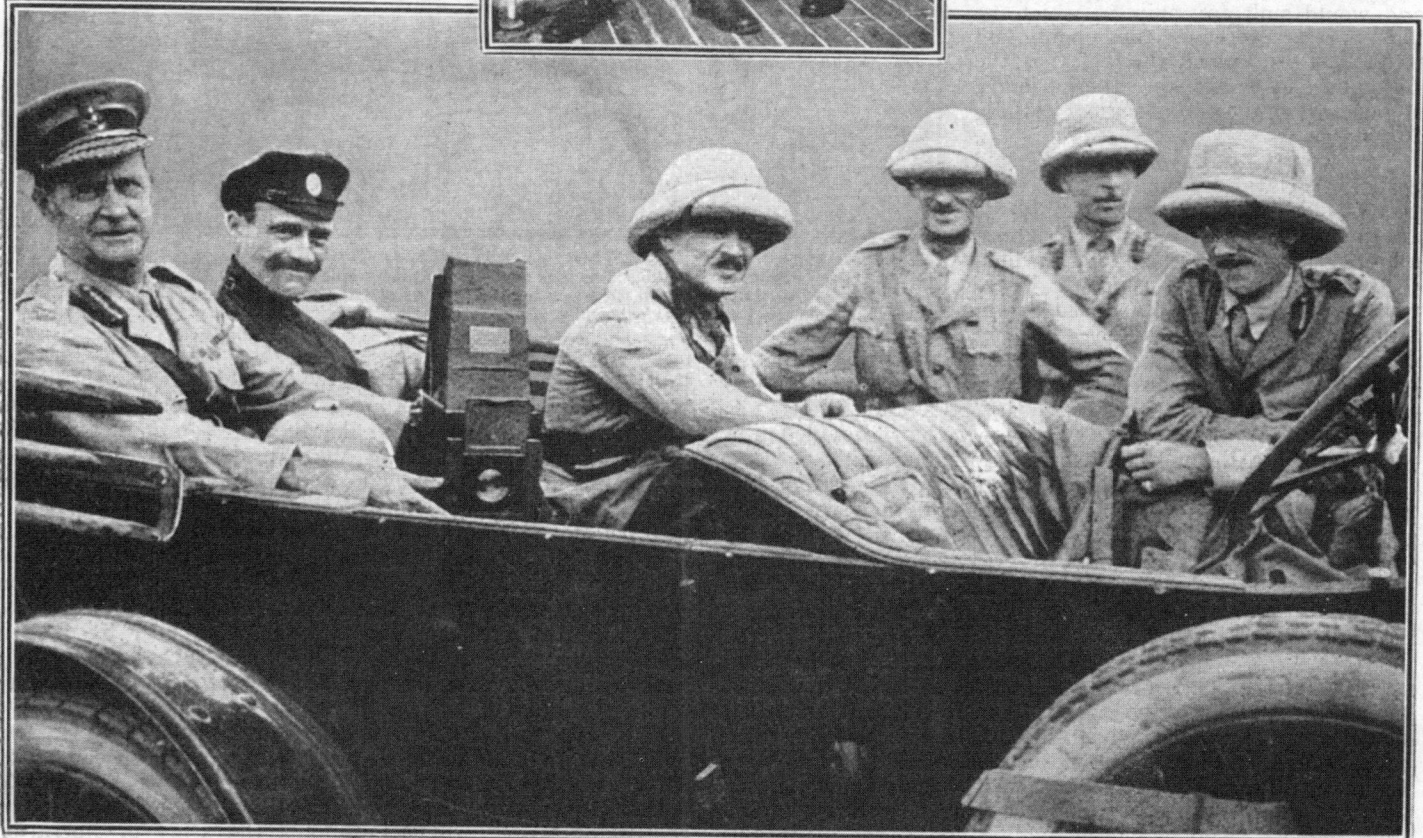

"STALKY" AND SOME OF HIS HELPERS IN THE "HUSH-HUSH PUSH" TO BAKU.

Major-General L. C. Dunsterville, C.B. (on extreme left) and Staff with an Armenian brigadier. Above : General Dunsterville and Commodore Morris, R.N. This general commanded the famous expedition from Mesopotamia to the Caspian Sea known as the "Hush-hush Push." In boyhood he was the model from whom Rudyard Kipling drew the hero of his school story, "Stalky and Co." The adventures of General Dunsterville and the small force with which he made his way from Bagdad through Kirmanshah to the Caspian Sea were among the most romantic episodes of the war.

REFEGEES AT DRILL.
Scene at Hamadan, the ancient Ecbatana, where Armenians and other refugees were armed and drilled by British instructors to render them capable of fighting their way back to their own country.

British general to attend before them, but he managed to induce the Soviet to call on him. He explained he was going to Tiflis in order to report to his Government on the situation in the Caucasus. The Bolshevists replied that they had a gunboat on the Caspian and would sink any ship in which he tried to sail. Moreover, they openly and frequently proclaimed the fact that the Germans and Turks were their friends, against whom they would allow nothing to be done.

"Of course you would not," said Stalky. "Naturally you would be their friends. You could not possibly be anything else. And now what about a drink?" Very pleasantly he provided the Bolshevists with refreshment. There were 3,500 Red Guards in the town, formed of remnants of the Russian Army of the Caucasus. The Britons did not number a score, but their commander managed the situation so admirably that the new allies of the Turk and Teuton not only allowed him and his party to depart but provided him with petrol for the journey back to Hamadan.

In the meantime General Bicherakhoff found that the Russian forces at Baku, forming part of his new command, were treacherous, and, being convinced that the fall of the town was inevitable, retired with his twelve hundred volunteers northward. General Dunsterville returned **Fifty thousand Assyrians rescued** to Enzeli with parts of three battalions of Worcesters, Warwicks, and North Staffords of the 39th Brigade, and with a thousand miles of communication between his port on the Caspian and his base at Basra on the Tigris. The Bolshevist forces had melted away, and an English officer with one platoon sailed across the sea to Baku to report on the situation there.

While waiting for news the British commander got in touch with a multitude of Assyrians, Nestorians, and other refugees, who had been holding out in the mountains by Urmia Lake against the exterminating Ottomans. By the middle of July the heroic resistance of the outcasts was weakening, more through lack of food and an epidemic of cholera than from any failure in courage. British aeroplanes

traced the fighting refugees, and a plan was made to send them a convoy with ammunition, machine-guns, and money.

The convoy arrived at the appointed spot on July 23rd, but the Assyrians were ten days late, and by the time they came the Turks had carried Urmia, and were driving out the collection of little independent races who had come together for defence down the road to Sain Kala.

There, however, the small British and Indian escort of the convoy checked a massacre, rescuing some fifty thousand men, women, and children, representing in the Assyrians the oldest people in the country, and in the Nestorians one of the most ancient of Christian sects, who in ancient days had spread their gospel as far as China. Even when saved from being murdered large

IN TRAINING TO WITHSTAND THE TURKS.
Armenian troops drilling at Baku. Previous to General Dunsterville's arrival in Baku, 7,500 Armenians and 3,000 loyal Russians garrisoned the town, but the victims of Ottoman oppression failed to rise to the occasion when the Turks attacked, and gave the small British defending force scarcely any assistance.

numbers died from cholera and the effects of hunger. Food was provided for all those who could take nourishment, and in batches of three thousands the broken mountaineers were carried down the Persian line of communications to a large camp at Bakuba, in Mesopotamia.

Here a remarkable tent city was made for them. Cholera was wiped out by disinfecting measures and medical treatment; food, clothing, and water supplies were provided. Schools were opened for the children, and work given to women and men, so that they could begin to save money. Then some 30,000 eager, angry fighting men—Armenians, Assyrians, Nestorians, and others—were armed and drilled by British instructors in the design to enable them to fight their way back to their own country with the aid of part of the Army of Mesopotamia.

This left, with other refugees, some 40,000 men, women, and children in about equal proportions in the city of tents. They exhausted all the food reserve which the British had collected for winter use. Had it not been for the magnificent revival of agriculture in Babylonia the army of liberation would have been starved by its rescue work in Persia. The food and clothing difficulty, however, was surmounted, and the refugees were ranged according to tribe and sect, with British officers and men supervising each tribal area and its special piped-water supply, communal kitchen, and washing-place. The manner in which the vast mob of refugees was defended, transported, and organised reflected great credit on Major-General L. C. Dunsterville and his Staff.

While this extraordinary and fine work was being undertaken in conjunction with the famine relief on the eastern side of the Bagdad-Caspian road, General Dunsterville decided to go with his men over the Caspian Sea to Baku. The lieutenant who had first explored the situation in the city with a platoon reported that the handful of British troops had had an electrifying effect upon the Armenians and Russians holding the town against a great Turkish force. The day after the first Britons arrived the townspeople met the Turks in high spirits and broke an assault in gallant fashion.

This was the reason why General Dunsterville sailed for Baku, with his detachment of Worcesters, Warwicks, and North Staffordshires. The number of men he was able to transport was restricted by the increasing length of his communications, but he managed to ferry a force of armoured cars over the great inland sea, together with some artillery and a small detachment of infantry. It was sufficient for the purpose of stiffening the 7,500 Armenians and 3,000 Russians garrisoning the town, and the British commander would have achieved one of the most romantic exploits in the war had the fighting townsmen, who had implored British aid, continued as they had begun.

But the Armenian volunteers especially could not rise to the occasion, though coming of a race that had reasons for fighting to the death. Both they and the Russians seemed to think it was no longer necessary for them to bear

ON THE LOOK-OUT FOR THE ENEMY.
British observer in a front-line trench with Armenian soldiers. The latter assisted the British in defending Baku against the Turks, but on September 14th, 1918, abandoned a strong line of hills. The British evacuated the town, September 18th, 1918.

the burden of battle when the British had arrived, so they gave General Dunsterville's little force scarcely any assistance.

On August 26th the Turks, who had command of the railway and were obtaining a constant stream of reinforcements, made a determined attack on an English company, whose large reserve of local Baku troops refused to help in the action. Against the odds of five to one the Englishmen met a massed Turkish bayonet charge, and only drew in from the salient in the line after suffering heavily and inflicting severe losses on the Turks. With large fresh forces the enemy again tried to carry the city by storm on August 31st. The first attack was beaten off, but in the second action some Armenian battalions broke and fled, exposing the British and Russian flank. Again the defending line was drawn in, and when on the following day the Turks again attacked, only the English troops met them. Consequently more ground was lost, but the Turks on the other hand were swept down in such masses by the guns, foot, and armoured cars of General Dunsterville that they made no further movement for a fortnight.

At this time General Bicherakhoff was two hundred miles north of Baku. The British commander sent a message to him urging that if his force would only return to the city the combined detachments of some two thousand regular British and Russian soldiers could save Baku. The Russian officer agreed with this plan, and the first small detachment of his men arrived on September 9th. They were Cossacks, belonging to the Army of Caucasus, who after the Revolution had volunteered to remain in touch with the British instead of returning to their homes and deserting their old allies.

TYPES OF ARMENIANS WHO MADE A STAND FOR FREEDOM.
Armenian soldier on outpost duty. Centre : The British G.O.C. talking to a youthful Armenian infantryman. Right : Armenian girl who fought in the front-line trenches. The Armenians who formed part of the British forces that advanced against Baku fought exceedingly well at the start, but their personal heroism evaporated gradually through lack of discipline and organisation, and the spread of the moral poison of Bolshevism.

General Bicherakhoff was lamed in one foot, his right arm was useless, and his left arm partly so. He carried a bullet lodged near his spine, and being often unwell by reason of his various wounds, he conducted operations from a stretcher. But he and his men were among the most hard-bitten soldiers in the war, and they knew their countrymen. The first Cossacks who returned to Baku did not like the tone of the town garrison, and discovered that some of them were negotiating a surrender. On September 14th the Turks, reckoning they had won the town by treachery within as well as with force without, closed down on it in great strength of both men and artillery. The Armenians, who had been

Grave disaster averted concerned in the treacherous negotiations, were given a strong line of hills to defend, which they abandoned in a manner that can only be termed blackguardly. The little British force had to save its flank by extending to the last ridge on the outskirts of the town. From this ridge the harbour could completely be dominated, and three very weak English companies held it all through the day and prevented a grave disaster.

In the centre the enemy was fought to a standstill by rifle fire, but a counter-attack failed. Well-handled Turkish guns so curtained off the ground that the British and Russians lost all their officers as well as many men, while the Armenians only saved themselves by drawing out of the attack at an early stage as soon as they came under shell fire. On the North Staffordshire Regiment and men from the Royal Warwick and Worcester Regiments fell all the burden of the struggle. They could not have fought the enemy to a standstill except for the aid given to them by the crews of the British armoured cars, who in boldly and skilfully executed movements put out of action great numbers of the attackers.

It must be remembered that Enver Pasha was collecting the last main force of the Ottoman Empire in the Caucasus, partly in the design to dominate the Germans in Georgia and partly with a view to developing a Turanian Empire stretching to the Chinese frontier. The more resistance he encountered round Baku, the Caspian bridge-head on the possession of which his scheme depended, the more divisions he ordered northward, beyond all range of possibility of influencing events in Palestine and Syria.

Furthermore, every defeat suffered by his troops, his Bolshevist allies, and his Austro-Hungarian assistants and obscure Moslem mercenaries near the far-extended British line caused him to increase the forces he was bringing to Baku for transport across the Caspian Sea. That is to say, Major-General Dunsterville, with a little band of Midlanders, armoured-car crews, and gunners, played no small part in North-Western Persia and at Baku in ensuring for Sir Edmund Allenby at Damascus the most decisive victory in modern history. He so completely diverted the last fine fighting reserves of the Ottoman Empire that, in happy co-operation with the ambitions and jealousies of the Young Turkish

party, he helped to overthrow one of the most warlike of races by a double operation at the remote ends of its territory, without the need for such a blow at its centre as had been attempted in the Dardanelles Campaign.

By four o'clock in the afternoon of September 14th the large Turkish forces round Baku, having fought since dawn without gaining their objectives, were exhausted. They could do little more than occupy the intermediate positions, which they had won through the cowardice and treachery of the Armenians. Had it been possible to counter-attack them they would have broken and fled. But General Dunsterville had no men left for a counter-offensive. Every British rifle was in the line, and neither the Russians nor Armenians, still numbering some 9,000, could be induced to attack. From the beginning they had been little more than a fighting mob, being so inflated with the licence of the revolutionary spirit, which they mistook for liberty, that neither Bicherakhoff nor Dunsterville could make an army

GUNS FOR THE DEFENCE OF THE GREAT OIL PORT OF THE CAUCASUS.
Guns being limbered up at the arsenal at Baku, and (in oval) interior of the arsenal, formerly a Mosque of the Persian shahs. A British detachment aided Armenians and other pro-Entente elements in defending Baku against the Turks, but lack of support caused General Dunsterville to evacuate it.

of them. Many of them were soldiers, but they had lost the sense of discipline that distinguishes the true soldier. The Armenians had started in a mood of heroic desperation, being ready to die if they could each take a Turk with them to the grave, by way of reprisal for the massacre of their race. But this spirit of personal heroism had evaporated gradually in the course of battle through lack of discipline and organisation. Tired men had begun to think for themselves, and had ended by thinking of saving their own lives.

With the enemy occupying high ground from which he could shell the shipping in the port at ranges of three and five thousand yards, nothing remained but for General Dunsterville to inform the Baku Government of his

CONTRASTING STREET SCENES IN TROUBLED BAKU.
Street scene in Baku, the famous oil port and former entrepot for Russo-Persian trade, which was occupied and evacuated by the British, August-September, 1918. The upper photograph shows Armenian and other troops drilling in one of the squares of the town.

decision to evacuate the town. By eight o'clock in the evening all sick and wounded were carried into ships. Two hours afterwards the rest of the troops were in the three vessels allowed for their use, and a fourth ship was laden with ammunition and explosive. This was hit by gun fire from the Russian guardship at the harbour mouth, but the other vessels, moving without lights, escaped untouched, and all four safely reached Enzeli.

For six weeks the British detachment had denied to the enemy the bridge-head of the Caspian Sea and oil-fields of grand importance, besides inflicting severe losses on the Turks and compelling them to bring up an overwhelming force before Baku could be captured. The Dunsterville adventure was a brilliant episode, representing a tactical failure and a strategic success. But for the demoralisation of the Armenians and some of the Russians it would have been a complete success, saving the lives of thousands of refugees.

With regard to the Armenians it must be remarked that many of their men had been fighting valiantly since the Russian Army dissolved into anarchy and treachery. Many had held the Ottomans from the Caucasus and Northern Persia from February to June, 1918, and though at last broken, bands maintained guerrilla warfare in the mountains, among them being Andranik and his men. In the early

part of the war it was mainly with Armenians that the Russians had captured Erzerum, and in the Foreign Legion at Verdun, and among the Indo-British forces in Palestine, Armenians had fought dauntlessly. Utter weariness combined with the moral poison of Bolshevism led to the sullying of the fame of the Armenian people in the last crisis of the war.

Baku was reoccupied by the 39th British Infantry Brigade, with Russian and Armenian troops under General Bicherakhoff, on November 7th, 1918, after the surrender of the Turks. By this time three hundred and forty miles of metalled road had been constructed from the Mesopotamian base to Hamadan, in Persia, allowing light motors to travel forty-eight hours after a rainfall. The better road from Hamadan to Enzeli was repaired, and on this improved line of communications operations continued against the Bolshevists.

Before the conclusion of the struggle with the Turk there were many skirmishes with him in the great mountain region between the Caspian Sea and the Kurdistan highlands. The British attacked in order to defend the Bagdad-Caspian road, and, mainly with aeroplanes and light-armoured motor-cars and cavalry, retained the enemy. These operations, however, were reduced to little importance by a devastating outbreak of influenza which enfeebled both forces. The Turks, who appeared to suffer most, retired so quickly that the British could not get in touch with them, and the British in turn were so stricken with the malady that they returned to get in touch with their doctors. Thus an influenza armistice obtained in Northern Persia some time before the general surrender of the Ottomans, but the epidemic at least served to safeguard the old road of conquest which the British had won.

Reoccupation of Baku

During the pause in the main operations of the Mesopotamian Expeditionary Force there was another great adventure by a British detachment connected with Sir William Marshall's divisions. It will be remembered that in March, 1916, Brigadier-General Sir Percy Sykes landed in the Persian Gulf with a force of five hundred rifles and two mountain guns, marched through Southern Persia, and, by admirable handling of the Persian tribesmen between Kerman, Ispahan, and Shiraz, raised a force of armed Persian police, replacing the Swedes and their men who had betrayed their trust and, joining the Germans, tried to force Persia into the war.

The native levies were increased in the course of two years to six thousand men, known as the South Persia Rifles. Led by British officers and non-commissioned officers, and stiffened by a hundred Indian troops, the new force began sternly to repress all brigandage in Southern Persia. This necessary measure excited the anger of some very strong tribes, that had won wealth and power by preying upon their weaker neighbours and taking toll of all the caravans crossing the baking highlands of the country. As soon as the Kashgais and other predatory tribes

BEFORE BAKU WAS ABANDONED.
British fixing up a military notice in Baku relative to the defence of the town. Despite every effort of the small British force Baku had to be abandoned.

IN THE REGION OF THE ETERNAL FIRE.
Typical scene in the famous petroleum fields of Baku, to save which from a threatened German and Turkish attack in the summer of 1918 two small expeditions were sent from the Mesopotamia armies across Persia.

grew restless, German and Ottoman agents and old members of the Swedish police entered into negotiations with the impoverished brigands. A confederacy was formed, headed by the Kashgais, to drive the British out of Southern Persia after the loyalty of the South Persian Rifles had been undermined.

Trouble started in January, 1918, when the highway between Shiraz and Ispahan, after a period of security lasting nearly a year, was attacked by Arabs. Two squadrons of Burma Mounted Rifles caught the tribe by means of a fine forced march from Shiraz, severely punished them, wringing from the Arab chief the admission that he had been stirred to rebellion by a Persian politician, Mukbir-u-Saltana, who

had been Governor-General of the southern province and also Persian Minister of the Interior.

Another Arab tribe raided a British caravan. Then a great plot was discovered very similar to that which led to the Indian Mutiny. It was arranged that at all the scattered outposts held by the South Persian Rifles, Britons of all ranks were to be murdered. At large centres, such as Shiraz, the native police were to go over to the enemy as soon as he attacked. Parties of the Rifles began to desert, but Sir Percy Sykes took stern measures to maintain discipline. He sent forces in pursuit of the renegades and shot all he captured. He obtained a small reinforcement of young Burmans and Baluchis, most of them only partly trained, amalgamated them with seasoned troops, quickly making good soldiers of them.

In May, 1918, just as the handful of reliable young troops arrived, the struggle for Persia opened in connection with Ludendorff and Enver's general scheme of operations in Central Asia. In the southern province of Fars the Kashgais had a leader of marked ability, Saulat. By energy, ferocity, and skill this nomad had won complete ascendancy over the people of Fars, and Court officials like Mukbir-u-Saltana, when acting as Governor-Generals, had found it well to compromise with the brigand chief.

Saulat proclaims a holy war

Saulat tried to get himself appointed Governor-General of the province which he had robbed and terrorised. Failing in his first attempt at this extraordinary scheme, he negotiated with the Britons on one side and the enemy on the other. From the British he wished to extract a great annual sum of blackmail as guardian of the mountain road between Shiraz and the Persian Gulf. From Germans, Turks, and pro-German Persians he wished to obtain the governorship of the province. He combined both schemes by an opening movement of envelopment against Shiraz on May 10th. The Kashgais came from their high winter pastures down towards Shiraz, in an apparently seasonable migration of an ordinary kind. Suddenly a British fort at Khan-i-Zinian, thirty miles west of the city, was invested by 2,000 tribesmen, while Saulat with 5,000 men approached the town. In small but increasing numbers the South Persian Rifles began to desert throughout Southern Persia, and in Shiraz the Mullahs and pro-German leaders started a fierce agitation. Still intending only to bring pressure on the British to obtain the large subsidy, Saulat proclaimed a holy war. The challenge was immediately taken up. With a column of 1,600 Indians and Persians,

Colonel E. F. Orton marched from the city into the plain, met Saulat on the road to the invested fort, and in an action lasting fourteen hours defeated him.

It was, however, impossible for the victors to relieve the small garrison in the fort. The Shiraz plain was only about eight miles wide at the western end, and topped by steep bare hills rising some 2,000 feet above the basin in which the blue-domed, picturesque city sparkled. At the end of the plain was a chain of mud villages with walled gardens and dense vineyards, into which Saulat, who was no mean tactician, threw a line of sniping skirmishers. They were picked marksmen in impregnable cover, and they enabled their chief to maintain good lines of retreat. The British forces also enjoyed excellent cover behind a circle of walled gardens, strengthened by towers and trenches, at a distance of a thousand yards from the city.

In the outlying fort at Khan-i-Zinian were Captain Will, Sergeant Coomber, and one hundred and sixty Persian officers and men. Captain Will had ample supplies, **Murder of** and reported on May 23rd that he could **Captain Will** hold out as long as was necessary. Saulat, however, won over the Persian garrison. They shot Captain Will before he could defend himself, but Sergeant Coomber held out single-handed for some hours, killing a considerable number of mutineers before he was wounded and captured. Both he and Captain Will were alive when the Kashgais entered the opened fort, but they were killed by Saulat's men.

By this time the tropic sun joined in the blockade, as Saulat had foreseen. The coast along the Persian Gulf was in summer the hottest in the world, the heat being of an intensity and physical effect quite unimaginable by natives of the temperate zone who had not been there. Even Punjabi troops from the fire-pit of Multan could not fight in the withering furnace on the road from the coast. In Shiraz life was not pleasant in the heat, with the mountain wall making the plain simmer like a cauldron, so that the European, with pith helmet and other protection, wanted a cooling roof above him and, if possible, a vaulted cellar with ventilation shafts to keep his mind in **Sir Percy Sykes** working order. Often in the heat of the **at Shiraz** open air the faculty of connected thought was suspended in the ablest European, who found himself reduced intellectually to a condition between that of imbecility and infancy.

But there was no lessening in energy of mind and strength of character among Sir Percy Sykes and his beleaguered force. They could expect no considerable movement in aid from Bushire until the heat decreased in the autumn of the year. A small force, consisting of a section of mountain artillery, two squadrons of cavalry, and a wing of infantry, left the Persian Gulf, at a spot four hundred and fifty miles away, at the beginning of July, and by great endurance managed to reach Saidrabad, two hundred miles inland, where it helped to guard the long lines of communication, but could not aid the besieged troops. Sir Percy Sykes had to withstand a siege in Shiraz in circumstances of difficulty even more serious than those that General Townshend struggled against in Kut.

The Shiraz garrison was less than 2,200 men. By far the

VICTIMS OF TURKISH BARBARITY WHO HAD TO BE CARED FOR BY THE BRITISH.

Inhabitants of a Persian town, swelled by refugees from districts overrun by the exterminating Turks, awaiting their daily water ration. In their campaign against the Turks and their Persian supporters the British were hampered by the necessity of feeding and doctoring large masses of people who would otherwise have died as the result of the Ottoman policy of oppression. This famine relief was a fine and memorable achievement.

larger part of it was composed of Persian officers and men, only watching for an opportunity to murder the British and Indians and repeat in the city on a larger scale the diabolical business of Khan-i-Zinian fort. The magnificently loyal Indian, Burman, and Baluchistan troops were distributed as a guard over the treacherous Persians, who were gradually dismissed. Saulat had cleverly timed his operations to prevent the harvest in the plain being reaped, and he cut off most of the irrigation canals to deprive the population of 50,000 of water supply. At one time only four days' fodder remained for the horses, and to complete the nightmare horrors of the siege, cholera broke out among both the townspeople and the garrison.

The most immediate pressing danger was that of a rising in the city. This possibility had not been overlooked during the construction of the British cantonments, which were

Gallant Indo-British sortie placed at long range from the Persian buildings. Yet the highest of these buildings commanded the British quarter. News of the great German thrusts into the British lines in France and Flanders were spread in highly exaggerated form by enemy agents among the Persians, together with legendary accounts of the submarine blockade of the British Isles.

Well it was for British prestige that a man with so wide and intimate a knowledge of Persian character and ways as Sir Percy Sykes commanded the besieged forces. His engineers provided the people with water by digging many new wells, and food was somehow obtained to keep the people from rising from sheer famine. Then on June 16th, as the emboldened Kashgais had approached within easy striking distance, and sent out another tribe to hold the garden quarter west of the city, an Indo-British column, secretly gathered for a sortie, broke the Kazerunis, the allies of Saulat, and when the Kashgais came up in support drove them back with heavy loss. The British had five men killed and twenty-four wounded, while the enemy losses amounted to two hundred killed and three hundred wounded.

Naturally, the sallying force returned to its fortified line. Thereupon the artful Kashgai chief sent messages to the Shiraz people, boasting that he had driven the British back with tremendous loss to them, while only one of his grooms had been killed in the action. The townsfolk were told that the capture of the city was only a matter of a few days, and that they would save themselves from being treated as allies of the British if they rose against the foreigners.

A great rising was therefore prepared, but before the main movement opened, some of the rougher elements among the townspeople began to plunder. Unfortunately for Saulat they attacked some of the houses of the South Persian Rifles. This gave Sir Percy Sykes an opportunity of displaying his diplomatic art. The Persian Rifles were ready to join with the rebellious people, but were awaiting the signal. Tactful British officers pointed out to the intending mutineers that they must protect their own officers from being plundered, and Persian officers who had suffered from

Popular reaction against Saulat the preliminary outbreak agreed to keep their men under arms during the critical night. Silently and swiftly the Indian troops surprised and occupied all the key positions in the city, while the disconcerted townspeople saw the armed Persian police apparently ready to attack them. By this means the city was overawed. The bazaars opened again, the hostile natives disappeared, and the anger of the people turned against Saulat and his associates for the suffering they caused by cutting off the water supply and stopping the corn mills.

On June 19th the British telegraph line was cut, but the general situation improved. The hereditary Mayor of Shiraz, Mohammed Ali Khan, was won over to the British side. He was a gallant leader with six hundred followers, and owing to his example other Persian chiefs began to change sides. The Kazerunis, who had lost heavily in the garden action, and secured none of the rich plunder Saulat had promised them, abandoned the siege, trailing home in silent anger against the Kashgais. Many of Saulat's

men also deserted him, and the Governor-General of Fars, his Highness the Farman Farma, who had never looked kindly upon the brigand lord's pretensions to usurp all power in the land, issued a proclamation by which Saulat was removed from the position of paramount chief of the Kashgais, a relative being nominally appointed in place of the bankrupt blackmailer.

Saulat's force dwindled by the first week in July, 1918, to one thousand men, and a scheme of combined attack was arranged against him. The new Persian forces that had joined the British, arranged to cross the hills south of the city and cut off the Kashgais, while an Indian column struck out across the plain westward and shepherded the tribesmen southward for capture. The Indian troops, under Lieutenant-Colonel Williams, carried out their part of the plan, storming ridge after ridge and driving the tribesmen into Saulat's main camp. The new Persian forces, however, were not successful in their movement. Saulat checked them, and the only important result of the action was that blood was spilt between the two Persian factions.

Immediately after this action Saulat and the medley of intriguers acting with him had a belated success in the north at Abadeh town. The South Persian Rifles there mutinied, and joining the Kashgais, combined in the besieging of the Indian post. The Indian column at Shiraz, which had carried the western ridges, took only thirty-six hours' rest after the pursuit, and then set out northward, in the hottest month of the year, and marched one hundred and eighty miles to the relief of the surrounded men at Abadeh.

Moving at an average pace of little more than one mile an hour up the mountain road—a wonderful speed in the circumstances—they passed the ruins of Persepolis and reached Abadeh. The mutineers and Kashgais fled rather than stand to fight, and without further trouble the loyal garrison was brought to headquarters.

Saulat spent some months soothing and menacing his scattered tribesmen. By October he won over those Kashgais who had joined the new paramount chief, and then attacked and besieged his suc- **Coming of the** cessor, who was his half-brother, in the **great sickness** town of Firuzabad, in the mountains some eighty miles south of Shiraz. Happily, a detachment of South Persian Rifles remained loyal to the new chief. The Kashgais lost some four hundred men in the new defeat, and Saulat was completely overthrown by a new foe—pneumonic influenza—which attacked both sides. The Kashgais lost at least thirty per cent. of their strength, and Saulat became a fugitive. The Indian troops suffered heavily, their losses amounting to eighteen per cent. of their strength, and the Shiraz people, recovering from the cholera epidemic, were more than decimated.

With the great sickness there came complete victory and peace. The coast route opened, relieving troops, fresh supplies, and adequate stores were sent across the mountains, and the siege of Shiraz, one of the high adventures of the Indo-British forces, ended in glory, thanks to the brilliant genius of General Sykes, the ability of his Staff, the devotion of his Indian troops, and the steady skill of the British non-commissioned officers.

Persia never struck a blow for herself. A considerable part of her sufferings during the war was inflicted upon her by her own tribesmen and the Swedish police. Persians invited the ravaging Turk continually to cross the frontier and live on the invaded country, and when the power of Russia was broken, some three small forces of British and Indian troops at Hamadan, in the Fars province, and by Meshed, saved Persia from complete ruin by plundering Turk, invading Bolshevists, and Austro-Hungarians. The political party in Persia which assumed the name of Democrats, and finally came forward as champions of the independence of their country, were originally so closely in league with the Germanic conspirators that the uninstructed countrymen at last concluded that a democrat was an organiser of assassins, ready to pay higher wages than used to be given by Omar Khayyám's friend the Old Man of the Mountains,

Arab Mounted Police who helped the British, crossing the dried=up bed of an ancient canal.

Company of the Staffordshire Regiment at Baladajar Station during the expedition to Baku.

H.M.S. Sedgefly in action on the Tigris, showing 'midships gun in full recoil.

Hoisting the Union Jack over the Turkish Headquarters at Kirkuk, occupied October 25th, 1918.

British monitor in action against the Turks on the banks of the Tigris.

Some of General Marshall's men bathing near Narin Kupri Bridge while sappers repaired it.

Harbour of Baku, showing Russian wireless station and (on immediate left) the naval jetty.

In ancient Babylonia, where the armies of freedom fought against the Turk.

whose secret refuge south of the Caspian Sea was passed by one of the small British expeditions.

The Ottoman appeal to religious prejudice in Persia failed almost as completely as the Teutonic gospel of democracy. There was a sharper difference in creed between Turk and Persian than obtains between Catholic and Protestant. The Turks lost all real hold upon the men whom they regarded as heretics in Islam when, in May, 1916, there was a rising in Kerbela, near Babylon, and Turkish guns were trained on the sacred shrine in the town containing the Tomb of Hussein. All the Persian holy places in Mesopotamia were at last brought under British protection in a reverent manner, with the result that Great Britain practically became guardian of the centres of the Persian faith as well as the fighting ally of the Sultan of the Hedjaz, who by right of birth was entitled to the Caliphate against the fallen Ottoman monarch.

The question of the Caliphate, however, remained a delicate problem. A considerable number of Indian Mohammedans, differing in sect from the Persians as did the Turks, seemed inclined to agitate for a continuance of the Ottoman Caliphate, claiming Constantinople and the ancient Christian Church of St. Sophia for the faith. Their disinclination to accept the Sultan of Hedjaz, whose claim as lineal successor to the Prophet was generally recognised before the war, appeared to be based upon the apprehension that his erection to the Caliphate would lose for Islam all that the Ottomans had gained and managed to hold. As the Indian Moslem had generally been loyal to the British Government, and contributed a very large number of excellent fighting men for the armies of the Empire, the Indian view weighed with the British authorities. But so did the Arabian view, for the Arabs had also helped, particularly the men of Mecca and the clans who gathered round the new Sultan and fought in alliance with his brilliant Emirs, more or less under the direction of the adventurous Oxford scholar, Colonel Lawrence. All this, however, was a matter left for settlement in the establishment of peace.

When the siege of Shiraz ended victoriously in October, 1918, the main Mesopotamian Expeditionary Force came into action in a final battle on the Tigris by the ruins of Asshur, the oldest city of the Assyrians, whose mouldering temple and walls stand by the modern site of Kalaat Shergat. The Sixth Turkish Army covered the approaches to Mosul by holding a position of great natural strength astride the Fatha gorge, where the rocky heights of the long Jebel Hamrin crossed the river and ran into the desert. In the gorge the rocks go sheer down into the water, leaving **Final battle** no space for a path, so that in days of **on the Tigris** peace caravans have to skirt the western slopes where there is no water. Here Ismail Hakki, the ablest of Ottoman commanders, had spent eighteen months in making entrenchments, prolonging his right flank through the waterless desert to Shergat, and placing batteries on the ranges of hills to sweep the road through the sand. On the left flank his men were entrenched for five miles on the crests, and by the junction of the Lesser Zab stream and the Tigris there was another series of works. The Ottoman commander had about 9,000 rifles and 59 guns placed around the gorge, and he was busy saving Sir William Marshall all further anxiety regarding the other part of the Bagdad-Caspian road by drawing a division—the

THE NEW AMID THE OLD.
Native workers repairing telegraph wires in New Street, Bagdad, a modern occupation that seemed strangely out of place in the old-world City of the Caliphs.

5th—from the Urmia region back towards Mosul. Other Turkish forces were also being hurriedly withdrawn in the first week of October from the Caucasus in a vain endeavour to prevent Sir Edmund Allenby's victory in Palestine from developing into complete disaster for the Ottoman Empire.

Immediately Sir William Marshall received news of the grand successes of Sir Edmund Allenby he made all preparations, and with great pleasure he received on October 7th a definite order to take the offensive. Much of his transport was scattered in Persia and in harvest work between the two great rivers. This prevented him from striking through Kirkuk, far north of the Hamrin range, and making the Turks fight on ground of his own choosing.

The British commander had already reached Kirkuk in the victorious advance, but had drawn back through lack of transport, which had been needed in Persia. In these circumstances nothing remained but a direct attack up the Tigris against the great fortress of the mountain gorge. A frontal attack was impossible in the nature of things. Even if successful it would have given no rapid road of advance along the river and would have been very costly. The manœuvre adopted was to turn the left of the Turkish stronghold and force a passage over the Lesser Zab, bringing the enemy's right positions under flanking fire and enabling them to be attacked with better chance of success.

Then it was intended to cut his line of retreat by means of cavalry working round on the left, while light-armoured motor-cars moved round on the right. There was, however, no room for any element of surprise in this scheme. The Turks and their Teutonic advisers had carefully foreseen every possible movement, and Ismail Hakki was well prepared on both sides of the gorge. The conduct of the main operations of assault was given to Lieutenant-General Sir A. S. Cobbe, commanding the 17th and 18th Divisions and 7th and 11th Cavalry Brigades. Protecting his right flank was a small column under Brigadier-General A. C. Lewin, whose task was to fend off Turkish forces on the higher reaches of the little Zab stream.

The attacking troops were suffering seriously from influenza, and many men had been removed to special influenza camps. Moreover, the forces were largely composed of new formations with no experience in **Turks abandon** war, most of the veterans of early **their stronghold** campaigns having been sent to Palestine, together with numerous officers and non-commissioned officers required for drilling General Allenby's recruits.

Generalship and fine regimental leading, with precise staff-work, had to supply the lack of experience in the men and absence of overwhelming strength. General Cobbe began by making repeated bold raids against the enemy's right flank in the hope of inducing a wasted concentration there. Then on October 23rd he got in touch with the Turks on both banks of the Tigris, and moved a column along the crest of the Jebel Hamrin against the Turkish left, while the 7th Cavalry Brigade carried out a wider enveloping movement in the same direction north of the barren hills. This manœuvre had the desired effect, and the Turks abandoned their great stronghold in the gorge during the night, blowing up the riverside road they had made.

British engineers at once began blasting a new path between the water and the rock. Meanwhile, another cavalry force, the 11th Brigade, had been making a forty-five-mile march through the northern desert, and about three o'clock in the afternoon of October 24th they reached a point on the Lesser Zab some twenty miles above the main battlefield. The horsemen found a ford covered by Turkish fire, but crossed through the deep water with remarkably slight loss, formed a strong bridge-head, ferried their transport over the stream, and sent a strong detachment riding down the tributary and clearing the bank of Turks.

Above them Brigadier-General Lewin's column carried Kirkuk, and below them the 7th Cavalry Brigade and the 53rd Brigade of Infantry battled across the stream near the confluence with the Tigris, meeting with strong opposition, yet conquering and extending bridge-heads. Under this pressure the Turkish forces on the left bank of the great river retreated across a bridge they had prepared at El Humr.

Main tussle for El Humr Then came the main tussle for the El Humr position. It was hard, forthright, wearing fighting for the untried 17th Division of young Indian troops and the British battalions. Through the deep ravines and up the steep sides of the Makhul mountain and the Khanuka mountain, on which the second Turkish position was based, the forces of the assault slowly worked, their transport following them up goat-tracks and breaking bulk from wheel to pack. Extreme was the difficulty of getting both light and heavy guns forward to support the clambering infantry, whose endurance was tested terribly by heat and thirst as well as by the enemy's bitter resistance.

The early successes on the left bank of the river told on the course of the struggle. Here the British artillery was able to enfilade the hostile stronghold. Steadily the gallant 17th Division worked upward and onward, and late in the evening the leading battalion of the 1st Highland Light Infantry made an heroic rush at the Turkish works covering the El Humr bridge. The wire entanglements protecting the entrenchments were uncut, but the Scotsmen themselves broke through the wire and stormed the trenches, and then held them throughout the night and the following morning, repulsing every counter-attack, in spite of their own bodily weakness and sadly thinned ranks.

The grand thrust they had delivered was continued on October 26th by the 17th Division. With the same slow, grinding effect, battalion after battalion came into action all through the day and night. At dawn on October 27th the decisive effect of the pressure became evident. While the Turks were intent upon the defence of their rocky mountain fortress, the 11th Cavalry Brigade of 7th Hussars, Guides Cavalry, 23rd Cavalry, and W Battery Royal Horse Artillery, under Brigadier-General Cassels, made a wide detour by the Tigris and found a ford some fourteen miles up the river. Through a strong current, some five feet deep, the leading regiment crossed and took at a gallop the Huwaish gorge in the Turkish rear, blocking the road of retreat to Mosul. The British armoured cars on the other side cut the telegraph line to Mosul, while another cavalry brigade distracted the enemy by a feint towards Shergat.

Road of Turkish retreat blocked The horsemen behind the trapped Turks began operations by bursting upon the enemy reserves south of Huwaish, and scattering them with the help of some light-armoured cars. This not only assisted the British and Indian infantry still fighting over the mountains but concealed in an uncommonly effective manner the weak strength of the Hussars and Guides and their comrades. The main Turkish force began to give under this surprise stroke at its rear, and while the enemy was still too confused to mass upon the single, tired cavalry brigade that barred the road, the 53rd Infantry arrived, with some guns and, after a march of thirty-three miles, moved into position at Huwaish.

Likewise, with a view to preventing the enemy from turning and throwing all his weight upon the 11th Cavalry Brigade, the tireless, undaunted infantrymen of the 17th Division continued their advance through difficult ground, maintaining such a menace of breaking through the Turks that the main hostile force had to act in shifts as rearguard. At three

o'clock in the morning of October 28th the 17th Division was still moving over a broken, arid, waterless waste, and at the end of eight hours it closed once more with the Turks holding a rearguard position three miles south of Shergat. The 2nd West Kents broke clean through in a most gallant and skilful attack, taking some two hundred prisoners and eleven machine-guns. By two o'clock in the afternoon the Ottoman was retiring from the field of battle.

The men of the 17th Division, under Major-General G. A. J. Leslie, could not pursue the foe they had beaten till he broke. They had been fighting since October 23rd. Men and animals were completely exhausted through great physical exertions, desert heat, and lack of water. They had to get to the river and drink.

The 11th Cavalry Brigade was reinforced by the advanced battalion of the 53rd Infantry Brigade, and by Hussars, Lancers, and Horse Artillery of the 7th Cavalry Brigade, who rode for seventeen hours from Fatha, and lost men and horses by drowning at the ford, in a determined effort to complete the envelopment movement. They took over the position on the right flank, where a fresh Ottoman force, the 5th Division from Urmia, speeded through Mosul, was trying to break into the British rear and so release the main body of the Sixth Turkish Army. On this side of the river Brigadier-General Cassels, who had executed the decisive manœuvre with the 11th Cavalry Brigade, was given charge of all the operations that closed and bolted the gate of escape to Mosul.

During the night of October 28th the Turks continued to attempt to break out, but were thrown back, and in the darkness over dreadful tracks the 17th Division, responding magnificently to the call, fought forward. Dawn came up, and the weary men still worked forward, and by eleven o'clock in the morning of October 29th they drove the enemy rearguard on to the main body, which in turn they attacked through lines of entrenchments and ravines by Shergat. Against a plunging fire Britons and Indians charged in the afternoon, falling back in places under fierce counter-charges, in which the 114th Mahrattas distinguished **Victory where Alexander failed** themselves by shattering the sallying enemy. Through the night, the terrible contest in pluck and endurance proceeded.

The Turks were heartened by the arrival of their 5th Division in force with artillery. The new troops occupied the high bluffs by the ford, but were dealt with by the 13th Hussars of the 7th Brigade. Led by their colonel, the Hussars galloped across the open, under artillery and machine-gun and rifle fire, dismounted by the bluffs, and carried the position with the bayonet. The remainder of the cavalry brigade rode in pursuit of other newly arrived Turks, and ended the menace from the north with the capture of a thousand prisoners.

Ismail Hakki's position was then hopeless. His men were packed in hollows that were raked by British gun fire, and, as at dawn on October 30th the attackers closed in for the final slaughter, white flags appeared all along the enemy lines, and Ismail Hakki surrendered later in person.

Eleven thousand three hundred and twenty-two prisoners were taken, with fifty-one guns, two thousand animals, and three steamers.

Exploiting fully and quickly the brilliant victory, Sir William Marshall sent a strong advanced force of foot, horse, and guns towards Mosul. On November 1st the Turks came out under a flag of truce.

Thus ended the campaign of four years that had begun in a small way by the capture of Fort Fao on November 6th, 1914, when the scheme was only to safeguard the Persian oil-field and protect friendly tribes round the Persian Gulf. The Briton, as was his way, had gone farther than he intended, and had only been spurred to put out his full strength by serious reverses. Some 114,000 square miles of territory had been conquered, 45,000 prisoners and 250 guns being taken, in one of the worst fields of operations in the world, where Alexander the Great had perished and the extension of the power of Rome had been checked when Julian fell with his army at Ctesiphon.

CHAPTER CCXCIX.

"THE RUMANIAN BLUNDER."

First Full Account of the Worst Error of the War.

By Hamilton Fyfe

(Who was in Rumania from August, 1916, until the end of that year as accredited correspondent with the Rumanian forces).

Reasons why Rumania Entered the War—The Lure of Transylvania—Military Unpreparedness not Generally Known—M. Bratiano's Defence at Jassy—The Moral of the Map—Rumania's 1,200-Mile Frontier—Co-operation Between Germany and Bulgaria—Colonel von Hammerstein's Proposal to Rumania to Join the Central Powers—What the Allies Did—Colonel Feyler's Criticism—Alleged Secret Understanding between Colonel Jostoff and M. Bratiano—Russian Faith in Bulgarians' Fidelity to their Brother-Slavs— M. Derussi's Warning—Russia Unjustly Blamed—General Zionchkovski's Limitations—His Recall—Rumania's Weakness in the Dobruja—The Disaster of Turtukai—General Iliesco's Advice Overruled by Politicians—Conflict of Counsellors—Attitude of General Alexeieff—Von Sturmer and M. Poklevski—Censorship of the Press—Fall of Constantsa—Rumanian Heroism in the Passes—Retreat of the First and Second Armies—100,000 Casualties—Avarescu's Bold Adventure—Nervousness of the Headquarters' Staff— What Mackensen Said to Avarescu Two Years Later—From Confidence to Despair—Rumanian Plans Fall Into Hands of the Enemy—Theory of Treachery—Spread of Panic—Capture of and Flight from Bukarest—Peasants Welcome the Invading Germans with Bread and Salt—Rumania not "Forced" to Come In—Ill-founded Charges against Russia—Responsibility Divided between Rumania's Rulers and the Allies.

A MONG the unexplained mysteries of the war that of Rumania's intervention, under conditions which, as we now see, made disaster certain, is the puzzle that has been found most difficult to solve. No explanation was allowed to be published so long as the war lasted. The military authorities who controlled the Press Bureau refused to permit any part of the truth to be told. Their excuse was that allied susceptibilities might be wounded. But perhaps a still stronger reason might be found in the official desire to shield some of those who were responsible for the blundering and lack of foresight which gave the Germans their success in Rumania and enabled them, by cheering up their peoples and persuading them that the German arms were invincible, to prolong the war for another two years.

I am now going to give as full an account as I can of the causes of the catastrophe. Whenever I think of them I think of the mild, grey morning of December

1st, 1916, when I walked up and down outside the village school, which housed the Operations Branch of the Rumanian Headquarters' Staff, and debated where the blame ought to be laid for what Mr. Lloyd George called later "the Rumanian blunder." I, who saw the pitifulness and misery of its consequences, prefer to call it the Rumanian tragedy. It was both.

Inside the schoolhouse, still hung with coloured wall-pictures of birds, beasts, flowers, and trees, orderlies were packing up papers and maps. Near by the Motor-car Department was hastily preparing all its automobiles for a long road journey, piling tyres and inner tubes, spare parts and accessories on vans. A train stood in the little railway-station, with steam up. The officers of the Staff and the Foreign Attachés were ready to leave at any moment. For-three months they had lived and worked in this village of Perish, forty miles north of Bukarest. It was conveniently placed between the northern and the southern fronts, between

HELP FOR HARD-PRESSED RUMANIA.

General Berthelot (left), head of the French Mission to Rumania, and General Avarescu, the Rumanian Commander-in-Chief. The famous French soldier arrived in Bukarest, October, 1916, to co-operate with the High Command of the Rumanian Army.

PATRIOTISM RUN RIOT.
Rumanian troops guarding a street in Bukarest against the violent demonstrations of the populace in favour of war against Austria.

WAR FEVER IN BEAUTIFUL BUKAREST.
Great demonstration of citizens of Bukarest in support of the entry of Rumania into the war on the side of the Allies. Banners were carried displaying " Down with Austria ! " Deceived and misled Rumania declared against Austria on August 27th, 1916.

this was a fancy picture. The British residents in the country—men who had lived there for a great many years and who had learned to know it intimately—were, without exception, I think, doubtful about the value of Rumania's military strength. No one thought of consulting them. The British Military Attaché, however, gave the home authorities the truth. Why was he not believed ?

The Rumanian War Office was warned from one British source. Six weeks before Rumania declared war a British armament firm received a visit from a Rumanian officer representing his Government. He asked them if they could supply ammunition for artillery of old patterns (the latest of the guns dated back to 1887). The firm replied that they had " ceased to make such ammunition," and that what the Rumanians needed was new artillery

the Carpathians and the Danube. When they went there nobody doubted but that their move, when it came, would be on to enemy territory. Now they were about to retire farther into the interior of their own country, for their country had been invaded. A large part of it was already in the hands of the enemy, and they knew that worse was to follow. The capital and the precious oil region were on the point of being abandoned. The high hope—nay, the certainty of success—with which Rumania began her war had been dashed to the ground.

As we walked up and down in the mild air under the grey, December sky we sorrowfully reviewed the stages which had led to this bitter disappointment, and we asked ourselves " Why ? " Why, first of all, did Rumania come in ?

She came in, after waiting patiently for two years, partly because she was pressed to come in ; but chiefly because her rulers thought the moment had arrived when they could without undue risk declare their sympathy with the Allies ; because these rulers believed that the offensive power of the enemy was broken ; because they imagined that the war was approaching its end, and argued that if they did not " march " now they could never realise their hope of uniting Transylvania, with its population of Rumanian blood, to the dominions of the Rumanian Crown.

Rumania's Army unprepared   In part they deceived themselves ; in part they were misled. They were told that the Austrians were exhausted ; that the Germans had no more available reserves. They were promised a vigorous offensive on the Salonika front. They were allowed, and even urged, to declare war, although their Army lacked almost everything that an army needs in the warfare of to-day. Their unpreparedness was not generally known. In Britain and in France the Rumanian Army was spoken of as a force ready at all point for battle. Its fighting strength was estimated at 800,000 men. It was described by writers who then enjoyed sure confidence as " one of the best small armies in Europe," both well-trained and well-equipped.

There were, of course, people in Rumania who knew that

of the latest pattern. But they could not deliver this for at least six months. " Postpone your offensive," they suggested. Unfortunately, the advice of the British armament firm was not taken. Six months later they began to deliver the new guns, according to contract ; but by that time Wallachia was in the hands of the enemy. (The guns did very useful work, by the way, in the campaign of 1917.)

Here another question will certainly be asked. Why was Rumania so ill-prepared for war ? The reply, by those who then ruled the country, is that no market for munitions and war material was open to her. " Neither side," they say, " trusted us. We could not buy what we required, because nobody would sell it." That was the defence offered by M. Bratiano to the members of his party at their meeting in Jassy just before Christmas, 1917. Many Rumanians said, " If that is true, how were the large sums voted for military preparation spent by the War Department ? " That is a question of internal politics. All that interests us is that these sums did not provide her with the necessities of modern war.

Besides being unfurnished with war material, Rumania found it difficult to frame a satisfactory plan of campaign. For many years she had been preparing to fight in an easterly direction—that is to say, against Russia. All her fortifications were upon her eastern frontier. When her rulers decided to join the Allies she had to make ready as best she could, in secret, for attack and defence upon the other side.

One glance at the map of Rumania, to those who do not recollect the shape of the country, will show the impossibly hard nature of this task. Its shape is that of the letter L turned backward. The frontier at the western end forms a salient. To the north and west lies Austria-Hungary; upon the south Bulgaria. For a small army to attempt to fight upon the whole of Rumania's 1,200-mile frontier, including this dangerous salient, was clearly out of the question. The Rumanian General Staff, therefore, decided, and made clear to the allied nations that it had decided

The moral of the map to content itself with operations against Transylvania and to leave the Bulgarian front alone. Let me repeat. The Rumanians gave the Allies clearly to understand that they did not propose to do anything upon their southern front. That I know. From this arise two insistent interrogatives:

I. WHY did Rumania suppose that she would be able to leave her southern frontier very lightly defended.

II. WHY did the Allies agree to the plan she proposed, instead of insisting that she should fight in close co-operation with General Sarrail's armies on the Salonika front, thus catching the enemy between two fires; stopping communication between the Central Empires and their vassals, Turkey and Bulgaria; dissolving for ever the German dream of a German Empire stretching from Hamburg to the Persian Gulf?

To this second query we were not able, that morning at Rumanian Headquarters, to suggest any answer; nor can I suggest one now.

Rumania's coming in, the cause of so much rejoicing in Britain and elsewhere, seems to me to have had a haphazard, unpremeditated character, which proved that somebody, somewhere, was not using his brains. Set alongside of it the careful manner in which the Germans arranged the entry of Bulgaria into the conflict. They knew months beforehand that "Fox" Ferdinand had made up his crafty mind. They fixed the date on which Bulgaria should begin operations; they said exactly what they wanted the Bulgarian Army to do.

Or, consider how the Germans would have acted if Rumania had taken their side. When Colonel von Hammerstein arrived at Bukarest, in the spring of 1916, as German Military Attaché,

he made a proposal to the Rumanians that they should join the Central Powers. He said:

We know all about your Army. As a small Army it was a good one. As you have enlarged it you have weakened it. You had not a sufficiency of good material for officers. You could not expand your equipment to meet the increased number of men and the needs of modern warfare. If you fight alone you will fare badly. What we suggest, if you will join us, is this: We will send you all the munitions you require. We will send also generals to assist your Headquarters Staff, and a number of officers skilled in the technical arts of war, as well as regimental officers, one or more to each regiment. Finally, we will give you two German army corps to stiffen your inexperienced troops.

The Allies did agree to provide Rumania with munitions, which had to pass through Russia, over the Russian railways, to reach her. They did propose to establish a park of heavy artillery in Bessarabia, so that she could be supplied with guns quickly when she decided to move—a proposal which was rejected. That was all they did, excepting the promise of Russia to put 50,000 men into the region south of the Danube. Rumania's coming in was a surprise. She was allowed to do just as she pleased. Disaster was the result.

It was as if a man should rush on to a football field and say to the captain of a team, " I have come to play for you "; and as if the captain, instead of inquiring whether he could play, and allotting him his place in the field, should say, " Hurrah! Come on! " all the team crying " Hurrah! " also; and as if the man should dash on to the field and try to kick a goal, but, in place of doing this, give the other side an opening and let them score heavily.

What had become of the Allied Military Council, sitting permanently in Paris, of which so much was hoped at the time (1916) when its formation was announced?

No longer, we were then told, would the **The Allied** allied armies suffer from that lack of co- **Military Council** ordinated direction which had hampered their gallant efforts up to that hour. On all fronts their activities would henceforward be regulated in accordance with a single plan. The enemy had gained very substantial advantages by reason of placing all the forces at his disposal under the supreme command of the German General Staff. Now the Allies were to benefit in the same direction.

Perhaps we did benefit. Perhaps the Allied Military Council did very useful work, which will be made clear some day; but of one thing I am certain, without waiting for the laboured volumes of the leisurely historians—the Allied

GALLANT SOLDIERS OF AN ALLY WHO WERE WRONGLY LED.

Rumanian infantry advancing in skirmishing order. The entry of Rumania into the war on August 27th, 1916, was hailed with extravagant hopes which were unfortunately not fulfilled. She believed that Bulgaria would desert the Central Powers, and consequently did not follow what was the true strategy of attacking vigorously in the direction of Constantinople. Instead, the Rumanian armies started an offensive against Austria across the Carpathian passes, which, it was held later, should have only been seized and fortified. The policy, at first successful, proved disastrous in the end.

Military Council did not do all the useful work which it might have done, and which, I imagine, it would have done if the Allied High Commands had considered it to be of value.

I speak only of that which I know. I speak of the activities of Rumania. She declared war at the end of August. It is not too much to say that, during the four or five weeks which followed, her operations were in a state of muddled uncertainty. It seems to me, as I think it must seem to all who have studied the military problem which the Allies had before them, that the action to be taken by Rumania in concert with the British, French, Russian, and Italian forces demanded the most careful consideration. So much depended upon it. So much, if it had fulfilled the hopes founded upon it by the popular imagination, might have been done by it to shorten the war.

Colonel Feyler's criticism
No doubt the popular imagination was too hopeful. It was not acquainted with the conditions of the case. But did those who were, or who ought to have been, in possession of all the facts, did they do all they could to make the entry of Rumania effective in a military sense? If so, then "all they could do" did not amount to much!

Colonel Feyler, of the Swiss Army, is, I believe, considered to be by far the soundest among the critics of military operations. He wrote of the Rumanian tragedy that it was an example of a punishment "frequently enough meted out to generals who do not order their movements sufficiently in conformity with the whole plan of campaign and who start out on business of their own."

What, according to Colonel Feyler, was their chief strategical error? It was, that they "embarked on a private expedition of their own instead of helping to destroy the principal enemy in the Balkans; they attacked Transylvania instead of Bulgaria."

For this there were two reasons. The rulers of Rumania wanted Transylvania, and they did not think Bulgaria would fight.

Why M. Bratiano supposed that the Bulgarians would forgo their chance of seeking revenge for what they called Rumania's "stab in the back" (1913), has never been explained. Many believe it can be explained by a secret understanding which he had with Colonel Jostoff, chief of the Bulgarian Headquarters Staff and virtually Commander-in-Chief of "Fox" Ferdinand's Army. Jostoff was known to be out of sympathy with the German leanings of his master. He was of opinion Bulgaria would do better to quit the side which, he was convinced, must lose in the end. He is said to have agreed with M. Bratiano that, as soon as Rumania gained certain successes, there should be a military revolution in Bulgaria. Ferdinand should be shot back into the rubbish-heap of minor unemployed Royalties from which he had come, and the Army should fight for the Allies instead of against them.

This fits in with a memorandum circulated by General Howell some months earlier, and it is the only hypothesis which can account for M. Bratiano's conviction that the Bulgarians would not fight.

The belief that it is a correct hypothesis is strengthened by

my knowledge that at Russian Head quarters it was said in July: "The Bulgarians are all right. They will not turn their arms against us, their brother-Slavs."

Presumably this notion was grown in the same soil as the persistent rumour pervading Petrograd at this time, to the effect that the Crown Prince Boris was to be substituted for his father, whose policy of alliance with the Central Powers would then be reversed. The soil which nourished these and other like stories must have been, I think, a vague knowledge of the Bratiano-Jostoff agreement.

Evidently the Germans also knew of it a few days after Rumania declared war. Jostoff either killed himself or was murdered. That awakened M. Bratiano from his dream of a friendly or, at any rate, a neutral Bulgaria. He had been warned for some weeks by M. Derussi, Rumanian Minister at Sofia, to expect an attack from the Bulgarians. Now he saw that these warnings, which had been disregarded, were only too well-founded. Almost at the same moment the attack was delivered. The

WHAT GERMANY COVETED IN RUMANIA'S CAPITAL.
Petrol tanks at Bukarest and (in oval) scene showing oil transport from a railway-station. A rich supply of petroleum, which they badly needed, fell to the invading Germans when they occupied Bukarest on December 6th, 1916, after the defeat of the Rumanian armies.

Bulgarians invaded the territory which they had been compelled to cede in 1913. The fortress of Turtukai (Tutrakan) fell. That was the first of the blows which ended in Rumania's defeat !

. . . .

I arrived in the country just when the news of the disaster to the Turtukai garrison was being whispered gloomily about. I recollect a very friendly Customs official shaking his head over it at the frontier station. There was a general disposition to blame the Russians for not sending their promised forces in time. This was unjust. As soon as Rumania had launched her declaration of war, 28,000 Russians were sent into the Dobruja. More followed within a few weeks. Unfortu-

PRECIOUS BOOTY FOR THE GERMANS.
The wharves and valuable accumulation of oil storage which the Germans found useful when they captured Constantsa, Rumania's Black Sea port, on October 22nd, 1916.

CORN FOR THE CONQUERORS.
German and Bulgarian soldiers in Veles, escorting donkeys carrying grain to be ground into flour. These ruthless conquerors of unhappy Rumania stripped her of all they could lay hands on.

nately, they were not commanded by a general of much energy or skill.

Correspondents were sent to see General Zionchkovski's army corps as a model of organisation. This officer certainly had the gift of organising, but there his ability stopped. His chief anxiety in the Dobruja was to have his trenches well-constructed, his lines of communication perfect, his rear positions all ready for a possible retirement. There were many generals of this stamp, among the Germans as well as among the allied forces. They did everything by the book. A vigorous commander, resolved to make his power felt by the enemy and willing to take a risk might have saved the position south of the Danube, even after Turtukai and Silistria were lost. Inactivity, with a commander of Mackensen's calibre on the other side, was the sure road to disaster. One consequence of the disaster was General Zionchkovski's recall.

The false hope based upon the belief that the Bulgarians would change sides, and thus separate Turkey from the Central Powers, accounts for the neglect of Russia to send a large force to the Dobruja, as well as for the weakness of Rumania in this region. If that hope had not been cherished, it would surely have been clear that the true strategy was to attack vigorously in the direction of Constantinople and of the railway which connected Turkey with its German masters. The Carpathian passes could have been seized and fortified. Small forces in each would have been

able to hold these naturally strong defensive positions. The Germans could not have sent large forces against them ; they would have been obliged hurriedly to throw the bulk of their available strength in the way of the advance towards Constantinople. No such advance being made, Falkenhayn was able to collect his armies and to plan his operations without haste.

He was assisted, moreover, by the confusion into which the disaster of Turtukai threw the Rumanian's plans. They had in the first days of their war made an easy and successful entry into Transylvania. Their dash through the mountains was cleverly schemed. The troops crossed by shepherds' and smugglers' paths ; or, hidden in trains supposed to contain merchandise, they sprang out at the Hungarian frontier stations and overpowered a weak resistance. They pushed on rapidly, driving the enemy's small forces before them.

Their object was to penetrate far enough into Transylvania to enable the Rumanian front to be shortened. Once in touch with General Prezan's Army of the North, they could have drawn a straight line from, say, Fogorash to a point in the mountains west of Roman. Had they **The disaster of Turtukai** resolutely followed this design, cutting their loss of territory in the south, they might have followed it with success.

General Iliesco, the clever soldier, who was actually Commander-in-Chief, although no more than a brigadier-general without any experience in the commanding of large bodies of troops, was in favour of keeping to the original plan and proceeding methodically with the invasion of Transylvania, in spite of the Turtukai reverse. His advice was overruled. The politicians were alarmed for the safety of the capital, which was in no danger at all, since the enemy had not enough men to put across the Danube as an invading force. Iliesco was not strong enough to resist political pressure. He was obliged to detach large forces from the two Transylvanian armies. General Avarescu was also transferred from the northern to the southern front. Thus began that unfortunate movement of troops from one point to another which continued all through and which was to be so important a contributory cause of the disaster which followed.

For, as soon as their original intention was abandoned the Rumanian General Staff found itself without any plan at all. It lived from hand to mouth, from hour to hour. Now was the moment when the Allied Military Council should, according to the scheme of its duties, have guided the Rumanians, inexperienced in warfare, to some fortunate decision. It offered them no guidance at all. What did happen was, according to Staff officers in close relation with the events of this period, ludicrous. The Rumanians received this advice from Russia, that advice from France; an admonition in one sense from Great Britain, and suggestions of a totally opposite character from somewhere else.

One day they would be influenced in one direction, next day would come doubts whether, after all, the contrary road

The conflict of counsellors

were not the more desirable. Even the wives of prominent personages took part in the hunt after ideas that might conceivably lead to victory. Chaos reigned instead of order. The operations of the allied armies were, as much as ever they had been, at the mercy of the misfortunes which always attend in warfare a divided command.

There can be no harm in relating this now. More important to us than any other factor, more important even than the steady output of munitions, was this factor of co-ordination, this need of a central command, the need of better general plans. I have shown by relating what happened in Rumania that our general plans had been dangerously defective. War cannot be conducted by the method of correspondence classes. That was the method employed while the fate of Rumania hung doubtful. Victories are won by taking decisions, not by offering advice.

There was also, I believe, in addition to the uncertainty about the general plans of the Allies, confusion as to the Allies' wishes for Rumania's entry. In Rumania I was told, for instance, that Russia presented in July an " ultimatum " to the Rumanian Government, which left the latter no alternative between " coming in " at once or staying out altogether. Russian Staff officers, on the other hand, who seemed to me to be in a position to know, told me that General Alexeieff, the Russian Chief of Staff, did not want Rumania to " come in " at that moment; he considered that she was doing useful work enough in " covering " his left flank.

Later, when I reached Petrograd on my way home, I learned the terms of General Alexeieff's letter which was regarded as an " ultimatum." He said, in effect, simply this: " If Rumania should be intending to join the Allies, please let me know in good time, since it will affect my plans." This letter was addressed to the Secretary-General of the Rumanian War Office, General Iliesco, not formally to the Rumanian Government.

To understand how it was possible for this to be considered an " ultimatum," you must please take into account the " raging, tearing propaganda," in favour of Rumania's immediate entry, which was carried on by the Russian

General Alexeieff's letter

Legation, under instructions from Von Stürmer, then, unluckily, Russian Minister for Foreign Affairs. This man, who was accused openly in the Russian Parliament of attempting to treat with Germany for a separate peace, and of personal corruption, and who made no reply to these charges, succeeded M. Sazonoff in the summer of 1916, and at once set to work to make Rumania move. Many people have since believed that he was working under German instructions and for German pay. I think it is far more likely that he aimed at a personal triumph; that he wished to be able to say: " What Sazonoff could not do, I have done." At all events, he spurred the Russian Minister in Bukarest, M. Poklevski, into vigorous action, which was supported by the British and French Legations, acting under precise instructions from London and from Paris.

Subjected to this violent pressure from M. Poklevski (who was later on dismissed for having done what Von Stürmer ordered him to do), the Rumanian Government may easily

have suspected in the letter of General Alexeieff a purpose quite at variance with the spirit in which it was written. Even the members of the Russian Legation were unaware of General Alexeieff's real attitude; one of the secretaries gave as the reason for their furious activity " that the Russian left flank was in danger of an attack from a new group of armies then being formed in Galicia, and that it needed Rumania's help to turn aside this blow." Thus the Headquarters Staff and the Foreign Office were out of touch. Poor Rumania appears to have been the victim of a tragic misunderstanding.

.   .   .   .   .   .

During the month of September I was in Bukarest. The First and Second Rumanian Armies continued to advance in Transylvania. In the Dobruja, after the painful episodes of Turtukai and Silistria, the Russo-Rumanian line became stronger and the enemy was stopped. The war seemed to be going well for Rumania.

But even in Bukarest, with only the official sources of information open to me, I could see that all was not well. I remember taking a telegram to the censor after I had been in the country a few weeks, a telegram in which I pointed out the danger ahead. I said it was clear from the appointment of the two ablest German commanders, Mackensen and Falkenhayn, that the enemy meant to try and reduce Rumania to the condition of Belgium and Serbia. I urged that the Allies must make every possible effort to avert this threatened disaster.

The Rumanian censor did not like to think even of the possibility of his country being treated like Belgium and Serbia. He asked me to strike that phrase out and generally to tone the telegram down. There came a time, not much later, when he was begging me every day to urge the need of help for his country in its agony and peril. But then it was too late.

If, in those early days when opinion was entirely misled at home, I and other correspondents—Braun, of the " Times," Donohoe, of the " Daily Chronicle," Ransome, of the " Daily News "—had been allowed to tell the truth as we saw it, the tragedy of Rumania might possibly not

Censorship of the Press

have been played. All through that hot month of September the Rumanian people were lulled into a false sense of security and the allied countries were equally deceived.

It was when I went to the Dobruja, early in October, that I understood the measure of Rumania's unpreparedness and the failings of General Zionchkovski. I travelled down with two French Staff officers, charming companions, as well as clear-sighted observers, one the possessor of a very old and very famous French title, the other a wit whose comedies have delighted the whole Western world. From them I heard much that I was afterwards to verify by experience. For example, the lack of aeroplanes, of field telephones, of trench-periscopes, of trench-mortars, of handgrenades, of wire-cutters. Barbed-wire entanglements, I found later, had frequently to be cut through with axes. Of heavy guns the Rumanian Army then had almost none. They were ill-provided with small arms. One cavalry regiment, the 10th, began the war with only 600 carbines for 1,100 men, 700 active and 400 reservists. That is an example I can vouch for personally. I heard of others as bad. The Rumanian fire-trenches were well made in the Dobruja, but were very ill-provided with communication trenches. In no way, except in courage, were the Rumanian troops the equals of the German, Bulgarian, and Turkish troops opposed to them under the brilliant leadership of Mackensen, for whom General Zionchkovski was no match at all.

Before a fortnight had passed these defects were apparent to all. Mackensen began his attack on October 18th. A Serbian division on the left flank did its best to hold the line, and was almost exterminated. The retreat of the survivors across the Danube to Reni was one of the most pitiful sights of the campaign. The whole of Zionchkovski's force, consisting of five divisions, was driven back with heavy loss. Constantsa was captured on the 23rd.

For some days the Headquarters Staff was without news of the retiring army, which had lost its big wireless telegraph plant. The enemy pressed on and on, and if at this time Falkenhayn had been able to make good his part in the German plan, it is probable that Mackensen would have pushed his army as far as Galatz.

The idea was that he and Falkenhayn should join hands across the narrowest strip of Rumanian territory between Galatz and the more northerly Carpathian Passes. By doing so they would have separated Wallachia from Moldavia and would have wiped out three of the four Rumanian armies. This plan failed. The Rumanians in the more northerly passes kept Falkenhayn's troops at bay.

Facing fearful odds, they fought magnificently. Falkenhayn concentrated the bulk of his forces in the valleys of the Oituz and Trotuz. He enjoyed a marked superiority in numbers, in heavy artillery, and in machine-guns. The Rumanians offered a dogged resistance. They got over the fear, which influenced their effort harmfully earlier in the campaign, that the Germans were irresistible. They found that at close quarters they were not nearly so terrible as they appeared from a distance. They quickly became hardened to the conditions of warfare.

Facing fearful odds

Their officers improved. The incompetents were weeded out, and those who were left gained in experience and initiative every day. Whenever counter-attacks were possible they delivered them with vigour. They took all advantage possible of the ground on which the battle was contested ; for the most part defiles, narrow valleys, rocky beds of streams, a mountainous region which made movements of troops very difficult and transport nigh impossible. In spite of all obstacles the Rumanian Army Service Corps, chiefly

figures I had from a Cabinet Minister. The forces which were defeated by Falkenhayn in the first week of October north of Brashov also lost large quantities of war material. They had a few howitzer batteries ; most of their howitzers were left behind. Many field-guns were abandoned. The First and Second Armies recovered later and changed commanders, but for the moment they were badly shaken, and their retirement opened the way for the passage of Falkenhayn's troops through the mountains into the Wallachian Plain.

The disaster was considered to be due to bad generalship even more than to the pressure of the fresh enemy forces. The commands were not in capable hands. There were dismissals afterwards, but the harm had been done. A small body of Bavarians worked round the flank of the First Army, which lay to westward of the Second, and caused a quite unnecessary panic. Help was called for from the Second Army, and was sent, with the result that the Second

Army, well on its way to make the junction with General Prezan, was obliged to retire. All that had been gained in Transylvania was abandoned. General Cortesco, who commanded the division which was leading the way, described to me dramatically his surprise and consternation at receiving orders to retire in the very moment of winning a battle.

There was a moment when it seemed possible, and even likely, that by a bold tactical enterprise the Rumanians might put the enemy in a bad position. This was when General Avarescu's engineers bridged the Danube with pontoons, and a large force, assembled for the purpose, began to march across into the rear of Mackensen's Dobruja lines. I do not think that episode of the war has ever been explained. The crossing gave cause for great hopes in Britain as well as in Rumania ; there was mystified wonder when it was known that the Rumanians had at once marched back again.

WHERE RUMANIA'S BRAVERY WAS UNAVAILING.
View in the Predeal Pass, between Rumania and Transylvania, which, despite the stout defence of the Rumanians, was captured by the Germans in October, 1916. Above : King Ferdinand of Rumania's shooting-box, used as Army Headquarters. The King and the Crown Prince accompanied the armies in the field and shared in the vicissitudes of their people.

dependent on bullock-carts, worked well. This was the department which failed badly in the war of 1913. It had been reorganised with good effect.

Unfortunately, while the more northerly passes were being so gallantly defended, the First and Second Armies had been driven back over the mountains. Their retreat had been hasty. They had lost heavily in men. Before the end of October the Rumanian Army, which consisted at the start of twenty-three divisions (460,000 men), had suffered over 100,000 casualties. At one period it was losing at the rate of 12,000 men put out of action every day. These

What happened was this. The Headquarters Staff were nervous about Avarescu's plan. They told him to make sure of his communications before he began to put his men across the river. According to them, he did not do so, and he was, therefore, ordered immediately to withdraw the division which had reached the other side. Avarescu's partisans maintained that this order was dictated by jealousy. They admit that the pontoon bridge was attacked by aeroplanes, and that mines were floated down the river towards it, but they deny that it was badly damaged ; if it had been, the troops could not have recrossed it.

HOME OF RUMANIAN STATESMAN.
Residence of M. Take Jonescu in Bukarest, occupied by Germans. This patriotic Rumanian statesman took a leading part in his country's intervention in the war on side of the Allies.

was no thought of defeat in the minds of the promenaders, no foreboding of evil troubled the blue and brilliant afternoon. Fourteen days later the well-to-do inhabitants of Bukarest were leaving the city in droves, terrified by the German advance, and the Government asked the Legations to be ready to leave at a moment's notice.

Then followed a period of anxious hope. I find in my diary during this period many entries like these :

October 17th.—Although *time is on the side of the Rumanians,* in view of the fact that Russian troops are on their way to help, the weather is unfortunately lending great assistance to the enemy. It is many years since an autumn was so hot and dry. The roads are all sand after a long drought. The movement of heavy guns is made easy. Day after day the sun shines steadily. Change is eagerly hoped for. In spite of this and other handicaps, however, the Rumanian troops are doing the best work they have done yet. They are fighting stubbornly in the Carpathian Passes against Falkenhayn's supreme effort to force his way into the plain. *If they can hold him for a short time longer, all will be well.*

The bridge was also open to attack from Austrian monitors. Avarescu's adventure was no doubt a risky one. But in war it is often the risky adventure which succeeds, while the cautious following of routine heads nowhere. Officers who were with the force which crossed the Danube assured me that there was good hope of success. They had four days' food and ammunition. They themselves had no fear of their bridge being destroyed. Certainly it would have been better to obtain command of the river, but then the plan was only feasible if carried out as a surprise. I do not venture to decide who was to blame for its failure, but I will quote what Field-Marshal Mackensen said to General Avarescu in 1918. They were discussing the operations of two years before, and Mackensen asked, "What made you get back across the Danube ? We should have had," he said, "a bad quarter of an hour there. You

Why Avarescu crossed the Danube had us between your four Rumanian divisions and Zionchkovski's eight Russian divisions. It looked bad for us, but we counted upon your civilians getting rattled

and saving us. That was why we told Falkenhayn to press on as hard as he could in the Predeal Pass, which he did with the result for which we hoped."

That result was the order to General Avarescu to withdraw and to abandon the move which, far more than anything the Rumanian armies had yet done, threatened serious danger to the enemy's positions, as Field-Marshal Mackensen admitted.

Thus the position which had appeared to be so favourable for Rumania at the beginning of October was in just over a fortnight changed so entirely that the Rumanians began already to fear the worst. On October 1st, a hot Sunday, I walked on the Chaussée Kisseleff, which serves Bukarest both as Champs Elysées and as Bois de Boulogne. There

BUKAREST IN THE HANDS OF THE ENEMY.
One of the principal squares in beautiful Bukarest during the German occupation. Enemy troops are seen marching through it watched by the inhabitants with fear and wretchedness in their hearts. The triumphant Von Mackensen took up his quarter in the Royal Palace.

October 19th.—Some snow has fallen in the mountains, but the weather is again obstinately warm and dry. The spirit of the Rumanian resistance is still fine and resolute. The feeling at Headquarters this morning was cheerful. They are confident *they can delay the progress of the enemy until the Russians arrive.*

October 25th.—A high military authority said to me one day : "We are in a better position than we were a week ago. We are still holding them in the Carpathian Passes. Our armies are unbeaten, and they are gaining strength and experience every day. The retirement in the Dobruja is, of course, unfortunate ; but the main thing is, that *we are a week nearer to the moment when the tremendous pressure which our troops are now bearing will be relieved.*"

October 28th.—Marked rise in cheerfulness. A Government organ, the "Indépendance Roumaine," says in its leading article, "Events are now wearing more and more satisfactory an aspect. Each day we continue to resist *brings nearer the hour when, thanks to operations in course of development, we shall have the advantage over the enemy and be able to resume* the offensive upon our whole front."

After all this encouragement to be hopeful of assistance arriving in time to save them, the Rumanians suffered badly when they realised that their capital and more than half their country must be lost. The swing-back from confidence to despair was natural enough, given a volatile, excitable race, but it was nevertheless painful to watch. The sufferings of the soldiers, tired out, unable to get any rest, fighting always on unequal terms, were tragic. They had held the passes longer than had been thought possible, but as soon as the enemy was in the plain they could make no stand against him at all for lack of the material of war.

Many people have said to me: "We cannot understand how the twenty-three full divisions which Rumania put into the field at the end of August were reduced to six weak ones by the middle of December." They were so reduced, and that terrible fact makes clear the extent of the disasters which befell them.

Their heaviest losses were at the Battle of the Argesul in the first week of December. Either through treachery or by reason of a lucky capture, the Rumanian order of battle and all the plans of the Rumanian General Staff fell into the hands of the Bavarian General Krafft von Delmingen.

The Rumanians had planned three general attacks, one to the south of Bukarest, another on the south-west, and another on the west. The Germans, knowing exactly what was intended, withdrew their forces at these points and advanced them at other points so as to form three "pockets." Into these three pockets they allowed the Rumanians to push their way, offering almost no resistance. Then they closed in, captured 100,000 Rumanians, killed a large number,

ordered, went out to his unit to be ready for the wounded, as they came back towards Bukarest. On the road he met troops retiring. The Germans had attacked them and driven them back.

Colonel Costinesco hurried into the city and told General Angelesco, who was in command there, that the capital could not long be considered secure. The general said: "Retreating? It is not possible. They were ordered to advance. They must be advancing." Colonel Costinesco, whose father was Minister of Finance, urged him to telephone to M. Bratiano. The Premier said the same thing as the general. "It is not possible. There must be some mistake."

Then a call was put through to General Headquarters. The reply given there was, "We have no news. We expect news at half-past eight this evening. We think it is probably all right."

Colonel Costinesco told me this, furiously indignant himself.

The bridge over the Argesul River was destroyed too soon, by order of the Headquarters Staff, and a very large number of troops were left on **The flight from** the wrong side of it. Those who escaped **Bukarest** scrambled through Bukarest. The streets were lighted for the first time in a week or so, and the inhabitants stood at their doors or windows, watching them go by, with fear and wretchedness in their hearts. Next day the Germans entered the city.

Panic spread through the land in more terrifying guise than it had worn earlier, when the flight from Bukarest began. Railway-stations were filled with fugitives, sitting on their bundles, waiting for trains to take them away. They waited entire days and nights, weary and hungry, for there was nothing to eat in the stations, and they dared not leave their places to go into the towns for fear a train might come and go without them.

Trains often came in filled to overflowing. I mean overflowing literally —people on the roofs, on the buffers between the coaches. I heard of many being killed by falling off. With my Rumanian Army pass as war correspondent, I could always call upon a station

drove the broken remains of the Army before them, and captured Bukarest.

The theory that treachery put the Rumanians at the mercy of the invading forces is supported by Mr. Ackerman, an American correspondent with the latter, who was told by one of Von Falkenhayn's general of divisions: "We have an army of spies behind the Rumanian lines. We know everything the Rumanians are going to do before their front-line officers know it themselves."

The confusion after the success of the German manœuvre founded upon exact knowledge of what the Rumanians were intended to do was pitiful. There was no order in the headlong flight. Headquarters was frequently in ignorance of what was happening. Colonel Costinesco, of the Rumanian Medical Service, knowing that in the early stage of the battle an advance had been

PRISONERS OF WAR IN THEIR OWN LAND.
German motor-vans of the field army postal service outside the Grand Hotel de Londres at Bukarest during the enemy occupation of the capital. In oval: Arrival of Rumanian prisoners of war in their lost metropolis. Bukarest was evacuated by the Rumanians after their Argesul defeat, December, 1916.

commandant to find room for me, which he did, if necessary, by turning someone out. But for this I should on many a platform have been left behind.

There was no order in the railway arrangements. Most of the carriages had broken windows. All were filthy. The engines were burning wood and making wretched time. Lines were constantly being blocked.

Jassy, the capital after Bukarest had been evacuated, had a small station and yard. No effort was made to improve it. Trains waited for hours outside unable to get in. The stationmaster had been superseded everywhere by military commandants, who were most of them inexperienced, incompetent, and helpless. In less than one month the railways fell to pieces, like every other institution in the land.

The peasants, by far the most numerous part of the population, were dazed and dumb. In many places they received the enemy in a friendly manner.

Germans welcomed by the peasants They did not know why their country had gone to war, and they saw no reason why they should not welcome Germans. Their old King had been a German. He had always boasted of it. So they carried out bread and salt to the invaders, the Eastern form of hospitable salutation, and went on tilling their land.

Rumanians of the educated, travelled class were divided in opinion. Some said that Carp and Marghiloman were right, and that it was madness of Bratiano to take sides against Germany. Old Carp, Rumania's veteran in politics, protested, at the Royal Council called for the purpose of declaring war, against what he called the "crime and folly" of Bratiano's decision. He declared that, although he had three sons in the Army (one was killed), he hoped to see his country beaten. Marghiloman was less emphatic in speech, but did not conceal his opinion that the country was moving towards certain disaster. It was significant that both these politicians stayed in Bukarest after the Government had gone to Jassy and after the Germans occupied it.

Other Rumanians blamed Russia for the misfortune which had fallen upon them. "We have been betrayed by our old enemy," they said. Russians and Rumanians disliked one another. The Rumanians, with their Latin culture, elaborated and over-refined, looked down upon the Russians as boors and "Orientals." The Russians despised the Rumanians for their lack of virility. The seizure of Rumanian Bessarabia by Russia after the war against Turkey in 1878, in which she and Rumania were allies, was bitterly resented. The insistence of Bratiano, in the negotiations about Rumania's price, upon the cession of Czernovitz, capital of the Bukovina, was equally the cause of ill-feeling in Russia. Russian troops had three times taken Czernovitz and lost heavily. The Government refused at first to throw it **Russo-Rumanian recriminations** in as part of Rumania's spoil. Rumania appealed to France, and France supported the demand. It was to be expected, therefore, as soon as Rumania came to grief, that she would blame Russia for the catastrophe, and that the Russians would say, "We never thought the Rumanians were any good." Both expectations were fulfilled.

All through the anguished period of hoping that "the Russian troops would come in time," the Rumanians cursed their neighbour for deliberate delay. More than one intelligent Rumanian told me they were convinced that Russia meant to keep Northern Rumania and let Germany have the rest. Even General Iliesco, after the Russian Revolution, lent his authority to the version that "Rumania had been betrayed."

All this is incoherent stuff. That Von Stürmer did what he could to hasten Rumania's entry I have admitted. But he did not "force Rumania into war." I was told all along at the Russian Foreign Office, where they were frank and open with me, that "Rumania had decided to come in for the last six months of the war." I heard this as early as the spring of 1915. I heard it as late as the summer of 1916. The truth is Bratiano decided to come in because he thought the last six months of the war were at hand.

If he had felt he was being "forced," he could have appealed to France and Great Britain. He could have said, "Our Army is not ready for war. It is not in a condition to do any serious fighting against German troops. We shall be a weakness to you, not an added force." Then France and Great Britain would certainly have replied, "Then, for God's sake, stay out!"

Bratiano had resisted pressure before. He could have done so again. That he did not struggle against Von Stürmer's influence was due to his belief that the moment had come for Rumania to dash in and seize what he wanted—Transylvania. General Alexeieff will be credited by history with giving good advice which was not taken, but which, if it had been taken, might have spared Rumania much of what she has suffered.

Alexeieff, when he was appealed to for troops to save Rumania, saw that at least five army corps would be required. The Russians are never able to do anything quickly. Their temperament and their railways alike said "No" to the proposal that they should "rush" their assistance, as France or Britain might have done in a like emergency. Therefore Alexeieff said to the Rumanians: "What you had better do is this. Evacuate all the southern part of your country, including Bukarest. Withdraw your armies from the positions they now occupy, positions which are impossible to defend, and place them on the line Ramnicu Sarat-Faurei-Babadag, defending your northern territory. I will send you five army corps. In the meantime you can save your troops from being defeated, and when we join forces we can advance and break the enemy's power, thus releasing your southern territory and striking a hard blow at Germany's prestige."

The reasoning was clear and keen. Alexeieff was a man whose vision and intellect were, I believe, above those of any general thrown up by the war, with the exception of Marshal Foch. If his counsel **Series of ghastly blunders** had been followed Rumania would, in all probability, have been cleared in the early part of 1917, Austria-Hungary and Bulgaria would have been taught that Germany was far from invincible, Turkey would have been overrun.

But the Rumanian Government and the Rumanian High Command, which was really General Iliesco, refused to consider such a plan of campaign. They refused to see things as they were. And when things grew worse they tried to throw the blame on to Russia. Rumania fell not by reason of Russia's negligence or unreadiness to help her, but because her rulers, civil and military, made a series of ghastly blunders.

On December 22nd I was watching a Russian division march through Jassy. In the big square I met Colonel Rossetti, who had been Chief of the Operations Department at Rumanian Headquarters. Iliesco had just been relieved of his command. Rossetti had fallen with him. He said gloomily, looking at the Russians: "If they had only come when they should have come, none of this would have happened." That was the general feeling. It was ill-founded and unjust. General Iliesco tried to throw the blame upon the Russians during the spring of 1917 after he had been sent to Paris (which was the Stellenbosch of Rumanian military failures), and after the Russian Revolution had relaxed the censorship upon spiteful slanders against that unfortunate country. Until then the charge had been only whispered. The Tsar knew what was being said, and spoke to General Hanbury-Williams about it.

The Rumanians (he said) asked us for a certain number of troops, and we sent them. It is utterly untrue that we failed to keep our promise.

This I have shown to be untrue, and I am glad to have been able to do justice to Russia in this direction. She has a heavy enough burden of crime and folly to bear, thanks to her incompetent rulers and her own incapacity for self-government on the large scale, without being made the scapegoat for others' faults. The responsibility for the Rumanian blunder rests upon all the Allies. The least guilty of all were the Russian military authorities. They did what they could to dissuade Rumania from taking the fatal step, and they did what they could to save her from its disastrous consequences. Nothing could do that. *Gegen Dummheit kampfen Gotter selbst vergebens.* ("Against folly even the gods fight in vain.") But it is only fair that the truth should be known.

U.S. WOUNDED IN HOSPITAL.

CHAPTER CCC.

AT RICHMOND, SURREY.

THE WONDERFUL WORK OF THE ROYAL ARMY MEDICAL CORPS AND THE MARVELS OF PREVENTIVE MEDICINE.

By Robert Machray.

Amazing Growth of the Corps—How It Became Larger than the Original Expeditionary Force—Early Developments in the War—Headquarters Temporarily Removed to Blackpool—Civilian Doctors as Officers—Procurement and Training of Nurses and Recruits—Twofold Work to be Done—The Care and Cure of the Wounded—The Prevention of Disease—Both Problems Splendidly Solved—Typhoid, the Scourge of Armies, Eliminated—Tetanus Conquered—Cholera and Dysentery Prevented—Efficient Precautions with Respect to "Carriers"—Malaria and the Mosquito Dealt With—Attacks of the Insect World Defeated—Trench Fever Taken in Hand—How Poison Gas Effects were Combated—Striking Figures of the Expansion of the Corps and Its Activities—Upwards of Two and a Half Million Patients Treated—Special Types of Hospitals—Magnificent and Successful Efforts in Various Departments—Wounded Men Given a Fresh Interest in Life—Mental Cases—Curative Value of Education—Impressive Summary of the Work of the Corps—Its Leaders.

"H OW the Wounded Were Brought Home" was the subject of Chapter CLXI. (Vol. 8, page 303). In a vivid and realistic fashion the various stages of the journey of the soldier from the trenches, in which he had been hit, to "Blighty," the haven of home, were described with a wealth of detail by an eyewitness. The narrative made frequent references to the Royal Army Medical Corps, and showed how it dealt with the wounded man all the way from the "aid-post," a little distance behind the firing-line, and the point at which he passed into its charge, to his arrival at the British hospital, where everything possible was done to make him fit again.

To treat of the R.A.M.C. as an organisation lay outside the scope of that chapter, and, indeed, the greatest development of that body took place after it was published. As the war continued, and drew into it more and more millions of men, so the Army Medical Service expanded to cope with the situation. In the whole story of the war there is no part of it more interesting, or amazing even, than that concerned with the work and growth of the R.A.M.C. And if out of all the evil of the colossal conflict much good has come, it may ultimately be seen that the more permanently beneficent results were achieved by that preventive medicine of which the corps made such

ARMY MEDICAL CHIEF IN FRANCE.
Lieutenant-General Sir C. H. Burtchaell, K.C.B., C.M.G., appointed Director-General Medical Services, British Armies in France, in succession to Lieut.-Gen. Sir A. T. Sloggett, May, 1918.

magnificent use in all the theatres of the struggle, and which, in mankind's age-long fight with disease—a foe far more terrible than Germany—holds out the finest promise of victory in the future. The present chapter takes up these subjects, and the information on which it is based has been obtained from authoritative sources.

At the outbreak of the war the total strength of the R.A.M.C., including nurses, was not quite 20,000. Of Regulars there were 1,279 officers and 3,811 other ranks; of Territorials 1,889 officers and 12,520 other ranks. The nurses, who belonged to Queen Alexandra's Imperial Military Nursing Service, numbered only 293. Many members of the corps, it must be remembered, were on duty with the forces in the far-flung Outer Empire, and these, of course, were Regulars. The large Territorial portion of the R.A.M.C. was not immediately available. Yet the units of the corps which formed part of the original Expeditionary Force that landed at Boulogne in August, 1914, were relatively strong, and the personnel was excellent. According to the ideas of the time the equipment was good. But experience of war on the great scale was lacking. In all the Empire the R.A.M.C. disposed of only 18,000 hospital beds.

In a word the Army Medical Service was proportionate and adequate to what were considered the British military requirements of the day—the day before the war. These

SURGICAL WORK IN MESOPOTAMIA.
First-aid for Indian wounded at a field dressing-station, Mesopotamia. In oval: Interior of the operating-room in the hospital at Amara, on the Tigris.

opened a fund on behalf of the Red Cross, and it grew into millions of pounds. A Red Cross Commission went to Belgium and France, its head being Sir Alfred Keogh, a former Director-General of the Army Medical Service, who again occupied that position in October, 1914, holding it till the end of February, 1918, with very great benefit to all concerned.

In countless ways the R.A.M.C. was helped in its work, and assisted to bear the enormous strain that it underwent in the opening months of the war. Many hospitals were opened, and V.A.D.'s sprang into existence, appreciably lightening the burden. Civilian doctors, at the instance of the British Medical Association, took various steps which made the services of many of them available. Men of eminence in the medical profession

requirements were summed up in the small striking force known as the Expeditionary Force, and French's first few divisions were that force. It was founded on knowledge derived from past wars, none of them in the least comparable with that which now had to be faced, as the Battle of Mons and the consequent retreat towards Paris soon disclosed. This was true in particular of its Medical Service, which was splendid within its limitations, as was every part of that glorious little Army. But limitations there were.

With Surgeon-General T. P. Woodhouse as Director of Medical Service, the R.A.M.C. had its first hospital base at Boulogne, but the retreat from Mons necessitated the evacuation of the hospitals at Boulogne and the opening of others at Havre, which in turn also had to be abandoned. Paris then became a great hospital centre, but with the advance of the Germans and the French Government's removal to Bordeaux it looked as if Paris were insecure. The First Battle of the Marne and the retreat of the Germans to the Aisne completely changed the situation. Paris was freed. Havre, Rouen and, later, Boulogne could and did become hospital bases again.

Meanwhile, the limitations of the Army Medical Service had become very apparent, and they were serious. Needs of all sorts made themselves felt terribly. More doctors, more orderlies, more nurses were required. Specialists of every kind were called for. Hospitals had to be established near the front. There was an insistent demand for more ambulance-cars and ambulance-trains and hospital-ships. But fortunately there was no shortage of drugs and dressings at any time.

Heroic work under fire

The Royal Army Medical Corps worked heroically both under fire and behind the lines, officers and men alike going with a minimum of food and sleep, and doing all in their power to the last ounce of their endurance. They were energetically supported by the Red Cross and the Order of St. John of Jerusalem, who provided, among many other things, large numbers of ambulance-cars. The "Times"

devoted themselves to special aspects of the difficult problems, such as the bacteriological, arising out of the war. It should perhaps be mentioned here that when the Indian troops went to the front the Indian Medical Service co-operated wherever possible with the R.A.M.C. The Medical Services of the Dominion Forces also were most helpful.

With the institution and development of the new British armies there went a corresponding expansion of the Army Medical Service. When the armistice was granted to Germany on November 11th, 1918, the total strength of the R.A.M.C. stood at 163,145. Of this large number—a number, it may be noted, which was greater than that of the whole original Expeditionary Force—11,385 were officers, including dental officers and quartermasters. The number of nurses had increased from fewer than three hundred to close upon twenty-four thousand. The exact figures for "other ranks" were 127,831. Of hospital beds there were upwards of 635,000. At the cessation of hostilities the corps was a vast, thoroughly-trained, and highly-competent organisation, with an equipment which was lacking in nothing. How was it all done?

First of all came the doctors—surgeons, physicians, and specialists—who formed the great majority of the officers of the corps. The Royal Army Medical Corps supplied many, but the bulk were taken from civil life on the basis which was proposed by the British Medical Association. This was that medical men under forty were to serve with the troops, while those over forty were to work in the hospitals. Such was the general basis, but as it was impossible to deprive the ordinary population of too many doctors, arrangements were made by which medical men at home gave part of their time to war work, undertook to attend officers' and soldiers' relatives in addition to their ordinary practice, or did part of the civil work of neighbouring practitioners who were engaged in military work. In this way hundreds and hundreds of doctors were added to the corps, but more were needed, as was indicated by a statement that after the war had been going on for nearly a year two thousand were still urgently required. To meet the emergency, doctors were obtained from the Dominions and even from America. The great thing was that in one way or another they were secured, though there

HOSPITAL WARDS AT KUT-EL-AMARA. Indian troops in hospital at Kut-el-Amara. In oval: Officers' ward in a hospital in the same town in which Townshend was besieged, December 3rd, 1915—April 29th, 1916.

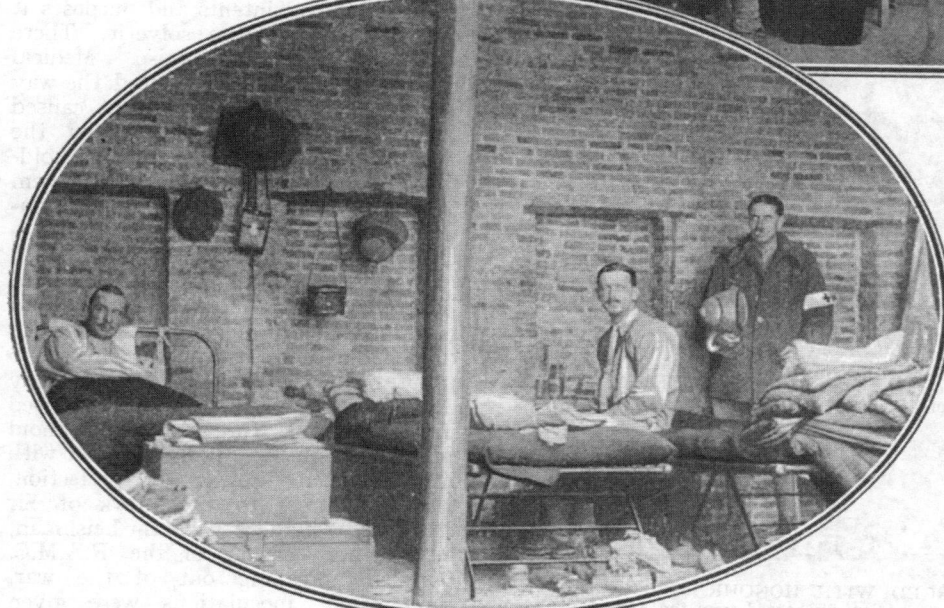

training of the field ambulances of the new divisions. There were five of these centres, but their designations were changed according as they were shifted from one locality to another. As the divisions of the New Armies were mobilised the field ambulances joined them, and the training centres then took on the functions of the depot, with the exception of not receiving returned Expeditionary Force men, who were posted to the provisional company of the depot which was formed for that purpose. The centres received and trained recruits, mobilised new units, and prepared drafts for overseas. Each centre was commanded by a Regular officer, and the training was carried out by special reserves and temporary commissioned officers, assisted by a few Regular N.C.O.'s.

were times when the R.A.M.C. could have done with many more.

At the R.A.M.C. temporary headquarters at Blackpool was established an Officers' School of Instruction, under the commandant, which provided a course of training spread over fourteen days in the duties of a regimental medical officer, in Army sanitation, in tropical diseases, in squad and stretcher drill, in equitation, and in gas conditions. There was a Gas School as well, capable of dealing with two thousand men a month.

Trained nurses were as necessary as doctors, and at the start and for a considerable time afterwards there was an equally marked shortage of them. Appeals made by the War Office brought in a fair number; but nothing like enough, though many responses came from the staffs of hospitals and infirmaries. Nearly two hundred arrived from Canada, Australia, and South Africa. Still more, many more, were wanted and the V.A.D., with other organisations stepped into the breach. The War Office for a while cancelled its order that sick and wounded soldiers were to be attended only by thoroughly trained and certificated nurses, the slight cases being cared for by probationers and V.A.D.'s. Eventually, just as the doctors were found, so were the nurses.

Before the war all R.A.M.C. recruits were trained at the R.A.M.C. Depot at Aldershot, and the depot provided all reserves and reinforcements. On the outbreak of the war it was necessary to form R.A.M.C. training centres for the

In 1916 it was decided that units could be more efficiently and economically administered if they were concentrated in one station. Ripon, Codford, and Sheffield training centres were transferred to Blackpool, and an administrative officer, with Headquarters Staff, was appointed. In April, 1917, the R.A.M.C. Depot was also moved to Blackpool, and placed under the same administrative officer. At the same time the Birr and Crookham training centres were absorbed. But as each centre retained its identity, and there was thus a considerable reduplication of work, accompanied by lack of system and centralisation of training, a fresh reorganisation took place in August and September, 1917. The depot was enlarged, two new companies being formed, and it was thus enabled to carry out completely the work of final training, mobilisation of units, and preparation of drafts for the R.A.M.C. in all the theatres of the war.

Reorganising the R.A.M.C.

The three training centres ceased to exist as such, and eight training battalions, each of 947 officers and men, were established, each having the same functions. They received recruits and transfers from other arms, vaccinated, inoculated, clothed and equipped them, and put them through a course of preliminary training for a month on squad and stretcher drill and first-aid. They were then posted to home hospitals for a course of two months' training in hospital duties, and afterwards returned to the depot to prepare for service overseas. The bulk of the recruits were selected on purely medical grounds. Men of certain medical categories and of fair intelligence were posted to the R.A.M.C. up to the number required. Special instructions were issued by the Army Council each month that all men with certain qualifications should be sent into the corps. In addition to these, men with particular qualifications were enlisted into the corps by the War Office, after these qualifications had been verified and approved.

All specialists after enlistment were examined, and when found satisfactory were registered as such by the officer in charge of the R.A.M.C. records. Masseurs were supplied by

FOR THOSE DISCHARGED WITH HONOUR.
Facsimile of the King's Certificate of Honour given to soldiers discharged from the Army on account of wounds or sickness contracted on service. The certificate for the Navy was almost identical, save that the figures standing represented the senior Service. Mr. Bernard Partridge designed these certificates.

the Almeric Paget Massage Corps. Courses of instruction for other ranks of the R.A.M.C. were given at the King's Lancashire Military Convalescent Hospital, Blackpool, and these courses were of a very comprehensive nature. Opticians were enlisted and posted where their services were needed. Mental attendants were trained by the R.A.M.C., and many of the staffs of the asylums which were taken over by the Army were specially enlisted into the corps. Cooks, too, were specially enlisted, and trained at the School of Cookery at the depot, Blackpool. Any specialists required in excess of those available were often obtained by transfer from other arms through the branch of the Department of the Adjutant-General known as "A.G.1." In all these ways was the personnel of the corps obtained and built up.

Importance of preventive work Properly to appreciate the wonderful work of the Army Medical Service, that work and the conditions in which it was performed must be understood. Its duty among the forces was twofold—first, to care for and heal the wounded; and second, to fight and conquer disease, or, what was better, to obviate disease by the use of the new preventive medicine.

At the start it was the wounded, as was natural, who held the chief place in the thoughts of most people, whether doctors or laymen. But the good health and fitness of the whole Army were even more important, and it soon was perceived that the general principle that must govern the work of the R.A.M.C. was the welfare of all the troops and not merely the treatment of the wounded. In former wars the losses suffered by armies from disease, from the ravages of plague and pestilence, had been far heavier than from actual casualties in the field, the proportion being estimated at something like four to one. This tremendous reduction in the strength of armies was extremely serious, and obviously it was pre-eminently desirable to take any measures that would prevent or at least lessen it. To take such measures was the business of the Medical Service of an Army, and according as these succeeded so the wastage was checked, and the Medical Service, by keeping more and more fit men in the Army, became endowed with a value which it had not possessed before.

To preserve health is better than to cure disease, and there is something to be said for the Chinese idea of paying one's doctor only so long as he keeps one well. To put it in another way, the problem is to prevent disease. This was the problem which the Army Medical Service set itself to solve, and to all practical intents and purposes it did in great measure solve it. There can be no higher praise. Medical science had already suggested the way by discovering the germs that caused some diseases, and by devising the means for killing these germs, or holding them at bay and making them innocuous. The human body was immunised against their attacks by vaccination or inoculation.

In the wars of the past typhoid had been one of the diseases that had scourged all armies, and there was no doubt that unless steps were taken to prevent an outbreak it would play havoc with the British troops engaged in the war. But an anti-typhoid vaccine was in use, and treatment with it had been brought to perfection, thanks largely to the work of Sir Almroth Wright, Sir William Leishman, and other officers of the R.A.M.C. On the breaking out of the war, immunising inoculations were given to the soldiers who were willing to undergo them; the vast majority were willing, and practically the whole British Army in the field was, to coin a word, anti-typhoided. In the course of the war the R.A.M.C. supplied upwards of fifteen million full doses of the prophylactic typhoid and paratyphoid vaccines, nearly all of which, with other vaccines to be mentioned later, were manufactured at the Army Medical College. With the elimination of "carriers"—*i.e.*, of men who carried the disease, and might give it to others—and with a strict supervision of water and food, in addition to the vaccine, which was the principal agent in this marvellous business, the result was that typhoid—though there were a few cases of it—never got the slightest hold on the British Army in France and Flanders.

Problem of "carriers"

At the outset the treatment of the wounded was necessarily the most pressing matter for the R.A.M.C., and one of the earliest discoveries was that a very large proportion of the wounds were infected. This infection took various forms. One of the most serious arose from the bacillus of tetanus, or lockjaw, which was present in the richly-manured soil of France. During the retreat from Mons soldiers slept on the ground as opportunity offered, and their muddy and dirty clothing was a breeding-ground for this and other organisms. If the men were wounded, the bullets or bits of shell drove these bacteria into their bodies, and infected them with the disease caused by these bacteria.

Pembroke Lodge, Kensington, residence of Mr. Bonar Law, loaned as a hospital for officers.

In Fulham Palace courtyard. The Palace was lent by the Bishop of London for wounded.

Staff of the "Aerochir," French aeroplane designed for Red Cross work. X-raying one patient while others await attention.

Compartment of Red Cross aeroplane containing surgical instruments and materials, and (centre) another view of the ambulance and staff. Right: Sterilising apparatus and dressings.

Red Cross Ambulance of the Air: Features of a remarkable French invention.

Ward of a New Zealand hospital on the western front, and (right) outside the huts of a temporary British hospital in France.

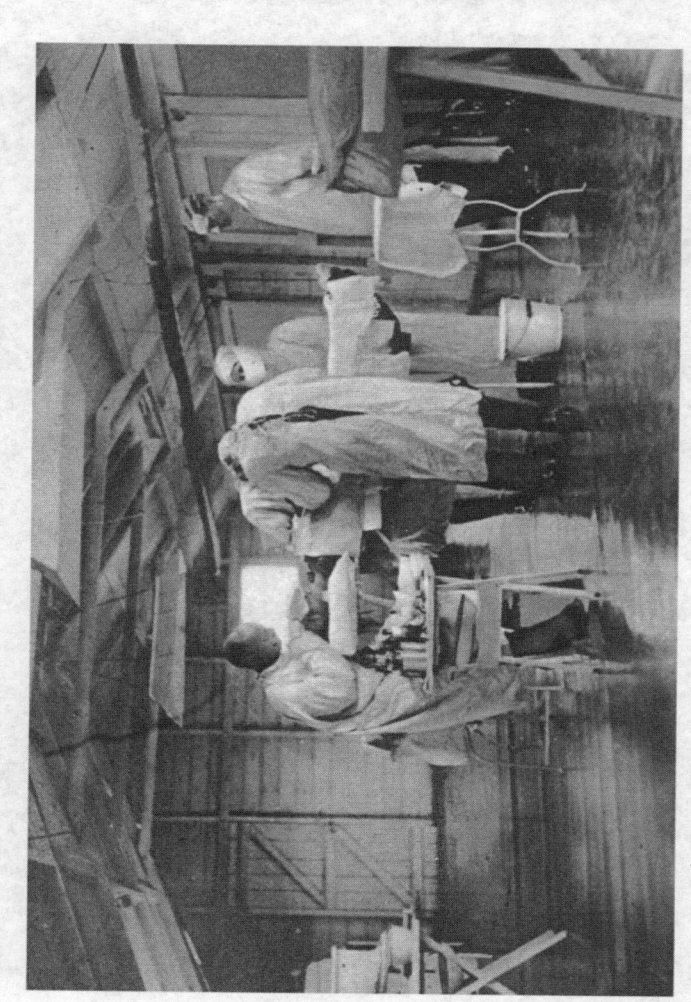

An operation in the theatre of a New Zealand hospital. Right: Grass-matting ward on roof of military hospital in Cairo where consumptive patients received open-air treatment.

Service under the Red Cross in varied scenes of war.

British hospital-ship leaving a French port at night time, with her symbolic crosses of red and white illumined by electric light.

The tetanus produced was of a severe and deadly type, and at the moment there appeared to be no cure for it. An anti-tetanus serum was in existence, but it had succeeded only in a few cases of treatment of the disease. In September, 1914, what may be called the tetanus situation was most serious and occasioned the greatest anxiety. The remedy, however, was found in administering the serum to every wounded man immediately after he had been hit, instead of some time afterwards to men when the symptoms of the disease were observed, as had been done previously. From that time on there was a marked improvement. All the wounded, as a matter of course, were given the serum at once, and by the beginning of 1915 tetanus ceased to occur. In brief, the serum prevented the disease and saved thousands of lives —a great achievement. During the war the R.A.M.C. issued nearly eleven million doses of the pro-phylactic tetanus antitoxin, as well as 27,500 much larger doses suitable for the treatment of the disease by the antitoxin.

Science also came forward to prevent two of the diseases that had ravaged armies—cholera and dysentery. Early in 1915 the Medical Research Committee of the National Insurance Act sent Dr. Freeman, of St. George's Hospital, to Galicia to procure the bacilli of cholera, and from these a cholera vaccine was prepared in the same way as the typhoid vaccine had been made. There are two types of dysentery, and against the form caused by bacilli a serum was used with excellent effect. During the war the R.A.M.C. furnished nearly four and a half millions of full doses of cholera vaccine, and about 144,000 of dysentery vaccine, as well as 275,000 treatment doses of anti-dysentery serum. Provision for dealing with possible outbreaks of cholera was made early in the war, and an outfit was devised containing sufficient apparatus, chemicals, drugs, and the like for dealing with one hundred cases of the disease. Of these outfits, 479 were furnished by the R.A.M.C.

The corps also supplied to the Army in the different theatres of the war many vaccines used in the prevention or treatment of various diseases. Among these vaccines were influenza and plague vaccines; of the former it issued 215,000 full doses of the prophylactic, and of the latter upwards of 122,000. In addition, it made use of 668,000 full doses of other prophylactic vaccines. Besides the sera already referred to, it supplied 90,000 doses of anti-meningo-coccus (spotted fever) serum, about 200,000 doses of anti-diphtheria serum, and nearly 190,000 doses of twelve varieties of other sera.

In all the R.A.M.C. furnished the Army with twenty million full doses of vaccines, and more than eleven million doses of sera.

Use of prophylactic vaccines To prevent disease, great precautions were taken by the R.A.M.C. with respect to " carriers." It was known that the organisms of enteric fever and of dysentery always originated from a human being who bred them in his body. This breeder or carrier might be an ordinary case of one of these diseases, probably the least dangerous type of carrier, as he was likely to be safely isolated in hospital before long. Or he might have the disease in so mild a form as to be unaware that there was anything seriously wrong with him. On the other hand, he might be a man who had got over his attack, but in whom the organisms still multiplied and passed out from his body. Then there was the chance that

[Photo : Russell.

SIR T. H. J. C. GOODWIN, K.C.B.,
Director-General of the Army Medical Service at the War Office.

a man might be infected and become a carrier without having shown any symptoms at all.

In the Army the number of carriers was reduced to a minimum by facilities for early bacteriological diagnosis of suspicious cases of disease. No person who had suffered from either of these diseases was employed in any capacity entailing the handling of food until he had been proved by repeated tests to be free from infection. In spite of all efforts, however, some carriers were sure to escape detection, but the authorities adopted stringent measures to render them harmless to their fellows. Even then it was possible that these measures, through carelessness or lack of discipline, might be ineffective, and infected material might gain access to food and water supplies. Therefore, in the field, all water was sterilised, generally by bleaching-powder. When a new area was taken over by the troops the various sources of water were rapidly tested, the best were selected, and directions posted up stating the quantity of bleaching-powder which had to be added to render the water fit for drinking.

The most common method of the infection of food was by flies, which fed on infected matter, and carried the organisms on their legs and bodies, in the crop—whence they were regurgitated while the insects were feeding—or passed through the intestine. To limit the spread of fly-borne diseases breeding grounds were destroyed as far as was possible. Flies were killed by " swatting," or in traps, of which various forms were designed. Poisons also were used, as were sprays for dealing with large collections of flies. Food was protected from infection by the provision of safes and by guard-ing it from contamination while in transit. Careful watch was kept for any sign of disease among the cooks, and cook-houses were maintained in a condition such as would not attract flies.

But always, if any of these precautions failed in protecting the soldier from disease, there was the prophylactic inoculation, the vaccine and the serum. Injections, generally two, were given of an emulsion of killed bacilli, which was tested and standardised before use. The systems of the soldiers re-sponded to these injections by producing " antibodies " which protected them against living bacilli of the nature of those used for the protective or preventive inoculation. It was the scientist's and the medical man's way of safeguarding the soldier by making him take " a hair of the dog that bit him "—or, rather, that was likely to bite him.

With respect to malaria, which was prevalent in some areas of the war—as, for instance, in Salonika and Macedonia—quinine prophylaxis against infection was largely used, but the results did not come up to expectation, for infection actually took place during the course of the preventive treatment. As against that, however, quinine prophylaxis against relapses was attended by very good results, the administration of large doses, combined with a general tonic treatment, preventing relapses in the majority of cases, and this permitted a definite policy to be fixed for the prevention of relapses in the Army. **Treatment of malaria**

Up to that time there had been no method of treatment which could be at all depended upon. Some years before the war the mosquito had been convicted, largely through the patient study of officers of the I.M.S. and R.A.M.C. in India, of being the carrier of malaria and its active propagator.

When the mosquito—the guilty one being the Anopheles variety—was destroyed, there was a cessation of the disease. Accordingly, in mosquito-infested localities measures were taken for the extermination, or at all events for the reduction, of the mosquitoes. These measures were of decided benefit to the troops, but naturally they could not be carried out in the front line. Mechanical protection by means of nets adapted to varying circumstances were extensively used, though in hot climates soldiers have an objection to the use of such nets. Further, various pomades, containing essential oils repellent to mosquitoes, were utilised, but they seldom afforded protection for more than two hours, and besides, it was difficult to persuade the men to anoint themselves with them.

The demand for quinine salts was very heavy. During 1916 the R.A.M.C. issued to the Army a total quantity exceeding twenty-one tons, or nearly sixty-six million five-grain doses. In the earlier part of the malaria season of 1917 the average amount supplied monthly was about five and a half tons.

Stamping out malaria The mosquito-malaria problem was solved sufficiently to permit the occupation by the British of such an infected area as the Struma Valley. In connection with the problem there arose a new phase. Many soldiers returned to the United Kingdom who were carriers of malaria in the sense that their bodies contained the parasite of that disease, and it only needed that the mosquito should exist in the country, bite these human reservoirs of the parasite, become the host of the parasite, and then pass it on again, for malaria to become prevalent in Great Britain once more. In the United Kingdom ague—which is but another name for malaria—might be said to have become non-existent, and such mosquitoes as existed there were harmless, as they had had no human reservoirs of the parasite to draw upon. But with men bringing the parasite from the Balkans, Palestine, Egypt, and elsewhere, there was a real danger of a general recurrence of malaria. But the War Office, with the assistance of the Medical Research Committee, took steps to meet it. Sir Ronald Ross, illustrious in the field of tropical medicine, acted as adviser, and special hospitals were opened. The steps taken were successful and the danger passed.

As carriers of disease, the fly and the mosquito by no means were alone in what may be called the insect world. The flea and the louse were equally guilty, the one as regarded bubonic plague and the other with respect to trench fever. Bubonic plague affected the Army to a very small extent, and, as mentioned above, the R.A.M.C. issued some 122,000 doses of the preventive plague vaccine, as against fifteen million doses of the typhoid vaccine, and nearly four and a half millions of the cholera vaccine. In past wars the plague, sometimes called the "rat plague"—before the war it had been discovered that the flea that induced the disease lived on rats—had been one of the worst terrors of armies, but science had found out its cause and how to defeat it. **The cause of trench fever** Therefore there were few cases of it during the war. But science had done nothing of the same kind with trench fever—for the very good reason that trench fever was something new; it was unknown before the war.

At first trench fever was thought to be a form of influenza, but presently it was recognised as a distinct disease. In some respects it resembled typhoid, but it was not typhoid. It increased in the Army, and though the men suffering from it did not die, they were incapacitated by it for so long a time, and were so numerous, that the authorities became very anxious. Doctors and men of science got to work upon it, but for a considerable period were baffled. One theory was that it was a gnat-borne disease, but this was disproved.

As the result of a series of investigations, involving the transmission of the disease to hale men—volunteers who nobly came forward and submitted to the ordeal for the sake of their comrades—it came to be suspected that the disease was spread in some way by the louse, but all efforts to find the parasite causing it failed.

As the matter grew more and more serious in its general effect on the health of the Army, the War Office in 1917 appointed a Trench Fever Committee, of which Sir David Bruce, Commandant of the Army Medical College, and well known for his work in connection with sleeping sickness and Malta fever, was made chairman. A committee also was formed in France, and it co-operated with U.S. Army Medical Service. The special hospital at Hampstead was the chief scene of the inquiry. Volunteers were again called for, and there was a splendid response. Finally it was proved that the disease was transmitted by the excreta of the louse, and not by the bite of the louse as had been supposed. But this was not known until well into 1918. Here again prevention of the disease lay in the extermination of the insect inducing the disease, no easy business in the case of the louse, which was ubiquitous in the Army in the trenches, but what could be done was done.

Of the developments of preventive medicine it might be said, in a word, that medical science combined with the entomologist and the sanitary engineer to defeat disease.

During the winter of 1914-15 there appeared in water-soaked Flanders what was called the "trench-foot" trouble. Men who had to remain for some length of time knee-deep in water in the trenches got their feet in such a condition that they became incapacitated. The water was cold, and there

STRETCHER CASES BEING TAKEN ABOARD THE TRAIN FOR HOME.
British wounded being taken on board the ambulance-train in France which was to convey them to the coast en route for England. Above: R.A.M.C. men giving first-aid to a wounded German prisoner.

was no protection; the feet turned blue or red and the skin seemed a mass of chilblains; sometimes gangrene set in. Various investigators took up the question how this troublesome and often dangerous affliction was to be treated, and finally a system of foot care—for in that lay prevention—was evolved. The men going into the trenches had their feet examined to see that the skin was in good order, and if it was, the feet were well greased, thick socks were drawn on, and then dry gum-boots or waders, coming well up the leg, completed the outfit. The R.A.M.C. officers saw to it that these precautions were strictly carried out. "Trench-foot" in the result markedly diminished.

One of the new and evil things with which the Army Medical Service had to deal was the gas poisoning of the soldiers from gas-clouds or gas-shells. The gas in use, at least in the early stages of the war, was a preparation of chlorine, and it was highly dangerous, fatal effects, preceded by horrible agony, often being caused. The medical men prevented these effects from occurring by the use of respirators which contained materials which combined with the gas and made it inert. Later, these respirators developed into masks so perfect that soldiers had every confidence in their complete protection. With regard to the treatment of men who had been gassed, methods were employed—after some experiments in treatment, for in this matter the doctors were on entirely new ground—which greatly reduced the pain and the danger. Thus oxygen inhalation and artificial respiration were used with advantage; sometimes, instead of oxygen, compressed air in medical "air-locks" was given to relieve the breathlessness incident to gassing.

No better general idea of the great work of the R.A.M.C. in the war could be given than by the following statement with respect to its hospitals. Before the **Magnificent record** war there were 7,000 beds in military **of service** hospitals in the United Kingdom. On the outbreak of hostilities provision was immediately made to increase this number, and as the sick and wounded from the Expeditionary Forces arrived, the expansion of the hospital accommodation continued, until in June, 1916, the number of beds increased to 200,000, and in June, 1917, to 300,000. At the time of the armistice the total number of hospital beds available in the British Isles for military patients was 364,133. In addition to these the number of hospital beds with the various Expeditionary Forces at the time of the armistice was: France, 155,897; Egypt, 48,363; Salonika, 42,040; Malta, 7,734; Italy, 9,045; Mesopotamia, 9,880; and North Russia (Murmansk-Archangel), 654, or a total of 273,613.

Before the war the number of military patients in hospital in the United Kingdom was 2,000. In June, 1916, the number had risen to 110,000, in June, 1917, to 230,000, and at the signing of the armistice was 333,074. The number of patients with the various Expeditionary Forces at the armistice was: France, 150,096; Egypt, 49,177; Salonika, 26,141; Malta, 5,178; Italy, 6,142; Mesopotamia, 7,815; and North Russia, 283. The grand total for all patients was

AN IMPROVISED AMBULANCE.
Perambulator used as carriage for stretcher case on the western front, and (above) scene at a field dressing-station, showing wounded in readiness for removal by the Red Cross ambulance.

577,906. At the time this chapter was written (May, 1919), the total number of patients—sick and wounded—received from overseas by the R.A.M.C. for treatment, including those of the Dominions, of allied and associated nations, and of German prisoners of war, amounted to the amazing figures of 130,000 officers and 2,500,000 men. What a magnificent record of service is implicit in this single statement.

A fleet of nearly one hundred ships was employed in the transportation of the sick and wounded during the days of heavy pressure. These vessels were distributed all over the world, and included the giant ships Aquitania, Mauretania, and Britannic. The total staffs on board these hospital-ships during the time of this pressure reached 400 medical officers, 900 nurses, and about 3,500 rank and file of the R.A.M.C. The Aquitania carried as many as 5,000 patients from the East on one voyage, and twenty ambulance-trains were employed in disembarking them. The largest cross-Channel hospital-ship was the Asturias, and she carried as many as 2,700 patients on one trip. The first convoy of invalids arrived at Southampton Docks on August 24th, 1914, and the first train-load of invalids left Southampton for Netley Hospital the same day. These patients were 107 in number, and the train was composed of W.D. coaches and ordinary corridor stock. Regular ambulance-trains, however, soon were running. The first, which arrived at Southampton Docks on August 24th, 1914, was one from the Great Central Railway Co.'s Dukinfield works; it made its first trip four days later, and carried 62 cot **Ambulance ships** and 125 sitting cases to Netley. The **and trains** R.A.M.C. had twenty permanent ambulance-trains and two vestibule ambulance-trains, the latter being made up of London and North-Western Railway Co.'s vestibule vans. During the war not more than six deaths occurred in the United Kingdom in ambulance-trains.

Dover and Southampton were the principal ports for the reception of the sick and wounded from the western front, but invalids from various areas also were embarked, disembarked, and distributed from Devonport, Avonmouth, Liverpool, Glasgow, Leith, Hull, Boston, London, Holyhead,

FROM TRENCHES TO BENCHES.
Boot and shoe making and repairing in the Australian Red Cross Hospital for Disabled Soldiers at Southall. These men, who had honourably served their country, gave evidence of their efficiency in a peaceful capacity.

Newcastle, Folkestone, and Weymouth. The heaviest month was July, 1916; in that period 118,496 patients arrived at Dover and Southampton. In the week July 3rd to 9th inclusive, 1916, upwards of 47,000 reached these two ports. In the middle of that week—on July 6th—10,112 sick and wounded men were landed, 7,902 at Southampton and 2,210 at Dover. All these were records. On July 6th, the heaviest day in this respect of the war, twenty-nine trains were despatched from Southampton and eight from Dover, and several of these trains performed two journeys during the day. It should be added that it was generally possible to remove serious cases from the train to the nearest hospital en route. The ambulance-trains were extremely well-equipped in all respects, and each had a staff of medical officers, two nursing sisters, and eleven other ranks of the R.A.M.C.

Very early in the war it was found to be necessary to allocate special hospitals, or sections of hospitals, for the treatment of large numbers of particular types of cases, experience of which was almost entirely limited to the Great War. Among these were orthopædic hospitals, or hospitals devoted to reparative surgical treatment of the later stages of wounds and injuries, hospitals for the treatment of facial and jaw injuries, for the treatment of heart cases, including what was called "soldier's-heart," or the "irritable heart of soldiers," for the treatment of malaria and dysentery cases, and for mental cases. These hospitals were established in order that the sufferers should receive treatment from R.A.M.C. officers who had given particular attention to the various types of cases.

It was not until the war had been in progress for some little time that the great importance of the reconstructive or reparative treatment of wounds in the later stages was fully realised. Suitable and efficient treatment of the wounded from the first was most essential, and that the wounded received. The ideal of the surgeon and the aim of the administrator was six hours from wound to operating unit. In France the time occasionally was reduced to four hours. But from the point of view of rendering a wounded man fit and able to earn a fair wage in the labour market the care exercised on his behalf had to be of the highest order.

Hospitals for special cases

Therefore, special hospitals, with appropriate staff and equipment, were provided, and each of them was supervised by inspecting officers who had made a life study of the subject. Examples of these hospitals were the Special Military Surgical Hospital at Shepherd's Bush, London, and at Alder Hey, Liverpool. In these and similar hospitals there was found everything known to modern surgical science—special plaster-rooms, splint-rooms, baths, electrical and gymnastic rooms, and curative workshops designed to restore the function in limbs and parts of the body where movement and sensation had been temporarily impaired. In these workshops disabled soldiers were taught to make splints for every type of injury and deformity, thus rendering these workshops productive as well as curative.

Nothing could be more important for a man who had been wounded than to recover his power to work; it was

DISABLED SOLDIERS QUALIFYING AS HANDICRAFTSMEN.
Carpenters and cabinet-makers at work. At the Australian Red Cross Hospital, Southall, disabled soldiers were taught various useful trades to enable them to earn their living on return to civil life.

like making a new man of him by giving him the capacity to make a fresh start in an occupation that ensured a livelihood.

Cases dealt with in orthopædic hospitals included injuries of bones, joints, nerves, and tendons, as well as deformities such as flat-foot and the like. All fractures which were "ununited" or "malunited," and all fractures of the femur, as well as "peripheral nerve" work, came within the scope of these institutions. These cases were segregated into orthopædic centres, which consisted of a large parent hospital and several annexes for convalescent treatment. The annexes were entirely in the charge of the parent hospital's staff, each patient being looked after by the surgeon who had attended him in the main establishment. The staff was composed of orthopædic surgeons, chief assistants and medical officers acting as house surgeons, and officers in charge of the special after-treatment departments.

The soldier on his admission was seen by the orthopædic surgeon, who outlined treatment. arranged what department or departments the patient was to go into, and saw him from time to time, in consultation with the officer in charge of such department or departments. The key to the successful treatment of the injured man lay in the team-work which existed in these splendid hospitals. The surgeon, the chief assistant and the medical officer, and the departmental officers formed the team, and with frequent consultations and exchange of ideas obtained in this way true continuity of treatment.

Of quite extraordinary interest were the departments, for it was through them that the finished results were obtained. The operation, if there was any, in connection with the wound was only an incident, although of course a very important incident. The suture of a nerve, or the union of a previously ununited fracture by means of a bone graft, was undertaken by the surgeon, but the whole after-treatment, on which the successful issue depended, of such a case demanded the co-operation and skilled handling of the departments. One of these was the Plaster Department, in which were made all necessary splints and casts, both for the cure of the disability and for the purpose of record. The plaster casts, used in making moulded leather appliances, foot-plates, and the like, were made in it. All the plaster work, manipulative, for fixation, and curative, was controlled by the surgeon and his assistants, but the cast for record purposes was usually one by an expert plaster moulder.

Massage and electrical cures

A second department was devoted to massage, and it was in the charge of an officer who gave his whole time to this speciality. In addition to massage the work of this department embraced remedial gymnastics during the earlier stages of recovery. Individual attention was given to each patient, the detail being carried out by the Military Massage Corps. A third department—the highly important Electrical Department, always in charge of a special officer—undertook the neurological side, or nerve-work, in connection with patients. All cases of definite or suspected nerve injury were examined completely, and a record was taken as soon as possible after admission to the hospital. This record included a chart of the sensory disturbances, the motor power, and the electrical findings, and it served not only as a record but provided data on which the diagnosis ultimately rested. The department

HUMANE TREATMENT FOR FRIEND AND FOE.

Canadian and German wounded lying on stretchers awaiting removal to a hospital in the rear. The shell-battered village had just been recovered from the enemy. Above: Orderlies of the R.A.M.C. carrying a wounded German from the field of battle. This photograph was taken during the great British offensive towards Cambrai, September-October, 1918, and furnishes clear proof of the British care for German wounded prisoners.

also carried out the after-treatment of peripheral nerve injury by "interrupted" or periodic galvanic stimulation and re-education as recovery advanced. A further part of its business was the regeneration and re-education of wasted muscle and atrophy of limbs without nerve lesions.

In intimate association with the Massage and Electrical Departments was the Hydrological (or Bath) Department. The preliminary heating of the limb of a patient before going into either of the other two departments was generally carried out in the baths. Massage and manipulation under water formed an important treatment. There were various methods pursued for heating the part. One was the paraffin bath, in which the limb was immersed in paraffin at a temperature of 130 degrees—a new and valuable method. Others were radiant heat baths, the "whirlpool" bath, douches of various kinds, and the hot and cold contrast baths. In brief, all the resources of the finest hydropathic establishments in the world, and much more, were brought into play on behalf of the wounded soldier.

Special baths for the limbs

In these hospitals a special department, known as the Psychotherapy Department, was set apart for the treatment of functional disabilities. It was presided over by a medical officer who had an aptitude for this kind of work, and he acted in consultation with the neurological section. Occasionally a masseuse was found who showed particular skill. The treatment was individual in the case of each patient. Each was reasoned with, and told how far the disability from which he suffered was functional and not organic. Common types of disability were functional drop wrists, functional paralysis of a limb, tilting of the pelvis, and spasmodic inversion of the feet, and in such cases excellent cures were achieved.

Many a man, who had thought that his disability was permanent and that he had no chance in life again, found that he had been mistaken, and took a new interest in everything. Further help was given in the gymnasium and in the curative workshops of these orthopædic hospitals.

In two ways the curative workshops were of particular benefit. The first had to do with moral. The patient was given a real interest in some specific thing, and prevented from wasting his time and developing the habits of idleness to which he was liable because of the prolonged stay in hospital that was generally necessary. The second was in the retraining and re-education of the damaged limbs so as to regain function. The articles produced in these workshops by the soldiers were of very considerable value, more especially from the point of view of the hospital. The making and fitting of splints and the repair and alteration of boots were done entirely in them. The carpenter's shop provided

THE SLEDGE-HAMMER SWING.
Demonstrating the use of the sledge-hammer swing with special appliance: A mechanical aid for soldiers with maimed arms at the Charterhouse Military Hospital.

frames and all the supports used in the treatment of fractures of the lower extremities, the leather shop produced other things, and a combination of the instrument shop and the leather workers made the more elaborate forms of leather and steel support used—knee cages, back

DEMONSTRATION IN THE USE OF ARTIFICIAL LIMBS.
One-armed man giving demonstration in use of a garden fork at Roehampton, and (centre) learning to use the "working arm" in the carpenter's shop. Right: A fretwork machine for armless soldiers at Blackrock Hospital, Dublin. In oval: The King and Queen and Princess Mary watching a disabled soldier chipping a log of wood with the aid of his artificial arm. The Queen Mary's Hospital, Roehampton, was established for the restoration of the limbless.

braces, and like articles. Another interesting and important branch of orthopædics was the fitting of artificial limbs. For this purpose special hospitals were arranged on a progressive system, the patient passing on from one to another, according to the shrinkage of the limb and the stage of repair. At the final hospital expert limb-makers had established workshops, in which the fitting in the last stage was carried out very expeditiously. Queen Mary's Convalescent Auxiliary Hospital at Roehampton, on the outskirts of London, was considered the standard type of this sort of hospital.

MECHANICAL AID TO PEN-MANSHIP.
At the Artificial Limb Manual Training Centre, Balham. Man with mechanical arm writing; another illustration of the marvels of war surgery.

Soldiers suffering from injuries to the face and jaw were mainly concentrated at Queen Mary's Hospital, Frognal, Sidcup, where most elaborate arrangements were made for the restoration of function and appearance to those who had received injuries of this kind. Considering the diffi-

culties involved, this phase of the work of healing and reconstruction was amazingly successful.

In addition to the problems which were concerned with wounds to the body, those that were raised by injuries to the mind of the soldier very soon engrossed the attention of the Army Medical Service. These injuries to the mind were generally summed up loosely in the term shell-shock, or simply shock. The phrase shell-shock was very much misused, and for that reason it was discarded in 1917 by the R.A.M.C. Very early in the war it was evident, unfortunately, that nervous diseases (neuroses) and abnormal mental states (psychoses) would form no small portion of the casualties and disabilities due to active service conditions and reduce the strength of the Army; but many keen investigators attacked the subject in its various and varying forms, such as the loss of memory, and all compendiously comprised under the heading of neurasthenia.

In the beginning it was decided to treat all these cases in the General Military Hospitals or in sections connected with them. It was manifest as time passed on, however, that the best results were not being obtained by this **Care of neurological cases** means, and in the early autumn of 1917 a conference of leading neurologists was called to see what could be done to better matters. As a result of their deliberations an administrative scheme was drawn up which included the opening of special neurological hospitals throughout the United Kingdom and the special training of medical officers to carry out the latest forms of psycho-therapeutic treatment.

The leading examples of hospitals of this kind were Maudsley Neurological Clearing Hospital, London; the Military Hospital, Maghull, Liverpool; the Craiglockhart War Hospital, Edinburgh; and the Special Hospital for Officers, Palace Green, Kensington, London. From the establishment of these and similar hospitals up to the time of the writing of this chapter most valuable work had been done in them, the recoveries effected being in many ways remarkable.

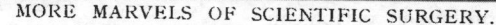
MORE MARVELS OF SCIENTIFIC SURGERY.

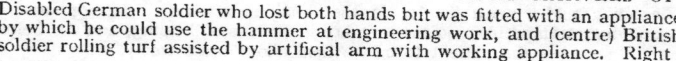
Disabled German soldier who lost both hands but was fitted with an appliance by which he could use the hammer at engineering work, and (centre) British soldier rolling turf assisted by artificial arm with working appliance. Right:

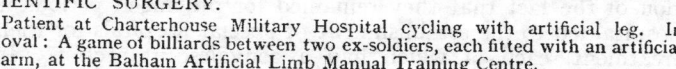
Patient at Charterhouse Military Hospital cycling with artificial leg. In oval: A game of billiards between two ex-soldiers, each fitted with an artificial arm, at the Balham Artificial Limb Manual Training Centre.

RESTORING ARMS AND HANDS.
Special bath treatment for wounded at Manor House Orthopædic Hospital, Hampstead. In circle: Making plaster casts of hands from which to make splints.

Treatment of patients in the neurological hospitals was variable and had to be adapted, as in other branches of medicine, to the particular requirements of each case. A notable thing was that psychotherapeutic conversation, or "persuasion," came increasingly into favour, this form of "suggestion" appearing to be more effective than the induction of hypnotic sleep, though the latter was of value in dealing with special varieties of nervous disturbances. It must be said that there was nothing new in the neuroses occasioned by the war, but the rapidity with which they were brought forward, and the vast number of men suffering from them, emphasised the important part played by functional nervous disorders in all branches of medicine and surgery. In other words, the fact was disclosed that in many types of disability there was

Psycho-therapeutic cure a functional nervous element which could rapidly be removed by psycho-therapeutic treatment. It came to be recognised on all sides that the study of war neuroses had drawn attention to a too long neglected field of medicine, and that the developments arising from this study would in time benefit the civil population in no small measure. Soldiers suffering from psychoses, or the more serious types of mental trouble, were treated in special sections of the General War Hospitals, and the results were most encouraging.

Another of the ailments from which the men at the front suffered was that called "soldier's heart," which was not in itself a new thing, for it had occurred in the Crimean War and was a good deal in evidence in the American Civil War. In 1864 the British Government of the day appointed a Commission to inquire into this subject, but in the end very little light was thrown upon it. In the Great War there were naturally large numbers of cases of this trouble, and recognition of the fact that they remained for prolonged periods in hospital led to the establishment of special hospitals for their treatment, each of which had a convalescent section. In

these hospitals, of which the pioneer was the Sobraon Military Hospital, at Colchester, the most up-to-date methods of testing the efficiency of the heart and of the treatment of disordered conditions were tried with very beneficial effects.

Throughout the hospitals there was in active operation a plan for the education, in the usual sense, of the patients. This had several good points. It hastened the recovery of the sick and wounded by occupying their minds and reviving mental interest. It continued, in the case of men who were likely to return to the ranks, the education given in the Army at home and abroad which had been found to have a valuable influence on military efficiency, and it provided a record of the educational courses that each man had followed during his service with the Colours. As regarded men who were likely to be discharged, it prepared them for civil life, and laid the foundation of the **Education for** vocational training which was given by the **patients** Ministry of Pensions and later by the Ministry of Labour to the discharged soldier unable to follow his old calling. The education given in the hospitals included English Grammar, Composition, and Literature, History, Geography, Modern Languages, Arithmetic, Economics, Lectures on Citizenship, Bookkeeping, Shorthand, Typewriting, Précis-writing, Commercial Correspondence, and Business Knowledge. Experience had shown that instrumental music and singing had a marked curative value in some cases, and music also was taught. There also was manual training. Where it was possible the patient was given some manual occupation while he was still confined to his bed, and after he had got up he went on with it in regular workshops.

As it was of primary importance to arouse interest, efforts were made by the teachers to make the personal experience of the soldiers in the field the starting-point of the teaching. Thus History and Geography were linked up with the war, while Economics and Citizenship were considered in connection with the national problems of resettlement and reconstruction. Of course, patients differed greatly in their educational attainments.

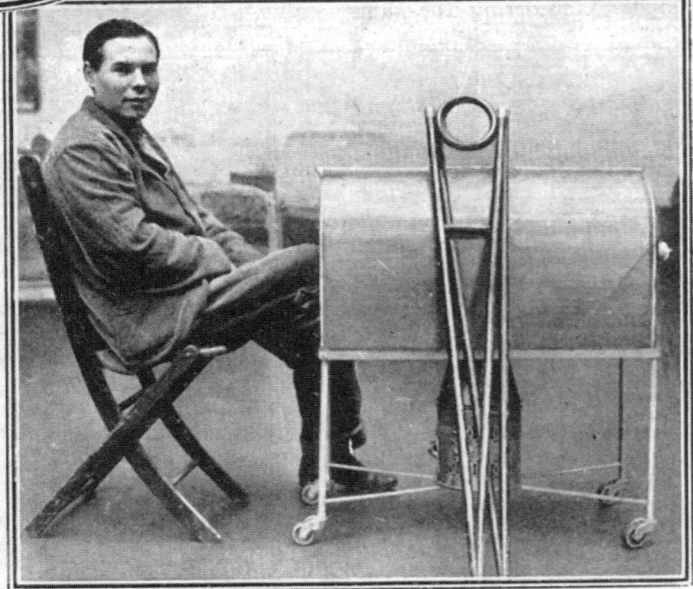

LEG DRILL FOR STIFF JOINTS.
Canadian soldier with his leg in the "baking machine," an appliance for removing stiffness from joints that are in process of healing, and for helping the patient to move them about more freely.

There were instances of men who had forgotten most of what they had learned at school, and could read and write but indifferently. For these special classes were formed to enable them to recover the ground they had lost, and they were urged to attend all general classes which they could follow, particularly those for training in Economics and Citizenship, as these were as important to them as to any others, and the fact that they were deficient in book-learning was no reason for assuming that they were not interested in questions of national significance.

The whole work of the Army Medical Service, whether at home or abroad, was nothing if not up to date; and, highly intelligent in every part of its wide-stretching activities, was, as it deserved to be, wonderfully successful. Many new inventions, remedies, and methods of treatment were tried, and if proved advantageous, adopted. One great difficulty which was

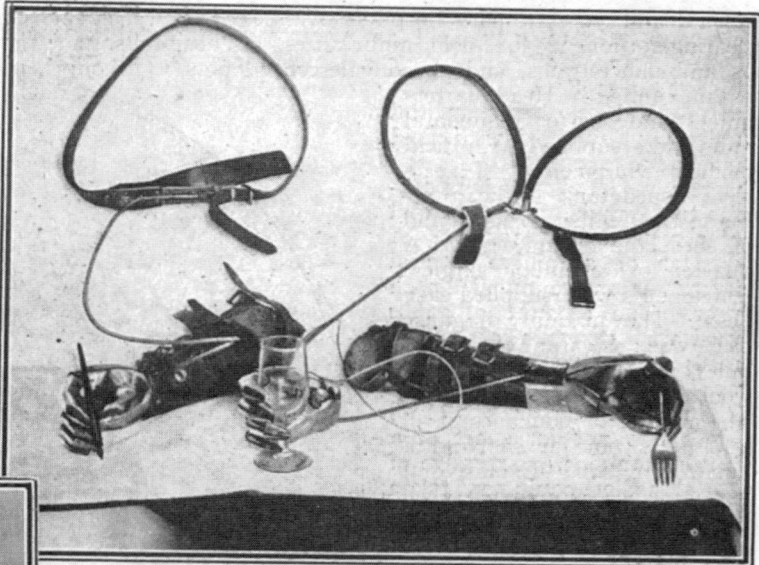

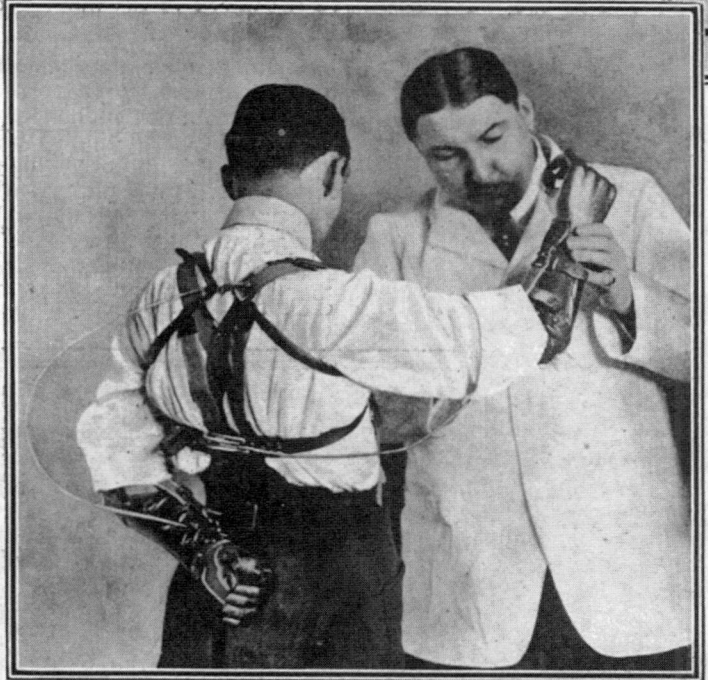

NEW ARMS FOR OLD:
Fitting on artificial arms with attachments to shoulder-straps. These attachments were manipulated by movements of the muscles of chest, back, and shoulders. They are seen more clearly in the top photograph where fingers are shown holding a fountain-pen, glass, and fork.

overcome was that of obtaining articles for which before the war Great Britain was largely dependent on enemy countries. Among these were such things as laboratory glassware, bacteriological stains and sugars, and certain drugs such as novocain, eucain, digitalis, bismuth and potassium salts, emetin, and belladonna. The R.A.M.C. built up a reserve of tablets of compressed drugs amounting to two hundred and fifty million tablets, the issues averaging about thirty million tablets a month.

At no time was there a shortage of anæsthetics, but steps were taken to have large supplies of them. The total quantities of ether and chloroform issued during the first three years of the war were 204,768 lb. and 180,772 lb. respectively. The monthly consumption of nitrous oxide was about 300,000 gallons during 1917, and was much larger in the following year. Nearly 10,000 nitrous oxide cylinders were in use. Large numbers of inhalers for the administration of gas and oxygen were supplied, the latest type, which was found very successful at casualty clearing-stations in France in cases suffering from severe shock, being an apparatus giving the gases alone or with ether. In 1917 the monthly consumption of oxygen was 80,000 cubic feet, and this figure was largely exceeded in 1918. Hundreds of sets of Haldane's inhalation apparatus were furnished

D 66

for the administration of oxygen in cases of gas poisoning. Perhaps there was no part of the equipment of the Army Medical Service more important in its way than X-ray apparatus, and no fewer than five hundred and twenty X-ray outfits were in use in the war. These outfits consisted of varying types, including the mobile outfit, mounted on a three-ton lorry chassis, the portable outfit, the trolly outfit, and the stationary outfit for hospital-ships and home hospitals. During one year upwards of a million X-ray plates were supplied. One of the things always needed in medicine was the clinical thermometer. Some difficulty was experienced in the early days of the war in obtaining a sufficient number of reliable instruments, but this difficulty, like other difficulties, was got over, and about a million of these thermometers, of proved reliability, were in use.

Spectacles and artificial eyes

Among other difficulties of the early days of the war with which the R.A.M.C. had to deal was the shortage of artificial eyes; before the war the manufacture of these had been in enemy hands. In 1916 the Service established at Clifford's Inn Hall, London, an Army Spectacle Depot for providing the troops with spectacles as required. The scope of this depot was developed, and eventually it produced not only spectacles but also artificial eyes, optical tools, and ophthalmological apparatus, besides carrying out repairs. It furnished the soldiers with nearly 302,000 pairs of spectacles and upwards of 14,000 artificial eyes.

The following statement of the number of medical units equipped showed, in summarised form but most impressively, the great range of work of the Army Medical Service: 16 base and 40 advanced depots of medical stores overseas; 122

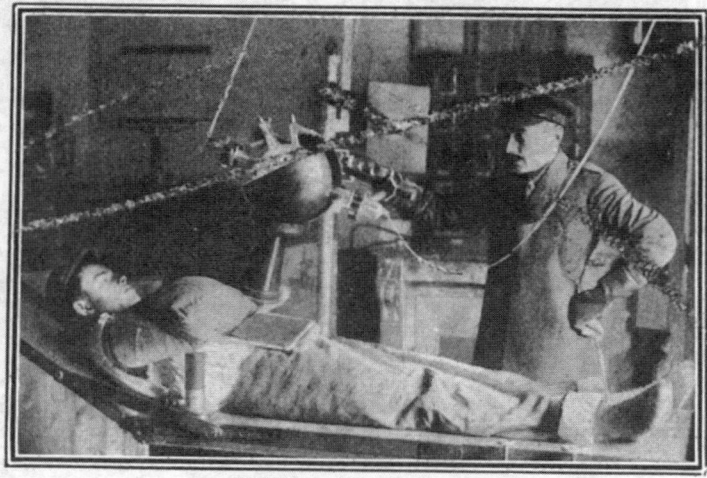

UNDER THE X-RAYS.
Locating a bullet in the arm of a French soldier in a Canadian hospital in France. The X-Ray process is seen in operation.

AA

general and 79 stationary hospitals overseas; 101 casualty clearing-stations; 394 field ambulances, 66 hospital-ships, 65 ambulance-trains, and 96 convalescent depots. Of combatant units 81 Headquarters units and 2,059 regimental units were supplied with field medical equipment. There were issued tank medical outfits to the number of 3,460, and of aeroplane outfits 1,774. A quarter of a million surgical instruments were supplied each year. The amount of gauze used was upwards of 75,000 miles in length, of lint and wool above 6,400 tons in weight. The number of bandages of all kinds was not far short of a hundred million. Exclusive of initial medical equipment taken by units, 525,000 cases and bales of medical stores were shipped overseas.

For the greater part of the duration of the war the chief administrator of the wonderful Army Medical Service was, as has been said, Sir Alfred Keogh, G.C.B., with headquarters at the War Office. For about the same period Sir A. T. Sloggett, K.C.B., was Director-

General in France. On the retirement of the former, early in 1918, Sir T. H. J. C. Goodwin, K.C.B., succeeded to the position at the War Office, and on the retirement of the latter in the same year, Sir C. H. Burtchaell, K.C.B., became Director-General in France. Men of distinguished ability and devoted to their work, they brought the Service to a high pitch of efficiency, as was warmly acknowledged by many thousands of grateful soldiers. In 1918 Sir William Leishman was brought from France to London, and acted at the War Office as adviser on pathology, doing a great work there. More than 4,600 officers, nurses, and men of the R.A.M.C. were killed in the war, and the number of wounded was very large in proportion to the numerical strength and particular work of the corps. In the distribution of honours the R.A.M.C. had its share, including V.C.'s and other high marks of distinction. Lord French, Sir Douglas Haig, and other commanders never failed to record in their despatches their appreciation of the splendid services of the corps.

METHODS FOR ENSURING A PURE WATER SUPPLY TO THE TROOPS IN FRANCE.
Sterilising drinking water for the troops in France. As a result of the process river water came out pure into the canvas cistern. Right : Pure water being pumped into a water-cart to be conveyed to the troops. Above : Lowering into a river pipes connected with the mobile de-poisoning machine seen on the motor-lorry. By these methods contaminated river water of the battle-areas was rendered innocuous, and typhoid practically non-existent.

RECORDS OF THE REGIMENTS: I. THE GUARDS.
By A. W. Holland.

This is the first of four chapters dealing with the services of various British regiments during the Great War. These chapters are confined, perforce, to the deeds of the infantry, on whom, when all is said and done, the brunt of the fighting fell. Various ways of dealing with the subject have been considered, and the one adopted is to divide them into groups. The Guards form a distinct unit, and can therefore easily be grouped together and their fortunes followed with ease; but the second group, that of the English regiments of the line, presents a more formidable problem, for they are so numerous and, during the Great War, were so ubiquitous. This difficulty, however, has been surmounted, and their deeds form the subject of the second and third chapters. The fourth deals with the Irish and the Welsh regiments, the sequence of the story being helped by the official arrangement of the Territorial and Service divisions according to nationality. The Scottish units are not included in the chapters immediately following, the reason being that their story has been told already in these pages by Dr. Neil Munro. The gallant deeds of the Canadian, Australian, New Zealand, South African, and Newfoundland units have also been related elsewhere in THE GREAT WAR.

N Saturday, December 15th, 1917, the Albert Hall, in London, was crowded with people. Surrounding the King and Queen were men from every part of the Empire, soldiers and civilians alike. They had come together for a purpose which may properly be called unique. They were there to commemorate the gallantry and devotion of the men of those seven divisions of the British Army who, in the autumn of 1914, sacrificed themselves that Britain and the cause of human freedom might live.

The commemoration was of an unusual character. There was a note of religion in it as when an eminent statesman read from the Apocrypha the passage beginning: " Let us now praise famous men," and when it concluded with the singing of the hymn, " For all the saints who from their labours rest." But it had a more secular, more purely military side, although this was not less inspiring, and there was certainly no incongruity between the two. In this the most important item was the reading by the Secretary for War, Lord Derby, of the Order of Battle of the Seven Divisions.

As one by one the names of the generals, battalions, and other units in that immortal Order of Battle were read out, there was a burst of cheers. Each brought vividly before the survivors who represented it at the commemoration a

vision of brave deeds and dead comrades; of wounds and thirst and other horrors; of retreat and helplessness; but above all, of the unconquerable and undying spirit of Britain's sons.

This chapter and two which will follow are intended to say something about the Order of Battle of the British Army during the Great War. It is a subject of absorbing interest, and one to which, for a variety of reasons, very inadequate attention was paid by those responsible for chronicling the war. The main reason for this, however, is one over which they had no control—the policy of secrecy adopted by the authorities. The bulk of us hardly realise how completely our real interests are local and circumscribed. We read of ten or sixty deaths in an air raid on London, and although in a general way we were sorry, it is absurd to assert that the mass of us were seriously moved. But when we knew, perhaps, that a man living in the same road was killed in one of those raids, when some houses in a neighbouring street were demolished, how much more real was our interest and how genuine our grief.

Similarly with our interest in the British Army. People are very proud of it, and are quite certain that it is the finest in the world, but their real enthusiasm and interest are reserved for one or other of its units. During the Great War the Army as a whole was too

THE PRINCE OF WALES WITH THE GUARDS.
General the Earl of Cavan and the Prince of Wales leaving Buckingham Palace to head the Guards' historic march through London, March 22nd, 1919.

DISTINGUISHED RECORDS OF SCOTS GUARDS.
Heroes of C Company, 1st Battalion Scots Guards, with a proud record for war decorations. Left to right (standing): Sergt. Leitch, Croix de Guerre; Sergt. Goldie, M.M.; C.-S.-M. McDonald, D.C.M.; C.-S.-M. Pyper, D.C.M.; Sergt. Rhodes, M.M. Seated: Sergt. F. McNess, V.C.; R. S. Cutler, M.C.; Sergt. J. McAulay, V.C., D.C.M. In addition Lieut. Boyd Rochford, V.C., belonged to the same company.

Historians tell us quite truly that the British Constitution is an organic growth. It was not, as the American was, written down on paper after full and ample inquiry and discussion. It developed as the nation did, adapting itself to the changing needs of each age. The same is true of the British Army. It was not suddenly called into being, after an elaborate scheme for its formation and regulation had been drawn up by a committee of experts. It developed from the warlike companions of Teutonic chieftains into the ceorls and huscarls of an Anglo-Saxon king; then from the knights and archers of mediæval warfare, through the pikemen of Tudor and Stuart times to the musketeers, fusiliers, and grenadiers who marched and conquered with Marlborough and won a terrible renown at Minden. Light infantry came into use during the Peninsular War, and then after more than half a century came the notable changes of the past forty years.

The use of the familiar word regiment reveals as by a flash of light the casual way in which the British Army has been built up. That word, as far at least as the

large, too varied, too scattered for their simple tastes; they wanted something smaller, something they could see, either mentally or physically, more easily; and so they preferred, perforce, to narrow their affections to a regiment in which a relative or friend was serving, or to one associated with the neighbourhood in which they lived.

It is hardly necessary to argue this point, but an illustration may be given. Compare the description given by Sir John French—as he then was—in his third despatch of the attack made by the Northamptonshire and Queen's Regiments on the hills above the Aisne, on September 17th, 1914, with the bald statements issued in 1917 to the effect that troops from the Midland counties gained their objective, or that Scottish troops advanced on the right. Again, how much local patriotism would have been lost had we not known that

Springs of local patriotism   it was the 2nd Worcesters that saved the day at Gheluvelt on October 31st, 1914, and if the account had just read: "By 2.30 p.m. a vital position had been retaken with the bayonet, an English battalion being to the fore in this enterprise."

Obviously, it is not possible in two or three chapters of THE GREAT WAR to deal separately with the various regiments of the British Army. They must be grouped, and the fortunes of each group described. These easily suggest themselves. The Guards form one such group, the Scottish regiments another—and their tale has been told already in these pages by Dr. Neil Munro—while others are the Irish and Welsh.

The English regiments of the line form another and larger group. Beyond these are the regiments from Greater Britain—Canadians, Australians, South Africans, Newfoundlanders, and the rest—but THE GREAT WAR has already had chapters on their exploits, and incidentally this is another reason for saying something about the regiments of the Homeland. The cavalry, artillery, engineers, and airmen, too, fall outside the scope of these chapters; the narrative therein will deal only with that astonishing infantry whose praise has been written for all time by Napier. It will not fail for lack of material.

Before passing on to describe the deeds of the Guards—for those of the infantry of the line must be reserved for later chapters—it will be well to say something about the extent to which the British Army is a local, or territorial, one, the nature of that connection and other kindred matters.

GRENADIER SURVIVORS OF THE "OLD CONTEMPTIBLES."
Thirteen members of the 2nd Grenadier Guards who returned to London in March, 1919, sole survivors of the battalion who accompanied the Expeditionary Force to France, August, 1914. Two won the D.C.M. and four had been wounded.

infantry is concerned, is not known upon the battlefield. During the Great War the Commander-in-Chief and his subordinates had before them plans showing the position of every unit in the Army, but one would look in vain for a regiment thereon. Army corps, division, brigade, battalion, company, platoon—all were there, but no regiments of foot.

Notwithstanding this, the British Army is a collection of regiments, and the regimental traditions are its life-blood. Before the Great War we knew nothing about the deeds of divisions or brigades or battalions, but a great deal about those of regiments, for every schoolboy had read of the Black Watch at Ticonderoga, the Middlesex at Albuera, the Gordon Highlanders at Waterloo, and the South Wales Borderers at Isandula. These were not the names of brigades or battalions, but of regiments.

Regiment was the name given in England to bodies of men which were raised, generally by some eminent soldier, to fight their country's battles. Thus in Cromwellian times there was Monk's Regiment of Foot and the Lord General's Regiment of Horse. After the restoration of Charles II., some of them, instead of being disbanded as had been the case previously when peace returned, were added to the standing Army, which then consisted only of the troops attached to the Royal household and troops on foreign service, "guards and garrisons," as the Act of 1661 called them. For purposes of convenience, as it became part of the Regular Army, each was given a number in very much the same way as the authorities numbered the various army corps, divisions, and brigades that were raised during the Great War. The Royal Scots became the 1st Regiment, the Tangiers Regiment the 2nd, the Holland Regiment the 3rd, and so on. Others were added later. At first independent bodies under the command of a colonel, who was responsible for their pay, clothing, and discipline, and who frequently bestowed his own name upon them, they were taken into the Royal service and given a number in the line. The 69th, for instance, part of the Army since 1760, was earlier known as Colville's Foot. The number borne to-day by a regiment, therefore, serves one useful purpose—it tells something about its age; the 10th is an older regiment than the 51st.

In addition to their numbers, certain regiments retained old titles or received new ones. The 1st could hardly be expected to give up the proud name of Royal Scots, a reminder of the time when Scotsmen served with distinction as the bodyguard of the kings of France, and fought under Hepburn for Gustavus Adolphus. The 2nd Regiment was soon known as the Queen's, and the 3rd, from the colour of the facings on its uniform, as the Buffs. The 4th became the King's Own, and the 8th the King's, and the practice was kept up, for in 1842 the 13th was called Prince Albert's. Other titles came in a variety of ways, and the result was a **Double system of** double system of nomenclature, of which **nomenclature** the 42nd, the Black Watch, and the 88th, the Connaught Rangers, are examples.

Next came the use of the word battalion, to denote a part of a regiment, or perhaps one should say a linked or related regiment. Occasionally it happened that someone connected with a particular regiment would obtain authority to raise another, and to get recruits he went among the neighbours and kinsfolk of those serving in the original regiment. Now and again this new body was not given a fresh number, but was known as the second battalion of the older one. There was no rule on these matters, but the word battalion was employed for what was in effect a second regiment, although one without a distinctive number in the line. Thus some regiments had two battalions, but until recent times the majority had only one. In 1756, for instance, when the Seven Years War opened, fifteen regiments were ordered to raise additional battalions, but two years later these were numbered as separate regiments.

Concurrent with this development, many of the regiments obtained in one way or another local associations, and in one or two cases these were worked into the name. One perhaps was raised by a Gloucestershire or Devon man in Gloucestershire or Devon, and its officers got into the habit of looking to that county for recruits. Others were raised among the Highland clans, Gordons and Camerons for example; while others were composed mainly of men from Yorkshire or Lancashire, the Borders or the West. Here again, without deliberate effort or plan, something of a territorial system arose in the British Army. Occasionally this territorial connection was formally **Origin of local** recognised, as when in 1782 the 9th was **associations** first styled the East Norfolk Regiment.

There were thus two customs, the outcome of chance—regiments with one battalion and regiments with more; regiments with local associations and regiments without. Another was that it was not regarded as necessary for the two battalions of a regiment, where they existed, to serve together in time of war. Now and again they did, as the records of the Napoleonic Wars show, but not always. In 1813 the Royal Scots had four battalions on foreign service; one was in Canada, one in India, one in France, and one in Germany.

In this connection it only remains to say a word about the Guards. They remained outside the territorial system, such as it was, and were never numbered among the regiments of the line, over which, as every "Army List" shows, they had precedence. But they adopted the idea of battalions, and there were 1st and 2nd Battalions of Grenadiers and Coldstreamers.

In 1881 the Army was reorganised, and on the whole wisely.

DAUNTLESS HEROISM OF BRITISH GUARDS THAT SAVED THE DAY.

During the second phase of the Battle of Cambrai the Germans launched a powerful attack on November 30th, 1917, and pushed their divisions very rapidly forward until they were stopped by the British Guards at Gouzeaucourt. At one place the heroic Guards saved some imperilled guns, dragging them back to safety by main force, while their comrades checked the oncoming Boches with the bayonet, and thus prevented a German break-through.

The new scheme, often known by the name of its author, Lord Cardwell, then Secretary for War, took account of the two main tendencies which had grown up since the Great Civil War—the relation between the regiment and the battalion, and the links which bound certain regiments to certain areas.

Uniformity was introduced in these matters into the Service. Every regiment of the line was henceforward to consist of at least two battalions of Regular soldiers, and every one was to be associated with a certain locality. Of the two battalions one was to stay at home and the other to serve abroad, the former acting as a feeder to the latter. To each battalions of Militia were attached, numbered after the Regular battalions (3rd, 4th, etc.), and these formed a reserve, liable to be called out for home defence in times of great national danger.

Effects of the Cardwell scheme Of the line regiments the first twenty-six already consisted of two battalions each, but most of the others had only one. The latter were, therefore, "linked" together in twos, care being taken to put together, as far as possible, regiments with common associations. Thus the 43rd and the 52nd, associated in glory in the stern battles of the Peninsular War, were united to form the Oxfordshire Light Infantry; the 72nd with the 78th, both raised by the Earl of Seaforth from among his clansmen, were joined to make the Seaforth Highlanders. There were one or two exceptions, but this was the general rule, and

it explains why some regiments have only one number—for instance, the 18th, the Royal Irish—while others have two. The former had two battalions before 1881; the latter were then made up of two distinct regiments.

Each regiment of the line received a new name, a territorial one, and here again, as far as possible, regard was paid to past associations. For instance, the 37th and 67th Regiments had been connected for a hundred years with Hampshire, and so they became together the new Hampshire Regiment. In some cases the association was less close, but in one way or other a regiment was allotted to every English county except two or three of the smallest, while Lancashire and Yorkshire had each several, and Staffordshire, Surrey, and Kent two each. Regiments were given to Scotland, Ireland, and Wales, and one, the Royal Fusiliers, to London.

Territorial system established

Each regiment, therefore, had a district, one county, or perhaps several, from which to draw its recruits, and in that county had a town as the depot, or headquarters. Thus Perth was the depot of the Black Watch, and Canterbury of the Buffs, or East Kents. In other words, a territorial system was established. This gave to each two titles, but in several cases there was a third. In various ways certain regiments had earned a distinctive name—Buffs or Black Watch, for example—and this, too, was kept. Thus the proper designation of one of these was: The King's (Liverpool) Regiment,

GUARDS' COLOURS, DESTINED FOR COLOGNE, TAKEN IN PROCESSION THROUGH LONDON STREETS.

Guards' colours being borne through London. An impressive military ceremony took place at Wellington Barracks, January 4th, 1919, when the Guards' colours destined for Cologne were paraded. Thence a procession was formed to Charing Cross Station, but the bearers had to abandon their journey owing to transport trouble at Folkestone. The trouble was, however, promptly settled, and the colours arrived at Cologne, January 7th. The colour parties each carried two colours, the ten parties representing the 1st, 2nd, 3rd Grenadier, 1st, 2nd, 3rd Coldstream, 1st and 2nd Scots, 1st Irish, and 1st Welsh Guards.

formerly the 8th Foot ; or the Middlesex Regiment (the Duke of Cambridge's Own), formerly the 57th and 77th Foot.

The next change took place in 1907, and this was the creation of the Territorial Army. Confining ourselves to the infantry, its backbone were the regiments with two Regular battalions each, although one or two—the Royal Fusiliers and the Rifle Brigade, for example—had four. Next to the Regulars came the old Militia, later called the Reserve, and the scheme was completed by the inclusion of the Volunteers in the regiment. A typical infantry regiment, therefore, between 1907 and the Great War in 1914, consisted of two battalions of Regulars, one of Reserve, and several of Volunteers, or Territorials as they were called from this time, numbered in that order.

Take an instance at random. The Northumberland Fusiliers had its two battalions of Regulars, the 1st at home and the 2nd in India, or vice versa ; the 3rd was a Reserve, or Militia, battalion; the 4th, 5th, 6th, and 7th were Volunteer, or Territorial, battalions, two with headquarters at Newcastle, one at Alnwick, and one at Hexham. The number of these Territorial battalions varied according to the population of the district, and there were none in Ireland.

In August, 1914, Lord Kitchener and his advisers had to decide what to do with the new recruits flocking in thousands to the Colours. Some joined the existing battalions, both Regular and Territorial, but there were far too many for their ranks, and the great majority were enrolled in special new battalions. For these the existing regimental organisation was used, and, called Service battalions, they were attached to each line regiment, the men enlisting in them usually joining one associated with their own district and receiving their early training at its depot. Thus the miners of the Glamorganshire valleys formed Service battalions of the Welsh Regiment, and recruits from Birmingham Service battalions of the Warwicks. These new battalions were numbered after the Territorial ones, so **Grouping the** in 1915 the Northumberland Fusiliers con- **Service battalions** sisted of those already mentioned and of Service battalions numbered from the 8th to the 27th. The proper designation of one of these was the 6th (Service) Battalion, Royal Welsh Fusiliers, or whatever the name of the regiment might be.

The next step was to put the battalions, new and old, together into groups suitable for service at the front. They were, therefore, made into brigades, each of four battalions, and divisions, each of three brigades. These brigades and divisions were numbered from one onwards, very much as the regiments had been in the Army's early days, and during the great German offensive of 1918 Sir Douglas Haig's reports made us familiar with many of the divisions—the 3rd and 51st for instance.

For some of the Regulars this process had been carried out already, and seventy-two battalions grouped into six divisions and eighteen brigades, the so-called Expeditionary Force, and incidentally the finest army probably the world has ever seen. In this grouping no account was taken of local associations. There was not an East Anglian or a Welsh division ; there was no case, excluding the Guards, of two battalions of a regiment serving together, and the same principle was observed when other divisions of Regulars were formed from troops serving abroad. Thus the famous 29th Division contained Royal Fusiliers (Londoners), South Wales Borderers, King's Own Scottish Borderers, Dublin

and Munster Fusiliers, Lancashire Fusiliers, Hampshire, Worcester, and Essex men. It was a mixed force representing all four nationalities and all parts of England.

Except for a time, for purposes of training in the field, the Territorials were not attached to the Regulars. They were formed into brigades and divisions of their own, as also were the Service men, and so it came about that there were soon three kinds of infantry divisions in the field. But

ARRIVAL OF GUARDS' COLOURS IN COLOGNE.
Proud bearers of the Guards' colours marching through Cologne, where they arrived on January 7th, 1919.
The colours were handed over with due ceremonial to the general commanding the British Army there.

the Territorial and Service men were grouped on a principle quite different from that of the Regulars. They were associated, in both brigades and divisions, with other battalions from the same locality. Thus the Territorials included a Highland division, an East and a West Lancashire division, a South Midland division, two London divisions, and so on. In like manner the Service battalions were formed into their larger units. Scotsmen formed one division of the " First Hundred Thousand," Irishmen formed one, and men from the North, West, and East of England formed one each.

A word should be said about the numbering of the divisions, for, as the war progressed, all armies began to regard this unit, one of twelve or thirteen battalions and anything from 10,000 to 16,000 men, as the most important of all. The first eight divisions, numbered one to eight, were composed of Regulars, forming the first six divisions of the Expeditionary Force and two others, the 7th and 8th ; these two were made up mainly of battalions brought from foreign stations, and one of them, the 7th, went across to Flanders in time to win a place, and that not the least **Numbering of** honourable one, among those that saved **the divisions** the Cause in the dreadful autumn of 1914.

Between these battalions, it may be repeated, there was no territorial link. There was no district to which the division as a whole could look for recruits.

To return to the numbering. From the 9th to the 26th, inclusive, the divisions were composed of Service battalions, eighteen divisions divided into three groups of six each, each one being, roughly speaking, a hundred thousand men. The first of each group, the 9th, 15th, and 21st, were Scottish divisions ; the 10th and 16th were Irish, and the English followed a like sequence. The 11th, 17th, and 23rd were made up of Northern troops; the 12th, 18th, and 24th of men from the Eastern; and the 13th, 19th, and 25th of men from the Western Counties; while the 14th, 20th, and 26th were mainly light infantry, a name which no longer meant any difference in arms or equipment. They may be regarded, therefore, as the miscellaneous divisions. After the 26th came three more divisions of Regulars, the 27th, 28th, and 29th, followed by more Service divisions which took the tale down to the 41st. Many of these had no special name, but the 36th was the Ulster and the 38th the Welsh Division.

The Territorial divisions began with the 42nd and continued until the 56th. Each had a name as well as a number. The 42nd was the East Lancashire, the 43rd the Welsh, the 46th the North Midland, the 47th and 56th the two London Territorial Divisions, and the 51st—so highly praised by Sir Douglas Haig in March and April, 1918—

Seventy divisions in the field was the Highland Division. After these were a few more Service and miscellaneous divisions, the 63rd, or Royal Naval Division, for instance, stretching well into the sixties, for during the German offensive of 1918 the 66th was mentioned. It was not possible to ascertain the exact number, but it was assumed, not without reason, that in 1917 and 1918 Great Britain had some seventy divisions in the field.

Without some such account as this it is not easy to follow the doings of the different regiments; indeed, in no case is it so. For instance, a regiment was not fighting in one place only, but perhaps in half a dozen. At one time some of them had several battalions in the West, one in Mesopotamia, and perhaps another in Gallipoli, while the North Lancashires had one in East Africa. At a later stage the battalions of a regiment like the Worcesters might be in a dozen places in France and Flanders. To follow their doings this should be remembered, and also the way they were grouped into divisions and brigades; the Regulars on one principle, the Territorials and Service men on another. The two subsequent chapters will illustrate this point more fully; the present one must confine itself to the deeds of the regiments of Guards, to which neither Territorial nor Service battalions were attached. For the purpose of maintaining a supply of recruits, however, each of these regiments had reserve battalions.

The very word Guards illumines the history of the British Army. Like most other armies it began with the men whose business it was to protect or guard the King, and for long no other kind of standing army was known. At some remote date these Guards were divided into Horse and Foot Guards, and the latter into regiments, 1st, 2nd, and 3rd, called after a time also Grenadier, Coldstream, and Scots Guards. This close connection with the Sovereign gave a special position to these Guards, which was intensified as a standing army came into being. They had certain privileges—immunity from duty abroad in time of peace, for instance. A higher physical standard was required from their recruits, and their terms of enlistment were somewhat different. Their system of training was not quite the same, either, and they were popularly regarded as men of special fitness and valour.

The Guards at Landrecies When the Great War broke out nine battalions of Guards were in existence. The Grenadiers and Coldstreamers had three each, and the Scots had two. The remaining one belonged to a new regiment, the Irish Guards, raised to perpetuate the valour shown by the Irish regiments in the Boer War. All of them were Regular soldiers, men of exceptional physique enlisted for a long period and trained by that intensive system of drilling "on the square," which proved its value in producing steadiness under the most critical conditions a thousand times during the Great War.

Six of these battalions, among them all three of the Coldstreamers, went at once to the front, four forming one of the brigades (the 4th) of the 2nd Division, and the other two being in the 1st Brigade and the 1st Division. It is, therefore, necessary to follow the doings of two brigades and two divisions—the 4th, or Guards, Brigade under General Scott-Kerr in the 2nd Division, which landed at Havre on August 13th,

1914, and the 1st under General Maxse in the 1st Division. Both were in Sir Douglas Haig's army corps.

This first corps was not at all heavily engaged at Mons on Sunday, August 23rd, but in the retreat the Guards fought at least three little battles—Landrecies, Maroilles, and Villers-Cotterets. Landrecies, fought on the night of the 25th, was solely the work of the Guards Brigade, upon which fell the onerous duty of protecting the rear of the corps. The tired men had received orders to bivouac for the night in this little French town, which stands on the edge of the Forest of Mormal, and in the late afternoon they reached it. There were rumours that the Germans were not far away and precautions were taken against a surprise.

Night was fast coming on when a party of soldiers emerged from the forest. Were they friend or foe, the sentries wondered, as the four battalions were called out and the 3rd Coldstreamers, the first on the spot, prepared to dispute the way along the road leading into the town. The Germans—for they were such—called out that they were French, but the ruse did not succeed, and the battle in the village street began. The houses were in the possession of the Guards, and their machine-guns commanded the street; so, in spite of the heavier guns which the enemy used and the arrival of fresh hordes, the Germans were unable to gain their objective. During the night they tried again and again, but the Coldstreamers were always in their way. Towards morning the Irish Guards relieved their comrades, and a little later the brigade was able to march unmolested away. In this engagement the losses fell nearly all upon the 3rd Coldstreamers. Lord Hawarden and the Hon. Archer Windsor-Clive, two of their officers, were killed, and about 170 altogether became casualties. An incident not reported for more than a year shows the nature of this fighting. In order to see the position of the foe the Germans set fire to some straw stacks. Lance-Corporal G. H. Wyatt, seeing the meaning of this, dashed out and extinguished the blaze. "Otherwise," said the notice by which the V.C. was awarded to Wyatt, "the position would certainly have been lost." On the same day the 1st Brigade was attacked at Maroilles, but some French troops came up to its help, and without any considerable losses it was able to move away. **In the woods of Villers-Cotterets**

Villers-Cotterets was another battle for the Guards Brigade. The retreat was not quite over, and early on the morning of September 1st the Germans came up with the rearguard of the brigade. This consisted of the Irish Guards and the 2nd Coldstreamers, and for some hours they kept up a ding-dong action in the woods near the village, rifles cracking amid the trees and each man playing a lone hand. There it was that General Scott-Kerr was wounded and the Irish Guards lost their colonel, the Hon. G. H. Morris, and several other officers. The command of the brigade passed from Scott-Kerr to Lord Cavan.

Events moved rapidly in the autumn of 1914, and the war was only just a month old when the Battle of the Marne began. It was wholly a manœuvre battle, and the successes won by the British cost a very moderate price indeed in human life. Without serious fighting the brigades crossed the Grand Morin, but the crossing of the Petit Morin was somewhat more difficult. However, the passage was forced, and a good share of the honours fell to the Guards. This was still more true when the Ourcq was passed, and pressing on, the six battalions, with the rest of the army, found themselves fronted by the Aisne.

The crossing of the Aisne was a more difficult operation, for the Germans had turned and were prepared to stand and fight. Yet the movement was tried and accomplished. The arrangements were made on September 13th, and the 1st Brigade got across without difficulty on a bridge at Bourg, which had been left undamaged. The Guards Brigade was less fortunate. One battalion was got across in boats at Chavonne, but when night came on the three others were still on the southern side of the river. They got over, however, on the next day, and then began the equally serious task of driving the enemy from the positions on the hillside, which he was feverishly strengthening. All the Guards were in this

Return of the Guards: 2nd Grenadiers at St. Pancras Railway Station, Feb. 25th, 1919.

1st Scots Guards marching past Buckingham Palace on the way to Wellington Barracks on their arrival from France, March 3rd, 1919.

230

Triumphant march of the Guards through London, March 22nd, 1919 : Some of the 8,000 who took part passing the laurelled pillars in the Mall.

Off to Cologne: Young Guards' inspection by the King, Hyde Park, March 1st, 1919.

Back from the war: Welcome to returning Guards, St. Pancras Station, March 3rd, 1919.

movement, the object of the First Corps being to seize the Ladies' Road, the famous Chemin des Dames. The movement was carefully planned. The 2nd Brigade was ordered to seize a sugar factory—by this time a fortress—at Troyon, and to assist them the 1st Coldstreamers came on from the 1st Brigade. In front of Troyon there was some costly fighting in which the Scots Guards did very good work.

Meanwhile the 4th Brigade was advancing from the river bank towards Ostel, its orders being to seize the woods around that village. The advance was difficult, for the day was wet and the numerous trees made it almost impossible for the artillery to lend effective support. However, some progress was made and, after a rest at noon, the march was resumed. By the end of the day an attempt to outflank the brigade had been thwarted, and although not on the Ladies' Road, the Guards were entrenched only a little way below it. The Irish Guards bore the brunt of this encounter, their killed including Lord Guernsey and Lord Arthur Hay.

The forward movement then stopped. Some weeks were passed in poor, wet trenches, whence a continuous succession of attacks was beaten back, and then suddenly and silently came one of the changes of the war—the transfer of the British Army to Flanders. The First Corps, in which all the Guards were, was the last of the three to go. On October 19th it left the train at St. Omer and marched towards the new front already reverberating loudly with the clamour of the guns. A great battle had just begun.

Two more battalions of Guards were by now at the front. A division of Regulars, numbered the 7th, had been hastily formed in England, put under Sir Henry Rawlinson, and hurried across to save Antwerp. In one of its brigades, the 20th, were the 1st Grenadiers and the 2nd Scots Guards. They landed at Ostend on October 6th, moved quickly to Ghent, but were unable to do anything for Antwerp; however, they were not too late to make the retreat less disastrous than it would otherwise have been. Acting as a rearguard to the Belgians, they marched from Ghent to Roulers, joined up with the main body of Sir John French's force, and were ordered by him to get possession of Menin.

The First Battle of Ypres

In this way the First Battle of Ypres began, the thin British line being just, but only just, in time to stem the heavy German onslaught—in plain English, to save Calais. In this struggle all the eight battalions of Guards were in the same neighbourhood. Six, as we have already seen, were in Haig's First Corps, which had just come up, and as regards the other two, those in Rawlinson's corps, French said : " I directed Sir Henry Rawlinson to endeavour to conform generally to the movements of the First Corps."

In the thickest of all this fighting were the Guards. On October 22nd those in the 1st Division, Scots and Coldstreamers, were almost surrounded, but managed to fight themselves free. Three days later, at Kruseik, the Germans broke through where the 2nd Scots Guards held the line. The position was restored by a counter-attack, but early the next morning the Germans came on again, and there was some more dreadful fighting. Although driven back, the Scots did not break, and at length the line was saved. The 1st Grenadiers were also in the struggle, and both they and the Scots had very heavy casualties.

The climax of the battle was yet to come. On the 29th Gheluvelt was attacked, and soon the Guards in the 1st and 7th Divisions were fighting against tremendous odds once more. Under cover of a fog the Germans broke through down the Menin road, and then, attacking the 1st Grenadiers from the rear, reduced the battalion to 150 fit men. Not far away the 1st Coldstreamers were nearly destroyed, no officer escaping unhurt, and some of the 1st Scots suffered a like fate. The Guards Brigade under Lord Cavan came to their help, and the 1st Irish and 2nd Grenadiers, sent into the front line, also distinguished themselves in those dire days. A little later the Irish, lying under a terrific fire of high-explosive shells, had 300 casualties, their colonel, Lord Ardee, being hit ; and in the attack on November 6th one of their companies was destroyed and another badly mauled.

The line had been saved, but at the cost of almost eight battalions of Guards, to say nothing of other soldiers. Of the 8,000 or 9,000 men who left England, only twelve or thirteen weeks before, very few now remained in the ranks. The 7th Division, in which were two battalions of Guards, had been reduced to 44 officers and 2,336 men, and the 1st Brigade, in which were the 1st Coldstreamers and 1st Scots, to eight officers and 500 men—battalions, that is, averaging two officers and 125 men each. The 1st Coldstreamers had been practically destroyed, 70 men only being left, and the other battalions suffered almost as heavily. Altogether it is not improbable that the Guards lost 6,000 men in those three months of war, and that the Coldstreamers lost more heavily than any other regiment.

Records of the Coldstreamers

The members and friends of the other three regiments of Guards will certainly pardon the writer if he pauses here for a moment to speak of the splendid record of the Coldstreamers. The historian of the British Army has told us that this is our " oldest national regiment and the sole survivor of the famous New Model." Its proud Latin motto means " second to none," and it lived up to it. Proof is at hand.

In Sir John French's first list of mentions no regiment save the Engineers had anything like as many names as had the Coldstreamers. Thereon are the colonels commanding its three battalions and many others, both officers and men, while the list referring to the Battle of Ypres is almost equally long. Men of this regiment won the first two Victoria Crosses earned in the war by Guardsmen—that of Wyatt has been mentioned already, while Lance-Corporal F. W. Dobson, of the 2nd Battalion, earned one on September 28th. It is equally evident if we consider the awards of Distinguished Conduct Medals. Down to June 11th, 1915, thirty-eight Coldstreamers had received this honour, the longest list of all.

But the final test is found in the Roll of Honour. Mr. J. W. Fortescue said, speaking of this very subject, that no name seemed to appear so frequently in the casualty lists as did the Coldstreamers, and his opinion on such a matter is no light one. Confining ourselves to the officers, what a roll it is ! In splendour of name it rivals that of the Scots who fell at Flodden or the Frenchmen who lay dead at Poitiers. Two peers of the realm, Viscount Hawarden and Lord Petre, were on it ; and so was a peer's heir, Viscount Northland, and a baronet, Sir Roland Corbet. Of the younger sons of peers may be mentioned on this roll of famous dead Archer Windsor-Clive, E. W. M. M. Brabazon, C. H. S. Monck, Vere D. Boscawen, C. W. Douglas-Pennant, and L. d' H. Hamilton. Percy Wyndham, Captain Banbury (a son of Sir Frederick Banbury, M.P.), and Nigel Legge-Bourke fell in these ranks, and so did men bearing the historic names of Tollemache, Beauchamp, Lambton, Adeane, Cottrell-Dormer, Graves-Sawle, De Winton, Pollock, Tritton, and Trotter. Scotland contributed a Murray, a Campbell, and a Stewart, and Wales a Williams-Wynn. The list of wounded Coldstreamers is too long for citation, but on it were the three colonels—Ponsonby, Feilding, and Pereira—who went out in command of the three battalions in August, 1914.

In the Cuinchy brick-fields

In January and February the Guards had another little battle almost alone. Where the line ran through some brick-fields near a village called Cuinchy the 1st Scots and 1st Coldstreamers were in trenches, and on January 25th these were suddenly and violently assailed. Something was done to recover them, but the enemy could not be altogether dislodged, and to improve matters the Guards Brigade came up from reserve. They took over the trenches, but soon the 2nd Coldstreamers were driven out, and a first attempt at recovery failed. Then a picked party of Irish and Coldstreamers tried their hand, and this time, careful preparations having been made for the attack, they were completely successful. It was on this day that the Irishman Michael O'Leary won the V.C. A few days later another bold enterprise drove the Germans from another such stronghold.

Bigger operations were at hand, for the wet and dismal winter was nearly over. Neuve Chapelle was fought on March 10th, 11th, and 12th, but it was only on the third day that any Guards were really in action. The 1st Grenadiers and 2nd Scots strove hard to seize Pietre Mill, and then it was that two Grenadiers, Barber and Fuller, won the V.C. Both battalions lost very heavily as they tried to storm cunningly-defended buildings, the killed including the Grenadier colonel, L. R. Fisher-Rowe.

When the Second Battle of Ypres was fought all the Guards were away to the south, holding the line where it stretched from Armentières to Arras. Just as the German assaults at Ypres were dying away the British struck on their part near Festubert. A first attack, made on Sunday, May 9th, did not yield the desired results, and another was fixed for the 16th. The 2nd Division, in which was the Guards Brigade, was in this movement, and so was the heroic 7th Division, with its Scots and Grenadiers.

In the northern section of the attack the Guards were in reserve, but farther south the 2nd Scots was one of the assaulting battalions, and it is of their fight that one of the epic tales of the war is told. One company of the Scots dashed on with such impetus that they soon became isolated in the German position. As far as their comrades knew, they were lost, and so they were; but the fine sequel was only revealed some days after, when our men won this forward ground. There they came upon the bodies of the Scots lying amid a ring of foes; they had died fighting. While they were thus so desperately employed the other companies had cut off the Germans, and, with the help of the supporting battalion, the 1st Grenadiers, had held and consolidated the ground.

Epic tale of the Scots

On the 17th the Guards, the supporting brigade on the other part of this battle, were needed. Under heavy fire they marched forward to relieve the battalions who had stormed some German trenches, and they themselves won several hundred yards of ground. The 1st Irish and 2nd Grenadiers led this attack, in which the former lost seventeen officers and several hundred men.

Soon after these events there was a notable change in the organisation of the British Army. This included the formation in August, 1915, of a division of Guards, the battalions already at the front being taken away from their comrades of the line and formed into a distinct unit, which was brought up to full strength by other battalions from England.

At this time a division consisted of thirteen battalions, twelve being in three brigades of four each, and one having been specially trained to serve as pioneers. Of the Guards eight were already in France, so five more came out to complete the division. Its 1st Brigade was the old Guards Brigade, the one composed of the 2nd and 3rd Coldstreamers, 2nd Grenadiers, and 1st Irish. Its 2nd Brigade contained the 1st Coldstreamers, 1st Scots, 2nd Irish, and 3rd Grenadiers, the two last named being new to the field. In the 3rd Brigade were the 1st Grenadiers and 2nd Scots from the 7th Division, the 1st Welsh, representing a new regiment of Guards, and the 4th Grenadiers. The 4th Coldstreamers were the pioneers. Lord Cavan commanded the division, and its brigades were under Generals G. P. T. Feilding, J. Ponsonby, and F. J. Heyworth.

This corps d'élite was held in reserve when the Battle of Loos opened on September 25th, 1915. It arrived on that evening at Nœux-les-Mines, about eight miles from the front, and from there was sent forward to share in the fray. On the Sunday some furious German attacks recovered part of the

ground near Loos itself, and Sir Douglas Haig decided that the Guards should be asked to regain these vital positions. The Guards reached the front trenches about mid-day on Monday, and the arrangements for the impending attack was soon made. One can imagine the activity at divisional headquarters as the three brigadiers motored up to discuss the matter with Lord Cavan. Each was told what was expected of his brigade, what was the time to start, while the nature of the artillery support, the strength and situation of the reserves and other vital matters were doubtless indicated. The brigadiers motored back to their headquarters and summoned their colonels. Again the process was repeated, although this time the plans were on a smaller scale, and so it was when the colonels conveyed their orders to the captains and the captains to their subalterns.

The plan of attack provided for the employment of all three brigades. The

INCIDENTS IN THE LIFE OF THE BRITISH ARMY OF THE RHINE.
Grenadier Guards, who formed part of the Army of the Rhine, passing the Hohenzollern Bridge, Cologne.
In oval: British Guards unloading hay in the famous Rhine city.

WITH THE IRISH GUARDS IN FRANCE.
Adjutant of the 1st Irish Guards reading the latest news to his men on the western front. This unit formed one of the six battalions of Foot Guards that landed in France on August 13th, 1914, and participated in most of the big fights there.

to advance up the slopes of Hill 70, famous for the deeds of the Highlanders on the previous Saturday. As they moved out of Loos they suffered a number of casualties from gas-shells, but the Welsh and the 4th Grenadiers, the leading battalions, marched majestically on. They reached the summit, which was swept by a hail of bullets, and the men were ordered to dig their trenches just below the crest. The 2nd Scots Guards had by this time relieved the Welsh, and the Guards remained in their new position until the following Thursday.

In this action the heaviest losses fell, perhaps, on the 2nd Irish, but the 1st Scots and the 1st Coldstreamers must have had nearly as many. The dead included more than one notable name, but none aroused more general grief than that of Mr. Rudyard Kipling's only son, a lieutenant in the Irish Guards. Another loss was that of the Hon. T. C. Agar-Robartes, a popular Cornish M.P.

For some months after this engagement very little was heard of the Guards, or, for that matter, of any British division, but the daily casualty lists bore tangible witness to the fact that they were still "somewhere in France," still holding some part of the scarred, long battle-line, still waiting for the great offensive of which all spoke though none knew its day or hour. As a matter of fact, they were in the neighbourhood of Loos until February, 1916, when they went back to the Ypres district.

The Battle of the Somme

The year was just half-way through when, on July 1st, the Battle of the Somme began. The authorities were singularly reticent about the doings of the various units. Something, however, did filter through; something was known about the corps, divisions, and battalions which were thrown into the fire, and as July and then August came to an end, and there was no word of the Guards having been

1st Brigade—General Feilding's—was on the left, linking up with the 7th Division, and it had the easiest task. This was to advance some little way and then to stand firm and prevent the enemy from troubling the other two brigades by a flank attack. It was soon accomplished, and these Guardsmen carried out the other part of their programme with equal success, including the letting off of smoke bombs and so feigning a big attack.

In front of the 2nd Brigade (Ponsonby's) were the wood and the chalk pit which the British had originally won, but from which one of their divisions had just been driven, while still farther to the right was Pit—or Fosse—14, really the headworks of a colliery. These had been hurriedly but, as events proved, by no means badly fortified by the Germans. After a preliminary bombardment had lasted for about an hour and a half, the men began the advance at four o'clock. They marched in artillery formation, clumps of half platoons with a fair space between each. The 2nd Irish, with the 1st Coldstreamers in support, were directed against the wood, and the 1st Scots against the colliery.

The former movement was quite successful. The ground was won, and the men dug themselves in, but around the colliery there was some desperate work. First of all the Scots, some of the Irish helping them, won the buildings, but they were driven out and forced back on the road they had just crossed. A second attack, in which two companies of Grenadiers assisted, was ordered, but again the casualties were frightfully heavy, and the Irish in front were in grave danger of destruction. A third attack was, therefore, made by some Coldstreamers. By this the chalk pit was firmly secured, and along this the new British line was made. During the evening it was heavily shelled, but it remained substantially unaltered, although a further assault failed to dislodge the enemy from the colliery.

The business of the 3rd Brigade was

IRISH GUARDS PASSING COLOGNE CATHEDRAL.
Irish Guards passing Cologne Cathedral on their way to relieve the guard on the bridges. The Irish Guards won fame early in the war by repulsing the Germans with heavy loss at Landrecies, and in the fighting near the Chemin des Dames and on the Menin Road.

engaged, some natural surprise was expressed. But when it came the surprise was on the other side. On September 15th the Tanks appeared in the battle, and so did the Division of Guards. It was a day to be remembered.

A word to get the setting of the battle. On September 9th an Irish division had captured Ginchy, but its environs had not been cleared of the enemy, who still held, among other

STAFF OFFICERS OF THE GRENADIER GUARDS.
[Photo: Bassano.
The above photograph shows (standing) : Sec.-Lieut. D. L. King, Lieut. R. W. Cornell, Sec.-Lieut. Hon. D. C. Grenfell. Seated : Capt. L. G. Fisher-Rowe, M.C., Capt. Lord Forbes, Lieut. J. C. H. Gordon-Lennox.

places, a strong position nearly half a mile away called the Quadrilateral. Three divisions were detailed for the new attack here. The Guards were directed to advance towards Lesbœufs, the Quadrilateral being on its right.

By easy stages the Guards had come from Ypres. Trains carried them on the earlier part of the journey, and soon they found themselves out of Belgium and in the pleasant land of France ; long white roads, pretty nestling villages, old châteaux, and clean, alluring auberges met their eyes. When they left the trains, motor-lorries carried them to villages, where they were billeted for two nights or so. Then, in the heat of August, marching began, after which some of them passed ten days in a delightful village, day and night, waking and sleeping in the open air. Later they were, for some days, in trenches in a quiet part of the line, after which they bivouacked for two days in and around a forest.

But if the men did not know whither all these marches were leading them, the officers at their head did, and no part of this tedious preparation was without an object. Especially this was so when they found themselves in a village through which passed a constant stream of military traffic, and in which the air was reverberant with the sound of gun fire. There, day after day, they were marched, sometimes only in platoons, at others by companies, at others by battalions, to a training ground where the coming attack was rehearsed in every detail. Night operations, conferences of officers, false alarms, and orders for immediate departure quickly cancelled helped to keep up the sense of expectancy.

After this there could only be one order, and that one soon came. The various battalions were to take up their positions at the front, some being in the advanced trenches, and others as supports behind them. These trenches were well in front of the old British line, for much ground had been won since July 1st, and they were by no means of the best type, while the journey to them was both dangerous and

Preparations for the attack

difficult. It lay through a tract of utter desolation, a land marked only with shell-holes and the wreckage of former fights. Landmarks hardly existed, and as one officer said of it, " What we shall want most is our compasses."

At this time the Guards formed one of the three divisions of the Fourteenth Corps, then under their old leader, Lord Cavan. The big attack was fixed for the 15th, but on the two days before some of the battalions lost heavily in endeavours to clear the way, if possible, by seizing the Quadrilateral. On the 13th the 2nd Brigade moved out towards this, and made some progress ; but, unable to get the full way, the men dug trenches and waited where they were. The 2nd Irish Guards were especially noticeable in this operation. On the 14th the 3rd Brigade made a similar effort, but again constant and destructive fire from the Quadrilateral held them up.

The next night—it was a Thursday— the remainder of the men were led up to the trenches wherein, their long, dark journey accomplished, they passed the night, officers and men sleeping as did the knights in Branksome Hall, who

Lay down to rest
With corslet laced,
Pillowed on buckler cold and hard.

In the morning all were awake early, for 6.30 was the hour fixed for the assault, and one who was there has told how the last tense moments of waiting for the whistles to blow were relieved by the strange sight of the new monsters of war crawling slowly forward to their task. To the Guards the sight was a delight, an omen of victory.

At last the whistles went. The 1st and 2nd Brigades — the 3rd was in reserve—had each two battalions in front and two in support, and so it came about that the attack was led by three units of Coldstreamers and one of Grenadiers, the Coldstreamers being together, a unique event even in the history of that famous regiment. Over the parapet the four battalions went, and those behind could see them slowly, but steadily, making their way up the long brown slope by Ginchy. One wave followed another, and soon the supporting battalions—the 1st and 2nd Irish, the 2nd Grenadiers, and the 1st Scots,—were also in the open.

Rallied by a hunting-horn

In the last stages of the advance the Coldstreamers lost heavily, but with a wild shout—the explosion, as it were, of the pent-up powder of months of waiting—they were among the foe. One battalion, checked for a moment by fire from some unsuspected trenches, had been rallied by blasts from the hunting-horn of their colonel, J. V. Campbell, D.S.O., who led a further charge in which other trenches were won.

But though the most superb gallantry was shown by the whole division, the attack was not an entire success. Some German trenches were taken, and for a time were held, but the Quadrilateral remained an enemy stronghold, and its fire was responsible for many deaths. A sunken road facing the line of advance was just a nest of machine-guns, and so complete was the wilderness that many lost their bearings entirely. Indeed, a war correspondent related how " at one point in the advance certain battalion commanders of the Guards held a conference in a shell-hole to try and locate precisely where they were."

One of these was Lieut.-Colonel Campbell, soon to be a V.C., and as the orders given to them were " the attack will be pushed with the utmost vigour," their duty was plain. That they were prepared to do it does not need stating. The scattered battalions, the men in the ruined trenches and numerous shell-holes, must be collected and led forward again. Eventually this was done, and in the afternoon some of them reached another line, and when they could get no farther, set to work to dig themselves in. Here they were in perhaps the greatest peril of the day. No one could be seen advancing to their support, although Germans were detected massing for an attack, while a powerful and accurate shell fire was making their numbers dangerously few. Worse still, in places the machine-guns were all useless, and, examining their revolvers, some of the officers quietly awaited the end.

A message indicating their peril was got through, however, to Headquarters, and from the 3rd Brigade the 2nd Scots Guards were sent forward to their relief. The barrage fire was heavy, and in passing through it the Scots lost very heavily, their colonel being among those **Death of** who fell; but the remnant pushed on, and **Raymond Asquith** the tired Coldstreamers were cheered by the report passing from mouth to mouth, " The Scots Guards are attacking ! "

So the counter-attack did not materialise. Instead, night came on, and with the darkness the arrival of food and letters, a delight which almost compensated for the horrors of the day. For one or two days and nights more the remnant of Guards held on to those trenches, and at last up came the men who were to relieve them. One by one the shrunken battalions were withdrawn, and in pleasant quarters behind the line they rested, bathed, shaved, and fed—civilised men once more. It was early in this battle, just as he was leading his Grenadiers past Ginchy, that Raymond Asquith, the eldest son of the statesman who was then Prime Minister, was killed. To him, far more than to most, the word brilliant could be applied, for his gifts were extraordinarily wide and complete, and his future assured of unbroken success. As an old friend said of him, " Many gave their all for the cause, but few, if any, had so much to give."

While in rest camps one important duty was not neglected. The reinforcements which had arrived from the base to fill the gaps were drilled and placed in the ranks, and it was while this work was proceeding that rumours came that the Guards were going to be sent forward again. They were true. Once more the men marched along the muddy roads, and, after a day or two behind the lines, were led in the darkness across the tractless wilderness of shell-holes to the trenches in front. This was on September 24th, and just after mid-day on the 25th the Guards were to " top the parapet " again.

This attack was not a big affair; the objectives were only local, but they were attained, the 3rd and 1st Brigades forming the attacking force. The left of the Guards, where the 4th Grenadiers were, lost heavily, but the division took Lesbœufs and materially advanced the British line in that direction. This done, they were soon relieved, and had no share in the later stages of the great Battle of the Somme.

The British successes of 1917 were substantial, but they were not, perhaps, so spectacular as were those of 1916. In a despatch dated January 7th, 1918, Sir Douglas Haig dealt with these operations, and in this document there are several mentions of the Guards.

From September to December, 1916, they were engaged in trench warfare and raids, holding the line about Lesbœufs, Combles, and Sailly-Saillisel **Trench warfare** during the unusually severe weather. After **and raids** a brief rest in the Somme back area the division was moved up in January, 1917, to hold sectors of the line between Combles and Péronne. The German retreat in March, from positions rendered untenable owing to the Somme advance, was followed up until the end of the month, when the division was withdrawn to engage in the construction of roads and railways to facilitate the advance. This work continued throughout April and May.

The Guards thus took no part in the British offensive near Arras, on April 9th, or in the one near Messines on June 7th, but in July they were in action. They were then right on the north of the allied line, not far from the sea. A new offensive was in preparation when it was discovered

SKIRL OF THE BAGPIPES IN COLOGNE.

Scots Guards marching past Cologne Cathedral, headed by their pipers. Along with other Guards units they formed part of the British Army of Occupation on the Rhine. The presence of British troops in their city was a source of never-failing interest to the inhabitants, who gazed with wonder at the men's smartness and keenness after years of campaigning. The boys of Cologne, after the manner of their kind, are seen keeping up with the soldiers.

OFFICERS OF THE IRISH GUARDS.—Group taken on St. Patrick's Day, 1919, at Warley. The names are, from left to right (back row): Lt. J. B. Dollar, Lt. L. D. Murphy, M.C., Sec.-Lt. P. H. Fitzgerald, Major T. F. Tallents, M.C., Capt. R. B. H. Kemp, Capt. D. S. Browne, M.C., Sec.-Lt. A. E. Taylor, Lt. D. A. B. Moodie, M.C., Sec.-Lt. G. M. Tylden-Wright, Capt. G. Gough, Lt. R. E. Coxon, Sec.-Lt. F. W. Burke. Sec.-Lt. S. L Bodenham, Sec.-Lt. R. E. Satchwell, Act.-Capt. J. W. Dalton. Fifth row : Sec.-Lt. A. W. Gray-Jamrack, Sec.-Lt. T. O'Brien, Sec.-Lt. R. Gamble, M.C., Sec.-Lt. A. L. W. Koch de Gooreynd, Sec.-Lt. F. C. Baggallay, Lt. T. Mathew, M.C., Sec.-Lt. C. E. McCausland, Sec.-Lt. T. E. Hacket-Pain, Sec.-Lt. E. R. Mahony ; Sec.-Lt. J. F. Ross, Sec.-Lt. A. R. Guillet, Sec.-Lt. A. G. St. P. Harris, Sec.-Lt. G. J. L. Leidig, Sec.-Lt. R. D. E. L. A. Bryne. Fourth row : Sec.-Lt. E. A. S. Alexander, Sec.-Lt. J. C Langton, Sec.-Lt. J. J. B. Brady, Capt. F. F. Graham, Sec.-Lt. A. E. Hutchinson, M.C., Lt. W. G. Rae, Sec.-Lt. J. C. Haydon, Lt. P. S. MacMahon, Sec.-Lt. C. L. Browne, Lt. G. E. F. Van der Noot, Sec.-Lt. J. Brooks, Lt. G. C. Vaughan-Morgan, Lt. E. H. Dowler, Sec.-Lt. the Hon. C. A. Barnewall. Third row : Capt. Sir Gerald Burke, Act.-Capt. D. J. B. Fitzgerald, Capt. A. H. Blom, Sec.-Lt. C. E. Maturin-Baird, Sec.-Lt. J. D. Duncan, Sec.-Lt. P. R. Barry, M.C., Act.-Capt. J. Black, M.C., Act.-Capt. W. C. Mumford, M.C., Act.-Capt. T. F. MacMahon, M.C., Act.-Capt. J. Orr, Lt. J. C. Zigomala, M.B.E., Sec.-Lt. T. B. Maughan, Sec.-Lt. E. C. Fitzclarence, Sec.-Lt. G. W. Repton. Second row : Capt. J. S. N. Fitzgerald, M.C., Capt. O. Hughes-Onslow, Lt. J. J. Kane, Act.-Major A. H. Boyse, Capt. K. E. Schweder, Act.-Capt. R. B. S. Reford, M.C., Capt. K. E. Dormer, Sec.-Lt. O. R. Baldwin, Lt. Lord Settrington, Act.-Capt. H. Bracken, M.C., Lt. T. R. Dames-Longworth, Act.-Major D. W. Gunston, M.C., Act.-Capt. J. B. Keenan, Act.-Capt. D. J. Hegarty, M.C., Act.-Capt. W. D. Faulkner, M.C., Act.-Capt. A. G. St. C. Bambridge, M.C., Lt. G. L. Crawford, Act.-Capt. G. R. L. Davison, Sec.-Lt. J. R. Reynolds, Capt. Viscount V. E. Castlerosse, Capt. W. S. P. Alexander, D.S.O. Front row : Major Rev. F. M. Browne, S.J., M.C., Major Rev. H. Rodgers, M.C., Capt. C. J. H. O'H. Moore, M.C., Major the Hon. A. C. S. Chichester, Act.-Lt.-Col. A. F. L. Gordon, M.C., Major C. A. Walker, Lt.-Col. the Hon. T. E. Vesey, Act.-Lt.-Col. R. R. C. Bagzallay, D.S.O., M.C., Major Broughton, Major C. F. Fleming, Act.-Major E. G. Nugent, M.C., Capt. H. Hickie, M.C., Capt. W. B. Stevens, Sec.-Lt. D. S. Woodbridge.

that in this neighbourhood the Germans had quietly fallen back. With some French troops, therefore, on July 27th, the Guards crossed the Yser, and along a front of nearly two miles settled themselves firmly in the enemy's front and support trenches. They were by no means undisturbed, but they beat back every attack, and during the night, to safeguard their communications, threw no less than seventeen bridges across the river or canal. This action, said Sir Douglas Haig, " greatly facilitated the task of the allied troops on this part of the battle-front, to whose attack the Yser Canal had previously presented a formidable obstacle."

The indicated attack was delivered on July 31st. The British troops started from the trenches defending Ypres, and, after certain objectives had been secured, battalions of Guards were brought forward to secure the crossings of the little River Steenbeek. This was held, and marked the new British line, at least, for the time being. This movement from Ypres consisted of a succession of attacks, an advance in a series of bounds, as Sir Douglas Haig expressed it, each having a certain limited objective. In one of these, on October 9th, the Guards, again in the company of French troops, had a great success. They crossed the flooded valley

OFFICERS OF 1ST BATTALION WELSH GUARDS.—The names are, from left to right (back row) : Sec.-Lt. W. A. Courtney, Sec.-Lt. T. B. Watson, Lt. A. W. Brawn, Lt. P. Llewellyn, M.C., Lt. H. A. Evan-Thomas, Lt. P. C. Trotter, Sec.-Lt. J. A. Davies, Lt. C. T. Browyer, Sec.-Lt. H. A. Spence-Thomas, Sec.-Lt. A. B. G. Stanier, M.C., Sec.-Lt. J. Jefferson, Sec.-Lt. R. M. V. Ponsonby, Sec.-Lt. R. W. Smith, Lt. R. C. R. Shand, M.C., Capt. W. Shipley. Centre row : Lt. H. A. H. G. Saunders, M.C., Lt. P. Coleman, D.S.O., Sec.-Lt. W. Morton, Sec.-Lt. C H. Adams, Sec.-Lt. H. Tatham, Sec.-Lt. C. Kemball, Lt. P. Dilberoglue, Lt. N. Harrip, Lt J. Jenkins, Lt. W. Arthur, M.C., Sec.-Lt. W. Holdsworth, Sec.-Lt. F. Mason. Front row : Capt. W. Dabell, M.C., Capt. J. Crawshay, Capt. W. Fox-Pitt, M.C., Capt. F. Copland-Griffiths, M.C., Capt. H. Allen, Lt.-Col. G. Gordon, D S.O. Capt. K. Menzies, M.C., Capt. B. Hambrough, Capt. H. Stokes, M.C., Capt. A. Price, Capt. H. Rice.

of the Broenbeek, captured four hamlets, some woods, and a great number of farmhouses and strong points on the outskirts of the Forest of Houthulst.

The Guards' most notable exploit of the year was yet to come. That brilliant feat, the surprise attack at Cambrai by Sir Julian Byng's army on November 20th, was followed by some fine fighting for the possession of Bourlon, both the village and the wood, and the former changed hands several times. On the 27th the adjacent village of Fontaine-Notre-Dame was captured by the Guards and the Tanks.

The unexpected reverse which is associated with the name of Cambrai opened with a strong German attack on the last day of November. At the moment the Division of Guards was in reserve, and when it was seen that the German thrust was dangerous the division was ordered forward. Its business was to win back some lost villages, and it attacked near Gouzeaucourt. Advancing with their customary élan, the Guards drove the enemy from this village and won their way along the ridge to the east of it.

The real glory of the Guards, however, was not so much in the seizure of this or that village, but in the fact that they stemmed the hostile tide. The enemy had broken through and was advancing with all the encouragement of success when they flung themselves across his path and drove him back. The British losses were heavy.

On January 1st, 1918, the division took over trenches in front of Arras, holding the line continuously in that sector until March 20th. The Guards were relieved on the night of March 20th, and were in Arras preparatory to going back to rest when the German offensive opened in the early hours of the 21st. Whereupon they were rushed off, leaving all spare kit in Arras, and took over the right of the Third Army in touch with the left of the Fifth Army, which was bearing the full weight of the German attack, with Amiens as its immediate objective. To conform with the line on its right, the division was slowly forced back a few miles until March 27th, after which the line it held remained firm until the German retreat.

In the meantime the 4th Guards Brigade—for the division had been by now divided into four—was moved farther north

to assist in the repulse of the attacks to the immediate south of the Ypres salient in the Bailleul sector, where it took part in extremely heavy fighting in April and greatly distinguished itself in action at Merris, suffering very considerable casualties, resulting in its withdrawal from the line. August again saw the division recalled to the line to the immediate south of Arras, and from then onwards it was continuously called upon to assist in driving back the enemy. Its efforts can best be summarised by an extract from a message, dated November 11th, 1918, addressed to the division :

Nothing in the record of the Brigade of Guards is finer than the performance of the three Guards brigades of this division since August 21st. From Moyenneville to Maubeuge they had advanced a distance of almost fifty miles. In the first week of this advance, from August 21st to 28th, in the face of very heavy fighting, they went forward a distance of five and a half miles. In the second phase, from September

OFFICERS OF THE BRIGADE OF GUARDS AT THE GUARDS DEPOT, CATERHAM.—Left to right (standing): Capt. R. W. Lewis, M.C., Welsh Guards; Lt. D. E. A. Horne, Grenadier Guards; Capt. and Adjt. J. C. Somers-Cocks, Coldstream Guards; Capt. E. Sheppard, D.S.O., M.C., Grenadier Guards; Capt. F. R. Harford, Scots Guards; Capt. A. E. Hardy, Coldstream Guards; Capt. S. D. Shafto, Grenadier Guards; Lt.-Col. F. M. Walker, Scots Guards; Major N. A. McNeill, Scots Guards; Sec.-Lt. A. M. Hollis, Guards Machine-Gun Regiment; Sec.-Lt. G. St. V. J. Vigor, Welsh Guards; Sec.-Lt. J. E. M. Bland, Scots Guards; Lt. T. Corry, D.C.M., Irish Guards; Left to right (sitting): Major P. S. Long Innes, M.C., Irish Guards; Lt.-Col. Sir William Ingilby, Scots Guards; Surg.-Lt.-Col. P. H. Whiston, Irish Guards.

3rd to 27th, during which they stormed the deep ditch of the Canal du Nord, broke through the Hindenburg system, and won the Flesquières Ridge, they penetrated into the enemy's lines a farther distance of eleven and a half miles. In the third phase, from October 9th to 22nd, at the end of which they forced the crossings of the River Selle, they advanced a distance of fourteen miles. And in their final advance, against still tenacious opposition and in constant rain and cold, they drove the enemy back a distance of nineteen miles before they reached their final goal, Maubeuge.

OFFICERS OF THE 1st BATTALION COLDSTREAM GUARDS AT CATERHAM AFTER RETURN FROM THE FRONT.—Back row (left to right): Major C. Boyd, M.C., Sec.-Lt. C. W. H. Sutton, Lt. M. V. Buxton, M.C., Capt. J. B. S. Bourne-May, Capt. F. C. R. Britten, Lt. W. G. Tatham, M.C., Sec.-Lt. V. V. R. Goodman, M.C., Lt. A. D. Bridge, M.C., Lt. O. Peake, Lt. Lord Hugh Kennedy, M.C., Sec.-Lt. J. N. S. Longe, Lt. A. de L. Cazenove, Sec.-Lt. J. H. W. Heney, M.C., Sec.-Lt. J. H. Simpson, Capt. C. C. Ibbetson, Sec.-Lt. A. J. B. Tickle, Sec.-Lt. A. E. C. Tennyson d'Eyncourt. Front row (left to right): Lt. T. A. Duff, Lt. W. G. Mappin, Sec.-Lt. Lord Romilly, Lt.-Col. J. C. Brand, D.S.O., M.C., Capt. and Adjt. Viscount Holmesdale, Sec.-Lt. S. V. Shaw, Sec.-Lt. A. T. Davies, Sec.-Lt. R. V. de Trafford, Lt. R. B. Pope.

THE RETURN OF THE LONDON RIFLES AFTER SPLENDID SERVICES IN FRANCE.

Cadre of the 1st Battalion London Rifle Brigade marching to the Mansion House, where the Lord Mayor took the salute, on their return from France, May 30th, 1919. The battalion was mobilised on August 5th, 1914, and reached France in November of that year. It specially distinguished itself at the Second Battle of Ypres and on the Somme. The honours gained by the battalion included one V.C., six D.S.O.'s (one with bar), eighteen D.C.M.'s, one hundred and fifty-five M.M.'s (one with bar), and five foreign decorations. On their arrival home several hundred old members of the regiment awaited them, and gave their comrades a hearty reception.

240

MEN OF THE WILTSHIRES

CHAPTER CCCII.

WEARING CAPTURED TROPHIES.

RECORDS OF THE REGIMENTS : II. ENGLISH, 1914-15.
By A. W. Holland.

The English Regiments Somewhat Neglected—Their Ubiquity—Their Share in the Mons Fighting—Feats in the Retreat—The Crossing of the Aisne—English Battalions Around Ypres—The 7th Division—The Worcesters at Gheluvelt—English Territorials at the Front—The Attack at Neuve Chapelle—The Losses of the Middlesex—Fighting Around St. Eloi—The English on Hill 60—In the Gap at Ypres—North Country Territorials—Second Part of the Ypres Battle—" Surrender be Damned ! "—The Aubers Ridge—The Kensingtons' Immortal Feat of Arms—Second Attack Fails—Rifle Battalions at Hooge—English Battalions in Africa and Asia—Increase in the Fighting Forces—The 29th Division in Gallipoli—The Lancashire Fusiliers—Lancashire Territorials—Lancashire's Share—The Battle of Loos—English Battalions in the Attack—Advance of the Londoners—Concluding Stages of the Battle—The 21st and 24th Divisions.

THE already extensive literature of the Great War contains quite a number of volumes describing the doings of Irish, Canadian and Australian troops, while the undying glory of the Scottish regiments has been noted by writer after writer. But the English regiments as a whole have as yet found no chronicler, no one who has made it his business to put together the story of the grand work they did for their country during the world-wide conflict.

On this subject some remarks made by Sir A. Conan Doyle in his History of the War may be fitly quoted. He says :

With that breadth and generosity of mind which make them the truly Imperial people of the world, the English and the English Press have continually extolled the valour of the Scots, Irish, Welsh, and men of the Overseas Dominions. There has hardly ever been a mention of the English as such, and the fact has given rise to some very false impressions. It is for the reader to bear in mind, none the less, that four-fifths of this great Army was purely English, and that the English divisions, be they North or South, had shown a sobriety of discipline and an alacrity of valour which place them in the very first place among fighting races.

He was speaking of the Army as it was in the middle of 1915, and he added : " The New Army, like the Old Fleet, was in the main a triumph of England. Of its first thirty-three divisions all but five were predominantly English."

In one of the early sentences of the " Memoirs " of Colonel Hutchinson, the writer, who was the wife of that model Puritan soldier, remarks that " to number his virtues is to give the epitome of his life." A somewhat similar idea must surely be in the mind of anyone who attempts to

give in any fullness the war story of the English infantry regiments. To do that is to cover little less than the full tale of the struggle ; and this, it may be, is the real reason why, in spite of their undoubted gallantry, these units have lacked their historian. Such, it might well be argued, would be a work of supererogation. Their record is in the ordinary histories of the Great War, for the enemies of England, whether on the Somme or the Lys, the Tigris or the Jordan, the Piave or the Struma, found them like that flaming sword " which turned every way, to keep the way of the tree of life."

In the first seven divisions there were eighty-four battalions, and in the four that stood at Mons on Sunday, August 23rd, 1914, there were forty-eight. Of those at Mons six were Guards, six were Scottish units, four were Irish, and two were Welsh. This accounts for eighteen, and the remaining thirty, something like two-thirds of the whole, were English. Four brigades, the 2nd, the 6th, the 14th and the 15th, were entirely English, while most of the others had each three English battalions of the line and only two—the 1st and 4th (Guards)—were without them. In the three other divisions that went out before the First Battle of Ypres this high proportion was more than maintained. Of their thirty-six battalions twenty-six were English, and three of their brigades—the 11th, 16th, and 18th — were entirely so. Indeed, except for one battalion, the 2nd Leinsters, the 6th Division was entirely English.

At Mons the heaviest part of the attack fell upon the 8th and 9th Brigades, which held the position formed by a loop of the

THE NEW GUARD AT BUCKINGHAM PALACE.
Posting a sentry at Buckingham Palace on February 19th, 1919. On this date the 3rd Battalion of the Bedfordshire Regiment took over the guard duties at the palace from the Brigade of Guards.

canal, and there the 4th Middlesex was entrusted with the task of guarding the three bridges across it. The 4th Royal Fusiliers and the 1st Northumberland Fusiliers were hard by, while other battalions hotly engaged on that day were the 1st Royal West Kents, the 1st Duke of Cornwall's Light Infantry, and the 1st East Surreys. The West Kents were, there is reason to believe, the first troops, apart from cavalry patrols, to suffer losses in the Great War. Upon these English and three Scottish regiments fell the bulk of the day's casualties.

The retreat then began, and during the next day there were some rearguard actions. The 1st Lincolns and 1st Northumberland Fusiliers fought a stubborn little battle at Frameries, in which both had heavy losses; the 2nd South Lancashires kept back the foe, also at a heavy cost, at Bavai, and the 2nd West Ridings, in a like encounter, lost three hundred men and all their officers save five. The 1st West Kents, in the same brigade, also suffered heavily, as did the 1st Norfolks and the 1st Cheshires in the 15th. The Cheshires, near Eloignes, were surrounded and practically destroyed; out of twenty-seven officers and 1,007 men, only five officers and

one hundred and ninety-three men were left to answer to their names. In fact, in this earlier and harder part of the retreat, the brunt of the fighting was done by Sir Charles Fergusson's 5th Division, in which, like the 6th, eleven of twelve battalions were English.

The Battle of Le Cateau was also something of a special ordeal for the English regiments, especially those in Fergusson's division. The 2nd Suffolks and the 2nd Manchesters on the right had the worst time, and when their part of the line had been destroyed the shock fell upon the 2nd Yorkshire Light Infantry and the 1st East Surreys. The former battalion lost six hundred men and twenty officers, and Major Yate led the nineteen survivors of his company in a last desperate charge.

At the other end of the battlefield the 4th Division, which had only just joined up with the rest of the force, felt the strain, especially its 11th and 12th Brigades, which were in front. The 1st Royal Lancasters, 2nd Lancashire Fusiliers, and 2nd Essex there behaved most gallantly, as did the battalions of the 11th Brigade. These, all English units, were protecting some quarries near Ligny, and from these they were four times driven out, but each time returned to renew the grim struggle. The brigade lost over one thousand men, while, when the retreat began again, the 1st Warwicks of the 10th Brigade had a bitter

experience. On September 1st the 1st Middlesex, marching to the succour of the heroic L Battery at Néry, captured some German guns.

The first five divisions forced the crossing of the Aisne, and one of the most daring exploits in that long encounter stands to the credit of the 2nd, one of the purely English brigades. The 2nd Sussex, 2nd King's Royal Rifles, 1st Northamptons, and 1st North Lancashires seized the sugar factory at Troyon, a building the Germans had turned into a fortress.

The 1st Division, in which these battalions were, crossed the river without very serious difficulty, for it found one unbroken bridge; but it was not so with those on its left. The 3rd, 4th, and 5th Divisions only crossed after tremendous exertions—boats, rafts, pontoons, and broken girders being used for the purpose. Once across, the second part of the fighting began. Some ground was gained, but the end was a stalemate, both sides being forced to remain **Brilliant feat of** in the trenches they had dug. The 2nd **Royal West Surreys** Brigade, General Bulfin's men, again distinguished themselves by their stout resistance to continuous German attacks; and of the others, although it is perhaps unfair to single out any one, certainly the 1st Queen's, or Royal West Surreys, one of those whose colonel was killed, deserves a word of praise. Their continual assistance to the Northamptons, holding an exposed position on the Ladies' Road, was one of the outstanding feats of those grim September days.

In the latter part of this battle the tired ranks were gladdened and helped by the arrival of a new division—the 6th—practically, as already stated, an English one. One of its brigades, the 18th, relieved the 2nd, and as soon as the battalions were in their new positions they were violently attacked. The 1st West Yorkshires in front were driven out, so General Congreve, V.C., ordered the 2nd Sherwood Foresters and the 2nd Durham Light Infantry to regain the ground. With a rush they came up the hill, the survivors of the West Yorkshires with them, and the 1st East Yorkshires and the 2nd Sussex of the relieved 2nd Brigade in support. For half a mile they advanced, and then with a whoop

WITH THE OLDEST TERRITORIALS IN AUSTRIA.
Members of the H.A.C., who formed part of the Allied Forces in Austrian territory, off for a joy-ride in their sleigh. Above: A bugler of this ancient British Territorial Regiment sounding the "Fall In," outside an Austrian pleasure resort.

they were among the Germans. The lost trenches were regained, but the brigade, only in action for an hour or two, had already lost a third of its strength.

The First Battle of Ypres began with the advance of Smith-Dorrien's Second Corps towards La Bassée, on October 12th. Eighteen English battalions were in this offensive movement, and among their many skirmishes may be mentioned the stand of the 1st Dorsets at Pont Fixe, near Givenchy. After

The Passing of Germany's Dream of World Dominion

Copyright

The Great War

Copyright

The Great War

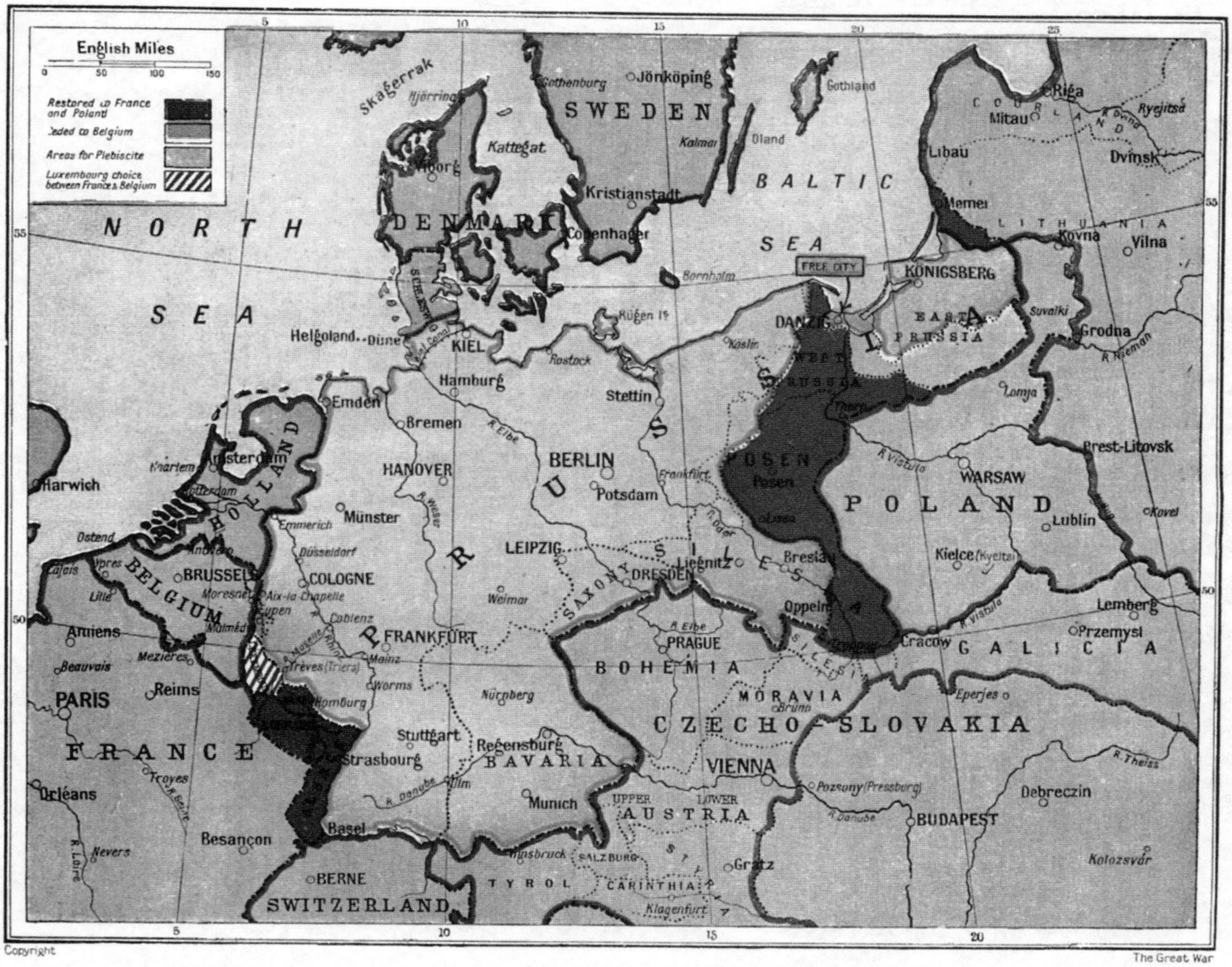

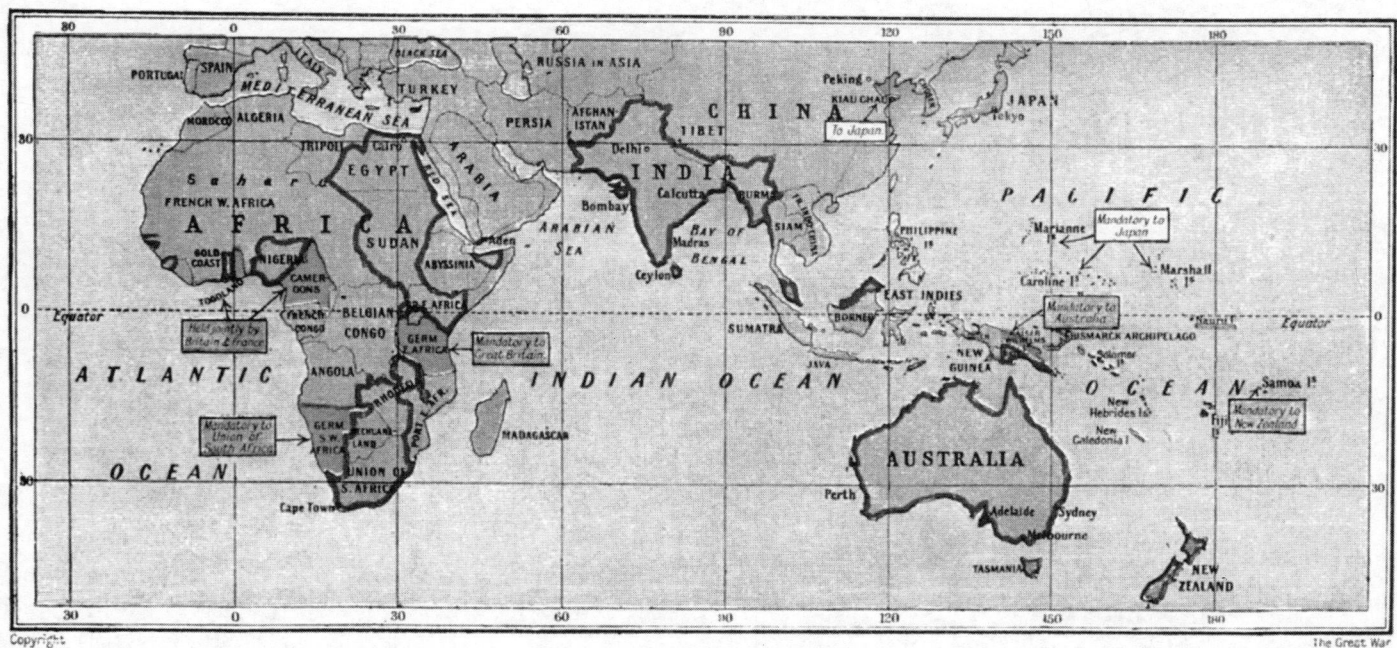

MAPS SHOWING TERRITORY LOST TO GERMANY UNDER THE TREATY OF PEACE.

The upper map, with explanatory inset, indicates the new frontiers of Germany in Europe. Below is shown Germany's former overseas possessions, and their future control according to the terms of the League of Nations Covenant.

The Passing of Germany's Dream of a World Dominion.

MAP SHOWING TERRITORY LOST TO GERMANY UNDER THE TREATY OF PEACE

The upper map, with coloring to show political frontier positions that marked the map. Below is shown Germany's controverted passages, and the map's coloring according to the terms of the League of Nations Dominion.

SPORT IN THE AUSTRIAN TIROL.
Soldiers belonging to the Honourable Artillery Company who found relief from guard duties in tobogganing in the Landeck Road, near Imst, between Bregenz and Innsbruck, Austria. In circle : Members of the H.A.C. learning to ski under shadow of snow-capped mountains.

and by two battalions which had just been in the thick of it at Lorgies—the 3rd Worcesters and the 1st Duke of Cornwall's Light Infantry. The 1st Wiltshires, 1st Norfolks, 4th Royal Fusiliers, and other English battalions were in some more fighting near Neuve Chapelle.

It was in these critical operations that the 1st West Kents and the 2nd Yorkshire Light Infantry held on for three days to some trenches, although, when relieved, the Kents had been reduced to two officers and about 150 men. About this event Sir Horace Smith-Dorrien said : " There is one part of the line which has never been retaken because it was never lost." This fighting around Neuve Chapelle cannot be left without mentioning the heroism of Lieutenant Leach and Sergeant Hogan, of the 2nd Manchesters, who, with ten volunteers, captured a German trench ; and the grand work done by the 1st Devons, who, having replaced a battalion in the 14th Brigade, held stoutly on to their post for sixteen days.

Across Belgium the 7th Division had marched to Ypres, and for some days had to stand alone before a vast host of Germans determined to break through before the thin British line was strengthened. Seven of its twelve battalions were English, and one of these, the **7th Division's** 2nd Bedfords, bore the brunt of an early **stand at Ypres** attack. In fact, before the 22nd, when a little of the pressure was taken off, every battalion was heavily engaged, and among those which lost several hundred men were the 2nd Wiltshires and 2nd Warwicks. It was at this time that the 2nd Yorkshires, like the Gloucesters at Aboukir over a century before, had one line firing in one and the other in the opposite direction.

These gallant battalions, however, had still to face more of the storm. On the 22nd, Lawford's brigade—the 22nd—fell back to Zonnebeke, and the few survivors of the 2nd Wiltshires were destroyed. The 2nd Warwicks, under Colonel Loring, who was killed in the charge, drove back the enemy, and splendid work was done by the 1st South Staffordshires and the 2nd Worcesters. A day or two later the division was

a check, the 8th and 9th Brigades had successful days on the 16th and 17th, when the 4th Middlesex, 4th Royal Fusiliers, 1st Lincolns, and 1st Northumberland Fusiliers were prominent. Meanwhile, the 1st Warwicks, in Pulteney's Third Corps, had helped to seize Bailleul, and the 2nd York and Lancasters and 1st Buffs had been prominent at Radinghen.

About the 21st the offensive passed to the Germans, and the village of Lorgies, where the 2nd South Lancashires joined hands with the 1st East Surreys in the 4th Brigade, was attacked in force. A gap was made in the line, the South Lancashires and the 3rd Worcesters beyond them being badly hit ; however, it was closed, largely through the efforts of the 1st West Kents and the 2nd Yorkshire Light Infantry.

Another attack was made at Violaines, where the 1st Cheshires suffered a fate like that of the South Lancashires at Lorgies. The 1st Dorsets shared in their resistance, and the enemy's advance was stopped by the 2nd Manchesters definitely attached to Haig's corps, and as part of that little force it stood at bay on October 29th, 30th, and 31st.

Sir Douglas Haig's two other divisions were in line by the 21st. For three weeks the Germans persisted in their assaults, and they were only stopped at tremendous cost. One of the earliest was made upon the British position round an inn on a road near Pilkem. It succeeded—for the time, anyhow—so Bulfin's fine 2nd Brigade was ordered forward, and with it were the 2nd South Staffords and the 1st Queen's. The Queen's, the 2nd King's Royal Rifles, and the 1st Loyal North Lancashires did the work, and did it well,

The Worcesters at Gheluvelt "capturing the trenches round the inn, besides releasing sixty Camerons and taking five hundred prisoners." A day or two later the 1st Liverpools and the 1st Berkshires met with heavy losses, although they seized two villages, and it was in a continuation of this movement, made by the 1st King's Royal Rifles, that Prince Maurice of Battenberg was killed.

In the fighting around Kruseik on October 29th, one of the critical days of this battle, only one English line regiment—the 2nd Border—was at first engaged, but others came up with the reserves, and soon the 1st and 2nd Queen's and the 1st Gloucesters were fighting hard. On the 30th the 2nd Bedfords and 2nd Yorkshires were almost overwhelmed as they fell back step by step, and then came the 31st.

The storm broke at dawn. In enormous force the Germans threw themselves upon the weary men at Gheluvelt. The 1st and 2nd Queen's (Royal West Surrey) were in the thick of it, and nothing could stop the rush, though the reserve battalions (1st Loyal North Lancashires and 2nd King's Royal Rifles) did more than their best. Disaster was impending. At 1.30 two of the divisional generals were wounded, and the whole line was falling back. But the day was not lost. The 2nd Worcesters, five hundred and fifty strong, went forward under heavy fire and closed the gap. They lost one hundred and eighty-seven of their number, but they performed a deed which will be remembered as long as English history is read.

If Gheluvelt was the most critical spot, and 2.30 p.m. the

most critical hour of that dreadful day, there were others where the tide of battle rolled almost as furiously. At Klein Zillebeke, a short distance to the south, the 1st Northamptons and 2nd Sussex held on grimly to a line hardly less vital than the one at Gheluvelt. Still farther south, at Wytschaete, where dismounted cavalry were facing the foe, the 1st Lincolns and 1st Northumberland Fusiliers lost heavily when going forward to help ; and at Messines, about five miles away, the 2nd Yorkshire Light Infantry, also from reserve, were engaged in some desperate street-fighting. The succeeding days, the first few of November, were not quite so strenuous, but the burden of defence was falling upon fewer and fewer men and those few more exhausted than ever. The English 2nd Brigade at this time, for example, only consisted of forty-three officers and 1,315 men, not much more than one strong battalion ; and the 22nd Brigade, in which were three English units, had been reduced to seven officers and 1,100 men.

The battle continued until November 17th, or thereabouts. On the 5th the 1st Gloucesters made a fine but costly advance, and on the 9th the 3rd Worcesters and 1st East Lancashires beat back a strong attack at "Plug Street." On the 7th the four battalions of the 22nd Brigade had performed, if possible, a finer feat of arms. Though each was only about a company —say, two hundred and fifty men—strong, they were ordered to retake some lost trenches, and it is said that in this wild enterprise they were led by **Wytschaete and** General Lawford himself with a cudgel in his **"Plug Street"** hand. They took the trenches and some machine-guns, but were reduced to three officers and seven hundred men. The English battalions in this affair were the 1st South Staffords, 2nd Warwicks, and 2nd Queen's.

With the German defeat on November 11th the campaigns of 1914 were virtually over, although to its end there was fighting on a smaller scale. On December 9th the 1st Lincolns made an unsuccessful attack upon a wood near Wytschaete, and five days later part of this was captured in an action in which the 4th Middlesex were prominent. A bigger affair took place on and around the 20th at Givenchy, when the

"NO SURRENDER!" STAND OF 13TH ESSEX MEN AT MŒUVRES.

During the German counter-attack at the Battle of Cambrai, November 30th, 1917, the enemy struck south-east of Mœuvres, isolating a company of the 13th Essex Regiment, 2nd Division, holding a trench along the west side of the Canal du Nord. Cut off, and realising the improbability of being relieved, this heroic company held a council of war, and unanimously determined to fight to the last. All attempts to extricate them failed, and the last that was known of the heroic band, to quote the words of an authoritative account, was "that it was heard fighting it out."

Indian Corps was attacked by the enemy. A counter-attack by the 1st Manchesters and 4th Suffolks regained the lost village; while on the 21st the 2nd English Brigade, ordered up from reserve, closed a dangerous gap in the line.

Everyone at this time was looking forward to the spring, and for the anticipated advance the British Army was being steadily strengthened; the first seven divisions were no longer to bear the strain alone. Three more, in addition to the two composing the Indian Corps, were soon at the front. The 8th had ten English battalions, and one of its brigades—the 24th—was entirely English. In Sir Herbert Plumer's Fifth Corps, consisting of the 27th and 28th Divisions, were seventeen English battalions out of twenty-four. The 83rd and 85th Brigades in the 28th Division, to which General Bulfin had been transferred, were wholly English, and in that whole division the 1st Welsh was the only battalion from outside. The 80th Brigade was also wholly English.

Moreover, many Territorial battalions were by this time at the front, and most of these were English. The 4th Suffolks have already been mentioned, and others were the 5th and 6th Cheshires, the London Rifle Brigade, the Honourable Artillery Company, the 8th Middlesex, the 5th Royal Lancasters, and battalions of Monmouthshire, Cambridgeshire, and Hertfordshire regiments, which were wholly made up of Territorials. Four more magnificent London units—the Kensingtons, the Queen's Westminsters, Queen Victoria's Rifles, and the Rangers—must not be forgotten.

For the time being these Territorial units were not brigaded together. To gain experience, one or two were assigned to each brigade of Regulars, and in this way these citizen soldiers received their baptism of fire. The H.A.C. joined the 7th Brigade, the London Rifles joined the 11th, and the Kensingtons the 25th. The 83rd Brigade had both the 3rd Monmouths and the 5th Royal Lancasters; the 84th Brigade had the 1st Monmouths and the London Rangers.

Fourth Corps at Neuve Chapelle

This was an intermediate stage in the organisation of the British armies at the front, and it may be said to have lasted until after the Second Battle of Ypres.

The fighting at Cuinchy, the most serious during the first two months of 1915, fell mainly upon the Guards, but the 2nd King's Royal Rifles, the 2nd Sussex, and the 1st Northamptons, of the incomparable 2nd Brigade, were also in it; while on January 25th the 1st Gloucesters had a hot time in Givenchy. The Fifth Corps, holding the line near Ypres, had difficult days, too, in those wet, cold months. On February 14th the 2nd Duke of Cornwall's Light Infantry were to the fore in regaining some lost trenches, while others to win repute were the 1st West Kents and the 2nd Royal Lancasters.

Something more spectacular was coming. On March 11th Sir John French sent to the expectant millions in England a brief but heartening message. On the previous day his troops had attacked at Neuve Chapelle, and so far the result had been successful. The details came later.

HERO PRISONERS OF KUT.
Group of the Hampshire Regiment outside headquarters at Winchester before marching to the Guildhall, where they were entertained. They were taken prisoners at the fall of Kut, April 29th, 1916.

350-MILE TRAMP TO SAFETY.
Capt. J. H. Harris, Hampshire Regiment, with his father. Taken prisoner at Kut, he escaped from the Turks, travelled 350 miles on foot, and crossed to Cyprus in a Turkish motor-boat.

The attack was entrusted to the Fourth Corps, made up of the 7th and 8th Divisions, and to the Indians. The Indian brigades had each one or two battalions of whites, including the 1st Manchesters, 2nd Leicesters, and 4th Suffolks. Four brigades were told off for the first assault. Each had two battalions in front and two in close support; and at five minutes past eight in the morning these for the first time had the experience of " going over the top." As far as the Fourth Corps was concerned, three of the four leading battalions were English. On the right the 2nd Berkshires and the 2nd Lincolns dashed victoriously into the enemy's trenches, seized the daze dsurvivors of the terrific opening bombardment, and then took up there a defensive position; while the 2nd Rifles together with an Irish battalion passed through their lines with a wild shout and swept into the village of Neuve Chapelle beyond.

The leading battalions of the other brigade were less fortunate. They found that the guns had failed to cut the terrible German wire, and as they hacked at it they were maimed and mangled in scores. One of the two was the 2nd Middlesex—the " Die-hards " of Albuera—and on that day its losses were greater than ever before in its history. At length a way was cleared through the wire, and the supporting battalions—the 2nd Devons and 2nd West Yorkshires—racing up, helped to hold ground gained, like the freedom of St. Paul's gaoler, at a great price. By this time the reserve brigade, one composed of four English battalions, had come up, and with their help the position was consolidated. At the same time the 2nd Leicesters and some London Territorials, both with an Indian brigade, had made their way through obstacles hardly less formidable, and before twelve o'clock had entered the village from the other side.

In the afternoon the attack was pressed further. The 21st Brigade, in which were the 2nd Bedfords, 2nd Yorkshires, and 2nd Wiltshires, got some way towards a hamlet to the northeast of Neuve Chapelle, while the 24th advanced as far as a small stream; but when darkness came on the other reserves had not been seriously engaged. This main attack was helped by secondary ones, the chief of these being at Givenchy. There the English 6th Brigade had an experience which, alas ! was far too common that March day and afterwards—the men found themselves confronted with uncut wire. The 1st Liverpools in front suffered the most, but the 2nd South Staffords and the 1st King's Royal Rifles had also heavy losses.

Territorials at St. Eloi The battle continued on the 11th, but not with its initial violence, although three English battalions and an Irish one seized the village of l'Epinette. On the 12th came a German counter-attack and an advance by the 20th Brigade. In the former the 2nd West Yorkshires recovered a lost trench, and in the latter the 2nd Borders took three hundred prisoners by capturing a fortified building, once a peaceful farmhouse. Another British diversion was at Wytschaete, where the 1st Wiltshires and 3rd Worcesters had heavy losses.

The real German reply to Neuve Chapelle was at St. Eloi, and in the first rush there the 1st Duke of Cornwall's Light Infantry were overwhelmed. Good work was done by the Cambridge Territorials, and later in the day—or, rather during the night—the 3rd and 4th King's Royal Rifles, the 4th Rifle Brigade, and the 2nd Shropshires attacked to recover the lost

ground. These battalions, especially perhaps the Shropshires, showed the most astounding gallantry, but they had not taken the key position when daylight put an end to the movement.

In this fighting the Territorials made good, and well it was for Britain that it was so. Consequently, Lord Kitchener and his advisers thought it possible to send them out in divisions of their own, and the first of these to arrive at the front were the 46th North Midlanders, from Nottingham, Derby, Leicester, Lincoln and Stafford counties, and the 48th South Midlanders. A division mainly of Northumberland and Durham men was soon out, and so was one of Londoners, the 47th.

On April 17th the West Kents, on the explosion of a tremendous mine, led the way in a wild rush which gave them the famous Hill 60. That opened a terrific fight, for the position was a vital one. The Germans won part of it back again, **West Kents carry Hill 60** but in a second British assault the 2nd West Ridings and the 2nd Yorkshire Light Infantry were the stormers. Again the crest was won, but the West Ridings had lost most of their officers and more than half their men in the effort. The defence was then handed over to other battalions, and these, too, were English. The 1st East Surreys, 1st Bedfords, and

HOME-COMING OF THE HONOURABLE ARTILLERY COMPANY.

Cadre of 1st Battalion Honourable Artillery Company marching up Queen Victoria Street, London, on arrival home, May 20th, 1919, after serving in France and Belgium since September 18th, 1914. In the procession were demobilised members of the regiment. The Honourable Artillery Company enjoys the time-honoured privilege of marching through the City of London with fixed bayonets, as shown in the photograph. The H.A.C. had seven units serving overseas in three continents, in addition to which it provided 4,000 officers for the Regular and Territorial Forces.

Queen Victoria's Rifles held on under a most furious bombardment, which continued through day and night alike, and there it was that G. H. Woolley, a young officer of the Victorias, won the first V.C. for the Territorials. The 1st East Surreys were noted, too, for the heaviness of their losses and the absolute steadiness of their defence, and so it was till the end. Hill 60 was an English victory.

The opening of the Second Battle of Ypres, in April, 1915,

belongs rather to the story of the Canadians, but as it progressed and extended English battalions were also involved. So dire was the danger after the first surprise that a number of odd battalions were collected from reserve stations, and, under Colonel Geddes, were sent to dam the field-grey tide flowing through a gap, five miles wide, made by the gas.

The 2nd Buffs (Geddes' own men), the 1st York and Lancasters, the 4th Rifle Brigade, the 2nd Cornwalls, and some Shropshires, as well as some Royal Lancaster Territorials, were among these battalions, and on the 23rd they took part in an attack. The 1st Suffolks leading and two Territorials—the 1st Monmouths and the London Rangers—made a desperate attack at Fortuin, which somewhat relieved the strain. A bigger effort was needed, however, and for this the 50th Territorial Division was brought up, the first occasion on which one was used as a unit. The plan was **Desperate attack** that on the 25th an attack should be **at Fortuin** made by these and other troops. The assault was led by the 10th Brigade and some Canadians, and when these had reached the limit of human endurance—for they were weak battalions assailing armies—the Northumberland Brigade of the 50th Division advanced, moving under fire for two miles towards St. Julien. Near Fortuin they came up with some Durham Territorials, the 9th battalion, who had previously advanced thus far, and there some trenches were dug and another German attack beaten off. On the same day, at Broodseinde, hard by, the 2nd East Surreys, the 1st Hampshires, and other English units had a strenuous time, in which they were greatly helped by the 8th Durhams, Territorials who, like the 9th, lost very heavily indeed in their first serious engagement.

The pressure was still intense, and accordingly another attack was arranged for the 26th. The Northumberland

Territorials had got forward to Fortuin, and from there they were ordered to capture St. Julien. All four battalions were Northumberland Fusiliers, the 6th and 7th in front, and the others in reserve, while behind them was a brigade of Durham Light Infantry. Crossing the fields, resting behind hedges for a moment, they got into the village; but they had lost their general, Julian Riddell, and half their strength, and they could not hold it, for events had made it necessary for the supporting Durhams to be sent elsewhere.

Other deeds of that day were the attack of the Indian troops, in which the 1st Manchesters won more glory, and the work of some English Territorials in going to the help of the 28th Division. On the 27th four English battalions went up to support the Indians, although in previous fighting they had been brought down to only 1,300 strong. Such an episode was typical of this battle, and throughout the thinned ranks the losses fell with terrible severity. No unit did better work in those awful days than the 1st Warwicks, the one English battalion in the 10th Brigade. **Lancs Fusiliers' heavy losses**

April ended with one or two more German attacks, in one of which the London Rifle Brigade lost one hundred and seventy men, and when May came in the British line was being made shorter and more defensible, while new—or at least rested—troops were replacing the survivors of the stricken battalions. Among these were the 12th Brigade—1st Royal Lancasters, 2nd Lancashire Fusiliers, 2nd Essex, and two Territorial units, the 5th South Lancashires and the 2nd Monmouths—and on May 2nd this was attacked with gas. It was on this occasion that the Lancashire Fusiliers lost three hundred men, one of them, Private Lynn, winning the V.C. for working his machine-gun while the poisonous fumes slowly destroyed his life. The 11th

FIGHTING WARWICKS AT HOME AND ABROAD.
Men of the Warwickshire Regiment marching through Vienna, headed by their band. Above: Soldiers of 2nd Warwicks unloading food supplies for starving Vienna at Matzleinsdorf Station. In oval: "Old Contemptibles" of the Warwicks passing by the saluting base on the occasion of King George's visit to Birmingham.

Brigade was next attacked, the 1st Somersets being the chief sufferers; but owing to the prompt arrival of reinforcements—Lancashire, Yorkshire, and Kentish men mainly—the enemy's advance was stopped. On Hill 60, too, the Germans had an initial success with their gas; there, on May 1st, some Dorsets

TWO OF ITALY'S FRIENDS IN NEED.
Trooper of the Northamptonshire Yeomanry giving his charger a well-earned drink in an Italian stream. The Northamptonshire Yeomanry were among the British troops that rendered splendid service to Italy in her hour of need.

were killed by it, and some Devons and Bedfords, sent up to relieve them, had also great losses. Another enemy attack followed on the 5th, and this time it was the turn of the 2nd West Ridings to suffer from the gas. Captain Robins, himself already poisoned beyond recovery, staggered to his colonel with the words, " The men are all up there—dead ! "

The second part of this battle began soon after the shortening of the British line, and, as usual, with a big German attack, the feature of which was the increasing strength and horror of the bombardments. Whatever was the case with the British, certainly at this time the Germans were not short of shells. The attack opened on the 8th, although before then the 5th South Lancashires and the 2nd Monmouths had been hard pressed, and the 3rd Monmouths, near Frezenberg, almost annihilated. The bigger attack of May 8th was beaten back in the north, where it came up against the battalions of the 11th and 12th Brigades, nearly all English ; but near Frezenberg the six—all English—units of the 83rd Brigade had an experience almost as ghastly as that of the Canadians.

Heroic stand of 1st Monmouths Out of 2,500 men, nearly 2,000 were put out of action by the gas or the shells, the 2nd East Yorkshires being perhaps the hardest hit. The brigade fell back—or, rather, its few survivors were forced back by sheer numbers—and then the 80th, entirely English except for Princess Patricia's Canadians, felt the full force of the storm.

The 84th Brigade fared as badly as the 83rd. The 1st Suffolks were surrounded and destroyed—at the time they were under three hundred strong ; and then the other battalions, endangered by this occurrence, found themselves faced by hordes of the foe. The 2nd Cheshires, 2nd Northumberland Fusiliers, 1st Monmouths, and London Rangers—for this brigade, too, had only one non-English battalion in it—were reduced to skeletons, and the few remains were brushed out of the way. In this mêlée the 1st Monmouths, although attacked on all sides, refused for long to budge an inch, and as the German stormers surrounded them, Captain Edwards cried out, " Surrender be damned ! " They lost, however, their colonel, C. L. Robinson, and perhaps six hundred men in this fine but hopeless resistance.

Meanwhile, the few regiments which had lost less heavily than the others were collected for a counter-attack. These, mainly English, took Frezenberg again, and on the next day the 1st Gloucesters made a forward move. The 4th Rifle Brigade and the 3rd and 4th King's Royal Rifles were in the thick of some later fighting, and indeed every battalion in the 27th and 28th Divisions, it is hardly an exaggeration to say, had been destroyed when this six days' fighting came to an end. The six battalions of the 83rd Brigade, for instance, were formed into one, and that not of excessive strength.

The 4th Division had similarly days and nights of loss and horror, thinned ranks getting still thinner, and weary men still wearier ; but with unshaken courage they held on, and the men were still confronting the Germans when, on the 24th, a last attack was made. This was preceded, as usual, by clouds of gas, but the Britons could not be moved. The 12th Brigade, we were told, was attacked on the front, the flank, and the right rear, and two of its battalions—the 1st Royal Lancasters and 2nd Essex, together with the 1st East Lancashires and 1st Rifle Brigade from the 11th Brigade—stuck to their places all the day, and even made efforts to counter-attack. In the evening they were ordered to form a new line five hundred yards behind, and this they did in perfect order, carrying their wounded with them. The long battle was now almost over, dying away, as did most of those in the Great War, from sheer exhaustion; but during May the Germans made several spasmodic assaults on the thin British line, the 2nd East Surreys, 2nd Buffs, 3rd Royal **Kensingtons' great feat of arms** Fusiliers, 3rd Middlesex, 2nd Cheshires, 2nd Northumberland Fusiliers, and some Durham Territorials being among the English battalions that added to their already high reputations.

Meanwhile, away to the south, the British on their part were conducting an offensive. This consisted of two frontal attacks on the German positions near Festubert—attacks which, owing to their very unsuccess, had important political results in Britain, for they revealed the terrible shortage of shells and led to the changes which quickly turned the country into one great arsenal.

Both attacks were made on a Sunday, May 9th and 16th, and both followed the same familiar tactics—a preliminary bombardment, and then a rush by certain selected battalions, with others after them at a stated interval. Three army corps shared in the first attack, made on a front between Richebourg and Festubert, these being the 1st, the 4th, and the Indian. The 8th Division, or rather two of its brigades, advanced against the terrible Aubers Ridge, whence the pitiless rain of lead mowed them down in hundreds. The 2nd Rifle Brigade, one of the leading battalions of the 25th Brigade, suffered in this way, as did the 2nd Lincolns and 2nd Berkshires behind them, but the palm was awarded by common consent to the Kensingtons. To these a distinct task was given, and in carrying it out they got right into the German lines. There they remained, but no aid could reach their dwindling numbers, and in the afternoon in ones and twos they began to make their way back. A few did so successfully, but the majority, including all the officers save four, lay dead or wounded in front. This was " a feat of arms," said Sir Henry Rawlinson, " surpassed by no battalion in the Great War." The 24th Brigade which, like the 25th, reached the first German trenches, suffered almost as heavily, the battalions here being the 2nd Northamptons, 1st Sherwood Foresters, and 2nd East Lancashires. The 2nd Devons also lost over two hundred men, but the casualties in the 2nd Rifle Brigade are said to have been twenty-one officers and five hundred and twenty-six men.

In the south the attack was equally unsuccessful and almost equally costly. Here the 2nd Brigade, that fine English unit which had done such grand work in the earliest days of the war, was heard of again, for it and the 3rd led the assault for the First Corps. It had now six battalions, two

Among the stones of Venice: British soldiers enjoying a gondola trip along one of the canals.

Colonel Cooper, commanding 1st Battalion Honourable Artillery Company, in his office at Cologne

Clerical staff of the 1st Battalion H.A.C. in the palatial room used as an office in Cologne.

Northamptonshire Yeomanry, who won honour on the Piave, crossing an Italian stream.

"A" Company, 5th Norfolk Regiment, a unit that achieved distinction in Gallipoli.

251

1st Battalion London Scottish marching through London on arrival from France, May. 16th, 1919. They received a great popular welcome.

of Territorials, the 5th Sussex and 9th Liverpools, having been added, and for the attack its formation was the 1st North-amptons and 2nd Royal Sussex in front, with the 2nd King's Royal Rifles and the 5th Sussex to follow. But the German fire was more devastating than ever, and the attack was a total failure. The brigade lost seventy officers and 1,800 men. The 3rd Brigade had a like fate, but this does not here concern us so much, as only one English battalion, the 1st Gloucesters, was engaged.

In spite of these discouragements, a second attack was arranged for a week later, the main change being that it was made in the dark instead of the day-light. This time the 2nd and 7th Divisions were selected for the work, the Indians, as before, assisting. As regards the 2nd Division, the men were led out in front of the trenches on the Saturday night, and there they lay down for an hour's rest. At 11.30 they rose and moved quietly forward. As before, most of the battalions were English. The 2nd Worcesters came up against some uncut wire, but the 1st King's Royal Rifles, 1st Berkshires, and 1st Liverpools got into the German trenches. There their lot was not unlike that of the Kensingtons a week before. Daylight made the ground behind them, swept as it was by machine-gun fire, impassable. The 5th and 7th Liverpools strove gallantly to reach them, but in vain.

The 7th Division's general sent forward the 2nd Borders and 2nd West Surreys, when at 3.30 a.m. his attack was made. After a temporary stoppage, both reached the enemy. The 1st South Sttaffords and the 2nd Warwicks did splendid work in supporing, and later in the day the 2nd Oxfordshire Light Infantry maintained its high reputation. The end of this battle, which lasted some days longer, was remarkable for the fact that the London Terri-torials of the 47th Division, one destined to win a renowned name in after days, came up to the front as a unit, and was involved in some heavy fighting near Givenchy. The 23rd London and 24th London very skilfully seized a German position, and under the heaviest fire they, with the help of the 21st London and 22nd London, held it—a fine feat of arms. One more piece of fighting and the first year of the war came to an end, although isolated en-

The fighting around Hooge counters were constant and numerous, in one of which the 4th Royal Lancasters and 4th Loyal North Lancashires were to the fore. The fighting around Hooge began on June 16th. The British command was anxious to improve the line by straight-ening it out, and to do this the 9th Brigade was brought up from its rest camp. In their usual impetuous fashion the 1st Northumberland Fusiliers and the 4th Royal Fusiliers dashed forward, and this time the attack succeeded. With the 1st Lincolns at their heels, the leading battalions made for the second, third, and even fourth German lines; while, following up, the 7th Brigade took over the captured ground. But they had gone too far, and had to fall back to the first line, where the 1st Wiltshires, 3rd Worcesters, and the H.A.C. had been under a steady and deadly fire. Around Ypres, about a fortnight later, the 1st Rifle Brigade and 1st Somersets won a distinct though small success, and the 2nd Lancashire Fusiliers showed equal gallantry in holding the ground.

To return to Hooge. The Germans were very reluctant to see their trenches in British hands, and, having found out how to make use of burning liquid as a weapon of offence, they decided to try and recover them. The place of trial was then held (July 30th) by four English battalions of Kitchener's men, the so-called New Army. They were all Rifles—the 7th and 8th K.R.R., and the 7th and 8th Rifle Brigade—and

upon them the flaming fire was hurled. Those in front were nearly all killed, and the remainder found shelter in a wood, while the artillery and the bombers stopped the Germans from coming farther.

A counter-attack was necessary, but for this very few troops were available. It had to be made, however, and the survivors of the Rifles, with the 9th K.R.R.C. and the 6th

CAPTORS AND CAPTIVES IN THE EAST.
Turkish gunners, glad to be out of the fighting, resting among their captors, men of the Lancashires. The latter won undying fame throughout the Mesopotamia Campaign. The forcing of the Diala in the Battle for Bagdad by sixty men of this regiment was a conspicuous example of their heroism.

Cornwalls, formed up for it. It failed with heavy losses. The men were killed or wounded immediately they emerged from the wood, and soon more than half their officers were on the ground. The liquid fire was then tried upon the wood, but this was held, the Cornishmen doing fine work here.

This brought to an end the first year of the war, but during that anxious and critical time English regiments had done a good deal of campaigning in other parts of the world, quite enough to make a considerable story even if France and Flanders had never existed. The Loyal North Lancashires had a battalion fighting the heat as well as the Germans, in East Africa; and the 2nd Dorsets, the 1st Oxford Light Infantry, and the 2nd Norfolks were marching along the Tigris with the Indians. On November 17th, 1914, the Dorsets, advancing over a bare and fiery plain, led an attack on a strong Turkish army near Basra, but the greatest of all these subsidiary enterprises was the attack on Gallipoli.

As the Great War grew in magnitude, and it became possible to count its fighters by the million, the method of recording it changed also. The scale, as it were, of our maps —or, to use another metaphor, the focus of our glass—was altered. So large did the operations become that battalions were of no more importance, relatively speaking, than companies had been, while later still they sank rather to the level of platoons. No **Growth of the** definite date can be assigned for this change, **British Army** but as far as Britain was concerned it may be said to have begun in the spring of 1915. By then the working idea of an Expeditionary Force of perhaps 200,000 men to aid France had been definitely abandoned in favour of a fighting army on the Continental scale.

This change, although it came gradually, meant that the battalion ceased, save in exceptional cases, to be the unit mentioned in despatches. Its place was taken by the division, a force twelve times its size, and from the early part of 1915 Britons were made familiar with the numbers and deeds of the various divisions.

The first division to make a name for itself was the 29th.

The first seven divisions had undoubtedly done superb work, had saved the Empire from destruction, but it was hardly by divisions that the heroes of the Expeditionary Force were popularly known. It was rather as battalions, and as there were only eighty-four of them, it was possible to deal with them as such; but a year later, so much more numerous were they, it was impossible. Two years later Britain had nearly eighty-four divisions in the field; so the size of her Army had almost exactly been multiplied by twelve.

The 29th Division was the one that, in April, 1915, landed on the beaches of Gallipoli, a feat probably unparalleled in military history, and one certainly that **29th Division at Gallipoli** only troops of the very highest quality could have even attempted. Just half of its twelve battalions were English. They were the 2nd Royal Fusiliers, 1st Lancashire Fusiliers, 1st Border Regiment, 2nd Hampshires, 4th Worcesters, and 1st Essex, and their names deserve to be remembered as are those of the six regiments that fought at Minden.

It is not easy, nor is it always desirable, to classify brave men into ranks of first, second, and third, but on this occasion one of the six battalions certainly stood out, remarkable for the heroism which it showed on a day when all men were heroes. It was the Lancashire Fusiliers, the old 20th, and a Minden regiment. The men came to the shore in thirty-two small boats, eight strings of four each. On landing, strong wire entanglements faced them, and while they hacked their way through they were mown down as with a scythe. Others, however, came along and at terrible cost the beach was won. As Lancashire Landing it is rightly known.

This was a case when every man deserved the Victoria Cross, but the officers responsible for the recommendations felt that they could not single out

A MISSILE FOR THE BOCHE. Men of the York and Lancaster Regiment in the trenches on the western front, with trench mortar. This regiment was attached to the 28th Division at Loos, September, 1915, and did excellent work.

any. To meet the dilemma, the War Office hit upon the expedient of leaving the matter to the men themselves. They were asked to name three of their number for the receipt of the crosses. The choice fell upon Captain R. R. Willis, Sergeant Alfred Richards, and Private W. Keneally. This was something, but it was inadequate and was felt to be inadequate. A year or so later, therefore, three more were given in the same unusual way, and this time the choice of the surviving Fusiliers fell upon Major Cuthbert Bromley and Sergeant F. E. Stubbs, both by then dead, and Corporal John Grimshaw.

It is not unfair to describe this 29th Division as the backbone of the Gallipoli enterprise. It was in all the savage fighting for Krithia, and later was sent round the coast to put new life into the failing attack at Cape Suvla. But it had comrades as devoted, even if they were not as hardened to warfare, and among these Lancashire men were prominent. At the beginning of May the first battalions of a Territorial division, the 42nd, or East Lancashire, landed on the Peninsula, and these, by a happy chance, belonged to the Lancashire Fusiliers. The division had **Lancs Fusiliers** volunteered for active service at once, **at Krithia** and had been for some time in Egypt.

These Lancashire Fusiliers took a leading part in the attack on Krithia which began on May 6th, and a few days later, when the forward move was again at a standstill, they were joined by the rest of the division. The Territorials were in the attack of June 4th, and the Manchester brigade "advanced magnificently." In five minutes the first line of Turkish trenches was captured, and by 12.30 the brigade had carried with a rush the second line. Elsewhere, however, the advance was less pronounced and the Manchesters had to withdraw, but, says Sir Ian Hamilton, "such was the spirit displayed by the brigade that there was great difficulty in persuading the men to fall back."

PRECAUTION AGAINST HUN GAS. Instructing members of the York and Lancaster Regiment in use of gas respirators. In oval: Soldiers of the same regiment in trenches on the western front. This unit did fine work in Second Battle of Ypres.

For a new plan, a landing at Cape Suvla and a general offensive everywhere else, five more divisions were sent to Sir Ian Hamilton. One of these, the 10th, except for a battalion of Hampshires, was Irish, though a good many Englishmen had been drafted into some of its battalions, and another was largely Welsh, but the other three—11th, 13th, and 54th—were, except for a Welsh battalion or two, English. The 13th—men from Lancashire and the Western counties—was sent to assist the Anzacs, and in the fight of August 8th the 7th Gloucesters performed the remarkable feat of fighting on for hours after all their officers had fallen. Other English battalions which distinguished themselves on those dreadful and indescribable days of heat and horror, disease and death, were the 6th South Lancashires and the 10th Hampshires. Heroism of a high order was also shown by the 9th Worcesters, 5th Wiltshires, and 6th North Lancashires, and a Warwickshire battalion which, like the Worcesters, lost all its officers. In all, the 13th Division lost 6,000 men out of 10,500, and had ten of its thirteen colonels killed or injured.

At Suvla Bay the landing of August 6th was led by the 11th Division, men from the Northern counties. The Turks were surprised by the move, and only one of the three brigades met with any opposition. At once the 9th West Yorkshires and 6th Yorkshires made a successful assault on a Turkish outpost, and the 11th Manchesters drove the enemy before them in fine style. This charge of the Manchesters was followed by another; on a hill of blazing gorse they and the 9th Lancashire Fusiliers routed some more of the enemy. The hill of Yilghin Burnu was seized meanwhile by the 6th Lincolns and 6th Borders, and the same two battalions were mentioned by Sir Ian Hamilton for gallantry on August 9th.

To a remarkable extent Lancashire contributed to this Gallipoli Campaign, so much so that in connection with it Lancashire and Anzac deserve to be bracketed. The Lancashire Fusiliers at the landing and after; the twelve battalions of the East Lancashire division in support; **Londoners' advance** the Lancastrians in the 13th Division aiding **at Loos** the Anzacs; and finally Lancashire battalions in the Suvla enterprise. It is indeed a deathless record, and, more than any other part of England, Lancashire must feel a swelling pride and a tragic sorrow when the story of that noble failure is told.

While the war in the East was thus languishing, that in the West was taking on new vigour. On September 25th the British attacked the German positions around Loos. For the main assault six divisions were employed. Two were Scottish, three were divisions of Regulars which had been at the front from the start, and the sixth was a division of London Territorials—the 47th. The London Division was wholly English save for the London Irish, and the three Regular divisions contained a majority of English battalions.

Where the 2nd Division attacked, the 2nd South Staffordshires and the 1st Liverpools lost heavily, the position in front of them being especially strong. The 7th Division on the right of the 2nd, but with the Scots between the two, was almost wholly composed of English battalions of the line, for the two of Guards formerly in one of its brigades had been replaced by the 8th and 9th Devons. The leading battalions, among them the 2nd Warwicks, 1st South Staffordshires, and 8th Devons, got well into the German trenches, but after a time the division was obliged to fall back.

A high road divided these divisions from the three in the Fourth Corps. In the 1st Division the rush of the 1st Brigade was led by the 8th Berkshires and the 10th Gloucesters, two Service battalions that had replaced the Guards. Some trenches were gained, but the losses were disproportionately heavy, as they were also where the four English units of the 2nd Brigade found some uncut wire. The whole four fought with all the heroism for which they were rightly noted, and at length they got to the German line and beyond, where they linked up with those on either side. Had they allowed the wire to stop them, as it would have done less determined men, the advance of this corps would have been in jeopardy.

While the Scots of the 15th Division were on their way to Loos, the Londoners' advance was as successful, and they, too, entered Loos itself. With the London Irish, the leading battalions were the 6th, 7th and 20th London. The whole of their gains was not maintained, but a good deal was, and in the critical days that followed the Londoners held on firmly to the captured German trenches of the second line.

Such was the fate of the main attack by the six divisions on September 25th, but there were also others intended to deceive and puzzle the foe. The 8th Division, the 2nd Rifle Brigade, 2nd Berkshires, and 2nd Lincolns in the van, carried some trenches; the 12th Rifle Brigade and 6th Shropshire Light Infantry assisted the Indian Corps near Neuve Chapelle, but **At the Quarries,** the biggest of the feints was one near **near Hulluch** Hooge; there an English division, the 14th, did excellent work, as did an English battalion in the 3rd Division, the 2nd South Lancashires.

With the advances and withdrawals the first day's work was over, but the enemy was in no sense beaten, and in one or two places the British line was drawn back a little under heavy pressure. However, two new English divisions—the 21st and 24th—were at hand from reserve, and it was hoped to follow up quickly the initial gain of ground. These reserves were sent to the aid of the weakened Scots of the 9th Division; while two battalions, the 8th Bedfords and 9th Norfolks, had heavy losses while attempting to retake the Quarries, a position near Hulluch lost the previous night.

The assault of September 26th was delivered by the 21st Division and part of the 24th on the enemy positions between Loos and Hulluch, where, for various reasons, the struggle had become most desperate. Six battalions of the 24th—men from Surrey, Kent, Essex and Suffolk—with the 10th Sherwood Foresters in support, got on for some distance, but about midday they found themselves faced with uncut wire and the target of bullets and shells innumerable.

The 21st Division, like the 24th, was fighting in sections. One of its brigades—8th East Yorkshires, 12th and 13th Northumberland Fusiliers, and 10th Yorkshires—was sent to support the Scots of the 15th Division, and these battalions, having got into the line there, were engaged stubbornly throughout the day. This left two brigades only for the main assault. The 8th Lincolns and 12th Yorkshires got well forward, and some men of the 10th York and Lancaster Regiment distinguished themselves, but in the Bois Hugo the two leading battalions crashed into a German attack, and after some most savage fighting were almost destroyed.

The 27th was another costly and critical day. The Hohenzollern Redoubt was practically regained by the Germans, but by this time the 28th Division was on the spot. One of its English battalions, the 2nd Buffs, delivered two gallant attacks, but in general it had to be content with defensive operations. In these the 1st Yorkshire Light Infantry and 1st York and Lancasters were prominent, and the 3rd Middlesex also did excellent work, as later did the 1st Suffolks.

On October 8th came the real German reply to the British attack. It took the form of a desperate infantry assault, delivered against four British divisions, three of which were mainly, if not wholly, of **A costly and** English infantry of the line. One of these **critical day** was the 12th, entirely English Service battalions, and in a successful resistance the 6th East Kents and 6th West Kents especially distinguished themselves.

The last big event in the Battle of Loos was the fine attack made by a division of English Territorials on the lost Hohenzollern Redoubt. This was the 46th, men from the Midlands, who on the 13th assaulted that destructive stronghold. But here again the most remarkable gallantry could do little. The 4th Leicesters, 5th Lincolns, 5th North Staffords, and 5th South Staffords were the attackers, and in superb fashion they reached their objective. But once there the Staffords on the right were shot down in scores; the Lincolns and Leicesters got somewhat farther, but met almost the same fate. The bombers, however, did deadly work in the trenches into which they made their way, and the action ended with a final attack delivered by four battalions of the Sherwood Foresters, which won a section of the coveted redoubt.

EAST SURREYS GIVE THREE CHEERS FOR THE KING.

The colonel of the East Surreys, mounted on an impromptu platform, in one of the sectors of the French front, calling for three cheers for the King, which were given with enthusiasm. The 1st Battalion of this fine county regiment greatly distinguished itself at Hill 60, April, 1915, for the defence of which three Victoria Crosses were given to the unit—Lieut. G. R. P. Roupell, Sec.-Lieut. B. H. Geary, L.-Cpl. Edward Dwyer. The 8th Battalion was conspicuous for gallantry at Loos, and the 2nd Battalion won praise from Lord French for staunchness at the Second Battle of Ypres.

SOUTH LONDON WELCOMES BACK ITS OWN REGIMENT.

Men of the 1st Royal West Surrey Regiment ("The Queen's"), known to South Londoners as "Southwark's Own," greeted at London Bridge Station on their return from France, May, 1919. The band leading the procession was formed of discharged soldiers, most of whom had served in the Regiment. The 2nd West Surreys were attached to the 7th Division in the fighting around Festubert in May, 1915, and earned praise for their heroism and endurance.

CHAPTER CCCIII.

RECORDS OF THE REGIMENTS: III. ENGLISH, 1916-18.

By A. W. Holland.

The Early Days of 1916—3rd Division at St. Eloi—Shropshires in a Sea of Mud—Opening of the Somme Battle—Gommecourt and Thiepval—The Strong Defences in the North—Successes in the South—The Well-drilled 18th Division—Fighting for Contalmaison—Trônes Wood—German Second Line Assailed—High and Delville Woods—English Battalions Around Pozières—Guillemont and Ginchy—Third Main Attack—Thiepval Taken at Last—Schwaben Redoubt—Fighting on the Ancre—Battle of Arras—Messines Ridge Captured—Gallantry on the Yser—British Attacks at Ypres—Houthulst Forest—British Successes at Cambrai and Bourlon—German Counter-Attack—The Critical Days of March and April, 1918—The Danger Over—Allied Advance Begins—The Battles of July and August—English Battalions Moving Forward—More Successes in September—End of the Struggle—Londoners and Yeomen in Palestine—English Battalions in Italy.

DURING the earlier part of 1916 there was plenty doing on the western front, as casualties to the extent of over 1,000 men a day certainly proved, but it was trench warfare only. The Germans were putting all their force into an attack on Verdun, while the British were training the armies which, it was hoped, would soon give the Allies a decisive victory.

The Germans, however, found time and energy now and again to keep the British front alert. On February 13th, for instance, they bombarded a part of the line near Ypres held by three English divisions, the 17th, the 24th, and the 50th. On the 17th the 10th Lancashire Fusiliers were nearly all killed by the explosion of powerful mines, and the 10th Sherwood Foresters had also heavy losses, but the 7th Borders and 7th Lincolns won back some of the lost ground. Against the 50th and 24th Divisions, however, the Germans had no success, the 3rd Rifle Brigade and the 9th Sussex looking after this.

On March 2nd a spirited assault gave back to the British the ground lost in this attack. The 2nd Suffolks, from the 3rd Division, won a marked success against a difficult position called the Bluff, and other English battalions helping were the 7th Lincolns, 8th Royal Lancasters, 9th West Ridings, and 12th West Yorkshires. To the same division, the 3rd, was entrusted another difficult operation, the capture of a valuable observation point near St. Eloi, and this was won on March 27th by two of its English battalions, veterans in the war, the 4th

Royal Fusiliers and the 1st Northumberland Fusiliers. The critical position in which the British in the captured trenches found themselves during the next few days was relieved by an equally gallant charge made by the 8th Royal Lancasters.

In April the 1st Shropshire Light Infantry, wading through mud, captured a lost trench near Langemarck, and in May the 11th Lancashire Fusiliers and 9th Loyal North Lancashires won some ground at Vimy. Along almost the whole line desperate German attacks were beaten back, sometimes only after heavy losses, and as July approached raids by the British battalions became more numerous. Finally, on June 20th, doubtless a feint, the 39th Division, represented by the 12th and 13th Sussex, rushed forward into a terrible fire, reached the German line, and then, with only three officers left, fell back.

The Battle of the Somme, the story of which has been fully narrated in Volume 8 of THE GREAT WAR, opened on July 1st, 1916, and lasted until November. On that bright summer morning the first attack was delivered by the men of thirteen divisions, with five others in close reserve. Six of the thirteen were wholly English, and there was only one, the 36th, that contained no English units. Four, the 4th, 7th, 8th, and 29th, were divisions of Regulars of mixed nationality, but with a majority of English battalions. The 18th, 21st, 30th, and 31st were composed entirely of Service battalions from the English counties; the 46th and 56th entirely of Territorial battalions of the same kind. The remaining two, the 32nd and 34th, contained Scottish

VETERANS OF THE LONDON SCOTTISH.
Five of the 1st Battalion London Scottish who went to France in 1914. Top row (left to right): Q.-M.-S. Lowe, M.M. and Medal Militaire; Sergt. Macnab. Bottom row: Capt. Valentine, Major Webb, D.S.O., Capt. W. B. Liebert.

SURVIVING OFFICERS OF THE BEDFORDS.
Seven officers of the 1st Battalion Bedfordshire Regiment who, of those who went to France, returned to England. They received an enthusiastic welcome on arriving at the historic town of Bedford in the spring of 1919.

The 8th Division included at this time a brigade, the 70th, raised mainly from the Yorkshire miners, and the four battalions of this lost heavily, many being killed before the advance began. When the whistle blew, however, the survivors went forward towards Ovillers, but the ground there was little more than a bare plain and only a few came back. Of the rest of this division the 2nd Middlesex was almost entirely destroyed, and the other leaders—2nd Devons, 2nd Berkshires, and 2nd Lincolns—fared little better. The 34th Division, next in the line, was only partially English. In it the 10th Lincolns and 11th Suffolks dashed through a terrific curtain of fire, and their gallantry did something to turn the fortunes of war in favour of the British.

The British attack was a failure in the north, but a success in the south.

as well as English units, but the majority were of the latter.

On the north, near Gommecourt, the attack was made by Territorials from Staffordshire, Nottinghamshire, and Derbyshire, and by some Londoners. The men advanced, six paces between each with smoke clouds in front, with splendid steadiness, and reached the German trenches. Unfortunately, however, these and their defenders appear to have escaped any serious damage ; the few unwounded Englishmen were too few to hold them, while machine-guns and barrage fire made it impossible to get supports forward.

This happened to both the Midlanders and the London men. The latter had the 12th London, Queen Victoria's Rifles, and the Queen's Westminsters in front, with the 2nd and 4th London, the Kensingtons, and the London Rifle Brigade following. To the south of the Londoners the Regulars of the 4th and 29th Divisions had no better luck, nor had those with them, the north country-

31st Division's terrible ordeal men of the 31st Division and some Warwick Territorials. The 31st Division had a terrible ordeal. The men advanced with superb determination, but nothing could live in that zone of fire ; the 12th York and Lancaster, men from Sheffield, was reduced to the colonel and six orderlies, while the 11th East Lancashires, who had shared their advance, were only slightly more numerous after the fight.

In the 4th Division the six leading battalions were all English, the 1st Somersets making the biggest advance ; but here again there was no decision. The famous 29th Division sent forward, with some Welshmen and some Irishmen, two of its hardened English battalions ; but once more the sad story was repeated—defences almost intact and gallant men going down in hundreds under the hail of shot and shell. In front of Thiepval the 32nd Division, English save for its battalions of Highland Light Infantry, suffered as heavily as did the Ulstermen on its left Among the battalions that won glory here were the 1st Dorsets, 11th Borders, and 15th Lancashire Fusiliers.

BACK IN THEIR NATIVE TOWN.
Duke of Bedford inspecting 1st Battalion of Bedfords on their return to their native town after splendid services in the war. Behind him, in mufti, is Lord Ampthill.

The success really began with the assault of the 21st Division, an entirely English unit, for, although its composition had been altered somewhat since its gruelling at Loos, this was only a case of like replacing like. The 9th and 10th Yorkshire Light Infantry led one of its brigades, and although the former lost its colonel and four captains, the men got into the German trenches ; then, having been joined by two other battalions from behind, they continued their way forward. They lost heavily, it is true, but they took many prisoners and some valuable ground. This particular brigade had got forward faster and farther than any other in that region, so the men made such shelter as they could and awaited events. After a time another brigade, also an English one, came alongside them, and the line was soon strengthened by a reserve brigade, 1st Lincolns and 10th Yorkshires leading, that put the finishing touch to a victory, important in itself but far more so for its influence on the rest of the battle. This 21st Division was aided by an attached brigade, the 50th, mainly composed of Yorkshire battalions, that did good work around Fricourt.

The 7th Division continued this success. Its four leading battalions, all English save the 2nd Gordons, had a somewhat easier task perhaps near Mametz, but it was only comparatively so. There was some sharp fighting in the village, where the

21st and 22nd Manchesters, two Service battalions, showed as much courage and dash as did the veteran Regulars with which they were associated.

Another English division came next in the line. The 18th, composed mainly of men from the Home and Eastern Counties, had been drilled to a high state of perfection by General Maxse, and on the day of trial this training told. All three of its brigades had battalions in the front line, a somewhat unusual formation, for generally one remained in reserve and only two attacked; and, dashing forward, they found the wire cut and the hostile trenches approachable. These were easily rushed, but loss came from isolated redoubts and from snipers, and it took time to reduce these to silence. The task, however, was accomplished, and the Englishmen of the 18th Division could congratulate themselves upon a distinct success. The hardest of its fighting fell upon some Londoners, the 8th East Surrey and the 7th Queen's, but all the battalions did splendidly, especially those who forced their way with bombs into Montauban Alley, and so made possible the successes of the division on their right.

This division, the one joining up with the French to the south, was the 30th, nearly all men from Manchester and Liverpool. On this occasion, however, it had exchanged a brigade with the 7th Division, and, as it formed up on that July morning, it consisted of eight battalions of Service men and four of Regulars. However, save for one battalion, it was entirely English. It attacked with two brigades, the third being ordered to go through and seize Montauban as soon as the initial assault was successfully launched. All went as arranged, although the losses in certain units, especially the 18th Liverpools, were very heavy indeed.

The first day of the battle was over, and much had been gained, but the issue was undecided. That depended largely upon the speed, endurance, and leadership of the reserves. The gaps made had to be widened, and this work occupied the British for nearly a fortnight. Then they were ready to move against the second line of the German defences.

The reserves immediately available amounted to seven or eight divisions, and one or two of them were in action before midnight on the 1st. Until the Welshmen of the 38th came up these were all English units, save for an odd battalion or two, and were numbered the 12th, 17th, 19th, 25th, and 48th, so **Fine charge at Ovillers.** the fighting that began on July 2nd and prepared the way for the general assault of the 14th was practically an English operation. It took place chiefly around Ovillers and Contalmaison, but near Thiepval some battalions of the 25th Division, 8th Borders, 11th Cheshires, and 2nd South Lancashires, had heavy losses whilst assisting the 32nd.

The 12th, 19th, and 25th Divisions made attack after attack upon Ovillers, and finally a charge, magnificently led by the 8th and 9th Royal Fusiliers, took possession of a part of it. This success was improved upon by other battalions, and the 48th Division, men from the South Midland Counties, shared in the final assault, afterwards clearing the enemy from the outskirts of the village.

Around Contalmaison the 17th and 23rd Divisions had come to the aid of the 21st and the 7th, and here was the most desperate fighting of those days. One

particular trench defied the gallantry of various battalions from the North of England, while others were equally unable to get into Contalmaison itself. Three attacks were delivered on the trench on the 6th, and on the 7th three others were made, but the result was the same. The Midlanders could do no more than the Northerners had done, and regiments from Lincoln, Derby, Nottingham and Stafford had long casualty lists to send home. Nothing daunted, however, Northumberland Fusiliers and Durham Light Infantry tried again, and this time got into the village. Their success turned the scale, and men of the 17th Division were now able to seize the trench that had defied them for so long. This work was done mainly by the 6th Dorsets and 7th East Yorkshires.

Farther to the south the 18th and 30th Divisions were battling for the possession of Trônes Wood, on which a first attack was made by the 2nd Yorkshires and other Regulars of the famous 7th Division. The Lancashire men of the 30th Division then came forward and won a footing in the wood, but not the whole of it; they were too weakened by their losses to continue. The men of the 18th Division completed the work, the 6th Northamptons and 12th Middlesex being, perhaps, the most prominent in this deadly task, although the stand by two hundred isolated West Kents in the recesses of the wood must not be forgotten.

The breaking of the German second line was not quite such a purely English performance as those just recorded. Leicester men of the 21st Division were successful near Bazentin-le-Petit, while close by some superb battalions of the 7th Division—8th Devons and 2nd Borders leading—got well into

LONDON TERRITORIALS RECLAIM THEIR COLOURS.
Colour party of 3rd Battalion London Regiment (Royal Fusiliers) outside the Union Jack Club with colours they took to France after the armistice. Left to right : Sgt. J. H. Cook, Lt. M. Middlemass, C.-S.-M. H. J. Hill, Sec.-Lt. P. F. Kimpton, Sgt. A. W. Wright. Inset : Lord Mayor (Sir Horace Marshall) handing back colours of Territorial Battalions London Regiment deposited in Guildhall during the war.

Bazentin-le-Grand Wood. The 2nd Warwicks cleared a village here, and High Wood, destined to prove another dreadful obstacle was attacked by the 2nd Queen's and 1st South Staffords. The attack on July 14th was shared by two other divisions, the 1st and the 3rd, both now combined of Regulars and Service men. Each met with success in the particular task, various English battalions, 12th and 13th West Yorkshires, 7th Shropshire Light Infantry, 13th Liverpools among the newer units, and 1st Northumberland Fusiliers and 1st Gloucesters among the older ones, participating therein with credit.

In the fighting that followed, the 1st Division continued to be heavily engaged, losing many men in an unsuccessful attack on the 23rd, when the chief sufferers were the 2nd Sussex, 2nd King's Royal Rifles, and 10th Gloucesters. The savage fighting for the possession of High Wood brought the 33rd Division to the front. This was of mixed nationality, but none did better than its English battalions, especially perhaps the 1st Queen's, 2nd Worcesters, 1st Middlesex, and 16th King's Royal Rifles. Later, the 20th Fusiliers, a battalion of public-school boys, helped materially in this costly fray. The 19th, an English division, was also battling for High Wood about this time, the 7th South Lancashires, 7th Royal Lancasters and 10th Warwicks showing marked gallantry and resolution.

After the South Africans and some Scots had passed dreadful days and nights in another bloodstained wood—Delville—two other divisions, the 3rd and the 18th, were sent there. Both carried the line forward, especially perhaps the battalions—8th Norfolks, 8th Suffolks and others—from the Eastern Counties. The village of Longueval, standing in the wood, was a terrible obstacle, even to the tried soldiers of the 3rd Division. With the help of the 5th Division they assailed it strongly on the 23rd, and made some progress, high praise being due to the 1st Norfolks, 1st East Surreys, and 1st Northumberland Fusiliers, and equally to those new but not less ardent units, the 17th West Yorkshires and 12th Gloucesters. The last and victorious assault on it was carried out mainly by Londoners, men of the 22nd and 23rd Royal Fusiliers and 17th Middlesex, although the 1st King's Royal Rifles and 1st Berkshires rendered no mean service on that day of strife.

Assault of Longueval Village

The German line of defence consisted of an elaborate arrangement of trenches with certain villages as bastions thereon. Until these were reduced no advance was possible, and two of the most formidable that faced the British after their first success were Guillemont and Pozières. The former had been attacked by the 36th Division without success, so a bigger assault was arranged for the 30th. That, too, failed, although Service battalions from Manchester—16th, 17th, 18th, 19th, and 20th—lost hundreds of valuable lives in crossing the fire-swept ground.

Pozières was an Australian success, but it was also attacked on June 23rd and later by Territorials from Warwickshire, Worcestershire, and the adjacent counties of Oxford, Gloucester, and Berkshire, and it speaks well for these men that they were able to go forward with the heroes of Gallipoli and so to share their undying glory. They, too, made good, the 4th and 6th Gloucesters showing special fighting qualities. When withdrawn, this 48th Division was replaced by the 12th, and these veterans from Surrey, Kent, and Sussex were equally determined to advance, their efforts culminating in a gain of ground on August 12th.

English battalions around Pozières

The Midlanders then returned and carried the matter a stage farther, the 5th and 6th Warwicks showing marked skill as raiders, and the Gloucesters their accustomed valour. North of Pozières, between that place and Thiepval, other English divisions were crashing into almost impregnable defences, and thereabouts the 11th Division, like the Australians transferred westwards from Gallipoli, captured the Wonder Work, a feat due entirely to Yorkshire battalions.

The August fighting on the Somme was almost as desperate as that of July. High Wood was once more attacked, this time on the 16th, by the 33rd and 1st Divisions. However, the gallantry shown by the 4th Liverpools, 4th Suffolks, and 20th Royal Fusiliers of the former was almost wasted; and although the four famous English battalions of the 2nd Brigade won some ground, the strong position remained, as a whole, untaken. In beating back a great German attack here the 1st Northamptons and 2nd King's Royal Rifles lost heavily. About the same time the 14th Division, English battalions all, was struggling forward from Delville Wood.

MANCHESTERS CHANGING GUARD ON THE BRIDGE-HEAD AT BONN.
Changing guard on the bridge-head at Bonn on the Rhine. The guard was provided by men of the 2nd Battalion of the Manchester Regiment, the old 96th Foot, which was among the first units to arrive in France in August, 1914. The Manchesters fought with great honour in France, in Gallipoli, and elsewhere.

At the Battle of Neuve Chapelle, March 10th-12th, 1915, the 1st Manchesters were among several battalions of white troops attached to the Indian Brigades. In one of the attacks on Krithia, Gallipoli, which began on May 6th, 1915, it was recorded that the Manchester brigade "advanced magnificently."

Another attempt had to be made to move the Germans from their stronghold, Guillemont, and this was entrusted to the 24th Division. The 9th East Surreys lost heavily in a preliminary assault on the 16th, and the 13th Middlesex in one two days later. The 7th Northamptons and 9th Sussex, however, won some ground, while the 3rd Rifle Brigade got possession of the railway-station here. The village itself was still untaken, although the assault was by no means a failure.

A larger and more general attack followed on the 24th, three divisions, practically all English, being employed. This attack was aimed at a stretch of the German line, and at one end of it the 1st Queen's, 2nd Worcesters, and 16th King's Royal Rifles made some ground. Near them the light infantry

THE KING'S ROYAL RIFLES IN FRANCE.
The Duke of Connaught taking the salute as a battalion of the King's Royal Rifles marched past, on the occasion of his visit to the west front, 1918. He also conferred a number of British decorations on Belgian officers and men.

AN INSPECTION ON THE WESTERN FRONT.
The Duke of Connaught inspecting a County regiment in France, which he visited in 1918. He mingled with troops from all parts of the Empire, and was received with immense enthusiasm.

battalions of the 14th Division, men from Yorkshire, Oxfordshire, and Shropshire, with a brigade of Rifles, were still more successful, and the movement was carried further by Durham, Somerset, and Cornwall men on the 27th.

Near Guillemont was Ginchy, and there the 1st South Staffords and other units of the noted 7th Division beat back a strong German attack, which shook also the men of the 20th Division. It failed, however, to move them, and in reply other battalions of the 7th assaulted Ginchy. The 20th Manchesters actually got into the village, but although finely helped by the 2nd Warwicks, they were too few to hold it. A second attack led by the 9th Devons was also ineffectual.

The two villages, however, fell at last to the determination and prowess of the British race. The main credit of Guillemont and of Ginchy belongs perhaps to the Irishmen; but they were greatly helped by an English brigade, one composed of the 10th and 11th Rifle Brigade and 10th and 11th King's Royal Rifles, who swept victoriously into the village from the south and west. Contributing also to this distinct success was the capture of two woods by another English brigade—1st Duke of Cornwall's Light Infantry, 1st Devons, 1st East Surreys, and 12th Gloucesters.

D 30

The third main attack on the German lines was made on September 15th. One of its features was the capture of High Wood by the Londoners of the 47th Division, the lead in this fine enterprise being taken by the 6th and 15th London. Between them and some equally victorious Scots, the Northumbrian Territorials of the 50th Division, now quite veteran soldiers, went forward with equal speed, valour, and success.

Farther to the south the attack was pressed home by other divisions, two out of three in Sir Henry Horne's corps being English. These were the 41st, men from the South of England, and the 14th, which had done so much of the recent fighting. The former did splendid work in helping the New Zealanders and the Tanks to capture Flers; then they pressed victoriously beyond that village, taking trench after trench, until, when relieved, the attacking battalions had lost more than half their officers and nearly half their men. As regards the 14th Division, its battalions of Rifles, followed by the light infantry of Oxfordshire and Shropshire, were equally successful.

To the south of these divisions was a corps under Lord Cavan, and this, too, like the one under Sir Henry Horne, had two of its three divisions composed mainly of English infantry. These were the 6th (Regulars) and the 56th (London Territorials), the former containing an Irish battalion and the latter the London Scottish. The Regulars were sent on the 15th against an exceptionally strong position called the Quadrilateral, and their first attack, a frontal one, failed with heavy losses to the 1st Buffs, 1st Leicesters, and 8th Bedfords. A more circuitous method of advance on the next day had happier results, and the trenches were entered by the 2nd Durham and 1st Shropshire Light Infantry. The Londoners had to fight equally hard. One of their brigades got into Bouleaux Wood, where the 7th Middlesex had heavy losses, but it was almost cleared of the enemy and the advance of the line was complete.

Formidable task at Thiepval

The next operation was the reduction of Thiepval, a position of enormous strength, and one to which the Germans attached the greatest value. This formidable task was entrusted to two English divisions, the 18th and the 11th, and on September 26th it was attacked. The consistent steadiness of the former—Suffolk, Essex, and Norfolk men leading—was again of the utmost service. They got into Thiepval and stayed there, while the men of the 11th helped them by seizing some dangerous positions on the right.

Two days later the same divisions made for the Schwaben Redoubt, a fortified maze of trenches which crowned a long

EE

upward slope. Some of its trenches were seized at the first onrush of these tried English troops, and for days there was desperate fighting. The 7th Bedfords were among the most persistent and successful of the attacking battalions; bit by bit the coveted ground was won until when, on October 5th, the 18th Division was withdrawn, the whole of the redoubt, except a small section, was British ground. The 6th Borders and battalions from the Midlands, all in the 11th Division, helped materially in this expensive but successful feat of arms. The 18th and 11th were relieved by two other English divisions, the 25th and 39th, and by the efforts of the 8th North Lancashires, 10th Cheshires, 16th Sherwood Foresters and others, a further advance was made. Finally, on October 21st, these and other English units assisted the Canadians to carry Stuff and Regina Redoubts, two of the most terrible defences in that region.

Farther along the line, in a northerly direction, there was also heavy fighting, this again being almost entirely an English affair. Of the three divisions engaged, the 1st, 23rd, and 50th, two were almost entirely drawn from

SAVING THE OIL-WELLS.
Staffords advancing under Turkish machine-gun fire towards the position of the Binagarley oil-wells which the Armenians had abandoned.

and 6th Divisions, such tried battalions as the 1st West Yorkshires, 2nd Durham Light Infantry, 1st Cheshires, 1st East Surreys, and 1st Devons performing Homeric deeds here.

Combles, another stronghold, fell to the combined operations of the London Territorials and the French. These Londoners, forming the 56th Division, were engaged in another grand assault, one made on October 7th, which was shared by three other English divisions, the 12th, the 20th, and the 41st. In this the most promising move was made by the light infantry battalions of the 20th; but the elements were by now fighting against the British, and the affair, although conducted with great gallantry, did not have the desired results.

The same was true when the attack was continued by the Regulars of the 4th, 6th, and 8th Divisions, except that the 8th won a certain amount of valuable ground near Le Transloy, where the trenches were especially strong and numerous. Other English divisions that did well in the same neighbourhood were the 33rd and the 17th. Yorkshire troops in the 17th were praised highly for valuable aid to the Australians—"never failing us once"; while in the 33rd the 16th King's Royal Rifles and 20th Royal Fusiliers were as useful to the French.

The offensive of 1916 ended with the Battle of the Ancre in November. Everyone knows of the gallant part taken by the naval men in the desperate work around Beaumont-Hamel, but apart from this the attack was largely performed by English infantry battalions. Three of these—the 1st H.A.C., the 4th Bedfords, and the 7th Royal Fusiliers—actually served in the Naval Division. The five other divisions in line on November 13th were the 2nd and 3rd, composed of Regulars, the 31st and 39th of English Service men, and the 51st of Highlanders.

In the northern area of attack, where the Yorkshiremen of

IN THE DUST OF THE DESERT.
Men of the Staffordshire Regiment advancing near Manjil, on the road between Kasvin and Enzeli. In oval: Cavalry of the same unit mounted on mules crossing the Persian desert in the British expedition to Baku in the summer of 1918.

Northumberland, Durham, and Yorkshire. During October they made their way surely and steadily into the German defences, one incident being when some Londoners of the 47th Division, having come up to help, broke into Eaucourt in the wake of a Tank.

Le Sars was only captured after a heavier fight, in which the 8th York and Lancasters won distinction and, incidentally, two Victoria Crosses, while battalions of Durham miners surged bravely forward and fell in scores near the Butte de Warlencourt. Leicestershire battalions of the 21st Division took Gueudecourt, and good work in the same region was done by the 55th Division, Territorials from West Lancashire. Lesbœufs and Morval were taken by the Regulars of the 5th

the 31st vied in gallantry with the Regulars of the 2nd and 3rd, some ground was gained, but the losses were very heavy. The 12th and 13th East Yorkshires showed remarkable skill and courage, and near them the 2nd Suffolks and 8th Royal Lancasters fell in scores before some uncut barbed-wire. In

Heroism at Beaumont-Hamel

the southern area, where greater success attended Britain's cause, a splendid deed was the capture of the village of St. Pierre Divion with its garrison by the 16th Sherwood Foresters and the 17th Rifle Brigade of the 39th Division, who advanced to it through a most appalling morass of mud.

When the naval men opened their memorable attack on Beaumont one of its brigades, composed of infantry of the line, three English and an Irish battalion, was in reserve, but it was soon thrown into the fight, as also was one from the 37th Division, and these were in the final assault, the H.A.C. and certain battalions of Rifles sharing the heroism and the success of the sailors. A day or two later the 32nd Division made an attack in which the 2nd Manchesters and 2nd Yorkshire Light Infantry met with only partial success, for they lost very heavily from lack of bombs when within the German trenches. Finally, the last attack of the year was carried out on November 18th by the 19th Division, but this, too, was a failure, although the 7th South Lancashires and 8th Gloucesters won part of Grandcourt.

The first months of 1917 were marked by the great German retreat, and then on April 9th came the British attack, generally known as the Battle of Arras. As regards the initial stroke we know on the authority of Sir Douglas Haig himself that " the greater part of the divisions employed in the attack were composed of troops drawn from the English counties," and that, with some other units, these won " a most striking success." The whistles blew at 5.30 in the morning, and by 12 o'clock, among other gains, men from the eastern counties had seized Observation Ridge, while London Territorials had taken Neuville Vitasse. Manchester and Liverpool troops were also mentioned for good work. An English division around Fampoux tore a wide gap in the German third line, and some North Countrymen took a strong position called the Point du Jour. Vimy Ridge was taken by the Canadians, but an English brigade was in the centre of the attack. On that memorable day of victory the English were ubiquitous.

On the 10th and 11th Monchy-le-Preux was a centre of resistance, and this fell at length to two English brigades, while on the latter of those days West Riding troops were deservedly praised for executing a very

Taking of the Messines Ridge

difficult attack across a wide extent of open country. English troops were also to the fore when the attack was renewed on a front of nine miles and some valuable ground was gained.

Preparations were then begun for another great effort, the Messines Ridge being selected for this, and during May there were various preparatory operations. Bullecourt was a specially strong obstacle, but after two weeks of almost constant fighting English troops got into it on May 7th, and London and West Riding Territorials completed its capture ten days later. The Londoners also took Cavalry Farm, while other English battalions helped to seize Rœux.

KING GEORGE VISITING A SCENE OF MIDLAND TROOPS' AMAZING VALOUR.

King George and General Rawlinson crossing ruined bridge over the Scheldt Canal, near St. Quentin, during his Majesty's visit to the front in December, 1918. The scene is that of the glorious exploit of the 46th (North Midland) Division, who, on September 29th, 1918, crossed the canal, provided with lifebelts and rafts, and stormed the main Hindenburg defences, notwithstanding the depth of the water and the enemy's murderous fire.

When Sir Herbert Plumer's army made its attack, almost a model operation, on June 7th, English brigades were almost certainly a majority of those that " pressed on up the slopes of the ridge to the assault of the crest line." The clearing of Grand Bois was done by men from the western counties, while a strong point known as the White Château could not permanently stop a rush of the Londoners. In Ravine Wood English battalions were fighting hard, and before night the Oosttaverne line had been taken and " our objectives gained." That line was first pierced by troops from the northern and western counties of England.

Before the third and longest of the year's great battles, that at Ypres, there was more preparatory work and also something

A WEST OF ENGLAND WELCOME.
Cadre of the Hereford Regiment marching through the town of Hereford on return from France, May, 1919. They had a magnificent reception.

in the nature of a disaster. In the former, English troops won a real success near Oppy, but the hardest fighting of this time was round Lens, where the Canadians were assisted by some North Midland Territorials, probably the famous 46th Division. On June 24th these Midlanders, by capturing a small hill near Lens, compelled a retirement on both sides of the Souchez, and on the 28th they helped the Canadians to win forward on a front of two miles and a half.

About this time the British took over from the French the defence of the stretch of the allied line nearest to the North Sea. Following a heavy bombardment, the Germans advanced there and the few British in front were isolated by a clever manœuvre which destroyed their communications

across the Yser. It did not, however, destroy the fighting spirit of the two English battalions there, one of Northamptons and the other of King's Royal Rifles, and the men of these won great renown by their obstinate and gallant resistance to an overwhelming number of foes.

When, on July 31st, the Second Army attacked at Ypres, four army corps were told off for the attack, and in these a majority of the battalions were English. On a front of seven miles and a half English troops were engaged almost everywhere, and at one point, the key to the German position —where, as was to be expected, the resistance was specially stiff—Lancashire men were prominent, as they had been many times before. Pommern Redoubt, a stronghold near Frezenberg, was taken by Territorials from West Lancashire, and later in the day English troops captured St. Julien with its memories of the earlier fighting at Ypres. When a successful day ended, English troops were also in Hollebeke and on the outskirts of the village of Westhoek. A week later they completed the capture of the latter place.

The battle was renewed on August 16th, and again English troops were in the van. Some brigades got forward as far as Langemarck, while West Lancashire Territorials, probably the 55th Division, were again mentioned for excellent work. **Pushing east from Ypres** Towards the end of that wet August, English troops were fighting along the famous Menin road, from which they won their way into Inverness Copse.

A third great attack was delivered on September 20th. Inverness Copse was completely secured by one English division. Men from the West Country and from the south-western counties attained their objective, as did a division of London Territorials, while once again the men of West Lancashire were mentioned for advancing finely over very wet and heavy ground near St. Julien. The positions were not only won but maintained against constant and furious efforts at recovery. Six days later other English troops took Zonnebeke, while North Midland and London Territorials seized a long line of strong German positions. This fighting took place around Polygon Wood, where English battalions helped to capture some fortified farms and to win useful ground, operations which were followed by strong counter-attacks, almost invariably beaten off.

The policy of giving the Germans no rest continued, another assault taking place on October 4th. The attack was made on a front of seven miles from the Menin road to the Ypres-

WAR-WORN HEROES RETURN TO NOTTINGHAM.
Welcome home of the 1st Notts and Derby Regiment (Sherwood Foresters) to Nottingham on May 17th, 1919. The Mayor of Nottingham and the Duke of Portland are seen welcoming them. A battalion of this regiment helped to carry the formidable Stuff and Regina Redoubts, October 21st, 1916.

Staden railway. On the right men from Kent, Devon, and Cornwall carried their objectives after heavy fighting; battalions from Yorkshire, Northumberland, Surrey, and Lincolnshire cleared the small enclosures east of Polygon Wood, and, although meeting with strong opposition, seized the village of Reutel; and on the left Surrey, Stafford, Devon, and Border men crossed the crest of the ridge and took a coveted hamlet. South Midland troops and "other English divisions" were also mentioned for their conduct in this victorious affair.

Houthulst Forest was the next British objective, and here, around places bearing the familiar names of Poelcappelle and

12th Division, men from the eastern counties, moved along the Bonavis Ridge, met with an obstinate resistance at Cateau Wood, and ended by taking the enemy's position and also his guns. Another English Service division, the 20th, having seized La Vacquèrie, stormed the strong defences of Welsh Ridge, while near it two other English divisions had a successful day. The 6th took the village of Ribécourt, and the 62nd that of Havrincourt, both showing their skill and bravery in fighting their way from street to street and from house to house. The work of the West Riding men was described as "a most gallant and remarkably successful advance." After it, moving out of Havrincourt to the north, they stormed

DURHAMS ON THE RHINE.
Guard of the 51st Durham L.I. on the great bridge, Cologne.

DORSETS AT COLOGNE.
Signal party of the Dorsets on one of the Rhine bridges at Cologne. Barbed-wire was in readiness for barricading the bridge had it been necessary.

FUSILIERS AT BONN.
Lancashire Fusilier on duty on the bridge over the Rhine at Bonn.

Passchendaele, English battalions were hard at work on October 9th. East Lancashire, Yorkshire, and once again South Midland Territorials were singled out for high praise, as were the Warwicks and the H.A.C., who regained a part of Reutel. The Canadians won the greatest glory in the concluding operations of November, 1917, but they were assisted by English troops hailing from Northumberland and both eastern and western counties. London Territorials and other English units were also fighting in the awful conditions which then prevailed around Passchendaele.

In his account of the fighting around Cambrai in November and December, 1917, Sir Douglas Haig reverted to the practice of mentioning by name the various divisions; for about a year previously he had contented himself with vague references to "Scottish Territorials," "troops from the western counties," and the like. Sixteen divisions were singled out by him in his despatch dated March 4th, 1918, but

Fighting around Cambrai of these two of cavalry and the one of Guards need not detain us here. Of the remaining thirteen only three, the 36th from Ulster, the 16th from Roman Catholic Ireland, and the 51st from the Highlands, were entirely non-English.

Of the ten remaining, four were divisions of Regulars in which English battalions predominated, this being especially true of the 6th. Three were divisions of Service men drawn from the English counties and towns, and the other three were divisions of English Territorials—the 47th and 56th, both of Londoners, and the 62nd from the West Riding.

In the sudden and successful attack of November 20th the

the German reserve line and seized Graincourt, making a total advance of four miles and a half. Meanwhile the 29th Division, half English, coming up, had entered Masnières, and at two villages had secured the passages across the Canal de l'Escaut. The 3rd Division helped by a subsidiary attack at Bullecourt. Less progress was made on the second day, but the 62nd Division was again mentioned.

The first surprise was over, but Sir Douglas Haig decided to press farther forward and secure, if possible, the important Bourlon Ridge. A few days were consumed in preparations, not the least noteworthy of these taking place on the 22nd, when a battalion of the Queen's Westminsters stormed a vital point in the Hindenburg line, contributing much to the success of the subsequent attack. In this new attack, made on the 23rd, were at least two English divisions, the 40th and the 56th. The former was engaged for four and a half hours in capturing Bourlon Wood, after which it got a foothold in the village, **Struggle about** while the latter was fighting around **Bourlon village** Moeuvres. The attack on Bourlon was renewed on the next day, November 24th, and this time it was taken by Englishmen of the 40th Division. It was lost on the 25th, but parties of the 13th East Surreys held out there for two days, and then the division was withdrawn. The valiant 62nd came up and entered it, but even they could not hold it.

Much, therefore, had been gained, but not everything that was intended, when on November 30th a sudden German attack came. Five divisions were defending the British line along a front of nearly ten miles, and of these, the 29th, beat back many powerful assaults and kept its grip intact.

Others, however, were less successful, and a surprise was undoubtedly effected by the enemy, who managed to turn the British positions and to recover much of his lost ground. A position called Limerick Post, however, gave the Germans a good deal of trouble, for its English defenders, two Lancashire battalions, kept them off for a whole day.

Such was the result of the attack near Masnières. Farther to the north, around Bourlon itself, the line was held by London Territorials and others. Both the London divisions were mentioned as greatly distinguishing themselves, as did

AWAITING THE ORDER TO ADVANCE.
Soldiers of a London regiment in France resting in a trench while awaiting instructions to advance. They were fully equipped with steel helmet, gas mask, Lewis gun and ammunition case.

the 2nd Division. It was here that a platoon of the 17th Royal Fusiliers won immortality. Four platoons were just being withdrawn when the German fury burst upon them. The commanding officer sent three of them on their way; with the fourth he held up the enemy's attack. All were killed. A company of the 13th Essex is worthy to rank with these heroes. Isolated in a trench they resisted throughout the day, and at four o'clock in a council of war the remaining officers decided on "no surrender." They, too, died fighting. Hard by a somewhat similar deed was done by a company of the 1st Berkshires.

The next great move in the war was the German attack of March 21st, 1918, and of the struggle, unprecedented for savagery and seriousness that followed that massive onrush, something was told officially about the deeds of the various British divisions. Up to April 23rd no fewer than twenty-seven of these were singled out for mention. Four of them hailed from Australia and New Zealand, but of the others the majority were English; one of these, the 31st, shared with the 3rd, predominantly English, the honour of being mentioned twice in quite a short time.

The 4th Division, also largely an English unit, performed especially gallant service on March 28th, **Gallantry of the** north of the Scarpe, in assisting to break **4th Division** up the attacks launched by the enemy on that day for the capture of Arras and the Vimy Ridge. This division also distinguished itself on the Lys battle-front on the night of April 14-15th, when, in an admirably executed counter-attack, it took the village of Riez du Vinage with one hundred and fifty prisoners, and again on April 18th, when it repulsed strong hostile attacks south-east of Robecq and took nearly two hundred prisoners.

During the first two days of the enemy's offensive south of Arras the 21st Division maintained its positions at Epéhy against all assaults, and only withdrew from the village under orders when the progress made by the enemy to the south rendered such a course necessary. Before this division withdrew it inflicted great loss on the enemy, and the German official reports acknowledged the bitterness of the fighting. In this work men from Lincoln and Northumberland were singled out for mention; rather than surrender they died by the score on Chapel Hill. The 25th Division was in close support when the German attack opened, and was at once sent into battle in the neighbourhood of the Bapaume-Cambrai road. Though constantly attacked, it was not dislodged from any position by the enemy's assaults. After this severe ordeal it was on these men that the blow of April 10th fell in Ploegsteert Wood, but they resisted finely here and also in and about Neuve Eglise.

On April 13th the 31st Division was holding a front of some 9,000 yards east of the Forest of Nieppe. The division was already greatly reduced in strength as the result of its fighting from March 24th onwards, and the enemy was still pressing his advance. The troops were informed that their line had to be held to the last to cover the detraining of reinforcements, and all ranks responded with magnificent courage and devotion to the appeal made to them. Throughout a long day of incessant fighting they beat off a succession of determined attacks. In the evening the enemy made a last great effort, and by sheer weight of numbers overran certain portions of the British line, the defenders of which died fighting but would not give ground. After severe fighting in the neighbourhood of Croisilles, at the commencement of the battle, the 34th Division took over the Armentières sector and was in the line there on April 9th. The division maintained its position intact throughout the first two days of the Lys battle, and when the enemy's advance on either flank made it necessary to order the evacuation of Armentières it withdrew from the town on the night of April 10-11th deliberately and in good order. Afterwards it fought throughout with the greatest gallantry, yielding ground reluctantly and counter-attacking frequently.

In the fierce fighting at the end of March and early in April around Bucquoy and Ablainzeville two Territorial divisions did superb work. These were the 42nd from East Lancashire and the war-worn **An unending and** 2nd from the West Riding. Of the former, **undying story** Lancashire Fusiliers, East Lancashires, and Manchesters used their bayonets to good effect in counter-attacks, and all contributed greatly to the successful maintenance of the British line in this important sector.

Another, the 50th, although but recently withdrawn from a week of continuous fighting south of the Somme, on April 9th and subsequent days held up the enemy along the line of the Lys, and by the stubbornness of its resistance at Estaires and Merville checked his advance until further reinforcements could be brought up.

There are many other such deeds to relate, for the valour of the English troops forms an unending as well as an undying story. For instance, in the first attack, that of March 21st, the 24th Division put up a splendid defence, holding La Verquier, where a body of the West Surreys fought until all were gone. In resisting the human torrent the 17th, 19th, and 40th English Divisions were among those mentioned, and later the 18th, 41st, 61st, and 66th were added to this roll of fame.

In the attack of March 28th the Londoners were in the midst of the storm. Some Queen's Westminsters showed the highest qualities of heroism, while equally some Essex men, with no word of surrender, fought to the last. In the 3rd Division, which held its position at Croisilles against repeated attacks, battalions of Suffolks and Northumberland Fusiliers proved their manhood. Finally, on April 9th, the 55th Division regained Givenchy by a fine action at a most critical hour for Britain. The Portuguese positions in that region had been breached, so these Lancashire men threw back their left to make a flank on that side, and began that defence of Givenchy which will be remembered as one of the brilliant incidents of the war. The ground here was of some importance, as being almost the only exception to the general flatness of the battle area. Three times, it is said, at least, the German masses succeeded in breaking a way into Givenchy, once during the course of the day, and twice during the evening and night, only to be thrown out again by the most dashing counter-attacks.

A lull, due on both sides to utter exhaustion, followed this desperate fighting. The casualties had been very heavy indeed, and here it may be mentioned that seventy-six per cent. of the British losses had fallen upon English units. Marshal Foch was working out his plans for a crushing and, as it proved, a final blow, while Sir Douglas

Lull in the great offensive Haig was training his new troops and resting his old ones. As he said in his despatch of December 21st, 1918, eight of his divisions had been written off as fighting units, while the forty-five remaining ones were mostly below establishment, so it was no wonder that he welcomed this opportunity for rest.

The rest, however, was only comparative. The line must be held, and that, moreover, in sufficient strength to resist further German attacks, which were far from unlikely.

The French were in like case with the British—nay, perhaps their position was even worse and their danger more real; for Sir Douglas Haig, weak as he was, allowed one of his corps,

the Ninth, to move south in order to strengthen the French line. This corps consisted of five divisions, and may be fairly described as an English unit, for, except one or two battalions in the 8th Division, it was certainly so. The 19th, 21st, and 25th Divisions were composed of Service battalions recruited in the English counties, and the 50th was one of Territorials from Northumberland and Durham. All had been but lately filled **Filling gaps** up with young drafts, and despite their **in the French line** high spirit and gallant record, were in no condition to take part in major operations until they had had a rest.

So great was the need of men, however, that during the first fortnight of May, three of them—8th, 21st, and 50th—were put into the line near Rheims. They held a front of about fifteen miles, and were there on May 27th, when the Germans launched a great attack on the Aisne front. The whole of the Ninth Corps was soon involved in this battle. Greatly reduced in numbers, it was forced across the Aisne and the Vesle, and was there pressed back, fighting grimly all the way. The 19th Division, the last British reserves here, was rushed up in omnibuses to close a gap in the French line, and these, mainly men from the West Country, deployed with great skill and steadiness and retook Bligny.

A few other details may be mentioned. The 8th Division had a trying time in this battle, for a very heavy fire was opened on its front between Craonne and Berry-au-Bac. Incidentally, it had thirty-four bridges to hold, and the nerve of the troops was highly tried by an abundance of gas-shells and a dense fog. The Germans got across the River Aisne, but they had to fight hard for every inch of the ground, the battalions which contested their progress including West Yorkshires, Berkshires, Sherwood Foresters, Cheshires, and Wiltshires. The 50th Division, on the left of the 8th, had an equally formidable task. The retreat of the French had left its flank unprotected, and it, too, was forced back step by

DAUNTLESS BUT UNAVAILING STAND OF THE DURHAMS AT MERVILLE.

Party of the Durhams and their comrades who made a gallant stand to save Merville, which the Germans captured on April 11th, 1918, in their great drive for the Channel ports. The British soldiers dug a line in front of it, and withdrew there under heavy fire, sternly fighting. One machine-gunner kept in action until all his comrades had got away. The enemy, who were in great strength, were " shot down like rabbits," wrote a war correspondent.

step. This was around Craonne, and these Territorials made a fine effort to retake the plateau there.

As the tide of battle seemed now to be definitely surging rather against the French than against the English, Marshal Foch asked for four more British divisions, and this request was agreed to, the Twenty-second Corps being accordingly sent down to the French front. In this there were two English divisions, the 34th and the 62nd, the noted West Riding Territorials ; and these were there on that great day, July 18th, when Foch launched the counter-offensive for which he had long been preparing on the front between Château-Thierry and Soissons. The Yorkshiremen attacked astride the River Ardre, near Rheims, and for ten days were engaged in continuous fighting of a most difficult and trying nature ; the 34th attacked near Soissons on July 23rd, and both won high praise for their behaviour at this time.

Before Rheims and Amiens

This operation was in the nature of a *ballon d'essai,* and having been successful, larger schemes were decided upon. For the British there several plans and theatres of attack were suggested, but eventually it was decided to throw all the resources into the freeing of Amiens from German pressure, and in August the Battle of Amiens opened. In this encounter Canadian and Australian divisions did much of the hardest work, but there were English divisions in the force that freed Amiens, captured 22,000 prisoners, and pushed forward the line for twelve miles.

A few instances may be cited. The Englishmen of the 12th Division took Morlancourt on August 9th, and south of this the Southerners of the 13th Division were also successful in their attacks. On the 13th the Londoners of the 47th Division took over the line here. These tried soldiers fought their way forward to St. Pierre Vaast Wood, which they cleared of the enemy, and took many prisoners and several guns. The 53rd Division was also mentioned for a successful move on the 9th.

On August 21st another strong attack, which has been called the Battle of Bapaume, was launched, wherein twenty-three British divisions turned the line of the Somme and took 34,000 prisoners. Three Regular divisions, in all of which English battalions predominated, were to the fore in this enterprise. The 2nd attacked at Ayette, and was constantly advancing for six days, during which time it took Ervillers and other villages ; the 3rd took Courcelles, and two days later Gomiecourt, and the 5th took Achiet-le-Petit. The Service men in the 12th Division fought their way forward for nine days and took Mametz ; while to the 17th, Englishmen from the North Country, fell the honour of seizing Thiepval, Courcelette, and the Stuff Redoubt. Combles, Montauban, and Trônes Wood fell to the 18th Division, and Beaucourt to the 21st, the exhilaration of a continuous and successful advance being tempered by the thought of the many brave lives sacrificed around those strongholds in the battles of 1916.

This success was exploited gloriously in September. On the 2nd the 4th Division, the 57th Division, which had just completed some splendid work, and the naval men of the 63rd, with the Canadians and the Scots of the 52nd Division, broke through the powerful Drocourt-Quéant line. On the right of the assault the 57th led the way, and the 63rd passed through them later to complete the tale. The 4th Division, on the left of the Canadians, did its share, and on the next day seized two villages.

Allies' great attack

A great combined attack by the French, British, American, and Belgian forces was then arranged, and it was in front of the British, who were to advance in the centre against Cambrai and St. Quentin, that the German defences were most highly organised. First were two heavily-wired lines of continuous trench ; behind this the Scheldt Canal, and across the canal the Hindenburg line proper.

Besides these main features, numerous other trench lines, switch trenches, and communication trenches had been constructed at various points to meet local weaknesses and to take advantage of local command of fire. At a distance of about 4,000 yards behind the most easterly of these trench lines was a second double row of trenches, known as the Beaurevoir-Masnières line, very thoroughly wired and holding numerous concrete shelters and machine-gun emplacements. The whole series of defences, with the numerous defended villages contained in it, formed a belt of country varying from 7,000 to 10,000 yards in depth, organised by the employment of every available means into a most powerful system, well meriting the great reputation attached to it.

The Battle of Cambrai opened on a seventeen-mile front in the early morning of October 8th. This is not the place to describe it in detail, for that has already been done in earlier chapters, but only to say something about the deeds of the English units engaged therein. As a preliminary, the 8th Division, on the preceding day, had seized Biache St. Vaast and Oppy, and this movement was continued on the 8th. The main attack was successful, and soon signs of a wholesale withdrawal on the part of the Germans began to show themselves. Some part of the credit for this belongs to English divisions, as it does for the success farther north, which led to the capture of Ostend and Lille.

On November 4th the last great attack was delivered by no less than three British armies. The Regulars of the 1st Division seized Catillon and got across the River Sambre, the 1st Northamptons being prominent here. The English 32nd Division was also mentioned for fine work, and the 10th, 25th, and 50th Divisions, forming the Thirteenth Corps, by capturing Landrecies, put a further feather in Old England's cap.

The 17th Division got into the Forest of Mormal, where also the 37th had a fine success. Other divisions mentioned included the West Riding, or 62nd, which, after hard fighting, captured Fresnoy, the 19th, 24th, 11th, and 56th (London) which, however, met with less desperate resistance. By now the German retreat was in full swing, and the story may fitly end with the entry of the 62nd Division into Maubeuge on November 9th.

Of the subsidiary campaigns carried on by Britain during the concluding period of the war the most important were those against Turkey and Austria, and in both Englishmen played a notable part. With Sir Edmund Allenby on his victorious advance from Egypt into Palestine were some Yeomanry and other English troops. In describing the action of November 16th, 1917, Sir Edmund mentioned also London troops, praising them highly for their dash, as he did also the yeomen, among whom regiments from Warwickshire and Worcestershire were prominent. In fact, right through the campaign which ended with the surrender of Jerusalem, these yeomen, clearly all Englishmen, did splendid work, and there were constant references both to them and to the Londoners in the official and unofficial accounts.

Against Turkey and Austria

The disaster at Caporetto in October, 1917, was a grave menace to the allied cause as a whole, and to assist Italy Sir Herbert Plumer was sent thither with an army almost at once. Having assisted the Italians to form a new line, Plumer and part of his force returned to France, but, under Lord Cavan, two divisions remained in Italy. These divisions were both wholly English—the 23rd, Service men from Northumberland and Durham, and the 48th, Territorials from the South Midland counties. These were in line with the Italians and the French on the Asiago Plateau when the Austrians attacked in June, 1918. The first shock fell most heavily upon the Territorials, and they gave way a little ; but they soon recovered, and in a day or two were able to advance and to share in the winter attack which delivered Italy. The two divisions remained there until the end, and did their part in recovering Italian soil from her ancient foe. Around Salonika, too, there were Englishmen fighting for the cause. One of the battalions there was the 12th Cheshires, and on September 18th, 1918, these men attacked a very strong position. They reached under the heaviest fire the third line of enemy trenches, and won the praise of the French as " a marvellous battalion." They were to the fore in another difficult undertaking and their deeds may be regarded as a sample of what many English battalions did in almost hidden corners of the world during the Great War.

British soldier looking on the war=made ruins in the pillared cloisters of Arras Cathedral.

Mametz, captured by British on first day of Battle of Somme, showing memorial to fallen.

Ruins of St. Léger village, captured by British in the Great Advance, August 24th, 1918.

Royal Munster Fusiliers on their way to attend a memorial service in France.

The same Irish troops at a solemn service held in memory of fallen comrades.

Captain Haggard, Welsh Regiment, mortally wounded, crying "Stick it, Welsh!" to his men, near Chivy, September 14th, 1914.

RECORDS OF THE REGIMENTS: IV. IRISH AND WELSH.
By A. W. Holland.

Irishmen as Fighters—The Irish Regiments—Irishmen in the Retreat from Mons—Ypres and Givenchy—Neuve Chapelle and Ypres—Ulstermen and Liverpool Irish—Irish Troops Land in Gallipoli—Dublins and Munsters Perform Immortal Deeds—A New Irish Division—The Landing at Suvla Bay—The Irishmen at Chocolate Hill—Some Dublin "Pals."—The Connaught Rangers Win Glory—The London Irish at Loos—The Ulster Men on the Somme—Their Wonderful Valour—Irish Troops Take Ginchy—Their Part at Salonika—The Assault on Messines—The Ulstermen at St. Quentin—Their Deeds in the Retreat—The Irish in Palestine—Welsh Regiments—Their Share in the Early Days—The South Wales Borderers at Gheluvelt—Welshmen in the Attacks—The Struggle in Gallipoli—A Welsh Division—The Battle of Loos—The Attack on the Somme—The Deeds of the 38th Division—Welshmen in Mesopotamia—The Welsh in Palestine.

FOR centuries Irishmen have had a great reputation for fighting. Indeed, it has been wittily said that an Irishman is never at peace unless he is at war. The large number of eminent soldiers who have hailed from Ireland—Wellington and Roberts, for example—has been frequently commented upon, and so has the large number of Irishmen who have served with distinction in foreign armies, especially that of France. The Irish soldier of fortune has been a favourite figure with novelists. Rudyard Kipling's creation of Terence Mulvaney—"the divil of a man I was fifteen years ago," in his own description — is typical of the Irish soldier at his best.

To Britain, during the Great War, Irish soldiers rendered great service, and it is proposed here to say something about their deeds, and also about those of the Welsh. It should be premised that, apart from the Irish Guards, whose record has been already described in Chapter CCI, (Vol. 13, page 223), together with those of the other regiments of Guards, there are eight distinctively Irish infantry regiments in the British Army, and battalions of all served in the Great War.

The senior of the eight is the Royal Irish Regiment, the old 18th of the Line. Then each of the four provinces has one. These are the Leinster Regiment, the Connaught Rangers—the old 88th and 94th of Peninsular fame—the Royal Munster Fusiliers, and, for Ulster, the Royal Inniskilling Fusiliers.

FIVE BROTHERS IN THE RANKS.
Five brothers of the 13th Service Battalion Welsh Regiment who served in the ranks. Left to right: Pte. H. Thomas, Pte. R. Thomas, Pte. O. Thomas (holding regimental pet goat "Punch"), Pte. T. Thomas and Pte. E. Thomas.

The three others are the Royal Dublin Fusiliers, the Royal Irish Rifles, whose headquarters are at Belfast, and the Royal Irish Fusiliers, with headquarters at Armagh. To round off the story, something should be said about the 18th County of London, generally known as the London Irish, and about certain battalions of Irishmen attached to the King's, or Liverpool, Regiment and the Northumberland Fusiliers.

In 1914 these eight regiments had among them sixteen battalions of Regulars, four of which were with Sir John French at Mons. The 2nd Royal Irish and the 2nd Irish Rifles were in the thick of the struggle on the canal, and the 2nd Connaught Rangers lost heavily in a little action near Pont-sur-Sambre. The battalion was cut off, but the men fought their way through their foes.

In the 4th Division, which came up to cover the retreat, there were three more Irish battalions, and the 10th Brigade, with the 1st Royal Irish and the 2nd Royal Dublin Fusiliers, was half Irish. All took part in the resistance at Le Cateau and suffered heavy losses.

The retreat ended without any serious disaster, but there were several small ones, and one of these affected the 2nd Munsters, of the 1st Brigade, a battalion which, on August 25th, had driven off some German Uhlans with the bayonet, and themselves dragged the rescued but horseless guns into safety. Its brigade formed the rearguard of the First Corps, and on the 26th it found the enemy too close to be comfortable. An action was fought, in which the Munsters got separated from the rest of the brigade, and an order to retire failed to reach their commanding officer. The result was that they stood at bay near Etreux, fighting in anticipation of relief that never came, until their leader, Major P. A. Charrier, and many others were killed. A few got through the enemy's ranks, but the majority could not do so, and a fine battalion was reduced to five officers and two hundred men. This put it for a time *hors de combat*, but the other Irish units shared in the Battles of the Marne and the Aisne, the 2nd Inniskillings taking part in a fine advance near Venizel, the 2nd Connaughts leading their brigade across the river on the remains of a broken bridge, and the 2nd Irish Fusiliers having a stiff fight one dark night with a force of German cavalry.

In the fighting around La Bassée in October the 2nd Irish Fusiliers cleared the enemy out of some trenches near Bailleul, and so made it possible for the British to seize that town, while the 2nd Royal Irish helped French cavalry to take Fromelles. On the 19th the same battalion, ordered to take the village of Le Pilly, gained their objective in fine style, advancing in skirmishing order for eight hundred yards. They entrenched themselves, but only to be assailed by a force stated to consist of three battalions. Within a circle of fire they were completely cut off from help, and like their commanding officer, Major E. H. E. Daniell, most of them fell while resisting the foe. A few days later the 2nd Irish Rifles beat back a savage German attack near Neuve Chapelle, while similar assaults were made upon trenches held by the 2nd Leinsters and the 2nd Inniskillings. Just previously the Leinsters had lost heavily at Premesque, where they held a position surrounded by Germans until relieved by the French.

The Irish battalions were not in the thick of the First Battle of Ypres, although the 2nd Inniskillings and the 1st Connaught Rangers, the latter serving with the Indian contingent, did good work therein, but they were in the great battles of 1915 both in Flanders and in Gallipoli. By then there were more Irish troops in the field, and **Irish defenders of Ypres** one brigade—the 82nd—in General Plumer's army corps was almost wholly Irish. Of its four Regular battalions, the only one recruited outside Ireland was the 2nd Duke of Cornwall's Light Infantry, and it was upon the corps to which it was attached that the defence of Ypres during the second battle largely fell. Before that, however, on April 14th, the Irish Brigade—for so it may be called—had made a spirited little attack on some trenches near St. Eloi, and still earlier there had been another sad but gallant episode in the career of the 2nd Munsters.

On December 20th, 1914, the Germans, by a sudden surprise, had driven the Indians from their trenches near Givenchy, and the First Corps, only just away in a rest camp, had been ordered to the front again. In this was the 2nd Munsters, brought up to strength again after their early disaster, and now attached to the 3rd Brigade. They succeeded in their task of recovering the lost ground near Festubert, but only at terrible sacrifices. For two whole days they were fighting, and, getting too far forward, they were for the second time practically destroyed.

At the Battle of Neuve Chapelle, the first of the greater encounters of 1915, the 1st Irish Rifles was one of the battalions engaged in the most successful move of the day—the dashing entry into the village itself; and an attack at St. Eloi on March 14th was carried out mainly by the Leinsters and the Royal Irish. There a sudden irruption of Germans had burst the British trenches, **Battle of Neuve Chapelle** and at night these two battalions went forward to regain the lost ground. They got in among the enemy, but after a night of desperate fighting the dawn showed that only part of the position had been rewon. This, however, was firmly held.

As far as this story is concerned, the Second Battle of Ypres is mainly, although not wholly, concerned with the doings of the 10th and 82nd Brigades. On April 22nd the latter, as part of the 27th Division, was somewhat to the south-east of the old Flemish town, holding a line which stretched from near Gheluvelt to Hill 60. The 10th Brigade, just after the first surprise, was brought up from reserve to face St. Julien, perhaps the worst position on the whole front. On the 25th the brigade attacked the German position near that village, and in this they were assisted by the 1st Royal Irish, sent up from the south.

Another successful movement carried out by this brigade, and in which again the Royal Irish were prominent, was the capture of Frezenberg early in May, after which the Irish and the 2nd Dublin Fusiliers suffered very heavy losses near Shell-trap Farm during a severe gas attack. Shells fell upon those who survived the gas, and both battalions lost their colonels. Of the Irish battalions outside these two brigades, the 1st Connaught Rangers, coming up hurriedly with the Indians, fought heroically in a counter-attack, and the 2nd Inniskillings were choked and dazed in their turn with gas.

All this time the 27th Division—or, rather, what was left of it—after sending away units to assist in keeping intact other vital parts of the line and suffering severe losses, had been holding grimly on. Before the end of April it had lost something like two thousand men, but it was able to beat back German attacks both on May 11th and on the next day.

While this battle was dying away the British were taking the offensive elsewhere, and on Sunday, May 9th, the 1st Royal Irish Rifles led an assault on Rouges Bancs. With the utmost gallantry they beat forward in the face of a storm of lead of intensity unknown to earlier fighters; but nothing could avail them, and that tragic day cost the battalion

YOUNG WELSH SOLDIERS OFF TO THE RHINE.

The 53rd Battalion of the Welsh Regiment entering Hyde Park for the great review of fourteen graduated and young soldier battalions, about to join the Army of Occupation in Germany, by his Majesty King George, March 1st, 1919. The bands—those of the Grenadier and Welsh Guards—struck up "Ap Shenkin" as these fine young soldiers passed by the King, who, in a message to the 10,000 men of all regiments present, praised their "steadiness on parade and general soldierly appearance," and expressed his confidence that the regiments' high reputation would always be maintained.

twenty-two officers and nearly five hundred men. In another part of the fight the 2nd Munsters, now for the second time brought up to strength after practical annihilation, was one of the attacking battalions, and they suffered quite as severely as the Rifles. Again they were destroyed, for only three unwounded officers and about two hundred men remained to be the nucleus of a new battalion.

In the second attack, the one made a week later, on May 16th, the 2nd Inniskillings were in the front of the assault. In the darkness these Ulstermen crawled silently through the mud until they were close upon the German trenches. There they lay for about three hours until midnight, when they rose and dashed into the enemy's trenches. The surprise was complete, and the first and second lines were speedily won. In this fight the

TAKING THE WELSH COLOURS TO FRANCE.
Men of the 6th Welsh Regiment marching through Christchurch, Hants, with their colours, which were deposited there in 1914. The colours were taken to France in November, 1918.

SYMBOL OF CELTIC COURAGE.
Parade of the 6th Welsh Regiment's colours at Christchurch. This unit, in which were many sturdy miners, won distinction on many battlefields in France and Flanders.

Liverpool Irish won renown. They were brought up from reserve to assault some trenches, not as part of the main attack, but as a diversion, and under Captain H. Finegan, who was shot in the fight, they topped the parapet and went across the open where the bullets were falling like hail. They did all that was asked of them and contributed to a considerable French success.

Before this time the British had made a landing on Gallipoli, and although the story of that daring feat of arms is an oft-told tale, a narrative such as the present cannot pass over the share taken in it by the Irish regiments.

In the 29th Division, which, with the naval men, was mainly responsible for the successful landing at the toe of the Peninsula, were three Irish battalions—the 1st Munster Fusiliers and 1st Dublin Fusiliers in the 86th, or Fusilier, Brigade, and the 1st Inniskillings in the 87th Brigade. The hardest part of the attack, the landing on Beaches V and W, was entrusted to these Fusiliers, Beach V falling to the lot of the two Irish units. The plan was for three companies of the Dublins to be towed to the shore in a string of small boats,

while the other company and the Munsters followed in the River Clyde.

The moment the boats grated on the sand a devilish storm of bullets met them. The sailors in charge and most of the Dublins were either killed or wounded, but a few of the soldiers managed to dash ashore, and found some slight shelter under cover of a bank of sand—much as one has often seen during a rainstorm a solitary pedestrian run from one shelter to another. After some little delay, due also to the terrific fire, a bridge of lighters was made between the River Clyde and the shore, and this ship began to disembark its human freight. A company of Munsters led the way, only, however, to be shot down; the second company was equally gallant but equally unfortunate, and those who were not struck by bullets were drowned through an unexpected movement of the lighters. The third company then rushed forward from the sheltering ship; but they, too, fell in scores, while those who landed found themselves faced by the Turkish wire entanglements, devised with peculiar cunning.

While a landing had been effected, the dead and dying in and around the boats afforded eloquent testimony as to its cost. For twenty-four hours the handful of men sheltering on the shore remained there, the guns from the battleships keeping down the Turkish fire, and at dawn on the next day, having during the night beaten back at close quarters an enemy attack, they got ready to assault the positions above them. Incredible as it may seem, they made their way into the village of Seddul Bahr, and early in the afternoon had seized the old castle there and the hill marked 141.

Heroism of the Gallipoli landing

So the 86th Brigade made good, and it was for the others to follow up their initial success. In the general attack on Krithia, which opened on April 28th, Sir Ian Hamilton stated that the Inniskillings, who reached a point about three-quarters of a mile from Krithia, got farther forward than any other unit. So stiff was the fighting that he was compelled to bring forward the tired remnant of the 86th Brigade, and it shared in the later stages of the attack.

When this advance stopped, the troops were ordered to hold the ground they had won, and there, in conditions of indescribable horror, they remained for some days. Early in May reinforcements arrived, and it was possible to take the Fusiliers out of the line, so the Inniskillings in the 87th Brigade were the only representatives of Ireland in the second attack on Krithia. They were, however, worthy representatives.

On May 7th they captured three Turkish trenches, and they did equally well throughout the whole battle.

A very short rest, however, was all that could be given to the Fusiliers, and on May 8th and 9th the Dublins and the Munsters were again in the fighting. But all chances of a quick success had by now vanished, and the struggle soon resolved itself into a succession of smaller attacks, especially after the bigger one which began on June 4th. On June 16th the 1st Dublins recovered some lost trenches, and on the 28th the 1st Inniskillings were prominent in a success which gave Sir Ian Hamilton three more lines. For something bigger, however, more troops were wanted, and their arrival and use is particularly an Irish story.

The men at this time training in England for the front were arranged in divisions mainly according to nationality, and one of these—the 10th—was entirely Irish. Its 29th Brigade consisted of the 5th Royal Irish, 5th Connaught Rangers, 6th Irish Rifles, and 6th Leinsters, men from every part of Ireland. Its 30th Brigade was the 6th and 7th Dublin Fusiliers, and the 6th and 7th Munster Fusiliers, once again to be comrades in glory; and its 31st Brigade was made up of Ulstermen entirely—the 5th and 6th Inniskilling Fusiliers and the 5th and 6th Irish Fusiliers. Finally, a fine Irish soldier, Sir Bryan Mahon, was in command.

The division was trained first in Ireland, when the men discussed eagerly the time and place of their participation in the great fray. No one knew anything definite, but about the time when the Irish Regulars were landing from the River Clyde the division was transferred to England. In and around Basingstoke they finished their training, and on May 28th were inspected by the King in Hackwood Park. Another month passed, and at the end of June it was known that the division was destined for service against the Turk. In July it was landed at Mitylene. In one particular only its units had been altered. The 5th Royal Irish had been trained to act as pioneer battalion to the division, and its place in the 29th Brigade had been taken by an English one—the 10th Hampshires.

The new movement included a landing at **Landing at Suvla Bay** Suvla Bay. The general plan at Suvla was that the 10th Division should support the 11th; but on August 5th one of its brigades, the 29th, was landed at Anzac and put into trenches by the side of the Australians. They were soon to gain a little experience of warfare, for they were in support when the Anzacs made a night assault on a Turkish position amid the hills. This took place on the 7th and 8th, and the Leinsters, detached from the others, went forward to the aid of the New Zealanders, who were holding on to Rhododendron Spur. There they came to close quarters with the Turk, and day and night alike there was some deadly work with the bayonet. The battalion did excellently, and a last charge of the foe was met by them running forward with a yell. The Turks turned and fled, and in one part of the field there was a temporary British success to record. The other two Irish battalions were equally active. On August 9th the Irish Rifles formed part of one of three columns of assault—the one that, led by General Baldwin, lost its way in the hills and suffered terribly from thirst and heat while on Chunuk Bair. There they were assailed by the Turkish hordes. In quick succession the officers of the Rifles were struck down, until only a few juniors remained. A retirement being decided on, the men fell back

in good order, as was proved by their readiness in responding to the call for a charge against the pursuing foe. Their spirit was as high as ever, but when they reached the beach their number looked pitifully few.

To save the situation the Connaught Rangers were hurried up. They had been sent off to act as reserves to another Australian brigade, but marched back again, and in the burning heat began the toilsome ascent of Chunuk Bair. They reached the summit, which fortunately the Turks had not yet occupied, collected all the wounded they could find, and then returned. By then, the evening of the 10th, nothing more could be done to assist by diversions the landing at Suvla.

Meanwhile, at Suvla Bay the 11th Division, having got ashore without serious opposition on August 6th, was followed on the 7th by six battalions of Irishmen—the four in the 31st Brigade, and two of Dublin Fusiliers from the 30th. They landed at Nibrunesi Point, and having been told to assemble under Lala Baba, they reached that spot in spite of an accurate and constant fire from the Turks on the hills above. The plan was for these hills to be assailed at once, but unfortunately there was delay owing to the landing having been made at the wrong beach. Later in the day the Irish battalions, four in number—for the other two remained behind—left Lala Baba and, skirting the Salt Lake, turned towards their objective, Chocolate Hill. In spite of bullets from unseen marksmen they advanced for some time without heavy losses, although the burning heat and the uneven ground tested the stamina of the strongest. The 6th Inniskillings and 5th Irish Fusiliers were in front with the 6th Irish Fusiliers and 7th Dublin Fusiliers in reserve, and in this order they continued until they were only three hundred yards from the hill. There at five o'clock, when they had marched for five miles carrying each a heavy load of arms and ammunition, they lay down for an earned and needed rest.

The final assault was made in traditional fashion. After a heavy bombardment by the big guns the leading companies dashed forward up the hill, and the men had the exultation of victory as their bayonets made the acquaintance of the Turks. In a trice the position was taken; but the more difficult part of the task then began, for it had to be made defensible during the night, while supplies of food, and especially water, must be obtained. In this work the 6th Dublins from reserve were most useful.

Two days later there was a fresh move. New troops were brought up for this, but they were assisted by the 6th Irish and 6th Dublin Fusiliers, two battalions whose part in the recent attack had been less strenuous than that of their comrades. These got on to the **Capture of Jephson's Post** hill which was their goal, but owing to the state of affairs elsewhere were ordered to fall back. The Irish battalions remained there for a few days longer acting as reserves, when another attack was made, and only left it when this enterprise was abandoned. Their losses, especially in officers, had been very heavy indeed.

For this next attack the 10th Division had been broken up. One brigade was at Anzac, and six battalions were on or near Chocolate Hill; the remaining three—two of Munsters and the 5th Royal Irish—really represented the division, for with them was its general, Sir Bryan Mahon. He landed with them, and at once ordered the Munsters to move forward

IRISH FUSILIERS IN GALLIPOLI.
Royal Irish Fusiliers in the trenches in Gallipoli. They distinguished themselves in the fighting following the new landing at Suvla Bay, August 6th, 1915.

towards the hills near the sea, a task originally detailed for the division as a whole.

Pushing forward through a country densely covered with scrub, the Munsters soon came up with an English battalion, the 11th Manchesters, who had been sent forward in that direction. They passed on, after ascertaining particulars about the enemy, and, following a night's rest, succeeded in capturing a strong position, called by them after their leader, Jephson's Post. Beyond this they could not go, but with the aid of the Royal Irish, who had come up, and later of the 5th Inniskillings, who came over from the other detachment, they stuck to their gains.

With the abandonment of Chocolate Hill more attention was paid to this position, Kiretch Tepe Sirt. The battalions from the former were given a few days' rest on the beach, and then marched up and joined those under Sir Bryan Mahon. Thus united, the 10th Division, now nine battalions strong, was ordered to make another attack on August 15th. In its initial stages it made but slow progress ; after a time, however, its direction was changed, and on the right, at least, the goal was won by a combined dash of Dublin and Munster Fusiliers. The Inniskillings, on the left, were less successful. The ground was unfavourable for skirmishing, the Turkish trenches, carefully hidden away, were untouched by the British guns ; and, consequently, before they reached the enemy, the 5th Inniskillings leading had lost nearly all their officers and most of their men. Some ground had been won, however, and with the aid of the reserves this was put into a state of defence before nightfall.

Battalions worn to a remnant

The counter-attacks began almost at once, and the Turks, having got back some of the lost trenches, were able to use their ample supply of bombs to good effect. Charges made with the highest courage failed to remove the intruders, and gradually the Irish battalions were worn to shadows. The remnant of the 5th and 6th Irish Fusiliers were relieved—not, however, by fresh men, but by those who had themselves only just gone away to rest, so dire was the need. But once again, alas ! gallantry proved helpless, and it was decided to vacate a position which, as men and munitions then were in small supply, was clearly untenable.

The 6th and 7th Dublin Fusiliers suffered as heavily as any on these sunburnt hills. Many of them, both officers and men, were known in the commercial and professional life of the Irish capital, and the 7th battalion was one of " pals." Its D Company consisted almost entirely of young men belonging to the professional classes, many of them with ample private means, and all distinguished in cricket, football, or some other form of sport. Its leader, Captain Poole Hickman, a barrister, was killed while leading on his men, and so were the battalion commander, Major Harrison, and many others, the unit being practically destroyed.

Dublin " pals " company losses

In two other parts of the Peninsula there were Irish troops. The 29th Brigade, really part of the 10th Division, was at Anzac, and the Irish battalions of the 29th Division was near Cape Helles. Of those at Anzac, the 5th Connaught Rangers alone were numerous enough for service, and they continued to face the Turks at Chunuk Bair until August 13th, when they were given four days' rest. Then they returned to the trenches and got ready for the desperate attack of August 21st.

Although the movement from Suvla had been a failure, it was decided to try again. The doughty Regulars of the 29th Division were brought round from Cape Helles, and arrangements were made for a simultaneous attack by the Anzacs and by the men at Suvla, the aim being for the two forces to join hands and so present a single front to the foe.

Of the Irish battalions the most deeply engaged in this new enterprise was the 5th Connaught Rangers, whose duty was to capture the two wells of Kaba Kuyu. General Godley's address to them before starting was evidently based on that short speech which Picton made to the Rangers under him before the storming of Badajoz. " Gentlemen, we will

HEROISM OF IRISH SOLDIERS NEAR HULLUCH.

Irish troops on the west front leaving their trenches and charging the Germans at the Chalkpit Salient, south of Hulluch, April, 1916. The regiments concerned were the Inniskillings and Dublin Fusiliers. Of this action the " Times " correspondent wrote : " The Irish troops at the front have had the opportunity of saying what they think of treason at home, and their message is there, in the German dead," alluding to the rebellion in Dublin, Easter week, 1916.

QUEEN ALEXANDRA'S SHAMROCK.
General Lord Cavan presenting Queen Alexandra's gift of shamrock to Irish Guards at Warley Barracks, on St. Patrick's Day, 1918. He also presented the twenty-six medals won by the 1st Battalion.

constant and desperate endeavours to retake. At last, having not surrendered an inch, they were relieved, and thanked for an action remarkable equally for its dash and its endurance.

In one of the later attacks—that of October 8th, near the Chalk Pit—the 2nd Munsters, in the 1st Division, did excellent service ; and away from the main fighting the 2nd Irish Rifles attacked, to make a diversion, near Bellewaarde Lake.

The story has now reached the opening of the Battle of the Somme. A number of Irish battalions were scattered throughout the divisions of Regulars as they had been from the first, but the greatest glory of all fell to the Ulster Division, new though it was to open warfare. The lesser incidents of July 1st may be described first. In the attack on Beaumont-Hamel the 2nd Dublin Fusiliers was one of the

do this business with the cold iron," and with this intention the men went forward, a platoon at a time, about four o'clock in the afternoon of August 21st. Dashing through a hail of bullets, they were soon in the Turkish trenches ; the Turks after a stubborn fight gave way, and the coveted wells belonged to the Rangers. The position was put into a state of defence, but many valuable lives were lost during the operation. On the next day they were relieved, twelve officers and over two hundred and fifty men less than at the outset, but cheered by the knowledge that they had been completely successful. They enjoyed a short rest, and on August 29th sent two hundred and fifty men, practically all their effectives, to take part in an attack on Hill 60. These men, weary though they were, said Sir Ian Hamilton, " excited the admiration of all beholders by the swiftness and cohesion of their charge." In five minutes they had carried their objective, the northern Turkish communications, and they at once set to and began a lively bomb
Gallipoli's glorious failure fight along the trenches against strong parties which came hurrying up. The Regulars, meanwhile, had assailed Scimitar Hill. There the 1st Inniskillings had charged into an inferno of fire, had gone forward a second and a third time, and had only desisted when the majority of them were dead or dying.

Before the end of September the offensive in Gallipoli was virtually abandoned. Reinforcements arrived to fill up the ranks of the stricken battalions, and at the end of September the 10th Division began to return to Lemnos. Its 29th Brigade went first and the concentration of the whole was completed in the early days of October. It was then transferred to another theatre of war.

By this time notable events were taking place on the western front. On September 25th the British attacked the Germans near Loos. Six divisions were in line for the assault, but in all there was only one Irish battalion leading. This performed one of the outstanding deeds of the day.

One of the brigades in the 47th (London) Division was led over the top by the London Irish. Before them went their regimental football, and, kicking this along, the men were soon in the German trenches, having shown in the rush the keenness that has always distinguished Irish forwards at the Rugby game.

They got into the first line of German trenches, and then followed Major Beresford to the second, which they cleared with their bombs. In these shelters they remained for the next three days, holding their gains, which the Germans made

MASCOT OF THE IRISH GUARDS.
Mascot dog of the Irish Guards on parade at Warley Barracks on St. Patrick's Day. They " made history," said Lord Cavan—in command of the Guards Brigade—of the Irish Guards' services at the First Battle of Ypres.

leading battalions of the 10th Brigade, and there the men sacrificed themselves recklessly in efforts to get through the deadly hurricane of fire. Near the Dublins were the battalions of the immortal 29th Division, and there the 1st Inniskillings were in the van. They, too, came out of action a mere remnant—not for the first time.

Attacking near La Boisselle was a brigade in which were two battalions of Northumberland Fusiliers, recruited from the Irishmen in and around Newcastle and known as the Tyneside Irish. At first they were in support, but they were soon needed in front, **Irish in** and they did their share of the bitter work. **Battle of the Somme** They dashed into the enemy's trenches, and although La Boisselle was untaken, they secured quite a lot of prisoners. In the vicinity of these operations the northern area of failure began to merge into the southern area of success.

Almost in the centre of the field was the Ulster Division. It was numbered the 36th, and consisted of nine battalions of Royal Irish Rifles—men from Belfast, three of Inniskilling Fusiliers, and one of Irish Fusiliers. It had finished its training at Seaford, and for nine months or so had been alternating duty in the trenches with rest in the areas behind. The ground now before it sloped upward to Thiepval, with the ridge behind it from which the German guns could sweep the whole long glacis of approach, and, as was truly said, it was a sector of ground which presented peculiar difficulties to its assailants.

The Irishmen did not flinch. Two brigades attacked on a front of about two miles, some battalions being on one side of the River Ancre and the rest on the other. Then was seen a spectacle for which the Great War had afforded few precedents—seven battalions of a single regiment, the Royal Irish Rifles, advancing together. Some of them, unfortunately, had been caught by shells as they formed up for the attack in Porcupine Wood; but, nevertheless, the whole line went sweeping steadily forward through the clouds of smoke, and, though many of them were hit, the rest moved on. The first, second, and third trenches were taken in turn, and finally the achievement was crowned by the seizure of the fourth.

The Schwaben Redoubt was now before them, and to take this the reserve brigade, mostly Inniskillings, came up. With the survivors of the earlier attack they dashed into its trenches, but that was the limit of their advance. There was no unit with which they could join hands, for no others in that region had won so far forward; moreover, there were no more reserves, and ammunition was running short. The guns from Thiepval were trained with merciless precision upon them, and at last they fell back to the German second line, where they remained until relieved. The Ulstermen in this memorable deed of arms are said to have lost half their strength, and certainly, with both sorrow and pride, none have more cause to remember July 1st than they.

Sorrow and pride of Ulstermen

Near the Ulstermen the 2nd Inniskillings (part of the 32nd Division) shared in the fight; and so, still farther south, did the 1st Irish Rifles in the 8th Division. But these Regulars would be the first to say that their comrades from civil life were, on that day of blood, equal to the best. As their general, Major-General O. S. W. Nugent, truly remarked,

"None but troops of the best quality could have faced the fire which was brought to bear on them, or the losses suffered during the advance." Four Victoria Crosses, in addition to many other honours, were further tributes to their gallantry. Private W. F. MacFadyean, of the Royal Irish Rifles, saved many lives, but lost his own by throwing himself upon some bombs just about to explode in a crowded trench. Lieutenant G. St. G. Cather, of the Irish Fusiliers, was killed after spending hours in searching for wounded men, while Private R. Quigg, of the Irish Rifles, the only survivor of the four, did similar hazardous work. Captain E. N. F. Bell, of the Inniskillings, won the cross for his superb gallantry in rallying and leading forward bombers and others until he was killed.

Four winners of the V.C.

In the fighting which followed the assault of the opening day various Irish battalions were engaged, these being mainly Regulars. The 2nd Royal Irish did good work at Mametz, and on the 7th the 2nd Irish Rifles lost heavily in charging forward to a nest of machine-guns near Ovillers. It was near there also that the 2nd Inniskillings made a successful move on the 10th.

On July 14th the time had come for a fresh attack on a grand scale. In the southern area the German first line had been taken, and the British were now confronted with the second. Bazentin-le-Petit, one of its bastions, was captured—a fine performance—by the 2nd Royal Irish, and the 2nd Munsters made a marked advance, although their attack on a German trench on August 24th was less successful.

At that time, like Ulster, the Roman Catholic provinces of Ireland had their own division in the west. This was the

BORDERS AND LINCOLNS BEFORE ACTION.

Men of the Border Regiment and the Lincolns in a village on the western front before going into action, during the great German offensive which opened on March 21st, 1918. The 21st Division, in which were men from Lincoln and Northumberland, had to withdraw from Epéhy after a fine defence, but not before inflicting great loss on the enemy, who acknowledge the bitterness of the fighting. These two fighting units were singled out for mention.

16th, the second Irish division of the New Armies, the 10th being the first. The earlier part of its training was got through in Ireland, and it was finished at Aldershot. Under Major-General W. B. Hickie, and with four Irish Members of Parliament in its ranks, this division had its first experience of the trenches in January, 1916, and did good service there during the ensuing six months, especially, perhaps, when two battalions of Dublins resisted a German attack on April 27th.

The division was not in the front line for the assault of July 1st, the units being then very much under strength, but it was brought up in order to make an attack on a selected part of the German line on September 3rd. One brigade, the 47th, was directed against Guillemont, and the afternoon was still young when the village was in British hands and its defenders in retreat. The Irish battalions, especially the 6th Connaught Rangers, lost heavily, but they showed once again the traditional Irish valour. On the same day the 2nd Royal Irish took part in the assault on Ginchy, and the 7th and 8th Irish Fusiliers supported an attack made by the 5th Division on the other side of Guillemont.

Glory of the 16th Division

The real task and glory of the 16th Division in those September days was the taking of Ginchy. There the main effort was left to it. Practically all the battalions were in front, and while the 6th Royal Irish and 8th Munster Fusiliers were fighting against the machine-gun defences, the 7th Irish Rifles and 7th Irish Fusiliers made their way into the German trenches. The 8th and 9th Dublin Fusiliers, following quickly, completed the work. The village was won and held against attacks made under cover of night. The Irish division was then withdrawn, and an officer of the Guards, who were marching up to replace them, has recorded how triumphant was their bearing when the two met on the road. Finally, as far as the campaigns of 1916 are concerned, the 10th Dublin Fusiliers in November helped the naval men when they made their notable attack along the Ancre.

When, in October, 1915, the 10th Division was taken from Gallipoli it was rested for a short time in Lemnos and then landed at Salonika. The Serbians were falling back through their own country, the Allies had marched out to help them, and on October 27th two Irish battalions took over a line between Kosturino and Lake Doiran. Other Irish battalions followed, and held a watching position in Serbia, until Sir Charles Monro ordered a retirement. While this was proceeding the Bulgars came on in great strength. The French, on the Irish left, were retiring, and on December 6th the Irish began to follow, and in so doing fought a stiff rearguard action against superior numbers. They won for their steadiness the commendation of their commanding officer, and when within thirty miles or so of Salonika took up a strong position from which no Bulgar army could drive them. For many months their duty was simply to hold it, although by then there were other British divisions to share the task. Only a little serious fighting, however, came their way. In August, 1916, there was a strong but unsuccessful Bulgarian attack on the front held by the allied troops, and in October one of the Irish brigades won the village of Yenikoi and held it against three strong counter-attacks, which lasted for a whole day and well into the night. In November, as reported by General Milne, some Dublin Fusiliers occupied certain villages and captured practically their whole garrison.

An all-Irish achievement

To return to the western front. Irish divisions were engaged in 1917 in the successful assault on Messines. At 3.10 in the morning of June 7th, Irish brigades moved out with the first line of attack, entered the German trenches, and climbed up the slopes of the ridge to its crest. Once there they went on again, and at 5.30 the Ulstermen, who probably belonged to the 36th Division, had reached the southern defences of Wytschaete. Their experiences, happily, were very different from those on that awful July day when they died in hundreds by Thiepval. Their casualties were very slight and they took over 1,000 prisoners.

This was an all-Irish achievement. On the left of the Northerners was a division composed of men from the rest of Ireland, and the two went forward side by side in fine

and friendly rivalry. Wytschaete Wood was the objective of the Southerners, and it was defended with both skill and valour, being full of machine-guns and wire, but these failed to check the Irishmen, who, with bayonets and grenades, were soon through the wood and in the village itself. There —or, rather, among the dust-heaps which represented it—they met one strong point that gave trouble, but it hardly checked them. The companies which went over first had the greatest opposition, but they went through every trench and stronghold as regularly as if at a rehearsal, and when the supporting companies took up the advance they moved against machine-gun positions and fortified posts in a way that no German could withstand. It was in the fighting in this wood that Major W. Redmond, M.P., of the Royal Irish, was killed, a death which for a variety of reasons aroused unusual sorrow.

On July 31st, when another great attack opened near Ypres, the Irish were again in the van, for Sir Douglas Haig mentioned them among those who delivered the main assault. These were evidently, however, battalions serving in mixed divisions, and their exploits consisted in fighting their way steadily forward through Shrewsbury Forest and Sanctuary Wood and capturing Hooge, Stirling Castle and the Bellewaarde Ridge. In the attack of October 4th also a few Irish battalions were engaged, but it is only with the Battle of Cambrai that they emerge again into the light of day.

The Ulster Division took a leading part in the sudden and striking success of November 20th. It was on the west side of the Canal du Nord, and, having swiftly seized a strong German position, its advance was carried forward in fine style. With some West Riding troops the Irishmen took the whole of the German trench system as far as the road running from Bapaume to Cambrai. This they crossed, and it was only when they reached Mœuvres that any halt was called. There they remained until the 23rd, when they renewed the attack, but this time the resistance was far more obstinate, and around Mœuvres and Bourlon there was severe fighting for several days. Some more ground was gained, but the surprise was over. **Ulstermen's fighting retirement** In this battle good work was also done by the 29th Division with its three Irish units, and by the 16th, the captors of Ginchy. The latter, on the 20th, made a subsidiary attack at Bullecourt, which was very successful, and on the 25th made further progress in that area.

Apparently, when the Germans in their turn scored a success at Bourlon, the Ulstermen had been withdrawn into reserve, but they were in front when St. Quentin was surprised in March, 1918. On the morning of March 21st the mist was very thick, and at 11.45 it was reported that the Germans were through the wire, had isolated the forward positions, and were creeping round on the right of the division. The Ulstermen flung back their flank, to meet the danger, and then began the retreat, fighting always with their faces to the foe.

At Douchy the Inniskillings made a brilliant counter-attack which drove the enemy back and gained a short respite, and men of the Royal Irish Rifles fought magnificently on several occasions. On the night of March 24th the men prepared to go into billets, but before they reached them they were called out again, and that night all hands, including the orderlies, fought with rifles. Again, on the night of the 27th, the men were to have been given a rest, but had again to turn out to cover the detrainment of other troops. Then it was that, though they were so tired that they could hardly move, they went in singing " Tipperary."

We already knew from their record on the Ancre and in Flanders how splendid the Ulster troops were in the attack, but they showed themselves no less formidable in retreat. It was a terrible test they were put to, and they never lost heart or fighting spirit, and to the end the Germans never once broke their front. Through long days they held impossible positions against the continuous pressure of overwhelming odds, and then at dusk, or as opportunity served, fell back to new positions, the enemy never finding them unprepared or unready to hit back.

This withdrawal was a fine feat for the Irishmen, and one incident, wherein the 1st Inniskillings fought a magnificent fight until the battalion was destroyed, has been recorded by Sir Douglas Haig. In general, however, the operations were on too grand a scale for battalions to be mentioned by name; but we know that the Irish Regular battalions in the 29th and other famous divisions were in the thick of this affray, as were the Irishmen with the London divisions. The same remark applies to the succeeding operations. The fact that there is no specific mention of Irish battalions does not mean that Irishmen were not advancing victoriously from July to November. They were fighting their way across the Somme battlefields into Belgium, but being mostly in mixed divisions their special part may at times have passed unnoticed. Of the full tale, however, the story of the Irish regiments is by no means its least honourable part.

There were thus Irishmen fighting on the west and also around Salonika, but there were also Irishmen in Palestine. In the list of mentions for good service in the campaign in the Holy Land, issued in June, 1918, by Sir Edmund Allenby, were the names of officers and men from the whole of the eight Irish regiments, indicating that he had with him a strong Irish contingent. These Irish troops were specially mentioned by him for excellent work against some trenches on November 6th, 1917, and they did good service until Jerusalem was occupied in December.

Turning to the records of the other section of our subject, the fact may be recalled that the assistance of Welshmen has always been welcomed by the leaders of the English Army. One of the notable events in the Battle of Crécy, as Froissart tells the story, was the execution done by the Welsh footmen armed with their terrible knives, and nearly a hundred years before, at Lewes, Henry III. had them in his host. Shakespeare was historically correct when in his " Henry V." he represented Welshmen as present at Agincourt, and Charles I. always looked to Wales for support.

In addition to the later regiment of Welsh Guards, Wales had three infantry regiments in the British Army. Two of them stand together in the list. The Royal Welsh Fusiliers, the regiment of North Wales, is the old 23rd of the Line, and the South Wales Borderers is the 24th, and incidentally one of the most famous regiments Britain possesses, ranking in glory with the Black Watch, the Oxfordshire Light Infantry, and one or two others. The third is the Welsh Regiment, made up of the old 41st and 69th Foot. This, with its headquarters at Cardiff, drew its recruits mainly from the sturdy miners of the Glamorgan valleys.

Each of the regiments had, in 1914, two Regular in addition to various Territorial battalions, and soon Service battalions were added. The first to come in serious **Welsh at** touch with the enemy was the 2nd **Le Cateau and Mons** Welsh Fusiliers, which formed part of an isolated brigade, the 19th. It took part in the Battle of Le Cateau and accompanied the Second Corps in its retreat to the Marne. With the First Corps at Mons were the 1st South Wales Borderers and the 2nd Welsh, both in the 3rd Brigade, but these did not come in for any very heavy fighting until the retreat was over and the Aisne reached in the advance.

Having crossed the river near Bourg the 3rd Brigade found the Germans almost wedged between the two divisions of Haig's corps. To prevent this its two Welsh battalions were thrown against them, and by their efforts the peril that the divisions would be divided was averted. The same

DUBLIN FUSILIERS HONOURED.
Heroes of the Royal Dublin Fusiliers who received the Military Medal of the Serbian Order of the White Eagle. Left to right : Sergeant Cummins, Sergeant Leonard, Lance-Corporal Carroll, Private Hayes. The last mentioned also received the French Croix de Guerre.

two battalions had another common experience on September 26th. A heavy German attack broke into the trenches occupied by a company of the Borderers and shot down all its officers. However, the reserves of the battalion with the Welsh regiment regained the lost ground and, in addition, drove the enemy from a wood in front of the position.

The Welshmen saw a good deal of fighting in the First Battle of Ypres. The 1st Welsh Fusiliers had crossed from England as part of Sir Henry Rawlinson's 7th Division, and on October 19th found itself confronted with a great new German force. On this day General Rawlinson decided to fall back to his original line, and it was at this stage that the Fusiliers had a mishap. The order to retire did not reach their colonel, and the men lost heavily. They remained, however, full of fight, and on the next day beat back another sturdy assault. But on the 21st, the third day of continuous fighting, the battalion was almost destroyed, having by then lost twenty-three of its officers. Its trenches were shelled with deadly precision, and, being in an exposed position, the men had little chance of escape.

When, about October 20th, Haig's corps came into line before Ypres, its task was to advance towards Bruges. The village of Poelcappelle was bravely attacked by the South Wales Borderers, but the movement forward could not continue; numbers were against it. The Borderers were assailed with great ferocity, but once again men of the Welsh Regiment came to their help in time. Near Gheluvelt a day or two later the same two units gained a little ground which had been lost.

The crisis of this grim struggle, however, was yet to come, and when it did come all the Welshmen were hard hit. On October 30th the Germans, by a tremendous effort, broke through where the line was very **Saving the** thin indeed, thus depriving one flank of the **British line** 7th Division of its supports. They then worked round this flank, where at the time were the Welsh Fusiliers, and the remainder of that fine battalion were nearly all killed or wounded. At dawn on the next day the 2nd Welsh felt the force of the storm. They were defending the Menin road, across which their trenches ran, and from these they were driven by a storm of shells followed by a burst of infantry. Half of them were down, but Captain Rees formed up the others in skirmishing order, and they protected a battery of guns behind them which were firing hard at the enemy and keeping him back. The battalion, however, was reduced to two officers and ninety-three men. Then came the turn of the Borderers.

English readers rightly know the story of how the 2nd Worcesters saved the British line about 2.30 on Saturday afternoon, October 31st, but there is an addition to be made to it. The Worcesters were ordered to close a dangerous gap that had been opened in the line, but the whole front had not given way, for the South Wales Borderers were still in their original trenches. The Worcesters made for the gap between the Borderers and Gheluvelt, and in the most gallant fashion closed it; but their deed would have been futile had not the Welshmen remained steadfast and immovable. The battle died away some days later, but before the end of the year some Welsh Fusiliers had won more distinction by raiding a German trench, and the Welsh and the Borderers of the 3rd Brigade, advancing to the support of the Indians on December 21st, had recovered some lost trenches near Festubert.

At Givenchy, on January 25th, 1915, the Germans made a determined attack upon the 1st Gloucesters, which was relieved by the strenuous courage of some men of the 2nd Welsh. A few of them charged forward while two of them captured a trench wherein were forty Germans. In this fighting the South Wales Borderers were also active.

The Second Battle of Ypres found another battalion of Welshmen at the front. This was the 1st Welsh, part of the 28th Division, and its brigade had a very **Eight Welshmen take 94 Germans** hot time on May 24th when attempting to regain some lost trenches. Into these they made their way in the darkness and fought by the fitful light of flares and bursting shells, but, having lost three-quarters of their numbers, were forced to retire at dawn.

Welshmen had a good deal to do with the great British attacks of May 9th and 16th. By this time they were backed by some of their Territorial battalions. The 3rd Brigade, which, in the first attack, dashed against the German line at Rue du Bois, had the 2nd Welsh in front, and the 1st South Wales Borderers and the 4th Welsh Fusiliers, Territorials from the Wrexham district, in support. The enemy's trenches were reached, but the attack failed because the British supply of ammunition was unequal to that of their foes. A second attempt, made later in the day, in which the Borderers led the line, met with a like fate. In the attack on the 16th the 1st

gallant effort to cross a smooth and bullet-swept area, and on June 28th were in a movement which captured three lines of Turkish trenches.

The second phase of the Gallipoli Campaign began with the arrival of fresh divisions, and in these, too, were Welshmen. In conjunction with the landing at Suvla Bay it was arranged that the Anzacs should make a grand attack on the hills above their camp, and in this they were assisted by other British and Indian troops. Among the British, presumably in the 13th Division, were the 4th South Wales Borderers and the 8th Welsh, the latter having been trained as a pioneer battalion. The first advance was made at night by two columns of assault and two covering columns, and the rapid success of the left covering column was due, we are told, to Lieut.-Colonel Gillespie, "a very fine man who commanded the advance guard consisting of his own regiment, the 4th South Wales Borderers, a corps worthy of such a leader. Every trench encountered was instantly rushed by the Borderers, until, having reached the predetermined spot, the whole column

IRISH CANADIANS IN BELFAST.
Group of the Irish Canadian Battalion of the Canadian Forces outside the cathedral at Belfast, inside the walls of which their colours were deposited during the duration of the war.

was unhesitatingly launched at a certain objective. There several Turkish trenches were captured at the bayonet's point, and by 1.30 a.m. the whole of the hill was occupied. This brilliant bit of work safeguarded the left rear of the whole Anzac attack. A day or two later, while the Borderers were repulsing two strong attacks, Gillespie was killed."

The troops were then reorganised for a fresh advance, and in this the 8th Welsh raced with other troops up a precipitous hill and were soon on the slopes and crest of Chunuk Bair. All this gallantry, however, was unavailing, for the position could not be held, and the operations at Suvla, in which the 2nd Borderers from Cape Helles also did good work, must be written down as a costly failure.

In the west the war was about to be marked by the Battle of Loos, which began on September 25th. On the left, where the 2nd Division attacked, two companies of Welsh Fusiliers, dashing forward to succour two isolated battalions, were almost destroyed, but the other Welsh **From Loos to the Somme** units were not seriously engaged on the first day. On October 1st, however, the 1st Welsh got into the trench famous as "Little Willie," and held it in spite of heavy losses for about a day, while in a subsidiary attack near Givenchy, intended to deceive the enemy, two new Welsh battalions, the 9th Welsh and the 9th Welsh Fusiliers, did extremely good work at heavy cost to themselves.

The New Armies were now fairly in the fight, and there were plenty of Welshmen among them. In March, 1916, the 10th Welsh Fusiliers were heard of during a great German attack, and among the many raids which preceded the Battle of the Somme one of the most successful was carried out by the 2nd Battalion of this regiment.

Coming to the opening day of the battle, the South Wales Borderers from Gallipoli were there, leading the charge of

CANADIAN COLOURS IN ULSTER'S CAPITAL.
Impressive scene outside Belfast Cathedral when the colours of the Irish Canadians were carried in solemn procession to be deposited within.

Welsh Fusiliers rushed the trenches before them, and one of their non-commissioned officers, with seven men, collected therein ninety-four Germans and led them back as prisoners. The battalion lost its colonel, R. E. P. Gabbett, in this fight. His predecessor, H. O. S. Cadogan, had fallen a short time before.

Wales was also represented in the ferocious struggle then being waged in Gallipoli. One of the battalions of the 29th Division was the 2nd South Wales Borderers, and on the memorable April 25th this got ashore from trawlers at Morto Bay and soon had a firm grip on the cliffs there. Their casualties amounted only to about fifty, and on the 27th they joined up with the other troops and made a line across the Peninsula. The division was now in front of Krithia, and in the thick of a series of assaults were the Borderers. On May 8th they were largely responsible for a specially

their division against the murderous fire from the strongholds around Beaumont-Hamel, while the 1st Welsh Fusiliers of the 7th Division fought with success around Mametz. On July 2nd the 9th Welsh Fusiliers were in a fierce struggle for the possession of the village of La Boisselle, one of great importance to the British plan, and on the 5th the 1st Fusiliers were attacking Mametz Wood, which the Germans had turned into a forest fortress. By now Wales could boast not merely of battalions but of a division at the front.

The Welsh division of the New Army was numbered the 38th, and this took the place of the 7th in the front line on July 5th, 1916. It had already been for some time in France and had gained experience in trench warfare, but it was now set a sterner task—that of clearing Mametz Wood. The 16th Welsh, men from Cardiff, and the 10th South Wales Borderers led a first attack on this formidable position, but it failed and another was planned for July 10th. The ground between the wood, dark and sinister, wherein the Germans lay concealed with their endless supplies of guns and bullets, and the British trenches was terribly exposed, but the attacking battalions reached it soon after the assault started at 4.30 a.m.

The fight, a desperately hard one, raged for hours. The German machine-guns were deadly, and in the tangle orderly formation was impossible. Small groups fought their way forward with undaunted courage, and early in the evening a good part of the wood had been cleared, and the two sections of the attacking force had joined hands.

The losses had been terrible. Fortunately the reserves were at hand, and while the pioneers, the 19th Welsh, strove frantically to put the place into a state for successful defence, the 13th Fusiliers captured a trench from which very heavy losses had been inflicted, and the 10th Welsh added numbers and vigour to the thin defending line in the wood. The 17th Welsh Fusiliers and 10th South Wales Borderers pressed on until only one end of the wood remained in the enemy's hands when at nightfall the attack ceased. In the morning the Welshmen, after a stiff fight with bayonets, seized a trench that had hitherto thwarted them, and after this the division was relieved. This capture of Mametz Wood by the Welshmen was a very fine performance—one of the heroic deeds of the Battle of the Somme.

Welsh capture Mametz Wood

In the attack launched on July 14th the 1st Welsh Fusiliers had a victory near Bazentin-le-Petit, and the 1st Borderers and 2nd Welsh were in a movement on the night of the 15th near Pozières. These two units lost many lives in trying to take Munster Alley, and the 2nd Welsh Fusiliers were fighting throughout another July day in High Wood, where their dash was of supreme value at a critical moment.

In August also there was deadly work in these blood-stained woods. The 1st Welsh Fusiliers fought hard near Delville Wood, and preceded the Irish in an attack upon Ginchy, while the two Welsh battalions of the 3rd Brigade were striving to win High Wood in September. Finally, as far as the Somme battles are concerned, the 16th Welsh Fusiliers did fine work near Lesbœufs on September 25th, and the 10th Battalion of the same regiment led one of those desperate attacks against uncut wire which made the November operations on the Ancre so costly in life.

The Welsh divisions, of which there were at least two in the field, one of Service men and the other of Territorials, do not appear to have been engaged in the Battle of Arras in April, 1917, and although there were undoubtedly Welsh units in some of the divisions responsible for that victory, it is impossible to disentangle their deeds from those of the associated battalions. The same is true of the capture of the Messines Ridge, but as regards the Ypres offensive it is otherwise.

The laconic statement about the opening of this encounter ran thus: "At 5.30 a.m. of the July 31st the combined attack was launched. English, Irish, Scottish and Welsh troops delivered the main assault on the British front." Evidently a Welsh division, almost certainly the 38th, was engaged here, and the reports of the fighting spoke highly of its gallantry. The objective of these Welshmen was the village of Pilkem, near which they met and routed the famous "Cockchafer" division of the Prussian Guard. They took Pilkem and, with some of the Guards, seized the crossings of the Steenbeek.

On September 20th the Welshmen had another successful day near Klein Zillebeke, and on the 26th were mentioned as fighting their way forward near Polygon Wood, where the Germans held some strongly fortified farm-houses. A few Welsh battalions were in the attack delivered on October 4th and in some fierce fighting for the possession of Bourlon in November. In this the 2nd South Wales Borderers of the 29th Division were also employed.

Welshmen also did good service in the raiding operations of 1916-17 near Salonika, between Lake Doiran and the River Vardar, where British and Bulgars faced each other in trenches not unlike those on the western front. General Milne remarked, referring to the autumn of 1916, that the most successful of these raids were carried out by battalions of the Welsh and Cheshire Regiments, and in the following spring, when these raiding tactics were further developed, some Welsh Fusiliers were among those who showed "conspicuous skill."

In the Balkans and Palestine

In December, 1916, Sir Stanley Maude began his advance in Mesopotamia, and on February 15th, 1917, there was some heavy fighting beyond Kut. About this encounter he said that, after a feint made on the Turkish position, "the Royal Welsh Fusiliers and the South Wales Borderers carried the enemy's right centre in dashing style on a front of 700 yards and extended their success by bombing to a depth of 500 yards on a frontage of 1,000 yards, taking many prisoners."

Most of the troops that left Gallipoli at the end of 1915 were taken to Egypt, and after a well-earned rest there some were sent to France, while others went to strengthen the force in Mesopotamia. Some, however, remained in the Land of the Pharaohs, ready to hit the Turk in a fresh place.

This new enterprise was the crossing of the Sinai Desert and the invasion of Palestine, and it began early in 1917. The advancing force contained some Welsh battalions, formed into a division of Territorials, and numbered the 53rd, and it fought on March 26th in the Battle of Gaza. Its brigades stormed most of a formidable position known as Ali Muntar and held it against obstinate assaults throughout the next day; but for some reason or other it was soon abandoned. Three weeks later the Welshmen fought in the Second Battle of Gaza. They were then on the left of the line, and after severe fighting took Samson Ridge; they advanced in spite of determined opposition and heavy casualties.

After this check there was a pause, but in the autumn General Allenby, who had been sent out to take command, moved swiftly forward. The information which came through about this campaign referred not infrequently to the doings of Welsh troops, evidently the 53rd Division.

On October 27th, they came up just in time to succour some outnumbered yeomen, and as soon as Beersheba was occupied they pushed out to the north; then in a severe fight on November 6th they won important positions on the way to Jerusalem.

It only remains now to say a few words about the Welshmen in the last stages of the war, which began with the British retreat, one incident of which was the defence of Bligny by the 9th Battalion Welsh Regiment, in the 19th Division. This division was involved in much more hard fighting during the later stages of the retreat, and in other hard-pressed divisions were Welsh battalions also doing nobly.

In the closing stages

The Welsh division, the 38th, was not so severely engaged in these spring battles as were many others, but it was one of those that took part in the forward movement that began in August. On the 21st it was fighting north of Albert, and on the night of the 23rd the men waded through the flooded waters of the Ancre, and as dawn was breaking stormed the German positions overlooking that river. Ovillers was taken, but only after hard fighting, as were La Boisselle and Pozières. Next day Contalmaison fell to it, and then came another hard spell around Longueval and Delville Wood. On September 2nd the division seized Sailly-Saillisel, and finally at the beginning of November it pushed far into the Forest of Mormal.

Part of the vast crowds which assembled at the port of Buenos Aires to accord a hearty welcome to the British Mission, headed by Sir Maurice de Bunsen, in May, 1918. In the background may be dimly seen something of the throngs of people who swarmed on to the loaded waggons of a stationary train.

Sir Maurice de Bunsen (in the foreground, with walking-stick) and the members of his party with the Argentine officials who had met them, passing through the thronging crowd which had gathered to welcome them on their arrival at Buenos Aires on May 31st, 1918.

BUENOS AIRES' GREAT WELCOME TO BRITAIN'S REPRESENTATIVES.

GERMAN LINERS

CHAPTER CCCV.

AT PERNAMBUCO.

LATIN AMERICA AND THE WAR.
By F. A. Kirkpatrick.

Latin America's part in the war has been dealt with already. In Chapter CCX. (Vol. 10) the course of events was traced down to the close of 1917. In the chapter now given, written at the moment when peace terms were being decided in Paris, it has been possible to make a general survey of the relations between Latin America and the United States and Europe; and the Editors regard themselves as specially fortunate in having been able to induce Mr. Kirkpatrick to undertake this survey. That Mr. Kirkpatrick writes with authority all who heard his lectures on "South America and the War" at King's College, London, in 1918, or have read these lectures in their revised form as published by the Cambridge University Press, can entertain no doubt. Nor can the importance of the subject be exaggerated, either from the commercial standpoint or in regard to the future of the League of Nations. In the ensuing pages Mr. Kirkpatrick shows very clearly that while the world-conflict caused a sharp shock to Latin America, particularly in the restriction of trade, immigration, and the flow of capital from Europe, the shock was followed by a remarkable recovery. Exports increased in value, prices rose, and a new spirit of independent nationhood was developed. In fact, as an Argentine writer expressed it, Latin America came to regard herself as "a constellation of peaceful republics moving up in the path of liberty, order, justice, and democracy," in harmony with the new movements in Western Europe and the United States. Mr. Kirkpatrick shows clearly also what Germany hoped to gain in Latin America, how she tried to secure and develop her influence there, and how and why she failed.

IN tracing the life of Latin America, history has marked with signal and conspicuous characters the three great epochs of birth, adolescence, and conscious growth to full stature in such a way that the intervening periods of slower movement have an unmerited reputation for stagnation or aimless activity.

The first of these arresting epochs is that movement of Spanish and Portuguese discovery and conquest which brought these lands into contact with Europe, and gave birth to the communities which now inhabit them. The second is the struggle for emancipation, through which, a century ago, those communities entered upon the path of independent existence. The third is the great crisis of our own day, which has put an end to their aloofness from outside politics, has forced them to shape their attitude in the play of world forces, has brought to them a sober consciousness of their growth to full stature, has assigned to them their due place in the family of nations, and has compelled the whole of civilised mankind to recognise the dignity and worth of these communities and their weight in the volume of human affairs.

In the past the world at large has been content with a somewhat dim and remote view of these countries, except when the momentous events just mentioned brought flashes of clearer vision. The marvellous tale of the *conquistadores*, with their aspirations, their crimes, and their valorous achievements, has imprinted itself upon the imagination of mankind, and thrown into the shade the less agitated but by no means dull centuries of Spanish dominion. Again, the movement of emancipation, the work of Bolivar and his fellows, focused itself upon the public vision, was a leading factor in the councils of Europe, and in that connection gave rise to Canning's famous exclamation, " I have called a new world into existence to redress the balance of the old." But in turn that conspicuous crisis depressed, by contrast, European opinion concerning the three succeeding generations, which, except by those directly interested in those lands, have been too often viewed with indifference or with an impatient pessimism which scarcely looked below the surface or sought enlightenment.

The third crisis, that of our own day, has not been to Latin America, like the two former epochs, a catastrophic upheaval. It brought, indeed, a certain shock and momentary interruption of normal life, but there was no destructive wave, to be followed by a process of painful reconstruction. Rather, the crisis has brought into relief the work already done, and has given a fresh

BRITISH DIPLOMATIC MISSION TO CHILE.
Sir Maurice de Bunsen driving through Santiago, the capital of Chile, on his way to present his credentials to the President of Chile. In 1918 Sir Maurice visited all the South American capitals as head of a Special Diplomatic Mission.

SIR MAURICE DE BUNSEN IN THE CHILEAN CAPITAL.
As head of the British Diplomatic Mission visiting Chile, Sir Maurice de Bunsen (standing) addressing members of the societies of mining, agriculture, etc., at Santiago in June, 1918.

direction, a new impetus and character to the continuation of that work. Yet the effects of the present war are as far-reaching and comprehensive as those of the two former great catastrophes. The rapid and striking events of to-day are moulding in decisive fashion the life of those countries, and in such a way that henceforth they claim more than a partial or episodical attention. They demand as their due, and they are receiving, a universal, sympathetic, and sustained interest. The present crisis has opened for Latin America a new era—social, political, and economic. Those countries stand upon the threshold of a fresh, more active, and more conspicuous existence. The way has been opened for them partly by external events, partly by the vigour with which they have availed themselves of their opportunities.

The European convulsion which broke out in August, 1914, remote though it seemed to be from the Transatlantic coasts of the Southern Hemisphere, shook the whole world. Its movements touched every shore of every ocean, and involved in varying degrees all the peoples

Economic aid to the Allies of all the continents. Brazilian warships acted with a British fleet in European waters. Cuba, Panama, and Brazil have been represented in the Council Chamber of the Allies in Paris. Out of the twenty Latin States of the New World eight declared war upon Germany, and five others severed diplomatic relations with that Empire.

But more important than belligerent or political action has been the economic aid furnished to the Allies by those lands, including those which remained neutral. A notable episode in the Great War and a damaging blow to Central Europe was the purchase of the Argentine and Uruguayan harvest of 1917-18 by the Allies. Exports from South America were a telling factor in the struggle. Nitrate and copper from the Pacific States supplied our munitions. Corn, meat, and wool from the Pampa fed and clothed our soldiers. Brazil sent rubber and manganese, besides varied foodstuffs. South America is the great producer of raw materials, the raw materials which feed guns and battalions as well as peaceful industries. And those resources were at our disposal, while our enemies were cut off from them. The Latin American peoples were not, it is true, ranged in the front line of the conflict, but they stood behind the fighting ranks and supplied their needs. It may be briefly said that hitherto Latin America had depended upon Europe. To-day Europe and Latin America are interdependent.

286

BRITISH DIPLOMATISTS IN THE ARGENTINE.
Members of the British Diplomatic Mission to Latin America, with some of their hosts, during their stay at the estancia of the Señora de Cobo, in Argentina.

The grouping of the nations in the recent trial brings out with vivid reality a fact already recognised as a theoretic truth—namely, that modern history, with all its eddies and side-currents, flows in a single broad stream, and that the New World, in character as well as in origin, is a part of that Old World which gave it birth. From the beginning these Transatlantic offshoots have been watched and fostered by Western Europe, and now these children have come home again to Europe with full hands. It can no longer be said to-day, as was said some years ago, that the countries of Latin America stand upon the margin of international life.

In estimating the effect of the war upon those lands it should be remembered that Latin America extends from the north temperate zone through the tropics and the south temperate zone to the shores of the Antarctic Ocean. It comprises twenty republics, which differ widely from one another in situation, products, and political methods, and even to some degree in ethnological origin. Thus any brief summary must necessarily be of a general and incomplete kind. Yet a comprehensive summary is possible and appropriate; for this group of Transatlantic peoples, which sprang, from the Iberian Peninsula, are rightly conscious of forming a world in themselves, a community of Ibero - American nations. Moreover, in thinking of Latin America, the European thinks first, reasonably enough, of the A B C countries —Argentina, Brazil, Chile— which possess between them half the population of Latin America and above three-fourths of its commerce.

In these three countries, as well as in the other Latin American States, the outstanding factor bearing on present conditions is the great creation of new wealth, the prodigious economic development of the past generation, a development which has favoured social and political consolidation, has aided in rescuing those republics from the half-century of turmoil succeeding the War of Independence, and has brought them into closer touch with Europe and European civilisation. The Pampa, intersected by railways, has become one of the great granaries of the world. Chile has been enriched by nitrate and copper, Brazil by rubber and coffee. And in the north, tropical hills, valleys, and coastal plains have yielded to rich cultivation. The Cordillera has once more been made to pour forth a stream of mineral wealth.

This economic development has been chiefly effected through European capital and enterprise. Moreover, the resultant products are food and raw materials, which find their chief market in Europe and are exchanged for European manufactured goods. Thus this great material advance, while on the one hand it has brought wealth, population, and vigour to those countries, on the other hand has

continued and emphasised their long-standing economic dependence upon Europe. Hitherto these young States have generally acquiesced in that dependence. Government loans floated in Europe, European capital for all public enterprises, importation of almost all manufactured articles from abroad—these have been regarded as the natural and inevitable conditions of life.

Thus the outbreak of the European War brought a sharp shock. The economic machine ceased to work. Immigration from Europe ceased. The flow of capital was stopped. Imports were restricted. Germany, which had ranked third among outside nations trading with the continent, dropped out altogether, but for some devious and limited efforts. The exportation of goods not indispensable for war purposes was diminished. The accustomed order of things was suspended. These countries were thrown upon their own resources, compelled to provide their own labour, to manage their own finances, and either to furnish for themselves or else go without many of the commodities hitherto obtained from Europe. The shock was severe, but it had wholesome results. It checked public over-borrowing and, in some degree, extravagance of public expenditure. It favoured domestic thrift and a more sober, graver view of life.

And the first shock was followed by a remarkable recovery. Foodstuffs and raw materials were urgently needed by the Allies for military purposes. Prices rose. While imports diminished, the value of exports increased. Hence a favourable trade balance and the increase of internal wealth. The result

BRAZIL'S CO-OPERATION IN THE WAR BY SEA AND AIR.

Captain Guilhon and crew of the Brazilian warship Belmonte, who secured the German mine shown in the picture, which delayed the arrival of the vessel at Portsmouth. Right: Rear-Admiral Pedro F. de Frontin and officers of the Brazilian flagship Bahia at Portsmouth on the occasion of the visit of the Brazilian squadron to England, January, 1919. In oval: Two Brazilian airmen who trained in England to help fight the Germans. Top picture: Officers of the Brazilian squadron that visited this country; they are in the engine-room of a captured German submarine. Brazil joined the Allies on October 26th, 1917, after the torpedoing of the Macao by a German submarine, the fourth Brazilian vessel to be sunk by the pirates.

was an important and very interesting industrial movement. For these countries, unable to purchase from abroad and having money at their disposal, proceeded in some degree to supply their own needs by home manufactures, particularly in the way of textiles and leather. The restriction of imports, the consequent falling-off in Customs receipts, and the urgent demands of the belligerents also brought about a more searching exploitation of local resources. Brazil was hard hit by the drop in coffee exports. But, whereas she had previously imported food for her own population, she has become with extraordinary rapidity a large exporter both of meat and of vegetable foodstuffs. She is also striving with considerable success to work her large southern coal deposits and to overcome difficulties of transport and of raising steam with soft coal. Argentina, wanting coal, is cutting fuel in her forests and is pushing forward the production of petroleum from the State oil-fields in Northern Patagonia. Chilean coal now mainly supplies Chilean needs, and the Chilean manufacturing industry has received a great impetus. The outbreak of the war and the temporary drop in the export of nitrates caused a momentary dislocation of Chilean trade and finance. Subsequently the high prices and increased export of nitrate and copper for war purposes brought great prosperity. But Chile has learnt her lesson—not to build her financial system too much upon export duties derived from a single commodity, and not to count upon the perpetual prosperity of one business. Thrift, foresight, industry, national self-dependence—these have been the lessons of the war for Latin America.

Lessons of the war

And this industrial movement has naturally favoured national consolidation, an increased sense of civic dignity and responsibility. Moreover, while thus strengthening their own internal structure, these republics have also been drawn closer together, and now feel themselves more than ever to constitute a world in themselves. For example, whereas Brazil and Chile are both taking steps to gather into their own hands their coastwise trade, they are at the same time promoting maritime communication with one another. Trade between the Latin American republics is increasing owing to the interruption of the former paths of commerce, and these States have been drawn to define and strengthen their relations with one another by the very fact that they have been obliged to abandon their comparative aloofness from extra-American politics and have been carried into the general current of world affairs. Moreover, gazing across the ocean with a kind of amazement at the spectacle of the great nations of the Old World convulsed with slaughter and destruction, Latin America might well congratulate herself, and feel herself to be, as an Argentine writer has expressed it, " a constellation of peaceful republics moving upon the path of liberty, order, justice, and democracy." The temporary contrast between the progressive tranquillity of Latin America and the destructive turmoil of Europe gave fresh point and significance to the current term *Nuestra América*—"Our America"—whereby Latin Americans proudly and affectionately designate that Ibero-American world which is in a large sense their home.

Germany's " economic war "

But in estimating the effects of the war there is of course a reverse side to the picture. The temporary economic crisis produced by the sudden cessation of hostilities and by the consequent abrupt changes in demand, requires no more than passing mention, since it need not involve any serious check to Latin-American prosperity. But the social unrest, the loud discontent with conditions of labour, the class jealousies, which in varying degrees have agitated all Europe, are rife in the New World also, particularly in Argentina, where the public welfare has suffered serious blows from a succession of disastrous strikes accompanied by destructive violence. The situation demands firmness as well as sympathy and tact on the part of the administration.

Since the States of Latin America were not actually dragged into the vortex of the conflict, it is obvious that in a review of Latin American affairs the actual incidents of the World War are of minor importance as compared with its general results. Moreover, in Chapter CCX. (Vol. 10) of this history the leading events down to the end of 1917 are traced. Nevertheless, in a general retrospect it is necessary to indicate briefly the attitude and the activities of the belligerents in relation to Latin America. It will be found that these activities generally tended to favour that moral, material, and political process of consolidation and national growth which has been already sketched.

With the exception of some breaches of neutrality on the Pacific coast, these countries never became the scene of active hostilities. But from the first they found themselves the object of a keen economic struggle on the part of the belligerents—that economic war of which the Germans had talked so confidently, and in which they now found their own weapons turned against them. By assiduous courtship, by an organised effort of solicitation and propaganda, by all kinds of devious and ingenious approaches, the German now aimed at the commercial conquest of Latin America. By embarking upon open war he had hoped to consolidate, extend, and erect into a kind of monopoly that remarkable position which he had won by years of patient, industrious, and intelligent observation and labour. The entry of Great Britain into the war, the exercise of her maritime power, and the strength of the economic weapon in the hands of the Allies thwarted those bellicose plans of commercial predominance. At first this weapon was not fully brought to bear, and considerable German trade was carried on with Europe. Moreover, while the United States remained neutral, the Germans took every advantage of that field of trade, while at the same time they strove to maintain their economic ground in Latin America by personal and collective efforts of every kind, and by a comprehensive, strenuous, and enormously costly campaign of propaganda, which mobilised all the powers of the printing-press in order to influence Latin American opinion and sentiment in favour of Germany and against her enemies.

In this campaign of solicitation, which treated the favour of Latin America as one of the prizes of war, the economic argument was particularly emphasised, and it was urged with incessant iteration that German efficiency and organisation made her the most capable purveyor and purchaser, and that after the exhaustion of war the Allies would be unequal to that task. The various organisations for furthering German influence abroad—particularly the Pan-German League, the League for Germanism Abroad, the German School League, and the newly-formed Foreign Museum—turned their attention particularly towards South America. Assiduous attempts were made to cultivate for Teutonic purposes the German-speaking settlements in Southern Brazil and Southern Chile. The South American Institute at Aix-la-Chapelle strove through its illustrated journal, printed in Spanish and Portuguese for South American circulation, to uphold the German cause ; and in the course of 1915-16 three new leagues were founded in Germany, which by every possible means aimed at cultivating Latin American friendship and advancing German influence in those lands. Clubs or reception-rooms were opened in Berlin and Hamburg for the purpose of bestowing hospitable attentions upon South American visitors to Germany, in order to send them home again as ardent Germanophil converts and missionaries. In every American republic branches were set up of the Economic League for South and Central America, which was founded in Berlin in the autumn of 1915 under the presidency of Herr Dernburg, and comprised among its numerous members the chief German banks, shipping companies, commercial associations, and industrial syndicates. Their efforts met with considerable success, and were vigorously supported by every German and every friend of Germany from California to Cape Horn.

A campaign of solicitation

But Germany had no monopoly of activity and foresight. Others strove by less equivocal methods to improve and strengthen their relations with Latin America. The events of the war, by intensifying the traditional Latin American sympathy and admiration for France, gave fresh life and significance to the efforts of societies such as the Alliance

Impressive French reception at Mainz of British naval patrol from Cologne.

Mounting guard at Mainz: Naval and military spectacle outside General Mangin's headquarters.

The Cross of Sacrifice: Memorial erected in every British military cemetery in France and Flanders.

Cemetery as designed by Imperial War Graves Commission for British dead in France.

Simple altar=like Stone of Remembrance erected in British cemeteries in France.

British naval contingent in Paris : President Poincaré presenting Grand Cross of Legion of Honour to Admiral Beatty, April 23rd, 1919.

Française, the Comité France-Amérique, and the Groupement des Universités et Grandes Ecoles de France pour l'Amérique Latine. In December, 1917, there was inaugurated at Lyons the " Latin American week," a yearly festival of intercourse and propaganda, to be held in some great French business centre, where Latin American delegates could meet representative Frenchmen in every walk of life.

After the very successful Latin American week celebrated in Bordeaux in October, 1918, a permanent and comprehensive organisation was founded, through the co-operation of the French Parliamentary Committee for Latin American affairs with the various associations which concern themselves with Latin America; and monthly meetings are held for the purpose of furthering commerce and every kind of intercourse. The reputation of France at the present time stands higher than ever in Latin America, where allied victory is viewed particularly as a triumph for France and for the principles of liberty embodied in French republicanism.

Nor has Britain been indifferent. In 1918 the King addressed an appeal to Britons in Latin America, acknowledging the achievements of individual enterprise in the past, and inculcating the spirit of collective effort for the future. A Special Diplomatic Mission was despatched under Sir Maurice de Bunsen to visit all the South American capitals. This marked attention on the part of the British Government was highly valued, and the Mission everywhere received an enthusiastic welcome. Several associations were founded in England, which aimed at extending social and commercial relations with Latin America. These are merely symptoms of a widespread interest, an interest which shows itself in the very large space given to Latin American affairs in British business journals. The Oversea Dominions are also taking their part, and Canada particularly is pushing forward her considerable industrial enterprises in that region.

The movement whereby Spain is cultivating closer relations with her daughter-republics demands particular mention. But, indeed, all the maritime peoples of Europe, by increasing their commercial and banking facilities, are **U.S.A. and** reaching after their share in the future pro- **Latin America** mise of Latin America. Nor is the movement confined to European peoples. Japan is carefully cultivating the Latin American field. Japanese steamship lines have long served the west coast; they now extend to Buenos Aires and Rio also. Japanese immigration to Southern Brazil is increasing. Japanese relations with Chile are particularly close and friendly. Japanese manufacturers are endeavouring, with considerable success, to substitute their own productions for commodities formerly imported from Germany.

But most remarkable of all are the advances of the United States towards Latin America. North Americans took full advantage of the interruption and changes caused by the war in European trade. American banks have been established in Latin American cities; American capital has been poured into those countries. American trade with them has enormously increased. American aid in the exploitation of local resources and in the furtherance of trade has led to much closer relations between North and South. The educational, social, commercial, linguistic, and historical cultivation of South America has gathered volume in the United States, and the Pan-American Union at Washington finds fresh opportunities for the vehement economic propaganda which is its principal business.

This world-wide interest and approach naturally strengthens and supports the movement of national growth and consolidation; for the external recognition of a national position is an indispensable condition of that position.

Among these many applicants the German has attempted to hold his ground. Although through the operation of the blockade German shipping has been excluded and German goods only arrived in limited measure and by devious routes, nevertheless the German trader in Latin America has been throughout as ubiquitous, as insinuating, as energetic, as accommodating as ever; and he has been vigorously supported by the German bank and the German capitalist. When in the course of 1916 the blockade became really effective and

the " Black List " restricted the scope of his activity, the German trader still struggled on to hold his post. He sold largely from accumulated stocks; he replenished his stocks by purchases of goods anywhere, no matter what their origin. He traded under the cover of cloaks or fictitious names; he imported German goods shipped in neutral vessels, and masquerading as neutral goods; and he despatched wool, coffee, cocoa, and rubber to Germany by the same means, hoping that such shipments might escape the vigilance of British cruisers and the ordeal of the British Prize Court. The parcel post and even the letter post were used with odd ingenuity for the same purpose. Large stocks of wool, coffee, and rubber were bought and stored with a view to future trade, and meantime the **Counter arguments** varied and ingenious propaganda, which has **of Germany** been already mentioned, strove incessantly to uphold in Latin American eyes the solidity of the German character, the excellence of German organisation, the efficiency of German methods.

These Teutonic efforts were not allowed to pass quite unnoticed and unanswered. But the German himself supplied a yet more potent counter-argument; and that was the German submarine, the sinking of unarmed South American trading ships, and the murder of South American sailors. A former chapter of this history narrates how the peoples of Latin America, at first holding aloof and disposed to a non-committal attitude in sentiment as well as in official relations, were gradually and inevitably drawn to a closer interest; how the German proclamation of unrestricted submarine warfare in February, 1917, brought the war to their gates, though not actually within their borders; how Cuba and Panama followed the United States into war; how the sinking of Brazilian ships and the violation of international law brought Brazil to sever relations with Germany and advance by successive steps to open belligerency; how the publication of the Luxburg despatches in September, 1917, raised a storm of indignation, not only in Argentina but throughout the Latin American world; how Brazilian action was supported by neighbour States through sympathetic assurances and, in some instances, through the severance of relations with Germany.

During the first half of 1918 Latin America threw herself more and more on the side of the Allies. During April and May of that year Guatemala, Nicaragua, Costa Rica, Haiti, and Honduras successively declared war upon Germany. After that date no change took place in the Latin American official attitude, which may be thus summarised:

Eight republics declared war with Germany—namely, Brazil, Cuba, Panama, Guatemala, Nicaragua, Costa Rica, Haiti, Honduras.
Uruguay broke off diplomatic relations with Germany, rescinded her edict of neutrality, offered the use of her ports to the warships of the Allies, and seized the German ships in her harbours.
Peru broke off relations with Germany, offered the use of her ports to the Allies, and seized the German ships at Callao.
Bolivia, Ecuador, and Santo Domingo broke off relations with Germany.
Mexico, Salvador, Venezuela, Colombia, Chile, Argentina, and Paraguay maintained neutrality and diplomatic relations with all the belligerents.

It will be noticed that, of the ten Latin American States which lie outside South America, no less than eight have ranged themselves against Germany. Out of this northern group two alone, Mexico **South America and** and Salvador, maintained uninterrupted **League of Nations** relations with the Central European Powers.

The United States had established, in effect if not in theory, a sphere of influence in the Caribbean region. Porto Rico is hers; Cuba is formally under her tutelage; Panama practically so. A semi-protectorate over Nicaragua secures the exclusive control of any possible canal route. In 1916 the administration of Haiti and Santo Domingo was taken over by United States officials. A year later the United States purchased the Danish Antilles.

It may be here incidentally noted that the war has brought into prominence a fact of great interest in its international bearings. The scheme of the League of Nations has been criticised in view of the possible preponderance of Great

Britain through the separate representation of the Oversea Dominions in the League. Recent events show that Cuba, Panama, Nicaragua, Haiti, and Santo Domingo are dependencies of the United States in a sense which cannot be predicated of Great Britain and the Dominions.

The predominance acquired by the United States in the Caribbean area, whereas it has met with general acquiescence

UNITED STATES COLONIAL TROOPS OFF TO THE WAR.
Porto Rican Regiment, the first of America's Colonial detachments to leave for duty, marching through the streets of San Juan, where the whole city turned out to give the soldiers a hearty send-off.

in other quarters, has been jealously assailed by Germany. That Empire had won a strong economic position in the same region, and aimed at pursuing by these means the path of political intrigue and military power. Thus the spontaneous adherence of these republics to the course traced by the United States was a crushing blow to German designs. These republics, by a deliberate and public decision, solemnly announced to all the world under which system they chose to live.

Thus the effect of the war has been to give a kind of charter to the United States in regard to the position which she has assumed in the Antillean and Isthmian republics. Moreover, not only in the Caribbean region but throughout Latin America the moral influence of the United States has been enormously enhanced by her entry into the war, by the aims which inspired her to that action, and by the vigour with which those aims have been pursued. The United States now stands out not merely as the theoretic propounder of a protection really depending on the assent of Great Britain, and on the strength of the British Fleet, but as the active champion of national independence and of democratic institutions. Her relation with her southern neighbours acquire fresh importance, from the fact that she is now, in a military as well as in a moral sense, a Great Power, fully armed, one of the chief victors in a world war, and one of the chief arbiters in the final issues of that war.

Obviously, the Caribbean relations of the United States and her relations with the South American republics, particularly those of the Southern Hemisphere, fall into quite different categories. Nevertheless, the closer intercourse, the shifting of political power, and the changes of international outlook produced by the war have forced into prominence the definition of her southern relations and their possible modification through the scheme known as Pan-Americanism. President Wilson, in an address to a party of Mexican journalists early in 1918, put the matter plainly. After solemnly disclaiming any aggressive intentions, he avowed the double weakness of the Monroe Doctrine—first that it was propounded by the United States without consulting her neighbours ; and secondly, that, although it protected Latin America from European aggression, it did not protect her from American aggression. Accordingly, he proposed a union of all the American republics to protect the "political independence and territorial integrity" of all ; so that, in case of aggression on the part of any State, including the United States, all the others should unite to **Pan-Americanism** "jump upon" the offender. In short, **and the future** the proposal is an anticipation, for the two Americas, of the later scheme of a general League of Nations. Obviously, in any purely Transatlantic League, one member would outweigh all the others put together in wealth, population, and power, as also in the directness of aim and speed of action which spring from national unity and from the impulse of a great historical expansion. Moreover, later events raise the question whether there is room or need for a purely American international group beside or within the general League.

As to this point South American opinion is divided. Some consider that the American republics can, by permanent agreement among themselves, secure peace, sovereignty, and territorial integrity for all. Others, who find cause for disquietude in some developments of the Monroe Doctrine, see a safeguard in the recognition by the United States of the authority of a general League of Nations, and expect greater national security in the decisions of a universal council and a world-wide tribunal.

At first sight the question may appear to be solved by the very interesting decision, reached at Paris, to include in the Covenant of the League of Nations a clause safeguarding the Monroe Doctrine. But in fact that decision, which abstains from defining the Monroe Doctrine, solves nothing, but remits to the two Americas the whole problem, including the interpretation of the doctrine which, in its various later phases baffles definition, as Mr. Bushnell Hart pointed out in his work on the subject. In short, Great Britain, out of deference to North American opinion, induces her Allies to join her in a formal undertaking that they will continue to observe the already well-established policy of leaving to the United States a free hand in the affairs of the Western Hemisphere—a policy gradually adopted by Great Britain, definitely followed by her since the Venezuelan question of 1896, and necessarily accepted by other nations. Thus in **Monroe Doctrine** the future, as heretofore, it remains for the **developments** republics of the Western Hemisphere to settle among themselves their position towards one another. In any case the future relation of the United States with her southern neighbours must largely depend on the question whether in her own external relations in the Western Hemisphere she is prepared to carry out whole-heartedly that abdication of national aims and of imperial methods which she demands of European Powers in the Eastern Hemisphere.

Meantime the relations of Latin America with the peoples of Western Europe follow their traditional path of friendly intercourse by a more sympathetic European recognition.

But the essential significance of the present situation lies rather in the effect of recent events upon Latin America herself, upon her character, her material position, her outlook upon the world, and the growth of her peoples. This chapter may fitly conclude by once more emphasising the fact that this development is the true matter which claims the observation of the student and the attention of the world.

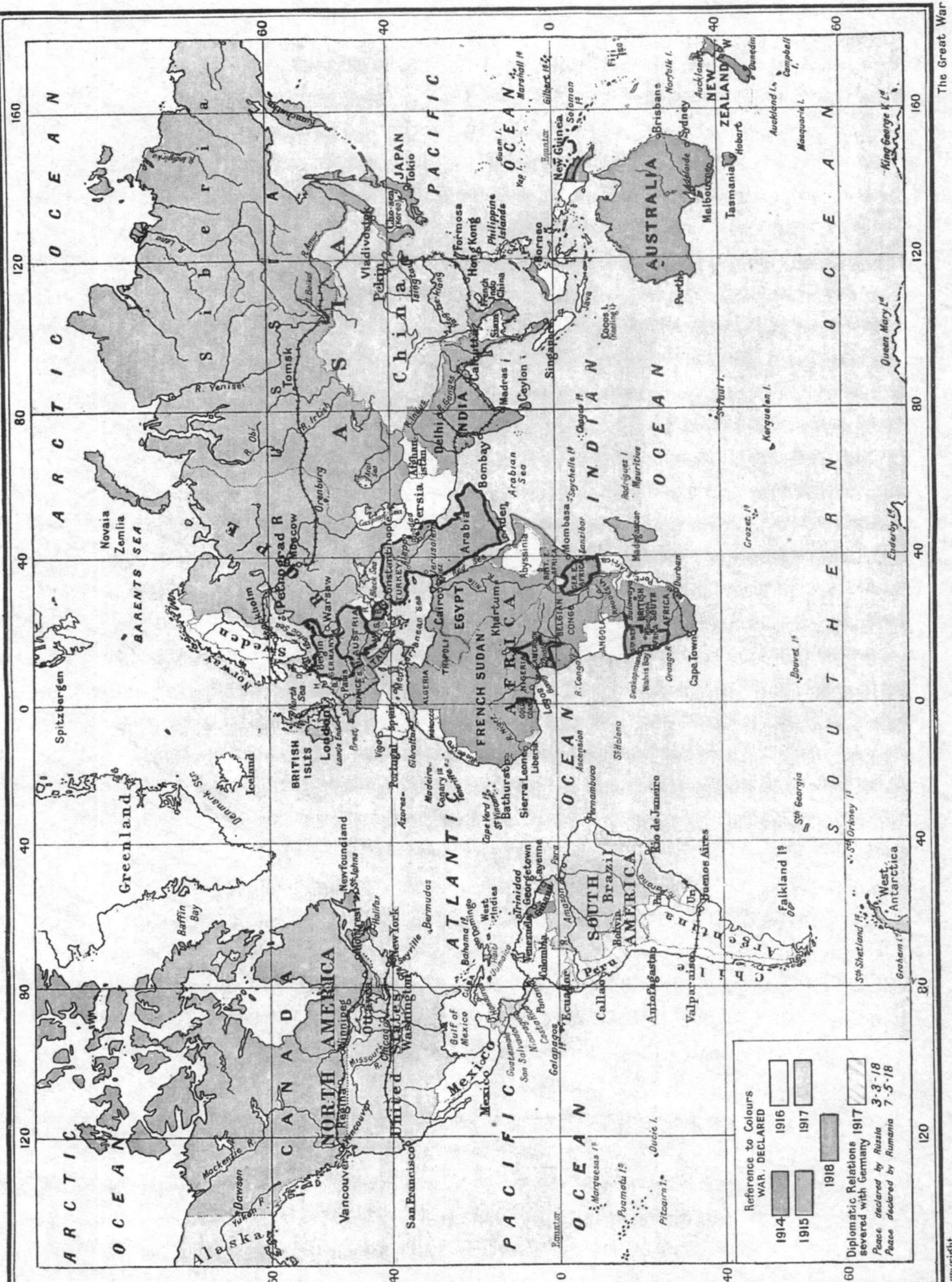

HISTORICAL MAP OF THE WORLD AT WAR, 1914-1918.

The above map shows the relations to one another of the countries of the world when the Armistice was signed by Germany, November 11th, 1918. It enables the reader to see at a glance how few

Copyright

The Great War

THE FOUNDING OF THE LEAGUE OF NATIONS.

By Hamilton Fyfe.

" A War to End War "—" Never Again ! "—How the Idea of the League of Nations Grew—American League to Enforce Peace—British League of Nations Society—The League of Free Nations Association—President Wilson's Intervention—International Charter of Right—History and the Sceptics—Attitude of the House of Lords—Lord Grey's Pamphlet—Debate in the Commons—Lord Robert Cecil's Lead—Views of General Smuts—Continental Hesitation—Public Opinion in the United States—Mr. Roosevelt and the Case Against the League—President Wilson and the Inter-Allied Conference—Criticism of the Draft Covenant—Opinion in Germany—Views of the British Trade Union Congress and the Labour Party—Fresh Outburst of Opposition in the United States—President Wilson and the Critics—Full Terms of the Amended Covenant.

FROM the earliest months of the war there went up from British hearts the cry that this must be the last time armed nations should face one another with all the resources of their civilisation turned to the purpose of slaughter. The horror of the conflict burned itself into the British soul all the more fiercely because we had among us so many who had persuaded themselves that humanity had outgrown war. When these saw that they were deceived they felt, after a period of stupefaction, an overmastering impulse to make their belief a reality. Out of this frame of mind grew such phrases as " a war to end war." Even professional soldiers, aghast at the proportions and the appalling nature of the struggle, joined in the chorus of " Never again ! "

The idea of a League of Nations pledged to live together in peace came to the surface of the national mind. It had often before filled the thoughts of thinkers and idealists. Now it took possession of the mass of people. Hitherto stigmatised as the dream of visionaries, it became, under the pressure of suffering and tortured imagination, a national policy.

From across the Atlantic came an answering cry. To the American people the war was like some hideous nightmare. They, too, were fed upon the delusion that the age of peace had arrived, though they knew quite well that two groups of nations in Europe were ever preparing themselves for hostilities.

LONDON HEADQUARTERS OF THE LEAGUE.
Sunderland House, Curzon Street, Mayfair, taken over from the Duchess of Marlborough. Formerly occupied by the Ministry of Blockade, this house was selected as the London headquarters of the League of Nations in June, 1919.

When war broke out the American people had no clear notion either of its immediate origin or of the deeply-rooted causes which had been leading up to this disastrous consummation. It was long before they formed correct conclusions, but from the very beginning they were moved by the generous and even passionate desire to make such a catastrophe impossible again. From this desire arose the League to Enforce Peace, which had Mr. Taft, formerly President of the United States, at its head, and many of the most honoured of American citizens among its members.

This society was formed in 1915. Before the end of the year its plan for a League of Nations was published and the American newspapers began to take notice of the movement. In Britain up to this time, and for some while after, little or nothing was heard of a movement destined to influence so deeply the course of events.

When, in the autumn of 1916, a branch office of the League to Enforce Peace was opened in London, the tenants of the building in which it had hired rooms sent a joint protest to the landlord against the appearance of its name on the door. They evidently thought it was a pacifist organisation, which aimed at stopping the particular war then raging. The landlord happened to know something about the League to Enforce Peace and explained matters, but the name had to be taken off the door.

295

MARSHAL FOCH AT SPA STATION.
Marshal Foch at Spa Station in April, 1919, after a conference which he
had had there with Herr Erzberger, Germany's plenipotentiary, regarding the
landing of Polish troops at Danzig.

of Nations Society, the idea of the
newer group being to form without delay
a League of such nations as were ready
to join, without awaiting the end of
the war. There were two opinions,
one that the Allies should establish the
League and admit Germany at some
later date; the other, that a League
without Germany would be incomplete
and therefore valueless. The discussion
of this point died away, so far as it
had any live interest, when President
Wilson declared himself, and laid it
down that the formation of the League
should be part of the work of the Peace
Conference. In October, 1918, it may be
added, the two British groups coalesced
into the League of Nations Union.

President Wilson's intervention began
in May, 1916. He then made a

A British League of Nations Society had been in existence
since 1914, but the first formal proposals which attracted
world attention came from Mr. Taft and his committee in
Washington. They were summarised in four articles :

Article 1.—All justiciable questions arising between the signatory
Powers (that is, the Powers belonging to the League of Nations),
which cannot be settled by negotiation, shall, subject to the limitations
of treaties, be submitted to a judicial tribunal for hearing and judgment,
both upon the merits of the question and upon any issue as to the
tribunal's jurisdiction.

2.—All other questions arising between the signatories and not
settled by negotiation shall be submitted to a Council of Conciliation
for hearing, consideration, and recommendation.

3.—The signatory Powers shall jointly use forthwith both their
economic and military forces against any one of their number that
goes to war or commits acts of hostility against another of the signatories
before any question arising shall be submitted as provided in the
foregoing.

4.—Conferences between the signatory Powers shall be held from
time to time to formulate and codify rules of international law which,
unless some signatory shall signify its dissent within a stated period,
shall thereafter govern the decisions of the judicial
tribunal mentioned in Article 1.

First League proposals The British League of Nations Society
stated its programme to be this :

1.—That a treaty shall be made as soon as possible whereby as
many States as are willing shall form a League binding themselves
to use peaceful methods for dealing with all disputes arising among
them.

2.—That such methods shall be as follows

(a) All disputes arising out of questions of international law
or the interpretation of treaties shall be referred to The Hague
Court of Arbitration or some other judicial tribunal whose decisions
shall be final and shall be carried into effect by the parties concerned.

(b) All other disputes shall be referred to and investigated
and reported upon by a Council of Inquiry and Conciliation,
the Council to be representative of the States which form the
League.

3—That the States which are members of the League shall unite
in any action necessary for ensuring that every member shall abide
by the terms of the treaty, and in particular shall jointly use forthwith
their economic and military forces against any one of their number
that goes to war or commits acts of hostility against another of the
signatories before any question arising shall be submitted as provided
in the foregoing articles.

4.—That the States which are members of the League shall make
provision for mutual defence, diplomatic, economic, or military, in
the event of any of them being attacked by a State not a member
of the League which refuses to submit the case to an appropriate
Tribunal of Council.

5.—That any civilised State desiring to join the League shall be
admitted to membership.

Later there was founded in London the League of Free
Nations Association, with the same objects as the League

AFTER THE CONFERENCE.
Herr Erzberger (seated on left) about to depart in a German car flying the
white flag after the conference on the Danzig question at Spa.

GERMANS DISCUSS THE ALLIES' TERMS.
German delegates who met Marshal Foch in a train at Spa. The portraits
are : Herr Erzberger, Dr. Heinrich Sahn, Burgomaster of Danzig, Freiherr
Langwerth von Simmern (Under-Secretary of State), Secretary de Driesen

speech in Washington at a meeting of two thousand prominent Americans called by the League to Enforce Peace. He had been thinking deeply about the state of the world, and he had been growing in statesmanship. He brought to the consideration of the world problem a mind trained by history, a grasp of the possibilities and the limitations of international law such as it was proposed to enact for the first time with any prospect of its being observed, an imagination warmed by sympathy and stirred by traditions of freedom. In his hands the plan of ending war by arbitration became a wider and vastly more stimulating scheme. He laid down these propositions:

That every people has a right to choose the sovereignty under which it will live.

LEADER OF POLAND'S ARMY.
General Haller (centre), the distinguished commander of the Polish Army Corps in France, with his Staff about to leave Paris for Poland.

OFF TO DEFEND THEIR NATIVE LAND.
Men of the Polish Army leaving Paris for Poland, April, 1919. It was finally settled by agreement that the Poles should not land at Danzig, but should cross Germany in closed trains.

That the small States of the world have a right to enjoy the same respect for their sovereignty and for their territorial integrity as that which the great and powerful nations expect and insist upon.

That the world has a right to be free from every disturbance to its peace which has its origin in aggression and in disregard of the rights of peoples and nations.

Putting forward these principles, Mr. Wilson left the details of machinery to be settled at a later date. But he made it clear that when these details were settled the American Government would be represented at the Conference table. He abandoned the view hitherto paramount in the United States that it was to the interest of that country to hold aloof from the political troubles of Europe, to avoid those "entangling alliances" against which Washington in his last public words solemnly warned his countrymen. This resolve, together with the Monroe Doctrine, had for over a century formed the basis of American foreign policy. "We leave the Old World alone. The Old World must leave us alone." The "hands off America" doctrine of President Monroe followed reasonably enough the line of action laid down by Washington.

Originally enunciated in order to prevent the European monarchs from sending troops to South America to support the rule of Spain, this doctrine had been extended by Mr. Wilson himself when he **U.S. President** told European capitalists that they need **and world-safety** not hope to exploit any longer the South American States, that the Washington Government would not allow concessions to be supported by force of arms, and that those who wished to invest money in South America must take the same course as they took in the United States.

Now, however, yielding to the call of the international spirit, and putting the safety of the world above merely national, above even Continental, interests, Mr. Wilson offered the abandonment of his country's isolation. He said that the United States was ready to assist in establishing a League of Peace, to enter it, and to lend its power for the enforcement of its decisions. In the settlement after the war it would aim, the President announced, at creating a "universal association of nations to maintain inviolate the security of the highways of the seas for the common unhindered use of all the nations of the world, and to prevent any war begun either contrary to treaty covenants or without warning and full submission of the cause to the opinion of the world." This, he pointed out, would be "a virtual guarantee of territorial integrity and political independence."

GREAT PIANIST AND PATRIOTIC PREMIER.
Poland's delegates at the Hôtel Wagram, Paris, where they arrived in April, 1919, to discuss their country's future. Left to right: M. Strakacz (Secretary), M. Paderewski (Prime Minister), M. Cilchanowski, Major Jwanenski.

Here was an unexpected ally for those who had been talking about a League of Nations. Here there was formulated in outline an international Charter of Right. Immediately the League came down from the heights of vague and misty idealism into the region of practical politics. By his Washington speech President Wilson opened a new era, and it became for the moment the one topic upon which newspapers commented and political discussion turned.

Amid a perfunctory chorus for the most part of agreement there were mingled some honest expressions of scepticism. History was called in to prove the fatuity of such plans. It was shown that all schemes of the kind in the past had been without effect. In the seventeenth century there was a French design for the establishment of universal peace.

DANZIG, CITY OF CONTENTION.
Striking view of the quays along the Vistula at Danzig. The Poles claimed this city, but the Peace Conference decided to constitute it a "Free City," under the guarantee of the League of Nations.

Drawn up by Sully, the Minister of Henry IV., its aim was the securing of that monarch's preponderance in Europe by the destruction of the power of the Hapsburgs, his chief rivals. France, England, Denmark, and Sweden were to form an alliance and to attack Austria, which would then be broken up. The impudence of calling this a "project for peace" did not conceal its true objective, the aggrandisement of France. It came to naught. No more fortunate was the plan elaborated about a hundred years later by the Abbé de St. Pierre. This, too, aimed at securing for France a preponderant influence in the affairs of Europe.

The French had been stirred by the memories of the *Pax Romana*, of that long period of "world-peace through world-empire" in which for nearly four hundred years the whole civilised society of Europe lived under uniform laws and institutions, with one common language, one currency, and one commercial system—the system, currency, language, laws, and institutions of Rome. The ambition to repeat the work of the Romans, no unworthy ambition, haunted the minds of the French. It did much to reconcile them to the cost and the bloodshed of the wars of Napoleon. It did seem at one time as if his Empire might do what Rome had done. In his Memoirs written at St. Helena he declared that this was his intent. He hoped to gather the **France and the** nations into a confederation held together **Pax Romana** by "unity of laws, principles, opinions, sentiments, and interests," with France at the head to watch over the "great European family." It is conceivable that such a *Pax Napoleonica* might have been a good thing for Europe, but by that date liberty had taken too firm a hold of men's minds to allow them even to consider a League on these lines.

Yet when Waterloo swept away the hopes of Napoleon there was set on foot another League which was quite as hostile to freedom as his could have been. The Emperors of Russia and Austria concocted with the King of Prussia, under the guidance of that fanatic for authority, Metternich,

a plot to crush all attempts at substituting constitutional systems for irresponsible despotism. This plot is very often called the Holy Alliance. That is incorrect. The Holy Alliance was an idea which occurred to the simple and on the whole kindly mind of the Emperor Alexander I. of Russia. He sent round to his fellow-sovereigns, including the King of England, George IV., a document filled with fine sentiments and windy aspirations. They none of them knew what to make of his strange proceeding. Metternich made the characteristic remark: "It seems quite clear that the Emperor's mind must be affected. Peace and goodwill engross all his thoughts, and I have found him of late friendly and reasonable on all points." Nothing came of this proposal, but at the Congress of Aix-la-Chapelle in 1818 the idea of the Holy Alliance was transformed into a basis for the league of monarchs against liberty which, though aimed in appearance at preventing war, filled Europe with trouble of one kind and another for a hundred years.

"Though no open declaration," wrote C. A. Fyffe in his "History of Modern Europe," "was made against constitutional forms, every sovereign and every Minister who attended the Conference left it with the resolution to draw the reins of government tighter." In the course of the strugggle between Imperialism or self-imposed authority and Democracy, the rule of the people, Napoleon III. was one of the sovereigns who consciously set himself to build up a system of international relationships similar to those of the "Roman Peace."

Again it was France which was to be Rome's successor. Again the plan came to an ignoble and disastrous end.

These failures to set up a European partnership in place of greedy and suspicious competition were used by those who disbelieved in a League of Nations as arguments to prove that President Wilson was, to borrow an expressive American slang-phrase, "talking through his hat." The reply to them was that in the past all schemes of the kind had been based upon the principle of authority, upon the theory that men must be driven like cattle, that they could not decide for and take care of themselves. That theory had crumbled. On another occasion Mr. Wilson replied to all such criticisms: **Why past** "There are two theories of Government," **schemes failed** he said, "which have been contending with each other ever since Government began. I am one of those who absolutely reject the trustee theory, the guardianship theory. I never found a man who knew how to take care of me, and, reasoning from that point out, I conjecture that there is not any man who knows how to take care of all the people of the United States. The concern of patriotic men is to put Government on its right basis by substituting the popular will for the rule of guardians, the processes of common council for those of private arrangement."

It was also pointed out that proposals for leagues in the past had been actuated by the desire of sovereigns to extend or, at all events, to keep their authority. It was left for the Great War to provoke a wish for a League, not of monarchs or Governments, but of peoples, and it was by President Wilson's speech at the meeting of the League to Enforce Peace on May 27th, 1916, that the wish first began to take shape as a practical possibility.

Up to this time no statesman of the first rank had openly proclaimed his belief that a League of Nations was attainable. From now on there was unceasing discussion of its possibility, though it did not attract wide attention from public men in Great Britain for nearly two years. In March, 1918, there was a debate on the scheme in the House of Lords. Lord

President Wilson, Father of the League of Nations, making his speech at the third full session of the Inter-Allied Conference, on February 14th, 1919, when he read the text of the historic and epoch-marking Covenant.

M. Venizelos (Greece) with M. Pichon (France), first President of the Organising Committee of the League of Nations which worked out the details of the world's Peace Charter, at the Hôtel de Crillon, Paris.

Members of the Committee that drew up the Covenant of the League of Nations, which was presented to the Peace Conference and adopted by it on April 28th, 1919. Seated (left to right): Viscount Chinda, Japan; next but one, M. Bourgeois, France; Lord Robert Cecil; Signor Orlando, Italy; next but one, M. Venizelos, Greece. Standing: Colonel House, U.S.A.; next but one, M. Vesnitch, Serbia; General Smuts, President Wilson, M. Hymans, Belgium; H. E. Wellington Koo, China. Inset: Sir Eric Drummond, First Secretary-General of the League of Nations.

MEN WHO FRAMED THE COVENANT OF THE LEAGUE OF NATIONS.

Parmoor opened it. The most weighty speech was made by Lord Loreburn, who said that, if Britain was to be a free country after the war, secret diplomacy must be abolished and a League of Nations must be set up. Again in June the House of Lords discussed the principle of the League and approved it. On this occasion Lord Curzon said he believed opinion in Britain was rather in advance of the opinion of any of our Allies, except in the United States. He thought we had better not go ahead too quickly or hurriedly or we might meet with a rebuff.

Shortly after this appeared a pamphlet by Lord Grey of Fallodon (Sir Edward Grey), in which he pleaded the cause of the League with vigour and persuasive argument. By degrees all the leaders of political groups made their professions of faith. Mr. Lloyd George was not until after the armistice very clear in his expressions. He said, on March 13th, 1918, that a real League of Nations would not come by talking about it. "That," he said, "is why it has not been given much prominence in our political speeches." And then he made his joke about the Kaiser's acceptance of the League idea and his offer to place Germany at the head of it being like "a dagger wrapped in the Sermon on the Mount." Later on Mr. Lloyd George said he was certainly one of those who believed in a League of Nations, but he hastened to add, "there are already two leagues of nations in existence—the first is the British Empire, and the second is the Great Alliance against the Central Powers." This left it doubtful whether he was with President Wilson and those who held that no League could be complete without Germany, or whether he favoured the formation

FIRST MEETING-PLACE OF THE LEAGUE.
Town Hall at Geneva where, it was announced, the first meeting of the League of Nations would take place in October, 1919, pending the erection of a suitable building as headquarters.

of a League by the Allied and Associated Governments, leaving Germany outside.

Mr. Balfour adopted the same enigmatic tone in the debate on the subject in the House of Commons on August 1st, 1918. He deprecated any attempt to formulate a League while the war continued. "The man who genuinely believes in a League of Nations," he said, "is, or ought to be, a most ardent advocate of pressing this war to a successful issue. It is only by our victory in this war that future wars can

be prevented ; only thus can we stabilise the machinery by which a League of Nations can be set up." Lord Robert Cecil was more encouraging. He agreed that the time to prepare a scheme had come, and that we ought to be ready with one for the end of the war. It was unfortunate that Lord Robert's opinion was not acted upon by the War Cabinet. The end of the war found them without any distinct or informed idea on the subject.

From that time onward Lord Robert Cecil became one of the mainstays of the League plan. When in November, 1918, he was installed as Chancellor of Birmingham University, he took this for the theme of his address. The Allies had in their hands, he told his audience, the political future of the whole world. The most glorious victory would be scarcely distinguishable from defeat unless thereby were laid the foundations of a lasting peace. It was more than questionable, he warned his hearers, whether permanent peace could be established on the basis of the world-domination of the Entente or any other group of Powers. World domination was only another term for international despotism, and, however benevolent such a despotism might be, it must be inconsistent with that liberty without which all other political advantages were insipid and not infrequently degrading. European civilisation, he declared, could hardly be relied on to withstand a repetition of four years of war. If, therefore, the League of Nations was a dream, it would be difficult to avoid despair.

The debate in the House of Commons proved that the public interest in the idea was strong. On July 18th Mr. Bonar Law had declined to give a day for a discussion ; but this decision was altered within a fortnight. This step was taken clearly in deference to popular desire. Mr. Asquith did not take part in the conversation at Westminster, but in speeches made by him outside the House of Commons he strongly supported the formation of a League. Before the war ended he asserted that, as a matter of practical reasoning and common-sense, a League of Nations stood on a more solid foundation than any of the transient combinations between the Great Powers in all history.

GENEVA : SHOWING ROUSSEAU'S ISLAND AND MONT BLANC.
Geneva, city of great historical associations, and headquarters of the League of Nations. In this beautiful picture is seen the clear-blue Lake with Rousseau's Island, named after the French writer who lived here and wrote about the city in his "Nouvelle Héloïse." In the background is the cathedral associated with the reformer Calvin, while at the extreme left rises the snow-capped peak of Mont Blanc, some sixty miles distant.

He recalled his declaration of September, 1914, " that our aim should be, not merely the defeat of our enemies, but to bring into existence, not as an abstraction or as an ideal, what Mr. Gladstone described as ' the assertion of public right as the law of Europe and the world.' " Mr. Asquith did not, however, claim to have forestalled Pre-

General Smuts on the League sident Wilson, to whom he gave credit " for having associated himself, and the great people of whom he was the spokesman, with the attainment of the ideal which now goes by the name of the League of Nations."

General Smuts was the member of the inner circle of government who took most interest in what he called " President Wilson's programme for a League of Nations for world peace." In a speech made just after the signing of the armistice he said that one of the circumstances which made the League " a sheer practical necessity " was the duty incumbent upon the Allies of providing with food all those countries which were threatened with disaster through

object of the Governments associated against Germany, and of the nations whom they govern, to achieve by the coming settlements a secure and lasting peace, it will be necessary that all who sit down at the peace table shall come ready and willing to pay the price, the only price, that will procure it ; and ready and willing also to create in some virile fashion the only instrumentality by which it can be made certain that the agreements of peace will be honoured and fulfilled. That price is impartial justice in every item of the settlement, no matter whose interest is crossed. That indispensable instrumentality is a League of Nations. And, as I see it, the constitution of that League of Nations, and the clear definition of its objects, must be a part—in a sense the most essential part—of the peace settlement itself. It cannot be formed now. If formed now, it would be merely a new alliance, confined to the nations associated against a common enemy. It is not likely that it could be formed after the settlement. It is necessary to guarantee the peace, and the peace cannot be guaranteed as an afterthought."

MEMBERS OF THE IMPERIAL WAR CONFERENCE IN LONDON, JUNE, 1918.
From left to right (standing) : Mr. A. Meighen, Canada ; Sir Joseph Ward, New Zealand ; Mr. N. W. Rowell, Canada ; Sir G. V. Fiddes ; Mr. W. A. S. Hewins ; Sir G. Aston ; Sir S. P. Sinha, India ; Mr. Burton, South Africa ; Mr. J. A. Calder, Canada ; Mr. Lambert ; and Mr. Harding. Seated : Mr. W. F. Lloyd, Newfoundland ; Mr. W. F. Massey, New Zealand ; the Maharajah of Patiala, India ; Sir Robert Borden, Canada ; Mr. W. Long ; Mr. W. M. Hughes, Australia ; General Smuts, South Africa ; Mr. (afterwards Sir Joseph) Cook, Australia ; and Mr. E. S. Montagu.

shortage of the necessaries of life. He suggested, also, that all countries, not only those of the Allies, but former neutrals and enemies as well, would have to be rationed with raw materials during the period of economic reconstruction. In a pamphlet which he issued early in 1919 he set forth in detail a scheme for a League, and made an earnest appeal to all thoughtful minds to realise that, unless the old conditions of statecraft were changed, " people simply will not stand it, and the menace of the great anti-State movement, now finding expression in Bolshevism, will become as great a danger as war itself. For there is no doubt," he continued, in an eloquent survey of the factors in world unrest, " that mankind is once more on the move. The very foundations have been shaken, and things are again fluid. The tents have been struck, and the great caravan of humanity is once more on the march. Vast social and industrial changes are coming, perhaps upheavals which may in their magnitude and effects be comparable to war itself. A steadying, controlling, regulating influence will be required to give stability to progress, and to remove that wasteful friction which has dissipated so much social force in the past, and in this war more than ever before."

Meantime, another speech on the subject of the League had been made by President Wilson. On September 27th, 1918, he said : " If it be, in deed and in truth, the common

Further, Mr. Wilson declared that within the general and common family of the League of Nations there could be no alliances or special covenants and understandings. Nor could there be within the League any special selfish economic combination, nor the employment of any form of economic boycott or exclusion, except as the power of economic penalty, by exclusion from the markets of the world, might be vested in the League of Nations itself, as a means of control and discipline.

On the Continent there was, as Lord Curzon had noted, a decided backwardness in falling into line with President Wilson's ideas. There were men in France, like M. Léon Bourgeois, who had been **Unity of confidence** advocates of a League for years, but it won **necessary** no sympathy from M. Clemenceau. Nor was it received with more than lukewarm interest in Italy. The Latin temperament is sceptical of new ideas, and inclines to the belief that bureaucracy is needed for the purposes of order, and that while democracy is useful in theory as a theme for speeches, it does not work well in practice. The smaller nations showed that they were following the development of the League principle with attention, and also with some fear as to how it would affect them. The Vatican approved. Japan's Foreign Minister, Viscount Uchida, welcomed the prospect, but warned the world that no League would be of

DUKE OF CONNAUGHT AT COLOGNE.
Visit of, the Duke of Connaught (second from the right) to some of the boats of the British Rhine Flotilla at Cologne in May, 1919.

from being overwhelmed by the tide of world ideas and humanitarianism."

Mr. Taft steadily resisted all efforts to detach him from support of the President. He travelled all over the country making speeches in favour of the League. In San Francisco he called Mr. Lodge and those who were associated with him " reactionaries." A voice from the auditorium shouted, " You were a reactionary once." Mr. Taft replied, good-humouredly, " I know more now." He insisted that the League was not a party issue, and, so far as could be seen, carried the mass of his hearers with him. Mr. Root said, in the spring of 1919, that he did not see much controversy among the American people as to the desirability of an effective or international organisation to preserve the peace of the

any use unless there was among its members a complete unity of confidence in one another. The *noblesse oblige* of the West or the *bushido* of the East must permeate and guide the action of any such association of peoples. Distrust and suspicion must be left outside the door.

In the United States there began to be, as time went on, two currents of opinion. One was strongly in favour of the President's plan. The other deprecated any haste, and was dubious about the wisdom of opening the door to any possibility of European nations interfering in American affairs. There were, indeed, four classes of objectors. There were those who held that the Monroe Doctrine must be maintained in its integrity. There were those who asked sceptically whether too much was not being expected from human nature. The Republican Party leaders were some of them prompted to oppose the scheme because it was put forward by a Democrat President, who had excluded them from any share in the management of the war. Finally, the pacifists disliked intensely the proposal to enforce the decrees of the League by armed might.

The case against the League was stated with characteristic vehemence by Mr. Roosevelt, and after his death was taken up by Senator Lodge, Senator Sherman, and **U.S. opponents** Senator Reed. " Who dares to take from **of the League** the American people," asked Mr. Reed, " its right to control America ? " The result of the November elections to Congress which gave the Republican Party a majority, encouraged the opposition, but it was suggested also that there was something more than party politics behind it.

A business man in California, writing in an English review, pointed out that Mr. Lodge and Mr. Sherman represented the special interests which had not been eliminated from American politics : " Lodge is from Massachusetts, controlled by the Woollen Trust, Rubber Trust, and what is left of the Hartford and Newhaven Octopus " (a railway company which had exercised a sinister influence). " Sherman is from Illinois, not yet freed from the grip of the Meat and Steel Trusts. They are grasping at anything to save them

BRITISH TANK IN OCCUPIED GERMANY.
On the Rhine bank at Cologne, showing one of the British Tanks attached to the Army of Occupation. The mechanical monster naturally excited the interest of German juveniles.

world, or of America doing her full share towards the establishment and maintenance of such an organisation. Of four hundred prominent ministers of religion who received circulars inviting their support only four refused to give it. Two were Quakers who could not agree to the employment of armed force by the nations composing the League. The other two said they thought the proposal was " inopportune." When President Wilson came to Europe in December he seemed, in spite of the Congressional elections, to have the bulk of the people with him.

He continued to put the creation of the League in the first place among the matters which the Peace Conference had to discuss. He explained with greater clearness what his proposal aimed at. At the Lord Mayor of London's luncheon in his honour he showed how wide he expected the scope of the League to be :

As I have conversed with the soldiers, I have been more and more aware that they fought for something which not all of them had defined, but which all of them recognised the moment you stated it to them. They fought to do away with the old order and to establish a new one. The centre and characteristic of the old order was that unstable thing which we used to call the balance of power. It is very interesting to observe how from every quarter, from every sort of mind, from every sort of counsel there comes the suggestion that there must be now, not the balance of power, not one powerful group of nations set off against another, but a single overwhelmingly powerful group of nations which shall be the trustee of the peace of the world. . . .

When war began the thought of a League of Nations was indulgently considered as an interesting thought of closeted students. Now we find the practical leading minds of the world determined to get·it. No such sudden and potent union of purpose has ever been witnessed in the world before.

A few days later, demanding that there should be open covenants of peace, the President threw a direct challenge to those who still clung to the old diplomatic methods. " The day of conquest and aggrandisement is gone by," he said. " So is also the day of secret covenants entered into in the interest of some particular Governments, and likely at some unlooked-for moment to upset the peace of the world. It is this happy fact," he went on, " now clear to the view of every public man whose thoughts do not still linger in an age that is dead and gone, which makes it **Peace Conference** possible for every nation whose purposes are **accepts the scheme** consistent with justice and the peace of the world to avow the objects it has in view."

The Inter-Allied Conference to decide what terms of peace should be presented to Germany and her supporters met in January, two months after the armistice had been signed. At the second meeting, on the 25th, Mr. Wilson proposed to the Conference to resolve that it was essential to the maintenance of the world settlement that a League of Nations should be created, that its creation must be treated as an integral part of the general Treaty of Peace, and that it should be open to every civilised nation which could be relied upon to promote its objects. In making this proposal Mr. Wilson once more set forth the far-reaching effect which he anticipated for the League.

We are here to see that the very foundations of this war are swept away. These foundations were (1) the private choice of small coteries

ALLIED ARMY LEADERS AT COLOGNE.
Marshal Foch with General Sir William Robertson, Commander-in-Chief of the British Army of Occupation on the Rhine, during the visit which the great French leader paid to Cologne in May, 1919.

BRITISH NAVAL VISIT TO PARIS.
Admiral Beatty, with General Berdoulat, Military Governor of Paris, at the march-past of British sailors during the visit of a detachment from the Grand Fleet to the French capital in April, 1919.

of civil rulers and military staffs, and (2) the power of a small body of men to work their will, using mankind as pawns in the game. Nothing less than the emancipation of the world from these things will accomplish peace.

The Conference accepted the League of Nations scheme in principle and named a Committee to work out the details.

This Committee met ten times in eleven days, and completed its task in a period of not more than thirty hours. Its meetings were held at the Hôtel Crillon, on the Place de la Concorde, in the salon of the suite of rooms occupied by Colonel and Mrs. House. Here at a big round table sat the nineteen members of the Committee ; in the corners of the room were smaller tables for secretaries and translators. Every speech was translated as it was being made. The translator followed the speaker only a sentence or two behind. That sounds as if the result might be confusing, but it worked well. All the arrangements were designed for getting the work done as quickly as **League of Nations** possible. Mr. Wilson had to go back to the **Committee** United States for a few weeks, and before he went he was anxious to present the report of the Committee to the Conference. He presided at all the meetings save one, and proved himself adept in smoothing the course of business and preventing unnecessary delay. He knew when to encourage speakers to go on, and when to suggest tactfully that they were wasting time. He was always good-humoured and often witty. When some proposal was made which seemed to him to aim at binding the hands of future ages, he remarked, with a smile : " Gentlemen, I have no doubt that the next generation will be made up of men as intelligent as you or I, and I think we can trust the League to manage its own affairs."

From the final meeting on February 13th the President was kept away by the necessity of attending somewhere else on matters of urgency. On this occasion his place was taken by Lord Robert Cecil. He, with M. Venizelos, M. Vesnitch,

Mr. G. N. Barnes, in the name of the workers of Great Britain, "salutes the dawn" heralded by the League of Nations. Prominent men in this picture (from right to left) include Lord Robert Cecil, Mr. Barnes (standing), Mr. A. J. Balfour, M. Dutasta (behind Mr. Balfour), M. Clemenceau, President Wilson, Mr. R. Lansing, Mr. H. White, and Colonel House.

M. Léon Bourgeois, addressing the Conference, said that there was reason to hope that the machinery of the League which was proposed would succeed in stopping war, because it was based on the principles of justice. Those present at the table included (from left to right) Baron Sonnino, Signor Orlando, M. Bourgeois (standing), M. Jules Cambon, M. André Tardieu, M. Klotz, and M. Pichon.

PLENARY SITTING OF THE PARIS PEACE CONFERENCE AT WHICH THE COVENANT OF THE LEAGUE OF NATIONS WAS PRESENTED, FEBRUARY 14TH, 1919.

Serbian Minister in Paris, and M. Larnaude, Dean of the Faculty of Law in the Sorbonne University, had made the final draft, and the Committee sat late to finish it. At a quarter to eight Lord Robert read out the last article of the proposed Covenant and asked, "Is there any objection to that?" A momentary pause followed. "If not, it is adopted," he said. And then, with a sigh of satisfaction and relief: "Gentlemen, our work is done."

Next day, February 14th, Mr. Wilson read the draft Covenant to the third full session of the Inter-Allied Conference. He drew attention to the number of human beings (twelve hundred millions) represented by the delegates of the fourteen States who had served on the Committee, and added, "When you think of the variety of circumstances among these fourteen nationalities, there is great significance in the fact that we have reached a unanimous result, for that means a union of will for our common purpose that cannot be resisted and one that, I dare say, no nation will ever take the risk of resisting." He warned the Conference that the world would not be satisfied with merely official guidance; the machinery of the League must not be composed entirely of officials. "A living thing is born in this document," he said, tapping the paper he held, "and we must see that the clothes we put on it do not hamper it." Finally, he pointed out that armed force was in the background of the constitution of the League. "If the moral force of the world will not suffice, physical force shall, but only as a last resource."

The draft Covenant provided for the setting up of two bodies, the first called the Body of Delegates, the second to be known as the Executive Council.

Each State which belonged to the League to send three delegates to the Body, and these delegates to admit other States to the League by a two-thirds majority vote; also to make amendments to the League constitution, and recommendations as to the settlement of disputes referred to it. This Body to meet as often as it desired and to be mainly an organ of discussion.

Action to be taken by the Executive Council, composed of representatives of America, France, Great Britain, Italy, and Japan, and of four other States to be selected by the Body of Delegates.

The signatory Powers to agree that they would in no case resort to war without submitting the matter in dispute either to arbitration or to the inquiry by the Executive Council. Three months to elapse between the announcement of the result of arbitration or inquiry and the declaration of war.

A Court of International Justice to be created for the consideration, of disputes. Any Power which disregarded its findings or broke faith in any way to be deemed to have committed an act of war against all the other members of the League, which would thereupon break off all relations and consider themselves at war.

Recognising the limitation of armaments to be desirable, the Covenant referred this matter to the Executive Council for the formulation of plans.

The German colonies and certain territories formerly part of the Turkish Empire to be administered by "advanced nations which by reason of their resources, their experience, or their geographical position could best undertake this responsibility." These nations to act under Mandates from the League, being known as Mandatory Powers.

"A living thing is born"

A permanent Bureau of Labour to be established for the securing and maintaining of fair and humane conditions of work for men, women, and children in all countries.

Freedom of transit and equitable treatment for the commerce of all States belonging to the League to be arranged for.

All treaties entered into by any member of the League to be registered forthwith with the Secretary-General of the League and as soon as possible published by him. All engagements inconsistent with the obligations of membership of the League to be considered as ceasing to exist.

The draft Covenant was at once published and called forth a great deal of criticism. The French demanded more safeguards against the possibilities of their being attacked again by Germany. The Germans described the draft as the result of a compromise, and as having, therefore, merely a provisional character. Many of those in Britain and in America who had been most eager in their support of the League as proposed by the President were inclined to say that the whole project had been wrecked by the "old gangs." Labour was frankly sceptical. Even Lord Bryce, who professed to be hopeful, pointed out that the scheme was

"in some points vague and in some obscure; that is to say, it is doubtful what precisely are the cases which the words are intended to cover, and it is not always clear what the words mean in their application to these particular cases."

Strong objection was raised at a Special National Conference arranged by the Trade Union Congress and the Labour Party to the constitution of the League as proposed by the Covenant. It was urged that the delegates should be chosen from the national Parliaments by some such method as proportional representation so as to secure an accurate reflection of public opinion; that the Executive Council should not be independent of the Body of Delegates; and that in all things the latter should be the more powerful organ of the League. As to armaments, it was suggested by the Conference that their manufacture should be under the direct control of the League,

AMERICAN PEACE MISSION IN PARIS.
The Hôtel de Crillon, on the Place de la Concorde, which was the Headquarters of the United States Peace Mission. It was there that the Committee appointed by the Peace Conference drafted the famous Covenant which was duly adopted.

that no armies should be raised by conscription, and that the Covenant should declare any security for peace which did not include national disarmament to be unreal. It was also claimed that, on the International Bureau of Labour, Labour should be directly and adequately represented, and the interests of women also. Finally, the Conference agreed that the Covenant of the League ought to form part of the preliminary Treaty of Peace.

In the United States there was a fresh outburst of opposition to the plan of a League in any form. Some denounced the whole idea. Some concealed their desire to destroy the scheme under a pretended anxiety to amend the Covenant. Senator Lodge called its provisions vague and loosely drawn, with numbers of loopholes which would cause misunderstandings, disputes, and other wars. He suggested that it ought to be altered so as to allow of the retention of the Monroe Doctrine; to prevent any interference in any country's internal affairs; to permit any nation to withdraw from the League, and to make clearer the language used about the use of troops for the enforcement of its decrees. Senator Borah appealed to the **President Wilson** distrust of Britain which lies deep in so **and his critics** many American — and especially Irish-American — hearts, and which has often proved useful for election purposes. The proposed constitution of the League was, he declared, "the greatest triumph that British diplomacy had won in three centuries of British diplomatic life."

During his short visit home in February and March, President Wilson replied to these and other criticisms, and appealed eloquently to the mass of his fellow-countrymen not to disappoint the expectations of Europe. Immediately after his arrival at Boston he addressed a meeting called to welcome him home. In this speech he said that American prestige had risen very high "because there is no nation in

Right : View of the same shop, taken from the same point, after the recovery of Lesquin. All the material and machines had been removed by the Germans, who when forced to retreat reduced the place to ruins.

One of the Thomson-Houston engineering workshops at Lesquin-lez-Lille as it was before the German invasion in October, 1914. The plant was of the most powerful kind, and over a thousand workpeople were employed.

Right : The devastation caused by the Germans when compelled to retreat. They stripped the zinc works, destroyed every one of the machines that could not be removed, and demolished all the chimneys by mines.

The largest zinc works in France, at Auby, near Douai, as they appeared when captured by the Germans in August, 1914. On October 1st, 1918, the buildings remained undamaged and the thirty-three chimney shafts still intact.

METHODICAL DESTRUCTION OF FRENCH FACTORIES BY THE GERMAN INVADERS.

Europe which suspects the motives of the United States," and because Europe had seen that America "not only held ideals, but acted ideals." This confidence which the people of the United States had won laid a burden upon them. Did they mean to take it up? If America failed the world now, men would be thrown back into the bitterness of despair, all nations would set up hostile camps again, the new States would be left unprotected and helpless. The arrangements which were being made in Paris could not stand for a generation unless they were guaranteed by the united force of the world.

Again, on March 6th, just before he returned to Europe, the President spoke at a meeting in the New York Opera House. His tone was triumphant, but it seemed to hide some doubt as to the light in which the nation regarded the League and to force the note of satisfaction so as to discourage its opponents. He declared his conviction that an overwhelming majority of the American people was in favour of the League with all its implications. He appealed from the politicians to the people.

The men who utter the criticisms, he urged, "have never felt the great pulse of the heart of the world. Those who suffer see. The only vision has been that of the people. What the peoples of Europe are thinking is this: If there is right in the world, stop thinking about the rival interest of nations and think about men, women, and children throughout the world. It would be fatal for Americans to ignore that. It would be a disaster if they did not help the world. We should of a sudden have become the most contemptible of nations. It is inconceivable that we should disappoint them, and we shall not. The day will come when Americans will look back

with pride that they have been privileged to make the sacrifice necessary in order to combine their might and their moral powers with the cause of justice for men of every kind everywhere."

With the idea of discovering whether the President was right in claiming that he had on his side "the overwhelming majority," the "Literary Digest" of New York inquired of 1,300 odd American editors, "Do you favour the proposed League?" Of the replies only 181 said "No." There were 718 editors who said "Yes," and 478 who said they were in favour of a League, but thought that the Covenant needed amending. In the work of amendment Mr. Wilson joined as soon as he reached Paris, and at the fifth plenary session of the Peace Conference, held at the Quai d'Orsay,

ALLIED ARBITERS BETWEEN THE POLES AND THE CZECHS.
Meeting of the Inter-Allied Commission appointed by the Paris Peace Conference early in 1919 to go to Teschen, in Austrian Silesia, to settle the differences between the Poles and the Czechs. Among those present were Mr. Lord and Gen. Kernan, U.S.; M. Noulens and Gen. Niessel, France; and Gen. Botha and Sir Esme Howard, Great Britain.

Paris, on April 28th, 1919, the amended Covenant of the League of Nations was, upon his motion, adopted.

COVENANT OF THE LEAGUE OF NATIONS.

PREAMBLE.—This defines the object of the League as the achievement of international peace and security by the acceptance of obligations not to resort to war, the prescription of open, just, and honourable relations between nations, the firm establishment of the understandings of international law as the actual rule of conduct among Governments, and the maintenance of justice and a scrupulous respect for all treaty obligations in the dealings of organised peoples with one another.

ARTICLE I.—The original members shall be those of the signatories named in the Annex, and such other States so named as shall accede unreservedly to the Covenant by a declaration deposited with the secretariat within two months of the Covenant coming into force. Any fully self-governing State, dominion, or colony may become a member, two-thirds of the Assembly agreeing, on giving effective guarantees of its intention to observe its international obligations and accepting such regulations as the League may prescribe regarding its military and naval forces and armaments. Withdrawal from the League is permissible after two years' notice and the fulfilment of all international obligations.

II.—The governing body shall consist of an Assembly and a Council with a permanent secretariat.

III.—The Assembly shall consist of members' representatives, meet at stated intervals as occasion may require, and may deal with any matter within the scope of the League or affecting the peace of the world, each member to have one vote and not more than three representatives.

IV.—The Council shall consist of representatives of the U.S.A., the British Empire, France, Italy, and Japan, with those of four other members selected by the Assembly from time to time. Pending this selection, representatives of Belgium, Brazil, Greece, and Spain shall be members of the Council. The majority of the Assembly approving,

the Council may name additional members of the League whose representatives shall always be members of the Council, and, with like approval, may increase the number of League members to be selected by the Assembly for representation on the Council. The Council shall meet as occasion may require and at least once a year, and may deal with any matter defined as within the scope of the Assembly.

Any League member not represented on the Council shall be invited to send a representative to sit as a member of the Council when any matter specially affecting that member's interests is under consideration. Each League member represented on the Council shall have one vote and not more than one representative.

V.—Except where the Covenant provides otherwise, decisions of Assembly or Council shall require the agreement of all representatives present. All matters of procedure, including appointment of committees, shall be regulated by Assembly or Council, and may be decided by a majority of representatives present. The first meetings of Assembly and Council shall be summoned by the President of the U.S.A.

VI.—The permanent secretariat at the seat of the League shall comprise a Secretary-General and secretaries and staff as required, the first Secretary-General being named in the Annex, his successors being appointed by the Council with the approval of the majority of the Assembly. The Council approving, the Secretary-General shall appoint secretaries and staff, and act at all meetings of Assembly and Council, the expenses of the secretariat being borne by League members according to the apportionment of expenses of the International Bureau of the Universal Postal Union.

VII.—The League's seat is at Geneva but the Council may establish it elsewhere, and all positions under it or in connection with it shall be open equally to men and women. Its representatives and officials, when on League business, shall enjoy

diplomatic privileges, and its occupied buildings or other property shall be inviolable.

VIII.—The Council, taking account of the geographical situation and circumstances of each League member, shall formulate plans for the reduction of armaments to the lowest point consistent with national safety and the common enforcement of international obligations, for consideration and action of the several Governments, such plans to be subject to revision at least every ten years and after adoption not exceeded without the Council's concurrence. The Council shall advise how the evil effects attendant upon private manufacture of munitions and implements of war can be prevented with due regard to the needs of League members unable to manufacture sufficient for their safety. League members undertake to interchange full and frank information as to their armaments, military and naval programmes, and industries adaptable to warlike purposes.

IX.—A permanent commission shall advise the Council on the execution of the provisions of Articles I. and VIII. and on military and naval questions generally.

X.—League members undertake to respect and preserve as against external aggression the territorial integrity and existing political independence of all members, and in case of aggression or threat or danger of it the Council shall advise upon the means by which this obligation shall be fulfilled.

XI.—Any war or threat of war is a matter of concern to the whole League, which shall act as may be deemed wise or effectual to safeguard peace; and on emergency the Secretary-General shall, on any member's request, summon the Council. Each member has the right to bring to the attention of Assembly or Council anything threatening international peace or the good understanding on which peace depends.

XII.—League members agree to submit any dispute between them likely to lead to a rupture to arbitration or the Council, and not to resort to var until three months after the arbitrators' award or the Council's report; the award to be made within a reasonable time and the report within six months after submission of the dispute.

XIII.—League members agree to submit to arbitration the whole subject matter of any dispute between them that diplomacy cannot satisfactorily settle. Disputes as to the interpretation of a treaty, any question of international law, any fact which if established would constitute a breach of international obligation, or the nature of reparation for any such breach are generally suitable for arbitration. The court for consideration of any such dispute shall be agreed on by the parties or stipulated in any convention existing between them. League members agree to carry out in full good faith any award and not to resort to war against a member complying therewith. The Council shall propose what steps should be taken to give effect to any award not carried out.

XIV.—The Council shall formulate and submit plans for a Permanent Court of International Justice competent to hear and determine any international dispute the parties submit to it, and advise upon any question referred to it by Council or Assembly.

XV.—League members agree to submit to the Council, through its Secretary-General, any critical dispute between them not submitted to arbitration, communicating to the Secretary-General, as promptly as possible, all relevant facts and papers, publication of which the Council may forthwith direct. If the Council effects a settlement, facts and explanations regarding it shall be made public as the Council may deem appropriate. In the event of no settlement the Council, unanimously or by a majority vote, shall issue a report and the recommendations deemed just and proper. Any League member represented on the Council may publish the facts and its conclusions. If only representatives on the Council of one or more of the parties refrain from agreement with the Council's report League members agree not to go to war with any party complying with the recommendations of the report, and if the Council fails to reach a report unanimously agreed to by its members other than representatives of one or more of the parties, League members reserve the right to take such action as they shall consider necessary to maintain right and justice.

If the dispute is claimed by one of the parties and found by the Council to arise out of a matter within the domestic jurisdiction of that party the Council shall so report and make no recommendation as to settlement. The Council may refer the dispute to the Assembly at the request of either party within fourteen days after the submission of the dispute to the Council. In any case referred to the Assembly all provisions of this Article and Article XII. relating to action and powers of the Council shall so apply to the Assembly, provided the Assembly's report, if concurred in by representatives of those League members on the Council and of a majority of other League members exclusive in each case of representatives of the parties, shall have the same force as a Council report concurred in by all its members other than representatives of one or more of the parties.

XVI.—Any League member resorting to war in disregard of Articles XII., XIII., or XV., shall be deemed to have committed an act of war against all other members of the League, which undertake immediately to subject it to severance of all trade or financial relations, prohibition of all intercourse between their nationals and nationals of the covenant-breaker, and the prevention of all intercourse between the nationals of the latter and those of any other State, whether League member or not; and the Council shall recommend to the Governments concerned what effective force League members shall severally contribute to the armed forces to be used to protect the League Covenants.

Members further agree mutually to support one another in financial and economic measures taken under this article to minimise loss and inconvenience from the above measures and in resisting any measures aimed at one of their number by the covenant-breaker, and to take steps to afford passage through their territory to forces of any League members co-operating to protect League Covenants. Any League member which has violated any League Covenant may be declared no longer a member by a vote concurred in by representatives of all other League members represented on the Council.

XVII.—In any dispute between a League member and a State not a member or between States not members, the State or States not members shall be invited to accept obligations or membership for the purposes of the dispute upon conditions the Council may deem just, and, the invitation being accepted, the provisions of Articles XII. to XVI. inclusive shall be applied with such modifications as the Council may deem necessary, the Council immediately instituting an inquiry and recommending such action as may seem best. In case a State refuses such invitation and resorts to war against a League member the provisions of Article XVI. shall be applicable against it; and if both parties refuse obligation of League membership the Council may take such measures and make such recommendations as will prevent hostilities and result in settlement.

XVIII.—Every treaty or international agreement hereafter entered into by any League member shall forthwith be registered with the secretariat, as soon as possible published by it, and not be binding until so registered.

XIX.—The Assembly may from time to time advise reconsideration by League members of treaties which have become inapplicable and consideration of conditions endangering peace.

XX.—League members severally agree that this Covenant abrogates all obligations or misunderstandings *inter se* inconsistent with its terms and solemnly undertake not hereafter to enter into any engagement inconsistent with its terms. Any member having before membership undertaken obligations inconsistent with the Covenant shall take immediate steps to procure release from such obligations.

XXI.—Nothing in the Covenant shall affect the validity of engagements such as treaties of arbitration or regional understandings like the Monroe Doctrine for maintaining peace.

XXII.—The well-being and development of colonies and territories inhabited by peoples unable to stand by themselves, which have ceased as a result of the late war to be under the States formerly governing them, form a sacred trust of civilisation, and their tutelage should be entrusted to advanced nations who, by reason of resources, experience, or geographical position, can best undertake this responsibility and are willing to accept it as mandataries of the League, the mandate differing according to development of the people, geographical situation, economic conditions, and similar circumstances.

Certain communities formerly of the Turkish Empire can be provisionally recognised subject to advice and assistance by a mandatary until such time as they are able to stand alone. Their wishes must be a principal consideration in the selection of the mandatary. Other peoples, especially of Central Africa, are at such a stage that the mandatary must be responsible for territorial administration under conditions guaranteeing freedom of conscience or religion subject only to maintenance of public order and morals, prohibition of abuses such as the slave trade, arms traffic, liquor traffic, and prevention of fortifications or military and naval bases and military training of natives for other than police purposes and territorial defence, and securing equal opportunities for the trade and commerce of other League members.

Territories such as S.W. Africa and certain of the S. Pacific Islands, owing to sparse population, small size, remoteness from centres of civilisation, geographical contiguity to territory of the mandatary and other circumstances, can be best administered under the laws of the mandatary as integral portions of its territory, subject to safeguards in the interests of the indigenous population.

Each mandatary shall annually report to the Council in reference to territory in its charge and its authority, control, or administration, if not previously agreed upon by League members, shall be explicitly defined in each case by the Council. A Permanent Commission shall receive and examine these reports and advise the Council on all matters relating to observance of the mandates.

XXIII.—Subject to and in accordance with the provisions of international conventions existing or hereafter agreed upon, League members will—

(*a*) Establish and maintain international organisations to secure and maintain fair and humane conditions of labour for men, women, and children in their own countries and all countries to which their commercial and industrial relations extend;

(*b*) Secure just treatment of natives of territories under their control;

(*c*) Entrust the League with general supervision over the execution of agreements with regard to traffic in women and children and traffic in opium and other dangerous drugs;

(*d*) Entrust the League with general supervision of trade in arms and ammunition with countries in which control of this traffic is necessary in the common interest;

(*e*) Make provision to secure and maintain freedom of communications and transit and equitable treatment for the commerce of all League members, the special needs of the regions devastated in the war of 1914-18 being borne in mind;

(*f*) Endeavour to take steps in matters of international concern for the prevention and control of disease.

XXIV.—The League shall direct all international bureaux already established by general treaties if the parties consent, and of all such bureaux and commissions for regulating matters of international interest hereafter constituted. In all such matters regulated by general conventions but not controlled by international bureaux or commissions the League secretariat, subject to consent of the Council and if desired by the parties, shall collect and distribute all relevant information and render any other assistance necessary or desirable. The Council may include as part of the expenses of the secretariat those of any bureaux or commission placed under League direction.

XXV.—League members agree to encourage and promote the establishment and co-operation of duly authorised voluntary national Red Cross organisations for the improvement of health, prevention of disease, and mitigation of suffering.

XXVI.—Amendments to this Covenant will take effect when ratified by members of the League whose representatives compose the Council and by a majority of such members whose representatives compose the Assembly. No such amendments shall bind any member which signifies its dissent therefrom, but in that case it shall cease to be a member of the League.

ANNEX.

1.—ORIGINAL MEMBERS OF THE LEAGUE OF NATIONS.

Signatories of the Treaty of Peace.

United States	Cuba.	Liberia.
of America.	Czecho-	Nicaragua.
Belgium.	Slovakia.	Panama.
Bolivia.	Ecuador.	Peru.
Brazil.	France.	Poland.
British Empire.	Greece.	Portugal.
Canada	Guatemala.	Rumania.
Australia,	Haiti.	Serbia.
South Africa.	Hedjaz.	Siam.
New Zealand.	Honduras.	Uruguay.
India.	Italy.	
China.	Japan.	

States Invited to Accede to the Covenant.

Argentine	Netherlands.	Spain.
Republic.	Norway.	Sweden.
Chile.	Paraguay.	Switzerland.
Colombia.	Persia.	Venezuela.
Denmark.	Salvador.	

2.—FIRST SECRETARY-GENERAL OF THE LEAGUE OF NATIONS.

The Hon. Sir James Eric Drummond.

Baron Makino, for Japan, proposed an amendment declaring that equality of nations should be a fundamental principle of the League; French amendments were also submitted in favour of an International Army Police Force, and of the verifying of the limited armaments of all nations. These, however, were withdrawn, the points being left to be decided by the League itself.

In the Peace Treaty the Covenant found a place, as President Wilson had from the beginning urged that it should.

On June 13th a campaign aimed at educating the British nation up to a just appreciation of the value of the League was opened at the Albert Hall, London. Lord Grey said the Governments had done their part. They had given the League form and substance. Now the peoples must make their attitude plain. The same causes which had brought about war in the past were already at work again. They could be seen in the news in the papers every day—the same jealousies, rivalries, suspicion, imputation of motives. The war had not killed them. Only an organisation such as the League could save us from future wars. Lord Robert Cecil, in his speech, said that Germany must be admitted into the League of Nations, and Russia also, and he appealed for crusaders to help on the attainment of an ideal not less high and not less holy than any which had ever moved men in the history of the world.

The Prince taking the salute at the march-past, outside the Admiralty, of nine hundred men of the Royal Naval Division on June 6th, 1919. In the upper photograph the Prince is seen on the Horse Guards Parade inspecting the men, who had just returned from abroad.

The Prince of Wales's welcome home to men of the Royal Naval Division.

Back to Bonnie Scotland : Arrival of the 4th Royal Scots in Edinburgh.

After service in Italy : First batch of British soldiers for demobilisation.

Hailing "home" with smiles and cheers: R.F.A. gunners arrive at Dover from Salonika.

Gunners of the R.F.A. landing at Dover after four and a half years' war service abroad.

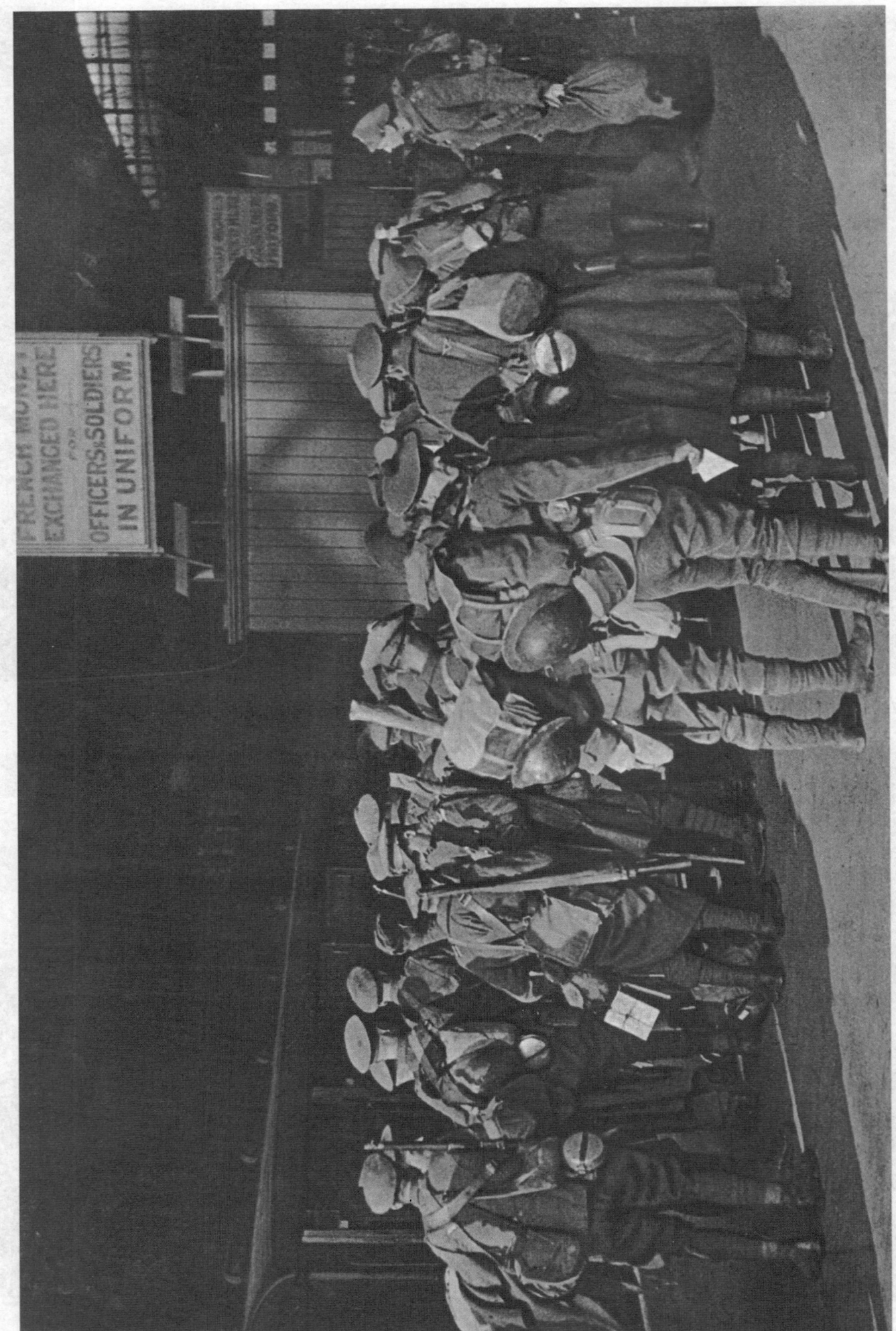

FRENCH MONEY EXCHANGED HERE FOR OFFICERS & SOLDIERS IN UNIFORM.

Homeward bound, with their great task greatly finished : Arrival of British troops at a London railway terminus.

SOLDIERS DEMOBILISED

CHAPTER CCCVII.

AT THE CRYSTAL PALACE.

THE DEMOBILISATION OF THE BRITISH ARMY.
A Gigantic Task and How it was Achieved.
By Eric N. Simons.

The Three Periods of Military Demobilisation—The Industrial Situation—Fourteen Complex Phases—The Original Scheme—The Order of Industrial Priority—How the Men Were Found—Demobilisation Benefits—Dispersal of Q.M.A.A.C., Nurses, and Prisoners of War—Repatriation of Dominion and Colonial Forces—Preparation—Release of Group 43—Demobilisation of Soldiers in Hospital—Suspension Order Affects Certain Services—Dispersal Stations Opened in the United Kingdom—Why the Scheme Failed—Sir Eric Geddes Given a Free Hand—Men Demobilised while on Leave—Adoption of "Contract" System—Percentage of Dispersal Drafts to Include Compassionate Cases—Delays Cause Dissatisfaction—Demonstration at Folkestone—Origin of the Disturbance—The Men's Claims Considered—R.A.S.C. Men Break Camp and Proceed to Whitehall—Protest in Other Parts of the Country—Cancelling of Suspension Order—The Disturbances Continue—The Prime Minister Tackles the Problem—The Contract System Abolished—Trouble with R.A.M.C. Men—Restrictions on this Corps Removed—Rate of Demobilisation—Organisation at Dispersal Stations—Abandonment of Industrial Scheme—Army of Occupation Formed—Sir Auckland Geddes Takes Over the Work of Demobilisation—Final Procedure.

EMOBILISATION proper may be said to date from November 11th, 1918. The signing of the armistice between Germany and the Allied Powers was the signal for wild scenes of joy in every country, but the beflagged crowds marching through the streets were not merely an expression of triumph. Partly they represented a vast relief, partly a legitimate and patriotic pride, but principally they expressed a joyous anticipation. The cessation of hostilities, somewhat prematurely regarded as peace itself by a large section of the public, caused millions of people to look forward on that day of rejoicing to the speedy return of their relatives and friends serving with the victorious armies. It was the task of the various Governments to release these men as quickly as was consistent with national security.

The history of military demobilisation in the United Kingdom may be divided into three periods. The first, extending from November 11th, 1918, to the middle of January, 1919, may be entitled the industrial period; the second, from the middle of January to the beginning of February, the period of acceleration; and the third, from February onwards, that of stabilisation.

During the summer and autumn months of 1918 the man-power situation prohibited anything in the nature of a general release of men from the forces, save only that a national shortage of coal led to the discharge of low-category miners when such could be traced. The armistice did not, however, find the authorities wholly unprepared to meet the enormous task which confronted them. For some time the War Office had had in preparation an extremely complex and comprehensive scheme for the demobilisation of all British and Colonial forces, auxiliary labour units, etc. As soon as the industrial position necessitated the release of men in fairly large numbers this scheme was brought into operation.

Before proceeding to describe the progress of demobilisation and the events accompanying it, it is essential that the immensity of the problem should be realised, and also that the methods elaborated to solve it successfully should be explained in detail. Only thus can a full understanding of subsequent happenings be achieved.

Demobilisation of the huge conscript armies of France and Italy was effected with comparative rapidity by the simple process of releasing men in yearly classes. It was felt, however, that such a system, while possessing the virtues of speed and simplicity, must lead inevitably to a serious disorganisation of the industrial life of a country such as Great Britain. In

RETURNING TO CIVIL LIFE.
Queue of soldiers, who had positions in civil occupations to which they could immediately return waiting at a Labour Exchange to have their papers endorsed for early demobilisation.

British soldiers from hospitals in France about to embark at Havre.

Kit inspection at the Crystal Palace preparatory to demobilisation.

Soldiers at the Crystal Palace for demobilisation handing in their papers.

consequence, it was decided that the chief factor in the demobilisation of the forces of the United Kingdom and the Dominions should be the ability of industry to absorb the labour released.

Industry itself, however, had first to be reorganised and placed upon a peace footing, and this involved not only the reconstruction of many factories which had been erected during the war for war purposes, but also the re-establishment on a peace basis of the transportation systems of the country. Other points that needed attention were the distribution of labour, and agricultural production.

The indiscriminate liberation of men would undoubtedly have resulted in considerable unemployment, and for this reason the War Office refrained from demobilising by military formations and units, which, when complete with their transport and regimental equipment, could only be dealt with at a very limited rate. Instead, it proposed to demobilise individuals on a selective basis, according to the requirements of fundamental trades. Industry, in short, was to be fed, and not flooded, with men.

It will thus be seen that the mere maintaining of this strict interdependence presented difficulties that required no little forethought and organising ability for their solution. To these had to be added the administrative problems arising out of the successive phases. These phases were fourteen in all, and each included many indispensable operations.

The first phase was, of course, the construction of the military machinery for the process of demobilisation, carrying with it the establishment of cadres for units of all arms, for the care of guns, transport, and equipment other than personal; the formation of units to deal with individuals and cadres in their various stages towards demobilisation.

The fourteen phases

The second phase—the reconstruction of the industries of the country for the absorption of labour—comprised among other things the earmarking of employers, supervisors, and labour required; arrangements for the prompt despatch of each individual to the district in which his services were required; and the compilation of an industrial priority list.

The third phase—transportation by sea—included not only the chartering of ships, but arrangements for wharfage accommodation, coaling, and supply. In addition, load-tables and time-tables had to be worked out. Transportation by land, the fourth phase, also involved the preparation of time-tables.

Of equal importance was the fifth phase, the organisation of a post-bellum army. This necessitated measures for recruiting, furlough arrangements, rejoining and refitting men at depots, as well as the working out of movements for the units composing the force.

The sixth phase was the care of those still unfit for civil life; and the seventh the storage of armaments, equipment, ammunition, etc. The latter phase included arrangements for accommodation, transportation, gradual storage, and the provision of personnel for custody.

Men who had been passed for demobilisation at the Crystal Palace being measured for their "civvies," and (right) demobilised soldiers handing in their rifles and equipment at the Wimbledon Dispersal Camp.

STAGES ON THE JOURNEY FROM MILITARY SERVICE TO CIVIL EMPLOYMENT.

Next came the disposal of surplus animals, vehicles, stores, etc. This formed the eighth phase, and comprised their sale (with a concomitant consideration of prices and preferential claims from Overseas Dominions and Allied Governments), the non-disturbance of trade prospects, and registration.

The ninth phase—the disposal of personnel on cessation of military employment—covered the return of the individual to the place selected by him, the collection of his arms and equipment, payment during furlough, reclothing, provision for him according to the terms of his enlistment, insurance against non-employment due to no fault of his own, registration for receipt of medals earned, and re-employment in civil life. It also carried with it the necessity of feeding him and providing for him should he fall sick en route.

The tenth phase—the disbandment of units no longer required—involved a decision as to which units should be maintained; the provision of personnel to form cadres for the care and safe custody of animals, equipment, guns, and vehicles until the cadre unit could be transported from its home or overseas station to the place of disbandment; the selection of places, and the proper disposal of arms, equipment, guns, and vehicles; the completion of documentary records and their handing in; and, finally, the closing down of accounts.

In the eleventh phase—the final settlement of payments to individuals—credits (furlough pay, separation allowances, family allowance, ration allowance, etc.), and debits for loss of arms or equipment, had all to be brought to account.

The twelfth phase was the final adjustment of the accounts of units, etc., and the thirteenth the preparation of plans for remobilisation should it be required. This **Forty-three** was an essential part of the vast scheme, **"industrial groups"** which could not have been initiated without every step being considered in conjunction with future possibilities, however improbable. It necessitated the critical examination of every arrangement from this point of view.

The fourteenth and final phase was the repatriation of prisoners of war, the evacuation of our enemies', and the return of our own. This called for special embarkation and transportation arrangements, and for our own men disembarkation, accommodation, and supply arrangements, the care of the individual, and his return to civil life.

The multitude of details covered by that simple and sometimes imperfectly understood word "demobilisation" having been indicated, it is now possible to examine the demobilisation scheme as originally devised.

A Special Army Order of October 21st, 1918, laid down that each individual should have his industrial group, his actual trade, and his condition, whether married or single, recorded in his Army Book 64. There were altogether forty-three industrial groups, as arranged by the Ministry of Labour. A system of consolidated returns by the Commanders-in-Chief of armies was then adopted, and by means of it the War Office was enabled to ascertain the exact

Demobilised soldiers leaving the Wimbledon Dispersal Camp for their homes.

Demobilised soldiers receiving their unemployment policies.

Demobilised men receiving their pay at the Wimbledon Dispersal Camp.

Girls packing civilian suits for those demobilised soldiers who chose a suit of "civvies" in preference to the alternative of a sum of money. Right : Demobilised men at the Wimbledon Dispersal Camp drawing their rations.
BRITISH SOLDIERS PASSING FROM UNIFORM KHAKI TO VARIETY OF "CIVVIES."

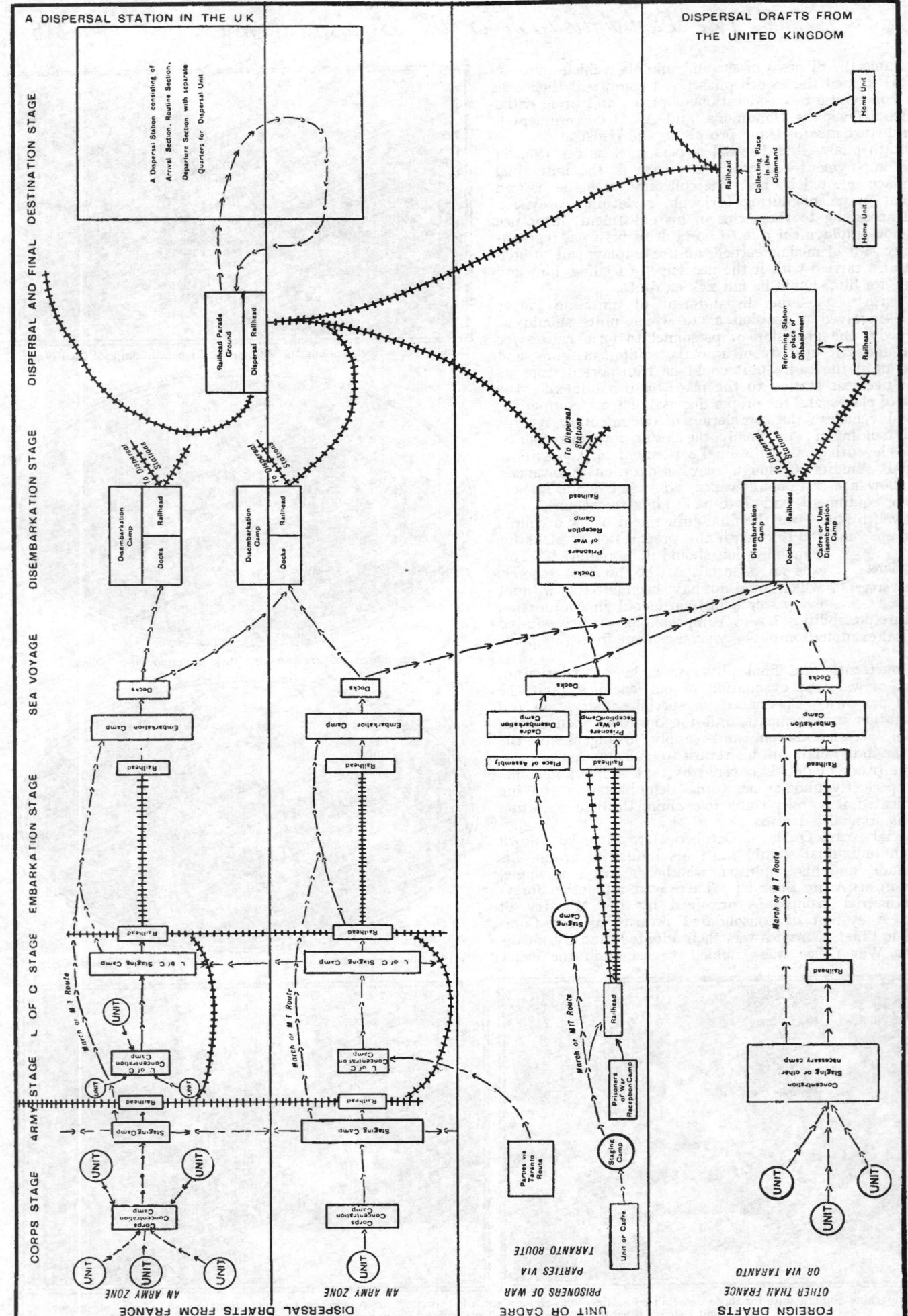

STAGES IN THE DEMOBILISATION OF THE BRITISH MILITARY FORCES SERVING ABROAD.

Diagram specially drawn to illustrate (1) the system by which men of the British Expeditionary Forces were drafted from the various army zones abroad to the dispersal stations in the United Kingdom; and (2) the repatriation, via Taranto, South Italy, of released prisoners of war.

composition by industrial groups of each army in the field and each command at home and abroad.

The United Kingdom was divided into nineteen areas for purposes of dispersal and distribution, and the Ministry of Labour was instructed to advise the War Office as to the order of priority of each industrial group. A daily allotment of men for dispersal was then made to expeditionary forces and commands at home and abroad, so as to ensure the return of approximately equal numbers from overseas and within the United Kingdom.

Men were demobilised in accordance with the requirements of industry, and in particular those for whom immediate civil employment could be found had preference. As a temporary measure the following order of industrial priority was fixed :

1. Coal-miners, who, as long as available, were to compose 50 per cent. of each draft, but not more than 50 per cent. except when there were insufficient men of categories 2 to 8 below to make up the draft.
2. Demobilisers—i.e., men needed by the Government for work in connection with demobilisation.
3. Pivotal men, or men whose release and return to work would enable employment to be found for others.
4. Men ordered for special release as being urgently wanted in the interests of industry.
5. Those for whom approved offers of employment were received.
6. Men over forty-one.
7. Soldiers discharged from hospital and convalescents.
8. Men of Group 43 (teachers, students, etc.).

This arrangement was made early in December, 1918, and the necessary instructions were issued to all officers commanding units. It was decided also that, in addition to demobilisers and pivotal men, the Ministry of Labour should be free to put forward for demobilisation the names of officers and men who had pre-war work or interrupted training to which they could immediately return.

The method of ascertaining the names of those who came under the eight categories above mentioned was ingenious and effective. To each officer and man a civil employment form was issued, and this when complete contained all the information desired. It gave the man's **Ingenious and** occupation, his former employer or em- **effective method** ployers, his age, condition, and also whether an employer had definitely promised him work, or whether he wished his name submitted to a particular employer. After the commanding officer had made his consolidated return to the War Office, these forms were sent on to the Appointments Department of the Ministry of Labour.

Correspondingly employers were instructed to make applications for the release of such men as they needed. Printed application forms were provided for demobilisers, pivotal men, and men whose early release was advisable on industrial grounds. Ordinary offers of employment for men who did not come under any special heading were recorded on official cards. These various forms and cards were examined and recommended by local advisory committees acting on behalf of the Ministry of Labour, and finally, after their official approval by the Ministry, they were registered, and instructions were transmitted to commanding officers regarding the release of individuals and their order of priority. A certain amount of latitude was, however, granted to officers in completing their dispersal drafts, to allow of a small proportion of long-service and time-expired men being released. Also, assuming other conditions to be equal, married men had preference over single.

Drafts for dispersal were sorted abroad and despatched to collecting camps, or, in the case of men serving in the United Kingdom, to military collecting places. From these they proceeded intact to dispersal stations, carrying with them dispersal certificates for the use of dispersal commandants and their staffs.

Each individual, with the exception of officers, who, as such, were entitled to special gratuities, received twenty-eight days' furlough with full pay and allowances. Further benefits under the scheme included the issue to every man of : (1) An out-of-work donation policy, valid for a period of one year from the date of discharge, and payable for not more than twenty weeks under certain conditions ; (2) a railway warrant home ; (3) a suit of plain clothes, or an allowance in lieu thereof ; (4) a protection certificate ; and (5) any gratuities earned. Men were also allowed to retain as their own property a uniform, one pair of boots, and all underclothing and small kit. The greatcoat had, however, to be returned before the expiration of the twenty-eight days' furlough, and £1 (deducted from the gratuity) was paid on its delivery to a railway-station. Payments were made by special money-orders or postal drafts in three weekly instalments. These were only cashable on production of the protection certificate issued at the dispersal station.

With certain minor differences the conditions governing the demobilisation of officers were similar to those of other ranks. The guiding principles, except in the case of Regular officers, were that they should have definite employment awaiting them, and should not be required for military reasons by the arm or branch of the Service to which they belonged. Officers were **Demobilising** demobilised in the proportion of three per **the officers** cent. of the strength of the dispersal drafts. In addition a limited number came independently of the men, and were dealt with either personally or by post at a special officers' dispersal station in London. R.A.M.C. officers were demobilised through the Ministry of National Service.

The members of Q.M.A.A.C. were formed into dispersal drafts and dispersed through dispersal hostels. In organisation their disbandment ran on the same lines as that of the combatant services, but the order of priority was decided by their ability to be spared, though domestic ties were also taken into consideration when necessary. The rate of release was slower, owing to many women being required to do clerical work.

Prisoners of war, after arrival in this country, were sent to Prisoners of War Reception Camps, where special facilities were afforded them for interviews with relatives and friends, and for the exchange of foreign moneys. Everything possible was done to secure their comfort, and they were demobilised as rapidly as possible.

Nurses were released under the superintendence of the Ministry of Labour, the conditions governing their demobilisation being the needs of the Army, civilian requirements, length of service, age and health, and domestic ties.

The demobilisation of Dominion and Colonial forces was largely affected by questions of transport and available tonnage. Repatriation at the public expense was given to all officers and soldiers of the Imperial Army who :

1. Joined or enlisted abroad after the outbreak of war, or who after that date proceeded to the United Kingdom and joined or enlisted.
2. Arrived in the United Kingdom on or after January 1st, 1914, and were temporarily resident therein, and joined or enlisted.
3. At the outbreak of hostilities were temporarily resident in the United Kingdom for purposes of attending a recognised educational or training course (including apprenticeship) whose recognised definite period does not exceed four years.

Officers and soldiers claiming repatriation were grouped as follows :

1. Those who wished to defer their embarkation from the United Kingdom and to terminate their service at the first opportunity.
2. Those who undertook to embark from the United Kingdom or Egypt at the first opportunity, remaining in the Service until such time as passages were available. **Dominion and**

A Repatriation Record Office was estab- **Colonial forces** lished temporarily at Winchester to deal with the above. They were conveyed to their own countries either direct or via the United Kingdom, under arrangements made by the Home Government in conjunction with the Government concerned. They did not pass through dispersal stations in the United Kingdom, but were dispersed under arrangements made by their own Governments.

The scheme also covered the disposal of medical stores and apparatus, and many other minute details, being in its way a splendid example of the organising ability latent in the British race. It completely standardised the process of dispersal on an industrial and selective basis. In fact, its weakness lay perhaps in being too complete, too closely worked out. It neglected the human element of error and the incalculable element of chance. It made no allowance for popular impatience or the pressure of public opinion, and it did not foresee—it could not possibly have foreseen—the extraordinarily complicated state of affairs that prevailed in Europe after the signing of the armistice, necessitating the maintenance for many months of a large Army of Occupation.

Marshal Foch had estimated that on a selective basis 10,000 men per day could be drafted from France to England for dispersal, or, on a non-selective basis, 23,000 per day, and as the selective method was that adopted, an effort was made to maintain the former figure.

HOMEWARD BOUND BY WAY OF THE RHINE.
British troops on the quayside at Cologne preparing to go aboard the steamer which was to convey them down the Rhine to Rotterdam on their return home to be demobilised.

November passed in preparation for the preliminary dispersal period, as it was termed to distinguish it from general demobilisation, which could only come with the signing of peace. Meanwhile the shortage of coal was still serious, and this, with its stultifying effect upon the industries of the country, rendered imperative the immediate release of coal-miners, and their group (No. 3) was given priority over all others.

Almost at the outset, however, unanticipated difficulties arose in connection with the scheme. As time progressed, hastily-framed resolutions were made and superimposed upon the original plan. On December 10th the War Cabinet Demobilisation Committee, formed to deal with the general policy of demobilisation, and presided over by General Smuts, approved the demobilisation of officers and men in command depots.

On the same date the Army Council decided that all Group 43 men who desired should be demobilised, providing they were not required for military reasons.
Men of Group 43 This instruction did not, however, apply to Regular soldiers on pre-war attestations with Colour service to complete. Group 43 was composed of professors, tutors, lecturers, examiners, inspectors, teachers, including pupil teachers, and all persons who were receiving tuition at a university, or college, or school, or technical college, or other similar institution.

The following day another important decision was made. It was announced that all soldiers who had been discharged fit for duty from hospital since November 11th, 1918, and on the date of discharge had undergone treatment for twenty-eight days consecutively, could be sent to the United

Kingdom for demobilisation by normal routes as soon as shipping permitted. Following upon this came orders for the release of all sick and wounded in command depots.

The force of circumstances was thus interfering at several points with the smooth working of the industrial scheme. Difficulties were also arising overseas and elsewhere, and led, on December 14th, to the issue of a suspension order to the effect that no more men of the R.A.S.C., R.A.V.C., R.A.O.C., Remounts, Transportation Services of the Royal Engineers, and the Army Pay Corps were to be demobilised until further notice. This, it was stated, was a temporary precaution until detailed arrangements for their relief had been completed, in order that the important services of these corps might not be dislocated.

Meantime dispersal stations were being opened all over the country, and by December 22nd no fewer than eleven were at work. The Scottish Command was served by dispersal stations at Duddingston and Georgetown, the Northern Command by Ripon and Harrowby, the Western and Irish Commands by Heaton Park and Oswestry, the Southern and Aldershot Commands by Chiseldon and Fovant, the Eastern Command by Shorncliffe and Purfleet, and the London District by Wimbledon. Later on Wimbledon was closed, and a much larger station opened at the Crystal Palace.

The weakness of the original selective scheme became, however, more and more evident with each day that passed. Elaborate and carefully planned as it was, it suffered from the defects of its qualities. It was too leisurely, and the rate of demobilisation was not quick enough to satisfy an eager and impatient public. Employers were inconvenienced by the failure of the authorities to release important men and by their apparent neglect of repeated applications. Relations and friends of absent soldiers failed in part to grasp the extreme complexity of the problem, and began to clamour for an immediate speeding-up of demobilisation. An agitation in the columns of the daily Press gave final expression to this popular dissatisfaction.

On December 20th the Prime Minister gave Sir Eric Geddes a free hand to organise and accelerate the demobilisation of the Army. Until then the War Cabinet Committee, under General Smuts, had had charge **Demand for** of the general policy, and the Department of **acceleration** Demobilisation, under Sir Stephenson Kent, had provided machinery. This arrangement was still continued, the actual mission of Sir Eric Geddes being to co-ordinate the activities of the various Government departments more or less directly concerned with demobilisation.

The appointment of the erstwhile First Lord of the Admiralty partly appeased the agitators, but trouble arose in another direction. Men were constantly arriving in the United Kingdom on leave from overseas, and among these were many " pivotal " and " special release " men, who claimed that it was only reasonable they should be demobilised while on their leave, rather than return overseas eventually to occupy valuable shipping space. A decision was made, therefore, that they should be allowed to return to work without going back to their units. Statements giving all necessary particulars had, however, to be sent to the Local Advisory Committees and then handed to the Military Records Offices at least five days before the leave expired ; or, in the case of officers, to the local District Director of the Appointments Department of the Ministry of Labour for endorsement.

Subsequently, in response to the growing pressure of public opinion, this concession was extended to include what came

Demobilising Army horses. Squadron waggons on the sale parade ground, drawn by heavy draught Shire and American horses and mules.

Sale of Army horses: three hunters, and a pair of heavy draught horses drawing a load of forty-four hundredweight.

Parade of draught horses roped together, so that four men could take charge of twenty-six animals. Inset: Men taking out mules and horses, some of the 25,000 demobilised animals that were sold out of the Army at Romsey and Swaythling Remount Depots during the first three months after the armistice.

HORSES AND MULES RELEASED FOR CIVIL EMPLOY AFTER ARMY SERVICE.

shortage of trains or shipping, or a deficiency of wharfage accommodation—it remained a fact that men were not being dispersed at the quickest possible rate.

The War Office, after collecting reports from various sources, came to the conclusion by the end of the year that the delay in releasing men was due to the following causes: a deficiency of Army forms, ignorance of orders issued, waiting for return of resettlement forms from the Ministry of Labour, the refusal of commanding officers and others to consider direct contracts to return to pre-war employment, or to verify a man's belonging to a group ordered for demobilisation, and, finally, to the lack of organisation in units.

Causes of the delay

The maximum possible rate of demobilisation was, of course, determined by the available shipping and wharfage accommodation and by the number of men sent daily for leave. Of these latter there were 7,000 passing every day between Calais and Folkestone. Of the Dominion Forces 1,500 men were also disembarked daily at Weymouth, and further accommodation had to be provided at Southampton for 1,485 men from Taranto, Italy.

On New Year's Day, 1919, it was decided that all cadets undergoing training in special cadet battalions should complete their course, upon which they would be gazetted, passed to the Special Reserve of Officers, and demobilised, without, however, drawing any pay or emoluments other than their regulation cadet pay and allowances while they were on furlough.

Three days passed, and then the smouldering fire of resentment burst into flame. About 10,000 soldiers who were returning from leave and staying in rest-camps at Folkestone made a remarkable demonstration against what they considered to be the slow demobilisation of the troops.

to be known as "contract" men. Any man on leave who could produce a written guarantee of employment from an employer in whose service he had been prior to August 4th, 1914, was entitled to claim an extension of leave, during which period his papers were examined and approved. A telegram was then sent to his commanding officer inquiring whether his return to the unit was required on military grounds, and if the answer were in the negative he was sent for demobilisation at once without having to return overseas.

As a natural consequence of these constant amendments large numbers of men were released without regard to the prearranged order of industrial priority, and individual grievances were bound inevitably to ensue. At this period the total daily allotment was 10,400, which, with a daily average of 1,000 men released while on leave, made a grand total of 11,400 soldiers demobilised per day.

The reaction of Continental affairs on demobilisation was indicated on December 27th, when instructions were issued that no men on leave from Archangel, Murmansk, Siberia, Caucasus, or North Persia were to be demobilised without reference having been made to the War Office.

Low rate of release

On December 28th yet another decision was made, and the Army Council instructed all commands to reserve a half per cent. of dispersal allotments for men released on compassionate grounds. It had to be clearly established that the soldier's demobilisation would be of material benefit to his family, but although the final decision was left in the hands of his commanding officer, a fairly clear idea was given as to what constituted a deserving application.

In spite of all these concessions the rate of release was still low enough to cause dissatisfaction. Invidious comparisons with America and France were made, both these countries having made considerable progress in the direction of general demobilisation. Indeed, after making all allowances for unavoidable delays—such as bad weather in the Channel preventing the departure of ships at the scheduled time, a

OFFICERS IN TRAINING FOR PEACE PROFESSIONS.
Officers in a Cambridge laboratory studying for a degree in science. In circle: Officers receiving instruction in the weaving industry at the Manchester College of Technology. Above: Another view in a Cambridge laboratory. Such educational work was instituted immediately after the armistice to fit demobilised young officers for positions in civil life.

Arrangements had been made to send the Brigade of Guards' colours to Cologne via Folkestone, but after being carried with full military ceremonial to Charing Cross Station, London, their departure was suddenly cancelled by the military authorities, Folkestone having been temporarily closed as a port.

The origin of the disturbance lay in a misunderstanding. A number of men had obtained an extension of leave in order to have time to complete the "contracts" with pre-war employers which qualified them for immediate demobilisation.

Protests against delays This caused discontent among the others, who declared they had never been informed that such a scheme was in force, and alleged that some were bogus contracts. In consequence they refused to allow the "contract" men to return to London, and also prevented their comrades from going on board ship.

The protest was quite orderly, and this greatly facilitated a settlement. The men were first seen by General Dallas, G.O.C. Canterbury, and subsequently by General Woolcombe, G.O.C. Eastern Command. It was promised that their cases should be dealt with individually. Those who had genuine contracts not yet in order could avail themselves of their week's extension of leave. A similar privilege was granted to men who could show reasonable grounds for claiming that they were in a position to obtain contracts, on condition that they returned to their units at the end of the period if they failed to do so. Men without contracts were to return at once. The examination of the men's claims was conducted by a number of officials of the Ministry of Labour sent down the following day with a strong staff of clerks. A similar difficulty arose at Dover, but the number of men concerned was smaller and the dispute was settled in the same way.

On Sunday, January 5th, it was announced that all officers over 51 years of age, or who

AT THE SPINNING-FRAMES.
Disabled and demobilised officers being trained in the textile industry at Bradford, Yorks.

attained that age, might be demobilised if they so desired.

The Folkestone incident was but the first of a series of similar occurrences. The tactful and sympathetic way in which the authorities had handled the situation, combined with the success of the negotiations, inspired other bodies of troops smarting under certain grievances to adopt equivalent tactics in order to draw attention to their claims.

The most spectacular demonstration took place on Monday, January 6th, 1919, when 200 men of the R.A.S.C. stationed at Osterley Park, Isleworth, broke camp and proceeded by lorry to Whitehall to state their case to the authorities. They represented for the most part time-expired infantrymen who had been drafted into the R.A.S.C. Many of them had been wounded after two or more years in France, and in view of the suspension order of December 14th, and a rumour that their corps would be the last branch of the Service to be demobilised, they demanded to be placed on an equal footing with the men of infantry regiments.

The outcome of this affair was that a deputation of six remained to lay the facts before a brigadier-general, while the remainder returned to camp, accompanied by a Staff major, who they insisted should go with them to investigate their grievance. **Not unnatural impatience**

On the same day 7,000 soldiers, leaving Shoreham Camp, marched into Brighton to protest against the demobilisation delay. They were joined by a detachment of Royal Marine Engineers from Southwick, but on a promise that the matter should be reported to the right quarter, and that no punishment should be meted out to them for their breach of discipline, they returned to camp.

In addition a number of men from the Shortlands Depot of the R.A.S.C. (M.T.) marched to the Central Hall, Bromley, and made a formal protest.

As a result of these various exhibitions of a not unnatural

OLD SOLDIERS LEARNING NEW TRADES.
Demobilised soldiers receiving instruction in the use of the lathe at the Technical Training School at Loughborough, Leicestershire; and (in circle) mastering the craft of welding at the same centre.

impatience and irritation, it was decided that the R.A.S.C. should be treated on the same lines as infantry, and further, that one-tenth of the dispersal drafts from France should consist of long-service men. On January 7th the Secretary of the War Office made the following announcement :

It is now, and always has been, necessary to retain a number of men, in proportion to the strength of the Army, in order to carry out the vital administrative work of feeding, clothing, housing, and moving the troops, and it must be realised that the more rapidly demobilisation proceeds the greater is the strain thrown upon the administrative services.

The demobilisation of the Army involves the continuous employment of men engaged in transportation, and it is on this account that it is impracticable to demobilise the administrative services as rapidly as the combatant branches. By transportation must be understood not merely the railway men, inland water transport men, dock employees, and mechanical transport drivers, but the men engaged in the repair and other shops connected with these services.

Every endeavour is being made to keep down the numbers of the administrative services to the minimum compatible with speedy demobilisation, and a beginning has already been made with the dispersal of the Royal Army Ordnance Corps, Royal Army Service Corps, Army Pay Corps, Remounts, Transportation, Royal Engineers, Royal Army Veterinary Corps, who have received a percentage of allotments which is as high as it possibly can be at present, and which will automatically increase as demobilisation proceeds.

By January 8th, 1919, some 300,000 men had been demobilised, and the release of pivotal men alone was proceeding at the estimated rate of 4,000 per day. Nevertheless, disturbances continued all over the country. On January 8th 4,000 R.A.S.C. men marched from Park Royal to Whitehall. A delegation was seen by Sir William Robertson, who gave assurances that their claims should be **Further outbursts** investigated, upon which the demonstrators **of discontent** marched back to camp.

Six hundred men of the Flying Service at Westerham Hill Aerodrome, Kent, demonstrated. Several hundred men of the Royal Air Force at Felixstowe marched to the headquarters of the Harwich Defence ; 500 members of the R.A.F. School of Imperial Gunnery at Hythe marched to the Hotel Imperial and protested ; 100 men belonging to the Highland Light Infantry marched to the headquarters of the Scottish Command in Edinburgh ; and finally, a large body of men representing the Queen's, Gloucesters, and Wiltshires in Maidstone, held a protest meeting in the High Street, and then marched to the Town Hall.

The trouble had now become sufficiently serious to receive the attention of the Prime Minister, who examined the situation in consultation with the military authorities. A long statement was published on January 9th appealing for patience on the part of soldiers and public, and declaring that sympathetic hearing would be given to all legitimate complaints, while everything possible was being done to quicken the pace of demobilisation.

As a preliminary it was decided to abolish the " contract " system by which men were enabled to obtain discharge while on leave. The Army Council gave notice to all units that " officers and soldiers who em- **" Contract " system** barked on and after January 12th for leave **abolished** in the United Kingdom are only permitted to proceed on leave to the United Kingdom on the distinct understanding that they are to return to their units on the expiration of their leave, and that they will not be demobilised under any pretext whatever while on leave. Experience," added the instruction, " has shown this order to be necessary to ensure the maintenance of the Army of Occupation, the personnel of which must receive leave in their turn. It is undesirable to release men in the order laid down by the leave rosters, which are prepared many weeks in advance. It has been found that in a high proportion of cases leave drafts from France now consist of men who have been overseas for six or nine months only, and the demobilisation of all men on leave would thus be unfair to long-service men still overseas, and in many cases would not lead to the release of men most urgently required in the national interest."

This somewhat belated explanation of the position, and the obvious sincerity of the efforts of the authorities, began to take effect, and the last flicker of indignation came on January 9th in the refusal of a large number of R.A.M.C. men in Blackpool to go on parade. The restrictions on this corps were, however, removed, and what has been referred to as the second period, that of acceleration, began.

January 12th saw the expiration of the contract system. By then the number of pivotal men released daily had risen to 6,000, and altogether 70,000 applications for such men had been received. Further, 125,000 miners had been demobilised. The daily allotment had risen to 20,000, and from January 15th the number of leave men was reduced to 6,000 daily. A fortnight later the daily figure had risen to

HOMEWARD BOUND AFTER DISTINGUISHED SERVICE IN THE HOLY LAND.
On the way from Egypt to England ; deck of a troopship carrying men from General Allenby's army on the first stage of their journey home. On that first stage to Italy, which occupied from five to eight days, much discomfort had to be put up with by the returning men owing to overcrowding.

"LEAVE MEN" IN WHITEHALL.
Some of the soldiers on leave who, on January 7th, 1919, marched to Whitehall to protest against being sent back to Salonika. An arrangement was made by which those who had work awaiting them should be at once demobilised.

30,000, and promised soon to reach 40,000. No less than 140,000 men per week were discharged from commands in the United Kingdom alone, and in view of the increasing strain on the personnel at dispersal stations it was decided that no dispersals should take place on Sundays.

The organisation at these centres was admirable. The regulation rate was originally fixed at 100 men per hour, but at many places this figure was exceeded, notably at Ripon and the Crystal Palace, where 2,400 men were discharged daily. Each man from overseas was provided with a clean shirt and socks, if necessary, given a hot bath and a hot meal, and had a short interview with an Army chaplain. The average time spent by the individual in the actual process of receiving his discharge was little more than an hour.

The third period was now rapidly approaching. Preparations for the establishment of a definite Army of Occupation were practically complete, and it was realised that the policy **Demobilisation's** of demobilisation in accordance with indus- **third period** trial requirements could no longer be strictly maintained. Desirable though it was to prevent unemployment and dislocation, European events had materially changed the situation. The probability that a large British Army would be required in Germany and elsewhere for many months rendered it advisable to create a stable force, and to demobilise as quickly as possible all who were not required to serve in it.

The Supreme War Council, after consultation with Marshal Foch, decided that the strength of the British contribution to the Allied Armies of Occupation should be 900,000 men of all ranks and arms. This announcement, together with a notification of the change in the method of demobilisation, and a statement of the conditions governing the new Army of Occupation, appeared on January 30th. It was also stated that no more applications for pivotal men would be considered unless they had been made prior to February 1st.

This definitely marked the end of the industrial scheme. The new arrangements promised demobilisation, as soon as the exigencies of the Service would permit, to the following warrant officers, non-commissioned officers, and men who:

1. Joined for immediate service prior to January 1st, 1916.
2. Were called up from the Reserve.
3. Belonged to the Territorial Force, and attested prior to January 1st, 1916.
4. Were serving under pre-war conditions of service and had completed their Colour service.
5. Were thirty-seven years of age, or subsequently attained that age.
6. Were entitled to wear three or more wound stripes.
7. Had been certified as pivotal men prior to February 1st, 1919.
8. Had, prior to February 1st, 1919, been recommended by the Ministry of Labour for special release.
9. Had been recommended for compassionate release

10. Were approved for return overseas to their pre-war homes or businesses.

The following classes were not immediately demobilised:

(a) Warrant officers, non-commissioned officers, and men, serving under pre-war conditions of service, who had not completed their term of Colour service.
(b) Warrant officers, non-commissioned officers, and men of the Non-Combatant Corps.
(c) Those required for the machinery of demobilisation.
(d) Those in overseas garrisons until they could be relieved.

The demobilisation of officers was similarly regulated. The selection of officers for the Army was made:

1. From those who volunteered.

TALKING IT OVER.
Lord Gort, V.C., discussing the situation with men of the R.A.S.C. who demonstrated in favour of immediate demobilisation on January 8th, 1919.

2. By promotion from lower ranks, if such officers were fit.
3. By compulsory retention.

Acting rank was not considered in selection. Officers under thirty-seven were not released at all if they were commissioned on or after January 1st, 1916, but officers passed to the Reserve on receipt of a commission were not retained. Increased rates of pay were introduced generally to compensate those whose retention in the force was compulsory.

From this time onward the rate and process of demobilisation were stabilised, and complaints, individual or collective, became noticeably less. The preference given to men with long service and wound stripes appealed to the popular sense of fairness, and the higher pay and other benefits largely appeased those whose demobilisation was indefinitely deferred.

Early in February the daily dispersal rate had risen to the excellent figure of 43,333, and on the third of that month the total number discharged from the British forces was 25,334 officers and 1,087,005 men. On the fifth of the same month Sir Auckland Geddes replaced his brother Sir Eric Geddes as general co-ordinator of demobilisation. On March 20th the grand total released was 57,082 officers and 2,052,460 other ranks.

The governing conditions continued to be age and length of service. Eventually the age of retention was reduced to thirty-six, then to thirty-five. Next, men with two wound stripes were released, and after that, soldiers of thirty-four. In this way the vast Army created slowly during four and a half years of war was whittled down until only the desired residuum of 900,000 men remained to form the Army of Occupation. Demobilisation was, broadly speaking, complete.

THE KING AND QUEEN WELCOMING A GREAT GATHERING OF WOMEN WAR WORKERS AT BUCKINGHAM PALACE IN JUNE, 1918.

Women war workers in the quadrangle of Buckingham Palace on June 29th, 1918, when many thousands of them marched to the palace to present an address of homage to King George and Queen Mary in connection with their silver wedding. All branches of women's work were represented. There were contingents from the various nursing organisations and from the many corps in which, under the stress of the war, women had proved their fitness for unaccustomed work as Queen Mary's Army Auxiliary Corps, Women's Royal Naval Service, Women's Land Army, and railway and omnibus employees.

324

KING GEORGE REVIEWING

CHAPTER CCCVIII.

LONDON SPECIAL CONSTABLES.

THE DEMOBILISATION AND RESETTLEMENT OF THE WAR WORKERS.

By Robert Machray.

From War to Peace—Demobilisation of All Great Britain—A Prodigious Undertaking—Vast Numbers Affected—Early Measures Taken by the Government—Position at the Armistice—Easing the Emergency—Employers Assisted to Resume Peace Work—Gradual Reduction of Workers in the National Factories—Unrestricted Discharges by Private Establishments—Critical Situation—Wages Stabilised—The Out-of-Work Donation Given to All the Unemployed—A Temporary Expedient Open to Abuse—How Abuse was Checked—Yet a Million Drawing the State's Bounty—Problem of Women War Workers—Attempt at Solution—Amount of Donation Decreased—Whole Question to be Investigated.

I N previous wars demobilisation was a comparatively simple affair, and called for little in the way of industrial reconstruction. Once the peace was ratified the fighting men who were not required for the standing army were disbanded and the extra war workers were discharged. Apart from pensions and gratuities they were left to shift for themselves. But their number, especially as regarded war workers, was relatively to the entire population not very great, and they were absorbed more or less readily into the ordinary life of the community. Very different was it with respect to the Great War, long before the end of which practically every person in the land was occupied in fighting or in the production of munitions and other supplies on which the fighting men depended.

With all Great Britain thus mobilised—either from the military or the industrial point of view—for the war, the problem of demobilisation became in effect one of transforming the United Kingdom from a war to a peace footing in every phase of its existence, of putting the whole country back on its former industrial basis. Though this was a prodigious undertaking it was in the highest degree urgent, because the British above everything were an industrial people, and their national prosperity was wrapped up in the success of their industries. Military demobilisation, which was the subject of the immediately preceding chapter, began by order, and was continued by regulation. Nor was it immediate or on a large scale. On the other hand industrial demobilisation in vast proportions started automatically, it might be said, from the moment the demand for destructive munitions stopped, and that was precisely the position as soon as

[Photo: Russell.
SIR ROBERT S. HORNE, K.C., M.P.
Appointed Minister of Labour in Mr. Lloyd George's second administration at the beginning of January, 1919.

the armistice was signed. The resettlement in industry of the war workers was therefore the first part of the general problem of reconstruction to be taken in hand and solved.

At the date of the armistice about forty thousand firms were engaged to a greater or less extent on war work for the Ministry of Munitions, the War Office, and the Admiralty. Upwards of five thousand six hundred establishments were definitely under Government control. The production of munitions at the outbreak of the war was limited to the State establishments, of which Woolwich Arsenal was the chief, and to a few large firms. The staff at Woolwich was little more than eight thousand, and the private armament concerns were for the most part employed on commercial work—in some cases, from lack of orders, the manufacture of munitions had almost reached the vanishing point. When the armistice was signed the State establishments, or national factories, numbered close on two hundred, and included enormous projectile, shell, and shell-filling works.

These national factories employed about 136,000 men and 170,000 women, or 306,000 in all. In private establishments the total number of workers engaged in munitions industries was 2,048,250, and of this huge aggregate about 730,000 were women. Between the national factories and the private establishments upwards of 900,000 persons were employed in the making of destructive munitions, and with the armistice their occupation was gone. To the general total of war workers there fell to be added nearly 900,000 men and women who were engaged on Admiralty work, making a grand total of nearly three millions. Of these, however, the Admiralty workers, as in the dockyards, were in a large measure non-demobilisable. Roughly the position was that upwards of a million people were required to change their work with the cessation of war manufactures, and of these more than half were men. The question was: What was to be done with or for this million of war workers?

Naturally the workers themselves were profoundly interested in the way the question was answered. To most of them the armistice came as a great surprise. Though in high quarters it was perfectly well known in October, 1918, that Germany was hopelessly beaten, and might ask for an armistice at any moment, this fact was not disclosed to the body of the public. In case knowledge of the favourable situation in the field might induce slackness among the war workers, and so cause the Germans to seek to prolong their resistance, the policy of the Government was to enjoin silence on the well informed, the result being that the general belief was that the fighting would continue much longer than it did. So unexpected, in the munition works, was the armistice that in several of them the announcement of it produced something in the nature of a panic, numbers of the workers fearing lest on the stoppage of hostilities they would be thrown into the streets and have to fend for themselves as best they could.

Ministry of Reconstruction

Of course it had been foreseen long before the armistice that dislocation of employment would inevitably follow the cessation of hostilities, and the Government had taken certain steps with a view to dealing with it. As far back as August 21st, 1917, the Ministry of Reconstruction had been constituted. It had carried out preliminary investigations, and issued a series of reports on various aspects of the industrial situation as it probably would be after the war, through an organisation known as the Civil War Workers' Committee. The first report of this body enunciated as a principle the proposition that the Government must assist munition and other war workers to return to their former employment or to find other work, and it stated that the

machinery for this object already existed in the Labour or Employment Exchanges, which should work in conjunction with the Labour Resettlement Committee and the Local Advisory (Labour) Committees. The second report considered the question of giving the munition workers a holiday at the expense of the State, and pronounced against it, on the ground that it was impossible to distinguish between munition and other workers. The fourth and most important report brought forward the plan of the " out-of-work donation," as it was called, or the paying of unemployment benefit by the State, to those demobilised workers who were unable to get work.

It had been suggested in some quarters that, to avoid the discharge of munition workers on a large scale, the production of destructive munitions should continue until the civil demand for labour had had time to grow and crystallise. Apart from the fact that this policy was nothing else than one of relief works, there was the still stronger objection to it that it involved the waste of an enormous quantity of raw material that was imperatively required for carrying on peace production. Obviously it was economically unsound to use, for example, steel for the **Problem of** manufacture of shell-cases for which there no **relief works** longer was any necessity, when that steel was urgently needed for the construction of ships or machinery. As Sir Robert Horne, the Minister of Labour, said quite rightly in a speech on the subject in the House of Commons on April 29th, 1919, it was impossible to imagine anything more demoralising than paying men to do what they knew was useless work, and with no other result than the waste of material. This policy, therefore, was ruled out—as a policy. But at the date of the armistice great contracts for munitions of every kind were still running, and though the expenditure on munitions actually reached its maximum about the end of September, 1918, the reduction thereafter to the armistice

DEPUTATION OF WOMEN MUNITION WORKERS TO THE MINISTRY OF LABOUR.
Scene outside the Ministry of Labour at the beginning of December, 1918, when about 1,000 women and girls employed at a London munition works marched to Whitehall to protest against their prospective discharge. This was one of several deputations, the leaders of which were received by the Minister of Labour, who in some instances made arrangements to postpone discharges pending discussion with the employers.

ACTIVITY ON THE CLYDE.
Men and women at work on the deck of a standard ship in a Clyde yard. The urgent demands for labour led to many people taking up unaccustomed work in connection with shipbuilding.

was very slight. Practically war production was at its top. A possible course for the Government to take was to stop dead, as in a moment, all this vast war production. It was plain that this was contrary to public policy, for it was bound to precipitate a highly dangerous industrial crisis, seriously affecting not only employers and employed but the whole nation. In any case a crisis was inevitable, and the Government decided to minimise it and tide the country over it. This was achieved partly by adjusting the contracts with the munitions manufacturers, partly by assisting them to get back to peace production, and partly by paying unemployment benefit to workers thrown out of employment by the upheaval in war industries.

Speaking generally, war production was continued where the work on the material was so far advanced that the result of that work could not be easily " scrapped." The production of shells was reduced gradually over a period of six weeks, at the end of which it ceased. The making of steel for munitions was stopped at once, and shell-filling also came to an abrupt termination. There was on balance a large immediate cessation of war production, and its complete cessation above normal Army requirements was only a question of time. Various employers were set free at once to readjust their programme to meet peace conditions, even though this course led to a considerable amount of unemployment instantly. Unemployment, however, was not so large as it might have been, because in the factories, **Relaxation of** particularly in the national factories, **controls** thousands of workers were kept on for the purpose of breaking-down filled ammunition, and for cleaning, overhauling, and repairing the guns, rifles, and other weapons which were sent back from the front.

To get the factories and works in which war work had ceased, or was ceasing, turned over as quickly as possible to peace production was the next thing, but in many cases this was difficult, and in some impossible—*e.g.*, shell shops had been standardised to such an extent that to change them into anything else was simply impracticable. Another difficulty was the shortage of certain raw materials, and still another was the not unnatural hesitation of the trading community to place orders in view of the uncertainty of prices. At the time of the armistice there was no free market. With respect to employers, the Government got out of the way of private enterprise by relaxing the various controls it had been forced to institute over materials and prices. Owing to the completeness of the victory over Germany the

process of relaxation of controls was fairly rapid. It took time, however, to re-establish a free market ; it was April, 1919, before the prime commodity—steel, for instance—ruled at an economic price.

Industrial demobilisation, so far as the employers were concerned, had to take all these things into account. Further, it had to be borne in mind that of all European countries which had been compelled to mobilise their industrial forces Great Britain suffered most by it. The United Kingdom was purely an industrial country, and as its industries were less prepared for war than those of any other belligerent they consequently underwent the greatest transformation. By advancing funds or giving an equivalent in credit, where deemed advisable, as well as by other means, the Government also helped the employers to get back to pre-war work.

DINNER HOUR ON THE TYNE.
Workers at one of the Tyne shipyards leaving the yard for the dinner-hour break in their day of strenuous labour, showing what a large proportion of young lads were employed.

Concurrently with the demobilisation of the war industries and the rebuilding of the old-time industries went the demobilisation of the workers and their resettlement in industry. As already noted, the Government eased the situation at the start of the demobilisation of the workers, and afterwards, by continuing to employ in various ways very considerable numbers of them. Thus at Woolwich, where upwards of 63,000 men and women were employed in October, 1918, there were still nearly 50,000 people, including more than 16,000 women, at work in the beginning of January, 1919. This, however, was a rather special case, for demobilisation at other national establishments had proceeded much farther. In the national projectile factory at Hackney, where about 4,500 were employed in October, 1918, the number was reduced to a few more than 1,500 by the beginning of 1919 ; the figures for the national shell-filling factory at Hayes on the same dates were, 8,700 and 1,800. In the huge national high-explosives factory or factory system of Gretna, a town created by war production, the figures similarly were 11,500 and 3,400.

As the months went past the process of demobilisation of civil war workers continued steadily until by May, 1919, there were 24,000 workers, of whom only 2,700 were women, at Woolwich ; not quite 600 at Hackney ; about

700 at Hayes; and rather more than 3,100 at Gretna. Proportionately to size, much the same thing occurred in the other national establishments. By the same date, too, a number of factories were closed, and the shutting down of others was certain. By the end of April, 1919, about 250,000 men and women had come into the labour market from national factories for re-absorption into peace-time employments.

At the date of the armistice private employers of war

THE MAKING OF KHAKI AT TROWBRIDGE.
Warping the cloth in the manufacture of khaki at one of the large factories established at Trowbridge, Wilts., for the manufacture of this material. Large numbers of women and girls were employed in the making of khaki, many millions of yards of which were required during each year of the war.

workers were set free at once to readjust their programme to meet peace conditions, as previously stated. In the matter of discharges of the workers the employers were in effect left to their own discretion. The Government confined itself to making general suggestions, and intervened directly in a few cases only. But at the same time it took such measures as it judged to be necessary, both to deal with the unemployment involved in this unrestricted return to peace conditions, and, as regarded those who remained at work, to prevent a serious fall in wages. On the day of the armistice the Government issued a circular to all firms engaged in munitions manufacture, suggesting that, as far as possible, there should be no immediate discharge of the workers, that all workers who wished to leave or could be absorbed readily elsewhere should be released at once, and that, to help to retain workers as long as possible, the production of certain munitions still being made should be slowed down by the abolition of overtime, the suspension where practicable of payment by result, and the reduction even of the normal working hours. No doubt this circular had some effect, but presently it was known that the discharge **Freeing the** of a very considerable number of workers **volunteer workers** was contemplated by the employers, and the Government sent out another circular, suggesting the order in which discharges of the workers should proceed.

Simultaneously, steps were taken to free from their obligations the various classes of workers who had worked under special conditions for State service. The enrolments of War Munition Volunteers were cancelled as from December 15th, 1918, or as from any earlier date at which the workman left his employment after giving or receiving the usual trade notice. The same step was taken with regard to War Work Volunteers, National Service Volunteers, and War Agricultural Volunteers. These workers thus recovered the freedom of movement they had given up for State purposes, and might either remain in their employment, if their employers desired

them to do so, or find work under ordinary conditions elsewhere. Steps were also taken for the general release of Army Reserve Munition Workers, and of serving soldiers temporarily withdrawn from the Colours, both from the terms of the agreements under which they had been transferred to civil work and from service with the forces. For the most part these men reverted at once to the position of ordinary civilian workers. All persons discharged were given free railway passes for their journey from the place of war employment to their homes, or to places where they had found new employment.

Further, to tide over the transition period from war to peace, the Government brought in some temporary measures with respect to the wages to be paid to the workers. Munition workers, whose work was slowed down immediately after the armistice, and whose reduced hours were put on a time-work basis, were guaranteed the following minimum rates: Men over eighteen, 30s., and boys under eighteen, 15s. a week; women over eighteen, 25s., and girls under eighteen, 12s. 6d. a week. Wherever the earnings of these classes fell below these amounts the Government undertook to make up these sums to employers, so as to enable them to pay the minima.

The general rates of wages were stabilised by the Wages (Temporary Regulation) Act, passed in November, 1918, and this Act gave statutory force to the rates of wages in operation on November 11th, 1918, for six months from that date. It further provided that the same statutory force should be extended to any new standard rates established by agreement between employers and Trade Unions, provided they were registered by the Ministry of Labour. The object of this Act was to give industry six months in which to get wages on a commercial basis. It did not settle the wages problem, but it facilitated a settlement by providing for definite and uniform rates in every industry during the period of transition. In its way it was a sort of armistice imposed in the war of wages.

After all these measures were taken to make the industrial demobilisation gradual and to provide for the resettlement in industry of the war workers, it was still plain that the demobilisation immediately subsequent to and consequent on the armistice **"Out-of-work** carried with it the certainty of the unemploy- **donation"** ment at once of hundreds of thousands of men and women. "The Government," to quote from the speech of Sir Robert Horne, referred to before, "was faced with the immediate prospect of great masses of workpeople being thrown out on the streets without any means of livelihood." The situation was highly critical, and called for some large measure of relief on the part of the Government, which alone could deal with it in a big way.

It happened that there was something of a precedent. Towards the end of 1915 the Government of the day had announced that upon demobilisation members of the forces would be entitled, in addition to other allowances, to receive an insurance policy, good for a year, against unemployment. In the same manner, but not at first for anything like the same length of time, the Government in existence in November, 1918, provided for the war workers thrown out of employment by a general scheme of unemployment benefit —the "out-of-work donation." As it was held to be impossible to discriminate between those who were engaged in war work and those who were not, the scheme was extended to include all industrial workers.

The benefits provided by the scheme were: For men over eighteen 24s., and for women over eighteen 20s., a

In occupied Cologne: British Tanks preceded by a guard of the Royal Navy.

British Tanks before Cologne Cathedral: An inspection by the Sixth Corps commander.

Under an armed guard: German prisoners stacking German trench stoves at a Namur dump.

Returning the loot: German prisoners unloading a barge of stolen furniture recovered for Belgium.

Gas shells at Luttre, Belgium: Part of a dump which the retreating Germans failed to destroy.

German booty dump in Belgium: Prisoners loading a barge with machinery to be restored.

Destroyed viaduct over the Scarpe at Athies, east of Arras, as it was on November 15th, 1918.

Rapid reconstruction by French engineers: The Athies Viaduct as it was on February 1st, 1919.

week; for boys between fifteen and eighteen 12s., and for girls of the same age 10s., a week. An allowance was given in respect of dependent children under fifteen of 6s. a week for the first child and 3s. for the others. The scheme came into operation on November 25th, 1918, and was to remain in operation for six months, but during that period the benefit could be drawn for a maximum time of thirteen weeks and no longer. Protests came from all parts of the country of the inadequacy of the amount of the unemployment donation. Demands were made sometimes for a "full maintenance allowance," and sometimes for a "50s. unemployment donation." The Government yielded to the extent of increasing the amount by 5s. in the case of adults, and 2s. 6d. in the case of juveniles, men and women thus getting 29s. and 25s. respectively a week, and boys and girls 14s. 6d. and 12s. 6d. respectively a week.

A system of contributory unemployment benefit—7s. a week—was in existence throughout the country, but it was not general in its incidence. Under the National Insurance Act of 1911 about two million workers were insured, and under the Munitions of War Act, 1917, one and a half millions were likewise insured. There were also many workers who were insured through their Trade Unions. When every allowance, however, was made for the number of those insured against unemployment, there remained about ten million workers who had no such provision. The new out-of-work donation was non-contributory; it was a free gift to all workers, war or otherwise, who showed that they were out of work, were willing to work, and could not find work—these were the conditions. The rules set up were those of the National Insurance (Unemployment) Acts.

Pains were taken by the Government to make everyone understand that the out-of-work donation was not intended to be permanent, but was a temporary expedient for minimising want and distress in the period of change from war to peace. From the public came few objections. The nation, exulting in the victory that was implicit in **Temporary expedient** the armistice, was in no mood to scan the **to minimise distress** scheme closely. At the moment its heart was fixed on peace, not on retrenchment. In the General Election, which took place shortly after the scheme was announced, no candidate for Parliament ventured to condemn what the Government had done. Yet from the beginning it was clear that the working out of the scheme in detail—in the case of each worker asking this help from the State—would have to be watched most carefully, otherwise workers who did not want to work might take advantage of the opportunity.

Perhaps it was not stated with sufficient plainness to the workers that to take the State's bounty, unless it was necessary, was an unpatriotic act, and that there was no place in the scheme for the "sponger." Provision was, in fact, made to prevent abuse. The applicant for the donation had first to go before a Labour Exchange; if the particular Exchange was not satisfied as to the *bona fides* of the application, he next applied to a Court of Referees—in all ninety-two of these courts, which consisted of employers and workers, with an independent chairman, were established; if he again failed, he could appeal to an umpire appointed by the Ministry of Labour, whose decision was final. In spite of this machinery there was abuse, as was evident enough as the weeks went by; but there was very little at the start. The number of applicants, however, constantly increased, the majority of them being women. At the beginning of May, 1919, 215,700 men and about 444,000 women war workers were drawing the donation.

The demobilisation of women war workers presented special features. Directly replacing men, nearly one and a half millions of women had entered industry during the Great War. Of these about 701,000 were engaged on munitions, and 774,000 on other Government work. The new increase of female workers employed outside their own homes during the period of the war was 1,200,000. In addition there were 79,300 women to be demobilised from the various women's

WAR-MADE BORDER TOWN.
Panoramic view of Gretna, a munition-making township of 16,000 workers which in two years grew upon a site that had been bare farmland.

corps. The extent to which women could be continued on men's work very largely depended on the attitude of the Trade Unions, and on the extent to which the men in the Army desired or were able to resume their former occupations; but it was feared that great numbers of women who had been engaged in women's work would be thrown out of employment during the time of transition. The fear was justified.

Leaving aside boys and girls, 45,000 women received the donation on November 29th, 1918, as against 16,600 men war workers. In the following week the numbers were: Women, 77,800; men, 31,700. By January 10th, 1919, the figures were: Women, **Free training** 265,400; men, 119,300. And on February **for new work** 7th: Women, 427,300; men, 191,300. By that date 26,800 girls were drawing the donation, as against 24,500 boys.

To assist in the demobilisation of the women war workers, and in transferring the women into peace occupations, an appeal was issued to women workers who intended marrying soldiers and sailors, and to war brides who purposed settling down with their husbands, to withdraw from industry altogether. Those to whom the remuneration received was not a necessity were also requested to withdraw. This, however, only dealt with the fringes of the matter, and the Ministry of Labour decided to assist women in search of fresh employment by arranging for free training for approved candidates in work for which there was a demand. The subjects selected for training were (1) domestic work and housewifery, and (2) work in factories or workshops which was recognised as women's work before the war. A maintenance allowance for a fixed period of training was given to the women while being trained, but not in supplement of the donation. Some private firms, realising the difficulty of getting experienced women in their particular trades, offered to train and did train some numbers of women.

One of the most serious difficulties encountered in finding employment for women war workers was the great reluctance of many women to re-enter domestic service. Mistresses blamed the out-of-work donation for this, and public opinion inclined to that view. The dearth of domestic servants, which was noticeable before the war, became greatly accentuated during the war, and after the armistice there was a keen demand for them which was far from being met. This, of course, fastened attention on the donation as a contributing cause of the scarcity, and unquestionably

Organisation of domestic service the donation did have an effect on the situation. But there were other factors, which had perhaps an even greater influence. Women had become accustomed for one thing to the much higher wages paid in the war factories, and for another to the freedom of factory life, compared with which domestic service appeared irksome and almost intolerable.

It became apparent to the authorities that if domestic service was to regain its place in women's estimation, and be undertaken by sufficient numbers of the demobilised war workers, the conditions of service would have to be more attractive than in the pre-war days. The matter was considered by the Women's Advisory Committee of the Ministry of Reconstruction, which published a report containing a series of recommendations on the organisation and conditions of domestic service. Efforts were made by many of the Local Advisory or Employment Committees and Employment Councils, actively at work all over the country, to have these recommendations carried out as far as practicable by means of conferences with mistresses and the demobilised women. The endeavours of the Government, through the Ministry of Labour, resulted, by the beginning of May, 1919, in the placing of upwards of 66,000 women in domestic, hotel, or charwoman service. On the other side of the account it had to be noted that women, rather than go back to or take up domestic service, threw up the donation.

With regard to the rapid re-absorption of the women war workers into general industry there was a circumstance that was found to militate against it. Many of the women, especially of the younger ones, had seen no industrial life except that in the munition factories. In them they had been accustomed to canteens, rest-rooms, decent cloak-rooms, and facilities for recreation. "Welfare" work had been a feature of the Ministry of Munitions, and employers had been induced to take it up on a large scale by the Government's permission to them to charge the major part of the costs of welfare departments against excess profits. Much of this welfare work was dropped by the employers after the armistice, even where women were still working. The Ministry of Labour continued its Welfare Department, and did its utmost to maintain interest in welfare among the employers. In thousands of cases where the women were demobilised this Welfare Department took

Women and welfare work charge of them, saw to their comfort, kept them when "stranded" at stations, and sent them on to their homes or to the places where there was employment.

At the outset of the industrial demobilisation the Government dealt *en bloc* with its various phases by creating a special department out of an amalgamation of the Labour Departments of the Ministry of Munitions, of the Admiralty, and of the Ministry of Labour. It was called the Department of Civil Demobilisation and Resettlement, and at its head, with the title of Controller-General, was placed Sir Stephenson Kent, a partner in the firm of Stephenson, Kent & Co., and a thorough business man, who had joined the Ministry of Munitions in 1915 and became the Director-General of its labour supply. From the beginning of the Ministry of Munitions he had been in the closest touch with very many of the war workers, and was intimately acquainted with the conditions both in the factories and in the labour market. Besides, dealing with the demobilisation and resettlement of the war workers, he also dealt with the demobilisation and resettlement of the Army, Navy, and Air Force. He was assisted by the Labour Resettlement Committee, which had been appointed in March, 1918, and which consisted of fifty-five members, representing employers and workpeople in all the chief industries, as well as several Government departments.

Any statement of the demobilisation and resettlement of the war workers would be very incomplete that did not at this point take into account the demobilisation and resettlement of the men of the forces, as the latter began to come into the open labour market in large and increasing numbers in January, 1919. Some of the demobilised soldiers, such as "pivotal men," no doubt helped demobilised war workers to find employment, but others to some extent competed with them for work, and made the obtaining of employment by the war workers so much the more difficult. On January 3rd, 1919, about 24,000 men from the forces could not get work, as was shown by that number of donations being paid; on January 10th the number was 31,500, and on January 31st it was upwards of 53,300. By the beginning of May the figure was about 380,000.

After the General Election of 1918 Mr. Lloyd George formed a new Cabinet, in which Sir Robert Horne, K.C., M.P., replaced Mr. G. H. Roberts as Minister of Labour. In February, 1919, the new Minister was faced with a critical situation. To quote his own words:

It became perfectly plain that a very large number of people had failed to find employment, and that at the same time they had drawn thirteen weeks' unemployment donation. The situation was very critical. At that time it seemed as if the whole world would be in a state of disturbance. But in any case, and apart altogether from the view one might take of the situation, the fact was that a large number of people who ought to have been in employment were without employment, and without the ordinary means of livelihood. It was plain, also, by that time that the figures of the previous donation **Abuse of the "donation"** were such as to induce certain people rather to remain idle than to look with great assiduity for work, and the Government had to make up its mind what it would do in these circumstances. What the Government decided to do was to reduce the donation, and make the rate of payment to men out of employment 20s. a week, instead of 29s., and the rate of payment to women 15s., instead of 25s.

Sir Robert went on to say that the reduction of the donation might be regarded as a compromise; but it had the result on the one hand of making the amount no longer a temptation to idle rather than to work if work was available, and on the other of providing, in case of those enduring real hardship, something towards their subsistence. While admitting that the donation had been abused, he stated that the amount of abuse was very greatly exaggerated, and that there was "a great deal of quite unwarranted talk in the matter." He pointed out that one of the causes of unemployment was that the employers made insufficient use of the Labour Exchanges, and that from one circumstance or another there were not nearly enough jobs to go round, while in some cases the wages offered were absurdly inadequate. But he laid down the principle that people who were drawing the bounty of the State were not entitled to discriminate as to what kind of work they were going to do. He mentioned that 22,000 women had been suspended from drawing the donation for refusing to enter domestic service, and that the Court of Referees had upheld this decision in 17,000 instances.

Declaring that in the circumstances of the time he could not think of any crime that was meaner than the attempt to obtain by fraud the State's money in the out-of-work donation, he said that investigators had been appointed, and that such criminals when detected would be prosecuted relentlessly. He announced the appointment of a committee to inquire into the whole administration of the unemployed benefit. This committee consisted of Lord Aberconway (chairman), and of Sir M. Barlow, M.P., Colonel G. Collins, Mr. G. R. Lane-Fox, M.P., Mr. T. Shaw, M.P., Sir W. Kinnear, Mr. T. G. Bowers, and Mr. T. W. Phillips, with Mr. G. C. Rickett, as secretary. No report had been issued by the committee when this chapter was completed; but when it came it was sure to be a document of remarkable public interest, for it would explain in detail why more than a million people were being paid the donation as late as six months after the armistice, and how the amount paid in donations had reached the enormous sum of nearly twenty-two millions sterling.

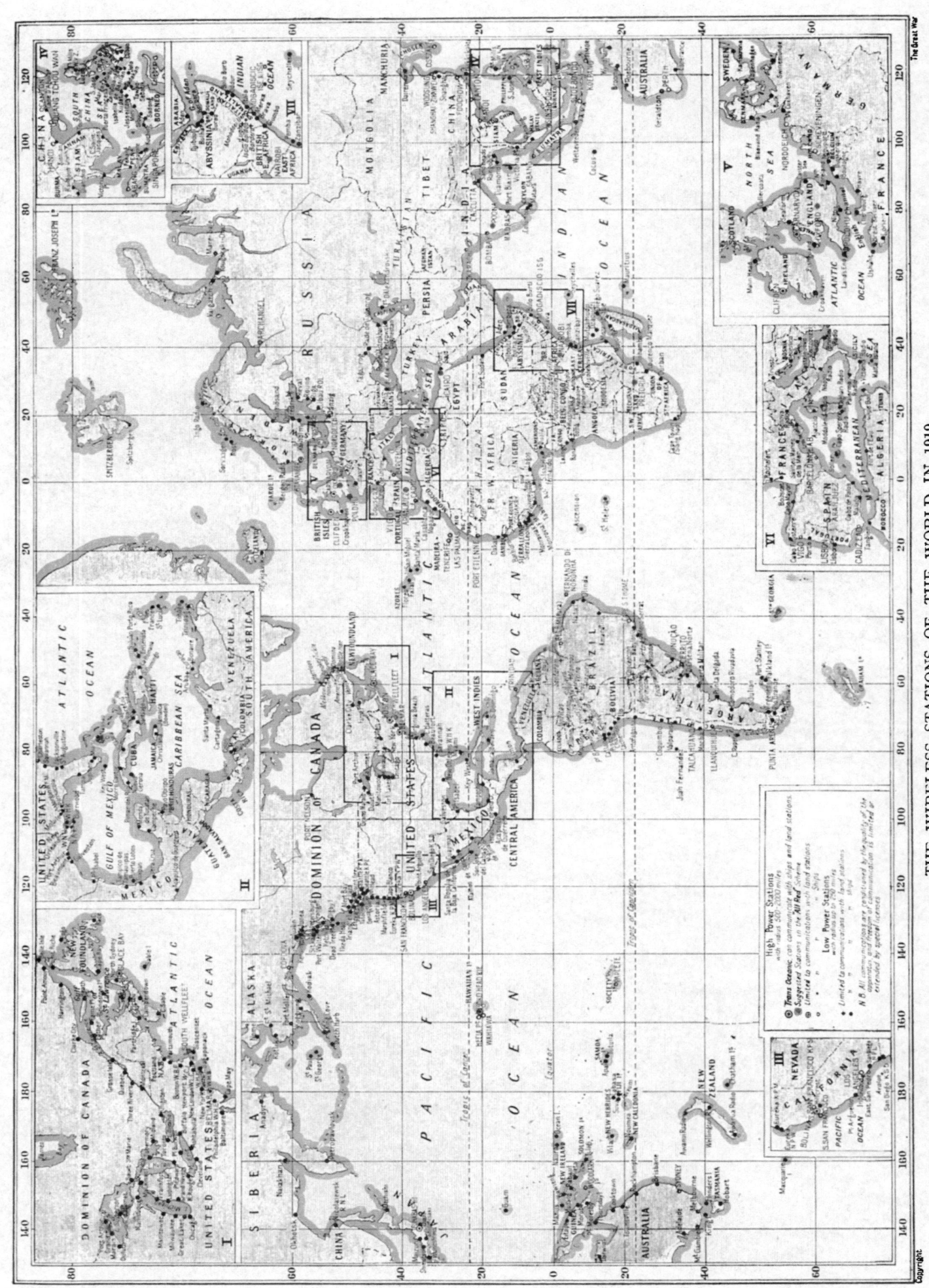

THE WIRELESS STATIONS OF THE WORLD IN 1919.

BRITISH OPERATORS AT | CHAPTER CCCIX. | GERMAN WIRELESS STATION.

THE WONDERS OF WIRELESS IN THE WAR.
By Edward Wright.

Extension of Wireless in 1915—German Attempt to Obtain Wireless Monopoly—Wireless Gunnery Control on Rufiji River—Heroic Conduct of "Spotting" Operator—Sayville Plotting Messages Discovered by American Wireless Detectives—Remarkable Decoding Feat Regarding Lusitania Plot—Enemy's Propaganda System Based on Electric-Wave Telegraphy—U Boats Use Wireless in Preparing their Attacks—Problem of Secret Hostile Wireless Plants—Lack of Directional Wireless in British Navy—Strange Tale of the Spider Web and the Triangulation of U Boats—Zeppelin Campaign Stopped by British Direction-Finders—British Wireless Makes Possible Long-distance Blockade of Enemy Ports—The New Electrical Nervous System of British Fleet.—Skill and Valour of Marconi Operators in Merchant Service—How Operator Duncan Smith Deceived the Leipzig Collier—Teutons' Horrible Use of S O S Decoy Calls—Development of Wireless in British Air Service—Invention of Aircraft Wireless Telephone and its Effect on Formation Tactics—The Wirelessing Tank in Smoke-Screen Attacks—British Army Uses German Wireless in Remarkable Fashion—Increase of Forward Wireless Work—Flexibility of Control of Multitudinous Forces with Wireless Equipment.

A T the outbreak of war all the principal elements of wireless systems of communication were worked out. The British Fleet had been using wireless control for some fifteen years, gradually extending the range of signalling, until both the Admiralty and the commander of the Grand Fleet could organise forces over great distances. Armies had practised wireless methods of command in the field by means of portable sets and motor-carried plant. Large airships had been equipped with far-ranging sending and receiving instruments, and experiments in wireless signalling from aeroplanes had been successfully conducted in 1913. In small naval craft, such as torpedo-boats and submarines, the range of wireless communication was at first about twenty-five miles, but in the early part of the war this was increased to sixty miles and afterwards further extended, especially at night time by sending up box-kites with an aerial wire, or even using jets of water as aerials. Great wireless stations were able to communicate over distances of more than 6,000 miles, and the Marconi Company, using improved Fleming valves and other devices, was preparing to make Transatlantic electric-wave telephony a practical commercial affair by the end of 1914.

By reason of their early fostering of the primary inventions of Senator Marconi, the British people should have been in a highly favourable position

in the matter of electric-wave communications. The British Navy had some four hundred and thirty-five ships equipped with wireless and about thirty shore stations, while some thousands of vessels of the British Mercantile Marine had the short-distance radio-telegraphy mechanism, as limited by the Berne Convention. This was a natural peaceful development due to the combination of Italian inventiveness and British enterprise, but there was a great gap in the British system of wireless stations. A proposal had been made by foresightful men for the erection of a chain of powerful stations, linking all the main settlements of the scattered British Commonwealth and supplementing the girdle of British submarine cables. The Liberal Government, however, did not have this vital scheme carried out, and the only immediate definite result was to enlighten and stimulate the more energetic German Government and lead it to spend some £2,000,000 in wireless preparations for the war.

The Teutons had the advantage of being the aggressors and fixing the date at which they would begin operations. They were thus able to build and organise to a programme, with no regard for ordinary economy and natural pacific development. At a cost three times as great as that with which the Marconi Company agreed to build the British Imperial chain of stations the Germans speeded up the erection and extension of the new methods of

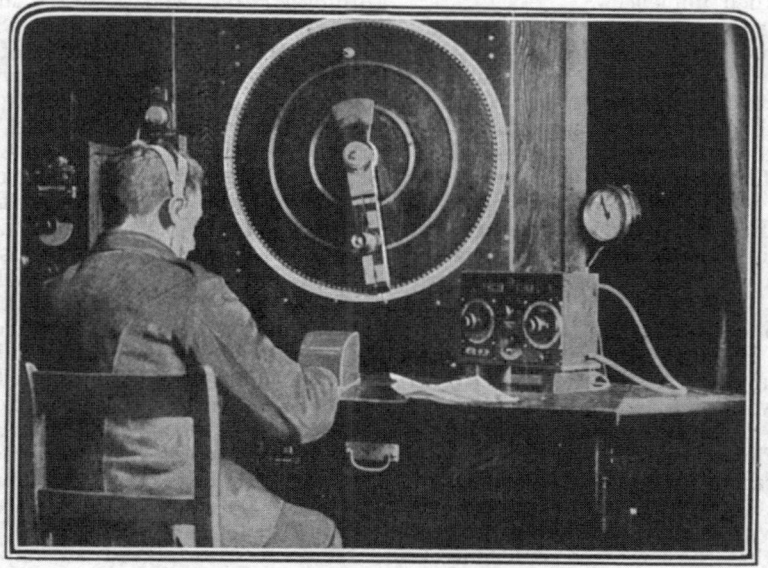

WIRELESS SIGNALLING FROM COLOGNE.
Operating one of the German instruments at the Cologne wireless station. When the British occupied Cologne this station was immediately taken over and utilised.

conducting war. In 1910 an extraordinary, subtle, and strong attempt was made to wreck the British Marconi Company and its undertakings, so as to make the German Telefunken Company and its associated corporations supreme in the world. The Germans had already imitated Marconi's master patents, and thus prevented the full expansion of **German Government** the British-Italian Company, and by **subsidises wireless** Government aid and Government direction the Telefunken Company sought to underbid the struggling, unaided British firm in erecting foreign shore stations and equipping foreign ships.

German ambassadors intrigued for orders, and the German Government provided financial help to the Telefunken Company, enabling it at need to build at a loss. Senator Marconi and his manager had at last to draw cheques on their private accounts to pay the weekly salaries of their staff. For some time it was only the aid given by Italian capitalists and by the Italian Government that kept the British Marconi Company from being wrecked and absorbed by the German imitators of the Marconi rights. When at last the British Cabinet was reluctantly convinced of the necessity for using its influence to prevent a universal German

ordinary signals. The Austrian wireless at Pola communicated with Spanish stations, and the Turks had a station outside Constantinople, which had already rendered important military service during the Balkan War, and maintained constant communication with Berlin.

In the first months of the war the enemy derived huge profit from the £2,000,000 he had spent in wireless preparations. He saved, for a time, a large part of the national fortune invested in shipping by sending out wireless instructions for all vessels at sea to make for neutral ports. The Pacific coast became the refuge of a large number of German ships, and until the United States entered the war many steamers of magnificent tonnage and power in American ports escaped capture by the Allies. To a considerable extent Senator Marconi became unwillingly the saviour of the German Mercantile Marine. Without his invention, German shipping on the high seas would, in large measure, have served to increase the carrying power of Great Britain, through being captured before many of the skippers became aware that the war had opened.

There can also be little doubt that the German China Squadron under Count von Spee would have been overtaken

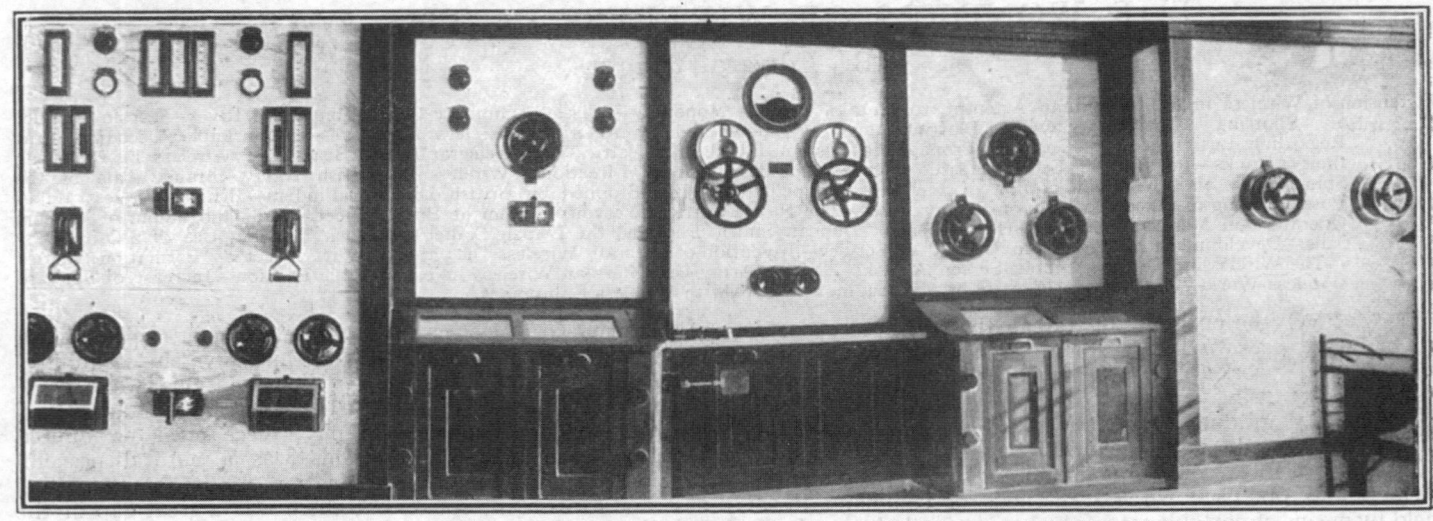

THE TWENTY-KILOWATT TRANSMITTING SWITCHBOARD FOR LONG-RANGE WIRELESS AT COLOGNE.
Both at home and abroad, in preparation for the war which they had willed, the Germans had indulged in lavish expenditure on wireless stations. For them wireless was primarily a military agent, and they organised it with no regard for economy or normal pacific development.

monopoly in wireless, the Teutons still remained able to cover a large part of the earth with stations, and attract such powerful foreign clients as the American Standard Oil Company into the sphere of their influence.

The Nauern station, near Berlin, was made the centre of the German world wireless system. The generating engines were increased from 35 h.p. to 1,000 h.p., giving a range of 6,200 miles. Under favourable electric conditions, signals could be heard at Windhoek, in South-West Africa, and there were connections and relays with the Togoland and Dar-es-Salaam stations. In the United States there was a German station at Sayville, Long Island, for which new and more powerful equipment was prepared. Between 1911 and 1913 the Germans attempted to obtain permanent land stations in Nicaragua, in connection with the Panama Canal, and also to acquire complete control of wireless plants in South and Central America, working in connection with Sayville. In the South Seas the Teutonic Rabaul station of New Guinea was a menace to Australia and New Zealand, and with other German-owned or German-worked plants had a deciding influence on naval operations in the outer seas.

The Teutons also had at Eilwese, in Hanover, a new kind of wireless station, communicating for some 4,000 miles with Tuckerton, in New Jersey. A novel system of continuous electric-wave transmission was employed in the Eilwese station, with the advantage that the messages could only be received by special detectors. Happily, the Marconi Company had acquired before the war rights in the Goldschmidt continuous-wave system, and read the messages as easily as

and destroyed in the absence of the power of wireless communication. The Scharnhorst, Gneisenau, and the enemy light cruisers were tracked by the Australian Squadron under Admiral Patey, who possessed in the battle-cruiser Australia and the cruisers Melbourne and Sydney a faster, heavier, and longer-ranged force than that of the German admiral. But while the Australians were carrying out elaborate operations for closing on the enemy in Simpsonshaven, the hostile wireless station at Rabaul informed Von Spee of the movements of the Australian ships. This not only frustrated the campaign of Admiral Patey, **Wireless strategy** but led to the British naval disaster off **of Von Spee** Coronel, lowering of British prestige in Chile and Argentina, and to loss and general hindrance of British shipping in the Southern Pacific.

Count von Spee practically usurped the Chile possession of Easter Island, and there erected a wireless station by means of which the movements of pursuing ships were communicated to him, and information regarding British merchant ships and collier vessels. On the South American coast were Telefunken stations with German operators, who also took part in the wireless strategy of the enemy admiral that led to the loss of the Good Hope and the Monmouth and to a threat to the Falkland Islands and British commerce with South America.

Wireless also played an important part in the raiding operations conducted by the German cruiser Emden, under Captain von Müller. It was given to Müller to show that electric-wave telegraphy, used by merchant ships for their protection, could be turned against them. Operators in the enemy raiding vessel picked up information with which Müller turned the Indian Ocean into a kind of vast echoing gallery, in which confidential whispers from unarmed merchantmen and their guiding shore stations could be overheard. With a knowledge of British codes the German raider was also able to pass herself off as one of her sunken victims, and so approach fresh prey. By combining false wireless signals with a disguise of false funnels the Emden in a remarkable manner surprised the allied warships at Penang, torpedoing the Russian cruiser Jemchug and sinking the French destroyer Mousquet. But, as described in Chapter XLVI. (Vol. 2, page 441), the career of the Emden was ended by a call sent out by a British wireless operator on Cocos (Keeling) Isles. This achievement was among the most remarkable examples of the direct warlike power of wireless telegraphy. The call for aid, flashed to the Australian cruiser Sydney at a speed of 186,400 miles a second, was among the first direct displays of the new power with which Senator Marconi had endowed the ocean Commonwealth.

CHANGING THE AERIAL.
British Army electrician changing the aerial on the Poulsen installation at the Cologne wireless station.

Wireless gunnery control from an aeroplane did much to quicken the destruction of the Königsberg, the second enemy raiding cruiser, in the Indian Ocean, in July, 1915. The windings of the Rufiji River and the thick high forests about it made range-finding difficult in the East African retreat of the German ship. The action became a contest between German telephone wire control and British wireless direction. The enemy had erected an observation tower by the river, in telephonic communication with the Königsberg. The British monitors Severn and Mersey began operations by bombarding the tower and destroying it, and then made a quick movement from their own positions. The blinded German gunners continued firing at the places the British warships had left, and meanwhile an aeroplane, carrying Flight-Commander Cull and a wireless operator, Mr. Arnold,

went up, spotted the enemy, and directed fire upon him. The aeroplane was hit and crashed into the water, throwing Arnold out; but, during the fall, he with admirable coolness continued his spotting work, his last message running, "Carry on, you are hitting her every time forward. We have been hit. Coming down on water. Send boat."

There would probably have been a different ending to the action if Mr. Arnold had not completely disregarded his own danger when the machine was falling, and kept the guns of the two monitors ranging exactly upon the Königsberg. Soon after, a German wireless message was intercepted, **Wireless and the Königsberg** giving the information that the hostile cruiser had been completely destroyed. In spite of the collier that had been sunk at the mouth of the river at the beginning of the autumn by H.M.S. Chatham, the Königsberg had not been bottled up. There were four other river mouths, along one or more of which the enemy could have put out to sea had circumstances been favourable. This was one of the things that gave high importance to the achievement of Flight-Commander Cull and Mr. Arnold.

When all enemy cruisers and early auxiliary steamers were destroyed on the open sea, the wireless stations remaining directly or indirectly under enemy control in foreign lands became serviceable for political and general ends. Also the enemy's campaign of submarine piracy was promoted by the various use of wireless communications. The U boats were at first unable to receive the large waves from the Sayville, on Long Island. This difficulty was overcome by the Nauern station, near Berlin, taking the messages in special code and transmitting information in shorter wave lengths suitable to the submarine apparatus.

The part which the Sayville apparatus played in the enemy submarine campaign and general policy of intrigue was remarkable. It was traced by Mr. John Rathom, an Australian editing the "Journal," of Providence, U.S.A., and by Mr. Charles Apgar, an

GENERATING CURRENT FOR LONG-DISTANCE WIRELESS.
Interior of the generating station at Cologne which supplied power for the twenty-kilowatt wireless communication between Cologne and Constantinople.

American owner of a private wireless station at Westfield, New Jersey. Mr. Rathom had wireless operators studying all messages sent and received by the Germans, and thereby discovered there was constant connection between many large commercial and shipping houses in the United States and the German Government. Code numbers and combinations of letters, which were used by the Germany Embassy in its messages to Berlin, were in many cases found in messages sent out by the Atlantic Communication Company of Sayville, the Siemens and Halske Company, of New York, the

ONE OF GERMANY'S CHIEF WIRELESS STATIONS.
View from one of the platforms of the southern tower of the wireless station at Nauern, in Germany, from which it was claimed communication could be carried on over a distance of 10,000 miles.

Hamburg-Amerika Line and North German Lloyd Line, and many other concerns. It became clear that the extraordinary strength of the German propaganda system in America was mainly due to the fact that the great German commercial houses were outposts of the German Government, heavily subsidised and acting directly under official orders.

From his wireless discoveries Mr. John Rathom found that various Central and South American Governments had, by accepting underpriced tenders from the Telefunken Company for the erection and operation of radio-telegraph stations, assisted unwittingly the Teutonic scheme for covering the world with German wireless. A branch of the Telefunken Company also intrigued for the erection of wireless stations in the Philippine Islands, being prepared to contract for the work at such an unprofitable price that no ordinary fair tender from wireless firms would be accepted.

Among the wireless messages received by the Germans at Sayville and recorded by the " Journal" operators, was one in connection with the Lusitania. The German message ran : " From Berlin Foreign Office. To Botschaft, Washington— 669. (44-W)—Welt nineteen-fifteen warne 175 29 1 stop 175 1 2 stop durch 662 2 4 stop 19 7 18 stop 11X 11 3 4 5 6." The deciphering of this message was an apparently impossible problem, as none of the known codes was used in it. But the "Journal" had an agent in the German Embassy at Washington, who remembered that on the morning of April 29th Prince Hatzfeldt, of the Embassy Staff, had been hunting for a " New York World Almanac" for 1915. The investigators obtained the almanac, for which the clue was given by " Welt nineteen-fifteen"—the first two words of the message. Following the numbers as representing page, line, and word in the publication, they decoded the order from the Berlin Foreign Office to the German Embassy at Washington. It ran:

Berlin and the Lusitania

Warne	—Warn	622 2 4	—Press
175 29 1	—Lusitania	19 7 18	—not
175 1 2	—Passengers	LIX 11, 3, 4, 5, 6,	—
durch	—through	Voyage across the Atlantic.	

The correctness of this decoding of the most secret wireless message sent across the Atlantic by the German Government was proved on May 1st, 1915, when there appeared in the " New York World" and the " New York Times" an advertisement by the German Embassy warning travellers across the Atlantic from sailing in any ship flying the British flag. Mr. John Rathom and his lieutenants continued to intercept and decode the messages sent to the Sayville station. They became so dangerous to the enemy that a council was held in the offices of the Hamburg-Amerika Line, in Broadway, at which Captain von Papen and his agent König advised that the offices of the "Journal" should be blown up. This murderous measure was, however, combated by the naval attaché, Captain Boy-Ed. Mr. Rathom became aware of this interesting affair and of many others of larger national importance, and continued to listen for months to the operations of both the Sayville and Tuckerton wireless stations, making discoveries on which were founded the "Journal's" startling exposures of German propaganda, intrigue, destruction, and murder.

Meanwhile, Mr. Charles Apgar, working at night with merely an amateur's instruments at Westfield, completed the evidence against the Teutons. It was suspected that the Sayville operators were continually sending out messages of a military character, under cover of ordinary commercial despatches in plain English and German. American naval censors stopped many communications on the ground that they were obviously not what they were intended to be.

For example, an attempt was made to send from Sayville an order to buy German cotton for an American firm. Other things were ordered from Germany which could not possibly be shipped to America. Such messages as these were stopped by the American authorities, but there continued a great stream of reasonable and apparently innocent words, from which the most expert and painstaking of American decoders could obtain **Ingenious secret messages** no evidence of secret messages. But Mr. Apgar had fitted phonographic records to his receiving instrument. He prevented gaps, while substituting a fresh record for a filled one, by using two machines, and switching the receiver from one phonograph to the other when necessary. His records showed that the Germans employed curious variations in their methods of transmission. The usual custom in long-distance sending is to repeat each word, so that if the first signal is faint the second will make all clear. For example, a message beginning with name and address such as : " Pr 3. W. 16 to, etc.," would be sent thus : " Pr 3. Pr 3. W. 16. W. 16. to to, etc." But in the Sayville communications it was found that messages often would run : Pr. Pr. 3. Pr. 3. Sometimes a word would be repeated three times instead of once. Sometimes there would be other variations in sending, that became apparent in the phonographic records. Official American operators at Arlington and Fire Island always listened carefully to the German messages, yet merely read them as what they purported to be. With their minds centred on getting the meaning, they regarded the repetitions as being merely intended to make the symbols clear. But every night, between 11 p.m. and 2 a.m., Mr. Apgar made his phonographic records. In the morning he transcribed them and either delivered them personally to the New York police or sent them to the Secret Service officer in Washington. With the exception of the

PORTABLE WIRELESS.
Testing a portable wireless installation at the Experimental Station, Somersham, with a view to ascertaining the limit of its range.

valve detector and the ordinary receiving telephones, all Mr Apgar's instruments were home-made. He had a 55-feet aerial on his house, and a 600-feet aerial running on neighbouring trees, and he could tune up to 10,000-metre wave lengths. He numbered his cylinders and made a complete index of message numbers, and in the course of two weeks gave the American Secret Service such material that the Sayville wireless station was, in July, 1915, taken over by the United States Government and operated only by American naval officers. As the Tuckerton station was already controlled by American authorities, the Teutons in America were left practically deaf and dumb.

The result of the double exposures of the German use of wireless in the United States showed the weakness of the new instrument of communication in the hands of a blockaded people. The lack of secrecy consequent upon the immense radius of the

Intellect pitted against intellect electric waves, laid all the messages open to permanent record and to intense examination both by the Allies and interested neutrals. The Marconi Company had been using the phonographic method of recording before the war, and during hostilities it was employed in Great Britain. The best experts in Great Britain and France constantly worked at decoding the enemy's far-flung wireless communications, including the millions of words sent out from the German stations. Therefore, in all military operations and in all political intrigues in foreign countries, directed by radio-telegraphy, the Germans and Austrians depended for safety on the inviolable secrecy of their various codes. Intellect was then pitted against intellect, and it was not the Teutons that won.

Before Mr. Apgar began his phonographic recording, the American Secret Service was warned by the Allies that the

Sayville messages were very suspicious. It was largely as a direct result of this warning that Mr. Apgar was asked to undertake the work he successfully carried out. German plots were discovered through the enemy's over-confident use of Transatlantic wireless codes, and the revelations thus made had no small effect upon bringing the United States into the war. Leading newspapers, such as the "Journal" and the "World," published astounding information regarding the enemy's use of wireless facilities, and directly aroused popular resentment before President Woodrow Wilson took any action. The welding of **Propaganda by** the national will of the United States **wireless** against the disruptive influences of Teutons, Fenian and Sinn Fein Irishmen, and anarchic organisations directed from Berlin and Vienna was partly accomplished by exposures derived from German wireless messages.

On the other hand it must be noted that the enemy's system of propaganda and intrigue in America, in Spain, and other countries within receiving range of the Nauern station, was greatly aided by the new means of direct and instant communication. When German cables were cut and all submarine telegraphs running through allied territory were brought under censorship, there remained free for a time only the American cable to the Azores. But for the power obtained from wireless methods of telegraphy the Central Empires would have been impotent to send the rapid and continual stream of reports necessary in maintaining their prestige among wavering neutral peoples. On particular occasions they would have been unable to forestall the Allies by coloured versions of military and naval actions, or counteract to some extent the natural and almost universal anger over their submarine operations against passenger and cargo steamers.

TRANSMITTING FROM A PACK STATION.
Signalling from a portable wireless telegraphy "pack station," that could be carried on the saddles of four horses.

Both with regard to their secret instructions to publicity agencies and to the news which they spread among neutrals, they would have been overwhelmed by the cabling advantages of the Allies had it not been for the development of electric-wave telegraphy.

As it was, the Teutons had a voice that rang across the Atlantic, and when their stations in the United States were taken by the American Government, a new system of communication was arranged by means of the American land lines to Mexico and long-distance stations in Mexico. This was countered by the American Government establishing censorship over telegraphic communications with Mexico. Mexican intriguers then remained in touch with the Germans, as they had done from the outbreak of hostilities, but their power of communicating useful knowledge to the enemy was considerably reduced. Alike in their period of vigilant neutrality and in their period of warfare the people of the

United States were favoured by geographical position and by temporary difficulties of extending the range of radio-telegraphy. They were near the fringe of the carrying power of the Nauern station, so that German operators could seldom make themselves clearly heard in daytime and were often in trouble during the better signalling conditions obtaining over the Atlantic at night time.

As a matter of fact, the experts of the Telefunken Company did not lead the way in devising means of extending the reach of wireless messages. When deprived by war of opportunities for adopting or adapting the latest refinements of the Marconi system, they proved distinctly inferior to the original inventor and his brilliant lieutenants. The British Company made remarkable practical progress, reaching direct to Australia with its messages, and conducting a large amount of long-distance signalling, while working to protect ships against the submarine menace and helping generally in wireless military affairs. The Germans did not lack inventiveness and patience in experiment, as they showed when they employed the Marconi device of the Fleming valve to tap the telephone wires along the British, French, and Russian fronts. They did not, however, achieve any great improvement in wireless transmission, such as might have extended their submarine operations across the Atlantic in a prolonged and dangerous campaign against American shipping.

Short-distance signals to U boats

In the intense attacks upon allied shipping round the British Isles, France, Spain, Portugal, and Italy, and throughout the Mediterranean, short-distance wireless signals were at times of remarkable service to the enemy. U boats had communication with points on the Irish coast, with places on the Spanish shore, with some Greek islands and other lonely spots.

The enemy craft could approach at night, and, while completely invisible, send a short-range signal in code, asking if the way were clear. There was often no need for the agent on the shore to reply by wireless. A lighted candle in a window, the glow of a lantern, or some other simple, old-fashioned way of answering was usually sufficient. Thus, all that was required on land was a small, concealed aerial wire running to a receiver, such as an amateur could make. It was the U boat's possession of wireless transmitting power that governed the situation.

Before the war the Germans arranged secret wireless stations in various countries. One of the most interesting of these hidden points of communication was the Island of Bréhat, off the Breton coast, south of the Channel Isles. A German professor bought a mill on rising ground, and engaged in scientific work. Not only were preparations made for a wireless station, but the plan included the formation of a base for receiving a large German force by transport from Bremen and Hamburg, and overrunning Northern Brittany. As the scheme depended upon the French Navy being left unaided against the German Navy, it failed from the outset, the British Grand Fleet intervening.

The abundance of both amateur and private scientific wireless installations in the lands of the Western Allies at the outbreak of war seemed to facilitate the erection of secret enemy plant of small transmitting power. But the danger from spies working with wireless soon became **Detecting sources of messages** less than that of signalling over short distances by lights, and far less than the peril from enemy agents communicating by coded cables abroad, by advertisements in exported newspapers, by letters secretly carried in ships, or sent openly, with hidden meanings, through the post. There was a way in which the exact position of a transmitting plant in operation could be calculated. So soon as the existence of a strange source of electric waves was discovered, two or more indicating instruments, that could be carried on a motor-lorry, were arranged to receive the signals at points some miles apart. Then, by a rapid collation of results, the wireless detectives could mark the place on the ordnance map from which the message had come.

The detective method was similar to the technique of directional wireless. If an airman loses his way in the air, but has his receiving and transmitting telegraph or telephone in order, he can send a message out to certain shore stations, and quickly receive from them a fairly precise calculation of his whereabouts. Indeed, so long as his instrument is sufficiently powerful to reach to the stations, he cannot use it and prevent his position from becoming known to the operators if they are expert in the use of their indicating instruments. This remarkable development went strongly against the use of radio-telegraphy for espionage purposes, and was turned directly against the Germans in a very subtle and successful manner.

The navigation of the submarine has many difficulties, especially in the North Sea, where the sun seldom shows and sights are infrequent. About fifty-two sea miles from Felixstowe and an equal distance from Zeebrugge there was moored the old, red, rusty North Hinder light vessel belonging to the Dutch Government. German submarines used to pass near the North Hinder light vessel in order to check their navigation. This was revealed by wireless "fixes" of the U boats.

They usually reported to Germany by electric-wave signals after making up safely through the Strait of Dover, and sometimes they communicated when south-bound. From the British point of view it did not much matter whether these enemy messages could be decoded or not.

The wireless signal was picked up by two widely separated direction-finding stations in England, and each of them obtained by indicating instruments a bearing of the submarine. What followed was a matter of simple triangulation. The base line between the two English stations was known, and when the bearings were plotted out a triangle was obtained. Its apex, where the two bearings crossed, gave the exact position of the U boat. German submarines took great precaution when sending these signals. No aerial mast was got up, as this would have attracted notice of the British air patrol. An auxiliary aerial was obtained by using the jumping wires, running from end to end of the vessel and over the conning-tower, and forming protection against nets, hawsers, and mines.

"The Spider Web"

The reduced visibility of the preying underwater craft did not save them. British operators made a chart showing the positions, dates, and times of day that German submarines were fixed by wireless. From this chart was made, between East Anglia and Holland, the Spider Web, in which the greatest of all defeats was inflicted upon U boats, at the time when they were threatening to win the war by the destruction of shipping. The Spider Web was based on the North Hinder light vessel. For thirty miles round, the water was divided into sectors by means of three imaginary circles and eight radial arms crossing and dividing the circles.

Flying-boats from Felixstowe flew along the radial arms and patrolled the sectors, according to the information provided by the British direction finders. With only a few flying-boats acting as spiders in the Spider Web, forty-seven German submarines were sighted from April, 1917, to April, 1918, and at least twenty-five of them were bombed.

Zeppelins, rising from sheds at Wittmundshaven, Nordholz, and Tondern, conducted a regular daylight reconnaissance course across the Bight of Heligoland, and as far south as the Terschelling Bank. They watched British destroyers and light cruisers, and occasionally dropped bombs on Harwich submarines running on the surface on patrol. The great aluminium-ribbed gasbags could outclimb a flying-boat, and as their crews kept a sharp look-out, only surprise attacks by British aircraft were successful; but the position, course, and speed of the Zeppelins were determined by British direction finders from the signals sent by the enemy's flying operators. The method of detection was the same as that used in the Spider Web.

Even some of the slow-flying, heavily-laden Porte flying-boats then became able to trap and destroy the giant rigid airships. When fast aeroplanes were carried by capital and cruising British ships, sweeping towards the Bight of Heligoland, within overtaking distance of a "fixed" Zeppelin, there was usually a spectacle of flaming destruction.

German airship control over the North Sea became increasingly difficult against the operations of the British direction finders and against the various kinds of aircraft to which they flashed their triangulated information. Enemy airships had to use their own wireless as little as possible, for fear of giving indications leading to a surprise attack. The Zeppelin and Schütte-Lanz were struck with deadly effect at what had been their strongest point. They were originally the best of instruments for naval reconnaissance. They possessed, by

British lack of wireless at Jutland reason of their great length, a powerful system of aerial wires, and afforded operators so steady a platform that during the first part of the war they were the only type of aircraft that could receive very long wave-length messages and themselves send out communications for hundreds of miles. In the latter part of 1917 a Zeppelin was flying over Khartoum, on the way to German East Africa, and taking direct orders from the Nauern station, near Berlin. In the Battle of Jutland only a single British seaplane was employed in finding the enemy forces and sending wireless information to the admiral commanding the Cruiser Fleet. The lack of British seaplanes with wireless sets, to work with the Grand Fleet on the misty day of battle, was a remarkable defect in organisation.

It was by means of wireless that reconnoitring German airships, after the fleet engagement, discovered the position occupied by Sir John Jellicoe's battle divisions, and helped to lead Admiral Scheer's fleet into harbour and safety. There can be little doubt that the fighting admirals of Great Britain were slower than the naval leaders of Germany to appreciate fully the use of wireless communication from aircraft. Neither for reconnaissance purposes nor for gunnery observation was the flying machine with wireless used in the first phases of the war in the complete way that was easily practical.

Aerial wireless gunnery direction could have been intensely developed during the bombarding operations along the Flemish shore, and brought to a degree of general utility during the campaign in the Dardanelles. But this was not done. Yet the British Navy had long led the way, alike in original research in methods of telegraphy without wires, and in the application of Marconi's discoveries to the development of power in handling a fleet. Before Senator Marconi found out how to use electric waves which were created by an electric spark, Admiral Jackson had experimented with induction effects produced at a short distance between electrified wires on a large ship and uncharged wires on a neighbouring vessel. Admiral Jackson's researches were merely the beginning of the system of overhearing ordinary telegraph and telephone messages, which came into use in Army listening-posts during trench warfare. Yet the eager researches into a new method of signalling which the British Navy conducted prepared the way for a quick and masterly use of the real electric-wave system established by Marconi.

With its powerful wireless stations, and warships in instant touch with each other and with the Admiralty plant, the British Navy greatly increased its power by increasing its flexibility and speed and scope of intercommunication. The Fleet remained united, with Admiral Jellicoe in Lough Swilly, Admiral Beatty in the Firth of Forth, Admiral Hood off Dover, Admiral Bayly off Portland, and the submarines and destroyers of Harwich on observation work in the North Sea.

In its general naval use wireless was an added advantage to the stronger sea Power, permitting an apparently loose deployment of secondary forces, and concentration of the main battle divisions in the remote regions of the Orkney Islands or northern Irish coast.

In the long-distance blockade of Germany the use of radio-telegraphy at least balanced the advantages acquired by the weaker Fleet. Owing to the increased range and striking power of guns and torpedoes, **The long-distance** to the menace of secretly and quickly-laid **blockade** mine-fields, and to the rapid organisation of submarine ambushes, the German naval defence was of extraordinary strength, especially in the fortified area of the Bight of Heligoland. A close watch by the enemy's naval bases was impossible, and in the absence of instantaneous means of communication between widely separated yet co-operating naval forces at sea, the work of holding the enemy in, while pressing him to come out, would have overtasked the ablest strategist.

In misty weather, when the divided forces of the Cruiser

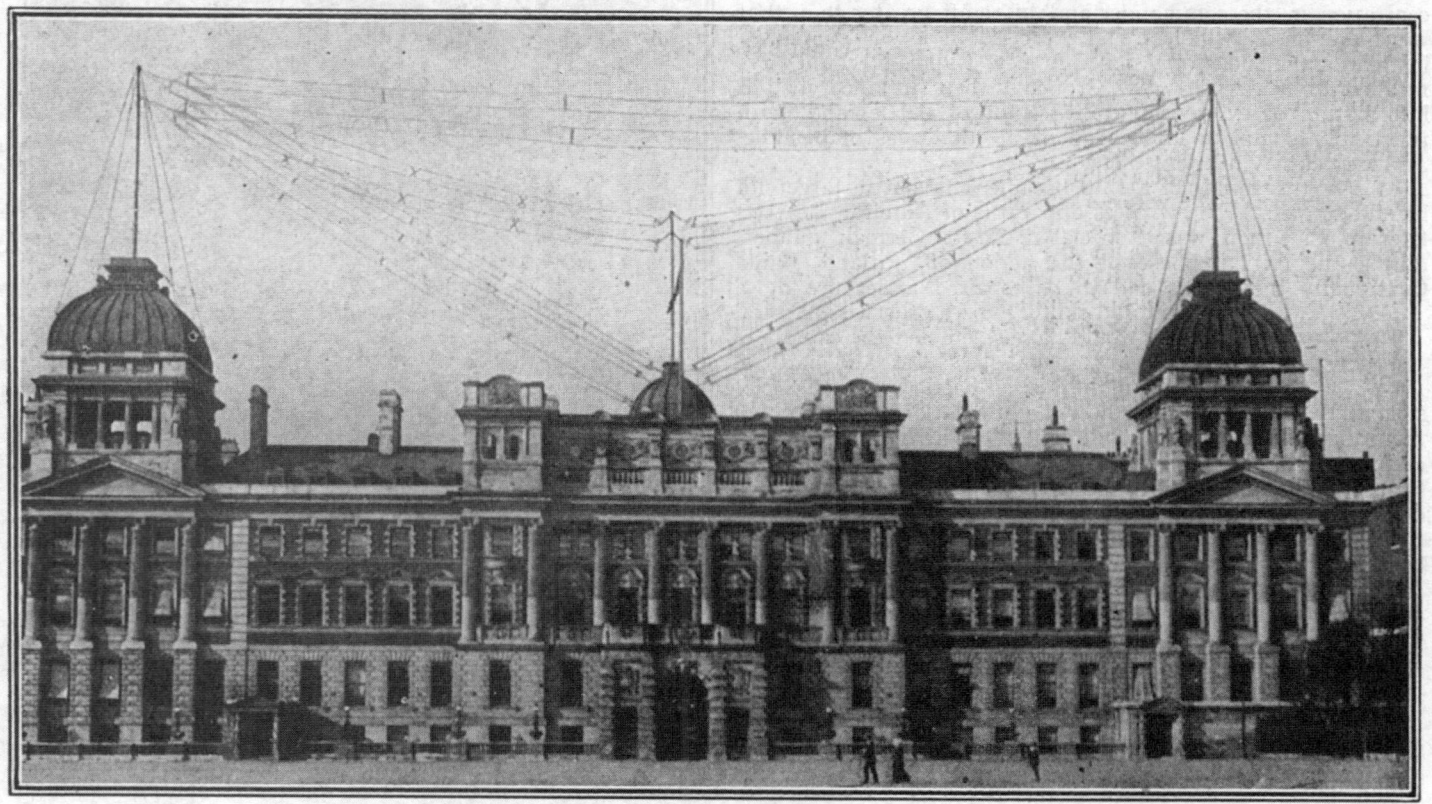

WIRELESS AERIAL ON THE BRITISH ADMIRALTY.

View of the Admiralty buildings seen from the Horse Guards Parade, showing the wires by means of which electric air waves were sent to or received from the British Navy. With its powerful wireless station and warships in instant touch with each other, though miles apart, the Navy greatly increased its flexibility and speed. The new invention had endowed the Fleet with a kind of electrical nervous system which more than doubled its mechanical striking strength.

Fleet and Grand Fleet co-operated in a sweep into the Bight, under a low-hung roof of cloud, through which reconnoitring enemy airships could not see, no flag or lamp signalling would have served the main purpose. It was Marconi's invention that enabled light forces to work when required at a considerable distance from capital ships, and yet remain sensitive to

FRENCH MOBILE WIRELESS.
Wireless operator with his installation on a motor-car engaged in transmitting a message while near the battle-front in France.

the commanding admiral's instructions, almost like fingers of an outstretched hand.

The new invention had indeed endowed the British Fleet with a kind of electrical nervous system which more than doubled its mechanical striking strength. All the intricate machinery of battle, which seemed to be growing beyond the personal control of a single man, was brought, when required, under the sway of one intellect. There was a personal concentration in the commander and his staff greater than that which Nelson or Napoleon had exercised in actions conducted in their actual field of vision. A new Napoleon could have recalled by wireless a new Grouchy, then obtained instant information of every important sector of battle, and, with practically complete knowledge of all that was happening, arranged clearly his next blow.

At sea the aerials of a ship became a favourite target for hostile gunners. The wireless apparatus of Admiral Beatty's flagship the Lion was a special mark for German gunners during the critical phase in the action off Jutland Bank. Continually the aerials had to be repaired under fire by a gallant and skilful expert, otherwise Admiral **Wireless aerials as** Beatty would have resembled the captain of **enemy targets** a company, made speechless and hard of hearing in the crisis of battle by a shell explosion, and left only with the power of gesticulation in a manœuvre requiring quick precision of direction. With flag signals the admiral might have been able to communicate with other ships in his command within telescopic range, as indeed was done. Yet in the fumes and smoke and mist of battle, with ropes being cut like aerial wires, flag-signalling was little better than gesticulation.

Had the naval struggle ended with another fleet engagement there would have been an opportunity for opening the attack in a scientific way by salvos of shell with vulcanite fuses, aimed at the aerials of opposing capital ships, and directed by wireless—using observers in aeroplanes launched from gun-turrets. No better means than this could be devised of opening an action at extreme range, with the preliminary aim of confusing the communication mechanism of the hostile command.

The aerial and Marconi cabin of merchant ships with wireless equipment were the first targets of gunners in German submarines. More than eight hundred Marconi operators were in merchantmen sunk by torpedo, gun fire, or mines.

One hundred and eighty-two lost their lives, and thirty-eight were severely injured. Most of them were young and inexperienced in the terrors of war, but there was already behind them the great tradition of keeping up wireless calls till the last possible moment in shipwreck and other general dangers of the sea. Under gun fire, in frail structures often without means of defence, the wireless men of the merchant service became, especially in the first period of submarine attack, the only hope of saving the ship. So long as their transmitting apparatus survived shell fire there was a fighting chance that the call for help would reach some armed patrolling vessel, or attract reconnoitring aircraft **Heroism in the** with bombing tackle, and compel the **Mercantile Marine** hyenas of the sea to hide and crawl away. There is a noble record of Marconi operators who lost their lives yet saved their ships. Equally noble is the long record of the young men who held to their work of calling for armed help, though no help came, and who died in agony in their shattered cabins and went down to a sailor's grave. The heroes of the wireless room on liners and cargo boats may justly rank in romantic heroism with fighting airmen, and those gallant submarine men who kept only hostile armed vessels under attack, and at times met their death fighting against heavy odds.

A MESSAGE OUT OF SPACE.
In the wireless operator's cabin on board ship. Taking down a message. Wireless operators on board ship established a great tradition of heroism and devotion to duty during the war.

Yet the wireless operator in the Mercantile Marine, during the period when merchantmen were neither armed nor convoyed, differed from the fighting airman and submarinist in that he had no source of any zest of battle. He and the crew he tried to save were unarmed men, attacked by human sharks, and possessing power only of calling for help. Still at times there were some highly dramatic scenes of fighting endurance. For instance, there was a merchantman who got into touch with a fast warship by wireless, while enemy submarine gunners were holing the hull and trying to destroy the radio-telegraphic apparatus. The naval operator in the warship sent messages that help was coming, and begged the crew to endure for a few minutes longer, so that the U boat might be kept in action and engaged at long range.

A romantic wireless story in the early days of the war was afterwards told by a Marconi operator, Mr. Duncan Smith. At the outbreak of hostilities he was working in the steamship Mazatlan, belonging to F. Jebsen, who was captain in the German Naval Reserve. In San Francisco the vessel was transferred to the Mexican flag, and a German wireless operator joined the ship, which left the American port with two hundred tons of coal. Mr. Smith was asked to inform Jebsen if a signalling call was heard with the letters "G. C. S. K." Jebsen, who was the worse for drink, boasted to the Marconi operator : " I may as well tell you right off that this coal is for the Leipzig ! " Mr. Smith refused to help in finding and coaling the raiding enemy cruiser ; but Jebsen and other officers threatened to shoot him **Coming of the** and throw him overboard if he did not **convoy system** obey orders.

He was told to explain the working of the Marconi apparatus to the German wireless man, who knew only the Telefunken system, and apparently did not know that very well. The Englishman took the German into the wireless room, but before so doing he tore out the wave-length markings, altered the clips, and shortened the coupling. This made the apparatus ineffective, and for three nights and two days the German operator vainly tried to call the Leipzig. When the enemy cruiser was met at an appointed rendezvous, Mr. Smith put the wireless apparatus back into working order, so that skilled enemy naval operators should not be able to discover why they had received no calls. When the Leipzig steamed away, Mr. Smith again put his wireless out of gear, and the German operator afterwards tried to communicate again with the cruiser, but naturally failed to do so.

With the establishment of the convoy system of protection against submarine attack the wireless men in the Mercantile Marine became a vital link of communication between the protecting force and the units of protected vessels. The

SIGNALLING FROM AN ARMOURED TRAIN.
Wireless railway-car, which was employed by the French on some parts of the western front. It was fitted with a tall detachable mast for carrying the aerial.

skippers had to keep formation in the manner of navigating lieutenants, and were without the years of practice of naval officers. Weather conditions were often too bad for flag or lamp signals, but most of the convoyed vessels were equipped with wireless, and it was easy to keep them together if there were no engine breakdowns or other trouble. It was the convoy system, with its wireless watch and wireless communications, that completed the active work of the wireless direction finders of U boats and scouting Zeppelins and saved the shipping of the Grand Alliance from being reduced to starvation limits.

In wireless work connected with submarines the Teutons began splendidly and ended badly. It was by wireless directions, sent out by an observing Zeppelin off the Netherlands coast, that the most famous of enemy submarine commanders, Lieutenant Weddigen, surprised the old British armoured cruisers Aboukir, Hogue, and Cressy, and sank all three ships with a loss **Germans' dastardly** of some sixty-two officers and 1,400 men. **use of the " S O S "** But by the development of British wireless such losses were at last ·inflicted upon enemy U boats, in a methodical, intricate, scientific way, that the German ratings began to rebel against being trained for submarine work, and so increased in mutinous spirit that they brought about a revolution rather than engage in another fleet action.

In spite of the German use of wireless in secret and dastardly ways, the new method of communication and defence was of more service to the stronger Power at sea than to the weaker. The horrible decoying calls of " S O S " which some German submarines sent out in order to bring merchantmen within sinking range should be held in historic remembrance as a supreme example of Teutonic perversity. The evidence in the matter is derived not only from allied operators and their seamen comrades, but also from men working in ships belonging to Spain and other neutral States which the Teuton did not wish to exasperate, and therefore in such cases he spared the witnesses of his " S O S " trick in murder.

KEEPING IN TOUCH.
Interior of a specially-constructed carriage used by the French for wireless signalling from the battle-front. After the armistice it was employed in the occupied territory.

To a considerable extent the submarine was the instrument of the weaker Power. Electric-wave communications, on the other hand, proved to be a source of new strength to the strong. Being a mechanism of a general, permanent, and broadening utility, the invention of Marconi—based on the experiments of a German man of science, Hertz, the far-reaching calculations of a Scotsman, Clerk Maxwell, and the lightning play of genius of the great Londoner, Faraday—became widely serviceable in warfare as well as in the peaceful intercourse of nations.

Aerial warfare developed in a remarkable manner through

NEWS FROM A FLYING MESSENGER.
Receiving a wireless message from an aeroplane on reconnaissance in India at a station set up in the open country. Remarkable advance was made before the close of the war in the means of wireless communication with aircraft.

the progress in wireless telegraphy and telephony. At the opening of hostilities reconnoitring and fire-controlling pilots of machines were little more than cavalrymen of the air. They flew over enemy forces, noted their movements, flew back to the nearest landing-place, found a telephone wire or motor wireless set, and communicated to General Henderson, who reported to Sir John French. In this slow, roundabout fashion were airmen's observations sent to Headquarters. When engaged in assisting guns to get on a target, airmen swooped and dropped a smoke-bomb, giving warning to the men they marked out for attack as well as informing their own artillery. When, in the early part of 1915, transmitting wireless sets began to be made for general use in reconnaissance and fire control, the power of the artillery became more terrible. Observation balloons, with telephone wires, and forward observation officers, also with wire means of communication, could direct the opening bombardment, conduct counter-battery work on known or suspected positions, and follow for a mile or so the advancing troops and the enemy's rallying and reinforced infantry.

But this was not sufficient, under conditions obtaining on the western front, to breach the lines of defence. The strength of the attack was exhausted by lack of wide and clear knowledge of preparations for counter-attacks proceeding behind the hostile zones. When, as happened on either side, the defence survived till nightfall, fresh and mighty dispositions were made under cover of darkness, and observers

for the attack in kite-balloons and new forward positions had to make a prolonged study of the new problems of the enemy's positions and arrangements.

With expert wireless reconnaissance and gunnery observation carried on during action and extended to the enemy's rail-heads and motor-transport centres, the power of military machines began to give promise of co-operating in a decisive victory. The German Staff under Falkenhayn was the first to make full use of an extraordinary number of heavy guns, directed on to distant targets by means of wireless messages from aeroplanes. Verdun became the struggle between Teutonic organisation and Gallic improvisation, the great gate to France being saved by the hill observation positions to which General Pétain held, and by the use of thousands of motor-trucks at night, during the period when flying wireless men had not learned to use parachute flares in nocturnal reconnaissances.

After the lesson at Verdun the French and British began to overtake the Teuton in the wireless method of conducting warfare. In airmanship expertness in working the signalling code became a matter of importance second only to skill in flying. Young officers usually worked as spotters for the guns, before being sent on long reconnoitring flights and rising to positions in fighting formations. The organisers of the Royal Air Force began to see new possibilities in electric-wave communications. A sound-proof headpiece was devised, with delicate microphone attachments for the ears, to enable airmen in flying machines to hear signals on short-wave lengths. This improvement promised to bring aeroplane and seaplane wireless to a practical level of efficiency with large airship radio-telegraphy. When a man flying over enemy territory could be asked questions regarding the information he sent and given fresh instructions, gunnery work and staff-work on ground improved in flexibility.

But this improvement was not the main end for which the experts of the Royal Flying Corps were working. At their experimental station on Biggin Hill, in Kent, they laboured intensely at the problem of making small wireless telephone sets for use in both small and large flying machines. The transmission of speech by electric waves had been accomplished a considerable time before the outbreak of war. In 1908 Danish, Italian, and French men of science had spoken by continuous wave systems across distances of hundreds of miles. In September, 1915, the U.S.A. Navy Department's wireless engineers succeeded in speaking from Arlington, in Virginia, to Mare Island, in San Francisco Bay. This was a distance of 2,500 miles. But before the end of the month the American experimenters claimed that they had been able to carry speech for 4,000 miles to Pearl Harbour, Honolulu.

Exceptionally favourable electrical conditions of the air were required to transmit wireless speech for thousands of miles. Very powerful electric arcs or other wave-producing means were also needed for the continuous stream of long electric waves that carried the modulations of speech and re-created them by vibrations in the receiving instrument. All the elements of wireless telephony were worked out for the Royal Flying Corps researchers. In particular they inherited the Fleming valve and its circuits, to which was added a modification that enabled operators to hear messages in spite of the deafening noise of the engines. The problem was reduced to improvements and refinements for making a wireless telephone set suitable for use in the small space of an ordinary machine. Portability was increased, better methods of fitting were worked out, and with other practical devices airmen were given the power of speaking and listening to speech while in flight.

Telephoning from aeroplanes

Under the Royal Air Force the work of the men on Biggin Hill was brought to successful completion. In the early spring of 1918 there were Sopwith and other machines on the western front which at first never crossed the German lines. They contained the new telephone set, or radiophone, and pilots flying them worked only over the British lines, so that if one of the new machines fell it would not present the Germans with the master key to the British command of the air.

The radiophone had a moulding influence upon aerial tactics. A formation leader rose to a position similar to

MARCONI CART-SET OF WIRELESS.
Transport of the plant of the 1½-2 kilowatt mobile wireless. Above: The interior of the operating-cart, and (below) the interior of the power-cart.

that of the commander of a destroyer flotilla. Being able to speak to every man flying under his command, he could direct in detail an attack upon an enemy force. The old "dog fight," that used to occur when formation met formation, began to be transformed into controlled team-work in attack, such as obtained on land and sea. The character of general aerial engagements was changed in so decisive a manner that the forces of General Salmond were able to hold all the main weight of the enemy air service, and after inflicting upon the Germans a series of defeats that saved the British lines from breaking, the British fighting formations ended by decisively breaking Teutonic air-power. Both Germans and Austrians felt the shattering strength of the Royal Air Force and its radiophone tactics. One British formation could speak to another within range, and make an overwhelming concentration of force. It became impossible for the greatest of German air fighters, such as Richthofen, to break a path for reconnaissance over British territory.

The British Commander-in-Chief and his Army leaders could conduct daring concentrations of armies without the enemy suspecting either the point of attack or the weight of it. In combination with a native gift for airmanship, excellent training, and a great output of good machines and engines and firing gear, the British Flying Corps invention of practical wireless telephone for flying machines ensured to the Royal Air Force that veritable mastery of the air which in the middle of the war had been regarded as an impossible attainment.

The benefit of the new technique in aerial tactics extended to the British Navy as well as to the British Army. If the war had lasted a few weeks longer it would also have been seen that the bombing squadrons of the Independent Force had grown in fighting strength by the development of the electric-wave transmission of speech. Indeed, it is scarcely extravagant to say that in November, 1918, the Royal Air Force was in process of becoming in its special field the peer of the British Navy. The Germans were beaten in one of the most important of inventions. They lagged behind in aerial tactics in the supreme crisis of the struggle, and their machines were destroyed faster than they could build new structures and train new men.

Tactics in Tank attacks were also improved by the invention of small and handy wireless sets, modified from those used on flying machines. When it became usual for Tanks to storm into the German lines under a smoke-screen, created by special shell by the British artillery, success largely depended upon the Tanks keeping in close touch with the infantry, artillery, aerial scouts, and, in a definite break-through, with the cavalry. Portable wireless of the telephonic kind, transmitting clear messages that could be heard through the noise of engines, permitted Tank manœuvres generally to be carried out with terrible precision. Tanks could be piloted by airmen to machine-gun nests, batteries could be ranged on hostile guns aiming at Tanks, openings could be indicated to infantry, and the various commanders and Staffs could be kept informed of progresses and checks.

As in the Royal Air Force and the Navy, the complete

practical realisation of all available possibilities of military wireless communication was not effected by the Army by the time the enemy broke and sued for an armistice. The Teuton did not wait for the entire power of the Britons to be organised into the general machinery of battle. The use of wireless among the British land forces began in a small but favourable manner. On August 26th, 1914, information was directly obtained from the enemy that his outflanking divisions were moving towards Cambrai, while the main forces of the First German Army were in movement towards Cattenières, Walincourt, and Le Cateau. This information was given in a German wireless message, intercepted by British operators and decoded. It confirmed the British Commander-in-Chief in his view of the position of forces in the Le Cateau action, and guided him during the difficult retreat after his Second Corps had been seriously weakened. The manner in which the Germans used wireless in the period of their first offensive in the west scarcely seems to have been judicious. Apparently the codes they used were known to Allied Staffs in France. Their messages became revelations of their forces in action and intending movements. Both the French and the British wireless signallers, on the other hand, worked in successful secrecy in spite of spies, secret wireless stations, carrier-pigeons, and

Tapping the enemy wireless interception of allied wireless messages. The Germans were ignorant of the rapid creation of the Sixth French Army on the exposed British flank, and of the unimpaired spirit of attack of the British Expeditionary Force. The allied manœuvres in the Battle of the Marne were not foreseen by the enemy, and when the race to the sea began he did not expect to meet the British again between Ypres and La Bassée.

The German wireless operators on the Ypres battlefield remained, until the winter of 1914, almost as frank in regard to the leading intentions of their chiefs as they had been in the summer. For example, at the end of October the British Army wireless took in a message that the Kaiser was at Courtrai and coming to Hollebeke, just by Ypres. His design was to make a triumphal entry into the city that was the gateway to the Strait of Dover. This information completed Sir John French's opinion of the importance and scope of the battle, nerving him to conduct to a victorious end one of the greatest defences in military history. British airmen profited by the intercepted wireless to arrange as warm a welcome as possible for the enemy Emperor, and from subsequent information received it appeared that the potentate changed his quarters at least once to escape from British pilots. All the British troops were told in an Order of the Day of the presence of the august visitor to their front, and urged to show him what "the contemptible little Army' could do. They did so. The intercepted German wireless served as a tonic to the tired British soldier, as well as affording the best of secret service to his chief.

The use of wireless in directing infantry during the long period of trench warfare developed somewhat slowly. The defect of the electric-wave method was that messages had to be sent in some sort of cipher, causing delay in transmission and reading, and requiring quick coders and decoders at either end, with a frequent change of code to prevent enemy experts from reading every message. It was thought that the telephone wire ensured secrecy. But this was not so, as we have already seen. In 1918, when the Fleming valve was improved into a "grid" of an extraordinary sensitiveness, German commanders, preparing to attack the Fifth and Third British Armies, gave orders that their own telephones should not be used for a distance of seven miles from the British lines. Telephone cables and telegraph lines also proved unreliable under the storms of shrapnel in the earliest trench battles. Armouring them made them heavier to draw over shell-holed ground, and digging protecting channels for them was slow work. Yet they continued in use, because the light portable wireless set for

Telephone and telegraph wires infantry signallers and for forward observation officers was long in being perfected. As military wireless improved for ordinary purposes, the detective direction finder improved with it. Thus operators, acting with hostile batteries, could triangulate the position of a wireless station on the other side, and direct a sudden tempest of gas-shell about it. The position was not usually fixed with bull's-eye precision, but wireless men within range, who sent out fairly regular messages, could not expect their position to remain unknown to the opposing forces.

When the battles of movement began again wireless stations, with portable instruments or travelling vehicles, increased in use. During the last great advance the British forward wireless was pushed onward against shell fire and machine-gun fire to link the advanced troops with Headquarters. There were times when all telegraph and telephone wires serving an attacking force were cut by German shell fire, and the entire traffic of communications was then conducted by the wireless station. The organisation of central electrical supplies, with the connecting, charging, and redistribution of heavy accumulators and the rapid removal of stations and their re-erection in more forward areas, were hard problems for forward wireless officers. Often they put up on ruined houses any kind of aerial that seemed to work, and operated in the cellar. Portable masts were carried and employed in the Somme region where a few buildings were left standing, but in the country beyond the Hindenburg line masts were not often needed, and more height was obtained by fixing the wire aerial to chimneys and roofs. Soon after a village or hamlet was conquered the forward wireless usually occupied a cellar and decorated two gables with an aerial.

Unimportant messages were transmitted in clear language, but everything likely to afford the enemy information was put into cipher, with the necessary small delays at both ends. Wooded country was bad for wireless work. Torn and dense forest trees broke up the electric waves and made a resistance seriously limiting the range to which messages can clearly be sent. Wherever possible, a line of fairly open country was chosen as operating terrain, and changes had to be made continually in the direction of aerials so as to increase the strength of signals received and transmitted.

In the first week of November, 1918, British wireless officers had reasons for judging that the main forces of the enemy were in flight. During the earlier stages of the final offensive the German stations worked most energetically, but in the last stage extremely few of them were to be heard working. Abandoned wireless material increased in quantity and quality, complete portable wireless sets being left intact and ready for use. Then from their lines British forward wireless officers, in pauses of their heavy work, found that eloquent eastward silence which marked the beginning of the great rout. The order **Speech with the speed of light** for "Cease fire" came through stations on the southern British front to give time to German delegates if they passed through the lines. Finally "forward wireless" received the best of all messages—announcing the hour of the armistice.

One result of this end of the struggle was that the British infantry generally did not go into action under the latest and most scientific of colours—the flag aerial. This was part of a wireless set for signallers, which had taken long to elaborate into a practical thing. It had the common wireless defect of emitting everything in an electric shout that enemy operators could overhear; cipher was required and trained operators. The method was more intricate than flash-lamp signalling and far less secret, and there was the peril that the cipher might be discovered by the enemy and used by him in a crisis. Yet this risk was run by the Fleet and the Royal Air Force, and some of their precautions could be adapted. Great were the advantages of having wirelessing signallers in the fighting-line linked with forward wireless stations and with intermediate stations connecting with Headquarters.

The multitudinous Army promised to become nearly as flexible to unified control as were the less numerous units of the Fleet. Standing at last, like the Fleet, so victorious that neither final battle nor closing manœuvre was necessary to reduce the enemy to terms, it possessed the peculiar glory of establishing the lines of future development of military technique. The wireless telephones of its airmen and Tankmen and other operators formed the growing part of the directive mechanism behind millions of men and machines. The progress in wireless communication helped to reduce the immense complexities of modern warfare into governable simplifications. It gave the speech of man the speed of light, while saving him on land the labour and cost of laying thousands of miles of insulated wire. It enabled him to speak to and from the sky and the surface of the sea, in flight and voyage, as no other device could. And practically nothing was lost in peace of all the wireless improvements in war.

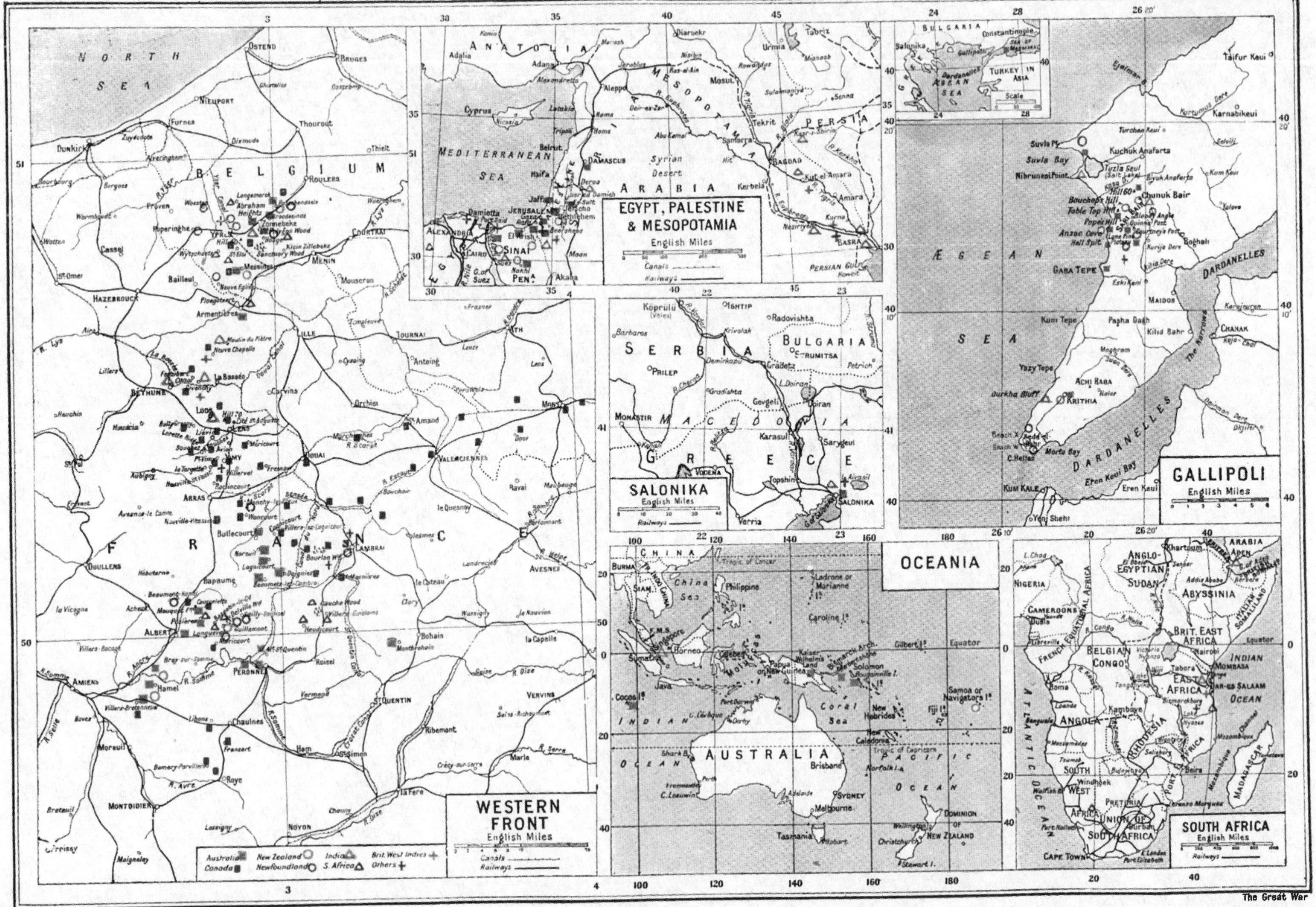
WESTERN FRONT
English Miles
EGYPT, PALESTINE & MESOPOTAMIA
English Miles
SALONIKA
English Miles
GALLIPOLI
English Miles
OCEANIA
SOUTH AFRICA
English Miles
Australia Canada New Zealand Newfoundland India S. Africa Brit. West Indies Others

Copyright

The Great War

[See Vol. xiii., p. 368.]

WHERE SOLDIERS OF BRITAIN'S OVERSEAS DOMINIONS FOUGHT IN THE GREAT WAR.

PRINCESS PATRICIA

CHAPTER CCCX.

INSPECTING THE P.P.C.L.I.

THE EMPIRE AND THE WAR: PROGRESS OF THE OVERSEAS DOMINIONS AND INDIA, 1914-18.

By Edward Wright.

How Canada was Better Prepared than any Other of the Belligerent Countries—Response of the Dominion to the Call for Men and Material—Problems Connected with the French-Canadian Population—Canada Emerged from the War with her Agriculture and Industry Greatly Expanded—Australian Dislike and Fear of the Teuton—Mr. W. M. Hughes' Prompt Action Against German Metal Control in Australia—Serious Effects of the Drought of 1914—Conscription Twice Negatived on Referendum—Australia Drew no Profit from the War but Built a Noble Tradition of Heroic Achievement—New Zealand and its Incomparable Work—Compulsory Training Followed by General Conscription—Military Effort no Check to Development of Productive Power—South Africa and its Varied Problems—Attempts at Rebellion—South African Difficulties Settled on the Battlefields of Europe—India's Magnificent Display of loyalty—Happy Effect in India of the Victories in Mesopotamia—Scheme of Reforms in Indian Administration.

PROFOUND was the effect of the war on nearly all countries that began, from the outbreak of hostilities, to throw their entire strength into the struggle. In the old settled lands of Europe, where life for centuries had run in channels slowly broadening under political and industrial changes, there were some deep modifications in the structure of society. In the new, sparsely-peopled Dominions of the British Commonwealth, possessing a looseness of organisation, answering instantly to war conditions, the war was in some cases an incomparable stimulus to development.

The Dominion of Canada was peculiarly favoured in meeting the stresses and demands of the struggle. Her population numbered only some eight millions; of these nearly two millions were new-comers arriving within the last twelve years. Nearly three million and a half persons of foreign stock went to form Canada's population, and of these there were more than half a million persons of German or Austrian nationality. In short, with the population little more than that of Greater London, occupying a land sixteen times larger than Germany, twice the size of British India, and larger by a quarter of a million square miles than the United States, there were only about four and a half million men and women and children of British stock to guide and mould its destinies.

Canada, however, was better prepared for the long, wearing struggle than any other belligerent nation.

TAPLOW MEMORIAL TO CANADIANS.
At the unveiling by Sir Robert Borden, in April, 1919, of the memorial to Canadian officers and men who died at the Duchess of Connaught's Red Cross Hospital at Taplow. The memorial was erected in the old Italian garden in the grounds of Cliveden, which had been consecrated as a cemetery for Canadians.

She had only a small militia whose exercises were commonly regarded as a social pastime, and she possessed neither rifles, ammunition, nor munition plants. The people were one of the most unwarlike in existence, being largely immersed in adventurous works of peace that made them look on a war between civilised countries as a dream of madness. Yet the Germans, with all their military preparations, were not so well equipped for the struggle as were the Canadians. Canada had been speculating for twelve years upon a great agricultural and industrial development. At heavy cost in borrowed money she had built railways, canals, and general works for her coming generation, and in the early part of 1914 there was grave danger of a decline in Canadian prosperity, owing to the adventurous way in which the country had mortgaged itself to build some thirty-one thousand miles of railway and provided advance for needs that did not then exist.

In industry Canada was apparently a vassal State of the United States. She exported scarcely any iron and steel manufactures, and even her meat trade seemed to have been undermined by the action of the American Meat Trust and the effect of the Underwood Bill, passed by Congress, that attracted into America a very considerable part of Canadian live-stock. Farmers of the prairie provinces then began to follow the disastrous American policy of making small, quick, personal fortunes by exhausting the fertility of the land, and moving on like human locusts to newly opened tracts of virgin soil. There was a great deal of the American spirit of winning individual gain at a national loss, yet with this fierce self-seeking enterprise there went generally a potential capacity for national sacrifice which the war elicited in a wonderful way.

The Canadian was indeed a born idealist. It was more from faith in the greatness of his country than from passion for financial speculation that he had built almost a generation ahead of his needs. The terrible war, that shortened the period of waiting for the grand development of Canada and made the Canadians the richest men in the world, gave the Dominion spiritual as well as material greatness. At first the native Canadian scarcely appreciated the scope of the war. To some extent there was a furtive reliance upon the Monroe Doctrine of the United States, combined with an unreflecting trust in the general security given by British sea-power.

The 1st Canadian Division obtained many of its privates from recent British immigrants. But with the opening of the German submarine campaign against shipping and the heroic tragedy of the enemy's gas attack upon the Canadian Division at Ypres, the British native-born of the Dominion saw that the war was their war, and began to conduct it with a productive energy and a military effort, which, in proportion to Canada's scanty man-power, exceeded the achievement of Ontario and the Eastern provinces during

THANKSGIVING SERVICE AT OTTAWA.
The Governor-General of Canada (the Duke of Devonshire), with the Duchess, proceeding to the Thanksgiving Service on Parliament Hill, Ottawa, on Armistice Day, November 11th, 1918 ; and (above) the great crowd at the service.

the conflict with America in 1812.

In the old frontier war the Canadian farmer and his sons fought while his wife and daughters tilled the land. Under modern conditions this heroic expedient would have been a dramatic folly. The Canadian was busy conquering the wilderness by means of the internal - combustion engine, and his tens of thousands of tractors required skilled men to work them to the utmost limit. All farms were already under - manned, and wives and daughters had to work with the farmer and his hired man in peace time in order to keep things going. The Canadians owed the British alone more than £500,000,000, and the agricultural exports required to pay the interest of this debt in London were calculated at £2,000,000 a month. Thus the Canadian was already working hard and long every week to win economic freedom when the war came and put him to one of the severest ordeals in history. Wheat was required to save the people of the British Isles from famine, and by reason of the short sea route between Liverpool and Lake Ontario, Canada could supply wheat when the Argentine and Australia were checked by shipping difficulties.

Yet the Canadian Army called for more men, and in addition to more than half a million soldiers there were required large numbers of munition workers of a skilled kind and makers of general equipment for the forces. Then it was that the Canadian farmer and his wife and daughters showed what inventive skill and tireless labour could accomplish. They produced crops of the value of thousands of millions of dollars,

CELEBRATING THE ARMISTICE IN THE CANADIAN CAPITAL.
The armistice of November 11th, 1918, was signed while Canada's Victory Loan was being pushed. Scene in Connaught Place, Ottawa, where an open-air cinema, a "Sand-bag Tea Hut," and captured guns were utilised in celebrating the triumph and helping the loan.

Prince of Wales giving colours to Canadians.

Princess Patricia decorating Canadian colours.

Inspection of the P.P.C.L.I.: Princess Patricia, honorary colonel-in-chief, taking the salute.

Anzac Day in London, April 25th, 1919: Australian cavalry marching down Fleet Street.

350

Triumphal march of Dominion troops in London, May 3rd, 1919: Artillery passing Australia House.

South African troops, headed by their mascot springbok, marching past the King.

King George and his Dominion troops, May 3rd, 1919: March-past of the Australians.

succouring the New Zealanders and Australians in a year of Southern drought, as well as making their farms the granary of Great Britain. Out of her small population Canada provided, in addition to her great Army and her food producers, some 350,000 war workers. Under an Imperial Munitions Board, basic steel plants were enormously extended by a development of the great water-power of Canada. Canada had little coal, but she constructed electric furnaces and used electric drives for much of her new machinery. By 1917 more than half the shrapnel for all British 18-pounder guns came from Canada, most of the supply consisting of complete rounds of ammunition that went direct to France, saving shipping during the great submarine crisis.

Canada also supplied 42 per cent. of the 4·5 in. shells, 27 per cent. of the 6 in. shells, 20 per cent. of the 60-pounder high-explosive shells, 15 per cent. of the 8 in., and 16 per cent. of the 9·2 in. shells. For the special steels used by the Allies, Canada possessed great resources of nickel and cobalt, which were worked with great energy. She also produced considerably more than 100,000,000 pounds of explosives and propellants, by means of seven large new factories working under the Munitions Board. Of shipping 360,000 tons were built and 2,500 aeroplanes, and in 1918, aero-motors of high quality were manufactured, together with bombing machines for the United States.

Canada's contribution in war material

From the forests of British Columbia came hundreds of millions of feet of spruce and fir for aeroplane factories in Britain and France. These logging operations were conducted by some forty-five camps over a region extending six hundred miles. The timber resources of Ontario, Quebec, and New Brunswick were also exploited, and at the same time fifteen thousand Canadian lumbermen worked in Great Britain and France, cutting down woodlands and milling the timber. Canada also supplied fifteen thousand railwaymen for building and repairing railways in France and Flanders and operating trains there, and tore up and transported to the main theatre of war some four hundred and fifty miles of her own railways, so as to help in forming the new strategic lines by means of which Sir Douglas Haig was able to make his sudden and finally decisive concentrations of overwhelming force.

Thus, out of a population of only eight million men, women, and children, that included more than half a million German and Austrian emigrants, Canada supplied at least one million soldiers, sailors, munition-makers, and general war workers. At the same time she brought more land into cultivation, until her cornland was nearly four times larger than that of the British Isles, though her farm hands were considerably less than half the number of those in the Motherland. While continually increasing her exports of food and munitions to Great Britain, Canada in 1918 found the means to help the Americans, and took great contracts for munitions and war supplies from the United States Government, beginning with orders for £14,000,000 of manufactures and metals.

Under their enormous increase in productive power and military strength the Canadians began to exercise a large influence upon American opinion. The plots hatched by Teutons in the United States to hinder grain export to the British Isles by blowing up the Welland Canal between the Great Lakes, and the strong suspicion of Germanic crime in the destruction by fire in June, 1916, of the Houses of Parliament at Ottawa, affected the American public as well as the Canadian people. But for the fiercely energetic example of Canada, the entrance into the war by the United States might have been disastrously delayed.

On the other hand, recent American immigrants into Canada played an important part in finally deciding Canadian policy during the war, and, together with a remarkably large number of British settlers in the United States who crossed the frontier, with gallant native American recruits, to enlist in the Canadian forces, the American new-comers saved Canada

WESTWARD HO!
Canadian soldiers from France leaving Southampton, homeward bound, on board the liner Olympic, March, 1919. They were interested in inspecting the paravane slung out in readiness for launching.

from the danger of civil war. On the wheatlands of the prairie provinces there were about 700,000 American farmers with their families and farm hands. They joined with the 2,000,000 French-Canadians in supporting the Liberal Party under Sir Wilfrid Laurier.

As a party truce obtained from the early months of the war, the Conservative Prime Minister, Sir Robert Borden, was for some time able to conduct affairs without serious opposition. The large Germanic population contained only 40,000 men or fewer, liable to disenfranchisement for suspected hostility.

Germans in the Dominion

The Germans as a rule voted for the French, made large profits out of the rising farm produce, and remained quiet, changing the name of one of their towns in Ontario from Berlin to Kitchener.

British Socialists of the Clyde school tried to cripple output by promoting labour unrest, and in more or less close co-operation with the great Germanic organisation known as the Industrial Workers of the World, they laboured, like the Bolshevists, in the enemy's interests. The Canadian Trade Unions, however, were closely united with the American Trade

Unions, having practically American leadership. They kept steadily on the side of the Allies, and in spite of a rise of 60 per cent. in the cost of living, there were no impeding labour troubles in Canada. All the really important work of unpatriotic opposition was carried out by the French Roman Catholic Party, under the nominal leadership of Mr. Bourassa and Colonel Armand Lavergne.

These two men were the political representatives of the Vatican, and immediately behind them were the French religious congregations, who had been driven out of France by a French anticlerical Ministry, and who were moved by extravagant bitterness of feeling towards France. They wished to see France beaten by a Germany in which the German Catholic Centre Party held power alongside Catholic Austria and Catholic Hungary. French parish priests

CANADIANS HOMEWARD BOUND.
Canadian soldiers on board the liner Olympic at Southampton, March, 1919. The vessel was just about to start, carrying five thousand N.C.O.'s and men and two hundred officers of the Canadian divisions to their western home.

BACK TO BRITAIN'S OLDEST COLONY.
"Good-bye to England!" Newfoundlanders waving farewell to friends at Liverpool, in May, 1919, when about one thousand men and officers of the Royal Newfoundland Regiment sailed for St. John's in the s.s. Corsican.

in Quebec and Ontario actively promoted the movement of hostility against France, and the French-Canadian Press generally spread the same movement in a more diplomatic manner.

The immediate result was that the French-Canadian population as a whole refused to enlist. In the first Canadian Contingent there were only 1,217 French soldiers, who came almost entirely from the English-speaking provinces. Even **French-Canadians** for home defence, against a possible raid of **and the Army** Germans from America, only one hundred Frenchmen enlisted. When Canada had completely exhausted the method of voluntary enlistment there were only about 13,000 French soldiers in the army. The 1,600,000 French people in Quebec province provided only 6,979 recruits, while the 400,000 English-speaking people in the same province furnished about 22,000 soldiers.

Where the French were in freer contact with the English-speaking settlers, French enlistment was greater, the 400,000 French people outside Quebec sending 5,904 men into the Army. As the French-speaking recruits included many adventurous, pioneering half-breeds, living outside the influence of the French-Canadian priesthood, the actual contribution by genuine Frenchman to the Army that was fighting to save France and Belgium was remarkably small.

Practically all the burden of enlistment fell upon the four and a half million people of British stock, the American settlers on the prairies who sympathised with them, and the Britons crossing the frontier. A strong popular movement for conscription started in the English-speaking provinces. It came directly from the people, **Language question** being discountenanced by the Government. **in Ontario** The Prime Minister would have liked to get through the war without an open racial division, and for the sake of internal peace he was willing to allow the French to grow rich on productive work while the British did the fighting.

The French, however, became aggressive, and the struggle opened in Ontario in the summer of 1916, over a local dispute regarding the use of the French language in elementary schools in the English province. For a generation the fertile French in Quebec had been overflowing into Ontario, into land left vacant by the movement of the descendants of the old Loyalists into the prairie wheatfields. Before the war began there had been a fierce struggle over the French language question in Ontario, but it had been decided by the intervention of an Irish Roman Catholic bishop, who strongly condemned the French schools for inefficiency and illiteracy.

In a new regulation the Government proposed that in the recent French centres in Ontario the French language should be used for two years as a medium of instruction, and that all further instructions should be given in English. Thereupon the French Nationalists arranged children's parades and children's strikes, and during the political agitation the Dominion Government narrowly escaped being overthrown by the loss of its French supporters. The British party was heavily defeated in provincial elections, and an attempt was made to cripple the export of grain by means of a railway strike, but this part of the plot was defeated by the patriotism of the Canadian railwaymen, who refused to strike for higher wages.

Sir Robert Borden, representing the governing power of the Eastern British party, maintained his position by a large vote, and went to London for the Imperial War Conference. When he returned, all the British provinces were in a mood of flaming indignation against the French. National service had become necessary to maintain the strength of the Canadian divisions.

Sir Robert Borden, whom his supporters had regarded as a man of timid compromises, then surprised friend and foe by his determination. Sir Wilfrid Laurier, a Liberal leader, was devoting himself in old age to educating his fellow-countrymen, the French-Canadians. Sir Robert proposed to him a Conservative-Liberal Coalition. This, however, Sir Wilfrid Laurier was obliged to refuse, for the reason that he knew that most of the French representatives would not follow him, and he thought that if he lost all control over his own people, Mr. Bourassa and the Clerical Party would seize all power in Quebec.

It was in these circumstances, in the autumn of 1917, that the 700,000 American settlers played a decisive part in determining the destinies of Canada. Owing largely to Canadian influence, their country had at last entered the war, and they returned the service that the Canadians had rendered their Motherland by steadying the course of Canadian policy. Under their impetus, combined with the awakened racial instinct of British settlers in the prairie province of British Columbia, the Western Liberals, who had followed Laurier, broke with him, and united with the Eastern Conservatives.

A case of historic irony

Thus was formed a complete alliance of all the English-speaking people of America against the French population. By the most amazing of historic ironies the Germanic element combined with the French element in opposition to national service for the salvation of France. There were probably about two million and a half French, German, and Austro-Hungarian peoples in the Dominion united against five million British and American peoples, with half a million German-directed anarchic Socialists, Sinn Feiners, and actively hostile

Germans indirectly supporting the men who were willing to rebel but yet afraid to be shot. The new Union Government came into power after a General Election, on December 17th, 1917, its home majority of forty-five representatives being increased by the overseas soldiers to seventy.

Female relatives of soldiers were granted the franchise, together with British and American recruits who had crossed the frontier in order to enlist, and some 35,000 German and Austrian settlers of recent arrival were prevented from influencing the elections by being disenfranchised. In all except six constituencies the French and German populations united to defeat the English-speaking candidate, and not a single man of British stock would have been elected in the French province but for the votes of soldiers on active service and the suffrages of their woman relatives.

Opposition to the Conscription Law

When, as a result of the verdict of the General Election, the measure for conscription was passed, there was rioting in Quebec. During the disorders the city police remained passive, and tribunals of Frenchmen would not give judgment against their countrymen. Out of the first Quebec draft of five thousand men there were three thousand five hundred men of British race, whereas the proportion, according to population, should have been three thousand five hundred French-speaking recruits and one thousand five hundred English-speaking recruits.

French conscripts had practically to be taken at first by armed force in Quebec province, where the State Government, administration, police, and juries were mainly French. Tribunals of Frenchmen discovered grounds of exemption with remarkable ease in the case of young, able-bodied Frenchmen, and although the French population were afraid to organise for a grand insurrection, with the United States fully engaged on the side of the Allies, they did as much as they could in the circumstances to impede the flow of reinforcements to the Canadian Army Corps.

OFFICERS OF THE CANADIAN 4TH DIVISION LEAVING LIVERPOOL FOR THE WEST.

Canadian officers who left Liverpool in the liner Empress of Britain in May, 1919, on their homeward journey. They all belonged to the "Fighting 46th" from Saskatchewan, which had on its battle-roll the names of Somme, Vimy, Passchendaele, Lens, Amiens, Arras, Cambrai, and Valenciennes, and had won immortal distinction in the capture of the Drocourt-Quéant "switch" on September 2, 1918, which led to the breaking of the Hindenburg line.

Meanwhile, the Canadian Army, brought up to more than half a million men, was enabled by the establishment of a system of national service to play a magnificent part in achieving complete victory over Germany, and thereby destroying the base of all the Franco-German system of intrigues in Canada. With France triumphant and the Vatican veering towards the victorious Latin Powers, with Marshal Foch, the Catholic warrior, pressing Protestant

CANADIAN COLOURS FOR MONS REWON.
Flag presented to the town of Mons by the 3rd Canadian Division, as a souvenir of their retaking of the town from the Germans on the very day on which the armistice was signed, November 11th, 1918.

Prussia under his foot, the position of the misleaders of the French-Canadian people became a sorry one.

After the victory the English-speaking Canadians as a whole were content to leave their French countrymen to recover from their shameful illusions. The French had drawn considerable profit from the war, and there was a certain amount of common greed in their dislike for sending their young farming hands and farming sons to the battle-fields at a time when fortunes could be made out of farm produce and the family be established on a prosperous basis of larger agricultural operations. Somewhat of the same feeling obtained among sections of English-speaking farmers, and it was only after information given by the Ministry at a secret session on April 20th, 1918, that Parliamentary consent was obtained for the revocation of agricultural exemptions. Deputations, reaching in one case to 5,000 farming men from Ontario and Quebec, tried to alter the policy established by Sir Robert Borden, but the strong, quiet leader of Canada held to his course, and relying upon the United States to make good any deficiency in the wheat supply, he conducted the Dominion along the

Canada's development glorious path of duty that ended in November, 1918, with the Canadian High-landers recovering Mons:

In spite of her tragic losses, Canada emerged from the war in a glory of material and spiritual power, with both her agriculture and industry expanded to a height that could scarcely have been attained in a generation of fluctuant, peaceful development. There were some labour troubles, engineered by the dark forces connected with the German-Russian-Jewish organisations for promoting anarchy among the victors, but these disturbances did not shake the high, strong position which the Canadian nation had won during the war. The time could be foreseen when Canada would be mightier than Great Britain and a friendly competitor with the United States. She had not found all the

coal required to supplement her electric water power in the creation of vast industries, but otherwise she possessed incomparable attractions for the best type of enterprising emigrants, whom she intended to invite across the ocean as soon as her soldiers were resettled in all her enlarging fields of employment.

During the war Australia resembled Canada in being a young nation with a great future imperilled by a division of races. The Roman Catholic Irish played in the Southern world a part like that of the French-Canadians in the Northern. At first, Australia with her smaller population raced Canada in military achievement. As long as the Sinn Fein movement of rebellion in Ireland was held in check by Mr. John Redmond and other Nationalist leaders, so that Erin seemed likely to emerge from the war united by a working compromise between Catholics and Protestants, Australia generally displayed a remarkable unity and warlike power. The governing Liberal Party made a bad mistake, however, in August, 1914, when it refused an offer of truce from the Labour Party, and, trusting to success at a General Election, was completely overwhelmed in the Senate and decisively overborne in the Lower House. At that time only a small, savage group of agitators, connected with the Germanic organisation of the Industrial Workers of the World, was averse to the resources of Australia being employed in the struggle against Germany.

For a generation the Teutons had been disliked and feared more in Australia than in any other country of the British Commonwealth. German New Guinea, New Pomerania, and other possessions in the South Seas were justly regarded by Australians as bases of attack on themselves, and most of the discontent with the British people was **Monroe Doctrine for** due to the purblind facility with which **the South Seas** Australian rights in the South Seas had been disregarded in the days of Bismarck to the advantage of the pushful and dangerous Teuton. The creation of a national Australian Navy had quickened the sense of responsibility in the people, who welcomed the outbreak of the struggle as giving them the opportunity of retrieving the mistakes of successive British Cabinets and establishing, with New Zealand, a protective Monroe Doctrine for the South Seas.

The Australian Fleet was only second in power in the Pacific to that of Japan, and the Australians, who had reluctantly contributed only £200,000 a year to the Imperial Navy, willingly spent £2,000,000 a year on their own Fleet. Only one in five hundred Australians was a person of German birth, and although the Teutons occupied some important positions in the social, commercial, agricultural, and political life of the country, their open influence was not great. Only when this influence was gradually subtly and indirectly exercised through discontented Labour agitators and Sinn Fein rebels did it become a directing factor in Commonwealth affairs.

The Australians had established before the war a system of compulsory training under a scheme of Lord Kitchener's. The training which the militia received did not make them ready to take the field, but it enabled an expeditionary force of 20,000 men to be rapidly prepared. The new Labour Party, under Mr. Andrew Fisher, was averse to conscription for overseas service, but it possessed in Mr. William M. Hughes, the new Attorney-General, and Senator G. F. Pearce, Minister for Defence, energetic and enlightened patriots who recognised that the war was Australia's war, and were ready to devote all the available power of the country to help in achieving decisive victory.

GERMAN DECORATIONS FOR CANADA'S WAR MUSEUM.
Some of the medals and orders collected from occupied Germany for Canada's War Museum. Colonel Beccles Willson, who had served with the British forces as Inspector of War Trophies, later rejoined the Canadian Corps on the Rhine to collect material for the Canadian War Museum.

prices. The stocks of some of the largest wheat dealers were seized, and the export of meat and wheat prohibited to any country save the United Kingdom. Serious unemployment occurred, especially in the mining industry, through the fact that the commerce in zinc and other important Australian base metals had been controlled by a world-wide organisation under German direction. As Attorney-General, Mr. W. M. Hughes was given the work of breaking the German metal trust and establishing Australian and British distilling plants. At the outbreak of war Australia produced half a million tons of zinc, of which only 15,000 tons were distilled in the country, while 30,000 tons were distilled in Great Britain, out of the 180,000 tons of spelter used in British industries.

Australia also possessed other valuable resources of wolframite, tantalite, and molybdenite; her lead mines furnished 20 per cent. of the world supply, and

There were, however, elements of disunion within the Labour Party itself. Against the old Trade Union leaders, who had organised the working classes and led them to the seat of Government, there were many younger men of ambitious temperament seeking to discredit the makers of the party so that they might win a controlling power. Like some of the new school of British Socialists, the younger men adopted the principles of German Social Democracy, the newer French Syndicalism, or the Bolshevism of the Industrial Workers of the World, as weapons against the old Trade Union movement leaders. Thus it happened that some of the most energetic groups in the governing party of the Commonwealth became liable to sinister suggestions from enemy intriguers, whose centre of propaganda was in the United States. One secretary of a small Trade Union received a ton of Industrial Workers of the World pamphlets in answer to a request for information.

The new movement had much in common with that which afterwards obtained in Russia under Lenin and Trotsky, but it would have had as little effect in **Australia's Military Effort** Australia as in Canada had it not been for a change of mood in the large Irish element in the Labour Party. The Coalition, first proposed by the elder Labour leaders, with the Liberal Ministry under Mr. Cook would have checked at the outset the expansion of the Revolutionaries and Sinn Feiners, by compelling them to engage at once in an open fight, at overwhelming disadvantage, when public opinion was almost entirely in the first flush of passionate patriotism. Therefore to the Liberal Party under Mr. Cook must largely be attributed the serious political misfortunes that ensued.

While the elder Labour leaders reigned, Australia, in spite of many difficulties, excelled Canada in direct military effort. In April, 1915, the percentage of men under arms in Australia in proportion to population was 1·4, and in Canada 1·3. For a time it seemed likely that the Commonwealth, with a united population of less than five millions, would surpass in enlistments the divided races of eight million Canadians, Britons, and Americans joining the Army from the United States. There was a widespread drought in Australia, causing grave financial depression, yet £100,000 was given for Belgium and £1,000,000 for a patriotic fund. The Labour Government tried to prevent any well-founded unrest by fixing maximum

FROM OTTOMAN TOMB TO OTTAWA MUSEUM.
Flag which the Kaiser placed on the tomb of the Sultan at Damascus when he made his ostentatious "pilgrimage" to the Holy Land in 1898. The flag, taken as a trophy when the British captured Damascus in October, 1918, was acquired for Canada's War Museum.

her copper mines, though comparatively small, could at least provide Great Britain with 35 per cent. of the quantity needed for ordinary requirements. Mr. Hughes went deeply into the German system of controlling Australian metals, and established a metal exchange and promoted the erection of refining plant. He became an eager advocate of an Imperial system of control of all the base metals, and a fierce opponent of German commercial aggression. His enlarging

PRESENTATION OF A SQUADRON OF AEROPLANES TO THE CANADIAN MILITARY AUTHORITIES.

General view of the ceremony at Hendon Aerodrome in February, 1919, when Lord Londonderry, on behalf of the British Government, presented to the Canadian military authorities a squadron of fifteen aeroplanes. The machines, which had been subscribed for as a gift to Canada through the Overseas Club and Patriotic League not only by residents in Canada but by British people in all parts of the world, were received by Sir Edward Kemp, K.C.M.G., Minister of the Overseas Military Forces of Canada, as representative of the Canadian military authorities.

view of the complexities of international commerce led him to adopt a tone of friendly compromise with Australian producers, manufacturers, and exporters, who seemed to him to be benefiting the nation generally. To some extent the war helped the development of Australia by throwing her back on her own resources, and when the lack of munitions became known, nearly every engineering firm in Australia concentrated on shell-making. New steel works were opened, and more wheat grown. Owing to defective means of communication with the Imperial Government, the Australian Ministry was imperfectly acquainted with the general scheme for prosecuting the war, and there was a delay of ten months in starting shell-making.

Mr. Andrew Fisher, the new Prime Minister, was disappointed that no arrangement was made in London for a conference of the representatives of the younger nations. **Australia and the shipping shortage** He remarked that most of the information he received in the matter came through the Press, in reports of answers to questions given by the Under-Secretary for the Colonies in the British Parliament. He expressed the opinion that the British Government did not yet fully realise the real position of the distant Dominions in matters very nearly affecting them.

Towards the end of 1915 a working arrangement between the Motherland and the young nation was arrived at. Mr. Andrew Fisher became High Commissioner for Australia in London in place of Sir George Reid. and Mr. W. M. Hughes came into power as Prime Minister. Thus the ruling Labour Party of Australia was well represented in Imperial affairs, and as Mr. Hughes also visited England afterwards to take part in an Imperial Conference, a close working arrangement was established.

Australia began seriously to suffer from a shortage of shipping in the early part of the war. The great length of the voyage between the Home Country and the Commonwealth drew steamers towards working in the quicker traffic between America and the British Isles. Some shipowners were also afraid that the Socialistic tendency of the Australian Labour Party would lead to ships being commandeered for Government commerce at low rates. The action of enemy raiding cruisers between Africa and South America, followed by the German naval victory at Coronel, interrupted Australasian shipping trade. When all raiding activities ceased for a time, the German submarine campaign opened round the British Isles, and an increasingly large number of cargo boats and liners were diverted from mercantile use into military employment. **Wheat waiting shipment**

In comparison with Canada, Australia suffered severely in commercial development by reason of her remoteness from the British people that wanted her wheat and meat. Mr. Hughes bought, in 1916, fifteen steamships of the Strath Line, at the good bargain price of little over £2,000,000. At that time there were two million tons of Australian wheat waiting shipment to Britain, and the Government steamers could only carry a quarter of a million tons of the corn in the course of twelve months. The result was that, while the British people grew seriously short of foodstuffs, great accumulations of Australian wheat wasted in the country in which it was grown, and fed mice and rats until they became a plague. Magnificent Australian horses, urgently needed at the front, ran wild and grew into natural herds, until an unbroken horse could be bought for eight shillings, but was not worth buying at that price. Men were finally engaged at considerable expense to shoot down the herds of horses so that the pasture could be given to cattle and sheep.

The drought of 1914 turned Australia into a buyer of wheat instead of a seller, and her trade fell by £33,000,000. Afterwards, the exports rose considerably in value, but the rise was rather due to increased prices than to greater volume. For example, on the basis of uniform prices, the value of Australian exports during 1916–17 would have been much below that of the years immediately preceding the war. At a time when Australian wool was one of the governing things in the world, upon which depended the health of armies and the comfort of nations, many sheep were killed by lack of water, seriously diminishing a quantity of the wool clip by more than one thousand million pounds. There was also a decline in the wool production of Cape Colony and the River Plate, and although the British Government, when engrossing the Australian wool clip, gave an increase of 55 per cent. on the pre-war price, the money received by the growers scarcely did more than balance the losses from drought and those which were produced by shortage of labour.

Having regard to the rising cost of living, increasing wages, and the tremendous price of many imported materials, the British Government did not deal over-generously with the Australian wool-grower. When the price of a wool suit in London was at last compared with the price given by the British Government for the Australian wool out of which the suit was made, the charge of general profiteering did not lie against the sheep farmers of the Commonwealth. Compared with the incomparably prosperous Canadian farmers, their lot was not a happy one.

Before the war Australia exported large quantities of chilled beef to United States territories, but most of this was diverted by 1916 to the British Isles, together with frozen lamb and mutton. About 97 per cent. of **Development** the output of Australian meat was taken **Checked** during the war by the British people. Yet again the drought greatly reduced exports for a time, and although the meat trade recovered in 1916, the price obtained was little more than that given in 1914. Altogether, the general development of the resources of Australia was checked by the war, and a tremendous new national debt incurred, without any of the new abounding strength that made Canada great both in agriculture and industry.

Yet the Australians enlisted 426,665 men, and despatched 337,060 troops overseas, who fought with an extraordinary casualty list of 212,376, after which the Australian divisions in France were prepared again to break through the enemy, if an armistice had not been arranged. It was amid bitter and destructive political feuds that the glorious Australian Army grew in strength. Agitation for compulsory service oversea was started in 1915, and developed in the following year. Mr. Hughes endeavoured to induce his party to pass a Bill for conscription, but was defeated at a Labour meeting, and one of his Ministers, Mr. F. G. Tudor, broke away from him and became the leader of a Socialist Party containing every variety of discontent, from the Sinn Fein priest to an alien revolutionary of the Russian school. A referendum on conscription produced a majority negative vote, and the forces of Sinn Fein and the Industrial Workers of the World combined in an attempt to weaken the Army of Australia and bedevil the social structure of the Commonwealth. Acts of incendiarism occurred at Sydney, and strikes spread in practically all important industries.

There was also a systematic discouragement to enlisting. One Irish Labour Minister of Queensland proclaimed that " Every Irish Australian who enlists for the war is merely helping England to oppress the Irish people." He was promoted in the Queensland Labour Cabinet after this incident. The Roman Catholic Archbishop of Melbourne was likewise distinguished by a fanatical bitterness that made him a very strange kind of disciple of Christ. He palliated the atrocities of the Teutons in Catholic Belgium, Catholic France, and Catholic Poland by the suggestion that the deeds of the British were as bad ; he denounced the struggle as a sordid trade war designed to free Britain from German competition, and advocated that Australia should transform herself into a Sinn Fein Republic.

Possessing great religious influence, this dignitary succeeded in turning the vote in Victoria twice against conscription. As in the Sinn Fein outbreak in Dublin, conservative Irish ecclesiastics were practically allied with anti-clerical communistic revolutionaries against the Government. Happily, all the Roman Catholic dignitaries of Australia were not leagued against the Australian soldiers and the British Commonwealth. The Archbishop of Western Australia vigorously supported the war against the Central Empires, and, using his influence, led his State to vote in favour of compulsory service. **Australia's Coalition**

In November, 1916, Mr. Hughes resigned, **Ministry** and then formed a new Ministry as head of a national Labour Party. Mr. F. G. Tudor became Leader of the Opposition forces of the Australian Labour Party, and the Prime Minister henceforward relied on the aid of the Liberal Party for all war measures. On February 15th, 1917, the Coalition Ministry was formed, containing six Labour members and five Liberal members, with Mr. W. M. Hughes as Prime Minister, Senator G. F. Pearce as Minister of Defence, and Mr. J. Cook as Minister for the Navy. Then in the spring a constitutional test was made of the loyal and disloyal forces in the country by means of a General Election. The Liberals had thirty-five members returned ; the National Labour Party, under Mr. Hughes, had fifteen members, while the disaffected Australian Labour Party, under Mr. Tudor, had twenty-five members elected. The question of conscription, however, was not fought out, Mr. Hughes promising that it would not again be raised unless some grave military disaster imperilled the cause of the Allies.

The country was thus free to rally entirely against the domestic peril of giving power to Labour revolutionaries and their Sinn Fein auxiliaries. Mr. Hughes decided in alliance with the Liberal leader to bid for the votes of the large number of people who neither desired any revolutionary changes, nor wanted Australia to take her full part in the war. There were men of more courage, and perhaps less political skill, who desired to put everything to the test and see the first great Labour democracy of the world emerge in triumph and fully armed, or fail and fall openly under the attacks of Sinn Fein rebels and Anarchist revolutionaries, to rise again when all the consequences were made clear. This grim, adventurous policy was not, however, adopted, and the Coalition Ministry of Liberals and patriotic Labour continued to direct affairs, while Mr. Hughes came to England, preaching against German intrigue and revolutionary treason with a passion that often amazed his British audiences. It was domestic troubles in Australia that directly inspired the old Trade Union leader.

He considered the downfall of Russia, and the arrangements made between the German Staff and the Russian Bolshevists, Ukrainian adventurers **Second referendum** and the Baltic barons, as a serious disaster **on Conscription** to the allied cause, requiring him to submit again to a referendum decision the problem of reinforcing the Army of Australia. By a majority of 166,588 the Australian people in 1917 once more refused to agree to establish compulsory military service oversea. The Roman Catholic Archbishop of Melbourne once more succeeded in turning the Victorian vote against aid to the soldiers ; the Irish Labour Ministers of Queensland carried their State against the measure, and only Western Australia, Tasmania, and the Territories gave a majority vote for the measure of necessity to reinforce the Army.

The troops in France could easily have swayed the event; but for a special reason they gave only a small majority vote for conscription. In the first place they were somewhat opposed to the question being put to the nation after one adverse referendum decision had been given. In the second place they were scarcely pleased that their democracy had generally lagged behind New Zealand in the matter of national service. But what weighed most with the large number of soldiers who voted against conscription was their view that they themselves were willing volunteers with a great tradition, and they did not want in their ranks any considerable body of discontented pressed men. Many of the soldiers who took this view wrote home asking their women folk to join with them in voting against conscription.

Thus, in ultimate analysis, it was the Australian Army that

ROYAL INSPECTION OF A.I.F.
Men of the Australian Imperial Forces in England formed up on their parade-ground in readiness for inspection by King George.

gallantly refused to be brought up to full strength by the compulsion of men who would not volunteer. The estimated number of reinforcements required to keep the divisions up to strength was about 7,000 a month, but the enlistments after the adverse vote of the second referendum fell at times as low as 400 a week. In April, 1918, when the seriousness of the situation in France was realised, the weekly enlistment rose to 450, and in the week ending May 19th, it reached 1,491. Had this figure been maintained, the volunteer system might have produced the reinforcements actually required to make good the casualties, but there was a considerable decline in the following week, indicating that the revolutionary influence was again predominant.

Mr. Hughes prosecuted Mr. T. J. Ryan, the Irish Labour Premier of Queensland, for publishing certain statements about military statistics in the Hansard Parliamentary Report, and was himself assailed by a Queensland mob. On January 8th, 1918, Mr. Hughes resigned as Prime Minister, but was requested to form another Ministry, and returned to office with all his Labour and Liberal Cabinet colleagues. As he and his Ministers had stated that they could not govern the country, and would not attempt to do so, without power of compulsion to ensure the reinforcements, the new position of Mr. Hughes was regarded as uncertain in the absence of a constitutional appeal to the country. A moral advantage was gained by the Opposition Labour Party, with a result that the sinister turmoil in the Commonwealth increased.

AN AUSTRALIAN GUARD OF HONOUR.
King George inspecting the Guard of Honour in the Strand, August 3rd, 1918, when his Majesty performed the opening ceremony at Australia House.

Australia was paying dearly for the magnificent work she directly accomplished in the war. In 1914 the Labour Party and Trade Union forces behind it had been pursuing an opportunist policy for better conditions and higher wages. It was this practical method that led the party to power. But largely under alien influence, exercised from centres of enemy propaganda in the United States, the elements of a war between classes had been introduced into Australian life, alongside the other disruptive movement of Sinn Fein, which, as had been seen in Ireland and America, owed much of its new virulence and sweep to Teutonic support and co-operation.

In the early summer of 1918, when Ludendorff ordered the German Foreign Minister, Admiral Hintze, to find new means of negotiating peace before the weakening German armies were broken, the Australian revolutionaries strangely answered the enemy's call for help. The Labour Councils of Melbourne and Brisbane decided to fly the Red Flag daily at their Trades Hall; the Sydney Trades and Labour Council passed a resolution against helping in the recruiting campaign; and in June, 1918, the Australian Labour Party agitated for an immediate peace. According to the peace proposals passed at an annual Labour Conference in New South Wales, and ratified by an Inter-State Conference in Western Australia, an allied victory could only be achieved by the impoverishment of the workers and the practical destruction of civilisation. So a settlement by arrangement with the military castes of the Central Empires was immediately demanded, together with separate representation for Ireland, at the Peace Conference.

Besides proposing peace with the Hohenzollern and Hapsburg, the new Labour Party of the Commonwealth agreed that working men should be trained for four years in their employers' time, without reduction of wages, and formed into an army of the Bolshevist type, with abolition of all military oaths and of distinctions between non-commissioned and commissioned officers. On conclusion of training, men were to retain their arms, presumably for use in the Red Army of the class war. Furthermore, Australia was practically to be severed from the British Crown in the matters of law appeals, the Royal assent to Bills passed by Parliament, and the general duties performed by the Governor-General.

The high cost of living and the revelation of some scandalous cases of profiteering would of themselves have produced unrest among the sensitive, alert, and strong working men of Australia. But these accidents of the long, wearing struggle were far from being the real cause of the troubles. So long as Ireland was the brightest spot in the war-clouded islands of the British Empire, all went well in Australia. When, however, the secret "boss" of Ireland, Mr. William Martin Murphy, completed his long duel with Mr. John Dillon and other Nationalist leaders, by preventing a working scheme of Home Rule being arranged, and by supporting with all his wealthy influence the development of the Sinn Fein movement to destroy the Nationalist Party, then the large Irish element in Australia, numbering nearly a million persons, became partially disaffected.

For the lay Irish people of the Commonwealth, with their increasing concern in the problem of Home Rule, Sinn Fein propaganda was used to destroy their reliance in the constitutional Nationalist work of effecting a compromise with Ulster. Finally, for the capable Irish working-class element in Australian cities, who were living in comfort with high wages and cheap meat and bread, there was provided the variety of Bolshevism spread by the Industrial Workers of the World organisation, largely created in the United States among the cheap immigrant labour from oppressed nationalities in Austria-Hungary.

Canadian Labour remained sound

It is worthy of remark that the American variety of Bolshevism was imported into Canadian Labour early in the war in order to check the transport of foodstuffs and the manufacture of war material. Though British agents were employed, the movement completely failed of effect among Canadian transport workers, miners, and factory hands so long as the struggle in Europe continued. In spite of the fact that the general cost of living was higher in the Dominion than in the Commonwealth, Canadian Labour remained the sounder. There was also propaganda of a Bolshevist type in New Zealand, combined with strife between men of Ulster stock and Catholic Irishmen of the Sinn Fein school; but the intrigues produced no disorder or weakness in the general effort of the New Zealand nation.

Australia alone among the Dominions allowed the strange alliance between the Sinn Feiners and Communist Revolutionaries to grow into an inhibiting force, stronger than that exerted in the United States by the union of Germans, Fenian, and Sinn Fein organisations and the Industrial Workers of the World. Yet, at the same time, Australia maintained in the field large forces of the highest quality, that greatly helped to mould the future of the world by victories in Flanders and France, Palestine and Syria. It was while the best of her men were away that the Commonwealth, injured by a great drought and loss of shipping, fell into bitter and anarchic domestic strife during the period in which she was becoming mistress of the South Pacific Ocean.

The fine Australian administration of Papua was evidence of the benign power of the greatest of Labour democracies, and with the home-coming of the victorious troops from the battlefields of France and Syria there was a happy prospect of fresh, softening, harmonising influences entering into play in the Commonwealth.

The way in which Australian soldiers in London welcomed their Prime Minister, Mr. W. M. Hughes, returning from the Peace Conference, was an augury of domestic peace in the continental Power of the South Seas. Only if the Teuton had been able to negotiate a settlement generally favourable to the development of his interests, might Australia have suffered seriously and permanently from the forces of disaffection which the enemy had directly or indirectly urged upon her. Like the Mother Country, Australia as a whole drew no profit whatever from the war. Her losses in life and wealth were beyond all compensation; but she had built,

against tremendous difficulties, a noble tradition of heroic achievement, which at least equalled that of the Athenians in the Persian War. She remained the light of Labour throughout the world.

Yet the smaller and more compact community of New Zealand, with a population of little more than one million, scattered in happy islands of larger extent than Britain, was incomparable in its way. New Zealand furnished 91,914 volunteer troops, and 32,270 conscript troops, making a total force of 124,184 engaged in home and oversea service, with a casualty list of 58,004, falling on practically half the entire force under arms. More than half the male population of military age in the islands was called up for service. In 1914 lads and men in New Zealand from nineteen to forty-five years old numbered 243,376, so that the total enlistment was about 51 per cent. of the then available manhood. But as the health and strength of the men taken as soldiers were unequalled by any other forces engaged in the war, the actual percentage of her male strength which New Zealand gave was more than can be estimated by the mere numbering of recruits.

Like the Australians, the men of Maoriland had a special reason for suspecting Teutonic aggression. The large German possessions and naval stations in the South Seas, by the Imperial trade routes, were a menace to both the Island Dominion and the Continental Commonwealth. During Bismarck's conquering intrigues in the South

MUNITION WORKERS FROM BENEATH THE SOUTHERN CROSS.
Arrival of men who came from Australia to Europe to help in the production of munitions, and (in circle) the workers listening to an address from Colonel Barraclough before their disembarkation.

Seas the New Zealanders tried to protect themselves by federating with Samoa, whose population was akin to the Maoris, and looked to them for help against the Teutons. Angrily and vainly did they protest against the Samoan Convention. On the outbreak of war the New Zealanders eagerly rushed to seize the German colony in which they felt their national honour was involved, and their Ministers forestalled peace discussions by declaring that Samoa must never go back to the enemy. From the beginning of the struggle it was also the intention of the New Zealand people to obtain for their leaders such a position in some Imperial Council that no British Cabinet would again be able to sacrifice South Sea interests to a foreign Power, without full consideration of all circumstances by Dominion representatives. New Zealand led in oversea affairs in war and peace. At the opening of the war she possessed merely five hundred and seventy-eight regular soldiers; but a system of compulsory training had furnished her with 25,902 militiamen, from whom was selected the force which swooped on Samoa. Her export trade rose to £27 6s. 5d. a head, which was the highest in the world in proportion to population, and some evidence of the wealth of the country was given in the totaliser records of wagers on horse-racing that amounted in a year to £4 9s. a head.

New Zealand and its leaders

The Government was in the hands of two middle-class parties, known as Liberal and Reform, who differed mainly on a land question that was losing its force. At the head of the Reform Party was Mr. W. F. Massey, an Irishman who had never seen England; while the leader of the Liberals, who were out of office, was Sir Joseph Ward, who had considerable experience in Imperial problems. There was a Labour group, touched with Revolutionary Socialism, and averse from compulsory training. It placed only seven members in the House of Representatives against the sixty-nine members of the Reform and Liberal Parties; and when a Coalition Government was arranged, after a General Election in August, 1915, the Labour group refused the offer of a seat in the Cabinet.

Mr. Massey remained Prime Minister, Sir Joseph Ward became Minister of Finance, and Colonel Sir James Allen continued as Minister of Defence. As the white population was mainly of English, Scottish, and Ulster stock, with only somewhat more than 100,000 Irish Roman Catholics, the spirit of the oversea Sinn Fein movement produced no violent effect on New Zealand politics. The only serious factor of unrest in the fortunate islands was an extraordinary rise in food prices in the land of exporting plenty. In 1915 bad weather and labour shortage led to

a failure of crops. New Zealand first imported wheat from Australia, then returned it, as the drought-stricken Australians became still shorter of breadstuff, and turned to Canada for help. Meanwhile, a general prosperity reigned, and sheep farmers and dairy farmers began to make remarkable profits. The working classes obtained more wages, and, as in the Motherland, only the professional class felt severely the financial strain of the war.

In the summer of 1916 a strong movement for conscription swept the country.

A lead in conscription

There was no need for any use of compulsion, as volunteers were still enlisting in numbers large enough to maintain the reinforcements required by the Expeditionary Force. But the general feeling grew that common compulsion was a juster system for a democratic country than was voluntary enlistment. So on August 1st, 1916, a Military Service Act was passed, giving the Government power to conscript men for service overseas. New Zealand thus led the Mother Country and Canada in enforcing democratic national service, by making common compulsion a matter of principle, instead of an emergency expedient. Voluntary recruiting was continued until November, 1916, when the first ballot for single men was held to fill vacancies in drafts. In October, 1917, the first ballot for married men was held. In all 135,184 men were balloted, of whom 32,270 were despatched to camp, and 6,732 were under orders at the date of the armistice. The training of Territorials and cadets, under the Home Defence scheme, continued throughout the war, 32,971 Territorials passing into the oversea Expeditionary Force.

The great direct military effort of New Zealand did not check the intense development of her productive power. Some large runholders combined with the Socialist Revolutionaries in complaining that the Imperial war was bleeding the country white; but a 40 per cent. excess profit tax brought in such additional revenue as showed that the wealth of the nation was greatly increasing. Allowances to soldiers' dependents were augmented, so that a private and his wife and child received £3 5s. a week, at a time when the cost of living had risen only 27 per cent. in the islands, against the rise of 102 per cent. in Britain. New Zealand began to borrow largely from her own people by the issue of 4½ per cent. bonds free of income tax, and promised soon to become like Canada, a creditor rather than a debtor nation.

Yet the increase of wealth among the farming class tended, in 1917, to excite the working man. The miners, who were labouring four and a quarter days a week, at an average wage approaching £7, adopted a policy of decreased output as a protest against national service, at a time when employed miners were exempted from conscription. There was a coal strike and a severe shortage of fuel during an exceptionally cold winter; and although the miners' wages were advanced beyond the additional cost of living, and some mines were shown to be running at a loss, or without any dividend return, the miners' new demand, backed by an overwhelming

VICTORIOUS ENERGY OF SOUTH AFRICA.
Entraining horses for service with the South African forces in the victorious campaign in "German South-West." In oval: Captured German guns on the end balcony of the Union Buildings overlooking Pretoria.

vote for a strike, was for the nationalisation of the mines. Yet the State mine, Point Elizabeth Colliery, which the agitators alleged was making an annual profit of £18,000, while selling coal cheaply, was proved to be getting coal by drawing pillars, paying no rents or royalties, and showing a balance of profit over loss of only £700 in an average of five years. The New Zealand miners seem to have deliberately starved the people of fuel in the coldest of winters in order to bring about an unprofitable nationalisation of coal resources, under their own management, as an introductory step towards complete communism of the Russian kind. In coal troubles, as in national service, New Zealand anticipated the Old Country.

Owing to the absence of the leaders of the Government in London, the Coalition Ministry began to lose some of its hold upon the people. In two by-elections a Syndicalist and also a professed Bolshevist were returned. In Wellington Central the man who stood for the party with "Bolshevism upon its banner" heavily defeated both a patriotic Labour candidate and a Government supporter. Lack of measures to cope with war profiteering was the general motive of discontent. Only the Labour Party had a definite programme, and there was by November,

SOUTH AFRICAN GUNNERS IN ENGLAND.
Men of the South African Heavy Artillery on the parade ground of their training camp in England. In spite of domestic peril fomented by enemy agents among the disaffected minority, South Africa had, before the end of 1916, 60,000 men on active service.

IN A DESERT CAMPAIGN.
Men and horses tired out, hungry, and thirsty in a desert tract of German South-West Africa, where General Botha's forces struggled heroically to a victorious end, often in the most terribly trying of conditions.

1918, a likelihood that if the Trade Unions could escape from the contagion of German and Russian diseases in politics, New Zealand would soon rank with Australia as a workers' democracy.

Meanwhile, the Conservative Premier and his Liberal colleague were playing no small part in trying to shape the course of evolution of the British Empire. In London it was found unsatisfactory to hold Imperial conferences at intervals, and the Prime Ministers of the Dominions were given the right to attend the sittings of the War Cabinet. Then the still more important proposal was made that any of the Dominions might appoint a resident Minister in Great Britain to watch permanently over the interests of his country from an Imperial point of view. At the end of the war there was to be an Imperial Cabinet sitting periodically when business required. There was to be no interference with the autonomy of any Dominion, and Imperial Federation, though keenly discussed, was regarded as much too advanced a policy.

South Africa, in particular, was far from being ready for any scheme of federation. The Union in which Boer and Briton lived remained throughout the war the miracle of the modern world, increasing the prestige of the British people in an incomparable way. Not without the patience of genius

was the finest of settlements maintained, and upon General Botha and General Smuts fell the main work of reconciling Dutch and British interests. The course of the struggle in South Africa during a war with Germany was largely decided in 1912. It was then that the Transvaal leaders, Botha and Smuts, separated from the Free State leaders, Steyn and Hertzog, by determining that the Union should not remain neutral in a struggle between Germany and Britain. Hertzog resigned from the Union Cabinet, and for two years preparatory to the outbreak of hostilities tried to win over the Transvaal Dutch to the dubious policy of the Orange Free State. The measure of success he obtained was seen in the rebellion of 1914 and in the speed and power with which General Botha quelled the rising.

While the old commander of the Transvaal Boers was engaged in the South-West Africa Campaign, with General Smuts directing domestic affairs, Hertzog conducted a virulent propaganda of calumny against the absent loyal leader. Hertzog was of German stock, with a Germanic talent for intrigue. He gained the support of the ubiquitous Industrial Workers of the World organisation, and with it tried to capture and annex to the disaffected Boer party the Labour groups in the mining towns. But the Labour leader, Mr. Cresswell, pledged his party to see the war through, and the I.W.W. aliens were expelled from the Trade Unions.

In the General Election that followed, General Botha's South African Party lost nearly half its strength, but yet held fifty-four seats against the twenty-seven seats won by the Nationalists under General Hertzog. With the forty British Unionist members, under Sir Thomas Smartt, and the patriotic Labour group, under Mr. Cresswell, there were, in October, 1915, one hundred and three supporters of the Union and the war in loose yet effective co-operation.

Situation in South Africa

The situation continued to give anxiety. General Hertzog and ex-President Steyn were dangerous exploiters of a difficult problem in Boer life. The Boers had formed in the old days an aristocracy living on great farmlands, worked with black labour, and drawing toll from gold and diamond mines run by impotent Outlanders. They were used to little restraint of law and government, being a kind of rude free barons, with black serfs, giving military service on commando, and maintaining a remarkable marksmanship.

When obliged to live in the more complex civilisation introduced by the Briton, the Boer of the back-veldt chafed and declined. He was angered by interferences under new regulations for combating stock diseases, and by the consideration shown to the blacks. He could not compete with the new scientific school of farmers, and with his Puritanism dissolving into laxity and his means growing scantier, he was in danger of degenerating into a position like that of the " mean whites " of the United States backwoods. The new influences might in time change and enlighten his sons, but he despairingly saw no other way out of degradation than to bring back the old free life by the use of his rifle.

The only important product he had to sell was wool, and his sheep were badly bred, giving wool of inferior quality that went before the war to Germany, as British spinners would not take so short a staple. When the British Government arranged to take the South African clip it paid 55 per cent. above the price before the war, but the Boers held they could have obtained in a free market a higher price from Japanese and American buyers. The commandeering of the wool clip, at a price which seemed at last to be astonishing when regard was had to the cost of British-made clothing, gave a widespread stimulus to Nationalist disaffection. As a matter of fact a large part of the old South African wool clip remained in Cape warehouses in 1917 when the new clip was being bought, the shortage of shipping making wool-buying a difficult problem for the British Government. But more generosity towards the poor back-veldt farmers would have been wise and soothing.

As it was there were two more attempts at a Boer rebellion. The Dutch did not volunteer for foreign service in proportion to their numbers, with the result that the more the Britons attempted directly to help the Imperial cause the greater the peril grew in South Africa. In 1916 the strength of the British settlers in the Union was seriously lessened by enlistments for the East Africa Campaign under General Smuts, for the South African Contingent in France under General Lukin, and for the garrison of the new Protectorate of South-West Africa. The Dutch loyalists who volunteered for foreign service were even a more serious loss than the British recruits, as their influence over their countrymen was greater. So they were retained as much as possible, but their numbers were not sufficient, and it was to General de Wet that much of the credit for the prevention of the second rebellion was due. When he was approached by some of the principal plotters he listened to what they said, and gave full information to the Government. The fierce old fighter had once been in a mind to shoot General Hertzog, and although he refrained from so doing after making peace with General Botha, he struck the hardest of blows against the crafty intriguers among the discontented Dutch.

Boer attempts at rebellion

A third and wider rebellion was arranged in the summer of 1918. General Hertzog conducted an oratorical campaign in the Transvaal and serious troubles occurred in his wake. By July attacks in considerable force were expected at Pretoria and Cape Town. It was the apparent successes of Ludendorff's offensives in France and Flanders that moved the old rebel party to arrange for a general rising throughout South Africa. The strain upon General Botha was tremendous. He made all his military preparations, and issued an eloquent manifesto calling for loyal support of all the enlightened progressive Dutch. The vigorous use of his power and influence held back the grand movement of rebellion for a few weeks. Then, before the racial struggle could break out on a scale larger than that of the South African War, Sir Douglas Haig began his last and decisive offensive. With the restoration of British military prestige there was a change of mood in the rebel camp. General Hertzog advocated the new doctrine that the destiny of South Africa would be settled on the battlefields of Europe. There was, in his view, no need for another bloody struggle between Boer and Britain— invincible Germany would arrange the settlement of South Africa in peace negotiations.

Hertzog's futile mission

When General Hertzog belatedly discovered that the Teuton was impotent to help the Boer drive the Briton from South Africa, he managed, after some trouble, to travel to Paris in order to convert President Woodrow Wilson into a champion of the oppressed Boer race, who had a Prime Minister of their own stock at the head of the Government, and another Boer commander, General Smuts, representing them brilliantly in the Peace Conference and leading the way in planning the structure of the League of Nations. The futility of the Hertzog mission was scarcely so remarkable as its ridiculousness. The rupture in 1912 between the Transvaal Party under Botha and Smuts and the Orange Free State Party under Hertzog and Steyn had arisen mainly from personal ambitions and animosities in the men of inferior calibre. In all Hertzog's intrigues he seems to have been moved less by the desire to create racial strife than by a wild quest for any instrument for striking down his former Cabinet colleagues. But the men he struggled against were stronger than he was, alike in powers of mind and character and in the command of resources of influence and main strength. The defeat of Hertzog was an event of brightest promise for the development of the union of races in South Africa.

In spite of her extreme domestic perils South Africa, by October, 1916, had 60,000 men on active service. With this enlistment a stratum of population was reached that could not be induced voluntarily to serve in the field, and with a large part of the people wholly neutral or openly hostile, any measure of conscription was not to be contemplated. The suggestion might have led to rebellion long before any empowering act was passed by the large loyal majority in Parliament. So delicate was the general situation that measures could not be taken in the way of restraint of German

RECRUITING IN THE HIMALAYAS.
Two views of a village gathering in the Himalayas in connection with a recruiting rally for the Indian Army during the Great War. The enlistment of Indians rose to over a million, and over half a million of Indian fighting men served overseas.

Men of the Australian Naval Brigade in the trenches of Madang, in German New Guinea. Madang had been known to the dispossessed Germans as Friedrich Wilhelmshafen.

Ships of the expedition for the attack on German New Guinea gathering at Port Moresby, the capital of British New Guinea.

Crews of Australian destroyers about to return to their ships after bathing from the beach at Deli, Timor, a Portuguese island west of New Guinea.
Inset : Men of the Australian Naval Brigade arranging the exploding of a German road mine in New Pomerania, Bismarck Archipelago.

AUSTRALIAN NAVAL FORCES AND THE CAPTURE OF GERMAN NEW GUINEA.

RULING PRINCES AND CHIEFS OF INDIA, WITH THE VICEROY (LORD CHELMSFORD), AT DELHI, JANUARY, 1919.

A great conference of the Ruling Princes and Chiefs of India was held at Delhi in January, 1919, and was addressed by the Viceroy. This photograph represents those who attended. From left to right the names are (front row, seated): H.H. the Maharajah of Navanager, H.H. the Maharajah of Alwar, H.H. the Maharajah of Kishengarh, H.H. the Maharao of Cutch, H.H. the Begum of Bhopal, H.E. the Viceroy, H.H. the Maharajah of Jaipur, H.H. the Maharao Rajah of Bundi, H.H. the Maharawal of Jaisalmer, H.H. Maharajah Bahadur Sir Pratap Singh of Jodhpur, H.H. the Maharajah of Sikkim. Second row : H.H. the Rajah of Jhabua, H.H. the Maharajah of Dattia, H.H. the Rajah of Sitamau, H.H. the Maharajah of Dhar, H.H. the Maharajah Scindia of Gwalior, H.H. the Maharajah of Kashmir, H.H. the Maharajah of Dewas (Senior Branch), H.H. the Rajah of Rajpipla, H.H. the Maharajah of Kapurthala, H.H. the Maharao of Kotah, H.H. the Maharajah of Kolhapur, H.H. the Maharajah of Dewas (Junior Branch). Third row : H.H. the Maharajah of Dharangadhara, H.H. the Nawab of Palanpur, the Thakur Sahib of Limbdi, H.H. the Raj Sahib of Wankaner, the Rajah of Sangli, the Thakur Sahib of Gondal, the Rajah of Baria, the Nawab of Loharu. Back row : H.H. the Rajah of Chamba, H.H. the Nawab of Malerkotla, H.H. the Rajah of Tehri, H.H. the Maharajah of Bharatpur, Kanwar Sahib of Limbdi, H.H. the Maharajah of Patiala, Rajah Sir Hari Singh of Kashmir, H.H. the Maharaj Rana of Dholpur, the Tika Sahib of Kapurthala, Nawabzada Aziz-ud-din Ahmed Khan of Loharu, the Hon. Sir John Wood, Col. R. E. Holland, Capt. C. M. G. Gordon Ives, Mr. J. C. B. Drake.

trade or the internment of the tens of thousands of Teutons intriguing among the Boers. In the opinion of General Botha and his lieutenants the Teutonic organisation was so strongly based on the sympathy of the back-veldt farming class that there would have been a rising if the Germans had been properly dealt with. So, although there was some rioting in towns of British settlement, no measures were taken to remove the German cancer from ramifying into the South African system. It was one of those operations that might have killed the patient. The only sure medicine was a complete allied victory over the enemy in Europe.

In all the disorders and troubles between the white races of the Union the natives remained intensely loyal. The old fighting tribes were indeed wonderfully eager to train for battle. **Loyalty of African natives**

From them could have been formed a great black force, with a traditional vehemence in attack superior to that of the 900,000 African natives enlisted in the armies of France. Against the Turk, in actions where artillery was not used so tremendously as in France, tribesmen trained to modern warfare could have charged, when well led, with probably over-whelming effect. The loyal Boer leaders, however, were averse to the enlistment of coloured men as infantry. There was one coloured combatant battalion that served in East Africa, but a far larger number of natives found their field of useful-ness in military labour. Ten thousand coloured men were recruited in a labour corps for France, and excelled Chinese, Indians, and natives from French possessions by their steady capacity for work. Forty thousand South African natives were employed in railway building and general labour in South - West Africa, and another **Industrial disputes** ten thousand native labourers served in German East Africa.

Being prevented from having their fill of fighting, many of the labouring races of the Union showed their unrest in industrial disputes as well as in the happier field for progress offered by social reforms. When the engineers of Johannesburg made a successful strike for a wage of £8 2s. a week, natives engaged in municipal employment also came out on strike, but were defeated on the technical ground that they could not quit work without a month's notice. It was a fact that the engineers were under short notice, while the natives could not leave under less than a month. But the black mind did not grasp this difference in legalities, and the feeling arose among the natives that there was no equality of justice between black and white workmen. Yet they generally remained finely loyal to the British Crown.

In India in the first months of the war there was a magnificent display of loyalty. Princes and peoples united in supporting the Government, and 200,000 troops were sent to five fields of war, from Flanders to China. In 1915, though the masses and native rulers of the vast Indian population of 315,000,000 continued to help in the war, signs of sinister agitation became evident. There were disorders in the Punjab and Bengal, trouble in Ceylon, and large schemes for a mutiny. The disaster at Kut and the failure of the Gallipoli Campaign seriously lowered British prestige, and wild rumours spread through the bazaars. An alliance between the Moslem League and the Hindu Congress was perhaps the most formidable evidence of the

RT. HON. EDWARD S. MONTAGU IN BENGAL.
The Secretary of State for India (centre) with a group of the leading men of Bengal by whom he was entertained during the visit which he paid to India in the autumn of 1917.

COMMANDER-IN-CHIEF AND HEADQUARTERS STAFF AT DELHI, 1919.
From left to right (on the ground) : Lieutenant Davy, Captain G. Mardan, Captain Khagendra, Lieut.-Colonel Gumbir Jung Thapa, Captain Narsing, Lieut.-Colonel Chundra Jung Thapa, Lieutenant Barker, Captain Scott. Seated : Colonel Indra Shum Shere Jung, Major-General T. E. Scott, Major-General Shere Shum Shere Jung, General Sir A. Barrett, General Sir Baber Shum Shere Jung, Sir C. C. Monro (Commander-in-Chief in India), General Sir Padma Shum Shere Jung, Lieut.-General Sir E. Altham, General Tej Shum Shere Jung, Lieut.-General Sir H. Hudson, Lieut.-Colonel Porteous. Third row : Conductor Chapman, Colonel Ghana, Captain Johanson, Lieut.-Colonel Shum Shere, Captain Rogers, Lieut.-Colonel Bhuban Bikram, Captain Weallens, Lieut.-Colonel Dumber Shum Shere Thapa, Lieutenant Feagon, Lieut.-Colonel Bhairub Shum Shere Jung. Back row : Lieut.-Colonel Madan, Captain Carpendale, Lieut.-Colonel Pratap, Captain Dent, Lieut.-Colonel Jit Jung Sahi, Captain Kemp, Lieut.-Colonel Molesworth, Major Baker, Major Uttam Bikram.

course of the undercurrents in Indian life.

The National Congress of the Hindus had been formed, under Government favour, to ventilate grievances and suggest improvements in administration. It helped to educate the Brahmin caste in the ways of modern politics, and after serving the Government became an organ of Brahmin ascendancy. Some of its leading men were prosecuted for sedition and convicted, but their wild methods were not without effect in spreading among Hindus the idea of Home Rule. Apprehensive of being submerged in a Hindu Government, the 70,000,000 Mohammedans of India formed a Moslem League to counter the Hindu Congress. This was sound and natural, and gave both the great Indian races means of organising public opinion and influencing the administration. Before the outbreak of the war, Lord Morley, as Secretary for India, laid the first foundations of Parliamentary

government in the medley of the great Dependency.

In the territory of the British administration the people elected members of municipal and rural Boards. The Boards sent some of their members to the Provincial Councils, and the Provincial Councils elected native representatives to sit with British administrators in the Legislative Council of the Viceroy. In 1915 one of the ablest of the Hindu members of the Viceroy's Council, Lord Sinha, acted as President of the Hindu Congress and managed to repress the extremists. But the agitators were already escaping from constitutional control and aiming at direct action, using the increasing strain of the war on Government and people to provoke disorders. An attempt was made by German-directed Hindus to suborn the Indian troops, and Turkish agents tried to bring about a rising among the Moslems of India. The new alliance

THE REFORM COMMITTEES AT DELHI, 1919.
From left to right (ground) : Mr. J. V. D. Hodge, Mr. P. C. Tallents. Seated : Maulvi Sir Rahim Bakhsh, Sahibzada Aftab Ahmed Khan, Mr. R. Feetham, Lord Southborough, Sir Frank Sly, Hon. Babu Surendranath Banerjea, Hon. Mr. M. E. Couchman. Standing : Captain M. Reader, Mr. A. C. Clauson, Mr. G. Rainy, Hon. Mr. N. Hogg, Sir Frabhushankar Pattani, Mr. J. P. Thompson, Hon. Mr. Srinivasa Sastri. Back row : Mr. W. M. Hailey, Mr. H. L. Stephenson, Hon. Dr. Tej Bahadur Sapru, and Sir Chimanlal H. Setalvad.

between the Moslem League and the Hindu Congress affirmed at Lucknow in 1916 was largely the result of Turkish and Teutonic intrigue.

The Indian Mohammedans seemed at first the more profoundly disaffected, though they contributed many fine soldiers to the enlarging Indian Army. The Ottoman Caliph was their religious chief, and his victories over the British strengthened the subtle and wide propaganda of the Young Turkish Party. Some Indian Moslems began to lose faith in the British Government and to regard a temporary union with the Hindu agitators as a working warlike policy.

Sir Stanley Maude's advance to Bagdad, with an army largely composed of Indians, had a happy effect upon the troubled Dependency. The war was bringing general prosperity to India, her war exports rising in value to more than £100,000,000 a year, while in addition **Effect of the** she became the base of supplies for **advance to Bagdad** Mesopotamia and other Eastern fields of battle. The appointment of Indian representatives at the Imperial Conference in London was recognised as testimony to her growing power, and the enlistment of Indians during the war rose at last to the extraordinary figure of 1,161,789 officers and men, of whom more than 750,000 were combatants. Of the Indian fighting men more than 500,000 served overseas, with nearly 400,000 Labour Corps men and other non-combatants. The total Indian casualties, in ten theatres of war, were 101,439 up to September, 1918.

Generally speaking, the waves of rebellious feeling in India were as shallow as they were wide. Even their width was limited, as two-fifths of the territory and nearly one-fourth of the population were under native princes who disliked and condemned the Brahmin agitators and the agents of the Ottomans. The disaffected Brahmins desired to recover their legendary power of rule by becoming the Parliamentary representatives of the people. In places they still would not permit an outcast to approach within forty yards of their sacred persons, yet they pretended a passionate love for Western democratic institutions, leading the violent clamour for Dominion self-government. Their veritable aim was to extend and reinforce the old, crippling caste system, against which the Buddha had vainly fought, by working the British out of India as they had the Buddhists.

Against them were the Indian men of action, the landowning warlike gentry, and the mass of peasantry, in addition to the native princes and chiefs. The Indian Moslems were also averse to a Brahmin oligarchy under a Parliamentary disguise.

Yet there was a feeling that Indians should have a larger place in the administration and government of their people. This was regarded as rightly earned by service and work in the Imperial cause, and as a due development of the political measures established by Lord Morley in 1909. The war had quickened feeling and aspirations, producing, a few years after the first essays in representative politics, a demand for a larger share of power. News of the Russian Revolution of March, 1917, had an extraordinary effect upon the people and Government of India. The dissolution of this Imperial bureaucracy was at first followed by some happy results; large forces of Russian Moslems, for example, **India and the** using their political freedom to draw away **Russian Revolution** from the Young Turkish Party and combine in federal government with the Russian Christians. The wealthy Turks in Baku, in closest touch with Ottoman intrigue, inclined rather to free government and co-operation with Christians than to military despotism under the Caliph.

In August, 1917, the Viceroy of India, Lord Chelmsford, proclaimed that a large part of the administrative work and the direction of Government policy would be given by the Crown to representatives of the Indian peoples. This strangely led, especially in Southern India, to a strong popular agitation against any grant of Parliamentary government. When Mr. Montagu, Secretary for India, came to the country to arrange with the Viceroy a scheme of political progress and study the general conditions obtaining, he was petitioned by large masses of peasantry to save them from Brahmin ascendancy. Many British administrators had an acute sense of the same danger, but in the report drawn up by Mr. Montagu and Lord Chelmsford as the basis of a Bill to be submitted to the Imperial Parliament, the problems of Hindu castes and outcasts and conflicting races were left unsolved. British India was to be established on a system of experimental free institutions, under the guidance of British officials, with the provincial assemblies as the first centres of Parliamentary government and the Viceroy's Legislative Council as the ultimate national chamber.

The Montagu-Chelmsford scheme had an appeasing effect upon the people by affording a large prospect of political and administrative careers to them. From a general point of view it was well that measures were taken to prepare British India for a controlled form of free government. The British reverses by Amiens and Ypres in the spring of 1918 had a disquieting effect upon native opinion. There were extraordinary rumours that German troops had forced the Khyber Pass, and that the British were evacuating India. The work of enemy agents who spread false rumours, however, helped rather than hindered the Government. The Indian peoples saw at last they were not fighting for the Empire or for European civilisation, but defending themselves. The harder they could press the Turks in Palestine and Mesopotamia the smaller grew the danger of an invasion in the direction of Peshawar. As was afterwards seen, when the Afghans murdered their Amir in order to become free to undertake an offensive against India, the peril along the frontier was serious. The best way in which the Indians could impress the restless Afghan chieftains was to enlist by the hundred thousand. This they did, while co-operation increased between British officials and Indian politicians of the moderate school.

Directly against the extremists in the Hindu Congress and the Moslem League the moderates gathered strongly in a new organisation—the National Liberal League. Thereby they acquired a remarkable influence upon the educated classes. As the tide of battle **Remarkable spirit** turned in France in the summer of 1918 **of nationality** and in early autumn the Ottoman Empire was overthrown in Palestine, Mohammedans joined with the Hindus in congratulations to the victorious armies. When the main struggle was over and the Afghans belatedly made an attack on India, they were met by a union of peoples of diverse tongues, races, and creeds, yet inspired by a remarkable spirit of nationality.

India was a continent rather than a country, but British genius seemed to have accomplished a miracle of welding it, under a continually enlightening and progressive scheme of government, into a growing unity. In spite of an increased cost of living, that pressed hard upon the poorer classes of the community, India emerged from the war purified, strengthened, and united by her great ordeal. Throughout the British Empire the enemy only strengthened that which he endeavoured to destroy. Both in regard to structure and in regard to mood the mighty Commonwealth of Nations, based on sea-power, was stronger in November, 1918, than it had been in August, 1914. Much was due to the fighting men, and to the men and women who armed and fed them; but much also was due to the wise, just founders of the expanding Commonwealth, who built it upon spiritual as well as material foundations.

On the accompanying coloured map, "Where Soldiers of Britain's Overseas Dominions Fought in the Great War," are shown the principal places associated with the exploits of troops from India and the outlying parts of the Empire in the various fields of conflict. In addition to the troops from Australia, Canada, Newfoundland, India, New Zealand, and South Africa, there were smaller bodies from other places, marked on the map as "Others"; for example, contingents from British Guiana served in Palestine, and from Ceylon in Egypt and Palestine; a Fijian platoon was at Ypres, Cambrai, and Salonika, while labour battalions from Malta, Mauritius, Seychelles, the Straits Settlements, the Cape, and elsewhere gave aid on many fronts.

GENERAL C. C. M. MAYNARD, C.B., C.M.G., D.S.O.

[Elliott & Fry

MAJOR-GEN. SIR WILLIAM IRONSIDE.

[Vandyk

BRIG.-GEN. L.W. de VERE SADLEIR-JACKSON, C.M.G., D.S.O.

BRIG.-GEN. GEORGE. ST. G. GROGAN V.C., D.S.O.

British generals in command of allied forces in Northern Russia.

In Archangel under allied occupation : Russian procession for encouraging recruiting.

With the North Russian Expeditionary Force : A wintry trail across an ice-bound lake.

With the British Cruiser Squadron in the wintry Baltic : Sentry on board H.M.S. Caradoc.

British cruiser in action in the Baltic : Firing the 6 in. after=gun of H.M.S. Caradoc.

Trotsky, Russia's Bolshevist Commissary for War, inspecting a regiment of the Letts, who formed the élite of the Red Army.

CHAPTER CCCXI.

RUSSIA UNDER THE RED TERROR.

By George Dobson,

Petrograd correspondent of the "Times" during the Revolution.

It is with considerable gratification that the Editors of THE GREAT WAR are able to include in their work this vivid and informing chapter concerning the condition of things in Russia under the Bolshevist regime. The writer of it is not only the doyen of British newspaper correspondents working in Russia, and one who for a quarter of a century represented the "Times" in Petrograd, but he was one of the last of the British residents to get away from the Russian capital after the terrorists had broken into the British Embassy and slain Captain Cromie, the Naval Attaché. Mr. Dobson already possessed a unique and intimate knowledge of the Russians, which, coupled with his first-hand knowledge of all that is meant by the reign of Bolshevism, give unchallengeable authority to this impression of Russia under the Red Terror. In the case of so personal a narrative it has seemed well to retain the present tense.

I T will probably be much more difficult for disrupted and lacerated Russia to recover and rehabilitate herself after the tornado of Bolshevism has spent itself than for the defeated Central European countries and their Eastern allies to bear the burdens imposed upon them by the Peace Treaty. Their condition after more than four years of useless slaughter and military failure was certainly much less calamitous than the state of Russia after a year and a half of boasted revolutionary freedom and so-called proletarian dictatorship. Had the Russians persevered with the campaign to the bitter end its evil effects would have been far less disastrous for them than they were in combination with the results of Bolshevist terrorism and national suicide.

Under the misguidance of a set of daring and unscrupulous adventurers, a party of political emigrants introduced by the Germans, Russia not only submitted to the enemy's conditions, but afterwards turned against her Allies in arms just when the latter were about to give the finishing stroke to the common foe. Influenced by these men of Bolshevist light and leading, the Russian troops deserted their friends by fraternising with the Germans, abolishing all discipline, murdering their officers, and breaking up their battle-front.

A few months later, after the British had been insolently summoned to join within ten days in what Lenin himself called "a disgraceful peace," the new Red Army, recruited from the lowest strata of

GENERAL SIR ALFRED KNOX, K.C.B.
Major-General Knox, who had been Military Attaché in Petrograd from 1908 to 1911, was appointed to the command of the British force sent to the aid of the Russians in Siberia.

the population, was taught to regard the British as downright enemies, and they were denounced as such in the most opprobrious terms possible on nearly every hoarding and house front in the main streets of Petrograd.

As soon as the dishonourable pact of Brest Litovsk had been concluded its violation was begun by both the Germans and the Bolshevists. The Germans continued to invade Russia, and the Bolshevists tried to undermine German authority and revolutionise the German prisoners. Although professedly exhausted and tired of fighting, the Russians were very soon revived and sufficiently energised by their Bolshevist leaders to fight among themselves and to turn Petrograd into something like a madhouse.

The force and vigour which they developed in plundering, shooting and reducing the bourgeoisie to starvation would have been better employed in helping to finish the campaign against the Huns. But they were out for bigger game than that. The People's Commissaries set to work to light the flame of civil war at home and foment disorder abroad by every means in their power. They sent propagandists and conspirators into other States, east and west, under all kinds of disguise, and hired the services of others already on the spot. They claimed to have 15,000 agitators in America alone, and this large number probably accounted a good deal for the endeavour of the Americans from the very beginning to propitiate the Bolshevist gang and bring them into negotiation with the Paris Peace Conference. Their principal representative in the United States was arrested in a police raid on the offices of the Russian Socialist Federal Republic in New York. This man, Ludwig Martens, was for years the business agent of the great Demidov Works and Factories, one of the largest capitalistic enterprises in Russia. He was described as being very rich and, personally, an avowed monarchist, so that he belonged to the very class which the Bolshevists set out to destroy. Nobody knew how he got his credentials from Lenin; but, of course, they were not accepted when he presented them to the Department of State. Nevertheless, Martens continued to act in his own way for the Russian Republic of Soviets, and as a security for

Bolshevist "legations" trading on the Republic's account he offered to deposit two hundred million dollars in a neutral bank. A similar incident occurred at Teheran in 1918. A legation of Soviet Russia, unrecognised by the Persian Government, was maintained there until October, when it was suddenly entered by a former Russian Consul with thirty Persian Cossacks. The legation staff was arrested, but the Bolshevist Minister escaped through one of the windows.

The British in Persia were declared responsible for that assault on the sacred premises of an unlawful Bolshevist headquarters, and were the object of a great deal of invective in the Bolshevist Press. It behoved that Press, however, to remember that only a month earlier a murderous raid was made by Bolshevist officials and Red Guards on the British Embassy in Petrograd, in which aggressive act Captain Cromie, the British naval representative, was shot dead, and all the members of the British Consulate were robbed and imprisoned.

CAPTURED BOLSHEVIST DESTROYER.
The Russian destroyer, Afritoil, manned by Bolshevists, which, after being fired at for a few minutes, surrendered to H.M.S. Caradoc in the Gulf of Finland. To the right of the Afritoil is H.M.S. Vortigern.

This is how the Bolshevists played the game. No fastidiousness worried them with regard to ways and means, and they openly proclaimed themselves the pioneers of a far greater struggle than the one with Germany. Their *ultima ratio* was a world struggle, in which the proletarians of every country were to overturn their respective Governments and destroy all other classes of society. This was the height of their egregious ambition, and the world was naïvely assured that it was absolutely altruistic, without the least suspicion of personal or party interest.

Inebriated with the immensity of their self-arrogated mission, which was not merely " the attainment of immediate

BRITISH WARSHIPS AT A FINNISH PORT.
On the quayside at Helsingfors during the stay there in the winter of 1918-19 of British war vessels. The two ships shown and partly shown in the photograph are H.M.S. Calypso and Caradoc.

aims and the enforcement of the momentary interests of the world's workers," but " the forcible overthrow of all existing social conditions," they remained blind to the abyss into which they were leading the Russian people. Had they kept to their own country—if, as Internationalists, they had one—and had they initiated sensible measures of evolutionary Socialism—beginning, for instance, by limiting the acquisition of vast property in land or capital by individuals, companies, and trusts, as recommended by President Roosevelt —they would have deserved well of the world's proletarians. But these frenzied fanatics of proletarian dictatorship—by which phrase they only disguised their **Frenzied fanatics and their aim** own despotism—professed that they would be satisfied with nothing less than the immediate and complete fulfilment, at all costs, of the gospel of Karl Marx.

Peter the Great, as Leroy-Beaulieu has said, was a great revolutionary; but he kept within decent bounds in comparison with the Bolshevists, who made a Bedlam of his " paradise " on the Neva, as he called his Petersburg, and proceeded to turn it into a city of the dead. Peter confined himself to the herculean task of trying to Europeanise Russia in the short span of a lifetime. Lenin's aim was to go one better. He wanted to revolutionise and remodel the whole world at once, and to accomplish it by a system of violence and cruelty much more frightful than Peter's practice in

HARBOUR OF FINLAND'S SEAPORT CAPITAL.
Helsingfors, the capital of Finland, where British warships were sent during the reign of Bolshevist terrorism in Russia, is a town which in a hundred years grew from being a place with 4,000 inhabitants to one with a population not far short of 200,000.

converting his semi-Asiatic subjects into full-fledged Europeans.

Neither the astonishing audacity of the Bolshevists' plan of universal upheaval—more pretentious than the world-conquering designs of the German militarists—nor the sophistical rhetoric of the People's Commissaries could hide the real facts of Russia's sorry plight from the outside world. The Paris journal "Le Temps" declared that Russia had to be counted among the vanquished. This could only mean that Russia had been vanquished by Marxism and Bolshevism imported from Germany. For, as far as an international Jew can have any nationality, the Hebrew author of "Das Kapital," the Bible of the German Socialists, was a German by birth and education, and Germany gave Bolshevism its introductory support in Russia. That placed Russia completely at the mercy of Germany until the Entente finally crushed the military supremacy of the Kaiser. When that was done, and Germany had to sue for terms, instead of dictating them, as at Brest Litovsk, the Bolshevists seized the opportunity to turn the tables on the discomfited neighbours who had helped them to gain a footing in Russia. Lenin said that he had taken German money to promote revolution in Russia, and would use Russian money to excite revolution in Germany. Accordingly, there was very soon an outbreak of Bolshevism in Berlin under the name of Spartacism, while a Soviet Government was established in Hungary. In its earlier stages, at least, the Bolshevist rule at Budapest seems to have been somewhat milder with regard to outrages and excesses than the Bolshevist tyranny in Russia, and therefore it did not excite so much execration in the world. The connection between the two, however, is only too evident. The international troops of Trotsky's Red Army —Letts, Finns, Chinese, and Germans,

the latter chiefly acting as officers—were supplemented by Hungarian mercenaries, some of whom helped to check Admiral Koltchak's advance towards Moscow. Admiral Koltchak, who had at one time commanded the Russian naval forces in the Baltic, in November, 1918, set up a provisional anti-Bolshevist Government in Siberia.

These foreign elements, especially the Letts and the Chinese, were the Prætorians of the Bolshevists, and they ruled Russia as a conquered land. They were more trusted by Lenin and Trotsky than the native Russians of the Red Guards, who originated in the dregs left by the collapse of the old Army.

Recruiting for a special international battalion, calculated to attract the world's malcontents and riffraff, was started in Petrograd in the early part of 1918. The first time I visited Trotsky in his lair at the Smolny Institute, which was bristling with machine-guns, I was surprised to be accosted in very good English by one of a knot of rough-looking men clad in civil dress and carrying rifles with fixed bayonets, who were lolling about in front of the celebrated Commissary's room door. They were guarding Trotsky in his room at one end of a long corridor, while a similar group of their comrades barred the entry to Lenin's chamber at the other end. Most of them, if not all, were Letts, including the one who spoke English. This man informed me that he had been a cabinet-maker in England for eighteen years, and that he had a British-born son serving in the British Army at the French front. He was receiving splendid pay (thirty shillings a day at pre-war rate of exchange), with full keep and opportunities of acquiring more.

In view of these facts, it cannot be too much emphasised that the Bolshevist movement was not essentially Russian, that it was not necessarily a part of the Russian Revolution, but was grafted on to

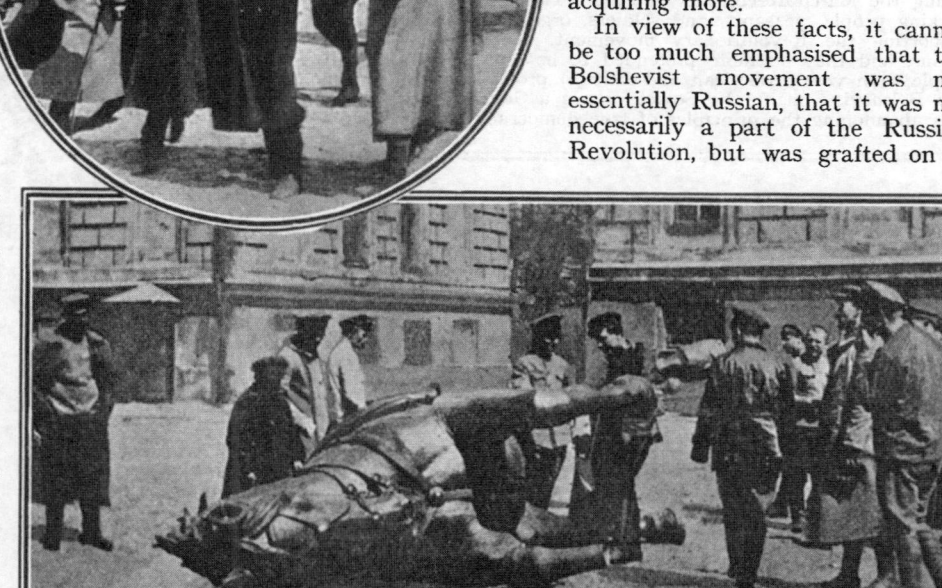

BOLSHEVIST DESTRUCTION OF NATIONAL MONUMENTS.
Statue of General Skobeleff thrown from its pedestal by the Red Revolutionaries, who destroyed large numbers of monuments and statues raised during the rule of the Tsars. In circle : Russian Red Guards in Moscow arresting a man suspected of counter-revolutionary plotting.

GUARDING RAILWAY WRECKAGE IN NORTH RUSSIA.
British bluejackets on duty at Soroka, on the Murmansk-Archangel Railway. They were guarding locomotives which had been damaged by Bolshevists before they retired from the place.

government. For the Bolshevist Soviets do not reflect the will of the people. Only the working class, the poorest peasants, and the Red Guards have the right to vote for the Soviet ; all other elements are excluded.

Other Russian Socialist writers went further than Avksyentiev in pointing out that the Soviets were completely over-ridden by the dictatorship of Lenin, Trotsky, Zinoviev, and others, and although Avksyentiev showed how the Bolshevists were damaging the prospects of the real Revolution in Russia, he did not refer to their pernicious and dangerous activities in other countries. These activities are indicated in one of their catch-phrases, " The international militant alliance of proletarians." Their Revolutionary ideas and aims were not Russian but international, and they used the Russian people, the most malleable and adaptable material in the world, for the execution of their far-reaching designs.

The educated and cultured classes, being a mere drop in the great ocean of the vast population, were frightened into exile, ruthlessly slaughtered, or starved and forced into unwilling submission. The rest were as clay in the hands of the potter. Russia was made the breeding-place of Bolshevist fermentation for inoculating other countries in Europe and Asia. Emissaries for the East were instructed in Eastern languages, and some of their work was seen in Afghanistan, Persia, and India.

To revolutionise the masses in all Imperialistic and bourgeois

it from without by a few extremists and Internationalist exiles, who were enemies of all existing social order, and hostile to all sensible democratic and even Socialist reform. For years previously they had nursed revenge for sufferings endured under the old Russian regime, and had carried on seditious propaganda everywhere.

An opinion expressed by Avksyentiev is worth quoting with regard to the kind of government set up and so much vaunted by these men. It appeared in an American periodical, and was reproduced in the " Russian Commonwealth." Avksyentiev was the ex-President of the All - Russian Directorate of Ufa, which was superseded by Admiral Koltchak's temporary dictatorship, and he was furthermore an old Socialist and Russian Revolutionary. He said :

Anti-Democratic Soviets

> The Soviet Republic is the direct opposite of Democracy, even as Bolshevism is the direct opposite of Socialism. The Soviets originated in Russia on the initiative of the Social Democrats, the Menshiviki and the Social Revolutionaries, during the first Revolution in 1905, and during the March Revolution of 1917. They constituted a union of working people, peasants, and soldiers, organised for the purpose of supporting the Revolutionary movement. They were not national organs, and they no more pretended to be representative of all the people than your (American and British) professional labour unions. The Bolshevists made the Soviet organs a Governmental authority, thus abandoning the principles of true democracy and representative

States was the chief end in view from the very beginning. As early as December, 1917, German prisoners in Petrograd were induced to take part in Bolshevist street processions, and publicly exhorted in their own language to march hand in hand with the Russian Revolutionary proletariat. After that it was not surprising that the German authorities detained their repatriated war prisoners from Russia in a sort of de-bolshevising quarantine. Lenin repeatedly announced in public that the success of Bolshevism in Russia depended upon a world revolution. The more the latter was delayed, the longer would he and his myrmidons have to keep going their horrible experiment at the cost of Russia's ruin.

They destroyed Russian patriotism within the sphere of their demoralising

ON LAND UNDER THE WHITE ENSIGN OF THE SEA.
British naval officers at the railway-station at Soroka, which became one of the British bases on the Murmansk-Archangel Railway. Above : British naval officers and bluejackets at Soroka, with the White Ensign flying above their railway train.

activity, or as much of it as existed; for the fatherland of the great bulk of the peasantry was bounded by their village districts; their love of country was very local. The cosmopolitan Bolshevist had no patriotism; the welfare of Russia was a secondary consideration for him.

One of Lenin's statements, reported in the "Freie Arbeiter," of Vienna, and reproduced in the Swiss "Volksrecht" of May 13th, 1919, ran: "The trivialities of Government and reconstruction interfere with the work of world revolution, which is the principal matter in hand."

The "Russkaya Jizn," a Russian journal published at Helsingfors, repeated another of Lenin's remarks to the effect that the only hope for Bolshevism was the spread of it throughout America, India, and Egypt, otherwise it would be conquered in Russia. Without the help of the world's proletarians Bolshevism would eke out a precarious existence, and after destroying everything within its grasp would probably end by destroying itself.

According to the Russian paper just mentioned, Bolshevism was already in a state of decomposition, and ought to be speedily liquidated by foreign intervention of some kind in order to save the world from the infection of its slow decay. Lenin, Trotsky, and their fellows ranted about saving the Revolution, but they did their utmost to nullify it by a system

READY FOR ALL EMERGENCIES.
British bluejackets, in land-fighting order, immediately after their arrival at one of the bases of the allied forces that were established along the Murmansk-Archangel Railway.

For a long time the Bolshevist chiefs attributed the evil consequences of their own misdeeds to the aftermath of the war, the horrible effects of which they were all the while intensifying and extending. Instead of more bread and peace, as promised in October, 1917—which promise helped the Bolshevists into power—there was a lessening of both from the moment that promise was first made.

There is another aspect of the international character of the Bolshevist Revolution in so far as the Jewish element in it is concerned, and the rôle played by that element is too important to be ignored. The **Prominence of** disguised names of the principal ringleaders **International Jews** are Jewish with the exception of Lenin's, which is Ulianov. This remarkable factor in the movement may unfortunately lead to more anti-Jewish pogroms in the event of its becoming thoroughly understood by the Russian masses in the course of the final suppression or downfall of the Bolshevist dictatorship. The British Embassy in Petrograd was raided and ransacked under the direction of a Jew commissary and his Jewish assistants.

It is no reflection whatever on the Jews as a race to call attention to this prominence of the International Jews, or Jewish Internationalists, in the tragedy of Russia. They are repudiated by the great Hebrew majority in all countries. They are also opposed by the Russian Zionists, or National

of tyranny, murder, and robbery such as Russia never knew before, not even in the worst days of her most autocratic Tsars. Russians of the olden time under the Tartars, the Muscovites at the mercy of the Oprichniki, or bodyguard of Ivan the Terrible, and the Armenians persecuted by the Turks, were not more terrorised and oppressed than the Russians in the power of the Bolshevists. The mad rule and exploits of these self-constituted champions of the world's workers turned the Russian Revolution into a "tempest of massacre and blood," and it was no argument or justification for them to retort, as they did, that millions of lives were sacrificed in repelling German aggression, which, it should be added, would have overcome Russia in six months if Britain had not taken the field.

IN ONE OF RUSSIA'S FORTIFIED SEAPORTS.
General view of Reval, on the south coast of the Gulf of Finland, in Russia's Baltic provinces. The building in the foreground, which had been used as a prison, was burnt by the Bolshevists. Above: Loyal Russian officers on a British cruiser; they were going to join General Denikin's army.

BRITISH SHIPS THAT WATCHED OVER BRITISH INTERESTS IN THE BALTIC.
H.M.S. Calypso passing through the ice. The photograph was taken from the deck of one of her sister ships as they left Helsingfors. A British cruiser force, sent to the Baltic during the Bolshevist Red Terror in 1918, was later relieved by the First British Light Cruiser Squadron under Rear-Admiral Cowan.

Jews, some of whom fired upon Bolshevist demonstrators in one of the South Russian towns. A similar Jewish element was conspicuous in the German and Hungarian Revolutions, but the results were somewhat different, owing to the character of the peoples of those countries.

Making due allowance for individual exceptions, the Russian Slavs, on the whole, are generally considered to lack the grit and perseverance necessary to carry through " enterprises of great pith and moment " to their legitimate conclusions. Their softness of nature and innate goodness of heart are sure to prevail sooner or later in the mass, unless they are egged on to desperation by individuals of strong and resolute will. Then they can be very fierce and cruel as long as the fit lasts.

Arnold White, in his book " The Modern Jew," refers to the Jewish race as one " that baffled the Pharaohs, foiled Nebuchadnezzar, thwarted Rome, defeated feudalism, circumvented the Romans, balked the Kaiser, and undermined the third French Republic." To this may now be added that the Jews very considerably helped to deform and disfigure the Russian Revolution.

Russian Jews were often heard to say after the October days of 1917, " *Rossia nasha* "—" Russia is ours." The tenacity of purpose and resourcefulness of the race were well displayed by the international Jews of the Bolshevist Government like Trotsky, Zinoviev, and a host of other Jewish commissaries and subordinates. It is very doubtful whether Lenin could have held sway so long without his Jewish colleagues, especially Trotsky. This is probably why the frequently reported differences of opinion between Lenin and Trotsky never led to any real separation.

Lenin and Trotsky

The Norwegian Consul Harnmer, who in 1919 returned from Petrograd and Moscow, was reported to have told an interviewer that there was no good feeling between Trotsky and Lenin, and that the former once interned the latter in the Kremlin for two days in order to force him to yield. Another statement attributed to the same informant was to the effect that Trotsky might be seen occasionally driving about, like the Tsar in former days, surrounded by hussars in gold-braided uniforms.

If Trotsky really had this kind of escort it only shows the importance to which he aspired and the danger which threatened him. He was pre-eminently a man of action and determination. Lenin often spoke in despondent tones and foresaw failure, but Trotsky never. He was also a good talker, but never wasted words like Kerensky. In two long interviews which I had with him in the Smolny Institute I was able to judge of his ready powers of speech in Russian and French, the French language being used for the benefit of a friend who was with me. Trotsky was a short, thick-set, big-headed, dark-complexioned man, and I should say that " the native hue of resolution " showing itself in the strong lines of his face was never " sicklied over with the pale cast of thought," which denotes hesitation or wavering. He suited the action to the word, and was not to be turned aside from his purpose. He gave us to understand, in the most peremptory manner, that he would not permit a single British subject to leave Russia unless his friends Chicherin and Petrov, detained in England by the British authorities, were allowed to leave England and return to Petrograd.

Everything or nothing

Thanks to the intervention of Mr. Bourchier, the well-known Balkan correspondent of the " Times," who was the friend above referred to, this demand was soon complied with, and Chicherin—who, Trotsky informed us, was a remarkable linguist and had spent a fortune in furthering Socialism—was at once appointed Chief Commissary for Bolshevist Foreign Affairs.

Although the Jews were so strong in the councils of the Bolshevists, they certainly did not spare their own race when they saw, or fancied they saw, any sign of opposition or even mere difference of opinion. They showed no favour or mercy to friend or foe. These Bolshevist tyrants were absolutely determined to have everything or nothing.

Not long ago the Russian Socialist Revolutionary Party took a Bolshevist orientation in so far as to give their support against Admiral Koltchak. This did not in the least mollify the Bolshevists towards them, and the Social Revolutionaries were imprisoned and persecuted more than before. In March, 1919, at a congress in Minsk, the Jewish Workers' Bund, which had previously held aloof, also decided to adopt a friendly attitude towards the Soviet Government without, however, approving of Bolshevist dictatorship over the Soviets and Bolshevist suppression of public opinion.

The Russian Jews of the Bund were not likely after this

to be treated any better than the Socialist Revolutionaries. The probability was that they would fare worse for attempting to split differences with such intransigent opponents. They had a warning in the fate of the Socialist Revolutionaries, who ventured to take advantage of their new leaning towards Bolshevism as against Koltchak to return to Moscow and reissue " Dyelo Naroda," the journal of their party. In a very short time they were all arrested, the editorial office of the paper was raided, and publication had to be discontinued.

A Jewess named Frumkin, who belonged to this Jewish Socialist organisation called the " Bund," and whose husband was an active member of it after 1896, gave an interesting account of Bolshevist terrorism and anarchy in a Russian province remote from Petrograd and Moscow. It is typical of what went on in most parts of the Russian interior. Mrs. Frumkin related her experiences and personal observations of the local Soviet and its agents in Krasnoufimsk (province of Perm) in the form of a signed declaration attested by witnesses.

One of the Krasnoufimsk Soviet, named Perevotchikov, had a false mandate as deputy, and tried to have the whole of the Executive Committee shot for their " flabbiness." A member of this same committee, named Scherbakov, made out lists of persons to be arrested when he was drunk, and sent for Red Guards to protect him in his orgies. A man named Pankevich, of the Military Revo-

The " terror " in the provinces lutionary Committee, who had been an ordinary workman, fraudently secured large quantities of sugar in the names of military prisoners already dead. In the summer of 1918 the peasants revolted against these men of the Soviets and threatened to burn down the town. No newspapers and no telegrams could be received, and even elementary education was stopped. An Extraordinary Commission was then formed with a preponderance of votes belonging to Yakovlev, who formerly kept a house of ill-fame, and Goldin, from the Supreme Extraordinary Examining Commission at Moscow. A whole series of arrests and shootings followed the establishment of this commission.

Citizen Goldin declared in front of the soldiers and hostages : " We don't require any proofs or examinations in order to shoot people ; we shoot when it suits us." There was no tribunal or consultation to decide about executions. Soldiers fetched prisoners from the gaol in the dead of night, ostensibly to take them to Perm. " Half an hour afterwards," says Mrs. Frumkin, who was in the prison at the time, "the sound of firing was heard, and the next morning the bodies were collected for burial."

This reminds me of my own experience in the prison of the fortress at Petrograd in September, 1918. The unbolting and clanging of the massive iron-bound doors of the cells along our corridor in the night often told of prisoners being taken out without knowing what fate awaited them, as the soldiers seldom imparted any information even if they knew anything. **" We shoot when it suits us "**

I heard of only one case in which prisoners were removed by Red Guards, who simply told them not to trouble to put on all their clothes, as they would not require them any more. When shooting was heard within the enceinte of the fortress, we concluded that somebody from amongst our fellow-prisoners had been shot.

Mrs. Frumkin had personal knowledge of the following executions : Vershinin, an old Revolutionary, Maximalist, and Social Democrat, who had worked in village Soviets and struggled against usurers and monopolists. A month before his execution he was obliged to leave the village of Sagin and join the Poverty Committees, or Committees of Poor People, in order to escape from the scamps and blackguards who tried to avenge themselves. Seiderikin, a peaceful employee, who had never taken any active part in politics. No accusation was made against him. It was enough that he was a personal enemy of Pankevich, of the Revolutionary Committee.

Klechelski, a dentist, was dragged out of his house and killed. The Notary Public Meder and his wife were shot because they refused to disclose the whereabouts of their son-in-law, who had been employed on the staff of the Red Guards. He ran away when they threatened to arrest him

BRITISH BASE DURING THE OPERATIONS IN NORTHERN RUSSIA.
Soroka, by the south-western shore of the White Sea. This town, on the railway to Murmansk, was made one of the bases for the allied forces in Northern Russia when Bolshevist excesses rendered intervention necessary, and allied troops were despatched to Murmansk and Archangel.

Meder and his wife were taken into a shed. The husband was forced on to his knees against a wall, and shots were fired right and left of him in order to frighten him into giving the required information. The next morning they were both shot. These facts were told to Mrs. Frumkin by Mrs. Meder while they were in one cell together the night before Mrs. Meder was taken out to execution. Several other victims were mentioned.

Mrs. Frumkin then recounted her own sufferings. She and her husband were arrested in September, released the next

ON DUTY IN THE FROZEN NORTH.
British soldier setting out on skis from one of the camps established in northernmost Russia during the winter of 1918-19.

day, and rearrested a week later without any charge or examination. When the town had to be evacuated, ten prisoners were chosen to be sent to Perm as hostages, including the Frumkins. Their children pleaded with a commissary on their behalf, and were told that one of their parents might be let off. This led to a hot dispute between Frumkin and his wife as to which of the two should die, for the hostages were informed that their lives would be safe only if their friends did no harm to the families of Red Guardsmen.

Mendelevitch, the commissary, would not wait for the question to be settled, but caught hold of Frumkin, the husband, and took him by force out of the prison, saying it did not matter which of them went away, and that he had better go.

Mrs. Frumkin was therefore one of the party of hostages, who now numbered nine. At the first stage of their march to Perm three of them, Loukanin, Povarov, and Seiderikin, were shot down. When the survivors reached Perm, Mrs. Frumkin was compelled to tramp two kilometres farther to the prison though suffering from excessive hæmorrhage. Her request to be allowed to ride in a cart was refused by the girl who conducted the convoy.

Shooting of hostages

Two weeks afterwards the Extraordinary Commission of Perm visited the prison. The secretary was asked to find the accusation against Mrs. Frumkin, and on consulting the papers he replied that there was nothing in the dossier. The next day the lady was liberated. Four days later three of her companions were also set free, one of them, a Mrs. Tsarensky, having lost her reason.

The aims of the Russian Revolutionary parties of the nineteenth century were moderate in contrast with the

outrageously destructive policy of the Bolshevists. These violent extremists spoiled the first Revolution of March, 1917, as well as the plans of the Allies. When the first Revolution overthrew the Imperial Autocracy, it consummated the efforts and sacrifices of several generations of Russian Revolutionists, and that might well have sufficed for the nonce, while Russia was still in the throes of the life-and-death struggle with Germany and Austria, without seeking to upset the very foundations of all civilised society into the bargain. But the Russians were always given to extremes, and they never had a finer opportunity of displaying their love of extravagance—their *shirokaya natura*, or expansiveness—than under the lawless regime of the Bolshevist party. The police force was destroyed, the old Army revolutionised and dissolved. All restraint was thus removed, and they were able to have their full fling.

The French Revolution was bad enough, and Trotsky at first thought of imitating its terror so far as openly to threaten to set up the guillotine, but that would have been a method of execution too open and above-board if practised as it was in Paris. The Bolshevist ruffians and dungeon villains preferred to shoot their victims in the back, or in the ear, without warning, wherever they found them, mostly at night, sometimes in the street, in houses, in prison yards and cells. It will be remembered how the Duma members Shingarov and Kokoshkin were foully done to death and mutilated while they were sleeping in their beds in the Mary Hospital at Petrograd.

Slaughter by caprice

In July, 1918, I witnessed an off-hand execution of the kind referred to in a yard next door to the Petrograd office of the "Times." The house sheltered the headquarters of the terrible Extraordinary Examining Commission under the fiendish Commissary Uritsky, who not long afterwards was killed there by a student. As I passed the open gateway several shots rang out, and looking into the yard I saw a man lying face downwards, and his executioners, half a dozen Red Guards, were standing a few paces off. The body was roughly dragged into the bottom of a droshky and driven away with two young soldiers sitting upon it, and smiling as if they were doing something amusing.

A few days later a newspaper mentioned it, and intimated that the soldiers had acted on their own initiative. In another case an old prisoner, in a batch of younger men who were being marched through the streets between the above-mentioned headquarters of the Extraordinary Commission and the fortress, was shot by one of the soldiers of the escort and thrown into the river simply because he was too feeble to keep pace with the rest. A particular friend of mine, an Englishman, living on the quay of one of the Petrograd canals, was one day looking out of his window, and he saw a Bolshevist soldier shoot a young cadet in the back and throw the body into the water. There was no provocation whatever; the young man did not even see his assassin. At that time the mere sight of a cadet was to a Bolshevist like a red rag in front of a mad bull.

About a month after the execution which I accidentally witnessed in the yard next door to the "Times" office, I was taken into that yard as a prisoner, in company with many more of my own countrymen. For three days before being sent to the fortress we were confined in a gloomy and filthy guard-room of the house entered from the yard, and when the chaplain of the English Church, who was with us, asked permission to read prayers in another chamber, where two or three of our number had been separated from the rest, the answer came back from the Commissaries of the Extraordinary Examining Commission: "This is the time for shooting, not for praying."

The individual who brought this answer to us, Professor Pissarev, was a rather remarkable man. He was also a prisoner, and had been there for a long time. He was chosen by his fellow-prisoners to act as intermediary between them and the Bolshevist Commissaries. When we asked him why he was in prison, he made the pithy reply: "When the wild beasts are let out of their cages, it is time for honest people to get behind the bars."

This reply had a special meaning for us, who had seen the worst criminals and human brutes placed in responsible positions by the Bolshevists. A young officer told me that one day in the street he met a soldier of his old regiment, who had been twice sentenced for murder and robbery. He was now an important Commissary of Soviet Russia, as he told the officer with an impudent sneer.

As to the comparative moderation of Russian Revolutionary parties of the last century, it is true that the Nihilists of Alexander the Second's time, although chiefly intent on destroying the autocracy and its bureaucratic Government, were also more or less engaged in Socialistic and agrarian propaganda, but they soon perceived the impossibility of any success on those lines as long as the autocratic power remained intact. The only Revolutionary attempt without any tendencies of a Socialistic or agrarian character was the one made under Nicholas the First by the Decembrists of 1825, who only demanded a constitution.

In 1905-6, before Bolshevism became known, but when its originators gave Russia a first taste of their quality, there were serious disorders among the peasantry, directed against the landlords, and among the working men in the towns. Mutiny also broke out in the Army and Navy, especially the latter. The war with Japan was the impelling cause on that occasion, and finally the Tsar was forced to concede an elected Duma.

But previous Revolutionary movements in Russia for more than two hundred years produced no leaders like Lenin and Trotsky and their coadjutors, and their **Hideous war of classes** immediate objective was of a different kind. If Lenin and Trotsky were engaged in the rising of 1905, they had no chance of becoming notorious before it was put down. The conspirators of the reign of Nicholas the First and the two Alexanders had as much as they could do in attacking the autocracy. When the Bolshevists fought themselves into power the autocracy had already gone, and they capped the war with Germany by creating another hideous war of classes while posing as the purveyors of peace and plenty.

Their murder of the dethroned Tsar, who was perfectly submissive and harmless, was an uncalled-for act of real savagery, whether ordered from the Bolshevist centre or decreed by a local Soviet.

We shall not find anything in former outbreaks of Russian revolution resembling the general plundering and class warfare of Lenin's work—without, of course, his mania for world revolution—unless we go back very far into Russian history—as far back, in fact, as the "Turbulent Period" (*Smootnae Vremya*) of the seventeenth century, and the reign of the second Tsar **Bolshevist of the 17th century** of the Romanoff dynasty. This is what the People's Commissioners themselves did at Moscow by reviving the memory of a former Cossack rebel and marauder, who was considered worthy of a monument in the centre of the ancient Russian capital.

In August, 1918, I saw a huge plaster-of-paris bust of Lassalle put on a very tall column in front of the Town Hall of Petrograd, and it was intended to erect a similar memorial to Karl Marx, the chief ideologist of the Bolshevist policy. Subsequently, the Bolshevist leaders appear to have bethought themselves that the Russian masses knew nothing of those two foreign philosophers. Their monuments in Petrograd may, in a sense, be appropriate, inasmuch as that city has always been the cradle of foreign ideas introduced into Russia, but in the Muscovite heart of the country it was advisable to monumentalise some native hero whose exploits thus brought to mind might appeal to the populace and encourage them in Bolshevism. They lighted upon such a hero and real practitioner of Bolshevist principles in the person of Stenka Razin, and on May 1st, 1919, as reported in "Folket's Dagblad Politiken," a monument was unveiled to him by Lenin and his colleagues on the Red Square in front of the Kremlin. The Russians had been taught to regard Stenka Razin as a celebrated Cossack adventurer and freebooter, but Lenin dubbed him the first champion of proletarian liberty—a seventeenth-century Bolshevist.

There ought no longer to be any necessity for asking the question, "What is Bolshevism?" It has been clearly answered by the great mass of data that has accumulated, and is perfectly damning in its indictment of the Russian

BRITISH SQUADRON IN ACTION AGAINST BOLSHEVIST SHIPS OFF PETROGRAD.

Naval action off Petrograd on May 18th, 1919, when, as Dr. Macnamara, Parliamentary Secretary to the Admiralty, announced in the House of Commons: "Bolshevist destroyers and four smaller craft, supported by a cruiser, came out to support their right flank and to attack Esthonian ships. An engagement ensued in which four of his Majesty's ships took part, and resulted in the Bolshevist vessels being driven back behind their mine-fields.

Bolshevists. Only one answer is possible in accordance with this wealth of evidence. The British White Book of a "Collection of Reports on Bolshevism in Russia" was alone enough to convince every impartial, unbiased reader. Yet there were still people who leaned towards this monstrous iniquity for various personal, political, or other reasons. They might be attracted by its ideals, which were dilated upon in Soviet wireless messages and in appeals to the world's proletariat, but its horrible methods were ignored,

WITH BRITISH TROOPS IN SIBERIA.
Colonel Franks, interpreter, translating a speech which Colonel John Ward (second from the right) had just addressed to Russian troops at Irkutsk, in Siberia. In circle : Colonel John Ward, C.B., C.M.G.

and these were just the very essence of Bolshevism as understood and felt in Russia. The pity is that people in Britain, as elsewhere, apparently became so callous after four years of killing that the Bolshevist atrocities did not seem to touch them. Bolshevist ideals and theories are marred by despotic cruelty, robbery, and murder ; Bolshevist decrees, which are mostly impossible of application without tyranny and injustice, are deeply stained with blood. Some persons found Bolshevism a useful weapon for agitation in Britain. One English friend I have was most shamefully ill-treated by the Bolshevists, and yet he favoured their ideas, and believed, not without good reason, that the British authorities were responsible for what he suffered before he was let out of Russia. Others there were who discovered two or three falsely reported items of news in the great batch of incriminating facts, and on that account they talked of the "campaign of lies" against Soviet Russia.

Then there was the attempt to explain the fact of the Bolshevists starving their enemies by blaming the Entente for the blockade. It was the latter, they said, that was starving the Russian people, and not the Bolshevists. As a matter of fact, however, the terrorism and chaos of Bolshevist rule prevented the Russian people from peacefully producing enough food for their own wants, to say nothing of the needs of others. Russia, besides being a self-supporting, self-sufficient (*samobuitnaya*) country, is likewise the "granary of Europe." This the Russians always maintained when there was no Bolshevism to interfere with the production of sufficient quantities of foodstuffs for both home consumption and export to foreign countries. And these countries suffered for the want of Russian produce through the nefarious doings of the Bolshevists.

Former famines, which affected only parts of the vast territories of Russia, were always aggravated, if not caused, by defects of transport, organisation, and distribution. The scarcity in 1919 was caused by something more than an increase of those defects in consequence of the war. The Bolshevists alone were responsible for complete disorganisation in all spheres of human activity. Production of everything was immensely reduced, and in many cases stopped altogether. What inducement was there to work in Bolshevist conditions ?

Shortage of food

When I was in Petrograd in the summer of 1918 there was a frightful scarcity of vegetables. On an average all round they cost, when obtainable, from twelve to sixteen shillings per pound, and yet there were hundreds of acres of more or less waste ground in all directions. A momentary fuss was made about allotments, but it came to nothing serious. Vegetables could not be cultivated with safety unless a man with a loaded rifle was stationed near to guard them while they grew. An English friend with a country house outside the city put his potatoes and other roots into an ensilage pit to be sure of something to eat in the winter. One night when he was absent in town they were all dug out and stolen by men from a neighbouring village.

The Petrograd Commune started a few garden plots, by which the Red Guards and workmen, the *nouveau riche* classes, principally benefited, but on the Yasili-Ostrov, the transpontine part of Petrograd, there were large waste gardens attached

PARADE OF MIDDLESEX MEN WHO FOUGHT AGAINST BOLSHEVISM IN SIBERIA.
Colonel John Ward inspecting the 25th Battalion of the Middlesex Regiment at Irkutsk, the capital town of the same province to the west of Lake Baikal, in Eastern Siberia. The Bolshevists tried to hold up the force of which Colonel Ward was in command, in the autumn of 1918, by engineering a strike on the Siberian Railway, but his decisive action put an end to an incident that might have left his battalion cut off both in rear and in front.

to hundreds of nationalised houses, in which not a vegetable was to be seen, except in one solitary instance, and in that garden a basement tenant had put up a high boarding round a tiny patch of soil in one corner, close to his door, so as to conceal it from the notice of thieves. Thieving of articles of food went on inside the houses as well as outside in the streets, particularly at railway-stations, when passengers brought provisions from the country. The Red Guards relieved travellers of what they considered any surplus of eatables under the pretext of confiscation or requisition.

When I reached the Russo-Finnish frontier, on leaving Russia, the "Reds" took away one of two loaves of bread which I had with me. Every small quantity of food had to be kept under lock and key when you left your house, otherwise it quickly disappeared. There was a plague of hungry rats and mice, which got on to the table as soon as you turned your back in the evening, and when they could get nothing better at night they gnawed your boots, which at that time cost about fifteen pounds a pair.

The famine in Petrograd was much intensified later, and

became gradually exhausted, and they finally died of malnutrition, or slow starvation.

On the other hand, many persons appeared to be well fed, and even stout, but on close examination they were seen to be simply bloated and swollen with a kind of dropsy from absorption of too much liquid food in default of anything more substantial.

BRITISH TROOPS ON THE MURMANSK COAST.
Carrying on in Arctic conditions. Soldiers belonging to the British force on the Murmansk Coast hauling a gun across snow-covered ground. The gun, mounted on sledge-runners, needed a goodly team to haul it along. Above : Train leaving the headquarters of the Finnish Legion in Northern Russia.

produced peculiar forms of psychical derangement and physical disease, in addition to the other concomitant evils of gradual starvation, such as hunger typhus and cholera.

According to the "Russkaya Jizn," a new kind of death from starvation revealed itself. In many cases of persons dying from hunger, hoards of food as well as money were found in their rooms. This was the result of the great fear and anxiety for the immediate future. As the quantity of food obtainable continued to dwindle and threaten to fail altogether, people stored up everything they could get and consumed too little each day, in order to make it last as long as possible. The consequence was that their systems

Besides the abundant literary evidence against Bolshevism there exists a great deal of personal testimony, which is still more important. There were many hundreds of British and Russian refugees in England in 1919 who bore witness to the facts. Most of them were members of the British Russian Club, which, under the presidency of Sir George Buchanan, and stimulated by its two secretaries, A. B. Stodart and A. Keay, did a great deal to sustain relations with Russia pending her return to more normal conditions. Another centre of living testimony to the effects of social destruction in Russia was at the Russian Embassy, where Lady Georgina Buchanan nobly devoted herself to the very difficult task of providing needlework for the relief of a constantly increasing number (by the summer of 1919 about one hundred and fifty) of women refugees of all grades in life, who had been rendered absolutely destitute through the devilries of Bolshevism.

British and Russian fugitives from the North and South of Russia continued to crowd into London and Paris. They escaped by hook or by crook through the Bolshevist lines and across the frontier, at the imminent risk of their lives, or else they were rescued from approaching hordes of Red Guards by British and French ships at Russian ports. A Russian arrived in London in 1919 with a bullet wound in

DOG-TEAMS EMPLOYED WITH THE ALLIED FORCES IN NORTH RUSSIA.
Sledge dogs tethered near an encampment on the shores of the White Sea. They were part of a Canadian dog detachment that was attached to the British North Russia Mobile Force. Right : Two officers setting out for a journey across the snow in a dog-drawn sledge.

one of his arms which he received on crossing into Finland. At that time no one was allowed to leave Soviet Russia. Those who managed to get away either ran the g a u n t l e t, used bribes, or had some Bolshevist acquaintance to befriend them. One Russian related how he started to escape over the boundary with five other men. The party was pursued through the woods b y R e d Guards, who kept up a running fire at them. My informant became faint, and fell down in some thickly-growing brushwood. Either his fall was not noticed by the soldiers in pursuit, or they thought they had shot him down, so that they passed by him and continued to chase the others. He was able, after recovering himself, to get away unseen and cross the frontier safely.

CHIEF LEADERS OF THE BOLSHEVISTS: LENIN AND TROTSKY.
Lenin (on the left), who was described as the life and soul of the whole Bolshevist movement, was an "hereditary noble" whose real name was Vladimir Ilytch Uliano. Lev Davidovitch Trotsky was a Jew of versatile talents whose real name was Leiba Bronstein.

shop and large store-rooms, with stocks of valuable goods, were nationalised—in plain E n g l i s h, they were stolen, as no compensation of any kind was given in such cases. Bolshevist employees were put into possession, he was relegated during business hours to the door-porter's lobby, and had to give the official robbers all the information they required. Thus plundered, humiliated, and not allowed to draw enough of h i s o w n m o n e y wherewith to buy sufficient food at t h e unconscionable prices then obtaining, Mr. B—— decided to abandon the little left to him in his living apartments, which had not yet been seized, and get clear of Soviet Russia, but the Bolshevists refused to let him go. He tried many devices without success,

In the early part of 1919 a British fellow-sufferer, and only succeeded at last after terrible experiences. long resident beyond Moscow, had very uncomfortable No baggage of any kind could be carried on these hazardous, experiences in making his escape. Although too old for military service, and not having committed any crime or misdemeanour, he was threatened with arrest by the local Commissaries. Presumably he was not to their liking as a British bourgeois, who had succeeded in saving up a little money by hard work all his life. They were not satisfied by confiscating his money in the bank, and seizing his house with a little land, but they wanted also his person. When he finally did get away his nerves were shattered, and he was obliged to break the homeward journey by resting for several weeks in a Finnish sanatorium. Had he been unable to smuggle a little of his money out of Russia this rest cure would have been impossible. His escape cost him 7,500 roubles (£750).

Another British resident in Russia, Mr. B——, who was at the head of a large business concern in Petrograd, had a still more perilous and nerve-racking experience in getting away from the tyrants. His

OVSEY HERSHON ZINOVIEV.
Zinoviev, whose real name was Apfelbaum, was a Jew who became virtual Dictator of Petrograd under the Bolshevist regime.

expeditions. The runaways were lucky if they escaped in dry clothes. Many swam across the stream which formed the boundary-line, while the rifle-shots of the Red Guards echoed through the birch trees along the Finnish bank. Woe to the unlucky wight unable to swim when no boat was at hand. Later the Finnish bank of the river was more strongly guarded, and yet, according to a Danish correspondent who came from the spot in 1919, fugitives managed to get across, somehow, nearly every night.

Many more would have risked the attempt if they had not been afraid of the vengeance that would have been wreaked upon their families and relatives left behind. Besides the Russian Red Guards, there was later a body of Bolshevist renegades from Finland on the Russian side of the frontier waiting for an opportunity to revive red terror and anarchy in their own country. On the Finnish side at Terioki was a motley crowd from all countries of the Entente—military,

SECRET POLICE PORTRAITS OF MEN WHO BECAME LEADERS AMONG THE BOLSHEVISTS.
These portraits are reproduced from the photographic records of the "Ochrana," or secret police system which was maintained under the rule of the Tsars. Each person on the record was photographed full face and in profile. On the left are those of Jacob Movshev Sverdlov, President of the Soviet Republic. Centre: Trotsky as a young man, and (right) Lev Borisovitch Kamenev, whose real name was Rosenfeldt, President of the Moscow Soviet.

civil, and Red Cross officials, marking time in expectation of the capitulation of Petrograd.

The state of lawlessness from which all these people ran away in thousands, or died in the attempt, is not easy to describe in such a way as to bring it home to the minds of law-protected Britons. There was never such a complete reversal of all the ordinary conditions of life, and new developments and complications set in every few days. An effort to represent Russian urban conditions for a cinema film was rejected on account of the scenes being too realistic and disgusting to suit the taste of the British public.

A poor girl arrived in London in 1919 who had one eye shot through in a Petrograd street, the bullet coming out near one of her ears. Russian Bolshevism means all this and much more. Schoolboys held soviets and dictated to old teachers and professors. Door porters and messengers in nationalised banks became Bolshevist bank commissaries in order to lord it over the former directors. Domestic servants slept in their employers' beds, and claimed to have as much right to all the rooms as anybody else, all property being in common; the people's authorities could compel anyone to keep servants in his employ if the reason for their discharge did not please them. A man, who was not allowed to dismiss his cook, got over the difficulty by marrying her and then getting a divorce, which became the easiest thing in the world amongst the Bolshevists. In short, all persons working with their brains had to become the hewers of wood and drawers of water for those who used to work with their hands and for the dregs of the population in general.

Something else was meant by Russian Bolshevism, and something which was too much left out of sight. Nationalisation, sequestration, requisition, socialisation, confiscation of property, and so forth, all these terms were mere euphemisms for robbery. This plundering of the rich for the so-called poor affected precisely the worthiest and most respectable of the poorer classes, whose savings in the different banks were invested to an enormous extent in Government stock and loans, which were annulled.

Assertions have been made in the Bolshevist foreign Press to the effect that Petrograd in 1919 was quiet and that order and tranquillity reigned there as it never did before. It was the kind of tranquillity which Verestchagin depicted in his famous ironical picture of a Russian sentinel on the heights of the Shipka Pass in the Balkans in the Russo-Turkish War of 1878. An isolated and cold-benumbed soldier on guard is seen at the top of the pass in a terrific snowstorm and gradually disappearing in the drift. That melancholy canvas was called "All Quiet at Shipka." When everybody with any spirit of resentment against injustice and tyranny was imprisoned, shot, or driven to take to flight, and those that remained—700,000 only out of 2,000,000—were so starved and poisoned that they could hardly crawl about, it was not surprising that Petrograd was quiet at last. As for public order, it was also quite easy of attainment by means of eighteen months of terrorism and wholesale executions. If tranquillity and order reigned on the Neva they were the signs of an expiring population.

But at the time of writing—July, 1919—the latest news from Russia did not confirm the idea of any repose in the sanguinary campaign against suspected counter-revolutionists. It was said that Zinoviev, the bloodthirsty President of the Petrograd Commune, who boasted of one thousand four

"All quiet at Petrograd"

hundred persons having been put to death in revenge for the murder of Commissary Uritsky, was giving orders to shoot all workmen who showed anti-Bolshevist tendencies. It appeared that many of them were agitating in favour of the White Army under General Yudenitch, which was expected to take Petrograd. From Moscow came news of serious labour disturbances in April, when the workmen started the cry: "Give us bread and work." The Red Guards were sent to quell the disturbances, and according to report several

AT A REVIEW OF BOLSHEVISM'S RED ARMY.
Karl Radek, in cloth cap and smoking, the Austrian Jew whose real name was Sobelsohn, at a review of the Red Army. He was Assistant Commissary for Foreign Affairs in the Bolshevist Administration.

thousands of the men (probably a mistake for hundreds) were shot. The "Warsaw Courier," which gave this news added the detail that the bodies were taken to the cemetery in carts, each cart being drawn by four bourgeois in the place of horses, as these animals had become scarce. Russian newspapers reported a Petrograd order to return to horse transport in default of any more petrol for motor-cars; but as horses had been dying of starvation in the streets for twelve months and the only meat for the inhabitants was horse-flesh, it seems that such an order was more than difficult to carry out.

Two kinds of terror existed in Russia, one Red and the other White. The White Terror was simply the consequence of the Red Terror, which was incomparably the worst of the two, because it formed part and parcel of the very principles of Bolshevist action. The White Terror was spasmodic, resulting from natural and inevitable fits of rage against the Bolshevists on the part of their adversaries. For instance, if any man was respected amongst the anti-Bolshevists it was the late General Korniloff, the first open and straightforward enemy of the Soviet Government. When the Red troops were in the district of Southern Russia where Korniloff was buried, they disinterred and decapitated the body and "played football with the head."

White Terror and Red Terror

On the other hand, when the Don Cossacks regained possession of the Donetz mining region at the end of 1918 they gave the population a spell of White Terror at Hughesovka, in the Batchmut district of the province of Ekaterinoslav. Hughesovka was named after John Hughes, a remarkable Welshman, who in the course of some forty years, with the aid of British capital and many skilled hands from Wales, created a great metallurgical works and a flourishing town of 50,000 inhabitants on a spot that was barren, uninhabited steppeland before he started the enterprise. I have lived there and in the surrounding country, and have a pretty good idea of the character of the population. Many of the criminal class and runaways from Siberia found a refuge there as coal-miners. It used to be said that the police in pursuit of some particular offender often had to chase him down one mine shaft and up another. They could be very wild and savage on occasion. I once saw several of them, for some reason or other, flog one of their fellows with a thin iron rod within an ace of his life. He was

stark naked, with the exception of the dirt and coal-dust that coated his body, and when they had done with him they pitched him into a cart and drove away.

Such a population would be sure to contain just the kind of elements to sympathise with Bolshevism, and the Cossacks seem to have put them down with the utmost severity.

In Hughesovka proper only five hundred of the ten thousand workmen voted for the Soviet when the Bolshevists were there. Besides workmen, the peasants in some of the neighbouring villages appear to have been hostile to the Cossacks. The way in which the latter terrorised the district may be seen from the following documents.

At Hughesovka, in December, 1918, Essaul (Cossack captain) Girov proclaimed the following order (No. 2,431), received from his superiors:

In the present telegram I communicate the despatches received by me: (1) I forbid the imprisonment of workmen, for I order them to be shot or hanged; (2) I order that all the workmen now in prison be taken out and hanged in the principal street, where they are to be left for three days. For every Cossack killed I order that ten inhabitants of the village of Stepanovka be hanged and a contribution levied of 200,000 roubles. For the imprisonment of an officer I order the most rigorous repression against the workmen; one in ten of those arrested must be hanged and left exposed for three days.

A further order (No. 3,151) from General Denisov, Commander of the Army of the Don, sent through the same Captain Girov to the mining region of Makeyevka, reads as follows:

I order pacification of the workmen to be carried out in the most implacable manner by shooting, or rather by hanging every tenth man of all those captured, and leaving them suspended during three days. Make it known at all the Works that the Cossacks will stand no more nonsense, and will show no mercy. Neither tears nor groans will save them from legally imposed punishment.

Besides these two kinds of terror, Russia was concerned with four armies of different imaginary colours—namely, a Red Army, a White Army, a Green Army, and a Black Army. The

Red and White Armies corresponded, of course, with the two terrors of those colours; the name of Green Army was given to bands of armed peasants who appeared to be opposing Bolshevist tyranny in the rural districts. A commissary was killed by some of these peasants while explaining to them that no right of inheritance in land existed under the Communist system. The Black Army consisted of a large number of civil officials whose business was to print and publish Bolshevist propaganda in pamphlets, books, leaflets, etc., for circulation throughout the world. These were printed in various languages. Another duty of the Black Army was the forging and uttering of foreign banknotes and paper money for the use of their emissaries and agents abroad. Machinery for this purpose was received from Germany.

After the danger of the fall of Petrograd became apparent to the Communist authorities in that city, they started a system of Bolshevist "frightfulness." Zinoviev declared that before the White troops of General Yudenitch entered Petrograd each Communist would be allowed to slaughter ten of the bourgeois inhabitants. Other threats equally terrible were launched abroad after the second evacuation of Petrograd began.

The most astonishing fact is that several Great Powers so calmly submitted to their embassies being violated or attacked, their representatives insulted, one even murdered, and their authority at home undermined by these treacherous enemies, whom they actually tried to placate instead of taking strong measures against them.

The Government of the small State of Finland, notwithstanding its home and foreign difficulties, set a good example in this respect. A short time ago Chicherin sent an

BRITISH CRUISERS AGAINST BOLSHEVISTS IN THE BALTIC.
Vessels at Reval, on the southern coast of the Gulf of Finland, bedecked with flags in honour of the British cruiser squadron which arrived there towards the end of 1918. In circle: Esthonian women clearing a path through the snow for the British landing. Above: British cruiser going into action against the Bolshevists.

unsubstantiated complaint of alleged Finnish aggression on the Russo-Karelian frontier, and in replying to it the Finnish Government concluded with the following trenchant paragraph:

A Government dissolving the National Assembly by force of arms, ordering the arrest and murder of citizens because of their political opinions, and preventing the issue of other parties' papers, is unworthy to represent true democracy. The Soviet Government, which does not include one single workman or peasant, represents, on the contrary, the most objectionable despotism existing. Tired of negotiating with a Government who seem to act on the principle of not keeping its word, the Finnish Government wishes to inform the Soviet that the patience of the Finlanders may come to an end, and that the Government considers it its right to take necessary measures without any further announcement to bring the Soviet to its senses.

The best way to form an idea of the disruption that has taken place in Russia is to glance at an ethnographical map of that country, for the racial distinctions tally pretty nearly with the independent political divisions, which, for the time being, constitute what was once the Russian Empire. These divisions were by no means clearly defined, and when the Bolshevist lease of power expires, some of them will probably undergo considerable modification as regards boundaries and relations with their neighbours. A few of the heterogeneous elements, who were stirred up by agitation for a separate political existence, such as the Asiatic nomads of Eastern Russia—Bashkirs, Buriats, Kirghiz, etc.—are mere relics of old and effete races. Bolshevist practice might coincide better with their wild and semi-barbarous habits than with the habits of more civilised citizens,

WITH WING AND WHEEL IN THE FAR NORTH.
British officer about to set out on a motor-cycle over snow-covered roadless country in Northern Russia, and (above) men belonging to the Royal Air Force engaged in the task of erecting a hangar for the housing of aeroplanes attached to the British North Russian Expeditionary Force.

but those tribes will hardly be able or permitted to maintain governments of their own.

When the Bolshevists launched their shibboleth, " the right of self-determination," it seemed to give the stamp of legality to secession movements amongst all the old races in Russia. It even produced a cleavage in the great family of Russian Orthodox Slavs, who, it might have been thought, had too much in common to cherish any serious desire for separation. This Bolshevist catchword, " self-determination," although flagrantly contradicted by Bolshevist action, caught on everywhere, and if everything else **" Right of** represented by Bolshevism is doomed to **self-determination "** disappear, this principle of everybody's right to determine their own destiny seems likely to survive as a stimulant to separatist movements all over the world.

On the basis of this principle the Socialistic Federated Soviet Republic of Great and Central Russia was hedged round by a ring of nine or ten offshoots in the form of republics and Soviet republics, the circle being nearly completed by the All-Russian Government of Admiral Koltchak, General Denikin, and Archangel. In this chain of republics were Finland, Esthonia, Latvia, Lithuania, White Russia, Poland, Ukraine, Bessarabia, and Georgia. There have been other short-lived Republics like that of the sailors of Cronstadt, who defied the Petrograd Commune and terrified the inhabitants of the capital for many months. Another specimen of

these ephemeral and miniature republics, not as big even as the principality of Monaco, was the " Anarchist Republic " of Berdyansk, on the Sea of Azov. In the Danish paper " Kjobenhavn " a Dr. Bronsted related how in trying to get away from Southern Russia he had been obliged to call at Berdyansk, where he was taken before President Makhno, head of the republic. The " Golos Rodiny " states that this man was once a convict. Makhno said to the Dane : " We are all thorough-going Anarchists and recognise neither the Commune, the Jewish Soviet Government, nor Denikin's bourgeois army ; we are decided anti-Semitics."

Of the small independencies above referred to, the most important, from the point of view of Western Europe, after Finland and Poland, were Esthonia and Latvia.

Esthonia, with the port of Reval, is inhabited by people of Finnish origin. On this account the Russians feared that the Esthonians might join their kinsmen, the Finlanders, on the **Esthonia and** opposite side of the gulf, which is not **Latvia** more than forty miles across from Reval to Helsingfors. In that event Russia would be shut out from the Finnish Gulf as she is from the Baltic Sea. If Peter the Great's " window into Europe," representing Russia's historical necessity of a waterway outlet to the West, should thus be blocked up, there would inevitably be serious trouble again in the future. A restored and recuperated Russia would never consent to be confined to the mouth of the Neva any longer than she could possibly help it.

Finland had more right, perhaps, to complete independence than any other component part of the Russian Empire, except Poland. She always strove to gain it, and preserved her autonomy against the attacks of Russian chauvinists during many years.

Latvia, or Lettland, formerly Livonia, includes part, if not all, of the old province of Courland, with the two important seaports of Riga and Libau. The Letts are regarded by the Russians as a diminishing race, which now number less than two million souls, but this is doubtful. There was no doubt, however, that they were infected with Bolshevism to a very great extent.

The Lettish Guards in the service of the People's Commissaries have been the mainstay of Lenin and Trotsky from the very beginning. Bolshevism was rampant in Lettland during the Revolutionary outbreak of 1905. Letts, Esthonians, and Finlanders continued to fight in the ranks of the Bolshevist troops as well as against them.

There has never been any real cohesion between the different races and peoples who were gathered together under the sceptre of the Tsars. The Autocratic Government never fostered any amalgamation ; the *divide et impera* policy was often only too apparent, while, on the other hand, attempt at forcible Russification only increased antagonism between the different peoples. Prince Gortchakoff called Austria-Hungary a mosaic, not a nation, and seemed proudly unconscious of the fact that his own country exhibited just the same characteristic.

Russia went to pieces as soon as autocratic pressure was removed. The few pessimistic Britons of forty years ago— who thoroughly understood Russia, and prophesied that she would fall to bits in such circumstances, whenever subjected to any great blow from outside—were right. The younger generation of enthusiastic students of "Holy and Glorious Russia," who conceived a poetical and fanciful Russia and influenced British authorities in favour of their brilliant ideas, were, for all practical purposes, egregiously wrong.

Under Bolshevism the whole population of Central Russia was groaning and starving under the most awful system of despotism that had ever been devised.

All attempts of the Bolshevists to break through their isolation by compromise with various Socialist groups and factions having completely failed, they continued to exterminate all differing and anti-Bolshevist elements with unabated ferocity. With regard to the proletarian socialisation of industry, which was one of the principal points of the Bolshevist programme, a reactionary tendency seemed to set in later under the direction of Commissary Krasin, who persuaded the Soviet that the workmen's control of factories had been fatally destructive of all production. The workmen's committees were therefore abolished, and factory management entrusted to engineers appointed by the Council of National Economy. Penalties and fines were reintroduced, and the six hours working day extended to one of eight hours, the old system being thus revived.

Russia in a state of flux

The whole of Russia passed into a state of flux in which Red and White Armies surged to and fro, evacuating towns and recapturing them, destroying each other's work, shooting hostages, and devastating the country.

Hordes of hooligans roamed about thieving. Bands of armed men, drawn from the lowest strata of society under leaders like Grigoriev and Makhno, seized towns and whole districts and sided with or against the Bolshevists as expediency suggested to them. Deserters from either of the contending forces became incorporated with the troops, going back to the "Reds" or the "Whites," as the case might be, just as it suited their purpose.

BRITISH CRUISER SQUADRON AGAINST THE BOLSHEVISTS IN THE BALTIC.
British fleet in the Baltic on its way to Reval, and (above) the departure from Libau for Reval. At the beginning of December, 1918, the activity of the Bolshevists in Esthonia was such that aid was urgently called for, and on December 12th a British squadron of three cruisers and three torpedo-boats reached Reval, arriving opportunely to protect the town against the advancing Bolshevists, from whom two destroyers and a cruiser were captured.

In Moscow under the Bolshevists: "No bread will be distributed to-day."

Mails for British troops at Archangel: H.M. icebreaker Alexander in the White Sea.

Opposing Bolshevism in the farthest East: Allied warships in the harbour of Vladivostok.

Ready to reinforce Britain's Russian Relief Force: Inspection by General Sir Henry Rawlinson.

Reinforcements for the Allies in North Russia: British troops being taken ashore at Archangel.

"Hands up!" Red Guard tyranny in the city streets.

Bartering personal belongings for food with peasants.

Victims of the Bolshevist food tyranny: A woman and her child collapse from starvation.

In Russia under the Red Terror, when food was monopolised for the Bolshevists' supporters.

A GERMAN TRENCH IN

CHAPTER CCCXII.

THE HINDENBURG LINE.

BRITISH PROPAGANDA AND HOW IT HELPED
THE FINAL VICTORY.

By Hamilton Fyfe.

For too long a time the weapon of propaganda was neglected by the Allied Governments. The departments charged with the work were kept short of money. Little importance was attached to their efforts. Not until 1918 was a really effective propaganda campaign undertaken. This chapter describes the methods adopted and the success that rewarded them. The writer was himself concerned in the work. It was Lord Northcliffe's appointment to be Director of an Enemy Propaganda Department which marked the change. First among the Austrians and then among the Germans there were introduced disintegrating forces. The Government was provided with policies which it had not been able to think out for itself. The Allies were brought into line. Energy and ingenuity and co-operation soon began to give the results aimed at. The best evidence of this was afforded by the angry protests and denunciations of the German leaders and newspapers. They abused Lord Northcliffe savagely. Field-Marshal Hindenburg paid a tribute to the value of his work by imploring the soldiers not to read the leaflets showered upon them. The Allied Governments recognised the value of enemy propaganda in hastening the end of the war.

PROPAGANDA was a word in everyone's mouth during the war. All knew that from very early days the Germans were using it as a weapon. Most people over-estimated the effect they produced with it. Of the Allies' propaganda little was heard; of the British effort in this direction scarcely a hint was given. For this there were good reasons so long as the war lasted. It was the open, blatant character of the German attempts to influence opinion which robbed them of their success. British propaganda proved in the end to have had more to do with ending the war than all the loudly-advertised campaigns of the Germans, whether in hostile or in neutral countries.

A German officer, discussing in the spring of 1919 the causes of his Fatherland's defeat in a German newspaper, said that what caused the revolution in Germany was the feeling that the Army was beaten, and that this feeling was largely due to the undermining of confidence in General Headquarters by British leaflets. This was admitted at the time no less freely. In the "Cologne Gazette" of October 31st, 1918, the statement was made by a high officer at the front that "what damaged us most of all" —during the retreat which broke down the fighting spirit of the German troops—"was the paper war carried on by the

enemy, who dropped daily among us 100,000 leaflets, which were extraordinarily well distributed and well edited."

This work went on in secret. If it had not been for the handsome testimonials given to its efficacy by Field-Marshal Hindenburg, General von Hutier, and other distinguished commanders, the British nation would have heard nothing of it. When these testimonials appeared, people asked one another what department was provoking the anger of the German Army leaders and who were concerned in its activities. But no information was then available. Not until now has it been thought advisable to tell the whole story.

It is not a story which reflects any credit upon those who directed the British effort during the war. What was done during the late summer and autumn of 1918 might have been done from the beginning. If, at the start, the value of vigorous propaganda had been understood by anyone in authority, the war could, in the opinion of a great many, have been shortened. Those who hold this opinion are men accustomed to study crowd-psychology. A German officer prisoner, sent to Switzerland in the latter part of 1918, remarked that " if the Entente knew what poison the leaflets were working in the minds of the German soldiers, they would give up lead and bombard only with paper in future." (Swiss Consular Report to the Foreign Office, September, 1918.)

VISCOUNT NORTHCLIFFE AT WORK.
Early in 1918, when the British Government made a belated attempt to shorten the war by means of propaganda, Lord Northcliffe was appointed Director of Propaganda in Enemy Countries, and his success was warmly acknowledged by the Prime Minister.

It would be absurd not to take into account the value of the allied advance in weakening the enemy's moral. So long as the Germans were, or thought they were, winning, the effect of propaganda could not be very great. But, as continual

dropping wears away even a big stone, so even small inroads made by steady and skilful suggestion would have amounted to something appreciable in the course of four years. If the appeals to the Germans to throw over the leaders who had worked for war and the dynasty which had blundered so clumsily, had been made unceasingly from 1914 onwards, they must have told upon the confidence and the endurance both of the Army and of the nation. Far too little was done to sow discord between the people and the ruling caste of Prussian Junkerdom, to drive in a wedge which should divide all who were democratically-minded in Germany from the reactionaries whose ideas were rooted in the past. A suggestion that this should be done systematically was made in the early part of 1915. It was rejected on the pretext that any attempt to influence Germans "would be interpreted as a sign of weakness." Thus the Government neglected a weapon of value and missed an opportunity of shortening the war by provoking (and perhaps assisting) the upheaval which was delayed until late in 1918.

In neutral countries the work of propaganda, that is to say, the explaining of our aims and of the reasons which forced us into the war, was seen to be desirable at an early date, and the Right Hon. Charles Masterman was put in charge of it. A department was created for the production and distribution of books, pamphlets, articles, maps, photographs of the destruction in Belgium, and all such matter as could enlist the sympathies of the neutral on our side. Many men of letters were employed in

TRUE NEWS FOR GERMAN SOLDIERS.
Copies of a journal printed in London for distribution by balloon post in the German trenches, and (middle) a map leaflet for the same purpose, to show the enemy soldiers on other parts of the front how effectually parts of their boasted Hindenburg line had been broken through by the British troops at the beginning of September, 1918.

these activities. Not all their efforts were of equal value. The influencing of the minds and the emotion of foreigners is a difficult task, and has to be learned. There was too great a reliance at first upon statements such as carried conviction and aroused indignation among our own people. There was too ingenuous an assumption that the foreigner would believe anything which told against the enemy and everything that was good and noble of the Allies.

Further, a pathetic illusion reigned in the Propaganda Department that neutral nations were hungry for pamphlets containing reports of speeches by British statesmen, translated sometimes with professorial exactitude, but without the enlivening touch of colloquialism which alone can make such efforts readable. Tons of such pamphlets were shipped abroad and lay about in the back rooms of Embassies, Legations, Consulates, accumulating dust.

Want of unity

The writer saw them so lying in Spain, in the Scandinavian countries, in America. He saw them also in Russia, for Mr. Masterman's department was charged with the enlightenment of our Allies as well as of neutral populations. No doubt it would have been able to make more impression upon both if the Government had considered it to be an important part of our war machinery.

There was a lack of co-operation between the department and the Foreign Office. The War Office treated it sometimes with contempt, sometimes with suspicion.

In Spain the Englishman in charge of propaganda did not know in the spring of 1917 what policy he was required to support. He could get no instruction as to whether the Foreign Office wished to keep Spain neutral, or to secure her as an ally, or to induce her to break off diplomatic relations with Germany. In another neutral country there was a War Office agent, an Admiralty agent, and an agent from the Propaganda Department, all three working in watertight compartments. Frequently the efforts directed from Wellington House were made of no account by utterances of British leaders taking an exactly opposite line. There was a complete lack of co-ordination, of united drive, in our attempts to keep neutral opinion favourable to the allied cause.

Such endeavours as were made in Russia to teach allied populations to value what we were doing were, for the most part, pitiful in their ineffectiveness. Mr. Hugh Walpole, the novelist, who was engaged in this work in Petrograd, has spoken of it in "The Secret City" with scornful amusement.

That Mr. Masterman's department managed, in spite of all obstacles thrown in its way, to accomplish so much, reflected the greatest credit upon the staff at Wellington House, most of them young men, enthusiasts, ready to devote all their time and energy to the work in hand, if only their energies could be given free play. After a time the Foreign Office also set up a propaganda section with Mr. John Buchan, the well-known writer and publisher, at its head. He had been employed at General Headquarters with the rank of lieutenant-colonel, and took up his new duties with eager hopefulness. But he, too, soon found that the official attitude was hostile to any wide and vigorous propaganda campaign. Lord Newton was another who for a while was entrusted with some supervision of the Foreign Office side of the work.

The Foreign Office share in propaganda was, on the whole, ineffective. This was due more to inherent defects in the machinery of the department and to the usual Foreign Office lack of imagination than to any fault or negligence on the part of those who were in charge. Wellington House did far more. Indeed, it may be said that whatever was achieved in the way of influencing neutral populations was the work of Mr. Masterman's staff.

First "Enemy Propaganda"

The most lamentable omission from the efforts which should have been made was the failure to appreciate justly the value of propaganda in enemy countries. The inception of this side of the work was due to the initiative of one man, supported by Mr. Masterman, but grievously hampered by official neglect in other quarters, and by Treasury unwillingness to allow money to be spent.

It was Mr. S. A. Guest, a young barrister in the National Insurance Department, who set up a little Enemy Propaganda Department in Victoria Street, and for two years worked almost single-handed at the task of making Germans understand how hopeless was their position and how notoriously they had been deceived.

This effort, which in the end developed into an offensive of such magnitude and such value, grew out of support given,

Eine Karte, die ihre Erklärung in sich birgt.

Deutsche Kriegsgefangene kommen hinter den englischen Linien an, wo sie von ihren Kameraden,

die sie einer guten Behandlung versichern, begrüßt werden.

ENLIGHTENING THE ENEMY.
Some of Britain's propaganda leaflets for German readers. Evident pleasure of German prisoners at the prospect of ample food and safety within the British lines. The leaflet on the left shows in diagrammatic form the increasing radius of Germany visited by British aircraft. In 1914 their bombs could only reach a very small area, but year by year, as this plan very graphically showed, this area was greatly extended, until by 1919 even Hamburg and Berlin would have been danger zones for the Germans. The leaflet on the right must have made plain to the dullest intellect among the Germans how the American Army was increasing from the little figure representing 100,000 men in 1917 to the giant of 3,500,000 in 1919.

the propaganda agencies, Mr. Guest, seeing how much might be done, was often tempted to throw up the work. But he hoped always that a time would come when his ideas would have larger scope. Little by little he built up the framework necessary, and when Lord Northcliffe took

him over and gave him a free hand, his faith and all the labour which he had expended were amply justified.

Within the limits imposed by official weakness of imagination and ill-judged parsimony the one-man Enemy Propaganda Section could point to useful results. General von Hutier, in his order to the Sixth German Army denouncing British efforts to lower the German morale, mentioned that " books and pamphlets were concocted which presented the appearance of having been printed in Germany and bore, for example, the title of the Reclam series." This was one of Mr. Guest's devices. A harmless-looking little volume with the name of a German classic on the cover would turn out to be a record of atrocities committed by the German Army in Belgium. Disguised as a school arithmetic book there would be smuggled into Germany a full account of the negotiations between Serbia and Austria and the subsequent exchange of despatches which ended with the declarations of war. Sometimes Mr. Guest had direct evidence that his labours were being rewarded. On the Danish frontier his emissaries were so

Evidence of effective work

at Mr. Guest's suggestion, to a Dutch gentleman who was smuggling into Germany printed matter setting forth the allied case.

After a time Mr. Guest began to do this himself through an agent in Holland. Later he worked through Denmark and Sweden, and created an organisation in Switzerland with a man at its head who proved himself a positive genius in this kind of work. It is a pity that his name cannot be mentioned, for he deserved well of his country.

Hampered by lack of funds, and condemned to periods of inactivity whenever there were changes in the direction of

successful in working among the German sentinels that the troops in this region had to be changed, their spirit, so an order stated, had been completely undermined.

What might have been the consequences of a vigorous propaganda campaign in 1915, 1916, or 1917 can now only be surmised, but it is not going beyond the bounds of probability to suppose that they would have brought the war to an end long before November, 1918. The production of leaflets on a large scale which began in July, 1918, was immediately followed by loud outcries and denunciations in the German Press. Instead of concealing the harm done by them, German Ministers and writers and even the German commanders in

PROPAGANDA BY BALLOON.
Inflating the British paper balloons which drifted across to the German lines on the western front and, by an ingenious arrangement, dropped propaganda literature at regular intervals.

the field paid tribute to their efficacy. We were told exactly how they were depressing the enemy's will and courage, and, of course, our efforts in the direction indicated increased tenfold. No doubt the propaganda campaign had the more effect because it synchronised with the allied successes in the field. No doubt it would have taken a longer time to enlighten the German people earlier in the war. But there is ground for the conviction that it could have been done. The neglect of any vigorous attempt to do it during three and a half years is a stain upon the record of those responsible for the conduct of the war.

It was not until early in 1918 that the War Cabinet gave sign of comprehending that propaganda, and especially propaganda in enemy countries, might be a means of shortening the war. Lord Northcliffe was asked to undertake the direction of an assault to be made upon the moral of our enemies. Lord Beaverbrook was put in charge of neutral countries. He became known as Minister of Propaganda, though no such office was, in fact, existent. He was in the Ministry as Chancellor of the Duchy of Lan-

Lord Beaverbrook's caster. The effect of the change, so far as the
propaganda work neutrals were concerned, was not great. The work had all been by this time organised under capable heads into sections which kept up a constant flow of material. Lord Beaverbrook appointed several business men as super-heads of certain sections, but they did not alter the course of activity, nor did they increase it. Indeed, Lord Beaverbrook's instructions from the Prime Minister seemed to be that he should cut down expenditure rather than enlarge the work, which was now being mainly done in the Howard Hotel close to the Temple, to which in a short time Horrex's Hotel across the street was added in order to accommodate the greater part of the Wellington House staff. There was now a very large export of what was called "literature" to Holland, Switzerland, Scandinavia, and Spain. Each of these countries was in charge of a "national," and there were "nationals" also for the allied countries, for the Dominions, for India, the United States, South America, and other parts of the world.

In the United States a propaganda mission was in permanent being under Mr. Geoffrey Butler. In each country there was a branch working under the "national" in London. Thus

close touch was kept with the developments of opinion and sentiment, and the supply of propaganda was restricted or increased, changed in character or maintained upon established lines, according to the counsel of the men on the spot. Twice a week the "nationals" met to discuss their work, to secure themselves against overlapping, to pick up hints from each other and from outsiders who volunteered advice, to keep each and all informed of what the department was doing as a whole. This meeting, known as the moot, was presided over with businesslike, and at the same time sympathetic, ability by Mr. Masterman; in a short space of time it got through a large and valuable amount of work.

Lord Northcliffe's first duty after accepting the appointment of Director of Enemy Propaganda early in February, 1918, was to find a home for his department. He was fortunate enough to secure, by the public-spirited consent of

RELEASING AN AERIAL MESSENGER.
Registering the direction of the wind for calculating whereabouts in the German lines the balloon being released would drop its truth-telling papers.

the Marquis of Crewe, Crewe House, in Curzon Street, Mayfair. Here there was ample room and, not less important, there was quiet. It was important that the work to be done should be done as secretly as possible. Many considered it an error of judgment to announce Lord Northcliffe's appointment, but this was proved by the event to have been a wise step, for the Germans and Austrians were so much disturbed by it that their nervousness was noticeably heightened. Henceforward they saw Lord Northcliffe's hand in every turn of the wheel that went against them. So much did they fear him that from this time onward they attributed to him all the growing dissatisfaction in Germany and Austria. Every disquieting rumour was said to have come direct from the "Northcliffe Lie Factory."

Upon settling in Crewe House, Lord Northcliffe gathered round him at once a number of men specially qualified to influence opinion among our enemies. Many of these were journalists accustomed to the persuasive setting forth of arguments, and fitted by intimate knowledge of the Central

Empires to choose the arguments most likely to appeal to their populations. Among them were Mr. Wickham Steed, later editor of the "Times," Mr. H. G. Wells, Sir Roderick Jones, managing director of Reuter's Foreign Telegram Agency, Mr. Robert Donald, then editor of the "Daily Chronicle," Sir Sidney Low, a publicist of large experience, Dr. Seton Watson, and Lieut.-Colonel Campbell Stuart, a young Canadian of marvellous energy and organising power, who in time became assistant-director of the department and rendered invaluable service.

The first campaign to be put in hand was that against Austria. In the spring of 1918 the Germans were apparently so confident of victory that for the moment direct propaganda in or against Germany appeared to offer few prospects of success. In Austria the conditions were different. Here, there had long been a promising field for energetic

AIR-BORNE TRUTH FOR GERMAN TRENCHES.
Sending off British balloons bearing papers and pamphlets that told the German soldiers the truth about the position of affairs in the autumn of 1918.

BOMBARDING THE ENEMY WITH PRINT.
The British propaganda organisation sent millions of papers across to the enemy trenches. Hindenburg described it as "a drum-fire of printed paper."

effort to detach from their allegiance to the Empire of the Hapsburgs those nationalities, comprising three-fifths of the entire population of Austria-Hungary, which longed for independence, and which were, therefore, either actually or potentially the friends of the Allies. Mr. Wickham Steed had urged that this effort should be made, but nothing had been done until the Crewe House organisation came into being. Now Mr. Steed was able to carry out his plan himself.

The one difficulty in the way of its success was the Treaty by which Britain, France, and Russia had bound themselves, before Italy came into the war, to allot to her certain territories inhabited by Southern Slavs. It was necessary to convince the Southern Slavs that the Allies would help them to determine their own form of government, and would guarantee to them the territories in which they had a decided majority of the inhabitants. Before this could be done the consent of Italy to these conditions had to be obtained. Mr. Steed's long residence in Rome as correspondent of the "Times," and his acquaintance with all the leading Italian politicians,

as well as those of South-Eastern Europe, made it easier for him than it would have been for any other negotiator to draw the two opposing views together. By means of a series of conferences—first in London, and later on in Rome—the differences between these views were whittled down until at a Congress of Hapsburg Subject Races in April, 1918, the Italian Government agreed to put no obstacle in the way of the attainment by the Southern Slavs with allied assistance of their national aims and legitimate ambitions.

The Rome Congress was really a remarkable act of constructive inter-allied propaganda. Nothing of this kind had been attempted before. Between the Scylla of alienating the Southern Slavs by allotting to Italy districts inhabited by them against the will of the inhabitants, and the Charybdis of arousing in Italy a sense of national loss and humiliation by abrogating the London Treaty, a way was found which satisfied the Slavs and yet left Italy without a grievance. She was given the leadership in the whole process of liberating the subject Hapsburg peoples, a rôle in tune with her best traditions. Unfortunately, Italy did not maintain during the Peace negotiations the **Lord Northcliffe's** attitude she took up at this period of the **policy** war, but at the moment it was felt that a great advance had been made, and from that time the work of detaching the subject races from the Austrian Empire went on with marked success.

The ground being thus cleared, it was possible to begin work. A general idea had already been drawn up and submitted to the War Cabinet for approval. In a letter to Mr. Balfour as early as February 24th, Lord Northcliffe had outlined two possible policies. One was to work for a separate peace with Austria-Hungary by undertaking not to interfere in the internal affairs of the Empire, and to leave its territories almost or quite intact. The objection to this was that, even if the Emperor and his advisers were inclined to make peace, they were under the control of Germany and had not the power to break away. Another objection was that, if we acted thus, we could not fulfil our obligations to Italy, to which we had promised Austrian territories inhabited mainly by Italians as the price of her coming into the war.

The alternative policy was to try to break the power of Austria by encouraging the nationalities which were eager for independence and which had no sympathy with the Germans, whether in Germany or in Austria itself. It was this which Lord Northcliffe recommended, and his letter to Mr. Balfour set forth methods which could be used in following it. Mr. Balfour's reply to what he called "this very lucid memorandum" was indecisive. He suggested that the two policies were not mutually exclusive, involving distinct and even opposite methods of propaganda. In fact, he showed plainly a desire to keep a free hand as regarded the first, while agreeing that the second should be tried. Lord Northcliffe, however, immediately pointed out that, while the two policies might not be mutually exclusive in the last resort, it was very important that one or other of them should be given absolute precedence. "It would place me in an awkward predicament," he said, "if after basing vigorous propaganda on the *b* policy, I were confronted with

aeroplanes, balloons, contact patrols, and rockets fired into the enemy's trenches. It published a news-sheet designed to persuade the nationalities concerned that their only hope of independence lay in turning against Austria and assisting the Allies to compass her downfall. It sent gramophones into the front-line Italian trenches to play Southern Slav and Czecho-Slovak national songs and turn the thoughts of those who heard them to their patriotic aspirations.

The result of these activities was seen in the increased number of desertions from the Austro-Hungarian ranks. Among the deserters were many junior officers—not professional soldiers, but men who had been lawyers, manufacturers, or merchants. They admitted that they were induced to desert by the prospect of liberation which the leaflets held out to them. Nearly all those who came over into the Italian lines to surrender had with them copies of these publications.

TO THE GERMANS IN CHILE.
German announcement in a Chilian newspaper, declaring to compatriots that the journal "drags our country daily through the dirt," and calling upon them to "act accordingly!"

some manifestation of the *a* policy on the part of the British or other Allied Government."

This decision, presented to the War Cabinet, put an end to the flickering notion which had all along been in the minds of a certain group in our Foreign Office that we might make a separate peace with Austria. They based this belief upon nothing in particular, and they never bestirred themselves to bring it to the test. Up to this time it had not hampered us in our conduct of the war. It had merely been an example of the absence from the minds of our governing men of any clear guiding ideas. But now that active efforts were about to be made to break up the Austrian Empire from within, it was necessary to make sure that no negotiations should be even thought of which contemplated the continued existence of that Empire with territories and allegiances unchanged. While the War Cabinet and the Foreign Office remained in a state of benevolent neutrality towards both policies indicated in Lord Northcliffe's letter to Mr. Balfour,
Aid to Austrian disintegration the Enemy Propaganda Department made up their minds for them, and a good step forward was taken, which might and should have been taken earlier, towards the dissolution of the Central Alliance.

Before the Rome Congress was held Mr. Wickham Steed had been sent to Italy by Lord Northcliffe at the head of a small special mission to establish an Inter-Allied Propaganda Organisation which should prepare and distribute among the Austro-Hungarian troops of subject nationalities leaflets inciting to revolt. After the Congress this organisation began work. It distributed millions of leaflets by means of

That the Austrian Army authorities were soon alarmed by the success of the new propaganda was made clear by references to it in Army orders and by articles in the Austrian and also in the German newspapers abusing Lord Northcliffe.

Machine-gun sections were detached for the purpose of turning their fire upon bodies of troops attempting to desert during an action. Yet in the Piave battle a company composed of Southern Slavs joined the Italians as a unit, led by the company commander. He discovered from talk which he overheard while he was going his rounds two hours before the company went into action that the men had decided to surrender. Being himself a fervent nationalist, he resolved that the best thing he could do was to put himself at their head. Even Hungarians were induced to desert by leaflets on their land grievances. Thus disorder increased so widely that when the British forces in Italy struck in October, 1918, they brought down the structure of Austria's military strength in a crumbling mass by one vigorous assault.

General Diaz, the Italian Commander-in-Chief, repeatedly expressed his sense of the services which had been rendered by the propagandists—especially by Lieut.-Colonel Granville Baker, Lord Northcliffe's representative at the front—and his testimonials were afterwards publicly confirmed by the admissions of the Austrian High Command. If the Allied Governments had earlier adopted a clear policy towards Austria-Hungary the war might have been sooner ended. It was in large part a consequence of the clearing-up of their indecision by the **Propaganda on the** Enemy Propaganda Department that **western front** Austria collapsed when she did, causing a similar debacle in Germany to follow within a very short time.

For the reason already explained, propaganda among the German troops on the western front and among the German people was, for some time after the creation of the Enemy Propaganda Department, left in the hands of those who had been carrying it on hitherto. Mr. Guest continued the work he had ably organised of securing the circulation in Germany of books, pamphlets, articles, and information in every form. A sub-section of the War Office went on preparing at Adastral House leaflets to be dropped by balloons over the German lines. In this task Captain Chalmers Mitchell, F.R.S., took the leading part. He had for a long period been studying German propagandist literature. Early in 1917 the War Office issued a valuable analysis from his pen of over two thousand books and pamphlets of enemy origin. His sub-section sent out reproductions of letters written by German prisoners of war describing the comfort in which they lived and the abundance of their diet; a weekly newspaper for French and Belgian civilians in districts occupied by the enemy, called " Le Courrier de l'Air "; and a series of leaflets, begun early in 1918, of which during six months some twelve millions were sent to France. These were distributed not by aeroplane, but by paper balloons, a method much employed by the enemy. For a short time in 1917 aeroplanes had been used by us, but two British airmen who were captured were tried by court-martial, and threats were offered that any others detected would be very severely treated. The British Army authorities then decided that aeroplane distribution of propaganda must cease.

During the late autumn and winter of 1917 efforts were made to hit upon some other system of dropping leaflets. The Aerial Inventions Board and the Munitions Inventions Department lent their aid. Every device which seemed to have in it any promise of value was taken to **Paper balloons** France by Captain Chalmers Mitchell and **for propaganda** discussed at G.H.O. At last, early in 1918, it was decided that paper balloons would give satisfactory results. Designs and apparatus had been tested in workshop and laboratory, also at experimental stations near London and on Salisbury Plain. Then the balloons were taken out to France and tried under actual conditions of war.

They were made of paper cut in ten longitudinal panels, with a neck of oiled silk about twelve inches long. The circumference was about twenty feet; the height, when inflated, just over eight. One hundred cubic feet of hydrogen gas could be pumped into the balloons, but they were not sent up quite full: ninety to ninety-five feet was the usual charge. For two or three hours there was no appreciable evaporation of the gas. The problem which caused the most labour of thought to the inventors was how to prevent escape. Hydrogen passes quickly through paper: it was necessary to hit upon a varnish which would make the paper gas-tight. This was at last found, and the balloons were thenceforward capable of floating for thirty-six hours. Each carried from five hundred to one thousand leaflets, according to size.

These were dropped by an ingenious **Ingenious** mechanical device, adopted after many **mechanical device** others had been tried and found wanting. Cotton wick of the kind used in flint pipe-lighters, which burns evenly at the rate of one inch every five minutes, was threaded to a wire; by the wire it was attached to the neck of the balloon. The leaflets were strung along the length of the fuse in small packets, which broke as soon as they began to fall. For work over the enemy's trenches the packets were arranged so as to fall every two minutes and a half. When the balloons were sent upon longer voyages, into Germany or across Belgium, the interval was much longer.

The balloon stations were placed a few miles behind our front line. The distribution units consisted of two motor-lorries containing a few men, the leaflets, and the cylinders of hydrogen. The weather was closely watched and the spots for sending off the balloons chosen by the meteorological officers. Fortunately, the wind was from the west nearly all the late spring and summer of 1918. If it had not been for this piece of good luck our propaganda would have been nothing like so effective as it was. For up to the late autumn

GERMAN DUG-OUTS OF THEIR GREAT HINDENBURG SYSTEM OF DEFENCES.
Wintry glimpse of infantry trenches of the Hindenburg line. It was to men in such trenches that the British propaganda was directed by balloon post. Hindenburg himself, a couple of months before the collapse of his armies, bemoaned that the British " bombard our front not only with a drum-fire of shells, but also with a drum-fire of printed paper. Besides bombs which kill the body, they drop from the air leaflets which are intended to kill the soul."

we had to depend upon balloon distribution. The use of aeroplanes was refused by the Army authorities until then.

As early as May 8th Lord Northcliffe wrote to Lord Milner, then Minister for War, suggesting that they should be again employed in this work. Lord Milner replied that Sir Douglas Haig had temporarily decided against it, but added: "We hold ourselves free at any moment to resume it." On June 11th the Committee of the Enemy Propaganda Department resolved to press the matter further. Lord Northcliffe wrote again to Lord Milner saying: "Our work is severely handicapped by our disuse of this method of distribution, and if, as I am informed, the Germans themselves continue to drop leaflets over our lines from aeroplanes, our attitude seems to me perfectly incomprehensible." The reply this time came from the War Cabinet,

Delay in employing aeroplanes and was to the effect that the General Staff did not consider it right to subject our airmen to the risk of reprisals with which they were still threatened.

During July the War Cabinet overruled the General Staff, and agreed that aeroplanes should be used, but now the Air Ministry (Lord Weir) raised further objection. For nearly three months this objection was maintained. The War Cabinet took no step to enforce its decision thus set at naught. Only in October was Lord Weir's opposition withdrawn. At once the preparation of leaflets for the interior of Germany was taken in hand. In one week five tons (3,000,000) were got ready and the distribution was started.

Propaganda in Germany and among the German troops came under the immediate direction of Lord Northcliffe's department in the month of May. Mr. Wells was then appointed to manage it with the assistance of Dr. J. W. Headlam-Morley, the historian of Germany. The first labour which they undertook was the drawing-up of a statement of policy. As in the case of Austria, it was felt that there must be some firm foundation upon which to build. The method of the Government was to decide nothing in advance, to eschew general principles, to settle difficult matters only when they became too urgent to be left alone. The directors of the Enemy Propaganda Department saw that they could do no service of any value unless they induced the War Cabinet to depart from this habit. Again a plan was prepared and presented for sanction.

This plan aimed at influencing the Germans both by hope and by fear. In his letter to Mr. Balfour explaining it, Lord Northcliffe wrote: "There is much evidence that the German people as a whole desire above all a cessation of the war. They acquiesce in the continuance of the present offensive chiefly because they are assured by their leaders that this is the only way in which a speedy peace can be achieved. It is therefore necessary to impress upon them that they are face to face with a determined and immutable will on the part of the allied nations to continue the war at whatever cost. Side by side with this we have another motive of the highest importance. One of the chief instruments of the German Government is the belief which they

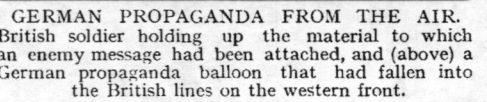

GERMAN PROPAGANDA FROM THE AIR.
British soldier holding up the material to which an enemy message had been attached, and (above) a German propaganda balloon that had fallen into the British lines on the western front.

foster that any peace that the Allies would, if they had their way, impose would mean the internal ruin of Germany. As against this it is necessary to impress on the German nation that these results might happen, but can be avoided. They can be avoided if the German nation will resign projects of domination openly avowed by the German Government, and consent to accept the allied scheme for a new organisation of the world."

Hitherto, Lord Northcliffe pointed out, allied policy and war aims had been defined too loosely to be comprehensible to the Germans, and there had been in them apparent inconsistencies of which the enemy had quickly taken advantage. It was obvious, therefore, that propaganda would be of little use unless it was supported by public and authoritative statements from the Allied Governments in favour of the plan suggested by the Enemy Propaganda Department. This plan included a League of Free Nations in which Germany would eventually be invited to take her place on condition that she accepted the principles of its foundation. Her admission would be in itself her guarantee against any hostile monopoly of raw materials.

"For the purposes of our work," Lord Northcliffe concluded, "it is of the most urgent importance that some statement of this kind should be put forward at the earliest possible date. Such a statement would be in effect an offer to the Germans of peace on stated conditions." If this offer had been made it might well have precipitated the changes which took place much later in the year, when the German Emperor decided to become a constitutional monarch and when, a few weeks afterwards, the monarchy was overthrown. But it was never made. The War Cabinet remained in a state of indecision. A step which might have spared us four months of war was not taken.

The proposed basis for propaganda having been accepted, Mr. Wells began work upon the lines laid down. He had already been engaged upon a useful collection of facts bearing upon the application in Great Britain of science to industry, his object being to show the Germans that we were emancipating ourselves from dependence upon them in the matter of products of scientific manufacture. He had also taken part in the preliminary work of outlining League of Nations schemes. But he did not find himself able to continue to give so much time to propaganda. Early in July he resigned, and his place was taken by the present writer. A few days later Crewe House took over the whole work **Daily bulletins for the enemy** of preparing leaflets hitherto left almost entirely to the sub-section of the War Office mentioned on an earlier page. Captain Chalmers Mitchell was transferred to the Enemy Propaganda Department, and continued his valuable services.

The printing arrangements, for example, now came under the direct control of the German Section, instead of being left to the Stationery Office. By the beginning of August daily bulletins of war news and leaflets explaining to the Germans the hopelessness of continuing the struggle were being produced with the speed of a daily newspaper, and despatched to France within forty-eight hours of their being written.

During August the number of leaflets dropped over the German lines reached a figure well over 100,000 a day. This was kept up until the end. Written in simple language, they aimed at letting the enemy troops know the truth, which was being concealed from them by their leaders. They gave information as to the progress of the Allies in all theatres of war; showed at a glance, by means of shaded maps, the territory gained. They laid stress upon the large numbers of Americans arriving daily. By diagrams the steadily progressive increase of the U.S. forces was strikingly illustrated. The heavy German losses were continually being chronicled, and the futility suggested of making further sacrifices in a losing cause. The leaflets were infinite in their variety. They appealed now to reason, now to the instinct of self-preservation, now to religious sentiment. They dealt also with political questions of interest to the German rank and file.

The general idea followed was to approach every matter handled as it would be approached by Germans of progressive mind. The British point of view was carefully suppressed. The writers of the leaflets did their best to penetrate German psychology. Many of their productions were got up to resemble the propaganda of German revolutionary groups, and purported to be issued by "the Committee for Freedom and Progress." A trench journal was issued, with a weekly circulation of a quarter of a million, so written and illustrated as to resemble a German production. The title was changed every week or two. Sometimes it was the "Heimatpost," sometimes "Herbstliche Blätter," and so on. The endeavour was to make it readable and amusing, as unlike the dreary "Continental Times" as possible (this was a paper which the Germans used to drop over our trenches, consisting mostly of immensely long and dull articles, quite unintelligible to the average soldier mind). A good deal of comic matter was included; the propaganda pills were thus carefully hidden in generous spoonfuls of jam.

In a very short while the German commanders showed that they were seriously disturbed by this "paper warfare." In the standing orders of the 11th Reserve Division appeared the following notice, which was typical of many: "The distribution of propaganda leaflets from English aeroplanes and balloons has of late considerably increased. It is the duty of every officer and man immediately to hand over such leaflets. Any officer or man found to be in possession of such leaflets or attempting to send them home is to be very severely dealt with." A great many, nevertheless, were sent by soldiers to their relations and friends in Germany. A little later, therefore, the offer of rewards was tried in place of threats. In the "Weissenbürger Zeitung" of August 29th

was published this announcement: "It is forbidden to keep pamphlets, books, leaflets, or pictures of the enemy propaganda. For fresh specimens given up to the military authorities will be paid: three marks (three shillings) for the first copy, thirty pfennigs (fourpence) for other copies, five marks (five shillings) for a book."

At the same time public opinion in Germany grew uneasy. Every day the newspapers attributed fresh triumphs to the British propaganda, and complained that there was nothing on the German side to approach it in cunning and effectiveness. In the Berlin "Morgenpost" the Minister for War, General von Stein, admitted that "in propaganda the enemy is undoubtedly our superior." The organ of Krupp's, the "Rheinische-Westfälische-Zeitung," wrote: "The British Propaganda Department has worked hard. Had we shown the same activity in our propaganda, perhaps many things would have been different now. But in this, we regret to say, we were absolutely unprepared." In the same strain of reproach the "Deutsche Tageszeitung" said: "We have a right to be proud of our General Staff. We have a feeling that our enemies' General Staff cannot hold a candle to it. But we have also the feeling that our enemies have a brilliant Propaganda Staff, whereas we have none."

North and south there grew an identical feeling of vague disquietude and distrust. In the Bavarian Lower House of Parliament the Bavarian Minister for War, General von Hellingrath, spoke angrily of rumours in circulation which, according to the Munich correspondent of the "Cologne Gazette," were "so wild and extravagant that one hardly understands how they can be credited." These rumours, the Minister said, were "nothing but the result of the industrious and determined agitation which our enemies carry on in the interior through their agents." In the Berlin "Lokalanzeiger," the editor, Herr von Kupffer, declared that these same rumours had produced in the north of Germany "a carnival of soulstorms, idiotic terror, and criminal irresponsibility.

"One would have to be blind," he continued bitterly, "not to see that these things radiate from that organisation in England formed to shatter the German nervous system by means of shameful and impudent lies. Is not the figure of Lord Northcliffe, the great propaganda chief of the English Home Army, pilloried in world history for all time?"

As to the effect of the Crewe House effort in and around Hamburg, the widely-read shipping journal "Hansa" said on September 14th: "At every step and turn we meet despondency, discontent, depression, hanging heads, grumbling. . . . Whence came they? Who brought them to us? To-day we know. To-day we can

MR. H. G. WELLS.
Appointed in May, 1918, to manage the department for carrying on propaganda in Germany and among German troops.

SIR CAMPBELL STUART.
Assistant director of the department for carrying on propaganda in the enemy countries.

CAPTAIN CHALMERS MITCHELL.
Experimented with the various suggested devices for dropping leaflets over enemy territory.

HOME OF THE ENEMY PROPAGANDA DEPARTMENT.
Crewe House, Curzon Street, Mayfair, lent by the Marquis of Crewe as headquarters for the Department of Enemy Propaganda, of which Lord Northcliffe was appointed Director in February, 1918.

recognise the origin of this depression of German will-power. It was the long-advertised publicity offensive of the Entente, directed against us under England's lead and under the special direction of that unprincipled, unscrupulous rascal, Northcliffe."

Testimony to the discouragement caused in the ranks was given in the " Kölnische Volkszeitung " of September 11th : " Leaflets calculated to cause low spirits and despair," said a letter from the front, " and to send deserters over to the enemy are being showered down in thousands. It is this combat, waged openly or secretly, which, particularly at home, produces depression and anxiety. In the leaflets you find statements that Hindenburg was once regarded as a divinity, but that his laurels are beginning to fade as the enemy advances farther every day; that our troops have lost heart; that whole companies surrender, and so on."

To such a length was moral lowered that, early in September, Field-Marshal Hindenburg issued a long and painfully anxious appeal to the nation and the Army. "The enemy knows," he said, " that Germany cannot be conquered by arms alone. The enemy knows that the spirit which dwells within our troops and our people makes us unconquerable. Therefore he has added to the struggle against German arms a struggle against the German spirit. . . .

German moral lowered by truth He bombards our front not only with a drum-fire of shells, but also with a drum-fire of printed paper. Besides bombs which kill the body, he drops from the air leaflets which are intended to kill the soul."

The number of leaflets had, Field-Marshal Hindenburg said, increased very largely during the summer. In May 84,000 had been handed to the authorities by " our field-grey men "; in June, 120,000; in July, 300,000. But this was nothing to the increase which was noticed during the autumn. In August the Enemy Propaganda Department issued 3,958,000; in September, 3,715,000; in October, 5,360,000. Passionately the German Commander-in-Chief implored his countrymen not to be " deceived." Fiercely General von Hutier, of the Sixth German Army, abused " the most thorough-paced rascal of the Entente, Lord Northcliffe, Minister for the Destruction of German Confidence," and asserted that the German soldiers could see through his machinations. It was too late for entreaty, too late for

belief in the German soldier's imperviousness to the truth. For it was the truth which was being told in the Crewe House leaflets. " Nothing but the truth " was the motto adopted for them.

Early in the war General Hindenburg said that the winners would be the side which had the better nerves. For years we had made no effort to shake the nerves of the Germans by the method which lay so plainly near to our hand. Now we were using this method, telling them the truth about the origin of the war, about the failure of the U boats, about the American numbers, about the crazy Junker schemes for dominating the world. The truth was prevailing. The German obstinacy kept up by lies was breaking down. **Dramatic collapse of the enemy**

Every possible way into Germany was used for the passage of the truth. From Holland, from Switzerland, and from Scandinavia there were secret avenues for books, pamphlets, newspapers, and newspaper articles. Neutral fishermen introduced packets of propaganda into German ports and on board German vessels. In the Army, although the German troops fought bravely until the end, there were thousands, convinced by our leaflets, who preached the truth to their fellows, and urged revolution as the one and only road to peace.

The endeavour to separate the Progressives from the Mediævalists in Germany, which had been recommended more than three years earlier by the journalist now conducting British propaganda among the German people, was now pressed with the most intense energy. There were no official hindrances, no Treasury " hold-ups." Ministers and other front-rank politicians gave out as interviews statements drawn up at Crewe House with the aim of dividing the enemy. The idea that arguments, delivered in the right way, might be as effective as bullets had at last penetrated to the minds of governing men. In his letter accepting Lord Northcliffe's resignation Mr. Lloyd George conveyed his gratitude for " the great services you have rendered to the allied cause while holding this important post," and added: " I have had many direct evidences of the success of your invaluable work and of the extent to which it contributed to the dramatic collapse of the enemy strength in Austria and Germany." The French Government gave a similar assurance. In the words used sorrowfully by the " Kölnische Volkszeitung," " Lord Northcliffe attained all his aims and left the political arena in triumph."

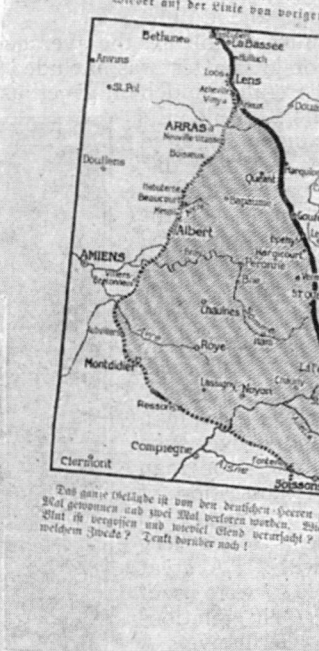

GERMAN DREAMS AND ALLIED REALITIES.
Some of the map leaflets by which the British Enemy Propaganda Department showed the Germans how events were moving against them. Left : A contrast between Germany's dream of a " Mittel Europa " and the reality of events. Centre : The wiping out of the St. Mihiel Salient. Right : Graphic evidence of the failure of Germany's great push of March, 1918, showing the line to which she had been driven back in the early autumn.

M. GEORGES CLEMENCEAU

The French Premier who led his country to the final victory

M. GEORGES CLEMENCEAU

The French Premier who led his country to the final victory

MARSHAL FOCH AND F.-M. HAIG

CHAPTER CCCXIII.

THE ORGANISERS OF VICTORY.
By Hamilton Fyfe.

Neutral Views as to the Prospects of Victory—The Dramatic Change in the Summer of 1918—Part Played by Organisation in the Final Triumph of the Allies—Preparatory Work of the British War Office Put to the Proof—Lord Kitchener and his Work as War Minister—Sir John French and the Shortage of Shells : His Brave Disregard of Formality—Mr. Lloyd George the Only Minister Capable of Fully Rousing his Countrymen—Sir Eric Geddes and Increased Vigour of Naval Strategy—Sir David Beatty as Energetic and Competent Commander —Inspiring Personality of " Papa Joffre "—M. Clemenceau's Confidence through the Darkest Hours—Britain's Notable Leaders of the Overseas Dominions—Sir Douglas Haig as British Commander-in-Chief on the Western Front—General Allenby as Resolute and Active Army Commander in Palestine—Sir Stanley Maude, a Commander who would not be Hurried—President Wilson and his Lieutenants— Lord Northcliffe's British War Mission in the U.S.—His Speeches to American Audiences.

LOOKING back over the course of the war we see that, broadly speaking, the Germans for nearly four years must have appeared to outsiders to be winning, while the victory of the Allies was accomplished in rather less than four months. There were ups and downs, of course. Germany had set-backs at Verdun, on the Somme, in the Battle of Jutland. But even into the early summer of 1918, when the French were forced to give up so wide a territory, there was excuse for those neutrals who imagined that the German forces were having the best of the struggle.

The writer was in touch all through the four years with a distinguished Scandinavian authority on war. It was not until after the first of the series of 1918 offensives by which the Germans were driven back and disorganised that this close observer began to believe in the possibility of their defeat. Up to that time, in spite of his sympathies being with the Allies, he had not been able to see how this could be compassed, even with American help. " Now," he wrote, " you will win, I am convinced. But it will take you a long time yet."

It did not, however, take the Allies a long time to win. Between the date of that letter and the request for an armistice not quite two months passed. Many, both at home and abroad, have been puzzled by the rapidity of the enemy's debacle. How was it that the armies which in the spring and early summer had been confident—full of vigour in attack and of

obstinacy in defence, handled with skill and coolness, supplied by careful staff-work, with accurate information, and ingenious plans—in the late summer and autumn could make no effective stand ?

The answer to that query is organisation. The entry of the Americans into the fight was, of course, of value. The assistance given by the British and French Tanks and the failure of the enemy to produce them in anything like the same numbers must also be taken into the account. But the chief factor in bringing about the allied victory between July and November was the work that had been going on, some of it for years, with the aim of creating such a powerful military machine that nothing could stand before it.

As soon as that machine had been created and had begun to show its power, the end, it was clear, could not be far off.

Generalship helped, but it had not the supreme value attributed to it by those who give all the credit of victory to Marshal Foch.

The single command was the vastly important change which made it possible to use the machine so as to get the best results out of it. In the exercise of that command any officer of intelligence and imagination would have been sure to follow pretty much the lines of Marshal Foch's strategy.

He must be praised very highly for delaying the offensive which was to end the war until everything was ready, and for timing his blows with such excellent judgment. T h e former of these merits

THE "BIG FOUR" AT THE PARIS CONFERENCE.
From left to right : Mr. Lloyd George, Great Britain ; Signor Orlando, Italy ; M. Clemenceau, France ; and President Woodrow Wilson, United States.

showed the character of the man, the latter proved his ability as a soldier. But neither character nor ability would have sufficed if the many other organisers of victory had not been at work for long beforehand. It was the sum total of what they accomplished that made it possible for Marshal Foch to administer the final blow. He was like the *espada* in the bull-ring who kills the bull and receives the applause of the multitude. But the bull has been worried and wearied by the *banderilleros* and the *picadores*. They have made the task of the *matador* far easier than it would have been without them.

Years before the war came, the organisers of victory had begun their work in the British War Office. It would be unjust not to begin with the compilers of the scheme for transporting an expeditionary force across the Channel.

Despatch of the B.E.F. When the moment arrived to test it, it worked perfectly and secured the appearance of British troops in the firing-line before the Germans thought it possible for them to be there. The officers employed in this scheme were too numerous to allow of their names being all mentioned here. Mr. Lloyd George has given the whole credit to Sir Henry Wilson.

He was in every way responsible for the despatch of the Expeditionary Force without noise, without fuss, without advertisement, and without hitch : that this was accomplished was due to the work of Sir H. Wilson, but none knew then to whom belonged the credit.

Mr. Lloyd George proved by these words, spoken in the summer of 1919, that he did not know, even then, where the credit truly belonged. The department "entirely responsible" for the despatch of the Expeditionary Force was the Quartermaster-General's, and Sir John Cowans, the Quartermaster-General, was complimented by Lord Kitchener, as Secretary of State for War, before it was made known that the landing had been completed. The Director of Movements Branch, under Colonel the Hon. R. Stuart-Wortley, should also be mentioned for its good work. Day and night these officers were at their posts until every man and every horse was safely ashore.

Justice also demands that the share of Lord Haldane in putting through so important a piece of work should be acknowledged. From many quarters and upon many counts Lord Haldane has been attacked, and much that is said

GREAT ARMY LEADERS IN LONDON'S PEACE CELEBRATIONS.
Marshal Foch, the victorious Commander-in-Chief of all the Allied Forces, riding past King George and Queen Mary near Buckingham Palace, and (above) Field-Marshal Haig at the head of the British troops, in the great procession of allied forces through London on July 19th, 1919.

Service campaigns undoubtedly stimulated the spirit of which the existence was made plain by the rush of volunteers from the very start. His object was not achieved, unfortunately, but his effort was not wasted.

The first name that demands mention among those of the organisers who began work after war had been declared is that of Lord Kitchener. Called to the War Office by a unanimous popular sentiment, to which the "Daily Mail" gave voice, he set in motion the forces which went to fill up the ranks of the New Army that it was necessary to create, and he laid down the lines on which its training and equipment should be carried out. As an organiser he did not succeed. He had been successful when it was possible for him to keep all strings in his own fingers and to manage every detail himself. The Sudan campaigns, and even the last stage of the South African War, were small enough to allow this method to be followed. The kind of organisation which consists in setting others to work and leaves the organiser's hands free of detail, so that he may devote his whole thought and energy to the general aspects and principles of his plan, Lord Kitchener did not understand. At the War Office he made confusion worse confounded by trying to look after everything himself. He took no one into his confidence except perhaps his private secretary. He concealed matters of urgent public importance even from the Prime Minister. This led to delays and disorders which culminated in the shells scandal.

But in recalling Lord Kitchener's limitations we must not allow ourselves to overlook the useful part he played by giving the enlisting campaign the prestige of his name and by laying the bases of the New Army upon the assumption that the war would be a long one, not the short and easy war which a great many people predicted at the outset. These were great services and will always be so regarded.

It was the short supply of the high-explosive shells needed for attacks upon fortified positions that gave Lord French

against him is true. All the more reason for admitting that he did good service when he permitted the officers at the War Office who were full of keenness for this work to get on with it, and when he bent his own mind to the perfecting of the mobilisation and transport arrangements. He even picked up some ideas in the German War Office, of which during an official visit to Berlin he was given the run by the Emperor, and worked them into the plan.

Another who helped before the war to lay the foundations for the edifice of victory was Lord Roberts. His Universal

the opportunity to take his place among the organisers of victory. He had already justified the confidence of the nation by the good judgment which he displayed during the German advance in August, 1914, and by his determined defence of the position in front of Ypres, which guarded the Channel ports. When his repeated requests for high-explosive were not met by the War Office, he established a firmer claim to the lasting gratitude of the British race by casting aside military tradition and etiquette and appealing direct to the nation.

Only a soldier of moral courage far beyond the ordinary would have decided upon this step. Technically he had done his duty when he asked for the shells with which to destroy the German trenches. Fortunately Sir John French was a man who could look beyond technicalities. He could not let his men die in heaps, as they did upon the Aubers Ridge, because shells were lacking, without making a further effort. He saw that defeat might be the consequence of doing nothing. So he determined, in his own words, " on taking the most drastic measures to destroy the apathy of a Government which had brought the Empire to the brink of disaster."

form a Coalition Ministry, whose first act was to acknowledge the first of the many great services which Lord Northcliffe rendered during the war by following his counsel and taking the supply of munitions out of Lord Kitchener's hands. A Ministry of Munitions was immediately established, and Mr. Lloyd George put at the head of it.

From this time onward Mr. Lloyd George became one of the most prominent organisers of victory. In the activities of his department there was much to criticise. The strength of the Minister did not lie, any more than that of Lord Kitchener, in organisation. His was not a business-like

KING GEORGE WITH FIELD-MARSHAL SIR DOUGLAS HAIG AND THE LEADERS OF THE FIVE BRITISH ARMIES.
This striking photograph was taken on the occasion of the triumphant home-coming of the British Commander-in-Chief and his famous Army leaders in December, 1918. From left to right : General Sir William R. Birdwood, General Sir Henry S. Rawlinson, General Sir Herbert C. O. Plumer, Field-Marshal H.M. the King, Field-Marshal Sir Douglas Haig, General Sir Henry Sinclair Horne, and General Sir Julian Byng.

No general ever deserved better of his country than did Sir John French when he resolved, no matter what the cost might be, to force the hand of the War Office and secure for the Army an essential requisite for the waging of trench warfare.

That he succeeded was due partly to his brave disregard of "formality" and partly to the lucky chance that there was a newspaper proprietor bold enough to support him without fear of consequences. It might have happened that all newspapers, from a mistaken sense of duty, would have declined to make public the facts which Sir John French wished to bring to light. So severe was the censorship of all statements which were not in agreement with official assurances, and so frequent were the appeals made to the newspapers not to publish anything which might " weaken the administration," that it did require as large an amount of courage as that which Sir John French displayed to publish and back up his appeal to the country. But as soon as

Sir John French and shell shortage Lord Northcliffe understood what was at stake, he decided at once to break the silence which he had imposed upon his newspapers from the moment war began and to make the nations of the Empire realise how acute the danger was.

The " Times " gave the facts. The " Daily Mail " pointed the moral, which was that Lord Kitchener's absolute authority over supplies must be brought to an end. There was an immediate unthinking outcry from the more hysterical sections of the public, but Mr. Asquith made great haste to

department. It wasted money by the million. It did not manage to deal tactfully with Labour. Yet there can be no two opinions as to the value of Mr. Lloyd George's work. His energy stimulated all who came into touch with him. His speeches made all over the country, for the purpose of letting people know how instant was the peril and how urgent the need for all to do their utmost to avert it, had an immediate effect. From that moment began **Mr. Lloyd George's** the whole-hearted and intensive preparation **great energy** of munitions which reached its highest point in the summer of 1918 and enabled the allied offensive to be launched.

Of all the more prominent Ministers of State during the war Mr. Lloyd George was the only one whose words roused his countrymen to a sense of the greatness of the issues and to a clearer understanding of the means that must be taken to make victory sure. He made mistakes, like the others. He agreed to the disastrous Dardanelles adventure. He cannot be absolved of responsibility with Mr. Asquith and the rest of the Liberal Cabinet for the deplorable lack of the ammunition so badly needed in France and Flanders. But whereas the mistakes of the others appeared to be those of men who failed for want of vigour, his were seen to be the mistakes of a man who errs because he is attempting to do a great deal. He failed in moral courage when he could not bring himself to dismiss officers whom he believed to be doing the allied cause harm. But he was not afraid to set his opinion against that of soldiers who affected to regard him as

between them to reform the methods of the department, which had fallen behind the age.

Sir Eric also earned the gratitude of the nation by the support he gave to the policy of adopting a more vigorous naval strategy. During Lord Fisher's stay in office as First Sea Lord this policy had been in favour. That distinguished officer did a great deal to organise victory at sea by far-sighted naval programmes and by his vigorous speeding-up of construction both before the war and after it began. He was alive also to the value of air-scouting for naval purposes, and helped by his encouragement and counsel to build up the brilliant Air Force which was formed

BRITISH SOLDIERS AND SAILORS IN THE FRENCH CAPITAL.
British flags borne in the great allied procession through Paris to celebrate the establishing of peace, July 14th, 1919. Above : Great reception accorded to the sailors of the Grand Fleet in Paris in April, 1919.

a meddler for daring to have an opinion at all about military matters.

The inflated claim put forward at the General Election of 1918 that he was "the man who won the war" was ridiculous, but he certainly deserves a forward place among those who organised in Great Britain the immense effort which, as soon as its full effect was felt, began the demoralisation of the enemy that in so short a period brought him to his knees.

Among those men distinguished outside politics for their capable conduct of great undertakings, who were called by Mr. Lloyd George to direct this effort, Sir Eric Geddes deserves prominent mention. The son of a Scottish clergyman, he had early sought fortune in the United States and found it on the Baltimore and Ohio Railroad. He was at first employed in some lowly position near a small station where the business was done mostly by a young woman. This young woman induced Geddes to take her place sometimes while she met her "young man." Once, while he was acting as **From railway office** substitute, the president of the road passed **to Admiralty** through the station and stepped off to make some inquiry. He was struck by the capable manner of the young fellow who answered him, and said, "You ought to have a bigger job than this, I guess."

"I guess I'm ready for it, sir," was Geddes' reply. So he was at once moved up. After some years with the B. and O., he went to India to manage a mill, then returned to England. At the time of the outbreak of war he was managing the North-Eastern Railway with intelligence, energy, and their usual concomitant success. The same qualities and the same result attended his control of the military railways on the British portion of the western front. To him was largely due the regularity with which the troops received their rations and their ammunition. A defective railway service would have been a disaster to our arms. Thanks to Sir Eric Geddes and those who worked devotedly under him, the railway transport worked very well indeed. Even in moments of crisis, as in March, 1918, it showed no signs of being overtasked. This duty performed, a higher post was found for Sir Eric as soon as Mr. Lloyd George took office as Prime Minister. He found at the Admiralty Mr. Balfour, who had succeeded Mr. Winston Churchill after the quarrel between the latter and Lord Fisher. He appointed Geddes to be First Lord, and there was never any reason to regret it. There was some grumbling in the Admiralty at the number of railway men brought in by one who was a famous railway man himself. But this was probably due to the fact that they managed

by officers and ratings of the Fleet. His temperament as well as his knowledge of naval history inclined him towards an active and even a daring strategy, as exemplified by his despatch of two battle-cruisers to wipe out the German vessels in the Pacific after their success against Admiral Cradock's command.

After Lord Fisher's resignation there was a slackening of energy in our naval warfare which was not entirely corrected until Sir David Beatty was given the supreme command at sea. He had played a part in the Battle of Jutland which would in any case have given him a place in history. The dashing manner in which he worked up the Grand Fleet after he succeeded Lord Jellicoe, entitles him to a niche in the temple of our great naval commanders. If the German Fleet had dared to come out against him he would have gained in all probability such a victory as would have set him beside Nelson and Camperdown. The knowledge that they would have to meet an admiral resolved to destroy them, and with a Fleet which he had brought up to the highest point of proficiency possible, made the German commanders prefer discretion to valour. Sir David Beatty's energy and competence, added to the feeling **Britain's great** of complete trust which he inspired in all **naval triumph** ranks of the Navy, gave the Germans no alternative but surrender. Never has an admiral celebrated a more striking triumph than that of Sir David Beatty when he received the enemy's ships. Never did any admiral better deserve it.

Going back now to the early days of the organisation of victory, we must acknowledge the worth of Marshal Joffre's personality in giving confidence not only to his own countrymen but to the nations of Britain as well. His name aroused the same respect and the same feeling of security as that of Lord Kitchener, and in a less degree the name of the Grand Duke Nicholas of Russia. This was exceedingly useful in the opening stages of the war. As a commander Marshal Joffre had to struggle against the unfortunate error of the French War Office in mobilising along the eastern frontier of France instead of on the front where it was certain the Germans would mass their principal striking force. At the time, however, so complete was the trustfulness of the allied peoples, the legend was believed that the retreat from the Mons and Charleroi line was "according to plan," and that Joffre was cunningly "drawing the enemy on." Even such imbecilities are sometimes useful in war time, and it so proved in this instance. It was not until long afterwards that the nature of the defeat sustained by the French and British forces in the first battle of the war was understood.

The Battle of the Marne, by which this defeat was avenged, proved Joffre's skill in choosing his ground **Influence of** and his ability to arrange a rapid concen- **Marshal Joffre** tration of troops. After that his rôle became mainly ornamental. He was employed, for instance, with most profitable results, to arouse enthusiasm for the war in the United States. But it must not be forgotten, though others went ahead of him in popular estimation, that the staying power displayed so magnificently by France was largely attributable to the magic of the name and legendary character of "Papa Joffre."

The enormously increased consumption of shells, and not only shells, but guns, machine-guns, rifles, and small-arms cartridges as well, which became at an early date a marked feature of the war, made it necessary for the French to follow Britain's example and establish a Ministry charged with the special task of keeping up a supply. The war also brought into everyday use new instruments of slaughter, such as trench-mortars, hand-grenades, bombs to be dropped from the air, and poison-gas cylinders. A new department was needed to secure the best designs for these and the manufacture of them in sufficient quantity. The first French Minister of Munitions was M. Albert Thomas, whose activity was often compared with that of Mr. Lloyd **M. Clemenceau's** George, and who certainly deserves credit **vigour and pertinacity** for calling in capable and experienced men to put the French output of munitions upon a sound and enduring basis.

But the one politician in France whose work towards the organisation of victory could fairly be set alongside that of Mr. Lloyd George was M. Clemenceau, who became Prime Minister in November, 1917, and from that date until the end of the war continued with energy surprising in a man of seventy-four to urge on the operations against Germany by every means in his power. He spoke even in dark hours with a certainty of success that calmed and steadied the nerve of the French people. He frequently visited the troops, seemed to court danger, tramped sturdily through trenches, and sowed confidence wherever he went.

His campaign against traitors within "the ranks" struck

TRIUMPHAL MARCH OF LONDON SOLDIERS THROUGH LONDON STREETS.
Scene in the Strand on July 5th, 1919, when nearly twenty thousand soldiers of London regiments marched past the King at Buckingham Palace, and thence through London to Tower Hill, where they dispersed. A notable feature of the march was the falling in of numbers of men who had already returned to civil life—a constant reminder that the regiments which had borne so great a part during the war were composed of citizen soldiers.

fear into the hearts of any who may have felt inclined to become what the French Press nicknamed "defeatists," though he did not manage to prove his charges against M. Caillaux, denounced as the head of the gang to which Bolo and others belonged. M. Clemenceau's vigour and pertinacity were just the qualities needed by France to carry her through the last year of the war. The "Tiger" had never before done his country such good service, or laid himself out with so single a mind to advance the national interest.

In the British Dominions victory was organised from the beginning chiefly by the large numbers who immediately volunteered for military service. To the Prime Ministers, however, we owe gratitude for taking the measures necessary to enable each Dominion to put forth its **General Botha** full strength in the common cause. General **and General Smuts** Botha must be named first, for he was the earliest to come into prominence. Taking the field again, he commanded in person the forces which drove the Germans out of South-West Africa. His plans were wise and soldierly; his execution of these left nothing to be desired, either in caution or in energy. He was greatly assisted by General Smuts, who later took over the command, and then came to England, joining the War Cabinet and making himself particularly useful.

General Botha had a more difficult, and certainly a more painful, piece of work to do when the South African Rebellion broke out. It gave little trouble. The man who had fomented the discontent of the back-veldt Boers, General Hertzog, stood aside when they put his precept into practice. As a fighting force the rebel army could not be taken seriously. But the impression made by this unfortunate event upon enemy and neutral opinion was deplorable. It was General Botha who rallied the South African nation and prevented, by a wise, statesman-like mixture of severity and mildness, any further outbreak.

In Canada, as has been told in Chapter CCCX. (Vol. 13, page 347), Sir Robert Borden at one period very nearly had a similar rising to deal with. All through the war Sir Robert proved himself a leader worthy of the race which set him at their head. He understood them and they trusted him. He had no doubt about their desire to do everything possible to bring victory nearer, and he took measures to make that desire of effect. Without parade or self-consciousness, with that modest dignity which he had always shown on great occasions, he gave all the assistance in his power to the British effort, and helped to make Canada's share in the final triumph a very substantial share indeed.

In Mr. Hughes the Australian people had a man of character, stiff in opinion, bold to encounter opposition, a man risen from lowly station, a man with his gaze fixed on the future, not on the past. They recognised his merits as a leader, even if they did not agree with all that he proposed. As has already been shown (Chapter CCCX., Vol. 13, page 347), he threw himself into the struggle with characteristic vehemence, and with the determination that no aid which Australia could give should remain ungiven. Australia's contribution to the final result was in con-
Canada and siderable measure due to his initiative and **Australasia** organisation; nor were the Prime Ministers of the States of the Commonwealth behind him in their zeal and vigour; Mr. Holman, of New South Wales, was specially commendable for his activity and eloquence.

When Field-Marshal French began to feel the strain of nearly eighteen months' command in the field, the most anxious eighteen months of the war, the choice of a successor to him was hardly in doubt. If General Grierson had lived, his was the name that would have occurred to those responsible for making the appointment. It was a misfortune that a sudden illness at the very start carried off this capable and quick-brained officer, who had, moreover, made a special study of German strategy.

General Grierson being gone, it was necessary to look for some commander who had proved his merit in the field, and whose name was sufficiently well known among the troops and among the nation generally to ensure his being given their confidence. When Field-Marshal Hindenburg said in the first year of the war that the side would win which had the stronger nerves, he showed that he had formed a perfectly accurate estimate of the factor that must determine more than any other the result of the war. When nations are arrayed against one another as solid units, not merely represented by their armies, as in wars gone by, the contest must be decided not so much by superior military dispositions, nor even by a preponderance in technical resources, as by the spirit that is manifested by the peoples as a whole. So long as a people believe in their leaders, and are confident of winning in the end, they will cheerfully endure losses and privations. As soon as they cease to feel that confidence they are at the mercy of their nerves—they are beaten.

The correctness of Field-Marshal Hindenburg's forecast was proved by what happened in his own country. While they trusted him, and General Ludendorff, and the Emperor, the German people resisted all temptations to abandon their hope of victory. When they were convinced, partly by the logic of events, partly by the propaganda calculated to produce this effect, that their leaders had deceived them, and that they could not possibly win, the end came quickly. Their nerves had given way.

No doubt the tightening of the blockade contributed to this breakdown. When people are half-starved they are not inclined to look at their situation hopefully. If after the Third and Fifth British Armies had been pushed back in the spring of 1918, the vitality of the British nations had been low through under-feeding, the dismay and depression of spirit caused by the success of the German offensive would have been vastly greater than they were. But, even so, they would, so far as one can judge possibilities, have held on grimly to the conviction that we should somehow "muddle through," because they trusted Field-Marshal Haig to pull them out of the mire. **Rise of**

They had never made of him an idol, **Sir Douglas Haig** as the Germans idolised Field-Marshal Hindenburg. They have never built statues of him, and paid to be allowed to knock in nails. They did not set his name alongside those of Marlborough and Wellington, but they felt that he was a safe man; they believed he was a man who would meet set-backs with a stiff upper-lip; they were easier in their minds for knowing very little about him—before the war not one in a thousand had so much as heard his name—and they were satisfied that if any one man could command success he was the man to do it.

He had, in the first battles of August, 1914, distinguished himself by his handling of the First Corps of the British Expeditionary Force during the retreat from Mons. At the War Office he had been opposed to sending out so small a force at the start, and the result of his earliest encounter with the enemy in largely superior numbers may have seemed to justify his attitude. It was his skill and coolness which in large measure saved the reverse from becoming a disaster. At the time Sir Horace Smith-Dorrien ranked equally high in popular esteem. He commanded the Second Corps, and was highly praised by Field-Marshal French, among others, in an official despatch, for his great and determined resistance to the oncoming enemy. But his decision to fight at Le Cateau, instead of continuing the retreat, was afterwards the subject of much controversy, and he was soon recalled. Sir Douglas Haig then remained the only commander in France who had made his name familiar to the public and the Army as a whole. He was plainly indicated as the new Commander-in-Chief.

It is too early yet to discuss at length and with complete frankness whether Field-Marshal Haig's strategy set him in the front rank among the famous soldiers of all time. Historians may ask themselves why, after Verdun, he attempted the same policy on the Somme. At Verdun, in the spring of 1916, the Germans tried to batter down a stone wall with their heads, and had to give up the effort with their heads all raw and bloody from their exertions. In July, 1916, Sir Douglas Haig began an attempt of the same character

Gathering of some of the great men who had led France through years of trial to triumph.

Marshal Foch (left) and Marshal Joffre at the head of the victory march through the French capital.

In Paris, July 14th, 1919 : Celebrating the Peace that had been won by the great victory of the Allies.

Great march of allied troops through Paris, in celebration of the Peace, July 14th,

ng under the Arc de Triomphe and by the cenotaph " Aux morts pour la Patrie."

President Poincaré decorating French heroes before the Hôtel de Ville, Paris, July, 1919.

American Independence Day, 1919, in Paris: French colours under which Lafayette fought in 1779.

on the Somme. His offensive ran the same course as the German offensive at Verdun. It gained ground, but it gained so slowly, and with such alarming losses, that after some months it " petered out."

The historian of the future may inquire also what gain could have rewarded the British Army for its losses in the Passchendaele offensive of 1917, and why that offensive was persisted in after the setting in of wet weather had made its success more than doubtful. " We have learnt," said Colonel von Hammerstein, speaking for the German High Command generally, when he was sent to Bukarest in the middle of 1916, " that attempts to break through lines entrenched and fortified as are those on the western front must be doomed to failure." How was it, the critical commentator of 1950 may be saying, that this lesson was lost upon the British Headquarters Staff ?

But in all probability the answers to those queries will by that time have become common property. It is more than likely that the historian will be able to point out that Field-Marshal Haig's strategy was the outcome of other than purely military calculation. He will show that in 1916, when France was exhausted after the heroic struggles of her troops at Verdun, and when Russia seemed, until the unexpected advance of Brussiloff, to be still paralysed by the long and terribly costly retreat of the year before, there was an insistent call for a British offensive. For political reasons Field-Marshal Haig was obliged to attack. Where and how could he have attacked otherwise than at the point and in the manner he did ?

Again, in 1917, it was a political exigency which dictated the Passchendaele offensive and which compelled it to be continued even when the weather turned so vilely against it. " Recall the circumstances," the historian may be in a position to write. " We know now that after the failure of the Champagne offensive, due in the first place to the faulty dispositions of General Nivelle, and secondly to the interference of politicians, who compelled it to be broken off, the French troops were mutinous. The French **Political exigency** leaders represented—quite accurately, no **and military acts** doubt—that only continual pressure on the enemy by the British Army, such pressure as would wear him down, even if no other advantage were obtained by it, could avert catastrophe. Mr. Lloyd George, when General Pétain told him this in the most solemn manner, was disinclined to believe it ; but when it was repeated and pressed by all the soldiers and statesmen responsible for France's effort in the war it was not possible to resist their entreaty. Orders were given to Sir Douglas Haig to make a move and to keep it up as long as he could."

It was due to pressure from the French also that our Fifth Army took over early in 1918 a long stretch of front held up to that time by our Allies. It was in a fair state of defence, but not strong enough to resist such an attack as the Germans loudly proclaimed their intention of launching in the spring. Field-Marshal Haig has been blamed for not insisting that better defences should be dug, in spite of the British soldier's well-known distaste for digging exercise. It is certainly likely that, if half the work which was done after the opening of the German offensive had been done before it, our troops would have been able to withstand the shock. But it had been agreed between the Commander-in-Chief and the commander of the Fifth Army (Sir Hubert Gough) that the better plan would be to retire on the Somme, in the event of the German offensive proving weighty enough to overrun our positions. The work of digging would have been very heavy ; the troops in the line had just come from an unpleasant sector in Flanders. Then needed rest ; spade-work would have been resented by them.

Retirement was therefore decided upon, and the front line was so arranged as to be held, for long stretches, by small bodies of men in machine-gun fortresses. It was not anticipated that they would be able to do more than delay the enemy, or that many of them would survive. " No great harm will be done," Sir Hubert Gough said to some war correspondents, the writer among them, at the end of January, " if the enemy gets to the Somme. If he were to get farther than that it would mean disaster." He must evidently have discussed this plan with the Commander-in-Chief and obtained his approval.

Unfortunately for Sir Hubert, it was he who became the scapegoat when the plan failed. The Germans did get across the Somme, and a long way beyond it. The retirement might have been turned into a disaster. We were saved from this only by the magnificent qualities of the British private soldier and his battalion and company officers. They " stuck it " because that expressed their nature and their code of duty, and also because they believed in the " C.-in-C." Some of those who were in the Passchendaele fighting had begun to doubt whether their faith was not misplaced ; but among the mass of British troops there was still the same confidence, and that was an enormous help.

That he was able to inspire this confidence was, indeed, Sir Douglas Haig's chief contribution to the organising of victory. Possessed of a sound, working acquaintance with military science, but not an original **F.-M. Haig, inspirer** mind, he was able to stimulate the minds **of confidence** of young soldiers ; those who came under his instruction often testified to the value and freshness of his observation, especially during Staff rides. His judgment is cool and balanced. He has generally been liked by those who have worked in close association with him ; upon those with whom he came into casual contact he left a pleasant impression of courtesy and competence, although he was plainly shy in the company of those who were not his intimates.

At General Headquarters he managed to soothe many pained susceptibilities, to smooth away many incipient quarrels, by pleasant good-nature and unassuming tact. There are some generals whose tact is as obvious and as irritant as a mustard poultice. They parade it, are proud of it, and make it a terror to their friends. Field-Marshal Haig is not among these. His tact was the outcome of a kindly, rather diffident nature, and a mind which regarded " fusses " not only as tiresome but as hindrances to getting on with the business in hand.

A good deal of the confidence felt in him was born of his dislike to advertising himself. Those who do advertise may gain popularity by this means, but they are seldom trusted. So little had Sir Douglas cultivated the art of pleasing, or studied the ways of the Press, that in his first talk with war correspondents he told them (with perhaps a Scotsman's humour), " I know just the sort of thing you want to send—something for Mary Jane in the kitchen to read." He made no effort to cultivate the war correspondents' interest in him. Indeed, he positively shunned them.

One quiet day he arrived at their headquarters while they were having lunch. They invited him to join them. He told his aide to say that he was much obliged, but that they had their lunch with them. They unfolded packets of sandwiches and ate them, sitting under a tree. The correspondents sent one of their number to say they hoped the Commander-in-Chief would do them the honour of taking coffee with them. The aide was instructed to reply that they had brought their coffee also, in a thermos flask. When they had drunk it they got back into their motor-car and drove on.

Other men might have done all that **The right man in** Field-Marshal Haig did in the way of **the right place** strategy. No other man could have held the Army and the nation together as he did. He became legendary, traditional. His handsome, expressionless face on picture postcards and in newspaper illustrations gave those who looked upon it the comfortable certainty that he was " the right man in the right place." He was one of the most important of the organisers of victory ; he kept the nerves of his troops and of the British people steady. He impressed them as being sure of himself, sure of the final result, serene, and not " too damned clever." History will not in all particulars confirm the popular judgment, but in most it will.

When there was some talk in the early summer of 1918 as to the advisability of recalling Sir Douglas Haig, two names were in the mouths of those who had watched closely the doings of British commanders in the field. The two names were Plumer and Allenby. Neither was himself a brilliant or even an outstandingly clever soldier; but both had the gift of being able to pick brilliant men to advise them. General Plumer's Chief of Staff to the Second Army was General Harington, later Assistant-Chief of the Imperial General Staff, and one of the ablest, acutest minds in the British Army. General Harington's lucid surveys of dispositions and objectives on the eve of an attack, or on the morrow of a stricken field, are among a war correspondent's most treasured memories.

While General Plumer's command did well in all engagements on the British front in Flanders, no such opportunity came to him as was offered to General Allenby when there was need of a resolute and active army commander in Palestine. In the western theatre of war General Allenby had shown the bustling, impetuous energy which earned for him the nickname of the "Bull." In Palestine this quality was badly wanted. The new commander, instead of directing operations from Egypt, some hundreds of miles away, pitched his camp in the desert, as near the front as seemed desirable, and instilled into the jaded troops a new spirit of enterprise and determination. Most important of all, he appointed to be his Chief of Staff, General Dawnay, a soldier of intellectual capacity far above the average, and not only permitted but encouraged him to make plans for the great turning and encircling movement against the Turkish forces which had been decided upon. The energy of General Allenby, the brains of General Dawnay, conceived and carried through without failure at any point one of the most completely successful campaigns of the whole war. The turning movement was skilfully planned and executed with exact punctuality. The Turks were surprised; their hurried retreat was every day more and more harassed; the efforts of their German officers to draw them together for a stand were unavailing. Retirement was rapidly turned into rout. The Turkish power of resistance was finally broken.

There was panic and disorder in Constantinople. The repercussion in Germany of the defeat further depressed spirits already in dismay at the pushing back of the German armies on the western front. The victory **In Palestine** organised in Palestine by General Allenby **and Mesopotamia** and his Chief of Staff was one of the sledge-hammer blows which brought crashing down in ruins the flimsy scaffolding upon which Prussian militarists dreamed they could build world-empire.

The Turks were, in truth, Germany's most useful allies. Austria never helped—she did much to hinder. The Turks, however, lent the Germans valuable assistance. They drew off large bodies of British troops to Gallipoli, to Mesopotamia, to Palestine. They obliged Britain to keep a considerable force in Egypt. They fought well, adapted themselves quickly to new conditions of warfare, convinced those who underrated their intelligence that they were foes who ought not to have been so lightly esteemed. To the wearing-down of their resistance, which culminated in the Palestine operations just noticed, the most effective contribution after General Allenby's was that of Sir Stanley Maude. Until he was given the command in Mesopotamia we had organised on that front not victory but defeat. The campaign was hastily planned and the advance pushed forward at a dangerous rate of speed. The advice of General Townshend, who commanded the expedition, was more than once disregarded. The medical supplies were utterly insufficient. Before the fall of Kut-el-Amara in May, 1916, while General Townshend and his force were doing their best to hold the place until relief came, the attempts to break

through the Turkish investment lines were inadequate and disappointing.

General Maude refused to make any move until he could make it with a force organically sound and complete, with full provision made for its continued nourishment and equipment. There were signs of impatience in Britain. "In the public eye," as Mr. Edmund Candler, the war correspondent, wrote in "The Long Road to Bagdad," "Mesopotamia had become a sink, a backwater; our troops had lost moral; we were for ever marking time." Maude would not be hurried. He laid his plans carefully and said nothing about them.

It was an organiser that the campaign needed. A Staff officer of large experience and sober judgment said of General Maude: "There are three things necessary for the carrying

GREAT ALLIED LEADERS AT OXFORD.
Marshal Joffre and General Pershing, followed by Field-Marshal Sir Douglas Haig and Admiral Beatty, passing from Trinity College to the Sheldonian Theatre at Oxford on June 25th, 1919, where they received the D.C.L. At the same time the same degree was granted to Gen. Sir William Robertson, Gen. Sir Henry Wilson, Admiral Sir Rosslyn Wemyss, Lieut.-Gen. Sir John Monash, Rear-Admiral Sir William Reginald Hall, M.P., Mr. Herbert C. Hoover, Rt. Hon. Robert Cecil, M.P., and Rt. Hon. J. R. Clynes, M.P.

on of a campaign—the fighting man who understands all about strategy and tactics, the man who is well up in staff-work, and the organising brain. The first two may be wasted if you have not the third. I never met a man who combined these three qualities until I met Sir Stanley Maude."

The result of the thoroughness of his preparations was seen directly the advance on Bagdad began towards the end of December, 1916. With steady, unremitting pressure the Turks were driven back, until in March, 1917, Bagdad was captured from them and the objective of the operations was reached.

When General Maude died of cholera in Bagdad during November, 1917, the British Army lost a commander of first-class ability. "Time in war is everything," was a favourite aphorism with him. "Every officer ought to have it over his shaving-glass," he used to say. He would leave nothing to chance, would attempt nothing which he was not reasonably sure of accomplish- **General Maude's** ing. When he took over the command in **aphorism** Mesopotamia his troops were beaten and disheartened troops, the enemy was swollen with success. He reversed these conditions, and contributed notably towards the eventual defeat of the Turk.

It is true that he had behind him a British Government ready to spend heavily in order to wipe out the disaster which the blunders both of statesmen and of soldiers had caused. He was given in all directions a fairly free hand; yet his task, nevertheless, was one which could only have been carried through by a clear and alert brain, allied with a great heart and a strong personality, all working day and night with no other aim in view.

Very soon after Bagdad fell the machine which was to overthrow the insane pretensions of German militarism was completed. The United States joined its power to the powers of the allied nations in Europe. The organisation of victory immediately became more intense. In this work the leading figure was at every stage President Wilson. He had prepared the way for America's entrance by his patient negotiations with the German Government. Each one of his Notes helped to convince the American people that Berlin was not to be trusted, and that, in addition to playing false, the Emperor and his advisers were intent upon flouting and humiliating their country.

His path was beset by difficulties. He was abused both by those who favoured intervention and by those who held

may be named as examples. Others failed to adapt themselves or their departments to novel conditions, and were dropped. On the whole the policy yielded excellent results. It was unfortunate that party bonds were too unyielding to allow Mr. Wilson to take into his Democratic Cabinet politicians from the Republican side, as he would almost certainly have done if he could have acted with an entirely free hand. Colonel Roosevelt was willing to give his services in any capacity, but his magnificent energy was left to expend itself upon occasional speeches and letters; even his request to be allowed to raise a division and take it to France had to be refused, partly because the allied army commanders were afraid his activity might be embarrassing to them. Mr. Taft threw his weight into the movement towards a League of Nations. Many leading Republicans took part in the Loan campaigns which followed one another in quick succession. But the party truce was not a genuine cessation of hostilities, and this inconveniently hampered the President's movements later on.

The man who was Mr. Wilson's principal lieutenant in the work of military preparation was Mr. Baker, Secretary of War. Born in humble station, and owing, therefore, his advancement entirely to his own efforts, this able lawyer had first made his mark as mayor of the great city of Cleveland. Small in stature and always looking young for his age, he had in his home-town days been mistaken for his own office-boy, and when he was asked to stand for mayor he was still surprisingly boyish in appearance. He was anything but immature, however, in his mental processes, and it soon became a general belief in Ohio that he would rise to high position in the Federal administration.

CAMBRIDGE HONOURS ALLIED LEADERS.
Leaving the Senate House at Cambridge on July 23rd, 1919, when the honorary degree of Doctor of Law was granted to twenty-seven of the distinguished war leaders. The photograph shows (from left to right) Admiral Sir Frederick Sturdee, Admiral Sir Herbert King-Hall, Admiral Sir Rosslyn Wemyss, General Pershing, General Sir Henry Rawlinson, General Sir William Birdwood, and General Sir Henry Wilson.

There was, however, some astonishment when he accepted the post of Secretary of War. He had made himself known as a pacifist of strong convictions. He was of the opinion that wars on a large scale had ceased. As the moment drew nearer for America's entrance there was much curiosity about the line Mr. Baker would take. He showed both character and good sense. The United States, he said, was obliged to fight in order to put an end to war. His principles were unchanged. He had been mistaken in supposing that mankind had outgrown war, but he was going to do his best to remove the cause which most often led to it—the ambition of hereditary rulers, claiming divine right, and of the castes upon whom they leaned for support.

The U.S. Secretary of War

that America would best consult its own advantage by staying out. These latter were not all sympathisers with Germany. The West did not take sides. Knowing little about Europe, and next to nothing about European politics, it considered that the United States was in no way concerned and need take no interest, save that of a dispassionate observer, in the causes or the issues of the war. The outrages upon American shipping stirred anger in the seaboard States of the East, but did not reach the Western imagination. It was not possible to light the flame of indignation, which could alone unite the country in a decision for war, either by rhetoric or by reasoning. The only hope lay in letting the people see for themselves how events were shaping, and how it was being made more and more difficult for a self-respecting and law-respecting nation to sit still under insult and injury.

It would have been perilous for the President to get ahead of the sentiment of any large section of the people while the issue—neutrality or war—was still in doubt. But as soon as he felt that he had the mass of the nation behind him he broke off diplomatic negotiations with Germany, followed this up, after a short interval, by declaring war, and then threw all his strength into the creation, training, and equipment of an Army that should, at the earliest possible moment, take the field alongside the Armies of France and Britain on the western front.

President Wilson's position

Men prominent in industry and business were at once invited to lend their experience and their initiative to the national effort. Some were towers of strength—Mr. Baruch, Mr. Stettinius, Mr. Bedford, of the Standard Oil Company,

Among the wonders which the American War Office accomplished the most spectacular was the building in a very short time of sixteen camps, which were really towns, for the reception of recruits. Each camp accommodated forty thousand men. The biggest contract firms all over the continent engaged themselves to erect modern buildings with light, heat, and water laid on, to put down tarred roads, to construct systems of drainage and sewage disposal, and to deliver the camps ready for their occupants within two months. The present writer saw some of these camps, and can bear witness to their comfortable and convenient character. They made him ashamed of British enterprise when he thought of the wretched conditions in which during the first winter of the war many of our unfortunate British recruits were housed.

For the rapid instruction of the American " draft " armies, and for their equipment within a shorter space of time than was at the outset thought possible, much credit must be given to Mr. Baker. Of Mr. McAdoo's labours at the Treasury and in other directions one must speak with respect. The advice of Mr. Justice Brandeis was frequently of value to the President. Upon Colonel House he relied in many a hour of difficulty for information and assistance. Yet when we have enumerated all those who did their separate parts in the organisation of victory, the figure of President Wilson stands out still immeasurably larger than any single one or than all put together. Lincoln is thought of as the man who made the Civil War for what he considered a necessary principle, as the man who organised the forces of the North against Secession, and who all through the war stood head and shoulders above all other Americans. So will Woodrow Wilson be reckoned the President who led his nation into the World War, who mobilised and set in order the strength of the United States, and who stood for his country in a peculiar sense, as did no other national leader, whether president, prime minister, or sovereign. Like Lincoln, he revealed himself as a noble idealist. He represented his people's soul.

When America took its place in the ranks of Germany's fighting antagonists it was clear that there **Anglo-American** must be close co-operation on the most **co-operation** business-like lines between the British and American Governments. Britain depended upon the United States for enormous quantities of supplies; she was also obliged to depend upon it for the means to keep up our payments for munitions, horses, mules, cotton, grain, leather, hogs, oil, and other necessaries. Good management was required to keep up the supplies and to keep down prices by a judicious and systematic purchasing system. In June, 1917, Lord Northcliffe was asked to undertake this management, and left at once for the United States, where he remained until November engaged in the work of this most necessary branch of the organisation of victory.

Lord Northcliffe had working under him upwards of ten thousand people. His offices in New York covered the whole of a floor in a building in Fifth Avenue; in Washington the British War Mission occupied the greater part of a floor in the largest business block of the city. In addition there were many local centres of activity, such as the Railway and Shipping Department, which had a vast range of rooms in Lower Broadway. One million pounds a day was the rate of expenditure for which the Mission was responsible. It had to be ready at any moment to take up any kind of business—financial, industrial, trading, or transportation, and smooth out wrinkles which were hindering Britain's effort in the war.

For example, there arrived one day a cablegram telling Lord Northcliffe that the stock of oil for our warships had got dangerously low. At once the Mission plunged into petroleum negotiations. The most influential oil men in the country were asked for their assistance; they gave it generously and with the most valuable effect. "We swam in oil," Lord Northcliffe told an American newspaper man long afterwards. "We breathed oil. The **Lord Northcliffe's** whole place seemed to reek of it. The **Mission to America** result was a steady shipment of oil across the Atlantic, and 'for this relief much thanks' came on the wings of the cable in return" ("New York Evening World").

That is but one illustration out of many which could be given of the work of the British War Mission. There was at the same time a personal side to Lord Northcliffe's duty as Envoy Extraordinary from the British to the American people. Mr. Balfour had visited Washington and New York just after the United States declared war. His speeches were listened to and read with admiration for their deft phrasing; his engaging manners won him immediate popularity with all whom he met. But to the American people Mr. Balfour represented Britain of tradition and caricature. He was a living proof that the British belonged to a past age. He was, in appearance, in speech, what an American, without any unkind or even humorous intention, called "an interesting survival."

What was needed in the summer of 1917 was that the American people should be convinced that they were to fight alongside a race not less virile, not less resourceful than themselves. A good many of them imagined they were going to the rescue of "an effete civilisation," thought of Britain as "played out," supposed that the British were timid, unenterprising, haters of innovation. Nothing could have done more to dissipate this illusion than the residence of Lord Northcliffe among them.

He had, to begin with, the advantage of being well known to them. He had paid their country some twenty visits, travelled from end to end of it, made hundreds of speeches there, given thousands of interviews. With his name Americans had long associated energy, ability, rapid thinking, fearless statement of unpalatable truths. In the years when Mr. Balfour, Mr. Asquith, Lord Haldane, and other British statesmen were prophesying smooth things and refusing to take into account the possibility of war, Lord Northcliffe told audiences all over the American Continent that war was certainly coming.

These warnings, offered as far back as 1908, were recalled in 1917. The memory of them lent added force to Lord Northcliffe's speeches during his residence in America as head of the British War Mission. He made several short tours, going as far west as Kansas City. Everywhere he was pressed to tell his audiences what he thought about the war. His words carried unusual weight. His introducers invariably spoke of him as the man who saved Britain from disaster by exposing the perilously inadequate supply of high-explosive shells; as the great journalist who had perpetually urged the British Government to more vigorous efforts, pointing out always the direction which these efforts should take; and as the power behind the scenes which had brought about the removal of the Asquith Ministry, often derided even there as the "old gang" or the "wait-and-see crew."

What Lord Northcliffe told those who crowded to hear him was not pleasant hearing. He could have won easy and cheap applause by **Lord Reading** giving them the assurances they would have **at Washington** liked to hear—that the war was almost won, that the submarine threat had failed, that the task of the United States would not be difficult, with abuse of Germany for seasoning, after the common form of politicians. Lord Northcliffe, however, was not seeking popularity; he was intent upon winning the war. He told them what he knew to be the truth. He spoke of the war as a calamity affecting everybody, a calamity which everybody could help to combat. He indulged in no glittering generalities. He addressed his hearers as responsible and intelligent human beings with vital interests at stake. He sent them away thoughtful, braced to the need for effort and sacrifice. Many of the best Americans thanked him for the stimulation of his words, and assured him they had notably helped to tune the American mind aright for engaging in the final stage of the terrific struggle.

Another Englishman who rendered most valuable service by assisting in the organisation of the joint effort which at last brought victory was Lord Reading. He went to Washington on a financial mission in the early autumn of 1917, was able to straighten out many awkward tangles, gained golden opinions from everybody, and was clearly indicated as the right man to act as temporary British Ambassador after the death of Sir Cecil Spring-Rice. For this appointment he left the Lord Chief Justice's bench in the Courts, and he held it until May, 1919, with the utmost success.

Shortly after his return to England Lord Northcliffe was asked by Mr. Lloyd George to undertake the direction of a new department which was being formed for carrying on propaganda in enemy countries. The story of the brilliant way in which his work in that direction helped to shorten the war has already been set forth in the preceding chapter.

The chief organisers of victory have now been passed in review. It only remains to add that their labours would have been fruitless but for the spirit of the peoples. To the great mass of undistinguished, unrewarded men who fought and worked day in, day out, with inexpressible courage, tenacity, and good-humour, to them the victory was in greatest part due. What individuals did was something. What the peoples did was all.

GETTING CANADIAN GUNS | CHAPTER CCCXIV. | INTO ACTION IN FRANCE.

THE STRATEGY OF THE WAR AND THE BLUNDERS OF THE GERMAN STAFF.

By H. W. Wilson.

Three Distinct Strategic Phases of the Struggle in the West: Manœuvring for the Advantage of Position, the War of Attrition, the Effort to Achieve Decisive Results—Germany's Blunder at the Outset—Alternative Ways of Striking at France. Over-Confidence of the French Staff—Belgium's Quixotic Strictness of Neutrality—The Threat to the British under Sir John French and General Lanrezac's Fifth French Army—Strategic Doctrine of "Imprudence as the Best of Safeguards"—The Retreat of August, 1914, and the Counter-stroke of the Battle of the Marne—That Counter-stroke Fatal to the German Plans—Two Days that Will Remain for Ever Memorable in the History of Our Country—Mistake in British Strategy: Wavering Between Two Objectives—A Campaign that Violated every Principle of Strategy—Rumania's Collapse and its Causes—A Psychological Offensive and its Strategic Effect—Germany's Neglect of the Moral Factor Repeated—German Attacks in Italy and on the West—The Unified Command under a Great Strategist—Franco-British Counter-strokes Lead to the Collapse of the Enemy before the Intended Final Blow.

THE Great War differed from all other wars in that it was fought by nations rather than by armies. In no previous struggle had such enormous masses of men been placed in the field backed by the organised force of whole peoples. From first to last the Germans mobilised 11,000,000 men out of a population of 70,000,000, or over one-seventh of their population, as against a total of 1,250,000 from a population of 39,000,000 mobilised by them in 1870, or one-thirtieth of that population. The French mobilised 7,900,000 men from a population of 37,800,000, or more than one-fifth of their population. Great Britain and the British Empire raised over 9,000,000 men for the Army, Navy, and Merchant Service. Russia, at the outset, mobilised 10,000,000 men, of whom, however, only a comparatively small proportion could be armed, equipped, and provided with officers.

The problem of strategy in earlier wars had been to break down the resistance of comparatively small armies by skilful manœuvres or a sudden blow. After the armies had been disposed of and decisively defeated, the Government which had placed them in the field yielded and made peace. But in this war the stake for the Allies was in actual fact national existence, because the

Germans had openly avowed their intention of destroying France, Great Britain, and Russia if they triumphed. And the German people had been persuaded by its Government during a long term of years that the Allies aimed at the destruction of Germany.

The real or supposed issue, therefore, affected every man, woman, and child in the nations engaged, and inspired them with such bitter determination that their resistance could only be crushed by ever-accumulating material loss, hardship, and prolonged and terrific slaughter. The problem of securing victory in such a war was a new one for generals. Nations in arms, fighting with stubborn fury, could not be defeated as professional armies, or as the relatively small conscripted armies of the Napoleonic age had been. Their man-power had to be exhausted before they would yield, and their material strength destroyed by the blockade. Both processes required time.

Thus the struggle in the west had three distinct phases from the strategic standpoint. There was, first, the opening stage in which the hostile forces manœuvred for advantage of position and obtained contact. The army which was most skilfully handled in this stage was able to transfer the struggle to its opponent's territory, and to inflict on its opponent all the immense material loss and misery which military

AFTER THE GUNS HAD CEASED.
Trenches of the German defences known as the Hindenburg line. The photograph was taken during the winter which immediately followed the cessation of fighting.

CAPTURED IN THE FINAL STAGES.
German soldiers taken prisoner by the Canadians during the closing months of the struggle on the western front in France.

The stopping power of the machine-gun, which the German had realised far more clearly than any other Staff, was a hindrance to manœuvring, and until it had been overcome by the provision of new weapons in the Tanks, and by the multiplication of heavy artillery, high-explosive shell, and aircraft, the difficulties of the strategist were immense. The American Civil War had proved that armies could entrench themselves in a few hours to such an extent that the attack on them, even by superior forces, rarely succeeded in breaking through, and the only course was to turn their flanks. But in this war the forces were so vast that at an early date in the west there were no flanks, and the Staffs on either side were driven to make frontal attacks, and face the full power of the machine-gun.

operations bring in their train—ruined villages, desolate countryside, cities wrecked beyond recognition, total suspension of economic life in the districts affected.

Success or failure in this initial stage depended on two chief factors —the readiness for war of the armies engaged and the numbers available in the first place, and the skill with which the plans were prepared in the second. In the first and preliminary stage Germany gained a prodigious military advantage—at the cost of bringing Great Britain into the field— by her violation of Belgian neutrality.

The second strategic stage was the war of attrition when the main armies were in contact—the destruction of the fighting power of one or the other group of combatants in a long series of battles. This stage may be said to have opened with the Battle of the Marne, and to have closed when the Germans began their great series of offensives in 1917-18. Sooner or later in all war a point is reached where mere manœuvring will effect little, and where the problem of victory becomes one of endurance and nerve.

The long second stage Through the three terrible years from September, 1914, to October, 1917, the plan of each side was the plan of General Grant in 1864 when confronted with the similar problem of crushing the American Confederacy. It was to break the military power of the opponent entirely, " to use the greatest number of troops practicable against the armed forces of the enemy; to hammer continuously against the armed forces of the enemy and his resources until, by mere attrition, if in no other way, there should be nothing left to him but submission."

The process might have been much accelerated if there had been less conservatism in the military commands, if such mechanical adjuncts as Tanks and aircraft had been earlier employed in sufficient number—for so far back as October, 1914, one of the ablest of British soldiers wished to construct Tanks by the thousand so soon as the design for them, which was then being prepared, should be completed. It was delayed by the time taken in training and equipping for the field the new British armies. But it was necessary, and it could not have been entirely eliminated.

LONG PROCESSION OF PRISONERS.
A column of German prisoners taken by the British forces in the course of the great forward movement which marked the definite turn of the tide on the western front during the early autumn of 1918.

The third stage, which came when one of the combatants was nearing exhaustion, was the effort in gigantic force to close, at whatever cost, and achieve decisive results. It opened with the German attack on Italy in October, 1917, which was followed by the stupendous German offensives of 1918; and, when those attacks were held, it was succeeded by the counter-offensive of the Allies which, brilliantly directed, fed with the large reserve forces of Great Britain, and the million of fresh American troops who were hurried to Europe, and supported by hundreds of Tanks and thousands of aircraft, issued at last in such complete and overwhelming victory that the armed strength of Germany and her moral were pulverised in a long series of battles. In that last stage of the war it seemed that nothing could stop the Allies. There comes a time in all struggles when the human element gives way, and that time was reached in the summer and autumn of 1918 as the result of the enormous losses which the Germans suffered in their final offensives and in Foch's counter-stroke.

The German aim at the outset, as German apologists have admitted since the war began, was to pulverise the fighting strength of Russia and to clear the German road to the East. This Germany achieved, though at stupendous cost to herself. Germany had no quarrel with France.

The Germans had conquered her in 1870, and did not fear her, for her Army, compared with theirs, was weak and ill-equipped, while her much smaller population, with its stationary birth-rate, was a guarantee against aggression on her part. They had defeated her when the numbers were nearly equal; now Germany had an advantage of more than 70 per cent. No French Government for twenty years had seriously contemplated war to recover Alsace-Lorraine. France might be said to have resigned herself to her mutilated condition, and was in no position to threaten any vital German interest.

If the Germans had been wise in their strategy they would have done their utmost to eliminate France from the war and isolate Russia. Then they might have triumphed swiftly. There was nothing to prevent them from massing their main armies on their eastern frontier and from adopting a defensive strategy against France. Their western frontier was strongly protected by the great fortress systems of Thionville, Metz, and Strasbourg, which before the war had been connected carefully by organised field defences. If they had left Belgium in peace, and stationed on the western

frontier 1,000,000 men to meet the 1,000,000 men whom France mobilised at the outset in her active Army, they would have been able to throw overwhelming masses of men—with the aid of the Austrians—in the east upon Russia.

If Belgium's neutrality had not been violated, if a defensive policy had been followed towards France, it is quite doubtful whether the British Government would have intervened at once. Russia would probably have suffered a series of decisive defeats, while the German armies, with their machine-guns, heavy artillery, entrenchments, and fortresses, would have been able to paralyse the French armies in the west. The German Navy could have been retained in the Baltic and have been used to strike at Petrograd and the Russian flank and rear. Its attention would not have been engrossed by the British Fleet. There would have been no blockade, except the German blockade of Russia, and Germany would have been able to import freely what she wanted. The

greatest danger that menaced Europe and the free world in July, 1914, was that Germany would follow this plan. Russia would almost certainly have been struck down, before the free Powers had grasped what was happening, at comparatively small cost to the German people.

Germany, when she decided to attack France with the main strength of her armies, had three courses open to her. There were three possible plans of war. She might have endeavoured to break through the French frontier in Lorraine, which, though strongly fortified, was far from impregnable. Some French officers, in the light of after events, hold that such a plan might have **Elbow-room for** succeeded, though history is against this **manœuvring** view. But if a speedy victory was to be won and a deadly attack delivered upon France, the German Staff had convinced itself that it must find space for the deployment of the vast forces which it could place in the field.

The French frontier from Longwy to Belfort was only one hundred and eighty miles long, and did not give the elbow-room required for manœuvring a force of two to three million men. To obtain space for such manœuvres the German Staff decided that the neutrality of the States bordering on France must be treacherously violated. There were three such States whose neutrality was guaranteed by the Great Powers, including Great Britain. They were Belgium, Luxemburg, and Switzerland.

A violation of Belgian neutrality was certain to alarm and estrange Great Britain, whose very existence depends on the Flanders coast being in the hands of friends, because of its proximity to London. But it was by no means certain that a hesitating and timid Government, such as that of Mr. Asquith, would have entered the war to uphold the neutrality of Switzerland. That Government never lifted a finger when the neutrality of Luxemburg — which Great Britain had guaranteed — was violated by German troops on August 1st, 1914.

WHERE THE TANKS WENT FORWARD ON THE WEST.
Two British Tanks in a wood behind the western front ready to press forward as soon as called upon.
Above : Tracks of a couple of British Tanks, showing where they had gone across the Hindenburg line.

For forty years before the war the French Staff had considered the various forms that the German attack, which it always foresaw, might take ; and some of its ablest officers believed that the violation of Swiss neutrality would give Germany most strategic advantage, and would be most dangerous to France. The Swiss Government, it is true, insisted on its determination to defend its neutrality, and the Swiss people was trained to arms. But the Swiss plan was known. It was to retire to certain prepared positions in the mountains with the great bulk of the Swiss forces, and there would have been nothing to meet such armies as Kluck's and Bülow's had they moved through Northern Switzerland into France. This line of attack had been followed in the Napoleonic Wars by Schwartzenberg. Had it been chosen in 1914, the Germans would have crossed the Rhine between Constance and Bâle, and have marched north of the mountainous region and the River Aar. Whereas with the plan followed in August, 1914, **Plan of attack** Kluck and Bülow turned the left French **through Switzerland** flank, with the violation of Swiss neutrality they could have turned the right. The Swiss territory through which they would have swept was well provided with railways and roads, and offered no special difficulties, though the Jura would have had to be passed. There were no fortifications of any strength. The way was open.

The German Staff seems actually to have considered the plan of attacking through Switzerland before the war, and, according to some accounts, finally decided against it in early 1914. Germany had not sufficient forces, even with the enormous number of men that she was able to place in the field, to violate the neutrality of Belgium and Switzerland and turn both the French flanks. It is a suggestive fact that on the outbreak of war reports came, possibly from German sources with the deliberate intention of misleading the French, that German troops had moved through Holland, Belgium, and Switzerland.

The first great mistakes were made by the impeccable German Staff, and they were the mistakes which lost Germany the war. But in the light of events the French Staff was also at fault. In its preparation long before the war it had always assumed, on insufficient evidence, that the Germans would attack only with their first-line troops, and that therefore they would only be able to give a limited and easily calculable extension to their front. The French only allowed for the deploy- **French** ment of twenty-two corps or 1,250,000 **anticipations** German troops, and therefore they decided to post their own first-line force of about 1,000,000 men from Mézières to Belfort on a front of about one hundred and eighty miles, whereas the Germans actually deployed thirty-four or thirty-five corps on a front of two hundred and fifty miles from Mézières to Belfort. When the Germans entered Belgium the French Staff did not immediately alter its dispositions. Four French armies were placed in line, and a fifth (the Fourth Army) was held in reserve.

The French Staff expected the Germans to march through Luxemburg. and the extreme south-eastern end of Belgium east of the Meuse. It did not believe that they would make a great sweep through Central Belgium west of the Meuse, as they did, because it did not imagine that they had troops enough for such a movement. On August 7th, 1914, General Lanrezac (who commanded the Fifth French Army on the French left) protested that there was grave danger of such a German manœuvre. He was told that he had no ground for his fear.

SOME OF THE GREAT GUN BOOTY CAPTURED BY THE CANADIANS ON THE WAY TO CAMBRAI.
Part of the gigantic total of guns of all kinds, arranged in a series of semicircles, that were taken by the Canadians in their great advance on Cambrai during the closing stages of the war. The large number of different kinds of machine-guns, forming the two inner circles, was especially remarkable.

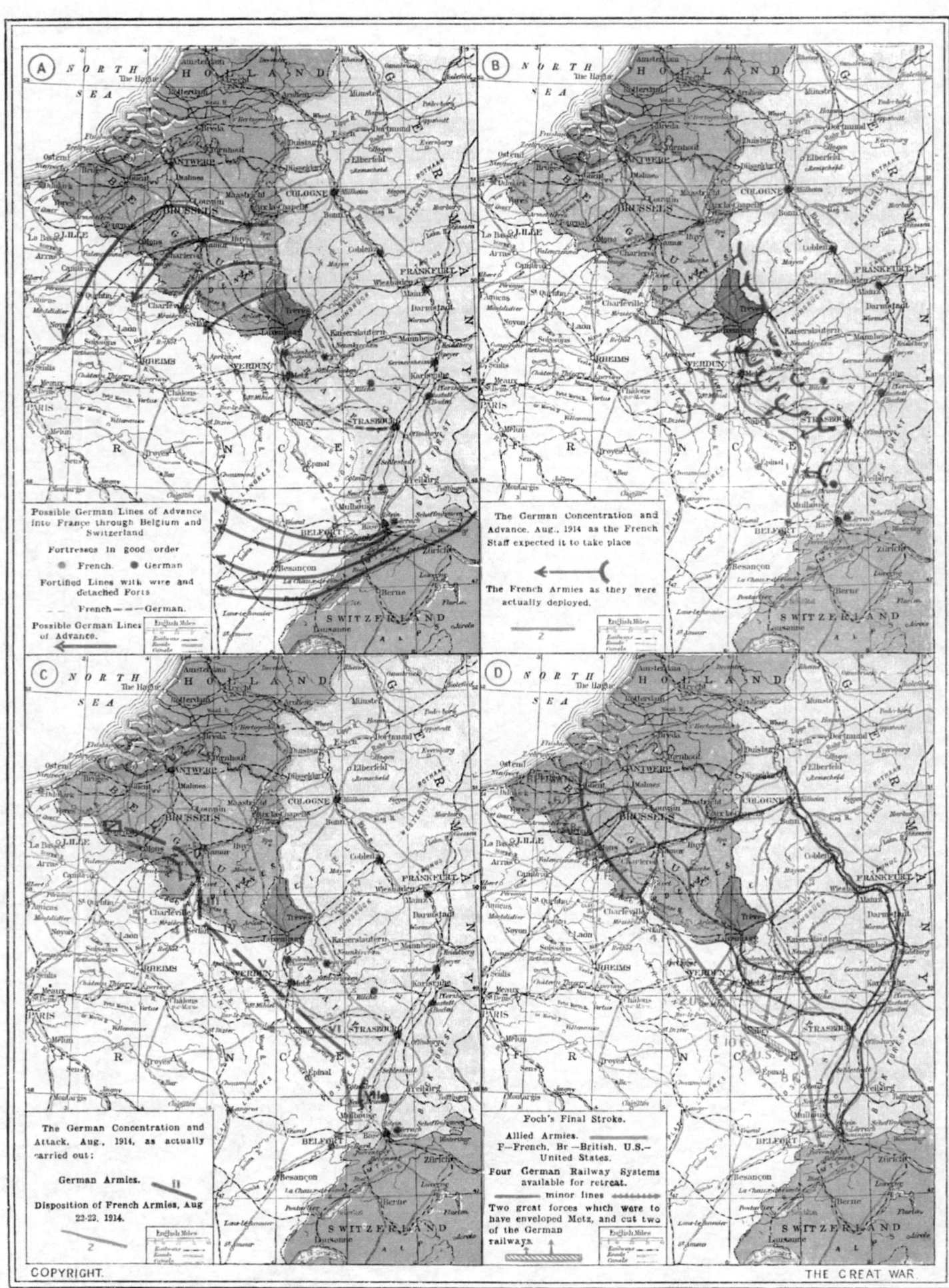

FROM THE GERMAN ADVANCE OF 1914 TO THE GERMAN RETREAT OF 1918.

On August 12th an official in the closest touch with the French Staff informed a deputy, who showed nervousness, that "the (French) Staff is not uneasy; it assures me that the western movement of the Germans is only dangerous to them." On August 14th General Lanrezac, who had now been ordered to move with his army to Charleroi, made a fresh appeal to General Joffre for precautions to be taken to protect his left, and was assured that "the Germans have nothing ready on that side." On August 15th the Belgian Staff at Namur sent a warning that the Germans were crossing the Meuse in masses. It **Mistaken theory** was disregarded. Yet it should have **and its results** been clear that the Germans were preparing to fall on General Lanrezac and the British Expeditionary Force in overwhelming strength.

It has been argued that the French Staff could not have met this vast turning movement, which was carried out by the German armies under Generals Kluck and Bülow, because it had not the men. But it had the men, only the men were not properly organised and equipped, because of the theory which was fashionable in France that reserve troops could not be employed in the initial battles. So far back as 1911 the French General Michel had protested against the danger of this theory, but in vain. A mistaken theory was thus one of the chief causes of the early defeats. It led directly

to the disasters of August, 1914, which were due to the fact that three powerful German armies, the First, Second, and Fourth, were flung upon Lanrezac and Sir John French, who were far too weak to meet them.

One of the mysteries of the early part of the war was the non-arrival of British and French help in Belgium. This, mystery could not be explained at the time, but the fact was that at the outset there was uncertainty as to the attitude of the Belgian Government. Its neutrality was so strict as to leave real doubt in the minds of the French Staff. Owing to very legitimate and intelligible scruples, it had refused before the war to consider the mere possibility of a German advance through Beligum, and therefore no arrangements could be made for the swift movement of British or French troops into Belgian territory.

Even when Germany's intentions were manifest to Great Britain and France, the Belgian Government remained unconvinced. On August 2nd, 1914, Germany sent her ultimatum to Belgium, and on the following day the French military attaché at Brussels, with the authority of his Government, offered the Belgians the aid of five French corps

(200,000 men). Had the offer been accepted, history might have been changed, and Belgium and Northern France been saved from years of misery.

The Belgian Government, however, declined the proposal. It refused all aid other than purely diplomatic support, and it maintained this position until August 5th. But even then the French Staff was not sufficiently certain what to expect. It issued instructions permitting French aircraft to fly over

GERMANY'S WAR LORD VISITING A BATTLE-FRONT.
The Kaiser with a number of his Staff officers on a visit to the front which had been endangered by the British thrust towards Cambrai in November, 1917 and (above) in a town behind that front with (left) Prince Rupert of Bavaria, and (right) General von der Marwitz.

Belgian territory, and cavalry to reconnoitre in Belgium, but it forbade the employment of strong detachments to support the French cavalry. In doing this it acted from political reasons, because it feared that the presence of a large French force on Belgian soil would be unwelcome to the Belgian Government. After August 5th it became more difficult to move large masses of men in Belgium; the French deployment had gone too far, and the precious time lost could not be regained.

As the German movement through Belgium became more and more pronounced, the French Staff still clung to its original plans and failed to modify them to meet the danger. The German strategy was always to avoid frontal attack, if possible, and to work round the enemy's flank. It ought to have been clear by mid-August that the German armies were carrying out a vast turning movement through Central and Western Belgium, and that the French dispositions must be drastically modified to parry and defeat such a movement. Yet the French Staff did not sensibly alter its distribution of force. It believed that the Germans had weakened their centre, between Mézières and Alsace, in order to provide troops for this turning movement, and it hoped to break through the German centre between these points and inflict a decisive defeat in a great offensive. Its calculations were based on its mistaken estimate of the German armies, which it supposed to be far weaker than they actually were.

In fact the French had some numerical superiority in Lorraine, but it was not sufficient to give them victory, in view of their great weakness in heavy artil- lery, aircraft, and machine-guns, against the **French defeats** Germans, who had the support of very **in Lorraine** strong positions, many of which had been carefully prepared before the war. An offensive in such condi- tions was bound to fail, and was quite contrary to the teaching of such masters of war as Napoleon and Foch. In a series of battles known as Virton, the Ardennes, Sarrebourg, and Morhange the French attacks broke down completely. The French infantry was thrown upon the German positions after an insufficient artillery preparation, and was generally repulsed with heavy loss. The French artillery, despite its admirable weapon, the "75," found itself under the fire of the German long-range heavy guns and howitzers, to which

in the east (in Lorraine) forces exceeding those necessary for a pure and simple defensive. It was still more unreasonable to attempt offensive movements in Alsace and Lorraine without any serious chance of success, when our troops were so greatly inferior numerically west of the Meuse.

This mistake was accentuated by the strategic doctrine which had been accepted in the French Army shortly before the war—that the offensive must be adopted at whatever cost, and that in it " imprudence was the best of safeguards." French soldiers knew that Russia would require time to bring her enormous masses into play ; they knew that time would be required to enable Great Britain to throw her colossal strength into the scale. There was nothing to be gained by rushing precipitately upon an admirably entrenched opponent.

" Imprudence the best safeguard "

It will always be a matter of speculation whether the war would not have taken an entirely different turn if the French Army had been taught to entrench, and if the French Staff at the outset had linked up its forces with the Belgian Army and held the line of the Meuse, which was defensible, with powerful field fortifications, such as proved so difficult to penetrate during the war. This was the strategy which the American Civil War, the South African War, and the Russo-Japanese War had shown to be advisable for the weaker army.

it could make no reply. The Germans, when the French attack failed, passed from the defensive to the offensive, and advanced, but without any great energy or speed. Had they pushed forward with resolution, or been handled by a Napoleon, they might have won a very great success. As it was they advanced sufficiently to add enormously to the danger which threatened General Lanrezac's Fifth French Army at Charleroi, and Sir John French at Mons. Lanrezac, in particular, was menaced with envelopment on both flanks, and a determined effort by the Third German Army, under General Hausen, would have cut off his line of retreat and have resulted in a new and far more disastrous Sedan.

General Mangin, then only a subordinate commanding a brigade in the Fifth French Army, by his energy and firmness drove back a very superior German force at the critical moment. The danger was so overwhelming that General Lanrezac had no alternative but to retreat with all possible speed, and though he was severely criticised

GERMANY'S MILITARY IDOL IN THE DAYS OF HIS SUCCESS.
Field-Marshal Paul von Beneckendorff und von Hindenburg, who at Tannenberg, in August, 1914, won one of the greatest of German victories in the campaign against Russia. Though sixty-seven years of age when the war broke out, he was, after his success on the eastern front, given the chief command of the German armies. Above : Hindenburg with his Staff on the eastern front.

at the time, there is no doubt that posterity will commend his retirement as necessary, judicious, and ably carried out. It was followed some hours later by Sir John French's retreat, which was equally necessary and judicious. The extrication of some 300,000 allied troops from the clutches of the 750,000 Germans who were closing upon them was a great feat of leadership. It saved the Allies.

Mistaken French strategy   The strategy which compelled such a retreat at the outset, such an abandonment of the richest part of France and all Belgium to German occupation, was clearly open to criticism. One of the ablest French military writers has thus pointed out its defects :

It was absurd on the part of our Headquarters not to have reckoned with the invasion of Belgium, which began on August 4th, and had been foreseen for years, in the concentration effected during the subsequent days. It was absurd to have obstinately closed the eyes to the obvious menace and postponed to the last extremity the measures which were indispensable to meet it. In the conditions in which France found herself in mid-August, 1914, in face of an attack which threatened her very national existence, it was unreasonable to maintain

This strategy was not adopted, and in consequence the Allies had to retreat after the bloody repulses of the offensive in Lorraine and the Ardennes. The retreat brought fearful misfortune on France, but it was a lesser evil than the loss of the two armies—Lanrezac's and the British—which played so important a part in the subsequent victory of the Marne. Even when the retreat became necessary, if fieldworks and positions had been prepared on the northern French frontier, the allied armies might have halted and delivered battle long before they reached the Marne. But the British, as they fell back, found ready nothing for them but a few straight trenches, altogether useless against shell fire.

Lille, which had works of an antiquated type, but of some strength, was ordered by the French Staff to be evacuated, though General Percin, who commanded troops there, was strongly in favour of holding it. Maubeuge, which was not better defended, and was poorly equipped, was certain to be isolated by the Germans when Lanrezac and Sir John French fell back. There were stronger arguments for its evacuation than for the abandonment of Lille. But General Fournier was ordered to hold it, and was given a garrison of forty thousand men, who were doomed to early capture, and would have been far more useful in the field. These forty thousand men, added to six territorial and reserve divisions—eighty thousand men—which were available near Lille, and to Sir John French's and Lanrezac's armies, both of which were intact on August 24th, would probably have been able to bring Kluck to a standstill, and cause the collapse of the whole vast German turning movement, if the French Staff had not concentrated its attention on Lorraine. In that case the vital mining and manufacturing district of Northern France and the Flanders coast would have been saved.

It is certain that the French Staff, in its plans, had never contemplated a general retreat such as that which took place in August, 1914. The retreat did, however, enable the French Staff to manœuvre and to meet the Germans by other methods than sheer frontal attacks on heavily entrenched positions. The general idea underlying the French counter-stroke dealt in the Battle of the Marne was to turn the flank of the German armies, which were turning the French front, by sweeping behind them and cutting their communications. For that purpose General Maunoury's Sixth Army was brought up from Lorraine and was launched at a favourable moment in a brilliant attack on Kluck. If it had had the support of a strong force at Lille—which the Germans did not occupy till many weeks later—its onslaught might have produced decisive results. Kluck's whole army might have been destroyed.

The Battle of the Marne did not issue in the complete defeat of the Germans for which the French Staff had hoped, but it was nevertheless fatal to the German plans. The Germans failed for two great reasons of strategy. Their famous Staff imagined that the French and British Armies were beaten and demoralised when they were nothing of the kind, and, filled with contempt for them, it failed to concentrate all possible force for the decisive battle. It allowed the German Emperor to waste troops in a futile attack on Nancy; it left other troops in Belgium engaged in duties of minor importance; and it also detached an army corps to East Prussia, where the advance of the Russians had caused panic. The corps sent to East Prussia played the rôle of Grouchy in the Waterloo campaign. It arrived in the east after the peril had passed, and the Russians had been decisively defeated at Tannenberg. Its presence might well have turned the scale on the Marne, where for days the issue was

GENERAL GEORG VON DER MARWITZ.
Commanded an army in the great German offensive of March, 1918. He was one of the first German generals to receive the Ordre Pour le Mérite in the Great War.

in suspense, and according to Kluck its absence was fatal to the success of his army. Thus, in the crisis of 1914, Russia helped to save France and Europe, though with better co-operation between the Russian armies the disaster at Tannenberg might have been averted.

After the Marne, the Battle of the Aisne proved conclusively that to break through a strongly entrenched line held by good troops a marked superiority in numbers and material was necessary. The Germans had now failed in their original plan, which was to outflank the French armies and swiftly crush France, but they still had superiority in numbers and an enormous advantage in their machine-guns, heavy guns, and strong positions. The French Staff attempted to dislodge them by working round their right flank with fresh troops brought from Lorraine and the British army which was transferred to Flanders. The effort failed, partly because it was made with insufficient force and partly because the German Staff had been quick to realise the position, and had simultaneously attempted to turn the French left flank by throwing in new formations and pushing with great determination for the Channel coast. By this strategy it hoped to strike a decisive blow.

By a strange coincidence each Staff struck at the other in the same quarter and at the same time, and the forces which they set in movement actually neutralised each other. The Germans had secretly organised four fresh reserve corps, the Twenty-first, Twenty-second, Twenty-sixth, and Twenty-seventh. These they hurried towards Eastern Flanders and the neighbourhood of Ypres in October, 1914. In this quarter there were now twelve German corps moving against seven allied corps, and the Germans were in such strength that disaster for the Allies seemed inevitable. The German plan was to break through the weak allied front near Ypres, cut off the French and Belgian troops to the north of that place, and to reach Dunkirk, Calais, and Boulogne. It was almost attained. In the words of Lord French, "October 31st and November 1st (1914) will remain for ever memorable in the history of our country, for during those two days no more than one thin and straggling line of tired-out British soldiers stood between the Empire and its practical ruin as a first-class Power." But at the fateful moment the British troops held, and French support was generously given. A second time Germany lost all hope of a speedy end of the war in the west when success seemed almost within her grasp.

General von Kluck.   F.-M. von Woyrsch.   The Crown Prince of Bavaria.   General Gröner.   General von Carlowitz.
SOME OF THE MEN WHO COMMANDED GERMANY'S MILITARY MIGHT.

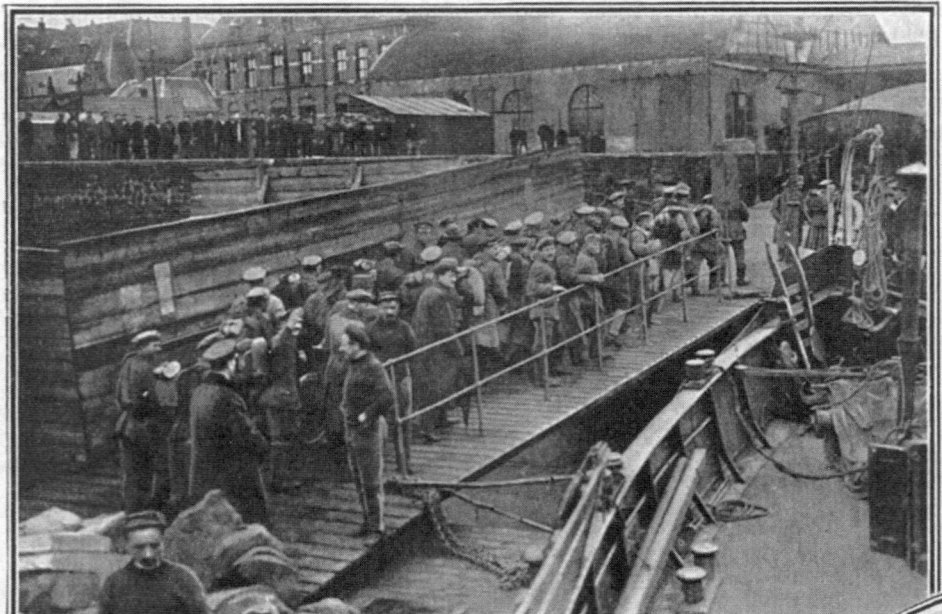

WHEN GERMANY'S ARMY WAS BREAKING.
German soldiers at Flushing in the autumn of 1918. They had deserted
from the Army and escaped into Holland, where they were put under arrest.
In circle : A group of soldiers escaping into Holland by boat shortly before
the armistice brought hostilities to an end.

when troops and ammunition were diverted to the Dardanelles that might have been better used on the western front. British strategy committed the same mistake as the German Staff; it wavered between two objectives, and struck at neither point with adequate force.

The French plan in 1915 was to break through the German front at Arras and in Champagne, but though repeated efforts were made to carry it out it was defeated because of the French lack of sufficient numbers and heavy guns. Only the gradual arrival of the new British armies, then slowly forming in Great Britain, could give the preponderance of strength required, and the concentration of great British forces in France was grievously delayed by the Dardanelles diversion. This was undertaken because the British Cabinet

One of the reasons why the Allies failed in their attempts to outflank the Germans and deal a crushing blow was that the Germans held the interior lines. Their front had already assumed the shape of a semicircle in France projecting into enemy territory, and they could move forces across it quicker than the Allies could move them round. This advantage they retained up to the very end of the war. It was an asset of enormous value to them, and one of the explanations of the constant failure of allied strategy.

When German troops were moved from Lorraine to Flanders — as the whole of Prince Rupert's army was transferred in 1914—the distance they had to cover was about two hundred miles, while the French troops which were moved from the same quarter to the same destination had to march or travel by train over three hundred miles. The Germans could always arrive first, and this enabled them to defeat many good plans. Again, the central position of their country and their forces, lying between the Allies in the west, Russia in the east, and the Balkan and Turkish fronts in the south-east, with direct communications and numerous railways, gave them the power of moving troops to and fro between these fronts as they were required. If the Allies decided to reinforce one of the eastern fronts, the Germans could always send countervailing reinforce-

Wavering British strategy ments quicker by their direct routes. By ably using this advantage they prevented the collapse of Turkey for three years, and upheld the tottering German dynasty in Bulgaria. With it they were able to crush Serbia before French and British troops could arrive in the necessary strength.

When the two opponents came to rest in the west, and when the trench lines ran from the sea near Ostend to the Swiss frontier, the question was raised what strategy was to be followed by the Allies. Sir John French was anxious for a strong offensive on the Flanders coast to clear that coast in combination with the British Navy. It was a project that had a real prospect of success if it had been pursued with the entire British strength. It would have signally hampered the Germans in their submarine war, and probably have prevented their aeroplane attacks upon Great Britain. The French Staff, however, was against this plan, for reasons which seemed excellent at the time, and the British Government was half-hearted in its support, arguing that sufficient troops and ammunition were not available for its execution. The answer to this argument was given a few months later

did not believe in the possibility of breaking the German entrenched line in the west. The repeated failures on the part of the Allies arose not only from want of tactical and strategical skill, but also in large part from lack of ammunition and the proper kind of ammunition — high-explosive shell—which was not provided until Lord Northcliffe, in 1915, boldly attacked the Asquith Cabinet and Lord Kitchener for their failure to comply with the demands of the Army at the front.

The Dardanelles Campaign was a failure because it violated every principle of strategy. Surprise is vital in an attempt of this kind, and the Turks were put on their guard by futile bombardments of the Gallipoli forts. To these bombardments Lord Fisher, the professional head of the Admiralty at that date, was strongly opposed, but instead of listening to its strategist the Government took other advice. An adverse report on any attempt to force the Dardanelles had been drawn up long before the war by the Imperial Defence Committee, based on careful military and naval study. This was disregarded. It is one of the axioms of naval war that ships cannot contend with forts; the Cabinet either knew nothing of the laws of war or thought they had no application in this case. An expeditionary force landing on an enemy's coast needs a harbour. There was none on the Gallipoli Peninsula, and the disembarkation of men and stores there was always carried out with difficulty; indeed, it became impossible in bad weather.

The British force which was employed in this unhappy operation was large—totalling 468,000 men, of whom from first to last over 200,000 were killed, wounded, or invalided. Though the attack on the Dardanelles was primarily undertaken to take Turkish pressure off Russia, and did this to some extent, the same result might have been more effectually obtained with far less sacrifice in other ways. There was no reason why Allenby's campaign should not have been carried out in 1915 with Egypt as a secure base. A violent attack on Palestine and Syria would have diverted Turkish armies from Armenia and would not have demanded so large a British force. Or, again, a determined offensive on a large scale in the west with the additional troops detached to Gallipoli, might have proved most effective of all by compelling the Germans to withdraw divisions from the Russian front.

The failure at Gallipoli, inevitable from the first in view of the manner in which the campaign was conducted, led directly to the entry of Bulgaria into the war, and, far from relieving the strain on the Allies, increased their danger. There is no stronger example in history of the misapplication

of resources. And it is probable that the diversion from Poland of a Russian army, which was to have co-operated with the British but never put in its appearance, was in part responsible for the disasters of 1915 in Galicia and Poland from which the Russian Army never really recovered.

The Dardanelles diversion was followed by the Salonika diversion, for which there was far better reason. Salonika was at least a fair harbour and a tolerable base, though the climate was bad, and it was no uncommon thing for half the strength of the battalions there to be on the sick list. But here there were vital strategic aims—to secure the support of the Serbian Army and to prevent Germany from pushing south in the Balkans and forcing Greece to join her with the complicity of that treacherous sovereign King Constantine. If Salonika had not been held by a strong allied force the Greek bases would have passed under German control and would have

been of inestimable service to the German submarines, enabling them to close the Adriatic and Eastern Mediterranean to allied shipping. Serbia would have been wiped out and her Army lost. Egypt would have been sundered from Great Britain by German and Austrian submarines in the Mediterranean.

So far back as the winter of 1914-15 the French Government was anxious for the despatch of an allied force to Salonika, to co-operate with the Serbians, who had just inflicted a crushing defeat on the Austrians. Its proposal was so to time the movements of the Allies that a great advance on Austria might begin at the moment when Italy entered the war. Had its plan been accepted the Bulgarians would hardly have ventured to join the Germans, and Rumania would probably have thrown in her lot with the Allies in the spring of 1915, before the defeat of Russia was complete. It is also possible that the Greek Government, despite the treachery of King Constantine, would have joined the Allies.

A landing at Salonika thus held out great prospects of important success in early 1915, and was a far more hopeful operation than the Dardanelles Campaign. The chief difficulty was the question of transport in the wild country of the Balkan peninsula. There, as in Spain, small armies were defeated and large armies were liable to starve. But in 1915 the Serbian railway system was intact, and by it communications could have been opened up with Rumania and Russia.

The French Government returned to its old project in August, 1915, when it decided to send a French force to Salonika and to place General Sarrail in command of it. General Joffre and Lord Kitchener were both hostile to the plan, as they were preparing great offensives in France and at Gallipoli for which they wanted all available troops; and in the end, when the Serbian retreat began, Sarrail found himself with only three divisions (two French and one British), a force which was inadequate to give effective aid to the Serbians.

The evacuation of Gallipoli after the unfortunate battles of August, 1915, was inevitable, and when it was carried out, Sarrail's army was strengthened with troops withdrawn from that bloodstained peninsula. Yet Lord Kitchener to the last opposed the Salonika Campaign, and, at the conference which took place at Calais on December 4th, 1915, between the heads

THE KAISER'S SUBTERRANEAN RETREAT AT SPA.,
One of the entrances to a subterranean passage made at the Kaiser's Castle, near Spa, when the War Lord was staying there, showing one of its massive iron doors. The passage was made for the Kaiser's safety in case of bombardment from the air. In circle: The other entrance to the tunnel.

of the British and French Governments and their military advisers, declared that he would resign rather than provide troops for it. His opposition was only overcome with great difficulty.

Having settled to send a force to Salonika, the Allies ought to have taken the necessary political measures to support it. Sarrail, the nominal Commander-in-Chief at Salonika, was not recognised as such by the British Government, so that there was no unity in the command. He saw clearly enough that his hands would be tied and that his force would be strategically useless unless he could be certain of the Greek Government, but his view, which after-events showed to be perfectly sound, was not accepted by the Allied Governments. Unity of command and unity of diplomacy were both necessary for allied victory; neither was attained for many months until a long series of reverses or repulses had driven home the need for concentrated effort and central control.

Sarrail's strategy was thus handicapped from the first. He was an able and daring soldier who had merited the admiration of the Allies by

Difficulty of Sarrail's position the tenacity with which he defended Verdun in the opening weeks of the war. But he had the reputation of being an extreme politician, and when he came into collision with the intriguing and treacherous Constantine it was supposed that he was dominated by republican or Socialist prejudices. The Russian Government vetoed Constantine's removal; the British Government was lukewarm and inert. Sarrail had hoped to secure the support of a purified Greece and of a powerful Greek army, whereas he found that his rear and his communications were threatened by Greek troops acting under Constantine's orders, and, as he had every reason to suspect, in close collusion with the German Staff. He was paralysed at the critical moment because the Allies could not understand that strategy and policy must march hand in hand.

In July, 1916, Sarrail's army had risen to respectable figures, even when allowance was made for the large number of men suffering from malaria and fever. He had rather over 300,000 effectives, of whom 100,000 were French, 96,000 British, 85,000 Serbians, 20,000 Italians, and 12,000 Russians, available for a determined effort to break the line from Berlin to Constantinople and Bagdad. Moreover, Rumania was preparing to enter the war, and she had nearly 500,000 men on

paper. The exact manner in which this force was to be employed was a strategic question of vital importance. The Allies proposed early in 1916 that Rumania should attack Bulgaria with her main forces and join hands with the Allied Army at Salonika. Thus the German route to the East would be broken and communications would be opened through the Balkans with Russia. Under this proposal a moderate Rumanian force, supported by ten Russian divisions, was to cover the north of Rumania from Austrian attack.

The Rumanians rejected the plan, which was undoubtedly

LOOTED MATERIAL RECOVERED FROM THE GERMANS.
General view of a dump of material collected by the British near Namur. Much of it had been looted by the Germans and had been either abandoned before the armistice or handed back after it.

sound. They insisted on invading and seizing Transylvania, and many weeks of fruitless discussion elapsed without any decision being reached. Finally, on July 1st, 1916, the rapid progress of the Russian armies under Brussiloff led the Rumanians to determine on immediate hostilities. On July 27th a treaty was signed by which a fatal half-measure was accepted. Rumania agreed to attack Bulgaria with 150,000 men, provided that fifteen days before this attack opened—it is said to have been timed to take place on August 25th—the Allied Army at Salonika began an offensive with all its force against the Bulgarians. The bulk of the Rumanian

GERMAN PRISONERS LENDING A HAND AT THE RESTORATION OF PLUNDER.
Bringing in some copper vessels which had been saved from the smelters, and (right) German prisoners helping at the unloading of a barge of picks and shovels at one of the dumps on the banks of the Meuse.

Army was still to invade Transylvania. Orders were given to General Sarrail to attack the Bulgarians on August 10th, but he did not move. His own explanation of his inaction was that the British and Italians would not remove Constantine, and that he could not advance unless his rear and lines of communication were secure, and that they could not be secure so long as Constantine's troops commanded vital strategic points near Salonika.

He also alleged that at the last moment the Rumanian Government refused to provide any troops for operations

CAMOUFLAGED MOTOR SEARCHLIGHT.
German prisoners hauling a seemingly derelict motor-car to a booty dump in Belgium. It was really a searchlight disguised to appear something other than it was, and capable of rapid movement to any required position.

against Bulgaria and decided to send all its forces into Transylvania.

The collapse of Rumania was thus due in part to her own faulty strategy and in part to the diplomacy of the Allies at Salonika. Though General Sarrail was removed from command subsequently, after he had obstinately refused to attack with vigour, and after the disasters to Rumania, and though his successor carried through with the most brilliant success the campaign against Bulgaria, the conditions had then vitally changed. Greece had been purified; Constantine had been deposed; M. Venizelos had returned to power and

had placed the aid of the Greek Army and Navy at the disposal of the Allies. The very measures which General Sarrail had urged had been carried out.

To return from the eastern diversions of the allied strategists to the west, when 1916 opened the Allies were at least rid of their Gallipoli commitments. But the new British armies were not yet ready for the field, and the wish was not to employ them until their training and equipment were complete. For that reason, though preparations for a great allied offensive were begun in the Somme region early in 1916, the date of the offensive was postponed till the summer. The Germans gained an inkling of what was coming, and determined to strike first, and once more to seize the initiative. About November, 1915, a council of war was held, at which, after much hesitation and against the advice of Hindenburg and Ludendorff, both of whom were for continuing the attack upon Russia and pulverising her, the Kaiser, at General Falkenhayn's instance, decided to attempt to break through the French front at Verdun.

The situation at Verdun had aroused great uneasiness in France. A very gallant and distinguished officer, Colonel Driant, who commanded a section on this front and died heroic- **Battle of** ally in the subsequent battle, visited **Verdun** Paris in November, 1915, and made it known that the defences there were in a most unsatisfactory condition. General Gallieni, who was then Minister of War, was so distressed by the news that he immediately urged General Joffre to make certain that two lines of defence were properly organised at Verdun. Two days later, on December 18th, 1915, he was assured by General Joffre that instructions had been given for the thorough organisation of the Verdun defences, and that, notwithstanding the shortage of barbed-wire, the two lines were adequate to arrest attacks. But on January 20th, 1916, when General Castelnau inspected Verdun, he found the works there quite inefficient, and ordered measures for their improvement to be taken without delay. It was too late. The arrival of French engineers and pioneers to reconstruct the fortifications accelerated the German attack. Thus, when the Battle of Verdun opened, there was really little to stop the Germans, though the world generally believed that Verdun was an impregnable fortress. The weakness of the defences became known in French political circles, and led to much criticism of General Joffre and the French Staff.

WORK AT SOME OF THE BOOTY DUMPS IN BELGIUM SET FREE.
German prisoners, under the direction of British soldiers, loading barges with timber from one of the big dumps established along the Meuse, and (right) prisoners stacking German trench stoves at another dump for war booty and recovered loot.

The losses of the two armies in the battles there were about equal, but the French, with their smaller population, suffered more acutely, especially as the German military offensive was accompanied by a psychological offensive, carried out by such agents as Bolo and Almeyreda, who insisted that France was bleeding to death while the British Army looked on. Both offensives were defeated—the one through the heroism of the French troops, the other through the noble steadfastness of the French nation, which under the heartbreaking strain never lost its faith in victory. But for a time the danger was appalling.

This offensive had a great strategic effect. It compelled the British Staff to use the new British armies before they were ready for the field and before the supply of ammunition was plentiful, so that throughout the Somme battle, in Sir Douglas Haig's words, "the expenditure of artillery ammunition had to be watched with the greatest care." But if Verdun was to be saved there was no choice. The pressure upon it must be relieved by an offensive at some other point. The British Staff would have preferred to attack the German positions from the north and from Arras, as they were attacked in August, 1918. The French Staff did not favour this plan, which would have rendered French co-operation more difficult. It therefore proposed to attack with twenty-eight British and thirty-nine French divisions on a front of forty miles from Hébuterne, nine miles north of Albert, to Lassigny.

Effect of German attack at Verdun

This attack on a wide front would have given a better chance of breaking through the German fortified lines than the offensive on a much narrower front, which was finally carried out. The reduction of the width of front was necessitated by the diversion of a large number of French units to Verdun, so that only twelve, instead of thirty-nine, French divisions, were available when the Battle of the Somme opened on July 1st, 1916. The prospect of decisive success was thus correspondingly diminished. The battle, nevertheless, had important results. It wore down the German forces. It enabled the British Staff to improve its methods, though the price paid—412,000 British casualties—was grievously high. It shook the German faith in the entrenched line and destroyed what prestige the German failure at Verdun had left to General Falkenhayn. It led to his replacement by Hindenburg, who chose Ludendorff as his right-hand man, and to a complete change in German strategy. William II. now resolved to stand on the defensive in the west and continue the offensive in the east. To enable the Germans to hold in the west, immense new works were constructed by Hindenburg with forced labour.

When the German Staff decided to stand on the defensive in the west, at the close of 1916, it does not seem to have understood that time was against it. It gave Great Britain the months she required to construct Tanks in large numbers, to increase her armies till they numbered 7,500,000 men, to augment her output of munitions, and, above all, to make the weight of her sea-power felt. The naval blockade had a cumulative effect. It required time to produce result, but with each month and year that passed it became more and more deadly and bore on the German people with greater weight, until its pressure finally forced them to their desperate submarine campaign. The supposed impregnability of the Hindenburg lines proved a complete delusion when they were vigorously attacked by skilled troops with Tanks and abundant artillery. But for the outbreak of the Revolution in Russia in early 1917, Germany must have sustained a decisive defeat in that year. As it was, the Russian collapse brought her temporary relief and enabled her to stave off fate.

German disregard of moral claims

In deciding upon the submarine war the German Staff repeated the immense error which it had made in violating Belgian neutrality. It disregarded moral claims, and its judgment was wrong. The German Admiralty argued that the internal situation of Germany was so difficult and dangerous owing to the blockade, that, whatever the risks of the submarine war, it must be pressed as the sure means of forcing Great Britain to conclude peace. It was supported in this view by many of the business leaders and professors. Thus one of the heads of the great Diskonto-Gesellschaft reported that war with the United States would probably follow, but the German position being so bad, that risk must be faced. He imagined that America's entry into the war would have little effect and would only lead to temporary estrangement. The German Admiralty guaranteed the German Army against the movement of American troops from the United States on any large scale, and it gave definite pledges that by a certain date Great Britain's power of resistance would be overcome and the British Government would be forced to sue for peace.

The entry of the United States into the war was treated with real or affected derision by the German Staff. That Staff placed childlike faith in the promises of the German Admiralty, and also argued that some years would elapse before America could train an effective army for operations in Europe. Strategists with a less prejudiced judgment recognised that the action of the United States rendered victory only a question of time for the Allies—if they could overcome the submarine.

The reason why allied strategy had so far failed to win decisive victory was that the Allies did not possess a sufficient superiority over the Germans in well-trained troops. To achieve success it is necessary to be stronger than the enemy at the point where the blow is delivered, and to be stronger to a considerable degree. In 1915 and 1916 the British forces were inferior in training and experience to the Germans, if the French were equal or superior to the Germans. By 1917 the British had reached the same level of skill as the French, and were superior man for man to the Germans. An ally with ample reserves of men could hold large parts of the line with comparatively inexperienced troops, and set free trained and experienced French and British troops for the strategic plans of a great soldier. The United States was such an ally, and the fact that American troops could be utilised on the western front—whereas Russian troops earlier in the war were tied down to the east by the inaccessibility of Russia—increased the value of American aid.

Significance of America's aid

For great strategic plans to be carried out with success central directions and unity of command are essential. Under General Joffre there was a working understanding between the British and French Armies, and the germ of a central command in the allied conferences which sat at Chantilly from 1915 onwards. But the authority of this conference was limited. Nor were the Allies prepared unreservedly to place their armies at the disposition of any French officer, however distinguished, who was himself subject to the pressure of the constantly changing Governments and parties in France. To take the case of Great Britain as typical, she had to defend India, Egypt, and the Persian Gulf, and to provide military support in the form of garrisons for her Navy at the naval bases. Her soldiers had for generations studied the special problems involved, and were familiar with them. If she had placed her Army unreservedly at the disposal of the French High Command, what security was there that proper attention would be paid to these needs of hers? She might fear a tendency to concentrate all the British forces in France, and to leave the Mediterranean and Near and Middle East bare, and the vital artery of the Suez Canal ill-protected.

The allocation of force in war between the various fields is one of the difficult and delicate questions of strategy, and in the Great War within the ranks of the British Army it led to endless controversies between the Western and Eastern Schools. The Western School was for the offensive in France and the stripping of the minor and secondary fields. The Eastern School emphasised the importance of striking down Germany from her rear by a vigorous offensive against Turkey, Bulgaria, and Austria, while economising force by standing generally on the defensive in France. It says much for the loyalty and comradeship of the French that there were so few difficulties between the two great armies in the west when the possibilities of disagreement were so serious.

The operations of 1917 in the west were marked by the growing mastery of the methods of war shown by the British Army. The German retreat on the Somme front was, it is true, carried out without molestation, owing to weather

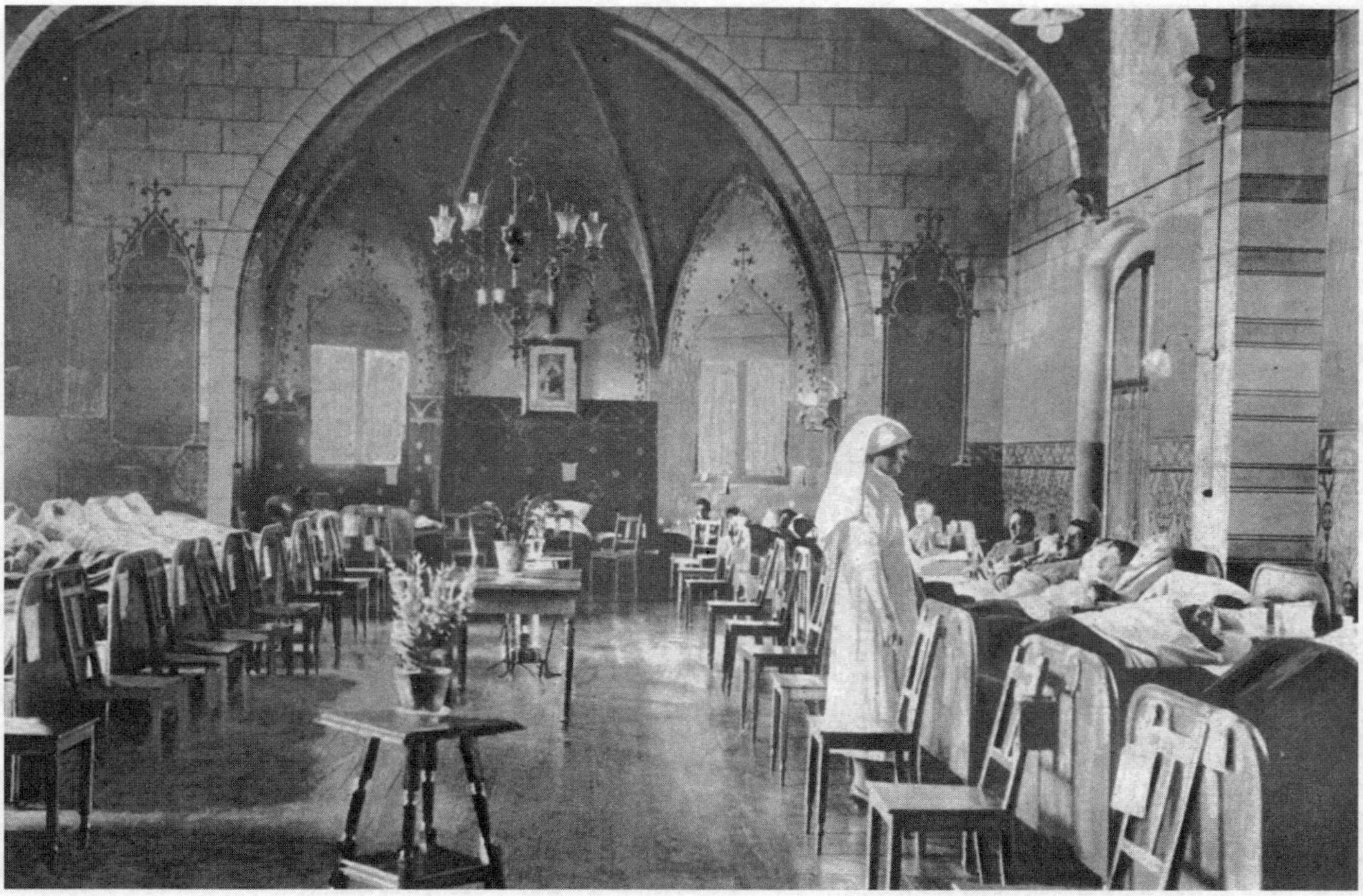

British wounded in a Bonn chapel: It had been converted into a hospital by the Germans.

Education in the British Army of Occupation, 1919: Learning chemistry at Bonn University.

British searchlight on the Rhine: For guarding against night smuggling across the river.

German carters showing their papers before being permitted to enter the British Rhine zone.

In case of need: British artillery parade on the banks of the occupied Rhine.

The British in Cologne: General Rogers inspecting the German police of that city.

Admiral Fremantle, Deputy Chief of Naval Staff, visiting the British flotilla at Cologne.

General Mangin (right) and Commander Acheson (third from right) at a naval review on the Rhine.

conditions. But the Battles of Arras and Messines were admirably conceived, brilliantly executed, and involved losses which were small in comparison with the result achieved. The French Army, however, at this precise moment was weakened by the campaign of sedition which the Germans had planned and financed, hoping doubtless that the French troops would collapse as the Russian Army had done. Nothing of the kind happened, but there were instances of indiscipline, and at Soissons two regiments marched on the station under the Red Flag, declaring their determination to go to Paris and overawe the Chamber. The outbreak was quickly got under by General Pétain, and order was re-established, but it reacted upon the operations.

As the year 1917 advanced the German Staff lost its faith in the submarine and was driven, as the only means of avoiding certain defeat, to a series of great offensives on land, for which it could now find men by withdrawing troops from the Russian front. Austria had been assured in January, 1917, that the ruthless submarine campaign would certainly end the war by the summer of that year. Her anxiety for peace was such that the first offensive had to be directed against the Italians, in the hope of crushing them and compelling them to come to terms. The German Staff finally decided to penetrate the Italian front at Caporetto, thus menacing the retreat of the Italian forces on the Carso, and then to turn on them and destroy them. Careful preparation for its attack was made by the German propaganda, which spread reports that the Italians were being exploited by the British. On the section which had been selected for the final attack, Austrian divisions from the Russian front with a Bolshevist spirit were stationed and encouraged to enter into communications with the Italian troops. The men on either side at this point agreed not to attack or fire upon each other, but if an offensive was ordered, to advance and throw down their arms.

On the eve of the attack the German Staff withdrew the Austrians and replaced them with Brandenburg divisions, who advanced against the Italians with fury, **Enemy offensive** and, when they acted as had been agreed, **in Italy** shot them down or had them marched off to prison camps and the mines. The Italians had never intended to sell their country, but the result of their conduct was that the Italian front was broken and the Italian armies were threatened with gigantic disaster. The Germans came near complete success. But at this critical moment the courage and devotion of picked Italian troops held up the advance of the Germans and Austrians, and gained time for a stand on the Piave, where the Italians fought with magnificent heroism, and stopped the Germans finally. After this great feat the arrival of eleven British and French divisions of high fighting quality removed any danger of a fresh German offensive on the Piave line.

It was natural that when the Allies moved not far short of 250,000 men to Italy, the Germans should determine to carry out a great offensive in France, where, they argued, that the allied forces must have been greatly weakened. From the moment when the Germans began their offensive in Italy, American troops ought to have been hurried to Europe to serve as a strategic reserve. No measure of the kind was taken. The offensive in Italy opened in October, 1917, in which month only 38,000 Americans were transported to Europe, and in the months immediately following the figures were 23,000 for November, 48,000 for December, 46,000 for January, and 48,000 for February, a total of 165,000 men for the four months, which may be compared with the 244,000 men embarked in May, 1918. The neglect of this important precaution was probably due to the absence of unity of command and imperfect appreciation of the danger in the United States. In Great Britain and France there was intense anxiety. Both had almost exhausted their last reserves of men, and, torn and bleeding, they could do little more.

The Germans in their great offensive of 1918 struck firstly at the British Army because they hoped to inflict on it an annihilating disaster, and thus to force Great Britain to make peace. As the submarine campaign had failed and the training of the American millions advanced steadily, the German Staff saw clearly enough that defeat was certain if the British could not be crushed on land. Ludendorff's strategy was simple; it was to drive "pockets" in the allied front and then to widen them till they joined and till the British and French Armies were forced apart or driven by retreat to uncover the Channel ports and Paris. He fatally underestimated the fighting power of the British Army, and left 200,000 men in the east, but he had a large force of specially trained divisions available, and he trusted to the effect of surprise. He complained afterwards that the main reason of the failure of his operations was the bad tactics of the German subordinate leaders, who attacked in too close formations and suffered enormous loss.

In the offensive of March 21st there was a moment when Ludendorff came very near success, and if he had resolutely pushed for Amiens he might have reached that great railway junction. As it was, the German onslaught melted away before the stubborn resistance of the British, and finally came to a standstill precisely as it had done at Ypres years before. There was this serious obstacle to a decisive German success.

A study of the later battles of the war leads to the conclusion that without a marked **Importance of** advantage in the air no great results can be **air-mastery** obtained. At no point did the Germans dominate the air, and the British aircraft in consequence worked such havoc with their communications and supply routes as to paralyse the energy of their advance and gain time when it was most vital.

The catastrophic retreat of the British Fifth Army was a blessing in disguise because it brought the Allies' acceptance of General Foch as supreme commander of the British, French, and American Armies on the western front on March 26th, and at last permitted a great strategist to deal with the problem of defeating Germany. The strong points in Foch were his knowledge of war and his heroic confidence and calm. In two decisive moments of the struggle he had earlier played a glorious part. At Ypres, if he did not, as has been alleged, persuade Sir John French to make the final stand which issued in the British victory, his energy and enthusiasm reacted on the British commander as did the confidence of Sherman on General Grant. On the Piave in November, 1917, his voice was raised for standing firm, and again exercised the same energising influence.

In the terrible strain of the German advance Foch maintained this unruffled calm. "His Headquarters," says a French friend, "was the temple of faith." And at Doullens, on the day when the news of his promotion was brought to him, he is said to have pointed with his stick to a certain position on a map of the front with the words "I shall stop them there." His strategy was, first, to gain time by fighting a defensive battle with the very minimum of force, thus exhausting the German armies and increasing his fresh reserves, and then, when the cream was skimmed off the German fighting divisions, to pass suddenly to the offensive at the right minute, after the maximum of American troops and of British reinforcements had **The man and** arrived. This, as Napoleon said, "is the most **the moment** delicate of all operations of war, and the proper moment is only perceived by a man of great talent." The history of the closing months of the war proves with what mastery Foch performed it.

He had, it is true, the finest instruments at his command. The British Army under Sir Douglas Haig was an incomparable weapon, now supplied with Tanks, artillery, ammunition, and aircraft in abundance, though its aeroplanes still left something to be desired in design. The French Army was only second to the British, equal in the superb quality of its troops and the magnificent standard of its generalship; inferior in nothing but its material equipment. The American Army was superlative in physique and in the eager spirit of its men, and its numbers were overwhelming; each month from 200,000 to 250,000 of its troops arrived. Foch did not engage his reserves prematurely. The second German offensive menaced Ypres and forced the British back in a vital sector; the third offensive threatened Paris as the first had threatened Amiens. But he held his head and waited patiently.

The supreme crisis of the war came in June, 1918, when the

Germans reached Château-Thierry. Never since the days before the First Battle of the Marne had they been so near the capital of France. Foch knew that their reserves were falling as fast as the allied reserves rose. The situation, though grave, was full of hope. As President Kruger once said, the tortoise must be allowed to put out its head in order to cut it off. The German fresh divisions in reserve were seventy-eight on March 21st; on May 27th the figures had fallen to sixty-two. It was still necessary to wait, but by July 15th, when Ludendorff ordered his last offensive, the total of fresh German reserve divisions was only forty-three, and Foch felt that once the Germans were well engaged, the hour had arrived for him to open the final counter-offensive.

With admirable prevision he judged where the new attack would come, and concentrated all his available reserve upon the counter-stroke. Judgment and faith—these are the secrets of strategy as of success in most other departments of human life—and he showed them. He allowed the Crown Prince to cross the Marne, and then on July 18th came his riposte, terrible and unexpected, on the flank of the German advance. At this moment, as the French Staff has since told the world, the Germans disposed of 12,500 field-guns and **Secrets of strategic success** 7,860 heavy guns, but already, owing to the enormous consumption of material in the previous offensives, it was becoming difficult for them to replace weapons and men. Their strength in machine-guns had fallen somewhat, but was still 95,000, of which 35,000 were of heavy pattern. Their railway material and their motor-lorries showed serious signs of wear and tear. It was the last effort of which they were capable, and it would not have been made if Ludendorff had not once more profoundly misjudged the situation of both the British and French Armies and believed that they were all but broken, and would collapse before another vigorous blow.

Foch's first counter-stroke on July 18th was a terrible surprise, but even more terrible was the second attack, which the British opened on August 8th. This had been planned by Sir Douglas Haig and Sir John Monash, the commander of the Australian Corps, and it showed the truth of Foch's saying, that "victory is an inclined plane and, provided that movement is not stopped, it advances with ever-increasing speed." Foch's strategy now was to engage the Germans on every part of the vast front, to leave them no quiet sectors, to wear and exhaust them to the uttermost, until new armies composed of American troops and French troops, which were held in reserve, could deal the crowning blow.

As it happened, that blow was never **Inclined plane** delivered. The preliminary battles so **of victory** shattered the Germans that they collapsed earlier than Foch had dared to hope. Under the continuous attacks their fresh divisions sank to twenty-one on September 26th, when their position was already desperate. A day later the British broke through the Hindenburg line in one of the most wonderful battles of the war; on September 29th Ludendorff telephoned to the German Chancellor warning him "of the extreme gravity of the military position, and inviting him to demand, as pressingly as possible, an armistice which might enable him to gain time and temporarily re-establish the situation."

One of the remarkable facts of the series of battles which followed Foch's counter-stroke was that in the war of movement the Allies showed a great superiority to the Germans. In some of the battles they had no advantage of numbers; but their equipment was so good, their spirit was so high, and the skill with which they were handled was so great that they seemed able to achieve impossibilities. By October 11th the number of fresh divisions in the German reserve had sunk to seven, and Foch then ordered the Allies to attack in every direction with the utmost determination, stating that it was "impossible" for the enemy with his worn and tired troops

AFTER THE TRIUMPHANT CONCLUSION OF THE MESOPOTAMIAN CAMPAIGN.
Grand-stand erected by a British bridging train on ground which a year earlier had been the scene of the Turks' last fight before they left Bagdad. The British troops, their great work as a fighting force accomplished, were able to seek recreation in the national sport of racing in novel surroundings.

ARRIVAL OF BULGARIA'S WHITE FLAG OF SURRENDER AT A BRITISH HEADQUARTERS.

Arrival of a Bulgarian envoy at a British corps headquarters towards the end of September, 1918. The episode was described by an eye-witness thus: "Early one morning a motor was heard approaching the camp, and a curious-looking vehicle presently made its appearance, driven by a Bulgarian chauffeur and flying a large white flag. The car had two passengers, a Bulgarian officer and a British infantry captain. . . The Bulgar had driven in under the white flag to our outposts at Kasturino, and was promptly escorted on to corps headquarters. . . The general arrived at this moment, and conferred for a few moments with the envoy. At the close of the conversation the latter saluted, which the general acknowledged by offering his hand."

to rally and meet any serious assault. By November 11th, the date of the armistice, the fresh German divisions had sunk to only two. Their companies had fallen from one hundred and twenty to fifty, though twenty-three of their divisions had been dissolved. The strength of their divisions had declined from 8,000 bayonets to 2,000, or even 1,000 men. Munitions were lacking; their artillery was reduced to 9,000 field and 4,500 heavy guns, many of which were in deplorable order. Their losses in prisoners alone had risen to 360,000 men, while their killed and wounded since the opening of the German offensive cannot have been much less than 1,000,000 men. Of their artillery, 6,500 guns had been taken, with vast quantities of material of all kinds.

It was at this juncture, when the German Government appealed for peace, that Foch was ready to deal his decisive blow. On a front east of the Moselle, between Pont-à-Mousson and Lunéville, he had assembled twenty fresh French divisions and six American divisions (each of these with the strength of about two French or British divisions), making a total force of over 400,000 men. They were to have advanced north-eastward, isolating Metz and striking the two great German lines of railway communication—Thionville-Saarbruck-Rastatt and Metz-Saarburg-Strasbourg—by which the beaten armies were retreating. Simultaneously, the Second American Army, 350,000 strong, was to have marched on a broad front from near Stenay to Verdun upon the railways north of Metz; and **Foch's great plan** on the rest of the front the Allies—British, Belgians, and French—were to have pressed the bruised and broken divisions of the German Army with the utmost determination, holding them while these two immense allied armies struck their rear.

The German High Command had nothing whatever of fighting value to oppose to Foch's new offensive in Lorraine, and in November, learning something of the French plans, it began to withdraw its troops and material from Metz. Had the war lasted a few days longer it would have been left with only two railways—the lines through Liège and through Visé—to withdraw its armies in Belgium and manœuvre them against Foch. Its task would have been impossible. The roads were choked with waggons, guns, and motor-lorries, evacuating material and plunder from Belgium. The railway plant was breaking down. The German troops were degenerating into mobs. It was in these conditions that Germany surrendered. Even when the armistice gave her rest from attack, order was not re-established for a week; the withdrawal of her troops **Triumph of** was only carried out with immense difficulty, **allied strategy** and a vast quantity of material (including property stolen from the Belgians) had to be transported over Dutch lines, by a singular complaisance of the Dutch Government, to get it away from the Allies.

Such was the issue of four months of attack directed by Foch's strategy in the west. It proved the utter falsity of the German Government's assertion that its surrender was due to political reasons. The German military situation on the western front was desperate. And, as if that was not enough to compel submission, the German Empire was suddenly menaced with attack on a new front through the collapse of its allies, at a time when it had lost all the advantages of the central position and interior lines through the defective condition of its railways. Had the Germans fought on they would have been invaded through Austria, and they would have been caught between two enormous allied armies —the Franco-British-American forces on the western front, and the Franco-British-Italian-Serbian-Greek Armies, advancing from Italy and the Balkans. They were unable to meet Foch in the west; they would have been able to spare only the merest handful of troops to resist the triumphant advance of Diaz's Italians and Franchet d'Esperey's half-million men from Salonika.

The allied victories in the west had prepared for the wonderful victories on the Italian and Balkan fronts by holding the German armies and completely demoralising

Germany's allies. Austria, Bulgaria, and Turkey had come to look to Germany for help in every emergency ; they had hitherto regarded the German Army as invincible and the German Staff as impeccable. Now the German Army was in retreat, beaten whenever it stood and delivered battle, and every plan of the German Staff was proved to be wrong. The famous German generals were outmanœuvred, and were helpless against Foch ; the allied campaigns were all co-ordinated and worked on a scientific plan, so that no army was left idle and no front silent.

By a masterly strategy the allied forces on the secondary fronts were held ready until all the German reserves should be involved, until Germany had been compelled to implore the aid of Austrian troops, which was very unwillingly given in September. In that month eight or nine Austrian divisions were moved to France, and there were quickly entangled in the disasters which were befalling the German Army. The withdrawal of these troops facilitated blows in the Near East, and prepared the way for the brilliantly daring a n d successful strategy w i t h w h i c h Franchet d'Esperey struck Bulgaria down and broke the line from Berlin to Constantinople.

Both the great offensives in the east in September, 1918, were intended to be decisive, and both achieved that aim. Franchet d'Esperey, with the Salonika Army, struck at the Bulgarian centre and pierced it at its very strongest point. So complete was the defeat, so great the panic which it caused in Berlin, that the German Staff most reluctantly had to direct seven German divisions upon the Bulgarian front in a last effort to save the Berlin-Constantinople line. The seven divisions arrived too late ; they were weak in number and poor in fighting quality, and they merely went down in the general collapse.

On September 30th Bulgaria abandoned the war, placing her territory and her railways at the disposal of the Allies, and on October 12th the allied armies reached and cut the vital railway. The crumbling of Bulgaria exposed Austria to attack from a new quarter—on the Danube front—and added terribly to the difficulties and anxieties of her command. She was perforce compelled to place there fourteen or fifteen divisions of troops whom she could ill spare, at a time when all her men were wanted on the Italian front.

Salonika and Palestine fronts With one army detached to France, a second army neutralised on the Danube, and her various races in ferment, she lay paralysed, and only waited the impending blow which was to end her existence.

In Palestine, Sir Edmund Allenby's strategy was of the same bold character as Franchet d'Esperey's ; but he struck at the Turkish right, because the country in that direction was best suited to the cavalry operations which he projected. He pierced the Turkish line and passed his cavalry through the gap. The cavalry, without troubling to deal with the remaining Turkish forces on the battle-front, rode straight for the rail-heads and bases well behind the line. It did not pursue, it intercepted. In no campaign had it been used with such insight and with such success. The British and Indian horsemen had reached the main Turkish supply centres and headquarters almost before the Turkish commanders knew what had happened. They moved with extraordinary rapidity, and in five weeks and two days covered no less than five hundred miles—the whole length of Syria.

Not less remarkable in this lightning campaign was the strategic use made of aircraft. It will ever be of importance

in the history of war, as showing what is possible when the command of the air has been secured. The British air force prevented the Turkish from ascertaining the British dispositions at a time when this was of vital importance, bombed all the telephone and telegraph exchanges, disorganised communications during the battle, and cruised continually over the hostile aerodrome, preventing the Turkish machines from leaving the ground. When the Turks broke, every available machine was used to attack them, and the British aircraft acted as a super-cavalry with the most demoralising effect. As the result of these operations the whole of Syria was liberated and the Turkish armies there utterly destroyed in less than six weeks.

What was not less important, Allenby's advance to the Bagdad Railway, o n October 26th, cut the main line of communication with the Turkish army in Mesopotamia, and placed that force in a hopeless position. Its surrender to the British army in Mesopotamia followed as a matter of necessity — one more example of the skilful strategy employed in the final stages of the war. By November 1st the two great British armies in the Near East, with perhaps 300,000 v e t e r a n combatants, led by one of the greatest generals and flushed with success, were available for transfer to Europe. Had the war lasted they, too, might have taken their

GENERAL ALLENBY IN JERUSALEM.
Reception of Sir Edmund Allenby by the Jewish community in Jerusalem on May 24th, 1918, when he was presented with a casket containing the Scroll of the Law.

place in the vast hosts converging on Germany to deal her the final blow. The collapse of the Turkish armies stunned the German public, which had never expected Great Britain to put forth such strength. There were sad comments in Berlin on the supreme skill with which British soldiers had organised and conducted **Increasing strain** this "colonial war." In a secondary **on Germany** campaign, and without drawing heavily on the resources of Great Britain, they had levelled in the dust the once great military power of Turkey.

As each of Germany's allies fell, the strain on her increased cumulatively, and also the difficulty of meeting that strain. It had always been maintained by the Eastern School of strategists in the British Army that the real road to peace lay through Constantinople, Sofia, and Vienna. And now Constantinople and Sofia were in allied hands. The collapse of Austria followed very quickly. Here again the strategy employed was of the boldest character, and resulted in the piercing of the Austrian centre. Lord Cavan's force, which formed the spear-head of the 800,000 Italian army on the Piave, followed Franchet d'Esperey's plan and struck where the Austrians seemed strongest, with even greater success than Franchet d'Esperey, and the Italian Army gained the most stupendous single victory of the war, capturing in one stroke 300,000 prisoners and thousands of guns. It was another Sedan on a far more gigantic scale, and it brought Austria down with a crash.

Thus, at the last, sound strategy, after years of mistakes and of futile efforts, after terrible sacrifices, brought with it one overpowering flood of victory—victory in every field and in every battle. Germany fell because she was surpassed in what she supposed to be her specialty and prerogative—the arts and science of war. She was beaten because the Allies had the better men and the better leaders, and also the clearer insight, which gave those leaders the better weapons. And her fall, once more, whatever her propagandists may profess, was a military, strategic, and tactical rout, and not due to any Machiavellian manœuvres of allied politicians.

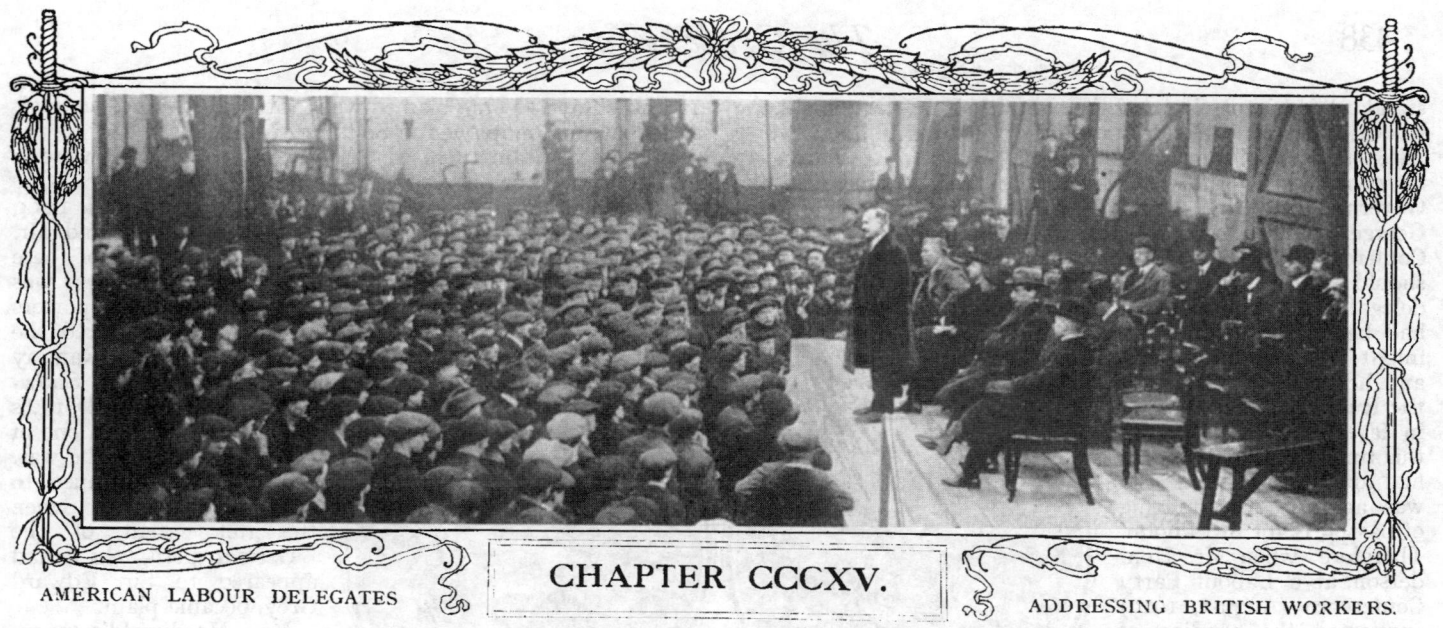

AMERICAN LABOUR DELEGATES

ADDRESSING BRITISH WORKERS.

LABOUR AND SOCIALISM IN GREAT BRITAIN DURING THE WAR.
By Hamilton Fyfe.

How Organised Labour Helped to Defeat Germany—Labour Representatives in the Cabinet—Mr. Arthur Henderson and the Proposed Stockholm Conference—Attitude of the Socialists—The House of Commons and Peace Prospects—Effect of Lord Lansdowne's Letter—" Labour's War Aims "—Inter-Allied Labour Conferences—Pacifist Defeat at the General Election of December, 1918—Increase in the Cost of Living—Strike Movements and the Supply of Munitions—Compulsory Arbitration—" Dilution " of Labour—Suppression of " Forward "—Conscription—Shells before Holidays—Waning Influence of the Trade Union Officials—Mr. Anderson s Warning—Seven Commissions of Inquiry into Labour Unrest—Women's Demand for " Equal Pay for Equal Work "—Grit and Self-Sacrifice of the Workers.

IF we take Labour to mean the mass of those who work with their hands as well as their brains, then we may say with truth, so far as Britain's effort was concerned, that " Labour won the war," for it would have been impossible that the British troops should have beaten the Germans, or even held the field, if Labour had not by severe and unrelaxed efforts provided them with the materials of war in immense and ever-increasing quantity.

In this chapter, however, " Labour " must be held to signify the representatives of organised labour ; the task before the writer is to show whether these representatives helped or hindered the prosecution of the war. It had better be said at once that of hindrance there was none worth mentioning. Such efforts as were made to hinder had so limited a circumference and were so coldly viewed by the community in general that they did not influence in the smallest degree the final result. The help that Labour gave was, on the contrary, of very great value, and certainly proved a substantial factor in securing Germany's defeat.

When war began the only representative of Labour in the Cabinet, Mr. John Burns, resigned his post. His motives were not made public, but it was clear that for some reason he disapproved of the war. At the same time Mr. Ramsay Macdonald resigned his chairmanship of the Labour Party in Parliament and was succeeded by Mr. Arthur Henderson.

If any anxiety was spread by these events as to the attitude that would be taken up by Labour, it was soon dispelled. Trade Union leaders on all sides displayed their public spirit. A number of disputes were brought rapidly to an end, so that the nation might be united.

There was much that might have justified severe criticism of the Government, and in particular of the War Office, during the early months of war—the scandalous lodging of recruits, for example ; the insufficiency, and in some cases the non-payment, of separation allowances ; the feeble handling by the Government of the profiteering scandal, with its consequence, the increase in the cost of living ; but the Labour Party observed the truce which had been proclaimed, and refrained from saying or doing anything which could hamper the authorities in their effort to repair the negligence of the past. Labour leaders took active part in the Recruiting Campaign.

When in June, 1915, Mr. Asquith formed a Coalition Cabinet a seat in it was offered to Mr. Henderson. He became the Minister of Education, and began the task of reconstructing the school system of the country. Before his efforts had time to bear fruit, however, he was, in August, 1916, asked to devote himself entirely to advising the Government on all matters connected with Labour. For this purpose he took the office of Paymaster-General. From that he was, in November, transferred to the Board of Pensions, and would have been Minister of Pensions but for his appointment by Mr. Lloyd George (December, 1916) to be a member of the War Cabinet of Four. In his stead Mr. Barnes became Pensions Minister. Mr. Hodge was also included in the Cabinet as Minister of Labour. Among the Under-Secretaries were Mr. G. H. Roberts and Mr. William Brace, while Mr. Stephen Walsh was appointed a Lord of the Treasury.

On the whole the representatives of Labour proved themselves to be as capable in the business of administration as the members of the older political parties ; the

MINISTER OF LABOUR.
[Bassano.
Right Hon. John Hodge, M.P., Minister of Labour in Mr. Lloyd George's Cabinet from December, 1916, to August, 1917.

standard was not, it must be admitted, a very high one to satisfy. Mr. Henderson did particularly good work. After the Revolution in Russia he was sent to Petrograd to confer with the Socialists who had taken over the Government of the country. Before he left, Mr. Lloyd George was in favour of the proposal to hold a Socialist Conference at Stockholm, in which Germans and Austrians should sit with British, French, Italian, and neutral delegates. When Mr. Henderson returned to London he had become convinced that a conference of this character might have useful results, and he brought word that the Russian Socialists were in favour of it. But by this time Mr. Lloyd George had altered his mind and was against the granting of passports for Stockholm. Therefore, when Mr. Henderson, at a Labour Party Conference (August, 1917) supported the sending of delegates from England to Stockholm, Mr. Lloyd George called upon him to resign.

[*Russell.*
RT. HON. J. H. THOMAS, P.C., M.P.
General Secretary of the National Union of Railwaymen. One of the few Labour Members of Parliament who opposed the Military Service Bill.

[*Russell.*
RT. HON. J. R. CLYNES, P.C., M.P.
President of the National Union of Workers, who was appointed Food Controller in 1918, but resigned after the signing of the armistice.

Mr. Henderson was succeeded in the War Cabinet by Mr. Barnes, Mr. Hodge becoming Minister of Pensions, Mr. Roberts Minister of Labour, and Mr. G. H. Wardle, another Labour member, Parliamentary Secretary to the Board of Trade. By a vote of six to one a Labour Party Conference had approved of the taking of office by Labour M.P.'s, and this approval was maintained until the summer of 1918, when the first conference of the Labour Party under its new constitution decided by a majority of two to one that the party truce must cease.

Just after the armistice a special conference, by a vote of 2,117,000 against 810,000, called upon all the Labour members of the Coalition Ministry to resign their offices. Mr. Barnes and Mr. Roberts decided to leave the party and remain in the Government. Others became independent members of Parliament. The most sharply regretted of the Labour Ministers was Mr. Clynes, who, after doing excellent service first in connection with soldiers' pensions and then at the Ministry of Food, as assistant to Lord Rhondda, became himself Food Controller, and continued, not only to deserve well of his country, but to retain the confidence and even the affection of his fellow-countrymen.

There was never at any period of the war a party openly opposed to carrying it on. There were small bodies of men— on the Clyde, for example—who tried to slow up the output of munitions. There were individuals who believed all war to be wicked. But among the Labour unions and societies, among the Socialist groups, among all the leaders of Labour and Socialism who occupied any place in the public eye, not one was found to denounce Britain as Karl Liebknecht denounced the German Government, or even to blame the British conduct of the war as Sir Henry Campbell-Bannerman

and Mr. Lloyd George blamed what they called the " methods of barbarism " employed in South Africa.

In Great Britain there were at the outset, as there were in Germany, meetings of Socialists to protest against war. One was held in Trafalgar Square on Sunday, August 2nd, 1914, Mr. Keir Hardie, Mr. Hyndman, Mr. Ben Tillett, and Mr. Barnes were the principal orators. The first-named of these was the only one who continued to believe that the war was unnecessary. The other three became ardent supporters of it. Many at the outset announced that they shared the view of Mr. Ramsay Macdonald and Mr. Snowden, that Sir Edward Grey's diplomacy had been one of the chief causes of the war. Scarcely any continued to support these two when the full extent of the " German peril," as it had appeared to Sir Edward Grey, became plain.

Mr. Macdonald's argument was that, by promising support to France and Russia, Sir Edward Grey had encouraged in France the fomenters of the desire for *la revanche*, and had put into the Russian War Office and Foreign Office the spirit which made them support Serbia so strongly and mobilise at a moment when there seemed still a faint prospect of settling the Austro-Serbian quarrel by negotiation. This view he repeated at intervals, in spite of its unpopularity, and a view very much like this Mr. Bernard Shaw expressed in a pamphlet which he published very soon after war began. But it was never held by more than a few persons, and had no influence whatever upon the course of events.

From time to time the possibility of peace negotiations was discussed in the House of Commons, usually upon the initiative of the Socialist-Labour group, which contended that the war was made by capitalists on each side, and that no benefit to the peoples could be expected to spring from it, no matter what the final result might be. The first occasion on which was expressed the anxiety of this group that no peace overtures should be rebuffed was in December, 1915. Mr. Snowden then asked for an assurance that no proposals for peace negotiations based upon the evacuation of conquered territory should be rejected by the Government without reference to Parliament. Mr. Asquith replied that the Allied Powers had agreed not to make peace

BRITISH AND CANADIAN LABOUR LEADERS IN PARIS.
Meeting of Labour representatives during the Peace Conference. Left to right : Mr. Stuart Bunning, British Trade Congress ; Right Hon. Arthur Henderson, P.C., M.P., British Labour Party ; Mr. Gustave Francq, Canada ; and Mr. P. M. Drape, Canada.

except in unison, but that it would be the desire of the Government to take Parliament into its confidence at the earliest possible moment after the making of any serious proposals.

Two and a half months later, on February 23rd, 1916, Mr. Snowden raised the question again. He declared his acceptance of the view that the motive of the British Empire in making war was disinterested, that the British people had not desired war, and that all they wanted was reparation for all the wrongs committed by Germany, with guarantees that they should not be committed again. The nation was united in believing that its cause was righteous. But with the object of arriving at a satisfactory and honourable conclusion of the war, it was necessary to study its development, and he affirmed that the situation in the field had now become one of stalemate. It was impossible for either side to win. If it were possible, it was not desirable that there should be a crushing military victory for either side, since this would lead

PROBLEMS OF TRANSPORT.
Conference of the Masters' Committee (on the extreme left, Sir Alfred Booth, chairman) at the Ministry of Labour in February, 1919, in connection with the trouble with the transport workers. Right · The Men's Committee under its president, Mr. Harry Gosling.

to a fresh war later on. Germany had shown, both by debates in the Reichstag and by articles in the newspapers, a certain readiness for peace, and he asked that the British Government should declare definitely the terms on which it would be willing to negotiate. Mr. Trevelyan supported this demand. The German Chancellor had declared his willingness to receive peace proposals, and Mr. Trevelyan considered that the Prime Minister ought to respond.

Mr. Asquith replied with a firm negative. He said that neither Mr. Snowden nor Mr. Trevelyan represented anybody but himself, and he repeated his declaration, made at the London Guildhall in November, 1914, as to the objects for which Britain was fighting. The House supported the Prime Minister by a vast majority.

Before the Whitsuntide recess in 1916 there was another discussion of the same kind. Mr. Ponsonby was this time the initiator. He moved that the time had come for peace negotiations to be opened. He argued that

Necessary step towards peace there was no difference between the statements of the British Foreign Secretary and the German Chancellor sufficient to justify a continuance of the war, and suggested that the British Government was in some way bound by secret promises made to its Allies as to what they should get out of the war. Sir Edward Grey said he could not regard the Chancellor's declarations as showing a disposition for peace. In his view the war was being prolonged by the German Government's assurances to the German people that they had won the war and that the Allies were beaten. The first step towards peace would be for the German Government to recognise that the Allies were not beaten.

Mr. Ramsay Macdonald supported Mr. Ponsonby on this occasion, and later in the year (November 14th) he spoke again in the same strain on Mr. J. H. Thomas's motion, censuring the Home Office for failing " to maintain freedom of speech and conscience " by allowing a mob to break up a Labour meeting at Cardiff, called to pass a resolution declaring that " the time had arrived when the objects for which the nations entered the war might be secured by negotiation." The mob had been led by Mr. Stanton, M.P., himself a Labour member, and he defended their right to prevent a meeting of notorious pro-German " pacifists."

Mr. Ponsonby and Mr. Snowden raised the question of peace by negotiation again in February, 1917. The latter said he believed twenty-five per cent. of the average opinion in all the constituencies was in favour of such a peace. Mr. Ponsonby urged that, whereas Britain entered the war for the purpose of protecting small nationalities, it seemed to be now committed to assisting the expansion of large Empires. Mr. Bonar Law's reply was received with strong approval by all save a very small minority.

A like reception was given to another effort made by Mr. Ramsay Macdonald and Mr. Trevelyan on July 26th, 1917, after the passing of the Reichstag resolution in favour of peace without annexations or indemnities. Mr. Asquith and Mr. Bonar Law pointed out the undesirability of stating any peace terms, and the proposal that they should be stated was lost by 148 votes to 19. Shortly before this Mr. Macdonald had taken part in a conference called by the Independent Labour Party at Leeds, which declared itself definitely against continuing the war, and in favour of declaring the allied war aims, which the Russian Republican Government had

asked the Allies, and especially Britain, to do. Mr. Smillie declared his conviction at this conference that peace could only come by negotiation.

Upon the appearance of Lord Lansdowne's letter urging an endeavour to make such a peace (November, 1917) his proposal was strongly supported by the organs of Labour which took the so-called " pacifist " view. But their views had no effect upon the mass of the nation. More importance was attached to the publication before the year 1917 ended of " Labour's War Aims." This document was drawn up for submission to a conference representing all the societies comprising the Labour Party and the Trade Union Congress. The conference met on December 28th, and by 343 votes to 12 adopted the memorandum. Mr. Henderson drew the loudest applause by his demand for " the destruction of militarism, not only in Germany, but universally." Mr. Havelock Wilson, who led the opposition to the War Aims declaration, was a good deal in the public eye during the war as a leader of sailors and stokers, in conflict with other Labour leaders.

Early in 1918 there began a series of Inter-Allied Labour Conferences, called as a substitute for Stockholm. To the War Aims memorandum Germany sent no reply, Austria's response was not discouraging, Bulgarian Socialists returned a favouring answer. This gave the " pacifist " wing little encouragement, and the jubilee meeting of the Trade Union Congress sent a unanimous message of congratulation to the British troops in the field. Twice in Parliament, in February and in June, there were further " pacifist " debates on the motion that the House of Commons regretted the decision

MR. LLOYD GEORGE RETURNING FROM PARIS.
The Prime Minister going on board H.M.S. Termagant at Boulogne when he returned from the Peace Conference to deal with the grave Labour unrest that had declared itself at home.

" that the prosecution of military effort was the only immediate task of the Government," Mr. Snowden, charged Mr. Balfour with not having read Dr. Hertling's and Count Czernin's replies to President Wilson's fourteen points before he discussed them. Mr. Anderson said that " if the intelligence of our rulers had equalled the courage of our soldiers the war would have been over long before this." But the motion was lost by 28 against 159.

On June 20th Mr. Snowden supported a motion asking for an assurance that no opportunity of settling the war by agreement would be neglected, but gained little or no ground. The feeling against the " pacifists " seemed, indeed, to grow stronger. Twice during 1918 Mr. Ramsay Macdonald was shouted down at meetings, and once had his platform stormed.

This feeling came out very strongly at the General Election, when all the " pacifists " lost their seats. In spite of this the Labour Party increased its strength. It put forward three hundred and seventy candidates and won fifty-nine seats, thus giving it the right to become the chief party in opposition. The Labour Programme was interesting. It included the following aims :

Peace of reconciliation, withdrawal from Russia, freedom for Ireland and India, no conscription, nationalisation of land, mines, railways, shipping, and electric power, a million new houses to be built at State expense, Free Trade, a levy on capital to pay off the war debt, minimum wages in all occupations, the right either to work or to maintenance, and equal pay for men and women.

That this programme was not regarded as fantastic shows how much ground Labour gained during the war. For this advance there were several reasons. One was the intensified consciousness of the power of the mass : another, the

socialisation of industries which the war made necessary ; a third, the insistence that the Allies were fighting for the rights of humanity. Why, asked Labour, should not these rights begin at home ?

Again, a powerful cause of the demands put forward with increasing urgency by Labour was the rapid rise in the cost of the necessaries of life. This was due to preventable as well as unavoidable causes. It is true that the Army made enormous demands upon the available supply of food, especially upon that of meat. Most of the men serving with the Colours consumed more than they had been accustomed to consume as civilians. But the rise in prices was due also to the block **Increased cost· of living** of goods at the ports and on the railways attributable to faulty management, and also to profiteering.

How large the increase in the cost of living was after six months of war was clearly brought out in the debate on the subject in the House of Commons during February, 1915. Wheat cost 72 per cent. more than it had cost twelve months earlier ; flour, 75 per cent. ; and sugar, 72 per cent. Coal showed an increase of only 15 per cent ; and meat (British), of 6 per cent., while foreign meat had only risen by 12 per cent. Mr. Ferens, however, who opened the debate, mentioned that coal as well as bread cost half as much again in London as it had cost before the war, and that poor people were obliged to pay two shillings a hundredweight to street sellers.

Mr. Asquith, in replying to the demand that the Government should " use every endeavour to prevent a continuance of the evil," pointed out that prices after the Franco-Prussian War were still higher (except for coal) than they were at this time. He said that hardships could not be avoided during war, and poured cold water upon all the suggestions made for Government action. Mr. Bonar Law agreed, but Mr. Clynes, for the Labour Party, expressed deep disappointment, and urged that measures should be adopted to stop " contractors and dealers from exploiting the needs of the people." Mr. W. C. Anderson also made a vigorous attack upon the Government for its inactivity. He said the purchasing power of the sovereign had dropped since 1900 to fifteen shillings. The poor asked for bread, and Mr. Asquith merely talked at them the abstract principle of supply and demand.

The Government managed to get the resolution calling upon it to take action " talked out." From the Labour benches there were repeated proposals that the closure should be

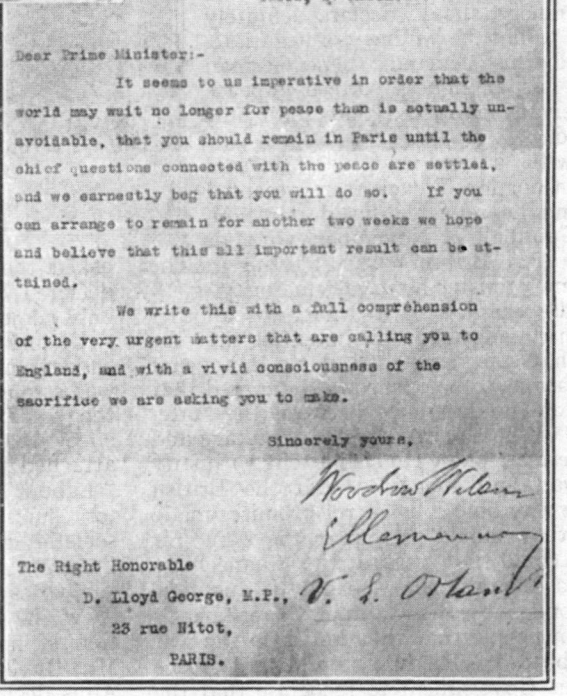

TRIBUTE TO THE BRITISH PREMIER.
Facsimile of the letter addressed to Mr. Lloyd George by President Wilson, M. Clemenceau, and Signor Orlando, in March, 1919, when the Labour troubles in Britain threatened to delay the work of the Peace Conference in Paris.

applied, but these the Speaker declined to accept. Prices continued to rise therefore ; profiteering went on.

This was in large part the cause of the strikes which at one time seemed as if they might threaten seriously the vigour of Britain's conduct of the war. Already, in January there had been trouble in the West Yorkshire coal-mines. This was settled by the men's demands being conceded " during the continuance of the war."

The railwaymen had also put forward a claim to a war bonus. In August, 1914, they had agreed to postpone the discussion of their programme of better conditions; now they felt the pinch of high prices and asked for five shillings a week bonus all round. What they received was: Three shillings a week for those who earned under thirty shillings, and two shillings a week for those earning thirty shillings or more.

Early in March there was a strike of engineers on the Clyde. They had asked for an increase of twopence an hour. The employers offered three farthings. After the men had been out for a short time the Government ordered them to go back to work, promising that the dispute should at once be referred to arbitration. The Strike Committee recommended that the order should be obeyed, but made the suggestion that, if the twopence asked for were not granted, the men should " ca' canny," or do as little work as they could. This provoked a good deal of indignation, and did much to prejudice the workers' cause, not only in this but in other disputes.

Increased wages demands The arbitration resulted in the men receiving only one penny an hour more for time work and 10 per cent. for piece work. Dissatisfaction among the workers became more inflamed. Almost every day some new trouble perplexed and dismayed the public mind. Shipyard strikes threatened at Southampton and at Barrow were turned aside by agreements that the men should have four shillings a week increase instead of the five shillings they had demanded.

So far the ordinary peace-time methods of bargaining had been followed, a process which involved both delays and irritation. When the Miners' Federation gave notice of a demand for an increase of 20 per cent. and the prospect was opened of another long and acrimonious haggle with the possibility of a disastrous strike at the end of it, the public demand that the Government should " do something " compelled Mr. Lloyd George, then Chancellor of the Exchequer, to call into conference the representatives of thirty-five Trade Unions and to put the danger of lessening the output of munitions before them.

Urgent need of munitions A few weeks before, at Bangor, Mr. Lloyd George had spoken earnestly on this theme. " This war," he said, " is not going to be fought mainly on the battlefields of Belgium and Poland. It is going to be fought in the workshops of France and Great Britain." He urged that during the war the Government ought to have power to settle all differences, and that workmen should never throw down their tools. " The country cannot afford it. It is disaster, and I do not believe, when this comes home to workmen and employers, that they will refuse for a moment to comply with the demand of the Government. There must be no delay."

Within ten days of this speech Mr. Lloyd George asked the House of Commons to give the Government power to take over any factories suitable for the manufacture of munitions. A Committee on Production, appointed early in February, to report on the best means of securing a full output, had reported that both from the Admiralty and the War Office they had received assurances as to " the present and continuously increasing need for shells and fuses." It laid stress upon the necessity of " a rapid and continuous increase " in the production of all munitions.

VISIT OF AMERICAN LABOUR DELEGATES TO SCOTLAND.

American representatives of Labour addressing a crowd of over five thousand shipyard workers in Scotland in April, 1918. A party of delegates from Labour organisations in the United States, invited over by the British Government that they might see something of Britain's efforts in the common cause, visited various parts of the country, and had a cordial reception from the vast gatherings of workers whom they addressed.

This warning was repeated by Lord Kitchener, who told the House of Lords, "We have, unfortunately, found that the output is not only not equal to our needs, but does not fulfil our expectations." The matter, he said, was causing him very serious anxiety, and he wished all those engaged in the manufacture and supply of these stores to realise "that every round of ammunition was of the utmost importance."

This appeal did not fail to move the Trade Union representatives in conference with Mr. Lloyd George. They agreed to recommend to their members " that there should in no case be any stoppage of work upon munitions and equipments of war." All disputes of demands for higher wages were to be freely discussed with employers, and, if no agreement was reached, to be submitted to arbitration. It was also settled that during the war certain Trade Union practices, concerning division of work and refusal to work with non-unionists, and the admission into factories of half skilled, or of women's labour, should be relaxed.

At this period an attempt was made to shift the blame for the unsatisfactory state of production off the shoulders of the Government on to the workers, who, it was now alleged, drank so persistently and excessively that their capacity was gravely impaired. Mr. Lloyd George put this argument picturesquely when he said, "We are fighting Germany, Austria, and drink, and as far as I can see the greatest of these three deadly foes is drink." A number of leading shipbuilders attributed four-fifths of the time lost in the shipyards to this cause, and urged total prohibition of the sale of excisable liquors during the war.

At the end of April the Government brought forward its plan for meeting the drink evil, but the country clearly did not believe that this was the chief reason for the munitions muddle, and what happened later proved that the country was right. The honest desire of the vast majority of workers to contribute their share to the war effort of the Empire was vigorously expressed by members of twenty-one engineering and shipbuilding societies who met at Newcastle and sent this message to Mr. Asquith :

> We do not want any more speeches about the failings of the workers, the employers, or the Government ; we want to pull together and get on with it. You may tell Lord Kitchener we shall deliver the goods.

Further steps in the direction of compulsory arbitration in Labour disputes were taken when the Munitions of War Act was passed during the summer. It had been suggested that the proper way to secure the workers needed for the munitions factories, upon whose working the lives of our soldiers depended, was to apply compulsion. What Mr. Lloyd George proposed was to depend upon volunteers for mobile munition corps of skilled men, and Mr. Hodge, for the Labour Party, pledged the Trade Unions **Suspension of** to do everything in their power to make the **Trade Union rights** plan a success. He also acquiesced in the suspension of the working classes' Trade Union rights. "It is better to give up such privileges as we have than to let the Germans be successful and have no liberties at all."

Mr. Snowden dissented ; denied that the Labour Party represented the mass of the Trade Unionists ; declared that the Government was trying to put on to the working classes the blame which was properly due to it for its inefficiency. An amendment moved by Mr. Snowden, providing that rises in prices should always be taken into account when applications for higher wages were under discussion, was supported by the Labour Party, but defeated. The miners' M.P.s, led by Mr. Stephen Walsh were successful, however, in alliance with

the cotton operatives, in persuading Mr. Lloyd George to agree that where existing machinery for the settlement of disputes was effective it should be made use of, instead of being superseded by the methods which the Bill proposed.

The miners' demand for a 20 per cent. increase, already mentioned, and the employers' offer of 10 per cent. were submitted by agreement to Mr. Asquith for decision. He gave no decision, merely stating that he considered a case had been made out for an immediate advance, and leaving the amount of it to be arranged by district committees and boards. This kept the peace until July, when the South Wales miners demanded that their existing wages agreement should be superseded by a new one which gave higher rates of pay all round. Notice of this demand had been given in April, but

LABOUR PARTY CONFERENCE AT WESTMINSTER, 1917.
Mr. Arthur Henderson, member of the Coalition Ministry, addressing a conference of Labour Party delegates, in August, 1917, when he supported the sending of delegates to the proposed Stockholm Conference. Subsequent to this speech he handed his resignation to the Prime Minister.

the Government paid no attention to the dispute until it became a source of serious danger. Mr. Runciman, as President of the Board of Trade, then made unavailing attempts to persuade the miners to reduce their terms, and having been told by a vote of 1,894 delegates against 1,037 that his efforts had come to naught, he issued a proclamation under the Munitions of War Act making it an offence to strike without referring the dispute to arbitration.

Of this proclamation the miners took **Miners demand** no notice. By 88,950 votes to 47,450 **higher wages** they decided to stop work, and 200,000 were for a week idle (the cost of this was reckoned at £1,500,000). Mr. Lloyd George now went down to Wales to try to arrange a settlement, and after exertions which, he said, left him " sick at heart," he induced the miners to agree to Mr. Runciman's terms with some additions. The men went back to work, but at the end of August men and employers were again quarrelling as to the date at which the increased pay granted in July should begin. This time Mr. Lloyd George, Mr. Runciman, and Mr. Henderson had to be called in to settle the dispute.

At a conference of 2,000 representatives of the mining industry Mr. Smillie, President of the Miners' Federation, said they would agree, if necessity were shown, to suspend the Eight Hours' Act and to reduce the age limit for boy labour, and to allow women to be employed in larger numbers. The necessity of producing more coal was clear from the falling off in the yield of 3,000,000 tons a month, due to the enlistment of a quarter of a million men from the pits.

That further " dilution " of labour was necessary, this being the phrase invented to cover the increased employment of women, boys, and unskilled men, was very seriously argued by Mr. Lloyd George in a speech which he made to 3,000 Trade Union officials and shop stewards at Glasgow towards the end of 1915. Mr. Henderson presided at the meeting, which was not unanimous even in its approval of the war. Mr. Lloyd George explained the need for the release of skilled men from work which could be done by the unskilled, so that the former might apply themselves to tasks in which skill was essential.

A report of the speech with all the interruptions and interjections was published by a weekly paper called " Forward," and when this paper was suppressed very soon afterwards the suppression was attributed in the House of Commons to the appearance of this report. Mr. Lloyd George

TRADE UNION CONGRESS AT DERBY, 1918.
Opening meeting of the Trade Union Congress at Derby, when powerful speeches by Mr. Hughes, the Australian Premier, and Mr. Gompers, the American Labour leader, emphasising the necessity of bringing German militarism to an end, were cordially acclaimed.

denied that there was any connection, but that " Forward " had been guilty of offences under the D.O.R.A. in discouraging men from joining the Army and in urging Clyde workmen not to turn out munitions. Mr. Anderson stated, nevertheless, that the suppression had had a bad effect on the Clyde, and that Mr. Lloyd George's visit had done more harm than good. Mr. D. A. Thomas (afterwards Lord Rhondda) suggested that there had been a difference between the treatment of Labour papers and others, which Labour thought very unfair.

Compulsory military service No sooner had the South Wales coal crisis been finally got rid of in August, 1915, than there began again to be ominous signs of restlessness among railwaymen. The extra sums which they had received as war bonus were no longer, they complained, sufficient to meet increased prices. Now, after some delay, the Executive Council of the National Union of Railwaymen met railway managers, and a further increase of pay was agreed to.

From now on until the early days of 1916 the controversy raged over the question whether compulsory military service should or should not be put in force. From the beginning of the war the Labour leaders, both in Parliament and throughout the country, had done a great deal to induce men to enlist of their own free will. For the most part they threw themselves into the recruiting campaign with patriotic energy. At a time when the supply of soldiers flagged, Mr. Henderson, as leader of the Labour Party, joined Mr. Asquith and Mr. Bonar Law in the issue of an appeal to householders to state how many members of their household were willing to enlist ; this appeal had very satisfactory results.

But, in general, Labour was opposed to any measure of compulsion, and as the demand for this grew louder, so did the attitude of Labour become stiffer in resisting it. The Trade Union Congress, meeting at Bristol, in September, 1915, passed by a unanimous vote a resolution which protested against " the sinister efforts of a section of the reactionary Press in . . . attempting to foist on this country conscription, which always proves a burden to the workers and will divide the nation at a time when absolute unanimity is essential." The resolution declared further that no sufficient evidence had been produced to show that the voluntary system was inadequate to meet all the Empire's requirements, and promised every aid to the Government in securing the men necessary to prosecute the war to a successful issue.

The speakers in support of this were loud in their denunciations of the " capitalist Junkers." Some said the British Empire should not undertake to provide a large Army ; it was enough to hold the seas, finance the Allies, and make munitions. Mr. Smillie urged the passing of a declaration that conscription would not be tolerated, and said, if the Government ignored that, it would be the duty of organised Labour to take measures to prevent conscription. A little later there was a conference in London of delegates from the chief bodies representing organised Labour. Mr. Henderson presided, and Lord Kitchener made a speech emphasising the needs of the military situation. The conference decided that it was still possible to obtain all the men required by the voluntary system, and undertook to carry through a special labour-recruiting effort all over the country.

Whether this attitude reflected the mind of the working classes concerning conscription still seemed doubtful, however, and doubt was increased by the result of the Merthyr Boroughs election. The seat was vacant through the death of Mr. Keir Hardie, who had said very little during the war. There were two candidates, both Labour men, Mr. Winstone, put forward by the Labour Party, and Mr. Stanton, who stood as an Independent, and professed to be more patriotic than the " official " candidate. Mr. Stanton was elected with a majority of over 4,000. Whether this had or had not an effect upon the counsels of the Labour members, their attitude, when the Military Service Bill was introduced, was seen to have changed. Only a few of them voted against it. Mr. Henderson, Mr. Hodge, Colonel John Ward, and others gave it their steady support. Mr. Thomas, Mr. Anderson and, of course, Mr. Snowden, opposed it, the last-named threatening organised resistance to the measure upon a large scale, of which nothing was ever heard after the Bill became law.

The attitude of the workers represented at the Conference of the Labour Party about this time seemed to be indicated pretty clearly by the results of three divisions taken during the discussion of the Military Service Bill. By a majority of 1,600,000 a protest was made against " any form of conscription." By a majority of **Conscription** 1,356,000 they registered their objection to **becomes law** the Bill then before Parliament. Then by 649,000 votes against 614,000 they decided against agitating for the repeal of the Bill after it became law. Thus they satisfied their consciences by registering their protests, and agreed as good constitutionalists to accept a law which they did not like, but which the vast majority of members of Parliament declared to be necessary for the safety of the Commonwealth.

The only workers who offered any serious resistance to the new Act and to the efforts being made to hasten the manufacture of munitions were a certain number on the Clyde. In March and April, 1916, a number of strikes broke out at munition works in that district. They were traced to the activities of a committee which aimed avowedly at stopping the production of our supplies and forcing the Government to repeal the Military Service Acts. Six of the members of this committee were arrested and the trouble soon afterwards subsided. The Amalgamated Society of Engineers had no part in it ; indeed the society did all it could to prevent the strikes and forbade its members to leave work in order to be present at a meeting of protest against the arrests. In the debate on the incident in the House of Commons the Labour members took scarcely any part, thus tacitly expressing their disapproval of the tactics of the new force which had arisen in the ranks of Labour—the shop stewards.

A long time passed, however, without any further manifestation of their force attracting public notice. The year 1916 was free from any further dangerous Labour troubles until very near its close. There was no unemployment in the country, it was stated in the House of Commons in July. The work of the munition factories went on steadily and with ever increasing output, it was announced in August. The workers gave up their Whitsuntide holiday in order to keep up the supply of shells to the Army, and they were promised two days instead of one in August as compensation.

MR. W. J. WEBB.
London District Secretary of the Electrical Trades' Union.

When August came, however, the needs of the troops were still too urgent to permit safely of any stoppage of production. Sir Douglas Haig asked the nation to " give up any idea of a general holiday until our goal had been reached." The meeting of employers and Labour representatives to which this was addressed replied that it would recommend the postponement of all holidays involving interrupted production until they could be taken without prejudice to the military position. This recommendation was loyally accepted. At the same time Mr. Henderson became chairman of a committee appointed by the Ministry of Munitions to suggest arrangements for letting workers take holidays in relays.

It was generally felt, therefore, that the President of the Trade Union Congress (Mr. H. Gosling) was justified in

claiming at Birmingham in September that " Labour had been the personification of real patriotism." This impression was not weakened by the debates and resolutions of the Congress. Earnest hopes found utterance that relations between employers and Labour would after the war be put upon a better footing than that of conflict by the admission of workmen to " some participation in the control of those matters which concerned them directly." The creation of a Labour Ministry was called for ; also State control of transport and food supplies. Detestation of German methods of warfare was shown by a refusal to agree that an International Labour Congress should meet at the same time and place as the Peace Conference. Two-thirds of the delegates were disinclined to meet enemies, even Socialists, when the war was over.

There was agreement, however, among all sections that compulsion to serve either in the Army or in industry was an evil which must be abolished as soon as war ended, and it was strongly urged that the danger of " a grave industrial peril " during the period of demobilisation, and of readjusting industry to peace conditions should be carefully considered and prepared against.

MR. CHARLES DUNCAN, J.P.
General Secretary of the Workers' Union.

The opinion appeared to be entertained by most of the delegates that no confidence could be placed in the promises of Ministers and employers that Trade Union rights and practices, surrendered in the national interest, should be restored as soon as fighting ceased ; but it was agreed that the unions should determine to restore them by their own power.

The close of 1916 was darkened by a strike of boilermakers at the Port of Liverpool. The men had applied to the Committee on Production, a body appointed by the Government, for a ten-shilling increase in their weekly wages to meet the rise in the cost of living. They were granted three shillings.

They gave notice then that they would " down tools " on December 9th. Their leaders urged them to apply for arbitration or to go into conference with the shipowners, but the men were in an obstinate temper and they ceased work. Mr. Hodge had at this time just been made Minister of

MR. PURDY AND MR. JOHN HILL.
Mr. Purdy (right), President of the Trade Union Congress, 1918, with Mr. John Hill (Boilermakers).

MR. BEN TILLETT.
General Secretary of the Dockers' Union, attending the Labour Conference at Nottingham, January, 1918.

MR. WILL THORNE, M.P.
General Secretary of the National Labourers' Union, formerly known as the Gasworkers' Union.

Labour. He declined to deal with the matter until the strikers went back to work; as soon as they did that, he said, he would hear their case and act at once. The men stayed out in spite of this, and the next step taken by the Government, in view of the delay to Admiralty work of the utmost national importance, was to announce its intention of exercising the special powers given to it by the Acts relating to munition production and the Defence of the Realm. Upon this the men met and decided by 827 votes to 74 to take up their tools again and, if necessary, do urgent work as overtime. Their grievances were then inquired into and their wages raised.

The Labour Party Conference at Manchester in January, 1917, was not less emphatic than the Trade Union Congress had been in its acceptance of Mr. Wardle's view that no peace was possible until Germany had renounced her war aims and in rejecting the proposal that the International Socialist Bureau should be re-established. The shop stewards' movement on the Clyde was condemned by the older members of the Labour Party with almost equal vigour. One of the engineers who had been arrested and deported from Glasgow appeared at the Conference; Mr. Henderson told him that " he and his friends were a danger to both Trade Unionism and to the nation," seeing that they had declined to listen to the officials of their own society, and had done their best to obstruct the rapid production of war material. The Party passed a resolution, however, demanding the immediate and unconditional return of the deported men.

Shop stewards' movement

It was clear from other incidents besides this that the Trade Union officials had lost their hold upon a great many of the members of Trade Unions. The year 1917 saw a tightening-up of war restrictions which caused a great deal of irritation and restless discontent. Food became scarcer and dearer. The necessity for regularly filling up the ranks of the Army swept into the recruiting net more and more of the men of military age. The danger of any slackening in the supply of munitions to the troops kept the factory workers on the stretch from Monday to Saturday without any of the relaxations of peace-time. War-weariness began to be noticeable, and one symptom of it was an increasing readiness to strike upon what often seemed to the general public slight provocation.

There was a most unfortunate stoppage of work in the Barrow district engineering shops during the

SOCIALIST CONFERENCE ON WAR AIMS.
Delegates to the Inter-Allied Socialist Conference on War Aims at Westminster, February, 1918. Left to right : Signor Arca, Italy ; Mr. W. H. Andrews, South Africa ; and M. Ostojich, Southern Slavs. Above : The Belgian delegates. Left to right : Messrs. W. Eekelers, Emile Vandervelde, V. Demenkmeester, Harry de Man, and (behind) M. Laboulle.

spring. The executive officials of the Amalgamated Society and other engineering unions twice tried to persuade the men to go back to work. Each time they were met by a refusal. When the Government threatened to enforce the Defence of the Realm Act unless work were resumed within twenty-four hours, the engineers proposed to nominate shop stewards to explain their case. Mr. Hodge said he would agree to this and discuss the matter with the shop stewards if the men would begin work again at once. This they did, and the questions in dispute was settled by negotiation after a fortnight had been wasted by the strike.

A month later the engineers in South Lancashire came out, again in defiance of their unions. The causes of this strike were complicated. One was the unreadiness of employers to discuss matters with the men's representatives. Another was the " dilution " practised by introducing larger numbers of women. A third, and perhaps the principal cause, lay in a change made in the arrangements for exempting men from military service. The Ministry of Munitions had decided that workers should be exempted only if they were highly skilled, and therefore indispensable. There had been

some lack of discretion in the manner of making the change; indeed, the dealings of the Ministry of Munitions with Labour were at no time tactful or discreet. The men had their " backs put up," and were in no mood to give way.

In the House of Commons, Mr. Anderson offered the nation a serious warning about Labour unrest. It was beginning, he said, to amount to a revolutionary feeling, and unless the Government were very careful, they would bring the country to the verge of revolution. This was the first mention of the ominous word in public; it had been spoken often in private for some months. An omnibus strike in London added to the depression of public feeling—but this was soon over. A cotton strike was threatened, but averted. Engineers in many other parts had followed the example of Lancashire, and the tension was not lessened by the refusal of the Minister of Munitions to negotiate with any but the " organised representatives " of Labour, meaning the Trade Unions. He was obliged to withdraw from this position, and to receive members of the " unofficial " Strike Committee, as well as officials of the Amalgamated Society. In the meantime, seven of the strike leaders had been arrested and charged under the Defence of the Realm Act with impeding the production of war material. In the general settlement they were released and work was resumed.

Hard upon this followed the setting up of seven Commissions throughout the country for the purpose of investigating Labour unrest and making suggestions to the Government. Each consisted of a representative of Labour, an employer, and an impartial third party with a casting vote. Of greater importance was the report on the relations between employers and employed of a sub-section of the Reconstruction Committee. Known as the Whitley Report, because Mr. J. H. Whitley, M.P., was Chairman of the Committee, this proposed the establishment in every large industry of a Joint Industrial

Council, which should settle general principles governing the conditions of employment, including wages, should endeavour to give the workpeople security of employment and earnings, and should encourage education, research, improvement of factory methods and machinery, and so on. District committees were also suggested, and works committees in each factory or workshop, representing both masters and men.

In August, 1917, the railwaymen again became restive, and pressed their demand for an eight hours' day through the Society of Locomotive Engineers and Firemen. The National Union of Railwaymen, with which the other railway unions had been amalgamated, opposed a strike, but the society was on the point of calling its members out when the Government, by proclamation, forbade a strike. It was stated, on the men's behalf, during the negotiations between the society and the Board of Trade, that "again and again engine-drivers and firemen had to work eighteen hours a day, and that for days together their hours ranged from twelve to fifteen. They did not ask for the rigid observance of an eight hours' day immediately, but they proposed that it should be introduced by degrees. Sir Albert Stanley, President of the Board of Trade, pledged the Government to keep the railways under control after the war long enough to give the men opportunity to make their demand for shorter hours, and promised that such a demand should meet with "immediate and sympathetic consideration."

That pledge was redeemed, and the eight hours' day arranged.

In November another railway crisis arose, this time over a demand for a ten-shilling rise in weekly wages by the National Union. The Railway Executive Committee offered five shillings. Thereupon the railwaymen in the Liverpool district resolved to "go slow" in the expectation that traffic would become utterly disorganised, and that the ten-shilling increase would have to be granted. But a meeting of delegates from all parts of the country urged the Liverpool men to abandon their plan, and they consented. In the end the men got a six-shilling rise, to date back three weeks.

That Labour would henceforward play a far greater part in politics than it had played before was made plain during the war by a multitude of signs. At the Trade Union Congress in the autumn of 1917 this was clearly foreshadowed by Mr. Hill, of the Boilermakers' Union. He said that hitherto the Trade Unionist prejudice against politics had kept Labour back, but in future industry and politics would never be separated. Other signs pointing in the same direction were : (1) The revised constitution of the Labour Party. Hitherto, membership had only been open to those who belonged to Trade Unions or Socialist societies. Now **War bonus on earnings** it was thrown open to individuals who need not be "working men" in the technical sense, or Socialists ; (2) the decision of co-operators that their movement should become a force in politics, with a programme of industrial, social, and economic reforms.

There were no strikes on a large scale during the early months of 1918. A number of small disputes arose over the granting of the 12½ per cent. war bonus on earnings, which, after the Government munition factory workers had received it, was demanded on all sides. These were soon settled. In May came the first perilous trouble of the year : in Wales 52,000 miners stayed out for nineteen days in order to force the employers to recognise a local workers' committee. In August three times as many Yorkshire miners left work over a dispute as to the hours to be worked by surfacemen.

They were only out, however, for a day or two. Arbitration was agreed to, and they went back.

Summer heats brought with them, as usual, a good deal of irritation—more than usual, because holidays were more difficult than in the time before the war. War-weariness was noticeable, especially in munition works, where the effort had to be kept up steadily without any relaxation. In July 35,000 munition workers in the Midlands came out for six days as a protest against further "dilution" of skilled labour. A Committee of Inquiry was promised, and they resumed their tasks. **"Equal pay for equal work"**

In August the girls and women employed as conductors on the London omnibuses and tramways struck because a five-shilling increase given to men was not given to them. "Equal pay for equal work" was their demand, and they secured it after the public had been put to a few days' inconvenience. More serious might have been the London Police strike during August if it had not been quickly settled by the concession to the men of increased pay, and by a promise that their union should be recognised, a promise which, so they complained later, had not been kept. Special Constables were called upon to perform certain police duties, but there was an increase of crime, especially in the form of burglary and housebreaking, during the few days the strike lasted.

September saw a partial railway strike. The regions affected were Wales, Monmouthshire, and London. The men had asked for a ten-shilling additional war bonus, and had been granted five shillings, which the railway directors considered to be enough—seeing that it brought the total war increase up to thirty shillings. The danger of a general hold-up of railway traffic was clearly apparent to most of the men, and the strike was therefore confined to certain localities. It ended by the men going back unconditionally, but upon the understanding that their demand for another five shillings a week should be sympathetically considered. It may be noted here that the eight hours' day for railwaymen was conceded before the end of the year, and that during the war the wages paid to this class of labour rose from 47 to 102 millions sterling a year.

Another strike in September was that of forty thousand textile workers in Lancashire and Cheshire. Their grievance was complicated, and an independent Government inquiry was agreed to. Later in the year there was a more serious strike in the same trade and the same districts. As many as one hundred thousand cotton spinners and weavers struck for a 40 per cent. increase on current pay. After nine days they went back with what amounted to a 30 per cent. increase. The year fortunately closed, as it had begun, with few Labour disputes outstanding, and none of them of any great importance.

In general, then, it may be said that the attitude of the representatives of Labour was a great help towards gaining the victory, and that the mass of workers stood by their country during the war with grit and self-sacrifice. A great deal was heard about the small number who were able to buy luxuries which had never been within their reach before. More should have been said about the very large number who laboured steadily at exhausting tasks for merely a living wage. Happily there is every reason to suppose that the country appreciated this. The changed mood of sympathy towards the demands for higher pay and shorter hours which took the place of former hostility and grudging concession was proof that Labour's share in killing Prussianism had not been overlooked.

[Russell.

RIGHT HON. J. H. WHITLEY, M.P.,
Chairman of the committee which proposed the establishing in every large industry of a Joint Industrial Council for settling the general conditions of employment.

RACIAL DISTRIBUTION OF THE PEOPLES OF CENTRAL EUROPE AND THE BALKAN STATES.

CHAPTER CCCXVI.

CENTRAL EUROPE IN REVOLUTION.
I.—Insurrections and Reactions in Germany.
By Edward Wright.

Southern Slavs Lead the Revolutionary Movement—German Independents Prepare Rising along German Coast—Liebknecht and "Red Rosa" Take the Road to Ruin—French Sailors Produce Mutiny in German Fleet—Kiel Outbreak and Spread of Insurrection—Linsingen Prepares to Save Berlin—Alexander Regiment of Guards Remember Kaiser's Speech—Quiet, Sudden Red-Flagging of German Capital—Scheidemann and Liebknecht Contend for Leadership—Guild Socialism as a Profit Producer in German Factories—Disbanded Troops Turn for Help to Liebknecht—Formation of Coalition—Socialist Government—Amazing Restoration of Kaiser's Ministers—Bernstorff Undertakes to Turn Defeat into Victory—Intrigue to Transform Holland and Switzerland into German Territories—Germany's Quick Change into the World's Defence against Bolshevism—German Revolution Ends with Return of Prussian Guard to Berlin—Eisner in Bavaria Tries to Save the Revolution—Revelations of Germany's War-making Plot—Spartacists Goaded into Fighting—First Battle of Berlin and Assassination of Spartacist Leaders—Success of Parties of Reaction in National Assembly Elections.

I N the last week of September, 1918, the practical surrender of the broken forces of Bulgaria clearly indicated to the peoples of Central Europe that the end of the war was near. There was then a great difference in the way in which Germany and Austria-Hungary reacted against the coming disaster. The Dual Monarchy fell to pieces almost without being touched. Bohemia and Greater Serbia at once completed their preparations for insurrection. Committees of Czechs, Slovaks, and Southern Slavs arranged for general risings among their peoples, and also for mutinies among the Slav troops at the front and for the capture of the Austro-Hungarian Fleet by the predominant Slav crews. The Austrian Emperor offered a system of federation to the Slav races, but the offer came a year too late. Even the Hungarian troops inclined to mutiny, nearly 200,000 of them being disaffected, and the attack opened by Lord Cavan on October 24th owed much of its rapid success to the fact that it was delivered partly against friendly rebels and breaking mutineers. The Austro-Hungarian Fleet might have been surrendered by the Southern Slavs in the middle of October, 1918, but for the measures taken by the Italian Foreign Minister, Baron Sonnino, to hinder the success of the plans of the Southern Slavs. In Germany there was no large

PRINCE MAX OF BADEN,
Appointed Imperial Chancellor early in October, 1918, and occupied that position at the outbreak of the Revolution.

genuine popular movement towards Revolution. Germany fell apathetically into a condition of moral and material bankruptcy. The only party with a policy of reconstruction was that of the Independent Social Democrats, who had broken with the Imperial Socialists and started organising a Revolution in 1916. Under Haase, Dittmann, Kurt Eisner, Kautsky, and other men, preparations were made for the establishment of a kind of Radical-Socialist republic upon the ruins of the Hohenzollern Empire. The Independent Socialists opened negotiations with the Imperial Socialists in the first week of October, 1918, and tried to arrange a scheme of common action. But Scheidemann, Ebert, David, Südekum, and the rest of the Majority Socialists of the Imperialist school were deeply involved with the military party, and could not recover their independence. Their leaders, Scheidemann and Ebert, elected to support the Royalties of the Empire, and assist Prince Max of Baden in carrying out Ludendorff's plan for forming a constitutional monarchy and negotiating a peace.

In these circumstances the Independents inclined to a temporary working alliance with the new German Communist organisation known as the Spartacists. The Spartacists were anarchic Revolutionaries of the Bolshevist sort. They obtained their name from Karl Liebknecht, the brilliant son of one of the founders of the

447

German Socialist movement, who had fought against the war-makers until persecution and imprisonment had driven him almost crazy with despair. Under the influence of a wild neurotic woman, Rosa Luxemburg, Liebknecht lost all the qualities of a statesman, and adopted the complete programme of Bolshevism. Under the *nom de guerre* of Spartacus, taken from the leader of the slave revolt in Italy in the first century B.C., Liebknecht published incitements to a class war, and found hundreds of thousands of followers among the German factory hands. Although he, like Rosa Luxemburg, was kept in prison, his influence over the urban working classes became apparently so great that he was generally known as the "Red Kaiser." The Imperial Government, however, cleverly managed to secure a measure of control over the Spartacist movement. This was done

GERMAN NATIONAL POSTAGE-STAMP DESIGNS.
Some of the thousands of designs sent in in a competition for postage stamps to be issued for the German Revolutionary Government. Nos. 1, 3, and 5 were among the approved designs.

by means of Secret Service men who professed to become converted to Spartacism. Prominent among these agents were many young and able military and naval officers who pretended to be followers of Captain von Beerfelde, the disillusioned aristocrat, who, after serving in an important position on the Great General Staff, had taken openly to working against the Government.

By reason of their organising ability, the Kaiser's men in the Spartacist movement won a peculiar power of direction. They were not able to betray the angry working men, because these were far too numerous and were armed with the weapons they had themselves made in the munition factories. From the Essen works to the Silesian shops the mechanics were ready for street battles. Moreover, many of the best troops kept in the country to break popular risings were found to be affected by the Revolutionary spirit. Yet the officers who had wormed their way into the centre of the arming mass of agitators were able to master it. Their method was to keep their mobs in hand until loyal and well-organised forces arrived, and then lead them into action in such a way **Imperial leaders** as would end in their being slaughtered. **of Spartacists** A certain Lieutenant Waltz, directing the Spartacists of Berlin, was among the most skilful of the agents of the counter-Revolution. When Liebknecht was released from prison, along with Rosa Luxemburg and some Independent Socialists, in the amnesty arranged by Prince Max and Scheidemann, Waltz was in control of the Red Guard of Berlin, so that General von Linsingen, the governor of the capital, looked forward only to a victorious street battle against the misguided Spartacists.

In essentials the counter-Revolutionary strategy of the German Government was similar to that of the Russian Government in the days of Protopopoff. The Teutonic

Bolshevists were secretly directed by the men who intended to defeat them, and in the meantime the wilder Revolutionary movement was cunningly employed as a means of frightening all the sober, sound progressive parties into submission to the military party. The main difference between the German and Russian methods was that the German governing class was determined, businesslike, and efficient. No doubt it was because Scheidemann and Ebert had at least an inkling of the realities of the situation that they refused on October 7th to co-operate with Haase and his Independents. It was against the Independents that the agents of the Government directed the Spartacist movement.

For three weeks the Independents worked at completing their organisation for a Radical republic with a cautious socialising tendency. Most of their arrangements had been made in 1917 at the time when a mutiny broke out in the German Fleet. Their influence was strongest round the seaboard of Northern Germany, but inland from the Westphalian coal-fields to the Silesian foundries the mechanics followed Liebknecht rather than Haase. In these centres of agitation the Independents appeared to have come to some arrangement with the Spartacists, employing men like Ledebour, who sympathised with Liebknecht's views, instead of drawing a clear line between a democratic Revolution and a bloody Communist reconstruction of society.

At Kiel and Wilhelmshaven there were special facilities for the Revolutionaries of both schools. Some 24,000 men from Alsace and Lorraine had been conscripted for service in the High Sea Fleet and its bases. Year after year deputies from Alsace-Lorraine had demanded in the Reichstag the reason why their inland people should contribute so excessive a number of recruits to the Navy. The official answer was that it had been found that Lorrainers and Alsatians suffered less in the tropical climates visited by German squadrons than did Teutons of the Empire. The real reason was that men from the conquered provinces could be kept under stricter discipline in the naval service than in the Army, but the result was that during the war German seamen tended strongly to mutiny more than a year before any signs of disorder were apparent among German soldiers.

The Independent Socialists had spread their views among the sailors before the Bolshevists rose to power in Russia, but by the autumn of 1918 they had to yield some ground to the Liebknecht agitators. Nevertheless, in the Fleet and the naval bases there were at **Revolution** first scarcely any Imperial agents acting as **at Kiel** misdirectors of the Spartacists. So when the great mutiny occurred in the battleship squadrons on October 31st, 1918 (as described in Chapter CCLXXVI., Vol. 12, page 555), the Imperialists had no means of controlling the men. After the mutineers were subdued and taken to prison, sedition spread among the Marines who had overcome the rebels. Then it was that the thousands of Alsatians and Lorrainers began to revolt, and one of their leaders—Thomas, of Wissemburg—played a leading part in starting a genuine Revolution at Kiel.

On Sunday, November 3rd, a meeting of sailors and workmen was held in the drill-ground of Kiel, and Independent Socialists addressed the arming multitude and took control. A procession was formed, and, as the demonstrators surged towards the military prison to release the mutineers of the Third Naval Squadron, a body of troops barred the way at the corner of Karlstrasse and Brunswick Street and shot down some of the Revolutionaries, dispersing them, but losing their own commander, who fell with a bullet in his head. All night the struggle went on, the Revolutionaries recruiting as they

Ready for action outside Berlin police station: Flame-throwers in civil warfare.

Berlin battle between Spartacists and Government troops: Barricade in the Potsdamer Platz.

Fighting on their home front: Berlin Government troops hurrying to encounter the Spartacists.

Berlin during the Spartacist insurrection: Barricade across one of the principal streets.

Government troops who had seized a Spartacist trench in the Frankfurter Allee, Berlin.

On the look=out for parties of Spartacists in one of Berlin's busy thoroughfares.

During a lull in civil strife in the Prussian capital : Appeal on behalf of the Government to a mass meeting of Berliners to maintain law and order.

fought, and spreading the movement again through the Fleet. The Revolutionaries conquered the harbour and arsenal, and by November 4th they were joined by all the Trade Unionists and dockyard workers, who came out on a general strike and armed themselves with weapons supplied by the sailors. The soldiers also were won over, and practically all the warships in Kiel Harbour were flying the Red Flag. The captain of the König battleship was killed, with two of his officers, while trying to prevent the hoisting of the ensign of Revolution, but on the whole there was little serious resistance. Admiral Souchon, the Governor of Kiel, agreed to the commands of the seamen, soldiers, and workmen forming the first Soviet in Germany, and by November 5th, though some desultory shooting went on, Kiel was generally quiet and orderly under its new Government of Independent Socialists.

The Marines held the main railway-station and general post-office, and the Council busily prepared to spread the movement through the country by the despatch of trainloads of seamen agitators. In the afternoon of November 5th the rising spread to Wilhelmshaven, where both ships' companies and dockyard hands welcomed the Revolution. By their foresight in swiftly seizing post and telegraph offices and wireless stations, the Fleet Revolutionaries won rapid means of communication with all ports and ships, and worked the railways for a considerable distance inland in a masterly manner. For instance, a train with five hundred Marines, escorting mutineers from Wilhelmshaven to Münster Camp, was directed to stop at Bremen. The Marines marched to Bremen Barracks, disarmed the sentries, and induced · the soldiers to join them.. Then mutineers, Marines, and soldiers walked at the head of an ever-growing mob to Bremen Town Hall, and with businesslike quickness set up a Soviet, which Liebknecht, hastily travelling from Berlin, was able to address in the evening of November 6th. Prisons were opened and officers disarmed, and while the alarmed **Revolutionaries** Senate of Bremen was still sitting in the **capture Bremen** House of Burgesses, discussing the problem of a democratic suffrage, the sailors pealed the cathedral bells to announce that the day of the new freedom had come.

Largely by means of telegraphic communications, but partly by emissaries sent in armoured motor-cars and trains, the Revolution spread along the North Sea and Baltic coasts on November 6th. Most of the submarine crews in German naval harbours refused to remain in their boats, and joined the Revolution. The garrisons of Heligoland and Borkum needed but little persuasion, and Hamburg was won by thousands of soldiers, sailors, and Russian prisoners of war, led by the Independent Socialist Dittmann, released from prison to which he had been sent as one of the leaders of the early mutiny of 1917.

One of the decisive strokes engineered by the Independent Socialists was a general peace demonstration, fixed for November 4th, and extending from the Southern German cities to the Northern ports. In many places these meetings were conducted with a good deal of rhetoric but little violence, and, being formed mainly by munition workers, they gave the working men who had the best opportunity for obtaining arms the growing sense of their power. It had, indeed, been the original design to transform the peace demonstration into a strong Revolution movement. At the last moment, however, both Liebknecht and Haase, ignorant of the course of events in Kiel, postponed the Revolution. In Berlin some of the Independents were arrested at the order of General von Linsingen, a fighting general from the eastern front, whose aim was to let the Spartacists loose while hampering the genuine Republican movement. He would not, however, have accomplished anything of importance, except to add fuel to fire, had it not been for the skilled and subtle aid given to the Government by the Imperial Socialists under Scheidemann.

Between the evening of November 5th and the morning of November 6th the Imperial Socialists, forming the mainstay of the Civil Administration of Prince Max of Baden, came to terms with the Independent Socialists. They agreed to the programme they had rejected on October 7th, and arranged for the establishment of a Republican Government, in which Majority and Minority Socialists were to be equally represented. The first measure taken was a brilliant example of policy of pacific penetration that led to the final success of the counter-Revolution. Herr Noske, an able, masterful Jew of the Scheidemann school, set out by train to Kiel as a Majority Socialist delegate to the Soviet. He arrived on November 6th, and made a flattering speech to the Marines, which was dramatically interrupted by an outburst of firing from one of the last bands of openly Royalist naval officers. Noske promised the Soviet that all its practical schemes would be immediately carried out. As he seemed the kind of man likely to carry them out, he was elected Governor of Kiel, and his election **" Pacific** was followed by an extraordinary general **penetration "** conversion of all naval and military officers.

They became miraculously eager to take part in the shaping of the new Social Democratic Republic of Germany. Among them were first-rate traffic managers, who performed miracles of ingenuity in bringing trains to the naval bases and dispersing the most violent of the ratings in missionary work hundreds of miles away. The Revolutionaries remaining in Kiel then became so tame that later they were decisively used in staying the Berlin Revolution. Noske had ability. The Alsatians and Lorrainers were cleverly tempted to travel home, with a programme for transforming their provinces into a little independent Bolshevist commonwealth. General von Lossberg, commanding the Army of Lorraine, was strangely and suddenly converted to Communism by telegraphic messages from naval officers at Kiel. He established a Soviet to work with the Revolutionary seamen.

But this trick of transforming a domestic difficulty into a frontier problem for the French was defeated by the men of Alsace and Lorraine. They refused to sit in a Soldier's and Workmen's Council with German troops, and Thomas returned to Germany and set up a Soviet in Oldenburg, and some of his followers settled in Düsseldorff and for months crippled the German steel industry. Other seamen went to Cologne, and led a mob that stormed the town-hall, post-office, and other public buildings, looted some shops and plundered clothing depots. There were scenes of disorders in other towns to which the most dangerous of the original mutineers were sent.

They it was who intensified down the lines of communication of Hindenburg's army the tendency to panic flight that came near to merging with the feeling of despair among the breaking combatant troops, and producing the greatest, wildest of disasters.

The plan of the counter-Revolutionary Coalition of Imperial Socialists and Imperial Ministers depended upon the fighting forces escaping from the contagion of the Independent Socialist movement. In Berlin, General von Linsingen continued confident that he could keep the picked garrison loyal to the Government so long as the Independents and their seamen missionaries were restrained from entering the capital. Field-Marshal von Hindenburg and his Army commanders were also hopeful of being able to turn the fighting-line troops against the revolting town garri- **Imperialists** sons, sailors, and working-class Spartacists. **versus Independents** He arranged his own Soldiers' Councils, to which tested men and non-commissioned officers were appointed in such strength that they were able to meet and talk down the wilder spirits who entered on the votes of their comrades.

The German governing class checked the Revolutionary movement at its outset with great skill, and then gradually modified it and changed it into a·weapon against the Allies. Rather than allow the movement for a Radical-Socialist republic to develop successfully, as the Independent Socialists might have developed it, they used the Spartacists as terrorisers of the reforming forces and of the Allies. General von Linsingen came near to losing the great game by reason of his strong-handed way of dealing with the most delicate of diplomatic situations. He would not act on the advice given to him by Scheidemann, Ebert, and Prince Max. On his orders, Berlin was isolated from all centres of disturbance, telegraphic and telephonic communications being stopped, as well as trains and motor traffic.

November 7th was the anniversary of the Bolshevist Revolution, and the Spartacists arranged to celebrate it by great gatherings. Linsingen forbade any popular meetings. All important points in the city were occupied by troops, strong bodies of police patrolled the streets, and the main thoroughfares were swept clear by armoured motor-cars, travelling to and fro at great speed. The working-class district of Moabit, where the Spartacists were in great strength, was guarded by military cordons. The crowds assembled, and, though continually broken up by the police, they re-formed

men were assembled into companies, and marched through the city to be drafted to their homes in the provinces.

But the Revolutionaries were able to work without arms. They spoke to the soldiers, telling them of what had taken place along the coast and down the Rhine and in Bavaria and Würtemberg. Fraternisation began between rebels and Royalists, and all the news of the Revolution spread by word of mouth to the capital. There was an intense period of preparation on November 8th, when Linsingen was defeated without fighting. The men of the Alexander Regiment of the Guard, occupying the barracks by the Imperial Palace, were among the first to go over to the people. When their new

GERMAN GOVERNMENT'S "LEAGUE FOR COMBATING BOLSHEVISM."

Three of the amazing posters which the German Republican Government had posted up all over the country early in 1919 as part of an organised campaign against the menace of Bolshevism. These graphic designs were devised to emphasise to the German people (left) "The Danger of Bolshevism," that (centre) "Bolshevism Means to Drench the World in Blood," and that (right) "Bolshevism Breeds War, Unemployment, and Famine."

in processions and tried to approach the Palace of the Chancellor. This movement was stopped, but all through the night the people thronged the streets, singing Revolutionary songs, and a conflict at last occurred as the mob refused to disperse, and were shot down with rifles and revolvers.

At dawn on November 8th, Linsingen still held the capital in apparently overwhelming strength, awaiting either the submission of the populace or their scientific slaughter when led by his Secret Service agents. The Independent Socialists exerted their influence to prevent a
Linsingen's attempt street battle, and took the best path to
to hold Berlin victory by personal pleading with the troops. Everything at the time was going in their favour from the Swiss frontier to the Polish border. They naturally desired that the capital should be won over by peaceful propaganda among the Guards and other garrisoning forces. A trainload of seamen was directed to Berlin. It was reckoned that the news they would bring to the isolated capital would complete the conversion of Linsingen's soldiers.

Linsingen learnt that the seamen were coming. Reckless of consequences he sent a trusted lieutenant and some sappers down the line with orders to wreck the train. This was one of the few serious mistakes made by the German military leaders, and it was averted by the young officer. He found that the train contained, in addition to the Revolutionary seamen, many women and children flying to Berlin for safety. He was ready to kill the sailors, but he would not sacrifice any innocent lives for a cause he believed to be almost hopeless. He let the train go on its way, and on the morning of November 8th the sailors arrived at Berlin.

Again Linsingen attempted to avoid the inevitable, instead of trying to ride the whirlwind in order to direct the storm. He met the Revolutionary seamen at the station with overpowering forces of infantry. Under the threat of annihilation, the

barracks were built, in 1901, the Kaiser addressed them in one of the most notorious of his speeches, saying that their quarters rose like a mighty fortress by his palace, in order that they might be at hand to repress and punish the unruly spirit of revolt if Berlin ever showed signs of rebellion against Royal authority.

It was because they remembered this speech that the Guardsmen of the Alexander Regiment refused to kill their fellow-countrymen. The Jäger Naumburg battalion also joined the Revolution, and other troops, sent to the capital for the express purpose of killing the populace, went over to the sailors and arming workmen. By the evening there seemed to be only some of the Guard Fusiliers, the Cockchafers, still determined to resist the will of the people. The Socialist leaders arranged a general strike for Saturday, November 9th, and some three thousand more sailors from Kiel entrained for the capital to ensure the popular victory.

On the morning of November 9th, Berlin appeared in a sudden, quiet transformation as a city of Red Flags. The Naumburg Jägers, Guardsmen, and other Revolutionary soldiers reversed Linsingen's dispositions by taking possession of the watch-house at the top of Unter den
Linden and other strategic places in the **Berlin a city of** city, from which they trained their **Red Flags** machine-guns. Socialist deputies went to all the barracks, and, except at the Cockchafers' quarters, the troops agreed to support the Revolution.

By noon the main streets were thronged with marching columns of soldiers and armed workmen, all moving to plan, and taking possession of the Government buildings. Scheidemann held a meeting outside the Reichstag and shouted:

The Kaiser has abdicated! The dynasty has fallen! It is a great and honourable victory for the German people. Herr Ebert has been given the task of forming a new Government in which both sections of the Socialist party are taking part. Orders by the Government are only valid when signed by Herr Ebert. Those by the Minister of War must be counter-signed by a Socialist delegate.

But it was not by the Reichstag, where the work of the counter-Revolution still went on, that the greatest excitement was seen. The main tide of the rejoicing multitudes swung towards the eastern end of Unter den Linden towards the Kaiser's palace. Down the balcony, from which William II. had been used to harangue the Berliners, there hung a red blanket, which some jester said was Augusta's petticoat. It was the only emblem of Revolution available, but its homeliness pleased the people better than a Red Flag would have done. On the balcony appeared the "Red Kaiser"—the spectacled, thin-faced Karl Liebknecht. After a tumult of welcoming cheers he spoke to the people in a different way from Scheidemann, cursing the Emperor and his Ministers for plotting the ghastly war that had brought Germany to ruin and degradation. Then for twenty minutes he declaimed, in the fashion of Lenin, against counter-Revolution, of which he had become unconsciously one of the chief agents. Disliking the cautious, democratic, pro-

Herr Erzberger, Minister of
Finance, June, 1919.

Herr Giesberts, Minister of Posts
and Telegraphs, June, 1919.

Dr. David, Minister of the
Interior, June, 1919.

of a paradise of peace, with little or nothing to pay for national wrongdoing, and the remaining capital of their country to draw upon for bettering themselves. The Junkers, industrial magnates, and Jewish capitalists had fallen with the Emperor, and the liberated working classes arranged to labour four hours a day, at something like four times their ordinary wages, upon the glorious work of social reconstruction.

Such were the ideas of the common followers of the new Spartacus. He also obtained tens of thousands of sinister recruits of the habitual criminal class by the opening of prisons and the call for determined men to form his Red Guard. Many demobilised soldiers, who could not find ordinary occupation, entered the ranks of the Spartacists. There was, indeed, at first a chance that Liebknecht might overwhelm those officers of his, who intended to betray him, by the extraordinary number of his trained soldier recruits.

Practically every shop, mill, and factory, that began to run on the lines of Guild Socialism, or Syndicalism,

Herr Scheidemann, Chancellor,
Feb.-June, 1919.

Herr Wissell, Minister of
Economics, June, 1919.

Herr Ebert, became President of
Republic, February, 1919.

Herr Schmidt, Minister of
Food, June, 1919.

Dr. Solf, delegate to the
Peace Conference.

gressive policy of the Independents more than the opposition of the Imperial Socialists, he did more than any other man to waste the working energy of the Revolution in bloodshed and impossible aims.

He was followed by a grey-bearded patriarchal figure, Adolf Hoffmann, who merely spoke in a vague poetic way of the glorious conquest of the citadel of autocracy and the sudden achievement of hopes beyond the wildest dreams. There were, unfortunately, many men of fine character in Liebknecht's following. By his early and decisive stand against all the war-makers and acquiescers in the war, Liebknecht had captured the minds of many of the younger generation of literary men, artists, and general intellectuals. There were, of course, obscure multitudes of the populace that looked with happy vacuity of mind for the immediate establishment

Herr Noske, Minister of Defence,
June, 1919.

Colonel Reinhardt, Minister of
War, January, 1919.
GERMAN LEADERS, 1918-19.

Herr Bauer, became Premier in
June, 1919.

became a recruiting force for the Spartacist army. The workmen in possession reduced owners, managers, and foremen to the rank of workmen, technicians drawing about the same wages as working hands. Then, as all weekly profits were shared among the governing workmen, there was a strong disinclination to give demobilised soldiers the positions they had left when joining the Army. Trade was not good, and the general stock of raw materials had to be husbanded in order to last six months. Therefore, if demobilised men were admitted to their old places, there would be less to share every week between the reigning Syndicalists.

The Ebert-Haase programme for restricting the day's work to four hours, so that all the returning soldier labour might be absorbed, did not meet with the approval of the Syndicalists. What they wanted was to keep their part of the machinery of production under their control, and maintain only the original number of profit-sharers. They did not mind huge taxes being imposed for unemployment pay. This, in their view, would fall on the discredited capitalists. They were the victorious proletariat, and all they wanted was a strong Government that would protect their newly-acquired interests.

The demobilised troops thus cheated out of civil employment were soon recognised as a grand source of danger by the old Army leaders. Partly to prevent Liebknecht from gaining all the recruits, but mainly to gather the discontented, disillusioned fighting men into a new Imperial force, the lieutenants of Hindenburg opened a recruiting campaign of enlistment for a frontier army that could be used either against the Poles, Spartacists, or Revolutionaries generally. The Imperial Socialists agreed with this scheme, afterwards obtaining the nomination of their comrade Noske as political chief of the new army when he had pacified and transformed Kiel.

Meanwhile, the situation in Berlin remained sufficiently dangerous to compel the Independent Socialists under Haase to come to terms with the Imperial Socialists under Scheidemann. Actual power fell into the hands of a Soviet, in which the Spartacist influence seemed to be strong. It was a Soldiers' and Workmen's Council of the Petrograd type, and, like its model, arrogated to itself the exercise of the power of the nation. The Reichstag might have been made into the organ of Government had it been changed from a sham into a veritable parliament when the Kaiser lost his autocratic privileges. But, even when the Kaiser abdicated, nobody of importance thought that had brought about the great change should control the country, by force if necessary, while completing the transformation of society. This was the way France had been governed during the Reign of Terror, with committees largely based on the Commune of Paris. It was a way that usually led to sanguinary tyranny, and the German people as a whole did not like it. While they quietly organised, the Soviet of Berlin tried to rule, but was shackled by the compromise between Haase and his Independents and Scheidemann and his Imperial Socialists. The Berlin Soviet was, likewise, gradually transformed by the secret agents of the counter-Revolution.

Meanwhile, a Provisional Government was formed, with three Imperial Socialist Ministers and three Independent Socialist Ministers. Friedrich Ebert, a tailor's son from Heidelberg, who first followed the trade of a saddler and became at the age of twenty-one a Socialist editor and Trade Union official, was the leader of the new Government. He was a silent, careful man, forty-seven years old, who succeeded to the presidency of the Imperial Socialist Democratic Party in 1916, and supported the Kaiser, after discussing matters with him in July, 1917. He had also strangely occupied the Bismarckian position of Imperial Chancellor in the brief interval between the fall of Prince Max of Baden and the rise of the Provisional Government.

Ebert controlled home affairs and the Army, while his more notorious colleague, Scheidemann, became Minister of Finance and the Colonies, and a third Imperial Socialist, Otto Landsberg, who had openly confessed since 1912 that he was a German Imperialist, was made Minister of Publicity, Art, and Literature. Landsberg was the Propagandist, and being, like Noske, a brilliant, strong-minded Jew, he was one of the principal shaping forces in the Government. The three Independent Socialist Ministers were Hugo Haase, a lawyer who became director of the foreign affairs, Wilhelm Dittmann, a cabinet-maker who rose through journalism into Socialist politics, and Herr Barth, who inclined to sympathise with Liebknecht and directed social policy. The Independents tried to bring Liebknecht and Ledebour into the Council, and make them equal to the other members, by retiring one Independent and one Imperialist. This measure would have completely reunited the Socialist parties,

Socialists fail to reunite

FIGHTING THE SPARTACISTS IN BERLIN.
Transporting the bodies of people killed in the street fighting. In circle: Inspecting passports at a street barrier, and (above) nurses bandaging wounded in the Frankfurter Allee.

of turning to the Reichstag for government. Not only was it elected on a class franchise, but most of its members were discredited as having acquiesced in the policy of Ludendorff.

The election, on a democratic suffrage, of a National Assembly seemed the easiest way out of the problem of forming a National Government. This immediately proved, however, to be the thorniest path of escape from the jungle of Soviet tyranny. All the Spartacists, and some of the extreme wing of the Independents, wished to follow the Bolshevist, or Jacobin, method of the direct rule by a few Revolutionary leaders, answerable to the local councils or clubs. In this view the active, daring, successful minority

certain exporters in America on business grounds. Germany required food, cotton, and other raw material to the value of three hundred million pounds sterling. She could pay a considerable sum down for the goods she most urgently needed, and thereby produce a grand increase in the price of commodities against the British, French, Italian, and neutral nations of Europe.

The Germans had learnt nothing from their defeat. Their directors based their calculations upon appeals to the selfishness of their opponents. They were answered by the United States Food Controller, Mr. Hoover, who stated that the needs of the starving people in the liberated territories came first, the allied populations second, and neutral countries third, while the object of extending the control to enemy supplies was to prevent mischievous competition in the food markets of the world. Mr. Hoover clinched his answer with the remark that the allied food controllers required to be satisfied that Germany's need for food was real, that her distribution organisation was efficient, and that a Government was established capable of making a lasting peace settlement.

and prevented the return of the Reactionaries to power. It proved, however, quite impracticable. Liebknecht would not compromise, and Scheidemann was too much afraid of him to share power.

After the fusion of the two constitutional Socialist parties had been arranged, the struggle over the form of government opened at a meeting of the Berlin Soviet in the Circus Busch on November 10th. Some of the extreme Independents joined with the Spartacists in trying to exclude the Imperial Socialists because of the dangers of reaction. When, however they endeavoured to force the rejection of the plan for a National Assembly, the officer members of the Council displayed their growing strength.

As a matter of fact, the Revolution in Germany was not caused by famine. To some extent it was provoked by an enormous system of profiteering and very unfair distribution of ordinary supplies among the poorest classes. There was a serious shortage of fats and milk, and in the towns especially children suffered from the milk shortage and the dearness of fruit and green vegetables. On a diet of potatoes, war bread, and other inferior food many poor women could not nourish their babies

They threatened to use the troops in establishing a military dictatorship, on the ground that the peril from reaction was insignificant in comparison with the danger of civil war. The Soviet discussion continued on November 11th, and the political victory of the Imperial Socialists was ensured.

The Independents were defeated in their scheme for a Socialist - Radical Republic, free from any reactionary influences. The main reason used against them was the theory that the Allies would refuse food supplies to Germany if none of the old Reactionaries were admitted to a share of power. The Secretaries of State and principal State officials who held office under the Kaiser were thereupon empowered to continue their duties in association with the two Socialist parties.

Bernstorff, master-intriguer

There followed an amazing restoration of the Kaiser's Ministers. Dr. Solf returned to the Foreign Office, with Kautsky vainly trying to control him. General von Scheuch became Minister of War, with Ebert assisting him, and other Kaiser politicians, with all the Prussian bureaucracy, resumed full control of the machinery of administration. Behind the men in office was the master intriguer, Count von Bernstorff, the former Ambassador to the United States, who rose secretly to power by reason of his presumed knowledge and influence in America. He it was who selected the policy of an immediate lifting of the blockade as the best means of dividing the United States and the British Empire by playing on the interests of the large exporting houses of the United States. While Dr. Solf sent imploring messages to the American Government to save the German people from immediate general famine, and elicited the sympathies of both American and British pacifists, Bernstorff appealed more quietly to

DAYS OF STRIFE IN PRUSSIA'S CAPITAL.
Trench dug across a street in preparation for an anticipated outbreak. In circle: Armoured car in the Alexander Platz during the Spartacist troubles, and (above) election posters of the Social Democrats.

by breast feeding. Corruption in the distribution of supplies and in the maintenance of unpatriotic high prices for the enrichment of the great landowners whose estates stretched from the Elbe to the Niemen, were the main causes of underfeeding among the urban poor. The German farm lands were in a high state of cultivation, and although an official statement was made in Berlin that the farm lands had decayed through the loss of all prisoners of war at the armistice, British officers observed, as late as in the summer of 1919, that hundreds of thousands of Russian prisoners were kept as cheap and skilled agricultural workers, and that the land was in a far better state of cultivation than in England.

DESTRUCTION OF INSURGENTS' PAPERS IN ONE OF THE STREETS OF BERLIN.

Papers belonging to the Spartacists thrown into the street by Government troops during the conflict in Berlin between the first Revolutionary administration and the Spartacist party formed by Liebknecht. The struggle, which was carried on between these opposing forces during December, 1918, and January, 1919, was more an affair of repeated street skirmishing than a pitched battle for a capital and a country.

The Americans at last took up the work of looking after the Russian prisoners, who were still working on the farms when the Peace Treaty was signed. It was the general knowledge of food conditions which the Americans thus obtained that made them harden against the dishonest manœuvres which Solf began and his successors continued. It is a question whether General Sir Herbert Plumer was not misled by a ghastly trick of the enemy when he found the suffering poor in Cologne a sight that moved him to indignant remonstrance with the Allied Council at Versailles. He and many of his officers could not bear to see men, women, and children wasting to death from lack of food. British naval officers visiting Hamburg and other northern ports were also moved by scenes of heart-breaking famine.

Yet some of the leading German food experts reckoned that, with the sugar saved from use as raw materials for munitions, and with the potatoes likewise saved from destruction for alcohol manufacture for war purposes, the harvest of 1918 was ample for feeding the population. There were reasons for believing that Hamburg was starved as a preliminary measure to its reduction by the Reactionary forces, and that things were made as uncomfortable as possible for all urban centres of Revolutionary feeling, while the provisioning of regions of the Rhineland bridge-heads was neglected, in order that there should be no pleasant memories of the period of allied occupation. It must be remembered that the old Prussian bureaucracy was in control of the leading of Revolution, and striving to get the blockade raised.

Starvation according to plan

In the first weeks of the Revolution the rations of the people were increased. This was a wise, preventive measure against the spread of disorders. It was a supreme necessity to keep the people hopeful and quiet, until Hindenburg

returned with picked loyal troops, trained to hate the Revolutionaries. There was a critical period of a month between the re-establishment of the old Government under a Socialist covering and the return of the Prussian Guard to Berlin. There was one very remarkable period of wavering among the Reactionaries themselves, between some form of controlled Socialism and the repression of all genuine Revolutionary feeling. Some of the Imperial Socialists, led by Scheidemann, considered that a Teutonic Socialist commonwealth might win Holland and Switzerland.

And M. Troelstra, the Dutch agent of **Socialist scheming** Imperial Socialism, and Herr Grimm, the **in Holland** Swiss agent of the same world-wide organisation, tried to provoke Socialist insurrections in their countries. At a Labour meeting at Rotterdam, on November 11th, Troelstra excited the working men to seize supreme power. The next day, in a speech in Parliament, he explained that he would be compelled to follow the example of the Berlin Revolutionaries. He claimed that the Army was on his side, and that most of the police were ready to help in the revolt, and he directly attacked the person of the Queen.

There was some disorder among the Hague garrison, and Revolutionary crowds demonstrated in the street. For a few hours the situation seemed to be perilous, and there was a report that Queen Wilhelmina had decided in the evening of November 13th to abdicate. Revolutionary disorders also occurred at Amsterdam, and some of the agitators of the Bolshevist sort began to form the usual Workmen's and Soldiers' Councils. Holland, however, was not to be overwhelmed by an artificial storm of unrest. In the provinces were strong forces of loyal troops, and the Volunteer Landstorm, composed of men who had freely offered their services, were called up. In the night the Loyalist forces marched into the

458

Hague in such overpowering numbers that the Revolutionaries gave up their arms, and the Germanising movement ended.

It took a good deal to move the stolid Dutch people, but when they were moved they were like their remote kinsmen the English, and acted quickly and strongly. A tidal wave of Royalist enthusiasm came from the peasant and middle classes, and submerged the fires of Revolution in the cities. Indignation meetings were held throughout the country, and practically to a man the Volunteers gathered for battle. Troelstra had merely been playing a game of bluff. Having been unable to organise the country, he agitated only in the principal cities, expecting that, in the capital, he could frighten the Government into surrendering to his demands, and win without a civil war. So complete was his overthrow that, on November 15th, his Socialist lieutenant in the Second Chamber condemned his action and his principles, and agreed to work with the constitutional parties. At the Dutch Labour Congress held at Rotterdam on the following day, Troelstra was again disavowed, and he at last came before the Congress and apologised with a kind of daring impudence, saying :

I admit that I have misjudged the existing relations of political power. We are not yet backed by the majority of the Dutch nation, and we shall act accordingly. But things move rapidly in these days, The Government must not underrate our importance, but recognise the inevitable necessity for fulfilling the demands on our programme.

The most enlightening observation on the enemy's intrigue against the Dutch people was made by a German soldier from the Minden Soviet. He asked one of the first British journalists who entered Germany for news of the Dutch Revolution. He was told it had collapsed. "That's a pity," he said. "If it had succeeded we should have united with

Attempts on Switzerland Holland, *and obtained colonies again.*" The Dutch nation was already educated in the system of democratic government, so that, as some of the sobered Labour men pointed out, German conditions for a struggle for freedom were wanting in Holland. It was the same in Switzerland. Here Grimm, working with the Russian Bolshevists and their German pay - masters, between whom he had been an intermediary when Lenin lived in Switzerland, promoted a general strike. The strike began at Zurich, and spread to the railway at Lausanne, in French Switzerland. The Government called out troops for the maintenance of order, and armed them with bombs. The overawed working men marched in procession in an orderly manner, and men in the post-offices and other Government places, who had been led into the movement by discontent over the high cost of living and scarcity of food, wisely decided at the last moment not to join the strikers.

Grimm thereupon endeavoured to induce the Federal authorities to withdraw the troops, in order not to provoke the workmen. It was his way of asking the Government to commit suicide. The Ministers not only maintained their forces, but collected the members of the Bolshevist legations and expelled them into German territory. The warlike peasantry of the most ancient Republic existing in the world showed themselves fiercely averse to any attempt at tyrannical Communism, and after some negotiation between the Government and the Workers' Union, the gross intrigue for the German conquest of Switzerland by means of a bogus revolution failed as completely as the attempt to absorb Holland.

There were vainer designs of the same character upon Denmark. Danish Jews of the Socialist school, who had formerly acted in the interests of Imperial Germany, proclaimed a general strike as a preliminary to disorders. Russian Bolshevist delegates in Copenhagen supplied funds, but so few men left their work in the land that was waiting the restoration of its stolen province of Schleswig, that the Scheidemann movement, after some rioting, expired at birth in ridiculous futility. In Sweden, to which Germanic ambitions had extended from the opening of the war, there was also a Communist ferment among the labourers of Stockholm. The Minority **Denmark and** Socialist Party talked of proclaiming a Soviet **Sweden** Government, with complete nationalisation and all factories under workman control. But M. Branting, the leader of the Majority Socialists, refused Revolutionary co-operation with the extremists, and kept his strong party in alliance with the Liberals, and sharing power with them.

In the Scandinavian countries there were differing conditions but a similar general aversion to revolt for the benefit of Prussia. In Denmark food was comparatively abundant, but work was scarce, owing to the lack of the raw materials of industry. Unemployed workmen induced their more fortunate mates to come out on strike, in the hope of compelling the Government to find more coal. In Sweden, rich in iron, wood, and water-power, there was abundant employment but a scarcity of wheat and meat. In Norway the great shipping traffic was wonderfully profitable, and both food and work were plentiful. In spite of the pressure of war conditions, no part of Scandinavia was a promising field for the last of the national German intrigues of conquest.

Probably the Teutons did not expect any great, permanent success in their scheme of annexation by a contagion of Revolution. Lenin and Trotsky had already so vaccinated neutrals with some of their stronger virus that the nations

CIVIL WAR IN THE STREETS OF BERLIN.
People running to cover in Berlin. Shooting took place in the spasmodic street fighting which marked the conflict between the first Revolutionary Government and the Spartacists at the end of 1918 and early in the following year.

Ich verzichte hierdurch für alle Zukunft auf die Rechte an der Krone Preussens und die damit verbundenen Rechte an der deutschen Kaiserkrone.

Zugleich entbinde ich alle Beamten des Deutschen Reichen und Preussens sowie alle Offiziere, Unteroffiziere und Mannschaften der Marine, des Preussischen Heeres und der Truppen der Bundeskontingente des Treueides, den sie Mir als ihrem Kaiser, König und Obersten Befehlshaber geleistet haben. Ich erwarte von ihnen, dass sie bis zur Neuordnung des Deutschen Reichs den Inhabern der tatsächlichen Gewalt in Deutschland helfen, das Deutsche Volk gegen die drohenden Gefahren der Anarchie, der Hungersnot und der Fremdherrschaft zu schützen.

Urkundlich unter Unserer Höchsteigenhändigen Unterschrift und beigedruckten Kaiserlichen Insiegel.

Gegeben Amerongen, den 28. November 1918.

THE FINAL SCRAP OF PAPER: RECORD OF THE ABDICATION OF THE KAISER.

Facsimile of the typescript document by signing which Wilhelm II. renounced for ever the Crown of Prussia and all rights connected with the Imperial German Crown. This historic document was signed by the Kaiser at Amerongen on November 28th, 1918, nine days after he had sought personal safety over the frontier of neutral Holland.

were practically immune against the artificial culture of a weaker kind exported from the Bernstorff-Scheidemann laboratories. There was a subtler and more diplomatic design underlying the manifold attempts to spread through Western Europe the German Revolutionary movement, just at the time when it was slackening and shallowing in Berlin.

By promoting an appearance of general unrest on the European continent, the leaders of the old German governing class turned their difficulties at home into advantages abroad. They exercised pressure upon allied statesmen, by making it appear that there was a strong tendency to Bolshevism, and that Western Europe would founder with Germany if the Germans were not freed from the blockade and given easy peace conditions. The scheme had a preliminary measure of success as was shown by speeches of President Wilson, Lord Milner, and other English-speaking leaders, who urged that the

Germans must be fed and saved from falling into complete anarchy if any part of war compensation and costs were to be obtained from them. Some of the Teutons then went too far, when Scheidemann became, on November 20th, the national publicity agent and director of propaganda. They stated that their propertied class would sacrifice all personal wealth in a genuine scheme of Communism, if an attempt were made to impose heavy indemnities and extend Polish territory to the Baltic shore.

With the return of the first multitudes of troops from the western front there was a resurgence of disorder from Düsseldorff to the North Sea ports. It was largely a matter of chance whether the Spartacists or Independents won control of the local Soviets, and in Brunswick and other towns there were cases of the wildest gutter rule. Even the Berlin Soviet, that claimed sovereignty and threatened to dismiss the Ebert-Haase Ministry, wavered a moment between a military dictatorship, a National Assembly, and Communism. Its hesitation was produced by the pressure of the fugitive part of the western armies on the one side, and on the other by the steady reinforcement of the Government forces, which were strengthened by the arrival of the Königsberg Army Corps and the reorganisation of a hundred other regiments collected in and about Berlin. As the main western armies moved forward, under the control of their officers, definite signs of their use for a counter-Revolution were clearly visible. General von Eberhardt, General von Böhn, General von der Marwitz, and General Sixt von Armin openly declared against the Soviets, forbade the use of red colours, and strongly moved the re-establishment of the old regime.

These commanders were honest in their intentions but lacking in diplomatic art. They soon adopted a subtler method of achieving their ends, under the advice of the Berlin bureaucracy, and helped in organising the packed Soldiers' Councils that met in congress at Ems. The troops were told that they had been prevented from winning the defensive campaign and robbed of a fair peace by cowardly seamen and "slackers" in munition factories. They were given a confused view of the Revolution, in which the Independents and the Spartacists were merged together as agents of a Bolshevist movement that would inflict more suffering on Germany than the civil wars of the seventeenth century. In this way the influence of Haase was undermined, and the Spartacists in Berlin, on November 21st, promoted the spirit of reaction in the western forces by vainly attempting to seize power by violence.

They were defeated in an action round the Police Presidency, but their influence extended along the North Sea coast, where a Communist republic was formed with Hamburg as its capital. The Berlin Soviet became in appearance more Spartacist in feeling, and prepared to hold a congress of delegates from all Soldiers' and Workmen's Councils, and from them to form an Executive General Council which should control the Provisional Ministry. Herr Barth, the most extreme of the Independent members of the Ministry, who had taken a leading part in the Berlin Revolution, pleaded with the Soviet for the rapid election of a Democratic National Assembly. But the Imperial Socialists and their reactionary allies had then no desire for an immediate General Election. Their plan was first to discredit and oust the Independents, so as to obtain complete control of the machinery of election.

As the Berlin Soviet at once abandoned directly to the old Prussian bureaucracy the exercise of all its executive powers, its pretence of being more Revolutionary than were the Independents was strangely weak. Yet its measures for summoning a Soviet Congress greatly alarmed the country. The North Sea ports agitated for an immediate National Assembly. Westphalia and the Rhineland threatened to secede, and Southern Germany also prepared to separate from Prussia. Bavaria then became the protagonist of the genuine Radical-Socialist-Republican movement, which the Independents had originated and directed. In the ordinary way the Catholic peasant country of Bavaria would have been a natural centre of Moderate Constitutionalism; but, at the opening of the Revolution a very able Galician Jew, Salomon Kusnowsky, who had risen to fame as a Socialist journalist under the nom de guerre of Kurt Eisner, organised a Trade Union rebellion in Munich and other Bavarian cities. Beginning with a demonstration for peace on November 4th, Eisner proceeded to win over the troops, and by November 7th he gained complete power over them through an error of the Bavarian Minister of War. This general took it upon himself to open a campaign against the victorious Italians by sending a strong force of troops over the southern frontier to Innsbruck.

They were the last soldiers in Bavaria who obeyed orders, and their despatch on a fruitless expedition left Bavaria undefended against the Revolutionaries. On November 7th Eisner filled the streets of Munich with another peace demonstration. In the night the multitudes surrounded the barracks and military prison. Only a few officers fought against the movement and, at light cost in dead and wounded, Kurt Eisner proclaimed the Republic of Bavaria, with himself as its Provisional President. He also formed a Provisional Parliament of the Socialist and peasant members of the old Diet, three Liberals, and with the support of some Catholic Trade Unions.

Kurt Eisner in Bavaria Eisner soon showed himself one of the best and fairest of Germans, possibly for the reason that he was not a German himself. He admitted into the Cabinet Herr Auer, an Imperial Socialist of the Scheidemann type, alongside some professors who had opposed or favoured the war. He maintained nearly all the old officials in the administrative services, and invited representatives of industrial interests to assist in the Government. Eisner himself was among the Socialist deputies who first acquiesced in the war, but he had repented, and had awaited the opportunity for overthrowing the war-makers and establishing a republic. Like other Independents, he worked for a National Assembly, with a Government that should proceed slowly and cautiously in the socialisation of

LEADERS OF THE GERMAN SPARTACISTS.
Rosa Luxemburg and Karl Liebknecht, leaders of the revolt against the first Revolutionary Government in Germany in the winter of 1918-19. They were assassinated in Berlin in January, 1919. Liebknecht had adopted the name of "Spartacus," and thus his followers came to be known as Spartacists.

large and profitable natural resources, such as coal and great landed estates. He was farther removed from Bolshevism than from Imperialism, but it was that latter that he feared more. He achieved the complete restoration of order in Bavaria within a week, and with other Independents arranged a scheme for a United States of Germany, including Austria, by which Prussia should be split up into Catholic and Protestant States, under federal control. The result would have been that the German Catholics, strengthened by the Austrians, would have outnumbered the German Protestants, and possessed the principal coal resources and other industrial advantages.

It was Eisner who took the first step in sharing power with the Imperial Socialists. Like Haase, his intention was that the two constitutional Socialist parties should combine in bringing Liebknecht to reason on the one side, and reducing the reactionaries to impotence on the other side. He was alarmed when Solf, Erzberger, and other upholders of the monarchy were admitted into the new Government. When he discovered the intricate scheme of the counter-Revolution, he fought gallantly for the Independent policy, and also for a true peace with the Allies.

In the hope of putting an end to all the intrigues of the war-makers, he published, in the last week of November, an official report in regard to the origin of the war. Using the Bavarian archives, he proved that on July 18th, 1914, the German Government made the outbreak of war certain, and fixed the beginning of operations for the time when the French President and Prime Minister would be at sea on their return voyage from Russia, and unable to cope with the situation. Other documents proved that the Kaiser's visit to Norway and the furlough of Moltke and Falkenhayn were arranged to delude France and Russia, and keep them from mobilising while in Germany and Austria preparations were being completed.

It was one of the most dramatic exposures in history. The German people were staggered by it, as their faith in the struggle having started as a war of defence after a Russian mobilisation had apparently been confirmed by Bolshevist revelations. Even the Imperial Socialists, **Exposure of Prussian duplicity** who were under no illusions, were compelled to make a show of indignant surprise, and to declaim against the wickedness of the men with whom they were working.

Haase and Kautsky, as Independents, then endeavoured to co-operate from Berlin with Eisner in Munich by arranging for the publication of a Government history of German secret policy from July, 1914, to November, 1918. As Dr. Solf, with a company of imperturbable Prussian bureaucrats of the Bernstorff school, was still working in the Foreign Office alongside Haase and Kautsky, the Berlin Independents found that the confidential documents they required had been strangely mislaid. They carried the matter before the Berlin Soviet, and some of the soldiers remarked that there had been a general destruction of documents likely to inconvenience the Imperial Government. The discussion became so wild and vain that the Bavarian delegates left the meeting with Alsace-Lorraine and Baden representatives.

By way of distracting public attention a proclamation was issued in the name of Hindenburg, with the disturbing news that Marshal Foch was preparing to overrun the country. Eisner got into telegraphic communication with General Headquarters, and discovered that Dr. Solf was one of the authors of the false proclamation. All the Independents then united in calling for the dismissal of Solf and Erzberger, with Scheidemann and David and other intriguing Majority Socialists. They tried to prevent Scheidemann from mis-informing foreign nations in regard to events in Germany and spreading vicious propaganda by seizing the great wireless stations, but they could not prevail against the strong, sinister forces they had admitted into the Revolutionary Government.

In the first week of December there was some fierce skirmishing in the streets of the capital. The Spartacists were led by some of the officers into action in the suburbs, and a larger force of a mysterious kind, containing seamen and soldiers, with Independent colours, marched to the Imperial Chancellory and tried to compel Ebert to summon a National Assembly at once, and proclaim himself President of the first German Social Republic. Ebert refused to do anything until the Soviet Congress met in the middle of the month.

Fighting in Berlin Thereupon a sergeant led some men to the building occupied by the Berlin Executive Soviet and arrested all the committeemen. The Independent Minister, Barth, intervened, and released the men who claimed to be the real governing force in Germany. Then there was a battle between Spartacists and Independents, the Spartacists wishing to hang Ebert and to rescue the Soviet Executive, who had already been set free. The next morning the extreme section of the Independent Party called for a general strike, and great crowds formed in street processions. Liebknecht sallied out in an armoured motor-car, and for some reason joined the men who had fought and scattered his followers.

This was the end of the Revolution, so far as related to the genuine reforming movement of the steadier sort of the Independents. Ebert brought more troops into Berlin to crush the Spartacists, and on December 9th the Guards Cavalry Division and Jäger Division arrived in Berlin. Two days afterwards the Prussian Guardsmen marched

ENTRANCE TO THE EX-KAISER'S PALACE.
Main doorway of the palace in Berlin as it appeared after the fight round the building. Though not structurally damaged, the palace had many windows and much ornamental work shattered, and a number of rooms wrecked.

through the Brandenburg Gate, the bands playing "Deutschland über Alles" and the Prussian anthem. Officers and men were decorated with flowers and wore the old black-white-and-red colours, and were welcomed by Ebert with flowers of rhetoric. They were told that no enemy had overcome them, that they had saved the country from invasion, and become the hope of German freedom. They retained their arms after the Independents had been defeated on the question of disarming the troops, and undertook to maintain order and to disarm riotous mobs. Cheered by their presence, the old Court Party, including the Empress, endeavoured to summon the old Reichstag. Liebknecht countered with a strike among the mechanics and electrical engineers, and with Rosa Luxemburg headed a great converging procession that massed round the building where the Soviet Congress sat. He tried to force his way into the assembly, but was kept out.

Triumph of Majority Socialists When the Spartacists were completely outvoted, the contest between Ebert and Haase was at last openly conducted. Independent after Independent attacked Hindenburg, Solf, Ebert, and Scheidemann. In as stormy a discussion as those of the Jacobin Club in Danton's days the Independents were outvoted, and Majority Socialists were alone chosen as members of the Executive Committee of the National Soviet. The issue had been decided beforehand, with the return of the Guards and the arrival of the multitude of delegates from the western armies.

The original mistake of the Independents was to allow the publicity and propaganda part of the Government to fall to Landsberg and Scheidemann. By trusting in the sincerity of their former comrades, Haase and his lieutenants were outvoted by well-meaning, ignorant soldiers, who had been taught to regard them as Bolshevists. The honest men resigned their positions in the Provisional Government which they had created. Scheidemann became Foreign Minister,

MACHINE-GUN IN A BERLIN PALACE.
One of the rooms in the Kaiser's palace in Berlin during the fighting between Government troops and Spartacists at the close of 1918. The palace was the centre of a sharp contest between the opposing parties.

BOMBS IN BERLIN FIGHTING.
House in one of the old streets of Berlin destroyed by a bomb in the course of one of the Spartacist outbreaks which occurred in the first few months of the Revolution in Germany.

Noske entered the Cabinet and climbed to the position of Civil Chief of the Army, and two other Majority Socialists entered the Government.

The Spartacists joined in condemning the Independents. Liebknecht and "Red Rosa," who regarded Haase as the new Kerensky, reckoned that the way was clear for them to follow the example of Lenin and Trotsky and enforce a Communist system. Their attempts at insurrection, that began at Christmas, were a tragedy of self-conceit and blind folly. In the first week of November, Liebknecht might have been dictator of Germany. He was admired by the disillusioned middle classes, as well as by the urban working men. He, however, refused to lead the Revolution on November 4th, the day fixed by the Independents, who had laboriously worked up their organisation since 1916. Then he paraded from city to city in as histrionic a manner as the Kaiser, and lost the support of steady men by refusing **A tragedy** to compromise with the Independents and **of folly** by adopting the Bolshevist programme which had failed in Russia. While Lenin was dragooning his factory hands, taking all power of control from them, and forcing them to work hard under expert overseers, Liebknecht, whose sufferings had disturbed his balance of mind, continued to charm the thoughtless and selfish section of the working classes with promises of a golden age for labour.

Largely under his influence, an economic Revolution went on beneath the political movements and counter-movements. In practically all large factories there was a Workers' Council that made crippling demands upon the employers. In one week a large electrical company in Berlin lost all its profits for the year, having to surrender £2,000,000 to its workmen. From smaller firms, too, huge sums were taken to prevent the workpeople from striking and agitating in the Soviet for the works to be taken over either by the

Council or by the State. At Christmas one month's salary was generally demanded as a Christmas gift, and the shop councils allowed no one to be dismissed or engaged without their consent. They appointed the book-keepers to study the profits and cash balances at the bank, and at times tried to direct all business operations.

There was scarcely a glimmer of true Communism in the system of extortion. Where firms had expanded as the result of the war the workmen never thought of giving the war profits to the State. Not only did they take the money required to place businesses upon a peaceful commercial footing, but they ruined undertakings of an ordinary kind that had not expanded during the war by making excessive demands upon them. The employing class would have supported a strong Radical-Democratic Government, and taken an interest in the nationalisation of coalfields and in the division of great landed estates of the nobility, besides submitting themselves to a capital levy to strengthen the national financial system. Their personal, practical experiences with the Spartacists, however, made them turn in desperate anger towards the most reactionary of the Reactionaries. They would have liked to have seen Hindenburg in Berlin and other Prussian towns sweeping the streets with travelling barrages of machine-gun fire, trench-mortar bombs, and shrapnel. In the end they had their wish fulfilled, but it was the Imperial Socialist Noske who smashed the wild working-class movement with gas shell, high-explosive projectiles, aerial bombs, and machine-gun fire.

Better robbers than fighters

Liebknecht boasted that he had in Berlin a hundred thousand armed men behind him. With them at Christmas-time he held the industrial suburb of Neukölln. Yet a single company of Royalist soldiers reduced Neukölln to order, without fighting, between dawn and breakfast-time. The armed members of the proletariat were better robbers than

BOLSHEVISM IN BERLIN.
One of the Berlin houses that were destroyed by bombs during a conflict between the Bolshevist extremists and the Government forces early in 1919. Twelve occupants of this house were killed.

fighters. They opened military stores of provisions, and bartered public goods in so general a way that corruption became more contagious than influenza. In Soviet politics any man who could talk himself into any position of control could make money, and, owing to the high price of everything, the general moral sense was blunted by strong temptations to purchase goods from the baser Revolutionaries. The police force had been virtually overthrown when the Revolution opened in Berlin, and criminals were liberated by the Spartacists, according to the Bolshevist method.

The people of Berlin danced the New Year in with as much festivity as if they had conquered the world. There was a brief period of fictitious abundance so long as the spoil from Government stores lasted. By hundreds new dancing-places opened, and the people set out in pursuit of pleasure like a pack of hungry wolves searching for sheep. Between dancing and street fighting, between the Red Flags and rows of bottles of imitation champagne, the Berliners celebrated the New Year of peace. The reactionaries had some cause for rejoicing. Having triumphed over the Independent Party and prepared a violent end for Liebknecht, they returned with masterful assurance and undivided attention to their manœuvre against the Allies.

At the suggestion of Scheidemann, Dr. Solf retired, and his place in the Foreign Office was taken by a cousin of Bernstorff, Count von Brockdorff-Rantzau, who had proved his ability as Ambassador at Copenhagen. Rantzau was a Holstein nobleman, who had served as an officer of the Guards before following a diplomatic career. In 1913 he became notorious through his action in forcing the Danish Government to alter the text of some school-books in which a reference had been made to the hope of recovering Schleswig by a friendly arrangement with Germany. During the war **Bernstorff and Rantzau** he was one of the directors of the intrigues with certain Danish Socialists and dealers in contraband, and a promoter of the Scandinavian League, directed against the Allies, which failed owing to Danish and Norwegian objections. The most famous of his ancestors had fought for France in the seventeenth century, which may have been one of the grounds for selecting him as the conductor of foreign policy. But, though he afterwards boasted of his own great scheme for making victory out of defeat, Bernstorff and other men were always close behind him, planning both outlines and details of the secret policy.

The outbreak of demobilisation troubles among British and French troops, increasing Labour unrest in France, Italy, and Britain, and the triumph of the Sinn Fein movement in Ireland at the General Election were among the foundations of the policy of Rantzau. Before engaging deeply in intrigues

FUNERAL OF SOME OF THE VICTIMS OF CIVIL WAR IN THE PRUSSIAN CAPITAL.
Crowds assembled in one of the streets of Berlin to witness the funeral of soldiers who had fallen in the course of the fighting against the Spartacists. In circle : Spartacist speaker addressing the people of Berlin in front of the Reichstag building.

for weakening the allied forces and producing general disorder in allied countries it was necessary to kill Liebknecht and Rosa Luxemburg. The Spartacist Red Guard in Berlin had to be brought into action, in spite of the reluctance it had displayed for two months to engage in anything but advertising skirmishes.

With the help of the officers who remained in the Spartacus camp, Liebknecht, Rosa Luxemburg, and other misguided fanatics were at last induced to make a grand attack before the National Assembly was arranged by the Government. Eichhorn, an associate of the Bolshevist emissaries

READY FOR ACTION AT A BERLIN BARRICADE.
Barricade outside the Naval Department in Berlin during the fighting against the Spartacists, with machine-guns in position. Above : An armoured train, decorated with the badge of piracy, used by the Spartacists in fighting at Eisenach, in Thuringia.

to Berlin, had seized the Police Presidency early in November, appointed himself President of Police, disarmed the policemen, and made the building a munition depot for fellow-Spartacists. When the Ebert Government ordered all civilians to deliver up their arms, Eichhorn issued a counter-order that the people should retain their weapons. The Government then removed Eichhorn from his office by another order, but he fortified himself in the Presidency, and the Spartacist forces came out on January 5th to make a second Revolution. Liebknecht's men began with a series of astonishing successes. They captured the office of the "Vorwärts," the Imperial Socialist newspaper, Wolff's Agency, the "Berliner Tageblatt," the propaganda offices of Scheidemann, and other buildings. In many places the Government troops were either overpowered or joined the Spartacists. Some of the Independent leaders tried to bring about a reconciliation between Liebknecht and Ebert, but neither side would make any sacrifices of persons and principles.

Liebknecht continued his remarkable success in winning over Government troops, or inducing them not to shoot their fellow-countrymen. Day and night the struggle went on in little skirmishes, and the Government politicians began to grow alarmed. As they were hesitating alike to strike with all their power or to arrange a settlement,

Noske, the Socialist from Kiel, too command of the forces of defence, with the help of Colonel Reinhardt, Minister of War, and a first-rate military staff. He brought troops from Potsdam and Kiel, while General Gröner, the former Quartermaster - General and successor to Ludendorff, marched on the capital with forty regiments. By January 8th the Berlin garrison, which had wavered between neutrality and Revolutionary activity, decided to return to Government service rather than fight the fresh forces marching towards Berlin. But the 3rd Guards Infantry Regiment and other troops still fought for Liebknecht, and the Red Guards and their allies occupied the suburban railway - stations in order to stay Gröner's and Noske's reinforcements.

No bread was baked for some days, and the feasting of Christmas and New Year was followed by food shortage in a darkened city with the water supply cut. In the night of January 9th the rallied Government troops and their large reinforcements began to turn the tide of battle by the capture of some of the most important railway-stations and central thoroughfares. With artillery, trench-mortars, flame-projectors, and armoured motor-cars the principal buildings occupied by the rebels were attacked. Bomb-dropping aeroplanes were also used, and machine-guns were brought to bear from a church tower upon

SPARTACIST PRISONERS UNDER AN ARMED GUARD.
A number of Spartacist prisoners taken by Government troops during the fighting in Berlin. They were guarded by several soldiers with rifles in case of any attempts being made to escape.

rebels on the housetops. The "Vorwärt's" building was shelled and then bombed with mortars until the garrison surrendered, but the Spartacists recaptured the office to prevent the paper being published.

Yet the struggle was more an affair of street skirmishing than a pitched battle for a capital and country. Many of the Junker officers were fiercely resolute, but their men were swayed by the feeling that they were fighting countrymen, and the Revolutionaries continued to try to win over the troops. The struggle was often an affair of excited propaganda, with machine-guns rattling out an accompaniment in the distance. At least on one occasion a naval force had to defend itself from attack, when its desire was to join the attackers. The attitude of the main body of the Prussian Guard, who were disinclined to risk their lives for either the Revolution or the counter-Revo-

Ludwig III., King of Bavaria.

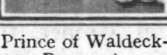
Prince of Waldeck-Pyrmont.   Gr. Duke of Mecklenburg-Schwerin.   Grand Duke of Oldenburg.

Prince Heinrich XXIV. of Reuss-Köstritz.   Prince Heinrich XXVII. of Reuss.

Prince of Schwarzburg-Rudolstadt.   Grand Duke of Saxe-Altenburg.   Prince Leopold IV. of Lippe.

lution, was an index of the general mood of the men of the western armies. They felt they had done their work, and that fighting battles in Berlin for politicians was not their business.

Victory rested with the side that could impress conviction on its forces. Noske succeeded by bringing from the country more fresh troops, who were hotly worked up to anger against the native Bolshevists by their officers, and sent into action before Liebknecht's followers could talk them over. Lads without battle experience were found to be best for this purpose. In gradual progress the capital was reconquered by January 20th, 1919, when the Police Presidency was shelled and stormed, and the Silesian railway-station was recovered. A considerable number of those who surrendered were killed without trial. This was the fate that befell Liebknecht and Rosa Luxemburg. They were tracked and arrested on January 15th. Soldiers brought them to the staff of the cavalry of the Prussian Guard, who pretended to send them, under preventive

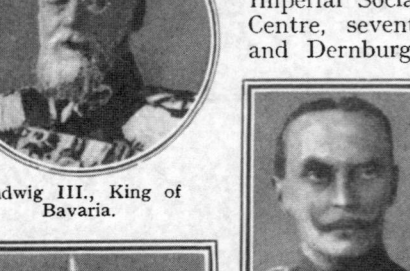

Wilhelm II., King of Prussia and German Emperor.

Wilhelm II., King of Würtemberg.
GERMANY'S DISCROWNED RULERS.

arrest, to Moabit Prison, and had them assassinated on their way. The officers put on their old arrogance, but the Socialists in the Government saw instantly the manifold ways in which the gross illegality might be avenged upon them both personally and politically.

Great pains were at once taken to convince the home public and foreign nations that Liebknecht had been shot while running away, and that Rosa Luxemburg had been lynched by the mob, though her guards tried to defend her. In spite of the industry of the Government publicity departments the truth came out. By this time, however, the General Election had taken place. Among the men returned for the National Assembly were one hundred and sixty-five Imperial Socialists, ninety-one Catholics of the Centre, seventy-five Democrats of a new Solf and Dernburg party, thirty-eight Junker Mili-

Duke Bernhard of Saxe-Meiningen.   Prince of Schaumburg-Lippe.   Grand Duke of Hesse.

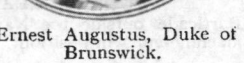
Friedrich August III., King of Saxony.   Ernest Augustus, Duke of Brunswick.

Grand Duke of Baden.   Grand Duke of Saxe-Weimar.   Duke of Saxe-Coburg-Gotha.

tarists, twenty-two National Liberals, representing large industrial interests, twenty-two Independent Socialists, and eight odd men.

Ebert and Scheidemann lost much less power than Haase and Eisner, yet they suffered a very considerable loss of authority. The new and rather dubious Democrats at first seemed to be the governing force, able to support or overturn the Majority Socialists or the Reactionary groups They elected to work with their old associates, Ebert and Scheidemann, but this arrangement was but a blind to the triumphant strength of the counter-Revolution. The militarists were actually in power, with Erzberger, of the Catholic Party, as balancing weight against the Imperial Socialists. Whenever these tried to recover their popularity by a programme of reconstruction they were checked. The way was clear for Count von Brockdorff-Rantzau to develop his scheme of intrigues against the Allies and Poles in a struggle that did not end until his strategy was defeated at the Peace Conference.

VIEW OF PEST

CHAPTER CCCXVII.

TAKEN FROM BUDA.

CENTRAL EUROPE IN REVOLUTION.
II.—Apathetic Republicanism in Austria and Active Bolshevism in Hungary.
By Edward Wright.

Empire that Consisted of an Army and a Bureaucracy—Maintenance of a Feudal Polity in the Twentieth Century—Bold Breakaway of the Bohemians—Mild Revolution in Vienna by the Constitutional Socialists—The Vorarlberg Proposes Joining Switzerland—Scheme for Uniting Austria with Germany—" Order before Socialism "—Hungary the Greatest Danger to Austria—Drifting Before the Storm—The Activities of Bela Kun—Struggle of the Oligarchs—Tisza and Karolyi : Fair and Foul Weather Figures—Assassination of Count Tisza : The Most Sinister of Reactionaries—Karolyi Arranges Armistice with General Franchet d'Esperey—Flight of the Emperor Charles to Switzerland—Internal Conditions Among the Magyars Go from Bad to Worse—Bolshevising Propaganda of Bela Kun's Agents—Erection of a Soviet Republic—Anarchy in Budapest—Hungary and Rumania—German Threats of Spreading Bolshevism—General Smuts' Visit to Budapest—The Patriotic Szeklers Between Two Fires—Advance of the Rumanians into Hungary—Bohemians Defeated by the Magyars—Serious Food Situation in Bohemia—Allied Missions Negotiate with the Vainglorious Bela Kun—Officers of the Landowning Class Rally to the Soviet—Moral and Military Successes of ·the Hungarian Communists a Reflection on Western Statesmen—Flight of Bela Kun and Arrival of Rumanians at Budapest.

WHILE Germany swayed in Revolution and counter-Revolution, with her structure holding firm amid the whirling movements, the allied Empire of Austria-Hungary fell completely to pieces. There has never been an Austro-Hungarian State. The Empire of the Hapsburgs consisted in an Army and a bureaucracy founded on the military force. It was an Empire that had grown out of a Bavarian legion of frontiersmen, recruited from a hardy Alpine peasantry to fight against successive hordes of Asiatic invaders. Mainly with the help of the warlike Polish nobility the Austrians crowned their work of a thousand years by repelling the Turks. But the Christian lands which they recovered were parcelled out in lordships for the Imperial nobility, and in the case of the Central Slav States the native gentry was largely dispossessed and alien lords set in dominion over serfs. In the struggle between Protestants and Catholics in the seventeenth century the Bohemians were conquered by the Austrian Emperor, who put to death hundreds of Bohemian noblemen and gave their estates to his Teutonic knights. Under Austrian influence Hungarian commoners lost their traditional freedom, and the Magyar peasant became the serf of his Magyar lord. Finally, by an arrangement promoted by Bismarck, the Magyar nobility joined with the Austrian aristocracy in sharing rule over the Slavs of Central Europe.

THE ARCHDUKE JOSEPH.

On the formation of the Hungarian Republic he took the oath of allegiance to it as Joseph of Hapsburg-Lorraine. When Bela Kun's Soviet Government was overthrown in the summer of 1919 the Archduke Joseph appointed a new Provisional Government.

In the old mountainous German territories of Austria the peasantry retained a tradition of freedom. The valleys of Tyrol, for example, were the nursery of Austrian power, and the mountaineers bred in such numbers that they were unable to feed themselves, and so emigrated and formed Germanic colonies in both Slav and Magyar territories. But the rest of the common people—Magyars as well as Bohemians or Czechs, Slovaks, Slovenes, Croats, Dalmatians, Bosnians, Rumanians, Little Russians, and outlying Serb stocks—were kept in as oppressed a condition in the twentieth century as they had been in the seventeenth.

There was a pretence of Parliamentary institutions, but the elections were strongly directed by the governing classes. Except for some Socialist representatives of working-class districts in large towns, who had little power except that of making a harmless noise, the polity of Austria-Hungary remained more feudal than that of the German Empire. When, therefore, the Army of the young Emperor Charles was seen to be seriously weakening, the oppressed races prepared to fall away and form new groups. The Bohemians had boldly met in Congress at Prague in May, 1918, and maintained, since 1917, a Provisional Independent Government in Paris. The Southern Slavs had arranged a congress at Laibach in August, 1918, and joined in proclaiming a Central Slav alliance between Bohemians, Slovaks, Poles, Croats, and other Jugo-Slavs.

By October 1st, 1918, the Hapsburg Monarchy was dissolving, and the Bohemians displayed remarkable boldness in the Imperial Parliament by announcing that the new States were formed, and that as the Imperial Government would not negotiate with the political representatives of the liberated peoples, when there had been an opportunity of so doing, they would have to conduct negotiations with the Bohemian and Slovak soldiers.

Having no longer any strong garrisons in the discontented countries, the governing classes were reduced to weak verbal protests. Great mutinies broke out behind the Italian front, and when the disaffected, broken Army scattered before the forces of General Diaz, the Empire of the Hapsburgs came to an end. The Austrian people did not revolt. It was against them that the other races were revolting. They were simply dazed by the complete overturn of their world, and entered upon the task of liquidating the bankruptcy of their Empire with quiet hopelessness. Directing power fell to the Socialists, under Dr. Victor Adler, because no other party was ready to accept responsibility. Many of the leaders of the former governing class were busy collecting jewellery and saleable securities with a view to flight to Switzerland, when, in the afternoon of October 29th, 1918, the Revolution was organised.

Austria's mild Revolution

It was a mild kind of Revolution, born of weakness rather than of energy. The Teutonic Deputies of the old Parliament met the following day, and passed a resolution declaring themselves the National Assembly of German Austria. Twenty members were elected to a Government Committee. Victor Adler was appointed President, Dr. Renner was made Minister of Supplies, and other Ministries were hastily erected and given mostly to Socialist leaders. Soldiers' and Workmen's Councils were in process of formation by Russian agents and returned prisoners of war from Russia. It was to counter this movement of anarchy that the Clericals and Nationalists allowed the Constitutional Socialists to spring unopposed into positions of authority.

There was a riot when a white-and-red flag was hoisted over the Parliament building. A mob, that vainly intended to become a Red Guard, wanted a red flag, but the Coalition forces, quickly formed under experienced officers, insisted on using the white-and-red flag, after pulling down the black-and-yellow colours of the Hapsburgs. In a sharp struggle, in which some ten men lost their lives, the Bolshevists were beaten. But the new white-and-red flag was flown only on the Parliament building and the Town Hall. General apathy prevailed in Vienna. The fact that the people mourned their downfall rather than celebrated their freedom was proof of the mildness of paternal rule in the Austrian capital, as contrasted with the harsh Hohenzollern methods that angered the Berliners. There was little anger against the fallen Emperor and aristocracy, and very little gladness in the advent of a reign of democratic freedom that reduced fair and lordly Vienna from the capital of a mighty Empire to the provincial town of some six million bankrupt, starving, isolated Teutons.

Vienna a parasitic capital

Lacking the corn, iron, coal, and other material supplied by her former tributary peoples, Vienna could not maintain her old population of some two million souls. Her now Germanic race could scarcely support itself, for it had failed, through indolent pride, to develop the water power and pastoral riches of its mountain valleys as its poorer but more industrious neighbours the Germanic Swiss had done. For many centuries it had lived on conquered peoples, and when reduced to separate independence it was for the time as helpless as a parasite that had lost its host.

The only Austrians possessing sufficient strength to react against the overwhelming disaster were the fine, manly mountaineers of the Alpine region of the Vorarlberg, adjoining Switzerland. In ancient times they had failed to unite with the Swiss in successful rebellion against the Hapsburgs, but free Switzerland had remained through the ages the country of their admiration. When they were at long last free to do as they wished, they proposed to form themselves into cantons for union with their neighbours. But the French and Italian Swiss immediately objected. The Germanic population of the old Republic was already predominantly large, and, rather short-sightedly perhaps, the Latin cantons would not allow it to be increased.

So the Austrians remained united in misfortune in spite of themselves. Then a scheme for union with Germany was arranged. In its origin this was a political trick. The ruling Socialists had no permanent base of power. The greater part of the electorate was formed of a Catholic peasantry, whose leaders were waiting for the raising of the blockade and the solution of urban problems of feeding and employment, in order to recover the means of government. Therefore, the Austrian Socialists, under Bauer, the successor to Adler, endeavoured to swing their country at once into confederation with Germany, so as to form a political alliance with the Social Democrats of Prussia and Bavaria. Bauer also tried to intrigue with the Italians against the French. His plan of a Germanic federation was attractive from various points of view. By bringing in the southern tribes it promised the Catholic States a predominant vote over Protestant Prussia. Erzberger, who took a principal part in the affair, designed a United States of Germany, with a strong Catholic majority outbalancing the Socialist and northern middle-class parties, and making Teutondom the greatest of Catholic powers, with certain advantages over anti-clerical France. Also, the official German Social Democrats were pleased at the prospect of being able to combine in a great Germanic union, in which the peasantry, after some concessions in the curtailing of great estates for their benefit, would assist in maintaining order against all Bolshevist tendencies. Austria was especially strong in her peasant power.

Drifting to an unknown end

On the other hand the Germans did not offer favourable terms to Austrian manufacturers. With their crippled resources the southerners would have been drowned in the aggressive competition of the great and highly-organised northern industries. What many Austrian manufacturers longed for was the recovery of their historic markets along the Danube by means of some economic Danubian federation among new and old States of the dissolved monarchy. There appeared strong reasons, when bitterness had died away, for the Danube countries to enter into some kind of economic arrangement. The decisive factor was the intervention of France. The French Government objected to the ancient enemy being strengthened in defeat by the gain of Austria. The French preferred some kind of Germanic division on religious lines, and there was a suggestion that the Catholics of the Rhine basin, possessing the greatest coalfield in Europe, would obtain quicker entrance into the League of Nations, and with this a working arrangement with the ironmasters of New France by drawing away from Protestant Prussia. An attempt made by Hoffmann, the Socialist Minister of Education in Germany, to repress religious instruction in elementary schools had a profound effect upon the anxious and hesitating Catholic population. Although the proposed measure was withdrawn, it served to show that the northern Socialists regarded themselves as the legatees of the traditions of their people in regard to the continuance of the domestic religious struggle between Teutons that had gone on from the age of Luther to the age of Bismarck.

By the end of November, 1918, the Austrians were more apathetic than ever. There was nothing for them to do but to await food supplies and peace terms. Hopeless listlessness was reflected in the elections, which somewhat unexpectedly left the Social Democrats in power but in alliance with the middle-class party and peasantry. " Order before Socialism " had become the watchword of the new governing party, whose moderation and readiness to adopt temporary compromises helped to still the anxieties of the other constitutional groups. Austria, with her little population of six millions, was like a sailing ship dismasted in a hurricane and drifting on unknown tides to an unknown end. All quarrelling stopped in the anxiety of a great common danger, and the helpless ship of State went on for months drifting and drifting. When, however, the Hungarians tried to seize the helm and guide

In Austria after the armistice: Men of the H.A.C. guarding a railway bridge near Imst.

British patrol in the Austrian Tyrol: Men of the H.A.C. passing through Tarrenz.

On the Austrian shore of the Adriatic: Church parade of British troops in Fiume.

Changing the guard at Imst, Tyrol, during the British occupation of the town.

In Austria's lost seaport: British sailors and soldiers marching through Fiume.

With the British forces in Austria: Transport of supplies on a hand=sleigh.

Visit of British destroyers to Pola, Austria's lost naval base on the Adriatic.

the vessel along their own dangerous course, the Austrians became alert. They hoped to drift into harbour rather than into a maelstrom.

It was by an extraordinary turn of events that Hungary became the greatest immediate danger to Austria. The Magyar peasantry had been for centuries as oppressed as the Russian peasantry. Their great landowning lords made little difference between their own humble countrymen and the Slovaks, Little Russians, Rumanians, Croats, and Outer Serbs, who had been reduced to serfdom in a thousand years of warfare. The Magyar clansmen had lost nearly all the common lands won in the early invasions, and their ruling families, in association with Polish, Turkish, and Teutonic aristocracies, had become a very selfish ruling class, intent entirely on the promotion of its personal and family interests.

Lenin and Trotsky were intelligent men who saw their opportunity in the deep discontent of the fighting Magyar peasant. Under a clever Galician Jew, Bela Kun, or Cohen, who deserted to the Russians early in the war and rose to Soviet fame as a fellow-Hebrew in the great Russian-Yiddish movements in Petrograd and Moscow, Hungarian prisoners of war were instructed in the methods of Bolshevism, and then released for home propaganda in scores of thousands. The Hungarian Jews had acted in the age of the oligarchy as the business managers for the Magyar noblemen, and had engrossed a large part of the trading affairs of the country. Circumstances thus had made them the natural managers of a Communist Revolution. They lost most of their means of livelihood when the great landowners fell on October 30th, 1918.

The oligarchs struggled and intrigued to the last moment. They offered reforms to their own people and federation to the oppressed nations, and tried to draw out of the war, and leave Austria to bear all blame and cost when the allied forces under General Franchet d'Esperey were about to invade Hungary. While negotiating for peace they still employed force.

Revolt and intrigue in Hungary The Archduke Joseph, a Magyarised member of the Hapsburg family, entered Budapest with a military force. His troops held the bridges with machine-guns, and shot down some of the leaders of the crowds that tried to demonstrate before the archduke's palace. In the popular reaction against this measure Soldiers' and Workmen's Councils were formed, largely under the direction of Bela Kun, and in the night of October 30th some Bosnian troops, supported by Croat regiments, broke into mutiny. News had reached them that their peoples had proclaimed their independence and set up a National Council. They would not then obey any foreign officers, and marched out under arms and called upon the Hungarians to revolt. By the morning of October 31st the Magyar troops and police had joined the Southern Slav garrison in Budapest, and a National Council was proclaimed under Count Michael Karolyi.

This gentleman was a relative of the great reactionary Count Andrassy, but during the war he had professed pacific and Liberal opinions, and become the organiser of an Independent Party. It is doubtful whether he was a sincere and outcast man of his caste or merely a subtle politician, acting in agreement with his kinsmen, and arranging a reinsurance policy for the Magyar oligarchy in the case of a lost war. Whenever things were going well with the Central Powers, Count Karolyi and his Independent Party shrank into gesticulating insignificancy. When things looked like going ill for Germany and her allies Karolyi became a figure of importance He and Count Stephan Tisza, the great war-maker in Hungary, resembled the two alternating figures in the old-fashioned Swiss weather-telling toys. In sunny weather Tisza was prominent, and Karolyi in the shadowy background. In bad weather Karolyi only was to be seen. There can be little doubt that he was the last hope of the Magyar landowners, who finally arranged for him to establish a democratic form of government in which there should be no general confiscation of great estates.

Karolyi relied for power upon coalition between the Hungarian Radicals, who were mainly professors and historical experts, and the Socialist Party that was supported by the working class of the capital. The urban proletariat was really only a small element in the rich agricultural State, and the course of events in the Revolution was mainly directed by the fears and passions of the land-hungry peasants and the desires of the Slav and Rumanian serfs. Karolyi and his Independent Party were designed to act as a safety-valve to the discontented Magyar farm-hands, but the new leader underestimated the influence among the peasantry of the scenes many of their soldier relations had witnessed in Russia. There in thousands of cases the Magyar peasants had helped Russians of the same class as themselves, in storming and dividing up the large landowners' estates. Bela Kun and his lieutenants were busy turning the national land problem into the spring of a Communist system by much the same method as Lenin and Trotsky had used in Russia.

Assassination of Count Tisza The beginning of the Revolution was marked by a significant assassination in Vienna on November 1st. Armed soldiers overcame the policemen guarding the house of Count Tisza and murdered him in the presence of his wife. Tisza met his fate with his usual courage, his last words being: "I knew this would be my end." He had been a master spirit of the Hungarian oligarchy, and had deliberately done more than any other man outside Germany to bring about the war. He seems, indeed, to have egged on the Teutonic war-makers, and led them to speed up their preparations by means of the historic levy on capital. He contemned popular government as a matter of principle, as well as a menace to his personal and class interests. He was the supreme enemy of the Slavs of Central Europe, being himself a curious fanatic of the Calvinist persuasion, who used every form of oppression for ends which he considered justified the means. He carried the doctrine of the elect into national ambitions. He wished to stamp out Slav speech and Slav traditions in all territory under Hungarian rule, and employed Austrian and German forces to break and absorb the Serb kingdom and definitely end Russian intrigues and threats to Middle Europe.

He hated the Russian with consuming hatred, arising from the sinister part played by Russian forces in breaking and capturing the Hungarian Revolutionary armies in 1848 and 1849, when the Austrian power was broken. He greatly helped to maintain the alliance between the Prussians and Hungarians, and, baffled by Italy in an attempt to launch the Great War immediately after the Serbo-Bulgarian victory over Turkey, he arranged the campaign of 1914. His aim was always to strike Russia though Serbia, and he cared not what happened in Western Europe so long as Germany was not there defeated. There were elements of greatness about Tisza, but his genius was perverted by inherited hatred and class interest, and he thoroughly deserved the end he met at the hands of murderers of his own race. One of the sternest of Protestants, leading one of the most backward of Catholic communities, he was the most sinister, because the most gifted, of Reactionaries in Europe.

National Council in Budapest His assassination alarmed all his fellow-oligarchs. The Soldiers and Workmen's Council in Budapest tried to profit by the confusion and the dismay by engrossing all power. But Karolyi cleverly countered this movement in sending representatives of the new National Council to act as civil commissionaries in every barracks on the pretence of guarding the rights of troops. Carried away by this preliminary success in tactics, Karolyi exceeded his doubtful measure of influence by endeavouring to erect a Hungarian monarchy, with the Archduke Joseph as sovereign. On assuming office, he took oath to the archduke, but provoked extreme agitation among the Socialists, who insisted that the oath should be taken to the National Council. Thereupon the archduke released him from the necessity of taking an oath at all, leaving it an open matter for a referendum decision whether the State should be a republic or a kingdom By way of winning popular favour the archduke, with his son, appeared in person before the National Council, and took the oath of allegiance to them. Joseph von Hapsburg swearing fealty to Hebraic Socialistic representatives of the slum-dwellers formed one of the memorable spectacles of the comedy of history.

FEEDING THE CHILDREN IN VIENNA.
Herr Seitz, President of the Austrian Republic, and American guests seeing the children of the Austrian capital at one of the daily meals provided for them by the American Mission of Help in the summer of 1919. Below : Officers of the Mission, which provided daily meals for 125,000 children in German Austria.

of the armistice of Belgrade were principally due to the Supreme Council of War at Versailles, which directed by telegraph General Franchet d'Esperey's line of action.

The chaos produced by the home-coming of the remnants of Hungarian forces from the Italian and Balkan fronts seemed likely at first to end in anarchy. The surrender of Germany and the flight of the Hohenzollern Kaiser led the young Hapsburg Emperor to renounce all share of power in German Austria and in Hungary, while carefully avoiding in either case any renunciation of the throne. Led by his Court advisers he bent before the popular storm, but hoped to return when the tempest abated. This young, well-meaning, but weak man was but a puppet in the hands of the great aristocratic families, many members of which fled to Switzerland, and there began

An attempt was then made to retain the lands of the Slovaks and Transylvanian Rumanians by coming to immediate terms with the Bohemians and Southern Slavs. In July, 1849, when the armies of the Russian Tsar were advancing in overpowering force upon the Hungarian Revolutionaries, Kossuth tried to win over the oppressed races by guaranteeing freedom to them. In November, 1918, the same deathbed act of repentance was performed by the defeated Magyars. The National Council appealed for reconciliation with the Slovaks and Rumanians. But on the day on which the appeal was made the Transylvanians erected their own National Council at Klausenburg, and organised themselves for union with Rumania. A few days afterwards the

Bohemia a republic

advance guard of the Bohemian Army penetrated into the Slovak lands, and the son of a Slovak blacksmith, Professor Thomas Masaryk, of King's College, London, hastened to Prague to take the position of President of the Republic of Bohemia and Slovakia. In Southern Hungary the Serbs occupied the famous Danubian wheatland of the Banat. After a thousand years of enslaving conquests the old invading Asiatic race of Magyars, whose power once extended to the South of France, the North Sea, and the Black Sea, were stripped of their ill-gotten and misused gains.

On November 8th Count Karolyi and one of his lieutenants met General Franchet d'Esperey at Belgrade and arranged an armistice. The French commander of the allied forces from the Salonika front was a better army leader than a statesman. He was outplayed completely by Karolyi, and he allowed the Magyars to withdraw to a line that gave them control over a large part of the Rumanian population of Transylvania. In their complete disarray and discouragement the Magyars would have accepted a definite retirement to their own territory. As it was they won the means of maintaining a hold upon the oppressed peoples on the Carpathian slopes, and prepared to resist by force the complete establishment of Slovak, Ruthene, and Rumanian independence. The allied commander obtained the disarmament by Magyar authorities of the army of Field-Marshal Mackensen, who was trying to withdraw from Rumania. In the ultimate event, however, this measure, which should have been carried out by the forces of the Allies, only served to introduce a considerable veteran German element into a new army of Hungary. The defects

working at a counter-Revolutionary movement in the hope of saving both the monarchy and their estates. After considerable hesitation at his hunting lodge at Eckartsau, near Vienna, Charles of Hapsburg joined his Court in Switzerland.

Meanwhile, the Magyar leaders, who remained in power as a Provisional National Government, tried to complete the arrangements they had made with General Franchet d'Esperey by inducing the Transylvanian Rumanians to remain under them. They offered a cantonal system like that of the Swiss, but the Rumanians required immediate and complete sovereignty, as did also all the Slovaks and Hungarian Ruthenes. In a menacing threefold movement Bohemian, Rumanian, and Southern Slav armies advanced to liberate their peoples. At the beginning of December the Council of Versailles intervened, and ordered the Magyars to retire completely from Slovakia. The mistake in regard to the subject Rumanians was also remedied towards the end of the year by the Versailles Council authorising the Rumanian forces to advance into the Rumanian districts of

Intrigues along new frontiers

Transylvania. Unfortunately, the appetite of the Magyars had been excited by two months of further power over Rumanians and Ruthenes, whom they alternately cajoled and terrified, until popular passion on either side was excited into battle fury.

Amid these incessant and tortuous intrigues along the new frontiers the internal condition of the diminished and restricted Magyar people went from bad to worse. The ruling race lost most of its material resources of coal, iron, salt, timber, and gold. Budapest, like Vienna, was completely dislocated as a centre of commercial exploitation. All that remained was an almost purely agricultural country, with a population of some eight millions and an overgrown, over-capitalised, over-peopled, provincial town that could not find work for most of its inhabitants. Magyar officials and Jewish middlemen fled from the lands of the resurgent nations into Budapest, and became a charge upon the small, bankrupt, new Republic. The Jews especially were moved by bitter resentment against the races which were shaking off both Jewish economic tyranny and Magyar political tyranny. With the loss of their helots and their protecting lords the Hungarian Jews were ready to bring down everything in their fall.

Directly inspired by the rôle which Jews were playing in the Soviet Government of Russia, the Hungarian Jews resolved to recover their position as agents of Bolshevism. Their leader, Bela Kun, appeared for the first time in a Communist insurrection in Budapest at the end of December. When this outbreak was put down, he provoked a strike of miners in the only coalfield left to the Hungarians, and Russian Bolshevists trooped to join him across the Carpathians, masquerading as Red Cross officials and returning prisoners of war. An intense propaganda was conducted among the Constitutional Socialists, who in increasing numbers went over to Bela Kun. Count Karolyi became afraid to arrange a General Election for a

Coming of the Bolshevists Constituent Assembly, for the reason that delay in dealing with the land problem had led the peasantry to incline towards the Socialist Party, who promised a general division of the great estates. The old Provisional National Council was reshuffled, but this futile essay in window-dressing an empty shop served only to embolden the Bolshevists. They fought for control of the Ministry of the Interior and the Ministry of War, and by January 10th, 1919, they won the principal means of power. A Communist, Wilhelm Böhm, was appointed political chief of the Army ; another Communist, Kunfi, became Director of Education, and abolished religious teaching in the schools, and moved for the confiscation of Church property.

For two months Karolyi remained the idle aristocratic ornament of a masked Soviet polity. He was no longer supported by his fellow-noblemen. These were losing all their property, and were inclined to carry out that staggering policy of revenge which the Prussian Junkers were threatening in appearance, but taking good care in reality not to follow. It was to join with Soviet Russia in throwing the rest of Europe into the tyrannic disorder of the wildest kind of Communism. What part Prussian intrigue played in launching the Magyars along this desperate course is hard to discern. It was certainly to the interest of the German governing class that the Associated Powers should be taught by the frightful example of Hungary that Germany could, as a last resource, adopt the same means of escaping a hard peace, while opening another world of dominion across Eastern Europe and Northern Asia to the Pacific.

Staggering policy of revenge

The Magyar nobleman agreed, reluctantly, slowly, to co-operate with his new friends. From the Magyar point of view, however, there was no permanent benefit in a Bolshevist alliance with Russia, unless the Germans, with their vast resources of technical knowledge, machinery, and material, were ready to follow the eastern road and undertake the main work of organising a vast Bolshevist Empire. After a long hesitation the Radicals of Hungary joined the Socialists, and members of the National Council strangely used their public position for preaching the doctrines of Lenin. Many of the younger members of the Magyar nobility rejoined the Army when the Revolutionary expert with the Germanic name of Wilhelm Böhm set to work to form a national Red Guard.

The plan of the old Magyar aristocracy and of the variegated kinds of politicians that rallied to it was similar in all essentials to the plan which the German nobility and bureaucracy reserved as a last resource. As commanding officers, with expert knowledge and experience, the Magyar gentry were able to look to recovering practical control of the people. The old heads of the families lost their revenues from their landed estates, but the land itself was a thing that could not be destroyed. Peasants could seize it and divide it, and

MEETING OF THE AUSTRIAN NATIONAL ASSEMBLY.
Opening session of the National Assembly at Vienna, where the Revolution had proved but a mild one, in the early part of 1919. A number of women members of the Assembly may be observed in the seats to the right of the photograph.

cultivate or neglect it, but whether they could permanently dispossess the capable class of traditional leaders, who were again exercising real power in the reorganising armies, was a problem of the future, admitting, the officer caste thought, of more than one solution.

At this time Lenin and Trotsky were placing under severe discipline the Russian working classes, compelling them to work more than they had done before in their lives, and also striving, with some small success, to compel the peasantry

of Russia, and of planning to reward Bohemian and Rumanian allies in the intended offensive by territory stolen from the Magyars.

The immediate result was the erection of a Yiddish-Magyar Soviet Republic, under the presidency of a Social Democrat of the German school, Alexander Garbai. Wilhelm Böhm undertook first the socialisation of the country, and then the creation of the Red Army, and Bela Kun, who was the veritable Soviet chief, looked first after foreign affairs and then also

HUNGARY'S BEAUTIFUL PARLIAMENT HOUSE.
Houses of Parliament at Budapest, on the left bank of the Danube. This fine group of buildings, the finest in a city famous for its handsome architecture, was erected during the closing years of the nineteenth century. Above : Liberty Square, Budapest, showing to the left the Exchange Buildings, and to the right the buildings of the Austro-Hungarian Bank.

helped to direct army organisation. In spite of the fact that 95 per cent. of the Magyar population was Christian, the new Soviet Government contained 80 per cent. of Jews. In subordinate official positions the proportion of Jews was still greater. They ran the Revolution as they had run the Magyar oligarchy, with this difference—that instead of being the clerks and stewards of the aristocracy they were now the equals, if not always the masters, of the former governing class. The noblemen had employed the Jews to prevent the rise and expansion of a Magyar middle class, and to keep the country peopled by supermen and serfs.

At first confusion and disorder reigned in Budapest, where the working class had established Soviets in large factories and business places, extracting all available money from the employers, while doing no work themselves and drawing unemployment pay. The greatest factory owner, Manfred Weiss, committed suicide, and his repentant Socialist workmen then came out rioting in the streets, and vainly tried to overthrow the Soviet Republic. Tens of thousands of men, though drawing unemployment pay, increased their means of enjoyment by highway robbery and housebreaking. When Bela Kun opened recruiting offices for the Red Guards, offering a fortnight's pay and a fortnight's leave to men who joined, he obtained in a week a paper army of some hundreds of thousands, and an actual force of rather less than ten thousand. The men made a complete tour of the recruiting offices, and after drawing a fortnight's pay from each, waited until the money was spent, and then under new names made another round trip in successive enlistments, and collected more advanced pay.

With the men who actually joined, the old regular officers could at first scarcely do anything. They had slow work in getting experienced sergeants. They had then to collect the scanty remnants of the Hungarian war material and organise Budapest into the main base of operations. Bela Kun entered into constant daily wireless communication with Lenin, and endeavoured immediately to arrange a combined Russian and Magyar offensive against Rumania. Lenin, however, openly expressed himself doubtful of the genuineness of Magyar Communism. In wireless messages, read by every receiving station in Europe, he suggested that the desperate Magyar nobility was engineering the new Revolution in their own interests. But when discomfited Bela Kun prepared to come to terms with the Versailles Council, Lenin changed his policy, and poured out promises in order to encourage the Magyars to remain Bolshevist.

Bela Kun's paper army

to raise an abundance of food on Communal lands. Bolshevism of this kind was not unsuited to the Hungarian and Prussian military castes in the year of the great defeat so long as they could resume a working command of large bodies of troops. They intended to spread the earlier, looser, anarchic form of Bolshevism among Bohemians, Moravians, Rumanians, and Southern Slavs.

The difference between the broken spirit of the German Austrians and the desperate resurgence of the old, fighting will-power of the Magyar race was very striking. While the Austrians remained sunk in apathy, the Magyars took the world by surprise by a general Revolution against the new League of Nations. Count Karolyi, having played his part, merely sought for some excuse to retire with a gesture of patriotism from the position he had already resigned to the Communist Revolutionaries. He found an excuse in an order from the Council of Versailles creating a neutral zone between the Magyar and Rumanian peoples, which zone was to be occupied by allied forces until the definite dividing line of languages was traced and established in the Treaty of Peace.

It was a just order, and expected by the Magyars, and would have been obeyed by them in November, 1918, but in March, 1919, it was angrily rejected. On March 21st Count Karolyi refused to allow the creation of the neutral inter-racial zone, and issued a proclamation for a Bolshevist Revolution. He accused the Associated Powers of arranging to convert Hungary into a base for military operations against the Soviet Government

Count Karolyi's resignation

All this wild comedy in Hungary was closely related to the tragedy of Odessa. General Franchet d'Esperey had been unable to hold the Black Sea port and advance and connect with General Denikin's Cossacks on his right and General Avarescu's Rumanians in Bessarabia on his left. There had been a serious mutiny in French warships in the Black Sea, and the French forces in Odessa were far from eager to fight. By the middle of March an allied evacuation of Odessa had become necessary. General Franchet d'Esperey's proposal to use new French and British troops in occupying a neutral zone in Transylvania was a sequel to the Odessa reverse. The French commander's design was to protect the Rumanians from a Hungarian attack, in view of the sudden disturbing menace of a Russian invasion of Bessarabia across the Dniester. The Bulgarians had, by the extraordinary kindness of the Versailles Council, been allowed to keep their arms. Every Bulgar soldier had his rifle and a hundred cartridges. Consequently, the Bulgars were hesitating between Sovietism and a new offensive, with Russian and Magyar help, and peace, with loss of territory and indemnities, with Rumania, Serbia, and Greece.

It was these grave difficulties, in which the allied commander in Eastern Europe was placed, that had directly led the old Magyar governing class to

Hungarian leaders' plans favour the establishment of Soviet rule and a fighting alliance with Soviet Russia. The immediate aim of the Magyar was to overwhelm Rumania with the help of Trotsky's armies, and the Bulgars, if possible, and then destroy the new Republic of Bohemia, and finally turn with the Bulgars upon the Serbians. The plan, however, failed, because Lenin and Trotsky were too weak to co-operate. Their main army between the Volga River and the Ural Mountains was broken by Admiral Koltchak's Siberian forces, and in order to save the loss of the Volga line, Red troops had to be hurried eastward. Moreover, some 20,000 Red Guards of Southern Russia went over to the Ukraine adventurer Petlura, and although the offensive against the Rumanians was pressed as far as the Dniester River, there was no longer any imminent peril of a Russian advance to the Carpathians.

The Rumanians under General Avarescu were therefore free to use their main forces against the Magyars. The Bohemians, under General Pellé, also prepared to strike southward against their old foes, and General Franchet d'Esperey planned a swift and overwhelming march on Budapest by French, British, and Serbian forces from Belgrade. In the condition in which the Magyars were at the end of March, 1919, the British and French divisions alone could have seized the Magyar capital within one week, and occupied Magyarland. The Supreme Council of Versailles, however, at **Advance on Budapest forbidden** first gave no answer to the proposal made by the French commander. Then, at the beginning of April, a command from France abruptly forbade the attack to be made. The Rumanian Government was also ordered, from Versailles, to desist from occupying Rumanian territory in Transylvania, and the Bohemian and Slovak forces were likewise commanded to cease chasing Magyars from the Slovak lands.

The fact was that Mr. Lloyd George, Lord Milner, and other British statesmen had fallen in the snare laid by Count von Bernstorff, Count von Brockdorff-Rantzau, Dr. Dernberg, and other master intriguers in Germany. At a secret meeting of the German National Assembly there was a fierce discussion over a certain enormous sum of money which Ebert and Scheidemann wished to use for Secret Service work. A majority of members refused to vote the money, until Count Brockdorff-Rantzau made a confidential explanation of the need for enlarging the already great espionage system established during the war. The most important passage in his long speech was communicated to the Allies by one of the few honest members of the National Assembly. It ran as follows :

The menace of Bolshevism is a good weapon for us to use against the Entente Powers, and we shall not cease from using it. For Bolshevism

WHEN HUNGARY BROKE AWAY IN REVOLUTION FROM THE AUSTRIAN EMPIRE.
Part of the vast crowd which gathered in one of the open spaces of Budapest to hear the proclamation of the Hungarian Republic on November 17th, 1918, nine days after the signing of the armistice with the Allies at Belgrade.

Council followed the line of least resistance. They did nothing, hoping that the Hungarian situation would be clarified by the interaction of its own ferments. But Bela Kun's lieutenants were not incapable. They had managed the business of the Magyar for more than a generation, and knew every current in Hungarian life.

The peasantry of the plain were appeased by a great food-production scheme. The land was left in their hands; but, instead of the noblemen's estates being divided into small-holdings, a system of co-operative agriculture was employed. The farm labourers formed themselves into a great trade union, and representatives of the urban working classes took over the distribution of farm produce. Shopkeepers became Soviet officials. The shopkeepers sold

is not dangerous to Germany. Furthermore, we must not think that the Bolshevist movement of two years ago is the same as the present Bolshevist movement. To-day we can arrive at an understanding with Bolshevists. We shall spread Bolshevism among all our enemies, with, I am afraid, the only exception of the French.

In England, Scotland, Wales, and Sinn Fein Ireland movements were then in train, supporting the boasts Rantzau made at the secret sitting of the new German Government. Mutinies among French forces and sinister Labour troubles in France seemed to indicate that for once the Teuton had underestimated the extent of his power in mischief-making. Italy was perilously balancing between aggressiveness towards the Southern Slavs and a general class warfare at home, which was one of the reasons why the Italian representatives at the Peace Conference preferred a dangerous foreign policy to a quiet compromise with Greater Serbia. Foreign trouble has always been the best counter-irritant remedy for domestic disorders. Of all the leading Powers in the new League of Nations the United States alone was beyond the reach of the Bolshevist weapon that Rantzau and Bernstorff were handling with such daring skill. Mr. Lloyd George was so intimidated by the success of the Teutonic intrigues that he opposed President Woodrow Wilson's Polish scheme, which was strongly backed by M. Clemenceau, and while temporarily forsaking the Poles, he gave diplomatic aid to the Magyars against the hard-pressed Rumanians, the endangered Bohemians, and the bankrupt, wasted Serbs. General Smuts, the confidential emissary of a section in the British Cabinet, who had tried in 1917 to arrange a peace with Austria-Hungary, travelled from Paris to Vienna and thence to Budapest. On April 4th, 1919, he had a conference with Bela Kun, the effect of which was merely to make the Soviet Jews of Hungary and their Magyar employers more insolently confident in their strength. They refused to allow British, French, and American troops to occupy the disputed line between Rumania and Magyarland, and General Smuts, seeing immediately the kind of men with whom he was trying to deal, broke off negotiations and returned to Paris.

Even then the Versailles Council would not allow General Franchet d'Esperey to capture Budapest, although this still could have been done with little loss of life. The Magyar peasantry were violently averse to the socialisation of the lands taken from the great noble landowners, and were prepared to revolt against the Revolution rather than become the economic serfs of the idle urban working classes. In Transylvania the Magyar elements among the Rumanians and Ruthenes were fiercely anti-Bolshevist, and prepared to march on Budapest. Weakly relying upon these symptoms of dissent among the Hungarians, the governors of the Versailles

General Smuts goes to Budapest

ELECTIONS IN REVOLUTIONARY VIENNA.
A maimed Austrian soldier carrying a poster inscribed, "The dead are at rest. Have we died without a cause? Vote for the Social Democrats who are the pioneers of freedom." Above: Demonstration of German Nationalists during the Austrian elections in the early part of 1919, bearing a banner with the legend "Long live the greater German Republic."

no goods for money, but only delivered them in rationed proportions to persons presenting Soviet tickets. Households were arranged in groups of fifty persons, over whom was placed a confidence man. He possessed Soviet tickets for everything obtainable, and gave them to his little group of subjects, according to his judgment of their needs. Over every five common confidence men there was a superior confidence man, and the overseers were again grouped under higher Soviet officials. By instituting a strict control of food and all articles of common use, Bela Kun reduced the Magyar cities to order in an astonishingly quick way.

The housing question was solved by taking inventories of all middle-class villas and aristocratic mansions, and apportioning rooms and furniture to persons of all stations in life according to the size of families. No servants were allowed, and all articles of jewellery were taken by the Government. Happy was the man who became a Soviet official, for, in spite of the socialisation of everything and everybody in urban centres, the hundreds of thousands of directors of the people lived very happily in the land of wheat, meat, wine, and accumulated military stores.

All the Hungarians lacked to make them a self-contained nation were coal and fat. The Magyars found that, at a pinch, they could live without lard and soap, but coal they had to win. Coal was the grand bribe which General Smuts had offered and Bela Kun rejected. The Magyars meant to get their coal by fighting against the Bohemians, and overrunning some of the Polish coalfields, in an arrangement with the reorganised German General Staff, who intended to break the Poles between Danzig and Posen. Towards the end of the first week in April the Jewish leaders of Magyarland overcame their recruiting difficulties. Recruits were at once placed in the Army without pay, and drilled by old non-commissioned officers and officers more vigorously than the Prussians dared to drill their men. Complete order reigned in the streets of Budapest, for armed guards, under young noblemen, shot, bayoneted, or bombed the robber bands, and also put down any Socialist movements among the workmen. As in Russia, workmen again had to work, for Jewish overseers who had often been experts in the art of sweating saw to it that every ordinary man earned his Soviet ticket for food and clothing for his family. The warm springtide solved the most difficult problem in domestic fuel supply, and communal kitchens helped to surmount the problem of cooking food

without wood or coal. The factories could not make enough power to keep all hands engaged, but this was not a national misfortune, as it released multitudes of men for the Army. Under the direction of Lenin an attack upon Rumania was organised to coincide with a Russian invasion of Bessarabia. Thereupon, the Rumanian Government asked for no orders or advice from the Versailles Council, but completed the remobilisation of the old Rumanian Army, and called out six classes of recruits among the Transylvanian Rumanes.

A far-reaching Bolshevist plot was discovered in the capital of Transylvania, where relatives of Bela Kun were striving to produce Soviet disorders. The Saxons of Hermannstadt and other old frontier towns were among those alarmed by the Jewish-Magyar intrigues, and went over to the side of the Rumanians. In one of the many little

ironies of modern history they formed into a division to combat the scheme of Bolshevist expansion, for which the German National Assembly was providing huge funds.

The Szeklers, or Translyvanian Magyars, on the other hand, remained passionate patriots. They changed their plan for marching against the Budapest Soviet into a more ambitious and impracticable operation. Their intention was first to defeat the Rumanians, and then change their own form of government. When the Rumanian advance began, the Russians were advancing on Bessarabia. But General Avarescu refused to strengthen his eastern front, and massing in the last week of April westward, his lieutenant, General Mardarescu, broke the combined Hungarian forces on a wide front by the town of Grosswardein. In places it was less a battle than a pursuit, for the Bolshevist forces of Magyarland refused to stand to action.

As they fled, the patriotic anti-Bolshevists of Transylvania stopped fighting against the Rumanians, and shot down their own fugitive countrymen, and then turned and continued the struggle against their half-friendly enemies. But for the Szeklers the Rumanian advance to Budapest   **Rumanian advance in Hungary** would have been little more than a skirmishing march. It was one of the tragedies that the gallant Szeklers should have been led to fight against the Rumanians. To a considerable extent the fault rested with the old Greek oligarchy of Rumania, under M. Bratiano, who, in the interests of the great alien landowning class of his country, had perilously delayed the election, on a democratic suffrage, of a genuine National Rumanian Assembly.

In Rumania some 4,000 men were possessed of about half of the best land. Most of these large landowners were Phanariot Greeks, who had remained in Constantinople when the city fell to the Ottomans, and entered the service of the conquering race. Descended from some of the oldest and noblest of Byzantine families, they brought a high degree of intelligence and a remarkable depth of cunning into their work of personal advancement. They crawled into some of the highest offices of State, and among other positions they occupied those of Hospodars of the Rumanian provinces. They held the Rumanian people down by the double weapon of tyrannic rule and Christian submissiveness, the Rumanian peasants being checked from revolting by the fear of losing fellow-Christians

PROCLAMATION OF THE HUNGARIAN REPUBLIC.
Count Karolyi, Hungarian Premier, who became President of the National Council, resigning the latter position and proclaiming the establishment of a Republic. He concluded his speech with " I resign, and hand over power to the proletariat of the Hungarian people." In circle : Count Karolyi (centre) with Countess Karolyi, and (right) the Revolutionary leader Wilhelm Böhm.

as their lords, and coming under the sway of Moslems as the Serbians did.

Naturally, the Phanariots showed little sympathy with the Greek struggle for independence and the Serbian victories over the Turk. It suited their family and personal interests rather to remain under an Ottoman suzerain than to help in any democratic Revolution that would endanger their hold on the land and the enslaved peasantry. It was the Russians who liberated the Rumanian provinces, but France and Great Britain restored them to Ottoman lordship. Soon afterwards a patriotic Rumanian colonel undid the work of the British and French and made his country independent, but he could not make the people free. For he was overthrown by the Phanariot lords, who found the kind of monarch they required in Prince Charles of Hohenzollern-Sigmaringen, a member of the elder line of the Imperial Hohenzollerns. Under Germanic organisation Rumania was governed in an old Prussian style, with the great landowning Greek lords in absolute possession of all real power, and maintaining the Rumanian people in illiterate servitude under a pretence of democratic govern-

Division of parties in Rumania ment. A little well-organised Socialism of a German kind was allowed in working-class districts in cities, where the Socialist leaders could be selected and controlled in various ways, but genuine political propaganda among the illiterate peasantry was rigorously discouraged. The unspoken, disconnected, brooding discontent of the people became the source of Rumania's weakness in the war.

Preparatory to taking any action in the war the Greek lords had already divided themselves into pro-German and pro-French parties. When General Falkenhayn and Field-Marshal Mackensen closed on Bukarest, with the aid of a Rumanian commander, the French party retired with the remnant of their forces. The German party thereupon came into power, as ready to serve the Teutons as their ancestors had been ready to serve the Ottoman. The price in each case was the same—continued lordship over the Rumanian people. This suited the Teutons. They asked and obtained full war costs, as a matter of business, and there the matter was settled. When, unexpectedly, from the Rumanian point of view, the entire power of the Central Europe Empires was overthrown the German political party retired, and the French political party under M. Bratiano resumed control.

There was then much discussion of concessions to the people, yet nothing of actual importance was done to transform Rumania from an oligarchic despotism into a democratic State. Otherwise the Szeklers **The Szeklers** might have been won over, the Budapest **of Transylvania** Soviet put down quickly by Magyars, while the intricate territorial problem of Transylvania might have been arranged by the mosaic of occupying races in friendly discussion. The Rumanian lords preferred to make a violent conquest of the whole of Transylvania. After winning the land by force they hoped to have opportunities of dispossessing the large masses of Magyar people, and thus obtaining land for settlement by their own soldiers without lessening their own great estates.

But the Szeklers baffled them. Though betrayed by their own Bolshevist countrymen, and far removed from their own homes, the small forces of Transylvanian Magyars fought a great fighting retreat towards Debreczen and the tributaries of the Tisza River, and won time for the old officers in the Red Guard army to reduce some of the troops to an iron discipline. The situation, however, remained for a time almost hopeless from the point of view of Bela Kun and his associates. Bohemians and Slovaks intervened in the struggle towards the end of April, and descended upon the upper bend of the Theiss River near Czap.

AUSTRIA'S CHIEF SEAPORT ON THE ADRIATIC SEA.
General view of Trieste, the Austrian seaport which was under the rule of Venice in the thirteenth and fourteenth centuries. Though long before the outbreak of the Great War it had passed under Austrian rule, its population consisted very largely of people of Italian origin and Southern Slavs.

The Rumanians forced the passage of the Middle Theiss on May 2nd, at Szolnok, about fifty miles east of Budapest. At the same time the Bohemian and Slovak forces camped victoriously in the town of Miskolcz, about ninety miles north-east of the Hungarian capital. In both cases Bela Kun frankly explained in wireless reports to the world that the reverses were due to the undisciplined condition of the Red Guards. On May 3rd the Rumanians were within forty miles of Budapest, and large numbers of the Bolshevist troops not only went over to the invader but offered to organise themselves in battalions and fight the Soviet mobs.

Bela Kun wavered between a bloodthirsty despair, in which he threatened to massacre a large part of the population, and apprehension regarding his own fate, that led him to make arrangements to escape to Russia by aeroplane. Bohemians and Rumanians united at Tokay, on the Theiss, and Rumanians, Serbs, and French troops joined at Arad, on the Maros stream, and at Szegedin, on the Lower Theiss. The Bohemians extended through the northern mountains towards Salgo-Tarjan—the only coalfield remaining to the Magyars, situated north-eastward of Budapest. The Serbo-French divisions extended westward from the Theiss River to the Danube, at a point some sixty miles below the enveloped capital.

So certain seemed the fall of the Magyar Soviet that the Hungarian noble class veered once more, and detached a considerable number of representatives to negotiate with the Associated Powers. In Vienna, where Magyar agents were endeavouring, with Teutonic aid, to promote a Communist Revolution, amid some serious street fighting, a party of reckless Hungarian officers kidnapped the Bolshevist delegates, imprisoned them in a monastery, and discovered incriminating papers, with a detailed plan of the insurrection. Apathetic as the Austrians remained, the papers showed them that the peril of Communism in the capital, with separation from Tyrol and Vorarlberg and their independent peasant communities, was serious and close. Henceforward they took more vigilant interest in Bolshevism, as Bavaria also became for a while a Soviet State.

At the same time, in Arad and Szegedin, a successor to Count Michael Karolyi appeared, in the person of Count Julius Karolyi, his cousin, who, under French protection, gathered a variety of the old Hungarian party men, including some Social Democrats, and established a second Provisional National Government. The new policy was one of friendship with all the Associated Powers, especially Rumania, Bohemia, and Jugo-Slavia, and the earliest possible erection of a constitutional form of State.

Julius Karolyi's brief power

The extreme, desperate stroke of the Magyar oligarchy had apparently failed abruptly and completely. So a Karolyi came forward in humble willingness to pick up what fragments of private and national property remained after two general defeats and three Revolutions.

Before Julius Karolyi could make all his rearrangements he went the way of his cousin into temporary obscurity. The third Revolution of Budapest was for a time postponed. For the ordinary Magyar found he had something worth fighting for. The peasant, especially, enjoying a free tribesman's right to a good share of land, for the first time since his Turanian forefathers conquered the Danubian wheatlands, was a man with a new spirit. Nothing like him had been seen since the French peasant of the Revolution, kindled by the possession of his master's estate, turned on the Prussians at Valmy.

The Magyar peasants were losing their newly-acquired farmsteads. All the invading forces had extended far beyond the line occupied by earlier Danube races surviving from exterminating conquests. The common Magyar was fighting for his farm against the common Rumanian who had no farm, against the French peasant who wanted only to return to his farm and against Serbs and Bohemians and Moravians, who had been taught by their own sufferings to be careful of the rights of other commoners.

In the surprising event that followed, Bela Kun and his gang of rogues were of less than no account. Men whose crimes in peace-time were publicly recorded, and who were denounced, on clear evidence for the basest of personal conduct, came forward as military leaders of an honest peasantry. For it cannot be imputed a crime to the Magyar tribesmen if they marked the end of their chieftains' tyranny and usurpation by the recovery of the common lands of the clans. War had made the Magyar peasant a veteran soldier. Although he had mutinied out of weariness of fighting for his masters, he was as great a fighting man as any in Europe when it came to defending his own farm. With a colonel of the regular Army and little more than sixty field-guns the Magyar people opened their offensive against enveloping numbers of enemies.

Magyar activity in May, 1919

The great action began in the middle of May, 1919. The French and Serbian troops, south of Budapest, were held merely by a light covering force, while General Franchet d'Esperey was organising his prolonged line of communications from Belgrade. Eastward the large Rumanian Army, of ragged, tired, and sadly-unprovisioned soldiers, was held by the Theiss River by only two Hungarian divisions numbering probably little more than ten thousand fighting men. These were sufficient to hold the Rumanians in check for more than a week, while, along the Rumanian rear, fierce, outworn, and hungry yet reckless bands of Szeklers harried the very long and weak Rumanian lines of supply. Then practically the entire available force of old regular Magyar soldiers, organised in seven divisions, attacked the Bohemians and Slovaks round the coalfield of Salgo-Tarjan that was the life of Budapest.

The Bohemians were led by an Italian commander, General Piccioni, with a French commander, General Pellé, as Chief

LEADERS OF THE SOCIALIST REGIME IN HUNGARY.
Bela Kun (second from right), who in 1919 rose to a brief term of power in Hungary as a Socialist with Bolshevist tendencies. Seated with him is Commissary Kurifi. Bela Kun had studied Bolshevist methods in Russia before the state of affairs in Hungary afforded him his opportunity for sinister leadership.

of Staff. They met with one of the greatest reverses in the war. The Magyars at first attacked on May 13th, 1919, in the centre by the Salgo-Tarjan coalfield, fifty miles from Budapest. While their centre advanced, they gave ground on their right wing at Eger. The battlefield was mountainous, and a great mountain block, the Matra, divided the Bohemian centre from its right wing. While giving ground south of the mountain, the Magyars shattered the Bohemian front north of the heights, and then pouring down the wide valley in the centre, they scattered the Bohemian forces. There were mutinies among Slovaks and Czechs, orders and counter-orders, confusion and flight over the hills to Miskolcz and the Upper Theiss Valley. Many guns were lost and many ammunition dumps. The link between the Bohemian and Rumanian Armies was broken, and an opportunity afforded the Hungarians for trying to join across the Carpathians with the Red Armies of Russia. The Ruthene corridor along the Carpathians, connecting Slovakia with Rumania, was seriously menaced.

The disarray of the army of the Republic of Bohemia and Slovakia was increased by insurrections in the rear of the defeated forces. Some of the Slovaks were discontented with the centralising administration of Prague. As their country, representing the ancient Moravian Empire, was as large as the younger Bohemian kingdom, they required co-operating equality with Bohemians instead of a centralised Prague rule. Undoubtedly, Magyar agents had done much to swell and envenom this **Bohemians and Moravians** quarrel between kindred people, but they did not start the fire which they fanned into something like a conflagration. Although the Bohemians had accepted a Slovak as President, they were inclined rather to regard the mountaineers of Old Moravia as poor relations. For a thousand years the Slovaks had been under Hungarian masters, who had reduced them to a condition that compared unfavourably with that of the beasts they tended on the hillsides. The Slovaks were deprived of schools, and had been compelled through centuries to rely on Bohemian missionaries of culture in keeping alive the flame of the ancient national spirit.

Moreover, things were not going very well even in Prague. The profiteering speculator in food and the greedy shopkeeper are types of original sin that obtain among the most patriotic of nations, and they were not absent from Bohemia in the months of her severest trial, when to her people the great statesmen of the Supreme Council of Versailles seemed, like the remote gods of Olympus, careless of the transient woes of mere mortals. As Hindenburg had concentrated his reorganised forces in the east, in order to fight for Danzig and break the Poles between his new army and a secretly allied force of Russian Red divisions, **Parlous state of Bohemia** Bohemia had no working port and railway of supply on the Baltic. She was victorious in Siberia and Italy, but dying of famine at home.

Her new army was recruited from families that knew as well as the Viennese what semi-starvation was, but, unlike the Viennese, they did not receive British and American food trains. So profiteers in food flourished hugely among them. As a German cynic put it, the Bohemians received from their allies, as the reward for victorious aid, starvation and officers. There was rioting in Prague, and an outcry against the unsuccessful Italian commander, General Piccioni. Towards the end of May the Versailles Council sent two new commanders, General Mitterhausen and General Hennocque, both of them experienced French leaders.

Meanwhile, British and American missions arrived at Budapest to continue negotiations with the triumphant and vainglorious Bela Kun. But the Jew made promises of friendship merely as a subterfuge to intended performances of a hostile kind. The Bohemians were driven back from Pressburg, near Vienna, to the foothills of the Carpathians. Then, at the beginning of June, the Magyar colonel, who was the veritable Commander-in-Chief, made another surprising concentration against the Rumanians, pressed them across the Theiss, and began to throw them back upon Transylvania.

By this time thousands of Magyar officers of the old land-owning class had rallied once more to the Jewish Soviet. Their patriotism was excited by the success of the peasantry, and they had more in common with the commoners of their

ON THE QUAYSIDE AT FIUME: THE DISPUTED ADRIATIC PORT.
Fiume was for centuries a bone of contention among several peoples. It was attached to Hungary in 1779, and several times detached, until 1870, when it became Hungarian again, and remained so until the Great War, when it was the object of the rival claims of Jugo-Slavs and Italians.

race than any Magyar nobleman had truly felt since the dim age of the early invasion. The spirit of the Revolution was unlike that of the national movement under Kossuth, in the middle of the nineteenth century, when the fighting nobility merely used the people for their own ends and kept them in practical serfdom as the disastrous issue of the struggle. The Magyar peasant at last knew his power, and, so long as Bela Kun and the other Jews did not bear too heavily upon the great farming class, they were able to experiment, almost as they pleased, in urban Bolshevism. Julius Karolyi's Provisional Government at Szegedin fell under the suspicion of being the landowners' instrument for the recovery of estates. Very slowly did the peasantry turn towards Szegedin, even when disillusioned regarding Budapest.

As in Russia, the ruling Jews were bitterly fierce against the organising element of the Christian religion. The Catholic Church of Hungary stood in need of reformation, and the accumulated ecclesiastical wealth, in both land and treasure, was an overwhelming temptation, especially to a bankrupt, outlawed State. There was a considerable secularisation of nuns and monks, and the popular benefits arising from the socialisation of Church estates appeared to make some of the peasantry willing to listen to a gospel of scientific materialism of the modern sort.

Yet the success of the new war and the revival of discipline tended to keep the Magyar people fairly submissive to Government control. There were risings, followed by sanguinary repression, but food held out sufficiently for the Hungarians to offer to feed the Austrians, on the condition that the latter became Bolshevists. Moreover, the new harvest was prepared and grown with a promise of plenty for the autumn. Meanwhile, Hungary, upon whom fell half the cost of the war made by the old Dual Monarchy, escaped attendance at the Peace Conference and the presentation of the bill of the expenses of defeat. So long as the Bolshevist form of Government lasted, it seemed to be one of the defences against anything in the nature of an indemnity. To many

Western leaders and the Hungarians Magyars it seemed permanently worth while going without soap and fat, and drawing closer to a victorious Red Empire of Russia, for the sake of such a result. Winter coal, however, was a perplexing problem, especially when the Rumanians recovered and resumed their advance on the Theiss.

To a very considerable extent, both the moral and military successes of the Hungarian Communists were a reflection upon the insight and resolution of Mr. Lloyd George and President Wilson. To them practically fell the supreme position of Commander-in-Chief of the forces of western civilisation, M. Clemenceau being placed in rather an awkward position by the aversion of white French troops to continue fighting against Oriental Communists when their own land was liberated and victorious. The event seemed to prove that representative, democratic statesmen of a high order do not make even tolerably good military chiefs. They sought to interpret the general will of their peoples in a matter on which they had not enlightened the public mind; they looked for the support of public opinion when they should have created it; and all this in circumstances in which instant decision in judgment and action were the essence of success.

General Smuts was overcome by the atmosphere of the Council Room of Versailles. He succumbed to the small accumulated effects of a petty revolt of some nervous, non-combatant American-Polish Jews on the Archangel front, of some transient discontent over disbandment muddles and low pay in the British Army, of similar discontent due to similar causes among French forces, and of all the sporadic and artificial spots of Bolshevism upon the surface of British life, which Count von Brockdorff-Rantzau secretly boasted he had created at great expense.

At a time when two divisions of British and native American troops, by a march from Belgrade, could have sent Bela Kun flying over the Carpathian Mountains, General Smuts vainly tried to win by words with a Galician Jew what the Jew admitted afterwards he had been ready to yield at a show of force.

The immediate world-wide consequences of the victories of the Soviet of the most warlike race of Middle Europe enable us to realise some of the importance of the obscure Battle of Salgo-Tarjan. The Magyar success helped the Rumanian peasantry in their struggle for land, education, and manhood suffrage. It led to better relations between Bohemians and Old Moravians, or Slovaks, and to a settlement of the agrarian problem among the Central Slavs, by measures for dividing the large estates of the nobility. As the modern Bohemian nobility was mainly an Austrian creation, by means of which foreign lords were enriched and empowered to hold down the people, confiscation of noble estates was a just and easy affair. The liberated groups of Southern Slavs could contemplate a similar solution to their problem of creating a large stock of yeoman farmers. Unfortunately, in Greater Serbia the Southern Slavs were concerned in serious domestic and foreign difficulties of a peculiar kind. In Poland also there were native obstacles to the erection of the natural, broad-based barrier of millions of free, landowning peasant farmers **Peasantry and the land** against the double inundations of Russian Bolshevism and German aggression. Wherever there was peril of wrecking explosions amid the frail, unfinished fabric of social reconstruction, the track of the German plotter could now faintly and now clearly be seen. Germany did not yet think she had lost dominion over Europe and Asia. Her strength of mind and character was as great as ever it had been, though changed in quality, like that of Milton's Lucifer when he became Satan. Into all the large and little Edens of the New Democracy that were being planned in the age of apparent victory, something with the spirit of a serpent insinuated itself by underground ways.

In the meantime Bela Kun and his gang, though serving the purpose of the Teutons down to the signing of the peace with Germany, weakened through domestic reaction among the Magyar people. The peasantry became more averse to any Communist limitation of their newly-won lands, and when murdering bands known as "Lenin's boys" were sent out under Szamuely to cow the small-holders, there were struggles in which the Jews were not always victorious. A peasants' blockade of all Soviet towns at last obtained. In May, 1919, the Trade Unions withdrew from the Soviet, and many old officers, keenly aware how things were tending, escaped from the Army and helped to train a new national force gathering under Julius Karolyi.

On June 24th there was a serious rising, and though it was put down, all popular energy evaporated from the Communist Revolution. After some attempts to arrange a settlement with the Council of Versailles, the Rumanian commander proposed to resume the drive on Budapest. Once more the movement was forbidden, but happily Bela Kun smoothed the road of advance for the Rumanians by ordering a general offensive that opened on July 20th, 1919. He hoped to solve all domestic problems by reviving the patriotic spirit of the May battle, but the Magyars were too deeply disillusioned about Hebraic Sovietism to fight once more for Bela Kun and Szamuely. On July 25th, after holding the attack from the Theiss River front, the reorganised **Collapse of Bela Kun** and well-supplied Rumanians turned the northern wing of the Magyars, completely enveloped it, captured the guns, and pursued with cavalry. By August 3rd, 1919, three Rumanian divisions were in the outskirts of Budapest. Bela Kun and his chief assistants had fled on August 1st, leaving in the capital some members of the Soviet, who tried to form a Provisional Government of a Democratic kind. They were arrested by agents of the Archduke Joseph, who assumed power, with the support of the Magyar nobility and the Rumanian Army, only to be deposed shortly after at the order of the Allies. Thus, nearly a year after the signing of the armistice, the country which had in effect been the predominant partner in the Austro-Hungarian Empire had not succeeded in stabilising itself to meet the new conditions brought about by the overthrow of the militaristic Powers of Central Europe.

Polytechnic Institute in Warsaw, one of the many fine buildings by which the Polish capital is distinguished. The Warsaw University, after suppression for a time, grew to be a highly important educational centre.

The old Town Hall of Warsaw, long the capital of the one-time Kingdom of Poland and capital of the Russian province of Poland after the partition of the ancient State.

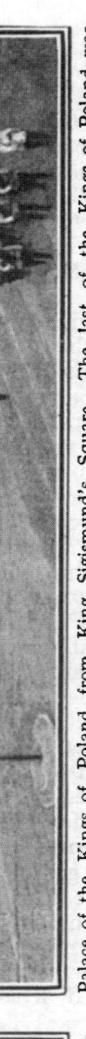

Palace of the Kings of Poland, from King Sigismund's Square. The last of the Kings of Poland was King Stanislas, who died in exile in 1798.

One-time Treasury of the Kingdom of Poland. The Kingdom was thrice partitioned among its neighbours—Germany, Russia, and Austria—in 1772, 1793, and 1795.

IN THE CAPITAL OF "THE FAIR LAND OF POLAND," ONCE MORE AN INDEPENDENT STATE.

CHAPTER CCCXVIII.

CENTRAL EUROPE IN REVOLUTION.

III.—The Turmoil in Poland and Bavaria and Defeat of Prussian Intrigue.

By Edward Wright.

Differences between Russian, Austrian, and German Poles—Polish Nobles and Revolutionaries Combine Against Entente—Warsaw Regency and the League of Landowners—Pilsudski and the Conversion of the Commoners—Problem of the Polish Jew—Hemming Poland between Bolshevism and a Peasants' Revolt—Lublin Revolution and Liberation of Pilsudski—A Dictator Who Could Not Dictate—Silesian Mineowners and their Sinister Propaganda—Poles Fight Back Russian Communists—Lithuania Struggles and Starves for Independence—Battles with Southern Russians and Bohemians—Teschen and the Coalfield Dispute—Paderewski's Attempts at Harmony—France Saves Poland as Rampart Against Teutondom—Campaign for Polish Manors in Ukraine—Germany Prepares an Eastern Offensive—Assassination of Eisner—General Strike in Germany—Counter-Revolution in Berlin—Terrible Scenes in Capital—Russian-German Alliance Established—Rhineland Magnates and Baltic Barons Averse to Russian Alliance—Carnival Revolution in Munich—Levien and Bavarian Soviet Rule—Defeat of Bavarian Government and Prussian Invasion—The Massacres in Munich—Germany Falls in Fragments—Scheidemann and Brockdorff-Rantzau Retire—Erzberger Prepares to Sign Peace Treaty.

POLAND was the most complicated of all countries menaced by the Revolutionary movement. Having been partitioned before the railway age, the different parts had become strongly linked with foreign industries and systems of communication. Moreover, Polish politicians, from German, Austrian, and Russian assemblies, inclined to different ways of looking at national problems. The chief source of complication was the ancient one of the noble land-owners' interests. Polish gentry, with descendants of Lithuanian chiefs who had amalgamated with them, possessed estates from the ryefields by the Baltic shore to the wheatlands by the Black Sea. These estates were mainly an in-heritance of old, conquests in the days when united Poland and Lithuania were supreme in Eastern Europe.

Amid centuries of defeats and disruptions the Polish noble families had guarded their great domains, and kept the peasantry in as complete a state of subjec-tion as foreign laws allowed. Under Russian rule the commoners of the villages in Polish, Lithuanian, and Southern Russian estates had been released from serfdom by the Tsar, but were left so landless that they largely existed by sup-plying the Prussian and Westphalian cheap labour markets. Under Austrian rule the Polish noblemen had things all their own

THE POLISH PRIME MINISTER AND HIS HELPERS.
M. Ignace Paderewski, the famous musician, who became Poland's Prime Minister, with (on his right) Major Joseph F. Kaslowski, and (on his left) Captain J. Marten.

way, and were therefore contented. They erected a modern stucco front to the ancient feudal system. In return for a free hand with their Polish and Ukrainian peasants, they not only kept order in Austrian-Polish territories, but arranged that the entire Polish nation should join Germany and Austria-Hungary in case of war.

Only in German-Polish territory was there anything like a veritable spirit of Slav independence and an approach to a fair union between noblemen and commoners. When thieves fall out honest men come by their own. The Prussian nobility and industrial magnates had fallen out with the Polish nobility in the Posen and Silesian provinces, and in fighting against the German scheme for buying up their estates and planting them with Teutons, the Polish landowners had united sincerely with the Polish peasantry. The result was the Poles of Posnania were the most enlightened, progressive, and democratic of their peoples, and far more in sympathy with French, British, and American democracy than were Rus-sian and Austrian Poles. Their influence, however, was of practically no effect upon the main course of events.

It had been arranged in 1906 that Poland should unite in a war against Russia and France. In this design the nobility entered into an alliance with the Socialist Revolutionaries.

Poland to become almost a purely agricultural country, with the large native landowners keeping their own people down, and making their fortunes by supplying food to German industrial centres. The Germans already had bought up the Cracow coalfields and kept these unworked, so as to prevent competition with the Silesian coalfields. By removing machinery and material and by forcibly deporting factory hands from Poland to Germany, the gradual ruin of Polish industry had been continued under the Regency Government.

The overthrow of the Central Powers was the greatest of all disasters which the Polish nobility had suffered in the course of a thousand years. Unlike issues of bygone battle, it directly and immediately exposed the leading men of the most brilliant of Slav races to the loss of their personal and family possessions. It reversed all the infinite, tortuous work achieved through the centuries when village communal systems had been transformed into the domains of lords of the manor, with some Polish adventurer in armour triumphant over men of his own stock, or over free Lithuanians and Ukrainians.

Power of the landowners

From the mediæval period there had obtained an unwritten agreement between German, Austrian, Magyar, Polish, and Russian lords of the manor. Among themselves they contended by arms and intrigue for larger possessions of serfs and land, but they held together when the vast manorial interests of Eastern and Middle Europe were threatened by any popular movement. They also agreed, through the dangerous period of the nineteenth century, in favouring the theory of Social Democracy, as a vent for the angry discontent of the dispossessed commoners. Karl Marx and his disciples seemed in the nineteenth century to turn the minds of the people away from effective methods of democratic reform, and, by giving them a new kind of earthly paradise to dream of, had retarded any practical organisation for the rapid attainment of a working liberty.

In the middle of November, 1918, the aristocracy of Poland was menaced by Bolshevism without and by democratic land reform within. The Lithuanian people took an independent attitude. Of old they had been united to the Poles by a dynastic marriage between their duke and a Polish princess; but this had led to the Polish nobility spreading themselves and their serf system into Lithuanian territory. The Lithuanians now wished for independence, in order to recover their ancient tribal lands. In the Ukraine, swaying between

POLITICAL MEETING IN POLAND'S CAPITAL.
Gathering in one of the streets of Warsaw, with the White Eagle of Poland freely displayed, after the Great War brought hopes of a reunited and independent Poland.

and when during the struggle a Polish Legion was formed to fight, according to agreement, for the Hohenzollerns and Hapsburgs, the working-class recruits were won over by the promotion of one of the most distinguished of their Revolutionary leaders, Joseph Pilsudski, to the position of commander. The Polish Legion played no small part in the defeat of Russia; but after the Brest Litovsk peace neither the Teutons nor the Polish aristocracy had any further use for Pilsudski and his Revolutionaries; but unlike most of his class, he was desperately sincere in his professions of political faith. He would not abandon his programme of land reform, and, much to the relief of his honourable associates, he was removed into Germany and imprisoned at Magdeburg.

The Polish nobility then arranged at Warsaw a Regency Government of a reactionary kind. There was some intention of forming a monarchy, preferably under the Hapsburgs, but the northern Teutons were naturally averse to allowing all Russian Poland to fall under the direct influence of the Dual Monarchy. After long negotiations regarding the way in which Poland could be brought into a Customs' Union with Germany, the final turn of the war suddenly upset arrangements between the Polish aristocracy and the Central Powers.

Partly by force and partly by persuasion the Teutons had arranged for

GERMAN CAVALRY IN WARSAW.
Poland, split up and divided among her more powerful neighbours, was certain to suffer when those neighbours went to war, and to a greater extent because her people remained a nation. The capital was more than once occupied by the Germans during the Great War.

Bolshevists and native marauder leaders, the Polish estates seemed lost, except for a fighting chance in Galicia. In the Polish parts of Old Prussia, running towards Danzig, only the common people were generally Polish, and here and elsewhere the Polish nation suffered from the old policy of its nobles, who had hindered the growth of a Polish middle class by engaging Teutons and settling them in commercial centres, in much the same way as the Magyar nobles engaged Jews as factors, so as to prevent strong native business municipalities from arising.

On the other hand the fertile Polish people had, in the long period between the death and resurrection of their nation, conquered new territory by the invincible law under which slaves overbreed their masters when the climate does not favour either side. The alert Teuton had long since been aware of this danger, and had done all he could to direct the ever-swelling numbers of the Polish proletariat against possible enemies, rather than against himself. In Old Prussia, Polish farm labour had been used as much as possible in a seasonal manner, so that the men did not settle with their women and inundate the country with children. But in the old crownland of the one-time kingdom of Bohemia, Silesia— taken from Bohemia by Austria and from Austria by Prussia— the Poles were encouraged to settle and breed, and so swamp the Bohemians. German coal and steel magnates directed this movement, until they were astounded by the growth of the Poles, who threatened to submerge old and new German settlers as well as the Bohemians.

Poles in Silesia

In 1917, when they were trying to arrange peace terms with the Western Powers, the Teutons found that their imported Polish labour in Silesia had given Poland, under the right of self-determination which President Wilson had

OLD POLISH TOWN HALL OF POSEN.
Posen Rathaus, as restored by the Germans. It was one of the few ancient Polish buildings left standing in the city that, since the partition of Poland, had become the capital of a Prussian province. Left : The Royal castle at Posen.

laid down, the power of acquiring the rich Silesian coalfields. The German Silesian coalowners immediately started a propaganda in America in the hope of preventing the Poles from mastering their masters. The method adopted was to accuse the Poles of arranging wholesale massacres of Jews, and then to engineer agitations among American and British Jews in favour of allowing the coal districts to remain in possession of the Teutonic magnates, who would become protectors of Israel.

The Polish Jews were the supreme complication in complicated Poland. They were not Jews by race, but only by religion, being descended from a Tatar tribe converted to the doctrine of Israel, and then degraded and toughened by centuries of Ghetto life. They lacked the fighting virility of their Mohammedan kinsmen, not from any fault of their own but from the effects of secular Christian oppression. In the Middle Ages the Poles generously gave them shelter, and for political reasons allowed them to become the middlemen between the lordly landowners and the enslaved

peasantry. When, in 1916, the Germans settled in Russian Poland as conquerors, the Jews were remarkably eager to serve their new masters. At the order of Hindenburg and Ludendorff they commandeered the machinery, food, and stock of the Poles. They served Ludendorff even better than they afterwards served Lenin.

Then, as the main shop-keeping class in the plundered, hungry country, they carried the craft of profiteering to an audacious height. Many honest Polish Jews began to incline to a fanatical Bolshevism as an only possible remedy. Yet these men could not keep their movement honest. They were joined by money-lenders' clerks and other strange converts to Communism, until the urban Revolutionary forces were little more than an instrument controlled by Bernstorff and Dernberg, and intended for blackmailing the Polish landowners.

This was a mistake on the part of the German schemers. They thought they had Poland hemmed between Bolshevism and a peasants' revolt, and compelled to purchase Prussian aid at the price of the Danzig corridor to the Baltic Sea and the Silesian coalfields. But there was one thing the Polish nobility never lacked, and that was courage. They equalled, if they did not excel, the Irish gentry in fighting spirit, and one reason why they continued to hold great estates in foreign lands after complete national disasters was that Tsar and Emperor found it unwise to provoke them to the last extremity. They were capable of anything—even of general patriotism—in such a case, as was seen in the Posen province.

Fighting spirit of the Poles

Some of the Reactionaries on the Regency Council at Warsaw appeared to have inclined to a continuance of the

Prussian alliance, on the base of class interests. The pro-Germans lost control of a peasants' rising against the invader, which had been long preparing, and was ready to break out in October, 1918, on a report that the Teutons were at last being broken in the west. A sham National Democratic Government was formed, that distinguished itself by sending extraordinary telegrams to Berlin and Vienna expressing a keen desire to remain on friendly terms with the Central Powers in the days when German and Austrian forces were breaking into disorder. The peasants' movement turned against the great nobles, such as Prince Czartoryski and Prince Lubomirski, who were preparing to form a monarchy. To prevent an outburst, the bolder, lesser gentry forced their views on the new Government, and had Poland proclaimed as a People's Republic.

This was a coup d'état that put an end to the Regency. But only for a few hours did the great landowners remain passive. They countered the stroke by dismissing the new Government, convoking a Constituent Assembly for December 1st, 1918, and appointing officials to carry on administrative work. This measure produced a real Revolutionary movement. Radical land reformers combined at Lublin with Socialists of the national kind, and proclaimed a People's Government. Only territory occupied by Poles was comprised in the Lublin scheme, but an outlet to the sea was required. The Lithuanians, White Russians, and Little Russians were welcomed as friendly neighbours, and Poles settled in frontier lands were invited to live in peace with their old associates, pending the solution of the problems of territorial settlement.

Revolution in Poland

Under the Lublin Government the men of the disbanded Polish Legion gathered for the task of expelling German troops from the country. Polish soldiers and officers from German, Russian, and Austrian forces joined the army of the new Republic, under a Revolutionary colonel holding temporary command, until Joseph Pilsudski appeared. Every Polish party moved for the release of the old commander of the Polish Legion. The Regency Council begged Dr. Solf to release Pilsudski, but Solf would not even discuss the matter. The first Warsaw Government implored Prince Max to liberate the great legionary, but Max required Pilsudski first to forswear all hostility to Germany and Pilsudski would submit to no conditions. A prison, he said, was not a place in which to discuss anything. He was finally released by German Revolutionaries in Magdeburg, and arrived in Warsaw on November 10th, just in time to save the life of his bitterest opponent, the Regent, Prince Lubomirski.

On November 14th General Pilsudski, at the head of forty thousand men, became the virtual Dictator of Poland. Between November 11th and November 15th his lieutenants cleared most of the country of armed Germans, and put an end to the systematic plundering of Poland. Polish Jews were stopped from requisitioning cattle for the Teutons, and the general destruction of forests and industries ceased. All the underground work for a rising against the Germans was completed by an open mobilisation of former legionaries and disbanded men and officers from Germany and Austria. A small force of three thousand regular soldiers, which had worked under German command, became the nucleus for the arming and equipping of the national forces. The leaders were dismissed, but the subordinate officers furnished the regular framework upon which the Volunteer Army was rapidly constructed.

Pilsudski as virtual Dictator

General Pilsudski at first concentrated his efforts upon the making of his army. In an early stage of the war he had preferred to destroy the legions he had created rather than see them take the oath to the Hohenzollern and the Hapsburg. He had first been duped by anger against the Tsar about the unsuccessful Baltic provinces rebellion in 1905; but when he saw he was a dupe, he entered a German prison rather than betray his own people. Released from prison, he became the hero of the Polish commoners and of the better part of the smaller Polish gentry, but by the great landowners he was for some time regarded as a deadlier enemy than Ludendorff had been.

Pilsudski wanted little to make him one of the most famous of nation-builders. What he wanted was a little more trenchancy and rigour in dealing with the men in and behind the Regency Council. He sacrificed too much to an impossible ideal of entire national unity. He tried to reconcile the interests of the great landowners with the interests of the land-hungry peasantry. After failing to combine oil and water, he governed with the moderate elements of his own Socialist Party, but refrained from carrying out the land reforms that would have made Poland a land of contented fighting peasants, against which any grandees' intrigue would have failed.

As the Dictator of Poland declined to dictate, and left everything of importance to a Constituent Assembly which was not elected, the mental atmosphere of the nation was perturbed. Paderewski, the famous pianist, was made President of Poland, but had difficulties in reconciling the malcontents during the months when the country was drifting into serious danger.

Germany had marked down Poland as her prey. The Poles both menaced Old Prussia by their claims to the Vistula outlet to the sea, and barred the way to German penetration of Russia by the fact of merely existing. The example of an independent Poland likewise had, from a Teutonic point of view, an inspiring influence upon Lithuania, Lettland, and Estland—the Baltic provinces where German baronial landowners were being upheld against the native peoples by a German army that pretended to fight the Muscovite Bolshevists. Three main methods of attack were employed —military, political, and religious—and the last was for a time the most effective. The Poles were discredited with all the Allies except France. This was done by exaggerating in a widespread propaganda the attacks made upon profiteering Jewish tradesmen and notorious Jewish traitors, until, in the British, American, and Scandinavian Press, the extermination of the Polish-Jews seemed to be the principal article of Polish Republican policy.

Invented tales of Jewish massacres

German landowners, coalowners, and industrialists in Upper Silesia spent about £500,000 between November, 1918, and February, 1919, in stirring feelings of hostility against the Poles among American, British, and Italian Jews. The engineers of the movement boasted that their tales of the wholesale massacre of Jews were affecting the views of some of the leading members of the Supreme Council at Versailles. An intimate Jewish friend of President Wilson was deeply moved by reports of atrocities that were not committed. In London a great demonstration of anti-Polish Jews was held at a time when Paderewski was arranging to visit the British capital. The pro-German Revolutionary forces in the British Labour movement were remarkably sympathetic towards the Jewish demonstration, on which part of the £500,000 given by the German capitalists of Upper Silesia had been spent. According to confidential Teutonic statements, the International Zionist movement, in return for contributions, gave promising support to German interests against Poland. Permanent propaganda delegations were established at The Hague, Berne, and Copenhagen. At St. Gall, in Switzerland, Dr. Solf assisted in person in the last elaboration of a scheme for enlisting the strong International forces of Israel against the Poles.

The Silesian tales of massacre became at last so greatly prejudicial to the interests of Polish Jews that leading representatives of the race came to London to protest to British Jews, and at first could scarcely obtain a hearing when they tried to defend their Christian fellow-countrymen. They had to live and work with the Poles, and, having considerable commercial interests, wanted a traffic outlet to the Vistula port. Very gradually, under their influence, the German propaganda scheme was killed, although it remained likely that in Polish-Jewish districts of London and New York such legends as the Vilna massacre of three thousand children of Israel would be current for a generation.

During the critical period in which Republican Poland

Victory March in London, July 19th, 1919: Troops entering the Mall through the Admiralty Arch.

490   To "The Glorious Dead," the men who died that civilisation might be saved to the world

erican troops passing the cenotaph in Whitehall in the great Victory March, July 19th, 1919 491

British sailors in Whitehall during the Victory March which celebrated the signing of peace.

displaced Tsarist Russia as the object of world-wide Jewish anger, the Polish aristocracy greatly assisted the Teutons in the scheme for discrediting the country in the judgment of President Wilson and Mr. Lloyd George. By means of experienced officers of their class who entered the small, new, under-armed, and under-horsed national army they made the Polish race appear extremely aggressive. German political agents from the Posen province also played a sinister part in provoking a frenzy of convulsive fighting.

With considerable and legitimate success the Poles engaged the German-led Bolshevist forces on their eastern frontier. Then they entered Lithuania, which was in December, 1918, still held by the Tenth German Army, under General Hoffmann, and moved to raise a Lithuanian militia for further action against Soviet Russia. It was very doubtful whether the Lithuanians as a whole wished to unite again with the Poles. The Lithuanians had nothing in common with Slav races, but, like their kinsmen, the Letts, were a curiously distinct stock using the oldest of Indo-European languages. In their pagan period they had overrun all the western provinces of Russia, and held most of them until 1793, but only for the profit of the Polish nobility, who remained in possession of large estates in the Ukraine until the Bolshevist Revolution in 1917.

Meanwhile, the Lithuanians had lost most of their native land to Polish manorial lords, and were tempted to unite with their kinsfolk, the Letts, against all alien immigrants, Poles as well as Baltic Germans. But the Tenth German Army prevented them from taking action against the Teuton lords, and they were not strong enough to resist the new Polish forces. Neither Germans nor Poles would provide the Lithuanians with arms and munitions for putting down marauders and defending the frontier against Bolshevist invaders. The Poles wished to sell protection at the price of loss of national independence, and the Lithuanians, who had formed at the end of December, 1918, a Government bent on land reform, struggled and starved rather than yield.

There was also a revival of the old, bitter **Position of the Ukrainians** feud between the Poles and the Ukrainians, otherwise known as Ruthenes or Little Russians, peopling part of Galicia and practically all Southern Russia. Under Germanic suggestion the Ukrainians, in November, 1918, seized Lemberg, a city for which they had vainly struggled for six centuries. Once more they were unequal to the task of attaining their object, and the old dominating Polish aristocracy summoned sufficient forces to retake Lemberg and make an effort to recover their large estates in the Ukraine, which their ancestors had acquired in the days of the Lithuanian Empire.

From the middle of the nineteenth century to the summer of 1914 the Ukrainians' discontent with their Polish landlords had been one of the most potent factors making for a Continental war. The Germans had promoted Ukrainian hostility against the Poles; the Poles had countered by making things uncomfortable for Austria, and by offering to come to an understanding with Muscovite Russia. For fifty years the Central Powers on one side and Russia on the other side had employed Polish landowners and Ukrainian peasants as pieces in warlike diplomacy. Bitterness had thus been artificially intensified in a situation that was naturally envenomed, and during the profound vicissitudes of the war the Ukrainian serf and his Polish lord had not learnt to like each other better.

Only the establishment of agrarian reform in Poland, and the Pilsudski scheme for restricting Polish rule to Polish people, could have ended the secular struggle between some thirty million Ukrainians and somewhat less than half that number of true Poles, and their immediate associates such as the Masurians.

There were fresh Polish divisions in France, under General Haller, which could have given the warlike aristocracy ample means of conducting their battles on all fronts. But in the circumstances it was perhaps well that General Pilsudski remained comparatively weak in troops and material in the months when he was being led into many unnecessary adventures. Had he been content with holding the Bolshevists and checking the ambitions of the Ukrainians, while maintaining a strong guard against the Germans, things might have gone more smoothly for Poland at Versailles.

He appeared to accept every suggestion from any party that gave him more work as a soldier. He intended originally, with the Polish Socialists, to work for a free and friendly Lithuanian nation and a liberated, neighbourly Ukrainian race. But, when he entered into a coalition with the Polish landowning party, Pilsudski had not the power and reach of mind required in a man in his position.

While injuring themselves by their conduct in Lithuania and Eastern Galicia, the Polish landowning caste achieved the complete encirclement of their unfortunate country by hostile Powers. Instead of patiently awaiting the decision of the Council of Versailles regarding the coalfields of Silesia, they sent out forces to fight the Bohemians and Slovaks for the possession of the coal resources of the Teschen Valley, in what had been Austrian Silesia.

This was another modernisation of a **Polish-Bohemian contentions** mediæval quarrel. It was a revival of the ancient Polish and Bohemian contentions over Silesia, which had ended in German settlements. The modern industrial movement of migrating cheap Polish labour and the grand enhancement of the economic importance of Silesian resources under German development were the reasons for renewing the struggle between the two Slav nations. Even as they had done in the Middle Ages, by fighting each other, Bohemian and Pole fought, without recognising it, for the Teuton.

In 1918 Bohemian and Polish leaders had agreed that the Teschen district should be regarded as neutral ground until the peace settlement. But as soon as the Bohemian Republic was proclaimed, the Poles occupied both the Polish and Bohemian parts of the Teschen duchy. When, in January, 1919, a commission of Entente officers came to Teschen and ordered the Polish commander to withdraw his troops from the disputed territory, the commander tried to obey, but his subordinate officers stood to action against the advancing Bohemian legionaries, and there was some heavy fighting. The Teschen affair served the interests of the German intriguers in the same way as the Lithuanian affair.

Direct hostilities between Germany and Poland had opened on December 17th, 1918, when the German Legation left Warsaw and the Polish Legation left Berlin. There was a triple scheme of operations against Poland. The Tenth German Army, withdrawing from the Dnieper River into East Prussia, arranged for Bolshevist forces to occupy immediately the country evacuated. General Hoffmann, notorious for his treatment of Trotsky in the Brest Litovsk negotiations, was the commander who concerted the plot with the Bolshevists. With Hoffmann was Falkenhayn, the former German Chief of Staff. When Poles and Lithuanians in towns about to be surrendered begged for arms to defend themselves, the Germans said they were under orders from Berlin to provide no means of resistance to the Russian Communists. More than one hundred thousand Russian prisoners of war were passed **Arrival of M. Paderewski** from the German to the Bolshevist lines to serve as recruits for Trotsky's Red Armies.

At the same time the Ukrainian forces fighting round Lemberg on Ukrainian territory were reinforced by Austrian gunners, so that the mobs of disbanded men again exerted formidable pressure upon the Polish troops, many of whom were but Boy Scouts.

Then, while serious internal Communist movements were occurring in Poland, the main Teutonic forces on the eastern front endeavoured to hold Posen city and province. Fierce fighting began on December 27th, 1918, when M. Paderewski, with Colonel Wade, arrived at Danzig in a British destroyer, and passed through Posen on the way to Warsaw. Ten thousand school-children welcomed Paderewski, and their display of British, American, and French flags angered a regiment of Prussian grenadiers, who started shooting at the children, at Paderewski, and at the British colonel. Armed Polish forces, composed of ex-German troops of Polish race, came out to protect M. Paderewski and avenge their

FIGHTING ON THE POLISH FRONTIER.
Patrol of the Polish frontier defence troops and of volunteers during the intermittent fighting that continued into the early months of 1919; and (in circle) a machine-gun with the same patrol.

affected by the German and Yiddish tales of massacres. It was the merit of the French commander and Premier that they studied the Polish problem from a European point of view. They needed Poland so much that, if she had not existed, they would have created her. In their view Poland was the eastern bulwark of the Western Powers, and also the western bulwark for a resurrected Russia. Great as was the military value of a strong Poland, her position as a barrier against a Teutonic policy of an economic, political, and intellectual penetration of a revived Russia was even more important.

A strong, aristocratic Poland would have suited the French leaders almost as well as a strong democratic Poland. Like the old French cardinals, when leaguing with Turk and Protestant

children. In a two days' battle the Poles recovered their city, but in the countryside were met by German reinforcements of gunners and infantry, hurried from Baltic ports.

There were a quarter of a million German troops available for immediate concentration against thousands of Pilsudski's legionaries and Boy Scouts. Hoffman in East Prussia had but to connect with Below near Posnania, and the Poles would have had as much chance of winning against the Germans as a rabbit has against a terrier. By way of assisting in the defence of their country, the reactionary Polish landowning party kidnapped, on January 5th, 1919, General Pilsudski and his Chief of Staff and principal Ministers. The troops in Warsaw freed their leaders, the kidnappers were pardoned, and the affair passed off as a fantastic comedy. But the suspicious peasants and urban workers inclined to a serious view of the matter. Pilsudski was their guarantee for eventual land and social reform, and some effective, lasting defeat of the landowning, Church-directing oligarchy. Where it was suspected that the Polish aristocracy was plotting an alliance with the old Prussian and Baltic aristocracies for a common defence of manorial domains, Polish Red Guards organised for action in a night, as happened again in Lublin.

M. Paderewski enjoyed a personal triumph in Warsaw, but he did not solve the agrarian difficulty though he formed a Coalition Cabinet. Only in Posnania, where the machinery of the German Civil Service was taken over, was there something of a businesslike air. British and French officers, who worked for months in the transport of General Haller's divisions through Germany into Poland, **Results of** were despondent over the seeming lack **long suffering** of business sense among their new allies. They put it down entirely to nervous exhaustion and to the prolonged underfeeding and suffering of the unhappiest of nations. But there was something more than that made for inefficiency. It was the thing that had led to the decay and dismemberment of Poland. The Polish lords wished things to drift, in the hope that they would once more float into positions of landed wealth and security.

M. Clemenceau and Marshal Foch proved the saviours of Poland. The French were not well informed on domestic Polish affairs, as the Polish Delegation at Paris was supposed to represent the reactionary, landowning party, and intrigued against the Pilsudski Government and the commoners' interests. British and American statesmen had no more knowledge than the French, and at times were apparently

against rival Catholic Powers, M. Clemenceau had no theoretic prejudices in international business. He sought only for practical remedies in pressing troubles. At Paris Mr. Lloyd George was the champion for a democratic Poland, and with the help of President Wilson, whose lieutenants fed the Poles from midwinter to harvesttime, and so prevented a hunger revolution and a German-Bolshevist triumph, he shaped the course of Polish development. It was not until July, 1919, that the Warsaw Diet passed, by the closest of divisions, governed by the single vote of a member, a measure for restricting the ownership of land to some four hundred acres. Thus tardily but constitutionally was the foundation laid for the erection of a strong, independent Polish middle class, for lack of which lord and peasant had failed to combine into a nation.

Meanwhile, the territorial ambitions of the Poles were not diminished. Intensely and bitterly the struggle continued for the Galician lands of the Ukrainians that stretched eastward from Przemysl. Eastern Galicia was native Ukrainian territory, being the ancient Red Russia for the conquest of which Lithuanians and Poles had contended at the time when the Russians were enfeebled by Mongol invasions. The dispossessed pariah class of Eastern Galicia accepted the leadership of the dancer Petlura and the help of his Germanic agents, who used them as pawns in the game being played for Posen, Silesia, and Danzig.

From the winter of 1918 to the summer of 1919 the struggle in Eastern Galicia went on, the Ukrainians gradually losing, through lack of an able general, sound organisation and supplies. The Council of Versailles made it a condition of the despatch of General Haller's divisions from France and America that these fresh and well-equipped forces should not be employed against the Ukrainians in Galicia, but used in defeating the Russian Bolshevist advance on Vilna.

General Pilsudski, who had started with the policy of a Little Poland, strangely became foremost in the savage fighting in Galicia. The latter retaliated cruelly. It was an internal affair, in which the moving spirit on the Polish side was the Prince Bishop of Cracow, an ecclesiastical noble-man, who fought for his landowning countrymen in the Ukraine, and also for the Catholic Church against the Uniat Church and Orthodox Church.

Although the Prussian nobility and German industrial magnates fiercely pressed the Polish landowners, and arranged an alliance with the Russian Bolshevists against them, there was some doubt of any real antagonism between the two aristocracies.

After the election of the German National Assembly, which

sources of information, estimated the organised German troops at six hundred thousand, with another two million and a half of veteran soldiers available for a desperate national struggle if their patriotic spirit could be revived.

From the point of view of the German Reactionaries the problem of reviving the national fighting spirit was a ticklish and delicate affair. The troops were intended for direct use on the western front if conditions became favourable, but this design could not be communicated to the rank and file. It was a Staff Office secret, for success depended upon the spread of disaffection among the allied armies holding the Rhine bridge-heads, and the creation of social disorder in Great Britain, Southern France, and Italy. All that could be publicly said in the great secret campaign for re-enlistment was that the life of the German people was menaced by Polish ambition in regard to Danzig and West Prussia.

Hundreds of guns were hidden for use in defending Berlin against an allied advance. Bohemian workmen discovered hidden batteries in Saxony and in Brandenburg, and passed their special knowledge on to the Versailles Council. German recruits were obtained at **German secret** the rate of thousands a day by the Bol- **military campaign** shevists' device of offering an abundance of good food, high rate of pay, and special family allowances. The masterful German Jew, Noske, who was nominally responsible for all the work of military organisation, was little more than the secretary of Hindenburg's able lieutenants. Colonel Reinhardt acted as Minister of War, and put forward General Lettow-Vorbeck, the national hero of the German East African compaign, as commander of the anti-Revolutionary forces. Better men even than Lettow-Vorbeck were behind the new movement. The former Chief of Staff to the Crown Prince, General von Lüttwitz, held the Berlin command. General von Below was organising in Pomerania.

In German Silesia a blacksmith, Hörsing, came forward as the popular champion of his race, and, as the figurehead of the mineowners, met with remarkable success round Breslau. In Old Prussia another civilian, Winnig, exercised a similar but less marked influence, and co-operated with Hörsing by means of Army Staffs working behind the civilian patriots. In Eastern Germany there was closer contact between the old Prussian landowners and German captains of industry,

was opened at Weimar in the first week of February, 1919, a Scheide-mann Government was formed under President Ebert. Haase and the Independent Socialists were deprived of all practical power in Imperial Germany, and a great reactionary movement was engineered by the Prussian landowners and the manu-facturers, bankers, and merchants who looked to the military class for protection. Count Bernstorff, Dr. Dern-berg, Dr. Solf, and Count Brockdorff-Rantzau, directly led the movement, while Scheidemann, Noske, Landberg, and other Imperial Socialists acted as responsible Ministers. Their activity was but a screen for the preparations for a civil war and a foreign war. Mr. Lloyd George stated, apparently on the authority of his military advisers, that the armed forces of Germany were being reduced to eighty thousand men. But Barth and Haase, the defeated Independent leaders, with their better

RESTORING POLAND TO THE MAP OF EUROPE.
In the Geographical Section of the British Peace Conference headquarters in Paris. Men of the R.E. at work on the map of Poland. In circle : M. A. Wagner and M. S. Filiproski, members of the Polish National Committee, who went through Russia and Siberia to protect Polish citizens suffering under Bolshevism.

both of them backed by hundreds of thousands of troops that Hindenburg's lieutenants directed from the new General Headquarters in the Baltic seaport of Kolberg. Kolberg was chosen as the centre of command, as being midway between the main front of civil war in Berlin and the intended line for an offensive against Poland. The spirit of the troops was strengthened and their obedience to discipline tested by means of countless little skirmishes against the Polish forces defending Posen. When a regiment was wrought into a loyal body by the hard and persuasive work of the officers, it could be railed westward for use in the civil war that Noske was conducting.

Entire army corps from the French front, however, remained rebellious to the Scheidemann Government, as also did the larger part of the naval forces that had started the first Revolution, and many of the Independent Socialists united with the Communist agitators and helped to provoke fresh outbreaks at Lübeck, Wilhelmshaven, and Bremen. At Brunswick there continued a rather ridiculous Soviet Government, under a tailor, which kept itself in power for several months owing to the Brunswickers' aversion to the Prussians. Sporadic Sovietism broke out in other towns, such as Augsburg, and Noske's troops—using Tanks, flame-throwers, and aeroplanes, in addition to heavy and light artillery—met with much opposition, and had considerable trouble in repressing the disorders.

The main source of the trouble was the frame of mind of millions of veteran troops. Care had to be taken not to provoke these men to revolt, while breaking and chasing the rebels. Here it was that the power which the Imperial active Socialists exercised in Trade Unions told gradually, yet strongly, upon the general situation. Amid all the rioting, an intense and personal propaganda was carried on among the working men by agents of the Scheidemann group. They had chiefly to contend with young men occupying similar positions to those of the British shop stewards, and inclined, often under direct Bolshevist influence, to a complete system of Soviet control in industry and commerce as well as in politics. Against these men the continuing allied blockade was skilfully used, until the majority of German working men were for the time convinced that President Wilson would not feed them and their families unless they obeyed the orders of the Imperial Socialists.

This was one of the most brilliant of moves of the reactionaries. The blockade was being maintained for the reason that the great plot of the new German Government was known at Versailles, and raw materials were withheld as a counter-measure to Revolutionary propaganda in allied countries and to the menace of the resumption of the ordeal of battle. The German Government was well aware that it could have had fair terms in the way of food and raw material had it thought fit to accept the peace settlement. As, however, the Bernstorff Party continued to gamble on outbreaks of Revolution in Great Britain and France, the blockade was maintained with a view to saving Marshal Foch the trouble of moving his armies.

Months were to pass before the German leaders lost all hope of achieving their purpose. In the middle of February

JOSEPH PILSUDSKI.
Towards the close of 1918, at the head of about forty thousand men, he became for a while virtual Dictator of Poland.

MEETING OF THE POLISH COUNCIL OF STATE.
First sitting of the Polish Council, in the Krassinsky Palace, Warsaw. At first Poland was proclaimed a kingdom under a Council of Regency, but before the close of 1918 it was decided to establish a Republic, with M. Paderewski as President. In February 1919, independent Poland was formally recognised by Great Britain.

Erzberger was standing aside, with all the powerful German Catholic interests, and allowing the bolder spirits of Protestant Prussia to make their desperate attempt to transform defeat into victory. Only the sane, moderate men among the diminishing Independent Socialist Party were still bent upon negotiating an honest peace. They were, however, growing more desperate, as all the forces of reaction were converging against them. Greatly embittered by loss of power, some of them became wild with the spirit of vengeance, and proclaimed that they would execute the war party, divide all large estates, and socialise every important industry. Approaching closer to the Russian Communists, the Independents strove to increase the power and scope of all Workmen's, Soldiers', and Peasants' Councils in Germany. One of their leaders, Adolf Hoffmann, succeeded Liebknecht as nominal controller of the principal Spartacist multitude of Berlin, and in Bavaria, where Kurt Eisner still uneasily reigned, there was also some understanding with the Spartacists.

In his campaign against the Reactionary Coalition, Eisner continued to use the same methods as were afterwards adopted by Erzberger. He tried to discredit the men in power by destroying the legend that Germany was guiltless of commencing the war. At the beginning of February, 1919, Eisner attended the International Socialist Conference at Berne, and produced a remarkable effect by admitting that Germany was guilty, while pleading for humane terms for a repentant people. His policy was probably sound from an enlightened German point of view, and an early peace might have been arranged had it been adopted by the German Government. It was, however, in conflict with the policy of the Weimar Cabinet, of which Scheidemann became Prime Minister early in February.

When Kurt Eisner returned from Switzerland to Munich, and prepared to make Bavaria the base for a movement against the Imperialists, he was struck down by the simplest of methods—assassination. In the morning of February 21st, as Eisner was walking from the Foreign Office to the Diet, two officers approached him. One of them was Count Arco-Valley, a young member of one of the oldest of noble Bavarian families. One member had married a famous British scholar, Lord Acton. Another kinswoman was the wife of Prince Lichnowsky, the German Ambassador in London at the outbreak of war. Another relative belonged to the Independent Socialist group, and sat in the first Revolutionary Cabinet in Berlin. Arco-Valley, dressed as a private soldier, approached Eisner and shot him twice through the brain, and was then shot himself, but not killed, by one of Eisner's followers.

An hour after the assassination a butcher entered the Bavarian Parliament and shot Auer, the Imperial Socialist, who had shared power with the Independents in Bavaria and had there served Scheidemann. Auer was notorious for the part he played during the war, in approaching the Socialist Mayor of Roubaix, M. Le Bas, and trying to induce this patriot to work with the invaders. When Le Bas refused Auer's advances the German accused him of high treason, and had him thrown in prison. Such was the man who was attacked but not killed by one of Eisner's angry disciples. Several other Imperial Socialists and bureaucrats were injured by the Revolutionary butcher, who afterwards walked about the streets boasting he had avenged Eisner. He certainly threw into considerable disorder the plans of the reactionary party in Munich.

It was reported that papers were discovered in the rooms of Arco-Valley giving indications of a counter-Revolutionary plot. The youngest son of the former Kaiser, Prince Joachim, who was in Bavaria, apparently awaiting the success of the Royalists, was compelled to flee. Just before the assassination of Eisner there had been a fierce dispute between the Independent Socialists and the Imperialists over the question of sending Bavarian troops to fight the Poles. The Bavarian Minister for War, belonging to the Scheidemann party,

CRACOW'S ANCIENT BARBICAN.
The barbican of Cracow, which originally served as part of the defences of the city. It was built in 1498, when Cracow was the capital of Poland. Above : Men of the German conscripted army in one of the streets of Warsaw.

arranged for the troops to be sent, without consulting Eisner. It was when Eisner returned from Switzerland, and supported the protests of the Munich Soldiers' and Workmen's Council, that he was assassinated.

His death merely provoked stronger opposition to the sinister scheme for placing Bavarian troops under Hindenburg's command. It became known that Herr Noske and the generals behind him were arranging to solve the question of Bavaria's relations with Prussia by sending strong forces to Munich. Thereupon, in the first week of March, 1919, the Independent Socialists, who were recovering control of the Berlin and other local Soviets, prepared a general strike in Central Germany that would stop communications between Berlin and Munich. They used this peaceful means of persuasion because they were again negotiating with some of President Ebert's followers for a reconciliation between the main Social Democrat parties on the basis of repudiation of Bolshevism and a cautious extension of State socialisation. Haase, the Independent leader, went to Bavaria to settle differences, and, repeating his old mistake at Berlin in November, 1918, he allowed the Imperial Socialists to obtain predominant power in Munich by means of a Coalition Government, in which Scheidemann's disciples obtained all the important offices. He helped to lessen the power of the Munich Soviet and its Russian-Jewish director, Levien, and to re-establish Constitutional Government.

During the pretence at reconciliation Brockdorff-Rantzau, Dernberg, and other directors of the grand reaction joined in making advances to the Independent Party. They stopped at times even to court the Spartacists, and loudly menaced

the Allies with a Russian-German movement in Communism that should sweep Western Europe and save Germany from indemnities and loss of territory. In Prussia a decree was made, under Socialist influence, that all great landed estates should be broken up into small holdings at the end of two years, if the landowners did not sell out to small farmers in the meantime. When, however, the creatures of the Junkers were seated in power in Munich, and the train laid for the Magyar rally to Bolshevism in Budapest, by the middle of March, 1919, the Weimar Government took sanguinary measures to prevent any genuine Socialist movement in their own country.

The general strike in Central Germany went on without violence, but increased in political scope. The Independent leaders apparently intended to use it to convince all honest followers of the Majority Party that the hacks of the Weimar National Assembly were powerless to meet the needs of the people. This was so. With little more than a show of a change of opinion, the puppets of the Kaiser's Reichstag had become the marionettes of the Weimar Assembly. But behind these petty personages were masterful, evil men who exercised real power. In a most deadly manner they displayed their strength by provoking a wild outbreak in Berlin.

For no reasonable cause the old Revolutionary garrison of the capital was attacked by the new troops led by General von Lüttwitz. The **Fresh fighting** Marine Division, the Alexander Regiment of **in Berlin** the Guards, and the Guards Fusiliers supported the Independent Party. These troops were not of Spartacist sympathy, but they wished to preserve the political changes they had helped to establish in the winter of 1918. They introduced more Independent delegates into the Berlin Council, and helped to prepare another Congress of Soviets that should exercise some general measure of control, so long as the Weimar Assembly tended to warlike Imperialism.

Once more the Secret Service officers in the Spartacist camp led out their working-men dupes in a foolish riot that was bound to end badly. Through some regimental quarrel the Marines began fighting with Lüttwitz's fresh troops and with the Guard Defence Division. It was one of those soldier fights that occur in the best conducted armies. The Marines were trained differently from the crack German riflemen of the Guards, and were contemned as inferior fighting men. They offered to prove in the street that they were as good men as those who jeered at them. During the riot the Spartacists came out, and Lüttwitz, who seemed to have staged the conflict, suddenly brought about another Battle of Berlin.

His object was completely to cow the Berlin populace by taking the Revolutionary forces unawares and subjecting them to merciless punishment. The trouble between Marines and Guards began on March 4th, 1919, and by March 5th there was a general engagement ranging from the centre of the city to the eastern suburbs. In the night Government aeroplanes whirred over Berlin, dropping flares, and machine-gunning rebels on the roofs of buildings. Other machines came out, rebel and Governmental, and used bombs upon crowded streets and upon buildings which were being besieged. Day and night the battle went on for a week and a half, Lüttwitz gaining the mastery by means of 5 in. howitzers, and reproduced in parts of Berlin scenes like those in Cambrai and Rheims. Noske, on an allegation that Government men were being shot when they sur-

"No quarter" in civil warfare rendered, proclaimed that no quarter would be given to anybody bearing arms. The massacres that followed kindled madness in the souls of the Spartacists, and their women especially fought to the death like human tigresses.

From the beginning to the end the Revolutionaries had no chance of victory, except by winning over the Government troops. This was prevented by Noske's diabolically clever trick of allowing no quarter. The Marines were annihilated by heavy gun fire, and the Alexander Guards and Guard Fusiliers siding with them suffered the same fate. All these were veteran troops, and Lüttwitz employed mostly lads, but behind the lads was the best machinery of destruction, and the youngsters were too much inflamed by tales of Spartacist atrocities against their comrades to listen to the appeals of Revolutionary women and girls.

Slowly and scientifically the former Chief of the Staff to the Crown Prince encircled Neukölln and Lichtenberg and other centres of battle, and with trench-mortars, field artillery, and heavy ordnance smashed roads of advance into the last positions of the insurgents. By March 13th the Lichtenberg suburb was stormed, and it was then found that the sensational tales of horrible cruelties practised by the

IN A POLISH VILLAGE.
Characteristic Polish village near the ancient town of Grodno, where the second partition of Poland took place in 1793. In oval: The new Market Square, and (above) Trinity Square, in the Polish town of Lodz.

Spartacists were without foundation. Scarcely ten men on the Government side had been shot after surrendering, and there were reasons for believing that most of these men had been killed because the surrender they offered, after fighting bitterly to the last minute, was not a fair one. The Teuton had not overcome his habit of using a machine-gun until he was doomed, and then trying to obtain mercy.

While the Berlin battle was raging in the suburbs, revelling went on in the central dancing-halls. Officers returning from battle with the Spartacists entered the crowded halls, with the dust and sweat of battle upon them, drank wine at high war prices, danced with wantons until daybreak, and then many of them went again into action. Here and there the orchestra and the whirling throng of merrymakers would be reduced to silence and standstill by a bomb or shell falling dangerously close, but in a general way Berlin danced between bankruptcy and death, while the Spartacists were trying to hold the railway by which the city was fed. Most of the money expended in orgies was ill-gotten, and the profiteers and dealers in stolen Government goods, with their trains of hangers-on, thought they had a short life before them, which they tried to make as merry as possible.

While Lüttwitz provoked and quelled the Revolutionary spirit in Berlin, other experienced commanders broke the general strike that interrupted communications between the capital and other important towns. General Märker, at the head of a division, stormed into Halle and restored railway traffic between Berlin and Weimar. Then he went to Brunswick and put an end to the Soviet which had been maintained there since the winter, owing to the people's dislike to Prussian rule. In Berlin an attempt was made to scatter the Workmen's Council in which the Independents ruled. Noske's soldiers occupied the Council Hall, but hundreds of thousands of work- **German Junkers and** men, who had taken no part in the **Russian Bolshevists** Spartacist fighting, threatened action, and compelled Noske to withdraw his troops and apologise.

As soon as the Berlin Revolutionaries were forced into insurrection and were defeated, an extraordinary intrigue began between the Soviet Government of Russia and the Coalition Government of Germany. German agents were sent to Moscow to arrange a secret alliance between the Bolshevists and Junkers. It was agreed that Russian manufacturers, especially those engaged in making arms and ammunitions, should be given more liberty by Lenin's lieutenants, so that their works could be restored to some efficiency. The Teutons undertook to help in rebuilding Russian railways, and to strengthen the Bolshevist armies by the despatch of thousands of military instructors.

In return for technical aid in industrial and military affairs,

Russia agreed not to come to any understanding with the Western Powers, and to export foodstuffs to Germany. The alliance was to last twenty years, and be binding on any successors of the Bolshevist Governments, though in what way that was to be ensured was not clear, but some attempt was made by the Germans to bring the patriotic Russian Socialist Parties into a working arrangement with Lenin.

The German Government did not intend to adopt a Bolshevist system in order to gratify the Communists of Moscow. All they offered the Russians was help of a capitalist sort in manufacturing and engineering affairs and army reorganisation, in return for Russian raw materials, food, and concessions in the development of the vast resources of Russia. Yet, at the same time, all German Ministers used the outbreak of Bolshevism in Hungary as a means of extorting easier terms from the Allies. Either by the natural force of suggestion, or by definite yet roundabout propaganda, Germany's troubles with her coalmines, railwaymen, transport workers, and engineers were balanced by apparently similar unrest in British mines, railways, and workshops.

British workmen, who allowed themselves to be led into imitating German workmen and to threaten direct action against their Constitutional Government, had not been tricked, cheated, and then terrorised by battles without quarter, conducted by Reactionaries. There was some excuse for the Independent German Socialist Party resorting to the general strike as a means of exerting political pressure upon the ruling Social Democrats who had betrayed their cause.

The Western Powers, however, were far from impotent against the supreme intrigue of the Teutonic reactionaries. On March 10th a mass meeting was held in the Casino of Cologne, where delegates from the Rhineland cities met to make arrangements for the establishment of a Republic of the Rhine. There was little doubt that the great coalfields of the Rhine basin would have been included in the new Republic. Western Germans saw that if they remained part of a German State engaged in over-running Poland and leaguing with Bolshevist Russia, their vineyards, factories, foundries, and coalmines would fall as ransom to the Western Powers. There was a report that Marshal Foch was preparing to move in overwhelming force, and that within ten days Europe would again be a great battlefield, while German emissaries of anarchy began work in both neutral and hostile countries, alongside Russian and Russian-Jewish Bolshevists and the agitators of the Industrial Workers of the World.

In these circumstances the Rhineland people publicly expressed their intention of forming themselves into an independent State, likely to side with France, Britain, America, Belgium, and Italy. Erzberger, representing more or less the permanent interests of Catholic **German intrigue in the east** Germany in which the Rhineland was included, became alarmed at the turn of events. By far the larger part of the mineral and agricultural wealth of Germany was in the Rhine basin, together with most of the heavy machinery plant. As Hindenburg could not guarantee to stay Marshal Foch's advance through the western front, it seemed to Erzberger the wildest of all new gambles to try to conquer Poland and unite with Russia at the cost of immediate loss of the Rhine country. Moreover, the Baltic coast of Germany was open to the combined attack of the allied navies and armies during the long period of clear water in 1919, so there was a strong possibility that German military operations in the east would be checked before Poland could be overrun.

The enemy scheme was thus impossible of execution under existing conditions. The master intriguers Count Bernstorff, Count Brockdorff-Rantzau, and their Social Democratic and Bolshevist co-operators, were unable to create in England, Scotland, and Wales the profound disorders required to disarm Great Britain. The French people also, though restless under

GENERAL HALLER.
In command of the Polish divisions that went from France to the assistance of Poland after the signing of the armistice.

profiteering and sinister agitation, were still mighty in arms, while the great military strength of the United States was practically unaffected by German-Russian propaganda. There were also domestic difficulties in the way of the master intriguers.

General von der Goltz, one of Ludendorff's lieutenants, came from Finland to the Baltic provinces to organise operations against the Bolshevist armies. He had defeated the Finnish Revolutionaries at the time when Germany seemed triumphant, and had tried to set a German monarch over the Finnish people. Now he had to work in the interests of the Allies, and naturally he did his best to aid the Baltic nobles of his own race against the native peasants, who were erecting democratic Governments with far-reaching schemes of land reform.

There were several counter-Revolutionary movements by the Baltic barons and the German troops—some of them serious, as at Libau; some comical, as at Grodno. When the first allied officer entered **German trick in Lithuania** Lithuania he asked to see the leading native representatives of Grodno. He was an American with some knowledge of Polish and Russian, and when, after considerable delay, a group of men was presented to him as the town notables, he tried to converse with them. He found conversation a very awkward affair, as the Lithuanians could not speak Polish or Russian, but they were ready to explain in German that they wished for union with Germany, owing to the way the town had prospered under German occupation. But the American officer was not lacking in shrewdness. He discovered that the town notables introduced to him were a squad of German troops dressed in ordinary clothes, and in the course of the day he found the real Lithuanian authorities, who completely exposed the plot. Tricks such as this and blows like that at Libau were but childish futilities, without lasting influence upon the main factors of the Baltic situation. The main fact remained that the Baltic barons were in their own interests averse to the Bolshevist intrigue. Nearly every native Baltic small-holder was ready to fight with the utmost personal bitterness against the pillaging communities of his own race. So the Baltic lords obtained a considerable number of armed native volunteers, and with German, British, Finnish and loyalist Russian help and Polish co-operation, they gradually pushed the Bolshevist forces back. That is to say, they directly worked against the scheme for a German-Russian attack on Poland. Sir Hubert Gough had to be sent to the Baltic to watch over Von der Goltz, and British warships intervened in domestic struggles in Lettland, but the main situation was adverse to a Bolshevist-Junker alliance during the critical months before the signing of the Peace Treaty.

While the Imperial Germans were wavering over their scheme for a Polish campaign and co-operation with the Bolshevists, Bavaria again became very independent. The Imperial Socialists and the new Bavarian Cabinet found themselves hindered by the Munich Soviet, the members of which were still strongly disinclined to allow troops to be sent to Poland. An order was made that every man passing the place where Eisner had been assassinated had to lift his hat, and every woman had to bow the knee. Many men who had followed the Independents in striving for a reconciliation with the Ebert Party reckoned they had been betrayed by the formation of the new Coalition Government in Munich and the massacres in Berlin. They therefore tended more towards the Spartacists' camp, and another great rising was organised in Southern Germany.

By way of forestalling the new Revolution the reactionaries prepared a kind of comic-opera experiment in Communist agitation. The art students and literary Bohemians of Munich were mobilised by much secret confabulation in taverns and studios. Under a young, erotic poet, Erich Toller, as dictator, an absinthe-crazed poet, Mühsam, and a lunatic, Dr. Lippe, they formed an artistic Communism. In the first week of April the poets and painters achieved their grand revolution by the easy method of giving drink to the men of the 1st Bavarian Regiment of Infantry, and showing them that it was better to undertake a little light skirmishing in Munich than to entrain under Prussian command for the Polish front.

With regular soldiers aiding the bands of armed working men, the capital was quickly won, and the Hoffmann Coalition Government fled into Northern Bavaria and collected loyal troops for operations against Munich. Scarcely any Bavarian troops, however, proved reliable when the new Revolutionaries taught them the plain facts that the reward for any Government victory would be a troop train towards Poland and a march to the new eastern battlefield under the direction of a cordon of Prussian machine-gunners and artillerymen.

A Russian-Jewish Spartacist leader, Dr. Levien, who had been agitating since the beginning of February to prevent Bavarian troops being sent against the Poles, entered into an alliance with Bolshevist emissaries. Levien was an old friend of Lenin, and had waited his time in attempting a real Communistic movement. There was also a mild, well-meaning pacifist party in Munich that endeavoured to change the art students' carnival into means of establishing a gentle, liberal form of government. But when Hoffmann's forces closed round the capital, Levien brought some fairly-well trained armed workmen into action together with regular soldiers, and Hoffmann's troops were partly beaten and partly persuaded that they were fighting against their own personal interests. In what devious ways the master minds of the Weimar Government worked behind the scenes of the Bavarian comedy would take too long to trace. They were connected with the poets' and painters' parade, but they did not intend that all Bavarian troops should become violently averse to serving under Prussian commanders. Their original desire was to promote such domestic difficulties in Bavaria as should compel the Hoffmann Cabinet to accept the aid of strong Prussian forces. That State was to be overawed by the Prussians, so that Bavarian troops could be removed in large numbers from their country, partly to increase the armies threatening Poland, but mainly to put an end to the new spirit of Bavarian independence that Eisner had fostered.

It took less than 30,000 Prussian troops to conquer distracted and divided Bavaria. Saxony was overrun by Prussians at the same time as Bavaria was invaded. It was found that the workmen of Leipzig and Dresden were preparing to assist the Bavarian Communists by cutting the lines of communication of the advancing Prussian forces. General Märker, the pacifier of Halle and Brunswick, made a surprise descent on Leipzig, and held the city so strongly that no rising took place.

Meanwhile the main Prussian force, under General Möhl, crossed the Danube and began to surround Munich. On April 25th the insurgents were driven into the city, and there broken in long and fierce street fighting. For a week the struggle went on, the Prussians using aeroplanes, heavy artillery, and all the mechanism of the latest kind of siege warfare that had been employed in the last battle in Berlin. It was estimated there were about 12,000 regular Bavarian soldiers holding the capital, with nearly thirty thousand armed working men assisting them.

But lack of generalship and of good staff-work exposed the Bavarian regulars and irregulars to piecemeal destruction. They held large shops, churches, and public buildings, and fought with much personal bravery, their courage being excited rather than diminished by the Prussian policy of giving no quarter. They could not, however, stand against the blasting power of the Prussian heavy guns. By May 1st Munich was stormed. For the first time in history the Northern German conquered the Southern German capital. Although desultory shooting went on for two weeks longer, it was not the nocturnal fighting of the last of the Communist troops that saved Bavaria.

It was the atrocious, inexcusable conduct of the victorious Prussians that produced a resurgence of Bavarian patriotism.

Communist rising in Bavaria

Prussian troops besiege Munich

The Prussian commanders proved themselves Reactionaries of an unsupportable kind. Suspected persons were shot without trial. Socialists of every kind, Imperial and Independent, as well as Spartacist, were indiscriminately executed. The Hoffmann Government recovered popular support by protesting against the savage massacres of the Prussians. Little was known in outer Europe at the time of the events that were happening in and around the Bavarian capital. A Prussian military censorship, as complete as that which Ludendorff used to exercise, was maintained at Bamberg and other towns to which newspaper men were confined.

There was a general movement throughout Bavaria against which the triumphant, brutally stupid Prussian could not prevail. The ordinary Bavarian found, by actual experience, that a reactionary Prussian was worse than the most violent of Jewish Spartacists. Levien, the Jewish Communist leader, found shelter, as did also the anarchist Swabian poet Toller. Under the disillusioned Imperial Socialist, Hoffmann, members of his own party, with Independent Socialists, Catholic politicians, and members of the Peasant Party, managed to form a new Coalition Government that resisted all the pressure of the Prussian commanders.

It was not until the end of May that the new Bavarian Government was able to recover power. In the meantime the angry people of Bavaria made their influence felt against all the Northern Germans with overwhelming, decisive effect. Movements for separating from Prussia gathered in force and intensity in all the Catholic States of the old Empire. Likewise in Northern Germany, Hanover once more renewed the struggle for freedom against the Prussians, and what seems strangest of all, Old Prussia, represented by the nobility of East and West Prussia, began to move for an independent existence, distinct from Brandenburg and Berlin.

On May 26th, 1919, German General Headquarters, at the seaport of Kolberg, made a searching inquiry through all military centres in the country as to the possibility of inducing the German peoples to agree to a resumption of war. Only in the German part of Silesia and among troops near the Polish border, under the command of General Hoffmann, was there found anything like popular support for a new war. In Wiesbaden a man with little influence Dr. Dorten, tried to establish the Republic of the Rhine, which many men of more weight and authority were considering but delaying to organise. Dorten's attempt was rather a ridiculous affair, and may indeed have been designed, like the carnival revolution in Munich, to anticipate and discredit a large and serious scheme.

German cross-currents

Southern and Western Germans of the Clerical school joined with many responsible leaders of the Independent Socialists in fighting against the mad plan for continuing the war. While these separatist movements were gaining ground, all the German working classes grew violently hostile to the Weimar gang of intriguers and war-makers, who by then had received the Treaty of Peace and were seeking some popular ground for rejecting it. Toller, the poet dictator of Munich, and Levien, the Russian Jewish Communist, who organised and led the Bavarian Soviet, were arrested, tried, condemned to death, and executed at the beginning of June, 1919.

Protest strikes at once occurred in Berlin and Westphalia, and spread through the country. At the same time the scandalous trial opened of the officers and privates of the Guard Defence Division, who had murdered Liebknecht and Rosa Luxemburg. After extraordinary and complete revelations of the details of the assassination, the officer who had killed Liebknecht was acquitted, and the officer who shot Rosa Luxemburg through the head was given a light sentence, from which he escaped. By the middle of June, 1919, Germany was dividing into Protestant and Catholic fragments, and was beginning to incline to a Government of the Soviet kind. Scheidemann, Brockdorff-Rantzau, and other intriguers, being too deeply implicated in their bankrupt scheme to draw from it, resigned. Under the nominal leadership of a man named Bauer, Erzberger became the ruler of Germany as representative of the Catholic States, and the way was cleared for the signing of the Treaty of Peace.

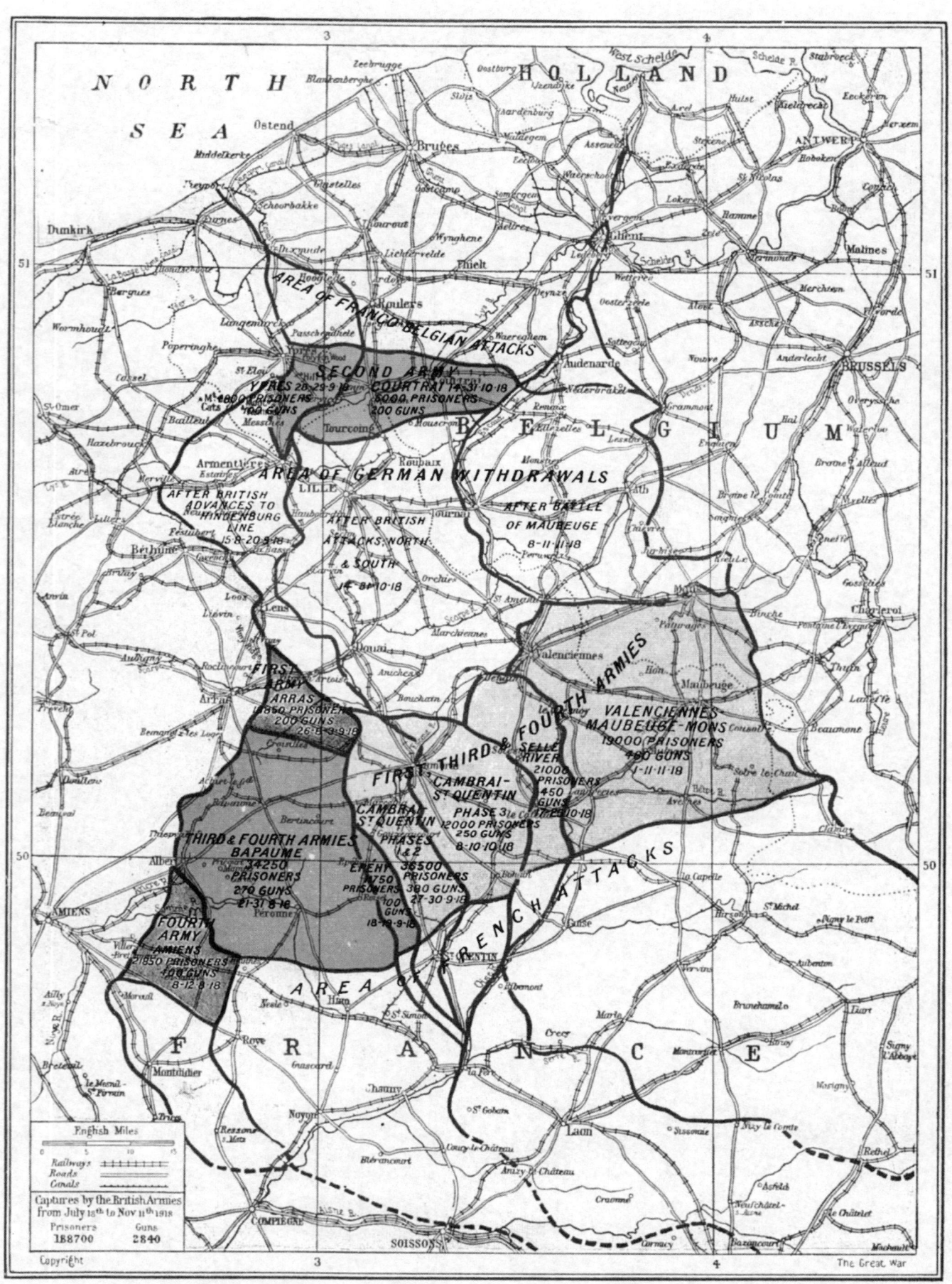

THE CROWNING ACHIEVEMENTS OF THE BRITISH ARMIES.

Map showing the ground won in the British battles, and yielded in German withdrawals, from August 8th to November 11th, 1918.

ARRIVAL OF ADMIRAL MEURER

CHAPTER CCCXIX.

ON ADMIRAL BEATTY'S FLAGSHIP.

FROM THE ARMISTICE TO THE PEACE: A GENERAL SURVEY.

By Robert Machray.

Germany Signs the Armistice—Thanksgiving and Rejoicing of the Allies—How the News was Received in London—Demonstrations at Buckingham Palace and in Downing Street—Speech by King George—His Happy Messages of Congratulation to the Navy, Army, and Air Force—Impressive Scene in the Palace of Westminster—Questions of Demobilisation and Reconstruction—General Election —Triumph of the Coalition—Close of the Fighting in German East Africa—British Fleet at Constantinople—Involved Situation in Asia Minor and Caucasia—March of Events in the Balkans and South-Eastern Europe—Chaos in Russia—The British Expeditions in Murmansk-Archangel—The Position in Siberia—Koltchak's Advance—German National Assembly at Weimar—The Peace Conference and the Covenant of the League of Nations—Troubles in Afghanistan and Egypt—Changes in Russia—British Safe in the North—Koltchak and Denikin's Campaigns—Peace Treaty Presented to Germany Slightly Revised and Signed by the Arch-Enemy—Sinking of the German Fleet at Scapa Flow—The Peace Celebrations in Paris and London.

I N all history there is no more significant date than that of the armistice of November 11th, 1918, which brought the bitter and bloody years of hostilities to a halt that, some months later, proved to be final. Fighting did not cease everywhere; in many areas both in Europe and in Asia little wars, and one that was not little, in what not long before had been the vast Russian Empire, were still waged, but the Great War itself came to an end. In every way its cost had been tremendous—far beyond that which even the most pessimistic had dreaded. Millions of lives, most of them young and hopeful lives, had been lost; millions of men had been incapacitated or seriously injured; millions more had to carry to their graves marks of the struggle, in disfigurements and disabilities British casualties alone were upwards of three millions. Unimaginable millions of treasure—about forty thousand millions sterling in money —had been spent, most of it clean gone, like the rivers of the East that bury themselves in the sands of the desert. Wide tracts of country had been devastated and left desolate. Famine and pestilence stalked through many lands.

But the essential fact remained that the war was over, and in the one and only way in which it should be over. Those who, without pity for others or misgivings for themselves, had loosed the thunderbolts in July-August, 1914, had

BRITISH NAVY LEADERS IN PARIS.
Admiral G. P. W. Hope (left) and Admiral Sir Rosslyn Wemyss, First Sea Lord, at the Hôtel Majestic during the Peace Conference.

been defeated and brought to the ground. The German dream of world domination, of "Deutschland über Alles," with all that it implied, was shattered. Liberty was re-established on a sure foundation, and justice upheld and magnified. Right had triumphed. Victory, snatched from the very mouth of the pit, had crowned the common cause. It had been bought at a heavy price, with enormous sacrifices, but was worth it and more.

To many the armistice appeared to come with such suddenness that they regarded it with suspicion. There were obstinate questionings as to the completeness of the downfall of the enemy, and especially as to the good faith of Germany in fulfilling any agreement to which she set her hand. The amazing arrogance and the truculent spirit of many Germans, even in defeat, gave point, it must be said, to these doubts. It soon became clear, however, that Germany was hopelessly beaten. Some weeks before the armistice her leaders realised that this was the case, and were casting about for some way of saving her face, chiefly by appeals to America that were a strange mixture of threats, cajolements, and whines, but which met with scant success.

Signed the armistice had to be, and signed it was. Its terms were drastic, but not too much so; some among the Allies thought that they were not drastic enough; in any case they were sufficient, and in all quarters of the globe not penetrated by German sentiment the hearts of the people overflowed with joy

THANKSGIVING FOR PEACE AT ST. PAUL'S CATHEDRAL.
Scene outside St. Paul's Cathedral on July 6th, 1919, on the occasion of the
Thanksgiving for Peace—the consummating Memorial Service for those who
had fallen—when King George and Queen Mary were leaving, and the great
crowds outside joined in the National Anthem. In circle: The Royal party
on the steps of the Cathedral.

the insistent cry arose, "We want King George!" About one o'clock their Majesties again appeared on the balcony, amid a roar of cheering such as London had not heard during the period of war. The band played and the vast throng sang the National Anthem, "Rule, Britannia," and other songs. Gripped by emotion, everyone recalled the early days of the war. Suddenly there was heard the call of "Speech, speech!" The band played and the people sang "The Old Hundredth," and next came various national airs, every voice taking part in singing the "Marseillaise." These finished, the King spoke.

"With you," he said, "I rejoice and thank God for the victories which the allied armies have won, bringing hostilities to an end and peace within sight."

and thanksgiving. "Joy," exclaimed Marshal Joffre, "not to be expressed in words." In a crowded House of Commons Mr. Lloyd George, in the afternoon of November 11th, read aloud the terms of the armistice, with the latest corrections, which he had received by telephone a few minutes before. After observing that an end had been put to the "most cruel and most terrible war that ever scourged mankind," and that this was "no time for words," he moved the adjournment in order that the Members of Parliament should proceed immediately to St. Margaret's, the parish church of Westminster, "to give humble and reverent thanks for the great deliverance of the world from its great peril." Headed by the Speaker, with Mr. Lloyd George, Mr. Asquith, and Mr. Whitley in the first line, Mr. Bonar Law, Mr. Balfour, and Mr. McKenna in the second, the Commons marched in impressive silence from the Chamber to give thanks in His house to the Lord God of Hosts.

Earlier in the day the good news had spread that the armistice was signed. In London and throughout the country it was received with fervent gratitude. Thanksgiving Services were hurriedly arranged in many churches, and were attended by deeply-moved crowds. Having expressed a wish to be present at a Thanksgiving Service at St. Paul's, the King attended one on the following day with the Queen and other members of the Royal Family, and the people, knowing what was toward, packed the huge cathedral to the doors long before his arrival, while above them surged the joyous clangour of its bells. On November 21st the King attended a Thanksgiving Service in St. Giles' Cathedral, Edinburgh. But on the ever-memorable November 11th thanksgiving was speedily almost swallowed up in manifestations of sheer jubilation. In London there were extraordinary scenes of joy and enthusiasm early at Buckingham Palace and in Downing Street. At eleven o'clock precisely a typewritten copy of the announcement of the signing of the armistice was hung on the Palace railings, and maroons were exploded as a general intimation. As if by magic a gigantic concourse gathered and swelled around the Queen Victoria Memorial, and presently the King, in admiral's uniform, accompanied by the Queen, stepped out on the balcony of the Palace, while the guard presented arms, the band crashed out the National Anthem, and the people cheered with might and main, half an hour elapsing before the demonstration concluded. A few minutes later a fresh crowd gathered in the same place, and

Thanksgivings and jubilation

One of the shortest speeches on record, it yet was one of the best, for everything was summed up in its well-chosen words. Perhaps they were not heard by many, as the crowd was so enormous, but all could see that the lips of the King were moving, and they knew that he was saying something to them. After he had spoken, the band played "Now thank we all our God," and on the conclusion of the hymn this wonderful, and indeed, historic scene closed in a last tumultuous burst of cheering, in which the King himself joined. Later in the afternoon the crowd outside the Palace was equally great, and there were occasional shouts for the King, with much singing of patriotic songs.

At half-past three the King and Queen, with Princess Mary, drove out in an open carriage, though by that time rain was falling. Slowly they went along the Mall, through the Strand, Fleet Street, Ludgate Hill, and Queen Victoria Street to the Mansion House, and thence back to the Palace by Holborn, Oxford Street, Shaftesbury Avenue, Trafalgar Square, and the Mall. Everywhere they were acclaimed with the utmost heartiness. A feature of the occasion was that in this drive the King drove through the old tradition that bade the Sovereign halt at Temple Bar. When their Majesties returned, another great crowd stood in front of the Palace in spite of the rain which continued to fall; the crowd was still there when the darkness of evening came, and once more the King and Queen, now with electric lights playing on them, stepped out on the balcony, again receiving a tremendous ovation. The "Court Circular" that night announced: "The King received with the utmost gratification the loyal greetings of the vast concourse of people assembled in the Mall to-day to celebrate the signing of the armistice."

Hardly less remarkable was the demonstration which took place on the morning of that great day in Downing Street. An effort was made to keep the street clear, but the pressure of the crowd was such that the effort was abandoned. A few minutes before eleven o'clock Mr. Lloyd George appeared at the door of No. 10, and instantly, as at a signal, a storm of cheering both deep and loud burst forth. He made a little speech which, however, was full of meaning. "At eleven o'clock this morning," said he, "the war will be over. We have won a great victory, and we are entitled to a bit of shouting."

Then, as one writer put it, the flood-gates were opened. The cheering might have been **Scene in Downing Street** heard over the greater part of the City of Westminster. The Prime Minister withdrew into the house, but as the people outside kept on demanding a speech he came to a window, opened it, and said: "You are entitled to rejoice. The people of this country and the peoples of the Dominions and of our Allies have won such a victory for freedom as the world has never seen. You have all had a share of it. Sons and daughters of the people have done it, and this is the hour for their rejoicing." After renewed cheering the Premier again withdrew, and the crowd dispersed.

Not only were there extraordinary scenes at Buckingham Palace and in Downing Street. All the central avenues of the capital swarmed with gay, happy, and enthusiastic people, not a few of them almost delirious with excitement. Within half an hour after the exploding maroons announced the armistice thousands of men, women, and children, wearing the emblems or carrying the flags of one or another of the Allies, were standing in masses on the pavements and across the breadth of the main streets cheering and shouting themselves hoarse. Omnibuses and **How London** taxi-cabs, with roaring loads, passed slowly **went wild** along. Army and Navy lorries, bearing on them as many soldiers, sailors, and girls as they could hold, moved more slowly still, to the accompaniment of volleys of cheering. Motor-cars, chartered by Dominion and American soldiers showing their respective flags and exhibiting enormous lung-power, pressed a way forward, while vehicles of other sorts struggled on. The cheering, if it stopped for a moment, was almost at once renewed; in effect it was continuous. Nightfall brought no cessation of the public jubilation. The drizzling rain had no effect on it. Inside the hotels and the restaurants the merry-making reached a height that somewhat lacked restraint, but was not surprising in the circumstances. If London went wild, the rest of the country was in much the same mood. Armistice Day was a Monday, and the celebrations were kept up in one way or other all the week.

In France there were great rejoicings. The Government ordered the bells to be pealed and all public buildings to be

REJOICING CROWD OUTSIDE BUCKINGHAM PALACE ON ARMISTICE DAY.

When it became known on the morning of November 11th, 1918, that the armistice had been signed there were extraordinary scenes of joy and enthusiasm at Buckingham Palace, and a gigantic concourse gathered about the Queen Victoria Memorial and cheered again and again when King George and Queen Mary appeared on the balcony of the Palace. All through that great day successive rejoicing crowds assembled outside the Royal residence.

beflagged and illuminated on the evening of the eleventh. The municipality of Paris issued a proclamation in which it said : " Let Paris depart from her proud reserve which has won for her the admiration of the world. Let us give free course to our joy and enthusiasm, and let us swallow our

EX-PRISONERS OF WAR AS GUARD OF HONOUR.
Arrival of Lieut.-General Sir Henry F. M. Wilson at Constantinople in November, 1918. General Wilson, who commanded the allied garrisons in the Bosphorus and Dardanelles, was received by a Guard of Honour consisting of several hundred British and Indian prisoners of war.

tears." In the Chamber of Deputies M. Clemenceau had a magnificent ovation after reading out, in a voice trembling with emotion, the terms of the armistice, and adding a few words in praise of the dead and the living who had fought for France and for humanity. He was hailed as the liberator of his country, and in the Senate a resolution was carried that a bust of him should be placed with the busts of the other great Frenchmen who had shed lustre on that historic Chamber. A proposal was also made to offer a sword of honour to Marshal Foch as a sign of the gratitude of the nation. In Italy and in all the allied lands there were great manifestations of joy. The United States took the occasion more quietly, but throughout America the thanksgiving was earnest and deep.

On the morning of November 12th the **King George and the** Press published messages, dated the previous **fighting services** day, which the King had addressed respectively to Sir Eric Geddes, First Lord of the Admiralty, Lord Milner, the Secretary of State for War, and Lord Weir, the President of the Air Council, expressing his praise and thankfulness to the officers, men, and women of the three great fighting Services. To the Royal Navy and Marines, with their comrades of the Fleet auxiliaries and the Mercantile Marine, the King said :

Ever since that fateful August 4th, 1914, I have remained steadfast in my confidence that, whether fortune frowned or smiled, the Royal Navy would once more prove the sure shield of the British Empire in the hour of trial. Never in its history has the Royal Navy, with God's help, done greater things for us, nor better sustained its old glories and the chivalry of the seas With full and grateful hearts

the peoples of the British Empire salute the White, the Red, and the Blue Ensigns, and those who have given their lives for the flag. I am proud to have served in the Navy. I am prouder still to be its head on this memorable day.

After expressing his heartfelt pride and gratitude to all ranks, he said to the Army :

Germany, our most formidable enemy, who planned the war to gain the supremacy of the world, full of pride in her armed strength and of contempt for the small British Army of that date, has now been forced to acknowledge defeat. I rejoice that in this achievement the British forces, now grown from small beginnings to the finest Army in our history, have borne so gallant and distinguished a part. Soldiers of the British Empire ! In France and Belgium the prowess of your arms, as great in retreat as in victory, has won the admiration alike of friend and foe, and has now by a happy historic fate enabled you to conclude the campaign by capturing Mons, where your predecessors of 1914 shed the first British blood. Between that date and this you have traversed a long and weary road ; defeat has more than once stared you in the face ; your ranks have been thinned again and again by wounds, sickness, and death ; but your faith has never faltered, your courage has never. failed, your hearts have never known defeat. With your allied comrades you have won the day. Others of you have fought in more distant fields—in the mountains and plains of Italy, in the rugged Balkan ranges, under the burning sun of Palestine, Mesopotamia, and Africa ; amid the snows of Russia and Siberia, and by the shores of the Dardanelles. Men of the British race who have shared these successes felt in their veins the call of the blood and joined eagerly with the Mother Country in the fight against tyranny and wrong. Equally those of the ancient, historic peoples of India and Africa, who have learned to trust the flag of Britain, hastened to discharge their debt of loyalty to the Crown. I desire to thank every officer, soldier, and woman of our Army for services nobly rendered, for sacrifices cheerfully given, and I pray that God, Who has been pleased to grant a victorious end to this great crusade for justice and right, will prosper and bless our efforts in the immediate future to secure for generations to come the hard-won blessings of freedom and peace.

To all ranks of the Royal Air Force the King said :

In this supreme hour of victory I send greetings and congratulations. Our aircraft have ever been in the forefront of the battle ; pilots and observers have consistently maintained the offensive throughout the ever-changing fortunes of the day, and in the war zones our gallant dead have lain always beyond the enemies' lines or far out at sea. Our far-flung squadrons have flown over home waters and foreign seas, the western and Italian battle-lines, Rhineland, the mountains of Macedonia, Gallipoli, Palestine, the plains of Mesopotamia, the forests and swamps of East Africa, the North-West Frontier of India, and the deserts of Arabia, Sinai, and Darfur. The birth of the Royal Air Force, with its wonderful expansion and development, will ever remain one of the most remarkable achievements of the Great War. Everywhere, by God's help, officers, men, and women of the Royal Air Force have splendidly maintained our just cause, and the value of their assistance to the Navy, the Army, and to home defence has been incalculable.

The King at Westminster

These eloquent and impressive messages to the fighting Services were reinforced and amplified in a reply made by the King to an address from each of the Houses of Parliament, unanimously voted on November 19th, congratulating him on the conclusion of the armistice and on the prospect of a victorious peace. In the afternoon of the next day the King, accompanied by the Queen, Queen Alexandra, the Prince of Wales, Princess Mary, the Duke of Connaught, and Princess Victoria, read his reply in the Royal Gallery of the Palace of Westminster to the Lords and Commons there assembled, distinguished representatives of the Dominions and India also being present. After thanking the Houses for their loyal addresses, the King continued, in a voice that was distinctly audible in every part of the huge gallery, by stating his desire to express to the Members of Parliament and the representatives of the Dominions and of India, and to the peoples represented by them, the thoughts that arose in his mind at a time so solemn and momentous. He gratefully recognised the spontaneous and enthusiastic expressions of loyalty and affection he had received, both personally in the metropolis and by messages from every quarter of the Empire. During the four years of national stress and anxiety his comfort had been faith in God and confidence in his people. Strengthened by the same help, he would strive to the utmost to perform his part in the days to come.

Remarking that the soil of Britain remained inviolate, the King spoke of the work of the Navy in holding the seas, overcoming the hidden menace of the submarines, and guarding food and munition ships. "Without that work," he said, "Britain might have been starved." And he declared : "The Fleet has enabled us to win the war." He spoke of the Army as it was in 1914, and of how, within a year, the organising genius and personal influence of Lord Kitchener had increased it tenfold. The "new soldiers," he said, "drawn from the civil population, displayed a valour equal to that of their ancestors who carried the flag of Britain to victory in so many lands in bygone times." He referred to the splendid response from the Dominions and India. To the Army and its commanders gratitude was due ; he made particular mention of Field-Marshal Sir Douglas Haig, General Sir Edmund Allenby, and General Sir Stanley Maude, as well as Field-Marshal Lord French ; he also named Admirals Lord Jellicoe and Sir David Beatty. Next he spoke of the services of the "keen-eyed and swift-winged knights of the air, a new type of daring and resourceful heroism." Nor did he forget the Mercantile Marine and the fishermen who patrolled the coasts, braving mine and torpedo. And then he spoke of the munition workers, and of non-combatants, such as surgeons, physicians, chaplains, and nurses, all of whom had borne their share in the struggle. This part of his reply closed with a touching allusion to the parents, wives, and children who had lost those who were the light and stay of their lives.

SURRENDER OF TURKEY.
Lieut.-Commander Tewfik Pasha (right), who, on behalf of Turkey, signed the armistice agreement with the Allies, with Commander Cottrell (seated) and Lieutenant H. P. Keeley, R.N.

Thereafter the King went on to observe that we had been associated with Allies whose spirit had been identical with our own, and who, amid sufferings in many cases exceeding our own, had devoted their united strength to the vindication of righteousness and freedom—France, whose final deliverance had been achieved by one of the greatest commanders, Marshal Foch ; Belgium, held in bondage for nearly five years, but now restored to liberty ; Italy, who had found her national unity ; and the remaining Allies, upon whose horizons, lately so dark, the light of emancipation was dawning. Next he spoke of direct association with the United States, "the great sister Commonwealth across the ocean," whose resources and valour had exercised so powerful an influence in the attainment of the high ideals that were her single aim.

What he next went on to say struck a new note :

Now that the clouds of war are being swept from the sky new tasks arise before us. We see more clearly some duties that have been neglected, some weaknesses that may retard our onward march. Liberal provision must be made for those whose exertions by land and sea have saved us. We have to create a better Britain, to bestow more care on the health and welfare of the people, and to ameliorate further the conditions of labour. May not the losses of war be repaired by a better organisation of industry, and by avoiding the waste which industrial disputes involve ? Cannot a spirit of reciprocal trust and co-ordination of effort be diffused among all classes ? May we not, by raising the standard of education, turn to fuller account the natural aptitudes of our people and open wider the sources of intellectual enjoyment ? How shall we achieve the victories of peace ? Can we

ARRIVAL OF VESSELS OF THE ALLIED FLEETS OFF CONSTANTINOPLE.
The first of the destroyers to pass through the Strait of the Dardanelles and arrive off Constantinople in November, 1918. It was on the last day of October that Turkey "went out of the war" on signing the armistice. On November 13th the allied fleets, having passed up the Strait of the Dardanelles, arrived off Constantinople, and on November 21st the first of the allied troops were landed at the Turkish capital.

FOOD FOR GERMANY AFTER THE ARMISTICE.
Loading up supplies of food from a British ship at Rotterdam for distribution among the civil population of the undisturbed parts of Germany during the spring of 1919, and (above) unloading flour for Germany from an American vessel.

do better than remember the lessons which the years of war have taught, and retain the spirit which they instilled? In these years Britain and her traditions came to mean more to us than they had ever meant before. It became a privilege to serve her in whatever way we could, and we were all drawn by the sacredness of the cause into a comradeship which fired our zeal and nerved our efforts. This is the spirit we must try to preserve. It is on a sense of brotherhood and mutual goodwill, on a common devotion to the common interests of the nation as a whole, that its future prosperity and strength must be built up. The sacrifices made, the sufferings endured, the memory of the heroes who have died that Britain may live, ought surely to ennoble our thoughts and attune our hearts to a higher sense of individual and national duty, and to a fuller realisation of what the English-speaking race, dwelling on the shores of all the oceans, may yet accomplish for mankind.

In addition to sending messages, making speeches, and showing himself frequently to his people in London during those wonderful days that followed the signing of the armistice, the King despatched telegrams of greeting and congratulation to Canada, Australia, New Zealand, South Africa, and Newfoundland, as well as India. He also sent telegrams to the King of the Belgians, President Poincaré, the Emperor of Japan, the King of Italy, the King of Serbia, President Wilson, the King of Rumania, the President of Portugal, the King of Montenegro, the Sultan of Egypt, the King of Greece, the President of China, the President of Brazil, the King of Siam, and the President of Cuba, offering his congratulations

Messages to all the Allies on the "glorious outcome" of the united efforts of the Powers who had been at war with the enemy. Frequent references in Parliament and in the Press to the work of the King at this time, and throughout the long period of strain that had preceded it, demonstrated how deeply that work was appreciated by the country. The Throne stood higher than ever—and that, too, when on the Continent monarchies and sovereignties, some of them old and apparently firmly established, had been swept away.

Though there were many who feared that the war was not really over, and that Germany was in no way to be trusted

to keep faith, the great majority of the British people believed that the conflict was ended. This was the view of the Government, and it was plainly the business of the Government, in that case, to take such measures as would most expeditiously and profitably place the nation on a peace footing, but with due regard to the fact that the Peace Treaty had still to be signed, and that this might cause delay. The day after the armistice was signed, Dr. Addison, the Minister of Reconstruction, made in Parliament a comprehensive statement on the plans of the Government for the demobilisation of the Army, the resettlement of officers and men in civil life, and the re-establishment of industry on a peace basis. Detailed accounts of the various steps that were taken, and of their working out, were given in Chapters CCCVII. and CCCVIII. (pages 313 and 325 of this volume).

The transference of the whole United Kingdom from war to peace—for it was nothing less than that—was a stupendous undertaking, and it was inevitable that in the process defects, shortcomings, and even injustices, would be manifested which would lead to protests and complaints. Besides, there was the unquiet state of Labour, industrially and politically, not only in Great Britain but in many other lands, to complicate the situation. Still, on the broad average, the prodigious business after some adjustments did proceed with tolerable smoothness and, weighing all the circumstances impartially, with considerable success. It was only natural that after the long war, with victory as the result, there should be a marked reaction—a keen desire for rest and refreshment—and as it was not realised as soon as it should have been that the words "from war to peace" were more adequately rendered "from war to work." This and problems connected with food, shipping, and trade generally the world over, all militated against the rapid fulfilment of the Government's schemes of resettlement and reconstruction. One piece of reconstruction the Government carried out quickly. Hardly was the armistice signed before preparations were set on foot for a General Election.

End of the "Long Parliament"

In the preceding July the War Parliament had passed an Act for prolonging its existence for six months. It had passed several Acts of a similar kind before, and had been sitting close on eight years. One of the reasons for the repeated extensions of its term had been the absence of a proper voters' roll, but the Representation of the People Act, 1918, yielded a register of the new electorate which was ready by October 1st. Some time before that there had been reports that Parliament was to be dissolved in November, and the signing of the armistice precipitated matters. On November 12th Mr. Lloyd George and Mr. Bonar Law summoned and attended meetings of their respective supporters, and put before them a common policy, which was the continuance of the Coalition Government during the peace negotiations and the period of reconstruction.

At his meeting Mr. Lloyd George outlined a great housing programme, and declared there must be an improvement of the conditions of labour and of wages and a reduction of hours. At the Unionist meeting Mr. Bonar Law read a letter he had received from the Prime Minister, who said in it that in his view the election should be a Coalition election, the country being definitely invited to return candidates who undertook to support the existing Government not only to prosecute the war to its final end and negotiate the peace, but to deal with the problems of reconstruction.

Mr. Bonar Law announced on November 14th that Parliament would be dissolved on the 25th of that month, the nominations and polls being held on December 4th and 14th respectively. The business of the session was speedily wound up, and the War Parliament, elected as a Peace Parliament in December, 1910, came to an end. The Government of Mr. Lloyd George had contained a strong Labour element, but during the summer the Labour Party had terminated the party truce with regard to by-elections, and it now decided to resume its independence and withdraw the Labour Ministers. Mr. Clynes, the Food Controller in succession to Lord Rhondda, at once resigned, and soon afterwards Messrs. Hodge, Brace, and Walsh followed his example, but Messrs. Barnes, Roberts, Wardle, and Parker stuck to their posts. Lord Robert Cecil resigned from the Ministry owing to the Government policy with regard to the Welsh Church. When, on November 22nd, the Government issued a manifesto to the electors, it was signed by Mr. Lloyd George and Mr. Bonar Law, the one representing a portion of the Liberal Party and the other the Unionists. Individual Labour leaders, however, appealed in the constituencies as supporters of the Coalition.

As the election campaign proceeded it became manifest

GERMAN GOLD FOR ALLIES' FOOD.
British soldiers removing bullion from the Rotterdam bank, where it had been deposited by the Germans in payment for foodstuffs supplied by the Allies during the armistice term.

that the voters held strong opinions about some matters that were not covered by the manifesto which had been issued by the Coalition leaders. For one thing they demanded that Germany should pay the cost of the war, and for another that the ex-Kaiser, who was a fugitive in Holland, should be brought to trial. They were determined that enemy agents should be given no opportunity of peacefully penetrating the country. But the result of the elections was never in doubt. On December 4th 107 members were returned unopposed—69 Coalition, and 38 (of whom 25 were Sinn Feiners) against. In the polls, held on December 14th, nearly eleven million men and women voted, or about 60 per cent. of the electorate. The new women voters, of whom there were about seven million, came forward in great strength. Seventeen women candidates appeared in the field at the polls. To give time for the collection of ballot papers from soldiers on the western front the votes were not counted till December 28th. Of these ballot papers 2,400,000 were issued, but only 830 000 were included in the count. The result of the poll, all told, was a sweeping, even sensational, triumph for the Coalition, which had a majority of 249 over all the non-Coalition members, the majority consisting of 334 Unionists, 134 Liberals, and 10 Labour men. Every Minister who had to stand a contest was returned, generally by a big majority. Next to the Coalition, Labour became the strongest British political combination in the House of Commons. Labour polled altogether about two and a half million votes, and though proportionately it should have done better, it succeeded in returning 63 members. Ireland, in which for the most part voting was on lines quite different from those in Great Britain, returned 73 Sinn Feiners, 6 Nationalists, and 25 Unionists,

SUPPLIES OF FOOD FOR GERMANY'S STARVING CIVILIANS.
Loading up sacks of potatoes on a German lighter at Rotterdam in accordance with the Allies' agreement to supply foodstuffs to the population of the undisturbed parts of Germany. It was announced that from centres where strikes were prevalent such supplies were withheld. Right : Scene at the quayside at Rotterdam, where cases of Army rations were being loaded up for distribution among German civilians.

Having carried the country, Mr. Lloyd George forthwith set about the reconstruction of the Ministry, and in January, 1919, the list of appointments was published. Having rearranged rather than reconstituted the Ministry, and leaving behind him Mr. Bonar Law as Leader of the House of Commons, the Prime Minister betook himself to Paris,

RETURN OF BRITAIN'S VICTORIOUS COMMANDER-IN-CHIEF.
Arrival of Sir Douglas Haig at Dover in December, 1918, after the conclusion of the great struggle in which he had borne the brunt of leadership for three years. For his great part in the great achievement he was a few months later raised to the peerage as Earl Haig of Bemersyde.

where the Peace Conference was officially inaugurated on January 18th, 1919.

While all these political developments had been occurring in the United Kingdom, the course of events in Central Europe continued to be of extraordinary interest, and much that was highly important was taking place in the war areas elsewhere.

At the first meeting of the Council which governed Germany after the abdication—the formal renunciation of the Crown of Prussia and of the German Empire was signed on December 1st—and flight of William II., and the resignation of the Chancellorship by Prince Max of Baden, Herr Ebert, the new Socialist Chancellor, stated that the first act of the Provisional Government had been to accept the conditions of the armistice, and that its next act would be to negotiate peace, and undertake the country's political and economic reorganisation. At the same time Dr. Solf, his Foreign Minister, appealed to President Wilson for a preliminary peace as early as possible, on the ground that there was pressing danger of famine in Germany. M. Clemenceau, answering indirectly, said that while the victors would do what they conveniently could to revictual Germany, the blockade must be maintained during the entire period of the armistice. Solf next sent out to the chief Allied Governments an appeal in which he whined about the menace of the terms of the armistice to economic conditions; but, as was pointed out at the time, it came with singularly ill-grace from the people who had ravished Belgium, Northern France, Poland, and Rumania, and boasted that they would starve Great Britain into submission. Naturally the Allies were not to be moved from conditions of armistice which guaranteed their own security against a repetition of these crimes. Germany learned but slowly to accommodate herself to her defeat, as also was shown by her ill-treatment of the British

Condition of Germany

prisoners returning, under the armistice, from her vile prison camps.

Hindenburg issued a statement that he remained at the head of the German Army, to lead the troops home in order and discipline, but even before the armistice large numbers of German soldiers were pressing back in disorder into Germany, and after the armistice some of them were guilty of barbarous acts of pillage and murder on the way. By November 17th the allied armies in the west had begun their forward movement along the whole front. By December 8th that portion of the armistice conditions which dealt with the occupation of German territory was fulfilled, and the beaten German Army was well on the far side of the Rhine. But before the German Army had thus been disposed of, the naval power of Germany had undergone total eclipse, for on November 21st the German Fleet had surrendered to the British—a full account of which appeared in Chapter CCLXXXVII. (Vol. 13, page 561). By land and sea Germany was humbled; she had, in fact, ceased to be a Great Power. Outside Europe the only distinctively German force that was still fighting at the time of the armistice was that under General Lettow-Vorbeck in East Africa. Chapter CCXXIV. (Vol. 10, page 577) brought up the story of the campaign in German East Africa to the close of November, 1917, when the whole colony was in the hands of the British, then commanded by General van Deventer, and Lettow-Vorbeck, with a remnant of his troops, was a fugitive in Mozambique. In compliance with the terms of the armistice, Lettow-Vorbeck surrendered on the morning of November 14th, on the Chambezi River, south of Kasama, in Northern Rhodesia. After his escape into Portuguese territory, he was hunted incessantly by various British forces, but his own skill and tenacity, the devotion of his native soldiers, and the difficulty of the country, kept him out of their hands, though he was driven south nearly to the Zambesi. Turning suddenly in his tracks and making rapidly northwards, he contrived to elude his pursuers, and he reappeared in September, 1918, in the neighbourhood of Songea, in what had been German East Africa. Attempts were made to round him up, but he managed to get away to Rhodesia, where the end came. Eventually he was taken to England, and permitted to return to Germany. In the summer of 1919 he was in command of German troops in the Hamburg area.

The end in "German East"

What may be called Armistice Week was full of great events, but in a way one of the most notable was the passage through the Dardanelles of the allied fleets on November 12th, and their arrival off Constantinople next day. In a sense this was the consummation of the war against Turkey, and marked, as perhaps nothing else could have done, the fall of her Empire. The forts on the Dardanelles had already been occupied by British and Indian troops, and the soldiers paraded as the great ships passed up the strait. First came the flagship Superb, and next was the Temeraire, with General Sir Henry F. M. Wilson on board; he was to command the garrisons of the allied forces in the forts of the Dardanelles and the Bosphorus. After the Temeraire steamed the Lord Nelson and the Agamemnon, followed by an imposing procession of cruisers, destroyers, and other craft. Half an hour behind them came first a French squadron, second an Italian, and third a Greek. The Superb and the Temeraire, with two French battleships, anchored near the European shore, with the Sultan's palace and the Chamber of Deputies within close view. On November 13th General Wilson landed, and

Opening meeting of the Peace Conference in Paris, January 18th, 1919 : The official interpreter reading in English M. Poincaré's address.

1. M. Dutasta (General Secretary).	18. Sir Robert Borden (Canada).
2. M. Ph. Berthelot (France).	19. Prince Charoon (Siam).
3. M. Pichon (France).	20. Sir J. Ward (New Zealand).
4. Col. E. M. House (United States).	21. M. Phya Bibadh Kosha (Siam).
5. Lieut.-Col. Hankey (Great Britain).	22. Mr. W. M. Hughes (Australia).
6. President Wilson (United States).	23. M. L. L. Klotz (France).
7. Mr. Lloyd George (Great Britain).	24. M. Benes (Czecho-Slovak Republic).
8. M. Clemenceau, President (France).	25. M. Bratiano (Rumania).
9. Mr. A. J. Balfour (Great Britain).	26. General Botha (South Africa).
10. Mr. H. White (United States).	27. M. Cambon (France).
11. General Bliss (United States).	28. M. Bourgeois (France).
12. Mr. R. Lansing (United States).	29. M. Vesnitch (Serbia).
13. Lord Milner (Great Britain).	30. M. Dmowski (Poland).
14. Mr. A. Bonar Law (Great Britain).	31. M. Paderewski (Poland).
15. Mr. G. N. Barnes (Great Britain).	32. Lieut.-Gen. Smuts (South Africa).
16. Lord Robert Cecil (Great Britain).	33. Mr. W. F. Massey (New Zealand).
17. M. A. Tardieu (France).	34. M. Burgos (Panama).

Plenary sitting of the Peace Con

the Ministry of Foreign Affairs in Paris, 1919.

mont.)

35. The Maharajah of Bikanir (India).	53. M. Guilbaud (Haiti).
36. Lord Sinha (India).	54. M. Barzilai (Italy).
37. The Emir Feisul (Hedjaz).	55. Marshal Foch (France).
38. M. Trumbitch (Serbia).	56. M. Politis (Greece).
39. M. Pàshitch (Serbia).	57. M. Blanco (Uruguay).
40. M. Haklar (Hedjaz).	58. M. Venizelos (Greece).
41. Signor Orlando (Italy).	59. M. Lou Tseng Tsiang (China).
42. Dr. Monitz (Portugal).	60. M. Sao Ke Alfred Sze (China).
43. Dr. Villela (Portugal).	61. M. de Bustamante (Cuba).
44. M. Matsui (Japan).	62. M. Montes (Bolivia).
45. Baron Makino (Japan).	63. M. Mendes (Guatemala).
46. Baron Sonnino (Italy).	64. M. O. de Magalhaes (Brazil).
47. Marquis Saionji (Japan).	65. M. Vandervelde (Belgium).
48. M. Dorn y de Alsua (Ecuador).	66. General Weygand (France).
49. Mr. C. D. B. King (Liberia).	67. M. Hymans (Belgium).
50. M. Calderon (Peru).	68. President E. Pessoa (Brazil).
51. M. Mantoux (Interpreter).	69. M. Van den Henvel (Belgium).
52. Marquis Salvago Raggi (Italy).	

Introduction of the German envoys, with Count Brockdorff-Rantzau at their head, into the salon of the Trianon Palace at Versailles, on May 7th, 1919.
They were introduced by M. William Martin (with outstretched hand), the Chef du Protocole.

" Messieurs les Plénipotentiares Allemands."

on the quay were drawn up several hundred British and Indian prisoners of war as a Guard of Honour, while in the background dense masses of the population of Constantinople gazed on the significant scene.

More than a week before Enver Pasha and Talaat Pasha had seen that the game was up so far as they were concerned, and had fled up the Black Sea in a German destroyer, which was said to have set them ashore—one to go into the Caucasus and the other to Berlin. Tewfik Pasha, a former Ambassador to London, was called on by the Sultan to form a Government which was likely to be looked on with favour by the Allies ; but the Turkish leaders had not yet absorbed the teaching of the war, and still carried on their old policy of procrastination and delay. They had to be brought up with a sharp turn or by a very strong hint, and that was what the guns of the allied fleets levelled on their capital supplied.

The conditions of the armistice granted to Turkey on October 30th had not been observed, and on November 15th the British War Office issued a statement to the effect that the Turkish Government had been required to evacuate Mosul and the Mosul vilayet, the Caucasus, and North-West Persia immediately, and by December 15th to withdraw in Asia Minor westward of Bozanti, north of Adana, in Cilicia, and to demobilise its troops. The armistice provided for the surrender of the Turkish garrisons in Syria, the Hedjaz, Asir, the Yemen, and Mesopotamia. Pressure, however, had to be applied by the presence of British and Indian soldiers in Caucasia,

Events in Caucasia North-West Persia, and elsewhere before the evacuations and surrenders were completed. Medina did not surrender till January, 1919, and then only because of a threat to shell Constantinople. Though its two chiefs had gone, the Committee of Union and Progress still exercised a baneful influence, and the plight of the Greeks, and far more of the Armenians, in Asiatic Turkey was nearly as wretched as before the armistice. It was not until well into 1919 that there was any change for the better, and the betterment then was but slight.

It was not generally understood by the British public— because the British Government, with its hands full at that time with the great German offensive in the west, said very little about it—that during the greater part of 1918 the Turks conducted a very strong and successful offensive of their own in Caucasia. They employed very considerable forces in that campaign, the result being, according to Liman von Sanders, that their remaining forces were insufficient to resist the British in Palestine, Syria, and Mesopotamia. As soon as the Russians, by order of the Bolshevist Government, withdrew from Armenia in the winter of 1917-18 the Turks pressed forward, retook Erzerum, in spite of the desperate efforts of the Armenians to hold it, and advancing into Caucasia, captured Batum, Ardahan, Kars, and Alexandropol. Nor did this campaign close until their taking of Baku in September, 1918, after General Dunsterville's retirement from that city.

The reason for the success of the Turks in this offensive was that the Armenians and Georgians were unable to offer an effective opposition and that the Tatars helped the invaders. In September-October, Germans and Turks—but mainly the latter—were in complete control of the Batum-Baku line and other Caucasian railways. Two things brought about a quick change. One was the capitulation of Bulgaria, which exposed the Turkish flank in Europe ; and the other was the sweeping triumph of General Allenby in Palestine and Syria (told in Chapter CCLXXIV., Vol. 12, page 341). Of less importance, but still of high value, was General

Marshall's campaign in Mesopotamia, which was described in Chapter CCXCVIII. (Vol. 13, page 175). As a matter of fact, allied forces were marching on Constantinople from the Macedonian side immediately after the surrender of Bulgaria, and would undoubtedly have captured the Turkish capital had the Turks not given in. The Turks did not hold Caucasia

AFTER THE CESSATION OF HOSTILITIES.
German officers in one of their cars bearing the white flag passing through the Canadian lines. Their errand was to point out places where mines had been laid in roads and elsewhere in the territory from which they had been driven during their great retreat that preceded the armistice.

very long, for the British were back in Baku on November 17th, General W. M. Thomson, C.B., C.M.G., being in command. Hostilities between the Georgians and the Armenians were stopped, and the Batum-Baku railway was taken over from the Turks. Early in December it was officially announced that the entry of the British into Baku, Batum, and other places in Caucasia implied no intention of permanent occupation. But the troops kept peaceful the country, which contained several little republics, each of which was eager to spring at the other's throat.

On the other side of the Black Sea events had marched in South-Eastern Europe. "The Balkans : from the Dethronement of Constantine to the Surrender of Bulgaria " formed the subject of Chapter CCLXXIII. (Vol. 12, page 321), the narrative breaking off as the Serbs and the other Allies were swooping down on the retreating Germans and Austrians. On October 12th the Serbs recaptured Nish, after heavy fighting, and the French on the west advanced into Upper Serbia. The Danube was reached within the next fortnight, and on November 1st Belgrade was once again in the possession of the Serbians, who farther west advanced into Bosnia, which, with Herzegovina, had already decided on union with them.

After the Revolution in Austria, Croatia, Slavonia and Dalmatia declared their independence, and a movement began for the formation of a Greater Serbia—Jugo-Slavia—by the combination with Serbia of **Triumph for** the Croatian and Slav parts of the defunct **Serbia** Austrian Empire and Montenegro. On December 29th, 1918, the first Ministry of the Kingdom of the Serbs, Croats, and Slovenes, as the new State was called, was formed under King Peter, who, after much tribulation of body and mind, had lived to see this splendid result of the war. What a triumph for Serbia, what glory for her unconquerable soldiers. Only three or four months before the prospects of the gallant little land had been apparently hopeless. Questions respecting Fiume and the Eastern Adriatic, in which Italy was deeply interested, soon engendered bitterness and strife. According to a semi-official statement issued in Rome, Italian troops with allied contingents on November 18th occupied Fiume, the reason given being the maintenance of order. Jugo-Slavia, looking on the port as its natural outlet, was greatly incensed, and there were collisions between Italian and Serb forces, but the matter was left to the Peace Conference for adjudication. On the north there were disputes with both Hungary and Rumania over territory which the Southern Slavs

In the Near East

claimed, and some fighting ensued. These differences the Conference had likewise to compose.

Greece reoccupied Eastern Macedonia, as the Bulgars after the surrender retired into their own country. The Greeks in Greece thereupon began to take steps to get into touch with the Greeks in Asia Minor, on the opposite side of the Ægean, with a view to political union — which came in June, 1919, with the occupation of Smyrna—and they agitated for the possession of Cyprus and of the Dodecanese Islands, the one held by Great Britain and the other by Italy. Nearly the whole of Albania was occupied by the Italians, but Greece looked to receive all Epirus, part of which they held. Besides taking full possession of

On the fringes of European Russia and in Siberia the position differed from that of Bolshevist Russia. In the north, in the Murmansk-Archangel area, the Allies occupied the territory and protected its inhabitants; while in the south the " Volunteer Army," which had been formed by Alexeieff and Korniloff in 1917-18, and now led by General Denikin, held the Bolshevist armies at bay in the Cossack region of the Don. In Siberia, which had been in a very confused condition in the first half of 1918, as was shown in Chapter CCLI. (Vol. 11, page 505), Admiral Koltchak had emerged as a great leader against Bolshevism and a capable governor of the country.

Cogent were the reasons that had induced the Allies to send forces to Northern Russia. In the spring of 1918 Finland had become practically a vassal State of Germany, which was forwarding the candidature of Duke Adolf Friedrich of Mecklenburg-Schwerin as its King; under German influence Prince Frederick Charles of Hesse was actually elected King in September. Months before that Germany had arranged with the Bolshevist Government that the Murman coast and the Murman Railway were to be included in an enlarged Finland. She thus would

GREAT GERMAN LINERS SURRENDERED TO THE ALLIES UNDER THE TERMS OF THE ARMISTICE.
The Hamburg-Amerika liner Imperator, and (right) the Kaiserin Auguste Victoria, of the same line, passing her sister ship the Vaterland in the Solent shortly before the outbreak of the war in 1914. These great vessels—the Imperator with a displacement of 70,000 tons—were taken over by the Allies from Germany in accordance with armistice terms. In oval: British naval officers questioning the German officers of surrendered mercantile vessels.

Trentino and some districts east of the Isonzo, Italy was pegging out claims in Dalmatia.

Shortly before the armistice granted to Germany, Rumania declared war on Germany, but as that armistice annulled the " Peace " of Bukarest which she had been compelled to accept some months earlier and gave her what she wanted, there were no operations. Field-Marshal Mackensen was permitted to march his army into Hungary, where it was interned by the Allies. Of all the German generals Mackensen had the greatest record of success, and here was the inglorious end of it all. His conquests of Serbia and Rumania had proved futile, and he and his soldiers became prisoners of war.

At the moment Russia was in a state of chaos. In this history of the Great War several chapters have been devoted to telling the story of the Russian Revolution and its subsequent developments in Europe and Asia, and Chapter CCCXI. (Vol. 13, page 373) recounted the experiences of one who had personally suffered from the Bolshevist regime.

be provided with a fine submarine base and another way of entry into Petrograd. Besides, it was the aim of the Allies at that time to reconstitute, so far as might be, the eastern front in order to prevent further withdrawals of German troops from that front to the west. Still another reason was that many Russians implored the Allies to come to their aid. Intervention was possible then only in the Murman-Archangel districts and in Siberia.

In July, 1918, the Germans were preparing to advance from Finland against the flank of the Murman Railway, but the

Murmansk and Archangel

Allies forestalled their designs by landing troops at Murmansk, on the Kola inlet, the Arctic terminus of the line, while simultaneously other of their forces were landed north of Archangel, that port itself being occupied in August.

In Murmansk the local Bolshevists of the regional council offered no opposition, but on the contrary entered into an agreement with the British and French authorities to co-operate for defence, the Allies on their part undertaking not to interfere in internal affairs. The agreement was ratified on July 7th and circulated by wireless by Lenin's Government. Shortly afterwards, however, the attitude of the Bolshevist Government, under German pressure, entirely changed, and there was some resistance at Archangel; but presently the Red Army, which numbered about 8,000 men, supported by Germans, withdrew to Obozerskaja, eighty miles south. It was driven out of this town a little later. By the end of 1918 the Allies held a crescent-shaped line, which stretched from the Onega on the west to the Pinega on the east, and crossed the railway to Vologda and the Northern Dwina. In the Murmansk region they occupied the railway for several hundred miles, thanks in a large measure to the help of the Karelians, who in September completely defeated a considerable force of Finns and Germans at Ukhtinskaya, some forty miles within the Russian frontier.

In both regions the first part of the winter passed quietly, but the Arctic climate bore heavily on the allied troops, particularly in the Archangel district, which was cut off by the ice from the outside world, except by reindeer sleigh transport. The majority of the men were British, but Americans, French, Italians, and even Serbs took part. There were besides many Russians. In March, 1919, according to a statement made in the French Chamber, the actual figures were: 13,100 British, 4,820 Americans, 2,350 French, 1,340 Italians, 1,280 Serbs, and 11,770 Russians. The last were to some extent drilled and led by officers from the other allied forces, and how far these men could be relied on was a question. The head of the Archangel Government was Nicholas Tchaikovsky, one of the leaders of the Russian co-operative movement and a pronounced anti-Bolshevist democrat; but there still were numbers of Bolshevists in the community, and they were active in propaganda. There was also a considerable monarchist element, which was as much opposed to Tchaikovsky as to the Bolshevists, and caused the Allies much trouble. The situation was not a comfortable one for the Allied Command. Somewhat similar uncertainty was felt at Murmansk, where the Red Finns were a dubious factor.

At the start of the operations in Northern Russia the Versailles Council had sent Major-General Poole to take the chief command of the allied forces, but later General C. S. M. Maynard, C.M.G., was in command in the Murmansk district, and General W. E. Ironside in the Archangel district. Ironside had fairly stiff fighting early in 1919, the Bolshevists attacking near Shenkursk so strongly that that place had to be abandoned by him on January 23rd-24th. In the beginning of March they attacked Yevsievskaya, on the Vaga, and compelled him to withdraw a mile from it. Thereafter the Bolshevists waited for the spring thaw. In the meantime Maynard gained possession of the Murman Railway for a length

UNDER NEW FLAGS.
American destroyer about to put aboard the surrendered Hamburg-Amerika liner Cleveland the crew which was to take her across the Atlantic. In oval: The Cap Finisterre and (beyond) the Patricia, two of the surrendered German liners in the Solent. Above: The Alexandra Woermann, one of the vessels of the German mercantile fleet which surrendered at Southend early in 1919.

WHEN THE KAISER FLED INTO HOLLAND.
Part of the luggage of the ex-Kaiser waiting to be forwarded to its
destination in Holland.

He pointed out that allied, not merely British, forces had been sent to Russia because the Bolshevists were assisting Germany in the war. Bolshevists had treacherously attacked the Czecho-Slovaks, and it was an obligation of honour for the Allies to save the latter. Further, it was a military necessity to prevent vast portions of Russia, struggling to escape the tyranny of the Bolshevists, from being overrun by them and thrown open as a source of supply to the enemy. He described the success of the intervention, but said that it was impossible to withdraw the allied forces and leave those who had fought on our side to the tender mercies of their enemies before they were strong enough to defend themselves. Still, the last thing the British Government desired,

from Murmansk of upwards of four hundred miles, and he established his headquarters at Kem, on the White Sea, which was open for ships in the summer.

After the departure of the German troops from Esthonia and Livonia, in consonance with the terms of the armistice, Bolshevism broke out in these regions, and a Red Army forced the Esthonians to retreat. That was early in December, 1918, and at that time a British squadron was in the Baltic, part of it being based on Libau. On December 12th three British cruisers with three torpedo-boats entered Reval. Along the shores of the Gulf of Finland British ships helped the Esthonians by bombarding the rear of the Bolshevist position, but soon the vessels were withdrawn because of the ice. Lord Milner about this time wrote a Note in defence of British policy in Russia, which was being criticised, and in some cases condemned, in the United Kingdom.

IN THE IMPERIAL EXILE'S DUTCH HOME.
View of the upper hall in Amerongen Castle, in Holland, the residence of his friend
Count Bentinck in which the ex-Kaiser found refuge.

he declared, was to leave any British soldiers a day longer than was necessary to discharge the moral obligations that had been incurred. When Lord Milner spoke of the success of the intervention of the Allies he had what had taken place in Siberia more particularly in his mind. Chapter CCLI. (Vol. 11, page 505) included in its survey a description of the occurrences in that enormous area up to the signing of the Sino-Japanese Convention on May 16th, 1918, and a reference was made to the march of the Czecho-Slovaks from the West to the Far East.

In the spring of 1918 Colonel Semenoff with a force of local Cossacks, carried on a single-handed struggle against the Bolshevists in Eastern Siberia with varying success, and, as the year wore on, the name of Koltchak, who had been the admiral in command of the Black Sea Fleet during the Kerensky period, began to appear in despatches from Vladivostok as the leader of a body of irregulars who were attacking the Bolshevists in the Amur Province. But Koltchak's opportunity had not yet come. The first great change in Siberia was made by the Czecho-Slovaks, of

MOTOR-CARS FOR THE EXILED KAISER.
Truckloads of motor-cars belonging to the ex-Kaiser. They had reached Rotterdam on their way to
Count Bentinck's castle at Amerongen, where Wilhelm II. sought safety on the collapse of the German
armies on the western front and the outbreak of Revolution in Berlin.

whom there were about 120,000 in Russia when Lenin and Trotsky seized the Government in November, 1917, but who would have nothing to do with Bolshevism. Originally they had served in the Austrian Army, and had gone over to the Russians, thereafter being incorporated in the Russian Army. The Treaty of Brest Litovsk provided for their exchange, but they refused to be exchanged, and ultimately the Allies arranged for them to go to the western front by way of Siberia and America. They started, but the Bolshevists

Great feat of the Czecho-Slovaks showed treachery, which resulted in the Czecho-Slovaks fighting a passage across Siberia. Defeating a Bolshevist force at Penza, they captured Kazan, where they found sixty-five millions sterling, and took Tcheliabinsk, the European terminus of the Siberian Railway, part of which was already in the hands of their forward detachments. In May, 1918, they helped a number of moderate Russians to form a Government at Omsk. In June 15,000 of them, under General Diterichs, a Russian but no Bolshevist, reached Vladivostok.

At that time the British Government recognised the Czecho-Slovak army as an allied belligerent, and it was decided that the force was to remain in Siberia, where the Allies were about to intervene. After many negotiations the United States made proposals to Japan, which were accepted; in sum these were that Japan should supply the bulk of the troops, the other Allies sending contingents. The Allies were careful to announce that the expedition was not to interfere in the internal affairs of the Russian people, and that there was no intention of impairing the territorial integrity of Russia. Commanded by Major-General A. W. F. Knox, a British force landed at Vladivostok on August 3rd, and a French detachment on the 9th, while considerable bodies of Japanese began arriving on the 12th. Japan put upwards of 60,000 men in all into Siberia, and the whole allied troops were commanded by General Otani, who had been at the head of the Japanese garrison at Tsingtau. In March, 1919, when half of the Japanese had returned home, the total strength of the expedition, exclusive of Russians, was 55,000 Czecho-Slovaks, 12,000 Poles, 4,000 Serbians, 4,000 Rumanians, 2,000 Italians, 1,600 British (Middlesex—under Colonel John Ward, the Labour M.P. for Stoke—and Hampshires), 760 French, 7,500 Americans, 4,000 Canadians, and 28,000 Japanese.

At the outset of the campaign the Japanese made short work of a body of Bolshevists who, crossing Lake Khanka, tried to cut the railway between Vladivostok and Harbin. A general forward movement began on August 24th, with the British, French, Czecho-Slovaks, and some Cossacks in the centre, and the Japanese on the flanks. Otani, advancing his left wing, captured two armoured trains, got behind the rear of the enemy and completely defeated him. On September 8th the Japanese captured Habarovsk, the Bolshevist headquarters, and took one hundred and twenty guns and much rolling-stock. On the west side of Manchuria, Semenoff, backed

by Japanese and Czecho-Slovak contingents, advanced, encountering little opposition; and presently there came into his camp a large number of Czecho-Slovaks, commanded by Colonel Gaida, who had been held up for some time by Bolshevist forces in the neighbourhood of Lake Baikal, and to rescue whom was one of the primary objects of the expedition. Gaida had succeeded in surmounting all opposition over a stretch of six hundred miles of hostile country—in itself an amazing adventure.

To obtain entire possession of the Siberian Railway was now the task of the Allies. The Czecho-Slovaks and non-Bolshevist Russians pushed forward, while British and other allied troops were quartered in the chief towns along the line, the eastern side being held by the Japanese. Ward's battalion of the Middlesex, joined later by the Hampshires, was stationed at Omsk in October, 1918, and settled down there for the winter. The presence of these allied detachments had a good effect on the population, and the result

was seen, after other Russian experiments had failed, in the formation of a fairly strong Siberian Government under Admiral Koltchak, who became Supreme Governor of Siberia in November, 1918. At first the Czecho-Slovaks looked askance at him, and some of them withdrew from the front; but their own General Stefanik, who fortunately at this juncture had just arrived from Europe, explained the situation, and the trouble passed. Koltchak set about building up an army, and in this he was much assisted by General Knox and the British.

His first effort with this army saved Ekaterinburg from the Bolshevists, and in December he began a vigorous offensive which gave him Perm, a military centre on the Kama, a tributary of the Volga, with several thousand Bolshevist prisoners, on December 23rd. In the course of these operations the Red Third Army was destroyed. Farther south, however, he was

THE EX-KAISER'S HEIR IN EXILE IN HOLLAND.
The German ex-Crown Prince on board the boat which carried him, accompanied by three officers of his Staff, to the island of Wieringen, in the Zuyder Zee, where he sought seclusion and safety. Above: The ex-Crown Prince taking his daily walk with a number of youngsters who became his frequent companions.

using armed force in many parts of Europe and the East to gain possession of territory the rightful claim to which the Conference was to decide. Yet though the situation was still so disturbed in Russia, Poland, the Ukraine, and elsewhere, demobilisation went on with great rapidity in Great Britain.

February began with an interesting event in the opening of the new German National Assembly at Weimar, Berlin having been barred on account of Spartacist outbreaks. In his inaugural address, Herr Ebert vehemently protested against the Allies' terms in the armistice, which had been renewed shortly before. **First President** He asserted that Germany ought to enter **of Germany** the League of Nations on equal terms, and he demanded the union of German Austria with the German Republic. Two or three days later Ebert was elected first President of Germany, and the Assembly was engaged in formulating and passing a provisional Constitution for Germany. Herr Scheidemann was appointed Chancellor. When the armistice came again to be renewed, which was from February 17th, on somewhat more stringent terms than before, the new German Government declined at first to sign it, but in the end did so.

unsuccessful, and the Bolshevists advanced into Turkestan, where they joined up with local Red forces. But in March, 1919, he made a fresh offensive, both from Perm, under Gaida, and from Birsk, in the south, recaptured Ufa, south-west of Tcheliabinsk, on the Siberian Railway, and pressing forward on a front four hundred miles long, recovered a large extent of the ground which had been lost ; but he was unable to regain Orenburg, large forces of the Reds having concentrated there. Then the spring thaw put a period to his operations, but on the whole the military position was very promising.

Among other movements of the Allies, and not covered by the preceding paragraphs dealing with Russia, it may be noted that shortly after the arrival of the allied fleets at Constantinople, an allied squadron sailed across the Black Sea to Sebastopol, where, on November 26th, 1918, it took over the remains of the Russian Black Sea Fleet there, and going on to Odessa seized the rest of them. Later the Allies occupied the Russian ports on the Black Sea, the British holding those on the eastern shore, while the French, with Greek and Rumanian troops, were in Odessa, Sebastopol, Kherson, and Nikolaieff. Primarily the business of the Allies in evacuation of German troops ; but it was preventing important ports from falling the Bolshevists. However, in the spring of 1919, the Bolshevists, after defeating the Ukrainians, advanced on Odessa and in the Crimea, and the Allies, who had no force for the defence of the ports there from the land side, abandoned them. But the British still held Batum, Poti, and Novo Rossik, the last-named being in the Kuban district, and used as a base of supplies for the Volunteer Army under Denikin, who was showing his quality as a fine fighting man in sharp, successful thrusts at the Bolshevists in South-Eastern Russia.

Turning back to the assembling of the Peace Conference in Paris in January, 1919, it may be remarked briefly here that from the first special interest attached to it because of the presence of President Wilson As the first week of the Conference was closing, a warning was issued to those who were

GERMANS WHO BROKE THE ARMISTICE.
Rear-Admiral von Reuter (left), chief officer of the German Fleet interned at Scapa Flow, who boasted that he was responsible for the scuttling of that Fleet on June 21st, 1919. Above : German officers from the sunken ships on board H.M.S. Ramillies.

On February 14th, at a plenary meeting of the Peace Conference, President Wilson read the League of Nations Covenant, which had been unanimously agreed to by the five Great Powers and by nine other belligerent States. He made a speech in explanation of its objects. Later in the day he left Paris for America. On his return home he proudly told his country how high its prestige now was in Europe, and he maintained that the confidence of Europe imposed obligations on America in the struggle for the liberty of the world which could not be evaded. An incident which caused a painful sensation about this time was the attempted assassination of M. Clemenceau by a youth named Cottin, who fired several shots at him, and wounded him in the shoulder, but happily not fatal. Among the Allies sympathy was universal with the veteran Premier of France, who, in spite of his great age, recovered.

that area was the also concerned with into the hands of

Mr. Lloyd George returned from the Conference on February 8th, and the new British Parliament met three days later.

In the debate in the House of Commons, in reply to the

GERMAN SAILORS SAVED FROM THEIR SCUTTLED SHIPS.
Group of men from the interned German Fleet who were taken on board a British vessel after the German ships had been treacherously scuttled on the eve of Germany's agreeing to the Allies' peace terms.

Germany's battle-cruiser Hindenburg resting on the bottom at Scapa Flow, and (right) another view of the same warship come to her ignominious end at the hands of those who had been compelled to yield her up to inglorious internment.

One of the German destroyers at the moment of capsizing.

Line of the interned destroyers sinking at their buoys.

Boatloads of German officers and men, with some of their belongings, coming alongside H.M.S. Ramillies after the scuttling of the interned Fleet, and (in oval above) part of the German crews of the sunken ships in a boat flying the white flag, making for safety on board the British ships.

SINKING OF THEIR INTERNED FLEET AT SCAPA FLOW BY FAITHLESS GERMANS, JUNE 21ST, 1919.

King's Speech, the Prime Minister touched on the Conference, which was "settling questions involving every continent," and referred to the punishment of those responsible for the war, the payment to be exacted from Germany, and the satisfactory progress of the League of Nations, a great experiment that was going to be tried with the full assent of all the nations represented at the Conference. At the moment, however, the industrial crisis held general attention, and at the end of the month a sign of the times was seen in a National Industrial Conference, convened by the Government, in London, which appointed a joint committee of employers and workmen to investigate the causes of industrial unrest and suggest remedies. In connection with the war there was little of interest in Parliament until well into April, when the Peace Conference had resumed in Paris, and was discussing the indemnity to be paid by Germany.

On February 20th Habibullah Khan, the Ameer of Afghanistan, was assassinated while sleeping in camp at a place

Trouble on the Afghan border

about forty miles from Kabul, and it was reported that his brother Nasrullah Khan had succeeded to the throne, but this proved to be incorrect, the new Ameer being Amanullah Khan, another relative of the murdered prince. Amanullah sent a letter to the Indian Government, from whom the former Ameer had had a large subsidy, announced his accession, and gave assurances of continuing Habibullah's policy of friendly relations with Great Britain, but within a few weeks these were completely falsified, the Afghans raiding across the frontier in May and attacking the British posts. Whether the action of the new Ameer was inspired by Bolshevists, as some said, or indicated a profound disturbance among the

Mohammedan peoples of the East because of the fall of Turkey, whose Sultan they regarded as the Caliph and head of their religion, as others alleged, was uncertain, but the latter hypothesis gained colour from a series of outbreaks which took place in Egypt in March, and which were believed to be caused in part by the Young Turks, cloaked under a demand for Egyptian "self-determination."

Nothing was farther from the thoughts of the British public than anything in the nature of a rising in Egypt, where it was understood that all was well. The first intimation that there was something wrong was given by the news that Zaghlul Pasha and Ismail Pasha, two Egyptian Ministers, as well as two other prominent Nationalists, had been arrested

Disturbances in Egypt

and deported to Malta. This intelligence was immediately followed by a statement that an agitation started by the adherents of these men had led to fatal riots in Cairo. The movement began with a strike by the pupils in the higher schools and some of the students of the Azhar University, and street demonstrations ensued with wrecking and pillage. Disorder became widespread throughout Egypt, and bedouins invaded the Beharia Oasis, where the Turkish flag was hoisted in some of the villages. British and Australian soldiers were insulted, attacked, and in some cases murdered. General Allenby was sent out to deal with the situation, and he arrived in Cairo towards the end of the month, but by that time the position, particularly in Cairo and Alexandria, had improved. Allenby brought the disturbances to an end, and instituted an inquiry into the causes of the trouble. Among other things he ordered the release of Zaghlul Pasha and his associates: the ringleaders of the rioters were tried and punished.

ALLIED NAVAL ARMISTICE COMMISSION: CONFERENCE WITH GERMAN OFFICERS ON H.M.S. HERCULES AT KIEL.

Shortly after the signing of the armistice an Allied Naval Commission, under Vice-Admiral Sir Montague Browning, K.C.B., M.V.O. (in centre, writing), was sent to German waters to see that the terms of the agreement in so far as they referred to naval matters were duly carried out. Arrangements for the necessary searching and inspecting of German warships and naval air stations were made at conferences with German officers, held on board Admiral Browning's flagship, H.M.S. Hercules. The scene depicted is that of the final conference before the Commission returned to England.

It was not only in Egypt that there was trouble. Grave riots occurred in India in the second week of April, the chief centres of disturbances being Amritsar, in the Punjab, and Ahmedabad, in Bombay Presidency. In the outbreak at Amritsar three British bank officials and a British railway guard were done to death; the Town Hall, bank buildings, and the telegraph office were wrecked. Between Amritsar and Lahore the country was in open rebellion, while at Viramjam, near Ahmedabad, an Indian Revenue officer was killed, and the Government offices were destroyed. In a riot at Delhi there were fifteen casualties. The disturbances continued for several days in the Punjab. Prominent features were the co-operation existing between Hindus and Mohammedans, and the strong anti-British feeling displayed by the mobs. Gradually the Indian Government got the situation in hand. Martial law was proclaimed in the Lyallpur district, in the Punjab, and flying columns visited the various places where unrest was most marked. Large numbers of British troops in India voluntarily undertook to remain there during the continuance of the trouble. The leaders of the rioters

were arrested, and, after trial, sentenced to long terms of imprisonment and transportation.

Scarcely were these trials concluded when armed bodies of Afghans, including regular troops of the Ameer, crossed the Indian frontier at several points near the Khyber Pass, and occupied three places in the hills on the British side. The Indian Government sent troops under General Barrett to expel the invaders, and the Viceroy called on the Ameer to control his subjects; but the Afghans advanced towards Landi Kotal, where, however, they were attacked and dispersed by British forces on May 9th. The British next occupied Dakka Fort, a strategic point within the Afghan frontier, about ten miles north-west of Landi Kotal, and there on May 16th they were assailed by the enemy, who was beaten off, attacked in turn, and driven into the hills, the fighting lasting for three days. But all along the Afghan frontier the Afghans were massing, and it looked as if Great Britain had another Afghan War on its hands, for the reply of the Ameer to the Viceroy was defiant

in tone. An ugly feature of this development was a sympathetic unrest in Peshawar, which had to be placed under martial law. It was well that by this time the rest of India had quieted down, or the situation would have been distinctly more serious. Those who thought that the Bolshevists were behind it all had their view confirmed by the Ameer's sending greetings to the Bolshevist Commissaries in Central Asia.

Under General Nadir Khan, the Afghans began an offensive in the Tochi and Gumal Valleys, in the south of the North-West Frontier. Various forward British posts had to be withdrawn. Farther north the Afghans suffered a sharp defeat at the hands of the Chitral forces, and an Afghan fort, on the border of Baluchistan, was captured by the British. A force of 3,000 Afghans was repulsed from Thal Fort, in the Kurram Valley, and another body driven back from Idak, in the Tochi Valley. Then, in a letter dated May 28th, the Ameer asked the Viceroy for peace. What probably brought about this change of mind so quickly was the incessant bombing by the British airmen of Kabul, Jalalabad, and other points, quite as much as his defeats in the field.

On the Afghan frontier

To revert to what was taking place in the United Kingdom. On April 14th Mr. Lloyd George somewhat suddenly returned from Paris, where he had been attending the Peace Conference, and made an important speech in the House of Commons two days afterwards. A week before, a telegram had been sent to him by nearly four hundred members of the House, expressing anxiety at the reports that the British delegates to the Conference were not formulating the complete financial claim of the British Empire on Germany. There was besides an impression that he had not shown himself as friendly to France as he should have. In his address he said the question of indemnities was not an easy one, and could not be settled by telegram; time was needed, and he asked that those who were trying to do their best should be left in peace. Speaking of Russia, he said that it was his conviction that military intervention would be the greatest act of stupidity; they were supplying, however, all countries bordering on Bolshevist territories with the means of resisting Bolshevist invasion. And he gave a positive assurance that every pledge they had given with regard to what they pressed for insertion in the Peace Terms had been included in the demand put forward by the Allies, who wanted a peace which, while not being vindictive, would be stern.

PEACE SOUVENIRS FOR THE BELGIANS IN EAST AFRICA.
Sacred cattle of the Watuzi given by Musinga, King of the Ruanda tribe, to General Malfeyt, the Belgian Royal Commissioner, in celebration of the coming of peace in East Africa. In circle : General von Lettow-Vorbeck (on right), the defender of German East Africa, after his surrender, talking with a British officer.

AT THE ROYAL DAIS ON JULY 19TH, 1919.
King George taking the salute at the Royal dais outside Buckingham Palace on the day of London's great Victory March. Behind his Majesty stand Marshal Foch, the Prince of Wales, Queen Mary, Queen Alexandra, and General Pershing. Above: The view from the Royal dais at the moment of Sir Douglas Haig's passing.

This assurance was what was wanted by most members of the House who had been returned to Parliament at the General Election. They had been afraid that Mr. Lloyd George had been "fluctuating" at Paris, and this speech of his was reassuring. On the whole the House gave him and it a very good reception.

As drawn up by the Conference, the Terms of Peace were presented to Count Brockdorff-Rantzau and the other German delegates on May 7th at Versailles. Opinion in the allied countries on the Peace Treaty was on the w h o l e favourable ; in Germany the terms were described as crushing and as "impossible." The German delegates were given fifteen days in which to reply to the allied offer, but the time was extended later. It was on May 7th that it was announced from Paris that Mr. Wilson and Mr. Lloyd George had pledged themselves to propose, to the United States Senate and the British Parliament respectively, an engagement—but subject to the approval of the Council of the League of Nations—immediately to go to the help of France in the event of an unprovoked attack by Germany. It was in this way that France looked to consolidate her position as against Germany.

While at Versailles the Germans were considering, with the usual mixture of whines and threats, the **Reburial of the** terms of the Treaty, and writing strange **martyred nurse** Notes to the Allies on the subject, the body of one of the most heroic victims of German brutality and frightfulness—Nurse Cavell—was brought from Belgium to Dover, whence it passed to London on May 15th. After a most moving and at the same time magnificent funeral service in Westminster Abbey, the body was taken to Norwich, where in the Cathedral an impressive service was also held, and there it was buried.

Towards the close of May it seemed possible that Germany would refuse to sign the Peace Treaty, and the Allies prepared for action if that should prove to be the case ; but they had

little real anxiety, for they had the power to compel the signature, and they were in complete accord as to the use of that power. Meanwhile, the very real apprehension which had been felt among the Allies, especially in Great Britain and America, regarding the safety of their forces in Northern Russia, had by this time been dissipated. A big Bolshevist offensive had been announced as soon as the spring thaw permitted operations, and reinforcements were prepared and sent out to General Ironside ; but when the offensive developed on May 2nd and 5th it turned out to be feeble, and was repulsed without much difficulty. The reasons for this failure of the Bolshevists in the north were not far to seek. Both Koltchak on the east and Denikin in the south were attacking their forces with remarkable success, and they had no men to spare for the Archangel front—which, in fact, they had to deplete. When the first contingent of the British reinforcements, under Brigadier-General Grogan, V.C., landed at Archangel on May 26th all immediate danger had passed away.

During that month of May the Bolshevist Government of Russia appeared to be tottering, and prophecies were made of its speedy downfall. An important advance in the direction of Petrograd was undertaken **Russia in** by the Esthonians, supported by a Russian **May, 1919** force ; Narva was reoccupied, and in the beginning of the fourth week detachments of the Esthonian Army were entrenching themselves on a line only thirty miles from the former capital of Russia. Somewhat earlier a British naval force, in response to an appeal for assistance by the Finnish batteries at Fort Ino, which had been shelled by a Bolshevist fleet, fought an action with that fleet near Kronstadt, in the Gulf of Finland, and sank an enemy cruiser, while an enemy gunboat was run ashore, the rest of the hostile ships taking to flight under cover of the guns of the fortress and the protection of the mine-fields. Lettish Government troops were marching on Riga, but were forestalled by the Germans, under General von der Goltz, with Baron von Manteuffel in local command, the latter entering the town on May 22nd. About the same time Denikin, with the Volunteer Army, conducted a successful offensive towards Tsaritsyn, on the Volga, in the south of Russia, and captured upwards of 10,000 Bolshevists. The situation was so alarming for the Lenin-Trotsky gang that they determined on a great military effort, and this they directed against Admiral Koltchak.

Koltchak's wonderful offensive had carried him well into European Russia; he had taken Perm and was advancing towards Kazan. Speaking in the House of Commons on May 29th, Mr. Winston Churchill, after remarking that the military weakness of Bolshevism had become very apparent, said that Koltchak's army had advanced to a maximum distance of three hundred miles on a front of seven hundred miles, and that it was hoped a junction would **Hopeful Russian** soon be effected between the admiral's and **outlook** the Archangel forces, with the result that the whole situation would be placed on a Russian —*i.e.*, a non-Bolshevist—basis before the summer was over. In these circumstances, continued Mr. Churchill, the five victorious Great Powers had obtained from the various anti-Bolshevist Governments in Russia an undertaking that their triumph—for which it was now permissible to hope—would be immediately followed by the summoning of a Constitutional

Assembly on a democratic franchise. Three days before it had been announced from Paris that the Allied and Associated Governments were prepared to extend recognition to Koltchak on condition that he agreed to call a Constituent Assembly and subscribed to the Covenant of the League of Nations. After much indecision and delay the Supreme Council had at last made up its mind to bar the Bolshevists from recognition, the reason for this being **Democracy's** the rejection by the Soviets of the principle **worst enemy** of the Constituent Assembly and their re-fusal to permit the one called to meet. Henceforth Bolshevism was to be regarded as the worst enemy of genuine democracy.

So far as it was known at the time, the position in Russia in the beginning of June appeared to confirm Mr. Churchill's views. There were successful attacks on the Reds in the Archangel and Murmansk areas. At Gatchina, in the neigh-bourhood of Petrograd, heavy fighting was going on, to the advantage, on balance, of the Esthonians and the Russians, partly under the leadership of General Yudenitch, the conqueror of Erzerum in 1916. British warships were active in support in the Gulf of Finland, and Petrograd, it was widely believed, was about to fall. General Sir Hubert Gough, at the head of a British Military Mission, was in Helsingfors and in close touch with Yudenitch. The Entente Powers sent a Note to Germany demanding the withdrawal of the German troops, who were suspected of co-operating with the Bolshevists, in the Baltic provinces to a line which was to be drawn, Von der Goltz being allowed to remain

LONDON'S GREAT VICTORY MARCH AS SEEN FROM BUCKINGHAM PALACE.
Men of the British Navy marching past the Royal pavilion—the roof of which can be seen immediately beyond the Victoria Memorial—on the day of London's great march of the allied forces in celebration of the conclusion of peace, July 19th, 1919.

south of that line on certain conditions. In the south of Russia, Denikin, who was receiving very considerable support in guns, Tanks, and other munitions from the British by way of the Black Sea, was continuing his advance northward with unbroken success. And Admiral Koltchak had accepted the conditions generally which the Supreme Council had laid down as necessary to the recognition of his Government. Thus all seemed to be well from the Allies' point of view. Bolshevism appeared to be waning fast—to be doomed. Then Koltchak was beaten and driven back by Trotsky, and Bolshevism revived.

It was not until well into June that what had taken place to Koltchak's army was understood among the Allies. Bolshevist wireless messages announcing victories over Koltchak about the middle of May had been looked on as

LONDON'S MARCH IN CELEBRATION OF PEACE.
Members of the Women's Royal Naval Service, familiarly known as the "Wrens," saluting the cenotaph to "The Glorious Dead" in the great march of July 19th, 1919; and (above) the colours of the men of the Mercantile Marine borne in the procession on the same occasion.

lies, but they were true enough. Even while the Supreme Council was negotiating with the admiral a large part of his forces was in full retreat. His offensive had been carried vigorously to within a hundred miles of the Volga, but there it was held by the counter-offensive of the Red Army under Trotsky, Koltchak's left wing being heavily defeated and its hasty withdrawal rendered inevitable. This serious set-back was occasioned by lack of trained reserves and the shrinkage in number of his troops owing to losses incurred in the advance. Some of Koltchak's men, who were ex-prisoners of war, were tempted with fair promises by the Reds, and deserted. The truth was that Koltchak's advance had been much too rapid. His troops were far outnumbered by the Reds, and were forced back to the River Bielya, a distance of about one hundred and fifty miles from the high-water mark they had reached in their attack. On the Koma, a tributary of the Volga, British bluejackets in two improvised gunboats, manned from the Suffolk and the Kent and flying the White Ensign, did all that was possible to save the situation by engaging the superior forces of the enemy and by preventing him from making use of the waterways. But on June 9th the Reds, after three days' most desperate fighting, took Ufa, an important railway centre which Koltchak had held for nearly three months, and this marked for them the recovery of more than half the ground they had previously lost to him in this part of the field.

While events in Eastern Russia were thus proceeding adversely to the desires of the Allies, the Peace Conference at Paris made further progress. On June 2nd the Terms of Peace for Austria were presented to the Austrian delegates at St. Germain, but in an incomplete form, as a number of questions were reserved for future consideration, among them being those connected with reparation and finance. The terms were commented on very angrily by the Vienna newspapers, which accused the four Great Powers of showing extreme partiality to the Czechs, Rumanians, and Jugo-Slavs.

In the first week in June reports were current that pressure had been brought to bear on Mr. Lloyd George to modify the Peace Terms on behalf of Germany. The matter came up in the House of Commons on June 5th, and Mr. Lloyd George authorised the denial that he had been in communication on the subject with pacifists, or that any pressure by persons of political or financial influence had been employed to cause him to modify the Terms of Peace in favour of Germany. In the meantime the committees appointed to consider the German counter-proposals had reported to the Supreme Council, and on June 16th the Allied and Associated Powers made a final statement to Germany in the shape of a detailed reply to the German counter-proposals and of a long covering **German disagreements and delays** letter dealing with the whole settlement. This statement was accompanied by a draft agreement with respect to the military occupation of the territories of the Rhine by the armed forces of the Allies and the appointment of a High Commission, a civilian body, as representing the Allies in that area.

Germany appealed for more time, but without avail. On June 20th the Scheidemann Government decided not to sign the Treaty, and subsequently resigned, whereupon a new Ministry was formed by Herr Bauer, with Herr Erzberger as Vice-Premier and Minister of Finance. Bauer, a Majority Socialist, had been Minister of Labour under Prince Max of Baden, as under Scheidemann. His policy was to sign the Treaty with certain reservations, but on his sending a Note to this effect he was promptly told that the time for discussion was past, that no reservations would be permitted, and that the German representatives must sign the Treaty as finally formulated, or refuse to sign it. The allied armies, in the latter alternative, were ready to advance into Germany; the Allies, in their reply, did not mention this fact, but the Germans were well aware of it, and it was doubtless for this reason that on June 23rd, Herr von Haniel, the Acting Chief of the German Delegation at Versailles, informed the Allies that Germany was ready to sign. Between 6.30 and 7 o'clock that evening guns and sirens announced to the people of Paris that the Germans had given in, and soon the streets were crowded with enthusiastic throngs. The news reached London by telephone about 6 o'clock, and created little excitement, though it was greeted in some of the theatres with cheering and the singing of the National Anthem.

Two days earlier an event had occurred which had caused not excitement so much as indignation and anger among the Allies—this was the scuttling of the German Fleet which was interned at Scapa Flow, in the Southern Orkneys, and perhaps it was this which made many indifferent to **German Fleet scuttled** the actual acceptance of the Treaty by Ger- **at Scapa Flow** many. In the afternoon of June 21st the British Admiralty issued a brief statement to the effect that in the morning certain of the German interned ships at Scapa Flow had been sunk and abandoned by their crews, who would be detained in safe custody. Later it was announced that all the German battleships and battle-cruisers were sunk, except the battleship Baden, which was still afloat, that five light cruisers likewise had been sunk and other three beached, and that eighteen destroyers had been beached, four were still afloat, and the rest were sunk. The German

Fleet had consisted of seventy-four vessels—ten battleships, six battle-cruisers, eight light cruisers, and fifty destroyers. Rear-Admiral von Reuter was in chief command, and it was by his orders that the Fleet was scuttled. He afterwards stated that he believed from a German newspaper that the armistice had terminated, and he gave the order personally to sink the ships in accordance with orders, issued early in the war by his superiors, that no German warship was to be surrendered.

That morning the British warships at **Von Reuter** Scapa Flow, under Vice-Admiral Sir Sydney **accepts responsibility** Fremantle, had put to sea for torpedo practice, and they were recalled when the British patrols noticed that the Germans were leaving their vessels, but before their return most of the German ships had been sunk. The German officers and crews were rounded up, a small number of Germans who refused to stop their boats when ordered to do so were killed and wounded. On the 24th Admiral Fremantle paraded in the Revenge the whole of the German personnel, and addressing Von Reuter, expressed his indignation at the deed which had been perpetrated, characterising it as " that of a traitor, violating the arrangements entered into with the Allies." It was not the first time, he remarked, that the Germans " had violated all the decent laws and rules of the sea." Von Reuter replied that he took entire responsibility for what had been done, and he declared he was sure that in similar circumstances every British sailor would have done the same. Speaking

NEARING THE END OF THE GREAT TRIUMPHAL MARCH IN LONDON.
Men of the Royal Navy at Hyde Park Corner on July 19th, 1919, after taking part in the Victory March through London. They had just passed under the arch from Constitution Hill, and were going on into Hyde Park, where they were disbanded.

in the House of Commons on the subject, on June 24th, Mr. Long, the First Lord, contradicted a report that the British Navy was to blame for the occurrence.

In a speech at Oxford, delivered about ten days later, Sir David Beatty, referring to the matter, maintained that all thinking people realised that no part of the blame for the fiasco, which deprived of the fruits of victory the men who had striven so nobly to obtain them, could rightly be laid to the charge of the British Navy. As a matter of historic fact, Mr. Long placed the blame where it belonged—on the shoulders of the Supreme Council. The sinking of the ships was widely hailed in Germany as meritorious, though there was no doubt that it was a clear breach of the armistice, and in truth an act of war. The subject was considered by the Peace Conference, but it did not affect the **A breach of the armistice** course of the peace negotiations, then nearing an end. A Note was sent to Germany telling her that it was open to the Allies to bring before military tribunals those responsible for the sinking of the Fleet, and to exact reparation, with such further measures as might be deemed appropriate. In the meantime, Von Reuter, his officers, and men had been removed to the mainland as prisoners of war.

German representatives, empowered to sign the Peace Treaty, having arrived at Paris, that Treaty was signed in the afternoon of Saturday, June 28th, 1919, in the Galerie des Glaces of the Château of Versailles, and thus was closed the greatest war the world had ever known. In a statement to the Press the German delegates declared that they signed the Treaty without any reservations whatsoever and with the sincere intention of carrying out its provisions to the best of their ability, but they expressed the hope that some of its conditions might still be modified.

News of the signing of the Treaty was received throughout the British Empire with great rejoicings. King George issued the following message to his peoples :

The signing of the Treaty of Peace will be received with deep thankfulness throughout the British Empire. This formal act brings to its concluding stages the terrible war which has devastated Europe and distracted the world. It manifests the victory of the ideals of freedom and liberty for which we have made untold sacrifices. I share my peoples' joy and thanksgiving, and earnestly pray that the coming years of peace may bring to them ever increasing happiness and prosperity.

In the evening of that historic Saturday great demonstrations were made outside Buckingham Palace, the King and Queen, with the Prince of Wales, the other princes, and Princess Mary appearing several times on the balcony. Twice the King briefly addressed the crowds, and the prince also made a short speech ; his Majesty expressed his thankfulness that the war was over, and his appreciation of the loyalty of his subjects ; the prince spoke of the magnificent reception accorded, and added : " I am very proud to have served with so many of you who are here." In Trafalgar Square many thousands assembled, and there was much cheering and singing, while processions of beflagged motor-cars moved along the adjacent streets. But it was noticeable that there were few or no evidences of that unrestrained and almost frantic rejoicing that followed on the signing of the armistice. There were joyous scenes in the theatres, hotels, and restaurants, but they never reached the **London's joy at peace** emotional height of Armistice Day. With the signing by Germany of the Treaty changes occurred in the Supreme Council. President Wilson returned to America. Mr Lloyd George came back to London, arriving on the evening of June 29th, and being met at Victoria Station by the King and the Prince of Wales, an unprecedented honour. When the Prime Minister appeared in the House of Commons next day he was given an enthusiastic welcome. The National Anthem was sung, all the " strangers " in the various galleries joining in, though such a proceeding was absolutely contrary to rule. On July 1st Mr. Bonar Law announced that Thanksgiving Services would be held throughout the country on the following Sunday, July 6th, and that Saturday, July 19th, had been set apart as the day of national rejoicing for the coming of peace. In Paris, M. Clemenceau, in the Chamber

on June 30th, tabled the Treaty, and the Franco-British and France-American Conventions establishing the security of France, and delivered a speech which, in the words of one who heard it, in the austerity of its terms and the lofty humanity of its inspiration placed it among the great orations of history.

With respect to the Treaty two points had to be noted, One was that the Treaty was negotiated by the Allied and Associated Powers with Germany alone, and that Treaties had still to be negotiated with Austria, Bulgaria, and Turkey ; the other was that China had declined, alone of the Allied and Associated Powers, to sign, her action being the result of what she considered the injustice of the Supreme Council in giving to Japan all the rights the Germans had held in Kiao-Chau and Shantung. It was plain that troublous times were still ahead, as was shown by the fall of the Orlando Ministry in Italy, and the fighting going on both in Europe and Asia.

On July 4th Mr. Lloyd George made his statement on the Treaty in the House of Commons, introduced the necessary Bills connected with the Treaty, and announced that the Allies had unanimously decided that William II. was to be tried by an Inter-Allied Tribunal sitting in London. On the 6th the King and Queen attended the Thanksgiving Service at St. Paul's Cathedral, and similar services were held in the churches of all denominations in the land. On July 10th President Wilson presented the Treaty to the American Senate, laying stress on the Covenant of the League of Nations as the solvent of difficulties, and declaring that it was a necessity for the new order of the world. On July 14th Paris celebrated the peace with great victory fêtes, marked by much enthusiasm. Marshals Foch, Joffre, and Pétain rode in a striking procession of troops, which included contingents from all the allied armies, the British contingent being commanded by Sir Douglas Haig.

But, as was natural, interest in the United Kingdom itself in the peace celebrations centred in the Victory March of British and allied troops through London on July 19th. The greatest military display ever seen in London, the march began at ten in the morning from the Albert Gate, Hyde Park, passed through the **Victory March in two capitals** Sloane Square and Belgrave Square districts into the Vauxhall-Kennington area, on the south side of the Thames, returned to the other side through Lambeth and the Westminster Bridge Road, thence reached Whitehall, where stood the cenotaph—the memorial erected " To the Glorious Dead," and reverently saluted—and next proceeded along the Mall to the Royal Pavilion, where stood the King and other members of the Royal Family, supported by many of the great men of the realm, the march coming finally to a halt at Hyde Park Corner. Leading the procession came the Americans, with General Pershing at their head ; next were Belgian soldiers, following their commander, General Bourremans. Two Chinese generals, Tang and Wan, succeeded, and close on them were the representatives of Czecho-Slovakia. The crowds cheered all these, but when next the French, with Marshal Foch and his Staff, appeared, the applause was tumultuous. After the French marched soldiers of Greece, Italy, Japan, Poland, Portugal, Rumania, Serbia, and Siam, the Serbians especially being heartily greeted.

Then came the British forces. First the Navy—officers and men all afoot. A great cheer went up for Admiral Beatty and his brother admirals, whose flags and those of the battle squadrons made an imposing display, and a continuous roar of cheering accompanied the bluejackets as they marched along. The men of the fringes of the Navy were there, too, and were duly acclaimed. And on the heels of the Navy was the Army, at whose head rode Field-Marshal Sir Douglas Haig. Followed the massed standards and colours of that wonderful and victorious Army, and then came the long lines of cavalry, artillery, and infantry, including gallant men from Canada, Australia, New Zealand, South Africa and other parts of the Empire. Last came a miscellany—Labour Corps, R.A.M.C., nurses, Tanks, and the Royal Air Force. A wonderful sight ! And as there were numerous bands, music was never wanting. London gave a magnificent welcome to the heroes. Throughout the country the day was celebrated with rejoicing. And so the curtain was rung down.

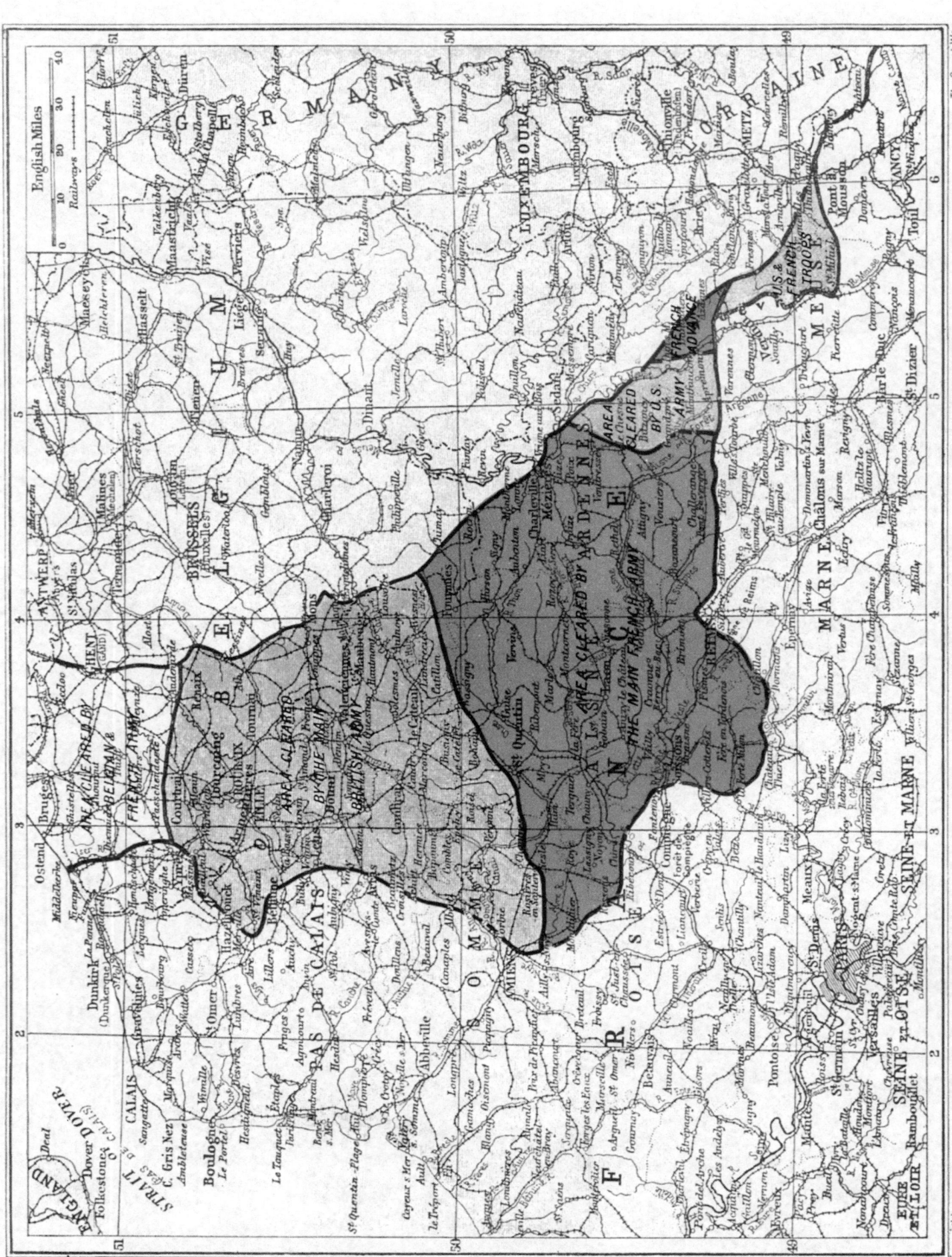

The Great War

TERRITORY RECOVERED BY THE ALLIED ARMIES ON THE WEST FRONT, JULY 18th to NOV. 11th, 1918.

In this map is clearly shown the area cleared by each of the Allies in the final triumphant advance which culminated in the collapse of the German armies and the signing of the armistice. British troops, it may be added, were in July and early August engaged in the French area near Soissons and Reims, though not in any great force.

Copyright.

PALACE OF VERSAILLES

CHAPTER CCCXX.

FROM THE GROUNDS.

HOW PEACE WAS MADE AT PARIS AND VERSAILLES.
By Edward Wright.

Two Months of Menacing Delay—President Wilson Fights Against Secret Treaties with Japan and Italy—British Sympathy with American View—League of Nations as Solution to Treaty Problems—President Wilson Opens Negotiations with Russian Bolshevists—M. Clemenceau's Success in Keeping Out Lenin's Delegates—Prince Feisul and the Struggle over Arabian Claims—M. Poincaré Adopts Wilsonian Programme of Peace—Attempted Assassination of M. Clemenceau—Conflict between United States and Japan over China—German Africa Handed over to Mandataries—Britain's Free Gift to Belgium—Mr. Balfour and Colonel House Induce President Wilson to Accept Japan's Terms—New Triple Alliance of France, Britain, and America—French Struggle for Saar Coal —Mr. Lloyd George Stands Against Polish Claim to Danzig—Scandal over Revelation of Conference Secrets—British Leadership in Making of Peace—Violent American and Italian Dispute over Eastern Adriatic—Italian Delegates Withdraw from Conference—Chinese Begin Agitation Against Japan—Bitter Contention over Arab and French Claims in Syria—British Consternation over Loss of Indemnity—Mr. Lloyd George as Master of Political Strategy—Americans Renew Negotiations with Bolshevist Russia—Opening of Peace Parley and Astonishing Attitude of Count Brockdorff-Rantzau—Allies Prepare to March to Berlin—Weimar Parliament Accepts Allies' Terms—Hohenzollern Empire is Buried in Its Birthplace at Versailles.

WHEN the Peace Conference opened in the Clock Room at the French Foreign Ministry in Paris, on January 18th, 1919, more than two months had passed since the signing of the terms of armistice with Germany. Disastrous as was the loss of time, the causes of the delay were still more menacing to the general interests of the war-wearied world. Profound differences between the Allied and Associated Powers had hindered the work of peacemaking. The long interval was vainly spent in preliminary discussions between the leading men of the victorious nations. No agreement could be made to serve as a basis for the rapid settlement of the main problems of Europe and Asia, and, as speeches by politicians and comments and reports by publicists revealed, there were two sharply-divided camps among the victors who met to shape the future of mankind.

It was the distinction of President Wilson to be the centre from which the main conflicts of opinions and interests radiated. Before the United States entered the war, Great Britain and France had made important concessions to Italy and Japan. In April, 1915, the Italian nation had been promised, by secret treaty, the possession of Teutonic land in Southern Tyrol and considerable territory peopled by the Southern Slavs in Dalmatia, besides the important Mediterranean dominating points of the Dodecanese Islands, of Greek population. Through Russian influence,

exercised on behalf of Serbia, the Adriatic port of Fiume had been exempted from Italian conquest in order that Southern Slavia should have the benefit of marine commerce. But the victorious Italians also claimed Fiume, and asked for coalfields in Asia Minor and extensions of territory in Africa.

In February, 1917, the Japanese Government obtained by secret treaty with Great Britain and France large interests in the rich Chinese province of Shantung, and exercised almost a dominating control over the policy of Northern China. By another secret treaty of 1916 the Rumanians acquired a general right over the finest wheatland in the world, the Banat, on the northern bank of the Danube opposite Belgrade, including territory peopled by the Serbs. There was also a secret treaty of 1917 between France and Russia, to which Great Britain was not a party, but this was happily invalidated by events. There was also a British-Arab treaty of 1915, which was not easy to reconcile with a British - French treaty of 1916. Finally, there was an understanding between the Western and Southern European Allies in regard to some of the Ottoman territory.

The American contention was that all secret treaties were abrogated by the terms of armistice with Germany. Furthermore, as the United States had been no party to the treaties and had generally entered the war without knowledge of them, President Wilson urged that his nation had

IN THE HALL OF MIRRORS AT VERSAILLES.
Busy scene at the gathering of the allied delegates in the Hall of Mirrors on June 28th, 1919, the day on which the German plenipotentiaries signed the Peace Treaty.

made such large contributions to the victorious issue, both by food and material supplies and by direct military and naval help, as to entitle the American people to some influence in the settlement of problems of territorial acquisition by European and Asiatic countries. The fact that the United States had suffered comparatively small loss in life, and had grown rich during the struggle that impoverished the European Powers, enabled the American people to take a generous view of the defeated countries and forgo territorial gains and indemnities. In

PRESIDENT AND PREMIER AT VERSAILLES.
In the central hall of the Trianon Palace at Versailles on the day that the terms of the Peace Treaty were presented to the German delegates. From left to right : President Wilson, Colonel House, General Bliss, Mr. Lloyd George (the British Premier), and Mr. Henry White.

regard to loss of life and strain on resources, the Japanese were in a position similar to that of the Americans. The war had enriched them and enlarged their field of power. The Japanese, however, were disinclined to a policy of disinterestedness, and intended to profit by the treaty with France and Great Britain, and move towards a mastery over China and a strong hold in the Northern and Southern Pacific. The Japanese policy was in direct conflict with American interests in the Pacific, yet honour bound Great Britain and France to the cause of Japan, against both the interests of their later Chinese and American allies. France and Great Britain were also in honour bound to the Italians, against the interests of their early allies the Serbs and their later allies the Greeks.

Italian and Japanese claims

In Italy, Signor Bissolati, the only leading statesman in the combatant nations who had fought in the trenches for many months before becoming a Minister, resigned from the Orlando Cabinet rather than take part in bringing Teutons of Tyrol and Dalmatians of Greater Serbia within the new frontiers of his country. In a remarkable speech at Milan on January 11th, 1919, Signor Bissolati attacked the secret treaty of 1915 and his countrymen's policy of annexation of Southern Slav, Tyrolean, and Greek lands. He suggested that Fiume, the great eastern Adriatic port, might be obtained by renouncing Dalmatia.

In Japan the frankly Imperialistic Government under Count

Okuma was succeeded by the first Cabinet under a commoner Prime Minister that had come into being in the country. It was thought that the new Premier, Mr. Hara, would be more democratic in home affairs than his predecessors and less bent upon bringing China virtually under Japanese control, and alarming Americans, Australians, and New Zealanders by enforcing claims over the Marshall and Caroline Islands in the South Pacific. There was, however, scarcely any change in the territorial ambitions of Italy and Japan.

The French also began to aspire to some German territory along the Rhine. The Saar coalfield was the immediate object of the French, but they had a grandiose plan for detaching practically all the Rhine basin from Prussia, helping the Rhinelanders to erect themselves into an independent State, inclining to friendship and alliance with France. In this plan Austria was also to be kept from uniting with Northern Germany, and it was hoped that Bavaria and other southern States would draw out of the Prussian system and enter into some combination with the Rhine basin and Austria.

The French scheme was designed for self-defence. With the help of Great Britain it could probably have been carried out by adjusting the apportioning of the war indemnities, opening immediate commerce with the separating States, and giving them other advantages over the Prussian part of the Germanic Empires. The French people on the whole were wonderfully tolerant, and their memories of the Westphalian kingdom of Napoleon would have made them gentle toward the Western Germans, who by their fertility would gradually have supplied the lack of children in twentieth-century France, as the Germanic stock of Alsace and Lorraine promised to do on a smaller scale. **French scheme for self-defence** The French believed they could hold, soothe, attract, and absorb the Western Germans, and, if the war had ended in complete success, without the entrance of the United States into the struggle, the French plan might have been carried out.

Italy then would have been given all the territory she asked for in the treaty of 1915, together with land in Asia Minor and probably Africa, so that she might become predominant in the Eastern Mediterranean and exert a balancing power beside an enlarged France. Great Britain in turn might have extended her possessions between Egypt and India and become the suzerain of the Turks, who were inclined to British protection and aid in developing the resources of their country.

On the other hand, British statesmen deeply sympathised with the main articles in the pacifying policy of President Wilson. Great Britain wanted lasting peace above everything else, and having no pretensions to annexing more land peopled by other European races, she was ready for considerable sacrifices, if these sacrifices were guaranteed to produce permanent settlement. France held the old Italian island of Corsica and the modern Italian territory round Nice, but gave no sign whatever of returning them to the Italians. Therefore the Italians pleaded, in regard to the Eastern Adriatic and the Greek islands off the Turkish coast, the same strategic necessities as the French urged with reference to Corsica and Nice and the British with reference to Gibraltar, Malta, and Cyprus.

Such were the problems for which solutions were vainly sought during nine weeks before the opening of the Peace Conference. President Wilson did all he could to induce the Italian Premier, Signor Orlando, and the Italian Foreign Minister, Baron Sonnino, to compromise on their claims to Southern Slav and Greek lands. He failed completely, and as France was relying on a new strategic frontier with a buffer State, rather than upon any League for maintaining perpetual peace, there was danger that the two Latin countries would draw together against the English-speaking countries.

Colonel House, as President Wilson's lieutenant, and Mr. Balfour, as chief lieutenant of Mr. Lloyd George, had to use all their fine skill in the arts of reconciliation to prevent an open breach being formed between the victorious nations. The dissensions, however, were so deep and notorious that the Northern Germans recovered the hope of emerging successfully from peace negotiations. Only by direct and overwhelming military threats was Marshal Foch able to keep the enemy

German delegates for receiving the Peace Treaty, at their table in the Trianon Palace, Versailles.

In the Hall of Mirrors at Versailles: Ready for the signing of peace on June 28th, 1919.

Germany's plenipotentiaries : 1. Prof. Schücking, 2. Herr
Giesberts, 3. Count Brockdorff-Rantzau, 4. Dr. Lansberg,
5. Herr Leinert.

Allies' representatives : 6. Sir R. Borden, Canada. 7. Sir J.
Ward, New Zealand. 8. Mr. G. N. Barnes, 9. Mr. Bonar Law,
10. Mr. A. J. Balfour, 11. Mr. Lloyd George, Great Britain.
12. M. Clemenceau, President, France. 13. President Wilson.
14. Mr. R. Lansing, 15. Mr. H. White, 16. Colonel House,
17. General Bliss, United States. 18. M. Pichon, 19. M. Klotz,
20. M. Tardieu, 21. M. J. Cambon, 22. Marshal Foch, France.
23. Signor Orlando, 24. Baron Sonnino, 25. Signor Crespi,
Italy. 26. M. Hymans, 27. M. Van den Heuvel, 28. M.
Vandervelde, Belgium. 29. M. F. Pessoa, 30. M. P. Calogeras,
31. Commandant Boulomaqué, Brazil.

Presenting the Terms of Peace to Germa

ric scene at Versailles, May 7th, 1919.

32. Chenting Thomas Wang, 33. Leo Tseng Tsiang, China. 34. M. de Bustamante, Cuba. 35. M. Joaquim Mendez, Guatemala. 36. M. Guilbaud, Haiti. 37. M. Bouilla, Honduras. 38. Mr. C. D. B. King, Liberia. 39. M. Chamorro, Nicaragua. 40. M. A. Burgos, Panama. 41. Prince Traidos Prabandhu, 42. Prince Charoon, Siam. 43. General Botha, 44. Lieut.-General Smuts, South Africa. 45. The Maharajah of Bikanir, 46. Lord Sinha, India. 47. M. R. Dmwoski, 48. M. Paderewski, Poland. 49. Senhor Affonso Costa, Portugal, 50. M. Pashitch, 51. M. Trumbitch, Serbia. 52. Marquis Saionji, Japan. 53. Mr. W. F. Massey, New Zealand. 54. Sir J. Cook, 55. Mr. W. M. Hughes, Australia. 56. Mr. A. L. Sifton, Canada.

Mr. Lloyd George signing the Peace Treaty, while the other members of the British Peace Delegation are filed up ready to append their signatures to the historic document. They are (from left to right): Mr. Bonar Law, Mr. A. J. Balfour, Lord Milner, Mr. W. M. Hughes, General Botha, and General Smuts. In the foreground are M. Dutasta, Secretary-General to the Peace Conference, and M. Arnavon, his co-secretary.

Britain's Prime Minister signing the Treaty of Peace with Germany in the Hall of Mirrors at Versailles, June 28th, 1919.

from reopening the war while the peacemakers in Paris were contending against each other, and national appetites were growing keener and larger, in the long, obscure, and troubled period of delay.

One important result of all the early, fruitless negotiations was that President Wilson succeeded in postponing the making of peace to the establishment of the League of Nations. The League was his solution for some of the chief difficulties in the annexation claims of France and Italy. This was one of the reasons why the Latin countries were not generally enthusiastic over the scheme for a League.

In general energy and special knowledge the British representatives were remarkable. Their chief, Mr. Lloyd George, however, compared neither with President Wilson in grasp of international law, nor with M. Clemenceau, Baron Sonnino, and many representatives of other States in vivid acquaintance with the ramifying complexities of European affairs. But he had good guidance. The British Foreign Minister, Mr. Balfour, was one of the masters of European diplomacy, and had been one of the directors of the old European Concert. Behind him were able men from the Foreign Office, Lord Hardinge and Sir William Tyrrell, with specialists for dealing with practically every affair of importance, and well-informed representatives of the great self-governing Dominions and India. British Labour was notably represented by Mr. Barnes.

The American representatives were distinguished more by open-mindedness than by special knowledge. President Wilson desired to establish in working order certain ideals, and in order to avoid the suspicion of being self-assertive, he left the planning of the League of Nations to the European Allies. In effect, President Wilson wished to act somewhat as the fosterer of the best ideas laid before the Conference. He therefore accepted the British plan for the League, as there was no other plan seriously challenging it. Thus, by simple hard work, Lord Robert Cecil and General Smuts became the authors of one of the most remarkable documents in the history of the human race. (See chapter on "The Founding of the League of Nations," page 295 of this volume).

Question of Russian representatives

Having come together in the actual work of making the Covenant of the League, the English-speaking nations endeavoured to find a way of making the Conference of Paris a universal affair by drawing in Russian representatives. Prince Lvov, Professor Miliukov, together with other leading men in the last Imperial and first Revolutionary Governments of Russia were assembled in Paris expecting to be entrusted entirely with the charge of Russian interests. They were, however, almost without power in their own country, and it was rather uncertain whether the Russian peasantry, having seized the landed estates of the aristocracy, would voluntarily accept the Russian statesmen in Paris as their leaders.

Through President Wilson, negotiations were opened with Lenin, Trotsky, and the Bolshevist rulers of Russia. It was reported that Mr. Lloyd George strongly supported the American President. With some difficulty, French and Italian statesmen were induced to agree to invite every organised group in European Russia and Siberia to send representatives to confer with leading men from the Associated Powers. There was to be a truce of arms among all Russian parties, and Princes' Island, in the Sea of Marmora, was appointed as the place of meeting between Bolshevists, Constitutional Democrats, Minority Socialists, and upholders of the old autocracy.

It was an extraordinary proposal, the Anglo-American idea underlying it being apparently that a purified and modified form of Soviet rule was probably the best thing for the Russian people in their circumstances. Scarcely had the decision been reached to invite the Bolshevists to the Conference than the scheme was wrecked by some of the men who had agreed to it. There was strange delay in sending the invitation to Moscow. It was belatedly delivered, unsigned, and with no impress of authenticity. Lenin and his Ministers seemed afraid they were being duped, and sent a wireless message to the extreme French Socialist, Jean Longuet, asking for information and advice. The French Government kept this

message back for a considerable time, and also refused to allow the Eiffel Tower wireless station to be used in despatching Longuet's reply.

An American journalist sent the reply as a piece of news to his country, and in roundabout fashion it reached the Moscow Soviet. The Bolshevists then agreed to meet representatives of other Russian parties and of the Associated Powers at the place appointed. Meanwhile, under French influence, the Russian statesmen in Paris declined to go to the meeting-place. Believing they were carrying out the secret desire of

THE "BIG THREE" AT VERSAILLES.
Mr. Lloyd George, M. Clemenceau, and President Wilson on their way to the Palace at Versailles for the signing of the Peace Treaty with Germany on June 28th, 1919.

the Allies by refusing to adopt the allied proposal, they declared they could not sit at the same table as the Bolshevists.

Mr. Lloyd George was attacked by some of the members of his Cabinet, Mr. Winston Churchill being especially eager to continue British operations against the Bolshevists. Mr. Lloyd George explained that he had supported President Wilson for the reason that the British Government doubted the truth of all the reports of Bolshevist atrocities, and wished to meet some of the leading Bolshevists, and, if possible, discover what was the actual state of affairs in Russia.

For good or ill, it was M. Clemenceau **French leaders'** and his Foreign Minister, M. Pichon, **change of view** who first agreed to the scheme for trying to end the war completely and then successfully worked against the proposal for including even Bolshevists in the Peace Conference. It was also strongly condemned by British public opinion. The mutinies that afterwards occurred among French soldiers and sailors sent to Odessa and the Black Sea to fight the Bolshevists, and the disorders that prevailed among other French troops who thought they were about to be sent to fight the Bolshevists, were disagreeable signs of a vague sympathy with Bolshevism even in France.

French African troops had mainly to be employed in anti-Bolshevist operations, and they were chiefly restricted to a passive watching rôle in the second Hungarian Revolution. The main burden of carrying out the Russian policy of the French bondholders fell upon British soldiers and sailors, and added greatly to the weight of British taxation. The Americans gave very little aid. The general effect of the Allies' uncertain Russian policy was strongly to increase German power and influence in both Communist Russia and Reactionary Russia, and again revive Teutonic hope of dominating the world by means of an understanding with Russia.

With regard to Russia, therefore, the Peace Conference was from the outset a failure. Peace was only to be given from Paris to part of the warring world, and grave difficulties faced the negotiators in avoiding the production of causes of new wars between Southern Slavs and Italians and between Chinese and Japanese.

There was considerable preliminary trouble in fixing the number of delegates allowed to each Power. In appearance the meeting in the Clock Room was a model of the Conference of the League of Nations. In reality the most powerful of victorious peoples—France, Great Britain, the United States, and Italy—exercised a governing influence so great that the later retirement of the Italian delegates made at the time no great difference in the main work of the representatives of the Atlantic nations. They adjudged the **Allotment of** number of seats allotted to each nation, **Conference seats** and began by giving Belgium fewer representatives than Brazil. The British were successful in obtaining representation for Canada, Australia, South Africa, New Zealand, India, and other parts of the Commonwealth.

The French were defeated in their counter-move to furnish delegates from Algeria, Cochin-China, and Morocco. Owing to strong Italian pressure, the Southern Slavs were refused a seat at the Conference, but room was found for other delegates from former Austrian territory, the Bohemians and Austrian Poles being ably represented.

The British also succeeded in obtaining a seat for the resurrected nation of Arabs, who sent Prince Feisul, the picturesque son of their new Sultan. The prince wanted the old Arab trading city of Damascus, while the French claimed Syria and also the desert city, and were worked up to a remarkable state of bitterness against Great Britain, who had created and armed the new **M. Poincaré's** Arab kingdom. In all some twenty-seven **splendid services** nations were represented in the assembly that met in the Clock Room of the French Foreign Ministry, at the Quai d'Orsay, on the forty-eighth anniversary of the proclamation of the Hohenzollern Empire at Versailles.

There was no spectacular effect in the scene of the Conference. The Clock Room was merely a large chamber in which persons calling on the Ministry of Foreign Affairs used to wait. It was remarkable for a clock of uncommon ugliness, and hangings of garish crimson set off with cream ; but it had the advantage of being large enough to accommodate the delegates and their secretaries and experts. The delegates sat at a large horse-shoe table, and their secretaries and special advisers were seated at smaller tables, while some two hundred and fifty journalists peered at the spectacle through the pillared arches of the ante-chamber. M. Poincaré, the greatest and quietest of all French Presidents, who shared with his famous kinsman, the mathematician, Henri Poincaré, the rare quality of genius, opened the Conference with a fine speech, marked by absence of rhetoric. There were thousands of politicians who could apparently speak better than Poincaré, who used no colour and little ornament and yet had more in common with Pericles and Demosthenes than had any contemporary orator. Throughout the war, M. Poincaré had been the incarnate mind of France, but the least known of

THE BRITISH PRIME MINISTER ADDRESSING AN EARLY MEETING OF THE MEMBERS OF THE PEACE CONFERENCE.
Gathering of the delegates of the Allies in the Clock Room of the French Foreign Office in January, 1919. Though there were complaints that the Conference was slow in settling the terms of the peace settlement which were to be dictated to Germany, it came to be recognised that the many conflicting interests to be reconciled made any really rapid progress impossible. In finding a way of conciliation among such conflicting interests the British Prime Minister, Mr. Lloyd George, who is here shown addressing his colleagues, proved particularly happy.

French leaders to the British and American peoples. Plain of face and unimposing in stature, he had gradually won his way through the gross corruption of plutocratic France to the position of Chief Magistrate. During the supreme crisis of the war he had mastered the sinister Caillaux group, that tried to use him as a weapon against Clemenceau, by forgetting his personal quarrel with the Vendèan and giving him power and loyal support.

In his speech to the first " Parliament of man," M. Poincaré showed that he was far more favourably inclined to regard the League of Nations as a practical scheme than was M. Clemenceau. He said to the delegates :

You will seek nothing but justice — justice that has no favourites, justice in territorial problems, justice in financial problems, justice in economic problems. Justice banishes the arbitrary exchange of provinces between States, as though people were but articles of furniture or pawns in a game. Gone is the time when diplomatists could meet and redraw with authority the map of empires on the corner of a table. If you are to redraw the map of the world, you will do so in the name of the peoples, on condition that you loyally interpret their thoughts and respect the rights of nations, little and great, to dispose of themselves, providing that they observe the equally sacred rights of racial and religious minorities.

In accordance with the fourteen propositions unanimously adopted by the Great Powers, you will establish a general League of Nations. This will be a supreme guarantee against any new attacks upon the rights of peoples. You do not intend this international association to be directed in future against anybody. Of set purpose it will not exclude any country, but having been formed by nations that have

DICTATING PEACE TERMS TO AUSTRIA.
Austrian delegates leaving the château at St. Germain after receiving the Peace Terms from the Allies, and (above) the meeting in the château, when M. Clemenceau addressed the Austrian delegates before handing over the Peace Terms to them on June 2nd, 1919.

sacrificed themselves to defend the right, it will receive from them its statutes and fundamental rules. Conditions will be laid down to which present or future adherents must submit ; and as the League will have as its essential aim the prevention of future war so far as is possible, it will endeavour to win respect for the peace settlement that you will establish.

President Wilson could not have spoken otherwise had he been asked to open the Conference. He found his most cherished ideas clearly set out by the President of the French Republic. It was a remarkable victory for the man who had exerted himself to the utmost of his energy to reduce the covenant to an accepted, practical thing. Between the American headquarters at the Hôtel de Crillon and the British offices in the Hôtel Majestic and Hôtel Astoria there was continual communication. The Americans compelled everybody to work harder. Many schemes were prepared, but none approached the British in completeness.

M. Léon Bourgeois, the French champion of the League, was urgent for the creation of an international police force to carry out the decisions of the common will. This proved much too complicated and dangerous an affair, as it invaded the sovereign rights of nations in a way likely to ruin the entire project. President Wilson was compelled for domestic reasons to oppose the establishment of a military Staff for the League. He had also to safeguard the Monroe Doctrine regarding European interference in Central and Southern

American affairs, and in turn he made concessions to foreign statesmen.

In February, President Wilson went to the United States with the first draft of the Covenant of the League, and Mr. Lloyd George travelled to England to deal with the wide and deep Labour unrest that threatened a national disaster. Only one of the three master figures of the Conference was left—M. Clemenceau—and he was struck down by the revolver of a young French anarchist, Cottin, while motoring to the Ministry of War on February 19th. M. Clemenceau had his shoulder pierced by a bullet, and, being nearly eighty years old, he was in danger of death. But after being kept on a low diet, with the bullet unremoved from his body, the vigorous old man recovered, and reduced the sentence on his attacker from the death penalty to ten years' imprisonment. During the interval at the Conference, caused by the absence of the leading men, a large number of Commissions divided the work of finding solutions for the problems of peace, and began to draw up reports on which the Supreme Council intended to come to decisions. The mental atmosphere of Paris became hot and stifling. The city was a hot-bed of infinite intrigues, movements, and counter-movements, making the Vienna of 1815 seem a quiet diplomatists' retreat.

At Paris in 1919 the problems of undoing the work of the Vienna Congress in regard to oppressed nationalities, and of righting the later wrongs done to France, Denmark, Italy, and the Balkan peoples, were complicated by universal difficulties. China was a more dangerous problem than even

Poland or Southern Slavia, in spite of the fact that French and Italian delegates were blind to the Oriental peril. During the war the French had been ready to give the Japanese practically everything they asked in return for strong military aid in Europe, and the Japanese had attempted by pressure in China to obtain all they wanted without sending an army to Europe.

While the United States stood out of the war, her leading men kept anxious watch over Japanese doings in China, and in the Marshall Islands and Caroline Islands, in the South Pacific. It was President Wilson personally who had finally induced the Chinese to enter the war on the side of the Allies at a time when Japan was reported to be striving strongly to prevent China from becoming a member of the Grand Alliance. The war had given the American nation the sea-power, military force, and equipment requisite for any struggle for mastery of the Pacific Ocean. And a friendly China was a permanent source of power for the maintenance of such mastery. In some of the territory which the Japanese had set themselves ultimately to win was the largest coalfield in the world, with iron ore lying beside the coal, and an abundance of the cheapest of intelligent labour. The Chinese themselves were pacific, and menaced the European and Northern American workmen only by their capacity for craftsmanship and their very low standard of wages.

Japan, on the other hand, was alert and aggressive, marching with wonderful strides in a generation from the conquest of Korea to the lordship of Manchuria, and beginning to envelop and penetrate the vast, disunited, helpless Chinese continent, apparently with a view to succeeding the Manchus as the governing, omnipotent Imperial clan. Alike from the point of economic interests and as a precaution of self-

GERMAN PEACE DELEGATES.
Four of the German delegates who went to Versailles to receive the Allies' Peace Terms at the beginning of May, 1919 : 1, Count Brockdorff-Rantzau ; 2, Herr Schücking ; 3, Herr Giesberts ; 4, Herr Melchior. Inset : Herr Bell (right), one of the German plenipotentiaries who signed the Peace Treaty, June 28th, 1919. The top photograph shows French and American soldiers watching some of the German delegates at Versailles in May returning from church.

defence, the United States could not permit Japan to reduce China to helotry.

The natural, fundamental Chinese peril was merely economic, and during the gradual training of millions of Chinese steel-makers and mechanics, who might threaten all high-living working classes of European stock with unemployment, there was likely to be ample time for readjustments. But the Japanese, with their astonishing swiftness in organisation and skilled energy in developing European methods of technique, might use the resources of China in a single generation in such a way as to make their position in the country almost impregnable.

Establishing the mandatory system

This was one of the reasons why President Wilson, while working on the Covenant of the League of Nations, vehemently pressed for the establishment of a mandatory system in the apportionment of German colonies and foreign possessions. In regard to Africa there was not any clear ground for giving the League the German possessions, and then designing South Africa, Great Britain, France, and Belgium as mandataries for the territories forming the spoil of war. To make the scheme logical and complete, all native Africa, in which there was no self-governing civilised people, should have been placed under the sovereignty of the League of Nations, with mandates to the Powers engaged in administering and developing the tropic treasure-house that Europe had seized. The Americans also could have put the Philippine Islands, Hawaii, and Cuba under the sovereignty of the League of Nations, and received a mandate to continue their work.

The partition of Africa, however, had occurred a generation before the war, and the use of the League in distributing the territories that Germany had acquired under Bismarck and Bülow was not of much importance. By a singular oversight, Belgium, whose forces had fought well in Central Africa, went unrewarded. The French, who owed the Belgians an incalculable debt, would not even yield the land which the victorious Congo troops had conquered from the common foe. The British were at first as grasping, but in characteristic fashion they had an attack of conscience afterwards, and, under the League, made a free gift of the best and most peopled provinces of East Africa to the Belgians. The gift was generous to an extreme degree, leaving East Africa almost wrecked, and hindering, through loss of land between Lake Tanganyika and Victoria Nyanza, Cecil Rhodes' scheme for a British Cape to Cairo railway. But as he who gives quickly gives double, so he who gives slowly gives half, and the joy in Belgium scarcely atoned for the disastrous British loss of linking territory.

The partition of German Africa was, however, followed by a prolonged dispute regarding the disposal of enemy possessions in China and the South Pacific. The Australians and New Zealanders received a mandate for what had been German New Guinea, German Samoa, and the islands south of the Equator. Then came the direct struggle between Japan and the United States over Shantung, the Marshall Islands, and the Caroline Islands. After the American victory over Spain the Caroline Islands had been hers to take, and also the Ladrone Islands, but she acquired only Guam, in the Ladrones, and was disconcerted when the Spaniards sold the other islands at a remarkably cheap price to Germany, and so placed a very menacing strong naval Power across the American Pacific trade route to the Philippines, Southern China, and India.

President Wilson, after months of fruitless discussion, was strongly inclined to use to the utmost the power he possessed at the Conference, and refuse to allow Japan to acquire Shantung. On this question he separated from Mr. Lloyd George and M. Clemenceau, and the Japanese delegates

GERMAN DELEGATES LEAVING VERSAILLES.
Count Brockdorff-Rantzau and his colleagues leaving Versailles after receiving the Allies' Peace Terms early in May, 1919. Above: Another view of the German delegates' departure.

countered by asking the French and British Governments to carry out the terms of their treaty of 1917. Early in that year the Japanese had sent destroyers and other warships to the Mediterranean to help in combating enemy submarines that had sunk some Japanese steamers. At the same time they had apparently lessened their pressure upon China, which had been overwhelming, and although this was done rather to quiet the Americans than to please the Western Allies, Japanese statesmen had managed to obtain in the 1917 treaty a forestalling advantage over President Wilson and his Cabinet.

The position of Great Britain became exceedingly difficult when America and Japan quarrelled. The Japanese delegation decided to retire from the Conference, and to call upon the British and French Governments to fulfil the treaty. The possible result might have been that Japan would have obtained all that she required from Great Britain and France, and that while the terms of the treaty were being carried out, the United States would have intervened as an independent and greatly interested third party. The American Fleet would have been concentrated in the Pacific, and with China in a fighting mood, the Western American States aflame, **Danger in the Pacific** and a new war spirit pervading the great Republic, the battle for the mastery of the Pacific Ocean might have opened while the universal Parliament to establish permanent peace on earth was still sitting.

Mr. Balfour, the British Foreign Minister, pleaded strongly with Colonel House, the confidential agent of President Wilson. Colonel House was at last convinced of the extreme danger of the situation, and in turn he won President Wilson to consent to the Japanese demands. Later in the year the strong Republican Party in the American Senate, during the

flagrant contradiction with the propaganda that French and Italians had maintained for more than a generation in regard to their own lost lands. M. André Tardieu, formerly foreign editor of "Le Temps," a French plenipotentiary of brilliant talent and deep knowledge of the minds of the English-speaking peoples, happily came forward as moderator. He was one of the best-informed Frenchmen of the new generation, appreciating keenly the · future course of events. To an alliance between France, Great Britain, and the United States, with the Channel Tunnel in working order, and the American mercantile marine increased sevenfold beyond its former size, he was passionately attached. To his doubting countrymen he pointed out that for the next fifteen years Germany would

discussions preliminary to the ratification of the Covenant of the League of Nations and the Treaty of Peace with Germany, refused to pass the concession of Shantung, and endeavoured to make over German territory and interest in China to the Chinese. Once more, therefore, the shadow of another great war hung over the world. The plans for the tremendous increase of the American Navy and the establishment of a permanent system of conscription in the United States were frankly and directly inspired by suspicion of Japan.

President Wilson became the most worried of the great leaders of the Conference. When he returned from his country, bringing back the draft of the Covenant, he seemed to have lost his buoyancy and vehement crusading spirit. He was the dreamer of a great dream who had knocked against some sharp, perilous actuality. He had not lost his dream and become a cynic. He was made of too good a texture of character for that, but he saw at last that he could no longer hope to mould Europe into a new way of life, as once he had hoped to do. Europe was no longer the most dangerous problem on earth. His own country was menaced by what seemed to many Americans an Imperialism directed by an ancient military caste that was more patient, subtle, and foresightful than the German nobility had

Triple Alliance of the West been. Against defeated Germany an alliance between France, Great Britain, and the United States favoured the two European Powers. The Americans were able to regard the matter with a kind of disinterested generosity. But in looking across the Pacific Ocean to the vast multitudes of hard-working, hard-living Chinamen, still ignorant of the enormous mineral wealth of their immense country, and studying the plans that had been clearly disclosed in the Japanese Press of 1915 and 1917, thoughtful Americans began to consider whether a new Triple Alliance between the conquerors of the Germans would not serve their interests even more than European interests, and become a main guarantee for peace.

M. Clemenceau was alert to the profound change in the situation. The weakness of his wounded body only seemed to make his extraordinary mind more active. Under the influence of Marshal Foch he proposed that France should be established in a position of permanent strength by the annexation of the left bank of the Rhine and some seven million Teutons, who could be transformed into friends. The Italian delegates were ready to support this measure, provided they had their way against the Serbian and Croatian stock along the Eastern Adriatic coast. Neither President Wilson nor Mr. Lloyd George, however, would consent to such a transformation of the Franco-German position. They refused to allow France and Italy to create a Germania Irredenta in

AT VERSAILLES, MAY 7TH, 1919.
Arrival of Marshal Foch at the Trianon Palace, Versailles, on the day on which the Allies' Peace Terms were handed to the German delegates, and (above) M. Clemenceau leaving the Palace at the close of the proceedings.

possess 120,000 reserve officers and some 5,000,000 trained soldiers, and that friction in the Rhine area might provoke a renewal of the secular struggle between Teuton and Gaul.

For more than a month M. Clemenceau, Mr. Lloyd George, and President Wilson, with their Foreign Ministers and military chiefs, contended over the Rhine problem. The French would not give way, but they were as firmly opposed by the British as by the Americans. In the end Mr. Lloyd George, who was becoming the leader of the Conference, found, with the help of Mr. Balfour, a natural solution. He won President Wilson over to a defensive alliance between the three Powers, and, on March 14th, 1919, he and President Wilson made the proposal that Great Britain and the United States should come to the aid of France in the event of a German attack. When this new union was accepted there was a dispute regarding the way in which the German Army should be restricted. The French wished for the maintenance of the German system of conscription on domestic French grounds. The British Government, on the other hand, wished to abolish obligatory military service in Germany on domestic British grounds. As a small professional army promised to provide the enemy with fewer trained soldiers, the British plan was adopted. This enabled Mr. Lloyd George to prepare to abandon conscription in Great Britain, but France and the United States maintained it.

When the principal question of the western frontier of Germany was settled, there remained the Saar coalfield problem. The French delegates hoped, at least, to obtain the Saar mining region as a consolation prize, after relinquishing the German left bank of the Rhine. Once more, however, the delegates of the English-speaking nations combined in opposition to the French claim, which was supported by some of the other delegates. Mr. Lloyd George, who had no knowledge of the Saar, had British experts to teach him all there was to know, and to him the fact that the region was then peopled by Germans decided the question. The utmost that he and President Wilson

AFTER A GREAT OCCASION.
Signor Orlando and (above) Mr. Lloyd George leaving the Trianon Palace after the handing over of the Allies' Peace Terms to the German delegates at historic Versailles on May 7th, 1919.

could allow their ally was to take a short occupation of the Saar coalfield as compensation for the enemy's destruction of the Lens mines, which could not be restored to working order for some years. At the end of the period of occupation the population of the Saar district was to vote for absorption into France or return to Germany.

It must be admitted that the French delegates were absorbed in the contemplation of their ruined provinces, weakened people, and emptied exchequer. Belgium, who had first met and checked the invader, and been almost completely overrun, and seen her little children perishing for years by famine, and her machinery of production broken or taken away, attracted very little active sympathy from France.

The French were ready to press their claims even against Belgium for the possession of the ironfield Duchy of Luxemburg. This was an old part of Belgium, lost through Prussian intrigue at the end of the Napoleonic Wars, and in the later successful rising of the Belgians against the Dutch. Belgium's claims remained unsettled after the peace with Germany was made. Although she had acted as the shield of the Western Allies, she was sadly neglected at the Conference of Paris.

Meanwhile, Poland attracted general attention, for the reasons stated in Chapter CCCXVIII. (page 485 of this volume).

The French delegates inclined to favour the Poles in every possible way, as a further insurance against Teutonic aggression. President Wilson, having spoken during the war on the need for giving outlets to the sea to the new States of Europe, was inclined to make Danzig a Polish seaport at the end of the Vistula corridor. But Mr. Lloyd George was hostile to the claims of the Poles. The British Foreign Office expert, Sir Eyre Crowe, endeavoured to overcome his chief's objections by arranging to narrow the seaward corridor. With his consent the Polish Commission unanimously decided to return Danzig to Polish suzerainty such as had obtained in the Middle Ages after the First Battle of Tannenberg.

To the consternation of the Conference, Mr. Lloyd George rejected the recommendation of Sir Eyre Crowe, who had signed the articles of agreement as member of the Polish Commission. The British Prime Minister had succeeded President Wilson as the incarnation of international justice. He definitely refused to be bound by Sir Eyre Crowe, and fought on single-handed until he made his view prevail. Danzig became a city of the League of Nations, serving both as a German connection between Central Germany and Eastern Prussia, and as the Baltic port for Polish commerce.

Some angry French member of the Conference communicated an outline of the incident to the French Press, and there were severe criticisms of the part that Mr. Lloyd George had played. Thereupon **Leakage of** Mr. Lloyd George astonished all foreign **information** delegates by a violent explosion of anger. He denounced the leakage of information, and threatened to retire from the Conference unless the person who had inspired the French Press was discovered and reprimanded.

As a matter of fact, one of the fourteen points of President Wilson's programme of peacemaking had been that all covenants should be openly arrived at. It had, therefore, been expected that the Conference would deliberate in public. The United States had sent some two hundred and fifty newspaper men to describe the historic proceedings, and the British Press was amply represented, together with other allied journalists and publicists from the keenly interested world of neutrals.

But two months of preliminary discussions had revealed such deep and determined conflicts of views and interests among the Associated Powers that secrecy in all-important deliberations seemed an urgent necessity. Had it not obtained, the peoples would have turned some of the diplomatic disputes into violent national quarrels, and in one or more cases there would have been danger of acute inflammation of popular temper provoking withdrawals from the Conference—such as happened in the case of Italy—and perhaps an outbreak of

La Galerie des Glaces
du Chateau de Versailles

Mr Lloyd George with his humble duty to Your Majesty has the honour to announce that the ~~great~~ long & terrible war in which the British Empire has been engaged with the German Empire for more than four years & which has caused such suffering to mankind has been brought to an end this afternoon by the Treaty of Peace just signed in this hall.

He desires on behalf of all the Plenipotentiaries of Your Majesty's Empire to tender their heartfelt congratulations to Your Majesty on the signature of a Treaty which marks the victorious end of the terrible struggle which has lasted so long & in which Your Majesty's subjects from all parts of the Empire have played so glorious a part

D Lloyd George

June 28th 1919 4 p.m.

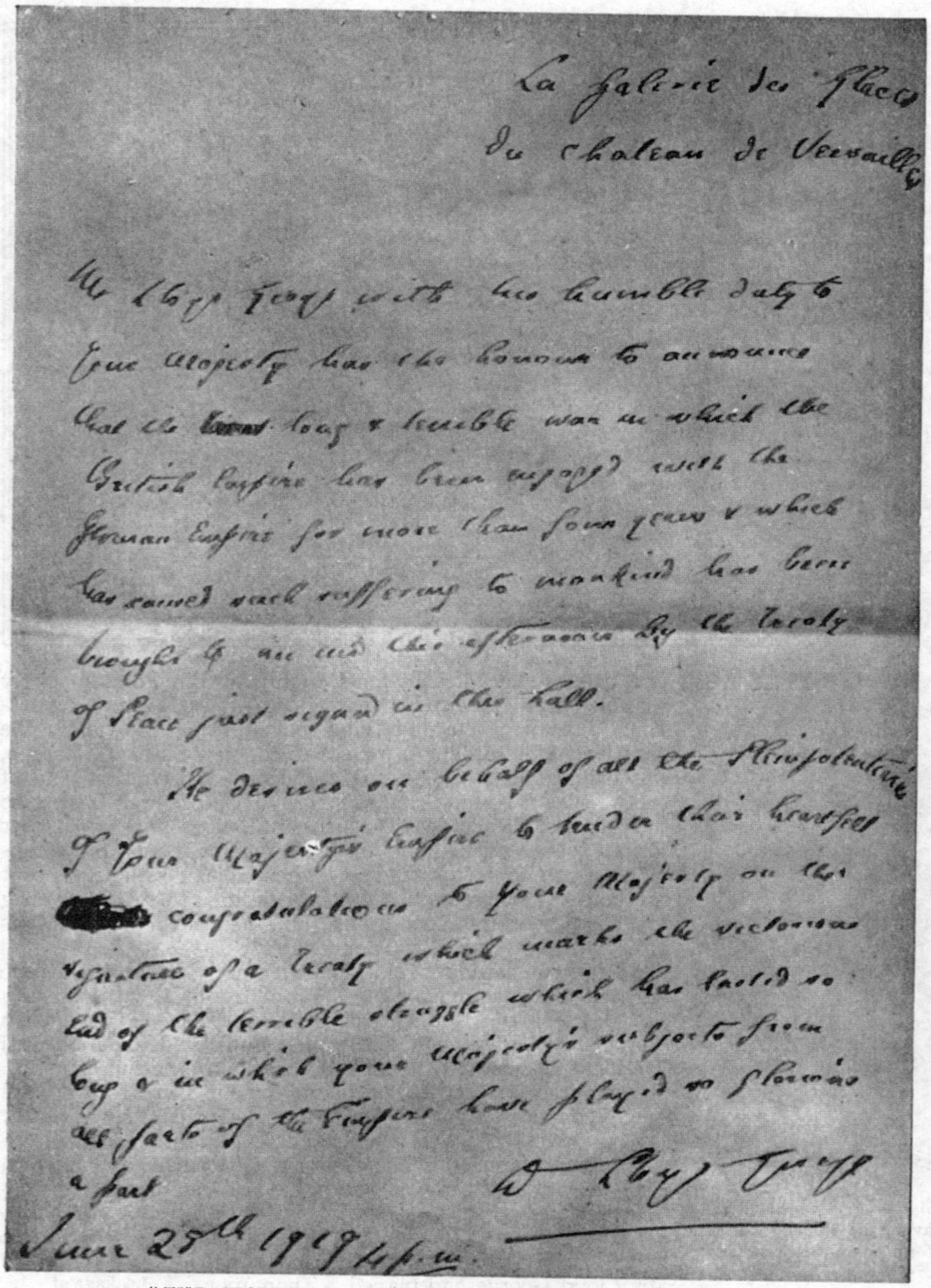

"THE VICTORIOUS END OF THE TERRIBLE STRUGGLE."
Facsimile of the letter to King George sent by Mr. Lloyd George, the British Prime Minister, immediately after the signing of the Peace Treaty with Germany on June 28th, 1919. The letter was sent from Paris to London by aeroplane.

war. In regard to the clash of interests between the United States and Japan, President Wilson recognised that covenants making for peace could not be openly arrived at by anything like a frank and full discussion in public of underlying difficulties.

Private diplomatic debate, lasting for more than half a year, was required to solve merely the problems of a peace settlement with Germany, leaving outstanding the reconciliation of Italians and Southern Slavs, the fate of the Ottoman Empire, decisions on disputed territory in the Balkans, and the Allies' general policy towards Bolshevist Russia.

There were, however, so many men of different stations taking large and small parts in the Conference and its Commissions that little veritable secrecy obtained. Great at times was the temptation for some lieutenant of a statesman, disappointed at not getting some idea accepted, to produce in the Press of his country a strong movement of disapproval of the course which the Conference seemed to be wrongly taking. With revelations made in anger by important personages, hints thrown out by secretaries, reports collected by interested national groups, and rumours started both loosely and deliberately, the gossiping annals of the Conference became one of the supreme marvels of the human mind. The Press observed a certain discretion, and the British Press in particular was loyal to both national and general interests. When, however, anything seriously went wrong, the news oozed from hotel to hotel and salon to salon, and there is little doubt that the espionage system of the enemy made him quickly acquainted with the secrets of the Conference.

Of the five master men in Paris, all except M. Clemenceau threatened at various times to withdraw from the Conference. President Wilson ordered his steamer the Washington, Mr. Lloyd George was ready to go back to London, Baron Makino prepared to leave for Japan, and Signor Orlando left for Rome. This was evidence enough of the extraordinary division of opinions and interests. Perhaps from one point of view it was as well that the Germans were not so crushed as to be unable to maintain against the Associated Powers the menace of a renewal of the war beside Russian and Hungarian Bolshevists.

In ultimate effect the Germans steadied what they intended to shake. Fear of them and of their universal intrigues preserved in the French a fund of soberness beneath a surface of excitement, and usually Mr. Lloyd George and his Ministers and officials acted as fly-wheel to all the racing machinery of national ambitions, jealousies, and apprehensions in the Conference, while President Wilson and his lieutenants served as brake.

The turn of events made the representatives of the British commonwealth of nations the most dispassionately impartial grand force in the Clock Room. The British system was already a little league of nations in being, and with the surrender of the German Navy and the creation of a mightily weaponed Commonwealth Army, it was in no danger of attack. Great Britain had played a considerable part in the development of the power of Japan, and did not fear a Mongolian mastery of the Pacific so keenly as did the United States and Australia. The proposed creation of a prepotent American Navy did not disturb the mind of the Briton. He came out of the war with great loss of life and waste of wealth, and the acquisition of more tropic land in which white men could not breed was no compensation to him as Alsace-Lorraine was to the Frenchmen and redeemed Italian lands and coveted Slav territory were to the Italians. Of all the great victorious Powers, Britain had permanently suffered most. She had as little cause of rejoicing in victory as a well-to-do middle-aged man would have if, when suddenly assailed by a foot-pad, he succeeded in killing his enemy at the cost of having to lay up for a year. Britain had escaped with her life and had learnt to put forth every ounce of sound power in her, but she was bruised, tired, and impoverished, and when she again set to work in peaceful ways, she could not equal her productiveness of 1913.

How Britain had suffered

She said little about her sufferings, but through the prestige and influence of her leaders she led the Conference. The main effort of her representatives was to make Germany surrender the territories of oppressed races, without giving the Teutons any just inspiration for the idea of another war of liberation. Though overthrown, the Germans were patient, tenacious, fertile, hard-working. Only by dealing justly with them could they be slowly brought, perhaps in the course of a generation to acquiesce in the enforced peace settlement. All that the strong Reactionary party in Germany wanted, to pull the nation together for another effort extending, if necessary, over a century, was a Germania Irredenta. By means of this they would be able to prove the cynical hollowness of all the oratory of the leaders of the Western democracies.

Germany escaped disruption, but the principle of the self-determination of peoples was modified in the French interests by the Associated Powers forbidding Austria to unite with Germany. This was one of the moves that helped to produce another crisis at the Conference. As the Austrians were hindered by British and Americans from confederating with the Catholic populations of the Rhine basin and Bavaria, and debarred by France from entering a general Teutonic union, an attempt was made to form a Danube economic league out of the fragments of the Hapsburg Empire.

Future of Austria This would have enabled Austrian urban labour and peasant craftsmen to keep their own old markets and earn sufficient money to purchase coal from Bohemia, wheat from Hungary, and bacon from Serbia. But the Italian delegates were alarmed at the Danubian scheme. They contended that it would leave them overshadowed by a more formidable neighbour than Austria-Hungary had been. There was certainly, as things then stood, some danger of Middle Europe and Slavic Balkania combining with Magyars and Austrians, in the course of a generation, to restrict the extended military and commercial power of Italy.

Many Serbs, Dalmatians, Bosnians, Croats, and Slovenes appeared to be ready to form alliances against Italy. The Serbian Premier, M. Pashitch, did not follow the popular movement. He wanted no confederation with the kinsmen and neighbours of the Old Serbs, and was apparently somewhat indifferent to Italian claims to Fiume and Dalmatia. But the younger generation of Serbs was enthusiastic for the creation of Jugo-Slavia, and bitterly angry with the Italians. In the new dominions to which they aspired the Italians could find little of the coal and iron they needed to give their engineering genius full play. Their new opponents were much better provided, and if all Slavs of Middle Europe made common cause in the future **Italians and** in a battle for an outlet to the Slav- **Slavs** peopled coast of the Adriatic, Italy would have been compelled to rely on her mercantile marine and her comparatively small financial power to stay the march of the retrievers of a Slavia Irredenta.

The Italians began to support the Austrians in the scheme for union with Germany. This was done to put pressure on France in the days when the French were definitely inclining towards the new Triple Alliance with the United States and Great Britain. President Wilson remained resolutely on the side of the Southern Slavs in the quarrel over Fiume and the Eastern Adriatic. Baron Sonnino, the Italian Foreign Minister, who was the grand Imperialist of his country, and Signor Orlando, who became Premier after the Caporetto reverse, proved to be as determined as was the American President. They fostered in their country an impassioned propaganda for annexation beyond the territory promised by the French and British Governments in the treaty of 1915. There were some dangerous incidents, French soldiers being attacked by Italian troops at Fiume, and little local struggles occurring between Italians and Southern Slavs. There was also trouble in working the Fiume line of supplies through Croatia to the inland Slav lands, and this served to convince the American Mission that Fiume was an absolutely necessary gate of commerce for the Southern Slavs.

As a matter of fact, the Slav people inhabited all the Eastern Adriatic from the Isonzo River to the Albanian highlands.

THE FRENCH PRESIDENT AT BELGIUM'S PEACE CELEBRATION.
President Poincaré in Brussels on the occasion of the celebration in the Belgian capital of the signing of the Peace Treaty. He arrived on the evening of July 21st, 1919, and one of his first acts was to journey on foot to lay a wreath on the cenotaph erected in honour of the dead on the Rue Royale side of the Parc. On the following day he was present at the Belgian Victory Review, and met with a great reception.

MEN OF 1914 IN THE VICTORY MARCH OF 1919.
Survivors from Britain's "contemptible little Army" of 1914 that helped to dam the flood of Prussian militarism in the hour of the world's great danger. They formed a special feature of London's great Victory March in July, 1919, and were fittingly acclaimed by the crowds that thronged the routes.

In the Middle Ages the enterprising Venetians established trading towns in Dalmatia, and held the country against the Turks, while treating the Slav highlanders like inferiors. The Venetians did not win Trieste, which remained an insignificant place until it was developed by the Austrians in direct rivalry against Venice. Fiume was also developed by the Hungarians as a sea outlet for the trade of their country and Croatia and Slavonia.

The Dalmatian fisher-folk had provided man-power in turn for the Venetian fleet, the Austro-Hungarian Navy, and the mercantile marine. The Italian element had increased in number in the coast towns of Southern Slavia. In Fiume they almost outnumbered the Slavs in the neighbouring suburb, but when the population of the Eastern Adriatic country was considered as a whole, the Italians formed generally small and segregated minorities. President Wilson remarked that there were more Italians in New York than in any city of Italy, but he did not see that was a reason why New York should be claimed by the House of Savoy.

Strategic necessity was the only sound basis for the Italian claim to Fiume, Dalmatia, and most of the Adriatic islands. The British possession of the strategic point of Malta, and the French possession of the strategic point of Italian Corsica, formed the real foundation of the claim upon outer Serbs and their fellow-countrymen. France and Great Britain had no answer to angry Italian complaints. They had injured Serbia at a time when the Serbians were fighting unaided against tremendous odds, but they had done this in the general interests of the Allies, hoping to help Serbia by bringing the war more quickly to an end, as well as to benefit themselves in the same way. But the fact that land belonging to the Serbian and related stock had been bartered away without the consent of the Serbian Government added another difficulty to the problem.

The Italians did not rest quietly under Serbian and Southern Slavian political attacks. They sought out every dissentient group in Jugo-Slavia, and were particularly successful in fostering the strength of King Nicholas' party in Montenegro. There were strong allegations that the Italians interfered with the movements of some Jugo-Slav leaders, and even put some of them in

prison, and some of the Maltese began to agitate for reunion with Italy.

Mr. Hoover's agents in the distribution of food to the starving people took to listening to complaints. It was no part of the Americans' business to take up political work, but from the Baltic to the Adriatic their vitally important work led them to secluded regions that the military and political missions of the Council of Versailles never reached. The American food suppliers were also brought more intimately in touch with the working people, and so learnt more about the true direction and strength of popular feeling than any Britons or Frenchmen.

In regard to some countries, Mr. Hoover practically became, by means of his network of agents and their stream of reports, the chief settlement officer for the English-speaking delegates at the Paris Conference. The love the Belgian nation bore him for his early work in food administration, that kept them alive, was supposed to be balanced by the dislike he aroused in Italy and in Rumania. They said he upheld the cause of the Magyar peasant against the Rumanian armies and the Southern Slavs against the Italians in some of the disputes over the Eastern Adriatic.

Dissatisfaction and unrest in Italy

He was feared in Italy in a way that made for frenzy. Some members of the Italian Government thought that Mr. Hoover would enforce his President's views by refusing to supply the Italians with food and raw material, and thus virtually establish an economic blockade. There was a considerable portion of the Italian people moving towards a dangerous state of unrest, and ready to attempt a Communist Revolution if a good opportunity offered. There was also a still powerful group of politicians of the old school, with a certain business-like kind of patriotism, who held that Baron Sonnino had seriously injured the country by entering the

SOLDIERS AND NURSES FROM SOUTH AFRICA.
Contingent of soldiers and nurses representing South Africa taking part in the great military spectacle with which London on July 19th, 1919, celebrated the end of the war. Representatives of the Overseas Dominions received hearty acclamation from the vast crowds assembled.

war against the Central Empires, and by helping strongly to overthrow them, thus leaving Italy wasted and impoverished, overshadowed by France, and with a new enemy of strong character in Jugo-Slavia.

Signor Orlando and Baron Sonnino became so uncertain of their position at home that they could not abate their claims. In their view the Italians had either to renew the Imperial traditions of Venice or fall headlong into the chaos of Bolshevism. They pointed out to the French delegates that, if Italy were driven to follow the example of Hungary, the temper of restless Southern France was such as to make for trouble throughout Western Europe.

Still President Wilson would not give

THE HEROES OF FRANCE GO BY.
French troops with their war-worn colours passing the Royal Pavilion on the great march of allied troops through London in celebration of peace, and (above) another view of the French contingent.

He pointed out that the enemy against whom the treaty was directed no longer existed, and that the liberated nations of the Eastern Adriatic were friends who were about to enter into the League of Nations. He insisted that Fiume was the outlet of the commerce of Jugo-Slavia, Hungary, Bohemia, and Rumania, and did not form an integral part of Italy. He also denied any strategic necessity regarding the Italian seizure of Dalmatia and many of the Eastern Adriatic islands.

Signor Orlando, Baron Sonnino, and other Italian delegates left the Conference. Italy rocked in an uproar. The Italian leaders professed that their people would withstand even the pressure of famine if the United States withdrew food supplies. This, however, was a flourish of rhetoric, for the plan of the Italian Ministers was to strengthen themselves in power by exciting popular patriotism, and then quietly to moderate their demands and negotiate a settlement. But Signor Orlando was unable to execute successfully his domestic strategy. He fell under the attack of a combination of Imperialists, Socialists, and Giolittists. The first attacked him because he had failed, and disappointed their hopes; the second assailed him because he had not **Complications** adopted the views of President Wilson; **at the Conference** and the third overthrew him because they were eager for office and power. Signor Nitti succeeded Signor Orlando, Baron Sonnino was compelled to resign, and under the astute direction of the old master politician of Italy, Signor Giolitti, who followed his customary method of exercising control without occupying any office, Italy continued for months to be antagonistic to the American programme.

Meanwhile, the Conference was in a condition of dismay and disorganisation. The German delegates had been summoned to attend at the end of April. It seemed there would be few Great Powers to receive them. For Baron Makino and other Japanese delegates used the Italian trouble as a means of enforcing their first large measure for the subjugation of China. Baron Makino threatened to follow the example of Signor Orlando and withdraw. The Chinese delegates would have been glad if this event had happened, as a considerable number of their immense population was ready for a fight for life with the Japanese, in spite of the military weakness of China, because of the practical assurance of obtaining some kind of American support. President Wilson, whom the Italians had excited into a mood of flaming combativeness, was personally eager to

way. At times he was so tired and disillusioned that he thought of retiring from the Conference. Then it was the turn for M. Clemenceau and Mr. Lloyd George to grow alarmed. Such was the unrest in Britain and France, fostered by enemy influences as well as by the strain of war and the new wealth spread partially among the employing and working classes, that the abrupt retirement of President Wilson might have brought about disaster to the structure of Europe. It might have led to the triumph of Germany, as well as to dire domestic trouble among the Western Allies.

President Wilson became once more master of the Conference in April, 1919. He used his power to insist on an abatement of Italian claims. The Italian Ministers would not yield. They reckoned they possessed one means of enforcing their views. Peace with Germany could not be made without Italy's acceptance and ratification. This point of view was perhaps based on diplomatic convention rather than upon the realities of the situation. The United States had but to make a separate peace with Germany and the Allies would be in danger. The crisis was **President Wilson** precipitated by the report that the Italian **and Fiume** Press was publishing news that Fiume had been definitely annexed.

There were movements of Italian troops pointing to this act of revolt against the Peace Conference. The Italian Ministers were apparently determined to confront President Wilson with an accomplished fact, but he was quick to make the first open stroke. In characteristic fashion he addressed the Italian people apart from their elected Government, claiming that the treaty between Great Britain, France, and Italy had been abrogated by the entrance into the war of many other Powers, great and small, which had no knowledge of the secret treaty.

American interference with their plans, together with the active resentment which the Chinese showed and the Koreans endeavoured to show, did not fully awaken them to an appreciation of the realities of the balance of power in the world in 1919.

The Peace Conference resolved itself into a whirl of quarrels. Poles argued and contended against Bohemians, Ukrainians, and Lithuanians. Serbs, Croats, and Greeks contended against Italians. Japanese manœuvred against Americans. Rumanians were bitter against Serbs, Americans, and Britons, and finally there arose a dispute of a dangerous sort between France, Arabia, and Great Britain. In a treaty of 1915 the British agent in Arabia, Colonel

back the cause of the Chinese, and, after letting the Japanese retire, intervene against the fulfilment of the secret treaty between Great Britain, France, and Japan, but, as already related, French and British diplomatists, whose predecessors had given Japan what they had no right to give, succeeded in convincing President Wilson that a great war in the Orient must be avoided. Yet although the agreed Terms of Peace made the German rights in Shantung over to the Japanese, peace in the Far East was not assured.

Throughout the Chinese ports there began a boycott of Japanese trade which seriously alarmed all Japanese merchants and manufacturers. The Chinese had successively lost to their island neighbours the overlordship of Korea, Kwantung, and Shantung. Shantung was the native country of Confucius, so that the loss of Shantung

ALLIES FROM THE FAR EAST.
Officers of the Japanese contingent saluting King George as they passed the Royal pavilion in London's Victory March of allied troops, and (above) General Tang at the head of the Chinese contingent.

to the Chinese hurt the religious feeling of the people of the most ancient of existing civilisations. Moreover, with her new possession and Korea and Kwantung, Japan enveloped and enclosed the country of which Peking was the centre. This was far from being all. The Japanese openly intended to bring all China under their rule, and with the Japanese-trained Chinese Army establish and enforce a Monroe Doctrine in the Orient.

The strange thing was that the Japanese regarded themselves as the noblest of champions of Asiatic interests. They appeared, indeed, to be blankly astonished when Koreans and Chinese attacked them and appealed for aid to Washington and Paris.

As a matter of fact, modern Japan had been largely modelled upon Prussia, possessing a similar kind of military oligarchy, working under a similar imitation of democratic institutions and possessed by a spirit of high-handed courage and immense ambitions of conquest. When the Western Allies had seemed, from the standpoint of Tokio, likely to lose the war, the Japanese had begun to veer towards the Germans, while preparing the campaign for the subjugation of China. Some French politicians had then been ready to give Cochin-China to the Japanese in return for aid of an army in Europe. Although Great Britain held a steadier course, she granted her Far Eastern ally concessions in the Pacific Ocean by a treaty that was afterwards abrogated.

All these events had increased in the Japanese an already acute sense of their superiority. They believed themselves to be potential masters of the larger part of Asia, and the

Ambition of the Japanese

Lawrence, arranged with the Sherif of Mecca for the establishment of a Kingdom of Arabia independent of Turkey. There were long and difficult negotiations with the princes of Arabia, and some Arab leaders, within reach of Ottoman German forces, remained on the enemy side. But the Kingdom of Arabia was recreated, so as to include Damascus and other Arab centres by the Mediterranean.

Sir Mark Sykes as agent of the British Foreign Office in 1916 arranged another secret treaty with France, giving the French Syria and cities that the new Arabian Power justly claimed by right of nationality. About the same time the Italians were given rights over Turkish-peopled parts of Turkey and some coastland of Asia Minor in which the Greek element was strong.

It must be remembered that, in 1915, Tsarist Russia had enforced upon France and Great Britain a claim to Constantinople, which she lacked power, in continually increasing degree, to conquer. Her vainly ambitious pretensions moved France to make far-reaching claims from Syria to the northern end of Mesopotamia, at the time when the Dardanelles expedition had failed.

Owing to General Allenby's extraordinarily complete victories, these treaties had now to be carried out. Russia was in no position to ask for the fulfilment of the arrangement regarding Constantinople, but Italians and Greeks clamoured for their share of Turkey, and France wanted Syria and the vilayets of Adana, Diarbekr, and Mosul. But Prince Feisul, son of the King of the Hedjaz, the most romantic personage at the Conference, put in his earlier title under the 1915 treaty, and met M. Clemenceau stubbornly in private debate.

But it was not on his debating powers that Prince Feisul relied. He had an excellent army, trained by British officers and towering in spirit with victorious experience of war. There was an abundance of arms and ammunition in Arabia, with which large additional forces could be raised. The prince held out against M. Clemenceau for Arab independence, and, returning to Damascus, found that an underground war had started, and sided with the strong movement against France. At the same time, Prince Feisul and his Royal father held Great Britain in honour bound by the 1915 treaty. The Turkish Committee of Union and Progress began to work in the interests of Arabia, in a way that promised internal peace in the Moslem world, by a reconcilement between the Ottoman Caliph and the Royal Mecca descendant of the Prophet. French Staff officers estimated that 100,000 of their best troops might be engaged for two years in a war against the Arabs for the conquest of Syria, with a possible renewal of trouble in Morocco.

Difficulties in Arabia

Through the summer of 1919 French Press attacks upon the good faith of Great Britain grew louder and occasionally envenomed. The legend of "perfidious Albion" was again revived. There was a considerable number of incidents liable to excite popular passion in France, especially when misreported by the French Press and further exaggerated by angry leader writers. One reassuring factor in the situation was the imperturbability of the British public. They seemed to take scarcely any interest in the affair. It was not until French newspapers, in September, 1919, made a general outcry over the arrest of a notorious Arab, who was strangely reported to be under the protection of France, that the Syrian drama

attracted attention in London and the provinces.

The cause of Egyptian independence spread through France and Italy. Revolutionary agitators crossed the Mediterranean and took part in fomenting troubles in Egypt, leading to murderous attacks upon loyal Egyptian Ministers and Europeans. Frenchmen of the standing of Anatole France and Emile Combes drew up petitions for the liberation of Egypt from British suzerainty. The remarkable fact in this connection was that the great French possessions in Northern Africa — Tunis, Algeria, and especially Morocco, which had been taken as compensation for old, lapsed partial rights in Egypt — were peopled by Moslems whom no Frenchman of importance dreamt of restoring to independence. Moreover, French territory in Morocco was not completely conquered, and comparatively few Moors had been induced to serve in the European War and fight for the salvation of France. As the Germans had shown, it was comparatively easy to produce in Morocco large native guerrilla forces ready to fight the French in the cause of national independence.

The main period of the Conference ended in the late summer of 1919, with the Germans still fighting the Poles and intriguing with Baltic barons and both Russian Reactionaries and Russian Bolshevists. Poland and Bohemia still contended over the Teschen coalfield, and there was a rather fragile truce between Polish armies, victorious in Galicia, and the Ukrainian forces, struggling for Kieff against Bolshevists, with uneasy relations with General Denikin's loyalist Russian army. Southern Slavs and Italians remained in conflict over Fiume and Dalmatia. Greeks and Italians disputed over Greek islands and the southern part of Albania. Montenegrins fought against Serbs. Armenians still struggled for life against Turks, and were not secure against Georgians. Kurds tried to rise against the British forces in Mesopotamia. Persia, menaced by plundering Turkish bands from the northwest, and by Russian Bolshevists of an aggressive sort on the north, and Afghan forces in a conquering mood on their eastern frontier, accepted the overlordship and help in industrial reconstruction of Great Britain.

This excited the jealousy of the Colonial party in France and the Imperial party in Italy, who wanted more compensation at the expense of Turkey and Arabia for the extension of British power in Asia. The protectorate of Armenia was urged upon the American people, but there was difficulty in inducing the Republican majority in Congress to agree to accept the proposal. President Wilson met with such opposition from his opponents in regard to the fundamental articles of the Covenant of the League of Nations, the Treaty of Peace with Germany, and Alliance with France that he refrained from submitting the Armenian problem to the judgment of his countrymen.

Menace of War Debt

Mr. Lloyd George, Mr. Balfour, and the other British delegates had to meet a domestic crisis as the time drew near for the German delegation to appear in Paris. From the popular British point of view, the question of the amount of indemnity obtainable from Germany was the supreme matter of interest in the peace settlement. The British war debt had grown so enormous that it menaced the Mother Country with economic servitude to the United States and with permanent difficulty in obtaining cheap food from the cattle ranches and wheatlands of South America. China and India exercised a financial superiority over Great Britain in the exchange of commodities, and practically throughout the

SERBIAN TROOPS IN LONDON'S VICTORY MARCH.
The Serbian contingent that took part in the great march of allied troops through London on July 19th, 1919, to celebrate the signing of peace. They are passing the Royal dais at foot of Victoria Memorial. Above: Rumanian contingent passing along one of the London streets on the same great occasion.

world, outside the war-wasted lands of Europe, the British people suffered from their crushing debt at home and the adverse balance of trade abroad produced by the war.

A large indemnity from Germany was generally expected by the victorious Britons as a relief to their disorganised industries and depleted exchequer. In the early part of April, 1919, news came from Paris that a high British authority regarded anything like a large indemnity from Germany as an impossibility. It was stated that the British people would be lucky if they obtained compensation for material damage caused by illegal acts of war and wanton destructiveness by the enemy. In private conversations with British correspondents some of the British delegates tried to prepare the British public for the shock over the practical loss of a real indemnity. When the revelation was made there was consternation in the general mind of the British people. Hundreds of Members of Parliament, who had pledged themselves at election time to obtain heavy indemnities, joined in sending a message of protest to Mr. Lloyd George. The Prime Minister returned to London and made a personal attack upon Lord Northcliffe in the House of Commons. His speech was described as a red herring trailed across the path of critics in full cry. The matter he discussed had no bearing whatever upon the problem of the indemnity and the threatened revolt of the Members of Parliament. But in the excitement he created Mr. Lloyd George managed with considerable skill to snatch the approval of the House of Commons for his policy at the Peace Conference. He had boasted some time before of his talent for political strategy, and he certainly managed to secure over a dazed people and their staggered political representatives a victory that left Great Britain handicapped for a century.

Question of indemnities

The Germans could not by any ordinary means pay the general costs of the war they had prepared and launched. Neither from their current wealth nor from the net income from their commerce did they appear able to meet the interest on the war expenses of the Western Allies and provide a sinking fund that would gradually discharge the capital debt. Full indemnities might have been obtained with the permanent enrichment of the mineral resources of Britain, Belgium, and France, by practically annexing the 200,000,000,000 tons of coal in the former German Empire. At the rate at which this coal was being extracted before the war it was reckoned that German coal resources would last thirteen hundred years. On the other hand, British coal resources, as estimated by Sir William Ramsay, were likely to be exhausted in one hundred and seventy years. Thus by a coal lien the British could have provided for the future power production of their race, and gradually have worked off their huge war debt by taking over, in partnership with France and Poland, the management of the Ruhr, Saar, and Upper Silesian coalfields.

The Ruhr basin was already growing into the largest city on earth, with a probable population of a hundred million souls. The German people were used to work above ground, as they thought coalmining on a large scale injured the national health. They employed mostly Polish and Italian labour in extracting the fuel that fed their foundries, generating stations, mills, and shops. The Western Allies could have followed the German method in Germany and brought capable Chinamen to work the Ruhr mines. The coal could then have been sold at a fair price to Germans, and the super-abundance exported to Italy, France, Holland, Switzerland, and Spain, with due regard to the interests of British coal exporters.

Germany's wealth in coal

German potash resources could have been worked in the same manner, and the German railway system, with cheap Chinese-produced coal, might have been restored into a dividend-paying system. German timber resources and a temporary measure of war taxation and bond issues could, with British, French, and American financial help at the beginning, have made the payment of full indemnities a practical though prolonged and intricate matter.

There were two obstacles. President Wilson was most strongly averse to placing the enemy in a permanent condition of helotry. He would have left the Conference and induced Congress to make a separate easy peace rather than concur in despoiling Germany of her minerals. Mr. Lloyd George and most of the British delegates, despite election pledges, were afraid of a desperate resistance from the Germans. It was estimated that the cost of maintaining adequate military control over the Germans would be too great. Men in large numbers would annually have to be withdrawn from productive work in Great Britain, in addition to the direct expense of maintaining a large army, which would diminish the paying power of Germany.

Moreover, the Teutons were prepared to set up something like a veritable Soviet Government and unite with Bolshevist Russia rather than lose their immense coal and potash resources, on which their industry, agriculture, resilient strength, and the entire future of the race depended. French statesmen believed they could counter this movement by detaching the Rhineland and Westphalia, and by giving cheap coal to the friendly Germans and allowing Protestant Germany to make such a trial of the Russian Communist system as would produce a reversal of opinion among the experimenters. But the members of the Conference as a whole were frightened by the menace of a sweeping Bolshevist movement in Germany, having seen how quickly Hungary followed the example of Russia. Neither Great Britain nor France seemed at the time safe from the contagion of revolutionary Communism.

President Wilson had his way in regard to indemnities, but to make a gentle slope along which French, British, and Belgian people could descend from the highest of hopes to the lowest of realities, some deliberately obscure articles regarding the payment of indemnities were inserted in the Treaty. Somewhat more than three hundred million tons of coal were to be given in the course of ten years to France, Belgium, and Italy, and one thousand million pounds sterling was payable by 1921, with a bond issue for two thousand million pounds and a possible later issue of bonds to the same amount.

From hopes to realities

As the French estimated the cost of repairing the damage to their agricultural interests in Flanders, Artois, Picardy, Ile de France, and Champagne at more than one thousand five hundred million pounds sterling, and the Belgians also had a tremendous bill for direct war damages, the vague amounts of indemnity scarcely covered the expense of restoring the war-wasted provinces. With the direct war damage done to Great Britain, and the responsibility of the Germans for a considerable part of the destruction wrought in Italy in the 1917 invasion, there was not sufficient money to pay for restoring buildings, impoverished farmlands, machinery, live-stock, merchant ships, roads, and railways.

The terrible losses in man-power could not be met by money compensation with which foreign labour might have been purchased, as the French intended doing, for no annual sums were exacted from the enemy for this purpose. In addition, there remained the actual war debts of the Western Allies. There was no hope whatever of reducing these by German contributions. It would probably have needed thirty thousand million pounds sterling from Germany to cover the allied war losses, and had any practical attempt been made to secure this almost inconceivable amount, no League of Nations would have been possible. In effect the war was finally regarded at the Paris Conference as a devastating general disaster. The nations half wrecked by it had to rebuild themselves mainly by their own efforts.

Having decided the question of indemnities and the allocation of former German colonies, the leaders of the Conference, at the time when the German delegation was expected, made one more attempt to establish universal peace by a reconciliation with Russia. Two Americans, Mr. W. C. Bullitt and Mr. Lincoln Steffen, went on a special mission to Moscow to examine the condition of the Bolshevist country. They returned in the middle of April, with a favourable report on the condition of affairs and an offer of peace from Lenin.

General Smuts had come to the conclusion that Sovietism of a constitutional kind would be better for Russia than Tsarism

and large landowners' rule. Mr. Lloyd George began to incline to the same point of view, and, at the suggestion of an English journalist, the American delegation formed a plan to feed Russia and open friendly relations with the Bolshevists. Lenin, who was then in difficulties, offered concessions to the Allies and the payment of Russian debts, with a pardon for all his political opponents, in return for the lifting of the blockade, the re-establishment of commercial and diplomatic relations, and help in the technical reconstruction of Russian manufactures.

The Bolshevists at that time had lost the Russian coalfields and three-quarters of the locomotives and trucks of the railways. Although there was no lack of food in Russia, the people starved in the towns from want of transport.

Mr. Lloyd George, President Wilson, and Signor Orlando signed a practical undertaking, arranged through the Norwegian explorer, Dr. Nansen, regarding relief work in Russia. M. Clemenceau, asked for time to consult his experts over matters of detail. For nearly a fortnight M. Clemenceau delayed to sign. President Wilson became angry with him, and Colonel House, usually the most imperturbable of men, threatened to issue the document without a French signature. Thereupon the French Premier signed, but negotiations with Lenin and Trotsky were still hindered by the refusal of the French Government to allow the Eiffel Tower wireless station to be used for rapid correspondence with Moscow.

By the time the courier reached Lenin, Admiral Koltchak made a sensational advance, and all the conservative forces in and about the Conference chamber used his temporary victory to put an end to the American-British scheme. Afterwards Admiral Koltchak retreated more quickly than he had advanced, and under a very serious defeat inclined more to establishment of a democratic form of Government. But in the Baltic provinces the German commander, General von der Goltz, acted as broker between Baltic barons and Russian leaders of the autocratic school, and something like an alliance obtained between Teutonic and Russian Reactionaries. The Russian Bolshevists, who were also aided by Germans, increased in strength and organisation, so that on neither side of the greatest of world problems did the conflicting peacemakers in Paris achieve anything of the slightest importance in the pacification and reconstruction of the people that had suffered most from the war.

When the enemy Foreign Minister, Count Brockdorff-Rantzau, and other German delegates arrived at the hotels at Versailles, prepared for them at the end of April, 1919, peace seemed farther off than it had been in November, 1918. The Germans came in the midst of an Italian crisis, a Japanese crisis, a French crisis, a Russian crisis, and a Franco-British dispute. There was Labour unrest of a serious kind in all the western lands of victory, with the exception of suffering, hardworking, and rather embittered Belgium. India was disturbed, Egypt was ready to revolt, and all the Moslem world was stirring to action through the Arabs of Mecca being angry with France. The fighting Moslems of India naturally supported the Sultan of Arabia and his brilliant son, Prince Feisul, and Great Britain swayed under the legitimate pressure which her numerous Moslem peoples exerted upon her. Count Brockdorff-Rantzau, a man of notable ability and daring courage, was confident that he could win the peace.

AMERICAN SOLDIERS IN THE VICTORY MARCH OF THE ALLIES.
American troops, with "Old Glory" and regimental colours, in the great march of allied troops through London on July 19th, 1919. Inset: General Pershing, who commanded the American forces in France, in London's Victory March; and (above) some of the American troops marching along the Mall.

Behind him was a great machine of intrigue worked by men of proved talent. He took the air in the Bois de Boulogne with calm assurance, shopped in Paris, and strolled in the park of Versailles, with his pretty girl typists and his inelegant male staff, some of whom, with their Tyrolean hats, capes, and tweed overcoats, looked like German tourists in caricature. His system of espionage worked in the troubled air of Paris. He knew the inner history of the conflicts between the Allies, and modelled his conduct accordingly.

Before the Germans were received Italy was induced to send her delegates back to the Conference. M. Barrère, French Ambassador in Rome, was energetic in conciliating action, and successful in preventing complete disunion. Although the Fiume problem remained unsettled, Signor Orlando returned to Paris, just before his Cabinet fell. Then, in a mood of sublime optimism, the peacemakers invited the Austrian delegation to attend, and made advances to the Bolshevist Jews of Hungary, apparently in the desire to obtain some Soviet colour in the Conference.

Opening scene at Versailles

Meanwhile, the business of preparing a separate peace with Germany was accelerated, and by an extraordinary general effort the lengthy articles of treaty were ready for presentation to the enemy eight days after Count Brockdorff-Rantzau arrived. M. Clemenceau would not allow the Palace of Versailles to be used for the preliminary negotiations for the peace. With a certain cynical disregard for spectacular effect, the leader of France appointed the dining-room of a modern commercial inn as the scene of the great hour of reckoning. It was in the Trianon Palace Hotel, built on the edge of the park in which Marie Antoinette used to play at pastoral life, that direct peace negotiations opened. The only definite touch of dramatic irony was the date fixed for the meeting—May 7th, 1919, the anniversary of the torpedoing of the Lusitania. With this exception in favour of British and American sentiment, one of the most important ceremonies in the annals of mankind was prepared in a simple, business-like way. The people of Paris did not come forth in multitudes to watch the arrival of the Teutons. A few policemen and soldiers were sufficient to preserve order among the sparse spectators when the cars of the German delegates stopped at the hotel door.

In the dining-room the members of the Grand Alliance were arranged at a horse-shoe table, and the Germans were placed facing them, like prisoners before their judges. Count Brockdorff-Rantzau was very pale, like a desperate gambler staking his life to win a fortune. The representatives of the League stood up courteously when the Teutons entered, and when everybody was seated M. Georges Clemenceau rose from his chair. The old man was still weak from the wound he had received from an assassin who had been inspired by German and Russian propaganda. With brilliant eyes in his pallid, parchment-like face he looked into the eyes in the thin, white visage of Brockdorff-Rantzau. Bending forward with his fists on the table, the former Mayor of Montmartre who had tried to induce his country to fight to the death after the fall of the third Napoleon, said that there could be no oral discussion, and that only fourteen days was allowed for written observations regarding the proposed Treaty. The second Treaty of Versailles, he remarked with grim irony, had cost the Allies too much for them to omit any precautions or guarantees for an enduring peace.

Clemenceau's grim irony

Then came the greatest triumph in the life of the man known as the "Tiger of France." A secretary handed the German envoy the voluminous Treaty of Peace bound in khaki. Brockdorff-Rantzau completely lost, in the duel of looks with Clemenceau, his talent in diplomacy. He made an angry remark to his companions and then, sitting in his chair, delivered a long and subtly insolent speech. He had been a Prussian officer before he became a diplomatist, and he used a harsh, rasping tone while denying that Germany was alone responsible for the war, and declaiming against the spirit of hate which he alleged was the inspiration of the allied terms.

An apology was afterwards issued regarding the Prussian leader's refusal to rise when speaking. It was said he was so overcome that he could not stand. The fact was he belatedly recognised that he had gone too far, and that a mere appearance of conventional politeness in attitude and tone of voice would have helped him in his ultimate manœuvre. He intended to reject the Treaty, but designed to keep on as good terms as possible with President Wilson. But Wilson became the most angry man in the allied circle of angry men. In effect Brockdorff-Rantzau's speech was a new declaration of war, a war of underground intrigue and plotting. As such it completed the life work of M. Clemenceau. Many of the associated delegates, and especially those of the English-speaking races, were new to the world of European politics, and inclined to believe in the conversion of the German people. But they saw the old Prussian spirit incarnate before them. In conjunction with the subsequent destruction of the German Navy at Scapa Flow, which was designed to embroil Great Britain with France and Italy, the attitude of Count Brockdorff-Rantzau so hardened the hearts of the allied delegates that certain terms which would have been mitigated to a repentant nation were strictly enforced.

In little under an hour the ceremony at Versailles was ended. No reply was made to the enemy Minister's speech. In eloquent silence the German delegates left the room, and everybody at once stood up, giving the Teutons another lesson in common courtesy. Brockdorff-Rantzau, after some attempts at negotiation, refused to sign the Treaty. Marshal Foch received the order from the Supreme Council to prepare an immediate advance, and completed his plans with General Sir William Robertson. The Royal Independent Air Force resumed its organisation for bombing Berlin. President Wilson refused to alter the Treaty either under American or British pressure. By a remarkable vicissitude of rôles it was Mr. Lloyd George who, alarmed at Brockdorff-Rantzau's policy of refusal, endeavoured to induce his associates to mitigate the terms. M. Clemenceau, uniting with President Wilson against the British Prime Minister, maintained the rigour of the agreed settlement.

Allies stand firm

The points on which Mr. Lloyd George was understood to be ready to give way were the Polish frontier in Upper Silesia, the amount of reparations, the length of the period of occupation, and the immediate admission of Germany into the League of Nations. It was owing to President Wilson's firmness that the arranged Treaty was not discarded and negotiations again begun in June as they might have been in January. He insisted that the terms should be maintained and the matter settled by June 13th. He had a superstitious liking for arranging events on the thirteenth day of any month. Twice he landed in France on the thirteenth, and he desired to finish the main work on the thirteenth. He practically succeeded, and after some details were settled the final firm reply of the Allies was delivered to Germany on June 16th. It was Marshal Foch that won.

There was an unhappy incident when Brockdorff-Rantzau and his party left Versailles for Weimar to consult the German Government regarding the Treaty. A French crowd, resenting the conduct of the German delegates at the meeting with the Associated Powers, hissed and stoned the departing delegation. Meanwhile General Mangin opened operations of a political kind to detach the Rhine provinces from Germany, and the allied armies awaited the order to move forward. Then it was that Herr Erzberger, representing the interests of Catholic Germany that were immediately menaced, obtained an admission from Hindenburg that he could not safeguard Western Germany.

Erzberger overthrew the Scheidemann Government, along with the Brockdorff-Rantzau and Bernstorff Junker clique. The British, French, and American naval forces arranged to blockade Germany, and neutral States neighbouring the enemy were approached by the Allies to take an active part in the intended blockade. Although the neutrals refused to do this, the general pressure upon Germany was overwhelming. The Weimar Parliament voted that the Treaty should be signed. A new Government was arranged, with Herr Bauer as nominal Premier, and after a last attempt to play for time, the Germans

British standards and colours borne in London's great Victory March of allied troops.

Bearers of British infantry colours in London's Peace March, July 19th, 1919.

Field=Marshal Sir Douglas Haig in the great march of allied troops through London.

Men of the Tank Corps, followed by four Tanks, in London's great Victory Pageant.

Band of the 1st Life Guards on London's day of rejoicing on the signing of peace.

Contingent of British heavy artillery passing along the Mail.

Nurses' contingents in the great Victory March of allied forces through London.

British infantry of the Southern Command in the London march of July 19th, 1919.

accepted the Treaty two hours before the armies of Marshal Foch were appointed to move.

There was some difficulty in finding Germans to perform the last act of humiliation at Versailles. But a Socialist, Herr Hermann Müller, and a Teuton of the Catholic Party with the English name of Dr. Bell, came to Versailles for the final ceremony on June 28th, 1919, the fifth anniversary of the Hungarian crime of Sarajevo that had plunged the world in war.

In the glittering Hall of Mirrors in the palace of Louis XIV., the conqueror of Alsace and Lorraine, the Hohenzollern Empire ended at the place of its arrogant birth. Where Hindenburg in his youth, with Bismarck and Moltke, led the cheers for the first Prussian Emperor, the German Socialist delegate came forward from between Japanese and Brazilian representatives and signed the Treaty of Peace, at twelve minutes past three, June 28th, 1919. President Wilson, shaking hands with friends as he passed to the table, followed the Germans in signing. Mr. Lloyd George, with the home and oversea British delegates, came forward. With a grave smile, M. Clemenceau accomplished his part in the act of victory, and at periods of three minutes all the other delegations, with the exception of the Chinese, signed the historic document. The two Chinese plenipotentiaries—Lou Tseng-Tsiang, Minister for Foreign Affairs, and Cheng Ting Wang, former Minister for Commerce—declined to attend the ceremony. The Chinese Foreign Minister called on M. Clemenceau in the morning, but could not at the last moment win any concession over Shantung, or get the problem excluded from the Treaty and reserved for future consideration.

The Chinese were not missed at the moment, though their absence was portentous. There was a democratic ending to the Peace Conference, by the terrace running down to the Grand Canal. All semblance of order maintained by troops and police disappeared, and M. Clemenceau, Mr. Wilson, and Mr. Lloyd George were surrounded by enthusiastic crowds of persons who wanted to pat or shake hands with the organisers of victory and the makers of the great peace. Mr. Wilson's guard of secret service police was scattered, along with the French and British private detectives, and in the homeliest fashion the rejoicing multitude captured their leaders, kissed them, and gave them an infinite choice of bouquets and garlands

Peace Treaty signed

Guns proclaimed the peace to Paris, and the heroic city spent the night in festival, the rejoicing crowds being so dense that the intended torchlight processions found no space in which to move. Great Britain and the United States took the news more calmly, for the reason perhaps that the people did not understand so well as did the French how near the Allies had been to disunion and a renewal of the war. Many serious difficulties remained after the mistakes in drawing up terms of armistice were partly remedied by the severe but just articles of peace.

The German Reactionaries continued unteachable and irrepressible, and, foiled in their main scheme, concentrated in Silesia and the Baltic provinces in pursuit of an eastward policy of aggression and intrigue. But the fighting strength went out of the general body of Germans. They slackened in industrial output and in political reconstruction. Austria, after another long period of delay, was presented with a Treaty of Peace. Bulgaria was neglected, and Turkey left in a turmoil of brigandage, riots, battles, and landings of allied and sometimes conflicting forces to occupy coveted zones of territory—all producing a dangerous ferment in the Moslem mind. But the war with Germany was over, and she, by her traditions, organisation, and immense industrial power, had been the grand power of evil. Lacking her aid and inspiration, her old associates could be reduced to peaceful ways if treated with both firmness and fairness. Russia and China were the principal new sources of peril to the war-wearied world, and the solution of their special difficulties was not in sight.

Unity of man asserted

To many thinking men of the English-speaking races, including the great Boer leaders, General Botha and General Smuts, the establishment of the Covenant of the League of Nations was an achievement of greater promise than the enforcing of the peace with Germany. French and Italian opinion remained rather sceptical in regard to the general benefit to mankind of the Anglo-American foundation for a future "Parliament of man." Yet, though there was opposition in America as well as on the Continent of Europe to some of the principles of the League, the Great War ended in a mood of hope different from the ending of all other victorious wars.

For the first time in the history of the half-animal and half-divine thing that was crawling through mud and blood to fellowship with God, the unity of mankind had been asserted in a grand and practical manner. Had it only been possible for all the strong, outer communities of the English-speaking race to overcome their prejudice against the Mongolian and Hindu, and accept the principle of race equality, the League of Nations would have been a scheme of larger and more generous design, with a stirring quality of appeal to Asia as well as to Europe, America, and Australasia. But the main thing was that the League, with all its hasty framework and colour prejudice, was born.

The war had ended without producing a leader of civilisation with a genius interpretative of the prophetic soul of the world. Yet there had gathered together men of goodwill and sincere energy of mind who had accomplished something of promise. It rested with the victorious nations to save themselves and their fellow-men.

SUMMARY OF TREATY BETWEEN THE ALLIES AND GERMANY, SIGNED AT VERSAILLES, JUNE 28th, 1919.

The Treaty signed with Germany consisted of 15 *Parts*, and the principal signatories of the Allies were the United States of America, the British Empire, France, Italy, and Japan. The following nations associated as allies against Germany also signed: Belgium, Bolivia, Brazil, Cuba, Ecuador, Greece, Guatemala, Haiti, the Hedjaz (of Arabia), Honduras, Liberia, Nicaragua, Panama, Peru, Poland, Portugal, Rumania, the Serb-Croat-Slovene State, Siam, Czecho-Slovakia, and Uruguay. China, although an associated ally, declined to sign.

The stated purpose of the Treaty was to replace by "a firm, just, and durable peace," the war which was originated by Austria-Hungary against Serbia, on July 28th, 1914, and by Germany against Russia on August 1st, and against France, August 3rd, 1914.

The League of Nations

Part I. of the Treaty is entirely concerned with the *League of Nations*, all the countries named above forming the original members of the League, and invitations to join the League being extended to the Argentine, Chile, Colombia, Denmark, Netherlands, Norway, Paraguay, Persia, Salvador, Spain, Sweden, Switzerland, and Venezuela. To withdraw from the League two years' notice must be given, and admission to the League is open to any self-governing State approved by two-thirds of the representative assembly of all the nations of the League. When this assembly meets, each member of the League has one vote, but the Council of the League, which is to meet once a year, is confined to representatives of the five principal signatories, and four representatives of the other nations. Until the latter four have been chosen Belgium, Brazil, Spain, and Greece are to be represented on the Council. The League is not only concerned with the reduction of armaments "to the lowest point consistent with national safety and the enforcement of international obligations," it also binds its members to exchange "full and frank information as to the scale of their armaments, and their military, naval, and air programmes," requires the Council to deal with any dispute likely to lead to a rupture between members of the League, proposes the establishment of a permanent Court of International Justice, and declares that any member that resorts to war without submitting the matter in dispute to the Council, or to arbitration, shall be regarded as at war with all the other nations of the League, and shall be opposed by the arms of these nations— all commercial and financial relations being completely broken off with the offending party. The same treatment shall be meted out to any country not in the League that makes war upon a member of the League without first submitting the dispute to arbitration. In every case there must be no resort to war until three months after the report of the arbitrators or of the Council, and such report is to be made within six months of the matter being brought to arbitration. Only in the event of the Council failing to come to an agreement are members of the League allowed "to take such action as they shall consider necessary for the maintenance of right and justice." If one nation accepts the report of the Council on a matter in dispute and the other refuses, then the rest of the League will remain at peace with the accepting nation.

Other important items in the Covenant of the League of Nations are: (1) All international treaties and engagements must be registered at the League of Nations and published, and are not binding unless they are registered; (2) Colonies and territories which have changed hands during the war and are not able to stand alone are to be placed under the care of one of the older nations, and such nation is called the Mandatary. The German colonies in Africa, certain territories of the Turkish Empire, and certain South Pacific Islands come under this article; the Mandatory Power will not have an entirely free hand, but will report and be subject to the Council of the League.

Finally, the League agrees to do its best to secure fair and humane conditions of labour for all men, women, and children, and just treatment for native races; it undertakes the responsibility of checking the traffic in women and children, and in opium and other dangerous drugs, and of supervising the trade in arms and ammunition in those countries where supervision is necessary.

The headquarters of the League of Nations are at Geneva; all its offices are open to men and women alike, and its first secretary is Sir James Eric Drummond.

Parts II. and III. are concerned with the boundaries of Germany and the new political arrangements of Central Europe.

Belgium and France

To *Belgium* are ceded small pieces of territory called Moresnet, Eupen, and Malmédy, lying between Aix-la-Chapelle and Luxemburg and west and south-west of Liège. But the inhabitants of Eupen and Malmédy are to be allowed within six months after the signing of the Treaty to register if they desire to remain part of Germany, and Belgium will accept the decision of the League of Nations as to the result of that registration.

Luxemburg, which was formerly a part of the German Empire as far as all trade and commerce were concerned, is no longer to be so included.

On the *left (i.e., the west) bank of the Rhine* Germany is neither to have any fortifications nor any troops.

France receives back the provinces of *Alsace-Lorraine* with their frontiers of 1871, and Germany is to pay all the civil and military pensions due to the inhabitants of those provinces in November, 1918. France also receives the mining district of the Saar Basin in compensation for the destruction of her coal-mines by Germany in the war. For fifteen years the mines of the Saar Basin shall be owned and administered by France, the League of Nations acting as trustee and appointing a Commission of Five with full powers of government. At the end of that time the inhabitants shall decide by a plebiscite whether they wish the existing regime to continue, or prefer union with France or with Germany. No military service of any kind is to be allowed in the Saar Basin, and the inhabitants will retain their local assemblies, religious liberties, schools and language. While France takes over the mines without payment, should the territory revert to Germany then Germany must repurchase the mines from France at a price payable in gold.

Austria is to be strictly independent of Germany, and only on the consent of the League of Nations may it become part of Germany.

Independence of Bohemia and Poland

The *independence of the Czecho-Slovak State* (consisting of the inhabitants of Bohemia, Moravia, and the Ruthenians, formerly in Austria-Hungary) is recognised, and a small territory in Silesia, east of Troppau, is ceded to it by Germany. The frontier line between Poland and Czecho-Slovakia to be decided on the spot by a Commission of the Allied Powers.

Poland is declared an independent State, and it will include the following territories which formerly were under Germany: Memel and the district north of the Niemen; a portion of West Prussia, including the sea-board of the Baltic; the province of Posen, including the cities of Posen and Lissa. The inhabitants of the remaining portion of West Prussia, of a large part of East Prussia, and of the territory of Upper Silesia are to decide by a plebiscite whether they wish to be under Germany or Poland, and these areas are to be occupied by the allied troops and governed by a Commission of the Allies until the plebiscite is taken. The German troops are to evacuate within fifteen days of the Treaty all the ceded territories, and Poland is to accord free access and full communications between East Prussia and the rest of Germany. The port of *Danzig* is declared a free city, included within the Polish Customs' frontier, and its constitution is to be drawn by its representatives in conjunction with a High Commissioner appointed by the League of Nations.

The people in the province of *Schleswig,* and of the adjacent islands, shall decide by a plebiscite whether they wish to be under Denmark or Germany, and an International Commission appointed by the Allies will administer the territory until the plebiscite has been taken and fix the frontier line.

Heligoland is to be entirely dismantled and its fortifications destroyed by the Germans under the supervision of the Allies.

All the treaties made with *Russia* during the war are annulled and the frontier is to remain as it was on August 1st, 1914.

Cession of German Colonies

Part IV. is concerned with the colonies and external interests of Germany, and requires the complete renunciation of all territories beyond her European frontiers. In addition to the loss of territory, Germany is required to give up all Government property in her colonies, to pay for damage done in French Cameroon, to annul all her treaties and conventions in Central Africa, and with China, Siam, Liberia, Morocco, and Egypt, and to renounce in favour of Japan all her rights at Shantung.

In *Part V.* the strict observance of certain military, naval, and aerial conditions is required "in order to render possible the initiation of a general limitation of the armaments of all nations."

By March 31st, 1920, the German Army must be reduced to seven divisions of infantry, and three divisions of cavalry, and must not exceed 100,000 men and 4,000 officers.

The Great German General Staff is to be abolished.

The manufacture of armaments is to be carried on only under the knowledge and approval of the Allied Powers, all armaments in existence beyond the amount permitted by the Allies are to be handed over to the Governments of the Allies, and all importation of armaments into Germany is forbidden.

Conscription must give way in Germany to voluntary enlistment.

All fortifications west and thirty-two miles east of the Rhine are to be dismantled.

Limitation of German Navy

The German Navy is strictly limited to six old battleships, six light cruisers, twelve destroyers, and twelve torpedo-boats—no submarines being permitted—while all the existing battleships and cruisers are to be handed over to the Allies and the auxiliary cruisers are to be disarmed and treated as merchant ships.

Germany is also required to sweep up the mines in the North Sea and to remove all guns and fortifications that threaten the free passage to the Baltic. She is not allowed any military or naval air force, and the aircraft of the Allies are to enjoy complete freedom in Germany until the evacuation of all allied troops. An Inter-Allied Commission of control is to sit in Germany—at Germany's expense—until March 31st, 1920, to see that these regulations are carried out. And Germany is given three months after the signing of the Treaty to bring her laws into conformity with the requirements of the Allies.

Part VI. enjoins the repatriation of prisoners of war and interned civilians—Germany to pay the costs of the repatriation—and the respect and maintenance of the graves of soldiers and sailors in all territories by the Allies and by Germany.

Kaiser to be Arraigned

Part VII. deals with the *penalties* imposed on Germany.

William II. of Hohenzollern is publicly arraigned "for a supreme offence against international morality and the sanctity of treaties," and is to be tried by a special tribunal of five judges, appointed by the United States of America, Great Britain, France, Italy, and Japan. This tribunal will fix the punishment to be awarded, and the Government of the Netherlands will be asked to surrender the ex-Emperor.

Germany also agrees to hand over to the Allies

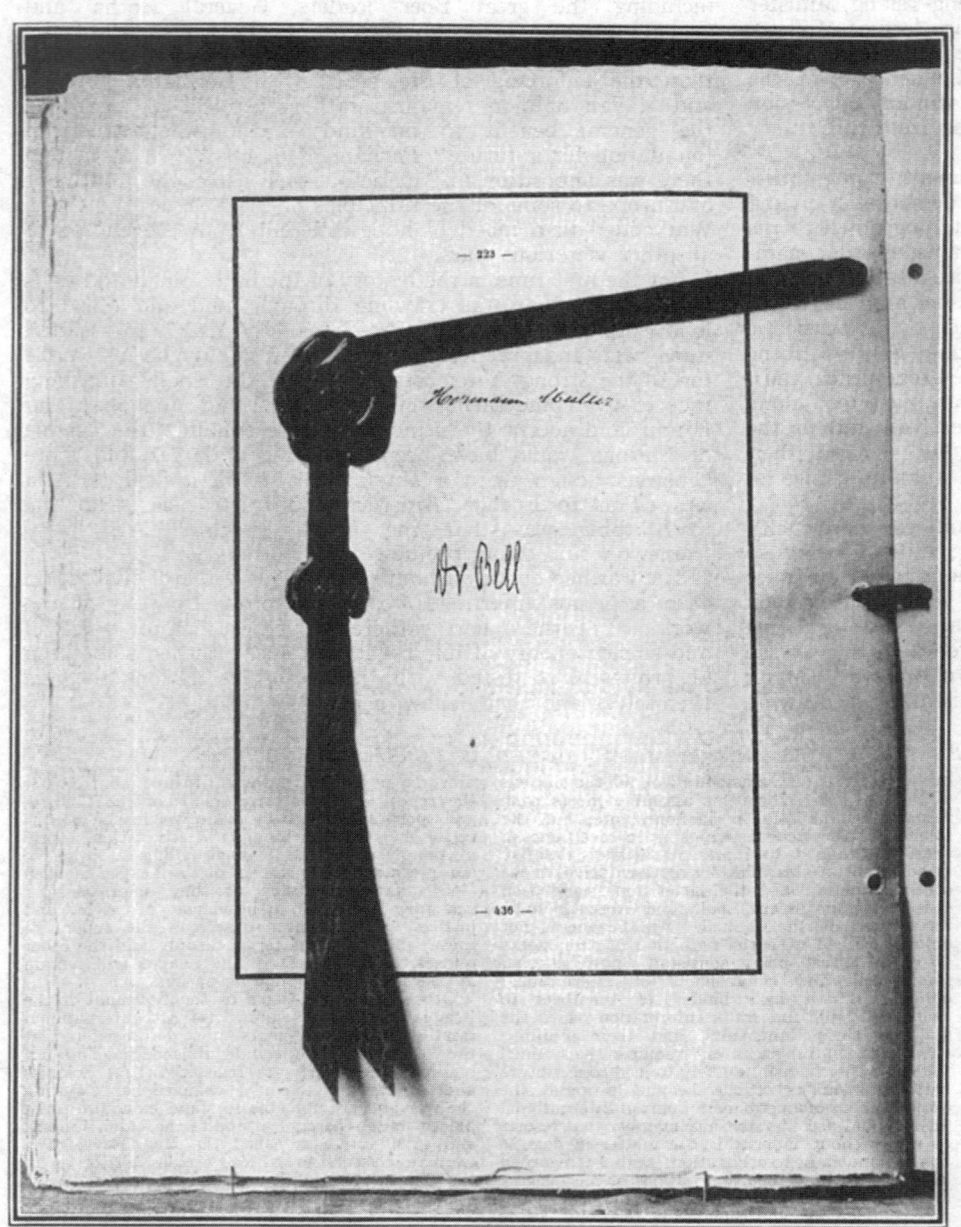

"WITHOUT MENTAL RESERVATION."
Last page of the Treaty of Peace, signed at Versailles on June 28th, 1919. It bears the signatures of the German delegates, Herr Müller and Dr. Bell, who said that they signed "without mental reservation." Though their signatures appear on the final page of the Treaty, Germany's delegates were the first to sign.

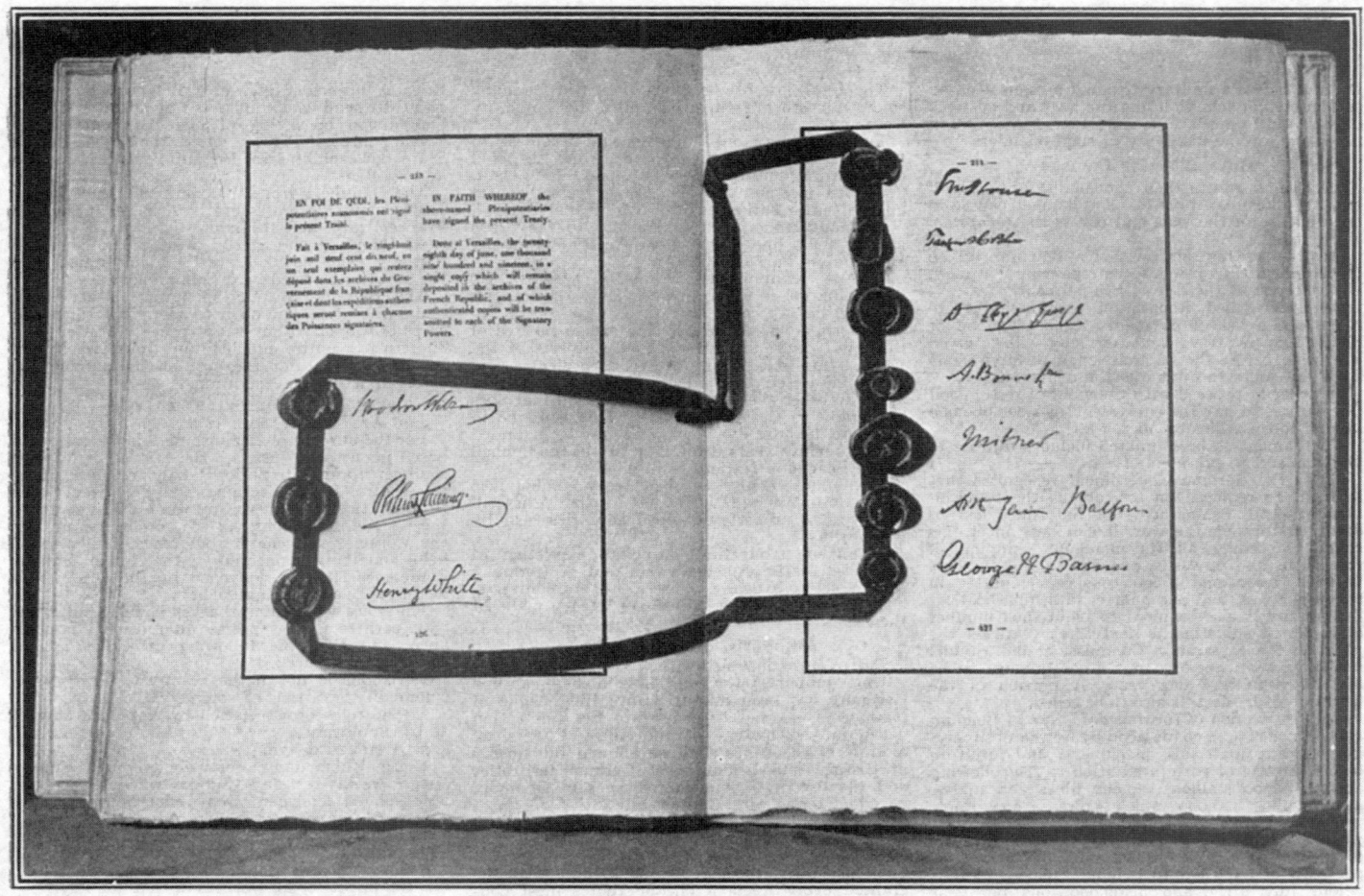

Signatures and seals of the American and British delegates to the Treaty. On the left page are those of President Wilson, Mr. Lansing, and Mr. White, and on the opposite one those of Colonel House, General Bliss, Mr. Lloyd George, Mr. Bonar Law, Lord Milner, Mr. Balfour, and Mr. Barnes.

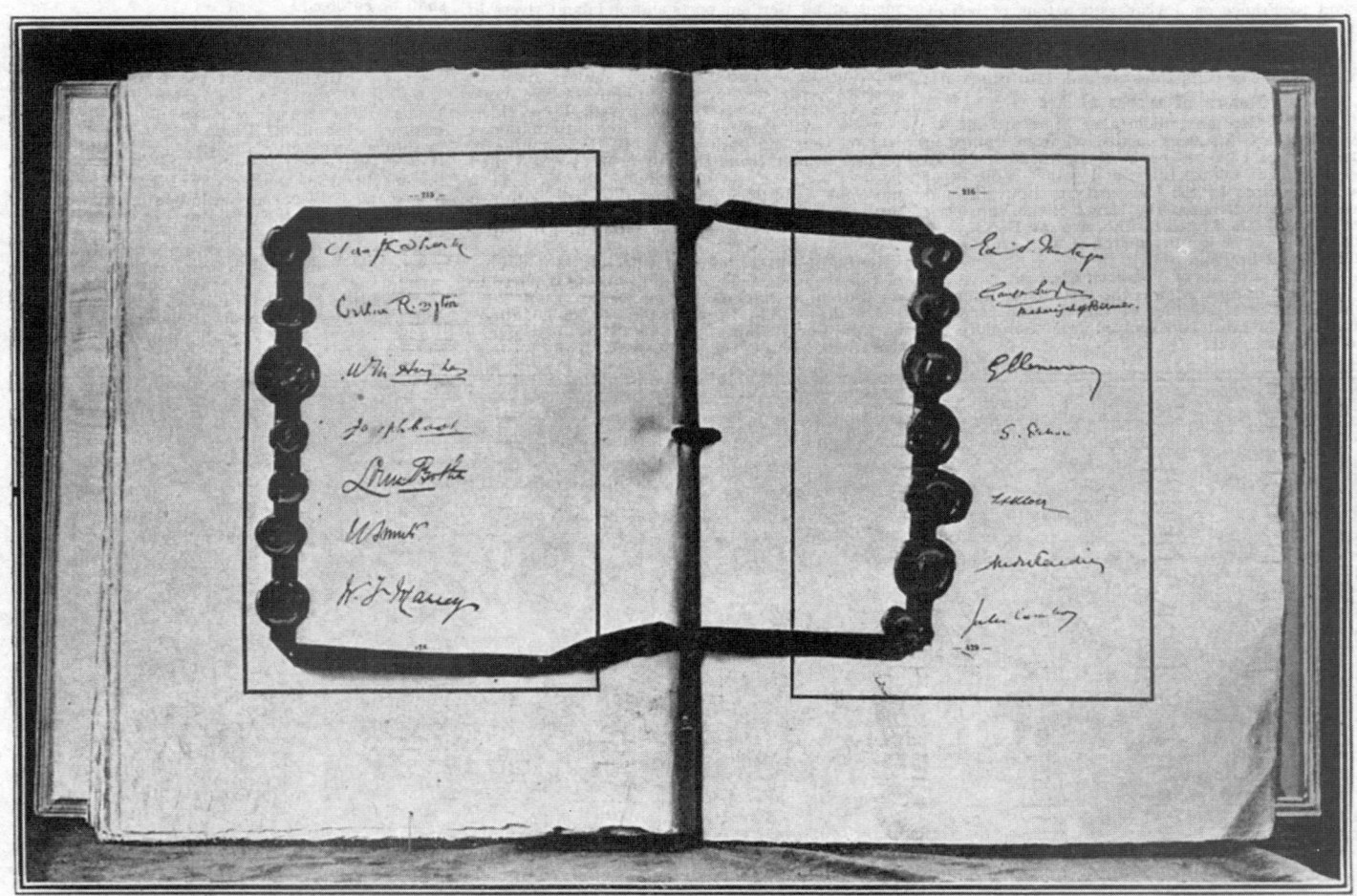

Signatures and seals of the delegates from the British Dominions and India, and the French delegates. On the left page are those of Mr. Doherty and Mr. Sifton, Canada ; Mr. Hughes and Sir Joseph Cook, Australia ; General Botha and General Smuts, South Africa ; Mr. Massey, New Zealand, On the right page are those of Mr. Montagu and the Maharajah of Bikaner, India ; and for France, M. Clemenceau, M. Pichon, M. Klotz, M. Tardieu, and M. Cambon.

THE GREAT VERSAILLES TREATY OF PEACE: AMERICAN, BRITISH, AND FRENCH SIGNATURES.

for trial before a military tribunal persons accused of committing acts violating the laws and customs of war, and to produce documents and information necessary for the discovery of such offenders.

Reparation for Damage

Part VIII. affirms the responsibility of Germany and her allies for all the loss and damage caused in consequence of the war, and orders the *reparation* to be made.

All the money borrowed by Belgium up to November 11th, 1918, is to be repaid by Germany, with interest at the rate of five per cent.

An Inter-Allied Reparation Commission is to make out a list of payments for damage on or before May 1st, 1921, and Germany will be given a hearing before the Commission, and thirty years from that date to discharge the debt.

In order to proceed with the work of restoration Germany is to pay the equivalent of 1,000,000,000 in gold to the Allies by May, 1921.

The damage to be estimated includes injuries to civilians and to prisoners of war.

While the German Government recognises that it ought to replace, ton for ton, all the *merchant shipping* and fishing-boats of the Allies lost or damaged through the war, it can only meet this claim by ceding all its merchant shipping of 1,600 tons and upwards, one half of this in ships between 1,000 and 1,600 tons, one quarter in steam-trawlers, and one quarter in fishing-boats.

Germany is also required to build such number of merchant ships in the next three years for the Allies as the Reparation Commission shall decide, not more than 200,000 tons gross tonnage to be laid down in any one year. A portion of the German river fleet is also to be ceded.

The destruction of the *invaded areas* of Belgium and France is to be made good by Germany supplying building materials, machinery, and furniture before the end of 1919 in addition to the following animals : 700 stallions, 40,000 fillies and mares, 4,000 bulls, 140,000 milch cows, 1,200 rams, 120,000 sheep, 10,000 goats, and 15,000 sows ; 7,000,000 tons of coal per year for ten years are to be sent to France from Germany, 8,000,000 tons per year for ten years to Belgium, 26,000,000 tons before July, 1923, and 8,500,000 tons per year from 1924 to 1929 to Italy.

For the three years ending 1922 Germany will send to France each year 35,000 tons of benzol, 50,000 tons of coal-tar, and 30,000 tons of sulphate of ammonia.

All submarine cables owned by the German Government or companies are ceded to the Allies.

Return of Works of Art

Finally, Germany undertakes to return all the works of art and flags carried off from France in the war of 1870-71, or in the present war ; to replace the manuscripts and other objects of value required by the University of Louvain, and to deliver to Belgium the leaves of the Van Eyck triptych of the Mystic Lamb, now at Berlin, and the leaves of the Bouts triptych of the Last Supper, formerly at Louvain.

Part IX. consists of *Financial Clauses.*

The cost of reparation is the first charge upon all the assets and revenues of the German Empire, and no gold must be exported from Germany up to May 21st, 1921.

The total cost of the allied troops in Germany since November 11th, 1918, must be borne by Germany.

From within a month after the Treaty comes into force Germany must pay to the Allies the gold deposited as security for the Ottoman Public Debt, and must pay annually for twelve years the gold guaranteed to Turkey as provision for that Debt.

Germany undertakes to transfer to the Allies all payments due to her from Austria, Hungary, Bulgaria, or Turkey.

Part X. contains the *Economic Clauses.* No discrimination is to be made against the imports of the Allies.

Imports from Alsace-Lorraine are to be free of Customs' duty for five years. Subjects of the Allies living in Germany are to be protected and to be subjected to no legislation that does not apply to other aliens, and to no taxation that does not apply to German citizens. This is to be in force for the next five years, and may be extended to another five years if the majority of the Council of the League of Nations so decide.

Within six months of the Treaty coming into force Germany will surrender to the Allies all securities of property in allied countries held by its subjects.

A mixed Arbitration Tribunal, consisting of nominees of the Allied Powers and of Germany shall be set up to deal with cases of debts, contracts, and property between subjects of Germany and of the Allies.

Air, Ports, and Transport

Part XI. is concerned with *Aerial Navigation.*

Until January 1st, 1923, unless in the meantime Germany has been admitted into the League of Nations or allowed to come into the Convention of Aerial Navigation of the Allied Powers, all aircraft of the Allies shall be allowed full liberty of passage and landing over German territories and the use of national aerodromes in Germany on equal terms with German aircraft.

Part XII. relates to *Ports, Waterways, and Railways.*

All goods in transit shall be carried free of Customs' duty through Germany, and shall be granted every freedom on the routes most convenient for international traffic. The vessels and property of the Allies shall enjoy the same treatment at all German ports and on inland rivers in Germany as German vessels and goods.

The German ports that were free on August 1st, 1914, shall be maintained, and goods and vessels entering these ports shall be subject only to necessary charges for the upkeep of the port. The navigable parts of the Rivers Elbe, Oder, Niemen, and Danube are declared international, and on them all nations shall be on a footing of perfect equality, and the only charges made shall be for the cost of maintaining the river in a navigable condition. A Convention will be drawn up by the Allies, with the approval of the League of Nations, concerning these international waterways.

Germany must cede to the Allies a certain number of tugs and boats, in addition to those required in reparation, for river navigation.

The Elbe shall be administered by an International Commission consisting of : German representatives, four ; Czecho-Slovak, two ; Great Britain, France, Italy, and Belgium, one each. The Oder shall be administered by an International Commission consisting of one representative of Poland, three of Prussia, one of the Czecho-Slovak State, one each of Great Britain, France, Denmark, and Sweden.

The Danube European Commission shall consist provisionally of representatives of Great Britain, France, Italy, and Rumania.

At Hamburg and Stettin areas are to be leased to the Czecho-Slovak State for ninety-nine years, the areas to be fixed by a Commission.

The Kiel Canal and its approaches are to be maintained free, and open to merchant ships and ships of war of all nations at peace with Germany on terms of entire equality, and no charges shall be made except for the cost of maintaining the canal in navigable condition.

Labour Problems

Part XIII. relates to *Labour.*

For the purpose of establishing " universal peace based upon social justice," the League of Nations shall set up an International Labour Office, under the control of a governing body of twenty-four persons, twelve representing the Governments of the League of Nations, six the employers, and six the workers. A general conference shall also be held, and the first meeting of the Annual Labour Conference shall be convened by the U.S.A. and held in 1919 at Washington.

The Allies declare that the well-being of industrial wage-earners is of supreme international importance, and that the following principles are of special importance :

1. Labour is not to be regarded merely as a commodity or article of commerce.
2. The right of association by employed as well as by employer.
3. A standard living wage.
4. Eight-hour day or forty-eight hour week.
5. A weekly rest-day—Sunday wherever practicable—of not less than twenty-four hours.
6. Abolition of child labour.
7. Equal pay to men and women for work of equal value.
8. Labour laws in each country to secure fair treatment for all workers in that country.
9. A system of State inspection, including women inspectors, in order that the Labour Laws shall be enforced.

These proposals are not to be considered as final, but are suitable for guiding the policy of the League of Nations.

Occupation of the Rhine

Part XIV. states the *Guarantees* of peace.

The allied troops will occupy the German territory west of the Rhine and the bridge-heads for fifteen years after the Treaty comes into force. If the Treaty is faithfully observed Cologne and the neighbouring territory will be evacuated in five years, Coblenz and neighbouring territory in ten years. If all the obligations of the Treaty are fulfilled by Germany, in less than fifteen years the occupying troops will be at once withdrawn.

Part XV. consists of *Miscellaneous Provisions.*

Germany recognises the new States set up and their frontiers as laid down by treaties between the Allies and Austria-Hungary, Bulgaria, and Turkey.

The present Treaty shall be ratified at Paris as soon as possible.

MEN OF THE MIDDLESEX HUSSARS IN A GREAT PARADE OF LONDON TROOPS.
Part of the mounted forces which took part on July 5th, 1919, in the great march of London Territorial troops. Horse and foot, nearly twenty thousand men, many of whom had already returned to civil life, marched past King George at Buckingham Palace, and thence through the City.

CHAPTER CCCXXI.

"FOR VALOUR": HEROES OF THE VICTORIA CROSS.

A Final Survey.

V.C. Winners One in Every Ten Thousand Fighters—Awards of the Cross in the Final Period of the War—Fuller Details Available of the Later Heroic Deeds that Won the V.C.—Coincidence in the Numbers Awarded to Canadian and Australian Forces—Seventy-three Won by the British Army—Twelve Added to the Naval Record—Winners of the Cross at Zeebrugge and Ostend—Lieutenant Auten and his Exploit with a Q Ship—Some Outstanding Deeds of Officers and Men of the Royal Naval Reserve—Some Heroes of the Air Service—Additions to the Guards' Wearers of the V.C.—Awards to Engineers who Greatly Distinguished Themselves in the Final Advance—V.C.'s Bestowed on Machine Gunners and Men of the Tank Corps—Achievements of the Infantry: Five V.C.'s to the Lancashire Fusiliers, Three to the Manchesters, and Two to the York and Lancaster Regiment—Other Regiments that Added Two New V.C.'s to their Roll—Twenty-three Regiments that Added One Apiece—Scottish and Irish Winners of the Cross—Heroes from the Far West and from Beneath the Southern Cross.

IN four preceding chapters have been provided a detailed and considered account of the deeds that won the Victoria Cross during the tremendous struggle. The award of the cross, partly on account of its comparative rarity, is a very special honour, and the men who won it, perhaps one in every 10,000 fighters, were a specially distinguished group. The plan adopted was to deal with those awarded during each year of combat, the year for this purpose running from August 4th to August 4th, and as in each twelve months the number of these distinctions granted to officers and men exceeded one hundred, there was no lack of material. The difficulty, indeed, was rather in the other direction. The most recent of these annual surveys dealt with the crosses awarded during the twelve months ending August 4th, 1918, the fourth year of the war; the present chapter, dealing with those awarded since that date, completes the whole story.

In this final period there were 154 grants of the Victoria Cross, although not all were won between August 4th, 1918, and the conclusion of the armistice in the November following. A fair number were won earlier in that year, in those anxious March days when the British were fighting with their backs to the wall around St. Quentin and elsewhere, and some were earned even earlier than that. At least one was awarded for a deed performed in 1915, and they represented, as it were, the final payments on account of liabilities that went back to August, 1914, and the landing of the Expeditionary Force. For a lengthened period of the war

the official accounts of the gallant deeds, that always accompany announcements of the bestowal of Victoria Crosses by the King, said nothing whatever about time or place, thus robbing the narratives of much of their value. But after the armistice there was no further need for this secrecy, and about many of the awards described in the present chapter full details are available. Moreover, on December 16th, 1918, the War Office issued a statement supplying omissions in earlier notices, and thus he who wrote on this subject after that date was in possession of the relevant facts.

There are various ways in which the 154 awards can be classified, but the best seems to be to adopt the distinctions between the fighting forces of the British Empire that are sanctioned by popular use. The three main divisions are, therefore, into Navy, Army, and Air Force. Numerically the Navy and Air Force are small, at least as compared with the Army, and in their case no further classification is necessary. But with the Army it is otherwise, and two lines of classification, overlapping somewhat it may be, suggest themselves. The one is territorial or national. The Canadians, the Australians, the New Zealanders, and other units from Overseas constitute distinct branches of the one great Army, and as such are entitled to distinct notice, thus leaving the way clear for the same method to be applied to those who, in the narrower sense, came from the Motherland.

Within these groups again lines of demarcation may be useful; between England and Scotland and Ireland, for instance, or between Ontario and Quebec, or between Queensland and Victoria. Finally, the persistence of

[Bassano.
VISCOUNT GORT, V.C., D.S.O., M.C., M.V.O.
It was when in command of the 3rd Brigade of Guards, on September 27th, 1918, that Viscount Gort, when badly wounded, gained the Victoria Cross by heroic leading of his men.

regimental traditions, which is one of the most vitalising influences at work in the British Army, demands some word about the records of the various regiments in this respect, for they are each and all quite as proud of their roll of Victoria Crosses as they are of the faded colours that were borne forward at Badajoz or waved defiantly at Inkerman.

Methods of classification The second method of classification groups men according to the arms with which they fight, and these arms are much more complicated now than they were half a century or less ago. It is no longer sufficient to speak of infantry, cavalry, and artillery, or to divide the infantry into Guards and regiments of the line. The Army has also its Engineers, and, of newer creation, its machine-gunners, and its Tank Corps. These and other units are worthy of a line to themselves. A further method of classification may occur to some, at least so far as the infantry are concerned. They may remember

Canadians had a slight advantage. They won 31 crosses against Australia's 25. But should an Australian remind us of his New Zealand colleagues and their share in the name and exploits of Anzac, we can only reply that there are six of these in our list, and so the totals are exactly equal—surely something of a coincidence.

Of the Canadians nine came from Ontario, and eight from Quebec, a fine record for both, but especially perhaps for the latter province, with its large population of home-keeping Frenchmen. Of the others, seven were from Manitoba, two each from British Columbia and Saskatchewan, and one each from Nova Scotia and Alberta. The last was an engineer not attached to any particular province. The other parts of the Empire, excluding Australia and New Zealand, were awarded three, two falling to India, and one to Newfoundland, making sixty-five Victoria Crosses for the soldiers from Overseas.

L.-CPL. W. AMEY, R. Warwick Regt. — SPR. A. ARCHIBALD, R.E. — LIEUT. H. AUTEN, R.N.R. — L.-CPL.T. L. AXFORD, A.I.F. — LT. J. C. BARRETT, Leicester Regt. — CDR. D. M. W. BEAK, R.N.V.R. — A.-CPT. BEAUCHAMP-PROCTOR, R.A.F.

LT. W. D. BISSETT, Argyll & Suth. H. — A.-CPL. A. BRERE-TON, Manitoba Regt. — LT. J. BRILLIANT, Quebec Regt. — SGT. M. V. BUCKLEY, A.I.F. — LT.-COL. D. BURGES, Gloucester Regt. — SGT. T. CALDWELL, R. Scots Fus. — SERGT. L. CALVERT, K.O.Y.L.I.

PTE. G. CART-WRIGHT, A.I.F. — A.-MAJ. B. M. CLOUT-MAN, R.E. — PTE. W. H. COLT-MAN, N. Staffs Regt. — CPL. F. G. COPPINS, Manitoba Regt. — PTE. J. CRICHTON, N.Z. — SGT. H. A. CURTIS, Dublin Fus. — DVR. H. DALZIEL, A.I.F.

their being divided into battalions and brigades—some of Regulars, others of Territorials, and others of Service men. In the early days of the war this line of demarcation was undoubtedly a clear one, and stood for real differences in training and experience, but as the struggle progressed it became less so. The handful of Regular soldiers, the highly-trained men of Mons and Ypres, were destroyed in a few months, and the ranks of all battalions alike were soon filled with men who were in effect civilians. Except as a matter of record, the earlier distinction vanished, and no useful purpose can be served by reviving it here. Finally, as far as these introductory remarks are concerned, we have classified a man as belonging to the unit with which he was serving when he won his V.C. Not infrequently it happened that a man was sent from one regiment to another without there being any permanent transfer of his name. Officially he was described as of his own regiment, attached to the other ; for instance, C. Wood, Yorkshire Regiment, attached East Surrey Regiment, was a Yorkshire soldier who, for some reason or other, had been drafted for the time being into the East Surreys.

To begin with a broad classification of our 154 men, it will surprise no one who followed, even superficially, the fighting of 1918 to learn that there were many awards to both Canadians and Australians. In their generous rivalry the

For the British Army proper the total is seventy-three, of which all save sixteen went to the infantry of the line. Of the sixteen, the Guards won five as did also the Engineers, the remaining six were given thus : Three to the Machine Gun Corps, two to the Tank Corps, and one to the Artillery. Those won by the infantrymen fell to men in almost every one of the regiments of the line, but the case of the Lancashire Fusiliers, with five crosses during the period, is specially notable. With the previous distinctions of this kind won by the Fusiliers in Gallipoli and elsewhere, this addition must surely place them at the head of the list of winners of the cross.

Distinguished regiments The Manchester Regiment won three in the same period, another distinction for Lancashire, and those that won two were the West Ridings, the York and Lancasters, the Northamptons, the Leinsters, the Sherwood Foresters, the Yorkshire Light Infantry, the Royal Scots, the Highland Light Infantry, the Northumberland Fusiliers, the South Wales Borderers, the Royal Inniskilling Fusiliers, the Royal Welsh Fusiliers, and the Royal West Kents.

Again, if we divide the 57 infantrymen according to nationality, we find that nine belonged to Scottish regiments, seven to Irish, and four to Welsh ones. England was left therefore with 37. Of the five Guardsmen two belonged to the

Grenadiers, two to the Coldstream, and one to the Scots. In fairness to the Irish Guards it should be said that one of their number won the cross, but at the time he was serving with the Lancashire Fusiliers. He was Lieut.-Colonel J. N. Marshall, M.C., then commanding the 16th Battalion. These soldiers account for a total of 138, and 16 therefore remain. Of these 12 were earned by naval men, and the remaining four went to the Air Force.

The more detailed part of the story must begin with the Navy, as the senior Service. As just stated 12 Victoria Crosses were awarded during the period to this Service, although not all were for valorous deeds on the water. Three were given for gallantry shown at Ostend on the night of May 9th, 1918, when the Vindictive was sunk between the harbour piers there. Lieut. Geoffrey H. Drummond, R.N.V.R., was in command of motor-launch 254, and Lieut. R. Bourke, D.S.O., of the same unit, in command of 276. Both followed

G. N. Bradford and A. L. Harrison, the latter known to thousands as an International footballer, were in command of storming-parties, the one from Iris II. and the other from Vindictive. They got on to the Mole after gigantic difficulties, and there Bradford was killed while making fast the anchor, an operation on which the whole enterprise, so far at least as his own ship was concerned, depended.

Harrison lived somewhat longer. Once on the Mole he led his men in a wild rush towards the guns that were commanding the Mole's length, only to fall dead at their feet.

V.C. "mysteries" revealed

On November 21st, 1918, ten days after the armistice, the Admiralty revealed the nature of the great deeds which had earlier won the V.C. for Commander Gordon Campbell and several other seamen. These were for actions with enemy submarines, and while the war was in progress it had been thought inadvisable to reveal the secrets. There were eight

PTE. P. DAVEY, A.I.F.	A.-SGT. J. B. DAY-KINS, Y. & Lanc. Regt.	LIEUT. D. J. DEAN, R.W. Kent Regt.	SEC.-LT. E. DE WIND, R. Irish Regt.	PTE. T. DINESEN, Quebec Regt.	C.-S.-M. M. DOYLE, R. Munster Fus.	LT.-COL. W. ELSTOB, Manchester Regt.

CAPT. C. H. FRISBY, Coldstream Guards.   LIEUT. M. F. GREGG, Novia Scotia Regt.   SGT. T. J. HARRIS, R.W. Kent Regt.   L.-CR. A. L. HARRISON, R.N.   PTE. J. HARVEY, London Regt.   CPL. N. HARVEY, R. Inniskilling Fus.   LT. F. W. HEDGES, Bedford Regt.

S.-LT. J. P. HUFFAM, W. Riding Regt.   CPL. D. F. HUNTER, H.L.I.   CPT. B. S. HUTCHESON, Canadian A.M.C.   LT. G. M. INGRAM, Australian Inf.   L.-CPL. T. N. JACKSON, Coldstream Gds.   SGT. W. H. JOHNSON, Notts & Derby Regt.   LIEUT. J. JOHNSON, Northumberland Fus.

the Vindictive into the harbour, and it was largely due to the skill and gallantry of these two officers that so many of her crew were saved. Drummond was wounded and his vessel damaged early in the fight, but nevertheless he laid her aside the Vindictive and took from her forty men. Bourke was equally intrepid in refusing, although his launch was seriously damaged, to leave the harbour until he was convinced that no one was left there in jeopardy.

The third of the trio, Lieut. V. A. G. Crutchley, D.S.C., known in days of peace as a county cricketer, took command of the Vindictive after his two superior officers had been disabled, the one killed and the other wounded, and was responsible for the final act of putting her in position. He then, satisfied that no one was left on the Vindictive, took charge of the motor-launch which rescued him, and by his tremendous exertions kept this damaged vessel afloat until H.M.S. Warwick found her in a sinking condition.

Ostend and Zeebrugge V.C.'s

Ostend reminds one of the earlier attempts made to close that port and also Zeebrugge, and the record before us contains two awards for gallantry in the latter operation. Both went to men who had given the final proofs of their valour, for both were killed while leading their men to attacks which meant almost certain death to those in front. Lieut.-Commanders

of them in this narrative, but only one concerns us here, for the remaining seven had been awarded previous to August 4th, 1918.

Lieut. H. Auten, D.S.C., of the R.N.R., was in command of H.M.S. Stock Force, when, on July 30th, 1918, she was torpedoed by an enemy submarine. Serious damage was done, practically everything, save only the nerves of the captain and his crew, being injured. As arranged previously, however, a panic-party left the ship in great haste, and began to row wildly about in their little boat. This manœuvre tempted the German submarine to come nearer, and when she was near enough Auten let fly with his two available guns. The shots took effect, and at length the submarine was sunk. The Stock Force was badly damaged, but she was kept afloat for some little time, and only sank when her crew were being rescued by torpedo-boats. This was described as "one of the finest examples of coolness, discipline, and good organisation in the history of Q ships."

Five other naval V.C.'s belonged to the R.N.R., and their deeds are more akin to those of soldiers. However, their connection with the Navy is too close to be interfered with, and their deeds must certainly come here. On October 31st, 1918, when the name of Chief Petty-Officer George Prowse was brought to public notice, it was only stated in vague terms how, during an advance, he collected some men from a disorganised section and led them against a strong post. Afterwards, he did a similar feat, on each occasion capturing the guns which were holding up the British advance, and bringing back prisoners. Later it was stated that Prowse belonged to the Drake Battalion of the R.N.V.R., and that his superb courage, as it was called, was displayed at Pronville on September 2nd, 1918.

To the same battalion belonged another hero, Commander D. M. W. Beak, D.S.O., M.C. On August 25th, 1918, he was fighting in the same neighbourhood as Prowse, and found himself suddenly in command, not of a battalion, but of a brigade. Four days earlier he had led his own men in a very successful attack on four hostile positions, and he was equally cool and alert when faced with a greater responsibility. He reorganised the brigade, led the men forward, and, when the rush was checked, dashed on and broke up the nest of machine-guns that was hindering the

SGT. R. S. JUDSON, N.Z.

LIEUT. G. F. KERR, Central Ontario Regt.

A.-SGT. G. KNIGHT, Alberta Regt.

SGT. H. J. LAURENT, N.Z.

PTE. F. LESTER, Lancashire Fus.

L.-CPL. A. LEWIS, Northampton Regt.

SGT. A. D. LOWER-SON, A.I.F. LT. L. D. McCARTHY, A.I.F. LT. D. S. McGREGOR, M.G.C.

advance. Early in September he gave another example of his powers as a leader, and contributed " very materially " to the success of the Naval Division in these operations.

The remaining three Victoria Crosses awarded to the R.N.R. were announced together on May 24th, 1919, but were for deeds widely separated in time and place, although alike as examples of the cool courage that British seamen invariably show in times of danger. All were in command of ships, one a submarine, one a transport, and one an ordinary steamer.

On July 4th, 1915, Lieut. F. Parslow, R.N.R., in command of the Anglo-Californian, a horse transport, was told that a submarine was in sight, and soon proof of this arrived in the form of shots. For a time Parslow kept in front of his enemy, and it was only when the latter was upon him that he prepared to obey the order to put the crew in boats and abandon the ship.

Heroes of the R.N.R. Just at that moment, however, he received a message by wireless saying that a destroyer was on the way to help him, so he remained on the bridge and under heavy fire got his ship moving again. While directing this, he was killed, but the destroyer arrived in time to save the ship and her cargo. For this the credit was rightly given to Parslow.

The next case was that of Lieut. A. B. Smith, also R.N.R. On March 10th, 1917, when in command of the Otaki, he met the German raider Möwe. He had one 4·7 in. gun against the raider's four heavier ones, but when ordered to stop he showed fight rather than obey. The unequal duel lasted for about twenty minutes. Smith went down with colours flying in the Otaki, and the Germans were moved to describe his action as " a duel as gallant as naval history can relate."

It is right and proper to find the name of a submarine commander among our heroes. Early in 1918, Lieut.-Commander G. S. White, in charge of E14, was sent off from Mudros to attack the

A.-SGT. L. McGUFFIE, K.O.S.B.

LT. D. L. MACIN-TYRE, Argy'l & S.H.

PTE. H. McIVER, Royal Scots.

CPL. J. MACNAMARA, E. Surrey Regt.

Goeben, then aground in the Dardanelles. In this particular matter he had no success, and when returning his ship was badly damaged, so badly in fact that she was obliged to travel on the surface. This brought her under constant fire from the Turkish forts, but White directed her course until he was killed, his last thought being to give his men a chance of escape by running her ashore.

The last of the naval honours was against the Bolshevists on June 17th, 1919, and, although earned after the armistice, should find a place here. Lieut. A. W. S. Agar, R.N., operating in the Baltic, got his vessel through a screen of destroyers, successfully attacked the cruiser Oleg, and got back again under heavy fire from both the land forts and the destroyers.

The deeds of the soldiers should be related next, but before turning to them we may be allowed to interpolate those of the newest Service — four airmen.

Captain F. M. F. West, M.C., was flying over the German lines when seven hostile machines turned upon him ; on tackling them, his leg was soon badly hit by an explosive bullet. Nothing daunted, he kept control of his machine and brought it safely into the British lines, where he fainted, but, on recovering consciousness, wrote his report. Captain A. W. Beauchamp-Proctor was a prince among air fighters, as the long record of his deeds, issued on November 30th, 1918, amply proved. Having won the D.S.O., D.F.C., M.C. and bar, he outdid his earlier deeds in the two months between August 8th and October 8th, 1918. Therein he was victor in twenty-six combats, and his record was fifty-four foes defeated, twenty-two enemy machines and sixteen kite-balloons destroyed, in addition to sixteen driven down out of control. For months his work was " almost unsurpassed in its brilliancy."

Captain W. G. Barker had won a batch of decorations very like those of Beauchamp-Proctor when he flew **Great victors in** out in the morning of October **air-fighting** 27th, 1918. Having disposed of two German machines, he found himself surrounded by others, and in the ensuing fight was rendered unconscious, obviously losing thereby control of his machine. However he recovered his senses and drove down another foe, only to be put again *hors de combat* by a serious injury to his elbow. Yet, strange to say, he went successfully through another combat, and finally crashed down in the British lines. He had disposed of four enemy machines, making a total of fifty.

Captain Edward Mannock's record was like unto these two. He had won the D.S.O. and two bars, and the M.C. and one bar, when he was killed in France on June 26th, 1918. His fighting career had been one long catalogue of victories, and as fifty of these were on record he was awarded, posthumously, the Victoria Cross in July, 1919, not for one or two deeds only, but " in recognition of bravery of the first order in aerial combat."

Having now reached the soldiers, a beginning may be made with the Guards. The Guards had one of their great days on September 27th, 1918. The division was advancing, and in front of it was the Canal du Nord. The 3rd Brigade was led by the 1st Battalion Grenadier Guards, and in command of this was Viscount Gort, an Irish peer, and a soldier who had already earned the D.S.O. and M.C. Under heavy fire he led up his men, but there was some unexpected obstacle to their progress. While dealing with this, Lord Gort was twice wounded, but he directed the final attack and organised the captured position before collapsing from his wounds.

Not far away was the 1st Battalion of the Coldstreamers, and this, too, met with very severe resistance on reaching the bank of the canal. Machine-guns, from one point of vantage especially, were doing very deadly work, so Captain C. H. Frisby, with three men who volunteered to follow him, rushed into the canal, got across it, and

CPL. J. McPHIE,
R.E.

CAPT. E. MANNOCK,
R.A.F.

being a cork-float bridge across the Canal de la Sensée. It was under fire and was damaged so much, that, when the infantry began to cross, it buckled up and began to break. Daylight was coming when McPhie dashed into the water and tried to make the bridge secure. He was unable to do this, but realising the vital necessity of keeping touch with his few comrades on the other side of the canal, he again led the way across the frail and tossing structure and this time was killed. However, the patrol on the other side was saved, thanks entirely to McPhie.

Captain A. H. S. Waters, D.S.O., M.C., was one of the three Engineers who won the cross on November 4th. He was on that day hard at work with his company bridging the Oise-Sambre Canal. Heavy fire was directed against the Engineers, and the operation was only completed after Waters himself had gone forward, all his subordinates having been killed or wounded, and taken charge of the surviving men, the group being held

A.-LT.-COL. J. N. MARSHALL, Lancs Fus.   SGT. J. MEIKLE, Seaforth Highrs.   L.-CPL. W. H. METCALF, Manitoba Regt.   PTE. F. G. MILES, Gloucester Regt.   SGT. W. MERRIFIELD, Cent. Ontario Regt.   PTE. M. MOFFATT, Leinster Regt.   L.-CPL. G. ONIONS, Devon Regt.

silenced the guns. Had this not been done, it is practically certain that the whole advance in this area would have been held up. Frisby was wounded, but he remained on duty; not only so, but he went to the aid of a neighbouring company that had lost all its officers, and encouraged the men to beat back a strong attack. One of the three who followed Frisby was Lance-Corporal T. N. Jackson, and after the first exploit he led the way into a German trench. Later in the day he was killed, and his cross, like that of so many others, was a posthumous one.

Another Grenadier and a Scots Guard remain to complete the five. The Grenadier was Private W. E. Holmes, of the 2nd Battalion, who was killed while saving life. He carried several wounded men out of danger, but his last errand of mercy was fatal. This happened on October 9th, 1918. The Scot was Lance-Sergeant H. B. Wood, of **A gallant** the 2nd Battalion, and his cross **Scots Guardsman** was won four days later. His company was then in the village of St. Python, trying to clear it of the enemy, and to win its way across the River Selle. The opposition was strong, but Wood was equal to the occasion. He himself lay down and dealt with the German snipers, while those under his orders worked their way forward. This done, he showed a like skill in keeping back the enemy, and it was recorded that the success of the day's operations was largely due to his " gallant conduct and initiative."

The five crosses won by the Engineers were all given for work done in the final advance, when rivers were bridged in hot haste, and the supreme consideration was to make a way for the men and guns to press hard on the retreating Germans. In such days the Engineers are invaluable, and never more so than in October and November, 1918, when Archibald, Cloutman, Findlay, McPhie, and Waters earned immortal fame.

In point of time the first of the five was Corporal James McPhie, of Edinburgh. On October 14th he was with some sappers whose task was to keep in

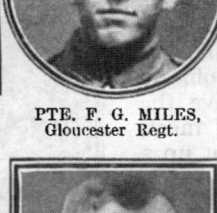

C.P.O. G. PROWSE,
R.N.V.R.

PTE. J. RICHARDSON,
Manitoba Regt.

PTE. T. RICKETTS,
Newfoundland Regt.

LT. C. S. RUTHERFORD, Quebec Regt.

up by cork floats. The success was " entirely due " to this example, for the officer and his assistants were fired at from point-blank range, and their escape from death was almost a miracle.

On the same day, Major G. de C. E. Findlay, D.S.O., M.C., was building or repairing bridges over the same canal. One of these was at the lock near Catillon, and here, too, the enemy's fire was very accurate and severe. Findlay, however, although wounded, got a bridge into position and was the first to cross it. Like Waters, his example was most valuable at a critical time.

The third of this trio was a sapper, Adam Archibald, of Leith. He was one of those who assisted Waters, working while standing on cork floats at building a bridge over the canal. This example, too, was of supreme value, and on the completion of his task he collapsed from gas poisoning, a bare **Splendid heroism** statement that reveals another **of Engineers** danger faced by these men.

Two days later, Major B. McK. Cloutman, M.C., of the 59th Field Company, R.E., saved a bridge, for the time being at least, from destruction. It was at Pont-sur-Sambre, and the retreating enemy had made all preparations for blowing it up at the right moment. However, quite alone, Cloutman swam out, and under heavy fire removed the leads from the charges. He returned safely.

Another five on our list may be made by grouping together the three machine-gunners and the two Tankmen. Sec.-Lieut. W. A. White was three times responsible for dealing successfully with hostile machine-guns. Alone he shot three gunners and took the gun, shot five gunners and took the gun ; he rushed an enemy position with a few assistants, and finally consolidated the captured position and severely damaged the enemy. This was done at Gouzeaucourt on September 18th, 1918.

The next machine-gunner was Lieut. D. S. MacGregor, a Territorial officer of the Royal Scots, who had joined the Machine Gun Corps. At

Hoogmolen, on October 22nd, he found himself in a position of difficulty and danger. In front of him was a bare stretch of ground swept by the German guns, but, nothing daunted, he got his men and his weapons forward, driving the horses across six hundred yards and getting the battery into action. The advance was thus resumed, but an hour later Mac-Gregor was killed.

In a very long statement the War Office, on September 5th, 1919, gave an account of the deeds that won the cross for Lieut. A. E. Ker, of the 61st Battalion Machine Gun Corps, and previously a Gordon Highlander. He was at St. Quentin on March 21st, 1918, the place and the day of the gravest danger, for there, as all know, the Germans got through. But in one place Ker, with a Vickers gun, held up the attack; and when this gun had been destroyed and the enemy was all around him, he and a few companions used their revolvers to beat back bayonet attacks. The wounded were collected in a small shelter, and then Ker and his men fought on, once taking from the Germans a rifle and some ammunition after a hand-to-hand encounter. For three hours

Two heroic Tank officers the attacks of five hundred men were held up by a few Britons, and no cross was ever more gallantly earned.

The two Tank officers received their award on the same day, October 30th, 1918. On September 2nd, Lieut.-Col. R. A. West, D.S.O., M.C., formerly of the North Irish Horse, was in charge of a battalion of light Tanks, which were waiting for the moment to advance. West went forward to find out the position and came up with an infantry battalion in sore straits. At once he took charge of this, for most of its officers were down. He reorganised the position, and to give the shaken men confidence went up and down in front of them, crying out : " Stick it, men," and " for God's sake put up a good fight." He could hardly escape being killed, and in a few minutes his gallant life came to an end. But the hostile attack was defeated.

Lieut. C. H. Sewell was in charge of some " whippet " Tanks at Fremicourt on August 29th, 1918. Under fire he got out of his own machine to rescue the crew of one that had overturned —and this he did, unaided, by digging a way to the door which was blocked in a shell-hole. Later he rescued one of his men who was lying wounded, and he was killed while assisting another.

The artilleryman in our list may fitly be mentioned here. He was Lieut. R. V. Gorle, R.F.A., who at Ledeghem on October 1st, 1918, took his gun into action in most exposed positions on four separate occasions, and afterwards galloped it in front of the leading infantry and knocked out some German machine-guns.

The record of the infantry may well begin with a group of five, those winners of the V.C. who belonged to the Lancashire Fusiliers, and we will follow them with a kindred group of the same size—three Manchesters and two men of the York and Lancaster Regiment.

Lance - Sergeant Edward Smith, of the 1/5th Battalion Lancashire Fusiliers, led his platoon to the capture of a machine-gun post, and then went off to the assistance of another platoon, where again he showed himself a resourceful leader. Next day he was to the fore in the critical operation of restoring a portion of the line, and his courage and example on August 21st, 22nd, and 23rd, 1918, were deservedly rewarded by a V.C. In the same list of awards was the name of another Fusilier, Sergeant H. J. Colley, who won the cross on the 28th. He, too, was in charge of a platoon, and it was owing to his courage and resource at Martinpuich that a dangerous attack was beaten back. Less fortunate than Smith, he was so badly wounded that he died.

Private Frank Lester, who, like Colley, belonged to the 10th Battalion, met his death in the noblest fashion on October 12th, 1918. The village of Neuvilly was being cleared by the British, and at one time the only chance of life was to keep to the houses. A clever sniper was steadily picking off the British soldiers, so Lester dashed into the street and shot him. Almost at once he fell himself mortally wounded, for German machine-guns were everywhere, but he had done his all—" to save their lives he sacrificed his own."

Sergeant James Clarke, of the 15th Battalion, a Rochdale man, comes next. On November 2nd, 1918, he was commanding a platoon which was held up by machine-gun fire. His action can easily be guessed. He dashed forward, seized the guns, and made the crew follow him as prisoners. But this was by no means all. Against some more guns he led a Tank, and two days later he was equally successful with a Lewis gun which he got into action very effectively, enabling his company to resume their advance.

The last of the five Fusiliers is an officer, and his description, Lieut. (acting Lieut.-Colonel), shows how severe was the fighting that caused such rapid promotion in those November days. He, John N. Marshall, transferred from the Irish Guards, was leading his battalion, the 16th, in the attack on the Sambre-Oise Canal near Catillon, on November 4th, 1918, an operation which has been already mentioned in connection with the Engineers. The bridge by which the Fusiliers were to cross was broken, so Marshall organised and led forward parties of volunteers to repair it. These were quickly killed or wounded, but he called for others, and, standing exposed on the bank, encouraged and assisted them at their work. So far he was unhurt, but he was killed when dashing at the head of his men across the repaired structure.

The first of the three Manchester names carries us back from the glad days of November to the dark ones of the previous March, for it was on March 21st and near St. Quentin

PTE. J. RYAN,   CPL. E. SEAMAN,   LIEUT. C. H. SEWELL,
A.I.F.   R. Inniskillings.   Tank Corps.

that Lieut.-Colonel W. Elstob, D.S.O., M.C., leading the 16th Manchesters, gave his life for the cause. He was at Manchester Redoubt, and the Germans were coming on in great force, so he dashed from point to point among his men, at one time beating back alone an attack of bombers, at another bringing up ammunition, and all the time assisting the defence in every possible way. The attack developed, and soon the redoubt was quite surrounded, but Elstob assured the general in command of the brigade that his men would fight to the last. " Here we fight and here we die," said he, and, as good as his word, he was killed when a final assault swept into the position.

Alfred Wilkinson was a private of the Manchesters, who won the cross for his gallantry in taking a message. When he volunteered, five men had been killed in attempts to do so, but happily he, although in extreme danger, completed his hazardous journey in safety. This was October 20th, and on November 4th, Sec.-Lieut. James Kirk, of the 2nd Battalion, won the cross, like **Daring deed on Oise Canal** Elstob, at the price of his life, for working a Lewis gun from a raft on the Oise Canal. He was only ten yards from the enemy, and his object was to protect a party who were working at making a bridge. He continued his daring work until killed.

The York and Lancaster heroes were both sergeants— F. C. Riggs and J. B. Daykins, the former belonging to the 6th Battalion, and the latter to the 2/4th. On October 1st, 1918, near Epinoy, Riggs led his platoon to the capture of several guns and fifty prisoners, being killed in a later enemy attack. Daykins, like so many, was successful in rushing a machine-gun, taking a number of prisoners and saving many casualties to his own side. He fortunately survived.

We may now deal with those other English regiments that won two Victoria Crosses each during the period. Of these there are six, making a group of twelve heroes : Northumberland Fusiliers, West Ridings, Yorkshire Light Infantry, Sherwood Foresters, Northamptons, and Royal West Kents.

The Northumberland Fusiliers were an officer and a private

and their deeds remind us of two facts worthy of mention in the recent history of the "Fighting Fifth." The officer, Lieut. James Johnson, belonged to the 36th Battalion, which indicates how great a number of Fusiliers were in the field, and the private, Wilfred Wood, won his cross in Italy, whither the 10th Battalion went to assist the Italians against Austria. On October 14th, 1918, Johnson was constant in bringing in wounded men under heavy fire, while Wood, working a Lewis gun at Casa Van on October 28th, 1918, compelled three hundred of the enemy to surrender in two groups.

An officer and a private also fill the bill for the West Ridings. Sec.-Lieut. J. P. Huffam, of the 2nd Battalion, twice led attacks against hostile machine-guns, and on four hard days was constantly to the front with gallant deeds. Henry Tandey, who had already won the D.C.M. and the M.M., was at Marcoing on September 28th, and his deeds there were somewhat remarkable, even in the Great War. As a preliminary, he knocked out a machine-gun, and under heavy fire restored a plank bridge, and then came his crowning deed. He and eight other men were surrounded by Germans and the position was truly hopeless, except to Tandey. He called for a bayonet charge and led it—with the unexpected result that thirty-seven of the enemy were driven on to the remainder of his company and became prisoners.

Sergeant Lawrence Calvert, of the Yorkshire Light Infantry, won the cross on September 9th, 1918. He belonged to the

L.-SGT. W. SIMPSON
Lincoln Regt.

L.-SGT. E. SMITH.
Lancs Fus.

SGT. P. C. STATTON
A.I.F.

5th Battalion, and at Havrincourt he dashed forward alone against two machine-guns, killed the crew, and so enabled the advance to proceed. Lieut.-Colonel Harry Greenwood, D.S.O., M.C., of the 9th Battalion, did like deeds on October 23rd at Ovillers, and on two days of hard fighting led his battalion with remarkable courage. Once he was almost surrounded, but he took his men forward, and the result was one hundred and fifty prisoners and some guns, and at other times on the two days his skilful and bold handling was productive of most important results.

The two Sherwood Foresters on our list won their crosses at almost the same time, and the awards appeared on the same day; both were among the thirty-two honours which were gazetted on December 14th, 1918. Lieut.-Colonel B. W. Vann was a remarkable man. He was a clergyman, but had given up his work to fight, and constant acts of courage had brought him to the command of his battalion—the 1/6th. On September 29th, 1918, he led this with great skill across the Canal du Nord, but soon the advance was stopped. Vann thereupon rushed up to the firing-line, and by his prompt action and absolute contempt for danger changed the whole situation. The line swept forward. Later, this officer rushed a field-gun quite alone, but on October 3rd, while leading another attack, he was killed. Sergeant W. H. Johnson was a Territorial in the 1/5th Battalion, and he won his cross on the day and place of Vann's death, October 3rd, at Ramicourt. The deeds — for he did it twice—were putting machine-guns out of action, which he did with remarkable efficiency, coming back with trophies in the shape of both guns and men. He was severely wounded.

Heroes of the Sherwood Foresters

The two Northamptons received their awards on the same day, and again one was an officer and the other in the ranks. Again one was taken and the other left, but this time it was the man, not the officer, who lost his life. Lance-Corporal A. L. Lewis, of the 6th Battalion, was at Rosny on September 18th, 1918, and there he crawled out alone, and came back

with prisoners, men who had been working two deadly machine-guns. Three days later he was killed, having again shown "great powers of command." Lieut. F. W. Hedges was serving with the same battalion about a month later, although he was really an officer of the Bedfords. He led forward his company with extraordinary success, and when it was stopped went on with only one follower and captured six machine-guns and fourteen prisoners. The great allied advance was just beginning when Sergeant T. J. Harris, described as late Royal West Kent Regiment, won his cross. On August 9th, 1918, he was with the 6th Battalion at Morlancourt, but all that need be said is that he was another of those who successfully tackled hostile machine-guns. Lieut. D. J. Dean, of the 8th Battalion, had rather a different task. From September 24th to 26th, 1918, he held an advance post near Lens, one that was not very secure, but under his leadership the enemy was five times driven back, and by his "valour, leadership, and devotion to duty" the position was saved.

Scotland, Ireland, and Wales had each two regiments with two recipients of the cross, and with this dozen brave men we will now deal. Lieut. D. L. Mac-Intyre was with the 1/6th Highland Light Infantry at Croisilles, in August, 1918, when the battalion was in a position of some danger. He was acting as adjutant and was constantly in the firing-line; at one time he was in command of it during an attack, and his courage was superbly shown when getting his force through entanglements of various kinds. Later he dealt, as did many others, with hostile machine-guns, raiding three "pill-boxes" in a redoubt, and single-handed capturing a machine-gun by sending its crew flying.

Two dauntless Highlanders

About the same time, or rather a little later, something was said in the Press about a certain non-commissioned officer who for two days held on to an isolated post. Later it turned out that this feat was performed by Corporal D. F. Hunter, of the Highland Light Infantry. Without food or water, subject not only to the fire of the enemy but to the British barrage also, he kept his post, showing, as we are told, a "determination, fortitude, and endurance" beyond all praise.

On August 23rd, 1918, Private Hugh McIver, of the 2nd Royal Scots, was serving as a runner to his company, then near Courcelles-le-Comte. Seeing an enemy scout, he chased him into a machine-gun post, where he had a fight with a number of Germans; this ended in McIver killing six and capturing twenty, with two guns, and the advance of his company being resumed. Later he stopped a Tank from firing by error on its own men, thus saving many lives, but later he lost his own. On October 15th, Corporal R. E. Elcock, of the 11th Battalion, then commanding a Lewis gun team, rushed his gun up at a critical moment, and by its prompt action "saved the whole attack from being held up." Later he rushed a German machine-gun and captured the crew.

Of the two Irish units we will take the junior, the Leinsters, first. Sergeant John O'Niell, M.M., and Martin Moffat, a private from Sligo, were both with the 2nd Battalion when it was doing its bit in the great advance on October 14th, 1918. O'Niell's company was checked by hostile fire, so with eleven men the sergeant dashed forward and captured four field-guns, two machine-guns, and sixteen Germans. Six days later, with only one man, he rushed a machine-gun, putting about one hundred of the enemy to flight, and altogether he showed "the most remarkable courage and powers of leadership." Moffat was crossing the open with five comrades, when they found themselves suddenly fired at from a house close by. Caring naught for the bullets, he dashed to it with some bombs, got round to the back door, and alone entered the building. The sight of this intrepid Irishman and his bombs was too much for the enemy, and, two having been killed, the remaining thirty surrendered.

At Terhand, in September, 1918, was the 2nd Battalion of that famous Irish regiment, the Inniskilling Fusiliers, and with it was Corporal E. Seaman. The advance was held up by hostile machine-guns, so he went forward alone with his

Lewis gun and destroyed the obstacle. He returned with two German machine-guns and twelve prisoners, and later repeated the feat, capturing another gun under heavy fire. It was entirely due to his gallant conduct that the company's further progress was possible, but unfortunately he was killed during the movement. The story of Private Norman Harvey, of the 1st Battalion, is very similar, save that he lived to receive the cross. On October 25th, 1918, he rushed forward alone against machine-guns, broke up the nest, and scattered the men in charge. He, too, repeated the feat a little later, and also did useful work by obtaining valuable information, the fruits of a night journey into the enemy's lines.

In the Army, North Wales is represented by the Royal

Lance-Corporal J. W. Sayer, of the 8th Battalion Royal West Surreys, belongs to the highest type of hero. He was killed just after performing superhuman deeds, not in the exhilaration of victory and advance, but on that dark day, March 21st, 1918, when all seemed lost. For two hours he held on to a small isolated post, beating off many attacks and killing many of the enemy who had loomed up in great numbers through the mist. Every kind of fire, as well as bomb and bayonet, was tried against him, but his skill enabled the post to hold out until nearly all the garrison had been killed, and he himself wounded and captured. He died subsequently as the result of wounds received at Le Cateau.

Sec.-Lieut. F. E. Young was with the 1st Hertfordshires

LIEUT. J. E. TAIT,　PTE. J. TOWERS,　LIEUT. TOWNER　A.-LT.-COL. B. W. VANN　SGT. W. WARING,　CPL. H. WEALE,　LT.-COL. C. WESLEY
Manitoba Regt.　Scottish Rifles.　A.I.F.　Notts and Derby Regt.　R. Welsh Fus.　R. Welsh Fus.　PECK, Manitoba Regt.

Welsh Fusiliers, and that fine regiment, so far as we are concerned here, by Corporal Henry Weale, of Shotton, Cheshire, and Sergeant William Waring, M.M., of Welshpool. Weale belonged to the 14th Battalion, and on August 26th, at Bazentin-le-Grand, he was deputed to deal with the machine-guns that were preventing an adjacent battalion from moving forward. He did this with such success that all the guns were captured, and the official notice described how the surviving members of the crew took to their heels with this gallant N.C.O. in hot pursuit. Waring, of the 25th Battalion, also led an attack on machine-guns, taking the guns and twenty prisoners. Later he was killed while re-organising the shaken ranks and leading them forward under very heavy fire.

The next award takes us to the Balkans where, in September, 1918, the 7th South Wales Borderers was serving. The battalion was under Lieut.-Colonel D. Burges, D.S.O., and having been assembled by him without loss, began an advance over very difficult ground. The enemy was in force, and the fire severe and accurate, so the colonel, although wounded, moved about the lines, and by his constant exertions kept it moving in the right direction and in good order. He then led the final stage of the advance until he was again wounded. Sergeant-Major J. H. Williams, D.C.M., M.M., of the 10th Battalion of the Borderers, rushed a machine-gun alone and took fifteen prisoners. One of these then turned on him, but after a sharp tussle, in which some of them were badly damaged, the Germans decided to follow the Welshman quietly to the prisoners' cages.

There were twenty-three regiments of the line in which there was one recipient of the Victoria Cross in the period under consideration. Fifteen of these were English, and a group of five from London and neighbourhood can be taken first. The London Regiment supplied one, Private Jack Harvey, of the 22nd Battalion—a Camberwell man. Although he rushed a machine-gun post near Péronne on September 2nd, 1918, he was not satisfied with his feat, so he continued his way along a German trench, reaching a well-populated dug-out, where he forced no fewer than thirty-seven of the enemy to surrender. By these two acts of great gallantry he saved his company from heavy casualties and enabled the whole of the attacking line to advance.

Each of the Surrey Regiments has one V.C. Corporal John McNamara, of the East Surreys, was with his battalion near Lens on September 3rd. This time the Germans were attacking, and the corporal, who was just then at the telephone, realising that the assault, a sudden one, was really being pressed, dashed to the nearest post and took the lead in holding it until reinforcements arrived.

at Havrincourt on September 18th, 1918, when a strong counter-attack developed. He did a good deal in warning the garrisons of this movement and encouraging them to resist it, and when it got really close he was prominent in the actual fighting. By his exertions the battalion was able to maintain a line of great tactical value, and after fighting hard for four hours he was last seen, still at it, "hand to hand against a considerable number of the enemy."

Lieut.-Colonel D. G. Johnson, D.S.O., M.C., is another case of a battalion leader earning the V.C. A captain in the South Wales Borderers, he was on November 4th, 1918, commanding the 2nd Battalion of the Royal Sussex. The order was for the men to cross the Sambre Canal, for the Germans were then in full retreat, but just where they came to it the fire was unusually severe. There was some confusion, but the colonel came forward and took the matter in hand. He got the parties, one of Engineers to make the bridges, and the other of infantry to dash across them into order again, and himself led a first assault. This failed, but he tried again, and this time the crossing was accomplished. By a miracle Johnson himself remained unwounded, and his conduct was entirely responsible for turning defeat into victory.

Yorkshire and Lancashire supply the British Army with many soldiers, and it is not therefore strange to find two more regiments recruited in those northern parts still to be mentioned—the Yorkshire and the Royal Lancaster.

Sergeant William McNally, M.M., of the 8th Yorkshires, apparently a collier, was in October, 1918, serving in Italy. He rushed a machine-gun on the 27th, thus enabling his company to advance, and two days later he performed a like feat. This did not, however, exhaust his capacity for gallant deeds, and " throughout the whole operations his innumerable acts of gallantry set a high example to his men, and his leading was beyond all praise."

Lance-Sergeant Thomas Neeley, M.M., of the 8th Royal Lancasters, was another of those who rushed dangerous machine-gun posts. He did it at Flesquières on September 27th, 1918, and his initiative and fighting spirit in dealing, at times alone, with a series of posts " were largely responsible for the taking and clearing of a heavily fortified and strongly garrisoned position, and enabled his company to advance three thousand yards along the Hindenburg support lines."

Moving in spirit across England, we come to Devonshire, and to Lance-Corporal George Onions, of the 1st Battalion of that county's regiment. He was out on a special errand when he saw a great body of Germans advancing. At once he fired on them, and, incredible as it sounds, with only one other man, he took two hundred of them prisoner and proudly marched them back to his company commander.

Readers of the awards of V.C.'s as they appeared in the daily papers might have looked in vain therein for the name of Arthur Evans, and yet this Lincolnshire man is among the winners of the cross. As Walter Simpson he enlisted, and it was as Lance-Sergeant Walter Simpson that he was known when serving with the 6th Battalion of the Lincolns on September 2nd, 1918, near Etaing. He swam across a river and disposed of a machine-gun's crew, and then, being on patrol work, went on his way. He was joined by an officer who was soon wounded, but Simpson got him back to safety, and the patrol brought back the information it was sent out to secure. Later on it was stated that his real name was Arthur Evans, which he had taken again.

Lieut. J. C. Barrett, of the Leicesters, 1/5th Battalion, was with an attacking force on September 24th, 1918. There was some confusion in the darkness and the smoke of the barrage, but Barrett, although in front of a very strong German position, was not unnerved. He got into the German trench and disposed of two of the machine-guns, and then, having been twice wounded, got out of it in order to ascertain the position. Having given the necessary orders to his few men, he found himself unable to move, and had to be carried away. Private Samuel Needham of the 1/5th Bedfordshires, won his V.C. in Palestine, on September 10th and 11th, 1918. He was with a patrol that was suddenly attacked, and it was his prompt action in dashing forward at the foe that enabled the other men to pull themselves together and eventually to get away with their wounded and their own lives.

Four more names and England's record is complete. Lance-Corporal William Amey, of the 1/8th Royal Warwicks, won the cross at Landrecies only a week before the armistice of November 11th, 1918.

V.C. won at Landrecies First leading, during a fog, his section against a nest of machine-guns, he captured fifty prisoners and several guns; later, quite alone, he rushed another post, and then another, returning the last time with twenty Germans.

Another lance-corporal was Alfred Wilson, of the 2/4th Battalion, Oxfordshire Light Infantry. At Laventie, on September 12th, 1918, he advanced on some machine-guns which were holding up an advance, and in a series of heroic deeds captured four guns, happily returning to his platoon without injury. Private (Actg. Lc.-Cpl.) W. H. Coltman, D.C.M., M.M., of the 1/6th North Staffordshire Regiment, won the cross at Mannequin Hill on October 3rd and 4th, 1918. Three times he carried wounded men into safety, and for forty-eight hours tended the injured unceasingly.

Sergeant John Meikle, of the Seaforth Highlanders, 4th Battalion, won the cross in France on August 20th, 1918, but at the price of his life. He rushed a nest of machine-guns alone, but on going forward against another he was killed. Those who followed him, however, finished the work.

Turning to the Lowlands we come to the Royal Scots Fusiliers, and Sergeant T. Caldwell, of its 12th Battalion. On October 31st, 1918, he cleared a farmhouse near Audenarde, and his section captured about seventy prisoners, eight machine-guns, and one trench-mortar. The sergeant himself took eighteen prisoners in a single-handed venture. **Clearing a farmhouse** Private James Towers, of the 2nd Scottish Rifles, volunteered to take a message, although five others had failed to carry it through. Going from cover to cover he succeeded, and his award was published on January 7th, 1919.

The last of the Scots bears the true Scottish name of McGuffie, a sergeant of the 1/5th Battalion, K.O.S.B., who hailed from Wigtown. He was in an advance on September 28th, 1918, and, with absolute fearlessness, entered dug-out after dug-out, returning with prisoners. Not only so, but he rescued some British prisoners and led a platoon in a further successful enterprise. Later he was killed by a shell.

When the Germans made their last great bid for victory, on March 21st, 1918, and won an initial success, the Ulstermen were in the centre of the danger zone. In the 36th Division was the 15th Royal Irish Rifles, and one of its officers, Sec.-Lieut. E. de Wind, for seven hours, although twice wounded and practically single-handed, held an important post. He beat back attack after attack and fought on until mortally wounded.

Company-Sergeant-Major Martin Doyle, M.M., of the 1st Munster Fusiliers, rescued a party surrounded by the enemy, helped a Tank that was in difficulty and danger, and silenced a machine-gun that was firing on it. He rescued a wounded officer, and, when his position was assailed, drove back the enemy and captured many prisoners. He set "the very highest example to all ranks by his courage."

Sergeant W. A. Curtis, of the 2nd Royal Dublin Fusiliers, was at Le Cateau on October 18th, 1918, and his story, although wonderful, is soon told. He rushed through the barrage, silenced six dangerous guns, and then, noticing some German reinforcements just coming up, captured over one hundred of them before his comrades joined him.

The Indians and the Newfoundlander may be placed together here, for truly East and West did meet in the ranks of Britain during the Great War. Badlu Singh was a ressaldar attached to the 29th Indian Lancers, then in Palestine, and on September 23rd, 1918, his squadron charged a strong position near the Jordan. He, noticing that heavy casualties were being caused by some machine-guns, got together six men, and

CAPT. F. M. F. WEST, R.A.F.   L.-CPL. A. WILCOX, Ox. and Bucks L.I.   PTE. A. WILKINSON, Manchester Regt.   S.-M. J. WILLIAMS, S.W. Borderers.   PTE. W. WOOD, Northumberland Fus.   SEC.-LT. F. YOUNG, Herts Regt.   SGT. R. ZENGEL, Saskatchewan Regt.

Private F. G. Miles, of the 1/5th Gloucestershire Regiment, was another of those who tackled the deadly machine-guns. Quite alone, he put two of these weapons out of action, and then, leading forward his company, he added another sixteen, to say nothing of fifty-one prisoners, to his bag. Had the advance here been seriously delayed the whole operation would have been in jeopardy.

Of the five Scottish regiments now to be mentioned two are Highland units. Lieutenant W. D. Bissett belonged to a Territorial battalion of the Argyll and Sutherland Highlanders, and on October 25th, 1918, he led his platoon with great dash near Maing; later, owing to casualties, he took control of the company, and his decision to charge with the bayonet at a critical moment saved a dangerous situation.

was killed just as the little party had successfully charged up to the position and had received the surrender of the guns and their crews. The other award was to a British officer, and goes back as far as December 19th, 1914, when the Indian troops were in action near Givenchy. Lieut. W. A. McC. Bruce, of the 59th Scinde Rifles, led a night attack and, although wounded, held his position against counter-attacks for some hours until he was killed. The Newfoundlander was Private Thomas Ricketts, who was instrumental in capturing five field-guns on October 14th, 1918.

The thirty-one Canadians can now be passed rapidly in review, as THE GREAT WAR has already dealt with the deeds of this corps, one that contributed so much to the final victory. Of these honours three were in the nature of arrears. That of Captain E. D. Bellew, of British Columbia, carries us back to April 24th, 1915, when the Germans were first using gas against the British lines near Ypres. There Bellew and Sergeant Peerless, in charge of two guns, were in the centre of the attack. All prospect of help had gone, but they decided to stay and fight it out. Bellew, fighting to the last, was taken prisoner.

On October 10th, 1916, Private (Piper) J. Richardson, of the 16th Battalion Manitoba Regiment, was in Regina Trench. During one of the attacks that marked the last stage of the long Battle of the Somme, he played his company "over the top," and later, when the men came up against some very strong wire, strode up and down playing his pipes there. The company got through, but Richardson was afterwards missed and his death presumed. On September 20th, 1917, Sergeant A. G. Knight, of the Alberta Regiment, led forward a bombing section, and, until fatally **Canadian piper** wounded, went several times against parties **on the Somme** of the enemy. One party he put to rout, from another he took twenty prisoners, and finally, also alone, he sent another group flying in disorder. This was done near Ypres.

The awards for 1918 are crowded together within quite a few weeks, and their number, and still more the deeds of outstanding valour which they describe, show how thoroughly the Canadians were sharers in the final victory of the Allies. The cross of Corporal Joseph Kaeble, Quebec Regiment, who belonged to a French-Canadian battalion, is dated June 3rd and 9th, but all the others were during the great offensive that started in August. Kaeble lost his life while resisting a most determined attack on some front trenches where he was with a Lewis gun. He fired his last shots when mortally wounded, and his final words to his companions were, "We must stop them." They did, and the attack was repulsed.

On August 8th, the opening day of the British attack, the Canadians won five crosses, and on the 9th two more. Lieut. James E. Tait, 76th Battalion, Manitoba Regiment, showed most conspicuous bravery and initiative in attack, leading his men until he was killed. Lieut. John Brillant, M.C., Quebec Regiment, led his company, with absolute fearlessness, for twelve miles, dealing with one obstacle after another, always himself taking the positions of danger; wounded again and again, he went on until nature asserted herself and he collapsed. Corporal H. J. Good, also of the Quebec Regiment, 13th Battalion, dashed forward alone against some machine-guns, and later captured the crews of three 5.9 in. guns. Private J. B. Croak, another Quebec man, had to his credit two daring feats against machine-guns when he was killed. Finally, so far as the five are concerned, Corporal H. G. B. Miner, of the Central Ontario Regiment, was killed after three heroic exploits against enemy defences.

These deeds were all done in the allied advance from Amiens that began at 4.30 on the morning of August 8th, and they serve to give some faint idea of the courage that alone made this forward movement possible. It was indeed no walk-over, but a stern struggle against a desperate and clever foe, and had there been none in the British **Allied advance** ranks ready to face almost certain death **from Amiens** by rushing against hidden machine guns and cunning defences of other kinds, there would have been no thrills of joy throughout the Empire, no British Army on the Rhine, no returning victoriously home for millions of soldiers.

On the 9th the advance continued. Two Manitoba men, Corporal F. G. Coppins, of the 3rd Battalion, and Corporal A. Brereton, of the 9th, dashed quite separately out to silence machine-guns. Both were successful and both happily escaped with their lives. The action of Coppins " enabled the advance to be continued "; that of Brereton saved many lives and " inspired his platoon to charge and capture the five remaining posts." Sergeant Raphael L. Zengel, M.M., of the 5th Battalion Saskatchewan Regiment, performed like deeds, showing, as did the others, " utter disregard for personal safety."

On August 18th two notable deeds are recorded in these awards. Sergeant Robert Spall, of Princess Patricia's Regiment, was killed while leading his platoon, which was isolated and overwhelmed. The men, however, were saved, as Spall " deliberately gave his life " in order to extricate them. Private T. Dinesen, of Quebec, went forward alone against hostile machine-guns no less than five times, put them out of action, and with bomb and bayonet accounted for twelve of the enemy. These deeds, one by a Quebec man and the other by an Ontario man, were both done at Parvillers.

On August 26th the Canadians, under Sir Arthur Currie, made a fresh and successful stroke. The historian of the war remarks that on this day Wancourt was taken, and the name of this place occurs in the V.C. records. Lieut.-Colonel W. H. Clark-Kennedy, C.M.G., D.S.O., was leading forward his battalion, 24th Quebecs, and it was in the centre of a brigade. The hostile fire was very heavy and there was some disorganisation, and here begins the long story of Clark-Kennedy's gallantry. He did everything that could be done until seriously wounded; leading in person parties against nests of machine-guns, improving during the night the positions won, inspiring and rallying the men, so that it was " impossible to overestimate the results achieved by the valour and leadership of this officer."

Lieut. C. S. Rutherford, M.C., M.M., was at Monchy on the 26th with his battalion, also one from Quebec. He was in charge of an assaulting-party, and came up against a German " pill-box." His men were behind, but undaunted he called to the Germans that they were his prisoners, and forty-five of them with three machine-guns surrendered to him. Later he led a section against another " pill-box " and returned with thirty-five Germans and some guns.

The next great day in the Canadian advance was September 2nd. Thereon the Canadian Corps, at 5 a.m., moved forward against a part of the Hindenburg line between Drocourt and Quéant, the key of the German position. They had a hard day, but a glorious one. They went right through one of the strongest possible positions, took six miles of the line, and 6,000 prisoners. Again the number of V.C.'s won on a single day by the Canadians was five, in addition one had been earned on the previous evening.

Private J. F. Young, of Quebec, won the cross for absolute fearlessness in searching for the wounded, dressing their injuries, and getting them into safety. He continued his work all through the two **Breaking the** succeeding days, September 3rd and 4th. **Hindenburg line** Private W. L. Rayfield, of the 7th British Columbia Regiment, rushed a trench quite alone, dealt with a dangerous sniper, took thirty prisoners from a trench, and finished by carrying in a wounded man.

Lieut.-Colonel C. W. Peck, D.S.O., commanded the 16th Battalion of the Manitoba Regiment in this attack, and its entire success was partly due to him. When the position was critical he made a personal reconnaissance, directed some Tanks to the right spot for a successful advance, and under the heaviest fire coolly made plans and gave directions which led to the victory of his brigade. W. H. Metcalf, M.M., was a lance-corporal in the same battalion, and was evidently a kindred spirit with his colonel. Although wounded, he walked under terrific fire in front of a Tank in order that it should strike the right spot. Captain B. S. Hutcheson, a doctor attached to the 75th Battalion 1st Central Ontario Regiment, won the cross for gallantry in attending to the wounded under heavy fire. " With utter disregard of personal safety he remained on the field until every wounded man had been attended to."

On September 1st, just before this attack, the Germans made a movement doubtless to upset it. Private C. J. P. Nunney, D.C.M., M.M., of the 38th Battalion Eastern Ontario Regiment, thereupon went from headquarters to the outposts of his company, and by his example showed the men how to see the matter through. In the attack on the next day he was equally daring, ending unfortunately with a severe wound.

Toward the end of the month the Canadians were again heavily engaged, and no less than four awards were made for gallantry on September 27th. Lieut. G. F. Kerr, M.C., M.M., 1st Central Ontario Regiment won one when commanding a company in Bourlon Wood, where also quite alone he rushed a strong post, returning with four machine-guns and thirty-one prisoners. Lieut. G. T. Lyall, also a Central Ontario man, was in these Bourlon Wood operations, and his wonderful deeds can only here be summarised. " During two days of operations Lieutenant Lyall captured in all three officers, one hundred and eighty-two other ranks, twenty-six machine-guns, and one field gun, exclusive of heavy casualties inflicted. He showed throughout the utmost valour and high powers of command."

The two others are Lieutenant M. F. Gregg, M.C., of Nova Scotia, and Lieut. S. L. Honey, D.C.M., M.M., of Manitoba. The former, in operations near Cambrai, made, by his skilful use of bombs, a remarkable haul of prisoners and guns, his deeds covering the period between September 27th and October 1st. The latter led his company when all the superior officers had been killed or wounded, carrying on until his death on the last day of the attack; in the interval he went out twice against enemy machine-guns.

Captain John McGregor, M.C., D.C.M., of the 1st Central Ontarios, should be linked with those, for he showed "most conspicuous bravery, leadership, and self-sacrificing devotion to duty near Cambrai from September 29th to October 3rd, 1918. Alone he went forward in broad daylight against enemy machine-guns, and then gallantly led the first waves of the attack.

Canada's final V.C. heroes

The four remaining awards to the Canadians carry the story to November 1st, practically to the end. On October 1st Sergeant W. Merrifield, 4th Battalion Central Ontario Regiment, showed great gallantry in attack near Abancourt, especially when going single-handed against two machine-gun emplacements. A week later an engineer, Captain C. N. Mitchell, M.C., found the Germans preparing to destroy a bridge over the Canal de l'Escaut, near Cambrai. By wondrous gallantry he cut away the wires and so saved an important bridge.

Lieut. W. C. Algie, of the 1st Central Ontario Regiment, was killed near Cambrai, after having settled two machine-guns, captured prisoners, and cleared the Germans from one end of a village. Lastly, Sergeant Hugh Cairns, D.C.M., of the 46th Battalion Saskatchewan Regiment, was mortally wounded on November 1st, after having performed a similar deed. He captured one gun, then two guns, and afterwards, with small parties, took many prisoners.

As regards the Australians, to whom the story may now turn, the twenty-five crosses awarded to them after August 4th, 1918, were all earned between June 26th and October 5th of that year, during an intense fourteen weeks for the Anzacs. This narrative, therefore, begins with an award issued from the War Office on August 17th, when four crosses were given—all to Australians. Corporal Philip Davey, M.M., of the 10th Battalion, A.I.F., was advancing with his platoon at Merris on June 26th. As usual, the most dangerous obstacle was machine-guns, one of which Davey silenced and captured, afterwards turning the same gun on to the Germans. Lance-Corporal T. L. Axford, M.M., of the 16th Battalion, performed a very similar feat on July 4th. There, too, during an advance, he rushed against machine-guns, and this is the result : " Unaided he killed ten of the enemy and took six prisoners ; he threw the machine-guns over the parapet and called out to the delayed platoon to come on."

Australia's twenty-five V.C.s

Driver Henry Dalziel, of the 15th Battalion, won his cross on the same day, and in the same area, Hamel Wood, as did Axford. He, too, dashed at a machine-gun and killed or captured the entire crew. Later he went under heavy fire to obtain ammunition, and kept on with that work until severely wounded. The last of the four was Corporal W. E. Brown, D.C.M., of the 10th Battalion, who, on July 6th, at Villers-Bretonneux, compelled the occupants of a dug-out to surrender to him as he stood, a terrible figure armed with bombs, at its door.

KING GEORGE VISITING THE MEN OF THE TANK CORPS ON THE WESTERN FRONT.
Inspection of men of the Tank Corps by King George during his visit to the western front after the great final offensive of the Allies had begun in the summer of 1918. During the closing months of the war two officers of the Tank Corps were awarded the V.C. for heroism which cost them their lives.

These incidents were evidently in operations preliminary to the great allied offensive that, so far as the British were concerned, began in August. They were part of a move under Rawlinson in which the Australians advanced for more than a mile south of the Somme and captured Hamel. The deed of Lieut. Albert Borella, M.M., of the 26th Battalion, was also performed before the great movements began, for it was on July 17th and 18th that he captured a machine-gun, seized a trench and thirty prisoners, and then, his men being in the proportion of one against ten, beat back some determined assaults.

On August 8th, Lieut. A. E. Gaby was at Villers-Bretonneux —the scene, too, of Borella's exploit. His company was checked in an advance, so he went forward alone against the strong position whence the trouble came, and there, firing his revolver, compelled fifty Germans with four guns to surrender. He then led forward his men to their objective, as he did two days later, his gallant life being ended on that day by a sniper's bullet. Private R. M. Beatham, of the 8th Battalion, lost his life on August 9th for a like deed. He had tackled the crews of four machine-guns and was killed when dashing forward against another.

Surrender of fifty Germans

Sergeant P. C. Statton belonged to the 40th Battalion, in which he commanded a platoon. Armed with only a revolver, in broad daylight, he at once—a battalion being held up rushed four enemy machine-gun posts in succession, disposing of two of them and killing five of the enemy. "The success of the attacking troops was largely due to his gallantry."

On August 23rd the Germans were counter-attacking on the Somme, and the Australians won two V.C.'s when beating them back. Both were by lieutenants—L. D. McCarthy, of the 16th Battalion, and W. D. Joynt, of the 8th. McCarthy, with two men, assailed a strong post that was holding up the advance; much of the work he did alone, for one reason or other, and the notice says that "single-handed" he killed twenty of the enemy and captured in addition five machine-guns and fifty prisoners. Joynt led a company in the attack on Herleville Wood. The position was very critical, so he dashed forward and led a magnificent frontal bayonet attack on the wood.

Lance-Corporal B. S. Gordon, of the 41st Battalion, led a section through heavy shell fire on August 26th near Bray, and then showed remarkable daring in attacking machine-guns. "Perfectly unaided, he captured in the course of these operations, two officers and sixty-one other ranks, together with six machine-guns, and displayed throughout a wonderful example of fearless initiative." Private G. Cartwright, of the 33rd Battalion, was another of those whose gallantry enabled an advance to proceed. He bombed a strong post, captured the gun and nine Germans, doing all under intense fire.

September 1st and 2nd were evidently great days for the Australians, for thereon they won no fewer than seven crosses. They attacked and took Mont St. Quentin, a village just north of Péronne, and there many fine deeds were done, of which these seven are outstanding. Private Robert Mactier, of the 23rd Battalion, showed "exceptional valour and determination" in dealing with strong enemy positions, and it was entirely due to him that the battalion was able to do its part in capturing the village of Mont St. Quentin. Lieut. L. T. Towner, M.C., an officer of the Machine Gun Corps, helped considerably in the same attack, showing like gallantry both in manipulating his own guns and in dealing with those of the enemy ; while Sergeant A. D. Lowerson, of the 21st Battalion, when his men met with severe opposition early in the attack, was equally daring. He led a storming-party of seven men against a strong post, which he captured.

Seven crosses in two days

Lance-Corporal L. C. Weathers, of the 48th Battalion, was with an advanced bombing-party on the following day. With three comrades he attacked a strong trench, himself mounted its parapet and bombed it, the result being one hundred and eighty prisoners and three machine-guns. Two corporals, A. C. Hall and A. H. Buckley, both of the 54th Battalion, were to the fore on these two days. Hall rushed a machine-gun post, carried a wounded man into safety, and, " continuously in advance of the main party," located posts of resistance and led small parties to assault them. Buckley was killed while trying to rush another of these obstacles ; he had just accounted for one of them, and throughout had displayed "great initiative, resource, and courage."

The last of the seven heroes of Péronne, as they may be called, is Private W. M. Currey, 53rd Battalion. Single-handed, he captured a field-gun which had proved very costly to the advance, then rushed a strong point, and finally went out with orders to an isolated company. In all these enterprises he was successful.

Sergeant Gerald Sexton, of the 13th Battalion, whose real name, it afterwards transpired, was Maurice Vincent Buckley, won the V.C. near Le Verguier on September 18th. He was, we are told, "to the fore, dealing with many machine-guns, rushing enemy posts, and performing great feats of bravery and endurance without faltering or for a moment taking cover." One or two of these feats are described later in the award, one of a long list published on December 14th, 1918. Private J. P. Woods also won his V.C. near Le Verguier on September 18th. He was in the 48th Battalion, and his deed was the capture of a formidable enemy post, which he held with two comrades again heavy counter-attacks.

By this time, the end of September, the Australians, like the Canadians, were crashing through the Hindenburg line. In this move Major B. A. Wark, D.S.O., showed great gifts of leadership, especially on the three critical days, September 29th, 30th, and October 1st. He went forward in front of his men through one village after another, at one time rushing a battery of guns with only a few men, and at another taking fifty prisoners. Private John Ryan, of the 55th Battalion, was in this attack. He was one of the first to rush into a German trench which was taken, but he showed perhaps higher qualities a little later, when he led three men against some bombers who were making his position untenable. He put those men out of action, and was then severely wounded.

The two last Australians to be mentioned are both young officers. Lieut. Joseph Maxwell, M.C., D.C.M., of the 18th Battalion, showed wonderful resource and courage in dealing with hostile machine-guns on October 3rd.

Great gifts of leadership

Lieut. G. M. Ingram, M.M., of the 24th Battalion, captured nine machine-guns and killed forty-two Germans, his platoon assisting, and later did more gallant work.

The deeds of the six New Zealanders cover very much the same period of time as do those of the Australians—to be exact, from July 24th, 1918, to September 30th ; it is worthy of note that five of the six were sergeants. Sergeant R. C. Travis, D.C.M., M.M., of the Otago Regiment, who was killed near Hébuterne, volunteered for a very dangerous piece of work—that of destroying a wire block with bombs. This he did successfully. After which he attacked two machine-guns, which he captured, killing four men single-handed during the operation. He was killed later when going from post to post encouraging his men.

Sergeant Samuel Forsyth was an engineer serving with the Auckland Regiment, and he also lost his life. On August 24th he was at Grévilers, and his award reveals a long record of almost incredible daring in dealing with machine-guns. He was wounded early in the day, and after doing good work in directing Tanks was killed by a sniper. Sergeant R. S. Judson, D.C.M., M.M., another Auckland man, was instrumental also in rushing machine-guns and putting their crews out of action. He won the V.C. near Bapaume on August 26th.

Sergeant J. G. Grant, of the 1st Battalion Wellington Regiment, led a platoon in an attack near Bancourt on September 1st. They came up against machine-guns, and it was owing to Grant's courage in dashing forward that the obstacles were overcome. He rushed other posts and "set a splendid example to all." Sergeant H. J. Laurent, of the New Zealand Rifle Brigade, 22nd Battalion, won his cross for charging a position, followed by his men, a move that completely disorganised the enemy.

The one New Zealand private awarded the V.C. was James Crichton, of the Auckland Regiment. On September 30th, during an advance, he was wounded, but he went forward. He swam across a river with a message, and saved a bridge from destruction.

Return of the victor of Palestine: Field=Marshal Lord Allenby in London, September 16th, 1919.

Arrival of Lord Allenby at Dover: With him are General Horne and Admiral Dampier.

Peace demonstration of the smoke screen: A British war device that baffled the U boats.

After-war difficulties of the Mercantile Marine: Ships held up at Gravesend awaiting unloading.

House in Ekaterinburg in which the Tsar and his family are said to have been murdered.

Where war kept on in Russia: Semenoff's armoured train for fighting Siberian Bolshevists.

Peace visitors to Flanders' scenes of war: In ruined Ypres of heroic and tragic memories.

"The Glorious Dead": Londoners placing tribute wreaths at the base of the Whitehall cenotaph.

CHAPTER CCCXXII.

THE SAVING OF CIVILISATION : BRITAIN'S CROWNING ACHIEVEMENT.

By H. W. Wilson.

Fighting on the Largest Possible Scale by Land, Sea, and Air—Two Great Factors in the Victory the Result of British Effort and Brains—Truth About the Retreat from Mons and About the British Part in the Battle of the Marne—Allegation that the British Army had Lost its Skill and Courage Magnificently Refuted—Wonderful Spirit of Confidence of the British Nation—If Great Britain had Kept Out of the Struggle the German Plans would have Succeeded—The Greatest Miracle of the War : British Acceptance of Conscription—The Great Development of British Gun-Power and Wonderful Growth of British Air-Power—Coming of the Tanks : Tribute from the Enemy to their Efficiency—British Ingenuity Equal to All Demands—Enormous Forces Raised within the Empire—Comparative Losses among the Allies—Great Britain's Financial Effort—Stubborn Devotion of the British Race Displayed in the Hour of Gravest Peril—Britain's Part in the Closing Great Offensives—High Achievement on Many Fronts—" A Great Example Belonging to Eternity."

OF the Great Powers which entered the war on the side of the Allies two only fought throughout from first to last. Those two were Great Britain and France. And of these two Powers one only fought on the largest possible scale both by sea and land, and in the closing months of the war by air. That Power was Great Britain. Because of the special part which she played in every field and in every element, because of the services which she rendered to the cause, she may claim, without injustice to her heroic comrades, that she was pre-eminent in this colossal conflict, and that she had the largest share in the overthrow of Germany and of the German allies. Her part is imperfectly known even to the British peoples, but the unanimous voice of German opinion, which on this subject is at least disinterested, is that Great Britain, in the four years' war with Germany, as in the twenty years' struggle with France in the Revolutionary age, was the soul and centre of the fight for freedom. In Tirpitz's words she was "the chief opponent, possessing the most ample resources and the greatest determination." From "a nation of shopkeepers " she developed into the greatest military Power of the world, while she maintained her naval ascendancy. She performed a feat which in no previous age had been accomplished by her people, for in the Napoleonic conflict they never placed large armies in the European field.

It had long been doubted whether democratic forms of Government were compatible with the strain and agony involved in persecuting a war to the death. The Britain of 1800 had been governed by an aristocracy. But in this war, democracy—even with many faults at home—proved its competence to hold its own against an autocratic antagonist of immense strength, who organised for a gigantic war during the previous half-century. It had long been alleged that the British peoples had lost something of their old high spirit of courage and fearlessness of death. But in this war half the whole able-bodied male British population was placed in the field and confronted bitter privation, torture, and death with unfaltering faith and determination.

No age and no generation can forget what the British Empire did, or the heights to which the British peoples rose in these days of trial. Not Athens in her noblest years, when men of one of her tribes died for her in such varied fields as Cyprus, Egypt, Phœnicia, Halieis, Megara, and Ægina, equalled the heroic record of those months of 1918 when, while the British armies in France beat back the German hordes, other British forces waged war in Italy, at Salonika, in Palestine, in Mesopotamia, in the Caucasus, on the Caspian, in Transcaspia, in Northern Persia, in Southern Persia, in East Africa, in Siberia, at Archangel, and on the Murman coast ; when the British Navy guarded the sea ; and when the British

AMERICAN DECORATIONS FOR BRITISH OFFICERS.
General Pershing investing the Earl of Cavan with an American decoration in Hyde Park. On the same occasion—when the Prince of Wales inspected the American troops who were to take part in London's Victory March of July 19th, 1919—General Pershing, as Commander-in-Chief of the United States forces in Europe, presented American decorations to several other distinguished British officers.

Merchant Service, in silent and deadly encounter defied and defeated the submarines.

The two factors to which the highest officers of the German Staff and Ludendorff ascribed the German defeat when the war was over were both the result of British effort and brains. The first was the blockade, the importance of which no one who understands sea-power and its silent workings will ignore. The blockade was the work of the British Navy, though it was aided by French warships at the outset, and by the Italian and American Fleets as Italy and the United States entered the war. Tanks were the invention of Great Britain alone; the idea was British; its working out was British; the tactics devised for the use of this new weapon were British; and the British armies used the Tank on a large scale with the most conspicuous success. The use of the Tank, and particularly of the heavy and powerful type which fought in the closing months of the war, demoralised the German infantry.

We now have, what was lacking at the outset, German evidence, which has not been manipulated, to show the peculiar qualities of the British soldier.

German tribute to British at Mons The very first battle fought by British troops —the action at Mons—was a terrible lesson to the Germans. Captain Bloem, of the 12th Brandenburg Grenadier Regiment, gives this account of the German attack, which was made, be it remembered, by overwhelmingly superior German forces:

A hellish fire broke loose, and the deadly leaden shower was pumped on our heads, chests, and knees, bringing us down in dense swathes. Wherever I looked, to right or left, there were nothing but dead and sobbing, writhing wounded, streaming with blood. . . . The regiment was shot down, smashed up, and only a mere handful was left. Heavy defeat—why not admit it? Our first battle was a heavy, unheard-of heavy defeat, and this from the British—the British at whom we jeered!

The total British force engaged against these three thousand German infantrymen numbered three hundred men of the famous "Old Contemptibles," and so violent was their fire, and so sustained, that the Germans then believed, and have ever since repeated, that the British had taken the field with masses of machine-guns, whereas the truth was that they had only two per battalion, and not always that. "They seem to understand war, these British," Captain Bloem concluded. They did understand war. The battle which they fought at Mons has since been described by an able French authority "as the first manifestation of the new form that war was going to take; the British had nothing to unlearn, and from the first moment of contact had grasped its meaning."

Two criticisms have been directed against the conduct

of these early and important operations. The first is that, by its slowness in reaching the position assigned to it, the British Expeditionary Force wrecked the whole French offensive plan. This is a criticism to which sanction was given by the French Headquarters in a report on the operations which it issued in 1914. But one of the latest and ablest French commentators, Colonel de Thomasson, has recently answered the charge conclusively. "It was getting the Fourth (French) Army into its place," he says, "which obliged us to delay the offensive in the centre by three or four days, and *not as Headquarters has stated—the wait for the British troops.* This offensive might have been ordered to open on August 17th, 1914, instead of on the 20th, if the Fourth Army had not been detrained far back

KING GEORGE IN FRANCE.
The King taking a trip on one of the military light railways on the western front in France during his visit to the troops in August, 1918, and (above) going by rail-motor to see British Forestry men at work in a French forest.

from the front. The second criticism is that Sir John French, by a precipitate retreat, compromised the whole French position. Here again there is a complete reply in the facts and in the verdict of able French soldiers, writing with full knowledge on those facts. General Palat, one of the best French military authorities, reaches this conclusion:

Field-Marshal French knew how to extricate himself cleverly from the difficult situation in which he had been placed by circumstances. Moved prematurely forward when his concentration was still incomplete, thrown into the midst of a great battle with inexact or very incomplete information, he saw himself on the night of August 23rd (the night of Mons) menaced by very superior forces, which obviously sought to envelop his left, while our (French) troops, after having lost the line of the Sambre, effected a retreat, which, however leisurely at the outset, soon became precipitate. . . . A prolonged resistance (in its positions) would have condemned the British Army to disaster. It was Field-Marshal French's great merit that he understood this in time, and immediately effected an indispensable retreat, while inflicting severe losses on the enemy.

Lord French has himself been guilty of an injustice to the able French soldier who commanded the Fifth French Army on his right, General Lanrezac, by blaming him for his retirement, though, as has already been pointed out in a previous chapter, but for that retirement the Fifth French

Army would have been surrounded and captured. There is a mystery about Lanrezac's retreat which requires to be cleared up. Lord French, in his book, states that he heard of it at 5 p.m. of the day on which Mons was fought (August 23rd), but actually the order for it was not issued till about 8 p.m. In any case, whatever the hour at which Lanrezac's decision was reached, the British Commander-in-Chief did not begin the great retreat. He fell back **British retreat** on a second line of positions south of Mons, **preceded by French** and continued the battle there, nor did he order his own general retreat until daybreak of August 24th, when the French Fifth Army was unquestionably retiring.

The British retreat (says M. Engerand, a very competent and generous French critic) followed our (French) retreat, and did not precede it. It is our duty as loyal men to state this, and to recognise that in these battles beyond our frontier the British Army, placed by its chief on the defensive, knew how to hold back the enemy.

A third criticism directed against the British Army is that it was slow in moving into position for the Battle of the Marne, and that, because of this slowness, the French plans were crowned with only partial success. But, as Lord French has pointed out, the original instructions for the battle issued by Joffre, were for a movement directly eastwards, as the retreat of Kluck's army was not then known. The British moved accordingly, whereas the proper direction of movement, in order to strike the Germans, was north-east. As soon as possible, the British Staff altered the direction of march, but time was necessarily lost, as Sir John French had to com-

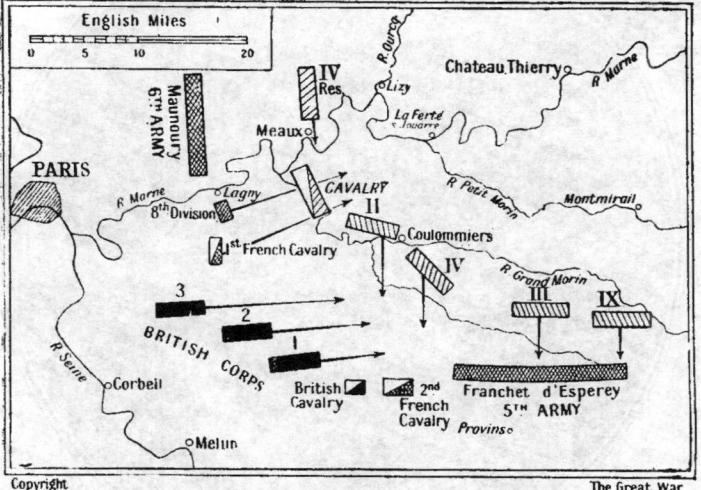

BRITISH AT THE MARNE: I.—AS PLANNED.
The Battle of the Marne, as it was planned by Joffre, so far as concerns the British. It was thought that Kluck's army, with the five German corps shown, would have continued to march south, when Maunoury and the British would have taken them in flank and rear. In that case the Germans would almost certainly have suffered a great disaster. The British and French corps are shown by figures 1, 2, 3, etc. ; the German by I., II., III., etc.

municate with Joffre, and did not receive his instructions "to continue the move in a rather more northerly direction" until very late on September 6th. Joffre's original plans "presupposed a continued German advance to the south and south-east, culminating in a great attack on the Fifth and Ninth French Armies"—on the British right. That Sir John French moved with all possible speed is shown by the fact that on September 7th his troops forced the crossing of the Grand Morin ; that on the 8th he crossed the Petit Morin, in the face of no contemptible resistance by the German cavalry and machine-guns ; that early on the 9th he crossed the Marne west of Château-Thierry, and that he intervened just in time to prevent Kluck from enveloping the left flank of Maunoury's Sixth Army. Sir John French, during the 9th, had received two pressing messages from Maunoury, whose troops, after a most desperate battle, and after heroic exertions, were very hard pressed.

A study of the map will show that the British intervention was most effective. It placed Kluck's rear in deadly peril, and before 11 a.m. of the 9th he began to withdraw towards the Aisne, as he was between Maunoury's army on the Ourcq

and the British, only twelve miles away, north of the Marne. The German resistance on the Marne near La Ferté-sous-Jouarre held back the British Third Corps for some hours, and on the British right the advance of the First Corps was delayed by the threat of a German flank attack from Château-Thierry. But the British troops in all marched in three days over thirty miles, crossing three rivers, in the face of German machine-guns and picked infantry, who formed a screen to stop them. The delaying power of the machine-gun was such throughout the war—until the Tank appeared—that this was

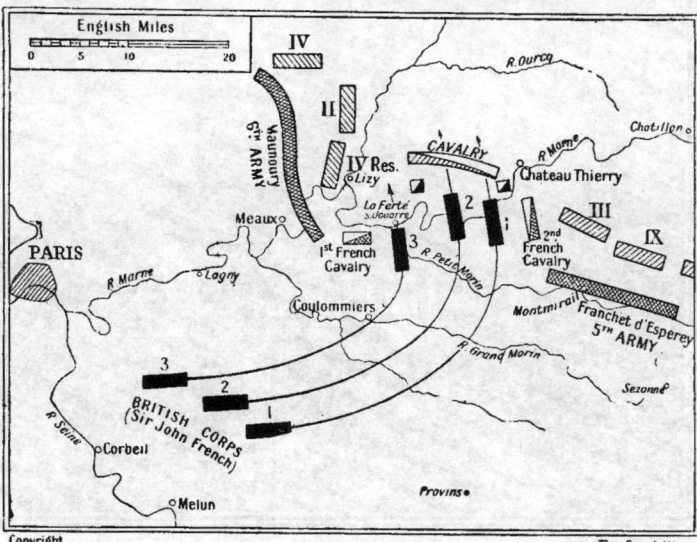

BRITISH AT THE MARNE: II.—AS FOUGHT.
The Battle of the Marne as it was actually fought. Kluck moved two of his corps back across the Marne and attacked Maunoury, while the British, obeying Joffre's instructions, were marching to fall on his flank. The moment the British detected signs of his movement they followed, but had, as the plan shows, to cover a considerable distance and to cross three rivers before they could effectively attack the Germans. Their crossing of the Marne forced Kluck to a hasty retreat and decided the battle.

a fine performance for soldiers who had been for three weeks continually marching and frequently fighting. Had Sir John French known exactly what Kluck was doing, he might possibly with the Sixth French Army have captured the greater part of Kluck's force. But such knowledge is not given in war to any commander. General Maurice's verdict will probably be endorsed by posterity :

It was the crossing of the Marne in the early hours of the 9th by the British Army which turned the scale against Kluck and saved Maunoury in an hour of crisis. This was (as he says) as wonderful an achievement as is to be found in the history of war.

Yet another criticism has been heard on Sir John French's conduct at the Marne. It is that he allowed Kluck to withdraw two corps from his own immediate front and to throw them upon the Sixth French Army, because he failed to attack with sufficient energy. The critical day on which Kluck began this movement was September 5th, 1914 ; but at that moment the British, after an all-night march, were fifteen miles south of these two German corps. They were south of these corps not for any want of fighting **Another criticism** spirit, but because at Joffre's request the **demolished** British Army had retired to give space for manœuvring and to link up with the Fifth French Army on the British right, which had been compelled to fall back. It would then clearly be unfair to blame the British Army for failing to hold back these two corps. The last criticism on the British share in the Battle of the Marne which shall be mentioned is that Sir John French crippled the attack delivered by the Sixth French Army by asking for the assistance of a fine French infantry division, the 8th, in crossing the River Marne, when this division was sorely needed to take the Germans in flank on the Ourcq. Lord French's answer to this is complete : " I can only say that no such request was ever made by me or my Headquarters Staff, nor had any other commander my sanction for such a demand." If there was any demand, which does not seem proved, it was unauthorised.

All these points are of great importance because they show

that not only was the fighting quality of the small British Army very high, but also that its leadership was excellent ; that throughout it acted in the finest spirit of comradeship with the French ; and that at no point did it " let Joffre down." Because these criticisms have been often printed and constantly repeated, they must be faced and answered, and the answer

to them is such as to enhance the glory of the " Old Contemptibles " and the British nation.

Above all, they supply the final refutation of the charge, often alleged after the Boer War, that the British Army had lost its skill and courage. So generous and so friendly an observer as the American Secretary of State, Mr. Hay, wrote in June, 1900 : " The serious thing is the discovery—now past doubt—that the British have lost all skill in fighting, and the whole world knows it, and is regulating itself accordingly. It is a portentous fact." The British Army had not lost its skill ; the British infantry had not lost its tenacity and its fearlessness of death. For in the early battles of the Great War divisions and battalions fought to almost actual extinction.

Great fighting tradition maintained The 7th Division, for example, in 1914, took the field with about 12,000 infantry, and after the Battle of Ypres it was left with only 2,000. One single battalion, nominally 1,000 strong, exhausted its strength three times, and in all by the close of 1915 had passed 4,000 men through its ranks, leaving 3,000 of them killed, wounded, and invalided. It was no uncommon thing for a battalion to go into action 800 or 900 strong and to come out with 80 or 90 men. In one typical instance, of 17 officers and 880 men, one officer and 150 men were left unhurt at the close of one of the early battles. The spirit was the same to the end. On the remote Salonika front, in the British holding attack of September, 1918, a South Wales battalion fought till, of its strength, only one wounded officer and 19 unwounded men remained.

Even in retreat before an overwhelming enemy the British soldier did not lose his moral. After Le Cateau most of the troops " marched in formation and were definitely under control." Where conditions were worst, discipline was not totally lost. " Down that Via Dolorosa," says a military authority of the Roman road, where the pressure of the Germans was most felt, " swirled a rudderless horde of men, guns, waggons, limbers without guns, carts, riderless horses. As units came into this stream they were engulfed in it, formations being broken up and cohesion lost. With nightfall it became harder to move and numberless long checks took place. Rain began to fall. The misery of hunger, thirst, and extreme fatigue could hardly be borne. Yet these men were soldiers still. Wounded and exhausted men were assisted along by their comrades, others were carried on waggons, guns, limbers, and carts. All kept their rifles and ammunition ; for

none had abandoned themselves to despair. In fact, it was not a rout or panic, merely extreme confusion."

In the dark hours of 1914 when the allied armies were falling back, as it seemed in great disorder, towards Paris and the Seine, the position superficially resembled that of late August, 1870. But there was this tremendous difference— that in 1914, behind France, stood the unexhausted strength and numbers of the British people. The French knew history, and history told them two things : That Great Britain's force has always been small at the outset but always prevails in the end, because it is never embarked in a wrong cause. They also knew from their own past the far-reaching influence of sea-power, which the Germans undoubtedly underestimated. Therefore they had no reason to despair when their armies were hurled reeling back from the frontier, and they showed so high and determined a spirit, even under all the miseries of invasion and actual peril to their capital, that their troops rallied brilliantly, and gained a

IN THE LAST OFFENSIVES IN FRANCE.
British Lewis gunners at a post commanding a canal during the German offensive of the spring of 1918. Above : British outposts on duty at the edge of a wood in Champagne during the subsequent allied offensive.

magnificent victory at the Marne. When we consider the odds against them in machine-guns, heavy artillery, and aircraft, that victory verges on the miraculous. In that battle, as has been seen, the British Army, despite its smallness, played a distinguished part, but the influence of the spirit of the British nation was even more marked. In war confidence reacts and generates confidence, and at no time did the British nation believe that **Victory that verged** defeat was possible. Local defeat, tem- **on the miraculous** porary reverses, these it was prepared for, but never for general and complete defeat. Indeed, this very courage and coolness of the British nation was at times a source of weakness because it led to delay in the efforts necessary to destroy the adversary.

So completely are man's views of the past changed by the present that it is difficult to-day to call up the situation which confronted Great Britain and her Allies in 1914 and to remember how formidable Germany was. She held that central position which Napoleon lacked, and which enabled her to turn first upon one and then upon another of her opponents. She had intact finances which Napoleon never enjoyed ; he was fettered throughout by the ruinous results of the Revolution, which rendered it impossible for him to raise any large loan or to make use of credit. She had for fifty years organised systematically for war, and had at the same time developed an industrial organisation which was unquestionably the most powerful in the world. She had provided an Army which, as events showed, was twice as strong as the French at the critical point in the critical moment. She had a Fleet of such efficiency that at Jutland, against a force nearly twice its strength, it was able to escape annihilation. In number of aircraft the

WITH THE BRITISH FORCES IN MESOPOTAMIA.
Indian cavalry at the Ramadie dump, established at the place where a notable battle had been fought in the autumn of 1917. Above : Turkish prisoners being brought in across the desert near Ramadie.

Allies had nothing to match or meet her. French estimates gave her strength of aeroplanes at the outset at 1,500, against 50 effective French machines and 66 British. She had in addition her airships. She acted, as has been pointed out in a previous chapter, by surprise. She violated all laws of civilisation and humanity, first by attacking through Belgium in defiance of solemn treaties and pledges, and then by using methods of the most barbarous brutality and such weapons as gas and the " spurlos versinken " of her submarines. Her ruthlessness, her violence, her injustice, cowed the weaker neutrals, and gave her immense advantages at the cost of alienating the moral sympathies of mankind. Yet against evil in its strongest and most terrible form Great Britain and France from the first stood resolutely, side by side, prepared to make any sacrifice rather than to capitulate before it.

At the very outset of the war there came two temptations to Great Britain. The first was to stand aside altogether, and, in the words of one of her false advisers, " to trade with all the belligerents (so far as the war allows of trade with them) ; to capture the bulk of their trade in neutral **Two temptations** markets ; to keep our expenditure down ; to **at the outset** keep out of debt ; to have healthy finances." This temptation the British nation rejected and preferred a desperate, bloody, and prolonged war to a dishonourable and cowardly peace. The temptation was great. It had been a British tradition for nearly a century to hold aloof from the Continent. British soil was not directly threatened. British interests, it might appear to a superficial observer, were not definitely assailed. Germany was ready to give treacherous pledges, and there were fools in Great Britain credulous enough to recommend their acceptance. Had Great Britain so acted, then the war was lost, and freedom in Europe would have perished for generations.

What is certain is that if Great Britain had not fought the German plans would have succeeded. As it was, even with her aid to France, they came within a hair's breadth of success. The French Army would have been weakened by the loss of the Algerian and Moroccan troops, which could not have been transported across the Mediterranean, and by the force which would have been required to man the coast fortifications and meet the attack of the German Navy. The two British corps would have been lacking to prevent the complete envelopment of the Fifth French Army at Charleroi on August 22nd and 23rd, 1914 ; the three British corps would have been absent at the Marne. Instead of the faith and determination which the British nation displayed in August, 1914, the French would have had for an example the soulless covetousness and shameful desertion of a friend. As good generates good, so evil generates evil. France would have foundered in a sea of blood.

The second great temptation was for Great Britain to spare herself and fight, not with her whole strength, but with limited forces. This, again, was a counsel given her. It was argued that she had promised only a **Great Britain's** limited force on land, and that, if she kept the **most heroic age** sea with her fleets and maintained a definite, very small total of men in France, she would have done her full duty. Again the spirit of the nation rejected this compromise, and by rejecting it entered upon the most heroic age that Great Britain has ever known, and rose to heights of which even those who loved their country most had scarcely believed it capable.

No one who lived through those immortal days can ever forget the rush to arms of the British youth and manhood—the enlistment of two million free volunteers, or the noble messages of encouragement and comradeship which came on every cable from every Dominion. The temptations that Great Britain had overcome had to be faced in an aggravated form by every one of the Dominions, with yet stronger arguments for inaction. In every case democracy rejected them, and once more in an ever-widening circle the influence of the faith and devotion of the oversea peoples reacted on the Mother Country and upon France, strengthening courage and determination, and animating with a new hope the troops then in the field, who were striving to hold off the adversary until help should arrive. When the need was felt for a more systematic supply of recruits than volunteering could give, the greatest miracle of the war took place. Great Britain, who had never, even in the Napoleonic conflict, adopted compulsory service, now accepted it for her manhood. More than this, the nation forced it upon its Government. It saw

BRITISH TROOPS IN THE GREAT CITY OF ORIENTAL ROMANCE.
Among the many achievements of British troops that specially touched the imagination was the brilliant advance of Sir Stanley Maude's troops on Bagdad after the capture of Kut. The taking of the City of the Caliphs, the centre of centuries of history and romance, marked a striking stage in the overcoming of the Turks.

the need ; it cheerfully faced the burden of "the blood tax" ; and by degrees it compelled the raising of the age limit to a point over fifty.

With the German people since Bismarck's day it had been an article of faith that the British Army "did not exist," and that a powerful British Army could not be quickly created. William II. said in 1905, when there was talk of a possible British landing on the German coast, in the event of a German attack on France, that he would follow Bismarck's plan and send for the German police to "lock up the British troops." Moltke told Tirpitz in 1914 : "We'll simply arrest the British troops." He tried that plan with results that wrecked the whole German war-plan. The adoption of compulsion by the British nation was perhaps the greatest shock which Germany experienced during the war, and we shall see the force which it produced.

Owing to the utter unpreparedness of Great Britain and the negligence of her Governments, the task of training, equipping, and arming the New Armies was one of peculiar difficulty. All the available stocks of military clothing were speedily exhausted. No boots could be obtained. The supply of weapons was quite inadequate, and the country was without the machinery to manufacture them. The total of rifles was only 800,000 in August, 1914, and of these many were of old pattern or slightly defective ; only 150,000 remained after the Expeditionary Force had been armed. Many **Want of Army** rifles were damaged, destroyed, or lost in the **material** marches and battles, and the total output of new weapons was only 2,000 a week. In March, 1915, the first of the New Armies was still incompletely armed. As regards artillery, the conditions were even worse. In March, 1915, many divisions of the First New Army had only two guns, instead of six, per battery. There was at the same time a great lack of skilled officers. During 1915 an average of 1,000,000 men was undergoing training in Great Britain. Only nine months after embodiment the First New Army was sent into the field, and was followed quickly by the Second and Third, and some selected divisions of the Fourth

578

and Fifth. These troops lacked experience and skill, yet none of them behaved badly on the battlefield. "The secret of this great triumph over difficulties," said the official account, "lay chiefly in the magnificent spirit of all ranks." The New Armies were engaged in the long and terrible struggle on the Somme, when it was noted during their attacks that "there were no stragglers." This is the supreme test of moral in troops. They endured fearful losses in the mud ; they were prodigal of their lives ; but though it was to certain death they went forward.

The losses of the British troops and their bitter trials were grievously aggravated by shortage of ammunition and the lack of equipment. The Germans, with a fore-sight which the French and British Govern- **Grave shortage** ments alike lacked, had provided themselves **of ammunition** with all the weapons needed for trench war.

They possessed bombs, trench-mortars, rifle-grenades, searchlights, and "sausage" observation balloons (said a British authority in early 1915) and, looking still farther ahead, they were, as we found to our cost, even then preparing their devilish gas and flame-throwers. We had none of these things, and for quite a considerable period our only bombs were those manufactured locally from empty jam-tins. In such conditions, and considering the thinness of our line, it is marvellous that it was kept intact during all these weary months. The Germans were to learn that the fine-drawn khaki line was whipcord ; it strained, it bent, but it never broke.

The full facts as to the shortage of ammunition could not be disclosed at the time because their publication would have involved danger to national interests ; but now they are known they supply the completest justification for the campaign which "the Northcliffe Press" conducted in 1915. From the Battle of the Aisne, and even before it, the British Army was hampered by want of shells.

So early as Le Cateau, one of the first battles of the war, battery commanders were warned to be "careful of ammunition," when abundance of ammunition would have saved life. The want of shells became so grave as to compel the restriction of operations to those sections of the front where the Germans were attacking, paralysing the

British and French troops elsewhere, and preventing them from relieving the pressure at critical points by a general offensive. To some extent the shortage of shells was felt by the Germans, but their plants were so much larger and their output so much greater that their supply was always in the earlier months of the war far in excess of both the British and French combined.

The feat of the British infantry in holding the fearful salient at Ypres was the more wonderful when it is remembered that the British guns were always short of shells, and often could not support the men in the trenches. During the First Battle of Ypres, when the fate of the Allies hung in the balance, it was necessary to issue an order restricting expenditure to twenty rounds per gun daily—less than one shot per hour—and to announce "that a further restriction to ten rounds would be necessary if the supply did not improve." This was a terrifying situation, and it persisted with little improvement until after the Battle of Loos in September, 1915. Battle after battle resulted in the repulse of the British troops because they had not the shells required for victory. Thus at Neuve Chapelle "the battle had to be broken off after three days' fighting because we were brought to a standstill through want of ammunition." In March, 1915, orders had to be issued limiting to two rounds per day the 3-pounders, forbidding 15-pounders to fire at all, allotting only three rounds per day to the 18-pounders, the normal

field-gun, and directing the heavy 9·2 in. and 15 in. howitzers to remain silent. What this meant to the British troops in the trenches an officer has told us : "I was in the line, and my trenches were so bombarded that they were beaten down to the ground during the day. All night my lads toiled to repair them, to save their lives, and again the bombardment continued. Men were maimed, blown out of existence—casualties, casualties, casualties. Our guns were strangely silent. I telephoned back to our batteries behind the line to retaliate, and then we crouched down behind our broken mass of trenches, waiting to hear the scream of our shells going over to protect us. We heard nothing. I telephoned again, 'Retaliate ; bombardment heavy ; casualties serious,' and we waited and waited, but heard nothing. Again I sent an even more urgent message, because we were almost beaten. Then the reply came : 'Carry on ; carry on ! Hold the line at all costs, but we can't retaliate ; we have got no shells.' "

Only troops of the highest fighting quality could have held a badly entrenched line against attack by greatly superior force in the face of all these difficulties and discouragements. For that reason the First Battle of Ypres was a decisive test of the moral in the two **Want of heavy** armies. In all, the Allies employed 267 **artillery** battalions against 402 German battalions, while the German artillery and ammunition superiority was simply overwhelming. "We did not succeed," says the German Staff in its recently published account of the battle, "in effecting the decisive break through the enemy's line, and the dreams of ending the campaign in the west in our favour in 1914 had to be consigned to the grave." The defeat which the Germans sustained is ascribed to the fact that the British and French "were equipped with every modern device"—which is not true—and to their overwhelming machine-gun fire, which was really the withering fire of the British and French infantry with the ordinary service rifle.

It was not only in ammunition and machine-guns that the British troops were handicapped in their struggle with the Germans. Their want of heavy artillery was hardly less serious. The French to some extent remedied their want of heavy guns by taking weapons from their old warships and coast defence vessels. The British could not do this,

FAMOUS BRITISH TRANSPORT SALVED AT THE DARDANELLES.
Senegalese soldiers landing ammunition from the transport River Clyde at V Beach, Gallipoli. This vessel was beached on April 25th, 1915, during the operations at the Dardanelles. Above : The same vessel is shown at Mudros Harbour, after having been successfully salved.

As with artillery and machine-guns so with aircraft. The development of the British Air Forces proceeded on such a scale in the later period of the war that the Royal Air Force at the armistice counted 25,000 machines (against a grand total for Army and Navy of 160 at the outset). With whatever fairy-tales the British people was fed by its officials, in the early battles the German Air Service was conspicuously superior, not in fighting quality, but in numbers. "Their supremacy in this respect," states Major Becke, "was due to their superior preparedness."

The Germans, therefore, knew the British dispositions, whereas the British could not always ascertain what the Germans were doing, though brilliant work was accomplished with its handful of machines by the Royal Flying Corps. It brought Sir John French information which showed that it would be suicide for him

because the Navy could not be weakened. In May, 1915, Lord French has stated that the British Army only possessed 71 guns of over 5 in. calibre, against 1,416 below that figure, whereas the French had one heavy gun to every 2 3 smaller guns, and the Germans were firing more shells of 5·9 in. calibre and upwards than small shells. Not until 1916 did the British artillery situation, in Sir Douglas Haig's words, "become even approximately adequate to the conduct of major operations." The want of ammunition still continued, and in 1917 the wear of the guns was such as to cause great uneasiness.

In the closing year of the war, 1918 at last it became possible " to conduct artillery operations independently of any limiting condition other than transport." Gradually the difficulties were overcome ; despite gigantic demands from almost every field—and the British Army was fighting on every front and had to meet claims which were not known by the French and American Armies—the total

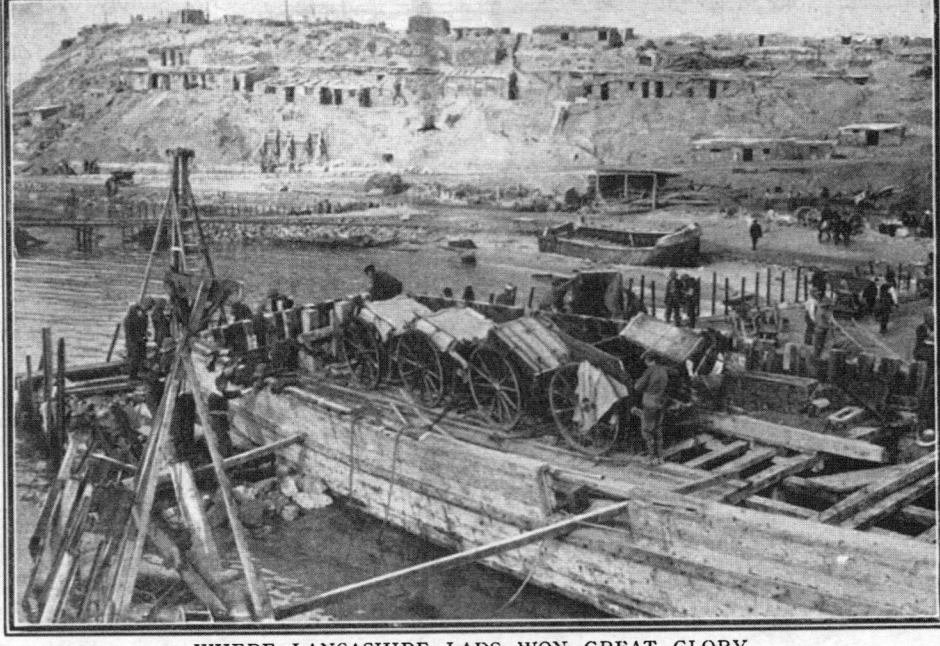

WHERE LANCASHIRE LADS WON GREAT GLORY.
Lancashire Landing, Cape Helles, at the western extremity of the Gallipoli Peninsula, where men of the Lancashire Fusiliers gained undying fame on April 25th, 1915. It was said by those who witnessed the exploit that there was not a man of the 1st Battalion who had not earned the V.C. half a dozen times on that murderous beach. Above : Wreckage caused by a westerly gale at Lancashire Landing.

of British guns on the western front had risen from 486 in August, 1914, to 6,437, and the total on all fronts to about 10,000 guns, a large proportion of which were of the heaviest pattern.

One of the secrets of the great victories which covered British arms with such glory in the last stage of the war was a sufficiency of guns and ammunition. Infantry attacks could be adequately prepared, and, supported by Tanks, no longer brought annihilating losses upon the assailant. At the same time the proportion of machine-guns had risen from 1 to every 500 infantry to 1 to every 20.

One secret of the closing victories

The British supplies of artillery and machine-guns were sufficient to assist in equipping the American Army, and to save it from the terrible experiences which had befallen the British infantry in the early years of the war, when it had to advance to the attack with a very imperfect assistance from its guns, and to make good with its blood the want of mechanical equipment.

to stand at Mons ; on the day after that battle it ascertained the German turning movements ; it detected Kluck's changes of movement during the days which preceded the Marne ; it brought the earliest news of his retreat when the British crossed the Marne. It was unsparing of itself, always resolutely attacking the Germans, though it was often equipped with machines inferior to theirs. Its casualties were fearful, because in the later stages of the war each offensive or great battle was preceded by an effort to gain command of the section of the front where the attack was to be delivered, and this could only be accomplished by hard fighting at the price of great sacrifices. Yet at the Battle of Arras in 1917 it controlled the front where the battle was being fought to a depth of twenty miles ; it hampered and checked the stupendous German offensive of March, 1918 ; and in the Palestine Campaign it prepared Allenby's surpassing victory by gaining such complete command of the air as was attained in no other theatre during the whole war, and this though it had no great numerical superiority.

Above all, the British Air Force contributed new tactical methods to the victory of the Allies. It introduced the use of contact patrols, supporting and operating with the infantry, and it perfected the co-operation of aircraft with Tanks, which in the closing stages of the war made these weapons almost irresistible whenever they were employed in any number.

Through the strange official secrecy which throughout the war concealed knowledge of the deeds of the British airmen, the impression was spread that the British Air Force lacked great champions. That is altogether incorrect, as the achievements of such pilots and fighters as Ball, McCudden, and Bishop

WITH THE BRITISH FORCE AT SALONIKA.
British artillery telephone operators in communication with their headquarters on the Salonika front, and (above) a British convoy crossing one of the Macedonian plains.

sufficiently prove. One of the greatest British triumphs of the war was the complete defeat of the Zeppelin, which was accomplished by British airmen with British devices. It is necessary to carry the memory back to understand what an achievement this was.

Down to 1916 the Zeppelin seemed a terrible weapon. Those who witnessed the comparative powerlessness against it of artillery and the helplessness of the towns which it threatened can alone realise all that its menace meant. The **Meeting the menace** first successful attack on a Zeppelin was **of the Zeppelin** delivered by Sub-Lieutenant Warneford with nothing more formidable than bombs, discharged by the crudest of contrivances. But with this feeble equipment by the most astonishing personal bravery he destroyed one of the best German airships, and for some weeks cowed the German airmen. Then followed in 1916 the manufacture of incendiary bullets, but it remained quite uncertain whether these would take effect, and until Lieut. Robinson had attacked and destroyed a Zeppelin the doubt remained. From the hour of his deed and of its repetition by other British airmen the Zeppelin lost its terror and fell into such disrepute that by 1919 men could scarcely believe that they ever feared it.

Even the night-raiding aeroplane—a far more terrible and dangerous antagonist—was in a fair way to be defeated when

the war closed. Methods had been worked out for its attack, as has been stated in a previous chapter, and raiding had been made too dangerous to be profitable. All the artillery appliances for dealing with it had been transformed, again by British skill and British ingenuity. At the opening of the war, for example, from ten to fifteen minutes were required to make the calculations and set the sights of powerful guns when attacking fast-moving aircraft. This rendered it almost useless to fire at them, except so far as the mere noise and concussion of the firing affected the airmen's nerve. By the close of the war devices had been introduced which made the setting of the sights practically instantaneous and enabled the guns to attack with great effect. They were only gradually applied because of the immense burden of work which was imposed on British factories and munition establishments, but their influence was beginning to be felt in the last air raid **Invention against** on London (that of May, 1918), which **air raiding** resulted in disastrous losses to the Germans.

At the end of the war the British Air Force was incontestably first—first in strength, first in numbers, first in organisation, first in excellence of its designs—though owing to official sluggishness and over-conservatism it had not, as we have had repeatedly to point out, the best available machines. In courage, in energy, in enterprise, it shortly after gave magnificent proof of its quality by achieving two of the most amazing feats yet performed by man—the crossing of the Atlantic both with aeroplane and airship, and in each case with aircraft built for the special purposes of the war and not for the different and even more exacting needs of immense ocean journeys. If, as seems probable, the future of war on land is with Tanks and aircraft, then Great Britain, when she excelled and led all other Powers in the development of these two new arms, showed an extraordinary power of adaptation to that future.

The first suggestion for the use of the Tank was made in the winter of 1914, and was welcomed by Sir John French, though not by Lord Kitchener. The design was worked out and improved in great secrecy, but there still were manifest imperfections when the new engine was first employed in September, 1916, during the Battle of the Somme. It was brought into the field prematurely, against the wishes and even the entreaties of its inventors, and consequently its effect, though marked, was nothing like that which would undoubtedly have been produced had it been employed at the outset in large numbers to deal some great stroke at the German front or carry out a break-through in decisive force. The Germans were thus given time to devise means of meeting it and to test defensive appliances of all kinds, including special anti-Tank guns, anti-Tank mines, anti-Tank traps, stockades of reinforced concrete, and hardened steel bullets. But its demoralising influence on the German infantry could not be destroyed. It grew with time and with the rapid improvement of the Tanks. The Mark V. machines, which broke the Hindenburg line in the great battle of September 27th, 1918, were terrible engines, and scarcely less terrible were the "whippets," or small fast Tanks, which appeared in ever increasing number. "Above all," says a German Staff officer, Major Bussche, "two facts have been decisive in forcing the issue of peace. First, the Tanks. The enemy has employed them in unexpectedly large numbers. Where, after a very liberal clouding of our positions with artificial mist, they effected a surprise, our men's nerves were often unequal to them. They broke through our front line, opened a way for their infantry, appeared in the rear, created local panics, and threw the control of the battle into confusion. When they had once been identified, our Tank-defence weapons and our artillery quickly settled with them. Then, however, the mischief had been done, and only the success of the Tanks can explain the large number of prisoners which so painfully reduced our strength and brought about a more rapid consumption of reserves than we had hitherto been accustomed to. We were not in a position to oppose to the enemy equal masses of German Tanks. Their construction would have exceeded the resources of our industry, which was strained to the uttermost."

Success of the Tanks

Behind this failure of the German Tanks lay the crippling effect of the blockade, which slowly paralysed German industry and deprived it of essential new materials, necessary for Tank construction, but also something which the German Staff officer did not admit—the failure of the German Staff to understand the potency of the new weapon. The British mind was quicker to invent, and, despite all handicaps of officialism, quicker to realise the importance of its invention. Had the

enabled the German Staff to attack at any point without special concentration and preparation of its artillery. The Tanks, moving in advance of infantry, could break down the wire and make smooth the path for the infantry. They needed an exact and careful artillery co-operation, but by 1918 the British artillery had attained the required degree of skill to come into action on a grand scale without any long preliminary process of registering, which warned the enemy. Here, again, the British artillery adopted and introduced new methods. It has already been noted that the most important artillery device of the war, the "creeping barrage," was introduced by a British general. It was immediately borrowed by every other allied army and by the Germans. It involved a very high degree of co-operation between the guns and Tanks and infantry, and, if it was to be used to the greatest profit, a remarkable development of the means of communication between them. But this again was achieved. In the great British attack of August 8th, 1918, one of the most brilliant and successful of the whole war, 2,000 guns took part, supporting a great array of Tanks, and all of them opened fire for the first time on the actual morning of the assault.

As in the air so in the Tank, the courage and determination of the British race asserted themselves. Those who have been in a Tank in peace conditions know the intense discomfort, heat, concussion, and uproar. But in battle the Tank officer had first to move up to the front with the greatest possible secrecy, the advance being usually covered by an intermittent fire to drown the roar and rattle of the engines— along roads which were almost invariably searched by the German artillery. A direct hit meant disaster. The Tank commander usually piloted his Tank in the darkness on foot, moving ahead of the great engine, which thundered along close behind him, and there was always risk that it might

How the Tanks worked

SPEED AND SMOKE ON GOING INTO ACTION.
View taken from a kite-balloon of H.M.S. Erin at full speed and putting up a smoke screen during battle manœuvres at sea. The photograph affords a very vivid impression of the speed of a warship.

overrun him. Then, when the "jumping off" point had been reached, he had to lay out tapes in the dark, showing the best route of advance on the hostile position, and this was not the least perilous part of his mission. Finally, when "zero" came, he had to lead the advance, now plunging as his engine reached trenches and dived into them, so that the sensation was that of a volplane in an aeroplane; now rising, as the runners caught the yielding ground and clawed a way up. As the grey side or snout of his Tank came into view through the cloud of the smoke, or mist-screen, the German fire opened on him with peculiar fury, yet he knew that so long as he kept in steady movement he and his crew were fairly safe. It was death to stop, for then the German artillery picked up the range. As the trenches were crossed, there was a scurry from them of frightened German infantry, who were swept down with blasts of fire from the machine-guns or with case from the 6-pounders.

Then came one of the hardest tasks —the hunting of the German machine-gun posts under a perpetual rattle of

German Staff suddenly turned to constructing Tanks it would have confessed that in foresight it had been surpassed by the despised islanders, and it would have dealt a blow at its own doctrine of German infallibility. When it tried to borrow the Tank it neglected some of the devices to which that weapon owed much of its value, and turned out indifferent machines.

The great value of the Tank was that it rendered surprise attacks possible, and indeed easy; and this without such an enormous artillery preponderance as the Germans possessed during the last weeks of 1917 and early months of 1918, owing to the Russian collapse. This artillery preponderance

bullets. Sometimes the anti-Tank bullets came through, and there was an end of the Tank; sometimes they struck fire as they smote the hardened steel of the side; within, in the earlier Tanks, there was a rain of splinters, so that the gunners were supposed to wear visors on their helmets. The crew worked in almost complete darkness when the flaps over the apertures were closed down. They had to trust to periscopes, which usually were shot away early in the fight, and then to tiny eye-holes. The Germans fired assiduously at the post of the commander, which they knew from their captured Tanks. Not infrequently the petrol container caught fire from incendiary bullets; sometimes

German infantrymen ran up behind and slipped bombs into the petrol, with terrible effect. But if the Tank drove through, as soon as it approached the German machine-gun nests the men in them surrendered. They had learnt in the later stages of the war the certain fate if they did not. To achieve that result the Tank Corps had to suffer cruelly. Its losses were very severe. As an example, one battalion which took the field in August, 1918, with sixty Tanks, had at the armistice only six left fit for service. But the corps did its work, and if it perished in doing it, that was the greater glory. It bequeathed to the nation a noble tradition of valour and endurance : its achievements are now the imperishable possession of our history.

In other directions British ingenuity made a gigantic contribution to the final victory. The British Admiralty solved the problem of building torpedo-proof ships by constructing the so-called "blister vessels," not one of which was sunk by a submarine. This fact was not generally known during the war, but the device was gradually applied to all the latest British battleships of the Royal Sovereign class, and to the great battle-cruisers Renown and Repulse. These two vessels were designed under Lord Fisher's administration in 1914-15. They represented as great a revolution as the conception of the Dreadnought, which is now known to have been the child of his fertile brain, and to have dated back to a period twenty years before the war. Under his control great efforts were made to strengthen the power of the British naval artillery. Enormous guns of 18 in. calibre, the largest ever made, were completed and mounted in monitors. They weighed nearly 200 tons, and fired shells of over 3,000 lb., stupendous projectiles, which were actually used in the bombardment of Zeebrugge towards the close of the war. Even larger guns were designed at his initiative ; a battle-cruiser to carry 20 in. weapons was planned, and was actually begun, when Mr. Balfour stopped its construction because labour could not be spared for the work. After he had left the Admiralty the whole British Navy had to be provided with a new type of fuse for the armour-piercing shells, as experience at Jutland showed that the British projectiles usually burst on striking the German armour, and did not go through it and explode inside. The devices with which the submarine was combated and finally **British ingenuity equal to all demands** defeated were almost exclusively of British invention. The paravane, the depth charge, the hydrophone, the floating barrage of nets and wires—all these were the product of British brains or were worked out and given practical form by British engineers. In short, in this period there was no demand to which British ingenuity was unequal.

All mechanical appliances depend ultimately on the skill and courage of the men who use them. There was no want of skill or courage in the men, though in most cases a prolonged training was necessary to get the best service out of the new weapons, a fact which explains the suddenness of the victory that came in every direction and in every field when the skill had been acquired. Yet while the increasing use of machinery in war economises the human material and makes it go farther, an ample supply of men is one of the first necessities of national war. The enormous forces which the British Empire raised during the struggle were employed piecemeal and in many directions. But their very immensity brought all the German calculations to the ground. Authoritative figures have at last been given (in an admirable article published by the "Round Table"), and they must be repeated

here, in order that future generations may know what the men of this generation did. The total white enlistments for the Army in the British Empire were 7,130,280, of whom 5,704,416 were drawn from the United Kingdom and 1,425,864 from the Empire outside it. In addition, 1,524,187 coloured troops were raised, 1,401,350 by India, and the rest in South Africa, the West Indies, and in various Colonies. The total strength of men thus provided reached 8,654,467 ; to whom had to be added the men raised for the Navy, who numbered about 500,000, and 300,000 required by the Merchant Service ; so that the grand total for the British Empire was over 9,450,000. Were the men included who were taken for various forms of service auxiliary to the Army, Navy, and Air Force, the total raised becomes well over ten millions,

SHIPS OF CONCRETE FOR MAKING GOOD WAR LOSSES.
Deck view of one of the first British sea-going vessels that were built of reinforced concrete. The building of such concrete ships was one of the devices hit upon for helping in making good the shortage of shipping owing to war service demands and losses from submarine attacks.

a larger figure than is shown by any of the Allies, and almost as large as the German total. This, too, though Great Britain was the principal, or indeed the only, great workshop that the Allies possessed in Europe, so that she had at one and the same time to provide shells, guns, rifles, aircraft, steel, warships, including all the vast quantity of special plant and craft for the defeat of the submarines, and merchant shipping, on which she and her Allies depended for their very existence. This, though she had to carry out in her shipyards constant repairs to her warships and to merchant vessels damaged in the struggle. No other ally in Europe had to maintain a great navy, and the United States, from its geographical position, after it entered the war, was able largely to rely on the protection which the British Fleet gave it. Its naval con- **Britain's man-power** struction in the critical period was **contribution** relatively small ; the main burden of naval defence always rested on the shoulders of Great Britain. In addition to men, the British Empire raised large numbers of women for auxiliary military and naval service, and such corps totalled over 250,000 women. Many of them faced terrible danger in the British hospitals and hospital-ships ; hundreds of them earned decorations by their signal gallantry and devotion.

The percentage of enlistments for the Army alone, excluding the Navy and Merchant Service, stood higher for England and for the United Kingdom than for any other part of the Empire. In England, according to the "Round Table" figures, 24·02 per cent. of the whole male population (including

the Dardanelles diverted a large part of the Turkish force, and finally absorbed and destroyed the whole Turkish Army with a completeness which was realised in no other field.

The troops from the British Dominions were uniformly good, and rendered superb service to the cause. The record of the Canadian Corps was one long roll-call of victories, after its troops had passed their first apprenticeship in arms. They excelled in the attack as in the defence; this was seen in their superlative fighting at Vimy Ridge, in their storming of the Drocourt-Quéant line, when they surpassed what men had thought possible, and in the long and deadly fight which raged about Cambrai. "It is impossible to serve with the Canadians and not to love them," said an Englishman who accompanied them in the field. The Australians

BRITISH TROOPS IN PALESTINE.
Cavalry passing through the streets of Haifa, the port on the Gulf of Acre which rapidly developed after the opening of railway connection with Damascus. Above: Mounting the first British guard in Jericho after its capture.

children) were enlisted from August, 1914, to the end of the war. The Welsh percentage of the male population was 21·52; the Scottish, 23·71; and the Irish only 6·14.

For the United Kingdom, excluding Ireland, the total enlisted, including the troops already serving on the outbreak of war, but not those raised by the Navy and Merchant Service, was 27·28 per cent. of the males; in Canada it was 13·48; in Australia, 13·43; in New Zealand, 19·35; and in South Africa, 11·12. These are figures of which the English, Scottish, and Welsh peoples, with the Dominions, have abundant reason to be proud. And they explain why it was that, towards the close of the war, British units were not always of such good physique as Dominion units.

Many foreign critics, who marked the comparatively small length of front held by the British in the early period of the war in France, ignored the other fronts on which the British nation maintained great armies. The work which those British forces on distant fronts accomplished cannot easily be overestimated. The total **Many fronts manned by British** employed by Great Britain in France was 5,399,000 men; in Italy, 145,000; at Salonika, 404,000; at the Dardanelles—though this drain on British man-power ceased in early 1916—468,000; in Mesopotamia, 889,000; in Palestine and Egypt, 1,192,000; and in other theatres, 475,000. In the last figure are included the troops that had to be detached for the garrisoning of India and the vital coaling stations, which could not be left exposed to the attack of German raiding cruisers or submarines, or to the possible onslaught of powerful German naval forces in case these managed to escape from the North Sea and Adriatic. The enormous forces maintained in Palestine and Mesopotamia late in the war were mainly recruited from India, and were largely supplied by her with munitions, but they had to be provided with British officers. It was a very wise application of the immense resources of the British Empire which thus brought the strength of India to bear in the decisive attack upon Turkey, and contributed so greatly to the victory of the Allies. From the moment when Turkey intervened in the war, Great Britain in Mesopotamia, in Egypt, and at

won the praise of Foch, who was not given to banal panegyrics, as "the best shock troops in the world." Their performance during the long series of battles which marked the German offensive of 1918 and the allied counter-offensive was one of singular and unbroken glory. If their discipline behind the fighting-line was lax, their behaviour in it endeared them to all their comrades. In physique and in appearance they were almost unmatched; the pure British type was theirs, but with a stature and perfection of feature which men bred in the sterner climate of the United Kingdom too often lack. The New Zealanders were also famous troops; they had the best qualities of the Australians, with an iron discipline which made them, if possible, more terrible to the enemy. The South Africans were few but fit, hard fighters, and excelling in the difficult business of colonial war; their conquest of South-West Africa was a brilliant achievement, admirably carried through. The Newfoundlanders, in the terrible struggle about Beaumont-Hamel in July, 1916, gave freely of their life-blood; and they also provided thousands of magnificent seamen for the Royal Navy. All these Dominion soldiers brought to war aptitudes which the city-bred British necessarily lacked, and their contribution to the victory was very great indeed. What would the history of the war have been if there had been no British Army, and no Canadian and no Australian Corps in the field ?

The total of men raised by Canada was 628,000 ; by Australia, 416,000 ; by New Zealand, 220,000 ; while the South African figure is not available, but was much smaller. Thus the Dominions alone provided more than a million and a quarter of the finest troops, gloriously answering the contention of Lord Morley, a generation before the war, that Canada would never fight for the protection of Belgium.

The enemy and neutral critics who professed that the British would " fight to the last Frenchman " or " to the last Belgian " or " to the last Russian "—for their phraseology changed from month to month and from year to year—were answered by the casualty roll of Great Britain and of her daughter States. From the date when the full strength of the British armies was engaged their losses were heavier than those of any of their Allies. The French, it is true, had a far heavier total death-roll, but that was due to the early battles, in which the French troops were flung upon intact entrenchments and machine-guns with little or no artillery preparation. It was due to an unscientific use of the admirable material in the French Army ; and when better tactics were adopted—they had been in practice from the first in the British Army—the French sacrifices, though terrible, were no longer upon the same scale. It is impossible to give in exact detail the British losses from year to year, but they were approximately as follows in France :

British losses year by year

August, 1914, to close of 1915	..	..	550,000
1916 ..	..	..	..	..	650,000
1917 ..	..	..	..	..	795,000
1918 ..	..	..	..	..	729,000

These figures, moreover, do not include the casualties to Indian or coloured troops, and are therefore far below the actual truth. For purposes of comparison with them, it may be stated that the French casualties in 1917 were about 700,000, and in 1918 about 650,000. Nor do they include the men who were invalided from sickness, fever, and such maladies as " trench foot." The total British killed on land,

excluding Indian and coloured troops, were 721,580, according to the " Round Table " figures ; the wounded, 2,068,727 ; the missing, 273,357 ; and the grand total, 3,063,664.

It was often alleged that the Dominion troops were used for service of special danger, and that their losses were correspondingly increased. This falsehood was insistently repeated by the German propaganda. It was conclusively answered by the percentages of casualties to the male population, which were as follows : For the United Kingdom, excluding Ireland, which scarcely took part in the war, 11·78 ; for Canada, 6·04 ; for Australia, 8·50 ; for New Zealand, 9·80.

Of the British losses, by far the largest part was incurred in France, where, according to the " Round Table," the casualties were 2,724,000. Then came the deplorable **Comparative losses of the Allies** Dardanelles Expedition, with casualties of 119,000 ; Mesopotamia, with 111,000 ; Egypt and Palestine, with 59,000 ; Salonika, with 28,000 ; East Africa, with 19,000 ; Italy, with 6,900 ; and various other theatres, with 3,748. One last fact in this connection is of importance as showing the high quality of the British troops. An excessive loss of officers is a sure sign that the men hang back. In the British Regular and Territorial Army there was no such excessive loss. The proportion of officers to rank and file in France was 1 to 21·4 ; the proportion of officer casualties, excluding the Royal Air Force, where the dangerous work was practically done by officers alone, 1 to 21.

To compare the efforts of the various Allies, the figures for killed and missing on land may be given. They were as follows, so far as they are known :

France (including coloured troops)	..	1,287,300
British Empire (excluding coloured troops)	994,937
Italy (including died of disease in captivity)	460,000
Serbia	..	..	..	..	127,535
United States	..	..	..	54,754
Belgium	..	..	..	..	38,172

The Russian figures cannot be given. Rumania's loss in killed and missing is stated to be 335,706. In addition to the above losses, Great Britain lost 22,258 killed, 23 missing,

OUTSIDE THE JAFFA GATE : ARRIVAL OF THE FIRST BRITISH TROOPS AT JERUSALEM.
The first of the British troops to reach the walls of Jerusalem were the centre of lively interest on the part of the inhabitants, who are here seen watching the new arrivals by the Jaffa Gate. Following on General Allenby's triumphant progress through Southern Palestine, the Holy City of Jerusalem was abandoned by the Turks on the approach of the British forces, and on December 9th, 1917, the city was taken by the British.

CELEBRATION IN CAIRO OF THE VICTORIOUS CAMPAIGN IN PALESTINE.
General Sir Edmund and Lady Allenby passing the Savoy Hotel, which was used as General Headquarters, Cairo, on the occasion of the victorious leader's official entry into Cairo after the signing of the armistice with Turkey had set the seal upon the great series of victories which he had achieved in Palestine.

and 4,894 wounded in the Navy; and in the Merchant Service, 14,661 killed and 30,000 severely injured in the submarine campaign; and she had 3,633 casualties among civilians in the air raids and naval bombardments to which her population was subjected.

At the close of the war the British Army was by far the strongest and by far the best trained and equipped in the field. Its mobilised strength on November 11th, 1918, was 5,680,247; while the corresponding figure for France was 5,075,000; for the United States, with a far larger white population, 3,707,132; for Italy, 3,420,000; for Germany, 4,500,000; for Austria-Hungary (on the eve of the great Italian offensive), 2,230,000; for Bulgaria (before the allied offensive), 500,000; for Turkey, at the armistice with her, 400,000. Once more the British effort on land stands out transcending everything that was accomplished in other countries, because it was accompanied by a similar naval effort, and by the effort of the British Mer-

Marshal Foch's tribute cantile Marine. And it deserves the verdict which Foch has rendered. "In every respect," he said, "the British Army has been superb. There was no branch of all its manifold departments in which it was not fully up to its work. This—for a nation with no obligatory military service and no military tradition behind it—is a marvellous accomplishment."

"It is a question of nerves; we have no nerves, and the British have none. We and the British shall fight it out," said a distinguished German Staff officer to Colonel Palmer, of the American Army, at the First Battle of Ypres. It was not quite just to the French, who bore strains as severe as the

British, and faced them with equal bravery, but as a general verdict on the war it was true. No amount of slaughter, no terrorism, no use of diabolical devices such as gas and flame-projectors, and systematic murder on the high seas, no brutality to British wounded or prisoners, could shake the constancy of the British troops. Many of the German units murdered the prisoners and wounded who fell into their hands. On that point there can be no dispute; it is proved by the damning diaries of German soldiers which during the war were captured by the Allies, and which have been photographed, translated, and reproduced. As to the cruel treatment of **Praise from pro-German neutral** British prisoners, that, again, has been established beyond controversy. "Among those ragged, verminous, emaciated creatures, the most miserable of all, the most cruelly used of all, were the British," said a French doctor in one of the German prison camps; "it was a sight to pierce the heart." And this, too, though even the Germans acknowledged that the British troops were gallant enemies. "All the Germans I spoke to," says Dr. Sven Hedin, whose sympathies were all with Germany and against Great Britain, "were of the same opinion respecting the individual bravery of the British—it was beyond all praise."

The great part which the British Merchant Service performed in the conflict has already been noticed in previous chapters. It is sufficient to say here that its conduct was incomparable. The Germans undoubtedly believed that its officers and men could be cowed by savagery, and once more they were disillusioned by events. But the strain was terrible, and the losses in tonnage were so heavy as to place Great Britain at a permanent disadvantage. Because she did not husband her ships, but placed them at the disposal of the Allies and employed them in waters where the submarine was most dangerous, because she devoted her naval forces to the task of convoying the American troops rather than to that of protecting her own priceless vessels, because she abandoned her old routes and markets, she opened the door to a formidable competition by neutrals and belligerents, who had not made her sacrifices, after the war and during it. But for the example which the British Merchant Service set, and but for the skill with which the British Navy worked the convoy system during the closing weeks of 1917 and the opening weeks of 1918, the United States would not have been able to send two million men to France, and Foch would not have had the reserves which he needed to deal the final crushing blows. The work of the British Merchant Service and the world's debt to it therefore stand very high. The price which the British paid was a fearful one—9,031,000 tons sacrificed —approached by no other Power that fought in the war.

Nor was the financial effort of Great Britain less than her effort in men and in ships. She raised during the war for war purposes down to March, 1919, £2,600,000,000 by taxation at home, and £4,600,000,000 by internal loans. She contracted a floating debt at home of £1,100,000,000 in addition to the above amounts, and she borrowed £1,300,000,000 abroad. Her total monetary contribution was £9,600,000,000, which enormously exceeded that of any other State. And these figures do not include a large part of the sums raised in the Dominions, whether by taxes or loans, and are quite incomplete. Australia, Canada, New Zealand, and Newfoundland raised by loans £656,000,000, and India also made a great contribution, both by gifts and by loans. Moreover, not only did Great Britain finance herself, providing the lenders in the United States with valuable British-owned securities against their advances, she also financed certain of the Allies with little or no security at all. She lent enormous sums to Russia by loans, and she aided France, Italy, Belgium, and Serbia.

In appreciating the financial effort of Great Britain and of other Allies, it is important to bring their outlay into relation with their national wealth, though it must always be remembered that Great Britain imposed heavier taxation than any other country, not even excepting the United States. A calculation published in the United States, and therefore free from any British bias, gives these figures :

	Estimated Total Wealth £	Debt (Jan., 1919). £	Percentage of Debt to Wealth.
U.S.A.	50,000,000,000	4,200,000,000	8·4
Great Britain ..	18,000,000,000	8,000,000,000	44·4
France	13,000,000,000	6,000,000,000	45·0
Russia	12,000,000,000	5,400,000,000	45·0
Italy	6,000,000,000	2,400,000,000	40·0
Germany..	17,000,000,000	8,000,000,000	47·0
Austria	8,000,000,000	4,800,000,000	60·0

And for the estimated annual incomes of these countries and the estimated taxes :

	Estimated Annual Income. £	Estimated Taxes. £	Per cent.
U.S.A.	8,000,000,000	420,000,000	5·2
Great Britain ..	2,400,000,000	680,000,000	28·3
France	1,500,000,000	600,000,000	40·0
Russia	1,400,000,000	640,000,000	45·5
Italy	850,000,000	220,000,000	26·0
Germany..	2,000,000,000	680,000,000	30·9
Austria	1,000,000,000	480,000,000	48·0

The figures for Russia and Austria are purely fanciful, and ignore, in the case of Russia, the repudiation of Russia's debt to Great Britain, which has greatly increased the burden on the British people. Nor do they make allowance for the debts prior to the war or the amounts raised by taxes in it. When all these factors are taken into account they establish the pre-eminence of Great Britain in financial sacrifice. She, for all the victory gained, was actually left by the peace in no better financial position than defeated Germany.

Great Britain not only sacrificed her finances, her manhood, her Merchant Service, and her industrial machinery, she also threw her railway system, on which the whole life of a modern State depends, into confusion. Enormous demands had to be made upon it to meet the enormous requirements of her immense armies. Two thousand miles of permanent way were torn up in Great Britain and bodily removed to France, together with more than a thousand locomotives and many thousands of trucks. The total of engines in France imported by the British Army in 1918 was 1,200, and of trucks 52,600, most of them drawn from the United Kingdom. In 1918 alone the British railway services in France built or reconstructed 2,340 miles of standard-gauge and 1,348 miles of narrow-gauge line. The weekly traffic of these lines was 530,000 tons. Some part of the lines and equipment was provided by Canada. As the result of the diminution in British rolling-stock, fares had to be raised 50 per cent. and

Sacrifice on the railways

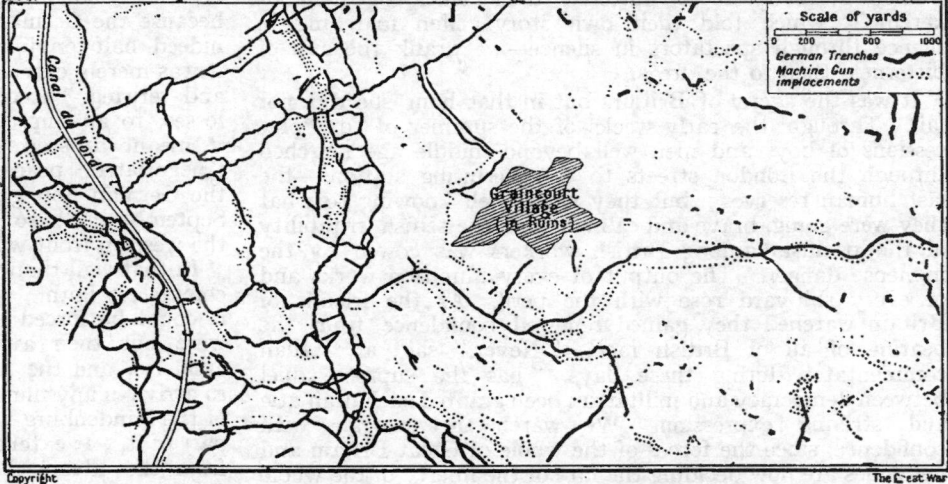

TYPICAL SECTION OF THE HINDENBURG LINE.
Map of the German first line and support line east of Bourlon Wood, where it was stormed on September 27th, 1918. The Canal du Nord, most of which was either dry or muddy, with little water, is on the left, and the ruins of Graincourt village near the centre, forming a mass of machine-gun nests. Only German works are marked ; the dots are machine-gun posts or gun-pits and positions. The lines are trenches, some of which were dug exceedingly deep. The troops attacking on this section were of the Seventeenth Corps in the northern half and of the Sixth Corps in the southern half. They advanced on the 27th beyond the right edge of the map, clearing the whole vast system. (From a British Staff map used in the fighting.)

the number of trains greatly reduced. This reacted on the comfort of the people, and directly affected their trade both during and after the war.

In the closing period of the war the German Government redoubled its efforts to sow discontent and stir up strife in Great Britain. It had achieved a brilliant success by demoralising and disorganising the Russian nation as the result of Revolutionary propaganda. That same propaganda was set to work to destroy the British nation. The Germans met with a certain measure of success. They undoubtedly caused grave anxiety. They stirred up strikes through their conscious or unconscious tools. They delayed the manufacture of aircraft at critical moments. But they never shook the determination of the vast majority of the British peoples. Though voices were raised for the conclusion of a premature peace, and though the assertion was made that an allied victory was out of the question, the British never relented from their deliberate purpose. What shines forth from the whole history of the British nation and its fighting forces during the war is their sublime tenacity. Their soldiers never retreated but they returned ; they never gave up a position but they recovered it. From Mons they retired at the very outset of the war, and to Mons they came back, but with millions where there had been some tens of thousands, with an immense artillery in place of some hundreds of guns, with aircraft in countless numbers in place of the few squadrons of machines in 1914. So it was also at Kut and at the Dardanelles.

Never was the stubborn devotion of the British race better shown than in the terrible weeks of March and April, 1918, when everything trembled in the balance, and when the German offensives on land and the action of the German submarines menaced Great Britain with the gravest peril which she had ever known. Among the many German miscalculations of the war, perhaps the greatest was the conclusion that the German offensives of those two months had destroyed the fighting power of the British Army. In May, William II. declared at Aix-la-Chapelle,

Stubborn devotion of the race " 600,000 British have now been put out of action, and 1,600 guns taken." Yet, as was abundantly proved, neither the nation nor the Army lost heart. " During the fight " (of April, 1918), says a British officer, " I had to take back 2,000 men to stop the breach. I marched those 2,000 men through one of our southern ports on a Sunday morning. The people were standing in the streets, there were thousands of them there; but I marched silent men through silent streets. The men were going to die, and they knew it, and others knew it. The women standing there fluttered their black-edged handkerchiefs, which told their own story. Men marching in silence through spectators in silence—we drank the cup of bitterness then to the dregs."

It was the agony of Britain, but in that hour she did not fail. Through the early weeks of the summer of 1918 processions of boys and men well beyond middle age marched through the London streets to the recruiting stations—the last human reserves; but they went, well knowing to what they were going, brave and calm. Even the selfish irritability of the pacifists among British workers was cowed by the immense danger. The output of every munition works and of every shipyard rose with the peril. As the friends of Britain watched they gained renewed confidence from the bearing of all of British race. " Never," said an Italian commentator during these days, " has the supreme duel between democracy and militarism been granted such dramatic and striking expression. We watch the struggle with confidence, since the forces of the whole of Great Britain and her Allies are now deciding the fate of the liberty of the whole world." The last British soldiers were in the fighting-line; Palestine, Mesopotamia, the Home Defence Army, had all been stripped of white troops for France. There was little or nothing left if the munition works, mines, and shipyards—all essential to the Allies—were not to be completely denuded.

The British offensive of 1918 came as a staggering surprise to the Germans, and startled the Allies and even men in the British Empire by its swift and dazzling success. In all history there is no such succession of victories as was won by Sir Douglas Haig and his troops in the three **Successes without precedent** months of continual battle which marked that offensive. Without rest or intermission the Germans were battered and pressed, blow following on blow. The record of these successive acts in the tremendous drama which preceded and brought the collapse of Germany may here be set forth from official sources :

Battle.	Armies Engaged.	Date.	Prisoners.	Guns Taken.	Divisions Brt.	Grm.
Amiens	.. 4th	Aug. 8-12	21,850	400	15	20
Bapaume	.. 3rd and 4th	Aug. 21-31 :	34,250	270	28	35
Arras	.. 1st	Aug. 26-Sept. 3	18,850	200	10	13
Epéhy	.. 3rd and 4th	Sept. 18-19	11,750	100	14	15
Cambrai	.. 1st, 3rd, and 4th	Sept. 27-30	36,500	380	40*	45
Ypres	.. 2nd	Sept. 28-29	4,800	100	9	5
Cambrai	.. 1st, 3rd, and 4th	Oct. 8-10	12,000	250	40*	45
Courtrai	.. 2nd	Oct. 14-31	6,000	200	7	6
Selle ..	.. 1st, 3rd, and 4th	Oct. 17-25	21,000	450	26	31
Valenciennes	1st, 3rd, and 4th	Nov. 1-11	19,000	460	26	32

Total taken by the British from July 18   188,700   2,840

* 2 American divisions included.

In the same period the French armies took 139,700 prisoners and 1,880 guns; the Americans, 43,300 prisoners and 1,421 guns; and the Belgians, 14,500 prisoners and 474 guns. The lion's share of the fighting and of the captures fell to the British armies. In that long series of battles British troops broke through the outer defences of the Hindenburg line; they broke through the Hindenburg line itself; they stormed the Canal du Nord; they cleared the Ypres salient; by sheer pressure at other points they compelled the Germans to withdraw from a zone stretching from the Lys to Ath; and by their final victory of Valenciennes-Maubeuge they sundered the German armies into two halves, driving one north and the other south of the Ardennes. When the armistice was signed the German forces in their front were little more than a rabble, and the fast British Tanks and cavalry were already moving to turn the retreat into a rout; the cavalry had indeed gained positions ten miles in front of the infantry outposts before they received the orders to stop. The Germans had nothing to meet them. The scale of the battles was in keeping with the result. At the opening of the offensive the British line was eighty-five miles long (as against the three-mile front of Waterloo), and at the armistice about fifty-five miles. At Waterloo thirty-seven tons of ammunition were fired, whereas on one day of the great offensive the British alone expended 18,680 tons.

But of all the operations of that fateful autumn the most critical, the most fruitful in result, was the British storming of the Hindenburg line. It was of peculiar importance because the German Staff had constantly repeated and had, indeed, half convinced the world that during its earlier defeats it was merely carrying out its principle of the " elastic front," and retiring " according to plan," after inflicting enormous losses, to an impregnable fortress. There it meant to stop while arranging for a **The " impregnable "** " negotiated peace." Admiral Hintze, **Hindenburg line** the German Foreign Minister, declared on September 24th to the Reichstag : " Our wall of bronze on the western front will not be broken."

In that wall the whole German Army and nation placed the completest faith. And many of the Allies doubted whether it could be forced except by overwhelming numbers, which were not then available, supported by an overwhelming artillery—and the American heavy guns had not then begun to arrive in any number. The trench map of a typical section of the Hindenburg line given on page 587 shows only the outer part of it. It extended for a distance of three to eight miles from the advanced trenches, and it was not so much one continuous trench as an unending series of trenches, gun-positions, machine-gun fortresses, concreted shelters, dug-outs of immense strength, and tunnels. Every art of the engineer had been exhausted to increase its resisting power, every device which science could suggest had been provided. The wire belts in front of it were not belts but literal jungles, extending at many points to a depth of hundreds of yards. The wire in them was not of ordinary pattern, but so thick and strong that the usual cutters would make little impression on it. Two great canals, wide and deep—the Canal du Nord and the Scheldt Canal—had been cleverly incorporated in this vast system of defence, rendering it so formidable where they passed in front of the trench maze that the German Staff believed an assault at those points to be impossible. The trenches and machine-gun forts were so arranged as to support one another, and behind every trench for miles was another so designed as to sweep it with fire. The line was manned by some of the best German troops in the field. They had been warned that their positions were their winter quarters, and must be held at all cost. They were quite confident of their ability to stand their ground, and expected to inflict a bloody defeat on the Allies.

Everything, therefore, was at stake on that September 27th when the British troops with two American divisions advanced to the attack on this gigantic fortress. A repulse would have encouraged the Germans and have correspondingly discouraged the Allies. The British had already taken the Hindenburg advanced system known as the Wotan line and some portions of the main Hindenburg line. But they had still to attack the main line at its strongest points. How the Tanks crossed the Canal du Nord (by a bridge, not on one another's backs, as the legend runs) is known, and how they went over the steep and deep Hindenburg trenches. It was one of the most gallant and glorious feats of the whole war, and it led up to surpassing victory, for the infantry who followed were as good as the Tanks. By nightfall of September 27th the German " wall of bronze " was in utter ruin. In one single day the British Tanks and infantry had stormed it to a depth of more than four miles, and administered to the German Army the most stunning blow that it received in the whole war. The effect was electrical. The collapse of this rampart brought the collapse of Ludendorff and the German Staff ; it evoked frantic messages from them urging the German Government to make peace ; it destroyed the fighting power of the German troops.

Astounding feat of Midlanders And this first stroke was followed by a yet more astounding feat, when the seemingly impossible was accomplished. The British 46th Division of North Midland troops climbed down the steep banks of the St. Quentin Canal, swam the water on a cold, misty day, and staggered up the opposite bank, carrying the tunnels and concrete fortifications at Bellenglise by storm in face of the stupefied garrison. Not even the landing of the British and Anzacs at Gallipoli, or the storming of Mont St. Quentin, which will go down to posterity as among the most splendid achievements accomplished by man, surpassed this heroic exploit. It was the more heroic because the Germans almost everywhere fought their machine-guns to the very last from their magnificent defences. In one such post, taken by the Australians, who also shared in the capture of the Hindenburg line with great glory, forty machine-guns were discovered, forty Germans were found dead, and sixty living prisoners were captured. " There are no words to describe the hellish power of a field fort like that," says an Australian witness. But the days

had passed when any fortifications devised by man could stop the advance of the British infantry.

The high achievements of the British armies in France were repeated by other British armies in Italy, at Salonika, in Palestine, and in Mesopotamia. In the first two theatres they made a great contribution to the victories gained there. In Palestine and Mesopotamia by their unaided efforts they brought Turkey down with a crash. Sir Edmund Allenby's campaign will always be studied as a model. It was the most brilliant and most breathless of the whole war. The

BRITISH SOLDIERS RESTORE THE SULTAN OF LAHEJ TO HIS THRONE.
General Beatty, who was in command of the Aden Field Force, and the Sultan of Lahej entering Lahej, the capital of the Aden hinterland, after it had been evacuated by the Turks. In circle : The Sultan, Sir Abdul Karim ibn Fadhl ibn Ali, K.C.I.E., at home. He succeeded to the throne of Lahej in January, 1918. Above : General Beatty leading the Sultan from the dais after his installation in his recovered capital.

to the curtailment of its liberties. It faced privations, which grew steadily, making of them a jest. In Great Britain alone of all European countries were the food rationing orders strictly enforced and obeyed. Her people had to endure a crushing load of taxation.

They continually skirted the precipice, but they did not fall. As in Rome of old, their constancy grew with their trials, and from their very danger they seemed to imbibe new strength. All the wealth that they had accumulated in long years of peace melted away and was devoted to the struggle. Long years of suffering and penury lay before them, but they persisted to the end. Discontents multiplied in a little noisy minority of the nation; it had to face sedition within, exactly as it had had before in the previous crisis of its existence, during the Napoleonic Wars, to resist mutiny, armed rebellion, and such upheavals as the Luddite riots. But it did its work calmly, coolly, and tenaciously, and it prevailed.

Thus to the British Empire it was given to triumph at the last. For whole years, in which each week was as a year of all earlier wars, to many sober and prudent observers victory had seemed beyond possibility and hope; yet through those times of stress and agony the British nation was borne, as it appeared, on the wings of an exaltation which no material force could destroy and no suffering daunt. The German Empire waxed and seemed to increase its power. It overshadowed all Europe; it held Belgium and Northern France in an iron grasp; it had gained a firm grip on the vast resources of Russia; it had broken up the unity of the Allies by the Bolshevist defection, at the very moment when the Allies stood on the verge of complete victory; it penetrated to far-off Persia and Afghanistan; it dominated the Baltic and the Black Sea. Yet always Great Britain stood erect. While she wept over the graves

resistance was not to be compared with that which the British armies had to encounter in France, but the Turk has always fought well, and if he collapsed it was because of the skill with which he was attacked and the extraordinary energy with which the initial British blow was followed up. Nor can it be forgotten that most of Sir Edmund Allenby's troops were new Indian levies. If they bore themselves like veterans it was because of the confidence which such leadership imparted and the care with which he laid his plans. The secrecy with which he prepared his thunderstroke was worthy of Napoleon or Lee; the execution of it recalls the handiwork of Stonewall Jackson. In the rush and tumult of tremendous events this campaign passed without its proper meed of praise, but its full value and importance was understood in Germany. It showed the high efficiency of the British Staff and proved that Great Britain had great strategists in her Army. And by a dramatic touch the close of the war in the East brought British troops over the very ground and through the famous cities which had been the scenes of Richard the Lionheart's exploits centuries before.

"In the storm of battle and calamity she has a secret vigour and a pulse like a cannon," said Emerson, more than half a century ago of England. It was true. Amidst all the dangers and discomforts of war, Britain persisted from first to last with growing strength. Her industries were dislocated from top to bottom. The machinery which had been provided in peace, or acquired in war with so much difficulty and expense, was worn out in munition working, so that at the close of the war most of it was verging on the unserviceable by reason of the strain.

What Britain endured

Her Merchant Service — the shipping which was as her very life-blood—was grievously depleted and reduced by losses which threatened her very existence. The submarine campaign struck directly at the sustenance of every man, woman, and child. The air raids, week after week, racked the nerve of her people. There was no trial to which she was not subjected by the German Staff, no means of war, however cruel and foul, which that Staff did not employ against her. One by one the lights of her life were extinguished, and there was no home in Great Britain that did not mourn its dead or tremble in daily apprehension for its living. Every form of insidious persuasion was tried to shake the British conviction that "the invincibility of right lies at the very heart of truth." The British nation submitted

THE SEVERED LINK BETWEEN SERBIA AND HUNGARY.
Destroyed bridge over the Save, where it flows into the Danube by Belgrade. Inset: King Alexander of Greece (left) visiting the British Macedonian front. Above: Men of the Serbian Army singing their national songs after their arrival on the allied front in Macedonia.

of her dead she drew from their offering fresh faith and constancy. She saw all her early hopes shattered and laid in the dust. "Baffled and beaten back she worked on still, Weary and sick of soul she worked the more, Sustained by her indomitable will!" She knew that she fought for the right, and she felt in all her sorrows and uncertainties that, if she quailed not, conclusive victory must in the end reward her faith.

Through what toil and suffering she might have to pass to her goal she no longer considered. In her soldiers burnt the flaming courage of the martyr. Day after day the leave trains carried back to France officers and men returning to the work of death, and every platform was saddened by the premonition of a final parting. Civilised life, it has been said, is only good so far as it presupposes and reveals such great fundamental virtues as love and courage and self-sacrifice, and here they were all shown in the highest degree and on the most tremendous scale. No tragedy was ever mounted on such a stage; everything else in human life seems trivial commonplace compared with the history of this war. One after another her noblest and her best were taken—men who were the hope of the rising generation, such as Raymond Asquith, who added to the highest gifts of intellect rare beauty of soul; Charles Lister, Socialist and heir to a peerage; Robert Palmer, of whom it was truly said that his very presence was a benediction; Rupert Brooke and Charles Hamilton Sorley, poets of the rarest promise; scholars such as Arthur George Heath—they passed down that road to death unflinchingly, only resolved that their duty should be done.

Honour above all honours

They lie on the fields of their sacrifice; and in thinking of them and of the tens of thousands who showed the same spirit it is well to remember that legend of Solon, which embodied all that was loveliest in Greek ideals, wherein Crœsus asked, "Who was the happiest man?"—supposing Solon should answer Crœsus himself—and was astonished to be told that it was Tellus the Athenian, as he died valiantly in battle for Athens, and had been granted the honour which was above all honours of old, that of burial on the scene of his glory. In death they left an inspiration shining across the centuries, and the nation which they so served and loved can never forget their memory and their example:

> Living they were the land, and dead
> Their souls shall be her soul.

All the legendary and historic heroism of Marathon and Thermopylæ, those names which have meant so much to mankind for thousands of years, was renewed and, indeed, exceeded in the epic struggles which marked the last desperate efforts of the Germans to break the will of the British in 1918.

Attack and defence on both sides were conducted with the utmost bravery and resolution, but the will of the British and their cause prevailed. No praise is too high, no human praise can adequately crown the magnificent behaviour of the British troops covering the retreats, whose mission it was to die fighting and inflicting on the enemy the heaviest possible loss.

They were well aware that their deeds might be for ever lost; as the telephones were cut and they were left engulfed in a sea of assailants who came on in overwhelming strength, night closed down upon them, and we know nothing more except from the German reports, though these show that they did something more than their duty.

Sacrifice that was not in vain

At each thrust the Germans found these stubborn British troops in their path, and found, too, that they were filled with the spirit of that gallant officer, Lieutenant Bethell, who, as the destroyer sank under him at Jutland, answered the question of his captain, "Where shall we go?" with the faithful words, "To heaven, I trust, sir!" So the shattered and worn British divisions at the Aisne died, surrounded and overpowered in a seemingly hopeless fight. No heroes of antiquity showed greater strength of soul. Over their bodies the allied armies a few weeks later were to march to a victory which they were not permitted to see in life; though in death, as there is a final justice for man, they must know that their labour and wounds have not been in vain. They were faithful to Sir Douglas Haig's famous order: "Victory belongs to the side which holds out longest. Every position must be held to the last man. There must be no retirement. With our backs to the wall and believing in the justice of our cause, each one of us must fight to the end."

And because they were faithful and endured to the end, so that scarcely a single battalion was left as a fighting unit after the battle—so that their conduct was the subject of special praise from General Mangin and French Army orders —and because there was the same spirit everywhere in the British fighting forces, their country prevailed. She conquered because she had borne such sons, and because as they faithfully served her so she served mankind. No State deserves to endure which does not leave a deep mark on history. It is not true, as has been foolishly said, that "blessed are the peoples which have no history," for in that case ants and bees would be nobler and greater than men. Rather we may say, looking at the history of this war, blessed is the nation which fights for a great ideal and whose sons flinch not before suffering and death. For peoples the right to live and be free is measured by the sum of the sacrifices they are willing to accept. The crown of glory is the crown of life.

Now it is finished. The British peoples fought for two great ends. They sought in the first instance to crush wrong and to liberate Belgium and the smitten minor States. That object they completely accomplished with the aid of their devoted Allies. They sought in the second instance what Pitt had sought a century before, security—"Security against a danger the greatest that ever threatened the world; security against a danger which never existed in any past period of society; security against a danger which in degree and extent was never equalled, against a danger which threatened all the nations of the earth." That security, so far as it is granted to human foresight to discern, they attained. But the interminable military cemeteries show the price. Over hundreds of acres stretches the array of graves, a silent witness to the valour and steadfastness of our race which only the slow hand of time can efface. The battlefields, where millions of men wrestled in agony for so many years in the fumes of gas and the presence of every terror, are already changing their shape.

British Empire's great example

The torn earth, the monstrous German trenches across which the Tanks charged, are vanishing fast. The immense aerodromes from which day after day the fighting and bombing machines rose humming on their mission of death are deserted and ruinous; the air no longer boils like a witches' cauldron. Already it seems that a whole age has elapsed since London day after day heard with a thrill of deep emotion the distant throb of battle—the pulse of the guns in Flanders beating like the grave, far-off murmur of the sea, and telling that Britons were suffering and dying that Britain might be free. The crash of the anti-aircraft barrage no longer breaks overhead on the nights when the wind is still and the moonlight intense. Yet the immaterial things remain—love, honour, patriotism, faith, so gloriously manifested in those days, as an abiding tradition of our people.

And because the British Empire was such in its supreme trial it deserves its place in the world. It is, as a foreign critic has said, "a great example belonging to eternity," and even if it were to collapse beneath the weight of its sacrifices none will be able to deny it "the pure glory of having, on the faith of solemn pledges, without thought of plunder or of gain, thrown itself into the hardest and most doubtful conflict of the ages and made itself the pivot of the grandest league of freedom in history." Now it remains for those who have lived through this war to prove in their lives that they are worthy of those who have died in it; and as they bow the head in gratitude to Heaven, remembering the splendid and solemn past, to resolve that the new world which is being reborn from this fearful convulsion shall be nobler, juster, and better than the old, and built upon some truer doctrine than that which, teaching that human society is a struggle between nation and nation or between class and class, brought the shipwreck of 1914.

| CHAPTER CCCXXIII |

WHAT LUDENDORFF DISCLOSED.

A Review of the Memoirs of the Enemy's Ablest Commander.

By H. W. Wilson.

Germany's Ablest Military Commander and his Memoirs—Indifference to Moral Factors—Effect of the Battles of 1916 on German Moral and Leadership—Inauguration of the Ruthless Submarine Campaign and Attitude Towards America—Personal Responsibility of the Kaiser Made Plain—Germany's Defeat Attributed to the British Blockade and British Tanks—Effect of the Battle of Arras in April, 1917—Tank Attack at Cambrai and the German Reaction—Approaching Collapse of Austria and Necessity for German Offensive—Result of the Great German Attack of March, 1918—Ludendorff's Views of American Troops and his Bitter Comment on British Propaganda under Lord Northcliffe—August 8th, 1918, the Blackest Day for Germany—Need For an Immediate Peace—Further "Black Days" and War Weariness—Hopelessness of More Resistance—Ludendorff's Last Interview with the Kaiser and his Resignation.

GENERAL LUDENDORFF, by the publication of his memoirs, "Meine Kriegserinneringen" (English Edition, Messrs. Hutchinson & Co., London), disclosed the aims and plans of the German Supreme Command, and revealed much that was mysterious in the closing act of the terrific drama. As Hindenburg's right-hand man and Chief of the Staff he became virtually supreme in the summer of 1916, after he had for two years conducted the operations on the eastern front with brilliant success. Never before has a soldier who has held so commanding a position in a gigantic struggle thus disclosed his thoughts while the events were still fresh in the memory of all. His book is a document of intense interest, though its statements cannot usually be accepted without verification. He displays bitter prejudice. He makes charges which he must well know are unfounded—as against the Belgians—and his aim is generally to prove that if his plans had been faithfully carried out and his advice followed the war would have been won. Napoleon frankly admitted his own mistakes. Not so Ludendorff. Yet for all his egotism he must hold a high position among the great soldiers of history, and he was indisputably the ablest commander that Germany ever produced.

He shows throughout his book the complete indifference to moral factors which made the German system and the German officer so terrible a menace to the peace of the world. Thus he takes the treacherous invasion of Belgium as a matter of course. It was planned, he says coldly, by Count Schlieffen, a famous German soldier, "in the event of Belgian neutrality being disregarded by France." The aim was to overpower and destroy the French Army quickly. He adds: "Countless games of Kriegspiel had

proved that in the actual military conditions the defensive against France, combined with an offensive against Russia, meant a long war. This was rejected by Count Schlieffen."

To carry out the swift stroke against France three more army corps were needed, and he states that he himself in 1912 had urged the organisation of these additional corps, which would, he believes, have given Germany a speedy victory.

When he and Hindenburg took over the supreme command all hope of a quick decision had been lost. The war, he says, had become "a struggle of Titans." The Allies had put forth unexpected strength and forced Germany to the defensive. Nothing is more impressive than his confession that the long and terrible battles of 1916 had shaken German moral and leadership. He reveals the secret that at Verdun the German Command had been half-hearted. "The Crown Prince very early urged the discontinuance of the attack," and expressed to Ludendorff "his desire for peace, though how we were to obtain it from the Allies he did not explain." To the allied offensive in the Battle of the Somme he ascribes far-reaching results:

The Allies had a colossal superiority on the ground and in the air. Our Supreme Command was at the outset surprised. We lost heavily in men and munitions. Our advanced trenches, for that reason, were not strongly held. Dug-outs and cellars filled under the enemy's shells. The enemy, attacking under the protection of his drum-fire, entered our trenches or villages before their garrisons could creep out of their burrows. The expenditure in moral and physical force was immense. Our divisions could only remain a few days in their positions. They had constantly to be withdrawn, to recover in quiet sections of the front.

September, 1916,

was a specially critical month. . . . Heavy was our loss. All was on the razor's edge. The strain on our nerves at Pless —where the Headquarters were then situated—was fearful.

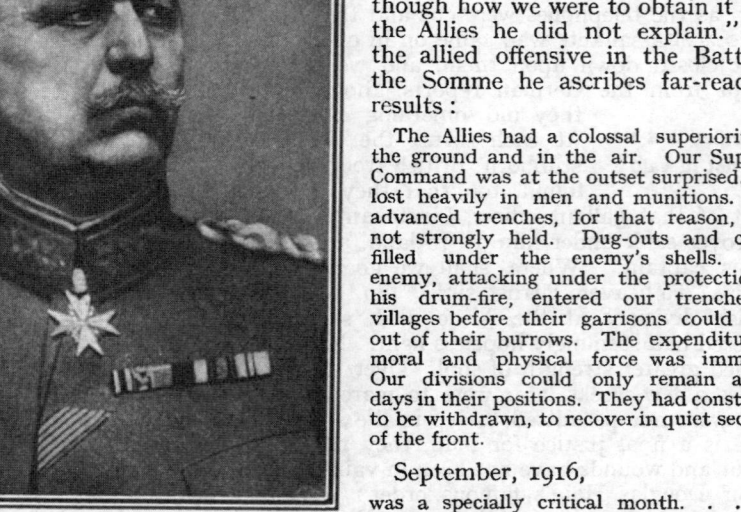

GENERAL VON LUDENDORFF.

German commander who, as Field-Marshal von Hindenburg's right-hand man and Chief of the Staff, became virtually supreme in the summer of 1916.

In November, 1916, the British attack on the Ancre increased the tension :

We had not regarded such an event as possible, least of all where our troops had good positions.

Then came the sudden French attack at Verdun in December, 1916, which resulted in the German loss of many men and of important positions. "On the western front we were completely exhausted."

Thus the German Colossus was tottering at the close of 1916, and not in vain had the British new armies made their prodigious sacrifice at the Somme. He comments on the decision and energy with which the Allies developed their war industries, and holds them up to Germany for admiration :

The Allies' technical equipment constantly increased in completeness and strength. The Allies were in a position to augment their numerical superiority on all their fronts by further formidable developments in all the technical departments of war, and to smash our troops on yet wider fronts than in the Battles of the Somme and Verdun.

The German Supreme Command was haunted by the dread that great battles such as that of the Somme might break out simultaneously on several sections of several fronts, and if so it felt that defeat was inevitable, perhaps even near at hand.

It was in these conditions that Ludendorff carried out the retreat from the Somme to the vast fortified positions which he and Hindenburg had prepared, and that the ruthless submarine campaign was sanctioned. This campaign was, he says, "the last means available by which the war could be ended in a reasonable time." To the question of its morality he paid no more attention than he had paid to the violation of Belgium. He declares that he was sceptical of the German Admiralty's calculation that Great Britain must collapse in six months. He was indifferent to the risk of America joining the Allies, which he anticipated and discounted. She would give them, he thought :

In the first year a reinforcement of five to six divisions, though later, if the U boat war was ineffective, she would increase the enemy's forces to an extent that would weigh very seriously **Attitude towards** in the scale. That America, when she entered the war, would arm as Britain had done, and **America** that the Allies would induce America to devote her whole intellect and energy to greater and even greater armaments, was not to be doubted.

But he hoped that the submarines would prevent the transport of any large force to Europe, and meantime Germany might compel the Allies to make peace.

One of the important disclosures of his memoirs is the personal responsibility of the ex-Kaiser for the great crimes of the war. Belgium, he states, was directly under William II., a fact which must be remembered when judging the executions of Captain Fryatt and Miss Cavell. The order for the ruthless submarine campaign, which meant death for thousands of non-combatants, was given by William II. After some earlier hesitation the final decision was reached at Pless on January 26th, 1917,

in one of the Kaiser's rooms with uncommon speed. His birthday presents lay about. I remember one of them, a fine picture of the cruiser Emden.

The Germans dragged Austria with them in their policy, though Count Czernin, it appears, afterwards protested that he had only acquiesced in it to avoid a conflict with Germany.

Tanks and the blockade figure frequently in the memoirs, but in previously published interviews Ludendorff has already attributed the German defeat largely to their influence. His excuse for failing to build Tanks in the winter of 1916-17 is that the Army was short of motor-waggons, and until they had been provided Tanks could not be taken in hand. He reveals incidentally the interesting fact that he prepared to meet attack coming through Holland and Denmark, and ordered defensive works to be constructed on their frontiers. He admits a remarkable sentence that "good defences later lost some of their strength because the Tanks were able to push across the broadest obstacles." But their great power had yet to be demonstrated, and he was full of not unreasonable satisfaction when in the early spring of 1917 the German armies safely retreated from the Somme to the Siegfried line. This retirement was known as the "Alberich movement" ·

the order for it was given by William II. on February 4th, and it began on March 16th. "The whole movement," he says, "was a brilliant performance on the part of leaders and troops," though for that peculiar weather conditions were mainly responsible. And thus time was gained.

At this juncture, when Germany was on the very edge of the precipice, when even her leaders saw little chance of staving off defeat, an unexpected event postponed her collapse for the best part of two years. That event was the Russian Revolution and the consequent demoralisation of the Russian Army. The joy with which the German Staff welcomed the news is vividly revealed in his words, "a load of lead fell from my heart ; that the Revolution would afterwards undermine our own power I then thought impossible." With the Revolution the sky darkened for the Allies. The spring of 1917, he thinks, was their most terrible period. The U boat campaign had not been effectively **An hour** met. Britain now, in his own earlier **of destiny** phrase, stood on the razor's edge. Yet in this hour of destiny she put forth all her resolution and her strength, and never did her Army fight more magnificently.

The Battle of Arras (in April, 1917), Ludendorff admits, renewed the crisis for the German Army. "The enemy early in the morning of April 9th broke into our artillery positions." Had the British pressed their advance, he thinks, the whole German Army would have been in danger. He does not notice that at this fateful moment, as so often in the war, the weather intervened to save the Germans. But his words emphasised Sir Douglas Haig's conclusion that it would be hard to "calculate the influence which a further period of fine weather might have had upon the course of the battle." The Germans had suffered a great defeat just as they imagined themselves secure. This was followed by the brilliant British local success at Messines and by the repetition at Ypres of the great Somme Battle in the prolonged, bloody, and terrible struggle for the Passchendaele Ridge. As Ludendorff speaks of it his words seem to grow graver. The British, he says, employed a more powerful artillery and a larger supply of ammunition than had before been seen :

Our troops no longer showed that steadiness in defence which the local command expected of them. . . . The waste of our forces was so great as to cause anxiety and exceed all anticipations. . . . The horror of the cratered ground at Verdun was surpassed. On that ground it was not life, but unspeakable suffering. And over the slimy surface the attackers worked forward, slowly but continuously, in dense masses. They often collapsed in the fore-field under the hail of our shells, and our lonely soldiers breathed more freely in their craters. Then on came the masses. Rifles and machine-guns clogged. It was man to man, and the masses only too often triumphed. . . . My impressions were exceedingly grave. . . . We knew that the enemy had incurred great expenditure of force. But we also knew he was extraordinarily strong and had, what was equally important, extraordinary power of will.

The only satisfactory point from the German side in the Battle of Flanders, the last and the most fearful of the great struggles round Ypres, was that in it the "Tank panic" among the German troops diminished, because there the Tanks in the slime could accomplish little. If at this moment the French Army had been able to attack with all its energy and with all the fire which it was later to display, Germany's fate might have been **First Tank attack** sealed that autumn. But it was hampered **at Cambrai** by the mutinies which had earlier in the year affected it. To these Ludendorff does not refer, possibly because the French kept their secret well.

The British Tank attack at Cambrai in November, 1917, is stated by Ludendorff to have achieved a "great initial success," but he adds, "the British Army commander (Sir Julian Byng) did not exploit it," and he asks, "What would have been the verdict on the German offensive in Italy had he done so ?" He regards the German counter-stroke which recovered much of the ground lost as of great importance. "We had won a complete victory over an imposing part of the British Army," and it was in truth the first such victory which the Germans had gained since 1915.

Throughout the later period of the war Ludendorff complains of the German civil authorities. The Reichstag, he says, abolished No. 1 field punishment, which existed in the

Allies' armies, and thus impaired discipline. The moral on the German home front was low, and he ascribes this to the skilful British propaganda, which accentuated the depression and weakened the resistance of the German soldier:

> Lloyd George knew what he was doing when, at the close of the war, he gave Lord Northcliffe the thanks of England for the propaganda he had carried out. He was a master of mass-suggestion. This propaganda was all the more effective against us, as we had to rely not on the strength but on the quality of our battalions. With the disappearance of our moral readiness to fight everything was completely changed. We no longer fought to the last drop of blood. Many Germans were no longer willing to die for their country.

His last two hundred pages recur again and again to the German failure to organise a corresponding propaganda, which, he naively argues, would have equalised matters. He forgets that Lord Northcliffe's leaflets and pamphlets simply told the truth, though until Lord Northcliffe took the matter in hand no one among the Allies had realised the importance of placing that truth in the proper way before the Germans and their allies.

Austria in sight of collapse The Germans had eliminated Russia by revolution. But though Ludendorff says that he yearned to employ the German troops thus set free on the western front, he had other claims to meet. In late 1917 the position of Austria became impossible. During the visit which the young Emperor Karl paid to William II. at Homburg, in April, 1917, the Austrian Staff had warned Ludendorff that, in consequence of the want of raw materials and the severe claims on Austrian man-power, the Austrian Army would " only be able to fight till the next winter." In the eleventh Battle of the Isonzo, fought in September, 1917, he says that the Austrian troops had been so severely handled that they could no longer be trusted to resist. Austria was in sight of the collapse which actually occurred a year later, and German forces had to be sent to save her. This was the history of the German offensive in Italy in October, 1917. It relieved Germany temporarily of anxiety for her ally's fidelity. It diverted British and French troops to the Italian front. But it achieved no decisive result, though Ludendorff with justice claims it as a great success for German arms.

While the Italians were beating back the Austrians on the Piave the trains were rolling west, carrying to the front in France the German troops that were, Ludendorff hoped, to end the war. The German situation in early 1918 was still difficult. The submarine campaign had failed to realise his hopes. The Austrian Army was worn out. Its colossal losses in prisoners, totalling, he says, 1,800,000, could not be replaced. The German Supreme Command every moment expected a warning that it could not fight longer, and with the collapse of the Austrian Army it feared the disappearance of Austria as a State. Bulgaria was weary of the war, and her people had begun an agitation, he says, against their Government and the continuance of the war.

> My conclusion was that the Bulgarians would remain true to us only so long as all went well with us. . . . Turkey was true to the alliance, but she was at the end of her strength.

Need of a German offensive . . . Her Army was in great part a paper force. . . . In Germany there was apparently a better spirit than among our allies, but there also it had greatly declined, and the tone of opinion had altered for the worse. I must admit that I formed a too favourable idea of the national energy still available. . . . The German Army had survived the year 1917 and had triumphed; but it had also showed that we could no longer be sure of holding the western front by a mere defensive in view of the Allies' enormous supply of munitions. . . . The enemy's fearful fighting equipment had given the attack an imposing superiority over our defence. . . . Our troops had been uncommonly and severely tried by our long persistence in the defensive. There were many skulkers. . . . The men shuddered at the prospect of fresh defensive battles and longed for the war of movement.

Ludendorff finally decided in favour of the war of movement and of a great offensive, mainly because it was, he states, less expensive than defence.

More than forty divisions were moved from Russia to the west, which gave the Germans a superiority of 25 to 30 per cent. against the Allies. This superior force was to be supported by every possible mechanical device. Tanks alone were wanting; he tells us that he might have

pressed more energetically for them, only he did not know which of the many needs of the German Army could have been sacrificed to their construction. One of the most remarkable points in the organisation of his offensive was his extraordinary concentration of artillery, so that there were to be 100 guns or more to each 1,000 yards of front attacked. On the whole front of forty miles where the great offensive actually opened the number of guns would thus have been about 6,000. On February 13th, 1918 (it is curious to note how the unlucky number recurs in his last campaign), he stated his views to William II.:

> It must not be supposed that we are going to have such an offensive as we carried out in Galicia or Italy; it will be a colossal struggle which will begin at one point, be continued at another, and will take a long time. It will be arduous, but victorious.

He decided to attack near the junction between the British and French Armies because:

> If we pierced the front there, the strategic success would be more gigantic, as we should sever the greater part of the British Army from the French and drive it up against the coast.

At the last it seemed that the weather would be unfavourable, but at noon of March 20th the conditions improved and the order was given to proceed. At 4 a.m. next morning " the gigantic struggle " began. He admits that the result fell far below his hopes, though he grossly overstates the number of unwounded prisoners at 90,000:

> Strategically, we did not win what we had hoped to win on March 23rd, 24th, and 25th. That Amiens was not reached was a special disappointment. . . . The overrunning of machine-gun nests in many places brought extreme difficulties and delayed our assaults. The initiative of infantry groups often failed, and also their co-operation with supporting arms. All the troops, and the mounted regiments in particular, suffered greatly from aircraft bombs.

The German infantry did not maintain sufficiently open formations in its attack. But just as it seemed that Ludendorff stood on the eve of tremendous success, with a curious instability of purpose he broke off his attack because, he says, he was determined to avoid a battle of **German attack** attrition. His troops now suffered from his **of March, 1918** brutal devastation of the Somme area in 1917. They found themselves with that desert behind them, and in front the shaken but still unbroken British Army.

He complains that while the Allies met the disaster with the extremest energy the German Government and nation did little to follow up his success. He admits that his offensive at Arras was a complete failure, " in spite of an extraordinary employment of artillery and munitions." His next blow came on the Lys, but though it caused intense anxiety among the Allies it failed from the German standpoint to achieve any great result, largely because of the determined resistance of the British troops at Festubert and Givenchy. Nevertheless, William II., waiting eagerly at the Headquarters at Avesnes, showed his approval of Ludendorff by sending as a birthday gift " his statuette in iron, by Betzner."

> There was much to estrange me from his Majesty—our natures were so different. . . . The monarch on whom rested so fearful a responsibility did not, like his Imperial grandfather, find men such as Bismarck and Roon, who were determined to obtain from the country all that the High Command required. And on this depended the fate of the Kaiser and the country in the war.

His next great attack was delivered on the Chemin des Dames on May 27th. It resulted, he says, " In a great tactical victory. . . . But it was a grave misfortune for us that we did not take Rheims, and here our armies might have pushed farther into the mountain region." It is characteristic of him that, as an excuse for his strategy which had forced the United States into war, he disparages the work of the American troops whenever it is possible. At Château-Thierry, he says, " Americans who had been a considerable time in France attacked our thinly-held line in dense masses, but without success. They were brave but they were badly led." At the close of the attack he admits that fifteen American divisions had been transported to France in April, May, and June, and that by the end of June there were twenty American divisions in the field, which is, he confesses, more than he had thought possible. Germany had lost her numerical advantage. But he did not despair:

> In our encounters with American divisions that had been a considerable time in France, we had been masters, though we were inferior in

numbers. There was no reason to suppose that new divisions thrown into the line with less training would fight better than the old divisions. . . . But it was a grave matter that these fresh American reinforcements could be used to set free French or British units on quiet sections of the front. This was a factor of immense importance. It illustrates the influence which the despatch of the American troops had upon the issue. America became therewith the Power that decided the war.

As these powerful reinforcements began to enter the field the German troops were unfavourably affected by a great outbreak of influenza. It was especially severe in Prince Rupert's army group, and was one of the reasons which led Ludendorff to employ the Crown Prince's armies and to strike in his last offensive towards Rheims. On the eve of this offensive he bitterly complains of the effect of the British propaganda on his troops. Lord Northcliffe, it seems, had scattered Prince Lichnowsky's damning indictment against the German Government broadcast. "The Army was literally drenched with the enemy's propaganda leaflets, the extreme danger of which was clearly recognised." The shaken moral of the troops was further weakened by a shortage of potatoes, by a growing desire for independence among the Bavarians, and by an increasing hatred for the Kaiser and both Crown Princes (German and Bavarian). The failure of the Austrians in their great offensive was another depressing factor, and he finds special fault with the confession of Baron Kühlmann, the German Foreign Secretary, that the war could not be ended by military means. His fall followed immediately, mainly through Hindenburg's and Ludendorff's influence. Germany then stood at the top of her power. A reasonable offer, the surrender of Belgium, the evacuation of Northern France, the payment of reparation, might have secured the peace which Ludendorff blames the German Government for failing to obtain. "Our leading statesmen," he says, "did not believe in victory, and could not find any way to peace. But they remained none the less in power."

If they hardened their hearts Ludendorff himself was in large measure to blame. In **Foch's first counter-stroke** mid-July, though he does not in his memoirs disclose this fact, he had answered Admiral Hintze's question, "Whether he was certain with his new offensive finally and decisively to defeat the enemy," with the words, "To that I reply with a decided ' yes.' "

This last offensive was originally timed to open on July 12th, but it was delayed by reports—which were true—that Foch was preparing a great Tank attack on the German flank near Villers-Cotterets. As this attack was not immediately delivered, and as perfect quiet apparently reigned on that front, the order was given for the offensive to begin on July 15th. As the world knows, it found the Allies on the alert. Ludendorff mentions the capture of prisoners by French patrols as the possible explanation. In actual fact Foch had other information, but on July 14th the French on Gouraud's front took several prisoners, and discovered from them that the German artillery preparation was to begin just after midnight on July 15th. At 11.30 p.m. of the 14th the French artillery on that whole front put down a terrific barrage, the sudden thunder of which wakened all Paris. So complete was the failure of the offensive that on July 16th Ludendorff ordered its suspension east of Rheims, and the transference of artillery and other units to Flanders. A day later he ordered the Germans south of the Marne to recross that river. Before these movements could be carried out Foch delivered his first counter-stroke, breaking on July 18th with numerous light Tanks into the German front near Soissons. The surprise was the more complete, as:

A well-known commander of a division informed me he had been on the 17th in our front line and had received the impression that the completest tranquillity prevailed in the enemy's positions. . . . July 19th was a critical day, but it closed passably. . . . In the direction of Château-Thierry, as on previous days, American attacks were shattered.

The offensive was abandoned, but not the idea of attempting yet another offensive. Ludendorff argued that if the Germans had suffered greatly, the Allies had also lost heavily:

The six American divisions which had been engaged had had specially severe losses without any result to show. In spite of the eager fighting spirit of the Americans individually, the low military value of the American troops was demonstrated by the fact that two valiant German divisions, which I had hitherto regarded as of only average

quality, had for several weeks repulsed the main attack of very superior American forces.

Such was the situation when on August 8th occurred:

The blackest day for the German Army in the history of the war. The only worse experience of my life was that caused by the events on the Bulgarian front from September 15th onwards, which sealed the destiny of the German alliance.

This " blackest day " was the result of the attack east of Amiens by the Fourth British Army, supported by the First French Army. To this event Ludendorff ascribes quite correctly—for Foch has since confirmed his statement—the complete change in the allied strategy which led to the rapid development of one stupendous battle along the whole front, bringing down the tottering German Empire in ruins. The British:

Broke deep into our front. Divisional staffs were surprised in divisional headquarters by the hostile Tanks. Our divisions allowed themselves to be completely overrun. . . . Six or seven divisions which had showed themselves good fighting troops were completely smashed. . . . . A fresh division, gallantly advancing, was greeted by the retreating troops with cries of " strike-breakers ! " and " prolongers of the war ! " . . . At many points the officers lost all control. . . . All that I feared, and all against which I had uttered so many warnings, were here realised in fact. Our fighting machine was no longer of high quality. . . . August 8th opened the eyes of both Supreme Commands. The great allied attack, the final battle of the war, began, and was from now on prosecuted by the enemy with ever increasing energy as he recognised ever more plainly our decline in strength.

Allied attack of August 8th, 1918

The first consequence of this grave disaster was that Ludendorff offered William II. his resignation. It was refused:

The Kaiser in those days showed special confidence in me. I was deeply moved, but I was anxious to know whether his Majesty really understood the general situation. I need not have been disturbed. The Kaiser told me later that after the shattering of our offensive in July, and the battle of August 8th, he knew that the war could no longer be won.

The second consequence was that he now called for peace. On August 13th a conference took place at the Hôtel Britannique, in Spa, where he told the heads of the German Government:

It was no longer possible to make the enemy willing to conclude peace by an offensive. By a defensive we could scarcely attain this aim. We must therefore bring about the ending of the war by diplomatic means.

It is noteworthy that the German Command had so far rendered peace impossible by refusing to give up Belgium, Poland, and the ironfields of French Lorraine. Next day Admiral Hintze again went over the military situation with the Kaiser :

He spoke with tears in his eyes. The Kaiser was very calm ; he agreed with Hintze, and charged him to open negotiations, if possible, through the Queen of Holland's mediation.

The disaster was followed by a warning from the Austrian Staff that the Austrian Army could " not hold out through next winter," and by alarming signs of defection in Bulgaria.

The British offensive continued, and on August 20th the French joined in, with the result that, " Here again we suffered grievous losses that we could not make good. August 20th was another black day." Before Ludendorff could recover from this defeat came another at the Wotan line, which, he says, had a violent repercussion in Austria and Bulgaria.

Gloomy German situation

On September 2nd a strong British Tank attack broke through the obstacles and trenches of this line, and opened a way for the British infantry.

So gloomy had the German situation become that :

The Supreme Command abandoned hope of making the enemy willing to conclude peace by bombing London and Paris. It would not permit the employment of a specially effective incendiary bomb, which was ready in August in sufficient quantity, and was designed for use against both capitals. The widespread destruction which was to be expected from this bomb would have had no more influence on the general course of the war. . . . Count Hertling had also warned the Supreme Command not to use these new incendiary bombs because of the reprisals which were to be expected against our own cities. . . . I wanted air attacks with ordinary bombs on London and Paris to continue, so as to tie down the enemy's defensive forces at points distant from the front and prevent our troops from noticing the decline in our power. But I no longer insisted. Paris was feebly attacked a few times after this date. We could not reach London in this period on account of the weather.

More terrible news followed. The Americans attacked at St. Mihiel and shattered a Prussian division; they opened their offensive in the Argonne, at which Ludendorff indulges in some ill-conceived sneers. Bulgaria collapsed.

We anticipated, as did the German leaders in Bulgaria, local reverses, but not a complete break-up of the Bulgarian Army. . . . As to the gravity of the position after the Bulgarian collapse, no one could have any illusions. Turkey, too, had a grievous burden thrown upon her. Her Palestine front was shattered beyond possibility of repair.

With desperate haste Ludendorff strove to concentrate troops on the Danube front; he had fresh warnings that the Austrian Army was failing, and yet the German Government had been unable to open negotiations. The last hope left him was that on the British front the German armies might hold the Siegfried (or Hindenburg) line sufficiently long to gain time for the conclusion of an armistice or peace, and this, too, failed him.

Before Cambrai on September 27th, the enemy by a violent thrust secured ground across the Nord Canal—and therefore behind the Hindenburg line—although there the best possible preparations had been made.

Snatching at every chance, he now imagined that the Germans might be goaded into desperate measures by learning the terms of the Allies. But though he declares that this was no Utopian dream, and that "France, Serbia, and Belgium had suffered far more than ourselves and held out," he deceived himself when he credited the Germans with their heroism. The storming of the Hindenburg line was followed by a council held at Spa, on September 28th, at which the Supreme Command expressed its desire for an armistice. Then Ludendorff, with other officials, went to William II. "His Majesty was unusually calm." He declared his consent to approaching Wilson, and that afternoon a proclamation was issued announcing the introduction of a Parliamentary system in Germany.

Independent observers at the German Headquarters reported that Ludendorff "lost his head" after the loss of the Hindenburg line. His alarm was certainly great. On October 2nd one of his officers gave this account of the military situation, at his orders, in Berlin. The account is not in the memoirs, but is contained in the recently issued German White Paper:

So far as human foresight goes, there is no more possibility of compelling the enemy to make peace. . . . The enemy, owing to American help, is able to replace his losses. The American troops are not in themselves of special quality or superior to our men. Where they have gained initial successes by employing masses we have repulsed them, despite their greater strength. . . . Hitherto our reserves have held the gaps in our line. Attacks of unprecedented violence have been repulsed. The battles have been of a fury which has not before been attained. Now our reserves are coming to an end. If the enemy again attacks, our situation will compel us to withdraw on wide stretches of the front.

Ludendorff adds that "the number of skulkers behind the front increased in terrifying manner; war weariness grew." His gloomy diagnosis of the military position and his sombre predictions did not evoke any outburst of supreme heroism. The truth was the German people had gone to war believing war would be a profitable speculation, and was now stunned by the unbroken series of defeats and disasters in every direction. It had lost all confidence in the German Staff, and at the best, if it fought on, saw that the war must be transferred to German soil. At the worst the German armies might at any moment be surrounded and compelled to surrender.

The breaking-point had been reached and German dismay was deepened by catastrophe to Austria. On October 24th Ludendorff, entirely misjudging the political situation, took a step which led to his immediate fall. He issued a proclamation to the Army about which there is some mystery, declaring that President Wilson required " a military capitulation."

That is unacceptable to us soldiers. . . . Wilson's answer— to the German Peace Note of October 20th—can only summon us soldiers to continue our resistance with all our possible strength.

He says that Hindenburg approved of this document, and that it was in accord with the views of the German Foreign Office. But from the German Headquarters an official warned the Government that:

The military position is now as hopeless as it was three weeks ago. No improvement is to be expected, and it is merely a question of weeks, or at the most of months, before the enemy will be in our country.

Of this warning Ludendorff probably knew nothing; he does not refer to it, nor to another message sent from Headquarters, that "the Gallwitz army group has expressed its anxiety as to the proclamation." Both appear in the German White Paper, which gives the clue to much in the later sections of the memoirs. The German Government realising that further resistance was hopeless, and that neither the Army nor the nation was prepared to fight on to certain disaster, required Ludendorff's removal and the suppression of the proclamation. On October 26th Ludendorff saw the Kaiser for the last time at the Bellevue Palace, in Berlin, a place haunted by the memories of Frederick the Great.

He seemed completely changed from what he had been previously. Speaking to me alone, he declared himself strongly against the proclamation of October 24th. There followed some of the bitterest minutes of my life. I said respectfully to his Majesty I had received the sorrowful impression that I no longer enjoyed his confidence, and therefore most humbly begged him to replace me. . . . I went away alone, and never saw his Majesty again.

Such was the end, after four years and three months of war, during two years of which Ludendorff had been well-nigh omnipotent. His domination collapsed when his strategy failed, and his strategy failed because it attempted too much and defied the deepest instincts of humanity. The German Staff was allowed by the German Government and people to defy all laws, to perpetrate unprecedented crimes, to disregard all pity and all ruth. Any measure which it said was to Germany's interest it was allowed to carry out. The great experiment whether any body of men or any nation can defy the moral law was tried in this case on the most stupendous scale. Ludendorff was the typical product of that Staff. He knew no circumspection and no moderation. Because he grasped at everything he lost all. Within his narrow lights he was a devoted servant of his Sovereign and his country, but the entire want of humanity and compunction in his character make him one of the grimmest and most repulsive figures in history. He stands directly inculpated with his "highest War Lord," William II., in the worst crimes which men have ever committed outside that hell known as Bolshevist Russia—in the wanton devastation of France, which he seeks to excuse, in the violation of Belgium, which he regards with satisfaction, in the frightful atrocities of the submarine campaign, which he takes as a matter of course. The judgment of history on him is already pronounced; the judgment of human justice has yet to come.

GERMANY'S WAR LORD AND SOME OF HIS LEADERS.
The King of Bavaria visiting the German western front in the days when the Kaiser and his war leaders still believed it possible to achieve a victory over the Allies. From left to right: the Emperor William II., Herr Bethmann-Hollweg, King Ludwig of Bavaria, and General Ludendorff.

THE END.